Random House Webster's
CROSSWORD PUZZLE DICTIONARY

 4TH EDITION

Random House Webster's
CROSSWORD PUZZLE DICTIONARY

 4TH EDITION

Stephen P. Elliott, Editor

Random House Reference

New York   Toronto   London   Sydney   Auckland

The Random House Webster's Crossword Puzzle Dictionary, Third Edition, published in 1999, was edited by Nancy Schuster. Earlier editions of this work were published as *Random House Crossword Puzzle Dictionary* in 1994 and 1989, prepared for Random House, Inc., by Sachem Publishing Associates, Inc., Stephen P. Elliott, President.

Please address inquiries about electronic licensing of any products for use on a network, in software or on CD-ROM to the Subsidiary Rights Department, Random House Information Group, fax 212-572-6003.

This book is available at special discounts for bulk purchases for sales promotions or premiums. Special editions, including personalized covers, excerpts of existing books, and corporate imprints, can be created in large quantities for special needs. For more information, write to Random House, Inc., Special Markets/Premium Sales, 1745 Broadway, MD 6-2, New York, NY 10019 or e-mail specialmarkets@randomhouse.com.

Library of Congress Cataloging-in-Publication Data is available.

Visit the Random House Reference Web site: www.randomwords.com

Paperback
ISBN-10: 0-375-72131-2
ISBN-13: 978-0-375-72131-1

Hardcover
ISBN-10: 0-375-42608-6
ISBN-13: 978-0-375-42608-7

Fourth Edition
May 2006

Printed in the United States of America

10 9 8 7 6 5 4 3 2

Preface

Although various word games and puzzles have existed almost since the beginnings of language, the modern crossword puzzle is a 20th-century innovation. The first newspaper crossword appeared on December 21, 1913, in the *New York World,* and this new type of word puzzle quickly captured the public's fancy. Within a decade, crossword puzzles were featured in most American newspapers, and they soon became the rage in England as well. Since the 1920s, crossword puzzles have been a standard feature of daily newspapers and have proved enormously popular when collected in book form.

Now found in almost every language and in variations ranging from theme puzzles to diagramless puzzles, crosswords are available for almost any age and vocabulary level. Those who solve crossword puzzles invariably relish the challenge of completing a puzzle, of "getting it right." When faced with a clue they cannot answer, they resist "cheating"—looking at the puzzle's solution. One way out of this difficulty is to consult a reference work— just as the puzzle's creator may have done in finding words or crafting clues. Yet neither a dictionary nor an encyclopedia nor an almanac contains the necessary information in a useful, quick-reference format. A standard dictionary might give a few synonyms for a word, an encyclopedia would give information about countries or historical figures, and an almanac usually has information about sports figures or the Academy Awards, but only a crossword puzzle dictionary combines in one handy volume the information that might be found in all three. Equally important, it does so without extraneous information and with the convenience of an arrangement by the number of letters in each word, and it includes the many words that are common in crossword puzzles but too obscure to be in other references.

Random House Webster's Crossword Puzzle Dictionary, drawing on the Random House Webster's line of dictionaries and thesauruses, with research into a host of other topics, answers the need of crossword puzzlers for one single-purpose reference work. In addition to general vocabulary and synonyms, there are entries covering history; the natural and physical sciences, literature; music, painting, and other arts; religion; mythology; sports; popular culture; and current affairs, among others. Longer items provide easy-to-find detailed information on the continents and countries of the world, states of the United States, U.S. presidents, the months of the year, and other facts of special interest. This Fourth Edition has been fully updated, with special emphasis placed on the pop cultural questions that are now such an important part of puzzledom—sports teams, TV characters, even sneaker manufacturers.

While *Random House Webster's Crossword Puzzle Dictionary*'s primary purpose is to meet the needs of the growing numbers of people who find crosswords both relaxing and challenging, even a cursory glance will demonstrate the book's usefulness as a reference for trivia buffs. From who won the Academy Award for best actress in 2004 (Hilary Swank) to the name of a coffee grown in Jamaica (Blue Mountain), it's all here.

How To Use This Book

The main entries in *Random House Webster's Crossword Puzzle Dictionary* are words or phrases likely to appear as crossword puzzle clues. Each entry consists of a clue word or phrase and a list of answer words, arranged first by the number of letters in each word and then alphabetically. For example, if the main entry—**banal**—is the clue for a five-letter answer, the answer—"trite"—will be found alphabetically listed under the five-letter answer words. For phrases, such as **contracted form,** the answer could be "digest," "summary," or "synopsis." Entries may also contain indented subheads and secondary subheads. If, for instance, the clue is a phrase, like **cotton fabric,** the word **cotton** will be found as a main entry in the dictionary, and **fabric** will be found as a subhead under it, with such possible answer words as "terry," "poplin," and "gingham." In some cases, the answer can be found in more than one place. For example, if the clue is **Mexican coin,** the answer could be found by looking under the main entry **Mexico** and the subhead **monetary unit,** or by looking under the main entry **coin/currency** and the subhead **of Mexico.**

There are also cross references for alternate spellings and very closely related items. Many terms that do not have explicit cross references may still have valuable additional answers at related entries. The reader is encouraged to look up synonyms even when there is no explicit cross reference. To take one example, the clue **canine** has a short entry in this book, but **dog** has a much longer list that could be examined as well.

The main entries, subheads, secondary subheads, and numbers all appear in boldface type; the answer words are in regular roman type. Most punctuation and accent marks have been omitted, since they are not used in puzzle answers; occasionally, apostrophes and other marks have been included in answers to make them more readable.

Random House Webster's
CROSSWORD
PUZZLE
DICTIONARY

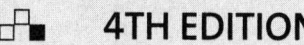 **4TH EDITION**

 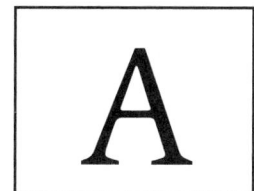 

aardvark
　also: 7 ant bear 8 anteater
　native to: 6 Africa
　food: 4 ants 8 termites
　name comes from: 9 Africaans
　　meaning: 8 earth hog, earth pig

Aaron
　brother: 5 Moses
　father: 5 Amram
　mother: 8 Jochebed
　sister: 6 Miriam
　son: 5 Abihu, Nadab 7 Eleazar, Itha-
　　mar
　wife: 8 Elisheba
　successor: 7 Eleazar
　Aaron's Rod 21 miraculously blos-
　　somed
　yielded: 7 almonds
　deathplace: 3 Hor 8 Mount Hor
　priestly descendant of: 8 Aaronite
　set up: 10 golden calf

Aaron, Henry (Hank)
　sport: 8 baseball
　position: 10 outfielder
　record: 8 homeruns
　team: 13 Atlanta Braves 15 Milwau-
　　kee Braves 16 Milwaukee Brewers

Aaron's Rod 21 miraculously blos-
　somed
　yielded: 7 almonds

Aatam *see* 4 Pima

Ab 16 fifth Hebrew month

Abaddon 4 hell 8 Appolyon

abaft 6 behind 11 to the rear of 12 to
　the stern of

Abagtha 6 eunuch
　served: 9 Ahasuerus

abandon 4 dash, drop, elan, jilt, junk,
　quit, stop 5 ardor, cease, forgo, gusto,
　leave, let go, scrap, verve, waive 6
　desert, give up, spirit 7 discard, for-
　feit, forsake, freedom 8 abdicate,
　evacuate, forswear, get rid of, re-
　nounce, run out on 9 animation, cast
　aside, repudiate, surrender 10 depart
　from, enthusiasm, exuberance, relin-
　quish, wantonness 11 discontinue,
　impetuosity, leave behind, spontane-
　ity, unrestraint 12 immoderation, in-
　temperance, recklessness, withdraw
　from 13 impulsiveness

abandoned 4 lewd, wild 5 loose 6 im-
　pure, jilted, sinful, vacant, wanton,
　wicked 7 debased, immoral 8 cast
　away, degraded, deserted, desolate,
　forsaken, marooned, rejected, un-

chaste 9 cast aside, debauched, discarded, dissolute, neglected, reprobate, shameless 10 dissipated, left
behind, licentious, profligate, unoccupied 11 unrepentant 12 disreputable,
incorrigible, irreformable, relinquished, unprincipled 13 irreclaimable

abandon oneself to 7 yield to 8 give
　in to, give up to 9 indulge in

Abaris
　origin: 5 Greek
　form: 4 sage

Abas
　mentioned in: 5 Iliad
　king of: 7 Argolis
　father: 6 Celeus 7 Lynceus 9 Euryda-
　　mas
　mother: 8 Metanira 12 Hypermnestra
　wife: 6 Aglaia
　son: 7 Proetus 8 Acrisius
　daughter: 7 Idomene
　changed into: 4 bird 6 lizard
　mocked: 7 Demeter
　protected by: 11 magic shield
　companion: 8 Diomedes
　killed by: 8 Diomedes

a bas 8 down with 11 to the bottom

abase 4 mock 5 shame 6 debase, de-
　fame, demean, humble, malign, vilify
　7 cheapen, degrade, mortify, put
　down, vitiate 8 badmouth, belittle, be-
　smirch, bring low, cast down, dis-
　grace, dishonor 9 denigrate, devalu-
　ate, discredit, downgrade, humiliate
　13 bring down a peg, cut down to
　size

abash 3 awe, cow 4 dash, faze 5
　daunt 6 deject, dismay 7 depress 8
　dispirit 9 discomfit, embarrass 10 dis-
　compose, disconcert, discourage, dis-
　hearten

abashed 3 shy 5 cowed, fazed 7
　ashamed, bashful, crushed, daunted,
　humbled, subdued 8 confused, dis-
　mayed, overawed 9 chagrined, morti-
　fied 10 bewildered, confounded, hu-
　miliated, nonplussed, taken aback 11
　dumbfounded, embarrassed, intimi-
　dated 12 disconcerted, disheartened
　13 self-conscious

abate 3 ebb 4 cool, dull, ease, fade,
　slow, wane 5 allay, blunt, lower,
　quell, quiet, slack 6 dampen, go
　down, lessen, pacify, recede, reduce,
　soften, soothe, temper, weaken 7 as-
　suage, curtail, decline, dwindle, fall

off, lighten, mollify, relieve, slacken,
subside 8 decrease, diminish, fade
away, fall away, mitigate, moderate,
palliate, restrain, restrict, slack off,
slow down, taper off 9 alleviate

Abba
　means: 6 father
　statesman: 4 Eban

abbey 6 cenoby, chapel, church, friary,
　priory 7 convent, nunnery 8 cloister,
　seminary 9 cathedral, hermitage,
　monastery

Abbott, Bud
　real name: 14 William A Abbott
　partner: 11 Lou Costello
　born: 12 Asbury Park NJ
　roles: 11 Who's on First 12 Buck
　　Privates 13 Hold That Ghost 33 Ab-
　　bott and Costello Meet Frankenstein

abbreviate 3 cut 4 clip, trim 6 reduce
　7 abridge, curtail, cut down, shorten
　8 boil down, compress, condense,
　contract, cut short, diminish, truncate
　9 summarize, synopsize

abbreviated 5 brief, short 7 limited,
　summary 8 abridged 9 condensed,
　curtailed, shortened 10 compressed,
　summarized

abbreviation 5 brief 6 digest 7 cut-
　ting, pruning, summary 8 abstract,
　clipping, synopsis, trimming 9 lessen-
　ing, reduction, short form 10 abridg-
　ment, diminution, shortening 11 ab-
　straction, compression, contraction,
　curtailment, cut-down form, reduced
　form 12 condensation 13 condensed
　form, shortened form 14 compressed
　form, contracted form

abdicate 4 cede, quit 5 forgo, waive,
　yield 6 abjure, give up, resign 7 aban-
　don 8 abnegate, renounce 9 surrender
　10 relinquish 15 vacate the throne

abdomen 3 gut, pot 5 belly, tummy 6
　paunch, venter 7 stomach 8 pot belly
　9 bay window 11 breadbasket

abduct 5 seize, steal 6 kidnap 7 bear
　off 8 carry off, take away 10 run off
　with 11 make off with

Abduction from the Seraglio, The
　also: 25 Die Entführung aus dem Se-
　　rail
　opera by: 6 Mozart
　character: 5 Osmin 6 Blonde 8 Bel-
　　monte, Pedrillo 9 Constanze 10 Pa-
　　sha Selim

Abdul-Jabbar, Kareem
 formerly: **11** Lew Alcindor
 sport: **10** basketball
 position: **6** center
 team: **8** LA Lakers **10** UCLA Bruins
  14 Milwaukee Bucks **16** Los Angeles
  Lakers
 shot: **7** sky hook

Abednego
 companion: **6** Daniel
 friend: **8** Meschach, Shadrach
 former name: **7** Azariah

Abel
 father: **4** Adam
 mother: **3** Eve
 brother: **4** Cain, Seth
 killer: **4** Cain

Abe Lincoln in Illinois
 author: **14** Robert Sherwood
 director: **12** John Cromwell
 cast: **10** Alan Baxter, Mary Howard,
  Ruth Gordon (Mary Todd Lincoln)
  11 Dorothy Tree, Minor Watson **12**
  Gene Lockhart **13** Howard da Silva,
  Raymond Massey (Abraham Lincoln)

aberrant 3 odd **7** unusual **8** abnormal,
 atypical, peculiar, uncommon **9**
 anomalous, eccentric, irregular

aberration 5 lapse, quirk **6** lunacy,
 oddity **7** anomaly, madness **8** delusion, illusion, insanity, mutation, rambling, straying **9** aberrance, aberrancy,
 curiosity, departure, deviation, exception, wandering **10** digression, distortion, divergence **11** abnormality, derangement, incongruity, mental lapse,
 peculiarity, singularity, strangeness

abet 3 aid **4** back, goad, help, spur,
 urge **5** egg on **6** assist, incite, lead on,
 second, uphold, urge on **7** advance,
 endorse, promote, support, sustain **8**
 advocate, join with, sanction **9** encourage, instigate

abettor 4 ally **6** cohort **7** partner **9** accessory, associate, colleague **10** accomplice **11** confederate **12** collaborator

abeyance 5 delay, on ice, pause **6** hiatus, recess **7** latency **8** deferral, dormancy, inaction **9** cessation, remission **10** quiescence, suspension **11**
 adjournment **12** intermission, postponement **13** in cold storage, on a
 back burner, waiting period **14** discontinuance

abhor 4 hate, shun **5** scorn **6** detest,
 eschew, loathe **7** despise, disdain, dislike **8** execrate, recoil at **9** abominate,
 can't stand, shudder at **10** shrink
 from **11** can't stomach **12** be revolted
 by **13** be nauseated by, find repulsive

abhorrence 4 hate **5** odium, scorn **6**
 hatred **7** disdain, disgust, dislike **8**
 aversion, contempt, distaste, loathing
 9 antipathy, revulsion **10** repugnance
 11 abomination

abhorrent 4 foul, vile **6** odious **7**

hateful **8** accursed **9** execrable, loathsome, repellent, repugnant, repulsive,
 revolting **10** abominable, despicable,
 disgusting, nauseating

abide 3 sit **4** bear, last, live, stay, stop
 5 brook, dwell, stand, tarry, visit **6**
 accept, endure, linger, remain, reside,
 suffer **7** sojourn, stomach **8** stand for,
 submit to, tolerate

abide by 4 obey **6** follow **8** accede to,
 adhere to, submit to **9** conform to **10**
 comply with **11** go along with

abiding 4 fast, firm **6** steady **7** durable, eternal, lasting **8** constant, enduring, unending **9** immutable, permanent, steadfast **10** changeless,
 continuing, unchanging, unshakable
 11 everlasting **12** indissoluble, wholehearted **13** unquestioning

Abidjan
 capital of: **10** Ivory Coast

Abigail
 husband: **5** David, Nabal
 brother: **5** David

Abihu
 father: **5** Aaron
 mother: **8** Elisheba
 brother: **5** Nadab **7** Eleazar, Ithamar
 killed with: **5** Nadab
 accompanied to Mt Sinai: **5** Moses

Abijah
 father: **8** Rehoboam
 grandfather: **7** Solomon
 grandmother: **6** Naamah

ability 4 bent, gift **5** flair, knack,
 power, skill **6** acumen, genius, talent
 7 faculty, knowhow, mind for **8** aptitude, capacity, facility **9** adeptness,
 expertise, potential **10** adroitness, capability, competence **11** proficiency
 12 potentiality **13** qualification

Abimelech
 king of: **5** Gerar
 means: **15** the father is king
 father: **6** Gideon **8** Abiathar
 brother: **6** Jotham
 army commander: **7** Phichol

Abinoam
 father: **4** Saul
 son: **5** Barak

abject 3 low **4** base, mean, vile **6** sordid **7** ignoble **8** complete, cringing,
 hopeless, horrible, terrible, thorough,
 wretched **9** groveling, miserable **10**
 deplorable, despicable, spiritless **11**
 inescapable **12** contemptible

abjure 6 desert, give up, recant, reject
 7 abandon, disavow **8** disallow, disclaim, forswear, renounce **9** repudiate
 10 relinquish

ablaze 5 afire, eager, fiery **6** aflame,
 alight, ardent, fervid, on fire, red-hot
 7 blazing, burning, excited, fervent,
 flaming, flushed, glowing, ignited,
 zealous **8** feverish, hopped-up, in
 flames, turned-on **10** passionate,

switched-on **11** conflagrant, impassioned, intoxicated

able 3 apt, fit **4** good **5** adept **6** adroit,
 expert, fitted **7** capable, equal to,
 learned **8** adequate, skillful, talented
 9 competent, effective, efficient, masterful, practiced, qualified **10** proficient **11** experienced **12** accomplished

able-bodied 5 beefy, hardy, husky,
 lusty, thewy **6** brawny, hearty, robust,
 rugged, strong, sturdy **8** athletic, muscular, powerful, stalwart, vigorous **9**
 herculean, strapping, well-built **15**
 broad-shouldered

ablution 4 bath, wash **7** bathing,
 washing **8** cleaning, lavation **9** cleansing **12** purification **13** ritual washing

Abnaki (Wabanaki)
 language family: **9** Algonkian **10** Algonquian
 tribe: **6** Micmac **8** Malecite **9** Penobscot **13** Norridgewock, Passamaquoddy
 location: **5** Maine **6** Canada, Quebec
  7 Old Town **9** Norumbega **10** New
  England **12** New Brunswick

abnegate 5 forgo, waive **6** abjure, eschew, give up, refuse **7** abstain, forbear **8** renounce **9** repudiate **10** relinquish **11** deny oneself

abnegation 7 refusal **8** eschewal, giving up **9** rejection, sacrifice, surrender
 10 abstinence, continence, forbearing,
 self-denial, temperance **11** forbearance, resignation **12** renunciation **14**
 relinquishment

Abner
 commanded: **9** Saul's army
 father: **3** Ner
 cousin: **4** Saul

abnormal 3 odd **4** rare **5** queer, weird
 7 bizarre, curious, deviant, strange,
 unusual **8** aberrant, atypical, deformed, freakish, peculiar, uncommon
 9 anomalous, eccentric, grotesque, irregular, monstrous, unheard of, unnatural **10** inordinate, outlandish, unexpected **11** exceptional **12**
 unaccustomed **13** extraordinary **14**
 unconventional

abnormality 6 oddity **7** anomaly **9**
 aberrance, curiosity, deformity, deviation **10** aberration, perversion **11** peculiarity **12** eccentricity, idiosyncrasy,
 irregularity, malformation, unconformity

abode 3 pad **4** home, nest **5** house **7**
 address, habitat, lodging **8** domicile,
 dwelling **9** residence **10** habitation **13**
 dwelling place **14** living quarters

abolish 3 end **5** annul, erase, quash **6**
 cancel, repeal, revoke **7** blot out, nullify, rescind, squelch, vitiate, wipe out
 8 abrogate, set aside, stamp out **9**
 eliminate, eradicate, extirpate, repudiate, terminate **10** annihilate, do away
 with, extinguish, invalidate, obliterate,

put an end to **11** exterminate **18** declare null and void

abolition 6 ending, repeal **9** annulment, vitiation **10** abrogation, extinction, rescinding, retraction, revocation **11** abolishment, dissolution, elimination, eradication, recantation, repudiation, termination **12** cancellation, invalidation **13** nullification

abominable 4 base, evil, foul, vile **5** awful, lousy **6** cursed, horrid, odious **7** hateful, heinous, hellish **8** accursed, damnable, horrible, infamous, terrible, wretched **9** abhorrent, atrocious, execrable, loathsome, miserable, repellent, repugnant, repulsive, revolting **10** deplorable, despicable, detestable, disgusting, unsuitable, villainous **11** ignominious **12** contemptible, disagreeable **13** reprehensible

abominate 4 hate **5** abhor, scorn **6** detest, loathe **7** despise **8** execrate **9** can't stand **10** recoil from, shrink from **11** can't stomach **12** be revolted by **13** find repugnant, find repulsive

abomination 4 evil, hate **6** hatred, horror, plague **7** bugbear, disgust, torment **8** anathema, aversion, disgrace, loathing **9** annoyance, antipathy, bete noire, obscenity, revulsion **10** abhorrence, affliction, defilement, repugnance **11** detestation

aboriginal 5 first, prime **6** native **7** ancient, endemic, primary **8** earliest, original, primeval **9** primitive **10** indigenous, primordial **13** autochthonous

aborigine 6 native **16** indigenous person **18** original inhabitant **19** primitive inhabitant

abort 3 end **4** fail, halt, stop **7** call off **8** miscarry **9** terminate

abortion 6 ending, fiasco **7** failure, halting **8** disaster **10** calling off **11** miscarriage, termination **16** fruitless attempt **19** unsuccessful attempt

abortive 4 vain **6** futile **7** sterile, useless **8** bootless **9** fruitless, nonviable, worthless **10** profitless, unavailing, unfruitful **11** ineffective, ineffectual, unrewarding **12** unproductive, unprofitable, unsuccessful **13** inefficacious

abound 4 gush, teem **5** swarm **6** thrive **7** run wild **8** be filled, be rich in, flourish, overflow **9** be flooded, luxuriate, spill over **10** be numerous **11** be plentiful, superabound, proliferate

abounding 4 rich, rife **5** ample **6** lavish, plenty **7** profuse, replete, teeming **8** abundant, brimming, swarming **9** bounteous, bountiful **11** overflowing, running over **14** more than enough

about 2 in, of, on **4** in re, near **5** astir, circa **6** abroad, almost, around, circum, nearby, nearly **7** close to **9** proximate, regarding **10** concerning, in regard to **13** approximately

about-face 5 shift **6** switch **7** reverse **8** reversal **9** disavowal, turnabout, volte-face **10** retraction, rightabout, turnaround **11** recantation **13** change of heart **14** tergiversation

above 4 atop, over **5** aloft, north, supra **6** before, beyond, dorsal, excess, heaven, higher **7** earlier **8** in heaven, overhead, superior, upstairs **9** exceeding **10** surpassing

aboveboard 4 just, open **5** blunt, frank, legal, legit, licit, moral, overt, plain **6** candid, direct, honest, public, square **7** artless, ethical, sincere, upright **8** revealed, straight, truthful, virtuous **9** disclosed, guileless, ingenuous, righteous **10** forthright, foursquare **11** unconcealed **12** on the up and up, plain-dealing, out in the open **13** square-dealing, undissembling **15** straightforward **16** straight-shooting

ab ovo 10 from the egg **16** from the beginning

abracadabra 5 charm, magic, spell **6** voodoo **7** sorcery **8** exorcism **10** hocus-pocus, invocation, magic spell, mumbo-jumbo, open sesame, witchcraft **11** incantation

abrade 3 rub **4** file, fray, sand **5** chafe, erode, grate, scour, scuff **6** scrape **7** scratch

Abraham
former name: **5** Abram
founded: **12** Hebrew nation
father: **5** Terah
wife: **5** Sarah, Sarai **7** Keturah
brother: **5** Haran, Nahor
son: **5** Isaac **6** Midian **7** Ishmael
nephew: **3** Lot
birthplace: **15** Ur of the Chaldees
received: **17** law of circumcision
sacrificed Isaac at: **6** Moriah
burial place: **6** Hebron
tomb in: **9** Machpelah

Abraham Lincoln
author: **12** Carl Sandburg

Abraham's bosom 6 heaven

Abram see **7** Abraham

abrasive 5 harsh, nasty, rough, sharp **6** biting, coarse **7** caustic, chafing, cutting, galling, grating, hurtful, rasping **8** annoying **10** irritating **11** excoriating **16** grinding material, scouring material, scraping material

abreast 6 in rank **7** aligned **8** arm in arm **10** side by side **11** in alignment

abridge 3 cut **4** trim **5** limit **6** digest, lessen, reduce **7** curtail, cut down, shorten **8** compress, condense, decrease, diminish, pare down, restrict, take away, truncate **9** scale down, telescope **10** abbreviate

abridgment 6 digest **8** decrease **9** lessening, reduction, restraint **10** diminution, limitation, truncation **11** curtailment, diminishing, restriction **12** abbreviation, condensation

abroad 3 out **4** rife **5** astir, forth **7** at large, outside **8** overseas **9** all around **10** out of doors **13** in circulation, out of the house, round and about **15** making the rounds, out in the open air, out of the country

abrogate 3 end **4** junk, undo, void **5** annul, quash **6** abjure, cancel, negate, recall, repeal, revoke **7** abolish, nullify, rescind, retract, reverse, vitiate **8** dissolve, override, renounce, set aside, throw out, withdraw **9** repudiate, terminate **10** do away with, invalidate, put an end to **11** countermand

abrupt 4 curt, rude **5** blunt, brisk, crisp, gruff, hasty, quick, rapid, rough, sharp, sheer, short, steep, swift **6** sudden **7** brusque, uncivil **8** impolite **9** impulsive **10** unexpected, unforeseen, ungracious **11** precipitate, precipitous, unannounced, unlooked for **12** discourteous **13** instantaneous, unanticipated, unceremonious

Absalom
father: **5** David
mother: **6** Maacah
half-sister: **5** Tamar
brother: **7** Solomon **8** Adonijah
half-brother: **5** Amnon
defeated at: **6** Gilead
killed by: **4** Joab

Absalom, Absalom!
author: **15** William Faulkner
character: **5** Henry **6** Judith **10** Charles Bon **13** Rosa Coldfield **14** Quentin Compson, Shreve McCannon **16** Goodhue Coldfield **19** Colonel Thomas Sutpen **20** Ellen Coldfield Sutpen

Absalom and Achitophel
author: **10** John Dryden

abscond 3 fly **4** flee, skip **5** split **6** escape, run off, vanish **7** make off, run away, take off **8** steal off **9** disappear, steal away **10** take flight

absence 3 cut **4** lack, want **6** dearth **7** truancy **8** scarcity **10** deficiency, scantiness **11** absenteeism, nonpresence

absent 3 cut, out **4** away, AWOL, gone **5** blank, empty, vague **6** dreamy, musing, truant, vacant **7** faraway, missing, out of it, removed, unaware **8** heedless, keep away, stay away, tuned out **9** not appear, not show up, oblivious **10** distracted, nonpresent, not present, out to lunch, play truant, unthinking **11** inattentive, preoccupied, unconscious **12** nonattendant

absentee 6 no show, truant **10** nonpresent **11** nonattendee, nonpresence **12** nonattendant **13** nonattendance

absenteeism 5 hooky **7** truancy **11**

nonpresence **13** nonappearance **19** absence without cause

absent-minded 5 blank, vague **6** dreamy **9** oblivious **10** abstracted, distracted **11** preoccupied **14** out in left field **17** out of it

Absent Without Leave
author: **12** Heinrich Boll

absinthe
ingredient: **8** licorice, wormwood **9** aromatics, star anise
color: **11** yellow green
substitute: **4** Ouzo **6** Pastis, Pernod **8** Anisette

absolute 4 full, pure, real, sure **5** sheer, total, utter **7** certain, genuine, perfect, supreme **8** complete, decisive, definite, outright, positive, reliable, thorough **9** confirmed, out-and-out, unbounded, unlimited **10** conclusive, consummate, infallible, undeniable

Absolute, Sir Anthony
character in: **9** The Rivals
author: **8** Sheridan

absolutely 3 yes **4** sure **5** truly **6** indeed, really, wholly **7** utterly **8** entirely **9** certainly, decidedly **10** completely, definitely, positively, thoroughly **11** indubitably, undoubtedly

absolution 5 mercy **6** pardon **7** amnesty, release **9** acquittal, clearance, quittance, remission **10** indulgence, liberation **11** deliverance, exculpation, exoneration, forgiveness, vindication **12** dispensation

absolve 4 free **5** clear, loose **6** acquit, exempt, pardon, shrive **7** deliver, forgive, release, set free **9** discharge, exculpate, exonerate, vindicate **10** excuse from **13** find not guilty, judge innocent

absolved 5 freed **6** exempt, spared **7** cleared, excused **8** forgiven, innocent, not guilty, pardoned, released, relieved **9** acquitted **10** discharged, exonerated, vindicated **13** found innocent

absorb 3 fix, get **5** grasp, rivet, sop up **6** arrest, digest, engage, enwrap, ingest, occupy, soak up, suck up, take up **7** consume, drink in, engross, immerse **8** sponge up **9** fascinate, preoccupy, swallow up **10** assimilate, understand **11** incorporate

absorbed 4 deep, rapt **8** immersed, involved, soaked up, sucked up **9** blotted up, engrossed

absorbent 6 porous, spongy **7** osmotic, thirsty **8** bibulous, pervious **9** permeable **10** absorptive, penetrable **12** assimilative

absorbing 8 engaging, exciting **9** thrilling **10** engrossing, intriguing **11** captivating, fascinating, interesting

abstain 5 avoid, forgo **6** desist, es-

chew, refuse, resist **7** decline, forbear, refrain

abstainer 3 dry **7** ascetic **10** nondrinker, self-denier, teetotaler

abstemious 3 dry **5** sober **7** ascetic, austere, sparing, spartan **8** teetotal **9** abstinent, continent, temperate **10** forbearing **11** abstentious, self-denying, straitlaced, teetotaling **12** nonindulgent **15** self-disciplined

abstention 7 refusal **8** eschewal **9** avoidance, desisting, eschewing **10** abstaining, refraining, resistance **11** forbearance, holding back **13** nonindulgence **14** denying oneself **16** nonparticipation

abstinence 8 chastity, sobriety **10** abstention, continence, discipline, self-denial, temperance **11** forbearance, self-control **13** nonindulgence, selfrestraint

abstinent 3 dry **5** sober **6** chaste **8** celibate, virginal **9** continent **10** abstemious, forbearing

abstract 4 take **5** brief **6** arcane, digest, precis, remote, remove, resume, subtle **7** abridge, extract, general, isolate, obscure, outline, summary, take out **8** abstruse, compress, condense, esoteric, profound, separate, synopsis, withdraw **9** imaginary, recondite, summarize, synopsize, theoretic, unapplied, visionary **10** abridgment, conceptual, dissociate, indefinite, intangible **11** generalized, impractical, nonspecific, theoretical **12** condensation, hypothetical, intellectual **14** recapitulation

abstruse 4 deep **6** arcane, remote, subtle **7** complex, obscure **8** abstract, esoteric, profound, puzzling **9** enigmatic, recondite **10** perplexing **11** complicated **12** unfathomable **16** incomprehensible

absurd 4 wild **5** crazy, funny, inane, kooky, silly **6** screwy, stupid **7** asinine, comical, foolish, idiotic **8** farcical **9** illogical, laughable, ludicrous, senseless **10** irrational, ridiculous **11** nonsensical **12** preposterous, unreasonable

absurdity 6 drivel, idiocy **7** fallacy, inanity **8** delusion, nonsense **9** asininity, falsehood, silliness **10** buffoonery **11** comicalness, foolishness **13** irrationality **14** ridiculousness **15** unbelievability **16** unreasonableness

Absyrtus see **8** Apsyrtus

Abu Dhabi
capital of: **18** United Arab Emirates

Abuja
capital of: **7** Nigeria

abundance 4 glut, heap **5** flood **6** bounty, excess, plenty, wealth **7** surfeit, surplus **8** plethora, richness **9** plenitude, profusion, repletion **10** cor-

nucopia **11** copiousness, full measure, sufficiency

abundant 4 rich, rife **5** ample **6** enough, galore, lavish, plenty **7** copious, profuse, replete, teeming **8** brimming, prolific **9** abounding, bounteous, bountiful, luxuriant **10** sufficient

ab urbe condita 24 from the founding of the city

abuse 4 harm, hurt, slur **5** curse, scold **6** berate, carp at, defame, deride, illuse, injure, injury, insult, malign, misuse, rail at, revile, tirade, vilify **7** assault, bawl out, beating, carping, censure, cruelty, cursing, exploit, harming, insults, railing, slander, torment, upbraid **8** badmouth, belittle, berating, denounce, derision, diatribe, ill-treat, maltreat, mistreat, reproach, ridicule, scolding, sneering, torments **9** castigate, criticism, criticize, denigrate, disparage, excoriate, invective **10** belittling, defamation, impose upon, imposition, oppression, speak ill of, upbraiding **11** castigation **12** exploitation, maltreatment, mistreatment, vilification **13** disparagement, misemployment, tongue-lashing **14** inveigh against, misapplication **15** take advantage of

abusive 4 rude, vile **5** cruel, gross, harsh **7** harmful, hurtful, obscene **8** critical, improper, reviling, scornful **9** injurious, insulting, maligning, offensive, vilifying **10** censorious, defamatory, derogatory, scurrilous, slanderous **11** acrimonious, castigating, deprecatory, disparaging, foulmouthed **12** vituperative

abusive word 5 curse **6** insult **7** epithet **9** blasphemy, expletive, invective, obscenity

abut 4 join, meet **5** touch **6** adjoin, border

abutment 4 prop, stay **5** brace, union **7** contact, meeting, support **8** buttress, junction, shoulder, touching **9** adjacency

abutting 6 next to **7** joining, meeting **8** adjacent, touching **9** bordering **10** contiguous, juxtaposed **12** conterminous

abysmal 4 deep, vast **7** endless, extreme, immense **8** complete, enormous, profound, thorough, unending **9** boundless **10** bottomless, incredible, stupendous **12** unfathomable, unbelievable, unimaginable

abyss 4 gulf, void **5** depth, gorge, gully, nadir **7** fissure **8** crevasse **9** vast chasm **13** bottomless pit

Abyssinia see **8** Ethiopia

Acacallis
father: **5** Minos
mother: **8** Pasiphae
son: **11** Amphithemis

acacia 9 gum arabic
  also called: 5 thorn **6** mimosa, wattle
academic 4 moot **6** remote, school **7**
  bookish, erudite, general, learned **8**
  abstract, educated, pedantic, studious
  9 scholarly **10** collegiate, scholastic,
  university **11** conjectural, educational,
  liberal-arts, presumptive, speculative,
  theoretical **12** hypothetical, ivory-
  towered, nontechnical, not practical
  13 nonvocational, suppositional **14**
  nonspecialized **18** college-preparatory
Academus
  origin: 8 Arcadian
  owned: 6 estate
    located in: 6 Athens
    served as meeting place for: 12
      philosophers
Academy Award
  also called: 5 Oscar
  1927-28:
    actor: 12 Emil Jannings
    actress: 11 Janet Gaynor
    director: 12 Frank Borzage **14**
      Lewis Milestone
    picture: 5 Wings
  1928-29:
    actor: 12 Warner Baxter
    actress: 12 Mary Pickford
    director: 10 Frank Lloyd
    picture: 14 Broadway Melody
  1929-30:
    actor: 12 George Arliss
    actress: 12 Norma Shearer
    director: 14 Lewis Milestone
    picture: 25 All Quiet on the West-
      ern Front
  1930-31:
    actor: 15 Lionel Barrymore
    actress: 13 Marie Dressler
    director: 12 Norman Taurog
    picture: 8 Cimarron
  1931-32:
    actor: 12 Fredric March
    actress: 10 Helen Hayes
    director: 12 Frank Borzage
    picture: 10 Grand Hotel
  1932-33:
    actor: 15 Charles Laughton
    actress: 16 Katharine Hepburn
    director: 10 Frank Lloyd
    picture: 9 Cavalcade
  1934:
    actor: 10 Clark Gable
    actress: 16 Claudette Colbert
    director: 10 Frank Capra
    picture: 18 It Happened One Night
  1935:
    actor: 14 Victor McLaglen
    actress: 10 Bette Davis
    director: 8 John Ford
    picture: 17 Mutiny on the Bounty
  1936:
    actor: 8 Paul Muni
    actress: 11 Luise Rainer
    director: 10 Frank Capra
    picture: 16 The Great Ziegfeld
  1937:

actor: 12 Spencer Tracy
actress: 11 Luise Rainer
director: 10 Leo McCarey
picture: 15 Life of Emile Zola
1938:
  actor: 12 Spencer Tracy
  actress: 10 Bette Davis
  director: 10 Frank Capra
  picture: 20 You Can't Take It with
    You
1939:
  actor: 11 Robert Donat
  actress: 11 Vivien Leigh
  director: 13 Victor Fleming
  picture: 15 Gone with the Wind
1940:
  actor: 12 James Stewart
  actress: 12 Ginger Rogers
  director: 8 John Ford
  picture: 7 Rebecca
1941:
  actor: 10 Gary Cooper
  actress: 12 Joan Fontaine
  director: 8 John Ford
  picture: 19 How Green Was My
    Valley
1942:
  actor: 11 James Cagney
  actress: 11 Greer Garson
  director: 12 William Wyler
  picture: 10 Mrs Miniver
1943:
  actor: 9 Paul Lukas
  actress: 13 Jennifer Jones
  director: 13 Michael Curtiz
  picture: 10 Casablanca
1944:
  actor: 10 Bing Crosby
  actress: 13 Ingrid Bergman
  director: 10 Leo McCarey
  picture: 10 Going My Way
1945:
  actor: 10 Ray Milland
  actress: 12 Joan Crawford
  director: 11 Billy Wilder
  picture: 14 The Lost Weekend
1946:
  actor: 12 Fredric March
  actress: 17 Olivia de Havilland
  director: 12 William Wyler
  picture: 22 The Best Years of Our
    Lives
1947:
  actor: 12 Ronald Colman
  actress: 12 Loretta Young
  director: 9 Elia Kazan
  picture: 19 Gentleman's Agreement
1948:
  actor: 15 Laurence Olivier
  actress: 9 Jane Wyman
  director: 10 John Huston
  picture: 6 Hamlet
1949:
  actor: 17 Broderick Crawford
  actress: 17 Olivia de Havilland
  director: 17 Joseph L Mankiewicz
  picture: 14 All the King's Men
1950:

actor: 10 Jose Ferrer
actress: 12 Judy Holliday
director: 17 Joseph L Mankiewicz
picture: 11 All About Eve
1951:
  actor: 14 Humphrey Bogart
  actress: 11 Vivien Leigh
  director: 13 George Stevens
  picture: 17 An American in Paris
1952:
  actor: 10 Gary Cooper
  actress: 12 Shirley Booth
  director: 8 John Ford
  picture: 19 Greatest Show on Earth
1953:
  actor: 13 William Holden
  actress: 13 Audrey Hepburn
  director: 13 Fred Zinnemann
  picture: 18 From Here to Eternity
1954:
  actor: 12 Marlon Brando
  actress: 10 Grace Kelly
  director: 9 Elia Kazan
  picture: 15 On the Waterfront
1955:
  actor: 14 Ernest Borgnine
  actress: 11 Anna Magnani
  director: 11 Delbert Mann
  picture: 5 Marty
1956:
  actor: 10 Yul Brynner
  actress: 13 Ingrid Bergman
  director: 13 George Stevens
  picture: 26 Around the World in
    Eighty Days
1957:
  actor: 12 Alec Guinness
  actress: 14 Joanne Woodward
  director: 9 David Lean
  picture: 23 The Bridge on the River
    Kwai
1958:
  actor: 10 David Niven
  actress: 12 Susan Hayward
  director: 16 Vincente Minnelli
  picture: 4 Gigi
1959:
  actor: 14 Charlton Heston
  actress: 14 Simone Signoret
  director: 12 William Wyler
  picture: 6 Ben-Hur
1960:
  actor: 13 Burt Lancaster
  actress: 15 Elizabeth Taylor
  director: 11 Billy Wilder
  picture: 12 The Apartment
1961:
  actor: 16 Maximilian Schell
  actress: 11 Sophia Loren
  director: 10 Robert Wise **13** Jerome
    Robbins
  picture: 13 West Side Story
1962:
  actor: 11 Gregory Peck
  actress: 12 Anne Bancroft
  director: 9 David Lean
  picture: 16 Lawrence of Arabia
1963:

actor: **13** Sidney Poitier
actress: **12** Patricia Neal
director: **14** Tony Richardson
picture: **8** Tom Jones
1964:
actor: **11** Rex Harrison
actress: **12** Julie Andrews
director: **11** George Cukor
picture: **10** My Fair Lady
1965:
actor: **9** Lee Marvin
actress: **13** Julie Christie
director: **10** Robert Wise
picture: **15** The Sound of Music
1966:
actor: **12** Paul Scofield
actress: **15** Elizabeth Taylor
director: **13** Fred Zinnemann
picture: **17** A Man for All Seasons
1967:
actor: **10** Rod Steiger
actress: **16** Katharine Hepburn
director: **11** Mike Nichols
picture: **19** In the Heat of the Night
1968:
actor: **14** Cliff Robertson
actress: **15** Barbra Streisand **16**
Katharine Hepburn
director: **12** Sir Carol Reed
picture: **6** Oliver!
1969:
actor: **9** John Wayne
actress: **11** Maggie Smith
director: **15** John Schlesinger
picture: **14** Midnight Cowboy
1970:
actor: **12** George C Scott
actress: **13** Glenda Jackson
director: **17** Franklin Schaffner
picture: **6** Patton
1971:
actor: **11** Gene Hackman
actress: **9** Jane Fonda
director: **15** William Friedkin
picture: **19** The French Connection
1972:
actor: **12** Marlon Brando
actress: **11** Liza Minnelli
director: **8** Bob Fosse
picture: **12** The Godfather
1973:
actor: **10** Jack Lemmon
actress: **13** Glenda Jackson
director: **13** George Roy Hill
picture: **8** The Sting
1974:
actor: **9** Art Carney
actress: **12** Ellen Burstyn
director: **18** Francis Ford Coppola
picture: **12** The Godfather (Part II)
1975:
actor: **13** Jack Nicholson
actress: **14** Louise Fletcher
director: **11** Milos Forman
picture: **25** One Flew Over the
Cuckoo's Nest
1976:
actor: **10** Peter Finch

actress: **11** Faye Dunaway
director: **13** John G Avildsen
picture: **5** Rocky
1977:
actor: **15** Richard Dreyfuss
actress: **11** Diane Keaton
director: **10** Woody Allen
picture: **9** Annie Hall
1978:
actor: **9** Jon Voight
actress: **9** Jane Fonda
director: **13** Michael Cimino
picture: **13** The Deer Hunter
1979:
actor: **13** Dustin Hoffman
actress: **10** Sally Field
director: **12** Robert Benton
picture: **14** Kramer vs Kramer
1980:
actor: **12** Robert De Niro
actress: **11** Sissy Spacek
director: **13** Robert Redford
picture: **14** Ordinary People
1981:
actor: **10** Henry Fonda
actress: **16** Katharine Hepburn
director: **12** Warren Beatty
picture: **14** Chariots of Fire
1982:
actor: **11** Ben Kingsley
actress: **11** Meryl Streep
director: **19** Richard Attenborough
picture: **6** Gandhi
1983:
actor: **12** Robert Duvall
actress: **15** Shirley MacLaine
director: **12** James L Brooks
picture: **17** Terms of Endearment
1984:
actor: **14** F Murray Abraham
actress: **10** Sally Field
director: **11** Milos Forman
picture: **7** Amadeus
1985:
actor: **11** William Hurt
actress: **13** Geraldine Page
director: **13** Sydney Pollack
picture: **11** Out of Africa
1986:
actor: **10** Paul Newman
actress: **12** Marlee Matlin
director: **11** Oliver Stone
picture: **7** Platoon
1987:
actor: **14** Michael Douglas
actress: **4** Cher
director: **18** Bernardo Bertolucci
picture: **14** The Last Emperor
1988:
actor: **13** Dustin Hoffman
actress: **11** Jodie Foster
director: **13** Barry Levinson
picture: **7** Rain Man
1988:
actor: **14** Daniel Day-Lewis
actress: **12** Jessica Tandy
director: **11** Oliver Stone
picture: **16** Driving Miss Daisy

1990:
actor: **11** Jeremy Irons
actress: **10** Kathy Bates
director: **12** Kevin Costner
picture: **16** Dances With Wolves
1991:
actor: **14** Anthony Hopkins
actress: **11** Jodie Foster
director: **13** Jonathan Demme
picture: **20** The Silence of the
Lambs
1992:
actor: **8** Al Pacino
actress: **12** Emma Thompson
director: **13** Clint Eastwood
picture: **10** Unforgiven
1993:
actor: **8** Tom Hanks
actress: **11** Holly Hunter
director: **15** Steven Spielberg
picture: **14** Schindler's List
1994:
actor: **8** Tom Hanks
actress: **12** Jessica Lange
director: **14** Robert Zemeckis
picture: **11** Forrest Gump
1995:
actor: **11** Nicolas Cage
actress: **13** Susan Sarandon
director: **9** Mel Gibson
picture: **10** Braveheart
1996:
actor: **12** Geoffrey Rush
actress: **16** Frances McDormand
director: **16** Anthony Minghella
picture: **17** The English Patient
1997:
actor: **12** Jack Nicholson
actress: **9** Helen Hunt
director: **12** James Cameron
picture: **7** Titanic
1998:
actor: **14** Roberto Benigni
actress: **14** Gwyneth Paltrow
director: **15** Steven Spielberg
picture: **17** Shakespeare in Love
1999:
actor: **11** Kevin Spacey
actress: **11** Hilary Swank
director: **9** Sam Mendes
picture: **14** American Beauty
2000:
actor: **12** Russell Crowe
actress: **12** Julia Roberts
director: **16** Steven Soderbergh
picture: **9** Gladiator
2001:
actor: **16** Denzel Washington
actress: **10** Halle Berry
director: **9** Ron Howard
picture: **14** A Beautiful Mind
2002:
actor: **11** Adrien Brody
actress: **12** Nicole Kidman
director: **13** Roman Polanski
picture: **7** Chicago
2003:
actor: **8** Sean Penn

actress: 14 Charlize Theron
director: 12 Peter Jackson
picture: 35 The Lord of the Rings: The Return of the King
2004:
  actor: 9 Jamie Foxx
  actress: 11 Hilary Swank
  director: 13 Clint Eastwood
  picture: 17 Million Dollar Baby

Accad
kingdom of: 6 Nimrod
location: 13 Plain of Shinar
captured by: 6 Sargon (I)

Acca Larentia
form: 7 goddess
corresponds to: 6 Dea Dia

accede 5 admit, grant **6** accept, permit **7** abide by, agree to, approve, concede, defer to, endorse, inherit, yield to **8** assent to, submit to **9** acquiesce, conform to, consent to, succeed to **10** comply with, concur with **11** acknowledge, subscribe to, surrender to

accede to the throne 4 keep **5** claim, usurp **6** ascend **7** possess, succeed **8** take over **9** be crowned **15** ascend the throne

accelerando
music: 15 becoming quicker

accelerate 4 rush, spur **5** hurry, impel **6** hasten, step up **7** advance, augment, further, promote, quicken, speed up **8** expedite **9** intensify **10** facilitate, to go faster **11** pick up speed, precipitate

accelerator 3 gas **4** goad, prod, spur **8** gas pedal **13** encouragement

accent 4 hint, tone **5** drawl, touch, twang **6** detail, stress **7** feature **8** emphasis, ornament, tonality, trimming **9** adornment, emphasize, highlight, punctuate, spotlight, underline **10** accentuate, inflection, intonation, modulation, underscore **11** enunciation **12** articulation **13** embellishment, primary stress, pronunciation

accentuate 6 accent, stress **7** feature, point up **9** emphasize, punctuate, underline **10** underscore

accentuation 6 accent, stress **8** emphasis

accept 3 buy **4** avow, bear **5** admit **6** assume **7** agree to, fall for, swallow **8** accede to, assent to **9** consent to, undertake **11** acknowledge, go along with

acceptable 4 fair, good, so-so **6** proper, worthy **8** adequate, passable, suitable **9** agreeable, allowable, tolerable **10** admissible **12** satisfactory

acceptable person
Latin: 12 persona grata

acceptance 6 belief, taking **7** consent, receipt **8** approval, sanction **9** accepting, agreement, receiving, reception **10** concession, permission **11** affirmation, approbation, endorsement, recog-

nition **12** acquiescence, confirmation **14** acknowledgment **15** stamp of approval

accepted 5 usual **6** common, normal **7** regular **8** approved, standard **9** confirmed, customary, universal **10** acceptable, agreed upon **11** established, time-honored **12** acknowledged, conventional

access 3 way **4** door, gate, path, road **5** entry **6** avenue, course, entree **7** gateway, passage **8** entrance **10** admittance

accessible 5 handy, on tap, ready **6** at hand, nearby, on hand **8** possible **9** available, reachable **10** attainable, obtainable **11** within reach **12** approachable

accession 7 seizure **9** induction **10** arrogation, assumption, investment, taking over, usurpation **11** inheritance **12** inauguration, installation

accessory 4 plus **6** accent, cohort, detail **7** adjunct, partner **8** addition **9** adornment, assistant, associate, auxiliary, colleague, component, extension **10** accomplice, attachment, complement, decoration, supplement **11** confederate, contributor **13** accompaniment

accident 4 fate, luck **5** crash, fluke, wreck **6** chance, mishap **7** smashup **8** fortuity **9** collision, mischance **10** misfortune **11** good fortune, serendipity **12** happenstance, misadventure

accidental 6 chance, random **9** haphazard, unplanned, unwitting **10** fortuitous, incidental, unexpected, unforeseen

acclaim 4 hail, laud **5** cheer, exalt, extol, honor, kudos **6** bravos, praise, salute **7** applaud, commend, ovation **8** applause, cheering, eulogize, plaudits **9** celebrate, rejoicing **10** compliment, enthusiasm **11** acclamation, endorsement

acclamation 6 cheers, homage **7** acclaim, hurrahs, ovation, tribute **8** cheering, hosannas, plaudits **9** adulation **10** salutation **11** approbation

acclimate 5 adapt, enure, inure **6** adjust, orient **8** accustom **9** get used to, habituate, reconcile **11** accommodate **16** become seasoned to

acclimation 9 seasoning **10** adaptation, adjustment **11** habituation

acclivity 4 hill, ramp, rise **5** slope **6** ascent **9** elevation **11** upward slope

accolade 5 award, honor, prize **6** praise, trophy **7** acclaim, tribute **8** applause, citation **10** admiration, compliment, decoration **11** recognition, testimonial **12** commendation

accommodate 3 aid, fit **4** help, hold **5** adapt, board, house, lodge, put up **6** adjust, assist, billet, modify, oblige, supply **7** bed down, conform, contain,

furnish, provide, quarter, shelter **8** accustom **9** acclimate, entertain, get used to, harmonize, lend a hand, reconcile

accommodating 4 kind **6** polite **7** helpful **8** friendly, gracious, obliging, yielding **9** courteous **10** hospitable, neighborly **11** considerate **12** conciliatory

accommodation 5 rooms **7** concord, housing **8** lodgings, quarters **9** agreement **10** adjustment, compromise, settlement **12** arrangements **14** reconciliation

accompaniment 6 escort **7** support **8** ornament **9** accessory, adornment **10** incidental

accompany 5 guard, usher **6** attend, back up, convoy, escort, follow **7** conduct, support **8** chaperon

accomplice 4 aide, ally **5** crony **6** cohort, helper, stooge **7** abettor, comrade, partner **8** henchman, sidekick **9** accessory, assistant, associate, colleague, supporter **11** confederate, participant, subordinate **12** collaborator **13** co-conspirator **14** partner-in-crime

accomplish 2 do **6** attain, finish **7** achieve, execute, fulfill, get done, perform, produce, realize **8** carry out, complete, expedite, knock off **9** succeed at **10** bring about

accomplished 3 apt **4** able, deft, fine **6** adroit, expert, gifted, proved, proven **7** capable, eminent, skilled **8** accepted, effected, existing, finished, masterly, polished, realized, seasoned, skillful, talented **9** brilliant, completed, concluded, practiced, qualified **10** cultivated, proficient **11** consummated, established, experienced, welltrained

accomplishment 3 act **4** deed, feat, gest, gift **5** skill, geste **6** talent **7** exploit, success, triumph, victory **9** execution **10** attainment, capability **11** achievement, carrying out, culmination, fulfillment, proficiency, realization, tour de force **12** consummation

accord 4 cede, give, jibe **5** agree, allow, award, grant, match, tally **6** bestow, concur, render, square, tender, unison **7** concede, concert, conform, entente, harmony, present, rapport **8** be in tune, bequeath, sympathy **9** agreement, harmonize, unanimity, vouchsafe **10** accordance, be in unison, comply with, conformity, consonance, correspond, uniformity **11** concurrence, go along with **19** mutual understanding

accordant 4 like **7** similar **8** parallel **10** consistent **11** homogeneous

accordingly 2 so **4** ergo, then, thus **5** hence **6** thence, whence **8** suitably **9** as a result, therefore, wherefore, whereupon **11** conformably, in due course, in which case **12** consequently **15** correspondingly

accost 3 nab **4** hail, halt, stop **5** greet **6** call to, salute, waylay **7** address, solicit **8** approach, confront **10** buttonhole **11** proposition

accouchement 10 childbirth **11** confinement

accoucheur 12 obstetrician **25** assistant during childbirth

accoucheuse 7 midwife **25** assistant during childbirth

account 3 IRA, use **4** deem, hold, note, rank, rate, sake, tale **5** basis, books, cause, count, gauge, honor, judge, merit, score, story, think, value, weigh, worth **6** esteem, import, reason, reckon, record, regard, report, repute, view as **7** believe, clarify, dignity, explain, grounds, history, justify, recital, version **8** appraise, consider, estimate, megillah, standing **9** calculate, chronicle, narration, narrative, statement **10** accounting, commentary, illuminate, importance

accountable 6 guilty, liable **7** at fault, to blame **8** beholden, culpable **9** obligated **10** answerable, chargeable **11** blameworthy, responsible

accountant 3 CPA **7** actuary, auditor **10** bookkeeper **25** certified public accountant

account for 6 excuse **7** explain, justify **9** answer for

accounting 5 cause **6** answer, motive, reason **7** warrant **10** motivation **11** explanation

account rendered
French: 11 compte rendu

accoutrements 4 gear **7** apparel **8** supplies **9** equipment, trappings **11** accessories, furnishings **13** paraphernalia

Accra, Akkra
capital of: 5 Ghana

accredit 6 assign, credit **7** ascribe, certify, empower, endorse, license **8** sanction **9** attribute, authorize, guarantee **10** commission **19** officially recognize **22** furnish with credentials

accredited 8 ascribed, assigned, endorsed, licensed **9** authentic, certified, empowered **10** attributed, authorized, recognized, sanctioned **12** commissioned **20** officially recognized

accretion 4 rise **6** growth **7** accrual **8** addition, increase **9** expansion, extension, increment **10** supplement **11** enlargement **12** accumulation, augmentation **13** amplification

accrue 4 grow **5** add up, amass **6** pile up **7** build up, collect **8** increase **10** accumulate

accumulate 4 grow **5** amass, hoard **6** accrue, garner, gather, heap up, pile up, save up **7** collect, store up **8** as-

semble, cumulate **9** aggregate **10** congregate **14** gather together

accumulation 4 heap, mass, pile **5** hoard, stack, stock, store **6** pile-up, supply **7** accrual **8** amassing, hoarding **9** acquiring, gathering, stockpile **10** assemblage, collecting, collection **11** aggregation **13** agglomerating **14** conglomeration

accuracy 5 truth **6** verity **8** fidelity **9** exactness, precision **10** exactitude **11** correctness **12** accurateness, faithfulness

accurate 4 true **5** exact, right **7** careful, correct, perfect, precise **8** faithful, truthful, unerring **9** authentic, faultless **10** meticulous, scrupulous **11** punctilious **12** without error

accursed 4 base, foul, vile **6** cussed, horrid, odious **7** hellish **8** damnable, horrible, infamous **9** abhorrent, atrocious, execrable, loathsome, revolting **10** abominable, despicable, detestable, disgusting **12** contemptible

accusation 6 charge **8** citation **9** complaint **10** allegation, imputation, indictment **11** insinuation **13** incrimination

accuse 4 cite **5** blame **6** charge, indict **7** arraign, upbraid **8** reproach **10** take to task **13** call to account **22** lodge a complaint against

accuser 8 attacker **11** complainant **13** finger pointer

accustomed 3 set **5** fixed, prone, trite, usual **6** cliche, common, inured, normal, used to, wonted **7** general, given to, regular, routine **8** everyday, expected, familiar, habitual, hardened, ordinary, seasoned **9** customary, hackneyed, ingrained, prevalent, well-known **10** acclimated, habituated, prevailing **11** commonplace, established **12** conventional, familiarized

ace 2 A-1 **3** top, one **4** A-one, star, tops **5** crack, pilot, super **6** expert, master, tip-top, victor, winner **7** one-spot **8** champion, medalist, terrific, top-notch, top-rated, **9** excellent, first-rate, headliner **10** first-class **11** crackerjack, outstanding **12** front-ranking

Aceldama
means: 12 field of blood
purchased by: 5 Judas

Acerbas *see* **8** Sychaeus

acerbity 7 acidity, sarcasm **8** acridity, acrimony, pungency, sourness, tartness **9** nastiness, sharpness **10** bitterness **11** astringency, brusqueness **12** irascibility

aces 2 A-1 **4** fine, tops **5** great, prime, super **6** grade-A, superb, tip-top **8** peerless, superior, terrific, top-notch **9** excellent, first-rate, marvelous, matchless, superfine, wonderful **10** first-class, tremendous **11** outstanding, superlative **13** extraordinary

Acesius
epithet of: 6 Apollo
means: 6 healer

Achaeus
founder of: 6 Achaea
father: 6 Xuthus
mother: 6 Creusa
brother: 3 Ion

Achan
punishment: 13 stoned to death

ache 4 hurt, need, pain, pang, want **5** covet, crave, mourn, smart, throb, yearn **6** be sore, desire, grieve, hanker, hunger, lament, sorrow, suffer, twinge **7** agonize, long for **8** soreness **10** discomfort

Achech
origin: 8 Egyptian
form: 8 creature
body of: 4 lion
wings of: 4 bird

Achelous
form: 3 god
habitat: 5 river
father: 7 Oceanus
mother: 6 Tethys
daughter: 6 Sirens **8** Castalia **10** Callirrhoe
defeated by: 8 Hercules
struggled over: 8 Deianira

Acheron
river in: 5 Hades
ferryman: 6 Charon
carries: 4 dead

Acheson, Dean
Secy. of State for: 6 Truman
author of: 20 Present at the Creation

a cheval 7 by horse **11** on horseback

achieve 2 do **3** get, win **4** earn, gain **5** reach **6** attain, effect, finish, obtain **7** acquire, fulfill, procure, realize **8** arrive at, carry out, complete, dispatch **9** succeed in **10** accomplish, bring about, effectuate **11** bring to pass

achievement 3 act **4** coup, deed, fear **5** skill **6** effort **7** command, exploit, mastery **9** expertise **10** attainment **11** acquirement, fulfillment, realization, tour de force **14** accomplishment

achieve recognition 6 arrive, make it **7** succeed **8** make good **10** be somebody **11** reach the top

Achilles
mentioned in: 5 Iliad
father: 6 Peleus
mother: 6 Thetis
foster father: 7 Phoenix
grandfather: 6 Aeacus
teacher: 6 Chiron
charioteer: 9 Automedon
friend: 9 Patroclus
warrior in: 9 Trojan War
vulnerability: 4 heel
killed: 6 Hector
killed by: 5 Paris

acid 4 sour, tart **5** acrid, harsh, nasty, sharp **6** biting, bitter, ironic **7** acerbic, caustic, crabbed, cutting, pungent **8** scalding, scathing, stinging, vinegary **9** aciduous, irascible, sarcastic, satirical, vitriolic **10** astringent, vinegarish **11** acrimonious

acidity 8 acerbity, pungency, sourness, tartness **9** sharpness **10** bitterness **11** astringency **13** nonalkalinity

Acis
lover: **7** Galatea
killed by: **10** Polyphemus

Acis and Galatea
opera by: **6** Handel

Acis et Galatee
opera by: **5** Lully

acknowledge 3 own **5** admit, allow, grant, yield **6** accede, accept, answer, assent, concur **7** concede, confess, own up to, reply to **8** call upon, thank for **9** recognize, respond to

acknowledgment 5 reply **6** answer, credit, thanks **8** response **9** admission, gratitude **10** concession, confession **11** affirmation, recognition **12** appreciation, recognizance

acme 3 top **4** apex, peak **5** crest, crown **6** apogee, climax, height, heyday, summit, zenith **8** pinnacle **9** flowering, high point **11** culmination **12** highest point
Latin: **11** ne plus ultra

Acmon
companion: **8** Diomedes
changed into: **4** bird
defied: **9** Aphrodite

acolyte 3 fan **6** helper, novice **7** admirer, devotee, groupie **8** adherent, altar boy, follower **9** assistant, attendant

Acoma
language family: **6** Pueblo
location: **3** Ako **4** Acus **8** Valencia **9** New Mexico
noted for: **7** pottery

acorn
from: **3** oak
shape: **8** balanoid

a couvert 9 sheltered **10** under cover

acquaint 4 meet, tell **6** advise, inform, notify, reveal **7** apprise **8** disclose **9** divulge to, enlighten, introduce, make aware **11** familiarize

acquaintance 8 dealings **9** awareness, knowledge **10** cognizance, friendship **11** association, conversance, familiarity **12** relationship

acquiesce 5 admit, agree, allow, bow to, grant, yield **6** accede, assent, comply, concur, give in, submit **7** concede, conform, consent **10** capitulate, fall in with **13** resign oneself **16** reconcile oneself

acquiescence 5 leave **7** consent **8** approval, giving in, sanction **10** permission, submission **11** concurrence

acquiescent 7 willing **8** amenable, yielding **9** agreeable **10** submissive

acquire 3 get, win **4** earn, gain **6** attain, obtain, pick up, secure **7** achieve, capture, procure, realize **9** cultivate

acquisition 4 gain **5** prize **8** property, purchase **10** attainment, obtainment, possession **11** achievement, acquirement, procurement

acquisitive 6 greedy **7** selfish **8** covetous, grasping **10** avaricious, possessive **13** materialistic

acquit 3 act **5** clear **6** behave, excuse, exempt, let off, pardon **7** absolve, comport, conduct, deliver, release, relieve, set free **8** liberate, reprieve **9** discharge, exculpate, exonerate, vindicate

Acraea
epithet of: **9** Aphrodite
means: **6** height

acre
one-fourth: **4** rood
one-half: **3** erf **5** erven
two-thirds: **5** cover
ten: **6** decare **7** furlong
one hundred: **7** hectare
one hundred twenty: **4** hide

Acres, Bob
character in: **9** The Rivals
author: **8** Sheridan

acrid 4 acid **5** harsh, nasty, sharp **6** biting, bitter, ironic, smelly **7** burning, caustic, pungent **8** stinging **9** sarcastic, satirical, vitriolic **10** irritating, malodorous **11** acrimonious **12** foul-smelling

acrimonious 4 sour **5** nasty, testy **6** biting, bitter **7** caustic, cutting, peevish **8** venomous, spiteful **9** corrosive, irascible, rancorous, sarcastic, splenetic, vitriolic **10** ill-natured

acrimony 5 anger, scorn, spite **6** animus, malice, rancor, spleen **7** ill will **8** asperity, derision **9** animosity, hostility, malignity **10** antagonism, bitterness, malignancy **12** hard feelings, spitefulness

Acrisius
king of: **5** Argos
father: **4** Abas
mother: **6** Aglaia
twin brother: **7** Proetus
daughter: **5** Danae
grandson: **7** Perseus
killed by: **7** Perseus

acrophobia
fear of: **7** heights

acrostic 6 cipher, puzzle **7** acronym

act 2 do **3** bit, gig, law **4** bill, deed, do it, fake, feat, move, play, pose, show, skit, step, work **5** edict, enact, feign, front, order, put-on **6** action, affect, behave, decree, stance **7** execute, exploit, go about, mandate, measure, operate, perform, portray, posture,

press on, routine, statute **8** carry out, function, pretense, put forth, simulate **9** enactment, ordinance, represent **10** pretension, resolution **11** achievement, affectation, counterfeit, impersonate, legislation, performance, pretend to be **14** accomplishment

Actaeon
form: **6** hunter
father: **9** Aristaeus
mother: **7** Autonoe
changed into: **4** stag
transformed by: **5** Diana
killed by: **6** hounds
killed at: **9** Gargaphia

acting 5 drama **6** deputy, ersatz, pro tem **7** interim, theater **8** the stage **9** dramatics, simulated, surrogate, temporary **10** dramaturgy, stagecraft, substitute, the theater **11** dramatic art, officiating, provisional, thespianism **12** stage playing

actinium *see* **8** elements

action 3 act **4** deed, feat, move, step, suit, work **5** force, power **6** battle, combat, effect, effort, motion **7** exploit, process, warfare **8** activity, conflict, endeavor, exertion, fighting, movement, progress **9** adventure, execution, influence, operation **10** enterprise, excitement, performing, production **11** achievement, functioning, performance, prosecution **14** accomplishment

Actis
father: **6** Helius
mother: **5** Rhoda
crime: **10** fratricide
taught: **9** astrology
fled to: **5** Egypt
memorial: **16** Colossus of Rhodes

activate 4 stir **5** drive, impel, start **6** prompt, propel, turn on **7** actuate **8** energize, mobilize, motivate, vitalize **9** stimulate

activated 5 began **7** started **8** impelled, in action, in effect, turned on **9** effective, energized, mobilized, operative, vitalized **10** stimulated **11** in operation

active 4 busy, spry **5** agile, alert, alive, peppy, quick **6** acting, at work, frisky, lively, nimble **7** engaged, in force, on the go, working, zealous **8** animated, diligent, forceful, occupied, spirited, vigorous **9** ambitious, assertive, effectual, energetic, go-getting, operative, sprightly, strenuous **10** aggressive, productive **11** functioning, imaginative, industrious **12** enterprising **13** indefatigable

active person 4 doer **6** beaver, dynamo **7** hustler **8** activist, go-getter

activist 4 doer **6** zealot **7** apostle **8** advocate, exponent **9** proponent, supporter

activity 4 fuss, stir, to-do **6** action,

bustle, flurry, hustle, tumult **7** project, pursuit, venture **8** endeavor, exercise, exertion, function, goings on, movement, vivacity **9** agitation, animation, avocation, commotion **10** assignment, enterprise, hurly-burly, liveliness, occupation **11** undertaking **13** sprightliness

act of the faith
Spanish: 8 auto da fe, auto de fe

act of war
4 raid **6** attack, strike **7** assault, offense **8** invasion **10** aggression, hostile act

actor
3 ham **4** doer, star **6** player, walk on **7** starlet, trouper **8** thespian **9** bit player, performer **11** functionary, participant, perpetrator **14** dramatic artist **15** supporting actor
type: 4 hero **5** cameo **7** feature, leading **9** character **10** supporting
hint: 3 cue

Actor
king of: 6 Phthia
father: 8 Myrmidon
mother: 8 Pasidice
brother: 6 Augeas
son: 7 Cteatus, Eurytus

actual
4 real, sure, true **7** certain, current, factual, genuine, present **8** bona fide, concrete, existent, existing, physical, tangible **9** authentic, confirmed, corporeal **10** legitimate, prevailing, true-to-life, verifiable

actual being
4 esse

actuality
4 fact, life **5** being, truth **6** effect, living, verity **7** reality **8** existing **9** existence, plain fact, substance **10** brutal fact **11** point of fact

actually
5 truly **6** indeed, in fact, really, verily **9** genuinely, literally
Latin: 7 ex facto

actually existing
Latin: 6 in esse **7** de facto

actuary
5 clerk **9** tabulator **12** statistician

actuate
4 move, stir **5** cause, drive, impel, rouse **6** arouse, excite, incite, induce, prompt **7** animate, inspire, trigger **8** activate, motivate **9** influence, instigate, stimulate **10** bring about

acumen
6 wisdom **7** insight **8** keenness, sagacity **9** acuteness, ingenuity, smartness **10** astuteness, cleverness, perception, shrewdness **11** discernment **12** intelligence, perspicacity **13** sound judgment **15** clearheadedness

acute
4 keen **5** sharp **6** clever, fierce, peaked, severe **7** intense, very bad **8** critical, piercing, powerful **9** agonizing, ingenious, intuitive, sensitive, very great **10** discerning, perceptive **11** distressing, penetrating **12** excruciating, needle-shaped **14** discriminating

acute suffering
5 agony **7** anguish, torment, torture **8** distress

A.D.
see **10** anno Domini

adage
3 saw **4** quip, wise **5** axiom, maxim, motto **6** cliche, dictum, old saw, saying, truism **7** epigram, precept, proverb **8** aphorism **9** platitude **11** observation

adagio
music: 4 slow

Adah
also: 9 Bashemath
husband: 4 Esau **6** Lamech
son: 5 Jabal, Jubal **7** Eliphaz

Adam
wife: 3 Eve
son: 4 Abel, Cain, Seth
home: 4 Eden
grandson: 4 Enas **5** Enoch

adamant
3 set **4** firm **5** fixed, rigid, tough **7** uptight **8** obdurate, resolute, stubborn **9** immovable, insistent, unbending **10** determined, hard as rock, inexorable, inflexible, unyielding **12** intransigent **14** uncompromising

Adam Bede
author: 11 George Eliot
character: 8 Seth Bede **11** Dinah Morris, Hetty Sorrel **12** Martin Poyser **17** Arthur Donnithorne

Adams, Henry
author of: 6 Esther **9** Democracy **14** Chapters of Erie **24** History of the United States (Under the Jefferson and Adams Administration), The Education of Henry Adams **26** Mont-Saint Michel and Chartres **34** The Degradation of the Democratic Dogma

Adams, John
nickname: 19 Atlas of Independence
presidential rank: 6 second
party: 10 Federalist
state represented: 2 MA
defeated: 9 Jefferson
vice president: 9 Jefferson
cabinet:
  state: 8 (John) Marshall **9** (Timothy) Pickering
  treasury: 6 (Samuel) Dexter **7** (Oliver) Wolcott
  war: 6 (Samuel) Dexter **7** (James) McHenry
  attorney general: 3 (Charles) Lee
  navy: 8 (Benjamin) Stoddert
born: 2 MA **9** Braintree
town now called: 6 Quincy
died/buried: 6 Quincy
education: 7 Harvard
religion: 9 Unitarian
author: 18 Discourses on Davila **20** Thoughts on Government
political career: 13 vice president **24** First Continental Congress **25** Second Continental Congress
  minister: 11 Netherlands **12** Great Britain
civilian career: 6 lawyer
notable events of lifetime/term: 9 XYZ Affair
  act: 9 Judiciary **16** Alien and Sedition
father: 4 John
mother: 7 Susanna (Boylston)
siblings: 5 Elihu **13** Peter Boylston
wife: 7 Abigail (Smith)
children: 7 Charles, Susanna **10** John Quincy (6th president) **13** Abigail Amelia **14** Thomas Boylston

Adams, John Quincy
nickname: 14 Old Man Eloquent
presidential rank: 5 sixth
party: 4 Whig **10** Federalist **20** Democratic-Republican
state represented: 2 MA
defeated: 4 (Henry) Clay **7** (Andrew) Jackson **8** (William H) Crawford
vice president: 7 (John C) Calhoun
cabinet:
  state: 4 (Henry) Clay
  treasury: 4 (Richard) Rush
  war: 6 (Peter Buell) Porter **7** (James) Barbour
  attorney general: 4 (William) Wirt
  navy: 8 (Samuel Lewis) Southard
born: 2 MA **9** Braintree
town now called: 6 Quincy
died: 2 DC **10** Washington
buried: 2 MA **6** Quincy
education:
  studied in: 5 Paris **9** Amsterdam **11** Latin School
  University of: 6 Leyden
  College: 7 Harvard
religion: 9 Unitarian
author: 7 Memoirs **14** Eulogy to Monroe, The Adams Papers **17** Eulogy to Lafayette **18** Letters from Silesia
political career: 8 US Senate **19** Massachusetts Senate **24** US House of Representatives
  secretary of: 5 state
  minister to: 6 Russia **7** Prussia **8** Portugal **11** Netherlands **12** Great Britain
civilian career: 6 lawyer
notable events of lifetime/term: 19 Pan-American Congress **20** Tariff of Abominations
father: 4 John
mother: 7 Abigail (Smith)
siblings: 7 Abigail, Charles, Susanna **14** Thomas Boylston
wife: 6 Louisa (Catherine Johnson)
children: 4 John **14** Charles Francis **15** Louisa Catherine **16** George Washington

Adams, Parson
character in: 13 Joseph Andrews
author: 8 Fielding

Adams, Richard
author of: 4 Maia **7** Shardik **12** Girl in a Swing **13** The Plague Dogs, Watership Down

Adam's Rib
director: 11 George Cukor

script by: 10 Ruth Gordon 11 Garson Kanin

cast: 8 Tom Ewell 9 Jean Hagen 10 David Wayne 12 Judy Holliday, Spencer Tracy 16 Katharine Hepburn

adapt 3 fit 4 suit 5 alter, frame, shape 6 adjust, change, modify, rework 7 conform, convert, fashion, make fit, remodel, reshape 8 attune to 9 acclimate, harmonize, recompose, reconcile, transform 10 assimilate, coordinate 11 accommodate, acculturate 12 make suitable

adaptable 6 pliant, usable 7 unrigid 8 amenable, flexible, obliging 9 alterable, compliant, easygoing, malleable, tractable 10 adjustable, applicable, changeable, open-minded 11 conformable, serviceable 13 accommodating, accommodative

adaptation 5 shift 6 change 8 revision 9 refitting, reshaping, reworking 10 adjustment, alteration, conversion, remodeling 12 modification 13 metamorphosis

Adar 18 twelfth Hebrew month

add 4 join 5 affix, sum up, total 6 append, attach, join on, reckon, tack on 7 combine, compute, count up, enlarge, include 8 figure up, increase 9 calculate, enlarge by 10 increase by, supplement

Addams, Frankie
character in: 19 A Member of the Wedding
author: 15 Carson McCullers

Addams Family, The
character: 5 Gomez, Lurch 7 Pugsley 8 Morticia 9 Cousin Itt, Grandmama, Wednesday 11 Uncle Fester
cast: 9 John Astin 10 Lisa Loring, Ted Cassidy 11 Blossom Rock 12 Carolyn Jones, Jackie Coogan 13 Ken Weatherwax

add details 6 expand 7 clarify 9 elaborate, embellish 13 particularize

added 5 bonus, extra 6 joined 7 totaled 8 appended, attached, computed, included, joined on, reckoned, summed up, tacked on 9 counted up 10 additional, enlarged by, enumerated 11 increased by 13 supplementary

addendum 7 codicil 8 addition 9 appendage 10 attachment, postscript, supplement 12 afterthought

addict 3 fan, nut 4 buff, head, hook, user 5 freak, hound 6 junkie, submit, turn on, votary 7 acolyte, devotee, druggie, habitue 8 adherent 9 dope fiend, indulge in, surrender

addiction 5 craze, mania, quirk 6 fetish, hangup 8 fixation 9 cocainism, obsession 10 alcoholism, compulsion, dipsomania, morphinism 11 barbiturism, enslavement 12 addictedness, enthrallment 13 preoccupation

adding machine
invented by: 6 Pascal 9 Burroughs

Addis Ababa
capital of: 8 Ethiopia

Addison, Joseph
author of: 4 Cato 9 The Tatler 12 The Spectator 13 The Freeholder
co-author: 13 Richard Steele

addition 4 wing 5 annex, extra 6 adding 7 adjunct, joining 8 addendum, additive, annexing, increase, totaling 9 adjoining, appendage, appending, attaching, embracing, expansion, extending, extension, including, increment, reckoning, summation, summing up 10 counting up, increasing 11 enlargement, enumeration 12 appurtenance, augmentation, encompassing

additional 5 added, extra, spare 7 added on 8 appended 12 over-and-above 13 supplementary

additional feature 5 extra 7 adjunct 10 attachment, complement, supplement 12 appurtenance 13 accompaniment

additive 5 extra 8 addition 10 adulterant, supplement 12 augmentation, preservative

addle 5 mix up 6 muddle 7 confuse, nonplus, stupefy 8 befuddle

addled 5 silly 7 foolish, mixed-up, muddled 8 confused 9 befuddled, nonplused 10 nonplussed

add on 5 affix 6 append, attach, tack on 7 include 10 increase by

address 4 talk 5 greet, orate 6 salute, speech, talk to 7 lecture, oration, speak to, write to 8 dwelling, locality, location 9 discourse, statement

Address to the Deil
author: 11 Robert Burns

add to 6 expand, extend, pad out 7 amplify, augment, bolster, enlarge 8 compound, increase, lengthen 10 strengthen, stretch out, supplement

Ade, George
author of: 13 Fables in Slang 15 The College Widow 17 The County Chairman

Aden
seaport of: 5 Yemen
Gulf in: Arabian Sea

adept 3 apt 4 able, good 6 adroit, expert, gifted, master 7 skilled 8 skillful 9 dexterous, ingenious, masterful, practiced 10 proficient 12 accomplished

adequacy 7 fitness 11 sufficiency 16 satisfactoriness

adequate 3 fit 4 so-so 5 ample 6 enough 7 fitting 8 passable, suitable 9 tolerable 10 sufficient 12 satisfactory

a deux 6 for two 10 two at a time

ad extremum 6 at last 7 finally 12 to the extreme

ad fin 8 at the end 12 toward the end

adhere 3 fix 4 glue, hold, keep 5 cling, paste, stick 6 be true, cement, cleave, fasten, glue on, keep to 7 abide by, be loyal, stand by 8 maintain 9 stick fast 10 be constant, be faithful

adherence 6 fealty 7 loyalty 8 adhesion, devotion, fidelity 9 constancy, keeping to, obedience 10 allegiance, attachment, observance, stickiness 12 adhesiveness, faithfulness

adherent 3 fan 4 ally 5 gummy, pupil 6 sticky, viscid 7 acolyte, devotee, viscous 8 adhering, adhesive, advocate, champion, clinging, disciple, follower, partisan, sticking, upholder 9 supporter

adhesion 9 adherence 10 attachment, sticking to

adhesive 4 glue 5 epoxy, gummy, paste 6 cement, gummed, mortar, solder, sticky 7 stickum 8 adherent, adhering, clinging, sticking 12 mucilaginous, rubber cement

ad hoc 17 with respect to this 18 for this purpose only

ad hominem 8 to the man 17 against an opponent 20 appealing to prejudice

adieu 4 by-by, ciao, ta-ta 5 adios, aloha 6 bye-bye, goodby, so long 7 a demain, cheerio, goodbye, good day 8 a bientot, au revoir, farewell, godspeed, toodle-oo 10 take it easy 11 leavetaking, see you later, valediction 14 Auf Wiedersehen

ad infinitum 9 endlessly 10 infinitely, to infinity, unendingly 11 boundlessly, ceaselessly, limitlessly, unceasingly 12 continuously, interminably, without limit

ad initium 14 at the beginning

ad interim 13 in the meantime

adios 4 by-by, ciao, ta-ta 5 adieu, aloha 6 bye-bye, goodby, so long 7 a demain, au revoir, farewell, godspeed, toodle-oo 10 take it easy 11 leavetaking, see you later, valediction 14 Auf Wiedersehen

adjacent 6 beside, next to 8 abutting, touching 9 bordering, proximate 10 contiguous, juxtaposed, next door to, tangential 12 conterminous

adjoining 6 joined 7 joining 8 next-door, touching 9 connected 10 contiguous 14 interconnected

adjourn 3 end 4 move 5 close 6 put off, recess, remove, repair 7 dismiss, suspend 8 break off, dissolve, postpone, withdraw 9 depart for, interrupt 11 discontinue

adjournment 6 recess 7 removal 8 abeyance 9 dismissal 10 suspension 12 postponement

adjudge 4 deem, rule 5 judge 6 decide, decree, ordain, rule on, settle, umpire **7** referee **8** consider **9** arbitrate, determine, pronounce **10** adjudicate

adjudicate 4 rule **5** judge **6** settle **7** adjudge **9** arbitrate

adjunct 9 accessory, auxiliary, secondary **10** complement, incidental, subsidiary, supplement **12** appurtenance

adjuration 4 oath, plea, suit **6** appeal **8** advising, entreaty **12** supplication

adjure 3 beg **5** plead **6** charge, enjoin, exhort **7** beseech, command, entreat, implore, solicit **8** appeal to, petition **9** importune **10** supplicate

adjust 3 fix, set **4** move **5** adapt, alter, order, reset **6** attune, change, modify **7** conform **8** accustom, regulate **9** acclimate, reconcile **11** accommodate

adjustable 7 movable **9** adaptable, alterable **11** rectifiable, regulatable **12** controllable

adjusting 8 adapting, altering **9** modifying **10** regulating **11** acclimating, controlling

adjusting device 5 lever, tuner, valve **6** handle **7** adapter **8** governor **9** modulator, regulator **11** control knob

adjustment 6 fixing **7** control, setting **8** adapting, focusing **9** adjusting, alignment, regulator **10** alteration, regulating, regulation, settlement, settling in **11** acclimation, orientation **12** modification **13** justification, rectification, straightening **14** reconciliation

adjutant 3 ADC **4** aide **9** assistant, right hand **10** aide-de-camp **12** right-hand man

ad-lib 6 make up **9** improvise **11** extemporize **13** improvisation **14** speak impromptu **15** speak off the cuff **21** speak extemporaneously **23** extemporaneous wisecrack

ad loc, ad locum 10 at the place, to the place

ad majorem Dei gloriam 23 for the greater glory of God

Admete
father: **10** Eurystheus
received: **12** golden girdle
belonged to: **4** Ares
received from: **8** Hercules
stolen from: **9** Hippolyte

Admeto, Re di Tessaglia
also: **21** Admetus King of Thessaly
opera by: **6** Handel

Admetus
king of: **8** Thessaly
member of: **9** Argonauts
father: **6** Pheres
wife: **8** Alcestis

administer 3 run **4** boss, give **5** apply **6** direct, govern, manage, tender **7** oversee **8** dispense **9** supervise **11** preside over, superintend **12** administrate

administering 7 bossing, running,

tending **8** managing **9** directing, executing **10** dispensing, governance, overseeing **11** carrying out, supervising, supervision **14** administration, superintending

administration 5 brass **8** officers **9** execution, governing, tendering **10** executives, government, leadership, management, overseeing **11** application **12** dispensation, distribution **13** administering, governing body **15** superintendence

administrative 9 executive **10** management, managerial **11** supervisory **14** organizational

administrative head 3 CEO **7** manager **8** chairman, director **9** executive, president **10** supervisor **13** administrator **14** superintendent

admirable 6 worthy **8** laudable **9** estimable, venerable **11** commendable **12** praiseworthy

Admirable Crichton, The
author: **12** James M Barrie

admiration 5 honor **6** esteem, praise **7** respect **8** approval **10** high regard, veneration **11** high opinion **12** commendation

admire 5 prize, value **6** esteem, praise **7** respect

admirer 3 fan **5** swain **6** suitor, votary **7** acolyte, devotee, groupie **8** adherent, advocate, champion, disciple, follower, partisan **9** attendant **10** aficionado

admissible 7 allowed **8** passable **9** allowable, permitted, tolerable, tolerated **10** acceptable, admittable, legitimate **11** permissible

admission 3 fee **5** entry **6** access, assent, charge, entree, tariff, ticket **8** entrance **10** admittance, concession, confession, profession **11** affirmation, declaration, entrance fee **14** acknowledgment

admit 3 let **5** allow, grant, let in, own up **6** induct, invest, permit **7** appoint, concede, confess, declare, profess, receive, welcome **8** let enter **11** acknowledge

admittable 7 allowed **9** allowable, permitted, tolerable, tolerated **10** acceptable, admissible **11** permissible

admittance 5 entry **6** access, entree **7** ingress **8** entrance **10** admission

admixture 4 mess, olio **5** blend **6** jumble, medley **7** amalgam, melange, mixture **8** compound, mishmash **9** composite, confusion, potpourri **10** commixture, hodgepodge, salmagundi **11** combination, commingling, gallimaufry **12** amalgamation, intermixture **13** intermingling **14** conglomeration

admonish 4 warn **5** chide, scold **6** advise, enjoin, rebuke, tip off **7** caution, censure, chasten, counsel, reprove,

upbraid **8** reproach **9** criticize, reprimand **10** put on guard, take to task **11** remonstrate **13** call to account **16** rap on the knuckles

admonition 6 advice, rebuke **7** chiding, warning **8** reproach, scolding **9** reprimand **11** mild reproof **12** remonstrance **16** rap on the knuckles

Adnah
deserted from: **4** Saul
deserted to: **5** David
fought against: **10** Amalekites
commander for: **10** Jehosaphat

ado 4 fuss, stir, to-do **5** furor **6** bother, bustle, flurry, fracas, furore, hubbub, pother, racket, tumult, uproar **7** flutter, trouble, turmoil **9** agitation, commotion, confusion **10** hurlyburly

adobe 3 mud **4** clay, silt, tile **5** brick, marly **6** earthy **7** clayish **13** sun-dried brick

adolescence 5 teens, youth **7** puberty **10** pubescence

adolescent 3 lad **4** lass, teen **5** minor, youth **6** boyish, callow, lassie **7** babyish, girlish, puerile **8** childish, immature, juvenile, teenager, young man, youthful **9** fledgling, pubescent, schoolboy, stripling, young teen **10** schoolgirl, sophomoric, young woman **11** undeveloped

Adolf Hitler 9 der Fuhrer **10** der Fuehrer

Adonai 3 God **6** my Lord

Adonijah
father: **5** David
mother: **7** Haggith
brother: **5** Amnon **7** Absalom, Chileab
executed by: **7** Solomon
conspired to overthrow: **5** David

Adonis
represents: **15** vegetation cycle
father: **7** Cinyras
mother: **6** Myrrha, Smyrna
favorite of: **9** Aphrodite
killed by: **4** boar
festival in honor of: **6** Adonia

adopt 3 use **4** take **6** accept, affect, assume, choose, employ, follow, take up **7** approve, embrace, espouse, utilize **9** conform to **11** acknowledge, appropriate

adorable 4 cute **6** divine **7** darling, likable, lovable, winsome **8** charming, engaging, fetching, pleasing, precious **9** appealing **10** delightful **11** captivating **12** irresistible

adoration 5 honor **7** worship **8** devotion **9** adulation, reverence **10** exaltation, veneration, worshiping **11** idolization **13** glorification, magnification

adore 4 like, love **5** exalt, fancy, prize **6** admire, dote on, revere **7** cherish, glorify, idolize, worship **8** hold dear, venerate

adorer 3 fan **5** lover **7** admirer **8** follower **9** worshiper

adorn 5 array **6** bedeck **7** bejewel, deck out, furbish **8** beautify, decorate, ornament **9** embellish

adornment 6 attire, finery **7** jewelry **8** ornament **10** decoration **13** embellishment, ornamentation

ad patres 4 dead

Adrammelech 13 Sepharvite god
father: 11 Sennacherib
killed: 11 Sennacherib

Adrastea
also: 7 Nemesis
origin: 5 Greek
goddess of: 17 divine retribution
father: 9 Melisseus
reared: 4 Zeus
entrusted by: 4 Rhea

Adrastus
also: 8 Adrastos
king of: 5 Argos
son: 8 Aegialus
leader of: 18 Seven against Thebes
companions: 6 Tydeus **8** Capaneus **9** Polynices **10** Amphiaraus, Hippomedon **13** Parthenopaeus
horse: 5 Arion

ad rem 9 pertinent **15** straightforward **17** without digression

Adrian, Edgar Douglas
field: 8 medicine **10** physiology
nationality: 7 British
discovered function of: 10 nerve cells
awarded: 10 Nobel Prize

Adriana
character in: 17 The Comedy of Errors
author: 11 Shakespeare

adrift 4 lost **5** at sea **6** afloat, aweigh **8** confused, drifting, unmoored, unstable **9** perplexed, uncertain, unsettled **10** bewildered, irresolute, unanchored

adroit 3 apt **4** deft **5** slick **6** artful, clever, expert, facile, nimble **7** cunning, skilled **8** skillful **9** dexterous, masterful **10** proficient

adroitness 7 aptness **8** deftness, facility **9** dexterity, handiness **10** cleverness **11** proficiency **12** skillfulness
French: 11 savoir-faire

adulation 7 fawning **8** flattery **9** adoration **11** fulsomeness **13** fulsome praise

adulatory 7 fulsome **8** admiring **10** flattering **13** complimentary

adult 3 big, man **5** elder, of age, woman **6** father, granny, mature, mother, parent, senior, x-rated **7** grandma, grandpa, grownup, oldster **8** seasoned **9** developed, full-grown **11** experienced, grandfather, grandmother **13** senior citizen

adulterate 3 cut **4** thin **5** water **6** dilute **9** water down **10** depreciate **11** contaminate

adulterated 3 cut **6** impure, watery **7** debased, diluted, thinned, watered **8** doctored, weakened **11** watered down

adultery 3 sin **9** carnality, cuckoldry **10** unchastity **11** fornication, promiscuity **14** unfaithfulness **17** marital infidelity **18** illicit intercourse **21** extramarital relations

adulthood 8 maturity, ripeness **10** full growth **11** age of reason

adumbrate 3 dim **6** darken, sketch **7** obscure, outline **8** intimate **9** prefigure **10** foreshadow, overshadow

adumbrated 3 dim **5** murky **7** shadowy **8** darkened **9** intimated **10** indistinct, prefigured **12** foreshadowed, overshadowed

advance 3 pre **4** gain, lend, loan, pass, step **5** add to, offer, prior **6** assign, binder, growth, move up, pay now, propel, send up **7** bring up, forward, further, improve, in front, lay down, press on, proffer, promote, upgrade, up front **8** foremost, increase, multiply, overture, previous, progress **9** go forward, promotion **10** furthering, move onward, prepayment, put up front **11** advancement, down payment, improvement, preliminary, proposition **12** breakthrough, bring forward, pay on account

advanced 7 extreme, far gone, radical **10** avant-garde **12** farther along, further along **14** industrialized

advanced in years 3 old **4** aged **5** hoary, older **7** ancient, antique, elderly **8** outmoded **9** senescent, venerable **10** antiquated, gray-haired

advancement 4 rise **5** boost **9** bettering, elevation, promotion **10** betterment, forwarding **11** improvement, progression

advance slowly 4 inch **5** crawl, creep

advantage 3 aid **4** boon, edge, help **5** asset, clout **6** profit **7** benefit, comfort, service, success, support **8** blessing **9** dominance, upper hand **10** precedence **11** convenience, superiority

advantageous 6 useful **7** helpful **8** enviable, superior, valuable **9** favorable, fortunate **10** auspicious, beneficial, dominating, profitable

advent 5 onset, start **6** coming **7** arrival **9** appearing, beginning, emergence, opening up **10** appearance, occurrence **12** commencement

adventitious 5 alien **6** exotic **7** foreign, strange **9** adventive, extrinsic **10** accidental

adventure 5 geste, quest **7** emprise, venture **8** escapade **10** enterprise **11** undertaking

adventurer 4 hero **7** heroine, upstart **8** romantic, vagabond **9** buccaneer, daredevil **11** giant-killer **12** dragonslayer, swashbuckler **16** soldier of fortune

Adventures of Robin Hood, The
director: 13 Michael Curtiz **15** William Keighley
cast: 8 Alan Hale (Little John) **10** Errol Flynn (Robin Hood) **11** Claude Rains (Prince John) **13** Basil Rathbone **17** Olivia de Havilland (Lady Marion)
Oscar for: 5 score (Erich Wolfgang Korngold)

Adventures of Sherlock Holmes
author: 16 (Sir) Arthur Conan Doyle
character: 9 Mrs Hudson **11** Irene Adler **12** Dr John Watson **13** Mycroft Holmes **14** Sherlock Holmes **17** Inspector Lestrade, Professor Moriarty **21** Baker Street Irregulars

adventuresome 4 bold **6** daring **9** audacious, daredevil **11** adventurous

adventurous 4 bold **5** brave, risky **6** daring **7** valiant **8** intrepid, perilous **9** audacious, dangerous, hazardous **10** courageous **11** challenging, venturesome

ad verbum 8 verbatim **9** to the word

adversary 3 foe **5** enemy, rival **8** opponent **10** antagonist, competitor

adverse 3 ill **4** evil **7** harmful, hostile **8** contrary, inimical, negative, opposing **9** difficult, injurious **10** pernicious, unfriendly **11** detrimental, unfavorable **12** antagonistic, unpropitious

adversity 3 woe **4** ills **5** trial **6** mishap **7** bad luck, trouble **8** calamity, disaster, distress, hardship **9** suffering **10** affliction, ill-fortune, misfortune **11** catastrophe, tribulation

advertise 4 show, tout **5** vaunt **6** reveal **7** display **8** proclaim **9** broadcast, publicize **11** noise abroad

advertisement 4 spot **5** blurb, flier, pitch, promo **6** notice, poster, want ad **7** leaflet, placard, trailer **8** circular, handbill **9** billboard, broadside, throwaway **10** commercial **12** announcement, classified ad, public notice

advice 4 news, view, word **6** report **7** account, counsel, message, opinion, tidings **8** guidance **10** advisement, suggestion **11** information **12** intelligence, notification **13** communication **14** recommendation

advisable 3 fit **4** best, wise **5** smart, sound **6** proper, seemly **7** fitting, prudent **8** a good bet, suitable **9** expedient, judicious **13** recommendable

advise 4 tell, urge, warn **6** enjoin, exhort, inform, notify, report **7** apprise, caution, commend, counsel, suggest **8** admonish **9** encourage, make known, recommend, suggest to **10** give notice **11** communicate

advise against 5 deter 8 dissuade 10 discourage, disincline

advisement 5 study 7 thought 12 deliberation 13 consideration

adviser, advisor 4 aide 5 coach, guide, tutor 6 egeria, mentor, nestor 7 monitor, teacher 8 Dear Abby, director 9 admonitor, assistant, counselor, preceptor, surrogate 10 Ann Landers, consultant, idea person, instructor

advisory 7 caution, guiding, warning 10 admonitory, cautionary, counseling 11 informative, instructive 12 consultative, consultatory 13 informational

advisory board 7 cabinet, council 8 ministry

advocaat
> type: 7 liqueur
> origin: 7 Holland

advocacy 4 egis 5 aegis 7 backing, defense, support 8 auspices, espousal 9 patronage, promotion 10 furthering, supporting 11 advancement, endorsement, pressing for, propagation, sponsorship 12 championship 14 campaigning for, recommendation

advocate 4 back, urge 5 favor 6 advise, backer, lawyer, patron 7 advance, apostle, counsel, endorse, espouse, further, pleader, promote, propose, push for, support 8 argue for, attorney, believer, champion, defender, press for, promoter, upholder 9 apologist, barrister, counselor, encourage, prescribe, propagate, proponent, recommend, solicitor, spokesman, supporter 10 mouthpiece, stand up for 11 campaign for, speak out for 12 legal adviser, propagandist, spokesperson 13 attorney-at-law

advocatus diaboli 14 devil's advocate

adz or **adze** 2 ax 3 axe 5 addis 7 hatchet

Aeacus
> descendants of: 8 Aeacides
> form: 5 judge
> habitat: 5 Hades
> father: 4 Zeus
> mother: 6 Aegina
> brother: 12 Rhadamanthys
> wife: 6 Endeis
> son: 6 Peleus, Phocus 7 Telamon
> grandson: 8 Achilles

Aeetes
> king of: 7 Colchis
> custodian of: 12 Golden Fleece
> father: 6 Helios
> mother: 5 Perse
> sister: 5 Circe 8 Pasiphae
> wife: 5 Idyia 9 Asterodea
> son: 8 Absyrtus, Apsyrtus
> daughter: 5 Medea 9 Chalciope

Aegaeon see 8 Briareus

Aegean Sea
> branch of: 13 Mediterranean
> islands: 5 Chios, Crete, Samos 6 Eu-
> boea, Lesbos, Rhodes 8 Cyclades 10 Dodecanese 16 Northern Sporades
> rivers into: 6 Struma, Vardar 7 Maritsa 8 Menderes
> surrounding countries: 6 Greece, Turkey

Aegeon
> character in: 17 The Comedy of Errors
> author: 11 Shakespeare

Aegeria see 6 Egeria

Aegesta see 6 Egesta

Aegeus
> king of: 6 Athens
> son: 6 Medeus 7 Theseus

Aegimius
> king of: 5 Doris 7 Dorians
> father: 5 Dorus
> son: 5 Dymas 9 Pamphylus

Aeginaea
> epithet of: 7 Artemis
> means: 11 goat goddess

Aegir
> origin: 6 Nordic
> form: 5 giant
> god of: 3 sea
> wife: 3 Ran

aegis 4 wing 5 favor, guard 6 surety 7 backing, shelter, support 8 advocacy, auspices, guaranty 9 patronage 10 protection 11 sponsorship 12 championship, guardianship

Aegis
> form: 6 shield
> shield of: 4 Zeus 6 Athena

Aegisthus
> father: 8 Thyestes
> mother: 7 Pelopia
> cousin: 9 Agamemnon
> daughter: 7 Erigone
> seduced by: 12 Clytemnestra
> killed by: 7 Orestes

Aegle
> member of: 8 Heliades 10 Hesperides
> mother of: 6 Graces

Aegyptus
> king of: 5 Egypt
> father: 5 Belus
> twin brother: 6 Danaus
> number of sons: 5 fifty

Aella
> form: 6 Amazon
> gift: 9 swiftness
> killed by: 8 Hercules

Aello
> member of: 7 Harpies

aelurophobia
> fear of: 4 cats

Aemilia
> character in: 17 The Comedy of Errors
> author: 11 Shakespeare

Aeneas
> hero of: 4 Troy
> father: 8 Anchises
> mother: 5 Venus

> grandfather: 5 Capys
> son: 5 Iulus 7 Silvius 8 Ascanius
> ancestor of: 6 Romans

Aeneas Silvius
> king of: 9 Alba Longa

Aeneid
> author: 6 Virgil
> character: 4 Gyas 5 Amata, Dares, Nisus 6 Arruns, Iarbas, Lausus, Pallas, Salius, Turnus 7 Acestes, Allecto, Camilla, Celaeno, Drances, Evander, Harpies, Helenus, Juturna, Latinus, Lavinia, Tarchon, Trojans, Venulus, Virbius 8 Ascanius, Entellus, Euryalus, Messapus 9 Cloanthus, Mezentius, Mnestheus, Palinurus, Sergestus 10 Andromache 12 Cumaean Sibyl
> gods: 4 Juno 5 Diana, Venus 6 Vulcan 7 Jupiter, Neptune
> Queen of Carthage: 4 Dido
> Aeneas' father: 8 Anchises
> Aeneas' mother: 9 Aphrodite
> Aeneas' wife: 6 Creusa
> Aeneas' son: 5 Iulus
> Aeneas meets in underworld: 6 Charon 8 Cerberus 9 Palinurus
> parts of the underworld: 7 Elysium 8 Tartarus 9 Ivory Gate
> river: 4 Styx 5 Lethe
> Aeneas plucks: 11 Golden Bough
> Aeneas visits: 5 Crete, Delos 6 Latium, Sicily, Thrace 8 Carthage

Aeolus
> other name: 5 Eolis
> ruler of: 5 winds
> founder of: 8 Aeolians
> father: 6 Hellen
> mother: 6 Orseis
> brother: 5 Dorus 6 Xuthus
> wife: 7 Enarete
> son: 5 Deion 6 Magnes 7 Athamas, Misenus 8 Cretheus, Macareus, Perieres, Sisyphus 9 Salmoneus
> daughter: 6 Calyce, Canace 7 Alcyone 8 Cleobule, Perimede, Pisidice

aerate 3 air 9 ventilate 10 mix with air 11 expose to air

aerial 3 air 4 airy 5 by air, lofty 6 dreamy, flying, unreal 7 antenna, elusive, soaring, tenuous 8 airborne, ethereal, fanciful, in the air 9 ephemeral, imaginary, visionary 10 by aircraft, from the air, of aircraft 11 atmospheric, impractical, wind-created 13 unsubstantial 15 capable of flight

aerobatic group 10 Blue Angels

aeronautics 6 flight, flying 8 aviation

Aerope
> father: 7 Catreus, Cerheus
> husband: 6 Atreus 10 Plisthenes
> sister: 9 Clymene
> son: 8 Menelaus 9 Agamemnon

aerophobia
> fear of: 6 flying

aeroplane 5 plane 8 aircraft, airplane

Aeschylus
   author of: 8 Oresteia 9 Agamemnon, Choephori (The Libation-bearers), Eumenides 11 The Persians 13 The Suppliants 15 Prometheus Bound 16 The House of Atreus 18 Seven Against Thebes

Aesculapius
   origin: 5 Roman
   god of: 7 healing 8 medicine
   corresponds to: 9 Asclepius

Aesir
   also: 4 Asar
   means: 9 chief gods
   origin: 12 Scandinavian
   leader: 4 Odin 5 Othin
   home: 6 Asgard
   conflicting with: 5 Vanir

aesthetic see 8 Esthetic

Aethalides
   member of: 9 Argonauts
   father: 6 Hermes
   trait: 6 memory

Aether
   origin: 5 Greek
   personifies: 3 air, sky

Aethra
   father: 8 Pittheus
   son: 7 Theseus

Aethylla
   brother: 5 Priam

Afars and the Issas see 8 Djibouti

affability 9 geniality 10 amiability, cordiality 11 sociability 12 friendliness, pleasantness 13 compatibility

affable 4 open, warm 5 civil 6 genial 7 amiable, cordial 8 friendly, gracious, mannerly, pleasant, sociable 9 agreeable, congenial, courteous, easygoing 10 compatible 11 good-humored, good-natured

affair 5 amour, event, party 6 effort, matter 7 concern, episode, liaison, pursuit, romance, shindig 8 activity, business, function, incident, interest, intrigue, occasion 9 adventure, festivity, happening, operation 10 love affair, occurrence, proceeding 11 celebration, transaction, undertaking 12 circumstance, relationship 14 social function 15 social gathering

affaire d'honneur 4 duel 13 affair of honor

affect 4 fake, move, stir 5 act on, adopt, alter, fancy, feign, put on, touch 6 assume, change, modify, regard 7 embrace, concern, imitate, impress 8 interest, relate to, simulate 9 impinge on, influence, pertain to, pretend to 10 tend toward 11 counterfeit

affectation 4 airs, sham 5 put-on 6 facade 8 false air, pretense 10 pretension 11 insincerity 13 artificiality, false mannerism

affected 4 vain 5 moved, phony, sorry, upset 6 harmed, la-di-da, un-

real 7 assumed, changed, grieved, injured, pompous, stirred, studied, touched 8 impaired, mannered, troubled 9 acted upon, afflicted, concerned, conceited, contrived, impressed, pertinent, sorrowful, unnatural 10 artificial, distressed, influenced, interested, not genuine 11 pretentious 12 vainglorious

affectedness 4 airs 7 hauteur, tension 9 formality 10 constraint 11 haughtiness, pretensions 12 affectations 15 pretentiousness

affection 4 love 6 liking, malady, warmth 7 ailment, disease, illness 8 disorder, fondness, sickness 10 proclivity, tenderness

affectionate 4 fond, warm 6 ardent, caring, doting, loving, tender 10 lovey-dovey 11 warmhearted 13 demonstrative, tenderhearted

affectionate term 3 hon 4 dear 5 cheri, honey, sugar 7 pet name, sweetie, darling, dearest 8 nickname 9 sobriquet 10 endearment

Affery
   character in: 12 Little Dorrit
   author: 7 Dickens

affettuoso
   music: 8 tenderly

affiance 6 engage, pledge 7 betroth 13 engage to marry 15 solemnly promise

affiancing 5 troth 8 pledging 9 betrothal 10 engagement

affiche 6 poster 12 public notice

affidavit 4 oath 8 document 11 affirmation 14 sworn statement

affiliate 3 arm 4 ally, join, part 5 merge, unite 6 branch 7 chapter, connect, consort 8 division 9 associate, colleague 10 amalgamate, fraternize 11 incorporate, subdivision 12 band together

affiliated 6 allied, joined, united 9 connected 10 associated 12 incorporated

affiliation 5 union 8 alliance 10 connection 11 association 12 relationship

affinity 4 bent 5 fancy 6 liking 7 leaning, rapport 8 fondness, homology, likeness, penchant, relation, sympathy, tendency 10 connection, partiality, proclivity, propensity, similarity 11 inclination, parallelism 13 compatibility

affirm 4 aver, avow, hold 5 claim 6 allege, assert, ratify, uphold 7 approve, confirm, contend, declare, endorse, profess, support, sustain, warrant 8 maintain, proclaim, validate

affirmation 6 avowal 7 consent 8 approval 11 declaration, endorsement 12 confirmation, ratification 13 certification

affirmative 3 yes 8 emphatic, positive 9 affirming, approving, assenting, rati-

fying 10 conclusive, concurring, confirming 11 affirmatory, categorical 12 confirmatory 13 corroborative

affix 3 fix, tag 4 glue, seal 5 add on, paste, put on, set to, stick 6 attach, fasten, tack on

afflict 5 beset 6 plague 7 oppress, torment 8 distress

afflicted 6 cursed 7 plagued 8 affected, troubled 9 tormented 10 distressed

affliction 4 pain 5 curse, trial 6 misery, ordeal 7 anguish, torment, trouble 8 calamity, distress, hardship 9 adversity 10 misfortune, oppression 11 tribulation 12 wretchedness

affluence 5 money 6 plenty, riches, wealth 7 success 10 prosperity 14 prosperousness, successfulness

affluent 4 rich 6 loaded 7 moneyed, wealthy, well-off 8 well-to-do 9 well-fixed 10 prosperous, well-heeled

afford 4 bear, give, lend, risk 5 grant, offer, yield 6 chance, impart, manage, supply 7 command, furnish, provide, support, sustain

affray 4 fray 5 brawl, melee 6 fracas 7 contest, scuffle 8 conflict 9 encounter 11 altercation

affright 4 fear 5 alarm, dread, panic, scare 6 dismay, fright, horror, terror 8 frighten

affront 4 slur 5 abuse, wrong 6 injury, insult, offend, slight 7 offense, outrage, provoke, put-down 8 disgrace, dishonor, ignominy, rudeness 9 indignity, insolence 11 discourtesy, humiliation 12 ill-treatment, impertinence 13 mortification 16 contemptuousness

afghan 5 shawl, throw 7 blanket 8 covering, coverlet

Afghanistan
   other name: 6 Ariana, Aryana
   capital/largest city: 5 Kabul
   others: 3 Rui 4 Jurm, Nani, Wama 5 Asmar, Balkh, Doshi, Farah, Herat, Kunar, Makur, Maruf, Matun, Pahra, Tagab, Tulak, Urgan 6 Chaman, Gardez, Ghazni, Haibak, Kunduz, Nauzad, Panjao, Rustak, Sangan, Sarobi, Tukzar, Washir 7 Andkhui, Baghlan, Bamiyan, Dilaram, Ghurian, Girishk 8 Charikar, Faizabad, Kandahar 9 Jalalabad 10 Daulatabad, Pul-i-Khumri, Shibarghan 12 Mazar-i-Sharif
   government:
      parliament: 10 Loya-Jirgah
      radical group: 7 Taliban
   leader: 4 amir, emir 5 ameer, emeer 6 sharif, sherif
   measure: 3 paw, sir 5 jerib, karoh 6 khurds 7 kharwar
   monetary unit: 3 pul 5 abaze, riyal, rupee 6 abbasi, amania 7 afghani
   weight: 3 pau, paw, ser, sir
   lake: 13 Hamud-i-Helmand

mountain: 3 Koh **5** Safeo **6** Chagai, Pamirs **7** Nowshak **8** Koh-i-Baba, Safed Koh, Sulaiman **9** Himalayas, Hindu Kush **11** Khwaja Amran, Paropamisus

highest point: 9 Istoro Nal

river: 4 Lora, Oxus **5** Cabul, Indus, Kabul, Kunar **6** Kokcha, Kunduz **7** Hari Rud, Helmand, Helmund, Murghab, Taleqan **8** Amu Darya, Farah Rud, Harut Rud, Khash Rud **9** Arghandab

sea: 5 Darya

physical feature:
  desert: 8 Registan
  panhandle: 6 Wakhan
  pass: 6 Khyber
  wind: 9 Afghanets

people: 5 Aimak, Aymak, Kafir, Nuris **6** Baloch, Baluch, Chahar, Durani, Hasara, Hazara, Kaffir, Kirgiz, Pathan, Tajiks, Uzbeks **7** Beluchi, Belucki, Ghilzai, Pakhton, Pakhtun, Pashtun, Pukhtun, Pushtun, Sistani, Taimani, Taimuri **8** Jamshidi, Siah Push **9** Firuzkuhi, Safed Push, Safid Push

  dynasty: 8 Barakzai
  leader: 5 Najib **6** Karzai **7** Mohmand **10** Najibullah **12** Babrak Karmal **14** Hafizullah Amin **17** Mohammad Zahir Shah, Mohammed Daoud Khan **18** Burhanuddin Rabbani Noor Mohammed Taraki

language: 4 Dari **5** Farsi **6** Afghan, Pashto, Pushtu **7** Balochi, Baluchi, Persian

religion: 5 Islam

place:
  dam: 6 Boghra **7** Kajakai **9** Arghandab
  feature:
    clothing: 7 chaderi
    coat: 6 chapan
    dance: 5 attan
    game: 8 buz-kashi
    guest room: 5 hujra
    hat: 7 karakul
    head-cloth: 7 chawdar
    house with tower: 4 qala
    medicinal plant: 9 asafetida
    wrestling: 6 ghosai
  food:
    potluck meal: 6 sohbat

aficionado 3 fan, nut **5** freak, pupil **7** devotee, pursuer, student **8** disciple

afield 5 amiss **6** abroad, astray **10** off the mark **11** out of the way **16** off the right track

afire 5 fiery **6** ablaze, aflame, alight, ardent, fervid, fuming, on fire **7** blazing, burning, fervent, flaming, flaring, glowing, ignited, smoking, zealous **8** aflicker, in flames, inspired **10** flickering, smoldering

afloat 5 at sea **6** adrift, wafted **7** sailing, wafting **8** drifting, floating

afoot 5 astir **8** underway **10** in the works

a fortiori 10 all the more

afraid 5 sorry **6** scared **7** alarmed, anxious, chicken, fearful, panicky, unhappy **8** cowardly, timorous **9** regretful, terrified **10** apologetic, frightened **11** lily-livered **12** apprehensive, disappointed, fainthearted **13** anxiety-ridden, panic-stricken **14** chicken-hearted, chicken-livered, terror-stricken

Afreet
  also: 5 Afrit
  origin: 7 Arabian
  form: 5 demon

afresh 4 anew **5** again **11** from scratch **16** from the beginning
  Latin: 6 de novo

Africa
  country: 4 Chad, Mali, Togo **5** Benin, Congo, Egypt, Gabon, Ghana, Kenya, Libya, Niger, Sudan, Zaire **6** Angola, Gambia, Guinea, Malawi, Rwanda, Uganda, Zambia **7** Algeria, Burundi, Comoros, Eritrea, Lesotho, Liberia, Morocco, Namibia, Nigeria, Reunion, Senegal, Somalia, Tunisia **8** Botswana, Cameroon, Djibouti, Ethiopia, Tanzania, Zimbabwe **9** Cape Verde, The Gambia, Mauritius, Swaziland **10** Ivory Coast, Madagascar, Mauritania, Mozambique, Seychelles **11** Burkina Faso, Sierra Leone, South Africa **12** Guinea-Bissau **13** Western Sahara **15** South-West Africa **16** Equatorial Guinea **18** Sao Tome and Principe **22** Central African Republic
  people: 2 Ga **3** Ibo, Kru, Luo, San, Tiv, Yao **4** Arab, Beja, Bobo, Boer, Fang, Hutu, Kota, Kuba, Luba, Nuba, Nuer, Nupe, Teda, Tibu, Zulu **5** Bemba, Dinka, Galla, Hausa, Kamba, Makua, Masai, Mende, Mongo, Negro, Pygmy, Rundi, Serer, Shona, Sotho, Swazi, Temne, Tigre, Tutsi, Wolof, Xhosa **6** Bateke, Berber, Fulani, Herero, Ibibjo, Kikuyu, Mau Mau, Nubian, Ovambo, Rwanda, Senufo, Sidamo, Somali, Tswana, Tuareg, Yoruba, Watusi **7** Ashanti, Baganda, Bambara, Bushmen, Chaamba, Makonde, Mashoma, Ndebele, Nilotic, Oshogbo, Songhai, Turkana **8** Khoikhoi, Mangbetu, Matabele **9** Africaner, Afrikaner, Hottentot
  desert: 5 Namib **6** Sahara **8** Kalahari
  island: 5 Bioko, Pemba **6** Canary **7** Comoros, Madeira, Mayotte, Reunion **8** St Helena, Zanzibar **9** Ascension, Cape Verde, Mauritius **10** Madagascar, Seychelles
  ancient people/empire: 3 Oyo **4** Kush, Mali, Toro **5** Aksum, Benin, Ghana, Kongo, Mossi, Nubia, Wadai **6** Ankole, Tekrur **7** Ashanti, Buganda, Bunyoro, Dahomey, Songhai **8** Baguirmi, Carthage **10** Kanem-

Bornu, Monomotapa **11** Ife and Benin
  ancient city: 5 Kilwa, Meroe **8** Timbuktu
  language: 4 Afar, Peul, Teda **5** Bantu, Bemba, Click, Hausa, Masai, Wolof **6** Arabic, Berber, French, Kanuri, Tsonga **7** Amharic, Khoisan, Lingala, Nilotic, Songhai, Swahili, Turkana **8** Cushitic, Mandingo **9** Afrikaans
  river: 4 Juba, Nile, Sudd **5** Congo, Kasai, Niger **6** Kwango, Orange, Ubangi **7** Senegal, Zambezi **8** Blue Nile **9** White Nile
  lake: 4 Chad, Kivu, Tana **5** Assal, Nyasa **6** Albert, Edward, Kariba, Malawi, Nassar, Red Sea, Rudolf **8** Victoria **10** Tanganyika **12** Chott Melrhir
  falls: 8 Victoria
  mountain/mountain range: 3 Air **4** Bihu, Meru **5** Atlas, Elgon, Kenya **6** Hoggar **7** Ahaggar, Crystal, Tibesti, Toubkal **8** Cameroon **9** Emi Koussi, Munchinga, Ruwenzori **10** Futa Jallon **11** Drakensberg, Kilimanjaro **13** Tibesti Massif
  lowest point: 17 Qattari Depression
  mineral/natural resource: 3 oil, tin **4** gold **5** ivory **6** cloves, copper, rubber **7** diamond, palm oil, uranium
  disease: 4 AIDS **5** Ebola **7** malaria **9** bilharzia **11** yellow fever **16** sleeping sickness
  homeland: 5 Venda **6** Ciskei **8** Transkei **14** Bophuthatswana
  game reserve: 5 Tsavo **6** Kruger **8** Amboseli **9** Serengeti
  tree: 4 cork, teak **5** cedar, ebony, olive **6** acacia, baobab, okoume, rubber **7** juniper, oil palm **8** date palm, mahogany, tamarisk **10** silk-cotton
  animal: 4 lion **5** bongo, hippo, hyena, zebra **6** jackal, monkey **7** buffalo, cheetah, giraffe, gorilla, leopard, wild pig **8** aardvark, antelope, elephant **9** crocodile **10** chimpanzee, rhinoceros **11** wildebeeste **12** hippopotamus
  bird: 5 heron, stork **6** falcon **7** bustard, ostrich, pelican **8** flamingo, hornbill **10** kingfisher
  fly: 6 tsetse
  snake: 5 cobra, mamba **6** python

Africaine, L'
  also: 14 The African Girl
  opera by: 9 Meyerbeer

African Queen, The
  director: 10 John Huston
  cast: 12 Robert Morley **14** Humphrey Bogart **16** Katharine Hepburn
  setting: 5 Congo
  Oscar for: 5 actor (Bogart)

Afrit *see* **6** Afreet

after 4 next, post **5** later **6** behind **9** afterward, following **10** conclusion, subsequent, succeeding

aftereffect 6 result **11** consequence

Afterlife
  god of: **4** Gwyn

aftermath 6 payoff, result, sequel, upshot **7** outcome **8** follow-up, offshoot **9** byproduct **11** consequence

afterpart 4 back, tail **5** stern **6** far end **7** back end, rear end, tail end **8** backside, hind part **9** posterior

after the fact 4 late **5** tardy **7** belated, delayed, too late **10** behindhand, behind time

After the Fall
  author: **12** Arthur Miller

after this, therefore because of it
  Latin: **21** post hoc ergo propter hoc
  describes: **14** logical fallacy

afterword 4 coda **8** addendum, epilogue **10** conclusion

Agacles
  king of: **9** Myrmidons

Agag
  king of: **10** Amalekites
  captured by: **4** Saul
  killed by: **6** Samuel

again 3 bis **4** also, anew, more **6** encore **7** besides **8** moreover, once more **10** in addition, repetition **11** another time, duplication, furthermore **12** additionally
  Latin: **6** de novo

against 7 adverse, opposed **8** conflict, contrary, opposite **10** opposition **11** unfavorable

against an opponent
  Latin: **9** ad hominem

against the property
  Latin: **5** in rem
  describes: **15** legal proceeding

against the thing
  Latin: **5** in rem

Agamemnon
  author: **9** Aeschylus
  mentioned in: **5** Iliad
  king of: **7** Mycenae
  leader of: **6** Greeks
  fought in: **9** Trojan War
  father: **6** Atreus
  brother: **8** Menelaus
  sister: **8** Anaxibia
  wife: **12** Clytemnestra
  daughter: **7** Electra **9** Iphigenia **12** Chrysothemis
  son: **7** Orestes
  cousin: **9** Aegisthus
  captive: **9** Cassandra
  Clytemnestra's lover: **9** Aegisthus
  killed by: **12** Clytemnestra

Aganippe 8 fountain
  location: **6** Greece **7** Helicon
  sacred to: **5** Muses

Aganus
  father: **5** Paris
  mother: **5** Helen

agape 4 agog **6** amazed, gaping **8** wide open **9** awestruck, stupefied **10** astonished, dumbstruck, spellbound **11** dumbfounded **12** wonderstruck **13** flabbergasted

Agassiz, Jean Louis Rodolphe
  field: **7** zoology
  worked on: **7** fossils **8** glaciers **14** classification

agate
  species: **6** quartz
  variety of: **10** chalcedony
  type: **3** eye **4** moss, onyx, ring **9** landscape **13** fortification
  source: **4** Ider **6** Brazil **7** Uruguay **9** Oberstein **14** Rio Grande de Sul

Agathon
  father: **5** Priam

Agathyrsus
  father: **8** Hercules

Agave
  father: **6** Cadmus
  mother: **8** Harmonia
  sister: **3** Ino **6** Semele **7** Autonoe
  husband: **6** Echion
  son: **8** Pentheus

age 3 eon, era **4** date **5** epoch, phase, ripen **6** mature, mellow, period, season **7** develop, forever, make old **8** life span, lifetime **9** adulthood, a long time, grow older, seniority **10** generation, millennium **11** stage of life, stage of time
  French: **6** siecle

aged 3 old **4** ripe **6** mature, mellow **7** ancient, as old as, elderly, ripened **8** enduring, grown old **9** developed, full-grown, long-lived

Agee, James
  author of: **10** Agee on Film **17** A Death in the Family **23** Let Us Now Praise Famous Men
  screenwriter for: **15** The African Queen **19** The Night of the Hunter

Agelaus
  mentioned in: **5** Iliad **7** Odyssey
  occupation: **8** herdsman
  father: **8** Hercules, Phradmon
  mother: **7** Omphale
  courted: **8** Penelope
  raised: **5** Paris
  employer: **5** Priam

ageless 7 classic, eternal **8** enduring, timeless

agency 5 force, means, power **6** action, bureau, charge **8** activity **9** influence, mediation, operation **10** department, instrument **12** intervention **15** instrumentality

agenda 6 docket **7** program **8** schedule **9** timetable

agent 4 doer **5** cause, envoy, force, means, mover, power **6** agency, author, deputy, worker **7** vehicle **8** advocate, emissary, executor, operator **9** go-between, performer **10** instrument, negotiator **11** perpetrator **12** intermediary, practitioner **14** representative

Age of Innocence, The
  author: **12** Edith Wharton
  character: **10** May Welland **12** Ellen Olenska **13** Newland Archer

age-old 4 aged **7** ancient, antique, very old **9** venerable

agglomerate 4 clot, mass **5** amass, bunch, clump, rally **6** gather, heap up, muster, pile up **7** cluster, collect **8** assemble, condense, mobilize **10** accumulate, collection **12** accumulation, conglomerate, heap together, lump together **14** conglomeration **15** gather into a mass

agglomeration 4 heap, mass, pile **5** bunch, clump **7** cluster **10** collection **12** accumulation **14** conglomeration

aggrandize 5 bloat, exalt, widen **6** beef up, blow up, dilate, expand, extend, puff up, step up **7** amplify, broaden, build up, distend, enhance, enlarge, inflate, magnify, stretch **8** escalate, increase **9** intensify **10** strengthen

aggrandizement 8 increase, widening **9** expansion, extension **10** broadening, escalation, exaltation, stepping up **11** enhancement, enlargement **13** amplification, magnification **15** intensification

aggravate 3 vex **4** rile **5** anger, annoy **6** nettle, worsen **7** affront, inflame **8** heighten, increase, irritate **9** intensify, make worse **10** exacerbate, exasperate

aggravating 7 irksome **9** inflaming, vexatious, worsening **10** irritating **11** heightening **12** exacerbating, exasperating, intensifying

aggregate 3 mix **4** mass **5** blend, union **7** mixture **8** amassing, compound **9** composite, gathering, summation **10** collection **11** combination **12** accumulation, conglomerate **14** conglomeration

aggregation 3 mob **4** army, band, bevy, crew, gang, host, mass, pack **5** crowd, horde, swarm **6** throng **7** cluster **9** multitude **10** collection

aggression 4 raid **7** assault, offense **8** act of war, invasion **9** hostility, pugnacity **11** viciousness **12** belligerence **13** combativeness

aggressive 4 bold **5** harsh, pushy **7** dynamic, hostile, intense, vicious, warlike, warring, zealous **8** forceful, militant **9** ambitious, assailant, assertive, attacking, combative, energetic **10** pugnacious **11** belligerent, competitive, contentious, quarrelsome **12** antagonistic, enterprising **13** self-assertive **15** tending to attack

aggressiveness 9 hostility, pugnacity **10** antagonism **12** belligerence **13** combativeness

aggressor 7 invader **8** attacker **9** assailant **11** belligerent **12** antagonistic

aggrieved 3 sad **4** hurt **5** stung **6** abused, pained **7** injured, put upon, tearful, wounded, wronged **8** grieving, mournful, offended, saddened, troubled **9** affronted, disturbed, sorrowful **10** distressed, ill-treated, maltreated, persecuted **11** imposed upon **13** grief-stricken

aghast 6 amazed **7** shocked, stunned **8** appalled **9** astounded, horrified, terrified **10** astonished, fear-struck, frightened **12** horror-struck **13** thunderstruck

agile 4 keen, spry **5** alert, fleet, lithe, quick, swift **6** active, clever, limber, nimble, supple **8** athletic, graceful **9** dexterous

agility 8 alacrity, spryness **9** dexterity, quickness, swiftness **10** limberness, nimbleness **12** gracefulness

agitate 3 jar, mix **4** beat, goad, rock, stir **5** alarm, churn, shake, upset **6** excite, foment, stir up, work up **7** disturb, provoke, shake up, trouble **8** disquiet

agitated 5 tense **6** uneasy **7** anxious, frantic, nervous, uptight **8** confused, seething **9** disturbed, perturbed, unsettled **10** disquieted, distracted, distraught **11** discomfited, discomposed **12** disconcerted

agitation 7 anxiety **9** confusion **10** discomfort, uneasiness **11** disquietude, distraction, nervousness **12** discomfiture, discomposure, perturbation

agitato
　music: **8** agitated

agitator 7 inciter **8** fomentor, inflamer, provoker **9** firebrand **10** incendiary, instigator **11** provocateur **12** rabble-rouser, troublemaker **13** mischief-maker, revolutionary **16** agent provocateur

Aglaia
　member of: **6** Graces
　father: **7** Jupiter
　mother: **8** Eurynome
　sister: **6** Thalia **10** Euphrosyne
　husband: **4** Abas
　son: **7** Proteus **8** Acrisius
　daughter: **7** Idomene

aglow 4 warm **5** fiery **6** ablaze, red-hot **7** blazing, glowing, radiant, shining

Agnes Grey
　author: **10** Anne Bronte
　character: **8** Mr Weston **13** Rosalie Murray

agnostic 5 pagan **7** atheist, doubter, heathen, heretic, infidel, skeptic **10** empiricist, free spirit, secularist, unbeliever **11** disbeliever, freethinker, nonbeliever **14** doubting Thomas

ago 4 gone, over, past **5** since **6** gone by **7** earlier **8** backward **15** retrospectively

agog 5 astir **7** excited **8** thrilled, worked up **9** awestruck **10** enthralled **11** openmouthed

Agon
　ballet by: **10** Stravinsky

agonize 5 labor, sweat, worry **6** strain, suffer **7** anguish, wrestle **8** struggle

agonizing 6 severe **7** painful, racking **8** grievous, worrying **9** suffering, torturous **10** tormenting, unbearable **11** distressing, intolerable, unendurable **12** excruciating, insufferable

agony 3 woe **4** pain **5** trial **6** effort, misery, sorrow, strain, throes **7** anguish, anxiety, torment, torture **8** distress, striving, struggle **9** suffering **10** affliction **11** tribulation

Agony and the Ecstasy, The
　author: **11** Irving Stone
　about: **12** Michelangelo

Agoraea
　epithet of: **6** Athena
　means: **16** of the marketplace

agoraphobia
　fear of: **10** open spaces

Agraeus
　epithet of: **6** Apollo
　means: **6** hunter

agrarian 5 rural **7** farming **8** pastoral **11** agronomical, crop-raising **12** agricultural

agree 4 jibe **5** admit, allow, chime, grant, match, tally **6** accede, accept, accord, assent, concur, settle, square **7** concede, conform, consent, support **8** coincide, side with **9** harmonize, subscribe **10** correspond, think alike

agreeable 4 nice **7** fitting **8** amenable, amicable, in accord, pleasant, pleasing, suitable **9** approving, complying, congenial **10** acceptable, concurring, consenting, gratifying **11** appropriate
　German: **9** gemutlich

agreeableness 7 amenity **9** geniality **10** amiability **11** sociability **12** pleasantness

agreed
　French: **7** d'accord

agreed upon 6 common, normal **8** accepted, approved **9** confirmed, customary **10** acceptable **11** established **12** acknowledged

agreement 4 deal, pact **6** accord **7** analogy, bargain, compact, concert, concord, harmony, promise **8** affinity, alliance, contract, covenant **10** accordance, compliance, conformity, settlement, similarity **11** arrangement, concordance, conformance **13** compatibility **14** correspondence

agricultural 4 farm **5** rural **7** farming **8** agrarian **9** gardening **11** agronomical, crop-raising **13** nonindustrial

agriculture 7 farming, tillage **8** agronomy **9** geoponics, husbandry **10** agronomics **11** crop-raising, cultivation **15** market gardening

Agriculture
　god of: **4** Dago **5** Dagan, Dagon, Pi-

cus **6** Saturn **12** Bonus Eventus
　goddess of: **5** Ceres **6** Brigit, Dea Dia, Vacuna **7** Demeter

Agriope *see* **8** Eurydice

Agrius
　member of: **8** Gigantes
　form: **7** centaur
　mother: **5** Circe
　father: **8** Odysseus
　son: **9** Thersites
　attacked: **8** Hercules

agronomics 7 farming, tillage **8** agronomy **9** geoponics **11** agriculture, crop-raising

agronomy 7 farming **9** gardening, husbandry **11** agriculture, cultivation

aground 5 stuck **6** ashore **7** beached **8** grounded, stranded **9** foundered

ague 5 chill, fever **7** malaria, shivers **12** sweating fits

Aguecheek, Sir Andrew
　character in: **12** Twelfth Night
　author: **11** Shakespeare

Agyius
　epithet of: **6** Apollo
　means: **15** god of the streets

Ah, But Your Land Is Beautiful
　author: **9** Alan Paton

Ah! Wilderness
　author: **12** Eugene O'Neill

Ahab
　character in: **8** Moby Dick
　author: **8** Melville
　rank: **7** captain
　feature: **6** pegleg

Ahab
　father: **4** Omri
　wife: **7** Jezebel
　son: **7** Ahaziah
　daughter: **8** Athaliah
　opposed: **6** Elijah
　killed by: **4** Aram

Ahasuerus
　known as: **6** Xerxes **8** Cyaxares
　wife: **6** Esther
　divorced: **6** Vashti
　son: **6** Darius
　eunuchs: **6** Biztha, Carcas, Zethar **7** Abagtha, Harbona, Mehuman
　servant: **7** Abagtha
　courtier: **5** Haman
　conqueror of: **7** Nineveh

ahead of time 5 early **6** before, in time, sooner **7** betimes, earlier **9** before now, in advance **10** beforehand, in good time **13** before the fact

Ahib 16 first Hebrew month

Ahithophel
　counseled: **5** David
　rebelled with: **7** Absalom
　granddaughter: **9** Bathsheba

aid 4 abet, alms, dole, help **5** serve **6** assist, foster, relief **7** advance, charity, further, promote, subsidy, support, sustain **8** donation, minister **9** allowance **10** assistance, contribute, facilitate **11** accommodate, helping hand **12** contribution

Aida 17 Ethiopian princess
   opera by: 5 Verdi
   character: 4 Aida **6** Ramfis **7** Amneris, Radames **8** Amonasro, Rhadames
   set in: 5 Egypt

aide 5 gofer **6** deputy, helper **7** abettor, acolyte **8** adherent, adjutant, follower, retainer, sidekick **9** assistant, associate, auxiliary, man Friday **10** aide-decamp, apprentice, girl Friday, lieutenant **11** helping hand, subordinate **12** right-hand man

aide-de-camp 3 ADC **4** aide **6** helper **8** adjutant **9** assistant, man Friday, right hand **12** right-hand man

aide memoire 4 memo, note **10** memorandum

aider 4 aide **6** helper **7** abettor **9** assistant **11** helping hand

Aiken, Conrad Potter
   author of: 6 Ushant **10** Blue Voyage **12** Reviewer's ABC **14** The Charnel Rose **15** Earth Triumphant

Aiken, Howard H
   field: 11 mathematics
   designed: 15 digital computer

ail 4 pain **5** annoy, be ill, upset, worry **6** be sick, bother, sicken **7** afflict, make ill, trouble **8** be infirm, be unwell, distress **12** be indisposed, fail in health

ailing 3 ill **4** sick **6** infirm, sickly, unwell **8** delicate

ailment 6 malady **7** disease, illness **8** disorder, sickness, weakness **9** complaint, infection, infirmity **10** affliction, disability, discomfort **13** indisposition

ailurophobia
   fear of: 4 cats

aim 3 end, try **4** beam, goal, mean, plan, seek, want, wish **5** essay, focus, level, point, sight, slant **6** aiming, design, desire, direct, intend, intent, object, scheme, strive, target **7** attempt, be after, purpose, take aim, train on **8** ambition, aspire to, endeavor **9** intention **10** aspiration, have in mind, have in view, work toward **11** have an eye to, line of sight **12** marksmanship

aim at 4 seek **6** pursue, target **8** aspire to, shoot for

aimless 6 chance, random **7** erratic, wayward **8** unguided **9** frivolous, haphazard, hit-or-miss, pointless, unfocus(s)ed **10** accidental, rudderless, undirected **11** purposeless, unorganized **12** inconsistent, unsystematic **13** directionless, unpredictable **14** indiscriminate

aine 5 elder **6** eldest

Ainsworth, William Harrison
   author of: 8 Boscobel, Crichton,

Rookwood **9** Guy Fawkes **10** Old St Paul's **12** Jack Sheppard **13** Windsor Castle **16** The Flitch of Bacon, The Tower of London **17** The Miser's Daughter, The South Sea Bubble **20** The Lancashire Witches

Ainu
   language spoken in: 8 Hokkaido, Sakhalin
   native of: 5 Japan

air, airs 3 lay, sky **4** aura, look, mood, puff, song, tell, tone, tune, vent, waft, wind **5** blast, carol, ditty, draft, ozone, style, swank, utter, voice, whiff **6** aerate, ballad, breath, breeze, expose, manner, melody, reveal, spirit, strain, zephyr **7** declare, display, divulge, exhibit, express, feeling, hauteur, quality **8** ambience, disclose, pretense, proclaim **9** arrogance, publicize, ventilate **10** appearance, atmosphere, make public **11** haughtiness, pretensions **12** affectations, affectedness, stratosphere **16** superciliousness
   god of: 5 Enlil
   goddess of: 6 Ninlil

airborne 5 aloft **6** aerial, Eolian **8** in flight **12** off the ground

aircraft 3 jet, SST **4** bird **5** blimp, crate, plane **6** copter, glider **7** balloon, chopper, prop-jet **8** airplane, jumbo jet, zeppelin **10** helicopter, whirlybird

air current 4 puff, wind **5** blast, draft, whiff **6** breeze, zephyr **11** breath of air

airdrome, aerodrome 7 airbase, airport, jet base **8** airfield **11** flying field **12** landing field

airfield 7 air base, airport, jet base **8** airstrip **11** flying field **12** landing field, landing strip

airfoil
   insect: 4 wing

airless 8 stifling **10** overheated, sweltering **16** poorly ventilated

airlines, American 3 ATA, Ted, TMA, TWA **4** Mesa, Reno, Song **5** Aloha, Delta, Pan Am, USAir **6** Alaska, Colgan, Spirit, United **7** Air Tran, Eastern, Jet Blue, Simmons, Sky West, ValuJet **8** American, Carnival, Frontier, Hawaiian, TowerAir **9** Allegiant, Northwest, Southwest **10** Horizon Air, Sun Country, Transworld **11** America West, Continental, Trans States **12** Air Wisconsin, Independence **13** Interstate Jet, Trans Meridian **14** Midwest Express, Western Pacific **16** American Trans Air **17** Atlantic Southeast **18** Continental Express **21** Continental Micronesia

airplane 3 jet **4** bird **5** crate, plane **7** airship, prop-jet **8** aircraft **9** aeroplane **11** flying jenny **19** heavier-than-air craft **20** propeller-driven plane
   invented by:
      automatic pilot: 6 Sperry

jet engine: 5 Ohain
   with motor: 12 Wilbur Wright **13** Orville Wright **14** Wright Brothers
   hydro: 7 Curtiss
first: 5 Flyer
part: 3 fin **4** flap, nose, tail, wing **5** cabin, cargo, pylon **6** rudder **7** aileron, cockpit, turbine **8** elevator, fuel tank, fuselage, throttle, turbofan, turbojet **9** empennage, propeller, turboprop **10** flight deck, power plant, stabilizer **11** landing gear **13** undercarriage
kind: 3 MIG **4** Zero **5** Eagle, Gotha, Piper, Sabre **6** Boeing, Cessna, Fokker, Mirage **7** Concorde, Piper Cub **10** Beechcraft, Dornier Do-X **11** Piper Navajo **12** Lockheed Vega, Sopwith Camel **13** Boeing Clipper, Messerschmitt, Piper Cherokee, Super Fortress **14** Cessna Citation, Flying Fortress, Grumman Hellcat, Stratofortress **15** Hawker Hurricane **16** De Havilland Comet
variation: 3 SST **4** STOL, VTOL **5** blimp, drone, VSTOL **6** bomber, glider **7** airship, fighter **8** zeppelin **10** hang glider, helicopter, supersonic
battle: 8 dog fight

airport 5 field **7** air base, jet base **8** airdrome, airfield, airstrip **9** aerodrome **11** flying field **12** landing field, landing strip
   Amsterdam: 8 Schiphol
   Bangkok: 8 Don Muang
   Berlin: 5 Tegel **9** Tempelhof **11** Schoenefeld
   Boston: 5 Logan
   Bucharest: 7 Baneasa, Otopeni
   Chicago: 5 O'Hare **6** Midway
   Dallas: 9 Love Field
   Houston: 5 Hobby **9** Ellington
   London: 7 Gatwick **8** Heathrow
   Madrid: 7 Barajas
   Milan: 6 Linate **8** Malpensa
   Montreal: 7 Mirabel, Trudeau
   Moscow: 12 Sheremetyevo
   Munich: 9 Flughafen
   New York: 3 JFK **9** La Guardia
   Paris: 4 Orly **15** Charles de Gaulle
   Pisa: 14 Galileo Galilei
   Rome: 8 Ciampino **9** Fiumicino
   Seoul: 5 Kimpo
   Shanghai: 6 Pudong
   Tokyo: 6 Narita
   Washington, DC: 6 Dulles, Reagan
   Airport Abbreviations:
      Albuquerque: 3 ABQ
      Anchorage: 3 ANC
      Atlanta: 3 ATL (Hartsfield International)
      Baltimore: 3 BWI
      Boston: 3 BOS (Logan International)
      Calgary: 3 YYC
      Charleston: 3 CHS
      Chicago: 3 ORD (O'Hare), MDW

(Midway)
Cincinnati: 3 CVG
Cleveland: 3 CLE
Columbus: 3 CMH
Dallas: 3 DAL (Love Field)
Dallas/Ft. Worth: 3 DFW
Denver: 3 DEN
Detroit: 3 DTW
Fairbanks: 3 FAI
Fargo: 3 FAR
Fort Lauderdale: 3 FLL
Green Bay: 3 GRB
Hartford: 3 BDL (Bradley)
Honolulu: 3 HNL
Houston: 3 EFD (Ellington), HOU
(Hobby), IAH
Las Vegas: 3 LAS (McCarran Inter-
national)
Little Rock: 3 LIT
Los Angeles: 3 LAX
Louisville: 3 SDF
Memphis: 3 MEM
Miami: 3 MIA
Minneapolis/St. Paul: 3 MSP
Montreal: 3 YMX, YUL
Nashville: 3 BNA
Newark: 3 EWR
New Orleans: 3 MSY
New York: 3 JFK (John F. Kennedy
International), LGA (LaGuardia)
Oakland: 3 OAK
Omaha: 3 OMA
Orlando: 3 MCO
Philadelphia: 3 PHL
Phoenix: 3 PHX (Sky Harbor Inter-
national)
Pittsburgh: 3 PIT
Providence: 3 PVD
Quebec: 3 YQB
St. Louis: 3 STL (Lambert St. Louis
International)
Salt Lake City: 3 SLC
San Diego: 3 SAN
San Francisco: 3 SFO
Savannah: 3 SAV
Seattle/Tacoma: 3 SEA
Toledo: 3 TOL
Toronto: 3 YYZ
Tuscon: 3 TUS
Tulsa: 3 TUL
Washington, DC: 3 IAD (Dulles),
DCA (Reagan)
airship 5 blimp **7** balloon **9** dirigible
19 lighter-than-air craft
airship, rigid dirigible
invented by: 8 Zeppelin
airstrip 6 runway **12** landing field,
landing strip
air weapon
German: 9 Luftwaffe
airy 5 light, merry, sunny, windy **6**
breezy, cheery, drafty, dreamy,
jaunty, lively **8** cheerful, ethereal, fanciful, gossamer, illusory, spacious **9**
idealized, imaginary, sprightly **10** frolicsome, immaterial **11** unrealistic **12**
lighthearted, light-of-heart **13** unsubstantial **14** well-ventilated

aisle 3 way **4** lane, path, walk **5** alley
6 avenue **7** passage, walkway **8** cloister, corridor **10** ambulatory, passageway
Aius Locutius
form: 5 voice
warned: 6 Romans
warned of: 14 Gallic invasion
ajar 4 open **5** agape **6** gaping **8** unclosed **10** partly open
Ajax
also: 4 Aias
called: 9 Great Ajax **10** Oilean Ajax
11 Locrian Ajax **13** Ajax the Lesser
14 Telamonian Ajax
king of: 7 Locrius
father: 6 Oileus **7** Telamon
mother: 8 Periboea
brother: 6 Teucer
author: 9 Sophocles
character: 8 Achilles, Odysseus
9 Agamemnon
son: 9 Eurysaces
slave: 8 Tecmessa
seer: 7 Calchas
rescued body of: 8 Achilles
violated shrine of: 6 Athena
killed in: 9 shipwreck
Akela
character in: 14 The Jungle Books
author: 7 Kipling
Akh
origin: 8 Egyptian
transfiguration of: 4 dead
Akihito
position: 7 emperor **11** crown prince
reign name: 6 Heisei **17** Establishing
Peace
family:
father: 5 Showa **8** Hirohito
mother: 6 Nagako
wife: 7 Michiko
children: 4 Hito **8** Narahito
schools: 6 Oxford **9** Gakushuin
akin 3 kin **4** like **5** alike **6** allied **7** kindred, related, similar, uniform **8**
agreeing, parallel **9** analogous, congenial, connected, identical **10** affiliated, comparable, resembling **11** correlative **13** corresponding **14**
consanguineous
Akkad see **5** Accad
Akutagawa, Ryunosuke
author of: 5 Kappa **8** Rashomon **13**
The Hell Screen
a la 9 in honor of **13** in the manner of
Alabama
abbreviation: 2 AL **3** Ala
nickname: 6 Cotton **12** Heart of
Dixie, Yellowhammer
capital: 10 Montgomery
largest city: 10 Birmingham
others: 5 Selma **6** Athens, Dothan,
Marion, Mobile **7** Decatur, Gadsden
8 Anniston **10** Huntsville, Tuscaloosa
colleges: 5 Miles **6** Auburn **7** Alabama **8** Tuskegee **9** Talladega **10**

Huntingdon
explorer: 12 Herman DeSoto
feature:
festival: 11 Azalea Trail
statue: 6 Vulcan
tribe: 5 Creek **6** Tohome **7** Alabamu,
Alibamu, Koasati **8** Tuskegee
people: 8 Joe Louis **9** Hank Aaron,
Hugo Black **10** Willie Mays **11** Helen
Keller, Nat King Cole **13** George
Wallace, William C Handy, William
Gorgas
lake: 12 Guntersville
land rank: 11 twenty-ninth
physical feature:
gulf: 6 Mexico
highest point: 6 Cheaha
highlands: 11 Appalachian
river: 3 Pea **5** Coosa **6** Mobile **7** Alabama **9** Tombigbee, Tennessee **10**
Tallapoosa **13** Chattahoochee
state admission: 12 twenty-second
state bird: 7 flicker **12** yellowhammer
state fish: 6 tarpon
state flower: 8 camellia **9** goldenrod
state motto: 21 We Dare Defend Our
Rights
state song: 7 Alabama
state tree: 20 southern longleaf pine
Alabama, Alibamu
language family: 9 Muskogean
location: 5 Texas **9** Louisiana **10** Polk
County **12** Alabama River
related to: 7 Koasati
alacrity 4 zeal **5** speed **6** fervor **7** agility, avidity **8** dispatch **9** alertness,
briskness, eagerness, readiness **10** enthusiasm, liveliness, nimbleness,
promptness **11** willingness **13** sprightliness
Aladdin
character in: 27 Arabian Nights' Entertainments
character: 13 Chinese sailor
Al Aiun, El Aaiun
capital of: 13 Western Sahara
a la mode 12 in the fashion, in the
style of **13** in the manner of
Alarcon, Pedro Antonio de
author: 10 The Scandal **12** Captain
Venom **14** El Nino de la Bola **19** The
Three-Cornered Hat
alarm 4 fear **5** alert, panic, scare **6** appall, dismay, fright, terror, war cry **7**
agitate, disturb, terrify, trouble, unnerve, warning **8** affright, distress,
frighten **9** agitation, hue and cry, misgiving **11** trepidation **12** apprehension, perturbation **13** consternation
alarmed 6 afraid, scared **7** anxious,
fearful, panicky, worried **8** dismayed
9 concerned, terrified **10** frightened
12 apprehensive **13** panic-stricken **14**
terror-stricken
alarming 5 awful, dread, scary **7** fearful **8** dreadful **10** horrifying, terrifying
11 frightening, hair-raising

alas
  expresses: **4** pity **5** grief **6** sorrow **7** concern **9** weariness **11** unhappiness **12** wretchedness
  phrase: **7** woe is me

Alaska
  abbreviation: **2** AK **4** Alas
  nickname: **9** Great Land, Sourdough **12** Last Frontier **20** Land of the Midnight Sun
  capital: **6** Juneau
  largest city: **9** Anchorage
  others: **4** Nome **5** Sitka **6** Barrow, Kodiak **7** Cordova, Douglas, Skagway **9** Fairbanks, Ketchikan
  feature: **5** Alcan **10** North Slope **13** Alaska Highway
    national park: **5** Sitka **6** Denali, Arctic, Katmai **9** Lake Clark **10** Glacier Bay **11** Kenai Fjords, Kobuk Valley **13** Mount McKinley **15** Wrangell-St. Elias **16** Klondike Gold Rush
  tribe: **3** Han **5** Aleut, Haida, Inuit **6** Ahtena, Akkhas, Eskimo, Karluk, Tetlin **7** Amerind, Ingalik, Kayukon, Khotana, Kutchin, Tanaina, Tlingit, Tlinkit, Venetie **9** Tsimshian, Unakalett
  island: **4** Adak, Atka **5** Aleut **6** Kodiak, Unimak **7** Diomede, Nunivak **8** Aleutian, Pribilof **9** Alexander
  lake: **6** Naknek **7** Iliamna **8** Becharof **9** Teshekpuk
  land rank: **5** first
  mountain: **3** Ada **4** Muir **5** Coast **6** Alaska, Brooks, Denali **7** Foraker, St Elias **8** Aleutian, Wrangell **9** Blackburn
    highest point: **8** McKinley
  physical feature:
    bay: **7** Glacier, Prudhoe
    channel: **9** Gastineau
    glacier: **9** Malaspina
    pass: **8** Chilkoot
    peninsula: **5** Kenai **6** Alaska, Seward
    rapids: **10** Whitehorse
    sea: **6** Arctic **8** Beaufort
    strait: **6** Bering
  river: **5** Kobuk, Yukon **6** Copper, Noatak, Tanana **7** Koyukuk, Susitna **8** Colville **9** Kuskokwim, Matanuska, Porcupine
  sled race: **8** Iditarod
  state admission: **10** forty-ninth
  state bird: **15** willow ptarmigan
  state fish: **10** king salmon
  state flower: **11** forget-me-not
  state motto: **16** North to the Future
  state song: **11** Alaska's Flag
  state symbol: **9** bald eagle
  state tree: **11** sitka spruce
  oil spill: **11** Exxon Valdez (ship)

Albania
  other name: **8** Shqiperi **9** Shqiprija, Shqyptare
  capital/largest city: **6** Tirana, Tirane

  others: **3** Opp **4** Fier, Klos, Puka, Puke **5** Berat, Dukat, Korce, Kruje, Pecin, Peqin, Qukes, Rubic, Spash, Vlore **6** Avlona, Bitsan, Dardhe, Durres, Karaje, Preshe, Valona **7** Chimara, Coritsa, Durazzo, Elbasan, Koritsa, Preyesa, Scutari, Shkoder **8** Tepeleni **11** Gjirokaster
  monetary unit: **3** lek **5** franc **6** qintar **7** quintar
  island: **6** Saseno
  lake: **4** Ulze **5** Matia, Ohrid **6** Prespa **7** Ochrida, Scutari, Shkoder **8** Ohridsko
  mountain: **5** Shala **6** Pindus **8** Koritnjk **12** Albanian Alps
  highest point: **10** Mount Korab
  river: **3** Mat **4** Arta, Drin **5** Byene, Erzen, Seman **6** Bojana, Bojane, Vijosa, Vijosa, Vijose **7** Drin-i-ci, Shkumbi
  sea: **6** Ionian **8** Adriatic
  physical feature:
    bay: **5** Vlore
    cape: **6** Glossa
    gulf: **4** Drin
    lagoon: **10** Kara Vastas
    peninsula: **6** Balkan
    promontory: **13** acroceraunium
    strait: **7** Otranto
    wind: **4** bora
  people: **3** Geg **4** Cham, Gheg, Gueg, Tosk **6** Arnaut, Arnout **8** Illyrian, Skipetar
    king: **3** Zog **9** Ahmet Zogu
    leader: **4** Alia **5** Hoxha **7** Berisha **10** Scanderbeg, Skenderbeg **13** Bishop Fan Noli
  language: **3** Geg **4** Cham, Gheg, Hish, Tosk **5** Greek **8** Albanian
  religion: **5** Islam **7** Bektash **13** Roman Catholic **15** Eastern Orthodox
  place:
    square: **10** Skenderbeg
  feature:
    lute: **6** luhata
    soldier: **7** palikar
    stone house: **4** kula
  food:
    cheese: **8** kackaval

Albanian
  language family: **12** Indo-European
  spoken in: **7** Balkans

Albee, Edward
  author of: **3** Box **7** All Over **8** Seascape, Zoo Story **9** Tiny Alice **10** The Sandbox **16** A Delicate Balance, The American Dream **18** The Lady from Dubuque **21** The Ballad of the Sad Cafe, The Death of Bessie Smith **25** Who's Afraid of Virginia Woolf?
  identified with: **18** theater of the absurd

Albeniz, Isaac
  born: **5** Spain **9** Camprodon
  composer of: **6** Iberia **12** The Magic Opal **13** Henry Clifford

Alberich
  origin: **8** Teutonic

  king of: **6** dwarfs
  possessed treasure of: **8** Niblungs **9** Nibelungs
  also possessed: **9** Tarnkappe

Albert, Eddie
  real name: **21** Eddie Albert Heimberger
  wife: **5** Margo
  born: **12** Rock Island IL
  roles: **8** Oklahoma **10** Brother Rat, Green Acres **11** Room Service **12** Roman Holiday **13** The Longest Day **16** The Heartbreak Kid **19** The Boys from Syracuse

Alberta
  abbreviation: **4** Alta
  capital/largest city: **8** Edmonton
  others: **7** Calgary, Reddeer **10** Lethbridge **11** Medicine Hat
  lakes: **5** Banff, Claire **6** Jasper **8** Waterton **9** Athabasca **11** Lesser Slave
  rivers: **3** Bow **4** Milk **6** Oldman, Wapiti **9** Athabasca **12** Saskatchewan
  religion: **13** Roman Catholic **20** United Church of Canada **22** Anglican Church of Canada
  people: **5** Dutch **6** French, German **7** British, English **9** Ukrainian **12** Scandinavian

Albert Herring
  opera by: **7** Britten

Alberti, Leon Battista
  architect of: **15** Palazzo Rucellai **18** Church of Sant' Andrea, Temple Malatestiano **20** Church of San Sebastian **25** Church of Santa Maria Novello

Albertson, Jack
  born: **8** Malden MA
  roles: **14** Chico and the Man **15** The Sunshine Boys **18** Days of Wine and Roses, The Subject Was Roses
  album **2** LP **4** book **6** record **8** register **9** portfolio, scrapbook

Alceste
  opera by: **5** Gluck

Alcestis
  author: **9** Euripides
  character: **6** Apollo **7** Admetus **8** Heracles, Thanatos

Alcestis
  father: **6** Pelias
  mother: **8** Anaxibia **10** Phylomache
  husband: **7** Admetus
  son: **7** Eumelus **8** Hippasus
  returned from: **5** Hades
  returned by: **8** Hercules

Alchemist, The
  author: **9** Ben Jonson
  character: **4** Face **5** Surly **6** Dapper, Subtle **7** Ananias, Drugger, Kastril, Love-wit **9** Dol Common **10** Dame Pliant **16** Sir Epicure Mammon **20** Tribulation Wholesome

  alchemy **5** magic **7** sorcery **8** wizardry **10** conversion, witchcraft **11** magic

appeal **13** transmutation **17** medieval chemistry
god of: 6 Hermes
purpose: 12 lead into gold

Alcimede
father: 8 Phylacus
mother: 7 Clymene
husband: 5 Aeson
son: 5 Jason

Alcimedon
origin: 8 Arkadian
mentioned in: 5 Iliad
father: 7 Laerces
daughter: 6 Philao
captain of: 9 Myrmidons

Alcina
opera by: 6 Handel
character: 6 Alcina **8** Ruggiero

Alcindor, Lew
former name of: 17 Kareem Abdul-Jabbar

Alcmaeon
father: 10 Amphiaraus
mother: 8 Eriphyle
brother: 11 Amphilochus
wife: 10 Callirrhoe
son: 7 Acarnan **10** Amphoterus
daughter: 9 Tisiphone
commanded: 7 Thebans

Alcmene
father: 9 Electryon
mother: 5 Anaxo
husband: 10 Amphitryon **12** Rhadamanthys
twin sons: 8 Hercules, Iphicles

alcohol 3 ale **4** beer, wine **5** drink **6** liquor **7** whiskey **9** the bottle
Latin: 9 aqua vitae

alcoholic 3 sot **4** hard, lush, soak **5** drunk, rummy, souse, toper **6** barfly, boozer, strong **7** guzzler, imbiber, tippler **8** drunkard **9** distilled, fermented, inebriate **10** spirituous **11** dipsomaniac, hard drinker, inebriating, inebriative, whiskey head **12** intoxicating

alcoholism 3 DT's **9** oenomania **10** dipsomania **12** intemperance **15** delirium tremens

Alcon
form: 6 archer, Trojan **7** warrior
aided: 8 Hercules
wounded: 8 Odysseus
abducted: 13 Geryons cattle
killed by: 8 Odysseus

Alcott, Louisa May
author of: 7 Jo's Boys **9** Little Men **11** Little Women **12** Eight Cousins, Flower Fables **15** Aunt Jo's Scrap-Bag **18** An Old-Fashioned Girl

alcove 3 bay **4** nook **5** niche **6** corner, recess **7** cubicle, opening **11** compartment

Alcyoneus
form: 5 giant
hurled: 5 stone
killed by: 8 Hercules

Alda, Alan
born: 9 New York NY
father: 10 Robert Alda
real name: 15 Alfonso D'Abruzzo
roles: 4 MASH **8** A New Life **9** Paper Lion, Playmates, White Nile **10** The Aviator **12** Sweet Liberty **13** Betsy's Wedding, Hawkeye Pierce, The Glass House **14** The Four Seasons **16** Same Time Next Year, The Mephisto Waltz **18** And the Band Played On

Alden, Roberta
character in: 17 An American Tragedy
author: 7 Dreiser

al dente 10 to the tooth

alder 5 Alnus
varieties: 3 Red **5** Black, Hazel, White, Witch **6** Oregon, Smooth, Yellow **7** Italian, Seaside **8** Japanese, Mountain, Speckled **9** Caucasian **10** Manchurian **13** American green, European green

Aldiss, Brian W
author of: 7 Non-Stop **9** Greybeard **13** The Saliva Tree **19** Frankenstein Unbound, The Billion Year Spree, The Eighty Minute Hour **20** The Trillion Year Spree

ale 4 beer, brew **5** stout **12** malt beverage **15** English festival

Alea
epithet of: 6 Athena
means: 9 sanctuary

Alecto
member of: 6 Furies

alehouse 3 pub **6** saloon, tavern **7** taproom **11** public house

Aleichem, Sholom
author of: 12 The Great Fair **14** Tevye's Daughter

Alembert, Jean le Rond d'
field: 11 mathematics
nationality: 6 French
studied: 13 fluid dynamics **18** celestial mechanics **28** partial differential equations

Aleph and Other Stories
author: 15 Jorge Luis Borges

alert 4 warn, wary **5** alarm, aware, quick, siren **6** active, inform, lively, nimble, notify, signal **7** careful, heedful, on guard, warning **8** diligent, forewarn, keen-eyed, vigilant, watchful **9** attentive, observant, sprightly, wideawake **10** perceptive **11** intelligent

alertness 8 alacrity, dispatch **9** awareness, readiness, vigilance **10** liveliness **12** watchfulness

Aleut
language family: 6 Eskimo
tribe: 4 Atka **8** Unalaska
location: 6 Alaska **15** Shumagin Islands **17** Aleutian Peninsula
noted for: 7 hunting

Aleutians

islands: 3 Fox, Rat **4** Attu, Near **5** Kiska **9** Andreanof **25** Islands of the Four Mountains
state: 6 Alaska
people: 6 Aleuts
language: 5 Atkan **9** Unalaskan

Alexander
director: 11 Oliver Stone
cast: 9 Jared Leto (Hephaistion), Val Kilmer (King Philip) **12** Colin Farrell (Alexander the Great) **13** Angelina Jolie (Queen Olympias), Rosario Dawson (Roxane) **14** Anthony Hopkins (Ptolemy) **18** Christopher Plummer (Aristotle)

Alexander, Jane
real name: 11 Jane Quigley
born: 8 Boston MA
roles: 9 Testament **17** The Great White Hope **18** Eleanor and Franklin **19** All the President's Men

Alexander's Feast
author: 10 John Dryden

Alexander the Great
battle: 5 Issus **9** Gaugamela
birthplace: 5 Pella
conquered: 6 Darius, Persia
father: 8 Philip II
founded: 10 Alexandria
friend: 11 Hephaestion
general: 7 Cleitus **8** Philotas **9** Parmenion
horse: 10 Bucephalus
mother: 8 Olympias
nationality: 10 Macedonian
tutor: 9 Aristotle
wife: 6 Roxana

alexandrite
species: 11 chrysoberyl
source: 8 Sri Lanka
color: 3 red **5** green

Alfheim
origin: 12 Scandinavian
dwelling place of: 5 elves
location: 11 above ground

Alfie
director: 12 Lewis Gilbert
based on play by: 12 Bill Naughton
cast: 12 Michael Caine **14** Shelley Winters

alga, algae 6 fungus **8** pond scum
contains: 4 agar **5** algin **11** carrageenan, chlorophyll
type: 3 red **5** brown, green **9** blue-green, euglenids **11** golden-brown, yellow-green **15** dinoflagellates
forms: 4 kelp **5** dulse **7** diatoms, seaweed **8** plankton, rockweed **9** Irish moss, stonewort

Alger, Horatio
author of: 10 Ragged Dick **11** Tattered Tom **12** Luck and Pluck
genre: 9 dime novel

Algeria
other name: 7 Algerie, Numidia, Pomaria **9** al-Djazair
capital/largest city: 7 Algiers

others: 4 Bona, Bone, Oran **5** Aflou, Arzew, Batna, Blida, Medea, Saida, Setif, Tenes **6** Abadla, Annaba, Aumale, Barika, Bechar, Bejaia, Benoud, Biskra, Bougie, Dellys, Djanet, Djelfa, Dzioua, Eloued, Frenda, Guelma, Skikda **7** Boghari, Mascara, Miliana, Negrine, Nemours, Ouargla, Tebessa, Tlemcen **8** Ghardaia, Laghouat **9** Touggourt **11** Constantine **12** Sidi-bel-abbes

division: 4 Oran **6** Annaba **7** Algiers **11** Constantine

leader: 3 bey, dey **6** disawa **9** beylerbey

measure: 3 pik **5** rebis, tarri **6** termin

monetary unit: 5 dinar **7** centime

weight: 4 rotl

lake: 5 Hodna **6** Sabkha **7** Cherqui, Fedjadj, Meirhir **10** Azzel Matti, Mekerrhane

mountain: 5 Aissa, Atlas, Aures, Dahra **6** Chelia **7** Ahaggar, Kabylia, Mouydir **8** Djurjura **9** Djurdjura, Tell Atlas **12** Saharan Atlas

highest point: 5 Tahat

river: 6 Shelif **7** Cheliff **8** Medjerda **15** Cheliffmedjerda

sea: 13 Mediterranean

physical feature: 14 Tropic of Cancer

  desert: 6 Sahara

  giant sand dune: 3 erg

  grass: 4 diss **7** esparto

  hill: 4 tell

  oasis: 4 Mzab

  oil field: 7 Edjeleh, El Gassi **10** Zarzaitine **13** Hassi Messaoud (happy spring), Tiguentourine

  plain: 7 Cheliff, Mitidja

  rocky plateau: 7 hammada

  salt basin: 5 chott, shatt

  wind: 7 sirocco

people: 4 Arab **6** Berber, Kabyle, Shawia, Tuareg **7** Haratin

  author: 3 Dib **5** Camus, Fanon **6** Yacine

  leader: 9 Bendjedid **10** Abd al-Qadir, Abd-al-Kadir, Abd-el-Kader **11** Boumedienne **13** Ahmed Ben Bella

  ruler: 8 Jugurtha **9** Masinissa

language: 6 Arabic, Berber, French, Zenata **7** Senhaja

religion: 5 Islam

place:

  monastery: 5 Ribat

  ruins: 7 Djemila

feature:

  camel: 6 mehari

  cavalry man: 5 spahi **6** spahee

  commune: 5 setif

  dwelling: 6 gourbi

  French settler/landowner: 5 colon **8** piednoir

  holy man: 8 marabout

  kingdom: 7 Numidia

  native quarter: 6 casbah, kasbah

  pirate: 7 corsair

  ship: 5 xebec, zebec

  slum: 10 bidonville

food:

  dish: 8 couscous

  fruit drink: 5 syrop

  seasoning: 4 mint **5** anise, cumin **6** cloves, fennel, ginger, pepper **7** parsley, pimento **8** cinnamon **9** coriander

Algiers

  Arabic: 8 al-Jazair

  building: 11 Great Mosque

  capital of: 7 Algeria

  center of city: 6 Casbah

  French: 5 Alger

  hills: 5 Sahel

  Roman: 7 Icosium

  ruled by: 5 Turks **6** French **7** Berbers **10** Free French **14** Barbary Pirates

  sea: 13 Mediterranean

Algonkian-Ritwan

  language family: 14 Algonkian-Mosan

  subgroup: 3 Fox **4** Cree, Sauk **5** Wiyot, Yurok **6** Ojibwa **7** Abenaki, Arapaho, Mohican **8** Cheyenne, Delaware, Menomini **9** Blackfoot

Algonkin, Algonquin

  language family: 9 Algonkian **10** Algonquian

  tribe: 7 Abitibi **8** Algonkin **9** Nipissing **11** Temiscaming

  location: 6 Canada **11** Ottawa River

  spirit of nature: 7 Manitou

Algonquian, Algonkian

  tribe: 3 Fox, Sac **4** Cree, Innu, Sauk **5** Miami **6** Abnaki, Atsina, Micmac, Ojibwa, Ottawa, Pequot **7** Arapaho, Mahican, Mohegan, Mohican, Ojibway, Shawnee **8** Algonkin, Cheyenne, Chippawa, Delaware, Haaninin, Iliniwek, Illinois, Kickapoo, Menomini, Merrimac, Powhatan, Puyallop **9** Algonquin, Blackfeet, Blackfoot, Massasoit, Menominee, Menomonie, Mesquakie, Pennacook, Penobscot, Pokanoket, Twightwee, Wampanoag **10** Leni-Lenape, Potawatomi **11** Gros Ventres **12** Narragansett **17** Montagnais-Naskapi

algophobia

  fear of: 4 pain

Algum 13 red sandalwood

Ali

  director: 11 Michael Mann

  cast: 9 Jamie Foxx (Drew "Budini" Brown), Jon Voight (Howard Cosell), Ron Silver (Angelo Dundee), Will Smith (Cassius Clay/Muhammad Ali) **15** Mario Van Peebles (Malcolm X)

Ali, Muhammad

  formerly: 11 Cassius Clay

  sport: 6 boxing

  class: 11 heavyweight

  won: 8 Olympics **16** heavyweight title

Alias

  network: 3 ABC

  creator: 8 J. J. Abrams

  cast: 9 Ron Rifkin (Arvin Sloan) **10** Carl Lumbly (Marcus Dixon) **12** Victor Garber (Jack Bristow) **13** Michael Vartan (Michael Vaughn) **14** Jennifer Garner (Sydney Bristow)

alias 9 pseudonym **11** assumed name, nom de guerre

Ali Baba

  character in: 27 Arabian Nights' Entertainments

alibi 3 out **6** excuse **7** pretext **11** explanation **13** justification

Alice Adams

  author: 15 Booth Tarkington

  character: 6 Mr Lamb **11** Virgil Adams, Walter Adams **13** Arthur Russell, Mildred Palmer

Alice's Adventures in Wonderland

  author: 12 Lewis Carroll **22** Charles Lutwidge Dodgson

  character: 5 Alice **7** Duchess **9** Mad Hatter, March Hare **10** Mock Turtle **11** Cheshire Cat, White Rabbit **13** Knave of Hearts, Queen of Hearts

Alice Sit-by-the-Fire

  author: 12 James M Barrie

alien 6 exotic, remote, unlike **7** distant, foreign, opposed, strange **8** contrary, newcomer, outsider, stranger **9** different, estranged, foreigner, immigrant, not native, outlander, separated, unrelated **10** dissimilar, outlandish **11** conflicting, incongruous, unconnected **12** incompatible, inconsistent **13** contradictory

  German: 9 Auslander

alienate 7 divorce **8** estrange, separate, turn away

alienation 5 exile **7** divorce **9** isolation **10** separation, withdrawal **13** repulsiveness

alight 4 land **6** get off **7** deplane, descend, detrain, get down **8** come down, dismount **9** climb down, disembark, thump down, touch down

align 4 ally, even, join, side **6** even up, line up **9** affiliate, associate **10** straighten

alignment 7 allying, evening **9** evening up **13** straightening

alike 4 akin, even, same **5** equal **6** evenly **7** equally, kindred, uniform **8** of a piece, parallel **9** analogous, identical, similarly, uniformly **10** equivalent, synonymous **11** homogeneous, identically **13** corresponding

Alisande (Sandy)

  character in: 36 A Connecticut Yankee in King Arthur's Court

  author: 5 Twain

alive 4 spry **5** alert, aware, eager, quick, vital **6** active, extant, lively, living, viable **7** animate, in force, not dead **8** animated, possible, spirited, vigorous **9** breathing, energetic, operative, vivacious **10** subsisting, unquenched **11** above ground, in existence, in operation **14** unextinguished

alive to 5 alert, awake, aware **7** heedful, mindful **8** watchful **9** attentive, conscious, wide-awake

alkaline 3 lye **5** salty **7** antacid **9** nonacidic

alkaloid 7 alkaline, codeine, guinine **8** morphine, nicotine **16** colorless complex

all 4 each, full, very **5** any of, every, fully, total, utter, whole **6** each of, entire, to a man, utmost, wholly **7** highest, perfect, totally, utterly **8** any one of, complete, entirely, everyone, greatest, the sum of, the total, the whole **9** every item **10** altogether, completely, every one of, everything, the total of, the whole of **11** every member, every part of, exceedingly, the entirety

All About Eve
  director: 17 Joseph L Mankiewicz
  cast: 10 Anne Baxter, Bette Davis **11** Celeste Holm, Gary Merrill **12** Thelma Ritter **13** George Sanders, Marilyn Monroe
  Oscar for: 7 picture **8** director **10** screenplay **15** supporting actor (George Sanders)

Allan-a-Dale, Alan-a-Dale
  character in: 9 Robin Hood

allargando
  music: 13 getting slower

all around 6 abroad **7** all over **10** everywhere, far and wide **15** making the rounds

all-around 5 broad **6** adroit, gifted **8** flexible **9** adaptable, many-sided, versatile **11** well-rounded **12** ambidextrous, multifaceted **13** comprehensive

allay 4 calm, dull, ease, hush **5** blunt, check, quell, quiet, slake **6** lessen, pacify, reduce, smooth, soften, soothe, subdue **7** appease, assuage, lighten, mollify, relieve, slacken **8** diminish, mitigate, moderate **9** alleviate, put to rest **14** cause to subside

all but 6 almost, nearly **7** close to **8** not quite **10** not far from, very nearly **14** except everyone, within an inch of **16** everything except

all by oneself 5 alone **7** unaided **9** on one's own **10** unassisted **13** unaccompanied

all-consuming 3 hot **5** fiery **6** ardent, fervid, raging, red-hot **7** burning, fanatic, fervent, frantic, glowing, intense, zealous **8** frenzied **10** passionate **11** impassioned

allegation 5 claim **6** avowal, charge **9** assertion, statement **10** accusation, contention, indictment, profession **11** declaration

allege 3 say **4** aver, avow **5** claim,

state **6** accuse, affirm, assert, charge, impugn, impute **7** contend, declare, profess **8** maintain

allegiance 6 fealty, homage **7** loyalty **8** devotion, fidelity **9** adherence, constancy, deference, obedience **12** faithfulness

allegory 5 fable **7** parable

allegro
  music: 4 fast

all-embracing 5 broad **6** all-out **7** general, overall **8** complete, sweeping, thorough **9** expansive, extensive, universal, unlimited **10** exhaustive, widespread **11** far-reaching, wide-ranging **12** all-inclusive, encyclopedic **13** comprehensive

Allen, Arabella
  character in: 14 Pickwick Papers
  author: 7 Dickens

Allen, Ethan
  served in: 16 Revolutionary War
  commander of: 17 Green Mountain Boys
  captured: 15 Fort Ticonderoga
  state: 7 Vermont

Allen, Fred
  real name: 20 John Florence Sullivan
  born: 11 Cambridge MA
  roles: 11 What's My Line **16** The Fred Allen Show

Allen, Steve
  real name: 12 Stephen Allen
  wife: 12 Jayne Meadows
  nickname: 10 Mr Midnight
  born: 9 New York NY
  roles: 13 I've Got a Secret **14** The Tonight Show

Allen, William Hervey
  author of: 7 Israfel **14** Anthony Adverse

Allen, Woody
  author of: 11 Getting Even, Side Effects **15** Without Feathers
  real name: 22 Allen Stewart Konigsberg
  wife: 12 Louise Lasser, Soon-Yi Previn
  born: 10 Brooklyn NY
  films: 5 Alice, Zelig **7** Bananas, Sleeper **9** Annie Hall, Interiors, Manhattan, Radio Days **10** Match Point **12** Anything Else, Casino Royale, Love and Death **14** New York Stories **15** Hollywood Ending, Mighty Aphrodite, Scenes from a Mall, Sweet and Lowdown **16** Husbands and Wives, Stardust Memories **17** Broadway Danny Rose **19** Bullets over Broadway, Hannah and Her Sisters **20** The Purple Rose of Cairo **21** Crimes and Misdemeanors **22** Manhattan Murder Mystery **25** The Curse of the Jade Scorpion

alleviate 4 dull, ease, quit **5** abate, allay, blunt, check, slake **6** lessen, quench, reduce, soften, subdue, tem-

per **7** assuage, lighten, mollify, relieve, slacken **8** diminish, mitigate, moderate

alleviation 6 easing, relief **9** lessening **10** palliation

alley 4 lane **5** byway **7** passage, pathway **10** passageway **16** narrow back street

Alley Oop
  creator: 14 Vincent T Hamlin
  character:
    girlfriend: 5 Ooola
    dinosaur: 5 Dinny
    king: 6 Guzzle
    scientist: 8 Dr Wonmug
  place:
    kingdom of: 3 Moo

All for Love
  author: 10 John Dryden
  character: 6 Antony, Caesar **7** Octavia **9** Cleopatra, Dolabella, Ventidius

All God's Chillun Got Wings
  author: 12 Eugene O'Neill
  character: 6 Mickey **9** Jim Harris **10** Ella Downey

alliance 4 pact **5** union **6** league, treaty **7** compact, company **9** agreement, coalition, concordat **10** federation **11** affiliation, association, confederacy, partnership **13** confederation **15** entente cordiale

allied 4 akin, like **5** alike, joint **6** united **7** cognate, kindred, related, similar **8** combined **9** corporate, federated **10** affiliated, associated, resembling **11** amalgamated **12** incorporated

all in 4 beat **5** spent, tired, weary **6** bushed, done in, pooped **7** drained, wearied, worn out **8** dog tired, fatigued, tired out **9** bone weary, dead tired, exhausted, played out

all in all 5 in sum **10** on the whole **20** when all is said and done

all-inclusive 5 broad **6** all-out, entire **7** general, overall **8** absolute, complete, sweeping, thorough **9** expansive, extensive, universal, unlimited **10** altogether, exhaustive, widespread **11** far-reaching, wide-ranging **12** all-embracing **13** comprehensive

All in the Family
  character: 10 Joey Stivic, Mike Stivic (Meathead) **11** Edith Bunker (Dingbat) **12** Archie Bunker **18** Gloria Bunker Stivic
  cast: 9 Rob Reiner **13** Jean Stapleton **14** Carroll O'Connor, Sally Struthers
  spinoffs: 5 Maude **12** Archie's Place **13** The Jeffersons

allocate 5 allot, allow **6** assign, budget **7** earmark **8** set aside **9** apportion, designate **11** appropriate

allocation 5 quota, share **7** measure, portion **8** division **9** allotment, meting out **10** dealing out **11** consignment, designation **12** apportioning, dispensation, distribution **13** apportionment

allot 4 dole, mete **5** allow, grant **6** assign **7** appoint, consign, dole out, earmark, give out, mete out, provide **8** allocate, dispense, divide up **9** apportion, parcel out **10** distribute, portion out

allotment 5 grant, quota, share **6** ration **7** measure, portion **9** allowance **10** allocation **11** consignment **12** dispensation **13** apportionment, appropriation

all-out 5 broad, total **7** full-out, maximum **8** complete, sweeping, thorough **9** extensive, full-scale **11** unqualified, unremitting **12** all-embracing, all-inclusive **13** comprehensive, thoroughgoing

all over 4 done **5** ended, kaput **8** finished **9** concluded **10** everywhere **11** universally

All Over
   author: 11 Edward Albee

allow 3 let **4** give **5** allot, grant **6** assign, permit **7** agree to, approve, concede, provide **8** allocate, sanction **9** authorize

allowable 7 allowed **8** accepted **9** permitted, tolerable, tolerated **10** acceptable, admissible, admittable, authorized, sanctioned **11** permissible

allowance 5 grant **6** bounty, income, ration **7** annuity, payment, pension, stipend, subsidy **8** discount **9** allotment, deduction, reduction **10** concession **11** subtraction

allow to go 4 free **5** let go **6** excuse, parole **7** dismiss, release, set free **8** liberate **9** discharge

allow to pass
   French: 13 laissez passer

alloy 3 mix **5** admix, blend **6** commix, dilute, fusion, impair **7** amalgam, combine, mixture **8** compound, intermix **9** admixture, composite, synthesis **10** adulterate, commixture, interblend **12** conglomerate

alloyed 5 mixed **6** impure **7** debased

All Quiet on the Western Front
   author: 18 Erich Maria Remarque
   character: 6 Muller, Tjaden **10** Paul Baumer **11** Albert Kropp, Haie Westhus **20** Stanislaus Katczinsky (Kat)
   director: 14 Lewis Milestone
   cast: 8 Lew Ayres **12** Louis Wolheim **14** Russell Gleason
   setting: 3 WWI
   Oscar for: 7 picture

all right 2 OK **3** yes **4** fair, hale, safe, sure, well **6** hearty **7** healthy **8** properly, unharmed **9** certainly, correctly, uninjured **10** absolutely, acceptably, unimpaired **14** satisfactorily
   Spanish: 5 bueno

All Said and Done
   author: 16 Simone de Beauvoir

allspice
   botanical name: 7 pimenta, p dioica **12** p officinalis
   also called: 7 pimento
   origin: 7 Jamaica **16** Caribbean Islands
   flavor: 5 clove **6** nutmeg **8** cinnamon
   use: 6 baking

Allston, Washington
   born: 10 Waccamaw SC
   artwork: 9 The Deluge **13** Uriel in the Sun **16** Belshazzar's Feast, Moonlit Landscape **20** Spanish Girl in Reverie

All's Well That Ends Well
   author: 18 William Shakespeare
   character: 5 Diana **6** Helena **7** Bertram **8** Parolles **12** King of France **14** Duke of Florence **19** Countess of Rousillon

All That Jazz
   director: 8 Bob Fosse
   cast: 9 Ben Vereen **11** Ann Reinking, Cliff Gorman, Roy Scheider **12** Jessica Lange, Leland Palmer

All the King's Men
   author: 16 Robert Penn Warren
   character: 9 Jack Burden, Judge Irwin, Sadie Burke **11** Adam Stanton, Willie Stark **12** Annie Stanton
   director: 12 Robert Rossen
   cast: 9 Joanne Dru, John Derek **11** John Ireland **17** Broderick Crawford **19** Mercedes McCambridge
   Oscar for: 5 actor (Crawford) **7** picture **17** supporting actress (McCambridge)

all the more
   Latin: 9 a fortiori

All the President's Men
   author: 11 Bob Woodward **13** Carl Bernstein
   subject: 16 Watergate scandal
   newspaper: 14 Washington Post
   director: 11 Alan J Pakula
   cast: 10 Jack Warden **11** Hal Holbrook **12** Jason Robards, Martin Balsam **13** Dustin Hoffman (Carl Bernstein), Jane Alexander, Robert Redford (Bob Woodward)
   Oscar for: 12 screenwriter **15** supporting actor (Robards)

all the same 5 alike **7** however, uniform **8** unvaried **9** identical **11** homogeneous

all together 7 en masse, in a body **8** as a group, in a group, in unison
   French: 12 tout ensemble

all told 5 in sum, total **6** in toto **7** totally **8** as a whole **10** altogether

allude 4 hint **5** refer **7** mention, speak of, suggest **8** intimate **9** touch upon

allure 4 bait, lure **5** charm, tempt **6** entice, lead on, seduce **7** attract, beguile, enchant, glamour **8** intrigue **9** captivate, fascinate **10** attraction, enticement, temptation **11** enchantment, fascination

allurement 4 draw, lure **5** charm **9** magnetism **10** attraction **11** fascination

alluring 4 sexy **8** charming, enticing, magnetic **10** attractive **11** fascinating

allusion 4 hint **7** mention **9** reference **10** suggestion

Allworthy, Squire
   character in: 8 Tom Jones
   author: 8 Fielding

ally 5 unite **6** league **7** combine, partner **8** confrere **9** accessory, affiliate, associate, colleague **10** accomplice, join forces **11** confederate **12** band together, bind together, collaborator, join together

Ally McBeal
   creator/writer: 11 David E Kelly
   actor: 10 Gil Bellows (Billy Alan Thomas) **11** Greg Germann (Richard Fish) **13** Jane Krakowski (Elaine Vassal), Peter MacNicol (John Cage) **16** Calista Flockhart (Ally McBeal), Lisa Nicole Carson (Renee Radick) **19** Courtney Thorne-Smith (Georgia)
   music: 13 Vonda Sheppard
   setting: 6 Boston

Allyson, June
   real name: 11 Ella Geisman
   husband: 10 Dick Powell
   born: 9 New York NY
   roles: 8 Good News **9** Interlude, The Shrike **11** Little Women **12** My Man Godfrey **16** The Stratton Story **19** The Glenn Miller Story

Almagest
   author: 7 Ptolemy
   title means: 11 the greatest
   subject: 9 astronomy

Al Maghrib see **7** Morocco

almandite
   species: 6 garnet
   color: 3 red

Almaviva, Count and Countess
   author: 12 Beaumarchais
   characters in: 18 The Barber of Seville **19** The Marriage of Figaro

Almayer's Folly
   author: 12 Joseph Conrad

almighty 7 supreme **8** absolute, infinite **9** sovereign, unlimited **10** invincible, omnipotent **11** all-powerful **12** transcendent

Almira
   opera by: 6 Handel

almond 12 Prunus dulcis
   varieties: 4 Wild **5** Earth, Green, Sweet **6** Bitter, Desert, Indian **8** Tropical **9** Flowering **12** Dwarf Russian
   candy: 8 marzipan
   liqueur: 6 orgeat **7** ratafia

almost 5 about **6** all but, nearly **7**

close to **8** not quite, well-nigh **9** just about **10** not far from, very nearly **11** practically, on the verge of **13** approximately **14** within an inch of

almost alike 5 close **7** similar **10** resembling **11** approaching, much the same **15** nearly identical

Almost Famous
director: **12** Cameron Crowe
cast: **8** Jason Lee (Jeff Bebe) **10** Kate Hudson (Penny Lane) **11** Billy Crudup (Russell Hammond) **12** Patrick Fugit (William Miller) **14** Zooey Deschanel (Anita Miller) **16** Frances McDormand (Elaine Miller)

alms 3 aid **4** dole, gift **5** mercy **6** relief **7** charity, handout, largess, present, subsidy, tribute **8** donation, gratuity, offering, pittance **9** baksheesh **10** assistance **11** benefaction, beneficence **12** contribution

almshouse 6 asylum **9** poorhouse, workhouse

almsman 5 tramp **6** beggar **9** mendicant **10** panhandler

Almug 13 red sandalwood

aloe 4 balm **5** succulent
full name: **8:** aloe vera
in: **6** lotion **7** shampoo

aloft 2 up **5** above, way up **6** high up, on high **7** skyward **8** in the air, in the sky, overhead **10** heavenward

Aloha State
nickname of: **6** Hawaii

alone 4 only, sole **6** lonely, single, singly, solely, unique **7** forlorn, unaided **8** deserted, desolate, forsaken, isolated, lonesome, peerless, singular, solitary, uniquely **9** abandoned, matchless, nonpareil, separated, unmatched, unrivaled **10** friendless, separately, singularly, solitarily, unassisted, unattended, unequalled, unescorted **11** unsurpassed, without help **12** incomparable, unchaperoned, unparalleled, without peers **13** unaccompanied, without others **14** singlehandedly
Latin: **4** sola **5** solus
French: **4** seul

along 2 on **4** over **6** beside, during, onward **7** abreast, forward, through

alongside 2 at, by **6** beside, next to **7** abreast, close by **9** at the side **10** parallel to **12** collaterally, parallelwise **13** equidistantly

aloof 3 icy **4** cold, cool **5** above, apart **6** chilly, formal, remote **7** distant, haughty, high-hat **8** detached, reserved **10** unsociable **11** at a distance, indifferent, standoffish, unconcerned **12** uninterested, unresponsive **13** unsympathetic **14** unapproachable

aloofness 7 reserve **8** coldness, coolness **9** formality **10** detachment, remoteness **11** haughtiness **12** indiffer-

ence **13** unsociability **15** standoffishness

aloud 7 audibly

alphabet 4 ABCs **6** schema **7** grammar, letters **8** elements **9** rudiments, tablature **10** characters, principles **13** writing system

Alphesiboea
also: **7** Arsinoe
form: **5** nymph
father: **4** Bias **7** Phegeus **9** Leucippus
mother: **9** Philodice
husband: **8** Alcmaeon
son: **6** Adonis
rejected: **8** Dionysus
nurse for: **7** Orestes

Alpheus
father: **7** Oceanus
mother: **6** Tethys
loved: **8** Arethusa
changed into: **5** river

Alphonse and Gaston
creator: **14** Frederick Opper
saying: **22** After you my dear Alphonse, No after you my dear Gaston

alpine 5 alpen, lofty **6** aerial **8** elevated, snow-clad, towering **9** subalpine **10** alpestrine, sky-kissing, snow-capped **11** cloud-capped, mountainous **13** cloud-piercing, cloud-touching **14** heaven-touching

Alps, Alpine
country: **5** Italy **6** France **7** Austria, Germany **10** Yugoslavia **11** Switzerland **13** Liechtenstein
range: **6** Carnic, Graian, Julian, Otztal **7** Bernese, Cottian, Pennine **8** Bavarian, Ligurian, Maritime, Rhaetian **9** Dolomites, Lepontine **10** Hohe Tauern
peak: **4** Rosa **5** Eiger, Monch **8** Jungfrau **10** Karawanken, Matterhorn, Piz Bernina **13** Grossglockner
highest point: **5** Blanc
pass: **7** Brenner, Simplon, Splugen, Stelvio **9** Semmering **10** St Gotthard **14** Great St Bernard
lake: **4** Como **6** Alpine, Geneva **7** Lucerne **8** Maggiore **9** Constance
phenomenon: **4** echo
resort: **7** Zermatt **8** Chamonix, Salzburg, St Moritz **9** Innsbruck **13** Berchtesgaden
singing: **5** yodel
wind: **5** foehn

already 5 early, so far **6** before **8** formerly, hitherto, until now **10** heretofore, previously

already seen
French: **6** deja vu

also 3 and, too **4** more, plus **5** extra **6** as well **7** besides **8** moreover **9** including **10** in addition **12** additionally

Altaic
language branches: **6** Turkic **8** Tungusic **9** Mongolian

altar 5 bomos **6** hestia, scribis **7** eschara **8** credence **9** holy table, prothesis **10** Lord's table

Altar
constellation of: **3** Ara

Altdorfer, Albrecht
born: **7** Germany **10** Regensburg
artwork: **16** Susanna at the Bath **20** St George and the Dragon, Susannah and the Elders **24** Landscape with a Footbridge **39** The Battle of Alexander and Darius on the Issus

alter 4 vary **5** amend **6** change, modify, recast, revise **7** convert, remodel **9** transform **13** make different

alterable 7 unfixed **8** variable **9** adaptable **10** adjustable, changeable, modifiable **11** convertible

alteration 6 change **10** adjustment, conversion, remodeling **12** modification **13** transmutation **14** transformation

altercation 3 row **4** spat, tiff **5** brawl, broil, fight, melee, scene **6** affray, fracas, rumpus, scrape **7** discord, dispute, quarrel, scuffle **8** argument **9** bickering, wrangling **10** falling-out **11** controversy **12** disagreement

alter ego 4 twin **5** match **6** double **9** duplicate, other self, semblable **10** complement, other image, second self, simulacrum **11** counterpart **12** Doppelganger

alternate 3 sub **4** vary **5** alter, proxy **6** backup, change, deputy, rotate, second **7** another, shoddy, stand-in **9** surrogate, take turns **10** every other, reciprocal, substitute, successive, understudy **11** alternating, consecutive, every second, interchange, intersperse, pinch hitter

alternative 6 choice, option, way out **8** recourse **9** selection **10** substitute **11** other choice

although 3 but, yet **4** even **5** still **7** however **11** nonetheless **12** nevertheless **15** notwithstanding

altitude 4 apex **6** height, vertex, zenith **8** eminence, tallness **9** elevation, loftiness, sublimity **10** prominence

Altman, Robert
director of: **4** Aria, MASH **6** Popeye **8** A Wedding **9** Short Cuts, The Player, Streamers, Nashville **10** Kansas City **11** Gosford Park, Ready to Wear **14** Cookie's Fortune, The Long Goodbye **17** The James Dean Story

altogether 5 fully, in all, in sum, quite **6** in toto, wholly **7** all told, totally, utterly **8** all in all, as a whole, entirely **9** in general, out and out, perfectly **10** absolutely, completely, in sum total, on the whole, thoroughly **12** all inclusive, collectively

altruism 7 charity **10** generosity **11** benevolence **12** philanthropy, public spirit **13** unselfishness **14** bigheartedness, charitableness **15** humanitarianism

altruistic 8 generous **9** unselfish **10** benevolent, charitable **12** humanitarian, largehearted **13** philanthropic **14** public-spirited

aluminum
 chemical symbol: **2** Al

alumni 5 grads

alumnus, alumna 4 grad **8** graduate **13** former student

Alverio, Rosita Dolores
 real name of: **10** Rita Moreno

always 7 forever **8** evermore **9** eternally, every time, regularly **10** for all time, invariably **11** continually, incessantly, perpetually, unceasingly **12** consistently **13** everlastingly, unremittingly **14** forever and ever

Amadan
 origin: **5** Irish
 form: **5** fairy

Amadeus
 director: **11** Milos Forman
 cast: **8** Tom Hulce (Wolfgang Amadeus Mozart) **14** F Murray Abraham (Antonio Salieri)
 choreography: **10** Twyla Tharp
 Oscar for: **5** actor (Abraham) **7** picture **8** director

Amadis of Gaul
 author: **16** Garcia de Montalvo
 character: **6** Oriana, Perion **7** Elisena **8** Garinter, Lisuarte

Amado, Jorge
 author of: **14** Tent of Miracles **15** Home Is the Sailor **19** Shepherds of the Night **24** Gabriela Clove and Cinnamon **25** Dona Flor and Her Two Husbands **30** The Two Deaths of Quincas Wateryell

Amahl and the Night Visitors
 opera by: **7** Menotti

Amalek
 father: **7** Eliphaz
 mother: **6** Timnah
 grandfather: **4** Esau
 descendant of: **9** Amalekite

amalgam 5 alloy, blend, combo, union **6** fusion, league, merger **7** joining, mixture **8** alliance, compound, mishmash **9** admixture, composite **10** assemblage, commixture **11** combination **12** amalgamation, intermixture

amalgamate 3 mix **4** fuse **5** blend, merge, unify, unite **7** combine **8** coalesce, federate **9** commingle, integrate **10** synthesize **11** consolidate, incorporate **12** join together

Amarcord
 director: **15** Federico Fellini
 cast: **10** Bruno Zanin, Magali Noel **13** Pupella Maggio

amaretto
 type: **7** liqueur
 origin: **5** Italy

flavor: **6** almond
 with vodka: **9** Godmother

Amaryllis
 character in: **9** Ecologues
 author: **6** Virgil
 represented: **11** shepherdess

amass 6 gather, heap up, pile up **7** acquire, collect, compile, round up **8** assemble **10** accumulate

amateur 4 tyro **6** novice, non-pro **7** dabbler **8** beginner, hobbyist, inexpert, neophyte **9** greenhorn, unskilled **10** dilettante, unpolished **13** inexperienced **14** unprofessional **15** nonprofessional

amateurish 5 inept **6** clumsy **7** awkward **8** inexpert, mediocre **9** unskilled, untrained **10** unskillful **11** incompetent, ineffective, unpracticed **13** inexperienced **14** unaccomplished, unprofessional

amatory 3 hot **4** fond, sexy **6** ardent, doting, erotic, loving, sexual, steamy, tender **7** adoring, amorous, devoted, fervent, sensual, sexed-up **8** lovesick, romantic, yearning **9** libidinal, loverlike, rapturous **10** infatuated, lascivious, passionate **11** impassioned, languishing

amaxophobia
 fear of: **7** driving **8** vehicles

amaze 3 awe **4** daze, stun **5** shock **7** astound, stagger, stupefy **8** astonish, surprise **9** dumbfound **11** flabbergast

amazement 3 awe **5** shock **6** wonder **8** surprise **9** disbelief **11** incredulity **12** astonishment, bewilderment, stupefaction

Amazing Race, The
 network: **3** CBS
 host: **11** Phil Keoghan
 winners: **10** Chip and Kim, Zach and Flo **12** Alex and Chris **13** Rob and Brennan **14** Chip and Reichen **15** Freddy and Kendra, Uchenna and Joyce

Amazon
 occupation: **7** warrior
 sex: **6** female
 queen: **9** Hippolyta
 river: **6** Brazil

amazonite
 species: **8** feldspar

Amazonomachia
 battle between: **6** Greeks **7** Amazons

ambassador 5 agent, envoy **6** consul, deputy, legate, nuncio **7** attache, courier **8** diplomat, emissary, minister **9** go-between **11** diplomatist **12** intermediary **13** consul general **14** representative

Ambassadors, The
 author: **10** Henry James
 character: **8** Strether, Waymarsh **10** Mrs Newsome **11** Mamie Pocock, Sarah Pocock **12** Maria Gostrey **15**

Chadwick Newsome **17** Comtesse de Vionnet

amber
 formed from: **5** resin
 color: **6** yellow
 Greek: **8** elektron

ambiance 3 air **4** aura, mood, tone **5** tenor **6** spirit, flavor, milieu, temper **7** climate, setting **9** character **10** atmosphere **11** environment **12** surroundings

ambiguity 9 vagueness **11** uncertainty **12** abstruseness, doubtfulness, equivocation **14** indefiniteness
 French: **13** double entente

ambiguous 5 vague **7** cryptic, unclear **8** doubtful, puzzling **9** enigmatic, equivocal, uncertain **10** indefinite, misleading

ambition 3 aim **4** goal, hope, plan, push, zeal **5** dream, drive **6** design, desire, intent **7** longing, purpose **8** striving, yearning **9** objective **10** aspiration

ambitious 4 avid **5** eager **6** ardent, intent **7** arduous, zealous **8** aspiring, desirous **9** difficult, energetic, grandiose, strenuous **10** determined **11** industrious **12** enterprising

ambivalent 5 mixed **7** warring **8** clashing, confused, opposing, wavering **9** equivocal, undecided, unfocused **10** wishy-washy **11** conflicting, fluctuating, vacillating **13** contradictory

amble 6 ramble, stroll **7** meander, saunter **15** wander aimlessly

Ambler, Eric
 author of: **11** The Levanter **12** A Kind of Auger **13** The Care of Time **14** The Night-Comers, Uncommon Danger **15** Journey Into Fear, The Dark Frontier **16** The Light of the Day **19** A Coffin for Dimitrios **22** The Siege of the Villa Lipp

Ambling Alp, The
 nickname of: **12** Primo Carnera

ambrosial 5 balmy **8** fragrant, luscious, perfumed **9** delicious **13** sweet-smelling

ambrosia of the gods 4 food **5** drink **6** nectar **7** perfume

ambulance chaser 4 beak **6** lawyer **8** attorney **9** counselor **10** mouthpiece **12** legal advisor

ambulatory 6 mobile, moving **7** walking **10** up and about **11** peripatetic

ambush 4 trap **5** blind, cover **6** attack, entrap, hiding, lay for, waylay **7** assault **8** hideaway, surprise **9** ambuscade **11** concealment, hiding place **13** stalking-horse

Ameche, Don
 real name: **17** Dominic Felix Amici
 born: **9** Kenosha WI
 roles: **4** Pais **5** Folks (Oscar) **6** Cocoon (Oscar) **12** Things Change **13**

Heaven Can Wait, Moon Over Miami, Silk Stockings, Trading Places **14** That Night in Rio **16** Down Argentine Way **18** The Three Musketeers **21** Harry and the Hendersons **29** The Story of Alexander Graham Bell

Amelia
author: 13 Henry Fielding
character: 10 Dr Harrison **11** Mrs Atkinson **12** Miss Matthews **19** Captain William Booth

ameliorate 4 heal, help, mend **5** amend, fix up **6** better, perk up, pick up, reform, remedy, revise **7** advance, correct, improve, patch up, promote, rectify **8** palliate, progress **9** come along, get better **10** grow better **11** improve upon

ameliorative 8 remedial **9** improving **10** corrective, palliative **11** therapeutic **12** compensatory

amen 5 truly **6** it is so, so be it, verily **8** hear hear **9** let it be so, yes indeed **11** so shall it be **17** would that it were so

Amen
also: 4 Amon **5** Ammon
origin: 8 Egyptian
king of: 4 gods
worshiped at: 6 Thebes
personifies: 3 air **6** breath
represented by: 3 ram **5** goose
patron of: 6 Thebes
corresponds to: 4 Jove, Zeus **6** Amen Ra, Amon Ra **7** Jupiter

amenable 4 open **7** cordial, willing **8** obliging, yielding **9** agreeable, tractable **10** open-minded, responsive, submissive **11** acquiescent, complaisant, cooperative, persuadable, sympathetic **17** favorably disposed

amend 3 fix **4** mend **5** alter, emend **6** better, change, modify, polish, reform, remedy, revise **7** correct, develop, enhance, improve, perfect, rectify

amendment 6 change, reform **7** adjunct **8** addition, revision **10** alteration, correction, emendation **11** improvement **12** modification **13** rectification

amends 7 apology, defense, payment, redress **8** requital **9** atonement, expiation **10** recompense, reparation **11** explanation, restitution, restoration, retribution, vindication **12** compensation, satisfaction **13** justification, peace offering **14** acknowledgment **15** indemnification

amenity, amenities 8 civility, mildness, niceties **9** geniality, gentility **10** affability, amiability, courtesies, gentleness, politeness, refinement **11** gallantries, good manners **12** friendliness, graciousness, pleasantness **13** agreeableness

Amen Ra

also: 6 Amon Ra, Amen Re
origin: 8 Egyptian
god of: 8 universe
corresponds to: 4 Amen, Amon, Jove, Zeus **5** Ammon **7** Jupiter

America
author: 19 Stephen Vincent Benet

America, North
country: 4 Cuba **5** Haiti **6** Belize, Canada, Mexico, Panama **8** Honduras **9** Costa Rica, Guatemala, Nicaragua **10** El Salvador **12** United States **17** Dominican Republic
island: 5 Banks **6** Baffin, Kodiak **7** Bahamas, Bermuda **8** Victoria **9** Alexander, Anticosti, Ellesmere, Greenland, Vancouver **10** Aleutians, Cape Breton, Long Island, West Indies **11** Southampton **12** Newfoundland, Prince Edward **13** Prince of Wales **14** Queen Charlotte
mountain: 4 Blue **5** Coast, Green, Kenai, Ozark, Rocky, White **6** Alaska, Brooks, Chuska, Diablo, Picket, Pocono **7** Cariboo, Cascade, Chugach, Klamath, Olympic, Purcell, St. Elias, Selkirk, Taconic **8** Catskill, Franklin, Ouachita, Santa Ana, Wrangell **9** Blue Ridge, Franconia, Mackenzie, San Rafael, Santa Cruz, Wenatchee **10** Adirondack, Bitterroot, Black Hills, Cumberland, Great Smoky, Kittatinny, Laurentian, San Jacinto **11** Appalachian, Grand Tetons, Santa Monica, Sierra Madre **12** Presidential, San Bernadino, Sierra Nevada
highest point: 6 Denali (National Park) **8** McKinley
lowest point: 11 Death Valley
river: 3 Red **4** Ohio **5** Yukon **6** Copper, Fraser, Hudson, Nelson **8** Arkansas, Colorado, Columbia, Delaware, Missouri **9** Mackenzie **10** Coppermine, Sacramento, San Joaquin, St Lawrence **11** Connecticut, Mississippi
lake: 4 Erie **5** Huron **6** Carson, Walker **7** Nipigon, Ontario **8** Manitoba, Michigan, Reindeer, Superior, Winnipeg **9** Athabasca, Champlain, Great Bear, Great Salt **10** Great Slave **11** Yellowstone
animal: 3 bat, rat **4** bear, lynx, puma, wolf **5** bison, moose, skunk **6** beaver, musk ox **7** bighorn, caribou **8** sewellel **9** pronghorn, white goat
bird: 4 hawk **5** eagle, snipe **8** bobwhite, woodcock, wood ibis **9** blue heron, ptarmigan
sea: 6 Bering **7** Chukchi, Lincoln **8** Beaufort **9** Caribbean
religion: 7 Judaism **10** Protestant **13** Roman Catholic **27** Eastern Orthodox Christianity
people: 6 Eskimo **8** European, Hispanic **12** African Negro **14** American Indian, *see also* Native American **15** African American

language: 6 French **7** English, Spanish

America, South
country: 4 Peru **5** Chile **6** Brazil, Guyana **7** Bolivia, Ecuador, Uruguay **8** Colombia, Paraguay, Suriname **9** Argentina, Venezuela
city: 4 Lima **5** Quito **6** Bogota, Recife **7** Caracas **8** Salvador, Santiago, Sao Paulo **10** Montevideo **11** Buenos Aires, Porto Alegre **12** Rio de Janeiro **13** Belo Horizonte
island: 6 Chiloe, Chonos, Marajo **9** Galapagos **10** Wellington **11** Madre de Dios **13** Juan Fernandez, Reina Adelaida **14** Tierra del Fuego
sea: 9 Caribbean
lake: 5 Patos, Poopo, Mirim **6** Viedma **8** Titicaca **9** Maracaibo, San Martin **10** Concepcion
mountain: 6 Andes **9** Pakaraima **12** Monte Fitz Roy **14** Cerro Aconcagua, Monte Sarmiento **15** Serra dos Parecis **16** Monte San Valentin, Serra do Espinhaco
highest point: 9 Aconcagua
lowest point: 15 Peninsula Valdes
river: 3 Ica **4** Beni, Iaco, Jari, Meta, Napo **5** Abuna, Cauca, Chico, Iriri, Ituxi, Jurua, Jutai, Negro, Palma, Pardo, Purus, Tiete, Tigre, Xingu **6** Amazon, Arauca, Branco, Chubut, Cumina, Curaco, Cuyuni, Grande, Gurupi, Iguacu, Japura, Javari, Mamore, Maroni, Mortes, Parana, Salado, Vaupes **7** Bermejo, Caqueta, Deseado, Guapore, Jamunda, Juruena, Madeira, Mapuera, Maranon, Orinoco, Oyapock, Ucayali, Vichada **8** Amazonas, Araguaia, Colorado, Guaviare, Jamachim, Paraguay, Parnaiba, Putumayo, Tapajoz, Urubamba, Uruguay **9** Essequibo, Jaguaribe, Paranaiba, Saladillo, Sao Manuel, Tocantins **10** Courantyne **12** Sao Francisco
animal: 3 bat **4** bear, deer **5** llama, sloth, tapir **6** alpaca, monkey, ocelot, weasel **7** opossum, peccary, raccoon **8** capybara, javelina **9** armadillo
bird: 3 owl **4** hawk, rhea **5** eagle **6** condor, falcon, jabiru **7** hoatzin **8** flamingo **11** hummingbird
people: 6 Indian **7** African, Chibcha, Mestizo, Mulatto, Spanish **10** Araucanian, Portuguese
religion: 7 Judaism **10** Protestant **13** Roman Catholic
language: 5 Dutch **7** English, Spanish **10** Portuguese

American, The
author: 10 Henry James
character: 8 Mrs Bread **10** Mr Tristram **11** Mrs Tristram **12** Noemie Nioche **13** Count Valentin **14** Claire de Cintre **17** Christopher Newman **25** Marquis Urbain de Bellegarde
setting: 5 Paris

American Beauty
director: 9 Sam Mendes
cast: 10 Mena Suvari (Angela Hayes), Thora Birch (Jane Burnham), Wes Bentley (Ricky Fitts) 11 Chris Cooper (Colonel Frank Fitts), Kevin Spacey (Lester Burnham) 13 Allison Janney (Barbara Fitts), Annette Bening (Carolyn Burnham) 14 Peter Gallagher (Buddy Kane)

American Caesar
author: 17 William Manchester

American Claimant, The
author: 9 Mark Twain

American Dreams
author: 11 Studs Terkel

American Dreams
network: 3 NBC
cast: 9 Tom Verica (Jack Pryor), Will Estes (J. J. Pryor) 10 Ethan Dampf (Will Pryor), Gail O'Grady (Helen Pryor), Sarah Ramos (Patty Pryor) 12 Brittany Snow (Meg Pryor) 13 Jonathan Adams (Henry Walker) 14 Arlen Escarpeta (Sam Walker), Vanessa Lengies (Roxanne Bojarski)

American Graffiti
director: 11 George Lucas
cast: 9 Paul Le Mat, Ron Howard 10 Candy Clark 11 Wolfman Jack 12 Harrison Ford 13 Cindy Williams 15 Richard Dreyfuss 17 MacKenzie Phillips

American Idol
network: 3 Fox
host: 12 Ryan Seacrest
judge: 10 Paula Abdul 11 Simon Cowell 12 Randy Jackson
winner: 13 Kelly Clarkson, Ruben Studdard 14 Fantasia Barino 15 Carrie Underwood

American Indian see under 14 Native American

American in Paris, An
director: 16 Vincente Minnelli
cast: 8 Nina Foch 9 Gene Kelly 11 Leslie Caron, Oscar Levant 14 Georges Guetary
score: 14 George Gershwin
Oscar for: 7 picture

Americanization of Emily
director: 12 Arthur Hiller
script by: 14 Paddy Chayefsky
cast: 11 James Coburn, James Garner 12 Julie Andrews 13 Melvyn Douglas

American Tragedy, An
author: 15 Theodore Dreiser
character: 12 Roberta Alden 14 Clyde Griffiths, Sondra Finchley 15 Samuel Griffiths
movie: 14 A Place in the Sun

America's Next Top Model
network: 3 UPN
host: 9 Tyra Banks
judge: 9 Jay Manuel, Kimora Lee, Nole Marin 10 J. Alexander 11 Nigel Barker 12 Beau Quillian 15 Janice

Dickinson
winner: 9 Naima Mora 10 Eva Pigford 11 Yoanna House 13 Adrianne Curry

America's Sweetheart
nickname of: 12 Mary Pickford

amethyst
species: 6 quartz
color: 6 purple
month: 8 February

Amfortas
leader of: 7 knights
in search of: 9 holy grail

ami, amie 6 friend

amiability 10 good nature, kindliness 12 agreeability, friendliness, pleasantness

amiable 6 genial, kindly, polite 7 affable, cordial, winning 8 amicable, charming, engaging, friendly, gracious, obliging, pleasant, pleasing, sociable 9 agreeable, congenial 10 attractive 11 good-natured

amicability 5 amity 7 concord 8 good will 9 affection 10 cordiality, friendship 12 friendliness 14 neighborliness

amicable 4 kind 5 civil 6 kindly, polite 7 amiable, cordial 8 amenable, friendly, sociable 9 agreeable, courteous, peaceable 10 benevolent, harmonious, neighborly 11 kindhearted

Amici, Dominic Felix
real name of: 9 Don Ameche

amicus curiae 17 a friend of the court

amigo, amiga 6 friend

Amis, Kingsley
author of: 8 Ending Up, Lucky Jim 10 Colonel Sun, Jake's Thing 11 I Like It Here, The Green Man 16 One Fat Englishman, Take A Girl Like You 18 Russian Hide-and-Seek, The Anti-Death League 20 That Uncertain Feeling
father of: 10 Martin Amis

amiss 4 awry 5 askew, false, wrong 6 astray, faulty 7 falsely, mixed-up, off base, wrongly 8 faultily, improper, mistaken, untoward 9 erroneous, incorrect, out of line 10 fallacious, improperly, mistakenly, out of order, unsuitable, unsuitably, untowardly 11 erroneously, incorrectly 12 inaccurately 13 inappropriate 15 inappropriately

Amistad
director: 15 Steven Spielberg
cast: 13 Djimon Hounsou (Cinque), Morgan Freeman (Joadson) 14 Anthony Hopkins (John Quincy Adams), Nigel Hawthorne (Martin Van Buren) 18 Matthew McConaughey (Baldwin)

Amittai
son: 5 Jonah

amity 6 accord 7 concord, harmony 8 good will, sympathy 9 agreement 10

cordiality, fellowship, fraternity, friendship 11 brotherhood, cooperation 13 understanding

Ammishaddai
son: 7 Ahiezer

Ammon
father: 3 Lot
descendants: 9 Ammonites

Ammonite god 6 Molech, Moloch

ammunition 4 ammo, arms 5 shell 6 bullet, rocket 7 missile, torpedo 9 artillery, cartridge, small arms 11 iron rations 13 powder and shot

ammunition dump 7 arsenal 8 magazine 18 military storehouse, munitions warehouse

amnesia 4 daze 5 fugue 6 stupor 7 agnosia 8 blackout 9 memory gap 11 anterograde, trance state

amnesty 6 pardon 8 immunity, reprieve 10 absolution 11 forgiveness 14 reconciliation

amoeba, ameba 4 dyad, germ, mold 5 spore, virus 6 fungus 7 ciliate, microbe 8 bacteria, reovirus 9 bacterium, echovirus 13 microorganism
part: 7 nucleus 8 membrane 9 pseudopod 10 protoplasm 11 food vacuole 18 contractile vacuole
reproduction by: 7 fission

amok see 5 amuck

Amon see 4 Amen

among 2 at 3 mid 4 amid, with 6 amidst 7 amongst, between, betwixt 12 in the midst of

among other persons
Latin: 10 inter alios

among others 8 attended, escorted, in a crowd, in a group, together 11 accompanied

among other things
Latin: 9 inter alia

among themselves
Latin: 7 inter se

Amon Ra see 6 Amen Ra

Amor see 5 Cupid

Amore dei Tre Re, L'
opera by: 10 Montemezzi

Amoretti
author: 13 Edmund Spenser

amoretto
art figure: 5 Cupid

amorous 4 fond 6 ardent, doting, loving, tender 8 enamored, lovesick 10 passionate 11 impassioned 12 affectionate

amorousness 4 love 5 ardor 6 warmth 7 passion

amor patriae 10 patriotism 13 love of country

amorphous 5 vague 8 formless, unshapen 9 anomalous, shapeless, undefined 11 nondescript 12 undelineated 13 characterless, indeterminate

Amos
  father: **4** Naum

Amos 'n' Andy
  character: **8** Lightnin' **9** Amos Jones,
  Andy Brown **13** George (the King
  Fish) Stevens **15** Sapphire Stevens
  cast: **8** Tim Moore **13** Ernestine
  Wade, Horace Stewart **14** Alvin Childress **15** Spencer Williams

amount 3 sum **4** bulk, mass **5** total **6**
extent, volume **7** measure **8** quantity,
sum total **9** aggregate, magnitude

amour 6 affair **7** liaison, romance **8** intrigue **10** love affair

amour propre 8 self-love **10** self-
esteem **11** self-respect

Ampelos
  form: **5** satyr

Ampere, Andre-Marie
  field: **7** physics **11** mathematics
  nationality: **6** French
  founded: **15** electrodynamics **16** electromagnetism

amphibian 8 seaplane **10** hydroplane,
vertebrate **14** aerohydroplane
  kind: **4** frog, newt, toad **9** caecilian
  10 salamander
  young: **6** larvae **7** tadpole **8** polliwog

Amphisbaena
  form: **7** serpent
  number of heads: **3** two

amphitheater 4 bowl **5** arena **7** gallery, stadium **8** coliseum **10** auditorium
  Roman: **9** Colosseum

Amphitrite
  origin: **5** Greek
  goddess of: **3** sea
  father: **6** Nereus
  mother: **5** Doris
  husband: **8** Poseidon

Amphitruo (Amphitryon)
  author: **7** Plautus
  character: **4** Zeus **7** Alcmena, Jupiter,
  Mercury **10** Amphitryon

Amphitryon
  father: **7** Alcaeus
  grandfather: **7** Perseus
  uncle: **9** Electryon, Sthenelus
  wife: **7** Alcmene
  son: **8** Iphicles
  daughter: **8** Perimede

Amphitryon 38
  author: **13** Jean Giraudoux

amphora 3 jar, jug, urn **4** vase

ample 3 big **4** huge, vast, wide **5**
broad, large, roomy **6** enough, plenty
7 copious, immense, liberal, profuse **8**
abundant, adequate, extended, generous, spacious **9** bountiful, capacious,
expansive, extensive, outspread, plentiful **10** commodious, sufficient, voluminous **11** substantial **12** satisfactory
14 more than enough

amplification 7 raising **8** increase,
widening **9** expansion, extension **10**

developing, filling out, increasing **11**
added detail, development, elaboration, enlargement, expatiation, flesh-
ing out, heightening, lengthening,
rounding out **12** augmentation **13**
magnification **14** aggrandizement **15**
supplementation

amplify 5 add to, raise, widen **6**
deepen, expand, extend **7** augment,
broaden, develop, enlarge, fill out **8**
complete, heighten, increase, lengthen
9 elaborate (on), expatiate, intensify
10 illustrate, strengthen, supplement

amplitude 4 bulk, mass, size **5** range,
reach, scope, sweep, width **6** extent,
volume **7** bigness, breadth, compass,
expanse **8** fullness, plethora, richness,
vastness **9** abundance, dimension,
largeness, magnitude, plenitude, profusion **11** copiousness **12** completeness, spaciousness **13** capaciousness

amply 5 fully **6** richly **8** lavishly **9** copiously, liberally, profusely **10** abundantly, adequately, completely, generously, thoroughly **11** bountifully,
plentifully **12** sufficiently, unstintingly
14 satisfactorily

amputate 5 sever **6** cut off, excise, lop
off, remove **9** dismember

Amram
  father: **4** Bani **6** Dishon
  son: **5** Aaron, Moses
  daughter: **6** Miriam

Amsterdam
  airport: **8** Schiphol
  canal: **11** Herengracht **13** Keizers-
  gracht, Prinsengracht
  capital of: **7** Holland **11** Netherlands
  landmark: **8** Oude Kerk **10** Nieuwe
  Kerk
  museum: **7** Van Gogh **9** Stedelijk **11**
  Rijksmuseum
  nickname: **16** Venice of the North
  waters: **6** Amstel **7** Ij River **9**
  Zuiderzee **10** Ijsselmeer **13** North
  Sea

amuck 4 amok, nuts **6** wildly **7** berserk, bonkers **8** crackers, insanely **9**
in a frenzy **10** frenziedly, maniacally
11 ferociously, murderously **14** uncontrollably

amulet 5 charm **6** fetish **8** talisman **10**
lucky piece

amuse 5 cheer **6** absorb, divert, occupy, please **7** beguile, engross, enliven, gladden **8** interest **9** entertain

amusement 3 fun **4** game, play **5**
hobby, revel **7** delight, pastime **8**
pleasure **9** avocation, diversion, enjoyment, merriment **10** recreation **11**
distraction **13** entertainment

amusing 5 droll, funny, witty **7** comical, waggish **8** cheering, farcical, humorous, pleasant, pleasing **9** absorbing, beguiling, diverting **10** delightful,
engrossing **11** interesting, pleasurable
12 entertaining

Amy, Gilbert
  composer of: **9** Alpha-Beth **10** Epi-
  grammes, Mouvements **11** Antipho-
  nies **12** Trajectories

anagram 4 code **6** cipher

Anakim 11 giant people

analects 8 extracts **9** gleanings **10** miscellany, selections **11** collectanea,
miscellanea

Analects of Confucius, The
  author: **9** Confucius

analeptic 9 stimulant **11** restorative

analgesic 4 drug **6** opiate **7** anodyne **8**
narcotic **10** anesthetic, painkiller

analogous 4 akin, like **7** similar **8** parallel **10** comparable, equivalent **11**
correlative **13** corresponding

analogy 6 simile **8** likeness, metaphor
10 comparison, similarity, similitude
11 correlation, equivalence, parallelism, resemblance **14** correspondence

analysis 4 test **5** assay, brief, study **6**
digest, precis, review, search **7**
breakup, inquiry, outline, summary,
therapy **8** abstract, judgment, synopsis, thinking **9** appraisal, breakdown,
diagnosis, partition, reasoning, reduction **10** dissection, estimation, evaluation, resolution, separation **11** examination, observation, speculation **12**
dissociation **13** investigation, psychotherapy **14** interpretation, psychoanalysis

analyst 5 judge **6** shrink, tester **8** examiner, observer **9** appraiser, estimator, evaluator **12** headshrinker, investigator **13** psychoanalyst

analytic, analytical 7 logical, testing
8 rational, studious **9** inquiring, organized, searching **10** diagnostic, systematic **14** problem-solving

analyze 5 assay, judge, study **6** search
7 examine **8** appraise, consider, diag-
nose, evaluate, question **9** reason out
11 investigate **12** think through

Ananais
  father: **8** Nebedeus
  wife: **8** Sapphira
  sent to: **4** Paul, Saul
  lied to: **5** Peter
  same as: **4** liar

anarchist 5 rebel **8** mutineer, nihilist **9**
insurgent, terrorist **11** syndicalist **13**
revolutionary

anarchy 5 chaos **6** utopia **8** disorder
11 lawlessness **13** the millennium **19**
absence of government

Anastasia
  director: **13** Anatole Litvak
  cast: **10** Helen Hayes, Yul Brynner **12**
  Akim Tamiroff **13** Ingrid Bergman
  (Oscar)

anathema 3 ban **5** curse, taboo **7** censure **11** abomination, malediction **12**
condemnation, denunciation, proscrip-

tion **13** unmentionable **15** excommunication

Anathema
author: **14** Leonid Andreyev

anathematize 4 damn **7** accurse, condemn **8** execrate, maledict **9** abominate **13** excommunicate **17** hold in abomination

Anatolia *see* **7** Armenia

Anatolian
language family: **12** Indo-European
includes: **6** Luwian Lycian Lydian **7** Hittite
spoken in: **9** Asia Minor
spoken by: **8** Hittites

anatomist 12 morphologist
American: **5** Allen, Evans **7** Herrick **8** Stockard
Arabian: **8** Avicenna
British: **4** Owen **5** Hooke **6** Harvey
Dutch: **10** Swammerdam
French: **6** Buffon, Cuvier
German: **5** Wolff **7** Schwann
Greek: **5** Galen **9** Aristotle **10** Herophilus **12** Erasistratus
Italian: **8** Malpighi
Scottish: **5** Brown

anatomize 7 analyze, dissect **18** separate into pieces

anatomy 4 body **8** analysis **9** structure **10** dissection **11** examination

Anatomy Lesson, The
author: **10** Philip Roth

Anatomy of a Murder
director: **13** Otto Preminger
cast: **8** Eve Arden **9** Lee Remick **10** Ben Gazzara **12** George C Scott, James Stewart, Kathryn Grant **14** Arthur O'Connell
score: **13** Duke Ellington

Anatosaurus
type: **8** dinosaur **10** ornithopod
period: **10** Cretaceous
characteristic: **10** duck-billed
location: **12** North America

Anaxibia
father: **6** Atreus
mother: **6** Aerope
brother: **8** Menelaus **9** Agamemnon
husband: **6** Nestor **9** Strophius
son: **7** Pylades

Anaximander
field: **11** mathematics
nationality: **5** Greek
doctrine: **11** single-world
first: **22** geometric universe model

ancestor 8 begetter, forebear **9** precursor, prototype **10** antecedent, forefather, forerunner, procreator, progenitor **11** predecessor

ancestry 4 line, race **5** house, stock **6** family, origin **7** descent, lineage **8** heredity, pedigree **9** ancestors, blood line, genealogy, parentage **10** derivation, extraction, family tree **11** progenitors

Anchisaurus
type: **8** dinosaur
location: **17** Connecticut Valley

Anchises
prince of: **4** Troy
father: **5** Capys
mother: **8** Themiste
grandfather: **9** Assaracus
uncle: **8** Laomedon
brother: **7** Laocoon
son: **5** Lyrus **6** Aeneas

anchor 3 fix **4** hook, moor **5** affix, basis **6** fasten, secure **7** bulwark, defense, mooring, support **8** mainstay, security **9** safeguard **10** foundation **12** ground tackle

anchorage 3 key **4** bund, dock, pier, port, quay, slip **5** berth, haven, jetty, wharf **6** harbor, marina **7** dockage, mooring, seaport **9** harborage, roadstead

ancient 3 old **4** aged **5** early, hoary, Greek, olden, passe, Roman **6** age-old, bygone, old hat, remote **7** antique, archaic, classic, very old **8** long past, obsolete, outmoded, primeval, timeworn **9** classical, out-of-date, primitive **10** antiquated, fossilized, Greco-Roman **11** obsolescent, prehistoric **12** old-fashioned, out-of-fashion

ancientness 8 great age **9** antiquity **11** advanced age

ancient times 9 antiquity **10** days of yore **12** the Golden Age

ancillary 5 minor **7** adjunct **8** inferior **9** accessory, auxiliary, dependent, secondary **10** additional, subsidiary **11** subordinate, subservient **12** contributory **13** supplementary

Ancius
form: **7** centaur

Ancus Marcius
king of: **4** Rome

and 3 too **4** also, more, plus **8** as well as **10** in addition **11** furthermore

andante
music: **4** even **14** moderately slow

Andean
language family: **16** Andean-Equatorial
group: **3** Ona **6** Aymara, Yahgan, Zaparo **7** Quechua **10** Araucanian

Andean-Equatorial
language branch: **6** Andean **10** Equatorial

and elsewhere 4 et al **7** et alibi

Andersen, Hans Christian
known for: **10** fairy tales
born: **7** Denmark
author of: **10** Thumbelina **11** The Red Shoes **12** The Snow Queen, The Swineherd, The Tinder Box **14** The Nightingale **15** The Ugly Duckling **16** The Little Mermaid **18** The Little Match Girl **20** The Princess and the Pea **21** The Emperor's New Clothes

22 The Steadfast Tin Soldier **25** The Shepherdess and the Sweep
played by: **9** Danny Kaye

Anderson, Frances Margaret
real name of: **14** Judith Anderson

Anderson, Judith
real name: **23** Frances Margaret Anderson
born: **8** Adelaide **9** Australia
roles: **5** Medea **6** Hamlet, Salome **7** Macbeth, Rebecca **8** Kings Row **16** Cat on a Hot Tin Roof

Anderson, Maxwell
author of: **7** High Tor **8** Key Largo **9** Winterset **11** Valley Forge **14** Both Your Houses, Lost in the Stars, Mary of Scotland, What Price Glory? **17** Elizabeth the Queen **20** Knickerbocker Holiday

Anderson, Sherwood
author of: **9** Poor White **12** Beyond Desire, Dark Laughter, Horses and Men **13** Many Marriages, Winesburg Ohio **15** Death in the Woods **18** The Triumph of the Egg

Anderson, Sparky (George Lee)
sport: **8** baseball
position: **7** manager
team: **9** Minnesota **14** Cincinnati Reds

Andersonville
author: **15** MacKinlay Kantor

Andersson, Bibi
born: **6** Sweden **9** Stockholm
roles: **14** The Seventh Seal **16** Wild Strawberries **19** Scenes from a Marriage **20** Smiles of a Summer Night

Andes
Spanish: **20** Cordillera de los Andes
peak: **6** Pissis, Sajama, Sorata **7** Illampu **8** Cotopaxi, Illimani **9** Huascaran **10** Chimborazo **14** Cristobal Colon
highest point: **9** Aconcagua
volcano: **6** Sangay, Tolima **8** Cotopaxi **10** Tungurahua
country: **4** Peru **5** Chile **6** Panama **7** Bolivia, Ecuador **8** Colombia **9** Argentina, Venezuela
river: **5** Cauca **6** Amazon, Parana **7** Orinoco, Ucayali **9** Magdalena
lake: **5** Poopo **8** Titicaca
animal: **5** llama **6** alpaca, condor, huemul **10** chinchilla

And I Worked at the Writer's Trade
author: **13** Malcolm Cowley

Andorra
other name: **13** Valls d'Andorra **16** Valleys of Andorra
capital/largest city: **14** Andorra-la-Vella
others: **3** Pal **5** Ramio **6** Ordino, Soldeu **7** Canillo, Certers **9** La Massana **11** Les Escaldes **16** San Julian de Loria
division: **6** Encamp, Ordino **7** An-

dorra, Camillo **9** La Massana, Sant Julia
heads of state: 13 Bishop of Urgel (Spain) **17** President of France
head of government: 11 First Syndic
monetary unit: 5 franc **6** peseta
lake: 11 Engolasters
location: 8 Pyrenees
mountain: 6 d'Etats **8** l'Estanyo, Pyrenees **10** Cataperdis
highest point: 11 Como Pedrosa
neighbors: 5 Spain **6** France
river: 6 Ariege, Valira
people: 7 Catalan **8** Andosian
language: 6 French **7** Catalan, Spanish
religion: 13 Roman Catholic
place: 12 Casa de la Vall
  Moorish ruin: 4 Ceca, Meka
feature:
  co-princes' representative: 7 vigueer, viguier
  fiesta: 13 Bal de Morratxa
  food payment to bishop: 9 la quistia

Andorra-la-Vella
capital of: 7 Andorra

and others 3 etc **4** et al **6** et alii **7** and so on **8** et cetera **10** and so forth, and the rest

And Quiet Flows the Don
author: 15 Mikhail Sholokov
character: 6 Piotra **7** Bunchuk, Natalia **14** Gregor Melekhov **16** Aksinia Astakhova

Andrea del Sarto
real name: 32 Andrea Domenico d'Agnolo di Francesco
born: 5 Italy **8** Florence
artwork: 7 Caritas **9** A Young Man **16** Birth of the Virgin, Journey of the Magi **19** Madonna of the Harpies, Portrait of a Sculptor

Andrea del Sarto
author: 14 Robert Browning

Andress, Ursula
husband: 9 John Derek
born: 5 Bern **11** Switzerland
roles: 3 She **4** Dr No **12** Casino Royale, Four for Texas

Andrew 7 apostle
brother: 5 Peter, Simon

Andrews, Dana
real name: 17 Carver Dana Andrews
brother: 12 Steve Forrest
born: 9 Collins MS
roles: 5 Laura **9** State Fair **12** Elephant Walk **13** A Walk in the Sun, Ox-Bow Incident **15** Two for the Seesaw **22** The Best Years of Our Lives

Andrews, Julie
real name: 19 Julia Elizabeth Wells
husband: 12 Blake Edwards
born: 7 England **14** Walton-on-Thames
roles: 5 Shrek (2) **10** My Fair Lady **11** Mary Poppins (Oscar) **14** Victor

Victoria **15** The Sound of Music **18** The Princess Diaries

Andreyev, Leonid Nikolaevich
author of: 3 S O S **5** Savva **7** Lazarus, Silence **8** Anathema **10** To the Stars **11** The Red Laugh **12** The Life of Man **16** He Who Gets Slapped **18** Love of One's Neighbor **19** Seven That Were Hanged

Andria
author: 7 Terence

Androcles
origin: 5 Roman
position: 5 slave

Androcles and the Lion
author: 17 George Bernard Shaw
removed: 5 thorn

androgenous 8 bisexual **14** hermaphroditic

Andromache
father: 6 Eetion
husband: 6 Hector
son: 6 Pielus **8** Astyanax, Molossus, Pergamus **9** Cestrinus
author: 6 Euripides
character: 6 Peleus, Thetis **7** Orestes **8** Menelaus
  mistress of: 11 Neoptolemus
  rival: 8 Hermione
  son: 8 Molossus
setting: 8 Thessaly

Andromaque
author: 18 Jean Baptiste Racine
character:
  son: 8 Astyanax
  king: 7 Pyrrhus
  setting: 6 Epirus

Andromeda
astronomy: 13 constellation
father: 7 Cepheus
mother: 10 Cassiopeia
husband: 7 Perseus
son: 6 Mestor, Perses **7** Alcaeus, Heleius **9** Electryon, Sthenelus
daughter: 10 Gorgophone
rescued from: 10 sea monster
rescued by: 7 Perseus

Andromeda Strain, The
author: 15 Michael Crichton

androphobia
fear of: 3 men

Androsphinx
form: 6 sphinx
head of: 3 man

and so forth 3 etc **7** and so on **8** et cetera **9** and others **10** and the rest

and so on 3 etc **8** et cetera **9** and others **10** and so forth, and the rest

And Then There Were None
director: 9 Rene Clair
based on novel by: 14 Agatha Christie
cast: 11 Roland Young **12** Louis Hayward, Walter Huston **15** Barry Fitzgerald
remade as: 16 Ten Little Indians

and thou, Brutus
Latin: 9 et tu Brute
spoken by: 12 Julius Caesar

Andvari
origin: 6 Nordic
form: 5 dwarf

Andy Capp
creator: 14 Reginald Smythe
character: 5 Vicar
  wife: 3 Flo
plays: 7 snooker

Andy Griffith Show, The
character: 10 Andy Taylor, Barney Fife, Goober Pyle, Helen Crump, Opie Taylor **11** Floyd Lawson **12** Otis Campbell **13** Aunt Bee Taylor, Howard Sprague
cast: 8 Hal Smith **9** Don Knotts, Ron (Ronny) Howard **10** Jack Dodson **12** Andy Griffith, Anita Corsaut, Howard McNear **13** Frances Bavier, George Lindsey
setting: 8 Mayberry
Andy's job: 7 sheriff

anecdote 4 tale, yarn **5** story **6** sketch **12** brief account, reminiscence
collection: 3 ana

anemic, anaemic 3 wan **4** dull, pale, weak **5** quiet **6** feeble, pallid **7** subdued **9** colorless **11** thin-blooded **13** characterless

anemone 4 lily **5** plant **6** flower

anesthesia, anaesthesia, anesthesis 6 stupor **8** numbness **11** insentience **13** loss of feeling **15** unconsciousness

anesthetic, anaesthetic 4 drug **5** ether, local **6** caudal, opiate, spinal **7** general **8** narcotic, procaine **9** analgesic, enflurane, halothane, lidocaine, peridural **10** chloroform, isoflurane, painkiller, tetracaine, thiopental **11** acupuncture, laughing gas **12** nitrous oxide **15** sodium pentothal

anesthetize 4 dope, drug, numb **6** deaden, sedate

anew 5 again, newly **6** afresh **8** once more **9** over again **11** from scratch
Latin: 6 de novo

a new order of the ages is born
Latin: 17 novus ordo seclorum
author: 6 Virgil
work: 8 Eclogues
motto of: 11 US great seal

Angel
network: 2 WB
cast: 8 Amy Acker (Winifred [Fred] Burkle) **10** Glenn Quinn (Allen Francis Doyle) **11** Andy Hallett (Lorne) **12** David Boreanz (Angel/Angelus) **13** Alexis Denisof (Wesley Wyndam-Pryce) **15** J. August Richards (Charles Gunn) **17** Charisma Carpenter (Cordelia Chase)

angel 3 gem **4** doll **5** jewel, power, saint **6** cherub, patron, seraph, throne, virtue **7** sponsor **8** cherabim, seraphim, treasure **9** archangel **10** benefactor, domination **11** underwriter **12** principality **14** celestial being, heavenly spirit, messenger of God **15** financial backer

Angel, fallen 5 Satan **6** Azazel **7** Lucifer

angelic 4 good, pure **5** ideal **6** divine, lovely **7** saintly **8** adorable, beatific, cherubic, ethereal, heavenly, innocent, seraphic **9** angel-like, beautiful, celestial, rapturous, spiritual **10** entrancing **11** enrapturing

Angelic Doctor
  nickname of: **15** St Thomas Aquinas

Angelico, Fra
  real name: **13** Guido di Pietro
  born: **7** Vicchio **14** Castell Vecchio
  artwork: **12** Annunciation **15** Madonna Annalena **19** Descent from the Cross **21** Coronation of the Virgin **29** Madonna of the Linen Drapers' Guild

Angelo
  character in: **17** Measure for Measure
  author: **11** Shakespeare

Angel of Fire, The
  also: **13** The Fiery Angel
  opera by: **9** Prokofiev

anger 3 ire, vex **4** bile, fury, gall, rage, rile **5** annoy, chafe, pique, wrath **6** choler, dander, enmity, enrage, hatred, madden, nettle, rankle, ruffle, spleen, temper **7** incense, inflame, outrage, provoke, umbrage **8** acrimony, embitter, irritate, vexation **9** animosity, annoyance, displease, hostility, hot temper, ill temper, infuriate, petulance **10** antagonism, antagonize, exacerbate, exasperate, irritation, resentment **11** displeasure, indignation **12** exasperation, make bad blood **14** disapprobation **15** get one's dander up **16** cause ill feelings **18** ruffle one's feathers

Angerboda
  also: **9** Angrbodha, Angurboda
  origin: **12** Scandinavian
  form: **8** giantess
  children: **3** Hel **6** Fenrir, Fenris **11** Iormungandr, Jormungandr **14** Midgard Serpent

angle 4 bend, cusp, edge, side, turn **5** focus, slant **6** aspect, corner **7** outlook **8** position **9** viewpoint **10** divergence, standpoint **11** perspective, point of view
  kind: **5** acute, right **6** obtuse **8** straight
  point: **6** vertex
  measure: **7** degrees

angled 4 bent **6** fished **7** crooked, slanted **8** diverged

Anglo-Frisian
  language family: **12** Indo-European
  branch: **8** Germanic

group: **15** Western Germanic
language: **7** English, Frisian

Angola
  other name: **7** Bakongo **20** Portuguese West Africa
  capital/largest city: **6** Luanda
  others: **5** Dundo **6** Ambriz, Huambo, Lobito **7** Cabinda, Kampala, Malange, Malanje, Salazar **8** Benguela, Cassinga, Vila Luso **9** Ambrizete, Mocamedes **10** Mossamedes, Nova Lisboa, Silva Porto
  division: **3** Bie **4** Uige **5** Huila, Lunda, Zaire **6** Cunene, Huambo, Luanda, Moxico **7** Cabinda, Malanje **8** Benguela **9** Cuanza Sul, Mocamedes **11** Cuanza Norte **13** Cuando Cubango
  monetary unit: **6** escudo, macuta, macute **7** angolar, centavo
  mountain: **5** Chela **6** Loviti **16** Humpata Highlands
  highest point: **4** Moco
  river: **4** Cuvo **5** Congo, Cuito, Longa **6** Cassai, Coanza, Cuando, Cuanza, Cunene, Kunene, Kwango, Kwanza, Luando **7** Chiumbe, Cubango, Zambezi **11** Lungue-Bungo
  sea: **6** Indian **8** Atlantic
  physical feature:
    basin: **8** Okavango
    desert: **9** Mocamedes
    falls: **15** Catarata Ruacana, Duque de Braganca
    plain: **8** Planalto
    plateau: **4** Rand **5** Huila **11** Benguela Bie, Lunda Divide
  people: **5** Bantu, Kongo, Lundu **6** Chokwe, Herero, Mbundu, Ovambo **7** Bakongo, Kangela, Kikongo **8** Kimbundu, Kwangare **9** Ovinbundu **12** Nyaneka-Humbi
    leader: **13** Agostinho Neto **20** Jose Eduardo dos Santos
  language: **5** Bantu **8** Kimbundu, Oumbundu **9** Ovimbundu **10** Portuguese
  religion: **7** animism **10** Protestant **13** Roman Catholic
  place:
    fortress: **9** Sao Miguel
  feature:
    mahogany: **5** khaya
    weed: **6** archil

angry 3 mad **5** huffy, irate, riled, vexed **6** fuming, galled, piqued, raging **7** annoyed, boiling, burnt up, enraged, furious, hateful, hostile, nettled **8** incensed, inflamed, offended, outraged, petulant, provoked **9** affronted, indignant, irascible, irritated, resentful, splenetic, turbulent **10** displeased, embittered, infuriated **11** acrimonious, exasperated, ill-tempered **12** antagonistic

angst 5 dread **6** unease **7** anxiety **10** foreboding, uneasiness **12** apprehension

angstrom
  abbreviation: **1** A

Angstrom, Anders Jon
  field: **7** physics **9** astronomy
  founded: **12** spectroscopy
  mapped: **11** solar system
  angstrom unit: **17** wavelength of light

Angstrom, Harry see **6** Updike

anguish 3 woe **4** pain **5** agony, grief **6** misery, sorrow **7** anxiety, despair, remorse, torment **8** distress **9** heartache, suffering

Anguish
  goddess of: **8** Angerona

anguished 6 pained **7** anxious, fearful **9** tormented **10** distressed **11** heartbroken

angular 4 bent, bony, lank, lean **5** gaunt, lanky, spare **6** jagged **7** crooked, scrawny **8** rawboned **13** sharp-cornered

Angus Og
  origin: **5** Irish
  god of: **4** love **5** youth **6** beauty

animadversion 4 flak **7** nagging, quibble **9** aspersion, criticism, pestering **12** faultfinding **14** censoriousness

animal 3 pet **5** beast, brute **6** mammal **8** creature, nonhuman, organism **9** quadruped
  group: **4** bird, fish, worm **6** insect, mammal, sponge **7** primate, reptile, rotifer **8** ruminant **9** amphibian **10** vertebrate **12** invertebrate

Animal Crackers
  director: **13** Victor Heerman
  cast: **5** Chico, Harpo, Zeppo **7** Groucho **11** Lillian Roth **12** Marx Brothers **14** Margaret Dumont
  song: **25** Hooray for Captain Spaulding

Animal Farm
  author: **12** George Orwell
  character: **5** Boxer **7** Mr Jones **8** Napoleon, Snowball

animate 4 fire, goad, move, stir, urge, warm **5** alive, impel, liven, set on **6** arouse, excite, fire up, incite, moving, prompt, spur on, vivify, work up **7** actuate, enliven, inspire, provoke, quicken **8** activate, energize, vitalize **9** instigate, make alive, stimulate **10** invigorate, make lively **11** add spirit to **12** give energy to

animated 3 gay, hot **4** airy **5** brisk, quick, vivid **6** active, ardent, blithe, breezy, bright, elated, lively **7** buoyant, dynamic, fervent, glowing, vibrant, zealous, zestful **8** exciting, spirited, sportive, vigorous **9** ebullient, energetic, sprightly, vivacious **10** passionate **12** invigorating

animation 3 vim **4** fire, glow, life, zest **5** ardor, verve, vigor **6** action, gaiety, spirit **7** elation **8** activity, alacrity, buoyancy, vibrancy, vitality, vivacity **9** alertness, briskness, eagerness, good cheer **10** brightness, ebullience, enthusiasm, excitement, liveliness **12** exhilaration, sportiveness **13** sprightliness

animosity 4 hate **5** anger **6** enmity, hatred, malice, rancor, strife **7** dislike, ill will **8** acrimony **9** antipathy, hostility, malignity **10** antagonism, bitterness, resentment **11** malevolence **14** unfriendliness

animus 5 anger, spite, venom **6** enmity, hatred, malice, rancor **7** disdain, dislike, ill will **8** acrimony, bad blood **9** animosity, antipathy, hostility **10** antagonism, bitterness, ill feeling, resentment **12** hard feelings

anise
botanical name: 16 Pimpinella Anisum
origin: 5 Egypt, India **13** Mediterranean
flavor: 8 licorice
use: 5 cakes, fruit, rolls **7** cookies
plant with similar flavor: 9 star anise
legend:
    safeguards against: 7 evil eye **10** nightmares **11** indigestion
    antidote to: 12 scorpion bite

anisette
type: 7 liqueur
origin: 6 France
flavor: 5 anise
drink: 17 Suissesse cocktail
with gin: 8 Snowball **11** Bachio Punch
substitute for: 8 Absinthe

Ankylosaurus
type: 8 dinosaur **10** ornithopod
location: 12 North America
period: 10 Cretaceous
characteristic: 7 armored

Anna
husband: 5 Tobit
daughter: 4 Mary
sister: 4 Dido
corresponds to: 11 Anna Perenna
died by: 8 drowning

Annabel Lee
author: 13 Edgar Allan Poe

Anna Christie
author: 12 Eugene O'Neill
character: 6 Marthy **8** Mat Burke **19** Chris Christopherson
ship: 14 Simeon Winthrop

Anna Karenina
author: 10 Leo Tolstoy
character: 12 Count Vronsky **13** Alexei Karenin **15** Konstantin Levin **19** Kitty Shcherbatskaya **20** Prince Stepan Oblonsky
setting: 6 Moscow, Russia **12** St Petersburg
director: 13 Clarence Brown
cast: 9 May Robson **10** Greta Garbo (Anna Karenina) **13** Basil Rathbone

(Karenin), Frederic March (Vronsky) **16** Maureen O'Sullivan **18** Freddie Bartholomew
earlier film version: 4 Love

annals 7 history, minutes, records **8** archives **9** registers **10** chronicles, chronology **13** yearly records **15** historical rolls **20** chronological records

Annam *see* **7** Vietnam

Anna Marie
character in: 16 Giants of the Earth
author: 7 Rolvaag

anneal 6 harden, temper **7** toughen

Anne of Geierstein (or, The Maiden of the Mist)
author: 14 Sir Walter Scott

annex 3 add **4** grab, join **5** affix, merge, seize **6** adjoin, append, attach, tack on **7** acquire, connect, subjoin **8** addition **9** appendage **10** attachment **11** appropriate, expropriate, incorporate

Annfwn
also: 5 Annwn
origin: 5 Welsh
means: 8 paradise

Annie Hall
director: 10 Woody Allen
cast: 9 Carol Kane, Paul Simon **10** Woody Allen **11** Diane Keaton, Tony Roberts **13** Shelley Duvall **15** Colleen Dewhurst
Oscar for: 7 actress (Keaton), picture **8** director (Allen) **10** screenplay

annihilate 3 end **5** erase, waste **7** abolish, destroy, wipe out **8** decimate, demolish, lay waste **9** eradicate, extirpate, liquidate **10** extinguish, obliterate **11** exterminate

annihilation 9 abolition, wiping out **11** destruction, extirpation, laying waste, liquidation **12** obliteration **13** extermination

anniversary 4 fete **7** holiday, name day **8** birthday, feast day **9** centenary **10** centennial **11** bicentenary, celebration **12** bicentennial **13** commemoration, golden jubilee **16** sesquicentennial

Ann-Margret
real name: 16 Ann-Margret Olsson
husband: 10 Roger Smith
born: 6 Sweden **9** Valsjobyn
roles: 5 Tommy **9** Scarlett **12** Bye-Bye Birdie **15** Carnal Knowledge, Grumpy Old Men **21** A Streetcar Named Desire

anno Domini 18 in the year of our Lord
abbreviation: 2 AD
alternative: 2 CE Common Era

anno mundi 19 in the year of the world

anno regni 19 in the year of the reign

annotate 5 gloss **6** remark **7** comment, explain, expound **8** construe,

footnote **9** elucidate, explicate, interpret **10** commentate

annotation 4 note **5** gloss **6** remark **7** comment **8** exegesis, footnote **10** commentary, marginalia **11** elucidation, explication, observation

announce 5 augur **6** herald, reveal, signal **7** betoken, declare, divulge, give out, portend, presage, publish, signify, trumpet **8** disclose, foretell, proclaim **9** advertise, broadcast, harbinger **10** promulgate **11** disseminate

announcement 9 broadcast, statement **11** declaration **12** proclamation

annoy 3 irk, nag, tax, vex **4** gall, rile **5** harry, tease, worry **6** badger, bother, harass, heckle, hector, nettle, pester, plague, ruffle **7** disturb, provoke, torment, trouble **8** distract, irritate **10** exasperate **13** inconvenience

annoyance 6 bother **8** irritant, nuisance, vexation **10** irritation **11** distraction, disturbance

annoyed 5 irked, upset, vexed **9** disturbed, irritated, perturbed **11** discomposed **12** disconcerted

annual 4 weed **5** plant **6** flower, serial **7** gazette, journal, reports **8** bulletin, magazine, notebook, periodic **9** vegetable **10** periodical, record book

annuity 6 income **7** pension, stipend **9** allowance

annul 4 undo, void **6** cancel, negate, recall, repeal, revoke **7** abolish, nullify, rescind, retract, reverse **8** abrogate, dissolve **10** invalidate

annulment 6 recall, repeal **7** undoing, voiding **8** reversal **9** abolition **10** abrogation, retraction, revocation **11** dissolution, repudiation **12** cancellation, invalidation **13** nullification

annus mirabilis 13 year of wonders

anodyne 4 balm **6** solace **7** comfort **9** comforter **10** palliative

anoint 3 oil **5** crown **6** ordain **8** put oil on **9** pour oil on

Anointed One 5 Jesus **7** Messiah

anomalous 3 odd **7** bizarre, strange **8** abnormal, atypical, peculiar **9** irregular, monstrous **11** incongruous **12** out of keeping

anomaly 6 oddity, rarity **9** deviation **10** aberration **11** abnormality, incongruity, peculiarity **12** eccentricity, irregularity **18** exception to the rule

anon 4 soon, then **5** again, later **7** by and by, shortly **8** tomorrow **9** afterward, presently **10** before long **11** immediately, in the future

anonymous 7 unnamed **8** nameless, unsigned **12** unidentified **13** bearing no name **14** unacknowledged **19** of unknown authorship

another 4 else, more **5** extra, other **7** further, renewed **9** accessory, otherwise **10** additional **12** supplemental

13 something else, supplementary **14** different thing

Anouilh, Jean
author of: **6** Becket **8** Antigone, Eurydice, Leocadia, L'hermine **11** Dear Antoine **14** Time Remembered **15** Le Bal des Voleurs, Thieves' Carnival **16** Point of Departure, Ring Round the Moon **19** Waltz of the Toreadors **20** L'Invitation au Chateau **23** Traveller Without Luggage

ansate 7 handled

anser 5 goose **6** stupid **7** foolish **8** anserine

answer 3 say **4** fill, meet, suit **5** reply, serve, solve, write **6** be like, rejoin, retort **7** conform, fulfill, react to, resolve, respond **8** be enough, response, solution **9** be similar, rejoinder **10** be adequate, correspond, pass muster, resolution **11** acknowledge, explanation **12** be correlated, be equivalent, be sufficient, do well enough **14** acknowledgment, be satisfactory

answerable 6 liable **8** beholden **10** chargeable **11** accountable, responsible

Answer as a Man
author: **14** Taylor Caldwell

ant
caste: **4** male **5** queen **6** worker **7** soldier
kind: **3** red **4** army, fire **5** dairy, thief **6** beggar, farmer, velvet, weaver **7** formica, janitor, pharaoh **8** honeypot, mushroom **9** Argentine, carpenter, cornfield, harvester, legionary **10** leaf cutter **11** little black **12** fungus grower, odorous house, southern fire **13** mound building **14** Texas harvester
group of: **6** colony

antagonism 5 spite **6** animus, enmity, hatred, rancor, strife **7** discord, dislike, rivalry **8** aversion, clashing, conflict, friction **9** animosity, antipathy, hostility **10** bitterness, dissension, opposition, resentment **11** detestation

antagonist 3 foe **5** enemy, rival **7** opposer **8** attacker, opponent **9** adversary, assailant, disputant **10** competitor, contestant

antagonistic 7 hostile **8** contrary, inimical **9** rancorous **10** antisocial, unfriendly **11** belligerent **12** antipathetic, disputatious

antagonize 5 repel **6** offend **8** alienate, estrange

Antananarivo, Tananarive
capital of: **10** Madagascar

Antarctica
division: **10** Wilkes Land **13** Marie Byrd Land, Queen Maud Land **14** Edith Ronne Land **17** Ellsworth Highland
explorers: **8** Tom Crean **9** James Ross **11** Richard Byrd **13** Charles Wilkes,

Roald Amundsen **16** Adrien de Gerlache, Ernest Shackleton **17** Robert Falcon Scott
island: **4** Ross **5** Peter, Scott **6** Biscoe, Hearst **7** Ballery, Charcot **8** Adelaide, Elephant **9** Alexander, Joinville, Roosevelt **10** Coronation, King George **11** South Orkney **13** South Shetland
mountain: **8** Sentinel **9** Pensacola **14** Transantarctic **23** Executive Committee Range
valley: **6** Wright
river: **4** Onyx
natural resource/mineral: **4** coal
plant life: **4** moss **5** algae, fungi **6** lichen, pollen **8** bacteria
animal: **4** lice, mite, tick **5** whale **7** fur seal **8** ross seal **9** crabeater **11** weddell seal, wingless fly
bird: **4** skua **6** fulmar, petrel **7** penguin **10** cape pigeon
sea: **4** Ross **5** Davis **6** Scotia **7** Weddell **8** Amundsen **14** Bellingshausen

ante 3 bet, pot **5** stake, wager **12** beginning bet

anteater 5 sloth **7** echidna **8** aardvark **9** armadillo

antecede 7 precede, predate **8** go before, preexist **10** anticipate

ante Christum 12 before Christ
abbreviation: **2** AC

antedate 7 precede, predate **8** antecede, go before **9** come first **10** anticipate **12** happen before

Antediluvian 14 before the flood

antediluvian 7 antique, archaic **8** obsolete **10** antiquated

antelope 8 ruminant
family: **7** Bovidae
kind: **3** doe, gnu **4** buck, deer, fawn, kudu, oryx, roan **5** bongo, eland, moose, sable **6** dik-dik, duiker, impala, lechwe, nilgai **7** gazelle, gemsbok, gerenuk **8** bluebuck, bontebok, steinbok **9** blackbuck, sitatunga, springbok, waterbuck **10** four-horned **12** Klipspringer
habitat: **4** Asia **6** Africa

Antelope State
nickname of: **8** Nebraska

antenna 6 aerial, feeler

anterior 5 front, prior **7** forward, in front **8** previous **9** precedent **10** antecedent **12** placed before

Anteros
brother: **4** Eros
avenger of: **14** unrequited love

Anthea
epithet of: **4** Hera
means: **7** flowery

Antheil, George
born: **9** Trenton NJ
autobiography: **13** Bad Boy of Music
composer of: **7** Volpone **12** Helen Retires, Jazz Symphony **13** Sonata Sauvage, Transatlantic **14** Airplane Sonata **15** Ballet Mecanique

anthem 4 hymn, song **5** carol, ditty, music, paean, psalm **6** ballad, sacred **7** cantata **8** doxology **11** church music

Anthesteria
origin: **5** Greek
festival of: **4** wine **6** spring **7** flowers

anthology 6 choice, digest **7** garland **8** analects, chapbook, extracts, treasury **9** gleanings, scrapbook **10** collection, compendium, miscellany, selections **11** collectanea, compilation, florilegium, miscellanea **15** commonplace book

Anthony, Susan B.
leader in: **14** women's suffrage
appears on: **12** silver dollar

Anthony Adverse
author: **18** William Hervey Allen

anthophobia
fear of: **7** flowers

anthropologist
American: **4** Boas, Mead **5** Lowie, Sapir **6** Geertz, Linton, Morgan **7** Kroeber **8** Benedict
British: **5** Leach, Tylor **6** Fortes, Leakey, Rivers **14** Evans-Pritchard, Radcliffe-Brown
French: **5** Mauss **8** Durkheim **11** Levi-Strauss
Polish: **10** Malinowski

anthropology
term: **4** myth **6** custom, ritual **7** culture, kinship **8** artifact **9** ethnology, evolution, field work **11** ethnography **16** natural selection
type/related study: **5** legal, urban **6** social **7** applied, medical **8** cultural, economic, physical **9** political **11** linguistics **12** human ecology **13** psychological **19** structural-symbolist
famous study: **3** San **4** Kung **7** Eskimos, Samoans, Tasaday **10** Aborigines **16** Pacific Islanders

anthropophobia
fear of: **6** people

antibiotic 4 drug **5** venom **6** poison **8** curative **9** antidotal, antitoxic, pesticide **10** wonder drug **11** insecticide, miracle drug
kind: **8** neomycin, subtilin **9** mycomycin **10** ampicillin, penicillin **12** erythromycin

antic, antics 5 larks, sport **6** pranks, tricks **9** escapades **10** buffoonery, skylarking, tomfoolery **11** shenanigans **12** clownishness, monkeyshines **14** practical jokes

anticipate 5 await **6** expect **7** count on, foresee, long for, look for, predict **8** envision, forecast, foretell **9** pin hope on **10** look toward **13** look forward

anticipation 4 hope **10** expectancy **11** expectation, preparation

anticlimax 7 letdown **8** comedown **14** disappointment

antidote 4 cure **6** remedy **9** antitoxin

10 antipoison, corrective **12** counteragent, countervenom **13** counterpoison **14** countermeasure

Antigone
author: **9** Sophocles **11** Jean Anouilh
character: **6** Ismene **8** Tiresias
 father: **7** Oedipus
 mother: **7** Jocasta
 brother: **8** Eteocles **9** Polynices
 sister: **6** Ismene
 uncle: **5** Creon
 cousin/lover: **6** Haemon
 defied: **5** Creon

Antigua and Barbuda
capital/largest city: **7** St John's
government:
 member of: **26** West Indies Associated States
head of state: **14** British monarch **15** governor-general
island: **4** Long **5** Guana **7** Antigua, Barbuda, Redonda
highest point: **9** Boggy Peak
sea: **9** Caribbean
physical feature:
 cove: **5** Royal
 harbor/harbour: **7** English
people: **7** African, British **8** Lebanese **10** Portuguese
language: **7** English
religion: **8** Anglican, Moravian **13** Roman Catholic
feature: **15** Nelson's Dockyard

anti-intellectual 5 yahoo **7** lowbrow **9** ignoramus, vulgarian **10** illiterate, philistine

antimony
chemical symbol: **2** Sb

Antinous
suitor of: **8** Penelope
killed by: **8** Odysseus

antipathetic 6 averse **7** hostile **8** inimical **9** rancorous **11** ill-disposed

antipathy 6 enmity, rancor **7** disgust, dislike, ill will **8** aversion, distaste, loathing **9** animosity, hostility, repulsion **10** abhorrence, antagonism, repugnance **14** unfriendliness

Antiphas
father: **7** Laocoon

Antipholus
character in: **17** The Comedy of Errors
author: **11** Shakespeare

antiphony 6 chorus **7** refrain **8** response

antipode 8 contrary, opposite **10** antithesis

Antiquary, The
author: **14** Sir Walter Scott

antiquated 5 dated, passe **7** antique, archaic **8** obsolete, outdated, outmoded **9** out-of-date **11** obsolescent **12** old-fashioned

antique 3 old **5** curio, relic **6** rarity **7** bibelot, trinket **9** objet d'art **10** antiquated, memorabile **11** memorabilia

antiquities 6 relics **8** artifact **9** monuments

antiquity 7 oldness **8** great age **11** ancientness **12** ancient times

antiseptic 6 iodine **7** aseptic, sterile **8** germ-free **9** germicide **10** germ killer **11** bactericide **12** disinfectant, prophylactic

antisocial 7 asocial, hostile **8** menacing, retiring, unsocial **9** alienated **10** disruptive, rebellious, unfriendly, unsociable **11** belligerent, sociopathic **12** antagonistic, misanthropic

antithesis 7 inverse, reverse **8** antipode, contrary, contrast, converse, opposite

antithetical 8 contrary, opposing, opposite **10** discrepant, refutatory **11** conflicting, disagreeing **13** contradictory **14** countervailing, irreconcilable

antitoxin 5 serum **8** antidote **9** antivenom **12** counteragent **13** counterpoison

antler 4 horn, knob, rack **5** spike **6** shovel **8** deerhorn, troching
part: **3** bay **4** brow **5** crown, royal

ant lion
also: **8** lacewing **9** doodlebug
kind: **6** owlfly **9** dusty wing, mantidfly **12** spongillafly **13** brown lacewing, giant lacewing, green lacewing **14** beaded lacewing **15** ithonid lacewing **16** pleasing lacewing

Antonello da Messina
born: **5** Italy **7** Messina
artwork: **8** Ecce Homo **11** Three Angels **13** Il Condottiere (Portrait of a Man), Salvador Mundi **21** Saint Jerome in his Study

Antonio
character in: **12** Twelfth Night **19** The Merchant of Venice
author: **11** Shakespeare

Antonioni, Michelangelo
director of: **6** Blow-up **8** The Night **10** The Eclipse **12** The Adventure, The Passenger **14** Zabriskie Point

Antony, Mark
also: **14** Marcus Antonius
member of: **11** triumvirate
other triumvirs: **7** Lepidus **8** Octavian (Caesar Augustus)
lover: **9** Cleopatra
cousin: **12** Julius Caesar
wife: **7** Octavia
battle: **6** Actium **8** Philippi **9** Pharsalus
invaded: **7** Parthia
died by: **7** suicide

Antony and Cleopatra
author: **18** William Shakespeare
character: **7** Octavia **9** Cleopatra **10** Mark Antony **14** Octavius Caesar
setting: **5** Egypt
Cleopatra bitten by: **3** asp

antonym 8 opposite **10** antithesis
abbreviation: **3** ant

Antrodemus
type: **8** dinosaur, therapod
also called: **10** Allosaurus
period: **8** Jurassic **10** Cretaceous

Anu
origin: **8** Akkadian
god of: **6** heaven
corresponds to: **2** An

Anubis
origin: **8** Egyptian
god of: **5** tombs **9** embalming
weigher of: **15** hearts of the dead
represented by head of: **6** jackal

anvil 5 block, incus **9** converter **11** transformer

anxiety 4 fear **5** alarm, angst, dread, worry **6** unease **7** anguish, concern, tension **8** disquiet, distress, suspense **9** misgiving **10** foreboding, solicitude, uneasiness **11** disquietude, fretfulness **12** apprehension

anxiety-ridden 7 anxious, fearful, nervous **10** distraught **11** worried sick **12** apprehensive

anxious 4 avid, keen **5** eager, tense **6** ardent, intent, uneasy **7** alarmed, earnest, fearful, fervent, fretful, itching, uptight, wanting, worried, zealous **8** desirous, troubled, yearning **9** anguished, concerned, disturbed, expectant, impatient **10** disquieted, distressed **11** overwrought **12** apprehensive

any 3 all, one **4** each, lone, sole, some **5** every **6** single, unique **8** anything, singular, solitary **9** something **10** individual, quantifier

anybody 3 any **6** anyone **8** anything

anyhow see **6** anyway

anything 3 any **4** some **5** aught **6** anyone **7** anybody

anyway 6 anyhow **8** sloppily **9** at any rate, in any case **10** carelessly, in any event, regardless **11** haphazardly, just the same, nonetheless **12** nevertheless **13** indifferently **14** without concern

anywhere 8 anyplace, wherever **11** wheresoever

A-1 3 ace **4** aces, fine, tops **5** great, prime, super **6** choice, grade-A, superb, tip-top **7** capital **8** sterling, superior, top-notch **9** excellent, first-rate, superfine **10** first-class, tremendous **11** crackerjack, outstanding, superlative

Aornis
tributary of: **4** Styx

Aornum
entrance to: **5** Hades
used by: **7** Orpheus

apace 4 fast **7** flat-out, hastily, quickly, rapidly, swiftly **8** speedily **9** posthaste **10** at top speed **11** double-quick, on the double **12** lickety-split **13** expeditiously, precipitately **18** hell bent for leather

Apache
  language family: 10 Athabascan, Athapaskan
  band: 9 Jacarilla, Mescalero, San Carlos **13** White Mountain
  location: 7 Arizona **8** Oklahoma **9** New Mexico
  leader: 7 Cochise **8** Geronimo
  noted for: 8 basketry

apart 4 afar **5** alone, aloof, aside **6** cut off **7** asunder, distant **8** by itself, divorced, isolated, separate **9** by oneself, into parts, to one side **10** into pieces, separately

apartment 3 pad **4** flat **5** rooms, suite

Apartment, The
  director: 11 Billy Wilder
  cast: 10 Jack Lemmon, Ray Walston **13** Fred MacMurray **15** Shirley MacLaine
  Oscar for: 7 picture

apathetic 4 cold **7** unmoved **9** impassive, unfeeling **10** disengaged, impossible, phlegmatic, spiritless **11** emotionless, indifferent, passionless, uncommitted, unconcerned, unemotional **12** uninterested, unresponsive

apathy 8 coolness, lethargy, numbness **9** lassitude, unconcern **11** impassivity, inattention, passiveness **12** indifference **13** impassibility, lack of feeling **14** lack of interest **15** emotionlessness **16** unresponsiveness

apatite
  source: 5 Burma, Mogok

Apatosaurus see **12** Brontosaurus

ape 4 copy, echo, mock **5** mimic **6** follow, mirror, monkey, parody, parrot **7** emulate, imitate, primate **8** travesty **9** burlesque **10** caricature
  family: 8 Pongidae
  combining form: 8 pithecus
  study of: 11 pithecology
  kind: 6 gibbon **7** gorilla, siamang **9** orangutan **10** chimpanzee
  famous: 8 Godzilla, King Kong

apercu 6 glance **7** glimpse, insight, outline, summary

aperture 3 gap **4** hole, rent, rift, slit, slot **5** chink, cleft, space **6** breach **7** fissure, opening, orifice **10** interstice

apex 3 cap, tip **4** acme, peak **5** crest, crown **6** apogee, climax, height, summit, vertex, zenith **8** pinnacle **11** culmination **12** consummation, highest point **13** crowning point

aphasic 4 dumb, mute **12** inarticulate **17** incapable of speech

aphid
  variety: 3 pea **4** pine, rose **5** apple, grape, peach, tulip **6** cereal, cotton, potato, spruce **7** adelgid, cabbage **8** pear root **9** elm woolly, plant lice, water lily **10** gall-making, phylloxera

aphorism 3 saw **5** adage, axiom, maxim **6** dictum, old saw, saying, slo-gan, truism **7** epigram, proverb **8** apothegm

aphrodisiac 4 sexy **6** carnal, erotic, turn-on **7** fleshly, philter, raunchy **8** prurient **9** cantharis **10** love potion **11** cantharides, magic potion, stimulating

Aphrodite
  also: 6 Urania **7** Cyprian, Paphian **8** Cytherea **10** Anadyomene
  origin: 5 Greek
  goddess of: 4 love **6** beauty
  husband: 10 Hephaestus
  lover: 4 Ares
  son: 5 Lyrus **6** Deimos, Phobus, Rhodus **7** Priapus
  daughter: 8 Harmonia
  corresponds to: 5 Venus
  epithet: 6 Acraea, Scotia **7** Doritis, Erycina, Limenia **8** Melaenis, Nymphaea, Pandemos **9** Migonitis **11** Aphrogeneia, Apostrophia

Apia
  capital of: 12 Western Samoa

apiary 4 hive **7** beehive

apiece 4 each **9** severally **12** individually, respectively

a pied 6 on foot **7** walking

Apis
  origin: 8 Egyptian
  also: 3 Hap **4** Hapi
  form: 4 bull
  from: 7 Memphis
  father: 6 Apollo **9** Phoroneus
  mother: 8 Teledice
  sister: 5 Niobe
  nephew: 5 Argus
  rid Argos of: 8 serpents
  killed by: 7 Aetolus
  worshipped at: 7 Memphis

aplomb 5 poise **7** balance **8** calmness, coolness **9** composure, sang-froid, stability **10** confidence, equanimity **11** intrepidity, savoir faire **13** self-assurance, self-composure **14** self-confidence, self-possession **15** level-headedness **16** imperturbability

Apocalypse Now
  director: 18 Francis Ford Coppola
  based on: 15 Heart of Darkness
  novel by: 12 Joseph Conrad
  cast: 11 Martin Sheen **12** Marlon Brando, Robert Duvall **16** Frederick Forrest
  setting: 7 Vietnam

apocalyptic 4 dire **7** ominous **8** oracular **9** far-seeing, ill-boding, ill-omened, prescient, prophetic, revealing **10** disclosing, eye-opening, foreboding, portentous, predictive, revelatory **11** prophetical **12** inauspicious, revelational **15** prognosticative

apocryphal 7 dubious **8** disputed, doubtful, mythical, spurious **10** fabricated, fictitious, unofficial, unverified **11** unauthentic, uncanonical **12** questionable, unauthorized **14** probably

untrue **15** unauthenticated, unsubstantiated

apogee 3 top **4** acme, apex, peak **5** crest, crown **6** climax, summit, vertex, zenith **8** meridian, pinnacle **9** high point **11** culmination **12** highest point

Apollo
  also: 7 Phoebus, Pythius **9** Musagetes
  origin: 5 Greek, Roman
  god of: 5 light, music **6** beauty, poetry **7** healing **8** prophecy
  father: 4 Zeus
  mother: 4 Leto
  twin sister: 7 Artemis
  sons: 3 Ion **5** Iamus **8** Laodocus **9** Aristaeus, Asclepius, Philammon **10** Polypoetes
  corresponds to: 5 Paeon **8** Hyperion
  epithet: 6 Loxias **7** Acesius, Agraeus, Agyieus, Carneus, Phyteus, Spodius **8** Grynaeus **9** Parnopius, Smintheus **10** Alexicacus, Archegetes, Boedromius, Delphinius **11** Argyrotoxus, Epibaterius **12** Platanistius

Apollo 13
  director: 9 Ron Howard
  cast: 8 Ed Harris (Gene Kranz), Tom Hanks (Jim Lovell) **10** Bill Paxton (Fred Haise), Gary Sinise (Ken Mattingly), Kevin Bacon (Jack Swigert) **15** Kathleen Quinlan (Marilyn Lovell)

Apollyon 4 hell **7** Abaddon

apologetic 5 sorry **8** contrite, penitent **9** defensive, regretful **10** excusatory, mitigatory, remorseful **11** exonerative, extenuatory, vindicatory **12** apologetical **13** justificatory, making excuses **15** self-reproachful

Apologia pro Vita Sua
  author: 15 John Henry Newman (Cardinal)

Apologie for Poetrie (Defense for Poetry)
  author: 15 Sir Philip Sidney

apologist 7 pleader **8** advocate, defender **9** supporter

apologize 9 beg pardon **11** make apology **13** express regret

apology 6 excuse **7** defense **11** explanation, vindication **13** begging pardon, justification

Apophis
  also: 5 Apepi
  form: 7 serpent
  habitat: 8 darkness
  destroyed daily by: 4 Dawn

Apophthegms New and Old
  author: 12 Francis Bacon

apostasy 7 atheism, perfidy **8** unbelief **9** defection, disbelief, recreancy **10** disloyalty, infidelity, irreligion **11** godlessness **13** double-dealing

apostate 6 bolter **7** heretic, seceder, traitor **8** defector, deserter, recanter, recusant, renegade, turncoat **9** dissenter, dissident, turnabout **10** backslider **13** nonconformist, tergiversator

apostle 5 envoy **6** zealot **7** pioneer, witness **8** activist, advocate, disciple, emissary, exponent, preacher **9** messenger, proponent, supporter **10** evangelist, missionary, propagator **12** propagandist, proselytizer, spokesperson

Apostle, The
    author: 10 Sholem Asch
    film by: 12 Robert Duvall

Apostles 4 John, Jude, Levi, Paul **5** Jacob, James, Peter, Simon **6** Andrew, Philip, Thomas **7** Matthew **8** Barnabas, Matthais **9** Nathanael, Thaddaeus **11** Bartholomew **12** James the Less **13** Judas Iscariot
    apostle to the Gentiles: 4 Paul
    apostle to the English: 9 Augustine
    apostle to the Irish: 7 Patrick
    apostle to the Goths: 7 Ulfilas
    apostle to the Germans: 8 Boniface
    apostle to the French: 5 Denis
    apostle to the American Indians: 9 John Eliot

apothegm 3 saw **5** adage, axiom, maxim, motto **6** dictum, slogan **7** epigram, proverb **8** aphorism **9** catchword, watchword

apotheosis 7 epitome, essence **9** elevation **10** embodiment, exaltation **11** deification **12** canonization, consecration, enshrinement, idealization, quintessence **13** dignification, glorification, magnification **15** immortalization

Appalachian Spring
    ballet by: 7 Copland

appall 4 stun **5** abash, alarm, repel, shock **6** dismay, offend, revolt, sicken **7** disgust, horrify, outrage, terrify, unnerve **8** frighten, nauseate **10** dishearten

appalled 6 aghast **7** alarmed, shocked **8** dismayed, outraged, repelled, revolted **9** disgusted, horrified, nauseated

appalling 4 dire, grim **5** awful **6** horrid **7** fearful, ghastly **8** alarming, dreadful, horrible, horrific, shocking, terrible **9** dismaying, frightful, repellent, repulsive, revolting, sickening **10** abominable, disgusting, horrifying, nauseating, outrageous, terrifying **11** frightening, intolerable **12** insufferable **13** disheartening

apparatus 4 gear **5** gismo, setup, tools **6** device, gadget, outfit, system, tackle **7** machine **8** material, utensils **9** appliance, equipment, machinery, materials, mechanism **10** implements **11** contraption, contrivance, instruments **12** organization **13** paraphernalia

apparel 4 duds, garb, gear, togs **5** array, dress, habit, robes **6** attire **7** clothes, costume, raiment, threads,

vesture **8** clothing, garments **9** equipment, trappings, vestments **13** accoutrements

appareled 4 clad **5** robed **6** garbed, suited **7** attired, clothed, covered, dressed

apparent 4 open **5** clear, overt, plain **6** likely, marked, patent **7** blatant, evident, obvious, seeming, visible **8** clear-cut, distinct, manifest, probable **10** clear as day, ostensible, presumable **11** conspicuous, discernible, perceivable, perceptible, self-evident, unequivocal **12** unmistakable **14** understandable

apparently
    Latin: 7 ex facie

apparition 5 ghost, shade, spook **6** spirit, wraith **7** phantom, specter **8** phantasm, presence, revenant **10** phenomenon **13** manifestation **15** materialization

appeal 3 beg, SOS **4** plea, pull, suit **5** apply, charm, plead, sue to, tempt **6** adjure, allure, engage, entice, excite, invite, invoke **7** attract, beseech, entreat, implore, request, solicit **8** call upon, charisma, entreaty, interest, petition **9** fascinate **10** adjuration, attraction, supplicate **11** fascination **12** solicitation, supplication

appealing 7 likable, lovable **8** adjuring, charming, engaging, enticing, fetching, inviting, pleading, pleasing, tempting **10** attractive, entreating, requesting, soliciting **11** charismatic, petitioning **12** irresistible, supplicating

appear 4 look, seem, show **5** arise **6** crop up, emerge, loom up, show up, turn up **7** be clear, be plain, come out, perform, surface **8** be patent **9** be evident, be obvious **10** be apparent, be manifest **11** be published, come to light, materialize

appearance 4 look **5** guise, image **6** advent, aspect, coming **7** arrival, pretext **8** pretense **9** appearing, emergence, showing up, turning up **10** impression **11** outward show **13** manifestation **15** materialization

appear at 6 attend, show up **9** perform at

appease 4 calm, dull, ease, lull **5** abate, allay, blunt, quell, quiet, slake, still **6** pacify, quench, solace, soothe, temper **7** assuage, compose, mollify, placate, relieve, satisfy **8** mitigate **9** alleviate **10** conciliate, propitiate **11** accommodate

appeasement 6 easing **7** abating, dulling **8** allaying, blunting, giving in **9** abatement, assuasion, quenching **10** mitigation, submission **11** alleviation, assuagement **12** conciliation, pacification, propitiation, satisfaction **13** accommodation, gratification, mollification

appellation 3 tag **4** name **5** title **6** handle **7** epithet, moniker **8** cognomen **9** sobriquet **11** designation, nom de guerre

append 3 add **4** join **5** affix **6** attach, hang on, tack on **7** subjoin, suspend **10** supplement

appendage 3 arm, leg **4** limb, tail **6** branch, feeler, member **7** adjunct **8** addition, offshoot, tentacle **9** accessory, auxiliary, extension, extremity **10** attachment, supplement

appendix 7 codicil **8** addendum, addition **10** back matter, postscript, supplement

appertain 7 apply to, concern, refer to **8** bear upon, be part of, belong to, inhere in, relate to **9** touch upon

appetite 4 zest **5** gusto **6** desire, hunger, liking, relish, thirst **7** craving, passion, stomach **8** fondness, penchant, yearning **10** proclivity **11** inclination

appetizer 6 canape, dainty, savory, tidbit **8** aperitif, cocktail, delicacy **9** antipasto **11** bonne bouche, hors d'oeuvre

appetizing 6 savory **8** alluring, enticing, inviting, tempting **9** appealing, palatable, succulent **10** attractive **11** tantalizing **13** mouth-watering

applaud 4 clap, hail, laud **5** extol **6** praise **7** acclaim, commend **8** eulogize **10** compliment **12** congratulate

applaudable 8 laudable **9** admirable, desirable, excellent **11** commendable, meritorious, outstanding **12** praiseworthy

applause 5 kudos **6** praise **7** acclaim, ovation **8** approval, clapping, plaudits **9** accolades **11** compliments

apple 5 Malus **15** Malus Sylvestris
    varieties/fruit: 4 Crab, Lodi **6** Pippin **7** Baldwin, Stayman, Winesap **8** Ben Davis, Cortland, Jonathan, McIntosh **9** Delicious **10** Rome Beauty **11** Granny Smith, Gravenstein, Northern Spy, Summer Rambo **12** Grimes Golden, York Imperial **13** Yellow Newtown **14** Stayman Winesap **15** Yellow Delicious **17** Esopus Spitzenberg, Yellow Transparent **19** Rhode Island Greening
    varieties/tree: 2 Wi **3** Kai, Kau, Sea, Wax **4** Cane, Java, Jew's, Pond, Rose, Star **5** Adam's, Baked, Belle, Blade, Chess, Conch, Malay, Melon, Thorn **6** Balsam, Indian, Mammee, Possum **7** Chinese, Custard, Dead Sea, Mexican **8** Elephant, Kangaroo, Otaheite, Paradise, Peruvian **11** Soulard crab, Toringo crab **12** Siberian crab
    beverage: 5 cider **8** Calvados **9** Applejack

apple brandy
drink: **8** Jack Rose **12** Jack-in-the-Box
with rum: **6** Bolero **8** Apple Pie

applejack
type: **6** brandy
origin: **6** Canada **10** New England
flavor: **10** apple cider
drink: **11** Frozen Apple **13** Harvard
Cooler

Apple of discord
color: **6** golden
thrown by: **4** Eris
awarded to: **9** Aphrodite
awarded by: **5** Paris
inscription: **13** for the fairest

apple of one's eye 11 pride and joy
15 light of one's life

applesauce 3 rot **4** bull, bunk **5** hokum, hooey **6** bunkum **7** baloney,
hogwash, spinach **8** tommyrot **9** poppycock **12** fiddlesticks **13** horsefeathers **16** stuff and nonsense

Apples of the Hesperides
color: **6** golden
given to: **4** Hera
kept by: **5** Ladon **10** Hesperides

appliance 4 gear **6** device **7** fixture,
machine **9** apparatus, equipment, implement, mechanism **11** contraption,
contrivance

applicable 3 apt, fit **6** useful **7** apropos, fitting, germane **8** relevant, suitable **9** adaptable, befitting, pertinent

applicant 7 hopeful **8** aspirant, claimant **9** candidate, job seeker, suppliant
10 petitioner

application 4 balm, form, suit, wash
5 claim, salve **6** appeal, lotion **7** request, unguent **8** dressing, entreaty,
industry, ointment, petition, poultice,
solution **9** assiduity, attention, diligence, emollient, putting on, relevance **10** commitment, dedication,
pertinence **11** germaneness, persistence, requisition, suitability **12** appositeness, perseverance, solicitation **13**
attentiveness

Appling, Luke (Lucius Benjamin)
nickname: **16** Old Aches and Pains
sport: **8** baseball
position: **9** shortstop
team: **15** Chicago White Sox

apply 3 fit, use **4** suit **5** adapt, lay on,
put on, refer **6** devote, direct, employ,
relate **7** address, pertain, request, utilize **8** dedicate, exercise, petition,
practice, spread on **9** implement

apply oneself 6 attend **10** buckle
down **13** give oneself to **15** give it all
one has **16** put one's heart into

appoint 3 fix, set **4** name **5** equip **6**
assign, choose, engage, fit out, select,
settle, supply **7** arrange, furnish, provide **8** decide on, delegate, deputize,
nominate **9** designate, determine, establish, prescribe **10** commission

appointment 3 job **4** date, post, spot

5 berth, place **6** naming, office **7**
meeting, station **8** choosing, position
9 placement, selection, situation **10**
assignment, engagement, nomination,
rendezvous **11** designation, meeting
time **13** commissioning

Appointment in Samarra
author: **9** John O'Hara
character: **8** Al Grecco, Caroline **11**
Harry Reilly **13** Julian English

appointments 4 gear **6** outfit **8** equip-
page **9** equipment, furniture **11**
furnishings **13** accoutrements

apportion 5 allot, share **6** divide, ration **7** consign, deal out, dole out,
mete out, prorate **8** allocate, disperse
9 parcel out, partition **10** measure out

apportioning 8 alloting, dividing **9**
doling out, meting out **10** allocating,
consigning, dealing out, dispensing **12**
distributing

apportionment 5 quota **6** ration **7**
measure, portion **8** division **9** allotment **10** allocation **11** consignment
12 distribution, pro rata share

apposite 3 apt **7** apropos, fitting, germane **8** material, relevant, suitable **9**
pertinent **10** applicable **11** appropriate

appositeness 9 relevance **10** pertinence **11** germaneness **15** appropriateness

appraisal 8 estimate, judgment **9** valuation **10** assessment, evaluation **14**
estimated value

appraise 5 assay, judge, value **6** assess, review, size up **7** examine, inspect **8** evaluate

appreciable 7 evident, obvious **8**
clear-cut, definite **10** detectable, noticeable, pronounced **11** discernible,
perceivable, perceptible, significant,
substantial **12** recognizable **13** ascertainable

appreciate 4 like **5** prize, savor, value
6 admire, esteem, relish **7** cherish, enhance, improve, inflate, realize, respect **8** perceive, treasure **9** recognize
10 comprehend, sympathize, understand **11** acknowledge

appreciation 4 rise **6** growth, liking,
regard, relish, thanks **7** advance **8**
sympathy **9** awareness, elevation,
gratitude **10** admiration, cognizance
12 gratefulness, thankfulness **13** comprehension, understanding

apprehend 3 bag, nab, see **4** know **5**
catch, grasp, seize, sense **6** arrest, collar **7** capture, discern, realize **8** perceive **9** recognize **10** comprehend, understand **12** take prisoner **15** take into
custody

apprehension 4 fear **5** alarm, dread,
worry **6** arrest, dismay **7** anxiety, capture, concern, seizure **8** disquiet, distress, mistrust **9** misgiving, suspicion
10 foreboding, perception, uneasiness
11 premonition **12** presentiment **13**

comprehension, understanding **16** apprehensiveness

apprehensive 6 afraid, scared, uneasy
7 alarmed, anxious, fearful, jittery,
nervous, worried **9** concerned, misgiving **10** disquieted, distressed, suspicious **11** distrustful

apprehensiveness 5 dread, worry **6**
dismay **7** anxiety **9** misgiving **10** foreboding, uneasiness **12** apprehension

Apprentice, The
network: **3** NBC
creator: **11** Mark Burnett
judge: **10** George Ross **11** Donald
Trump **14** Carolyn Kepcher
winner: **10** Bill Rancic, Kendra Todd
11 Kelly Perdew

apprentice 4 tyro **5** pupil **6** novice **7**
learner, student **8** beginner, neophyte
19 indentured assistant

apprise 4 tell **6** advise, inform, notify
8 disclose **9** enlighten, make aware

approach 3 way **4** come, near, road **5**
begin, equal, match **6** access, avenue,
be like, method, system **7** advance,
compare, passage, solicit **8** attitude,
come near, draw near, embark on,
gain upon, initiate, resemble, set
about, sound out **9** come close, enter
upon, procedure, technique, undertake **10** move toward, passageway **11**
approximate

approachable 9 available, reachable
10 accessible

approbation 6 praise **7** acclaim, support **8** applause, approval, sanction **9**
laudation **10** acceptance, compliment
11 endorsement **12** commendation,
ratification **14** congratulation

appropriate 3 apt **4** take **5** allot, seize
6 assign, proper, seemly **7** apropos,
correct, earmark, fitting, germane **8**
allocate, relevant, set apart, suitable **9**
apportion, befitting, belonging, congruous, opportune, pertinent **10** confiscate, to the point, well-chosen,
well-suited **11** expropriate **12** to the
purpose **14** characteristic

appropriateness 7 aptness, fitness **9**
congruity, propriety, relevance **10** pertinence **11** correctness, suitability

appropriation 6 taking **9** allotment
10 allocation, arrogation, usurpation
12 confiscation **13** expropriation,
money set aside **16** misappropriation

approval 5 favor, leave **6** esteem, liking, regard **7** acclaim, consent, license, mandate, respect **8** sanction **9**
agreement **10** acceptance, admiration,
compliance, permission **11** approbation, concurrence, countenance, endorsement, good opinion **12** acquiescence, appreciation, confirmation **13**
authorization **14** acknowledgment

approve 4 like, pass **5** allow **6** accept,
affirm, defend, esteem, permit, praise,
ratify, second, uphold **7** condone,

confirm, endorse, respect, sustain **8** accede to, advocate, assent to, concur in, sanction **9** authorize, consent to **10** appreciate **11** countenance, go along with, rubber-stamp, subscribe to

approved 8 official **9** canonical **10** authorized, sanctioned

approving 9 endorsing, favorable **10** concurring **11** affirmative, sanctioning **12** appreciative

approximate 5 guess, rough **6** reckon **7** inexact, verge on **8** approach, border on, estimate, look like, relative, very near **9** estimated

approximately 5 circa **6** almost, around **7** close to **9** generally, just about **10** more or less, not far from, very nearly

appurtenance 4 wing **5** annex, extra **7** adjunct **8** addendum, addition **9** accessory, appendage, extension **10** attachment

APR
abbreviation for: **14** above prime rate **20** annual percentage rate

Apres-midi d'un Faune, L' (The Afternoon of a Faun)
author: **16** Stephane Mallarme
(prelude) ballet music: **7** Debussy

April
event: **9** income tax (15) **11** Black Monday (13)
flower: **5** daisy **8** sweet pea
French: **5** Avril
gem: **7** diamond
German: **5** April
holiday: **6** Easter **11** All Fool's Day (1) **13** April Fool's Day (1)
Italian: **6** Aprile
Latin: **7** Aprilis
number of days: **6** thirty
origin of name: **4** aper (wild boar) **6** aparas (following) **7** aperire (to open) **9** Aphrodite
place in year:
    Gregorian: **6** fourth
    Roman: **6** second
saying: **24** April is the cruellest month **27** April showers bring May flowers
Spanish: **5** Abril
zodiac signs: **5** Aries **6** Taurus

April Fool's Day
French: **9** April Fish

a priori 6 theory **7** opinion **11** of reasoning

apron 3 bib **5** smock **8** covering **10** stagefront

apropos 3 apt **6** seemly **7** correct, fitting, germane, related **8** relevant, suitable **9** befitting, congruous, opportune, pertinent **10** applicable, to the point, well-suited **11** appropriate **12** just the thing

apry
type: **7** liqueur

origin: **6** France
flavor: **7** apricot

Apsyrtus
also: **8** Absyrtus
father: **6** Aeetes
sister: **5** Medea
killed by: **5** Medea

apt 5 prone **6** bright, clever, gifted, liable, likely, proper, seemly **7** apropos, fitting, germane, given to **8** inclined, relevant, suitable **9** befitting, congruous, opportune, pertinent **10** disposed to, well-suited **11** appropriate, intelligent, predisposed

aptitude 4 bent, gift, turn **5** flair, knack, skill **6** genius, talent **7** ability, faculty, leaning **8** capacity, facility, penchant, tendency **9** endowment, proneness, quickness **10** capability, cleverness, proclivity, propensity **11** inclination, proficiency **12** predilection **14** predisposition

aptness 4 bent, gift **5** flair, knack **6** talent **7** ability, faculty **8** aptitude, facility **11** suitability **15** appropriateness

Apuleius
author of: **12** The Golden Ass **13** Metamorphoses

aqua 4 blue **5** water **6** bluish **9** turquoise **10** aquamarine **12** greenish-blue

aquamarine 4 aqua, blue **5** beryl **9** turquoise **12** greenish-blue
color: **9** blue-green

aquaphobia
fear of: **5** water

aquarelle 10 watercolor

Aquarius
symbol: **11** water bearer **12** water-carrier
planet: **6** Saturn, Uranus
rules: **5** hopes **7** friends
born: **7** January **8** February

aquatic 6 marine **7** abyssal, fluvial, neritic, oceanic, pelagic **8** littoral **9** thalassic **10** fluviatile, lacustrine

aquavit
type: **6** spirit
origin: **11** Scandinavia
flavor: **4** dill **7** caraway **9** coriander
drink: **5** Glogg

aqua vitae 7 alcohol **11** water of life

aqueduct 4 duct, race **7** channel, conduit **11** watercourse **18** artificial waterway

aqueous 4 damp **5** moist **6** liquid, serous, watery **7** hydrous **8** waterish **9** lymphatic

Aquinas, St Thomas
nickname: **13** Angelic Doctor
followers: **8** Thomists
author of: **15** Summa Theologica **21** Summa Totius Theologiae **34** Summa Catholicae Fidei contra Gentiles

Arab
clothing: **3** fez **4** veil

country: **4** Iraq, Oman **5** Egypt, Libya, Qatar, Sudan, Syria, Yemen **6** Jordan, Kuwait **7** Algeria, Bahrain, Lebanon, Morocco, Tunisia **11** Saudi Arabia **18** United Arab Emirates
demon: **5** afrit **6** afreet
habitat: **6** desert
Holy City: **5** Mecca **6** Medina
holy war: **5** jihad
language: **6** Arabic
people: **7** Semitic
religion: **6** Muslim **7** Islamic
television station: **9** al-Jazeera (Qatar)
tribe: **4** Kurd **6** Berber, Nubian, Tuareg

Arabella
opera by: **7** (Richard) Strauss

Arabia
ancient name: **14** Jazirat al-Arab
ancient people: **6** Sabean **8** Egyptian **10** Babylonian
bounded by: **4** Iraq **5** Syria **6** Jordan, Red Sea **10** Gulf of Aden, Gulf of Oman **11** Indian Ocean, Persian Gulf
country: **4** Oman **5** Qatar, Yemen **6** Kuwait **7** Bahrain **11** Saudi Arabia **18** United Arab Emirates
highest peak: **11** Jabal Shayib
holy book: **5** Koran
Holy City: **5** Mecca **6** Medina
island: **7** Bahrain, Socotra **9** Laccadive
language: **6** Arabic
mineral/natural resource: **3** oil **4** goat **5** sheep, wheat **6** barley, millet **7** iron ore, granite **8** porphyry **9** manganese, petroleum
nomadic tribe: **5** Maaza **6** Ababda
prophet: **8** Muhammad
religion: **6** Muslim **7** Islamic
river: **4** Nile, Oxus **5** Indus **6** Tigris **9** Euphrates
sea: **3** Red **7** Arabian **11** Persian Gulf **13** Mediterranean

Arabian Nights
director: **17** Pier Paolo Pasolini
based on: **20** Thousand and One Nights
cast: **11** Franco Citti **13** Ninetto Davoli **14** Ines Pellegrina

Arabian Nights' Entertainments, The (The Thousand and One Nights)
author: **7** unknown
storyteller: **12** Scheherazade
character: **3** Roc **5** Ahmed **6** Fatima, Sinbad **7** Aladdin, Ali Baba, Sindbad **9** Abu Hassan

Arabic
national language in: **4** Iraq, Oman **5** Egypt, Libya, Qatar, Sudan, Syria, Yemen **6** Jordan, Kuwait **7** Algeria, Bahrain, Lebanon, Morocco, Tunisia **10** Mauritania **11** North Africa, Saudi Arabia **16** Arabian Peninsula **18** United Arab Emirates
also spoken in: **6** Israel **12** North

America, South America **17** Soviet Central Asia, Sub-Saharan Africa
language of: 5 Koran

arable 6 fecund **7** fertile **8** farmable, fruitful, plowable, tillable **10** cultivable, productive

Arachne
origin: 6 Lydian
challenged: 6 Athena
contest: 7 weaving
changed into: 6 spider

arachnid
class: 4 mite, tick **6** spider **8** scorpion **13** daddy-long-legs
phylum: 9 Arthropod
pairs of legs: 4 four
respiratory organ: 12 pulmonary sac, tracheal tube
dwelling: 4 land **5** water
body part: 15 anterior prosoma **20** posterior opisthosoma
way of feeding: 8 parasite, predator **9** scavenger

arachnophobia
fear of: 7 spiders

Aram *see* **5** Syria

Aramis
character in: 18 The Three Musketeers
author: 5 Dumas (pere)

Arapaho
language family: 9 Algonkian **10** Algonquian
tribe: 6 Atsine **11** Gros Ventres **15** Northern Arapaho, Southern Arapaho
location: 6 Plains **8** Colorado, Red River
related to: 8 Cheyenne
ceremony: 8 sun dance

Arawak
language family: 8 Arawakan
tribe: 5 Taino **6** Igneri, Lucayo
location: 4 Cuba **5** Haiti **6** Guyana **8** Antilles, Colombia **9** Venezuela **12** South America

Arawakan
tribe: 6 Arawak **8** Boriquen **9** Borinquen

arbiter 5 judge **6** pundit, umpire **7** referee **9** authority **10** arbitrator **11** connoisseur

arbitrary 6 chance, random **7** summary, willful **8** absolute, despotic, fanciful, personal **9** frivolous, imperious, unlimited, whimsical **10** autocratic, capricious, peremptory, subjective **12** inconsistent, uncontrolled, unrestrained

arbitrate 5 judge **6** decide, settle, umpire **7** adjudge, mediate, referee **9** reconcile **10** adjudicate **12** bring to terms **13** sit in judgment

Arbitration, The
author: 8 Menander

arbitrator 5 judge **6** umpire **7** arbiter, referee **8** mediator **9** go-between,

moderator **10** negotiator **11** adjudicator **12** intermediary

arbor 5 bower, folly, kiosk **6** gazebo, grotto **7** pergola **8** pavilion **9** belvedere **10** shaded walk **11** summerhouse

arc 3 bow **4** arch **5** curve **8** crescent, half-moon **10** semicircle

arcade 6 loggia, piazza **7** archway, areaway, gallery, skywalk **8** cloister, overpass **9** breezeway, colonnade, peristyle, underpass

Arcadia, The
author: 15 Sir Philip Sidney
character: 5 Mopsa **6** Pamela **7** Dametas, Gynecia, Zelmane **8** Basilius, Cecropia, Pyrocles **9** Amphialus, Musidorus, Philoclea, Plexistus

Arcadian stag *see* **8** Cerynean

Arcanan
father: 8 Alcmaeon
mother: 10 Callirrhoe
brother: 10 Amphoterus

arcane 6 mystic, occult **7** obscure **8** abstruse, esoteric, hermetic, mystical **9** enigmatic, recondite **10** mysterious

arch 3 arc, bow, sly **4** bend, dome, main, span, wily **5** chief, curve, major, saucy, vault **7** cunning, primary, roguish **8** bow shape **9** curvature, designing, principal **10** curved span **11** mischievous

archaeologist
American: 7 Bingham **8** Douglass, Stephens
British: 5 Evans **6** Carter, Childe, Layard, Leakey, Petrie, Wooley **7** Lubbock, Ventris, Wheeler **9** Rawlinson **10** Pitt-Rivers **13** Caton-Thompson
Danish: 7 Thomsen, Worsaae
French: 5 Botta **8** Cousteau **11** Champollion
German: 5 Conze **7** Curtius **8** Dorpfeld, Koldewey **9** Grotefend **10** Schliemann **11** Winckelmann
Italian: 8 Fiorelli
Swedish: 4 Geer **9** Montelius

archaic 5 passe **6** bygone **7** ancient, antique **8** obsolete **9** out-of-date **10** antiquated **11** obsolescent **12** old-fashioned

archangel 5 Satan, Uriel **7** Gabriel, Michael, Raphael

arched 4 bent **5** bowed **6** curved

archenemy 3 foe **7** archfoe, bugbear, nemesis, scourge **8** opponent **9** adversary, assailant, bete noire, combatant, disputant **10** antagonist

archeology
term: 3 dig **6** midden **9** earthwork **11** burial mound **17** aerial photography
type: 7 salvage **8** American, medieval **9** classical, text-aided **10** Egyptology, industrial, underwater **11** Assyriology, prehistoric **12** Mesopotamian
ages: 4 Iron **6** Bronze

Old Stone Age: 11 Paleolithic
Middle Stone Age: 10 Mesolithic
New Stone Age: 9 Neolithic
dating method: 5 cross **8** absolute, carbon-14 **13** geochronology **16** dendrochronology **18** thermoluminescence **28** potassium-argon varved deposits
site/artifact: 2 Ur **4** Giza, Troy **5** Copan, Crete, Delos, Minos **6** Amarna, Carnac, Nimrud, Nippur, Tiryns **7** Alalakh, Babylon, Ephesus, Knossos, Mycenae, Nineveh, Olympia, Pompeii, Rio Azul **8** Behistun, Kuyunjik, Pergamum, pyramids **9** Arikamedu, Hissarlik, Khorsabad, New Grange, Tarquinia, Woodhenge **10** Carchemish, Persepolis, Samothrace, Stonehenge **11** Herculaneum, Machu Picchu, Mohenjodaro **12** Easter Island, Hadrian's Wall, Olduvai Gorge, Rosetta Stone **13** Avebury Circle, Zimbabwe Ruins **14** Dead Sea Scrolls, Laocoon statues **15** temple of Artemis **16** Valley of the Kings **18** Ostrava-Petrokovice, Royal Palace of Minos
tomb: 11 Tutankhamen **15** Ch'in Shih Huang Ti

archer 6 bowman **8** spearman
famous: 5 Cupid **9** Robin Hood **11** William Tell

Archer
constellation of: 11 Sagittarius

Archer, Isabel
character in: 18 The Portrait of a Lady
author: 5 James

Archer, Lew
created by: 13 Ross Macdonald
role: 10 private eye
played by: 10 Paul Newman (as Harper)
on TV: 10 Brian Keith

Archer, Miles
character in: 16 The Maltese Falcon
author: 7 Hammett

Archer, Newland
character in: 17 The Age of Innocence
author: 7 Wharton

Archer in Jeopardy
author: 13 Ross MacDonald

archery
athlete: 10 Linda Myers, Luanne Ryon **11** Darrell Pace

archetypal 5 model **7** classic **8** original **9** classical, exemplary **10** definitive, prototypal, protypical

archetype 5 model **7** classic **8** exemplar, original **9** prototype **12** prime example

Archias
founder of: 8 Syracuse
location: 6 Sicily
descendant of: 8 Hercules

Archie
creator: **10** Bob Montana **13** John Goldwater
character: **5** Betty, Moose **6** Reggie **7** Sabrina **8** Big Ethel, Veronica **11** Mr Weatherby **12** Jughead Jones
place: **9** Riverdale

Archimago
character in: **15** The Faerie Queene
author: **7** Spenser

Archipenko, Alexsandr
born: **4** Kiev **6** Russia
artwork: **8** Medranos **9** Gondolier, Medrano II, Pregnancy, The Bather **11** Boxing Match **12** Archipentura, Walking Woman **15** Geometric Statue **18** Wilhelm Furtwangler **19** Woman Combing Her Hair

architect 6 author, shaper **7** creator, deviser, founder, planner **8** designer, engineer **9** artificer, contriver, draftsman, innovator **10** instigator, originator, prime mover **13** master builder **16** building designer
name **3** Pei **4** Hunt, Mead, Pope, Root, Wren **5** Hoban, IM Pei, Jones, Le Vau, McKim, Mills, Roche, Stone, Tange, White, Wyatt **6** Breuer, Fuller, Owings, Smirke, Wright **7** Bernini, Burnham, Gilbert, Gropius, Johnson, Latrobe, Mansart, Merrill, Renwick **8** Bramante, Harrison, Palladio, Saarinen, Skidmore, Sullivan, Yamasaki **9** Jefferson **10** Richardson **11** Le Corbusier **12** Brunelleschi, Michelangelo **14** Mies van der Rohe **15** Hardouin-Mansart
legendary first: **8** Daedalus
designed: **18** Minotaur's Labyrinth
Roman: **9** Vitruvius

architecture 5 style **6** design **11** structuring **12** construction **14** architectonics **16** structural design

archives 6 annals, museum, papers **7** library, records **9** documents **10** chronicles, depository **11** memorabilia

arctic 3 icy **5** gelid, polar **6** bitter, frigid, frozen **7** glacial, ice-cold **8** freezing, icebound **9** North Pole **10** frostbound **11** far-northern, hyperborean **13** septentrional

Arden, Eve
real name: **13** Eunice Quedens
born: **12** Mill Valley CA
roles: **13** Mildred Pierce, Our Miss Brooks

ardent 4 keen **5** eager, fiery, lusty **6** fierce **7** earnest, fervent, intense, zealous **8** feverish, spirited, vehement **10** passionate **11** impassioned, tempestuous **12** enthusiastic

ardor 4 love, zeal **5** gusto, verve, vigor **6** fervor, spirit **7** feeling, passion, rapture **8** devotion **9** eagerness, intensity, vehemence **10** enthusiasm, excitement, fierceness **11** amorousness **12** feverishness

Ardrey, Robert
author of: **17** The Social Contract

arduous 4 hard **5** heavy, tough **6** severe, tiring, trying **7** onerous **8** toilsome, vigorous **9** difficult, energetic, fatiguing, Herculean, laborious, strenuous, wearisome **10** burdensome, exhausting, formidable **11** troublesome

arduousness 5 trial **8** tough job **10** difficulty, rough going, uphill work **12** hard sledding, toilsomeness **13** laboriousness, wearisomeness

area 4 turf, zone **5** arena, field, range, realm, scope, space, tract **6** domain, extent, region, sphere **7** expanse, portion, section, stretch, terrain **8** district, locality, precinct, province **9** territory

Areithous
origin: **5** Greek
mentioned in: **5** Iliad
king of: **7** Arcadia
son: **10** Menesthius
nickname: **7** maceman
weapon: **8** iron mace
killed by: **8** Lycurgus

Areius *see* **5** Areus

arena 4 area, bowl, ring **5** field, lists, realm, scene, stage **6** circus, domain, sector, sphere **7** stadium, theater **8** coliseum, platform, province **9** gymnasium, territory **10** hippodrome **11** battlefield, marketplace **12** amphitheater, battleground, playing field

Arendt, Hannah
author of: **10** On Violence **12** On Revolution **13** Life of the Mind **17** The Human Condition **19** Crises of the Republic, Eichmann in Jerusalem **27** The Origins of Totalitarianism

Arene
son: **4** Idas **7** Lynceus

Arensky, Anton Stepanovich (Antony)
born: **6** Russia **8** Novgorod
composer of: **7** Tempest **13** Egyptian Night **18** Variations on Legend

Areopagitica
author: **10** John Milton

Ares
also: **8** Theritas
origin: **5** Greek
god of: **3** war
father: **4** Zeus
mother: **4** Hera
sister: **4** Hebe
son: **5** Molus **6** Cycnus, Deimos, Phobos, Tereus **8** Diomedes, Eurytion, Meleager, Oenomaus, Phlegyas, Thestius **10** Ascalaphus
daughter: **7** Alcippe **8** Harmonia **9** Melanippe **11** Penthesilea
nurse: **5** Thero
corresponds to: **4** Mars
epithet: **8** Enyalius **14** Gynaecothoenas

Arete
father: **8** Rhexenor
husband: **8** Alcinous
daughter: **8** Nausicaa
personifies: **7** courage

Arethusa
form: **5** nymph
changed into: **6** spring
saved from: **7** Alpheus

Aretus
father: **5** Priam
killed by: **9** Automedon

Areus
also: **6** Areius
father: **4** Bias
mother: **4** Pero
brother: **6** Talaus **8** Leodocus
member of: **9** Argonauts
epithet of: **4** Zeus
means: **7** warlike

Argades
father: **3** Ion

Argeiphontes
also: **11** Argiphontes
epithet of: **6** Hermes
means: **13** slayer of Argus

argent 5 white **6** silver **7** shining, silvery

Argentina
name means: **6** silver
capital/largest city: **11** Buenos Aires
others: **4** Acha, Azul, Goya, Oran, Puan, Rosa **5** Jujuy, Junin, Lanus, Lujan, Metan, Monte, Salta, Tigre **6** Parana, Rufino, Zarate **7** Bolivar, Caseros, Cordoba, Dolores, Formosa, LaBanda, LaPlata, LaRioja, Mendoza, Neuquen, Posadas, Quilmes, Rafaela, Rosario, San Juan, Santa Fe, Tucuman **9** Catamarca, Rio Cuerto **10** Avellaneda, Corrientes **11** Bahai Blanca, Mar del Plata, Resistencia **17** Santiago del Estero **20** San Carlos de Bariloche
division: **5** Andes, Chaco, Pampa **9** Patagonia **11** Mesopotamia **14** Tierra del Fuego
measure: **4** sino **5** legua **6** cuadra, lastre **7** manzana
monetary unit: **4** peso **7** centavo **9** argentino
weight: **4** last **5** libra **7** quintal **8** tonelada
island: **14** Tierra del Fuego
lake: **6** Viedma **7** Cardiel, Fagnano, Musters **11** Buenos Aires, Mar Chiquita, Nahuel Huapi
mountain: **4** Toro **5** Andes, Chato, Laudo, Potro **6** Bonete, Conico, Pissis, Rincon **8** Famatina, Murallon, Olivares, Tronador, Zapaleri **9** Aconcagua, Tupungato **10** Cordillera **13** Ojos del Salado **15** Cerro Mercedario, Sierra de Cordoba
highest point: **9** Aconcagua
river: **4** Sali **5** Atuel, Chico, Coyle, Dulce, Limay, Negro, Plata, Teuco **6** Blanco, Chubut, Cuarto, Flores, Grande, Iguazu, Parana, Quinto, Sa-

lado **7** Bermejo, Deseado, Iguassu, Mendoza, Tercero, Tunuyan, Uruguay **8** Colorado, Paraguay, Picomayo, Senguerr **9** Pilcomayo

sea: **8** Atlantic

physical feature:

falls: **6** Grande, Iguazu **7** Iguassu

lowland: **5** chaco

plains: **6** pampas

plateau: **4** Puna **6** Parana

salt flat: **14** Salinas Grandes

volcano: **5** Lanin, Maipo **6** Domuyo **7** Peteroa

wind: **5** Zonda **7** Pampero

people: **3** Api **4** Lule **5** Vejoz **6** Abipon, Vilela **7** Guarani, Puelche, Ranquel, Taluhet **8** Querandi, Querendy

artist: **6** Borges

author: **4** Wast **6** Banchs, Borges **7** Lugones **9** Guiraldes, Hernandez **10** Echeverria

leader: **4** Roca **5** Illia, Menem, Mitre, Peron, Rosas **6** Videla **7** Urquiza **8** Aramburu, Belgrano, Eva Peron (Evita), Frondici, Galtieri **9** San Martin, Sarmiento **11** Isabel Peron

language: **7** Spanish

religion: **13** Roman Catholic

place:

opera house: **11** Teatro Colon

world's southernmost town: **7** Ushuaia

feature:

bird: **6** chunga

cowboy: **6** gaucho **7** vaquero

dance: **5** samba, tango, zamba **6** cuando, gaucho **7** milonga **9** chacarera

farm: **6** quinta

knife: **5** facon

metal straw: **8** bombilla

ranch: **8** estancia

school smock: **9** delantale

shawl: **6** poncho

trousers: **9** bombachas

weapon: **4** bola

food:

cocktail: **7** clarito

dish: **4** luna **7** criollo, puchero **8** chivitos, empanada **10** parrillada

Arges

member of: **8** Cyclopes

Argia

also: **5** Aegia

father: **7** Oceanus

mother: **6** Tethys

husband: **7** Polybus

son: **5** Argus

Argiope

form: **5** nymph

father: **8** Teuthras

husband: **6** Agenor **8** Telephus

son: **6** Cadmus

daughter: **6** Europa

Argiphontes *see* **12** Argeiphontes

Argive

pertaining to: **5** Argos

Argo

built by: **5** Argus

ship of: **4** Argo

argon

chemical symbol: **2** Ar

Argonauts

crew: **6** Castor, Mopsus, Peleus, Pollux **7** Acastus, Orpheus, Telamon **8** Atalanta, Heracles, Hercules, Melampus, Meleager **10** Polydeuces

searchers for: **12** Golden Fleece

leader: **5** Jason

ship: **4** Argo

sailed to: **7** Colchis

pilot: **6** Tiphys

argot 4 cant **5** idiom, lingo, slang **6** jargon, patois **10** vernacular

arguable 7 at issue **9** debatable **10** disputable **12** questionable **13** controversial, problematical

argue 4 hold, show **5** claim, imply, plead **6** assert, bicker, debate, denote, evince, reason **7** contend, display, dispute, exhibit, express, point to, quarrel, quibble, wrangle **8** indicate, maintain, manifest **11** demonstrate, expostulate, remonstrate

argument 3 row **4** case, gist, plot, spat, tiff **5** clash, fight, story **6** debate, reason **7** dispute, outline, quarrel, summary **8** abstract, contents, squabble, synopsis **9** bickering, imbroglio **10** war of words **11** altercation, central idea, controversy, embroilment **12** disagreement

argumentation 6 debate **7** dispute **8** argument **10** discussion

argumentative 5 testy **7** peevish, scrappy **8** contrary, petulant, snappish **9** combative, fractious, litigious, querulous **11** belligerent, contentious, quarrelsome **12** cantankerous, disputatious

aria 3 air **4** solo, song, tune **6** melody, number **7** arietta, excerpt, section **9** selection **10** canzonetta **13** aria cantabile

Ariadne

also: **7** Ariadna

father: **5** Minos

mother: **8** Pasiphae

husband: **8** Dionysus

son: **8** Oenopion

gave thread to: **7** Theseus

deserted by: **7** Theseus

Ariadne auf Naxos

also: **14** Ariadne on Naxos

opera by: **7** (Richard) Strauss

character: **7** Bacchus, Theseus **8** Composer **10** Zerbinetta

Ariana *see* **11** Afghanistan

Ariane et Barbe-Bleu

also: **19** Ariadne and Bluebeard

opera by: **5** Dukas

character: **7** Ariadne **9** Bluebeard

Arianrhod

origin: **5** Welsh

form: **7** goddess

brother: **7** Gwydion

mistress of: **7** Gwydion

son: **14** Llew Llew Gyffes

cursed: **14** Llew Llew Gyffes

arid 3 dry **4** dull **5** vapid **6** barren, dreary, jejune **7** dried-up, parched, tedious **8** lifeless, pedantic **9** colorless, dry as dust, waterless **10** desertlike, uninspired **13** unimaginative, uninteresting **15** drought-scourged

aridity 6 dearth **7** drought, dryness **8** aridness, dullness **10** barrenness **12** lifelessness, rainlessness **17** unimaginativeness

aridness 6 dearth **7** aridity, drought, dryness **8** dullness **10** barrenness **12** lifelessness, rainlessness **17** unimaginativeness

arid region 6 desert **9** wasteland **16** barren wilderness

Ariel

author: **11** Shakespeare, Sylvia Plath

character in: **10** The Tempest

Aries

symbol: **3** ram

planet: **4** Mars

rules: **11** personality

born: **5** April, March

Arimaspians

member of: **9** Scythians

number of eyes: **3** one

Arion

form: **11** winged horse

father: **8** Poseidon

mother: **7** Demeter

Ariosto, Ludovico

author of: **14** Orlando Furioso

arise 4 dawn, go up, rise, wake **5** awake, begin, climb, ensue, get up, mount, occur, set in, start **6** appear, ascend, crop up, emerge, result, wake up **7** emanate, stand up **8** commence, spring up, stem from **9** originate **11** come to light

arista 3 awn **7** bristle

aristocracy 5 elite **6** gentry **7** peerage, society **8** nobility **9** beau monde **10** patricians, upper class, upper crust **11** high society

aristocrat 4 duke, earl, lady, lord, peer **5** noble **7** Brahmin, duchess, grandee, marquis **8** countess, marquess, nobleman **9** blue blood, gentleman, patrician **10** noblewoman **11** gentlewoman **12** silk stocking

aristocratic 5 noble, regal, royal **6** lordly, titled **7** courtly, genteel, refined **8** highborn, highbred, wellborn **9** dignified, patrician **10** of high rank, upper-class **11** blue-blooded, gentlemanly **12** silk-stocking **13** of gentle blood

Aristophanes

author of: 6 Plutus 8 The Birds, The
Frogs, The Peace, The Wasps 9 The
Clouds 10 Lysistrata, The Knights 13
Ecclesiazusae, The Acharnians

Aristotle
  author of: 7 Physics, Poetics 8 On
  Plants, Politics, Rhetoric, Sophisms 9
  On the Soul 10 Generation 11 Metaphysics 12 On the Heavens 14 Parts
  of Animals, Prior Analytics 17 Nicomachean Ethics 18 Posterior Analytics 23 On Beginning and Perishing

Arizona
  abbreviation: 2 AZ 4 Ariz
  nickname: 11 Grand Canyon
  capital/largest city: 7 Phoenix
  others: 3 Ajo 4 Eloy, Mesa, Naco,
  Yuma 5 Globe, Leupp, Tempe 6 Bis-
  bee, McNary, Salome, Toltec, Tucson
  7 Cortaro 8 Chandler, Glendale,
  Prescott 9 Flagstaff 10 Scottsdale
  college: 7 Arizona 11 Grand Canyon
  12 Arizona State, Southwestern
  explorer: 8 Coronado 12 Marcos de
  Niza
  feature:
    dam: 6 Hoover 8 Coolidge 9 Roose-
    velt
    national park: 11 Grand Canyon
    15 Petrified Forest
  tribe: 4 Hano, Hopi, Pima 6 Apache,
  Navaho, Navajo, Papago
  people: 7 Cochise 8 Geronimo 10
  John McCain 14 Barry Goldwater
  lake: 4 Mead 6 Havasu, Mohave,
  Mormon, Powell 9 Roosevelt
  land rank: 5 sixth
  mountain: 5 White 6 Lemmon 7
  Hualpai 8 Mazatzal 9 Baldy Peak 13
  Santa Catalina
    highest point: 13 Humphreys Peak
  physical feature:
    canyon: 5 Grand
    desert: 6 Sonora 7 Painted
    forest: 9 Petrified
  river: 4 Gila, Salt, Zuni 5 Verde 6
  Puerco 8 Colorado 12 Bill Williams
  14 Little Colorado
  state admission: 11 forty-eighth
  state bird: 10 cactus wren
  state flower: 13 saguaro cactus
  state motto: 11 God Enriches
  state song: 7 Arizona
  state tree: 9 palo verde
ark 3 box 4 ship 5 barge, chest 8 flatboat 9 houseboat 10 Noah's boat
Ark
  built by: 4 Noah
  landing place: 6 Ararat
  groups: 5 pairs
Arkansas
  abbreviation: 2 AR 3 Ark
  nickname: 4 Bear 9 Bowie Land 17
  Land of Opportunity
  capital/largest city: 10 Little Rock
  others: 3 Coy, Cuy, Keo, Ola, Roe,
  Ulm 4 Alma, Bono, Casa, Dell, Diaz,
  Moro 5 Enola, Perla, Rondo 6 Alicia,

Camden 8 El Dorado 9 Fort Smith,
Jonesboro, Pine Bluff, Texarkana 10
Hot Springs 11 Blytheville 12 Fayetteville
  feature:
    national park: 10 Hot Springs
  tribe: 5 Caddo, Osage 6 Quapaw 7
  Choctaw, Wichita 8 Cherokee
  people: 8 Alan Ladd 9 Sam Walton
  10 Dick Powell 11 Bill Clinton 16
  Douglas MacArthur
  lake: 6 Beaver, Chicot, Conway, Nimrod 7 Greeson, Norfork 8 Maumelle,
  Ouachita 10 Bull Shoals 11 Greers
  Ferry 12 Blue Mountain
  land rank: 13 twenty-seventh
  mountain: 4 Blue 5 Ozark 6 Boston,
  Gaylor 7 Fourche 8 Magazine,
  Ouachita
    highest point: 8 Magazine
  river: 3 Red 5 Black, White 6 Saline
  7 Buffalo, Current 8 Arkansas, Cos-
  satot, Ouachita 9 St Francis 11 Mississippi
  state admission: 11 twenty-fifth
  state bird: 11 mockingbird
  state flower: 12 apple blossom
  state motto: 13 (Let) The People
  Rule
  state song: 8 Arkansas
  state tree: 13 shortleaf pine
Arkin, Alan
  born: 9 New York NY
  roles: 5 Simon 6 Havana 7 Catch-22
  9 The In-Laws, Rocketeer 12 Indian
  Summer, The 13 Wait Until Dark 16
  Grosse Point Blank 17 Glengarry
  Glen Ross 21 Last of the Red-Hot
  Lovers 23 The Heart Is a Lonely
  Hunter 40 The Russians Are Coming
  The Russians Are Coming
Ark of the Covenant
  gold covering: 9 mercy seat 12 pro-
  pitiatory
arm, arms 4 guns 5 brace, crest,
equip, prime 6 branch, outfit, sector 7
forearm, fortify, prepare, protect, section, weapons 8 armament, blazonry,
division, firearms, insignia, materiel,
offshoot, ordnance, weaponry 9 appendage, make ready, upper limb 10
coat of arms, department, detachment,
obtain arms, projection, strengthen,
take up arms 12 anterior limb 13 prepare for war 14 heraldic emblem 18
furnish with weapons
armada 4 navy 5 fleet 8 flotilla,
squadron 10 escadrille
armadillo 4 a par
  family: 11 Dasypodidae
  order: 8 Edentata
  body: 5 armor 6 plates
  habitat: 9 South America, United
  States 14 Central America
  habit: 9 nocturnal
Armageddon 8 doomsday 11 final
battle 13 great conflict
  author: 8 Leon Uris

armagnac
  type: 6 brandy 7 liqueur
  origin: 6 France 7 Gascony
armament 4 arms, guns 7 weapons 8
ordnance, weaponry 9 equipment,
munitions 10 outfitting 13 military
might 16 war-making machine
Armenia
  other name: 5 Minni 6 Urartu 8 Anatolia
  former name: 31 Armenian Soviet
  Socialist Republic
  capital/largest city: 6 Erivan 7 Yerevan
  ancient capital: 3 Ani 8 Artashat, Ar-
  taxata
  others: 3 Van 5 Sivas 7 Trabzon 9
  Kirovakan, Leninakan, Trabizond 13
  Bitlisarzurum
  head of state: 9 President
  monetary unit: 5 ruble
  lake: 3 Van 5 Sevan, Urmia 8 Urumiyah
  mountain: 6 Ararat, Taurus 7 Aladagh 8 Karabakh
  highest peak: 12 Mount Aragats
  river: 3 Ara 4 Aras, Kura 5 Araks,
  Cyrus, Halys, Zanga 6 Araxes, Raz-
  dan, Tigris 9 Euphrates 10 Kizil-
  Irmak
  physical feature:
    volcano: 7 Aragats
  people: 5 Armen, Ermyn, Gomer,
  Hadji
    apostle: 7 Gregory
    gypsy: 5 bosha
    hero: 4 haik 6 vartan
    leader: 26 Levon Akopovich Ter
    Petrosyan
    me: 3 ara
    saint: 5 Sahak 6 Mesrop
  language: 7 Russian 8 Armenian
  religion: 16 Armenian Orthodox
  feature:
    cap: 6 calpac
    fortress: 7 erebuni
    game: 7 barbout
    kingdom: 6 Urartu, Vannic 7 Cili-
    cia, Sophene 8 Ardsruni
  food:
    bread: 4 peda
    cucumber: 4 guta
    dish: 7 lahvosh 9 paraghazt, sou-
    beoreg
Armenian
  language family: 12 Indo-European
  spoken in: 4 USSR 6 Russia 7 Armenia
Armida
  opera by: 5 Gluck, Haydn, Lully 6
  Dvorak 7 Rossini 10 Eszterhazy
Armies 7 Sabaoth
Armies of the Night
  author: 12 Norman Mailer
armistice 5 peace, truce 9 cease-fire
23 suspension of hostilities
armlet 6 bangle 8 bracelet, ornament

arm of the sea 5 bight, firth, fjord (fiord), inlet 6 strait 7 channel, estuary, narrows

armoire 8 cupboard, wardrobe 12 clothespress

armor 4 mail 5 chain 6 shield 7 bulwark 10 coat of mail, protection 11 suit of armor 18 protective covering

armorial bearings 4 arms 5 crest 10 coat of arms, escutcheon

armory 7 arsenal 9 arms depot 13 ordnance depot

Arms and the Man
author: 17 George Bernard Shaw

arms depot 6 armory 7 arsenal 13 ordnance depot 18 military storehouse

Armstrong, Henry
sport: 6 boxing
class: 11 lightweight 12 welterweight

army 3 mob 4 band, bevy, crew, gang, host, mass, pack 5 crowd, force, horde, swarm 6 legion, throng, troops 7 legions, militia 8 military, soldiers, soldiery 9 land force, multitude 10 land forces 11 aggregation, fighting men 12 congregation 13 military force 15 military machine

Arnaeus
also: 4 Irus
origin: 5 Greek
mentioned in: 7 Odyssey
form: 6 beggar 9 errand boy
errandboy for: 16 Penelope's suitors

Arne
son: 6 Aeolus 7 Boeotus
foster father: 9 Desmontes

Arne, Thomas Augustine
born: 6 London 7 England
composer of: 6 Alfred, Judith 8 Rosamond, Tom Thumb 10 Artaxerxes 13 Rule, Britannia 14 Love in a Village, Thomas and Sally

Arness, James
real name: 12 James Aurness
brother: 11 Peter Graves
born: 13 Minneapolis MN
roles: 8 Gunsmoke 10 Matt Dillon

Arnold, Matthew
author of: 7 Thyrsis 10 Dover Beach 15 Sohrab and Rustum, The Scholar-Gypsy 16 Empedocles on Etna 17 Culture and Anarchy, Essays in Criticism 18 On Translating Homer

aroma 4 odor 5 savor, scent, smell 7 bouquet 9 fragrance, redolence

aromatic 5 spicy 7 odorous, piquant, pungent, scented 8 fragrant, perfumed, redolent 11 odoriferous

around 4 near 5 about, circa 10 encircling, on all sides, roundabout 11 surrounding

Around the World in Eighty Days
author: 10 Jules Verne
director: 15 Michael Anderson
character: 11 Phileas Fogg 12 Passepartout

cast: 10 Cantinflas, David Niven 12 Robert Newton 15 Marlene Dietrich, Shirley MacLaine
score: 11 Victor Young
Oscar for: 5 score 7 picture

arouse 3 fan 4 goad, move, spur, warm, whet 5 pique, rouse, waken 6 awaken, bestir, excite, foment, foster, heat up, incite, kindle, stir up, wake up 7 provoke, quicken, sharpen 8 summon up 9 stimulate

Arowhena
character in: 7 Erewhon
author: 6 Butler

arpeggio 5 chord, scale 8 flourish 13 musical device

arraign 6 accuse, charge, impute, indict 7 censure 8 denounce 9 criticize

arrange 4 file, plan, plot, pose, rank, sort 5 adapt, array, fix up, group, order, range, score 6 assort, design, devise, lay out, line up, map out, set out, settle 7 agree to, marshal, prepare, provide 8 classify, contrive, organize, schedule 9 methodize 11 orchestrate, systematize

arrangement 5 order 8 arraying, disposal, grouping, ordering 10 assortment 12 distribution, organization 13 methodization 14 categorization, classification 15 systematization
German: 9 Ausgleich
flower: 7 ikebana

arrangements 5 plans, score, terms 7 compact 8 measures 9 agreement 10 adaptation, provisions, settlement 12 preparations 13 orchestration

arrant 4 rank 5 utter 7 extreme 8 flagrant, outright, thorough 9 confirmed, downright, egregious, notorious, out-and-out 11 undisguised, unmitigated 13 thoroughgoing

array 4 deck, garb, pose, rank, robe, show, wrap 5 adorn, align, dress, group, order, place, range 6 attire, bedeck, clothe, deploy, finery, fit out, outfit, parade, set out, supply 7 apparel, arrange, display, marshal, raiment 8 clothing, garments, organize 9 pageantry 10 assortment, collection, exhibition, marshaling 11 arrangement, disposition

arrears 5 debit 9 liability 10 balance due, obligation, unpaid debt 11 overdue debt 12 indebtedness 15 outstanding debt

arrest 3 end, fix, nab 4 bust, halt, hold, slow, stay, stop 5 block, catch, check, delay, pinch, rivet, roust, seize, stall 6 absorb, collar, detain, engage, hinder, occupy, retard, secure 7 attract, capture, engross, inhibit, seizure, slowing, staying 8 blocking, checking, hold back, restrain, stoppage, stopping, suppress 9 apprehend, interrupt, retention 10 inhibiting 11

holding back 12 apprehension, take prisoner

Arrested Development
network: 3 Fox
narrator: 9 Ron Howard
cast: 8 Tony Hale (Byron "Buster" Bluth) 10 David Cross (Tobias Funke), Will Arnett (George Oscar "Gob" Bluth II) 11 Alia Shawkat (Mae "Maeby" Funke), Michael Cera (George-Michael Bluth) 12 Jason Bateman (Michael Bluth) 13 Jeffrey Tambor (George Bluth, Sr./Oscar Bluth), Jessica Walter (Lucille Bluth), Portia de Rossi (Lindsay Bluth Funke)

Arrhenius, Svante August
field: 7 physics 9 chemistry
nationality: 7 Swedish
theory of: 24 electrolytic dissociation

arriere pensee 12 hidden motive 17 mental reservation

arrival 5 comer 6 advent, coming 7 entrant, visitor 8 approach, arriving, entrance, newcomer, visitant 10 appearance

arrive 4 come, near 5 get to, occur, reach 6 appear, befall, happen, show up, turn up 7 succeed 8 approach, make good

arrivederci, a rivederci 7 goodbye 8 farewell 16 until we meet again

arrogance 5 scorn 6 egoism, vanity 7 bluster, conceit, disdain, swagger 8 contempt 9 assurance, insolence, loftiness, vainglory 10 lordliness, pretension 11 braggadocio, haughtiness, presumption 13 imperiousness 14 self-importance

arrogant 4 vain 6 lordly 7 haughty, pompous 8 insolent, scornful 9 conceited, imperious 10 disdainful, egoistical, swaggering 11 egotistical, overbearing, overweening, pretentious 12 contemptuous, presumptuous, self-assuming, supercilious, vainglorious 13 high-and-mighty, self-important

arrogate 5 adopt, claim, seize, usurp 6 assume 7 preempt 8 take over 10 commandeer 11 appropriate

arrogation 6 taking 7 seizure 10 assumption, usurpation 12 confiscation 13 appropriation, expropriation

arrow 3 bow 4 bolt, dart, nock 5 shaft 7 pointer 9 direction 12 pointed shaft

Arrow
constellation of: 7 Sagitta

Arrowsmith
author: 13 Sinclair Lewis
character: 10 Leora Tozer 11 Max Gottlieb 12 Terry Wickett 14 Capitola McGurk 15 Gustaf Sondelius 16 Martin Arrowsmith 18 Dr Almus Pickerbaugh

arroyo 4 wadi 5 gorge, gully 6 ravine, trench

arsenal 6 armory **7** weapons **8** magazine **9** arms depot **11** arms factory **13** ordnance depot **14** ammunition dump

arsenic
  chemical symbol: **2** As

Arsenic and Old Lace
  director: **10** Frank Capra
  cast: **9** Cary Grant **10** Jack Carson, Peter Lorre **13** Josephine Hull, Priscilla Lane, Raymond Massey

Arsinoe *see* **11** Alphesiboea

Arsinous
  son: **8** Aecamede

Arsippe
  father: **6** Minyas
  mocked: **8** Dionysus

ars longa, vita brevis 18 art is long, life short

Ars Poetica
  author: **5** Homer

art, arts 5 craft, knack, skill **6** genius **7** finesse, mastery, methods **8** artistry, facility, strategy **9** dexterity, expertise, technique **10** fine points, humanities, principles, subtleties, virtuosity
  goddess of: **6** Athena, Athene, Pallas, Saitis **7** Minerva **11** Tritogeneia **12** Pallas Athena **18** Alalcomenean Athena

Artegall
  character in: **15** The Faerie Queene
  author: **7** Spenser

Artemis
  also: **7** Cynthia **9** Astrateia
  origin: **5** Greek
  form: **6** virgin **7** goddess **8** huntress
  habitat: **4** moon
  mother: **4** Leto
  twin brother: **6** Apollo
  companion: **4** Opis **5** Oread
  corresponds to: **5** Diana **6** Phoebe, Selene **11** Britomartis
  epithet: **6** Orthia **7** Eurippa, Laphria, Limnaea, Pyronia **8** Aeginaea, Agrotera, Calliste, Caryatis, Daphnaea **9** Hemerasia, Lygodesma **10** Polymastus **11** Leucophryne

artery 3 way **4** path, road, vein **5** aorta **6** street **7** channel, highway **11** blood vessel

artful 3 apt, sly **4** able, deft, foxy, wily **5** adept, quick, sharp, smart **6** adroit, astute, clever, crafty, gifted, shifty, shrewd, subtle, tricky **7** cunning, knowing, politic **8** masterly, scheming, skillful, talented **9** deceitful, deceptive, designing, dexterous, ingenious, inventive, strategic, underhand **10** contriving, diplomatic, proficient **11** imaginative, machinating, maneuvering, resourceful **12** disingenuous

artfulness 5 guile **6** deceit **7** cunning, slyness **8** artifice, foxiness, scheming, subtlety, trickery, wiliness **10** craftiness **11** machination

Arthur
  director: **11** Steve Gordon
  cast: **11** Dudley Moore, John Gielgud **12** Liza Minnelli **19** Geraldine Fitzgerald
  Oscar for: **15** supporting actor (Gielgud)

Arthur
  began: **10** Round Table
  buried: **6** Avalon
  chronicler: **4** Wace **6** Malory **8** Chretien
  father: **14** Uther Pendragon
  half-sister: **11** Morgan le Fay
  home: **7** Camelot
  island: **6** Avalon
  knights: **3** Kay **6** Gareth, Gawain **7** Geraint **8** Bedivere, Lancelot, Percival, Tristram **9** Launcelot
  knights sought: **9** Holy Grail
  mother: **7** Igraine, Ygaerne
  nephew: **6** Modred **7** Mordred
  sword: **9** Excalibur
    given by: **13** Lady of the Lake
  wife: **9** Guinevere
  wizard: **6** Merlin
  women, Arthurian: **4** Anna, Enid **5** Nimue **6** Elaine, Gyneth, Iseult, Isolde **7** Igraine, Ygaerne **9** Bellicent, Guinivere **11** Morgan le Fay

Arthur, Chester Alan
  nickname: **4** Chet **16** The Gentleman Boss
  presidential rank: **11** twenty-first
  party: **10** Republican
  state represented: **2** NY
  defeated: **5** no-one
    succeeded upon death of: **8** Garfield
  vice president: **4** none
  cabinet:
    state: **6** (James Gillespie) Blaine **13** (Frederick Theodore) Frelinghuysen
    treasury: **6** (Charles James) Folger, (William) Windom **7** (Walter Quintin) Gresham **9** (Hugh) McCulloch
    war: **7** (Robert Todd) Lincoln
    attorney general: **8** (Benjamin Harris) Brewster, (Isaac Wayne) MacVeagh
    navy: **4** (William Henry) Hunt **8** (William Eaton) Chandler
    postmaster general: **4** (Timothy Otis) Howe **5** (Thomas Lemuel) James **6** (Frank) Hatton **7** (Walter Quinton) Gresham
    interior: **6** (Henry Moore) Teller **8** (Samuel Jordan) Kirkwood
  born: **2** VT (or Canada) **9** Fairfield
  died: **2** NY **11** New York City
  buried: **2** NY **6** Albany
  education:
    college: **5** Union
    studied: **3** law
  religion: **12** Episcopalian
  interests: **8** good food (an epicure) **13** salmon fishing
  political career: **13** vice president **26** customs collector for New York
  civilian career: **6** lawyer **7** teacher
  military service: **8** Civil War
    quartermaster general of: **12** state militia (New York)
  notable events of lifetime/term: **5** Panic (of 1883)
    Act: **9** Pendleton **16** Chinese Exclusion **19** Edmunds Anti-Polygamy
  father: **7** William
  mother: **7** Malvina (Stone)
  siblings: **4** Jane, Mary **6** Almeda, George, Regina **7** Malvina, William **8** Ann Eliza
  wife: **5** Ellen (Lewis Herndon)
    nickname: **4** Nell
  children: **11** Chester Alan **12** Ellen Herndon **19** William Lewis Herndon

artichoke 14 Cynara Scolymus
  varieties: **5** Globe **7** Chinese **8** Japanese **9** Jerusalem **14** White Jerusalem

article 4 item, part, term **5** count, essay, paper, piece, point, story, theme, thing **6** clause, detail, matter, object, review, sketch **7** portion, product, proviso, write-up **8** division **9** commodity, condition, paragraph, provision, substance **10** commentary, particular **11** proposition, stipulation

articulate 4 join **5** hinge, state, utter, voice **6** convey, facile, fluent, hook up **7** connect, enounce, express **8** eloquent, organize **9** enunciate, formulate, pronounce **10** enunciated, expressive, meaningful, speechlike **12** intelligible

articulation 5 hinge, joint **7** diction **8** juncture **9** elocution, utterance **10** connection **11** enunciation **13** pronunciation

artifact 4 tool **7** manmade **9** arrowhead

artifice 4 hoax, ruse, trap, wile **5** blind, dodge, feint, guile, trick **6** deceit, device, tactic **7** cunning, slyness **8** foxiness, intrigue, maneuver, scheming, trickery, wiliness **9** deception, duplicity, falsehood, imposture, ingenuity, invention, stratagem **10** artfulness, cleverness, craftiness, subterfuge **11** contrivance, machination **13** inventiveness

artificer 7 artisan, deviser **9** contriver, craftsman

artificial 4 fake, mock, sham **5** bogus, false, phony, stagy **6** ersatz, forced **7** feigned, labored, specious, spurious **8** affected, mannered, specious, spurious **9** imitation, insincere, pretended, simulated, synthetic, unnatural **10** factitious, non-natural, theatrical **11** counterfeit **12** manufactured

artillery 6 cannon **7** big guns **8** ordnance **11** mounted guns

artisan 6 master **9** craftsman **10** technician **14** handicraftsman

art is long, life short
  Latin: 18 ars longa vita brevis
artist 6 expert, master 8 virtuoso
artistic 7 elegant, stylish 8 graceful, handsome, tasteful 9 aesthetic, exquisite 10 attractive
artistic ability 6 talent 7 mastery 8 artistry 10 virtuosity
artistry 5 taste, touch 6 talent 7 mastery 10 virtuosity 11 proficiency, sensibility 14 accomplishment
artless 4 naif, open, pure, true 5 crude, frank, naive, plain 6 candid, honest, humble, simple 7 natural, sincere 8 innocent, trusting 9 guileless, ingenuous, primitive, unadorned 10 inartistic, lacking art, unaffected, untalented 11 open-hearted, undesigning 13 unpretentious 15 straightforward, unselfconscious, unsophisticated
artlessness 6 candor 7 honesty, naivete 8 openness 9 frankness, sincerity 10 simplicity 11 naturalness 13 guilelessness, ingenuousness 14 unaffectedness
art object
  French: 9 objet d'art
Art of Living, The
  author: 11 John Gardner
Art of Love, The (Ars Amatoria)
  author: 4 Ovid
arty 6 dainty 7 foppish 8 affected, high-brow, overnice, precious 9 dandified, overblown 10 effeminate 11 overrefined, pretentious 12 artsy-craftsy, bluestocking, high-sounding
Aryan
  modern name: 13 Indo-European
  origin: 10 North India 11 Central Asia
  family of languages: 5 Hindi 7 Bengali, Panjabi 9 Sinhalese
  religion: 8 Hinduism
  originated: 11 caste system
Aryana *see* 11 Afghanistan
as 4 that, when 5 while 7 because, equally
Asa
  father: 6 Abijah
  grandfather: 8 Rehoboam
  grandmother: 6 Maacah
  deposed: 6 Maacah
  defeated: 6 Baasha
as above
  Latin: 7 ut supra
as a group 7 en masse, in a body 8 as a whole, together 11 all together
as a matter of form
  Latin: 8 pro forma
Asar *see* 5 Aesir
as a result 2 so 5 due to 7 because 9 therefore, wherefore, whereupon 11 accordingly 12 consequently 13 in consequence
as a whole 6 in toto 8 all in all 10 al-

together 19 all things considered
  French: 6 en bloc
as below
  Latin: 7 ut infra
Ascalaphus
  occupation: 6 sentry 8 gardener
  location: 10 underworld
  father: 4 Ares
  brother: 8 Ialmenus
  member of: 9 Argonauts
  killed by: 9 Deiphobus
  changed into: 3 owl
  changed by: 7 Demeter
Ascanius
  also: 5 Iulus
  father: 6 Aeneas
  mother: 6 Creusa
  founder of: 9 Alba Longa
ascend 4 rise 5 climb, mount, scale 7 inherit 9 succeed to
ascendancy, ascendance 4 edge, rule, sway 5 power, reign 7 command, control, mastery 8 whip hand 9 advantage, authority, dominance, influence, supremacy, upper hand 10 domination, leadership 11 preeminence, sovereignty, superiority 12 predominance
ascension 6 ascent, rising 7 scaling 8 climbing, mounting 10 ascendancy
ascent 4 rise 5 climb, grade, slope 6 rising 7 advance, incline, scaling, upgrade 8 climbing, gradient, mounting, progress 9 ascension 11 advancement, progression
ascertain 5 learn 6 detect, verify 7 certify, find out, unearth 8 discover 9 determine, establish, ferret out
ascertainable 10 detectable 11 discernible, perceivable, perceptible
ascetic 3 nun 4 monk, yogi 5 fakir, stern 6 essene, hermit, strict 7 austere, dervish, eremite, recluse, Spartan 8 celibate, cenobite, rigorous, solitary 9 abstainer, anchorite, religious 10 abstemious, flagellant, self-denier 11 self-denying 13 self-mortifier 14 self-mortifying
Asch, Sholem
  author of: 4 Mary 5 Moses 8 A Village 10 The Apostle, The Prophet 11 The Nazarene, Three Cities 15 Song of the Valley 17 The God of Vengeance
Asclepius
  origin: 5 Greek
  god of: 7 healing 8 medicine
  father: 6 Apollo
  mother: 7 Coronis
  wife: 6 Epione
  son: 7 Machaon 10 Podalirius
  daughter: 4 Iaso 6 Hygeia
  nurse: 6 Trygon
  corresponds to: 11 Aesculapius
  epithet: 8 Cotyleus
ascribe 6 assign, credit, impute, relate

7 trace to 8 accredit, charge to 9 attribute
asea 4 lost 6 addled, adrift 7 puzzled 8 confused 10 bewildered
Asgard
  home of: 4 Asar 5 Aesir
  origin: 12 Scandinavian
  connected to earth by: 7 bifrost 13 rainbow bridge
  location of: 8 Valhalla
ash 4 dust 6 cinder 7 residue 12 powdered lava
  family: 5 olive
  genus: 8 Fraxinus
  climatic zone: 17 northern temperate
  varieties: 3 Pop, Red, Sea 4 Blue 5 Black, Green, Manna, Texas, Wafer, Water, White 6 Alpine, Ground, Shamel, Syrian, Velvet 7 Arizona, Modesto, Prickly 8 Carolina, Stinking 9 Evergreen, Flowering 10 Manchurian, Montebello 18 Yellow-topped mallee
  use: 4 fuel 6 timber 7 barrels 8 landscape 9 furniture 10 motor parts, sport goods
  most common species: 8 white ash
ashamed 3 shy 7 abashed, bashful, prudish 9 chagrined, mortified, squeamish 10 chapfallen, distressed, humiliated, shamefaced 11 crestfallen, discomfited, embarrassed 12 disconcerted 13 guilt-stricken 18 conscience-stricken
Ashby, Hal
  director of: 10 Being There, Coming Home
ashen 3 wan 4 gray, pale 5 livid, pasty 6 anemic, leaden, pallid 8 blanched
Asher
  father: 5 Jacob
  mother: 6 Zilpah
  brother: 3 Dan, Gad 4 Levi 5 Judah 6 Joseph, Reuben, Simeon 7 Zebulun 8 Benjamin, Issachar, Nephtali
  sister: 5 Dinah
  city in: 8 Manasseh
  descendant of: 8 Asherite
Ashkenaz
  father: 6 Japhet
  mother: 5 Gomer
Ashley, Lady Brett
  character in: 15 The Sun Also Rises
  author: 9 Hemingway
ashore 6 on land 7 aground 9 on dry land
Ashton-Warner, Sylvia
  author of: 5 Three 6 Myself 7 Teacher 8 Spinster 10 Greenstone
Ashtoreth
  origin: 7 Semitic
  corresponds to: 6 Inanna, Ishtar 7 Astarte, Mylitta
Ash Wednesday
  author: 7 T S Eliot
ashy 3 wan 4 pale 5 ashen, pasty,

white **6** pallid, sallow **7** ghastly, ghostly **8** blanched **9** colorless

Asia

country: 4 Iran, Iraq, Laos, Oman **5** Burma, China, India, Japan, Macao, Nepal, Qatar, Syria, Tibet, Yemen **6** Bhutan, Brunei, Cyprus, Israel, Jordan, Russia, Sikkim, Taiwan, Turkey **7** Armenia, Bahrain, Georgia, Kashmir, Lebanon, Myanmar, Vietnam **8** Cambodia, Hong Kong, Malaysia, Maldives, Mongolia, Pakistan, Sri Lanka, Thailand **9** East Timor, Indonesia, Kirghizia, Singapore **10** Azerbaijan, Bangladesh, Kazakhstan, Kyrgyzstan, North Korea, South Korea, Tajikistan, Uzbekistan **11** Afghanistan, Saudi Arabia **12** North Vietnam, South Vietnam, Turkmenistan **13** Inner Mongolia **14** Papua New Guinea **15** Sinkiang-Uighur **18** United Arab Emirates

desert: 4 Gobi, Thar **6** Syrian **7** Arabian, Karakum **8** Kyzylkum **10** Takla Makan

island: 5 Kuril, Japan **6** Taiwan **7** Hainan **8** Sri Lanka **9** Indonesia: **3** Aru **4** Java, Sulu **5** Ceram, Sumba, Timor **6** Borneo, Flores **7** Celebes, Sumatra **8** Moluccas, Tanimbar **9** Halmahera, New Guinea **11** Philippines

ancient people/empire: 4 Elam, Thai **5** Akkad, Aryan, Indus, Khmer, Media, Shang **6** Mongol, Ohoman, Semite **7** Amorite, Assyria, Hwang Ho, Parthia, Persian **8** Sumerian **9** Babylonia, Dravidian, Sassanian **11** Hephthalite, Mesopotamia

ancient city: 2 Ur **5** Pagan, Sumer **6** Anyang **7** Ayuthia, Harappa **8** Mandalay **12** Mohenjo-daro

ancient leader: 5 Asoka, Kassi **6** Darius **9** Anawratha, Zoroaster **13** Cyrus the Great **17** Alexander the Great

religion: 5 Islam **6** Muslim, Shinto, Taoism **7** Jainism, Judaism **8** Buddhism, Hinduism **12** Christianity, Confucianism **13** Protestantism **16** Roman Catholicism

language: 5 Hindi, Malay **6** Arabic, French, Korean **7** Chinese, English, Russian, Spanish **8** Japanese **10** Indonesian, Portuguese

   Chinese dialects: 2 Wu **3** Min **5** Hakka **8** Mandarin **9** Cantonese

river: 2 Ob **3** Amu, Hsi, Syr **4** Amur, Lena **5** Indus **6** Ganges, Mekong, Tigris **7** Hwang Ho, Salween, Yangtze, Yenisei **9** Euphrates, Irrawaddy **10** Brahmaputra **16** Tigris-Euphrates

lake: 6 Baikal **7** Aral Sea **8** Balkhash **10** Caspian Sea

mountain/mountain range: 5 Altai, Urals **6** Kunlon, Pamirs, Taurus, Zagros **8** Caucasus, Sulaiman, Tien Shan **9** Himalayas, Hindu Kush, Karakoram **10** Arakan Yoma

highest point: 12 Mount Everest

lowest point: 7 Dead Sea

mineral/natural resources: 3 oil, tin **4** coal, mica, talc, zinc **7** bauxite, iron ore, mercury **8** chromium, graphite, selenium, tungsten **9** manganese **10** natural gas

largest city: 8 Shanghai

vegetation: 3 fir, sal **4** moss, pine, teak **5** larch **6** bamboo, lichen, spruce **8** ironwood

animal: 3 elk, yak **4** bear, wolf **5** camel, panda, sable, takin, tiger **6** ermine, kuland **7** markhor **8** antelope, elephant, reindeer **9** arctic fox, polar bear

people: 4 Huis, Kurd, Thai, Turk **5** Aryan, Khmer, Malay, Tungu **6** Buryat, Chuang, Kalmyk, Mongol, Semite, Vighor **7** Baluchi, Burmese, Chinese, Chukchi, Persian, Russian, Tadzhik, Tibetan **8** Armenian, Filipino, Japanese **9** Dravidian **10** Han Chinese, Indonesian, Vietnamese

aside 4 away **5** apart **6** aslant, beside **7** whisper

As I Lay Dying

author: 15 William Faulkner

character:

   Bundren family: 4 Anse, Cash, Darl **5** Addie, Jewel **9** Dewey Dell

Asimov, Isaac

author of: 6 I Robot **10** Foundation (trilogy) **12** Caves of Steel, Robots of Dawn **17** The Gods Themselves

character: 12 Elijah Bailey **13** R Daneel Olivaw

asinine 5 silly **6** absurd, insane, stupid **7** foolish, idiotic, moronic, witless **9** brainless, imbecilic, senseless **10** halfwitted, irrational, muddlehead, ridiculous **11** lamebrained, thickheaded, thick-witted **12** dunderheaded, feebleminded, simpleminded, thick-skulled

asininity 5 folly **8** dumbness **9** silliness, stupidity **10** imbecility **11** doltishness, foolishness **16** simplemindedness

as it should be

French: 11 comme il faut

Asius

origin: 5 Greek

mentioned in: 5 Iliad

king of: 7 Percote

father: 8 Hyrtacus

killed by: 9 Idomeneus

ask 3 beg, bid, sue **4** call, pump, quiz, seek, urge **5** apply, claim, grill, plead, press, query **6** appeal, charge, demand, desire, expect, invite, summon **7** beseech, entreat, implore, inquire, request, solicit **8** petition, question, sound out **10** supplicate **11** interrogate

askance 11 skeptically **12** disdainfully, suspiciously **13** distrustfully, mistrustfully **14** disapprovingly

askew 4 awry **6** aslant **7** crooked **8** cockeyed, lopsided, sleeping **9** crookedly

Askkimey see **6** Eskimo

aslant 4 awry **5** askew **7** crooked **8** cockeyed, lopsided **9** crookedly, obliquely, slantwise

asleep 6 dozing **7** napping **10** slumbering **13** taking a siesta **14** dead to the world

as much as this

Latin: 8 quoad hoc

Asner, Ed

born: 12 Kansas City KS

roles: 5 Roots **6** Daniel **8** El Dorado, Lou Grant **12** A Case of Libel, The Gathering, Silent Motive **14** Rich Man Poor Man **18** Mary Tyler Moore Show

asocial 8 unsocial **9** nonsocial, reclusive **10** antisocial **12** misanthropic

Asopus

form: 3 god

habitat: 5 river

father: 7 Oceanus

mother: 6 Tethys

wife: 6 Metope

son: 7 Ismenus, Pelagon

number of daughters: 6 twenty

asparagus

varieties: 4 Cape **6** Common, Garden, Smilax **7** Cossack **8** Prussian, Sprenger

aspect 3 air **4** look, side **5** angle, facet, point **7** feature **10** appearance **13** consideration

aspen 7 Populus

varieties: 7 Chinese, quaking **8** European, Japanese **9** trembling **12** largetoothed

asperity 5 rigor **6** rancor **8** acrimony, hardship, severity **9** harshness, hostility, roughness **10** difficulty

Aspern Papers, The

author: 10 Henry James

aspersion 4 slur **5** abuse, smear **7** calumny, censure, obloquy, railing, slander **8** reproach, reviling **10** defamation, detraction **11** deprecation **12** vilification **13** disparagement

Asphodel Fields

meadow of: 10 dead heroes

asphyxiate 5 choke **6** stifle **7** smother **9** suffocate **11** strangulate

aspirant 7 hopeful, nominee **9** applicant, candidate **10** competitor, contestant

aspiration 3 end **4** hope, mark, wish **6** design, desire, intent, object **7** craving, longing, purpose **8** ambition, daydream, endeavor, yearning **9** hankering, intention, objective

aspire 4 seek **5** aim at, covet, crave **6** desire, pursue **7** hope for, long for, pine for, wish for **8** yearn for **9** pant after **10** hunger over **11** hanker after, thirst after

ass 3 oaf **4** dolt, fool, jerk **5** booby, burro, dunce, idiot, moron, ninny **6** donkey, dum-dum, nitwit **7** half-wit, jackass **8** bonehead, imbecile, lunkhead, numskull **9** blockhead, lamebrain **10** dunderhead, nincompoop

assail 5 fly at **6** attack **7** assault, lunge at, set upon **9** pitch into **11** descend upon

assailant 6 mugger **8** assailer, attacker, molester **9** aggressor, assaulter

assailer 8 attacker **9** aggressor, assailant, assaulter

Assamese
   language family: 12 Indo-European
   branch: 11 Indo-Iranian
   group: 5 Indic
   spoken in: 5 (northern) India

Assaracus
   origin: 5 Greek
   mentioned in: 5 Iliad
   father: 4 Tros
   son: 5 Capys
   founder of: 10 royal house

assassin 6 hit man, killer, slayer **8** murderer **11** executioner

assassinate 4 kill, slay **6** murder, rub out **7** bump off **9** do to death, liquidate **10** put to death **11** exterminate

assault 4 push, raid **5** drive, fly at, foray, lunge, sally, siege, storm **6** assail, attack, charge, invade, strike, thrust **7** besiege, bombard, lunge at, offense, set upon **8** fall upon, invasion, storming, strike at, thrust at **9** assailing, lash out at, onslaught **10** aggression **11** bombardment

assaulter 6 mugger **8** assailer, attacker **9** aggressor, assailant

assay 3 try **4** rate, test **5** essay, prove **6** assess **7** analyze, attempt **8** appraise, endeavor, estimate, evaluate **9** undertake

assemblage 4 body, heap, herd, mass, pack, pile **5** batch, bunch, clump, flock, group, stock, store **6** throng **7** cluster, company **8** assembly, conclave **9** aggregate, amassment, gathering **10** collection **11** aggregation **12** accumulation, congregation

assemble 4 join, meet **5** amass, flock, rally **6** gather, heap up, muster, pile up, summon **7** collect, compile, connect, convene, convoke, marshal, round up **9** construct, fabricate **10** accumulate, congregate **11** fit together, put together **12** call together, come together **13** bring together, group together

assembly 4 body, herd, mass, pack **5** crowd, flock, group, troop **6** throng **7** cluster, company, council **8** conclave, congress **9** aggregate, gathering **10** assemblage, collection **11** aggregation, convocation, legislature **12** congregation

assembly hall 8 auditory **10** auditorium **11** concert hall, lecture hall, meeting hall

assent 5 agree, allow, grant, yield **6** accept, accord, comply, concur, permit **7** approve, concede, consent, defer to **8** approval, sanction **9** acquiesce, admission, agreement **10** acceptance, compliance, concession, fall in with **11** affirmation, approbation, concurrence, endorsement, recognition, subscribe to **12** acquiescence, confirmation, ratification, verification **13** corroboration **14** acknowledgment

assent to 4 okay **5** allow **6** accept, permit **7** approve **8** sanction, say yes to **9** agree with, authorize **11** acquiesce to, go along with

assert 4 aver, avow **5** argue, claim, state, swear **6** accent, affirm, avouch, insist, stress, uphold **7** advance, contend, declare, profess **8** advocate, maintain, propound, set forth **9** emphasize **10** put forward

assertion 5 claim **6** avowal, dictum **8** argument, averment **9** statement, upholding **10** allegation, contention **11** declaration, maintaining **12** protestation

assertive 5 pushy **8** cocksure, decisive, emphatic, forceful, positive **9** confident, insistent, outspoken **10** aggressive **11** domineering, self-assured **12** strong-willed

assertiveness 10 insistence **11** forwardness **12** cocksureness, forcefulness, positiveness **13** aggressiveness, outspokenness **14** self-confidence

assess 3 tax **4** levy **5** judge, value **6** charge **8** appraise, consider, estimate, evaluate, look over

assessment 3 fee, tax **4** dues, fine, rate, toll **6** charge, impost, tariff **8** judgment **9** appraisal **10** estimation, evaluation

asset 3 aid **4** boon, help, plus **7** benefit, service **9** advantage

assets 4 cash **5** goods, means, money **6** wealth **7** capital, effects **8** property, reserves **9** resources **10** belongings **11** possessions

asseverate 4 aver, avow **5** state, swear **6** affirm, assert, attest, avouch, insist **7** certify, contend, declare, protect **8** maintain, proclaim **9** emphasize, pronounce

as shown below
   Latin: 7 ut infra

assiduity 8 industry, tenacity **9** diligence **10** dedication, doggedness **11** application, persistence **13** determination

assiduous 6 dogged **7** earnest **8** constant, diligent, sedulous, tireless, untiring **9** laborious, steadfast, tenacious **10** determined, persistent, unflagging **11** hardworking, industrious, persevering, unremitting **13** indefatigable

assign 3 fix, set **4** give, name **5** allot, grant **6** charge, choose, invest **7** appoint, consign, entrust, mete out, specify **8** allocate, delegate, dispense, set apart **9** apportion, designate, determine, prescribe, stipulate **10** commission, distribute

assignation 4 date **5** tryst **7** meeting **10** rendezvous **11** appointment

assignment 3 job **4** duty, post, task **5** chore **6** lesson **8** exercise, homework **9** allotment **10** allocation, commission **11** appointment, designation **12** distribution **13** apportionment

assimilate 6 absorb, digest, imbibe, ingest, take in **9** integrate **10** metabolize **11** incorporate

Assiniboine, Assiniboin
   language family: 6 Siouan
   location: 9 Minnesota **12** Lake Winnipeg, Saskatchewan
   related to: 7 Dakotas

assist 3 aid **4** abet, hand, help **5** boost, serve **6** back up, uphold, wait on **7** benefit, support, sustain **9** cooperate, lend a hand, reinforce **11** accommodate, collaborate, helping hand

assistance 3 aid **4** alms, help **6** relief **7** charity, service, stipend, subsidy, support **10** sustenance **11** cooperation, helping hand **12** contribution **13** collaboration, reinforcement **16** financial support

assistant 3 aid **4** aide, ally **5** aider **6** helper **7** partner **8** adjutant, co-worker, sidekick **9** accessory, associate, auxiliary, colleague, subaltern, supporter **10** accomplice, apprentice, cooperator, lieutenant **11** confederate, helping hand, subordinate **12** collaborator **15** second-in-command

associate 3 mix, pal, tie **4** ally, bind, chum, club, join, link, mate, pair, peer, yoke **5** buddy, crony, merge, unite **6** allied, couple, fellow, friend, hobnob, league, mingle, relate **7** combine, comrade, connect, consort, hang out, partner, related **8** confrere, co-worker, identify, intimate, sidekick **9** affiliate, colleague, companion, confidant, correlate, pal around, rub elbows, run around **10** accomplice, affiliated, fraternize **11** confederate, subordinate **12** collaborator

associated 6 allied, joined, united **9** connected **10** affiliated **11** amalgamated

association 3 tie **4** body, bond, club, meld **5** blend, group, union **6** clique, league **7** combine, company, linkage, mixture, society **8** alliance, intimacy, mingling, relation **9** coalition, community, relations, syndicate **10** assemblage, connection, federation, fellowship, fraternity, friendship, membership **11** affiliation, camaraderie, combination, confederacy, corporation, correlation, familiarity, partnership **12** acquaintance, friendliness, organization, relationship **13** collaboration, companionship, confederation, participation **14** fraternization, identification

assorted 5 mixed **6** motley, sundry, varied **7** diverse, various **9** different **11** diversified **13** heterogeneous, miscellaneous

assortment 5 array, stock, store **6** medley, motley **7** melange, mixture, sorting, variety **8** grouping, quantity **9** arranging, assorting, diversity, potpourri, selection **10** collection, hodgepodge, miscellany **11** arrangement, classifying, disposition **14** classification, conglomeration

assuage 4 calm, ease **5** allay, quiet, still **6** lessen, pacify, soften, soothe, temper **7** appease, lighten, mollify, relieve **8** mitigate, tone down **9** alleviate **14** take the edge off

assuagement 6 easing, relief, solace **7** comfort **8** blunting, easement **9** abatement, lessening, tempering **10** mitigation **11** appeasement **13** mollification

assume 4 take **5** fancy, guess, infer, judge, seize, think, usurp **6** accept, deduce, gather, take on, take up **7** believe, imagine, presume, suppose, surmise, suspect **8** arrogate, shoulder, take over, theorize **9** postulate, speculate, undertake **10** commandeer, conjecture, understand **11** appropriate, expropriate, hypothesize **14** take for granted

assumed 4 fake **5** bogus, false, phony **6** made-up **8** presumed, supposed **9** falsified **10** fictitious **11** make-believe, presupposed, pseudonymic **12** pseudonymous

assumed name 5 alias **7** pen name **9** pseudonym **13** false identity
French: 10 nom de plume **11** nom de guerre

assuming 4 bold **5** nervy, pushy **6** brazen, cheeky **7** forward, haughty **8** arrogant, insolent **9** audacious, presuming **11** overbearing **12** presumptuous **13** self-assertive

assumption 6 belief, taking, theory **7** premise, seizure **8** assuming, taking on, taking up **9** accepting, postulate **10** acceptance, arrogation, hypothesis, usurpation **11** postulation, presumption, shouldering, supposition, undertaking **13** appropriating **14** presupposition

assurance 3 vow **4** oath **5** poise **6** binder, pledge **7** promise **8** averment, boldness, coolness, sureness, warranty **9** certainty, certitude, guarantee **10** confidence, profession **11** affirmation, assuredness, word of honor **12** self-reliance **14** aggressiveness, self-confidence, self-possession

assure 5 vow to **6** clinch, ensure, secure **7** confirm, promise **8** pledge to **9** guarantee **11** make certain **14** give one's word to

assured 4 sure **5** fixed **6** poised, secure **7** certain, settled **8** positive **9** confident, undoubted **10** dependable, guaranteed **11** indubitable, irrefutable **12** indisputable **13** self-confident, self-possessed **14** unquestionable

Astaire, Fred
real name: 19 Frederick Austerlitz
partner: 12 Ginger Rogers
born: 7 Omaha NE
roles: 6 Top Hat **9** Funny Face, Let's Dance, Swing Time **10** Holiday Inn **12** Easter Parade, Royal Wedding, Shall We Dance **14** The Gay Divorcee

Astarte
origin: 7 Semitic
goddess of: 9 fertility **12** reproduction
habitat: 4 moon
corresponds to: 6 Inanna, Ishtar **7** Mylitta **9** Ashtoreth

aster 12 Callistephus
varieties: 4 Tree **5** Black, China, Heath **6** Annual, Golden, Mojave, Stoke's **7** Italian **8** Blue-wood **9** Tartarian, White wood **10** New England **11** White upland

Asteria
form: 8 Titaness
father: 5 Coeus
mother: 6 Phoebe
sister: 4 Leto
husband: 6 Perses
son: 8 Paropeus
daughter: 6 Hecate
changed into: 5 Delos **6** island

Asterius
also: 8 Asterion
form: 5 giant **8** minotaur
king of: 5 Crete
father: 4 Anax **8** Tectamus **10** Cretan Bull, Hyperasius
mother: 8 Pasiphae
wife: 6 Europa
adopted sons: 5 Minos **8** Sarpedon **12** Rhadamanthys
daughter: 5 Crete
member of: 9 Argonauts

astern 3 aft **5** abaft **6** behind

asteroid 6 debris **9** planetoid

Asteropaeus
origin: 5 Greek
mentioned in: 5 Iliad
father: 7 Pelegon
ally of: 4 Troy
killed by: 8 Achilles

Asterope *see* **7** Sterope

astir 2 up **5** afoot, awake **6** active, roused **8** in motion, out of bed **10** up and about

astonish 4 daze, stun **5** amaze, shock **6** dazzle **7** astound, confuse, perplex, stagger, startle, stupefy **8** bewilder, confound, dumfound, surprise **9** electrify, overwhelm, take aback **10** strike dumb **11** flabbergast **18** take one's breath away

astonishing 7 amazing **8** dazzling, shocking, striking **9** confusing, startling **10** astounding, impressive, perplexing, staggering, stupefying, surprising **11** bewildering, confounding **12** breathtaking, electrifying, overpowering, overwhelming

astonishment 3 awe **5** shock **6** wonder **8** surprise **9** amazement, confusion **10** perplexity, wonderment **12** bewilderment, stupefaction

Astor, Mary
real name: 28 Lucille Vasconcellos Langhanke
born: 8 Quincy IL
roles: 6 Marmee **11** Little Women, The Great Lie **15** Meet Me in St Louis **16** The Maltese Falcon **17** The Palm Beach Story **18** The Prisoner of Zenda

astound 4 daze, stun **5** amaze, shock **6** dazzle **7** stagger, startle, stupefy **8** astonish, dumfound, surprise, take back **9** electrify, overwhelm **10** strike dumb **11** flabbergast **15** make one's eyes pop **18** take one's breath away

Astrabacus
origin: 5 Greek **7** Spartan
form: 6 prince
found: 11 wooden image
hidden by: 7 Orestes
co-finder: 8 Alopecus

Astraea
also: 6 Astrea
goddess of: 7 justice
father: 4 Zeus
mother: 6 Themis

Astraeus
form: 5 Titan
consort of: 3 Eos
father of: 4 wind **5** stars

astral 6 starry **9** celestial **12** astronomical

Astrateia *see* **7** Artemis

astray 3 off **5** amiss **6** afield **10** off the mark **12** off the course **16** off the right track

Astrea *see* **7** Astraea

astringent 4 acid, keen, sour, tart **5** brisk, sharp, stern, tonic **6** biting, severe **7** acerbic, austere, bracing, puckery, styptic **8** curative, incisive, piercing, salutary, stabbing, vinegary **10** antiseptic, salubrious **11** contracting, penetrating, restorative **12** invigorating

astrology 6 Zodiac **9** horoscopy, star-

craft **10** astromancy, astrometry, stargazing **11** genethliacs **13** mathematicals **14** astrodiagnosis
belief in: 8 siderism
term: 4 sign **5** house, trine **6** alnath, apheta, aspect **7** almuten, anareta, mansion, mundane, sextile **8** alkahest, nativity, quartile, synastry **9** planetary **10** opposition **11** conjunction

astronomer 4 Bode, Bopp, Gold, Hale **5** Adams, Baade, Bayer, Bethe, Gould, Hoyle, Royer **6** Bessel, Halley, Hubble, Jansky, Kepler, Newton, Piazzi **7** Bradley, Celcius, Galileo, Huggins, Huygens, Kapteyn, Laplace, Ptolemy, Russell, Shapley, Slipher **8** Angstrom, Einstein, Herschel, Hevelius, Lacaille, Lemaitre, Mercator **9** Eddington, Leverrier **10** Copernicus, Hipparchus, Tycho Brahe **11** Aristarchus, Hertzsprung **13** Petrus Apianus

astronomy
term: 5 comet, orbit **6** apogee, meteor, nebula, parsec, quasar **7** azimuth, eclipse, equinox, perigee, transit **8** aphelion, asteroid, ecliptic, meridian, solstice **9** meteorite, satellite **10** perihelion, precession **11** declination, occultation **12** perturbation, spectroscopy **16** celestial equator
type/related study: 9 cosmogony, cosmology **10** astrometry, photometry **12** astrophysics **18** celestial mechanics
see also **4** star

Astrophel and Stella
author: 15 Sir Philip Sidney
astute 3 sly **4** able, foxy, keen, wily **5** acute, sharp, smart **6** adroit, artful, bright, clever, crafty, shrewd, subtle **7** cunning, knowing, politic **9** designing, sagacious **10** discerning, keen-minded, perceptive **11** calculating, intelligent, penetrating **13** Machiavellian, perspicacious
astuteness 6 acumen **8** keenness **9** acuteness, smartness **10** cleverness, shrewdness **12** perspicacity

Astyanax
also: 11 Scamandrius
father: 6 Hector **9** Strophius
mother: 10 Andromache
thrown from: 11 Trojan walls
thrown by: 6 Greeks
slain by: 8 Menelaus

Asuncion
capital of: 8 Paraguay
asunder 4 rent **5** apart **8** in pieces, to shreds **9** torn apart **11** broken apart
asylum 4 home **5** haven **6** harbor, refuge **7** retreat, shelter **8** madhouse, preserve **9** almshouse, orphanage, poorhouse, sanctuary **10** sanatorium, sanitarium **11** institution **13** children's home, state hospital **14** mental hospi-

tal **15** place of immunity **17** mental institution **23** eleemosynary institution

Asynjur
origin: 12 Scandinavian
goddesses of: 4 Asar **5** Aesir
leader: 3 Fri **5** Frigg, Frija **6** Frigga

As You Like It
author: 18 William Shakespeare
character: 5 Celia (Aliena) **6** Audrey, Jaques, Oliver **7** Orlando **8** Rosalind (Ganymede) **9** Frederick **10** Touchstone

Atabyrian *see* **4** Zeus
at a distance 4 afar, away **5** above, aloof, apart **6** far off **9** separated

Atala
author: 21 Francois Chateaubriand

Atalanta
also: 8 Atalante
form: 6 virgin **8** huntress
father: 5 Iasus
mother: 7 Clymene
son: 13 Parthenopaeus
wounded: 14 Calydonian boar
lost race to: 10 Hippomenes

Atalanta in Calydon
author: 24 Algernon Charles Swinburne

at any rate 6 anyhow, anyway **9** in any case **10** in any event
at cross purposes 7 counter, opposed **8** contrary, converse, inimical, opposite **9** disparate **10** at variance, discordant **11** conflicting **12** antithetical, incompatible **13** contradictory

Ate
origin: 5 Greek
form: 7 goddess
personifies: 12 recklessness **16** divine punishment
at ease 4 calm, cool **6** at rest, serene **7** content, relaxed, unmoved **8** composed **9** at leisure, confident, unruffled **10** complacent, nonchalant, unbothered, untroubled **11** comfortable, unconcerned

a tergo 9 at the back **10** from behind
at fault 6 guilty **8** culpable **10** implicated **11** blameworthy, responsible
at full length
Latin: 9 in extenso

Athabascan, Athapascan (Slave Indians)
language family: 10 Athabascan, Athapaskan
location: 6 Canada **14** Great Slave Lake
dominated by: 4 Cree
related to: 9 Chipewyan
tribe: 4 Dine **5** Slave **6** Apache, Navaho, Navajo **9** Mescalero **10** Athabascan

Athalie
author: 18 Jean Baptiste Racine
Athamas
king of: 6 Thebes

father: 6 Aeolus
wife: 3 Ino **7** Nephele
son: 5 Ptous **6** Leucon **7** Phrixus **8** Learchus **10** Melicertes
daughter: 5 Helle

at hand 4 near, nigh **5** close, handy, on tap, ready **6** nearby **7** close by **8** imminent **9** available, impending **10** accessible, convenient **11** at one's elbow, forthcoming **14** at one's disposal **15** within arm's reach
atheism 8 apostasy, unbelief **9** disbelief **10** irreligion **11** godlessness
atheist 7 infidel **10** unbeliever **11** disbeliever, nonbeliever

Athena
also: 6 Athene, Pallas, Saitis **11** Tritogeneia **12** Pallas Athena **18** Alalcomenean Athena
origin: 5 Greek
goddess of: 4 arts **6** wisdom **7** warfare **9** fertility
father: 4 Zeus **6** Triton
mother: 5 Metis
sprang from head of: 4 Zeus
raised by: 12 Alalcomeneus
symbol: 3 owl
corresponds to: 7 Minerva
epithet: 4 Alea **5** Meter, Xenia **6** Ergane, Itonia, Polias **7** Agoraea, Cissaea, Paeonia, Pronaus, Pronoea **8** Anemotis, Poliates, Zosteria **9** Oxyderces, Parthenia, Poliuchus, Promachus **10** Axiopoenus, Chalinitis, Cyparissia **11** Promachorma

Athens
capital of: 6 Greece
Greek: 7 Athinai
hills: 9 Acropolis **14** Hagios Georghios
landmark: 4 Stoa **9** Areopagus, Parthenon **10** Erechtheum, Propylaeum **17** Theater of Dionysus
marketplace: 5 Agora
mountain: 6 Parnes **8** Aigaleos, Hymettus **10** Pentelikon
named for: 6 Athena
port: 7 Piraeus
river: 7 Ilissus
sea: 6 Aegean **11** Saronic Gulf
square: 8 Syntagma (Constitution)
event: 8 Olympics **12** Olympic Games

Athens Graces 4 Auxe **8** Hegemone
athirst 4 avid, keen **5** eager **6** raring **7** longing, panting **8** yearning
athlete 4 jock **8** champion **9** contender, sportsman **10** contestant, game player
athletic 5 burly, hardy, husky, manly **6** brawny, robust, strong, sturdy, virile **8** muscular, powerful, stalwart, vigorous **9** masculine, strapping **10** able-bodied
athletics 5 games **6** sports **8** exercise **9** exercises **10** gymnastics
at home 6 at ease, inside, shut in **7** indoors **8** confined **10** in the house

11 comfortable
French: 4 chez

Athos
character in: 18 The Three Musketeers
author: 5 Dumas (pere)

athwart 6 across **7** astride **8** sideways,
sidewise **9** crossways, crosswise **12**
transversely

Atlanta
baseball team: 6 Braves
basketball team: 5 Hawks
football team: 7 Falcons
hockey team: 9 Thrashers

Atlantean
pertaining to: 5 Atlas

Atlantic City
director: 10 Louis Malle
cast: 8 Kate Reid **13** Burt Lancaster,
Michel Piccoli, Susan Sarandon

at large 5 astir, loose **6** abroad **8** as a
whole, at length **9** at liberty, in general **10** on the loose, unconfined **11**
out and about **13** in circulation **14**
around and about **15** making the
rounds

Atlas
form: 5 Titan
father: 7 Iapetus
mother: 7 Clymene
brother: 9 Menoetius **10** Epimetheus,
Prometheus
wife: 7 Pleione
daughters: 6 Hyades **7** Calypso **8**
Pleiades **10** Hesperides
supported: 3 sky
identified with: 14 Atlas Mountains

Atlas Shrugged
author: 7 Ayn Rand
character: 8 John Galt **11** Hank Reardon **12** Dagny Taggart, James Taggart

at last
Latin: 10 ad extremum

at leisure 4 idle **7** off duty **8** inactive
9 at liberty **10** unemployed, unoccupied

Atli
origin: 12 Scandinavian
sister: 8 Brynhild
wife: 6 Gudrun, Kudrun **7** Guthrun
killed by: 6 Gudrun, Kudrun **7**
Guthrun
represents: 6 Atilla

atmosphere 3 air **4** aura, feel, mood,
tone **5** color **6** spirit **7** feeling, quality
8 ambience **11** environment **12**
surroundings

atmospheric 3 air **4** airy **8** ethereal

at odds 6 unlike **8** contrary **9** different
10 at variance, discordant, discrepant,
dissimilar **11** contrasting

at odds with 9 counter to **10** contrary
to **14** at variance with

atoll 6 island
made of: 5 coral

pool: 6 lagoon
famous: 6 Bikini **8** Eniwetok

atom 3 bit, dot, jot **4** iota, mite, mote,
whit **5** crumb, grain, scrap, shred,
speck, trace **6** morsel, tittle **7** smidgen
8 fragment, particle **9** scintilla **10**
smithereen

atomic 6 cobalt **7** fission, neutron, nuclear, uranium **8** hydrogen **9** molecular, plutonium, subatomic, unseeable
10 impalpable **11** fissionable, microcosmic, microscopic, superatomic **13**
imperceptible, indiscernible, infinitesimal, thermonuclear

atom part 6 proton **7** neutron **8** electron

at once
French: 11 tout de suite

atone 6 pay for, redeem, repent, shrive
7 expiate **9** make up for **10** compensate, recompense, remunerate **12** do
penance for **13** make amends for **17**
make reparation for

atonement 6 amends, shrift **7** penance, redress **9** expiation **10** recompense, redemption, reparation, repentance **12** compensation, satisfaction **14**
penitential act

at one's disposal 5 handy **6** at hand,
on hand **9** available **10** accessible,
convenient **11** at one's elbow, ready
for use **13** at one's service

at one's elbow 5 handy **6** at hand,
nearby **9** available **10** accessible, convenient

at rest 5 quiet, still **6** asleep, at ease,
serene **7** at peace, content **8** in repose
9 quiescent **10** motionless

Atreus
father: 6 Pelops
mother: 10 Hippodamia
sister: 7 Nicippe
wife: 6 Aerope
son: 8 Menelaus **9** Agamemnon **10**
Plisthenes
daughter: 8 Anaxibia
killed: 6 Aglaus

Atridae
descendants of: 6 Atreus
family name of: 8 Anaxibia, Menelaus **9** Agamemnon **10** Plisthenes

atrium 4 hall **6** cavity **7** auricle **8** entrance **13** Roman entrance

atrocious 3 bad, low **4** dark, evil,
rude, vile **5** black, cruel **6** brutal, savage, tawdry, vulgar **7** heinous, hellish,
inhuman, uncouth, vicious **8** dreadful,
enormous, fiendish, flagrant, grievous,
horrible, infamous, infernal, pitiless,
ruthless, terrible **9** barbarous, execrable, merciless, monstrous, nefarious,
tasteless **10** diabolical, outrageous,
villainous

atrociousness 6 infamy **7** cruelty **8**
enormity, vileness **9** barbarity, brutality, depravity **11** heinousness, vicious-

ness **13** monstrousness, offensiveness
14 outrageousness

atrocity 6 horror **7** outrage **8** enormity, savagery, villainy **9** barbarism,
barbarity, brutality **10** inhumanity **11**
heinousness

atrophy 7 decline **8** decaying, drying
up **9** lack of use, withering **10** emaciation, shriveling **11** wasting away **12**
degeneration **13** deterioration

Atropos
member of: 5 Fates
cuts thread of: 4 life

Atsina (Gros Ventres, Haaninin)
language family: 9 Algonkian **10** Algonquian
location: 6 Canada **7** Montana **9** Milk
River **12** Saskatchewan **13** Missouri
River
related to: 7 Arapaho

attach 3 fix **4** join **5** affix, allot, annex
6 append, assign, couple, detail, secure **7** connect, destine, earmark **8** allocate, be fond of, fasten to, make fast
9 affiliate, associate, designate

attache 4 aide **5** envoy **6** consul **8** adjutant, diplomat, emissary, minister **9**
assistant **10** ambassador, vice consul
11 diplomatist, subordinate **12** ambas-
sadress **13** consul general

attachment 4 bond, love **6** fixing, liking, regard **7** adjunct, fixture, respect
8 addendum, addition, affinity, affix-
ing, appendix, coupling, devotion,
fondness, securing **9** accessory, affection, appendage, attaching, fastening
10 connection, friendship, supplement, tenderness **12** predilection

attack 3 fit **4** damn, go at **5** abuse,
blame, fault, fly at, onset, spasm,
spell **6** assail, charge, impugn, strike,
stroke, tackle **7** assault, censure,
lunge at, offense, seizure **8** denounce,
fall upon, invasion, paroxysm **9** criticism, criticize, denigrate, disparage,
incursion, offensive, onslaught, pitch
into, undertake **10** aggression, impugnment **11** denigration **13** disparagement

attacker 6 mugger **7** accuser **8** assailer, opponent **9** adversary, aggressor, assailant **10** antagonist **11** belligerent

attain 3 win **4** earn, gain, reap **5** reach
6 effect, obtain, secure **7** achieve, acquire, procure, realize **10** accomplish

attainable 6 at hand **9** available,
reachable **10** accessible, achievable,
realizable **11** within reach

attainment 5 skill **6** talent **7** earning,
gaining, getting, mastery, success,
winning **8** securing **9** acquiring, at-
taining, obtaining, procuring **10** competence **11** achievement, acquirement,
acquisition, fulfillment, procurement,
proficiency, realization **14** accomplishment

attempt 3 aim, try **4** seek **5** essay **6** attack, effort, hazard, strive, tackle, work at **7** assault, venture **8** endeavor **9** have a go at, onslaught, undertake **11** undertaking **12** make an effort, take a crack at, take a whack at

Attenborough, Richard
director of: 6 Gandhi (Oscar) **7** Chaplin **10** Cry Freedom **11** A Chorus Line, Shadowlands **12** In Love and War, Young Winston **13** A Bridge Too Far
roles: 10 Wavelength **12** Jurassic Park **14** The Great Escape **15** Doctor Doolittle **16** Ten Little Indians

attend 4 go to, heed, mark, mind, note **5** serve, usher, visit **6** convoy, escort, follow, show up, squire, tend to **7** care for, conduct, observe, oversee, service **8** appear at, consider, frequent, harken to, listen to, wait upon **9** accompany **11** superintend
French: 4 oyez
cry used by: 10 court crier
preceded: 12 proclamation

attendance 4 gate **5** crowd, house **8** audience, presence **10** appearance, assemblage, being there

attendant 3 aid **6** escort, flunky, helper, lackey, menial **7** related, servant **8** adherent, chaperon, follower **9** accessory, assistant, companion, underling **10** associated, consequent **12** accompanying

attention 4 care, heed, mind, note, suit **5** court **6** homage, notice, regard, wooing **7** concern, respect, service, thought **8** civility, courtesy, devotion, wariness **9** alertness, deference, diligence, vigilance **10** observance, politeness **11** assiduities, compliments, gallantries **12** deliberation **13** concentration, consideration, contemplation **14** thoughtfulness

attentive 5 alert, awake **6** intent, polite **7** devoted, heedful, mindful, zealous **8** diligent, obliging **9** courteous, dedicated, listening, observant, wide awake **10** respectful, thoughtful **11** considerate, deferential, painstaking **13** accommodating

attentiveness 7 concern **8** devotion, industry **9** alertness, attention, diligence **10** commitment, dedication **11** application, devotedness, heedfulness, mindfulness **14** thoughtfulness

attenuate 6 dilute, impair, lessen, reduce, weaken **7** draw out, spin out **8** decrease, diminish, enervate, enfeeble **9** water down **10** adulterate

attest 4 show **5** prove **6** affirm, assert, assure, evince, verify **7** bear out, certify, confirm, declare, display, exhibit, support, swear out, testify, warrant **8** vouch for **11** bear witness, corroborate, demonstrate **12** substantiate

attestation 9 testimony **10** deposition **11** declaration
at the back
Latin: 6 a tergo
at the beginning
Latin: 9 ad initium
at the bottom
French: 6 au fond
at the end
Latin: 5 ad fin
at the place
Latin: 5 ad loc **7** ad locum
attic 4 loft **6** garret **7** mansard **8** cockloft **10** clerestory
French: 7 grenier
German: 9 Dachboden
Spanish: 9 guardilla

attire 3 don **4** duds, garb, gown, robe, togs **5** array, dress **6** bedeck, clothe, finery, fit out, invest, outfit, rig out **7** apparel, clothes, costume, deck out, raiment, turn out **8** clothing, garments, glad rags, wardrobe **9** vestments **11** habiliments

Attis
also: 4 Atys
form: 5 youth
home: 7 Phrygia
loved: 6 Cybele
driven mad by: 6 Cybele

attitude 3 air **4** pose **6** manner, stance **7** outlook, posture **8** demeanor, position **11** disposition, frame of mind, perspective, point of view

attorney 4 beak **6** lawyer **7** counsel **8** advocate **9** barrister, counselor, solicitor **10** mouthpiece **12** legal adviser **14** member of the bar **15** ambulance chaser

attract 4 draw, lure, pull **5** cause, charm, evoke **6** allure, beckon, entice, induce, invite **7** bewitch, enchant, provoke **8** appeal to, interest **9** captivate, fascinate **11** precipitate

attraction 4 lure, pull **5** charm **6** allure, appeal **7** glamour **8** affinity, charisma, tendency **9** magnetism **10** enticement, inducement, temptation **11** captivation, enchantment, fascination **12** drawing power

attractive 4 chic, fair, foxy, sexy **6** lovely, pretty **7** elegant, likable, sightly, winning **8** alluring, becoming, charming, engaging, enticing, fetching, handsome, inviting, pleasant, pleasing, tasteful, tempting **9** agreeable, appealing, beautiful, seductive **10** bewitching, delightful, enchanting **11** captivating, charismatic, fascinating

attractiveness 5 charm **6** beauty **9** good looks **11** pulchritude **12** handsomeness

attribute 4 gift **5** facet, grace, lay to, trait **6** aspect, assign, credit, impute, talent, virtue **7** ability, ascribe, blame on, cause by, faculty, feature, quality,

trace to **8** charge to, property **9** character, endowment, set down to **10** account for, attainment, derive from, saddle with **11** acquirement, bring home to, distinction **14** accomplishment, characteristic

attrition 4 loss **7** erosion **8** abrasion, decrease, friction, grinding, scraping **9** reduction **10** decimation **11** wearing away, wearing down **14** disintegration

attune 5 adapt **6** adjust, tailor **8** accustom **9** acclimate **11** acclimatize

attune to 3 fit **5** adapt **6** adjust **7** conform **9** harmonize **11** accommodate

at variance 7 counter, opposed **8** contrary, converse, inimical, opposite **9** disparate **10** discordant **11** conflicting **12** antithetical, incompatible **13** contradictory **15** at cross purposes

Atwood, Margaret
author of: 7 Cat's Eye **8** Survival **9** Surfacing **10** Alias Grace, Bodily Harm, Lady Oracle **11** Second Words **13** Bluebeard's Egg, Life Before Man, Power Politics, The Circle Game **14** The Robber Bride **16** The Handmaid's Tale

at work 4 busy **5** in use **6** active **7** engaged, working **8** occupied

Atymnius
mentioned in: 5 Iliad
companion of: 8 Sarpedon
killed by: 10 Antilochus

atypical 7 unusual **8** abnormal, contrary, uncommon **9** anomalous, irregular, unnatural, untypical **10** nontypical **11** uncustomary, unlooked for **12** out of keeping **16** unrepresentative

Atys *see* **5** Attis

Auber, Daniel Francois Esprit
born: 4 Caen **6** France
composer of: 6 Haydee **7** La Macon **10** Fra Diavolo **12** Le Domino Noir **14** The Bronze Horse **16** Le Cheval de Bronze, The Crown Diamonds **17** La Muette de Portici **19** La Bergere Chatelaine **20** The Dumb Girl of Portici **22** Le Premier Jour de Bonheur

auberge 3 inn **6** tavern

auburn 5 henna, tawny **6** russet **8** cinnamon, nut-brown **11** golden-brown, rust-colored **12** reddish-brown **13** copper-colored **15** chestnut-colored

Aucassin and Nicolette
author: 7 unknown

Auchincloss, Louis
author of: 10 Watchfires **11** The Dark Lady, The Partners **12** Second Chance, The Embezzler **14** A World of Profit **16** Powers of Attorney, Tales of Manhattan, The Country Cousin **17** The Rector of Justin **19** The Winthrop Covenant **20** Portrait in Brownstone

au contraire 13 on the contrary
au courant 8 up-to-date

auction 3 sale **7** bidding **8** offering

audacious 4 bold, pert, rash, rude, wild **5** bossy, brave, fresh, gutsy, risky, saucy **6** brazen, cheeky, daring, plucky **7** defiant, forward, valiant **8** assuming, fearless, heedless, impudent, insolent, intrepid, reckless, stalwart, unafraid, valorous **9** breakneck, daredevil, dauntless, desperate, foolhardy, hotheaded, imprudent, shameless, unabashed **10** courageous, outrageous, self-willed **11** adventurous, impertinent, injudicious, lionhearted, venturesome **12** death-defying, devil-may-care, discourteous, enterprising, presumptuous, stouthearted **13** disrespectful

audaciousness 6 daring **8** audacity, boldness **11** forwardness **13** assertiveness **14** aggressiveness **15** adventurousness

audacity 4 gall, grit, guts **5** brass, cheek, nerve, pluck, spunk, valor **6** daring, mettle **7** bravery, courage **8** backbone, boldness, chutzpah, rashness, temerity **9** brashness, derring-do, impudence, insolence **10** brazenness, effrontery **11** forwardness, presumption **12** fearlessness, impertinence, recklessness **13** bumptiousness, foolhardiness, shamelessness **15** venturesomeness

Auden, W H
author of: 11 Another Time, Thank You Fog **12** Homage to Clio, The Dyer's Hand **13** About the House, Journey to a War **15** For the Time Being, The Age of Anxiety **16** City Without Walls, Epistle to a Godson **17** In Memory of W B Yeats, Musee des Beaux Arts **20** The Dog Beneath the Skin **22** Forewords and Afterwords

Audhumbla
also: 8 Audhumla
origin: 12 Scandinavian
form: 3 cow
owner: 4 Ymir
birth from: 3 ice
uncovered: 4 Buri

audible 5 clear, heard **8** distinct **11** discernible, perceptible

audience 4 talk **5** house **6** market, parley, public **7** hearing, meeting **8** assembly, audition **9** following, interview, listeners, onlookers, reception **10** conference, discussion, readership, spectators **12** congregation, constituency, consultation

audit 5 check **6** go over, review, verify **7** balance, examine, inspect **10** inspection, scrutinize **11** examination, investigate, take stock of **12** scrutinizing, verification **13** investigation

audition 6 tryout **7** hearing **15** test performance

auditor 8 listener **10** accountant, book-

keeper **11** comptroller **17** financial examiner

auditorium 4 hall **5** arena **7** theater **8** auditory, coliseum **11** concert hall, lecture hall, meeting hall **12** assembly hall

Audrey
character in: 11 As You Like It
author: 11 Shakespeare

Audubon, John James
born: 8 Les Cayes **12** Santo Domingo
artwork: 14 Birds of America **34** Viviparous Quadrupeds of North America

Auel, Jean M
author of: 15 Plains of Passage **17** The Mammoth Hunters, The Valley of Horses **18** The Shelters of Stone **20** The Clan of the Cave Bear

Auerbach, Arnold (Red)
sport: 10 basketball
position: 5 coach
team: 13 Boston Celtics

au fait 6 expert, versed **11** experienced **13** knowledgeable

Aufklarung 13 enlightenment **16** the Enlightenment

au fond 9 basically, in reality **11** at the bottom

auf Wiedersehen 7 goodbye **8** farewell **16** until we meet again

Auge
priestess of: 6 Athena
father: 9 King Aleus
mother: 6 Neaera
son: 8 Telephus
assaulted by: 8 Hercules

Augean stables
owned by: 10 King Augeas
number of oxen: 13 three thousand
cleaned by: 8 Hercules
river running through: 7 Alpheus

auger 4 bore **5** drill **6** pierce **10** boring tool

aught 3 all, zip **4** love, nada, null, zero **6** naught **7** a cipher, nothing **8** goose egg **11** horse collar

augment 5 add to, boost, raise, swell, widen **6** deepen, expand, extend **7** amplify, build up, enlarge, inflate, magnify **8** flesh out, heighten, increase, lengthen **9** intensify

augmentation 5 boost, extra, raise **8** addition, increase, swelling, widening **9** deepening, expansion, extension, inflation **10** supplement **11** elaboration, enlargement, heightening, lengthening **13** amplification, magnification **15** intensification

augur 4 bode, seer **6** herald, oracle **7** diviner, portend, predict, presage, promise, prophet, signify **8** forecast, foretell, forewarn, intimate, prophesy **9** be a sign of **10** be an omen of, foreshadow, soothsayer **13** prognosticate **14** prognosticator

augury 4 omen, sign **5** token **6** herald **7** auspice, portent, promise, warning **8** prophecy **9** harbinger, precursor, sortilege **10** divination, forerunner, indication **11** forewarning, soothsaying **14** fortunetelling **15** prognostication

august 5 grand, lofty, noble, regal **6** solemn, superb **7** eminent, exalted, stately, sublime, supreme **8** glorious, imposing, majestic **9** dignified, estimable, grandiose, venerable **10** impressive, monumental **11** high-ranking, illustrious, magnificent **12** awe-inspiring **13** distinguished

August
Anglo-Saxon: 10 Weod-Monath
characteristic: 7 dog days
flower: 5 poppy
French: 4 Aout
gem: 7 peridot **8** sardonyx **9** carnelian
German: 6 August
holiday:
  England/Scotland: 11 Harvest Home (1)
Italian: 6 Agosto
number of days: 9 thirty-one
original name: 8 Sextilis **12** Metageitnion
origin of name: 6 Augere (Latin to open) **8** Augustus (Roman emperor)
place in year:
  Roman: 5 sixth
  Gregorian: 6 eighth
Spanish: 6 Agosto
zodiac sign: 3 Leo **5** Virgo

Augustine, St (of Hippo)
author of: 10 Civitas Dei **11** Confessions, Enchiridion **12** The City of God

augustness 7 dignity, majesty **8** eminence, nobility **9** loftiness **11** distinction **13** monumentality **15** illustriousness

August 1914
author: 23 Aleksandr Solzhenitsyn Jr

au naturel 4 nude **8** uncooked **15** in a natural state

Auntie Mame
author: 13 Patrick Dennis

Aunt Jo's Scrap-Bag
author: 15 Louisa May Alcott

Aunt Julia and the Scriptwriter
author: 16 Mario Vargas Llosa

au pair 4 maid **5** nanny **9** governess **13** mother's helper

aura 3 air **4** feel, mood **5** aroma **7** essence, feeling, quality **8** ambience **9** character, emanation **10** atmosphere, suggestion

Aura
companion of: 7 Artemis
bore: 5 twins
  fathered by: 9 Dionysius
changed into: 6 spring
  changed by: 4 Zeus

au revoir 7 goodbye 8 farewell 16 until we meet again

Aurora
  origin: 5 Roman
  goddess of: 4 dawn
  corresponds to: 3 Eos

Aurora Leigh
  author: 24 Elizabeth Barrett Browning

Ausgleich 10 compromise 11 arrangement 12 equalization

Auslander 5 alien 9 foreigner, outlander

auspice 4 omen, sign 6 augury 7 portent, warning 10 indication 15 prognostication

auspices 4 care, egis 5 aegis 6 charge 7 control, support 8 advocacy, guidance 9 authority, influence, patronage 10 protection 11 countenance, sponsorship 12 championship

auspicious 4 good 5 happy, lucky 6 benign, timely 7 hopeful 9 favorable, fortunate, opportune, promising, red-letter 10 felicitous, heartening, propitious, reassuring, successful 11 encouraging

Austen, Jane
  author of: 4 Emma 10 Persuasion 13 Mansfield Park 15 Northanger Abbey 17 Pride and Prejudice 19 Sense and Sensibility

austere 5 rigid, spare, stark, stern 6 chaste, severe, simple, strict 7 ascetic, Spartan 8 rigorous 10 abstemious, forbidding 11 self-denying, strait-laced

Austerlitz, Frederick
  real name of: 11 Fred Astaire

Australia
  other name: 9 Down Under
  name means: 19 unknown southern land
  capital: 8 Canberra
  largest city: 6 Sydney
  others: 3 Ayr 4 Yass 5 Dubbo, Perth 6 Albury, Cairns, Casino, Coburg, Darwin, Hobart 7 Bendigo, Geelong, Kogarah, Mildura, Mitcham, Whyalla 8 Adelaide, Ballarat, Bathurst, Brighton, Brisbane, Essendon, Randwick, Ringwood 9 Melbourne, Newcastle, Port Pirie, Toowoomba 10 Broken Hill, Kalgoorlie, Waggawagga, Wollongong 11 Collingwood, Rockhampton 12 Alice Springs
  division: 8 Tasmania, Victoria 10 Queensland 13 New South Wales 14 South Australia 16 Western Australia 17 Northern Territory 26 Australian Capital Territory
  head of state: 14 British monarch 15 governor general
  measure: 4 arna, naut, saum
  monetary unit: 4 dump, tray, zack 5 pound 6 dollar 8 shilling
  island: 4 Cato, King 5 Cocos, Green, Timor 6 Barrow, Koolan 7 Coringa,

Keeling, Neptune, Norfolk 8 Flinders, Kangaroo, Lacepede, Melville, Rottnest, Tasmania, Thursday 9 Admiralty
  lake: 4 Eyre 5 Carey, Cowan, Frome, Moore, Wells 6 Austin, Barlee, Bulloo, Dundas, Harris, Mackay 7 Amadeus, Blanche, Everard, Torrens 8 Carnegie, Gairdner 9 MacDonald 10 Yammayamma 14 Disappointment
  mountain: 3 Ise 4 Blue, Olga, Ossa, Zeil 5 Bruce, Snowy 6 Cradle, Doreen, Garnet, Gawler, Magnet, Morgan 7 Bongong, Gregory, Herbert 8 Augustus, Brockman, Cuthbert, Jusgrave, Mulligan, Surprise 9 Murchison, Woodroffe 14 Australian Alps 15 New England Range 18 Great Dividing Range
  highest point: 9 Kosciusko
  river: 3 Hay 4 Avon, Daly, Swan, Yule 5 Bullo, Comet, Drava, Naomi, Paroo, Roper, Yarra 6 Barcoo, Barwon, Bulloo, Culgoa, Degrey, Hunter, Isaacs, Murray, Norman 7 Darling, Derwent, Fitzroy, Georges, Gilbert, Lachlan, Staaten, Warrego 8 Belyando, Brisbane, Burdekin, Clarence, Drysdale, Flinders, Gascoyne, Georgina, Mitchell, Thompson, Victoria, Weeribee, Wooramel 9 Ashburton, Fortescue, Hawksbury, MacKenzie, Macquarie, Murchison, Saltwater 10 Diamantina, Shoalhaven 12 Murrambidgee
  sea: 5 Coral, Timor 6 Indian, Tasman 7 Arafura, Pacific
  physical feature:
    bay: 5 Bight, Shark 6 Botany 7 Moreton 11 Port Phillip
    cape: 4 Howe, York 5 Byron 9 Southeast
    channel: 5 Cowal 9 Anabranch, Billabong
    desert: 6 Arunta, Gibson, Stuart, Tanami 7 Simpson 10 Great Sandy 13 Great Victoria
    gulf: 8 Spencers 9 Van Dieman 11 Carpentaria 15 Joseph Bonaparte 20 Great Australian Bight
    peninsula: 4 Eyre
    reef: 12 Great Barrier
    strait: 4 Bass
  people: 3 Abo 4 Koko, Mara, Wong 5 Anzac, Binge, Dieri, Maori, Myall 6 Aranda, Arunta, Aussie, Binghi, Digger, Kipper, Papuan 7 Arawong, Ilpirra 8 Antipode, Barkinji, Billijim, Euahlayi, Warragal, Warrigal 9 Aborigine 10 Australoid, Melanesian, Sandgroper
    actor: 8 Eric Bana 9 Judy Davis, Mel Gibson, Paul Hogan 10 Bryan Brown 11 Heath Ledger, Hugh Jackman 12 Geoffrey Rush, Nicole Kidman, Russell Crowe, Toni Collette 13 Cate Blanchett

    author: 4 West 5 White 7 Russell 10 Richardson
    explorer: 4 Bass, Cook 6 Mawson, Tasman 7 Wilkins
    leader: 4 Holt 5 Hawke 6 Howard 7 Keating, Menzies, Whitlam
    nurse: 11 Sister Kenny
  language: 7 English
  religion: 7 Judaism 8 Anglican 10 Protestant 13 Roman Catholic
  place: 7 outback 9 billabong 11 back country
    aborigine area: 9 Arhemland
    beach: 5 Manly
    dam: 4 Hume
  possession: 12 Cocos Islands 13 Norfolk Island 16 Christmas Islands
  feature:
    animal: 5 dingo 6 kelpie 7 wallaby 8 anteater, kangaroo 9 koala bear 18 duckbilled platypus
    bird: 3 emu 10 kookaburra
    cowboy: 6 waddie 8 jackaroo
    dance: 6 dreher
    song: 15 Waltzing Matilda
    flower: 7 boronia, fuchsia, waratah 9 coachwood 12 kangaroo paws
    game: 3 sye 10 tambaroora
    tree: 3 gum 10 eucalyptus
    weapon: 5 kiley, kyley 7 wommera 9 boomerang
    food: 3 kai 6 tucker
    cake: 6 damper 7 brownie
    dish: 8 coolamon
    drink: 9 arkaloola
    fruit: 5 nonda 7 kumquat 11 desert-lemon

Austria
  other name: 10 Osterreich
  name means: 12 eastern state
  capital/largest city: 6 Vienna
  others: 4 Enns, Graz, Lech, Linz, Ried, Wels 5 Krems, Steyr, Traun 6 Leoben 7 Bregenz, Modling, Spittal, Villach 8 Bad Ischl, Dornbirn, Salzburg 9 Innsbruck, Semmering 10 Kapfenberg, Klagenfurt 11 Sankt Polten 14 Wiener Neustadt
  division: 5 Tirol, Tyrol 6 Istria, Styria, Triest 7 Bohemia, Galicia, Moravia, Silesia 8 Bukowina, Dalmatia, Earniola, Gradisca 9 Earinthia 10 Burgenland, Vorarlberg 12 Lower Austria, Upper Austria
    Roman province: 6 Raetia 7 Noricum 8 Pannonia
  government:
    legislature: 9 Bundesrat, Reichsrat 10 Herrenhaus, Reichsrath
  head of government: 10 Chancellor
  other leader: 7 emperor 12 burgomeister
  measure: 4 fass, fuss, joch, mass, muth, yoke 5 halbe, linie, meile, metze, pfiff, punkt 6 achtel, becher, leipoa, seidel 7 dlafter, viertel 8 dreiling 12 futtermassel
  monetary unit: 4 lira 5 crown, ducat,

krone **6** florin, gulden, heller, zehner **8** albertin, groschen, kreutzer **9** schilling

weight: 4 marc, unze **5** denat, karch, stein **7** centner, pfennig **8** vierling **9** quantchen

lake: 6 Almsee **7** Fertoto, Mondsee **8** Bodensee, Traunsee **9** Constance **10** Neusiedler

mountain: 4 Alps **6** Stubai, Tirols, Tyrols **8** Eisenerz, Rhatikon **9** Dolomites, Kitzbuhel **10** Hohe Tauern **14** Silvretta Group

highest point: 13 Grossglockner

river: 3 Inn, Mur **4** Drau, Elbe, Enns, Iser, Kamp, Lech, Murz, Raab **5** Donau, Drava, Drave, March, Salza, Thaya, Traun **6** Danube, Moldau

physical feature:
  basin: 7 Styrian
  canal: 6 Danube
  mountain pass: 7 Brenner
  wind: 6 Foehen
  woods: 6 Vienna

people: 5 Poles **6** Croats, Czechs **7** Germans, Gypsies **8** Slovenes **10** Hungarians
  botanist: 6 Mendel
  composer: 5 Haydn **6** Czerny, Mahler, Mozart, Webern **7** Amadeus, Strauss **8** Bruckner, Schubert **9** Beethoven **10** Schoenberg
  emperor: 7 Charles, Francis **9** Ferdinand, Habsburgs, Hapsburgs **10** Franz Josef
  philosopher: 12 Wittgenstein
  psychiatrist: 5 Adler, Freud, Reich
  statesman: 10 Metternich **12** Kurt Waldheim

language: 5 Czech **6** German, Magyar **8** Croatian **9** Slovenian

religion: 7 Judaism **10** Protestant **13** Roman Catholic

place:
  boulevard: 3 Kai **11** Ringstrasse
  cathedral: 9 St Stephen
  city hall: 7 Rathaus
  fortress: 13 Hochosterwitz, Hohensalzburg
  imperial palace: 7 Hofburg
  monastery: 4 Melk **8** Gottweig **14** Klosterneuburg
  museum: 6 Mozart **9** Johanneum
  people's garden: 11 Volksgarten
  resort: 5 Baden **7** Bregenz **8** Bad Ischl **9** Innsbruck, Semmering

feature: 8 yodelers **11** ice grottoes

clothing: 5 loden **10** lederhosen

dance: 5 waltz **6** dreher **7** landler **13** schuhplattler **14** grand polonaise

festival: 8 Salzburg

horse: 10 Lippizaner

pastry shop: 12 konditoreien

food:
  breaded veal cutlet: 15 Wiener schnitzel

  cake: 11 linzer torte, sacher torte
  cookie: 7 kipferl
  roll: 10 golatschen

Austroasiatic

language subfamily: 5 Khasi, Munda **8** Annamite, Mon-Khmer **9** Palaung-Wa **10** Nicobarese **11** Semang-Sakai **13** Annamite-Muong

spoken in: 5 Burma, India **7** Nicobar, Vietnam **8** Cambodia, Malaysia **9** Kampuchea

authentic 4 pure, real, true **5** valid **6** actual **7** factual, genuine **8** accurate, attested, bona fide, faithful, original, reliable, verified **9** veritable **10** accredited, dependable, legitimate **11** trustworthy **12** unquestioned **13** authoritative, unadulterated

authenticate 6 attest, avouch, verify **7** certify, confirm, endorse, warrant **8** document, validate, vouch for **9** guarantee **11** corroborate **12** substantiate

authenticated 7 genuine **8** attested, verified **9** validated **10** accredited, vouched for **13** substantiated

authentication 7 voucher **10** validation **11** certificate **12** verification **13** authorization, certification

author 4 poet **5** maker **6** father, framer, writer **7** creator, founder, planner **8** essayist, inventor, novelist, producer **9** initiator, innovator, organizer **10** originator, playwright, prime mover **16** short-story writer
see author under each country

authoritarian 5 harsh **6** severe, strict, tyrant **7** austere, fascist **8** autocrat, dogmatic, martinet **9** by the book, by the rule **10** inflexible, tyrannical, unyielding **11** dictatorial, doctrinaire **12** disciplinary, rule follower **14** disciplinarian, little dictator, uncompromising

authoritative 5 sound, valid **6** lordly, ruling **7** factual, learned **8** arrogant, decisive, dogmatic, imposing, official, reliable **9** authentic, masterful, scholarly, sovereign **10** autocratic, commanding, definitive, dependable, imperative, impressive, peremptory, sanctioned, tyrannical **11** dictatorial, trustworthy **14** administrative

authoritativeness 6 belief **9** authority **10** conviction **11** credibility **14** conclusiveness

authorities 6 expert, police, pundit **7** scholar **10** mastermind, specialist **11** connoisseur, officialdom **12** powers that be

authority 4 rule, sway **5** clout, force, might, power **6** esteem, weight **7** command, control, respect **8** dominion, prestige, strength **9** influence, supremacy **10** domination, importance **12** jurisdiction **14** administration

authorization 7 license **8** approval, sanction **10** commission, imprimatur, permission **11** entitlement **12** confir-

mation, legalization **13** accreditation, certification

authorize 5 allow **6** enable, invest, permit **7** approve, certify, charter, confirm, empower, entitle, license, warrant **8** accredit, sanction, vouch for **9** give leave **10** commission

authorized 8 approved, official **9** canonical **10** sanctioned

Autobiography of Alice B Toklas
  author: 13 Gertrude Stein

Autobiography of Miss Jane Pittman, The
  author: 13 Ernest J Gaines

autochthonous 5 first **6** native, primal **7** ancient **8** earliest, original, primeval **10** aboriginal, indigenous, primordial

autocracy 7 czarism, tyranny **8** autarchy, monarchy **9** Caesarism, despotism, Hitlerism, kaiserism, monocracy, Stalinism **10** absolutism **11** Bonapartism **12** dictatorship **14** tyrannical rule **15** totalitarianism

autocrat 5 ruler **6** despot, tyrant **7** monarch **8** dictator, overlord **13** absolute ruler

autocratic 8 despotic **9** czaristic, imperious, tyrannous **10** iron-handed, oppressive, repressive, tyrannical **11** dictatorial, monarchical **13** authoritarian

auto da fe, auto de fe 13 act of the faith **17** burning of heretics
  from: 18 Spanish Inquisition

autograph 4 mark, sign **5** x-mark **9** John Henry, signature **11** endorsement, handwriting, inscription, John Hancock **16** countersignature

Autolycus
  character in: 14 The Winter's Tale
  author: 11 Shakespeare

Autolycus
  form: 5 thief
  father: 6 Hermes
  mother: 6 Chione
  half-brother: 9 Philammon
  wife: 9 Amphithea
  daughter: 8 Anticlea
  grandson: 8 Odysseus
  gift: 12 invisibility **13** shape changing

automated 9 automatic **10** mechanical, mechanized **15** machine-operated

automatic 6 reflex **7** natural, routine **8** electric, habitual, inherent, unwilled **9** automated **10** mechanical, push-button, self-acting, self-moving **11** instinctive, involuntary, spontaneous, unconscious **12** uncontrolled **13** nonvolitional, self-operating **14** self-propelling

automaton 4 pawn, tool **5** golem, patsy, robot **6** puppet, stooge **7** android, cat's-paw, fall guy, machine **10** fantoccino, marionette

automobile
  invented by:

differential gear: 4 Benz
electric: 8 Morrison
gasoline: 6 Duryea **7** Daimler
muffler: 5 Maxim
self-starter: 9 Kettering
see also **3** car

automobiles
Buick: 7 Century, LeSabre **10** Park Avenue
Cadillac: 7 DeVille **8** Escalade
Chevrolet: 5 Astro **6** Blazer, Impala, Lumina, Malibu **7** Beretta, Corsica, Equinox **8** Cavalier, Colorado, Corvette, Suburban **9** Silverado **10** Monte Carlo
Chrysler-Plymouth: 7 LeBaron, Sebring **8** Pacifica **9** PT Cruiser
Dodge: 3 Ram **4** Neon **5** Viper **6** Dakota **7** Caravan **8** Intrepid
Ford: 5 Focus, Tempo **6** Escape, Escort, Ranger, Taurus **7** Mustang **8** Explorer **9** Excursion **11** Thunderbird
Honda: 5 Civic **6** Accord
Hummer
Hyundai: 6 Accent, Sonata, Tucson **7** Elantra, Santa Fe, Tiburon
Kia: 3 Rio **6** Amanti, Optima, Sedona **7** Sorento, Spectra **8** Sportage
Lexus
Lincoln: 7 Aviator, Town Car **9** Navigator
Mazda: 5 Miata **7** Tribute
Mercury: 5 Sable **7** Mariner, Montego **8** Monterey **11** Mountaineer **12** Grand Marquis
Mini: 6 Cooper
Mitsubishi: 6 Galant, Lancer **7** Eclipse, Montero **8** Endeavor **9** Outlander
Nissan: 5 Quest, Titan **6** Altima, Armada, Maxima, Murano, Sentra, Xterra **8** Frontier **10** Pathfinder
Oldsmobile: 5 Ciera **7** Achieva **11** Ninety-Eight
Pontiac: 4 Vibe **5** Aztec **7** Grand Am, Montana, Sunfire, Trans Am **8** Firebird **9** Grand Prix **10** Bonneville
Porsche: 7 Boxster, Carrera, Cayenne
Saturn: 3 Ion, Vue **5** Relay
Scion
Subaru: 4 Baja **6** Legacy **7** Impreza, Outback **8** Forester
Suzuki: 4 Reno **5** Aerio **6** Verona **7** Forenza **11** Grand Vitara
Toyota: 3 Rav (4) **4** Echo **5** Camry, Prius **6** Avalon, Celica, Matrix, Sienna, Tacoma, Tundra **7** Corolla, Sequoia **10** Highlander
Volkswagen: 4 Golf **5** Jetta **6** Beetle, Passat **7** Phaeton, Touaveg
nickname: 3 Bug

Autonoe
father: 6 Cadmus
mother: 8 Harmonia
sister: 3 Ino **5** Agave **6** Semele
husband: 9 Aristaeus

son: 7 Actaeon
daughter: 6 Macris

autonomous 4 free **9** sovereign **11** independent, self-reliant **13** self-governing **14** self-determined, self-sufficient

autonomy 7 freedom **8** home rule, self-rule **10** liberation **11** sovereignty **12** independence **14** self-government **17** self-determination

auto racing
driver: 6 A J Foyt **7** Al Unser **8** Tom Sneva **9** Niki Lauda **10** Bobby Unser, Jeff Gordon, Juan Fangio **11** Jack Brabham **12** Bobby Allison, Janet Guthrie, Richard Petty **13** Jackie Stewart, Mario Andretti **14** Barney Oldfield, Cale Yarborough, Craig Breedlove **16** Johnny Rutherford

Autry, Gene
horse: 8 Champion
born: 7 Tioga TX
roles: 11 Melody Ranch **16** The Singing Cowboy **19** Tumbling Tumbleweeds **22** Springtime in the Rockies

autumn 4 fall **11** harvest time **12** Indian summer **15** autumnal equinox

auxiliary 6 backup, helper **7** partner, reserve **9** accessory, ancillary, assistant, associate, companion, emergency, secondary **10** accomplice, subsidiary, supplement **11** subordinate **13** supplementary

avail 3 aid, use **4** help **5** serve **6** assist, profit **7** benefit, purpose, service, success, utilize **9** advantage

available 4 free, open **5** handy, on tap **6** at hand, on hand **9** in reserve **10** accessible, convenient, obtainable

avalanche 4 heap, mass, pile **5** flood **6** deluge **7** barrage, cascade, torrent **8** blizzard **9** cataclysm, rockslide, snowslide **10** earthslide, inundation **11** bombardment

Avalon
island of: 8 Paradise
burial place for: 6 heroes **10** King Arthur

avant-garde 7 leaders **8** pioneers, vanguard **10** innovators **11** forerunners, originators, tastemakers **12** advance guard, trailblazers, trendsetters

avarice 5 greed **6** penury **8** rapacity, venality **9** parsimony **10** greediness, stinginess **11** miserliness **12** covetousness, graspingness **13** money-grubbing, niggardliness, penny-pinching **15** close-fistedness

Ave Maria 8 Hail Mary

avenge 5 repay **6** injure, punish **7** revenge **9** retaliate

Avengers, The
character: 8 Emma Peel, Tara King **9** John (Jonathan) Steed

cast: 9 Diana Rigg **12** Linda Thorson **13** Patrick Macnee
movie cast: 10 Uma Thurman **12** Ralph Fiennes

avenue 3 way **4** gate, path, road **5** means, route **6** access, chance, course, outlet **7** gateway, parkway, passage, pathway **8** approach **9** boulevard, concourse, direction, esplanade **10** passageway **11** opportunity **12** thoroughfare

aver 4 avow **5** state, swear **6** affirm, assert, avouch, insist, verify **7** certify, contend, declare, profess, protest **8** maintain, proclaim **9** emphasize, guarantee, pronounce, represent **10** asseverate

average 3 par **4** fair, mean, norm, so-so **5** ratio, usual **6** common, medial, median, medium, normal, not bad **7** the rule, typical **8** mediocre, midpoint, moderate, ordinary, passable, standard, standing, the usual **9** tolerable **10** mean amount **11** indifferent, rank and file **12** run-of-the-mill

averment 5 claim **6** avowal **8** argument **9** assertion, assurance **10** allegation, contention, profession **11** affirmation

averse 5 loath **7** opposed **8** inimical **9** reluctant, unwilling **10** indisposed, unamenable **11** disinclined, ill-disposed, unfavorable **12** antipathetic, recalcitrant

aversion 6 hatred, horror **7** disgust, dislike **8** distaste, loathing **9** animosity, antipathy, hostility, prejudice, repulsion, revulsion **10** abhorrence, opposition, reluctance, repugnance **11** detestation **13** unwillingness **14** disinclination

avert 4 turn **5** avoid, deter, shift **7** beat off, deflect, fend off, keep off, prevent, ward off **8** preclude, stave off, turn away **9** forestall, frustrate, keep at bay, sidetrack **11** nip in the bud

aviary 4 cage **9** birdhouse, enclosure

aviation 6 flight, flying **11** aeronautics **12** aerodynamics

Aviator, The
director: 14 Martin Scorsese
cast: 7 Ian Holm (Professor Fitz), Jude Law (Errol Flynn) **8** Alan Alda (Senator Ralph Owen Brewster) **11** Alec Baldwin (Juan Trippe), Gwen Stefani (Jean Harlow), John C. Reilly (Noah Dietrich) **13** Cate Blanchett (Katharine Hepburn) **14** Kate Beckinsale (Ava Gardner) **16** Leonardo DiCaprio (Howard Hughes)

aviator, aviatrix 4 bird **5** flyer, pilot **6** airman, fly-boy **7** birdman

avid 4 keen **5** eager, rabid **6** ardent, greedy, hungry **7** anxious, devoted, fanatic, intense, zealous **8** covetous, desirous, grasping **9** rapacious, voracious **10** avaricious, insatiable **11** acquisitive **12** enthusiastic

avidity 4 zeal **5** greed **6** fervor, hunger **8** rapacity, voracity **9** eagerness **10** enthusiasm, fanaticism, greediness **12** covetousness **15** acquisitiveness

Avignon Papacy 15 Babylonian Exile **19** Babylonian Captivity

avocado 9 dark green **13** alligator pear, tropical fruit
origin: 6 Mexico **12** South America **14** Central America
family: 9 Lauraceae
used to make: 9 guacamole

avocation 5 hobby **7** pastime **8** sideline **9** diversion **10** recreation **11** distraction **13** entertainment

Avogadro, Amedeo
field: 7 physics **9** chemistry
nationality: 7 Italian
formulated: 19 molecular hypothesis

avoid 4 shun **5** avert, dodge, elude, evade, skirt **6** escape, eschew **7** boycott, forbear, forsake **8** sidestep **10** fight shy of **11** refrain from **12** steer clear of

avoidance 7 eluding, evasion **8** shirking, shunning, skirting

avoid the issue 4 duck **5** dodge, evade, hedge, stall **10** equivocate **17** beat around the bush

a votre sante 5 toast **12** to your health

avouch 5 argue, swear **6** affirm **7** declare **8** advocate, maintain

avow 3 own **4** aver **5** admit, state, swear **6** affirm, assert, reveal **7** confess, declare, profess **8** announce, disclose, proclaim **11** acknowledge

avowal 4 word **8** averment **9** admission, assertion, assurance, statement **10** confession, profession **11** affirmation, declaration **12** proclamation, protestation **14** acknowledgment

avowed 5 sworn **8** admitted, declared **9** confessed, professed **12** acknowledged, self-declared **14** self-proclaimed

await 6 attend, expect **7** look for **10** anticipate

awake 5 alert, aware, spark **6** arouse, awaken, bestir, excite, incite **7** alive to, heedful, inspire, mindful, provoke **8** open-eyed, vigilant, watchful **9** attentive, conscious, stimulate

Awake and Sing!
author: 13 Clifford Odets

awaken 3 fan **4** fire **6** arouse, excite, kindle, revive, stir up **9** stimulate

awakening 7 arising, arousal **8** sparking, stirring **11** stimulation

award 4 give **5** allot, allow, grant, honor, medal, prize **6** accord, assign, bestow, decree, trophy **7** appoint,

concede, laurels, tribute **8** citation, confer on **10** decoration

aware 6 with it **7** alert to, alive to, awake to, mindful **8** apprised, informed, sensible, sentient **9** cognizant, conscious, tuned in to **10** conversant **11** enlightened **12** familiar with **13** knowledgeable

awareness 9 acuteness, alertness, appraisal, knowledge **10** cognizance, perception **11** familiarity, information, mindfulness, realization, recognition, sensibility **12** acquaintance **13** consciousness, understanding

away 3 far **4** gone **6** absent, at once, way off **8** distance **9** elsewhere

awe 3 cow **4** fear **5** abash, alarm, amaze, dread, panic, shock **6** dismay, fright, horror, terror, wonder **7** perturb, quaking, respect, terrify **8** astonish, disquiet, frighten **9** abashment, adoration, amazement, quivering, reverence, solemnity, trembling **10** exaltation, intimidate, veneration **11** disquietude, trepidation **12** apprehension, astonishment, perturbation **13** consternation

awe-inspiring 5 giant, grand, great, noble **6** august, mighty **7** eminent, exalted, mammoth, sublime, supreme, titanic **8** colossal, enormous, gigantic, glorious, imposing, majestic, wondrous **9** excessive **10** impressive, incredible, monumental, prodigious, stupendous, tremendous **11** astonishing, extravagant, illustrious, magnificent, spectacular **12** breathtaking, overwhelming

awesome 6 solemn **7** amazing, fearful **8** alarming, dreadful, fearsome, majestic, wondrous **9** inspiring **10** formidable, perturbing, stupefying, terrifying **11** astonishing, disquieting, frightening, magnificent **12** breathtaking, intimidating, overwhelming

awestruck 6 humble **8** overcome **11** reverential

awful 3 bad, low **4** base, dire, mean, ugly **5** lousy **6** solemn **7** amazing, awesome, fearful, ghastly, heinous, hideous **8** alarming, dreadful, fearsome, gruesome, horrible, majestic, shocking, terrible, wondrous **9** appalling, frightful, monstrous, revolting **10** deplorable, despicable, formidable, horrendous, horrifying, stupefying, terrifying, unpleasant **11** displeasing, disquieting, distressing, redoubtable **12** awe-inspiring, contemptible, disagreeable **13** reprehensible

awfully 4 very **5** quite **8** horribly, terribly **9** extremely, immensely **10** dreadfully **11** excessively **13** exceptionally

awkward 5 inept **6** clumsy, touchy, trying **7** unhandy **8** bungling, delicate, inexpert, ticklish, ungainly, unwieldy

9 difficult, graceless, maladroit **10** blundering, cumbersome, unpleasant, unskillful **11** troublesome **12** embarrassing, inconvenient, unmanageable **13** disconcerting, uncomfortable, uncoordinated
French: 6 gauche

Awkward Age, The
author: 10 Henry James

awkwardness 9 gaucherie **10** clumsiness, difficulty, ineptitude **12** ungainliness, unwieldiness **13** embarrassment, inconvenience

awl 4 nail **6** gimlet **11** leather tool, sharp device

awning 4 hood **6** canopy **7** marquee **8** covering, sunshade

awry 5 amiss, askew, wrong **6** astray, uneven **7** crooked, twisted **8** unevenly **9** crookedly, obliquely **11** out of kilter

axe, ax 3 can **4** chop, fire, oust, sack **5** let go, split **6** bounce, cut out, delete, remove **7** cut down, dismiss **8** get rid of, tomahawk **9** discharge, terminate **11** send packing
type: 4 pick **6** poleax **7** hatchet **8** tomahawk

Axelrod, Julius
field: 9 chemistry
studied: 24 nerve-impulse transmission
awarded: 10 Nobel Prize

axiom 3 law **5** basic **7** precept **9** postulate, principle **10** assumption **14** fundamental law

axiomatic 5 banal, given **6** cliche **7** assumed **8** accepted, manifest **9** apodictic **10** aphoristic **11** self-evident **12** demonstrable, epigrammatic, indisputable, unquestioned **13** incontestable, platitudinous

axis 4 stem **5** pivot, shaft **7** compact, entente, spindle **8** alliance **9** alignment, coalition **10** center line **11** affiliation **12** pivotal point **13** confederation **14** line of rotation, line of symmetry

axle 3 bar, pin **5** shaft, wheel **7** spindle **8** crossbar **10** turning bar

ayah 4 maid **5** nurse

aye 3 yea, yes **11** affirmative

Aykroyd, Dan
born: 6 Canada, Ottawa **7** Ontario
roles: 6 My Girl **7** Dragnet **8** Sgt. Bilko **9** Coneheads **11** Spies Like Us **12** Ghostbusters **13** Doctor Detroit, Trading Places **16** The Blues Brothers, Driving Miss Daisy, The Great Outdoors, Grosse Point Blank **17** Saturday Night Live

Aymara
location: 4 Peru **7** Bolivia **12** South America

Ayres, Lew
wife: 8 Lola Lane **12** Ginger Rogers
born: 13 Minneapolis MN

roles: 7 Holiday, The Kiss **9** Dr Kildare **25** All Quiet on the Western Front

azalea 12 Rhododendron

varieties: 4 Cork, Mock, Snow **5** Coast, Dwarf, Early, Flame, Hiryu, Hoary, Luchu, Royal, Sims's, Swamp, Sweet, Torch **6** Alpine, Balsam, Clammy, Indian, Korean, Kurume, Kyushu, Oconee, Pontic, Smooth, Spider, Summer, Yellow **7** Alabama, Chinese, Maries's, Mt Amagi, Oldham's, Western **8** Fiveleaf, Japanese, Piedmont, Rusticum, Yodogawa **9** Kirishima, Mayflower, Pink-shell, Rose-shell, Wild-thyme **10** Cumberland, Macranthum, Plumleaved, White swamp **11** Gable hybrid, Ghent hybrid, Molle hybrid **12** Arnold hybrid, Florida flame, Sander hybrid **13** Indicum hybrid **15** Glenn Dale hybrid, Kaempferi hybrid, Knapp Hill hybrid **16** Rutherford hybrid **24** Rusticum Flore Pleno hybrid

Azan

father: 5 Arcas

mother: 5 Erato

Azariah

also: 6 Uzziah

father: 4 Jehu **5** Ethan **6** Nathan **7** Hilkiah, Jehoram, Johanan **11** Jehoshaphat

son: 4 Joel

known as: 8 Abednego

companion: 6 Daniel

friend: 7 Meshach **8** Shadrach

succeeded: 5 Zadok

Azazel 9 scapegoat **11** fallen angel

Azerbaijan

capital/largest city: 4 Baku

others 9 Kirovabad

division 24 Nagorno-Karabakh Territory **29** Nakhichevan Autonomous Republic

head of state: 9 president

government: 8 republic

monetary unit: 5 manat

mountain: 8 Caucasus

sea: 7 Caspian

people: 5 Azeri **11** Azerbaijani

language: 6 Turkic

religion: 6 Muslim

Aziz, Dr

character in: 15 A Passage to India

author: 7 Forster

Aztec (Nahua, Mexica)

language family: 7 Nahuatl **10** Uto-Aztecan

location: 6 Mexico, Puebla **8** Guerrero, Veracruz **9** Guatemala, Michoacan **11** Lake Texcoco **14** Central America

leader: 9 Montezuma

worshipped: 12 Quetzalcoatl

capital: 12 Tenochtitlan

conquerer: 6 Cortes, Cortez

Azuela, Mariano

author of: 8 The Flies **9** The Bosses **12** The Underdogs **26** Trials of a Respectable Family

azure 4 blue **5** lapis **6** cobalt **7** sky blue **8** cerulean **9** clear blue, cloudless **11** lapis lazuli

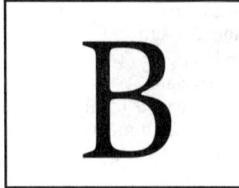
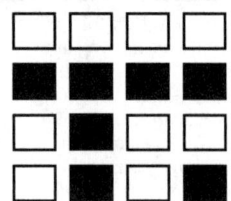

Baade, Walter
field: **9** astronomy
discovered: **15** Hidalgo asteroid

Baal 3 god **5** deity

Baal Merodach *see* **6** Marduk

Babbage, Charles
field: **11** mathematics
nationality: **7** British, English
first: **15** actuarial tables
inventor of: **13** adding machine **18** calculating machine
invented forerunner of: **15** digital computer
planned: **10** calculator

Babbitt 9 bourgeois **10** conformist, middlebrow, philistine

Babbitt
author: **13** Sinclair Lewis
character: **9** Myra Babbitt, Seneca Deane **12** Paul Riesling **15** Mrs Tanis Judique **22** George Folansbee Babbitt

babble 3 coo, din, gab, hum **4** blab, talk **5** prate **6** burble, clamor, drivel, gabble, gibber, gurgle, hubbub, jabber, murmur **7** blabber, blather, chatter, prattle, twaddle **8** chitchat, rattle on **9** jabbering, murmuring **14** chitter-chatter

babbling 6 drivel, hubbub **7** blabber, twaddle **8** burbling, gabbling, gurgling, nonsense **9** clamoring, gibberish, jabbering, murmuring

babe 3 tot **4** baby **5** child **6** infant

babe in arms 4 baby **6** infant **7** neonate, newborn

babe in the woods 8 innocent **9** fledgling, greenhorn **10** tenderfoot

babel, Babel 3 din **6** bedlam, clamor, hubbub, tumult, uproar **7** turmoil **9** confusion **10** hullabaloo **11** pandemonium

Babel, Isaac
author of: **9** Benia Krik **11** Odessa Tales **13** The Red Cavalry

Babe Ruth
nickname of: **16** George Herman Ruth

Babe the Blue Ox
character in: **10** Paul Bunyan

baboon 6 monkey
breeding: **9** year round
characteristic: **4** mane, pads **6** muzzle
diet: **6** plants **8** scorpion **12** small animals
dwelling: **5** Egypt, Sudan **6** Africa, Arabia **7** Somalia **8** Ethiopia
family: **15** cercopithecidae
habitat: **5** hills **6** plains
largest genus: **6** Chacma
most sacred: **6** Anobis
smallest genus: **7** Western

babushka 4 baba, veil **5** scarf, stole **8** kerchief **11** grandmother

baby 3 wee **4** babe, tiny **5** dwarf, humor, pygmy, small, spoil, young **6** bantam, coddle, coward, infant, little, midget, minute, pamper, petite **7** crybaby, indulge, neonate **8** dwarfish, sniveler **9** miniature, youngster **10** babe in arms, diminutive **11** mollycoddle, overindulge, pocket-sized

Baby
nickname of: **12** Lauren Bacall

baby carriage 4 cart, pram **6** cradle **12** perambulator

babyish 7 puerile **8** childish, immature, juvenile **9** infantile

babylike 3 wee **4** tiny **5** small **9** infantile **10** diminutive

Babylonian Captivity 13 Avignon Papacy **15** Babylonian Exile

Babylonian god 3 Bel **6** Marduk

Babylonian Mythology
chief of gods: **6** Marduk **8** Merodach **12** Baal Merodach
demon: **6** Namtar
goddess of air: **6** Ninlil
goddess of death: **10** Ereshkigal
goddess of love/war/ fertility: **6** Ananna, Inanna, Ishtar **7** Astarte, Mylitta **9** Ashtoreth
god of air: **5** Enlil
god of dead: **6** Nergal
god of fire: **5** Ishum
god of heaven: **2** An **3** Anu
god of moon: **3** Sin
god of pastures/vegetation: **6** Dumuzi
god of pestilence: **4** Irra
god of shepherds: **6** Tammuz
god of sun: **3** Utu **7** Shamash
god of wisdom: **4** Enki
hero: **5** Ninib **7** Ninurta
king: **9** Gilgamesh
king of gods: **5** Enlil
mother of gods: **5** Nammu
queen of heaven: **6** Ishtar
world of dead: **3** Kur

Baby Roo
character in: **13** Winnie-the-Pooh

author: **5** Milne
mother: **5** Kanga

Baby Snooks 10 Fanny Brice

Baby Snookums
character in: **12** The Newlyweds

Bacall, Lauren
real name: **15** Betty Joan Perske
husband: **12** Jason Robards **14** Humphrey Bogart
nickname: **4** Baby
born: **9** New York NY
roles: **8** Applause, Key Largo **11** Dark Passage, The Big Sleep **12** Cactus Flower **16** To Have and Have Not **22** How to Marry a Millionaire

Bacchae
form: **11** priestesses
attendants of: **7** Bacchus
participants in: **11** Bacchanalia

Bacchae, The
author: **9** Euripides
character: **4** Zeus **5** Agave **6** Cadmus, Semele **8** Dionysus, Pentheus, Tiresias

bacchanal 4 orgy **5** feast, revel, spree **6** frolic **7** carouse, debauch, revelry, wassail **8** carnival, carousal, festival **10** debauchery, Saturnalia **11** merrymaking

Bacchanalia
festival honoring: **7** Bacchus

Bacchant
priest who worships: **7** Bacchus

Bacchante
also: **6** Thyiad
priestess who worships: **7** Bacchus

Bacchus
also: **5** Evius **8** Dionysus
god of: **4** wine **5** drama **9** fertility
father: **4** Zeus
mother: **6** Semele
son: **6** Phlias **7** Narcaus, Priapus **8** Oenopion
epithet: **6** Lyaeus **7** Bromius, Cresius **8** Thyoneus, Triambus **9** Pyrigenes **11** Dithyrambus, Mitrephorus

Bach, Carl (Karl) Philipp Emanuel
born: **6** Weimar **7** Germany
father: **19** Johann Sebastian Bach
composer of: **14** Prussian Sonata **19** Wurtembergian Sonata

Bach, Johann Sebastian
born: **7** Germany **8** Eisenach
composer of: **8** Chaconne **10** Giant Fugue, Inventions, Magnificat,

Wedge Fugue **11** Dorian Fugue, Fiddle Fugue, Little Fugue **12** Corelli Fugue, French Suites, Fuga alla Giga, German Suites, St Anne's Fugue **13** Coffee Cantata, English Suites, St John Passion **14** Alla Breve Fugue, Easter Oratorio, Peasant Cantata, Wedding Cantata **15** Jesu Meine Freude, Musical Offering **16** St Matthew Passion, The Art of the Fugue **17** Christmas Oratorio **18** Goldberg Variations **20** Brandenburg Concertos **22** The Well-Tempered Clavier **24** The Wise and Foolish Virgins **30** The Dispute Between Phoebus and Pan

Bach, Richard
  author of: **9** Illusions **12** A Gift of Wings **16** Messiah's Handbook **22** The Bridge Across Forever **25** Jonathan Livingston Seagull

Bachelor, The
  network: **3** ABC
  host: **13** Chris Harrison
  bachelor: **9** Bob Guiney **10** Alex Michel **11** Aaron Buerge, Jesse Palmer **12** Byron Velvick **15** Andrew Firestone, Charlie O'Connell
  winner: **10** Jen Schefft, Sarah Brice **11** Amanda Marsh, Mary Delgado **13** Jessica Bowlin **16** Estella Gardinier **17** Helene Eksterowicz

bachelor 6 single **9** single man, unmarried **12** unmarried man

Bachelorette, The
  network: **3** ABC
  host: **13** Chris Harrison
  bachelorette: **10** Jen Schefft, Trista Rehn **16** Meredith Phillips
  winner: **8** Ian McKee **10** Ryan Sutter

Bachelor Father
  character: **9** Peter Tong **10** Kelly Gregg **12** Bentley Gregg **13** Ginger Farrell
  cast: **10** Sammee Tong **12** John Forsythe **14** Noreen Corcoran **17** Bernadette Withers

bachelorhood 8 celibacy **13** baccalaureate **14** unmarried state

bacillus 3 bug **4** germ **7** microbe **8** pathogen **9** bacterium **13** microorganism

back 3 aid, ebb **4** abet, gone, help, hind, late, past, rear, tail **5** after, guard, minor, rural, spine, tardy **6** affirm, assist, attest, behind, bygone, caudal, dorsal, dorsum, far end, former, hinder, hold up, praise, recede, recoil, remote, retire, return, revert, second, succor, tergal, uphold, verify **7** belated, bolster, certify, confirm, delayed, distant, earlier, elapsed, endorse, expired, far side, finance, not paid, overdue, promote, protect, rear end, rebound, retract, retreat, reverse, sponsor, support, sustain, tail end, warrant **8** advocate, backbone, hind part, hindmost, maintain, move away,

obsolete, previous, sanction, secluded, turn tail, validate, vouch for, withdraw **9** afterpart, encourage, in arrears, out-of-date, patronize, posterior, reinforce, subsidize **10** retrogress, testify for, underwrite, untraveled **11** bear witness, corroborate, countenance, countrified, countryside, farthermost, furthermost, reverse side, undeveloped, unimportant, unpopulated **12** beat a retreat, hindquarters, spinal column, substantiate **13** take sides with

back away from 7 back off **11** retreat from **12** draw back from, withdraw from

backbiter 5 scold **6** carper, critic **7** reviler **8** vilifier **9** slanderer

backbiting 5 abuse, catty **6** gossip, malice **7** abusive, calumny, gossipy, hurtful, obloquy, slander **8** libeling, reviling **9** aspersion, cattiness, censuring, contumely, injurious, invective, malicious, maligning, vilifying **10** belittling, bitchiness, calumnious, defamation, defamatory, derogating, detracting, detraction, scandalous, scurrility, slanderous, traduction **11** badmouthing, denigrating, deprecating, disparaging, traducement **12** backstabbing, calumniation, vilification, vituperation **13** disparagement, maliciousness **16** scandal-mongering

backbone 4 grit, guts, sand **5** basis, chine, nerve, pluck, spine, spunk **6** dorsum, mettle, spirit **7** bravery, courage, resolve **8** firmness, mainstay, strength, tenacity **9** character, fortitude, manliness, vertebrae **10** foundation, resolution **11** intrepidity **12** resoluteness, spinal column **13** dauntlessness, steadfastness **15** vertebral column **19** strength of character

back-country 4 farm **5** rural **6** rustic **7** farming **10** provincial

back down 7 back off **8** draw back, move away **9** withdrawn

backdrop 4 flat **7** curtain, scenery **10** background

backer 4 ally **5** angel **6** patron **7** sponsor **8** adherent, advocate, champion, follower, investor, promoter **9** financier, guarantor, supporter **10** well-wisher **11** underwriter

backfire 4 flop, miss **5** crash **6** fizzle, go awry **8** backlash, lay an egg, miscarry, ricochet **9** boomerang **10** bounce back, disappoint **11** come to grief, fall through **12** come to naught **13** come to nothing

background 3 set **4** past, rear **5** flats **6** milieu **7** context, history, rearing, setting **8** backdrop, breeding, distance, heritage, training **9** education, grounding, landscape, life story **10** experience, upbringing **11** antecedents,

credentials, environment, mise-en-scene, preparation **13** circumstances

backhanded 7 awkward **8** reversed **9** insincere

backing 3 aid **4** core, help **5** aegis **6** succor **7** support **8** advocacy, interior, sanction **9** patronage, prompting **10** assistance, inner layer, sustenance **11** championing, cooperation, endorsement, helping hand, sponsorship **13** encouragement

backlash 4 flop, snag **5** crash, ravel **6** fizzle, go away, recoil **7** rebound **8** backfire, kick back, miscarry, ricochet, snap back **9** animosity, boomerang, hostility, reversion **10** antagonism, bounce back, opposition, resistance **11** come to grief, fall through **12** come to naught **13** come to nothing, counteraction, recalcitrance

backlog 5 hoard, stock, store **6** assets, excess, supply **7** nest egg, reserve, savings **9** abundance, amassment, inventory, reservoir, stockpile **12** accumulation **13** reserve supply **14** superabundance

back matter 5 index **8** addendum, appendix **10** supplement **12** bibliography

back off 7 retreat **8** back down, pull back, withdraw

backpack 4 hike, load **5** pouch **6** bundle **8** knapsack

backside 3 can **4** buns, butt, duff, prat, rear, rump, seat, tail **5** fanny **6** behind, bottom, settee, setter, sitter **7** keister, rear end **8** buttocks, derriere **9** fundament, posterior

backslide 5 lapse **6** revert **7** relapse **10** recurrence, regression **11** deteriorate **14** slip from virtue

back street 5 alley, byway **8** alleyway **13** secondary road

Back Street
  director:
    1941 version: 15 Robert Stevenson
    1961 version: 11 David Miller
  based on story by: **11** Fannie Hurst
  cast:
    1932 version: 9 John Boles **10** Irene Dunne
    1941 version: 12 Charles Boyer **16** Margaret Sullavan
    1961 version: 9 John Gavin, Vera Miles **12** Susan Hayward

back talk 3 jaw, lip **4** gall, guff, rude, sass **5** cheek **8** pertness, rudeness **9** impudence, insolence, sassiness, sauciness **12** impertinence

Back to the Future
  director: **14** Robert Zemeckis
  cast: **11** Lea Thompson, Michael J Fox **16** Christopher Lloyd

backup 6 second **7** reserve, standby, stand-in **9** alternate, auxiliary, emergency, secondary **10** substitute, understudy **11** pinch-hitter **13** supplementary

back up 4 abet **6** assist, uphold **9** reinforce **11** corroborate

backward, backwards 3 shy **4** dull, slow **5** dense, tardy, timid, wrong **6** behind, ebbing, remiss, toward **7** bashful, impeded, laggard, messily, reverse, the rear **8** inverted, rearward, receding, reserved, retarded, reticent, reversed, sluggish **9** in retreat, in reverse, inside out, returning, slow-paced, to the past, to the rear, withdrawn **10** disorderly, improperly, regressive, retreating, retrograde, slow-witted, topsy-turvy, upside down **11** chaotically, undeveloped, withdrawing **12** wrong side out **13** retrogressive **15** uncommunicative
French: **9** en arriere

backwash 4 burg, wake **6** result, sticks, upshot **7** boonies, outcome **8** frontier, tank town **9** aftermath, backwater, boondocks, provinces, upcountry **10** hinterland **11** aftereffect, backcountry, consequence

backwater 3 ebb **5** slack **7** retreat, reverse **8** holdback, stagnant, withdraw

backwoods 5 rural, wilds **6** rustic, simple, sticks **7** boonies, country **8** woodland **9** boondocks, rural area **10** hinterland, provincial **11** backcountry, countryside, hinterlands **15** unsophisticated

bacon 3 pig **4** pork **6** gammon **8** porkslab **10** smoked pork **11** porkbellies
measure: **6** rasher

Bacon, Francis
author of: **6** Essays **11** New Atlantis **12** Novum Organum **14** Maxims of the Law **16** Instauratio Magna **17** History of Henry VII **18** De Sapientia Veterum **20** Apophthegms New and Old **21** Advancement of Learning **25** Reading on the Statute of Uses

Bacon, Francis
born: **6** Dublin **7** Ireland
artwork: **15** Henrietta Moraes **35** Three Studies at the Base of a Crucifixion **44** Studies After Velazquez' Portrait of Pope Innocent X

Bacon, Henry
architect of: **15** Lincoln Memorial

Bacon, Kevin
born: **14** Philadelphia PA
wife: **12** Kyra Sedgwick
roles: **3** JFK **5** Diner **7** Tremors **8** Apollo 13, Sleepers **9** Footloose, Hollow Man **10** Flatliners **11** A Few Good Men, Animal House, Mystic River, The Woodsman **12** The River Wild **13** He Said She Said **16** Murder in the First

bactericide 9 germicide **10** antiseptic, germ killer **12** disinfectant

bacteriologist
American: **4** Reed

British: **7** Fleming
German: **4** Koch **7** Behring, Ehrlich **10** Wassermann
Japanese: **7** Noguchi **8** Kitasato

bacterium 3 bug **4** germ **5** virus **7** microbe **8** bacillus, pathogen **13** microorganism

bad 3 ill, sad, sin **4** base, dire, evil, foul, glum, grim, mean, poor, rank, sick, sour, vile **5** acrid, acute, angry, awful, cross, false, fetid, grave, harsh, lousy, moldy, nasty, risky, sorry, unfit, wrong **6** ailing, bitter, crimes, faulty, gloomy, guilty, infirm, odious, putrid, rancid, rotten, severe, sickly, sinful, touchy, tragic, turned, unwell, wicked, wrongs **7** baneful, beastly, corrupt, decayed, harmful, hurtful, immoral, joyless, lacking, naughty, not good, noxious, painful, searing, serious, spoiled, tainted, unsound, useless **8** below par, contrite, criminal, dreadful, grievous, inferior, menacing, mildewed, offenses, polluted, terrible, troubled, villainy, wretched **9** agonizing, dangerous, defective, deficient, erroneous, frightful, hazardous, imperfect, incorrect, injurious, irascible, irritable, loathsome, miserable, nefarious, obnoxious, offensive, regretful, repugnant, repulsive, revolting, sad events, sickening, troubling, unethical, unhealthy, unnerving, unwelcome, valueless **10** calamitous, decomposed, deplorable, detestable, disastrous, disgusting, distressed, disturbing, fallacious, immorality, inadequate, indisposed, melancholy, misfortune, nauseating, not correct, perfidious, putrescent, remorseful, second-rate, unpleasant, villainous, wickedness **11** detrimental, discouraged, distasteful, distractive, distressing, ineffective, inefficient, opprobrious, regrettable, substandard, troublesome, unpalatable **12** contaminated, disagreeable, discouraging, disreputable, excruciating, questionable, unprincipled, unproductive **13** below standard, disappointing, disheartening, harmful things, nonproductive, reprehensible, short-tempered **14** disappointment **15** disadvantageous, under the weather **18** conscience-stricken

bad faith 7 perfidy, treason **8** betrayal **9** falseness, treachery, two-timing **10** disloyalty **11** double-cross **13** breach of faith, double-dealing **14** unfaithfulness

badge 4 mark, seal, sign, star **5** brand, stamp, token **6** device, emblem, ensign, shield, symbol **7** earmark **8** hallmark, insignia **9** medallion

badger 3 nag, vex **4** bait, goad **5** annoy, beset, bully, chafe, harry, hound, tease **6** coerce, harass, hector, nettle, pester, plague **7** provoke, torment,

trouble **8** irritate **9** persecute
group of: **4** cete

Badger State
nickname of: **9** Wisconsin

badinage 5 chaff **6** banter, joking **7** jesting, joshing, kidding, ragging, ribbing, waggery **8** chaffing, raillery, repartee, word play

bad judgment 5 folly **10** imprudence **11** foolishness **12** carelessness **13** senselessness **15** thoughtlessness **16** shortsightedness, unperceptiveness

bad luck 6 mishap **7** ill wind **8** bad break **9** adversity, mischance **10** ill fortune, misfortune

badly 3 ill **5** wrong **6** basely, poorly, sorely, vilely **7** acutely, greatly, ineptly, not well, wrongly **8** faultily, horribly, severely, shoddily, sinfully, sloppily, terribly, very much, wickedly **9** corruptly, extremely, immorally, intensely, unsoundly **10** carelessly, criminally, dreadfully, improperly, wretchedly **11** defectively, deficiently, desperately, erroneously, exceedingly, frightfully, imperfectly, incorrectly, nefariously, offensively, unethically **12** disreputably, inadequately, villainously **13** incompetently, in the worst way **16** unsatisfactorily

bad manners 8 rudeness **9** surliness **10** incivility **11** boorishness, discourtesy **12** impoliteness

bad mark 4 blot **7** demerit **9** poor grade

badminton
racket: **10** battledore
racket used to hit: **4** bird **7** shuttle **11** shuttlecock
Indian version: **5** poona
stroke: **4** drop **5** clear, smash **7** service **13** backhand drive, forehand drive

badmouthing 5 barbs **7** dissing, insults, slander **9** criticism, insulting **10** slandering **11** criticizing

bad taste 9 crudeness, vulgarity **10** coarseness, garishness, tawdryness

bad tasting 4 sour **5** nasty **6** bitter **7** spoiled **9** medicinal, revolting **10** disgusting **11** unpalatable

bad-tempered 5 cross, testy **6** grumpy **7** grouchy **8** choleric, churlish **9** difficult, irascible, irritable **10** ill-natured **11** acrimonious **12** disagreeable

bad times 4 bust **5** slump **9** hard times, recession **10** depression

bad turn 4 harm, hurt **5** wrong **6** injury **7** ill turn **8** disfavor **9** injustice **10** disservice **11** discourtesy

Baekleland, Leo Hendrik
field: **9** chemistry
invented: **8** Bakelite **32** artificial light photographic paper

Baer, Max (Maximillian Adalbert)

nickname: 17 Livermore Larruper
sport: 6 boxing
class: 11 heavyweight

Baeyer, Johann Friedrich Wilhelm Adolph von
field: 9 chemistry
nationality: 6 German
synthesized: 6 indigo
discovered: 13 phthalein dyes
awarded: 10 Nobel Prize

baffle 3 bar 4 daze, dull, foil, stop 5 amaze, check, stump 6 deaden, muddle, puzzle, reduce, thwart 7 astound, confuse, inhibit, mystify, nonplus, perplex 8 astonish, befuddle, bewilder, confound, dumfound, minimize, restrain, surprise 10 disconcert

baffling 7 elusive 8 puzzling 9 confusing, enigmatic 10 mysterious, mystifying, perplexing 11 confounding 16 incomprehensible

bag 3 get, sag 4 hunt, kill, sack, take, trap 5 bulge, catch, droop, pouch, purse, shoot, snare 6 bundle, entrap, obtain, packet 7 acquire, capture, collect, ensnare 8 paper bag, protrude, suitcase 10 receptacle

bagatelle 6 trifle 7 nothing, trinket 10 knickknack, light music 11 unimportant

baggage 4 bags, gear 5 grips 6 trunks 7 bundles, effects, luggage, valises 8 movables, packages 9 apparatus, equipment, suitcases, trappings 10 belongings 11 impedimenta 13 accoutrements, paraphernalia

baggy 4 limp 5 loose, slack 6 droopy, flabby, puffed 7 bloated, bulbous, flaccid, paunchy, sagging, swollen 9 unpressed, unshapely 12 loose-fitting

Baghdad
capital of: 4 Iraq
founder: 8 (Caliph) al-Mansur
landmark:
  minaret: 10 Suq al-Ghazi
  mosque: 8 Madrasah 14 al-Mustansiriya
means: 8 God-given
river: 6 Tigris

Bagheera
character in: 14 The Jungle Books
author: 7 Kipling

bagnio 4 bath, stew 5 house 6 bordel, prison 7 brothel 8 bordello, cathouse 10 bawdy house, fancy house, whorehouse 13 sporting house 14 house of ill fame 16 house of ill repute 19 house of prostitution

Bagnold, Enid
author of: 14 National Velvet, The Chalk Garden 23 The Chinese Prime Minister

Bagstock, Joe
character in: 12 Dombey and Son
author: 7 Dickens

Bahamas
capital/largest city: 6 Nassau

others: 8 Freeport 9 Rock Sound 10 George Town 11 Mastic Point 12 Spanish Wells
head of state: 14 British monarch 15 governor general
island: 3 Cat 4 Long 5 Berry, Exuma 6 Andros, Bimini, Caicos, Rum Cay 7 Crooked, Harbour, Watling 9 Eleuthera, Mayaguana 10 Great Abaco 11 Grand Bahama, Great Inagua, Great Ragged, San Salvador 13 New Providence
sea: 8 Atlantic 9 Caribbean
physical feature:
  strait: 7 Florida
  swamp: 8 mangrove
people: 5 black 7 Haitian
language: 6 Creole 7 English
religion: 12 Christianity
place:
  harbor: 9 Governors
  naval base: 9 Mayaguana
feature:
  key: 3 cay
  native: 5 conch

Bahrain
capital/largest city: 6 Manama
others: 5 Rifaa 7 Jidhafs 8 Muharraq
head of state/government: 4 emir
monetary unit: 4 fils 5 dinar
island: 5 Hawar, Jidda 6 Sitrah 7 Bahrain 9 Umm Nassan 10 al-Muharraq 11 An Nabi Salih
physical feature:
  gulf: 7 Bahrain, Persian
people: 4 Arab 6 Indian 7 Persian 8 American, European 9 Pakistani
  ruling family: 9 al-Khalifa
language: 4 Urdu 5 Farsi 6 Arabic 7 English, Persian
religion: 5 Islam

bail 3 dip 4 bond, lade 5 ladle, scoop, spoon 6 surety 9 guarantee 11 post bond for

bailiff 6 deputy 8 marshall, overseer 9 assistant, constable 12 court officer

bailiwick 4 area, beat, turf 5 arena, orbit, place, realm 6 domain, sphere 7 compass 8 dominion, province 9 territory 10 department 12 neighborhood

Baird, Spencer Fullerton
field: 7 zoology
authority on: 5 birds 7 mammals
established: 30 US Commission of Fish and Fisheries
laboratory at: 11 Woods Hole MA

bait 3 vex 4 lure, ride, worm 5 annoy, bribe, harry, hound, tease, worry 6 allure, badger, come-on, harass, heckle, hector, magnet, needle 7 provoke, torment 9 put bait on, tantalize 10 allurement, antagonize, attraction, enticement, inducement, temptation

bake 3 fry 4 boil, burn, cook, sear, stew 5 grill, roast, saute, toast 6 braise, pan-fry, scorch, simmer 7 parboil, swelter

Baked Bean State
nickname of: 13 Massachusetts

Baker, Norma Jean Mortenson
real name of: 13 Marilyn Monroe

Balaam
father: 4 Beor
brother: 4 Bela
lived at: 4 Aram 6 Pethor
commanded by: 5 Balak
killed by: 6 Israel
rebuked by: 3 ass

Balak
father: 6 Zippor
commanded: 6 Balaam

Balakiref, Mily
born: 6 Russia 13 Nijni-Novgorod
member of: 7 Kutchka, The Five
composer of: 6 Russia, Tamara, Thamar 7 Islamey 8 King Lear (overture)

balance, balances 3 pay 4 cool, mean, rest 5 poise, ratio, scale, sum up, tally, total, tot up, weigh 6 aplomb, equate, offset, parity, ponder, reckon, scales, set off, square, steady, weight 7 compare, compute, harmony, opinion, reflect, remnant, residue 8 cogitate, consider, contrast, coolness, equality, estimate, evaluate, judgment, leftover, level off, parallel, presence, symmetry 9 appraisal, calculate, composure, equipoise, juxtapose, make level, remainder, stability, stabilize 10 amount owed, comparison, counteract, deliberate, equanimity, evaluation, keep steady, neutralize, proportion, steadiness 11 equilibrium 12 counterpoise, equalization, middle ground 13 compensate for, consideration, judiciousness 14 amount credited, self-possession, unflappability 15 level-headedness 16 imperturbability
constellation of: 5 Libra

balanced 4 fair, just 9 equitable, impartial 12 unprejudiced 13 disinterested

balance out 6 cancel, offset 9 make up for 10 neutralize 13 compensate for 14 counterbalance

Balanchine, George
choreographer of: 4 Agon 6 Jewels 8 Episodes, Ivesiana, Serenade 15 Concerto Barocco 16 Allegro Brillante

balcony 4 deck 5 boxes, foyer, loges 6 loggia 7 portico, terrace, veranda 9 mezzanine

bald 4 bare, flat, open 5 blunt, naked, plain, stark, utter 6 barren, simple, smooth 7 denuded, obvious 8 flagrant, glabrous, hairless, outright, treeless 9 depilated, out-and-out, unadorned 11 categorical, undisguised, unqualified, unvarnished 12 without cover 13 unembellished, unequivocable 15 straightforward

Balder
  also: 5 Baldr **6** Baldur
  origin: 6 Nordic
  god of: 6 beauty **8** radiance
  father: 4 Odin **5** Othin
  mother: 3 Fri **5** Frigg, Frija **6** Frigga
  twin brother: 5 Hoder, Hodur
  killed by: 5 Hoder, Hodur

balderdash 3 rot **4** bosh, bull, bunk **5** crock, trash **6** bunkum, drivel, hot air **7** twaddle **8** buncombe, claptrap, flummery, nonsense, tommyrot **9** gibberish, poppycock **10** double-talk, tomfoolery **11** obfuscation **16** stuff and nonsense

baldheaded 8 hairless **9** baldpated, depilated **10** skin-headed **11** chrome-domed

Baldr *see*
  6 Balder

Baldung Grien, Hans
  born: 6 Alsace **10** Weyersheim
  artwork: 9 Todentanz **17** Death and the Maiden **19** Death Kissing a Maiden **21** The Bewitched Stable Boy **24** Rest on the Flight into Egypt

Baldur *see*
  6 Balder

Baldwin, James
  author of: 13 Giovanni's Room, The Amen Corner **14** Another Country **15** Just Above My Head, The Fire Next Time **17** Going to Meet the Man, Nobody Knows My Name, No Name in the Street **21** Blues for Mister Charlie, Go Tell It on the Mountain

Bale, Christian
  born: 5 Wales **13** Haverfordwest
  wife: 10 Sibi Blazic
  roles: 7 Newsies **9** Swing Kids **11** Little Women, The New World **12** Batman Begins, The Machinist **14** American Psycho, Empire of the Sun **18** The Portrait of a Lady

bale 4 case, load, pack **6** bundle, packet, parcel **7** package **11** bound bundle

balefire 6 beacon **9** watchfire **10** signal fire

baleful 3 icy **4** cold, dire, evil **6** deadly, malign **7** baneful, furious, harmful, hurtful, ominous **8** sinister, spiteful, venomous **9** malicious, malignant **10** malevolent **11** coldhearted, threatening

Balfe, Michael William
  born: 6 Dublin **7** Ireland
  composer of: 15 The Bohemian Girl, The Maid of Artois **17** I rivali di se stessi **18** The Siege of Rochelle

Balfour, David
  character in: 9 Kidnapped
  author: 9 Stevenson

Bali
  province of: 9 Indonesia
  capital: 8 Denpasar
  city: 10 Singaraja

  island: 11 Lesser Sunda
  highest peak: 6 Agoeng
  climate: 3 dry **7** monsoon
  tree: 8 waringin
  animal: 4 deer **5** tiger
  people: 7 Malayan
  religion: 8 Hinduism
  agriculture: 3 pig **4** corn, rice **6** cattle, coffee **7** tobacco

Balius
  horse of: 8 Achilles
  gift: 11 immortality

balk 3 bar **4** foil, shun **5** block, check, demur, evade, shirk, spike, stall **6** baffle, defeat, derail, eschew, hinder, impede, recoil, refuse, resist, stymie, thwart **7** inhibit, prevent **8** draw back, hang back, hesitate, obstruct **9** forestall, frustrate **10** shrink from

Balkan 16 Forested mountain
  agriculture: 5 grain **6** cotton, grapes, olives **7** tobacco
  ancient people: 4 Slav **5** Greek, Roman **8** Illyrian, Thracian
  language: 9 Slovenian **10** Macedonian **14** Serbo-Croatian
  mountain: 6 Balkan, Massif **7** Rhodope **10** Carpathian **11** Dinaric Alps **13** Transylvanian
  religion: 5 Islam **8** Orthodox **13** Roman Catholic
  river: 6 Danube, Morava, Vardar
  sea boundary: 5 Black **6** Aegean, Ionian **8** Adriatic **13** Mediterranean
  state: 6 Greece, Turkey **7** Albania, Croatia, Romania **8** Bulgaria, Slovenia **9** Macedonia **10** Yugoslavia **19** Serbia and Montenegro **20** Bosnia and Herzegovina

balky 6 mulish, ornery, unruly **7** restive, wayward, willful **8** contrary, perverse, stubborn **9** fractious, obstinate, pigheaded **10** rebellious, refractory **11** disobedient, intractable **12** recalcitrant, unmanageable

ball 3 hop, orb **4** prom, shot **5** dance, globe **6** pellet, soiree, sphere **7** bullets, globule **8** spheroid **9** cotillion, promenade **11** projectiles

Ball, Lucille
  husband: 9 Desi Arnaz
  children: 4 Desi **5** Lucie
  born: 11 Jamestown NY
  roles: 9 Here's Lucy, I Love Lucy **11** The Lucy Show

Balla, Giacomo
  born: 5 Italy, Turin
  artwork: 8 The Sewer **11** The Mad Woman **18** Speeding Automobile **20** Rhythm of the Violinist **22** Dynamism of a Dog on a Leash **26** The Street Light Study of Light **29** Mercury Passing in Front of the Sun **40** Swifts Paths of Movement and Dynamic Sequences

ballad 3 lay **4** song **5** carol, ditty **6**

chanty **8** folk song **12** rhyming story **13** narrative poem **14** narrative verse

Ballad of Reading Gaol, The
  author: 10 Oscar Wilde

ballast 6 weight **7** balance, control **9** equipoise **10** ballasting, dead weight, makeweight, stabilizer **12** counterpoise **13** counterweight **14** counterbalance **19** stabilizing material

Ballesteros, Severiano
  nickname: 4 Seve
  sport: 4 golf
  nationality: 7 Spanish

ballet 4 Agon **5** Manon, Rodeo **6** Apollo, Parade **7** Giselle, Orpheus **8** Coppelia, Episodes, Ivesiana, Les Noces, Serenade, Swan Lake, The Doves **9** Anastasia, Fancy Free, Interplay, Petrushka, The Jewels **10** La Sylphide, Petrouchka **11** Billy the Kid, Lilac Garden, Soccer Dance, Symphony in C, The Firebird **12** Pillar of Fire, Sailor's Dance, Spring Waters, The Partisans **13** The Nutcracker **14** Romeo and Juliet **15** Concerto Barocco, Fall River Legend, The Rite of Spring **16** Allegro Brillante, La Fille Mal Gardee, Specter of the Rose **17** The Sleeping Beauty **18** Raymonda Variations **19** The Afternoon of a Faun, The Four Temperaments **24** Stravinsky Violin Concerto
  ballet company: 5 Kirov, Royal **7** Bolshoi, Joffrey **9** Mariinsky, Maryinsky **11** New York City **13** Ballets Russes **20** Dance Theater of Harlem **21** American Ballet Theater **22** National Ballet of Canada
  choreographer: 9 Hanya Holm, Lev Ivanov **10** John Weaver **11** Jules Perrot **12** Agnes de Mille, Igor Moiseyev, Marius Petipa, Michel Fokine **13** Jean Duberval, Jerome Robbins, Leonid Massine **15** Arthur Saint-Leon **16** George Balanchine, Kenneth MacMillan **18** August Bournonville, Bronislava Nijinska, Jean Georges Noverre, Sir Frederick Ashton
  chorus: 8 ensemble **13** corps de ballet
  dancer: 9 Karen Kain **10** Anton Dolin, Marie Lieta, Serge Lifar, Wayne Sleep **11** Allegra Kent, Anna Pavlova, Anthony Blum, Lucile Grahn, Lynn Seymour, Nadia Nerina **12** Agnes Letestu, Angel Corella, Edwaard Liang, Ethan Stiefel, Fanny Cerrito, Joaquin de Luz, Marie Camargo, Peter Martins, Ross Stretton, Stephen Hanna **13** Alicia Markova, Andre Eglevsky, Anthony Dowell, Carlotta Grisi, Darcey Bussell, Frank Augustyn, Galina Ulanova, Margot Fonteyn, Marie Taglioni, Melissa Hayden, Patricia Neary, Rudolf Nureyev **14** Arthur Mitchell, Augustus Damian, Cynthia Gregory, Edward Villella, Gelsey Kirkland, Leonide Massine, Maria Tallchief, Suzanne

Farrell, Vaslav Nijinsky **15** Fernando Bujones, Jacques D'Amboise, Martine Van Hamel, Maya Plisetskaya, Natalia Makarova, Patricia McBride, Tamara Karsavina **16** Antoinette Sibley, Olga Spessivtseva **17** Alexandra Danilova, Marina Kondratieva **18** Mikhail Baryshnikov

fast movement: 7 allegro

first ballet: 22 Ballet Comique de la Reine

impresario: 12 Marie Rambert **15** Ninette de Valois, Sergei Diaghilev

kick: 9 battement

modern dancer/choreographer: 8 Ted Shawn **9** Eliot Feld **10** Mary Wigman, Paul Draper, Twyla Tharp **11** Anna Sokolow, Antony Tudor, Eric Hawkins, Ruth St Denis **12** Martha Graham **13** Alwin Nikolais, Doris Humphrey, Isadora Duncan **14** Charles Weidman **15** Merce Cunningham

position/step: 4 jete, plie, tour **5** saute **6** releve **7** en avant, fouette, on point, pas seul, turnout **8** batterie, cabriole, en dedans, en dehors, glissade **9** arabesque, developpe, en arriere, entrechat, pas de chat, pas-de-deux, pirouette **10** demi-pointe, port de bras, tour en l'air **11** rond de jambe, terre-a-terre **12** pas de bourree, saut de basque **17** changement de pieds

principal female dancer: 6 etoile **9** ballerina **14** prima ballerina

principal male dancer: 12 danseur noble

skirt: 4 tutu

slow movement: 6 adagio

term: 4 coda **5** barre **6** ballon **14** divertissement

Ball of Fat
author: 15 Guy de Maupassant

balloon 4 grow **5** belly, bloat **6** billow, blow up, dilate, expand **7** distend, enlarge, fill out, inflate, puff out **8** increase, swell out

ballot 4 poll, vote **5** slate **6** ticket, voting **7** polling **13** round of voting **16** list of candidates

ballyhoo 4 hype, puff, push, tout **6** herald, hoopla **7** buildup, promote, puffery, trumpet **8** proclaim **9** advertise, promotion, publicity, publicize **10** hullabaloo, propaganda **11** advertising **15** public relations

balm 5 cream, salve **6** balsam, lotion, solace **7** anodyne, comfort, unguent **8** curative, narcotic, ointment, sedative **9** comforter, emollient **10** palliative **11** restorative **12** tranquilizer

balmy 3 odd **4** calm, fair, mild, soft, warm **5** bland, kooky, weird **6** easing, gentle **7** calming, clement, summery **8** aromatic, fragrant, perfumed, pleasant, redolent, soothing **9** agreeable,

ambrosial, eccentric, temperate **10** refreshing, salubrious

Balnibari
fictional land in: 16 Gulliver's Travels
author: 5 Swift

baloney 3 rot **4** bull, bunk **5** hokum, hooey, stuff **6** bunkum, hot air, humbug **7** hogwash, sausage, spinach **8** claptrap, nonsense, tommyrot **9** poppycock **10** applesauce **11** foolishness

Baloo
character in: 14 The Jungle Books
author: 7 Kipling

balsam 3 fir **4** balm **5** cream, salve **7** unguent **8** ointment **9** Impatiens
varieties: 2 He **3** Fir, She **4** Rose, Wild **6** Garden **8** Zanzibar

Balsam, Martin
born: 9 New York NY
roles: 6 Psycho **7** Catch-22 **15** A Thousand Clowns, On the Waterfront

Baltic
language family: 12 Indo-European
group: 11 Balto-Slavic
subgroup: 7 Latvian **10** Lithuanian
canal: 4 Kiel
port: 4 Kiel, Riga **6** Danzig, Gdansk **7** Tallinn

Baltimore
baseball team: 7 Orioles
football team: 5 Stars **6** Ravens

Baltimore, David
field: 12 microbiology
studied: 11 animal cells **13** viral genetics
awarded: 10 Nobel Prize

Balto-Slavic
language family: 12 Indo-European
branch: 6 Baltic, Slavic

baluster 4 post, rail **6** column, pillar **7** support, upright **8** pilaster

balustrade 7 railing **8** baluster, banister, handrail

Balzac, Honore de
author of: 7 Gobseck **10** La Vendetta **11** Cousin(e) Bette **12** Father Goriot, Le Cousin Pons, Le Pere Goriot **13** Lost Illusions **14** Eugenie Grandet, The Human Comedy **15** The Wild Ass's Skin **16** La Comedie Humaine **23** The Physiology of Marriage

Bamako
capital of: 4 Mali

Bambi
author: 11 Felix Salten
character: 3 Ena **6** Faline, Flower **7** Thumper
film made by: 6 Disney
directed by: 9 David Hand

bamboo 4 Sasa **7** Bambusa **9** Shibataea **10** Pseudosasa **11** Arundinaria **13** Phyllostachys **14** Chimonobambusa **15** Semiarundinaria
varieties: 4 Moso **5** Arrow, Black, Dwarf, Giant, Hardy, Hedge, Henon,

Meyer, Pygmy, Simon, Stake **6** Buddha, Common, Forage, Oldham, Sacred, Sickle, Square, Tonkin **7** Allgold, Beechey, Mexican **8** Calcutta, Feathery, Heavenly, Narihira **9** Canebrake, Castillon **10** Red-berried, Square-stem **11** Punting-pole **12** Alphonse Karr, Yellow-groove **13** Dwarf fern-leaf, Fern-leaf hedge, Oriental hedge **14** Chinese-goddess **16** Dwarf white-stripe **17** Silver-stripe hedge **18** Stripe-stem fern-leaf

bamboozle 3 con, gyp **4** coax, dupe, fool, gull, hoax, lure, rook, take **5** cheat, cozen, trick **6** delude **7** beguile, deceive, defraud, mislead, swindle **8** hoodwink **9** victimize

ban 3 bar **5** debar, taboo **6** banish, enjoin, forbid **7** barring, embargo, exclude **8** disallow, prohibit, stoppage, suppress **9** exclusion, interdict, proscribe, restraint **10** banishment, censorship **11** forbiddance, prohibition, restriction **12** interdiction, proscription

banal 4 dull **5** corny, stale, stock, tired, trite, vapid **6** jejune **7** humdrum, insipid, prosaic **8** bromidic, everyday, ordinary, shopworn **9** hackneyed **10** pedestrian, threadbare, unexciting, unoriginal **11** commonplace, stereotyped **12** cliche-ridden, conventional **13** platitudinous, unimaginative, uninteresting

banality 6 cliche **7** bromide **9** platitude, staleness, triteness **10** insipidity

banana 4 Musa
varieties: 3 Fe'i **4** Fehi, Koae **5** Dwarf **6** Edible **7** Chinese **9** Flowering **10** Abyssinian, Ladyfinger **12** Canary Island, Chinese dwarf
similar to: 8 plantain

Bananas
director: 10 Woody Allen
cast: 10 Woody Allen **12** Howard Cosell, Louise Lasser **15** Carlos Montalban

Bancroft, Anne
real name: 23 Anna Maria Louise Italiano
husband: 9 Mel Brooks
born: 7 Bronx NY
roles: 4 Antz (voice) **11** Mrs Robinson, The Graduate **12** Up at the Villa **15** The Pumpkin Eater, The Turning Point, Two for the Seesaw **16** The Miracle Worker (Oscar)

band 3 set **4** belt, body, club, crew, gang, hoop, join, pack, ring, sash **5** bunch, crowd, group, junta, party, strap, strip, swath, thong, troop, unite **6** caucus, circle, clique, collar, fillet, gather, girdle, league, ribbon, streak, stripe, throng **7** bandeau, binding, circlet, company, society **8** assembly, cincture, ensemble **9** multitude, orchestra, surcingle **10** fellowship, sisterhood **11** association, brotherhood, confederacy, consolidate **13** confederation

bandage 4 bind **5** dress **7** binding, plaster **8** compress, dressing

bandanna, bandana 5 scarf **8** kerchief **10** silk square **11** neckerchief **12** handkerchief

Bandar Seri Begawan
  capital of: **6** Brunei

bandeau 3 bra **4** band **6** fillet **7** binding, circlet **9** brassiere

Banderas, Antonio
  real name: **18** Jose Antonio Bandera
  born: **5** Spain **6** Malaga
  wife: **7** Ana Leza **15** Melanie Griffith
  mother-in-law: **11** Tippi Hedren
  roles: **5** Evita, Frida, Shrek (2, 3) **7** Spy Kids **9** Desperado **11** Original Sin **12** Philadelphia **13** Miami Rhapsody, The Mambo Kings **14** The Mask of Zorro **16** The Legend of Zorro **21** Once Upon a Time in Mexico **23** Interview with the Vampire

bandit 4 thug **5** crook, thief **6** badman, outlaw, robber **7** brigand, burglar, footpad, ladrone **8** blackleg **9** desperado, road agent **10** highwayman

bandleader 6 master **7** maestro **8** director **9** conductor
  famous: **11** Glenn Miller, Tommy Dorsey **12** Lawrence Welk

Band of Merry Men
  followers of: **9** Robin Hood

band together 5 unify, unite **6** league **7** combine **10** join forces **11** consolidate

bandy 4 swap **5** trade **6** barter **7** shuffle **8** exchange **9** toss about **11** interchange **16** toss back and forth

bandying 4 swap **5** trade **8** exchange **9** tit for tat **10** quid pro quo **11** give and take

bane 3 woe **4** ruin **5** curse, toxin, venom **6** blight, burden, canker, plague, poison **7** scourge, torment, tragedy **8** calamity, disaster, downfall, nuisance **9** destroyer, detriment, ruination **10** affliction **13** pain in the neck **14** thorn in the side **16** fly in the ointment

baneful 4 evil **6** deadly, malign, woeful **7** harmful, noxious **8** venomous **9** injurious, malignant, poisonous **10** malevolent **11** destructive

bang 3 box, hit, pop, rap, tap **4** beat, blow, boom, clap, cuff, kick, lick, slam, slap, sock **5** burst, clout, crash, knock, smack, thump, whack **6** buffet, charge, report, thrill, thwack, wallop **7** delight **8** good time, headlong, pleasure, suddenly **9** enjoyment, explosion **10** crashingly, excitement

Bangkok
  also: **9** Krung Thep
  capital of: **8** Thailand
  landmark: **5** Wat Po **11** Grand Palace **16** Wat Emerald Buddha
  means: **12** City of Angels
  nickname: **15** Venice of the East
  port: **8** Klongtoi
  river: **10** Chao Phraya

Bangladesh
  other name: **10** East Bengal **12** East Pakistan
  capital/largest city: **5** Dacca
  others: **6** Khulna, Sylhet **7** Comilla, Jessore, Rangpur, Saidpur **8** Jamalpur, Rajshahi **9** Madaripur **10** Chittagong **11** Narayanganj **12** Brahmanbaria
  monetary unit: **4** taka **5** paisa
  island: **10** Sundarbans
  mountain: **15** Chittagong Hills
  highest point: **10** Keokradong
  river: **5** Padna **6** Ganges, Meghna **10** Burhi Ganga, Karnaphuli **11** Brahmaputra
  physical feature:
    bay: **6** Bengal
  people: **7** Bengali
    guerrillas: **11** muktibahini
    leader: **6** Ershad **11** Ziaur Rahman **19** Sheikh Mujibur Rahman
  language: **6** Bihari **7** Bengali, English
  religion: **5** Hindu, Islam
  feature:
    clothing: **4** sari **5** lungi

bangle 3 fob **5** chain, charm **6** armlet, bauble, gewgaw, tinsel **7** bibelot, fribble, trinket **8** bracelet, gimcrack, ornament, wristlet **10** knickknack **11** junk jewelry **14** costume jewelry

Bangui
  capital of: **22** Central African Republic

banish 3 ban, bar **4** drop, oust **5** eject, erase, evict, exile, expel **6** deport, dispel, outlaw, reject, remove **7** cast out, discard, dismiss, exclude, put away, shut out, turn out **8** cast away, dislodge, drive out, get rid of, send away, shake off **9** discharge, eliminate, eradicate, extradite **13** excommunicate **14** send to Coventry

banished person 5 exile **6** emigre, pariah **7** outcast **8** deportee, expellee **10** expatriate **14** deported person **15** displaced person

banishment 3 ban **5** exile **6** ouster **7** removal **8** eviction **9** dismissal, exclusion, expulsion **11** deportation **12** expatriation **14** transportation **15** excommunication

Banjo Eyes
  nickname of: **11** Eddie Cantor

Banjul, Bathurst
  capital of: **6** Gambia

bank 3 bar, row, tip **4** dike, dune, edge, file, flat, fund, heap, hill, keep, line, mass, pile, rank, reef, rise, save, side, tier, tilt **5** amass, array, brink, chain, knoll, mound, ridge, shelf, shoal, shore, slant, slope, stack, store, train **6** barrow, line up, margin, pile up, series, strand, string, supply **7** deposit, parapet, reserve, savings, shallow, terrace **8** keyboard, sandbank **9** exchequer, reservoir, stockpile **10** depository, embankment, repository, storehouse, succession **12** accumulation, trust company **14** savings and loan

Bank Dick, The
  director: **10** Eddie Cline
  cast: **8** W C Fields **9** Una Merkel **15** Cora Witherspoon

Bankhead, Tallulah
  father: **16** William B Bankhead
  born: **12** Huntsville AL
  roles: **8** Lifeboat **14** The Little Foxes **17** The Skin of Our Teeth

banknote 4 bill **5** greenback **11** certificate, legal tender **12** currency note, treasury note **17** silver certificate

bank of pity
  French: **11** mont-de-piete
  literal name for: **10** pawnbroker

bankrupt 5 broke **6** busted, failed, ruined **8** depleted, indigent, in the red, wiped out **9** destitute, exhausted, insolvent, penniless **12** impoverished, without funds

Banks, Ernie
  nickname: **5** Mr Cub
  sport: **8** baseball
  noted for: **7** hitting
  team: **11** Chicago Cubs

banner 4 flag **6** burgee, colors, ensign, record **7** leading, notable, pendant, pennant, winning **8** standard, streamer **9** red-letter **10** profitable **11** outstanding **14** most successful

Bannock
  language family: **10** Shoshonean
  location: **5** Idaho

banquet 4 dine **5** feast, revel **6** dinner, repast **9** symposium

Banquo
  character in: **7** Macbeth
  author: **11** Shakespeare

bantam 3 hen, wee **4** cock, fowl, tiny **5** dwarf, pygmy, runt, small, teeny, weeny **6** little, midget, minute, petite **7** chicken, dwarfed, rooster, stunted **9** miniature **10** diminutive, pocket-size, teeny-weeny **11** Lilliputian, pocket-sized

banter 3 kid, rib **4** dish, josh, mock, ride, twit **5** chaff, jolly, taunt, tease **6** joking, needle **7** jesting, joshing, kidding, ragging, ribbing, teasing, waggery **8** badinage, chaffing, raillery, repartee, word play

Banting, Frederick Grant
  field: **8** medicine
  nationality: **8** Canadian
  extracted: **7** insulin
  awarded: **10** Nobel Prize

Bantu
  means: **9** the people

dwelling: 6 Africa
tribe: 5 Xosas, Zulus **6** Swazis **7** Basutos, Kalanga

baptism 9 beginning, immersion, sacrament **10** initiation, sprinkling **11** christening **12** introduction, purification **13** rite of passage **16** spiritual rebirth

baptize 3 dub **4** name **8** christen

bar 3 ban, pub, rib, rod **4** band, bank, beam, belt, bolt, cake, curb, flat, line, lock, oust, pale, pole, rail, reef, snag, spar, spit, stay, stop **5** block, catch, check, court, debar, eject, evict, exile, expel, forum, ingot, jimmy, lever, limit, shelf, shoal, slice, sprit, stake, stick, strip, taboo **6** banish, enjoin, fasten, forbid, impede, lounge, paling, ribbon, saloon, secure, streak, stripe, stroke, tavern **7** barrier, block up, canteen, cast out, close up, crowbar, exclude, grating, lock out, measure, prevent, sandbar, shallow, shut out, taproom **8** alehouse, crossbar, disallow, judgment, obstacle, obstruct, preclude, prohibit, restrain, restrict, tribunal **9** barricade, blackball, blacklist, hindrance, long table, lunchroom, restraint, speakeasy **10** constraint, crosspiece, impediment, injunction, limitation **11** obstruction, public house, restriction **14** cocktail lounge, serving counter, stumbling block **15** legal profession

Bara, Theda
real name: 16 Theodosia Goodman
nickname: 7 The Vamp
born: 12 Cincinnati OH
roles: 6 Carmen, Salome **7** Camille **8** The Vixen **9** Cleopatra **13** A Fool There Was, Madame Du Barry

Barabbas 6 robber **8** murderer

Barak
father: 7 Abinoam
summoned by: 7 Deborah
defeated: 6 Sisera

barb 3 cut, dig, nib **4** cusp, jibe, snag, spur, tine **5** point, prong, spike **6** insult **7** affront, barbule, bristle, prickle, putdown, sarcasm, spicule **9** complaint, criticism **11** badmouthing

Barbados
capital/largest city: 10 Bridgetown
others: 7 Oistins **8** Boscabel, Crab Hill, Hastings, Holetown, Portland, Worthing **9** Bathsheba **10** Martin's Bay **11** Belleplaine **12** Speightstown
school: 10 Codrington
head of state: 14 British monarch **15** governor general
mountain: 6 Chalky
highest point: 7 Hillaby
river: 12 Constitution
sea: 8 Atlantic **9** Caribbean
physical feature:
bay: 4 Foul, Long **8** Carlisle
beach: 5 Crane

gully: 12 Welchman Hall
hill: 10 Cherry Tree
point: 5 North, South **6** Ragged **8** Harrison, Kitridge
people: 5 Bajan **9** Barbadian
leader: 5 Adams
language: 7 English
religion: 8 Anglican
place:
airport: 7 Seawell
castle: 8 Sam Lords
church: 7 St Johns
feature:
sea crab: 7 shagger

barbarian 4 boor, hood, lout, punk **5** alien, bully, crude, rowdy, tough, yahoo **6** savage, vandal **7** boorish, hoodlum, lowbrow, peasant, ruffian, uncouth **8** hooligan **9** ignoramus, outlander, roughneck, vulgarian **10** delinquent, illiterate, philistine, provincial, troglodyte, uncultured **11** knownothing **12** uncultivated **15** unsophisticated **16** anti-intellectual

barbaric 4 rude, wild **5** crude **6** coarse, savage, vulgar **7** boorish, uncouth, untamed **9** barbarian, barbarous **10** unpolished **11** ill-mannered, uncivilized

barbarism 7 cruelty **8** savagery **9** brutality **10** inhumanity **11** viciousness

barbarity 7 cruelty **9** brutality **10** savageness **12** ruthlessness

barbarous 4 mean **5** crass, crude, cruel, harsh, rough **6** brutal, coarse, vulgar **7** inhuman, vicious **8** barbaric, impolite **10** outrageous

barber 3 cut **4** trim **5** dress, shave, style **6** Figaro **7** arrange, stylist, tonsure **10** haircutter **11** hairdresser

Barber, Samuel
born: 13 West Chester PA
composer of: 7 Vanessa **10** Dover Beach **16** Adagio for Strings **17** Capricorn Concerto **19** Anthony and Cleopatra, The School for Scandal

Barber of Seville, The
author: 12 Beaumarchais
opera by: 7 Rossini
character: 6 Bazile, Figaro, Rosine, Rosina **8** Almaviva, Bartholo **9** Dr Bartolo **13** Count Almaviva

barbette 5 mound **7** bastion, rampart **8** platform **9** earthwork **10** breastwork

barbiturate 8 euphoria, hypnotic, sedative **10** depressive **13** anesthesiatic **14** barbituric acid
kind: 7 seconal **10** thiopental **11** amobarbital **12** secobarbital **13** phenobarbital

barbule 4 barb **11** feather part

Barchester Towers
author: 15 Anthony Trollope
sequel to: 9 The Warden
character: 7 Mr Slope, Mrs Bold **8** Mr Arabin **9** Dr Proudie, Mr Harding **10** Mrs Proudie **11** Mr Quiverful **13** Ca-

non Stanhope **17** Archdeacon Grantly **18** Signora Vesey-Neroni

bard 4 poet **6** rhymer, writer **8** epic poet, minstrel, poetizer **9** poetaster, rhymester, troubador, versifier **10** poet-singer **13** narrative poet

Bardell, Mrs
character in: 14 Pickwick Papers
author: 7 Dickens

Bardot, Brigitte
husband: 10 Roger Vadim
born: 5 Paris **6** France
roles: 18 And God Created Woman

bare 4 bald, mere, nude, open, show, thin, void, worn **5** basic, blank, empty, naked, offer, plain, scant, stark, strip **6** denude, divest, expose, meager, peeled, reveal, simple, unclad, unmask, unveil, vacant **7** austere, exposed, hapless, uncover, undrape, undress, unrobed **8** disrobed, in the raw, marginal, stripped **9** endurable, essential, unadorned, unclothed, uncolored, uncovered, undressed, unsheathe **10** elementary, just enough, threadbare **11** fundamental, supportable, undecorated, undisguised, unvarnished **12** unelaborated, unornamented **13** unembellished **15** straightforward

barefaced 4 bald, bold, flip **5** brash, fresh, sassy **6** brazen, cheeky, snotty **7** forward **8** flippant, impudent, insolent, palpable **9** shameless, unabashed **11** transparent

barefoot 6 unshod **8** shoeless **9** discalced **11** discalceate

Barefoot Boy
author: 21 John Greenleaf Whittier

Barefoot in the Park
director: 8 Gene Saks
based on play by: 9 Neil Simon
cast: 9 Jane Fonda **12** Charles Boyer **13** Robert Redford

barely 4 just **6** almost, hardly **7** faintly, scantly **8** meagerly, only just, scarcely, slightly **9** almost not, just about, sparingly **10** no more than **20** by the skin of one's teeth

bareness 6 nudity **9** bleakness, emptiness, nakedness **10** barrenness

Baresark
origin: 12 Scandinavian
form: 7 warrior
trait: 7 courage

Baretta
character: 7 Rooster **11** Billy Truman, (Det) Tony Baretta, (Lt) Hal Brubaker
cast: 8 Tom Ewell **11** Robert Blake **12** Edward Grover **15** Michael D Roberts
Tony's pet: 8 cockatoo
named: 4 Fred

barfly 3 sot **4** lush, soak **5** drunk, rummy, souse, toper **7** tippler **8** drunkard **9** alcoholic **11** dipsomaniac

bargain 4 deal, pact **5** steal **6** accord, barter, dicker, haggle, higgle, pledge, treaty **7** compact, entente, good buy, promise **8** contract, covenant, good deal **9** agreement, negotiate **10** settlement **11** arrangement, transaction **13** understanding
French: 9 bon marche

bargain for 6 expect **7** foresee **8** envision, reckon on **11** contemplate

barge 4 bust, scow, ship **6** launch, vessel **7** freight, intrude

barium
chemical symbol: 2 Ba

bark 3 bay, cry, rub, yap, yip **4** flay, hide, howl, hull, husk, peel, rind, roar, skin, woof, yell, yelp **5** crust, scale, shout, strip **6** abrade, arf-arf, bellow, bow-wow, casing, cry out, holler, scrape **7** howling **8** covering, periderm **9** sheathing

Barker, Lex
real name: 25 Alexander Crichlow Barker Jr
wife: 10 Arlene Dahl, Lana Turner
born: 5 Rye NY
roles: 6 Tarzan **11** La Dolce Vita

Barkis
character in: 16 David Copperfield
author: 7 Dickens

Barkley, Catherine
character in: 15 A Farewell to Arms
author: 9 Hemingway

Barlach, Ernst
born: 5 Wedel **7** Germany **8** Holstein
artwork: 9 Expellees **10** Seated Girl, Singing Man **11** Man in a Stock **13** Mater Dolorosa **14** Crippled Beggar, The Hovering One **16** Man Drawing a Sword **25** The Community of the Holy Ones

barn 4 mews **6** corral, stable

Barnabas
companion: 4 Paul

Barnaby Jones
character: 7 J R (Jedediah Romano) Jones **8** Lt Biddle **10** Betty Jones
cast: 9 Mark Shera **10** Buddy Ebsen, John Carter **13** Lee Meriwether

Barnaby Rudge
author: 14 Charles Dickens
character: 8 Mrs Rudge **9** Miss Miggs **10** John Willet **11** Dolly Varden **12** Emma Haredale **13** Edward Chester, Gabriel Varden **14** Reuben Haredale, Simon Tappertit, Sir John Chester **16** Dennis the Hangman, Geoffrey Haredale
subject: 11 Gordon riots

Barnard, Christiaan
field: 7 surgery **8** medicine
nationality: 12 South African
performed first: 15 heart transplant

Barnard, Edward Emerson
field: 9 astronomy
named for him: 12 red dwarf star

Barnes, Jake
character in: 15 The Sun Also Rises
author: 9 Hemingway

Barney Google
creator: 11 Billy DeBeck
character: 11 Snuffy Smith
baby: 5 Bunky
horse: 9 Spark Plug

Barney Miller
character: 8 (Det) Phil Fish **9** (Det) Ron Harris **10** (Det Wojo) Wojohowicz, (Det) Nick Yamana, (Officer) Carl Levitt **14** Inspector Luger, (Det) Arthur Dietrich
cast: 7 Jack Soo **8** Ron Carey, Ron Glass **9** Abe Vigoda, Hal Linden **11** Maxwell Gail **12** James Gregory **15** Steve Landesberg

Barnstock see **9** Branstock

Baroja y Nessi, Pio
author of: 15 Caesar or Nothing **23** The Struggle for Existence **26** Memorias de un Hombre de Accion

barometer
invented by: 10 Torricelli

baroque 6 florid, ornate **10** flamboyant **11** extravagant

Barrack-Room Ballads
author: 14 Rudyard Kipling

barracks 3 BOQ **4** base, camp **7** lodging **8** garrison

barrage 5 blast, burst, salvo, spray **6** ack-ack, deluge, shower, stream, volley **7** battery, torrent **8** shelling **9** cannonade, fusillade **10** outpouring **11** bombardment

barrel 3 keg, tub, tun, vat **4** butt, cask, drum, tube **8** hogshead
abbreviation: 3 bar, bbl

barren 3 dry **4** arid, dull **5** stale, waste **6** farrow, futile **7** austere, prosaic, sterile, useless **8** depleted, desolate, infecund **9** fruitless, infertile **10** lackluster, unfruitful **11** ineffectual, uninspiring, unrewarding **12** unproductive **13** uninformative, uninstructive, uninteresting

barrenness 8 bareness **9** bleakness, emptiness **10** desolation

barren wilderness 6 desert **9** wasteland

barricade 5 block, fence **7** barrier, bulwark, rampart **8** blockade, obstacle, obstruct **10** impediment **11** obstruction

Barrie, Sir James M
author of: 7 The Will **8** Mary Rose, Peter Pan **10** Dear Brutus **13** Quality Street **15** Margaret Ogilvie, The Wedding Guest **17** Alice Sit-By-the-Fire, The Little Minister **18** A Kiss for Cinderella, The Twelve-Pound Look **19** What Every Woman Knows **20** Shall We Join the Ladies?, The Admirable Crichton
character: 8 Peter Pan **10** Tinkerbell

11 Captain Hook
Darling children: 4 John **5** Wendy **7** Michael
nurse/Newfoundland dog: 4 Nana
setting: 14 Never-Never Land

barrier 3 bar **4** moat, wall **5** ditch, fence, hedge **6** hurdle, trench **7** rampart **8** blockade, handicap, obstacle **9** barricade, hindrance **10** difficulty, impediment, limitation **11** obstruction, restriction **13** fortification **14** stumbling block

Barrier, The
author: 8 Rex Beach

barring 3 but **4** save **6** except, saving **7** besides **9** excepting, excluding, other than **11** exclusive of

barrister 6 lawyer **7** counsel **8** advocate, attorney **9** counselor **10** mouthpiece **13** attorney-at-law

barroom 3 bar, pub, **6** bistro, lounge, saloon, tavern **7** taproom

barrow 4 heap, pile **5** mound **7** tumulus **8** handcart, pushcart **11** wheelbarrow

Barrow, Joe Louis
real name of: 8 Joe Louis

Barry, Gene
real name: 11 Eugene Klass
born: 9 New York NY
roles: 9 Burke's Law **11** Thunder Road **12** Bat Masterson **16** The Name of the Game **17** The War of the Worlds

Barry, John
served in: 16 Revolutionary War
commander of ship: 7 Raleigh **8** Alliance **9** Effingham, Lexington
ship captured: 6 Edward

Barry, Redmond
character in: 11 Barry Lyndon
author: 9 Thackeray

Barry, Sir Charles
architect of: 8 Cliveden **14** City Art Gallery (Manchester) **18** Houses of Parliament (London)

Barry Lyndon
author: 25 William Makepeace Thackeray
character: 12 Redmond Barry **14** Lord Bullingdon **17** Lady Honoria Lyndon (Countess of Lyndon) **19** Chevalier de Balibari
director: 14 Stanley Kubrick
cast: 9 Ryan O'Neal **11** Hardy Kruger **12** Patrick Magee **14** Marisa Berenson

Barrymore, Drew
born: 12 Culver City CA
husband: 8 Tom Green **12** Jeremy Thomas
roles: 2 ET **6** Scream **9** Ever After, Home Fries, Poison Ivy **11** Donnie Darko, Firestarter **13** Batman Forever, Boys on the Side **14** Charlie's Angels **15** Fifty First Dates, Never Been Kissed **16** The Wedding Singer

Barrymore, Ethel
real name: **14** Ethel Mae Blythe
brother: **4** John **6** Lionel
born: **14** Philadelphia PA
roles: **11** A Doll's House **14** The Corn Is Green **16** Portrait of Jennie **19** Trelawney of the Wells **21** None But the Lonely Heart, Rasputin and the Empress

Barrymore, John
real name: **10** John Blythe
brother: **6** Lionel
sister: **5** Ethel
son: **17** John Drew Barrymore
daughter: **14** Diana Barrymore
granddaughter: **4** Drew
nickname: **12** Great Profile
born: **14** Philadelphia PA
roles: **6** Hamlet **7** Don Juan **8** Moby Dick, Svengali **9** Richard IV **10** Grand Hotel **11** Beau Brummel **13** Dinner at Eight **17** Dr Jekyll and Mr Hyde **21** Rasputin and the Empress

Barrymore, Lionel
real name: **12** Lionel Blythe
brother: **4** John
sister: **5** Ethel
born: **14** Philadelphia PA
roles: **7** The Jest **9** A Free Soul (Oscar), (friend of) Dr Kildare **11** Dr Gillespie **13** Peter Ibbitson, The Copperhead **21** Rasputin and the Empress

Barsabbas *see* **6** Joseph

Barstad, John
character in: **16** A Tale of Two Cities
author: **7** Dickens

Bart, Lily
character in: **15** The House of Mirth
author: **7** Wharton

barter 4 swap **5** trade **8** exchange **11** interchange

Bartered Bride, The
opera by: **7** Smetana
character: **5** Jenik, Kecal, Micha, Vasek **7** Marenka

Barth, John
author of: **7** Chimera, Letters **10** Coming Soon!!!, Friday Book, Sabbatical **12** Giles Goat-Boy **14** Further Fridays **15** The End of the Road **16** The Floating Opera, The Sot-Weed Factor **17** Lost in the Funhouse, The Tidewater Tales

Barthelme, Donald
author of: **7** Sadness **8** City Life **9** Great Days, Snow White **14** Sixty Stories **13** The Dead Father **15** Guilty Pleasures **18** Come Back Dr Caligari **33** Unspeakable Practices Unnatural Acts

Bartholdi, Frederic-Auguste
born: **6** Alsace, Colmar
artwork: **13** Lion of Belfort **26** Liberty Enlightening the World (Statue of Liberty)

Bartholo, Dr
character in: **18** The Barber of Seville

19 The Marriage of Figaro
author: **12** Beaumarchais

Bartholomew 7 apostle
also called: **9** Nathanael

Bartholomew Fair
author: **9** Ben Jonson

Bartok, Bela
born: **7** Hungary **15** Nagyszentmiklos
composer of: **9** Wrestling **11** Mikrokosmos **12** Divertimento **14** Cantata Profana **15** The Wooden Prince **20** Duke Bluebeard's Castle **21** The Miraculous Mandarin

Bartolommeo, Fra
born: **5** Italy **8** Florence
real name: **31** Bartolommeo di Pagolo del Fattorino
artwork: **5** Jonah **6** Isaiah **13** Salvator Mundi **15** The Last Judgment **17** Vision of St Bernard **24** Madonna della Misericordia **30** The Mystic Marriage of St Catherine

Barton Fink
director: **8** Joel Coen **9** Ethan Coen
cast: **9** Jon Polito (Lou Breeze), Judy Davis (Audrey Taylor) **11** John Goodman (Charlie Meadows), John Mahoney (W. P. Mayhew) **12** John Turturro (Barton Fink), Steve Buscemi (Chet), Tony Shalhoub (Ben Geisler) **13** Michael Lerner (Jack Lipnick)

Bartram, John
field: **6** botany
noted for first American: **12** hybrid plants

Baruch
father: **5** Judah **6** Neriah
friend and scribe of: **8** Jeremiah

Baruch, Bernard 9 statesman, financier

basal 3 key **4** easy **5** basic, vital **6** simple **7** initial, minimal, primary **8** cardinal **9** beginning, essential, intrinsic, necessary **10** elementary, lower-level, simplified **11** fundamental, rudimentary **12** prerequisite **13** indispensable

bas bleu 12 bluestocking

base 3 bad, bed, key, low **4** camp, core, foul, mean, post, root, vile **5** basis, dirty, gross, heart, petty, place, stand **6** abject, billet, bottom, craven, ground, impure, locate, scurvy, sinful, sneaky, sordid, source, vulgar, wicked **7** alloyed, corrupt, debased, essence, found on, ignoble, immoral, install, model on, scrubby, situate, station, support **8** backbone, cowardly, degraded, depraved, garrison, infamous, inferior, pedestal, rudiment, shameful, spurious, unworthy **9** dastardly, dissolute, establish, faithless, insidious, nefarious, principle **10** degenerate, derive from, despicable, detestable, evilminded, foundation, groundwork, iniquitous, villainous **11** adulterated, disgraceful, ignominious, poor quality,

scoundrelly **12** black-hearted, contemptible, dishonorable, disreputable, installation, substructure, underpinning, unprincipled **13** discreditable, reprehensible

baseball
term: **3** bag, ERA, fan, RBI, run **4** balk, base, bunt, bush **5** choke, curve, error, fungo, liner, pop-up, slide **6** assist, batter, cellar, double, dugout, duster, inning, on deck, relief (pitcher), rookie, single, slider, triple, umpire, windup **7** blooper, bullpen, catcher, cleanup, fly ball, home run, infield, pickoff, pitcher, rhubarb, rundown, shutout, slugger **8** bean ball, changeup, grounder, keystone, no hitter, outfield, pitchout, southpaw, spitball **9** bleachers, brushback, grand slam, hot corner, infielder, line drive, sacrifice, shortstop **10** bush league, gopher ball, infield fly, outfielder, passed ball **11** bases loaded, knuckleball, pinch hitter, triple crown, World Series **12** Texas leaguer **16** designated hitter, earned run average

Hall of Fame:
1936: 4 Cobb (Ty), Ruth (Babe) **6** Wagner (Honus) **7** Johnson (Walter) **9** Mathewson (Christy)
1937: 4 Mack (Connie) **5** Young (Cy) **6** Lajoie (Nap), McGraw (John), Wright (George) **7** Johnson (Ban), Speaker (Tris) **8** Bulkeley (Morgan)
1938: 8 Chadwick (Henry) **9** Alexander (Grover) **10** Cartwright (Alexander)
1939: 5 Anson (Cap), Ewing (Buck) **6** Gehrig (Lou), Keeler (Willie), Sisler (George) **7** Collins (Eddie) **8** Comiskey (Charlie), Cummings (Candy), Spalding (Albert) **9** Radbourne (Old Hoss)
1942: 7 Hornsby (Rogers)
1944: 7 Kenesaw (M. Landis)
1945: 5 Duffy (Hugh), Kelly (King) **6** Clarke (Fred) **7** Collins (Jimmy), O'Rourke (Jim) **8** Jennings (Hughey), Robinson (Wilbert) **9** Bresnahan (Roger), Brouthers (Dan), Delahanty (Ed)
1946: 5 Evers (Johnny), Plank (Eddie), Walsh (Ed) **6** Chance (Frank), Tinker (Joe) **7** Burkett (Jesse), Chesbro (Jack), Waddell (Rube) **8** Griffith (Clark), McCarthy (Tommy) **9** McGinnity (Joe)
1947: 5 Grove (Lefty) **6** Frisch (Frankie) **7** Hubbell (Carl) **8** Cochrane (Mickey)
1948: 7 Pennock (Herb), Traynor (Pie)
1949: 5 Brown (Mordecai) **7** Nichols (Kid) **9** Gehringer (Charlie)

1951: 3 Ott (Mel) **4** Foxx (Jimmie)
1952: 5 Waner (Paul) **8** Heilmann (Harry)
1953: 4 Dean (Dizzy), Klem (Bill) **6** Barrow (Ed), Bender (Chief), Wright (Harry) **7** Simmons (Al), Wallace (Bobby) **8** Connolly (Tom)
1954: 5 Terry (Bill) **6** Dickey (Bill)
1955: 5 Baker (Frank), Lyons (Ted), Vance (Dazzy) **6** Schalk (Ray) **8** DiMaggio (Joe), Hartnett (Gabby) **10** Maranville (Rabbit)
1956: 6 Cronin (Joe) **9** Greenberg (Hank)
1957: 8 Crawford (Sam), McCarthy (Joe)
1959: 5 Wheat (Zach)
1961: 5 Carey (Max) **8** Hamilton (Billy)
1962: 5 Roush (Edd) **6** Feller (Bob) **8** Robinson (Jackie) **9** McKechnie (Bill)
1963: 4 Rice (Sam), Eppa (Rixey) **5** Flick (Elmer) **8** Clarkson (John)
1964: 4 Ward (Monte) **5** Faber (Red), Keefe (Tim) **6** Grimes (Burleigh), Manush (Heinie) **7** Appling (Luke), Huggins (Miller)
1965: 6 Galvin (Pud)
1966: 7 Stengel (Casey) **8** Williams (Ted)
1967: 5 Waner (Lloyd) **6** Rickey (Branch) **7** Ruffing (Red)
1968: 6 Cuyler (Kiki), Goslin (Goose) **7** Medwick (Joe)
1969: 4 Hoyt (Waite) **6** Musial (Stan) **9** Coveleski (Stan) **10** Campanella (Roy)
1970: 5 Combs (Earle), Frick (Ford) **6** Haines (Jesse) **8** Boudreau (Lou)
1971: 5 Paige (Satchel), Hafey (Chick), Weiss (George) **6** Hooper (Harry), Kelley (Joe) **7** Beckley (Jake) **8** Bancroft (Dave), Marquard (Rube)
1972: 4 Wynn (Early) **5** Berra (Yogi), Gomez (Lefty) **6** Gibson (Josh), Koufax (Sandy), Youngs (Ross) **7** Leonard (Buck) **8** Harridge (Will)
1973: 5 Evans (Billy), Irvin (Monte), Kelly (George), Spahn (Warren), Welch (Mickey) **8** Clemente (Roberto)
1974: 4 Bell (Cool Papa), Ford (Whitey) **6** Conlan (Jocko), Mantle (Mickey) **8** Thompson (Sam) **9** Bottomley (Jim)
1975: 5 Kiner (Ralph) **6** Harris (Bucky), Herman (Billy) **7** Averill (Earl), Johnson (Judy)
1976: 5 Lemon (Bob) **6** Connor (Roger) **7** Hubbard (Cal), Roberts (Robin) **9** Lindstrom (Fred) **10** Charleston (Oscar)
1977: 5 Banks (Ernie), Lloyd (Pop), Lopez (Al), Rusie (Arnos) **6** Di-

higo (Martin), Sewell (Joe)
1978: 4 Joss (Addie) **7** Mathews (Eddie) **8** MacPhail (Larry)
1979: 4 Mays (Willie) **5** Giles (Warren) **6** Wilson (Hack)
1980: 5 Klein (Chuck) **6** Kaline (Al), Snider (Duke), Yawkey (Tom)
1981: 4 Mize (Johnny) **6** Foster (Rube), Gibson (Bob)
1982: 5 Aaron (Hank) **7** Jackson (Travis) **8** Chandler (Happy), Robinson (Frank)
1983: 4 Kell (George) **6** Alston (Walter) **8** Marichal (Juan), Robinson (Brooks)
1984: 5 Reese (Pee Wee) **7** Ferrell (Rick) **8** Aparicio (Luis), Drysdale (Don) **9** Killebrew (Harmon)
1985: 5 Brock (Lou) **7** Vaughan (Arky), Wilhelm (Hoyt) **9** Slaughter (Enos)
1986: 5 Doerr (Bobby) **7** McCovey (Willie) **8** Lombardi (Ernie)
1987: 6 Hunter (Jim "Catfish") **8** Williams (Billy) **9** Dandridge (Ray)
1988: 8 Stargell (Willie)
1989: 7 Bench (Johnny) **7** Barlick (Al) **11** Yastrzemski (Carl) **12** Schoendienst (Red)
1990: 6 Morgan (Joe), Palmer (Jim)
1991: 5 Carew (Rod), Perry (Gaylord), Veeck (Bill) **7** Jenkins (Ferguson), Lazzeri (Tony)
1992: 6 Seaver (Tom) **7** Fingers (Rollie), McGowan (Bill) **9** Newhouser (Hal)
1993: 7 Jackson (Reggie)
1994: 7 Carlton (Steve), Rizzuto (Phil "Scooter") **8** Durocher (Leo)
1995: 5 Day (Leon) **6** Willis (Vic) **7** Ashburn (Richie), Hulbert (William), Schmidt (Mike)
1996: 6 Foster (Bill), Hanlon (Ned), Weaver (Earl) **7** Bunning (Jim)
1997: 3 Fox (Nellie) **5** Wells (Willie) **6** Niekro (Phil) **7** Lasorda (Tommy)
1998: 4 Doby (Larry) **5** Davis (George), Rogan (Joe) **6** Sutton (Don) **8** MacPhail (Lee)
1999: 4 Ryan (Nolan) **5** Brett (George), Selee (Frank), Yount (Robin) **6** Cepeda (Orlando), Chylak (Nestor) **8** Williams (Joe)
2000: 4 Fisk (Carlton) **5** Perez (Tony) **6** McPhee (Bid) **7** Steames (Turkey) **8** Anderson (Sparky)
2001: 5 Smith (Hilton) **7** Puckett (Kirby) **8** Winfield (Dave) **10** Mazerowski (Bill)
2002: 5 Smith (Ozzie)
2003: 6 Carter (Gary), Murray (Eddie)
2004: 7 Molitor (Paul) **9** Eckersley (Dennis)
2005: 5 Boggs (Wade) **8** Sandberg (Ryne)

other player/manager/owner: 7 Jim Rice **8** Joe Torre, Pete Rose, Vida Blue **9** Bowie Kuhn, Cal Ripken, Gil Hodges, Luis Tiant, Ralph Houk, Ron Guidry, Sammy Sosa, Ted Turner, Tommy John, Tony Gwynn **10** Barry Bonds, Boog Powell, Derek Jeter, Maury Wills, Mike Piazza, Roger Maris, Sparky Lyle **11** Billy Martin, Frank Thomas, Jason Giambi, Jeff Bagwell, Mark McGwire, Rich Gossage **12** Albert Pujols, Dennis McLain, Dick Williams, Elston Howard, Ken Griffey Jr, Randy Johnson, Roger Clemens **13** Alex Rodriguez, Mariano Rivera, Pedro Martinez, Rocky Colavito, Thurman Munson, Walter O'Malley **14** Keith Hernandez, Peter Ueberroth **15** Rickey Henderson **18** George Steinbrenner

baseball leagues
National: 11 Chicago Cubs, New York Mets **13** Atlanta Braves, Houston Astros **14** Cincinnati Reds, Florida Marlins, San Diego Padres **15** Colorado Rockies **16** Milwaukee Brewers, St Louis Cardinals **17** Los Angeles Dodgers, Pittsburgh Pirates **18** San Francisco Giants **19** Arizona Diamondbacks, Washington Nationals **20** Philadelphia Phillies
American: 9 Oakland A's **12** Boston Red Sox, Texas Rangers **13** Anaheim Angels, Detroit Tigers **14** Minnesota Twins, New York Yankees **15** Chicago White Sox, Seattle Mariners, Toronto Blue Jays **16** Baltimore Orioles, Cleveland Indians, Kansas City Royals, Oakland Athletics **17** Tampa Bay Devil Rays

baseball team
Atlanta: 6 Braves
　stadium: 11 Turner Field
Arizona 12 Diamondbacks
　stadium: 15 Bank One Ballpark
Baltimore: 7 Orioles
　stadium: 11 Camden Yards
Boston: 6 Red Sox
　stadium: 10 Fenway Park
Chicago: 4 Cubs
　stadium: 12 Wrigley Field
Chicago: 8 White Sox
　stadium: 12 Comiskey Park
Cleveland: 7 Indians
　stadium: 11 Jacobs Field
Cincinnati: 4 Reds
　stadium: 21 Great American Ball Park
Colorado: 7 Rockies
　stadium: 10 Coors Field
Detroit: 6 Tigers
　stadium: 12 Comerica Park
Florida: 7 Marlins
　stadium: 8 Dolphins
Houston: 6 Astros
　stadium: 14 Minute Maid Park
Kansas City: 6 Royals

stadium: 8 Kauffman
Los Angeles: 6 Angels **7** Dodgers
　　stadium: 5 Angel **6** Dodger
Milwaukee: 7 Brewers
　　stadium: 10 Miller Park
Minnesota: 5 Twins
　　stadium: 9 Metrodome **24** Hubert
　　H Humphrey Metrodome
New York: 4 Mets **7** Yankees
　　stadium: 4 Shea **6** Yankee
Oakland: 2 A's **9** Athletics
　　stadium: 14 McAfee Coliseum
Philadelphia: 8 Phillies
　　stadium: 16 Citizens Bank Park
Pittsburgh: 7 Pirates
　　stadium: 7 PNC Park
St Louis: 9 Cardinals
　　stadium: 5 Busch **9** Cardinals
San Diego: 6 Padres
　　stadium: 9 Petco Park
San Francisco: 7 Giants
　　stadium: 7 PNC Park
Seattle: 8 Mariners
　　stadium: 11 Safeco Field
Tampa Bay: 9 Devil Rays
　　stadium: 14 Tropicana Field
Texas: 7 Rangers
　　stadium: 11 The Ballpark **15**
　　Ameriquest Field
Toronto: 8 Blue Jays
　　stadium: 7 Sky Dome **12** Rogers
　　Centre
Washington (DC): 9 Nationals
　　stadium: 3 RFK
baseless 7 unsound **9** unfactual, unfounded **10** groundless, ungrounded **11** unjustified, unsupported **12** without basis **13** unjustifiable **14** uncorroborated **15** unsubstantiated
basement 5 below **6** bottom, cellar **15** underground room
baseness 7 lowness **8** meanness, vileness **9** depravity **11** ignobleness **14** iniquitousness **16** contemptibleness
base of operations
　　Greek: 6 pou sto
bash 4 blow **5** blast, clout, crack, knock, party, whack **7** clopper **8** wingding **9** bacchanal
Bashemath *see* **4** Adah
bashful 3 shy **5** timid **6** demure, modest **8** blushing, reserved, reticent, retiring, sheepish, skittish, timorous **9** diffident, shrinking, uncertain **10** shamefaced **11** constrained, unconfident
bashfulness 7 shyness **10** diffidence **12** sheepishness **14** self-effacement **15** unassertiveness
basic 3 key **4** base, core **5** prime, vital **7** bedrock, primary **8** rudiment **9** essential, intrinsic **10** elementary, foundation **11** fundamental, rudimentary **12** foundational, prerequisite, underpinning
basically
　　French: 6 au fond

basic ideas 6 basics **7** essence, factors, origins **8** elements, features **9** rudiments **10** principles **11** foundations
basic need 9 essential, necessity, requisite, vital part **10** key element, sine qua non
basic part 4 unit **7** element **9** component **10** ingredient **11** constituent **13** building block
basic quality 6 nature **7** essence **9** principle, substance **12** quintessence
basics 4 ABCs **8** elements **9** rudiments **10** principles **11** nitty-gritty **12** fundamentals
basil
　　also called: 6 tulasi
　　botanical name: 6 Ocimum **8** O minimum **10** O basilicum
　　means: 5 royal **6** kingly, lizard (basilisk)
　　nickname: 14 kiss-me-Nicholas
　　origin: 5 India
　　sacred to: 6 Vishnu **7** Krishna, Lakshmi
　　symbol of: 4 hate, love
　　use: 5 pasta, pesto, sauce **10** vegetables
basilica 6 church **10** house of God **14** house of worship
Basilisk
　　form: 6 dragon
basin 3 pan, tub, vat **4** bowl, dale, dell, font, glen, sink **5** gulch, gully, stoup **6** crater, hollow, lavabo, ravine, tureen, valley **7** dishpan, washtub **8** lavatory, sinkhole, washbowl **9** porringer, washbasin, washstand **10** depression, finger bowl
basis, bases 4 base, root **6** ground **7** bedrock **9** essential, principle **10** foundation, touchstone **11** cornerstone, fundamental **12** underpinning **13** starting point
bask 5 revel, savor **6** relish, wallow **7** delight **8** sunbathe **9** luxuriate **11** warm oneself **12** soak up warmth, toast oneself
basket 5 cesta, crate **6** barrel, hamper **7** carrier, pannier **8** bassinet, canister
basketball
　　term: 3 key **4** dunk, hoop, pick, post, trap, zone **5** court, guard, lay-up, pivot, point, press, steal **6** assist, basket, center **7** dribble, forward, palming, rebound, referee **8** charging, hook shot, jump shot, sixth man, turnover **9** backboard, backcourt, fast break, field goal, free throw, give-and-go, traveling **11** goal tending, pick-and-roll **12** three-pointer
　　organizations: 3 NBA **4** NCAA, WNBA
　　Hall of Fame:
　　　　1959: 5 Allen (Phog; Forrest Clare), Hyatt (Charles), Mikan (George),

Olsen (Harold), Stagg (Amos Alonzo), Tower (Oswald) **6** Gulick (Luther), Hickox (Edward), Morgan (Ralph) **7** Carlson (Henry), Kennedy (Matthew) **8** Luisetti (Hank), Meanwell (Walter E), Naismith (James), Schommer (John) **15** Original Celtics
1960: 5 Blood (Ernest) **6** Hanson (Victor), Keaney (Frank), Murphy (Charles), Porter (Henry), Wooden (John) **7** Hepbron (George), Lambert (Ward) **8** Macauley (Ed) **9** McCracken (Branch)
1961: 4 Hoyt (George) **5** Sachs (Leonard), Tobey (David), Walsh (David) **6** Keogan (George), O'Brien (John), Roosma (John) **7** Kurland (Bob), Phillip (Andy), Quigley (Ernest), Trester (Arthur), Wachter (Edward) **8** Borgmann (Bernhard) **9** Steinmetz (Christian) **10** DeBernardi (Forrest), Schabinger (Arthur) **14** Buffalo Germans
1962: 4 Page (Harlan) **6** Sedran (Barney), St John (Lynn) **8** Thompson (John) **9** McCracken (Jack) **10** Morgenweck (Frank)
1963: 4 Reid (William) **7** Gruenig (Robert) **11** New York Rens
1964: 4 Bunn (John) **5** Irish (Ned), Jones (R William) **6** Foster (Harold), Holman (Nat) **7** Russell (John) **8** Loeffler (Kenneth)
1965: 5 Brown (Walter) **6** Hinkle (Paul), Hobson (Howard), Mokray (William)
1966: 4 Dean (Everett) **8** Lapchick (Joe)
1967: 3 Bee (Clair) **4** Cann (Howard), Gill (Amory) **6** Julian (Alvin)
1968: 3 Iba (Hank; Henry P) **4** Rupp (Adolph F) **6** Taylor (Charles H) **7** Denhart (Henry G) **8** Auerbach (Red; Arnold J)
1969: 6 Davies (Bob) **9** Carnevale (Bernard L)
1970: 5 Cousy (Bob) **6** Pettit (Bob) **10** Saperstein (Abe)
1971: 5 Wells (W R Clifford) **6** Diddle (Edgar A) **7** Douglas (Robert L) **8** Endacott (Paul), Friedman (Max), Gottlieb (Edward)
1972: 5 Drake (Bruce) **6** Ripley (Elmer H), Wooden (John) **7** Beckman (John), Lonborg (Arthur C), Schayes (Dolph)
1973: 6 Fisher (Harry A) **7** Schmidt (Ernest) **8** Podoloff (Maurice)
1974: 6 Liston (Emil) **7** Brennan (Joseph), Russell (Bill) **9** Vandivier (Robert)
1975: 4 Gola (Tom) **6** Krause (Edward W) **7** Litwack (Harry), Sharman (Bill)
1976: 4 Gale (Lauren) **6** Baylor (Elgin), Cooper (Charles T) **7** Johnson (Wiliam C), McGuire (Frank)

1977: 5 Fulks (Joe), Hagan (Cliff) **6** Arizin (Paul) **7** Pollard (Jim) **8** Nucatola (John P)

1978: 5 Barry (Sam; Justin M), Meyer (Raymond J) **6** Hickey (Edgar S), Newell (Peter F) **7** Enright (James E) **8** McLendon (John B) **11** Chamberlain (Wilt)

1979: 4 West (Jerry) **5** Lucas (Jerry) **7** Shelton (Everett), Shirley (J Dallas) **8** Harrison (Lester) **9** Robertson (Oscar)

1980: 4 Hepp (Ferenc) **6** Barlow (Thomas B) **7** Kennedy (J Walter) **9** McCutchan (Arad A)

1981: 4 Case (Everett N), Duer (Alva O), Reed (Willis) **5** Greer (Hal) **6** Gaines (Clarence E), Martin (Slater), Ramsey (Frank)

1982: 5 Leith (Lloyd R), Smith (Dean E), Wilke (Louis G) **6** Twyman (Jack) **7** Bradley (Bill) **11** DeBusschere (Dave)

1983: 5 Fagan (Clifford B), Jones (Sam) **6** Steitz (Edward S) **7** Gardner (Jack) **8** Havlicek (John)

1984: 4 Wade (L Margaret) **5** Cervi (Al) **6** Abbott (Senda Berenson), Teague (Bertha F) **8** Anderson (W Harold), Harshman (Marv K), Thurmond (Nate)

1985-1986: 5 Watts (Stanley H) **6** Taylor (Fred R) **7** Holzman (Red), Mihalik (Red) **8** Heinsohn (Tom) **10** Cunningham (Billy)

1986-1987: 5 Barry (Rick) **6** Wanzer (Bobby) **7** Frazier (Walt) **8** Houbregs (Robert J), Maravich (Pete)

1987-1988: 6 Miller (Ralph H), Unseld (Wes) **9** McDermott (Robert), Lovelette (Clyde)

1988-1989: 5 Gates (William "Pop"), Jones (K C) **7** Wilkens (Lenny)

1989-1990: 4 Bing (Dave) **5** Hayes (Elvin) **6** Monroe (Earl) **8** Johnston (Neil)

1990-1991: 6 Cowens (Dave), Knight (Bobby), O'Brien (Lawrence F) **8** Fleisher (Lawrence), Gallatin (Harry) **9** Archibald (Nate), Stankovic (Borislav)

1991-1992: 5 Belov (Sergei), White (Nera) **6** Lanier (Bob), Ramsay (Jack) **7** Hawkins (Connie), McGuire (Al) **8** Woolpert (Phillip) **10** Carnesecca (Louie) **13** Harris-Stewart (Lusia)

1992-1993: 5 Issel (Dan) **6** Erving (Julius), Meyers (Ann), Murphy (Calvin), Walton (Bill) **7** Bellamy (Walter), McGuire (Dick) **9** Semjonova (Uljana)

1994: 4 Crum (Denny), Daly (Charles J) **6** Rubini (Cesare) **9** Jeannette (Buddy) **11** Blazejowski (Carol)

1995: 5 Strom (Earl) **6** Kundla (John), Miller (Cheryl), Walton (Bill) **7** Donovan (Anne) **8** Gomelsky (Aleksandr) **9** Mikkelsen (Vern) **10** Abdul-Jabbar (Kareem)

1996: 5 Cosic (Kresimir) **6** Gervin (George) **7** Yardley (George) **8** Goodrich (Gail), Thompson (David) **9** Lieberman (Nancy)

1997: 5 Curry (Denise) **6** Carril (Pete), Howell (Bailey) **7** English (Alex), Haskins (Dan) **8** Crawford (Joan) **10** Diaz-Miguel (Antonio)

1998: 4 Bird (Larry) **5** Risen (Arnie) **6** Hannum (Alex), Haynes (Marques) **7** Conradt (Jody), Nikolic (Aleksandar), Wilkins (Lenny, as coach)

1999: 5 Embry (Wayne), Moore (Billie) **6** McHale (Kevin) **7** Zollner (Fred) **8** Thompson (John)

2000: 6 McAdoo (Bob), Newton (Charles), Thomas (Isiah) **7** Biasone (Danny), Summitt (Pat), Wootten (Morgan)

2001: 6 Chaney (John), Malone (Moses) **7** Krzyzewski (Mike)

2002: 3 Yow (Kay) **5** Brown (Larry), Olson (Lute) **7** Johnson (Earvin "Magic") **8** Petrovic (Drazen) **19** Harlem Globetrotters

2003: 5 Hearn (Chick), Lemon (Meadowlark), Lloyd (Earl) **6** Parish (Robert), Worthy (James) **7** Barmore (Leon) **8** Meneghin (Dino)

2004: 6 Stokes (Maurice) **7** Drexler (Clyde), Sharman (Bill, as coach), Woodard (Lynette) **9** Colangelo (Jerry), Dalipagic (Drazen)

2005: 5 Brown (Hubie) **6** Gunter (Sue) **7** Calhoun (Jim), Boeheim (Jim), Marcari (Hortencia)

other player/coach: 7 Yao Ming **8** Pat Riley **9** Grant Hill, Jason Kidd, Larry Bird, Tim Duncan **10** Danny Ainge, Karl Malone, Kobe Bryant **11** Bernard King, Bill Lambeer, Chris Webber, Dick Barnett, LeBron James, Phil Jackson **12** Dirk Nowitzki, Kevin Garnett, Manu Ginobili, Patrick Ewing, Reggie Miller, Tracy McGrady **13** David Robinson, Michael Jordan, Scottie Pippen, Terry Cummings **14** Charles Barkley, Hakeem Olajuwon, Shaquille O'Neal

basketball team

league: 3 NBA **29** National Basketball Association

Atlanta: 5 Hawks
Boston: 7 Celtics
Charlotte: 7 Bobcats
Chicago: 5 Bulls
Cleveland: 9 Cavaliers
Dallas: 4 Mavs **9** Mavericks
Denver: 7 Nuggets
Detroit: 7 Pistons
Golden State: 8 Warriors
Houston: 7 Rockets
Indiana: 6 Pacers
Los Angeles: 6 Lakers **8** Clippers
Memphis: 9 Grizzlies
Miami: 4 Heat
Milwaukee: 5 Bucks
Minnesota: 12 Timberwolves
New Jersey: 4 Nets
New Orleans: 7 Hornets
New York: 14 Knickerbockers
Orlando: 5 Magic
Philadelphia: 5 76ers **13** Seventy-Sixers
Phoenix: 4 Suns
Portland: 12 Trail Blazers
Sacramento: 5 Kings
San Antonio: 5 Spurs
Seattle: 11 SuperSonics
Toronto: 7 Raptors
Utah: 4 Jazz
Washington: 7 Wizards
WNBA
Charlotte: 5 Sting
Connecticut: 3 Sun
Detroit: 5 Shock
Houston: 6 Comets
Indiana: 5 Fever
Los Angeles: 6 Sparks
Minnesota: 4 Lynx
New York: 7 Liberty
Phoenix: 7 Mercury
Sacramento: 8 Monarchs
San Antonio: 11 Silver Stars
Seattle: 5 Storm
Washington: 7 Mystics

Basque

language spoken in: 5 Italy, Spain **6** France

bas-relief

Italian: 12 basso-rilievo

bass 3 low **4** alto **5** basso **7** harmony **8** baritone, bass clef

bass

types: 3 sea **4** rock **5** black **6** calico **7** striped, sunfish **10** largemouth, smallmouth
characteristic: 10 forked-tail **12** spiny-finned

Bassanio

character in: 19 The Merchant of Venice
author: 11 Shakespeare

Bassett, Angela

born: 9 New York NY
husband: 14 Courtney B. Vance
roles: 7 Contact **8** Malcolm X **10** City of Hope **12** Boyz n the Hood **15** Music of the Heart, Waiting to Exhale **17** The Rosa Parks Story, Vampire in Brooklyn **22** What's Love Got to Do with It **25** How Stella Got Her Groove Back

basso-rilievo 9 bas-relief

bastard 6 impure **8** inferior, spurious **9** imperfect, irregular, love child **12** natural child **17** illegitimate child

bastardize 6 debase, weaken 7 degrade 9 downgrade

baste 3 sew 4 drip 5 roast 6 cudgel, flavor, stitch, thrash 7 moisten 15 temporary stitch

bastinado 4 beat, blow, cane, drub 5 whale 7 beating 8 drubbing

bastion 4 fort 5 tower 6 pillar 7 bulwark, citadel, rampart 8 barbette, fortress 10 breastwork, stronghold

bat 3 hit, rod 4 cane, clip, club, cuff, mace, slug, sock 5 baton, billy, knock, smack, staff, stick, whack 6 buffet, cudgel, mallet, strike, thwack, wallop 7 clobber 8 bludgeon 9 blackjack, truncheon 10 shillelagh

batch 3 lot 5 bunch, crowd, group, stock 6 amount, number 8 quantity 9 aggregate 10 collection

Bates, Alan
　　born: 7 England 9 Allestree 10 Derbyshire
　　roles: 6 Hamlet 8 The Fixer 10 Duet for One, Georgy Girl 12 King of Hearts 13 A Kind of Loving, The Collection, Zorba the Greek 16 An Unmarried Woman 18 An Englishman Abroad, A Prayer for the Dying 22 Far From the Madding Crowd

Bates, Kathy
　　born: 9 Memphis TN
　　roles: 6 Misery 7 Titanic 10 Diabolique, Used People 12 About Schmidt, The Late Shift, Men Don't Leave 18 Fried Green Tomatoes

Bates, Miss
　　character in: 4 Emma
　　author: 6 Austen

Bateson, William
　　field: 7 biology
　　nationality: 7 British
　　founded: 8 genetics

bath 3 dip, tub 4 wash 5 sauna 6 douche, shower 7 washing 8 ablution, lavement 9 cleansing, immersion, steam bath 10 irrigation
　　type: 3 hip, mud 4 sitz 5 steam 6 shower, sponge 7 Turkish bath

bathe 3 dip, tub, wet 4 lave, soak, wash 5 douse 6 douche, shower, sponge 7 cleanse 8 irrigate

bathing 3 dip, tub 6 laving, plunge 7 washing 8 swimming 9 ablutions, immersion

bathos 4 corn, mush 5 slush 8 schmaltz 9 mushiness, soppiness 10 maudlinism, slushiness 11 false pathos, mawkishness 14 sentimentalism, sentimentality

bathroom 2 W C 3 can, loo 4 head, john 5 biffy 6 toilet 7 commode, latrine 8 facility, lavatory, men's room, restroom, washroom 10 ladies' room, powder room 11 water closet 14 little boys' room 15 little girls' room

Bathsheba
　　also: 8 Bathshua
　　father: 5 Eliam
　　husband: 5 David, Uriah
　　son: 7 Solomon
　　grandfather: 10 Ahithophel

Batman
　　character: 6 Alfred 7 Egghead, King Tut 8 Catwoman, The Joker 10 Bruce Wayne (Batman), Chief O'Hara, The Penguin, The Riddler 11 Dick Grayson (Robin) 13 Barbara Gordon (Batgirl) 17 Aunt Harriet Cooper 24 Police Commissioner Gordon
　　cast: 8 Adam West, Burt Ward 9 John Astin 10 Alan Napier, Eartha Kitt, Madge Blake 11 Cesar Romero, Julie Newmar, Victor Buono, Yvonne Craig 12 Frank Gorshin, Neil Hamilton, Stafford Repp, Vincent Price 13 Lee Meriwether 15 Burgess Meredith
　　city: 10 Gotham City
　　nickname: 9 Boy Wonder 10 Dynamic Duo 13 Caped Crusader
　　gimmick: 6 Batlab 7 Batcave 8 Batphone 9 Batmobile, Batsignal

Batman
　　director: 9 Tim Burton
　　cast: 9 Pat Hingle (Commissioner Gordon) 11 Kim Basinger (Vicky Vale) 12 Michael Gough (Alfred) 13 Jack Nicholson (Joker), Michael Keaton (Batman/Bruce Wayne)

Batman and Robin
　　director: 14 Joel Schumacher
　　cast: 9 Pat Hingle (Commissioner Gordon) 10 Uma Thurman (Poison Ivy/Dr. Pamela Isley) 12 Michael Gough (Alfred) 13 Chris O'Donnell (Robin/Dick Grayson), George Clooney (Batman/Bruce Wayne) 17 Alicia Silverstone (Batgirl/Barbara Wilson) 20 Arnold Schwarzenegger (Mr. Freeze/Dr. Victor Fries)

Batman Begins
　　director: 16 Christopher Nolan
　　cast: 10 Gary Oldman (Jim Gordon), Liam Neeson (Ducard) 11 Katie Holmes (Rachel Dawes), Rutger Hauer (Earle) 12 Michael Caine (Alfred), Tom Wilkinson (Carmine Falcone) 13 Christian Bale (Batman/Bruce Wayne), Morgan Freeman (Lucius Fox)

Batman Forever
　　director: 14 Joel Schumacher
　　cast: 9 Jim Carrey (Riddler), Pat Hingle (Commissioner Gordon), Val Kilmer (Batman/Bruce Wayne) 12 Michael Gough (Alfred), Nicole Kidman (Dr. Chase Meridian) 13 Chris O'Donnell (Robin/Dick Grayson), Tommy Lee Jones (Harvey Two-Face)

Batman Returns
　　director: 9 Tim Burton
　　cast: 9 Pat Hingle (Commissioner Gordon) 11 Danny DeVito (Penguin) 12 Michael Gough (Alfred) 13 Michael Keaton (Batman/Bruce Wayne) 16 Michelle Pfeiffer (Catwoman/Selina Kyle) 17 Christopher Walken (Max Shreck)

Bat Masterson
　　cast: 9 Gene Barry

baton 3 bat, rod 4 club, mace, wand 5 billy, crook, staff, stick 6 cudgel, fasces 7 crosier, scepter, war club 8 bludgeon, caduceus 9 billy club, truncheon 10 nightstick, shillelagh

batter 4 beat, lash, maul 5 break, crush, pound, smash, smite 6 beat up, buffet, mangle, pummel 7 clobber, shatter

battercake 6 waffle 7 biscuit, pancake

battered 4 shot 6 beat-up, ruined, shabby 8 decrepit 11 dilapidated 12 disreputable

battery 3 set 4 army, band, pack, team 5 block, cadre, force, group, suite, troop 6 caning, cannon, convoy, legion, lineup, outfit, series 7 beating, brigade, company, hitting, hurting, maiming, phalanx, section 8 armament, cannonry, clubbing, division, drubbing, flogging, ordnance, squadron, whipping, wounding 9 cudgeling, spearhead, strapping, thrashing

battle 3 war 4 bout, duel, feud, fray, meet 5 argue, brawl, clash, fight, siege 6 action, affray, combat, debate, engage, tussle 7 contend, contest, crusade, dispute, quarrel, warfare 8 campaign, conflict, skirmish, struggle 9 agitation, encounter, firefight 10 engagement 11 altercation, controversy 13 confrontation

Battle, final
　　place: 10 Armageddon

battle cry 6 war cry 8 Geronimo, war whoop 9 Rebel yell

Battle Cry
　　author: 8 Leon Uris

battlefield 5 arena, lists 8 the front, war arena 9 front line 10 battle line, no man's land 11 battlefront 12 battleground

battleground 5 arena, lists 11 battlefield, battlefront

Battle of the Books
　　author: 13 Jonathan Swift

battle-ready 5 armed 7 arrayed 8 prepared 9 fortified

battleship 4 Iowa 5 Maine 6 Oregon 7 carrier, warship 8 Missouri 9 Ironsides, New Jersey, Wisconsin 10 bluish-gray 11 Dreadnought 12 Constitution
　　first: 7 Gloire
　　largest: 6 Yamato
　　German: 8 Graf Spee

Battus
　　ruler of: 5 Libya
　　form: 7 peasant

witness to: 11 cattle theft
thief: 6 Hermes
turned to: 5 stone
cured of: 16 speech impediment

batty 4 nuts **5** crazy, loony, queer, wacko, wacky **6** cuckoo, crazed **7** bat-like, cracked

bauble 3 toy **4** bead **6** geegaw, trifle **7** trinket **8** gimcrack, ornament

Baucis
form: 7 peasant
home: 7 Phrygia
husband: 8 Philemon
offered hospitality to: 4 Zeus **6** Hermes

Baudelaire, Charles
author of: 13 Flowers of Evil **14** Les Fleurs du Mal

Baugh, Sammy
nickname: 13 Slinging Sammy
sport: 8 football
position: 11 quarterback
team: 18 Washington Redskins

Baum, Lyman Frank
author of: 13 The (Wonderful) Wizard of Oz **18** Father Goose His Book, Mother Goose in Prose

Baum, Vicki
author of: 8 Shanghai **10** Grand Hotel, Grand Opera **12** Men Never Know **13** A Tale from Bali, And Life Goes On

Baumgarner, James
real name of: 11 James Garner

bawdy 4 blue, lewd, sexy **5** dirty, gross, lusty **6** coarse, earthy, ribald, risque, sexual, vulgar **7** raunchy **8** immodest, improper, indecent, off-color **10** indecorous, indelicate, licentious, suggestive

bawdy house 7 brothel **8** bordello, cathouse **10** fancy house, whorehouse **13** sporting house **14** house of ill fame **16** house of ill repute **19** house of prostitution

bawl 3 cry **4** call, howl, roar, wail, weep, yell, yowl **5** shout **6** bellow, clamor, cry out, squall **7** blubber, call out

bawling out 6 rebuke **7** censure, chiding, reproof **8** reproach, scolding **9** reprimand **10** chewing out, upbraiding **11** castigation, reprobation **12** dressing-down, remonstrance **13** tongue-lashing

bawl out 5 scold **6** berate, rail at, rebuke, yell at **7** censure, chew out, reprove, upbraid **8** admonish, reproach **9** castigate, dress down, reprimand **10** take to task, tongue-lash **14** read the riot act

Bax, Arnold Edward Trevor
born: 6 London **7** England
composer of: 8 Tintagel **13** November Woods **14** Mater Ora Filium **15** The Garden of Fand **27** Overture to a Picaresque Comedy

Baxter, Anne
grandfather: 16 Frank Lloyd Wright
born: 14 Michigan City IN
roles: 8 Applause **11** All About Eve **13** The Razor's Edge

Baxter, Jody
character in: 11 The Yearling
author: 8 Rawlings

bay 3 cry, yap **4** bank, bark, cove, gulf, howl, nook, road, yelp **5** basin, bayou, bight, fiord, firth, inlet, niche, sound **6** alcove, bellow, clamor, lagoon, recess, strait **7** barking, estuary, howling, narrows, yapping, yelling, yelping **9** bellowing **11** compartment **13** natural harbor

bay (at bay) 7 trapped **8** cornered

bay leaf
botanical name: 12 Pimenta acris
expression: 16 to win one's laurels
from tree: 9 bay laurel
transformation of: 6 Daphne
tree sacred to: 6 Apollo
laurel berries called: 10 bacca lauri
source of: 13 baccalaureate
gives gift of: 8 prophecy
helps girls win back: 12 errant lovers
origin: 5 Italy
protects against: 5 death **6** poison **7** sorcery **11** evil spirits
symbol of: 7 victory (laurel wreath)
use: 4 fish, fowl, meat, soup, stew

bayou 4 slew **5** creek, inlet, marsh, river, swamp **6** outlet, slough, stream **9** backwater **13** stagnant marsh

Bayou State
nickname of: 9 Louisiana **11** Mississippi

Bay Psalm Book
author: 9 John Eliot

Bay State
nickname of: 13 Massachusetts

bazaar 4 fair, mart **6** market **8** carnival, exchange **11** charity fair, charity sale, marketplace

Bazile
character in: 18 The Barber of Seville
author: 12 Beaumarchais

Bazzard, Deputy
character in: 22 The Mystery of Edwin Drood
author: 7 Dickens

BC see **12** before Christ

B C
creator: 10 Johnny Hart
character: 3 Tor **4** Grog **5** Peter **8** anteater **10** Clumsy Carp **11** the Fat Broad
poet: 5 Wiley
era: 11 Neanderthal, prehistoric

BCE 15 before Common Era

be 4 last, live, stay **5** exist, occur **6** befall, endure, happen, remain **7** persist, subsist **8** continue **9** be present, take place **10** come to pass

be absent 4 miss **12** fail to attend

beach 5 coast, shore **6** strand **8** littoral, seashore **10** water's edge

Beach, Rex
author of: 6 The Net **7** Oh Shoot **8** Pardners **9** Going Some **10** Jungle Gold, The Barrier **11** Don Careless, The Spoilers **12** Son of the Gods **13** The Goose Woman, The Ne'er-dowell **15** The Auction Block **17** Alaskan Adventures

beached 7 aground **8** grounded, stranded **11** shipwrecked **12** washed ashore

beacon 4 beam **5** light **6** pharos, signal **7** seamark **8** bale-fire, landmark **9** watch fire **10** lighthouse, watchtower **11** lighted buoy

bead 3 dot **4** blob, drop, pill **5** speck **6** bubble, pellet **7** droplet, globule **8** particle, spherule

be adequate 2 do **6** answer **8** be enough **10** pass muster **12** be sufficient, do well enough **14** be satisfactory

be afraid of 4 fear **5** dread **7** cower at **8** cringe at **10** shrink from

beak 3 neb, tip **4** bill, nose, pike, prow **5** lorum, snout, spout **7** process, rostrum, snozzle **8** hooknose **9** headmaster, proboscis **10** magistrate

beaker 3 cup **5** glass **6** vessel **9** container

beam 3 ray **4** emit, glow, prop, spar, stud **5** brace, glare, gleam, glint, joist, shine, width **6** girder, rafter, streak, stream, timber **7** breadth, expanse, glimmer, glitter, radiate, trestle **8** transmit **9** broadcast, radiation

bean 9 Phaseolus
varieties: 3 goa, pea, soy, wax, yam **4** fava, jack, lima, moth, mung, rice, seim, snap, soja, soya, tick, wild **5** azuki, black, broad, civet, coral, field, green, horse, lubia, pinto, salad, screw, sewee, sieva, snail, sword, tonka **6** butter, castor, common, French, Indian, kaffir, kidney, lablab, locust, manila, mescal, nicker, potato, romano, runner, sacred, string, tepary, velvet, winged, wonder **7** cluster, English, sarawak, Windsor **8** bovanist, bush lima, Carolina, Cherokee, European, Egyptian, hyacinth, yard-long **9** algarroba, asparagus, bonavista, dwarf lima, Java glory **10** dwarf sieva, giant stock, Hottentot's **12** Italian queen, scarlet flame **13** African locust, Florida velvet, scarlet runner **14** Dutch caseknife **16** white Dutch runner
bean curd: 4 tofu

be a party to 3 aid **4** abet **7** support **9** connive in **11** cooperate in **13** be accessory to, participate in

be apparent 6 appear **7** be clear, be

plain **8** be patent **9** be evident, be obvious **10** be manifest

bear 4 bend, drop, give, haul, have, lead, push, show, take, tend, tote, turn, wear **5** abide, admit, allow, apply, brace, brave, bring, brook, carry, curve, drive, force, hatch, press, refer, spawn, stand, whelp, yield **6** affect, aim for, convey, convoy, create, endure, escort, go with, harbor, invite, permit, relate, render, suffer, take on, uphold **7** bolster, cherish, concern, conduct, contain, deliver, develop, deviate, display, diverge, exhibit, pertain, possess, produce, stomach, support, sustain, undergo, warrant **8** bear down, engender, generate, maintain, manifest, shoulder, submit to, tolerate, transfer, underpin **9** accompany, appertain, encourage, germinate, hold close, propagate, put up with, reproduce, touch upon, transport **10** bring forth, keep in mind **11** give birth to, hold up under

bear
combining form: 4 arct, ursi **5** arcto
constellation: 4 ursa **9** ursa major, ursa minor
family: 7 Ursidae
group of: 6 sleuth
kind: 3 sun **5** black, brown, koala, malay, panda, polar, sloth **6** kodiak, wombat **7** grizzly **9** roachback, silvertip **10** spectacled, thalarctos
male: 4 boar
mythological: 8 Callisto
order: 9 carnivora
young: 3 cub
famous: 6 Smokey

beard 4 dare, defy, face, trap **5** brave **6** corner **7** stubble **8** bristles, confront, whiskers **10** bring to bay **16** five-o'clock shadow

bearded 5 bushy, hairy **6** shaggy **7** bristly, hirsute **8** unshaven **9** whiskered **11** bewhiskered

bear down 4 push **5** press **13** apply pressure

bear down upon 6 assail, attack, come at **7** assault **11** descend upon

Beardsley, Aubrey Vincent
born: 7 England **8** Brighton
artwork: 6 Salome **10** Lysistrata **12** Morte d'Arthur

Beard's Roman Women
author: 14 Anthony Burgess

bearer 5 Atlas **6** holder, porter **7** carrier **8** conveyer, producer **9** messenger **13** beast of burden **16** one holding a check
Spanish: 8 escudero, portador

bear fruit 4 bear **6** mature **7** develop, prosper **8** fructify

bearing 3 air **4** mien, port **5** sense **6** import, manner **7** concern, meaning **8** attitude, behavior, breeding, carriage, demeanor, presence, relation **9** producing, reference, relevance **10** conception, connection, deportment, importance, pertinence **11** application, association, comportment, germination, giving birth, procreation, propagation, reproducing **12** relationship, reproduction, significance **13** applicability

bearing no name 7 unnamed **8** unsigned **9** anonymous

bearings 3 way **6** course **8** position **9** direction **11** orientation **16** sense of direction

bearish 5 cross, gruff, surly, testy **6** crusty, sullen **7** brusque, crabbed, grouchy **8** churlish **9** crotchety, irascible **10** ill-humored, out of sorts **11** ill-tempered, pessimistic **12** cantankerous

bear off 5 seize, steal **6** abduct, convey, kidnap

bear out 5 prove **6** verify **7** confirm **11** corroborate **12** substantiate

Bear State
nickname of: 8 Arkansas

bear up under 4 bear, take **5** abide, brave, brook, stand **6** endure, suffer **7** stomach, undergo, weather **9** go through, withstand

bear witness 4 back **6** attest **7** confirm, testify **11** corroborate, demonstrate **12** give evidence, substantiate

beast 3 cad, cur, pig, rat **4** ogre **5** brute, swine **6** animal, mammal, savage **8** creature **9** barbarian, quadruped

beastly 3 bad **4** vile **5** awful, cruel, gross, lousy, nasty **6** brutal, coarse, savage **7** bestial, brutish, inhuman, swinish **8** degraded, dreadful, terrible **9** barbarous, loathsome, monstrous **10** abominable, deplorable, disgusting, unpleasant **12** contemptible, disagreeable

beat 3 bat, hit, mix, rap, tap, way **4** area, bang, best, blow, cane, club, drub, flap, flog, flop, lick, maul, path, rout, slap, time, whip, zone **5** clout, count, crush, flail, knock, meter, outdo, pound, pulse, punch, quake, quell, realm, repel, route, shake, smack, smite, strap, throb, whack **6** accent, batter, course, defeat, domain, hammer, master, pummel, quiver, rhythm, rounds, stress, strike, stroke, subdue, switch, thrash, thwack, twitch, wallop **7** cadence, circuit, clobber, conquer, destroy, eclipse, flutter, pulsate, put down, repulse, scourge, shellac, surpass, trounce, vibrate, win over **8** overcome, vanquish **9** excel over, fluctuate, go pit-a-pat, overpower, palpitate, pulsation, territory **10** win out over **11** predominate, prevail over, triumph over **14** stir vigorously

beat a retreat 6 beat it **7** back off **8** turn tail, withdraw **10** high tail it

beat around the bush 5 dodge, evade, hedge, stall **10** equivocate, mince words

beatific 4 rapt **6** divine, serene **7** angelic, exalted, saintly, sublime **8** blissful, ecstatic, glorious, heavenly **9** rapturous **10** enraptured **14** transcendental

beat it 2 go **3** out **4** away, scat, shoo **5** be off, leave, scram **6** begone, cut out, depart, get out, go away **7** get lost, vamoose **10** hit the road, make tracks

beatitude 5 bliss **7** ecstasy, rapture **8** euphoria, felicity **10** exaltation **11** blessedness, exaltedness, saintliness **13** transcendence **15** transfiguration

Beatles 10 John Lennon, Ringo Starr **13** Paul McCartney **14** George Harrison
Songs: 6 Taxman **7** Hey Jude, Get Back **10** Nowhere Man, Drive My Car, Revolution **12** Come Together, Dear Prudence, Eleanor Rigby, Rocky Raccoon **13** Twist and Shout **14** A Hard Day's Night, Eight Days A Week **23** Strawberry Fields Forever **24** Lucy in the Sky with Diamonds
albums: 4 Help **7** Hey Jude, Let It Be **8** Revolver **9** Abbey Road **10** Rubber Soul, White Album **14** A Hard Day's Night, Meet the Beatles **15** Yellow Submarine **17** Yesterday... and Today **18** Magical Mystery Tour **30** Sgt. Pepper's Lonely Hearts Club Band

be at loggerheads 5 clash **7** quarrel **8** disagree

be at odds 6 differ **7** dispute, diverge **8** conflict, disagree

beat rhythmically 3 rap, tap **4** drum **6** tattoo **7** pulsate

Beatrice
character in: 12 Divine Comedy
author: 5 Dante

Beatrice
character in: 19 Much Ado About Nothing
author: 11 Shakespeare

Beatrice et Benedict
opera by: 7 Berlioz

Beat the Clock
host: 10 Bud Collyer

Beattie, Ann
author of: 11 Distortions **14** Falling in Place **15** The Burning House **19** Secrets and Surprises **20** Chilly Scenes of Winter

Beatty, Ned
born: 12 Louisville KY
roles: 3 Spy **4** Rudy **9** The Affair, Sweet Land **10** The Big Easy, Black Water, Hear My Song **11** Deliverance **14** Prelude to a Kiss

Beatty, Warren
real name: 11 Warren Beaty
sister: 15 Shirley MacLaine
born: 10 Richmond VA

wife: 13 Annette Bening
roles: 4 Reds **5** Bugsy **6** Ishtar **8** Bulworth **9** Dick Tracy **10** Love Affair **11** All Fall Down **13** Heaven Can Wait **14** Bonnie and Clyde, Town and Country **18** Splendor in the Grass **24** The Roman Spring of Mrs Stone
director of: 4 Reds (Oscar) **8** Bulworth **9** Dick Tracy

beat up 3 mug **4** lick, maul, whip **6** batter, pummel **7** assault, clobber

beat-up 4 shot **6** shabby **7** worn-out **8** battered **10** broken-down **11** dilapidated

Beaty, Shirley MacLean
real name of: 15 Shirley MacLaine

Beaty, Warren
real name of: 12 Warren Beatty

beau, beaux 3 fop, guy, nob **4** buck, dude, love, stud, toff **5** blade, dandy, flame, lover, Romeo, spark, swain, swell, wooer **6** adorer, escort, fellow, fiance, garcon, squire, steady, suitor **7** admirer, beloved, courter, coxcomb, cupidon, Don Juan, gallant, playboy **8** cavalier, courtier, gay blade, Lothario, paramour, popinjay, true love, young man **9** betrothed, boyfriend, courtesan, gentleman, inamorato, ladies' man **10** sweetheart, young blood **15** gentleman caller, gentleman friend
nickname of: 14 George Brummell

Beauchamp's Career
author: 14 George Meredith

Beau Geste
author: 6 P C Wren **15** Christopher Wren
director: 14 William Wellman
cast: 10 Gary Cooper, Ray Milland **12** Brian Donlevy, Susan Hayward **13** Robert Preston
  silent version starred: 12 Ronald Colman
setting: 19 French Foreign Legion

Beaumarchais, Pierre Augustin Caron de
author of: 18 The Barber of Seville **19** The Marriage of Figaro

beau monde 3 elite **6** gentry **7** society **10** upper class, upper crust **11** aristocracy, high society **15** beautiful people

Beauregard, P G T (Pierre Gustave Toutant)
served in: 8 Civil War
side: 11 Confederate
rank: 7 general
ordered firing on: 8 Ft Sumter
battle: 7 Bull Run

beaut 4 lulu, oner **5** daisy, dandy **6** beauty **7** stunner **8** knockout **10** good-looker

beautification 9 adornment **10** decoration **13** embellishment, ornamentation

beautiful 4 fair, fine **5** bonny, great **6** comely, lovely, pretty, seemly, superb,

worthy **7** radiant **8** alluring, gorgeous, handsome, pleasing, splendid, very good **9** admirable, beauteous, enjoyable, estimable, excellent, exquisite, first-rate, ravishing, wonderful **10** attractive, stupendous **11** captivating, commendable, fine-looking, good-looking, resplendent **15** pulchritudinous

Beautiful Mind, A
director: 9 Ron Howard
cast: 8 Ed Harris (Parcher) **9** Josh Lucas (Hansen) **11** Paul Bettany (Charles) **12** Adam Goldberg (Sol), Russell Crowe (John Nash) **16** Jennifer Connelly (Alicia Nash) **18** Christopher Plummer (Dr. Rosen)

beautify 4 do up **5** adorn, grace **7** dress up, enhance, gussy up, improve **8** ornament **9** embellish, glamorize

beauty 4 boon, doll **5** asset, beaut, belle, grace, Venus **6** eyeful, looker **7** benefit, feature, goddess, stunner **8** knockout, radiance, splendor **9** advantage, good looks, good thing **10** attraction, excellence, good-looker, loveliness **11** pulchritude **12** handsomeness, magnificence, resplendence **14** attractiveness
goddess of: 6 Graces **7** Gratiae **9** Aphrodite, Charities
god of: 5 Baldr **6** Apollo, Balder, Baldur **7** Angus Og, Phoebus, Pythias **9** Musagetes

Beauvoir, Simone de
author of: 12 The Mandarins, The Second Sex **14** A Very Easy Death, All Said and Done, The Coming of Age, The Prime of Life **17** Ethics of Ambiguity **22** The Force of Circumstance **25** Memoirs of a Dutiful Daughter **34** Brigitte Bardot and the Lolita Syndrome

beaver
young: 3 kit

Beaver State
nickname of: 6 Oregon

be blessed with 3 own **4** have **5** enjoy **7** possess **16** have the benefit of

because 2 so **3** for **4** that, then, thus **5** cause, hence, since **6** whence **7** whereas **8** inasmuch **9** therefore **10** seeing that **11** considering

Bechuanaland
now called: 8 Botswana

Bechuanland see **8** Botswana

beck 3 bid **4** call **7** bidding, summons **9** summoning

Becker
network: 3 CBS
cast: 9 Ted Danson (John Becker) **10** Alex Desert (Jake Malinak) **11** Jorge Garcia (Hector), Nancy Travis (Chris Konnors) **12** Shawnee Smith (Linda), Terry Farrell (Reggie Kostas) **13** Hattie Winston (Margaret Wyborn), Saverio Guerra (Bob)

Becket
author: 11 Jean Anouilh **18** Alfred Lord Tennyson
director: 14 Peter Glenville
cast: 11 John Gielgud, Peter O'Toole (King Henry II) **13** Richard Burton (Becket)

Beckett, Samuel
author of: 4 Not I, Play, Watt **6** Embers, Molloy **7** Endgame **8** That Time **9** Footfalls, Happy Days **10** Malone Dies **11** All that Fall, The Lost Ones **13** The Unnameable **15** Waiting for Godot **16** Mercier and Camier **20** Murphy Krapp's Last Tape **25** Stories and Texts for Nothing

Beckmann, Max
born: 7 Germany, Leipzig
artwork: 6 Kasbek **7** Perseus **8** Acrobats, The Night **9** The Actors **11** View of Genoa **12** Charnel House, The Argonauts, The Departure **13** Blindman's Buff, Family Picture **14** Double Portrait **17** David and Bathsheba **18** Odysseus and Calypso **19** Sinking of the Titanic **20** Destruction of Messina **22** The Descent from the Cross

beckon 4 call, coax, draw, lure, pull **6** allure, entice, invite, motion, signal, summon, wave at, wave on **7** attract, gesture **11** gesticulate **14** crook a finger at

be clear 6 appear **7** be plain **8** be patent **9** be evident, be obvious **10** be apparent, be manifest

becloud 3 fog **4** blur, hide, veil **5** befog, cloud **6** muddle, screen, shroud **7** confuse, cover up, eclipse, obscure **8** confound, make hazy, overcast **9** obfuscate **10** camouflage, overshadow **14** make indistinct

become 3 get **4** grow, suit, turn **6** go with **7** enhance, flatter, get to be **8** come to be **9** agree with, begin to be **10** complement **11** be reduced to, turn out to be

become apparent 4 dawn, loom **5** arise **6** appear, crop up, emerge, turn up **7** develop, surface

become bigger 4 grow **5** swell **6** expand **7** develop, enlarge, inflate **8** increase

become irrational 5 break, crack **7** crack up **9** break down, fall apart, go berserk **10** go to pieces **11** lose control **12** lose one's mind

become one 3 wed **4** fuse **5** blend, marry, merge, unite **7** combine **8** coalesce **10** amalgamate **11** consolidate

become seasoned to 5 adapt, inure **6** adjust **8** accustom **9** acclimate, get used to, habituate **15** learn to live with

become smaller 6 lessen, shrink **7**

decline, dwindle, shrivel **8** decrease, diminish

become visible 4 loom, show **6** appear, crop up, emerge, show up, turn up **7** surface **11** come to light **12** come into view

becoming 3 apt, fit **4** meet **6** pretty, proper, seemly, worthy **7** fitting **8** suitable **9** befitting, congenial, congruous, enhancing, in keeping **10** attractive, compatible, consistent, flattering, harmonious **11** appropriate, good-looking

Becquerel, Antoine Henri
    field: **7** physics
    nationality: **6** French
    discovered: **13** radioactivity
    awarded: **10** Nobel Prize

bed 3 cot, hay **4** band, bank, base, belt, bunk, crib, lode, plot, sack, seam, zone **5** berth, floor, layer, patch **6** bottom, cradle, pallet **7** deposit, stratum **8** bedstead **10** foundation

bedazzle 4 daze **6** dazzle **7** astound, confuse, enchant, fluster, nonplus, stagger, stupefy **8** befuddle, bewilder, confound, dumfound **9** captivate, overpower, overwhelm **10** disconcert **11** flabbergast **19** sweep one off one's feet

bed chamber 7 bedroom, boudoir

bed down 5 sleep **7** lie down, sack out **8** doss down **10** hit the hay, settle down **11** accommodate, hit the sack

bedeck 4 deck, trim **5** adorn, array **7** garnish **8** decorate, ornament **9** embellish

be deficient in 4 fail, lack, want **7** be scant **9** be short of **10** have too few

be deprived of 4 lack, lose, want

be deserving of 4 earn, rate **5** merit **7** deserve **10** be worthy of **12** be entitled to

bedevil 3 dog **5** annoy, hound, worry **6** badger, harass, pester, plague **9** beleaguer

be devoted to 4 love **5** adore **6** dote on **7** cherish **8** be fond of

bedim 4 blur **6** darken **7** obscure

Bedivere
    character in: **16** Arthurian romance

bedizen 5 adorn, array **6** bedeck, rig out **7** bejewel, costume

bedlam 5 chaos **6** tumult, uproar **7** turmoil **8** madhouse **11** pandemonium

bed of justice
    French: **12** lit de justice

Bedouin, Beduin
    also: **4** Absi, Arab **5** nomad **7** bedawee
    Arabic: **6** badawi
        means: **13** desert dweller
    found in: **5** Egypt, Syria **6** Arabia **11** North Africa
    religion: **5** Islam

bedraggled 4 limp **5** dirty, dowdy,

messy, seedy, soggy, tacky, tatty **6** blowsy, frowsy, frumpy, matted, ragtag, sloppy, soiled, untidy **7** unkempt **8** frumpish, sluttish, tattered **10** disarrayed, disordered, disheveled, slatternly, threadbare **11** disarranged **13** draggletailed **14** down-at-the-heels, out-at-the-elbows

bedridden 7 invalid **8** disabled, immobile **13** incapacitated

bedroom 7 boudoir, chamber **10** bedchamber

bedspread 5 quilt **8** bedcover, coverlet **9** comforter

bedstead 3 bed **8** bed frame **10** four poster

bee
    caste: **5** drone, queen **6** worker
    classification: **6** social **8** solitary
    communication: **13** dance language
    family: **6** Apidae **7** Apoidea **8** Bombidae **10** Andrenidae, Halictidae **11** Meliponidae, Xylocopidae **12** Megachilidae
    group of: **5** grist, swarm
    order: **11** Hymenoptera
    scent: **10** pheromones
    variety: **5** mason, miner **6** alkali, cuckoo **8** burrower, honeybee **9** bumblebee, carpenter, plasterer **10** leaf-cutter **11** yellow-faced

beech 5 Fagus
    varieties: **4** blue **5** water **6** copper, purple **7** cut-leaf, weeping **8** American, European, fern-leaf, Japanese

Beedle, William Franklin, Jr,
    real name of: **13** William Holden

beef 4 heft, kick, meat **5** brawn, gripe, steer **6** cattle, grouch, grouse **7** grumble **8** complain **9** bellyache, complaint, criticize, find fault

Beef State
    nickname of: **8** Nebraska

beefy 5 bulky, burly, hefty **6** brawny, robust **8** thickset **9** strapping

beehive 4 hive **6** apiary **9** busy place **10** powerhouse

Beehive State
    nickname of: **4** Utah

Beekeeping
    god of: **9** Aristaeus

Beelzebub
    character in: **12** Paradise Lost
    author: **6** Milton

be enough 2 do **6** answer **7** suffice

be entitled to 4 rate **5** merit **7** deserve **10** be worthy of **13** be deserving of

beer 3 ale, keg, mum **4** bier, bock, brew, dark, faro, flip, gail, grog, gyle, hops, kvas, malt, mild, quas, scud, suds **5** chang, chica, draft, grout, kvass, lager, light, quass, scuds, stout, weiss **6** bitter, chicha, double, gatter, porter, spruce, stingo, swanky, swipes, wallop, zythum **7** bottled, cer-

veza, pangasi, pharaoh, Pilsner, tankard, taplash, tapwort **8** bock beer, cervisia, near beer, pilsener **9** microbrew **10** malt liquor
    add to beer: **7** krausen
    bad/inferior beer: **4** tack **5** belch **6** swanky **7** taplash
    brand: **3** Bud **5** Beck's, Coors, Pabst, Piels **6** Corona, Miller, Molson, Stroh's **7** Schlitz **8** Bud Light, Michelob **9** Budweiser, Lowenbrau **10** Miller Lite, Molson Gold **11** Samuel Adams **13** Guinness Stout **14** Pete's Wicked Ale **15** Pabst Blue Ribbon
    cask: **4** butt
    cup: **3** mug **4** toby **5** glass, stein **6** flagon, seidel **7** tankard **8** schooner **9** blackjack
    hot beer and gin: **4** purl
    ingredient: **4** hops, malt **5** yeast **6** barley
    maker: **6** brewer **8** brewster, maltster
    mythological inventor: **9** Gambrinus
    quantity of: **3** keg **4** case **7** six-pack
    small beer: **4** tiff **5** grout
    sour beer: **4** kuas, kvas **5** quash, quass **8** beeregar
    thin beer: **6** pritch, swipes
    Tibetan beer: **5** chang
    warm beer and oatmeal: **6** storry
    with whiskey: **11** Boilermaker

beer-bust 4 toot **5** binge, drunk, spree **6** bender **8** carousal **9** bacchanal

Beery, Noah
    brother: **7** Wallace
    son: **6** Noah Jr
    born: **12** Kansas City MO
    roles: **7** Lord Jim, The Dove **9** Beau Geste **10** The Sea Wolf **14** The Mark of Zorro

Beery, Wallace
    brother: **4** Noah
    nephew: **6** Noah Jr
    wife: **13** Gloria Swanson
    born: **12** Kansas City MO
    roles: **8** The Champ (Oscar) **9** The Bowery, Viva Villa **10** Grand Hotel **11** The Big House **13** Dinner at Eight **14** Treasure Island **15** The Mighty Barnum **16** A Message to Garcia

beet 12 Beta vulgaris
    varieties: **3** Red, Sea **4** Leaf, Wild **5** Sugar **6** Garden, Yellow **7** Spinach
    base for: **6** borsch **7** borscht

Beethoven, Ludwig van
    born: **4** Bonn **7** Germany
    composer of: **5** Laube (sonata) **6** Egmont, Eroica (symphony no 3), Spring (sonata) **7** Fidelio, Leonore **8** Coriolan, Dramatic (sonata), Kreutzer (sonata), Pastoral (symphony no 6), The Storm **9** Moonlight (sonata), Pastorale (sonata), Waldstein (sonata) **10** Bagatellen, Great Fugue (no 133), Pathetique (sonata), Spirit Trio **11** Grosse Fugue (no 133), Harp Quartet (no 74), Namensfeier **12** Appassionata (sonata), Archduke Trio,

beetle

Konig Stephan **13** Hammerklavier (sonata), Missa Solemnis **15** Emperor Concerto (No 5) **16** Christus am Olberg, The Mount of Olives, The Ruins of Athens **17** Die Ruinen von Athen, Die Weihe des Hauses **18** An die ferne Geliebte, Rage over a Lost Penny **20** Rasoumoffsky Quartets (no 59) **24** The Creatures of Prometheus **25** Die Geschopfe des Prometheus

beetle
   variety: **3** bog, may, sap **4** bark, bean, flea, leaf, mold, moss, pill, rove, sand, stag **5** cedar, click, flour, grain, marsh, penny, tiger, water **6** beaver, diving, flower, fungus, ground, hister, lizard, scarab, spider, weevil **7** bessbug, blister, burying, carrion, firefly, goldbug, goliath, ladybug, soldier **8** elephant, glowworm, hercules, Japanese, ladybird, tortoise **9** ant loving, bombadier, burrowing, checkered, fruitworm, goldsmith, grassroot, scavenger, tumblebug, whirligig **10** deathwatch, false clown, longhorned, mammal nest, shiptimber **11** reticulated, trout stream **12** antlike stone, lightning bug **13** feather winged, horseshoe crab

Beetle Bailey
   creator/artist: **9** Dik Browne **10** Mort Walker **12** Bob Gustafson
   character: **5** Cosmo, Plato **6** Killer, Lt Flap, Lt Fuzz **10** Miss Buxley **12** Gen Halftrack **17** Sgt Orville Snorkel
      chef: **6** Cookie
   place: **10** Camp Swampy

be evident 6 appear **7** be clear, be plain **8** be patent **9** be obvious **10** be apparent, be manifest

befall 5 ensue, occur **6** betide, chance, follow, happen **10** come to pass **11** materialize

befitting 3 apt, fit **5** right **6** decent, proper, seemly **8** becoming, relevant, suitable **11** appropriate

be fond of 6 dote on **11** be devoted to **12** be in love with

before 3 ere, yet **5** afore, ahead, prior **6** rather, sooner **7** already, earlier, vis-a-vis **8** erewhile, until now **9** in advance, in front of, in sight of **10** face-to-face, previously

before Christ
   abbreviation: **2** BC
   alternative: **3** BCE **15** before Common Era
   Latin: **2** AC **12** ante Christum

beforehand 6 in time, sooner **7** earlier **9** in advance **11** ahead of time

before now 6 in time, sooner **7** earlier **9** in advance

before the fact 6 in time **9** in advance **10** beforehand **11** ahead of time

before the public
   Latin: **11** coram populo

befoul 4 soil **5** dirty, smear, stain, sully, taint **6** defile, poison **7** blacken, corrupt, pollute, tarnish **8** besmirch **9** desecrate **11** contaminate

befriend 4 help **6** assist, defend, succor, uphold **7** comfort, embrace, help out, protect, stand by, stick by, support, sustain, welcome **8** side with **9** give aid to, look after **10** minister to **11** consort with **13** associate with **14** fraternize with, sympathize with **17** take under one's wing

be friends 7 consort **9** associate, pal around **10** fraternize

befringe 3 hem **4** bind, edge, trim **6** border **7** festoon **8** decorate

befuddle 4 daze **5** addle, mix up **6** baffle, muddle, puzzle, rattle **7** confuse, fluster, perplex, stupefy **8** bewilder, confound, unsettle **9** disorient, inebriate, make drunk, make tipsy **10** intoxicate, make groggy **11** disorganize

beg 3 bum, sue **4** pray, shun **5** avert, avoid, cadge, dodge, evade, mooch, parry, plead, shirk **6** escape, eschew, hustle, sponge **7** beseech, entreat, fend off, implore, solicit **8** appeal to, petition, sidestep **9** importune, panhandle **10** supplicate

beg, bey 4 lord **6** prince **8** governor

beget 3 get **4** sire **5** breed, cause, spawn **6** effect, father, lead to **7** produce **8** engender, generate, occasion, result in **9** call forth, procreate, propagate **10** bring about, give rise to

begetter 4 sire **6** father **7** creator **9** generator **10** progenitor

beggar 3 bum, guy **4** chap **5** devil, tramp **6** baffle, fellow **7** almsman, moocher, sponger, surpass **8** be beyond **9** challenge, mendicant **10** panhandler

Beggar 7 Lazarus

Beggar's Opera, The
   author: **7** John Gay
   form: **11** ballad opera
   character: **6** Lockit **10** Lucy Lockit **12** Polly Peachum **15** Captain Macheath

begin 5 arise, found, start **6** be born, crop up, emerge, launch, set out **8** break out, commence, embark on, initiate **9** establish, institute, introduce, originate, undertake **10** burst forth, inaugurate **11** set in motion **16** take the first step

beginner 4 babe, tyro **6** author, father, novice, rookie **7** creator, founder, learner, starter, student **8** freshman, neophyte **9** fledgling, greenhorn, initiator, organizer **10** apprentice, originator, prime mover, tenderfoot **11** inaugurator **14** babe in the woods

beginning 3 new **4** germ, seed **5** birth, onset, start **6** embryo, novice, origin, outset, source, spring **7** kick-off, student, untried **8** neophyte, zero hour **9** embryonic, inception, incipient, launching **10** foundation, wellspring **11** preliminary, springboard **12** commencement, fountainhead, inauguration, introduction **13** inexperienced, starting point
   Latin: **12** terminus a quo

Beginnings
   god of: **5** Janus

begone 3 out **4** away, scat, shoo **5** be off, leave, scram **6** beat it, depart, get out, go away **7** get lost, vamoose

begonia
   varieties: **3** Rex, Wax **4** Fern, King, Star, Wild **5** Hardy, Trout **6** Bamboo, Kidney, Shrimp, Winter, Zigzag **7** Bedding, Dewdrop, Elm-leaf, Eyelash, Fuchsia, Leopard, Lily-pad, Swedish **8** Climbing, Fern-leaf, Fire-king, Lorraine, Palm-leaf, Pond-lily, Star-leaf, Trailing **9** Alder-leaf, Angel-wing, Beefsteak, Calla-lily, Christmas, Crazy-leaf, Grape-leaf, Grapevine, Hollyhock, Holly-leaf, Honey-bear, Iron-cross, Maple-leaf, Miniature, Pennywort, Trout-leaf, Whirlpool **10** Bronze-leaf, Castorbean, Finger-leaf, Guinea-wing, Seersucker, Strawberry **11** Fairy-carpet, Lettuce-leaf, Painted-leaf **12** Blooming-fool, Elephant's Ear, Metallic-leaf **13** Peanut-brittle **14** Hybrid tuberous, Nasturtium-leaf, Youth-and-old-age **15** Winter-flowering **16** Manda's woolly-bear, Philodendron-leaf **17** Miniature pond-lily **18** Trailing watermelon

beg pardon 6 excuse **9** apologize **13** express regret, say one is sorry

be grateful 9 be obliged **10** appreciate, be beholden, be thankful **11** be obligated

begrime 4 soil **5** dirty, muddy, smear, stain, sully **6** smudge, soot up **7** besmear, tarnish

begrimed 5 dirty, grimy, muddy **6** filthy, grubby, soiled **7** unclean **8** unwashed **9** tarnished

begrudge 4 envy **5** covet **6** grudge, resent **11** be jealous of, hold against

beguile 4 dupe, hoax, lull, lure **5** amuse, charm, cheat, cheer, trick **6** delude, divert, occupy, please **7** bewitch, deceive, enchant, ensnare **8** distract, hoodwink **9** bamboozle, captivate, entertain **10** lead astray

beguiling 7 winning, winsome **8** charming, magnetic **9** appealing, disarming **10** bewitching, entrancing **11** captivating **12** ingratiating, irresistible

behalf 3 aid, for **4** part, side **5** favor **7** benefit, by proxy, defense, in aid of, support **8** interest

Behan, Brendan
author of: **10** Borstal Boy, The Hostage **12** The Scarperer **14** The Quare Fellow **25** Confessions of an Irish Rebel

be handed down 4 pass **7** descend **11** be inherited

behave 3 act **13** acquit oneself, deport oneself **14** comport oneself, conduct oneself, control oneself

behavior 4 acts **5** deeds **6** action, habits, manner **7** actions, bearing, conduct, control **8** activity, attitude, demeanor, practice, reaction, response **9** operation **10** deportment **11** comportment, functioning, performance, self-control

behead 9 decollate **10** decapitate, guillotine **15** bring to the block

behest 4 fiat **5** edict, order, say-so **6** charge, decree, ruling **7** bidding, command, dictate, mandate **9** direction, ultimatum **10** injunction **11** instruction

behind 4 rump, seat, slow **5** abaft, after, fanny **8** backward, buttocks, in back of **9** fundament, in arrears **11** to the rear of **12** hindquarters

behind closed doors 7 sub rosa **8** in secret, secretly **9** in private, privately

behindhand 4 late, slow **5** tardy **7** belated **8** backward **10** unpunctual

behind the times 5 passe **7** archaic **9** out-of-date **10** antiquated **12** old-fashioned

behind time 4 late, slow **5** tardy **7** belated, delayed **12** after the fact

behold 3 see **4** heed, look, mark, note, scan, view **5** watch **6** attend, gaze at, look at, notice, regard, survey **7** discern, examine, inspect, observe, stare at, witness **8** look upon **10** scrutinize **11** contemplate **12** pay attention

beholden 5 bound **6** liable **7** obliged **8** indebted **9** obligated **10** answerable, in one's debt **11** accountable, responsible **15** under obligation

behold the man
Latin: **8** ecce homo
said by: **13** Pontius Pilate
spoken of: **7** Christ

behoove 4 suit **5** be apt, befit **6** become, be wise **7** benefit **8** be proper **9** be fitting **11** be advisable, be necessary **13** be appropriate **14** be advantageous

Behring, Emil Adolph von
field: **12** bacteriology
nationality: **6** German
developed: **19** diphtheria antitoxin
awarded: **10** Nobel Prize

beige 3 tan **4** ecru, fawn **6** greige **8** brownish

Beijing
also: **7** Peking
means: **15** northern capital

capital of: **5** China
landmark: **9** Bell Tower, Drum Tower, Ming Tombs **10** Pei-hai Park **12** Palace Museum **13** Forbidden City **14** Hall of Classics, Temple of Heaven **15** Marco Polo Bridge **17** Temple of Confucius **18** Old Legation Quarter **19** Temple of Agriculture **20** Great Hall of the People, Hall of Supreme Harmony **21** Mausoleum of Mao Tse-tung **22** Palace of Heavenly Purity **26** Monument to the People's Heroes **32** Revolutionary and Historical Museum

mountain: **7** Taihang
river: **3** Hai **7** Ch'ao-pai **8** Yungting
square: **9** T'ien-an Men
university: **8** Tsinghua
walled city: **5** Inner, Outer, Tatar

be ill 3 ail **6** be sick **8** be unwell **12** be indisposed **13** be in ill health

be in a class with 5 equal, match **6** be up to **7** compare **8** approach **10** be as good as **11** compete with **12** be comparable, be on a par with **13** hold a candle to **14** bear comparison

being 4 core, life, soul **5** human **6** living, mortal, nature, person, psyche, spirit **7** essence, persona, reality **8** creature, existing **9** actuality, existence **10** individual, occurrence **11** subsistence

Being John Malkovich
director: **10** Spike Jonze
cast: **9** Orson Bean (Dr. Lester) **10** John Cusack (Craig Schwartz), Ned Bellamy (Derek Mantini) **11** Cameron Diaz (Lotte Schwartz) **12** Mary Kay Place (Floris) **13** John Malkovich (John Malkovich) **15** Catherine Keener (Maxine Lund)

be inherited 4 pass **7** descend **12** be handed down

be in short supply 4 lack, want **8** be scanty, be scarce **9** fall short

be intemperate 7 carouse, debauch **9** dissipate **11** overindulge

be in tune 4 jibe **5** agree, match, tally **6** accord, square **7** conform **9** harmonize

Beirut, Beyrouth
capital of: **7** Lebanon
Phoenician name: **7** Berytus
sea: **13** Mediterranean
settled by: **11** Phoenicians
square: **15** Place des Martyrs

be jealous of 4 envy **6** resent **8** begrudge

Bekesy, Georg von
field: **7** physics
researched: **3** ear **7** cochlea, hearing
awarded: **10** Nobel Prize

Bel 3 god **5** deity

belabor 6 rehash, repeat **7** dwell on **9** reiterate **11** pound away at **12** hammer away at, recapitulate **14** beat a dead horse, go on and on about

Bel-Ami
author: **15** Guy de Maupassant

Belarus
other name: **10** Belorussia **11** Byelorussia, White Russia
capital/largest city: **5** Minsk
head of state: **9** president
government: **8** republic
monetary unit: **5** ruble
river: **5** Dvina **7** Dnieper
physical feature: **13** Pripet Marshes
people: **12** Byelorussian
leader: **8** Sidorsky **10** Lukashenko

Belasco, David
author of: **7** DuBarry **15** Madame Butterfly **21** The Return of Peter Grimm **22** The Girl of the Golden West

belated 4 late, slow **5** tardy **6** behind **7** delayed, overdue, past due **8** deferred **10** behindhand, behind time, unpunctual **12** after the fact

belch 4 burp, emit, gush, spew, vent **5** eject, eruct, erupt, expel, issue, spout, spurt, vomit **7** cough up, issuing **8** disgorge, ejection, emission, eruption **9** discharge, roar forth, send forth **10** eructation

Belch, Sir Toby
character in: **12** Twelfth Night
author: **11** Shakespeare

beleaguer 3 vex **5** annoy **6** assail, badger, bother, harass, hector, pester, plague **7** besiege, bombard **8** blockade, surround

bel-esprit 3 wit **12** intellectual

belfry 4 dome **5** spire **7** steeple **9** bell tower, campanile

Belgian Congo see **5** Congo

Belgium
other name: **13** Gallia Belgica **15** Cockpit of Europe **16** Koninkrijk Belgie **17** Royaume de Belgique
capital/largest city: **8** Brussels **9** Bruxelles
others: **2** As **3** Aat, Ans, Ath, Hal, Huy, Mol, Spa **4** Aath, Amay, Asse, Boom, Bree, Doel, Gaud, Geel, Genk, Gent, Hoei, Lier, Looz, Mons, Vise, Waha, Zele **5** Aalst, Alost, Arlon, Ciney, Ecklo, Essen, Eupen, Evere, Genck, Ghent, Heist, Ieper, Jette, Jumet, Liege, Namur, Ronse, Tielt, Uccle, Vorst, Wezet, Ynoir, Ypres **6** Aarlen, Anvers, Bergen, Bilzen, Bruges, Deurne, Izegem, Leuven, Lierre, Merxem, Opwijk, Ostend **7** Antwerp, Ardooie, Berchem, Brabant, Hainaut, Herstal, Hoboken, Ixelles, Leliven, Limburg, Louvain, Malmedy, Mechlin, Roulers, Seraing, Tournai **8** Bastogne, Courtrai, Doorwick, Flanders, Kortrijk, Mouscron, Turnhout, Verviers, Waterloo **9** Antwerpen, Charleroi **10** Anderlecht, Borgerhout, Luxembourg, Quatrebras, Schaerbeek
school: **7** Louvain

division: 5 Liege, Namur **7** Antwerp, Brabant, Hainaut, Limburg **8** Flanders, Wallonia
head of state: 4 king
measure: 3 vat **4** aune, pied **5** carat **6** perche **8** boisseau
monetary unit: 5 belga, franc **7** brabant, centime, crocard
weight: 4 last **5** carat, livre **6** charge **7** chariot **8** esterlin
mountain: 8 Ardennes
highest point: 16 Signal de Botrange
river: 3 Lys **4** Dyle, Leie, Maas, Mark, Yser **5** Boucq, Demer, Lesse, Meuse, Nethe, Rupel, Senne **6** Dender, Escaut, Manjel, Ourthe, Sambre, Semois, Vesdre, Warche **7** Ambleve, Schelde, Scheldt
sea: 5 North
physical feature:
  canal: 4 Yser **5** Union **6** Albert **7** Campine
  cave: 7 Furfooz **8** Grenelle
  forest: 8 Ardennes
  plateau: 8 Hohevenn
people: 4 Remi **6** Nervii **7** Belgian, Fleming, Flemish **8** Walloons **9** Bellovaci
  artist: 5 Ensor **6** Rubens **7** Delvaux, Van Dyke, Van Eyck **8** Brueghal, Magritte
  author: 6 Coster **7** Simenon **9** Verhaeren **10** Conscience, Ghelderode **11** Maeterlinck
  composer: 6 Franck
  king: 6 Albert **7** Leopold **8** Baudouin
  leader: 5 Spaak **9** Tindemans **11** Verhofstadt
language: 5 Dutch **6** French, German **7** Flemish
religion: 13 Roman Catholic
place:
  battleground: 5 Bulge **8** Waterloo
  breadhouse: 9 Broodhuis
  castle: 5 Steen
  cathedral: 5 Ghent **13** Saint Rombauts
  city hall: 12 Hotel de Ville
  home for elderly women: 9 Beguinage
  museum: 9 Beaux Arts
  palace: 10 Gruuthuuse
features:
  horse: 9 Brabancon
  lace: 5 fichu **6** Bruges **7** Malines, Mechlin **8** Brussels
  lawn bowling: 6 boules
  linen: 7 brabant
  musical instrument: 8 carillon
  religious procession: 9 Holy Blood
  tapestry: 9 oudenarde
headquarters of: 2 EU **4** NATO **13** European Union
food:
  cheese: 9 Limburger
  gingerbread: 12 pain d'espices

raisin bread: 8 cramique
soup: 9 Waterzooi
Belgrade, Beograd
capital of: 6 Serbia **10** Yugoslavia
landmark:
  fortress: 10 Kalemegdan
  parliament house: 9 Skupstina
name means: 11 white forest
river: 4 Sava **6** Danube
Roman fort: 10 Singidinum
Serbian: 7 Beograd
Belial
character in: 12 Paradise Lost
author: 6 Milton
belie 4 defy, deny, mask **5** cloak **6** betray, negate, refute **7** conceal, falsify, gainsay **8** disguise, disprove **9** repudiate **10** camouflage, contradict, controvert, invalidate **12** misrepresent
belief 4 view **5** faith, guess, trust **6** theory **7** feeling, opinion **8** judgment, reliance **9** assurance, certitude, deduction, inference **10** assumption, conclusion, confidence, conviction, firm notion, hypothesis, impression, persuasion **11** expectation, presumption, supposition
beliefs 5 canon, creed, dogma, faith, tenet **6** ethics, gospel, morals **8** doctrine, morality **9** principle, teachings **10** conviction, persuasion
believable 8 credible, knowable, possible **9** plausible, thinkable **10** acceptable, convincing, imaginable, supposable **11** conceivable, perceivable
believe 4 hold **5** guess, infer, judge, think, trust **6** assume, credit, deduce, rely on **7** count on, fall for, imagine, presume, suppose, surmise, suspect, swallow, swear by **8** be sure of, consider, depend on, maintain, theorize **9** speculate **10** conjecture, presuppose, put faith in **11** hypothesize
believe in 5 trust **6** accept, esteem **7** approve, go in for, respect **11** have faith in **16** have confidence in
Believe It or Not
author: 13 Robert L Ripley
believer 7 admirer **8** advocate, disciple, partisan **9** supporter **16** faithful adherent
be like 5 equal, match **8** approach, resemble
Bel-Imperia
character in: 17 The Spanish Tragedy
author: 3 Kyd
Belinda
character in: 16 The Rape of the Lock
author: 4 Pope
belittle 5 knock, scorn **6** deride, malign **7** disdain, put down, run down, sneer at **8** minimize, mitigate, play down, pooh-pooh **9** deprecate, disparage, underrate **10** depreciate, undervalue **11** make light of **13** underestimate **16** cast aspersions on

belittling 5 snide **10** derogatory **11** deprecating, disparaging, unfavorable **12** depreciating **15** uncomplimentary
Belize
other name: 15 British Honduras
capital: 8 Belmopan
largest city/former capital: 10 Belize City
head of state: 13 prime minister **14** British monarch **15** governor-general
monetary unit: 6 dollar
island: 8 Turneffe
mountain range: 4 Maya
highest point: 12 Victoria Peak
river: 3 New **4** Moho **6** Belize, Monkey
sea: 9 Caribbean
physical feature:
  gulf: 8 Honduras
  peninsula: 7 Yucatan
  swamp: 8 mangrove
people: 5 Mayan **6** Indian, Syrian **7** African, Chinese **15** Spanish-American
language: 7 English, Spanish
bell 4 gong, peal **5** chime **6** tocsin **7** ringing **8** carillon **16** tintinnabulation
Bell, Alexander Graham
born: 8 Scotland
inventor of: 9 telephone **14** record cylinder
saying: 24 Mr Watson come here I want you
Bellamann, Henry
author of: 8 King's Row
Bellamy, Edward
author of: 8 Equality **15** Looking Backward
Bellamy, Ralph
born: 9 Chicago IL
roles: 11 Ellery Queen, Mike Barnett **13** The Awful Truth **14** Detective Story **15** Man Against Crime, State of the Union **19** Sunrise at Campobello
Bellarius
character in: 9 Cymbeline
author: 11 Shakespeare
Bellaston, Lady
character in: 8 Tom Jones
author: 8 Fielding
bell buoy 5 float **6** signal **13** channel marker
belle 4 star **5** queen **6** beauty **7** charmer **12** heart-stopper
Belle Dame Sans Merci, La
author: 9 John Keats
Bellefleur
author: 15 Joyce Carol Oates
Belle Helene, La
also: 14 Beautiful Helen
operetta by: 9 Offenbach
Bellerophon
form: 4 hero
brother: 8 Deliades
son: 11 Hippolochus
home: 7 Corinth

rode: 7 Pegasus
killed: 7 Chimera

Bell for Adano, A
   author: 10 John Hersey
   director: 9 Henry King
   cast: 10 John Hodiak **11** Gene Tierney **13** William Bendix

bellicose *see* **11** belligerent

belligerence, belligerency 9 animosity, hostility, pugnacity **10** aggression, antagonism **11** bellicosity **12** warmongering **13** combativeness **14** aggressiveness, unfriendliness

belligerent 7 fighter, hostile, martial, warlike, warring **8** attacker, inimical **9** adversary, aggressor, bellicose, combatant, combative, irascible, irritable, truculent **10** aggressive, antagonist, pugnacious, unfriendly **11** bad-tempered, contentious, quarrelsome **12** antagonistic, cantankerous

belligerent state 3 foe **5** enemy **9** aggressor **13** hostile nation

Bellini, Gentile
   born: 5 Italy **6** Venice
   father: 6 Jacopo
   brother: 8 Giovanni
   artwork: 24 The Miracle of the True Cross **26** A Procession in St Mark's Square, The Miracle at Ponte di Lorenzo **27** St Mark Preaching in Alexandria **38** A Procession of Relics in the Piazza San Marco

Bellini, Giovanni (Giambellino)
   born: 5 Italy **6** Venice
   father: 6 Jacopo
   brother: 7 Gentile
   artwork: 8 St Jerome **16** Venus with a Mirror **18** St Francis in Ecstasy, The Madonna and Child **19** Allegory of Purgatory, The Agony in the Garden, The Barberini Madonna

Bellini, Jacopo
   born: 5 Italy **6** Venice
   son: 7 Gentile **8** Giovanni
   artwork: 11 Crucifixion **16** Christ on the Cross **35** The Madonna and Child with Lionello d'Este

Bellini, Vincenzo
   born: 5 Italy **7** Catania
   composer of: 5 Norma, Zaira **8** Il Pirata **9** I Puritani **11** La Straniera **12** La Sonnambula **15** Bianca e Fernando

Bell Jar, The
   author: 11 Sylvia Plath

bellow 4 bawl, roar, yell **5** shout, whoop **6** holler, scream, shriek

Bellow, Saul
   author of: 6 Herzog **11** It All Adds Up **13** Dean's December, Humboldt's Gift, Mosby's Memoirs **15** The Last Analysis **16** Mr Sammler's Planet **18** To Jerusalem and Back **25** The Adventures of Augie March

Bellows, George Wesley
   born: 10 Columbus OH

artwork: 8 Lady Jean **11** Billy Sunday, Edith Cavell, Floating Ice, Up the Hudson **12** Forty-Two Kids **13** Men of the Docks **14** Rain on the River, Stag at Sharkey's **16** The Cliff Dwellers **18** Emma and her Children **21** Both Members of This Club

Bells Are Ringing
   music: 5 Styne
   lyric: 5 Green **6** Comden
   director: 16 Vincente Minnelli
   cast: 9 Fred Clark **10** Dean Martin **12** Judy Holliday
   song: 10 Just in Time **13** The Party's Over

Bells in Winter
   author: 13 Czeslaw Milosz

Bells of St Mary's, The
   director: 10 Leo McCarey
   cast: 10 Bing Crosby (Father O'Malley) **12** Henry Travers **13** Ingrid Bergman
   sequel to: 10 Going My Way
   song: 20 Aren't You Glad You're You

bell tower 5 spire **6** belfry **7** steeple **9** campanile

Belluschi, Pietro
   architect of: 21 Bank of America Building (San Francisco) **22** Juilliard School of Music (NYC) **31** Pan American World Airways Building (NYC, with Gropius)

bellwether 4 lead **5** doyen, guide, pilot **6** leader **8** director, shepherd **9** conductor, guidepost, precursor **10** forerunner, pacesetter **14** standard-bearer

belly 3 abs, gut, yen **4** guts **5** taste, tummy **6** bowels, depths, desire, hunger, liking, paunch, vitals **7** abdomen, insides, midriff, stomach **8** appetite, interior, recesses **11** breadbasket

bellyache 4 beef, kick **5** gripe **6** grouch, grouse, squawk **7** grumble **8** complain **9** tummy ache **11** stomach ache **12** upset stomach

belong 6 go with **7** concern **8** attach to, be held by, be part of **9** be owned by, pertain to **10** be allied to **11** be a member of **12** be included in **15** be connected with, be the property of

belongings 4 gear, junk **5** goods, stuff **6** things **7** effects **8** movables **11** possessions **13** accoutrements, paraphernalia **16** personal property

Beloved
   author: 12 Toni Morrison

beloved 4 beau, dear, love, wife **5** loved, lover **6** adored, fiance, spouse, steady **7** admired, darling, dearest, fiancee, husband, revered **8** endeared, esteemed, loved one, precious **9** betrothed, boyfriend, cherished, respected, treasured **10** girlfriend, sweetheart

below 4 less **5** lower, under **6** in hell **7** beneath, on earth, short of **8** infe-

rior, unworthy **9** at a low ebb, downwards **10** downstairs, downstream, second-rate, underneath **11** at a discount, at the foot of, indifferent, subordinate, underground

below par 3 bad **4** poor **8** inferior **9** imperfect **10** second-rate **12** below average, not up to snuff

below standard 3 bad **4** poor **5** lousy **6** faulty, shoddy **8** below par, inferior, slipshod, terrible **9** imperfect **10** second-rate **12** not up to snuff

belt 4 area, band, land, sash, zone **5** cinch, layer, strip **6** circle, girdle, region, stripe **7** country **8** district, encircle **9** waistband **10** cummerbund

Belushi, James
   born: 7 Chicago
   roles: 8 Curly Sue **9** Mr. Destiny **13** Working Stiffs **14** About Last Night **15** Jumpin' Jack Flash **19** Little Shop of Horrors

Belushi, John
   born: 9 Chicago IL
   roles: 9 Neighbors **11** Animal House **16** The Blues Brothers **17** Saturday Night Live

be manifest 6 appear **7** be clear, be plain **8** be patent **9** be evident, be obvious **10** be apparent

bemoan 3 rue **5** mourn **6** bewail, lament, regret **7** cry over **8** weep over **9** whine over **10** grieve over

bemused 5 dazed, fuzzy **7** muddled, stunned **8** confused **9** engrossed, stupefied **10** bewildered, dull-witted, thoughtful **11** preoccupied **12** absent-minded

be nauseated by 4 hate **5** abhor **6** detest, loathe **7** despise **8** execrate **9** abominate **11** can't stomach **13** be disgusted by, find repulsive, find revolting

Benbow, Horace
   character in: 9 Sanctuary
   author: 8 Faulkner

Ben Casey
   character: 12 Dr David Zorba, Dr Ted Hoffman **13** Nick Kanavaras **14** Dr Maggie Graham
   cast: 8 Sam Jaffe **10** Nick Dennis **12** Harry Landers, Vince Edwards **14** Bettye Ackerman

bench 3 pew **4** banc, seat **5** board, court, stool, table **6** settee **7** counter, take out, trestle **8** sideline, tribunal **9** judiciary, workbench, worktable **10** second team **11** judge's chair, substitutes **12** second string

Benchley, Peter
   author of: 4 Jaws **5** Beast **7** The Deep **12** Shark Trouble

Benchley, Robert
   author of: 14 From Bed to Worse **21** Benchley Beside Himself, My Ten Years in a Quandary

benchmark 4 norm 5 gauge, guide, model 7 example, measure 8 exemplar, paradigm, standard 9 criterion, principle, prototype, reference, yardstick 10 touchstone

bend 3 arc, bow 4 flex, hook, lean, loop, mold, sway, turn, warp, wind 5 crook, curve, defer, force, shape, stoop, twist, yield 6 accede, attend, buckle, coerce, compel, crouch, give in, relent, submit 7 bow down, contort, control, succumb 9 genuflect, influence, surrender 10 buckle down, capitulate 11 make crooked

Bend in the River, The
   author: 9 V S Naipaul

Bendix, William
   born: 9 New York NY
   roles: 8 Hostages, Lifeboat 11 The Hairy Ape 13 A Bell for Adano 14 The Life of Riley 16 Guadalcanal Diary, The Babe Ruth Story

bend to one's own will 4 tame 5 break, train 6 master, subdue 8 overcome 10 discipline 12 show who's boss 18 have under one's thumb

beneath 5 below, lower, under 9 covered by 10 inferior to, underneath, unworthy of 11 subordinate, underground 16 below one's dignity

Benedick
   character in: 19 Much Ado About Nothing
   author: 11 Shakespeare

Benedict 5 groom 8 newlywed

Benedict XVI, Pope
   real name: 15 Joseph Ratzinger

benedictine
   type: 6 brandy, cognac 7 liqueur
   flavor: 4 herb
   with brandy: 5 B and B
   with bourbon: 9 Twin Hills 13 Brighton Punch
   with whiskey: 10 Frisco Sour

benediction 6 prayer 7 benison 8 blessing 10 invocation 12 consecration 13 closing prayer

benefaction 4 alms, gift 5 grant 7 charity 8 bestowal, donation, offering 9 endowment 10 almsgiving 12 contribution, dispensation, philanthropy

benefactor 5 angel, donor 6 backer, friend, helper, patron 7 sponsor 8 upholder 9 supporter 11 contributor 14 fairy godmother

beneficent 6 benign, kindly 7 liberal 8 generous, salutary 10 beneficial, benevolent, charitable 11 magnanimous 13 philanthropic

beneficial 6 useful 7 good for, healing, helpful 8 valuable 9 favorable, healthful 10 productive, profitable, propitious 12 advantageous, contributive

beneficiary 4 heir 7 grantee, heiress, legatee 8 receiver 9 inheritor, recipient

benefit 3 aid, use 4 gain, good, help 5 asset, avail, serve, value, worth 6 assist, behalf, better, profit 7 advance, be aided, service 8 be helped, be served, blessing, interest 9 advantage, do good for 10 be useful to, betterment, profit from 13 charity affair 18 charity performance

Benet, Stephen Vincent
   author of: 7 America 8 Tiger Joy 11 Western Star 14 John Brown's Body, Thirteen O'Clock, Young Adventure 16 Five Men and Pompey 19 Tales Before Midnight, The Headless Horseman 20 The Beginning of Wisdom 24 The Devil and Daniel Webster

benevolence 7 charity 8 good will, kindness 9 benignity 10 compassion, generosity, kindliness, liberality 13 bountifulness 14 charitableness 15 humanitarianism, kindheartedness

benevolent 3 kin 6 benign, humane, tender 7 liberal 8 generous 9 benignant, bounteous, bountiful, unselfish 10 bighearted, charitable 11 considerate, kindhearted, warmhearted 12 humanitarian 13 compassionate, philanthropic

Bengali
   language family: 12 Indo-European
   branch: 11 Indo-Iranian
   group: 5 Indic
   spoken in: 5 (northern) India

Ben-Hur
   author: 10 Lew Wallace
   character: 4 Iras, Isas 5 Jesus 6 Esther 7 Messala 9 Balthasar, Simonides 11 Judah Ben-Hur
   director: 12 William Wyler
   cast: 11 Jack Hawkins, Stephen Boyd 12 Hugh Griffith 14 Charlton Heston (Judah Ben-Hur)
   setting: 9 Palestine
   Oscar for: 5 actor (Heston) 7 picture 8 director 14 cinematography 15 supporting actor (Griffith)

benighted 4 dumb 5 crude, unhip 8 backward, ignorant, untaught 9 primitive, untutored 10 illiterate, uncultured, uneducated, uninformed, unlettered, unschooled 11 empty-headed, know-nothing, uncivilized 12 uncultivated 14 unenlightened

benign 4 good, kind, mild, nice, soft 5 balmy, lucky 6 genial, gentle, humane, kindly, tender 7 affable 8 gracious, harmless, pleasant, salutary 9 favorable, healthful, innocuous, temperate 10 auspicious, benevolent, propitious 11 encouraging, kindhearted, soft-hearted 13 tender-hearted

benignant 4 kind 6 benign, humane, kindly, tender 9 forgiving 10 benevolent 11 kindhearted 13 compassionate, tenderhearted

benignity 8 good will, kindness 10 compassion, kindliness 11 benevolence 15 kindheartedness

Benin
   other name: 17 Republic of Dahomey
   capital: 9 Porto-Novo
   largest city: 7 Cotonou
   others: 4 Pobe 5 Kandi, Kerou, Ketou, Porga 6 Abomey, Ouidah 7 Parakou, Savalou 8 Aplahoue
   government: 30 Military Council of the Revolution
   monetary unit: 5 franc 7 centime
   lake: 5 Aheme 6 Nokoue
   mountain: 7 Atakora
   river: 4 Mono 5 Niger, Oueme 6 Couffo
   sea: 8 Atlantic
   physical feature:
      gulf: 6 Guinea
      plains: 6 Borgou
   people: 3 Fon, Pla 4 Adja, Aizo, Mina, Peul 5 Pedah, Peuhl, Somba 6 Bariba, Fulani, Yoruba 8 Pilapila 9 Dahomeyan
   language: 3 Fon 5 Dendi 6 Bariba, French, Fulani, Yoruba
   religion: 5 Islam 6 tribal 7 animism 13 Roman Catholic
   food:
      tapioca: 4 gari

Bening, Annette
   born: 8 Topeka KS
   husband: 12 Warren Beatty
   roles: 5 Bugsy 7 Valmont 8 In Dreams, The Siege 10 Being Julia, Love Affair, Richard III 11 Mars Attacks!, The Grifters 14 American Beauty, Regarding Henry 20 The American President

Benito Cereno
   author: 14 Herman Melville

Benjamin
   father: 5 Jacob
   mother: 6 Rachel
   also known as: 6 Benoni
   brother: 3 Dan, Gad 4 Levi 5 Asher, Judah 6 Joseph, Reuben, Simeon 7 Zebulun 8 Issachar, Naphtali
   sister: 5 Dinah
   descendant of: 11 Benjaminite

Bennet family
   characters in: 17 Pride and Prejudice
   members: 4 Jane, Mary 5 Kitty, Lydia 9 Elizabeth
   author: 6 Austen

Bennett, Arnold
   author of: 8 Accident 10 Clayhanger, Lord Raingo, Milestones, These Twain 11 Buried Alive 13 Hilda Lessways, Riceyman Steps 15 The Old Wives' Tale 18 Anna of the Five Towns

Benny, Jack
   real name: 16 Benjamin Kubelsky

born: 10 Waukegan IL
roles: 12 Charley's Aunt **13** Jack Benny Show, To Be or Not To Be **16** Artists and Models

Benoni *see* **8** Benjamin

Benson
character: 5 Kraus **12** (Lt Gov) Benson DuBois **13** (Gov) Eugene Gatling
cast: 10 James Noble **11** Inga Swenson **15** Robert Guillaume

bent 4 bias, gift, mind **5** bowed, flair, knack **6** angled, arched, curved, genius, liking, talent **7** ability, aptness, crooked, faculty, hunched, leaning, stooped, twisted **8** aptitude, capacity, facility, fondness, penchant, tendency **9** contorted, endowment **10** attraction, partiality, proclivity, propensity **11** disposition, inclination **12** predilection **14** predisposition

bent into folds 6 fluted, ridged **7** creased, grooved, pleated **8** crinkled, furrowed, puckered, wrinkled **10** corrugated

Benton, Robert
director of: 8 Twilight **13** Billy Bathgate, The Human Stain **14** Kramer vs Kramer (Oscar) **16** Places in the Heart

Benton, Thomas Hart
born: 8 Neosho MO
artwork: 7 Bubbles **8** Boomtown **9** Homestead **12** American Life **13** Arts of the West, Cotton Pickers **14** Threshing Wheat **19** Louisiana Rice Fields, The Lord Is My Shepherd

Benue-Congo
language family: 16 Niger-Kordofanian
group: 10 Niger-Congo
includes: 3 Tiv **4** Zulu **5** Bantu, Jukun **6** Chwana, Nyanja **7** Kikongo, Luganda, Swahili

benumb 4 daze, dull **5** blunt **6** deaden **7** stupefy **15** make insensitive

Benvolio
character in: 14 Romeo and Juliet
author: 11 Shakespeare

Benz, Karl
nationality: 6 German
inventor of: 22 electric ignition engine **26** differential gear automobile
built first practical: 10 automobile

be obvious 6 appear **7** be clear, be plain **8** be patent **9** be evident **10** be apparent, be manifest

be off 2 go **5** leave, scram **6** beat it, begone, cut out, depart, go away, set out **8** set forth, withdraw **10** make tracks

be of one mind 5 agree **6** accord, concur **10** think alike **11** see eye to eye

be of use 3 aid **4** help **5** serve **6** assist **7** benefit

be on a par with 5 equal **6** be up to

7 compare **10** be as good as **12** be comparable **14** be in a class with

be on the sick list 3 ail **5** be ill **6** be sick **8** be unwell **12** be indisposed **13** be in ill health **17** be under the weather

Beor
son: 4 Bela **6** Balaam

Beothuk (Red Indians)
location: 6 Canada **12** Newfoundland
intermixed with: 7 Naskapi

Beowulf
author: 7 unknown
character: 4 Finn **5** Breca, Hnaef, Oslaf, Scyld **6** Wiglaf **7** Beowulf, Guthlaf, Hengest, Higelac, Hrethel, Unferth **8** Aeschere, Heardred, Hondscio, Hrothgar **9** Hildeburh
great hall: 6 Heorot
monster: 7 Grendel **14** Grendel's mother
tribe: 5 Danes, Geats **8** Frisians
Beowulf tears from Grendel: 3 arm

be part of 4 form **6** make up **8** belong to **9** appertain, pertain to **10** constitute

be patent 6 appear **7** be clear, be plain **9** be evident, be obvious **10** be apparent, be manifest

be pertinent to 4 bear **5** apply, refer **6** affect, relate **7** concern, pertain **9** appertain, touch upon

be plain 6 appear **7** be clear **8** be patent **9** be evident, be obvious **10** be apparent, be manifest

be pleased with 4 like **5** favor **7** approve

bequeath 4 will **5** endow, leave **6** impart **7** consign **8** hand down

bequest 6 legacy **8** bestowal **9** endowment **10** settlement **11** inheritance

berate 5 scold **6** rail at, rebuke **7** bawl out, chew out, reprove, upbraid **8** reproach **9** castigate, criticize, reprimand **10** take to task, tongue-lash

Berber
language family: 11 Afro-asiatic **13** Hamito-Semitic
spoken in: 6 Sahara **11** North Africa

bereave 3 rob **5** strip **6** divest **7** deprive **10** dispossess

Berenice's Hair
constellation of: 13 Coma Berenices

be resigned to 6 accept **8** tolerate

Beret
character in: 16 Giants of the Earth
author: 7 Rolvaag

be revolted by 4 hate **5** abhor **6** detest, loathe **7** despise **8** execrate **9** abominate **10** recoil from, shrink from **11** can't stomach **13** find repulsive

berg 4 floe **7** glacier, iceberg, icefloe
South African: 8 mountain
French: 4 neve **5** serac

Berg, Alban

born: 6 Vienna **7** Austria
composer of: 4 Lulu **7** Wozzeck

Bergen, Candace
father: 11 Edgar Bergen
born: 14 Beverly Hills CA
roles: 8 The Group **11** Murphy Brown **15** Carnal Knowledge
husband: 10 Louis Malle

Berger, Thomas
author of: 7 The Feud **9** Neighbors **10** Vital Parts **11** Best Friends, Killing Time **12** Little Big Man, Sneaky People **13** Crazy in Berlin, The Houseguest **14** Reinhart in Love, Reinhart's Women **15** Regiment of Women

Bergman, Ingmar
director of: 14 The Seventh Seal **16** Cries and Whispers, Wild Strawberries **17** Fanny and Alexander **19** Scenes from a Marriage **20** Smiles of a Summer Night

Bergman, Ingrid
born: 6 Sweden **9** Stockholm
children: 12 Pia Lindstrom **18** Isabella Rossellini
roles: 8 Gaslight (Oscar) **9** Anastasia (Oscar), Golda Meir, Joan of Arc, Notorious **10** Casablanca, Intermezzo, Spellbound **17** A Woman Called Golda, The Bells of St Mary's **19** For Whom the Bell Tolls **24** Murder on the Orient Express **25** The Inn of the Sixth Happiness

Berith, Berit, Bris, Brith, Brit 8 covenant **12** circumcision

Berle, Milton
real name: 15 Milton Berlinger
nickname: 11 Uncle Miltie **12** Mr Television
born: 9 New York NY
roles: 17 The Texaco Star Hour **18** Who's Minding the Mint **23** Always Leave Them Laughing

Berlin
landmark: 14 Humboldt Castle **15** Gruenwald Castle **16** Berlin Opera House, Markisches Museum **21** Scharlottenburg Castle **29** Kaiser-Wilhelm-Gedachtniskirche
river: 5 Spree
square: 14 Alexander-Platz

Berlin, Elaine
real name of: 9 Elaine May

Berlinger, Milton
real name of: 11 Milton Berle

Berlioz, (Louis) Hector
born: 6 France **13** La Cote St Andre
composer of: 6 Rob Roy, Te Deum **7** Requiem, **8** Herminie, King Lear, Waverley **9** Cleopatra, Nuits d'Ete **10** Le Corsaire, Les Troyens, The Trojans **11** Sardanapale **13** Harold in Italy **14** Les Francs Juges, Romeo and Juliet **16** Benvenuto Cellini, Damnation of Faust, Le Carnaval Romain, L'Enfance du Christ **18** Beatrice et

Benedict **20** Symphonie Fantastique **28** Symphonie Funebre et Triomphale

Bermuda
  other name: **13** Somers Islands
  capital/largest city: **8** Hamilton
  others: **8** St George
  head of state: **14** British monarch **15** governor general
  island: **4** Boaz **5** Coney **7** Bermuda, Ireland, Watford **8** Somerset, St Davids **9** St Georges
  highest point: **8** Town Hill
  sea: **8** Atlantic
  physical feature:
    harbor: **6** Castle
    hill: **5** Gibbs
  people:
    discoverer: **14** Juan de Bermudez
  language: **7** English
  religion: **8** Anglican **10** Protestant **15** Church of England
  feature:
    dancers: **6** Gombey

Bermuda Triangle
  bounded by: **7** Bermuda, Florida **9** Melbourne **10** Puerto Rico
  site of: **24** mysterious disappearances
  of: **5** ships **9** airplanes

Bern, Berne
  capital of: **11** Switzerland
  landmark: **10** Clock Tower **12** Nydegg Church
  river: **3** Aar **4** Aare

Bernard, Henriette-Rosine
  real name of: **14** Sarah Bernhardt

Bernhardt, Sarah
  real name: **22** Henriette-Rosine Bernard
  nickname: **11** Divine Sarah
  born: **5** Paris **6** France
  roles: **6** Phedre **7** Hernani, Ruy Blas **8** King Lear **14** Queen Elizabeth **17** La Dame aux Camelias

Bernini, Gianlorenzo (Giovanni Lorenzo)
  born: **5** Italy **6** Naples
  father: **6** Pietro
  artwork: **7** Montoya **8** Louis XIV, Vigevano **10** Bellarmine, St Longinus **13** Cathedra Petri, Francis I d'Este, The Assumption **15** Apollo and Daphne **18** Costanza Buonarelli **19** The Rape of Proserpina **21** Saints Andrew and Thomas, The Ecstasy of St Theresa **24** Blessed Lodovica Albertoni **25** Aeneas Anchises and Ascanius
  architect of: **12** Santa Bibiana **16** Piazza of St Peter's (Rome) **19** Palazzo Montecitorio **21** Sant' Andrea al Quirinale **22** Palazzo Chigi-Odescalchi **23** Fountain of the Four Rivers **24** Santa Maria dell' Assunzione

Bernoulli, Daniel
  field: **11** mathematics
  nationality: **5** Swiss
  theory of: **5** gases **6** fluids **18** Bernoulli's Equation

Bernstein, Carl
  author of: **12** The Final Days (with Bob Woodward) **19** All the President's Men (with Bob Woodward)
  newspaper reporter for: **14** Washington Post
  ex: **10** Nora Ephron

Bernstein, Leonard
  born: **10** Lawrence MA
  composer of: **4** Mass **7** Candide, Kaddish **8** Jeremiah **9** Facsimile, Fancy Free, On the Town **13** West Side Story, Wonderful Town **15** The Age of Anxiety, Trouble in Tahiti **16** Chichester Psalms

Beroe
  father: **6** Adonis
  mother: **9** Aphrodite
  nurse of: **6** Semele

Berowne
  character in: **16** Love's Labour's Lost
  author: **11** Shakespeare

Berra, Yogi (Lawrence Peter Berra)
  sport: **8** baseball
  position: **5** coach **7** catcher, manager
  team: **14** New York Yankees
  saying: **18** deja vu all over again **21** it ain't over till it's over **28** it ain't over til the fat lady sings

Berry, Halle
  born: **11** Cleveland OH
  husband: **9** Eric Benet **12** David Justice
  roles: **2** X2 **4** X-Men **5** Queen **7** Gothika **8** Bulworth, Catwoman **9** Swordfish **12** Losing Isaiah, Monster's Ball (Oscar) **13** Die Another Day **14** The Flintstones **24** Their Eyes Were Watching God **27** Introducing Dorothy Dandridge

berry 3 egg **4** seed **5** fruit, grain, grape **6** dollar, kernel, tomato, banana **7** currant **8** allspice, bayberry, mulberry **9** blueberry, cranberry, raspberry **10** blackberry, gooseberry, peppercorn, strawberry **11** boysenberry, huckleberry, pomegranate **12** checkerberry
  poisonous: **9** baneberry

Berryman, John
  author of: **8** Recovery **9** Delusions **11** Love and Fame **12** 77 Dream Songs **13** The Dream Songs **16** Berryman's Sonnets **19** The Freedom of the Poet **21** His Toy His Dream His Rest **26** Homage to Mistress Bradstreet

berserk 4 amok, wild **5** crazy **6** insane **7** frantic, violent **8** demented, deranged, frenzied, maniacal, wild-eyed **9** desperate **10** distracted, distraught **12** out of control

Berserker
  origin: **6** Nordic
  form: **7** warrior

berth 3 bed, job **4** bunk, dock, pier, post, quay, slip, spot **5** haven, niche, place, wharf **6** billet, employ, office **8** position **9** anchorage, situation **11** appointment **12** resting place **13** sleeping place

Berthollet, Claude Louis
  field: **9** chemistry
  nationality: **6** French
  researched: **7** ammonia **8** chlorine

Bertram
  character in: **20** All's Well That Ends Well
  author: **11** Shakespeare

Bertram family
  characters in: **13** Mansfield Park
  members: **3** Tom **5** Julia, Maria **6** Edmund **9** Sir Thomas
  author: **6** Austen

beryl
  color: **5** green **6** yellow

Berzelius, Jons Jakob
  field: **9** chemistry
  nationality: **7** Swedish
  developed: **15** chemical symbols
  discovered: **6** cerium **7** silicon, thorium **8** selenium, titanium **9** zirconium
  founded: **15** modern chemistry

be satisfactory 2 do **6** answer **7** suffice **8** be enough **10** be adequate, pass muster **12** be sufficient, do well enough

be scant 4 lack, want **8** be skimpy **9** fall short **14** be insufficient **15** be in short supply

beseech 3 beg **4** pray **6** adjure **7** entreat, implore **9** plead with **10** supplicate

beset 3 dog, set **4** bead, deck, stud **5** annoy, array, hem in, hound, worry **6** assail, badger, harass, pester, plague **7** bedevil, besiege, set upon **8** surround **9** beleaguer, embellish

be sick 3 ail **5** be ill **8** be unwell **12** be indisposed **13** be in ill health

beside 2 by **4** near **5** saved **6** except, nearby, unless **7** abreast, barring, without **8** let alone **9** adjoining, alongside, aside from, other than **10** on a par with, side by side **12** compared with, in addition to

beside oneself 4 wild **5** elated, joyful, joyous, raging **7** berserk, exalted, frantic, furious, ranting **8** agitated, blissful, distrait, ecstatic, frenetic, frenzied **9** delirious, in a frenzy, overjoyed, rapturous **10** distracted, distraught, distressed, enraptured **11** carried away, overwrought, transported **13** out of one's wits

besides 3 but **4** also, save **6** as well, except, saving **7** barring **8** moreover **9** excepting, excluding, other than **11** exclusive of, furthermore

besiege 3 dog **5** annoy, beset, hound **6** assail, badger, harass, pester, plague

7 assault, bedevil **9** beleaguer **10** lay siege to

besmear 4 soil **5** dirty, muddy, smear, stain, sully **6** mess up, slop up, smudge **7** begrime, tarnish **8** besmirch

besmeared 5 dirty, grimy, messy **6** grubby, smudgy **7** muddied, sullied **8** begrimed **10** besmirched

besmirch 4 soil **5** smear, stain, sully, taint **6** defame, defile **7** blacken, corrupt, debauch, degrade, slander, tarnish **8** discolor, disgrace, dishonor **9** discredit

besotted 5 drunk **6** sodden, soused, wasted, zapped, zonked **7** smashed **9** plastered **10** inebriated, infatuated **11** intoxicated **17** under the influence **20** three sheets to the wind

bespangle 3 dot **4** gild, star, stud **5** adorn, jewel **6** bedeck **7** dress up, festoon, garnish **8** decorate, ornament **9** embellish **10** illuminate

bespatter 4 blot, soil, spot **5** decry, dirty, libel, smear, stain, sully, taint **6** debase, defame, defile, smudge, splash **7** condemn, slander, smotter, tarnish **8** denounce, reproach **9** deprecate, fling dirt **10** calumniate, disapprove

Bessemer, Sir Henry
  nationality: 7 English
  inventor of manufacturing process for: 5 steel

best 3 top **4** most, pick **5** cream, elite **6** choice, finest, nicest, utmost **7** hardest, largest **8** foremost, greatest, superior, topnotch **9** greetings, loveliest, most fully, most of all, unequaled, unrivaled **10** unexcelled **11** compliments, unsurpassed **13** most competent, most desirable, most excellent **14** highest quality, kindest regards

Best, Charles Herbert
  field: 10 physiology
  nationality: 8 Canadian
  discovered: 7 insulin

best group 3 top **5** cream, elite **6** choice **9** chosen few **10** select body **14** cream of the crop, creme de la creme

bestial 5 cruel **6** brutal, savage **7** beastly **8** barbaric, depraved, inhumane, ruthless **9** barbarous, merciless

bestir 4 goad, spur, stir, urge **5** rouse, speed **6** arouse, excite, hasten **7** quicken **8** activate **9** get moving

bestir oneself 5 rouse **8** be active **9** make haste **10** get up early, lose no time **11** keep moving **15** make short work of **19** seize the opportunity

bestow 3 use **4** give, mete **5** apply, award, grant, lay on, spend **6** accord, confer, devote, donate, employ, expend, impart, occupy, render **7** consign, consume, deal out, deliver, hand out, present, utilize **8** dispense, give

away **9** apportion **10** settle upon, turn over to

bestowal 4 alms, gift **5** bonus, favor, grant **6** reward **7** charity, present, tribute **8** donation, gratuity, offering **9** endowment **10** conferment, recompense **11** benefaction **12** contribution, dispensation

best society
  French: 10 grand monde

Best Years of Our Lives, The
  director: 12 William Wyler
  based on story by: 15 MacKinlay Kantor
  script: 14 Robert Sherwood
  cast: 8 Myrna Loy **11** Dana Andrews **12** Teresa Wright, Virginia Mayo **13** Frederic March, Harold Russell **15** Hoagy Carmichael
  Oscar for: 5 actor (March) **7** picture **8** director

be sufficient 6 answer **7** suffice **8** be enough **10** be adequate, pass muster **12** do well enough **14** be satisfactory

bet 4 ante, risk **5** stake, wager **6** chance, gamble, hazard, plunge **7** venture **8** make a bet **9** speculate **11** speculation

bete noir 5 bogey **6** plague **7** bugaboo, bugbear **8** anathema, bogeyman **9** annoyance **10** black beast

be thankful 8 thank God **10** appreciate **11** thank heaven **19** thank one's lucky stars

Bethe, Hans Albrecht
  field: 7 physics
  developed: 8 atom bomb
  awarded: 10 Nobel Prize

be the same 5 agree, equal, match **6** equate **7** balance **11** be identical

betide 4 fall **5** occur **6** befall, chance, happen **10** come to pass

betimes 5 early **10** in good time

betoken 4 show **5** augur **6** attest, denote **7** portend, presage, signify **8** foretell

betray 4 dupe, fink, jilt, show, tell **5** rat on, trick **6** expose, reveal, squeal, tell on, unmask **7** abandon, deceive, divulge, lay bare, let down, let slip, sell out, two-time, uncover, violate **8** blurt out, disclose, give away **9** play Judas **10** be disloyal **11** double-cross **12** be unfaithful **13** inform against, play false with **14** break faith with

betrayal 7 perfidy, telling, treason **8** bad faith, sedition, trickery **9** chicanery, deception, duplicity, falseness, treachery, two-timing, violation **10** disclosure, disloyalty, divulgence, revelation **11** double-cross **13** breach of faith, double-dealing **14** unfaithfulness

betrayal of trust 7 falsity, perfidy **8** apostasy, cheating **9** falseness, recreancy **10** disloyalty, infidelity **11** inconstancy **13** deceitfulness, double-

dealing, faithlessness **14** unfaithfulness

Betrayer 13 Judas Iscariot

betroth 6 commit, engage, pledge **7** espouse, promise **8** affiance, contract

betrothal 5 troth **8** espousal **10** affiancing, betrothing, engagement

betrothed 6 fiance **7** engaged, fiancee **8** promised **9** affianced

Bettelheim, Bruno
  author of: 15 Love Is Not Enough **16** The Informed Heart **20** The Uses of Enchantment

better 3 top **4** more **5** finer, outdo, raise **6** bigger, enrich, exceed, fitter, larger, longer, refine, uplift **7** advance, elevate, enhance, farther, forward, further, greater, improve, mending, promote, surpass, upgrade **8** heighten, improved, increase, outstrip, stronger, superior **9** cultivate, healthier, improving **10** preferable, recovering, strengthen **11** more healthy, progressing

bettering 9 elevation **10** betterment **11** advancement, improvement

betterment 4 good **6** reform **7** benefit **8** revision **9** advantage, amendment, promotion **10** correction, enrichment **11** advancement, improvement **12** amelioration, regeneration **13** rectification **14** reconstruction

better than average 2 A-1 **3** A-OK **4** aces, a-one, fine, good, tops **5** great, prime, super **6** choice, grade-A, superb **7** capital, special **8** peerless, sterling, superior, terrific, top-notch **9** excellent, first-rate, marvelous, matchless, wonderful **10** first-class, inimitable, preeminent, remarkable, tremendous **11** exceptional, outstanding, superlative **12** incomparable **13** extraordinary

between 4 amid **5** among, entre **6** amidst, atwixt, shared **7** betwixt, joining **9** in the midst **10** connecting

between ourselves
  French: 9 entre nous
  Latin: 8 inter nos

between themselves
  Latin: 7 inter se

between us 9 entre nous, privately **14** confidentially **15** between you and me **16** between me and thee, between ourselves

betwixt and between 4 so-so **7** average **8** confused **9** in between, undecided **14** halfway between **21** neither one nor the other

Beulah, Land of
  place in: 16 Pilgrim's Progress
  author: 6 Bunyan

be unlike 4 vary **6** differ **7** deviate, diverge **8** conflict, disagree **12** be at variance, be discordant, be dissimilar

be unwell 3 ail **5** be ill **6** be sick **12** be indisposed **13** be in ill health

be unwilling to pursue
Latin: **13** nolle prosequi

bevel 4 blow, cant, ream, tool **5** angle, bezel, miter, mitre, slant, slope, snape, splay **6** aslant **7** incline, oblique **8** slanting

beverage 3 ade, ale, cup, nog, pop, tea **4** beer, brew, cafe, dram, grog, milk, soda, soup, wine **5** broth, caffe, cider, cocoa, draft, drink, juice, julep, lager, latte, leban, punch, toddy, water **6** bishop, coffee, cordial, eggnog, liquid, liquor, potion **7** limeade, seltzer, spirits, wassail **8** aperitif, cocktail, espresso, expresso, highball, lemonade, libation, potation **9** champagne, chocolate, orangeade **10** cappuccino

Beverley, Constance de
character in: **7** Marmion
author: **5** Scott

Beverly Hillbillies, The
character: **11** Jed Clampett **12** Jane Hathaway, Jethro Bodine **14** Granny Clampett, Milton Drysdale **16** Ellie May Clampett
cast: **9** Irene Ryan, Max Baer Jr, Nancy Kulp **10** Buddy Ebsen **12** Donna Douglas **13** Raymond Bailey

Beverly Hills Cop
director: **11** Martin Brest
cast: **11** Eddie Murphy **13** Judge Reinhold, Lisa Eilbacher

bevy 4 band, body, herd, host, pack **5** brood, covey, crowd, drove, flock, group, horde, party, shoal, swarm **6** clutch, flight, gaggle, school, throng **7** company, coterie **9** gathering, multitude **10** assemblage, collection

bewail 3 rue **5** mourn **6** bemoan, lament, regret **7** cry over, deplore **8** moan over, weep over **10** grieve over

beware 4 mind **6** be wary **7** look out **8** take care, take heed **9** be careful **11** take warning, watch out for **12** be on the alert, guard against **15** take precautions

beware of the dog
Latin: **9** cave canem

bewhiskered 5 bushy, hairy **6** shaggy **7** bearded, bristly, hirsute **8** unshaven **11** mustachioed

bewilder 5 addle, mix up **6** baffle, bemuse, muddle, puzzle **7** confuse, fluster, mystify, nonplus, perplex, stupefy **8** befuddle **10** disconcert

bewildered 7 at a loss, up a tree **8** all at sea, confused **9** perplexed **10** confounded, nonplussed **12** disconcerted

bewilderment 9 confusion **10** perplexity, puzzlement **11** frustration **13** mystification

bewitch 4 jinx **5** charm, spook **6** turn on **7** bedevil, beguile, delight, enchant **8** entrance **9** captivate, enrapture, fascinate **12** cast a spell on **14** put under a spell

bewitched 7 charmed, seduced **8** beguiled **9** bedeviled, enchanted, entranced **10** captivated, enraptured, fascinated, spellbound **11** under a spell

Bewitched
character: **6** Endora, Serena **7** Maurice **9** Aunt Clara, Esmerelda, Larry Tate **11** Uncle Arthur **12** Abner Kravitz **13** Gladys Kravitz **14** Darrin Stephens **15** Tabitha Stephens **16** Samantha Stephens
cast: **8** Dick York **9** Paul Lynde **10** David White **11** Dick Sargent, Marion Lorne, Sandra Gould **12** George Tobias, Maurice Evans **13** Alice Ghostley **14** Agnes Moorehead **19** Elizabeth Montgomery
film director: **10** Nora Ephron
film cast: **11** Will Ferrell (Jack Wyatt/Darren) **12** Michael Caine (Nigel Bigelow), Nicole Kidman (Isabel Bigelow/Samantha) **15** Shirley MacLaine (Iris Symthsm/Endora)

bewitching 8 alluring, charming, enticing, fetching, tempting **9** appealing, beguiling, disarming, seductive **10** enchanting, entrancing **11** captivating, fascinating **12** irresistible

be worthy of 4 earn, rate **5** merit **7** deserve

bey, beg 4 lord **6** prince **8** governor

beyond 2 by **4** over, past **5** above, later, ultra **6** abroad, except, yonder **7** beneath, besides, farther, further, outside, passing **8** superior **9** exceeding, hereafter **10** out of range, out of reach **11** at a distance, in addition to

Beyond Desire
author: **15** Maxwell Anderson

beyond hope 8 hopeless **9** desperate **10** despairing

Beyond Human Power
author: **20** Bjornstjerne Bjornson

beyond one's means 10 immoderate **11** extravagant **15** too high on the hog

beyond question 4 sure **6** surely **7** certain, decided, settled **9** certainly, decidedly **10** absolutely, positively **12** without doubt

Bharat (Varsha) see **5** India

Bhot see **5** Tibet

Bhutan
other name: **7** Druk-Yul **15** Kingdom of Bhutan, Land of the Dragon
capital/largest city: **6** Thimbu **7** Thimphu
others: **4** Paro **12** Phuntsholing **14** Wangdu Phedrang
government:
assembly: **7** Tsongdu
head of state/ government:
hereditary king: **10** dragon king, druk gyalpo

other leader:
spiritual leader: **10** dharma raja
temporal ruler: **7** deb raja
monetary unit: **5** paisa, rupee **8** chetrums, ngultrum
mountain: **5** Black **9** Himalayas **10** Chomo Lhari
highest point: **10** Kula Kangri
river: **4** Kuru, Paro **5** Machu, Manas, Pachu, Torsa **6** Amochu, Raidak, Tongsa **7** Sankosh, Thinchu
physical feature:
plain: **5** Duars
people: **5** Monpa **6** Bhutia **7** Tibetan **8** Assamese, Nepalese
dragon people: **7** Drukpas
leader: **5** Zimba **9** Wangchuck
language: **5** Hindi, Lhoke **7** Tibetan **8** Dzongkha, Nepalese
religion: **15** Tibetan Buddhism
place:
fortress (dzong): **4** Paro **6** Bya Kar, Tongsa **8** Tashi Cho
feature:
pony: **6** Tangun

Bianca
character in: **10** Kiss Me Kate **19** The Taming of the Shrew
author: **11** Shakespeare

Bianchi, Mose
born: **5** Italy, Milan
artwork: **11** Snow in Milan **21** Return from the Festival

bias 4 bent, sway **5** angle, slant **7** bigotry, feeling, leaning **8** tendency **9** fixed idea, prejudice, proneness **10** narrow view, partiality, predispose, proclivity, propensity, unfairness **11** inclination, intolerance **12** diagonal line, one-sidedness, predilection **13** preconception **16** narrow-mindedness, preconceived idea

biased 6 unfair, unjust **7** bigoted, slanted **8** inclined **9** arbitrary **10** intolerant, prejudiced **11** close-minded, opinionated **12** narrow-minded

bibelot 5 curio **7** trinket **8** ornament **9** objet d'art

bible 5 guide **6** manual **8** handbook **9** authority, guidebook **13** reference book

Bible 6 Gospel **7** the Book **8** good book, Holy Writ **9** Scriptures **11** bibliotheca, the Good Book **13** holy scripture **14** Holy Scriptures, sacred writings

Bible, books of
Old Testament: **3** Job **4** Amos, Ezra, Joel, Osee, Ruth **5** Hosea, Jonah, Jonas, Josue, Kings, Micah, Nahum, Tobit **6** Abdias, Aggeus, Baruch, Daniel, Esdras, Esther, Exodus, Haggai, Isaiah, Isaias, Joshua, Judges, Judith, Psalms, Samuel, Sirach, Tobias, Wisdom **7** Ezekiel, Genesis, Habacuc, Malachi, Micheas, Numbers, Obadiah **8** Ezechiel, Habakkuk, Jere-

miah, Jeremias, Nehemiah, Proverbs **9** Leviticus, Maccabees, Machabees, Malachias, Sophonias, Zacharias, Zechariah, Zephaniah **10** Chronicles **11** Deuteronomy, Song of Songs **12** Ecclesiastes, Lamentations **13** Paralipomenon, Song of Solomon **14** Ecclesiasticus **19** Canticle of Canticles

New Testament: 4 Acts, John, Jude, Luke, Mark **5** James, Peter **6** Romans **7** Hebrews, Matthew, Timothy **9** Ephesians, Galatians **10** Colossians, Revelation **11** Corinthians, Philippians **13** Thessalonians, Titus Philemon

first five books called: 3 Law **5** Torah **10** Pentateuch

first seven books called: 10 Heptateuch

Bible scholar 7 biblist **9** biblicist

Bible version 5 Douay **6** The Way **7** Vulgate **8** Peshitta **9** Gutenberg, Jerusalem, King James **10** Authorized, New English **11** New American, Rheims-Douay **14** The Living Bible **15** American revised, revised standard

Biblical animal 7 unicorn

Biblical gemstone 6 ligure **7** sardius **8** sardonyx

Biblical instrument 7 sackbut

Biblical length
   reed: 9 six cubits

Biblical measure 3 cab, cor **4** epah, omet, reed, seah **5** cubit, epheh, homer **6** shekel **9** half homer

Biblical personage 9 patriarch

Biblical plant 6 hyssop **12** Rose of Sharon

Biblical precept
   Hebrew: 7 mitsvah, mitzvah

Biblical tree 5 algum, almug **6** storax **7** juniper **8** sycamire **10** gopherwood **11** shittim wood **12** opobalsammum **13** red sandalwood

Biblical weed 4 tare **6** darnel

Biblical weight 6 talent

Biblicist 12 Bible scholar

Bibliotheca 5 Bible **14** sacred writings

Biblist 12 Bible scholar

Bickel, Ernest Frederick McIntyre
   real name of: 13 Frederic March

bicker 4 spar, spat **5** argue, fight **6** haggle **7** dispute, quarrel, wrangle **8** disagree, squabble

bickering 4 spat **5** fight **7** arguing, dispute, quarrel **8** argument, fighting **9** wrangling **10** quarreling, squabbling **12** disagreement

Bickford, Charles
   born: 11 Cambridge MA
   roles: 12 Anna Christie **13** Johnny Belinda **16** Song of Bernadette **18** The Farmer's Daughter

bicycle 4 bike, ride **5** cycle, moped **10** two-wheeler
   invented by: 7 Starley

Bicycle Thief, The
   director: 14 Vittorio De Sica
   cast: 14 Lianella Carell **18** Lamberto Maggiorani

bid 3 ask, say, try **4** call, tell, wish **5** greet, offer, order **6** beckon, charge, demand, direct, effort, enjoin, insist, invite, ordain, summon, tender **7** attempt, command, proffer, propose, request, require **8** call upon, endeavor, instruct, offering, proposal **10** invitation

bidding 4 beck, call **5** offer, order **6** behest, charge, demand, offers **7** command, dictate, mandate, request, summons **8** offering, proposal **9** direction, summoning, tendering **10** injunction, invitation, proffering **11** instruction

bide 4 stay, wait **5** abide, dwell, stand, tarry **6** endure, linger, remain, suffer **8** tolerate **9** put up with

Bierce, Ambrose
   author of: 15 Can Such Things Be? **16** In the Midst of Life **19** The Devil's Dictionary

Bierstadt, Albert
   born: 7 Germany **8** Solingen
   artwork: 11 Laramie Park **13** Mount Corcoran **17** The Rocky Mountains **20** Discovery of the Hudson, Storm on the Matterhorn **21** Sunrise Yosemite Valley **22** Settlement of California **31** Thunderstorm in the Rocky Mountains

bifocal lenses
   invented by: 8 Franklin

Bifrost
   origin: 12 Scandinavian
   form: 6 bridge
   bridge of: 4 gods
   made of: 7 rainbow
      from: 6 Asgard
      to: 5 earth

bifurcate 4 fork **5** split **6** branch, divide **7** diverge **8** separate

big 3 top **4** head, high, huge, just, kind, main, vast **5** adult, ample, bulky, chief, great, grown, heavy, husky, large, major, noble, prime, vital **6** heroic, humane, mature **7** eminent, grown-up, haughty, hulking, immense, leading, liberal, mammoth, massive, notable, pompous, sizable, weighty **8** abundant, arrogant, boastful, bragging, colossal, enormous, generous, gigantic, gracious, princely **9** conceited, grandiose, honorable, important, momentous, prominent, strapping **10** benevolent, chivalrous, high-minded, monumental, prodigious **11** magnanimous, pretentious, significant, substantial **12** considerable **13** consequential

Big Apple
   nickname of: 11 New York City

Big Bend State
   nickname of: 9 Tennessee

Big Brother
   network: 3 CBS
   host: 9 Julie Chen
   winner: 7 Jun Song **9** Will Kirby **10** Drew Daniel, Eddie McGee **11** Lisa Donahue

Big Chill, The
   director: 14 Lawrence Kasdan
   cast: 8 Meg Tilly **10** Glenn Close, Kevin Kline **11** Tom Beringer, William Hurt **12** Jeff Goldblum

Big Daddy
   character in: 16 Cat on a Hot Tin Roof
   author: 8 Williams
   played by: 8 Burl Ives

Big E
   nickname of: 10 Elvin Hayes

Bigfoot 4 Yeti **9** Sasquatch **17** Abominable Snowman

big guns 4 VIPs **5** brass **6** cannon **7** bigwigs, top dogs **8** big shots, ordnance **9** artillery **14** heavy artillery, high muck-a-mucks **15** important people

bighearted 6 lavish **7** liberal **8** generous, handsome, princely, prodigal **9** bounteous, bountiful, unselfish **10** beneficent, benevolent, charitable, freehanded, open-handed, unstinting **11** magnanimous, open-hearted **12** humanitarian

bight 3 bay **4** bend, cave, road

Biglow Papers
   author: 18 James Russell Lowell

Big Money, The
   author: 13 John Dos Passos

bigness 4 bulk **8** enormity, hugeness **9** amplitude, great size, greatness, largeness, magnitude **11** massiveness

Big O, The
   nickname of: 14 Oscar Robertson

bigoted 6 biased **10** intolerant, prejudiced **12** closed-minded, narrow-minded

bigotry 4 bias **6** racism **9** prejudice **10** unfairness **11** intolerance **14** discrimination **16** closed-mindedness, narrow-mindedness

Big Parade, The
   director: 9 King Vidor
   cast: 11 John Gilbert, Renee Adoree **14** Hobart Bosworth

big shot 3 VIP **4** name **5** mogul, nabob, wheel **6** big gun, bigwig, fat cat, tycoon **7** big deal, magnate, notable **8** somebody **9** big cheese, dignitary, personage **13** high muck-a-muck, wheeler-dealer

Big Six
   nickname of: 16 Christy Mathewson

Big Sky, The
   author: 11 A B Guthrie Jr

Big Sky State
   nickname of: 7 Montana

Big Sleep, The
author: **15** Raymond Chandler
hero: **13** Philip Marlowe
director: **11** Howard Hawks
cast: **12** Elisha Cook Jr, Lauren Bacall **13** Dorothy Malone, Martha Vickers **14** Humphrey Bogart (Philip Marlowe)
setting: **10** Los Angeles

Big Train
nickname of: **13** Walter Johnson

Big Unit
nickname of: **12** Randy Johnson

Big Valley, The
character: **11** Nick Barkley **12** Audra Barkley, Heath Barkley **13** Jarrod Barkley **15** Victoria Barkley
cast: **9** Lee Majors **10** Linda Evans, Peter Breck **11** Richard Long **15** Barbara Stanwyck

bigwig 3 VIP **7** big shot, notable **9** dignitary, personage

bikini 8 two-piece **11** bathing suit
top: **3** bra
bottom **5** thong
topless: **8** monokini
type: **6** string

Bikini 5 atoll **9** Namu islet **10** West Pacific **15** Marshall Islands

bile 4 gall, rage **5** anger, venom, wrath **6** choler, spleen

bilge 3 rot **4** bosh, bull, bunk, tosh **5** hooey, tripe **6** drivel, humbug, jabber, piffle **7** baloney, hogwash, rubbish, twaddle **8** malarkey, nonsense **9** gibberish **10** balderdash **11** foolishness, jabberwocky **13** horsefeathers **16** stuff and nonsense

bilious 4 sick **5** angry, cross, huffy, nasty, testy **6** crabby, cranky, grumpy, queasy, sickly, touchy **7** grouchy, peevish **8** bile-like, greenish, nauseous, petulant, snappish **9** irritable, sickening **10** ill-humored, out of sorts **11** ill-tempered **12** cantankerous **13** short-tempered **15** green at the gills

bilk 3 gyp **4** dupe, gull, rook, take **5** cheat, cozen, trick **6** fleece, rip off **7** deceive, defraud, swindle **8** hoodwink **9** bamboozle, victimize

bill 3 act, fee, law **4** card, chit, list **5** tally **6** agenda, charge, decree, docket, poster, roster, ticket **7** account, catalog, charges, invoice, leaflet, measure, placard, program, statute **8** banknote, brochure, bulletin, calendar, circular, handbill, proposal, register, schedule **9** greenback, inventory, ordinance, reckoning, statement **10** regulation **12** treasury note **13** advertisement **17** silver certificate

billet 3 job **4** base, bunk, camp, digs, note, post **5** berth, house, lodge, place, put up **6** letter, office **7** bed down, lodging, quarter, shelter **8** domicile, dwelling, lodgment, position, quarters **9** residence, situation **11** accommodate, appointment **13** accommodation

billfold see **6** wallet

billiards
player: **11** Willie Hoppe **13** Minnesota Fats, Willie Mosconi

Bill of Divorcement, A
director: **11** George Cukor
cast: **11** Billie Burke **13** John Barrymore **16** Katharine Hepburn

billow 4 roll, wave **5** belly, cloud, crest, surge, swell **6** puff up **7** balloon, breaker

Billy Budd
author: **14** Herman Melville
character: **8** Claggart **11** Captain Vere
opera by: **7** Britten

billyclub 3 bat **5** billy, stick **8** bludgeon **9** truncheon

bin 3 box **4** cart, crib, silo **5** crate, frame, hatch **6** barrel, basket, bunker, hamper, holder, trough, vessel **9** container, inclosure **10** receptacle

binate 4 dual **6** double **7** coupled, two fold **14** growing in pairs

bind 3 rim, tie **4** edge, gird, glue, join, lash, rope, trim, wrap **5** affix, chafe, cover, cramp, force, frame, hitch, paste, stick, strap, tie up, truss **6** attach, border, coerce, compel, encase, fasten, fringe, oblige, secure, swathe **7** bandage, confine, require **8** encumber, obligate **9** prescribe **11** necessitate

binder 4 glue, roux **5** paste **6** cement **8** notebook **9** assurance, guarantee **11** down payment **12** earnest money **17** looseleaf notebook

binding 4 band, face, tape **5** valid **6** edging, ribbon **7** styptic **8** fastener, ligative **9** stringent **10** compulsory, obligatory, peremptory **12** constricting

binge 3 jag **4** bust, orgy, tear, toot **5** blast, drunk, fling, revel, spree **6** bender **7** carouse **8** beer-bust, carousal **11** bacchanalia **12** drunken spree

Bingham, George Caleb
born: **15** Augusta County VA
artwork: **13** Stump Speaking **17** The Trapper's Return **18** Verdict of the People **19** The Jolly Flatboatman **20** Raftsmen Playing Cards **31** Fur Traders Descending the Missouri

Bingley, Mr
character in: **17** Pride and Prejudice
author: **6** Austen

biochemist 17 biological chemist
American: **4** Cori **5** Bloch, Moore, Ochoa **7** Axelrod, Lipmann **8** Kornberg
English: **5** Krebs **6** Porter, Sanger **8** Mitchell
French: **5** Monod **7** Duclaux
German: **5** Lynen

biogenesis
discoverer: **12** Louis Pasteur

biography 3 bio **4** life, vita **6** memoir **7** account, history **9** life story

biologist
American: **6** Carson, Yerkes **7** Burbank **8** Delbruck
British: **6** Darwin, Huxley **7** Bateson, Medawar
French: **5** Jacob, Monod **7** Lamarck
German: **7** Schwann
Swiss: **6** Haller

biology
branch: **6** botany **7** zoology
classification: **15** Carolus Linnaeus

birch 6 Betula
varieties: **3** Low, Red **4** Fire, Gray **5** Black, Canoe, Dwarf, Paper, River, Swamp, Sweet, Water, White **6** Cherry, Yellow **7** Monarch **8** Mahogany, Old-field **10** West Indian **13** European white, Japanese white, Young's weeping **14** Japanese cherry

Birches
author: **11** Robert Frost

bird
anatomy: **3** bec, neb, nib **4** beak, bill, cere, crop, lora, lore, mala, nape, rump, tail, tuft, wing **5** alula, crest, crown, flank, larum, lorum, pilea, rosta **6** breast, gullet, pecten, pileum, pinion, syrinx, tarsus **7** ambiens, crissum, gizzard, rostrum **8** gigerium, pectines, scapular **9** auchenium, gastraeum **10** cordylanus
aquatic/water: **3** auk, cob, ern, mew **4** cobb, coot, duck, erne, gony, gull, ibis, loon, rail, shag, skua, sora, swan, teal, tern **5** booby, cahow, crane, diver, goose, grebe, heron, murre, ousel, rotch, snipe, solan, stilt, stork **6** avocet, curlew, cygnet, dipper, fulmar, gannet, godwit, hagdon, jabiru, jacana, osprey, petrel, plover, puffin, rotche, scoter, wigeon **7** anhinga, bidcock, bittern, bustard, dovekey, dovekie, finfoot, mallard, moorhen, pelican, penguin, seriema, skimmer, widgeon **8** alcatras, baldpate, dabchick, flamingo, murrelet, umbrette **9** albatross, baptornis, cormorant, gallinule, guillemot, kittiwake, phalarope, snakebird, spoonbill **10** gaviformes, kingfisher, shearwater, sheathbill, yellowlegs **13** whooping crane
bird cage/home: **4** cote, mews, nest **5** roost **6** aviary, volary, volery **7** rookery
bird of freedom: **9** bald eagle
bird of ill-omen: **5** raven
bird of Jove: **5** eagle
bird of June: **7** peacock
bird of Minerva: **3** owl
bird of peace: **4** dove
bird of prey: **3** owl **4** gled, hawk, kite **5** buteo, eagle, glead, glede, harpy, saker **6** condor, elanet, elenet,

falcon, musket, osprey, raptor **7** buzzard, goshawk, harrier, kestrel, stooper, vulture **8** caracara **9** accipiter, gyrfalcon, peregrine **11** accipitrine, lammergeier

bird of wonder/rebirth: 7 phoenix

carrion-eater: 4 aura **5** urubu **6** condor **7** buzzard, vulture

class: 4 Aves

combining form: 3 avi **4** orni **5** ornis **6** ornith **7** ornitho **8** ornithes

crow family: 3 daw, jay, kae **4** crow, rook **5** crake, raven **6** chough, corbie, magpie **7** corvine, jackdaw

duck family: 4 clee, coot, lory, smew, teal, wood **5** eider, goose **6** scoter **7** gadwall, mallard, Muscovy, pintail, pochard **8** baldpate, redshank, shoveler **9** merganser **10** bufflehead, canvasback

extinct: 3 auk, jib, moa **4** dodo, jibi, mamo **5** didus **8** Diatryma **9** aepyornis, apatornis, gastornis, hespornis, solitaire **11** archaeornis

flightless: 3 emu, ihi, moa **4** dodo, gorb, kagu, kiwi, rhea, weka **5** nandu **6** callow, kakapo, moorup, ratite, takahe **7** apteryx, horling, ostrich, peacock, penguin, roatelo **8** notornis **9** cassowary

game: 4 duck, guan, rail, sora, teal **5** brant, goose, quail, snipe **6** chukar, colima, grouse, pigeon, plover, turkey **7** bustard, chicken, flapper, gadwall, mallard, pintail, prairie, widgeon **8** baldpate, bobwhite, moorfowl, pheasant, shoveler, tragopan, wildfowl, woodcock **9** merganser, partridge, ptarmigan **10** canvasback

group of birds: 3 nye **4** bank, bevy, cast, nide, sord **5** aerie, brood, covey, drove, flock, plump **6** covert, flight, gaggle, litter, spring

largest: 7 ostrich **11** lammergeier

legendary: 3 roc **6** simurg **7** phoenix, simurgh **9** feng-huang, feng-hwang

loss of feathers: 7 molting

nocturnal: 3 owl **5** cahow, owlet, potoo **7** bullbat, dorhawk **8** guacharo, nightjar **9** nighthawk, thickknee **10** goatsucker **11** nightingale

pet: 4 myna **5** mynah **6** canary, parrot, pigeon **8** cockatoo, lovebird, parakeet

plumage: 8 ptilosis

poultry: 3 hen **4** duck **5** goose **6** pigeon, turkey **7** chicken, rooster **8** pheasant **14** Cornish game hen

smallest: 11 hummingbird

talking: 4 myna **5** mynah **6** parrot

wingless: 4 kiwi, weka **7** apteryx

young: 4 eyas, gull **5** chick, piper, poult, squab **6** gorlin, pullus **7** flapper, nestler **8** birdikin, nestling **9** fledgling

of Africa: 4 coly, fink, taha, tock **5** crane, paauw **6** barbet, bulbul, cuckoo, jabiru, quelea, whidah **7**

courser, finfoot, marabou, ostrich, touraco **8** hornbill, oxpecker, parakeet, umbrette **9** beefeater, parabill, francolin, napecrest, trochilus **10** hammerhead, weaverbird

of Antarctic/Arctic: 3 auk **4** gull, knot, skua, xema **5** brant, murre, rotch **6** dunlin, falcon, fulmar, jaeger, rotche **7** dovekey, dovekie, penguin **8** grayling **9** guillemot, gyrfalcon, ptarmigan **10** sheathbill

of Asia: 4 kora, myna, ruff, smew **5** mynah, pewit, pitta **6** bulbul, chukar, drongo, dunlin, hoopoe, linnet **7** boobook, courser, hill tit, lapwing, peacock, sirgang **8** accentor, dotterel, hornbill, leaf bird, parakeet, tragopan, wheatear **9** brambling, francolin, muted swan

of Australia: 3 emu **4** kahu, kiwi, koel, koil, lory **5** arara, galah, lowan, pitta **6** drongo, leipoa **7** boobook, bustard, figbird, grinder, waybung **8** bellbird, bushlark, cockatoo, ganggang, lorikeet, lyrebird, megapode, manucode, morepork, parakeet, platypus **9** bowerbird, cassowary, coachwhip, cockatiel, frogmouth, pardalote, thornbird **10** kookaburra

of Central America: 4 guan, ibis **5** booby, macaw **6** barbet, jabiru, quezal, toucan **7** bittern, cotinga, jacamar, quetzal, tinamou **8** curassow, puffbird, troupial

of Cuba: 6 trogon **8** tocororo **14** bee hummingbird

of England: 4 kite, rook **9** cormorant **11** carrion crow

of Europe: 3 dar, mag, mew, nun **4** clee, gled, mall, merl, pope, rook, ruff, shag, smew, wren **5** amsel, crake, egret, finch, glede, merle, ousel, ouzel, pewit, pipit, stilt, stork, swift, tarin, terek, whaup **6** cuckoo, dunlin, godwit, grouse, hoopoe, linnet, martin, merlin, missel, redleg, roller, siskin, thrush **7** bittern, bustard, jackdaw, kestrel, lapwing, martlet, ortolan, redwing, ruddock, skylark, sparrow, starnel, wagtail, wryneck **8** bee eater, blackcap, brantail, daychick, dotterel, garganey, nightjar, nuthatch, peesweep, redstart, reedling, starling, throstle, wheatear, whimbrel, whinchat, whinshat, woodcock **9** brambling, chaffinch, crossbill, field fare, gallinule, sheldrake, stonechat **10** chiffchaff, goatsucker, kingfisher, lammergeir, turtledove **11** lammergeier, nightingale, wallcreeper **12** capercaillie

of Hawaii: 2 io **3** ava, ioa, iwa, poe **4** nene, iiwi, koae, mamo, moho, omao **6** parson **7** frigate

of India: 4 baya, kala, koel, koil **5** sarus, shama **6** argala, bulbul, homrai, luggar **7** peacock **8** adjutant, am-

adavat, pheasant, tragopan **11** red hornbill

of Jamaica: 7 vervain

of Java: 7 sparrow **8** rice bird **9** fruit dove

of Madagascar: 6 drongo **7** anhinga, kirombo, roatelo

of Mexico: 6 jacana

of New Guinea: 9 cassowary **14** bird of paradise

of New Zealand: 3 ihi, kea, moa, poe, tui **4** huia, kaka, kaki, kiwi, koko, kuku, ruru, titi, weka **6** kakapo **7** apteryx **8** morepork, notornis

of North America: 3 ani, auk, tit **4** coot, crow, dove, ibis, lark, loon, pape, rook, sora, stib, swan, tern, wamp, wren **5** booby, brant, colin, crane, egret, finch, grebe, junco, murre, quail, robin, snipe, swift, veery, vireo **6** chebec, cuckoo, curlew, darter, dunlin, fulmar, grouse, hagdon, magpie, martin, oriole, phoebe, plover, shrike, thrush, towhee, turkey, verdin, willet **7** anhinga, bittern, blue jay, catbird, flicker, goshawk, grackle, lapwing, pelican, sparrow, swallow, tanager, warbler **8** bluebird, bobolink, bobwhite, cardinal, grosbeak, killdeer, nuthatch, poorwill, starling, thrasher, titmouse, wheatear **9** blackbird, chickadee, crossbill, goldfinch, gyrfalcon, nighthawk, partridge, sandpiper, snakebird **10** bufflehead, kingfisher, meadowlark, woodpecker **11** hummingbird, mockingbird **12** whippoorwill

of South America: 3 ara, hia **4** anna, guan, jacu, loro, mitu, rhea, soco, toco, yeni **5** egret, macaw, potoo, sylph **6** barbet, chatja, chunga, cracid, jabiru, motmot, sappho, toucan **7** cariama, cotinga, hoatzin, jacamar, limpkin, manakin, seriema, tinamou, warrior **8** boatbill, caracara, curassow, guacharo, hoactzin, screamer, tapacolo, tapaculo, terutero, troupial **9** campanero, trumpeter **11** scarlet ibis

of West India: 3 ani **4** tody

Bird, Larry
sport: 10 basketball
position: 5 coach **7** forward
team: 13 Boston Celtics, Indiana Pacers
from: 7 Indiana

Birdman of Alcatraz
director: 17 John Frankenheimer
cast: 10 Karl Malden **12** Edmond O'Brien, Neville Brand, Thelma Ritter **13** Burt Lancaster (Robert Stroud)

Bird of Paradise
constellation of: 4 Apus

Birds, The
author: 12 Aristophanes
character: 4 Iris **5** Meton **8** Basileia, Cinesias **9** Euelpides **10** King Tereus, Prometheus **12** Peithetairos

Birds, The
  director: **15** Alfred Hitchcock
  based on story by: **15** Daphne du Maurier
  cast: **9** Rod Taylor **11** Tippi Hedren **12** Jessica Tandy **16** Suzanne Pleshette
  setting: **10** California

Birds Fall Down, The
  author: **15** Dame Rebecca West

Birkin, Rupert
  character in: **11** Women in Love
  author: **8** Lawrence

Birmingham
  football team: **9** Stallions

Birmingham, Stephen
  author of: **8** Our Crowd **11** The Grandees **14** The Right People **15** Life at the Dakota

Birnbaum, Nathan
  real name of: **11** George Burns

birth 5 blood, start, stock **6** family, origin, source, strain **7** bearing, descent, genesis, lineage **8** ancestry, breeding, delivery **9** beginning, being born, emergence, genealogy, inception, parentage **10** background, beginnings, childbirth, derivation, extraction **11** confinement, parturition **12** commencement

Birth of a Nation, The
  director: **10** D W Griffith
  cast: **8** Mae Marsh **11** Lillian Gish **14** Henry B Walthall

Birth of Tragedy, The
  author: **18** Friedrich Nietzsche

birthstones
  January: **6** garnet
  February: **8** amethyst
  March: **6** jasper **10** aquamarine, bloodstone
  April: **7** diamond **8** sapphire
  May: **5** agate **7** emerald
  June: **5** pearl **7** emerald **9** moonstone **11** alexandrite
  July: **4** onyx, ruby **8** star ruby
  August: **7** peridot **8** sardonyx **9** carnelian
  September: **8** sapphire **10** chrysolite **12** star sapphire
  October: **4** opal **5** beryl **10** aquamarine, tourmaline
  November: **5** topaz
  December: **4** ruby **6** zircon **9** turquoise

biscuit 3 bun **4** cake, roll **5** cooky, scone, wafer **6** bisque, cookie, muffin, parking, simnel **7** cracker, dogbone **8** hardtack, zwieback **9** pale-brown **10** crisp bread, quick bread **15** unglazed pottery

bisect 5 cross, split **8** cut in two **9** cut in half, intersect

bishop 4 abba, pope **5** punch **6** cleric, despot, priest **7** pontiff, prelate, primate **8** overseer **9** clergyman, patriarch **10** chesspiece, high priest

  of Rome: **4** pope
  Greek: **9** episkopos
    means: **8** overseer
  district: **7** diocese
  headdress: **5** miter, mitre

Bismarck, Otto von
  nickname: **14** Iron Chancellor
  unified: **7** Germany
  chancellor/minister for: **15** Emperor William I
  policy: **12** "iron and blood"

bison 4 urus **6** wild ox, wisent **7** aurochs, buffalo
  native to: **6** Europe **12** North America

Bissau
  capital of: **12** Guinea-Bissau

bistro 3 bar **4** cafe **6** tavern **7** cabaret **9** nightclub **10** supper club
  French: **9** estaminet

bit 3 dab **4** chip, drop, iota, mite, snip, whit **5** crumb, grain, pinch, scrap, shred, speck, spell, trace **6** dollop, moment, morsel, paring, trifle **7** droplet, granule, shaving, smidgen **8** fragment, particle **9** short time **10** short while, small piece, smithereen, sprinkling
  type: **5** auger, drill **6** gimlet, wimble **7** bradawl **11** brace and bit

bitch 3 nag **5** botch, brood, cheat, fault, shrew, spoil, witch, whine **6** kvetch, virago **7** blunder, bungle, grouse **8** complain, harridan **9** complaint, female dog, termagant

bitchy 4 mean **5** catty, cruel, nasty **6** wicked **7** hateful, vicious **8** spiteful **9** heartless, malicious **10** backbiting, malevolent, vindictive

bite 3 bit, dab, dig, nip **4** gnaw, grip, snip **5** champ, crumb, gnash, prick, scrap, shred, smart, speck, sting, taste **6** morsel, nibble, pierce **7** eat into **8** mouthful, stinging, take hold **10** small piece, tooth wound **12** small portion

biting 5 harsh, sharp **6** bitter **7** caustic, cutting, mordant, nipping **8** piercing, scathing, smarting, stinging **9** sarcastic, trenchant, withering **12** sharptongued

bit player 5 extra **6** walk on **14** minor character

bitte 6 please **12** you're welcome **14** I beg your pardon

bitter 4 acid, mean, sour, tart **5** acrid, angry, cruel, harsh, sharp **6** biting, morose, severe, sullen **7** acerbic, caustic, crabbed, painful **8** grievous, piercing, scornful, smarting, spiteful, stinging, wretched **9** rancorous, resentful **10** astringent **11** distressing

bitterness 5 anger, scorn, spite **6** animus, rancor, spleen **7** ill will **8** acerbity, acrimony, sourness **9** animosity, harshness, hostility, malignity, sharpness **10** antagonism, malignancy **11**

astringency **12** hard feelings, spitefulness **14** unpleasantness

bitters
  type: **6** spirit
  flavor: **6** orange **7** gentian
  brand: **9** Angostura, Peychaud's

bivalve 4 clam **5** pinna **6** cockle, mussel, mollusk, scallop **8** mollusca **9** pelecypod **13** lamellibranch

bivouac 4 camp **5** tents **10** campground, encampment

bizarre 3 odd **5** kinky, kooky, queer, weird **7** strange, unusual **8** freakish **9** fantastic, grotesque **10** outlandish

Bizet, Georges
  real name: **26** Alexandre Cesar Leopold Bizet
  born: **5** Paris **6** France
  composer of: **4** Roma (suite) **6** Carmen, Patrie **8** Djamileh **11** Don Procopio, L'Arlesienne **12** Jeux d'enfants, Pearl Fishers **14** Children's Games **15** Ivan the Terrible **16** Le Docteur Miracle **18** The Fair Maid of Perth

Bjornson, Bjornstjerne
  author of: **4** Arne **7** The King **8** Magnhild **9** A Happy Boy, In God's Way, Lame Hulda, The Editor **10** King Sverre **11** A Bankruptcy, The Bankrupt **12** Sigurd Slembe **14** Arnljot Gelline, Beyond Our Power **15** The Fisher Maiden, The Newly Married **16** Beyond Human Might, Sigurd the Bastard **17** Between the Battles **20** Mary Stuart in Scotland **24** Paul Lange and Tora Parsberg **27** Flags Are Flying in Town and Port

blab 3 rat **6** babble, tattle **7** blabber, prattle **9** tell tales **13** spill the beans **20** let the cat out of the bag

blabber 3 gab, gas, yak **4** blab, bull **5** prate **6** babble, drivel, gabble, gibber, gossip, jabber **7** blather, chatter, palaver, prattle, twaddle **8** blah-blah, chitchat, idle talk **9** jabbering **10** mumbo-jumbo **12** gobbledegook **14** chitter-chatter

blabbermouth 6 gabber, gossip, prater **7** blabber **8** bigmouth, busybody, gossiper, informer, jabberer, liverlip, prattler, quidnunc **9** chatterer **10** chatterbox, talebearer, tattletale **11** rumormonger **12** gossipmonger **13** scandalmonger

black, Black 3 bad, dim, jet **4** dark, evil, grim, inky **5** angry, ebony, murky, Negro, raven, sable **6** dismal, gloomy, somber, sullen, wicked **7** colored, furious, hostile, stygian, sunless, swarthy **8** moonless **9** coal-black, lightless, nefarious, unlighted **10** calamitous **11** dark-skinned, threatening **12** Afro-American **13** unilluminated

Black Arrow, The
  author: **20** Robert Louis Stevenson

blackball 3 ban, bar, cut **4** snub **5** debar **6** banish, outlaw, reject **7** boycott, exclude, keep out, shut out **8** pass over, turndown **9** blacklist, ostracize, proscribe **11** vote against **12** cold-shoulder **14** send to Coventry

black beast
French: **9** bete noire

blackberry 5 Rubus
variety: **4** Sand **5** Swamp **7** Cut-leaf, Pacific, Running, Sow-teat **9** Evergreen **13** Parsley-leaved **18** Evergreen thornless

Blackberry Winter
author: **12** Margaret Mead

blackbird 3 ani **4** crow, rook **5** raven, slave **6** thrush **7** cowbird, grackle, redwing **8** song bird **9** slave ship **11** slave trader **17** kidnapped islander, plantation laborer
kind: **9** red-winged **12** yellow-headed
family: **8** Turdidae **9** Icteridae

Blackboard Jungle, The
director: **13** Richard Brooks
based on novel by: **10** Evan Hunter
cast: **9** Glenn Ford, Vic Morrow **11** Anne Francis **12** Louis Calhern, Paul Mazursky, Richard Kiley **13** Sidney Poitier **14** Warner Anderson

Black Boy
author: **13** Richard Wright

blacken 5 libel, smear, stain, sully **6** befoul, darken, defame, defile, revile, vilify **7** slander, tarnish **8** besmirch, disgrace, dishonor **9** denigrate, discredit **10** stigmatize

Blackfoot, Blackfeet
language family: **9** Algonkian **10** Algonquian
tribe: **6** Bloods, Kainah, Piegan, Pikuni **7** Siksika
location: **6** Canada **7** Alberta, Montana **12** Saskatchewan

blackguard 3 cad, rat, SOB **5** knave, louse, rogue, scamp **6** rascal **7** bastard, villain **9** miscreant, scoundrel

blackhearted 4 base, vile **6** sinful, wicked **7** ignoble **10** despicable, evil-minded, villainous **11** scoundrelly **12** unprincipled **13** reprehensible

blackjack
also known as: **9** twenty-one
French: **9** vingt-et-un
play against: **6** dealer
additional card: **3** hit

Black Lamb and Grey Falcon
author: **15** Dame Rebecca West

Black Land, The see **5** Egypt

blackleg 7 cheater **8** swindler **9** trickster

blacklist 3 ban, bar **4** shun **5** debar **6** reject **7** exclude, lock out, shut out **8** preclude **9** blackball, ostracize

blacklisting 7 boycott **8** spurning **9** exclusion, ostracism, rejection **12** blackballing

black magic 7 sorcery **10** witchcraft

blackmail 5 force **6** coerce, extort, payoff **7** squeeze, tribute **8** threaten **9** extortion, hush money, shakedown

black mark 4 blot **5** stain **6** bruise **7** blemish, demerit **9** contusion

Blackmore, Richard Doddridge
author of: **10** Lorna Doone **11** Springhaven **13** The Maid of Sker

black mountain see **10** Montenegro

Black Narcissus
author: **11** Rumer Godden
director: **13** Michael Powell **17** Emeric Pressburger
cast: **4** Sabu **11** David Farrar, Deborah Kerr, Jean Simmons
setting: **9** Himalayas

blackness 4 dark **5** gloom, shade **7** dimness **8** darkness

Blackpool, Stephen
character in: **9** Hard Times
author: **7** Dickens

Black Prince 6 Edward (Prince of Wales)
battles: **5** Crecy **8** Poitiers

Black Prince, The
author: **11** Iris Murdoch

Blackstone, Sir William
author of: **12** Commentaries (on the Laws of England)

Black Uhlan
nickname of: **12** Max Schmeling

Blackwater State
nickname of: **8** Nebraska

Blackwell, Elizabeth
first American: **11** woman doctor

bladder 3 bag, sac **4** cyst **5** pouch **7** blister, pustule, saccule, utricle **10** receptacle

blade 4 epee, leaf **5** frond, knife, razor, saber, sword **6** cutter, needle, switch **7** scalpel **10** sled runner **11** cutting edge, skate runner

blah 4 bosh, dull, flat, guff, so-so **5** bland, ho-hum, hooey, vapid **6** boring, bunkum, dreary, hot air, humbug **7** blather, eyewash, humdrum, nothing, tedious, twaddle **8** claptrap, lifeless, listless, nonsense **9** gibberish **10** balderdash, monotonous, pedestrian **11** uninspiring **13** characterless, unimaginative, uninteresting, unstimulating

Blaik, Earl H
sport: **8** football
position: **5** coach
team: **4** Army **9** Dartmouth
military rank: **7** colonel

Blair, Eric Arthur
real name of: **12** George Orwell

Blake, Robert
real name: **28** Michael James Vijencio Gubitosi
born: **8** Nutley NJ
wife: **14** Bonny Lee Bakley
tried for: **6** murder
verdict: **9** not guilty

roles: **7** Baretta, Our Gang **8** Red Ryder **11** In Cold Blood **12** Little Beaver **23** Tell Them Willie Boy Is Here **24** The Treasure of Sierra Madre

Blake, William
born: **6** London **7** England
author of: **6** Milton, Tiriel **9** Jerusalem **13** The Book of Thel **14** Prophetic Books **15** The Book of Urigen **16** Songs of Innocence **17** Songs of Experience **21** Little Lamb Who Made Thee **23** Marriage of Heaven and Hell, Tiger Tiger Burning Bright
artwork: **6** Milton **8** Book of Job, Jerusalem **11** The Four Zoas **12** Book of Urizen, Divine Comedy **16** Songs of Innocence **17** Songs of Experience **23** Marriage of Heaven and Hell

blamable 10 censurable, deplorable, punishable, reprovable **11** blameworthy **12** reproachable **13** reprehensible

Blamauer, Karoline
real name of: **10** Lotte Lenya

blame 4 onus **5** fault, guilt **6** accuse, burden, charge, rebuke **7** censure, condemn, reproof, reprove **8** reproach **9** castigate, criticism, criticize, liability **10** accusation, disapprove **11** castigation, culpability **12** condemnation, denunciation, remonstrance **13** find fault with, recrimination **14** accountability, responsibility **15** hold responsible

blameless 5 clear **8** innocent, spotless **9** guiltless, not guilty, unspotted, unstained, unsullied, untainted **10** inculpable, not at fault, unblamable **11** unblemished, uncorrupted **13** unimpeachable **14** irreproachable, not responsible

blameless in life
Latin: **12** integer vitae

blame on 7 trace to **8** charge to **9** set down to **11** attribute to **14** lay at the door of

blameworthy 8 blamable **10** censurable, deplorable, punishable, reprovable **12** reproachable **13** reprehensible

blanch 4 fade **6** bleach, whiten **7** lighten **8** turn pale

blanched 3 wan **4** pale **5** ashen, faded **6** chalky, pallid **8** bleached **9** bloodless

Blanchett, Cate
real name: **18** Catherine Blanchett
born: **9** Australia, Melbourne
husband: **11** Andrew Upton
roles: **9** Elizabeth, Parklands **10** Pushing Tin, The Aviator (Oscar), The Missing **12** Paradise Road **13** Charlotte Gray **14** Veronica Guerin **15** Oscar and Lucinda, The Shipping News **17** The Lord of the Rings **19** The Talented Mr. Ripley

bland 4 blah, calm, dull, even, flat, mild **5** balmy, quiet, vapid **6** benign, smooth **7** calming, humdrum, nothing, prosaic, tedious **8** moderate, peaceful, soothing, tiresome, tranquil **9** peaceable, temperate, unruffled **10** monotonous, unexciting, untroubled **11** uninspiring **13** nonirritating, uninteresting, unstimulating

blandish 4 coax, lure, urge **5** charm, tempt **6** cajole, entice, prompt **7** blarney, flatter, wheedle **8** inveigle, persuade

blandishment, blandishments 7 blarney, coaxing **8** cajolery, flattery **9** sweet talk, wheedling **12** ingratiation, inveiglement

Blandois, Monsieur
character in: **12** Little Dorrit
author: **7** Dickens

blank 3 gap **4** dull, idle, void **5** clean, clear, empty, inane, plain, space **6** futile, hollow, unused, vacant, vacuum, wasted **7** useless, vacancy, vacuous **8** unmarked **9** emptiness, fruitless, valueless, worthless **10** empty space, hollowness, profitless **11** meaningless, thoughtless, unrewarding **12** inexpressive **14** expressionless

blanket 4 coat, film **5** cloak, cover, quilt, throw **6** afghan, carpet, mantle, veneer **7** coating, overlay **8** covering, coverlet **9** comforter

blare 4 honk, peal, roar **5** blast **6** bellow, scream **7** resound, trumpet

blarney 4 fibs, line **5** pitch, spiel **6** hot air **7** coaxing, fawning, snow job, stories **8** cajolery, flattery **9** hyperbole, wheedling **10** inveigling, overpraise, sweet words **12** exaggeration, honeyed words **13** blandishments, overstatement

blase 4 full **5** bored, jaded **6** gorged **7** glutted **9** apathetic, satisfied, saturated, surfeited, unexcited, unmovable **10** insouciant, nonchalant, spiritless, world-weary **11** indifferent, unconcerned **12** uninterested **14** unenthusiastic

Blasko, Bela
real name of: **10** Bela Lugosi

blaspheme 5 curse, swear **6** revile **7** profane **10** take in vain

blasphemous 7 godless, impious, profane, ungodly **10** irreverent **11** irreligious **12** sacrilegious

blasphemy 7 cursing, impiety **8** swearing **9** profanity, sacrilege **11** impiousness, irreverence, profanation

blast 4 bomb, boom, bore, gale, gust, honk, peal, roar, rush, toot **5** blare, bleat, burst, level, shell, surge **6** bellow, blow up, report, scream, shriek **7** explode, resound, torpedo **8** dynamite, eruption **9** discharge, explosion, loud noise **10** detonation **11** sound loudly

blasting material 3 TNT **8** dynamite **9** explosive

blatant 4 loud **5** cheap, clear, crass,

crude, gross, harsh, noisy, overt **6** brazen, coarse, tawdry, vulgar **7** blaring, glaring, obvious, uncouth **8** flagrant, piercing, unsubtle **9** clamorous, deafening, obtrusive, offensive, prominent, tasteless, ungenteel, unrefined **10** indelicate, unpolished **11** conspicuous, ill-mannered, undignified **12** earsplitting, unmistakable

blather 4 stir **7** chatter, prattle **8** nonsense **9** commotion

Blatty, William P
author of: **11** The Exorcist

Blaue Reiter 10 Blue Riders
group of: **13** German artists

blaze 3 ray **4** beam, burn, fire, glow, rush **5** blast, burst, flame, flare, flash, glare, gleam, shine **6** flames **7** glisten, glitter, shimmer, torrent **8** eruption, outbreak, outburst, radiance **9** explosion **10** brightness, brilliance, effulgence **12** resplendence **13** conflagration

blazer 4 coat **6** jacket **12** sports jacket

blazing 3 hot **5** fiery, afire **6** firing, on fire **7** burning, flaming, flaring, glaring, glowing, intense, shining **8** bursting, bleaming, shooting, shouting **9** brilliant

Blazing Saddles
director: **9** Mel Brooks
cast: **9** Mel Brooks **10** Alex Karras, Dom DeLuise, Gene Wilder **11** Slim Pickens **12** Harvey Korman, Madeline Kahn **13** Cleavon Little, John Hillerman **15** David Huddleston

blazon 4 blare, boast **7** trumpet **8** proclaim **10** coat of arms, make public **16** armorial bearings

blazonry 4 arms **5** crest **6** blazon **8** insignia **10** coat of arms **14** heraldic emblem **16** heraldic bearings

bleach 4 fade **6** blanch, whiten **7** lighten, wash out **8** make pale

bleak 3 raw **4** bare, cold, grim **5** chill **6** barren, biting, bitter, dismal, dreary, frosty, gloomy, somber, wintry **7** nipping **8** desolate, piercing **9** cheerless, windswept **10** depressing, forbidding **11** distressing, unpromising **13** weather-beaten

Bleak House
author: **14** Charles Dickens
character: **2** Jo (the crossing sweeper) **4** Nemo **5** Guppy, Krook **6** Bucket, Guster **7** Snagsby **8** Ada Clare, Chadband **9** Miss Flite **10** Mrs Jellyby, Turveydrop **11** Dr Woodcourt, Lady Dedlock, Tulkinghorn **12** John Jarndyce **13** Captain Rawdon **14** Harold Skimpole **15** Esther Summerson, Richard Carstone **19** Sir Leicester Dedlock
satire of: **3** law **6** courts **8** chancery
case: **19** Jarndyce and Jarndyce

bleakness 8 bareness, grimness **10**

barrenness, desolation, dreariness, gloominess **13** cheerlessness

bleat 3 baa, cry, maa **5** whine **7** whimper

bleb 6 bubble **7** blister

bleed 3 run, tap **4** leak, soak **5** drain, valve **6** fleece, suffer **7** diffuse, extract, **8** let blood **9** draw blood, sacrifice **10** hemorrhage, overcharge **12** phlebotomize

Blefuscu
fictional land in: **16** Gulliver's Travels
author: **5** Swift

blemish 3 mar, zit **4** blot, blur, flaw, mark, spot **5** spoil, stain, sully, taint **6** blotch, defect, smirch, smudge **7** tarnish **9** disfigure **12** imperfection **13** disfigurement

blend 3 mix **4** fuse **5** merge, unite **6** fusion, go well, merger, mingle **7** amalgam, combine, mixture **8** coalesce, compound, mergence, mingling **9** harmonize **10** amalgamate, complement, concoction **11** combination, incorporate, intermingle

bless 4 give **5** endow, favor, grace, guard, honor **6** anoint, bestow, hallow, oblige, ordain **7** baptize, benefit, protect, support **9** dedicate, sanctify **9** watch over **10** consecrate

blessed 4 holy **5** happy, lucky **6** adored, graced, joyful, joyous, sacred **7** endowed, favored, revered **8** blissful, hallowed **9** fortunate, venerated, wonderful **10** felicitous, sanctified **11** consecrated

Blessed Damozel, The
author: **20** Dante Gabriel Rossetti

blessedness 5 bliss **8** felicity **9** beatitude **11** saintliness

blessing 4 boon, gain, gift, good **5** favor, grace, leave **6** bounty, profit, regard **7** backing, benefit, consent, support **8** approval, sanction **9** advantage, hallowing **10** dedication, good wishes, invocation, permission **11** benediction, concurrence, good fortune **12** consecration, thanksgiving **14** sanctification

blessings 4 joys **5** gifts **6** favors **7** success **8** benefits, delights **10** advantages **11** good fortune

Blifil, Master
character in: **8** Tom Jones
author: **8** Fielding

Bligh, Captain William
character in: **17** Mutiny on the Bounty
authors: **4** Hall **8** Nordhoff

blight 3 pox, rot **4** harm, kill, ruin, rust **5** blast, crush, curse, decay, smash, spoil, wreck **6** cancer, canker, dry rot, fungus, injure, mildew, plague, thwart, wither **7** cripple, destroy, scourge, shrivel **8** demolish **9**

frustrate **10** affliction, corruption, pestilence **12** plant disease **13** contamination

Blimber, Dr
character in: **12** Dombey and Son
author: **7** Dickens

blind 4 dull, ruse **5** cover, dodge, front, shade **6** hidden, insane, obtuse, screen **7** obscure, pretext, unaware **8** disguise, heedless, ignorant, mindless, unseeing **9** concealed, deception, senseless, sightless, sun shield, unfeeling, unknowing, unmindful, unnoticed **10** camouflage, insouciant, irrational, masquerade, neglectful, subterfuge, unthinking **11** inattentive, incognizant, indifferent, insensitive, smoke screen, unconcerned, unconscious, unobservant, unobserving **12** imperceptive, uncontrolled, undiscerning, uninterested, unnoticeable, unperceptive, unreasonable **13** unenlightened **14** uncontrollable **15** uncomprehending

blind alley 7 closure, dead-end, impasse **8** blockade, cul-de-sac, dead lock, no escape **9** hindrance, stone wall **10** impassable, standstill **11** obstruction

blinder 4 hood **5** blind, shade **6** screen **7** blinker **9** blindfold

blindfold 6 darken **7** bandage, blinder, obscure **8** covering heedless, reckless **11** strike blind

blind seer 8 Tiresias

blink 4 wink **5** flash, shine, waver **6** falter, flinch, squint **7** flicker, glimmer, shimmer, sparkle, twinkle **9** nictitate, vacillate

blinker(s) 3 eye **6** peeper **7** blinder, flasher, goggles **8** black eye **13** warning signal

blintz, blintze 4 blin **5** crepe **6** blints **7** pancake

blip 3 dot, tap **4** spot **5** bleep, image **6** censor **7** replace

bliss 3 joy **4** glee **6** heaven, luxury **7** delight, ecstasy, rapture **8** gladness, paradise **9** cloud nine, happiness **10** exaltation, jubilation **12** exhilaration

blissful 5 happy **6** divine, joyful, joyous **7** blessed, sublime **8** beatific, ecstatic, glorious, heavenly **9** rapturous

blithe 3 gay **4** airy, glad **5** blind, happy, jolly, merry, sunny **6** casual, cheery, jaunty, jovial, joyous, lively **7** gleeful, radiant **8** carefree, careless, cheerful, debonair, exaltant, heedless, mirthful, uncaring **9** ebullient, sprightly, unfeeling, unmindful **10** blithesome, frolicking **11** indifferent, insensitive, thoughtless, unconcerned, unconscious **12** light-hearted **13** inconsiderate

Blithedale Romance, The
author: **18** Nathaniel Hawthorne

blithesome 3 gay **5** light, merry, sunny **6** breezy, jaunty, lively **7** buoyant **8** animated, carefree, cheerful **11** free and easy

Blixen-Finecke, Karen
real name of: **11** Isak Dinesen

blizzard 4 blow, gale **5** blast **6** flurry, squall **7** tempest **8** snowfall **9** snowstorm **11** winter storm

Blizzard State
nickname of: **11** South Dakota

bloat 5 swell **6** blow up, dilate, expand, puff up **7** balloon, distend, enlarge, inflate

blob 3 dab **4** daub, drop, glob, mass **7** globule, splotch

bloc 4 body, ring, wing **5** cabal, group, union **6** clique **7** combine, faction **8** alliance **9** coalition **11** combination

Bloch, Ernest
born: **6** Geneva **11** Switzerland
composer of: **7** Macbeth, Solomon **8** Baal Shem, Schelomo **13** Sacred Service **14** Avodath Hakdesh, Israel Symphony **16** American Symphony **19** Concerto Symphonique **20** Voice in the Wilderness

block 3 bar, jam **4** cube, form, halt, mold **5** brick, check, choke, shape **6** hinder, impede, re-form, square, stop up, thwart **7** barrier, prevent, reshape **8** blockade, blockage, obstacle, obstruct **9** hindrance **10** impediment **11** obstruction **12** interference

blockade 3 bar, dam **4** dike **5** block, check, levee **6** hurdle **7** barrier, parapet, rampart **8** blockage, obstacle, obstruct, stockade, stoppage **9** barricade, hindrance, roadblock **10** checkpoint, earthworks, impediment **11** obstruction, restriction **13** fortification

blockage 3 jam **8** obstacle **9** hindrance **10** impediment **11** obstruction

blockhead 3 ass, oaf **4** clod, dolt, dope, fool, yutz **5** booby, dummy, dunce, idiot, klutz, moron, ninny **6** dum-dum, nitwit **7** fathead, half-wit, jackass **8** bonehead, dumb-dumb, dummkopf, imbecile, lunkhead, mushhead, numskull **9** harebrain, lamebrain, simpleton **10** chowerhead, dunderhead, nincompoop, noodlehead **12** featherbrain

block out 3 hew **5** carve **6** chisel, devise, map out, sculpt, sketch **7** outline **8** indicate **9** formulate

block up 3 bar **4** clog **6** stop up **7** brick up **9** barricade

blond, blonde 4 fair, gold, pale **5** light **6** flaxen, golden, yellow **8** light tan **9** yellowish **10** fair-haired **11** fair-skinned **12** light-colored

Blonde Bombshell
nickname of: **10** Jean Harlow

Blondell, Joan
husband: **8** Mike Todd **10** Dick Powell
born: **9** New York NY
roles: **8** The Champ **11** Blonde Crazy, Gold Diggers, The Blue Veil **14** Blondie Johnson, The Public Enemy **20** A Tree Grows in Brooklyn

Blondie
creator: **9** Chic Young
character:
husband: **15** Dagwood Bumstead
children: **6** Cookie **9** Alexander **12** Baby Dumpling
boss: **6** Julius **9** Mr Dithers
boss's wife: **4** Cora
neighbor: **11** Herb Woodley **14** Tootsie Woodley
dog: **5** Daisy

blood 4 gore **5** birth, stock **6** family, source, spirit, temper **7** descent, lineage, passion **8** ancestry, heritage, vitality **9** lifeblood **10** extraction, family line, vital fluid, vital force **11** temperament **13** consanguinity **14** vital principle

Blood, field of 8 Aceldama

bloodless 4 pale **5** ashen **6** anemic, pallid **7** insipid **8** blanched, lifeless, peaceful **9** colorless, deathlike, washed out

bloodline 6 family **8** ancestry, pedigree **9** genealogy **10** family tree

bloodshed 4 gore **6** murder, pogrom **7** carnage, killing, slaying **8** butchery, massacre **9** blood bath, blood feud, slaughter **10** mass murder **12** bloodletting, manslaughter **15** spilling of blood

Bloodsmoor Romance, A
author: **15** Joyce Carol Oates

bloodstone
month: **5** March

Blood, Sweat and Tears
author: **17** Winston S Churchill

blood system
part: **5** blood, liver **6** spleen **9** lymph node **10** bone marrow

bloodthirsty 5 cruel **6** bloody, brutal, fierce, savage **7** bestial, demonic, inhuman, vicious **8** barbaric, demoniac, fiendish, pitiless, ruthless **9** atrocious, barbarous, cutthroat, heartless, homicidal, merciless, murdering, murderous **10** demoniacal, sanguinary **11** sanguineous

blood vessel 4 vein **5** aorta **6** artery **7** carotid **9** capillary
prefix: **5** angio

Blood Wedding
author: **19** Federico Garcia Lorca

bloody 3 red **4** gory, rude, vevy **5** cruel, lurid **6** cursed, damned **7** crimson, scarlet **8** bleeding **9** merciless, murderous **10** sanguinary

Bloody Shame see **10** Virgin Mary (drink)

bloom 3 bud **4** glow, grow, zest **5**

flare, flush, prime, shine, vigor **6** beauty, flower, heyday, luster, sprout, thrive **7** blossom, burgeon, develop, prosper, succeed **8** fare well, flourish, fructify, radiance, rosiness, strength **9** bear fruit, flowerage, flowering, germinate **10** blossoming **11** florescence, flourishing

Bloom, Claire
real name: **11** Claire Blume
husband: **10** Rod Steiger
born: **6** London **7** England
roles: **6** Charly **9** Limelight **10** Richard III **15** Look Back in Anger **26** The Spy Who Came in from the Cold

Bloom, Leopold and Molly
characters in: **7** Ulysses
author: **5** Joyce

Bloom, Orlando
born: **7** England **10** Canterbury
roles: **4** Troy **5** Haven, Wilde **8** Ned Kelly **13** Black Hawk Down **15** Kingdom of Heaven **17** The Lord of the Rings **21** Pirates of the Caribbean

bloomers 8 knickers, trousers **9** plus fours, underwear **10** underpants **15** knickerbockers

blooming 3 fit **4** pert, rosy **5** utter **6** abloom, robust, strong **7** healthy **8** vigorous **9** healthful **10** blossoming **11** flourishing **12** efflorescent, fit as a fiddle **15** picture of health

blooper 4 goof, slip **5** boner, botch, error, fluff, gaffe, lapse **6** bobble, booboo, slip-up **7** blunder, mistake, screwup

blossom 4 grow **5** bloom **6** flower, thrive **7** burgeon, develop **8** flourish, progress

Blossomed miraculously 9 Aaron's rod

blossoming 5 bloom **8** blooming, thriving **9** flowering **10** burgeoning, developing **11** florescence, flourishing

blot 3 dry **4** flaw, mark, spot **5** smear, stain, taint **6** absorb, blotch, remove, smirch, smudge, soak up, stigma, take up **7** bad mark, blemish, splotch **8** besmirch **13** discoloration

blotch 4 blot, mark, spot **7** splotch

Blot on the 'Scutcheon, The
author: **14** Robert Browning

blot out 5 erase **6** remove, rub out **7** abolish, eclipse, expunge **9** eliminate, eradicate **10** obliterate

blotting out 7 eclipse, erasing **9** expunging, wiping out **11** eradicating, eradication **12** annihilation, obliterating, obliteration **13** overshadowing

blouse 4 coat **5** drape, tunic, shirt, smock **6** camise, billow **7** blouson **8** casaquin

blow 3 box, hit, jab, pop **4** bang, bash, belt, cuff, gale, gust, honk, jolt, play, puff, sock, toot, wind **5** blast, burst, clout, crack, knock, punch, shock, smack, sound, storm, thump, upset, whack **6** exhale, rebuff, squall, wallop **7** breathe, explode, tempest, tragedy, whistle **8** calamity, disaster, expel air, reversal **9** detriment, windstorm **10** affliction, misfortune **11** catastrophe **14** disappointment

blow from the hand
French: **10** coup de main

blowhard 6 gascon **7** boaster, bragger, egotist **8** braggart **9** big talker **11** braggadocio

blow of mercy
French: **11** coup de grace

blow out 5 burst **7** rupture **10** extinguish

blowsy, blowzy 5 messy **6** frowzy, mussed, sloppy, untidy **7** unkempt **10** disarrayed, disheveled, disordered, disorderly, in disorder **11** disarranged

blow up 5 bloat, burst **6** billow, dilate, expand **7** balloon, distend, enlarge, explode, inflate, puff out **8** dynamite, swell out **12** lose one's cool **14** lose one's temper

Blow-up
director: **21** Michelangelo Antonioni
cast: **8** Verushka **10** Sarah Miles **13** David Hemmings **15** Vanessa Redgrave

blowy 5 gusty, windy **6** breezy **7** squally **8** blustery

blubber 3 cry, fat, sob **4** bawl, flab, wail, weep **6** boohoo

bludgeon 3 bat, hit **4** club **5** billy, clout, stick **6** cudgel **7** clobber **9** billy-club, truncheon

blue 3 low, sad **4** aqua, down, navy **5** azure **6** bluish, cobalt, gloomy, indigo, morose **7** doleful **8** cerulean, dejected, downcast, sapphire **9** depressed, turquoise **10** aquamarine, despondent, melancholy **11** downhearted, lapis lazuli, ultra-marine **12** disconsolate **14** down in the dumps, down in the mouth

Blue Angel, The
director: **17** Josef von Sternberg
based on novel by: **12** Heinrich Mann
cast: **10** Kurt Gerron **12** Emil Jannings **15** Marlene Dietrich (Lola-Lola)
song: **18** Falling in Love Again

Bluebeard
characteristic: **9** many wives

bluebell 9 Mertensia **18** Mertensia Virginica **21** Campanula rotundifolia
variety: **7** English, Spanish **8** Virginia **10** Australian, California **11** Clanwilliam

blueberry 9 Vaccinium
variety: **3** Low **4** Male **5** Swamp **7** Lowbush, Sourtop, Western **8** Creeping, Elliott's, Highbush, Low sweet **9** Late sweet, Rabbit-eye **10** Velvet-leaf **13** Black highbush

blueblood 4 peer **5** noble **8** nobleman **9** patrician, socialite **10** aristocrat, noblewoman **14** peer of the realm

blue-blooded 5 noble, regal, royal **6** titled **7** courtly **8** highbred, wellborn **9** patrician **10** upper-class **12** aristocratic, of royal blood

blue bloods 5 elite, toffs **8** nobility **9** haut monde **10** patricians **11** aristocracy, high society **14** creme de la creme

bluegrass 3 Poa
varieties: **3** Big **4** Wood **5** Rough, Texas **6** Annual, Canada **7** Bulbous, English **8** Kentucky, Sandberg **10** Rough-stalk

Bluegrass State
nickname of: **8** Kentucky

Blue Hen State
nickname of: **8** Delaware

Blue Knight, The
author: **14** Joseph Wambaugh

Blue Law State
nickname of: **11** Connecticut

blue-pencil 3 cut **4** edit, trim **6** censor, cut out, delete, digest, reduce **7** abridge, shorten **8** boil down, condense, pare down **9** expurgate **10** abbreviate

blueprint 4 plan **5** chart **6** design, scheme **7** diagram **9** schematic

Blue Riders
German: **11** Blaue Reiter
group of: **7** artists

blues 5 dumps **8** doldrums **10** depression, low spirits, melancholy **11** despondency

bluestocking
French: **7** bas bleu

bluff 3 lie **4** bank, bold, crag, curt, dupe, fake, fool, hoax, liar, open, peak, sham **5** blunt, boast, cliff, faker, frank, fraud, ridge, rough **6** abrupt, candid, crusty, delude, direct, humbug **7** bluffer, boaster, brusque, deceive, fake out, mislead, pretend **8** bragging, headland, headlong, palisade, pretense **9** bamboozle, deception, idle boast, outspoken, precipice, pretender **10** escarpment, forthright, promontory, subterfuge **11** braggadocio, counterfeit, plainspoken **13** unceremonious, straightforward

bluffer 5 bluff, faker, fraud, phony **6** humbug **9** pretender

bluish 7 off-blue **12** somewhat blue

Blume, Claire
real name of: **11** Claire Bloom

Blume, Judy
author of: **5** Wifey **6** Deenie **7** Blubber, Forever **9** Tiger Eyes **10** Smart Women, Superfudge **13** Summer Sisters **19** Then Again Maybe I Won't **22** It's Not the End of the World **26**

Tales of a Fourth Grade Nothing **27**
Are You There God? It's Me Margaret

Blumenbach, Johann Friedrich
   field: 7 anatomy **10** physiology
   nationality: 6 German
   father of: 20 physical anthropology

blunder 4 goof, slip **5** boner, error, gaffe **6** booboo, bumble, bungle, slip up **7** faux pas, mistake, stagger, stumble **8** flounder **9** gaucherie **11** impropriety, make a booboo **12** indiscretion

blunt 4 curt, dull, numb, open **5** frank, rough, thick **6** abrupt, benumb, candid, deaden, dulled, soften, weaken **7** brusque, lighten, stupefy **8** edgeless, explicit, mitigate, moderate, tactless **9** outspoken, unpointed **10** to the point **11** insensitive, unsharpened **15** straightforward

bluntness 6 candor **10** directness **14** forthrightness **15** plainspokenness

blur 3 dim, fog, run **4** blot, haze, veil **5** bedim, befog, cloud, smear **6** blotch, darken, smudge, spread **7** becloud, obscure, splotch **9** confusion, obscurity

blurb 2 ad **4** rave, spot **5** brief **10** commercial **13** advertisement

blurred 3 dim **5** vague **6** blurry **7** smeared **10** ill-defined, indefinite, indistinct

blurt out 4 blab, sing **7** confess, divulge, let slip **8** give away **9** come clean

blush 5 color, flush **6** redden **7** grow red, turn red **8** rosy tint **9** reddening

blushing 3 coy, red **4** rosy **5** fresh, timid **6** demure, modest **7** colored, bashful, flushed, glowing **8** blooming, sheepish **9** rosaceous **10** embarrassed **11** flourishing

bluster 4 brag, crow, rant **5** bluff, boast, bully, gloat, noise, storm **7** bombast, bravado, crowing, protest, ranting, swagger **8** boasting, gloating, threaten **9** noisy talk **10** swaggering **14** boisterousness

blustery 5 blowy, gusty, windy **6** breezy **7** squally

Blythe, Ethel Mae
   real name of: 14 Ethel Barrymore

Blythe, John
   real name of: 13 John Barrymore

Blythe, Lionel
   real name of: 15 Lionel Barrymore

Boadicea
   Latin name: 8 Boudicca
   queen of: 5 Iceni
   husband: 10 Prasutagus
   ruled: 7 Norfolk (England)
   fought: 6 Romans
   died: 7 suicide

Boanerges
   means: 13 sons of thunder
   name given to: 4 John **5** James

boar
   group of: 7 sounder

board 3 bed **4** deal, feed, food, slat **5** enter, get on, house, lodge, meals, panel, plank, put up **6** batten, billet, embark, go onto **7** council, quarter **8** tribunal **9** clapboard, directors **10** daily meals

board game 4 Clue, Life, ludo **5** chess **7** Othello **8** checkers, cribbage, dominoes, draughts, fanorona, Monopoly, Scrabble **9** Alquerque **10** backgammon **14** Trivial Pursuit **15** Chinese checkers
   Egyptian: 5 Senat
   Korean: 5 Nyout, Pa-tok
   Indian: 7 pachisi **8** parchesi, shatranj **9** ashtapada **10** shaturanga
   Japanese: 2 Go **3** I-go **5** Shogi
   Chinese: 6 Ma-jong, wei-ch'i **7** Mahjong, Ma-jongg **8** Mah-jongg
   Swedish: 6 tablut

boast 4 brag, crow, have **5** vaunt **6** flaunt **7** contain, exhibit, possess, show off, talk big **15** blow one's own horn

boaster 6 gascon **7** bragger, egotist **8** blowhard, braggart **9** big talker **11** braggadocio

boastful 5 cocky **7** crowing, pompous, swollen **8** bragging, cocksure, inflated, puffed up, vaunting **9** conceited **11** braggadocio, exaggerated, pretentious **12** vainglorious

boastfulness 7 conceit, egotism **8** bragging **9** cockiness, immodesty, pomposity, vainglory **10** self-praise **11** braggadocio **12** cocksureness

boastful soldier
   Latin: 14 miles gloriosus

boat 4 ship **5** craft **6** vessel

Boaz
   father: 5 Salma **6** Salmon
   wife: 4 Ruth
   son: 4 Obed
   kinsman of: 5 Naomi **9** Elimelech

bob 3 cut, hop, nod **4** clip, crop, dock, duck, leap, trim **5** dance, shear **6** bounce **7** shorten

Bobadill
   character in: 19 Every Man in His Humour
   author: 6 Jonson

bobbin 3 pin **4** coil, cord, reel **5** quill, spool **6** piping **7** ratchet, spindle, torchon **8** cylinder

bobcat 3 cat **4** lynx **7** wildcat

Bob Cummings Show, The
   later name: 11 Love That Bob
   character: 10 Bob Collins **14** Chuck MacDonald **15** Charmaine (Shultzy) Shultz **17** Margaret MacDonald
   cast: 9 Ann B Davis **11** Bob Cummings **13** Dwayne Hickman **14** Rosemary DeCamp

Bob Newhart Show, The
   character: 12 Elliot Carlin, Emily Hartley, Howard Borden **13** Jerry Robinson, Robert (Bob) Hartley **20** Carol Kester Bondurant
   cast: 9 Bill Daily, Jack Riley **11** Peter Bonerz **13** Marcia Wallace **16** Suzanne Pleshette

Boccaccio, Giovanni
   author of: 10 Filostrato, Filocopo **11** Life of Dante **12** The Decameron

Boccherini, Luigi
   born: 5 Italy, Lucca
   composer of: 8 La Divina **9** The Aviary **10** Clementina **11** L'Uccelliera

Boccioni, Umberto
   born: 5 Italy **10** Reggio Emilia **16** Reggio di Calabria
   artwork: 10 Elasticity **12** The City Rises **15** Charge of Lancers **18** Dynamism of a Cyclist, The Forces of a Street **21** Fusion of Head and Window **30** Unique Forms of Continuity in Space

Bock, Hier
   field: 6 botany
   nationality: 6 German
   founded: 12 modern botany
   classified: 6 plants
   author of: 15 Neu Kreutterbuch

Bocklin, Arnold
   born: 5 Basel **7** Germany
   artwork: 13 Pan in the Reeds **16** The Isle of the Dead

Bod see **5** Tibet

bode 4 omen **5** augur **6** herald **7** betoken, ominate, point to, portend, predict, presage, signify **8** forecast, foretell, precurse **9** foreshadow, prefigure

bodega 9 warehouse **12** grocery store

bodice 3 top **5** stays, waist **6** bolero, corset, girdle **7** corsage **8** camisole, corselet **9** stomacher **10** underwaist

bodily 8 corporal, physical

bodkin 3 awl **4** pick, tool **5** auger, borer, drill, point, probe **6** dagger, lancet, needle, reamer **7** hair pin, piercer **8** puncheon, stiletto

body 3 mob **4** bloc, bulk, form, mass **5** being, build, force, frame, group, shape, stiff, thing, torso, trunk **6** corpse, corpus, figure, league, person, throng **7** cadaver, carcass, combine, council, faction, remains, society **8** assembly, cohesion, congress, deceased, main part, majority, physique, quantity **9** coalition, multitude, stiffness, thickness **10** federation **11** brotherhood, consistency **13** confederation

Body and Soul
   director: 12 Robert Rossen
   cast: 10 Anne Revere **11** Hazel Brooks, Lilli Palmer **12** John Garfield **13** William Conrad

bodybuilder 12 Charles Atlas **20** Arnold Schwarzeneger

Boeotus
father: **8** Poseidon
mother: **4** Arne

Boer, Boor 6 farmer **9** Afrikaner
language: **9** Afrikaans
ancestry: **5** Dutch
inhabitants of: **9** Transvaal **11** South
Africa **15** Orange Free State

Boffin
character in: **15** Our Mutual Friend
author: **7** Dickens

bog 3 fen **4** mire, sink **5** marsh,
swamp **6** morass **7** be stuck **8** quagmire, wetlands **9** marshland, swamp-
land

Bogaerde, Derek Van den
real name of: **11** Dirk Bogarde

Bogarde, Dirk
real name: **19** Derek Van den Bogaerde
born: **6** London **7** England **9** Hamp-
stead
roles: **6** Victim **7** Darling **10** The
Servant **13** Death in Venice **14** Song
Without End, The Night Porter **16** A
Tale of Two Cities
author of: **7** Jericho **9** Backcloth **12**
An Orderly Man, Closing Ranks **16**
Snakes and Ladders **27** Postillion
Struck by Lightning

Bogart, Humphrey
nickname: **5** Bogie
wife: **12** Lauren Bacall
born: **9** New York NY
roles: **8** Key Largo **10** Casablanca,
High Sierra **11** The Big Sleep **14** The
Caine Mutiny **15** The African Queen
(Oscar) **16** The Maltese Falcon, To
Have and Have Not **18** The Petrified
Forest **27** The Treasure of the Sierra
Madre

Bogdanovich, Peter
director of: **4** Mask **7** Targets, The
Trip **9** Paper Moon, Saint Jack **10**
Texasville **14** They all Laughed, Pic-
ture Windows **18** The Last Picture
Show
roles: **7** Targets, The Trip **9** Saint
Jack

bogey
term in: **4** golf
song: **18** Colonel Bogey's March

boggle 3 shy **4** balk, muff **5** botch, demure, hover, waver **6** bungle, shrink,
wobble **7** blunder, stumble **8** flounder, frighten, hesitate, hold back **9**
overwhelm **11** make a mess of

boggy 3 wet **4** soft **5** foggy, mossy,
soggy **6** marshy, spongy, swampy **7**
squashy

Bogie
nickname of: **14** Humphrey Bogart

Bogota
capital of: **8** Colombia

bogus 4 fake, sham **5** dummy, false,
phony **6** ersatz, forged, pseudo **7**
feigned, pretend **8** spurious **9** imita-

tion, simulated, synthetic **10** artificial,
fraudulent **11** counterfeit, make-
believe

Boheme, La
also: **12** Bohemian Life
opera by: **7** Puccini
character: **4** Mimi **7** Colline, Musetta,
Rodolfo **8** Marcello **9** Schaunard

bohemian, Bohemian 6 hippie **7**
beatnik **10** unorthodox **13** nonconformist **14** unconventional

Bohr, Niels
field: **7** physics
nationality: **6** Danish
developed: **8** atom bomb **13** quantum theory, uranium theory

Boiardo, Matteo Maria
author of: **17** Orlando Innamorato

boil 4 brew, burn, foam, fume, rage,
rant, rave, sore, stew, toss **5** chafe,
churn, froth, storm **6** bubble, fester,
quiver, seethe, simmer, sizzle, well up
7 abscess, bristle, parboil, pustule,
smolder **8** furuncle **9** carbuncle, fulminate

boil down 3 cut **6** reduce **7** abridge,
cut down, shorten **8** condense, contract **10** abbreviate

boiler 6 copper, geyser, heater, kettle **7**
alembic, caldron, furnace

Boilermaker, the
nickname of: **20** James Jackson Jeffries

boisterous 4 loud, wild **5** noisy,
rowdy **6** unruly **9** clamorous, out-of-
hand **10** disorderly, uproarious **12** obstreperous, uncontrolled, unrestrained

boite, boite de nuit 7 cabaret **9**
nightclub

Bojer, Johan
author of: **12** Folk by the Sea, The
Emigrants **14** The Great Hunger, The
Power of a Lie **16** Last of the Vikings

bold 3 hot **4** loud, rude **5** brash, brave,
fiery, fresh, saucy, vivid **6** brazen,
cheeky, daring, flashy, heroic **7** defiant, forward, valiant **8** colorful, creative, fearless, impudent, insolent, intrepid, spirited, stalwart, striking,
unafraid, valorous **9** audacious, daredevil, dauntless **10** courageous **11**
eye-catching, imaginative, impertinent,
indomitable, lionhearted, unshrinking
12 stouthearted **13** adventuresome

boldfaced 5 brash, saucy **6** brassy,
brazen **7** forward **8** immodest, impudent, insolent **9** audacious, barefaced,
shameless, unabashed

boldness 4 grit **5** nerve, pluck, spunk
6 daring, mettle **7** bravery, courage **8**
audacity **9** brashness, hardihood **10**
brazenness **13** audaciousness, determination, self-assurance **14** courageousness **15** adventurousness

Bolger, Ray

born: **12** Dorchester MA
roles: **9** Scarecrow **10** On Your Toes
13 The Wizard of Oz, Where's Charley

Bolivia
named for: **12** Simon Bolivar
capital:
administrative: **5** La Paz
legal: **5** Sucre
largest city: **5** La Paz
others: **3** Ivo **4** Icla, Itau, Mojo, Saya,
Yaco, Yato, Yura **5** Cliza, Llica,
Oruro, Quime, Uyuni, Zongo **6**
Guaqui, Potosi, Tiraja, Tupiza **8**
Pulacayo, Santa Cruz **10** Chuqui-
saca, Cochabamba **11** Vallegrande,
Villa Montes
government: **8** republic
school: **6** Xavier **8** St Andrew **12** San
Francisco
division: **6** Valles **7** Oriente, Valleys **8**
Montanas **9** Altiplano
measure: **6** league **7** celemin
monetary unit: **7** centavo **13** peso
boliviano
weight: **5** libra, marco
lake: **5** Poopo **7** Allagas, Coipasa, Rogagua **8** Titicaca **10** Desaguader
mountain: **4** Jara **5** Andes, Cusco,
Cuzco **6** Pupuya, Sajama, Sorata,
Sunsas **7** Illampu **8** Illimani,
Mururata, Sansimon, Santiago, Zapaleri **12** Eastern Range, Western
Range **18** Cordillera Oriental **20** Cordillera Occidental
highest point: **8** Ancohuma
river: **4** Beni, Yata **5** Abuna, Lauca,
Orton **6** Blanco, Ichilo, Itenez,
Madidi, Mamore, Mizque, Yacuma **7**
Guapore, Machupo **8** Inambari,
Itonamas **9** Pilcomayo, Rio Grande,
San Miguel **11** Desaguadero, Madre
de Dios
physical features:
lowlands: **6** Llanos
plateau: **9** Altiplano
swamp: **6** Izozog
valley: **5** Yunga
volcano: **7** Ollague
people: **6** Aymara **7** mestizo,
Quechua
author: **7** Mendoza **8** Arguedas **11**
Costa du Rels
leader: **5** Busch, Sucre **6** Candia,
Ortuno, Zamora **7** Bolivar **9** Mel-
garejo, Paz Zamora, Santa Cruz
10 Barrientos, Estenssoro **11** Mesa
Gisbert
language: **6** Aymara **7** Quechua,
Spanish
religion: **13** Roman Catholic
place:
church: **9** St Francis, St Michael **10**
San Lorenzo
monument: **11** La Coronilla
ruins: **10** Tiahuanaco
tower: **6** Chulpa
feature:

animal: 5 llama **6** alpaca, vicuna
bar/club: 7 boliche
boat: 5 balsa
dance/song: 5 cueca **7** huainos, pasillo **8** morenada **9** taquirari **10** palla-palla **11** cacharpayas, wakatokonis
devil dance: 8 Diablado
guitar: 8 charango
skirt: 7 pollera
wind instrument: 4 kena, sicu **5** erque, quena, tarka **6** pututu **9** pinquillo
food:
chicken dish: 14 picante de pollo
corn: 4 mote
corn drink: 3 api **14** chicha taratena
dish: 11 plato paceno **14** sajta de gallina
dried meat: 7 charque
pancakes: 7 bunulos
potato: 5 chuno

Bolkonsky, Andrei
character in: 11 War and Peace
author: 7 Tolstoy

Boll, Heinrich
author of: 8 The Clown **12** The Safety Net **11** The Casualty **14** The Silent Angel **18** Absent Without Leave **21** Group Portrait With Lady **23** Billiards at Half-Past Nine **27** The Lost Honor of Katharina Blum **28** Missing Persons and Other Essays

bolster 3 aid **4** help **5** add to, brace **6** assist, cradle, hold up, pillow, prop up, uphold **7** cushion, shore up, support, sustain **8** buttress, maintain, shoulder **9** reinforce **10** strengthen

bolster one's spirits 5 cheer **7** cheer up, comfort, hearten **8** inspirit **9** buoy one up, encourage

bolt 3 bar, fly, peg, pin, rod, run **4** dart, dash, flee, gulp, jump, leap, lock, roll, rush, tear, wolf **5** bound, brand, catch, dowel, flash, hurry, latch, rivet, scoot, shaft, speed **6** fasten, gobble, hasten, hurtle, length, secure, spring, sprint, stroke **8** fastener **12** swallow whole

bolt down 4 wolf **5** scarf **6** devour, gobble **8** gulp down

bomb 3 dud, egg **4** bust, fail, flop, mine **5** lemon **6** fiasco, fizzle, turkey **7** bombard, grenade, failure, washout

bombard 5 beset, hound, shell, worry **6** assail, attack, batter, harass, pepper, pester, strafe **7** assault, barrage, besiege **8** fire upon **9** cannonade

bombardment 5 blitz, siege **7** air raid, assault, barrage, bombing **10** blitzkrieg

bombast 3 pad **4** puff, rant **6** cotton **7** bluster, fustian, palaver **8** boasting, flummery, rhapsody, tall talk, verbiage **9** bavardage **10** balderdash **12** braggadocio, exaggeration **13** magnilo-

quence, overstatement **14** grandiloquence **17** sesquipedalianism

bombastic 5 tumid, windy, wordy **6** padded, turgid **7** pompous, verbose **8** inflated **12** magniloquent **13** grandiloquent

Bombay *see* **6** Mumbai

Bona Dea
also: 5 Fauna
origin: 5 Roman
goddess of: 8 chastity **9** fertility
worshipped by: 5 women
father: 6 Faunus
brother: 6 Faunus
husband: 6 Faunus

bona fide 4 real, true **5** legal **6** actual, honest, lawful **7** genuine, sincere **9** authentic, honorable **10** legitimate **11** in good faith

bon ami 5 lover **8** cleanser. **10** good friend

bonanza 8 gold mine, windfall

Bonanza
character: 3 Ben **4** Adam, Hoss **5** Candy **7** Hop Sing **9** Little Joe
family: 10 Cartwright
cast: 10 Dan Blocker **11** David Canary, Lorne Greene **13** Michael Landon, Victor Sen Yung **14** Pernell Roberts
ranch: 9 Ponderosa

Bonanza State
nickname of: 7 Montana

bon appetit 14 hearty appetite

Bonario
character in: 7 Volpone
author: 7 Jonson

bonbon 5 candy, sweet **7** fondant **9** sweetmeat **10** confection, sugar candy **13** confectionery **14** chocolate cream

bond, bonds 3 tie **4** cord, knot, link, rope **5** irons, scrip, union **6** chains, pledge **7** compact, fetters, promise **8** affinity, bindings, manacles, security, shackles **9** agreement, guarantee, handcuffs **10** allegiance, attachment, connection, fastenings, obligation **11** certificate, stipulation

Bond, James
actor: 10 Roger Moore **11** Sean Connery **12** Peter Sellers **13** George Lazenby, Pierce Brosnan, Timothy Dalton
appears in: 4 Dr No **9** GoldenEye, Moonraker, Octopussy **10** Goldfinger **11** Thunderball **12** A View To A Kill **13** Die Another Day, Licence to Kill, Live and Let Die **15** For Your Eyes Only **16** The Spy Who Loved Me, You Only Live Twice **17** Tomorrow Never Dies **18** Diamonds Are Forever, From Russia with Love, Never Say Never Again, The Living Daylights **19** The World Is Not Enough **22** The Man with the Golden Gun **26** On Her Majesty's Secret Service

author: 10 Ian Fleming
drink: 12 vodka martini **16** shaken not stirred
employer: 3 MI-6 **20** British Secret Service
foe: 7 Blofeld, SPECTRE
office staff: 1 M, Q **14** Miss Moneypenny
university: 6 Oxford
wife: 5 Tracy

bondage 4 yoke **6** chains **7** fetters, serfdom, slavery **8** shackles **9** captivity, servitude, vassalage **11** enslavement

bone
comprise: 8 skeleton
contain: 6 marrow **9** cartilage **11** blood vessel
fitted together by: 5 joint
held by: 8 ligament
pulled by: 6 muscle
specific: 3 rib **4** ulna **5** femur, skull, tibia **6** carpal, fibula, pelvis, radius, sacrum, tarsal **7** humerus, patella, scapula, sternum **8** clavicle, vertebra **9** vertebrae

bone chilling 3 icy **4** cold **5** harsh, sharp **6** arctic, biting, bitter, frigid **7** cutting, glacial **8** piercing, stinging **11** penetrating **15** teeth-chattering

bonehead 3 ass **4** clod, dolt, fool **5** booby, dunce, idiot, moron, ninny **6** dimwit, nitwit **7** fathead, half-wit **8** dumb-dumb, imbecile, lunkhead **9** blockhead, lamebrain, numbskull **10** dunderhead, nincompoop **11** chowderhead

boner 4 goof, slip **5** error **6** boo-boo, slip-up **7** blooper, blunder, mistake

boneyard 4 dump **7** ossuary **8** Boot Hill, cemetery, junkyard **9** graveyard **10** churchyard **12** burial ground **13** burying ground

Bonheur, Rosa
real name: 19 Marie Rosalie Bonheur
born: 6 France **8** Bordeaux
artwork: 12 The Horse Fair **23** Ploughing in the Nivernais

bonjour 5 hello **7** good day

Bonjour Tristesse
author: 14 Francoise Sagan

bon marche 7 bargain

bon mot 4 quip **7** epigram **9** witticism

Bonn
former capital of: 11 West Germany
landmark: 10 Bundeshaus **11** Munsterkerk
museum: 18 Ludwig van Beethoven
river: 5 Rhine
Roman fort: 15 Castra Bonnensia

Bonnard, Pierre
born: 6 France **16** Fontenay-aux-Roses
artwork: 8 Intimist, Luncheon **9** The Review **13** Nude in the Bath, The Open Window, Women with a Dog **14** After the Shower, Farm at Le

Cannet **16** The Breakfast Room **17** The Terrasse Family **22** Figure Before a Fireplace

bonne amie 5 lover **6** friend **10** good friend

bonne nuit 9 good night

bonnet 3 cap, hat **4** cowl, hood, sail **5** cover, toque **7** chapeau, commode **8** headgear **9** headdress

Bonnie and Clyde
   director: **10** Arthur Penn
   cast: **11** Faye Dunaway (Bonnie Parker), Gene Hackman **12** Warren Beatty (Clyde Barrow) **15** Michael J Pollard

bonny 4 fair **6** comely, lovely, pretty, seemly **7** winning, winsome **8** engaging, fetching, handsome, pleasing **9** beautiful, exquisite, ravishing **10** attractive

bon soir 9 good night **11** good evening

bonus 4 gift **5** prize **6** bounty, reward **7** benefit, premium **8** dividend, gratuity **10** honorarium

Bonus Eventus
   also: **7** Eventus
   origin: **5** Roman
   god of: **4** luck **10** prosperity **11** agriculture

bon vivant 7 epicure, gourmet **8** gourmand, sybarite **10** gastronome

bony 4 lean **5** gaunt, lanky, spare **6** skinny **7** angular, scrawny **11** full of bones **12** skin-and-bones

boo 3 pan **4** hiss **5** taunt **6** deride, heckle, revile **7** catcall **8** ridicule **9** criticize, shout down **11** give the bird **16** give the raspberry

boo-boo 4 goof, slip **5** boner, error **6** slip-up **7** blunder, mistake

boobtube 2 TV **3** box **5** telly **8** idiot box **13** television set

booby 4 bird, dope, fool **5** dummy, dunce, idiot, moron, ninny **6** dimwit, gannet, nitwit **7** fathead, halfwit **8** bonehead, dumb-dumb, imbecile, lunkhead, numskull **9** blockhead, lamebrain, simpleton **10** nincompoop **11** chowderhead

Booby, Lady
   character in: **13** Joseph Andrews
   author: **8** Fielding

boodle 4 loot, swag **5** booty, bribe, crowd, graft, group **7** plunder **10** collection **11** stolen goods

Boog
   nickname of: **10** John Powell

Boogie Nights
   director: **18** Paul Thomas Anderson
   cast: **10** Don Cheadle (Buck Swope), Luis Guzman (Maurice Rodriguez) **12** Burt Reynolds (Jack Horner), Mark Wahlberg (Dirk Diggler), William H. Macy (Little Bill) **13** Heather Graham (Brandy), Julianne Moore (Amber Waves)

boohoo 3 cry, sob **4** bawl, weep **7** blubber **9** shed tears

book 4 bill, file, list, note, opus, post, tome **5** album, enter, index, slate **6** accuse, charge, engage, enroll, indict, insert, line up, record, tablet, volume **7** catalog, procure, program, put down, reserve **8** mark down, notebook, register, schedule, treatise **9** bound work, write down **10** arrange for **11** publication, written work **16** make reservations

bookish 7 erudite, learned, stilted **8** academic, educated, informed, literary, pedantic, studious, well-read **9** scholarly **11** pedagogical, impractical **12** intellectual

bookkeeper 5 clerk **7** auditor **10** accountant **11** comptroller

booklet 5 folio **7** leaflet, program **8** brochure, circular, pamphlet

Book of Common Prayer
   author: **10** Joan Didion

Book of Lights, The
   author: **10** Chaim Potok

Book of Manuel
   author: **13** Julio Cortazar

Book of Odes
   author: **9** Confucius

Book of psalms 12 psalter

Book of Sand, The
   author: **15** Jorge Luis Borges

Book of the Duchess, The
   author: **15** Geoffrey Chaucer

boom 3 bar **4** bang, beam, gain, grow, push, roar, spar **5** blast, boost, shaft, spurt **6** growth, rumble, thrive, thrust, upturn **7** advance, develop, prosper, thunder, upsurge **8** flourish, increase **9** expansion, good times

Boom Boom
   nickname of: **15** Bernie Geoffrion

boomerang 5 kalie, kiley, kylie, wango **6** atlatl, recoil **7** rebound, womerah, woomera **8** backfire, ricochet, trombush **9** bound back, solitaire **10** projectile

Boomer State
   nickname of: **8** Oklahoma

boon 3 fun, gay **4** gift **5** favor, jolly, merry **6** kindly **7** benefit, bequest **8** blessing, donation, offering, pleasant **9** advantage, congenial, convivial, endowment **11** full of cheer, good-natured

boon companion 3 pal **4** chum **5** buddy, crony **6** friend **7** comrade **8** confrere, intimate **9** confidant **10** bosom buddy

boondocks 4 bush, veld **6** Podunk, sticks **7** boonies, country, outback **8** frontier **9** backwater, backwoods, provinces **10** hinterland **11** backcountry, countryside **12** squaresville **13** nowheresville **14** wide open spaces

Boone, Richard

born: **12** Los Angeles CA
roles: **5** Medic **6** Hombre **7** Paladin **8** The Alamo **11** The Shootist **12** Ten Wanted Men, The Desert Fox **17** Have Gun Will Travel

boonies 6 sticks **7** country **9** backwoods, boondocks, provinces **10** hinterland **11** countryside

boor 3 oaf **4** hick, lout, rube **5** brute, churl, yokel **6** rustic **7** bumpkin, hayseed, peasant **9** vulgarian **10** clodhopper, philistine **11** guttersnipe

boorish 4 rude **5** crude **6** coarse, gauche, oafish, rustic, vulgar **7** loutish, uncouth **9** unrefined **10** unpolished **11** peasantlike

boorishness 8 rudeness **9** surliness, vulgarity **10** bad manners, coarseness, incivility, oafishness **12** churlishness, impoliteness

boost 4 hike, laud, lift, plug, push, rise **5** add to, extol, heave, hoist, pitch, raise, shove, steal, swipe **6** expand, foster, free ad, growth, pickup, praise, upturn, urge on **7** acclaim, advance, develop, elevate, enlarge, forward, further, improve, nurture, promote, root for, support, sustain, upsurge, upswing **8** addition, applause, good word, increase, propound, shoplift **9** expansion, increment, promotion **10** compliment, give a leg up, stick up for **11** development, enlargement, improvement, speak well of

boot
   French: **9** chaussure

booth 3 pen **4** coop, nook, tent **5** hutch, stall, stand, table **7** counter **9** cubbyhole, enclosure **11** compartment

Booth, Shirley
   real name: **15** Thelma Booth Ford
   born: **9** New York NY
   roles: **5** Hazel **13** The Matchmaker **19** Come Back Little Sheba (Oscar)

bootleg 5 hooch **7** illegal, illicit **8** unlawful **9** moonshine **12** football play

bootless 6 futile **7** useless **11** ineffective, ineffectual **12** unproductive, unprofitable

bootlick 4 fawn **5** toady **6** cringe, grovel **7** flatter, truckle

bootmaker 7 cobbler **9** shoemaker

booty 4 gain, loot **5** prize **6** boodle, spoils **7** pillage, plunder, takings **8** pickings, winnings

booze 4 bout, soak **5** drink, hooch, spree **6** guzzle, liquor, tipple **7** alcohol, spirits, swizzle **8** cocktail **10** intoxicant **14** drink like a fish
   type: **3** gin, rum, rye **4** beer, wine **5** vodka **6** scotch **7** bourbon, whiskey

boozer 3 sot **4** lush **5** drunk, souse, toper **7** tippler **8** drunkard **9** alcoholic, inebriate **11** hard drinker

bordello, bordel 4 stew **5** house **6** bagnio **7** brothel **8** cathouse **10**

bawdy house, fancy house, whore-house **13** sporting house **14** house of ill fame **16** house of ill repute **19** house of prostitution

border 3 hem, rim **4** abut, bind, brim, curb, edge, join, line, pale, trim **5** brink, flank, frame, limit, skirt, touch, verge **6** adjoin, fringe, margin **8** befringe, be next to, boundary, frontier, outskirt **9** extremity, perimeter, periphery **13** circumference

borderline 4 open **5** vague **7** halfway, inexact, obscure, unclear **8** marginal **9** ambiguous, equivocal, uncertain, undecided, unsettled **10** ambivalent, indefinite **11** indefinable, problematic **13** indeterminate

bore 4 drag, drip, sink, tire **5** drill, drive, weary **6** burrow, pierce, tunnel **7** caliber, exhaust, fatigue, wear out **8** gouge out **9** hollow out **10** wet blanket **14** inside diameter

Boreal
pertaining to: **6** Boreas

Boreas
origin: **5** Greek
personifies: **9** north wind
father: **8** Astraeus
mother: **3** Eos
twin sons: **5** Zetes **6** Calais
daughter: **6** Chione **9** Cleopatra

bored 5 jaded **7** wearied **12** discontented, uninterested

boredom 5 ennui **6** tedium **8** doldrums, dullness, monotony **9** weariness **11** tediousness

Borges, Jorge Luis
author of: **8** The Aleph **10** Labyrinths **11** Dreamtigers **13** The Book of Sand **18** A Personal Anthology, In Praise of Darkness **19** Doctor Brodie's Report, Fervor of Buenos Aires **25** A Universal History of Infamy
nationality: **9** Argentina

Borghild
origin: **12** Scandinavian
mentioned in: **8** Volsunga
husband: **7** Sigmund

Borgia, Alfonso de 16 Pope Callistus III

Borgia, Rodrigo de 15 Pope Alexander VI

Borglum, (John) Gutzon
born: **10** Bear Lake ID
artwork: **7** Lincoln **18** Mt Rushmore Memorial, The Mares of Diomedes

Borgnine, Ernest
real name: **18** Ermes Effron Borgnine
wife: **11** Ethel Merman
born: **8** Hamden CT
roles: **5** Marty (Oscar) **8** Barabbas **11** McHale's Navy **12** The Wild Bunch **13** The Dirty Dozen **17** Bad Day at Black Rock **18** From Here to Eternity **20** The Poseidon Adventure

boring 4 dull, flat **5** stale **6** tiring **7** humdrum, insipid, tedious **8** tiresome **9** wearisome **10** monotonous, unexciting **11** repetitious **13** uninteresting

boring tool 3 bit **5** auger, drill **11** brace and bit

Borinquen *see* **10** Puerto Rico

Boriquen, Borinquen
language family: **8** Arawakan
location: **10** Puerto Rico
related to: **5** Taino

Boris Godunov
author: **16** Alexander Pushkin
opera by: **10** Mussorgsky **12** Shostakovich **14** Rimsky-Korsakov
role: **4** czar, tsar
character: **6** Dmitri, Feodor, Maryna **7** Gregory, Grigory **8** Basmanov, Otrepyev

born 6 innate **7** natural **9** delivered, intuitive **12** brought forth

Born, Max
field: **7** physics
nationality: **7** British
worked on: **13** quantum theory
awarded: **10** Nobel Prize

borne 6 afloat, braved **7** carried, endured **8** put up with, tolerated **11** gone through, went through **12** given birth to

Borneo
other name: **10** Kalimantan
largest city: **12** Bandjermasin
others: **5** Kumai **6** Sambas, Sampit **7** Malinau, Pagatan, Sanggau, Sintang, Tarakan **8** Ketapang **9** Pontianak **10** Balikpapan
division of island:
  independent: **6** Brunei
  Malaysian state: **5** Sabah **7** Sarawak
  part of Indonesia: **10** Kalimantan
measure: **7** gantang
weight: **4** para **6** chapah
mountain: **4** Iran, Raja **5** Saran **6** Kapuas, Muller, Nijaan, Tebang **8** Kinibalu, Schwaner
highest point: **8** Kinabalu
river: **4** Arut, Iwan **5** Bahau, Berau, Kajan, Padas, Pawan **6** Barito, Kapuas, Rajang, Sebuku **7** Kahajan, Mahakam, Mendawi **8** Pembuang
sea: **4** Java, Sulu **7** Celebes **10** South China
physical feature:
  bay: **5** Adang, Kumai **6** Sampit
  cape: **3** Aru **4** Datu **5** Lojar **6** Puting, Sambar **7** Selatan
  port: **4** Miri **5** Balik, Papan **6** Brunei **9** Pontianak **12** Bandjermasin
  strait: **8** Macassar
people: **4** Iban **5** Bukat, Dajak, Dayak, Dusan, Malay, Punan **6** Ilano **7** Bakatan, Chinese, Illanun
language: **5** Malay **6** tribal **7** Chinese, English
religion: **5** Islam **7** animism **12** Christianity

feature:
  tree: **5** kapor, kapur **7** billian

Born Yesterday
director: **11** George Cukor
cast: **12** Judy Holliday **13** William Holden **17** Broderick Crawford
Oscar for: **7** actress (Holliday)

Borodin, Alexander
born: **6** Russia **12** St Petersburg
member of: **7** The Five
composer of: **8** Bogatyri **10** Prince Igor **25** In the Steppes of Central Asia

boron
chemical symbol: **1** B
compound: **5** borax

borough 4 burg, town **5** borgo, shire **6** county, parish **7** village **8** district, precinct, province, township **12** municipality
of New York City: **5** Kings, Bronx **6** Queens **8** Brooklyn, Richmond **9** Manhattan **12** Staten Island

Borromini, Francesco
architect of: **10** San Carlino **17** Palazzo Falconieri **20** Sant' Ivo della Sapienza **23** Oratory of San Filippo Neri **24** Collegio di Propaganda Fide **26** San Carlo alle Quattro Fontane (Rome)

borrow 3 get, use **4** copy, take **5** filch, steal, usurp **6** obtain, pilfer, pirate **7** acquire **10** commandeer, plagiarize, take on loan **11** appropriate

Borrow, George Henry
author of: **8** Lavengro **9** Romany Rye, Wild Wales **10** The Zincali **15** The Bible in Spain

Bors, Sir
character in: **16** Arthurian romance

Bosch, Hieronymus
real name: **13** Jerome van Aken **14** Jerome van Aeken **17** Jeroen Anthoiszoon
artwork: **7** HayWain **11** Ship of Fools **14** The Crucifixion **19** Adoration of the Kings **21** The Crowning with Thorns **26** The Garden of Earthly Delights

bosh 3 rot **4** bunk **6** bunkum, drivel **7** twaddle **8** claptrap, nonsense, tommyrot **10** balderdash, tomfoolery **11** foolishness **16** stuff and nonsense

bosky 5 bushy, drunk, shaded, tipsy, treed **6** wooded

Bosnia and Herzegovina
capital/largest city: **8** Sarajevo
others: **4** Neum **5** Tuzlal **6** Citluk, Kupres, Lenica, Mostar **8** Prijedor **9** Banja Luka, Bijeljina **10** Srebrenica **12** Bosanski Brod, Siroki Brijeg
head of state: **9** president
monetary unit: **5** dinar
mountain: **11** Dinaric Alps
river: **3** Una **4** Sava **5** Bosna, Drina, Vrbas **7** Neretva
sea: **8** Adriatic

people: 4 Serb **5** Croat **6** Muslim **8** Yugoslav
language: 13 Serbo Croatian
religion: 11 Sunni Muslim **15** Serbian Orthodox

bosom 4 bust, core, dear, soul **5** chest, close, heart, midst **6** breast, center, spirit **8** beloved, nucleus **8** intimate **9** cherished **11** inner circle

bosom buddy 4 chum **5** crony **6** cohort **7** best pal, comrade **8** alter ego, intimate, sidekick **9** companion, confidant **10** best friend

bosomy 5 busty, buxom **6** zaftig **11** full-figured **13** large-breasted

boss 4 head, push **5** chief, order **6** leader, master **7** command, foreman, kingpin, manager **8** employer **9** big cheese, executive **10** supervisor **13** administrator **14** superintendent

bossy 3 cow **9** imperious **10** commanding, tyrannical **11** dictatorial, domineering

Boston
airport: 5 Logan
area/landmark: 7 Back Bay **10** Beacon Hill, Bunker Hill, Fenway Park **11** Faneuil Hall **14** Kennedy Library, Old North Church
baseball team: 6 Red Sox
basketball team: 7 Celtics
dish: 10 baked beans
hockey team: 6 Bruins
leader: 7 Brahmin
nickname: 8 Bean town
project: 6 Big Dig
river: 7 Charles

Bostonians, The
author: 10 Henry James

Boston Legal
network: 3 ABC
creator: 12 David E. Kelley
cast: 8 Lake Bell (Sally Heep) **10** Mark Valley (Brad Chase), Rhona Mitra (Tara Wilson) **11** James Spader (Alan Shore) **12** Monica Potter (Lori Colson) **13** Candice Bergen (Shirley Schmidt) **14** William Shatner (Denny Crane) **15** Rene Auberjonois (Paul Lewiston)

Boston Public
network: 3 FOX
creator: 12 David E. Kelley
cast: 8 Jeri Ryan (Ronnie Cooke) **9** Nicky Katt (Harry Senate) **10** Chi McBride (Steven Harper), Sharon Leal (Marilyn Sudor) **12** Anthony Heald (Scott Guber), Fyvush Finkel (Harvey Lipschultz) **13** Loretta Devine (Marla Hendricks) **14** Jessalyn Gilsig (Lauren Davis) **15** Michael Rapaport (Danny Hanson)

Boston Strong Boy
nickname of: 13 John L Sullivan

Boswell, James
author of: 22 The Life of Samuel Johnson

botanist
American: 6 Barton, Carver, Torrey **7** Bartram
Austrian: 6 Mendel
Dutch: 7 DeVries
German: 4 Bock, Cohn
Scottish: 5 Brown
Swedish: 8 Linnaeus
Swiss: 6 Bauhin

botch 3 err, mar **4** blow, fail, flop, flub, goof, hash, mess, muff, ruin **5** spoil **6** bungle, foul up, fumble **7** blunder, butcher, failure, louse up **8** butchery **9** mismanage **11** make a mess of

bother 3 ado, irk, nag, tax, try, vex **4** care, drag, fret, fuss, load, onus, stir **5** annoy, harry, trial, upset, worry **6** dismay, flurry, harass, pester, racket, rumpus, strain, stress, tumult **7** attempt, disturb, problem, trouble **8** disquiet, distress, hardship, headache, irritate, nuisance, vexation **9** aggravate, commotion, hindrance **10** affliction, difficulty, impediment, irritation **11** aggravation, disturbance, encumbrance **12** make an effort **13** inconvenience, pain in the neck **14** responsibility

bothersome 6 taxing, vexing **8** annoying **9** worrisome **10** disturbing **11** aggravating, disquieting, distressing, troublesome **12** inconvenient

Botswana
other name: 12 Bechuanaland
capital/largest city: 8 Gaborone **9** Gaberones
others: 5 Kanye, Orapa, Tsane **6** Serowe **7** Lobatse, Lobotsi, Mochudi, Palapye, Thamaga **10** Molepolole **11** Francistown, Selebi-Pikwe
monetary unit: 4 pula, rand
lake: 3 Dow, Xau **5** Ngami
highest point: 11 Tsodilo Hill
river: 4 Nata, Okwa **5** Chobe, Nosob **6** Cuando, Molopo, Shashi **7** Cubango, Limpopo **8** Botletle, Okovango **9** Okovanggo
physical feature:
desert: 8 Kalahari
salt pans: 10 Makarikari
swamp: 8 Okavango
people: 5 Bantu **6** Tswana **7** Bakatla, Bakwena, Bushman **8** Bamalete, Baralong, Batawana, Batlokwa, Botswana **10** Bamangwato **11** Bangwaketse
language: 5 Bantu, Click **6** Tswana **7** English, Khoisan **8** Setswana
religion: 7 animism **10** Protestant **12** Christianity

Botticelli, Sandro
real name: 30 Alessandro di Mariano dei Filipepi
born: 5 Italy **8** Florence
artwork: 12 Birth of Venus **14** Mystic Nativity **16** Calumny of Apelles **18** Adoration of the Magi **22** Pallas Sub-duing a Centaur **25** The Madonna of the Magnificat

bottle 3 jar **4** vial **5** flask, phial **6** carafe, flagon, vessel **7** canteen

bottleneck 3 bar, jam **4** clog, stop **5** block **6** detour **7** barrier, embolus **8** blockage, embolism, gridlock, obstacle, stoppage, thrombus **10** congestion, impediment, infarction **11** costiveness, obstruction

bottom 3 can **4** base, core, foot, gist, root, rump, seat, sole **5** basis, belly, cause, fanny, heart, lower **6** center, deeper, depths, ground, lowest, origin, source, spring **7** deepest, essence **8** backside, buttocks, pedestal, riverbed **9** beginning, fundament, principle, rudiments, substance, underpart, underside **10** foundation, mainspring, wellspring **12** quintessence

Bottom
character in: 21 A Midsummer Night's Dream
author: 11 Shakespeare
turned into: 3 ass

bottomless 4 deep **7** abysmal **8** profound **11** measureless **12** immeasurable, unfathomable

Boucher, Francois
born: 5 Paris **6** France
artwork: 9 The Rising **13** Madame Boucher, Reclining Girl **16** Evening Landscape, Rinaldo and Armida, The Toilet of Venus **17** Chinese Tapestries, The Triumph of Venus **18** The Setting of the Sun

boudoir 7 bedroom **10** bedchamber **12** dressing room

bough 4 limb **6** branch

bougie 3 dip, wax **5** light, taper **6** candle, cierge, tallow

boulder, bowlder 3 nob **4** crag, knob, rock **5** block, stone **6** gibber **7** dornick **8** megalith

boulevard 6 avenue **7** parkway **9** concourse

bouleversement 7 turmoil **9** confusion, upsetting **11** overturning

bounce 3 bob, hop, pep **4** bump, life **5** bound, thump, verve, vigor **6** energy, jounce, recoil, spirit **7** rebound **8** dynamism, ricochet, vitality, vivacity **9** animation **10** liveliness

bouncing 3 big **4** full **5** jolly, large, lusty, plump **6** chubby, lively, robust, strong **7** healthy **8** animated, vigorous **12** in good health

bound 3 bob, orb, rim **4** area, edge, jump, leap, line, mark, pale, romp, sure, tied **5** dance, fated, hedge, limit, orbit, range, realm, vault **6** border, bounce, define, domain, doomed, forced, fringe, gambol, liable, prance, region, spring, tied up **7** certain, compass, confine, covered, encased, enclosed, flounce, going to, in bonds, limited, obliged, rebound, secured, trussed, wrapped **8** beholden, boundary, confined, destined, district, encircle, fastened, province, required, resolute, resolved, surround, tethered **9** bailiwick, committed, demarcate, extremity, periphery, territory **10** determined, restrained **11** demarcation **12** circumscribe

boundary 3 rim **4** edge, line, pale **6** border, margin **7** barrier **8** frontier, landmark **9** extremity, periphery **11** demarcation **12** dividing line

boundary line 4 edge **5** bound **6** border **8** sideline

bounder 3 cad, rat **4** heel **5** knave, louse, rogue **6** rascal, rotter **7** caitiff, dastard, villain **9** scoundrel **10** blackguard

Bounderby, Mr
  character in: **9** Hard Times
  author: **7** Dickens

boundless 4 vast **7** endless, immense **8** infinite, unending **9** limitless, perpetual, unbounded, unlimited **10** without end **11** everlasting, measureless **12** immeasurable, incalculable, unrestricted **13** inexhaustible

bounteous, bountiful 4 free, full, rich **5** ample, large **6** lavish **7** copious, liberal, profuse, teeming **8** abundant, generous, prolific **9** abounding, plenteous, plentiful, unsparing **10** beneficent, benevolent, charitable, munificent, unstinting **11** magnanimous, overflowing

Bountiful, Lady
  character in: **17** The Beaux Stratagem
  author: **8** Farquhar

bountifulness 10 liberality, generosity **11** benevolence, magnanimity, munificence **14** charitableness **15** humanitarianism

bounty 3 aid **4** gift, help **5** bonus, favor, grant **6** giving, reward **7** charity, present, tribute **8** bestowal, donation, gratuity **9** endowment **10** almsgiving, assistance, generosity, liberality, recompense **11** benefaction, benevolence, munificence **12** contribution, philanthropy **14** charitableness, openhandedness

bouquet 4 odor **5** aroma, scent, spray **7** essence, garland, nosegay, perfume **9** fragrance **11** boutonniere

bouquet garni
  ingredient: **5** basil, thyme **6** celery, savory **7** bay leaf, chervil, parsley **8** rosemary, tarragon

bourbon
  variety of: **7** whiskey
  origin: **7** America
  ingredient: **4** corn
  type: **7** blended **8** straight
  drink: **9** Mint Julep **10** Boston Sour **11** John Collins **12** Old Fashioned
  with Benedictine: **9** Twin Hills

with brandy and Benedictine: **13** Brighton Punch
  with Cointreau: **10** Temptation
  with rum: **14** Artillery Punch
  with sloe gin: **9** Black Hawk
  with Southern Comfort: **14** Blended Comfort
  with triple sec: **10** Chapel Hill
  with vermouth: **9** Allegheny

bourgeois 6 square **7** Babbitt, burgher **8** commoner, ordinary **11** middle-class **12** conventional **13** unimaginative

Bourgeois Gentleman, The
  author: **7** Moliere
  character: **6** Lucile, Nicole **7** Cleonte, Dorante **8** Covielle, Dorimene **14** Madame Jourdain **16** Monsieur Jourdain

Bourget, Charles Joseph Paul
  author of: **11** The Disciple **12** A Cruel Enigma **14** The Night Cometh

Bourgh, Lady Catherine de
  character in: **17** Pride and Prejudice
  author: **6** Austen

Bourjaily, Vance
  author of: **11** The Violated **14** The End of My Life **18** Brill Among the Ruins **22** Now Playing at Canterbury

Bourne Identity, The
  director: **9** Doug Liman
  author: **12** Robert Ludlum
  cast: **8** Brian Cox (Ward Abbott) **9** Clive Owen (the Professor), Matt Damon (Jason Bourne) **11** Chris Cooper (Alexander Conklin), Julia Stiles (Nicky Parsons) **13** Franka Potente (Marie Helena Kreutz)

Bourne Supremacy, The
  director: **14** Paul Greengrass
  based on novel by: **12** Robert Ludlum
  cast: **8** Brian Cox (Ward Abbott), **9** Joan Allen (Pamela Landy), Karl Urban (Kirill), Matt Damon (Jason Bourne) **11** Gabriel Mann (Danny Zorn), Julia Stiles (Nicky Parsons) **13** Franka Potente (Marie Helena Kreutz)

bout 4 fray, term, tilt, turn **5** brush, clash, cycle, fight, match, set-to, siege, spell, spree **6** affair, battle, course, period, series **7** contest, go-round, scuffle, session, tourney **8** conflict, interval, skirmish, struggle **9** encounter **10** contention, engagement **11** boxing match, embroilment

boutonniere 4 posy **7** nosegay **16** buttonhole flower

bow 3 arc **4** bend, knot, prow, stem **5** agree, curve, defer, front, stoop, yield **6** archer, comply, curtsy, give in, kowtow, relent, salaam, submit, weapon **7** concede, succumb, crescent **9** acquiesce, genuflect, surrender **10** capitulate, forward end **12** genuflection, knuckle under

Bow, Clara

nickname: **6** It Girl
  born: **10** Brooklyn NY
  roles: **2** It **7** Mantrap **12** The Wild Party

bowdlerize 6 censor **9** expurgate **10** blue-pencil

bow down 5 yield **6** give in, submit **9** surrender **10** capitulate **12** knuckle under

bowed 4 bent **6** arched, curved, nodded **7** hunched, stooped

bowels 3 gut, pit **4** core, guts, womb **5** abyss, belly, bosom, heart, midst **6** depths, hollow, vitals **7** innards, insides, stomach, viscera **8** entrails, interior, recesses **10** intestines **11** vital organs **13** innermost part

Bowen, Elizabeth
  author of: **8** Eva Trout, The Hotel **10** To the North **11** Bowen's Court, Little Girls, The Cat Jumps **12** A World of Love **15** The Heat of the Day, The House in Paris **18** The Death of the Heart

Bowen's Court
  author: **14** Elizabeth Bowen

bower 4 jack, joker, nook **5** arbor **6** alcove, anchor, pandal **7** bedroom, chamber, cottage, enclose, retreat, sanctum, shelter **8** dwelling, snuggery

Bowie, David
  real name: **16** David Robert Jones
  born: **6** London **7** England
  roles: **9** Cat People, Labyrinth, The Hunger **20** The Man Who Fell to Earth **24** Merry Christmas Mr Lawrence
  wife: **4** Iman
  Personae: **11** Aladdin Sane **13** Ziggy Stardust

Bowie Land, Bowie State
  nickname of: **8** Arkansas

bowl 4 boat **5** arena, basin **6** cavity, hollow, tureen, valley, vessel **7** dishful, helping, portion, stadium **8** coliseum, deep dish **9** container, porringer **10** depression, receptacle **12** amphitheater

bowler 11 Earl Anthony

bowling
  variation: **7** tenpins **8** duckpins, fivepins **10** candlepins
  term: **4** miss **5** frame, spare, split **6** strike **10** gutterball
  perfect score: **12** three hundred

bow-shape 3 arc **4** arch, bend **5** curve **9** curvature

bow to 5 yield **6** give in, give up, submit **9** acquiesce

box 3 bat, hit, rap **4** belt, cuff, slap, spar **5** booth, caddy, chest, crate, fight, punch, stall, whack **6** buffet, carton, coffer, strike, thwack **8** thumping **9** container **10** receptacle **11** compartment **13** exchange blows

boxer 7 Max Baer **8** Joe Louis **9** Mike

Tyson **10** Barney Ross, Cory Spinks, Gene Tunney, Joe Frazier, Joe Walcott, Leon Spinks, Roy Jones Jr **11** Archie Moore, Jack Dempsey, Jack Johnson, Jake LaMotta, Larry Holmes, Lennox Lewis, Muhammad Ali, Sonny Liston **12** Benny Leonard, James Corbett, John Sullivan, Johnny Dundee, Max Schmeling, Mickey Walker, Primo Carnera, Roberto Duran, Thomas Hearns **13** Carmen Basilio, Ezzard Charles, Felix Trinidad, George Foreman, Hector Camacho, James Jeffries, Oscar de la Hoya, Rocky Graziano, Rocky Marciano **14** Bob Fitzsimmons, Floyd Patterson, Henry Armstrong **15** Maxie Rosenbloom, Sugar Ray Leonard **16** Evander Holyfield, Sugar Ray Robinson

boy **3** lad **5** youth **8** man child **9** male child, stripling, youngster
French: **6** garcon

Boy
character in: **6** Tarzan
author: **9** Burroughs

boycott **5** spurn **6** reject **7** exclude **8** spurning **9** blackball, blacklist, exclusion, ostracism, ostracize, rejection **12** blackballing, blacklisting

Boyd, James
author of: **5** Drums **8** Long Hunt **9** Roll River **10** Marching On

Boyd, William
born: **13** Hendrysburg OH
roles: **15** Hopalong Cassidy

Boyer, Charles
born: **6** Figeac, France
roles: **7** Algiers **8** Conquest, Gaslight **10** Back Street **11** Lost Horizon **16** The Garden of Allah **19** All This and Heaven Too

boyfriend **3** man **4** beau, date **5** flame, lover, swain, wooer **6** escort, fellow, old man, squire, steady, suitor **7** admirer, beloved, Don Juan **8** cavalier, Lothario, paramour, truelove, young man **9** companion, inamorato **10** sweetheart **15** gentleman caller

boyish **5** boyey, fresh **6** callow, tender **7** boylike, puerile **8** childish, immature, innocent, juvenile, youthful **9** childlike **10** sophomoric

Boylan, Blazes
character in: **7** Ulysses
author: **5** Joyce

Boyle, Robert
field: **9** chemistry
nationality: **7** British
father of: **9** chemistry
advocated: **20** experimental approach
established: **9** Boyle's Law

boylike **5** fresh, young **6** boyish, callow **7** puerile **8** childish, immature, innocent, juvenile, youthful **9** childlike

Boys Town
director: **12** Norman Taurog

cast: **9** Henry Hull **12** Mickey Rooney, Spencer Tracy (Father Flanagan)
Oscar for: **5** actor (Tracy)
sequel: **13** Men of Boys Town
near: **5** Omaha

Boy Wonder
nickname of: **5** Robin **6** Mel Ott

brace **3** duo **4** pair, prop, stay **5** shore, strut, truss **6** bracer, couple, hold up, prop up, steady **7** bolster, bracket, fortify, prepare, shore up, support, sustain, twosome **8** buttress **9** reinforce, stanchion **10** strengthen **13** reinforcement

bracelet **6** armlet, bangle

bracer **10** stiff drink, stimulator, wristguard **11** invigorator **12** strengthener, strong drink

Brachiosaurus
type: **8** dinosaur, sauropod
location: **10** East Africa **12** United States
period: **8** Jurassic

bracing **8** arousing, reviving **10** energizing, fortifying, refreshing **11** restorative, stimulating **12** exhilarating, invigorating **13** strengthening

Brack, Judge
character in: **11** Hedda Gabler
author: **5** Ibsen

bracken **4** fern **5** brake, brush, ferns **10** underbrush **11** undergrowth

bracket **4** prop, rank, stay **5** brace, class, group, range, shore, strut, truss **6** prop up, status **7** shore up, support **8** category, classify, division, grouping **9** designate, stanchion **10** categorize **11** designation **14** classification

brackish **4** salt **5** briny, salty **6** saline

Bracknell, Lady Augusta
character in: **27** The Importance of Being Earnest
author: **5** Wilde

bract **4** leaf

Bradbury, Ray
author of: **13** Dandelion Wine, Fahrenheit 451 **17** The Illustrated Man **20** The Martian Chronicles **27** Something Wicked This Way Comes

Bradford, Barbara Taylor
author of: **17** A Woman of Substance

Bradford, Richard
author of: **15** Red Sky at Morning

Bradley, Bill (William Warren)
nickname: **10** Dollar Bill
sport: **10** basketball
college: **6** Oxford **9** Princeton
team: **13** New York Knicks
elected: **7** Senator
from: **9** New Jersey

Bradstreet, Anne
author of: **35** The Tenth Muse Lately Sprung Up in America

Brady Bunch, The
character: **3** Jan **4** Greg **5** Alice, Bobby, Cindy, Peter **6** Marcia **9** Mike

Brady **10** Carol Brady
cast: **8** Eve Plumb **9** Ann B Davis **10** Robert Reed, Susan Olsen **13** Barry Williams **14** Mike Lookinland **16** Maureen McCormick **17** Christopher Knight, Florence Henderson

brag **4** crow **5** boast, vaunt **7** big talk, crowing, talk big **8** boasting, bragging **10** exaggerate, self-praise **12** boastfulness, exaggeration **15** blow one's own horn **19** pat oneself on the back

Brage see **5** Bragi

Bragg, William Henry and William Lawrence
field: **7** physics
nationality: **7** British
determined: **16** crystal structure
by: **15** X-ray diffraction
established: **9** Bragg's Law
awarded: **10** Nobel Prize

braggadocio **5** pride **6** egoism, vanity **7** bluster, conceit, swagger **9** cockiness, vainglory **10** pretension **14** self-importance

braggart **7** boaster, bragger **8** blowhard **9** big talker

Bragi
also: **5** Brage
origin: **6** Nordic
god of: **5** music **6** poetry
father: **4** Odin **5** Othin
wife: **4** Idun **5** Iduna, Ithun **6** Ithunn
mother: **3** Fri **5** Frigg, Frija **6** Frigga

Brahe, Tycho
field: **9** astronomy
nationality: **6** Danish
built: **11** observatory

Brahman
country: **5** India
religion: **8** Hinduism
system: **5** caste
rank: **7** highest
function: **6** leader, priest **7** teacher

Brahms, Johannes
born: **7** Germany, Hamburg
composer of: **7** Rinaldo **10** Rain Sonata **11** Triumphlied, Volkslieder **12** Thuner-Sonate **13** German Requiem, Song of Destiny, Song of Triumph **14** Schicksalslied, Song of the Fates, Tragic Overture **15** Gesang der Parzen, Hungarian Dances **19** Liebeslieder Waltzes, Meistersinger Sonata **24** Academic Festival Overture **31** Variations on the St Anthony Chorale

braid **4** knit, lace **5** plait, ravel, twine, twist, weave **7** entwine, wreathe **9** interlace **10** intertwine

brain
part: **7** medulla **8** cerebrum **9** pituitary **10** cerebellum

brainchild **8** creation **9** invention **12** original work **15** imaginative work

braininess **6** genius **9** smartness **10** brightness, brilliance, cleverness **12** intelligence

brainless **4** dumb **6** stupid **7** asinine,

foolish, idiotic, moronic, witless **8** mindless **9** imbecilic **10** half-witted **11** lamebrained **12** feeble-minded, simple-minded

brain power 4 mind **9** intellect **12** intelligence **14** mental capacity

Brainworm
character in: **19** Every Man in His Humour
author: **6** Jonson

brainy 5 smart **6** bright, clever **9** brilliant **11** intelligent

brainy group 5 Mensa

brake 4 curb, drag, halt, rein, slow, stay, stop **5** check **6** arrest **7** control **9** restraint **10** constraint **11** reduce speed

Bramante, Donato
architect of: **9** Tempietto **14** Belvedere Court (the Vatican), Palazzo Caprini **19** Santa Maria della Pace **21** Santa Maria della Grazie

bramble 4 bush, vine **5** rough, shrub **7** thicket **8** prickers **13** raspberry bush **14** blackberry bush

Bramble, Matthew
character in: **14** Humphry Clinker
author: **8** Smollett

Bran
origin: **5** Welsh
giant king of: **7** Britain
habitat: **3** sea
saint in: **12** Christianity
brother: **9** Evnissyen **10** Manawyddan
sister: **7** Branwen
head buried in: **6** London

branch 3 arm, leg **4** fork, limb, part, wing **5** bough, prong, spray **6** agency, bureau, divide, feeder, member, office, ramify **7** channel, chapter, diverge, radiate, section, segment **8** division, offshoot, separate, shoot off **9** bifurcate, component, extension, tributary **10** department **11** subdivision **12** ramification

branched 6 forked, parted **7** divided **8** extended **9** spread out

Brancusi, Constantin
born: **7** Romania **13** Pestisani Gorj
artwork: **4** Fish **7** Chimera, The Kiss, The Seal **9** Sorceress **10** Adam and Eve, Prometheus **11** Bird in Space, Prodigal Son **12** Flying Turtle, Sleeping Muse **13** Endless Column **20** Sculpture for the Blind

brand 4 blot, kind, make, mark, sear, sign, slur, sort, spot, type **5** class, grade, label, smear, stain, stamp, taint **6** burn in, emblem, smirch, stigma **7** blemish, quality, variety **8** besmirch, disgrace **9** discredit, trademark **10** imputation, stigmatize **11** manufacture

brandish 4 wave **5** shake, swing, wield **6** flaunt, waggle **7** display, exhibit, show off **8** flourish

brand new 4 mint **5** fresh, young **6** unused

Brando, Marlon
born: **7** Omaha NE
roles: **8** Sayonara **10** The Wild One, Viva Zapata **12** Julius Caesar, The Godfather (Oscar refused) **13** Apocalypse Now **15** On the Waterfront (Oscar) **16** Last Tango in Paris **17** Mutiny on the Bounty **21** A Streetcar Named Desire

brandy 6 cognac, grappa, kahlua, kirsch, metaxa **8** Armagnac, Calvados, Tia Maria **9** applejack, Slivovitz **12** Grand Marnier, Peter Heering **14** forbidden fruit
French: **8** eau de vie

Brangwen, Ursula and Gudrun
characters in: **11** Women in Love
author: **8** Lawrence

Branstock
also: **9** Barnstock
origin: **12** Scandinavian
mentioned in: **8** Volsunga
form: **3** oak **4** tree
location: **7** Volsung
house of: **7** Volsung
Odin (Othin) thrusts: **4** Gram **5** sword

Brant, Captain Adam
character in: **22** Mourning Becomes Electra
author: **6** O'Neill

Branwen
origin: **5** Welsh
brother: **4** Bran
husband: **10** Matholwych
son killed by: **9** Evnissyen

Braque, Georges
born: **6** France **18** Argenteuil sur Seine
artwork: **7** Atelier, Grand Nu (Great Nude), The Echo **8** The Table **13** The Portuguese **14** Man with a Guitar **16** Violin and Palette, Violin and Pitcher **18** Woman with a Mandolin

brash 4 bold, rash, rude **5** fresh, hasty, sassy **6** brazen, cheeky, madcap **7** forward **8** careless, heedless, impudent, reckless **9** foolhardy, impetuous, imprudent, know-it-all **10** incautious **11** impertinent, precipitous, smart-alecky **12** unconsidered **13** overconfident

brashness 4 gall **5** brass, cheek, nerve **8** audacity, boldness, chutzpah, temerity **10** brazenness, effrontery **11** forwardness, presumption

Brasilia
capital of: **6** Brazil

brass 4 gall, sand, VIPs **5** cheek, nerve **8** audacity, boldness, chutzpah, officers, temerity **9** impudence **10** brazenness, effrontery **11** forwardness, presumption

Brass, Sampson
character in: **19** The Old Curiosity Shop
author: **7** Dickens

brass instrument 4 tuba **5** bugle **6** cornet **7** trumpet **8** trombone **9** euphonium **10** French horn, sousaphone
ancient: **3** lur **7** Alphorn, buisine, serpent **10** ophicleide

brass tacks 4 crux, meat **7** details **9** realities, substance **10** essentials **11** nitty-gritty **15** sum and substance

brassy 4 bold, loud **5** brash, cheap, cocky, sassy, saucy, showy **6** brazen **7** blaring, forward **8** arrogant, impudent, insolent, overbold **9** barefaced, outspoken, shameless, unabashed **10** unblushing **11** impertinent

brat 3 imp **4** chit **5** whelp **6** hoyden, rascal **9** rude child **10** holy terror **12** spoiled child

Brauhaus 6 tavern **7** brewery

Brautigan, Richard
author of: **15** Sombrero Fallout **18** The Hawkline Monster **21** Trout Fishing in America **38** The Pill Versus the Springhill Mine Disaster

bravado 7 big talk, blowing, bluster, bombast, bravura, crowing, puffery, swagger **8** boasting, bragging **9** cockiness **10** swaggering **11** braggadocio **12** boastfulness **13** show of courage

brave 4 bear, dare, defy, face, game, take **5** abide, brook, gutsy, stand **6** breast, endure, gritty, heroic, plucky, spunky, suffer **7** doughty, stomach, sustain, undergo, valiant, weather **8** confront, fearless, intrepid, stalwart, tolerate, unafraid, valorous **9** challenge, dauntless, outbrazen, put up with, stand up to, undaunted, withstand **10** courageous **11** lionhearted, unflinching, unshrinking **12** stouthearted

brave deed 4 feat, gest **5** geste **7** exploit **9** heroic act **11** achievement

Braveheart
director: **9** Mel Gibson
cast: **8** Brian Cox (Argyle Wallace) **9** Mel Gibson (William Wallace) **10** James Cosmo (Campbell), Sean Lawlor (Malcolm Wallace) **11** Sandy Nelson (John Wallace) **12** Sean McGinley (MacClannough) **13** James Robinson (young William Wallace), Sophie Marceau (Princess Isabelle) **15** Patrick McGoohan (Edward I of England)

Brave New World
author: **12** Aldous Huxley
character: **4** John **11** Bernard Marx **12** Lenina Crowne, Mustapha Mond

bravery 4 grit **5** pluck, spunk, valor **6** daring, mettle, spirit **7** courage, heroism **8** audacity, boldness **11** intrepidity **12** fearlessness **13** dauntlessness

Bravo, The
author: **19** James Fenimore Cooper

brawl 3 row **4** fray, tiff **5** broil, clash,

fight, melee, scrap, set-to **6** battle, fracas, ruckus, rumpus, uproar **7** dispute, quarrel, scuffle, wrangle **8** squabble **9** imbroglio **11** altercation, embroilment

brawn 5 might, power **7** muscles, stamina **8** strength **9** beefiness, huskiness **10** robustness, ruggedness, sturdiness **19** muscular development

brawny 5 burly, husky **6** mighty, robust, rugged, strong, sturdy **8** muscular, powerful **9** strapping

Bray, Madeline
  character in: 16 Nicholas Nickleby
  author: 7 Dickens

brazen 4 bold, open **5** brash, saucy **6** brassy, cheeky **7** forward **8** arrogant, immodest, impudent, insolent **9** audacious, barefaced, boldfaced, shameless, unabashed

brazenness 4 gall **5** brass, cheek, nerve **8** audacity, boldness, chutzpah **9** impudence **10** effrontery, fowardness **11** presumption

Brazil
  capital: 8 Brasilia
  former capital: 12 Rio de Janeiro
  largest city: 8 Sao Paulo
  others: 5 Bahia, Belem **6** Recife, Sabara, Santos **7** Vitoria **8** Salvador **9** Ouro Preto, Paranagua **10** Diamantina **11** Porto Alegre **13** Belo Horizonte, Cruzeiro do Sul
  government: 18 federative republic
  school:
    junior high: 7 ginasio
    senior high: 7 colegio
  measure: 2 pe **4** moio, sack, vara **5** braca, legoa, milha, tonel **6** canada, cuarto, quarto, tarefa **7** garrafa **8** alqueire
  monetary unit: 3 joe **4** reis **5** dobra **7** centara, halfjoe, milreis **8** cruzeiro
  weight: 3 bag **4** onca **5** libra **6** arroba, oitava **7** quilate, quintal **8** tonelada
  island: 6 Maraca, Marajo **7** Bananal, Cardoso, Caviana, Mexiana **8** Comprida
  lake: 4 Aima, Feia **5** Mirim **13** Logo dos Platos
  mountain: 3 Mar **5** Geral, Organ, Piaui **6** Acarai, Gurupi, Parima, Urucum **7** Amambai, Carajas, Gradaus, Oragaos, Roraima **8** Bandeira, Itatiaja, Roncador, Tombador **9** Pacaraima, Sugar Loaf **10** Tumuc-Humac
  highest point: 7 Neblina
  river: 3 Apa, Ica **4** Doce, Geio, Ivai, Jari, Para, Paru, Sono, Tefe **5** Abuna, Anaua, Apore, Capim, Claro, Corua, Icana, Iriri, Itapi, Jurua, Jutai, Manso, Negro, Pardo, Piaui, Preto, Tiete, Turvo, Urubu, Verde, Xingu **6** Ajuana, Amazon, Arinos, Balsas, Branco, Canuma, Contas, Cuiaba, Demini, Grajau, Grande, Gurupi,

Ibicui, Iguacu, Japura, Javari, Mearim, Mortes, Mucuri, Parana, Purpus, Ronuro, Sangue, Tacutu, Tibagi, Uatuma, Uaupes **7** Corumba, Iguassu, Madeira, Madiera, Orinoco, Paraiba, Sucuriu, Tapajos, Taquari, Teodoro, Uruguai, Uruguay, Velhass **8** Araguaia, Padauiri, Paracatu, Paraguay, Parnaiba, Solimoes, Tarauaca **9** Tocantins **12** Sao Francisco
  sea: 8 Atlantic
  physical feature:
    bay: 9 All Saints
    cape: 4 Frio **6** Blanco, Buzios, Gurupy, Orange **7** Saotome **8** Saoroque
    dam: 6 Furnas **7** Peixoto
    estuary: 4 Para
    rain forest: 5 selva
    waterfall: 6 Guaira, Iguacu **7** Iguassu **11** Paulo Afonso
  people: 2 Ge **4** Anta **5** Acroa, Arara, Araua, Bravo, Carib, Guana, Negro **6** Arawak, Caraja **7** Carayan, Javahai, Tariana **8** Botocudo, Chambioa **9** Caucasian, mamelucos, mulattoes **10** Portuguese **11** Tupi-Guarani
    architect: 8 Niemeyer
    artist: 6 Segall **9** Portinari **10** Cavalcenti
    author: 5 Amado, Bilac, Ramos **6** Freyre
    composer: 10 Villalobos
    discoverer: 6 Cabral
    leader: 6 Aranha, Branco, Collor, Franco, Geisel, Medici, Vargas **7** Goulart
    sculptor: 11 Aleijadinho
  language: 10 Portuguese
  religion: 10 Protestant **13** Roman Catholic
  place:
    beach: 7 Ipanema **9** Boa Viagem **10** Copacabana
  feature:
    bird: 4 mitu **5** mitua
    dance: 5 frevo, samba **6** maxixe **9** bossa nova
    fish: 7 piranha
    gourd: 4 cuia
    plantation: 7 fazenda
    slums: 7 favelas
    tree: 5 icica **6** ucuuba **7** arariba
  food:
    dish: 6 vatapa **8** feijoada
    dried salted beef: 7 charque
    drink: 4 acai **9** cafezinho
    tea: 4 mate
    turtle soup: 16 cas quinho de mucua

Brazil
  director: 12 Terry Gilliam
  cast: 8 Ida Lowry **9** Kim Greist **12** Robert De Niro **13** Jonathan Pryce

Brazilian Bombshell
  nickname of: 13 Carmen Miranda

Brazzaville
  capital of: 5 Congo

breach 3 gap **4** gash, hole, rent, rift, slit **5** break, chink, cleft, crack, split **7** crevice, failure, fissure, neglect, opening, rupture **8** defiance, trespass **9** disregard, violation **10** infraction **11** dereliction **12** disobedience, infringement **13** noncompliance, nonobservance, transgression

breach of faith 7 perfidy **8** bad faith, betrayal **9** falseness, treachery, two-timing **10** disloyalty **11** double-cross **13** double-dealing

breach of order 4 riot **6** fracas, mutiny, ruckus, uproar **7** turmoil **8** uprising **9** commotion, rebellion **10** dissension **11** disturbance, pandemonium **18** disturbance of peace

breach of trust 7 falsity, perfidy **9** falseness, treachery **10** disloyalty, infidelity **13** deceitfulness, double-dealing

bread 3 rye **4** food, pita **5** bucks, dough, money, wheat, white **6** staple **9** sourdough **10** livelihood, sustenance **11** staff of life **12** pumpernickel

bread and butter 3 job **6** career, living **7** calling **8** business, vocation **9** life's work **10** livelihood **14** means of support

Bread and Wine
  author: 13 Ignazio Silone

breadbasket 3 gut **5** belly, tummy **6** paunch **7** abdomen, labonza, midriff, Midwest, stomach **11** solar plexus

breadth 4 area, size, span **5** range, reach, scope, width **6** extent, spread **7** compass, expanse, measure, stretch **8** latitude, wideness **9** broadness **10** dimensions **13** extensiveness

break 3 cap, end, fly, gap, off, run, top **4** beat, bust, chip, dash, defy, flee, gash, halt, hole, rend, rent, rest, rift, rive, ruin, snap, stop, tame, tear, tell **5** burst, cease, cleft, crack, crush, erupt, excel, lapse, occur, outdo, pause, sever, shirk, smash, split, train **6** appear, better, breach, chance, cleave, detach, divide, escape, exceed, happen, hiatus, ignore, inform, lessen, master, powder, recess, reveal, soften, subdue, sunder, weaken **7** control, cushion, destroy, disobey, divulge, eclipse, fissure, fortune, give out, lighten, neglect, opening, pull off, respite, run away, rupture, shatter, surpass, suspend, tear off, violate, wipe out **8** announce, bankrupt, burst out, cracking, demolish, diminish, disclose, disjoint, division, fracture, fragment, go beyond, interval, outstrip, overcome, proclaim, renege on, separate, shut down, slip away, splinter **9** dismember, disregard, granulate, interlude, interrupt, make a dash, pulverize, splitting, transcend **10** discipline, disconnect, fall back on, fly the coop, fracturing, impoverish, infringe on, make public, overshadow, separation,

shattering, take flight, wrench away
11 discontinue, get away from, opportunity, pay no heed to **12** be derelict
in, disintegrate, intermission, interruption, make a getaway, stroke of luck
13 strap for funds **14** bend to one's
will, take the force of **15** take to one's
heels

breakable 5 frail, shaky **6** flimsy **7**
brittle, crumbly, fragile **8** delicate

break apart 7 crumble, shatter **8** collapse **9** fall apart **12** disintegrate, fall
to pieces

breakdown 6 mishap **7** crackup, decline, failure **8** analysis, collapse, disorder, division **12** detailed list **13** deterioration **14** categorization

break down 6 divide **7** dissect **8** collapse, separate **9** decompose **11** deteriorate

breaker 4 cask, wave **6** comber **7**
crusher **8** boat cask **9** destroyer

break faith with 6 betray **7** do wrong
9 play false **11** double-cross **12** be unfaithful **13** be treacherous **16** sell
down the river

Breakfast at Tiffany's
   author: 12 Truman Capote
   director: 12 Blake Edwards
   cast: 10 Buddy Ebsen **12** Mickey
      Rooney, Patricia Neal **13** Audrey
      Hepburn (Holly Golightly), George
      Peppard
   score: 12 Henry Mancini
   song: 9 Moon River

Breakfast Club, The
   director: 10 John Hughes
   cast: 10 Ally Sheedy, Judd Nelson **13**
      Emilio Estevez, Molly Ringwald **18**
      Anthony Michael Hall

Breakfast of Champions
   author: 12 Kurt Vonnegut

break free 4 bolt, flee, skip **6** escape
7 get away, make off, run away **9** cut
and run **10** fly the coop **12** make a
getaway

breakfront 5 hutch **7** cabinet **8** bookcase, cupboard **12** china cabinet

break in 5 train **7** intrude **8** accustom,
initiate **9** acclimate, interrupt **10** burglarize **12** indoctrinate

break-in 5 theft **7** robbery **8** burglary,
stealing **12** burglarizing **13** housebreaking **19** breaking and entering

Breaking Away
   director: 10 Peter Yates
   screenplay: 11 Steve Tesich
   cast: 10 Paul Dooley **11** Daniel Stern,
      Dennis Quaid **13** Barbara Barrie **16**
      Jackie Earle Haley **17** Dennis Chris-
      topher
   setting: 7 Indiana **11** Bloomington

break loose 4 bolt, flee, skip **6** escape
7 get away, make off **9** cut and run
10 fly the coop **12** make a getaway

breakneck 4 rash **5** risky **8** reckless,

very fast **9** dangerous, daredevil **12**
death-defying

break of day 4 dawn **5** sunup **7**
dawning, sunrise **8** daybreak **11** crack
of dawn

break off 3 end **4** halt **5** cease **6** recess **7** adjourn, snap off, suspend **8**
conclude, shut down **11** discontinue

breakout 6 escape, flight **7** getaway
10 decampment

break out 4 bolt, skip **5** begin, erupt **6**
escape **7** bust out, get away **10** burst
forth, fly the coop **12** make a getaway

Break the Bank
   host: 9 Bert Parks **10** Bud Collyer

break the habit 4 kick, quit, stop **6**
eschew, give up **8** renounce, withdraw **14** quit cold turkey

breakthrough 7 advance **11** advancement, improvement, penetration, step
forward

breakup 5 split **7** crackup **9** dispersal,
splitting **10** separation **14** disintegration

break with 5 leave **8** be untrue, part
from **10** be disloyal **11** divorce from
12 fall away from, separate from

breast 4 bust, core **5** bosom, chest,
heart **10** very marrow
   Italian: 5 petto

breastwork 7 bastion, rampart **8** barbette **9** earthwork **13** fortification

breath 4 wind **6** spirit **9** animation,
breathing, lifeblood, life force **10** exhalation, inhalation, vital spark **11** divine spark, respiration, vital spirit **12**
vitalization

breathe 4 gasp, huff, pant, puff **5** utter
6 impart, murmur **7** respire, whisper
9 draw in air **10** draw breath **15** inhale and exhale

breathe in 6 inhale **7** inspire, respire

breathe out 4 huff, pant, puff **6** exhale, expire **7** respire

breathing 4 live **5** alive **6** living **7** animate **11** respiratory **13** drawing
breath

Breathless
   director: 14 Jean-Luc Goddard
   written by: 16 Francois Truffaut
   cast: 10 Jean Seberg **16** Jean-Paul
      Belmondo
   setting: 5 Paris

breathtaking 7 amazing, awesome **8**
exciting **9** startling **10** surprising **11**
astonishing

Brecht, Bertolt
   author of: 13 Mother Courage **15**
      Drums in the Night **18** The Three-
      penny Opera **21** St Joan of the
      Stockyards **23** The Caucasian Chalk
      Circle **27** The Resistable Rise of Ar-
      turo Ui **29** The Private Life of the
      Master Race

Breck, Alan

character in: 9 Kidnapped
   author: 9 Stevenson

breech 4 rump, seat **6** behind **8**
buttocks, haunches, hind part **9** fundament, posterior **12** hindquarters

breeches 5 pants **8** trousers

breed 4 bear, grow, kind, race, sire,
sort, type **5** beget, cause, order, raise,
spawn, stock **6** family, father, foster,
lead to, mother, strain **7** develop, nurture, produce, promote, species, variety **8** generate, multiply, occasion **9**
cultivate, give forth, procreate, propagate, reproduce **10** bring forth, give
rise to **11** proliferate **16** produce offspring

breeding 4 line **5** grace **6** mating, polish **7** bearing, descent, growing, lineage, manners, raising, rearing **8** ancestry, courtesy, hatching, heredity,
pedigree, spawning, training **9** begetting, bloodline, genealogy, gentility,
parentage, producing **10** background,
extraction, family tree, generation, politeness, production, refinement, upbringing **11** cultivation, germination,
multiplying, procreation, propagation
12 reproduction

breeze 4 flit, pass, sail, snap, waft **5**
coast, float, glide, sweep **6** zephyr **9**
light gust, light wind **10** gentle wind,
puff of wind

breezy 3 gay **4** airy, pert, spry **5**
blowy, brisk, fresh, gusty, light,
merry, peppy, sunny, windy **6**
bouncy, casual, frisky, jaunty, lively **7**
buoyant, squally **8** animated, blustery,
carefree, cheerful, debonair, spirited **9**
energetic, resilient, sprightly, vivacious, windswept **10** blithesome **11**
free and easy

Brennan, Walter
   born: 12 Swampscott MA
   roles: 8 Kentucky **12** Come and Get
      It, The Westerner **13** The Real Mc-
      Coys **16** To Have and Have Not

Brent, George
   real name: 18 George Brendan Nolan
   wife: 11 Ann Sheridan **14** Ruth Chat-
      terton
   born: 7 Ireland **14** Shannonsbridge
   roles: 7 Jezebel **11** Dark Victory, The
      Great Lie **17** Forty-Second Street

Bres
   origin: 5 Irish
   king of: 7 Ireland

Breton, Andre
   author of: 5 Nadja **21** Manifesto of
      Surrealism

Breuer, Marcel
   architect of: 17 IBM Research Center
      (La Gaude France) **18** UNESCO
      headquarters (Paris) **25** St John's
      Abbey and University (Collegeville
      MN) **26** Whitney Museum of Ameri-
      can Art (NYC)
   designed: 5 chair

brevity 9 briefness, pithiness, quickness, shortness, terseness 10 transience 11 conciseness 12 ephemerality, impermanence, succinctness

brew 3 ale 4 beer, boil, cook, form, make, plan, plot, soak, suds 5 begin, drink, hatch, ripen, start, steep, stout 6 cook up, devise, foment, gather, porter, scheme, seethe 7 arrange, brewski, concoct, ferment, mixture, prepare, produce, think up 8 beverage, contrive, initiate 9 formulate, germinate, originate 10 concoction, malt liquor

brewery
German: 8 Brauhaus

Brian de Bois, Sir
character in: 7 Ivanhoe
author: 5 Scott

bribe 3 sop 5 graft 6 buy off, grease, pay off, payola, suborn 9 hush money 10 inducement 11 illegal gift 15 grease the hand of, grease the palm of
French: 7 douceur

bric-a-brac 7 baubles, gewgaws 8 bibelots, trinkets 9 gimcracks, kickshaws, ornaments 11 knickknacks

Brick
character in: 16 Cat on a Hot Tin Roof
author: 8 Williams

Bricks
god of: 5 Kulla

bridal 7 nuptial, wedding 8 marriage 11 matrimonial

Bridehead, Sue
character in: 14 Jude the Obscure
author: 5 Hardy

Bride of Lammermoor, The
author: 14 Sir Walter Scott
character: 10 Lady Ashton, Lucy Ashton, Ravenswood 14 Laird of Bucklaw 16 Sir William Ashton

Brideshead Revisited
author: 11 Evelyn Waugh
character: 5 Celia, Julia 8 Cordelia 9 Sebastian 10 Brideshead (Bridey), Rex Mottram 12 Boy Mulcaster, Charles Ryder 13 Lady Marchmain, Lord Marchmain 14 Anthony Blanche

bridge 3 tie 4 band, bind, bond, link, span 5 cross, unify, union 6 go over 7 catwalk, connect, liaison, viaduct 8 alliance, overpass, traverse 9 cross over 10 connection, passageway 11 association, reach across 12 extend across

bridge
derived from: 5 whist
type: 7 auction 8 contract
partnership: 9 East/West 11 North/South
cards/hand: 8 thirteen
no cards of a suit: 4 void
one card of a suit: 9 singleton
two cards of a suit: 9 doubleton

rule book by: 5 Goren
position: 4 east
action: 3 bid 4 pass
term: 4 slam 5 trump 6 double, renege, tenace

Bridge of San Luis Rey, The
author: 14 Thornton Wilder
character: 5 Clara, Jaime 6 Manuel, Pepita 7 Esteban, Viceroy 8 Uncle Pio 11 La Perichole 14 Brother Juniper 20 Marquesa de Montemayor

Bridge on the River Kwai, The
director: 9 David Lean
based on story by: 12 Pierre Boulle
cast: 11 Jack Hawkins 12 Alec Guinness 13 William Holden 14 Sessue Hayakawa
Oscar for: 5 actor (Guinness) 7 picture

Bridges, Beau
real name: 21 Lloyd Vernet Bridges III
father: 5 Lloyd
brother: 4 Jeff
born: 12 Los Angeles CA
roles: 5 Space 8 Norma Rae 11 Signs of Life, The Landlord, The Wild Pair 17 The Fifth Musketeer 20 The Fabulous Baker Boys 25 The Other Side of the Mountain

Bridges, Jeff
father: 5 Lloyd
brother: 4 Beau
born: 12 Los Angeles CA
roles: 4 Tron 7 Starman 8 King Kong 9 The Moguls 10 Jagged Edge, Seabiscuit 12 The Vanishing 13 Kiss Me Goodbye, The Fisher King 14 Against All Odds, The Big Lebowski 17 The Door in the Floor 18 The Last Picture Show 20 The Fabulous Baker Boys

Bridges, Lloyd
sons: 4 Beau, Jeff
born: 12 San Leandro CA
roles: 7 Sea Hunt 8 Airplane, High Noon

Bridges at Toko-ri, The
author: 13 James Michener

Bridget
character in: 19 Every Man in His Humour
author: 6 Jonson

Bridge Too Far, A
author: 13 Cornelius Ryan

Bridgetown
capital of: 8 Barbados

bridle 3 gag 4 curb, rule 5 check 6 arrest, direct, draw up, flinch, hinder, manage, master, muzzle, rear up, recoil 7 control, harness, inhibit, repress 8 draw back, restrain, restrict, suppress 9 constrain, restraint 11 bit and brace, head harness

brief 4 case 5 hasty, pithy, quick, short, swift, terse 6 advise, inform, precis, resume 7 capsule, compact,

concise, defense, limited, prepare, summary 8 abridged, abstract, argument, fill in on, fleeting, instruct, succinct 9 condensed, curtailed, momentary, shortened, temporary, thumbnail, transient 10 abridgment, compressed, contention, describe to, short-lived, summarized, transitory 11 abbreviated 12 legal summary

brief account 6 precis, sketch 7 outline, summary 8 anecdote

brier, briar 4 Rosa 5 Rubus, thorn 6 Smilax 7 bramble
varieties: 3 Cat, Dog, Hag, Saw 4 Bull 5 Green, Horse, Sweet 7 Jackson 8 Austrian 9 Sensitive 14 Austrian copper

brigade 4 crew, team, unit 5 corps, force, group, squad 6 legion, outfit 7 company 9 regiments, squadrons 10 army groups, battalions, contingent, detachment

Brigadoon
director: 16 Vincente Minnelli
based on Broadway hit by: 14 Lerner and Loewe
cast: 9 Gene Kelly 10 Van Johnson 11 Cyd Charisse
setting: 8 Scotland

brigand 5 thief 6 bandit, gunman, looter, outlaw, pirate, robber, vandal 7 corsair, hoodlum, ruffian, rustler, spoiler 8 marauder, pilferer, pillager 9 buccaneer, cutthroat, desperado, despoiler, plunderer, privateer 10 highwayman

bright 3 gay 4 glad, good, keen, rosy, sage, warm, wise 5 acute, alert, aware, grand, great, happy, jolly, merry, quick, sharp, smart, sunny, vivid 6 astute, blithe, brainy, clever, gifted, joyful, joyous, lively, shrewd 7 beaming, blazing, capable, glowing, healthy, hopeful, intense, lambent, radiant, shining 8 cheerful, dazzling, exciting, gleaming, luminous, lustrous, profound, splendid, talented 9 brilliant, competent, effulgent, excellent, favorable, ingenious, inventive, masterful, promising, sagacious, sparkling, wide-awake 10 auspicious, discerning, glittering, optimistic, perceptive, proficient, propitious, prosperous, remarkable, shimmering, successful 11 clearheaded, illuminated, illustrious, intelligent, light-filled, magnificent, outstanding, quick-witted, resourceful, resplendent 12 exhilarating

brighten 4 lift 5 boost, cheer, light 6 buoy up, lift up, perk up 7 animate, enliven, gladden, lighten 9 make happy, stimulate 10 illuminate

bright-eyed 5 alert, awake 9 wideawake 12 on the qui vive

brightness 4 glow 5 glare, gleam, shine 6 dazzle, luster 7 glitter, sparkle

8 radiance 9 lightness 10 brilliance, luminosity 12 intelligence

bright spot 3 joy 6 solace 7 comfort 8 pleasure 13 consolation

Brigit
origin: 5 Welsh
goddess of: 4 fire 6 wisdom 9 fertility, household 11 agriculture

Brigitte Bardot & the Lolita Syndrome
author: 16 Simone de Beauvoir

brilliance, brilliancy 4 gift, glow 5 blaze, eclat, gleam, sheen, shine 6 acuity, dazzle, genius, luster, talent, wisdom 7 glitter, shimmer, sparkle 8 grandeur, keenness, radiance, sagacity, splendor 9 alertness, awareness, greatness, ingenuity, intensity, quickness, sharpness, smartness, vividness 10 braininess, brightness, capability, cleverness, competence, effulgence, excellence, luminosity, perception, profundity, shrewdness 11 discernment, distinction, proficiency 12 intelligence, magnificence, resplendence 13 inventiveness, masterfulness 15 clearheadedness, illustriousness, resourcefulness

brilliant see 6 bright

brim 3 fill, lip, rim 5 brink, flood, ledge, verge 6 border, fill up, margin, well up 8 overflow

brimless hat 3 cap 5 beret 6 beanie 11 stocking cap, tam o'shanter

brimming 4 full 7 flooded, teeming 8 overfull, swarming 11 overflowing

Brimo
origin: 5 Greek
form: 7 goddess
corresponds to: 6 Hecate 7 Demeter 10 Persephone

brine 6 the sea 8 sea water 9 salt water 12 salt solution 14 saline solution 16 pickling solution

bring 4 bear, make, take, tote 5 begin, carry, cause, fetch, force, start 6 compel, convey, create, effect, induce 7 deliver, produce, sell for, usher in 8 convince, engender, generate, initiate, persuade, result in 9 accompany, institute, originate, transport 10 bring about

bring about 2 do 4 form, open 5 begin, cause, found, set up, start 6 attain, create, effect, lead to 7 achieve, execute, produce 8 carry out, generate, initiate, organize 9 establish, institute, succeed at 10 accomplish, effectuate, inaugurate 11 bring to pass, precipitate 18 bring into existence

bring back 6 return 7 restore 8 recreate 9 surrender 10 return with

bring down a peg 5 abase 6 humble 7 mortify 9 humiliate 13 cut down to size

bring down to earth 10 disenchant

11 disenthrall, disillusion, open the eyes 13 break the spell 14 burst the bubble 20 shatter one's illusions

bring forth 4 bear 5 breed, elicit, evoke, hatch, spawn, whelp 7 deliver, produce 9 reproduce 10 make appear 11 give birth to

bring home to 7 blame on, clarify 11 attribute to 15 place emphasis on

bringing together 7 joining, wedding 8 amassing 9 combining, gathering, including 10 assembling, collecting 12 accumulating 13 incorporating

Bringing Up Baby
director: 11 Howard Hawks
cast: 9 Cary Grant 14 Charlie Ruggles 16 Katharine Hepburn
"Baby": 7 leopard

Bringing Up Father
creator: 13 George McManus
character: 5 Jiggs 6 Maggie
daughter: 5 Rosie
brother-in-law: 5 Bimmy
place: 11 Dinty Moore's
favorite dish: 20 corned beef and cabbage

bring into being 4 bear, form, make 5 erect, hatch, spawn, whelp 6 create, design, devise, invent, render 7 concoct, deliver, develop, fashion, produce 8 contrive, generate 9 construct, fabricate, formulate, originate 10 bring forth 11 give birth to

bring into existence 4 form 5 begin, set up, start 6 create 8 organize 9 establish, institute 10 bring about, inaugurate

bring into line 5 adapt 6 adjust 7 conform, shape up 9 harmonize, reconcile 10 discipline 11 accommodate 13 whip into shape

bring into question 11 cast doubt on 18 throw suspicion upon

bring into relief 6 accent, stress 7 dwell on, feature, point up 9 emphasize, press home, underline 10 accentuate, underscore

bring low 5 abase, shame 6 humble 8 cast down 9 denigrate, humiliate

bring off 4 gain 6 attain, effect, secure 7 achieve 10 accomplish

bring to an end 5 cease 6 finish 8 break off, conclude 9 call a halt, terminate 11 discontinue

bring to a standstill 3 end 4 halt, stay, stop 5 block, check 6 arrest 12 bring to a halt

bring to bay 4 trap, tree 6 corner 8 confront, hunt down

bring to bear 5 apply 6 employ 7 utilize 9 implement

bring together 5 amass 6 gather, muster 7 collect, marshal, round up 8 assemble 10 accumulate

bring to light 6 expose, reveal, unveil 7 clarify, divulge, explain, uncover 8

disclose 9 explicate, make known, make plain 10 illuminate, make public

bring to one's senses 3 jar 5 alarm, alert, shock 9 make aware

bring to pass 5 cause 6 create, effect 8 carry out 10 bring about, effectuate

bring to terms 6 settle 7 mediate 9 arbitrate, reconcile

bring to view 5 dig up 6 reveal 7 exhibit, uncover, unearth 8 disclose, retrieve 10 come up with

bring word 4 tell 6 advise, convey, inform, notify, relate, reveal 7 divulge, publish 8 announce, disclose, proclaim 9 apprise of, broadcast, make known, publicize 11 communicate

brink 3 rim 4 bank, brim, edge 5 point, shore, skirt, verge 6 border, margin 9 threshold

briny 4 salt 5 salty 6 saline

brio, con
music: 9 with vigor 10 with spirit

Briseis
origin: 5 Greek
mentioned in: 5 Iliad
father: 18 Briseus of Lyrnessus
husband: 5 Mynes
captured by: 8 Achilles
caused: 7 quarrel
between: 8 Achilles 9 Agamemnon

Briseus
origin: 5 Greek
mentioned in: 5 Iliad
daughter: 7 Briseis
death by: 7 suicide

Brisingamen 8 necklace
origin: 12 Scandinavian
trait: 5 magic
owned by: 5 Freia, Freya

brisk 4 busy, spry 5 alert, fresh, peppy, quick, swift 6 active, breezy, lively, snappy 7 bracing, chipper, dynamic, rousing 8 animated, bustling, spirited, stirring, vigorous 9 energetic, sprightly, vivacious, vivifying 10 refreshing 11 stimulating 12 exhilarating, invigorating

briskness 3 pep 5 vigor 6 energy 8 alacrity, spryness 9 quickness, swiftness 13 sprightliness

bristle 4 hair, seta 5 quill 7 stiffen, whisker

bristles 5 barbs, setae 6 quills 7 stubble 8 prickles, whiskers

bristletail
variety: 7 jumping 8 firebrat 9 primitive 10 nicoletiid, silverfish

bristly 5 rough 6 barbed, coarse 7 prickly, stubbly 8 unshaven 9 whiskered 11 bewhiskered

Britannia see 7 England

British 6 Breton, Briton 7 English 8 Brittany

British Columbia
  bordered by: **5** Idaho, Yukon **6** Alaska **7** Alberta, Montana **10** Washington **12** Pacific Ocean, United States **20** Northwest Territories
  country: **6** Canada
  Indian: **5** Haida **6** Nootka, Salish **8** Kwakiutl **9** Tsimshian **10** Bella Coola
  island: **9** Vancouver **14** Queen Charlotte
  mountain: **5** Coast, Rocky **7** Cascade **8** Columbia **11** Cordilleran **14** Cassiar Omineca
  nickname: **2** BC
  park: **7** Glacier
  rank in size: **5** sixth
  river: **6** Fraser
  section: **8** province
British Guiana see **6** Guyana
British Honduras see **6** Belize
British Mythology
  god of rebirth/afterlife: **4** Gwyn
  chief of gods: **5** Woden
  island of paradise: **6** Avalon
Britomart
  character in: **15** The Faerie Queene
  author: **7** Spenser
Britomartis
  origin: **6** Cretan
  goddess of: **7** hunters, sailors **9** fishermen
  father: **4** Zeus
  mother: **5** Carme
  corresponds to: **7** Artemis **8** Dictynna
Briton **4** Celt **6** Celtic **7** British
Brittany
  coast: **5** Armor
  country: **6** France
  inhabitant: **5** Celts **6** French, Romans
  interior: **6** Argoat
  land form: **9** peninsula
  language: **6** Breton
  other name: **5** Breiz **6** Breton **8** Bretagne
Britten, (Edward) Benjamin
  born: **7** England **9** Lowestoft
  composer of: **8** Gloriana **9** Billy Budd **10** Paul Bunyan, War Requiem **11** Curlew River, Peter Grimes, Winter Words **12** Owen Wingrave, The Poet's Echo **13** Albert Herring, Death in Venice **14** The Prodigal Son, Turn of the Screw **15** Phantasy Quartet **17** A Ceremony of Carols, A Charm of Lullabies, Sinfonia da Requiem, The Rape of Lucretia **18** Holderlin Fragments **20** Cantata Misericordium **21** A Midsummer Night's Dream, Sonnets of Michelangelo **22** The Burning Fiery Furnace
brittle **7** crumbly, fragile, friable **9** breakable, frangible
broach **4** pose **6** launch, open up, submit **7** advance, bring up, mention, propose, suggest, touch on **9** institute, introduce

broad **4** full, open, wide **5** ample, clear, large, plain, rangy, roomy, thick **7** general, immense, obvious, sizable **8** extended, spacious, sweeping **9** capacious, expansive, extensive, inclusive, outspread, universal, unlimited **10** undetailed **11** far-reaching, nonspecific, wide-ranging **12** all-embracing, encyclopedic **13** comprehensive
broadcast **4** beam, show, talk **5** cable, radio, relay **7** program, send out **8** televise, transmit **9** statement **10** distribute **11** disseminate, put on the air **12** announcement
broaden **5** boost, raise, swell, widen **6** dilate, expand, extend **7** advance, amplify, augment, build up, develop, distend, enlarge, improve, stretch **8** increase **9** intensify, reinforce, spread out **10** strengthen, supplement
broadened **7** dilated, swelled, swollen, widened **8** enlarged, expanded, extended **9** distended, spread out
broad-minded **7** liberal **8** amenable, catholic, flexible, tolerant, unbiased **9** receptive, unbigoted **10** charitable, open-minded, undogmatic **11** magnanimous **12** unprejudiced, unprovincial
Broadway Joe
  nickname of: **9** Joe Namath
Brobdingnag
  fictional land in: **16** Gulliver's Travels
  author: **5** Swift
Brobdingnagian **4** huge **5** giant **7** immense, mammoth **8** colossal, enormous, gigantic **10** gargantuan, tremendous **11** elephantine
broccoli **9** vegetable **12** Brassica rapa **16** Brassica oleracea (Botyris Group) **17** Brassica septiceps
  variety: **6** Turnip **7** Italian **9** Asparagus, Sprouting
brochure **5** flier **6** folder **7** booklet, leaflet **8** circular, handbill, pamphlet **9** throwaway
Brockton Blockbuster
  nickname of: **13** Rocky Marciano
Broglie, Louis Victor de
  field: **7** physics
  nationality: **6** French
  developed: **13** wave mechanics
  awarded: **10** Nobel Prize
broil **3** fry **4** bake, burn, cook, sear **5** parch, roast, toast **6** scorch **7** blister
broiler **3** hot, pan **4** rack **5** grill **6** cooker **8** scorcher **12** young chicken
broke **8** bankrupt, strapped, wiped out **9** insolvent, penniless **10** down and out **12** impoverished, on one's uppers, without funds **16** strapped for funds
broken **4** torn **5** rough, split, tamed **6** ruined, uneven **7** crushed, damaged **8** bankrupt, in pieces, ruptured **9** frac-

tured, separated, shattered **10** incomplete **11** fragmentary, interrupted
Broken Commandment, The
  author: **14** Toson Shimazaki
broken-down **6** beat-up, ruined **7** rickety, worn-out **8** battered, decrepit **10** ramshackle **11** dilapidated **12** deteriorated
broken-hearted **3** sad **6** gloomy, woeful **7** crushed, doleful, forlorn, unhappy **8** dejected, desolate, downcast, mournful, wretched **9** depressed, long-faced, miserable, sorrowful, woebegone **10** despairing, despondent, melancholy **11** heartbroken **12** disconsolate, inconsolable
Brom Bones
  also: **12** Brom Van Brunt
  character in: **23** The Legend of Sleepy Hollow
  author: **6** Irving
Bromfield, Louis
  author of: **11** Early Autumn, Malabar Farm **12** The Rains Came **13** Mrs Parkington, Night in Bombay **14** Wild Is the River **15** The Green Bay Tree **31** The Strange Case of Miss Annie Spragg
bromide **6** cliche **8** banality **9** platitude **10** stereotype **11** trite phrase **19** hackneyed expression
bromidic **4** dull **5** banal, corny, stale, tired, trite, vapid **6** jejune **7** humdrum, insipid **8** ordinary **9** hackneyed **10** pedestrian, unexciting, unoriginal **13** platitudinous, unimaginative
bromine
  chemical symbol: **2** Br
Bromius
  epithet of: **8** Dionysus
  means: **7** thunder
Bronson, Charles
  real name: **16** Charles Buchinsky
  wife: **11** Jill Ireland
  born: **11** Ehrenfeld PA
  roles: **9** Death Wish **13** The Dirty Dozen **14** The Great Escape **16** Battle of the Bulge, The Valachi Papers **19** The Magnificent Seven
Bronte, Anne
  author of: **9** Agnes Grey **23** The Tenant of Wildfell Hall
  pseudonym: **9** Acton Bell
Bronte, Charlotte
  author of: **7** Shirley **8** Jane Eyre, Villette **12** The Professor
  pseudonym: **10** Currer Bell
Bronte, Emily
  author of: **16** Wuthering Heights
  pseudonym: **9** Ellis Bell
Brontes
  member of: **8** Cyclopes
brontophobia
  fear of: **7** thunder
Brontosaurus
  also: **11** Apatosaurus

type: 8 dinosaur, sauropod
period: 8 Jurassic

Bronx Bull
   nickname of: 11 Jake La Motta

bronze 3 tan **5** metal **8** brownish, chestnut **10** reddish-tan **12** reddish-brown **13** copper-colored

brooch 3 pin **5** clasp

brood 4 chew, fret, mope, mull, sulk **5** cover, dwell, hatch, spawn, worry, young **6** chicks, family, litter **7** agonize, sit upon **8** children, incubate **9** offspring **10** hatchlings

brook 3 run **4** bear, rill, take **5** abide, allow, creek, stand **6** accept, endure, stream, suffer **7** rivulet, stomach **8** tolerate **9** put up with, streamlet

Brooks, Gwendolyn
   author of: 4 Riot **10** Annie Allen **14** Family Pictures

Brooks, James L
   director of: 9 Spanglish **13** Broadcast News **14** As Good As It Gets **17** Terms of Endearment (Oscar)

Brooks, Mel
   real name: 14 Melvin Kaminsky
   wife: 12 Anne Bancroft
   born: 10 Brooklyn NY
   director of/roles: 7 Dracula **10** Life Stinks, Spaceballs **11** High Anxiety, Silent Movie **12** The Producers **14** Blazing Saddles **17** Young Frankenstein **20** The History of the World

Brooks, Richard
   director of: 10 Fever Pitch **11** Elmer Gantry, In Cold Blood **16** Cat on a Hot Tin Roof, Sweet Bird of Youth **19** Looking for Mr. Goodbar, The Blackboard Jungle **20** The Brothers Karamazov, The Last Time I Saw Paris

broom 4 bush **5** besom, brush, whisk **7** sweeper

broth 5 stock **8** bouillon, consomme **9** clear soup

brothel 4 stew **5** house **6** bagnio, bordel **8** bordello, cathouse **10** bawdy house, fancy house, whorehouse **11** maison close **13** maison de passe, sporting house **14** house of ill fame **16** house of ill repute **19** house of prostitution

brother 3 pal **4** chum, monk, peer **5** buddy, friar **6** cleric **7** comrade, kinsman, partner, sibling **8** confrere, landsman, monastic, relative, relation **9** associate, colleague, companion, fellowman **10** countryman **11** male sibling **12** fellow member **13** fellow citizen
   French: 5 frere

brotherhood 4 club **5** amity, lodge **10** fellowship, fraternity, friendship **11** association

Brother Juniper
   character in: 21 The Bridge of San

Luis Rey
   author: 6 Wilder

Brothers Karamazov, The
   author: 10 Dostoevsky **17** Fyodor Dostoyevsky
   character: 4 Ivan **6** Dmitri **7** Alyosha (Alexey), Zossima **8** Katerina **9** Grushenka **10** Smerdyakov **15** Fyodor Karamazov

brougham 3 car **8** carriage **10** automobile

brought 6 caused **7** carried, fetched, sold for **8** conveyed **9** conducted, convinced, persuaded

brow 3 rim **4** brim, edge, side **5** brink, verge **6** border, margin **8** boundary, forehead **9** periphery

browbeat 4 cow **5** abash, bully, cower **6** badger, harass, hector **7** henpeck **8** bulldoze, domineer, frighten, threaten **9** terrorize, tyrannize **10** intimidate

browbeater 5 bully **6** despot **7** coercer **9** oppressor, tormenter, tormentor **11** intimidator, petty tyrant

browbeating 8 bullying **11** threatening, tyrannizing **12** intimidation

brown 3 bay, dun, fry, tan **4** buff, cook, drab, fawn, puce, roan, rust **5** beige, camel, cocoa, hazel, khaki, saute, tawny, toast, umber **6** auburn, bronze, brunet, coffee, copper, ginger, russet, sorrel, walnut **8** brunette, chestnut, cinnamon, mahogany **9** chocolate, olive drab **10** terra-cotta **11** dirt-colored, sand-colored **12** liver-colored

Brown, Angeline
   real name of: 14 Angie Dickinson

Brown, Berenice Sadie
   character in: 19 A Member of the Wedding
   author: 9 McCullers

Brown, Charles Brockden
   author of: 6 Ormond **7** Wieland **11** Edgar Huntly **12** Arthur Mervyn

Brown, Claude
   author of: 16 The Children of Ham **25** Manchild in the Promised Land

Brown, Dee
   author of: 15 Creek Mary's Blood **24** Bury My Heart at Wounded Knee

Brown, Helen Gurley
   author of: 19 Sex and the Single Girl
   editor of: 12 Cosmopolitan

Brown, Helen Hayes
   real name of: 10 Helen Hayes

Brown, Jim (Jimmy)
   sport: 8 football
   position: 8 fullback
   team: 15 Cleveland Browns
   actor in: 10 Dirty Dozen

Brown, Robert
   field: 6 botany
   nationality: 8 Scottish
   established: 16 Brownian movement

Brown Bomber
   nickname of: 8 Joe Louis

Browne, Dik
   creator/artist of: 9 Hi and Lois **12** Beetle Bailey **16** Hagar the Horrible

Browne, Sir Thomas
   author of: 9 Urn Burial **12** Hydriotaphia **13** Religio Medici **16** The Garden of Cyrus

brownie 3 elf **4** cake, puck **5** fairy, pixie **6** sprite **9** girl scout **10** leprechaun

Browning, Elizabeth Barrett
   author of: 11 Aurora Leigh **14** How Do I Love Thee **16** Casa Guidi Windows **24** Sonnets from the Portuguese

Browning, Robert
   author of: 8 Sordello **10** Paracelsus **11** Pippa Passes **13** Fra Lippo Lippi, My Last Duchess **14** Andrea del Sarto **17** The Ring and the Book **20** The Pied Piper of Hamlin **29** Soliloquy of the Spanish Cloister **30** Childe Roland to the Dark Tower Came

brownish 3 tan **5** taupe **6** bronze **8** chestnut **13** copper-colored

Brownlow, Mr
   character in: 11 Oliver Twist
   author: 7 Dickens

Brownmiller, Susan
   author of: 14 Against Our Will

browse 3 eat **4** feed, scan, skim, surf **5** graze **6** nibble, peruse, survey **7** dip into, pasture **8** look over **9** check over **11** look through **13** glance through

Bruckner, Anton
   born: 7 Austria **9** Ansfelden
   composer of: 6 Te Deum **7** Psalm CL **11** Grosse Messe **16** Romantic Symphony **26** Intermezzo for String Quartet

Brueghel, Pieter (the Elder)
   born: 5 Breda **8** Flanders
   nickname: 14 Peasant Bruegel
   sons: 3 Jan **6** Pieter
   artwork: 9 Blue Cloak, The Months **10** Dulle Griet (Mad Meg) **12** Fall of Icarus, Peasant Dance, Tower of Babel **14** Children's Games, The Misanthrope **15** Return of the Herd **16** Hunters in the Snow **17** The Triumph of Death **19** Peasant Wedding Dance **21** Peasant Wedding Banquet, The Magpie on the Gallows **22** Massacre of the Innocents **23** The Blind Leading the Blind, The Fall of the Rebel Angels

Brueghel, Jan
   born: 8 Brussels, Flanders
   nickname: 6 Velvet
   father: 13 Pieter Bruegel
   artwork: 12 Four Elements **13** Village Street **15** The Garden of Eden (with Rubens) **17** The Battle of Arbela

Brueghel, Pieter (the Younger)
   born: 8 Brussels, Flanders

Brugh, Spangler Arlington
nickname: **12** Hell Brueghel **19** The Infernal Brueghel
father: **13** Pieter Bruegel (the Elder)
artwork: **11** Village Fair **14** The Crucifixion **16** The Burning of Troy

Brugh, Spangler Arlington
real name of: **12** Robert Taylor

bruise 3 mar **4** hurt, mark **5** abuse, wound **6** damage, injure, injury, offend **7** blacken, blemish **8** discolor **9** black mark, contusion **13** discoloration

bruit 3 din **5** noise, rumor **6** clamor, hubbub, racket, report, uproar **7** clangor **10** clattering, noise about **11** voice abroad

Brunei
capital/largest city: **17** Bandar Seri Begawan
others: **4** Labi **5** Badas, Danau, Muara, Seria **6** Bangar, Tutong **7** Kampong **10** Kuala Abang, Kuala Balai **11** Kuala Belait
head of state/government: **6** sultan
island: **6** Borneo **8** Sipitang
mountain: **6** Teraja **9** Ulu Tutong
highest point: **10** Pagon Priok
river: **6** Belait, Brunei, Tutong **9** Temburong
sea: **10** South China
physical feature:
  bay: **6** Brunei
people: **4** Iban **5** Dayak, Malay **7** Chinese, Kadazan
language: **4** Iban **5** Malay **7** Chinese, English
religion: **5** Islam **6** Taoism **7** animism **8** Buddhism **12** Christianity
feature: **3** oil

Brunelleschi, Filippo
architect of: **10** San Lorenzo **11** Pazzi Chapel (Santa Croce), Pitti Palace **12** Santo Spirito **14** Badia Fiesolana **15** Duomo of Florence **16** Palazzo Quaratesi **21** Santa Maria degli Angeli **22** Ospedale degli Innocenti **23** Dome of Florence Cathedral

brunet, brunette 4 dark **5** black **9** brown-eyed, dark brown **10** dark-haired **11** brown-haired, dark-skinned **12** olive-skinned **16** dark-complexioned

Brunhild
origin: **8** Germanic
Scandinavian: **8** Brynhild
character in: **14** Nibelungenlied
queen of: **8** Isenland
husband: **7** Gunther
won by: **9** Siegfried

brunt 5 force **6** impact, stress, thrust **8** violence **9** full force, main shock

brush 4 bush, dust, fern, wash **5** clean, copse, flick, graze, groom, paint, run-in, scrub, sedge, set-to, shine, sweep, touch, whisk **6** battle, bushes, caress, duster, forest, fracas, polish, shrubs, stroke **7** bracken, cleanse, dusting, grazing, meeting, scuffle, thicket, varnish **8** skirmish, woodland **9** encounter, shrubbery, woodlands **10** engagement, underbrush, whisk-broom **11** bush country, undergrowth **12** bristled tool **13** confrontation
type: **4** hair, nail, shoe, wash **5** paint, scrub, tooth **7** clothes

brush aside 6 slight **7** neglect **8** pass over **9** disregard

brush-off 3 cut **4** snub **5** brush **6** rebuff, slight **7** put-down, squelch **9** disregard, rejection **11** repudiation **12** cold shoulder

brusque 4 curt, rude, tart **5** bluff, blunt, gruff, harsh, rough, short **6** abrupt, crusty **7** bearish **8** impolite, ungentle **10** ungracious **12** discourteous **13** unceremonious

Brussels
canal: **9** Charleroi **10** Willebroek
capital of: **7** Belgium
cathedral: **26** Saint Michel and Sainte Gudule
early name: **10** Bruocsella
  means: **16** marshy settlement
Flemish: **7** Brussel
French: **9** Bruxelles
headquarters of: **2** EU **3** EEC **4** NATO **12** Common Market **13** European Union **25** European Economic Community
landmark: **11** Royal Palace **15** Palace of Justice **17** Palace of the Nation
province: **7** Brabant
river: **5** Senne, Zenne
square: **11** Grande Place

brutal 5 crude, cruel, harsh **6** bloody, coarse, fierce, savage **7** brutish, hellish, inhuman, vicious **8** barbaric, pitiless, ruthless **9** atrocious, barbarous, heartless, merciless, unfeeling **10** demoniacal **11** hardhearted, remorseless **12** bloodthirsty

brutality 7 cruelty **8** ferocity, savagery **9** barbarity, harshness **10** inhumanity, savageness **11** brutishness, viciousness **12** ruthlessness

brute 5 beast, demon, devil, fiend, swine **6** animal, savage **7** monster **9** barbarian **10** wild animal **11** cruel person **12** dumb creature

brutish 5 cruel, feral **6** bloody, brutal, fierce, savage **7** inhuman **8** barbaric **9** barbarous, ferocious, unfeeling **11** remorseless

brutishness 8 ferocity, savagery **9** barbarity, brutality **10** bestiality, coarseness, inhumanity, savageness **11** viciousness **15** remorselessness

Brutus
also: **12** Marcus Brutus
character in: **12** Julius Caesar
author: **11** Shakespeare

Bruxelles see **8** Brussels

Bryan, C D B
author of: **12** Friendly Fire **24** Ugly Scenes Beautiful Women

Bryant, Bear (Paul)
sport: **8** football
position: **5** coach
team: **7** Alabama **11** Crimson Tide

Brynhild
origin: **12** Scandinavian
Germanic: **8** Brunhild
husband: **6** Gunnar
won by: **6** Sigurd
position: **8** Valkyrie

Brynhildr Sigrdrifa see **9** Sigrdrifa

Brynner, Yul
real name: **10** Taidje Khan
born: **14** Sakhalin Island
roles: **9** Anastasia, West World **11** The King and I (Oscar) **18** The Ten Commandments **19** The Magnificent Seven **20** The Brothers Karamazov **23** Invitation to a Gunfighter

Brythonic
language family: **12** Indo-European
group: **5** Welsh **6** Breton **7** Cornish, Pictish

Bschliessmayer, Oskar Josef
real name of: **11** Oskar Werner

Bubba Smith
nickname of: **17** Charles Aaron Smith

bubble, bubbles 4 bleb, boil, fizz, foam **5** froth **6** burble, fizzle, gurgle, seethe **7** air ball, blister, droplet, globule, sparkle **9** percolate **10** effervesce **13** effervescence

bubbliness 9 fizziness, foaminess **10** ebullience, enthusiasm, frothiness, liveliness **11** high spirits **13** effervescence

bubbling 5 fizzy, foamy **6** frothy **7** fizzing, foaming **9** sparkling **12** effervescent

bubbly 5 fizzy, foamy **6** frothy, lively **7** fizzing, foaming **9** champagne, sparkling **12** effervescent, high-spirited

buccaneer 6 pirate **7** corsair **9** privateer **10** freebooter

Buchan, John (Baron Tweedsmuir)
author of: **10** John Macnab **11** Greenmantle, Pilgrim's Way **17** John Burnet of Barns **18** The Thirty-Nine Steps

Buchanan, Daisy
character in: **14** The Great Gatsby
author: **10** Fitzgerald

Buchanan, Edgar
born: **13** Humansville MO
roles: **5** Shane, Texas **7** Arizona **8** Cimarron **9** McLintock **13** Penny Serenade **17** Petticoat Junction **18** Ride the High Country

Buchanan, James
nickname: **7** Old Buck
presidential rank: **9** fifteenth
party: **8** Democrat
state represented: **2** PA
defeated: **7** (John Charles) Fremont **8**

(Millard) Fillmore
vice president: 12 (John Cabell) Breckinridge
cabinet:
  state: 4 (Lewis) Cass **5** (Jeremiah Sullivan) Black
  treasury: 3 (John Adams) Dix **4** (Howell) Cobb **6** (Philip Francis) Thomas
  war: 4 (Joseph) Holt **5** (John Buchanan) Floyd
  attorney general: 5 (Jeremiah Sullivan) Black **7** (Edwin McMasters) Stanton
  navy: 6 (Isaac) Toucey
  postmaster general: 4 (Horatio) King, (Joseph) Holt **5** (Aaron Venable) Brown
  interior: 8 (Jacob) Thompson
born: 11 Cove Gap PA (near Mercersburg)
died/buried: 11 Lancaster PA
education:
  Academy: 8 Old Stone
  College: 9 Dickinson
  studied: 3 law
religion: 12 Presbyterian
political career: 13 state assembly **24** US House of Representatives
  secretary of: 5 State
  minister: 6 Russia **12** Great Britain
civilian career: 6 lawyer
notable events of lifetime/term: 5 Panic (of 1857) **11** English Bill, Pony Express
  raid by: 9 John Brown
  raid on: 12 Harper's Ferry
  Supreme Court case: 9 Dred Scott
father: 5 James
mother: 9 Elizabeth (Speer)
siblings: 4 Jane, John, Mary **5** Maria, Sarah **7** Harriet **9** Elizabeth **11** Edward Young **12** William Speer **16** George Washington
wife: 4 none
children: 4 none

Bucharest
  capital of: 7 Romania, Rumania
  founder: 5 Bucur
  landmark: 8 Scinteia **13** Village Museum
  river: 9 Dimbovita
  Rumanian: 9 Bucuresti

Buchinsky, Charles
  real name of: 14 Charles Bronson

buck 3 man **4** beau, deer, dude, kick, male **5** dandy **6** dollar, oppose **7** coxcomb **8** cavalier, gay blade **9** go against **10** young blood

Buck
  character in: 16 The Call of the Wild
  author: 6 London

Buck, Pearl S
  author of: 8 The Exile **9** Other Gods **10** Dragon Seed **12** The Good Earth **13** A House Divided

bucket 3 can, hod, tub **4** cask, pail **5**

scoop **6** vessel **7** pailful, pitcher, scuttle **9** container **10** receptacle

Buckeye State
  nickname of: 4 Ohio

buckle 3 sag **4** bend, clip, curl, hasp, hook, warp **5** bulge, catch, clasp **6** cave in, couple, fasten, secure **7** contort, crinkle, crumple, distort, wrinkle **8** belly out, collapse, fastener

buckle down 6 attend **12** apply oneself

Buckley, William F Jr
  author of: 11 Who's on First? **15** God and Man at Yale, God Save the Queen
  editor of: 14 National Review
  wife: 3 Pat
  son: 11 Christopher

Buck Rogers
  creator: 14 Richard Calkins
  character: 5 Alura, Buddy, Dercu, Kayla, Wilma **6** Ardala **10** Killer Kane

bucolic 4 idyl, poem **5** idyll, rural **6** poetic, rustic **7** eclogue, idyllic, peasant **8** pastoral, shepherd

bud 4 open **5** shoot **6** flower, sprout **7** blossom, burgeon, develop

Bud, Rosa
  character in: 22 The Mystery of Edwin Drood
  author: 7 Dickens

Budapest
  area: 4 Buda, Pest **5** Obuda
  capital of: 7 Hungary
  cathedral: 13 Saint Matthias
  hill: 10 Castle Hill
  island: 6 Csepel
  river: 6 Danube
  Roman town: 8 Aquincum

Buddenbrooks
  author: 10 Thomas Mann

Buddha
  also called: 5 Butsu
  born: 11 Kapilavastu
  father: 11 Suddhodhana
  founded: 8 Buddhism
  means: 15 enlightened one
  message: 6 dharma
  name for: 17 Siddhartha Gautama
  son: 6 Rahula
  tree: 2 bo **5** bodhi
  wife: 9 Yasodhara

Buddhism
  action: 5 karma
  branch: 3 Zen **8** Mahayana **9** Theravada **12** Great Vehicle **14** way of the elders
  doctrine: 6 duhkha **7** nirvana **9** suffering **13** eightfold path **15** four noble truths **17** pratityasamutpada
  founded by: 6 Buddha **17** Siddhartha Gautama
  monk: 7 bhikshu
  nun: 9 bhikshuni
  rebirth: 7 samsara
  religious community: 6 sangha

buddy 3 pal **4** chum, mate **5** amigo, crony **6** cohort, fellow, friend **7** brother, comrade, partner **8** confrere, intimate, playmate, sidekick **9** associate, colleague, companion, confidant **10** playfellow **11** confederate

buddy-buddy 5 close, palsy **6** chummy **8** friendly, intimate **10** palsy-walsy

budge 4 move, push, roll, stir, sway **5** shift, slide **6** change **8** convince, dislodge, persuade **9** dislocate, influence

budget 4 cost, plan **5** funds, means **6** moneys, ration **7** arrange **8** allocate, schedule **9** allotment, allowance, apportion, resources **10** allocation, portion out **12** spending plan **13** financial plan

budgetary 6 fiscal **8** economic, monetary **9** financial, pecuniary

buenas noches 9 good night

bueno 4 good

Buenos Aires
  capital of: 9 Argentina
  landmark: 11 Teatro Colon **16** Saavedra Monument, San Martin Theater **17** Wildestein Gallery, Witcomb Art Gallery **18** Church of El Salvador **27** Christopher Columbus Monument
  park: 7 Palermo
  people: 8 portenos
    means: 15 people of the port
  river: 12 Rio de la Plata

buff 3 bug, fan, nut, rub, tan **4** swab **5** freak, hound, maven, mavin, sandy, straw, tawny **6** addict, dauber, polish, smooth, the raw **7** admirer, burnish, devotee, leather **8** bare skin, follower, polisher **9** nakedness, yellowish **10** aficionado, enthusiast **11** buffalo hide, connoisseur **14** yellowish-brown

buffalo 5 bison **6** puzzle **7** mystify **10** intimidate
  kind: 7 African **10** Asian water
  African: 14 syncerus caffer
  Asian water: 14 bubalus bubalis

Buffalo
  football team: 5 Bills
  hockey team: 6 Sabres

buffer 6 bumper, fender, shield **7** cushion **9** protector

buffet 3 box, hit, jab, rap **4** bang, beat, bump, cuff, meal, push, slap **5** baste, knock, pound, shove, thump **6** pummel, strike, supper, thrash, thwack, wallop **7** cabinet, counter **8** credenza **9** cafeteria, sideboard **11** smorgasbord

Buffone, Carlo
  character in: 22 Every Man out of His Humour
  author: 6 Jonson

buffoon 3 wag **4** fool, zany **5** clown, comic, joker, mimic, Punch **6** jester, madcap **7** Pierrot **8** comedian, funnyman **9** harlequin, pantaloon, prankster, trickster **10** Scaramouch, silly-billy **11** merry-andrew, punchinello, Scaramouche

buffoonery 6 antics, comedy **7** foolery, inanity **8** zaniness **9** asininity, horseplay, silliness, slapstick **10** tomfoolery **11** foolishness, loutishness **12** clownishness, monkeyshines, prankishness **14** clowning around, playing the fool

Buffy the Vampire Slayer
  network: 2 WB **3** UPN
  creator: 10 Joss Whedon
  cast: 9 Seth Green (Oz) **10** Marc Blucas (Riley Finn) **11** Amber Benson (Tara), Eliza Dushku (Faith) **13** David Boreanaz (Angel/Angelus), Emma Caulfield (Anya/Anyanka), James Marsters (Spike) **14** Alyson Hannigan (Willow Rosenberg) **15** Nicholas Brendon (Xander Harris) **17** Charisma Carpenter (Cordelia Chase) **18** Anthony Stewart Head (Rupert Giles), Kristine Sutherland (Joyce Summers) **19** Sarah Michelle Gellar (Buffy Summers) **20** Michelle Trachtenberg (Dawn Summers)

bug 3 nag **4** flaw, germ **5** annoy, fault, virus **6** badger, bother, defect, insect, pester **7** wiretap **8** drawback, listen in, weakness **9** eavesdrop, Hemiptera **11** Heteroptera
  variety: 3 bat, bed, red **4** gnat, lace, leaf, seed, toad **5** negro, plant, shore, stilt, stink, water **6** ambush, damsel, fungus, pirate, ripple **7** boatman, stainer **8** assassin, burrower, creeping **9** royal palm **10** leaf footed **11** ashgray leaf, backswimmer, broadheaded, jumping tree, velvet water **12** velvety shore, water strider, water treader **13** jumping ground, water measurer, water scorpion **14** scentless plant **17** terrestrial turtle

bugaboo 4 ogre **5** scare **6** fright **7** anxiety

bugbear 4 ogre **5** bogey **6** goblin **7** bugaboo **8** bogeyman **9** bete noire

buggy 4 cart **5** wagon **7** vehicle **8** carriage **10** conveyance

bugle 4 horn **10** instrument

Bugs Bunny
  creator: 15 Leon Schlesinger
  character: 9 Elmer Fudd
  voice of: 8 Mel Blanc
  saying: 10 what's up doc

build 4 body, form, make, mold, open **5** begin, brace, erect, forge, found, put up, raise, renew, set up, shape, start, steel **6** create, extend, figure, harden, launch **7** amplify, augment, develop, enhance, enlarge, fashion, greaten, improve, produce **8** embark on, increase, initiate, multiply, physique **9** construct, establish, fabricate, institute, intensify, originate, reinforce, structure, undertake **10** inaugurate,

strengthen, supplement **11** manufacture, put together **12** construction

building 7 edifice **9** structure **12** construction

building front 6 facade **8** frontage

build up 5 amass **7** develop, promote **8** increase **10** accumulate

Bujold, Genevieve
  born: 6 Canada **8** Montreal
  roles: 4 Coma **9** Monsignor, Obsession **12** King of Hearts **21** Anne of the Thousand Days

Bujumbura
  capital of: 7 Burundi

Bul 17 eighth Hebrew month

bulb 3 bud **4** corm, seed **5** plant, tuber **8** swelling

Bulfinch, Charles
  architect of: 7 Capitol (Washington DC) **16** Hartford City Hall (CT) **23** Massachusetts State House (Boston)
  style: 7 Federal

Bulgakov, Mikhail
  author of: 9 Black Snow **13** The White Guard **14** The Heart of a Dog **19** The Days of the Turbins **21** The Master and Margarita

Bulgaria
  capital/largest city: 5 Sofia
  others: 3 Lom **4** Rila, Ruse **5** Aytos, Butan, Byclu, Elena, Iskra, Stara, Varna **6** Bleven, Burgas, Devnia, Dulovo, Levsky, Pernik, Pleuna, Pleven, Plevna, Shumen, Shumla, Sliven, Slivno, Widden, Yambol, Zagora **7** Gabrovo, Karlovo, Plovdiv, Sistova, Tirnova **8** Khaskovo, Rustchuk, Svishtov **9** Ruse Vidin, Silistria **11** Kolorovgrad **12** Dimitrovgrad
  school: 5 Sofia **7** Plovdiv **13** Veliko Turnovo
  measure: 3 oka, oke **5** krine, lekhe, likhe
  monetary unit: 3 lev **8** stotinki
  weight: 3 oka, oke **5** tovar
  mountain: 3 Kom **5** Botev, Pirin, Sapka **6** Balkan, Sredna **7** Vikhren **11** Rila-Rhodope
  highest point: 6 Musala **8** Musallah
  river: 3 Lom, Vit **4** Arda, Osma **5** Isker, Iskur, Mesta **6** Danube, Marica, Ogosta, Struma, Yantra **7** Maritsa, Stryama, Tundzha
  sea: 5 Black
  physical feature:
    cape: 5 Emine, Sabla **7** Kuratan
    gulf: 5 Burga
    plateau: 6 Danube
    resort: 9 Pyassatzi **13** Slunchev Bryav
    valley: 7 Maritsa
  people: 4 Slav, Turk **5** Gypsy, Pomak, Tatar **6** Bulgar, Slavic **7** Chuvash **9** Cheremiss **10** Macedonian
  language: 9 Bulgarian
  religion: 5 Islam **24** Bulgarian Eastern

Orthodox
  place:
    church: 9 St Nedelja
    monastery: 4 Rila **6** Rilski
    monument: 7 Red Army
    mosque: 10 Banya Bashi
    museum: 21 Revolutionary Movement
    square: 5 Lenin
    valley of roses: 8 Kazanluk
  feature:
    dance: 4 horo
    holiday: 12 St Georges Day
    newspaper: 17 Rabot Nichesko Delo
  food:
    stew: 8 giuvetch

bulge 3 bag, sag **4** bump, lump **5** curve, swell **6** excess **7** distend, project, puff out, sagging **8** protrude, stand out, stick out, swelling, swell out **9** bagginess **10** projection, prominence, protrusion **12** protuberance

bulk 4 body, mass, most, size **6** extent, volume, weight **7** bigness, measure **8** enormity, hugeness, main part, majority, quantity **9** amplitude, greatness, largeness, magnitude, major part, plurality, substance **10** better part, dimensions, lion's share **11** greater part, massiveness, proportions **13** preponderance

bulky 3 big **4** huge **5** large **6** clumsy **7** awkward, hulking, immense, lumpish, massive, sizable, unhandy **8** enormous, ungainly, unwieldy **9** capacious, extensive **10** cumbersome, voluminous **12** unmanageable

bull 2 ox **4** male
  male of the: 3 elk **4** seal **5** moose, whale **6** bovine **8** elephant
  constellation of: 6 Taurus
  Spanish: 4 toro

bulldoze 3 cow **4** bump, fell, push, rage, raze **5** abash, bully, drive, force, level, press, shove **6** coerce, hector, jostle, propel, subdue, thrust **7** buffalo, dragoon, flatten **8** bludgeon, browbeat, domineer, shoulder **9** push about, tyrannize **10** intimidate

Bullen, Frank T
  author of: 19 Told in the Dry Watches **22** The Cruise of the Cachalot

bullet 4 ball, lead, shot, slug **7** missile **8** buckshot

bulletin 4 note **6** report **7** account, message, release **8** dispatch **9** statement **10** communique, news report **12** notification **13** communication

Bullet Park
  author: 11 John Cheever

bullfighter 6 torero **7** matador, picador **8** Manolete, toreador **9** Escamillo **10** El Cordobes (Manuel Benitez Perez) **15** Miguel Dominguin

Bullion State
nickname of: **8** Missouri

Bullitt
director: **10** Peter Yates
cast: **9** Don Gordon **12** Robert Duvall,
Robert Vaughn, Steve McQueen **16**
Jacqueline Bisset
setting: **12** San Francisco

Bullock, Sandra
born: **11** Arlington VA
roles: **5** Crash, Speed **6** The Net **8**
Loverboy **10** Hope Floats **14** Practical Magic, Two Weeks Notice **15**
Murder by Numbers **16** Miss Congeniality **20** While You Were Sleeping
32 Divine Secrets of the Ya-Ya Sisterhood

bullock 2 ox **4** beef, bull **5** steer

bullocks 4 kine, oxen **5** beefs, bulls **6**
beeves, cattle, steers

bull session 3 rap **4** talk **7** gabfest,
palaver **8** dialogue **9** discourse **10** discussion **12** conversation **13** confabulation

bull's-eye 5 black **6** center **7** exactly **8**
on target **9** dead center, precisely

bully 3 cow **4** good **5** annoy, swell,
tough **6** cheers, coerce, despot, harass, hurrah, hurray **7** coercer, right
on, ruffian, tread on **8** browbeat, bulldoze, domineer, frighten, ride over,
well done **9** oppressor, terrorize, tormentor, tyrannize **10** browbeater, intimidate **11** intimidator

bullying 7 torment **8** coercion **9** despotism **10** harassment, tormenting **11**
browbeating, domineering, tyrannizing
12 intimidation

bulrush 5 plant, sedge **7** cattail, papyrus

bulwark 5 guard **7** barrier, parapet,
rampart, support, defense **8** mainstay
9 earthwork **10** embankment

Bulwer-Lytton, Edward
author of: **6** Harold, Pelham, Rienzi
9 Richelieu **13** The Coming Race **16**
Kenelm Chillingly **18** The Last of the
Barons **20** The Last Days of Pompeii

Bulworth
director: **12** Warren Beatty
cast: **9** Sean Astin (Gary) **10** Don
Cheadle (L.D.), Halle Berry (Nina)
11 Oliver Platt (Dennis Murphy) **12**
Joshua Malina (Bill Feldman), Warren Beatty (Senator Jay Billington
Bulworth) **13** Ernie Lee Banks (Leroy) **17** Christine Baranski (Constance Bulworth) **19** Kimberly Deauna Adams (Denisha)

bum 3 beg **4** grub, hobo **5** cadge, idler,
mooch, tramp **6** borrow, loafer,
sponge **7** drifter, vagrant **8** derelict,
vagabond

bumble 6 bungle **7** blunder, stagger,
stumble **8** flounder

Bumble

character in: 11 Oliver Twist
author: **7** Dickens

bumcombe, bunkum 3 rot **4** bosh,
bunk **6** drivel **7** twaddle **8** nonsense,
tommyrot **10** balderdash **16** stuff-and-
nonsense

bump 3 hit, jar, rap **4** bang, blow,
butt, hump, jolt, knob, knot, lump,
node, poke, slam, slap, sock **5** bulge,
clash, crack, crash, gnarl, knock,
punch, shake, smack, smash, thump,
whack **6** bounce, buffet, impact, jostle, jounce, nodule, rattle, strike, wallop **7** collide, run into **8** swelling **9**
collision, crash into, smash into **11**
excrescence **12** protuberance

bump into 4 meet **7** collide, run into
9 encounter

bumpkin 3 oaf **4** boor, lout **5** churl,
yokel **8** ship beam **10** clodhopper

bump off 4 do in, kill, slay **6** murder,
rub out **7** execute, gun down **8** dispatch **11** assassinate **12** take for a
ride

bumptious 4 bold **5** cocky, pushy **6**
brazen **7** forward, haughty **8** arrogant,
boastful, cocksure, impudent, insolent
9 bodacious, conceited, obtrusive **10**
aggressive, swaggering **11** impertinent, overbearing **12** presumptuous
13 overconfident, self-assertive

bumptiousness 4 gall **5** cheek **8** audacity, boldness **9** impudence **11** forwardness, presumption **12** impertinence **13** obtrusiveness **17** self-
assertiveness

bumpy 5 lumpy, rocky, rough **6** uneven **10** undulating

bun 4 coil, knot, roll **8** soft roll **9** sweet
roll

Bunaea
epithet of: **4** Hera
refers to: **6** temple

bunch 3 lot, mob **4** band, bevy, gang,
heap, herd, host, knot, mass, pack,
pile, team **5** array, batch, clump,
crowd, flock, group, shock, stack,
tribe, troop **6** amount, bundle, gather,
huddle, number, string **7** cluster, collect, company **8** assemble, assembly,
quantity **9** gathering, multitude **10** assortment, collection, congregate **12** accumulation

bundle 3 lot **4** bale, bind, heap, mass,
pack, pile, wrap **5** array, batch,
bunch, group, sheaf, stack, truss **6**
amount, packet, parcel **7** package **8**
quantity **9** multitude **10** assortment,
collection **11** tie together **12** accumulation

Bundren family
characters in: **11** As I Lay Dying
member: **4** Anse, Cash, Darl **5** Addie,
Jewel **9** Dewey Dell
author: **8** Faulkner

bungalow 5 cabin, house, lodge **7** cottage

bungle 3 mar **4** flub, goof, miff, ruin **5**
botch, spoil **6** foul up, mess up, muddle **7** blunder, butcher, do badly,
louse up, screw up **8** misjudge **9** mismanage, misreckon **10** miscompute
11 make a mess of, misestimate **12**
miscalculate

Bunin, Ivan Alekseyevich
author of: **10** The Village **15** The
Elagin Affair **17** The Life of Arseniev
28 The Gentleman from San Francisco

bunk 3 bed, cot, rot **4** bull **5** berth, hokum, hooey, stuff **6** bunkum, hot air,
humbug, pallet **7** baloney, blather,
bombast, hogwash, inanity, malarky,
spinach **8** claptrap, nonsense, tommyrot **9** poppycock **10** applesauce, balderdash **11** foolishness **16** stuff and
nonsense

Bunsen, Robert Wilhelm
nationality: **6** German
inventor of: **9** gas burner **10** photo
meter **12** Bunsen burner, spectroscope **24** electromechanical battery

Bunshaft, Gordon
architect of: **10** Lever House (NY) **23**
Beinecke Rare Book Library (Yale)
33 Hirshhorn Museum and Sculpture
Garden (Washington DC) **34** Lyndon
Baines Johnson Memorial Library
(Austin TX)

Bunyan, John
author of: **10** The Holy War **16** Pilgrim's Progress **25** The Life and
Death of Mr Badman **33** Grace
Abounding to the Chief of Sinners

buona notte 9 good night

buona sera 11 good evening

buon giorno 7 good day **11** good
morning

Buono, Victor
born: **10** San Diego CA
roles: **11** The Stranger **12** Four for
Texas **22** Hush Hush Sweet Charlotte
26 Whatever Happened to Baby Jane

buoy 4 bell, lift **5** boost, cheer, float,
raise **6** beacon, uplift **7** cheer up, elevate, gladden, lighten **8** brighten **10**
keep afloat **14** floating marker

buoyancy, buoyance 4 glee **6** gaiety
7 jollity **8** gladness, vivacity **9** animation, good humor, joviality, lightness,
sunniness **10** brightness, cheeriness,
enthusiasm, floatiness, joyousness **11**
good spirits **12** cheerfulness, exhilaration, floatability **14** weightlessness **16**
lightheartedness

buoyant 3 gay **4** glad **5** happy, jolly,
light, merry, peppy, sunny **6** afloat,
breezy, bright, elated, joyful, joyous,
lively **7** hopeful **8** animated, carefree,
cheerful, floating, sportive **9** energetic,
floatable, sprightly, vivacious **10**
blithesome, optimistic, weightless **11**
exhilarated, free and easy **12** enthusiastic, lighthearted

buoyed 6 elated 7 exalted, pleased 8 elevated 9 confident, heartened, reassured 10 inspirited

buoy up 4 warm 6 assure, uplift 7 comfort, hearten, inspire 8 inspirit, reassure 9 encourage

Burbank, Luther
field: 7 biology
developed: 13 plant breeding

burble 6 babble, bubble, gurgle, murmur 8 babbling

Burce, Suzanne
real name of: 10 Jane Powell

burden 3 tax, try, vex 4 care, load, onus, pack 5 cargo 6 hamper, hinder, strain, stress, weight 7 afflict, anxiety, freight, oppress, trouble 8 encumber, handicap, hardship, load with, obligate, overload 9 press down, weigh down 10 saddle with 11 encumbrance 14 responsibility

burden of proof
Latin: 12 onus probandi

burdensome 4 hard 5 heavy 6 tiring 7 arduous, onerous 8 wearying 9 Herculean, laborious 10 exhausting

bureau 6 agency, branch, office 7 cabinet, commode, dresser, service, station 8 division 10 chiffonier, department 14 administration, chest of drawers

bureaucrat 8 mandarin, official, politico 9 penpusher 10 politician 11 apparatchik, functionary, rubber stamp 12 civil servant, officeholder 13 public servant

burgee 4 flag 6 banner, colors, ensign 7 pennant

burgeon 3 wax 4 blow, grow, open 5 bloom 6 expand, flower, spread, thrive 7 augment, blossom, develop, enlarge, prosper, shoot up, succeed 8 escalate, flourish, fructify, increase, mushroom, spring up 9 bear fruit 10 effloresce 11 proliferate

Burgess, Anthony
author of: 2 MF 5 Byrne 13 Man of Nazareth, Time for a Tiger 14 Enderby Outside, The Wanting Seed 16 A Clockwork Orange, Beard's Roman Women 17 Nothing Like the Sun 18 A Dead Man in Deptford 20 The End of the World News
series: 7 Enderby

burgher 7 citizen 9 bourgeois 11 townsperson

burglar 3 cat 4 yegg 5 thief 6 robber 7 prowler 8 pilferer 9 cracksman, purloiner 12 housebreaker 14 second-story man

burglary 5 theft 6 felony 7 break-in, larceny, robbery 8 filching, stealing 9 pilfering 10 purloining 13 housebreaking 19 breaking and entering

burgundy 3 red 4 wine 5 color 13 reddish-purple

Burgundy
ancient city: 5 Autun
city: 5 Dijon
district: 5 Youne 6 Nievre 7 Cote d' Or 12 Saone-et-Loire
French: 9 Bourgogne
location: 6 France
river: 5 Rhone, Saone
tribe: 9 Burgundii

Buri
origin: 12 Scandinavian
first: 3 god
revealed by: 8 Audhumla 9 Audhumbla

burial 5 rites 7 funeral 9 interment, obsequies 10 entombment, inhumation

burial ground 7 ossuary 8 boneyard, Boot Hill, catacomb, cemetery 9 graveyard 10 churchyard, necropolis 12 potter's field

buried 4 laid, sunk 6 hidden 7 covered, inhumed, immured 9 concealed, deep sixed 10 laid to rest 11 underground

Burke, Francis
character in: 21 The Master of Ballantrae
author: 9 Stevenson

Burkina Faso
other name: 10 Upper Volta
capital/largest city: 11 Ouagadougou
others: 4 Kaya 7 Banfora 9 Koudougou 10 Ouahigouya
division: 7 Yatenga 9 Tenkodogo 11 Fada Ngourma
monetary unit: 5 franc 7 centime
mountain: 4 Tema
highest point: 8 Nakourou 10 Tenakourou, Tenekourou
river: 5 Komoe 6 Mekrou, Sourou 8 Pendjari, Red Volta 10 Black Volta, White Volta
physical feature:
  plateau: 5 Sahel 7 Sikasso, Voltaic
  wind: 9 harmattan
people: 4 Bobo, Lobi, Samo 5 Bella, Bissa, Dyula, Fulbe, Hausa, Mande, Marka, Mossi, Puehl 6 Fulani, Senufo, Tuareg 7 Grunshi, Voltaic, Yatenga 8 Mandingo 9 Gourounsi 15 Bunsansi Gambaga
  French governor: 7 Hesling
  god: 4 Wuro 5 Tenga
  king: 4 Naba 5 Mogho
  leader: 5 Oubri, Zerbo 7 Yameogo 8 Lamizana 9 Mogho Naba
language: 4 Bobo, Lobi, More, Samo 5 Dyula, Mande, Mossi 6 French
religion: 5 Islam 7 animism 12 Christianity
place:
  game reserve: 11 Arlyand Pama
feature:
  animal: 5 hyena 6 duiker, jackal 7 gazelle, warthog 10 hartebeest
  tree: 4 shea 6 acacia, baobab, karite, locust

burlap 3 bag 4 hemp, jute 5 cloth 6 fabric 8 material

burlesque 5 farce, spoof 6 comedy, parody, satire 7 mockery, takeoff 8 ridicule, travesty 10 buffoonery, caricature 15 slapstick comedy

burly 3 big 5 beefy, bulky, hefty, large 6 brawny, stocky, strong, sturdy 7 hulking, sizable 8 thickset 9 ponderous, strapping

Burma see 7 Myanmar

burn 3 nip, tan 4 bite, char, fire, glow, hurt, pain, sear, skin 5 be hot, blaze, brown, chafe, flame, flare, flash, parch, prick, scald, singe, smart, smoke, sting 6 abrade, bronze, flames, ignite, kindle, nettle, scorch, scrape, suntan, tingle, wither 7 blister, consume, cremate, flicker, oxidize, prickle, shrivel, smolder, sunburn, swelter 8 abrasion, be ablaze, be on fire, charring, irritate, kindling 9 be flushed, reddening, set fire to, set on fire, use as fuel 10 be feverish, be in flames, blistering, incandesce, incinerate, irritation, smoldering 12 incineration 13 reduce to ashes

burnable 9 flammable, ignitable 10 combustive 11 combustible, inflammable 13 conflagrative

Burne-Jones, Sir Edward Coley
born: 7 England 8 Birmingham
artwork: 11 Laus Veneris 15 The Golden Stairs 16 The Mirror of Venus 18 The Star of Bethlehem 28 King Cophetua and the Beggar Maid

burner, gas
invented by: 6 Bunsen

Burnett, Carol
born: 12 San Antonio TX
roles: 14 The Four Seasons 19 The Carol Burnett Show

Burnett, Frances H
author of: 20 Little Lord Fauntleroy

Burney, Fanny
author of: 7 Camilla, Diaries, Evelina

Burnham, Daniel Hudson
partner: 16 John Wellborn Root
architect of: 7 Rookery 12 Union Station (Washington DC) 15 Calumet Building 16 Flatiron Building (NYC), Reliance Building 17 Monadnock Building 25 World's Columbian Exposition

burning 3 hot 5 acrid, afire, aglow, eager, fiery, sharp 6 aflame, ardent, biting, fervid, heated, raging, red-hot 7 blazing, boiling, caustic, earnest, fanatic, fervent, flaming, flaring, frantic, glowing, ignited, intense, kindled, painful, pungent, sincere, smoking, zealous 8 flashing, frenzied, piercing, resolute, sizzling, smarting, stinging, tingling 9 corroding, prickling 10 astringent, compelling, flickering, irritating, passionate, smoldering 11 impassioned 12 all-consuming

burnish 3 wax 4 buff 5 rub up, shine 6 polish, smooth

burnished 5 shiny 6 bright, buffed, shined 8 lustrous, polished, smoothed

burnoose 4 cape, robe 5 cloak 6 mantle 7 pelisse

burn out 3 pop 4 blow 7 exhaust 10 exhaustion, extinguish

Burns, George
real name: 14 Nathan Birnbaum
wife: 11 Gracie Allen
born: 9 New York NY
roles: 5 Oh God 12 Going in Style 15 The Sunshine Boys 17 Burns and Allen Show

Burns, Robert
author of: 8 To a Louse, To a Mouse 11 A Red Red Rose, Tam O'Shanter 12 Auld Lang Syne 16 Address to the Deil, Coming Thro the Rye 17 Holy Willie's Prayer 20 Flow Gently Sweet Afton 22 My Heart's in the Highlands 23 The Cotter's Saturday Night 32 Poems Chiefly in the Scottish Dialect

Burnt Norton
author: 7 T S Eliot

burp 5 belch, eruct 10 eructation

burr 4 buhr, rock 5 notch, stone 9 whetstone 13 pronunciation

Burr
author: 9 Gore Vidal

Burr, Aaron 13 vice president
event: 4 duel
victim: 17 Alexander Hamilton

Burr, Raymond
born: 6 Canada 14 New Westminster 15 British Columbia
roles: 8 Ironside 10 Perry Mason, Rear Window

burro 3 ass 4 mule 6 donkey, onager 7 jackass

Burroughs, Edgar Rice
author of: 15 Tarzan of the Apes

Burroughs, William S
author of: 5 Junky, Queer 6 Junkie 13 The Naked Lunch
member of: 14 Beat Generation

Burroughs, William Seward
nationality: 8 American
inventor of: 13 adding machine
grandson: 17 William S Burroughs (author)

burrow 3 den, dig 4 cave, hole, lair 6 covert, dugout, furrow, tunnel 8 excavate, scoop out 9 hollow out

Burrows, Abe
author of: 41 How to Succeed in Business without Really Trying

bursa 3 bag, sac 5 pouch, purse 6 cavity

bursar 6 purser 7 cashier 9 paymaster, treasurer 10 cashkeeper

burst 3 fly, pop, run 4 bang, bust, rend, rush 5 barge, blast, break, crack, erupt, split, spout 6 blow up,

detach, divide, sunder 7 disjoin, explode, rupture, shatter, torrent 8 breaking, break out, cracking, crashing, detonate, eruption, fly apart, fracture, fragment, outbreak, separate, splinter 9 break open, discharge, explosion, gush forth, pull apart, splitting, tear apart 10 detonation, disconnect, outpouring, shattering 11 spring forth 12 disintegrate

burst forth 5 arise, begin, erupt, start 6 arrive, emerge 8 break out, commence

Burstyn, Ellen
real name: 14 Edna Rae Gillooly
born: 9 Detroit MI
roles: 11 The Exorcist 16 Same Time Next Year 18 The Last Picture Show 26 Alice Doesn't Live Here Anymore (Oscar)

Burton, Richard
real name: 22 Richard Walter Jenkins Jr
wife: 15 Elizabeth Taylor
born: 5 Wales 11 Pontrhydfen Wales
roles: 6 Becket, Hamlet 7 Camelot, The Robe 9 Cleopatra 14 My Cousin Rachel 19 The Night of the Iguana, The Taming of the Shrew 21 Anne of the Thousand Days 25 Who's Afraid of Virginia Woolf 26 The Spy Who Came in from the Cold

Burton, Robert
author of: 22 The Anatomy of Melancholy

Burundi
capital/largest city: 9 Bujumbura
others: 6 Ngozi 6 Bururi, Gitega, Kitega, Rutana, Ruyigi 7 Kibumbu, Muyinga
monetary unit: 5 franc 7 centime
lake: 7 Rugwero 8 Tshohoha 10 Tanganyika
mountain: 9 Nyamisana
highest point: 8 Nyarwana
river: 6 Akanya, Ruvuvu, Ruzizi 8 Rukagera 10 Malagarasi
people: 3 Twa 4 Hutu 5 Bantu, Batwa, Pygmy, Tutsi 6 Bahutu, Watusi 7 Barundi
language: 6 French 7 Kirundi, Swahili
religion: 5 Islam 7 animism 10 Protestant 13 Roman Catholic
feature:
  king: 4 mwam
food:
  coffee: 7 Arabica

Burushaski
language spoken in: 7 Kashmir

bury 4 hide 5 cache, cover, inter 6 encase, engulf, entomb, inhume 7 conceal, cover up, enclose, immerse, secrete 8 submerge, submerse 13 lay in the grave 17 consign to the grave

Bury My Heart at Wounded Knee
author: 8 Dee Brown

bush 4 veld 5 brush, hedge, plant, shrub, woods 6 forest, jungle 7 barrens 9 shrubbery, woodlands

Bush, George Herbert Walker
presidential rank: 10 forty-first
party: 10 Republican
state represented: 2 TX 5 Texas
defeated: 7 (Michael) Dukakis
defeated by: 7 (Bill) Clinton
vice president: 6 (James Danforth) Quayle
born: 8 Milton MA
education: 4 Yale 7 Andover
religion: 12 Episcopalian
vacation spot: 5 Maine 13 Kennebunkport
political career: 13 vice president 14 representative 21 Ways and Means Committee
  ambassador to: 2 UN 13 United Nations
  chairman of: 27 Republican National Committee
  head of: 3 CIA
  liaison with: 5 China
civilian career: 3 oil 14 Zapata Offshore
military career: 5 pilot 6 US Navy
vice president under: 12 Ronald Reagan
notable events of lifetime/term: 7 Gulf War 14 Persian Gulf War 20 Operation Desert Storm
  Supreme Court appointments: 11 David Souter 14 Clarence Thomas
  invasion of: 6 Panama
father: 15 Prescott Sheldon
mother: 13 Dorothy Walker
wife: 13 Barbara Pierce
children: 4 John, Neil 5 Robin (died 1953) 6 George, Marvin 7 Dorothy

Bush, George Walker
presidential rank: 10 forty-third
party: 10 Republican
state represented: 2 TX 5 Texas
defeated: 6 Al Gore 9 John Kerry
vice president: 10 Dick (Richard) Cheney
born: 10 New Haven CT
education: 4 Yale 7 Andover, Harvard
religion: 7 Baptist
home: 10 Crawford TX
political career: 8 governor (TX)
civilian career: 3 oil 8 baseball
ownership in: 12 Texas Rangers
military career: 5 pilot 13 National Guard
notable events of lifetime/term: 7 tsunami (Asia), Iraq War, Katrina 14 Afghanistan War 15 terrorist attack
  destruction of: 10 Twin Towers 16 World Trade Center
father: 19 George Herbert Walker
mother: 13 Barbara Pierce
wife: 10 Laura Welch
children: 5 Jenna 7 Barbara

bush country 5 scrub, wilds 7 outback 10 wilderness

bushed 4 beat 5 all in, spent, tired, weary 6 done it, pooped 7 drained, wearied, worn out 8 dog tired, fatigued, tired out 9 dead tired, exhausted, played out

bushel
abbreviation: 2 bu 4 bush

bushes 5 brush 6 shrubs 9 brushwood, shrubbery 10 underbrush 11 undergrowth

bushy 5 hairy 6 fluffy, shaggy 7 hirsute 9 overgrown

business 3 job 4 case, duty, firm, line, shop, task, work 5 chore, field, place, point, store, topic, trade 6 affair, career, living, matter, office, racket 7 affairs, calling, company, concern, dealing, factory, mission, problem, pursuit, subject, venture 8 activity, commerce, function, industry, position, province, question, vocation 9 procedure, situation, specialty 10 assignment, bargaining, employment, enterprise, livelihood, occupation, profession, walk of life 11 corporation, negotiation, partnership, transaction, undertaking 13 establishment, manufacturing, merchandising 14 bread and butter, responsibility

businesslike 7 careful, correct, orderly, regular, serious 8 diligent, sedulous, thorough 9 assiduous, efficient, organized, practical 10 methodical, systematic 11 industrious, painstaking 12 professional

Busiris
king of: 5 Egypt
father: 8 Poseidon
mother: 10 Lysianassa

Busoni, Ferruccio
born: 5 Italy 6 Empoli
composer of: 8 Turandot 10 Arlecchino 11 Doctor Faust, Doktor Faust 12 Die Brautwahl 14 Comedy Overture 25 Fantasia Contrappuntistica

bus station 5 depot 8 terminal, terminus

Bus Stop
director: 11 Joshua Logan
cast: 9 Don Murray 10 Betty Field 13 Eileen Heckart, Marilyn Monroe 14 Arthur O'Connell

bust 3 nab 4 head, raid 5 bosom, chest, seize 6 arrest, breast, collar 7 capture 9 apprehend, sculpture 12 take prisoner 15 take into custody

Buster Brown
creator: 10 RF Outcault
bulldog: 4 Tige
trademark: 9 sailor hat 10 wide collar

bustle 3 ado, fly 4 dash, flit, fuss, rush, stir, tear, to-do 5 hurry 6 bestir, flurry, hustle, pother, scurry, tumult 7 be quick, fluster, flutter, press on,

scamper, scuttle 8 activity, be active, scramble 9 agitation, commotion, make haste 10 excitement, hurly-burly

busy 4 full 6 active, employ, engage, intent, occupy, on duty, work at 7 engaged, labor at, slaving, toiling, working 8 absorbed, bustling, employed, laboring, occupied 9 engrossed, in harness, strenuous 10 hard at work 11 industrious 12 be absorbed in, keep occupied 13 be engrossed in

busybody 3 pry 5 snoop 6 gossip 7 blabber, meddler, Paul Pry 8 telltale 10 chatterbox, newsmonger, talebearer, tattletale 12 blabbermouth 13 scandalmonger

busy place 4 hive 6 warren 7 anthill, beehive

but 3 yet 4 save, than that 5 if not, still 6 except, saving, unless 7 however, outside, that not 9 excepting, other than, otherwise 10 except that 14 on the other hand

Butch Cassidy and the Sundance Kid
director: 13 George Roy Hill
cast: 10 Paul Newman (Butch) 13 Katharine Ross (Etta Place), Robert Redford (The Kid)
score: 13 Burt Bacharach
Oscar for: 5 score
song: 27 Raindrops Keep Fallin' on My Head

butcher 4 goof, kill, muff, ruin, slay 5 botch, purge, spoil 6 boggle, bungle, fumble, hack up, hit man, killer, mess up, murder 7 louse up, screw up 8 assassin, decimate, homicide, massacre, murderer 9 liquidate, manhandle, mishandle, slaughter 10 annihilate, hatchet man, liquidator 11 assassinate, exterminate, make a mess of, slaughterer 12 exterminator, massmurderer 15 homicidal maniac

butchery 4 flop, mess 5 botch 8 massacre 9 slaughter

Butes
father: 6 Boreas 7 Pandion
mother: 8 Zeuxippe
brother: 8 Lycurgus 10 Erechtheus
sister: 6 Procne 9 Philomela
son: 4 Eryx
priest of: 6 Athena 8 Poseidon
member of: 9 Argonauts
stricken with: 8 insanity
enticed by: 6 Sirens
leaped into: 3 sea
rescued by: 9 Aphrodite

Butkus, Dick (Richard Marvin)
sport: 8 football
position: 10 linebacker
team: 12 Chicago Bears

Butler, Rhett
character in: 15 Gone With the Wind
author: 8 Mitchell

Butler, Samuel
author of: 7 Erewhon 8 Hudibras 16

The Way of All Flesh 20 The Elephant in the Moon

butt 3 end, hit, jab, ram, rap 4 buck, bump, bunt, dupe, goat, mark, push, slap, stub 5 knock, shank, shove, smack, stump, thump 6 bottom, buffet, jostle, object, strike, target, thrust, thwack, victim 8 blunt end 13 laughingstock

buttercup 10 Ranunculus
variety: 4 Tall 5 Early 6 Common 7 Bermuda, Bulbous, Persian 8 Colombia, Creeping 11 Yellow water

butterfingered 5 inept 6 clumsy 7 awkward 8 bungling 9 maladroit 10 ungraceful

butterfly
pupa: 9 chrysalis 10 chrysalids 11 chrysalides
variety: 4 blue 5 giant, nymph, satyr, snout, tiger, zebra 6 alpine, apollo, arctic, kalima 7 alfalfa, budwing, dogface, monarch, peacock, viceroy 9 Baltimore, bathwhite, brimstone, christmas, metalmark, orange tip, wood nymph 10 Parnassian 11 painted lady, spring azure 12 blue mountain, cabbage white, clouded white, silver stripe, white admiral 13 chalkhill blue, mourning cloak, pearl crescent 14 American copper, gulf fritillary, tailed birdwing 15 longtail skipper, regal fritillary 16 black swallowtail, black-veined white, camberwell beauty, green-veined white, Leonardus skipper, red-spotted purple 18 orchard swallowtail 19 European swallowtail 20 spicebush swallowtail, variegated fritillary 21 great purple hairstreak, questionmark anglewing, white admiral wood nymph

butter up 4 coax 6 cajole 7 flatter, wheedle 8 soft-soap

buttocks 4 buns, butt, rear, rump, seat 5 fanny, nates 6 behind, bottom 7 keister, rear end 8 backside, derriere, haunches 9 fundament, posterior 12 hindquarters

buttonhole 4 halt, slit, stop 6 accost, waylay 7 solicit 8 approach, confront

button one's lip 7 keep mum 10 keep silent 16 keep one's trap shut 18 keep one's lips sealed

Buttons, Red
real name: 11 Aaron Chwatt
born: 9 New York NY
roles: 8 Sayonara 13 The Longest Day 20 The Poseidon Adventure 23 They Shoot Horses Don't They

buttress 4 arch, prop, stay 5 boost, brace, shore, steel 6 prop up 7 bolster, shore up, support 8 abutment, shoulder 9 reinforce, stanchion 10 strengthen

buxom 5 plump 6 bosomy, chesty, robust, zaftig 9 strapping 10 voluptuous 13 large-breasted, well-developed

buy 3 get 4 deal, gain 5 bribe 6 buy
off, obtain, pay for, suborn 7 acquire,
bargain, corrupt, procure 8 invest in,
purchase 9 influence

buy and sell 4 deal 5 trade 6 market

buy off 5 bribe 6 pay off 13 grease the
palm

Buzi
son: 7 Ezekiel

Buz Sawyer
creator: 8 Roy Crane
sidekick: 7 Sweeney

Buzuhov, Pierre
character in: 11 War and Peace
author: 7 Tolstoy

buzz 3 hum 4 whir 5 drone 6 murmur
7 whisper

by 4 near, over, past 5 along 6 beside,
beyond, during, toward 7 through 9
alongside 10 concerning, on or before
11 according to, no later than

by air
French: 8 par avion

Byam, Roger
character in: 17 Mutiny on the
Bounty
authors: 4 Hall 8 Nordhoff

Byblis
father: 7 Miletus
mother: 6 Cyanea
twin brother: 6 Caunus
loved: 6 Caunus
changed into: 8 fountain

by few words
Latin: 12 paucis verbis

bygone 4 past 5 olden 6 former, gone
by, of yore 7 ancient, earlier 8 departed, obsolete, previous 10 antiquated

by horse
French: 7 a cheval

Byington, Spring
born: 17 Colorado Springs CO
roles: 7 Jezebel 11 Little Women 13
December Bride, Heaven Can Wait
17 Mutiny on the Bounty 20 The
Devil and Miss Jones, You Can't
Take It with You 26 The Charge of
the Light Brigade

by itself 4 solo 5 alone, aloof, apart 8
isolated 13 unaccompanied

Byng, Admiral
character in: 7 Candide
author: 8 Voltaire

by oneself 4 solo 5 alone, aloof 8 isolated 10 solitarily 13 unaccompanied
Latin: 4 sola 5 solus

by operation of law
Latin: 8 ipso jure

bypass 4 go by 5 avert, avoid, dodge 8
go around 10 circumvent 12 detour
around

bypath 3 way 4 lane 5 alley, byway,
track, trail 6 bypass 7 footway, pathway, towpath, walkway 8 back road,
dirt road, footpath, shortcut, side road
10 beaten path, bridle path, garden
path

by-product 8 offshoot 9 aftermath 16
incidental result

by right
Latin: 6 de jure

Byron, Lord (George Gordon)
author of: 7 Don Juan, Manfred 10
The Corsair 19 The Vision of Judgment 20 The Prisoner of Chillon 23
Childe Harold's Pilgrimage

byrrh
type: 8 aperitif
origin: 6 France
flavor: 6 orange 7 quinine

bystander 6 viewer 7 watcher, wit-

ness 8 attender, beholder, looker-on,
observer, onlooker, passerby 9 spectator

by the book 9 by the rule 13 authoritarian 16 according to Hoyle

by the fact itself
Latin: 9 ipso facto

by the grace of God
Latin: 9 Dei gratia

by the law itself
Latin: 8 ipso jure

by the month
Latin: 9 per mensem

by the rule 9 by the book 11 as specified 13 authoritarian

by the skin of one's teeth 6 barely,
hardly 8 only just, scarcely 11 by an
eyelash

by the very nature of the deed
Latin: 9 ipso facto

by the way
French: 9 en passant

by virtue and arms
Latin: 13 virtute et armis
motto of: 11 Mississippi

byway 4 lane 5 alley 6 detour, street 8
shunpike

by what right?
Latin: 7 quo jure

byword 3 law, saw 4 rule 5 adage, axiom, maxim, motto, truth 6 dictum,
saying, slogan 7 precept, proverb 8
aphorism, apothegm 9 catchword, pet
phrase, principle, watchword 10 shibboleth

Byzantine 6 complex 8 scheming 9
expedient, intricate 13 Machiavellian

Byzas
founder of: 9 Byzantium
father: 8 Poseidon

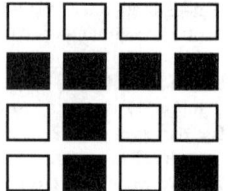 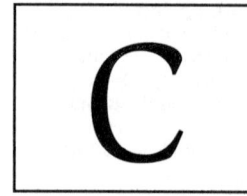 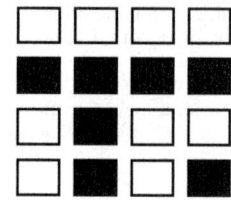

Caan, James
 born: 9 New York NY
 roles: 3 Elf 6 Misery 8 Dogville, Las Vegas 9 Dick Tracy, Funny Lady 10 Brian's Song, For the Boys, Rollerball 11 Bulletproof, The Gamblers 12 Brian Piccolo, The Godfather 13 Sonny Corleone 17 Cinderella Liberty

cab 4 hack, taxi 7 taxi cab

Cab 15 Biblical measure

cabal 4 band, plan, plot, ring 5 junta 6 design, league, scheme 7 faction 8 intrigue 10 connivance, conspiracy 11 combination, machination

cabalistic 6 arcane, mystic, occult, secret 7 cryptic, obscure, strange 8 abstruse, esoteric, mystical 10 mysterious, unknowable 11 inscrutable 12 impenetrable, supernatural, unfathomable 16 incomprehensible

cabaret 4 cafe, club 6 bistro 9 nightclub 10 supper club
 French: 5 boite 11 boite de nuit

Cabaret
 director: 8 Bob Fosse
 based on stories by: 20 Christopher Isherwood
 cast: 8 Joel Grey 11 Fritz Wepper, Helmut Griem, Michael York 12 Liza Minnelli (Sally Bowles) 14 Marisa Berenson
 Oscar for: 7 actress (Minnelli) 8 director 15 supporting actor (Grey)
 song: 12 The Money Song

cabbage 16 Brassica oleracea (Capitata Group)
 varieties: 3 Cow 4 Deer, Head, Wild 5 John's, Savoy, Skunk 6 Celery 7 Chinese 9 Flowering, Tronchuda 10 Portuguese 11 Yellow skunk 12 Western skunk

Cabecar
 language family: 10 Talamancan
 location: 9 Costa Rica 12 Sixaola River 14 Central America, Talamanca Plain
 intermixed with: 6 Bribri

Cabell, James Branch
 author of: 6 Jurgen 12 The High Place 14 Figures of Earth 17 The Cream of the Jest

cabin 3 hut 4 room 5 hutch, lodge, shack 6 shanty 7 cottage 8 bungalow, log cabin, quarters 9 stateroom 11 compartment

cabinet 3 box 4 case, file 5 chest 6 bureau 7 council 8 advisors, cupboard, ministry 10 breakfront, counselors, receptacle 11 china closet 13 advisory board 14 chest of drawers

cable 4 cord, line, rope, wire 5 chain, wires 6 hawser 7 mooring 8 wire line, wire rope 12 electric wire 16 overseas telegram

Cable, George W
 author of: 8 Dr Sevier 13 Old Creole Days 15 The Grandissimes

cablegram 4 wire 5 cable 7 message 8 wireless 16 overseas telegram

Cabot, Ephraim
 character in: 18 Desire Under the Elms
 author: 6 O'Neill

Caca
 origin: 5 Roman
 goddess of: 6 hearth
 corresponds to: 5 Vesta

Cacambo
 character in: 7 Candide
 author: 8 Voltaire

cache 4 heap 5 hoard, stock, store 8 hideaway 9 stockpile 11 hiding place, secret place

cachet 4 mark, seal 5 stamp, wafer 6 design, slogan 7 capsule

cackle 7 chatter 10 harsh laugh 11 shrill laugh
 sound made by: 3 hen 4 chicken

cacophonous 5 harsh 6 off-key 7 grating, jarring, raucous 8 off-pitch, screechy, strident 9 dissonant, out of tune, unmusical 10 discordant 11 unmelodious 12 inharmonious, nonmelodious 13 disharmonious

cacophony 3 din 5 noise 7 discord 9 harshness 10 disharmony, dissonance

cactus
 varieties: 3 Cob, Sun 4 Ball, Cane, Chin, Claw, Club, Comb, Crab, Hook, Lace, Leaf, Moon, Rose, Star, Toad, Vine, Yoke 5 Agave, Apple, Brain, Chain, Coral, Crown, Devil, False, Giant, Leafy, Melon, Paper, Plain, Prism, Snake, Spice, Torch 6 Barrel, Button, Cholla, Dagger, Dollar, Easter, Hatpin, Hot-dog, Myrtle, Nipple, Old-man, Orchid, Peanut, Pencil, Ribbon, Spider 7 Cushion, Eve's pin, Feather, Hatchet, Hat-rack, Jumping, Old-lady, Popcorn, Rain-

bow, Rattail, Redbird, Serpent, Thimble, Whisker 8 Cinnamon, Dumpling, Fishbone, Fishhook, Flapjack, Gold lace, Golf-ball, Hedgehog, Old-woman, Polka-dot, Pond-lily, Snowball, Snowdrop, Starfish, Tortoise, Turk's-cap 9 Bird's nest, Chain-link, Christmas, Cow-tongue, Electrode, Fire-crown, Hairbrush, Lamb's-tail, Mistletoe, New old-man, Organ-pipe, Porcupine, Red orchid, Sea-urchin, Spineless, Teddy-bear, Toothpick, Totem-pole, Turk's-head, White chin 10 Bluebarrel, Candelabra, Cottonpole, Easter-lily, Golden ball, Golden-star, Living-rock, Powder-puff, Silver ball, Strawberry, Unguentine, White torch, Wickerware 11 Frilled lace, Grizzlybear, Joseph's coat, Large barrel, Scarlet ball, Woolly torch 12 Dancing-bones, Golden barrel, Mule-crippler, Scarlet crown, Thanksgiving 13 Colombian ball, Creeping-devil, Dutchman's pipe, Peruvian apple, Peruvian torch, Silver cluster 15 Golden bird's nest 16 Mexican dwarf tree 17 Burbank's spineless 18 Fishhook pincushion

Cacus
 form: 5 giant
 father: 6 Vulcan
 eats: 3 men
 killed by: 8 Hercules

cad 3 cur, rat 4 heel, lout 5 churl, knave, louse, rogue 6 rascal, rotter 7 bounder, caitiff, dastard, villain 9 scoundrel

cadaver 4 body 5 stiff 6 corpse 7 remains 8 dead body, deceased

cadaverous 4 pale 5 ashen, gaunt 6 chalky, pallid 7 deathly, ghastly 8 blanched 9 bloodless, deathlike 10 corpselike

caddisfly
 variety: 5 micro 8 northern 9 finger-net, primitive, snailcase 10 long-horned, trumpetnet, tubemaking 11 netspinning

Caddoan
 tribe: 6 Pawnee 14 Chahiksichhiks

caddy 3 box, can, tin 5 chest 6 coffer

cadence 4 beat, lilt 5 meter, pulse, swing, tempo, throb 6 accent, rhythm 7 measure

Caderousse
character in: **21** The Count of Monte
Cristo
author: **5** Dumas (pere)
cadet 5 plebe **7** recruit, student **11**
youngest son **14** military student
cadge 3 beg, bum **5** mooch **6** hustle,
peddle, sponge **7** solicit, scrounge **9**
panhandle
cadmium
chemical symbol: **2** Cd
Cadmus
form: **6** prince
realm: **9** Phoenicia
father: **6** Agenor
mother: **10** Telephassa
brother: **5** Cilix **7** Phoenix
sister: **6** Europa
wife: **8** Harmonia
son: **8** Illyrius **9** Polydorus
daughter: **3** Ino **5** Agave **6** Semele **7**
Autonoe
introduced to the Greeks: **7** writing
founded: **6** Thebes
planted: **12** dragons teeth
caduceus
staff of: **7** Mercury
Caeneus
also: **6** Caenis
member of: **9** Argonauts
gift: **15** invulnerability
former identity: **6** Caenis
Caenis
also: **7** Caeneus
father: **6** Elatus
violated by: **8** Poseidon
changed into: **3** man
subsequent identity: **7** Caeneus
caesar, Caesar 5 ruler **6** despot, kaiser, tyrant **7** emperor **8** autocrat, dictator
Caesar, Julius
adopted son: **8** Octavian **14** Caesar
Augustus
author of: **13** On the Civil War **14**
On the Gallic War
battle: **4** Zela **5** Munda **7** Durazzo,
Thapsus **8** Mytilene **9** Pharsalus **11**
Dyrrhachium
conquered: **4** Gaul
crossed: **7** Rubicon (river)
defeated: **6** Pompey
lover: **9** Cleopatra
member of: **16** First Triumvirate
murdered by: **5** Casca **6** Brutus **7**
Cassius
murdered on: **11** Ides of March
other triumvirs: **6** Pompey **7** Crassus
saying: **9** Et tu Brute? (Even you Brutus?) **12** Veni vidi vici (I came I saw
I conquered)
wife: **7** Pompeia **8** Cornelia **9** Calpurnia
Caesar, Sid
partner: **11** Imogene Coca
born: **9** Yonkers NY
roles: **15** Your Show of Shows

Caesar and Cleopatra
author: **17** George Bernard Shaw
Caesar or Nothing
author: **9** Pio Baroja
caesura 5 break, pause **6** hiatus **12** interruption
cafe 3 bar, inn **5** diner **6** bistro, eatery,
nitery, tavern **7** automat, beanery,
cabaret **9** cafeteria, chophouse, hash
house, lunchroom, nightclub **10** restaurant, supper club **11** bar and grill,
coffeehouse, discotheque **12** luncheonette
French: **9** estaminet
cafe au lait 10 light brown **14** coffee
with milk
cafe noir 11 black coffee
cage 3 pen **4** coop **5** pen in **6** coop up,
encage, lock up, shut in **7** confine,
impound **8** imprison, restrain, restrict
9 enclosure
cagey 3 sly **4** foxy, keen, wary, wily **5**
alert, chary, leery, sharp **6** artful,
crafty, shifty, shrewd **7** careful, cunning, heedful, prudent **8** cautious, discreet, watchful
Cagliari
capital of: **8** Sardinia
Cagney, James
nickname: **5** Jimmy
born: **9** New York NY
roles: **7** Ragtime **14** The Public Enemy **17** Yankee Doodle Dandy (Oscar) **19** Man of a Thousand Faces
Cagney and Lacey
cast: **8** Tyne Daly **11** Sharon Gless
Cain
father: **4** Adam
mother: **3** Eve
brother: **4** Abel, Seth
home: **4** Eden
son: **5** Enoch
killed: **4** Abel
traveled to: **3** Nod
Caine, Michael
real name: **24** Maurice Joseph Micklewhite
born: **6** London **7** England
honor: **10** knighthood
roles: **4** Zulu **5** Alfie **6** Sleuth **9**
Deathtrap **11** Little Voice **13** Educat-
ing Rita, Jack the Ripper, Jekyll and
Hyde **14** The Ipcress File **16** The
Quiet American **17** A Shock to the
System **18** The Cider House Rules **19**
Hannah and Her Sisters **20** The Man
Who Would Be King **21** Dirty Rotten
Scoundrels
Caine Mutiny, The
author: **10** Herman Wouk
director: **13** Edward Dmytryk
cast: **7** May Wynn **9** Lee Marvin **10** E
G Marshall, Jose Ferrer, Van Johnson
13 Fred MacMurray, Robert Francis
14 Humphrey Bogart (Captain
Queeg)
Caingua see **7** Guarani

Cairo
Arab camp: **8** al-Fustat
Arabic: **9** al-Qahirah
capital of: **5** Egypt
island: **5** Rodah **7** Zamalik
landmark:
mosque: **7** al-Azhar **11** Muhammed
Ali
statue: **8** Ramses II
museum: **8** Egyptian
river: **4** Nile
Roman fortress: **7** Babylon
rulers: **5** Turks **7** British, Saladin **8**
Fatimids **9** Mamelukes **11** Ismail Pasha, Muhammed Ali **12** Ottoman
Turks
university: **7** Al-Azhar **8** Ain Shams,
American
Cairo, Joel
character in: **16** The Maltese Falcon
author: **7** Hammett
played by: **10** Peter Lorre
caitiff 3 cad, cur, rat **4** heel **5** churl,
knave, louse, rogue **6** rascal, rotter **7**
bounder, dastard, villain **9** scoundrel
10 blackguard
cajole 4 coax **7** beguile, deceive, flatter, wheedle **8** blandish, inveigle, persuade
cajolery 7 blarney, coaxing, fawning **8**
flattery, promises, soft soap **9** adulation, sweet talk, wheedling **10** enticement, inveigling, persuasion **11** be-
guilement **12** blandishment
cake 3 bar, bun, dry **4** lump, mass **5**
block, crust, tort **6** cookie, eclair, gateau, harden, pastry, **7** congeal, cup-
cake, thicken **8** compress, solidify **9**
coagulate, sweet roll **11** consolidate
Cakes and Ale
author: **16** W Somerset Maugham
cakewalk 5 cinch, dance **9** promenade
12 dance contest
calaboose 3 pen **4** jail, stir **6** prison **7**
slammer **8** hoosegow
Calah
founder: **6** Nimrod
Calais
origin: **5** Greek
member of: **9** Argonauts
father: **6** Boreas
mother: **8** Orithyia
twin brother: **5** Zetes
calamitous 5 fatal **6** tragic, woeful **7**
adverse, baleful, harmful, ruinous, unlucky **8** dreadful **9** blighting **10** disastrous, pernicious **11** cataclysmic, deleterious, destructive, detrimental,
distressful, unfortunate **12** catastrophic
calamity 3 ill, woe **4** blow, ruin **5** trial
6 misery, mishap **7** bad luck, failure,
ill wind, reverse, scourge, tragedy,
trouble, undoing **8** disaster, distress,
downfall, hardship **9** adversity, cataclysm, mischance **10** affliction, ill fortune, misfortune **11** catastrophe, trib-

ulation **13** sea of troubles **15** stroke of ill luck

calando
music: **22** getting weaker and slower

calcium
chemical symbol: **2** Ca

calculate 4 mean, plan **5** add up, aim at, count, judge, sum up **6** design, devise, figure, intend, reckon **7** compute, measure, predict, project, surmise, work out **8** estimate **9** ascertain, determine **10** conjecture

calculated 7 planned **10** deliberate, purposeful, thought out **11** intentional, prearranged **12** premeditated

calculating 3 sly **4** foxy, wily **6** artful, crafty, shrewd, tricky **7** cunning, devious **8** plotting, scheming **9** designing **10** contriving, intriguing **12** manipulative **13** Machiavellian

calculating machine
invented by: **7** Babbage

calculation 6 answer, result **8** figuring, judgment **9** reckoning **10** estimation **11** computation

calculator 6 abacus **7** counter, thinker **8** computer, reckoner

Calcutta
alternate name: **7** Kolkata
captured by: **5** Clive
founded by: **23** British East India Company
landmark: **10** Jain Temple **12** Howrah Bridge, Indian Museum **16** Botanical Gardens, Victoria Memorial **17** Zoological Gardens **18** Dakshineswar Temple
opposite city: **6** Howrah
river: **7** Hooghly
state: **10** West Bengal

Calder, Alexander
born: **14** Philadelphia PA
sculptures also called: **7** mobiles **8** stabiles
artwork: **3** Man **5** Whale **6** Spiral **10** Teodelapio **12** Ticket Window **13** La Grande Voile **14** The Brass Family **23** Lobster Traps and Fish Tail

Calderon de la Barca, Pedro
author of: **12** Life Is a Dream

caldron, cauldron 3 pot **6** boiler, kettle

Caldwell, Erskine
author of: **10** Georgia Boy **11** Tobacco Road **14** God's Little Acre

Caldwell, Taylor
author of: **12** Answer as a Man **13** A Pillar of Iron **14** Great Lion of God **17** Testimony of Two Men, The Devil's Advocate **19** Bright Flows the River **20** Glory and the Lightning **22** The Captains and the Kings **24** Dear and Glorious Physician

Caleb Williams
author: **13** William Godwin

Caledonia *see* **8** Scotland

calendar 4 list **5** chart, diary, table **6** agenda, docket **7** day book, program **8** register, schedule

calf 4 veal **5** dogie **6** weaner **7** leg part
young of: **3** cow **4** bull, seal **5** whale **8** elephant

Calgary
hockey team: **6** Flames

Calhern, Louis
real name: **13** Carl Henry Vogt
born: **10** Brooklyn NY
roles: **8** King Lear **12** Julius Caesar **15** Annie Get Your Gun **16** The Asphalt Jungle **20** The Magnificent Yankee

Calhoun, Rory
real name: **20** Francis Timothy Durgin
born: **12** Los Angeles CA
roles: **8** The Texan **21** Treasure of Pancho Villa **22** How to Marry a Millionaire, Requiem for a Heavyweight

Caliban
character in: **10** The Tempest
author: **11** Shakespeare

caliber 4 bore, rank **5** gifts, merit, place, power, scope, skill, worth **6** repute, talent **7** ability, quality, stature **8** capacity, diameter, eminence, position, prestige **10** capability, competence, estimation, excellence, importance, prominence, reputation **11** achievement, distinction

California
abbreviation: **2** CA **3** Cal **5** Calif
nickname: **6** Golden **8** Eldorado **12** Promised Land
capital: **10** Sacramento
largest city: **10** Los Angeles
others: **4** Lodi **5** Azusa, Chico, Chino, Indio **6** Blythe, Carmel, Covina, Eureka, Fresno, Lompoc, Merced, Oxnard, Pomona, Sonoma, Tulare **7** Alameda, Anaheim, Burbank, Gardena, Needles, Oakland, Salinas, Vallejo, Visalia **8** Altadena, Berkeley, Palo Alto, Pasadena, Redlands, San Diego, Stockton **9** Cucamonga, Long Beach **11** Palm Springs, Santa Monica **12** Beverly Hills, San Francisco, Santa Barbara
college: **3** USC **4** UCLA **5** Mills **6** Pitzer, Pomona **7** Caltech, Chapman, Scripps **8** Stanford, Whittier **10** Occidental, Pepperdine
explorer: **6** Cortez
feature:
   amusement park: **10** Disneyland **15** Knotts Berry Farm
   area: **9** Hollywood **15** Fishermans Wharf
   dam: **6** Hoover, Shasta **7** Boulder
   island prison: **8** Alcatraz
   mill: **7** Sutters
   national park: **7** Redwood, Sequoia **8** Yosemite **11** Kings Canyon **14** Channel Islands, Lassen Volcanic

   parade: **4** Rose
   prison: **6** Folsom **10** San Quentin
   tribe: **4** Hupa, Pomo, Yana, Yuki **5** Karok, Maidu, Miwok, Wappo, Wiyot, Yurok **6** Patwin, Shasta, Tolowa, Yokuts **7** Chumash, Luiseno, Salinan, Serrano **8** Diegueno
people: **6** Sutter **10** Earl Warren, Jerry Brown **11** Robert Frost **13** George S Patton, John Steinbeck **14** William Saroyan **20** Arnold Schwarzenegger
island: **4** Goat, Mare **7** Anacapo, Channel **8** Alcatraz, Catalina, Coronado **9** Farallone
lake: **4** Mono, Soda **5** Clear, Eagle, Owens, Tahoe **6** Salton, Tulare **7** Almanor **8** Elsinore **9** Berryessa
land rank: **5** third
mountain: **4** Muir **5** Coast **6** Lassen, Shasta, Wilson **7** Cascade, Klamath, Palomar, Whitney **10** Peninsular, Transverse **12** Sierra Nevada
   highest point: **7** Whitney
physical feature:
   bay: **8** Monterey, San Diego **12** San Francisco
   cape: **9** Mendocino
   desert: **6** Mohave, Mojave **8** Colorado
   fault: **10** San Andreas
   glacier: **8** Palisade
   sea: **6** Cortez **7** Pacific
   tree: **7** redwood
   valley: **5** Death
   volcano: **6** Lassen
   wind: **7** Collada **8** Santa Ana
president: **13** Richard M Nixon, Ronald W Reagan
river: **3** Eel, Mad, Pit **4** Kern **5** Kings, Owens, Putah, Smith, Stony **6** Little, Merced, Salmon **7** Feather, Klamath, Rubicon, Russian, Salinas, Trinity, Truckee **10** Sacramento, San Jacinto, San Joaquin, Stanislaus
state admission: **11** thirty-first
state bird: **21** California Valley quail
state fish: **21** California golden trout
state flower: **11** golden poppy
state motto: **6** Eureka (I have found it)
state song: **18** I Love You California
state symbol: **11** grizzly bear
state tree: **17** California redwood
baseball team: **6** Angels, Giants, Padres **7** Dodgers **9** Athletics
basketball team: **6** Lakers **8** Clippers **19** Golden State Warriors
football team: **7** Raiders **8** Chargers **11** Forty-Niners

Calinieff, Martin
real name of: **13** Michael Callan

Calinky State
nickname of: **13** South Carolina

calisay
type: **7** liqueur
origin: **5** Spain **9** Catalonia
flavor: **5** herbs **7** quinine

Calkins, Richard
  creator/artist of: **10** Buck Rogers
call 3 ask, bid, cry, dub, tag **4** bawl, buzz, hail, name, need, plea, ring, roar, stop, term, yell **5** cause, claim, label, order, phone, rally, right, shout, style, title, visit **6** appeal, ask for, bellow, charge, clamor, cry out, decree, demand, direct, drop in, excuse, gather, halloo, holler, invite, invoke, know as, muster, notice, outcry, pray to, reason, scream, stop by, summon **7** collect, command, contact, convene, convoke, declare, entitle, entreat, grounds, refer to, request, require, specify, stop off, summons, warrant **8** announce, appeal to, assemble, christen, entreaty, identify, instruct, look in on, occasion, petition, proclaim **9** crying out, designate, direction, pay a visit, telephone **10** describe as, invitation, supplicate **11** declaration, instruction **12** announcement, call together, characterize, proclamation, supplication **13** justification
Callan, Michael
  real name: **15** Martin Calinieff
  born: **14** Philadelphia PA
  roles: **9** Cat Ballou **10** The Interns **18** Gidget Goes Hawaiian, The Flying Fontaines **23** The Magnificent Seven Ride
call for 4 need **6** demand, pick up **7** request, require
call forth 4 spur **5** evoke, raise **6** arouse, awaken, excite, incite, invoke, kindle, stir up **7** command, conjure, provoke **8** summon up **9** make aware, stimulate **10** make appear
calling 3 job **4** line, work **5** craft, field, forte, trade **6** career, crying, living, metier, outcry **7** hailing, mission, passion, yelling **8** activity, business, devotion, function, province, shouting, vocation **9** bellowing, crying out, first love, hallooing, life's work, screaming, specialty **10** assignment, attachment, dedication, employment, enthusiasm, livelihood, occupation, profession, walk of life **14** bread and butter, means of support, specialization
calling off 6 ending **7** halting **8** giving up **11** termination **12** backing out of, cancellation
calling oneself thus
  French: **9** soi-disant
Calliope
  member of: **5** Muses
  presided over: **10** epic poetry
  father: **4** Zeus
  mother: **9** Mnemosyne
  son: **7** Orpheus
Callisto
  form: **5** nymph
  attended: **7** Artemis
  loved: **4** Zeus

changed into: **4** bear
  killed by: **7** Artemis
call off 3 end **4** halt **5** abort **6** cancel, give up **8** postpone **9** back out of, terminate **10** summon away **12** dispense with
Call of the Wild, The
  author: **10** Jack London
  dog: **4** Buck
  master: **12** John Thornton
callous 4 cold, hard **5** cruel, horny, tough **6** inured **8** hardened, uncaring **9** apathetic, heartless, unfeeling **11** hard-hearted, indifferent, insensitive **12** thick-skinned, unresponsive **13** dispassionate, unsympathetic **14** pachydermatous
call out 3 cry **4** bawl, hail, yell **5** shout **6** bellow, cry out, holler, summon **9** challenge
callow 3 raw **5** crude, green, naive **7** artless, awkward, puerile, shallow, untried **8** childish, ignorant, immature, juvenile **9** infantile **10** sophomoric, uninformed, unschooled, unseasoned **11** uninitiated **13** inexperienced **15** unsophisticated
call to 4 hail **5** greet **6** accost, salute **7** address, shout at
call to account 5 chide, scold **6** accuse, charge, rebuke **7** arraign, bawl out, censure, chasten, reprove, upbraid **8** admonish, denounce, reproach **9** criticize, dress down, reprimand **10** take to task **11** remonstrate
call to arms 6 war cry **9** battle cry **11** rallying cry
call to order 4 open **6** muster **7** convene, convoke
call upon 3 ask, bid **4** urge **5** visit **6** charge, enjoin, exhort, invite, invoke **7** beseech, entreat, request, require **8** appeal to, petition, summon up **9** encourage **11** acknowledge
callused 4 hard **5** horny, tough **8** hardened **12** thick-skinned **14** pachydermatous
calm 4 cool, ease, mild **5** allay, balmy, bland, quell, quiet, still **6** becalm, gentle, lessen, pacify, placid, reduce, repose, sedate, serene, smooth, soothe, subdue **7** assuage, collect, compose, cool off, halcyon, mollify, pacific, placate, relaxed, relieve **8** composed, coolness, diminish, mitigate, moderate, peaceful, serenity, tranquil, unshaken **9** alleviate, collected, composure, impassive, placidity, quietness, stillness, unexcited, unruffled **10** cool-headed, motionless, simmer down, smoothness, unagitated, untroubled **11** impassivity, passionless, restfulness, self-control, tranquility, tranquilize, undisturbed, unflappable, unperturbed **12** peacefulness, tranquillity, windlessness **13** imperturbable, self-possessed, stormless-

ness **14** self-possession **16** imperturbability
calmness 5 poise **6** aplomb **8** coolness, serenity **9** composure, placidity, sangfroid, stillness **10** equanimity, steadiness **11** self-control, tranquility **12** peacefulness, tranquillity **14** presence of mind, self-possession **16** imperturbability
Calpurnia
  character in: **12** Julius Caesar
  author: **11** Shakespeare
calumnious 8 libelous **9** maligning, vilifying **10** defamatory, derogatory, slanderous **11** disparaging
calumny 4 barb, slur **5** libel, smear **6** malice **7** slander **8** innuendo **9** aspersion **10** backbiting, defamation, derogation, revilement **11** denigration, deprecation, insinuation **12** backstabbing, calumniation, depreciation, vilification **13** animadversion, disparagement, malicious lies
calvados
  type: **6** brandy
  origin: **6** France **8** Normandy
  flavor: **5** apple
  aged in: **3** oak
Calvary 8 Golgotha
  means: **10** skull place
Calydonian boar
  sent by: **5** Diana
  killed by: **8** Meleager
Calydonian hunt
  pursuit of: **4** boar
Calypso
  form: **5** nymph
  home: **6** Ogygia
  father: **10** Titan Atlas
  detained: **8** Odysseus
  for: **10** seven years
calyx 4 husk **5** sepal
cam 3 cog **4** disk **8** cylinder **10** projection
  located on: **5** shaft, wheel
  motion: **7** rocking **8** circular **12** back and forth
camaraderie 7 jollity **8** bonhomie, good will **10** affability, clubbiness, fellowship, friendship **11** brotherhood, comradeship, sociability **12** congeniality, conviviality, friendliness **13** companionship, esprit de corps **14** goodfellowship
Camarasaurus
  type: **8** dinosaur, sauropod
  location: **12** United States
  period: **8** Jurassic
Cambodia
  other name: **7** Camboja **8** Cambodge **9** Kampuchea
  capital/largest city: **8** Pnom-Penh
  others: **3** Som **4** Ream **5** Takeo **6** Kampot, Kratie, Pursat **7** Kohnieh, Kompong, Kracheh, Rovieng, Samrong **8** Siem Reap, Sisophon **10** Battambang, Stung Treng **11** Kompong

Cham **12** Krungkoh Kong **13** Si-
hanoukville
head of state: 4 King
monetary unit: 3 sen **4** quan, riel **6**
puttan **7** piaster
weight: 4 mace, tael
island: 4 Kong, Rong
lake: 8 Tonle Sap
mountain: 3 Pan **7** Dangrek, Dong
Rek **8** Cardamom, Elephant
highest point: 10 Phnom Aoral, Phnom Aural
river: 3 San, Sen **5** Sreng **6** Bassac,
Chinit, Mekong, Porong, Pursat,
Srepok **7** Kamlong, Sekhong **8** Tonle
Sap
physical feature:
bay: 10 Kompongsom
cape: 5 Samit
gulf: 4 Siam **8** Thailand
people: 4 Cham, Thai **5** Khmer **7**
Chinese **10** Vietnamese
leader: 6 Pol Pot **8** Sihanouk
language: 5 Khmer **6** French **9** Cambodian **10** Vietnamese
religion: 7 animism **8** Buddhism **12**
Christianity
places:
ruins/temple: 6 Angkor **9** Angkor
Wat
feature:
Communist group: 10 Khmer
Rouge

Cambria *see* **5** Wales

cambric 5 cloth, linen **6** cotton, fabric
8 material

camel
called: 13 beast of burden **15** ship of
the desert
chews: 3 cud
group: 4 herd
habitat: 4 Asia **6** Africa, desert
kind: 7 Arabian **8** Bactrian **9** dromedary
number of humps: 3 one, two
species: 6 mammal
type of: 8 ruminant
young: 4 calf

camellia
varieties: 5 Silky **6** Common **8** Mountain, Sasanqua

Camenae
means: 11 foretellers
form: 6 nymphs **7** deities
gift: 8 prophecy
names: 6 Egeria **8** Carmenta **9** Antevorta, Postvorta
habitat: 8 fountain
correspond to: 5 Muses

camera 3 APS, SLR **4** 35mm, view **6**
manual **7** digital, plastic **8** panorama,
Polaroid, twin lens **9** automatic **11**
large format, range finder **12** medium
format **13** point-and-shoot
brand: 4 Fuji **5** Canon, Kodak, Leica,
Nikon, Ricoh **6** Konica, Pentax, Rol-
lei **7** Bronica, Minolta, Olympus **8**
Polaroid **10** Hasselblad

invented by:
Kodak: 6 Walker **7** Eastman
Polaroid: 4 Land
photography: 6 Niepce, Talbot **8**
Daguerre
film, celluloid: 6 Edison
11 Reichenbach
film, transparent: 7 Eastman,
Goodwin
color photo: 4 Ives

Cameroon
capital: 7 Yaounde
largest city: 6 Douala
others: 3 Wum **4** Bali, Buea, Edea,
Tiko **5** Kumba, Lomie, Mamfe **6**
Garona, Maroua **7** Batouri, Dschang,
Ebolowa, Foumban **8** Victoria **10**
N'Gaoundere, N'Kongsamba
monetary unit: 5 franc **7** centime
island: 5 Nanny **8** Fernando
lake: 4 Chad
mountain: 5 Mbabo **7** Bambuto, Kapsiki, Mandara **8** Batandji **9** Atlantika
highest point: 8 Cameroon
river: 3 Dja, Lom **4** Faro, Mbam, Vina
5 Benue, Campo, Cross, Kadei,
Mbere, Nyong, N'Goko, Sanga, Shari
6 Djerem, Ivindo, Logone, Sanaga
sea: 8 Atlantic
physical feature:
cape: 10 Debundscha
gulf: 6 Guinea
plateau: 7 Adamawa **8** Mambilla
people: 3 Abo, Edo, Ibo **4** Beti, Bulu,
Ekoi, Ijaw, Sara **5** Bantu, Bassa,
Kirdi, Pygmy, Tikar **6** Bamoun, Donala, Ewondo, Fulani, Ibibio **7** Bakweri **8** Bamileke
Fulani chief: 7 Lamidos
language: 4 Bulu **5** Bantu, Bassa,
Hausa **6** Douala, Ewondo, French,
Fulani **7** English **8** Bamileke, Fulfulde
religion: 5 Islam **7** animism **12** Christianity
places:
home of prime minister: 7 Schloss

Camille
also: 17 La Dame aux camelias
author: 14 Alexander Dumas (fils)
character: 6 Nanine **11** Armand Duval **17** Marguerite Gautier (Camille)
director: 11 George Cukor
cast: 10 Greta Garbo (Camille) **12**
Henry Daniell, Robert Taylor (Armand) **14** Elizabeth Allan, Laura
Hope Crews **15** Lionel Barrymore

Camillo
character in: 14 The Winter's Tale
author: 11 Shakespeare

Camirus
origin: 5 Greek
grandfather: 6 Helios, Helius

camisole 3 top **4** slip **6** jacket **10** underwaist

camouflage 4 hide, mask, veil **5**
blind, cloak, cover, front **6** screen,
shroud **7** conceal, cover up **8** disguise

10 masquerade, subterfuge **11** concealment

camouflaged 6 hidden, masked **7**
cloaked **8** shrouded **9** concealed, disguised

camp 4 tent **5** tents **7** bivouac, lodging,
rough it **8** army base, barracks,
quarters **10** pitch a tent

campaign 3 run **4** push **5** drive,
stump **6** action, effort **7** crusade **8** endeavor, movement **9** offensive, operation **11** electioneer, whistle-stop **12**
battle series, beat the drums, solicit
votes

campanile 6 belfry **9** bell tower

Campari
type: 7 bitters **8** aperitif
origin: 5 Italy

campground 7 bivouac **8** tent city **16**
temporary shelter

Campin, Robert
born: 8 Flanders
also known as/identified with: 14
Master of Merode **16** Master of Fle-
malle
artwork: 10 St Veronica, The Trinity
13 The Entombment **16** Merode Altarpiece (Merode Triptych) **17** The
Virgin and Child **18** The Thief on the
Cross

Camptosaurus
type: 8 dinosaur **10** ornithopod
location: 12 North America
period: 8 Jurassic
characteristic: 10 duck-billed

Camus, Albert
author of: 4 L'ete **6** Summer **7** The
Fall **8** Caligula, The Rebel **9** The
Plague **11** A Happy Death, The
Stranger **12** Cross Purpose **17** The
Myth of Sisyphus

can 3 tin **4** buns, fire, rump, seat **5**
fanny, put up **6** bottom **8** backside,
buttocks, preserve **9** container, fundament, give the ax

Canaan
father: 3 Ham
brother: 4 Cush
grandfather: 4 Noah
known as: 12 promised land
see also **6** Israel

Canada
capital: 6 Ottawa
largest city: 8 Montreal
others: 4 Hull **5** Banff, Laval **6** Dawson, Guelph, London, Oshawa, Que-
bec, Regina, Sarnia, Val d'or **7** Calgary, Halifax, Moncton, Nanaimo,
Sudbury, Toronto, Welland, Windsor
8 Edmonton, Hamilton, Kingston,
Moose Jaw, Victoria, Winnipeg **9**
Saskatoon, Vancouver **10** Port Arthur, Sherbrooke **11** Fredericton **12**
Niagara Falls, Peterborough, Prince
Albert, Prince George **13** Charlottetown **21** St Catherines Stratford
school: 3 UBC **5** Laval **6** McGill,

Queens **7** Toronto **8** McMaster, Montreal **9** Concordia, Dalhousie **11** Simon Fraser

division: 5 Yukon **6** Quebec **7** Alberta, Nunavut, Ontario **8** Manitoba **10** Nova Scotia **12** Newfoundland, New Brunswick, Saskatchewan **15** British Columbia **18** Prince Edward Island **20** Northwest Territories

head of state: 14 British monarch **15** governor general

measure: 3 ton **5** minot, perch, point **6** arpent **7** chainon

island: 4 Read **5** Banks, Bylot, Coats, Devon, Grand, Manan, Parry, Sable **6** Baffin, Breton, Mansel, Middle **7** Belcher **8** Bathurst, Magdalen, Victoria **9** Anticosti, Ellesmere, Vancouver **10** Campobello, Manitoulin **15** Southampton **14** Queen Charlotte

lake: 4 Cree, Erie, Gras, Seul **5** Garry, Huron, Rainy **6** Louise, St John **7** Abitibi, Dubawnt, Nipigon, Ontario, Testlin **8** Kootenay, Manitoba, Okanagan, Reindeer, Superior, Winnipeg **9** Athabaska, Great Bear, Nipissing **10** Great Slave, Mistassini **12** Winnipegosis

mountain: 5 Coast, Royal **6** Robson, Skeena **7** Cariboo, Cascade, Purcell, Rockies, Selkirk, St Elias **8** Columbia, Hazelton, Monashee **9** Mackenzie, Notre Dame, Tremblant **10** Laurentian, Richardson, Shickshock **14** Jacques Cartier

highest point: 5 Logan

river: 3 Hay, Red **4** Peel **5** Liard, Peace, Slave, Yukon **6** Albany, Fraser, Nelson, Nicola, Ottawa, Skeena, St John, Thames, Thelon **7** St Marys **8** Columbia, Gatineau, Kootenay, Petawawa, Saguenay **9** Athabasca, Athapaska, Churchill, Mackenzie, Richelieu **10** Coppermine, St Lawrence **11** Assiniboine, **12** Saskatchewan

sea: 6 Arctic **7** Pacific **8** Atlantic, Labrador

physical features:
bay: 5 Basin, Fundy, Hecla, James, Minas **6** Baffin, Griper, Hudson, Ungava **8** Georgian
canal: 3 Soo **7** Welland **10** Wellington
cape: 5 Canso
falls: 7 Niagara **9** Horseshoe
gulf: 10 St Lawrence
pass: 8 Chilkoot
peninsula: 5 Gaspe **7** Boothia **8** Labrador, Melville
plain: 11 Barren lands
port: 6 Quebec **7** St Johns **8** Hamilton, Victoria **9** Churchill
strait: 5 Cabot, Davis, Dease **6** Hecate, Hudson **7** Georgia **9** Belle Isle **10** Juan de Fuca

people: 5 Inuit **6** Canuck, Eskimo, French **7** English

explorer: 5 Cabot **6** Fraser, Joliet **7** Cartier, LaSalle, Selkirk **8** Thompson **9** Champlain, MacKenzie, Marquette

leader: 4 King, Riel **5** Clark **6** Borden, Martin **7** Laurier, Trudeau **8** Campbell, Chretien, Mulroney **9** Macdonald, St Laurent **11** Diefenbaker

language: 6 Eskimo, French **7** English

religion: 8 Anglican **13** Roman Catholic **20** United Church of Canada

places:
battlefield: 15 Plains of Abraham
national park: 4 Yoho **5** Banff **6** Jasper **7** Glacier **8** Kootenay **9** Elk Island **10** La Mauricie, Revelstoke **11** Wood Buffalo **12** Prince Albert **13** Waterton Lakes
resort: 5 Banff **10** Lake Louise

feature:
emblem: 9 maple leaf
fish: 5 charr, trout
flower: 10 Juneflower
police: 8 Mounties **12** Royal Mounted

food:
soup: 7 rubaboo

canaille 6 proles, rabble **8** riffraff **9** commoners, hoi polloi **11** proletariat **13** great unwashed

canal 4 duct, Erie, Kiel, Suez, tube **5** Grand **6** Panama **7** channel, conduit, passage **8** aqueduct

Canaletto
real name: 20 Giovanni Antonio Canal
born: 5 Italy **6** Venice
artwork: 18 The Stonemason's Yard

canard 4 hoax **5** rumor **7** slander **9** falsehood **12** exaggeration

Canary Islands
other name: 14 Fortunate Isles **15** Isles of the Blest
named for: 3 dog **5** canis **6** canine
capital: 9 Las Palmas **19** Santa Cruz de Tenerife
largest city: 9 Las Palmas
others: 4 Icod **6** Laguna **7** Orotava **8** Arrecife, Valverde **12** San Sebastian
government: 16 overseas province
of: 5 Spain
measure: 8 fanegada
monetary unit: 6 peseta
island: 4 Roca **5** Clara, Ferro, Lobos, Rocca **6** Gomera, Hierro **7** Inferno, La Palma **8** Graciosa, Tenerife **9** Lanzarote **10** Lanzarotte **11** Gran Canaria **13** Fuerteventura
mountain: 6 La Cruz **8** El Cumbre, Tenerife
highest point: 5 Teide, Teyde
sea: 8 Atlantic
people: 7 Spanish
language: 7 Spanish
religion: 13 Roman Catholic

canasta

number of players: 4 four
cards/hand: 6 eleven
meld: 12 three of a kind
wild card: 5 deuce, joker

Canberra
capital of: 9 Australia
territory: 13 New South Wales **26** Australian Capital Territory
lake: 13 Burley Griffin

cancel 4 undo, void **5** abort, annul, erase, quash, scrub **6** delete, offset, recall, recant, repeal, revoke **7** abolish, call off, nullify, rescind, retract, vitiate **8** abrogate, call back, set aside **9** repudiate **10** balance out, blue-pencil, do away with, invalidate, neutralize **11** countermand **12** dispense with **13** compensate for **14** counterbalance **18** declare null and void

cancellation 6 repeal **9** abolition **10** abrogation, effacement, rescinding, revocation **11** abolishment, eradication, repudiation, termination

cancer 3 rot **4** crab **6** plague **7** sarcoma, scourge **8** neoplasm, sickness **9** carcinoma **10** malignancy **14** malignant tumor **15** malignant growth

Cancer
symbol: 4 crab
planet: 4 Moon
rules: 4 home **6** family
born: 4 July, June

Cancer Ward, The
author: 21 Aleksandr Solzhenitsyn

candelabrum 7 menorah **8** dikerion **9** girandole, trikerion **11** candlestick **12** candleholder

Candia *see* **5** Crete

candid 4 fair, free, just, open **5** blunt, frank, plain **6** direct, honest **7** genuine, natural, relaxed, sincere, unposed **8** informal, outright, truthful **9** downright, impromptu, outspoken **10** forthright, impromptu, outspoken **10** forthright **11** plain spoken, spontaneous, unvarnished **14** extemporaneous **15** straightforward

Candida
author: 17 George Bernard Shaw

candidate 7 hopeful, nominee **8** aspirant, eligible **9** applicant, contender, job seeker **10** competitor, contestant **11** possibility **12** office seeker

Candid Camera
host: 9 Allen Funt
co-host: 11 Bess Myerson **12** Durward Kirby **13** Arthur Godfrey
tag: 5 smile

Candide
author: 8 Voltaire
character: 6 Martin **7** Cacambo **8** Pangloss **9** Cunegonde **11** Admiral Byng **17** Thunder-ten-Tronckh

candidness 6 candor **7** honesty, openess **9** frankness, sincerity **10** directness **12** truthfulness **13** guilelessness

candle 3 dip, wax 5 light, taper 6 bougie, cierge, tallow 9 rush light

candleholder, candlestick 6 sconce 7 menorah 8 dikerion 9 girandole, trikerion 10 chandelier 11 candelabrum

candor 7 honesty 8 fairness, justness, openness 9 bluntness, frankness, sincerity 10 directness 11 artlessness 12 impartiality, truthfulness 14 forthrightness 15 plainspokenness 19 straightforwardness

candy 3 bar 4 kiss 5 cream, fudge, jelly, sweet, taffy 6 bonbon, comfit, dainty, nougat, sweets, toffee 7 brittle, caramel, fondant, gumdrop, praline 8 lollipop 9 chocolate, jellybean, sweetmeat 10 confection 12 all-day sucker 13 confectionery, peanut brittle

cane 3 hit, rap, rod, tan 4 beat, drub, flog, lash, whip 5 baste, flail, smite, staff, stick, whack 6 strike, switch, thrash, wallop 7 trounce 12 walking stick

cane 11 Arundinaria
  varieties: 4 Dumb, Wild 5 Arrow, Sugar 6 Rattan, Switch, Tobago, Tonkin 7 Tsingli 8 Southern 11 Spotted dumb 12 Chinese sweet 14 Yellow-leaf dumb

Canea
  capital of: 5 Crete

Canetti, Elias
  author of: 8 Auto da Fe 12 Tower of Babel 14 Crowds and Power 15 The Torch in My Ear 16 Kafka's Other Trial, The Tongue Set Free

Caniff, Milton
  creator/artist of: 10 Dickie Dare 11 Steve Canyon 14 The Gay Thirties 18 Terry and the Pirates

canine 3 cur, dog, fox, pup 4 mutt, wolf 5 hound, hyena, puppy, tooth 6 coyote, cuspid, jackal 7 mongrel 8 eyetooth

canker 4 sore 5 ulcer 6 blight, cancer, lesion 9 mouth sore 12 inflammation

Cannibal Galaxy, The
  author: 12 Cynthia Ozick

cannon 3 bit, gun 4 bone 5 carom 6 mortar 7 battery 8 field gun, howitzer, ordnance 9 artillery 10 field piece, mounted gun, pickpocket

Cannon
  character: 11 Frank Cannon
  cast: 13 William Conrad

Cannon, Dyan
  real name: 19 Samille Diane Friesen
  husband: 9 Cary Grant
  born: 8 Tacoma WA
  roles: 6 Shamus 9 Deathtrap 10 Ally McBeal 13 Heaven Can Wait 15 Such Good Friends 19 Bob & Carol & Ted & Alice 23 Revenge of the Pink Panther

cannonade 5 burst, salvo 6 volley 7 barrage, battery 8 shelling 9 fusillade 11 bombardment

canny 4 foxy, wary, wily, wise 5 cagey, sharp 6 artful, astute, clever, crafty, shrewd, subtle 7 careful, cunning, knowing 8 skillful 9 judicious, sagacious 10 convincing 11 circumspect, intelligent 13 perspicacious

Cano, Alonso
  born: 5 Spain 7 Granada
  artwork: 16 Granada Cathedral (facade) 18 Madonna of the Rosary 20 Immaculate Conception 23 The Seven Joys of the Virgin

canoe 4 boat 5 bungo, kayak 6 dugout 7 pirogue

canoeing
  athlete: 11 Marcia Smoke

canon 3 law 4 code, rule 5 dogma, edict, model, order 6 decree 7 pattern, precept, statute 8 doctrine, standard 9 bench mark, criterion, ordinance, principle, yardstick 10 regulation, touchstone

canonical 6 proper 8 accepted, approved, official orthodox 9 authentic, customary 10 authorized, legitimate, recognized, sanctioned 12 conventional 13 authoritative

Canonization, The
  author: 9 John Donne

canopy 4 hood 5 cover 6 awning, tester 8 covering

Canova, Antonio
  born: 5 Italy 8 Possagno
  artwork: 7 Perseus 12 Venus Victrix (Pauline Bonaparte Borghese) 14 Cupid and Psyche 16 Letizia Bonaparte 17 Daedalus and Icarus

Cansino, Margarita Carmen
  real name of: 12 Rita Hayworth

cant 4 sham, talk 5 argot, lingo, slang 6 humbug, jargon 8 parlance, pretense 9 hypocrisy 10 lip service, vernacular 11 insincerity 15 pretentiousness 17 sanctimoniousness

cantabile
  music: 7 flowing, singing 8 songlike

cantaloupe 5 fruit, melon 9 muskmelon

cantankerous 4 mean 5 cross, huffy, short, sulky, surly, testy 6 crabby, cranky, crusty, grumpy, morose, ornery, sullen, touchy 7 bearish, crabbed, fretful, grouchy, peevish, waspish 8 choleric, churlish, contrary, snappish 9 irascible, irritable, splenetic 10 ill-humored, ill-natured 11 contentious, ill-tempered, quarrelsome 12 disagreeable 13 argumentative

cantatrice 6 singer 9 chanteuse 10 songstress 18 professional singer

canteen 2 PX 4 club 5 flask 6 bottle 10 commissary 11 pocket flask 12 post exchange

canter 4 gait, lope, pace, trot 6 gallop, singer, whiner

Canterbury Tales, The
  author: 15 Geoffrey Chaucer
  starting point: 9 Southwark, Tabard Inn
  goal:
    tomb of: 6 Becket
  character/tale: 3 Nun 4 Cook, Dyer, Monk 5 Canon, Friar, Reeve, Webbe 6 Knight, Miller, Parson, Squire, Yeoman 7 Shipman, Tapicer 8 Franklin, Manciple, Merchant, Pardoner, Prioress, Summoner 9 Carpenter, Ploughman 10 Wife of Bath 11 Haberdasher 13 Clerk of Oxford, Sergeant of Law 14 Doctor of Physic

Cantor, Eddie
  real name: 21 B Edward Israel Iskowitz
  nickname: 9 Banjo Eyes
  wife: 9 Ida Tobias
  born: 9 New York NY
  roles: 7 Whoopee 8 Kid Boots 9 Banjo Eyes

cantor of a synagogue
  Hebrew: 5 hazan 6 chazan

Cantos
  author: 9 Ezra Pound

can't stand 4 hate 5 abhor 6 detest, eschew, loathe 7 despise 8 execrate 9 abominate, can't abide 11 can't stomach 14 hate the sight of

canvas 4 duck 7 painting 8 painting 9 sailcloth, tarpaulin, tent cloth

canvass 4 poll, scan, sift 5 study, tally 6 survey 7 analyze, discuss, examine, explore, inquiry, inquire, inspect, solicit 8 analysis, campaign, scrutiny 10 evaluation, scrutinize 11 enumeration, exploration, inquire into, investigate, take stock of 13 give thought to, investigation

canyon 3 col, cut, gap 4 draw, pass, wadi, wash 5 break, chasm, cleft, crack, gorge, gulch, gully, notch 6 arroyo, coulee, defile, divide, ravine, valley 7 fissure, opening 8 corridor, crevasse, water gap

cap 3 fez, lid, tam, top 4 acme, seal 5 beret, cover, limit, outdo 6 better, exceed, top off 7 surpass 8 headgear, out-strip 9 headdress 10 visored hat

capability 3 art 4 gift 5 flair, knack, power, skill 6 talent 7 ability, faculty, know-how 8 capacity, efficacy, facility 9 potential 10 attainment, competence, competency 11 proficiency 12 potentiality 13 qualification

capable 3 apt 4 able, deft 5 adept 6 adroit, artful, clever, expert, gifted 7 skilled 8 masterly, skillful, talented 9 competent, effective, ingenious 10 proficient 11 efficacious, intelligent 12 accomplished

capable of assuming legal responsibility
  Latin: **8** sui juris
Capable of Honor
  author: **10** Allan Drury
capable of managing one's own affairs
  Latin: **8** sui juris

capacious 3 big **4** huge, vast, wide **5** ample, broad, large, roomy **7** mammoth, massive **8** gigantic, spacious **9** expansive, extensive **10** commodious, expandable, tremendous, voluminous **13** amplitudinous

capaciousness 9 amplitude, roominess **12** spaciousness **14** commodiousness

capacitate 5 allow **6** enable, permit **7** empower, qualify **8** make able

capacity 4 mind, role, room, size **5** gifts, limit, might, power, range, scope, space **6** extent, talent, volume **7** ability, faculty **8** aptitude, facility, function, judgment, position, sagacity, strength **9** amplitude, endowment, intellect, potential **10** brain power, capability **11** discernment **12** intelligence, perspicacity **15** maximum contents

caparison 5 adorn, equip **6** bedeck **9** equipment, trappings

cape 4 spit **5** cloak, manta, point, shawl **6** mantle, poncho, serape, tabard, tongue **7** pelisse **8** headland **9** peninsula **10** promontory

Capek, Karel
  author of: **3** R U R **8** Hordubal, Krakatit **9** The Mother **13** Power and Glory **18** The War with the Newts

caper 3 hop **4** jape, jump, lark, leap, romp, skip **5** antic, bound, fling, frisk, prank, spree, stunt, trick **6** bounce, cavort, frolic, gambol, prance **7** caprice **8** escapade **9** adventure, high jinks **10** carrying on **11** shenanigans **14** monkey business

capital 4 cash, fine **5** great, money, super **6** center, riches, superb, wealth **7** supreme **9** excellent, financing, first-rate, majuscule, matchless, principal, resources **10** cash on hand, first-class **11** large letter, wherewithal **12** headquarters **13** working assets **14** available means **15** investment funds, upper-case letter

capital city (of countries)
  of **Afghanistan: 5** Kabul
  of **Albania: 6** Tirana, Tirane
  of **Algeria: 7** Algiers
  of **Andorra: 14** Andorra-la-Vella
  of **Angola: 6** Luanda
  of **Antigua and Barbuda: 7** St John's
  of **Argentina: 11** Buenos Aires
  of **Armenia: 6** Erivan **7** Yerevan
  of **Australia: 8** Canberra
  of **Austria: 6** Vienna
  of **Azerbaijan: 4** Baku
  of the **Bahamas: 6** Nassau

of **Bahrain: 6** Manama
of **Bangladesh: 5** Dacca
of **Barbados: 10** Bridgetown
of **Belarus: 5** Minsk
of **Belgium: 8** Brussels **9** Bruxelles
of **Belize: 8** Belmopan
of **Benin: 9** Porto-Novo
of **Bermuda: 8** Hamilton
of **Bhutan: 6** Thimbu **7** Thimphu
of **Bolivia: 5** La Paz, Sucre
of **Bosnia-Herzegovina: 8** Sarajevo
of **Botswana: 8** Gaborone **9** Gaberones
of **Brazil: 8** Brasilia
of **Brunei: 17** Bandar Seri Begawan
of **Bulgaria: 5** Sofia
of **Burkina Faso: 11** Ouagadougou
of **Burundi: 9** Bujumbura
of **Cambodia: 8** Pnom-Penh
of **Cameroon: 7** Yaounde
of **Canada: 6** Ottawa
of the **Canary Islands: 9** Las Palmas **19** Santa Cruz de Tenerife
of **Cape Verde: 5** Praia
of the **Central African Republic: 6** Bangui
of **Chad: 8** Fort-Lamy, N'Djamena
of **Chile: 8** Santiago
of **China: 6** Peking
of **Colombia: 6** Bogota
of **Comoros: 6** Moroni
of the **Congo: 11** Brazzaville
of **Costa Rica: 7** San Jose
of **Crete: 5** Canea **8** Iraklion
of **Croatia: 6** Zagreb
of **Cuba: 6** Havana **8** La Habana
of **Cyprus: 7** Nicosia
of **Czechoslovakia/Czech Republic: 6** Prague
of **Denmark: 10** Copenhagen
of **Djibouti: 8** Djibouti
of the **Dominican Republic: 12** Santo Domingo **14** Ciudad Trujillo
of **Ecuador: 5** Quito
of **Egypt: 5** Cairo
of **El Salvador: 11** San Salvador
of **England: 6** London
of **Equatorial Guinea: 6** Malabo
of **Eritrea: 6** Asmara
of **Estonia: 7** Tallinn
of **Ethiopia: 10** Addis Ababa
of **Fiji: 4** Suva
of **Finland: 8** Helsinki **11** Helsingfors
of **France: 5** Paris
of the **Gabon Republic: 10** Libreville
of **The Gambia: 6** Banjul **8** Bathurst
of **Georgia: 7** Tbilisi
of **Germany (East): 10** East Berlin
of **Germany (West): 4** Bonn
of **Germany (reunited): 5** Berlin
of **Ghana: 5** Accra, Akkra
of **Greece: 6** Athens
of **Greenland: 3** Nuk **8** Godthaab, The Point
of **Grenada: 9** St Georges
of **Guatemala: 13** Guatemala City
of **Guinea: 7** Conakry
of **Guinea-Bissau: 6** Bissau

of **Guyana: 10** Georgetown
of **Haiti: 12** Port-au-Prince
of **Honduras: 11** Tegucigalpa
of **Hong Kong: 8** Victoria
of **Hungary: 8** Budapest
of **Iceland: 9** Reykjavik
of **India: 8** New Delhi
of **Indonesia: 7** Jakarta **8** Djakarta
of **Iran: 6** Tehran **7** Teheran
of **Iraq: 7** Baghdad
of **Ireland: 6** Dublin
of **Israel: 9** Jerusalem
of **Italy: 4** Roma, Rome
of the **Ivory Coast: 7** Abidjan
of **Jamaica: 8** Kingston
of **Japan: 3** Edo **5** Tokyo
of **Java: 7** Jakarta **8** Djakarta
of **Jordan: 5** Amman
of **Kazakhstan: 7** Alma-Ata
of **Kenya: 7** Nairobi
of **Kiribati: 6** Tarawa
of **Korea (North): 9** Pyongyang
of **Korea (South): 5** Seoul
of **Kuwait: 10** Kuwait City
of **Kyrgyzstan: 7** Bishkek (Frunze)
of **Laos: 9** Viengchan, Vientiane
of **Latvia: 4** Riga
of **Lebanon: 6** Beirut **8** Beyrouth
of **Lesotho: 6** Maseru
of **Liberia: 8** Monrovia
of **Libya: 7** Tripoli
of **Liechtenstein: 5** Vaduz
of **Lithuania: 5** Vilna **6** Kausas **7** Vilnius
of **Luxembourg: 10** Luxembourg
of **Macedonia: 6** Skopje
of **Madagascar: 10** Tananarive **12** Antananarivo
of **Malawi: 8** Lilongwe
of **Malaysia: 11** Kuala Lumpur
of **Maldives: 4** Male
of **Mali: 6** Bamako
of **Malta: 8** Valletta
of **Mauritania: 10** Nouakchott
of **Mauritius: 9** Port Louis
of **Mexico: 10** Mexico City
of **Moldova: 16** Chisinau, Kishinev
of **Monaco: 11** Monaco-Ville
of **Mongolia: 9** Ulan Bator
of **Montenegro: 7** Cetinje **8** Titograd **9** Podgorica
of **Morocco: 5** Rabat **6** Rabbat
of **Mozambique: 6** Maputo **15** Lourenco Marques
of **Myanmar: 6** Yangon **7** Rangoon
of **Namibia: 8** Windhoek
of **Nauru: 13** Yaren District
of **Nepal: 8** Katmandu **9** Kathmandu
of **Netherlands: 8** The Hague **9** Amsterdam
of **New Guinea: 11** Port Moresby
of **New Zealand: 10** Wellington
of **Nicaragua: 7** Managua
of **Niger: 6** Niamey
of **Nigeria: 5** Abuja, Lagos
of **Northern Ireland: 7** Belfast
of **Norway: 4** Oslo **11** Christiania
of **Oman: 6** Masqat, Muscat

of Pakistan: **9** Islamabad
of Panama: **10** Panama City
of Paraguay: **8** Asuncion
of Peru: **4** Lima
of the Philippines: **6** Manila
of Poland: **6** Warsaw
of Portugal: **6** Lisbon
of Puerto Rico: **7** San Juan
of Qatar: **4** Doha **7** al-Dawha
of Romania: **9** Bucharest
of Russia: **6** Moscow
of Rwanda: **6** Kigali
of Samoa (American): **8** Pago Pago
of Samoa (Western): **4** Apia
of San Marino: **9** San Marino
of Sao Tome and Principe: **7** Sao Tome
of Sardinia: **8** Cagliari
of Saudi Arabia: **6** Riyadh
of Scotland: **9** Edinburgh
of Senegal: **5** Dakar
of Seychelles: **8** Victoria
of Sicily: **7** Palermo
of Sierra Leone: **8** Freetown
of Sikkim: **7** Gangtok
of Singapore: **9** Singapore
of Slovakia: **10** Bratislava
of Slovenia: **9** Ljubljana
of the Solomon Islands: **7** Honiara
of Somalia: **9** Mogadishu **10** Mogadiscio
of South Africa: **8** Cape Town, Pretoria **12** Bloemfontein
of Spain: **6** Madrid
of Sri Lanka: **7** Colombo
of the Sudan: **8** Khartoum
of Suriname: **10** Paramaribo
of Swaziland: **7** Mbabane
of Sweden: **9** Stockholm
of Switzerland: **4** Bern
of Syria: **8** Damascus
of Taiwan: **6** Taipei
of Tajikistan: **8** Dushanbe
of Tanzania: **11** Dar es Salaam
of Thailand: **6** Bankok **7** Bangkok **8** Thonburi **9** Ayutthaya
of Tibet: **5** Lassa, Lhasa
of Togo: **4** Lome
of Tongo: **9** Nukualofa
of Trinidad and Tobago: **11** Port of Spain
of Tunisia: **5** Tunis
of Turkey: **6** Ankara
of Turkmenistan: **9** Ashkhabad
of Tuvalu: **8** Funafuti
of Uganda: **7** Kampala
of Ukraine: **4** Kiev
of United Arab Emirates: **8** Abu Dhabi
of United States: **12** Washington DC
of Uruguay: **10** Montevideo
of Uzbekistan: **8** Tashkent
of Vanuatu: **4** Vila
of Venezuela: **7** Caracas
of Vietnam: **5** Hanoi **6** Saigon
of Wales: **7** Cardiff
of Western Sahara: **6** Al Aiun **7** El Aaiun

of Western Samoa: **4** Apia
of Yemen: **4** Sana, Aden **5** Sanaa
of Yugoslavia: **7** Beograd **8** Belgrade
of Zaire: **8** Kinshasa
of Zambia: **6** Lusaka
of Zimbabwe: **6** Harare **9** Salisbury
capital city (of states) *see* state capitals
capitalism 14 free enterprise
capitalist 5 mogul **6** tycoon **8** investor **9** financier, plutocrat **14** businessperson
capitalize 4 back, fund **5** stake **7** exploit, finance, support, trade on, utilize **8** bankroll, cash in on, profit by **9** subsidize **11** foot the bill **13** make the most of **17** turn an honest penny **23** strike while the iron is hot **24** make hay while the sun shines
capitalize on 7 exploit, utilize **8** profit by **13** turn to account **14** use to advantage
capitol 10 statehouse **11** legislature **15** government house
capitulate 5 yield **6** accede, give in, give up, relent, submit **7** succumb **8** cry quits **9** acquiesce, surrender **11** come to terms, sue for peace **15** lay down one's arms **17** acknowledge defeat, hoist the white flag
capitulation 8 giving in, giving up, quitting, yielding **9** surrender **10** submission
Capote, Truman
    author of: **11** In Cold Blood **12** A Tree of Night **19** Breakfast at Tiffany's **21** Other Voices Other Rooms
    character: **14** Holly Golightly
Capp, Al
    real name: **18** Alfred George Caplin
    creator/artist of: **13** Li'l Abner Yokum
Cappotas
    epithet of: **4** Zeus
    means: **8** reliever
Capra, Frank
    director of: **11** Lady for a Day, Lost Horizon **15** State of the Union **17** Arsenic and Old Lace, It's a Wonderful Life, Mr Deeds Goes to Town (Oscar) **18** It Happened One Night (Oscar) **20** You Can't Take It with You (Oscar) **23** Mr Smith Goes to Washington
caprice 3 fad **4** lark, whim **5** antic, caper, craze, fancy, fling, prank, quirk, spree, stunt **6** notion, oddity, vagary **7** impulse **8** crotchet, escapade **10** erraticism **11** peculiarity **12** eccentricity, idiosyncrasy
capricious 6 fickle, fitful, quirky, uneven **7** erratic, faddish, flighty **8** fanciful, skittish, unstable, unsteady, variable, wavering **9** eccentric, impulsive, mercurial, uncertain, undecided **10** changeable, indecisive, irresolute **11**

vacillating **12** inconsistent **13** irresponsible **15** shilly-shallying
capriciousness 7 caprice **10** fickleness **11** instability **12** irresolution **13** impulsiveness, inconsistency **15** shilly-shallying
Capricorn
    symbol: **4** goat
    planet: **6** Saturn
    rules: **6** career
    born: **7** January **8** December
capsicum peppers
    origin: **15** tropical America
    color: **3** red **5** green, white **6** violet, yellow
    variety: **5** ancho, chile **7** cayenne, paprika, serrano **8** chipotle, habanero, jalapeno **9** red pepper **11** chili pepper, chili powder, curry powder, sweet pepper
    flavor: **3** hot
    use: **5** chili, curry, pizza **8** barbecue **9** paprikash
capsize 5 upset **6** invert **7** tip over **8** flip over, keel over, overturn, turn over **10** turn turtle
capsule 4 case, pill **6** ampule **7** cockpit **8** covering **9** spore case **12** condensation
captain 4 boss, head **5** chief, pilot **6** leader, master, old man **7** headman, skipper **9** chieftain, commander **10** commandant **12** chief officer **16** company commander **17** commanding officer
    famous: **4** Ahab, Andy, Hook, Kirk, Nemo
Captain Blood
    director: **13** Michael Curtiz
    cast: **10** Errol Flynn **12** Lionel Atwill **13** Basil Rathbone **17** Olivia de Havilland
Captain Carpenter
    author: **15** John Crowe Ransom
Captain Craig
    author: **22** Edwin Arlington Robinson
Captain Hook
    character in: **8** Peter Pan
    author: **6** Barrie
    henchman: Smee
Captain Horatio Hornblower
    author: **10** C S Forester
Captains Courageous
    author: **14** Rudyard Kipling
    director: **13** Victor Fleming
    cast: **12** Mickey Rooney, Spencer Tracy **13** John Carradine, Melvyn Douglas **15** Lionel Barrymore **18** Freddie Bartholomew
    Oscar for: **5** actor (Tracy)
Captain's Daughter, The
    author: **16** Alexander Pushkin
Captain Video and His Video Rangers
    character: **7** Dr Pauli **9** The Ranger **12** Captain Video
    cast: **7** Al Hodge **10** Hal Conklin **11**

Don Hastings **13** Richard Coogan
slogan: 29 Guardian of the Safety of
the World
villain: 4 Atar **7** Nargola **8** Dahoumie,
Kul of Eos **9** Dr Clysmok **12** Heng
Foo Seeng **14** Mook the Moon Man
gimmick: 5 Tobor **9** Discatron **11**
Atomic Rifle **16** Barrier of Silence,
Radio Scillograph **17** Cosmic Ray Vi-
brator **18** Opticon Scillometer **19**
Cloak of Invisibility, Trisonic Com-
pensator
spaceship: 6 Galaxy

caption 5 title **6** legend **7** heading,
subhead **8** headline, subtitle **11** explanation

captious 4 mean **5** picky, testy **6** ornery **7** carping, cutting, peevish **8**
caviling, contrary, niggling, perverse,
petulant, picayune, snappish **9** fractious, querulous **10** belittling, censorious, nitpicking **11** deprecating **12** cantankerous, faultfinding **13**
hypercritical

captivate 4 lure **5** charm **6** dazzle, enamor, seduce **7** attract, bewitch, delight, enchant, win over **8** enthrall **9**
carry away, enrapture, fascinate, hypnotize, infatuate, mesmerize, transport
13 turn the head of **14** take the fancy
of

captivated 7 charmed, pleased **9** delighted, enchanted **10** enraptured, enthralled, spellbound

captivating 7 winning, winsome **8**
adorable, charming, dazzling, engaging, fetching, magnetic **9** appealing,
beguiling, disarming **10** attractive, bewitching, delightful, enchanting, entrancing **11** enthralling, fascinating,
mesmerizing **12** ingratiating, irresistible

captive 3 POW **5** caged **6** penned **7**
hostage **8** confined, enslaved, interned, locked up, prisoner **9** oppressed **10** imprisoned, subjugated **12**
incarcerated

captivity 7 bondage, holding, slavery
9 servitude **10** detainment **12** imprisonment

capture 3 bag, nab **4** bust, grab, snag,
take, trap **5** catch, grasp, pinch, seize,
snare **6** arrest, collar, taking **7** bag-
ging, ensnare, procure, seizure, snar-
ing **8** catching, trapping **9** apprehend,
collaring, ensnaring, lay hold of **12**
apprehension, laying hold of, take
prisoner **14** taking prisoner **15** take
into custody

Capulet family
characters in: 14 Romeo and Juliet
author: 11 Shakespeare

Capys
father: 9 Assaracus
son: 7 Laocoon **8** Anchises
grandson: 6 Aeneas

founded: 5 Capua
warned against: 11 Trojan horse
car 4 auto, heap **5** buggy, coach, diner,
motor **6** boxcar, hot rod, jalopy,
wheels **7** flivver, machine, sleeper, vehicle **8** carriage **9** tin lizzie **10** automobile **12** motor vehicle
kind: 4 coal **5** cable, horse, motor **6**
cattle, dining, parlor, street **7** baggage, freight, Pullman, railway **8**
sleeping

carabiniere 9 policeman

Caracas
birthplace of: 12 Simon Bolivar
capital of: 9 Venezuela
founder: 13 Diego de Losada
museum: 7 Bolivar **8** Criolan **11** Colonial Art, Raul Santana
river: 6 Guaire

carafe 5 flask **6** bottle, vessel **9** container

carapace 4 case **5** shell **6** lorica, shield
7 carapax **8** calipash, covering **11** turtle shell

**Caravaggio, Michelangelo Merisi
da**
born: 5 Italy **10** Caravaggio
artwork: 12 Young Bacchus **14** Burial
of St Lucy **16** Raising of Lazarus **17**
The Supper at Emmaus **18** Calling of
St Matthew, The Life of St Matthew
20 St Matthew and the Angel **21** The
Conversion of St Paul **23** The Crucifixion of St Peter **30** The Beheading
of St John the Baptist

caravan 4 band, file, line **5** queue,
train, troop **6** coffle, column, convoy,
parade, string **7** company, cortege,
retinue, trailer **9** cavalcade, chain
gang, entourage, motorcade **10** procession, wagon train

caravansary 3 inn **5** hotel **8** hostelry

caraway
botanical name: 10 Carum carvi
origin: 6 Europe **9** Asia Minor **14** the
Netherlands
liqueur: 6 Kummel
candy-covered caraway seeds: 6
comfit **12** whisky-killer
use: 4 pork, soup, stew **8** rye bread

carbohydrate
consists of: 5 water **6** carbon, oxygen
8 hydrogen **13** carbon dioxide
kinds: 5 sugar **6** simple, starch, xy-
lose **7** complex, glucose, lactose,
maltose, sucrose **8** dextrose, fructose
9 cellulose

carbon 4 coal, coke, copy **8** charcoal **9**
lampblack
chemical symbol: 1 C

carbon copy 5 clone **7** replica **9** duplicate, facsimile **12** reproduction

carbonize 4 burn, char, sear **5** singe **6**
scorch **10** incinerate

carbuncle 4 boil, sore **11** excrescence
12 inflammation

carcass 4 body, bouk, husk, wall **5**
shell, stiff, trunk **6** corpse **7** cadaver,
carrion, remains **8** dead body, fireball,
skeleton **9** framework

carcinoma 5 tumor **6** cancer **8** neoplasm **10** malignancy **15** malignant
growth

card 4 bill **6** ticket **7** program **8** postcard
kind: 7 calling, get-well, playing **8**
birthday, business, greeting **9** Christmas, Valentine

cardamon
botanical name: 19 Elettaria carda-
momum
origin: 4 Asia **5** India **13** southeast
Asia
related to: 6 ginger
color: 5 black
use: 5 curry **7** dessert **12** Danish pastry

Cardew, Cecily
character in: 27 The Importance of
Being Earnest
author: 5 Wilde

card game 3 loo, war **4** brag, faro,
fish, skat, vint **5** ombre, poker,
rummy, whist **6** Boston, bridge, casino, chemmy, ecarte, euchre, go fish,
hearts, memory, piquet, pocher **7** bezique, canasta, cooncan, Old Maid,
plafond, primero **8** baccarat, conquian, cribbage, gin rummy, napoleon, patience, pinochle, slapjack **9**
blackjack, pelmanism, solitaire, spoil
five, twenty-one, vingt-et-un **11**
chemin de fer, crazy eights **13** concentration **14** contract bridge **16** beggar-my-neighbor, trente et quarante
card names: 3 ace **4** fool, jack, king,
trey **5** deuce, joker, queen
combination of cards: 4 meld
one hand or round: 5 trick
rulebook by: 5 Hoyle
suits: 4 club **5** heart, spade **7** diamond
French: 5 coeur, pique **6** trefle **7**
carreau
German: 4 grun, herz, piks **5** ka-
ros, treff **6** eichel **7** schelle
Italian: 5 coppa, cuori, fiori, spada
6 denaro, picchi, quadri **7** bastone
Spanish: 3 oro **4** copa **5** basto **6**
espada

Cardiff
capital of: 5 Wales

Cardiff Giant 4 hoax **5** relic

cardigan 5 corgi **6** jacket, wampus **7**
sweater **10** Welsh corgi

cardinal 3 key, top **4** head, main **5** basic, chief, first, prime, vital **6** cherry,
claret, red hat **7** carmine, central,
deep-red, highest, leading, primary,
scarlet **8** blood-red, dominant, foremost, greatest **9** essential, intrinsic,
necessary, paramount, principal, uppermost **10** elementary, preeminent,

underlying **11** fundamental, outstanding, predominant, wine-colored **13** indispensable, most important
number suffix: 3 eth

care 3 TLC **4** heed, load, mind, want, wish **5** grief, pains, worry **6** bother, charge, desire, effort, misery, regard, sorrow, strain, stress **7** anguish, anxiety, caution, concern, control, custody, keeping, sadness, thought, trouble **8** distress, give a rap, hardship, nuisance, pressure, vexation **9** annoyance, attention, be worried, diligence, exactness, give a hoot, heartache, vigilance **10** affliction, management, precaution, protection, solicitude **11** application, be concerned, bother about, carefulness, supervision, tribulation, unhappiness **12** ministration, trouble about, watchfulness **13** attentiveness, consideration **14** be interested in, circumspection, discrimination, fastidiousness, meticulousness, responsibility, scrupulousness **17** conscientiousness

Careas 6 eunuch

careen 3 tip, yaw **4** lean, list, sway, tilt, veer **5** heave, slant, slope **7** capsize **8** lean over, overturn

career 3 job **4** line, work **7** calling, pursuit **8** activity, business, lifework, vocation **10** employment, livelihood, occupation, profession, walk of life

care for 4 like, mind, tend **5** fancy **7** oversee **8** attend to, wait upon **9** look after, watch over **10** minister to, provide for

carefree 3 gay **4** glad **5** happy, jolly, sunny **6** breezy, elated, jaunty, joyous **7** buoyant, gleeful, radiant, relaxed, smiling **8** careless, cheerful, jubilant, laughing **9** easygoing **10** full of life, optimistic, untroubled **11** free-and-easy **12** happy-go-lucky, light-hearted, without worry **13** in high spirits **23** without a worry in the world
French: 9 sans souci

careful 4 fine, nice, wary **5** alert, chary, exact, fussy **7** correct, guarded, heedful, mindful, on guard, precise, prudent, tactful **8** accurate, cautious, diligent, discreet, vigilant, watchful **9** attentive, concerned, judicious, observant, regardful **10** fastidious, meticulous, particular, scrupulous, solicitous, thoughtful **11** circumspect, painstaking, punctilious **13** conscientious

carefulness 7 caution **10** steadiness **12** deliberation **14** circumspection

careless 3 lax **4** rash **5** messy, slack **6** casual, sloppy, untidy **7** inexact, offhand **8** heedless, mindless, slapdash, slipshod, slovenly **9** forgetful, imprecise, incorrect, negligent, unmindful **10** disorderly, inaccurate, neglectful, nonchalant, unthinking, untroubled

11 indifferent, thoughtless, unconcerned **12** absent-minded, devilmay-care **13** inconsiderate, lackadaisical

carelessness 6 laxity **7** neglect **9** messiness, slackness **10** inaccuracy, negligence, sloppiness, untidiness **11** imprecision, inexactness **12** heedlessness, indiscretion, slovenliness **13** unmindfulness **14** disorderliness **15** thoughtlessness **16** absentmindedness, irresponsibility

Care of Time, The
author: 10 Eric Ambler

caress 3 hug, pat, pet **5** clasp, touch **6** cuddle, fondle, stroke **7** embrace, petting, toy with **8** fondling, stroking **11** gentle touch

caretaker 6 keeper, porter, warden **7** curator, janitor, steward **8** overseer, watchman **9** concierge, custodian **10** gatekeeper **14** superintendent

careworn 7 haggard, worried **8** fatigued, troubled **11** pessimistic

cargo 4 load **5** goods **6** burden, lading **7** freight **8** shipment **11** consignment, merchandise

Carib
language family: 7 Cariban
location: 7 Guianas **9** Caribbean, Venezuela **12** South America
alleged custom: 11 cannibalism

Cariban
tribe: 5 Carib **6** Acawai, Akawai

Caribbean 3 sea
channel: 7 Yucatan
city: 6 Havana **7** San Juan **8** Santiago **10** Guantanamo **12** Port au Prince **13** Santo Domingo **15** Charlotte Amalie
Indian: 5 Carib **6** Arawak
island: 4 Cuba **5** Aruba, Haiti, Nevis **6** Cayman, Nassau, Tobago, Virgin **7** Antigua, Bahamas, Barbuda, Curacao, Grenada, Jamaica, Leeward **8** Anguilla, Dominica, Trinidad, Windward **9** Saint John **10** Guadeloupe, Hispaniola, Martinique, Montserrat, Puerto Rico, Saint Kitts, Saint Lucia **11** Saint Thomas **12** Saint Vincent **14** Lesser Antilles **15** Greater Antilles **19** Dominican Republic, Netherlands Antilles
language: 6 gullah **10** papiamento
product: 3 rum **5** fruit, spice, sugar **6** coffee

caricature 4 mock **6** parody, satire **7** lampoon, mockery, takeoff **8** satirize, travesty **9** absurdity, burlesque **10** distortion **12** exaggeration

Carker
character in: 12 Dombey and Son
author: 7 Dickens

Carlisle, Kitty
real name: 13 Katherine Conn
husband: 8 Moss Hart
born: 12 New Orleans LA
roles: 13 She Loves Me Not **14** To

Tell the Truth **16** A Night at the Opera **19** Murder at the Vanities

Carlton, Steve (Steven Norman)
nickname: 5 Lefty
sport: 8 baseball
position: 7 pitcher
team: 20 Philadelphia Phillies

Carlyle, Thomas
author of: 8 Cromwell **14** Sartor Resartus **17** Frederick the Great **19** The French Revolution **20** Heroes and Hero Worship

Carmen
author: 14 Prosper Merimee
opera by: 5 Bizet
setting: 7 Seville
character: 7 Don Jose **9** Escamillo, Frasquita
song: 8 Habanera

Carmen Jones
director: 13 Otto Preminger
based on opera by: 5 Bizet (Carmen)
adaptation by: 18 Oscar Hammerstein II
cast: 11 Pearl Bailey **14** Harry Belafonte **16** Dorothy Dandridge

carmine 3 red **6** cherry **7** crimson, deep red, scarlet **8** blood red **9** bright red

carnage 8 butchery, massacre **9** blood bath, slaughter

carnal 4 lewd **6** erotic, impure, sexual, sinful, wanton **7** fleshly, immoral, lustful, sensual **8** prurient, sensuous, unchaste, venereal **9** lecherous, salacious **10** lascivious, libidinous, voluptuous

Carnegie, Dale
author of: 33 How To Win Friends and Influence People

carnelian
species: 6 quartz

Carnera, Primo
nickname: 13 the Ambling Alp
sport: 6 boxing
class: 11 heavyweight

Carney, Art
real name: 26 Arthur William Matthew Carney
partner: 13 Jackie Gleason
born: 13 Mount Vernon NY
roles: 8 Ed Norton **13** Harry and Tonto (Oscar) **15** The Honeymooners

carnival 4 fair, fete, gala **6** circus **7** holiday, jubilee **8** festival, jamboree, sideshow **9** Mardi Gras **11** celebration

Carnivale
network: 3 HBO
cast: 8 Toby Huss (Stumpy) **9** Nick Stahl (Ben Hawkins) **10** Amy Madigan (Iris), Carla Gallo (Libby), Clea DuVall (Sofie) **11** Clancy Brown (Brother Justin) **14** Patrick Bauchau (Lodz) **15** Adrienne Barbeau (Ruthie), Cynthia Ettinger (Rita Sue) **16** Michael J. Anderson (Samson) **19** Debra Christofferson (Lila)

carnivore 3 cat, dog, fox **4** bear, lion, lynx, mink, puma, wolf **5** civet, dingo, fossa, hyena, otter, panda, skunk, tayra, tiger **6** badger, bobcat, coyote, ferret, grison, hyaena, jackal, jaguar, marten, olingo, weasel **7** polecat, raccoon, suricat **8** aardwolf, kinkajou, mongoose **9** meat eater, wolverine **10** cacomistle, coatimundi, flesh eater

carnivorous 9 predatory **10** meat-eating, predaceous **11** flesh-eating

carol 4 hymn, noel, sing **5** paean **6** warble **8** canticle **9** song of joy **12** song of praise

Caroline Islands
  district: 3 Yap **4** Truk **5** Palau **6** Ponape
  inhabitant: 10 Polynesian **11** Micronesian
  island: 3 Yap **6** Ponape, Ulithi **8** Nukuroro **10** Babelthuap **14** Kapinamarangi
  language: 7 English **10** Polynesian **11** Micronesian
  ocean: 7 Pacific

carom 6 bounce, strike **7** collide, rebound, **8** billiard, ricochet **9** bounce off

Caron, Leslie
  born: 6 France **19** Boulogne-Billancourt
  roles: 4 Gaby, Gigi, Lili **5** Fanny **11** Father Goose **13** Daddy Longlegs **14** The L-Shaped Room **17** An American in Paris

Carothers, Wallace Hume
  field: 9 chemistry
  discovered: 5 nylon

carousal 4 orgy **5** binge, drunk, spree **7** debauch **9** bacchanal **10** debauchery, saturnalia

carouse 5 drink, party, quaff, revel **6** guzzle, imbibe, tipple **7** roister, wassail **8** live it up **9** make merry **10** go on a binge **11** make whoopee

Carousel (film)
  director: 9 Henry King
  based on: 6 Liliom
    adaptation by: 21 Rodgers and Hammerstein
  cast: 12 Gordon MacRae (Billy Bigelow), Shirley Jones **15** Cameron Mitchell
  song: 9 Soliloquy **11** If I Loved You **19** You'll Never Walk Alone

carp 3 nag **5** cavil, chide, decry, knock **6** deride, impugn, jibe at, pick on **7** censure, condemn **8** belittle, complain, reproach **9** criticize, deprecate, disparage, fault-find, find fault **10** disapprove

Carpaccio, Vittore
  born: 5 Italy **6** Venice
  artwork: 13 Two Courtesans **18** The Dream of St Ursula **19** The Legend of St Ursula **21** St Augustine in his Study **24** St George Killing the Dragon **28** St Augustine's Vision of St Jerome **29** The Arrival of St Ursula at Cologne

carpal
  bone of: 5 wrist

carpe diem 11 seize the day **15** enjoy the present

carpenter 6 fitter, joiner **7** builder **8** repairer **10** woodworker **12** cabinetmaker
  ant: 10 camponotus
  bee: 8 xylocopa
  bird: 10 woodpecker
  fish: 10 hammerhead
  moth: 10 prinoxysus

Carpenter, Harlean
  real name of: 10 Jean Harlow

carper 6 critic **7** caviler **9** nit-picker **11** fault-finder

carpet 3 mat, rug **4** shag **5** cover, layer, sheet **7** blanket, matting **8** covering

Carpetbaggers, The
  author: 13 Harold Robbins

Carr, Emily
  born: 6 Canada **8** Victoria **15** British Columbia
  artwork: 3 Sky **8** Big Raven **14** Blunden Harbour, Kispiax Village **15** Woods and Blue Sky **17** Forest Landscape II **36** Cape Mudge An Indian Family with Totem Pole

Carra, Carlo
  born: 5 Italy **9** Quargneto
  artwork: 13 Lot's Daughters **16** Metaphysical Muse **20** Patriotic Celebration **29** The Funeral of the Anarchist Galli

Carradine, David
  father: 4 John
  half-brothers: 5 Keith **6** Robert
  born: 11 Hollywood CA
  roles: 6 Kung Fu **8** Kill Bill **13** Bound for Glory **14** The Serpent's Egg

Carradine, John
  real name: 21 Richmond Reed Carradine
  son: 5 David, Keith **6** Robert
  born: 18 Greenwich Village NY
  roles: 9 Cleopatra, Kidnapped **10** Stagecoach **12** Count Dracula **15** The Invisible Man **18** Captains Courageous, The Three Musketeers

Carradine, Keith
  father: 4 John
  brother: 6 Robert
  half-brother: 5 David
  born: 10 San Mateo CA
  roles: 9 Nashville **10** Pretty Baby **11** Into the West

Carraway, Nick
  character in: 14 The Great Gatsby
  author: 10 Fitzgerald

Carrere, John Merven
  partner: 14 Thomas Hastings
  architect of: 19 House Office Building (Washington DC) **20** New York Public Library, Senate Office Building (Washington DC) **21** Henry Clay Frick mansion (now Frick Collection NYC)
  style: 18 French neo-classical, Spanish Renaissance

carriage 3 air, rig **4** mien **5** buggy, coach, poise, wagon **6** aspect, manner **7** bearing, posture, vehicle **8** attitude, behavior, demeanor, presence **10** appearance, conveyance, deportment **11** comportment

Carrie
  author: 11 Stephen King

carried away 7 excited, frantic, seduced **8** ecstatic, frenzied, overcome **9** delirious **10** fascinated, infatuated **11** transported

carrier 3 bus, car **4** rack, wave **5** agent, barge, plane, coach, drain, ferry, train, truck, wagon **6** bearer, boxcar, pigeon, porter **7** airline, channel, mailman, postman, trucker, vehicle **8** airplane, aircraft, carriage, catalyst, railroad **9** messenger **11** transmitter, wheelbarrow

carrion 5 bones, offal, waste **6** corpse, refuse **7** cadaver, carcass, garbage, remains, wastage **8** crowbait, dead body, leavings

Carroll, Leo G
  born: 6 Weedon **7** England
  roles: 6 Topper **7** Rebecca **9** Suspicion **10** Spellbound **11** Cosmo Topper **15** A Christmas Carol, The Man from UNCLE, The Paradine Case **16** Father of the Bride, North by Northwest

Carroll, Lewis
  real name: 22 Charles Lutwidge Dodgson
  author of: 11 Jabberwocky **20** The Hunting of the Snark **22** Through the Looking Glass **28** Alice's Adventures in Wonderland

carrousel 4 ride, tray **8** conveyor **9** quadrille, whirligig **10** tournament **12** merry-go-round

carry 3 lug, run **4** bear, cart, haul, lift, move, prop, ship, take, tote **5** brace, bring, fetch, offer, print, shift, stock **6** convey, hold up, supply, uphold **7** conduct, deliver, display, publish, release, support, sustain **8** displace, maintain, shoulder, transfer, transmit **9** broadcast, transport **10** keep on hand **11** communicate, disseminate

carry away 4 lure **6** abduct, kidnap, seduce **7** attract **9** captivate, fascinate, infatuate, transport

carry off 5 seize, steal **6** abduct, kidnap **7** bear off **9** succeed at **11** get away with

carry out 2 do **6** effect, wind up **7** achieve, execute, fulfill, perform, realize **8** complete, conclude, dispatch **9**

discharge, dispose of, succeed at **10** accomplish, bring about **11** bring to pass

carry through 6 effect, finish **7** achieve, develop, execute, fulfill, perform, realize **8** complete, conclude **9** discharge **10** accomplish, consummate, effectuate, perpetuate **13** put into effect

Carson, Rachel Louise
 field: **7** biology
 studied: **9** pollution
 author of: **12** Silent Spring **14** The Sea Around Us **15** The Edge of the Sea

Carstone, Richard
 character in: **10** Bleak House
 author: **7** Dickens

cart 3 gig, lug **4** bear, dray, haul, move, take, tote, trap **5** bring, carry, fetch, truck, wagon **6** barrow, convey **7** schlepp, trundle, tumbrel **8** curricle, transfer, transmit **9** transport **10** handbarrow, transplant, two-wheeler **11** wheelbarrow
 kind: **2** go **3** dog, tip **4** dump, hand, push

carte blanche 7 license **9** a free hand, free reign **10** blank check **12** open sanction **13** full authority **18** unconditional power

cartel 4 OPEC, pool **5** chain, trust **7** combine **8** monopoly **9** syndicate **10** consortium, federation **11** corporation

Carter, Charles
 real name of: **14** Charlton Heston

Carter, James Earl, Jr
 nickname: **3** Hot **5** Jimmy **7** Hotshot
 presidential rank: **11** thirty-ninth
 party: **10** Democratic
 state represented: **2** GA **7** Georgia
 defeated: **4** (Gerald R) Ford **8** (Eugene) McCarthy
 vice president: **7** (Walter Frederick "Fritz") Mondale
 cabinet:
  state: **5** (Cyrus R) Vance **6** (Edmund S) Muskie
  treasury: **6** (G William) Miller **10** (W Michael) Blumenthal
  defense: **5** (Harold) Brown
  attorney general: **4** (Griffin B) Bell **9** (Benjamin R) Civiletti
  interior: **6** (Cecil D) Andrus
  agriculture: **8** (Robert S) Bergland
  commerce: **5** (Juanita Morris) Kreps **9** (Philip M) Klutznick
  labor: **8** (F Ray) Marshall
  HEW: **6** (Patricia Roberts) Harris **8** (Joseph A) Califano (Jr)
  HUD: **6** (Patricia Roberts) Harris **8** (Moon) Landrieu
  transportation: **5** (Brockman) Adams **11** (Neil E) Goldschmidt
  education: **10** (Shirley) Hufstedler
 born: **2** GA **6** Plains
 education: **14** US Naval Academy **26**

Georgia Southwestern College **28** Georgia Institute of Technology
 religion: **15** Southern Baptist
 interests: **5** track **6** tennis **7** fishing, hunting **8** football, softball **10** basketball **12** cross country **13** square dancing **17** collecting bottles
  music: **8** folk rock **9** classical
 author: **11** Living Faith **12** Keeping Faith **13** Why Not the Best? **14** The Hornet's Nest **16** Everything to Gain, Sharing Good Times **17** The Blood of Abraham
 political career: **12** state senator
  governor of: **7** Georgia
 civilian career: **12** peanut farmer
 military service: **6** US Navy
 notable events of lifetime/term: **6** SALT II **9** Love Canal, recession **18** Habitat for Humanity
  deaths at: **9** Jonestown
  eruption of: **13** Mount St Helens
  first baby from: **8** test tube
  hostages taken in: **4** Iran
  nuclear accident: **15** Three Mile Island
  pipeline: **5** Alcan
  prize: **5** Nobel **10** Nobel Peace
  scandal/investigation: **6** Abscam **9** Bert Lance, Koreagate **11** Billy Carter
  Supreme Court case: **5** Bakke
  treaty: **11** Panama Canal **16** Camp David Accords
 father: **11** James Earl Sr
 mother: **7** Lillian (Gordy)
  nickname: **11** Miss Lillian
 siblings: **6** Gloria **17** William "Billy" Alton **19** Ruth Carter Stapleton
 wife: **8** Rosalynn (Smith)
 children: **7** Amy Lynn **11** John William (Jack) **12** James Earl III (Chip) **13** Donnel Jeffrey (Jeff)
 first lady: **36** Presidential Commission on Mental Health
  author: **19** First Lady from Plains

Carthage see **7** Tunisia

carton 3 box **4** case **5** crate **9** container **11** packing case **12** cardboard box, packing crate **18** cardboard container

Carton, Sydney
 character in: **16** A Tale of Two Cities
 author: **7** Dickens

cartoon 5 comic **6** design, satire, sketch **7** drawing, funnies, picture **8** animated **10** caricature, comic strip

cartoonist 6 artist, drawer **7** gagster **12** caricaturist
 famous: **6** Al Capp, C C Beck, Ted Key **7** Bob Kane, Stan Lee **8** Herblock (Herbert L. Block), Jim Davis, Roy Crane **9** Bud Fisher, Chic Young, Dik Browne, Frank King, Hal Foster, Ham Fisher, Walt Kelly **10** Bob Montana, Gary Larson, Harold Gray, Jimmy Hatlo, Johnny Hart, Joe Shuster, Mort Walker, Paul Conrad,

Thomas Nast, Walt Disney **11** Alex Raymond, Bill Mauldin, Dale Messick, David Levine, Ding Darling, Elzie C. Segar, Hank Ketcham, Max Beerbohm, Rollin Kirby **12** Al Hirschfeld, Brad Anderson, Chester Gould, Garry Trudeau, James Thurber, Jeff MacNelly, Jules Feiffer, Milton Caniff, Rube Goldberg, Rudolph Dirks, Virgil Partch **13** Bill Watterson, Charles Addams, Charles Schulz, George McManus, Honore Daumier, Joseph Keppler, Saul Steinberg **14** Homer Davenport, William Hogarth **15** Ernie Bushmiller, Patrick Oliphant, Richard Outcault **16** Benjamin Franklin, George Cruikshank

cartridge 3 dud **4** case, tape **5** blank, shell **6** holder **7** capsule, package **8** cassette, cylinder **9** container

Cartwright, Edmund
 nationality: **7** English
 inventor of: **9** power loom **18** wool-combing machine

carve 3 hew, saw **4** etch, form, hack, mold, rend, turn, work **5** allot, cleve, cut up, model, shape, slash, slice, split **6** chisel, divide, incise, sculpt **7** engrave, fashion, pattern, quarter **8** block out, dissever **9** apportion, sculpture

Carver, George Washington
 field: **9** chemistry
 worked in: **11** agriculture
 studied: **6** peanut **7** soybean **11** sweet potato

carving 5 cameo **8** intaglio, triptych **9** sculpture

caryatid 6 column
 shape of: **12** female figure

Casablanca
 director: **13** Michael Curtiz
 cast: **10** Peter Lorre **11** Claude Rains (Louis), Conrad Veidt, Paul Henreid (Victor Laslo) **12** Dooley Wilson (Sam), **13** Ingrid Bergman (Ilsa Lund) **14** Humphrey Bogart (Rick) **17** Sydney Greenstreet
 Oscar for: **7** picture
 song: **12** As Time Goes By

Casanova 3 cad, rip **4** beau, lech, roue, wolf **5** lover, Romeo, swain, wooer **6** chaser, lecher, suitor **7** admirer, bounder, Don Juan, gallant, rounder **8** cavalier, Lothario, lover boy, paramour **9** ladies' man, libertine, womanizer **10** lady-killer, profligate **11** philanderer

Casby
 character in: **12** Little Dorrit
 author: **7** Dickens

cascade 4 fall, gush, pour, rush **5** chute, falls, surge **6** plunge, rapids, tumble **7** Niagara **8** cataract **9** waterfall

Cascade Range
location: **9** northwest
highest peak: **9** Mt. Rainier

case 3 bin, box **4** plea, suit, tray **5** cause, chest, cover, crate, event **6** action, affair, appeal, carton, debate, injury, jacket, matter, sheath, victim **7** cabinet, concern, disease, dispute, episode, example, hearing, housing, inquiry, invalid, lawsuit, overlay, patient, wrapper **8** argument, business, covering, envelope, incident, instance, sufferer **9** condition, container, happening, incidence, sheathing, situation **10** litigation, occurrence, proceeding, protection, receptacle, sick person **11** controversy **12** circumstance, illustration

case in point 7 example **8** instance **12** illustration

Case of Sergeant Grischa, The
author: **11** Arnold Zweig

Casey
nickname of: **20** Charles Dillon Stengel
team: **7** Yankees
role: **7** manager

Casey at the Bat
author: **6** Thayer
town: **8** Mudville

Casey Jones 8 engineer, folksong, railroad

cash 5 bills, bread, coins, dough, money **6** change, redeem **8** currency, exchange **9** bank notes **10** paper money **11** legal tender **13** turn into money **14** coin of the realm

cashier 6 banker, bursar, purser, teller **9** treasurer **10** bank teller

cash register
invented by: **4** till **5** Ritty
sign: **6** no sale

casing 4 skin **5** frame **9** sheathing

Casino
director: **14** Martin Scorsese
cast: **8** Alan King (Andy Stone), Joe Pesci (Nicky Santoro) **10** Don Rickles (Billy Sherbert), James Woods (Lester Diamond) **11** Kevin Pollak (Phillip Green), Sharon Stone (Ginger Rothstein) **12** Robert De Niro (Sam Rothstein)

Casino Royale
author: **10** Ian Fleming

cask 3 keg, tub, tun, vat **4** butt, pipe **6** barrel **8** hogshead

casket 4 case, pall **5** chest **6** coffer, coffin **8** jewel box **11** sarcophagus

Cask of Amontillado, The
author: **13** Edgar Allan Poe
character: **9** Fortunato, Montresor

Cassandra 7 seeress
also: **9** Alexandra
father: **5** Priam
mother: **6** Hecuba
brother: **5** Paris

concubine of: **9** Agamemnon
son: **6** Pelops **9** Teledamus
cursed by: **6** Apollo
violated by: **4** Ajax
killed by: **12** Clytemnestra

Cassatt, Mary
born: **15** Allegheny City PA
artwork: **6** La Loge **7** The Bath **11** The Cup of Tea **12** After the Bath, Woman Bathing **14** Gathering Fruit **15** Reading Le Figaro **20** Girl Arranging Her Hair, Woman and Child Drawing

Cassavetes, John
wife: **12** Gena Rowlands
born: **9** New York NY
roles/films: **8** Husbands **10** The Tempest **13** Rosemary's Baby, The Dirty Dozen **23** A Woman Under the Influence

casserole 4 dish, food, mold **6** tureen, vessel **8** saucepan

Cassio
character in: **7** Othello
author: **11** Shakespeare

Cassiopeia 13 constellation
husband: **7** Cepheus
daughter: **9** Andromeda
offended: **7** Nereids

Cassius
also: **12** Caius Cassius
character in: **12** Julius Caesar
author: **11** Shakespeare

Cass Timberlane
author: **13** Sinclair Lewis
character: **11** Bradd Criley **24** Jinny Marshland Timberlane

cast 3 set, sow **4** fire, form, hurl, look, mien, mint, mold, pick, shed, toss **5** fling, heave, model, pitch, shape, shoot, sling, stamp, throw **6** actors, assign, casing, choose, direct, launch, let fly, propel, sculpt, spread, troupe **7** appoint, company, deposit, diffuse, pattern, players, project, scatter **8** catapult, disperse **9** broadcast, circulate, discharge, launching, semblance **10** appearance, distribute, impression, performers, propulsion **11** disseminate, give parts to **16** dramatis personae

Castalia
origin: **5** Greek
sacred: **6** spring
location: **14** Mount Parnassus
sacred to: **5** Muses **9** Apollo
source of: **11** inspiration

cast aside 4 junk, shed **6** desert, reject **7** abandon, discard, forsake, neglect **8** get rid of, renounce, throw out **9** repudiate, throw away **11** discontinue

cast a spell on 3 hex **4** jinx **5** charm **7** bewitch, conjure, enchant **8** entrance **11** work magic on

cast aspersions on 5 knock, scorn **6** deride, malign **7** disdain, put down, run down, sneer at **8** belittle, pooh-

pooh **9** criticize, disparage **13** find fault with

castaway 3 bum **4** hobo, waif **5** exile, leper, nomad, rover, stray **6** outlaw, pariah **7** Ishmael, outcast, vagrant **8** deportee, derelict, renegade, unperson, vagabond, wanderer **9** foundling, nonperson **10** expatriate **11** beachcomber, offscouring, untouchable **12** down-and-outer **15** knight-of-the-road

cast away 4 junk **6** launch, propel, reject **7** abandon, discard, toss out **8** get rid of, pitch out, throw out **9** throw away

cast down 5 abase, droop, lower **6** abased, deject, droopy, humble, sadden **7** depress, humbled, lowered **8** bring low, dejected, disgrace, saddened **9** depressed, disgraced, humiliate **10** brought low, dishearten, humiliated **11** crestfallen **12** disheartened

caste 4 rank **6** status **7** lineage, station **8** position **9** condition
Hindu: **5** sudra, varna **6** vaisya **7** brahman **9** kshatriya

castigate 5 chide, scold **6** berate, punish, rebuke **7** bawl out, censure, chasten, chew out, correct, reprove, upbraid **8** admonish, chastise, penalize, reproach **9** criticize, dress down, reprimand **10** discipline, take to task **15** call on the carpet **16** haul over the coals

castigation 9 reprimand **10** chastening, correction, discipline, penalizing, punishment **12** chastisement

Castiglione, Baldassare
author of: **20** The Book of the Courtier

castle 4 hall, keep, rook **5** manor, tower, villa **6** palace **7** chateau, citadel, mansion **8** fortress **10** stronghold

Castle, Vernon
wife: **5** Irene **15** ballroom dancers
invented: **10** Castle Walk

Castle, The
author: **10** Franz Kafka
character: **1** K

Castle of Otranto, The
author: **13** Horace Walpole
character: **6** Conrad **7** Alfonso, Manfred, Matilda **8** Isabella, Theodore **12** Father Jerome

Castle Rackrent
author: **14** Maria Edgeworth

cast off 4 shed **6** reject **7** discard, set sail, toss out **8** throw off, throw out **9** repudiate, throw away **11** weigh anchor

Castor and Pollux
also: **6** Gemini **8** Dioscuri **10** Polydeuces, Tyndaridae
form: **8** twin sons
mother: **4** Leda
father: **4** Zeus
sister: **5** Helen **12** Clytemnestra

members of: 9 Argonauts
protectors of: 6 seamen

cast out 4 oust **5** eject, evict, exile, expel **6** banish, reject **7** discard, dismiss, turn out **8** drive out, send away, throw out

cast up 4 spew **5** eject, expel, vomit **6** spew up **7** cough up, throw up **8** disgorge

casual 4 cool, so-so **5** blase, vague **6** chance, random, sporty **7** offhand, passing, relaxed **8** informal **9** easygoing, haphazard, non-dressy, unplanned **10** accidental, fortuitous, incidental, nonchalant, unarranged, undesigned, undirected, unexpected, unforeseen **11** half-hearted, indifferent, unlooked for **13** lackadaisical, serendipitous, unintentional **14** indiscriminate, unpremeditated

casualty 4 loss **6** injury, victim **7** injured **8** fatality

casuistry 5 guile **6** deceit **7** fallacy, sophism **8** subtlety **9** Jesuitism, quibbling, sophistry **10** nitpicking **12** equivocation, pettifoggery, speciousness **13** deceptiveness, hair-splitting **14** sophistication

casus belli 10 cause of war

Casy, Jim
character in: 16 The Grapes of Wrath
author: 9 Steinbeck

cat 3 pet **4** puss, whip **5** kitty, pussy, tabby **6** feline, kitten, mouser, tomcat
anatomy: 3 paw **4** loin, nape, rump, tail **5** break, flank, shank **6** feeler **7** dewclaw, leather, whisker **8** vibrissa **10** metatarsus
breed/kind: 3 tom **4** coon, Eyra, lion, lynx, Manx, puma **5** alley, civet, hyena, kitty, Korat, tabby, tiger **6** Angola, angora, bobcat, cougar, jaguar, ocelot, serval **7** Burmese, caracal, cheetah, leopard, linsang, Maltese, panther, Persian, polecat, Siamese, Turkish, wildcat **8** Balinese, Cheshire, Egyptian, ringtail **9** Himalayan, shorthair **10** Abyssinian, chinchilla **11** Russian blue **13** tortoise-shell
combining form: 5 aelur, ailur, felin **6** aeluro, ailuro, felino
Egyptian goddess of: 4 Bast
extinct: 10 saber-tooth
family: 7 Felidae
famous: 6 Morris **8** Cheshire, Garfield, Kilkenny **9** Mehitabel **10** Heathcliff
fastest: 7 cheetah
fear of: 12 aelurophobia, ailurophobia
female: 5 queen **7** lioness, tigress **8** wheencat **9** grimalkin
genus: 5 Felis
grinning: 8 Cheshire
group: 7 clowder, clutter
group of kittens: 6 kendle, kindle
lover: 11 aelurophile, ailurophile

male: 3 gib, tom **6** tomcat
ring-tailed: 6 serval **10** cacomistle
tailless: 4 Manx
young: 6 kitten

cataclysm 4 blow **7** debacle **8** calamity, disaster, upheaval **11** catastrophe, devastation

cataclysmic 4 dire **6** tragic **7** ruinous **10** calamitous, disastrous **12** catastrophic, earth-shaking

catacomb 4 tomb **7** ossuary **8** cemetery **10** passageway **12** burial ground

catafalque 3 box **4** pall **6** casket, coffin

catalog, catalogue 4 file, list, post, roll **5** index **6** record, roster **7** listing **8** classify, register, syllabus, tabulate **9** directory, enumerate, inventory, mail order

Catamitus see **8** Ganymede

Cat and Mouse
author: 11 Gunter Grass

catapult 4 cast, hurl, toss **5** fling, heave, pitch, shoot, sling, throw **6** hurtle, onager, propel **9** slingshot **13** hurling engine

cataract 5 falls, flood **6** deluge, rapids **7** cascade, torrent **8** downpour **9** lens cover, waterfall **10** inundation

catastrophe 4 blow **5** havoc **6** mishap, ravage **7** debacle, scourge, tragedy **8** calamity, disaster **9** cataclysm **10** affliction, misfortune **11** devastation

catastrophic 6 tragic **7** ruinous **10** calamitous, disastrous **11** cataclysmic

catcall 3 boo **4** gibe, hiss, hoot, jeer, razz **7** whistle **8** heckling **9** raspberry **10** Bronx cheer

catch 3 bag, bat, get, hit, nab **4** bait, bang, belt, bump, bust, dupe, feel, find, fool, grab, hasp, haul, hoax, hook, lock, lure, make, snag, snap, spot, take, trap **5** booty, break, charm, clasp, crack, get to, grasp, hitch, latch, prize, reach, seize, sense, smack, smite, snare, trick, whack, yield **6** allure, arrest, betray, buffet, collar, corner, corral, dazzle, deceit, delude, descry, detect, expose, fasten, fathom, kicker, snatch, strike, take in, turn on, unmask **7** attract, bewitch, capture, closure, deceive, delight, discern, enchant, ensnare, find out, gimmick, mislead, rasping, seizure **8** catching, come upon, contract, coupling, discover, drawback, enthrall, hoodwink, overtake, perceive, pickings, surprise **9** apprehend, bamboozle, captivate, carry away, enrapture, fastening, intercept, lay hold of, play false, recognize, transport **10** comprehend, understand **11** take captive **12** break out with, come down with, disadvantage, seize and hold, take off guard **14** stumbling block **15**

take into custody **18** become infected with

catch-as-catch-can 7 cursory **9** haphazard, hit-or-miss, unplanned **10** disorderly, incomplete **11** superficial, unorganized **12** disorganized, unsystematic

Catcher in the Rye, The
author: 10 J D Salinger
character: 15 Holden Caulfield Phoebe Caulfield

catching 10 contagious, infectious **12** communicable **13** transmittable

Catch Me If You Can
director: 15 Steven Spielberg
cast: 8 Amy Adams (Brenda Strong), Tom Hanks (Carl Hanratty) **11** James Brolin (Jack Barnes), Martin Sheen (Roger Strong) **12** Nathalie Baye (Paula Abagnale) **16** Leonardo DiCaprio (Frank Abagnale, Jr.) **17** Christopher Walken (Frank Abagnale, Sr.)

catch on to 3 get **5** grasp, savvy **6** absorb, digest, fathom, pick up **10** assimilate, comprehend, get the idea, understand

catch sight of 3 see **4** espy **6** behold, descry, detect, notice **7** discern, make out, observe, pick out **8** perceive

Catch-22
author: 12 Joseph Heller
character: 9 Yossarian
means: 7 paradox

catchword 5 motto **6** byword, cliche, slogan, war cry **8** password **9** battle cry, guide word, pet phrase, watchword **10** shibboleth

categorical 4 flat, sure **7** certain, express **8** absolute, definite, emphatic, explicit **10** pronounced, unreserved **11** unequivocal, unqualified **12** unmistakable **13** unconditional

categorically 10 absolutely, definitely, positively **12** conclusively

categorization 5 order **11** arrangement **14** classification

category 5 class, group **8** division, grouping **14** classification

cater 5 humor **6** pamper, pander, please **7** gratify, indulge, satisfy

caterpillar 4 moth, worm **5** larva **7** cutworm, tractor, webworm **8** hangworm, silkworm, wortworm **9** butterfly, woolybear **10** astragalus

caterwaul 3 cry **4** bawl, howl, wail, yelp **5** whine **6** clamor, scream, shriek, squawk, squeal **7** screech **10** rend the air

catfish 4 barb **5** banjo **6** dorado, madtom, mudcat, sucker **7** ariidae, bluecat **8** bagridae, bullhead, claridae, electric, flathead **9** siluridae **10** channel cat, cuttlefish, mochocidae, plotosidae, spotted cat **11** ictaluridae, pimelodidae, schilbeidae **12** aspredinidae, ostariophysi **14** malapteruridae **16** trichomycteridae

Catfish
nickname of: **9** Jim Hunter

Catfish Row
setting of: **12** Porgy and Bess

catharsis 7 purging, release, venting **9** cleansing **12** purification

Catharsius
epithet of: **4** Zeus
means: **8** purifier

cathartic 5 purge **6** physic **8** aperient, evacuant, laxative **9** castor oil, purgative, purifying

cathedral 3 see **6** church, temple **7** lateran **8** basilica, official **9** authority **10** pontifical
Italian: **5** duomo

Cather, Willa
author of: **9** A Lost Lady, My Antonia, One of Ours, O Pioneers! **13** My Mortal Enemy **16** Shadows on the Rock, The Song of the Lark **18** The Professor's House **23** Sapphira and the Slave Girl **26** Death Comes for the Archbishop

cathode ray tube
abbreviation: **3** CRT
invented by: **7** Crookes

catholic, Catholic 5 broad **7** liberal **9** universal, worldwide **12** all-embracing, all-inclusive **13** comprehensive

cathouse 4 stew **5** house **6** bagnio, bordel **7** brothel **8** bordello **10** bawdy house, fancy house, whorehouse **13** sporting house **14** house of ill fame **16** house of ill repute **19** house of prostitution

Cat Jumps, The
author: **14** Elizabeth Bowen

catlike 5 catty, lithe **7** sinuous **8** stealthy **14** light on the feet

Catlin, George
born: **13** Wilkes-Barre PA
artwork: **16** Gallery of Indians

catnap 3 nap **4** doze **6** siesta, snooze **10** forty winks, light sleep

Cato 5 Roman
Elder: **6** Censor
younger (grandson): **5** Stoic

Cato
author: **13** Joseph Addison

Cat on a Hot Tin Roof
author: **17** Tennessee Williams
director: **13** Richard Brooks
cast: **8** Burl Ives (Big Daddy) **10** Jack Carson, Paul Newman (Brick) **14** Judith Anderson **15** Elizabeth Taylor (Maggie)

cats-eye
species: **11** chrysoberyl
source: **8** Sri Lanka

cat's paw 4 dupe, pawn, tool **5** patsy **7** fall guy

cattle 4 cows, kine, oxen **5** beefs, bulls, stock **6** beeves, calves, dogies, steers **8** bullocks, milk cows **9** livestock
family: **7** Bovidae
group of: **5** drove
kind: **2** ox **3** yak **4** Zebu **5** Angus **6** Ankole, Jersey **7** Brahman **8** Ayrshire, Guernsey, Hereford, Highland, Holstein **9** Charolais **12** water buffalo **13** Texas Longhorn **16** English Shorthorn, Holstein-Friesian
young: **4** calf **6** heifer **8** yearling

Catton, Bruce
author of: **22** A Stillness at Appomattox

catty 4 mean **7** catlike **8** spiteful **9** malicious, malignant **10** malevolent

catwalk 6 bridge **7** walkway **10** passageway

Caucasian
language branch: **5** Ubykh **9** Daghestan **10** Circassian **11** Khartvelian

Caucon
brought mysteries to: **8** Messenia

caucus 6 parley, powwow **7** council, meeting, session **8** assembly, conclave **10** conference

caudal 4 back, tail **7** tail-end

cauldron see **7** caldron

Caulfield, Holden
character in: **18** The Catcher in the Rye
author: **8** Salinger

Caulfield, Joan
real name: **21** Beatrice Joan Caulfield
born: **8** Orange NJ
roles: **8** Dear Ruth **17** My Favorite Husband

causation 4 root **5** cause **6** author, origin, reason, source **7** creator, genesis **8** etiology, inventor, stimulus **9** generator, invention **10** antecedent, conception, mainspring, originator **11** determinant, inspiration, origination

cause 4 goal, make, root, side **5** ideal, impel, tenet **6** belief, create, effect, incite, lead to, motive, object, origin, reason, source, spring, stir up **7** genesis, grounds, incline, inspire, produce, provoke, purpose **8** etiology, generate, motivate, occasion, stimulus **9** incentive, principle, stimulate **10** aspiration, bring about, conviction, foundation, give rise to, inducement, initiation, mainspring, motivation, persuasion, prime mover **11** bring to pass, inspiration, instigation, precipitate, provocation

cause of war
Latin: **10** casus belli

cause to appear 6 expose, reveal **7** uncover **8** disclose **12** bring to light **13** bring into view

caustic 3 lye **4** tart **5** acrid, harsh, sharp **6** biting, bitter **7** burning, cutting, erosive, gnawing **8** scathing, stinging **9** corroding, corrosive, sarcastic **10** astringent **11** acrimonious

caution 4 care, heed, warn **5** alarm, alert **6** advise, caveat, exhort, notify, regard, tip-off **7** concern, thought, warning **8** admonish, forewarn, prudence, wariness **9** alertness, restraint, vigilance **10** admonition, discretion, precaution **11** carefulness, forewarning, guardedness, heedfulness, mindfulness **12** deliberation, watchfulness **14** circumspection, put on one's guard

cautionary 7 warning **8** advisory **10** admonitory **11** admonishing

cautious 4 wary **5** alert, cagey **7** careful, guarded, prudent **8** discreet, vigilant, watchful **9** attentive, judicious **11** circumspect

cavalcade 5 troop **6** column, parade **7** caravan, retinue **10** procession

Cavalcade
director: **10** Frank Lloyd
based on play by: **10** Noel Coward
cast: **10** Clive Brook **11** Ursula Jeans **12** Diana Wynyard **13** Herbert Mundin **15** Margaret Lindsay
Oscar for: **7** picture

cavalier 3 fop **4** beau **5** blade, cocky, dandy, swell **6** hussar, lancer **7** cursory, dragoon, gallant, haughty, offhand, playboy **8** arrogant, courtier, gay blade, horseman, uncaring **9** easygoing, cavalryman, disdainful, nonchalant **11** indifferent, thoughtless

cavalry 7 hussars, lancers **8** dragoons **10** mounted men **11** horse troops **13** horse soldiers, mounted troops

cavalryman 6 hussar, lancer **7** dragoon **8** cavalier, horseman **12** horse soldier, horse trooper **14** mounted soldier

cave 3 den **4** lair, sink **6** burrow, cavern, cavity, dugout, grotto, hollow
growth: **10** stalactite, stalagmite
explorer: **9** spelunker

caveat 5 alarm, alert, aviso **6** tip-off **7** caution, red flag, warning **8** high sign, red light **10** admonition, danger sign, yellow jack **11** forewarning **12** admonishment, flea in the ear **13** word to the wise **20** handwriting on the wall

caveat emptor 17 let the buyer beware

cave canem 14 beware of the dog

cave in 6 buckle, fall in, give up, submit **7** crumple, give way, implode **8** collapse **10** capitulate **12** fall to pieces

Cavendish, Henry
field: **7** physics **9** chemistry
nationality: **7** British
discovered: **8** hydrogen
determined composition of: **3** air **5** water **10** nitric acid
method: **19** Cavendish experiment

cavernous 4 huge, vast **5** roomy **6**

gaping **7** chasmal, immense, yawning **8** cavelike, enormous, spacious **10** tremendous

cavil 6 deride **7** nitpick, quibble **8** belittle, complain **9** criticize, deprecate, discredit, disparage, faultfind, find fault **12** pick to pieces

cavity 3 dip, pit **4** bore, dent, hole, sink **5** basin, niche **6** burrow, crater, hollow, pocket, tunnel **7** opening, orifice, vacuity **8** aperture **9** concavity **10** depression, excavation

cavort 4 play, romp **5** bound, caper, frisk **6** frolic, gambol, prance

Cawdor
   author: 15 Robinson Jeffers

Caxtons, The
   author: 12 Bulwer-Lytton

Cayuga
   language family: 9 Iroquoian
   location: 4 Ohio **6** Canada **7** New York **8** Oklahoma **9** Wisconsin
   branch of: 10 Six Nations **19** Iroquois Confederacy, League of the Iroquois

CE 9 Common Era

cease 3 end **4** halt, pass, quit, stop **5** abate, pause **6** desist, finish **7** adjourn, die away, forbear, suspend **8** break off, conclude, leave off **9** terminate **11** abstain from, discontinue, refrain from **12** bring to an end

cease-fire 5 truce **9** armistice

ceaseless 7 endless, eternal **8** constant, enduring, unending **9** continual, incessant, permanent, perpetual, unceasing **10** continuous, protracted **11** everlasting, never-ending, unremitting **12** interminable **13** uninterrupted

cease to be 3 die, end **6** die out, expire, vanish **9** disappear, evaporate **13** become extinct

Cecilia (Memoirs of an Heiress)
   author: 11 Fanny Burney

Cecrops
   also: 8 Cecropia
   form: 3 man **6** dragon
   founder of: 6 Attica
   king of: 6 Attica
   father: 14 King Erechtheus
   brother: 6 Metion, Orneus
   wife: 8 Aglaurus
   son: 11 Erysichthon
   daughter: 5 Herse **8** Aglaurus **9** Pandrasos
   renamed Attica: 8 Cecropia

cedar 6 Cedrus
   varieties: 3 red **4** pink, salt **5** Atlas, giant, white **6** Alaska, Cyprus, ground, Mlanje **7** Bermuda, incense, Russian, Spanish **8** Barbados, cigarbox, creeping, Japanese, stinking **10** Ozark white, Port Orford, swamp white, western red, West Indian, Willowmore **11** Clanwilliam, Colorado red, southern red **13** Atlantic white, southern white **14** Chilean in-

cense, Formosa incense **17** California incense

cede 4 give **5** grant, leave, yield **6** tender **7** abandon, deliver, release **8** hand over, transfer **9** deliver up, surrender **10** relinquish

cedez
   music: 8 slow down

Cedric the Saxon
   character in: 7 Ivanhoe
   author: 5 Scott

ceiling 3 top **4** roof **5** cover, limit **6** canopy, cupola, lining **7** maximum **8** altitude **10** upperlimit

Celebes
   also: 8 Sulawesi
   bordered by: 6 Borneo **8** Moluccas **10** Celebes Sea, Kalimantan **12** Flores Strait **14** Makassar Strait
   city: 4 Poso **6** Manado **7** Kendari, Madjene **8** Bonthain, Donggala, Makassar **9** Gorontalo
   location: 9 Indonesia
   people: 4 Bugi, Laki, Mori, Muna, Napu, Palu, Peso, Seko, Wana **5** Besoa, Buton, Toala **6** Bungku, Butung, Parigi, Sadang, Sangir, Toland **7** Banggai, Bolaang, Kabaena, Loinang, Toradja **8** Balantak, Buginese, Mongondu, Rongkong, Sanghike **9** Gorontalo **11** Makassarese
   province: 13 North Sulawesi, South Sulawesi **15** Central Sulawesi **17** Southeast Sulawesi

Celebes ox 4 anoa

celebrate 4 laud **5** bless, cheer, exalt, extol, honor **6** hallow, praise, revere **7** acclaim, applaud, commend, glorify, observe **8** proclaim, sanctify, venerate **9** broadcast, ritualize, solemnize **10** consecrate **11** commemorate **13** ceremonialize

celebrated 5 famed, feted, noted **6** famous, prized **7** eminent, honored, notable, revered **8** lionized, renowned **9** acclaimed, important, prominent, respected, treasured, venerable, wellknown **11** illustrious, outstanding **13** distinguished

Celebrated Jumping Frog of Calaveras County, The
   author: 9 Mark Twain

celebration 4 fete, gala **5** feast, party **6** ritual **7** jubilee, revelry **8** carnival, ceremony, festival **9** festivity, hallowing **10** ceremonial, observance **13** commemoration, solemnization **14** sanctification **15** memorialization

celebrity 3 VIP **4** fame, name, note, star **5** glory, wheel **6** bigwig, renown **7** big shot, notable, stardom **8** eminence, luminary **9** dignitary, notoriety, personage **10** notability, popularity, prominence **11** distinction, personality **12** famous person, person of note

celerity 5 haste, hurry, speed **6** hustle **8** alacrity, dispatch, fast clip, fastness,

legerity, rapidity **9** briskness, quickness, swiftness **10** expedition, snappiness, speediness **12** precipitance **14** lightning speed **15** expeditiousness

celery seed
   also called: 8 smallage
   origin: 13 Mediterranean
   use: 4 soup **5** salad, sauce **6** pickle **10** vegetables

celestial 3 sky **5** solar **6** astral, divine **7** angelic, elysian, stellar, sublime **8** beatific, blissful, empyrean, ethereal, hallowed, heavenly, seraphic **9** planetary, unearthly **12** astronomical, otherworldly, paradisiacal

celestial being 3 god **5** angel, deity **7** goddess **8** divinity **11** divine being

Celestial City
   place in: 16 Pilgrim's Progress
   author: 6 Bunyan

Celia (Aliena)
   character in: 11 As You Like It
   author: 11 Shakespeare

celibacy 6 purity **8** chastity **9** virginity **10** abstinence, continence **12** bachelorhood, spinsterhood

celibate 4 pure **5** unwed **6** chaste, single **8** bachelor, spinster, virginal **9** abstinent, continent, unmarried

Celine, Louis-Ferdinand
   author of: 12 Guignol's Band **25** Death on the Installment Plan, Journey to the End of the Night

cell
   part: 7 nucleus **8** membrane **9** cytoplasm
   made of: 3 fat **4** salt **5** water **7** protein **9** compounds **12** carbohydrate
   theory of: 7 (Rudolf) Virchow, (Theodor) Schwann

cellar 3 den **4** cave **6** dugout **8** basement **10** downstairs **14** wine collection

Cellini, Benvenuto
   born: 5 Italy **8** Florence
   artwork: 7 Cosimo I, Perseus **13** Bindo Altoviti **18** The Crucified Christ **20** Nymph of Fontainebleau
   autobiography: 22 Life of Benvenuto Cellini

Celsius
   abbreviation of: 1 C

Celt 4 Gaul, Kelt, Manx, Pict, Scot **5** Irish, Welsh **6** Breton, Briton, chisel **8** Scottish **10** Highlander

Celtic 4 Erse
   language group: 6 Gaelic **9** Brythonic
   family: 12 Indo-European
   language of: 5 Gauls

cement 3 fix, set **4** bind, fuse, glue, join, seal, weld **5** paste, stick, unite **6** mortar, secure **8** concrete

cemetery 7 ossuary **8** boneyard, Boot Hill, catacomb **9** graveyard **10** churchyard, necropolis **12** burial ground, memorial park, potter's field **13** bury-ing ground

Cenci, The
  author: 18 Percy Bysshe Shelley

cenobite 4 monk **7** ascetic **8** celibate **9** religious

censor 4 blip, edit **5** amend, bleep, judge, purge **6** critic, delete, excise **7** amender, Bowdler, clean up **8** black out, examiner, reviewer, suppress **9** expurgate, inspector **10** blue-pencil, bowdlerize, expurgator, suppressor **11** bowdlerizer, faultfinder, scrutinizer **12** investigator **17** custodian of morals **25** guardian of the public morals

censorious 5 picky **7** abusive, carping **8** critical **10** defamatory **12** faultfind-ing

censurable 8 blamable **10** deplorable, punishable, reprovable **11** blamewor-thy **12** reproachable **13** reprehensible

censure 3 pan, rap **5** chide, scold **6** berate, rebuke **7** bawl out, chew out, chiding, condemn, reproof, reprove, upbraid **8** admonish, denounce, re-proach, scolding **9** castigate, com-plaint, criticism, criticize, reprehend, reprimand **10** admonition, bawling-out, chewing-out, disapprove, up-braiding **11** castigation, disapproval, reprobation **12** condemnation, dress-ing-down, remonstrance **13** tongue-lashing **14** disapprobation **16** rap on the knuckles, take over the coals
  god of: 5 Momos, Momus

census 3 tax **4** data, list, poll **5** count **6** amount, number **11** enumeration **12** registration

Centaur
  form: 3 man **5** horse **7** monster **16** half-man half-horse
  constellation of: 9 Centaurus
  famous: 6 Chiron
  represents: 11 Sagittarius

Centennial
  author: 13 James Michener

Centennial State
  nickname of: 8 Colorado

center, centre 3 fix, hub, mid **4** axis, core, crux **5** focus, heart, pivot, point **6** direct, gather, middle **7** address, es-sence, nucleus **8** converge, interior **9** middle **10** focal point **11** concentrate

centered 4 even, true **5** right **7** fo-cused **8** straight **10** pinpointed **12** concentrated

centigrade 5 scale **6** degree **7** celcius **11** thermometer

centigram
  abbreviation of: 2 cg

centiliter
  abbreviation of: 2 cl

centimeter
  abbreviation of: 2 cm

centipede 4 boat **5** shrub **6** earwig,

insect **8** chilopod, multiped **9** arthro-pod **13** Muehlenbeckia

central 3 key **4** core, main **5** basic, chief, focal, inner, major, prime **6** in-most, middle **7** leading, midmost, piv-otal, primary **8** dominant, foremost, interior **9** essential, paramount, princi-pal **10** middlemost **11** fundamental, predominant **13** most important

Central African Republic
  other name: 11 Ubangi-Chari **20** Cen-tral African Empire
  capital/largest city: 6 Bangui
  others: 3 Obo **4** Bria, Ippy **5** Birao, Bouar, Kembe, Ndele, Ngoto, Paoua, Rafai, Zemio **6** Baboua, Bakala, Bo-zoum, Mbaiki **7** Bambari, Grimari, Zemongo **9** Bangassou, Berberati, Bossangoa, Fort-Sibut
  monetary unit: 5 franc **7** centime
  lake: 4 Chad
  mountain: 5 Karre, Tinga **6** Mongos **9** Dar Challa
  highest point: 11 Kayagangiri
  river: 4 Bomu, Nana **5** Chari, Kotto, Mbari, Mpoko, Ouaka **6** Chinko, Lo-baye, Mbomou, Ubangi **11** Upper Sangha
  people: 4 Baya, Sara **5** Banda, Bwaka, Sango **6** Azande, Yakoma **7** Banziri, Mandjia, Nzakara
  language: 5 Sango, Zande **6** French
  religion: 5 Islam **7** animism **12** Chris-tianity **13** Roman Catholic
  food:
    tapioca: 6 manioc **7** cassava

Central America
  land form: 7 isthmus
  countries: 6 Belize, Panama **8** Hon-duras **9** Costa Rica, Guatemala, Nica-ragua **10** El Salvador
  bordered by: 6 Mexico, **8** Colombia **12** Caribbean Sea, North America, Pacific Ocean, South America
  capital city: 7 Managua, San Jose **8** Belmopan **10** Panama City **11** San Salvador, Tegucigalpa **13** Guatemala City
  river: 3 New **4** Axul, Coco, Sico, Tuma, Ulua, Wawa **5** Aguan, Chepo, Hondo, Lempa, Wauks **6** Chixoy, Grande, Pasion, Patuca, Sulaco, Waspuk **7** Motagua, Paulaya, San Juan, Sarstun, Segovia **8** Kukalaya **9** Choluteca, Escondido **10** Chucunague **11** Prinzapolca
  lake: 5 Gatun, Guija, Yojoa **7** Atitlan, Managua **9** Nicaragua, Peten Itza
  mountain: 4 Maya, Pija **5** Colon, Huapi, Minas, Pando **6** Blanco **7** Dipilto, Gongora, San Blas **8** Brew-ster, Dariense, Isabelia, San Pablo, Santa Ana **9** Esperanza **14** Chirripo Grande
  people: 3 Mam **5** Zambo **6** Indian, Ladino, Quiche **7** mestizo **8** Miskitas **10** Black Carib, Cakchiquel
  animal: 5 tapir **6** agouti **7** opossum,

peccary **8** anteater, kinkajou, mar-moset **9** armadillo, porcupine, tree sloth **12** howler monkey, spider monkey **14** capuchin monkey

Central Amerind
  language branch: 9 Oto-Mangue **10** Uto-Aztecan **11** Kiowa-Tanoan

central city 8 core city, downtown **9** inner city, urban area **10** metropolis **16** business district, metropolitan area

central idea 3 nut **4** core, crux, gist, meat **5** heart, theme **6** kernel **7** es-sence **9** main point

centralization 5 focus **11** convergence **13** concentration, consolidation

centralize 5 focus, unify **6** center, gather **7** collect, compact **8** center on, coalesce, converge, pinpoint **9** inte-grate **10** congregate **11** concentrate, consolidate

central part 4 core, crux, gist, pith **5** heart **6** center, kernel **7** nucleus

century
  abbreviation of: 4 cent
  French: 6 siecle

cephalopod 5 squid **7** mollusk, octo-pus **8** nautilus **10** cuttlefish

ceramic ware 5 china, glass **7** pottery **8** crockery **9** chinaware, glassware, porcelain, stoneware **10** enamelware **11** earthenware

ceratopsid
  type of: 8 dinosaur
  member: 10 Torosaurus **11** Mono-clonius, Triceratops **13** Protocera-tops, Styracosaurus **14** Psittacosaurus

Ceratosaurus
  type of: 8 dinosaur
  period: 8 Jurassic

Cerberus
  form: 3 dog
  father: 6 Typhon
  mother: 7 Echidna
  sibling: 5 Hydra **7** Orthrus **8** Chi-maera **10** Nemean lion **12** Theban Sphinx
  number of heads: 5 three
  guarded: 10 Underworld

Cercopes
  race of: 6 Gnomes

cereal 4 bran, corn, oats, rice, seed **5** grain, grass, gruel, plant, wheat **6** bar-ley, pablum **7** oatmeal, pabulum **8** porridge

cerebellum
  part of: 5 brain
  controls: 7 balance **8** movement

cerebrum
  part of: 5 brain
  controls: 6 seeing **7** hearing, tasting **8** deciding, feelings, learning, smelling, thinking, touching **9** awareness **11** remembering

ceremonial 4 rite **6** formal, ritual **7** lit-urgy, service **8** ceremony **9** formality, sacrament **10** liturgical, observance **11** celebration, ritualistic

ceremonialize 7 observe **9** celebrate, ritualize **11** commemorate

ceremonious 5 exact, fussy, rigid, stiff **6** formal, proper, solemn **7** careful, correct, pompous, precise **8** starched **9** dignified **10** methodical, meticulous **11** punctilious

ceremony 4 rite **6** custom, nicety, ritual **7** amenity, decorum, pageant, service **8** function, protocol **9** etiquette, formality, propriety **10** observance, politeness **11** celebration, formalities **13** commemoration

Cerenkov, Pavel Alekseevich
    field: 7 physics
    nationality: 7 Russian
    discovered: 12 cause of light **14** Cerenkov effect

Ceres
    origin: 5 Roman
    goddess of: 11 agriculture
    corresponds to: 7 Demeter

certain 4 sure **5** valid **6** secure **7** assured, express, settled, special **8** absolute, cocksure, definite, positive, reliable, specific **9** confident, convinced, satisfied **10** conclusive, individual, inevitable, particular, undeniable, undisputed, undoubtful, undoubting, unshakable **11** indubitable, inescapable, irrefutable, unalterable, unequivocal, unqualified **12** indisputable, unchangeable, unmistakable, well-grounded **13** bound to happen, incontestable **14** unquestionable **16** incontrovertible

certainly 5 truly **6** indeed, surely **7** for sure **8** of course **9** decidedly **10** absolutely, definitely, positively **11** indubitably, undoubtedly **13** unequivocally, without a doubt **14** unquestionably **21** beyond a shadow of a doubt

Certain Smile, A
    author: 14 Francoise Sagan

certainty 4 fact **5** faith, trust **6** belief, surety **7** reality, sure bet **8** sureness **9** actuality, assurance, certitude, sure thing **10** confidence, conviction **11** presumption **12** positiveness **13** inevitability **14** conclusiveness, inescapability **17** authoritativeness

certificate 4 deed **6** permit **7** diploma, license, voucher **8** document, warranty **9** affidavit **10** credential **11** testimonial **13** authorization **14** authentication

certification 7 voucher **8** approval **10** validation **11** endorsement **12** confirmation, ratification, verification **13** authorization, corroboration **14** authentication, substantiation

certify 4 aver **5** swear, vouch **6** assure, attest, ratify, second, verify **7** confirm, declare, endorse, support, warrant, witness **8** notarize, sanction, validate

9 authorize, guarantee, testify to **10** underwrite **11** corroborate **12** authenticate, give one's word, substantiate

certitude 5 faith, trust **6** belief, surety **8** reliance, sureness **9** assurance, certainty **10** confidence **12** positiveness **14** conclusiveness

cerulean 4 blue **5** azure **6** cobalt **7** sky blue **9** clear blue

Cervantes Saavedra, Miguel de
    author of: 20 Don Quixote de la Mancha

Cesar Birotteau
    author: 14 Honore de Balzac

cessation 3 end **4** halt, stay, stop **5** pause **6** ending, recess **7** ceasing, halting, respite **8** quitting, stopping, surcease **9** desisting **10** concluding, leaving off, suspension **11** adjournment, breaking off, termination **12** interruption **13** coming to a halt, discontinuing **14** discontinuance

c'est la vie 9 that's life **10** such is life

Cestus
    girdle of: 5 Venus

cetacean 4 apod, orca **5** whale **6** beluga, mammal **7** cetacea, dolphin, dowfish, grampus, narwhal **8** porpoise, sturgeon **9** blue whale **11** baleen whale, killer whale

Cetinje
    capital of: 10 Montenegro

Ceylon *see* **8** Sri Lanka

Cezanne, Paul
    born: 6 France **13** Aix-en-Provence
    artwork: 7 Bathers **11** Card Players **13** The Black Clock, The Railway Out **14** Uncle Dominique **15** La Maison du Pendu **16** The Suicide's House **17** Grandes Baigneuses **19** Woman with a Coffee Pot **36** Mont-Sainte-Victoire with Large Pine Trees

Chabrier, (Alexis) Emmanuel
    born: 6 Ambert, France
    composer of: 6 Espana **7** L'Etoile **10** Gwendoline **12** Marche Joyeuse **14** Le Roi Malgre Lui **18** King Despite Himself **19** Une Education Manquee

Chad
    other name: 5 Tchad
    capital/largest city: 8 Fort-Lamy, N'Djamena
    others: 3 Ati, Bol, Lai, Mao **4** Fada, Faya, Sarh **5** Mongo **6** Abeche, Bongor **7** Largeau, Moundou **8** Moussoro
    monetary unit: 5 franc **7** centime
    lake: 4 Chad
    mountain: 7 Tibesti, Touside
    highest point: 9 Emi Koussi
    river: 5 Chari **6** Logone **8** Bahraouk
    physical feature:
        plateau: 6 Ennedi
    people: 4 Arab, Daza, Maba, Sara, Teda, Tubu **5** Barma, Hakka, Kreda, Massa **6** Fulani, Kotoko, Toubou, Wadaii **7** Kamadja, Kanembu, Moundan

    language: 4 Sara **5** Turku **6** Arabic, French
    religion: 5 Islam **7** animism **12** Christianity

Chadband
    character in: 10 Bleak House
    author: 7 Dickens

Chadic
    language family: 11 Afro-Asiatic **13** Hamito-Semitic
    includes: 5 Hausa
    spoken in: 6 Africa **8** Lake Chad

Chadwick, James
    field: 7 physics
    nationality: 7 British
    discovered: 7 neutron
    awarded: 10 Nobel Prize

chafe 3 rub **4** boil, burn, foam, fume, rage, rasp **6** abrade, rankle, scrape, seethe **7** scratch **9** be annoyed **11** be irritated

chaff 3 bug, kid, rag, rib **4** josh, junk, pods, razz, ride, slag, twit **5** dross, hulls, husks, jolly, trash, waste **6** banter, debris, litter, refuse, rubble, shells, shoddy, shucks **7** kidding, ragging, remnant, residue, ribbing, rubbish, waggery **8** badinage, chaffing, leavings, raillery, ridicule **9** sweepings **9** give and take

chaffing 6 banter **7** jesting, joshing, kidding, ragging, ribbing, waggery **8** badinage, raillery

chafing 5 harsh **6** fuming **7** rasping, rubbing **8** abrading, abrasive **10** irritating

Chagall, Marc
    born: 6 Liosno, Liozno, Russia
    artwork: 8 Birthday, Cockcrow **9** The Circus, The Red Sun **10** The Juggler **11** Over Vitebsk **12** The Violinist **14** Double Portrait, I and the Village **16** The Jewish Wedding **17** Lovers with Rooster **20** Paris Through My Window

chagrin 5 shame **6** dismay **8** distress **11** humiliation **13** embarrassment, mortification

chagrined 7 abashed, ashamed **9** mortified **10** humiliated **11** embarrassed

Chahiksichhiks *see* **6** Pawnee

chain 3 fob **5** cable, links **7** shackle **8** necklace **10** metal links **11** linked cable
    abbreviation: 2 ch

Chain, Ernst Boris
    field: 12 biochemistry
    nationality: 7 British
    discovered: 10 penicillin
    worked with: 6 Florey **7** Fleming
    awarded: 10 Nobel Prize

Chained Lady
    constellation of: 9 Andromeda

chains 3 tie **4** bind, lash, moor **5** bonds, irons, tie up, train **6** fasten, fetter, secure, series, string, tether **7**

bondage, fetters, manacle, serfdom, shackle, slavery **8** leg irons, manacles, sequence, shackles **9** handcuffs, servitude, thralldom **10** put in irons, succession **11** enslavement, subjugation

chair 4 seat **5** bench, couch, sedan stool **6** chaise, lounge, rocker, settee, throne **7** conduct, ottoman **11** preside over **16** presiding officer

chairman 4 head **5** chair, emcee **6** leader **7** manager, preside, speaker **8** director **9** chairlady, executive, moderator **10** chairwoman, supervisor **11** chairperson, toastmaster **13** administrator **16** presiding officer **18** master of ceremonies

Chair of Forgetfulness
    form: 4 seat
    made of: 5 stone
    location: 10 Underworld

chaise 3 gig **4** shay **5** chair **6** daybed, longue, lounge **7** calesin **8** carriage, duchesse

chalcedony 3 gem **4** onyx, opal, sard **5** agate, prase **6** jasper, plasma, quartz, silica **7** catseye, mineral, opaline, sardius **8** hematite, sardonyx **9** carnelian **10** bloodstone, heliotrope **11** chrysoprase **12** semiprecious **14** silicon dioxide

Chaldean 4 seer **5** magic **6** Syriac **7** Aramaic, semitic **8** magician **9** astrology, enchanter, Nabonidus **10** astrologer, Babylonian, soothsayer **12** Nabopolassar **14** Nebuchadnezzar

chalice 3 cup **5** grail **6** goblet, vessel

chalk 4 draw **6** crayon, pastel, sketch **9** limestone

chalk up 4 earn **5** score **6** attain, charge, credit **7** achieve, ascribe

chalky 3 wan **4** pale **5** ashen, white **6** pallid **7** powdery **8** blanched **9** bloodless

challenge 3 bid, tax, try **4** dare, defy, gage, test **5** doubt, trial **6** demand, impute, summon **7** defiant, dispute, summons **8** question **15** take exception to **20** fling down the gauntlet

chamber 4 diet, hall, room **5** board, court, house, salon **6** office, parlor **7** bedroom, boudoir, council **8** assembly, congress **9** apartment

Chamberlain, Owen
    field: 7 physics
    developed: 8 atom bomb
    awarded: 10 Nobel Prize

Chamberlain, Richard
    real name: 24 George Richard Chamberlain
    born: 12 Los Angeles CA
    roles: 6 Shogun **9** Dr Kildare **10** Wallenberg **13** The Thorn Birds **17** The Bourne Identity **21** The Count of Monte Cristo

Chamberlain, Wilt (Wilton Norman)

nickname: 6 Dipper **12** Wilt the Stilt
sport: 10 basketball
position: 5 coach **6** center
team: 16 Los Angeles Lakers **17** Philadelphia 76ers **20** Philadelphia Warriors, San Francisco Warriors **21** San Diego Conquistadors

chambermaid
    French: 14 femme de chambre

chambord
    type: 7 liqueur
    origin: 6 France
    flavor: 14 black raspberry

chameleon 4 newt **6** lizard **8** renegade, turncoat **10** fickleness **14** changeableness

champ 4 bite, chew, gnaw **5** chomp, crush, grind, munch **6** crunch **8** champion

champagne 4 fizz **6** bubbly
    type: 4 wine
    drink: 7 the Pope
    with white wine: 8 Cold Duck
    with orange juice: 6 Mimosa
    measure: 6 magnum **8** jeroboam, rehoboam **9** balthazar **10** methuselah, salmanazar **14** Nebuchadnezzar

Champaigne, Philippe de
    born: 7 Belgium **8** Brussels
    artwork: 6 Ex Voto **17** Cardinal Richelieu **26** The Adoration of the Shepherds

champion 3 aid **4** abet, back **6** backer, defend, master, uphold, victor, winner **7** espouse, paladin, paragon, promote, support **8** advocate, defender, fight for, laureate, promoter, speak for, upholder **9** battle for, conqueror, protector, supporter **10** stand up for, vanquisher **11** protagonist, title holder

Champion
    constellation of: 7 Perseus

championship 3 cup **5** crown, title **7** backing, defense, support, winning **8** advocacy, espousal

Chan, Charlie
    creator: 15 Earl Derr Biggers
    actors: 7 E. L. Parks **10** George Kuwa **11** Warner Oland, Sidney Toler **13** Roland Winters, Kamiyama Sojin
    films: 7 The Trap **8** Jade Mask **11** Dead Men Tell **13** Shanghai Cobra, The Chinese Cat, The Black Camel **16** House Without a Key **17** Castle in the Desert, Behind that Curtain

chance 3 try **4** fall, fate, luck, risk **5** lucky, occur **6** befall, danger, gamble, happen, hazard, random **7** attempt, destiny, fortune, turn out, venture **8** accident, jeopardy, occasion **9** come about, fortunate, unplanned **10** accidental, fortuitous, likelihood, likeliness, providence, undesigned, unexpected, unforeseen **11** opportunity, possibility, probability, speculation, unlooked for **12** happenstance **13** unintentional **14** unpremeditated

chance upon 4 find, meet **7** learn of, run into **8** come upon, discover **9** encounter, light upon **10** happen upon **11** stumble upon

chancy 4 iffy **5** dicey, risky **6** touchy, tricky **7** dubious, erratic, unsound **8** doubtful **9** hazardous, uncertain, whimsical **10** capricious, precarious **11** speculative, venturesome **13** problematical, unpredictable

chandelier 11 hanging lamp **12** candleholder **15** lighting fixture

Chandler, Jeff
    real name: 10 Ira Grossel
    born: 10 Brooklyn NY
    roles: 7 Cochise **11** Broken Arrow **17** Merrill's Marauders

Chandler, Raymond
    author of: 11 The Big Sleep **14** The Long Goodbye **16** Farewell My Lovely
    born: 7 England
    character: 13 Philip Marlowe
    screenplay: 13 The Blue Dahlia **15** Double Indemnity **17** Strangers on a Train

Chaney, Lon
    real name: 12 Alonso Chaney
    son: 9 Creighton (Lon Chaney Jr)
    nickname: 19 Man of a Thousand Faces
    born: 17 Colorado Springs CO
    roles: 14 The Unholy Three **18** Tell It to the Marines **20** Hunchback of Notre Dame, The Phantom of the Opera

Chaney, Lon Jr
    real name: 9 Creighton
    father: 3 Lon
    born: 14 Oklahoma City OK
    roles: 6 Lennie **8** The Mummy **10** The Wolf Man **12** Of Mice and Men, Son of Dracula **20** Frankenstein's Monster

change 4 swap, turn, vary **5** alter, coins, shift, trade **6** modify, mutate, recast, reform, silver, switch **7** convert, novelty, remodel, replace, restyle, shuffle, variety, veering **8** pin money, swapping, transfer **9** deviation, diversion, exception, restyling, transform, transmute, turn about, variation **10** alteration, conversion, difference, remodeling, reorganize, revolution, small coins, substitute **11** fluctuation, pocket money, reformation **12** metamorphose, modification, substitution, transmogrify **13** make different, metamorphosis, revolutionize, transmutation, transposition **14** reorganization, transformation **15** transfiguration

changeable 6 fickle, fitful **7** erratic, flighty, mutable, varying **8** unstable, unsteady, variable, volatile **9** deviating, irregular, mercurial, uncertain **10** capricious, inconstant, modifiable, reversible **11** alternating, convertible, fluctuating, vacillating **13** transformable

change in plan
French: **8** demarche

changeless 4 fast **5** fixed **6** stable **7** abiding, certain, durable, eternal, lasting **8** constant, enduring **9** immutable, steadfast, unvarying **10** unshakable **11** everlasting, unalterable **12** indissoluble

changelessness 9 certainty, constancy, stability **10** durability, permanence **12** immutability **13** steadfastness

change of heart 10 conversion **16** change of attitude

changeover 10 conversion

channel 3 cut **4** gash, lead, send **5** guide, route, steer **6** convey, course, direct, furrow, groove, gutter, strait, trough **7** narrows, passage **11** watercourse **21** avenue of communication

Channing, Carol
born: **9** Seattle WA
roles: **10** Hello Dolly **22** Gentlemen Prefer Blondes, Thoroughly Modern Millie

chanson 4 song

Chanson de Roland
also: **12** Song of Roland
author: **7** unknown
character: **4** Aude **6** Turpin **7** Ganelon, Marsile, Olivier **11** Charlemagne, Twelve Peers
foe: **8** Saracens
knight: **7** paladin

chant 2 om **3** ode **4** hymn, lied, sing, song **5** carol, croon, dirge, elegy, psalm, theme, trill, troll **6** chorus, intone, melody, monody, strain **7** chanson, chorale, descant **8** canticle, doxology, threnody, vocalize **9** homophony, monophony, offertory, plainsong **11** Gloria Patri **14** Gregorian chant

chanteuse 6 singer (female)

chaos 4 mess **5** furor **6** bedlam, jumble, muddle, tumult, uproar **7** turmoil **8** disarray, disorder, upheaval **9** agitation, commotion, confusion **10** turbulence **11** pandemonium **12** discomposure **14** disarrangement **15** disorganization

Chaos
origin: **5** Greek
personifies: **9** confusion

chaotic 7 jumbled, mixed-up, muddled, tangled **8** confused **9** confusing, illogical, turbulent **10** disjointed, incoherent, in disarray **11** unorganized **12** disorganized **13** disharmonious

chap 3 boy, dry, guy, jaw, lad, man, rap **4** chop, gent **5** bloke, buyer, crack, knock, split **6** fellow, redden,

split, stroke **7** fissure, roughen **8** customer **9** purchaser

chapbook 7 garland **8** treasury **9** anthology **10** collection **11** florilegium

chapeau 3 hat

chapel 6 church, shrine **7** oratory **9** sanctuary **10** house of God, tabernacle **14** place of worship

chaperon, chaperone 5 guard, watch **6** duenna, escort **7** oversee **8** guardian, shepherd **9** accompany, attendant, custodian, protector, safeguard **11** keep an eye on

chaperoned 7 oversaw **8** attended, escorted **10** supervised **11** accompanied

chapfallen 6 droopy **8** cast down, dejected **9** depressed

chaplain 4 abbe **5** padre, rabbi, vicar **6** cleric, curate, father, parson, pastor, priest, rector **7** Holy Joe **8** minister, preacher, reverend, sky pilot **9** churchman, clergyman **12** ecclesiastic

chaplet 4 band **6** fillet, wreath **7** circlet, coronet

Chaplin, Charlie
real name: **24** Sir Charles Spencer Chaplin
nickname: **14** the Little Tramp
wife: **10** Oona O'Neill **15** Paulette Goddard
daughter: **9** Geraldine
born: **6** London **7** England
director of/roles: **6** The Kid **8** The Tramp **9** Limelight **10** City Lights **11** Modern Times, The Gold Rush **15** Monsieur Verdoux **16** The Great Dictator

Chaplin, Geraldine
father: **14** Charlie Chaplin
mother: **17** Oona O'Neill Chaplin
born: **13** Santa Monica CA
roles: **12** The Hawaiians **13** Doctor Zhivago

chapter 3 era **4** body, part, span, unit **5** group, phase **6** branch, clause, period **7** episode, portion, section **8** division **9** affiliate **11** subdivision

char 4 burn, sear **5** singe **6** scorch **9** carbonize **10** incinerate

character 4 part, role, self **5** being, honor **6** makeup, nature, person, traits, weirdo **7** honesty, oddball, persona **8** goodness, morality, original, specimen **9** eccentric, integrity, odd person, qualities, rectitude **10** attributes, individual, one-of-a-kind **11** personality, uprightness **13** individuality, moral strength **15** distinctiveness **16** dramatis personae

characteristic 4 mark **5** trait **6** aspect **7** earmark, feature, quality, typical **8** property, symbolic **9** attribute, mannerism, specialty, trademark **10** emblematic, indicative **11** distinctive, peculiarity **14** distinguishing, representative

characterization 8 portrait **9** depiction, picturing, portrayal **11** delineation, description **12** representing **14** representation

characterize 4 mark **5** class **6** define, depict, typify **7** earmark, portray **8** classify, describe, indicate **9** designate, represent **11** distinguish

characterless 4 weak **5** vague **6** anemic **11** nondescript **13** indeterminate **14** expressionless

Characters of Shakespeare's Plays, The
author: **14** William Hazlitt

Charcot, Jean Martin
nationality: **6** French
father of: **9** neurology

Chardin, Jean Baptiste Simeon
born: **5** Paris **6** France
artwork: **7** The Kiss **8** The Grace **14** Young Governess **16** The Copper Cistern **17** Attributes of Music **19** Attributes of the Arts **28** Rayfish Cat and Kitchen Utensils

charge 3 ask, bid, fee **4** care, cost, duty, fill, heap, lade, levy, load, pack, pile, rate, rush, toll **5** beset, blame, debit, exact, onset, order, price, stack, storm, stuff **6** accuse, advice, amount, assail, assess, assign, attack, come at, demand, direct, enjoin, impute, indict, sortie, summon **7** ascribe, assault, bidding, command, control, custody, dictate, expense, keeping, payment, require **8** call upon, instruct, storming **9** attribute, complaint, direction, enjoining, onslaught **10** accusation, allegation, assessment, indictment, injunction, management, protection **11** arraignment, incriminate, instruction, safekeeping, supervision **12** delay payment, guardianship, jurisdiction **14** administration, lay the blame for, request payment **15** superintendence **16** put on one's account

chargeable 6 liable **10** answerable **11** responsible

charged 5 taxed, tense **6** blamed, filled, levied, loaded, priced **7** accused, ordered, uptight **8** assessed, attacked, exhorted, mandated, prepared **9** commanded, entrusted **10** accusation, allegation, indictment

Charge of the Light Brigade, The
author: **18** Alfred Lord Tennyson
director: **13** Michael Curtiz
cast: **10** David Niven, Errol Flynn, Nigel Bruce **11** Donald Crisp **13** Patric Knowles **15** Henry Stephenson **17** Olivia de Havilland
setting: **6** Russia

charger 5 horse, mount, steed **6** vessel **7** accuser, platter **8** warhorse

charge with 5 trust **6** assign, commit **7** consign, entrust **8** delegate, hand over, turn over **9** authorize

chariot 3 car **5** buggy **7** phaeton, vehicle **8** carriage

Charioteer
  constellation of: **6** Auriga

Chariots of Fire
  director: **10** Hugh Hudson
  cast: **7** Ian Holm **8** Ben Cross (Harold Abrahams) **11** John Gielgud, Nigel Havers **12** Ian Charleson (Eric Liddell)
  Oscar for: **5** score (Vangelis) **6** script **7** picture

charisma 5 charm **6** allure, appeal **7** glamour **8** presence, witchery **9** magnetism, sex appeal **10** bewitchery **11** enchantment, fascination **14** attractiveness

charitable 4 kind **6** giving, kindly **7** lenient, liberal **8** generous, gracious, tolerant **9** bounteous, bountiful, forgiving, indulgent **10** almsgiving, benevolent, munificent, open-handed **11** considerate, kindhearted, magnanimous, sympathetic, warmhearted **12** eleemosynary, sympathizing **13** philanthropic, understanding

charitableness 10 generosity, liberality **11** benevolence **12** philanthropy **13** bountifulness **14** openhandedness **15** humanitarianism

Charites *see* **6** Graces

charity 3 aid **4** alms, fund, gift, help, love **6** bounty, giving **7** handout **8** altruism, donating, good will, goodness, humanity, kindness, offering, sympathy **9** benignity, donations, endowment, tolerance **10** alms-giving, assistance, compassion, generosity **11** benefaction, benevolence, fundraising, munificence **12** graciousness, philanthropy **13** contributions, financial help, love of mankind **14** openhandedness

charlatan 4 fake **5** cheat, fraud, quack **7** cozener **8** deceiver, imposter, impostor, swindler **9** trickster **10** mountebank **16** confidence artist

Charles, Nick and Nora
  characters in: **10** The Thin Man
  author: **7** Hammett
  pet dog **4** Asta

Charleston 5 dance **13** ballroom dance
  capital of: **9** W Virginia

Charlie's Angels
  character: **10** Jill Monroe, John Bosley, Kris Munroe **12** Kelly Garrett **13** Sabrina Duncan **15** Charlie Townsend
  cast: **10** Cheryl Ladd, David Doyle **11** Jaclyn Smith, Kate Jackson **18** Farah Fawcett-Majors
  voice of Charlie: **12** John Forsythe

Charlotte's Web
  author: **7** E B White
  Charlotte: **6** spider
  saved: **6** Wilbur (piglet)

Charly
  director: **11** Ralph Nelson
  based on story by: **11** Daniel Keyes (Flowers for Algernon)
  cast: **10** Leon Janney, Lilia Skala **11** Claire Bloom **13** Dick van Patten **14** Cliff Robertson
  Oscar for: **5** actor (Robertson)

charm 4 draw, grip, lure, take **5** magic, spell **6** allure, amulet, bauble, cajole, engage, please, seduce, turn on **7** attract, beguile, bewitch, conjure, delight, enchant, gratify, sorcery, trinket, win over **8** charisma, enthrall, entrance, ornament, talisman **9** captivate, enrapture, fascinate, magnetism **10** allurement, attraction, cast a spell, lucky piece **11** conjuration, enchantment, fascination, incantation, work magic on

Charmed
  network: **2** WB
  cast: **10** Drew Fuller (Chris Halliwell) **11** Brian Krause (Leo), Rose McGowan (Paige Matthews) **12** Alyssa Milano (Phoebe Halliwell), Finola Hughes (Patty Halliwell) **13** Dorian Gregory (Darryl Morris), Julian McMahon (Cole Turner) **14** Shannen Doherty (Prue Halliwell) **15** Holly Marie Combs (Piper Halliwell)

charmer 4 vamp **5** belle, siren **9** enchanter, temptress **11** enchantress, femme fatale, spellbinder

charming 6 lovely **7** likable, winning, winsome **8** alluring, engaging, enticing, fetching, graceful, magnetic, pleasing **9** agreeable **10** attractive, bewitching, delightful, enchanting, entrancing **11** captivating, charismatic, enthralling, fascinating **12** irresistible

charmless 4 dull **5** blunt **6** dreary **9** repulsive, unlikable, unlovable **10** unpleasant **12** disagreeable, unattractive

Charon
  father: **6** Erebus
  mother: **3** Nyx
  occupation: **8** ferryman
  river: **4** Styx

Charops
  epithet of: **8** Hercules
  means: **14** with bright eyes

Charpentier, Gustave
  born: **6** Dieuze, France
  composer of: **6** Julien, Louise **18** Impressions of Italy

chart 3 map, pie **4** plan, plot **5** draft, graph, table **6** design, draw up, lay out, map out, scheme, sketch **7** diagram, outline **8** tabulate **9** blueprint, delineate **10** tabulation

charter 3 let **4** deed, hire, rent **5** grant, lease **6** employ, engage, permit **7** compact, license **8** contract, covenant, sanction **9** agreement, authority, authorize, franchise **10** commission, concession

Charterhouse of Parma, The
  author: **23** Marie Henri Beyle Stendhal
  character: **8** Marietta **10** Count Mosca **11** Clelia Conti **14** Gina Pietranera **16** Fabrizio del Dongo

chartreuse
  type: **7** liqueur
  origin: **6** France **15** Carthusian monks
  flavor: **4** herb
  color: **5** green **6** yellow
  with apricot brandy: **13** Golden Slipper
  with gin: **5** Bijou **9** Green Lady

chary 3 shy **4** wary **5** alert, cagey, leery **7** careful, guarded, heedful, prudent, sparing **8** cautious, hesitant, vigilant, watchful **10** economical, suspicious **11** circumspect, distrustful

Charybdis
  form: **7** monster
  father: **8** Poseidon
  mother: **4** Gaea
  identified with: **9** whirlpool

chase 3 dog **4** hunt, oust, rout, shoo, tail **5** drive, evict, hound, quest, stalk, track, trail **6** dispel, follow, pursue, shadow **7** cast out, go after, hunting, pursuit, repulse, scatter **8** pursuing, run after, send away, stalking, tracking **9** drive away, following **11** put to flight, send packing

Chase, Chevy
  real name: **19** Cornelius Crane Chase
  born: **9** New York NY
  roles: **4** Hero **6** Fletch **8** Foul Play, Vacation **10** Caddyshack **11** Spies Like Us, Three Amigos **17** Saturday Night Live

chasm 3 gap, pit **4** gulf, hold, rift **5** abyss, break, cleft, crack, gorge, gulch, split **6** breach, cavity, crater, divide, ravine **7** fissure **8** crevasse

chasseur 6 hunter

chaste 4 pure **5** clean **6** decent, modest, severe, strict **7** austere, classic, precise, sinless **8** virginal, virtuous **9** continent, righteous, unadorned, unsullied, untainted, wholesome **10** immaculate, restrained **11** clean-living, uncorrupted **12** unornamented **13** unembellished

chasten 5 chide, scold **6** berate, punish, rebuke **7** censure, reprove, upbraid **8** admonish, chastise, reproach **9** reprimand **10** discipline, take to task

chastened 7 humbled **8** contrite, penitent **9** repentant **10** remorseful **18** conscience-stricken

chastise 4 beat, flog, whip **5** chide, roast, scold, spank, strap **6** berate, punish, rebuke, thrash **7** censure, chasten, correct, reprove, scourge, upbraid **8** admonish, call down, penalize, reproach **9** castigate, criticize, reprimand **10** discipline, take to task,

chastisement tongue-lash **15** call on the carpet **16** fulminate against, haul over the coals

chastisement 10 correction, discipline, punishment **11** castigation **12** reprimanding

chastity 6 purity **8** celibacy **9** innocence, virginity **10** abstinence, continence, singleness **12** bachelorhood, spinsterhood **14** abstemiousness
goddess of: **5** Diana, Fauna **7** Artemis, Bona Dea

chasuble 6 casual **7** garment **8** vestment

Chasuble, Reverend Canon
character in: **27** The Importance of Being Earnest
author: **5** Wilde

chat 3 gab, rap **4** talk **5** prate **7** chatter, palaver, prattle **8** chitchat, converse **10** chew the fat, chew the rag, rap session **11** talk session **12** conversation **13** confabulation **16** heart-to-heart talk

chateau 4 wine **6** castle, estate **7** mansion **8** chatelet **12** country house

Chateaubriand, Francois Rene
author of: **4** Rene **5** Atala **10** Los Natchez, The Martyrs **19** Memoires d'Outre-tombe **24** Memoirs from Beyond the Tomb

Chateau d'If
prison in: **21** The Count of Monte Cristo
author: **5** Dumas (pere)

Chateaupers, Phoebus de
character in: **23** The Hunchback of Notre Dame
author: **4** Hugo

chattel 4 gear **6** things **7** effects **8** movables **9** trappings **10** belongings **13** accoutrements, paraphernalia **15** personal effects **19** personal possessions

chatter 3 gas **4** blab, talk **5** clank, click, prate **6** babble, gabble, gibber, gossip, jabber, patter **7** blabber, blather, clatter, palaver, prattle, talking, twaddle **8** blabbing, chitchat, idle talk, talk idly **11** confabulate **14** chitterchatter

chatterbox 6 gabber, gasbag, gossip, talker **7** babbler, tattler, windbag **8** jabberer, prattler, tell tale **9** chatterer **10** talebearer, tattle tale **12** blabbermouth, blatherskite, hot-air artist **13** chatterbasket

chatty 5 gabby, gassy, gushy, talky, windy **7** gossipy, gushing, prating, verbose, voluble **8** babbling, chatting, effusive **9** garrulous, jabbering, talkative **10** blabbering, long-winded, loquacious **11** loose-lipped **12** loose-tongued **13** tongue-wagging

Chaucer, Geoffrey
author of: **18** The Canterbury Tales, Troilus and Criseyde **19** The Book of the Duchess **20** The Legend of Good Women, The Parlement of Fowles

Chauchoin, Claudette Lily
real name of: **16** Claudette Colbert

chauffeur 6 driver

chaussure 4 boot, shoe **8** footwear

chauvinism 8 jingoism **10** flag-waving, militarism, patriotism **11** nationalism **15** ethnocentricity, superpatriotism

cheap 4 base, easy, mean, poor **5** close, gaudy, petty, tacky, tight **6** common, flashy, meager, paltry, shabby, shoddy, sordid, stingy, tawdry, trashy, two-bit, vulgar **7** ignoble, immoral, miserly **8** costless, gimcrack, indecent, inferior, wretched **9** inelegant, low-priced, penurious, worthless **10** despicable, economical, effortless, in bad taste, reasonable, second-rate **11** inexpensive, tightfisted **12** contemptible

Cheaper by the Dozen
author: **14** Frank B Gilbreth (with Ernestine Gilbreth Carey)

cheat 3 con, gyp **4** bilk, dupe, fake, foil, fool, gull, hoax, rook, take **5** cozen, crook, fraud, quack, shark, trick **6** baffle, betray, defeat, delude, dodger, escape, fleece, humbug, outwit, thwart **7** deceive, defraud, mislead, swindle **8** chiseler, deceiver, hoodwink, imposter, impostor, swindler **9** bamboozle, charlatan, con artist, frustrate, trickster, victimize **10** circumvent, mountebank **11** shortchange **13** break the rules, double-crosser

check 3 bar, end, fit, gag, tab **4** curb, halt, hold, jibe, mesh, rein, slow, stay, stop, test **5** agree, block, brake, chime, choke, limit, probe, stall, study, tally **6** arrest, bridle, impede, look at, muzzle, peruse, rein in, retard, review, search, survey, thwart **7** barrier, conform, control, examine, explore, harness, inhibit, inspect, perusal, prevent, smother **8** hold back, look into, look over, obstacle, obstruct, restrain, scrutiny, stoppage, suppress **9** cessation, constrain, frustrate, harmonize, hindrance, restraint **10** circumvent, constraint, correspond, impediment, inspection, limitation, prevention, repression, scrutinize **11** examination, exploration, investigate, obstruction, prohibition, restriction, take stock of **13** investigation **18** bring to a standstill

checkered 4 pied **6** fitful, motley, seesaw, uneven, varied **7** checked, dappled, mottled, piebald **9** irregular, up-and-down **10** inconstant, variegated **11** fluctuating, vacillating **12** particolored

checkmate 4 rout, stop **6** corner, defeat, outwit, stymie, thwart **8** chess

win, deadlock **9** frustrate, overthrow **11** countermove

cheder, heder 12 Jewish school

cheek 4 jowl **5** brass, nerve **8** audacity, boldness, temerity **9** arrogance, brashness, impudence, insolence **10** brazenness, effrontery **11** forwardness **12** impertinence

cheep 4 peep **5** chirp, tweet **7** chirrup, chitter, twitter

cheer 3 cry, fun, joy, ole, rah **4** glee, hail, hope, root, warm, yell **5** bravo, shout **6** assure, buoy up, gaiety, hooray, hurrah, huzzah, shriek, uplift **7** acclaim, animate, comfort, delight, enliven, fortify, gladden, hearten, inspire, revelry **8** brighten, buoyance, buoyancy, gladness, optimism, pleasure, reassure, vivacity **9** animation, assurance, encourage, festivity, geniality, joviality, merriment, rejoicing **10** joyfulness, jubilation, liveliness **11** acclamation, high spirits, hopefulness, merrymaking, reassurance **13** encouragement

cheerful 3 gay **4** airy, glad **5** happy, jolly, merry, sunny **6** blithe, breezy, bright, cheery, elated, jaunty, jovial, joyful, joyous, lively **7** buoyant, gleeful **8** gladsome, pleasant **9** agreeable, sparkling, sprightly **10** optimistic **11** in high humor **12** high-spirited, lighthearted

cheerfulness 5 gaity **7** jollity **8** buoyancy, optimism **9** joviality, merriment **10** brightness, cheeriness **11** high spirits **16** lightheartedness

cheerless 3 sad **4** dull, glum, gray, grim **5** bleak **6** dismal, dreary, gloomy, morose, rueful, solemn, somber, sullen, woeful **7** austere, doleful, forlorn, joyless, sunless, unhappy **8** dejected, desolate, dolorous, downcast, funereal, mournful **9** miserable, saturnine, woebegone **10** depressing, despondent, dispirited, lugubrious, melancholy, spiritless, uninviting **11** comfortless, downhearted **12** disconsolate, heavy-hearted

Cheers
location: **3** bar **6** Boston
character: **4** Norm **5** Cliff, Coach, Woody **5** Lilith **7** Rebecca **9** Sam Malone **13** Carla Tortelli, Diane Chambers
cast: **9** Ted Danson **11** George Wendt, Rhea Perlman, Shelley Long **12** Kirstie Alley **13** Kelsey Grammer **14** Woody Harrelson **16** John Ratzenberger

cheer up 5 elate, pep up **6** buoy up **7** comfort, enliven, hearten **8** brighten, inspirit **9** bolster up, encourage **18** bolster one's spirits

cheery 3 gay **5** happy, jolly, merry, sunny **6** bright, joyful **9** sprightly **12** lighthearted

cheese
  French: **7** fromage
  kind: **4** bleu, blue, brie, edam, feta, jack **5** brick, colby, cream, gouda, Swiss **6** romano, samsoe **7** cheddar, cottage, fontina, gjetost, gruyere, limburg, munster, ricotta, sapsago, stilton **8** American, bel paese, cheshire, emmental, muenster, parmesan, port wine, raclette **9** camembert, jarlsberg, limburger, port salut, provolone, roquefort **10** caerphilly, Danish blue, Gloucester, gorgonzola, mozzarella, neufchatel **11** emmenthaler, liederkranz, petit suisse, port du salut, wensleydale **12** monterey jack

Cheever, John
  author of: **8** Falconer **10** Bullet Park **16** The Enormous Radio, The World of Apples **17** The Wapshot Scandal **19** The Wapshot Chronicle **20** The Way Some People Live **22** Oh What a Paradise It Seems

Chekhov, Anton
  author of: **6** Ivanov **10** The Sea Gull, Uncle Vanya **15** The Three Sisters **16** The Cherry Orchard

chemical compound 4 acid, base, enol **5** amide, amine, ester, imide **6** isomar, ketone **8** aldehyde

chemical symbols
  actinium: **2** Ac
  aluminum: **2** Al
  antimony: **2** Sb
  argon: **2** Ar
  arsenic: **2** As
  barium: **2** Ba
  boron: **1** B
  bromine: **2** Br
  cadmium: **2** Cd
  calcium: **2** Ca
  carbon: **1** C
  chlorine: **2** Cl
  chromium: **2** Cr
  cobalt: **2** Co
  columbium: **2** Cb
  copper: **2** Cu
  fluorine: **1** F
  gold: **2** Au
  hafnium: **2** Hf
  helium: **2** He
  hydrogen: **1** H
  iodine: **1** I
  iron: **2** Fe
  krypton: **2** Kr
  lead: **2** Pb
  lithium: **2** Li
  magnesium: **2** Mg
  manganese: **2** Mn
  mercury: **2** Hg
  molybdenum: **2** Mo
  neon: **2** Ne
  nickel: **2** Ni
  nitrogen: **1** N
  oxygen: **1** O
  phosphorus: **1** P
  platinum: **2** Pt
  plutonium: **2** Pu

  potassium: **1** K
  radium: **2** Ra
  radon: **2** Rn
  rhodium: **2** Rh
  rubidium: **2** Rb
  silicon: **2** Si
  silver: **2** Ag
  sodium: **2** Na
  sulfur: **1** S
  thorium: **2** Th
  tin: **2** Sn
  titanium: **2** Ti
  tungsten: **1** W
  uranium: **1** U
  xenon: **2** Xe
  zinc: **2** Zn
  zirconium: **2** Zr

chemise 4 slip **5** dress, shift, shirt, smock **6** blouse **7** garment **8** camisole, lingerie, unbelted **12** undergarment

chemist
  American: **4** Urey **5** Tatum **6** Carver **7** Axelrod, Lipmann, Pauling **8** Kornberg, Langmuir, McMillan **9** Carothers **10** Baekleland
  British: **4** Davy **5** Boyle, Chain, Soddy **6** Dalton, Ramsay **7** Faraday **8** Smithson **9** Cavendish, Priestley, Wollaston
  Dutch: **4** Hoff
  French: **5** Curie, Le Bel **6** Cuvier, Dulong **7** Pasteur **9** Gay-Lussac, Lavoisier **10** Berthollet **11** Joliot-Curie
  German: **4** Hahn **5** Krebs **6** Baeyer, Wohler **7** Glauber, Ostwald
  Italian: **8** Avogadro
  Russian: **9** Mendeleev **10** Mendeleyev
  Scottish: **5** Dewar
  Swedish: **7** Scheele **9** Arrhenius, Berzelius
  Swiss: **6** Muller

Chemosh 10 Moabite god

Chennault, Claire L
  served in: **4** WWII **15** Sino-Japanese War
  commander of: **12** Flying Tigers
  general in: **12** Army Air Force
  air advisor to: **13** Chiang Kai-shek

cherchez la femme 15 look for the woman

cheri, cherie 4 dear **10** sweetheart

cherish 4 love **5** honor, nurse, prize, value **6** dote on, esteem, revere, succor **7** care for, idolize, nourish, nurture, shelter, sustain **8** hold dear, treasure, venerate **10** appreciate, take care of

cherished 4 dear **5** loved **7** beloved, darling, dearest **8** favorite, held dear, precious **9** treasured

Cherokee
  language family: **9** Iroquoian
  location: **7** Alabama, Georgia **8** Oklahoma, Virginia **9** Tennessee **13** North Carolina, South Carolina

  associated with: **12** Trail of Tears
  scholar: **7** Sequoya

cherry
  varieties: **3** pie, pin, rum **4** bing, bird, duke, fire, sand, sour, wild **5** black, brush, choke, dwarf, Higan, Naden, sweet **6** bitter, Brazil, ground, Indian, Madden, Oregon, Taiwan, winter **7** bastard, Cayenne, Morello, Nanking, Potomac, prairie, rosebud, sargent, Spanish, St Lucie, wild red, Windsor, Yoshino **8** Barbados, Catalina, oriental, perfumed, Suriname **9** christmas, cornelian, evergreen, Jerusalem, wild black **10** west indian **11** downy ground, Hansen's bush, holly-leaved, western sand **12** clammy ground, European bird, Japanese bush, purple ground **13** European dwarf **14** European ground, false Jerusalem, purple-leaf sand **15** Australian brush **17** Japanese cornelian, Japanese flowering, north Japanese hill
  drink: **6** kirsch

cherry brandy 6 kirsch **12** Peter Heering

Cherry Orchard, The
  author: **12** Anton Chekhov
  character: **4** Anya, Gaev **5** Fiers, Varya, Yasha **7** Pischin **8** Dunyasha, Lopakhin, Trofimov **9** Charlotta **16** Madame Ranevskaya

cherub 4 amor **5** angel, child, cupid, youth **6** moppet **8** amoretto, cherubim **13** heavenly being

cherubic 7 angelic **8** innocent **9** spiritual

Cherubin
  character in: **19** The Marriage of Figaro
  author: **12** Beaumarchais

chervil
  botanical name: **20** Anthriscus cerefolium
  origin: **6** Europe, Russia
  use: **4** soup **5** salad **11** fines herbes, potato salad

Chesapeake
  author: **13** James Michener

Cheshire Cat
  character in: **28** Alice's Adventures in Wonderland
  author: **7** Carroll

chess
  also called: **9** Royal Game
  chess champion: **3** Tal **4** Euwe, Fine **6** Karpov, Lasker, Morphy **7** Fischer, Kashdan, Smyslov, Spassky **8** Alekhine, Kasparov, Philador, Steinitz **9** Anderssen, Botvinnik, Petrosian, Reshevsky **10** Capablanca
  French: **6** echecs
  German: **11** schachspiel
  horizontal rows: **4** rank
  international chess federation: **4** FIDE

patron goddess/muse: 6 Caissa
piece: 4 king, pawn, rook **5** queen **6** bishop, castle, knight **8** chessman, material
Russian: 8 shakhmat
Spanish: 7 Ajedrez
term: 3 pin **4** fork, hole **5** check, tempo **6** center **7** isolani, outpost **8** castling, majority, open file, queening, zugzwang **9** checkmate, en passant, promotion **10** fianchetto **11** zwischenzug
tied game: 4 draw **9** stalemate
vertical rows: 4 file

chest
Italian: 5 petto

chesterfield 4 coat, sofa **5** couch **8** overcoat **9** davenport

Chesterton, G K (Gilbert Keith)
author of: 20 The Man Who Was Thursday **24** The Napoleon of Notting Hill **25** The Innocence of Father Brown

chestnut 8 Castanea
varieties: 4 Cape, Wild **5** Horse, Water **6** Guiana, Marron **7** Chinese, Spanish **8** American, Eurasian, European, Japanese, Red horse **10** Dwarf horse, Moreton Bay **11** Common horse **12** Chinese water **13** European horse, Japanese horse **15** California horse

chestnut-colored 6 auburn, russet, sienna **8** cinnamon, nut-brown **11** golden-brown, rust-colored **12** reddish-brown

chest of drawers 5 chest **6** bureau, lowboy **7** cabinet, commode, dresser, highboy, tallboy **10** chiffonier

cheval 5 horse

chevalier 4 lord **5** cadet, noble **6** knight **7** gallant **8** cavalier

Chevalier, Maurice
born: 5 Paris **6** France
roles: 4 Gigi **5** Fanny **6** Can-Can **13** The Love Parade, The Merry Widow **18** Love in the Afternoon

chew 4 gnaw **5** champ, crush, grind, munch **6** crunch, nibble **8** ruminate **9** masticate

Chew
character in: 21 The Master of Ballantrae
author: 9 Stevenson

chewing-out 6 rebuke **7** censure, chiding, reproof **8** reproach, scolding **9** reprimand **10** bawling-out, upbraiding **11** castigation, reprobation **12** dressing-down, remonstrance **13** tongue-lashing

chew noisily 4 gnaw **5** chomp, gnash, grind, munch **6** crunch

chew out 5 scold **6** berate, rail at, rebuke **7** bawl out, reprove, upbraid **8** reproach **9** castigate, reprimand **10** take to task, tongue-lash **14** read the riot act

chew the fat 3 gab, gas, jaw, rap, yak **4** blab, chat, chin, talk **5** prate **6** gossip, patter **7** blather, chatter, palaver, prattle, twaddle **8** chitchat, converse, talk idly **10** chew the rag **11** confabulate **14** chitterchatter

chew the rag 4 talk

Cheyenne
language family: 9 Algonkian **10** Algonquian
location: 6 Platte **7** Montana, Wyoming **8** Oklahoma, Red River **9** Minnesota **11** South Dakota
allied with: 7 Arapaho

Cheyenne
character: 6 Smitty **13** Cheyenne Bodie
cast: 7 L Q Jones **11** Clint Walker

chez 4 with **11** at the home of

Chiang Kai-shek
leader of: 5 China **6** Taiwan
ally: 9 Sun Yat-sen
party: 10 Kuomintang **11** Nationalist
defeated by: 10 Communists
wife: 12 Soong Mei-ling

Chibcha (Muisca)
location: 6 Bogota, Panama **8** Colombia **12** South America
associated with: 8 El Dorado

Chibchan
language family: 13 Macro-Chibchan
group: 4 Cuna, Paya, Rama **5** Lenca, Xinca **7** Chibcha

chic 4 tony **5** natty, ritzy, smart, swank **6** classy, modish, snazzy, swanky **7** elegant, stylish, voguish **11** fashionable

Chicago
author: 12 Carl Sandburg

Chicago
airport: 5 O'Hare **6** Midway
baseball team: 4 Cubs **8** White Sox
basketball team: 5 Bulls
downtown area: 4 Loop
football team: 5 Bears
fort: 8 Dearborn
hockey team: 10 Black Hawks
lake: 4 Wolf **7** Calumet **8** Michigan
landmark: 10 Meigs Field, Sears Tower **12** Board of Trade, Comiskey Park, Humboldt Park, Soldier Field, Wrigley Field **13** Shedd Aquarium **15** Lincoln Monument, Merchandise Mart, Newberry Library, Wrigley Building **16** Adler Planetarium **17** Holy Name Cathedral, John Hancock Center **18** Mercantile Exchange, Prudential Building **20** Midwest Stock Exchange **21** Art Institute of Chicago **23** Museum of Contemporary Art **26** Museum of Science and Industry **27** Field Museum of Natural History
mayor: 5 Byrne, Daley **10** Washington
nickname: 9 Windy City
river: 7 Chicago **10** Des Plaines
street: 11 Wacker Drive **13** Chicago Skyway **14** Lake Shore Drive
university: 6 DePaul, Loyola **9** Roosevelt **12** Northwestern **19** University of Chicago **29** Illinois Institute of Technology

Chicago
director: 11 Rob Marshall
cast: 9 Colm Feore (Martin Harrison) **11** John C. Reilly (Amos Hart), Richard Gere (Billy Flynn) **12** Queen Latifah (Mama Morton) **14** Renee Zellweger (Roxie Hart) **18** Catherine Zeta-Jones (Velma Kelly)

chicanery 4 ruse, wile **5** craft, fraud, guile **6** deceit, duping **7** cunning, gulling, knavery, roguery **8** artifice, cozenage, trickery, villainy **9** deception, duplicity, rascality, sophistry **10** craftiness, hocus-pocus, humbuggery, subterfuge **11** hoodwinking **12** pettifoggery **13** double-dealing

chichi 4 arty **5** fussy, showy **6** flashy, frilly, garish, prissy, vulgar **7** finical, pompous, splashy **8** affected, gimcrack, overnice, precious, sissyish **9** arty-tarty, grandiose, nasty-nice **10** flamboyant **11** overrefined, pretentious **12** artsy-craftsy, ostentatious

chick
group of: 5 brood **6** clutch

Chickasaw
language family: 10 Muskhogean
location: 8 Oklahoma **9** Tennessee **11** Mississippi
related to: 7 Choctaw
member of: 19 Five Civilized Tribes

chicken, chickenhearted 3 hen **4** cock, fowl **5** layer, timid **6** afraid, coward, craven, pullet, scared, yellow **7** caitiff, dastard, fearful, gutless, rooster **8** cowardly, poltroon, timorous **9** flinching, fraidy-cat, shrinking **11** lily-livered, yellow-belly **12** fainthearted **13** pusillanimous, yellow-bellied **22** showing the white feather

chickenheartedness 8 timidity **9** cowardice **10** yellowness **11** fearfulness, poltroonery **12** timorousness **13** pusillanimity **16** faintheartedness

chide 5 scold **6** berate, rebuke **7** censure, chasten, reprove, upbraid **8** admonish, denounce, reproach **9** criticize, find fault, reprimand **10** take to task

chief 3 key **4** boss, head, lord, main **5** first, major, prime, ruler **6** leader, master, ruling **7** captain, highest, leading, monarch, primary, supreme **8** cardinal, chairman, crowning, director, dominant, foremost, greatest, overlord, overseer **9** chieftain, commander, governing, number-one, paramount, potentate, principal, sovereign, uppermost **10** prevailing, ringleader, supervisor **11** outstanding, predominant **12** preponderant **13** administrator

chief good
Latin: **11** summum bonum
chiefly 5 first **6** mainly, mostly **8** above all **9** expressly, in the main, most of all, primarily **10** especially **11** principally **12** particularly **13** predominantly
chieftan 4 boss, head **6** leader **7** captain, head man
chiffonier 6 bureau **7** dresser **8** cupboard **14** chest of drawers
chignon 3 bun **4** knot, roll **6** hairdo **9** hairpiece, hairstyle
child 3 boy, kid, lad, son, tad, tot **4** baby, girl, lass, tyke **5** youth **6** infant, moppet, rug rat **7** toddler **8** daughter, juvenile **9** little one, offspring, youngster
childbearing 5 birth **11** parturition
childbirth 8 delivery **11** confinement, parturition
French: **12** accouchement
goddess of: **4** Upis **5** Parca **6** Lucina, Matuta **7** Artemis **8** Ilithyia **10** Eileithyia
Childe Harold's Pilgrimage
author: **21** George Gordon Lord Byron
Childe Roland to the Dark Tower Came
author: **14** Robert Browning
childhood 5 youth **7** boyhood **8** girlhood **10** school days **11** adolescence, nursery days
childish 5 naive, silly **6** callow, simple **7** asinine, babyish, foolish, puerile **8** immature, juvenile **9** infantile **10** adolescent
childlike 8 childish, immature, innocent **9** ingenuous
child prodigy 7 quiz kid, whiz kid
German: **10** Wunderkind
children 4 boys, kids, sons, tads, tots **5** girls, issue, young **6** babies, result, youth **7** infants, product, progeny **9** daughters, juveniles **11** descendants
Children of Paradise
director: **11** Marcel Carne
cast: **7** Arletty **11** Albert Remay **14** Pierre Brasseur **17** Jean-Louis Barrault
Child's Garden of Verses, A
author: **20** Robert Louis Stevenson
Chile
other name: **6** Tchile
name means: **21** deepest part of the Earth
capital/largest city: **8** Santiago
others: **4** Boco, Cuya, Lebu, Lota, Ocoa, Tome **5** Angol, Arica, Cobya, Talca **6** Arauco, Calama, Curico, Gatico, Osorno, Ovalle, Serena, Temuco, Vicuna, Yumbel, Yungay **7** Caldera, Chillan, Copiapo, Iquique, Valdiva **8** Coquimbo, Rancagua, Santiago, Vallenar **9** Cauquenes **10** Concepcion, Coquembana, Valparaiso, Vina del Mar **11** Antofagasta, Puerto Montt, Punta Arenas, San Bernardo
measure: **4** vara **5** legua, linea **6** cuadra, fanega
monetary unit: **4** peso **5** libra **6** condor, escudo
weight: **5** grano, libra **7** quintal
island: **3** Luz **4** Prat **5** Byron, Guafo, Hoste, Mocha, Nueva, Nunez, Vidal **6** Chiloe, Chonos, Dawson, Easter, Lennox, Piazzi, Picton, Quilan, Riesco, Stosch, Talcan **7** Angamos, Campana, Hanover, Hermite, Pajaros, Refugio, Tranqui **8** Chauques, Clarence, Huamblin, Nalcayec, Navarino, Traiguen **13** Juan Fernandez **14** Tierra del Fuego
lake: **5** Ranco **6** Yelcho **7** Puyehue, Rupanco **8** Cochrane **10** General Paz, Llanquihue **11** Buenos Aires
mountain: **4** Maca, Toro **5** Chato, Maipo, Maipu, Paine, Potro, Pular, Torre, Yogan **6** Apiwan, Burney, Conico, Jervis, Poquis, Rincon **7** Chaltel, Copiapo, Fitzroy, Palpana, Velluda **8** Cochrane, Tronador, Yanteles **9** Tupungato
highest point: **13** Ojos del Salado
river: **3** Loa, Laja, Yali **5** Alhue, Azapa, Bravo, Bueno, Elqui, Lauca, Lluta, Maipo, Maule, Puelo, Rahue, Rapel, Stata, Vitor **6** Biobio, Camina, Choapa, Choros, Cisnes, Colina, Huasco, Limari, Morado, Palena, Poscua, Tolten **7** Copiapo **8** Valdivia
sea: **7** Pacific
physical features:
bay: **4** Cook, Eyre, Nena, Tarn **5** Lomas, Otway, Sarco **6** Darwin, Inutil, Moreno, Stokes, Tongoy **7** Dyneley, Inglesa, Skyring **8** Desolate
cape: **4** Dyer, Horn **6** Choros, Falsos, Hornos, Quilan, Tablas **7** Deseado **10** Tres Montes
channel: **5** Ancho, Cheap **6** Beagle **8** Cockburn, Moraleda
desert: **7** Atacama
gulf: **5** Ancud, Guafo, Penas **6** Arauco
isthmus: **5** Ofqui
peninsula: **5** Hardy, Lacuy **6** Taitao, Tumbes
point: **4** Toro **5** Gallo, Liles, Lobos, Loros, Morro, Talca, Tetas, Vieja **6** Cachos, Galera, Molles **7** Angamos, Lavapie
strait: **6** Nelson **8** Magellan
volcano: **5** Lanin, Maipo **6** Antuco, Llaima, Oyahue, Tacora **7** Peteroa, Socomap
people: **3** Ona **4** Auca, Inca, Onan **6** Arauca, Chango, Yahgan **7** Mapuche, mestizo, Moluche, Pampean, Patagon, Puegian, Ranquel **8** Alikuluf, Picunche, Tsonecan
author: **5** Bello **6** Donoso, Neruda
7 Mistral
conqueror: **7** Valdiva
explorer: **8** Magellan
leader: **7** Allende **8** O'Higgins, Pinochet **9** San Martin **10** Alessandri
language: **7** Spanish
religion: **13** Roman Catholic
places:
copper mine: **12** Chuquicamata
resort: **8** Portillo **10** Vina del Mar
possession: **12** Easter Island **20** Juan Fernandez Islands
feature:
cowboy: **5** huaso
dance: **5** cueca **6** pequen **9** resbalosa
shrub: **5** litre
slum: **9** callempas
tree: **5** rauli
wind instrument: **4** sicu
food:
drink: **5** pisco **6** chicha
hot red pepper: **3** aji
meat pie: **8** empanada
soup: **7** cazuela **8** caldillo
chile peppers see **15** capsicum peppers
chill, chilly 3 icy, nip, raw **4** bite, cold, cool, keen **5** aloof, brisk, crisp, fever, harsh, nippy, sharp, stiff, stony **6** arctic, biting, bitter, frigid, frosty, frozen, wintry **7** callous, coolish, cutting, glacial, hostile, iciness, rawness, shivery **8** coolness, uncaring **9** crispness, frigidity, sharpness, unfeeling **10** forbidding, frostiness, unfriendly **11** indifferent, passionless, penetrating **12** unresponsive
chilled 4 cold, iced **6** cooled, frozen **7** frosted **8** hardened **10** dispirited **11** discouraged **12** refrigerated
chilling 3 icy, raw **5** nippy, on ice **6** frigid **7** bracing, cooling **10** unfriendly
Chillingworth, Roger
character in: **16** The Scarlet Letter
author: **9** Hawthorne
chime 4 gong, peal, ring, toll **5** knell, sound **6** jingle, tinkle **7** pealing, ringing **8** carillon, ding-dong, tinkling, tollings **10** set of bells **14** tintinnabulate **16** tintinnabulation
Chimene
character in: **6** The Cid
author: **9** Corneille
chimera 5 dream, fancy **6** bubble, mirage **7** fantasy, monster, phantom **8** daydream, delusion, idle whim, illusion **9** pipe dream **10** self-deceit, shemonster **12** will-o'-the-wisp **13** castle in Spain, fool's paradise, hallucination, self-deception **14** castle in the air **24** figment of one's imagination
Chimera
form: **7** monster
father: **6** Typhon

mother: 7 Echidna
breathes: 4 fire

Chimera
  author: 9 John Barth

chimerical 6 absurd, unreal 7 utopian 8 delusive, ethereal, fabulous, fanciful, illusory, mythical, quixotic 9 fantastic, imaginary, visionary 10 impossible, phantasmal 11 nonexistent

chimney 4 flue, tube, vent 5 cleft, gully, spout, stack 6 funnel, hearth 7 opening 9 stovepipe 10 smokestack

chimpanzee 3 ape 6 animal, baboon, monkey

chin 3 gab, jaw, rap 4 chat, talk 7 chatter, palaver 8 chitchat, converse 10 chew the fat, chew the rag 11 confabulate

china 6 dishes, plates 7 pottery 8 crockery 9 chinaware, porcelain, stoneware, tableware 11 ceramicware, earthenware 14 cups and saucers

China
  other name: 3 PRC 13 Middle Kingdom 14 Flowery Kingdom 22 People's Republic of China
  capital: 6 Peking 7 Beijing
  largest city: 8 Shanghai
  others: 3 Bai, Noh 4 Ahpa, Amoy, Fuyu, Guma, Hami, Huma, Ipin, Kian, Kisi, Lini, Loho, Luta, Moho, Moyu, Niya, Noho, Omin, Rima, Saka, Sian, Taku, Tali, Tayu, Wuhu, Yaan 5 Chiai, Fusin, Kirin, Koklu, Linyu, Macao, Penki, Shasi, Soche, Taian, Talai, Tihwa, Tuyun, Wuhan, Wusih, Yenan, Yenki, Yulin, Yumen 6 Anshan, Antung, Canton, Dairen, Fuchau, Fuchow, Fushun, Hankow, Harbin, Ilhasa, Kalgan, Loyang, Lushun, Mukden, Nanhai, Ningpo, Singan, Sining, Taipei, Tsinan, Yangku, Yunnan 7 Fuskhih, Hanyang, Kunming, Lanchow, Lioyang, Mengtze, Nanking, Nanning, Paoshan, Peiping, Soochow, Taiyuan, Tatshan, Urumchi, Urumsti, Waichow, Wuchang, Yenping 8 Chinchow, Fengkiek, Fengtien, Hangchow, Kingchow, Nanchang, Shanghai, Shenyang, Siangtan, Tientsin, Tungchow, Wanchuan, Wanhsien 9 Chungking, Kiangling, Tsingyuan 10 Chiangling, Port Arthur
  school: 5 Futan 6 Peking 7 Nanking 8 Hangchow 9 Sun Yat-sen 16 Chengtu Technical
  division:
    province: 5 Honan, Hunan, Hupei, Kansu 6 Anhwei, Fukien, Shansi, Shensi, Yunnan 7 Kiangsi, Kiangsu 8 Chekiang, Kweichow, Shantung, Szechwan, Tientsin, Tsinghai 9 Kwangtung, Manchuria
    measure: 3 cho, fan, fen, pau, tou, tun, yan, yin 4 chek, chih, fang, kish, papa, quei, teke, tsan,

tsun 5 catty, chang, ching, sheng, shing 6 chupak, gungli, kungho, kungmu, tching 7 kungfen, kungyin 8 kungchih, kungshih, 9 kungching
    monetary unit: 4 cash, cent, fyng, mace, tael, tiao, yuan 5 sycee 12 jen nin piao pu
    weight: 3 fan, fen, hao, kin, ssu, tan, yin 4 chee, chin, dong, shih, tael, tsin 5 catty, chien, picul, tchin, tsien 6 kungli 7 haikwan, kungfen, kungssu, kungtun 8 kungchin 9 candareen 10 kupingtael

island: 4 Amoy 5 Macao, Matsu, Namki, Taipa 6 Chusan, Hainan, Pratas, Quemoy, Taiwan, Tinian, Yuhwan 7 Coloane, Formosa, Hungtow, Tungsha 8 Ching Hai, Chouchan, Kulangsu

lake: 3 Tai 4 Chao, Namu 5 Kaoyu, Oling, Telli 6 Bamtso, Bornor, Ebinor, Erhhai, Khanka, Lopnor, Namtso, Poyang 7 Chaling, Hungtse, Karanor, Kokonor 8 Hulunnor, Montcalm, Taroktso, Tellinor, Tienchih, Tsinghai, Tungting

sea: 6 Yellow 9 East China 10 South China

physical features:
  bay: 7 Laichow 8 Hangchow
  cape: 7 Olwanpi
  channel: 5 Bashi
  desert: 4 Gobi 5 Ordos, Shamo 7 Alashan 10 Takla Makan
  dry lake: 6 Lopnor
  gulf: 5 Pohai 6 Chihli, Tonkin 7 Pechili 9 Liaotung
  peninsula: 6 Leichu 7 Luichow 8 Liaotung
  plateau: 5 Loess 7 Tibetan
  port: 4 Amoy, Wuhu 5 Aigun, Shasi 6 Antung, Canton, Chefoo, Dairen, Ichang, Ningpo, Pakhoi, Swatow, Wuchow 7 Foochow, Hunchun, Luichow, Nanking, Samshui, Santuao, Soochow, Wenchow, Yinkkow, Yungkia 8 Changsha, Hangchow, Kiukiang, Kongmoon, Shanghai, Tengyueh, Tientsin, Tsingtao, Wanhsien 9 Kwangchow, Weihaiwei 10 Tsingkiang
  strait: 6 Hainan, Taiwan 7 Formosa
  people: 3 Han, Yis 4 Huis, Lolo, Miao, Puis 5 Hakka, Hoklo, Seres, Sinic 6 Cataia, Chuang, Johnny, Korean, Manchu, Mongol, Serian, Uighun 7 Sinaean, Tibetan
  leader: 8 Hu Jintao 9 Hu Yaobang, Mao Zedong, Sun Yat-sen, Zhou Enlai 10 Jiang Zemin, Kublai Khan, Mao Tse-tung, Zhao Ziyang 11 Genghis Khan 12 Deng Xiaoping 13 Chiang Kai-shek
  philosopher: 6 Lao-tzu 9 Confucius
  language: 7 Chinese 8 Mandarin, Shanghai 9 Cantonese
  religion: 5 Islam 6 Taoism 8 Bud-

dhism 12 Christianity, Confucianism
  place:
    palace: 6 Summer 8 Imperial 13 Forbidden City
    ruins: 9 Ming Tombs
    square: 9 Tiananmen
    wonder: 9 Great Wall
  event: 9 Long March 16 Great Leap Forward 18 Cultural Revolution 23 T'ien-an Men Square Massacre
  feature:
    boat: 4 junk
    conspirators: 10 Gang of Four
    dynasty: 3 Han, Sui 4 Chou, Ch'in, Ming, Sung, T'ang 5 Ch'ing, Shang 6 Manchu
    military academy: 7 whompoa
    watercolor: 8 shan shiu

China Syndrome, The
  director: 12 James Bridges
  cast: 9 Jane Fonda 10 Jack Lemmon, Scott Brady 14 Michael Douglas
  setting: 17 nuclear power plant

Chinatown
  director: 13 Roman Polanski
  cast: 10 John Huston 11 Faye Dunaway 13 Jack Nicholson
  Oscar for: 10 screenplay

chinaware 6 dishes, plates 7 pottery 8 crockery 9 porcelain, stoneware, tableware 11 ceramicware, earthenware 14 cups and saucers

chine 5 spine 6 dorsum 8 backbone

Chinese book of divination 6 I Ching

Chingachgook
  character in: 13 The Pathfinder 20 The Last of the Mohicans
  author: 6 Cooper

chink 3 cut, gap 4 gash, hole, rent, rift, ring, slit 5 break, clank, cleft, clink, crack, fault, split 6 breach, jangle, jingle, rattle, tinkle 7 crevice, fissure, opening 8 aperture

Chinook (Flathead)
  language family: 9 Chinookan
  location: 7 Pacific 10 Washington
  ritual: 15 head deformation

Chinookan
  tribe: 7 Chinook 8 Flathead

chintzy 5 cheap, close, dowdy, tacky, tatty, tight 6 frowzy, frumpy, shabby, sleazy, stingy 7 miserly 8 grudging, schlocky, stinting 9 niggardly, penurious 11 closefisted 12 parsimonious 13 penny-pinching

chip 3 bit, cut, hew 4 chop, gash, hack, nick 5 chunk, crumb, flake, scrap, shred, slice, split, wafer 6 chisel, morsel, paring, sliver 7 cutting, shaving, whittle 8 fragment, splinter

chipmunk 4 Chip, Dale 6 chippy, gopher, rodent 8 chipmuck, squirrel 14 ground squirrel 16 chipping squirrel

chipper 3 gay 4 pert, spry 5 alive, brisk, peppy 6 frisky, jaunty, lively 8 animated, carefree, cheerful, spirited 9 easygoing, energetic, sprightly, vivacious **12** high-spirited, light-hearted

Chippewa (Ojibwa, Ojibway)
language family: **9** Algonkian **10** Algonquian
tribe: **4** Cree **6** Ottawa **8** Chippewa **10** Missisauga
location: **6** Canada **9** Lake Huron **11** North Dakota **12** Lake Superior, Niagara Falls
leader: **7** Pontiac

CHiPS
character: **8** (Officer) Jon Baker **10** (Sgt) Joe Getraer **16** (Officer) Frank (Ponch) Poncherello
cast: **10** Robert Pine **11** Erik Estrada, Larry Wilcox

Chirico, Giorgio de
born: **5** Volos **6** Greece
artwork: **15** Enigma of the Hour **19** Enigma of an Afternoon **21** Enigma of an Autumn Night **22** Nostalgia of the Infinite **32** The Melancholy and Mystery of a Street

Chiron
also: **7** Cheiron
form: **7** centaur
father: **6** Cronos, Cronus, Kronos
mother: **7** Philyra
wife: **8** Chariclo
daughter: **6** Endeis
grandson: **6** Peleus
occupation: **7** teacher

chirp 4 peep, sing **5** cheep, chirr, tweet **7** chirrup, chitter, peeping, twitter **8** cheeping

chirrup 4 peep **5** cheep, chirp, tweet **7** chitter, twitter

chisel 3 cut, gyp **4** gull, hoax, rook, tool **5** blade, cheat, slice **6** incise
type: **4** cape, cold, wood **7** v-shaped

Chisel
constellation of: **6** Caelum

chiseler 4 fake **5** cheat, fraud, quack **7** cheater **8** swindler

Chislev 16 ninth Hebrew month

chit 3 IOU, tab **4** note **5** check **7** voucher

chitchat 3 gab **4** chat **5** prate **6** drivel, gossip **7** chatter, palaver, prattle **8** converse **9** small talk **10** chew the fat, chew the rag **11** confabulate **13** confabulation

Chitimacha
language family: **6** Tunica
location: **9** Louisiana
noted for: **8** basketry

chitter 4 peep **5** cheep, chirp, tweet **7** chatter, chirrup, twitter

chitter-chatter 3 gab **4** blab **6** babble, drivel, gabble, jabber **7** blabber, prattle, twaddle **8** chitchat **9** jabbering **16** idle conversation

chivalrous 6 polite **7** courtly, gallant **8** mannerly

chivalry 8 courtesy **9** gallantry **10** knighthood, politeness **11** courtliness

Chivery, Young John
character in: **12** Little Dorrit
author: **7** Dickens

chivy 3 nag **4** hunt, race **5** annoy, chase, chevy, hound, trail, worry **6** badger, bother, harass, pursue **7** scamper, torment

Chlidanope
form: **5** Naiad

Chloe
epithet of: **7** Demeter
means: **5** green

chloride 7 muriate **8** chemical, compound

chlorine
chemical symbol: **2** Cl

chocolate 5 brown, candy, cacao, cocoa, drink **6** bon bon **10** confection

Choctaw
language family: **10** Muskhogean
location: **7** Alabama **11** Mississippi
related to: **9** Chickasaw

Choephoroe
author: **9** Aeschylus
character: **6** Furies **7** Electra, Orestes, Pylades **9** Aegisthus **12** Clytemnestra

choice 3 say **4** A-one, best, fine, pick, vote **5** array, elite, prime, prize, stock, store, voice **6** better, opting, option, select, supply, tip-top **7** display, special, variety **8** choosing, deciding, decision, superior **9** excellent, exclusive, first-rate, preferred, selection, top drawer **10** assemblage, assortment, collection, consummate, discretion, first-class, preferable, preference, well-chosen **11** alternative, appointment, exceptional, superlative **13** determination, extraordinary

choice food 5 treat **8** delicacy

choicest part
French: **14** creme de la creme

choir 4 band **5** quire **6** angels, chorus **7** chorale, singers **10** choristers

Choirboys, The
author: **14** Joseph Wambaugh

choke 3 dam, gag **4** clog, plug **5** block, check, dam up, stuff **6** arrest, bridle, hamper, hinder, impede, plug up, retard, stifle, stop up **7** congest, garrote, inhibit, repress, smother **8** blockade, hold back, obstruct, restrain, strangle, suppress, throttle **9** constrain, constrict, suffocate **10** asphyxiate

choler 3 ire **4** fury, rage **5** anger, wrath **6** spleen, temper

choleric 3 mad **5** angry, irate, testy, vexed **6** cranky, grumpy, shirty, touchy **7** enraged, furious, grouchy, peevish, waspish **8** snappish, wrathful **9** dyspeptic, indignant, irritable, irascible, splenetic **10** infuriated, short-fused **11** contentious, hot-tempered, ill-tempered, thin-skinned **12** cantan-

kerous, sour-tempered **13** quick-tempered, short-tempered

choose 3 opt **4** like, pick, take, wish **5** adopt, elect **6** decide, desire, intend, opt for, prefer, see fit, select **7** call out, embrace, espouse, extract, fix upon, pick out, resolve **8** decide on, settle on **9** determine, single out **10** be inclined **13** commit oneself **14** make up one's mind

choosy 5 fussy, picky **7** finicky **9** selective **10** fastidious, particular **14** discriminating

chop 3 cut, hew, hit, lop **4** blow, chip, crop, cube, dice, fell, gash, hack **5** cut up, mince, slash, slice, split, swipe, whack **6** cleave, cutlet, stroke, sunder **8** fragment, rib slice **9** cotelette, pulverize

Chopin, Frederic Francois
born: **6** Poland **12** Zelazowawola
companion: **10** George Sand
composer of: **5** Etude **7** Ballade **8** Berceuse, Cat Valse, Dog Valse, Fantasie **9** Ecossaise **10** Barcarolle **11** Minute Valse **15** Andante Spianato, Heroic Polonaise (No 6), Raindrop Prelude, Winter Wind Etude **16** Shepherd Boy Etude **17** Impromptu Fantasie, Rondo a la Krakowiak **18** Revolutionary Etude **20** Butterfly's Wings Etude

choral ode
Greek: **7** parodos **8** stasimon

chord 4 cord, line, note, tone **5** music, triad **6** accord, string, tendon **7** cadence, emotion, feeling, harmony **9** harmonize

chore 3 job **4** duty, task, work **5** stint **6** burden, errand, strain **8** farm task, small job **10** assignment **13** household task **14** responsibility

choreography 5 dance **12** stage dancing **16** dance composition

chorister 6 singer **7** changer **8** choirboy

chortle 5 laugh **7** chuckle

chorus 5 choir, unity **6** accord, unison **7** concert, concord, refrain **8** glee club, one voice, response **9** antiphony, consensus, unanimity **11** concordance **12** singing group

chosen 5 elite **6** picked, sorted **7** elected **8** selected **9** picked out

Chosen, The
author: **10** Chaim Potok

Chosen see **5** Korea

Chouans, The
author: **14** Honore de Balzac

chough
group of: **10** chattering

Chowbok
character in: **7** Erewhon
author: **6** Butler

Christ, the see **5** Jesus

christen 3 dip, dub **4** name **6** launch **7**

baptize, immerse **8** dedicate, sprinkle **9** designate

Christian
character in: **16** Pilgrim's Progress
author: **6** Bunyan

Christian, Fletcher
character in: **17** Mutiny on the Bounty
authors: **4** Hall **8** Nordhoff

Christian, Linda
real name: **16** Blanca Rosa Welter
husband: **11** Tyrone Power **12** Edmund Purdom
born: **6** Mexico **7** Tampico
roles: **6** Athena **15** Slaves of Babylon **18** Green Dolphin Street

Christiania
capital of: **6** Norway
now called: **4** Oslo

Christie, (Dame) Agatha
author of: **7** Curtain **12** The Mousetrap **14** Death on the Nile **15** The Mirror Crack'd **16** Ten Little Indians **19** Murder at the Vicarage **20** And Then There Were None **22** What Mrs McGillicuddy Saw! **23** The Murder of Roger Ackroyd **24** Murder on the Orient Express, Witness for the Prosecution **27** The Mysterious Affair at Styles
character: **6** Mr. Pine **10** Jane Marple **13** Hercule Poirot

Christie, Julie
born: **5** Assam, India **6** Chukua
roles: **7** Darling (Oscar), Shampoo **9** Billy Liar **11** Heat and Dust **13** Doctor Zhivago, Fahrenheit 451, Heaven Can Wait **18** McCabe and Mrs Miller **22** Far From the Madding Crowd

Christine
author: **11** Stephen King

Christmas
also: **4** Noel, Yule **8** Yuletide
feature/symbol: **4** bell, star, tree **5** angel, gifts, holly **6** candle, carols, creche, manger, sleigh, wreath **7** Yule log **8** presents **9** evergreen, mistletoe, snowflake, stockings **10** Santa Claus

Christmas, Joe
character in: **13** Light in August
author: **8** Faulkner

Christmas Carol, A
author: **14** Charles Dickens
character: **7** Tiny Tim **8** Fezziwig **11** Bob Cratchit **12** Marley's Ghost **15** Ebenezer Scrooge
ghosts of: **13** Christmas Past **15** Christmas Future **16** Christmas Present
director: **17** Brian Desmond Hurst
cast: **10** Jack Warner **11** Alastair Sim (Ebenezer Scrooge), Mervyn Johns **14** Michael Hordern **16** Kathleen Harrison

Christopher Robin

character in: **13** Winnie-the-Pooh
author: **5** Milne

chromium
chemical symbol: **2** Cr

chronic 7 abiding, lasting **8** constant, enduring, habitual, periodic **9** confirmed, continual, ingrained, perennial, recurrent, recurring **10** continuous, deep-rooted, deep-seated, inveterate, persistent, persisting **12** intermittent, longstanding

chronicle 3 log **4** epic, list, note, post, saga **5** diary, enter, story **6** annals, docket, record, relate, report **7** account, history, journal, narrate, recount, set down **8** archives **9** narrative **10** chronology

chronological 5 dated **6** serial **7** ordered, sequent **10** sequential, succeeding, successive **11** consecutive, progressive, time-ordered **12** chronometric, chronoscopic **13** chronographic

chronology 6 annals, record **7** history **9** chronicle **13** order of events

chronometer 5 clock **8** horologe **9** timepiece

chrysanthemum
varieties: **3** Max **4** Corn **5** Daisy, Tansy **6** Nippon **7** Garland **8** Florist's, Tricolor **10** Portuguese

chrysoberyl
variety: **7** cat's-eye **11** alexandrite

chrysolite 4 iron, lava **5** beryl, green, stone **6** yellow **7** mineral, olivine, peridot **8** silicate **9** magnesium **10** aquamarine

chrysoprase
species: **6** quartz
color: **5** green

Chrysothemis
father: **9** Agamemnon
mother: **12** Clytemnestra
brother: **7** Orestes
sister: **7** Electra **9** Iphigenia
daughter: **5** Rhoeo

Chthonian
form: **5** deity **6** spirit
habitat: **10** underworld

Chthonius
member of: **6** Sparti
epithet of: **4** Zeus
means: **15** of the underworld

chubby 3 fat **5** buxom, plump, podgy, pudgy, stout, tubby **6** chunky, flabby, fleshy, portly, rotund, stocky, zaftig **7** paunchy **8** heavyset, roly-poly, thickset **9** corpulent **10** overweight **15** pleasingly plump

chuck 3 pat, pet, tap **4** cast, toss **5** fling, heave, pitch, sling, throw **6** tickle

chuckle 5 cluck, laugh **6** clumsy **7** cackle, chortle, snicker

chum 3 pal **4** bait **5** buddy, crony **6** cohort, friend **7** comrade **8** intimate,

playmate, sidekick **9** companion, confidant **10** bosom buddy, playfellow **11** close friend

chummy 5 close, palsy **7** devoted **8** familiar, friendly, intimate **9** congenial **10** buddy-buddy, palsy-walsy **12** affectionate

chump 4 dolt, dupe, fool, goof, goon, head **5** champ, munch **6** sucker **9** blockhead

chunk 3 gob, wad **4** clod, hunk, lump, mass **5** batch, block, piece **6** nugget, square

chunky 5 beefy, dumpy, lumpy, pudgy, squat, stout, thick **6** chubby, portly, stocky, stodgy, stubby **7** squabby **8** heavyset, thickset **11** thick-bodied

church 4 cult, sect **5** faith **6** belief, chapel, mosque, temple **7** service **8** basilica, religion **9** cathedral, devotions, synagogue **10** house of God, Lord's house, persuasion, tabernacle **11** affiliation **12** denomination **13** divine worship **14** house of worship

Church, Frederick Edwin
born: **10** Hartford CT
artwork: **14** Andes of Ecuador, Falls of Niagara (Niagara Falls) **18** The Heart of the Andes **19** Morning in the Tropics

Churchill, Frank
character in: **4** Emma
author: **6** Austen

Churchill, Sarah
father: **19** Sir Winston Churchill
born: **6** London **7** England
roles: **12** Royal Wedding

Churchill, Winston Spencer
born: **7** England **14** Blenheim Palace
father: **8** Randolph
mother: **12** Jennie Jerome
wife: **16** Clementine Hosier
daughter: **5** Sarah
school: **6** Harrow **9** Sandhurst
captured by: **5** Boers
position: **13** prime minister
author of: **11** Marlborough, My Early Life **14** The World Crisis **17** The Second World War **35** A History of the English-Speaking Peoples
won: **10** Nobel Prize

churchly 8 clerical, pastoral, priestly **9** parochial **11** ministerial **14** ecclesiastical

churchman 5 vicar **6** bishop, cleric, curate, deacon, parson, pastor, priest, rector **7** prelate **8** chaplain, minister, preacher **9** clergyman **12** ecclesiastic

church official 5 elder **6** beadle, deacon **9** presbyter

churchyard 8 cemetery **9** graveyard **12** burial ground **13** burying ground

churl 3 cad, oaf **4** boor, lout **7** bounder

churlish 4 rude, sour, tart **5** crude, surly, testy **6** crusty, sullen **7** bearish, bilious, boorish, brusque, crabbed, grouchy, ill-bred, uncivil, uncouth, waspish **8** arrogant, captious, choleric, impolite, impudent, insolent, petulant **9** dastardly, insulting, irascible, irritable, obnoxious, rancorous, splenetic **10** unmannerly **11** ill-mannered, ill-tempered, quarrelsome **12** contemptible, discourteous

churn 4 beat, foam, rage, roil, roll, toss, whip **5** heave, shake, swirl, whisk **6** stir up **7** agitate, disturb, pulsate, shake up, vibrate **8** convulse **9** palpitate

chute 5 rapid, slide, slope **7** incline, passage **9** parachute

chutzpa, chutzpah 4 gall **5** brass, cheek, nerve **8** audacity, boldness, temerity **9** brashness, impudence **10** brazenness, effrontery **11** forwardness, presumption

Chwatt, Aaron
  real name of: 10 Red Buttons

ciao 2 hi **5** hello **6** so long **7** goodbye **11** see you later

Cicero, Marcus Tullius
  lived in: 11 ancient Rome
  noted as: 6 author, lawyer, orator **9** statesman **11** philosopher **12** letter writer
  position: 6 aedile, consul **7** praetor
  author of: 9 De finibus, De oratore **10** De amicitia, De officiis **11** De republica, De senectute, In Catilinam **14** De natura deorum, Pro lege Manilia **23** Tusculanae Disputationes

cicerone 5 guide, pilot **8** conductor **9** explainer

cicisbeo 5 lover

Cid, The
  also: 11 Poema del Cid
  author: 7 unknown **15** Pierre Corneille
  character: 7 Chimene **8** Rodrigue
  Cid also called: 14 el Cid Campeador **18** Rodrigo Diaz de Bivar
  horse: 7 Babieca

Cider House Rules, The
  author: 10 John Irving
  director: 14 Lasse Hallstrom
  cast: 8 Paul Rudd (Wally Worthington), Kathy Baker (Angela) **11** Delroy Lindo (Mr. Rose) **12** Michael Caine (Dr. Wilbur Larch), Tobey Maguire (Homer Wells) **13** Jane Alexander (Edna) **14** Charlize Theron (Candy Kendall)

ci-devant 6 former **7** retired **10** heretofore

cierge 3 dip, wax **5** light, taper **6** bougie, candle, tallow

cigar 4 toby **5** claro **6** corona, havana, maduro, stogie **7** cheroot **8** panatela, panetela, perfecto **9** cigarillo, panatella
  ingredient: 11 tobacco leaf
  part: 6 binder, filler **7** wrapper

  made in: 4 Cuba **6** Havana
  kept in: 7 humidor

cigarette, cigaret 3 cig, fag **4** biri, rett, weed **5** smoke **6** gasper, grette, reefer **10** coffin nail
  ingredient: 3 tar **7** menthol, tobacco **8** nicotine

Cimabue
  real name: 11 Cenni di Pepi
  born: 5 Italy **8** Florence
  artwork attributed: 18 The S Trinita Madonna **29** Madonna Enthroned with St Francis **45** Madonna and Child Enthroned with Angels and Prophets

Cimarron
  author: 10 Edna Ferber
  director: 13 Wesley Ruggles
  cast: 10 Irene Dunne, Richard Dix **13** Estelle Taylor
  Oscar for: 7 picture **10** screenplay

Cimarron Strip
  character: 8 (US Marshal) Jim Crown **9** Mac Gregor **12** Francis Wilde **17** Dulcey Coopersmith
  cast: 10 Randy Boone **12** Jill Townsend, Percy Herbert **13** Stuart Whitman

Cimino, Michael
  director of: 11 Heaven's Gate **13** The Deer Hunter (Oscar)

Cimmerian
  mentioned by: 5 Homer
  form: 10 Westerners
  live in: 8 darkness

cinch 4 band, snap **5** girth **6** clinch, ensure, girdle, shoo-in **8** lead-pipe **9** pull tight, sure thing **11** piece of cake

Cincinnati
  baseball team: 4 Reds
  football team: 7 Bengals

cincture 4 band, belt, cord, sash **6** girdle

cinder 3 ash **4** slag **5** ashes, dross, ember **6** embers, scoria **8** clinkers, iron slag **10** burned coal, burned wood

Cinderella
  author: 7 unknown
  source: 8 Perrault
  character: 14 Fairy Godmother, Handsome Prince **15** Ugly Stepsisters **16** Wicked Stepmother
  coach: 7 pumpkin
  horses: 9 white mice
  footman: 4 frog
  loses: 12 glass slipper

cinema 5 films **6** flicks, movies **7** theater **14** motion pictures, moving pictures

cinnamon 5 spice
  botanical name: 20 Cinnamomum zeylanicum
  variety: 6 cassia, Ceylon **10** zeylanicum
  color: 4 buff **5** tawny **6** auburn **8** nut-brown **11** golden-brown, yellow-brown **12** reddish-brown **13** chest-

nut-brown **14** yellowish-brown
  origin: 5 China **7** Vietnam **9** Indonesia **10** East Indies

Cinyras
  king of: 6 Cyprus
  son: 5 Melus
  daughter: 6 Myrrha
  introduced worship of: 9 Aphrodite
  crime: 6 incest
  death by: 7 suicide

cipher 3 nil, zip **4** code, zero **5** aught **6** naught, nobody **7** anagram, nothing, nullity **8** acrostic, goose egg **9** nonentity, obscurity **10** cryptogram **11** cryptograph

Circe
  form: 11 enchantress
  father: 6 Helios
  mother: 5 Perse
  brother: 6 Aeetes
  son: 6 Agrius **7** Latinus **9** Telegonus
  home: 5 Aeaea
  turned men into: 4 pigs **5** swine

circle 3 orb, set **4** belt, curl, gird, girt, halo, hoop, knot, loop, reel, ring, turn **5** arena, bound, cabal, crowd, curve, cycle, field, girth, group, hem in, orbit, pivot, range, reach, realm, round, sweep, swing **6** border, bounds, clique, cordon, corona, course, domain, girdle, region, sphere **7** circlet, circuit, company, compass, coterie, enclose, envelop, hedge in, revolve, ringlet, society, theater **8** dominion, encircle, province, sequence, surround **9** bailiwick, encompass, territory, wind about **10** move around, revolution, ring around **11** curve around, progression **12** circumrotate, circumscribe **13** revolve around **14** circumnavigate

Circle 6 gilgal

circlet 4 band, halo, ring **5** tiara **6** diadem, fillet, wreath **7** chaplet, coronet, ringlet

circuit 3 lap, run **4** area, beat, edge, tour, trek, walk **5** jaunt, limit, round, route **6** border, bounds, course, margin, sphere **7** compass, confine, journey **8** circling, frontier, orbiting, pivoting **9** excursion, extremity, perimeter, revolving, territory **10** revolution **13** circumference **14** distance around

circuitous 7 devious, turning, winding **8** circular, indirect, rambling, tortuous, twisting **10** meandering, roundabout, serpentine **12** labyrinthine **14** circumlocutory

circular 4 bill **5** flier, round **6** curved, notice, rotary **7** coiling, curling, leaflet, rocking, rolling, rounded, turning, winding **8** bulletin, gyrating, handbill, pivoting, spinning, twirling **9** revolving, spiraling, swiveling, throwaway **10** circuitous, ring-shaped **12** announcement **13** advertisement

circulate 4 flow **5** issue, strew **6** circle,

course, spread, travel **7** give out, go forth, journey, publish, radiate, scatter **8** announce, disperse, go around, put about **9** broadcast, get abroad, make known, move about, publicize **10** distribute, make public, move around, pass around, put forward **11** disseminate, pass through, visit around **13** make the rounds

circulation 4 flow **6** motion **7** flowing **8** circling, rotation **9** diffusion, radiation **10** dispersion **11** propagation **12** distribution, promulgation, transmission **13** dissemination

circulatory system
part: 4 vein **5** heart **6** artery **9** capillary **15** lymphatic vessel
carries: 6 plasma **9** platelets **13** red blood cells **15** white blood cells

circumcision
Hebrew: 4 Bris, Brit **5** Berit, Brith **6** Berith
performed by: 5 Mohel

circumference 3 rim **4** edge **5** girth **6** border, bounds, fringe, girdle, limits, margin **7** circuit, compass, outline **8** boundary **9** extremity, perimeter, periphery **14** distance around

circumlocution 8 rambling, verbiage **9** garrulity, verbosity, wordiness **10** digression, meandering **14** discursiveness, long-windedness, roundaboutness

circumlocutory 5 wordy **7** diffuse, verbose **8** rambling **9** wandering **10** digressive, discursive, maundering, roundabout

circumnavigate 5 skirt **6** bypass, circle **8** encircle, go around **10** circumvent

circumnavigation 8 circling, skirting **9** bypassing **11** going around **12** encirclement **13** circumvention

circumscribe 3 fix **4** curb **5** check, hem in, limit **6** bridle, circle, corset, define, impede **7** confine, enclose, outline **8** encircle, restrain, restrict, surround **9** constrain, delineate, encompass, proscribe

circumscribed 6 narrow **7** limited **10** restricted

circumscription 5 limit **7** outline **9** hemming in, restraint **10** constraint **11** confinement **12** encirclement **14** restrictedness

circumspect 4 sage, wary **5** alert **7** careful, guarded, prudent **8** cautious, discreet, vigilant, watchful **9** judicious, sagacious, wide-awake **10** deliberate, discerning, particular, thoughtful **13** contemplative, perspicacious **14** discriminating

circumspection 4 care, heed **7** caution **8** prudence **10** discretion, precaution, steadiness **11** carefulness, heedfulness, mindfulness **12** deliberation

circumstance 4 fact, item **5** event,

point, thing **6** detail, factor, matter, ritual **7** element **8** ceremony, incident, splendor **9** condition, formality, happening, pageantry **10** brilliance, occurrence, particular, phenomenon **11** vicissitude **12** happenstance, magnificence, resplendence **14** state of affairs

circumstances 5 state **9** situation **11** environment **16** living conditions

circumstantial 4 full **6** minute **7** deduced, hearsay, implied, precise **8** accurate, complete, detailed, explicit, inferred, presumed, thorough **9** secondary **10** blow-by-blow, evidential, exhaustive, extraneous, incidental, particular, unabridged **11** conjectural, inferential, provisional **12** nonessential

circumvent 4 miss, shun **5** avoid, dodge, elude, evade, skirt **6** bypass, circle, escape, outwit, thwart **8** go around **9** frustrate **12** keep away from **14** circumnavigate

circumvention 7 dodging, ducking, eluding, evasion **9** avoidance, bypassing **11** frustration **12** sidestepping

circus 4 ring **5** arena **6** big top, circle, uproar **8** carnival, coliseum **9** spectacle **10** exhibition, hippodrome **11** amphitheater **12** intersection
act: 5 clown, flyer **7** acrobat, juggler, trapeze **8** side show **9** lion tamer, menagerie **10** equestrian **13** flying trapeze
famous: 6 Astley **12** Cirque d'Hiver **15** Barnum and Bailey **16** Ringling Brothers

Cist
form: 9 sacred box
used for: 8 utensils

cistern 3 box, tub, vat **4** tank, well **6** cavity, vessel **8** aqueduct **9** reservoir

citadel 4 fort **7** bastion, rampart **8** fortress **10** stronghold **13** fortification

citation 4 cite **5** award, honor, kudos, medal, quote **7** example, excerpt, extract, passage **8** instance **9** quotation **12** commendation, illustration **14** official praise

cite 4 name, note **5** honor, quote **6** praise **7** advance, commend, mention, present, refer to, specify **8** allude to, document, indicate **9** enumerate, exemplify **12** bring forward **13** give as example

Cithaeronian *see* **4** Zeus

citified 5 urban **6** urbane **12** cosmopolitan **13** sophisticated

citizen 6 native **7** denizen, subject **8** national, resident **10** inhabitant
French: 7 citoyen

Citizen Kane
director: 11 Orson Welles
script: 11 Orson Welles **17** Herman J Mankiewicz
cast: 11 Orson Welles **12** Joseph Cot-

ten **13** Everett Sloane **14** Agnes Moorehead
score: 15 Bernard Herrmann
sled: 7 Rosebud

citizenry 4 folk **6** people, public **7** society **8** populace **9** community **10** population

citoyen 7 citizen

citrine
species: 6 quartz
color: 6 yellow

citron 3 rue **4** lime, rind **5** lemon **6** cedrat, orange, yellow **8** Rutaceae **9** tangerine **10** watermelon **12** citrus medica
Jewish: 6 ethrog

city 4 burg, town **7** big town **8** denizens, township **9** residents **10** metropolis **11** inhabitants, megalopolis, townspeople **12** municipality **16** incorporated town, metropolitan area

city hall
French: 12 hotel de ville

City Life
author: 15 Donald Barthelme

City Lights
director: 14 Charles Chaplin
cast: 8 Hank Mann **10** Harry Myers **14** Charlie Chaplin **16** Virginia Cherrill

City of God, The (De Civitate Dei)
author: 11 St Augustine

City of the Lion *see* **9** Singapore

city slicker 4 dude **8** urbanite **11** cosmopolite **12** sophisticate

Ciudad Trujillo
capital of: 17 Dominican Republic

Civ 17 second Hebrew month

civic 5 local **6** public **8** citizen's, communal **9** community

civil 3 lay **4** city **5** civic, state **6** genial, polite, public **7** affable, amiable, citizen, cordial, secular **8** citizen's, communal, decorous, gracious, mannerly, obliging **9** civilized, community, courteous, municipal **10** individual, neighborly, respectful **11** gentlemanly, nonmilitary **12** conciliatory, well-mannered

Civil Disobedience
author: 17 Henry David Thoreau

civilian 9 lay person **14** private citizen **17** nonmilitary person **18** nonuniformed person

civility 4 tact **7** manners, respect **8** courtesy **10** affability, amiability, cordiality, good temper, politeness **11** good manners **12** graciousness, pleasantness **13** agreeableness, courteousness **14** respectfulness

civilization 7 culture, society **10** refinement **11** cultivation, worldliness **13** enlightenment **14** sophistication

civilize 5 edify, teach, train **6** inform, polish, refine **7** culture, develop, educate, elevate **8** humanize, instruct **9**

cultivate, enlighten **11** acculturate **12** sophisticate

civil law
  Latin: **9** jus civile

Civil War
  admirals: **6** DuPont, Semmes
  battles: **6** Shiloh **7** Bull Run **8** Antietam **9** Nashville, Vicksburg **10** Cold Harbor, Gettysburg **11** Chattanooga, Chickamauga **14** Fredericksburg
  coin: **10** copperhead
  Confederate commanders: **3** Lee **4** Hill, Hood **5** Bragg, Early, Ewell, Mosby, Smith **6** Stuart, Toombs **7** Buckner, Hampton, Jackson **10** Beauregard **12** Breckinridge
  Union commanders: **5** Banks, Buell, Grant, Logan **6** Butler, Custer, Hooker, Porter **7** Sherman, Hancock **8** Sheridan

clad 6 garbed **7** arrayed, attired, clothed, dressed **9** outfitted

Claggart
  character in: **9** Billy Budd
  author: **8** Melville

claim 3 ask **4** avow, call, plea, take **5** exact, right, title **6** access, affirm, allege, assert, avowal, charge, demand, pick up **7** call for, collect, command, declare, profess, request **8** exaction, insist on, maintain, proclaim **9** assertion, ownership, seek as due, statement **10** allegation, lay claim to, pretension, profession **11** affirmation, declaration, postulation, requirement **12** proclamation, protestation

claimant 6 suitor **9** applicant, pretender **10** petitioner

clairvoyant 7 psychic **8** divining, oracular **9** prescient, prophetic **10** telepathic **11** foreknowing, telekinetic **12** extrasensory, precognitive, psychometric **13** psychokinetic, second-sighted

clam 4 vise **5** clamp, clasp **6** dollar, marine **7** bivalve, mollusk
  kind: **5** pismo, razor **6** butter, quahog **7** geoduck, steamer **10** little neck **11** cherrystone
  part: **4** foot, palp **5** gills, shell, valve **6** mantle, siphon **7** sinuses **8** ligament
  habitat: **3** mud **4** sand
  relative: **6** mussel, oyster

clamber up 5 climb, mount, scale **10** scramble up, struggle up

clamminess 4 damp **7** wetness **8** dampness, dankness **10** stickiness, sweatiness

clammy 3 wet **4** damp **5** pasty, slimy **6** sticky, sweaty **10** perspiring **11** cold and damp

clamor 3 cry, din **4** call, howl, yell **5** blast, chaos, noise, shout, storm **6** bedlam, bellow, cry out, hubbub, jangle, outcry, racket, rumpus, tumult, uproar **7** bluster, call out, clangor, thunder **8** brouhaha, shouting **9** com-

motion, hue and cry **10** hullabaloo, vociferate, wild chorus

clamorous 4 loud **5** noisy **10** boisterous, uproarious

clamp 4 clip, grip, vise **5** brace, clasp **6** clench, clinch, fasten, secure **7** bracket **8** fastener

clan 4 gang, knot, line, ring **5** breed, cabal, crowd, group, guild, house, party, stock **6** circle, league, strain **7** company, dynasty, lineage, society **8** alliance, pedigree **10** fraternity **11** affiliation, association, brotherhood, family group, lineal group **12** tribal family

clandestine 6 covert, hidden, masked, secret, veiled **7** cloaked, furtive, private **8** secluded, sneaking, stealthy **9** concealed, secretive, underhand **10** undercover, unrevealed **11** underground, underhanded, undisclosed **12** confidential **13** surreptitious

clang 3 din **4** bong, gong, peal, toll **5** chime, clank, clash, knell **6** jangle **7** clangor, resound, ringing, tolling **8** clashing **10** resounding, ring loudly

clangor 3 din **5** noise **6** clamor, hubbub, jangle, racket, uproar

clank 5 chink, clang, clash, clink **6** jangle, rattle **7** clangor, clatter **8** clashing

clannish 4 cold **5** aloof **6** narrow **7** distant, insular **8** cliquish, snobbish **9** exclusive, parochial, sectarian **10** provincial, restricted, unfriendly **11** unreceptive

Clan of the Cave Bear, The
  author: **9** Jean M Auel

clap 3 bat, hit, rap, tap **4** bang, bump, cast, cuff, dash, hurl, peal, push, roar, rush, slam, slap, swat, toss **5** burst, clack, crack, drive, fling, force, pitch, shove, smack, smite, thump, whack **6** buffet, plunge, propel, strike, thrust, thwack, wallop **7** applaud, clatter **9** explosion **11** set suddenly

claptrap 3 rot **4** bosh, bull, bunk, sham, **5** bilge, hokum, hooey, stuff, trash, tripe **6** bunkum, drivel, hot air, humbug, tinsel **7** baloney, blarney, fustian, hogwash, spinach, twaddle **8** buncombe, nonsense, quackery, tommyrot **9** gaudiness, poppycock, staginess **10** applesauce, flapdoodle, tawdriness, tomfoolery **11** foolishness **15** pretentiousness **16** stuff and nonsense

claque 10 sycophants **15** cheering section

claret 3 red **5** blood **7** carmine, deep red, red wine **8** blood-red, Bordeaux, cardinal **11** purplish red, wine-colored

clarification 10 commentary **11** elucidation, explanation, explication **14** further comment
  French: **15** eclaircissement

clarify 5 clear, purge, solve **6** purify, refine **7** clear up, explain, lay open,

resolve **9** elucidate, explicate, make clear, make plain **10** illuminate **11** disentangle, shed light on **12** bring to light **18** make understandable

clarinet 4 wind **8** woodwind **11** transposing **13** licorice stick
  mouthpiece: **4** reed
  ancestor: **9** chalumeau
  musician: **12** Benny Goodman

clarion 5 acute, clear, sharp **6** shrill **7** blaring, ringing **8** distinct, piercing, resonant, sonorous, stirring **10** commanding, compelling, imperative **11** high-pitched

Clarissa Harlowe
  author: **16** Samuel Richardson
  character: **8** Miss Howe **11** John Belford **14** Robert Lovelace **20** Colonel William Morden

clarity 6 purity **8** lucidity, radiance **9** clearness, exactness, plainness, precision **10** brightness, brilliance, directness, effulgence, glassiness, luminosity, simplicity **12** explicitness, translucence, transparency **15** intelligibility **17** comprehensibility

Clark, Mark W
  served in: **3** WWI **4** WWII **9** Korean War
  rank: **22** allied commander in Italy **24** commander of forces in Korea **30** chief of staff of army ground forces
  president of: **7** Citadel

Clark, Walter Van Tilburg
  author of: **16** The Ox-Bow Incident

Clarke, Arthur C
  author of: **10** (2010) Odyssey Two **13** (2001) A Space Odyssey, Childhood's End **18** Rendezvous with Rama

clash 4 bang, boil, feud, fray, tiff **5** argue, clang, clank, crash, fight, set-to **6** battle, combat, fracas, jangle, rattle, tussle **7** clangor, clatter, contend, contest, discord, dispute, grapple, jarring, quarrel, wrangle **8** conflict, crashing, friction, skirmish, squabble, struggle **9** altercate, encounter, lock horns **10** antagonism, difference, disharmony, dissidence, opposition **11** cross swords **12** disagreement **13** exchange blows

clash of arms 5 fight **6** battle, combat **8** conflict, skirmish, struggle **9** encounter **10** engagement

clash with 9 fight with **12** do battle with **14** contend against **15** cross swords with

clasp 3 hug **4** bolt, clip, grip, hasp, hold, hook, link, lock, snap **5** catch, clamp, grasp, latch, press **6** buckle, clinch, clutch, couple, fasten, secure **7** coupler, embrace, grapple, squeeze **8** fastener **9** fastening

clasp in the arms 3 hug **4** hold **6** enfold **7** embrace

class 3 set **4** form, kind, rank, rate,

size, sort, type **5** brand, breed, caste, genre, genus, grade, group, index, label, order, state **6** circle, clique, codify, course, lesson, number, sphere, status **7** arrange, catalog, section, session, species, station, variety **8** category, classify, division, pedigree, position **9** condition, designate **10** categorize, pigeonhole, social rank **11** set of pupils **13** social stratum **14** classification **15** departmentalize, graduating group

classic, classical 4 epic **5** model **6** heroic **7** ageless, paragon **8** absolute, accepted, enduring, masterly **9** archetype, excellent, exemplary, first-rate, prototype **10** archetypal, consummate, definitive, first-class, Greco-Roman, prototypal **11** masterpiece, outstanding, traditional **12** ancient Greek, ancient Roman, standard work **13** authoritative, distinguished **14** distinguishing **17** first-class example

classification 4 kind, rank, sort, type **5** class, genus, group, order **6** family, series **7** section, species **8** category, classing, division, grouping, labeling, ordering, taxonomy **9** arranging, gradation **10** assortment, organizing **11** arrangement, designation, disposition **12** categorizing, codification, organization **14** categorization **15** systematization

classified 5 secret **6** sorted **7** classed **8** assorted **10** restricted **11** categorized **12** confidential

classify 3 tag **4** list, rank, rate, size, sort, type **5** brand, class, grade, group, index, label, order, range **6** assort, codify, number, ticket **7** arrange, catalog **8** organize **9** segregate **10** categorize, pigeonhole **11** distinguish

classy 4 chic, posh, tony **5** nifty, nobby, ritzy, smart, swank, swell **6** dressy, modish, spiffy, swanky **7** elegant, genteel, opulent, refined, stylish **8** cultured, polished, tasteful **9** high-class **10** ultrasmart **11** fashionable, in good taste **12** aristocratic, well-mannered

clatter 4 bang **5** clack, clang, clank, clash, clink, clump, crash **6** clamor, jangle, racket, rattle **7** chatter **8** crashing, rattling

clattering 3 din **6** clamor, hubbub, racket, uproar **7** clangor

Claude
real name: **12** Claude Gellée
also called: **14** Claude Lorraine
born: **6** France **9** Champagne
artwork: **7** The Mill **16** Hagar and the Angel **18** Ascanius and the Stag, The Enchanted Castle **27** The Rest on the Flight into Egypt **31** The Embarkation of the Queen of Sheba

Claudel, Paul
author of: **6** L'Otage **10** The Hostage

13 Partage de Midi **15** The Satin Slipper **20** Tidings Brought to Mary

Claudia Quinta
freed: **12** grounded ship
feat proved: **8** chastity

Claudio
character in: **17** Measure for Measure **19** Much Ado About Nothing
author: **11** Shakespeare

Claudius
character in: **6** Hamlet
author: **11** Shakespeare

Claudius the God
author: **12** Robert Graves
sequel to: **9** I, Claudius

clause 4 term **7** article, proviso **8** covenant **9** condition, provision **11** proposition, stipulation **13** specification **14** simple sentence

claustrophobia
fear of: **12** closed spaces **14** confined spaces

Clavell, James
author of: **6** Gai Jin, Shogun, Tai-Pan **7** King Rat **9** Whirlwind **10** Noble House

clavicle
bone of: **10** collarbone

claw 3 paw **4** foot, grip, maul, tear **5** seize, slash, talon **6** clutch, pincer, scrape **7** scratch **8** lacerate **10** animal nail

Clay, Cassius
former name of: **11** Muhammad Ali

Clayburgh, Jill
born: **9** New York NY
husband: **9** David Rabe
roles: **9** Semi-Tough **10** Never Again **12** Starting Over **14** Going All the Way **16** An Unmarried Woman, North Dallas Forty **21** I'm Dancing as Fast as I Can

Clayhanger Trilogy, The
author: **13** Arnold Bennett

clean 3 mop **4** dust, fine, neat, pure, tidy, trim, wash **5** bathe, clear, fresh, moral, order, scour, scrub, sweep **6** bathed, chaste, decent, neaten, tidy up, vacuum, washed **7** cleaned, cleanse, healthy, launder, orderly, perfect, scoured, shampoo, upright **8** cleansed, decorous, flawless, innocent, sanitary, scrubbed, spotless, unsoiled, virtuous, well-made **9** exemplary, faultless, honorable, laundered, stainless, undefiled, unspotted, unstained, unsullied, untainted, wholesome **10** immaculate, uninfected, unpolluted **11** unblemished **13** unadulterated **14** uncontaminated

cleaner, cleanser 4 soap **5** borax **6** washer **7** ammonia, janitor **8** purifier, scrubber **9** detergent **14** scouring powder

cleaning 7 bathing, washing **8** scour-

ing **9** cleansing, going-over, scrubbing, tidying up **10** laundering

cleanse 3 rid **4** free, wash **5** bathe, clean, clear, erase, flush, scour, scrub **7** absolve, deliver, expunge, launder, release, shampoo **8** sweep out, unburden **9** expurgate

clean-shaven 6 smooth **9** unbearded **11** unwhiskered **12** smooth-shaven

cleansing 7 bathing, healing, purging, washing **8** flushing, scouring **9** expunging, purifying, scrubbing **10** absolution

cleanup 4 gain **6** profit **8** windfall
baseball: **12** fourth batter

clear 3 rid **4** fair, free, keen, make, open **5** alert, clean, empty, gauzy, lucid, plain, sharp, sunny **6** acquit, bright, patent, remove, serene, unstop, wholly **7** absolve, audible, audibly, certain, clearly, evident, express, fly over, glowing, halcyon, hop over, lighten, obvious, plainly, radiant, unblock **8** apparent, brighten, clear-cut, dazzling, definite, distinct, entirely, explicit, gleaming, leap over, luminous, manifest, pass over, pellucid, positive, skip over, unhidden **9** all the way, bound over, brilliant, cloudless, exculpate, exonerate, sparkling, unblocked, unclouded, unimpeded, unmuddled, vindicate, wide-awake **10** articulate, become fair, completely, diaphanous, discerning, distinctly, glistening, pronounced, unconfused, undeniable, unobscured **11** crystalline, inescapable, self-evident, translucent, transparent, unambiguous, unconcealed, undisguised, unequivocal, unqualified **12** articulately, intelligible, recognizable, unencumbered, unmistakable, unobstructed **14** comprehensible **15** distinguishable, straightforward

clearance 4 room, sale **6** margin, permit **7** removal **8** clearing **10** offsetting **11** elimination **13** authorization, certification

clear as day 5 plain **7** obvious **8** apparent, clear-cut, manifest **11** self-evident

clear-cut 4 open **5** exact, lucid, plain **6** patent **7** evident, express, obvious, precise **8** definite, detailed, distinct, explicit, manifest **10** clear as day, unconfused, undeniable **11** appreciable, conspicuous, self-evident, substantial, unambiguous, undisguised, unequivocal, well-defined **12** crystal-clear, unmistakable **14** comprehensible, understandable **15** straightforward

clearheaded 5 acute, alert, awake, aware, sharp **6** astute **8** rational, sensible **9** on the ball, practical, realistic, wide-awake **10** discerning, insightful, on one's toes, on the stick, perceptive **13** perspicacious

clearheadedness 7 insight 8 sagacity 9 alertness, sharpness 10 perception 11 discernment 12 perspicacity

clearing 5 glade

clearly 6 surely 7 plainly 8 markedly, palpably, patently 9 assuredly, certainly, decidedly, evidently, obviously 10 distinctly, manifestly, noticeably, observably, undeniably 11 beyond doubt, indubitably, perceptibly, undoubtedly 12 recognizably, unmistakably 13 unequivocally 14 beyond question, unquestionably

clearly expressed 8 coherent 10 articulate 11 unambiguous 12 intelligible

clearness 7 clarity 10 brightness, brilliance 12 explicitness 15 unmistakability

clear-sighted 4 sage, wise 5 acute, sharp 6 astute, shrewd 8 piercing 9 judicious, sagacious, sensitive 10 discerning, perceptive 11 intelligent, keen-sighted, penetrating 12 sharp-sighted 13 perspicacious

clear up 6 settle 7 clarify, unsnarl 8 untangle 11 disentangle 12 uncomplicate 13 straighten out

Cleary, Beverly
author of: 6 Ramona 7 Fifteen 12 Henry Huggins 13 Jean and Johnny 15 Beezus and Ramona 16 Sister of the Bride

cleat 5 block, chock, spike, wedge 6 batten 7 bollard

cleavage 3 gap 4 rent, rift, slit 5 cleft, crack, notch, split 6 furrow, trench, trough 7 crevice, fissure, opening 8 crevasse

cleave 3 cut, hew 4 chop, fuse, hack, hold, open, part, plow, rend, rive, slit, tear 5 cling, crack, halve, sever, slash, slice, split, stick, unite 6 adhere, be true, bisect, cut off, detach, divide, furrow, sunder, uphold 7 abide by, chop off, disjoin, lay open, stand by 8 be joined, break off, hold fast, separate 9 disengage, dismember

cleaver 3 axe 4 tool 5 knife ridge

cleft 3 gap 4 rent, rift, slit 5 break, crack, notch, split 6 breach, cloven, cranny, divide, forked, furrow, trench, trough 7 crevice, divided, fissure, notched, opening, slotted 8 aperture, bisected, branched, cleavage, crevasse, division 10 separation 11 indentation

clemency 5 mercy 7 charity 8 humanity, kindness, leniency, mildness, softness, sympathy 9 tolerance 10 compassion, indulgence, moderation, temperance 11 benevolence, forbearance, magnanimity 12 mercifulness, pleasantness 13 forgivingness

clement 4 kind, mild, warm 5 balmy 6 benign, gentle, humane 7 lenient 8

merciful, tolerant 9 not severe, not strict 10 benevolent 13 compassionate

clench 3 set 4 grip 5 clasp, tense 6 clinch, clutch 7 stiffen, tighten 8 fasten on, hold fast 11 grasp firmly, strain tight 12 close tightly

Cleopatra
queen of: 5 Egypt
father: 7 Ptolemy
brother/husband: 7 Ptolemy
lover: 10 Mark Antony 12 Julius Caesar
son: 9 Caesarion 15 Alexander Helios 19 Ptolemy Philadelphos
daughter: 15 Cleopatra Selene
death by: 3 asp 7 suicide

Cleopatra
director:
1934 version: 13 Cecil B DeMille
1963 version: 17 Joseph L Mankiewicz
cast:
1934 version: 13 Henry Wilcoxon, Warren William 16 Claudette Colbert
1963 version: 11 Rex Harrison 13 Richard Burton, Roddy McDowall 15 Elizabeth Taylor

clergy 6 rabbis 7 clerics, pastors, priests 8 ministry, prelates, the cloth 9 churchmen, clergymen, clericals, ministers, pastorate, preachers, rabbinate, the church, the pulpit 10 priesthood 14 the first estate

clergyman 5 padre, rabbi 6 cleric, father, parson, pastor, priest 7 prelate 8 chaplain, minister, preacher, reverend, sky pilot 9 churchman 13 man of the cloth

cleric 6 parson, pastor 8 chaplain, preacher 9 churchman, clergyman 13 man of the cloth

clerical 6 cleric, filing, office, typing 7 clerkly 8 churchly, of clerks, pastoral, priestly 10 accounting, rabbinical 11 bookkeeping, ministerial 13 record-keeping 14 ecclesiastical

clerical worker 5 clerk 6 typist 9 file clerk 10 bookkeeper, keypuncher 12 office worker 13 data processor

clerk 6 typist 8 salesman 9 file clerk 10 bookkeeper, salesclerk, saleswoman 11 salesperson 12 office worker

Clerks
director: 10 Kevin Smith
cast: 10 Jason Mewes (Jay), Kevin Smith (Silent Bob) 12 Jeff Anderson (Randal Graves) 14 Brian O'Halloran (Dante Hicks), Lisa Spoonhauer (Caitlin Bree) 17 Marilyn Ghigliotti (Veronica Loughran)

Cleta
member of: 6 Graces
worshipped at: 6 Sparta

Cleveland
baseball team: 7 Indians

basketball team: 9 Cavaliers
football team: 6 Browns

Cleveland, Grover
name at birth: 22 Stephen Grover Cleveland
nickname: 5 Grove
presidential rank: 12 twenty-fourth, twenty-second
party: 8 Democrat
state represented: 2 NY
defeated: 4 (Simon) Wing 6 (Benjamin Franklin) Butler, (James Baird) Weaver, (James Gillespie) Blaine, (John Pierce) St John 7 (John) Bidwell 8 (Belva Ann Bennett) Lockwood, (Benjamin) Harrison
vice president: 9 (Adlai Ewing) Stevenson, (Thomas Andrews) Hendricks
cabinet:
state: 5 (Richard) Olney 6 (Thomas Francis) Bayard 7 (Walter Quinton) Gresham
treasury: 7 (Daniel) Manning 8 (John Griffin) Carlisle 9 (Charles Stebbins) Fairchild
war: 6 (David Scott) Lamont 8 (William Crowninshield) Endicott
attorney general: 5 (Richard) Olney 6 (Judson) Harmon 7 (Augustus Hill) Garland
interior: 5 (Hoke) Smith, (Lucius Quintus Cincinnatus) Lamar, (William Freeman) Vilas 7 (David Rowland) Francis
born: 2 NJ 8 Caldwell
died/buried: 2 NJ 9 Princeton
education:
high school: 16 Liberal Institute
religion: 12 Presbyterian
interests: 7 fishing 8 shooting 13 gun collecting
political career:
mayor of: 7 Buffalo
governor of: 7 New York
civilian career: 6 lawyer
notable events of lifetime/term: 5 Panic (of 1893) 10 gold crisis (of 1895)
Act: 6 Tariff 14 Dawes Severalty 18 Interstate Commerce
strike: 7 Pullman
father: 13 Richard Falley
mother: 4 Anne (Neal)
siblings: 7 Ann Neal 9 Mary Allen 11 Susan Sophia, William Neal 12 Richard Cecil 13 Rose Elizabeth 14 Lewis Frederick 20 Margaret Louise Falley
wife: 7 Frances (Folsom)
children: 4 Ruth 6 Esther, Marion 13 Francis Grover, Richard Folsom

clever 4 able, cute, deft, keen 5 acute, quick, sharp, smart, witty 6 adroit, artful, astute, bright, crafty, expert, shrewd 8 creative, humorous, original 9 ingenious, inventive 11 imaginative, intelligent, quick-witted, resourceful

cleverly 6 deftly 7 sharply, smartly,

wittily **8** adroitly, artfully, craftily, expertly **10** creatively, humorously **11** ingeniously, inventively **13** imaginatively, intelligently

cleverness 3 wit **6** acumen **8** ableness, deftness, keenness **9** expertise, ingenuity, quickness, sharpness, smartness **10** adroitness, artfulness, astuteness, brightness, craftiness **12** intelligence, skillfulness **13** inventiveness **15** imaginativeness, quick-wittedness

clew *see* **4** clue

Clew
    thread in: 9 Labyrinth
    showed way to: 7 Theseus
    given by: 7 Ariadne

cliche 3 saw **6** old saw **7** bromide **8** banality, old story **9** platitude **10** stereotype **11** trite phrase

cliche-ridden 5 corny, stale, tired, trite, vapid **6** jejune **8** bromidic **9** hackneyed **10** unoriginal **13** platitudinous, unimaginative

click 3 tap **4** clap, snap **5** clack, clink, crack **6** rattle **7** crackle

client 5 buyer **6** patron **7** advisee, shopper **8** customer **9** purchaser **17** person represented

cliff 3 tor **4** crag **5** bluff, ledge **8** palisade **9** precipice **10** promontory

Cliff Dwellers *see* **6** Pueblo

Clift, Montgomery
    real name: 21 Edward Montgomery Clift
    nickname: 5 Monty
    born: 7 Omaha NE
    roles: 9 The Search **10** The Heiress, The Misfits **14** A Place in the Sun **18** From Here to Eternity, Suddenly Last Summer

climactic 7 crucial **8** critical, dramatic **11** sensational, suspenseful

climate 3 air **4** mood, tone **5** pulse **6** spirit, temper **7** quality, weather **8** ambience, attitude **9** character, condition **10** atmosphere **11** disposition, frame of mind, weather zone **12** usual weather **13** weather region **14** general feeling, weather pattern

climax 4 acme, apex, peak **5** crown **6** crisis, height, summit **8** best part, pinnacle **9** high point **10** denouement **11** culmination **12** highest point, turning point **13** critical point, crowning point, decisive point, supreme moment **18** moment of revelation

climb 4 go up, rise **5** mount, scale **6** ascend, ascent, come up **8** climbing **9** clamber up **10** scramble up

climb down 6 go down **7** descend **8** back down, come down

clinch 3 cap, fix, win **4** bind, bolt, grip, nail **5** cinch, clamp, clasp, close, crown, grasp, screw **6** assure, clutch, couple, decide, fasten, obtain, secure, settle, verify, wind up **7** confirm,

grapple **8** complete, conclude, make fast, make sure **9** culminate, establish, finish off **10** grab hold of, hold firmly **12** seize and hold **13** ensure victory

cling 3 hug **4** fuse, grip, hold **5** clasp, grasp, stick **6** adhere, be true, cleave, clutch **7** stand by **8** hang on to, hold fast, hold on to, maintain **9** stay close **10** be constant, be faithful, grab hold of

clinging 6 sticky **7** holding **8** adherent, adhering, adhesive, clasping, cleaving, grasping, gripping, sticking **9** hanging on, holding on **11** holding fast **12** grabbing hold

clinic 9 infirmary **10** polyclinic **13** medical center **15** outpatients' ward

clink 4 ting **5** clack, clank, click **6** jangle, jingle, rattle, tinkle **11** ring sharply

clinkers 4 duds, slag **5** dross, flops **6** cinder, scoria **8** failures

Clinton, William Jefferson
    original last name: 6 Blythe
    nickname: 4 Bill
    presidential rank: 11 forty-second
    party: 10 Democratic
    state represented: 2 AR **8** Arkansas
    defeated: 4 (George) Bush, (Bob) Dole
    vice president: 4 (Albert) Gore
    cabinet:
        state: 11 (Warren) Christopher
        treasury: 7 (Lloyd) Bentsen
        attorney general: 4 (Janet) Reno
        interior: 7 (Bruce) Babbitt
        labor: 5 (Robert) Reich
        HUD: 8 (Henry) Cisneros
    born: 2 AR **4** Hope
    education: 6 Oxford **7** Yale Law **10** Georgetown
        honor: 13 Rhodes Scholar
    political career:
        governor of: 7 Arkansas
        attorney general of: 7 Arkansas
    notable events of lifetime/term: 4 Waco **5** NAFTA **10** Whitewater **11** impeachment **13** Anticrime Bill, Rhodes Scholar **15** Branch Davidians **17** Health Security Act **20** Monica Lewinsky Affair
        Supreme Court appointments: 13 Stephen Breyer **17** Ruth Bader Ginsburg
    father: 13 William Blythe
    mother: 12 Virginia Cassidy Blythe
    stepfather: 12 Roger Clinton
    sibling: 12 Roger Clinton
    wife: 13 Hillary Rodham
    children: 7 Chelsea

Clio
    muse of: 7 history

clip 3 bob, cut, fix **4** crop, grip, hook, snip, trim **5** clamp, clasp, shear **6** attach, buckle, clinch, couple, cut off, cut out, fasten, paring, secure, staple **7** cutting, shorten **8** clipping, crop-

ping, cut short, fastener, shearing, snipping

clipper 4 boat, ship **6** cutter, shears **8** aircraft, airplane, sailboat, scissors **9** racehorse

clipping 7 cutting, pruning, snippet **8** trimming

clique 3 set **4** clan, gang **5** crowd, group **6** circle **7** coterie, faction

cliquish 4 cold **5** aloof **7** distant **8** clannish, snobbish **9** exclusive **10** unfriendly **11** unreceptive

cloak 4 cape, hide, mask, robe, veil, wrap **5** cover, tunic **6** mantle, screen, shield, shroud **7** conceal, curtain, pelisse, secrete **8** burnoose, disguise **10** camouflage **11** concealment

cloaked 7 covered, muffled, wrapped **9** disguised

cloaking 7 masking, veiling **8** covering **9** obscuring **10** disguising

cloakroom 8 anteroom, coatroom

clobber 3 hit **4** beat, belt, drub, lick, maul, rout, slug, sock, trim, whip **5** clout, pound, punch, smash, smear, whack **6** batter, beat up, strike, subdue, thrash, wallop **7** conquer, shellac, trounce **8** beat up on, lambaste

clock 5 watch **8** horologe **9** timepiece **11** chronometer

Clockwork Orange, A
    author: 14 Anthony Burgess
    director: 14 Stanley Kubrick
    cast: 12 Patrick Magee **13** Adrienne Corri **15** Malcolm McDowell
    protagonist: 4 Alex

clod 3 oaf, wad **4** boor, dolt, dope, glob, hunk, lout, lump, rube **5** chunk, clown, clump, dummy, dunce, moron, yokel **7** bumpkin, fathead **8** imbecile, numskull **9** blockhead, ignoramus, simpleton

clodhopper 3 oaf **4** boot, clod, hick, lout, rube, slob **5** booby, clown, yokel **6** galoot, lubber, lummox, rustic **7** bumpkin, hayseed, peasant, plowboy, redneck **8** clodpole, lunkhead **9** heavy shoe, hillbilly **10** provincial

clog 4 stop **5** block, check, choke, close, dam up **6** stop up **7** barrier, congest **8** blockage, obstacle, obstruct, stoppage **9** restraint **10** impediment **11** obstruction

clogged 6 choked, halted, jammed **7** clotted, impeded **8** choked up, filled up, hampered, hindered, restrained **10** encumbered, obstructed, overloaded

cloister 4 stoa, walk **5** abbey, aisle **6** arcade, closet, coop up, friary, hole up, immure, shut up, wall up **7** conceal, confine, convent, embower, gallery, nunnery, passage, portico, seclude, walkway **8** shut away **9** colonnade, courtyard, monastery, promenade, sequester **10** ambulatory, passageway

cloistered 5 alone, aloof, apart **6** hidden **7** immured, recluse **8** closeted, confined, detached, isolated, secluded, secreted, separate, solitary **9** concealed, insulated, sheltered, withdrawn **11** dissociated, sequestered

clone 4 copy **5** robot **6** double **7** android, replica **9** automaton, duplicate, replicate **10** carbon copy **12** doppelganger **13** identical copy

close 3 end, hot, pen **4** akin, clog, fast, fill, firm, fuse, halt, join, keen, link, near, neat, nigh, plug, shut, stop, trim, warm **5** alert, block, cease, dense, fixed, humid, muggy, pen in, sharp, short, solid, stuff, tight, unite **6** allied, at hand, clog up, coop up, couple, ending, fill in, fill up, finale, finish, hard by, intent, jammed, loving, narrow, nearby, next to, plug up, recess, secure, shut in, shut up, smooth, stingy, stop up, stuffy, windup **7** adjourn, careful, close up, closing, compact, confine, connect, cramped, crowded, devoted, dismiss, enclose, intense, miserly, pinched, seal off, shut off, similar, stuffed, suspend, teeming **8** attached, blockade, break off, conclude, confined, familiar, friendly, grudging, imminent, intimate, leave off, obstruct, populous, shut down, squeezed, stagnant, stifling, stinting, swarming, thorough, vigilant, watchful **9** attentive, congested, impending, niggardly, penurious, scrimping, terminate **10** almost like, completion, compressed, conclusion, nearly even, nip-and-tuck, resembling, restricted, sweltering, ungenerous **11** almost alike, approaching, approximate, close-fisted, discontinue, forthcoming, impermeable, in proximity, inseparable, nearly equal, neighboring, suffocating, termination, tight-fisted, well-matched **12** bring to an end, impenetrable, parsimonious, unventilated **13** bring together, near to the skin, penny-pinching, uncomfortable **14** thick as thieves

closed 6 secret **7** private **9** exclusive

closed-minded 5 rigid **7** adamant, uptight **8** obdurate, stubborn **9** hidebound, obstinate, pig-headed, unbending **10** inflexible, unyielding **12** intransigent **14** uncompromising

Close Encounters of the Third Kind
director: **15** Steven Spielberg
cast: **8** Teri Garr **13** Melinda Dillon **15** Richard Dreyfuss **16** Francois Truffaut
score: **12** John Williams

closefisted 4 mean **5** cheap, close, mingy, tight **6** stingy **7** miserly **8** grudging **9** niggardly, penurious **10** economical, ungenerous **11** close-handed, tightfisted **12** parsimonious **13** penny-pinching

close-fitting 4 snug **5** tight **9** skintight **11** constricted, form-fitting **12** constricting, tight-fitting **15** like a second skin

close friend 3 pal **4** chum, mate **5** buddy, crony **6** cohort **7** best pal **8** alter ego, intimate **9** companion, confidant **10** bosom buddy **17** intimate confidant

close loudly 4 bang, clap, slam

closely 6 keenly **7** alertly, sharply **8** intently **9** carefully, heedfully, intensely **10** diligently, vigilantly, vigorously, watchfully **11** attentively

close-mouthed 3 shy **4** cool **5** terse **7** bashful, distant **8** reserved, reticent, retiring, taciturn **9** diffident, secretive, withdrawn **11** tight-lipped **15** uncommunicative

closeness 8 meanness, nearness **10** stinginess **11** familiarity, miserliness **15** tightfistedness

close of day 3 eve **4** dusk, even **6** sunset **7** evening, sundown **8** eventide, gloaming, twilight **9** nightfall

Closer
director: **11** Mike Nichols
cast: **7** Jude Law (Dan) **9** Clive Owen (Larry) **12** Julia Roberts (Anna) **14** Natalie Portman (Alice)

closet 2 WC **4** eury, safe **5** ambry, cuddy **6** covert, hidden, locker pantry, secret, toilet **7** armoire, cabinet, private **8** coatroom, cupboard, imprison, secluded **9** cloakroom, storeroom, visionary **11** speculative, theoretical, unpractical, water closet

close tightly 3 set **4** seal, slam **5** latch **6** clench, secure **13** press together

close to 4 near **6** almost, around **9** just about **12** on the point of **13** approximately

closure 3 lid, tap **4** bung, cork, plug, stop **5** cover **6** ending, faucet, finish, spigot **7** barring, bolting, closing, cloture, locking, sealing, stopper **8** securing, shutting, stoppage **9** cessation **10** conclusion, stoppering **11** termination **14** discontinuance **15** discontinuation

clot 3 gob **4** lump, mass **7** congeal, thicken **8** embolism, solidify, thrombus **9** coagulate, occlusion **11** coagulation

Cloten
character in: **9** Cymbeline
author: **11** Shakespeare

cloth 5 goods **6** fabric **7** textile **8** dry goods, material **9** yard goods **10** piece goods

clothe 3 don **4** case, coat, deck, garb, robe, veil, wrap **5** array, cloak, cloud, cover, drape, dress **6** attire, bedeck, encase, enwrap, outfit, rig out, screen, shroud **7** bedizen, costume, deck out, envelop, sheathe, swaddle **8** accouter

clothed 4 clad **5** robed **6** draped **7** cloaked, couched, covered, dressed, mantled, wearing **8** equipped, provided **9** expressed, furnished

clothes 4 duds, garb, rags, togs, wear **5** dress **6** attire, finery **7** apparel, costume, raiment, regalia **8** clothing, ensemble, garments, wardrobe **11** habiliments

clotheshorse 3 fop **4** dude **5** dandy, model **12** Beau Brummell, fashion plate, man of fashion, sharp dresser **14** woman of fashion

clothing see **7** clothes

Clotho
member of: **5** Fates
spinner of: **12** thread of life

cloud 3 dim, mar **4** blur, hide, veil **5** blind, cloak, cover, muddy, shade, sully, upset **6** darken, impair, muddle, screen, shadow, shroud **7** conceal, confuse, curtain, distort, disturb, eclipse, obscure, tarnish **8** overcast **9** discredit, make vague **10** overshadow **11** cast doubt on **14** call to question **19** place under suspicion

cloudburst 6 deluge **8** downpour, rainfall **9** rainstorm

clouded 3 dim **5** dusky, murky **7** blurred, obscure, sullied, tainted, unclear **8** confused, darkened, obscured **10** ill-defined, indistinct

cloudless 4 fair **5** clear, sunny **6** bright **7** halcyon **8** sunshiny **9** unclouded **10** unobscured

Clouds
goddess of: **3** Fri **5** Frigg, Frija **6** Frigga

Clouds, The (Nephelai)
author: **12** Aristophanes
character: **8** Just Plea, Socrates **10** Unjust Plea **11** Strepsiades **12** Pheidippides

cloudy 4 dark, gray, hazy **5** murky, vague **6** dreary, gloomy, leaden, veiled **7** clouded, obscure, sunless, unclear **8** confused, nebulous, overcast **9** confusing, undefined **10** indefinite, mysterious **11** overclouded

Clouet, Jean
born: **8** Flanders
artwork attributed: **13** Guillaume Bude **16** Madame de Canaples, Man with Gold Coins **17** The Count of Brissac, The Dauphin Francis **22** Man with a Book by Petrarch

clout 3 box, hit, jab **4** bash, belt, blow, pull, sock **5** crack, knock, punch, smack, thump, whack **6** wallop **9** influence **10** importance

clove
botanical name: **16** Eugenia aromatica **18** Syzygium aromaticum
origin: **5** Pemba **7** Far East **8** Moluc-

cas, Zanzibar **9** Mauritius **10** Madagascar
use: 3 ham **8** pickling, pomander **16** yellow vegetables

cloven 5 cleft, split **7** divided, notched, slotted **8** bisected

clover 9 Trifolium
varieties: 3 bur, elk, hop, low, pin, red **4** bush, holy, Kura, musk, owl's, tick **5** Alyce, Hubam, lucky, sweet, water, white **6** Alsike, cow hop, indoor, Korean, Ladino, yellow **7** Bukhara, crimson, Italian, mammoth, Mexican, Persian, prairie **8** four-leaf, Japanese, large hop, reversed, small hop, stinking **9** Hungarian **10** strawberry, toothed bur, white Dutch, white sweet **11** yellow sweet **12** silky prairie, subterranean, white prairie **13** European water **16** strawberry-headed

clown 3 wag, wit **4** card, fool, jest, joke, mime, zany **5** comic, cut up, joker **6** jester, madcap **7** buffoon **8** comedian, humorist **9** harlequin, kid around **10** comedienne, fool around **11** funny person, merry-andrew

Clown, The
author: 12 Heinrich Boll

clownishness 6 antics **10** buffoonery, tomfoolery **12** monkeyshines **14** playing the fool

cloy 3 gag **4** bore, glut, pall, sate, tire **5** choke, weary **6** benumb, overdo **7** exhaust, satiate, surfeit **8** nauseate, saturate

cloying 5 sweet **6** sugary **9** excessive, satiating **10** saccharine

club 3 bat, hit **4** bash, beat, flog, slug **5** billy, flail, group, guild, lay on, lodge, stick, union **6** batter, buffet, cudgel, league, pommel, pummel, strike **7** society **8** alliance, bludgeon, sorority **9** billyclub, clubhouse, truncheon **10** fraternity, shillelagh, sisterhood **11** affiliation, association, brotherhood, country club

clubhouse 4 club, hall **5** lodge **11** locker rooms **12** meeting house

clue 3 cue, key **4** clew, hint, mark, sign **5** guide, scent, trace **7** glimmer, inkling, pointer **9** evidence **9** indicator, inference **10** indication, intimation, suggestion **11** insinuation

clump 4 bulb, bump, knob, knot, lump, mass, plod, thud **5** batch, bunch, clomp, clunk, copse, group, grove, plunk, shock, stamp, stomp, thump, tramp **6** lumber **7** cluster, thicket **8** aggregate **10** assemblage, collection

clumsiness 9 gawkiness **10** ineptitude **11** awkwardness **12** carelessness, ungainliness **13** gracelessness, maladroitness

clumsy 5 bulky, crude, gawky, inept, rough **6** klutzy **7** awkward, unhandy

8 bungling, careless, ungainly, unwieldy **9** graceless, makeshift, maladroit, unskilled **10** blundering, cumbersome, ungraceful **11** heavy-handed **12** ill-contrived, unmanageable **14** butterfingered **21** like a bull in a china shop

cluster 4 band, bevy, heap, herd, knot, mass, pack, pile **5** amass, batch, block, bunch, clump, crowd, flock, group, sheaf, shock, swarm **6** gather, muster, throng **7** collect, company **8** assemble, converge **9** aggregate **10** accumulate, assemblage, collection, congregate **12** accumulation, congregation **13** agglomeration **14** conglomeration

cluster around 6 gather **7** collect **10** congregate **12** herd together **13** flock together

clutch 3 hug **4** grip, hold **5** clasp, grasp **6** clench **7** cling to, embrace, squeeze **8** hang on to

clutter 4 fill, heap, mess, pile **5** chaos, strew **6** jumble, litter, tangle **7** scatter **8** disarray, disorder **9** confusion **10** hodgepodge

cluttered 5 messy **7** chaotic, crowded, jumbled, muddled **8** confused, littered **9** scattered **10** disordered, disorderly

Clytemnestra
father: 9 Tyndareus
mother: 4 Leda
brother: 6 Castor, Pollux
sister: 5 Helen **8** Timandra
cousin: 8 Perilaus
husband: 9 Agamemnon
son: 7 Orestes
daughter: 7 Electra, Erigone **9** Iphigenia **12** Chrysothemis
lover: 9 Aegisthus
killed: 9 Agamemnon
killed by: 7 Orestes

Coach
network: 3 ABC
cast: 8 Kris Kamm (Stuart Rosebrock) **10** Clare Carey (Kelly Fox) **12** Craig T. Nelson (Coach Hayden Fox), Jerry Van Dyke (Luther Van Dam) **14** Bill Fagerbakke (Dauber Dybinski), Kenneth Kimmins (Howard Burleigh), Shelley Fabares (Christine Armstrong Fox) **16** Katherine Helmond (Doris Sherman)

coach 3 bus **5** drill, guide, sedan, stage, teach, train, tutor **6** advise, direct, mentor **7** omnibus, trainer **8** carriage, instruct **9** limousine, preceptor **10** automobile, four-in-hand, motor coach, stagecoach **11** four-wheeler, second class **12** economy class **14** private teacher **16** athletic director

coachman 3 fly **4** jehu, whip **5** pilot **6** driver **10** charioteer

Coactrice 14 poisonous snake

coagulate 3 gel, set **4** clot, jell **6** curdle, harden **7** congeal, jellify, thicken **8** solidify

coagulation 3 gob **4** clot, mass **8** clotting, curdling, thrombus **10** thickening

coal 4 ash, bass, char, coke, coom, culm, dust, fuel, slag, smut, swad **5** ember **6** cannel, cinder **7** lignite, clinker **8** charcoal **10** fossil fuel **11** charred wood
box: 3 hod **7** scuttle
made from: 6 carbon
type: 4 hard, soft **7** lignite **10** anthracite, bituminous
mining method: 4 deep **8** opencast **10** strip auger **11** underground
mine: 5 drift, shaft, slope, strip
size: 3 egg, nut, pea **5** stove

coal-black 3 jet **4** dark, inky **5** black, ebony, raven, sable **9** pitch-dark

coalesce 3 mix **4** ally, form, fuse, join, meld **5** blend, merge, unify, unite **6** cohere **7** combine **9** become one, integrate **10** amalgamate, join forces **11** agglutinate, consolidate **12** band together, come together **14** form an alliance

coalition 5 union **6** fusion, league **7** society **8** alliance **9** syndicate **10** federation **11** affiliation, association, combination, confederacy, partnership **12** amalgamation **13** agglomeration, consolidation **14** conglomeration

Coal Miner's Daughter
director: 12 Michael Apted
cast: 9 Levon Helm **11** Sissy Spacek (Loretta Lynn) (Oscar) **13** Tommy Lee Jones **14** Beverly D'Angelo
Oscar for: 7 actress (Spacek)
screenplay: 10 Tom Rickman

Coaluitecan
tribe: 6 Payaya

coarse 4 lewd, rude, vile **5** crass, crude, dirty, gross, harsh, rough **6** common, nubbly, odious, ribald, shaggy, sordid, vulgar **7** boorish, bristly, brutish, ill-bred, loutish, obscene, prickly, uncouth **8** impolite, improper, indecent, scratchy **9** bristling, inelegant, offensive, repulsive, revolting, sandpaper, unrefined **10** disgusting, indecorous, indelicate, lascivious, licentious, scurrilous, unladylike, unpolished **11** foul-mouthed, ill-mannered **12** lacking taste **13** rough-textured, ungentlemanly

coarse-grained 5 crude, harsh, nubby, rough **6** coarse, grainy, shaggy **7** bristly **8** scratchy **9** unrefined **13** rough-textured

coarseness 9 crudeness, grossness, roughness, vulgarity **10** indelicacy, inelegance **11** boorishness **16** lack of refinement

coast 4 skim, slip, waft **5** drift, float, glide, shore, slide, sweep **6** strand **7** seaside **8** glissade, littoral, seaboard, seacoast, seashore **9** shoreline

coaster 3 mat **4** ship, sled, tray **5** wagon **6** cradle, glider, slider **8** toboggan **9** tray stand **13** decanter stand, roller coaster

coat 3 fur **4** hair, hide, pelt, wrap **5** cover, glaze, layer, paint, smear **6** blazer, enamel, encase, jacket, spread **7** coating, encrust, envelop, lacquer, overlay, plaster, slicker, topcoat **8** covering, laminate, mackinaw, overcoat, raincoat **9** whitewash **10** mackintosh, sports coat

coating 4 coat, film, skin **5** layer, sheet **6** veneer **7** overlay **8** covering, envelope

coat of arms 4 arms **5** crest **6** creast **8** insignia **9** blaconwry **10** escutcheon **14** heraldic emblem **16** armorial bearings

coat of mail 4 mail **5** armor **9** chain mail **11** suit of armor

Coat of Varnish, A
   author: 6 C P Snow

coax 6 cajole **7** wheedle **8** butter up, inveigle, soft-soap, talk into **9** sweet-talk

cobalt 4 blue **5** azure **7** element, sky blue **10** bright blue **12** greenish blue
   chemical symbol: 2 Co

Cobb, Lee J
   born: 9 New York NY
   roles: 10 Willy Loman **12** The Virginian **14** Twelve Angry Men **15** On the Waterfront **16** Death of a Salesman

Cobb, Ty (Tyrus Raymond)
   nickname: 12 Georgia Peach
   sport: 8 baseball
   position: 8 outfield
   noted for: 7 hitting **12** base stealing
   team: 13 Detroit Tigers

cobbler 3 pie **9** bootmaker, shoemaker **12** shoe repairer **16** deepdish fruit pie

cobra
   also: 3 asp **5** mamba **11** hooded snake
   native to: 4 Asia **6** Africa
   kind: 4 king **6** hooded, Indian **8** Egyptian
   enemy: 8 mongoose

Coburn, Charles
   born: 10 Savannah GA
   roles: 9 Boss Tweed **17** The More the Merrier

Coburn, James
   born: 8 Laurel NE
   roles: 10 Hudson Hawk **11** In Like Flint, Our Man Flint **14** The Great Escape, The Muppet Movie **17** The Nutty Professor **19** The Magnificent Seven

Coca, Imogene
   partner: 9 Sid Caesar
   born: 14 Philadelphia PA
   roles: 15 Your Show of Shows

cock 3 tip **4** knob **5** raise, valve **6** faucet, handle, perk up **7** rooster, stand up **8** cockerel, male bird, set erect **9** bristle up **11** chanticleer **13** turn to

one side **16** raise the hammer of **17** draw back the hammer

cockade 4 knot **5** badge **6** ribbon **7** rosette **8** ornament **10** party badge

Cockade State
   nickname of: 8 Maryland

cock-and-bull story 3 fib, lie **4** myth, yarn **5** fable **7** fiction, untruth, whopper **9** fairy tale, falsehood, fish story, invention, tall story **11** fabrication **13** prevarication

Cockcroft, John Douglas
   field: 7 physics
   nationality: 7 British
   developed: 24 Cockcroft-Walton generator
   worked with: 6 Walton
   awarded: 10 Nobel Prize

cockeyed 3 mad **4** awry, wild **5** askew, crazy, goofy, inane, nutty, weird **6** absurd, aslant, insane, tilted **7** crooked, foolish, twisted **8** lopsided, sideways **9** irregular, off-center, senseless **10** cockamamie, out of whack, ridiculous, unbalanced **11** nonsensical **12** asymmetrical, preposterous

Cockpit of Europe *see* **7** Belgium

cockscomb 4 comb **5** crest **7** celosia, coxcomb **8** amaranth, caruncle

cocksure 4 pert, smug, vain **5** brash, cocky, pushy **6** cheeky, snooty **8** arrogant, positive **9** assertive, audacious, bumptious, conceited **10** aggressive, swaggering **11** overbearing, self-assured, swell-headed **13** overconfident, self-confident

cocktail 5 drink, fruit, horse **6** shrimp **10** docked tail, semi-formal
   type: 4 grog **6** brandy, gibson, gimlet, mai tai, rob roy, zombie **7** Bellini, gin fizz, martini, negroni, sidecar, stinger **8** daiquiri, highball, hot toddy, pink lady **9** cuba libre, hurricane, gin rickey, manhattan, margarita, mint julep, rusty nail **10** bloody mary, tom collins **11** boilermaker, gin and tonic, grasshopper, screwdriver, sloe gin fizz **12** black russian, cosmopolitan, old-fashioned, tom and jerry, whiskey sour **13** planter's punch **15** brandy alexander
   mixer: 4 soda **5** tonic, water **7** bitters, seltzer **9** ginger ale
   garnish: 4 lime **5** lemon, olive, orange, twist **16** maraschino cherry
   stirrer: 7 muddler

cocktail lounge 3 bar **6** saloon, tavern **7** gin mill, taproom

cocky 5 brash, saucy **6** jaunty **8** arrogant, cocksure, impudent **9** conceited, egotistic **10** swaggering

Coco, James
   born: 9 New York NY
   roles: 11 Sancho Panza **13** Man of La Mancha **21** Last of the Red Hot Lovers

cocoa 5 brown, cacao **9** chocolate **12** hot chocolate

cocoon
   covering for: 5 larva
   stage: 5 pupal
   made of: 4 silk

Cocteau, Jean
   author of: 7 Orpheus **8** Antigone **12** Blood of a Poet **18** The Infernal Machine **19** Les Enfants Terribles, Les Parents Terribles **20** The Beauty and the Beast

Cocytus
   river in: 5 Hades

coddle 3 pat, pet **4** baby **5** humor, spoil **6** caress, cuddle, dote on, fondle, pamper **7** indulge **11** mollycoddle

code 4 laws **5** rules **6** cipher **7** statute **8** precepts **9** ordinance, standards **10** cryptogram, guidelines, principles **11** cryptograph, proprieties, regulations **13** secret writing **14** secret language

codger 5 crank, miser **6** geezer, oddity, old man **9** eccentric, odd person

codicil 5 rider **8** addendum, addition, appendix **9** extension, subscript **10** postscript, supplement **11** added clause

codify 4 rank, rate **5** grade, group, index, order **7** arrange, catalog **8** classify, organize, tabulate **9** methodize **10** categorize, coordinate, regularize **11** systematize

coelenterate 5 coral, hydra, polyp **6** Medusa **7** acaleph, radiate **8** acalephe **9** jellyfish **10** sea anemone
   habitat: 5 ocean **9** salt water

Coelophysis
   type: 8 dinosaur, therapod
   location: 7 Arizona
   period: 8 Triassic

coequal 5 equal **10** coordinate **16** equally important

coequality 6 parity **8** equality, evenness, sameness **10** uniformity **11** equivalency **14** correspondence

coerce 3 cow **4** make **5** bully, drive, force **6** compel, oblige **7** dragoon **8** browbeat, bulldoze, pressure, threaten **9** constrain, strong-arm **10** intimidate

coercer 5 bully **9** oppressor, tormenter, tormentor **10** browbeater **11** intimidator, petty tyrant

coercion 5 force **6** duress **7** threats **8** bullying, pressure **10** compulsion, constraint **11** browbeating **12** intimidation

coercive 8 enforced, forcible **10** compulsory, obligatory **11** threatening

coexist with 12 go hand in hand, go side by side, live together **13** go hand in glove

coffee 6 Coffea **13** Coffea arabica
   varieties: 4 Java, Kona, Wild **5** Irish, Mocha **6** Almond, Common **7** Arabian, Arabica, Robusta, Vanilla **8** Li-

berian, Liberica, Zanzibar **9** Colombian **11** French Roast, Wild robusta **13** Decaffeinated **20** Jamaican Blue Mountain
beverage: 5 decaf, latte **6** kahlua **8** espresso **10** cafe au lait, cappuccino
small cup: 9 demitasse

coffee (black)
French: 8 cafe noir **10** cafe nature

coffee brandy 6 Kahlua **8** Tia Maria

coffee with milk 5 latte
French: 10 cafe au lait

coffer 3 box **4** case **5** chest **9** strongbox **10** depository, repository **13** treasure chest

coffers 5 safes **6** vaults **8** treasury **9** cash boxes **11** money supply

coffin 3 box **4** pall **6** casket **10** catafalque **11** sarcophagus

cog 3 cam, lie **4** gear **5** cheat, cozen, tenon, tooth, wedge, wheel **8** small boat **10** projection

cogent 5 sound, valid **6** potent **7** weighty **8** forceful, powerful **9** effective, trenchant **10** compelling, convincing, persuasive, undeniable **11** meritorious, well-founded **12** well-grounded **16** incontrovertible

cogitate 5 study, think, weigh **6** ponder **7** reflect **8** meditate, mull over, ruminate **9** think over **10** deliberate, think about **11** contemplate, reflect upon **18** consider thoroughly

cogito ergo sum 18 I think therefore I am
said by: 9 Descartes

cognac
type: 6 brandy **7** liqueur
origin: 6 France
brand: 7 Bisquit, Martell **8** Hennessy **10** Remy Martin **11** Courvoisier
label: 2 VO (very old), VS (very special), XO (extra old) **3** XXO (extra extra old) **4** VSOP (very superior old pale) **8** Napoleon (5 year premium)
drink: 9 Andalusia
with Cointreau: 10 Rolls Royce
with Triple Sec: 7 Chicago **10** Rolls Royce
with vodka: 7 Cossack

cognate 4 akin, like **5** alike, close **7** kindred, related, similar **8** familial, parallel, relative **9** affiliate **10** derivative **11** consanguine

cognition 7 knowing **9** awareness, knowledge **11** familiarity **13** comprehension, understanding

cognizance 4 heed, note **5** grasp **6** notice, regard **8** scrutiny **9** attention, awareness, cognition, knowledge **10** perception **11** familiarity, observation, recognition, sensibility **12** apprehension **13** comprehension, consciousness, understanding

cognizant 5 aware **6** posted **7** knowing, mindful **8** familiar, informed,

versed in **9** conscious **10** acquainted, conversant, instructed **11** enlightened **13** knowledgeable, understanding

cognomen 4 name **6** handle **7** epithet, moniker, surname **11** appellation, designation

cognoscenti 6 judges **7** experts **8** insiders **11** authorities **12** connoisseurs **14** those in the know

cohere 3 fit, set **4** bind, fuse, glue, hold, jibe, join **5** agree, cling, match, stick, tally, unite **6** cement, concur, square **7** combine, conform, congeal **8** coalesce, coincide, dovetail, solidify **9** coagulate, harmonize **10** correspond **11** consolidate, synchronize **12** hold together **13** stick together

coherence 5 logic, unity **7** clarity, concord, harmony **8** cohesion **9** congruity **10** accordance, conformity, consonance **11** consistency, rationality **12** organization

coherent 5 clear, lucid **7** logical, orderly **8** cohesive, rational **9** congruous, connected, in keeping, organized **10** articulate, consistent, harmonious, meaningful, systematic **11** in agreement **12** intelligible **13** corresponding **14** comprehensible, understandable

cohesion 4 bond **5** union, unity **7** bonding **8** adhesion **10** attraction, solidarity

cohesive 3 set **5** solid **6** sticky **7** viscous **8** cemented, coherent, cohering, sticking **9** connected **11** indivisible, inseparable **12** consolidated **13** agglutinative

Cohn, Ferdinand Julius
field: 6 botany
nationality: 6 German
founded: 12 bacteriology

Cohn, Robert
character in: 15 The Sun Also Rises
author: 9 Hemingway

cohort 3 pal **4** chum **5** buddy, crony **6** fellow, friend **7** comrade **8** follower, myrmidon **9** associate, companion **10** accomplice

coif 3 cap **4** hood, veil **6** beggin, burlet, hairdo **8** biggonet, coiffure, skull cap **9** head-dress

coiffed 6 capped, styled **7** dressed **8** arranged

coiffeur 7 stylist **11** hairdresser **15** male hairdresser

coiffure 2 DA, GI **3** bob, bun **4** Afro, coif, perm, shag, trim, updo, wave **6** hairdo **7** beehive, blowcut, comb-out, flattop, haircut, pageboy, upsweep **8** cold wave, cornrows, ducktail **9** hairstyle, permanent, pompadour

coil 4 curl, loop, ring, roll, wind **5** braid, twine, twist **6** circle, spiral, writhe **7** entwine **8** encircle

coin 4 mint **5** hatch, money, piece **6** change, create, devise, invent, make

up, silver, strike **7** concoct, dream up, think up **8** conceive **9** fabricate, originate

coin/currency
of Afghanistan: 3 pul **5** abaze, riyal, rupee **6** abbasi, amania **7** afghani
of Albania: 3 lek **5** franc **6** qintar **7** quintar
of Algeria: 5 dinar **7** centime
of Andorra: 5 franc **6** peseta
of Angola: 6 escudo, kwanza, macuta, macute **7** angolar, centavo
of Argentina: 4 peso **7** centavo **9** argentino
of Armenia: 5 ruble
of Australia: 4 dump, tray, zack **5** pound **6** dollar **8** shilling
of Austria: 4 lira **5** crown, ducat, krone **6** florin, gulden, heller, zehner **8** albertin, groschen, kreutzer **9** schilling
of Azerbaijan: 5 manat
of Bahrain: 5 dinar
of Bangladesh: 4 taka **5** paisa
of Belarus: 5 ruble
of Belgium: 5 belga, franc **7** brabant, centime, crocard
of Benin: 5 franc **7** centime
of Bhutan: 5 paisa, rupee **7** chetrum **8** ngultrum
of Bolivia: 4 peso **7** centavo **9** boliviano
of Bosnia-Herzegovina: 5 dinar
of Botswana: 4 pula, rand
of Brazil: 3 joe **4** reis **5** dobra **7** centara, halfjoe, milreis **8** cruzeiro
of Bulgaria: 3 lev **8** stotinki
of Burkina Faso: 5 franc **7** centime
of Burundi: 5 franc **7** centime
of Cambodia: 3 sen **4** quan, riel **6** puttan **7** piaster
of Cameroon: 5 franc **7** centime
of Canada: 6 loonie, toonie
of Canary Islands: 6 peseta
of Cape Verde: 6 escudo **7** centavo
of Central African Republic: 5 franc **7** centime
of Chad: 5 franc **7** centime
of Chile: 4 peso **5** libra **6** condor, escudo
of China: 4 cash, cent, fyng, mace, tael, tiao, yuan **5** sycee **12** jen nin piao pu
of Colombia: 4 peso, real **6** condor, peseta **7** centavo
of Comoros: 5 franc **7** centime
of Congo: 5 franc **7** centime
of Costa Rica: 5 colon **6** colone **7** centimo
of Crete: 7 drachma
of Croatia: 5 dinar
of Cuba: 4 peso **7** centavo **8** cuarenta
of Cyprus 4 para **5** pound
of Czechoslovakia/ Czech Republic: 5 crown, ducat **6** heller, koruna
of Denmark: 3 one, ora, ore **4** fyrk **5** krone **8** frederik, skilling **9** rigsdaler
of Djibouti: 5 franc **7** centime

of Dominican Republic: 3 oro **4** peso **6** franco
of Ecuador: 5 sucre **7** centavo
of Egypt: 4 fils, kees, para **5** asper, dinar, fodda, gersh, girsh, medin, pound, riyal **6** ahmadi, dirham, foddah, guinea, junayh, maidin, medine, medino **7** piaster, piastre, tallard **8** bedidlik, millieme
of El Salvador: 4 peso **5** colon **7** centavo
of England: 3 ora **4** rial **5** achey, crown, groat, noble, pence, penny, pound **6** bawbee, florin, guinea **7** angelet, hapenny **8** farthing, shilling, sixpence, tuppence, tuppenny **13** pound sterling
of Equatorial Guinea: 6 ekuele, peseta **7** centimo
of Estonia: 3 lat **4** sent **5** kroon **7** estmark
of Ethiopia: 4 besa, birr, harf **5** amole, girsh **6** dollar, kharaf, levant, pataca, talari **7** ashrafi, menelik, plaster, tallero **12** maria theresa
of European Union: 4 euro
of Fiji: 6 dollar
of Finland: 4 mark **5** penni **6** markka **7** markkaa
of France: 5 franc **7** centime **8** napoleon
of Gabon Republic: 5 franc **7** centime
of the Gambia: 5 pound **6** butbut, dalasi
of Georgia: 5 ruble
of Germany: 4 mark **7** Ostmark, pfennig **12** Deutsche mark
of Ghana: 4 cedi, cidi **5** ackey
of Greece: 5 lepta **7** drachma
of Greenland: 3 ore **5** krone
of Guatemala: 4 peso **7** centavo, quetzal
of Guinea: 4 iliy, syli **5** franc **6** cauris
of Guinea-Bissau: 4 peso **6** escudo **7** centavo
of Haiti: 6 gourde **7** centime
of Honduras: 4 peso **7** centavo, lempira
of Hungary: 4 gara **5** balas, krone, pengo **6** filler, forint, gulden, korona, ongara, ungara
of Iceland: 5 aurar, eyrir, krona **6** kronur
of India: 3 lac, pie **4** anna, fels, lakh, pice, tara **5** abidi, crore, paisa, rupee
of Indonesia: 3 sen **6** rupiah
of Iran: 3 pul **4** asar, gran, lari, rial **5** bisti, daric, dinar, larin, shahi, toman **6** stater **7** ashrafi, kasbeke, pahlavi
of Iraq: 4 fils **5** dinar
of Ireland: 3 rap **4** real **5** pence, pound **6** turney **8** shilling
of Israel: 3 mil **5** agora, agura, pound, pruta **6** agorot, shekel
of Italy: 4 lira, lire, tara **5** grano, paoli, paolo, scudo, soldo **6** danaro, denaro, ducato, sequin **7** testone **8** zec-

chino **9** centesini
of Ivory Coast: 5 franc **7** centime
of Jamaica: 7 quattie
of Japan: 2 bu **3** mon, rin, rio, sen, shu, yen **4** cash, mibu, oban **5** koban, obang, tempo **6** cobang, ichebu, ichibu, itzebu, kogang **7** itzeboo, itziboo
of Jordan: 4 fils **5** dinar
of Kazakhstan: 5 ruble
of Kenya: 4 cent **5** pound **8** shilling
of Kiribati: 4 cent **6** dollar
of Korea: 3 woh, won **4** chun, hwan, kwan
of Kuwait: 4 fils **5** dinar
of Kyrgyzstan: 3 som
of Laos: 2 at **3** att, kip
of Latvia: 3 lat **4** latu **6** rublis, santim **7** kapeika, santima
of Lebanon: 5 livre, pound **7** piastre
of Lesotho: 4 cent, rand **6** maloti
of Liberia: 4 cent **6** dollar
of Libya: 5 dinar
of Liechtenstein: 5 franc **6** rappen **7** franken
of Lithuania: 3 lit **5** litas, marka **6** centas, fennig **7** ostmark, skatiku **8** auksinas, skatikas
of Luxembourg: 5 franc **7** centime
of Macao: 3 avo **6** pataca, pataco
of Macedonia: 5 denar
of Madagascar: 5 franc **7** centime
of Malawi: 6 kwacha **7** tambala
of Malaysia: 3 sen, tra **4** taro, trah **7** ringgit, tampang
of Maldives: 5 laree, rupee **7** rufiyaa
of Mali: 5 franc **7** centime
of Malta: 4 cent **5** grain, grano, pound
of Mauritania: 5 khoum **7** ouguiya
of Mauritius: 4 cent **5** rupee
of Mexico: 4 onza, peso **5** adobe, claco, tlaco **6** azteca, cuarto, dinero **7** centavo, piaster
of Moldova: 5 ruble
of Monaco: 5 franc **7** centime
of Mongolia: 5 mongo, mungo **6** tugrik **7** tughrik
of Montenegro: 4 para **6** florin **7** perpera
of Morocco: 4 flue, okia, rial **5** floos, franc, okieh, ounce **6** dirham, miskal **8** mouzouna
of Mozambique: 6 escudo **7** centavo, metical
of Myanmar: 3 pya **4** kyat
of Namibia: 4 cent, rand
of Nauru: 4 cent **6** dollar
of Nepal: 4 anna, pice **5** mohar, rupee
of the Netherlands: 4 doit, oord, raps **5** crown, daler, rider, ryder **6** florin, gulden, stiver, suskin **7** daalder, ducaton, escalan, escalin, guilder, stooter, stuiver **8** albertin, ducatoon **9** dubbeltje **12** rijksdaalder **13** albertustaler
of New Guinea: 4 kina, toea

of New Zealand: 4 cent **6** dollar
of Nicaragua: 4 peso **7** centavo, cordoba
of Niger: 5 franc **7** centime
of Nigeria: 4 kobo **5** naira
of Norway: 3 ore **5** krone **6** kroner
of Oman: 3 gaj, gaz **4** rial **5** baiza, ghazi **7** mahmudi
of Pakistan: 4 anna, pice **5** paisa, rupee
of Panama: 4 cent **6** balboa **9** centesimo
of Paraguay: 4 peso **7** centimo, guarani
of Peru: 3 sol **5** libra **6** dinero, reseta **7** centavo
of the Philippines: 4 peso **6** conant, peseta **7** centavo
of Poland: 4 abia **5** dalar, ducat, grosz, marka, zloty **6** fening, groszy, gulden, halerz, korona **8** groschen
of Portugal: 3 avo, joe **4** peca, real **5** conto, crown, dobra, indio, justo, rupia **6** escudo, macuta, octave, pataca, testad, tostao, vintem **7** angalar, centavo, crusado, miereis, moidore, testone **8** equipaga, johannes
of Qatar: 5 riyal **6** dirham
of Rumania: 3 ban, lei, leu, lev, ley **4** bani **5** uncia **6** triens
of Russia: 5 altin, bisti, copec, genga, grosh, kopek, ruble, shaur **6** abassi, copeck, grivna, kopeck, piatak, rouble **7** poltina, valiuta **8** auksinas, deneshka, imperial, polushka **9** poltinnik **10** altininink, chervonets
of Rwanda: 5 franc **7** centime
of San Marino: 4 lira, lire **9** centesimi
of Samoa: 4 tala
of Sao Tome and Principe: 5 dobra **6** escudo **7** centavo
of Sardinia: 7 carline
of Saudi Arabia: 5 girsh, gursh, pound, riyal
of Scotland: 3 ecu **4** demy, doit, lion, mark, rial, ryal **5** bodle, broad, groat, plack, rider, turne **6** bawbee, folles **7** unicorn **8** atchison, hardhead **9** halfpenny **11** bonnetpiece
of Senegal: 5 franc **7** centime
of Sicily: 5 litra, oncia, uncia **6** carlin **7** carline, oncetta
of Sierra Leone: 4 cent **5** leone
of Singapore: 4 cent **6** dollar
of Slovakia: 6 koruna
of Slovenia: 5 tolar
of Solomon Islands: 4 cent **6** dollar
of Somalia: 4 besa **6** somalo **8** shilling **9** centesimi
of South Africa: 4 cent, pond, rand **5** pound **6** florin **7** daalder **9** krugerrand
of Spain: 3 cob **4** duro, peso, real **5** dobla **6** cuarto, dinero, doblon, escudo, peseta **7** alfonso, centimo, pistole, realdor **8** doubloon
of Sri Lanka: 4 cent **5** rupee

of **Sudan:** 5 pound 7 piastre
of **Suriname:** 4 cent 7 guilder
of **Swaziland:** 4 rand 9 lilangeni
of **Sweden:** 3 ore 5 krona, krone 7 carolin 8 skilling 9 rigsdaler
of **Switzerland:** 5 franc, rappe 6 hallar, rappen 7 angster, centime, duplone 8 baetzner, blaffert
of **Syria:** 4 lira 5 pound 6 talent 7 piaster
of **Taiwan:** 4 yuan 6 dollar
of **Tajikistan:** 5 ruble
of **Tanzania:** 4 cent 8 shilling
of **Thailand:** 2 at 3 att 4 baht 5 cutty, fuang, tical 6 pynung, salung, satang 11 bullet money
of **Tibet:** 5 tanga
of **Togo:** 5 franc 7 centime
of **Tonga:** 6 paanga, seniti
of **Trinidad and Tobago:** 4 cent 6 dollar
of **Tunisia:** 5 dinar 6 dollar 7 millime
of **Turkey:** 4 lira, para 5 akcha, asper, attun, kurus, pound, rebia 6 akcheh, sequin, zequin 7 aetilik, beshlik, pataque, piaster 8 medjidie, zecchino
of **Turkmenistan:** 5 ruble
of **Tuvalu:** 4 cent 6 dollar
of **Uganda:** 4 cent 8 shilling
of **Ukraine:** 6 grivna 10 karbovanet
of **United Arab Emirates:** 3 fil 6 dirham
of **Uruguay:** 4 peso 9 centesimo, centisimo
of **Uzbekistan:** 5 ruble
of **Vanuatu:** 5 franc 6 dollar
of **Venezuela:** 4 peso, real 5 medio 6 fuerte 7 bolivar, centimo 8 morocota 10 venezolano
of **Vietnam:** 2 xu 4 dong 7 piaster
of **Western Samoa:** 4 sene, tala
of **Yemen:** 4 fils, rial 5 dinar, riyal
of **Yugoslavia:** 4 para 5 dinar
of **Zaire:** 5 zaire 6 makuta
of **Zambia:** 5 ngwee 6 kwacha
of **Zimbabwe:** 4 cent 6 dollar

coincide 3 fit 4 jibe, meet 5 agree, cross, match, tally 6 accord, concur, square 7 conform 8 converge, dovetail 9 harmonize 10 correspond 11 synchronize 12 be concurrent, come together 19 occur simultaneously

coincidence 4 fate, luck 6 chance 8 accident 11 concurrence, synchronism 12 happenstance 22 simultaneous occurrence

coincident 10 coexistent, concurrent 12 contemporary, simultaneous 15 contemporaneous

coincidental 6 chance 9 unplanned 10 accidental, contiguous, synchronal 11 concomitant, synchronous 12 happenstance, simultaneous

Cointreau
type: 7 liqueur
variety: 7 curacao 9 triple sec
origin: 6 France

flavor: 6 orange
drink: 8 Applecar
with bourbon: 10 Temptation
with brandy: 7 Sidecar
with cognac: 10 Rolls Royce
with gin: 7 Florida 9 White Lady 13 Sweet Patootie 14 Flying Dutchman
with rum: 8 Acapulco 10 Casa Blanca 11 Beachcomber 12 Blue Hawaiian
with rye: 10 Temptation
with tequila: 9 Margarita
with whiskey: 16 Canadian Cocktail

Colavito, Rocky (Rocco Domenico)
sport: 8 baseball
team: 16 Cleveland Indians

Colbert, Claudette
real name: 22 Claudette Lily Chauchoin
born: 5 Paris 6 France
roles: 8 Tovarich 9 Cleopatra 14 Palm Beach Story 18 It Happened One Night (Oscar)

cold 3 icy, old 4 cool, dead, flat, hard 5 aloof, brisk, chill, crisp, cruel, faded, faint, gelid, harsh, nippy, polar, sharp, stale, stiff, stony 6 arctic, biting, bitter, chilly, cooled, frigid, frosty, frozen, inured, numbed, remote, severe, snappy, steely, wintry 7 callous, chilled, cutting, distant, frosted, glacial, haughty, nipping, passive, unmoved 8 chilling, coolness, detached, freezing, hardened, piercing, reserved, reticent, stinging, uncaring, unheated, unloving, unwarmed 9 apathetic, heartless, impassive, insensate, unfeeling, unstirred 10 disdainful, forbidding, impervious, insensible, phlegmatic, unfriendly 11 frozen stiff, indifferent, passionless, penetrating, unconcerned, unconscious, unemotional, unexcitable 12 antipathetic, bone-chilling, inaccessible, supercilious, uninterested, unresponsive 13 uninteresting, unsympathetic 14 marrow-chilling, unapproachable 15 teeth-chattering, uncommunicative, undemonstrative 16 chilled to the bone, unimpressionable 18 chilled to the marrow

cold-blooded 4 evil, hard 5 cruel, harsh, stiff, stony 6 brutal, flinty, formal, frigid, inured, savage, steely 7 callous, demonic, inhuman, passive, satanic, unmoved 8 detached, fiendish, hardened, inhumane, pitiless, reserved, ruthless, uncaring 9 barbarous, heartless, impassive, merciless, unfeeling, unpitying, unstirred 10 deliberate, diabolical, disdainful, impervious, implacable, unfriendly, unmerciful, villainous 11 calculating, hardhearted, indifferent, insensitive, passionless, unconcerned, unemotional, unexcitable 12 bloodthirsty, contemptuous, uninterested, unresponsive 13 disinterested, unimpas-

sioned, unimpressible, unsympathetic 16 unimpressionable

Cold Case
network: 3 CBS
cast: 8 John Finn (John Stillman) 9 Danny Pino (Scotty Valens), Thom Berry (Will Jeffries) 13 Kathryn Morris (Lilly Rush) 15 Jeremy Ratchford (Nick Vera)

cold-hearted 5 cruel 9 heartless, unfeeling 11 hard-hearted 13 unsympathetic

Cold Mountain
director: 16 Anthony Minghella
author: 14 Charles Frazier
cast: 7 Jude Law (Inman) 11 Ray Winstone (Teague) 12 Eileen Atkins (Maddy), Nicole Kidman (Ada Monroe) 14 Natalie Portman (Sara), Renee Zellweger (Ruby Thewes) 16 Donald Sutherland (Reverend Monroe) 20 Philip Seymour Hoffman (Reverend Veasy)

coldness 5 chill 7 iciness 9 aloofness 10 chilliness, frostiness 12 indifference 13 unfeelingness 14 unfriendliness 15 hardheartedness

Cole, Janet
real name of: 9 Kim Hunter

Cole, Thomas
born: 7 England 13 Bolton-le-Moors
artwork: 8 The Ox-Bow 15 The Voyage of Life 17 The Course of Empire

coleoptera
class: 8 hexopoda
phylum: 10 arthropoda
group: 6 beetle, weevil

Coleridge, Samuel Taylor
author of: 9 Kubla Khan 10 Christabel 14 Dejection An Ode, Lyrical Ballads (with Wordsworth) 19 Biographia Literaria 26 The Rime of the Ancient Mariner

Colette (Sidonie)
author of: 4 Gigi, Sido 5 Cheri 8 Claudine 11 La Vagabonde 14 The Evening Star

coliseum 4 bowl 5 arena 6 circus 7 stadium, theater 9 Colosseum 10 hippodrome 12 amphitheater 14 exhibition hall

collaborate 4 join 5 unite 6 assist, team up 7 collude 9 cooperate 10 join forces 12 work together 14 work side by side

collaborationist 6 puppet 7 traitor 8 quisling

collaborator 4 ally 6 puppet 7 traitor 8 co-worker, quisling, teammate 9 associate, colleague, co-partner 11 confederate

collapse 4 coma, fail, fall, flop, fold 5 faint, swoon 6 attack, buckle, cave-in, fizzle 7 break up, crack-up, crumple, failure, give way, seizure 8 be in vain, buckling, downfall, flounder, keel over, take sick 9 become ill, break down **10** be stricken, break apart, run aground **11** fall through **12** disintegrate, falling apart, fall helpless, fall to pieces **13** come to nothing, sudden illness **14** disintegration **17** become unconscious

collapsed 4 limp **7** caved in, compact **8** deflated, fallen in, folded up **13** disintegrated

collapsible 7 folding **8** foldable **10** deflatable

collar 3 nab **4** eton, grab **5** catch, fichu, pinch, seize **6** arrest, bertha **7** capture **9** apprehend, neckpiece **12** take prisoner **15** take into custody

collate 5 order **6** bestow, verify **7** compare **8** assemble, organize **9** integrate **11** put together

Collateral
    director: **11** Michael Mann
    cast: **9** Jamie Foxx (Max), Tom Cruise (Vincent) **11** Mark Ruffalo (Fanning) **16** Jada Pinkett Smith (Annie)

collateral 4 bond **5** extra **6** pledge, surety **7** warrant **8** parallel, security, warranty **9** accessory, ancillary, auxiliary, guarantee, insurance, secondary **10** additional, incidental, supporting, supportive **11** endorsement, subordinate **12** contributory **13** supplementary

collation 3 tea **4** meal **5** lunch **6** brunch, repast, sermon **7** address, reading **8** hotchpot, luncheon, treatise **10** comparison **11** description

colleague 4 mate **6** fellow **7** partner **8** confrere, co-worker, teammate **9** associate, co-partner **11** confederate **12** collaborator, fellow worker

collect 3 get **4** calm, meet **5** amass, raise, rally **6** gather, heap up, muster, obtain, pick up, pile up, summon **7** call for, compile, compose, control, convene, marshal, prepare, receive, solicit **8** assemble, gather up, scrape up **9** aggregate, get hold of **10** accumulate, congregate **11** concentrate, get together

collectanea 8 analects, treasury **9** anthology, gleanings **10** collection, miscellany, selections **11** miscellanea

collected 4 calm, cool **5** quiet **6** placid, poised, serene, steady **8** composed, peaceful, tranquil **9** confident, unruffled **10** cool-headed, restrained **11** level-headed, self-assured, undisturbed, unemotional, unflappable, unperturbed **12** even-tempered **13** self-possessed **14** self-controlled

collection 3 mob **4** bevy, body, gift, heap, mass, pack, pile **5** array, bunch, clump, crowd, drove, flock, group, hoard, store, swarm **6** corpus, jumble, muster, throng **7** cluster, clutter, variety **8** amassing, assembly, oblation, treasury **9** anthology, gathering, offertory, receiving **10** assemblage, assort-

ment, hodgepodge, miscellany, soliciting **11** aggregation, compilation **12** accumulating, accumulation

collective 5 joint **6** common, mutual, united **7** unified **8** combined, gathered **9** aggregate, composite **10** cumulative, integrated **11** accumulated, cooperative

collector 6 grouper **7** dustman **8** antiquer, compiler, composer, gatherer, zamindar **9** assembler **10** garbageman **11** anthologist

Collector, The
    author: **10** John Fowles

college 7 academy **8** seminary **9** institute **10** university **11** institution

college-preparatory 4 prep **8** academic **11** liberal-arts **12** nontechnical **13** nonvocational

collegiate 8 academic **10** scholastic, university **11** educational

collide 3 hit **4** meet **5** clash, crash, smash **7** crack up, diverge, run into **8** bump into, conflict, disagree **9** knock into **10** meet head on **11** beat against **13** hurtle against, strike against

Collier, Lucille Ann
    real name of: **9** Ann Miller

Collins, Mary Catherine
    real name of: **7** Bo Derek

Collins, Mr
    character in: **17** Pride and Prejudice
    author: **6** Austen

Collins, Wilkie
    author of: **6** No Name **12** The Moonstone **15** The Woman in White

collision 4 bump **5** clash, crash, fight, smash **6** battle, combat, impact **7** smash-up **8** accident, conflict, skirmish, struggle **9** encounter **10** engagement **11** clash of arms

colloquial 5 homey, plain **6** casual, chatty, common, folksy **8** everyday, familiar, homespun, informal, ordinary, workaday **9** idiomatic **10** vernacular **14** conversational **15** unsophisticated

colloquy 4 chat, talk **6** caucus, parley **7** council, palaver, seminar **8** commerce, congress, converse, dialogue **9** communion, discourse **10** conference, discussion, rap session **11** interchange, intercourse **12** conversation **13** confabulation

collude 4 plot **7** connive **8** conspire, intrigue **9** cooperate **11** collaborate

collusion 5 fraud **7** treason **8** intrigue **10** complicity, connivance, conspiracy **13** collaboration **15** secret agreement **17** guilty association

Colman, Ronald
    born: **7** England **8** Richmond
    roles: **9** Beau Geste **10** Arrowsmith **11** A Double Life (Oscar), Lost Horizon **16** A Tale of Two Cities

cologne 5 scent **7** essence, perfume **9** fragrance **11** toilet water

Colomba
    author: **14** Prosper Merimee

Colombia
    other name: **6** Darien **10** New Granada
    capital/largest city: **6** Bogota
    others: **3** Ten **4** Amza, Buga, Cali, Mitu, Muzo, Paez, Sipi, Tado, Tolu, Yari **5** Bello, Chinu, Guapi, Neiva, Pasto, Tulua, Tunja **6** Cucuta, Ibaque, Lorica, Quibdo, Sangil, Tumaco **7** Cartago, Ipiates, Leticia, Palmira, Pereira, Popayan **8** Girardot, Maganque, Medellin, Monteria **9** Cartagena, Manizales **10** Santa Marta **11** Bucaramanga **12** Barranquilla, Buenaventura
    school: **5** Andes, Valle **20** Instituto Caro y Cuervo **21** Industrial de Santander
    measure: **4** vara **7** azumbre, celemin
    monetary unit: **4** peso, real **6** condor, peseta **7** centavo
    weight: **3** bag **4** saco **5** libra **7** quintal
    island: **4** Baru **5** Naipo **6** Fuerte **7** Gorgona, Malpelo **8** Cusachon **9** San Andres **11** Providencia
    lake: **4** Tota
    mountain: **5** Abibe, Andes, Baudo, Chita, Cocuy, Huila, Pasto **6** Ayapel, Perija, Purace, Tolima, Tunahi **7** Chamusa, del Ruiz **8** Oriengal **10** Santa Marta **17** Central Cordillera, Eastern Cordillera, Western Cordillera
    highest point: **14** Cristobal Colon
    river: **3** Uva **4** Bita, Meta, Muco, Sinu, Tomo, Yari **5** Cauca, Cesar, Isana, Mesai, Nechi, Pauto, Sucio **6** Amazon, Arauca, Ariari, Atrato, Atroto, Caguan, Pattia, Yapura **7** Apapois, Caqueta, Guainia, Inirida, Truando, Vichada **8** Casanare, Guaviara, Putumayo **9** Magdalena
    sea: **7** Pacific **9** Caribbean
    physical feature:
      cape: **4** Vela **5** Aguja, Marzo, Punta **7** Augusta **8** Gallinas
      falls: **10** Tequendama
      gulf: **5** Uraba **6** Cupica, Darien, Tibuga **8** Tortugas
      inlet: **6** Tumaco
      plains: **6** Ilanos
      point: **6** Cruces, Lacruz, Solano **8** Caribana, Gallinas
    people: **4** Boro, Cuna, Duit, Hoka, Macu, Muso, Muzo, Paez, Tama, Tapa **5** Carib, Catio, Choco, Cofan, Cogui, Cubeo, Guane, Haida, Mocoa, Paeze, Pijao, Seona, Yagua **6** Arawak, Betoya, Calima, Colima, Ingano, Mirana, Saliva, Tahami, Ticuna, Tucano, Tunebo, Witoto, Yahuna **7** Achagua, Andaqui, Chibcha, Chimila, Churoya, Guahibo,

Guajiro, Panches, Puinave, Puitoto, Quechua, Shuswap, Tairona, Telembi **8** Coconuco, Guarauno, mestizos, Motilone, Puinavis, Quimbaya, Sinsigas **9** Cocanucos, Coconucan, mulattoes, Panaquita **10** Bellacoola
  leader: 7 Bolivar
language: 7 Spanish
religion: 13 Roman Catholic
place:
  museum: 4 Gold **8** Colonial
  palace: 11 Inquisition
feature:
  dance: 7 bambuco **8** merengue
  game: 4 tejo
  guitar: 5 tiple
  poncho: 5 ruana
  shoes: 10 alpargatas
  shoulder bag: 7 carriel
  tree: 8 arboloco
  woven hat: 5 jipas

Colombo
  capital of: 8 Sri Lanka

colon 4 coin **6** farmer, vitals **7** pioneer, planter, settler, viscera **9** hemistich, intestine **15** plantation owner, punctuation mark

colonize 5 found, plant **6** gather, settle **7** migrate **8** establish **10** infiltrate

colonnade 3 row **4** stoa **5** porch **6** arcade, piazza **7** portico, terrace **8** cloister **9** peristyle

colony 3 set **4** band, body **5** flock, group, swarm **7** mandate **8** dominion, province **9** community, territory **10** dependency, possession, settlement **12** protectorate **14** satellite state

colophon 6 design, device, emblem **7** insigne **8** insignia **11** inscription

color 3 dye, hue **4** bias, burn, cast, glow, mood, tint, tone, warp, wash **5** bloom, blush, chalk, drift, flame, flush, force, paint, sense, shade, slant, stain, taint, tinge, twist **6** affect, aspect, crayon, effect, import, intent, redden, spirit, stress **7** distort, feeling, meaning, pervert, pigment, redness, skin hue **8** dyestuff, rosiness **9** go crimson, influence, intention, prejudice **10** intimation **11** connotation, implication, insinuation **12** become florid, pigmentation, significance **17** natural complexion

Colorado
  abbreviation: 2 CO **4** Colo
  nickname: 10 Centennial
  capital/largest city: 6 Denver
  others: 4 Vail **5** Aspen, Delta, Lamar, Ouray **6** Arvada, Aurora, Denver, Golden, Pueblo, Salida **7** Alamosa, Boulder, Durango, Greeley, Manassa, Manitou **8** Gunnison, Loveland, Trinidad **9** Purgatory, Silverton, Telluride **11** Central City **12** Cripple Creek **13** Grand Junction **15** Colorado Springs
  college: 5 Regis **6** Denver **7** Boulder **17** US Air Force Academy

feature: 11 Four Corners **15** Garden of the Gods **17** Continental Divide
  national monument: 8 Dinosaur **14** Great Sand Dunes
  national park: 5 Estes **9** Mesa Verde **13** Rocky Mountain
  tribe: 3 Ute **7** Arapaho **8** Cheyenne
  people: 9 John Elway **11** Jack Dempsey **12** Ralph Edwards **14** Scott Carpenter **18** Douglas Fairbanks Sr
  lake: 6 Frozen
  land rank: 6 eighth
  mountains: 5 Longs, Rocky **7** San Juan **9** Pikes Peak **14** Sangre de Cristo
    highest point: 6 Elbert
  physical feature:
    canyon: 5 Black
    gorge: 5 Royal
    plains: 5 Great
    wind: 7 Chinook
  pro teams:
    baseball: 7 Rockies
    basketball: 7 Nuggets
    football: 7 Broncos
    hockey: 9 Avalanche
  river: 4 Gila **5** Yampa **6** Platte **7** Dolores **8** Apishapa, Arikaree, Arkansas, Gunnison **9** Rio Grande **10** Purgatoire
  state admission: 12 thirty-eighth
  state bird: 11 lark bunting
  state flower: 22 Rocky Mountain columbine
  state motto: 24 Nothing Without Providence
  state song: 22 Where the Columbines Grow
  state tree: 18 Colorado blue spruce

colored 4 dyed, hued **5** dusky **6** biased, shaded, tinged, tinted **7** blushed, excused, flushed, glossed, labeled, painted, stained **8** affected, labelled, reddened **9** chromatic, distorted, pigmented **10** influenced, prejudiced **12** complexioned **13** characterized **14** misrepresented

colorful 3 gay **4** loud **5** showy, vivid **6** bright, florid, unique **7** dynamic, graphic, unusual, vibrant, zestful **8** animated, forceful, spirited, vigorous **9** brilliant, full-toned, vivacious **10** compelling, variegated **11** distinctive, interesting, many-colored, picturesque **12** multicolored, particolored

coloring 3 dye **4** tint **5** color, shade, stain **10** coloration, complexion

colorless 3 wan **4** ashy, drab, dull, flat, pale **5** ashen, dingy, faded, pasty, vapid, white **6** anemic, boring, dreary, grayed, pallid, sallow, sickly, undyed **7** ghastly, ghostly, insipid, natural, neutral, prosaic **8** blanched, bleached, lifeless, ordinary, whitened **9** bloodless, washed out **10** cadaverous, lackluster, monotonous, spiritless, unanimated, unexciting, uninspired **11** commonplace **13** uninteresting

Color Purple, The
  author: 11 Alice Walker
  director: 15 Steven Spielberg
  cast: 11 Danny Glover **12** Adolph Caesar, Oprah Winfrey **13** Margaret Avery **14** Whoopi Goldberg

colors 4 flag, jack **6** banner, ensign, pennon **7** pennant **8** standard

colossal 4 huge, vast **5** giant, grand, great **6** mighty **7** extreme, immense, mammoth, massive, titanic **8** enormous, gigantic, imposing **9** exceeding, excessive **10** incredible, inordinate, monumental, prodigious, tremendous **11** extravagant, spectacular **12** awe-inspiring, overwhelming

Colossus of Rhodes
  statue of: 6 Apollo

colt 4 foal **5** horse **6** novice **8** equuleus, yearling **9** fledgling, youngster
  constellation of: 8 Equuleus

columbium
  chemical symbol: 2 Cb

Columbo
  character: 9 Lt Columbo
  cast: 9 Peter Falk

column 3 row **4** file, line, post **5** pylon, queue, shaft, train **6** parade, pillar, string **7** caravan, phalanx, support, upright **8** pilaster **9** cavalcade, formation **10** procession **11** vertical row **12** vertical list

columnist 6 writer **7** analyst
  famous: 7 Heloise **9** Dear Abby, Herb Caen **9** HL Mencken, Jack Smith **10** Ann Landers **11** Miss Manners **15** Abigail van Buren

coma 6 stupor, torpor **8** collapse **15** unconsciousness

Comanche
  language family: 10 Shoshonean
  location: 5 Texas **6** Kansas, Mexico **8** Oklahoma
  noted as: 8 horsemen

comatose 3 lax **4** dull, idle, lazy **5** inert **6** leaden, torpid **7** drugged, languid, passive **8** inactive, indolent, lifeless, listless, slothful, sluggish **9** apathetic, catatonic, lethargic, stuporous **10** cataleptic, insensible, narcotized, phlegmatic, spiritless **11** indifferent, unconcerned, unconscious **12** unresponsive

comb 4 card, tuft **5** curry, dress, groom, plume, scour, style **6** search **7** arrange, explore, panache, ransack, topknot **8** head tuft, hunt over, untangle **9** cast about, cockscomb, currycomb **11** look through **14** rummage through

combat 5 clash, fight **6** action, attack, battle, oppose, resist **7** contest, go to war, wage war **8** conflict, fighting, skirmish, struggle **9** encounter **10** contention, engagement, war against **11** come to blows, grapple with, make warfare, work against **12** do battle with, march against **13** confrontation **14** military action

Combat
character: **4** Caje (Caddy Cadron) **5** Kirby **8** (Pvt) Braddock **9** Doc Walton, (Lt) Gil Hanley **12** (Sgt) Chip Saunders
cast: **9** Jack Hogan, Rick Jason, Vic Morrow **12** Shecky Greene, Steven Rogers **13** Pierre Jalbert

combatant 7 fighter, soldier, warrior **9** man-at-arms **10** serviceman **11** fighting man

combating 8 battling, clashing, fighting, opposing **9** waging war **10** contention, contesting, opposition, struggling **11** doing battle **13** grappling with **17** coming to blows with

combative 6 bantam **8** militant **9** agonistic, bellicose **10** aggressive, pugnacious **11** belligerent, contentious **12** antagonistic

combativeness 9 hostility, pugnacity **10** antagonism **12** belligerence **14** aggressiveness **15** contentiousness

combination 3 mix **5** alloy, blend, union **6** fusion, league, medley, merger, mixing **7** amalgam, joining, mixture, pooling, variety **8** alliance, blending, compound **9** coalition, composite, synthesis **10** assortment, coalescing, federation **11** association, composition, confederacy **12** amalgamation **13** confederation

combine 3 mix **4** fuse, join, pool **5** blend, merge, unify, unite **6** couple, league, mingle **8** compound **9** commingle **10** amalgamate, synthesize **11** consolidate, incorporate

combo 4 band **5** group **11** aggregation, combination

comb out 4 curl **5** dress **7** arrange, unsnarl **8** untangle

combustible 8 burnable **9** flammable, ignitable **10** combustive, incendiary **11** inflammable **13** conflagrative

combustion 6 firing **7** burning, flaming **8** ignition, kindling **12** incineration **13** conflagration

combustive 8 burnable **9** flammable, ignitable **11** combustible, inflammable **13** conflagrative

come 2 be, go **3** bud **4** fall, loom, rise **5** arise, issue, occur, range, reach **6** appear, arrive, be made, drop in, emerge, extend, follow, happen, impend, show up, spread, spring, turn up **7** advance, descend, emanate, stretch **8** approach, draw near, go toward, grow to be **9** be a native, germinate, take place **10** be imminent, move toward **11** be a resident, be in the wind, materialize, originate in, spring forth

come about 5 occur **6** chance, happen **7** turn out **10** come to pass

come afterward 5 ensue **6** derive, follow, result **7** succeed

come apart 6 detach **7** disjoin, unstick **8** separate

come back 5 rally **6** answer, retort, return **7** rebound **8** recovery

Come Back Little Sheba
director: **10** Daniel Mann
based on play by: **11** William Inge
cast: **10** Terry Moore **12** Shirley Booth **13** Burt Lancaster
Oscar for: **7** actress (Booth)

come clean 4 sing **5** own up **7** confess **14** unbosom oneself **18** make a clean breast of

come close to 7 verge on **8** approach, border on **11** approximate, nearly equal

comedian 3 wag **4** fool, zany **5** clown, comic, cutup, joker **6** jester, madcap **7** buffoon **8** humorist, jokester **9** prankster **10** comedienne, comic actor **14** practical joker

comedown 4 drop **8** lowering **10** anticlimax

come down 4 dive, drop, fall, sink **6** plunge, tumble **7** descend, plummet **8** decrease

come down a peg 5 deign, stoop **6** unbend **7** descend **10** condescend **12** lower oneself **13** humble oneself

comedy 3 fun, wit **5** farce, humor **6** banter, joking, pranks, satire **7** foolery, jesting **8** drollery, raillery, travesty **9** burlesque, cutting up, horseplay, silliness **10** buffoonery, pleasantry, tomfoolery **13** fooling around

Comedy of Errors, The
author: **18** William Shakespeare
character: **6** Aegeon, Dromio **7** Adriana, Aemilia, Luciana, Solinus **10** Antipholus

come face to face with 4 meet **8** confront **9** encounter

come first 7 precede, predate **8** antecede, antedate, go before **10** anticipate

come into being 4 dawn, show **5** arise, begin, occur, set in, start **6** appear, be born, crop up, emerge, sprout **8** commence, spring up **9** germinate, originate **11** come to light

come into port 4 dock **5** berth

come into view 4 show **6** appear, come up, emerge, show up **7** surface **11** come to light **13** become visible

come loose 5 let go **6** detach, loosen **7** slip off **8** break off, separate, unfasten **9** break away **10** come undone, come untied, disconnect **11** come unglued, come unstuck

comely 4 fair, nice **5** bonny **6** pretty, proper, seemly, simple **7** correct, fitting, natural, sightly, winning, winsome **8** becoming, blooming, charm-

ing, decorous, engaging, fetching, pleasant, pleasing, suitable, tasteful **9** agreeable, appealing, wholesome **10** attractive, unaffected **11** well-favored

come near 4 loom, near **6** appear **8** approach **9** draw close **10** move toward

come-on 4 bait, hook, lure, trap **5** decoy, snare **6** magnet **9** seduction **10** allurement, attraction, bewitchery, enticement, inducement, seducement, temptation **12** inveiglement

comestibles 5 foods **7** edibles **8** victuals **10** foodstuffs, provisions

come to a decision 6 decide, settle **7** resolve **8** conclude **9** determine

come to an understanding 5 agree **6** settle **11** come to terms **12** agree to marry **16** reach an agreement

come to a standstill 4 halt, quit, stop **5** abate, cease **7** die away **8** quit cold

come to blows 5 fight **7** contest **8** do battle **9** square off **12** start to fight

come together 4 meet **5** flock, group, rally **6** gather **7** collect, convene **8** assemble **10** congregate **11** get together

come to light 4 dawn **5** arise **6** appear, crop up, emerge, evolve, show up, turn up, unfold **7** develop, surface, turn out

come to nothing 4 fail, flop, fold **6** fizzle **8** be in vain, collapse **9** break down **11** fall through **12** come to naught **17** fail to materialize

come to pass 5 ensue, occur **6** arrive, befall, follow, happen **9** take place

come to terms 5 agree, yield **6** give up, settle **8** succumb **8** contract, cry quits **9** make a deal, negotiate, surrender **10** capitulate, compromise **11** come to grips, meet halfway, sue for peace **13** resign oneself **14** strike a bargain **15** lay down one's arms **16** reach an agreement **17** acknowledge defeat, hoist the white flag **18** split the difference

come unglued 6 detach, loosen **8** separate **9** fall apart **11** come unstuck

come unstuck 4 lift **6** detach, loosen **8** break off, unfasten **9** break away, come apart, come loose, fall apart **11** come unglued

come up 4 rise **5** arise **7** quicken, sharpen **8** heighten, increase **9** intensify **10** accelerate, strengthen **12** be referred to

come upon 4 find, meet **7** learn of, run into **8** discover **9** encounter

comfit 5 candy, sweet **9** sweetmeat **10** confection, sugar candy **13** confectionery

comfort 4 calm, ease, help **5** cheer, peace, quiet **6** luxury, relief, solace, soothe, succor, warmth **7** cheer up, compose, console, hearten **8** coziness, opulence, pleasure, reassure, serenity, snugness **9** bolster up, comforter, composure, encourage, well-being **10** cheering up, relaxation **11** consolation, contentment, reassurance **12** satisfaction **13** encouragement, gratification **14** quiet one's fears

Comfort, Alex
author of: **11** The Joy of Sex **12** More Joy of Sex

comfortable 4 cozy, easy **6** at ease, at home, serene **7** relaxed **8** adequate, pleasant, suitable **9** agreeable, congenial, contented **10** giving ease, gratifying, untroubled **11** pleasurable, undisturbed **12** satisfactory **16** free from distress

comforter 4 balm, puff **5** quilt, scarf **6** afghan, solace **7** anodyne, blanket, comfort, soother **8** coverlet **10** palliative

comic, comical 4 rich **5** droll, funny, merry, silly, witty **6** absurd, jocose, jovial **7** amusing, jocular, risible **8** farcical, humorous, mirthful **9** facetious, laughable, ludicrous, whimsical **10** ridiculous **11** nonsensical **12** nimble-witted

coming 4 next **6** advent, future, in view, to come **7** arrival, nearing **8** approach, arriving, imminent, on the way **9** advancing, emergence, imminence, impending, in the wind, proximity **10** appearance, occurrence, subsequent **11** approaching, forthcoming, prospective **12** on the horizon **13** materializing

Coming Home
director: **8** Hal Ashby
cast: **9** Bruce Dern, Jane Fonda, Jon Voight **15** Robert Carradine
Oscar for: **5** actor (Voight) **7** actress (Fonda) **10** screenplay

Coming into the Country
author: **10** John McPhee

Coming of Age, The
author: **16** Simone de Beauvoir

Coming of Age in Samoa
author: **12** Margaret Mead

Coming Race, The
author: **18** Edward Bulwer-Lytton

command 3 bid, get **4** boss, call, draw, fiat, grip, head, hold, lead, rule **5** edict, evoke, grasp, guide, order, power **6** adjure, behest, charge, compel, decree, demand, direct, elicit, enjoin, govern, incite, induce, kindle, manage, ordain, prompt, summon **7** call for, conduct, control, deserve, extract, inspire, mastery, provoke, receive, require, summons **8** call upon, instruct, motivate **9** authority, call forth, direction, directive, governing, knowledge, ordinance, supervise, ultimatum **10** administer, be master of, domination, injunction, leadership, management **11** familiarity, instruc-

tion, superintend, supervision **12** have charge of **13** comprehension, understanding **14** administration **17** have authority over

commandant 7 captain **9** commander **12** chief officer

commandeer 4 take **5** seize, usurp **8** shanghai **11** appropriate, expropriate

commander 4 boss, head **5** chief, ruler **6** leader **7** manager **8** director **9** conductor

commanding 4 head **5** chief, grand, lofty **6** ruling, senior, strong **7** dynamic, leading, ranking, stately **8** forceful, gripping, imposing, powerful, striking, towering **9** arresting, directing, governing, important, prominent **10** compelling, dominating, impressive **11** controlling, significant **13** authoritative, distinguished, overshadowing

commandment
Hebrew: **7** mitsvah, mitzvah

comme il faut 6 proper **7** fitting **12** as it should be

commemorate 4 hail, mark **5** extol, honor **6** hallow, revere, salute **7** acclaim, glorify, observe **8** venerate **9** celebrate, solemnize **11** acknowledge, memorialize, pay homage to **12** pay tribute to

commence 5 begin, start **8** get going, initiate **10** get started, inaugurate, originated

commencement 4 dawn **5** birth, onset, start **6** outset **7** genesis, morning **9** beginning, first step, inception **10** graduation, initiation **11** origination **12** inauguration **13** graduation day **20** graduation ceremonies

commend 2 OK **4** back, give, laud **5** extol **6** commit, confer, convey, praise **7** acclaim, approve, consign, endorse, entrust, stand by, support **8** delegate, give over, hand over, pass over, relegate, transfer **13** speak highly of

commendable 6 worthy **7** notable **8** laudable **9** admirable, deserving, estimable, exemplary, honorable **10** creditable **11** meritorious **12** praiseworthy

commendation 5 honor **6** praise **7** support **8** approval **10** acceptance **11** acclamation, approbation

commendatory 8 admiring, praising **9** laudatory, praiseful **10** plauditory **13** complimentary **14** congratulatory

commensurate, commensurable 4 even, meet **5** equal **6** square **7** fitting **8** balanced, in accord, parallel, relative, suitable **10** comparable, compatible, consistent, equivalent **11** appropriate, in agreement **13** corresponding, proportionate **14** on a proper scale

comment 4 note, word **6** remark **7** clarify, discuss, explain, expound **8** expand on **9** assertion, criticism, elu-

cidate, shed light, statement, talk about, touch upon, utterance **10** annotation, expression, reflection **11** elucidation, explanation, explication, observation **13** clarification **15** exemplification

commentary 6 review **8** critique, scholium, treatise **9** criticism **10** exposition **11** explanation, explication **12** dissertation **14** interpretation **16** explanatory essay

commentator 6 critic, writer **7** speaker **8** panelist, reporter, reviewer **9** columnist, explainer **10** newscaster **11** interpreter, news analyst

comment upon 7 clarify, clear up, explain **8** spell out **9** delineate, elucidate, explicate, interpret, make plain **10** illuminate, illustrate **14** throw light upon

commerce 5 trade **6** barter **7** trading, traffic **8** business, exchange, industry **12** mercantilism **16** buying and selling
god of: **6** Hermes **7** Mercury

commercial 2 ad **5** sales, trade **8** business **10** mercantile, sales pitch **12** profit-making **13** advertisement **16** buying-and-selling

commingle 3 mix **4** fuse **5** blend, merge, unify **7** combine **10** amalgamate

commiserate 7 feel for **8** show pity **10** grieve with, lament with **13** express sorrow **14** sympathize with **15** share one's sorrow **17** have compassion for

commiseration 4 pity **8** sympathy **10** compassion, tenderness **13** fellow feeling

commission 3 act, bid, cut, fee **4** duty, hire, name, rank, role, task **5** board, doing, order, piece, power, proxy, trust **6** agency, assign, charge, direct, employ, engage, office **7** appoint, certify, charter, conduct, council, empower, license, mandate, mission, portion, rake-off, stipend, warrant **8** capacity, contract, delegate, dividend, document, exercise, function, position **9** acting out, allotment, allowance, authority, authorize, committal, committee **10** assignment, commitment, committing, delegation, deputation, entrusting, percentage, performing **11** appointment, carrying out, certificate, performance, transacting **12** officer's rank, perpetration **13** authorization, written orders **14** give the go-ahead **15** representatives **16** piece of the action

commissioner 5 envoy, trier **7** officer, pristaw **8** delegate, official **9** authority, commissar

commissioning 10 assignment, delegation **11** appointment, designation, entrustment **13** authorization

commit 2 do **3** act, put **4** bind, pull **5**

enact, place **6** assign, decide, effect, engage, intern, pursue **7** confine, consign, deliver, deposit, entrust, execute, perform, pull off, resolve **8** carry out, give over, obligate, practice, transact, transfer **9** determine **10** make liable, perpetrate **13** participate in **16** institutionalize

commitment 3 vow **4** bond, word **5** stand **6** pledge **7** promise **8** decision, delivery, transfer, warranty **9** assurance, detention, guarantee, liability, restraint **10** assignment, giving over, internment, obligation, resolution **11** confinement, consignment, dispatching **12** imprisonment **13** determination, incarceration **14** responsibility **18** institutionalizing

commit oneself 3 act **7** resolve **8** dedicate, obligate **9** determine

committed 6 active, liable **8** confined, detained, interned **9** concerned, delivered, entrusted, obligated **10** interested, responsive **11** responsible **17** institutionalized

committee 4 body, jury **5** bench, board, group, junta, table **6** bureau, soviet **7** cabinet, council **9** gathering, syndicate **10** assemblage **12** organization

commode 6 bureau, toilet **7** cabinet, dresser **9** washstand **14** chest of drawers

commodious 5 ample, large, roomy **8** spacious **9** capacious, uncramped **11** unconfining

commodity 4 ware **5** asset, goods, stock **6** staple **7** chattel, holding, product **8** property **9** advantage, belonging **10** possession **11** convenience, merchandise **14** article of trade **17** article of commerce

common 3 bad, low **4** base, lewd, mean, rude, vile **5** brash, cheap, crass, crude, gross, joint, lowly, minor, plain, stock **6** brazen, brutal, coarse, lesser, normal, old-hat, public, ribald, shared, simple, smutty, tawdry, vulgar **7** average, boorish, callous, general, ignoble, ill-bred, loutish, low-bred, obscene, obscure, popular, prosaic, regular, routine, settled, uncouth, unknown, worn-out **8** communal, everyday, familiar, frequent, homespun, impolite, informal, mediocre, middling, nameless, ordinary, plebeian, shameful, standard, workaday, worn thin **9** bourgeois, customary, deficient, household, low-minded, motheaten, obnoxious, offensive, pervasive, shameless, tasteless, unexalted, universal, unnoticed, unrefined, wellknown **10** collective, colloquial, despicable, dime-a-dozen, inglorious, threadbare, unblushing, uncultured, unpolished, widespread **11** disgraceful, established, ill-mannered, insensi-

tive, middle-class, oft-repeated, subordinate, traditional, unimportant, widely known, without rank **12** contemptible, conventional, disagreeable **13** garden-variety, insignificant **15** undistinguished

commoners 5 plebs **6** masses **8** plebians

common law
Latin: **13** lex non scripta

commonly 5 often **6** widely **7** as a rule, usually **8** normally, of course **9** generally, in general, most often, popularly, regularly, routinely **10** by and large, familiarly, frequently, habitually, informally, ordinarily, repeatedly **11** customarily **13** traditionally **14** by force of habit, conventionally, for the most part **15** in most instances **17** generally speaking

common people 5 demos, plebs **6** masses **8** populace **9** hoi polloi, plebeians **11** bourgeoisie

commonplace 3 old **4** dull **5** adage, banal, stale, trite, usual **6** cliche, old-hat, truism **7** bromide, general, humdrum, regular, routine, worn-out **8** banality, everyday, familiar, ordinary, standard, worn thin **9** customary, hackneyed, moth-eaten, platitude **10** pedestrian, threadbare, un original, widespread **11** oft-repeated, stereotyped, traditional **12** received idea, run-of-the-mill **13** unimaginative, uninteresting

commonplace book 9 anthology, gleanings, scrapbook

Common Sense
author: **11** Thomas Paine

common-sense 5 sound **8** everyday, sensible **9** mother wit, practical, pragmatic, realistic **10** no-nonsense **11** down-to-earth, levelheaded, serviceable, utilitarian **12** matter-of-fact

commonwealth 5 state **6** nation **8** republic
Latin: **10** res publica

commotion 3 ado **4** fuss, stir, to-do **5** furor **6** bustle, racket, ruckus, tumult, uproar **7** clatter, turmoil **9** agitation **10** excitement, hullabaloo **11** disturbance **12** perturbation

communal 5 joint **6** common, mutual, public, shared **9** community **10** collective

commune 3 gab, rap, yak **4** chat, chin, farm, talk, town **5** visit **6** babble, confer, gossip, parley, powwow **7** chatter, palaver, prattle **8** converse, schmooze **9** discourse **10** chew the fat, chew the rag **11** communicate, confabulate **14** shoot the breeze

communicable 8 catching **10** contagious, infectious **12** transferable **13** transmissible, transmittable

communicate 3 say **4** give, show, talk, tell **5** state, write **6** advise, con-

vey, impart, notify, pass on, relate, reveal **7** declare, divulge, exhibit, mention, publish, signify **8** announce, converse, disclose, inform of, proclaim, transmit **9** apprise of, bring word, broadcast, make known, publicize **10** correspond

communication 4 news, note, wire **5** cable **6** letter, missal, report **7** liaison, message, missive, notices, rapport, writing **8** bulletin, dispatch, document, speaking, telegram **9** broadcast, cablegram, directive, statement **10** communique **11** declaration, information **12** conversation, intelligence, proclamation, radio message **13** telephone call **14** correspondence

communicative 4 open **5** frank **6** candid, chatty **7** voluble **8** friendly, outgoing, sociable **9** revealing, talkative **10** expressive, forthright, freespoken, loquacious, revelatory, unreserved **11** informative

communion, Communion 6 accord **7** concord, harmony, rapport, sharing **8** affinity, sympathy **9** agreement **12** the Eucharist **13** communication, contemplation

communique 4 note, wire **5** aviso, cable, flash **6** report, letter, notice **7** epistle, message, missive, release, telegram **8** bulletin, dispatch **9** directive, statement **10** memorandum **12** announcement, intelligence, notification **13** communication

Communist 3 red **6** soviet **7** comrade, marxist **8** Leninist **9** Bolshevik, socialist **10** Bolshevist **12** totalitarian

Communist Manifesto
author: **8** Karl Marx **15** Friedrich Engels

community 4 area, folk, town **5** arena, field, group, range, realm, scope **6** locale, people, public, sphere, suburb **7** quarter, society **8** affinity, district, environs, likeness, populace, province, sameness, vicinity **9** agreement, citizenry **10** population, similarity **11** environment, social group **12** commonwealth, neighborhood, surroundings

commute 4 ride, trip **5** alter **6** adjust, change, redeem, soften, switch, travel **7** convert, journey, replace, reverse **8** diminish, exchange, mitigate **9** alleviate, supersede, transform, transmute, transpose **10** substitute **11** transfigure **12** metamorphose, transmogrify

comodo
music: **9** leisurely

Comoros
other name: **26** lost pearls of the Indian Ocean
capital/largest city: **6** Moroni
others: **6** Bambao **7** Fomboni **8** Dzaoudzi **9** Mutsamudu **11** Mitsamiouli

monetary unit: 5 franc **7** centime
island: 6 Moheli **7** Anjouan, Mayotte **12** Grande Comoro
highest point: 7 Kartala **8** Karthala
sea: 6 Indian
physical feature:
  channel: 10 Mozambique
people: 4 Arab **5** Bantu, Malay **7** African **8** Malagasy
language: 6 Arabic, French **7** Swahili **8** Malagasy
religion: 5 Islam **13** Roman Catholic

compact 4 bond, cram, deal, pack, pact, snug, tidy **5** close, dense, press, small, stuff **6** little, treaty **7** bargain, crammed, pressed, squeeze, stuffed **8** alliance, compress, contract, covenant **9** agreement, clustered, concordat **10** compressed **11** arrangement, pack closely **12** concentrated **13** tightly packed, understanding

compactness 7 density **8** snugness **9** smallness **10** littleness **11** compression **13** concentration

companion 3 pal **4** chum, mate **5** buddy, crony **6** escort, friend, helper **7** comrade **9** assistant, associate, attendant

companionable 6 social **7** amiable, cordial **8** friendly, sociable **9** agreeable, congenial, convivial

companionate 4 warm **6** genial **7** cordial **8** amicable, friendly, platonic, suitable **9** accordant, agreeable, consonant, easygoing, nonsexual, spiritual, unfleshly **10** compatible, concordant, harmonious **11** nonphysical, passionless, warm-hearted **12** affectionate **13** companionable

companionship 4 pals **5** chums **7** buddies, company, friends **8** comrades **10** associates, companions, fellowship, friendship **11** camaraderie, comradeship, familiarity, sociability **17** close acquaintance, friendly relations

company 3 mob **4** band, firm, gang **5** bunch, group, guest, party **6** guests, outfit, people, throng **7** callers, concern, friends, society, visitor **8** assembly, comrades, presence, visitors **9** gathering, multitude, syndicate **10** assemblage, companions, fellowship, friendship **11** camaraderie, comradeship, corporation, sociability **12** conglomerate, congregation **13** companionship, establishment **15** business concern

comparable 4 like, up to **5** close, equal **6** akin to **7** similar **8** as good as, parallel **9** a match for, analogous **10** equivalent, on a par with, tantamount **11** approaching, approximate **12** commensurate, in a class with **13** commensurable

comparative 4 near **8** relative **11** approximate

compare 5 equal, liken, match **6** be up

to, equate, relate **7** vie with **8** approach, contrast **9** correlate **11** compete with **12** be on a par with **13** hold a candle to **14** be in a class with **20** draw a parallel between

compare notes 6 confer **7** consult **8** talk over **13** exchange views

comparison 7 analogy, kinship **8** contrast, equality, likeness, parallel, relation **10** connection, similarity **11** correlation, resemblance **13** comparability

compartment 3 box, pew **4** brig, cell, crib, hold, hole, nook, room **5** berth, booth, cabin, crypt, niche, stall, vault **6** alcove, bunker, closet **7** chamber, cubicle, section **8** anteroom, roomette **9** cubbyhole **10** pigeonhole **11** antechamber

compass 5 bound, range, reach, scope, sweep **6** domain, extent **8** boundary, province **13** circumference

Compass, Mariner's Compass
constellation of: 5 Pyxis

Compasses, Pair
constellation of: 8 Circinus

compassion 4 pity **5** heart **7** empathy, feeling **8** humanity, sympathy **10** tenderness **13** commiseration, fellow feeling **17** tender-heartedness
  Latin: 12 misericordia

compassionate 4 kind **6** humane **7** pitying **8** merciful **10** benevolent, charitable **11** kindhearted, sympathetic **13** tender-hearted

compatibility 6 accord **7** concord, harmony, rapport **8** affinity **9** agreement, unanimity **12** congeniality **14** like-mindedness

compatible 3 apt, fit **6** seemly **7** fitting **8** in accord, suitable **9** congenial, in harmony, in keeping **10** like-minded **11** appropriate

compel 4 make **5** drive, force **6** oblige **7** require **11** necessitate

compelled 4 must **5** bound, urged **6** driven, forced **7** coerced, obliged, pressed **8** commanded, dragooned, enforced, impelled, obsessed, pressured, required **11** constrained, overpowered

compelling 7 driving, dynamic **8** forceful **10** commanding **12** overwhelming

compel obedience to 5 force **6** coerce **7** enforce **8** carry out, insist on **10** administer

compendium 4 list **5** brief **6** apercu, digest, precis, survey **7** abstract, capsule, catalog, epitome, summary **8** syllabus, synopsis **9** catalogue **11** abridgement, compilation **12** condensation

compensate 3 pay **5** cover, repay **6** make up, offset, redeem, square **7** balance, pay back, redress **9** indem-

nify, reimburse **10** make amends, recompense, remunerate **14** counterbalance **15** make restitution

compensation 3 fee, pay **4** gain **5** wages **6** income, profit, return, reward, salary **7** payment, redress **8** benefits, earnings, gratuity **9** indemnity, repayment **10** recompense, settlement **11** restitution **12** remuneration, satisfaction **13** consideration, reimbursement

compete 3 vie **5** fight **6** battle, combat, oppose **7** contend, contest **8** be rivals **9** lock horns, match wits

competence 5 skill **7** ability, know-how, mastery **8** ableness **9** expertise **10** capability, competency, expertness **11** proficiency

competent 3 fit **6** expert, versed **7** skilled, trained **8** skillful **9** efficient, practiced, qualified **10** dependable, proficient **11** experienced, responsible, trustworthy

competition 4 game **5** event, match, rival **7** contest, rivalry, tourney **8** conflict, opponent, struggle **9** contender **10** contention, opposition, tournament

competitive 8 fighting, opposing, striving **9** combative **10** aggressive, contending

competitor 5 rival **7** fighter **8** opponent **9** adversary, contender **10** contestant, opposition

compilation 4 body **5** group **9** collating, garnering, gathering, mustering **10** assemblage, assembling, assortment, collecting, collection, compendium, marshaling **11** aggregating, aggregation, marshalling **12** accumulating, accumulation

compile 5 amass **6** garner, gather, heap up, muster **7** collate, collect, marshal **8** assemble **10** accumulate

complacent 4 smug **6** at ease **7** content **9** contented **10** self-secure, unbothered, untroubled **13** self-satisfied

complain 3 nag **4** beef, carp, kick, moan, pick **5** cavil, gripe, whine **6** grouch, grouse, squawk **7** grumble **9** bellyache, criticize, find fault **15** state a grievance

complaint 4 beef, kick **5** gripe **6** malady, squawk, tirade **7** ailment, illness, protest **8** debility, disorder, sickness **9** criticism, grievance, infirmity, objection **10** impairment **12** faultfinding **15** dissatisfaction

complaisance 7 pliancy **8** docility **10** affability, amiability, compliance **12** acquiescence

complaisant 4 warm **7** affable, amiable, cordial **8** friendly, gracious, obliging, pleasant, pleasing **9** agreeable, compliant, congenial, easygoing **10** solicitous **11** good-humored, good-natured

Compleat Angler, The
author: **11** Izaak Walton

complement 3 cap **5** crown, match, total, whole **7** balance, perfect **8** ensemble, entirety, parallel, round out **9** aggregate, companion **10** completion, consummate, full amount, full number, supplement **11** counterpart, rounding-out **12** consummation **14** required number

complementary 7 matched **8** integral, opposite **9** companion **10** additional, compatible, completing **11** correlative **12** interrelated, supplemental **13** correspondent, corresponding

complete 3 cap, end **4** full **5** crown, total, utter, whole **6** entire, finish, intact, settle, wrap up **7** achieve, execute, fulfill, perfect, perform, plenary, settled **8** absolute, achieved, carry out, conclude, executed, round out, thorough, unbroken **9** discharge, make whole, performed, polish off, terminate, undivided **10** accomplish, carried out, complement, conclusive, consummate, unabridged **11** consummated **12** accomplished

completed 4 done **5** ended, whole **6** closed, entire, filled **7** matured, through **8** achieved, finished, realized **9** concluded, executed, fulfilled, perfected **10** terminated, wrapped up **11** consummated **12** accomplished

completeness 8 fullness, richness **9** wholeness **10** perfection **12** thoroughness

completion 3 end **5** close **6** ending, finish, windup **7** closing **9** finishing **10** concluding, conclusion, expiration **11** fulfillment, terminating, termination **12** consummation

complex 4 maze **5** mixed **6** knotty, system **7** network, tangled **8** compound, involved, manifold, multiple, puzzling **9** aggregate, composite, difficult, enigmatic, fixed idea, intricate, obsession **10** perplexing, variegated **11** bewildering, complicated **12** conglomerate, labyrinthian, labyrinthine, multifarious **13** preoccupation

complexion 3 hue **4** look, tone **5** color, guise, image, slant **6** aspect **7** outlook **8** coloring **9** character **10** appearance, coloration, impression **11** countenance, skin texture **12** pigmentation, skin coloring

complexity 6 puzzle **9** intricacy, obscurity **10** bafflement, involution, perplexity **11** crabbedness, elaboration, involvement **12** complication, entanglement **15** inextricability **17** unintelligibility **19** incomprehensibility

compliance 6 assent **7** pliancy **8** docility, giving in, meekness, yielding **9** deference, obedience, passivity **10** conforming, conformity, submission

compliance 12 acquiescence, complaisance **13** nonresistance

compliant 8 flexible, yielding **9** agreeable **10** submissive

complicate 4 knot **5** ravel, snarl **6** muddle, tangle **7** confuse, involve **8** confound, entangle **11** make complex **13** make difficult, make intricate

complicated 7 complex **8** involved **9** elaborate, intricate

complication 4 snag **5** hitch **7** dilemma, problem **8** drawback, handicap, obstacle, quandary **9** hindrance **10** difficulty, impediment, perplexity **11** aggravation, obstruction, predicament **12** disadvantage **14** stumbling block

complicity 8 abetment, intrigue, plotting, schemery, scheming **9** collusion, finagling **10** connivance, conspiracy **11** confederacy, contrivance, implication, involvement **12** entanglement

compliment 5 honor, kudos **6** homage, praise **7** tribute **8** flattery **9** adulation, laudation **11** acclamation **12** commendation **14** congratulation

complimentary 4 free **6** gratis **8** admiring, praising **9** adulatory, extolling, laudatory, panegyric, praiseful **10** flattering, gratuitous, plauditory **12** appreciative, commendatory **13** without charge **14** congratulatory

compliments 4 best, laud **5** exalt, extol, toast **6** homage, praise, salute **7** applaud, commend, regards **8** respects **9** greetings **10** best wishes, good wishes **11** salutations **13** felicitations **15** congratulations

comply 3 bow **4** bend, meet, mind, obey **5** defer, yield **6** accede, adhere, follow, give in, submit **7** abide by, conform, consent, fulfill, observe, satisfy **9** acquiesce, surrender

component 4 item, part **5** piece **6** detail, member, module **7** element, modular, segment **8** material **9** composing, elemental, essential, intrinsic **10** elementary, ingredient, particular **11** constituent, fundamental **13** component part

component part 4 item, part **5** piece **6** detail, member **7** element **10** ingredient, particular **11** constituent, fundamental

comport 3 act **4** bear **5** carry **6** acquit, behave, deport **7** conduct

comportment 7 bearing, conduct **8** attitude, behavior, carriage, demeanor, presence **9** acquittal **10** appearance, deportment

comport oneself 3 act **6** behave **13** acquit oneself **14** conduct oneself

compose 4 calm, form, lull, make **5** frame, quell, quiet, relax, shape, write **6** create, devise, make up, pacify, settle, soothe **7** collect, fashion, placate

compose 8 be part of, belong to, comprise, conceive, modulate **9** formulate **10** constitute

composed 4 calm, cool **5** quiet **6** at ease, placid, poised, sedate, serene, steady **8** peaceful, tranquil **9** collected, quiescent, unexcited, unruffled **10** controlled, cool-headed, restrained, unagitated, untroubled **11** levelheaded, undisturbed, unemotional, unflappable, unperturbed **12** eventempered **13** dispassionate, imperturbable **15** undemonstrative

composer 4 bard, poet **6** author, writer **7** creator **8** musician, producer **10** compositor, typesetter

composite 6 mosaic **7** blended **8** combined, compound **10** compounded

composition 4 form, opus, work **5** essay, etude, piece **6** design, layout, make-up, making **7** forming, framing, product, shaping **8** creating, creation, devising, exercise **9** framework, structure **10** concoction, fashioning, organizing, production **11** arrangement, combination, compilation, formulation, preparation **12** constitution, organization **13** configuration

compos mentis 4 sane **13** mentally sound

composure 4 calm, cool, ease **5** poise **6** aplomb **7** control, dignity **8** calmness, coolness, patience, serenity **9** sang-froid **10** equanimity **11** selfcontrol **13** self-assurance, self-restraint **14** cool-headedness, self-possession, unexcitability, unflappability **15** levelheadedness

compound 3 mix **4** fuse, make **5** add to, alloy, blend, boost, mixed, union, unite **6** devise, fusion, mingle **7** amalgam, amplify, augment, blended, combine, complex, concoct, enlarge, magnify, mixture, prepare **8** combined, heighten, increase **9** composite, fabricate, formulate, reinforce **10** synthesize **11** combination, complicated, composition, incorporate, put together **12** conglomerate **14** conglomeration

comprehend 3 dig, get **5** catch, grasp, savvy **6** absorb, digest, fathom **7** make out **8** conceive, perceive **9** penetrate **10** appreciate, assimilate, understand

comprehensible 5 clear, plain **7** evident **8** apparent **11** unambiguous **12** intelligible

comprehension 5 grasp **7** insight **9** awareness **10** conception, perception **11** realization **12** acquaintance, appreciation, apprehension **13** consciousness, understanding

comprehensive 4 full **5** broad **7** copious, general, overall **8** complete, sweeping, thorough **9** expansive, extensive, universal **10** exhaustive, widespread **11** compendious **12** all-embracing, all-inclusive

compress 4 cram, pack **5** press **6** reduce, shrink **7** abridge, bandage, compact, curtail, plaster, shorten, squeeze **8** condense, dressing **10** abbreviate

compressed 5 dense **6** jammed, packed **7** crowded **8** squashed, squeezed **9** compacted **12** concentrated

compressed form 6 digest **7** summary **8** cake form, synopsis **10** shortening **11** abridgement, contraction, curtailment **12** abbreviation, condensation

compression 9 narrowing, squeezing, stricture, tightness **10** compaction, constraint **12** constriction

compressor 4 pump **7** presser, reducer **8** squeezer **9** compactor, condenser

comprise 4 form **6** make up **7** compose, contain, include **8** be made of **9** consist of **10** constitute **12** be composed of

compromise 4 risk **5** agree, truce **6** settle **7** balance, compact, imperil **8** endanger, undercut **9** agreement, discredit, embarrass, implicate, make a deal, prejudice **10** adjustment, jeopardize, settlement **11** arrangement, come to terms, happy medium, make suspect, meet halfway **12** conciliation **13** accommodation, rapprochement **14** make vulnerable, strike a bargain **16** mutual concession **18** split the difference **21** come to an understanding
German: 9 Ausgleich

compromising 7 risking **8** settling **9** adjusting **10** bargaining **11** give and take, making a deal **12** embarrassing, jeopardizing **13** accommodating, coming to terms **14** meeting halfway

Compsognathus
type: 8 dinosaur, theropod
characteristic: 8 smallest
location: 6 Europe **7** Bavaria
period: 8 Jurassic

Compson, Quentin
character in: 14 Absalom Absalom **18** The Sound and the Fury
author: 8 Faulkner

Compson family
characters in: 18 The Sound and the Fury
member: 5 Benjy, Caddy, Jason **7** Candace, Quentin **8** Benjamin
author: 8 Faulkner

compte rendu 6 record, report, review **7** account **15** account rendered

comptroller 7 auditor **9** treasurer **10** accountant, bookkeeper, controller

compulsion 5 force **6** demand, duress, urging **8** coercion, pressure **9** necessity **10** obligation **11** domineering, requirement

compulsive 6 driven, hooked **7** driving, fanatic **8** addicted, habitual **9** compelled, obsessive **10** compelling **14** unable to resist, uncontrollable

compulsory 7 binding **8** coercive, demanded, enforced, forcible, required **9** mandatory, requisite **10** compulsive, imperative, obligatory **11** unavoidable **12** prescriptive

compunction 5 demur, qualm, shame **6** regret, unease **7** anxiety, concern, remorse, scruple **9** misgiving **10** contrition **16** pang of conscience

computation 6 tally, total **8** figuring **9** numbering, reckoning **10** numeration **11** calculation, enumeration

compute 3 add **5** add up, sum up, tally, total **6** figure, reckon **7** count up, work out **9** ascertain, calculate, figure out

computer 5 adder **9** processor **10** calculator
language: 3 Ada, APL, XML **4** Java, LISP, HTML, LOGO, SGML **5** ALGOL, BASIC, COBOL **6** Pascal **7** FORTRAN
term: 2 PC **3** bit, bug, bus, CAD, CAM, CPU, DOS, FAQ, PDA, pdf, RAM, ROM, web, www **4** beta, blog, boot, byte, chip, file, hack, icon, Java, link, spam, Unix **5** CD-Rom, crash, debug, drive, e-mail, input, Linux, modem, mouse, pixel, pop-up, queue, virus **6** adware, analog, applet, avatar, backup, cookie, cursor, domain, glitch, hacker, laptop, memory, online, output, read me, server, window, wizard **7** ActiveX, blogger, browser, digital, keyword, network, offline, program, spyware **8** banner ad, bookmark, chat room, database, download, emoticon, firewall, handheld, hardware, homepage, internet, lightpen, notebook, printout, software, terminal, wireless **9** bandwidth, broadband, hyperlink, hypertext, interface, IP address, mainframe, trackball **10** binary code, cyberspace, Cold Fusion, floppy disk **11** application, interactive, plug and play, spreadsheet, text message, trojan horse **12** minicomputer, World Wide Web **13** microcomputer, word processor **14** microprocessor **17** desktop publishing
see also **8** Internet

comrade 3 pal **4** ally, chum **5** buddy, crony **6** friend **7** partner **8** confrere, co-worker, helpmate, intimate **9** associate, colleague, companion, confidant **10** bosom buddy **11** confederate **12** collaborator **13** boon companion
Russian: 8 tovarich

comradeship 8 alliance **10** fellowship, friendship **11** association, camaraderie **13** companionship

comte 5 count

Comte Ory, Le
also: 8 Count Ory
opera by: 7 Rossini
character: 13 Countess Adele

Comus
author: 10 John Milton
subtitle: 7 A Masque

Comus
origin: 5 Roman
god of: 7 revelry **8** drinking

con 3 gyp **4** anti, bilk, coax, fool, gull, hoax, lure, rook **5** cheat, cozen, felon, trick **6** delude **7** against, beguile, convict, defraud, mislead, swindle **8** hoodwink, jailbird, prisoner, yardbird **9** bamboozle

Conakry
capital of: 6 Guinea

concatenation 4 link **5** union **6** hookup **7** joining, linking, reunion **8** coupling, junction **10** bracketing, confluence, connection **11** conjunction **12** interlinking **15** interconnection

concave 6 hollow, sunken **8** indented **9** depressed **13** curving inward

conceal 4 hide, mask **5** cloak, cover **6** screen, shield **7** cover up, obscure, secrete **8** disguise **10** camouflage, keep secret

concealed 5 blind, doggo **6** covert, hidden, latent, masked, perdue, secret, veiled **7** cloaked, covered, obscure, unknown, wrapped **8** abstruse, shrouded, ulterior **9** disguised, incognito **11** clandestine

concealment 5 cover **6** hiding **7** hideout, masking **8** covering, hideaway **9** screening, secreting, secretion **10** covering up, under cover

concede 3 own **4** cede **5** admit, agree, allow, grant, yield **6** accept, give up, resign, tender **7** abandon, confess, deliver **8** hand over **9** acquiesce, recognize, surrender, vouchsafe **10** relinquish **11** acknowledge, be persuaded

conceit 3 ego **5** pride **6** vanity **7** ego trip, egotism **8** bragging, self-love **9** vainglory **10** self-esteem **12** boastfulness **14** self-importance

conceited 4 smug, vain **7** stuck-up **8** arrogant, boasting, bragging, puffed up **9** bombastic, overproud, strutting **11** egotistical, swellheaded **12** vainglorious **13** self-important

conceivable 8 credible, knowable, possible **9** thinkable **10** believable, imaginable, supposable **11** perceivable

conceive 4 form **5** frame, hatch, start **6** create, ideate, invent **7** concoct, dream up, imagine, produce, think of, think up **8** consider, contrive, envisage, envision, initiate **9** originate **10** comprehend, understand

concentrate 4 mass **5** amass, bunch, focus, hem in **6** center, gather, heap up, reduce **7** close in, cluster, pay heed, thicken **8** assemble, attend to, condense, converge, fasten on **10** accumulate, congregate **11** bring to bear **12** direct toward

concentrated 5 dense **7** crowded, focused, thought **8** centered **10** compressed

concentration 4 mass **5** focus **7** cluster **9** diligence, gathering, reduction **10** absorption, assemblage, collection, intentness, thickening **11** aggregation, boiling down, convergence, deep thought, engrossment **12** accumulation **13** concentrating, consolidation **14** centralization

concept 4 idea, view **5** image **6** belief, notion, theory **7** opinion, surmise, thought **9** postulate **10** conviction, hypothesis, impression **11** supposition

conception 4 idea **5** birth, image, start **6** notion **7** forming, genesis, inkling, picture **8** creating, devising, hatching **9** beginning, formation, imagining, inception, invention, launching **10** conceiving, concocting, initiation, perception **11** envisioning, formulation, originating **12** apprehension **13** fertilization, understanding **16** becoming pregnant

conceptual 8 abstract **9** visionary **11** conjectural, ideological, speculative, theoretical **12** experimental, hypothetical **15** impressionistic

concern 3 job **4** care, duty, firm, heed **5** chore, house, store, touch, worry **6** affair, affect, charge, matter, occupy, regard **7** anxiety, apply to, company, disturb, involve, mission, trouble **8** bear upon, business, distress, interest, relate to **9** attention, pertain to **10** disconcert, enterprise, solicitude **11** appertain to, corporation, disturbance, involvement, undertaking **12** apprehension **13** consideration, establishment **14** thoughtfulness

concerned 5 upset **6** active, caring, uneasy **7** alarmed, anxious, engaged, fearful, worried **8** involved, troubled **9** attentive, committed, disturbed **10** disquieted, distressed, interested, solicitous **12** apprehensive **13** participating

concerning 2 of, on, re **3** for **4** as to, over, upon **5** about, anent **7** apropos **8** engaging, touching, worrying **9** affecting, involving, mattering, regarding **10** relating to, respecting

concert 5 union, unity **6** accord, settle **7** concord, harmony **8** teamwork **9** agreement, congruity, unanimity **10** accordance, complicity **11** association, cooperation **13** collaboration **14** correspondence **18** musical performance

concerted 5 joint **6** united **7** planned **8** by assent **10** agreed upon **11** coop-

erative, prearranged **12** premeditated **13** predetermined

concert hall 5 odeum **6** lyceum **7** theater **9** music hall **10** auditorium **12** symphony hall

concession 5 lease **6** assent **8** giving in, yielding **9** admission, franchise, privilege **10** adjustment, compromise, indulgence **12** acquiescence, modification **14** acknowledgment

Conch
  form: **7** trumpet
  made of: **5** shell
  owned by: **7** Tritons

Conchobar
  origin: **5** Irish
  king of: **6** Ulster
  nephew: **10** Cuchulainn

concierge 7 janitor **9** custodian **10** doorkeeper

conciliate 6 pacify **7** appease, placate **9** make peace, reconcile **11** accommodate

conciliation 11 appeasement, peacemaking **12** propitiation **13** accommodation **14** reconciliation

conciliatory 8 friendly **9** appeasing, pacifying, placatory **10** mollifying, reassuring **11** peacemaking, reconciling **13** accommodative

concise 5 brief, pithy, short, terse **7** compact **8** succinct **9** condensed **10** to the point **11** abbreviated

conciseness 7 brevity **9** terseness **11** compactness **12** condensation, succinctness

conclave 6 parley, powwow **7** council, meeting, session **8** assembly **10** conference, convention **11** convocation **13** secret council

conclude 3 end **4** halt, stop **5** close, infer, judge **6** decide, deduce, effect, finish, gather, reason, settle **7** arrange, resolve, surmise **8** break off, carry out, complete **9** determine, terminate **10** accomplish **11** bring to pass, discontinue **12** draw to a close

concluded 5 bound, ended, guess **6** closed, judged **7** decided, deduced, expired, settled, wound up **9** completed **10** culminated, determined, restrained, terminated

conclusion 3 end **5** close **6** finale, finish, result, upshot, windup **7** finding, outcome **8** decision, judgment **9** agreement, deduction, final part, inference, summation **10** completion, denouement, resolution, settlement, working out **11** arrangement, presumption, termination **13** determination

conclusive 5 clear **6** patent **7** certain, obvious **8** absolute, decisive, definite, manifest, palpable **9** clinching **10** compelling, convincing, undeniable **11** categorical, determining, inescapable,

irrefutable **12** demonstrable, unanswerable **13** incontestable, unimpeachable **14** unquestionable **16** incontrovertible

concoct 3 mix **4** brew **5** frame, hatch **6** cook up, create, devise, invent, make up **7** think up **8** compound, contrive **9** fabricate, formulate

concoction 4 brew **5** blend **6** jumble, medley **7** mixture **8** compound, creation **9** invention, potpourri **11** contrivance, fabrication **14** conglomeration

concomitant 7 related **9** accessory, attendant, connected, corollary, secondary **10** additional **12** accompanying, contributing, supplemental **13** complementary

concord 5 amity, peace **6** accord **7** harmony **8** goodwill **9** agreement **10** friendship **11** amicability, cooperation **16** cordial relations **19** mutual understanding

concordance 5 index **6** accord **7** concord **9** agreement, consensus, unanimity **17** meeting of the minds

concordant 6 unison **7** calming **8** agreeing, unifying **9** assenting, consonant **10** concurrent, harmonious

concordat 4 pact **8** covenant **9** agreement

Concorde 3 jet, SST **10** supersonic airline **9** Air France **14** British Airways

Concordia
  origin: **5** Roman
  goddess of: **5** peace **7** harmony

concourse 7 conflux, joining, linkage, meeting **8** junction **9** amassment **10** assembling, concursion, confluence **11** aggregation, association, convergence **12** congregation, focalization **13** concentration **14** conglomeration **15** flowing together **16** flocking together

concrete 4 real **5** solid **6** cement **7** express, factual, precise **8** definite, distinct, explicit, material, specific, tangible **10** particular **11** fused stones, substantial **12** alloyed rocks

concupiscence 4 itch, lust **6** desire **7** craving, lechery, longing, passion **8** appetite, hot pants, lewdness, satyrism **9** horniness, lubricity, prurience, randiness **10** wantonness **11** goatishness, libertinism, lustfulness **12** sexual desire **13** lecherousness **14** lasciviousness, libidinousness

concur 5 agree, match, tally **6** square **7** conform **8** coincide, hold with **9** be uniform **10** be in accord, correspond **11** go along with **12** go hand in hand

concur in 7 approve **9** agree with **11** go along with

concurrence, concurrency 6 accord **7** concord, consent, harmony **8** approval **9** agreement, consensus, unanimity **10** acceptance, conformity **11**

affirmation, coexistence, coincidence, conjuncture, cooperation, synchronism **12** acquiescence **13** collaboration, mutual consent **14** correspondence **15** working together **17** meeting of the minds **22** simultaneous occurrence

concurrent 5 at one **6** allied **7** aligned **8** agreeing, matching **9** congenial, congruous, consonant **10** coexisting, coincident, coinciding, compatible, harmonious **11** in agreement, sympathetic, synchronous **12** commensurate, contemporary, in accordance, simultaneous **13** correspondent, of the same mind **15** contemporaneous

concurring 8 agreeing **10** consenting **11** affirmative, in agreement, synchronous **12** coincidental, simultaneous **13** corresponding

concussion 3 jar **4** blow, bump **5** clash, shock **6** buffet, impact **7** shaking **8** pounding **9** agitation, collision **11** brain injury

condemn 4 damn, doom **5** decry **6** rebuke **7** censure **8** denounce, sentence **9** criticize, proscribe, reprehend **10** disapprove

condemnation 6 rebuke **7** censure, reproof **8** judgment, reproach, sentence **9** criticism **10** conviction, punishment **11** disapproval **12** denunciation, reprehension **14** disapprobation **20** pronouncement of guilt

condensation 6 digest **9** reduction **10** abridgment **13** shortened form **16** condensed version

condense 3 cut **4** trim **6** digest, reduce **7** abridge, compact, liquefy, shorten, thicken **8** boil down, compress, contract, pare down **10** abbreviate, blue-pencil **11** concentrate, consolidate, precipitate

condensed form 6 digest, precis **7** summary **8** synopsis **10** shortening **11** abridgement, compression, contraction, curtailment **12** abbreviation

condescend 5 deign, stoop **6** submit, unbend **7** descend, disdain **9** patronize **10** look down on, talk down to **12** come down a peg, lower oneself **13** humble oneself

condescending 7 high-hat **8** superior **10** disdainful **11** overbearing, patronizing

condescension 4 airs **7** disdain, hauteur, modesty **8** humility **9** deference, loftiness **10** humbleness **11** haughtiness **12** graciousness **13** self-abasement **14** self-effacement **19** patronizing attitude **20** assumption of equality **21** high-and-mighty attitude

condign 3 due **4** fair, just, meet **5** right **6** earned, proper, worthy **7** fitting, merited **8** deserved, suitable **9** warranted **11** appropriate

condiment 4 herb **5** sauce, spice **8** dressing, flavorer, seasoner **9** seasoning

kind: 3 bay **4** dill, mace, mint, sage, salt **5** caper, clove, curry, onion, thyme **6** catsup, garlic, ginger, nutmeg, pepper, pickle, relish **7** caraway, chutney, ketchup, mustard, parsley, oregano, paprika, pimento, tabasco, vinegar **8** cardamon, marjoram, turmeric **9** pimpernel **10** bell pepper, mayonnaise

condition 3 fit **4** term **5** adapt, equip, ready, shape, state, train **6** demand, fettle, malady, status, tone up **7** ailment, prepare, problem, proviso **8** accustom, position, standing **9** agreement, complaint, provision, requisite, situation **10** limitation, make used to, put in shape **11** arrangement, contingency, malfunction, reservation, restriction, stipulation **12** prerequisite **13** circumstances, qualification, state of health **14** state of affairs **15** physical fitness

conditional 7 limited **9** dependent, qualified, tentative **10** contingent, restricted **11** provisional, stipulative **16** with reservations

condolence 4 pity **6** solace **7** comfort **8** sympathy **10** compassion **11** consolation **13** commiseration

Condon, Richard
author of: **11** Winter Kills **18** Death of a Politician **22** The Manchurian Candidate

condonation 11 forgiveness, overlooking **12** disregarding **13** putting up with

condone 6 excuse, forget, ignore, pardon, wink at **7** absolve, forgive, justify, let pass **8** overlook **9** disregard, put up with

conduce 3 aid **4** help, lead, tend **5** bring, favor, guide **6** effect **7** advance, forward, further, promote **10** contribute

conducive 7 helpful **8** salutary **9** favorable, promotive **10** beneficial **11** expeditious **12** contributive, contributory, instrumental **19** calculated to produce **22** helpful in bringing about

conduct 3 act **4** bear, lead, rule, ways **5** carry, chair, deeds, enact, guide, pilot, steer, usher **6** action, attend, behave, convey, convoy, direct, escort, govern, manage, manner **7** carry on, comport, control, execute, marshal, operate, perform **8** behavior, carry out, dispatch, guidance, regulate, transact **9** accompany, direction, discharge, look after, supervise **10** administer, deportment, government, leadership, management **11** comportment, generalship, preside over, superintend, supervision **14** administration

conduct oneself 3 act **6** behave **13** acquit oneself **14** comport oneself

conductor 3 cad **5** guide **6** carman, escort, leader **7** cathode, channel, maestro, manager **8** aqueduct, batonist, cicerone, conveyor, director, operator, stickman, trainman **9** collector, drum major **10** impresario, supervisor **11** choirmaster, transmitter **13** concert master

conduit 4 duct, main, pipe, tube **5** canal, drain, flume, sewer **6** gutter, trough **7** channel, passage **8** aqueduct **11** watercourse

cone 5 bevel, shape, spire **6** bobbin, conoid, funnel **7** pyramid, volcano **8** pyramid
kind: 3 fir **4** pine **5** larch **7** conifer, retinal **8** ice cream

confabulate 4 chat, talk **6** confer, patter **7** chatter, discuss **8** chitchat, converse, talk idly

confabulation 4 chat, talk **8** chitchat **10** conference, discussion **12** conversation

confection 3 jam **5** candy **6** pastry **7** dessert **8** conserve, delicacy **9** preserves, sweetmeat **10** sugar candy

confectionery 5 candy **6** sweets **7** goodies, pasties **10** sugar candy, sweetmeats

confederacy, Confederacy 3 CSA **4** band, bloc **5** guild, union **6** fusion, league **7** combine, society **8** alliance, the South **9** coalition, syndicate **10** federation **11** association **13** confederation **14** Southern states **18** secessionist states **26** Confederate States of America
states: 5 Texas **7** Alabama, Florida, Georgia **8** Arkansas, Virginia **9** Louisiana, Tennessee **11** Mississippi **13** North Carolina, South Carolina
capital: 8 Richmond **10** Montgomery
leader: 14 Jefferson Davis
flag: 12 Stars and Bars
See also **8** Civil War

confederate 4 ally **5** merge, unite **6** cohort, helper **7** abettor, comrade, partner **8** coalesce, coworker **9** accessory, affiliate, associate, colleague, companion **10** accomplice, cooperator, join forces **11** consolidate, helping hand **12** band together, collaborator, right hand man **17** fellow conspirator

Confederates
author: **14** Thomas Keneally

confederation 4 band **5** guild, union **6** fusion, league **7** combine, society **8** alliance **9** coalition, syndicate **10** federation **11** association, confederacy

confer 4 give **5** award **6** accord, parley **7** consult, discuss, palaver **8** converse **9** present to **10** bestow upon **12** compare notes, talk together **15** hold a conference **18** deliberate together

conference 4 talk **6** parley **7** council, meeting, seminar **8** conclave **9** symposium **10** convention, discussion **12** consultation, deliberation

conferment 4 gift **5** award **8** bestowal **12** presentation

confess 3 own **4** avow, sing **5** admit, own up **6** expose, reveal **7** declare, divulge, lay bare **8** blurt out, disclose **9** come clean, make known **11** acknowledge **12** bring to light **14** unbosom oneself **18** make a clean breast of

confessed 6 avowed **8** admitted **9** professed **12** self-declared **14** self-proclaimed

confession 6 avowal, shrift **9** admission **10** disclosure, divulgence, revelation **11** declaration **12** confessional **14** acknowledgment

Confessions of an English Opium Eater
author: **15** Thomas DeQuincey

Confessions of Nat Turner, The
author: **13** William Styron

confidant, confidante 5 crony **6** friend **8** intimate **10** bosom buddy **15** trusty companion

confide 6 impart, reveal **7** confess, divulge, lay bare, let in on, let know **8** disclose **9** make known **12** tell secretly **13** tell privately **14** unbosom oneself

confidence 4 grit, guts **5** faith, nerve, pluck, spunk, trust **6** belief, daring, mettle, secret, spirit **7** courage **8** audacity, boldness, credence, intimacy, reliance **9** certainty, certitude **10** conviction **11** intrepidity **12** self-reliance **13** private matter, self-assurance **14** faith in oneself **17** inside information

confidence man 5 cheat **6** con man **8** swindler **9** charlatan, trickster **10** mountebank

confident 4 bold, sure **5** cocky **6** daring, secure **7** assured, certain **8** cocksure, intrepid, positive **9** convinced, dauntless, expectant **10** optimistic **11** self-assured, self-reliant **13** sure of oneself

confidential 5 privy **6** secret **7** private **8** hush-hush **9** top-secret **10** classified **11** undisclosed **12** off-the-record **16** not to be disclosed

confidentially 7 sub rosa **8** in secret, secretly **9** privately **16** between ourselves **17** behind closed doors
French: **9** entre nous

confiding 6 trusty **7** reliant **8** trustful, trusting **9** confident **11** trustworthy

configuration 4 form **6** design, makeup **11** arrangement, composition

confine 3 pen, tie **4** bind, cage, hold, jail, keep **5** limit **6** coop up, govern, keep in, lock up, shut in, shut up **7** fence in, impound **8** imprison, regulate, restrain, restrict **9** sequester **11** incarcerate **13** hold in custody

confined 4 pent **5** close, tight **6** jailed, narrow **7** cramped **8** locked up **10** imprisoned, restricted

confinement 7 custody, lying in **9** cooping up, detention, restraint **10** childbirth, constraint, limitation, shutting in **11** parturition, restriction **12** accouchement, imprisonment **13** incarceration **15** circumscription

confines 4 edge **6** border, bounds, limits **7** margins **8** precinct **10** boundaries **13** circumference

confirm 5 prove **6** accept, clinch, ratify, uphold, verify **7** agree to, approve, bear out, certify, sustain **8** make firm, validate **9** authorize, establish **11** acknowledge, corroborate, make binding, make certain **12** authenticate, substantiate

confirmation 5 proof **6** assent **8** approval, sanction **9** agreement **10** acceptance, validation **11** affirmation, endorsement **12** ratification, verification **13** corroboration **14** authentication, substantiation

confirmed 3 set **5** fixed **7** chronic **8** hardened, verified **9** ingrained, validated **10** deep-rooted, deep-seated, inveterate, proven true **11** established **12** corroborated **13** authenticated, dyed-in-the-wool, substantiated

confiscate 4 take **5** seize **7** impound, possess, preempt **8** take over **9** sequester **10** commandeer **11** appropriate, expropriate

confiscation 7 seizure **10** impounding, preemption **13** appropriation, commandeering, expropriation

conflagration 4 fire **5** blaze **7** bonfire, inferno **8** conflict, fighting, wildfire **9** brush fire, firestorm, holocaust **10** forest fire, raging fire, wall of fire **11** sea of flames **12** sheet of flame

conflagrative 8 burnable **9** flammable, ignitable **10** combustive, incendiary **11** combustible, inflammable

conflict 4 fray **5** clash, fight, melee, set-to **6** action, battle, combat, fracas, oppose, strife, tussle **7** collide, discord, dissent, scuffle, warfare **8** disagree, division, friction, skirmish, struggle, variance **9** encounter, hostility **10** antagonism, be contrary, difference, dissension, engagement **12** disagreement **13** confrontation **14** be inharmonious **15** be contradictory
Spanish: **9** mano a mano

conflicting 7 warring **8** clashing, opposing **10** ambivalent **13** contradictory

confluence 5 union **7** conflux, joining, linkage, meeting **8** junction, juncture **9** concourse, gathering **10** assembling, concursion **11** association, convergence **13** concentration **14** coming together **15** flowing together

conform 3 fit **4** obey **5** adapt **6** adjust,

follow **8** adhere to, jibe with, submit to **9** agree with, reconcile, tally with **10** be guided by, comply with, fall in with, square with **11** acquiesce in **12** correspond to

conformable 8 amenable **9** agreeable, malleable **10** submissive **12** in compliance

conformance 7 harmony **9** agreement **10** accordance, compliance, conformity **13** compatibility

conformation 4 form **5** build, shape **6** figure **7** anatomy **9** formation, framework, structure **11** arrangement **13** configuration

conformist 12 well-adjusted **13** unadventurous

conformity 6 accord, assent **7** harmony **8** likeness **9** agreement, obedience **10** compliance, observance, similarity, submission, uniformity **11** resemblance **12** acquiescence **14** correspondence **15** conventionality

confound 5 amaze, mix up **6** baffle, puzzle, rattle **7** astound, confuse, fluster, mystify, nonplus, perplex, startle **8** astonish, bewilder, dumfound, surprise, unsettle **10** disconcert **11** flabbergast **16** strike with wonder, throw off the scent

confounded 8 confused **10** bewildered, nonplussed **11** dumbfounded **12** disconcerted

confraternity 4 body **5** guild, union **7** society **8** sodality **9** confrairy **11** association, brotherhood

confrere 3 pal **4** ally, chum **5** buddy **6** friend **7** brother, comrade, partner **9** associate, colleague

confront 4 dare, defy, face, meet **5** brave **8** cope with, face up to **9** challenge, encounter, withstand

confrontation 5 clash, run-in, set-to **6** battle, combat, debate **7** contest, dispute, face-off **8** conflict, showdown, skirmish **9** encounter **10** engagement, opposition **11** controversy **17** face-to-face meeting
Spanish: **9** mano a mano

Confucius
author of: **10** Book of Odes **11** The Analects

confuse 5 addle, befog, mix up, stump **6** baffle, muddle, puzzle, rattle **7** fluster, mistake, mystify, nonplus, perplex **8** befuddle, bewilder, confound, unsettle **10** discompose, disconcert **11** make unclear **12** make baffling **14** make perplexing **17** throw into disorder

confused 5 fazed **6** addled **7** abashed, baffled, chaotic, jumbled, mixed-up, muddled, tangled **8** rambling **9** befuddled, illogical, perplexed, unsettled **10** bewildered, disjointed, distracted, incoherent, nonplussed **11** dumb-

founded 12 disconcerted, disorganized 13 disharmonious, heterogeneous

confusing 7 addling 8 baffling, blinding, blurring, dizzying, jumbling, mixing up, muddling 9 deranging, mistaking 10 befuddling, disorderly, flustering, mystifying, perplexing, stupefying 11 bewildering, confounding 13 disconcerting, unintelligible

confusion 4 mess, riot 5 chaos, snarl 6 bedlam, hubbub, jumble, muddle, tangle, tumult, uproar 7 clutter, ferment, turmoil 8 disarray, disorder, madhouse, shambles, upheaval 9 abashment, commotion 10 bafflement, hodgepodge, hullabaloo, perplexity, puzzlement, untidiness 11 disturbance, pandemonium 12 bewilderment, discomposure, stupefaction 13 mystification 14 disarrangement, disconcertment 15 disorganization
French: 14 bouleversement

confutation 6 denial 7 counter 8 negation, rebuttal 10 refutation 13 contradiction

confute 4 deny 5 rebut 6 impugn, oppose, refute 7 counter, gainsay 10 contradict, controvert 12 be contrary to

congeal 3 set 4 clot, jell 6 curdle, freeze, harden 7 stiffen, thicken 8 solidify 9 coagulate 10 gelatinize

congenial 4 like 6 genial, social 7 affable, cordial, kindred, related, similar 8 agreeing, amenable, gracious, pleasant, pleasing, sociable 9 agreeable, convivial 10 compatible, consistent, harmonious, well-suited 11 sympathetic 13 companionable, corresponding
French: 9 en rapport
German: 9 gemutlich

congeniality 7 harmony, rapport 8 affinity 11 sociability 12 conviviality, friendliness, pleasantness 13 compatibility 14 like-mindedness

congenital 6 inborn, inbred, innate, native 7 natural 8 inherent 9 ingrained, inherited, intrinsic 10 hereditary

congested 6 filled, gorged, jammed, packed 7 crowded 9 saturated 11 overcrowded

congestion 3 jam, mob 4 mass 5 snarl 6 pile-up 8 crowding 10 bottleneck 11 obstruction 12 overcrowding

conglomerate 4 heap, mass, pile 5 amass, blend, stack 7 mixture 8 assemble 9 aggregate 10 accumulate, assemblage 12 accumulation 16 large corporation

conglomeration 6 jumble, medley 7 mixture 8 mishmash 9 aggregate, potpourri 10 assortment, collection, hodgepodge 11 aggregation, combination 13 agglomeration

Congo, Democratic Republic of the
other name: 5 Zaire 12 Belgian Congo 13 Congo-Kinshasa 17 Congo-Leopoldville
capital/largest city: 8 Kinshasa
others: 4 Baya, Boma, Lebo 5 Aketi, Ilebo 6 Banana, Kamina, Kasaji, Kikwit, Matadi, Sandoa 7 Butembo, Kananga, Kolwezi 8 Bakwanga, Yangambi 9 Kisangani 10 Lubumbashi, Luluabourg, Mutshatsha 12 Port Francqui, Stanleyville 14 Elisabethville
school: 5 Zaire 8 Lovanium
division: 4 Kivu 5 Kasai, Shaba 7 Equator, Katanga 8 Oriental
monetary unit: 5 zaire 6 makuta
lake: 4 Kivu 5 Mweru, Tumba 6 Albert, Edward, Upemba 9 Mai-Ndombe 10 Tanganyika
mountain: 7 Crystal, Mitumba, Virunga 9 Ruwenzori 10 Nyaragongo 18 Mountains of the Moon
highest point: 10 Margherita
river: 4 Ruki, Uele 5 Congo, Dengu, Ibina, Kasi, Lindi, Zaire 6 Likati, Lomami, Lukuga, Ubangi 7 Aruwimi, Lualaba, Lulonga
sea: 8 Atlantic
physical feature:
falls: 4 Kiva 6 Tshopo 7 Stanley
forest: 5 Ituri
valley: 9 Great Rift
people: 4 Kuba, Luba, Yaka 5 Bantu, Bashi, Bemba, Kongo, Lulue, Lunda, Mongo, Pygmy 6 Azande, Baluba, Watusi 7 Bakongo, Nilotes, Tshokwe 8 European, Mangbetu, Sudanese
explorer: 3 Cao 7 Stanley
leader: 6 Mobutu (Sese Seko) 7 Lumumba, Tshombe 8 Kasavubu
ruler: 7 Belgium, Leopold
language: 5 Bantu 6 French 7 Chiluba, Kikongo, Lingala, Swahili 8 Sudanese, Tshiluba
religion: 5 Islam 7 animism, Kimbang 10 Protestant 13 Roman Catholic
place:
dam: 4 Inga 9 Le Marinee 10 Del Commune
national park: 6 Albert, Upemba 7 Garamba
feature:
animal: 5 hyena, okapi 7 giraffe, gorilla 10 rhinoceros
fish: 11 electric eel

Congo, Republic of the
other name: 10 Moyen Congo 11 Middle Congo
capital/largest city: 11 Brazzaville
others: 3 Ewo 4 Boko 5 Epena, Kayes, Kelle, Okoyo, Sembe 6 Dongou, Komono, Makoua, Matadi, M'Binda, M'Vouti, Ouesso, Sibiti, Zanaga 7 Cabinda, Dolisie, Etoumbi, Gamboma, Kinkala, Loubomo, Loudima, Madingo, Mossaka, So-

uanke 8 Djambala, Impfondo, Kibangou, Madingou, Mindouli 9 Mossendjo 11 Fort-Rousset, Pointe-Noire 17 Mayombe Escarpment
school: 13 Marien Ngoubai
monetary unit: 5 franc 7 centime
lake: 5 Mweru, Tumba 6 Albert, Nyanza, Upemba 7 Leopold 11 Stanley Pool
highest point: 6 Leketi
river: 3 Dja 4 Uele 5 Alima, Congo, Kasal, Kwilu, Lulua, Ngoko, Niari, Sanga, Swilu, Wamba, Zahir, Zaire 6 Kwango, Kwenge, Loange, Lobaye, Lomami, Ogooue, Ubangi 7 Aruwima, Kouilou, Lualaba, Luapula, N'Gounie 8 Itimbiri, Likouala, Lubilash
sea: 8 Atlantic
physical feature:
plateau: 6 Bateke
people: 3 Rua 4 Akka, Susa, Teke, Vili 5 Amadi, Bantu, Figot, Kongo, Mantu, Pygmy, Sanga, Warua, Zambi 6 Ababua, Bafyot, Bateke, Mbochi, Nzambi, Wabuma 7 Bacongo, Bakongo, Bangala, Batetla, Manyema 10 Binga Pygmy
discoverer: 3 Cam
language: 4 Susu 5 Bantu, Fiote 6 French, Kituba 7 Bangala, Lingala
religion: 5 Islam 7 animism 10 Protestant 13 Roman Catholic
place:
church: 9 Saint Anne
stadium: 5 Eboue
feature:
tree: 5 limba

congratulate 4 hail 6 salute 10 compliment, felicitate, wish one joy 11 rejoice with 18 give one's best wishes 28 wish many happy returns of the day

congratulations 6 salute 8 mazel tov 9 blessings, greetings 10 best wishes, good wishes 11 well-wishing 13 felicitations

congregate 4 mass 5 amass, flock, swarm 6 gather, throng 7 cluster, collect 8 assemble 12 come together 13 crowd together

congregation 5 crowd, flock, group, horde, laity 6 parish, throng 8 assembly, audience, brethren 9 gathering, multitude 12 parishioners 16 church membership 17 religious assembly

congress, Congress 4 diet 6 caucus 7 council 8 assembly 9 delegates, gathering 10 conference, convention, parliament 11 legislature 14 federal council 15 discussion group, legislative body, national council, representatives 17 chamber of deputies

Congreve, William
author of: 11 Love for Love 15 The Double-Dealer 16 The Mourning Bride, The Way of the World

congruity 7 harmony **9** agreement, coherence **10** consonance **11** consistency **12** congeniality **13** compatibility **14** correspondence **15** appropriateness

congruous 4 meet **6** seemly **7** apropos **8** becoming, relevant, suitable **9** congenial, consonant, in keeping **10** harmonious **11** appropriate, in agreement **13** corresponding

conifer
  means: 11 cone-bearing
  order: 11 coniferales
  class: 10 gymnosperm
  kind: 3 fir, yew **4** pine **5** cedar, larch, pinal **6** ginkgo, pinale, spruce, torrey **7** cypress, hemlock, juniper, redwood, sequoia **8** softwood **9** evergreen

Coningsby
  author: 16 Benjamin Disraeli

conjectural 7 reputed **8** abstract, academic, doubtful, putative, supposed, surmised **11** inferential, speculative, theoretical **12** hypothetical **13** suppositional **14** supposititious

conjecture 4 idea, view **5** fancy, guess, infer, judge, think **6** augury, notion, reckon, theory **7** imagine, opinion, presume, suppose, surmise **8** estimate, forecast, judgment, theorize **9** calculate, deduction, guesswork, inference, speculate, suspicion **10** assumption, guestimate, hypothesis, presuppose **11** guesstimate, hypothesize, speculation, supposition **13** shot in the dark

conjoin 4 join, knit, link **5** touch, unite **7** combine, connect, overlap **8** together **9** associate

conjoined 6 joined, linked, united **7** knitted, meeting **8** combined, touching **9** connected **10** associated **11** overlapping **14** joined together

conjugal 6 wedded **7** marital, married, nuptial, spousal **9** connubial **11** matrimonial

conjugate 4 join, pair, yoke **5** mated, unite, yoked **6** couple, joined, paired, united **7** connect, coupled, related **9** connected **10** paronymous

conjunction 3 and, but **5** union **7** joining, meeting **11** association, coincidence, combination, concurrence

conjuration 5 charm, spell, trick **11** incantation

conjure 5 allay, charm, raise **6** invoke, summon **7** bewitch, command, enchant **8** call away, call upon **9** call forth **10** cast a spell, make appear **13** make disappear **15** practice sorcery

conjurer 6 wizard **8** magician

conk 3 die, hit **4** bean, blow, fail, head **5** decay, faint, sleep, stall **6** fungus, strike **7** bracket **8** knock out **9** break down **10** straighten

Conn, Katherine
  real name of: 13 Kitty Carlisle

connect 3 tie **4** join **5** hinge, merge, unite **6** attach, couple, relate **7** combine, compare **9** associate, correlate **14** fasten together

connected 4 tied **6** joined, merged, united **7** coupled **8** abutting, adjacent, attached, combined, touching **9** bordering, proximate **10** connecting, contiguous, juxtaposed **12** conterminous **16** fastened together

connected group 5 cycle **6** series **8** sequence **11** progression

Connecticut
  abbreviation: 2 CT **4** Conn
  nickname: 6 Nutmeg **7** Blue Law **9** Freestone **12** Constitution **18** Land of Steady Habits
  capital/largest city: 8 Hartford
  others: 4 Avon **6** Bethel, Canaan, Cos Cob, Darien, Hamden, Mystic, Sharon, Storrs **7** Ansonia, Bristol, Danbury, Enfield, Madison, Meriden, Milford, Niantic, Norwalk, Norwich, Shelton, Tolland, Windsor **8** Guilford, New Haven, Simsbury, Stamford, Westport **9** Greenwich, Naugatuck, New London, Stratford, Waterbury **10** Bridgeport, Manchester, New Britain, Torrington **11** Wallingford
  college: 4 Yale **7** Trinity **8** Hartford, St Joseph, Wesleyan **9** Fairfield **10** Quinnipiac **11** Connecticut, Sacred Heart **12** U S Coast Guard
  feature: 10 Charter Oak
    museum: 8 PT Barnum
    seaport: 6 Mystic
    theater: 27 American Shakespeare Festival
  tribe: 6 Pequot **7** Mohegan, Niantic **10** Quinnipiac
  people: 8 PT Barnum **9** John Brown **10** Ella Grasso, Nathan Hale **11** John Rowland, Noah Webster **12** Thomas Hooker **19** Harriet Beecher Stowe
  lake: 10 Candlewood
  land rank: 11 forty-eighth
  mountain: 4 Bear **7** Taconic
    hills: 10 Berkshires
    highest point: 8 Frissell
  physical feature: 15 Long Island Sound
  river: 6 Thames **9** Naugatuck **10** Housatonic **11** Connecticut
  state admission: 5 fifth
  state bird: 5 robin
  state flower: 14 mountain laurel
  state motto: 30 He Who Transplanted Still Sustains
  state song: 12 Yankee Doodle
  state tree: 8 white oak

Connecticut Yankee in King Arthur's Court, A
  author: 9 Mark Twain
  character: 5 Sandy **6** Merlin **8** Alisande, Clarence **11** Morgan le Fay **12** Hello-Central **18** Sir Kay the Seneschal

connection 3 kin, tie **4** bond, link **5** nexus **6** family, friend **7** contact, coupler, kinfolk, kinsman, linkage **8** affinity, alliance, coupling, junction, kinsfolk, relation, relative **9** associate, connector, fastening **10** attachment, kith and kin **11** association, correlation **12** acquaintance, relationship **13** flesh and blood, interrelation

Connelly, Marc
  author of: 16 The Green Pastures
    with Frank Elser: 19 The Farmer Takes a Wife
    with George S Kaufman: 5 Dulcy **11** To the Ladies **17** Beggar on Horseback, Merton of the Movies

Connery, Sean
  real name: 13 Thomas Connery
  born: 8 Scotland **9** Edinburgh
  honor: 10 knighthood
  roles: 6 Marnie **7** The Rock **10** Entrapment, Highlander **14** Robin and Marian **15** The Untouchables **16** The Molly Maguires **20** The Great Train Robbery, The Man Who Would Be King **28** Darby O'Gill and the Little People **29** Indiana Jones and the Last Crusade **33** The League of Extraordinary Gentlemen
    James Bond: 4 Dr No **10** Goldfinger **11** Thunderball **16** You Only Live Twice **18** Diamonds Are Forever, From Russia with Love, Never Say Never Again

connivance 4 plot **5** cabal **6** design, scheme **8** intrigue **9** collusion **10** complicity, conspiracy **11** machination

connive 3 aid **4** abet, plan, plot **5** allow **6** wink at **7** collude **8** conspire **10** be a party to **13** be accessory to, lend oneself to **14** shut one's eyes to **17** be in collusion with, cooperate secretly

conniving 4 wily **6** artful, crafty **7** cunning **8** plotting, scheming **9** designing **10** intriguing **11** calculating

connoisseur 5 judge, maven, mavin **6** expert **7** epicure, gourmet **9** authority **11** cognoscente **17** person of good taste

Connolly, Maureen
  nickname: 8 Little Mo
  sport: 6 tennis

Connor, Dale
  creator/artist of: 9 Mary Worth

connotation 5 drift **6** import, spirit **8** coloring **9** evocation, undertone **10** intimation, suggestion **11** implication, insinuation **12** significance

connote 5 imply **6** hint at **7** suggest **8** intimate **9** insinuate **11** bring to mind

connubial 6 wedded **7** marital, married, nuptial **8** conjugal **11** matrimonial

conquer 4 beat, best, drub, lick, rout,

rule, trim, whip **5** floor, quell **6** defeat, humble, master, occupy, subdue, thrash **7** possess, win over **8** overcome, surmount, vanquish **9** overpower, rise above, subjugate **11** prevail over, triumph over **14** get the better of

conqueror 6 victor, winner **7** subduer **8** champion **10** subjugator, vanquisher **12** conquistador

conquest 3 fan **4** sway **5** lover **6** adorer, defeat **7** captive, mastery, triumph, victory, winning **8** adherent, follower, whip hand **9** upper hand **10** ascendancy, conquering, domination, overcoming **11** acquisition, subjugation **12** vanquishment **17** captured territory

Conrad, Joseph
real name: 29 Josef Teodor Konrad Korzeniowski
author of: 6 Chance **7** Lord Jim, Typhoon, Victory **8** Nostromo **13** Almayer's Folly **14** The Secret Agent **15** Heart of Darkness **16** Under Western Eyes **21** An Outcast of the Islands **23** The Nigger of the Narcissus

consanguine 4 akin **7** cognate, kindred, related **8** relative

consanguineous 3 kin **4** akin **7** kindred, related **9** connected **21** having a common ancestor

conscience 8 scruples **10** moral sense, principles **15** ethical feelings **20** sense of right and wrong

conscience-stricken 6 guilty **7** ashamed **8** contrite, penitent **9** chastened, regretful, repentant **10** remorseful **13** guilt-stricken

conscientious 5 exact **6** honest **7** careful, dutiful, ethical, upright **10** fastidious, meticulous, particular, scrupulous **11** painstaking, responsible, trustworthy **12** conscionable **14** high-principled

conscious 5 aware **7** alert to, alive to, awake to, studied **8** noticing, sensible, sentient **9** cognizant, in the know, observing **10** calculated, deliberate, discerning, perceiving **12** apperceptive, premeditated **13** knowledgeable

consciousness 4 mind **6** senses **8** feelings, thoughts **9** awareness **10** cognizance, perception **11** discernment, sensibility

conscript 3 PFC **4** boot, hire, levy **5** draft **6** call up, employ, engage, enlist, enroll, induct, muster, rookie, seaman, select, take on **7** draftee, impress, private, recruit **8** enlistee, inductee, mobilize, register, selectee, shanghai **9** conscribe **11** buck private

consecrate 5 bless **6** hallow **7** glorify **8** sanctify **10** make sacred **11** immortalize **13** declare sacred

consecrated 4 holy **7** blessed **8** hallowed **10** sanctified

consecutive 6 in turn, serial **8** unbroken **10** continuous, sequential, successive **11** progressive **13** uninterrupted **19** following one another

consensus 6 accord **7** concord **9** unanimity **11** concurrence **13** common consent **14** general opinion **15** majority opinion **16** general agreement

consent 5 agree, allow, yield **6** accede, accept, accord, assent, concur, permit, ratify, submit **7** approve, concede, concord, confirm, endorse **8** approval, sanction **9** acquiesce, agreement **10** acceptance, fall in with, permission **11** concurrence, endorsement, willingness **12** acquiescence, confirmation, ratification

consent to 2 OK **4** okay **6** permit **7** approve **8** accede to **10** concur with **11** acquiesce to, go along with **14** give the go-ahead

consequence 3 end **4** note **5** avail, fruit, issue, value, worth **6** import, moment, result, sequel, upshot **7** account, gravity, outcome **9** aftermath, influence, magnitude, outgrowth **10** importance, notability, prominence, usefulness **11** development, distinction, seriousness **12** significance

consequent 7 ensuing **8** eventual **9** following, resulting

consequential 7 crucial, epochal **8** historic **9** important, momentous **10** meaningful **11** significant

consequently 2 so **4** ergo, then **5** and so, hence, later **9** as a result, therefore **11** accordingly **12** subsequently

conservation 4 care **6** upkeep **9** husbandry **10** careful use, protection **11** maintenance, safekeeping **12** preservation

conservative 5 quiet **6** square **7** oldline **8** cautious, moderate, undaring **9** right-wing **10** nonliberal, unchanging **11** reactionary, right-winger, traditional **13** unprogressive **15** middle-of-the-road **16** opponent of change **17** middle-of-the-roader **22** champion of the status quo

conservatoire 11 music school **12** conservatory, music academy

conservatory 7 nursery **8** hothouse **9** arboretum **10** glasshouse, greenhouse **11** music school **12** music academy **13** conservatoire

conserve 4 save **5** guard **7** care for, cut back, husband, use less **8** maintain, not waste, preserve **9** safeguard **12** use sparingly

consider 4 deem, hold, note **5** gauge, honor, judge, opine, study, think, weigh **6** ponder, regard, review **7** believe, examine, pay heed, respect **8** appraise, envision, hold to be, mull over **9** be aware of, reflect on **10** bear

in mind, cogitate on, think about **11** contemplate **12** deliberate on **17** make allowances for **18** turn over in one's mind

considerable 4 tidy **5** ample, great, large **6** goodly **7** notable, sizable **8** not small **9** estimable, important **10** impressive, noteworthy, noticeable, of some size, remarkable **11** a good deal of, significant, substantial

considerably 5 amply **7** greatly, largely, notably, sizably **9** estimably **10** abundantly, noticeably, remarkably **13** significantly, substantially

considerate 4 kind **6** kindly **7** mindful **8** obliging **9** attentive, concerned **10** solicitous, thoughtful

consideration 4 heed, tact **5** cause, honor, point, study **6** factor, ground, motive, notice, reason, regard, review **7** concern, respect, thought **8** interest, judgment **9** attention **10** advisement, cogitation, inducement, kindliness, meditation, reflection, solicitude **11** examination **12** deliberation **13** contemplation **14** thoughtfulness **15** considerateness

consider closely 7 pay heed **11** concentrate **12** pay attention **13** put one's mind to **21** give one's full attention

considered 5 mused **6** deemed, heeded, judged, mulled **7** advised, express, honored, noticed, studied, thought, weighed, willful **8** believed, esteemed, looked on, pondered, regarded, supposed **9** reflected, respected, ruminated **10** deliberate, looked upon, thought out **11** deliberated, entertained, intentional **12** contemplated, premeditated, thought about

consign 5 remit **6** assign, commit, convey, remand **7** deliver, entrust **8** delegate, hand over, relegate, transfer **9** commend to **11** deposit with

consignment 8 delivery, shipment, transfer **10** assignment, committing, consigning, delegation, depositing, entrusting, relegation **11** handing over **12** goods for sale, goods shipped **19** goods sent on approval

consist 3 lie **6** reside **7** contain, include **10** be made up of **11** to be found in **13** be comprised of **14** to be composed of

consistency, consistence 4 body **5** unity **6** makeup **7** density, harmony, texture **8** firmness **9** agreement, coherence, congruity, stiffness, structure, thickness, viscosity **10** accordance, conformity, connection, uniformity **11** compactness, composition, persistence **12** construction, faithfulness, steady effort **13** compatibility, steadfastness **14** correspondence **16** uniform standards

consistent 4 meet **6** steady **7** regular,

unified **8** agreeing, constant, of a piece, suitable **9** congenial, congruous, consonant **10** compatible, harmonious, persistent, unchanging **11** in agreement, undeviating **13** correspondent **16** conforming to type

consolation 4 help **5** cheer **6** relief, solace, succor **7** comfort, support **8** easement, soothing, sympathy **10** condolence **11** alleviation, assuagement **13** encouragement

console 4 calm, ease **5** cheer **6** soothe, succor **7** comfort, support, sustain **10** lament with, sympathize **11** condole with **13** express sorrow **15** commiserate with **18** express sympathy for

consolidate 4 fuse, join **5** merge, unify, unite **6** league **7** combine, fortify **8** coalesce, compress, condense, federate, make firm, make sure, solidify **9** integrate, make solid **10** amalgamate, centralize, strengthen **11** concentrate, incorporate **12** band together **13** bring together

consolidation 5 union **6** fusion, merger **8** alliance **9** coalition **11** unification **12** amalgamation **13** agglomeration **14** conglomeration

consomme 4 soup **5** broth **9** madrilene

consonance 5 amity, unity **6** accord, unison **7** concord, harmony, oneness **9** agreement, coherence, congruity, unanimity **10** accordance, conformity, congruence, consonancy **11** concordance, consistency, homogeneity **13** compatibility **14** correspondence, likemindedness

consonant 8 in accord **9** agreeable, congruous, in harmony **10** concordant, consistent **11** in agreement

consort 3 mix **4** club, mate, wife **6** mingle, spouse **7** hang out, husband, pair off, partner **8** go around, sidekick **9** accompany, associate, companion, other half, pal around, rub elbows **10** fraternize **11** keep company

conspicuous 5 clear, great, overt, plain **6** famous, patent **7** eminent, evident, glaring, notable, obvious **8** distinct, flagrant, glorious, manifest, renowned, splendid, striking **9** arresting, brilliant, memorable, notorious, prominent, well-known **10** celebrated, easily seen, remarkable **11** illustrious, outstanding, standing out **13** distinguished, easily noticed, highly visible

conspicuousness 9 celebrity, flagrance, notoriety **10** prominence, visibility **11** obviousness **13** noticeability

conspiracy 4 plot **7** treason **8** intrigue, sedition **9** collusion, treachery **10** connivance, secret plan **11** machination **12** criminal plan **14** treasonous plan

conspirator 7 plotter, schemer, traitor **8** conniver **9** intriguer **10** subversive

conspire 5 unite **6** concur, scheme **7** collude, combine, connive **8** intrigue **9** cooperate, machinate **11** plot treason **12** work together

Constable, John
  born: 7 England **12** East Bergholt
  artwork: 10 The Haywain **12** Cloud Studies **14** Hadleigh Castle **39** Salisbury Cathedral from the Bishop's Grounds

constancy 6 fealty **7** loyalty **8** devotion **9** fixedness, stability **10** allegiance, permanence **12** faithfulness, immutability **13** dependability, invariability, steadfastness **15** trustworthiness **16** unchangeableness

constant 4 even, true **5** fixed, loyal **6** stable, steady, trusty **7** abiding, devoted, endless, eternal, regular, staunch, uniform **8** diligent, enduring, faithful, resolute, stalwart, unbroken, unvaried **9** ceaseless, continual, immutable, incessant, permanent, perpetual, steadfast, sustained, unceasing, unfailing **10** dependable, invariable, persistent, unchanging, unflagging, unswerving, unwavering **11** everlasting, never-ending, trustworthy, unalterable, undeviating, unrelenting **12** interminable, tried-and-true **13** uninterrupted

Constant Nymph, The
  director: 14 Edmund Goulding
  cast: 11 Alexis Smith **12** Charles Boyer, Joan Fontaine **14** Brenda Marshall

constellation 4 host **5** group, rally **6** circle, galaxy, nebula, spiral, throng **7** cluster, company, pattern **9** gathering **10** assemblage, collection **12** spiral nebula **13** configuration **14** island universe
  name: 3 Ara, Leo **4** Apus, Crux, Grus, Lynx, Lyra, Pavo, Vela **5** Aries, Cetus, Draco, Hydra, Indus, Lepus, Libra, Lupus, Mensa, Musca, Norma, Orion, Pyxis, Virgo **6** Antlia, Aquila, Auriga, Bootes, Caelum, Cancer, Carina, Corvus, Crater, Cygnus, Dorado, Fornax, Gemini, Hydrus, Octans, Pictor, Pisces, Puppis, Scutum, Taurus, Tucana, Volans **7** Cepheus, Columba, Lacerta, Pegasus, Perseus, Phoenix, Sagitta, Serpens, Sextans **8** Aquarius, Circinus, Equuleus, Eridanus, Hercules, Leo Minor, Scorpius, Sculptor **9** Andromeda, Centaurus, Delphinus, Monoceros, Ophiuchus, Reticulum, Ursa Major, Ursa Minor, Vulpecula **10** Canis Major, Canis Minor, Cassiopeia, Chamaeleon, Horologium, Triangulum **11** Capricornus, Sagittarius, Telescopium **12** Microscopium **13** Canes Venatici, Coma Berenices **14** Camelopardalis, Corona Borealis **15** Corona Australis, Piscis Austrinus **18** Triangulum Australe

consternation 5 alarm, panic, shock **6** dismay, fright, horror, terror **11** trepidation **12** apprehension

constituent 4 atom, part **5** piece, voter **6** factor, member **7** elective, element, essence **8** electing, integral, making up **9** component, formative, principal, supporter **10** appointing, ingredient

constitute 4 form, make, name **5** found, set up **6** create, invest, make up **7** appoint, compose, empower, produce **8** compound, delegate **9** authorize, establish, institute **10** commission

constitution 6 figure, health, make-up, mettle **7** charter, stamina, texture **8** physique, strength, vitality **9** basic laws, formation, structure **10** figuration **11** composition **12** construction **13** configuration **16** governing charter **17** physical condition **21** fundamental principles

constitutional 4 turn, walk **5** basic **6** inborn, ramble, stroll, vested **7** natural, organic **8** inherent, internal, physical **9** chartered, intrinsic **10** congenital **11** fundamental

Constitution State
  nickname of: 11 Connecticut

constrain 4 curb, urge **5** check, crush, drive, force, quash **6** coerce, compel, oblige, subdue **7** confine, enforce, put down, repress, squelch **8** hold back, pressure, restrain, restrict, suppress **9** fight down, necessity, strong-arm **14** put the screws on

constrained 3 shy **5** timid **6** forced **7** bashful **8** reserved, reticent **9** compelled, diffident **10** restricted **11** embarrassed

constraint 5 force **6** duress **7** reserve **8** coercion, pressure **9** restraint **10** compulsion, diffidence, inhibition, obligation **11** enforcement **13** necessitation

constrict 4 bind **5** choke, cramp, pinch **6** shrink **7** squeeze **8** compress, contract, strangle **11** strangulate

constriction 7 binding, choking **8** cramping, pinching **9** narrowing, shrinking, squeezing, stricture, tightness **10** constraint, strangling **11** compression, contraction

construct 4 form, make **5** build, erect, frame, set up, shape **6** create, design, devise **7** arrange, fashion **8** organize **9** fabricate, formulate

construction 4 form, make **5** build, style **6** format **7** edifice, raising, reading, rearing, version **8** building, creation, erecting **9** rendition, structure **10** fashioning, production **11** composition, elucidation, explanation, explication, fabrication, manufacture **12** conformation, constructing **13** configuration **14** interpretation **15** putting together

constructive 5 handy 6 useful 7 helpful 8 valuable 9 practical 10 beneficial, productive 12 advantageous

construe 4 read, take 7 explain, make out 8 decipher 9 elucidate, figure out, interpret, translate 10 comprehend, understand

Consuelo
author: 10 George Sand

consul 5 envoy 8 emissary, minister 14 foreign officer, representative 15 diplomatic agent

Consul, The
opera by: 7 Menotti
character: 10 Magda Sorel

consult 6 confer, parley, regard 7 refer to 8 consider, talk over 9 inquire of 11 ask advice of, have an eye to 12 compare notes 13 exchange views 15 discuss together, seek counsel from, take into account 16 seek the opinion of 18 deliberate together

consultant 6 expert 7 adviser, advisor, counsel 9 discusser

consultation 7 council, hearing, meeting, palaver 9 interview 10 conference, discussion 12 deliberation

consumable 6 edible 7 eatable 10 comestible

consume 3 eat 4 gulp 5 drain, eat up, spend, use up, waste 6 absorb, devour, expend, guzzle, ravage 7 deplete, destroy, drink up, engross, exhaust 8 demolish, lay waste, squander 9 devastate, dissipate, swallow up 10 annihilate

consumed 4 used 5 burnt, drank, drunk, eaten, spent 6 used up, wasted 7 drained, outworn 8 absorbed, burned up, expended, perished 9 destroyed, engrossed, exhausted, swallowed 10 squandered 11 annihilated

consume greedily 5 eat up, snarf 6 devour, inhale 7 stuff in 8 bolt down, gobble up, gulp down, wolf down 12 swallow whole 13 eat ravenously 14 eat voraciously

consumer 4 user 5 buyer, drain 6 client, patron, waster 7 spender 8 customer 9 purchaser 10 dissipater, squanderer

consummate 2 do 5 sheer, total, utter 6 effect, finish 7 achieve, execute, fulfill, perfect, perform, realize, supreme 8 absolute, carry out, complete, finished, thorough 9 faultless 10 accomplish, bring about, undisputed 11 unmitigated 12 accomplished, unquestioned 13 unconditional 17 through-and-through

consummation 3 end 5 close 6 finish 9 execution 10 attainment, completion, conclusion 11 achievement, culmination, fulfillment, realization 14 accomplishment

consumption 2 TB 3 use 7 using up

9 consuming, depletion 10 exhaustion 11 expenditure, utilization 12 exploitation, tuberculosis

Consus
origin: 5 Roman
god of: 11 good counsel, horse racing
protector of: 5 grain
corresponds to: 3 Ops

contact 4 join, meet 5 reach, touch, union 7 connect, meeting 8 abutment, junction, touching 9 adjacency, get hold of 10 connection 11 association 13 communication 14 get in touch with 15 communicate with

contagion 7 disease 8 epidemic, outbreak 9 infection, spreading 13 contamination

contagious 8 catching 9 spreading 10 infectious, spreadable 12 communicable 13 transmittable

contain 4 curb, hold 5 check 6 embody, hold in 7 control, embrace, enclose, include, inhibit, involve, repress 8 hold back, keep back, restrain, suppress 11 accommodate, incorporate 12 keep the lid on 16 keep within bounds

container 3 bag, box, can, jar, vat 4 pail 6 barrel, bottle, bucket, carton, holder, vessel 10 receptacle

containment 7 control 9 restraint, retention

contaminate 4 foul, soil 5 dirty, spoil, taint 6 befoul, blight, debase, defile, infect, poison 7 corrupt, pollute 8 besmirch 10 adulterate, make impure

contamination 5 filth 7 fouling, soiling 8 dirtying, foulness, impurity, spoiling 9 dirtiness, poisoning, polluting, pollution, putridity 10 defilement 11 uncleanness 12 adulteration

Conte, Richard
real name: 18 Nicholas Peter Conte
born: 12 Jersey City NJ
roles: 8 Barabbas 13 A Bell for Adano 24 The Greatest Story Ever Told

contemplate 4 note, plan, scan 5 weigh 6 expect, gaze at, intend, ponder, regard, survey 7 examine, imagine, inspect, observe, project, stare at, think of 8 aspire to, envision, mull over, ruminate 9 muse about 10 anticipate, cogitate on, have in view, meditate on, think about 11 reflect upon 12 deliberate on 13 consider fully, look at fixedly, look forward to 14 speculate about

contemplation 5 study 6 gazing, musing, seeing, survey 7 looking, reverie, thought, viewing 8 scanning, thinking 9 pondering 10 cogitation, inspection, meditation, reflection, rumination 11 examination, observation 12 deliberation 13 consideration

contemplative 6 musing 7 pensive 8 studious 9 engrossed 10 cogitative, meditative, reflective, ruminating,

thoughtful 11 speculative 13 introspective, lost in thought

contemporaneous 6 coeval 10 coexistent, coincident, concurrent 11 synchronous 12 contemporary, simultaneous

contemporary 3 new 4 late 6 modern, recent, with-it 7 current 8 advanced, brand-new, up-to-date 10 coexistent, coincident, concurrent, newfangled, present-day 11 ultramodern 12 simultaneous 13 of the same time, up-to-the-minute 15 contemporaneous

contempt 4 hate 5 scorn, shame 6 hatred 7 disdain, disgust 8 aversion, derision, disfavor, disgrace, dishonor, distaste, ignominy, loathing, ridicule 9 antipathy, disregard, disrepute, revulsion 10 abhorrence, repugnance 11 detestation, humiliation

contemptible 3 low 4 base, mean, vile 5 cheap 6 abject, paltry, shabby 8 shameful, unworthy, wretched 9 miserable, repugnant, revolting 10 despicable, detestable, disgusting 11 ignominious

contemptuous 6 lordly 7 haughty, pompous 8 arrogant, derisive, insolent, scornful, snobbish 10 disdainful 12 supercilious 13 condescending, disrespectful

contemptuousness 5 scorn 7 disdain 8 contempt, rudeness 9 arrogance, insolence

contend 3 vie, war 4 aver, avow, hold, spar 5 argue, claim, clash, fight 6 allege, assert, battle, combat, debate, insist, jostle, strive, tussle 7 compete, contest, declare, dispute, grapple, quarrel, wrestle 8 be a rival, maintain, propound, skirmish, struggle 10 put forward

content 4 area, core, gist, load, size, text 5 cheer, happy, heart, ideas, peace 6 at ease, at rest, matter, please, serene, thesis, volume 7 appease, comfort, essence, gratify, insides, meaning, pleased, satisfy, suffice, unmoved 8 capacity, make easy, pleasure, serenity, thoughts 9 contented, gratified, happiness, satisfied, set at ease, substance 10 complacent, untroubled 11 comfortable, contentment, peace of mind, unconcerned 12 satisfaction 13 gratification

contented 5 happy 6 at ease, serene 7 at peace, content, pleased 9 gratified, satisfied 11 comfortable

contentedness 4 ease 5 peace 7 comfort, content 8 pleasure, serenity 9 happiness 11 contentment 12 satisfaction 13 gratification

contention 5 clash, fight 6 battle, combat, strife 7 contest, discord, dispute, rivalry 8 argument, conflict, disunity, fighting, friction, skirmish, struggle, variance **9** assertion, encounter, wrangling **10** dissension, quarreling **11** competition, discordance **12** disagreement **13** confrontation

contentious 5 angry, cross **7** hateful, scrappy **8** captious **9** bellicose **10** pugnacious **11** belligerent, competitive, quarrelsome **12** cantankerous, disputatious **13** argumentative, controversial

contentment 4 ease **5** peace **7** comfort, content **8** pleasure, serenity **9** happiness **12** satisfaction **13** contentedness, gratification

conterminous 8 abutting, adjacent, touching **9** bordering **11** right beside **14** contiguous with

contest 3 war **4** bout, game **5** fight, match **6** battle, combat, debate, oppose, vie for **7** dispute, rivalry, tourney **8** conflict, fight for, object to, struggle **9** battle for, challenge, combat for, encounter **10** compete for, contend for, controvert, engagement, tournament **11** competition, struggle for **12** argue against **14** call in question

contestant 5 rival **6** player **7** entrant, fighter **8** competer, prospect **9** combatant, contender **10** challenger, competitor

context 6 milieu **7** climate, meaning, setting **8** ambience **9** framework, precincts, situation **10** atmosphere, background, conditions, connection **11** environment **12** relationship, surroundings **13** circumstances **16** frame of reference

contiguous 5 close, handy **6** nearby **7** close-by, tangent **8** abutting, adjacent, next-door, touching **9** adjoining, bordering, in contact **10** juxtaposed **11** neighboring **12** conterminous

continence 6 purity **8** chastity, sobriety **10** abstinence, moderation, temperance **11** forbearance **13** self-restraint

continent 4 Asia, pure **6** Africa, chaste, Europe **7** Eurasia **8** celibate, land mass, mainland, virginal **9** abstinent, Australia, temperate **10** abstemious, Antarctica **12** North America, South America

contingency 7 urgency **8** accident **9** emergency, extremity **10** likelihood **11** possibility, predicament **15** unforeseen event

contingent 9 dependent, subject to **11** conditioned **12** controlled by

continual 7 endless, eternal **8** constant, frequent, habitual, unbroken, unending **9** ceaseless, incessant, perennial, perpetual, recurring, unceasing **10** continuous, persistent **11** everlasting, never-ending, oft-repeated, unremitting **12** interminable **13** uninterrupted

continually 3 aye **4** ever **6** always, steady **7** endless, eternal, forever, on and on **8** steadily **9** recurring **10** constantly, frequently, repeatedly

continuance 4 stay, term **6** extent, period **7** lasting **8** duration **9** extension **10** continuing, permanence **11** adjournment, persistence, protraction **12** continuation, perseverance, prolongation

continuation 6 sequel **8** addition, sequence **9** extension **10** continuing, supplement **11** continuance, protraction **12** prolongation

continue 4 go on, last, stay **5** abide **6** drag on, endure, extend, keep on, keep up, remain, resume, stay on **7** carry on, persist, proceed **9** persevere

continued 6 kept on, kept up, lasted, went on **7** endured **8** extended **9** carried on, persisted, proceeded, prolonged **10** persevered, protracted

continuing 6 steady **7** abiding, eternal, ongoing **8** constant, enduring, extended, unbroken, unending **9** ceaseless, incessant, perpetual, prolonged **10** dragged out, persistent, protracted **11** persevering, unremitting **12** interminable **13** uninterrupted

continuity 4 flow **5** chain **9** continuum **10** succession **11** continuance, progression **12** continuation

continuous 6 linked, steady **7** endless, eternal, lasting **8** constant, enduring, unbroken **9** ceaseless, connected, continual, extensive, incessant, perpetual, prolonged, unceasing **10** continuing, persistent, protracted, successive **11** consecutive, everlasting, persevering, progressive, unremitting **12** interminable **13** uninterrupted

continuum 4 flow **5** chain **8** sequence **10** continuity, succession **11** continuance, progression **12** continuation

contort 4 bend, warp **5** twist **6** deform **7** distort **11** be misshapen

contorted 4 bent **7** crooked, twisted **8** deformed **9** distorted

contortion 7 bending **8** twisting **10** distortion **11** crookedness

contour 4 form **5** lines, shape **6** figure **7** outline, profile **10** silhouette **11** physiognomy

contraband 11 bootlegging **13** smuggled goods **14** illegal exports, illegal imports **15** unlicensed goods **17** black-marketeering **18** prohibited articles **19** unlawful trafficking

contract 3 get **4** pact, take **5** agree, incur **6** absorb, assume, narrow, pledge, reduce, shrink, treaty **7** acquire, compact, develop, dwindle, promise, shorten, tighten **8** compress, condense, covenant, engender **9** constrict, enter into, negotiate, undertake **11** arrangement, come to terms **12** draw together, make a bargain **13** become

smaller, legal document **15** sign an agreement **16** written agreement

contracted form 6 digest **7** summary **8** synopsis **9** short form **11** abridgement, compression **12** abbreviation, condensation

contraction 8 decrease **9** drawing in, lessening, narrowing, reduction, shrinkage **10** shortening, shriveling, tightening **11** compression **12** abbreviation, condensation, constriction

contradict 4 deny **5** belie, rebut **6** impugn, oppose, refute **7** confute, counter, dispute, gainsay **8** disprove **10** controvert **12** be contrary to, disagree with

contradiction 6 denial **7** counter **8** negation, rebuttal **10** refutation **11** confutation **12** disagreement

contradictory 8 contrary, opposing **10** discrepant, dissenting, refutatory **11** conflicting, disagreeing **12** antithetical, inconsistent **14** countervailing, irreconcilable

contradistinction 8 contrast **10** difference **13** dissimilarity

contraption 6 device, gadget **9** apparatus, invention **11** contrivance

contrariety 9 deviation **10** difference, divergence **13** contradiction

contrary 5 balky **6** ornery **7** adverse, counter, froward, hostile, opposed, wayward, willful **8** converse, inimical, opposite, stubborn, untoward **9** disparate, obstinate, unfitting **10** at variance, discordant, headstrong, refractory, unsuitable **11** conflicting, disagreeing, intractable, unfavorable **12** antagonistic, antithetical, disagreeable, inauspicious, incompatible, recalcitrant, unpropitious **13** contradictory **15** at cross purposes, unaccommodating

contrast 6 depart, differ **7** deviate, diverge **8** variance **9** disparity **10** comparison, difference, divergence, unlikeness **11** distinction **12** disagree with **13** differentiate, dissimilarity **15** differentiation, set in opposition

contrasting 8 clashing, dividing, opposing **9** comparing, differing **10** discordant, juxtaposed **14** distinguishing **15** differentiating

contravene 4 deny **5** annul, fight, spurn **6** abjure, breach, combat, disown, negate, offend, oppose, reject, resist **7** disobey, exclude, gainsay, infract, nullify, violate **8** abrogate, disclaim, overstep **9** overreach, repudiate **10** act against, contradict, infringe on, transgress **12** encroach upon **15** trespass against

contretemps 4 spat **5** clash, set-to **7** dispute, quarrel **8** argument, squabble **10** difference, falling out **12** disagreement **18** embarrassing mishap

contribute 4 give **5** endow, grant **6**

bestow, confer, donate, lead to **7** advance, forward, hand out, present **9** bear a part, influence **11** have a hand in **13** be conducive to **14** help bring about

contribution 4 alms, gift **5** grant **7** charity, subsidy **8** bestowal, donation, offering **9** endowment **11** benefaction **12** dispensation

contributive 8 valuable **9** favorable **10** beneficial

contributory 9 accessory, ancillary, auxiliary **13** supplementary

contrite 6 rueful **7** humbled **8** penitent **9** chastened, regretful, repentant, sorrowful **10** apologetic, remorseful **18** conscience-stricken

contrition 6 regret **7** penance, remorse **9** atonement, penitence **10** repentance **11** compunction **12** self-reproach **18** qualms of conscience

contrivance 4 plan, plot, tool **5** gizmo, trick **6** design, device, doodad, gadget **7** machine, measure **8** artifice, intrigue **9** apparatus, implement, invention, mechanism, stratagem **10** instrument **11** contraption, machination, thingamajig **12** Rube Goldberg

contrive 4 plan, plot **6** create, design, devise, invent, manage, scheme **7** concoct **8** maneuver **9** improvise **11** devise a plan **17** effect by stratagem

contrived 7 labored, studied **8** mannered **9** unnatural **10** artificial

contriver 7 creator, deviser **8** designer, inventor **9** architect

control 4 curb, rule, sway **5** brake, steer **6** bridle, charge, govern, manage, master, subdue **7** command, contain, mastery, repress **8** dominate, dominion, regulate, restrain, restrict **9** authority, direction, reign over, restraint, supervise **10** domination, management, manipulate, regulation **11** superintend, supervision, suppressant **12** have charge of, jurisdiction

controlled 5 ruled **6** curbed, steady, swayed **7** checked, managed, powered, servile, subdued **8** directed, governed, held back, kept down, reserved, verified **9** commanded, contained, dominated, moderated, regulated, repressed **10** authorized, regimented, restrained, supervised **11** manipulated

controlling 6 ruling **8** dominant **9** governing **10** commanding **11** influencing, predominant **13** predominating

controversial 7 at issue **8** arguable **9** debatable, polemical **10** disputable **12** questionable **13** causing debate **15** widely discussed **16** open to discussion

controversy 6 debate **7** dispute, quarrel, wrangle **8** argument, squabble **10**

contention, discussion, dissension **11** altercation **12** disagreement

controvert 4 deny **5** belie, rebut **6** negate, oppose, refute **7** confute, dispute, gainsay, protest **8** confound, disprove, question **9** challenge, disaffirm **10** contradict, contravene, invalidate **12** give the lie to

contumacious 6 unruly **7** froward **8** contrary, factious, insolent, mutinous, perverse **9** fractious, seditious **10** headstrong, rebellious, refractory **11** disobedient, intractable **12** ungovernable, unmanageable **13** disrespectful, insubordinate

contumely 5 abuse, insult, scorn **7** disdain, obloquy **8** contempt, diatribe, reproach, rudeness **9** arrogance, insolence, invective, pomposity **10** opprobrium, scurrility **11** brusqueness, haughtiness **12** billingsgate, vituperation **15** overbearingness

contusion 4 hurt, mark, sore **5** mouse **6** bruise, injury, shiner **7** blemish **8** abrasion, black eye **9** black mark **13** discoloration **16** black-and-blue mark

conundrum 5 poser, rebus **6** enigma, puzzle, riddle **7** arcanum, mystery, paradox, problem, puzzler, stopper, stumper **11** brain-teaser **13** Chinese puzzle

convalesce 4 mend **5** rally **6** revive **7** improve, recover, restore **8** progress **9** get better **10** recuperate

convalescence 7 recruit **8** recovery **11** restoration **12** recuperation **14** return to health

convene 6 gather, muster, summon **7** collect, convoke, round up **8** assemble **12** call together, come together, hold a session **13** bring together

convenience 3 use **4** ease **6** chance **7** benefit, comfort, service, utility **8** facility, pleasure **9** appliance, enjoyment, handiness, work saver **10** usefulness **11** opportunity **12** availability, satisfaction, suitable time **13** accessibility, accommodation

convenient 5 handy **6** at hand, nearby, suited, useful **7** adapted, helpful **8** suitable **9** easy to use **10** beneficial **11** serviceable **12** advantageous **16** easily accessible

convent 7 nunnery **8** cloister **13** society of nuns

convention 4 code **6** caucus, custom **7** meeting, precept **8** assembly, conclave, congress, practice, propriety, protocol, standard **9** formality, gathering **10** conference, social rule **11** convocation

conventional 5 usual **6** common, normal, proper **7** regular, routine **8** accepted, orthodox, standard **9** customary **11** traditional

converge 4 meet **5** focus **8** approach

11 concentrate **12** come together **13** bring together

convergence 6 accord **8** junction **9** congruity **10** confluence **12** meeting place **14** correspondence

conversant 4 up on **5** aware **6** au fait **7** erudite, privy to, skilled, tutored **8** familiar, informed, sensible, sentient **9** au courant, cognizant, practiced **10** acquainted, proficient **12** wellinformed **13** knowledgeable

conversation 3 rap **4** chat, talk **7** gabfest, palaver **8** chit-chat, dialogue **9** discourse, tete-a-tete **11** bull session **13** confabulation
Italian: **13** conversazione

**Conversation, The
director: 18** Francis Ford Coppola
cast: 10 John Cazale **11** Gene Hackman **13** Allen Garfield

conversational 6 casual, chatty **8** everyday, informal **9** idiomatic **10** colloquial, vernacular

conversazione 12 conversation

converse 3 gab, jaw, rap **4** chat, chin, talk **7** palaver, reverse **8** chitchat, contrary, opposite **10** antithesis, chew the fat, chew the rag **11** confabulate **13** speak together **14** shoot the breeze

conversely 12 contrariwise **14** antithetically, on the other hand

conversion 6 change **10** changeover **12** modification **13** change of heart, metamorphosis, transmutation **14** transformation **15** change in beliefs, transfiguration **16** change of religion

convert 4 turn **6** change, modify, novice **8** neophyte **9** proselyte, transform **11** proselytize

convex 7 bulging, rounded **11** protuberant **13** curved outward

convey 4 bear, cede, deed, give, move, tell, will **5** bring, carry, grant, leave **6** impart, relate, reveal **7** conduct, consign, deliver, divulge **8** bequeath, disclose, dispatch, transfer, transmit **9** confide to, make known, transport **11** communicate

conveyance 3 bus, car, rig, van **4** cart **5** buggy, truck, wagon **7** vehicle **8** carriage, carrying, movement, transfer **9** conveying, transport **12** transmission **14** transportation

convict 3 con **4** doom **5** felon **7** condemn **8** jailbird, prisoner, yardbird **10** find guilty **11** prove guilty **13** declare guilty

conviction 4 view, zeal **5** ardor, creed, dogma, faith, fever, tenet **6** belief, fervor **7** opinion **8** doctrine, judgment, position **9** assurance, certainty, certitude, intensity, principle, viewpoint **10** persuasion **11** earnestness **13** steadfastness

convince 4 sway **6** assure **7** satisfy,

win over **8** persuade **9** influence **11** bring around, prevail upon

convincing 5 sound, valid **6** cogent, potent **7** evident **8** assuring, forceful, powerful **9** plausible **10** persuading, persuasive, satisfying

convivial 5 merry **6** genial, jovial **7** affable, festive **8** friendly, sociable **9** agreeable, fun-loving **10** gregarious **13** companionable

convocation 6 caucus, muster, roster **7** council, meeting, roundup **8** assembly, conclave, congress **9** gathering **10** conference, convention **11** ingathering

convoke 4 meet, open **6** gather, muster **8** assemble, converse **11** call to order **12** call together

convolute 4 coil, wave, wavy, wind **5** twirl, twist **6** coiled, rolled, spiral, tangle **7** contort, sinuous, twisted **8** involved, spiraled **9** intricate **11** complicated **12** turn and twist

convolution 4 coil, maze **5** twist **7** coiling, winding **8** twisting **9** labyrinth, sinuosity **10** contortion, undulation **11** sinuousness **12** tortuousness

convoy 5 fleet, usher **6** column, escort **7** conduct **9** accompany, formation, safeguard **10** armed guard, protection

convulse 4 rock, stir **5** laugh, shake, spasm, wring **6** excite **7** agitate, disturb, perturb, trouble **8** double up

convulsion 3 fit **5** spasm **6** tumult **7** seizure **8** outburst, paroxysm **9** agitation, commotion **10** contortion **11** disturbance

convulsive 6 fitful **7** hurtful, rending, shaking **8** exciting, stirring **9** agitating, epileptic, spasmodic, troubling **10** disturbing

Conway, Tim
  real name: 18 Thomas Daniel Conway
  born: 12 Willoughby OH
  roles: 11 McHale's Navy **16** Carol Burnett Show **17** The Steve Allen Show

coo 4 bill **6** babble, gurgle, murmur **20** whisper sweet nothings

Coogan, Jackie
  real name: 16 Jack Leslie Coogan
  wife: 11 Betty Grable
  born: 12 Los Angeles CA
  roles: 6 The Kid **9** Tom Sawyer **11** Oliver Twist, Peck's Bad Boy **15** Huckleberry Finn

cook 3 fix **4** chef, fire, heat, make **5** occur **6** cookie, doctor, happen, seethe **7** concoct, falsify, prepare, process **8** work well **9** improvise
  method: 3 fry **4** bake, boil, brew, sear, stew **5** baste, broil, grill, poach, roast, saute, scald, shirr, steam **6** braise, coddle, simmer **7** parboil, stir-fry **8** barbecue **9** fricassee

Cooke, Alistair
  author of: 14 One Man's America **18** A Generation on Trial **26** Around the World in Fifty Years
  TV host of: 18 Masterpiece Theatre

cooked sufficiently 4 done **5** ready **7** al dente **11** done to a turn

cookie 3 bar, gal, gul **4** cake, cook **5** wafer **6** person **7** biscuit, brownie **10** shortbread
  type: 4 oreo **5** sugar **7** oatmeal **8** macaroon, molasses **9** Girl Scout, tollhouse **10** gingersnap, Lorna Doone **12** peanut butter **13** chocolate chip

cooking, fine/gourmet
  French: 12 haute cuisine

cooking term 3 a la, cut, dot, fry **4** bake, beat, boil, chop, coat, cube, dice, dust, flan, fold, lard, roux, sear, snip, stew, toss, whip **5** aspic, au jus, baste, blend, bread, broil, brush, candy, cream, crepe, devil, dough, flake, glace, glaze, grate, grill, knead, plank, puree, roast, saute, scald, score, shirr, steep, stock, swear, torte **6** au lait, blanch, braise, coddle, devein, dredge, fillet, flambe, fondue, render, simmer, skewer, sliver **7** a la mode, compote, crouton, garnish, goulash, liquefy, parboil, precook, preheat, rissole, scallop, stir-fry **8** aperitif, au gratin, barbecue, conserve, consomme, julienne, marinate, pot roast **9** brochette, demitasse, drippings, forcemeat, fricassee, lyonnaise, macedoine **10** caramelize, cracklings
  boneless strips of meat/ fish: 6 fillet
  clear soup: 8 bouillon, consomme
  cubed toasted bread: 7 crouton
  food cooked and served in foil or paper: 11 en papillote
  fruit preserve with nuts/raisins: 8 conserve
  fruits in syrup: 7 compote
  in the fashion: 7 a la mode
  remove veins: 6 devein
  skewered meat: 5 kebab **9** brochette
  small cup of black coffee: 9 demitasse
  thin strips: 6 sliver **8** julienne
  with cheese: 8 au gratin
  with ice cream: 7 a la mode
  with juice/with its own juices: 5 au jus
  with milk: 6 au lait

cook up 3 mix **4** brew **5** hatch **6** create, devise, invent, make up **7** concoct, think up **8** compound, contrive **9** fabricate, formulate

cool 3 icy **4** calm, cold **5** aloof, chill **6** chilly, frosty, offish, serene **7** distant, not warm **8** composed, lose heat, make cool, reserved **9** collected, impassive, uncordial, unexcited **10** become cool, cool-headed, deliberate, nonchalant, unfriendly, unsociable,

untroubled **11** indifferent, standoffish, undisturbed, unemotional, unflappable **12** slightly cold, somewhat cold, unresponsive **13** dispassionate, imperturbable, self-possessed

cooler 3 ade, can, fan, jug **4** coop, icer, jail **5** drink, icier **6** calmer, icebox, lockup, prison **11** refrigerant **12** refrigerator **14** air conditioner

Cool Hand Luke
  director: 15 Stuart Rosenberg
  cast: 8 J D Cannon **10** Jo Van Fleet, Lou Antonio, Paul Newman **12** Anthony Zerbe, Dennis Hopper **13** George Kennedy **14** Strother Martin
  Oscar for: 15 supporting actor (Kennedy)

Coolidge, Calvin
  name at birth: 18 John Calvin Coolidge
  nickname: 9 Silent Cal
  presidential rank: 9 thirtieth
  party: 10 Republican
  state represented: 2 MA
  succeeded: 7 Harding
  defeated: 5 (Frank Thomas) Johns, (Herman P) Faris, (John William) Davis **6** (William Zebulon) Foster **7** (Gilbert O) Nations, (William James) Wallace **10** (Robert Marion) La Follette
  vice president: 4 none (first term) **5** (Charles Gates) Dawes
  cabinet:
    state: 6 (Charles Evans) Hughes **7** (Frank Billings) Kellogg
    treasury: 6 (Andrew William) Mellon
    war: 5 (Dwight Filley) Davis, (John Wingate) Weeks
    attorney general: 5 (Harlan Fiske) Stone **6** (Charles B) Warren **7** (John Garibaldi) Sargent **9** (Harry Micajah) Daugherty
    navy: 5 (Edwin) Denby **6** (Curtis Dwight) Wilbur
    postmaster general: 3 (Harry Stewart) New
    interior: 4 (Hubert) Work, (Roy Owen) West
    agriculture: 4 (Howard Mason) Gore **7** (Henry Cantwell) Wallace, (William Marion) Jardine
    commerce: 6 (Herbert Clark) Hoover **7** (William Fairfield) Whiting
    labor: 5 (James John) Davis
  born: 2 VT **13** Plymouth Notch
  died: 2 MA **11** Northampton
  buried: 2 VT **8** Plymouth
  education:
    College: 7 Amherst
    later studied: 3 law
  religion: 17 Congregationalist
  vacation spot: 10 Black Hills
  author: 32 The Autobiography of Calvin Coolidge
  political career: 13 vice president

state senator/lieutenant governor/governor of: **2** Ma **13** Massachusetts

civilian career: **6** lawyer **17** bank vice president **18** newspaper columnist

notable events of lifetime/term: **22** Pennsylvania coal strike

Act: **8** Volstead **10** Boulder Dam **11** Immigration **17** Japanese Exclusion

bribery case: **8** Elks Hill

conference: **11** Geneva Naval

flight by: **16** Charles Lindbergh

Lindbergh's plane: **15** Spirit of St Louis

Pact: **13** Kellogg-Briand

trial: **6** Scopes **12** Scopes monkey

quote: **35** (After all) the chief business of America is business **43** Spend less than you make and make more than you spend

father: **10** John Calvin

mother: **8** Victoria (Josephine Moor)

stepmother: **8** Caroline (Brown)

sibling: **13** Abigail Gratia

wife: **5** Grace (Anna Goodhue)

children: **4** John **6** Calvin

coolness 5 chill **7** dislike, reserve **8** distance **9** aloofness, composure, sangfroid **10** chilliness, detachment, frostiness **11** impassivity **12** indifference **13** lack of emotion, lack of feeling **14** unfriendliness **15** emotionlessness, standoffishness **16** imperturbability, unresponsiveness

coop 3 mew, pen, sty **4** auto, cage, cote **5** cramp, hutch, roost **6** encase, prison **7** confine **8** imprison **9** enclosure **11** cooperation, cooperative

Cooper, Gary

real name: **16** Frank James Cooper

born: **8** Helena MT

roles: **8** High Noon (Oscar) **9** Beau Geste **12** Sergeant York (Oscar), The Virginian **15** A Farewell to Arms **17** Mr Deeds Goes to Town **19** For Whom the Bell Tolls, The Cowboy and the Lady **20** The Pride of the Yankees **22** North West Mounted Police

Cooper, James Fenimore

author of: **6** The Spy **8** The Bravo, The Pilot **9** Wyandotte **10** The Prairie **11** The Pioneers, The Red Rover **13** The Deerslayer, The Pathfinder, The Water-Witch **20** Leatherstocking Tales, The Last of the Mohicans

character: **4** Cora **5** Alice, Magua, Uncas **7** Hawkeye **11** Natty Bumppo **12** Chingachgook

cooperate 4 join **5** unite **7** go along, pitch in, share in **8** take part **9** join hands **10** act jointly, bear part in, join forces **11** collaborate, participate **12** pull together, work together **14** work side by side

cooperation 7 concert, detente **8** teamwork **9** agreement **10** accordance **11** concurrence, cooperating, give and take, joint action **13** collaboration, participation **15** pulling together, working together

coop up 3 pen **4** cage **5** pen in **6** closet, encage, shut in **7** confine, impound **8** restrain, restrict

coordinate 4 mesh **5** equal, match, order **6** relate **7** arrange, coequal **8** organize, parallel **9** correlate, harmonize **11** correlative, systematize **16** equally important

coordination 4 bond **5** skill **6** accord **7** harmony, liaison **10** adaptation, adjustment **12** equalization, organization **15** synchronization

cop 3 bag, nab, rob, win **4** bull, grab, take **5** bobby, catch, filch, pinch, snare, steal, swipe **6** peeler, pilfer, snatch **7** capture **8** flat foot, gendarme, purchase **9** policeman **11** acquisition, policewoman **13** police officer

cope 4 face, spar **6** handle, hurdle, manage, strive, tussle **7** contend, wrestle **8** struggle **11** hold one's own

copious 4 full **5** ample **6** lavish **7** liberal, profuse **8** abundant, generous **9** bountiful, extensive, plenteous, plentiful

copiousness 6 bounty, plenty, wealth **7** surfeit **8** fullness, plethora **9** abundance, ampleness, plenitude, profusion **10** lavishness, oversupply

Copland, Aaron

born: **10** Brooklyn NY

composer of: **5** Rodeo **9** Quiet City **10** Statements **11** Billy the Kid **12** Connotations **13** Dance Symphony, El Salon Mexico, The Tender Land **15** Outdoor Overture **17** Appalachian Spring **18** Music for a Great City, Music for the Theater

Copley, John Singleton

born: **8** Boston MA

artwork: **11** Samuel Adams **19** The Siege of Gibraltar **21** The Boy with the Squirrel **22** Brook Watson and the Shark, The Death of Major Pierson **26** The Death of the Earl of Chatham

copper

chemical symbol: **2** Cu

copper-colored 5 henna **6** auburn, russet **11** golden-brown, rust-colored **12** reddish-brown

coppice 4 bosk, wood **5** bluff, copse, firth, grove **6** forest, growth **7** boscage, thicket

Coppola, Francis Ford

director of: **7** Dracula **12** The Godfather (Part I) (Part II, Oscar), The Rainmaker **13** Apocalypse Now, The Cotton Club **15** The Conversation

copse 5 brush, clump, grove **6** forest **7** coppice, thicket **8** woodland

copy 3 ape **4** fake, sham, text **5** clone, mimic, story, Xerox **6** follow, mirror, parody, repeat **7** emulate, forgery, imitate, replica **8** likeness **9** duplicate, facsimile, imitation, photostat, reportage, reproduce **10** carbon copy, manuscript **11** counterfeit, make a copy of **12** reproduction **14** representation **15** written material

coquette 4 vamp **5** flirt, tease **12** heart-breaker

coquettish 3 coy **9** kittenish **11** flirtatious

coral 3 red **4** fire, pink, rose **5** horny, polyp, snake **6** orange, sea fan **8** acropora, hydrozoa, staghorn **9** gorgonian **10** sea feather **12** coelenterata

coram populo 8 publicly **15** before the public

corban 8 offering

Corbett, James (John)

nickname: **12** Gentleman Jim

sport: **6** boxing

class: **11** heavyweight

cord 5 braid, twine **8** thin rope **11** heavy string

abbreviation: **2** cd

Cordelia

character in: **8** King Lear

author: **11** Shakespeare

cordial 4 warm **6** genial, hearty **7** affable, amiable, sincere **8** friendly, gracious **9** heartfelt **11** good-natured **12** affectionate, wholehearted

cordiality 6 warmth **8** goodwill **9** affection, geniality, sincerity **10** affability, amiability, heartiness **11** amicability, earnestness **12** friendliness, graciousness, pleasantness **13** agreeableness

cordial relations 5 amity **6** accord **7** concord, harmony **8** goodwill **9** agreement **10** friendship **11** amicability **15** entente cordiale

cordon 4 cord, ring, rope **6** circle **8** encircle

cordon bleu 4 bird **5** finch **7** waxbill **10** red cheeked **11** estrildidae

school for: **5** chefs **7** cooking

where: **5** Paris **6** France

founded by: **13** Marthe Distell

means: **10** blue ribbon

core 3 nub, nut **4** crux, gist, guts, meat, pith **5** heart **6** center, kernel **7** essence, nucleus **9** substance **10** brass tacks **11** central part, nitty-gritty **13** essential part, innermost part **15** sum and substance

Corelli, Arcangelo

born: **5** Imola, Italy

composer of: **7** La Folia (sonata No 12) **14** Concerti Grossi

coriander

botanical name: **17** Coriandrum sativum

origin: **13** Mediterranean

color: **5** brown, white **6** yellow

flavor: **4** sage **5** cumin **7** caraway **9** lemon peel
candy: **6** comfit

Corinth, Lovis
born: **6** Tapiau **7** Prussia
artwork: **6** Salome **8** Ecce Homo **10** Apocalypse **29** The Walchensee with a Yellow Field

Coriolanus
author: **18** William Shakespeare
character: **8** Cominius, Virgilia, Volumnia **12** Junius Brutus, Titus Lartius **14** Tullus Aufidius **15** Menenius Agrippa, Sicinius Velutus **22** Caius Marcius Coriolanus

cork 3 bob, oak **4** bark, bung, plug, seal, stop **5** check, close, float **7** confine, filling stopper, stopple **8** restrain, suppress **10** insulation

corker 3 ace **4** lulu, oner, whiz **7** stopper **8** clencher, striking, top notch **9** excellent, humdinger **10** remarkable **11** astonishing

corkscrew 4 coil, curl **5** twist **6** spiral **7** winding **10** serpentine **12** bottle opener

Corleone family
characters in: **12** The Godfather
author: **4** Puzo **9** Mario Puzo
member: **5** Fredo, Sonny **6** Connie **7** Don Vito, Freddie, Michael

corn 4 cure **5** grain **6** callus **7** Zea Mays **8** preserve, schmaltz **9** vegetable
varieties: **3** Pod **4** Crow, Dent, Rice, Sand **5** Broom, Flint, Kafir, maize, Sugar, Sweet **6** Indian, Turkey **8** Egyptian, Squirrel
bread/cake: **4** pone **7** hoecake **8** tortilla **9** hushpuppy **10** johnnycake
beverage: **7** bourbon, whiskey

Corncracker State
nickname of: **8** Kentucky

Corneille, Pierre
author of: **5** Cinna, Le Cid, Medea, Medee **6** Horace, The Cid **8** Nicomede **9** Polyeucte

Cornelius, Peter von (van)
born: **7** Germany **10** Dusseldorf
artwork: **12** Last Judgment **24** The Wise and Foolish Virgins **30** The Four Horsemen of the Apocalypse

Cornell, Katherine
nickname: **21** first lady of the theater
born: **6** Berlin **7** Germany
roles: **8** Dear Liar **9** Saint Joan **18** Antony and Cleopatra **26** The Barretts of Wimpole Street

corner 3 fix, jam, nab **4** bend, grab, hole, nail, nook, spot, trap **5** angle, seize **6** collar, pickle, plight, scrape **7** dead end, dilemma, impasse **10** blind alley, pigeonhole **11** predicament

cornerstone 4 base **5** basis **9** principle **10** foundation **11** fundamental

cornet 4 cone, horn **7** trumpet **9** cornopean

Cornhusker State
nickname of: **8** Nebraska

cornice 4 drip **5** ancon, crown **7** molding, valance **8** astragal

Cornwallis, Charles
also: **10** second Earl **13** first Marquess
nationality: **7** British
served in: **5** India **7** Ireland **18** American Revolution
battle: **8** Yorktown **10** Brandywine
captured: **10** Charleston **12** Philadelphia
surrendered at: **8** Yorktown

Cornwell, David
real name of: **11** John Le Carre

corny 5 banal, hokey, inane, stale, tired, trite, vapid **6** jejune, square **7** fatuous, insipid **8** bromidic, ordinary, shopworn **9** hackneyed **10** threadbare, unoriginal **11** commonplace, stereotyped **12** cliche-ridden, old-fashioned **13** platitudinous, unimaginative **15** unsophisticated

corona 4 halo, ring **5** cigar **6** circle, nimbus

coronet 5 tiara **6** diadem **7** chaplet, circlet **10** small crown

Corot, Jean-Baptiste-Camille
born: **5** Paris **6** France
artwork: **9** Pastorale **11** Ville d'Avray, Woman in Blue **15** Woman with a Pearl **16** The Farnese Garden, Woman in the Studio **21** Memory of Mortefontaine **23** Souvenir de Mortefontaine

corporal 3 NCO **6** bodily **8** physical **9** corporeal

corporation 7 combine, company **9** syndicate **11** association **14** conglomeration

corporeal 6 bodily, mortal **7** worldly **8** material, physical **11** perceptible **12** nonspiritual

corps 4 band, crew, team **5** force, party, squad, troop **6** outfit

corpse 4 body **5** stiff **7** cadaver, remains **8** dead body

corpselike 4 pale **5** ashen **6** pallid **9** bloodless, deathlike **10** cadaverous

corpulent 3 fat **5** dumpy, hefty, obese, plump, pudgy, stout **6** chubby, chunky, fleshy, portly, rotund **7** lumpish, well-fed **8** roly-poly **10** overweight, well-padded

corral 4 herd **5** pen in **6** shut in **7** enclose, fence in, round up

correct 3 fit, fix **4** true **5** alter, amend, chide, emend, exact, right, scold **6** adjust, berate, change, modify, proper, punish, rebuke, remedy, repair, revamp, revise, rework, seemly **7** censure, chasten, factual, fitting, improve, lecture, perfect, precise, rectify, reprove **8** accurate, admonish, becoming, chastise, flawless, regulate, suita-

ble, unerring **9** castigate, dress down, faultless, make right, reprimand **10** acceptable, discipline, take to task **11** appropriate **12** conventional **16** haul over the coals, read the riot act to

correction 6 change **8** revision **10** adjustment, alteration, discipline, emendation, punishment **11** castigation, improvement, reformation **12** chastisement, modification **13** rectification

corrective 7 counter **8** remedial **9** improving **10** palliative, rectifying **11** reformatory, restorative, therapeutic **12** ameliorative, compensatory **13** counteractive **16** counterbalancing

correctness 8 accuracy **9** exactness, precision, propriety, rightness **10** exactitude, seemliness **11** suitability **12** becomingness, flawlessness **13** acceptability

Correggio
real name: **14** Antonio Allegri
born: **5** Italy **6** Emilia **9** Correggio
artwork: **5** Danae **12** Jupiter and Io **14** Leda and the Swan **17** The Rape of Ganymede **21** The Madonna of St Francis **23** Adoration of the Shepherds **28** Mystic Marriages of St Catherine

correlate 7 compare, connect **8** parallel **10** correspond

correlation 8 parallel **10** comparison, connection **14** correspondence

correlative 4 akin **7** related **8** agreeing, parallel **9** analogous **10** comparable, connecting, equivalent **13** corresponding

correspond 3 fit **4** jibe, suit **5** agree, match, tally **6** accord, be like, concur, equate, square **7** conform **8** coincide, dovetail, parallel **9** harmonize **11** communicate, drop a line to, keep in touch

correspondence 4 mail **7** analogy, letters **8** epistles, missives, relation **9** bulletins **10** dispatches, similarity **11** association, communiques, resemblance

corresponding 4 akin **5** alike, equal **7** similar **8** agreeing, matching, tallying **9** according **10** equivalent **11** correlative **12** proportional

corridor 3 way **4** hall, road **5** aisle **6** artery **7** hallway, passage **8** approach **10** passageway

corroborate 4 back **5** prove **6** affirm, back up, uphold, verify **7** bear out, certify, confirm, endorse, support, sustain **8** validate **9** vindicate **12** authenticate, substantiate

corroborated 6 backed, proved, proven, upheld **7** factual **8** affirmed, backed up, borne out, verified **9** certified, confirmed, supported, sustained, validated **10** vindicated **11** wellfounded **12** well-grounded **13** authenticated, substantiated

corroboration 5 proof **7** support **8** evidence **10** validation **11** affirmation, endorsement, vindication **12** confirmation, verification **13** certification, documentation **14** authentication, substantiation

corroborative 7 proving **9** affirming, backing up, upholding, verifying **10** bearing out, concurring, confirming, supporting, validating **11** affirmative **12** confirmative **14** substantiating

corrode 4 rust **7** oxidize **12** disintegrate

corrosive 4 acid **7** burning, caustic, erosive, mordant **8** abrasive **9** corroding **11** destructive

corrugated 6 fluted, ridged **7** creased, grooved, pleated **8** crinkled, furrowed, puckered, wrinkled **10** crenulated

corrupt 3 low **4** base, evil, mean **5** shady **6** debase, poison, seduce, sinful, wicked **7** crooked, debased, debauch, deprave, immoral, pervert, subvert **8** depraved **9** dishonest, unethical **10** fraudulent, iniquitous **11** contaminate **12** dishonorable, unprincipled, unscrupulous

corruption 4 vice **5** fraud, graft **7** bribery **8** iniquity **9** decadence, depravity, looseness, turpitude **10** debauchery, degeneracy, dishonesty, immorality, perversion, sinfulness, wickedness, wrongdoing **11** malfeasance

corsair 6 pirate, sea dog, Viking **7** brigand, sea wolf **8** marauder, picaroon, sea rover **9** buccaneer, plunderer, privateer, sea looter, sea robber **10** Blackbeard, freebooter **11** Captain Kidd **14** Long John Silver

corset 5 laces **6** girdle **8** corselet **17** foundation garment

Corsica 6 island
　located in: 16 Mediterranean Sea
　capital: 7 Ajaccio
　colony of: 4 Rome
　purchased by: 6 France
　birthplace of: 8 Napoleon
　industry: 7 tourism **10** wine making **12** sheep raising, cheese making

Corsican Brothers, The
　author: 14 Alexandre Dumas (pere)

Cortazar, Julio
　author of: 7 Rayuela **9** A Model Kit, Bestiario, Hopscotch **10** The Winners **12** Book of Manuel, End of the Game **15** All Fires the Fire **18** We Love Glenda So Much

cortege 4 line **5** court, staff, suite, train **6** column, escort, parade, string **7** caravan, company, retinue **9** cavalcade, entourage, following, motorcade **10** attendants, procession **17** funeral procession

corundum
　variety: 4 ruby **8** sapphire, star ruby **12** star sapphire

coruscate 4 beam **5** flash, gleam **7** glimmer, glitter, shimmer, sparkle

Corybant
　attendant of: 6 Cybele

Corythosaurus
　type: 8 dinosaur **10** ornithopod
　period: 10 Cretaceous
　characteristic: 10 duck-billed

Cosby, Bill
　born: 14 Philadelphia PA
　roles: 4 I Spy **8** Ghost Dad **12** The Cosby Show **19** Mother Juggs and Speed, Uptown Saturday Night
　cartoon: 24 Fat Albert and the Cosby Kids
　author: 9 Childhood **10** Fatherhood **11** I Am What I Ate **15** Love and Marriage
　nickname: 3 Cos

Cosby Show, The
　character: 4 Rudy, Theo **6** Denise, Sondra **7** Vanessa **13** Clair Huxtable, (Dr) Cliff (Heathcliff) Huxtable
　cast: 9 Bill Cosby, Lisa Bonet **14** Sabrina LeBeauf **15** Tempestt Bledsoe **18** Malcolm Jamal-Warner **19** Keshia Knight Pulliam, Phylicia Ayers-Rashad

Cosi fan tutte
　also: 11 So Do They All **16** Women Are Like That
　opera by: 6 Mozart
　character: 7 Despina **8** Ferrando **9** Dorabella, Guglielmo **10** Don Alfonso, Fiordiligi

cosmetic 5 blush, liner, paint, rouge **6** makeup, powder **7** mascara, surface **8** artifice, eyeliner, lipstick **9** cold cream, eye shadow **10** foundation, nail polish **11** beautifying **13** eyebrow pencil

cosmic 4 vast **7** immense **8** colossal, enormous, infinite **9** grandiose, universal **10** stupendous, widespread **12** interstellar **14** interplanetary **16** extraterrestrial

cosmopolitan 5 suave **6** urbane **7** worldly **8** traveler **11** broad-minded, worldly-wise **12** globetrotter, sophisticate **13** international, sophisticated

cosmos 5 stars **8** universe **9** macrocosm **10** starry host **13** vault of heaven
　book by: 5 Sagan

Cossack 7 czarist, Russian, trooper **8** horseman **10** cavalry man

cosset 3 pet **6** caress, coddle, fondle, pamper

cost 3 fee, run, tab **4** bill, harm, hurt, loss, pain, take, toll **5** fetch, go for, price, value, worth **6** amount, burden, charge, come to, damage, injure, injury, outlay **7** bring in, expense, penalty, sell for, set back **8** amount to, distress **9** face value, sacrifice, suffering, valuation, weigh down **11** expenditure, market price

Costa-Gavras, Constantine
　director of: 7 Missing

Costard
　character in: 16 Love's Labour's Lost
　author: 11 Shakespeare

Costa Rica
　name means: 9 rich coast
　other name: 19 Land of Eternal Spring
　capital/largest city: 7 San Jose
　others: 5 Canas, Limon, Vesta **6** Boruca, Nicoya **7** Cartago, Golfito, Heredia, Liberia, Negrita **8** Alajuela, Colorado, Guapiles **9** Turrialba **10** Puntarenas
　measure: 4 vara **5** cafiz, cahiz **6** fanega, tercia **7** cajuela, cantaro, manzana **10** caballeria
　monetary unit: 5 colon **7** centimo
　weight: 3 bag **4** caja **5** libra
　island: 4 Cano, Coco
　lake: 6 Arenal
　mountain: 4 Poas **5** Barba, Irazu **6** Blanco **7** Central, Gongora **9** Talamanca, Turrialba **10** Guanacaste
　highest point: 14 Chirripo Grande
　river: 4 Poas **5** Irazu **6** Matina **7** San Juan, Sixaola, Tenoria **8** Tarcoles
　sea: 7 Pacific **9** Caribbean
　physical feature:
　　bay: 7 Salinas **8** Coronada
　　cape: 5 Velas **6** Blanco **8** Matapalo **10** Santa Elena
　　crater: 4 Poas
　　gulf: 5 Dulce **6** Nicoya **8** Papagayo
　　hot springs spa: 12 Agua Caliente
　　peninsula: 3 Osa **6** Nicoya
　　point: 5 Judas **6** Blanca, Burica, Quepos **7** Cahuito, Galonos, Guionos, Llerena
　　valley: 8 Tarcoles **10** Reventazon
　people: 4 Voto **6** Boruca, Bribri, Guaymi **7** Guatuso, mestizo, Spanish
　　explorer: 8 Columbus, Coronado
　language: 7 Spanish
　religion: 13 Roman Catholic
　place:
　　shrine: 18 Our Lady of the Angels
　　theater: 14 Teatro Nacional
　feature:
　　barbecue: 5 asado
　　dance: 6 torito **9** botijuela, zapateado **11** baile suelto **17** punto guanacasteco
　　drum: 8 quijonga
　　gourd: 4 caro
　　outdoor concerts: 7 retreta
　　plantation: 5 finca
　　wind instrument: 8 chirimia
　food:
　　hearts of palm salad: 7 palmito
　　pudding: 10 tamal asado

Costello, Lou
　real name: 21 Louis Francis Cristillo
　partner: 9 Bud Abbott
　born: 10 Paterson NJ
　roles: 11 Who's on First

costly 4 dear **5** steep, stiff **7** harmful **8**

damaging, precious **9** expensive **10** disastrous, exorbitant, high-priced **11** deleterious, extravagant **12** catastrophic

Costner, Kevin
  born: 2 CA **10** Los Angeles
  films: 3 JFK **6** Tin Cup **9** Dragonfly, Open Range, Silverado, Wyatt Earp **10** Bull Durham, The Postman, Waterworld **12** The Bodyguard, Thirteen Days **13** Field of Dreams, A Perfect World **15** The Untouchables **16** Dances With Wolves **24** Robin Hood: Prince of Thieves

costume 4 garb **5** dress **6** attire, livery, outfit **7** apparel, clothes, raiment, uniform **8** clothing, garments

costuming 8 disguise **10** masquerade

cot 3 bed, hut, pen **4** coop, crib **5** cover, stall **7** cottage

cotelette 3 cut **4** chop **5** slice **6** cutlet

coterie 3 set **4** band, camp, clan, club, crew, gang **5** crowd, group **6** circle, clique **7** faction

cottage 3 cot, hut **5** lodge, shack **6** chalet **8** bungalow

Cotten, Joseph
  born: 12 Petersburg VA
  roles: 8 Gaslight **11** Citizen Kane, The Third Man **12** Duel in the Sun **14** Shadow of a Doubt **15** Journey into Fear **16** Portrait of Jennie **23** The Magnificent Ambersons

cotton 9 Gossypium
  varieties: 3 bog **4** tree, wild **6** kidney, levant, upland **8** lavender **9** sea island **11** Arizona wild
  fabric: 4 duck, jean, lawn, pima **5** baize, chino, denim, drill, khaki, lisle, pique, scrim, terry, twill **6** burlap, calico, canvas, chintz, dimity, madras, muslin, nankin, oxford, poplin, sateen **7** batiste, buckram, cambric, flannel, fustian, gingham, holland, jaconet, oilskin, organdy, percale, ticking **8** chambray, cretonne, sheeting **9** crinoline, sailcloth **10** broadcloth, hopsacking, printcloth, seersucker, terrycloth **11** cheesecloth, dotted Swiss

Cotton Club, The
  director: 18 Francis Ford Coppola
  cast: 9 Diane Lane **11** Richard Gere **12** Gregory Hines

cotton gin
  invented by: 7 Whitney

Cotton State
  nickname of: 7 Alabama

cottonwood 7 Populus **16** Populus deltoides
  varieties: 5 black, Jack's, swamp **7** Fremont **9** Rio Grande **10** Wislizenus **11** Great Plains

Cotyleus
  epithet of: 9 Asclepius
  means: 13 of the hip joint

couch 3 put **4** sofa, word **5** divan, draft, frame, state, utter, voice **6** daybed, draw up, lounge, phrase, settee **7** express **8** love seat, set forth **9** davenport **12** chesterfield

couch potato
  activity: 7 viewing
  loves: 10 television

cougar 3 cat **4** lion, puma **7** panther **9** catamount **12** mountain lion

cough 4 hack **6** tussis **9** pertussis

cough up 3 pay **5** eject, expel **7** deliver **8** disgorge, hand over **9** surrender **11** regurgitate

Coulomb, Charles Augustin de
  field: 7 physics
  nationality: 6 French
  invented: 14 torsion balance
  discovered: 16 inverse square law

council 5 board, panel, synod **7** cabinet, chamber **8** assembly, colloquy, conclave, congress, ministry **9** committee, gathering, sanhedrin **10** conference, convention **11** convocation **12** congregation **15** representatives

counsel 4 urge, warn **6** advice, advise, charge, lawyer, prompt **7** call for, caution, opinion, suggest **8** admonish, advocate, attorney, guidance, instruct **9** barrister, counselor, recommend, solicitor **10** advisement, suggestion **12** consultation **14** recommendation

counsel house
  German: 7 Rathaus

Counsellor-at-Law
  director: 12 William Wyler
  based on play by: 9 Elmer Rice
  cast: 11 Bebe Daniels, Doris Kenyon **12** Isabel Jewell **13** John Barrymore, Melvyn Douglas, Onslow Stevens

counselor, counsellor 5 tutor **6** lawyer, mentor **7** adviser **8** advocate, attorney, minister **9** barrister, solicitor **10** instructor

counselor-at-law 6 lawyer **8** advocate, attorney **9** barrister, solicitor **10** mouthpiece

count 4 deem, hold, lord, rate, tell **5** add up, judge, noble, tally, total **6** impute, look on, matter, number, reckon, regard **7** ascribe, include, tick off **8** consider, estimate, look upon, numerate **9** attribute, enumerate, numbering, reckoning **10** numeration **11** calculation, computation, enumeration
  German: 4 Graf
  French: 5 comte
  Italian: 5 conte
  famous: 7 Dracula **8** Almaviva **11** Monte Cristo

countenance 3 aid, air **4** back, face, help, look, mien **5** build, favor **6** aspect, permit, traits, uphold, visage **7** advance, approve, condone, endorse, forward, further, profile, promote, support, work for **8** advocacy, advo-

cate, approval, auspices, champion, contours, features, presence, sanction **9** promotion **10** appearance, assistance, expression, silhouette **11** approbation, physiognomy **12** championship, moral support **13** encouragement

counter 3 bar, man **4** defy, disk **5** piece, stand, table **6** buffet, contra, offset, oppose, resist **7** against, get even, hit back, opposed, pay back, reverse **8** contrary, fountain, opposite **9** fight back, retaliate **11** conflicting **13** contradictory

counteract 4 curb, undo **5** check, fight **6** defeat, hinder, negate, offset, oppose, resist, thwart **7** assuage, nullify, repress **8** overcome, restrain **9** alleviate, frustrate, overpower **10** annihilate, contravene, neutralize

counteraction 8 negation **10** offsetting, opposition **13** contravention, nullification **14** neutralization

counteractive 7 adverse **8** inimical **10** corrective **11** unfavorable **12** antagonistic, neutralizing

counteractor 7 negator **9** nullifier, offsetter **11** neutralizer

counteragent 3 spy **4** mole **8** antidote **9** antitoxin **10** antipoison **11** double agent

counterbalance 5 amend, check **6** cancel, offset, redeem, set off **7** correct, rectify **8** atone for, equalize, make good, outweigh **9** make up for **10** balance out, neutralize, outbalance, recompense **12** compensation

counterfeit 4 copy, fake, sham **5** bogus, fraud, phony **6** ersatz, forged **7** feigned, forgery **8** spurious **9** facsimile, imitation, simulated **10** artificial, fraudulent, substitute **11** make-believe

Counterfeiters, The
  author: 9 Andre Gide

countermand 4 void **5** annul, quash **6** cancel, recall, repeal, revoke **7** abolish, nullify, rescind, retract, reverse **8** abrogate, call back, disenact, override, overrule, set aside, withdraw, write off **12** disestablish

counterpart 4 copy, mate, twin **5** equal, match **6** double, fellow **8** parallel **9** duplicate **11** correlative **12** doppelganger **13** correspondent, spitting image

counterpoise 7 balance **9** stability **11** equilibrium

countersign 4 sign **7** certify, confirm, endorse **8** validate **9** authorize **11** corroborate **12** authenticate

countess
  French: 8 comtesse
  Italian: 8 contessa

countless 6 myriad, untold **7** endless **8** infinite **9** limitless, unlimited **10** numberless, unnumbered **11** innumerable, measureless **12** immeasurable, incalculable **13** multitudinous

Count of Monte Cristo, The
author: **14** Alexandre Dumas (pere)
character: **6** Albert, Haydee, Morrel **7** Fernand (Comte de Morcerf) **8** Danglars, Mercedes **9** Abbe Faria, Valentine, Villefort **10** Caderousse, Maximilian **12** Edmond Dantes
prison: **10** Chateau d'If

count on 6 expect **7** hope for **10** anticipate

countrified 5 rural **6** rustic **9** backwoods **15** unsophisticated

country 4 area, farm, land **5** realm, rural, state **6** nation, people, public, region, rustic, simple, sticks **7** boonies, farming, kingdom, natives, scenery, terrain **8** citizens, district, homeland, populace **9** backwoods, boondocks, community, landscape, territory **10** fatherland, native land, native soil, population, provincial, rural areas **11** farming area, hinterlands, inhabitants, nationality **12** commonwealth **15** unsophisticated

Country Girl, The
director: **12** George Seaton
based on play by: **13** Clifford Odets
cast: **10** Bing Crosby, Grace Kelly (Oscar) **11** Anthony Ross **13** William Holden
Oscar for: **7** actress (Kelly)

countryman 4 hick, rube **5** yokel **6** farmer, rustic **7** bumpkin, hayseed, peasant **8** landsman **10** clodhopper, compatriot, provincial

country place 4 farm **5** manor **6** estate

countryside 6 sticks **7** boonies **9** backwater, backwoods, boondocks, rural area **10** hinterland

count up 3 add **5** tally, total **6** reckon **7** compute **9** calculate

count upon 6 expect **7** foresee **10** anticipate

coup 3 act **4** blow, deed, feat **6** stroke **12** master stroke

coup de grace 9 deathblow **11** mercy stroke **12** decisive blow **15** finishing stroke
literally: **11** blow of mercy

coup de main 14 surprise attack **17** sudden development
literally: **15** blow from the hand

coup d'etat 6 mutiny **8** uprising **9** overthrow, rebellion **10** revolution, subversion

coup de theatre 15 theatrical trick

coup d'oeil 11 quick glance
literally: **14** stroke of the eye

Couperin, Francois (Le Grand)
born: **5** Paris **6** France
composer of: **9** La Sultane, Les Fastes (de la grande et ancienne) **13** Concert Royaux **16** Apotheose de

Lulli, Pieces de Clavecin **17** Lecons des Tenebres **20** Les Follies Francoises **31** Le Parnasse on l'Apotheose de Corelli

couple 3 duo, tie **4** bind, join, link, pair, yoke **5** hitch **6** fasten **7** connect, doublet, twosome **10** man and wife **11** man and woman **14** husband and wife

coupler 4 link, lock **5** clasp, hitch **6** buckle **8** fastener **9** fastening

Couples
author: **10** John Updike

coupling 5 clasp, hatch **6** hookup, yoking **7** joining, pairing **8** hitching **9** attaching, fastening **10** attachment, connecting, connection

courage 4 grit, guts, sand **5** nerve, pluck, spunk, valor **6** daring, mettle **7** bravery **8** boldness **9** derring-do, fortitude **11** intrepidity **12** fearlessness **13** dauntlessness **16** stout-heartedness

courageous 4 bold **5** brave, manly **6** dogged, heroic **7** dashing, doughty, gallant, valiant **8** fearless, intrepid, resolute, stalwart, unafraid, valorous **9** dauntless **10** chivalrous **11** indomitable **12** bold-spirited **13** strong-hearted

Courbet, Jean Desire Gustave
born: **6** France, Ornans
artwork: **16** The Artist's Studio, The Stonebreakers **17** The Burial at Ornans **19** The Peasants of Flagey **25** Self-Portrait with a Black Dog

courier 4 mule **5** envoy **6** herald, legate, runner **7** Gabriel, mailman, Mercury, postman **8** emissary **9** go-between, harbinger, messenger, postrider **11** herald angel, internuncio

course 3 run, way **4** flow, gush, mode, path, pour, race, road **5** march, orbit, round, route, surge, track **6** action, circle, method, policy, stream **7** channel, circuit, classes, conduct, lessons, passage, subject **8** behavior, lectures, sequence **9** direction, procedure, unfolding **10** curriculum, racecourse, trajectory **11** development, progression

court 3 bar, woo **4** hall, quad, seek, suit, yard **5** bench, manor, plaza, staff, train **6** atrium, castle, homage, induce, invite, palace, pursue, wooing **7** address, attract, chateau, cortege, council, flatter, hearing, meeting, provoke, retinue, session **8** advisers, assembly, audience, blandish, fawn upon, respects, run after **9** entourage, following **10** attendants, quadrangle **13** solicitations

Courtenay, Tom
born: **4** Hull **7** England
roles: **9** Billy Liar **10** The Dresser **12** Let Him Have It **13** Doctor Zhivago **36** The Loneliness of the Long Distance Runner
honor: **10** knighthood

courteous 4 kind, mild **5** civil **6** polite **7** refined, tactful **8** gracious, mannerly, well-bred **10** diplomatic, respectful, soft-spoken **11** considerate, well-behaved **12** well-mannered

courtesy 5 favor **7** manners, regards, respect **8** civility, kindness, respects **9** deference, gallantry, gentility **10** indulgence, politeness, refinement **11** cultivation **12** graciousness **13** consideration

courtier 4 beau **7** gallant **8** cavalier **9** attendant **18** gentleman-in-waiting

Courtier, The
author: **21** Baldassare Castiglione

Court Jester
director: **11** Melvin Frank **12** Norman Panama
cast: **9** Danny Kaye **11** Glynis Johns **13** Basil Rathbone **14** Angela Lansbury

courtly 5 suave **6** polite **7** elegant, gallant, genteel, refined, stately **8** debonair, decorous, highbred, ladylike, mannerly, polished **9** civilized, courteous, dignified **10** chivalrous **11** blue-blooded, gentlemanly **12** aristocratic **14** silk-stockinged

courtship 4 suit **6** wooing **14** keeping company

Courtship of Eddie's Father, The
character: **4** Tina **10** Tom Corbett **12** Eddie Corbett, Norman Tinker **13** Mrs Livingston
cast: **9** Bill Bixby **11** Brandon Cruz, James Komack **12** Miyoshi Umeki **15** Kristina Holland

Courtship of Miles Standish, The
author: **24** Henry Wadsworth Longfellow
character: **9** John Alden, Priscilla

courtyard 4 area, quad **6** atrium **9** curtilage, enclosure **10** quadrangle

cousin 7 kinsman **8** relation, relative **9** kinswoman

Cousin Bette
author: **14** Honore de Balzac
character: **6** Crevel **7** Adeline **10** Baron Hulot **11** Mme Marneffe **13** Hortense Hulot, Marechal Hulot **14** Lisbeth Fischer **23** Count Wenceslas Steinbock

Cousy, Bob
nickname: **12** Mr Basketball
sport: **10** basketball
position: **5** guard
team: **13** Boston Celtics

couturier, couturiere 8 designer **9** midinette **10** dressmaker, seamstress

cove 3 bay **5** inlet **6** lagoon **7** estuary

covenant 3 vow **4** bond, oath, pact **6** pledge, treaty **7** bargain, promise **8** contract **9** agreement **15** solemn agreement
Hebrew: **4** Brit **5** Berit, Brith **6** Berith

Covenant, The
author: **13** James Michener

cover 3 cap, lid, top **4** case, hide, hood, mask, veil, wrap **5** cloak, cross, guard, lay on, put on, quilt **6** asylum, clothe, defend, embody, enwrap, jacket, refuge, report, screen, sheath, shield, shroud, take in, tell of **7** binding, blanket, conceal, contain, defense, embrace, envelop, include, involve, obscure, overlay, protect, put over, secrete, sheathe, shelter, wrapper, write up **8** comprise, deal with, describe, disguise, envelope, pass over, traverse **9** chronicle, comforter, eiderdown, encompass, sanctuary **10** camouflage, comprehend, encasement, protection **11** concealment, hiding place

coverage 7 payment **8** analysis **9** indemnity, reporting **10** protection, publishing **11** description **12** broadcasting **13** reimbursement

covered 4 clad **6** hidden **7** aimed at, cloaked, guarded, insured **8** included, overlaid, screened **9** blanketed, concealed, protected, sheltered, traversed **10** overspread

covering 6 casing, sheath **7** wrapper **8** envelope, wrapping **11** descriptive, explanatory **12** introductory

coverlet 5 quilt, throw **6** afghan, spread **7** blanket **9** bedspread, comforter

Coverly, Sir Roger de
character in: **12** The Spectator
authors: **6** Steele **7** Addison

covert 6 hidden, secret, veiled **7** sub rosa, unknown **9** concealed, disguised **11** clandestine **13** surreptitious

cover up 4 hide, mask, veil **6** hush up **7** conceal **8** disguise, keep back, suppress, withhold **9** gloss over, whitewash

cover-up 4 mask **5** blind **6** screen **8** disguise **9** whitewash **11** concealment

covet 4 want **5** crave, fancy **6** desire **7** long for

covetous 6 greedy **7** craving, envious, jealous, lustful, selfish **8** desirous, grasping, yearning **9** mercenary, rapacious **10** avaricious

covetousness 4 envy **5** greed **7** avarice **8** jealousy, rapacity **10** greediness **12** graspingness **13** mercenariness

covey 4 bevy **5** flock, group **6** family

cow 4 beef **5** abash, Bossy, bully, deter, Elsie, scare **6** bovine, cattle, dismay **7** terrify **8** browbeat, bulldoze, frighten, threaten **9** terrorize **10** discourage, dishearten, intimidate, make cringe
young: **4** calf **6** heifer

coward 3 cad **5** sissy **6** craven **7** caitiff, chicken, dastard, milksop **8** poltroon **11** Milquetoast, mollycoddle, yellow-belly

Coward, Sir Noel
author of: **8** Hay Fever **9** Cavalcade **10** Sigh No More **12** Blithe Spirit, Private Lives **14** In Which We Serve, Nude with Violin **15** Design for Living

cowardliness 8 timidity **10** yellowness **12** irresolution **13** pusillanimity, spinelessness **18** chicken-heartedness

cowardly 5 shaky, timid **6** afraid, craven, yellow **7** anxious, chicken, fearful, gutless, nervous **8** timorous **9** dastardly, tremulous **10** frightened **11** lily-livered **12** apprehensive, fainthearted, uncourageous **13** pusillanimous, yellow-bellied **14** chickenhearted

Cowardly Lion
character in: **13** The Wizard of Oz
author: **4** Baum
played by: **8** Bert Lahr

cowboy 6 drover, gaucho **7** vaquero **8** buckaroo **10** roughrider **12** broncobuster, cattle-herder

cowed 5 fazed **7** abashed, crushed, subdued **8** dismayed **11** intimidated **12** disconcerted **14** under one's thumb

cower 5 crawl, quail, toady **6** cringe, flinch, grovel, recoil, shrink **7** tremble, truckle **8** bootlick, draw back

cowl 4 cope, hood **5** cloak

Cowley, Malcolm
author of: **12** Exile's Return **16** A Second Flowering **27** And I Worked at the Writer's Trade **28** The Dream of the Golden Mountains

coworker 7 partner **8** teammate **9** associate, colleague **10** accomplice **11** confederate **12** collaborator

Cowper, William
author of: **7** The Task **11** The Cast-Away

Cowperwood, Frank
character in: **8** The Titan **12** The Financier
author: **7** Dreiser

coxcomb 3 fop **4** beau **5** dandy **8** popinjay

coy 3 shy **5** timid **6** demure, modest **7** bashful, prudish **8** blushing, sheepish, skittish, timorous **9** diffident, kittenish, shrinking **10** coquettish, overmodest

Coyote State
nickname of: **11** South Dakota

cozen 3 con, gyp **4** bilk, coax, dupe, gull, rook **5** cheat, trick **6** fleece **7** deceive, defraud, swindle, wheedle **9** bamboozle, victimize

cozener 4 fake **5** cheat, fraud, quack **6** con man **8** deceiver, swindler **9** charlatan, trickster **10** mountebank **13** confidence man

coziness 6 warmth **7** comfort **8** intimacy, snugness **11** contentment

cozy 4 easy, snug **5** comfy, homey **7** restful **8** homelike, relaxing **9** gemutlich, simpatico **11** comfortable **16** snug as a bug in a rug
French: **6** intime

Cozzens, James Gould
author of: **12** Guard of Honor **15** By Love Possessed

CPA 7 auditor **10** accountant, bookkeeper **25** certified public accountant

crab 4 carp **5** crank, gripe, grump **6** grouch, grouse **8** complain, sourball **9** shellfish **10** crustacean, curmudgeon
constellation of: **6** Cancer

Crabbe, Buster
real name: **20** Clarence Linden Crabbe
nickname: **16** King of the Serials
born: **9** Oakland CA
roles: **6** Tarzan **10** Buck Rogers **11** Flash Gordon **15** King of the Jungle

crabbed 4 mean, sour **6** cranky, morose **7** grouchy, peevish, pinched **8** churlish, spiteful **9** irascible, irritable, rancorous

crabby 5 cross, testy **6** cranky, touchy **7** grouchy, peevish **8** petulant, snappish **9** irritable **10** ill-humored, out of sorts **11** ill-tempered **12** cantankerous

crack 3 gag, jab, pop **4** chip, clap, gash, gibe, jest, joke, quip, rent, rift, slit, snap **5** break, burst, cleft, split, taunt **6** cleave, insult, report **7** crackle, crevice, fissure, give way, rupture, thunder **8** fracture, splinter **9** break down, wisecrack, witticism **10** go to pieces

cracked 3 mad **4** daft, nuts **5** crazy, nutty **6** crazed, insane **8** demented, deranged, unhinged **10** unbalanced **12** mad as a hatter **13** off one's rocker, out of one's head **14** off one's trolley **15** mad as a March hare

cracker 5 snack, wafer **7** biscuit, redneck **10** party favor **11** backsettler **12** backwoodsman

crackerjack 2 A-1 **3** ace **4** a-one, fine **5** super **6** superb, tip-top **8** splendid, terrific **9** excellent, fantastic, first-rate, wonderful **10** first-class

Cracker State
nickname of: **7** Georgia

crackle 4 snap **5** craze, crink **9** crepitate

crackpot 3 nut, odd **4** fool, kook **5** balmy, crank, flake, freak, kinky, kooky, loony, nutty, wacko **6** freaky, insane, looney, madman, maniac, weirdo **7** dingbat, foolish, lunatic, oddball **9** character, eccentric, screwball **11** impractical

cracksman 4 yegg **7** burglar **10** cat burglar **14** second-story man

crackup 5 crash, smash, split, wreck **6**

mishap, pileup **7** breakup, debacle, smashup **8** accident, calamity, collapse, disaster **9** breakdown, collision, splitting **10** exhaustion, shellshock **11** catastrophe, prostration **14** disintegration

cradle 3 hug **4** crib, font, rock **6** cuddle, enfold, origin, source, spring **7** nursery, snuggle **8** bassinet, fountain **10** birthplace, wellspring **12** fountainhead

craft 3 art **4** boat, ruse, ship, wile **5** guile, knack, plane, skill, trade **6** deceit, vessel **7** ability, calling, cunning, know-how, mastery, perfidy, pursuit **8** airplane, artifice, business, commerce, deftness, fineness, industry, intrigue, trickery, vocation **9** adeptness, chicanery, deception, duplicity, expertise, technique **10** adroitness, artfulness, competency, craftiness, employment, expertness, handicraft, occupation **11** proficiency

craftiness 4 ruse, wile **5** guile **7** cunning, slyness **8** artifice, foxiness, scheming, trickery, wiliness **9** chicanery **10** artfulness **11** machination

craftsman 4 hand **5** smith **6** worker, wright **7** artisan **8** mechanic

crafty 3 sly **4** foxy, wily **5** canny, sharp **6** artful, astute, shifty, shrewd, tricky **7** cunning, devious **8** guileful, plotting, scheming **9** deceitful, deceptive, designing, dishonest, underhand, unethical **10** intriguing, perfidious, suspicious **11** calculating

crag 3 tor **4** rock **5** bluff, cliff **9** precipice

craggy 5 rocky, rough, sheer, steep, stony **6** abrupt, jagged, ragged, rugged, snaggy **7** scraggy **8** bouldery **9** rockbound **10** rock-ribbed **11** precipitous

Crain, Jeanne
born: **9** Barstow CA
roles: **5** Pinky **6** Margie **9** State Fair **17** Cheaper by the Dozen **19** A Letter to Three Wives

cram 3 jam **4** fill, pack **5** crowd, force, grind, press, stuff **7** congest, squeeze **8** compress **9** overcrowd, study hard

Cram, Ralph
architect of: **17** US Military Academy (West Point) **29** Cathedral of Saint John the Divine (NYC)
style: **13** Gothic Revival

crammed 4 full **6** filled, packed **7** studied, stuffed **9** jam-packed **11** overflowing, well-stocked

cramp 4 pang **5** block, check, crick, limit, spasm **6** hamper, hinder, stitch, stymie, thwart **7** prevent, seizure **8** handicap, obstruct, restrain, restrict **9** frustrate **12** charley horse

cramped 5 close, tight **6** narrow **7** compact, pinched **8** confined **10** compressed, restrained, restricted

Cranach, Lucas (Lukas) (the Elder)
born: **7** Kronach, Germany
artwork: **6** Luther **10** Adam and Eve **11** Crucifixion **14** Apollo and Diana **15** Rest on the Flight **18** The Judgment of Paris **22** Duke and Duchess of Saxony

Cranaus
king of: **6** Athens, Attica
wife: **6** Pedias
daughter: **6** Atthis, Cranae
renamed Athens: **6** Attica

cranberry 9 Vaccinium **19** Vaccinium vitis-idaea **20** Vaccinium macrocarpon
varieties: **3** bog **4** rock, tree **5** large, small **8** American, European, highbush, mountain **10** Australian

crane 4 bird, boom **5** davit, heron **7** derrick **10** wading bird
group of: **5** sedge, siege
constellation of: **4** Grus

Crane, Bob
born: **11** Waterbury CT
roles: **12** Colonel Hogan, Hogan's Heroes

Crane, Hart
author of: **9** The Bridge **14** White Buildings

Crane, Ichabod
character in: **23** The Legend of Sleepy Hollow
author: **6** Irving

Crane, Roy
creator/artist of: **9** Buz Sawyer, Wash Tubbs **11** Captain Easy

Crane, Stephen
author of: **11** The Open Boat **20** The Red Badge of Courage **23** Maggie: A Girl of the Streets **24** The Bride Comes to Yellow Sky

Cranford
author: **10** Mrs Gaskell

cranium 4 head **5** skull **6** noggin **8** brain box, brainpan **9** brain case

crank 4 turn, whim **5** brace, winch **6** grouch, handle **7** fanatic **8** crotchet **9** eccentric

cranky 5 cross, testy **6** crabby, touchy **7** bearish, grouchy, peevish, waspish **8** captious, petulant **9** crotchety, irascible, splenetic **10** ill-humored, out of sorts **11** ill-tempered **12** cantankerous

cranny 3 gap **4** nook, slit **5** break, chink, cleft, crack, notch, split **7** crevice, fissure **8** cleavage

crash 3 din **4** bang, boom, bump, dash, ruin **5** crack, slump, smash, wreck **6** hurtle, invade, pileup, plunge, racket, slip in, topple, tumble **7** bumping, clangor, clatter, collide, crackup, decline, failure, hitting, intrude, setback, shatter, smashup, sneak in **8** accident, smashing, toppling, tumbling **9** collision, recession **10** bankruptcy, depression, shattering

crass 5 crude, cruel, gross **6** coarse,

oafish, vulgar **7** boorish **8** uncaring **9** inelegant, unfeeling, unrefined **10** unpolished **11** hardhearted, insensitive **13** unsympathetic

crassness 9 crudeness, grossness, vulgarity **10** coarseness, inelegance, oafishness **11** boorishness **13** insensitivity

Cratchit, Bob
character in: **15** A Christmas Carol
author: **7** Dickens
son: **7** Tiny Tim

crate 3 box, car **4** auto, case, pack **5** plane **6** jalopy, pallet **8** airplane **9** container

crater 3 pit **4** hole **6** cavity **10** depression

cravat 3 tie **5** ascot, scarf, stock **7** necktie **11** neckerchief

crave 4 need, want **5** covet **6** desire **7** hope for, long for, pine for, require, sigh for, wish for **8** yearn for **9** hunger for, lust after, thirst for **11** hanker after, have a yen for **13** have a fancy for

craven 3 low **4** base **5** timid **6** scared, yellow **7** fearful, lowdown **8** cowardly, timorous **9** dastardly **10** frightened **11** lily-livered **12** mean-spirited **13** pusillanimous **14** chicken-hearted

craving 3 yen **4** need **6** desire, hunger, thirst **7** longing **9** hankering

Crawford, Broderick
real name: **24** William Broderick Crawford
wife: **11** Jan Sterling
born: **14** Philadelphia PA
roles: **6** The Mob **10** The Interns **12** Of Mice and Men **13** Born Yesterday, Highway Patrol **14** All the King's Men (Oscar)

Crawford, Henry
character in: **13** Mansfield Park
author: **6** Austen

Crawford, Joan
real name: **17** Lucille Fay Le Sueur
husband: **12** Franchot Tone **18** Douglas Fairbanks Jr
daughter: **6** Cheryl **9** Christina
born: **12** San Antonio TX
biography: **13** Mommie Dearest
roles: **8** The Women **10** Grand Hotel **13** Mildred Pierce (Oscar) **26** What Ever Happened to Baby Jane

crawl 4 drag, inch, poke, worm **5** creep, mosey **6** squirm, wiggle, writhe **7** slither, wriggle

Crawley, Rawdon
character in: **10** Vanity Fair
author: **9** Thackeray

crayon 5 chalk, draft **6** pastel, pencil, sketch **7** drawing **8** charcoal

craze 3 fad **4** rage **5** furor, mania **6** dement **7** derange, passion, unhinge **11** infatuation

crazed 3 mad 6 insane 7 cracked, lunatic 8 demented, deranged

crazy 3 mad, odd 4 avid, daft, gaga, keen, nuts, wild 5 nutty, rabid, silly, weird 6 absurd, far-out, insane, stupid, unwise 7 berserk, bizarre, cracked, excited, foolish, frantic, idiotic, strange, touched, unusual, zealous 8 demented, deranged, maniacal, peculiar, uncommon, unhinged 9 fanatical, foolhardy, imprudent, laughable, senseless 10 hysterical, infatuated, outrageous, passionate, ridiculous, unbalanced 11 smitten with 12 enthusiastic, mad as a hatter 13 out of one's head 15 mad as a March hare

creak 4 rasp 5 grate, grind 6 scrape, screak, squeak 7 screech

Creakle
character in: 16 David Copperfield
author: 7 Dickens

cream 3 top 4 beat, best, drub 5 elite 6 choice, flower 7 the pick, trounce 8 greatest, off-white 14 creme de la creme

Cream, Arnold Raymond
real name of: 10 Joe Walcott

cream of the cream
French: 14 creme de la creme

creamy 5 thick, foamy 6 smooth, yellow 8 emulsive

crease 4 fold 5 crimp, pleat, ridge 6 furrow, pucker, ruffle, rumple 7 crimple, crinkle, wrinkle 9 corrugate 11 corrugation

create 4 form, make, mold 5 cause, erect, found, set up 6 design, devise, invent 7 appoint, concoct, develop, fashion 8 conceive, contrive, organize 9 construct, establish, fabricate, formulate, institute, originate

creation 5 world 6 making, nature 8 building, devising, erection, founding 9 all things, formation, handiwork, invention 10 brainchild, conception, concoction, fashioning, production 11 development, fabrication, institution, origination 12 construction 13 establishment

Creation
author: 9 Gore Vidal

creative 8 fanciful, original 9 ingenious, inventive 11 imaginative, resourceful

creator 5 maker 6 author, father, framer 7 founder 8 begetter, designer, inventor, producer 9 architect, generator, initiator 10 originator

creature 3 man 4 bird, fish 5 beast, human 6 animal, insect, mammal, mortal, person 7 critter, reptile 9 earthling, quadruped 10 individual, vertebrate 12 invertebrate

credence 5 faith, trust 6 belief, credit 8 reliance 9 certainty, certitude 10

confidence 11 reliability 13 believability 14 acceptableness, dependableness 15 trustworthiness

credentials 6 permit 7 diploma, license, voucher 9 reference 11 certificate, testimonial 13 authorization

credenza 5 shelf, table 6 buffet 8 bookcase 9 sideboard

credible 6 likely 7 tenable 8 possible, probable, reliable 9 plausible, thinkable 10 believable, dependable, imaginable, reasonable 11 conceivable, trustworthy

credit 3 buy 4 time 5 glory, honor, trust 6 accept, assign, esteem, rely on 7 acclaim, ascribe, believe, fall for, swallow 9 allowance, attribute, recognize 10 prepayment 11 acknowledge, recognition 12 commendation 14 acknowledgment

creditable 6 worthy 8 laudable 9 admirable, estimable, reputable 11 commendable, meritorious, respectable 12 praiseworthy

credo 4 code, rule 5 maxim, motto, tenet 8 doctrine 10 philosophy

credulous 5 naive 8 gullible, trusting 9 believing 10 overtrustful, unsuspecting, unsuspicious 13 unquestioning 15 unsophisticated

Cree
language family: 9 Algonkian 10 Algonquian
tribe: 10 Plains Cree 13 Woodlands Cree
location: 6 Canada 8 Manitoba
related to: 8 Chippewa

creed 5 dogma 6 belief, canons, gospel 8 doctrine

creek 3 run 4 rill 5 brook 6 branch, spring, stream 7 freshet, rivulet 10 millstream, small river

Creek
language family: 10 Muskhogean
location: 7 Alabama, Florida, Georgia 11 Mississippi
leader: 8 Red Eagle 15 William McIntosh 20 Alexander McGillivray

creep 4 inch, worm 5 crawl, sneak, steal 6 dawdle, squirm, writhe 7 slither, wriggle

creeper 3 ivy 4 bird, iron, vine, worm 5 snake 7 climber, crawler, grapnel, trailer

creepy 4 eery 5 eerie, scary 6 crawly, spooky, uneasy 12 apprehensive

cremate 4 burn, char, fire, sear 5 roast 6 ignite, kindle, scorch 8 enkindle 10 incinerate 11 conflagrate 17 consume with flames

creme de banane
type: 7 liqueur
flavor: 6 banana
color: 6 yellow

creme de cacao
type: 6 brandy 7 liqueur

origin: 6 France
flavor: 9 chocolate
color: 5 brown, white
drink: 11 Fifth Avenue
with rum: 6 Panama
with tequila: 8 Toreador
with vodka: 9 Ninotchka 11 Russian Bear 12 Velvet Hammer, White Russian

creme de cassis
type: 7 liqueur
origin: 6 France 8 Burgundy
flavor: 12 black currant
with gin: 8 Parisian

creme de fraise
type: 7 liqueur
flavor: 10 strawberry

creme de framboise
type: 7 liqueur
flavor: 9 raspberry

creme de la creme 3 top 4 best 5 cream, elite 6 choice, flower 8 choicest, very best 12 choicest part 15 cream of the cream

creme de menthe
type: 7 liqueur
flavor: 4 mint
color: 5 green, white
with brandy: 7 Stinger
with cream: 11 Grasshopper
with gin: 6 Caruso, Virgin

creme de noyau
type: 7 liqueur
flavor: 6 almond

creme de violette
type: 7 liqueur
flavor: 7 violets
color: 8 lavender

creme Yvette
type: 7 liqueur
origin: 12 United States
flavor: 7 violets
with gin: 9 Union Jack

Crenna, Richard
born: 12 Los Angeles CA
roles: 9 Death Ship 13 Our Miss Brooks, The Real McCoys

Creole 6 patois 7 criollo, dialect, Haitian 10 West Indian

Creole State
nickname of: 9 Louisiana

Creon
king of: 6 Thebes 7 Corinth
father: 9 Lycaethus, Menoeceus
sister: 7 Jocasta
daughter: 6 Creusa, Glauce
nephew: 7 Oedipus 8 Eteocles 9 Polynices
niece: 6 Ismene 8 Antigone
defeated: 18 Seven against Thebes

crescendo
music: 22 gradually getting louder
abbreviation: 5 cresc

crescent 3 arc, bow 4 arch 5 curve 8 half-moon

crescit eundo 15 it grows as it goes
  motto of: 9 New Mexico

Cressida
  also: 8 Criseyde 9 Crisseyde
  based on characters of: 7 Bryseis 8 Chryseis
  setting: 9 Trojan War
  loved: 7 Troilus
  deserted Troilus for: 8 Diomedes

crest 3 tip, top 4 apex, arms, comb, peak, tuft 5 crown, plume 6 emblem, height, summit 7 topknot 8 pinnacle 10 coat of arms, escutcheon

crestfallen 8 dejected, downcast 9 depressed, woebegone 10 despondent, dispirited 11 discouraged, downhearted, low-spirited 12 disappointed, disheartened

Cretaceous period
  dinosaur from: 9 Euhelopus, Iguanodon 10 Allosaurus, Antrodemus 11 Anatosaurus, Ankylsaurus, Deinonychus, Gorgosaurus, Triceratops 12 Lambeosaurus, Ornithomimus 13 Albertosaurus, Corythosaurus, Hypselosaurus, Hypsilophodon, Palaeoscincus, Protoceratops, Struthiomimus, Styracosaurus, Tyrannosaurus 14 Psittacosaurus, Thescelosaurus 15 Parasaurolophus, Procheneosaurus

Cretan bull
  also: 15 Marathonian bull
  form: 4 bull
  son: 8 Minotaur
  captured on: 5 Crete
  captured by: 8 Hercules
  roamed: 8 Marathon
  recaptured by: 7 Theseus

Cretan Mythology
  goddess of fishermen/hunters/
    sailors: 11 Britomartis
    corresponds to Greek: 7 Artemis
  goddess of the sea: 8 Dictynna
  maze: 9 labyrinth
  monster: 8 Minotaur

Crete
  other name: 5 Kriti 6 Candia
  capital/largest city: 5 Canea 8 Iraklion
  others: 3 Hag 4 Lato 5 Khora, Sitia, Zakro 6 Anoyia, Candia, Khania, Lisamo, Mallia, Meleme, Retimo 7 Malerni 8 Kastelli, Nikolaos, Sphakion 9 Heraclion, Heraklion, Rethymnon, Tympakion 11 Palaiophora
  government:
    division of: 6 Greece
  monetary unit: 7 drachma
  mountain: 3 Ida 5 Dikte, Phino 6 Juktas 7 Lasithi, Madaras 8 Leuka Ori, Theodore, Thriphte 9 Psiloriti
  highest point: 3 Ida
  sea: 5 Crete 6 Aegean 13 Mediterranean
  physical feature:
    bay: 4 Suda 5 Kanca 6 Kisamo,

Mesara
  cape: 4 Buza 5 Liano 6 Salome, Sidero, Spatha 7 Stavros 8 Lithinon, Sidheros
  gulf: 6 Khania 9 Merabello
  people: 7 Candiot, Cretans, Minoans 9 Caphtorim, Sphakiots 11 Philistines
    artist: 7 El Greco
    author: 11 Kazantzakis
    conqueror: 8 Metellus
    king: 7 Minos
  language: 5 Greek 6 Minoan 7 Linear A, Linear B
  religion: 14 Greek Orthodoxy
  place:
    ruins: 15 Palace at Knossos

Creusa
  also: 6 Glauce
  father: 5 Creon, Priam 8 Cychreus 10 Erechtheus
  mother: 6 Hecuba
  husband: 6 Aeneas 7 Telamon
  son: 3 Ion 8 Ascanius
  bride of: 5 Jason
  killed by: 5 magic, Medea

crevasse 3 gap 4 rift 5 abyss, break, chasm, cleft, gorge, gulch, gully, split 6 breach, divide 7 fissure

crevice 4 rent, rift, slit 5 chasm, cleft, crack, split 6 breach 7 fissure 8 crevasse, fracture

crew 3 men, mob 4 band, body, herd, mass, pack, team 5 corps, force, group, hands, horde, party, squad, troop 6 seamen, throng 7 company, haircut, sailors 8 mariners 9 multitude, seafarers 10 assemblage, complement

crib 3 bed, bin, cot, hut, key 4 pony, trot 5 cheat, shack, stall, steal 6 creche, manger 7 purloin 8 bassinet 10 plagiarize

cribbage
  scorer: 3 peg
  score kept on: 5 board
  points/game: 8 sixty-one
  third hand: 4 crib
  jack: 7 his nobs

Crichton, Michael
  author of: 4 Coma, Prey 5 Congo 6 Sphere 8 Airframe, Timeline 9 Lost World, Rising Sun 10 Disclosure 11 State of Fear 12 Jurassic Park 14 The Terminal Man 15 Eaters of the Dead 18 The Andromeda Strain 20 The Great Train Robbery

cricket
  players/team: 6 eleven
  equipment: 3 bat 4 bail, ball 5 stump 6 wicket
  position: 5 gully, mid on, slops 6 bowler, long on, mid off 7 batsman, fine leg, long off 8 third man 9 mid wicket, square leg 10 cover point, extra cover, silly mid on 11 silly mid off 12 wicket keeper 13 deep mid

wicket 16 backward short leg
  lines: 7 creases
  period of play: 4 over 7 innings
  championship game: 9 test match
  England/Australia match: 8 the Ashes

cricket
  variety: 4 bush, cave, fair, sand, tree 5 camel, field, house 6 ground 9 Jerusalem, pygmy mole

Cries and Whispers
  director: 12 Ingmar Bergman
  cast: 10 Liv Ullmann 12 Ingrid Thulin 16 Harriet Andersson

crime 3 sin 4 tort 5 wrong 6 felony 7 misdeed, offense, outrage 8 foul play, iniquity, villainy 10 misconduct, wrongdoing 11 abomination, lawbreaking, malfeasance, misdemeanor 13 transgression

Crime and Punishment
  author: 16 Fyodor Dostoevsky
  character: 5 Sonya 6 Dounia 7 Porfiry 9 Razumihin 11 Raskolnikov

criminal 4 hood 5 crook, felon, wrong 6 guilty, outlaw 7 crooked, culprit, illegal, illicit, lawless 8 culpable, offender, unlawful, wasteful 9 felonious, senseless, wrongdoer 10 abominable, delinquent, indictable, lawbreaker, malefactor, outrageous, villainous 11 blameworthy, disgraceful, lawbreaking 12 transgressor

crimp 4 curl, fold, kink, wave 5 clamp, flute, frill, frizz 7 crinkle, frizzle, wrinkle 8 obstacle

crimple 4 curl 6 pucker 7 crinkle, crumple, wrinkle 9 corrugate

crimson 3 red 4 ruby 5 blush, flush 6 redden 7 carmine, scarlet

cringe 4 duck 5 cower, dodge, quail, toady 6 blench, flinch, grovel, recoil, shrink 7 truckle

cringing 6 abject 7 fawning, ignoble, servile, wincing 8 cowering, toadying 9 flinching, groveling, shrinking, sniveling

crinkle 5 crush 6 rumple, rustle 7 crumple, wrinkle

crinkly 4 wavy 5 curly, kinky 6 crimpy, frizzy 7 cockled, crimped, crimply, puckery, ruffled, rumpled, twisted, wrinkly 8 crimpled, frizzled, puckered, wrinkled 9 shriveled

crinoline 4 hoop 5 skirt 9 hoopskirt, petticoat 10 underskirt

cripple 4 gimp, halt, harm, maim, stop 6 damage, impair 7 disable 8 make lame, paralyze 9 hamstring 10 debilitate, inactivate 12 incapacitate

crisis 6 climax 9 emergency

crisp 5 brisk, fresh, nippy, sharp, terse, witty 6 candid, chilly, crispy, lively, snappy 7 bracing, brittle, crunchy, pointed 8 incisive 9 energetic, sparkling, vivacious **10** potato chip, refreshing **12** invigorating

crisscross 4 awry **5** cross **8** confused, traverse

Crisseyde *see* **8** Cressida

Cristillo, Louis Francis
real name of: **11** Lou Costello

criterion 3 law **4** norm, rule **5** gauge, model **7** example, measure **8** standard **9** guidepost, precedent, principle, yardstick **10** touchstone

critic 5 judge, mavin, scold **6** carper, censor, expert, rapper **7** analyst, arbiter, knocker, reviler **8** attacker, reviewer, vilifier, virtuoso **9** authority, backbiter, detractor, evaluator **10** antagonist, criticizer **11** cognoscente, commentator, connoisseur, faultfinder

critical 5 fussy, grave, hairy, picky, risky, vital **6** urgent **7** carping, crucial, finicky, judging, nagging, serious **8** caviling, decisive, perilous, pressing **9** dangerous, harrowing, hazardous, judicious, momentous, sensitive **10** analytical, censorious, derogatory, diagnostic, nitpicking, precarious **11** disparaging **12** disapproving, faultfinding

critical situation 3 jam **4** mess **6** crisis, pickle **7** straits, trouble **8** hot water **9** deep water **10** difficulty **11** predicament

critical stage 5 H-hour **6** climax, crisis **9** emergency

critical success
French: **13** succes d'estime

criticism 4 fire, flak, slam **5** blame, knock **6** review **7** censure, comment **8** analysis, critique, judgment **9** aspersion, stricture **10** commentary, evaluation **12** faultfinding

criticize 4 carp, fuss, pick **5** cavil, nag at **7** censure, nitpick, reprove **8** denounce, reproach **9** disparage

critique 6 review **8** analysis

Crna Gora *see* **10** Montenegro

croak 3 caw, die **4** kill, moan, roup **7** grumble, kick off **8** complain, harsh cry **13** kick the bucket

Croatia
capital/largest city: **5** Zagreb
others: **4** Knin **5** Split, Zadar **6** Osijek, Rijeka (Fiume) **7** Vukovar, Sibenik **8** Karlovac, Varazdin, Vinkovci **9** Dubrovnik **10** Kostajnica
head of state: **9** president
government: **9** democracy
monetary unit: **5** dinar
mountain: **10** Julian Alps **11** Styrian Alps
sea: **8** Adriatic
people: **5** Serbs **6** Croats **7** Muslims **9** Yugoslavs
language: **8** Croatian **10** Serbo Croat
religion: **17** Catholic Christian, Orthodox Christian

Crocetti, Dino Paul
real name of: **10** Dean Martin

crock 3 jar, pot **4** olla **9** container

crockery 5 china **6** dishes, plates **7** pottery **8** clayware **9** chinaware, tableware **11** ceramic ware, earthenware **14** cups and saucers

Crock of Gold
author: **13** James Stephens

crocodile 4 croc **6** cayman, gavial, lizard **7** reptile, asurian

crocus
varieties: **4** fall, wild **5** dutch **6** autumn, scotch **7** Chilean, saffron **8** tropical **9** celandine **12** iris-flowered

Crome Yellow
author: **12** Aldous Huxley

Crommyonian sow
also: **5** Phaea
killed by: **7** Theseus

Cromwell, Oliver
also: **13** Lord Protector
served in: **15** English Civil War
fought against: **8** Charles I **9** Cavaliers
fought for: **10** Parliament, Roundheads
regiment: **9** Ironsides
battle: **6** Naseby, Oxford **7** Preston **11** Marston Moor

crone 3 hag **5** witch **6** beldam **7** beldame, old wife

Cronus
also: **6** Cronos, Kronos
form: **5** Titan
father: **6** Uranus
mother: **4** Gaea
sister: **4** Rhea
wife: **4** Rhea
son: **4** Zeus **5** Hades **8** Poseidon
daughter: **4** Hera **6** Hestia **7** Demeter
corresponds to: **6** Saturn

crony 3 pal **4** ally, chum, mate **5** buddy **6** bunkie, cohort, friend **7** comrade **8** bunkmate, intimate, shipmate, sidekick **9** accessory, associate, companion, old friend **10** accomplice, bosom buddy **11** confederate **12** acquaintance, collaborator **13** coconspirator

Cronyn, Hume
wife: **12** Jessica Tandy
born: **6** London **7** Canada, Ontario
roles: **13** The Fourposter **17** Phantom of the Opera **19** Sunrise at Campobello

crook 3 arc, bow **4** bend, hook, thug, turn **5** angle, cheat, curve, knave, thief, twist **6** bandit, outlaw, robber **7** burglar **8** criminal, swindler **9** curvature, embezzler

crooked 4 awry, bent, wily **5** askew, bowed, shady **6** crafty, curved, hooked, shifty, sneaky, spiral, warped, zigzag **7** corrupt, sinuous, twisted, winding **8** criminal, deformed, tortuous, twisting, unlawful **9** deceitful,

deceptive, dishonest, distorted, nefarious, unethical **10** fraudulent, meandering, perfidious, serpentine **11** underhanded **12** dishonorable, unscrupulous

crookedness 10 dishonesty **11** deviousness **13** deceitfulness, double-dealing

Crookes, William
nationality: **7** British
invented: **8** thallium **10** radiometer **11** Crookes tube

croon 3 hum **4** sing **6** murmur, warble

crop 3 bob, cut, lop **4** clip, snip, trim **5** prune, shear, yield **6** growth **7** harvest, reaping **8** cut short, gleaning **9** gathering **10** production

crop-raising 7 farming, tillage **11** agriculture **12** agribusiness, truck farming **15** market gardening

crop up 5 arise, ensue, occur **6** appear **7** develop, surface **11** come to light

croquet
equipment: **4** ball, hoop **6** mallet, wicket
variation: **5** roque
term: **5** rover
site: **4** lawn

Crosby, Bing
real name: **17** Harry Lillis Crosby
partner: **7** Bob Hope **10** Hedy Lamarr **13** Dorothy Lamour
nickname: **8** Der Bingle
wife: **8** Dixie Lee **12** Kathryn Grant
born: **8** Tacoma WA
roles: **10** Going My Way (Oscar), Holiday Inn **11** High Society **14** The Country Girl, White Christmas **17** The Bells of St Mary's **22** Christmas in Connecticut
Road to: **3** Rio **4** Bali **7** Morocco **8** Hong Kong, Zanzibar **9** Singapore

cross 3 mad, mix, tau **4** crux, ford, meet, rood **5** angry, blend, erase, gruff, surly, testy, trial **6** burden, cancel, cranky, delete, go over, hybrid, ordeal, shirty, touchy **7** amalgam, annoyed, athwart, grouchy, oblique, peevish, trouble, waspish **8** captious, choleric, churlish, contrary, crucifix, distress, intermix, pass over, petulant, snappish, traverse **9** adversity, crotchety, half-breed, hybridize, intersect, irascible, irritable, querulous, splenetic, strike out, suffering **10** affliction, difficulty, ill-humored, interbreed, misfortune, obliterate, out of sorts, transverse **11** combination, ill-tempered, intractable, tribulation **12** cantankerous, disagreeable, intersecting

crossbar 3 bar **4** spar **5** sprit **6** stripe

crossbreed 3 mix **8** intermix **9** hybridize **10** interbreed

cross-fertilize 9 hybridize

crossing 4 pass **7** mixture, passage **8** blocking, opposing, traverse **9** thwarting **10** traversing **11** hybridizing, intersection **13** hybridization

cross over 4 span **5** cross **6** bridge **8** traverse

crosspiece 3 bar **4** spar **5** sprit

cross-pollinate 9 hybridize

crossroad 12 intersection, turning point

cross swords 5 clash, fight **6** battle, combat, tussle **7** contend, contest **8** skirmish

crossways 7 athwart **12** transversely

crosswise 6 across **7** athwart **8** sideways, traverse **10** transverse

crotchet 3 tat **4** bent, whim **5** habit, quirk, trait **6** foible, hang-up, oddity, vagary, whimsy **7** caprice **8** quiddity **9** mannerism **10** erraticism **11** peculiarity **12** eccentricity, idiosyncrasy, irregularity **14** characteristic

crotchety 3 odd **5** fussy **6** cranky **7** erratic, grouchy **8** contrary, peculiar **9** eccentric

crouch 4 bend, duck **5** cower, squat, stoop **6** cringe, recoil, shrink **9** hunch over **10** hunker down **11** scrooch down, scrunch down

Crouching Tiger, Hidden Dragon
director: 6 Ang Lee
cast: 9 Chen Chang (Lo "Dark Cloud"), Zhang Ziyi (Jiao Long) **10** Chow Yun Fat (Master Li Mu Bai) **12** Michelle Yeoh (Yu Shu Lien)

crow 3 daw, jay, kae **4** blow, brag, rook **5** boast, crake, exult, gloat, raven, strut, vaunt **6** cackle, chough, corbie, magpie **7** corvine, jackdaw, rejoice, swagger, triumph, trumpet **8** jubilate **14** cock-a-doodle-doo
group of: 6 murder

Crow
constellation of: 6 Corvus

Crow
language family: 6 Siouan
tribe: 9 River Crow **12** Mountain Crow
location: 7 Montana, Wyoming
related to: 7 Hidatsa

crowbar 3 bar, pry **5** jimmy, lever

crowd 3 jam, mob, set **4** cram, gang, herd, host, mass, push **5** crush, flock, group, horde, press, shove, surge, swarm **6** circle, claque, clique, gather, huddle, legion, throng **7** cluster, coterie, elbow in, squeeze **8** assemble **9** gathering, multitude **10** assemblage, congregate **11** concentrate **12** congregation

Crowd, The
director: 9 King Vidor
cast: 9 Bert Roach **11** James Murray **15** Eleanor Boardman

crowded 4 full **6** filled, jammed, mobbed, packed **7** crammed, teeming **8** swarming, thronged **9** congested, jampacked **11** overflowing

crowd out 8 displace **9** overwhelm

crown 3 cap, top **4** acme, apex, head, pate, peak **5** crest, tiara **6** climax, diadem, noggin, noodle, summit, top off, wreath, zenith **7** chaplet, circlet, coronet, fulfill, garland, perfect, royalty **8** complete, monarchy, pinnacle, round out **11** sovereignty

crowning point 3 cap, tip **4** apex, peak **6** summit, vertex, zenith **8** pinnacle

crown of thorns 4 bane **5** cross **6** burden, ordeal **7** torment **8** vexation **10** affliction **11** tribulation

crow over 5 gloat **9** brag about **10** boast about

crucial 5 grave **6** knotty, urgent **7** serious, weighty **8** critical, decisive, pressing **9** essential, important, momentous **11** determining, significant

Crucible, The
author: 12 Arthur Miller

crude 3 raw **5** crass, gross, rough **6** coarse, vulgar **7** obscene, sketchy, uncouth **9** imperfect, tasteless, unrefined **10** incomplete, unfinished, unpolished, unprepared **11** uncompleted, undeveloped, unprocessed

crudeness 7 rawness **8** bad taste **9** crassness, grossness, obscenity, vulgarity **10** coarseness, indelicacy **13** tastelessness

cruel 6 brutal, savage **7** inhuman, vicious **8** inhumane, pitiless, ruthless, sadistic **9** heartless, merciless, unfeeling **10** unmerciful **11** cold-blooded, hardhearted, remorseless **15** uncompassionate

cruelty 6 sadism **8** ferocity, savagery **9** barbarity, brutality **10** bestiality, inhumanity **11** viciousness **12** ruthlessness **13** heartlessness

cruet 3 jar, jug **6** bottle **7** urceole **9** dispenser

cruise 4 sail, scud, skim **5** coast, drift, float, glide, sweep **6** stream, voyage **7** seafare **8** navigate

Cruise, Tom
original name: 21 Thomas Cruise Mapother
born: 10 Syracuse NY
wife: 10 Mimi Rogers **12** Nicole Kidman
companion: 11 Katie Holmes
films: 4 Taps **6** Top Gun **7** The Firm, Rain Man **8** Cocktail **10** Far and Away **11** Endless Love, A Few Good Men **12** Eyes Wide Shut, Jerry Maguire, The Outsiders **13** Days of Thunder, Risky Business **14** The Last Samurai, War of the Worlds **15** The Color of Money **16** All the Right Moves **17** Mission Impossible **21** Born on the Fourth of July, Interview with a Vampire

crumb 3 bit, ort **5** grain, scrap, shred, speck **6** morsel, sliver **8** fragment, particle

crumble 5 crush, decay, grate, grind **6** powder **8** fragment, splinter **9** decompose, pulverize **12** disintegrate

crumbly 7 brittle, friable **9** breakable

crummy 5 awful, lousy **6** rotten **8** terrible

crumple 4 fall **5** crush **6** cave in, crease, pucker, rumple **7** crimple, crinkle, wrinkle **8** collapse **9** corrugate

crunch 4 chew, gnaw **5** chomp, gnash, grind, munch **7** squeeze **8** showdown **9** masticate

crunchy 3 dry **5** crisp **6** crispy **7** crackly

crusade 5 drive, rally **8** campaign, movement

Crusader 6 knight, zealot **7** pilgrim, Templar **8** champion **11** Hospitaller

Crusades
time: 10 Middle Ages
cry: 8 deus vult
foe: 4 turk **7** infidel, Saladin, saracen
leader: 5 Louis **7** Baldwin, Richard, Tancred **9** Frederick **10** Saint Louis
port: 4 Acre
named: 9 Children's

crush 4 mash **5** break, press, quash, quell, smash **6** enfold, quench, squash, subdue **7** crumble, crumple, embrace, put down, shatter, squeeze, squelch **8** compress, overcome, suppress **9** granulate, overpower, overwhelm, pulverize **10** extinguish

crushed 3 sad **5** cowed **6** broken, mashed, woeful **7** abashed, doleful, forlorn, pressed, put down, quashed, quelled, smashed, subdued **8** crumbled, crumpled, dejected, desolate, overcame, overcome, quenched, squashed, squeezed, wretched **9** flattened, miserable, squelched, woebegone **10** compressed, despondent, pulverized, suppressed **11** overpowered, overwhelmed **12** disconsolate, extinguished, inconsolable **13** brokenhearted

crushing 7 mashing **8** decisive, quelling, smashing **10** shattering **11** humiliating, putting down, stamping out, suppression **12** obliterating, overwhelming **13** pulverization

crust 4 coat, gall, hull, rind, scab **5** brass, nerve, shell **6** harden **7** coating **8** chutzpah, covering, pie shell **9** impudence **11** pastry shell

crustacean 4 crab, flea **5** louse, prawn **6** isopod, shrimp **7** lobster **8** barnacle, crawfish, crayfish **9** shellfish, water flea

crusty 4 curt **5** blunt, gruff, rough, short, stern, surly, testy **6** abrupt, crabby, cranky, shirty, snippy, sullen **7** brusque, peevish, waspish **8** choleric, snappish, snippety **9** irascible, splenetic **10** ill-natured **11** ill-tempered **13** short-tempered

crux 3 nub **4** core, gist **5** basis, heart **7** essence **9** essential **10** brass tacks **11** nitty-gritty

cry 3 beg, sob, sue **4** bawl, call, hawk, howl, keen, moan, plea, roar, wail, weep, yell, yelp **5** blare, cheer, groan, mourn, plead, shout, utter, whoop **6** appeal, bellow, blazon, boohoo, clamor, hurrah, huzzah, lament, outcry, prayer, scream, shriek, snivel **7** blubber, call out, exclaim, implore, request, screech, trumpet, whimper **8** entreaty, petition, proclaim **9** advertise, importune **10** adjuration, promulgate **11** exclamation **12** solicitation, supplication

Cry, the Beloved Country
author: **9** Alan Paton
locale: **11** South Africa

cry out 4 bark, bawl, call, howl, roar, yell **5** shout **6** bellow, clamor, holler **7** exclaim **8** proclaim **9** ejaculate

cry over 5 mourn **6** bemoan, bewail, lament

crypt 4 tomb **5** vault **8** catacomb **9** mausoleum, sepulcher

cryptic 4 dark **5** vague **6** arcane, hidden, occult, secret **7** obscure, strange **8** esoteric, mystical, puzzling **9** ambiguous **10** cabalistic, mysterious, perplexing **11** enigmatical

cryptogram 4 code **6** cipher

cryptograph 4 code **6** cipher, encode

crystal 3 ice **5** clear, flake, glass, lucid **6** quartz **7** diamond **8** stemware **9** glassware, snowflake, watch part **10** rhinestone **11** transparent

crystallize 3 fix, gel **4** firm, jell **5** candy **6** harden **8** solidify **9** granulate

CSI: Crime Scene Investigation
network: **3** CBS
cast: **8** Jorja Fox (Sara Sidle) **10** George Eads (Nick Stokes) **11** Eric Szmanda (Greg Sanders), Gary Dourdan (Warrick Brown) **13** Paul Guilfoyle (Jim Brass) **15** William Petersen (Gil Grissom) **16** Marg Helgenberger (Catherine Willows)

CSI: Miami
network: **3** CBS
cast: **9** Kim Delany (Megan Donner) **10** Sofia Milos (Yelina Salas) **11** David Caruso (Horatio Caine) **12** Emily Procter (Calleigh Duquesne), Jonathan Togo (Ryan Wolfe), Rory Cochrane (Tim Speedle) **13** Adam Rodriguez (Eric Delko) **15** Khandi Alexander (Alexx Woods)

CSI: New York
network: **3** CBS
cast: **10** Gary Sinise (Mac Taylor), Hill Harper (Dr. Sheldon Hawkes) **11** Eddie Cahill (Don Flack) **14** Vanessa Ferlito (Aiden Burn) **17** Carmine Giovinazzo (Danny Messer), Melina Kanakaredes (Stella Bonasera)

Csonka, Larry (Lawrence Richard)
nickname: **9** Lawnmower
sport: **8** football
position: **8** fullback
team: **13** Miami Dolphins, New York Giants

cub 3 boy, pup **4** bear, lion **5** scout, whelp **6** novice **8** reporter **9** youngling, youngster **10** apprentice

Cuba
other name: **18** pearl of the Antilles
capital/largest city: **6** Havana **8** Le Habana
others: **5** Bauta, Colon, Duabi, Guane, Manes **6** Baines, Bayamo, Gibara, Guines, Mayari **7** Antilla, Baracoa, Fomento, Holguin, Holquin, Jiguani, Niquero, Palmira, Sanhuis **8** Artemisa, Camaguey, Cardenas, Guaimaro, Guayabal, Marianao, Matanzas, Nuevitas, Varadero, Yaguajay **9** Cabaiguan, Camajuani, Cienfuego **10** Cienfuegos, Guanabacoa, Guantanamo, Manzanillo, Santa Clara **11** Campechuela, Pinar del Rio, Puerto Padre **12** Ciego de Avila **13** Sagua de Tanamo **14** Sancti Spiritus, Santiago de Cuba **17** Aguada de Pasajeros, Consolacion del Sur
measure: **4** vara **5** bocoy, cocoy, tarea **6** cordel, fanega **10** caballeria
monetary unit: **4** peso **7** centavo **8** cuarenta
weight: **5** libra **6** tercio
island: **5** Pines, Pinos **6** Sabana **8** Camaguey, Juventud **9** Canarreos **17** Jardines de la Reina
  cay: **4** Coco **5** Largo **6** Romano **7** Guajaba, Rosareo, Sabinal **8** Cantiles **9** San Felipe **10** Santa Maria
mountain: **6** Copper **7** Cristal, Maestra, Organos **8** Camaguey, Trinidad **9** Las Villas **11** Pinar del rio **12** Guaniguanico **14** Sancti-Spiritus
highest point: **8** Turquino
river: **4** Zaza **5** Cauto **8** San Pedro
sea: **8** Atlantic **9** Caribbean
physical feature:
  bay: **4** Nipe, Pigs **6** Jiguey **8** Cochinos **10** Buena Vista, Guantznamo
  cape: **4** Cruz **5** Maisi **8** Lucrecia **10** Corrientes, San Antonio
  channel: **8** Nicholas **9** Old Bahama
  falls: **3** Toa **7** Agabama, Caburni
  gulf: **6** Mexico **7** Cazones **8** Anamaria, Batabano **12** Guancanayabo
  inlet: **4** Broa **10** Corrientes
  peninsula: **6** Zapata
  point: **7** Guarico
  swamp: **6** Zapata
people: **5** Carib, Negro, Taino, white **6** Arawak **7** Ciboney, mestizo **8** Ciboneye
  conqueror: **9** Velazquez
  explorer: **8** Columbus

leader: **6** Castro **7** Batista **10** Che Guevara
language: **7** Spanish
religion: **13** Roman Catholic
  cult: **6** Chango, Yemaya
places:
  castle: **5** Morro
  cathedral: **8** Santiago
feature:
  dance: **5** conga, rumba **6** danzon, rhumba **8** guaracha, pachanga
  harvest: **5** zafra
  peasant: **7** guajiro
  tree: **5** jique, jiqui
  witch doctor: **7** nanigos
food:
  dish: **6** paella
  drink: **4** pina

cubbyhole 4 nook **5** niche **6** cranny **10** pigeonhole **11** compartment

cube of deep-fried pork
American Spanish: **10** cuchifrito

cubic centimeter
abbreviation: **4** cu cm

cubic dekameter
abbreviation: **5** cu dkm

cubic foot
abbreviation: **4** cu ft

cubic inch
abbreviation: **4** cu in

cubicle 3 bay **4** cell, nook **5** booth, niche **6** alcove, carrel, recess

cubic meter
abbreviation: **3** cu m

cubic millimeter
abbreviation: **4** cu mm

cubic yard
abbreviation: **4** cu yd

cubit 15 Biblical measure

cuchifrito 19 cube of deep-fried pork

Cuchulainn
origin: **5** Irish
hero of: **6** Ulster
uncle: **9** Conchobar
guarded house of: **10** Smith Culan
killed by: **6** Lugaid

cuckoo 3 ani **4** bats, bird, fool, gaga, nuts **5** balmy, batty, crazy, daffy, dotty, goofy, loony, nutty, silly, wacky **6** screwy **7** idiotic **9** screwball **12** crackbrained **13** off one's rocker **14** off one's trolley

cucumber 14 Cucumis sativus
varieties: **3** bur **4** mock, star, wild **6** bitter, pickle **7** prickly, serpent **9** squirting **13** African horned

cuddle 3 hug, pet **5** clasp **6** caress, curl up, fondle, huddle, nestle, nuzzle **7** cling to, embrace, lie snug, snuggle

Cuddly Dudley
nickname of: **11** Dudley Moore

cudgel 4 club **5** baton, staff, stick **8** bludgeon **9** billy club, blackjack, truncheon **10** shillelagh **12** quarterstaff

cue 3 key, tip **4** clue, hint, sign **6** signal **7** inkling **10** intimation, sugges- tion **11** insinuation

cuff 3 box, hit, rap **4** blow **5** clout, smack, thump, whack **6** thwack, wal- lop

cui bono 10 for what use, of what good **15** for whose benefit

cuisine 4 fare, food, menu **5** table **6** viands **7** cookery, cooking, edibles **8** victuals, vittles **11** comestibles

Cukor, George
   director of: 7 Camille **8** Adam's Rib, Gaslight, The Women **10** My Fair Lady (Oscar) **11** A Double Life, A Star Is Born, Little Women **13** Born Yesterday, Dinner at Eight **14** Romeo and Juliet **16** David Copperfield **18** A Bill of Divorcement **20** The Philadel- phia Story

cul-de-sac 6 pocket **7** dead-end, im- passe **10** blind alley

cull 4 junk, pick, sift, take **5** dross, glean, scrap, trash, waste **6** choose, divide, garner, gather, jetsam, reject, second, select, winnow **7** castoff, col- lect, discard, excerpt, extract, leaving **8** abstract, scouring, separate **9** segre- gate

culminate 3 cap, end, top **5** crown, end up **6** climax, finish, result, top off, wind up **8** complete, conclude **9** terminate **10** consummate

culmination 4 acme, apex, peak **6** ap- ogee, climax, height, zenith **7** epitome **8** pinnacle **10** conclusion **11** fulfill- ment, realization **12** consummation

culpability 4 onus **5** blame, fault, guilt **9** liability **14** accountability, responsi- bility

culpable 6 guilty, liable **7** at fault, to blame **8** blamable **10** censurable **11** blameworthy

culprit 5 felon **6** sinner **8** criminal, evildoer, offender **9** miscreant, wrong- doer **10** lawbreaker, malefactor **12** transgressor

cult 4 sect **7** faction, zealots **8** admir- ers, devotees, devotion **9** disciples, followers **10** admiration

cultivable 6 arable **7** fertile, friable **8** farmable, plowable, tillable

cultivate 3 dig, hoe, sow **4** farm, grow, plow, seek, till, weed **5** court, plant, spade **6** enrich, garden **7** ac- quire, advance, develop, elevate, en- hance, improve

cultivated 3 dug **4** fine, grew, hoed **6** farmed, forked, sought, spaded, tilled, weeded **7** courted, planted **8** ad- vanced, cultured, elevated, enhanced, enriched, finished, improved, polished **9** developed

cultivation 5 grace **6** polish, sowing **7** farming, manners, tilling **8** agronomy, planting **9** elevation, gardening, gentil-

ity, good taste, husbandry **10** refine- ment **11** agriculture

culture 3 art **5** music **7** the arts **8** learning **9** erudition, knowledge **10** enrichment, literature, refinement **12** civilization **13** enlightenment **15** accomplishments

Culture and Anarchy
   author: 13 Matthew Arnold

cultured 7 elegant, erudite, genteel, learned, refined **8** polished, well-bred, well-read **11** enlightened **12** accom- plished, well-educated **13** sophisti- cated

culture medium 4 agar **8** agar-agar

culvert 5 ditch, drain, sewer **6** trench **7** channel, conduit, fox-hole

cumbersome 5 bulky, hefty **6** clumsy **7** awkward **8** cumbrous, ungainly, un- wieldy **9** ponderous **12** unmanageable

cum grano salis 15 not too seriously **16** with a grain of salt

cumin
   botanical name: 14 Cuminum cyminum
   other name: 6 comino, jiraka, kum- mel
   origin: 5 Egypt
   family: 7 parsley
   symbol of: 5 greed
   guards against straying: 7 pigeons **8** chickens, husbands
   use: 4 fish, meat, rice, soup, stew **5** bread, curry **6** cheese **7** pickles, sau- sage **8** potatoes **11** chili powder

cum laude 10 with praise

Cummings, E. E. (Edward Estlin)
   author of: 12 in just spring **15** The Enormous Room **17** Tulips and Chimneys **18** Chansons Innocentes

Cummings, Robert
   real name: 29 Clarence Robert Orville Cummings
   born: 8 Joplin MO
   roles: 8 King's Row **14** Dial M for Murder **18** The Bob Cummings Show

cumulate 5 amass **6** gather, heap up, pile up **10** accumulate

cumulative 7 amassed, piled up **8** ad- ditive, heaped up **9** aggregate **10** col- lective **12** accumulative, conglomerate

Cunegonde
   character in: 7 Candide
   author: 8 Voltaire

cunning 3 art, sly **4** foxy, wily **5** canny, craft, guile, knack, skill **6** art- ful, crafty, deceit, genius, shifty, shrewd, talent, tricky **7** ability, devi- ous, finesse, slyness **8** aptitude, arti- fice, deftness, foxiness, guileful, sub- tlety, trickery, wiliness **9** chicanery, deceitful, deception, deceptive, dexter- ity, duplicity, ingenious, underhand **10** adroitness, artfulness, cleverness, craftiness, expertness, shrewdness **11**

deviousness **13** Machiavellian
   god of: 6 Hermes

Cunning Little Vixen, The
   opera by: 7 Janacek

cup 3 cup **5** glass, grail, stein **6** beaker, goblet, vessel **7** chalice, tankard **8** half pint, schooner
   abbreviation: 1 c

Cup
   constellation of: 6 Crater

cupbearer of gods 8 Ganymede

cupboard 6 buffet, bureau, closet **7** ar- moire, cabinet **9** sideboard, storeroom **10** chiffonier **11** china closet **12** clothespress

Cupid 6 cherub
   also: 4 Amor
   origin: 5 Roman
   god of: 4 love
   mother: 5 Venus
   corresponds to: 4 Eros
   features: 3 bow **5** arrow, wings

cupidity 5 greed **7** avarice, avidity **8** rapacity **10** greediness **11** selfishness **12** covetousness, graspingness **13** con- cupiscence, insatiability, rapaciousness **14** avariciousness **15** acquisitiveness

cupola 4 dome, roof **5** tower, vault **6** belfry, turret **7** ceiling

cur 3 cad **4** mutt **5** rogue **6** rascal, var- let, wretch **7** mongrel, varmint, villain **9** scoundrel **10** blackguard

curacao
   type: 7 liqueur
   origin: 19 Netherlands Antilles
   flavor: 6 orange
   with gin: 8 Blue Moon, Napoleon **9** Blue Devil **14** Flying Dutchman
   with rum: 6 Mai-Tai **8** Blue Lady **12** Blue Hawaiian
   with vodka: 8 Aqueduct

curate 5 vicar **6** cleric, deacon, parson, pastor, priest, rector **8** minister, preacher **9** churchman, clergyman **12** ecclesiastic

curative 4 balm **7** healing **11** restora- tive

curator 5 doyen **6** keeper **7** steward **8** director, overseer **9** caretaker, custo- dian

curb 3 rim **4** edge, rein **5** brink, check, ledge, limit **6** border, bridle, halter, retard, slow up **7** control, harness, in- hibit, repress, slacken **8** hold back, moderate, restrain, restrict, slow down, suppress **9** curbstone, hin- drance, restraint **10** decelerate, limita- tion **11** restriction, retardation

Curb Your Enthusiasm
   network: 3 HBO
   cast: 10 Jeff Garlin (Jeff Greene), Larry David (Larry David) **11** Cheryl Hines (Cheryl David), Susie Essman (Susie Green) **12** Richard Lewis (Richard Lewis)

curdle 3 rot **4** clot, curd, sour, turn **5**

decay, go bad, go off, spoil **7** clabber, congeal, ferment, putrefy, thicken **8** putresce, solidify **9** coagulate **11** deteriorate

cure 3 dry **4** heal, salt **5** smoke **6** remedy **8** antidote, make well, preserve **10** corrective

cure-all 4 balm **6** elixir, remedy **7** panacea **10** catholicon

cured 5 dried **6** healed, mended, smoked **8** made well, remedied **9** preserved, recovered

Curie, Marie Sklodowska and Pierre
  field: 7 physics **9** chemistry
  discovered: 6 radium **8** polonium **13** radioactivity
  awarded: 10 Nobel Prize
  daughter: 5 Marie (Joliot-Curie, Nobelist)

curio 7 bibelot, trinket **9** bric-a-brac, objet d'art

curiosity 5 freak, sight **6** marvel, oddity, prying, rarity, wonder **7** novelty **8** interest, nosiness **10** phenomenon, rare object **11** questioning **15** inquisitiveness

curious 3 odd **4** nosy, rare **5** funny, novel, queer, weird **6** prying, quaint, unique **7** bizarre, strange, unusual **8** peculiar, singular, snooping, uncommon **9** inquiring, searching **11** inquisitive, questioning

curl 4 coil, lock, wave, wind **5** crimp, frizz, swirl, twirl, twist **6** spiral **7** frizzle, ringlet, scallop **8** curlicue **9** corkscrew

curled 3 set **5** kinky, waved, wound **6** coiled, frizzy, permed, spiral **7** crimped, frizzed, twisted **8** crinkled, scrolled **9** curlicued

curlicue 4 coil **5** twist **6** spiral **8** flourish

curly 4 wavy **5** kinky **6** frizzy **7** rippled **8** crinkled **9** ringleted

curmudgeon 4 crab **5** crank, grump **6** grouch **8** grumbler, sourball

currant 5 Ribes
  varieties: 3 red **5** black, fetid, skunk, squaw, stink **6** alpine, cherry, common, garden, Indian, Sierra **7** Buffalo **8** Missouri, mountain, swamp red **9** chaparral, wild black **11** northern red **12** bristly black **13** American black, European black, northern black, white-flowered **15** California black

currency 4 cash, coin **5** bills, money, vogue **6** specie **7** coinage **9** bank notes **10** acceptance, popularity, prevalence **12** predominance, universality

current 3 now **4** flow, flux, mood, tide **5** draft, drift, trend **6** modern, spirit, stream, with-it **7** feeling, in style, in vogue, popular, present **8** existing, tendency, up-to-date **9** prevalent, zeit-

geist **10** atmosphere, present-day, prevailing **11** inclination **12** contemporary, undercurrent

current of air 4 wind **5** draft **6** breeze, zephyr

curricle 3 gig **4** cart, trap **6** chaise **8** carriage

curry powder
  origin: 5 India
  ingredient: 5 cumin **6** cloves **8** capsicum, turmeric **9** coriander, fenugreek, red pepper **13** cayenne pepper
  use: 5 kebab, kebob, kofta, malai **6** kormas **7** curries **8** meat loaf, vindaloo, zucchini **11** potato salad

curse 3 vex **4** bane, cuss, damn, oath **5** blast, cross, swear, trial **6** burden, ordeal, plague, whammy **7** afflict, condemn, evil eye, scourge, swear at, torment, trouble **8** anathema, denounce, execrate, swearing, vexation **9** annoyance, blasphemy, damnation, evil spell, expletive, obscenity, profanity **10** affliction, execration, misfortune **11** imprecation, malediction, tribulation **12** anathematize, denunciation

cursory 5 brief, hasty, quick, swift **6** casual, random **7** hurried, offhand, passing **8** careless **9** desultory, haphazard **11** inattentive, perfunctory, superficial

curt 4 rude **5** bluff, blunt, gruff, short, terse **6** abrupt, crusty, snappy **7** brusque, summary **8** petulant **10** peremptory

curtail 3 cut **4** clip, trim **6** reduce **7** abridge, shorten **8** condense, contract, cut short, decrease, diminish, pare down **10** abbreviate

curtailed 3 cut **7** checked, concise, cut back, reduced, slashed **8** abridged, cut short **9** shortened **10** retrenched

curtailment 7 cutback, cutting, halting, pruning **8** clipping, decrease, trimming **9** lessening, reduction, restraint **10** limitation, shortening **11** abridgement, contraction **12** abbreviation, condensation

curtain 3 end **4** mask, veil **5** blind, cover, drape, shade, sheet **6** screen, shroud **7** conceal, drapery, hanging **8** portiere

Curtis, Tony
  real name: 15 Bernard Schwartz
  wife: 10 Janet Leigh
  daughter: 8 Jamie Lee
  born: 9 New York NY
  roles: 7 Houdini, Trapeze **12** The Great Race **13** Some Like It Hot **14** The Defiant Ones **16** The Great Imposter **18** The Boston Strangler **22** The Sweet Smell of Success

Curtius
  also: 6 Marcus
  volunteered as: 17 sacrificial victim

Curtiz, Michael
  director of: 10 Casablanca (Oscar),

The Sea Hawk **12** Captain Blood **13** Mildred Pierce **14** Life with Father **17** Yankee Doodle Dandy **24** The Adventures of Robin Hood (with William Keighley) **26** The Charge of the Light Brigade **34** The Private Lives of Elizabeth and Essex

curtsy, curtsey 3 bob, bow, dip **5** honor **6** homage **9** obeisance, reverence **11** bend the knee

curvature 3 arc **4** arch, bend **5** crook **6** bowing

curve 3 arc, bow, ess **4** arch, bend, coil, hook, loop, turn, wind **5** crook, twist **6** spiral, swerve

curved 4 bent **5** bowed **6** arched, looped, turned

curved span 3 bow **4** arch, dome **5** vault **6** bridge

curving 4 bent **5** bowed **6** arched **7** bending, looping, turning, winding **8** twisting

curving inward 6 hollow, sunken **7** concave **8** hollowed **9** depressed

curving outward 5 bowed **6** convex **7** bulging, rounded **8** bellying **11** protuberant

Cuscatlan see **10** El Salvador

Cush
  father: 3 Ham
  grandfather: 4 Noah
  brother: 6 Canaan
  son: 6 Nimrod
  Hebrew for: 8 Ethiopia

cushion 3 mat, pad **4** damp **5** quiet **6** dampen, deaden, muffle, pillow, soften, stifle **7** bolster **8** suppress

Cushitic
  language family: 11 Afro-Asiatic **13** Hamito-Semitic
  branch: 6 Somali **8** Gallinya
  spoken in: 7 Somalia **8** Ethiopia, Tanzania

cusp 4 apex, barb, horn, peak **5** angle, point, tooth **6** corner

custard 4 flan, fool **5** creme **6** junket **7** dessert, pudding **8** flummery **10** blanc-mange, zabaglione

Custer, George A
  served in: 8 Civil War **10** Indian Wars
  side: 5 Union
  battle: 13 Little Big Horn
  defeated: 11 Black Kettle
  defeated by: 10 Crazy Horse

custodian 6 duenna, keeper, warden **7** janitor, chaperon, guardian, watchman **9** attendant, caretaker, chaperone, concierge **14** superintendent

custody 4 care **5** watch **6** charge **9** detention **10** possession, protection **11** confinement, safekeeping, trusteeship **12** conservation, guardianship, preservation

custom 4 form, mode **5** habit, usage **7** fashion **10** convention

customarily 7 as a rule, usually **8** commonly, normally **9** generally, regularly **10** frequently, habitually, ordinarily **13** traditionally

customary 5 usual **6** common, normal, wonted **7** general, regular, routine, typical **8** everyday, habitual, ordinary **10** accustomed **11** traditional **12** conventional

customer 5 buyer **6** client, patron **7** habitue, shopper **9** purchaser

customs 4 duty, levy, toll **6** excise, tariff **9** import tax **10** assessment

cut 3 mow, saw **4** chop, clip, crop, cube, dice, fall, gash, hack, move, nick, pare, part, rent, rive, slit, snip, snub, trim **5** carve, cross, lance, mince, piece, prune, sever, share, shave, shear, slash, slice, split, wound **6** bisect, course, delete, divide, furrow, hollow, ignore, incise, pierce, reduce, sunder, trench **7** abridge, channel, curtail, decline, dissect, opening, passage, portion, section, segment **8** condense, contract, decrease, diminish, incision, lacerate **9** abatement, intersect, lessening, reduction, shrinkage **10** abbreviate, diminution, excavation, shortening **11** contraction, curtailment, indentation

cut and run 4 bolt, flee, skip **6** escape **7** abscond, get away, make off, run away **8** slip away **9** break free **10** break loose, fly the coop **12** make a getaway

cut apart 7 dissect **9** anatomize

cutback 8 decrease, trimming **9** reduction **11** abridgement, curtailment

cut back 4 trim **5** prune **6** reduce **7** abridge, curtail **8** decrease

cut costs 4 save **5** skimp, stint **6** scrimp **7** husband **8** conserve, downsize **9** economize **15** tighten one's belt

cut down 4 kill, trim **5** limit **6** lessen, reduce **7** abridge, curtail, destroy, disable, remodel, shorten **8** condense, decrease, diminish, restrict **10** abbreviate

cut-down form 6 digest, precis **7** summary **8** synopsis, trimming **10** shortening **11** abridgement, contraction, curtailment **12** abbreviation, condensation

cut down to size 5 abase **6** humble **7** mortify **8** belittle, bring low, disgrace **9** humiliate **13** bring down a peg

cute 5 sweet **6** dainty, pretty **7** darling, lovable **8** adorable, handsome, precious **9** beautiful **10** attractive

cut expenses 4 save **5** skimp, stint **6** scrimp **8** conserve **9** economize **12** pinch pennies **15** tighten one's belt

cut in half 5 halve **6** bisect

cut in two 5 halve, sever **6** bisect

cutlet 3 cut **4** chop **5** slice **9** cotelette, croquette

cut off 4 dock, trim **5** apart, sever **6** detach, remove **7** chop off, divorce, isolate **8** amputate, divorced, isolated, separate **10** disconnect

cut out 2 go **4** blow, exit **5** be off, erase, leave, scram, split **6** beat it, delete, depart, escape, excise, go away, remove, set out **7** abolish **8** designed, get rid of, set forth **9** eliminate **10** do away with, hit the road, make tracks **11** exterminate, take a powder

cut short 4 clip, crop, dock, trim **7** abridge, shorten **8** truncate **10** abbreviate

cutter 4 boat **5** blade, hewer, knife **6** sledge, sleigh, tailor **11** cutting edge

cutthroat 5 cruel **6** outlaw **7** brigand, hoodlum, ruffian **8** ruthless **9** merciless

cutting 3 raw **4** acid, cold **5** harsh, nasty, sharp **6** biting, bitter **7** acerbic, caustic, nipping, pruning, searing **8** clipping, derisive, piercing, scathing, smarting, snubbing, stinging, trimming **9** reduction, sarcastic, stringent **11** abridgement, acrimonious, compression, contraction, curtailment, disparaging, penetrating **12** abbreviation, condensation

cutting edge 5 blade **8** vanguard **9** forefront

cutting off 8 severing **9** severance **10** detachment, separation **13** disconnection, disengagement

cutting remark 3 dig **4** gibe, jeer **5** taunt

Cuttle
    character in: 12 Dombey and Son
    author: 7 Dickens

cut up 4 chop, hack, maim, rend **5** caper, carve, halve, mince, slash, slice, split **6** cleave, deface, deform, divide **7** portion, quarter **8** dissever, mutilate **9** apportion, kid around **10** fool around **11** clown around, play the fool

Cuvier, Georges
    field: 7 geology, zoology
    nationality: 6 French
    founded: 12 paleontology **18** comparative anatomy

Cybele
    also: 9 Dindymene **10** Berecyntia, Magna Mater **11** Great Mother **12** Mater Turrita **17** Great Idaean Mother
    origin: 8 Phrygian **9** Asia Minor
    goddess of: 6 nature
    priest: 5 Galli **10** Corybantes
    corresponds to: 3 Ops **4** Rhea
    epithet: 6 Antaea

Cyclades 3 Dos, Zea **4** Keos, Nios, Sira, Syra **5** Delos, Melos, Naxos, Paros, Siros, Syros, Tenos, Tinos **6**

Andros **7** Amorgos, islands, Kythnos **13** Aegean islands

cycle 3 run **6** series **8** sequence **10** succession **11** progression **14** connected group

cyclone 4 gale, gust, wind **5** storm **7** tornado, twister, typhoon **9** whirlwind, windstorm
    Australian: 10 willy-nilly

Cyclone (Cy)
    nickname of: 15 Denton True Young

Cyclops, Cyclopes
    form: 5 giant
    number of eyes: 3 one
    father: 6 Uranus
    mother: 2 Ge
    blinded by: 8 Odysseus

Cycnus
    father: 4 Ares
    killed in: 4 duel
    killed by: 8 Hercules
    changed into: 4 swan

cylinder 3 can, tin **4** drum, pipe, roll, tube **5** spool **6** barrel, column, pillar, piston, platen, roller **13** piston chamber

cylindrical 5 round **6** tarete **7** tubular **8** columnar

Cymbeline
    author: 18 William Shakespeare
    character: 6 Cloten, Imogen **7** Iachimo, Pisanio **9** Bellarius **17** Leonatus Posthumus

Cymru see **5** Wales

cynic 7 scoffer, skeptic **9** pessimist **10** misogynist **11** faultfinder, misanthrope

cynical 8 derisive, sardonic, scoffing, scornful, sneering **9** misogynic, sarcastic, skeptical **12** misanthropic

cypress 8 Taxodium **9** Cupressus
    varieties: 3 toy **4** bald, berg, pond **5** false, Gowen, Modoc, Piute **6** Bhutan, Hinoki, Lawson, MacNab, Nootka, Sawara, summer, Tecate **7** African, Arizona, Italian, Mexican, Sargent **8** Cuyamaca, golf-ball, Monterey, mourning, Siskiyou, standing **9** Guadalupe, Mendocino, Montezuma, red summer, Santa Cruz **10** Portuguese, tennis-ball **12** Chinese swamp **18** rough-barked Arizona **19** smooth-barked Arizona

Cyprian see **9** Aphrodite

Cyprus
    biblical name: 6 Kittim
    capital/largest city: 7 Nicosia
    city: 6 Paphos **7** Kyrenia, Larnaca **8** Limassol **9** Famagusta
    monetary unit: 4 para **5** pound
    mountain: 7 Kyrenia, Troodos
    highest point: 7 Olympus
    river: 6 Pedias
    sea: 13 Mediterranean
    physical feature:
        bay: 8 Episkopi
        cape: 4 Gata **5** Greco **7** Andreas, Arnauti **9** Kormakiti

peninsula: 6 Karpas
plain: 8 Mesaoria **9** Messaoria
people: 5 Greek, Turks **9** Cypriotes
ruler: 5 Turks **6** Greeks, Romans **7**
British **9** Egyptians, Lusignans,
Venetians **10** Byzantines **11** Phoenicians
language: 5 Greek **7** Turkish
religion: 5 Islam **6** Muslim **13** Greek
Orthodoxy **16** Eastern Orthodoxy

Cyrano de Bergerac
director: 13 Michael Gordon
author: 13 Edmond Rostand
cast: 10 Jose Ferrer (Cyrano), Mala
Powers **13** William Powers
character: 6 Roxane **22** Christian de
Neuvillette
setting: 5 Paris
Oscar for: 9 best actor (Ferrer)

Cyrano de Bergerac, Savinien
author of: 25 Voyages to the Moon
and the Sun
play based on his life by: 13 Edmond Rostand

cytology
study of: 5 cells

czar, tsar 4 king **5** ruler **6** caesar, despot, tyrant **7** emperor, monarch **8** dictator, overlord **9** potentate, sovereign

czarina 7 empress

czaristic 10 autocratic **11** all-powerful,
dictatorial, monarchical

Czechoslovakia/Czech Republic
see also **8** Slovakia
capital/largest city: 5 Praha **6** Prague
others: 2 As **4** Asch, Brno, Cheb,
Most **5** Brunn, Nitra, Opava, Plzen,
Tabor, **6** Aussig, Bilina, Kladno, Kosice, Pilsen, Presov, Sadowa, Trnava,
Vsetin **7** Budweis, Jihlava, Liberec,
Olomouc, Ostrava, Teplitz **8** Carlsbad, Jachymov, Karlsbad **9** Press-
burg **10** Austerlitz, Bratislava, Konig-
gratz **11** Reichenberg
university: 7 Charles
division: 7 Bohemia, Moravia, Silesia
8 Ruthenia, Slovakia
measure: 3 Lan **4** Mira **5** Korec, Liket, Stopa **6** Merice, Strych
monetary unit: 5 crown, ducat **6**
heller, Koruna
mountain: 3 Erz, Ore **5** Giant, Tatra
6 Sumava **7** Sudeten, Sudetes **8**
Krkonose **10** Carpathian
highest point: 7 Gerlach **11** Gerlachovka
river: 2 Uh, **3** Mze, Vag, Vah **4** Dyje,
Eger, Elbe, Gran, Hron, Ipel, Iser,
Labe, Nisa, Oder, Odra, Ohre, Olse,
Waag **5** Becva, Dunaj, March, Nitra,
Slana, Tisza **6** Danube, Moldau, Morava, Ondava, Sazava, Torysa, Vltava
7 Laborec, Luznice **8** Berounka

physical feature:
plateau: 8 Bohemian **11** Sudeten-
land
people: 4 Slav **5** Czech **6** Slovak **8**
Bohemian, Moravian
author: 5 Capek, Hasek, Havel **7**
Kundera, Seifert
composer: 6 Dvorak **7** Janacek,
Martinu, Smetana
director: 11 Milos Forman
philosopher/reformer: 8 Come-
nius, John Huss
language: 5 Czech **6** German, Magyar, Slovak **7** Russian **9** Hungarian
religion: 6 Uniate **8** Lutheran **9** Orthodoxy **13** Roman Catholic
place:
castle: 8 Hradcany
cathedral: 7 St Vitus **10** St Nicholas
resort/spa: 8 Carlsbad, Piestany **9**
Marienbad **10** Luhacovice **11** Kar-
lovy Vary **14** Marianske Lazne
square: 9 Wenceslas
feature:
dance: 5 polka **6** redowa, talian **7**
furiant
gymnastics festival: 11 spartakiada
song: 7 Ma Vlast
food:
beer: 6 pilsen
sausage: 5 parky **6** vursty

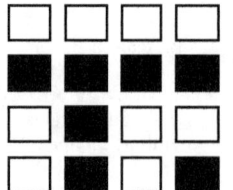
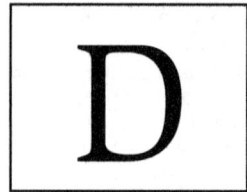
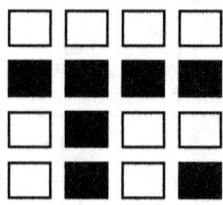

dab 3 bit, pat, tap 6 stroke 7 smidgen, soupcon

dabble 5 slosh 6 fiddle, putter, splash 7 spatter, toy with 8 sprinkle

dabbler 7 amateur, trifler 10 dilettante 12 experimenter 15 nonprofessional

da capo
music: 22 repeat from the beginning
abbreviation: 2 DC

Dacca
capital of: 10 Bangladesh

d'accord 2 OK 6 agreed 7 granted

Dactyls
also: 7 Daktyls
dwellers of: 8 Mount Ida

dad 2 da, pa 3 pop 4 papa, pops, sire 5 daddy, pappy, pater 6 father, parent 11 the old man

Daedalus
occupation: 9 architect
father: 6 Metion
son: 5 Iapyx 6 Icarus
nephew: 5 Talos 6 Perdix
killed: 5 Talos
built: 9 labyrinth
for: 5 Minos
made: 5 wings

Daedalus, Stephen see 30 Portrait of the Artist as a Young Man

daffodil 9 Narcissus 24 Narcissus pseudonarcissus
varieties: 3 sea 6 winter 8 Peruvian 9 petticoat 13 hoop-petticoat

daft 3 mad 4 loco 5 balmy, batty, crazy, daffy, dizzy, goofy, loony, nutty, silly, wacky 6 cuckoo, insane, screwy 7 foolish, lunatic, witless

Dagan
origin: 12 Mesopotamian
god of: 5 earth 11 agriculture
corresponds to: 5 Dagon

dagger 4 dirk, snee 5 blade, knife 6 weapon 7 poniard 8 stiletto 11 snickersnee

Dagon
origin: 10 Philistine, Phoenician
god of: 5 earth 11 agriculture
corresponds to: 5 Dagan

Daguerre, Louis J M
nationality: 6 French
inventor of: 11 photography 13 daguerreotype

Dagwood 8 sandwich
see also 7 Blondie

dahlia

varieties: 3 sea 4 tree 6 common, garden 7 bedding 8 bell tree 10 candelabra

Dahomey, Republic of see 5 Benin

daily 7 diurnal, per diem 9 circadian, quotidian

Daimler, Gottlieb
nationality: 6 German
inventor of: 10 carburetor, motorcycle 14 gasoline engine 18 gasoline automobile 25 compression ignition engine

daimyo 4 lord 10 feudal lord

dainty 4 fine 5 fussy, tasty 6 choice, choosy, lovely, pretty, savory 7 choosey, elegant, refined 8 delicate, pleasing 9 beautiful, delicious, exquisite 10 attractive, fastidious, particular

Daira
father: 7 Oceanus

dais 5 stage 6 podium 7 rostrum 8 platform

daisy 6 Bellis 23 Chrysanthemum frutescens 25 Chrysanthemum leucanthemum
varieties: 4 blue, cape, high, lazy 5 crown, giant, globe, oxeye, Paris, veldt, white 6 butter, Easter, Nippon, shasta, sleepy, Tahoka 7 African, English, painted, seaside, turfing 8 Dahlberg, mountain, panamint 9 Barberton, Englemann, Swan River, Transvaal 10 Kingfisher, Michaelmas, Portuguese 11 Clanwilliam, Livingstone, Namaqualand 12 Boston yellow, double orange 15 blue-eyed African

Daisy Miller
author: 10 Henry James
character: 10 Giovanelli 12 Winterbourne

Dakar
capital of: 7 Senegal

Dakota (Sioux)
language family: 6 Siouan
tribe: 5 Teton 6 Lakota, Nakota, Santee 7 Yankton 8 Sisseton, Wahpeton, Wiciyela 9 Wahpekute, Yanktonai 11 Mdewakanton
location: 7 Montana 9 Minnesota 11 North Dakota, South Dakota
leader: 4 Gall 10 Crazy Horse 11 Sitting Bull 13 Jashunca-Uiteo
noted for: 15 military prowess
deity: 10 Wakan Tanka

dale 4 dell, dene, glen, vale 6 dingle, hollow, valley

D'Alembert
author of: 12 Encyclopedia

Dali, Salvador
born: 5 Spain 7 Figuras
artwork: 10 Last Supper 17 Atomic Leda and Swan 19 Persistence of Memory 22 Accommodations of Desire 24 Christ of St John of the Cross

Dalibor
opera by: 7 Smetana
character: 6 Milada

Dallas
airport: 9 Love Field 23 Dallas-Fort Worth Regional
basketball team: 4 Mavs 9 Mavericks
football team: 7 Cowboys
hockey team: 5 Stars
landmark: 15 Turtle Creek Park 16 Museum of Fine Arts 19 Dallas Theater Center 25 Margo Jones Memorial Theater
river: 7 Trinity
stadium: 10 Cotton Bowl
university: 3 SMU 17 Southern Methodist

Dallas
character: 7 JR Ewing 9 Jack Ewing, Jenna Wade, Jock Ewing, Miss Ellie, Ray Krebbs 10 Bobby Ewing 11 Christopher, Cliff Barnes, Mandy Winger, Mark Graison 12 Digger Barnes 13 Clayton Farlow, John Ross Ewing, Sue Ellen Ewing 16 Donna Culver Krebs 17 Pamela Barnes Ewing 22 Eleanor Southworth Ewing
cast: 8 John Beck 9 Dack Rambo, Linda Gray 10 Howard Keel 11 Larry Hagman, Steve Kanaly, Susan Howard 12 Ken Kercheval, Patrick Duffy 16 Barbara Bel Geddes, Priscilla Presley 17 Victoria Principal
ranch: 9 Southfork
business: 3 oil 8 Ewing Oil

dalliance 6 affair, toying 7 romance 8 fiddling, trifling 10 flirtation, lovemaking

dally 3 toy 4 play 5 flirt 6 dawdle, loiter, trifle

Dalmatia see 10 Yugoslavia

Dalmatian (dog) 5 spots 12 firehouse dog 13 black and white

Dalton, John
field: 7 physics 9 chemistry
nationality: 7 British

formulated: 12 atomic theory
first: 18 atomic weights table
described: 14 color blindness

dam 3 bar, cow **4** clog, mare, plug, stop, wall **5** bitch, block, check **6** bridle, hinder, hold in, impede, plug up, stanch, stop up **7** barrier, block up, confine, congest, inhibit, repress, stopper, stuff up **8** blockade, hold back, obstruct, restrain **9** barricade, hindrance **11** obstruction

damage, damages 3 mar **4** cost, harm, hurt, loss **6** impair, injure, injury, ravage **10** impairment, reparation, settlement **11** destruction **12** compensation, despoliation

damaging 7 harmful, hurtful, ruinous **9** injurious **11** destructive, detrimental

Damascus
ancient kingdom: 8 Aramaean
Arabic: 7 Dimashq
capital of: 5 Syria
monastery: 22 Suleiman the Magnificent
mosque: 5 Great **7** Umayyad
mount: 6 Qasyun
museum: 8 National **9** Qasr al-Azm
river: 4 Awaj **6** Barada
rulers: 5 Arabs, Timur **6** Romans **7** Mongols, Saladin **8** Assyrian **9** Caliphate, Seleucids **12** Ottoman Turks **15** Byzantine Empire **17** Alexander the Great
tomb: 7 Saladin

Damastes see **10** Procrustes

Dame Pliant
character in: 12 The Alchemist
author: 6 Jonson

Damia
spirit of: 9 fertility

damn 4 doom **5** blast **6** rail at **7** censure, condemn **8** denounce **9** criticize, disparage

damned 4 lost **6** cursed, darned, doomed, fallen **7** doggone, dratted, godless **8** accursed, doggoned **9** condemned, execrated, reprobate **12** unregenerate

Damocles
of: 8 Syracuse
offended: 9 Dionysius
seated under: 14 suspended sword

Damon
friend: 7 Pythias

damp 3 wet **4** curb, dank, dash, dewy, dull, mist **5** check, foggy, humid, misty, moist, muggy, rainy, soggy, spoil **6** clammy, deaden, hamper, hinder, reduce, soaked, sodden **7** depress, drizzly, inhibit, sopping, wettish **8** dankness, diminish, dripping, humidity, moisture, restrain **9** mugginess, restraint **10** clamminess, discourage **14** discouragement

dampen 3 wet **4** mute **7** moisten, wet down

dampen one's spirits 5 daunt, un-

man **6** deject **7** depress **10** discourage, dishearten

damper 4 curb, mute **8** obstacle **9** hindrance, restraint **10** constraint, impediment, wet blanket **14** discouragement

damsel 4 girl, lass **6** maiden **9** young lady

damselfly
varieties: 8 forktail **10** civilbluet **11** black-winged, broad-winged **12** narrow-winged, spread-winged, violet dancer

dam up 4 clog, plug **5** block, choke **6** plug up, stop up **7** congest **8** obstruct

Dan
means: 5 judge
father: 5 Jacob
mother: 6 Bilhah
brother: 3 Gad **4** Levi **5** Asher, Judah **6** Joseph, Reuben, Simeon **7** Zebulun **8** Benjamin, Issachar, Naphtali
sister: 5 Dinah
descendant of: 6 Danite

Dana see **4** Danu

Dana, Richard Henry
author of: 21 Two Years Before the Mast

Danae
form: 6 maiden
father: 8 Acrisius
mother: 8 Eurydice
imprisoned by: 8 Acrisius
lover: 4 Zeus
son: 7 Perseus

Danai
members of: 6 Greeks **7** Argives

Danaides
daughters of: 6 Danaus
number of daughters: 5 fifty

Dan August
character: 9 (Sgt) Joe Rivera **14** (Sgt) Charles Wilentz **16** (Chief) George Untermeyer
cast: 9 Ned Romero **10** Norman Fell **12** Burt Reynolds **15** Richard Anderson

Danaus
ruler of: 5 Argos
father: 5 Belus
twin brother: 8 Aegyptus
daughters called: 8 Danaides
number of daughters: 5 fifty

dance 3 hop, jam **4** ball, jump, leap, prom, reel, skip **5** lindy, party, polka, twist **6** bounce, cavort, frolic, gambol, prance, square **7** fox-trot, perform **8** cakewalk **9** jitterbug **10** Charleston **11** Boston waltz **12** choreography, Virginia reel **15** hesitation waltz
Renaissance/17th century: 3 jig **5** galop, gigue **6** branle, pavane, redowa **7** bourree, gavotte, lancers, lavolta, mazurka **8** canaries, chaconne, courante, galliard, rigadoon, rigaudon, tourdion **9** allemande, passepied, polonaise, sarabande **10** danse basse, danse haute

18th century: 6 minuet **9** cotillion **11** contre danse **12** country dance
19th century: 5 waltz **9** quadrille
early 1900's: 7 foxtrot, one-step, two-step **8** bunny hug **10** turkey trot **11** grizzly bear
1920's: 5 tango **6** shimmy, toddle **10** Charleston **11** black bottom
1930's: 4 shag **5** conga, rumba, samba, Suzy-Q **7** pecking **8** big apple, lindy hop, trucking **9** jitterbug
1940's: 5 mambo **6** cha-cha
1950's and 1960's: 4 frug, go-go **5** twist **6** monkey **9** rock'n'roll
1970's: 5 disco
1980's: 7 lambada
1990's: 8 macarena
Argentine: 5 tango
Austrian: 13 schuhplattler
Balinese: 6 legong
Brazilian: 5 samba **6** maxixe **7** lambada
Cuban: 5 conga, rumba **6** cha-cha
Czech: 5 polka
Dominican: 8 marengue, merengue
folk: 6 Morris **7** maypole
French: 6 can-can **8** galliard **9** ecossaise
German: 11 schottische
Indian: 6 kathak **9** manipuri **9** kathakali **13** bharata nat yam
Japanese: 6 bugaku **7** dengaku **8** sarugaku
dance/theater: 2 no **3** noh **6** kabuki
Mexican: 3 hat
Polish: 7 mazurka **9** krakoviak, polonaise **11** varsovienne
Scottish: 5 sword
Siamese: 10 wayang wong
Spanish: 4 jota **6** bolero **8** flamenco **9** sevillana **10** seguidilla
modern dancer/choreographer: 4 Juba **8** Ted Shawn **9** Eliot Feld, Gene Kelly, Ray Bolger **10** Alvin Ailey, Mary Wigman, Paul Draper, Twyla Tharp **11** Anna Sokolow, Antony Tudor, Eric Hawkins, Fred Astaire, Irene Castle, Ruth St Denis **12** Bill Robinson, Ginger Rogers, Martha Graham, Vernon Castle **13** Alwin Nikolais, Doris Humphrey, Isadora Duncan **14** Charles Weidman **15** Merce Cunningham
see also **6** ballet

dance of death
French: 12 danse macabre

Dances with Wolves
director: 12 Kevin Costner
cast: 12 Graham Greene (Kicking Bird), Kevin Costner (John Dunbar), Rodney A. Grant (Wind in His Hair) **13** Mary McDonnell (Stands with a Fist) **14** Tantoo Cardinal (Black Shawl) **16** Robert Pastorelli (Timmons) **21** Floyd Red Crow Westerman (Ten Bears)

dander 3 ire **5** anger, Irish **6** temper

Dandie Dinmont terrier 24 soft-coated wheaten terrier, Staffordshire bull terrier, West Highland white terrier

dandy 3 fop 4 beau, dude, fine 5 beaut, great, super, swell 6 beauty, superb 7 coxcomb, peacock 8 terrific 9 excellent 12 clotheshorse

danger 4 risk 5 peril 6 hazard, menace, threat 8 jeopardy 12 endangerment

dangerous 5 hairy, risky 6 chancy, unsafe 8 menacing, perilous 9 hazardous 10 precarious 11 threatening, treacherous

danger signal 5 alarm, alert 7 red flag, warning

dangle 3 sag 4 drag, hang, sway 5 droop, swing, trail 6 depend 7 draggle, hang out, suspend 8 hang down, hang over 9 oscillate

Daniel
　　Babylonian name: 12 Belteshazzar
　　companion: 7 Meshach 8 Abednego, Shadrach

Daniel Boone
　　character: 5 Mingo 6 Yadkin 11 Cincinnatus, Israel Boone, Jemima Boone 12 Rebecca Boone
　　cast: 6 Ed Ames 10 Fess Parker 11 Albert Salmi, Dal McKennon, Darby Hinton 13 Patricia Blair 18 Veronica Cartwright

Danielovitch, Issur
　　real name of: 11 Kirk Douglas

dank 3 wet 4 cold, damp 5 humid, moist, muggy, soggy 6 chilly, clammy, sodden, sticky

danke 8 thank you

danke schon 16 thank you very much

dankness 4 damp 7 wetness 8 dampness, humidity 9 humidness, moistness, mugginess 10 clamminess

Danner, Blythe
　　born: 14 Philadelphia PA
　　roles: 8 Betrayal 14 Mr and Mrs Bridge, Meet the Fockers, Meet the Parents 15 The Great Santini 16 Man Woman and Child 16 The Prince of Tides
　　children: 11 Jake Paltrow 14 Gwyneth Paltrow

Danny Deever
　　story in: 18 Barrack-Room Ballads
　　author: 14 Rudyard Kipling

Danny Thomas Show, The
　　character: 6 Clancy 12 Uncle Tonoose 13 Danny Williams, Linda Williams, Rusty Williams, Terry Williams 16 Mrs Kathy Williams 18 Uncle Charley Halper
　　cast: 9 Sid Melton 10 Rusty Hamer 11 Hans Conried 12 Marjorie Lord, Penney Parker 13 Sherry Jackson 16 Angela Cartwright

danse macabre 12 dance of death

Dante (Alighieri)
　　author of: 9 Vita Nuova 15 The Divine Comedy
　　　　Divine Comedy Part I: 10 The Inferno
　　　　Divine Comedy Part II: 9 Purgatory 10 Purgatorio
　　　　Divine Comedy Part III: 8 Paradise, Paradiso
　　heroine: 8 Beatrice
　　guide: 6 Virgil

Dantes, Edmond
　　character in: 21 The Count of Monte Cristo
　　author: 5 Dumas (pere)

Danton, Ray
　　born: 9 New York NY
　　roles: 14 I'll Cry Tomorrow 18 The George Raft Story 27 The Rise and Fall of Legs Diamond

Danu
　　also: 4 Dana
　　origin: 5 Irish
　　mother of: 14 Tuatha De Danann

Danvers, Mrs
　　character in: 7 Rebecca
　　author: 9 Du Maurier
　　played by: 14 Judith Anderson

Daphnaea
　　epithet of: 7 Artemis
　　means: 11 of the laurel

Daphne
　　form: 5 nymph
　　father: 5 Ladon 6 Peneus
　　pursued by: 6 Apollo 9 Leucippus
　　changed into: 7 bay tree

Daphnis
　　occupation: 7 cowherd 8 shepherd
　　father: 6 Hermes
　　originated: 14 pastoral poetry
　　blinded by: 5 Nomia

Daphnis and Chloe
　　characters in: 12 Greek romance
　　author: 6 Longus

Daphnis et Chloe
　　ballet by: 5 Ravel
　　choreographer: 12 Michel Fokine

dapper 4 neat, trim 5 natty, smart 6 jaunty, modish, spiffy, sporty, spruce 7 stylish

dapple 3 dab, dot 4 spot 6 mottle

dappled 7 flecked, mottled, spotted 10 variegated

Darcy, Fitzwilliam
　　character in: 17 Pride and Prejudice
　　author: 6 Austen

Dardanus
　　father: 4 Zeus
　　mother: 7 Electra
　　twin brother: 6 Iasion
　　wife: 6 Myrina
　　son: 12 Erechthonius
　　ancestor of: 7 Trojans

dare 3 bet 4 defy 5 taunt 7 venture 9 challenge 11 provocation

daredevil 4 bold, rash 5 risky 8 heedless, reckless, stuntman 9 audacious, breakneck, risk-taker 11 adventurous, Evel Knievel 12 death-defying, devil-may-care 13 adventuresome

daredevilry 6 daring 8 rashness 9 derring-do 10 imprudence 12 carelessness, heedlessness, recklessness 13 foolhardiness

Dar es Salaam
　　former capital of: 8 Tanzania

Darien *see* 8 Colombia

daring 4 bold, game 5 brave 6 plucky 7 bravery, courage, gallant, valiant 8 audacity, boldness, intrepid 9 audacious, dauntless, undaunted 10 courageous 11 adventurous, venturesome 13 audaciousness 15 adventurousness

daring deed 4 feat 7 exploit 11 achievement

dark 3 dim 4 deep, evil, inky 5 angry, black, bleak, dingy, dusky, murky, night, shady 6 dismal, dreary, gloomy, hidden, opaque, secret, somber, sullen, wicked 7 evening, joyless, obscure, ominous, shadowy, sunless 8 eventide, frowning, hopeless, overcast, sinister, twilight 9 concealed, nightfall, nighttime, sorrowful 10 forbidding 11 threatening 12 discouraging 13 disheartening

darken 3 dim 4 dye 4 tint 5 cloud, color 6 sadden 7 blacken, obscure 8 dispirit

darkened 3 dim 5 dusky, unlit 6 cloudy, gloomy 7 clouded 9 blackened, tenebrous, unlighted 10 blacked out 13 unilluminated

darkening 7 eclipse, shading 8 clouding, lowering 9 obscuring, shadowing 10 blackening 12 clouding over

dark-hued 5 black, dusky, ebony, raven 6 somber 7 swarthy

Dark Is Light Enough, The
　　author: 14 Christopher Fry

Dark Lady, The
　　author: 16 Louis Auchincloss

Dark Laughter
　　author: 16 Sherwood Anderson

darkness 4 dusk 5 night, shade 7 dimness, evening 8 eventide, twilight 9 blackness, nightfall, nighttime

Darkness at Noon
　　author: 14 Arthur Koestler

Darkness Visible
　　author: 14 William Golding

Dark Victory
　　director: 14 Edmund Goulding
　　cast: 10 Bette Davis 11 George Brent 12 Ronald Reagan 14 Humphrey Bogart 19 Geraldine Fitzgerald
　　remade as: 11 Stolen Hours

darling 4 cute, dear, love 5 loved, sweet 6 adored, lovely 7 beloved, dearest, lovable 8 adorable, charming, precious 9 cherished 10 attractive, enchanting, sweetheart 11 captivating

Darling
director: **15** John Schlesinger
cast: **11** Dirk Bogarde **13** Julie Christie **14** Laurence Harvey
Oscar for: **6** script **7** actress (Christie)

Darling, Wendy
character in: **8** Peter Pan
author: **6** Barrie

darn 4 damn, dang, dash, drat, mend **5** blast, patch, sew up **6** hang it, stitch **7** consarn, doggone, goldang **8** confound **10** confound it

Darnay, Charles
character in: **16** A Tale of Two Cities
author: **7** Dickens

darnel 12 Biblical weed

Darnell, Linda
real name: **20** Monetta Eloyse Darnell
born: **8** Dallas TX
roles: **12** Blood and Sand, Forever Amber **14** The Mark of Zorro **17** Unfaithfully Yours

Darren, James
real name: **13** James Ercolani
born: **14** Philadelphia PA
roles: **6** Gidget **13** The Time Tunnel

dart 3 run **4** bolt, dash, flit, jump, leap, race, rush, tear **5** bound, fling, hurry, spear, spurt **6** hasten, spring, sprint **7** javelin, missile **10** projectile

D'Artagnan
character in: **18** The Three Musketeers
author: **5** Dumas (pere)

Darwin, Charles
author of: **15** The Descent of Man **18** The Origin of Species **20** The Voyage of the Beagle
studied: **16** Galapagos Islands
field: **6** nature **7** biology
nationality: **7** British
theory of: **9** evolution **16** natural selection
ship: **6** Beagle

dash 3 bit, run, zip **4** bolt, dart, drop, elan, foil, hurl, race, ruin, rush, slam, tear, zeal **5** bound, crash, flair, fling, hurry, oomph, pinch, smash, speed, spoil, throw, touch, verve, vigor **6** dampen, energy, hasten, pizazz, spirit, splash, sprint, thrust, thwart **7** a little, panache, shatter, soupcon, spatter **8** splatter, splinter, vivacity **9** animation, frustrate **10** disappoint, discourage

dashing 4 bold **5** brave **6** daring, plucky **7** gallant **8** fearless, spirited, unafraid **9** audacious, impetuous **10** courageous **13** swashbuckling

dash one's hopes 5 daunt, unman **6** deject **7** depress **8** dispirit **10** discourage, dishearten

Dashwood, Elinor and Marianne
characters in: **19** Sense and Sensibility
author: **6** Austen

Da Silva, Howard
real name: **17** Harold Silverblatt
born: **11** Cleveland OH
roles: **8** Oklahoma **12** Sergeant York **14** The Great Gatsby **20** Abe Lincoln in Illinois

Dass, Secundra
character in: **21** The Master of Ballantrae
author: **9** Stevenson

dastard 3 cad **6** coward, craven **7** bounder, caitiff, chicken **8** poltroon **11** yellow-belly

dastardly 3 low **4** base, mean, vile **6** sneaky **8** cowardly, shameful **9** atrocious **10** despicable

data 4 dope, info **5** facts, input **7** dossier, figures **8** evidence **9** documents **11** information

date 3 age, era **5** court, epoch, stage **6** escort, period **7** partner, take out **9** companion, originate **10** engagement, rendezvous **11** appointment

date 18 Phoenix dactylifera
varieties: **5** cliff **6** Ceylon **7** Chinese **9** Jerusalem **12** Canary Island

dated 5 passe **6** old hat **8** obsolete, outmoded **9** out-of-date **10** antiquated **12** old-fashioned **13** unfashionable

daub 4 blot, coat, soil, spot **5** cover, dirty, paint, smear, stain **6** blotch, smirch, smudge **7** splotch

Daudet, Alphonse
author of: **6** Sappho **15** The Woman of Arles **17** Letters from My Mill **18** Tartarin of Tarascon

Daughter of the Regiment, The
opera by: **9** Donizetti

Daumier, Honore
born: **6** France **10** Marseilles
artwork: **7** Bathers **9** Gargantua **12** Men of Justice **13** Bluestockings **14** The Washerwoman **16** The Good Bourgeois **18** The Legislative Body **19** Professors and Pupils **20** Stories from Antiquity **21** The Third-Class Carriage

daunt 3 cow **4** dash, faze **5** abash, alarm, scare **6** deject, dismay, menace, subdue **7** depress, unnerve **8** affright, browbeat, frighten, threaten **10** discourage, dishearten, intimidate

dauntless 4 bold **5** brave, gutsy **6** daring, heroic **7** gallant, valiant **8** fearless, resolute, unafraid, valorous **10** courageous **12** stouthearted

dauntlessness 4 grit, guts, sand **5** nerve, pluck, spunk, valor **6** daring, mettle **7** bravery, courage, resolve **8** boldness **9** fortitude **10** resolution **12** fearlessness, resoluteness **16** stoutheartedness

David 6 statue
by: **12** Michelangelo
site: **8** Florence
size: **6** heroic

David
king of: **6** Israel
father: **5** Jesse
wife: **6** Maacah, Michal **7** Abigail, Ahinoam, Haggith **9** Bathsheba
son: **5** Amnon **7** Absalom, Chileab, Solomon **8** Adonijah
daughter: **5** Tamar
brother: **5** Eliab **7** Shammah **8** Abinadab
sister: **7** Abigail
friend: **5** Abner **8** Jonathan
nephew: **5** Amasa
city of: **9** Bethlehem, Jerusalem
anointed by: **6** Samuel
killed: **7** Goliath
wrote: **6** Psalms
comforter: **7** Abishag
conspirators against: **4** Joab **8** Abiathar, Adonijah
pertaining to: **7** Davidic

David, Jacques-Louis
born: **5** Paris **6** France
artwork: **13** Mme de Verninac **15** The Death of Marat **19** The Oath of the Horatii **23** The Coronation of Napoleon **26** View of the Luxembourg Gardens **31** The Intervention of the Sabine Women

David Copperfield
author: **14** Charles Dickens
character: **3** Ham **6** Barkis, Mr Dick **7** Creakle **8** Traddles **9** Mr Spenlow, Uriah Heep **10** Aunt Betsey, Little Em'ly, Mr Micawber, Rosa Dartle, Steerforth **11** Dora Spenlow, Little Emily, Mr Murdstone, Mr Wickfield, Mrs Gummidge **13** Clara Peggotty **14** Agnes Wickfield, Betsey Trotwood
director: **11** George Cukor
cast: **8** W C Fields **10** Madge Evans **11** Frank Lawton, Roland Young **13** Basil Rathbone, Edna May Oliver **15** Lionel Barrymore **16** Maureen O'Sullivan **18** Freddie Bartholomew

David Harum
author: **19** Edward Noyes Westcott

Davies, Arthur Bowen
born: **7** Utica NY
artwork: **5** Dream **8** Unicorns **9** Crescendo **13** Every Saturday **15** Dancing Children, Sacramental Tree **17** Along the Erie Canal **18** Leda and the Dioscuri

Davies, Marion
real name: **19** Marion Cecilia Douras
lover: **21** William Randolph Hearst
born: **10** Brooklyn NY
roles: **12** Cain and Mable **13** Runaway Romany **15** Tillie the Toiler

Da Vinci, Leonardo
born: **5** Italy, Vinci
artwork: **8** Mona Lisa **10** La Gioconda **13** The Last Supper **15** The Annunciation **19** The Battle of Anghiari **21** The Adoration of the Magi

Davis, Bette
real name: **18** Ruth Elizabeth Davis
husband: **11** Gary Merrill
born: **8** Lowell MA
roles: **7** Jezebel (Oscar) **9** Dangerous
(Oscar), The Letter **10** Now Voyager,
The Old Maid **11** All About Eve,
Dark Victory **14** Of Human Bondage,
The Little Foxes **18** The Petrified
Forest **22** Hush Hush Sweet Char-
lotte **26** What Ever Happened to
Baby Jane?

Davis, H L
author of: **14** Honey in the Horn

Davis, Ossie
wife: **7** Ruby Dee
born: **9** Cogdell GA
author: **16** Purlie Victorious
roles/films: **7** Jamaica **15** A Raisin in
the Sun **18** No Time for Sergeants
19 Cotton Comes to Harlem

Davis, Sammy Jr
wife: **8** May Britt
group: **7** Ratpack **14** Will Master Trio
born: **9** New York NY
autobiography: **7** Yes I Can
roles: **11** Mr Wonderful **12** Porgy and
Bess **20** The Benny Goodman Story

Davis, Stuart
born: **14** Philadelphia PA
artwork: **4** Visa **9** Eggbeater **11**
Lucky Strike, Ready to Wear **11**
Owh! In Sao Pao **12** The Mellow Pad
14 Colonial Cubism **15** Cigarette
Papers

Davy, Humphrey
field: **9** chemistry
nationality: **7** British
isolated: **5** boron **6** barium, sodium **7**
calcium **8** chlorine **9** magnesium, potassium, strontium
invented: **8** Davy lamp **10** miner's
lamp

dawdle 4 idle, loaf **5** dally, delay **6** loiter **10** dillydally **12** putter around **13**
procrastinate

dawdler
French: **7** flaneur

dawdling
French: **8** flanerie

dawn 4 rise **5** begin, birth, occur, start,
sunup **6** advent, appear, Aurora,
emerge, origin, strike, unfold **7** develop, sunrise **8** commence, daybreak,
daylight **9** beginning, emergence, inception, unfolding **12** commencement
god of: **8** Heimdall
goddess of: **3** Eos **6** Aurore, Matuta

dawning 5 sunup **7** morning, sunrise
8 daybreak, daylight

Dawn Patrol, The
director: **14** Edmund Goulding
cast: **10** David Niven, Errol Flynn **11**
Donald Crisp **13** Basil Rathbone **14**
Melville Cooper **15** Barry Fitzgerald

day 3 age, era **4** date, time **5** epoch **6**
period

Day, Clarence (Jr)
author of: **14** God and My Father,
Life with Father, Life with Mother

Day, Doris
real name: **18** Doris von Kappelhoff
born: **12** Cincinnati OH
autobiography: **19** Doris Day Her
Own Story
roles: **10** Pillow Talk **12** Calamity
Jane **13** The Pajama Game **15** Move
Over Darling, The Doris Day Show
23 Please Don't Eat the Daisies

daybed 5 couch **6** lounge **12** chaise
longue

day book 3 log **5** diary **6** agenda **7**
journal **8** calendar, schedule

daybreak 4 dawn, morn **5** sunup **7**
sunrise

daydream 4 muse **5** fancy **7** fantasy,
imagine, reverie **9** fantasize **10** wool-
gather **14** castle in the air

Day for Night
director: **16** Francois Truffaut
cast: **15** Jean-Pierre Leaud **16** Francois Truffaut, Jacqueline Bisset, Jean-
Pierre Aumont
Oscar for: **11** foreign film

daylight 4 dawn **5** sunup **7** morning,
sunrise **8** full view, openness, sunlight, sunshine

Days and Nights
author: **17** Konstantin Simonov

day's end 3 een, eve **4** dusk, even **6**
sunset **7** evening, sundown **8** gleaming, twilight **9** nightfall

Days of Heaven
director: **14** Terrence Malick
cast: **9** Linda Manz **10** Sam Shepard
11 Brooke Adams, Richard Gere
Oscar for: **14** cinematography

Days of Wine and Roses
director: **12** Blake Edwards
cast: **9** Lee Remick **10** Jack Lemmon
11 Jack Klugman **15** Charles Bickford
score: **12** Henry Mancini

daze 4 numb, stun **5** amaze, shock **6**
benumb, dazzle, excite, muddle, stupor **7** astound, confuse, stagger, startle, stupefy **8** astonish, bewilder, surprise **9** disorient, electrify **11**
flabbergast **12** astonishment, bewilderment, blow one's mind **14** discombobulate

dazed 5 woozy **6** groggy **7** confused,
dazzled, stunned **9** befuddled, stupefied **10** bewildered, punch-drunk

dazzle 3 awe **4** blur, daze **5** blind **6**
excite **7** confuse, overawe **9** electrify,
overpower, overwhelm

dazzling 7 radiant **8** blinding **9** sparkling **10** impressive, staggering **11**
coruscating **12** breathtaking, electrifying, overwhelming **14** flabbergasting

deacon 6 cleric **9** churchman, clergyman **12** ecclesiastic

deactivate 6 defuse **9** switch off **10**
neutralize

Dead, The
author: **10** James Joyce

dead, the dead 4 beat, cold, dull, flat
5 depth, exact, midst, quiet, spent,
tired, total, utter, vapid **6** entire, middle, unused **7** defunct, expired, extinct, insipid, precise, useless, utterly,
worn-out **8** abruptly, absolute, complete, deceased, entirely, inactive, lifeless, obsolete, perished, stagnant, suddenly, thorough, unerring **9** exhausted, inanimate, inorganic **10** absolutely, completely, lackluster, unemployed, unexciting **11** ineffectual, inoperative **12** unproductive,
unprofitable
Latin: **8** ad patres
god of: **6** Osiris **7** Veiovis

dead body 5 stiff **6** corpse **7** cadaver,
remains

deaden 4 dope, drug, dull, mute,
numb **5** abate, blunt **6** lessen, muffle,
soothe, subdue, weaken **7** assuage,
smother **8** diminish, mitigate, moderate **9** alleviate **11** anesthetize

deadened 5 muted **6** dulled, numbed
7 muffled, subdued

Dea Dia
origin: **5** Roman
goddess of: **11** agriculture
corresponds to: **13** Acca Laurentia

deadlock 7 impasse **8** standoff **9** stalemate **10** standstill

deadly 3 wan **4** dull **5** ashen, awful,
fatal, fully, undue **6** boring, lethal,
mortal, pallid **7** awfully, baneful, destroy, extreme, ghostly, tedious, totally **8** dreadful, entirely, horribly, terrible, terribly, tiresome **9** excessive,
malignant, wearisome **10** cadaverous,
completely, implacable, inordinate, relentless, thoroughly **11** destructive,
unrelenting

Dead Man Walking
director: **10** Tim Robbins
author: **12** Helen Prejean
cast: **8** Sean Penn (Matthew Poncelet)
9 R. Lee Ermey (Clyde Percy) **11**
Celia Weston (Mary Beth Percy) **12**
Robert Prosky (Hilton Barber) **13**
Raymond J. Barry (Earl Delacroix),
Susan Sarandon (Sister Helen Prejean) **14** Roberta Maxwell (Lucille
Poncelet)

deadpan 5 sober **8** detached **9** impassive **10** poker-faced **11** unemotional
13 straight-faced

dead ringer 4 copy, mate, twin **6** double **9** duplicate **11** counterpart **12**
doppelganger **13** spitting image

Dead Souls
author: **12** Nikolai Gogol

dead to the world 6 asleep **7** out
cold **9** konked out **10** fast asleep,
slumbering **11** sound asleep

dead weight 7 ballast 9 inert mass

Deadwood
   network: 3 HBO
   cast: 8 Anna Gunn (Martha Bullock) 9 Jim Beaver (Ellsworth) 10 Ian McShane (Al Swearengen), John Hawkes (Sol Star) 11 Molly Parker (Alma Garret) 12 Dayton Callie (Charlie Utter), Robin Weigert (Calamity Jane) 14 Paula Malcomson (Trixie) 15 Timothy Olyphant (Seth Bullock) 16 William Sanderson (E. B. Farnum)

Dead Zone, The
   author: 11 Stephen King

deal 3 act 4 give, hand 5 round, see to, trade, treat 6 behave, handle, market 7 bargain, concern, deliver, dole out, give out, mete out, oversee 8 consider, dispense 9 agreement, apportion 10 administer, distribute 11 arrangement 12 distribution 13 apportionment

dealer 5 agent 6 monger, trader, vendor 8 merchant 10 trafficker 11 distributor

dealing, dealings 5 trade 7 traffic 8 business, practice 9 relations, treatment 12 transactions

dealing out 8 dividing 9 allotting, bestowing 10 conferring, consigning, dispensing 12 apportioning, distributing

Dea Marica *see* 6 Marica

Dean, Dizzy (Jay Hanna)
   sport: 8 baseball
   position: 7 pitcher
   team: 16 St Louis Cardinals
   part of: 12 Gashouse Gang
   brother: 4 Paul

Dean, James (Jimmy)
   real name: 14 James Byron Dean
   born: 8 Marion IN
   roles: 5 Giant 10 East of Eden 18 Rebel Without a Cause

Deane, Seneca
   character in: 7 Babbitt
   author: 5 Lewis

Dean's December
   author: 10 Saul Bellow

dear 4 love 5 angel, loved 6 costly 7 beloved, darling 8 esteemed, favorite, precious 9 cherished, expensive, respected 10 sweetheart
   French: 5 cheri 6 cherie

Dear Brutus
   author: 12 James M Barrie

dearest 7 beloved, darling

dearth 4 lack 7 paucity 8 scarcity, shortage 10 deficiency

death, Death 5 dying 6 demise 7 decease, passing 9 departure 10 expiration, grim reaper
   goddess of: 3 Hel 7 Berchta, Perchta 10 Ereshkigal

Death Be Not Proud
   author: 9 John Donne

death blow
   French: 11 coup de grace

Death Comes for the Archbishop
   author: 11 Willa Cather
   character: 7 Jacinto 9 Kit Carson 16 Bishop Jean Latour 20 Father Joseph Vaillant

death-dealing 5 fatal 6 lethal, mortal 7 killing 11 destructive

death-defying 4 bold, rash 5 risky 6 daring 8 reckless 9 audacious, breakneck, daredevil

Death in the Family, A
   author: 9 James Agee
   filmed as: 13 All the Way Home

Death in Venice
   director: 15 Luchino Visconti
   author: 11 Thomas Mann
   cast: 9 Mark Burns 11 Dirk Bogarde 14 Marisa Berenson

deathless 7 eternal 8 immortal 9 perpetual 11 everlasting

deathlike 3 wan 4 pale 5 ashen 6 pallid 7 ghastly 9 bloodless 10 cadaverous, corpselike

deathly 4 very 7 extreme, intense 8 terrible 9 extremely 12 overwhelming 15 resembling death

Death of a Salesman
   director: 12 Laslo Benedek
   author: 12 Arthur Miller
   character: 4 Biff 5 Happy, Linda 7 Bernard, Charley 8 Uncle Ben 10 Willy Loman
   cast: 13 Frederic March, Kevin McCarthy 14 Mildred Dunnock 15 Cameron Mitchell

Death of Ivan Ilyich, The
   author: 10 Leo Tolstoy

Death on the Nile
   author: 14 Agatha Christie

Death Takes a Holiday
   director: 14 Mitchell Leisen
   cast: 11 Guy Standing 13 Evelyn Venable, Frederic March (Death)

Death Valley Days
   host: 12 Robert Taylor, Ronald Reagan 13 Dale Robertson 14 Stanley Andrews

debacle 4 rout, ruin 5 havoc, wreck 8 collapse, disaster, downfall 9 breakdown, cataclysm, overthrow, ruination 10 bankruptcy 11 catastrophe, devastation, dissolution 12 vanquishment 14 disintegration

debar 3 ban 6 reject 7 exclude, keep out 8 preclude, prohibit 9 blackball, blacklist

debark 4 land

debarment 7 removal 8 omission 9 exception, exclusion, exemption, rejection 11 elimination, prohibition 12 nonadmission

debase 5 lower 6 befoul, defile 7 corrupt, degrade 8 disgrace, dishonor 9 desecrate 10 adulterate 11 deteriorate 16 impair the worth of 18 reduce the quality of

debased 4 vile 6 impure 7 corrupt, defiled, lowered 8 degraded, depraved 9 debauched, disgraced, dissolute, perverted 10 degenerate, dissipated 11 adulterated

debasement 9 decadence, depravity 10 corruption, debauchery, degeneracy, immorality, perversion 13 dissoluteness

debatable 4 iffy 6 unsure 7 dubious 8 arguable, doubtful 9 uncertain, undecided 10 disputable 12 questionable 13 problematical

debate 5 argue 6 ponder 7 discuss, dispute, reflect 8 argument, cogitate, consider, hash over 10 cogitation, deliberate, discussion, meditation, reflection, think about 12 deliberation, meditate upon 13 consideration

debauch 4 orgy 5 revel, spree 6 debase 7 carouse, corrupt, deprave, revelry, subvert 8 carousal 9 bacchanal 10 lead astray, saturnalia

debauched 4 lewd 6 wanton 7 corrupt, debased, immoral 8 degraded, depraved, perverse, vitiated 9 abandoned, corrupted, dissolute, lecherous, led astray, perverted, reprobate, shameless 10 degenerate, dissipated, lascivious, libidinous, licentious, profligate 12 disreputable

debauchery 6 excess 11 dissipation 12 immoderation, intemperance 14 self-indulgence

DeBeck, Billy
   creator/artist of: 12 Barney Google 20 Parlor Bedroom and Sink

debilitate 6 weaken 7 wear out 8 enervate 10 devitalize, make feeble 17 deprive of strength

debilitated 5 frail 6 feeble, infirm 7 worn out 8 delicate, weakened 9 enervated 11 devitalized

debilitation 8 handicap, weakness 9 infirmity 10 affliction, disability, impairment, inadequacy 11 disablement

debility 7 fatigue, frailty 8 asthenia, handicap, senility, weakness 9 infirmity, lassitude, weakening 10 affliction, enervation, exhaustion, feebleness, impairment, invalidism, sickliness 11 decrepitude, prostration

debit 4 debt 6 red ink 7 account, payable 9 liability 10 balance due, obligation 11 ledger entry, shortcoming

debonair 5 suave 6 dapper, jaunty, urbane 7 buoyant, elegant, genteel, refined 8 carefree, charming, gracious, well-bred 9 sprightly 11 free and easy 12 lighthearted 13 sophisticated

Deborah 11 Hebrew judge

companion: 7 Rebekah
summoned: 5 Barak

debouch 5 drain 6 emerge, let out 7 flow out 9 discharge

debris 4 crap, junk 5 dreck, dregs, dross, ruins, scrap, trash, waste 6 litter, rubble, shards 7 clutter, garbage, rubbish 8 detritus, wreckage 9 fragments

debt 4 bill 5 debit 7 arrears 9 liability 10 obligation 15 deferred payment, that which is owed

debunk 4 bare 5 strip 6 expose, send up, show up, unmask 7 deflate, lampoon, take off, uncloak, uncover 8 ridicule, satirize 9 burlesque, demystify, disparage 13 demythologize

Debussy, Claude Achille
born: 6 France 15 St Germain-en-Laye
composer of: 5 La Mer 6 Gigues, Iberia, Images 8 Estampes 9 Nocturnes, Printemps 11 Clair de Lune 13 En Blanc et Noir 15 Children's Corner, L'Enfant prodigue 16 La Demoiselle Elue, Suite Bergamasque 17 Rondes de Printemps, The Blessed Damozel 18 Pelleas et Melisande 24 The Girl with the Flaxen Hair 26 Prelude a l'apres-midi d'un faune 28 Prelude to the Afternoon of a Faun

debut 9 coming out 12 presentation

decadence 5 decay 7 decline 10 corruption, debasement, degeneracy, immorality 12 degeneration 13 deterioration

decadent 7 corrupt, debased, immoral 8 decaying, depraved, perverse 9 debauched, dissolute, perverted 10 degenerate
French: 11 fin de siecle

Decalogue 15 Ten Commandments

Decameron, The
author: 17 Giovanni Boccaccio

decamp 7 move off, run away, take off 8 march off, sneak off

decampment 6 escape, flight 7 getaway

decant 4 pour 7 draw off, pour out

decanter 6 bottle, carafe, vessel

decathlon winner 11 Bruce Jenner

Decatur, Stephen
served in: 11 Algerine War, Barbary Wars 13 Tripolitan War 19 War of Eighteen Twelve
commander of ship: 12 United States
defeated ship: 10 Macedonian (British)
saying: 22 "Our country right or wrong"

decay 3 rot 5 spoil 7 corrode, putrefy, rotting 8 spoiling 9 decompose 12 disintegrate, putrefaction 13 decomposition
goddess of: 4 Hour 5 Horae

decayed 3 bad 6 putrid, rotted, rotten, ruined 7 corrupt, gone bad, spoiled 10 decomposed 12 deteriorated 13 disintegrated

deceased *see* 4 dead

deceit 5 fraud 8 cheating, trickery 9 duplicity 10 dishonesty, trickiness 11 fraudulence 13 double-dealing 15 underhandedness 17 misrepresentation

deceitful 5 false 6 crafty, sneaky, tricky 7 cunning 9 dishonest, insincere 11 duplicitous, treacherous, underhanded 12 hypocritical 13 double-dealing, untrustworthy

deceive 3 con 4 fool 5 cheat, put on, trick 6 delude 7 defraud, mislead, swindle

deceiver 4 fake 5 cheat, fraud, quack 6 con man 7 cozener 8 impostor, swindler 9 charlatan, trickster 10 mountebank 13 confidence man

decelerate 5 brake 8 slow down

deceleration 7 braking, slowing

December
event: 11 Pearl Harbor (7), Winter solstice (21, 22)
flower: 5 holly 9 narcissus
French: 8 Decembre
gem: 4 ruby 6 zircon 9 turquoise
German: 8 Dezember
holiday: 7 Kwanzaa (26-Jan 1) 8 Hanukkah 9 Boxing Day (26), Christmas (25) 16 Saint Nicholas Day (6)
Italian: 8 Dicembre
number of days: 9 thirty-one
origin of name: 5 decem (Latin meaning ten)
place in year:
  Gregorian: 7 twelfth
  Roman: 5 tenth
  Julian: 7 twelfth
Spanish: 9 Diciembre
Zodiac sign: 9 Capricorn 11 Sagittarius

decency 7 decorum, modesty 9 propriety 14 respectability 15 appropriateness

decent 4 fair, nice 5 ample 6 proper, seemly 7 correct, fitting 8 adequate, gracious, obliging, passable, suitable 9 courteous 10 acceptable, sufficient 11 appropriate 12 satisfactory 13 accommodating

deception 3 con 4 scam 5 fraud, sting, trick 7 cunning, slyness 8 artifice, illusion, trickery 9 duplicity, falseness, hypocrisy, treachery 10 craftiness, dishonesty, sneakiness, trickiness 11 fraudulence, insincerity 13 deceitfulness, double-dealing 15 underhandedness 17 untrustworthiness

deceptive 5 phony 9 dishonest 10 fraudulent, misleading

decibel
abbreviation: 2 dB

decide 4 rule 5 elect, judge 6 choose, decree, select, settle 7 resolve 9 determine

decided 4 firm 7 certain 8 clear-cut, definite, emphatic, resolute 9 assertive 10 deliberate, determined, unwavering 12 indisputable, strong-willed, unhesitating, unmistakable 14 unquestionable

decidedly 9 certainly 10 absolutely 11 indubitably, undoubtedly 12 indisputably, unmistakably 13 unequivocally 14 unquestionably

decidedness 7 purpose, resolve 10 resolution 12 resoluteness 13 determination 14 purposefulness

decide on 5 adopt, elect 6 choose, opt for, select, settle 7 appoint, arrange, embrace, espouse, pick out 8 settle on 9 determine, establish, single out

decigram
abbreviation: 2 dg

deciliter
abbreviation: 2 dL

decimate 6 reduce 7 destroy 8 massacre 9 slaughter 13 greatly reduce

decimeter
abbreviation: 2 dm

decipher 4 read 5 solve 6 decode, deduce, render 7 decrypt, dope out, explain, make out, unravel 8 construe, untangle 9 interpret, translate 12 cryptanalyze

decision 6 decree, ruling 7 finding, outcome, purpose, resolve, verdict 8 judgment 10 conclusion, resolution 12 resoluteness 13 determination 14 purposefulness

decisive 4 firm 5 final 8 absolute, definite, positive, resolute 10 conclusive, convincing, definitive, determined, undeniable 12 indisputable

decisive blow 9 deathblow 11 coup de grace

decisiveness 7 purpose, resolve 10 resolution 12 resoluteness 14 purposefulness

decisive point 3 nut 4 core, crux, gist 5 basis, heart 6 kernel 7 essence 9 essential

deck 4 garb, trim 5 adorn, array, dress, prank 6 clothe, doll up, enrich, outfit, tog out 7 apparel, bedizen, festoon, furbish, garnish, gussy up 8 accouter, beautify, ornament, spruce up 9 embellish

Decker, Mary
sport: 7 running
married name: 6 Slaney

deck out 5 adorn, array, dress 6 attire, clothe, fit out, outfit, rig out 7 costume

declaim 4 rail 5 orate 6 recite 7 inveigh 9 sermonize 11 pontificate

declaration 6 avowal, notice 8 document 9 assertion, statement, testimony 10 deposition 11 affirmation, attestation, publication **12** announcement, notification, proclamation **14** acknowledgment

declare 4 show **6** affirm, reveal **7** express **8** announce, proclaim **9** pronounce

declare null and void 6 cancel, repeal, revoke **7** abolish, rescind, retract **8** abrogate, set aside **9** repudiate **10** invalidate **11** countermand

declare untrue 4 deny **9** repudiate **10** contradict

decline 3 ebb **4** drop, fail, flag, sink, wane **5** decay, slump, spurn **6** balk at, eschew, lessen, refuse, reject, weaken, worsen **7** dwindle **8** decrease, diminish, downfall **9** downgrade, downswing **11** deteriorate **13** deterioration

Decline and Fall
　author: **11** Evelyn Waugh

Decline and Fall of the Roman Empire, The
　author: **12** Edward Gibbon

declivity 4 drop **5** slant, slope **6** plunge **7** descent

decompose 3 rot **5** decay, spoil **7** putrefy **8** separate **10** go to pieces **12** disintegrate

decomposed 6 putrid, rotted, rotten **7** decayed, spoiled **9** putrefied **13** disintegrated

decontaminate 6 purify **9** disinfect, sterilize

decor 13 ornamentation

decorate 4 trim **5** adorn, array, honor **7** festoon, garnish **8** beautify, ornament **9** embellish

decorated 5 fancy **6** decked, ornate **7** adorned, trimmed **8** bedecked **9** bemedaled, bedizened, garnished **10** ornamented **11** embellished

decoration 4 trim **5** award, badge, medal **6** emblem, ribbon **7** garnish **8** ornament, trimming **9** adornment **13** embellishment, ornamentation **14** beautification

decorous 3 fit **6** decent, polite, proper, seemly **7** correct **8** becoming, mannerly, suitable **9** dignified **10** respectful **11** appropriate

decorum 4 tact **5** taste **7** dignity **8** good form **9** gentility, propriety **10** politeness **14** respectability

decoy 4 bait, lure **5** plant, snare **6** allure, come-on, entice **10** enticement, inducement **11** smoke screen

decrease 4 drop, ease, loss **5** abate, taper **6** lessen, reduce **7** cutback, decline, dwindle, fall-off, slacken, subside **8** diminish **9** abatement, dwindling, lessening, reduction **10** deescalate, diminution **12** de-escalation

decree 3 law **5** edict, order **6** dictum, ruling **7** command, mandate, statute **8** proclaim **9** authorize **12** proclamation

decrepit 7 rickety **8** battered **10** broken-down **11** dilapidated

decrescendo
　music: **22** gradually getting softer
　abbreviation: **4** decr

decry 7 censure, condemn **8** denounce **9** criticize, deprecate, disparage

Dedalus, Stephen
　character in: **7** Ulysses **30** Portrait of the Artist as a Young Man
　author: **5** Joyce

dedicate 6 commit, devote, launch, pledge **7** address, present **8** inscribe

dedication 8 devotion **10** commitment **11** devotedness **16** prefatory address **20** prefatory inscription

Dedlock, Sir Leicester and Lady
　characters in: **10** Bleak House
　author: **7** Dickens

deduce 5 infer **6** gather, reason **8** conclude **10** comprehend, understand

deduct 4 take **6** remove **8** subtract, take from, withdraw **10** decrease by

deduction 5 guess **6** belief, credit, rebate **7** removal **8** analysis, decrease, discount, judgment, markdown, rollback **9** abatement, allowance, exemption, gathering, inference, lessening, reasoning, reduction **10** assumption, concession, conclusion, diminuition, hypothesis, reflection, taking away, withdrawal **11** calculation, presumption, speculation, subtraction, supposition **13** comprehension, consideration, understanding **14** interpretation

Dee, Ruby
　real name: **14** Ruby Ann Wallace
　husband: **10** Ossie Davis
　born: **11** Cleveland OH
　roles: **15** A Raisin in the Sun **16** Purlie Victorious

Dee, Sandra
　real name: **13** Alexandra Zuck
　husband: **10** Bobby Darin
　born: **9** Bayonne NJ
　roles: **6** Gidget **12** A Summer Place **15** Tammy Tell Me True

deed 3 act **4** feat **5** title **6** action, effort **11** achievement **14** accomplishment

deeds are manly, words are womanish
　Italian: **24** fatti maschii parole femine
　motto of: **8** Maryland

deem 4 hold, view **5** judge, think **6** regard **7** believe **8** consider

de-emphasize 8 play down **9** underplay

deep 3 far, sea **4** dark, late, lost, rich, wise **5** far in, midst, ocean, vivid **6** astute, strong **7** extreme, intense, learned **8** absorbed, immersed, involved, profound, resonant, sonorous **9** engrossed, sagacious **10** discerning **11** intelligent **13** philosophical

Deep, The
　author: **13** Peter Benchley

deeply 6 richly **7** acutely, gravely, greatly, vividly **8** entirely **9** intensely, seriously **10** completely, profoundly, resonantly, sonorously, thoroughly **12** passionately

deeply felt 6 ardent, fervid **7** earnest, fervent, intense, sincere, zealous **9** heartfelt **10** passionate **11** impassioned **12** wholehearted

deepness 10 profundity

deep-rooted 7 abiding, lasting **8** enduring **9** confirmed, ingrained

deep-seated 7 abiding, lasting **8** enduring **9** confirmed, ingrained

deep thought 10 absorption, brown study, intentness **11** engrossment **13** concentration

deep water 3 jam **4** mess **5** ocean **6** pickle **7** trouble **8** distress **10** difficulty **11** dire straits, predicament **12** over one's head

deer
　young: **4** fawn
　female: **3** doe
　male: stag

Deer Hunter, The
　director: **13** Michael Cimino
　cast: **10** John Cazale, John Savage **11** Meryl Streep **12** Robert De Niro **17** Christopher Walken
　Oscar for: **7** picture **8** director **15** supporting actor (Walken)

Deerslayer, The
　author: **19** James Fenimore Cooper
　first of: **20** Leatherstocking Tales
　character: **4** Hist **5** Hetty **6** Judith **10** Hurry Harry **11** Natty Bumppo (Deerslayer) **12** Chingachgook, Thomas Hutter

de-escalate 5 limit **6** lessen, narrow **8** contract, minimize

deface 3 mar **4** mark, scar **5** spoil **6** bruise, damage, impair, injure **9** disfigure

de facto 4 real **6** actual, really **8** actually

defalcate 8 embezzle **14** misappropriate

defamation 5 libel **7** calumny, slander **12** vilification **13** disparagement

defamatory 8 libelous **9** vilifying **10** calumnious, derogatory, slanderous **11** disparaging

defame 5 libel **6** malign, vilify **7** degrade, slander **8** derogate **9** denigrate, discredit, disparage **10** calumniate

Defarge, Madame
　character in: **16** A Tale of Two Cities
　author: **7** Dickens

default 10 nonpayment

defeat 4 foil, loss, rout **5** cream, crush, elude, quell **6** baffle, thwart **7** conquer, setback, shellac, trounce **8** confound, overcome, vanquish **9** frustrate, overpower, overthrow, overwhelm, thwarting **11** frustration **14** disappointment

defeated 4 beat **5** upset **6** beaten, bested, licked, routed **7** outdone, whipped, worsted **8** overcame **9** conquered, overthrew, put to rout **10** frustrated, overthrown **11** overpowered, overwhelmed **12** hors de combat

defect 4 flaw, scar, spot **5** break, crack, fault, stain **6** blotch, foible **7** blemish, default, failing, frailty **8** omission, weakness **10** deficiency **11** shortcoming **12** imperfection **14** incompleteness

defective 6 broken, faulty, flawed **7** lacking, wanting **8** abnormal, impaired **9** deficient, imperfect, subnormal **10** inadequate, out of order **11** inoperative **12** insufficient

defend 5 guard **6** secure, shield, uphold **7** endorse, protect, shelter, stand by, support, sustain **8** advocate, champion, maintain, preserve **9** safeguard

defender 8 advocate, champion, guardian, upholder **9** protector, supporter

Defender of the Faith
Latin: **13** Fidei Defensor
title of: **17** English sovereigns

Defenders, The
character: **10** Joan Miller **14** Helen Donaldson, Kenneth Preston **15** Lawrence Preston
cast: **10** E G Marshall, Robert Reed **11** Joan Hackett, Polly Rowles

defense 4 care **5** guard **7** custody, support **8** advocacy, security **9** barricade, safeguard, upholding **10** protection, stronghold **11** maintenance, safekeeping **12** preservation **13** fortification, justification

defenseless 7 unarmed **8** helpless **10** on one's back, vulnerable, weaponless **11** unprotected, unresisting

defensible 3 fit **5** valid **6** proper **7** tenable **8** sensible, suitable **9** allowable, excusable **10** admissible, condonable, forgivable, pardonable, vindicable **11** justifiable, permissible, supportable, warrantable

defer 4 obey **5** delay, table, yield **6** accede, give in, put off, shelve, submit **7** respect, suspend **8** postpone **10** capitulate

deference 5 honor **6** esteem, regard **7** respect **9** obedience, reverence **12** capitulation **13** consideration

deferential 5 civil **6** polite **7** dutiful **8** obedient, reverent **9** courteous, regardful **10** respectful, submissive **11** acquiescent, considerate, reverential

deferment 4 stay **5** delay **9** extension **12** postponement

deferral 5 pause **6** hiatus, recess **8** abeyance **10** suspension **12** postponement **14** discontinuance

defiance 9 hostility, obstinacy, rebellion **12** disobedience **14** rebelliousness

defiant 4 bold **9** truculent **10** aggressive, rebellious **11** disobedient, provocative

Defiant Ones, The
director: **13** Stanley Kramer
cast: **10** Tony Curtis **11** Lon Chaney Jr **12** Cara Williams **13** Charles McGraw, Sidney Poitier, Theodore Bikel
Oscar for: **10** screenplay

deficiency 4 flaw **6** defect **7** failing, frailty **8** shortage, weakness **10** inadequacy **11** shortcoming **12** imperfection **13** insufficiency

deficient 4 weak **6** flawed **7** lacking, short on **8** inferior **9** defective **10** inadequate **11** substandard **12** insufficient **14** unsatisfactory

deficit 8 shortage **9** shortfall **10** deficiency

de fide 10 of the faith

defile 4 soil **5** dirty, smear, spoil, stain, taint **6** befoul, debase **7** degrade, profane, tarnish **8** besmirch, disgrace, dishonor **9** desecrate

defiled 5 dirty **6** fouled, impure, soiled **7** debased, dirtied, stained, sullied, tainted, unclean **8** befouled, polluted, ravished, smirched, violated **9** blackened, corrupted, tarnished **10** besmirched **12** contaminated

define 5 state **7** clarify, explain, specify **8** describe, spell out **9** delineate, designate

definite 3 set **4** sure **5** exact, fixed **7** certain, precise **8** clear-cut, positive

definitely 5 truly **6** indeed, surely **7** for sure, no doubt **9** assuredly, certainly, decidedly, doubtless, expressly **10** absolutely, decisively, explicitly, positively, undeniably **11** indubitably, inescapably, unavoidably, undoubtedly **12** unmistakably **13** categorically, unequivocally **14** unquestionably **16** incontrovertibly

definiteness 8 sureness **9** certainty, precision **10** exactitude **11** unambiguity

definition 6 limits **7** clarity, purpose **11** description **15** distinctiveness

definitive 5 exact **7** decided, perfect **8** complete, decisive, reliable **10** conclusive, consummate

deflate 6 reduce **7** flatten **8** contract **9** devaluate

deflect 6 divert, swerve

Defoe, Daniel
author of: **6** Roxana **11** Colonel Jack **12** Moll Flanders **14** Robinson Crusoe **23** A Journal of the Plague Year

DeForest, Lee
invented/worked on: **10** audion tube, television **13** sound pictures

deform 3 mar **4** maim **5** twist **6** mangle **7** blemish, contort, distort **9** disfigure

deformation 9 deformity **10** distortion **12** malformation **13** disfigurement

deformed 6 marred, warped **7** defaced, mangled, spoiled, twisted **8** crippled **9** misshapen, monstrous **10** disfigured

defraud 3 con **4** bilk, rook **5** cheat **6** fleece, rip off **7** swindle

defray 3 pay **5** cover **11** foot the bill

deft 3 apt **4** able, sure **5** quick **6** adroit, expert **8** skillful **9** dexterous

deftness 5 knack, skill **7** ability **8** facility **9** adeptness, dexterity, handiness **10** adroitness, competency **11** proficiency **12** skillfulness

defunct 4 dead **7** extinct

defy 5 spurn **6** oppose, resist **7** disdain **8** confront **9** challenge, disregard, withstand

degage 4 easy **8** detached **10** disengaged **13** unconstrained

Degas, (Hilaire Germain) Edgar
born: **5** Paris **6** France
artwork: **14** The Ballet Class, The Morning Bath **15** Ballet Rehearsal **16** The Millinery Shop **17** The Glass of Absinth **23** Woman with Chrysanthemums **30** The Little Fourteen-Year-Old Dancer

degeneracy 9 decadence, depravity **10** debasement, debauchery, immorality, perversion **11** dissolution

degenerate 3 rot **4** base, sink, vile **5** decay **6** revert, wanton, wicked, worsen **7** corrupt, debased, decline, go to pot, immoral, pervert, vicious **8** decadent, degraded, depraved **9** abandoned, backslide, debauched, dissolute, perverted **10** dissipated, go downhill, profligate, retrograde, retrogress **11** deteriorate, hit the skids **12** disintegrate

degeneration 7 decline **9** depravity **10** corruption, debasement, immorality, perversion **11** degradation, dissolution, viciousness **13** deterioration

degradation 8 disgrace **11** humiliation

Degradation of the Democratic Dogma, The
author: **10** Henry Adams

degrade 5 lower, shame **6** debase, demote **7** corrupt **8** disgrace, dishonor

degraded 4 vile **6** wicked **7** corrupt, debased, lowered **8** depraved, shameful, unworthy **9** debauched, perverted, reprobate **10** degenerate **11** undignified **12** unregenerate

degrading 3 low **6** menial **8** shameful **11** humiliating

degree 4 mark, step, unit **5** grade, level, order, phase, point, stage **8** division, interval
abbreviation: **3** deg

De Guiche, Lillian
    real name of: **11** Lillian Gish
de gustibus non est disputandum
    29 there is no disputing about tastes
De Havilland, Joan de Beauvoir
    real name of: **12** Joan Fontaine
De Havilland, Olivia
    sister: **12** Joan Fontaine
    born: **5** Japan, Tokyo
    roles: **7** Melanie **10** The Heiress (Oscar) **11** The Snake Pit **12** Captain Blood, To Each His Own (Oscar) **14** Anthony Adverse, My Cousin Rachel **15** Gone With the Wind, Hold Back the Dawn **16** Light in the Piazza **22** Hush Hush Sweet Charlotte **24** The Adventures of Robin Hood
dehydrate 3 dry **5** parch **6** dry out
dehydrated 3 dry **7** parched, thirsty **8** dried-out **9** shriveled **10** desiccated
deification 7 worship **8** idolatry **10** exaltation **13** glorification
deify 5 exalt **7** glorify, idolize, worship
Deighton, Len
    author of: **4** Hope, SS-GB **5** Faith **7** Charity **14** The Ipcress File **15** Funeral in Berlin **16** Catch a Falling Spy
    characters: **11** Harry Palmer **13** Bernard Samson
deign 4 deem **5** stoop **6** see fit **7** consent **8** think fit **10** condescend
Dei gratia 15 by the grace of God
Deiphobus
    father: **5** Priam
    mother: **6** Hecuba
    brother: **6** Hector
    wife: **5** Helen
    killed by: **8** Menelaus
Deirdre
    origin: **5** Irish
    husband: **6** Naoise
    father-in-law: **6** Usnach
    uncle: **9** Conchobar
Deirdre of the Sorrows
    author: **19** John Millington Synge
deity, the Deity 3 god **4** idol **7** goddess, godhead, Jehovah **8** Almighty, divinity, immortal, Olympian
deja vu 11 already seen
dejected 3 low, sad **4** blue, down **7** doleful, unhappy **8** desolate **9** depressed, sorrowful **10** despondent, dispirited, spiritless **11** discouraged, downhearted, low-spirited **12** disconsolate, disheartened
dejection 5 gloom **7** sadness **10** depression, low spirits, melancholy **11** despondency **15** dispiritedness, downheartedness
dejeuner 5 lunch
de jure 7 by right **14** according to law
dekagram
    abbreviation: **3** dkg
dekaliter
    abbreviation: **3** dkL

dekameter, decameter
    abbreviation: **3** dkm
Dekker, Thomas
    author of: **11** Westward Ho! (with John Webster) **20** The Shoemaker's Holiday
de Kooning, Willem
    born: **9** Rotterdam **14** The Netherlands
    artwork: **5** Woman **8** Painting **15** Woman and Bicycle
Delacroix, Eugene
    born: **6** France **18** Charenton-St Maurice
    artwork: **8** Paganini **14** Women of Algiers **15** Massacre at Chios **16** The Barque of Dante **19** Chopin and George Sand **20** Dante and Virgil in Hell **22** Liberty at the Barricades, The Death of Sardanapalus
Delaroche, Paul
    born: **5** Paris **6** France
    artwork: **24** The Death of Queen Elizabeth, The Death of the Duke of Guise **26** The Execution of Lady Jane Grey **36** Children of Edward Imprisoned in the Tower
Delaunay, Robert
    born: **5** Paris **6** France
    artwork: **5** Disks **6** Cities, Rhythm **7** Runners, Windows **10** Cathedrals **11** City of Paris, Eiffel Tower **14** The Cardiff Team **19** Cosmic Circular Forms **28** Simultaneous Prismatic Windows
Delaware
    abbreviation: **2** DE **3** Del
    nickname: **5** First **7** Blue Hen, Diamond
    capital: **5** Dover
    largest city: **10** Wilmington
    others: **5** Acoma, Lewes **6** Easton, Newark, Smyrna **7** Briston, Elsmere, Milford **8** Claymont **9** New Castle **10** Georgetown
    college: **6** Wesley **10** Brandywine, Wilmington **12** Goldey Beacom
    feature: **10** Winterthur **15** Old Swedes Church **17** E I du Pont de Nemours
    tribe: **4** Leni **5** Lenni **6** Lenape, Munsee
    people: **8** Joe Biden **10** Howard Pyle
    island: **7** Fenwick
    land rank: **10** forty-ninth
    physical feature:
        bay: **8** Delaware, Rehoboth
        sea: **8** Atlantic
    river: **8** Delaware **9** Christina, Nanticoke **10** Brandywine
    state admission: **5** first
    state bird: **14** blue hen chicken
    state flower: **12** peach blossom
    state motto: **22** Liberty and Independence
    state song: **11** Our Delaware
    state tree: **13** American holly

Delaware (Lenni-Lenape)
    language family: **9** Algonkian **10** Algonquian
    tribe: **5** Munsi, Unami **6** Munsee **11** Unalachtigo
    location: **7** New York **8** Delaware **9** Manhattan, New Jersey **10** Long Island **12** Pennsylvania, Staten Island
    leader: **7** Tamanen, Tammany
    deity: **11** Kitanitowet
delay 4 slow, stay **5** check, table, tarry **6** dawdle, detain, hamper, hinder, hold up, impede, linger, put off, retard, shelve **7** inhibit, slowing, suspend **8** dawdling, obstruct, postpone, reprieve, stoppage, tarrying **9** deferment, lingering, loitering **10** suspension **12** postponement, prolongation **13** procrastinate
delayed 4 late **6** put off, slowed **7** held up, stalled, tarried **8** arrested, deferred, detained, retarded **9** postponed, slackened **12** dillydallied **14** procrastinated **15** dragged one's feet
Delbruck, Max
    field: **7** biology **17** molecular genetics
    researched: **20** genetic recombination
    awarded: **10** Nobel Prize
delectable 5 tasty, yummy **8** pleasant **9** agreeable, delicious, enjoyable **10** delightful, gratifying **11** pleasurable
delegate 3 rep **4** give, name **5** agent, envoy, proxy **6** assign, charge, deputy **7** entrust **8** give over, transfer **9** authorize, designate **10** commission **14** representative
delegation 11 designation, entrustment **13** authorization, commissioning
delete 3 cut **4** omit **5** erase **6** cancel, remove
deleterious 7 harmful, hurtful, ruinous **9** dangerous, injurious **11** destructive, detrimental
Delia
    festival of: **6** Apollo
deliberate 4 easy, slow, wary **5** weigh **6** confer, debate **7** careful, discuss, examine, express, planned, prudent, willful **8** cautious, cogitate, consider, measured, meditate, mull over **9** leisurely, unhurried **10** calculated, considered, purposeful, thoughtful **11** circumspect, contemplate, intentional, prearranged **12** premeditated
deliberate together 6 confer **7** consult, discuss
deliberation 4 care **6** debate **10** conference, discussion, steadiness **11** calculation, carefulness, forethought **13** premeditation **14** circumspection
Delibes, C P (Clement Philibert) Leo
    born: **6** France **14** St Germain-du-Val
    composer of: **5** Lakme **6** Sylvia **8** Coppelia **10** Le Roi l'a dit
delicacy 4 tact **5** taste **7** frailty **8** accuracy, elegance, fineness, softness,

weakness **9** fragility, frailness, lightness, precision **10** perfection, smoothness **11** savoir-faire, sensibility, sensitivity, unsoundness **13** consideration, exquisiteness, sensitiveness **14** discrimination

delicate 4 fine, soft **5** frail, muted **6** ailing, dainty, feeble, flimsy, infirm, minute, savory, sickly, touchy, unwell **7** careful, elegant, fragile, refined, subdued, tactful **8** detailed, luscious, tasteful, ticklish, weakened **9** breakable, delicious, difficult, exquisite, palatable, sensitive, toothsome **10** appetizing, diplomatic, fastidious, perishable, precarious, scrupulous **11** debilitated

Delicate Balance, A
  author: **11** Edward Albee

delicious 5 tasty, yummy **6** joyful, savory **8** charming, luscious, pleasant **9** palatable **10** appetizing, delectable, delightful **11** pleasurable **13** mouthwatering

delight 3 joy **5** amuse, charm, cheer, revel **6** please **7** enchant, gratify, rapture **8** pleasure **9** enjoyment, fascinate, happiness **13** gratification

delighted 6 elated **7** pleased, psyched **8** ecstatic **9** enchanted **10** captivated, enraptured, enthralled **11** on cloud nine

delightful 6 peachy **7** amiable, amusing **8** charming, engaging, pleasing **9** agreeable, congenial, enjoyable **10** enchanting **11** pleasurable **12** entertaining

delight in 4 love **5** adore, eat up, enjoy, fancy, savor **6** dote on, relish **7** cherish **8** treasure **10** appreciate

Delilah
  lover: **6** Samson
  betrayed: **6** Samson

delineate 4 draw **5** draft **6** define, depict, design, lay out, sketch **7** outline, portray **8** describe **9** represent **12** characterize

delineation 9 depiction, portrayal **11** description **12** illustration **14** representation **16** characterization

delineavit 6 he drew (this) **7** she drew (this)

delinquency 7 misdeed **10** misconduct, negligence **11** dereliction, misbehavior **19** neglect of obligation

delinquent 3 due **4** late **6** remiss **7** hoodlum, misdoer, overdue **8** derelict **9** in arrears, miscreant, negligent, wrongdoer **10** neglectful

delirious 6 raving **7** excited, frantic **8** ecstatic, frenzied **10** incoherent **11** carried away **13** hallucinating

delirium 5 fever **6** frenzy, raving **7** madness, ranting **8** insanity **10** brain fever

Deliro

character in: **22** Every Man Out of His Humour
  author: **6** Jonson

Delisle, Guillaume
  field: **9** geography
  nationality: **6** French
  founder of: **15** modern geography

Delius, Frederick
  born: **7** England **8** Bradford
  composer of: **5** Paris **6** Koanga **7** Eventyr, Irmelin **8** Sea-Drift **9** Brigg Fair **10** Appalachia **11** A Mass of Life, Sur les Cimes **17** Fennimore and Gerda **20** North Country Sketches **22** A Village Romeo and Juliet, Over the Hills and Far Away

deliver 3 aim, say **4** bear, deal, free, give, save **5** bring, carry, throw, utter **6** convey, direct, launch, rescue, strike **7** release, set free **8** give over, hand over, liberate, proclaim, turn over **9** surrender **10** emancipate

deliverance 6 rescue **7** release **9** salvation **10** liberation **12** emancipation

Deliverance
  director: **11** John Boorman
  author: **11** James Dickey
  cast: **8** Ronny Cox **9** Jon Voight, Ned Beatty **12** Burt Reynolds
  song: **13** Dueling Banjos

deliver up 4 cede, give **5** grant, yield **8** fork over, hand over, transfer **9** surrender **10** relinquish

delivery 8 transfer **11** transferral, transmittal **12** transmission

delivery service 3 DHL, UPS **4** USPS **5** FedEx **8** Airborne **11** Express mail

dell 4 dale, dene, glen, vale **5** glade **6** dingle, hollow, valley

Della Robbia, Luca
  born: **5** Italy **8** Florence
  artwork: **8** Cantoria (Singing Gallery) **12** The Ascension **13** Altman Madonna **15** Madonna and Child, The Resurrection

Dello Joio, Norman
  born: **9** New York NY
  composer of: **7** The Ruby **12** Psalm of David **15** New York Profiles, The Trial at Rouen, Triumph of St Joan **20** Proud Music of the Storm, The Lamentation of Saul

Delon, Alain
  born: **6** France, Sceaux
  roles: **10** Purple Noon, The Leopard **13** The Black Tulip **14** Is Paris Burning? **19** Rocco and His Brothers

Delphic
  pertains to: **6** Apollo, Delphi

Delphic oracle
  oracle of: **6** Apollo
  located at: **6** Delphi
  priestess: **6** Pythia

Delphinia
  festival of: **6** Apollo

Del Rio, Dolores

real name: **21** Lolita Dolores Negrette
  born: **6** Mexico **7** Durango
  roles: **11** The Fugitive **13** Madame duBarry **15** Flying Down to Rio, Journey into Fear, Maria Candelaria

Delta Wedding
  author: **11** Eudora Welty

delude 3 con **4** dupe, fool **5** put on, trick **7** deceive, mislead

deluge 4 bury, glut **5** drown, flood, spate, swamp **6** engulf **7** barrage, torrent **8** inundate, overflow, submerge **10** inundation

DeLuise, Dom
  born: **10** Brooklyn NY
  roles: **5** Fatso **6** The End **11** Silent Movie **14** An American Tail, Blazing Saddles **16** Breaking the Fifth
  co-star pal: **12** Burt Reynolds

delusion 8 illusion **9** misbelief **10** aberration **11** derangement **13** hallucination, irrationality, misconception, self-deception

Delusions, Etc. of John Berryman
  author: **12** John Berryman

deluxe 4 fine, posh **5** grand **6** choice, classy **7** elegant **8** splendid **9** luxurious

delve 5 probe **6** search **7** examine, explore **8** look into

demagogue 6 ranter **7** hothead, spouter **8** agitator, fomenter, inflamer **9** firebrand, haranguer **10** incendiary, malcontent, tub-thumper **12** rabble-rouser, troublemaker

demand 4 call, need, want **5** exact, order **7** command, require **11** requirement

demanding 4 hard **5** harsh, rigid **6** strict **8** exacting **9** difficult

demantoid
  species: **6** garnet

demarche 4 gait, plan

demean 5 lower, shame **6** debase, humble **7** degrade **8** disgrace **9** humiliate

demeanor 4 mien **6** manner **7** bearing, conduct **8** behavior, presence **10** appearance, deportment **11** comportment

demented 3 mad **4** nuts **5** crazy **6** crazed, cuckoo, insane **7** lunatic **8** deranged

dementia praecox 13 schizophrenia

dementophobia
  fear of: **8** insanity

demesne 4 land **5** realm **6** domain, estate **8** property

Demeter
  origin: **5** Greek
  goddess of: **5** earth **9** fertility
  protectress of: **8** marriage **11** social order
  father: **6** Cronus
  mother: **4** Rhea
  daughter: **10** Persephone

corresponds to: 5 Brimo, Ceres **8** Despoena
epithet: 5 Chloe, Lusia, Mysia **6** Antaea, Erinys, Stiria **7** Chamyne, Thesmia **8** Stiritis **9** Anesidora, Thermasia **11** Carpophorus **13** Thesimophorus

Demetrius
character in: 21 A Midsummer Night's Dream
author: 11 Shakespeare

De Mille, Agnes
choreographer of: 5 Rodeo **15** Fall River Legend

DeMille, Cecil B
director of: 9 Cleopatra **18** The Ten Commandments **22** The Greatest Show on Earth
niece: 5 Agnes (choreographer)

Demiphon
form: 4 king
sacrificed: 7 maidens
to prevent: 6 plague

demise 3 end **4** fall, ruin **5** death **7** decease, passing **8** collapse **10** expiration

demobilization 7 release **9** discharge **10** disbanding

demobilize 7 disband, release **9** discharge

Democoon
father: 5 Priam
birth: 12 illegitimate
killed by: 8 Odysseus

democracy 8 equality, fairness

Democracy
author: 10 Henry Adams

Democracy in America
author: 19 Alexis de Tocqueville

Democratic Party
symbol: 6 donkey
president belonging to: 4 Polk **6** Carter, Pierce, Truman, Wilson **7** Clinton, (Lyndon Baines) Johnson, Jackson, Kennedy **8** Buchanan, Van Buren **9** Cleveland, (Franklin D) Roosevelt

Democratic Republican Party
president belonging to: 5 (John Quincy) Adams **6** Monroe **7** Madison **9** Jefferson

demode 8 outmoded **13** unfashionable

demoiselle 4 girl

demolish 4 raze, ruin **5** level, total, wreck **7** destroy **9** devastate

demolition 6 razing **8** leveling, wrecking **11** destruction

demon 3 imp **4** jinn, ogre **5** afrit, devil, fiend, genie, harpy, jinni, lamia, satan, troll **6** afreet, dybbuk, goblin **7** incubus, monster, vampire, warlock **8** go-getter, succubus

demonic, demoniacal 6 hectic **7** frantic, hellish **8** devilish, fiendish, frenzied

demonstrable 7 evident **8** apparent, manifest, palpable **11** supportable

demonstrate 4 show **5** march, prove, teach **6** parade, picket, reveal **7** display, exhibit, explain **8** describe, manifest **9** establish **10** illustrate

demonstration 5 march, rally **6** parade **7** display **9** picketing **10** exhibition, exposition, expression **12** illustration, presentation **13** manifestation

demonstrative 7 gushing **8** effusive **12** affectionate

demonstrativeness 9 gushiness **12** effusiveness, emotionalism

demoralize 8 dispirit **9** undermine **10** disconcert, discourage, dishearten **11** disorganize

de mortuis nil nisi bonum 26 of the dead say nothing but good

demos 5 plebs **6** masses, people **7** commons **8** populace **9** commoners

demote 4 bust **5** abase **7** degrade

Dempsey, Jack (William Harrison)
nickname: 13 Manassa Mauler
sport: 6 boxing
class: 11 heavyweight

demur 5 qualm **6** object **7** protest, scruple **8** disagree **9** misgiving, objection **10** hesitation **11** compunction

demure 3 shy **4** prim **6** modest **7** bashful **8** reserved

demurrer 5 doubt, qualm **7** dissent, protest, scruple **8** objector, question, rebuttal **9** challenge, exception, misgiving, objection, protester, protestor, stricture **11** compunction **12** remonstrance

den 4 lair **5** haunt, study **6** hotbed **7** hangout, library, retreat, shelter **9** sanctuary

denial 7 refusal **9** disavowal, disowning, rejection **10** disclaimer

denigrate 4 soil **5** abuse, smear, sully **6** defame, dump on, malign, revile, vilify **7** asperse, blacken, degrade, run down, slander, traduce **8** backbite, badmouth, belittle, besmirch, tear down **9** call names, discredit, disparage, downgrade **10** calumniate, stigmatize

De Niro, Robert
born: 9 New York NY
roles: 4 Heat **6** Brazil **8** Cape Fear, Sleepers **9** Wag the Dog **10** A Bronx Tale, Angel Heart, Awakenings, Goodfellas, Raging Bull (Oscar), Taxi Driver **11** Analyze This, Hide and Seek, Mean Streets **13** The Deer Hunter **14** Meet the Fockers, Meet the Parents, New York New York, The Godfather II **15** The King of Comedy, The Untouchables, True Confessions **17** Bang the Drum Slowly
film festival: 7 Tribeca

denizen 7 dweller **8** resident **10** inhabitant

Denmark
other name: 17 Kongeriget Danmark
capital/largest city: 9 Kobenhavn **10** Copenhagen
others: 3 Hov **4** Hals, Koge, Nibe, Ribe, Soro **5** Arhus, Kosor, Vejle **6** Aarhus, Abenra, Alborg, Dorsor, Dragor, Nyberg, Odense, Skagen, Struer, Viborg **7** Aalborg, Esbjerg, Horsens, Kolding, Morsens, Randers **8** Ballerup, Elsinore, Gentofte, Glostrup, Hillerod, Naestred, Roskilde, Slagelse **9** Haderslev, Helsingor, Svendborg **10** Fredericia **13** Frederikshavn
school:
   university institute of: 18 Theoretical Physics
   folk high school: 14 folkehojskoler
   continuation school: 11 efterskoler
division: 3 Fyn **7** Jutland, Lolland **9** Schleswig, Sjaelland
measure: 3 ell, fod, mil, pot **4** alen, favn, last, rode **5** album, anker, kande, linje, paegl, tomme **6** achtel, paegel, skeppe **7** landmil, oltonde, ortonde, skieppe, viertel **8** fjerding **9** ottingkar **10** korntonmde
monetary unit: 3 one, ora, ore **4** fyrk **5** krone **8** frederik, skilling **9** rigsdaler
weight: 2 es **3** lod, ort, vog **4** last, mark, pund, unze **5** carat, kvint, pound, quint, tonde **7** centner, lispund, quintin **8** lispound, skippund **9** skibslast, skippound **10** bismerpund
island: 2 Oe **3** Als, Fyn, Mon, Rum, Thy **4** Aaro, Aero, Fano, Fohr, Moen, Mors, Romo **5** Baago, Faero, Faroe, Funen, Laeso, Samso, Sando **6** Amager, Sandoy, Sejero, Sudero **7** Faeroes, Falster, Hesselo, Laaland, Lolland, Seeland, Zealand **8** Bornholm, Eysturoy, Sudhuroy **9** Greenland, Langeland, Sjaelland **10** Vendsyssel
lake: 6 Arreso
hill: 12 Ejer Bavnehoj **14** Himmelbjaerget
highest point: 12 Yding Skovhoj
river: 3 Asa **4** Holm, Omme, Stor **5** Skive, Susaa, Varde **6** Gelsaa, Gudena, Vorgod **7** Gudenaa, Lilleaa, Lonborg
sea: 5 North **6** Baltic **7** Oresund **8** Atlantic, Kattegat **9** Skagerrak
physical feature:
   fjord: 3 Ise **4** Isse **5** Lamme
   inlet: 3 Ise **5** Fjord, Vejle **6** Nissum, Odense **7** Horsens, Logstor **8** Limfjord, Mariager
   peninsula: 7 Jutland
   strait: 7 Otesund **8** Kattegat **9** Skagerrak
people: 4 Dane, Jute **5** Angle **6** Cimbri, Eskimo, German, Ostmen, Teu-

ton, Viking **12** Scandinavian
astronomer: 10 Tycho Brahe
author: 11 Isak Dinesen **21** Hans Christian Andersen
founder: 4 Axel **7** Absalon
king: 4 Hans, Knud **6** Canute **8** Frederik **9** Christian **10** Gorm the Old **15** Harold Bluetooth
philosopher: 11 Kierkegaard
physicist: 9 Niels Bohr
queen: 9 Margrethe **12** Thyra Danebod
sculptor: 11 Thorvaldsen
teacher: 4 Kold
language: 4 Odan **6** Danish, German **8** Faeroese **11** Greenlander
religion: 19 Evangelical Lutheran
place:
  airport: 7 Kastrup
  castle: 7 Egeskov **8** Kronborg **13** Frederiksborg
  museum: 6 Rebild **9** Glyptotek **11** Thorvaldsen **15** Rosenborg Castle
  park: 10 Langelinie **13** Tivoli Gardens
  royal palace: 11 Amalienborg
  statue: 13 Little Mermaid
  stock exchange: 5 Borse **6** Borsen
feature:
  dance: 6 sextur
  drink: 5 glogg **7** aquavit
  beer: 6 Tuborg **9** Carlsberg
food:
  cheese: 3 Ost **4** Blue, Tybo **5** Esrom, Samso **6** Samsoe **7** Havarti, Mycella
  meat patty: 11 frikadeller
  pudding: 15 rodgrod med flode
Dennis, Patrick
  author of: 10 Auntie Mame
Dennis, Sandy
  real name: 16 Sandra Dale Dennis
  born: 10 Hastings NE
  roles: 12 Any Wednesday **15** A Thousand Clowns **18** Up the Down Staircase **25** Who's Afraid of Virginia Woolf?
Dennis the Hangman
  character in: 12 Barnaby Rudge
  author: 7 Dickens
Dennis the Menace
  creator: 11 Hank Ketcham
  character: 9 Mrs Elkins **10** John Wilson **12** Eloise Wilson, George Wilson, Joey McDonald, Martha Wilson **13** Alice Mitchell, Henry Mitchell, Tommy Anderson **14** Dennis Mitchell
  dog: 4 Ruff
  cast: 8 Gil Smith, Jay North **10** Billy Booth, Gale Gordon, Sara Seeger **11** Gloria Henry, Irene Tedrow, Sylvia Field **12** Joseph Kearns **15** Herbert Anderson
denomination 4 name, sect, size **5** class, value **8** category, grouping **10** persuasion **11** designation
denotation 4 mark, name, sign **6** symbol **7** meaning **10** indication

denote 4 mark, mean, name **6** signal **7** signify **8** indicate
denouement 3 end **6** finale, upshot **7** outcome **8** solution **10** conclusion **11** termination
denounce 6 accuse, vilify **7** censure, condemn **9** criticize
denouncement 7 censure **12** condemnation, denunciation
de novo 4 anew **5** again **6** afresh **16** from the beginning
dense 4 dull, dumb, slow **5** close, heavy, thick **6** stupid **7** compact, crowded, intense **8** ignorant **9** dimwitted **10** compressed **11** thickheaded **12** concentrated, impenetrable
Densher, Merton
  character in: 17 The Wings of the Dove
  author: 5 James
density 4 mass **6** weight **7** opacity **8** dullness, solidity **9** stupidity, thickness **10** obtuseness, opaqueness **11** compactness
dent 3 pit **4** nick **6** hollow **10** depression **11** indentation
denude 4 bare **5** strip **6** divest **7** lay bare **8** unclothe
denuded 4 bare **5** naked **6** barren **8** stripped **9** unclothed, uncovered
denunciation 7 censure **12** condemnation, denouncement **13** attack against
Denver
  basketball team: 7 Nuggets
  football team: 4 Gold **7** Broncos
deny 6 refuse, refute **7** disavow **8** disallow, disclaim **9** disaffirm **10** contradict
deny oneself 5 avoid, forgo **6** eschew, give up, refuse **7** abstain, forbear **8** renounce **9** sacrifice
deny responsibility 7 disavow
Deo gratias 13 thanks be to God
Deo volente 10 God willing
DePalma, Brian
  director of: 6 Carrie **8** Scarface **11** Carlito's Way, Femme Fatale, Raising Cain **13** Dressed to Kill, Mission to Mars **15** The Untouchables **17** Mission: Impossible **20** Bonfire of the Vanities
depart 2 go **4** exit **5** leave **6** embark **7** deviate, digress, entrain
departed 4 dead, gone, late, left, past, went **6** at rest, bygone **7** gone off **8** gone away **10** passed away **11** gone to glory **12** late-lamented **20** gone the way of all flesh
depart for 8 leave for **9** adjourn to, set off for, set out for **10** head toward, move toward
depart hastily 3 fly **4** flee **5** elope **6** decamp, escape **7** abscond **9** skedaddle

department 4 unit **6** branch, bureau, sector **7** section **8** district, division, province
departure 4 exit **5** going **6** exodus **7** leaving **9** deviation **10** digression, divergence
depend 4 rely, rest **5** count, hinge **6** hang on
dependable 4 sure, true **5** loyal **6** steady, trusty **7** trusted **8** faithful, reliable **9** steadfast, unfailing **11** trustworthy
dependence 5 trust **8** reliance **10** confidence, dependency
dependency 10 dependence
dependent 7 reliant
depict 4 draw, limn **5** carve, chart, draft, paint **6** define, detail, map out, recite, record, relate, sculpt, sketch **7** diagram, narrate, picture, portray, recount **8** describe **9** chronicle, delineate, dramatize, represent, verbalize **10** illustrate **12** characterize
depiction 6 sketch **7** drawing, picture **8** portrait **9** picturing, portrayal **11** delineation **12** illustration **14** representation **16** characterization
deplete 5 drain, use up **6** lessen, reduce **7** consume, exhaust **8** decrease **10** impoverish
depleted 5 empty, spent, waste **6** barren, used up **7** drained, emptied, reduced, worn out **8** bankrupt, consumed, expended, lessened **9** exhausted, infertile **10** unfruitful
deplorable 5 awful **8** wretched **9** miserable **11** blameworthy **13** reprehensible **17** deserving reproach
deplore 5 mourn **6** bemoan, bewail, lament **7** censure, condemn **9** grieve for **12** disapprove of
deport 3 act **4** oust **5** carry, exile, expel **6** banish, behave **7** cast out **10** expatriate **14** conduct oneself
deported person 2 DP **5** exile **8** deportee **10** expatriate **14** banished person
deportment 7 conduct **8** behavior, demeanor **11** comportment
depose 4 oust **6** unseat **8** dethrone **16** remove from office
deposit 3 put **4** pile **5** place **7** put down, set down **8** sediment **10** accumulate **11** down payment, give in trust, installment **12** accumulation **14** partial payment
deposition 7 deposit **9** statement, testimony **11** declaration **12** accumulation
depository 4 bank, safe **5** vault **6** museum **7** library **8** archives **10** storehouse
depot 4 dump **7** station **8** terminal, terminus **10** bus station **15** railroad station **20** military storage place
depraved 4 vile **6** wicked **7** corrupt,

debased **8** degraded **9** debauched, perverted **10** degenerate

depravity 8 vileness **9** decadence **10** corruption, debasement, debauchery, degeneracy, immorality, perversion, wickedness **11** degradation, dissolution

deprecate 6 insult **7** condemn, protest **8** belittle, object to, play down **10** depreciate **15** take exception to

deprecated 7 defamed, put down **8** despised **9** belittled, derogated, disdained

deprecation 4 slur **5** abuse **7** protest, put-down **9** aspersion **10** aspersions, belittling, defamation, derogation **11** disapproval **12** condemnation **13** disparagement

deprecatory 8 critical **9** insulting, maligning, vilifying **10** belittling, defamatory, derogatory, slanderous **11** disparaging **12** disapproving

depreciate 5 scorn **7** run down **8** belittle, diminish **9** denigrate, disparage, downgrade, lose value **13** reduce in value, lower the value

depreciation 5 scorn **7** disdain **8** contempt **9** criticism, deflation **10** belittling, disrespect **11** devaluation **13** disparagement

depredation 4 sack **6** rapine, ravage **7** looting, pillage, plunder, robbery, sacking **8** spoiling **9** marauding **10** brigandage, ravishment, spoliation **11** desecration, devastation, freebooting, laying waste

depress 5 lower **6** deject, lessen, reduce, sadden, weaken **7** cut back **8** diminish, dispirit **9** press down **10** dishearten **14** lower in spirits

depressed 3 sad **4** blue **7** unhappy **8** dejected, downcast **10** despondent, dispirited, melancholy **11** low-spirited **12** disconsolate, inconsolable

depressing 3 sad **6** gloomy **8** lowering **9** dejecting, saddening **10** oppressing **11** casting down, dispiriting, melancholic, pushing down **12** discouraging, pressing down, weighing down **14** causing sadness

depression 5 gloom **6** dimple, hollow **7** sadness **9** dejection, recession **10** desolation, melancholy **11** despondency, indentation, melancholia **14** discouragement **15** downheartedness, economic decline

deprive 5 strip **6** divest **8** take from **10** confiscate, dispossess

deprived 8 divested, stripped **11** handicapped **12** dispossessed, impoverished **13** disadvantaged **15** underprivileged

deprive of honor 5 abase, shame, sully **6** defame **7** blacken, tarnish **8** disgrace, dishonor **9** discredit **10** stigmatize

deprive of strength 6 hinder, weaken **7** disable, wear out **8** enervate, enfeeble, handicap **10** debilitate, devitalize

de profundis 13 from the depths

depth 6 timbre **8** deepness **10** profundity **19** downward measurement **24** perpendicular measurement

depths 4 deep **6** bowels **8** interior, recesses

deputation 9 committee **10** commission, delegation **15** representatives

deputize 6 assign **7** appoint **8** delegate **10** commission

deputy 4 aide **5** agent, envoy, proxy **6** second **8** delegate, emissary, minister **9** alternate, assistant, go-between, messenger, middleman, surrogate **10** ambassador, substitute **11** pinch hitter **12** spokesperson **14** representative **15** second-in-command

DeQuincey, Thomas
author of: **19** The English Mail-Coach **31** On the Knocking at the Gate in Macbeth **32** Confessions of an English Opium-Eater

derail 3 bar **4** balk, foil **5** block, check, spike **6** hinder, impede, thwart **7** inhibit, prevent **8** obstruct **14** throw off course

deranged 3 mad **5** crazy **6** insane **8** demented **10** irrational, unbalanced

derangement 6 lunacy **7** madness **8** insanity **9** craziness **11** peculiarity **13** irrationality, mental illness **14** mental disorder

Der Bingle
nickname of: **10** Bing Crosby

Derby 4 race
site: **5** Epsom **8** Kentucky **14** Churchill Downs

Derek, Bo
real name: **11** Mary Collins
husband: **4** John
roles: **3** Ten (10) **6** Bolero, Tarzan **8** Tommy Boy

derelict 3 bum **4** hobo **5** tramp **6** remiss **7** outcast, vagrant **8** careless, deserted **9** abandoned, negligent **10** delinquent, neglectful

dereliction 7 failure, neglect **9** disregard **10** negligence **11** delinquency **13** noncompliance, nonobservance

De rerum natura
author: **9** Lucretius

deride 4 mock **5** scoff, scorn **7** sneer at **8** ridicule

de rigueur 11 fashionable **16** strictly required

derision 5 scorn **7** disdain, mockery **8** ridicule, sneering

derivation 5 stock **6** origin, source **7** descent, getting, lineage **8** ancestry, deriving, heritage **9** acquiring, etymology, parentage **10** background,

beginnings, extraction **21** historical development

derive 4 gain **5** arise, enjoy, glean **6** obtain **7** descend **8** stem from **9** originate

dermaptera
class: **8** hexapoda
phylum: **10** arthropoda
group: **6** earwig

dermatitis 4 rash **6** eczema **9** psoriasis **12** inflammation

Dern, Bruce
born: **9** Chicago IL
wife: **9** Diane Ladd **12** Andrea Becker
daughter: **9** Laura Dern
roles: **6** Marnie, Tattoo **7** Madison, Monster **10** Coming Home, Family Plot **11** Black Sunday **13** The Wild Angels **14** The Great Gatsby **22** The King of Marvin Gardens

dernier 4 last **5** final **8** ultimate

dernier cri 9 latest cry **10** latest word **13** latest fashion

derogate 4 blot **5** taint **6** smirch **8** disgrace **9** disparage

derogation 4 blot **5** odium, stain **7** blemish **8** contempt, disfavor, disgrace, ignominy **9** disesteem, disrepute **10** disrespect **11** humiliation **13** disparagement

derogatory 9 injurious **10** belittling **11** disparaging, unfavorable **12** unflattering **15** uncomplimentary

derrick 3 rig **5** crane, hoist, tower **9** framework
kind: **3** oil **6** sheers **7** gin-pole
part: **3** gin, leg **4** boom, mast **6** pulley **7** guy line

derring-do 6 daring **8** audacity, boldness **11** daredevilry **12** daredeviltry, recklessness **15** venturesomeness

dervish 5 fakir **6** Muslim **7** ascetic

De Sapientia Veterum
author: **12** Francis Bacon

Descartes, Rene
author of: **17** Discourse on Method
field: **11** mathemathics
nationality: **6** French
developed: **18** analytical geometry
quote: **13** Cogito ergo sum **18** I think therefore I am
pertaining to: **9** Cartesian

descend 3 dip **4** drop, pass **5** slant, slope, swoop **6** go down, invade **7** incline **8** come down, inherited **11** come in force **12** be handed down, move downward

descendant 5 issue, scion **7** progeny **9** offspring

descend upon 6 assail, attack, charge **7** assault, set upon **12** bear down upon

descent 4 drop, fall, raid **5** slant, slope **6** origin **7** assault, decline, lineage **8** ancestry **9** declivity, incursion **10**

coming down **11** sneak attack, sudden visit

describe 4 draw **5** trace **6** depict, detail, recite, relate **7** explain, mark out, narrate, outline, portray, recount, speak of **9** delineate **10** illustrate **12** characterize

description 3 ilk **4** kind, sort, type **5** brand, class, genus **6** manner, nature **7** account, species, variety **9** depiction, narration, portrayal **12** illustration **16** characterization

descry 3 see **4** spot **6** behold, notice **7** discern, observe, pick out **8** discover **12** catch sight of

Desdemona
character in: **7** Othello
author: **11** Shakespeare

desecrate 6 defile **7** profane, violate **8** dishonor

desecration 8 dishonor **9** violation **10** defilement **11** profanation

desert 3 dry **4** arid, wild **5** leave, waste **6** barren **7** abandon, forsake **8** desolate, untilled **9** infertile, wasteland **10** arid region **11** run away from, uninhabited **12** uncultivated **16** barren wilderness
world: **4** Gobi, Thar **6** Gibson, Libyan, Mohave, Nubian, Sahara, Syrian **7** Arabian, Atacama, Kara Kum, Painted, Sonoran **8** Kalahari **9** Patagonia **10** Great Sandy **11** Death Valley
watering spot: **5** oasis

deserted 4 AWOL, left **5** empty **6** lonely, vacant **7** cast off, forlorn, reneged **8** defected, desolate, forsaken, marooned **9** abandoned, absconded **12** quit one's post **14** left in the lurch

desertedness 7 emptiness **10** desolation **13** uncrowdedness

Deserted Village, The
author: **15** Oliver Goldsmith

desertion 8 quitting **9** forsaking **11** abandonment **14** relinquishment

desertlike 3 dry **4** arid, sere **5** sandy **6** barren **7** dried up, parched **9** waterless

deserts 3 due **5** worth **6** reward **7** payment

deserve 4 rate **5** merit **7** warrant **9** earn as due **10** be worthy of, qualify for **12** be entitled to **13** be deserving of

deserving 6 worthy **9** qualified

deserving reproach 8 blamable **10** deplorable, punishable, reprovable **11** blameworthy **12** reproachable **13** reprehensible

De Sica, Vittorio
director of: **15** The Bicycle Thief **27** The Garden of the Finzi-Continis

desiccate 5 dry up, parch **6** wither **7** shrivel **9** dehydrate

design 3 aim, end **4** draw, form, goal, plan, plot **5** draft, motif, set up **6** devise, intend, scheme, sketch, target **7** destine, diagram, drawing, fashion, outline, pattern, project, purpose **8** conceive, intrigue **9** blueprint, intention, objective **11** arrangement **14** draw up plans for

designate 4 call, name, term **5** elect, label **6** assign, choose, select **7** appoint, signify, specify **8** identify, indicate, nominate, pinpoint

designation 5 label **6** naming **10** delegation **11** appointment **13** specification **14** identification

designer 7 creator, deviser, planner **9** contriver **10** originator

designing 4 wily **6** artful, crafty **7** cunning **8** plotting, scheming **9** conniving

desirable 4 fine **8** in demand, pleasing **9** advisable **10** beneficial **11** worth having **12** advantageous

desire 3 yen **4** need, urge, want, wish **5** crave **6** ask for, hunger, thirst **7** craving, longing, long for, request **8** yearning, yearn for **9** hunger for, thirst for

Desire Under the Elms
author: **12** Eugene O'Neill
character: **4** Eben **5** Peter **6** Simeon **11** Abbie Putnam **12** Ephraim Cabot

desirous 4 avid, keen **5** eager **7** hopeful, longing, wishful **8** yearning

desist 4 stop **5** cease **6** lay off **7** suspend **8** leave off **11** discontinue, refrain from

Desk Set
director: **10** Walter Lang
cast: **8** Gig Young **11** Dina Merrill **12** Joan Blondell, Spencer Tracy **16** Katharine Hepburn

desolate 3 sad **4** bare, ruin **5** bleak, empty **6** barren, grieve, ravage, sadden **7** depress, destroy, forlorn **8** dejected, demolish, deserted, distress, downcast, forsaken, lay waste, wretched **9** abandoned, depressed, devastate, miserable, sorrowful **10** despondent, discourage, dishearten, melancholy **11** downhearted, uninhabited

desolating 6 tragic **7** ruinous **8** dreadful, grievous, terrible **10** calamitous, horrendous **11** devastating **12** catastrophic

desolation 4 ruin **6** misery, sorrow **7** sadness **8** bareness, distress, solitude **9** bleakness, dejection, emptiness, seclusion **10** barrenness, depression, dreariness, loneliness, melancholy, wilderness **11** destruction, devastation, unhappiness **12** solitariness

despair 5 gloom, trial **6** burden, ordeal **9** lose heart **10** depression, have no hope **11** despondency, lose faith in **12** hopelessness **14** discouragement

despair of 5 doubt **8** give up on **10** have no hope

desperado 4 thug **5** rowdy **6** bandit, gunman, outlaw **7** brigand, convict, hoodlum, ruffian **8** criminal, fugitive, hooligan **9** terrorist **10** lawbreaker

desperate 4 dire, rash, wild **5** grave, great **6** daring, urgent **7** extreme, frantic, serious **8** critical, hopeless, reckless, wretched **9** dangerous, incurable **10** beyond hope, despairing, despondent

Desperate Hours, The
director: **12** William Wyler
cast: **8** Gig Young **11** Dewey Martin, Martha Scott **13** Arthur Kennedy, Frederic March **14** Humphrey Bogart

Desperate Housewives
network: **3** ABC
cast: **9** Cody Kasch (Zach Young), Mark Moses (Paul Young) **10** Doug Savant (Tom Scavo), Steven Culp (Rex Van De Kamp) **11** Andrea Bowen (Julie Mayer), Eva Longoria (Gabrielle Solis), James Denton (Mike Delfino), Marcia Cross (Bree Van De Kamp), Teri Hatcher (Susan Mayer) **12** Brenda Strong (Mary Alice Young) **13** Jesse Metcalfe (John Rowland) **14** Ricardo Chavira (Carlos Solis) **15** Felicity Huffman (Lynette Scavo) **18** Nicollette Sheridan (Edie Britt)

Desperately Seeking Susan
director: **14** Susan Seidelman
cast: **7** Madonna **15** Rosanna Arquette

desperation 7 despair **12** hopelessness, recklessness

despicable 4 base, mean, vile **10** detestable, outrageous **11** disgraceful **12** contemptible **13** reprehensible

despise 5 abhor, scorn **6** detest, loathe **7** contemn, disdain, dislike **10** look down on

despoil 3 rob **4** loot **6** ravage **7** pillage, plunder

despoiler 6 looter, robber, vandal **7** brigand **8** pillager **9** plunderer

despondency 5 gloom **6** dismay **7** despair, sadness **9** dejection, pessimism **10** depression, desolation, low spirits, melancholy **11** melancholia **12** hopelessness **14** discouragement **15** downheartedness

despondent 3 low **4** blue, down **8** dejected, downcast, hopeless **9** depressed **11** discouraged, downhearted **12** disconsolate, disheartened

despot 4 czar, tsar **6** tyrant **8** autocrat, dictator **9** oppressor

despotic 9 imperious **10** autocratic, tyrannical **11** dictatorial **13** authoritarian

despotism 7 tyranny **9** autocracy **10** absolutism

dessert 3 pie 4 cake, nuts, tart 5 fruit, sweet, treat 6 pastry 7 cobbler 8 ice cream 11 final course

destination 3 aim, end 4 goal, plan 6 object, target 7 purpose 8 ambition 9 objective 11 journey's end

destiny 3 lot 4 fate 5 karma, moira 6 future, kismet 7 fortune 9 necessity
goddess of: 5 Fates, Morae, Parca 6 Moerae, Moirai, Parcae

destitute 4 poor 5 broke, needy 6 busted 8 indigent 9 penniless 15 poverty-stricken

destitution 4 lack, want 6 penury 7 beggary, poverty 9 indigence, privation 11 extreme want 13 pennilessness 14 impoverishment

destroy 4 ruin 5 waste, wreck 6 ravage 8 demolish 9 devastate

destroy completely 3 end 4 rase, raze 5 total 7 abolish, wipe out 8 lay waste 9 eradicate, extirpate, liquidate 10 annihilate, obliterate 11 exterminate

destroyer 4 bane 6 blight, killer 7 gunboat, warship 10 affliction 11 annihilator

destruct 3 gut 4 raze, ruin 5 wreck 7 despoil, destroy, wipe out 8 decimate, demolish, desolate, pull down, tear down 9 devastate 10 lay in ruins

destruction 4 ruin 5 havoc 8 wreckage, wrecking 10 demolition 11 devastation

destructive 7 harmful, hurtful, ruinous 8 damaging 9 injurious 11 detrimental, devastating 15 not constructive

Destry Rides Again
director: 14 George Marshall
based on a story by: 8 Max Brand
cast: 12 Brian Donlevy, James Stewart 15 Marlene Dietrich 16 Charles Winninger
song: 35 See What the Boys in the Back Room Will Have

desultory 4 idle 6 casual, chance, fitful, random 7 aimless, cursory 9 haphazard 10 without aim 11 unconnected

detach 5 sever 6 loosen 7 unhitch 8 separate, unfasten 9 disengage 10 disconnect 11 disentangle

detached 4 fair 5 aloof 7 distant, neutral, severed 8 reserved, unbiased 9 impartial, objective, separated, uncoupled, unhitched 10 disengaged, fairminded, unfastened 11 indifferent, unconnected 12 disconnected, unprejudiced 13 disinterested, dispassionate
French: 6 degage

detachment 4 unit 5 force 8 coolness, fairness, severing 9 aloofness, isolation, severance 10 cutting off, neutrality, separation 11 objectivity 12 impartiality, indifference 13

disconnection, disengagement, preoccupation 16 special task force

detail 4 fact, iota, item 6 aspect, relate 7 appoint, feature, itemize, recount, respect, specify 9 component, delineate, designate, enumerate 10 detachment, particular 11 special duty 13 assign to a task, particularize 14 special service 20 particular assignment

detailed 6 minute 8 itemized, thorough 10 item by item 12 point by point

detailed list 9 breakdown 11 itemization 14 categorization

detain 4 hold, slow, stop 5 delay 6 arrest, hinder, retard, slow up 7 confine 8 slow down 13 keep in custody

detainment 7 custody, holding 9 detention 11 confinement 12 imprisonment 13 incarceration

detect 3 see 4 espy, note, spot 5 catch 6 notice 7 observe, uncover 8 discover, perceive

detectable 10 noticeable 11 appreciable, discernible, perceivable, perceptible 13 ascertainable

detective 2 PI 3 tec 6 shamus, sleuth 7 gumshoe 10 private eye 12 investigator 19 special investigator

detectives 5 Kojak 7 Columbo, Matlock 8 Magnum P.I., Sam Spade 9 Hardy Boys, James Bond, Nancy Drew 10 Bertha Cool, Goldfinger, Harry Bosch, Mike Hammer, Miss Marple, Perry Mason 11 Charlie Chan, Ellery Queen 12 Father Dowling, Hercule Poirot, Philip Marlowe 14 Lucas Davenport, Sherlock Holmes 15 Jessica Fletcher

detention 7 custody, holding 9 keeping in 10 detainment 11 confinement, holding back 12 imprisonment 13 incarceration

deter 4 stop 5 daunt 6 divert, hinder, impede 7 prevent 8 dissuade 10 discourage

deteriorate 3 ebb 4 fade, wane 5 decay, lapse 6 worsen 7 crumble, decline, fall off 10 degenerate 12 disintegrate

deteriorated 6 shabby 7 rickety 8 decaying, worsened 9 crumbling 10 broken-down, tumble-down 11 dilapidated, in disrepair 13 disintegrated

deterioration 5 decay, lapse 6 fading, waning 7 decline 9 crumbling, decadence, worsening 12 degeneration, dilapidation 14 disintegration

determination 4 grit 5 pluck, power, spunk 6 fixing 7 finding, resolve, verdict 8 boldness, decision, judgment, settling, solution, tenacity 9 reasoning, resolving 10 conclusion, resolution 11 determining, persistence 12 perseverance, resoluteness 13 act of

deciding, steadfastness 16 stick-to-itiveness

determine 5 learn 6 affect, decide, detect, settle 7 control, find out, resolve 8 conclude, discover, regulate 9 ascertain, establish, figure out, influence 15 come to a decision, give direction to

determined 7 dead set, decided, settled 8 found out, obdurate, resolute, stubborn 9 obstinate, tenacious 10 figured out 11 ascertained, established 15 come to a decision

deterrent 4 curb 5 check 9 hindrance, restraint 14 discouragement

detest 4 hate 5 abhor 6 loathe 7 despise 10 recoil from 16 dislike intensely

detestable 4 vile 6 odious 7 hateful 9 abhorrent, loathsome, obnoxious, offensive, repulsive, revolting 10 disgusting, unpleasant 12 disagreeable

detestation 4 hate 6 hatred 7 disgust, dislike 8 aversion, distaste, loathing 9 antipathy, repulsion, revulsion 10 abhorrence, repugnance

dethrone 4 oust 6 depose, unseat

detonate 4 fire 5 blast, burst, erupt, go off, shoot 6 blow up, ignite, report, set off 7 explode 8 touch off 9 discharge, fulminate

detonation 5 blast, burst 6 report 9 discharge, explosion

detour 5 skirt 6 bypass, byroad, divert 7 digress 9 deviation, diversion 10 digression

detract 5 lower 6 lessen, reduce 8 diminish 12 subtract from, take away from

detraction 4 flaw 11 shortcoming 12 disadvantage

detractor 5 enemy 6 critic 8 opponent 9 adversary, belittler, slanderer 10 antagonist, bad mouther, disparager

detriment 4 harm, loss 6 damage, injury 10 impairment 12 disadvantage

detrimental 7 adverse, harmful 8 damaging 9 injurious 10 pernicious 11 deleterious, destructive, unfavorable 15 disadvantageous

Detroit
baseball team: 6 Tigers
basketball team: 5 Shock 7 Pistons
football team: 5 Lions
hockey team: 8 Redwings

de trop 7 too many, too much 8 in the way 9 not wanted

Deucalion
father: 10 Prometheus
mother: 7 Pronoia
wife: 6 Pyrrha
son: 6 Hellen
founded: 9 human race
after: 6 deluge

deus ex machina 15 god from a machine 18 improbable solution

Deus vobiscum 12 God be with you

Deus vult 8 God wills (it)
   cry of: 9 Crusaders

devaluate 6 lessen, reduce 7 deflate, degrade 10 depreciate

devaluation 4 drop 7 decline 12 depreciation

devalue 5 lower, taint 6 debase, defile, infect 7 cheapen, corrupt, degrade, pervert, pollute, revalue 8 mark down 9 devaluate, underrate, write down 10 adulterate, degenerate, demonetize, depreciate, remonetize 11 contaminate

devastate 4 ruin 5 level, spoil, waste, wreck 6 ravage 7 despoil, destroy 8 demolish, desolate, lay waste

devastating 7 ruinous 8 damaging 9 injurious 10 calamitous, disastrous 11 cataclysmic, destructive, detrimental 12 catastrophic

devastation 4 ruin 9 ruination 10 demolition 11 destruction

develop 4 grow 5 print, ripen 6 evolve, expand, finish, flower, mature, pick up, unfold 7 acquire, advance, amplify, augment, broaden, build up, convert, enlarge, improve, process, turn out 8 contract, energize 9 cultivate 10 come to have 11 come to light, elaborate on

development 5 event 6 growth, result 7 advance, history 8 progress 9 evolution

deviant 4 warp 5 shift 7 deviate, pervert 8 aberrant, abnormal 9 deflected, divergent

deviate 4 part, vary, veer 5 stray 6 depart, swerve, wander 8 go astray 9 sidetrack, turn aside

deviation 6 change 7 veering 8 rambling, straying 9 wandering 10 aberration, digression, divergence 11 abnormality, fluctuation

device 4 plan, plot, ploy, ruse, wile 5 angle, trick 6 design, gadget, scheme 7 gimmick 8 artifice, strategy 9 apparatus, invention, mechanism, stratagem 11 contraption, contrivance

devil, the Devil 3 guy 5 rogue, Satan, thing 6 Azazel, fellow, wretch 7 hellion, Lucifer, ruffian, serpent, villain 8 creature 9 Archfiend, Beelzebub, scoundrel 11 unfortunate 12 spirit of evil 13 mischief-maker 16 prince of darkness

Devil and Daniel Webster, The
   author: 19 Stephen Vincent Benet
   director: 15 William Dieterle
   character: 5 Devil 7 Webster 9 Mr Scratch
   cast: 10 James Craig 11 Anne Shirley 12 Edward Arnold, Walter Huston
   score: 15 Bernard Herrmann
   Oscar for: 5 score
   also titled: 18 All That Money Can Buy

devilish 4 evil 6 wicked 7 demonic, heinous, impious, satanic, vicious 8 demoniac, fiendish 9 nefarious 10 demoniacal, diabolical, villainous

devil-may-care 4 bold, rash, wild 5 risky 6 daring, rakish 8 heedless, reckless 9 audacious, daredevil

devil's advocate
   Latin: 16 advocatus diaboli

Devil's Advocate
   author: 14 Taylor Caldwell

Devil's Disciple, The
   author: 17 George Bernard Shaw

Devine, Andy
   real name: 16 Jeremiah Schwartz
   born: 11 Flagstaff AZ
   roles: 7 Jingles 9 Andy's Gang 14 Wild Bill Hickok

devious 3 sly 4 wily 6 sneaky, tricky 7 crooked 9 deceitful, dishonest 11 treacherous 12 dishonorable 13 double-dealing

devise 4 plot 5 forge, frame 6 design, invent, map out 7 concoct, prepare, think up 8 block out, conceive, contrive 9 construct, formulate

deviser 6 author, framer 7 creator, planner 8 inventor 9 architect, contriver 10 originator

devitalize 4 kill 6 deaden, weaken 8 enervate 10 debilitate

DeVito, Danny
   born: 9 Neptune NJ
   wife: 11 Rhea Perlman
   roles: 4 Taxi 5 Hoffa, Twins 6 Be Cool, Tin Men 7 Matilda, Screwed 9 Get Shorty 11 Mars Attacks 13 Batman Returns, War of the Roses 14 Ruthless People 22 Throw Mamma From the Train

devoid 5 empty 6 barren 7 lacking, wanting, without 8 bereft of 9 destitute 11 unblest with

devote 5 apply 6 direct 7 address, utilize 8 dedicate 10 consecrate, give over to 11 concentrate 15 give oneself up to 22 center one's attentions on

devoted 4 fond, true 5 loyal 6 ardent, loving 7 earnest, staunch, zealous 8 adhering, faithful 9 dedicated, steadfast 10 passionate, unwavering 17 strongly committed

devotedness 8 devotion 10 commitment, dedication 13 attentiveness 17 earnest attachment

devoted to luxury 9 epicurean, sybaritic 10 hedonistic, voluptuous

devotee 3 fan 6 rooter 7 booster, groupie 8 adherent, advocate, champion, disciple, follower 10 aficionado, enthusiast

devotion, devotions 4 love, zeal 5 ardor, piety 6 fealty, regard 7 loyalty 8 fondness, holiness 9 adherence, godliness, reverence 10 allegiance, commitment, concern for, dedication,

devoutness, meditation 11 religiosity 12 faithfulness, spirituality 13 attentiveness, prayer service 15 religious fervor 17 earnest attachment 19 religious observance

De Voto, Bernard A
   author of: 21 Across the Wide Missouri

devour 7 stuff in 8 bolt down, gobble up, gulp down, knock off, wolf down 9 go through 10 read widely 14 eat voraciously 15 absorb oneself in, consume greedily 16 read compulsively, take in ravenously 17 become engrossed in

devout 5 pious 6 ardent 7 earnest, fervent, intense, serious, zealous 8 orthodox, reverent 9 religious 10 passionate, worshipful

devoutness 5 piety 8 devotion, holiness 9 godliness, reverence 12 spirituality 15 religious fervor

DeVries, Hugo
   field: 6 botany
   nationality: 5 Dutch
   researched: 8 heredity, mutation

DeVries, Peter
   author of: 16 Consenting Adults 24 Slouching Toward Kalamazoo

dew 8 moisture 12 condensation 18 droplets of moisture

Dewar, James
   field: 7 physics 9 chemistry
   nationality: 8 Scottish
   liquified: 8 hydrogen
   solidified: 8 hydrogen
   developed: 7 cordite 10 Dewar flask 12 liquid oxygen

Dewey, George
   served in: 18 Spanish-American War
   battle: 9 Manila Bay
   destroyed: 12 Spanish fleet

Dewhurst, Colleen
   husband: 12 George C Scott
   born: 6 Canada 8 Montreal
   roles: 12 The Nun's Story 18 Desire Under the Elms 22 A Moon for the Misbegotten

De Wilde, Brandon
   born: 10 Brooklyn NY
   roles: 3 Hud 5 Shane 11 All Fall Down

dewy 4 damp 5 moist 7 bedewed

dexterity 8 deftness, facility 9 handiness 10 adroitness, nimbleness 11 manual skill, proficiency

dexterous 4 able, deft 5 agile, quick 6 active, adroit, gifted, nimble 8 skillful 9 efficient, ingenious 11 resourceful

diabolic, diabolical 4 evil, foul 6 wicked 7 baleful, demonic, heinous, impious, satanic, vicious 8 devilish, fiendish 9 monstrous, nefarious 10 malevolent, villainous

diadem 4 halo 5 crown, tiara 7 circlet, coronet 8 headband

diagnosis 5 study **8** analysis, scrutiny **11** examination **13** investigation, medical report **16** scientific report **22** conclusion from symptoms, specification of illness

diagonal line 4 bias **5** angle, slant

diagram 3 map **4** plan **5** chart **6** sketch **7** drawing, outline **9** breakdown **11** line drawing **12** illustration **14** representation **15** rough projection

dialect 5 argot, idiom, lingo **6** accent, jargon, patois **8** localism **10** vernacular **11** regionalism **13** colloquialism, provincialism **15** language variety

Dial M for Murder
   director: **15** Alfred Hitchcock
   based on play by: **14** Frederick Knott
   cast: **10** Grace Kelly, Ray Milland **14** Robert Cummings

dialogue, dialog 4 talk **5** lines **6** parley, speech **8** conclave **10** conference **12** conversation **14** verbal exchange **15** personal meeting **16** formal discussion

diamond
   characteristic: **7** hardest
   color: **4** blue, pink **9** blue-white **12** canary yellow
   element: **6** carbon
   famous: **4** Hope **6** Jonker **8** Cullinan, Idol's Eye, Koh-i-Noor **9** Excelsior **12** Star of Africa **13** Star of the East **17** Star of Sierra Leone
   quality: **3** cut **4** fire **5** color **7** clarity **10** brilliance
   source: **5** Congo, India **6** Africa, Borneo, Brazil, Guyana, Russia **7** Namibia **8** Tanzania **9** Australia, Venezuela **11** Sierra Leone, South Africa, Soviet Union **12** South America **15** South West Africa
   weight: **5** carat, point

Diamond State
   nickname of: **8** Delaware

Diana
   origin: **5** Roman
   goddess of: **4** moon **6** slaves **7** hunting
   protectress of: **5** women
   corresponds to: **6** Phoebe **7** Artemis
   epithet: **10** Nemorensis
     means: **10** of the grove

Diana of the Crossways
   author: **14** George Meredith
   character: **9** Mr Warwick **11** Diana Merion, Percy Dacier **12** Lady Dunstane **14** Thomas Redworth **15** Lord Dannisburgh

diaphanous 5 filmy, gauzy, lucid, sheer **6** flimsy, limpid **8** gossamer, pellucid **11** translucent, transparent

diary 3 log **7** daybook, journal **9** chronicle **12** daily journal **14** day-to-day record

Diary of Anne Frank, The
   author: **9** Anne Frank
   director: **13** George Stevens

   cast: **6** Ed Wynn **9** Lou Jacobi **10** Diane Baker **13** Millie Perkins, Richard Beymer **14** Shelley Winters (Mrs Van Daan) **17** Joseph Schildkraut (Father Frank)
   Oscar for: **17** supporting actress (Winters)

Diasia
   festival of: **4** Zeus

diatribe 6 tirade **9** contumely, invective **11** castigation **12** vituperation **13** stream of abuse **14** bitter harangue **18** accusatory language **19** violent denunciation

dice 4 chop, cube **5** bones, cubes, cut up, mince
   singular: **3** die

Dick, Mr
   character in: **16** David Copperfield
   author: **7** Dickens

Dickens, Charles
   author of: **9** Hard Times **10** Bleak House **11** Oliver Twist **12** Barnaby Rudge, Dombey and Son, Little Dorrit **14** Pickwick Papers **15** A Christmas Carol, Our Mutual Friend **16** A Tale of Two Cities, David Copperfield, Martin Chuzzlewit, Nicholas Nickleby **17** Great Expectations **19** The Old Curiosity Shop **22** The Mystery of Edwin Drood

dicker 4 deal **6** haggle, higgle, outbid **7** bargain, chaffer, quibble, wrangle **8** beat down, talk down, underbid **9** negotiate **17** drive a hard bargain

Dickey, James
   author of: **9** The Zodiac **11** Deliverance **14** The Whole Motion **16** Strength of Fields **17** Buckdancer's Choice

Dickinson, Angie
   real name: **13** Angeline Brown
   husband: **13** Burt Bacharach
   born: **6** Kulm ND
   roles: **8** Rio Bravo **10** Big Bad Mama **11** Police Woman **13** Dressed to Kill **19** The Sins of Rachel Cade

Dick Tracy
   creator: **12** Chester Gould
   character: **9** BO Plenty, Moonmaid **12** Gravel Gertie **13** Sparkle Plenty **16** Jeremiah Truehart
     wife: **12** Tess Truehart
     daughter: **11** Bonny Braids
     assistant: **9** Pat Patton
     protege: **6** Junior
     villain: **5** Itchy **6** B-B Eyes **7** Flattop, Flyface, Measles, Mumbles, The Brow, The Mole **8** The Blank **9** Pruneface, The Midget, The Rodent
   equipment: **16** two-way wrist radio

Dick Van Dyke Show, The
   character: **9** Alan Brady, Rob Petrie **11** Jerry Helper, Laura Petrie, Sally Rogers **12** Buddy Sorrell, Melvin Cooley, Millie Helper **13** Ritchie Pe-

trie
   cast: **9** Rose Marie **10** Carl Reiner, Jerry Paris **13** Larry Matthews, Richard Deacon **14** Mary Tyler Moore, Morey Amsterdam **17** Ann Morgan Guilbert

dictate 4 rule **5** edict, order **6** decree, dictum, direct, enjoin, impose, ordain, ruling, urging **7** bidding, counsel, lay down, mandate **8** set forth **9** determine, ordinance, prescribe, prompting, pronounce, stricture **11** exhortation, inclination, requirement

dictator 4 czar, duce, tsar **6** caesar, despot, fuhrer, kaiser, tyrant **7** emperor **8** autocrat **13** absolute ruler
   Argentinian: **5** Peron
   German: **6** Hitler
   Italian: **9** Mussolini
   Russian: **5** Lenin **6** Stalin
   Spanish: **6** Franco
   Ugandan: **7** Idi Amin

dictatorial 6 lordly **7** haughty, willful **8** absolute, arrogant, despotic **9** arbitrary, imperious, unlimited **10** autocratic, peremptory, tyrannical **11** categorical, domineering, magisterial, overbearing **12** supercilious, unrestricted **13** authoritative **17** inclined to command

diction 7 wording **8** delivery, rhetoric, verbiage **9** elocution **10** intonation, use of idiom, vocabulary **11** enunciation, phraseology, verbal style **12** articulation **13** choice of words, pronunciation **16** turn of expression **17** command of language **18** manner of expression

dictum 3 saw **4** fiat **5** adage, axiom, edict, maxim, order **6** decree, saying, truism **7** dictate, precept, proverb **11** commandment **13** pronouncement **15** dogmatic bidding **22** authoritative statement

Dictys
   occupation: **9** fisherman
   found: **5** chest
     containing: **5** Danae **7** Perseus

didactic 7 donnish, preachy **8** academic, edifying, pedantic, tutorial **9** doctrinal, homiletic, pedagogic **10** expository, moralizing **11** educational, instructive, lecturelike, overbearing **12** prescriptive **17** inclined to lecture

didactics 8 teaching **9** education, teachings **10** pedagogics **11** instruction

Diderot, Denis
   author of: **12** Encyclopedia **13** Rameau's Nephew

Didion, Joan
   author of: **8** Salvador **10** White Album **14** Play It as It Lays **19** A Book of Common Prayer **24** Slouching Toward Bethlehem

Dido
   queen of: **8** Carthage

father: 5 Mutto
brother: 9 Pygmalion
sister: 4 Anna
husband: 8 Sychaeus
lover: 6 Aeneas
corresponds to: 6 Elissa

Dido and Aeneas
opera by: 7 Purcell
character: 4 Dido (Queen of Carthage) **6** Aeneas

die 3 ebb, rot **4** ache, fade, fail, long, pass, stop, wane **5** croak, yearn **6** depart, expire, go flat, pass on, perish, recede, run out, wither **7** be eager, decline, die away, go stale, run down, subside **8** fade away, melt away, pass away, pass over, wear away **9** be anxious, break down, lose force, lose power, meet death **10** degenerate, want keenly **11** come to an end, suffer death **12** wish ardently **13** come to one's end, desire greatly, go to one's glory, kick the bucket **14** leave this world, pine with desire, become inactive **15** slowly disappear **17** become inoperative
plural: 4 dice

die away 4 fade **5** abate, cease **8** diminish

die down 5 abate **7** subside **8** diminish, slack off

die out 6 vanish **9** cease to be, disappear **13** become extinct

Diesel, Rudolf
field: 11 engineering
invented: 12 Diesel engine

diet 5 board, synod **7** edibles, nurture **8** congress, victuals **9** nutriment, nutrition **10** assemblage, convention, parliament, provisions, sustenance **11** comestibles, convocation, legislature, nourishment, subsistence **12** eating habits, eat sparingly **13** eating regimen, lawmaking body **14** eat judiciously **15** eat abstemiously, eat restrictedly, general assembly **16** limitation of fare, regulate one's food **17** bicameral assembly **18** nutritional regimen, representative body, restrict one's intake

Dietrich, Marlene
real name: 22 Maria Magdalene Dietrich
born: 7 Germany
roles: 8 Lola Lola **11** Blonde Venus **12** The Blue Angel **15** Rancho Notorious **16** Destry Rides Again, The Garden of Allah **17** The Scarlet Empress **24** Witness for the Prosecution

Dietrich von Bern
origin: 8 Germanic
king of: 10 Ostrogoths
Latin name: 9 Theodoric

Diety 3 Bel, God **4** Baal **6** Marduk, Molech, Moloch, Yahweh **7** Chemosh, Jehovah **10** Anammelech **11** Adrammelech

Dieu et mon droit 13 God and my right
motto of: 18 royal arms of England

differ 5 demur **7** dispute, dissent **8** be unlike, contrast, disagree **9** take issue **10** be distinct, depart from, stand apart **11** be disparate, deviate from, diverge from **12** be at variance, be dissimilar, stand opposed

difference 4 spat **5** clash, set-to **7** dispute, quarrel **8** argument, contrast, squabble **9** deviation, disparity, variation **10** divergence, falling out, unlikeness **11** contrariety, contretemps, discrepancy, distinction **12** disagreement **13** contradiction, dissimilarity, dissimilitude

different 4 rare **6** divers, sundry, unique, unlike **7** bizarre, diverse, foreign, several, strange, unusual, various **8** aberrant, atypical, distinct, manifold, not alike, peculiar, separate, singular, uncommon **9** anomalous, disparate, divergent, other than, unrelated **10** dissimilar, individual, variegated **11** contrasting, distinctive, diversified, not ordinary **12** not identical **13** miscellaneous **14** unconventional

differential 8 contrast **11** distinction

differentiate 6 set off **8** contrast, separate, set apart **11** distinguish, draw the line **12** discriminate **13** make different

differentiation 8 contrast **10** comparison, separation **11** discernment, distinction

Different World, A
network: 3 NBC
cast: 9 Lisa Bonet (Denise Huxtable), Mary Alice (Lettie Bostic) **10** Cree Summer (Freddie Brooks), Dawnn Lewis (Jaleesa Taylor), Jasmine Guy (Whitley Gilbert Wayne) **11** Darryl M. Bell (Ron Johnson), Jada Pinkett (Lena James), Marisa Tomei (Maggie Lauten) **13** Charnele Brown (Kim Reese), Loretta Devine (Stevie Rallen) **14** Kadeem Hardison (Dwayne Wayne)

differing 6 unlike **7** variant **8** distinct, opposing **9** deviating, disparate, dissident, divergent **10** dissenting, dissimilar **11** contrasting, disagreeing

difficult 4 grim, hard **5** hairy, rough, tough **6** knotty, thorny, trying, unruly, uphill **7** arduous, complex, forward, not easy, onerous, tedious, willful **8** critical, exacting, perverse, stubborn, ticklish, toilsome **9** demanding, enigmatic, fractious, Herculean, intricate, laborious, obstinate, Sisyphean, strenuous, wearisome **10** burdensome, exhausting, fastidious, formidable, inflexible, perplexing, unyielding **11** bewildering, complicated, hard to solve, intractable, troublesome **12** hard to manage, hard to please, ob-

streperous, rambunctious, recalcitrant, unmanageable **13** hard to satisfy, problematical, unpredictable **14** hard to deal with **15** unaccommodating

difficulty 3 jam, rub **4** mess, snag **5** trial **6** crisis, muddle, pickle, puzzle **7** barrier, dilemma, problem, straits, trouble **8** hot water, obstacle, quandary, tough job **9** deep water, hindrance, intricacy **10** impediment, perplexity, rough going, uphill work **11** arduousness, obstruction, predicament **12** hard sledding **13** laboriousness **14** stumbling block **15** troublesomeness **17** critical situation

diffidence 7 reserve, shyness **8** meekness, timidity **9** hesitancy, timidness **10** constraint, humbleness, insecurity, reluctance **11** bashfulness **12** introversion, sheepishness, timorousness **14** extreme modesty **15** unassertiveness **19** lack of self-assurance, retiring disposition

diffident 3 shy **6** modest **7** anxious, bashful **8** doubtful, hesitant, reserved, reticent, retiring **11** distrustful, unassertive **12** apprehensive

diffuse 5 wordy **7** verbose **8** rambling **9** desultory, dispersed, scattered, spread out, wandering **10** digressive, discursive, disjointed, long-winded, maundering, meandering, roundabout **14** circumlocutory, extended widely, unconcentrated, vaguely defined **15** not concentrated **18** lacking conciseness

diffuseness 8 rambling **9** prolixity, verbosity, wandering, wordiness **10** dispersion **11** indirection **14** circumlocution, long-windedness

diffusion 6 spread **8** rambling, verbiage **9** dispersal, prolixity, verbosity, wordiness **10** maundering, scattering **11** indirection, profuseness **14** circumlocution, discursiveness, disjointedness, roundaboutness

dig 3 jab **4** gibe, jeer, like, poke, prod, slur **5** aside, drive, gouge, punch, taunt **6** exhume, thrust **7** put-down, salvage, unearth **8** disinter, excavate, pinpoint, retrieve, scoop out **9** extricate, find among, hollow out **10** come up with, excavation, wry comment **11** bring to view **12** verbal thrust **13** cutting remark, search and find

digest 3 dig **5** grasp **6** absorb, fathom, precis, resume **7** realize, summary **8** abstract, dissolve, synopsis **10** abridgment, appreciate, assimilate, comprehend, understand **12** condensation, take in wholly **14** take in mentally

digestive system
component: 5 liver, mouth, teeth **6** tongue **7** stomach **8** appendix, pancreas **9** esophagus, intestine **11** gall bladder **13** salivary gland

dig in 3 eat **4** root **5** begin, embed, imbed, plant **6** anchor **7** pitch in **8** entrench, go to work **10** begin to eat **12** apply oneself

digit 3 one, six, two, toe **4** five, four, nine, unit, zero **5** light, seven, three **6** cipher, figure, finger, number **7** integer, numeral

dignified 5 proud **6** august, proper **7** upright **8** decorous, reserved **9** honorable **10** upstanding **11** circumspect **13** distinguished **14** self-respecting

dignify 5 raise **6** uplift **7** elevate, inflate, promote

dignitary 3 VIP **7** notable **8** luminary **9** personage **12** person of note

dignity 5 honor **7** decorum, majesty, station **9** loftiness, solemnity **10** augustness, importance **11** comportment, stateliness **12** high position, lofty bearing **13** proud demeanor **14** self-possession

digress 5 stray **6** back up, wander **7** deviate **8** divagate **9** turn aside **15** go off on a tangent **17** depart from subject

digression 6 detour **8** straying **9** departure, deviation, diversion, wandering **10** divagation, divergence, side remark **12** obiter dictum

digressive 7 diffuse **9** wandering **10** disjointed, maundering, roundabout **11** off the point **14** circumlocutory

dig up 6 locate **7** find out, root out, uncover, unearth **8** discover **9** ferret out **12** bring to light

dike 4 bank **5** levee, ridge **10** embankment

Dike *see* **4** Dice

dikerion 11 candelabrum, candlestick **12** candleholder

dilapidated 4 shot **6** beat-up, ruined, shabby **7** rickety, run-down, worn-out **8** battered, decaying, decrepit **10** broken-down, ramshackle, tumble-down **11** in disrepair **12** deteriorated, falling apart **15** falling to pieces

dilate 5 swell, widen **6** expand, extend **7** broaden, distend, enlarge, inflate, puff out **10** make wider

dilation 8 swelling, widening **9** expansion **10** broadening, distension, distention

dilatory 4 lazy, slow **5** tardy **6** remiss **8** dawdling, indolent, slothful, sluggish **9** negligent, reluctant **10** phlegmatic **13** lackadaisical **15** inclined to delay, procrastinating

dilemma 4 bind **6** crunch, plight **7** impasse, problem **8** deadlock, quandary **9** stalemate **11** predicament **13** Hobson's choice **15** difficult choice

dilettante 7 amateur, dabbler, trifler **12** experimenter **16** cultured hobbyist

diligence 4 zeal **8** industry **10** commitment, dedication **11** persistence **12** perseverance

diligent 6 active **7** careful, earnest, patient, zealous **8** plodding, sedulous, studious, thorough, untiring **9** assiduous, concerted **10** persistent **11** hardworking, industrious, painstaking, persevering **12** pertinacious **15** well-intentioned

dill 4 anet
   botanical name: 17 Anethum graveolens
   origin: 9 Asia Minor **13** Mediterranean
   family: 7 parsley
   guards against: 7 Evil Eye **10** witchcraft
   use: 6 sauces **7** pickles **10** vegetables

Dillon, Matt
   roles: 3 Tex **8** Factotum **10** Rumblefish **12** The Outsiders **18** Employee of the Month

dillydally 3 lag **4** idle, loaf **5** dally, delay **6** dawdle, loiter **8** kill time **9** waste time **10** fool around **13** procrastinate

Dilsey
   character in: 18 The Sound and the Fury
   author: 8 Faulkner

dilute 4 thin, weak **6** reduce, temper, watery, weaken **7** diffuse, diluted, thin out **8** decrease, diminish, make weak, mitigate, weakened **9** attenuate, liquidify, water down **10** add water to, adulterate, thinned out **11** adulterated, make thinner, watered down

diluted 4 weak **6** dilute, watery **8** weakened **10** thinned out **11** adulterated, watered down

dilution 8 thinning **9** weakening **12** watering down

dim 3 low **4** hazy, soft, weak **5** dusky, faint, foggy, murky, muted, vague **6** blurry, feeble, gloomy, remote **7** blurred, clouded, muffled, shadowy **8** darkened, nebulous, obscured **9** not bright, tenebrous **10** adumbrated, ill-defined, indefinite, indistinct, intangible **13** unilluminated

DiMaggio, Joe
   nickname: 9 Joltin Joe
   sport: 8 baseball
   position: 8 outfield
   team: 14 New York Yankees
   wife: 13 Marilyn Monroe

dime-a-dozen 6 common **7** humdrum **8** ordinary, workaday **9** plentiful **10** ubiquitous **11** commonplace **12** easy to come by **13** garden-variety **15** undistinguished

dimension, dimensions 4 bulk, mass, size **5** range, scope, width **6** extent, height, length, volume, weight **7** measure **9** amplitude, greatness, magnitude, thickness **10** importance, proportion **11** massiveness **12** measurements **14** physical extent

diminish 3 ebb **4** wane **5** abate, lower

6 lessen, narrow, reduce, shrink **7** decline, dwindle, fall off, shorten, shrivel, subside **8** decrease, peter out **9** be reduced **11** make smaller **13** become smaller

diminuendo
   music: 22 gradually getting softer
   abbreviation: 3 dim

diminution 6 ebbing, waning **7** decline **8** decrease, lowering **9** dwindling, lessening, reduction, shrinkage **10** falling off, shortening, shriveling, subsidence **11** petering out, slacking off

diminutive 3 wee **4** tiny **5** elfin, short, small, teeny **6** little, minute, petite, slight **7** pet name, stunted **8** dwarfish, half-pint, nickname **9** miniature, short form **10** pocket-size, undersized, vest-pocket **11** lilliputian, small-scale, unimportant **13** insignificant **14** inconsiderable

Dimmesdale, Arthur
   character in: 16 The Scarlet Letter
   author: 9 Hawthorne

dimness 4 dusk **5** gloom, shade **8** darkness **14** indistinctness

dimwit 4 fool **5** dummy, dunce, idiot, moron **6** cretin, nitwit **7** dingbat, dullard, dumbell, pinhead **8** dumbbell, dummkopf, imbecile, meathead, numskull **9** birdbrain, blockhead, ding-a-ling, lamebrain, numbskull, simpleton **11** chowderhead, knucklehead

dim-witted 4 dull, dumb **5** dense **6** stupid **7** foolish, idiotic, moronic, witless **8** retarded **9** cretinous, imbecilic

din 4 stir, to-do **5** bruit **6** babble, clamor, hubbub, racket, ruckus, tumult, uproar **7** clangor **9** commotion **10** clattering, hullabaloo

Dinah
   father: 5 Jacob
   mother: 4 Leah
   brother: 3 Dan, Gad **4** Levi **5** Asher, Judah **6** Joseph, Reuben, Simeon **7** Zebulun **8** Benjamin, Issachar, Naphtali
   violated by: 7 Shechem

dine 3 eat, sup **4** feed **5** feast, lunch **6** fall to, supper **7** banquet, partake **9** breakfast, eat dinner **10** break bread, gluttonize, have dinner **11** gourmandize **14** take sustenance

Dine *see* **6** Navajo

Dinesen, Isak
   real name: 18 Karen Blixen-Finecke
   author of: 9 Last Tales **11** Out of Africa **12** Winter's Tales **16** Seven Gothic Tales

dinghy 5 skiff **7** rowboat **8** sailboat **9** small boat

dingy 4 dull **5** dusty, grimy, murky, tacky **6** dismal, dreary, gloomy, shabby **12** dirty and drab

dining room
French: **12** salle a manger

dinner 4 food, meal **5** feast **6** repast, supper **7** banquet
French: **8** dejeuner **10** table d'hote

Dinner at Eight
director: **11** George Cukor
author: **10** Edna Ferber **14** George S Kaufman
cast: **8** Lee Tracy **10** Jean Harlow **11** Billie Burke **12** Wallace Beery **13** John Barrymore, Marie Dressler **15** Lionel Barrymore

dinosaur
means: **14** fearfully great, terrible lizard
subclass: **11** Archosauria
characteristic: **7** diapsid **14** teeth in sockets, two-arched skull **18** three-element pelvis
group: **11** Saurischian **13** Ornithischian
  flesh-eating biped: **8** therapod
  plant-eating quadruped: **8** sauropod
  plant-eating biped: **10** ornithopod
  armored: **10** ceratopsid
of Africa: **9** Iguanodon **13** Brachiosaurus **17** Heterodontosaurus
of Asia: **13** Hypselosaurus, Protoceratops
of Europe: **9** Iguanodon **12** Plateosaurus **13** Compsognathus, Hypselosaurus, Hypsilophodon
of North America: **10** Diplodocus, Edmontonia, Nodosaurus **11** Anatosaurus, Anchisaurus, Gorgosaurus, Monoclonius, Saurolophus, Scolosaurus, Stegosaurus, Triceratops **12** Ankylosaurus, Camarasaurus, Camptosaurus, Coelophysics, Lambeosaurus, Paleoscincus **13** Brachiosaurus, Styracosaurus, Tyrannosaurus **14** Thescelosaurus **15** Parasaurolophus, Procheneosaurus
of South America: **12** Pisanosaurus
fictional: **4** Puff **6** Barney **12** Jurassic Park

dint 4 push, will **5** drive, force, labor, might, power **6** charge, effort, energy, strain, stress **8** endeavor, exertion, strength, struggle **10** insistence **12** forcefulness **13** determination **14** relentlessness

diocese 3 see **7** eparchy **9** bishopric **14** church district
jurisdiction of: **6** bishop

Diomedes
king of: **6** Thrace
father: **4** Ares **6** Tydeus
mother: **6** Cyrene **7** Deipyle
member of: **7** Epigoni
kept: **9** wild mares
fed mares on: **10** human flesh
death planned by: **8** Hercules

Dione
consort of: **4** Zeus

Dionysia
festival of: **8** Dionysus

Dionysus see **7** Bacchus

Dioscuri see **15** Castor and Pollux

dip 4 bail, dish, dunk, sink, skim, soak **5** droop, ladle, scoop, slope, spoon **6** dabble, dish up, peruse, shovel **7** decline, descend, dish out, run over **8** drop down, glance at, submerge, turn down **13** study slightly **14** immerse briefly, lift by scooping, try tentatively **15** incline downward

dip into 4 scan, skim **5** ladle **6** browse, peruse **7** deplete **8** look over **13** glance through, make inroads in

Diplodocus
type: **8** dinosaur, sauropod
period: **8** Jurassic
location: **12** North America

diplomacy 4 tact **5** craft, skill **7** finesse **8** delicacy, prudence, subtlety **10** artfulness, discretion **11** maneuvering, savoir-faire **13** statesmanship **14** foreign affairs **16** artful management **18** foreign negotiation **21** international politics

diplomat 5 envoy **6** consul **7** attache **8** emissary, minister **9** statesman **10** ambassador, negotiator **12** interlocutor **13** tactful person
acceptable: **12** persona grata
unacceptable: **15** persona non grata

diplomatic 5 adept, suave **6** artful, urbane **7** attuned, politic, prudent, tactful **8** discreet **9** sensitive, strategic **13** ambassadorial **14** foreign-service **15** state-department

Dipper
nickname of: **15** Wilt Chamberlain

Dipsas
form: **7** serpent

dipsomaniac 3 sot **4** lush, soak, wino **5** drunk, rummy, souse, toper **6** barfly, boozer **7** tippler **8** drunkard **9** alcoholic, inebriate

diptera
class: **8** hexapoda
phylum: **10** arthropoda
group: **7** true fly

Dirae see **6** Furies

dire 4 grim **5** awful, grave **6** dismal, urgent, woeful **7** crucial, extreme, fearful, ominous, ruinous **8** critical, dreadful, horrible, terrible **9** appalling, desperate, harrowing, ill-boding, ill-omened **10** calamitous, disastrous, portentous **11** apocalyptic, cataclysmic **12** catastrophic, inauspicious

direct 3 aim **4** head, lead, urge **5** blunt, clear, focus, frank, guide, order, pilot, usher **6** advise, candid, charge, enjoin, handle, head-on, honest, manage **7** address, command, conduct, control, earmark, forward, level at, oversee, pointed, sincere, train at **8** explicit, indicate, instruct, navigate,

personal **9** conduct to, designate, firsthand, intend for, supervise **10** administer, face-to-face, forthright, point-blank, show the way, unmediated **11** plain-spoken, point the way, point toward, preside over, superintend **15** straightforward

direction 3 aim, ENE, ESE, NNE, NNW, SSE, SSW, way, WNW, WSW **4** bent, care, east, path, west **5** drift, north, order, route, south, track, trend **6** charge, course, recipe **7** bearing, command, control, current **8** guidance, headship, tendency **9** alignment **10** guidelines, leadership, management, regulation **11** inclination, instruction, line of march, supervision **12** line of action, prescription, surveillance **13** line of thought **14** administration, point of compass **15** superintendence

directive 5 ukase **8** bulletin **9** statement **10** communique **11** declaration **12** instructions, proclamation **13** communication

directly 4 soon **6** at once, openly **7** exactly, frankly **8** candidly, honestly, in person, promptly, straight **9** forthwith, precisely, presently, right away **10** face-to-face, in a beeline, personally **11** immediately, momentarily **12** in plain terms, not obliquely, unswervingly **13** unambiguously, unequivocally **14** as the crow flies **15** in a straight line **16** as soon as possible **17** on a straight course, straightforwardly

directness 6 candor **9** bluntness, frankness **10** candidness **14** forthrightness **19** straightforwardness

direct opposite 7 reverse **8** converse **10** antithesis

director 4 boss, head **5** chief **6** leader, master **7** curator, foreman, manager **8** chairman, governor, overseer **9** commander, conductor, organizer **10** controller, supervisor **13** administrator **14** superintendent

dirge 6 lament **7** requiem **8** threnody **9** death song **10** burial hymn, death march **11** funeral song **13** mournful sound **19** mournful composition

dirigo 7 I direct
motto of: **5** Maine

dirk 3 sny **4** snee, stab **5** knife, skean **6** dagger, skiver **7** poniard
origin: **8** Scotland

Dirks, Rudolph
creator/artist of: **12** Hans and Fritz **17** Captain and the Kids **19** The Katzenjammer Kids

dirt 3 mud **4** dust, loam, mire, muck, scum, slop, smut, soil, soot **5** dross, earth, filth, grime, humus, offal, rumor, slime, trash **6** gossip, ground, refuse, sludge, smudge **7** garbage, rubbish, scandal, slander **8** impurity, leavings, vileness **9** excrement, indecency, obscenity, profanity, sweepings **10** foul matter, moral filth, scurrility **11** pornography, scuttlebutt, squalidness **12** scabrousness **13** salaciousness **14** defamatory talk **15** filthy substance, unclean language **17** sensational expose

dirt-cheap 6 a steal **7** bargain **11** inexpensive **14** very reasonable **15** bargain-basement

dirty 4 base, foul, hard, lewd, mean, soil, spot, vile **5** grimy, messy, muddy, nasty, smear, stain, sully **6** coarse, filthy, grubby, mess up, muck up, risque, rotten, shabby, slop up, smudge, smudgy, smutty, soiled, sordid, untidy, vulgar **7** begrime, besmear, blacken, corrupt, crooked, devious, illegal, illicit, immoral, lowdown, muddied, obscene, pollute, squalid, sullied, tarnish, unclean **8** befouled, begrimed, indecent, off-color, polluted, prurient, scabrous, unwashed **9** besmeared, deceitful, difficult, dishonest, tarnished, unsterile **10** despicable, fraudulent, licentious, perfidious, unpleasant, villainous **11** distasteful, treacherous **12** contemptible, disagreeable, dishonorable, pornographic, unscrupulous **14** morally unclean

Dirty Dozen, The
    director: 13 Robert Aldrich
    cast: 8 Jim Brown **9** Lee Marvin **10** Robert Ryan, Trini Lopez **11** Clint Walker **13** George Kennedy **14** Charles Bronson, Ernest Borgnine, John Cassavetes, Richard Jaeckel **16** Donald Sutherland

Dis
    also: 8 Dis Pater
    means: 5 Hades
    god of: 10 underworld
    corresponds to: 5 Orcus, Pluto

dis 6 insult **9** disparage

disability 5 minus **6** defect **8** handicap, weakness **9** infirmity, unfitness **10** affliction, impairment, impediment, inadequacy **11** shortcoming **12** debilitation, disadvantage **16** disqualification

disable 6 damage, hinder, impair, weaken **7** cripple **8** handicap **12** incapacitate

disabled
    French: 12 hors de combat

disabuse 8 set right **9** relieve of **10** disenchant **11** disillusion, set straight

disaccord 7 discord **10** disharmony **12** disagreement **15** incompatibility

disacknowledge 4 deny **6** disown **7** disavow **8** disallow, disclaim **9** repudiate

disadvantage 4 flaw **6** burden **7** trouble **8** drawback, handicap, hardship, nuisance, weakness **9** detriment, hindrance, in arrears, weak point **10** impediment **12** weak position **13** inconvenience **16** fly in the ointment

disadvantaged 8 deprived, emergent, emerging, troubled **10** struggling **11** handicapped **12** impoverished **14** underdeveloped **15** underprivileged

disadvantageous 7 harmful **9** injurious **11** detrimental, inadvisable, inexpedient, undesirable, unfavorable, unfortunate

disaffect 4 wean **8** alienate, estrange **10** drive apart

disaffected 5 upset **7** hostile **8** agitated, inimical **9** alienated, disturbed, estranged, withdrawn **10** unfriendly **11** belligerent, discomposed, disgruntled, quarrelsome **12** antipathetic, discontented, dissatisfied **14** irreconcilable

disaffection 7 dislike **8** aversion, distaste **9** antipathy **10** alienation, discontent, disloyalty **12** estrangement

disaffirm 4 deny **5** annul **6** disown **7** decline, disavow **8** abnegate, disclaim, forswear, renounce **9** repudiate **15** wash one's hands of

disaffirmation 6 denial **9** annulment, disavowal **10** abnegation, disclaimer **11** repudiation **12** renunciation **13** contradiction

disagree 4 vary **5** clash, upset **6** depart, differ **7** deviate, diverge, make ill **8** be unlike, conflict, distress **9** discomfit **10** disconcert, stand apart **11** be injurious, fail to agree, not coincide **12** be at variance, be discordant, be dissimilar **13** cause problems **14** be unreconciled **15** be at loggerheads, differ in opinion **16** oppose one another, think differently

disagreeable 5 cross, harsh, nasty, surly, testy **7** grating, grouchy, peevish **8** churlish, petulant **9** difficult, irascible, irritable, obnoxious, offensive, repellent, repugnant, repulsive, unamiable, unwelcome **10** disgusting, ill-natured, uninviting, unpleasant **11** acrimonious, bad-tempered, displeasing, distasteful, ill-tempered, uncongenial, unpalatable **13** uncomfortable

disagreeing 6 at odds **7** deviant, varying **8** clashing **9** deviating, differing, disputing **10** quarreling **11** conflicting **13** at loggerheads

disagreement 5 clash, fight **7** discord, dispute, quarrel **8** argument, squabble, variance **9** deviation, disaccord, disparity, diversity **10** difference, divergence, falling-out, unlikeness **11** discrepancy, incongruity **13** dissimilarity, dissimilitude, lack of harmony **15** incompatibility **16** misunderstanding

disallow 4 deny, veto **6** abjure, forbid, refuse, reject **8** prohibit **9** repudiate

disallowance 4 veto **6** denial **7** refusal **9** rejection **11** prohibition, repudiation

disallowed 6 vetoed **7** abjured, refused **8** rejected **9** forbidden **10** repudiated **12** inadmissible, unacceptable

disappear 2 go **3** end **4** exit, fade, flee **5** leave **6** be gone, depart, die out, retire, vanish **8** be no more, fade away, melt away, withdraw **9** evaporate **12** be lost to view, cease to exist, leave no trace **13** cease to appear, cease to be seen **14** become obscured, cease to be known, pass out of sight **15** vanish from sight

disappearance 9 vanishing **11** evanescence **16** passing from sight

disappoint 4 foil **6** hinder, sadden, thwart **7** chagrin, let down, mislead **9** frustrate **10** dishearten **11** disillusion

disappointing 11 frustrating **12** unfulfilling **13** dissatisfying **14** unsatisfactory

disappointment 3 dud **4** bomb, loss **6** defeat, fiasco, fizzle **7** failure, letdown, setback, washout **8** disaster **9** the knocks **11** frustration **13** unfulfillment, unrealization **15** disillusionment, dissatisfaction

disapprobation 7 censure **8** disfavor **9** criticism, disesteem, objection **11** disapproval, displeasure **12** condemnation **15** dissatisfaction

disapprove 4 veto **5** decry **6** refuse, reject **7** censure, condemn, deplore, dislike **8** denounce, disallow, object to, turn down **9** criticize, deprecate, disparage, frown upon **10** think ill of **13** look askance at, regard as wrong **14** discountenance, refuse assent to **15** take exception to **16** find unacceptable, view with disfavor

disapprove of 7 censure, condemn, deplore **8** object to

disarm 4 move, sway **5** charm **6** entice **7** attract, bewitch, enchant, win over **8** convince, persuade **9** captivate, fascinate, influence, prevail on

disarming 7 melting, winning, winsome **8** charming, magnetic **9** appealing, beguiling, ingenuous, seductive **10** bewitching, entrancing **11** captivating **12** ingratiating, irresistible

disarrange 5 mix up, upset **6** jumble, mess up, muddle, ruffle, rumple **7** confuse, scatter **8** disarray, dishevel, disorder, displace, put askew, scramble **11** disorganize **13** put out of order **14** turn topsy-turvy

disarranged 5 messy **6** mussed, sloppy, untidy **7** jumbled, ruffled, rumpled, tousled, unkempt **8** uncombed **9** cluttered **10** disarrayed, disheveled, disordered, disorderly, in disorder **11** in a shambles

disarrangement 4 mess **5** chaos, mix-up, upset **6** jumble, mixing, muddle **7** clutter **8** disarray, disorder, scramble, shambles **9** confusion, messiness, messing up **10** disharmony, disruption, sloppiness, untidiness **12** dishevelment **14** disorderliness **15** disorganization, heaping together

disarray 5 chaos, mix-up, upset **6** jumble **7** clutter **8** disorder, scramble, shambles **9** confusion, messiness **10** disharmony, sloppiness, untidiness **12** dishevelment **14** disarrangement **15** disorganization

disarrayed 5 messy **6** mussed, sloppy, untidy **7** chaotic, jumbled, mixed up **10** disheveled, disordered, disorderly, in disorder **11** disarranged

disarticulate 6 detach **7** unhinge **8** disjoint, disunite, separate **9** disengage, dislocate **10** disconnect **13** put out of joint

disarticulated 5 apart **7** divided **8** unhinged **9** disunited, separated **10** disengaged, disjointed, dislocated, unattached **11** unconnected **12** disconnected **13** helter-skelter

disassemble 7 disband, scatter **8** disperse **9** knock down, take apart

disassociate 7 divorce **8** separate **10** disconnect **12** disaffiliate

disassociation 5 break, split **6** schism **7** divorce **8** division **10** separation

disaster 4 harm **5** wreck **6** blight, fiasco **7** scourge, tragedy, trouble **8** accident, calamity **9** adversity, cataclysm, ruination **10** misfortune **11** catastrophe, great mishap **12** misadventure

disastrous 4 dire **5** fatal **6** tragic **7** adverse, hapless, harmful, ruinous **8** dreadful, grievous, ill-fated, terrible **9** harrowing **10** calamitous, desolating, horrendous, ill-starred **11** destructive, devastating, unfortunate **12** catastrophic, inauspicious

disavow 4 deny **6** abjure, disown, recant, reject **7** gainsay, retract **8** denounce **9** repudiate **10** contradict

disavowal 6 denial **8** demurrer **9** rejection **10** abjuration, disclaimer, refutation **11** repudiation **13** contradiction

disband 7 adjourn, dismiss, scatter **8** disperse, dissolve **11** disassemble

disbelief 5 doubt **7** dubiety **8** distrust, mistrust, unbelief **10** skepticism **11** incredulity **12** doubtfulness **14** lack of credence

disbelieve 5 doubt **6** refuse, reject **7** suspect **8** discount, distrust **9** discredit, unbelieve **10** misbelieve

disbeliever 7 atheist, skeptic **8** apostate

disbursable 7 payable **9** available, spendable **10** expendable

disburse 6 lay out, pay out **7** fork out **8** allocate, shell out **10** distribute

disbursement 6 outlay **7** payment **8** spending **9** paying out **10** dispensing

11 expenditure **12** dispensation, distribution

discard 4 drop, dump, junk, shed **5** scrap **6** remove, shelve **7** abandon, weed out **8** get rid of, jettison, throw out **9** cast aside, dispose of, eliminate, throw away **10** relinquish **11** thrust aside **12** dispense with, have done with **14** throw overboard

discarded 6 dumped, junked **7** cast off, dropped **8** deserted, forsaken, rejected, scrapped **9** abandoned, cast aside, tossed out **10** jettisoned, left behind, thrown away

discern 3 see **4** espy **6** behold, descry, detect, notice **7** make out, observe, pick out **8** perceive **9** ascertain **12** catch sight of

discernible 7 visible **8** apparent **10** detectable, noticeable **11** perceivable, perceptible

discerning 4 sage, wise **5** acute, sharp **6** astute, shrewd **8** piercing **9** judicious, sagacious, sensitive **10** perceptive **11** intelligent, keen-sighted, penetrating **12** clear-sighted, sharp-sighted **13** perspicacious **14** discriminating

discernment 6 acumen, senses **7** insight **8** feelings, sagacity, thoughts **10** cognizance, discretion, perception **11** distinction **13** consciousness, judiciousness **14** discrimination **15** differentiation

discharge 3 axe, can **4** emit, fire, flow, free, gush, ooze, oust, sack, shot **5** blast, burst, eject, expel, exude, issue, let go, shoot **6** bounce, firing, launch, lay off, let fly, propel, report, set off **7** cashier, dismiss, explode, fire off, project, release, seepage, set free, trigger **8** activate, detonate, drainage, emission, get rid of, liberate, throw off, touch off **9** allow to go, exploding, explosion, firing off, fusillade, give forth, pour forth, secretion, send forth, terminate **10** activating, detonating, detonation, triggering **11** send packing, suppuration **13** give the gate to, walking papers **14** demobilization

disciple 3 nut **5** freak, pupil **7** admirer, convert, devotee, pursuer, student **8** adherent, believer, follower, neophyte, partisan **9** proselyte, supporter **10** aficionado **11** afficionado

Disciples *see* **8** Apostles

disciplinarian 8 martinet **13** authoritarian **16** stickler for rules, strict taskmaster

disciplinary 8 punitive **9** punishing **10** corrective **13** authoritarian

discipline 5 drill, prime, rigor, train **6** method, punish **7** break in, chasten, regimen **8** chastise, drilling, instruct, practice, training **9** schooling **11** preparation **14** indoctrination **15** prescribed habit, teach by exercise **16** course of exercise

disclaim 4 deny **6** disown **7** decline, disavow **8** abnegate, forswear, renounce **9** disaffirm, repudiate

disclaimer 6 denial **8** demurrer **9** disavowal **10** abnegation **11** repudiation **12** renunciation

disclose 4 bare, leak, show, tell **6** expose, impart, reveal, unveil **7** divulge, lay bare, publish, uncover **9** broadcast, make known **10** make public **11** communicate **12** bring to light **13** allow to be seen, bring into view, cause to appear

disco 4 club **5** a-go-go, dance **7** cabaret **9** dance club, nightclub

discolor 4 spot **5** stain, tinge **6** bleach, streak **7** tarnish

discoloration 4 blot, mark, spot **5** smear, stain **6** blotch, bruise, smudge **7** blemish **9** contusion

discolored 4 doty **5** dingy, dirty, faded, livid **6** soiled, tinged **7** bruised, stained **9** tarnished

discomfit 5 upset **6** thwart **7** chagrin **8** confound, distress **9** embarrass, frustrate **10** disconcert

discomfited 5 upset **6** uneasy **7** ashamed **8** thwarted **9** chagrined, ill at ease **10** distressed **11** embarrassed **12** disconcerted

discomfiture 7 anxiety **9** agitation, confusion **10** uneasiness **11** disquietude, distraction, nervousness **12** discomposure, perturbation **13** embarrassment

discomfort 3 try **4** ache, hurt, pain **5** trial **6** misery **7** malaise, trouble **8** disquiet, distress, hardship, nuisance, soreness, vexation **9** annoyance, discomfit, embarrass **10** affliction, discompose, irritation, make uneasy **11** disquietude

discompose 5 abash, upset **6** rattle **7** agitate, confuse, disturb, fluster, nonplus, perturb, trouble, unnerve **8** disquiet, distract, distress, unsettle **9** discomfit, embarrass **10** disconcert

discomposed 5 upset **6** jolted, rocked, shaken, uneasy **7** anxious, nervous, worried **8** agitated, confused, troubled **9** disturbed, flustered, perturbed **10** disquieted, distracted **11** discomfited, uncollected

discomposure 6 flurry **7** anxiety **8** disquiet **9** agitation, confusion **10** discomfort, uneasiness **11** awkwardness, disquietude, distraction, nervousness **12** discomfiture, perturbation **13** embarrassment **17** self-consciousness

disconcert 5 abash, annoy, upset **6** raffle, ruffle **7** agitate, confuse, disturb, nonplus, perturb, trouble **8** unsettle **10** discompose

disconcerted 5 fazed, upset **7** annoyed, rattled, ruffled **8** agitated, confused, troubled **9** disturbed, perturbed, thrown off, unsettled **10** distracted, nonplussed

disconcertment 8 rattling **9** abashment, agitation, confusion **11** disturbance **12** discomposure

disconnect 6 detach **8** separate, uncouple **9** disengage

disconnected 5 split **6** cut off **7** jumbled, mixed-up, severed **8** confused, detached, rambling **9** illogical, separated, uncoupled **10** disengaged, disjointed, incoherent, irrational, unattached, unfastened **12** disorganized

disconnection 8 severing **9** severance **10** cutting off, detachment, separation **13** disengagement

disconsolate 3 sad **4** blue, down **6** woeful **7** crushed, doleful, forlorn, unhappy **8** dejected, desolate, downcast, wretched **9** depressed, miserable, sorrowful, woebegone **10** despondent, dispirited, melancholy **11** discouraged, low-spirited, pessimistic **12** heavyhearted, inconsolable **13** brokenhearted **14** down in the dumps, down in the mouth

discontent 9 displease **10** discomfort, disgruntle **11** displeasure, unhappiness **15** dissatisfaction

discontented 5 bored **7** fretful, unhappy **9** miserable, regretful **10** displeased, malcontent **11** disgruntled **12** dissatisfied

discontinuance 3 end **4** halt, stop **6** ending, recess **7** ceasing, halting **8** abeyance, giving up, quitting, stoppage, stopping, surcease **9** cessation, desisting **10** concluding, leaving off, suspension **11** abandonment, breaking off, termination

discontinue 3 end **4** drop, quit, stop **5** cease **6** desist, give up **7** abandon, abstain, suspend **8** break off, leave off **9** interrupt, terminate **10** put an end to

discontinuous 8 discrete, episodic, sporadic **9** segmented, spasmodic **10** occasional **11** interrupted **12** disconnected, intermittent

discord 6 strife **7** dispute **8** clashing, conflict, disunity, division, friction **9** cacophony, harshness, wrangling **10** contention, disharmony, dissension, dissonance, quarreling **11** being at odds, differences, discordance **12** disagreement, grating noise **13** lack of concord **15** incompatibility **16** unpleasant sounds
  goddess of: 4 Eris **9** Discordia

discordance 6 strife **7** discord, dispute **8** clashing, conflict, disunity, division, friction **9** wrangling **10** contention, disharmony, dissension, quarreling **12** disagreement **15** incompatibility

discordant 6 at odds **9** disparate, dissonant **10** at variance, discrepant **11** conflicting, disagreeing **12** unharmonious

Discordia
  origin: 5 Roman
  goddess of: 7 discord
  corresponds to: 4 Eris

discount 3 cut **5** break **6** rebate **7** cut rate **9** abatement, allowance, deduction, exemption, reduction **10** concession **11** subtraction

discountenance 7 condemn, despise, disdain, dislike **8** object to **9** frown upon **10** disapprove, think ill of **12** look down upon **13** look askance at, regard as wrong **14** hold in contempt **15** take exception to

discourage 4 do in **5** daunt, deter, unman **6** deject, dismay **7** depress, unnerve **8** decimate, dispirit, dissuade, keep back, restrain **9** disparage, prostrate **10** dishearten, disincline, divert from **13** advise against, dash one's hopes **17** dampen one's spirits

discouraged 3 low **7** daunted **8** dejected, downcast, hopeless **9** depressed, dispirited **10** despondent, dispirited **11** downhearted, pessimistic **12** disconsolate, disheartened

discouragement 4 curb **5** gloom, worry **6** damper, dismay **7** despair **8** obstacle **9** dejection, hindrance, pessimism, restraint **10** constraint, depression, impediment, low spirits, melancholy, moroseness **11** despondency **12** hopelessness, lack of spirit **13** consternation **15** downheartedness

discourse 3 gab **4** chat, talk **5** essay **6** confer, sermon, speech **7** address, discuss, lecture, oration **8** colloquy, converse, dialogue, diatribe, harangue, treatise **10** discussion **11** intercourse **12** conversation, dissertation, talk together **16** formal discussion

Discourse on Method
  author: 13 Rene Descartes

discourteous 4 rude **5** fresh, surly **6** cheeky **7** boorish, ill-bred, uncivil, uncouth **8** impolite, impudent, insolent **9** uncourtly, ungallant **10** ill-behaved, ungracious, unladylike, unmannerly **11** ill-mannered, impertinent **13** disrespectful, ungentlemanly

discourtesy 8 rudeness **9** impudence, insolence **10** incivility **11** boorishness **12** impoliteness

discover 3 see **4** find, spot **5** dig up **6** detect, locate, notice **7** discern, find out, learn of, realize, root out, uncover, unearth **8** come upon, perceive **9** ascertain, determine, ferret out, light upon, recognize **10** chance upon **11** gain sight of, stumble upon **12** bring to light

discredit 4 deny, slur **5** abuse, smear, sully, taint **6** debase, defame, demean, reject, smirch, vilify **7** degrade, dispute, tarnish, vitiate **8** disallow, disgrace, dishonor, disprove, question **9** challenge, disparage, undermine **10**

prove false, stigmatize **16** shake one's faith in **17** drag through the mud

discreditable 8 shameful, shocking **9** appalling **10** outrageous, scandalous **11** disgraceful, ignominious **12** dishonorable, disreputable

discreet 6 polite **7** careful, politic, prudent, tactful **8** cautious **9** judicious, sensitive **10** diplomatic, thoughtful **11** circumspect

Discreet Charm of the Bourgeoisie, The
  director: 10 Luis Bunuel
  cast: 11 Fernando Rey **14** Delphine Seyrig, Stephane Audran
  Oscar for: 11 foreign film

discrepancy 3 gap **8** variance **9** disparity **10** difference, divergence **11** discordance, incongruity **12** disagreement **13** dissimilarity, inconsistency

discrepant 6 at odds **8** contrary, opposing **9** disparate **10** at variance, discordant, dissimilar, refutatory **11** conflicting, contrasting, disagreeing **12** antithetical, inconsistent **13** contradictory **14** countervailing, irreconcilable

discrete 7 several, various **8** detached, distinct, separate **9** different **10** unattached **11** disjunctive, independent **12** disconnected, unassociated **13** discontinuous

discretion 4 tact **6** acumen, option **8** judgment, prudence, sagacity, volition **9** good sense **10** preference **11** discernment, inclination **12** good judgment, predilection **13** judiciousness, sound judgment **14** discrimination **15** power of choosing **16** individual choice

discretionary 8 optional **9** voluntary **10** nonbinding **11** nonrequired, unnecessary **12** nonrequisite, unimperative **13** nonobligatory

discriminate 7 disdain **8** separate **11** distinguish **12** disfranchise **13** differentiate

discriminating 5 acute **6** astute, biased, shrewd **7** bigoted, refined **9** judicious, sensitive **10** cultivated, discerning, fastidious **11** intelligent, prejudicial **13** perspicacious **15** differentiating

discrimination 4 bias **5** taste **6** acumen **7** bigotry **8** inequity, judgment, keenness, sagacity **9** prejudice **10** astuteness, discretion, favoritism, refinement, shrewdness **11** discernment, distinction **12** perspicacity **21** differential treatment

discursive 7 diffuse **8** rambling **9** wandering **10** circuitous, digressive, longwinded, meandering, roundabout

discursiveness 8 rambling **10** digression, meandering **14** circumlocution

discuss 6 debate, parley, review **7** dissect, examine, speak of **8** consider, talk over **9** talk about **13** converse about, exchange views **14** discourse about

discussion 3 rap **4** talk **6** debate, parley, powwow, review **7** inquiry **8** analysis, argument, colloquy, dialogue, scrutiny **9** discourse **10** hashing-out **11** disputation **12** deliberation **13** consideration, investigation

disdain 4 snub **5** abhor, scorn, spurn **6** deride, detest, loathe **7** despise, dislike **8** contempt, distaste **9** frown upon **10** abhorrence, brush aside, disrespect **11** intolerance **12** icy aloofness, look down upon **14** deem unbecoming, discountenance

disdained 7 derided, scorned, spurned **8** abhorred, despised **10** deprecated, disparaged **14** held in contempt

disdainful 4 cold **5** aloof **7** haughty, high-hat **8** derisive, scornful, superior **11** overbearing, patronizing **12** contemptuous, supercilious **13** condescending

disease 6 malady **7** ailment, illness **8** sickness **9** ill health, infirmity **10** affliction **15** morbid condition **16** physical disorder

disembark 4 land **7** deplane, detrain, pile out **10** leave a ship **11** get off a ship

disenchant 6 put off **7** turn off **8** alienate, disabuse, turn away **9** undeceive **11** disenthrall, disillusion **12** open one's eyes **13** break the spell **15** burst one's bubble

disencumber 3 rid **8** unburden **9** disburden, extricate **11** disentangle

disengage 5 sever **6** detach **7** disjoin **8** separate **9** extricate **10** disconnect

disengaged 7 unmoved **8** detached **9** apathetic, disjoined, separated **11** indifferent, uncommitted, unconcerned **12** disconnected, unresponsive French: **6** degage

disengagement 6 apathy **8** severing **9** severance, unconcern **10** detachment, separation **12** indifference **13** disconnection **16** unresponsiveness

disentangle 4 free **6** detach, loosen, remove **7** unravel **9** extricate

disenthrall 9 undeceive **10** disenchant **11** disillusion **12** open one's eyes **13** break the spell **15** burst one's bubble **16** bring down to earth

disesteem 7 dislike **8** disfavor **9** disrepute **11** disapproval, displeasure **14** disapprobation

disfavor 5 odium **7** dislike, ill turn **8** disgrace, ignominy **9** disesteem, disregard **10** disrespect, disservice, harmful act **11** disapproval, discourtesy, displeasure **14** disapprobation **15** dissatisfaction **16** unacceptableness

disfigure 3 mar **4** maim, scar **5** cut up **6** damage, deface, deform, impair **7** blemish, scarify **8** make ugly, mutilate

disfigurement 4 blot, flaw, mark, scar, spot **6** blotch, defect **7** blemish **12** imperfection

disfranchise, disenfranchise 15 deprive of a right **19** discriminate against

disgorge 4 spew **5** eject, expel, spout, vomit **6** cast up, spew up **7** cough up, throw up **8** dislodge **9** discharge **10** vomit forth **11** regurgitate

disgrace 4 blot **5** abase, shame, stain, taint **6** debase, smirch **7** blemish, degrade, eyesore, scandal, tarnish **8** contempt, derogate, disfavor, dishonor, ill favor, reproach **9** discredit, disparage, disrepute, embarrass, humiliate **13** embarrassment, in the doghouse **14** bring shame upon

disgraceful 3 low **4** base, mean, vile **6** odious **8** infamous, shameful, shocking, unseemly, unworthy **9** appalling, detestable, obnoxious **10** despicable, detestable, inglorious, outrageous, scandalous, unbecoming **11** ignominious, opprobrious **12** dishonorable, disreputable **13** discreditable, reprehensible

disgruntled 5 sulky, testy, vexed **6** grumpy, shirty, sullen **7** grouchy, peevish **8** petulant **9** irritated **10** displeased, malcontent **12** discontented, dissatisfied

disguise 4 garb, hide, mask, pose, sham, veil **5** blind, cloak, cover, feign, getup, guise **6** facade, muffle, screen, shroud, veneer **7** conceal, cover-up, dress up, falsify **8** pretense, simulate **9** costuming, dissemble, gloss over **10** camouflage, false front, masquerade **11** concealment, counterfeit **12** misrepresent **13** false identity **15** false appearance

disguised 6 masked, veiled **7** cloaked **9** dressed up, incognito **10** undercover **11** camouflaged **14** unrecognizable

disgust 5 repel **6** appall, hatred, offend, put off, revolt, sicken **7** dislike **8** aversion, contempt, distaste, loathing, nauseate **9** antipathy, disrelish, repulsion, revulsion **10** abhorrence, repugnance **11** detestation, displeasure **12** disaffection **13** be repulsive to, cause aversion **15** turn one's stomach

disgusting 4 vile **5** hasty **6** horrid, odious **7** hateful **9** abhorrent, appalling, loathsome, offensive, repellent, repugnant, repulsive, revolting, sickening **10** abominable, despicable, nauseating **13** reprehensible

dish 4 dole, fare, food **5** ladle, place, plate, scoop, serve, spoon **6** recipe, saucer, vessel **7** bowlful, dishful, edibles, helping, platter, portion, serving **8** dispense, plateful, transfer, victuals **10** comestible **11** shallow bowl

dishabille 7 undress **8** bathrobe, disar-

ray, disorder, informal, negligee **9** housecoat

disharmonious 7 chaotic **8** clashing, confused **9** dissonant, illogical **10** discordant, incoherent **11** conflicting, contentious **12** incompatible **13** heterogeneous

disharmony 5 chaos **6** strife **7** discord **8** clashing, conflict, disarray, disunity, division, friction **9** cacophony, confusion, disaccord, harshness **10** contention, dissension, dissonance **11** discordance **12** disagreement, grating noise **15** disorganization, incompatibility

dishearten 4 dash, faze **5** abash, crush, daunt **6** deject, dismay, sadden **7** depress **8** dispirit **10** discourage

disheartened 3 low **6** dismal **8** dejected, desolate, downcast **9** depressed **10** despondent, dispirited **11** discouraged **12** disconsolate

disheartening 4 dark **7** adverse **8** hopeless **11** dispiriting **12** discouraging, inauspicious

disheveled 5 messy **6** blowsy, frowzy, mussed, sloppy, untidy **7** ruffled, rumpled, tousled, unkempt **8** uncombed **10** bedraggled, disarrayed, disorderly, in disorder **11** disarranged

dishevelment 5 chaos, mix-up, upset **6** jumble **7** clutter **8** disarray, disorder, scramble, shambles **9** messiness **10** sloppiness, untidiness **14** disarrangement **15** disorganization

dishonest 5 false **7** corrupt, crooked **8** cheating, specious, spurious, two-faced **9** deceitful, disarray, faithless, insincere, not honest **10** fraudulent, mendacious, misleading, perfidious, untruthful **11** underhanded **12** disingenuous, false-hearted, unprincipled, unscrupulous **13** untrustworthy

dishonesty 8 cheating **9** duplicity, falseness, mendacity **10** corruption **11** crookedness **12** speciousness **14** untruthfulness

dishonor 4 blot **5** abase, odium, shame, stain, sully **6** debase, defame, infamy, insult, slight, stigma **7** affront, blacken, blemish, degrade, offense, scandal, tarnish **8** disfavor, disgrace, ignominy **9** discredit, disparage, disrepute, humiliate, ill repute **10** derogation, stigmatize **11** discourtesy, humiliation **12** bring shame on **14** public disgrace

dishonorable 4 base **7** debased, ignoble **8** shameful **10** despicable **12** contemptible, disreputable **13** reprehensible

dishonorableness 4 blot **5** odium, shame, stain **6** stigma **7** blemish **8** disfavor, disgrace, ignominy **9** discredit, disrepute, ill repute **10** derogation **11** humiliation

dishonoring 8 disgrace **10** debasement **11** degradation, humiliation

dish up 3 dip **5** ladle, serve, spoon **7** dish out, serve up

disillusion 6 clue in **8** disabuse **9** undeceive **10** disenchant **11** disenthrall **13** break the spell, open the eyes of **14** burst the bubble **16** bring down to earth

disinclination 8 aversion **9** hesitancy **10** reluctance **13** indisposition, unwillingness

disincline 5 deter **8** dissuade, keep back, restrain **10** discourage, divert from **13** advise against **16** attempt to prevent

disinclined 5 loath **6** averse **8** hesitant **9** reluctant, unwilling **10** indisposed

disinfect 6 purify **7** cleanse **8** sanitize **9** kill germs, sterilize **13** decontaminate **15** destroy bacteria

disinfectant 9 germicide **10** antiseptic, germ killer **11** bactericide

disinherit 6 cut off, disown **15** deprive of rights

disintegrate 7 break up, crumble, shatter **8** splinter **9** fall apart **10** break apart, go to pieces

disintegration 4 ruin **5** decay **7** breakup, erosion **8** biolysis **9** crumbling **10** dispersion, dissolving, separation **11** decomposing **12** falling apart **13** decomposition, deterioration, pulverization

disinter 5 dig up **6** exhume **7** unearth

disinterest 6 apathy **9** disregard, unconcern **12** indifference

disinterested 7 neutral, outside **8** unbiased **9** impartial **10** impersonal, uninvolved **12** free from bias, unprejudiced **13** dispassionate

disinterment 9 digging up **10** exhumation, unearthing

disjecta membra 15 disjointed parts **16** scattered members

disjoin 4 part, undo **5** break, sever **6** detach, divide **8** disunite, separate **9** disengage

disjoint 6 detach **7** unhinge **8** disunite, separate **9** dislocate **10** disconnect **13** disarticulate

disjointed 5 apart, split **7** chaotic, divided, jumbled, mixed-up, tangled **8** confused, detached, rambling **9** illogical, spasmodic **10** incoherent, irrational, unattached **11** unconnected **12** disconnected, disorganized **13** discontinuous, disharmonious, helter-skelter, heterogeneous **14** disarticulated

disjointedness 8 rambling **11** indirection **14** discursiveness **16** disconnectedness

disjointed parts
Latin: **14** disjecta membra

disk, disc 3 cam **4** aten, coin, dial, face, plow, puck **5** plate, wafer, wheel **6** harrow, record, sequin **7** discuss **8** diskette **9** cultivate, videodisc **11** discotheque

type: 4 hard **5** fixed **6** floppy **8** magnetic **10** Winchester

dislike 4 hate **5** abhor, scorn **6** animus, detest, enmity, hatred, loathe, malice, rancor **7** despise, disdain, disgust, not like **8** aversion, distaste, loathing, object to **9** abominate, animosity, antipathy, hostility, repulsion, revulsion **10** abhorrence, antagonism, repugnance **11** abomination, detestation **12** disaffection

disliked 5 hated **7** loathed, unloved **8** abhorred, despised, detested **10** abominated

dislike intensely 4 hate **5** abhor **6** detest, loathe **7** despise **9** abominate **10** recoil from

dislocate 6 uproot **7** unhinge **8** disjoint, disunite, separate **9** disengage **10** disconnect **13** disarticulate, put out of joint

dislodge 4 oust **5** eject, expel **6** dig out, dispel, remove, uproot **7** disturb **8** displace, force out **9** extricate **11** disentangle

disloyal 6 untrue **8** recreant **9** faithless, seditious, undutiful **10** inconstant, perfidious, subversive, traitorous, unfaithful **11** treacherous, treasonable **12** dishonorable

disloyalty 7 falsity, perfidy, treason **8** apostasy, betrayal, sedition **9** falseness, rebellion, recreancy, treachery **10** infidelity, subversion **11** inconstancy **12** insurrection **13** breach of trust, deceitfulness, double-dealing, faithlessness **14** lack of fidelity, perfidiousness, unfaithfulness **15** betrayal of trust, breaking of faith **18** subversive activity

dismal 3 sad **4** drab, grim, poor **5** awful, bleak **6** dreary, gloomy, morbid, rueful, somber, woeful **7** abysmal, doleful, forlorn, joyless, unhappy, very bad, visaged **8** dejected, desolate, dolorous, downcast, dreadful, hopeless, horrible, mournful, terrible **9** cheerless, depressed, long-faced, sorrowful, woebegone **10** abominable, despondent, in the dumps, lugubrious, melancholy **11** pessimistic **12** disconsolate, disheartened, heavy-hearted **13** unmentionable **14** down-in-the-mouth

dismantle 5 strip **6** denude, divest **9** take apart

dismay 3 cow **5** abash, alarm, daunt, dread, panic, scare **6** appall, fright, horror, put off, terror **7** anxiety, concern, horrify, unnerve **8** affright, distress, frighten **10** disappoint, discourage, dishearten, intimidate **11** disillusion, trepidation **12** apprehension, exasperation, intimidation, perturbation **13** consternation **14** disappointment, discouragement **15** disillusionment

dismayed 7 abashed, daunted **8** appalled **10** confounded, nonplussed **12** disconcerted

dismember 4 limb **6** hack up **8** disjoint **16** tear limb from limb

dismiss 3 can **4** fire, free, oust, sack **5** let go **6** bounce, excuse, reject **7** adjourn, cashier, disband, discard, release **8** disclaim, disperse, dissolve, lay aside, liberate, pink-slip, set aside **9** disregard, eliminate, repudiate, send forth, terminate **10** permit to go **11** send packing **12** allow to leave, put out of a job, put out of mind **14** give the heave-ho **17** remove from service, give walking papers **19** discharge from office

dismissal 6 firing **7** release **9** discharge, dispersal, disregard **10** disclaimer **11** adjournment, repudiation

Disney
theme parks **10** Disneyland, EuroDisney **15** Disneyland Paris, Tokyo Disneyland, Walt Disney World

Disney, Walt
creator/artist of: **5** Goofy, Pluto **10** Donald Duck **11** Mickey Mouse, Minnie Mouse

disobedience 8 defiance **9** rebellion **10** resistance **13** noncompliance, nonconformity **14** rebelliousness

disobedient 6 unruly **7** defiant, forward, haughty, wayward **8** contrary, mutinous, perverse, stubborn **9** fractious, insurgent, obstinate, seditious, undutiful **10** disorderly, rebellious, refractory, unyielding **11** intractable **12** noncompliant, recalcitrant, ungovernable, unmanageable, unsubmissive **13** insubordinate

disobey 4 defy **5** break **6** ignore, resist **7** violate **8** overstep **9** disregard **10** infringe on, transgress **11** go counter to **12** rebel against

disoblige 5 annoy **6** bother **7** trouble **13** inconvenience

disobliging 4 rude **8** churlish **9** unhelpful **13** inconsiderate

disorder 4 mess, riot **5** chaos **6** fracas, jumble, malady, muddle, ruckus, uproar **7** ailment, clutter, disease, illness, turmoil **8** disarray, sickness **9** commotion, complaint, confusion **10** affliction, disruption, dissension **11** disturbance **13** indisposition, minor uprising **14** disarrangement **15** disorganization

disordered 7 jumbled **8** confused, messed up **9** haphazard **11** disarranged **12** disorganized

disorderliness 4 mess **5** chaos **6** muddle **8** disarray **9** confusion **10** disruption **14** disarrangement **15** disorganization

disorderly 3 bad 4 awry, wild 5 amiss, messy, noisy, rowdy 6 sloppy, unruly, untidy 7 chaotic, jumbled, lawless, riotous, unkempt, wayward 8 careless, confused, improper, pell-mell, rowdyish, slipshod, slovenly, unlawful, unsorted 10 boisterous, disheveled, disordered, disruptive, rebellious, straggling, topsy-turvy 11 disarranged 12 disorganized, disreputable, obstreperous, unrestrained, unsystematic 13 helter-skelter, undisciplined 14 rough-and-tumble, unsystematized

disorganization 4 mess 5 chaos, upset 6 jumble, muddle 7 clutter 8 disarray, disorder, shambles 9 confusion, messiness 10 disharmony, disruption, sloppiness, untidiness 12 dishevelment 14 disarrangement, disorderliness

disorganize 5 mix up, upset 6 jumble, mess up, muddle 7 confuse, scatter 8 disarray, disorder, put askew, scramble 10 disarrange 13 put out of order 14 turn topsy-turvy

disorganized 5 messy, upset 7 chaotic, jumbled, mixed-up, muddled 8 confused, rambling 9 haphazard, illogical 10 disordered, disorderly, incoherent, in disarray, irrational 12 unsystematic 16 at sixes and sevens

disoriented 7 mixed-up 8 confused, unstable 10 distracted, out of joint, out of touch 11 not adjusted

disown 4 deny 6 reject 7 cast off, disavow, forsake 8 denounce, disclaim, renounce 9 repudiate 10 disinherit 17 refuse to recognize 19 refuse to acknowledge

disparage 4 mock 6 demean, slight 7 put down, run down 8 belittle, derogate, ridicule 9 denigrate, discredit, underrate 10 depreciate, undervalue 11 detract from

disparagement 5 abuse, libel 7 slander 8 ridicule 9 criticism 10 belittling, defamation, derogation, detraction 11 denigration, putting down 12 vilification 17 defamatory remarks

disparaging 5 snide 10 belittling, derogatory 11 unfavorable 15 uncomplimentary

disparate 6 at odds, unlike 9 different 10 at variance, discordant, discrepant, dissimilar 11 contrasting

disparity 3 gap 8 contrast, imparity, variance 10 difference, divergence, inequality, unlikeness 11 discrepancy, incongruity 12 disagreement, dissemblance 13 contradiction, disproportion, dissimilarity, dissimilitude, inconsistency

dispassion 6 apathy 8 coolness 10 detachment 12 indifference

dispassionate 4 calm, cool, fair 6 serene 7 neutral, unmoved 8 composed, detached, unbiased 9 collected, impar-tial, unexcited, unruffled 10 impersonal, uninvolved 11 levelheaded, undisturbed, unemotional 12 unprejudiced 13 disinterested, imperturbable

dispatch 4 item, kill, post, slay 5 flash, haste, piece, speed, story 6 finish, letter, murder, report, settle, wind up 7 bump off, execute, forward, message, missive, send off 8 alacrity, bulletin, carry out, celerity, complete, conclude, expedite, massacre, rapidity 9 finish off, quickness, slaughter, swiftness 10 communique, expedition, promptness, put an end to, put to death 11 assassinate, news account 12 send on the way 14 execute quickly, summarily shoot, swift execution 15 make short work of, transmit rapidly 16 carry out speedily, dispose of rapidly

Dis Pater *see* 3 Dis

dispel 4 rout 5 allay, expel, repel 6 banish, remove 7 diffuse, dismiss, resolve, scatter 8 drive off 9 dissipate, drive away, eliminate 10 put an end to 11 disseminate 13 make disappear

dispensable 8 nonvital 9 accessory, extrinsic, secondary 10 disposable, expendable, extraneous 11 superfluous, unessential, unimportant, unnecessary 12 nonessential

dispensation 6 decree 8 approval, bestowal, division 9 allotment, diffusion, exemption, meting out 10 allocation, conferment, credential, dealing out, dispensing, permission, reparation 11 consignment, designation 12 apportioning, distribution, remuneration 13 authorization, dissemination

dispense 6 confer 7 dole out, mete out 8 allocate 9 apportion 10 administer, distribute

dispense with 4 drop, dump, junk, shed 5 scrap 6 shelve 7 abandon, discard 9 dispose of

dispensing 9 bestowing, doling out, meting out 10 allocating, conferring 12 distributing

dispersal 7 breakup, parting 9 dismissal 10 breaking up, scattering 12 distributing, distribution

disperse 4 rout 6 dispel 7 diffuse, disband, scatter, send off 8 drive off 9 dissipate 10 distribute 11 disseminate 13 send scurrying 16 spread throughout

dispersed 7 diffuse 9 scattered, spread out 10 dissipated 11 distributed 14 extended widely, unconcentrated

dispersion 9 dispersal 10 disbanding, scattering 11 dissipation 12 distribution

dispirit 5 cloud 6 darken, deject, sadden 7 depress 10 demoralize, dishearten

dispirited 3 sad 4 blue, down, glum 5 moody 6 morose 7 forlorn, unhappy 8 dejected, downcast, listless 9 cheerless, depressed 10 melancholy 11 crestfallen, demoralized, discouraged, downhearted, pessimistic 12 disconsolate, disheartened 14 down in the dumps, down in the mouth, unenthusiastic

dispiriting 4 cold, dark 6 chilly, dismal, gloomy 9 dampening 10 depressing 12 discouraging 13 disheartening

displace 4 bump, move, oust 5 shift 6 unseat 7 replace 8 crowd out, dislodge, force out, supplant 9 dislocate, supersede

displaced person 2 DP 5 exile 6 emigre 7 refugee 8 expellee 10 expatriate

display 4 show 6 reveal 7 exhibit 8 manifest 10 exhibition 11 demonstrate, make visible 12 presentation 13 bring into view, demonstration, manifestation 15 put in plain sight

display case 7 cabinet, vitrine 8 showcase

displease 3 irk 5 annoy, pique 6 offend 7 disturb, incense, provoke 8 irritate

displeasing 8 annoying 9 loathsome, offensive, repellent, repugnant 10 irritating 11 distasteful, distressing 12 disagreeable

displeasure 5 wrath 7 dislike 8 vexation 9 annoyance 10 irritation 11 disapproval, indignation 15 dissatisfaction

disport 3 act 4 play, romp 5 amuse, caper, sport, frolic, gambol 7 display, pastime 9 amusement, entertain 10 recreation 13 entertainment

disposal 5 array, order, power 7 command, control, dumping, junking, pattern, ridding 8 grouping, riddance 9 authority, clearance, direction, placement 10 discarding, government, management, regulation, settlement 11 arrangement, destruction, disposition, supervision 12 distribution, organization, throwing away 13 authorization, configuration, juxtaposition

dispose 4 rank 5 array, order, place 7 arrange, deal out, incline 8 classify, get rid of, motivate, organize 9 be willing 10 distribute

dispose of 4 dump 5 scrap 6 unload 7 discard 8 get rid of, throw out 9 cast aside, throw away

disposition 6 nature, spirit 7 control 8 bestowal, grouping, tendency 9 placement 11 arrangement, inclination, temperament 12 distribution, organization 14 predisposition 15 final settlement

dispossess 4 oust 5 evict, expel 8 take away, take back 9 deprive of

disproportionate 7 unequal 9 disparate 10 dissimilar, unbalanced

disprove 6 refute 9 discredit 10 controvert

disputable 7 dubious 8 doubtful 9 debatable, uncertain 12 questionable 14 controvertible

disputant 5 rival 7 opposer 8 opponent 9 adversary 10 antagonist, competitor, contestant

disputation 6 debate, review 8 argument, dialogue 10 discussion

dispute 4 feud 5 argue, clash, doubt 6 debate, impugn 7 quarrel, wrangle 8 argument, question, squabble 9 bickering, challenge 10 contradict 11 altercation, controversy 12 disagreement

disputed 6 argued 8 wrangled 9 debatable, in dispute, quarreled 10 in question, unverified 12 questionable 13 controversial 15 unsubstantiated

disqualification 5 minus 8 handicap 10 disability 11 shortcoming 13 ineligibility

disqualify 7 disable 9 make unfit 17 declare ineligible, deny participation

disquiet, disquietude 3 awe 6 unease 7 anxiety 8 distress 9 agitation 10 uneasiness 11 fretfulness, trepidation 12 apprehension, discomposure, perturbation 13 consternation

disquieted 6 uneasy 7 anxious, worried 9 concerned 10 distressed 12 apprehensive

disquieting 6 vexing 8 annoying 9 troubling, upsetting 10 bothersome, disturbing, irritating, perturbing, unsettling 11 distressing 13 disconcerting

disquisition 8 tractate, treatise 9 discourse, monograph 12 dissertation

disregard 6 ignore 8 overlook 11 pay no heed to 13 lack of respect 14 take no notice of 15 lack of attention 16 willful oversight

disregardful 8 careless, heedless 9 unmindful 11 insensitive, thoughtless 13 inconsiderate

disreputable 5 shady 8 infamous, shameful, shocking 9 notorious 10 scandalous 11 disgraceful 12 dishonorable, unprincipled 14 not respectable, of bad character

disrespect 6 insult 8 contempt, dishonor, rudeness 9 disregard 11 discourtesy, irreverence 12 impoliteness

disrespectful 4 rude 8 impolite 11 impertinent 12 contemptuous, discourteous

disrobe 5 strip 7 undress 16 divest of clothing

disrupt 5 upset 9 interrupt 13 interfere with 17 throw into disorder

disruption 5 upset 8 disorder 9 confusion 11 disturbance 12 interference, interruption 14 disarrangement 15 disorganization

dissatisfaction 4 veto 7 protest 9 rejection 10 discontent 11 disapproval, displeasure, unhappiness

dissatisfied 7 unhappy 10 displeased 12 discontented

dissect 5 study 7 analyze, lay open 8 cut apart, separate 9 anatomize, break down

dissemble 4 hide, mask 5 feign 7 conceal 8 disguise 10 camouflage 11 dissimulate

disseminate 6 spread 7 diffuse, scatter 8 disperse 9 broadcast, circulate

dissemination 9 diffusion, dispersal, spreading 10 scattering 12 broadcasting, distribution

dissension 7 discord, dispute 8 conflict, disunity, division 9 rebellion 10 contention, disharmony, quarreling 11 discordance 12 disagreement 14 rebelliousness

dissent 6 object, oppose 7 discord, protest 8 disagree 10 difference, dissension, opposition 12 disagreement 14 withhold assent 16 withhold approval

dissenter 5 rebel 9 dissident, protester 13 nonconformist

dissenting 9 differing, dissident 11 disagreeing

dissertation 6 memoir, thesis 8 tractate, treatise 9 discourse, monograph 12 disquisition

disservice 4 harm, hurt 5 wrong 6 injury 7 bad turn 9 injustice

dissever 3 saw 4 hack, rend 5 carve, sever, slash, slice, split 6 cleave, divide 8 disunite, separate

dissident 5 rebel 8 agitator, opposing 9 differing, dissenter 10 dissenting 11 disagreeing

dissimilar 6 unlike 8 distinct 9 different, disparate

dissimilarity 8 contrast, variance 9 disparity 10 difference, dissonance, divergence, inequality, unlikeness 11 discrepancy 12 disagreement 13 inconsistency 17 lack of resemblance

dissimilitude 8 variance 9 disparity 10 difference, unlikeness 11 incongruity 12 disagreement 17 lack of resemblance

dissimulate 4 hide, mask 7 conceal 8 disguise 9 dissemble 10 camouflage

dissipate 5 waste 6 dispel 7 carouse, deplete, scatter 8 disperse, misspend, squander 11 fritter away, overindulge 13 be intemperate 14 spend foolishly

dissipated 6 wasted 8 misspent 9 abandoned, debauched, dispelled, dispersed, dissolute, scattered 10 squandered 11 intemperate 12 disreputable 13 frittered away

dissipater 5 waste 7 wastrel 8 prodigal 10 profligate, squanderer 11 spendthrift

dissipation 6 excess 7 wasting 9 dispersal 10 debauchery, dispelling, scattering 11 dissolution, loose living 12 immoderation, intemperance 14 disintegration, frittering away, self-indulgence

dissociate 8 separate 10 disconnect 12 break off with

dissociation 7 breakup 10 separation

dissolute 5 loose 7 corrupt, immoral 9 abandoned, debauched 10 dissipated 12 unrestrained

dissolution 9 annulment 10 separation 11 termination 14 disintegration

dissolve 3 end, run 4 fade, melt, thaw, void 5 annul, sever 6 finish, render, soften, vanish 7 break up, disband, liquefy, thaw out 8 abrogate, conclude, evanesce 9 disappear, dissipate, terminate 10 deliquesce 12 disintegrate 13 dematerialize

dissonance 5 clash 7 discord 9 cacophony, harshness 10 difference, disharmony 11 discordance 12 disagreement 13 dissimilarity

dissonant 5 harsh 7 grating, hostile, jarring, raucous, warring 8 clashing, jangling 10 discordant, discrepant 11 cacophonous, disagreeing, incongruent, incongruous, unmelodious 12 incompatible, inconsistent, inharmonious 13 contradictory 14 irreconcilable

dissuade 9 urge not to 10 discourage 13 advise against, persuade not to

distance 3 gap 4 span 7 reserve, stretch 8 coldness, coolness, interval 9 aloofness, formality, restraint, stiffness 11 reservation 16 intervening space

distant 3 far 4 cold, cool 5 aloof 6 far-off, remote 7 faraway 8 detached, reserved 10 far-removed, restrained, unfriendly 11 standoffish 17 not closely related

Distant Mirror, A
    author: 15 Barbara W Tuchman

distaste 7 disgust, dislike 8 aversion 9 antipathy 10 repugnance 11 displeasure

distasteful 9 loathsome, repugnant 10 disgusting, unpleasant 11 displeasing 12 disagreeable

distastefulness 13 offensiveness 14 unpleasantness 16 disagreeableness

distasteful work 8 drudgery 11 menial labor

distend 5 bloat, bulge, swell 6 billow, expand 7 inflate, puff out 8 swell out

distended 4 full, taut 5 puffy, tumid 7 blown up, bloated, dilated, swelled, swollen 8 enlarged, expanded, extended, inflated, patulant 9 edematous, stretched

distill 7 draw out, extract 8 condense, vaporize 9 draw forth, evaporate

distillate 7 essence, extract 11 concentrate 13 concentration

distilled 9 condensed, extracted, vaporized 10 evaporated

distinct 5 clear, lucid, plain 7 diverse, supreme 8 clear-cut, definite, explicit, separate 9 different 10 dissimilar, individual 11 unmitigated, well-defined 12 not identical, unmistakable 13 extraordinary 14 unquestionable

distinction 6 renown 8 contrast, eminence 9 greatness 10 difference, excellence, importance, notability, prominence, separation 11 discernment, preeminence, superiority 12 differential 14 discrimination 15 differentiation

distinctive 6 unique 7 special 8 atypical, original, singular, uncommon 9 different 10 individual 13 extraordinary 14 characteristic

distinctiveness 7 clarity 9 character 10 definition, uniqueness 11 personality 13 individuality

distingue 13 distinguished

distinguish 6 decide, define 7 discern 8 set apart 9 single out 10 make famous 12 characterize, discriminate 13 differentiate, make prominent, make well known 14 make celebrated 15 make distinctive, note differences

distinguished 5 grand, great 6 famous, superb 7 elegant, eminent, notable, refined 8 renowned, splendid 9 acclaimed, dignified, distingue, prominent 10 celebrated 11 illustrious, magnificent
French: 9 distingue

distort 6 deform 7 contort 8 misshape 9 disfigure 11 misconstrue 12 misrepresent 15 twist out of shape, twist the meaning

distorted 4 awry 5 askew 6 belied, loaded, warped 7 altered, colored, crooked, twisted 8 cockeyed, deformed, wrenched 9 contorted, falsified, grotesque, irregular, misshapen, misstated, perverted 13 unsymmetrical 14 misrepresented 15 misproportioned

distortion 7 skewing 8 twisting 10 aberration, caricature 11 crookedness, deformation 12 malformation 17 misrepresentation

distract 5 amuse, craze, worry 6 divert, madden 7 agitate, confuse, disturb, perplex, torment, trouble 8 bewilder, disorder 9 entertain

distracted 3 mad 4 wild 6 amused, crazed, insane, raving 7 frantic, pleased, puzzled 8 agitated, confused, deranged, diverted, frenzied, harassed, heedless, occupied 9 disturbed, stirred up 10 bewildered, distraught, irrational 11 entertained, turned aside

distraction 5 fazed, upset 6 frenzy 7 frantic, madness, pastime, rattled, ruffled 8 agitated, confused 9 amusement, diversion, unsettled 10 distraught, distressed, nonplussed, recreation 11 desperation 12 disconcerted 13 entertainment 14 mental distress

distractive 9 confusing 10 disturbing, unsettling 11 distressing, troublesome

distraught 3 mad 7 anxious, frantic 8 agitated, frenzied, seething 10 distracted, distressed 13 beside oneself

distress 4 need, pain, want 5 agony, upset 6 danger, grieve 7 anguish, disturb, torment, torture, trouble 14 acute suffering

distressed 5 upset 7 anxious, fearful, frantic, grieved, unhappy, worried 8 agitated, troubled 9 anguished, concerned, disturbed, tormented 10 distracted, distraught

distressing 5 acute 7 nagging, painful 8 grievous 9 agonizing, upsetting 10 disturbing, tormenting, unpleasant 11 displeasing, troublesome, unfortunate 13 uncomfortable

distribute 5 allot, class 6 divide, parcel 7 arrange, catalog, deliver, dole out, give out, scatter 8 classify, dispense, disperse, separate, tabulate 9 apportion, circulate, methodize, spread out 11 disseminate, systematize

distribution 7 sorting 8 division, grouping 9 allotment, spreading 10 allocation, dispersion, scattering 11 arrangement, circulation, disposition 12 organization 13 apportionment, dissemination

distribution center
French: 8 entrepot

district 4 area, ward 6 parish, region 8 precinct 12 neighborhood

distrust 5 doubt 7 suspect 8 question 9 misgiving, suspicion 11 lack of faith

distrustful 3 shy 4 wary 5 leery 7 dubious, jealous 8 cautious, doubtful, doubting 9 diffident 10 suspicious, untrusting 11 incredulous, mistrustful 12 disbelieving

disturb 5 annoy, upset, worry 6 bother 7 disrupt, perturb, trouble 8 distress, unsettle 9 dislocate, interrupt, intrude on 10 disarrange 11 disorganize

disturbance 5 upset, worry 6 bother, hubbub, ruckus, tumult, uproar 7 rioting, turmoil 8 disorder, distress, outbreak 9 annoyance 11 distraction 12 interruption, perturbation

disturbance of peace 4 riot 6 fracas, ruckus, uproar 7 turmoil 8 disorder 9 commotion 13 breach of order

disturbed 5 upset 6 uneasy 7 annoyed, anxious, nervous, rattled 8 agitated, confused, troubled 9 perturbed 10 disquieted 11 discomfited 12 disconcerted

disunion 7 divorce 8 division 9 secession 10 separation 14 disintegration

disunite 4 part 6 divide 7 divorce 8 separate 9 disengage 10 disconnect 12 disintegrate 13 disarticulate

disunited 6 parted 8 diverged, divorced, unallied 9 came apart, dispersed, separated 10 uncombined 13 disassociated

disunity 6 strife 7 discord 8 clashing, conflict, division, friction 9 wrangling 10 contention, dissension, separation 11 being at odds, discordance 12 disagreement 15 incompatibility

ditat Deus 11 God enriches
motto of: 7 Arizona

ditch 3 pit 4 junk 5 scrap 6 hollow, trench 7 abandon, discard 8 get rid of 10 excavation

dither 4 flap, fuss 5 tizzy, waver, whirl 6 bother, flurry, lather, quiver, shiver, thrill 7 fluster, tremble, twitter 8 hesitate 9 agitation, commotion, confusion, vacillate, vibration 10 excitement

Dithyrambus
epithet of: 8 Dionysus
means: 20 child of the double door

ditty 3 lay 4 song, tune 6 ballad 7 refrain

Dius Fidius
origin: 5 Roman
god of: 5 oaths 11 hospitality 20 international affairs
corresponds to: 6 Sancus 10 Semo Sancus

divagation 8 straying 9 wandering 10 digression, divergence

divan 4 book, hall, poem, room, salon, seat, sofa 5 couch, court 6 canape, daybed, leewan, lounge, settee 7 chamber, council, ottoman, davenport

dive 4 dash, fall, jump, leap 5 lunge 6 plunge 7 gin mill 9 honky-tonk, shabby bar 15 sleazy nightclub

Diver, Dick and Nicole
characters in: 16 Tender Is the Night
author: 10 Fitzgerald

diverge 6 differ, swerve 7 deflect, deviate 8 be at odds, conflict, disagree, separate, split off

divergence 7 parting 8 conflict, rambling, straying, variance 9 deviation, disparity, wandering 10 difference, separation 11 discrepancy, incongruity 13 dissimilarity, inconsistency

divergent 8 separate 9 different 11 conflicting, disagreeing 12 drawing apart, splitting off

diverse 6 sundry, varied 8 eclectic, far-flung, opposite 9 different, differing, disparate 10 dissimilar 11 conflicting, of many kinds 13 contradictory

diversified 6 divers 7 various 8 manifold 9 different, unrelated 13 miscellaneous

diversify 4 vary 7 diffuse 8 divide up 9 spread out, variegate

diversion 5 hobby 7 pastime 9 amusement, avocation 10 deflection 11 distraction, drawing away 12 turning aside
French: 14 divertissement

diversity 7 variety 8 variance 10 assortment, difference 13 heterogeneity

divert 5 amuse 7 deflect 8 distract 9 entertain, sidetrack, turn aside

diverting 7 amusing 10 deflecting 11 distracting 12 entertaining, sidetracking

divertissement 9 diversion 13 entertainment

divest 3 rid 4 free 5 strip 7 deprive, disrobe, peel off, take off 8 get out of 10 dispossess 14 remove clothing

divest oneself of 6 give up 7 take off 8 get rid of, give over, hand over, put aside, strip off 9 surrender 10 relinquish

divide 4 part, sort 5 share, split 7 arrange, deal out, divvy up 8 allocate, classify, disunite, separate 9 apportion, partition 10 distribute, put in order

divide and rule
Latin: 14 divide et impera
maxim of: 11 Machiavelli

divided 5 apart, split 6 parted 8 meted out 9 disunited, separated 10 unattached 11 apportioned 12 disconnected, portioned out

divide et impera 13 divide and rule
maxim of: 11 Machiavelli

divide in two 5 halve, split 6 bisect 8 cut in two, separate 9 cut in half 10 break in two 11 split in half 18 split down the middle

dividing line 4 edge 5 brink, verge 6 border, margin 8 boundary 9 threshold

divination 5 guess 6 augury 8 prophecy 10 conjecture, foreboding, prediction, prescience 11 premonition, soothsaying 15 prognostication

divine 4 holy 5 guess 6 fathom, sacred 7 predict, surmise, suspect 8 forecast, foretell, heavenly, prophesy 9 admirable, celestial, excellent, marvelous, wonderful

divine being 3 god 5 deity 7 goddess 8 divinity 14 celestial being

Divine Comedy
author: 14 Dante Alighieri
part: 7 Inferno 8 Paradiso 10 Purgatorio
guide: 6 Virgil 8 Beatrice

diviner 4 seer 5 augur 10 soothsayer 14 prognosticator

Divine retribution
goddess of: 7 Nemesis 8 Adrastea

Divine Sarah
nickname of: 14 Sarah Bernhardt

divining rod 4 twig, wand 5 dowse 9 doodlebug

divinity 3 god 5 deity 7 goddess 8 holiness, religion, theology 9 theosophy 12 science of God 14 celestial being

division 4 part, unit, wing 5 split 6 branch 7 discord, divider, section 8 disunion, variance 9 partition 10 department, difference, divergence, separation 11 splitting up 12 disagreement

divorce 4 rift 5 split 6 breach, divide 7 rupture 8 disunite, separate 9 segregate 10 dissociate, separation

divulge 4 tell 6 impart, relate, reveal 8 disclose 9 make known 11 communicate

divulgence 7 telling 8 exposure 9 imparting 10 disclosure, giving away, laying open, revelation 13 communication 15 bringing to light 17 bring out in the open

divulge to 4 tell 6 advise, inform, notify, reveal 7 apprise 8 acquaint, disclose 9 enlighten, make aware 11 familiarize 13 spill the beans 20 let the cat out of the bag

Dix, Otto
born: 7 Germany 11 Unterhausen
artwork: 6 The War 7 The City 12 The Procuress 15 Sylvia von Harden 18 Parents of the Artist 39 Prague Street Dedicated to My Contemporaries

Dixie Dugan
creator: 8 J P McEvoy 13 John H Striebel

dizzy 5 fleet, giddy, quick, rapid, shaky, swift 6 whirly 7 confuse, reeling 8 bewilder, unsteady 9 make giddy 11 lightheaded, vertiginous 12 make unsteady

Djawa see 4 Java

Djebel al-Tarik see 9 Gibraltar

Djibouti
other name: 16 French Somaliland 39 The French Territory of the Afars and the Issas
capital/largest city: 8 Djibouti
others: 5 Obock 6 Dikhil 8 Tadjoura 9 Ali-Sabieh
monetary unit: 5 franc 7 centime
lake: 4 Abbe 5 Assal
mountain: 5 Gouda
highest point: 9 Moussa Ali
sea: 3 Red
physical feature:
gulf: 4 Aden 8 Tadjoura
strait: 11 Bab el-Mandeb
people: 4 Afar, Arab 5 Issas 6 French 8 European
language: 4 Afar 6 Arabic, French, Somali
religion: 5 Islam

do 3 act 4 fare 5 clean, cover, get on, serve, visit 6 behave, finish, look at, stop in 7 achieve, arrange, carry on, conduct, execute, fulfill, make out,

perform, prepare, proceed, suffice 8 be enough, carry out, complete, conclude, organize 10 accomplish, administer, bring about, put in order 13 travel through 14 be satisfactory, comport oneself, conduct oneself

do a favor 4 help 6 assist, oblige 7 help out 11 accommodate, do a kindness

do away with 3 end 4 junk, kill, void 5 erase, quash 6 banish, cancel, cut out, give up, remove, repeal, revoke, rub out 7 abolish, blot out, nullify, rescind, weed out, wipe out 8 abrogate, stamp out, throw out 9 eliminate, eradicate, terminate 10 annihilate, put an end to 11 exterminate

Dobie Gillis, The Many Loves of
character: 11 Zelda Gilroy 13 Maynard G Krebs 14 Herbert T Gillis, Milton Armitage, Winifred (Winnie) Gillis 15 Thalia Menninger 19 Chatsworth Osborne Jr
cast: 9 Bob Denver 11 Frank Faylen, Sheila James, Tuesday Weld 12 Warren Beatty 13 Dwayne Hickman 14 Florida Friebus, Stephen Franken
Dobie imitated pose of: 7 Thinker

do business 4 deal 5 trade 10 buy and sell

docile 4 tame 7 willing 8 obedient, obliging 9 agreeable, compliant, tractable 10 manageable 11 complaisant

docility 7 pliancy 8 meekness 9 passivity 10 placidness 12 acquiescence, complaisance 13 nonresistance

dock 4 crop, join, pier, quay 5 berth, wharf 6 couple, cut off, deduct, hook up, link up 7 landing 8 cut short 10 waterfront 12 come into port 13 subject to loss 14 fasten together

dock 5 Rumux
varieties: 3 Bur 4 Sour 5 Green 6 Golden 7 Prairie, Spinach, Tanner's, Western 8 Patience 9 Purple-wen 10 Giant water

docket 4 bill, card, list 5 slate 6 agenda, lineup, roster 7 program 8 calendar, schedule 9 timetable 14 things to be done 15 order of business

doctor 2 GP, MD 3 PhD 5 alter, treat 6 change 7 dentist, falsify, surgeon 9 internist, osteopath, physician 10 podiatrist, tamper with 11 pathologist 12 gynecologist, obstetrician, pediatrician, psychiatrist, veterinarian 15 ophthalmologist 17 apply medication to 19 general practitioner, medical practitioner

Doctor Faustus
author: 10 Thomas Mann 18 Christopher Marlowe

Doctor J
nickname of: 12 Julius Erving

Doctorow, E L
author of: 7 Ragtime 8 Loon Lake,

The March **9** City of God **10** World's Fair **13** Billy Bathgate, The Waterworks **15** The Book of Daniel **18** Welcome to Hard Times

Doctor's Dilemma, The
  author: **17** George Bernard Shaw

Doctor Zhivago
  director: **9** David Lean
  author: **14** Boris Pasternak
  cast: **10** Omar Sharif (Zhivago), Rod Steiger **12** Alec Guinness, Tom Courtenay **13** Julie Christie (Lara) **14** Rita Tushingham **15** Ralph Richardson **16** Geraldine Chaplin

doctrinaire 5 rigid **6** mulish **8** absolute, dogmatic, stubborn **9** arbitrary, imperious, pigheaded **10** bullheaded, inflexible, pontifical **11** dictatorial, opinionated, overbearing, stiff-necked **12** narrow-minded **13** authoritarian **14** disciplinarian

doctrinal 8 didactic, dogmatic, edifying, tutorial **11** educational, instructive **12** prescriptive

doctrine 5 dogma, tenet **6** belief, gospel **7** precept **8** teaching **9** principle **10** conviction, philosophy

document 6 back up, record, verify **7** certify, support **9** legal form **10** instrument **12** give weight to, substantiate **13** official paper

documentation 5 proof **7** support **8** evidence **12** verification **13** corroboration **14** substantiation

doddering 4 weak **6** feeble, senile **7** shaking **8** decrepit **9** tottering, trembling

dodge 4 duck, wile **5** avoid, elude, evade, hedge, trick **6** device, swerve **7** fend off **8** sidestep **9** jump aside, stratagem, turn aside **10** equivocate **11** machination

dodging 7 ducking, eluding, evading **8** shunning **12** sidestepping **13** circumventing

Dodgson, Charles Lutwidge
  real name of: **12** Lewis Carroll

Dodoma
  capital of: **8** Tanzania

Dodsworth
  director: **12** William Wyler
  author: **13** Sinclair Lewis
  character: **4** Fran **12** Arnold Israel **14** Edith Cortright, Renee de Penable **15** Samuel Dodsworth **16** Kurt von Obersdorf **17** Major Clyde Lockert
  cast: **9** Mary Astor, Paul Lukas **10** David Niven **12** Walter Huston **14** Ruth Chatterton

doer 6 dynamo **7** hustler **8** activist, go-getter **12** active person

doff 4 bare, drop, junk, shed **5** scrap, strip **6** put off, remove **7** abandon, cast off, discard, disrobe, take off, toss off, undress **8** throw off, throw out **9** eliminate, step out of **10** do away with

dog 3 cur, pup **4** heel, mutt **5** beast, puppy **6** canine **7** mongrel, villain **9** scoundrel **10** blackguard
  Alaskan: **5** husky **8** malamute, malemute
  anatomy: **3** hip, lip, pad, paw, toe **4** arch, back, hock, loin, rump, stop **5** cheek, crest, croup, flews, skull **6** carpus, dewlap, muzzle, stifle, tarsus **7** brisket, cushion, knuckle, occiput, pastern, withers **8** heelknob, shoulder **10** metacarpus, metatarsus
  Australian: **5** dingo **8** warragal
  barkless: **7** basenji
  breed:
    herding group: **4** puli **6** briard, canaan, collie **12** border collie **13** bearded collie **14** German Shepherd **15** Belgian malinois, Belgian sheepdog, Belgian tervuren **16** Shetland sheepdog **18** Australian shepherd, Bouvier des Flandres, Cardigan Welsh corgi, Old English sheepdog, Pembroke Welsh corgi **19** Australian cattle dog **21** Polish Lowland Sheepdog
    hound group: **6** beagle, borzoi, saluki **7** basenji, harrier, whippet **9** dachshund, greyhound **10** bloodhound, otter hound **11** Afghan hound, basset hound, Ibizan hound **12** pharaoh hound **14** Irish wolfhound **15** English foxhound **16** American foxhound **17** Norwegian elkhound, Scottish deerhound **18** Rhodesian ridgeback **20** black and tan coonhound **25** petit basset griffon vendeen
    nonsporting group: **6** poodle **7** bulldog, lowchen **8** chow chow, keeshond, Shiba ina **9** dalmatian, lhasa apso **10** schipperke **11** Bichon frise **12** Finnish spitz **13** Boston terrier, French bulldog **14** American Eskimo, Chinese Sharpei, Tibetan spaniel, Tibetan terrier
    sporting group: **6** vizsla **7** pointer **8** Brittany **10** weimaraner **11** Irish setter **12** field spaniel, Gordon setter **13** cocker spaniel, English setter, Sussex spaniel **14** Clumber spaniel **15** golden retriever, Spinone Italiano **17** Irish water spaniel, Labrador retriever **19** flat-coated retriever **20** American water spaniel, curly-coated retriever, English cocker spaniel, Welsh springer spaniel **22** Chesapeake Bay retriever, English springer spaniel **23** German wirehaired pointer **24** German shorthaired pointer **25** wirehaired pointing griffon **30** Nova Scotia duck tolling retriever
    terrier group: **10** fox terrier **11** bull terrier, Skye terrier **12** Cairn terrier, Irish terrier, Welsh terrier **13** border terrier **14** Norfolk terrier, Norwich terrier, wire fox terrier **15** Airedale terrier, Lakeland terrier, Scottish terrier, Sealyham terrier **16** Kerry blue terrier, smooth fox terrier **17** Australian terrier, Bedlington terrier, Manchester terrier **18** Glen of Imaal terrier, Jack Russell Terrier, miniature schnauzer **20** Dandie Dinmont terrier, miniature bull terrier, Parson Russell terrier **24** soft-coated wheaten terrier, Staffordshire bull terrier, West Highland white terrier **28** American Staffordshire terrier
    toy group: **3** pug **7** Maltese, shih tzu **8** Havanese, papillon **9** chihuahua, pekingese, toy poodle **10** pomeranian **12** Japanese chin, silky terrier **13** affenpinscher, toy fox terrier **14** Chinese crested **15** Brussels griffon **16** Italian greyhound, Yorkshire terrier **17** English toy spaniel, Manchester terrier, miniature pinscher **26** Cavalier King Charles Spaniel
    working group: **5** akita, boxer **7** mastiff, samoyed **8** komondor, kuvaszok **9** great Dane, St Bernard **10** komondorok, rottweiler **11** bullmastiff **12** Newfoundland **13** great Pyrenees, Siberian husky **14** German pinscher, giant schnauzer **15** Alaskan malamute **16** doberman pinscher **17** Anatolian shepherd, standard schnauzer **18** Bernese mountain dog, Portuguese water dog **23** Greater Swiss mountain dog
  Bill Clinton's: **5** Buddy
  Buster Brown's: **4** Tige
  Charles, Nick and Nora's: **4** Asta
  Chinese: **7** shih tzu
  coach: **9** dalmatian
  combining form: **3** cyn **4** cani, cyno
  constellation: **12** Canis Majoris
  Dorothy's: **4** Toto
  family: **7** Canidae
  FDR's: **4** Fala **5** Falla
  female: **3** dam, gip, gyp **4** slut **5** bitch, brach **7** brachet
  genus: **5** Canis
  George Bush's: **4** Spot **6** Barney
  group: **4** pack **5** leash **6** kennel
  "His Master's Voice": **6** Nipper
  Hungarian: **4** puli **6** kuvasz, vizsla
  Indian: **5** dhole
  Japanese: **5** akita
  Little Orphan Annie's: **5** Sandy
  male: **3** dog
  movie/TV: **4** Asta, Lady **5** Benji, Tramp **6** Lassie **9** Old Yeller, Rin Tin Tin
  mythical: **8** Cerberus
  Nixon's: **8** Checkers
  Punch and Judy's: **4** Toby

Russian: 6 borzoi 7 samoyed
star: 6 Sirius 8 Canicula
Thin Man movies, in: 4 Asta
Welsh: 5 corgi
wild: 5 adjag, dhole, dingo, guara, rabid 6 jackal 7 agouara 8 cimarron
young: 3 pup 5 puppy, whelp

Dogberry
  character in: 19 Much Ado About Nothing
  author: 11 Shakespeare

Dog Day Afternoon
  director: 11 Sidney Lumet
  cast: 8 Al Pacino 10 John Cazale 14 Charles Durning

dogged 8 stubborn 9 tenacious 10 determined, persistent 11 unremitting

dogie 4 calf 14 motherless calf

dogies 6 calves, cattle 16 motherless calves

dogma 5 credo, tenet 7 beliefs 8 doctrine 9 teachings 10 philosophy, principles 11 convictions

dogmatic 6 biased 8 stubborn 9 arbitrary, doctrinal, imperious, obstinate 10 prejudiced 11 dictatorial, domineering, opinionated

Dog Star
  constellation of:
    Hunting Dogs: 13 Canes Venatici
    Larger Dog: 10 Canis Major
    Smaller Dog: 10 Canis Minor

dogwood 6 Cornus
  varieties: 5 Brown, Creek, False, Giant, Silky, Stiff 6 Pagoda, Poison 7 Chinese 8 American, Jamaican, Mountain, Panicled, Redosier, Siberian, Tatarian 9 Blood-twig, Flowering, Tartarian 10 Golden-twig, West Indian 11 Round-leaved 13 White Mountain

Doha, al-Dawha
  capital of: 5 Qatar

do in 4 kill 6 murder 7 destroy, exhaust, tire out

Doktor Faust
  opera by: 6 Busoni
  character: 5 Faust 14 Duchess of Parma 14 Mephistopheles

dolce
  music: 7 sweetly

dolce far niente 18 pleasing inactivity 20 it is sweet to do nothing

dolce vita 9 sweet life

Dol Common
  character in: 12 The Alchemist
  author: 6 Jonson

doldrums 5 blues, dumps, gloom 10 depression, melancholy

dole 4 deal, give 5 share 6 parcel 7 charity, handout, welfare 9 allotment 10 allocation 13 apportionment

doleful 3 sad 6 dismal, dreary, gloomy, woeful 7 joyless, unhappy 9 sorrowful

dolente
  music: 9 sorrowful

dole out 4 give, mete 5 allot 6 parcel 7 portion 8 allocate, dispense 9 apportion 10 distribute

doling out 7 dealing 9 allotment, parceling 10 allocation, assignment 12 distribution 13 apportionment

doll 5 dolly, dummy, honey 6 beauty, puppet 7 darling, rag doll 8 baby doll, figurine, golliwog 9 teddy bear 10 marionette, sweetheart 11 pretty child

dollar 3 one 4 bean, bill, buck, coin, note, skin, yuan 5 money, tater, token 6 single 7 ironman, smacker 8 cartwheel, simolean

Dollar A Second
  host: 9 Jan Murray

Dollar Bill
  nickname of: 11 Bill Bradley

dollop 3 dab 4 blob, dash, lump 11 small amount

Doll's House, A
  author: 11 Henrik Ibsen
  character: 8 Krogstad 10 Nora Helmer 13 Torvald Helmer

dolly 3 toy 4 cart, doll 9 plaything 15 wheeled platform

dolor 5 grief 6 sorrow 7 anguish, sadness

dolorous 3 sad 6 rueful, woeful 7 doleful, tearful, unhappy 8 dejected, downcast, grievous, mournful, pathetic, pitiable, wretched 9 anguished, cheerless, harrowing, miserable, sorrowful, woebegone 10 calamitous, despondent, lamentable, melancholy 11 distressing 12 disconsolate, heavyhearted 13 grief-stricken

Dolphin
  constellation of: 9 Delphinus

Dolphin, The
  author: 12 Robert Lowell

dolt 4 clod, fool, jerk 5 idiot, moron 6 nitwit 7 half-wit, jackass 8 bonehead, imbecile, numskull 9 blockhead

doltish 4 dumb, slow 5 thick 6 simple, stupid 7 asinine, foolish, idiotic, moronic, witless 8 ignorant, retarded 9 brainless, imbecilic 10 half-witted, slow-witted 12 dunderheaded, muddleheaded, simple-minded 13 rattlebrained 14 featherbrained

domain 4 area, fief, land 5 field 6 empire, estate, region, sphere 7 kingdom 8 dominion, property, province 9 bailiwick, territory

Dombey and Son
  author: 14 Charles Dickens
  character: 4 Paul 5 Toots 6 Carker, Cuttle 8 Florence, Mr Dombey 9 Dr Blimber, Walter Gay 11 Joe Bagstock, Susan Nipper 12 Cousin Feenix, Edith Granger, Solomon Gills

dome
  Italian: 5 duomo

Domenichino
  real name: 16 Domenico Zampieri
  born: 5 Italy 7 Bologna
  artwork: 11 Hunt of Diana 16 Monsignor Agucchi 18 The Four Evangelists, The Life of St Cecilia 23 Last Communion of St Jerome 30 Landscape with Tobias and the Angel

domestic 4 cook, maid, tame 6 au pair, butler, native 7 endemic, servant 8 homemade, houseboy 9 attendant, home-grown 10 indigenous, not foreign 11 houseborne, native-grown, not imported 12 domesticated, hearthloving 13 household help

domesticated 4 tame 11 housebroken

domicile 4 home 5 house 8 dwelling 9 residence 14 legal residence

dominance 4 edge 8 hegemony 9 advantage, authority, upper hand 10 precedence 11 preeminence, superiority

dominant 5 chief, major 6 ruling 8 superior 9 principal 10 commanding 11 controlling, outstanding 13 authoritative, most important, most prominent

dominate 4 rule 5 dwarf 6 direct, govern 7 command, control 8 domineer 9 tower over 11 preside over

dominating 6 lordly, ruling 7 topmost 8 dominant 9 directing, governing, principal, prominent 10 commanding 11 controlling, domineering, outstanding 12 advantageous 13 authoritative, most important 15 most outstanding

domination 4 rule 5 power 7 command, control, mastery 9 authority 11 superiority

domineer 7 control 8 dominate, lord over 9 dictate to, tyrannize

domineering 8 arrogant, despotic, dogmatic 9 imperious 10 commanding, oppressive, tyrannical 11 dictatorial, overbearing 13 authoritative

Dominican Republic
  capital/largest city: 12 Santo Domingo 14 Ciudad Trujillo
  others: 4 Azua, Bani, Moca, Pena, Polo 5 Bonao, Cotui, Nagua, Neiba, Nizao, Sosua 6 Higuey, La Vega, Oviedo 7 Sanchez 8 Barahona, Santiago 11 Puerto Plata 17 San Pedro de Macoris 21 San Francisco de Macoris
  measure: 3 ona 5 tarea 6 fanega
  monetary unit: 3 oro 4 peso 6 franco
  island: 5 Beata, Saona 8 Altovelo, Catalina 10 Hispaniola
  lake: 10 Enriquillo
  mountain: 4 Tina 5 Gallo, Neiba 7 Baoruco, Central 8 Bahoruco, Oriental 13 Sententrional
  highest point: 6 Duarte
  river: 4 Yuna 5 Ozama 11 Yaque del Sur 13 Yaque del Norte
  sea: 8 Atlantic 9 Caribbean
  physical feature:

bay: 4 Ocoa, Yuma 5 Neiba 6 Rincon, Samana 7 Isabela 8 Calderas, Escocesa

cape: 5 Beata, Falso 6 Cabron, Engano 7 Caucedo, Isabela, Macoris

valley: 4 Real 5 Neyba

people: 5 Negro, Taino 6 Indian 7 mulatto, Spanish 9 Caucasian

discoverer: 8 Columbus

language: 6 French 7 English, Spanish

religion: 13 Roman Catholic

feature:

dance: 8 merengue

religious pilgrimage: 8 romerias

sport: 8 baseball

food:

dessert: 8 pinonate

fish/meat pastry: 10 pastelitos

stew: 8 sancocho

dominion 4 land, rule 5 realm 6 domain, empire, region 7 command, mastery 9 authority, supremacy, territory 11 sovereignty 12 jurisdiction

Hindu: 3 raj

Dominus 3 God 4 Lord

Dominus vobiscum 16 the Lord be with you

don 4 wear 5 put on 6 pull on 7 dress in, get into

Don

origin: 5 Welsh

form: 7 goddess

son: 7 Gwydion

daughter: 8 Arianrod

dona 4 lady 5 madam

Dona Flor and Her Two Husbands

author: 10 Jorge Amado

Donalbain

father: 6 Duncan

brother: 7 Malcom

Donald Duck

creator: 10 Walt Disney

character:

girlfriend: 5 Daisy

nephew: 4 Huey 5 Dewey, Louie

uncle: 7 Scrooge

Donar

origin: 8 Germanic

god of: 7 thunder

donate 4 give 6 bestow 7 present 8 bequeath 10 contribute 11 make a gift of

Donatello

real name: 15 Donato di Niccolo

born: 5 Italy 7 Florence

artwork: 5 David 6 St Mark 7 Zuccone 8 Jeremiah, St George 11 Gattamelata 12 Mary Magdalen 19 Judith and Holofernes, St John the Evangelist 22 Cavalcanti Annunciation

donation 4 gift 7 present 12 contribution

Don Carlos

author: 14 Johann Schiller

opera by: 5 Verdi

character: 7 Rodrigo 8 Philip II 9 Don Carlos 13 Princess Eboli 15 Grand Inquisitor 17 Elizabeth de Valois

Dondi

creator: 8 Gus Edson 10 Irwin Hasen

dog: 7 Queenie

done 5 ready 8 finished, prepared 9 completed 12 cooked enough 18 cooked sufficiently

done for 4 dead, gone, over, sunk 5 all up, ended, kaput, spent 6 beaten, doomed, ruined 7 all over, damaged, through 8 finished 9 exhausted

done in 4 beat 5 all in, slain, spent, tired, weary 6 bushed, killed, pooped 7 drained, wearied, worn out 8 dog tired, fatigued, murdered, tired out 9 bone weary, dead tired, played out 10 knocked off

Don Giovanni

also: 7 Don Juan 15 The Rake Punished

opera by: 6 Mozart

setting: 7 Seville

character: 7 Masetto, Zerlina 9 Donna Anna, Leporello 10 Don Ottavio 11 Donna Elvira 15 The Commendatore

Donizetti, Gaetano

born: 5 Italy 7 Bergamo

composer of: 10 Anna Bolena, La Favorita 11 Don Pasquale 12 Elixir of Love, Maria Stuarda 13 L'elisir d'amore, Marino Faliero, Torquato Tasso 14 Lucrezia Borgia 15 Roberto Devereux 16 Linda di Chamounix 17 Lucia di Lammermoor 21 Daughter of the Regiment

Don Juan 3 man 4 beau, wolf 5 Romeo, swain, wooer 6 fellow, squire, steady, suitor 7 admirer, courter, gallant, pursuer 8 Casanova, lothario, lover boy, paramour, young man 9 boyfriend, Lochinvar 10 lady-killer 15 gentleman caller

Don Juan

author: 21 George Gordon Lord Byron

character: 6 Haidee 9 Donna Inez 10 Donna Julia

donkey 3 ass 4 fool, mule 5 burro, idiot 7 jackass

Donlevy, Brian

wife: 12 Marjorie Lane

born: 7 Ireland 9 Portadown

roles: 9 Beau Geste 15 The Great McGinty 21 Two Years Before the Mast

Donn, Arabella

character in: 14 Jude the Obscure

author: 5 Hardy

donna 4 lady 5 madam

Donna Reed Show, The

character: 9 Jeff Stone, Mary Stone 10 Donna Stone 11 Dr Alex Stone, Midge Kelsey, Trisha Stone 12 Dr Dave Kelsey

cast: 8 Bob Crane, Carl Betz 9 Ann McCrea, Donna Reed 12 Paul Peterson 13 Patty Peterson 14 Shelley Fabares

Donne, John

author of: 7 Sermons 10 The Ecstasy, The Extasie 11 Holy Sonnets 15 Death Be Not Proud, Songs and Sonnets, The Canonization 20 Paradoxes and Problems 30 A Valediction Forbidding Mourning

donnish 7 preachy 8 academic, didactic, pedantic 9 pedagogic

donnybrook 3 row 4 fray 5 brawl, fight, melee, set-to 6 affray, dustup, fracas, ruckus, rumpus 7 ruction, scuffle 8 skirmish 10 free-for-all 19 knock-down-and-drag-out

donor 5 giver 10 benefactor 11 contributor 12 humanitarian 14 philanthropist

do-nothing 5 idler 6 loafer 14 good-for-nothing

do not prosecute

Latin: 13 nolle prosequi

do not repeat

Latin: 12 non repetatur

Don Pasquale

opera by: 9 Donizetti

character: 6 Norina 7 Ernesto 11 Dr Malatesta

Don Quixote de la Mancha

also: 38 El ingenioso hidalgo Don Quijote de la Mancha

author: 17 Miguel de Cervantes (Saavedra)

character: 10 Pedro Perez 11 Sancho Panza 17 Dulcinea del Toboso

horse: 9 Rosinante

musical: 13 Man of La Mancha

doodad 5 gizmo 6 device, gadget 8 ornament 9 doohickey 10 decoration 11 contraption, contrivance, thingamabob, thingamajig 15 whatchamacallit

doohickey 5 gizmo, thing 6 device, dingus, gadget, object, widget 7 dojiggy, whatsis 8 dojigger 9 thingummy 11 thingamabob, thingamajig 14 thingamadoodle 15 whatchamacallit

Dooley, Thomas Anthony

founded: 6 MEDICO 31 Medical International Corporation

worked in: 13 Southeast Asia

doolie 4 USAF 8 freshman

Doolittle, Eliza

character in: 9 Pygmalion 10 My Fair Lady

author: 4 Shaw

doom 3 end, lot 4 fate, ruin 5 death, judge 7 condemn, convict, destiny, portion, verdict 8 judgment 10 Armageddon 11 destruction, Judgment Day 13 consign to ruin, end of the world, pronouncement 15 resurrection day, the Last Judgment 17 mark for demolition

doomed 5 fated 6 damned, ruined 8 ill-fated 9 condemned

doomsday 11 Judgment Day 13 Day of Judgment, end of the world 15 the Last Judgment

do one's best 3 try 6 strive 7 attempt 8 endeavor, go all out 9 take pains 12 make an effort 13 give all one has 15 knock oneself out

Doonesbury
creator: 12 Garry Trudeau
character: 2 B D 5 Honey, Rufus 6 Calvin, Zonker 7 Boopsie 9 Uncle Duke 12 Joanie Caucus 14 Mark Slackmeyer 18 Michael J Doonesbury

door 4 exit 5 entry 6 egress, portal 7 hallway, ingress 8 entrance 11 entranceway

doorway 5 entry 7 ingress, opening 8 entrance

Doorways
god of: 5 Janus

dope 3 pot, tip 4 drip, drug, fool, jerk, junk, nerd, news 5 creep, drugs, dummy, klutz, scoop 6 heroin, sedate, uppers 7 downers, opiates 8 additive 9 narcotics, narcotize, substance 10 antiseptic, astringent, medication 11 anesthetize, preparation 12 disinfectant 17 inside information

dope fiend 4 head, user 5 doper, freak 6 addict, junkie 7 hophead 8 cokehead 10 dope addict, drug abuser, drug addict

do penance 5 atone 7 expiate 10 make amends

dopey 4 dumb 6 leaden, stupid, torpid 7 asinine, idiotic, witless 8 comatose, mindless, sluggish 9 brainless, lethargic 10 dull-witted, slow-witted, slumberous 11 block-headed, thickheaded 12 simple-minded

Doppelganger 6 double 13 ghostly double
literally: 12 double-walker

Doppler, Christian Johann
field: 7 physics
nationality: 8 Austrian
discovered: 13 Doppler Effect

Dorcas
also called: 7 Tabitha
revived by: 5 Peter
hometown: 5 Joppa

Doris
father: 7 Oceanus
mother: 6 Tethys
husband: 6 Nereus
mother of: 7 Nereids

dormancy 7 latency 8 inaction 10 inactivity, quiescence, somnolence 11 hibernation

dormant 4 idle 8 inactive, sleeping 9 quiescent, somnolent 11 hibernating

Dorothy
character in: 13 The Wizard of Oz

author: 4 Baum
dog: 4 Toto

dorsum 5 chine, spine 8 backbone

dose 2 OD 3 cut, nip 4 dram, pill, shot, slug 5 quota, share, slice 6 amount, needle, ration, tablet 7 capsule, measure, portion, section, segment 8 division, overdose, quantity 9 allotment, allowance, daily dose, injection 10 percentage

Dos Passos, John
author of: 3 U S A 11 The Big Money 13 Three Soldiers 16 Nineteen Nineteen 17 Manhattan Transfer 22 The Forty-Second Parallel

dossier 4 file 5 brief 6 record 9 portfolio 14 detailed report

Dostoevsky, Fyodor Mikhailovich
author of: 8 The Idiot 9 The Double 10 The Gambler 12 The Possessed 18 Crime and Punishment 20 The Brothers Karamazov 23 Notes from the Underground

dot 3 dab 4 mark, spot 5 fleck, point, speck 6 dapple, period 7 stipple 9 small spot

dotage 8 senility 15 second childhood 16 feeblemindedness

dote 8 be senile, fuss over

dote on 5 adore, prize, spoil, value 6 pamper 7 cherish, indulge 8 fuss over, treasure 15 lavish affection

doting 4 fond 6 loving 9 indulgent, pampering 12 affectionate

double 4 dual, twin 5 clone 6 paired 7 replica, two-part 8 two-sided 9 ambiguous, duplicate 10 dead ringer 11 again as much, counterpart, meant for two, twice as much 12 twice as great 13 multiply by two, spitting image 15 increase twofold
German: 12 Doppelganger

Double, The
author: 16 Fyodor Dostoevsky

double-cross 5 rat on 6 betray, do dirt, tell on, turn in 7 abandon, deceive, let down, sell out, two-time 8 denounce, inform on, run out on, snitch on 9 play Judas 10 be disloyal 13 be treacherous, inform against, play false with 14 break faith with 16 blow the whistle on, sell down the river

double-crosser 5 cheat 7 traitor 8 betrayer, deceiver, informer

Double-Dealer, The
author: 15 William Congreve

double-dealing 5 false 6 deceit, sneaky, tricky 7 crooked, devious, perfidy 8 bad faith, betrayal, disloyal 9 deceitful, duplicity, falseness, treachery, two-timing 10 disloyalty, perfidious, sneakiness 11 crookedness, double-cross, duplicitous, treacherous 12 dishonorable 13 breach of faith, faithlessness

double entendre 12 off-color joke, risque remark 18 ambiguous statement

double entente 9 ambiguity

Double Indemnity
director: 11 Billy Wilder
cast: 13 Fred MacMurray 15 Barbara Stanwyck, Edward G Robinson
script: 9 James Cain 15 Raymond Chandler

Double Life, A
director: 11 George Cukor
cast: 10 Signe Hasso 12 Edmond O'Brien, Ronald Colman 14 Shelley Winters
Oscar for: 5 actor (Colman)
script: 10 Ruth Gordon 11 Garson Kanin

double meaning 9 ambiguity
French: 13 double entente 14 double entendre

doublet 4 pair 5 tunic 6 couple, jacket 10 two of a kind

double-talk 4 bunk, jazz 5 hokum 6 bunkum, drivel, gabble, jabber 7 baloney, blather, palaver, prattle, twaddle 8 flimflam, flummery, nonsense 9 gibberish 10 balderdash, hocus-pocus, mumbo jumbo 11 obfuscation 12 gobbledygook

double-walker
German: 12 Doppelganger

Double X
nickname of: 9 Jimmy Foxx

doubt 5 qualm 6 wonder 7 suspect 8 distrust, mistrust, question 9 misgiving, skeptical, suspicion 10 be doubtful, indecision 11 uncertainty 12 apprehension 14 feel uncertain 14 waver in opinion 15 have doubts about 16 lack confidence in, lack of conviction

Doubter see 6 Thomas

doubtful 5 vague 7 dubious, obscure, suspect, unclear 9 tentative, uncertain, undecided, unsettled 10 hesitating, irresolute, suspicious 11 unconvinced 12 inconclusive, questionable

doubtfulness 5 doubt 7 dubiety 8 distrust, mistrust, unbelief 9 disbelief, suspicion 10 skepticism 11 incredulity 14 lack of credence

Doubting see 6 Thomas

doucement
music: 6 gently

douceur 3 tip 5 bribe 8 gratuity 9 sweetness

dough 4 cash, duff, spud 5 bread, crust, money, paster 6 batter, change, leaven, noodle 8 doughboy 11 infantryman

doughnut 4 cake, tire 5 bagel, torus 6 cymbal, dunker, sinker 7 beignet, cruller, twister

doughty 4 bold 5 brave 6 strong 8 fearless, intrepid, unafraid 9 confi-

dent, dauntless **10** courageous, determined **12** stout-hearted

Douglas, Archibald
character in: **7** Marmion
author: **5** Scott

Douglas, Kirk
real name: **17** Issur Danielovitch
son: **7** Michael
roles: **8** Champion **9** Spartacus **10**
The Vikings **11** Lust for Life **14** De-
tective Story, Seven Days in May **17**
The Glass Menagerie, It Runs in the
Family, Young Man with a Horn **18**
Letter to Three Wives **22** Mourning
Becomes Electra

Douglas, Lloyd C
author of: **7** The Robe **23** The Magnificent Obsession

Douglas, Melvyn
real name: **23** Melvyn Edouard Hesselberg
wife: **12** Helen Gahagan
born: **7** Macon GA
roles: **3** Hud **9** Ninotchka **10** Being
There

Douglas, Michael
father: **4** Kirk
wife: **18** Catherine Zeta-Jones
roles: **4** Coma **7** The Game **9** The In-
Laws **10** Disclosure, Wall Street (Oscar) **11** Star Chamber **13** Basic Instinct **14** Jewel of the Nile **15** Fatal
Attraction **16** The China Syndrome,
The Perfect Murder, The War of the
Roses **17** It Runs in the Family, Romancing the Stone **20** The American
President

dour 4 sour **6** gloomy, morose, solemn,
sullen **9** cheerless **10** forbidding, unfriendly

Douras, Marion Cecilia
real name of: **12** Marion Davies

douse 4 soak **5** souse **6** drench **7** immerse **8** saturate, submerge **15** plunge
into water

Dove, Noah's
constellation of: **7** Columba

Dover Beach
author: **13** Matthew Arnold

dovetail 4 jibe, join **5** match, tally,
unite **8** coincide **9** harmonize **11** fit
together **12** interlocking

dowager 5 widow **6** relict **7** elderly

dowdy 4 drab **5** tacky **6** frumpy,
shabby, sloppy **8** slovenly **12** unattractive

dowel 3 peg, pin, rod **4** pole **5** stick **7**
spindle

down 3 ill **4** blue, deck, drop, fell,
gulp, sick **5** drink, floor **6** ailing **7** put
away, swallow **8** dejected, downcast,
feathers **9** depressed **10** dispirited **12**
disheartened

down-and-out 4 sick **5** broke **9** penniless **12** impoverished, on one's

uppers **13** incapacitated **15** under the
weather

downcast 3 low, sad **4** blue **7** unhappy **8** dejected **9** cheerless, depressed **11** discouraged **12** disconsolate, disheartened

downfall 4 fall, ruin **6** shower **8** collapse, downpour **9** rainstorm, ruination **10** rain shower **11** destruction

downgrade 4 drop **5** lower **6** debase
7 decline, descent, way down **8** belittle, minimize **9** declivity, denigrate,
devaluate **10** depreciate

downhearted 3 sad **7** unhappy **8** dejected, downcast **9** depressed, sorrowful **10** dispirited **11** discouraged **12**
disheartened

downheartedness 5 gloom **6** dismay
7 despair, sadness **9** dejection, pessimism **10** depression, low spirits, melancholy **11** despondency **12** hopelessness **14** discouragement

down in the dumps 4 blue, glum **6**
gloomy **7** in a funk **9** depressed **10**
despondent **13** in the doldrums

down in the mouth 3 sad **6** dismal,
woeful **7** joyless, unhappy **8** dejected,
downcast **9** depressed, sorrowful,
woebegone **10** lugubrious **12** disconsolate

downpayment 6 binder **7** advance,
deposit **9** money down

downpour 6 shower **9** rainstorm **10**
cloudburst, rain shower

downright 4 open **5** blunt, frank, total, utter **6** candid, direct, honest, really **7** in truth, plainly, sincere, utterly
8 absolute, actually, complete **9** out-
and-out **10** aboveboard, completely,
thoroughly **12** unmistakably **13** thoroughgoing, unequivocally **15** straightforward

Downright
character in: **19** Every Man in His
Humour
author: **6** Jonson

downstairs 5 below **6** cellar **8** basement **10** first floor **11** ground floor

down the drain 4 gone, lost **9** up in
smoke **12** out the window

down-to-earth 5 crass, plain, sober,
solid **6** casual, coarse, earthy, simple
7 relaxed **8** informal, sensible **9** practical, pragmatic, realistic **10** hardheaded, hard-boiled, no-nonsense **11**
plain-spoken, substantial **12** matter-of-
fact, unidealistic **13** unsentimental

downtown 9 inner city, urban area **10**
center city, metropolis **16** business
district, metropolitan area

downtrodden 9 exploited, oppressed
10 tyrannized **11** subservient **12**
harshly ruled

downturn 3 dip, sag **4** drop, fall, skid,
slip **5** slide, slump **6** plunge, waning
7 decline, reverse, setback **8** decrease

9 downslide, downswing, downtrend,
dwindling, recession **10** depression,
diminution **12** degeneration **13** deterioration

Down Under see **9** Australia

down with
French: **4** a bas

downy 4 soft **5** fuzzy, nappy, plumy,
quiet **6** fleecy, fluffy **7** cunning,
knowing **8** feathery **9** featherbed

do wrong 3 err, sin **8** go astray **9** misbehave **10** transgress

Doyle, Sir Arthur Conan
see also **14** Holmes, Sherlock
author of: **13** The Sign of Four **15** A
Study in Scarlet, The White Company **25** The Hound of the Baskervilles **26** Adventures of Sherlock
Holmes
character: **10** Irene Adler **12** Dr John
Watson **13** Mycroft Holmes **14** Sherlock Holmes **17** Inspector Lestrade,
Professor Moriarty

doze 3 nap **6** catnap, siesta, snooze **10**
forty winks, light sleep **12** sleep
lightly

dozy 4 lazy **6** drowsy, sleepy **7** languid
9 lethargic, somnolent

D P 5 exile **6** emigre **7** outcast, refugee
8 deportee **10** expatriate **14** banished
person, deported person **15** displaced
person **16** political refugee

drab 4 dull, gray **5** dingy **6** dismal,
dreary, gloomy, somber **9** cheerless,
dull brown **10** lackluster

drabness 8 dullness **9** dinginess **10**
dreariness, gloominess **13** colorlessness

Dracula
author: **10** Bram Stoker
character: **8** Dr Seward **10** Mina Murray **12** Count Dracula, Dr Van Hels-
ing, Lucy Westenra **14** Arthur Holm-
wood, Jonathan Harker

draft 4 drag, gulp, haul, pull, wind **5**
drink **6** breeze, induct, sketch **7** diagram, outline, swallow **9** conscript,
induction **10** money order **11** postal
order, rough sketch **12** conscription,
current of air **15** military service **16**
drawing from a cask **18** preliminary
version **22** call for military service

drafty 6 breezy, chilly

drag 3 lug **4** bore, haul, pull **5** bring,
crawl, trail **6** dredge **7** be drawn **9**
inch along **10** creep along, move
slowly, spoilsport, wet blanket **11**
party-pooper

Dragnet
character: **8** (Sgt) Ed Jacobs **9** (Sgt)
Ben Romero, (Sgt) Joe Friday **10** (Of-
ficer) Bill Gannon, (Officer) Frank
Smith
cast: **8** Jack Webb **9** Herb Ellis **11**
Harry Morgan **12** Ben Alexander **14**
Barney Phillips **16** Barton Yarbor-

ough
setting: 10 Los Angeles

Dragon 14 Leviathan
constellation of: 5 Draco

drag on 4 last **6** endure, keep on, keep up **7** persist **8** continue **9** persevere

drag one's feet 5 crawl, creep **6** dawdle **9** waste time **10** move slowly **13** procrastinate

dragonfly
varieties: 5 biddy **6** darner **7** skimmer **8** clubtail, grayback **9** amberwing **12** Elisa Skimmer

Dragon Seed
author: 10 Pearl S Buck

Dragon's teeth
sown by: 6 Cadmus
location: 6 Thebes
grew into: 8 warriors

dragoon 5 bully, force **6** coerce, compel **7** trooper **8** browbeat, bulldoze, cavalier, horseman, pressure **9** strongarm **10** cavalryman **12** horse soldier, horse trooper **14** mounted soldier

drag through the mud 5 smear, sully, taint **6** debase, defame, smirch, vilify **7** degrade, tarnish, vitiate **8** disgrace, dishonor **9** discredit, disparage **10** stigmatize

drain 3 sap **4** drag, pipe, tube **5** empty, sewer, use up **6** outlet, strain **7** channel, conduit, debouch, deplete, flow out, pump off **8** empty out **9** depletion, discharge, dissipate **10** impoverish

drainage 4 flow **9** discharge

drained 4 beat **5** all in, empty, spent, tired, weary **6** bushed, done in, pooped, used up **7** emptied, wearied, worn out **8** consumed, depleted, dog tired, expended, fatigued, finished, tired out **9** dead tired, enervated, exhausted, played out

Drake, Stan
creator/artist of: 21 The Heart of Juliet Jones

Drake, Temple
character in: 9 Sanctuary
author: 8 Faulkner

dram
abbreviation: 2 dr

drama 4 play **6** acting **8** the stage **9** direction, vividness **10** excitement, the theater **11** mise-en-scene **15** dramatic quality, intense interest, theatrical piece
god of: 7 Bacchus

dramatic 8 striking **9** climactic, emotional **10** theatrical **11** sensational, suspenseful **12** melodramatic **13** for the theater

dramatics 6 acting **7** emoting **9** theatrics **10** dramaturgy, stagecraft **11** hamming it up, histrionics, thespianism

dramatis personae 4 cast **6** actors **7**

players **10** performers **16** cast of characters, list of performers

dramaturgy 5 drama **7** theater **10** stagecraft **11** dramatic art

Drambuie
type: 7 liqueur
origin: 8 Scotland
flavor: 5 herbs, honey
with scotch: 9 Rusty Nail

drape 4 deck, garb, veil, wrap **5** adorn, array, cloak, cover, dress **6** attire, bedeck, enrobe, enwrap, shroud, swathe, wrap up **7** apparel, bedight, envelop, festoon, sheathe, swaddle **8** enshroud, enswathe

drastic 4 dire, rash **7** bizarre, extreme, radical **8** dreadful **9** dangerous **10** outlandish **11** deleterious

Dravidian
language group: 3 Kui **5** Ghond, Tamil **6** Teluga **8** Kanarese **9** Malayalam
spoken in: 5 India **6** Ceylon **8** Sri Lanka

draw 3 get, tie, tow **4** drag, etch, haul, limn, lure, pick, pull, take **5** charm, draft, drain, evoke, infer, write **6** allure, come-on, deduce, elicit, entice, extend, make up, siphon, sketch **7** attract, distort, draw out, extract, make out, pick out, pull out, pump out, stretch, suck dry, take out, wrinkle **8** contract, deadlock, elongate, protract **9** attenuate, pull along, stalemate **10** attraction, bring forth, enticement, inducement, make appear **14** make a picture of

draw away 2 go **5** leave **6** go back, shrink **7** retreat **8** withdraw

drawback 8 handicap, obstacle **9** detriment, hindrance **10** impediment **12** disadvantage **14** stumbling block

draw back 6 flinch, recoil **7** back off, retreat **8** move away, withdraw

draw close 3 hug **4** come, near **6** arrive, enfold **7** embrace **8** approach, come nigh, gain upon **10** move toward

drawers 5 pants **6** shorts **7** panties **8** bloomers, calzoons, trousers **9** pantalets, underwear **10** underpants

draw forth 5 evoke **6** elicit **7** distill, extract

drawing 5 study **6** sketch **7** lottery, picture **9** depiction, selection **11** delineation **12** illustration

drawing apart 8 dividing **9** diverging **10** separating **12** splitting off

drawing out 9 expansion, extension **10** elongation, stretching **11** attenuation, lengthening, protraction **12** prolongation

drawing power 4 pull **6** allure, appeal **9** magnetism **10** attraction, enticement **11** fascination

drawing room 5 salon **6** parlor **10**

living room **11** sitting room **13** reception room

drawn out 4 long **7** lengthy **8** extended **9** elongated, prolonged **10** lengthened, protracted

draw out 5 educe, evoke **6** elicit, expand, extend, extort **7** distill, enlarge, extract, prolong, spin out, stretch **8** elongate, lengthen, protract **9** attenuate, call forth **10** stretch out

draw the line 5 limit **8** contrast, separate **12** fix a boundary **13** differentiate

draw to a close 3 end **6** finish **8** conclude **11** come to an end

draw together 4 herd, mass, pack **5** bunch, crowd, flock, group **6** gather, huddle **7** cluster, collect, tighten **8** assemble, compress, contract **9** constrict **10** congregate

draw up 3 map **5** draft **6** make up, map out **7** charter, diagram, outline **9** blueprint

draw up plans 5 draft **6** design, sketch **7** outline

dray 4 cart **5** wagon **7** tipcart, tumbrel **8** dumpcart

dread 4 fear **5** awful **6** fright, terror **7** anguish, anxiety, cower at, fearful **8** alarming, cringe at **10** be afraid of, horrifying, shrink from, terrifying **11** fearfulness, frightening, trepidation **12** apprehension **20** anticipate with horror

dreaded object
French: 9 bete noire

dreadful 5 awful **6** tragic **7** fearful **8** alarming, horrible, shocking, terrible **9** frightful **11** distressing

dream 3 joy **4** goal, hope, muse, wish **5** think **6** desire, vision **7** delight, fantasy, hope for, incubus, reverie, think up **8** consider, pleasure, prospect **9** nightmare **11** expectation, have as a goal **13** look forward to, lost in thought

Dream of the Golden Mountains, The
author: 13 Malcolm Cowley

Dreams
god of: 6 Icelus, Oniros **7** Oneiros **8** Morpheus **9** Phantasus

Dream Songs, The
author: 12 John Berryman

dream up 5 frame, hatch **6** create, invent **7** concoct **8** conceive, contrive

dreamy 4 airy **5** blank, empty, vague **6** absent, musing, unreal **8** ethereal, fanciful, illusory, soothing **9** fantastic, wonderful **10** delightful **11** preoccupied, unrealistic **13** unsubstantial **14** out of this world

dreariness 9 bleakness **10** desolation, dismalness, gloominess, melancholy **13** cheerlessness

dreary 3 sad **4** drab **5** bleak **6** dismal,

gloomy **7** forlorn **8** mournful **9** cheerless **10** depressing, melancholy

dregs 6 rabble **7** deposit, grounds, residue **8** canaille, riffraff, sediment **9** settlings, worst part **11** lower depths

Dreiser, Theodore
 author of: **8** The Titan **12** Sister Carrie, The Financier **17** An American Tragedy

drench 3 wet **4** soak **5** douse **8** saturate

dress 4 curl, deck, do up, garb, gown, robe, trim **5** adorn, frock, groom, treat **6** attire **7** apparel, arrange, bandage, cleanse, clothes, comb out, costume, garnish **8** clothing, decorate, ornament **9** disinfect, embellish **12** put on clothes **13** clothe oneself

Dressed to Kill
 director: **12** Brian De Palma
 cast: **10** Nancy Allen **11** Keith Gordon **12** Michael Caine **14** Angie Dickinson

dressed up 7 adorned, duded up **8** costumed, dolled up, tarted up **9** decorated, disguised, in costume **10** ornamented **11** embellished

dresser 6 bureau **7** cabinet, commode **8** cupboard **10** chiffonier **14** chest of drawers

dressing-down 6 rebuke **7** censure, chiding, reproof **8** reproach, scolding **9** reprimand **10** bawling-out, chewing-out, upbraiding **11** castigation, reprobation **12** remonstrance **13** tongue-lashing

dressing-gown
 French: **13** robe-de-chambre

dressmaker 9 couturier, midinette **10** couturiere, seamstress

dress up 5 adorn **6** doll up **7** enhance, improve **8** beautify, ornament, spruce up **9** embellish, embroider, smarten up **10** exaggerate

Dreyfuss, Richard
 roles: **4** Jaws **6** Tin Men **8** Stakeout **9** Stand by Me, The Big Fix **10** Silver City **12** What About Bob **14** Mr. Holland's Opus, The Goodbye Girl (Oscar) **15** Moon Over Parador **16** American Graffiti **20** Postcards from the Edge **24** Down and Out in Beverly Hills **29** Close Encounters of the Third Kind **31** The Apprenticeship of Duddy Kravitz

dribble 4 drip, kick **6** bounce **7** drizzle, trickle **11** fall in drops, run bit by bit

driblet 4 drip, drop, tear **7** droplet, globule

dried up 4 arid **7** drained, parched **9** prunelike, shriveled **10** dehydrated, desiccated

drift 3 aim **4** flow, gist, heap, mass, pile **5** amass, amble, sense **6** course, gather, object, pile up, ramble, stream, wander **7** current, meander, meaning, purpose, scatter **8** movement **9** direction, intention, objective **10** accumulate **11** implication, peregrinate **12** accumulation, be borne along

drifter 3 bum **4** hobo **5** idler, tramp **6** loafer **8** derelict, vagabond **16** ne'er-do-well

drill 4 bore **5** punch, train **6** pierce **8** exercise, practice, puncture, training, work with **10** boring tool, repetition **11** instruction **17** repeated exercises
 type: **4** hand **7** twist **8** electric

drilling 4 rote **6** boring **8** practice, training **9** schooling **10** discipline **11** preparation

drink 3 sip **4** gulp, swig **5** booze, taste, toast **6** absorb, imbibe, ingest, salute, take in **7** alcohol, swallow **8** beverage, libation **9** partake of, the bottle **10** alcoholism **11** drunkenness **15** alcoholic liquor **17** liquid refreshment
 type of: **3** cup, fix **4** fizz, flip, mull, puff, sour **5** daisy, julep, punch, shrub, sling, smash **6** cooler, frappe, rickey **7** cobbler, stinger **8** highball

drinker 3 sot **4** lush, wino **5** dipso, drunk, rummy, souse **6** bibber, boozer, sponge **7** guzzler, imbiber, tippler, waterer **8** drunkard **9** alcoholic, inebriate

drink in 6 absorb, digest, soak up, take in **10** assimilate **14** immerse oneself

drinking
 god of: **5** Comus

drinking spree 4 orgy, toot **5** binge, drunk **6** bender **8** beer-bust, carousal **9** bacchanal

drink up 4 gulp **5** quaff **6** absorb, guzzle, soak up **7** consume, swallow

drip 3 ass **4** bore, jerk, nerd **5** creep, dummy, klutz **6** splash **7** dribble, drizzle, trickle **8** sprinkle

dripping 3 wet **4** damp **5** soggy **6** soaked, sodden **10** soaking wet

drive 4 goad, lead, mean, move, prod, push, ride, rush, spur, urge **5** force, guide, impel, motor, press, steer, surge **6** coerce, compel, incite, intend, outing **7** advance, conduct, go by car, impulse, operate, suggest **8** ambition, campaign, motivate **9** excursion, insinuate, trip by car, urge along **10** motivation

drive apart 8 alienate, estrange **9** disaffect

drive away 4 rout, shoo **5** chase, deter, repel **6** rebuff **7** repulse **8** alienate **11** put to flight, send packing

drive home 7 impress **8** hammer at

drivel 4 drool **6** babble, ramble, slaver **7** dribble, slobber **8** babbling, nonsense, rambling **9** gibberish **12** talk nonsense **13** senseless talk, talk foolishly

drive out 4 fire **5** chase, depel, eject, evict, exile, expel, force, roust **6** compel, remove **7** dismiss, repulse **8** discharge, exorcise

driver 6 cowboy, drover **8** herdsman **9** chauffeur

drizzle 3 fog **4** mist, rain **7** dribble **8** sprinkle

drizzly 3 wet **4** damp **5** foggy, misty, rainy

Dr Jekyll and Mr Hyde
 author: **20** Robert Louis Stevenson
 character: **5** Poole **10** Mr Utterson **13** Dr Henry Jekyll **14** Dr Hastie Lanyon

Dr Kildare
 character: **14** Dr James Kildare **18** Dr Leonard Gillespie
 cast: **13** Raymond Massey **18** Richard Chamberlain
 hospital: **12** Blair General

Dr No
 author: **10** Ian Fleming

droll 5 funny **7** offbeat, strange **8** humorous **9** eccentric, laughable, whimsical **12** oddly amusing

drollery 3 wit **5** humor **6** banter, comedy, whimsy **7** jesting

Dromio
 character in: **17** The Comedy of Errors
 author: **11** Shakespeare

drone 3 hum **4** buzz, whir **5** idler **6** loafer **7** vibrate **8** parasite **9** murmuring, vibration **10** lazy person

drool 6 drivel, slaver **7** dribble, slobber **8** salivate **15** water at the mouth

droop 3 dim, sag **4** flag, sink **5** lower **6** weaken, wither **8** diminish, hang down **9** lose vigor **14** hang listlessly **15** incline downward

droopy 4 bent, blue, down, limp **5** baggy, bowed, slack **6** dashed, pining **7** doleful, sagging, subdued **8** cast down, dangling, dejected, downcast **9** depressed **10** despairing, despondent, dispirited, spiritless, world-weary **11** downhearted, hanging down, languishing **14** down in the mouth

drop 3 can, dab **4** bead, dash, deck, dive, drip, fall, fell, fire, omit, sack, sink, tear **5** abyss, floor, leave, lower, pinch, slide, slope, smack, trace **6** give up, lessen, plunge **7** abandon, decline, descend, descent, dismiss, dribble, driblet, dwindle, forsake, globule, plummet, slacken, smidgen, soupcon, trickle **8** decrease, diminish, leave out, lowering **9** declivity, discharge, knock down, precipice, terminate **10** sprinkling **12** bring to an end **13** fail to include **15** cease to consider, fail to pronounce

drop anchor 4 dock, moor **5** tie up

drop in 4 call, come **5** visit **6** appear, come by, look in, show up, stop by, turn up **7** stop off **9** pay a visit

droplet 4 bead, drip, tear **7** driblet, globule **8** spherule

droplets of moisture 3 dew, fog **4** mist **5** sweat **12** condensation

drop out 4 quit **5** leave **6** resign, retire

dross 4 scum, slag **5** waste **6** cinder, scoria **8** clinkers, impurity

drought, drouth 4 lack, need, want **6** dearth **7** aridity, paucity **8** scarcity, shortage **10** deficiency, dry weather, lack of rain **13** insufficiency

drover 6 cowboy, driver **7** cowpoke **8** herdsman, shepherd **10** cowpuncher

drown 4 soak **5** flood **6** deluge, drench, engulf **7** immerse **8** inundate, overcome, submerge **9** overpower, overwhelm, suffocate, swallow up **10** asphyxiate

drowse 3 nap, nod **4** doze, laze **5** dover, drone, sleep **6** snooze **7** slumber **8** languish **10** sleepiness

drowsy 4 dozy, lazy, slow **5** tired **6** sleepy **7** languid **8** hypnotic, listless, sluggish, soothing **9** lethargic, somnolent, soporific

Dr Strangelove or How I Learned to Stop Worrying and Love the Bomb
  director: 14 Stanley Kubrick
  cast: 9 Peter Bull **10** Keenan Wynn **11** Slim Pickens **12** George C Scott, Peter Sellers **14** James Earl Jones, Sterling Hayden

drub 3 hit **4** beat, cane, flog, whip **5** whale **6** thrash **9** bastinado

drubbing 6 caning **7** beating, licking, tanning **9** trouncing **11** shellacking

drudge 4 grub, hack, plod, toil **5** labor, slave **6** lackey, menial, toiler **7** grubber **8** inferior, struggle **9** underling **11** subordinate

drudgery 4 toil **5** grind **7** travail **8** hack work **11** menial labor **15** distasteful work

Druk-Yul see **6** Bhutan

drum 3 din, keg, rap, tap, tub **4** beat, cask, roar, roll **5** expel, force **6** barrel, harp on, rumble, tattoo **7** dismiss, pulsate **8** drive out, hammer at **9** discharge, drive home, reiterate **11** beat a tattoo, din in the ear, reverberate

Drums
  author: 9 James Boyd

Drums Along the Mohawk
  author: 14 Walter D Edmonds
  character: 4 Lana **9** Blue Black, John Wolff **11** Joseph Brant, Mark Demooth **12** Mrs McKlennan **13** Gilbert Martin **20** Magdelena Borst Martin

drunk 3 sot **4** bust, lush, soak **5** binge, rummy, souse, tipsy, toper **6** barfly, bender, looped, sodden, soused, stewed, zapped, zonked **7** smashed **8** beer-bust, besotted, carousal **9** alcoholic, plastered **10** inebriated **11** dip-somaniac, intoxicated **13** drinking spree, under the influence

drunkard 3 sot **4** lush, soak, wino **5** rummy, souse, toper **6** barfly **9** alcoholic **11** dipsomaniac

drunkenness 10 alcoholism **11** inebriation **12** intoxication

Drury, Allen
  author of: 9 Public Man **14** Capable of Honor, Return to Thebes **15** The Promise of Joy **16** Advise and Consent **18** Preserve and Protect **19** Come Nineveh Come Tyre

Druse 5 Syria **6** Muslim **7** Lebanon

dry 4 arid, blot, dull, wipe **5** droll **6** boring, low-key **7** deadpan, parched, tedious, thirsty **8** rainless **9** dehydrate, desiccate, shrivel up, wearisome **10** dehydrated, monotonous **13** uninteresting

Dryad
  form: 5 deity, nymph
  location: 5 woods

dry as dust 4 arid, dull, sere **7** parched **8** pedantic, withered **9** shriveled **13** unimaginative

Dryden, John
  author of: 10 All for Love **11** Mac Flecknoe **14** Annus Mirabilis **15** Alexander's Feast, Marriage-a-la-Mode **20** Absalom and Achitophel, Essay on Dramatic Poesy, The Hind and the Panther **22** Fables Ancient and Modern

dry goods 5 cloth, goods **6** fabric **8** material **9** yard goods **10** piece goods

dryness 7 aridity, drought **8** aridness **11** dehydration

Dry Salvages
  author: 7 T S Eliot

dry up 6 wither **7** shrivel **9** dehydrate, desiccate, evaporate

Dr Zhivago
  author: 14 Boris Pasternak
  character: 4 Lara
  setting: 17 Russian Revolution

dual 6 double **7** twofold, two-part

dub 4 call, name **5** label **6** knight **7** baptize **8** christen, nickname **9** designate

Dubai see **18** United Arab Emirates
  part of: 3 UAE

dubiety 5 doubt **8** unbelief **9** disbelief **10** skepticism **11** incredulity **12** doubtfulness **14** lack of credence

Dubin's Lives
  author: 14 Bernard Malamud

dubious 5 shady **6** unsure **7** suspect **8** doubtful **9** skeptical, uncertain **10** suspicious, unreliable **11** unconvinced **12** questionable, undependable **13** untrustworthy

Dublin
  brewery: 8 Guinness
  capital of: 7 Ireland
  Irish: 8 Dubh Linn (black pool) **15** Baile Atha Cliath (town of the Hurdle Ford)
  landmark: 10 Four Courts **11** Custom House **12** Abbey Theater, Christ Church, Dublin Castle **13** Leinster House **18** Kilmainham **19** St Patrick's Cathedral
  mountain: 7 Wicklow
  museum: 8 National **10** James Joyce
  park: 7 Phoenix
  river: 6 Liffey
  rulers: 7 English, Vikings
  scene of: 12 Easter Rising (1916)
  university: 14 Trinity College

Dubliners
  author: 10 James Joyce

DuBois, Blanche
  character in: 21 A Streetcar Named Desire
  author: 8 Williams

Du Bois, W E B
  founded: 5 NAACP
  author of: 19 The Souls of Black Folk

Dubonnet
  type: 8 aperitif
  origin: 6 France
  ingredient: 7 quinine, red wine
  with gin: 3 BVD **8** Napoleon
  with rum: 10 Bushranger

duc 4 duke

Duccio di Buoninsegna
  born: 5 Italy **6** Sienna
  artwork: 6 Maesta **18** The Rucellai Madonna (attributed)

duce, il duce 6 despot, leader, tyrant **8** dictator **9** Mussolini

Duchamp, Marcel
  born: 6 France **8** Normandy **10** Blainville
  artwork: 5 LHOOQ **9** Given That **11** Etant Donnes **12** Bicycle Wheel **13** The Large Glass (The Bride Stripped Bare by Her Bachelors Even) **24** Nude Descending a Staircase **37** The King and Queen Surrounded by Swift Nudes

Duchess of Malfi, The
  author: 11 John Webster
  character: 6 Bosola **7** Antonio **8** Giovanna **9** Ferdinand **11** The Cardinal

duck 4 clee, coot, lory, smew, teal, veer **5** avoid, dodge, drake, eider, elude, evade, goose, ruddy, shirk, stoop **6** canard, canvas, crouch, gannet, Peking, scoter, swerve **7** gadwall, mallard, Muscovy, pintail, pochard **8** baldpate, freckled, redshank, shelduck, shoveler, sidestep, submerge **9** merganser, whistling **10** bufflehead, canvasback **11** wood steamer **13** give the slip to
  male: 5 drake
  group of: 5 brace

Duck Soup
  director: 10 Leo McCarey
  cast: 5 Chico, Harpo, Zeppo **7**

Groucho (Rufus T Firefly) **12** Louis Calhern, Raquel Torres **14** Margaret Dumont
setting: 9 Freedonia

duct 4 pipe, tube **6** vessel **7** channel, conduit

ductile 6 docile, pliant, supple **7** elastic, plastic, pliable, tensile **8** amenable, bendable, flexible, formable, moldable, shapable, swayable **9** adaptable, compliant, malleable, tractable **10** extensible, manageable, submissive **11** complaisant, manipulable, stretchable, susceptible

dud 3 dog **4** bomb, bust, flop, hash **5** botch, lemon, loser **6** bummer, fiasco, fizzle **7** clinker, debacle, failure, washout **11** lead balloon, miscarriage **14** disappointment

dude 3 fop **4** beau **5** dandy **7** peacock **11** city dweller, city slicker **12** Beau Brummell

Dudevant, Aurore
real name of: 10 George Sand

duds 4 togs **5** flops **6** attire **7** apparel, clothes, fizzles, threads **8** clothing, failures, garments

due 4 owed **5** ample, owing **6** enough, proper, unpaid **7** fitting, merited **8** adequate, becoming, deserved, expected, plenty of, rightful, suitable **9** in arrears, scheduled **10** sufficient **11** appropriate, outstanding

duel
French: 15 affaire d'honneur

Duel, The
author: 15 Alexander Kuprin

duenna 8 guardian **9** attendant, chaperone, custodian, protector

dues 4 fees **7** charges **10** assessment

Duessa
character in: 15 The Faerie Queene
author: 7 Spenser

duet 3 duo, two **4** pair **6** couple **7** twosome

Dufy, Raoul
born: 6 France **7** Le Havre
artwork: 7 The Palm **15** Riders in the Wood **16** Chateau and Horses **18** Deauville Racetrack, Posters at Trouville

dugout 3 den **4** cave **5** canoe **6** cavity, hollow **7** shelter

Dukas, Paul
born: 5 Paris **6** France
composer of: 6 La Peri **18** Ariane et Barbe-Bleue **19** Ariadne and Bluebeard **22** The Sorcerer's Apprentice

duke
French: 3 duc

Duke
nickname of: 9 John Wayne

Duke, Patty (Patty Duke Astin)
real name: 13 Anna Marie Duke
husband: 9 John Astin
born: 10 Elmhurst NY

roles: 11 Helen Keller **16** The Miracle Worker, The Patty Duke Show, Valley of the Dolls
author of: 10 Call Me Anna **17** A Brilliant Madness

Dukenfield, William Claude
real name of: 8 W C Fields

Duke Snider
nickname of: 11 Edwin Snider

dulcet 7 lyrical, musical, tuneful **8** pleasing, sonorous **9** melodious **11** mellifluous

Dulcinea del Toboso
character in: 10 Don Quixote
author: 9 Cervantes

dull 4 slow **5** blunt, dense, muted, quiet, thick, trite, vapid **6** boring, obtuse, stupid **7** muffled, not keen, prosaic, subdued, vacuous **8** deadened, inactive, not brisk, not sharp **9** dimwitted **10** indistinct, lackluster, uneventful **13** unimaginative, uninteresting

Dull
character in: 16 Love's Labour's Lost
author: 11 Shakespeare

dullard 4 dolt **5** dummy, dunce **6** nitwit **7** halfwit **8** dumbbell, imbecile

Dullea, Keir
born: 11 Cleveland OH
roles: 12 David and Lisa **18** Butterflies Are Free **27** Two Thousand One: A Space Odyssey

dullness 6 idiocy, tedium **8** dumbness, lethargy, monotony, slowness **9** bluntness, ignorance, stupidity, vapidness **10** boringness, imbecility, obtuseness **11** tediousness **13** dim-wittedness **15** thick-headedness

dull-witted 5 dazed, fuzzy **7** bemused, muddled, stunned **8** confused **9** stupefied

Dulong, Pierre-Louis
field: 7 physics **9** chemistry
nationality: 6 French
discovered: 19 nitrogen trichloride
studied: 4 heat **13** atomic weights

duly 6 on time **8** properly, suitably **9** correctly **10** deservedly, punctually, rightfully **13** appropriately **15** at the proper time

Dumaine
character in: 16 Love's Labour's Lost
author: 11 Shakespeare

Dumas, Alexandre (fils)
author of: 7 Camille **11** Le Demi-Monde **17** La Dame aux Camelias **21** The Lady of the Camellias
Camille inspired: 10 La Traviata
opera by: 5 Verdi

Dumas, Alexandre (pere)
author of: 17 The Queen's Necklace **18** The Three Musketeers **19** The Man in the Iron Mask **21** The Count of Monte Cristo **22** The Vicomte de Bragelonne

Du Maurier, Daphne
author of: 7 Rebecca **10** Jamaica Inn **11** Don't Look Now **14** My Cousin Rachel **15** Frenchman's Creek **19** The House on the Strand

Du Maurier, George
author of: 6 Trilby **10** The Martian **13** Peter Ibbetson

dumb 3 mum **4** dull, mute **5** dense, dopey **6** silent, stupid **7** foolish, aphasic **8** aphasiac **9** dim-witted **13** unintelligent **17** incapable of speech

dumbbell 3 ass, oaf **4** clod, dolt, dope, fool **5** booby, clown, dummy, dunce, idiot, moron, ninny **6** dimwit, nitwit **7** dullard, halfwit **8** dumb-dumb, dummkopf, imbecile, lunkhead, meathead, numskull **9** birdbrain, blockhead, ignoramus, lamebrain, numbskull, simpleton **10** noodlehead

dumbfound, dumfound 4 stun **5** amaze **7** startle **8** astonish **11** flabbergast

dumbfounded 5 agape **6** amazed **7** stunned **9** astounded, stupefied **10** astonished, speechless **11** open-mouthed **13** flabbergasted

dumbness 6 idiocy **8** dullness **9** asininity, stupidity, thickness **10** imbecility **11** witlessness **12** wordlessness **14** speechlessness **15** thickheadedness

dumbstruck 5 agape **6** amazed, gaping **7** riveted **9** awestruck, stupefied **10** speechless **11** electrified, open-mouthed **13** flabbergasted

dump 3 hut **4** hole, toss **5** empty, hovel, shack **6** shanty, unload **8** get rid of, junkyard **9** dispose of **10** refuse pile **11** rubbish heap

dumpy 5 squat **7** lumpish **13** short and stout

Dunaway, Faye
real name: 18 Dorothy Faye Dunaway
born: 8 Bascom FL
roles: 6 Barfly, Milady **7** Network (Oscar) **8** The Champ **9** Chinatown **13** Mommie Dearest **14** Bonnie and Clyde **15** Towering Inferno **16** The Handmaid's Tale **17** The Four Musketeers **18** The Three Musketeers

Duncan
character in: 7 Macbeth
author: 11 Shakespeare

Duncan, Sandy
born: 11 Henderson TX
roles: 8 Peter Pan **9** Funny Face **12** The Boyfriend

dunce 4 fool **5** dummy, idiot, moron **6** dimwit, nitwit **8** imbecile, numskull **9** blockhead, numbskull, simpleton

Dunciad, The
author: 13 Alexander Pope

dune 4 bank **5** mound **8** sandbank, sandpile

dunk 3 dip, sop **4** duck, soak **5** bathe, douse, drown, slosh, souse, steep **6** deluge, drench, engulf, plunge **7** baptize, immerse **8** inundate, saturate, submerge

Dunne, John Gregory
  author of: 5 Vegas **11** Dutch Shea Jr, Nothing Lost **15** True Confessions **18** Quintana and Friends

Dunnock, Mildred
  born: 11 Baltimore MD
  roles: 8 Baby Doll **12** The Nun's Story **14** The Corn Is Green **16** Butterfield Eight, Cat on a Hot Tin Roof, Death of a Salesman

duo 4 pair **5** combo **6** couple **7** twosome **11** combination

duomo 4 dome **9** cathedral

dupe 4 fool, pawn **5** patsy, trick **6** humbug, sucker **7** cat's paw, deceive, fall guy, mislead **8** hoodwink **9** bamboozle

duplicate 4 copy **5** clone, match **6** repeat **7** replica **8** parallel **9** facsimile, imitation, make again, photocopy, photostat **10** carbon copy **12** reproduction

duplicity 5 fraud, guile **6** deceit **7** cunning **9** deception, falseness **10** dishonesty **13** deceitfulness

Du Pont Labs
  founder: 17 E I du Pont de Nemours
  inventor of: 5 nylon **6** Teflon **7** Gore-Tex

Duquesnoy, Francois
  born: 8 Brussels, Flanders
  nickname: 11 Il Fiammingo
  artwork: 8 St Andrew **9** St Susanna

dur
  musical term: 5 major **8** major key

durability 7 stamina **8** strength **9** endurance, toughness **10** sturdiness

durable 5 sound, tough **6** strong, sturdy **7** lasting **8** enduring **11** long-wearing, substantial

Durand, Asher Brown
  born: 18 Jefferson Village NJ
  artwork: 14 Kindred Spirits

Durante, Jimmy
  real name: 19 James Francis Durante
  nickname: 10 Schnozzola **15** Inka Dinka Doo Man
  born: 9 New York NY
  roles: 5 Jumbo **21** It's a Mad Mad Mad Mad World

duration 4 term **6** extent, period **11** continuance **12** continuation

Durdles
  character in: 22 The Mystery of Edwin Drood
  author: 7 Dickens

Durer, Albrecht
  born: 7 Germany **9** Nuremberg
  artwork: 10 Adam and Eve, Apocalypse, The Triumph **11** Wehlsch Pirg

12 Four Apostles, Large Passion, Melancholia I **13** Castle of Trent **15** Life of the Virgin **18** St Jerome in his Study **19** Virgin with the Siskin **21** Christ Among the Doctors **22** Knight Death and the Devil **24** Crowned Death on a Thin Horse **25** The Feast of the Rose Garlands **28** The Festival of the Rose Garlands

duress 5 force **6** threat **8** coercion, pressure **10** compulsion, constraint

Durgin, Francis Timothy
  real name of: 11 Rory Calhoun

during litigation
  Latin: 12 pendente lite

Durocher, Leo
  nickname: 9 Leo the Lip
  sport: 8 baseball
  position: 7 manager
  team: 11 Chicago Cubs **13** New York Giants **15** Brooklyn Dodgers
  saying: 18 Nice guys finish last

Durrenmatt, Friedrich
  author of: 5 Traps **8** The Visit **9** The Pledge, The Quarry **13** The Physicists **21** The Judge and His Hangman **27** The Marriage of the Mississippi

Durrie, James and Henry
  character in: 21 The Master of Ballantrae
  author: 9 Stevenson

dusk 6 sunset **7** sundown **8** twilight **9** nightfall

dusky 3 dim **4** dark **5** murky **6** cloudy, gloomy, veiled **7** swarthy **8** dark-hued

dust 4 dirt, lint **5** brush, motes **8** sprinkle

duster 3 rag **4** coat, robe **5** brush, cloth, whisk **9** housecoat **10** whisk broom

Dutch Guiana *see* **8** Suriname

Dutch Shea, Jr
  author: 16 John Gregory Dunne

dutiful 5 loyal **8** diligent, faithful, obedient **9** compliant **13** conscientious

duty 3 tax **4** levy, onus, task **6** charge, excise, tariff **7** customs **8** business, function, province **10** assignment, obligation **14** responsibility

Duval, Armand
  character in: 7 Camille
  author: 5 Dumas (fils)

Duvall, Robert
  born: 10 San Diego CA
  roommate: 13 Dustin Hoffman
  roles: 4 MASH **10** The Apostle **11** Falling Down, Godfather II, The Lost City **12** A Civil Action, Lonesome Dove, The Godfather **13** Apocalypse Now, Days of Thunder, Tender Mercies (Oscar) **15** The Great Santini, True Confessions **16** The Handmaid's Tale, The Scarlet Letter **18** To Kill a Mockingbird

Duvall, Shelley
  born: 9 Houston TX
  roles: 6 Popeye **9** Nashville **10** The Shining, Three Women **15** Brewster McCloud

Dvorak, Antonin
  born: 11 Nelahozeves **14** Czechoslovakia
  composer of: 5 Dumky **6** Hymnus, Te Deum **8** Carnival (overture) **10** St Ludmilla **11** Stabat Mater **15** American Quartet, From the New World (Symphony in E Minor) **16** The Specter's Bride **17** The Bells of Zlonice

dwarf 3 dim, elf, imp **4** baby, tiny **5** fairy, gnome, pixie, pygmy, small, troll **6** bantam, goblin, petite, sprite **8** diminish **9** miniature **10** diminutive, leprechaun, overshadow

dwarfish 3 wee **4** tiny **5** pygmy, short, small **6** bantam, little, midget **7** compact, squatty **10** diminutive, undersized **13** foreshortened

dweeb 4 fool, geek, nerd, wonk **5** grind

dwell 4 live **5** abide **6** harp on, reside **7** inhabit **10** linger over

dwelling 4 home **5** abode, house **8** domicile **9** residence **10** habitation

dwelling place 4 home **5** abode, house **7** habitat, lodging **8** domicile **9** residence **10** habitation **14** living quarters

dwell on 6 accent, stress **7** feature, iterate **9** emphasize, press home

dwindle 4 fade, wane **6** lessen, shrink **7** decline **8** decrease, diminish **13** become smaller

dye 4 tint **5** color, shade, stain **8** coloring **10** coloration

dyed-in-the-wool 9 confirmed, ingrained **10** deep-rooted, inveterate **11** established

dyestuff 14 coloring matter

dynamic 5 vital **6** active **7** driving **8** forceful, powerful, vigorous **9** energetic

dynamism 3 pep **4** life **5** verve, vigor **6** energy, spirit **8** vitality, vivacity **9** animation **10** liveliness

dynamite 4 raze, ruin **5** blast, trash, wreck **6** blow up, charge **7** destroy, shatter, wipe out **8** decimate, demolish **9** devastate, dismantle, eradicate, explosive **10** annihilate, extinguish, obliterate **11** exterminate

dynamo 4 doer **7** hustler **8** activist, go-getter **9** generator **12** active person **14** bundle of energy, mover and shaker

Dynasts, The
  author: 11 Thomas Hardy
  subject: 17 Napoleon Bonaparte
dynasty 4 line 5 crown, reign 6 regime 7 lineage, regency 8 dominion, hegemony, kingship, monarchy, regnancy 9 authority 10 government, suzerainty 11 ruling house 12 jurisdiction 14 administration

Dynasty
  character: 9 Dex Dexter, Jeff Colby 12 Alexis (Morel Carrington Colby) Dexter 14 Adam Carrington 15 Blake Carrington 16 Amanda Carrington, Steven Carrington 17 Krystle Carrington 18 Dominique Devereaux, Krystina Carrington 21 Fallon Carrington Colby
  cast: 9 John James 10 Linda Evans 11 Joan Collins 12 John Forsythe
  setting: 6 Denver 8 Colorado
  hotel: 8 La Mirage

dyspeptic 4 mean 6 crabby, grumpy, ornery, shirty, touchy 7 grouchy, waspish 8 choleric 9 crotchety, fractious, irascible, irritable 10 ill-humored, ill-natured 11 bad-tempered, contentious, hot-tempered 12 cantankerous, sour-tempered 13 short-tempered

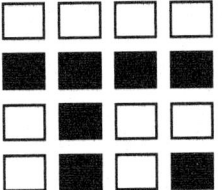
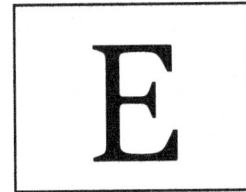
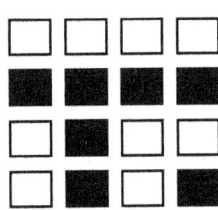

each **3** per **4** a pop **5** every **6** apiece **7** that one, this one **8** everyone, separate **12** respectively

Eagels, Jeanne
born: **12** Kansas City MO
roles: **4** Rain **8** Jealousy **9** The Letter **13** Sadie Thompson **14** Man Woman and Sin

eager **3** hot **4** agog, avid, keen **6** ardent, fervid, intent, raring **7** athirst, earnest, excited, fervent, intense, longing, zealous **8** desirous, diligent, resolute, spirited, yearning **9** ambitious, hungering, impatient, thirsting **10** aggressive, passionate **11** hardworking, impassioned, industrious, persevering **12** enterprising, enthusiastic

eagerly **6** avidly, keenly **8** ardently, desiring, fervidly, intently **9** anxiously, earnestly, fervently, zealously **16** enthusiastically

eagerness **4** zeal, zest **5** ardor **6** fervor **7** avidity **9** readiness **10** enthusiasm **11** willingness

eagle
young: **6** eaglet

Eagle
constellation of: **6** Aquila

Eakins, Thomas
born: **14** Philadelphia PA
artwork: **11** Agnew Clinic **13** Mrs Edith Mahon **14** The Gross Clinic **24** Max Schmitt in a Single Scull

ear
section: **5** inner, outer **6** middle
part: **4** drum **5** anvil, canal **6** hammer **7** cochlea, stirrup **8** hair cell **14** eustachian tube

earl **4** lord, peer **5** noble **8** nobleman
wife: **8** countess

earlier **6** before, in time, sooner **9** before now, in advance **10** beforehand **11** ahead of time **13** before the fact

earliest **5** first **6** oldest, primal **7** ancient, initial, primary, soonest **8** original, primeval **9** beginning, primitive **10** aboriginal, indigenous **11** fundamental

Earl of Baltimore
nickname of: **10** Earl Weaver

Earl the Pearl
nickname of: **10** Earl Monroe

early **5** first **6** primal **7** ancient, archaic, betimes, initial, too soon, very old **8** primeval **9** in advance, premature, primitive **10** beforehand, in good time, primordial **11** ahead of time, prehistoric, prematurely

Early Autumn
author: **14** Louis Bromfield

early man **6** Peking **9** Cro-Magnon, Steinheim **11** Neanderthal **18** Trobriand Islanders **24** Australopithecus robustus **25** Australopithecus africanus

earmark **3** tag **4** band, hold, sign **5** allot, label, stamp, token, trait **6** aspect, assign, dog-ear **7** feature, put away, quality, reserve **8** allocate, property, set aside **9** attribute, designate **11** peculiarity, singularity **14** characteristic

earn **3** get, net **4** draw, gain, make, rate, reap **5** clear, merit **6** attain, pick up, secure **7** achieve, collect, deserve, realize, receive, warrant **9** bring home **12** be entitled to

earn as due **4** rate **5** merit **7** deserve **10** be worthy of **12** be entitled to **13** be deserving of

earnest **4** firm **5** eager, fixed, grave, sober, staid **6** ardent, fervid, honest, intent, sedate, solemn, stable, steady, urgent **7** devoted, fervent, intense, serious, sincere, zealous **8** constant, diligent, resolute, spirited, vehement **9** ambitious, assiduous, heartfelt, insistent **10** deeply felt, determined, passionate, purposeful, thoughtful **11** hard-working, impassioned, industrious, persevering **12** enthusiastic, wholehearted

earnest request **4** plea **6** appeal **8** entreaty, petition **11** importunity **12** supplication

earnings **3** pay **5** wages **6** income, salary **7** payment, profits **8** proceeds, receipts, take-home **12** compensation

Earnshaw, Catherine
character in: **16** Wuthering Heights
author: **6** Bronte

ear-splitting **7** blaring **8** piercing **9** clamorous, deafening **10** thunderous

earth **3** sod **4** clay, dirt, dust, land, loam, soil, turf **5** terra **6** ground **7** topsoil
god of: **3** Geb, Keb **5** Dagan, Dagon **10** Trophonius
goddess of: **2** Ge **4** Gaea, Gaia **6** Hecate, Hekate, Tellus

earthen pot
Spanish: **4** olla

earthenware **5** china **7** pottery **8** clayware, crockery **11** ceramic ware

earthly **6** bodily **7** mundane, secular, ungodly, worldly **8** feasible, material, physical, possible, temporal **9** corporeal, practical **10** imaginable **11** conceivable, terrestrial **12** nonspiritual **13** materialistic

earthquake **5** quake, seism, shock **6** tremor **8** tremblor, upheaval **11** earth tremor

earth tremor **5** quake, seism, shock **6** tremor **8** tremblor, upheaval **10** earthquake

earthy **5** bawdy, crude, dirty, funky, gross, lusty, rough **6** coarse, filthy, ribald, robust, smutty, vulgar **7** obscene, peasant, raunchy **8** indecent **9** primitive, unrefined **10** unblushing, uncultured **12** uncultivated

Earwicker family
characters in: **13** Finnegans Wake
author: **5** Joyce

earwig
variety: **5** black **6** little **10** long horned

ease **4** calm, rest, slip **5** abate, allay, poise, quiet, slide, still **6** aplomb, lessen, luxury, pacify, plenty, relief, repose, solace, soothe **7** assuage, comfort, console, leisure, lighten, mollify, relieve **8** diminish, easement, easiness, facility, maneuver, mitigate, palliate, security, serenity **9** abundance, affluence, alleviate, composure, disburden, readiness **10** confidence, prosperity, relaxation **11** assuagement, naturalness, peace of mind, restfulness **12** tranquillity, unconstraint **13** luxuriousness, move carefully, relaxed manner **14** effortlessness, handle with care, unaffectedness

easel **5** frame, stand **6** tripod

easement **4** ease **6** relief, solace, succor **7** comfort **8** soothing **10** right of way **11** assuagement

easily **5** by far **6** freely, surely **7** clearly, handily, lightly, plainly, readily **8** facilely, smoothly, with ease **9** certainly **10** far and away, undeniably **11** beyond doubt, undoubtedly **12** effortlessly, with facility **13** without a hitch **14** beyond question, without trouble **17** without difficulty **23** beyond the shadow of a doubt

easily embarrassed 3 shy 5 timid 7 bashful 8 blushing, skittish, timorous 9 diffident, shrinking 11 constrained, unconfident

easily noticed 5 clear, plain 6 patent 7 evident, glaring, obvious, visible 8 flagrant, striking 9 arresting, prominent 10 noticeable 11 conspicuous, outstanding

easily ruffled 9 emotional, excitable 11 hot-tempered 13 quick-tempered

easiness 4 ease 10 equanimity, simplicity 11 naturalness 12 indifference 13 impassiveness

East, the 4 Asia 9 the Orient 10 the Far East 11 the Near East 17 Eastern Hemisphere

East Bengal *see* 10 Bangladesh

East Berlin
former capital of: 11 East Germany

East Coker
author: 7 T S Eliot

Eastern Slavic
language family: 12 Indo-European
group: 11 Balto-Slavic
branch: 6 Slavic
language: 7 Russian 9 Ukrainian 12 White Russian

Easter Parade
director: 14 Charles Walters
based on musical by: 12 Irving Berlin
cast: 9 Ann Miller 11 Fred Astaire, Judy Garland 12 Peter Lawford

East Germany *see* 11 Germany, East

East Indies *see* 8 Malaysia 9 Indonesia

Eastman, George
nationality: 8 American
founder of: 14 Eastman Kodak Co
inventor of: 9 Kodak film 11 Kodak camera 20 transparent photo film

East of Eden
author: 13 John Steinbeck
director: 9 Elia Kazan
cast: 8 Burl Ives 9 James Dean 10 Jo Van Fleet 11 Julie Harris 13 Raymond Massey
Oscar for: 17 supporting actress (Van Fleet)
characters: 4 Abra, Adam, Aron 5 Caleb, Trask

East wind
associated with: 5 Eurus 9 Volturnus

Eastwood, Clint
born: 14 San Francisco CA
roles: 7 Firefox, Rawhide 10 Dirty Harry, Hang Em High, Unforgiven 11 Magnum Force, The Dead Pool 12 Coogan's Bluff, Kelly's Heroes, Space Cowboys, Sudden Impact 13 Absolute Power, A Perfect World 14 Play Misty for Me 15 In The Line of Fire, Where Eagles Dare 17 A Fistful of Dollars, Any Which Way You Can, High Plains Drifter, Million Dollar Baby 18 Escape from Alcatraz, For a Few Dollars More 21 Two Mules for Sister Sara 23 The Good the Bad and the Ugly 25 The Bridges of Madison County
director of: 10 Unforgiven (Oscar) 11 Mystic River 12 Sudden Impact 13 Absolute Power, A Perfect World 14 Play Misty For Me 17 Million Dollar Baby (Oscar) 25 The Bridges of Madison County 32 Midnight in the Garden of Good and Evil
mayor of: 6 Carmel

easy 4 calm, mild, open, soft 5 cushy, frank, light, naive 6 benign, calmly, candid, docile, easily, gentle, secure, serene, simple 7 lenient, natural, not hard, relaxed, restful, wealthy 8 affluent, carefree, composed, friendly, gracious, gullible, informal, outgoing, painless, peaceful, pleasant, scarcely, serenely, tranquil, unforced, well-to-do, yielding 9 compliant, indulgent, leisurely, luxurious, tractable, unworried 10 effortless, peacefully, permissive, unaffected, untroubled 11 comfortable, comfortably 12 not difficult, unsuspicious 13 accommodating, unconstrained

easygoing 4 calm 6 casual 7 offhand, patient, relaxed 8 carefree, laidback 9 unruffled, unworried 10 insouciant, nonchalant 11 unconcerned, unexcitable 12 even-tempered, happy-go-lucky, mild-tempered

Easy Rider
director: 12 Dennis Hopper
cast: 10 Karen Black, Peter Fonda 11 Luana Anders 12 Dennis Hopper, Robert Walker 13 Jack Nicholson

easy to use 7 adapted, helpful 9 adaptable 10 convenient 11 serviceable 12 advantageous, user friendly

eat 3 sup 4 bolt, dine, feed, gulp, rust, take 5 feast, lunch 6 devour, gobble, ingest, nibble 7 consume, corrode 8 dispatch, dissolve, wear away, wolf down 9 breakfast, take a meal, waste away 10 break bread, gormandize 14 take sustenance 15 take nourishment

eatable 4 food 6 edible 8 fit to eat 10 comestible, consumable

eat away 4 rust 5 erode 7 corrode, oxidize

eating habits 4 diet 7 regimen

eat into 4 bite 5 erode 6 nibble 7 consume, corrode 8 wear away 9 swallow up

eat one's fill 5 feast, gorge 6 pig out 7 banquet 12 stuff oneself

eat rapidly 4 bolt, gulp, wolf 5 scarf 6 gobble 12 swallow whole

eat up 5 enjoy, savor 6 devour, relish 7 consume, swallow 9 delight in, rejoice in 13 be pleased with, get a kick out of 14 take pleasure in

eat voraciously 6 cram in, devour, gobble 7 stuff in 8 bolt down, gulp down, wolf down 10 gormandize 12 swallow whole

eau, eaux 5 water

eau de vie 6 brandy 11 water of life

eaves 8 overhang

eavesdrop 3 bug, pry, spy, tap 5 snoop 6 attend, harken 7 monitor, wiretap 8 listen in, overhear 9 bend an ear 11 cock one's ear 14 strain one's ears 15 prick up one's ears

ebb 5 abate, go out 6 go down, lessen, recede, shrink, weaken 7 decline, dwindle, retreat, slacken, subside 8 decrease, diminish, fade away, fall away, flow away, flow back, move back, withdraw 9 waste away 10 degenerate 11 deteriorate

ebony 3 jet 4 dark, inky 5 black, raven, sable 8 hardwood 9 coal-black 15 Diospyros Ebenum
varieties: 5 green, Texas 8 Macassar, mountain 10 East Indian, Queensland

Ebsen, Buddy
real name: 23 Christian Rudolph Ebsen Jr
born: 12 Belleville IL
roles: 12 Barnaby Jones, Davy Crockett 21 The Beverly Hillbillies

ebullience 3 zip 7 elation 8 buoyancy 9 animation 10 enthusiasm, exuberance, joyousness, liveliness 11 high spirits 12 exhilaration 13 effervescence

ebullient 6 elated, joyful, joyous 9 exuberant 11 exhilarated 12 effervescent, enthusiastic, high-spirited

ecce homo 12 behold the man
said by: 13 Pontius Pilate
spoken of: 6 Christ

eccentric 3 nut, odd 4 kook, rash, sick 5 curio, flake, funny, kooky, nutty, queer, weird 6 freaky, insane, quaint, unique, weirdo 7 bizarre, curious, erratic, oddball, offbeat, strange, unusual, weirdie 8 aberrant, abnormal, crackpot, freakish, peculiar, quixotic, singular, uncommon 9 character, irregular, odd person, off center, parabolic, psychotic, screwball, unnatural, whimsical 10 capricious, elliptical, outlandish, unorthodox 13 extraordinary 14 unconventional

eccentricity 6 oddity, whimsy 7 caprice 9 deviation, queerness 10 aberration 11 abnormality, peculiarity, strangeness 12 idiosyncrasy, irregularity

ecclesiastic, ecclesiastical 5 rabbi, vicar 6 cleric, curate, deacon, parson, pastor, priest, rector 7 prelate 8 chaplain, churchly, clerical, minister, pastoral, preacher 9 churchman, clergyman, episcopal, parochial, religious

echelon 4 file, line, rank, rung, tier 5 grade, level 6 office 8 position 9 authority, hierarchy

Echidna 8 anteater
  feature: 5 snout
echinoderm 9 sea animal
  characteristic: 10 spiny shell
  form: 6 radial
  kind: 6 cystid 7 crinoid 8 starfish 9 sea urchin 10 basket star 11 sea cucumber
echo 3 ape 4 copy, ring 5 match 6 follow, mirror, parrot, repeat 7 imitate, reflect, resound 8 parallel, simulate 9 duplicate, reproduce, take after 11 reverberate 13 reverberation
Echo
  form: 5 nymph
  location: 8 mountain
  loved: 9 Narcissus
  loved by: 3 Pan
  changed into: 4 echo
eclair 6 pastry 7 dessert 9 creampuff
eclaircissement 11 explanation 13 clarification, (the) Enlightenment
eclat 4 fame, pomp 5 glory, honor 6 praise, renown, repute 7 acclaim, display, success
eclipse 3 dim 4 hide, loss, mask 5 cloak, cover, excel, outdo 6 darken, exceed 7 blot out, conceal, erasing, masking, obscure, surpass, veiling, wipe out 8 cloaking, clouding, covering, outrival, outshine 9 darkening, shadowing, transcend 10 obliterate, overshadow, tower above 11 blotting out, diminishing, eradicating, obscuration 12 annihilation, obliteration 13 overshadowing
eclogue 4 idyl, poem 5 idyll 7 bucolic 8 dialogue, pastoral
Eclogues
  author: 6 Vergil, Virgil
ecole 6 school
economic 6 fiscal 8 material, monetary 9 budgetary, financial, pecuniary 10 productive 12 distributive
economical 5 chary, cheap 6 frugal, modest, saving 7 careful, prudent, sparing, spartan, thrifty 8 economic 9 low-priced, niggardly, penurious, scrimping 10 reasonable 11 closefisted, tightfisted 12 parsimonious
economic decline 8 downturn 9 recession 10 depression
economics
  term: 3 GNP 5 labor 7 capital, Marxism, surplus 8 property 9 commodity, Communism, inflation, Keynesian, recession 10 capitalism, monetarist, supply-side 11 bourgeoisie, central bank, competition, consumption, marketplace, proletariat, stagflation 12 distribution, econometrics, fiscal policy, interest rate, laissez-faire, mercantilism 14 federal deficit, macroeconomics, microeconomics, monetary policy 17 trickle-down theory

economist
  American: 6 George, Hansen, Sumner, Veblen 7 Commons 8 Friedman, Laughlin 9 Greenspan 10 Schumpeter
  British: 4 Mill 5 Smith 6 Keynes 7 Malthus, Ricardo 8 Marshall
  French: 3 Say 7 Quesnay
  German: 4 Marx 7 Schacht
  Italian: 6 Pareto
  Scottish: 5 Smith
economize 4 save 5 pinch, skimp, stint 6 scrimp 7 husband 8 be frugal, conserve, cut costs 9 be prudent 10 avoid waste 11 cut expenses 12 be economical, use sparingly 14 be parsimonious 15 practice economy, tighten one's belt
economizing 10 conserving 11 cutting down 13 penny-pinching 14 belt-tightening 15 pinching pennies 18 tightening one's belt
economy 6 thrift 8 prudence 9 frugality 10 providence 11 thriftiness 15 financial status, productive power
ecstasy 3 joy 5 bliss 6 frenzy, thrill, trance 7 delight, emotion, madness, rapture 8 delirium, gladness, pleasure 9 cloud nine, happiness, transport 10 enthusiasm, exultation
ecstatic 4 glad, rapt 5 happy 6 elated, joyful, joyous 7 exalted, excited 8 blissful 9 delighted, delirious, ebullient, entranced, overjoyed, rapturous 10 enraptured 11 transported 12 enthusiastic 13 beside oneself
Ecuador
  name means: 7 equator
  other name: 5 Quito
  capital: 5 Quito
  largest city: 9 Guayaquil
  others: 4 Jama, Loja, Napo, Puyo, Tena 5 Guano, Manta, Pajan, Pinas, Piura, Pojan, Yaupi 6 Ambato, Cuenca, Ibarra, Tulcan, Zaruma 7 Azogues, Cayambe, Guamote, Guapulo, Machala, Pelileo, Pillaro, Salinas 8 Riobamba 10 Esmeraldas, Portoviejo
  division: 5 Costa 6 Sierra 7 Oriente
  measure: 5 libra 6 cuadra, fanega
  monetary unit: 5 sucre 7 centavo
  weight: 5 libra
  island: 4 Puna, Wolf 5 Colon, Mocha, Pinta 6 Baltra, Chaves, Darwin, Pinzon, Rabida, Wenman 7 Isabela, La Plata, Sante Fe, Tortuga 8 Espanola, Floreana, Genovesa, Marchena, Santiago 9 Culpepper, Galapagos, Santa Cruz 10 Fernandina, Santa Maria 11 San Salvador 12 San Cristobal
  mountain: 5 Andes 6 Condor, Sangay 7 Cayambe 8 Antisana, Cotopaxi 9 Cotacachi, Pichincha
  highest point: 10 Chimborazo
  river: 4 Coca, Mira, Napo 5 Cocoa, Daule, Paute, Pindo, Tigre 6 Blanco, Guayas, Tumbes, Zamora 7 Con-

ambo, Curaray, Jubones, Pastaza, Puyango 8 Aguarico, Bobonaza, Cononaco, Naranjal, Putumayo 9 San Miguel 10 Esmeraldas, Nangaritza 12 Guaillabamba
  sea: 7 Pacific
  physical feature:
    bay: 5 Manta 7 Isabela 9 Elizabeth 11 Santa Elenas 15 Ancon de Sardinas
    cape: 4 Rosa 6 Pasado 8 Marshall, Puntilla 10 San Lorenzo
    channel: 7 Jambeli
    gulf: 9 Guayaquil, Pichincha
    peninsula: 10 Santa Elena
    point: 4 Jama 5 Essex 6 Galera 9 Albemarle 10 Christobal
  people: 4 Cara, Cixo, Inca 5 Ardan, Aucas, Macoa, Maina, Palta, Quitu, Yumbo 6 Canelo, Jibaro, Jivaro, Puruha 7 Cayapas, Jivaros, mestizo, mulatto 8 Barbacoa, Colorado, Montuvio, Serranos 9 Montubios
    artist: 4 Egas 8 Santiago 9 Caspicara 10 Guayasamin
    author: 6 Espejo 14 Carrera Andrade
    conqueror: 7 Pizarro 10 Benalcazar 11 Huayna-Capac
    god: 5 umina
    leader: 6 Alfaro, Flores 10 Plaza Lasso, Rocafuerte 12 Garcia Moreno 13 Velasco Ibarra
  language: 6 Jibaro 7 Quechua, Spanish
  religion: 13 Roman Catholic
  feature:
    animal: 6 vicuna
    dictator: 8 caudillo
    estate: 8 hacienda
    festival: 5 Yamor
    hat: 6 Panama 8 jipijapa, toquilla
    tree: 5 balsa
  food:
    baked guinea pig: 3 cuy
    corn tamale: 6 humita
    drink: 6 chicha
    marinated raw shrimp/fish: 7 ceviche, seviche
    potato/cheese patty: 11 llapingacho
    potato soup: 5 locro
ecumenical 6 global 7 general 8 catholic 9 communist, planetary, universal, worldwide 10 heavenwide 11 communalist 12 all-embracing, all-including, all-inclusive, all-pervading, collectivist, cosmopolitan 13 communitarian, comprehensive, international
eczema 4 rash 8 eruption 10 dermatitis 12 inflammation
eddy 6 vortex 9 maelstrom, whirlpool 14 countercurrent
Eddy, Nelson
  partner: 17 Jeanette MacDonald
  born: 12 Providence RI
  roles: 9 Rose Marie 15 Naughty Marietta 16 Northwest Outpost

Eden 8 Paradise
see also 4 Adam

Eden, Anthony 10 Earl of Avon 13 prime minister

Eden, Barbara
role: 7 Jeannie
TV: 15 I Dream of Jeannie
costar: 11 Larry Hagman

edentate 5 manis, sloth 7 antbear 8 aardvark, anteater 9 armadillo, toothless

Edgar Huntly
author: 20 Charles Brockden Brown

edge 3 hem, rim 4 bind, inch, line, side, trim 5 bound, brink, creep, limit, sidle, slink, sneak, steal, verge 6 border, fringe, margin 7 contour, outline 9 extremity, periphery, threshold 12 boundary line, dividing line, move sideways

Edgeworth, Maria
author of: 7 Belinda 11 The Absentee 14 Castle Rackrent

edging 3 hem 4 trim 5 limit 6 border, fringe, margin, ruffle 7 binding, curbing, salvage 8 boundary, fringing, trimming

edgy 5 sharp, testy 7 anxious, nervous 8 snappish 9 excitable, impatient, irascible, irritable 10 high-strung

edible 7 eatable 10 comestible, consumable, digestible 12 fit to be eaten, nonpoisonous 13 safe for eating

edict 3 law 4 bull, fiat 5 order, ukase 6 decree, dictum, ruling 7 command, dictate, mandate, statute 9 enactment, manifesto, ordinance, prescript 10 injunction, regulation 12 proclamation, public notice 13 pronouncement 14 pronunciamento

edification 8 guidance, teaching 9 direction, education, elevation, uplifting 11 advancement, information, instruction 13 enlightenment 14 indoctrination

edifice 8 building 9 structure 12 construction

edify 5 teach 6 inform 7 educate, improve 8 instruct 9 enlighten

edifying 8 didactic, tutorial 11 educational, instructive 12 enlightening

Edinburgh
bay: 12 Firth of Forth
capital of: 8 Scotland
Celtic: 11 Dune-eideann (Eidin's Fort)
church: 7 St Giles
landmark: 14 Holyrood Palace 15 Edinburgh Castle
port: 5 Leith
rocks: 10 Castle Rock 11 Arthur's Seat

Edison, Thomas Alva
nickname: 17 Wizard of Menlo Park
home: 11 Menlo Park, NJ
inventor of: 6 (wax cylinder) record 9 light bulb, (quadruplex) telegraph 10 phonograph 11 kinetoscope, stock ticker 14 movie projector 16 incandescent lamp 18 automatic telegraph (transmitter and receiver) 21 flexible celluloid film 22 alkaline storage battery

edit 5 adapt, emend 6 censor, polish, redact, revise 7 abridge, clean up, correct, expunge, rewrite, touch up 8 annotate, condense, copy-edit, rephrase 9 expurgate 10 blue-pencil, bowdlerize

edition 4 book, copy, kind 5 issue 6 number 7 imprint, version 8 printing 9 redaction

editor 2 ed 6 writer 7 newsman, reviser 8 compiler, redactor 10 journalist

Edmonds, Walter D
author of: 8 Rome Haul 19 Drums Along the Mohawk

Edmonton
football team: 7 Eskimos
hockey team: 6 Oilers

Edmontonia
type: 8 dinosaur 10 ornithopod
location: 12 North America

Edmund Campion
author: 11 Evelyn Waugh

Edom
name given: 4 Esau
descendants: 8 Edomites

Edson, Gus
creator/artist of: 5 Dondi 8 The Gumps

Ed Sullivan Show, The
regular cast: 17 June Taylor Dancers 23 Ray Bloch and His Orchestra
noted appearances: 7 Beatles, Bob Hope 9 Topo Gigio (mouse) 10 Walt Disney 11 Senor Wences 12 Elvis Presley 14 Martin and Lewis

educate 5 coach, edify, teach, train, tutor 6 inform, school 7 develop 8 civilize, instruct 9 enlighten

education 5 study 7 culture 8 learning, pedagogy, teaching, training, tutelage 9 didactics, erudition, knowledge, schooling 10 pedagogics 11 cultivation, edification, information, instruction, scholarship 13 enlightenment

Education of Henry Adams, The
author: 10 Henry Adams

educe 5 evoke 6 elicit, extort 7 draw out, extract 8 bring out 9 draw forth 12 bring to light

Edward II
author: 18 Christopher Marlowe

Edwards, Blake
director of: 3 SOB, Ten 14 The Pink Panther, Victor Victoria 18 Days of Wine and Roses 19 Breakfast at Tiffany's
wife: 12 Julie Andrews

Edwards, Vince
real name: 18 Vincent Edward Zoimo roles: 8 Ben Casey 13 Devil's Brigade 14 The Desperadoes 15 Three Faces of Eve

Edwin Drood, The Mystery of
author: 14 Charles Dickens
character: 7 Durdles, Mr Tatar, Rosa Bud 8 Mr Sapsea 10 John Jasper, Mr Datchery 11 Mr Grewgious 12 Mr Crisparkle 13 Deputy Bazzard 14 Helena Landless, Miss Twinkleton, Mr Honeythunder 15 Neville Landless

eel 6 conger
young: 5 elver

eerie 3 odd 5 queer, weird 6 creepy, spooky, uneasy 7 bizarre, fearful, ghostly, ominous, strange, uncanny 10 mysterious, portentous 11 frightening 12 apprehensive

Eeyore 6 donkey
character in: 13 Winnie-the-Pooh
author: 5 Milne

efface 4 raze 5 erase 6 cancel, delete, excise, rub out 7 blot out, destroy, expunge, wipe out 9 eradicate, extirpate 10 annihilate, obliterate

effect, effects 4 fact, gist, make 5 cause, drift, force, goods, power, tenor, truth 6 action, assets, attain, create, impact, import, intent, result, sequel, things, upshot, weight 7 achieve, essence, execute, meaning, outcome, perform, produce, purport, reality, realize 8 carry out, chattels, efficacy, function, holdings, movables, validity 9 actuality, aftermath, execution, furniture, influence, intention, operation, outgrowth, trappings 10 accomplish, bring about, impression 11 commodities, consequence, development, enforcement, general idea, implication, possessions 12 significance 14 accomplishment

effective 4 real 6 active, actual, cogent, moving, potent, strong, useful 7 capable, current, dynamic, telling 8 a reality, eloquent, forceful, forcible, incisive, powerful, striking 9 activated, competent, effectual, efficient, operative 10 compelling, convincing, impressive, persuasive, productive, successful 11 efficacious, influential, in operation, serviceable

effectiveness 5 power 6 effect, impact 7 potency 8 efficacy, strength 9 influence 10 efficiency, usefulness 14 serviceability

effectual 6 acting, active, useful 7 working 8 adequate 9 effective, efficient, operative 11 efficacious, functioning

effectuate 6 effect 7 achieve, execute, realize 8 carry out, complete 9 discharge 10 accomplish, consummate, perpetrate 12 carry through 13 put into effect

effeminate 7 unmanly **8** sissyish, womanish **9** sissified

effervesce 4 fizz, foam **5** froth **6** bubble, fizzle **7** sparkle

effervescence 3 zip **4** dash, fizz, life **5** froth, vigor **6** fizzle, gaiety, spirit **7** foaming **8** bubbling, buoyancy, vitality, vivacity **9** animation, fizziness **10** bubbliness, bubbling up, ebullience, enthusiasm, liveliness

effervescent 3 gay **5** fizzy, merry **6** bubbly, lively **7** fizzing, foaming **8** animated, bubbling **9** ebullient, exuberant, sparkling, vivacious **13** irrepressible

effete 5 spent **6** barren, wasted **7** sterile, worn-out **8** decadent, depraved **9** enervated, exhausted **10** degenerate, unprolific **12** unproductive

efficacious 9 effective, effectual, efficient

efficacy 6 impact **10** efficiency **13** effectiveness

efficiency 5 skill **6** energy **8** efficacy, facility **9** apartment **10** competence **11** proficiency **13** effectiveness

efficient 3 apt **7** capable **8** skillful **9** competent, effective, effectual **10** productive, proficient, timesaving, unwasteful, work-saving **11** crackerjack, efficacious, workmanlike **12** businesslike

effigy 4 doll **5** dummy, image **6** puppet, statue **8** likeness, straw man **9** mannequin, scarecrow **10** marionette **14** representation

effluence 6 efflux **7** outflow, outpour **8** effluent **9** discharge

effluent 5 waste **6** efflux, sewage **7** outflow **9** effluence

effluvium 4 aura, odor, ooze, reek **5** vapor **6** efflux, flatus **8** outgoing

efflux 7 outflow **8** effluent, emission **9** discharge, effluence

effort 3 try **4** toil, work **5** force, labor, pains, power **6** energy, strain, stress **7** attempt, travail, trouble **8** endeavor, exertion, industry, struggle **11** elbow grease

effortless 4 easy **6** facile, simple, smooth **8** graceful, painless **12** not difficult **13** uncomplicated

effortlessness 4 ease **8** easiness, facility **9** readiness **12** painlessness

effrontery 4 gall **5** brass, cheek, nerve **8** audacity, temerity **9** arrogance, brashness, impudence, insolence **10** brazenness **11** presumption **12** impertinence **13** shamelessness
  Yiddish: 7 chutzpa **8** chutzpah

effulgence 6 dazzle **8** radiance, splendor **10** brilliance **12** resplendence

effulgent 6 bright **7** radiant **8** dazzling, splendid **9** brilliant **11** resplendent

effusive 5 gushy **6** lavish **7** copious,
gushing, profuse **9** ebullient, expansive, exuberant **10** unreserved **11** extravagant, free-flowing, overflowing **12** unrestrained

eft 4 newt **5** again **6** lizard **9** afterward

egalitarian 10 democratic **11** equal-rights **14** constitutional

egalite 8 equality

Egeria
  instructed: 4 Numa **5** nymph **7** advisor

egg 3 ova, roe **4** bomb, goad, mine, oval, ovum, seed, spur **6** embryo, fellow, incite, person **7** albumen **9** instigate, stimulate

Eggar, Samantha
  born: 6 London **7** England
  roles: 12 The Collector, Walking Stick **15** Doctor Doolittle, The Lady in the Car **16** The Molly Maguires

egghead 8 highbrow **13** intellectual

Eggleston, Edward
  author of: 15 The Circuit Rider **19** The Hoosier Schoolboy **22** The Hoosier Schoolmaster

egg on 4 abet, back, goad, spur **6** exhort, incite **8** talk into **9** encourage

egg-shaped 4 oval **5** ovoid **7** oviform **10** elliptical

Egmont
  author: 12 Johann Goethe

egocentric 8 egoistic **11** egomaniacal, egotistical, on an ego trip, self-seeking, self-serving **12** narcissistic, self-absorbed, self-centered, self-involved, self-obsessed **13** self-concerned **14** megalomaniacal, stuck on oneself **18** wrapped up in oneself

egoism 6 vanity **8** self-love **10** narcissism **14** self-absorption, self-importance **16** overweening pride, self-centeredness

egoist 10 narcissist, selfish one **13** selfish person **18** self-centered person

Egoist, The
  author: 14 George Meredith

egoistic 7 selfish **12** narcissistic, self-centered

egotism 6 vanity **7** conceit **8** bragging, smugness **9** arrogance, immodesty, vainglory **10** self-praise **11** braggadocio **12** boastfulness

egotist 6 gascon **7** boaster, peacock **8** blowhard, braggart **9** swaggerer **11** braggadocio

egotistic 4 vain **10** egocentric **12** self-centered **13** self-important

egregious 5 gross **7** extreme, glaring, heinous **8** flagrant, grievous, shocking **9** monstrous, notorious **10** outrageous **11** intolerable **12** insufferable

egress 4 exit, vent **5** issue **6** escape, outlet, way out **7** leakage, outflow, seepage **8** aperture **9** departure, discharge **10** passage out, withdrawal

Egypt
  other name: 3 UAR **5** Kemet **6** Tomeri **11** The Two Lands **12** The Black Land
  capital/largest city: 5 Cairo
  others: 3 Tor **4** Edfu, Gaza, Giza, Idfu, Said, Suez **5** Altur, Aswan, Tanta **6** Boolak, Dumyat, Faiyum, Quseir, Safaga, Sallum **7** Alemein, Memphis, Raschid, Rosetta, Zagazig **8** Damietta, Hurghada, Ismailia, Mansurah **10** Alexandria
  school: 5 Cairo **7** Al-Azhar **8** American
  division: 5 Lower, Nubia, Upper
  measure: 3 apt, dra, hen, rob **4** arab, dira, draa, khet, nief, ocha, roub, theb, wudu **5** abdat, ardab, cubit, farde, fedan, keleh, kerat, kilah, sahme **6** artaba, aurure, baladi, kantar, keddah, robhah, schene **7** choryos, daribah, malouah, roubouh, toumnah **8** kassabah, kharouba **10** diramimari, diribaladi
  monetary unit: 4 fils, kees, para **5** asper, dinar, fodda, gersh, girsh, medin, pound, riyal **6** ahmadi, dirham, foddah, guinea, junayh, maidin, medine, medino **7** piaster, piastre, tallard **8** bedidlik, millieme
  weight: 3 kat, ket, oka, oke **4** dera, heml, khar, okia, rotl **5** artal, artel, deben, kerat, minae, minas, okieh, pound, ratel, uckia **6** hamlah, kantar **7** drachma, quintal
  island: 4 Roda **6** Philae **7** Shadwan **11** Elephantine
  lake: 4 Edku, Idku **5** Qarun **6** Maryut, Moeris, Nasser **7** Manzala **8** Burullus, Mareotis
  mountain: 5 Sinai, Uekia **6** Gharib **13** Shayib al-Banat
  highest point: 8 Katerina **9** Katherina
  river: 4 Bahr, Nile
    Nile branch: 7 Rosetta **8** Damietta
  sea: 3 Red **13** Mediterranean
  physical feature:
    cape: 4 Sudr **5** Banas **8** Rasbanas
    desert: 3 Tih **5** Dakla, Scete, Sinai, Skete **6** Libyan, Nubian, Sahara **7** Arabian
    gulf: 4 Suez **5** Aqaba
    isthmus: 4 Suez
    oasis: 4 Siwa **6** Dakhel, Dakhla, Kharga **7** Farafra, Khargeh **8** Bahariya **9** Bahariyeh **12** Wahel-Khargeh
    peninsula: 5 Sinai **6** Pharos
    plain: 7 Asaseff
    plateau: 3 Tih
  people: 3 Kem **4** Arab, Copt, Misr, Wafd **5** Gippy, Gyppy, Gypsy, Nilot **6** Ababda, Berber, Hyksos, Nubian, Tasian **7** Mizraim, Pharian **8** Badarian, Bisharin, Memphian
    leader: 5 Jawar, Sadat **6** Nasser **7** Mubarak, Saladin **10** King Farouk **11** Ismail Pasha, Mohammed Ali,

Tawfiq Pasha

pharaoh: 5 Khufu, Menes, Zoser **6** Khafre, Ptulol, Ramses **8** Horemheb, Menkaure **9** Akhenaten, Amenemhet, Amenhotep **10** Mentuhotep **11** Tutankhamen

queen: 9 Cleopatra, Nefertari, Nefertiti **10** Hatshepsut, Hetepheres

language: 6 Arabic, French **7** English
for liturgy: 6 Coptic

religion: 5 Islam **18** Coptic Christianity

ancient god: 2 Ra **3** Geb, Nut, Shu **4** Aton, Atum, Isis, Ptah, Seth **5** Horus, Thoth **6** Anubis, Hathor, Osiris, Tefnut **8** Nephthys

place:

dam: 4 Sadd, Sudd **5** Aswan **6** Assuan

mosque: 5 Rifai **9** Alabaster **11** Sultan Hasan

palace: 6 Kubbeh

pyramids: 4 Giza **5** Khufu **6** Cheops **7** Saqqara

ruins: 5 Miroe **6** Abydos, Sphinx, Thebes **7** Memphis **8** Berenice **9** Abu Simbel **13** Valley of Kings, Valley of Tombs

temple: 4 Idfu **5** Edoon, Luxor, Thoth **6** Abydos, Karnak, Osiris **7** Dendera

feature:

dynasty: 5 Saite **7** Ayyubid, Fatimid **8** Mameluke **9** Ptolemaic

long robe: 10 gallabiyea

peasant: 6 fellah **8** fellahin **9** fellaheen

sacred bird: 4 benu, ibis **5** bennu

sailboat: 7 felucca

statue: 6 Sphinx **15** Colossi of Memnon

food:

bean: 5 lotus

beer: 6 zythum

bread: 6 herisa

dish: 3 ful

drink: 4 bosa, boza **5** bozah

Egyptian

language family: 11 Afro-Asiatic **13** Hamito-Semitic

later form: 6 Coptic

Egyptian cross 4 ankh

Egyptian Mythology

deities: 6 Ennead

eight gods: 3 Heh **6** Ogdoad

goddess of evil: 7 Sekhmet

goddess of fertility: 2 Io **4** Isis

goddess of law/righteousness: 4 Maat

goddess of love/joy/music/dance: 6 Hathor

goddess of sky: 3 Nut

goddess personifying sky: 6 Hathor

god of bricks: 5 Kulla

god of creation: 4 Ptah

god of dead/Nile: 6 Osiris

god of earth: 3 Geb, Keb

god of ocean: 3 Nun **4** Nunu

god of sun: 2 Ra, Re **5** Horus
corresponds to Greek: 10 Harcorates

god of tombs/embalming: 6 Anubis

god of wisdom/magic/learning: 5 Thoth
corresponds to Greek: 6 Hermes

immortal spirit: 2 Ka

judge of dead: 6 Osiris

king of dead: 6 Osiris

king of gods: 4 Amen, Amon **5** Ammon **6** Amen Ra, Amon Ra
corresponds to Greek: 4 Zeus
corresponds to Roman: 4 Jove **7** Jupiter

personification of femininity: 5 Neith
corresponds to Greek: 6 Athena

ram god: 5 Khnum

vulture: 7 Nekhbet

Ehrlich, Paul

field: 12 bacteriology

nationality: 6 German

studied: 6 toxins **8** immunity **10** antitoxins

discovered: 9 salvarsan

coined term: 12 chemotherapy

awarded: 10 Nobel Prize

Eichmann in Jerusalem

author: 12 Hannah Arendt

eiderdown 4 puff **5** cover, quilt **8** coverlet **10** featherbed

Eight and a Half, 8 1/2

director: 15 Federico Fellini

cast: 10 Anouk Aimee **16** Claudia Cardinale **19** Marcello Mastroianni

Eijkman, Christiaan

nationality: 5 Dutch

discovered: 19 antineuritic vitamin

researched: 8 beriberi

awarded: 10 Nobel Prize

Einstein, Albert

birthplace: 3 Ulm

field: 7 physics

theory of: 10 relativity **14** uranium fission

awarded: 10 Nobel Prize

Eire *see* **7** Ireland

Eisenhower, Dwight David

nickname: 3 Ike
changed name from: 21 David Dwight Eisenhower

presidential rank: 12 thirty-fourth

party: 10 Republican

state represented: 2 NY

defeated: 4 (Eric) Hass, (Harry Flood) Byrd **5** (Farrell) Dobbs **6** (Darlington) Hoopes, (William Ezra) Jenner **7** (Stuart) Hamblen, (Thomas Coleman) Andrews **8** (Enoch Arden) Holtwick, (Vincent William) Hallinan **9** (Adlai Ewing) Stevenson

vice president: 5 (Richard Milhous) Nixon

cabinet:
state: 6 (Christian Archibald) Herter, (John Foster) Dulles

treasury: 8 (George Magoffin) Humphrey, (Robert Bernard) Anderson

defense: 5 (Thomas Sovereign) Gates (Jr) **6** (Charles Erwin) Wilson **7** (Neil Hesler) McElroy

attorney general: 6 (William Pierce) Rogers **8** (Herbert) Brownell (Jr)

postmaster general: 11 (Arthur Ellsworth) Summerfield

interior: 5 (Douglas) McKay **6** (Frederick Andrew) Seaton

agriculture: 6 (Ezra Taft) Benson

commerce: 5 (Sinclair) Weeks **7** (Frederick Henry) Mueller, (Lewis Lichtenstein) Strauss

labor: 6 (Martin Patrick) Durkin **8** (James Paul) Mitchell

HEW: 5 (Oveta Culp) Hobby **6** (Marion Bayard) Folsom **8** (Arthur Sherwood) Flemming

born: 9 Denison TX

died: 12 Washington DC

buried: 9 Abilene KS

education: 9 West Point **17** US Military Academy

religion: 12 Presbyterian

interest: 4 golf **6** flying **7** fishing, hunting **8** football, painting

vacation spot: 10 Gettysburg **11** Palm Springs

author: 11 Waging Peace **15** Crusade in Europe **16** Mandate for Change **27** At Ease: Stories I Tell to Friends

civilian career:
president of: 18 Columbia University

military service: 7 general **9** World War I **10** World War II **16** Army Chief of Staff

supreme commander of: 6 Allies **15** European Defense (NATO) **18** US occupation forces (Europe)

head of: 18 Joint Chiefs of Staff

notable events of lifetime/term: 4 D-Day, NATO

Acts: 11 Civil Rights

battle of the: 5 Bulge

conference: 7 Big Four **10** NATO Summit **11** Paris Summit

Cuba taken over by: 11 Fidel Castro

invasion: 8 Normandy

trial/execution of: 14 Ethel Rosenberg **15** Julius Rosenberg

USSR shot down: 9 U-Two plane

father: 10 David Jacob

mother: 3 Ida (Elizabeth Stover)

siblings: 3 Roy **4** Earl, Paul **5** Edgar **6** Arthur, Milton

wife: 5 Marie (Geneva Doud)
nickname: 5 Mamie

children: 10 Doud Dwight **15** John Sheldon Doud

ejaculate 4 howl, yell, yelp **5** shout **6** bellow, cry out **7** exclaim **10** vociferate

ejaculation 3 cry **4** howl, yell, yelp **5** shout **6** bellow, outcry, shriek, squeal **7** screech **11** exclamation **12** vociferation

eject 4 emit, oust, spew **5** evict, exile, expel, exude, spout **6** banish, bounce, deport, remove **7** cast out, kick out, spit out, turn out **8** disgorge, drive out, force out, throw out **9** discharge **10** dispossess

ejection 4 gush **5** spurt **6** ouster **7** issuing, removal **8** emission, eruption, eviction **9** dismissal, expelling, expulsion **10** banishment **11** throwing out

eke 3 add **4** also **7** augment, enlarge, stretch **8** increase, lengthen, likewise, moreover **10** in addition, supplement

elaborate 5 fancy, gaudy, showy **6** expand, flashy, garish, ornate **7** clarify, complex, elegant, labored, specify **8** involved, overdone **9** embellish, intricate **10** add details **11** complicated, painstaking **12** ostentatious **13** particularize

elaborate on 6 expand **7** amplify, develop **9** embellish **10** supplement **11** expatiate on

elaboration 11 added detail, rounding out **12** augmentation **13** amplification, embellishment

Elaine
character in: 16 Arthurian romance
called: 8 lily maid
home: 7 Astolat
lover: 8 Lancelot
son: 7 Galahad
father: 6 Pelles

Elais
father: 5 Anius
mother: 7 Dorippe
changed things into: 3 oil

elan 4 dash, zeal **5** flair, verve, vigor **6** energy, spirit **8** vivacity **9** animation **10** enthusiasm

eland 3 elk **8** antelope **11** taurotragus

elapse 4 go by, pass **5** lapse **6** pass by, roll by, slip by **7** glide by, slide by **8** slip away **9** intervene

elastic 6 pliant, supple **7** pliable, rubbery, springy **8** flexible, tolerant, yielding **9** adaptable, recoiling, resilient **10** rebounding, responsive **11** complaisant, stretchable **12** recuperative **13** accommodating

elate 5 cheer, exalt **6** excite, lift up, please **7** animate, delight, elevate, enliven, gladden, gratify, inspire **10** exhilarate

elated 4 glad **5** happy, proud **6** joyful, joyous **7** exalted, excited, gleeful, pleased **8** animated, blissful, ecstatic, jubilant **9** overjoyed, rejoicing **10** delightful **11** exhilarated **13** in high spirits **18** flushed with success

elation 3 joy **4** glee **5** pride **7** triumph **8** gladness **9** happiness **10** excite-ment, exultation, jubilation **12** cheerfulness

elbow grease 4 work **5** force, labor **6** effort, energy, muscle **8** exertion, hard work **11** application

elbow in 4 push **5** force, press, shove **6** horn in **7** crowd in

El Cordobes (Manuel Benitez Perez)
sport: 12 bullfighting

elder 4 head **5** older **6** senior **8** old-timer **9** firstborn, patriarch, presbyter **14** church official **15** church dignitary **French: 4** aine

elder, elderberry 8 Sambucus
varieties: 3 Box **4** Blue **5** Dwarf, Sweet **6** Ground, Poison, Yellow **8** American, European, Stinking **10** Red-berried **11** American red, European red **15** Pacific Coast red

elderly 3 old **4** aged **9** venerable **11** over the hill **13** past one's prime

Eldorado
nickname of: 10 California

Eleanor and Franklin
author: 11 Joseph P Lash

Eleazar
father: 4 Dodo **5** Aaron, Elind, Mahli **6** Parosh **7** Phineas **8** Abinadab
mother: 8 Elisheba
brother: 5 Abihu, Nadab **7** Ithamar
succeeded: 5 Aaron

elect 4 pick **5** adopt **6** choose, opt for, select, take up **7** embrace, espouse, fix upon, pick out **8** decide on, settle on **9** single out

election 4 poll, vote **6** choice, option, voting **7** resolve **8** decision **9** balloting, selection **10** resolution **11** alternative **13** determination

electioneer 3 run **5** stump **8** campaign **11** whistle-stop **12** beat the drums, solicit votes

elective 8 optional **9** selective, voluntary **11** not required **12** open to choice, passed by vote **13** discretionary, not obligatory

Electra
author: 9 Euripides, Sophocles
character: 7 Orestes, Pylades **8** Dioscuri **9** Aegisthus **12** Clytemnestra
father: 9 Agamemnon
mother: 12 Clytemnestra
brother: 7 Orestes
sister: 9 Iphigenia **12** Chrysothemis
husband: 7 Pylades
son: 5 Medon **9** Strophius

electric 7 dynamic, rousing **8** exalting, exciting, spirited, stirring **9** inspiring, thrilling **10** full of fire **11** galvanizing, power-driven, stimulating **12** electrifying, soul-stirring

electric battery
invented by: 5 Volta

electricity measure 3 ohm **4** volt, watt **5** joule **6** ampere **10** horsepower

Electric Kool-Aid Acid Test, The
author: 8 Tom Wolfe

electrify 4 daze, stir, stun **5** amaze, rouse **6** dazzle, excite, fire up, thrill **7** animate, astound, quicken, startle **8** astonish, surprise **9** fascinate, galvanize, stimulate **18** take one's breath away

electrifying 8 dazzling, shocking, stunning **10** astounding, stupefying **11** astonishing

electromagnet
invented by: 8 Sturgeon

Electryon
king of: 7 Mycenae
father: 7 Perseus
mother: 9 Andromeda
brother: 6 Mestor **9** Sthenelus
wife: 5 Anaxo
son: 9 Licymnius
daughter: 7 Alcmene
grandson: 8 Hercules

eleemosynary 10 altruistic, beneficent, benevolent, charitable **13** philanthropic **15** non-profitmaking

elegance 5 class, grace, taste **6** purity **7** balance **8** delicacy, grandeur, richness, symmetry **10** refinement **12** gracefulness **13** exquisiteness, luxuriousness, sumptuousness

elegant 4 fine, rich **5** grand **6** classy, dapper, lovely, ornate, polite, urbane **7** classic, courtly, genteel, refined, stylish **8** artistic, charming, debonair, delicate, graceful, gracious, handsome, polished, tasteful, well-bred **9** beautiful, dignified, exquisite, luxurious, sumptuous **10** attractive, cultivated **11** fashionable, symmetrical **16** wellproportioned

elegiac 3 sad **8** funereal, mournful **10** melancholy

elegy 7 requiem, sad poem **11** funeral song **14** melancholy poem **16** lament for the dead **17** poem of lamentation, song of lamentation **22** melancholy piece of music

Elegy Written in a Country Churchyard
author: 10 Thomas Gray

Elektra *see* **7** Electra

element, elements 3 air **4** fire **5** earth, water **6** basics, member, milieu **7** essence, factors, origins **8** original **9** basic part, basic unit, component, rudiments **10** basic ideas, ingredient, principles, simple body **11** constituent, environment, foundations, native state, subdivision **13** building block, component part, natural medium **14** natural habitat

elemental 5 basal, basic **10** elementary **11** fundamental, rudimentary

elementary 4 easy **5** basal, basic, crude, first, plain **6** simple **7** primary **8** original **9** elemental, primitive **11**

fundamental, rudimentary, undeveloped **13** uncomplicated

elephant
group of: **4** herd
types: **5** Asian **7** African
features: **5** trunk, tusks
famous: **5** Babar, Dumbo
elephant boy: **4** Sabu **6** mahout
extinct: **7** mammoth **8** mastodon
produce: **5** ivory

elephantine 4 huge **7** immense, mammoth, titanic **8** colossal, enormous, gigantic **9** ponderous **10** gargantuan, tremendous **14** Brobdingnagian

Elephant Man, The
director: **10** David Lynch
cast: **8** John Hurt **11** John Gielgud, Wendy Hiller **12** Anne Bancroft **14** Anthony Hopkins

Eleusinian mysteries
in memory of: **10** Persephone
in honor of: **7** Bacchus, Demeter
celebrated at: **6** Athens **7** Eleusis
founded by: **8** Eumolpus
god of: **7** Bacchus

elevate 4 lift **5** boost, cheer, elate, heave, hoist, raise **6** better, excite, lift up, move up, perk up, refine, uplift **7** advance, animate, dignify, enhance, ennoble, improve, inspire, promote, upraise **8** heighten **9** place high **10** exhilarate, raise aloft

elevated 4 high **5** lofty **6** raised **7** exalted **8** improved, uplifted **9** prominent **10** heightened

elevation 4 hill, lift, rise **5** boost **6** ascent, height **8** altitude, mountain **9** acclivity, bettering, high place, promotion **10** prominence, refinement **11** advancement, cultivation, improvement

elevator 4 cage, lift, silo, wing **5** hoist **7** granary **10** dumbwaiter
inventor: **4** Otis

elevator brake
invented by: **4** Otis

Elf
director: **10** Jon Favreau
cast: **9** James Caan (Walter) **10** Bob Newhart (Papa Elf) **11** Edward Asner (Santa), Will Ferrell (Buddy) **14** Zooey Deschanel (Jovie) **15** Mary Steenbergen (Emily)

elf 4 puck **5** fairy, gnome, pixie, troll **6** goblin, sprite **7** brownie, gremlin **9** hobgoblin **10** leprechaun

elfin 3 fey, wee **4** tiny **7** pixyish **9** fairylike **10** diminutive

Elgar, Sir Edward William
born: **7** England **10** Broadheath
composer of: **8** Falstaff **9** Cockaigne, Froissart **10** Caractacus, The Kingdom **11** The Apostles **14** The Black Knight, The Light of Life **16** Enigma Variations **19** Pomp and Circumstance, The Banner of St George, The

Dream of Gerontius **30** Scenes from the Bavarian Highlands

Eli
son: **6** Hophni **7** Phineas
home: **6** Shiloh **10** high priest
teacher of: **6** Samuel

Eli, Eli, Lama sabachthani
means: **31** My God My God why hast thou forsaken me?

Elia see **11** Lamb, Charles

elicit 5 cause, educe, evoke, exact, fetch, wrest **6** derive, extort **7** draw out, extract **9** call forth, draw forth **10** bring forth **12** bring to light

elide 4 omit, slur **5** annul **6** delete **7** neglect **8** slur over, suppress **9** eliminate, strikeout **10** abbreviate

Eliezar
father: **5** Moses
mother: **8** Zipporah
brother: **7** Gershom

eligible 6 proper **7** fitting **8** suitable **9** desirable, qualified **10** acceptable, applicable, authorized, worthwhile **11** appropriate

Elihu
brother: **5** David
friend: **3** Job **6** Bildad, Zophar **7** Eliphaz

Elijah 7 prophet
opposed: **4** Ahab, Baal **7** Jezebel
successor: **6** Elisha

Elimelech
wife: **5** Naomi

eliminate 4 drop, omit, oust **5** eject, erase, exile, expel **6** banish, cut out, delete, except, reject, remove, rub out **7** abolish, cast out, dismiss, exclude, weed out **8** get rid of, leave out, stamp out, throw out **9** eradicate **10** annihilate, do away with **11** exterminate

Eliot, George
real name: **13** Mary Anne Evans
author of: **6** Romola **8** Adam Bede **11** Middlemarch, Silas Marner **17** The Mill on the Floss

Eliot, John
author of: **12** Bay Psalm Book

Eliot, T S
author of: **9** East Coker, Gerontion, Hollow Men **11** Burnt Norton, Dry Salvages **12** Ash Wednesday, Four Quartets, The Waste Land **13** Little Gidding, The Sacred Wood **16** The Family Reunion **20** Murder in the Cathedral **27** Sweeney Among the Nightingales **28** The Love Song of J Alfred Prufrock
inspiration for: **4** Cats

Eliphaz
father: **4** Adah, Esau
friend: **3** Job **5** Elihu **6** Bildad, Zophar

Elisabeth see **9** Elizabeth

Elisha 7 prophet

home: **11** Abelmeholah
succeeded: **6** Elijah

elite 3 top **4** best **5** cream **6** choice, flower **7** bigwigs, society, the pick, wealthy **8** big shots, notables **9** haut monde **10** blue bloods, personages, select body, upper class **11** aristocracy, celebrities, high society **14** creme-de-la-creme

elixir 6 potion, remedy **7** essence, extract, panacea, spirits **8** tincture **11** concentrate **17** alcoholic solution

Eliza
character in: **14** Uncle Tom's Cabin
author: **5** Stowe

Elizabeth
director: **12** Shekhar Kapur
cast: **10** Kathy Burke (Queen Mary) **11** John Gielgud (the Pope) **12** Geoffrey Rush (Sir Francis Walsingham), Terence Rigby (Bishop Gardiner) **13** Cate Blanchett (Elizabeth), Joseph Fiennes (Robert Dudley, Earl of Leicester), Rod Culbertson (Master Ridley) **14** George Yiasoumi (King Philip) **19** Richard Attenborough (Sir William Cecil)

Elizabeth
husband: **9** Zacharias, Zechariah
son: **14** John the Baptist

Elizabeth I
queen of: **7** England
father: **10** Henry Tudor **14** Henry the Eighth
mother: **10** Anne Boleyn
sister: **4** Mary **10** Bloody Mary
brother: **14** Edward the Sixth
advisor: **5** Cecil **8** Burghley **10** Walsingham
suitor: **5** Essex **6** Dudley **9** Leicester
victory over: **13** Spanish Armada

Elizabeth II
father: **14** George the Sixth
mother: **9** Elizabeth
husband: **17** Philip Mountbatten
son: **6** Andrew, Edward **7** Charles
son-in-law: **11** Mark Philips **15** Timothy Laurence
daughter: **4** Anne
daughter-in-law: **5** Diana, Sarah (Fergie) **6** Sophie **7** Camilla

Elizabeth the Queen
author: **15** Maxwell Anderson

elk
group of: **4** gang

Ellas see **6** Greece

Ellen
network: **3** ABC
original title: **18** These Friends of Mine
cast: **9** Clea Lewis (Audrey Penney) **11** Alice Hirson (Lois Morgan), Jeremy Piven (Spence Kovak), Joely Fisher (Paige Clark) **13** Steven Gilborn (Harold Morgan) **14** Ellen DeGeneres (Ellen Morgan) **19** David Anthony Higgins (Joe Farrell)

Ellerbee, Linda 6 writer **10** newscaster
  book: 11 And So It Goes
Ellice Islands *see* **6** Tuvalu
Ellington, Duke
  real name: 22 Edward Kennedy Ellington
  born: 12 Washington DC
  composer of: 10 Mood Indigo **14** Creole Love Call, Creole Rhapsody, Hot and Bothered **17** Concerto for Cootie **18** Black and Tan Fantasy
Elliot family
  characters in: 10 Persuasion
  member: 4 Anne **7** William **9** Elizabeth, Sir Walter
  author: 6 Austen
Ellison, Harlan
  author of: 7 Paingod **10** Spider Kiss **13** A Boy and His Dog **16** Deathbird Stories **19** Approaching Oblivion **20** Alone Against Tomorrow
Ellison, Ralph
  author of: 12 Invisible Man
elm 5 Ulmus
  varieties: 3 red **4** bush, cork, rock, vase, wych **5** cedar, Dutch, dwarf, globe, wahoo, water, white **6** Exeter, horned, Jersey, moline, Scotch, willow, winged **7** Belgian, Chinese, Cornish, English, Holland **8** American, fern-leaf, Guernsey, Japanese, Siberian, slippery, tabletop, wheatley **9** September **10** camperdown, Chichester, Huntingdon, smooth-leaf **11** small-leaved **13** European white
Elmer Gantry
  author: 13 Sinclair Lewis
  director: 13 Richard Brooks
  cast: 10 Dean Jagger **11** Jean Simmons **12** Shirley Jones **13** Arthur Kennedy, Burt Lancaster
  Oscar for: 5 actor (Lancaster) **17** supporting actress (Jones)
elocution 7 speech **7** diction, oratory **10** intonation **11** enunciation **12** articulation **13** pronunciation **14** public speaking
Elohim 3 God
Eloisa to Abelard
  author: 13 Alexander Pope
Elon 11 Hebrew judge
elongate 6 extend **7** draw out, prolong **8** lengthen, protract **10** stretch out
elongated 4 long **8** drawn out, extended **9** prolonged **10** attenuated, lengthened, protracted **12** stretched out
eloquence 5 force, grace **7** fluency, oratory **8** rhetoric **9** elocution, speakwell, vividness **10** expression **12** silver tongue
  god of: 4 Ogma **6** Ogmios **7** Mercury
eloquent 5 vivid **6** moving, poetic **8** emphatic, forceful, spirited, stirring,

striking **10** articulate, passionate, persuasive **11** impassioned
El Salvador
  other name: 9 Cuscatlan
  capital/largest city: 11 San Salvador
  others: 6 Cutuco, Izalco **7** Corinto, Metapan **8** Acajutla, Libertad, Santa Ana, Usulutan **9** San Miguel, Sonsonate **10** San Vicente, Santa Tecla **11** Union-Cutuco **12** Chalatenango
  school: 15 Jose Simeon Canas **16** Alberto Masferrer
  measure: 4 vara **5** cafiz, cahiz **6** fanega **7** batella, botella, cantara, manzana
  monetary unit: 4 peso **5** colon **7** centavo
  weight: 3 bag **4** caja **5** libra
  lake: 5 Guiha, Guija **8** Ilopango **10** Coatepeque
  mountain: 6 Izalco
  highest point: 8 Santa Ana
  river: 5 Jiboa, Lempa, Lopaz **6** Torola **7** de la Paz **9** Goasoaran **17** Grande de San Miguel
  sea: 7 Pacific
  physical feature:
    bay: 10 Jiquilisco
    coast: 6 Balsam
    gulf: 7 Fonseca
    point: 7 Amapala **8** Remedios
    valley: 7 Hamacas
  people: 5 Lenca, Pipil **6** Indian, Mangue **7** mestizo, Spanish **9** Matagalpa
    artist: 8 Salarrue **10** Mejia Vides
    author: 8 Salarrue **14** Antonio Gavidia
    conqueror: 8 Alvarado
    leader: 6 Osorio **8** Jose Arce **13** Matias Delgado **15** Manuel Rodriguez **17** Hernandez Martinez
    philosopher/journalist: 9 Masferrer
  language: 7 Spanish
  religion: 13 Roman Catholic
  place:
    ruins: 7 Tazumal
  feature:
    blouse: 9 volcanena
    dance: 7 pasillo **15** los historianes
    drum: 8 huehuetl
    estate: 5 finca
    musical instrument: 7 caramba
  food:
    bread: 10 quesadilla
    cheese pancake: 6 pupusa
Elscheimer, Adam
  born: 7 Germany **15** Frankfurt am Main
  artwork: 17 Tobias and the Angel **21** The Stoning of St Stephen **24** Rest on the Flight into Egypt
else 3 and, too **4** also, more **5** if not, other **7** besides, instead **9** different, otherwise **10** additional, contrarily, in addition
elsewhere 4 away **6** except **7** absence, not here

Elsinore
  castle in: 6 Hamlet **7** Denmark
  author: 11 Shakespeare
Elton, Mr
  character in: 4 Emma
  author: 6 Austen
elucidate 6 detail **7** clarify, clear up, explain, expound **8** describe, spell out **9** delineate, explicate, interpret, make plain **10** illuminate, illustrate **11** comment upon **14** throw light upon
elucidation 7 account **10** commentary **11** description, explanation, explication **13** clarification **14** interpretation **15** exemplification
elude 4 shun **5** avoid, dodge, evade **6** escape, slip by **10** circumvent, fight shy of **11** get away from, keep clear of
eluding 7 dodging, ducking, evading, evasion **8** avoiding **9** avoidance **12** escaping from, sidestepping **13** circumventing **15** getting away from
Elul 16 sixth Hebrew month
elusive 4 foxy, wily **6** crafty, shifty, tricky **7** evasive **8** baffling, puzzling, slippery **11** hard to catch, hard to grasp
elusory 4 wily **6** shifty **7** devious, dodging, elusive, evasive, hedging **8** slippery **9** ambiguous, deceitful, deceptive, equivocal **10** misleading **12** equivocating
Elvsted, Thea
  character in: 11 Hedda Gabler
  author: 5 Ibsen
elysian 7 sublime **8** blissful, empyreal, empyrean, ethereal, heavenly **9** celestial, unearthly **12** otherworldly, paradisiacal
Elysium
  also: 17 islands of the blest
  afterworld of the: 7 blessed
Elytis, Odysseus
  real name: 19 Odysseus Alepoudelis
  author of: 10 Seemly It Is **20** Heroic and Elegiac Song
emaciated 4 lank, lean, thin **5** gaunt **6** sickly, skinny, wasted **7** haggard, scrawny, wizened **8** skeletal, starving, underfed **10** cadaverous **14** undernourished
emanate 4 flow, rise, stem, well **5** exude, issue **6** spring **7** give off, proceed **8** come from **9** come forth, originate, send forth
emanation 6 coming **7** arising, flowing, issuing **8** effusion **9** effluence, radiation, springing **10** exhalation **11** coming forth
emancipate 4 free **7** manumit, release, set free, unchain **8** liberate, unfetter **9** unshackle **12** set at liberty
emancipation 7 freedom, liberty **10** liberation **11** manumission **12** independence

emasculate 4 geld **5** alter **6** soften, weaken **8** castrate **9** undermine **10** devitalize

Emaux et Camees
author: **16** Theophile Gautier

Embalming
god of: **6** Anubis

embankment 4 bank, dike, wall **5** levee

embargo 3 ban **8** shutdown, stoppage **10** impediment, inhibition, injunction, quarantine, standstill **11** prohibition, restriction **12** interdiction, proscription **16** restraint of trade

embark 5 begin, board, start **6** launch, set out **7** enplane, entrain **8** commence, go aboard **9** board ship, enter upon

embark on 5 begin, start **8** approach, commence, initiate, set about **9** enter upon, undertake

embarras de richesses 13 overabundance **21** embarrassment of riches

embarrass 4 faze **5** abash, shame, upset **6** rattle **7** agitate, chagrin, confuse, fluster, mortify, nonplus **8** distress **9** discomfit **10** discompose, disconcert **13** make ill at ease **14** discountenance **17** make self-conscious

embarrassed 7 abashed **8** red-faced **9** chagrined, mortified **10** nonplussed **11** discomfited **13** self-conscious

embarrassing 7 awkward **8** confused, crushing **9** bothering **10** disturbing, mortifying, unpleasant **12** demoralizing, discomfiting **13** discomforting, disconcerting, uncomfortable

embarrassment 4 blot **5** stain **6** smirch **7** blemish, scandal, tarnish **8** disgrace **9** discredit **19** financial difficulty

embattled 8 fighting **9** embroiled, fortified **11** battle-ready, hard-pressed

embed 3 fix, set **4** bond **5** plant **6** fasten **8** ensconce **9** establish

embedded 3 set **5** fixed **6** bonded **7** engaged, planted **8** immersed, inserted **9** ensconced **11** established

embellish 4 gild **5** adorn, color **6** set off **7** dress up, enhance, fancy up, garnish, gussy up **8** beautify, decorate, ornament **9** elaborate, embroider **10** exaggerate

embellished 6 ornate **7** adorned, flowery **8** brocaded **9** decorated **10** beautified, elaborated, ornamented, rhetorical **11** embroidered

embellishment 5 frill **6** accent **7** garnish **8** furbelow, ornament, trimming **9** adornment **10** decoration, embroidery **11** elaboration **14** beautification **15** fuss and feathers

ember 3 ash **4** slag **6** cinder **7** clinker **8** live coal

embezzle 4 bilk, rook **5** cheat, filch **6** fleece **7** defraud, swindle **9** defalcate **14** misappropriate

embezzler 5 cheat, crook, thief **8** swindler

embitter 4 sour **6** rankle **7** envenom **10** make bitter **11** make cynical **13** make rancorous, make resentful **15** make pessimistic

Embla
origin: **12** Scandinavian
first: **5** woman
made by: **4** gods
made from: **4** tree

emblem 4 sign **5** badge **6** design, device, symbol **8** colophon, hallmark, insignia

emblematic 7 typical **8** symbolic **10** indicative **11** distinctive **14** characteristic, representative

embodiment 6 avatar **7** epitome, essence **14** representation **15** exemplification, personification

embody 4 fuse **5** blend, merge **6** typify **7** collect, contain, embrace, express, include, realize **8** manifest, organize **9** exemplify, personify, represent, symbolize **10** assimilate **11** consolidate, incorporate **12** substantiate

embolden 7 fortify, hearten, inspire **8** inspirit **9** encourage

emboldened 6 poised **7** assured, unfazed **9** confident, heartened, unabashed **10** courageous, encouraged, inspirited

embonpoint 9 plumpness, stoutness **15** in good condition

emboss 4 knob, knot, stud **5** adorn, chase **6** indent **7** engrave, exhaust **8** decorate

embossed 4 bold **6** raised **7** adorned, antique, knotted **8** engraved, indented **9** decorated, exhausted

embrace 3 hug **5** adopt, clasp, cover, grasp **6** accept, embody **7** contain, espouse, include, involve **8** comprise **9** encompass **10** comprehend **11** consolidate, incorporate

embroider 5 color **7** dress up **9** elaborate, embellish, fabricate **10** exaggerate **11** romanticize

embroidery 8 tapestry **9** adornment, gros point **10** crewelwork, decoration, needlework, petit point **11** imagination **12** exaggeration **13** ornamentation

embroil 4 trap **6** enmesh **7** ensnare, involve **8** entangle **10** complicate

embroiled 8 enmeshed **9** embattled, entangled **11** hard-pressed

embroilment 3 row **4** fray, tilt **5** brawl, brush, clash, melee **6** fracas, ruckus, rumpus, uproar **7** scuffle **8** conflict, disorder, struggle **9** confusion, imbroglio **10** contention **11** altercation **12** entanglement

embryo 3 bud, egg **4** germ **5** fetus, larva, ovule **6** budding, source **8** immature, rudiment **9** beginning **11** rudimentary, undeveloped

embryonic 5 rough **6** unborn **7** nascent **8** immature, inchoate **9** beginning, imperfect, incipient **10** incomplete, unfinished **11** rudimentary, undeveloped

emend 4 edit **6** change, revise **7** correct, improve, rectify

emendation 8 revision **10** alteration, correction **11** improvement

emerald
species: **5** beryl
source: **4** Muzo **5** Egypt, India **6** Chivor **8** Colombia, Rhodesia, Zimbabwe **11** South Africa, Soviet Union **13** Ural Mountains
color: **5** green

Emerald City
setting in: **13** The Wizard of Oz
author: **4** Baum

Emerald Isle *see* **7** Ireland

emerge 3 run **4** dawn, emit, flow, gush, loom, pour, rise **5** arise, issue **6** appear, come up, crop up, escape, stream, turn up **7** develop, surface **9** come forth, discharge **11** come to light **12** come into view **13** become visible **14** become apparent, become manifest

emergence 4 dawn **7** dawning **10** appearance **11** development **13** coming to light, manifestation **15** materialization

emergency 5 pinch **6** crisis **7** urgency **8** exigency **11** contingency, predicament **16** unforeseen danger

Emergency
character: **8** (Dr) Joe Early, (Paramedic) John Gage **9** (Paramedic) Roy DeSoto **11** (Nurse) Dixie McCall **13** (Dr) Kelly Brackett
cast: **10** Bobby Troup, Kevin Tighe **11** Julie London **12** Robert Fuller **16** Randolph Mantooth

Emerson, Ralph Waldo
nickname: **13** Sage of Concord
author of: **4** Fate **6** Brahma, Nature **10** Friendship, The Rhodora **12** Compensation, Self-Reliance **14** The Concord Hymn **18** The American Scholar
philosophy: **17** Transcendentalism

emeute 4 riot

emigrant 6 emigre **8** wanderer, wayfarer **10** expatriate

Emigrants, The
author: **10** Johan Bojer

emigrate 4 move, quit **5** leave **6** depart, remove **7** migrate

emigration 5 exile **6** exodus **12** expatriation

emigre 2 DP **5** alien, exile **7** evacuee, refugee **8** defector, emigrant, expellee, fugitive **9** immigrant **10** expatriate **15** displaced person **16** political refugee

Emile
author: **19** Jean Jacques Rousseau
treatise on: **9** education

Emilia
character in: **7** Othello
husband: **4** Iago
author: **11** Shakespeare

eminence 4 fame, hill, note, peak, rise **5** bluff, cliff, glory, knoll, ridge **6** height, repute, summit, upland **7** hillock, hummock **8** mountain, standing **9** celebrity, elevation, greatness, high place, high point **10** excellence, importance, notability, prominence, promontory, reputation **11** distinction, preeminence **12** elevated rank, high position, public esteem **15** conspicuousness

eminence grise 15 unofficial power
literally: **12** gray eminence

eminent 3 top **5** grand, great, noted **6** famous, signal, utmost **7** exalted, notable, unusual **8** elevated, esteemed, glorious, imposing, laureate, renowned **9** important, memorable, paramount, prominent, well-known **10** celebrated, noteworthy, preeminent, remarkable **11** high-ranking, illustrious, outstanding **13** distinguished, extraordinary

emir 4 amir, Arab, Turk **5** chief, emeer, ruler **6** leader, prince **9** chieftain, commander, dignitary

emissary 5 agent, envoy **6** deputy, herald, legate **7** courier **8** delegate **9** go-between, messenger **10** ambassador **14** representative

emission 5 fumes, smoke, waste **8** ejection, emitting, impurity, issuance, voidance **9** discharge, emanation, excretion, expulsion, extrusion, pollutant **10** sending out **11** throwing out **12** transmission

emit 4 beam, give, shed, vent **5** expel, issue **7** cast out, excrete, secrete, send out **8** dispatch, throw out, transmit **9** discharge, give forth, pour forth

Emma
author: **10** Jane Austen
character: **7** Mr Elton **9** Miss Bates, Mrs Weston **11** Jane Fairfax **12** Harriet Smith, Robert Martin **13** Emma Woodhouse **15** Frank Churchill George Knightley

Emmanuel 7 Messiah **11** Jesus Christ
means: **9** God with us

emollient 3 oil **4** balm **5** balmy, cream, salve **6** lotion **7** calming, easeful, healing, unguent **8** allaying, lenitive, ointment, relaxing, soothing **9** assuasive, lubricant, relieving **10** palliative **11** alleviative, restorative

emolument 3 fee, pay **4** gain, wage **6** income, profit, salary **7** benefit, stipend **9** advantage **10** honorarium **12** compensation, remuneration

emotion 4 fear, hate, heat, love, zeal **5** anger, ardor, pride **6** fervor, sorrow, warmth **7** concern, despair, passion, sadness **8** jealousy **9** agitation, happiness, sentiment, vehemence **10** excitement **12** satisfaction

emotional 4 warm **5** fiery **6** ardent, moving **7** fervent, zealous **8** stirring, touching **9** excitable, impetuous, thrilling, wrought-up **10** high-strung, hysterical, passionate, responsive, vulnerable **11** impassioned, sentimental, tear-jerking **12** enthusiastic, heart-warming, heart-rending, soul-stirring **13** demonstrative, temperamental **14** hypersensitive

emotionalism 8 hysteria **9** gushiness, hysterics, melodrama, theatrics **11** mawkishness **13** melodramatics, show of emotion **14** sentimentality **17** demonstrativeness

emotionless 6 stolid **7** unmoved **9** apathetic, impassive, unfeeling **11** passionless, unemotional

emperor, empress 4 czar, king, shah **5** queen, ruler **6** caesar, kaiser, mikado, sultan **7** czarina, monarch, sultana **9** sovereign **14** dowager empress

Emperor Jones, The
author: **12** Eugene O'Neill
character: **4** Jeff **8** Smithers **11** Brutus Jones

Emperor's New Clothes, The
author: **21** Hans Christian Andersen

emphasis 9 accent, stress, weight **7** feature **10** focal point **12** accentuation, underscoring

emphasize 6 accent, stress **7** dwell on, feature, iterate, point up **9** press home, punctuate, underline **10** accentuate, underscore

emphatic 4 flat **6** marked, strong **7** certain, decided, express, telling **8** absolute, decisive, definite, distinct, forceful, striking, vigorous **9** assertive, insistent, momentous **10** pronounced, undeniable, unwavering, unyielding **11** categorical, conspicuous, significant, unequivocal, unqualified **12** unmistakable

empire 4 rule **5** realm **6** domain **8** dominion, imperium **11** sovereignty **12** commonwealth

Empire State
nickname of: **7** New York

Empire State of the South
nickname of: **7** Georgia

Empire Strikes Back, The
director: **13** Irvin Kershner
cast: **10** Kenny Baker, Mark Hamill (Luke Skywalker) **11** David Prowse, Peter Mayhew **12** Alec Guinness, Carrie Fisher (Princess Leia), Harrison Ford (Han Solo) **14** Anthony Daniels (C3PO) **16** Billy Dee Williams (Lando Calrissian)
sequel to: **8** Star Wars
sequel: **15** Return of the Jedi

empirical 9 firsthand, practical, pragmatic **12** experiential, experimental

employ 3 use **4** hire **5** apply **6** devote, engage, occupy, retain, take on **7** service, utilize **8** exercise, keep busy, put to use **9** make use of **10** commission, employment **12** retainership

employee 6 member, worker **8** hireling **9** job holder, underling **10** wage earner

employer 4 boss, firm **6** outfit **7** company **8** business **10** proprietor **12** organization **13** establishment

employment 3 job, use **4** line, task, work **5** chore, field, trade, using **6** employ **7** calling, pursuit, service **8** business, exercise, exertion, vocation **9** employing **10** engagement, occupation, profession **11** application, utilization **13** preoccupation

emporium 5 store **6** bazaar, market **9** warehouse **10** large store **12** general store **15** department store

empower 4 vest **5** allow, endow **6** enable, invest, permit **7** license **8** delegate, sanction **9** authorize **10** commission

empress 5 queen, ruler **7** czarina, monarch, sultana, tsarina **9** sovereign

emprise 7 venture **9** adventure **10** enterprise **11** undertaking

emptied 6 used up **7** drained, vacated **8** consumed, depleted, finished **9** evacuated, exhausted

emptiness 4 void **6** vacuum **7** vacancy **8** bareness **10** barrenness, desolation, hollowness

empty 4 bare, dump, flow, idle, void **5** banal, drain, inane **6** futile, hollow, vacant **7** aimless, debouch, insipid, pour out, shallow, trivial, vacuous **8** evacuate **9** discharge, frivolous, worthless **10** unoccupied **11** meaningless, purposeless, unfulfilled, uninhabited **13** insignificant

empty space 3 gap **4** void **5** blank **6** cavity, lacuna, vacuum **7** vacancy

empyrean 7 elysian, sublime **8** blissful, heavenly **9** celestial **12** paradisiacal

emu
also: **4** emeu
form: **4** bird
habitat: **9** Australia
characteristic: **9** nonflying, three-toed

emulate 3 ape **4** copy **5** mimic, rival **6** follow **7** imitate

emulative 5 model **9** exemplary

enable 3 aid **5** allow **6** assist, permit **7** benefit, empower, qualify, support **8** make able **10** capacitate, facilitate **15** make possible for

enact 4 pass **6** decree, ratify **7** approve

8 proclaim, sanction **9** authorize, institute, legislate **11** pass into law **12** vote to accept

enactment 3 law **4** bill **5** canon, edict, ukase **6** decree **7** statute **9** ordinance, prescript **11** legislation **12** proclamation, ratification

enamel 4 coat **5** paint **7** coating **10** nail polish **12** glossy finish, tooth coating

enamor 5 charm **6** allure, attach, draw to, excite **7** bewitch, enchant **8** enthrall, entrance **9** captivate, enrapture, fascinate, infatuate **12** take a fancy to

enamored 6 in love **7** amorous **8** lovesick **10** infatuated

en arriere 8 backward

en avant 6 onward **7** forward

en bloc 8 as a whole

encage 3 pen **4** cage **5** pen in **6** coop up, lock up, shut in **7** confine **8** restrain **11** incarcerate

encamp 4 camp **7** bivouac **9** set up camp **10** pitch a tent

encampment 4 camp **5** tents **7** bivouac **8** tent city

encase 4 wrap **5** cover **6** enfold, enwrap **7** enclose, envelop, sheathe

enceinte 8 pregnant

Enceladus
  form: 5 giant
  hit by: 5 stone
  stone flung by: 6 Athena
  location: 6 Sicily
  buried under: 9 Mount Etna

enchain 7 enslave, shackle **8** enthrall **11** put in chains **13** hold in bondage

enchant 3 hex **5** charm **7** bewitch, delight **8** enthrall, entrance **9** captivate, enrapture, fascinate, hypnotize, mesmerize, transport **14** cast a spell over **16** place under a spell

enchanted 7 charmed, pleased **9** bewitched, delighted, entranced **10** captivated, enraptured, enthralled, spellbound **11** under a spell

enchanting 8 charming, pleasant **9** agreeable, wonderful **10** bewitching, delightful, entrancing **11** captivating, enthralling, fascinating, hypnotizing **12** spellbinding **15** casting a spell on **17** casting a spell over

enchantment 5 spell **6** allure, appeal **9** magnetism **10** attraction **11** captivation, fascination

enchantress 4 vamp **5** siren, witch **7** charmer, vampire **9** sorceress, temptress **10** seductress **11** femme fatale

Enchiridion
  author: 11 St Augustine

encircle 4 gird, ring, wall **5** fence, hem in **6** circle, girdle **7** enclose, wreathe **8** surround **9** encompass **12** circumscribe

enclose, inclose 4 ring **6** circle, gir-

dle, insert, wall in **7** close in, fence in, include **8** encircle, surround **9** encompass, send along **12** circumscribe

enclosed area 4 quad **5** court, patio **6** atrium **9** courtyard **10** quadrangle

enclosure 3 sty **4** cage, coop, jail, wall **5** fence, hedge, stall **6** corral, kennel, pigsty **7** paddock, wrapper **8** envelope, stockade **9** cartridge, inclosure **10** receptacle

encomium 5 kudos, paean **6** eulogy **7** plaudit, tribute **8** citation **9** laudation, panegyric **11** acclamation

encompass 4 hold, ring **5** cover, hem in **6** circle, embody, girdle, take in, wall in **7** contain, embrace, enclose, fence in, include, involve, touch on **8** comprise, encircle, surround **11** incorporate **12** circumscribe

encounter 4 bout, face, meet **5** brush, clash, fight **6** affray, battle, combat, endure, fracas, suffer **7** run into, sustain, undergo **8** come upon, confront, meet with, skirmish **9** clash with **10** chance upon, engagement, experience **11** grapple with **12** do battle with, meet and fight, skirmish with **13** confrontation **14** contend against, engage in combat, hostile meeting **18** come face to face with

encourage 3 aid **4** help, spur, sway **5** boost, cheer, egg on, favor, impel, rally **6** assist, exhort, foster, induce, prompt **7** advance, forward, further, hearten, inspire, promote **8** embolden, inspirit, reassure **10** give hope to

encouragement 4 lift **5** boost **6** praise **7** backing, support **11** approbation, encouraging, reassurance **12** shot in the arm **13** reinforcement

encroach 6 invade **7** impinge, intrude, overrun, violate **8** infringe, overstep, trespass **9** break into, interfere **10** transgress **11** make inroads

encumber 3 tax **4** lade, load **6** burden, hinder, impede, saddle **8** handicap, load down, obstruct, slow down **9** weigh down **13** inconvenience

encumbrance 4 load, onus **6** burden **9** hindrance **10** impediment **11** obstruction **13** inconvenience

Encyclopedia
  author: 9 D'Alembert **12** Denis Diderot

encyclopedic 5 broad **7** erudite **9** scholarly, universal **10** exhaustive **11** wide-ranging **13** comprehensive **15** all-encompassing

end 3 aim **4** edge, goal, halt, kill, ruin, stop **5** cease, close, death, issue, limit, scrap **6** border, demise, design, effect, ending, finale, finish, object, result, run out, upshot, windup **7** destroy, outcome, purpose, remnant **8** boundary, conclude, fragment, leave off, leftover, terminus **9** cessation, eradicate, extremity, finish off, intention,

objective, terminate **10** annihilate, completion, conclusion, denouement, expiration, extinction, extinguish, put an end to, settlement **11** consequence, culmination, destruction, exterminate, fulfillment, termination **12** annihilation, consummation, draw to a close **13** extermination **19** bring down the curtain

endanger 4 risk **6** expose, hazard **7** imperil **8** threaten **10** compromise, jeopardize **11** put in danger

endear 4 make dear **10** ingratiate **11** make beloved

endearment 7 pet name **9** sweet talk **10** loving word **12** sweet nothing **13** fond utterance

endeavor 3 aim, job, try **4** seek, work **5** essay, labor **6** aspire, career, effort, strive, work at **7** attempt **8** exertion, interest, striving, struggle, vocation **9** take pains, undertake **10** do one's best, enterprise, occupation **11** undertaking **12** make an effort **13** preoccupation

ended 4 done, over **6** ceased, closed, halted, runout **7** expired, stopped, wound up **8** finished, over with, resulted **9** completed, concluded, destroyed **10** terminated **11** annihilated **12** discontinued, exterminated

Enderby
  author: 14 Anthony Burgess

end from which
  Latin: 12 terminus a quo

ending 3 end **5** close **6** finale, finish, windup **9** cessation **10** completion, conclusion, expiration **11** culmination, termination **12** consummation

ending point
  Latin: 14 terminus ad quem

endless 7 eternal **8** constant, infinite, unbroken, unending **9** boundless, continual, perpetual, unlimited **10** continuous, persistent, without end **11** everlasting, measureless, never-ending **12** interminable **13** uninterrupted

endlessly 7 forever **10** constantly **11** ceaselessly, continually, perpetually **12** continuously
  Latin: 11 ad infinitum

endocrine system
  component: 5 ovary **6** testes, thymus **7** adrenal, thyroid **9** pituitary **11** parathyroid

endocuticle
  consists of: 6 chitin

end of the century
  French: 11 fin de siecle

End of the Road, The
  author: 9 John Barth

end of the world 8 doomsday **10** Armageddon **11** Judgment Day **13** Day of Judgment **15** the Last Judgment

endorse, indorse 2 OK **4** back, sign **6** affirm, ratify, second **7** approve, certify, support **8** advocate, champion, sanction, validate, vouch for **9** authorize, recommend **11** countersign, stand behind, subscribe to **14** lend one's name to

endorsement 2 OK **7** support **8** approval **9** signature **10** acceptance **12** commendation, ratification **14** seal of approval **16** official sanction

endow 4 will **5** award, bless, equip, favor, grace, grant, leave **6** accord, bestow, confer, invest, supply **7** furnish, provide **8** bequeath, settle on

endowed 6 graced **7** blessed, favored **8** bestowed, enriched, provided **10** bequeathed

endowment 4 gift **5** award, flair, grant **6** legacy, talent **7** ability, bequest, faculty **8** aptitude, donation **9** attribute **10** capability **11** benefaction, natural gift

end to which
    Latin: 14 terminus ad quem

endue 5 dress, endow, equip, indue, put on **6** bestow, clothe, outfit, supply **7** furnish

endurable 8 bearable **9** tolerable **11** sustainable

endurance 7 stamina **8** strength, tenacity **9** fortitude, hardihood, stability **10** durability, permanence, resolution **11** durableness, persistence **12** immutability, perseverance, staying power **13** tenaciousness **14** changelessness **16** stick-to-itiveness

endure 4 bear, last, live **5** brave, brook, stand **6** live on, remain, suffer **7** persist, prevail, sustain, undergo, weather **8** continue, cope with, tolerate **9** go through, withstand **10** experience **11** bear up under, countenance

enduring 7 abiding, durable, eternal, lasting **8** constant, unending **9** immutable, permanent, steadfast **10** changeless, continuing, unchanging **11** everlasting, long-lasting **12** indissoluble

Endymion
    author: 9 John Keats
    form: 5 youth
    father: 8 Aethlios
    mother: 6 Calyce
    loved by: 4 Moon **6** Selene
    son: 5 Epeus, Paeon **7** Aetolus
    number of daughters: 5 fifty
    granddaughter: 7 Hyrmina

enemy 3 foe **5** rival **7** nemesis **8** armed foe, attacker, opponent **9** adversary, assailant, detractor **10** antagonist, competitor

Enemy of the People, An
    author: 11 Henrik Ibsen

energetic 5 alert, brisk, peppy, zippy **6** active, lively, robust **7** dynamic **8** animated, forceful, restless, spirited, vigorous **9** go-getting **11** hardworking, high-powered, industrious, quick-witted **12** enthusiastic

energize 7 animate, enliven, quicken **8** vitalize **9** galvanize, stimulate **10** invigorate, strengthen

energy 2 go **3** pep, vim, zip **4** elan, zeal, zest **5** drive, force, power, verve, vigor **6** hustle **8** dynamism, vitality, vivacity **9** animation **10** enterprise, liveliness

enervate 3 fag **4** bush, tire **5** weary **6** tucker, weaken **7** deplete, disable, exhaust, fatigue, wash out **8** enfeeble **9** prostrate **10** debilitate, devitalize **13** sap one's energy

enervated 5 spent **6** effete, wasted **7** languid, worn-out **8** fatigued, listless, sluggish, unmanned, unnerved, weakened **9** enfeebled, exhausted, lethargic, washed out **11** debilitated, devitalized, emasculated

enervation 7 fatigue **9** tiredness, weariness **10** exhaustion

en famille 11 in the family

Enfants Terribles, Les
    author: 11 Jean Cocteau

enfant terrible 16 indiscreet person **17** incorrigible child **19** irresponsible person

enfeeble 3 sap **6** impair, weaken **8** enervate **10** debilitate

enfin 7 finally **8** in the end **12** in conclusion

enfold 4 veil, wrap **5** cloak, cover **6** encase, enwrap, shroud **7** blanket, contain, embrace, enclose, envelop, sheathe **8** surround

enforce 5 apply, exact **6** defend, impose **7** execute, support **8** carry out, insist on **9** implement **10** administer

enforcement 5 force **6** duress **7** defense, support **8** coercion, pressure **9** execution **10** compulsion, constraint, imposition, obligation **11** carrying out **13** necessitation, strengthening **14** implementation

engage 4 hire **6** absorb, combat, employ, occupy, pledge, retain, secure, take on **7** betroth, engross, involve, partake, promise, war with **8** affiance, embark on, set about, take part **9** enter into, fight with, undertake **10** commission **11** busy oneself, participate **12** give battle to **15** take into service

engaged 5 hired, in use **6** active, took on **7** partook, pledged, secured **8** absorbed, employed, involved, occupied, promised, retained, took part **9** affianced, betrothed, engrossed, undertook **10** embarked on **11** entered into, particpated **15** took into service

engagement 3 gig, job **4** bout, date, duty, fray, post **5** banns, berth, brush, fight, troth **6** action, battle, billet, combat **7** contest, meeting, scuffle **8** conflict, position, skirmish **9** betrothal, encounter, situation **10** affi-

ancing, commitment, employment, obligation **11** appointment, arrangement

engage pleasantly 5 amuse, charm **6** divert, please **7** beguile, delight **8** enthrall, interest **9** entertain

engaging 7 likable, lovable, winning, winsome **8** charming, fetching, pleasing **9** agreeable, appealing, disarming **10** attractive, enchanting **11** captivating **12** ingratiating

engender 5 beget, breed, cause **7** produce **8** generate, occasion **10** bring about, give rise to **11** precipitate

engine
    inventor:
        of compression ignition: 7 Daimler
        of electric ignition: 4 Benz
        of gas (compound): 10 Eickemeyer
        of gasoline: 7 Brayton, Daimler
        of piston steam: 4 Watt **8** Newcomen

engineer 5 pilot **6** driver, hogger **7** builder, hoghead, planner **8** maneuver, motorman, operator **10** accomplish

England
    other name: 6 Albion **7** Britain **9** Britannia
    capital/largest city: 6 London
    others: 3 Ely **4** Bath, Deal, Hull, Ryde, Ware, York **5** Blyth, Brent, Derby, Dover, Erith, Flint, Leeds, Ripon, Truro, Wigan **6** Barnet, Bolton, Bootle, Camden, Durham, Ealing, Exeter, Henley, Jarrow, Leyton, Oldham, Oxford, Yeovil **7** Bristol, Bromley, Burnley, Chelsea, Croydon, Enfield, Grimsby, Halifax, Hornsey, Ipswich, Lambeth, Newport, Norwich, Preston, Salford, **8** Bradford, Brighton, Cornwall, Coventry, Dewsbury, Hastings, Plymouth **9** Cambridge, Greenwich, Liverpool, Newcastle, Sheffield **10** Birmingham, Manchester **15** Stratford-on-Avon
    school: 4 Eton **5** Leeds, Rugby **6** Harrow, London, Oxford **9** Cambridge, Sandhurst **23** London School of Economics
    division: 4 Avon, Kent **5** Devon, Essex, **6** Dorset, Durham, Surrey, Sussex **7** Norfolk, Suffolk **8** Cheshire, Cornwall, Somerset **9** Hampshire, Wiltshire, Yorkshire **10** Derbyshire, East Sussex, Humberside, Lancashire, Merseyside, Shropshire, West Sussex **11** Oxfordshire, Tyne and Wear **12** Bedfordshire, Lincolnshire, Warwickshire, West Midlands **13** Hertfordshire, Staffordshire, West Yorkshire **14** Cambridgeshire, Leicestershire, Northumberland, North Yorkshire, South Yorkshire **15** Buckinghamshire, Gloucestershire, Nottinghamshire **16** Northamptonshire **20** Hereford and Worcester
    head of state: 4 king **5** queen **7** monarch

measure: 3 cut, lea, pin, rod, ton, tun, vat 4 acre, bind, butt, comb, coom, foot, gill, goad, hand, hank, heer, hide, inch, last, line, mile, nail, pace, palm, peck, pint, pipe, pole, pool, rood, rope, sack, seam, span, trug, typp, wist, yard, yoke 5 bodge, chain, coomb, cubit, digit, float, floor, fluid, hutch, jugum, minim, ounce, perch, point, prime, quart, skein, stack, truss 6 barrel, bovate, bushel, cranne, fathom, firkin, gallon, hobbet, hobbit, league, manent, oxgang, pottle, runlet, square, strike, sulung, thread, tierce 7 auchlet, furlong, kenning, quarter, rundlet, seamile, spindle, tertian, virgate 8 carucate, chaldron, hogshead, landyard, puncheon, quadrant, standard
monetary unit: 3 ora 4 rial 5 ackey, crown, groat, noble, pence, penny, pound, sprat, unite 6 bawbee, florin, guinea, seskin 7 angelet, hapenny 8 farthing, shilling, sixpence, tuppence
weight: 3 bag, kip, tod, ton 4 keel, last, mast, maun 5 barge, fagot, grain, pound, score, stone, truss 6 bushel, cental, fangot, fother, fotmal, pocket 7 quarter, sarpler
island: 3 Man 4 Holy 5 Farne, Lundy, Wight 6 Coquet, Mersea, Scilly, Thanet, Tresco, Walney 7 Bardsey, Channel, Hayling, Ireland, Sheppey 8 Anglesea, Anglesey, Foulness, Holyhead
lake: 8 Grasmere 9 Ennerdale, Ullswater, Wastwater 10 Buttermere, Windermere 12 Derwentwater 13 Coniston Water
mountain: 5 Black 7 Pennine, Snowdon 8 Cambrian, Cumbrian
  hill: 6 Formby, Lizard, Mendip 7 Brendon, Cemmaes, Trevose
highest point: 11 Scafell Pike
river: 3 Cam, Dee, Don, Esk, Exe, Lea, Nen, Ure, Wye 4 Aire, Avon, Eden, Lune, Nene, Nidd, Ouse, Penk, Tame, Tees, Till, Tyne, Wear, Yare 5 Anker, Colne, Deben, Stour, Swale, Tamar, Tawar, Trent, Tweed 6 Humber, Kennet, Mersey, Rother, Severn, Thames, Wharfe, Witham 7 Derwent, Parrett, Waveney, Welland 8 Torridge 9 Yorkshire 12 Wensum Ribble
sea: 5 Irish, North 6 Celtic 8 Atlantic
physical feature:
  bay: 3 Tor 4 Lyme, Wash 5 Start 6 Mounts 7 Bigbury 8 Bideford, Cardigan, Falmouth, Tremadoc, Weymouth
  chalk cliffs: 5 Dover
  channel: 6 Solent 7 Bristol, English 8 Spithead
  firth: 6 Solway
  forest: 5 Arden 6 Exmoor 8 Dartmoor, Sherwood
  point: 4 Naze 5 Lynas, Morte,

Sales 6 Dodman, Lizard, Prawle 8 Hartland, Landsend
region: 5 Weald 8 Midlands 10 West Riding 11 North Riding 12 Lake District
valley: 4 Coom, Eden, Tees, Tyne 5 Combe, Coomb 6 Coquet
people: 4 Celt, Pict 5 Jutes, Norse, Saxon 6 Angles, Briton, Norman, Viking
  artist: 6 Romney, Turner 7 Hogarth 8 Reynolds, Rossetti 9 Constable 12 Gainsborough
  author: 3 Kyd 4 Bede, Hume, Pope, Shaw 5 Auden, Bacon, Blake, Burke, Byron, Defoe, Donne, Eliot, Hardy, Joyce, Keats, Scott, Swift, Waugh, Wilde, Woolf 6 Austen, Bronte, Bunyan, Conrad, Dryden, Gibbon, Jonson, Milton, Newton, Ruskin, Sterne, Thomas 7 Boswell, Chaucer, Dickens, Kipling, Marlowe, Shelley, Spenser, Walpole 8 Browning, Fielding, Lawrence, Sheridan, Smollett, Tennyson, Trollope 9 Churchill, Coleridge, Stevenson, Thackeray 10 Galsworthy, Richardson, Thomas More, Wordsworth 11 Shakespeare
  king: 3 Hal 4 Cnut, John, Lear 5 Henry, James 6 Alfred, Arthur, Canute, Edmund, Edward, Egbert, George, Harold 7 Charles, Richard, Stephen, William 9 Cymbeline 18 Richard Coeur de Lion 19 Richard the Lionheart
  leader: 4 Eden, Grey, Lamb, Peel, Pitt 5 Blair, Heath, Major 6 Attlee, Wilson 7 Baldwin, Balfour, Canning, Fitzroy, Spencer, Stanley, Walpole 8 Disraeli, Stanhope, Thatcher 9 Cavendish, Churchill, Gladstone, Grenville, MacDonald, Macmillan 10 Palmerston, Wellington 11 Chamberlain, Douglas-Home, Lloyd George
  queen: 3 Mab 4 Anne, Bess, Jane, Mary 7 Eleanor 8 Boadicea, Victoria 9 Catherine, Charlotte, Elizabeth, Guinevere 10 Bloody Mary 11 Jane Seymour
language: 7 English
religion: 6 Jewish 8 Anglican 9 Methodist, Unitarian 13 Roman Catholic 15 Church of England
place:
  bridge: 5 Tower 6 London 11 Westminster
  cathedral: 4 York 6 Exeter 7 St Pauls 8 St Albans 9 Salisbury 10 Canterbury, Winchester 16 Westminster Abbey
  clock: 6 Big Ben
  fortification: 12 Hadrian's Wall
  museum: 4 Tate 7 British 9 Ashmolean 17 Madame Tussaud's Wax
  palace: 7 St James, Windsor 10

Buckingham 12 Hampton Court
  racetrack: 5 Ascot
  ruins: 10 Stonehenge
  street: 4 Grub 5 Fleet 12 Threadneedle 16 Piccadilly Circus
  tower: 6 London
feature:
  dance: 6 morris
food:
  bacon: 6 gammon, rasher 7 streaky
  beer: 5 grout, stout
  cookie: 7 biscuit
  dessert: 6 trifle 11 plum pudding
  dish: 12 fish and chips 14 Cornish pasties 15 bubble and squeak 16 Yorkshire pudding
  drink: 3 ale, tea 6 squash

English Mail-Coach, The
  author: 15 Thomas DeQuincey
English Patient, The
  director: 16 Anthony Minghella
  cast: 10 Colin Firth (Geoffrey Clifton) 11 Willem Dafoe (Caravaggio) 12 Ralph Fiennes (Almasy) 13 Naveen Andrews (Kip) 15 Juliette Binoche (Hana) 18 Kristin Scott Thomas (Katharine Clifton)
engrave 3 cut 4 etch 5 carve, stamp 6 chisel 7 decorate, stipple
engraving 3 cut, die 5 print, stamp 7 etching, gravure 9 woodblock 11 copperplate, lithography 12 photogravure
engross 4 hold 6 absorb, arrest, engage, occupy, take up 7 immerse, involve 9 preoccupy
engrossed 4 busy, deep 6 intent 7 engaged 8 absorbed, immersed, involved, occupied 11 preoccupied
engrossing 8 engaging, exciting 9 absorbing, arresting, thrilling 10 intriguing 11 captivating, fascinating, interesting
engrossment 9 immersion 10 absorption, intentness 11 involvement 13 concentration, preoccupation
engulf 4 bury 5 swamp 6 deluge 7 envelop, immerse, overrun 8 inundate, submerge 9 swallow up
enhance 4 lift 5 add to, boost, raise 7 augment, elevate, magnify 8 heighten, redouble 9 embellish, intensify 10 complement
enhancement 11 heightening, improvement 15 intensification
Enid
  character in: 12 The Mabinogion 15 Idylls of the King 16 Arthurian romance
  husband: 7 Geraint
  known for: 9 constancy
  author: 8 Tennyson
enigma 6 puzzle, riddle, secret 7 mystery 8 question 9 conundrum 10 perplexity
enigmatic, enigmatical 7 cryptic, elusive 8 baffling, puzzling 9 ambiguous, equivocal, secretive 10 mysteri-

ous, perplexing **11** inscrutable, paradoxical **12** unfathomable **14** indecipherable

Eniwetok 5 atoll
  location: 15 Marshall Islands
  known for: 5 A bomb, H bomb (tests)

enjoin 3 ask, ban, bar, beg, bid **4** urge, warn **6** advise, charge, direct, forbid **7** command, counsel, entreat **8** admonish, call upon, instruct, prohibit, restrain, restrict **9** interdict, proscribe

enjoy 3 own **4** have, like **5** eat up, fancy, savor **6** admire, relish **7** possess **9** delight in, rejoice in **10** appreciate **11** think well of **13** be blessed with, be pleased with, get a kick out of **14** take pleasure in **16** have the benefit of

enjoyable 8 pleasant, pleasing **9** agreeable, fun-filled, rewarding **10** delightful, gratifying, satisfying **11** pleasurable

enjoyment 3 fun, joy **4** zest **5** gusto, right **6** relish **7** benefit, delight **8** blessing, exercise, good time, pleasure **9** advantage, amusement, diversion, happiness, privilege **10** possession, recreation **11** prerogative **12** satisfaction **13** entertainment, gratification

enlarge 4 grow **5** add to, swell, widen **6** expand, extend **7** amplify, augment, broaden, develop, expound, inflate, magnify **8** elongate, increase, lengthen, multiply **9** discourse, elaborate, expatiate

enlarged 7 swollen, widened **8** expanded, extended, inflated **9** amplified, broadened, distended, elongated, magnified

enlargement 6 growth **8** addition, increase, swelling, widening **9** expansion, extension, inflation **10** broadening, elongation **11** development, elaboration, expatiation, lengthening **12** augmentation **13** amplification, magnification **14** multiplication

enlighten 5 edify **6** advise, inform, wise up **7** apprise, clarify, educate **8** civilize, instruct **9** make aware **10** illuminate **12** sophisticate

enlightenment 8 learning **9** erudition, knowledge **11** edification, instruction
  French: 15 Eclaircissement
  German: 10 Aufklarung

enlist 4 join **6** engage, enroll, join up, obtain, secure, sign up **7** procure, recruit **8** register **9** volunteer **19** gain the assistance of

enlistment 9 signing up **10** admittance, enrollment, recruiting

enliven 4 fire **5** pep up, renew **6** excite, vivify, wake up **7** animate, cheer up, quicken **8** brighten, vitalize **10** make lively, rejuvenate

enlivened 7 revived **8** animated, vivified **9** refreshed **11** invigorated

---

en masse 7 in a body **8** as a group, as a whole, in a group, together **11** all together

enmesh 4 trap **5** catch, snare, snarl **6** tangle **7** embroil, ensnare, entwine, involve **8** entangle

enmity 6 animus, hatred, malice, rancor, strife **7** ill will **8** acrimony, bad blood **9** animosity, antipathy, hostility **10** bitterness

Ennead 7 dieties
  origin: 8 Egyptian
  number: 4 nine

ennoble 5 raise **6** refine **7** dignify, elevate

ennui 6 apathy, tedium **7** boredom, languor **9** lassitude, weariness **12** indifference, listlessness
  Latin: 12 taedium vitae

Enoch
  father: 4 Cain **5** Jared
  son: 10 Methuselah
  grandfather: 4 Adam

Enoch Arden
  author: 18 Alfred Lord Tennyson
  character: 8 Annie Lee **9** Philip Ray **10** Miriam Lane

enology *see* **8** oenology

enormity 8 baseness, evilness, hugeness, vastness, vileness, villainy **9** depravity, immensity, largeness, malignity **10** wickedness **11** heinousness, viciousness **12** enormousness **13** atrociousness, monstrousness, offensiveness **14** outrageousness

enormous 4 huge, vast **7** immense, mammoth, massive, titanic **8** colossal, gigantic **10** gargantuan, prodigious, tremendous **11** elephantine **14** Brobdingnagian

enormousness 8 enormity, hugeness, vastness **9** amplitude, immensity, largeness **11** massiveness

Enormous Room, The
  author: 10 e e cummings

Enos
  father: 4 Seth
  grandfather: 4 Adam

enough 5 ample, amply **6** plenty **7** copious **8** abundant, adequate, passably **9** tolerably **10** abundantly, adequately, competence, plentitude, reasonably, sufficient **11** ample supply, full measure, sufficiency **12** sufficiently **14** satisfactorily

enounce 8 set forth **9** enunciate **10** articulate

en passant 8 by the way **9** chess term, in passing

enrage 5 anger **6** madden **7** incense, inflame **9** aggravate, infuriate **11** make furious **13** make one see red **14** throw into a rage **17** make one's blood boil

enraged 3 mad **5** angry, irate **7** angered, furious, violent **8** incensed, in-

---

flamed, maddened, provoked **9** irritated **10** aggravated, infuriated **11** exasperated

en rapport 8 in accord **9** congenial **10** in sympathy **11** in agreement

enrapture 5 charm **6** thrill **7** beguile, bewitch, delight, enchant **8** enthrall, entrance, hold rapt **9** captivate, transport

enraptured 4 rapt **8** beatific, blissful, ecstatic **9** delighted, enchanted **10** enthralled **11** transported

enravel 5 snare, snarl, twist **6** enmesh, tangle **7** ensnare, ensnarl, entwine **8** entangle **10** intertwine

enrich 5 adorn, endow **6** refine **7** elevate, enhance, fortify, improve, upgrade **8** make rich **9** embellish **10** ameliorate **11** make wealthy **15** feather one's nest

enroll 4 join **5** admit, enter **6** accept, engage, enlist, join up, sign up, take on **7** recruit **8** register

enrollment 6 roster **9** enrolling, signing up **10** admittance, enlistment, recruiting **12** registration **13** matriculation

en route 8 on the way **9** in transit, on the road

ensconce 4 bury, hide, seat **5** lodge **6** settle **7** conceal, secrete, shelter **9** establish

ensemble 5 getup **6** attire, outfit, troupe **7** company, costume **8** assembly, entirety, grouping, totality **9** aggregate

ensign 4 flag, jack, mark, sign **5** badge **6** banner, colors, emblem, pennon, symbol **7** pennant **9** insignia, standard

enslave 6 addict, subdue **7** capture, control, enchain, shackle **8** dominate, enthrall **9** indenture, subjugate **13** hold in bondage, put in shackles

enslavement 4 yoke **6** chains, thrall **7** bondage, serfdom, slavery **9** captivity, servitude, thralldom, vassalage **11** subjugation

ensnare 4 trap **5** catch **6** enmesh, entrap, tangle **7** enravel **8** entangle

Ensor, James
  born: 6 Ostend **7** Belgium
  artwork: 8 Intrigue **19** Bourgeois Living Room **25** Entry of Christ into Brussels **26** The Tribulations of St Anthony **29** Self-Portrait Surrounded by Masks

enstatite
  source: 5 Burma, Mogok

ensue 6 derive, follow, result **7** succeed **10** come to pass **13** come afterward

ensuing 8 eventual **9** following, resulting **10** consequent, succeeding

en suite 6 in a set **9** in a series **12** in succession

ensure, insure 5 guard **6** assure,

clinch, secure **7** protect, warrant **8** be sure of, make safe, make sure **9** guarantee, safeguard **13** make certain of

entail 6 demand **7** call for, include, involve, require **8** occasion **11** incorporate, necessitate

entangle 4 trap **5** catch, mix up, snare, snarl **6** enmesh, foul up, muddle, tangle **7** confuse, embroil, enravel, ensnare, involve **8** encumber **9** embarrass, implicate **10** complicate, compromise, intertwine

entanglement 5 mixup, snarl **6** foul-up, muddle **7** problem **9** confusion, imbroglio **10** difficulty, entrapment **11** embroilment **12** complication

entente 4 pact **6** accord, treaty **7** compact **8** alliance, covenant **9** agreement, consensus, unanimity **10** consortium **12** conciliation **13** rapprochement, understanding **14** likemindedness

entente cordiale 21 friendly understanding

enter 4 go in, join, list, post **6** arrive, come in, record **8** enlist in, enroll in, inscribe, pass into, set out on, trespass **9** penetrate, sign up for **10** embark upon, take part in

enterprise 4 push, task, zeal **5** drive, vigor **6** daring, effort, energy, spirit **7** attempt, program, project, venture **8** ambition, boldness, campaign, endeavor, industry **9** alertness, eagerness, ingenuity, operation **10** enthusiasm, initiative **11** undertaking, willingness **14** aggressiveness **15** adventurousness

enterprising 4 bold, keen **5** alert, eager **6** active **7** earnest, zealous **8** intrepid **9** ambitious, energetic, inventive, wide-awake **10** aggressive **11** hardworking, industrious, self-reliant, up-and-coming, venturesome **12** enthusiastic

entertain 4 heed **5** admit, amuse, charm **6** absorb, divert, foster, harbor, please, ponder, regale **7** beguile, delight, dwell on, engross, imagine, nurture, support **8** consider, enthrall, interest, muse over, play host **10** cogitate on, give a party, have guests, keep in mind, think about **11** contemplate **13** keep open house

entertainer 4 host **5** actor **6** amuser, artist, dancer, singer **7** hostess **8** magician, musician **9** performer

entertaining 3 fun **7** amusing, hosting **8** charming, pleasing **9** beguiling, diverting, enjoyable **10** delightful, hostessing **11** playing host **12** having guests **14** having people in

entertainment 3 fun **4** play **7** novelty, pastime **8** good time, pleasure **9** amusement, diversion, enjoyment **10** recreation **11** distraction **12** satisfac-

tion
French: 14 divertissement

enter upon 5 begin **6** assume **9** undertake

enthrall, enthral 5 charm, rivet **6** seduce, thrill **7** beguile, bewitch, enchant, enslave **8** entrance, intrigue, transfix **9** captivate, enrapture, fascinate, hypnotize, overpower, spellbind, subjugate, transport **13** keep in bondage **14** put into slavery

enthralled 4 rapt **8** beguiled, enslaved **9** bewitched, enchanted, entranced, in bondage, intrigued **10** captivated, enraptured, fascinated, hypnotized, spellbound, subjugated

enthusiasm 4 love, rage, zeal, zest **5** ardor, craze, hobby, mania **6** fervor, relish **7** elation, passion **8** devotion, interest, keenness **9** diversion, eagerness **10** excitement, exuberance, hobbyhorse **11** distraction, pet activity **12** anticipation

enthusiast 3 bug, fan, nut **4** buff **5** freak **6** addict **7** devotee, fanatic **10** aficionado

enthusiastic 5 eager **6** ardent, fervid **7** fervent, zealous **8** spirited **9** exuberant **10** passionate, unstinting **11** unqualified **12** wholehearted

entice 4 coax, lure **5** tempt **6** allure, incite, induce, seduce **7** attract, beguile, wheedle **8** inveigle, persuade

enticement 4 bait, draw, lure **6** allure **9** seduction, siren song **10** attraction, temptation

entire 4 full **5** gross, total, whole **6** in toto, intact **8** absolute, complete, thorough, unbroken **9** undamaged **10** unimpaired **12** all-inclusive

entirely 5 fully **6** wholly **7** totally, utterly **10** absolutely, altogether, completely, thoroughly **12** unreservedly **13** unqualifiedly
French: 9 tout a fait

entitle 3 dub, tag **4** call, name **5** allow, label, style, title **6** enable, permit **7** qualify **9** authorize, designate **12** make eligible

entity 4 body **5** being, thing **6** matter, object **7** article **8** creature, presence, quantity **9** real thing, structure, substance **10** individual

entomb 4 bury **5** inter **7** confine

entombment 6 burial **9** interment **10** inhumation

Entommeures, Frere Jean des
character in: 22 Gargantua and Pantagruel
author: 8 Rabelais

entourage 5 court, staff, suite, train **6** convoy, escort **7** cortege, retinue **9** followers, following **10** associates, attendants, companions

entrails 4 guts **5** offal **6** bowels **7** innards, insides, viscera **10** intestines

entrance 4 door, gate **5** charm, entry, way in **6** access, entree, portal **7** beguile, bewitch, delight, doorway, gateway, gladden, ingress, opening **8** approach, coming in, enthrall **9** captivate, enrapture, fascinate, hypnotize, mesmerize, spellbind, transport **10** admittance, appearance, passageway **12** introduction

entranced 4 rapt **7** charmed **8** beguiled **9** entralled, rapturous **10** enraptured, fascinated, spellbound **11** carried away, transported

entranceway 5 entry, foyer, way in **7** doorway, ingress **8** entryway **9** front hall, vestibule

entrancing 6 lovely **8** adorable, charming **9** appealing, beautiful, beguiling, disarming **10** bewitching, delightful **11** captivating, fascinating **12** irresistible

entrap 3 bag, nab **4** hook, land, nail **5** catch, snare, tempt **6** allure, collar, drag in, draw in, entice, rope in, seduce, suck in **7** beguile, capture, ensnare **8** inveigle

entreat 3 beg **6** adjure, enjoin, exhort **7** beseech, implore, request **8** appeal to, petition **9** importune, plead with **10** supplicate

entreaty 4 plea **6** appeal, prayer **8** petition **11** importunity **12** supplication

entree 4 pull **5** entry **6** access **7** ingress **8** entrance, main dish **9** admission **10** acceptance, admittance, main course

entremets 8 side dish

entrench, intrench 3 fix, set **4** root **5** dig in, embed, plant **6** anchor **7** implant, ingrain, install, solidly **8** ensconce **12** establish

entrenched leaders 11 ruling class **12** powers that be **13** Establishment **14** power structure

entre nous 9 between us, privately **14** confidentially **15** between you and me **16** between me and thee, between ourselves **18** in strict confidence

entrepot 5 depot **9** warehouse **18** distribution center

entrepreneur 7 manager **8** director **9** organizer **10** impresario **11** coordinator

entrust, intrust 5 trust **6** assign, commit **7** consign **8** delegate, hand over, turn over **9** authorize **10** charge with

entrustment 10 delegation **13** authorization, commissioning

entry 3 way **4** door, gate, item, memo, note **5** foyer, way in **6** access, entree, minute, portal, record **7** account, doorway, gateway, ingress, jotting **8** approach, entrance **9** admission, vestibule **10** admittance, appearance, competitor, contestant, memorandum, passageway **11** entranceway **12** entrance hall, introduction, registration

entwine, intwine 4 fold, lace, wind **5** braid, plait, twine, twist, weave **9** interlace **10** interweave

enumerable 6 finite **7** limited **11** denumerable

enumerate 3 add **4** cite, list **5** add up, count, sum up, tally, total **6** detail, number, relate **7** count up, recount, specify, tick off **8** numerate, spell out, tabulate

enumeration 4 list **5** tally **7** account, listing **8** adding up, addition, citation, tallying, totaling **9** checklist, detailing, numbering, reckoning, summing up **10** counting up, recounting, tabulation, ticking off **11** spelling out

enunciate 5 sound, speak, voice **8** vocalize **10** articulate **15** utter distinctly **16** pronounce clearly

enunciation 6 accent, speech **7** diction **9** utterance **12** articulation **13** pronunciation

envelop 4 hide, veil, wrap **5** cloak, cover **6** encase, enfold, engulf, enwrap, shroud, swathe **7** blanket, conceal, contain, enclose, obscure, sheathe, swaddle **8** encircle, surround **9** encompass

envelope 5 cover **6** jacket **8** covering, wrapping

envenom 4 sour **6** rankle **8** embitter **13** make poisonous

enviable 5 lucky **8** salutary **9** agreeable, covetable, desirable, excellent, fortunate **10** beneficial **12** advantageous

envious 5 green **7** jealous **8** covetous, grudging, spiteful **9** jaundiced, resentful

enviousness 4 envy **8** jealousy **10** resentment **12** covetousness **13** resentfulness **19** the green-eyed monster

environment 5 scene **6** locale, medium, milieu **7** climate, element, habitat, setting **8** ambience **9** situation **10** atmosphere, background **12** surroundings **13** circumstances
French: 11 mise en scene

environs 6 exurbs **7** suburbs **8** vicinity **9** outskirts, precincts **11** outer limits **12** outlying area **15** surrounding area

envisage 5 fancy **7** dream of, dream up, imagine, picture **8** conceive, envision **9** conjure up, visualize **11** contemplate **13** conceptualize **14** have a picture of, picture to oneself

envoy 5 agent **6** deputy, legate **7** attache, courier **8** delegate, emissary, minister **9** messenger, middleman **10** ambassador **12** intermediary **14** representative

envy 5 greed, spite **6** resent **8** begrudge, grudging, jealousy **10** resentment **11** be jealous of, enviousness,

malevolence **12** covetousness **13** resentfulness **16** be spiteful toward **19** the green-eyed monster

enwrap 6 absorb, engage, enrobe **7** engross, envelop **9** preoccupy

Enyo
origin: **5** Greek
goddess of: **3** war
companion of: **4** Ares
member of: **6** Graeae, Graiae
corresponds to: **7** Bellona

enzyme 7 protein **8** molecule **13** macromolecule
function: **8** catalyst
acts on: **9** substrate
kind: **5** amino, malic **6** lactic, lipase, pepsin, rennin, urease **7** amylase, glucose, trypsin **8** aldehyde, glutamic, glycolic, lipozyme, thrombin, xanthine **9** cellulase **12** ribonuclease

eon 3 age, era **8** eternity, long time **9** many years **15** one billion years

Eos
origin: **5** Greek
goddess of: **4** dawn
father: **8** Hyperion
mother: **5** Theia
brother: **6** Helios
sister: **6** Selene
husband: **8** Astraeus, Tithonus **10** Eosophorus
son: **6** Memnon **8** Phaethon, Zephyrus **10** Eosophorus
horse: **6** Lampos **8** Phaethon
mother of: **5** stars, winds
corresponds to: **6** Aurore **7** Hermera

Epha, Ephah, Epheh 15 Biblical measure

ephemeral 5 brief **7** passing **8** fleeting, flitting, fugitive, temporal **9** fugacious, momentary, temporary, transient **10** evanescent, fly-by-night, inconstant, nondurable, short-lived, transitory, unenduring **11** impermanent **21** here today gone tomorrow

ephemeroptera
class: **8** hexapoda
phylum: **10** arthropoda
group: **6** mayfly

Ephraim
father: **6** Joseph
mother: **7** Asenath
brother: **8** Manasseh
blessed by: **5** Jacob
descendant of: **10** Ephraimite

Ephraimi 16 Greek unical codex

epic 4 saga **5** drama, great, noble **6** fabled, heroic **7** exalted, storied **8** fabulous, imposing, majestic **9** legendary **10** heroic poem, superhuman **14** larger than life

Epicaste see **7** Jocasta

epicure 7 glutton, gourmet **8** gourmand, hedonist, sybarite **9** bon vivant **10** gastronome

epicurean 4 rich **6** lavish **7** gourmet,

sensual **8** hedonist, Lucullan, sybarite **9** libertine, luxurious, sybaritic **10** hedonistic, sensualist, voluptuary, voluptuous **11** intemperate **13** self-indulgent

epidemic 4 rife **6** plague **7** rampant, scourge **8** catching, outbreak, pandemic **9** contagion, infection, pervasive, prevalent **10** infectious, pestilence, prevailing, widespread **11** far-reaching

Epigoni
sons of: **18** Seven Against Thebes

epigram 4 quip **5** adage, maxim **6** bon mot **8** aphorism, apothegm **9** witticism

epilogue 4 coda **5** rider **7** codicil **8** addendum **9** afterword **10** supplement **12** final section

Epione
husband: **9** Asclepius

episcopal 8 churchly, diocesan, pastoral **12** ecclesiastic(al)

episode 4 part **5** event, scene **6** affair, period **7** chapter, passage, section **8** incident **9** adventure, happening, milestone **10** experience, occurrence **11** installment

Episode of Sparrows, An
author: **11** Rumer Godden

episodic 7 halting **8** rambling **9** segmented, wandering **10** digressive, discursive, meandering **13** discontinuous

epistle 6 letter **7** message, missive **10** encyclical

Epistle to Dr Arbuthnot
author: **13** Alexander Pope

Epithalamion
author: **13** Edmund Spenser

epithet 5 curse **6** insult **8** nickname **9** blasphemy, expletive, obscenity, sobriquet **10** ascription **11** appellation, designation

Epithet
of Aphrodite: **6** Acraea, Scotia **7** Doritis, Erycina, Limenia **8** Melaenis, Nymphaea, Pandemos **9** Migonitis **11** Aphrogeneia, Apostrophia
of Apollo: **6** Loxias **7** Acesius, Agraeus, Agyieus, Carneus, Phyteus, Spodius **8** Grynaeus **9** Parnopius, Smintheus **10** Alexicacus, Archegetes, Boedromius, Delphinius **11** Argyrotoxus, Epibaterius **12** Platanistius
of Ares: **8** Enyalius **14** Gynaecothoenas
of Argus: **8** Panoptes
of Artemis: **6** Orthia **7** Eurippa, Laphria, Limnaea, Pyronia **8** Aeginaea, Agrotera, Calliste, Caryatis, Daphnaea **9** Hemerasia, Lygodesma **10** Polymastus **11** Leucophryne
of Asclepius: **8** Cotyleus
of Athena: **4** Alea **5** Meter, Xenia **6** Ergane, Itonia, Polias **7** Agoraea, Cissaea, Paeonia, Pronaus, Pronoea **8**

Anemotis, Poliates, Zosteria **9** Oxyderces, Parthenia, Poliuchus, Promachus **10** Axiopoenus, Chalinitis, Cyparissia **11** Promachorma
of Cybele: 6 Antaea
of Demeter: 5 Chloe, Lusia, Mysia **6** Antaea, Erinys, Stiria **7** Chamyne, Thesmia **8** Stiritis **9** Anesidora, Thermasia **11** Carpophorus **12** Thesmophorus
of Dionysus: 6 Lyaeus **7** Bromius, Cresius **8** Thyoneus, Triambus **9** Pyrigenes **11** Dithyrambus, Mitrephorus
of Hera: 6 Anthea, Bunaea **8** Henioche **9** Prodromia
of Hercules: 7 Charops **8** Buphagus **9** Ipoctonus
of Hermes: 6 Dolius **8** Agoraeus **9** Spelaites **10** Criophorus **11** Argiphontes **12** Argeiphontes, Psychopompus
of Icelus: 8 Phobetor
of Juno: 6 Moneta **7** Curitis, Pronuba, Sospita
of Jupiter: 5 Ultor **7** Elicius, Pluvius
of Mopsus: 9 Ampycides
of Nestor: 7 Nelides
of Odin: 7 Alfader, Alfadir
of Odysseus: 10 Laertiades
of Persephone: 11 Carpophorus
of Pheriphetes: 9 Corynetes
of Poseidon: 11 Ennosigaeus, Hippocurius **12** Prosclystius
of Rhea: 6 Antaea
of Sinis: 12 Pityocamptes
of Vulcan: 8 Mulciber
of Zeus: 5 Areus, Soter **6** Aqueus, Areius, Nemean, Philus **7** Alastor, Apemius, Ctesius, Lycaeus, Polieus, Stenius **8** Agoraeus, Aphesius, Apomyius, Cappotas, Cosmetas, Dodonian, Herceius, Leucaeus, Tropaean **9** Aegiochus, Chthonius, Coccygius, Hecaleius, Lecheates, Mechaneus **10** Cataebates, Catharsius, Coryphaeus, Homagyrius, Laphystius, Meilichius **11** Eleutherius **12** Panhellenius

epitome 4 peak **5** ideal, model **6** height **7** essence, summary **9** summation **10** embodiment **12** typification **14** representation **15** exemplification, sum and substance

e pluribus unum 12 out of many one
motto of: 12 United States

epoch 3 age, era **4** time **6** period **8** interval

epochal 7 weighty **8** historic **9** important, momentous **11** significant **13** consequential

Eppie
character in: 11 Silas Marner
author: 5 Eliot

Eppie
nickname of: 10 Ann Landers

Epstein, Sir Jacob
born: 9 New York NY

artwork: 4 Adam **7** Genesis **8** Ecce Homo, Einstein **9** Rock Drill **10** Visitation **11** Night and Day, Paul Robeson **12** Behold the Man, Joseph Conrad **13** Haile Selassie **14** Consummatum Est **19** Social Consciousness **20** Monument to Oscar Wilde, St Michael and his (the) Devil

equable 4 calm, even **5** sunny **6** placid, serene, stable, steady **7** regular, uniform **8** constant, pleasant, tranquil, unvaried **9** agreeable, easygoing, unruffled **10** consistent, dependable, unchanging **11** goodnatured, predictable, unexcitable, unflappable **12** even-tempered **13** imperturbable

equably
Latin: 9 pari passu

equal 4 even, like, peer **5** match **7** matched, the same, uniform **8** balanced, be even to, equalize, jibe with, of a piece, parallel **9** agree with, identical, tally with **10** accord with, comparable, equate with, equivalent, square with, tantamount **11** balance with, be the same as, correlative, counterpart, symmetrical **12** commensurate, correspond to, proportional **13** be identical to, corresponding, evenly matched, one and the same

equality 6 parity **7** balance, justice **8** evenness, fair play, fairness, sameness **10** similarity, uniformity **11** equivalency **12** impartiality **13** fair treatment **14** correspondence
French: 7 egalite

Equality
author: 13 Edward Bellamy

Equality State
nickname of: 7 Wyoming

equalization 7 balance **9** stability **11** equilibrium **14** counterbalance
German: 9 Ausgleich

equalize 7 balance **9** make equal **11** make uniform **10** compensate for

equal to 3 fit **4** able, up to **5** adept **7** capable **8** adequate, master of **9** competent, qualified

equanimity 4 cool **5** poise **6** aplomb **8** calmness, coolness **9** composure, sangfroid **10** steadiness **11** selfcontrol, tranquility **12** tranquillity **14** presence of mind, self-possession **16** imperturbability

equate 5 liken, match **7** average, balance, compare, even out **8** equalize, equal out **9** think of as **10** consider as **14** be commensurate, be equivalent to **17** be proportionate to

Equatorial
language family: 16 Andean-Equatorial
group: 8 Arawakan **11** Tupi-Guarani

Equatorial Guinea
other name: 13 Spanish Guinea
capital/largest city: 6 Malabo

others: 4 Bata **9** Rio Benito
division: 5 Bioko **7** Rio Muni
monetary unit: 6 ekuele, peseta **7** centimo
island: 5 Bioko **6** Pagalu **7** Corisco **11** Chico Elobey **12** Grande Elobey
mountain: 5 Mitra
highest point: 11 Santa Isabel
river: 5 Mbini
physical feature:
gulf: 6 Guinea
people: 4 Bubi, Fang **5** Benge, Combe **6** Bujeba **10** Fernandino
explorer: 2 Po
leader: 12 Nguema Biyogo
language: 4 Bubi, Fang **7** Spanish **13** pidgin English
religion: 7 animism **10** Protestant **13** Roman Catholic

equilibrium 7 balance **8** symmetry **9** equipoise, stability **14** sense of balance

equip 3 rig **5** stock **6** fit out, outfit, supply **7** appoint, furnish, prepare, provide **8** accoutre **9** caparison, provision

equipage 4 gear **6** outfit **8** carriage **9** equipment **13** accoutrements

equipment 4 gear **5** stuff **6** tackle **8** equipage, material, materiel, supplies **9** apparatus **11** furnishings, outfittings **13** accoutrements, paraphernalia

equipoise 7 balance **9** stability **11** equilibrium

equitable 3 due **4** fair, just **6** proper **8** unbiased **9** impartial **10** evenhanded, reasonable **12** unprejudiced

equity 4 cash **5** value **6** assets, profit **7** justice **8** fairness, justness **9** cash value **10** investment **12** fair dealings, impartiality **14** evenhandedness, fairmindedness, reasonableness

equivalency 6 parity **7** balance **8** equality **9** coequality, uniformity **14** correspondence

equivalent 4 even, peer **5** equal, match **8** of a piece, parallel **9** the same as **10** comparable, tantamount **11** correlative, counterpart, equal amount

equivocal 4 hazy **5** vague **7** dubious **9** doubtful **9** ambiguous, enigmatic, imprecise, qualified, uncertain, undecided **10** ambivalent, indefinite, suspicious **11** nonspecific **12** undetermined **13** indeterminate

equivocate 5 dodge, evade, fudge, hedge, stall **9** pussyfoot **10** mince words **11** be ambiguous, prevaricate **13** avoid the issue **16** straddle the fence **17** beat around the bush

equivocating 6 shifty **7** devious, dodging, elusive, elusory, evasive, hedging **8** stalling **9** ambiguous, deceptive, equivocal **10** misleading **11** dissembling

ER
  network: 3 NBC
  creator: 15 Michael Crichton
  hospital: 17 Cook County General
  cast: 6 Ming-Na (Jing-Mei "Deb" Chen) **8** Noah Wyle (John Carter) **9** Shane West (Ray Barnett) **10** Laura Innes (Kerry Weaver) **11** Eriq La Salle (Peter Benton), Mekhi Phifer (Gregory Pratt), Paul McCrane (Robert Romano) **12** Alex Kingston (Elizabeth Corday), Goran Visnjic (Luka Kovac), Maura Tierney (Abby Lockheart), Sharif Atkins (Michael Gallant) **13** George Clooney (Doug Ross) **14** Abraham Benrubi (Jerry Markovic), Anthony Edwards (Mark Greene), Parminder Nagra (Neela Rasgotra) **15** Linda Cardellini (Sam Taggart) **17** Julianna Margulies (Carol Hathaway), Sherry Stringfield (Susan Lewis)

ERA
  abbr. for: 16 earned run average (baseball) **20** equal rights amendment (failed)

era 3 age **4** time **5** epoch **6** period **8** interval

eradicate 5 erase **6** remove **7** abolish, blot out, destroy, expunge, wipe out **8** get rid of **9** eliminate, extirpate, liquidate **10** annihilate, do away with, extinguish, obliterate **11** exterminate

eradication 7 erasure, removal **9** abolition **11** blotting out, destruction, elimination **12** obliteration

erase 6 delete, remove, rub out **7** expunge, scratch **8** wipe away **9** eliminate, eradicate, strike out

Erasistratus
  field: 10 physiology
  nationality: 5 Greek
  described: 5 brain, heart

Erasmus, Desiderius
  author of: 14 Encomium Moriae **16** The Praise of Folly

Erato
  muse of: 10 love poetry

Ercolani, James
  real name of: 11 James Darren

erect 5 build, put up, raise, rigid, stiff **6** unbent **7** stand up, upright **8** straight, vertical **9** construct, unstooped **12** place upright

erection 7 raising **8** building **9** putting up **11** fabrication **12** construction

eremite 4 monk **6** essene, hermit **7** ascetic, recluse **9** anchorite, religious

Erewhon
  author: 12 Samuel Butler
  title spelled backwards, modified: 7 nowhere
  character: 5 Higgs **6** Strong **7** Chowbok **8** Arowhena

erg
  metric unit of: 4 work **6** energy

ergo 4 work **6** hence **7** because **9** therefore **11** accordingly

Eriboea
  husband: 6 Aloeus

Ericson 4 Leif
  son of: 10 Eric the Red
  discovered: 7 Vinland
  home: 6 Norway

Erie 4 lake, port **5** canal **9** Iroquoian

Erigone
  father: 7 Icarius **9** Aegisthus
  mother: 12 Clytemnestra
  brother: 6 Aletes
  death by: 7 suicide

Erin *see* **7** Ireland

Erin Brockovich
  director: 16 Steven Soderbergh
  cast: 11 Peter Coyote (Kurt Potter) **12** Aaron Eckhart (George), Albert Finney (Ed Masry), David Brisbin (Dr. Jaffe), Dawn Didawick (Rosalind), Julia Roberts (Erin Brockovich) **14** Erin Brockovich (Julia, the waitress) **15** Conchata Ferrell (Brenda) **16** Marg Helgenberger (Donna Jensen), Valente Rodriguez (Donald)

Erin go bragh 14 Ireland forever

Erinys
  also: 6 Furies
  epithet of: 7 Demeter
  means: 4 fury

Eris
  origin: 5 Greek
  goddess of: 7 discord
  brother: 4 Ares
  threw: 14 apple of discord
  corresponds to: 9 Discordia

Eritrea
  capital/largest city: 6 Asmara
  others: 5 Assab, Keren **6** Ghinda **7** Massawa
  formerly division of: 8 Ethiopia
  river: 5 Mareb
  highest point: 5 Soira
  strait: 11 Bab el Mandeb
  sea: 3 Red
  language: 7 Amharic
  religion: 5 Islam **6** Coptic, Muslim

Erlking
  origin: 8 Germanic **12** Scandinavian
  form: 6 spirit
  personifies: 6 nature
  works: 8 mischief
  poem by: 6 Goethe
  song by: 8 Schubert

ermine 3 fur **4** duty, rank **6** weasel **7** ermalin **8** position

Ernani
  opera by: 5 Verdi
  setting: 6 Aragon
  character: 6 Ernani **11** Donna Elvira

Ernst, Max
  born: 5 Bruhl **7** Germany
  co-founder of: 7 Dadaism **10** Surrealism
  artwork: 7 Moon Man **8** Lady Bird **11** A Little Calm, Femme Oiseau **12**

The Whole City **13** The Table Is Set, Totem and Taboo **14** Lunar Asparagus

erode 3 eat **5** spoil, waste **6** ravage **7** corrode, despoil, eat away **8** wear away **12** disintegrate

Eros
  origin: 5 Greek
  god of: 4 love
  mother: 9 Aphrodite
  corresponds to: 4 Amor **5** Cupid

erosion 8 abrasion, ravaging **9** corrosion **10** eating away **11** wearing away, wearing down

erosive 7 burning, caustic **9** corrosive

erotic 3 hot **4** lewd, sexy **5** bawdy, lusty **6** ardent, carnal, impure, ribald, risque, sexual, wanton **7** amatory, amorous, obscene, raunchy **8** immodest, indecent, unchaste **9** salacious **10** lascivious, passionate, suggestive

err 3 sin **6** mess up, slip up **7** blunder, do wrong **8** go astray **9** be in error, misbehave **10** transgress **12** make a mistake, miscalculate **13** slip from grace

errand 4 duty, task **6** office **7** mission **10** assignment

errant 5 wrong **6** arrant, astray, erring, roving **7** erratic, wayward **8** mistaken, straying **9** incorrect, wandering, wayfaring **11** adventurous

errare humanum est 12 to err is human

erratic 3 odd **5** queer **6** fitful **7** strange, unusual, wayward **8** aberrant, abnormal, peculiar, shifting, unstable, variable **9** eccentric, unnatural **10** capricious, changeable **11** vacillating **12** inconsistent **13** unpredictable

erroneous 5 false, wrong **6** all wet, faulty, untrue **7** off base, unsound **8** mistaken, spurious **9** incorrect, unfounded **10** fallacious, inaccurate **12** full of hot air **13** unsupportable

error 4 flaw **5** boner, botch, fault **6** boo-boo, bungle, howler **7** blooper, fallacy, mistake **9** oversight **10** inaccuracy **13** misconception **14** miscalculation **15** misapprehension **16** misunderstanding **17** misinterpretation

ersatz 4 fake, sham **5** bogus, phony **9** imitation, pretended, synthetic **10** artificial, not genuine **11** counterfeit

Erse 4 Celt, Gael, Scot **5** Irish **6** Celtic, Gaelic **7** Ireland **8** Scottish **10** Highlander

erstwhile 2 ex **4** past **6** bygone, former **7** onetime **8** previous

eruct 4 burp **5** belch

eructation 4 burp **5** belch

erudite 4 wise **7** learned, sapient **8** cultured, literate, well-read **9** scholarly **10** cultivated, thoughtful, well-versed **11** intelligent **12** well-educated, well-informed, well-reasoned

erudition 5 skill 7 culture 8 learning, literacy 9 education, expertise, knowledge, schooling 10 refinement 11 cultivation, learnedness, scholarship 12 book learning 13 enlightenment

Erulus
king of: 5 Italy
mother: 7 Feronia
gift: 10 three lives

erupt 4 emit, gush, vent 5 eruct 6 blow up 7 explode 8 break out, throw off 9 be ejected, discharge, flow forth, pour forth 10 belch forth, burst forth

eruption 4 rash 6 eczema 7 flare-up, gushing, venting 8 ejection, emission, outbreak, outburst 9 blowing up, discharge, explosion, festering 10 dermatitis, outpouring 11 breaking out 12 flowing forth, inflammation, pouring forth 13 belching forth, bursting forth

Erving, Julius
nickname: 7 Doctor J
sport: 10 basketball
position: 7 forward
team: 11 New York Nets 15 Virginia Squires 25 Philadelphia Seventy-Sixers

Erymanthian boar
form: 4 boar
plagued: 7 Arcadia
captured by: 8 Hercules

erythrophobia
fear of: 8 blushing

Esau
also called: 4 Edom
father: 5 Isaac
mother: 7 Rebekah
twin brother: 5 Jacob
wife: 6 Judith 8 Makalath
son: 7 Eliphaz
birthright sold to: 5 Jacob

escadrille 6 armada 8 flotilla, squadron

escalate 4 rise 5 boost, mount, swell 6 ascend, expand, extend, step up 7 advance, amplify, broaden, elevate, enlarge, magnify 8 increase 9 intensify 10 accelerate, aggrandize

Escalus
character in: 17 Measure for Measure
author: 11 Shakespeare

escapade 4 lark 5 antic, caper, fling, prank, revel, spree, trick 7 caprice 8 mischief 9 adventure 11 high old time

escape 3 lam 4 bolt, exit, flee, flow, gush, leak, seep, shun, skip 5 avert, avoid, dodge, elude, issue, skirt 6 efflux, egress, emerge, eschew, exodus, flight, stream 7 abscond, emanate, getaway, leakage, make off, outflow, outpour, run away, seepage 8 breakout, emission, outburst, slip away, steal off 9 be emitted, break free, cut and run, discharge, diversion, effluence, pour forth 10 break loose, decampment, fly the coop 11 avoid danger, deliverance, distraction,

extrication, safe getaway 12 make a getaway

escargot 5 snail

escarpment 4 bank, crag 5 bluff, cliff, ridge, slope 8 headland, palisade 9 precipice 10 promontory

eschew 4 shun 5 avoid, forgo 6 give up 7 forbear 9 keep shy of 11 abstain from 12 steer clear of

eschewal 7 refusal 8 forgoing, shunning 9 avoidance 10 abnegation, abstention, self-denial 11 forbearance 13 nonindulgence 16 nonparticipation

Escoffier, Auguste
nationality: 6 French
profession: 4 chef
worked in: 4 Ritz 6 London

escort 4 date, take 5 guard, guide, train, usher 6 squire 7 company, conduct, cortege, retinue 8 chaperon 9 companion, conductor, entourage 10 attendants, lead the way

escritoire 4 desk 5 table 9 secretary 10 secretaire 11 writing desk

escutcheon 4 arms 5 crest 6 shield 10 coat of arms 16 armorial bearings
see also 8 Heraldry

Eskimo (Eskimantsic, Askkimey, Inuit, Yuit)
tribe: 5 Aleut
location: 6 Alaska, Arctic, Canada 9 Greenland
noted for: 7 fishing 9 mechanics

Eskimo-Aleut
language branch: 5 Aleut, Yupik
spoken in: 6 Alaska 7 Siberia 15 Aleutian Islands

Esmeralda
character in: 23 The Hunchback of Notre Dame
author: 4 Hugo

esoteric 6 arcane, covert, hidden, occult, secret, veiled 7 cloaked, cryptic, obscure, private 8 abstruse, mystical 9 concealed, enigmatic, recondite 10 inviolable, mysterious 11 inscrutable, undisclosed 12 confidential 16 incomprehensible

ESP 7 insight 9 foresight, intuition 10 sixth sense 11 premonition, second sight 12 clairvoyance 22 extrasensory perception

espanol 7 Spanish 13 Spanish person 15 Spanish language

especial see 7 special

especially 6 really 7 notably 9 expressly, intensely, primarily, unusually 10 singularly, uncommonly 11 exclusively, principally 12 particularly, specifically 13 exceptionally, outstandingly 15 extraordinarily

espiegle 7 playful, roguish

espieglerie 12 playful trick

esplanade 4 mall, path, walk 5 drive 9 boardwalk 10 quadrangle

espousal 7 backing, support, wedding

8 adoption, advocacy, marriage, taking up 9 betrothal, promotion 10 supporting 12 championship

espouse 3 wed 4 back, tout 5 adopt, boost, marry 6 take up 7 embrace, further, promote, support 8 advocate, champion, side with 10 stand up for

espressivo
music: 12 expressively
abbreviation: 4 espr

esprit de corps 10 fellowship, group pride, group unity, high morale, solidarity, team spirit 11 camaraderie

espy 3 see, spy 4 spot, view 6 behold, descry, detect, locate, notice 7 discern

essay 3 try 5 paper, theme, tract 6 effort, take on 7 article, attempt, venture 8 critique, endeavor, treatise 9 editorial, undertake 10 commentary, experiment 11 make a stab at, undertaking 12 dissertation, take a crack at, take a fling at 14 make an effort at 16 short composition

Essay on Criticism, An
author: 13 Alexander Pope

Essay on Man, An
author: 13 Alexander Pope

Essays
author: 12 Francis Bacon

esse 5 being 9 existence

essence 4 core, germ, gist, pith, soul 5 heart, point, scent 6 elixir, nature, spirit 7 cologne, extract, meaning, perfume, spirits 8 tincture 9 fragrance, lifeblood, principle, substance 11 concentrate, toilet water 12 basic quality, quintessence, significance 15 sum and substance

essential, essentials 3 key 4 main 5 basic, vital 6 basics, needed 7 crucial, leading 8 cardinal, inherent 9 basic need, important, ingrained, intrinsic, necessary, necessity, principal, requisite, rudiments, vital part 10 key element, principles 11 fundamental, nitty-gritty 12 fundamentals 13 indispensable

essential ingredient 9 necessity 10 sine qua non 22 indispensable component

establish 3 fix 4 form, open, show 5 begin, found, prove, set up, start 6 create, settle, uphold, verify 7 confirm, implant, install, justify, situate, sustain, warrant 8 initiate, organize, validate 9 institute 10 bring about, inaugurate, make secure 11 corroborate, demonstrate 12 authenticate 16 win acceptance for 18 bring into existence

established 6 common 7 regular 8 accepted, familiar 9 customary 10 recognized

establishment, Establishment 4 firm 5 plant 6 office, outfit, system 7 company, concern, factory 8 building, business, creation, founding 9 formation, setting up **10** foundation **11** corporation, development, instituting, institution, ruling class **12** organization, powers that be **13** bringing about

estaminet 4 cafe **6** bistro

estate 4 rank, will **5** class, grade, manor, money, order, state **6** assets, legacy, status, wealth **7** bequest, fortune, station **8** compound, holdings, property **9** condition, situation **10** belongings, plantation **11** inheritance **12** country place

esteem 4 deem, hold **5** honor, judge, prize, think, value **6** admire, reckon, regard, revere **7** believe, cherish, respect **8** approval, consider, estimate, look up to, treasure, venerate **9** calculate, reverence **10** admiration, set store by, veneration **12** appreciation **13** think highly of **16** favorable opinion, hold in high regard **18** attach importance to

esteemed 5 great, noted **6** prized, valued, worthy **7** admired, eminent, honored, notable, revered **9** admirable, important, respected **10** looked up to, preeminent **11** illustrious **13** distinguished, well thought of **14** highly regarded

Estella
   character in: 17 Great Expectations
   author: 7 Dickens

Estevez, Ramon
   real name of: 11 Martin Sheen

Esther
   author: 10 Henry Adams

Esther
   Persian name of: 8 Hadassah
   father: 7 Abihail
   grandfather: 6 Shimei
   cousin: 8 Mordecai
   husband: 9 Ahasuerus
   displaced: 6 Vashti
   enemy: 5 Haman
   holiday: 5 Purim

Esther Waters
   author: 11 George Moore

esthetic 7 refined **8** artistic **9** sensitive **10** cultivated, fastidious **12** aesthetic **14** discriminating

estimable 4 good **6** prized **7** admired, revered **8** laudable **9** admirable, honorable, important, reputable, respected, treasured **10** worthwhile **11** commendable **12** praiseworthy **14** highly regarded

estimate 4 view **5** assay, guess, judge, opine, think, value **6** assess, belief, figure, reckon **7** believe, opinion, surmise **8** appraise, conclude, consider, evaluate, judgment, thinking **9** appraisal, calculate, reckoning **10** assessment, conjecture, evaluation **11** calculation

estimation 4 view **6** belief, esteem, regard **7** opinion, respect **8** approval, judgment **9** appraisal, reckoning **10**

admiration, evaluation **13** consideration

estimator 7 analyst **8** assessor **9** appraiser, evaluator **10** calculator

Estonia
   capital/largest city: 7 Tallinn
   others: 5 Narva, Paide, Parnu, Tartu, Valga **6** Dorpat **7** Petseri **8** Paldiski **11** Kohtla-Jarve
   government: 8 republic
   measure: 3 tun **4** elle, liin, sund, toll, toop **5** verst **6** sagene, versta **7** kulimet **8** tonnland
   monetary unit: 3 lat **4** sent **5** kroon **7** estmark
   weight: 4 lood, nael, puud
   island: 4 Dago, Muhu **5** Kihnu, Oesel, Saare **6** Sarema, Vormsi **7** Hiiumaa **8** Saaremaa
   lake: 5 Pskov **6** Peipus **9** Vortsjarv
   highest point: 8 Munamagi
   river: 3 Ema **5** Narva, Parnu
   sea: 6 Baltic
   physical feature:
     gulf: 4 Riga **5** Parnu **7** Finland
     strait: 4 Irbe
   people: 4 Esth, Finn **5** Aesti **6** Jewish **8** Estonian **9** Ukrainian **11** Belorussian
   language: 5 Tartu **10** Finno-Ugric
   religion: 8 Lutheran

estop 3 bar **4** fill, plug, stop **7** prevent **8** obstruct

esto perpetua 17 may she live forever
   motto of: 5 Idaho

Estragon
   character in: 15 Waiting for Godot
   author: 7 Beckett
   French for: 8 tarragon

estrange 4 part **8** alienate **9** disaffect **10** antagonize, dissociate, drive apart

estranged 5 aloof **6** cut off **7** distant **8** detached, divorced **9** alienated, separated **10** unfriendly

estrangement 8 coolness **10** alienation **12** disaffection

estuary 5 firth, inlet **10** river mouth, tidal basin

eta 10 Greek vowel **22** estimated time of arrival

etagere 7 whatnot **11** open shelves

etc (&c) 4 et al **7** and so on, whatnot **8** et cetera, whatever **9** and others **10** and so forth, and the rest

etch 3 cut, fix **5** carve, stamp **7** corrode, engrave, impress, scratch

Eteocles
   father: 7 Oedipus
   mother: 7 Jocasta **10** Euryganeia
   uncle: 5 Creon
   brother: 9 Polynices
   sister: 6 Ismene **8** Antigone
   son: 8 Laodamas
   slain by: 9 Polynices

eternal 7 abiding, endless **8** constant,

immortal, infinite, timeless, unending **9** ceaseless, continual, perpetual **10** persistent, relentless, without end **11** everlasting, never-ending **12** interminable **13** uninterrupted

Eternal Sunshine of the Spotless Mind
   director: 12 Michel Gondry
   cast: 9 Jane Adams (Carrie), Jim Carrey (Joel Barish) **10** David Cross (Rob), Elijah Wood (Patrick) **11** Kate Winslet (Clementine Kruczynski), Mark Ruffalo (Stan) **12** Kirsten Dunst (Mary), Tom Wilkinson (Howard Mierzwiak) **13** Thomas Jay Ryan (Frank)

eternity 4 Zion **6** Heaven **7** forever, nirvana **8** infinity, paradise **11** ages and ages, endlessness, eons and eons, immortality **12** New Jerusalem, the hereafter, the next world **13** the afterworld **14** the world to come, time without end **15** everlasting life

Ethan Frome
   author: 12 Edith Wharton
   character: 5 Zeena **7** Zenobia **12** Mattie Silver

Ethanim 18 seventh Hebrew month

ether 5 ester, ethyl, ozone, vapor **7** diethyl, solvent **10** anesthetic **11** refrigerant

ethereal 4 airy, rare **6** aerial **7** elusive, refined, sublime **8** delicate, rarefied **9** celestial, exquisite, unearthly, unworldly

ethical 4 fair, just **5** moral, right **6** decent, kosher, proper **7** correct, fitting, upright **8** virtuous **9** honorable **10** aboveboard, scrupulous **15** straightforward **17** open and aboveboard

ethical feelings 9 integrity **10** conscience, moral sense **16** incorruptibility

ethics, ethic 8 morality **9** integrity, moral code **10** conscience, principles **11** moral values, sense of duty **14** moral standards, rules of conduct

Ethiopia
   Biblical name: 4 Cush
   other name: 9 Abyssinia
   capital/largest city: 10 Addis Ababa
   others: 3 Edd **4** Axum, Bako, Dori, Goba, Gore, Thio **5** Adola, Adowa, Aduwa, Aksum, Assab, Awash, Dimtu, Elfud, Harar, Jidda, Jimma, Kecha, Meroe, Mojjo **6** Antalo, Asmara, Dessye, Dunkur, Gondar, Harrar, Makale, Napata **7** Ankober, Gambela, Gardula, Magdala, Massawa, Nakamti **8** Dire Dawa, Lalibala, Mustahil
   school: 13 Haile Selassie
   division: 5 Tigre **6** Amhara, Ogaden
   former division: 7 Eritrea
   measure: 3 tat **4** cubi, kuba **5** derah, messe **6** cabaho, sinjer, sinzer, tanica **7** entelam, farsakh, farsang,

ghebeta

monetary unit: 4 besa, birr, harf **5** amole, girsh **6** dollar, kharaf, levant, pataca, talari **7** ashrafi, menelik, plaster, tallero **12** Maria Theresa

weight: 3 pek **4** kasm, natr, oket, rotl **5** alada, artal, mocha, neter, ratel, wakea **6** wogiet **8** farasula **9** mutagalla

island: 6 Dahlak

lake: 3 Abe **4** Tana **5** Abaya, Shola, Tanna, Tsana, Tzana, Zeway **6** Dambea, Dembea **7** Rudolph **8** Stefanie **11** The Blue Nile

mountain: 4 Amba, Batu, Guge, Guna, Talo **5** Ahmar, Choke **9** Rasdashan

highest point: 9 Ras Deshen

river: 3 Omo **4** Baro, Dawa, Gibe, Gila, Juba **5** Abbai, Akoho, Albai, Awash, Fafan, Mareb, Mofer, Rahad, Webbe **6** Tekeze **7** Tacazze, Takkaze **8** Gashgash, Shebante **11** The Blue Nile

sea: 3 Red

physical feature:
  desert: 17 Danakil Depression
  falls: 7 Tisisat **8** Blue Nile
  valley: 4 Rift

people: 4 Afar, Agau, Beja, Doko, Kafa, Kala, Saho, Shoa **5** Afara, Agows, Galas, Galla, Negro, Tigre **6** Abigar, Amhara, Annuak, Gondar, Hamite, Harari, Sidama, Sidamo, Somali, Tigrai, Wolamo **7** Cushite, Danakil, Donakus, Falasha, Somalis **8** Assamite, Blemmyes **10** Abyssinian, Troglodyte

leader: 7 Menelik **8** Mengistu **13** Haile Selassie

language: 3 Giz **4** Afar, Agow, Geez, Saho **5** Geeze, Ghese, Smali, Tigre **6** Arabic, Harari **7** Amharic, English, Italian, Russian **8** Gallinya, IrobSaho, Tigrinya

religion: 5 Islam **7** Falasha, Judaism **18** Ethiopian Orthodoxy

place:
  cathedral: 8 St George
  hall: 6 Africa
  palace: 7 Jubilee **9** Menelik II
  park: 4 Lion

feature:
  flower: 7 brayera
  game: 5 dulla **8** shum-shir
  garment: 4 toga **5** kamis **6** barnos, chamma, netela, shamma
  tree: 4 koho, koso **5** cusso

food:
  banana: 4 musa **6** ensete
  beer: 5 talla
  bread dish: 6 injera
  cereal: 4 teff
  honey liquor: 3 tej
  spicy sauce: 3 wat

ethnic 6 native, racial, unique **8** cultural, national, original **10** indigenous

ethnic group

of Afghanistan: 5 Aimak, Aymak, Kafir, Nuris **6** Baloch, Baluch, Chahar, Durani, Hasara, Hazara, Kaffir, Kirgiz, Pathan, Tajiks, Uzbeks **7** Beluchi, Belucki, Ghilzai, Pakhton, Pakhtun, Pashtun, Pukhtun, Pushtun, Sistani, Taimani, Taimuri, Taliban **8** Jamshidi, Siah Push **9** Firuzkuhi, Safed Push, Safid Push

of Albania: 3 Geg **4** Cham, Gheg, Gueg, Tost **6** Arnaut, Arnout **8** Illyrian, Skipetar

of Algeria: 4 Arab **6** Berber, Kabyle, Shawai, Tuareg **7** Haratin

of Andorra: 7 Catalan

of Angola: 5 Bantu, Kongo, Lundu **6** Chokwe, Herero, Mbundi, Ovambo **7** Bakongo, Kangela, Kikongo **8** Kimbundu, Kwangare **9** Ovinbundu **12** Nyaneka-Humbi

of Antigua and Barbuda: 7 African, British **8** Lebanese **10** Portuguese

of Argentina: 3 Api **4** Lule **5** Vejoz **6** Abipon, Vilela **7** Guarani, Puelche, Ranquel, Taluhet **8** Querandi, Querendy

of Armenia: 5 Armen, Ermyn, Gomer, Hadji

of Australia: 3 Abo **4** Koko, Mara, Wong **5** Anzac, Bieri, Binge, Maori, Myall **6** Aranda, Arunta, Aussie, Binghi, Digger, Kipper, Papuan **7** Arawong, Billjim, Ilpirra **8** Antipode, Barkinji, Euahlayi, Warragal, Warrigal **9** Aborigine **10** Austroloid, Melanesian, Sandgroper **12** Jindyworobak

of Austria: 4 Pole **5** Croat, Czech, Gypsy **6** German **7** Slovene **9** Hungarian

of Azerbaijan: 5 Azeri **11** Azerbaijani

of the Bahamas: 5 black **7** Haitian

of Bahrain: 4 Arab **6** Indian **7** Persian **8** European **9** Pakistani

of Bangladesh: 7 Bengali

of Barbados: 5 Bajan **9** Barbadian

of Belarus: 12 Byelorussian

of Belgium: 4 Remi **6** Nervii **7** Belgian, Fleming, Flemish, Walloon **9** Bellovaci

of Benin: 3 Fon, Pla **4** Adja, Aizo, Mina, Peul **5** Pedah, Peuhl, Somba **6** Bariba, Fulani, Yoruba **8** Pilapila **9** Dahomeyan

of Bhutan: 5 Monpa **6** Bhutia **7** Tibetan **8** Assamese, Nepalese

of Bolivia: 6 Aymara **7** mestizo, Quechua

of Borneo: 4 Iban **5** Bukat, Dajak, Dayak, Dusan, Malay, Punan **6** Illano **7** Bakatan, Chinese, Illanum

of Bosnia-Herzegovina: 4 Serb **5** Croat **8** Yugoslav

of Botswana: 5 Bantu **6** Tswana **7** Bakatla, Bakwena, Bushman **8** Bamalete, Baralong, Batawana, Batlokwa, Botswana **10** Bamangwato **11** Bangwaketse

of Brazil: 2 Ge **4** Anta **5** Acroa, Ar-

ara, Araua, Bravo, Carib, Guana, Negro **6** Arawak, Caraja **7** Carayan, Javahai, mulatto, Tariana **8** Botocudo, Chambioa, mameluco **9** Caucasian **10** Portuguese **11** TupiGuarani

of Bruneii: 4 Iban **5** Dayak, Malay **7** Chinese, Kadazan

of Bulgaria: 4 Slav, Turk **5** Gypsy, Pomak, Tatar **6** Bulgar, Slavic **7** Chuvash **9** Cheremiss **10** Macedonian

of Burkina Faso: 4 Bobo, Lobi, Samo **5** Bella, Bissa, Dyula, Fulbe, Hausa, Mande, Marka, Mossi, Puchl **6** Fulani, Senufo, Tuareg **7** Grunshi, Voltaic, Yatenga **8** Mandingo **9** Gourounsi **15** Bunsansi Gambaga

of Burundi: 3 Twa **4** Hutu **5** Bantu, Batwa, Pygmy, Tutsi **6** Bahutu, Watusi **7** Barundi

of Cambodia: 4 Cham, Thai **5** Khmer **7** Chinese **10** Vietnamese

of Cameroon: 3 Abo, Edo, Ibo **4** Beti, Bulu, Ekoi, Ijaw, Sara **5** Bantu, Bassa, Kirdi, Pygmy, Tikar **6** Bamoun, Donala, Ewondo, Fulani, Ibibio **7** Bakweri **8** Bamileke

of Canada: 6 Canuck, Eskimo, French, Innuit **7** English

of the Canary Islands: 7 Spanish

of Cape Verde: 6 Creole **7** African, mulatto **8** European **10** Portuguese

of Central African Republic: 4 Baya, Sara **5** Banda, Bwaki, Sango **6** Azande, Yakoma **7** Banziri, Mandjia, Nzakara

of Chad: 4 Arab, Daza, Maba, Sara, Teda, Tubu **5** Barma, Hakka, Kroda, Massa **6** Fulani, Kotoko, Toubou, Wadaii **7** Kamadja, Kanembu **8** Moundang

of Chile: 3 Ona **4** Auca, Inca, Onan **6** Arauca, Chango, Yahgan **7** Mapuche, mestizo, Moluche, Pampean, Patagon, Puegian, Ranquel **8** Alikuluf, Picunche, Tsonecan

of China: 3 Han, Yis **4** Huis, Lolo, Miao, Pu-is **5** Hakka, Hoklo, Seres, Sinic **6** Cataia, Chuang, Johnny, Korean, Manchu, Mongol, Serian, Uighun **7** Sinaean, Tibetan

of Colombia: 4 Boro, Cuna, Duit, Hoka, Macu, Muso, Muzo, Paez, Tama, Tapa **5** Carib, Catio, Choco, Cofan, Cogui, Cubeo, Guane, Haida, Mocoa, Paeze, Pijao, Seona, Yagua **6** Arawak, Betoya, Calima, Colima, Ingano, Mirana, Saliva, Tahami, Ticuna, Tucano, Tunebo, Witoto, Yahuna **7** Achagua, Andaqui, Chibcha, Chimila, Churoya, Guahibo, Guajiro, mestizo, mulatto, Panches, Puinave, Puitoto, Quechua, Shuswap, Tairona, Telembi **8** Coconuco, Guarauno, Motilone, Puinavis, Quimbaya, Sinsigas **9** Cocanucos, Coconucan, Panaquita **10** Bellacoola

of Comoros: 4 Arab **5** Bantu, Malay **7** African **8** Malagasy

of Congo, Republic of the: 3 Rua **4** Akka, Susa, Teke, Vili **5** Amadi, Bantu, Figot, Kongo, Mantu, Pygmy, Sanga, Warua, Zambi **6** Ababua, Bafyot, Bateke, Mbochi, Nzambi, Wabuma **7** Bacongo, Bakongo, Bangala, Batetla, Manyema **10** Binga Pygmy

of Congo, Democratic Republic of the: 4 Kuba, Luba, Yaka **5** Bantu, Bashi, Bemba, Kongo, Lulue, Lunda, Mongo, Pygmy **6** Azande, Baluba, Watusi **7** Bakongo, Nilotes, Tshokwe **8** European, Mangbetu, Sudanese

of Costa Rica: 4 Voto **6** Boruca, Bribri, Guaymi **7** Guatuso, mestizo, Spanish

of Crete: 6 Cretan, Minoan **7** Candiot **8** Sphakiot **9** Caphtorim **10** Philistine

of Croatia: 4 Serb **5** Croat **8** Yugoslav

of Cuba: 5 Carib, Negro, Taino **6** Arawak **7** Ciboney, mestizo **8** Ciboneye **9** Caucasian

of Czechoslovakia/Czech Republic: 4 Slav **5** Czech **6** Slovak **8** Bohemian, Moravian

of Denmark: 4 Dane, Jute **5** Angle **6** Cimbri, Eskimo, German, Ostmen, Teuton, Viking **12** Scandinavian

of Djibouti: 4 Afar, Arab **5** Issas **6** French **8** European

of Dominican Republic: 5 Negro, Taino **6** Indian **7** mulatto, Spanish **9** Caucasian

of Ecuador: 4 Cara, Cixo, Inca **5** Ardan, Aucas, Macoa, Maina, Palta, Quitu, Yumbo **6** Canelo, Jibaro, Jivaro, Puruha **7** Cayapas, Jivaros, mestizo, mulatto **8** Barbacoa, Colorado, Montuvio, Serranos **10** Montubious

of Egypt: 3 Kem **4** Arab, Copt, Misr, Wafd **5** Gippy, Gyppy, Gypsy, Nilot **6** Ababda, Berber, Hyksos, Nubian, Tasian **7** Mizraim, Pharian **8** Badarian, Bisharin, Memphian

of El Salvador: 5 Lenca, Pipil **6** Indian, Mangue **7** mestizo, Spanish **9** Matagalpa

of England: 4 Celt, Jute, Pict **5** Norse, Saxon **6** Angles, Briton, Norman, Viking

of Equatorial Guinea: 4 Bubi, Fang **5** Benge, Combe **6** Bujeba **10** Fernandino

of Estonia: 4 Esth, Finn **5** Aesti **6** Jewish **8** Estonian **9** Ukrainian **11** Belorussian

of Ethiopia: 4 Afar, Agau, Beja, Doko, Kafa, Kala, Saho, Shoa **5** Afara, Agows, Galas, Galla, Negro, Tigre **6** Abigar, Amhara, Annuak, Gondar, Hamite, Harari, Sidama, Sidamo, Somali, Tigrai, Wolamo **7** Cushite, Danakil, Donakus, Falasha **8** Assamite, Blemmyes **10** Abyssinian, Troglodyte

of Fiji: 6 Fijian, Indian **7** Chinese **10** Melanesian, Polynesian **11** Micronesian

of Finland: 3 Jew, Vod, Vot, Yak **4** Avar, Finn, Hame, Lapp, Turk, Veps **5** Fioun, Gypsy, Ijore, Inger, Suomi, Vepse, Zyrin **6** Magyar, Ostiak, Ostyak, Tarast, Tavast, Ugrian **7** Lappish, Mordvin, Permiak, Samoyed, Uralian **8** Cheremis, Estonian, Karelian, Livonian, Swekoman **9** Tavastian **11** Karjalaiset, Suomalaiset

of France: 5 Frank

of the Gabon Republic: 4 Fang **6** Adouma, Bakota, Bateke, Echira, Okande, Omyene **7** Eshiras **8** Bandjabi, Bapounou

of The Gambia: 4 Fula, Jola **5** Foula, Wolof **6** Fulani **8** Mandingo, Serahuli **9** Seranuleh

of Georgia: 5 Azeri **7** Russian **8** Armenian, Georgian, Ossetian

of Germany: 3 Hun **4** Slav, Sorb, Wend **5** Saxon

of Ghana: 2 Ga **3** Ewe **4** Akan, Akim, Akra, Aksa **5** Ahafo, Brong, Inkra **7** Akwapim, Ashanti, Dagomba, Maprusi **11** Mole-Dagbani

of Gibraltar: 6 Jewish **7** British, Italian, Maltese, Spanish **10** Portuguese

of Greece: 5 Greek **6** Achean, Dorian, Ionian **7** Aeolian, Hellene

of Greenland: 3 Ita **6** Eskimo **8** European

of Grenada: 5 Negro **6** Indian

of Guatemala: 3 Mam **4** Chol, Itza, Ixil, Maya **5** Xinca **6** Caribe, Quiche **7** ladinos, mestizo, Pocomam **13** Guatemaltecos

of Guinea: 4 Koma, Loma, Nalu, Susu, Toma **5** Kissi, Manon **6** Fulani, Guerzi **7** Landoma, Malinke **8** Kouranke, Landuman **11** Kissi-Sherbo **12** Guerze-Kpelle

of Guinea-Bissau: 6 Fulani **7** Balanta, Balante, mulatto **8** Mandingo, Mandyako

of Guyana: 6 Akawai, Arawak, Creole, Taruma **7** African, Chinese, mulatto **10** Portuguese

of Haiti: 5 Taino **7** African, mulatto

of Honduras: 4 Maya, Paya, Sumo, Ulva **5** Carib, Lenoa, Pipil **6** Tauira **7** Jicaque, mestizo, Miskito **8** Mosquito

of Hong Kong: 5 Hakka, Haklo, Punti, Tanka **7** British, Chinese **8** American, Japanese **9** Cantonese **10** Portuguese

of Hungary: 3 Hun **4** Serb **5** Croat, Gypsy **6** Cigany, Magyar, Slovak, Ugrian

of Iceland: 6 Celtic, Viking **8** Norseman **9** Norwegian

of India: 2 Ao **3** Gor **4** Bhil **5** Aryan **6** Badaga, Pathan **7** Sherani **9** Dravidian **10** Andamanese

of Indonesia: 4 Dyak **5** Batak, Dayak, Malay **6** Battak, Papuan, Toraja **7** Chinese, Igorots **8** Acehnese, Achinese, Balinese, Javanese, Madurese, Sudanese **11** Minang Kabau

of Iran: 3 Lur, Tat **4** Arab, Kurd, Turk **5** Medes **6** Galcha, Gilani, Jewish, Shugni **7** Baluchi, Persian **8** Armenian, Bactrian, Bartangi, Parthian, Scythian **9** Bakhtiari **11** Azerbaijani, Mazandarani

of Iraq: 4 Arab, Kurd **7** Bedouin

of Ireland: 4 Celt, Erse, Gael **5** Irish **6** Celtic **9** Hibernian

of Israel: 3 Jew **4** Arab **5** Druze **10** Circassian

of Italy: 5 Latin **6** Sabine **7** Italian, Lombard **8** Etruscan

of Ivory Coast: 3 Abe, Dan, Kru, Kwa **4** Akan, Bete, Dida, Guro, Koua, Lobi, Wobe **5** Abron, Abure, Attie, Baule, Guere, Mande, Mossi **6** Baoule, Lagoon, Senufo, Senufu **7** Kroumen, Malinke, Voltaic **8** Dan-Gouro **10** Anyi-Baoule **11** Lobi-Kulango **12** Agnis-Ashanti

of Jamaica: 7 African, Chinese **10** East Indian

of Japan: 3 Eta **6** Korean **8** Japanese, Okinawan **10** Buramkumin

of Java: 5 Krama, Kromo **6** Kalang **8** Javanese, Madurese, Sudanese

of Jordan: 4 Arab, Kurd **7** Bedouin, Checher **8** Armenian, Assyrian **10** Circassian **11** Palestinian

of Kazakhstan: 6 Kazakh

of Kenya: 3 Luo **4** Arab, Meru **5** Bantu, Elgey, Galla, Kamba, Kisii, Luhya, Masai, Nandi, Tugen **6** Kikuyu, Ogaden, Somali **7** Baluyha, Hamitic, Hilotic, Kipsigi, Swahili, Turkana **8** Kalenjin, Marakwet

of Kiribati: 8 Banabans **10** Polynesian **11** Micronesian

of Korea: 6 Korean

of Kuwait: 4 Arab **5** Iraqi, Saudi **6** Indian **7** Bedouin **8** Egyptian **9** Pakistani **11** Palestinian

of Kyrgyzstan: 5 Uzbek **6** Kyrgyz **7** Kirghiz

of Laos: 2 Lu **3** Kha, Lao, Man, Meo, Tai, Yao, Yun **4** Miao, Thai **5** Hmong **8** Lao Teung **10** Phoutheung

of Latvia: 3 Kur, Liv **4** Balt, Cour, Lett **7** Latgale, Latvian, Russian, Zemgale

of Lebanon: 4 Arab **9** Canaanite **10** Phoenician **11** Palestinian

of Lesotho: 4 Zulu **5** Bantu, Tembu **6** Basuto **7** Basotho

of Liberia: 2 Gi **3** Gio, Kra, Kru, Kwa, Vai, Vei **4** Gola, Kroo, Krou, Loma, Mano, Toma **5** Bassa, Gibbi, Gissi, Grebo **6** Gbande, Kpelle, Kpuesi, Krooby, Kruman **7** Krooboy, Krooman **8** Mandingo **15** Americo-Liberian

of Libya: 4 Arab, Tebu **6** Berber, Tuareg **7** Gaetuli **8** Getulans, Harratin

of Liechtenstein: 8 Alamanni, Alemanni

of Lithuania: 4 Balt, Lett, Pole **5** Zhmud **6** Jewish, Litvak **7** Aistian, Russian, Yatvyag **10** Lithuanian, Samogitian **11** Belorussian

of Luxembourg: 6 French, German **12** Luxembourger

of Macao: 6 Macaon **7** Chinese **10** Portuguese

of Macedonia: 4 Turk **8** Albanian **10** Macedonian

of Madagascar: 4 Arab, Bara, Hova **5** Malay **6** Merina, Tanala **7** African **8** Betsileo, Mahafaly, Malagasy, Sakalava **9** Antaimoro, Antaisaka, Antandroy, Tsimihety **10** Indonesian, Polynesian **13** Betsimisaraka

of Malawi: 3 Yao **4** Sena **5** Bantu, Lomwe, Ngoni **6** Cheiva, Maravi, Ngonde, Nyanja **7** Tumbuka

of Malaysia: 4 Iban **5** Dayak, Malay **6** Indian **7** Chinese, Kadazan **9** Pakistani, Sri Lankan **10** Bangladesh, Indonesian

of Maldives: 4 Arab **6** Indian **9** Sinhalese **10** Singhalese

of Mali: 3 Bwa **4** Fula, Kyan, Moor, Peul **5** Dogon, Dyula, Fulbe, Marka **6** Berber, Dognon, Fulani, Senufo, Tuareg **7** Bembara, Fellata, Malinke, Miniaka, Songhai, Soninke **8** Khasonke, Mandingo, Senoulfo

of Malta: 7 Maltese

of Mauritania: 4 Arab, Fula, Moor **5** Black, Fulbe, Wolof **6** Bafour, Berber, Fulani **7** African, Soninke, Tukulor **8** Sarakole **9** Sarakolle **10** Toucouleur **12** Halphoolaren

of Mauritius: 6 Creole, French, Indian **7** African, Chinese **8** European **13** Indo-Mauritian

of Mexico: 3 Ixe, Mam, Mie, Ser **4** Chol, Cora, Jova, Meco, Mixe, Pame, Pima, Roto, Seri, Teca, Teco, Texo, Xova **5** Aztec, Chizo, Chora, Mayan, Nahua, Opata, Otomi, Zoque **6** Eudeve, Indian, Mixtec, Pueblo, Toltec, Zotzil **7** Chincha, mestizo, Nahuatl, Nayarit, Spanish, Tehueco, Tepanec, Totonac, Zacatec, Zapotec **8** Lagunero, Mazateca, Tezcucan, Totonaco, Tzapotec, Yucateco, Zacateco, Zapoteca **9** Tlascalan **10** Coahuiltec, Cuitlateco, Tarahumara

of Moldova: 7 Gagauzi **8** Moldovan **9** Moldovian

of Monaco: 6 French **7** Italian **10** Monegasque

of Mongolia: 5 Oirat, Tungu **6** Buryat, Darbet, Khoton, Mongol **7** Kazakhs, Khalkha **8** Tuvinian **9** Dariganga

of Montenegro: 4 Serb, Slav **11** Montenegrin

of Morocco: 4 Arab, Moor **6** Berber, French **7** Spanish

of Mozambique: 3 Yao **5** Bantu, Chopi, Lomue, Lomwe, Macua, Makua, Ngoni, Nguni, Shona **6** Maravi, Thouga **7** Maconde, Makonde **10** Portuguese

of Myanmar: 4 Shan **7** Burmese, Siamese

of Namibia: 4 Nama **5** Bantu **6** Damara, Herero, Ovambo, Tswara **7** Bushman, Colored **8** Okavango **9** Hottentot

of Nauru: 7 Chinese **10** Melanesian, Polynesian **11** Micronesian

of Nepal: 3 Rai **4** Aoul **5** Limbu, Magar, Murmi, Newar, Tharu **6** Gurkha, Gurung, Nepali, Sherpa, Tamang **7** Bhutias, Kiranti **8** Gorkhali, Nepalese

of the Netherlands: 5 Dutch **7** Frisian **9** Hollander **10** Surinamese **12** Netherlander **13** South Moluccan

of New Guinea: 5 Pygmy **6** Papuan **7** Negrito **10** Melanesian

of New Zealand: 3 Ati **5** Arawa, Dutch, Maori **7** British, Ringatu **10** Polynesian

of Nicaragua: 4 Mico, Mixe, Rama, Smoo, Ulva **5** Cukra, Diria, Lenca, Sambo, Toaca **6** Mangue **7** mestizo, Miskito **8** Mosquito **9** Matagalpa

of Niger: 4 Daza, Idjo, Idyo, Idzo, Peul, Teda **5** Hausa, Warri **6** Djerma, Fulani, Kanuri, Songha, Toubou, Tuareg **13** Djerma-Songhai

of Nigeria: 3 Abo, Aro, Djo, Ebo, Edo, Ibo, Ijo, Tiv, Vai **4** Beni, Bini, Eboe, Efik, Egba, Ejam, Ekoi, Idyo, Igbo, Ijaw, Nupe **5** Angas, Benin, Gwari, Hausa **6** Chamba, Fulani, Ibibio, Kanuri, Yoruba **11** Hausa-Fulani

of Norway: 4 Lapp **5** Samme **6** Nordic, Viking

of Oman: 4 Arab

of Pakistan: 5 Sindi, Wazir **6** Afridi, Bengal, Mahsud, Pathan, Puktun, Sindhi **7** Baluchi, Brahuis, Punjabi, Pushtun, Sherani **8** Khattack, Shinwari, Yusefazi **11** Mohammedzai

of Panama: 4 Cuna **5** Choco **6** Guaymi **7** mestizo

of Qatar: 4 Arab **6** Pushtu, Yemeni **7** Baluchi, Iranian **9** Pakistani

of Romania: 6 Dacian **8** Romanian, Rumanian

of Russia: 4 Slav **5** Kulak **6** Jewish, Soviet, Velika **7** Chukchi, Latvian, Russian, Turkmen **8** Armenian, Estonian, Georgian, Siberian, Ukrainian **10** Lithuanian **11** Belorussian

of Rwanda: 3 Twa **4** Hutu **5** Batwa, Pygmy, Tutsi **6** Bahutu, Watusi **7** Batutsi

of Samoa: 6 Samoan **10** Polynesian

of San Marino: 7 Italian **11** San Marinese

of Sao Tome and Principe: 7 African **10** Portuguese **11** Cape Verdean

of Saudi Arabia: 4 Arab **7** Bedouin

of Scotland: 4 Gael, Pict, Scot **5** Norse

of Senegal: 4 Lebu, Peul, Soce **5** Diola, Dyola, Foula, Laobe, Peulh, Serer, Wolof **6** Fulani, Serere **7** Bambara, Malinke, Tukuler, Tukulor **8** Mandingo

of Seychelles: 5 Asian **6** Creole, French, Indian **7** African, Chinese

of Sicily: 5 Elymi, Sican, Sicel **6** Sicani, Siculi

of Sierra Leone: 3 Vai **4** Kono, Loko, Susu **5** Bulom, Kissi, Limba, Mande, Mendi, Temne **6** Creole, Fulani, Syrian **7** Gallina, Koranko, Kuranko, Sherbro, Yalunka **8** Lebanese, Mandingo

of Sikkim: 4 Rong **5** Bhote **6** Bhotia, Bhutia, Indian, Lepcha **7** Tibetan **8** Nepalese **9** Mongoloid

of Singapore: 5 Malay **6** Indian **7** Chinese **9** Malaysian, Pakistani, Sri Lankan

of Slovakia: 5 Czech **6** Slavic, Slovak **9** Hungarian

of Slovenia: 7 Slovene

of the Solomon Islands: 7 Chinese **8** European **10** Melanesian, Polynesian

of Somalia: 3 Sab **4** Asha **5** Galla **6** Hawiya, Isbaak, Somali **7** Danakil, Hamitic, Marehan, Samaale, Shuhali **8** Rahanwin

of South Africa: 4 Boer, Yosa, Zulu **5** Asian, Bantu, Namas, Nguni, Pondo, Sotho, Swazi, Tembu, Venda **6** Damara, Kaffir **7** African, British, Bushmen, English, Swahili **8** Bechuana, Coloured, Khoikhoi, San Xhosa **9** Afrikaner, Hottentot

of Spain: 4 Pict **5** Diego, Gente, Latin **6** Basque, Espana **7** Catalan, Espanol, Iberian **8** Galician, Gallegos, Maragato

of Sri Lanka: 5 Malay, Tamil, Vedda **6** Veddah, Weddah **7** Burgher, Mahinda, Malabar **8** Eurasian **9** Cingalese, Dravidian, Sinhalese **10** Ginghalese **12** Bandaranaike

of the Sudan: 3 Bor, Dor, Fur **4** Arab, Bari, Beri, Bobo, Daza, Egba, Fula, Golo, Nuba, Nuer, Poul, Sere **5** Anuak, Bongo, Dinka, Fulah, Hausa, Joluo, Junje, Mosgu, Mossi, Negro, Tibbu, Volta **6** Acholi, Azande, Gurusi, Hamite, Lotuho, Makari, Nilote, Nubian, Senufo, Surhai, Taureg **7** Balante, Baqqara, Gubayna, Jaaliin, Nilotes, Shilluk, Songhai, Songhay, Songhoi, Sourhai **8** Kababish, Mandingo, Menkiera **9** Sarakille **10** Gurmantshi, Shaiquiyya

of Suriname: 4 Boni, Bush, Trio **5** Djuka, Dutch **6** Creole, Wayana **7** African, Chinese **10** Amerindian, Boschneger, West Indian **11** Asian Indian

of Swaziland: 5 Asian, Bantu, Swazi **10** Eurafrican

of Sweden: 4 Lapp **5** Norse, Swede **6** Viking

of Switzerland: 5 Swiss, **6** Franks **8** Alamanni, Alemanni, Italians **12** Rhaeto-Romans

of Syria: 4 Arab, Kurd, Turk **5** Alawi, Aptal, Druse, Druze **6** Afshar, Aissor, Aushar, Avshar, Awshar **7** Amorite, Ansarie, Bedouin, Nosaris, Saracen, Shemite **8** Ansarieh, Armenian **9** Ansariyah **10** Circassian **12** Khachaturian

of Taiwan: 4 Yami **5** Hakka, Hoklo **7** Chinese, Malayan **9** Fukienese, Taiwanese **10** Indonesian, Polynesian **12** Kwangtungese

of Tajikistan: 5 Tajik, Uzbek **7** Tadzhik

of Tanzania: 2 Ha **4** Arab, Gogo, Goma, Haya, Hehe **5** Asian, Bantu, Masai **6** Arusha, Chagga, Sukuma, Wagogo, Wagoma **7** African, Makonde, Sambara, Sandawe, Shirazi, Swahili, Wabunga, Zongora **8** Nyakyusa, Nyamwezi

of Thailand: 3 Lao, Mon **4** Lawa, Shan, Thai **5** Malay **6** Indian, Khymer **7** Chinese, Siamese **9** Cambodian **10** Vietnamese

of Tibet: 5 Asian, Balti, Bodpa, Drupa **6** Bhotia, Champa, Drokpa, Khamba, Khambu, Mongol, Panaka, Sherpa, Tangut **7** Bhotiya, Bhutani, Gyarung, Taghlik, Tibetan

of Togo: 3 Ana, Ewe, Twi **4** Mina **5** Hausa **6** Akposa, Kabrai **7** Bassari, Cabrais, Kabrais, Ouatchi **8** Konkomba, Kotokoli, Lotokoli

of Tongo: 10 Polynesian

of Trinidad and Tobago: 5 Irish **6** French, Indian, Syrian **7** African, Chinese, English, Spanish **8** European, Lebanese **10** East Indian, Portuguese, Venezuelan **11** Asian Indian **13** Latin American

of Tunisia: 4 Arab **6** Berber, Jewish

of Turkey: 4 Arab, Kurd, Turk **6** Seljuk

of Turkmenistan: 7 Turkmen **10** Turkmenian

of Tuvalu: 6 Samoan **10** Polynesian

of Uganda: 4 Alur, Gisu, Soga, Teso **5** Ateso, Bantu, Chiga, Ganda, Langi, Lango, Nkole, Pygmy **6** Acholi, Ankole, Bagisu, Bakega, Basoga, Batoro **7** Baganda, Banyoro, Bunyoro, Hamitic, Lugbara, Nilotic, Sudanic **9** Nyoro-Toro **10** Banyankole, Karamojong

of Ukraine: 7 Russian **9** Ukrainian

of United Arab Emirates: 4 Arab **6** Indian **7** African, Iranian **9** Pakistani **10** South Asian

of Uruguay: 4 Yaro **5** Swiss **6** Indian **7** Italian, mestizo, Russian, Spanish **8** Charruas

of Uzbekistan: 5 Uzbek

of Vanuatu: 8 European **10** Melanesian, Polynesian **11** Micronesian

of Venezuela: 4 Bare, Pume **5** Bello,

Carib, pardo, zambo **6** Arawak, Creole, Timote **7** Charoya, Guahibo, Kaliana, mestizo, mulatto, Otomaca, Timotex **8** Caquetio, Guarauno, Matilone **11** Maquiritare

of Vietnam: 3 Hoa, Man, Meo, Tai, Tay **4** Cham, Kinh, Nung, Thai **5** Khmer, Malay, Muong **7** Chinese **8** Annamese, Annamite **9** Cambodian **10** montagnard, Vietnamese

of Wales: 4 Celt, Kelt **5** Cymry, Kymry, Welsh **7** Brython, Silures, Taffies **8** Awabokal, Cambrian **9** Siluridan

of Western Sahara: 4 Arab **6** Berber

of Western Samoa: 6 Samoan **10** Melanesian, Polynesian

of Yemen: 4 Arab **5** Zaidi **6** Shafai, Yemeni **8** Yemenite

of Yugoslavia: 4 Serb, Slav **5** Croat **7** Bosnian, Slovene **8** Albanian, Croatian **9** Hungarian **10** Macedonian **11** Montenegrin **13** Herzegovinian

of Zambia: 4 Lozi **5** Bantu, Bemba, Ngoni, Tonga

of Zimbabwe: 3 Ila **4** Sena **5** Asian, Bantu, Bemba, Sotho, Tongo, white **6** Indian **7** Barotse, Chinese, English, Mashona, Mashona, Ndebele **8** Coloured, Japanese, Matabele **9** Afrikaner **10** Balakwakwa

etiquette 5 usage **7** decorum, manners **8** behavior, courtesy, good form, protocol **9** amenities, gentility, good taste **10** civilities, politeness **11** conventions, proprieties **15** rules of behavior

etoile 4 star **9** ballerina

Etruscan
native of: (ancient) **7** Etruria
location: 7 Tuscany
king: 7 Tarquin **11** Lars Porsena

Ettarre
character in: 16 Arthurian romance

ET The Extra-Terrestrial
director: 15 Steven Spielberg
cast: 10 Dee Wallace **11** Henry Thomas, Peter Coyote **13** Drew Barrymore **17** Robert MacNaughton

et tu, Brute 13 and thou Brutus
spoken by: 12 Julius Caesar

etymology 7 history **10** derivation

Etzel
origin: 8 Germanic
mentioned in: 14 Nibelungenlied
represents: 6 Attila
wife: 9 Kriemhild

Eucharist 8 viaticum **9** Communion, sacrament **13** Holy Communion

euchre
number of players: 3 two **4** four **5** three
derived from: 8 triomphe
five tricks won: 5 march
jack of trump: 10 right bower
second highest trump: 9 left bower

Euclid
field: 11 mathematics

nationality: 5 Greek
founder of: 8 geometry
author of: 8 Elements

Eugene Onegin
author: 16 Alexander Pushkin
opera by: 11 Tchaikovsky
character: 4 Olga **6** Lensky, Onegin **7** Tatyana **12** Prince Gremin, Tatyana Larin **14** Vladimir Lensky

Eugenie Grandet
author: 14 Honore de Balzac
character: 5 Nanon **7** Charles, Eugenie **11** Mme d'Aubrion

Euhelopus
type: 8 dinosaur, sauropod
period: 10 Cretaceous

Euler, Leonhard
field: 7 physics **11** mathematics
nationality: 5 Swiss
first: 12 calculus book

eulogize 4 hail, laud, tout **5** boost, exalt, extol **7** acclaim, commend, glorify, magnify **9** celebrate **10** compliment, panegyrize **12** pay tribute to, praise highly

eulogy 5 paean **6** homage **7** hosanna, plaudit, tribute **8** citation, encomium **9** laudation, panegyric **10** high praise **11** acclamation

Eumenides
author: 9 Aeschylus
character: 6 Apollo, Athene, Furies **7** Orestes
see **6** Furies

Eunice
son: 7 Timothy

Eunomia
member of: 5 Horae
personifies: 5 order

Eunuch 6 Biztha, Careas, Zethar **7** Abagtha, Harbona, Mehuman **8** castrato

Eunuch, The
author: 7 Terence

euphemism 11 prudishness, refined term **12** delicate term, overdelicacy **13** prudish phrase **14** mild expression, overrefinement

euphoria 7 ecstasy, elation, rapture **9** well-being

Euphrosyne
member of: 6 Graces

Euphues
character in: 20 Euphues and His England **22** Euphues The Anatomy of Wit
author: 4 Lyly

Euripides
author of: 3 Ion **5** Medea **6** Hecuba **7** Electra, Orestes **8** Alcestis, Heracles **10** Andromache, Heraclidae, Hippolytus, Phoenissae, The Bacchae **13** The Suppliants **14** The Trojan Women **16** Iphigenia in Aulis **17** Iphigenia in Tauris **21** The Children of Heracles

Europa
 also: **6** Europe
 father: **6** Agenor
 mother: **10** Telephassa
 brother: **5** Cilix **6** Cadmus **7** Phoenix
 son: **5** Minos **8** Sarpedon **12** Rhadamanthus
 daughter: **5** Crete
 abducted by: **4** Zeus
Europe see **6** Europa
Europe
 country: **5** Italy, Malta, Spain, Wales
 6 France, Greece, Latvia, Monaco,
 Norway, Poland, Russia, Sweden **7**
 Albania, Andorra, Armenia, Austria,
 Belarus, Belgium, Croatia, Denmark,
 England, Estonia, Georgia, Germany,
 Hungary, Iceland, Ireland, Romania,
 Ukraine **8** Bulgaria, Portugal, Scot-
 land, Slovakia, Slovenia **9** Lithuania,
 Macedonia, San Marino **10** Azerbai-
 jan, Luxembourg, Yugoslavia **11** Bye-
 lorussia, Netherlands, Switzerland,
 Vatican City **13** Czech Republic,
 Liechtenstein **14** Czechoslovakia **17**
 Bosnia Herzegovina
 city: **4** Bern, Bonn, Oslo, Rome **5**
 Paris, Sofia, Vaduz **6** Athens, Dublin,
 Lisbon, London, Madrid, Monaco,
 Moscow, Prague, Tirana, Vienna,
 Warsaw **7** Cardiff **8** Belgrade, Brus-
 sels, Budapest, Helsinki, Valletta **9**
 Amsterdam, Bucharest, Edinburgh,
 Reykjavik, San Marino, Stockholm
 10 Bratislava, Copenhagen, Luxem-
 bourg **14** Andorra la Vella
 river: **3** Don **4** Ebro, Elbe, Oder **5**
 Loire, Neman, Rhine, Rhone, Seine,
 Tagus, Volga **6** Danube, Thames **7**
 Dnieper, Pechora, Vistula **8** Dniester
 island: **3** Man **4** Skye **5** Crete, Malta
 6 Faeroe, Sicily **7** Corsica, Iceland,
 Ireland **8** Balearic, Sardinia **12** British Isles
 mountain/mountain range: **4** Alps **7**
 Balkans **8** Caucasus, Pyrenees **9** Apennines **11** Carpathians **12** Sierra
 Nevada
 highest point: **11** Mount Elbrus
 lowest point: **10** Caspian Sea
 sea: **4** Aral, Azov, Kara **5** Black,
 North, White **6** Aegean, Baltic **7** Caspian, Marmara **8** Adriatic **13** Mediterranean
 people: **3** Hun **4** Gael, Pict, Serb **5**
 Celts, Croat, Danes, Dutch, Jutes,
 Kymry, Marur, Poles, Scots, Slavs,
 Tatar, Welsh **6** Czechs, Franks **7**
 Basques, Britons, Gypsies, Iberian,
 Magyars, Slovaks, Slovene **8** Alamanni, Cossacks, Tyrolean, Walloons
 language: **5** Czech, Irish **6** Basque,
 Danish, French, Gaelic, German, Polish, Slovak **7** English, Italian, Ro-
 mance, Russian, Spanish, Swedish **8**
 Germanic **9** Bulgarian, Portugese **11**
 Balto-slavic
 religion: **5** Islam **6** Jewish, Muslim **8**

Anglican, Lutheran **9** Methodist **10**
 Protestant **12** Presbyterian **13** Dutch
 Reformed, Greek Orthodox, Roman
 Catholic **15** Church of England, Eastern Orthodox
 holiday: **11** Bastille Day, National
 Day **12** Guy Fawkes Day **13** Liberation Day, St Patricks Day **14** Queens
 Birthday **15** Independence Day **19**
 Heroes of the Republic
European Union 2 EU
 currency: **4** euro
 members: **5** Italy, Malta, Spain **6** Cyprus, France, Greece, Latvia, Poland,
 Sweden **7** Austria, Belgium, Denmark, Estonia, Finland, Germany,
 Hungary, Ireland **8** Portugal, Slovakia, Slovenia **9** Lithuania **10** Luxembourg **11** Netherlands **13** Czech Republic, United Kingdom
 predecessor organizations: **3** EEC **25**
 European Economic Community **29**
 European Coal and Steel Community
Eurus
 origin: **5** Greek
 personifies: **8** east wind **13** southeast
 wind
Euryale
 member of: **7** Gorgons
Euryanthe
 opera by: **5** Weber
 character: **6** Adolar **7** Lysiart **9** Eglan-
 tine
Euryclea
 nurse of: **10** Telemachus
Eurydamas
 member of: **9** Argonauts
Eurydice
 also: **7** Agriope
 form: **5** dryad
 husband: **7** Orpheus
 daughter: **8** Themiste
 pursued by: **9** Aristaeus
Eurynome
 father: **7** Oceanus
 mother: **6** Tethys
 sister: **6** Thetis
 daughters: **6** Graces
Eurysthenes
 origin: **7** Spartan
 father: **11** Aristodemus
 twin brother: **7** Procles
 shared: **6** throne
 shared throne with: **7** Procles
Eurystheus
 king of: **6** Tiryns **7** Mycenae
 father: **9** Sthenelus
 mother: **7** Nicippe
 cousin: **8** Hercules
 son: **9** Perimedes
 imposed: **6** labors
  number of labors: **6** twelve
  imposed on: **8** Hercules
Euterpe
 member of: **5** Muses
 muse of: **5** music **11** lyric poetry
evacuate 4 quit **5** leave **6** desert, re-

move, vacate **7** abandon, forsake,
move out, take out **8** order out **12**
withdraw from
evade 4 duck, shun **5** avoid, dodge,
elude, hedge, parry **6** escape, eschew
7 fend off **8** sidestep **10** circumvent,
equivocate **12** steer clear of
evaluate 4 rate **5** assay, gauge, judge,
value, weigh **6** assess, size up **8** appraise, estimate
evaluation 4 test **8** analysis, judgment
9 appraisal **10** assessment, estimation
evaluator 5 judge **6** critic, tester **7** analyst, arbiter **8** assessor, reviewer **9**
appraiser, estimator
evanesce 6 vanish **8** fade away, pass
away **9** disappear, dissipate, evaporate
evanescence 9 vanishing **10** fading
away **12** ephemerality **13** disappearance **14** transitoriness
evanescent 8 fleeting **9** ephemeral,
transient **10** short-lived, transitory
evangel 6 gospel
Evangeline
 author: **24** Henry Wadsworth Longfellow
 character: **17** Gabriel Lajeunesse **23**
 Evangeline Bellefontaine
evangelist 4 John, Luke, Mark **7** apostle, Matthew **8** disciple, minister,
preacher, reformer **9** apostolic, mis-
sioner, soul-saver **10** missionary, revivalist **12** Bible Thumper, propagandist, proselytizer **17** religious crusader
Evan Harrington
 author: **14** George Meredith
 character: **6** Louisa **10** Jack Raikes
 11 Rose Jocelyn **12** Tom Cogglesby
 13 Count de Saldar, Juliana Bonner
 14 Caroline Strike **15** Andrew Cogglesby, Ferdinand Laxley, Melville
 Jocelyn **16** Countess de Saldar, Harriet Cogglesby **21** Melchisedek Harrington
Evans, Dame Edith
 born: **6** London **7** England
 roles: **8** Tom Jones **11** A Doll's House
 13 The Whisperers **14** The Chalk
 Garden **27** The Importance of Being
 Earnest
Evans, Mary Anne
 real name of: **11** George Eliot
Evans, Maurice
 born: **6** Dorset **7** England **10** Dorchester
 roles: **9** Saint Joan **13** Rosemary's
 Baby **14** Man and Superman, Romeo
 and Juliet **15** Heartbreak House,
 Planet of the Apes **17** The Devil's
 Disciple **18** Gilbert and Sullivan **19**
 Androcles and the Lion
evaporate 5 dry up **6** dispel, vanish **7**
scatter **8** dissolve, evanesce, fade
away, melt away, vaporize **9** dehydrate, desiccate, disappear, dissipate
evasion 7 dodging, ducking, eluding **8**

shunning **9** avoidance **12** sidestepping **13** circumventing, shrinking from **15** attempt to escape

evasive 6 shifty **7** devious, dodging, elusive, elusory, hedging **9** ambiguous, deceitful, deceptive, equivocal **10** misleading **11** dissembling **12** equivocating

eve 4 dusk **6** female, sunset **7** evening, sunset **8** eventide **9** day before

Eve
   husband: **4** Adam
   son: **4** Abel, Cain, Seth
   home: **4** Eden

Evelina
   author: **11** Fanny Burney

even 4 calm, fair, flat, just, true **5** equal, flush, level, plane, plumb **6** placid, smooth, square, steady **7** balance, equable, flatten, regular, the same, uniform **8** balanced, constant, equalize, matching, parallel, straight, unbiased **9** equitable, identical, impartial, make flush, unruffled, unvarying **10** straighten, unwavering **11** make uniform, unexcitable **12** even-tempered, make parallel **13** dispassionate

evening 3 e'en, eve **4** dusk, even **6** sunset **7** day's end, sundown **8** eventide, gloaming, twilight **9** nightfall **10** close of day

evenly matched 5 equal **8** of a piece **9** identical **10** well suited **13** one and the same

evenness 7 balance **8** calmness, equality, fairness, flatness, sameness **9** placidity **10** regularity, smoothness, steadiness, uniformity **11** equivalency

event 4 bout, game **7** contest, episode **8** incident, occasion **9** happening, milestone **10** experience, occurrence, tournament **11** competition

even-tempered 5 calm **6** serene **7** equable, patient **11** good-natured, unflappable **12** mild-tempered, well-adjusted

eventful 7 crucial, epochal, fateful, notable, weighty **8** critical, exciting, historic **9** important, memorable, momentous, thrilling **10** noteworthy **11** significant **13** consequential, unforgettable

eventide 4 dusk **6** sunset **7** evening, sundown **8** gloaming, twilight **9** nightfall

eventual 5 final, later **6** coming, future **7** ensuing **8** imminent, ultimate, upcoming **9** following, impending, resulting **10** consequent, subsequent **11** prospective

eventually 6 one day **7** finally **8** in the end, sometime **10** ultimately **12** in the long run **13** sooner or later **17** in the course of time **20** when all is said and done

even up 3 tie **5** align **8** make even **10** straighten

Eve of St Agnes, The
   author: **9** John Keats

ever 5 at all **6** always **7** forever **9** at any time, eternally, in any case **10** at all times, constantly **11** incessantly, perpetually **12** continuously

Everglade State
   nickname of: **7** Florida

evergreen 3 fir, yew **4** pine **5** heath, holly **6** jujube, laurel, myrtle, needle, privet **7** arbutus, casiope, conifer, jasmine, juniper **8** camellia, hawthorn, oleander, rosemary **9** mistletoe, sugarbush **11** conebearing **12** rhododendrum

Evergreen State
   nickname of: **10** Washington

everlasting 7 durable, endless, eternal, lasting, tedious, undying **8** constant, immortal, infinite, timeless, tiresome **9** ceaseless, continual, incessant, perpetual, unceasing, wearisome **10** continuous, ever-living **11** long-lasting, never-ending **12** imperishable, interminable **14** indestructible

evermore 6 always **7** forever **9** eternally **10** for all time **13** everlastingly

ever upward
   Latin: **9** excelsior
   motto of: **7** New York (state)

Everwood
   network: **2** WB
   cast: **9** Sarah Drew (Hannah), Scott Wolf (Jake Hartman) **10** Chris Pratt (Bright Abbott), Tom Amandes (Harold Abbott) **11** Debra Mooney (Edna Abbott Harper), John Beasley (Irv Harper) **12** Emily VanCamp (Amy Abbott), Gregory Smith (Ephram Brown), Merrilyn Gann (Rose Abbott) **13** Treat Williams (Andy Brown), Vivien Cardone (Delia Brown) **15** Stephanie Niznik (Nina Feeney)

everybody
   French: **11** tout le monde

Everybody Loves Raymond
   network: **3** CBS
   cast: **9** Ray Romano (Ray Barone) **10** Peter Boyle (Frank Barone) **11** Brad Garrett (Robert Barone), Monica Horan (Amy MacDougall Barone) **12** Doris Roberts (Marie Barone) **14** Patricia Heaton (Debra Barone)

everyday 4 dull **5** daily, stock, trite, usual **6** common, square **7** mundane, regular, routine **8** familiar, ordinary, workaday **9** customary, hackneyed, quotidian **11** commonplace, day after day, established, stereotyped **12** conventional, run-of-the-mill **13** unimaginative

Everyman
   author: **7** unknown
   character: **3** God **5** Death, Goods **6** Beauty **7** Kindred **8** Strength **9** Good Deeds, Knowledge, Messenger **10** Fellowship

every man for himself
   French: **12** sauve qui peut

Every Man in His Humour
   author: **9** Ben Jonson
   character: **6** Kitely **7** Bridget **8** Bobadill, Wellbred **9** Brainworm, Downright **13** Edward Knowell **14** Justice Clement

Every Man out of His Humour
   author: **9** Ben Jonson
   character: **6** Deliro **7** Fungoso, Sordido **9** Macilente, Sogliardo **10** Puntarvolo **12** Carlo Buffone **15** Fastidious Brisk

everyone
   French: **11** tout le monde

everywhere 7 all over **10** every place, far and near, far and wide, throughout **11** extensively, in all places, universally **12** the world over, ubiquitously **14** to the four winds

evict 4 oust **5** eject, expel **6** remove **7** kick out, turn out **8** dislodge, get rid of, throw out **10** dispossess

evidence 4 fact, sign **5** proof, token **7** exhibit, grounds **9** testimony **10** indication **11** affirmation **12** confirmation, illustration **13** corroboration, documentation, material proof **14** authentication, substantiation **15** exemplification

evident 5 clear, plain **6** patent **7** certain, obvious, visible **8** apparent, manifest, tangible **10** noticeable, undeniable **11** conspicuous, perceptible **12** demonstrable, unmistakable **14** unquestionable **24** plain as the nose on your face

evidently 7 clearly, plainly **9** assumedly, certainly, doubtless, obviously **10** apparently, undeniably **11** doubtlessly **12** unmistakably **14** unquestionably **16** to all appearances

evil 3 bad, sin **4** base, vice, vile **5** venal **6** sinful, wicked **7** heinous, immoral, vicious **8** baseness, iniquity, sinister **9** depravity, malicious, malignant, nefarious, turpitude **10** corruption, immorality, iniquitous, malevolent, pernicious, villainous, wickedness, wrongdoing **12** blackhearted, unprincipled, unscrupulous
   goddess of: **7** Sekhmet

evildoer 6 sinner **7** culprit, villain **9** miscreant, wrongdoer **10** malefactor **12** transgressor

evil-minded 4 base **5** nasty **6** wicked **7** ignoble, immoral **8** depraved **10** despicable, iniquitous, villainous **12** dishonorable, unprincipled

evilness 6 malice **7** cruelty **8** villainy **9** barbarity, malignity **10** sinfulness, wickedness

evince 4 show **6** convey, reveal **7** display, exhibit, express **11** communicate, demonstrate **12** give evidence

Evius *see* **7** Bacchus

Evnissyen
   origin: **5** Welsh
   brother: **4** Bran **10** Manawyddan
   sister: **7** Branwen
   caused: **3** war
      between: **5** Irish **7** British
   killed: **6** nephew

evoke 4 stir **5** rouse, waken **6** arouse, awaken, call up, elicit, excite, induce, invite, invoke, summon **7** produce, provoke, suggest **9** call forth, conjure up, stimulate **10** bring forth

evolution 4 rise **6** change, growth **8** fruition, increase **9** expansion, unfolding **10** maturation **11** development, enlargement, progression **13** metamorphosis
   founder of theory: **13** Charles Darwin
   forerunner of theory: **12** Charles Lyell **18** Chevalier de Lamarck

evolve 4 grow **5** ripen **6** expand, mature, unfold, unroll **7** develop, enlarge **8** increase

Ewell, Tom
   real name: **14** Yewell Tompkins
   born: **11** Owensboro KY
   roles: **8** Adam's Rib **9** State Fair **14** The Great Gatsby **16** Tender Is the Night, The Seven Year Itch

ewer 3 jug, urn **5** basin **6** vessel **7** pitcher

Ewing, Patrick
   sport: **10** basketball
   team: **13** New York Knicks **15** Georgetown Hoyas

exacerbate 3 irk **5** anger **6** deepen, worsen **7** inflame, magnify, provoke, sharpen **8** heighten, increase, irritate **9** aggravate, intensify **10** exaggerate **12** fan the flames **16** pour oil on the fire **17** add insult to injury **18** add fuel to the flames **19** rub salt into the wound

exact 4 take, true **5** claim, force, mulct, right, wrest **6** compel, demand, extort, strict **7** careful, correct, extract, literal, precise, require, squeeze **8** accurate, clear-cut, exacting, explicit, specific **9** on the head, on the nose **10** methodical, meticulous, scrupulous, systematic **11** painstaking, punctilious, to the letter, unequivocal

exacting 4 hard **5** harsh, rigid, stern, tough **6** severe, strict, trying **7** arduous **8** critical **9** demanding, difficult, hard-nosed, strenuous, unbending, unsparing **10** hard-headed, meticulous, no-nonsense

exactly 4 just **5** fully, quite, truly **6** indeed, just so, wholly **7** quite so **8** entirely, of course, strictly **9** assuredly, certainly, correctly, literally, precisely

10 absolutely, accurately, definitely, explicitly, that's right **12** specifically

exactness 8 accuracy **9** precision **10** exactitude **12** accurateness

exact satisfaction 6 avenge, punish **7** get back, get even, revenge **9** retaliate **14** get one's own back

exaggerate 5 boast **6** overdo **7** amplify, lay it on, magnify, stretch **9** embellish, embroider, enlarge on, overstate **11** hyperbolize

exaggerated 7 extreme, intense **10** inordinate, overstated **14** overemphasized

exalt 4 laud **5** cheer, elate, extol, honor **6** praise, uplift **7** acclaim, applaud, commend, elevate, ennoble, glorify, inspire, magnify, worship **8** venerate **9** celebrate, stimulate **10** exhilarate, make much of **12** pay tribute to

exaltation 4 high **5** bliss, glory, honor **6** praise **7** dignity, ecstasy, elation, rapture, tribute, worship **8** grandeur, nobility, praising **9** happiness, panegyric, transport **10** eulogizing, exultation, veneration **11** celebration, deification **12** exhilaration

exalted 2 up **5** grand, happy, lofty, noble **6** august, elated, lordly **7** excited, notable **8** blissful, ecstatic, elevated, glorious, inspired, uplifted **9** dignified, honorable, rapturous, venerable **10** heightened **11** high-ranking, illustrious, magnificent

exaltedness 5 bliss **6** height **7** ecstasy, elation, heights, rapture **8** highness, nobility **9** elevation, loftiness, transport

examination 4 exam, quiz, test **5** assay, audit, final, orals, probe, study **6** review, survey **7** midterm, perusal **8** analysis, scrutiny **10** inspection **11** looking over **13** investigation **15** physical checkup

examine 4 pump, quiz, scan, test, view **5** audit, grill, probe, query, study **6** peruse, ponder, review, survey **7** explore, inspect, observe **8** consider, look into, look over, question **10** scrutinize **11** inquire into, interrogate, investigate, take stock of

examiner 6 tester **8** inquirer, reviewer, surveyor **12** interrogator, investigator

example 5 ideal, model **6** sample **7** paragon, pattern **8** exemplar, specimen, standard **9** archetype, prototype **11** case in point **12** illustration **14** representation **15** exemplification

exasperate 3 bug, irk, vex **4** rile **5** anger, annoy, chafe, pique **6** bother, enrage, harass, madden, offend, rankle, ruffle **7** incense, provoke, turn off **8** irritate **9** aggravate, infuriate **15** try one's patience

exasperating 7 irksome **8** annoying **9** vexatious **10** irritating **11** infuriating

Excalibur 5 sword
   drawn from: **5** stone
      by: **6** Arthur
   given by: **5** Nimue **7** Viviane **13** Lady of the Lake

ex cathedra 12 from the chair **13** with authority **22** from the seat of authority

excavate 3 dig **4** mine **5** dig up, gouge **6** burrow, cut out, dig out, furrow, groove, quarry, tunnel **7** uncover, unearth **8** scoop out **9** hollow out **11** make a hole in

excavation 3 dig, pit **4** hole, mine, sump **5** ditch, grave, shaft, space **6** cavity, dugout, trench, trough **7** digging, opening

exceed 4 pass **5** excel **6** go over, outrun, overdo **7** outpace, outrank, surpass **8** go beyond, outreach, outrival, outstrip, surmount **9** come first, overshoot, transcend **10** be superior **11** predominate

exceedingly 4 very **6** vastly **7** greatly, notably **9** amazingly, eminently, extremely, supremely, unusually **10** enormously, especially, unwontedly, very highly **11** excessively **12** immeasurably, impressively, inordinately, preeminently, surpassingly **13** astonishingly, outstandingly, superlatively **15** extraordinarily

excel 4 outdo **6** exceed **7** prevail, surpass **8** outrival, outstrip **9** rank first **10** tower above **11** predominate, take the cake **20** walk off with the honors

excellence 5 merit **7** quality **8** eminence **9** greatness **10** perfection **11** distinction, high quality, preeminence, superiority **13** transcendence

excellent 4 aces, A-one, fine, tops **5** great, nifty, prime, super, swell **6** bang-up, choice, grade A, superb **7** capital, classic, notable **8** peerless, sterling, superior, terrific, top-notch **9** admirable, exemplary, first-rate, matchless, superfine, wonderful **10** first-class, preeminent, tremendous **11** exceptional, outstanding, superlative

excelsior 10 ever upward
   motto of: **7** New York (state)

Excelsior State
   nickname of: **7** New York

except 3 ban, bar, but **4** omit, save **6** enjoin, excuse, exempt, reject, remove, saving **7** barring, besides, exclude, shut out **8** count out, disallow, pass over **9** eliminate, excepting, excluding, other than **11** exclusive of

excepted 6 exempt **7** excused **8** excluded **11** not included

exception 6 oddity, rarity **7** anomaly, removal **8** omission **9** debarment, deviation, exclusion, exemption, isolation, rejection, seclusion **10** difference, leaving out, separation **11** elimination, peculiarity, repudiation, segregation, shutting out, special case **12** disallowment, irregularity, renunciation **13** inconsistency

exceptional 3 odd **4** rare **5** great, queer **6** unique **7** special, strange, unusual **8** aberrant, abnormal, atypical, freakish, peculiar, singular, superior, terrific, uncommon, unwonted **9** anomalous, excellent, irregular, marvelous, unheard of, unnatural, wonderful **10** first-class, inimitable, noteworthy, out-of-sight, phenomenal, remarkable **11** outstanding **12** incomparable **13** extraordinary, unprecedented

exception to the rule 7 anomaly **11** abnormality **12** irregularity

excerpt 4 part **5** piece **7** extract, portion, section **8** abstract, fragment **9** quotation, selection **13** quoted passage

excess 4 glut **5** extra, flood, spare **7** residue, surfeit, surplus, too much **8** fullness, overflow, plethora **9** avalanche, excessive, profusion, remainder, repletion **10** inundation, lavishness, oversupply **11** undue amount **13** overabundance **14** superabundance

excessive 5 undue **6** excess **7** extreme, profuse, too much **8** needless **9** senseless **10** immoderate, inordinate **11** exaggerated, extravagant, superfluous, unnecessary **12** overabundant, unreasonable **16** disproportionate

excessively 5 enorm **7** greatly **9** extremely, intensely **11** exceedingly, fanatically **12** boisterously, exorbitantly, inordinately **14** overabundantly

exchange 4 swap **5** trade **6** barter, switch **8** bandying, trade off **9** tit for tat **10** quid pro quo **11** convert into, give-and-take, interchange, reciprocate, reciprocity

exchange blows 3 box **5** clash, fight **6** battle, combat, tussle **7** contend, contest, grapple **8** skirmish **11** cross swords

exchange of viewpoints 6 debate, parley **8** dialogue **10** conference, discussion

exchange premium 4 agio

exchange views 6 confer, debate **7** consult, discuss **8** consider, talk over **12** compare notes

excise 3 tax **4** duty **6** cut off, cut out, impost, remove **7** extract **8** pluck out **9** eradicate, surcharge

excitable 4 edgy **5** jumpy **7** jittery, nervous **8** feverish, frenzied, skittish **9** flappable, hotheaded **10** highstrung, passionate **11** combustible, inflammable

excite 4 fire, move, whet **5** evoke, pique, rouse, waken **6** arouse, awaken, elicit, foment, incite, kindle, spur on, stir up, thrill **7** agitate, animate, inflame, provoke **8** energize **9** electrify,

galvanize, instigate, stimulate, titillate **13** get a kick out of

excited 4 daft **5** afire, astir **6** ablaze **7** aroused **8** agitated, ecstatic, frenzied, inflamed, turned on **9** disturbed, stirred up **10** magnetized **11** electrified

excitement 3 ado **4** flap, stir, to-do **5** furor, kicks **6** action, flurry, frenzy, hoopla, thrill, tumult **7** elation, ferment, flutter, turmoil **8** activity, brouhaha, interest **9** adventure, agitation, animation, commotion, fireworks **10** enthusiasm **11** stimulation

exciting 5 spicy **6** moving, risque **7** rousing, zestful **8** dazzling, stirring **9** affecting, impelling, inspiring, thrilling **11** hair-raising, provocative, sensational, stimulating, titillating **12** breathtaking, electrifying **13** spinetingling

exclaim 4 howl, yell **5** shout **6** bellow, cry out **7** call out **8** proclaim **9** ejaculate **10** vociferate

exclamation 3 cry **4** howl, yell, yelp **5** shout **6** bellow, outcry, shriek, squeal **7** screech **9** expletive **11** ejaculation **12** interjection, vociferation

exclamation of:

approval: 3 ole, rah **5** bravo

despair: 4 alas **5** alack **7** woe is me

dicovery: 3 aha, oho

disdain: 3 duh, hah, tsk **4** bosh, bunk, pooh

disgust: 3 bah, ugh **4** damn, darn, drat, pfui, rats **5** shoot **6** humbug, phooey

joy: 3 yay **4** whee, yeah **6** hooray, hurrah, hurray **7** whoopie

pain: 4 ouch **5** yipes

relief: 4 phew, whew

other: 3 fie, hah, hey, tut, wow **4** oops, scat, shoo, ta-da **5** voila **6** hoopla

bacchanalian cry: 4 evoe

exclude 3 ban, bar **4** omit, oust **5** eject, evict, expel **6** banish, except, forbid, refuse, reject, remove **7** boycott, keep out, rule out, shut out **8** disallow, leave out, prohibit, set aside, throw out **9** blackball, repudiate **13** shut the door on

excluding 3 but **4** save **6** except, saving **7** banning, barring, besides **9** excepting, other than **10** keeping out

exclusion 6 ouster **7** barring, refusal, removal **8** ejection, eviction **9** debarment, dismissal, expelling, expulsion, rejection, restraint **10** banishment, keeping out, preclusion, prevention **11** prohibition, throwing out **12** nonadmission

exclusive 4 full, posh, sole **5** aloof, total **6** closed, entire, single **7** private **8** absolute, clannish, cliquish, complete, snobbish, unshared **9** undivided, selective **10** restricted **11** restrictive

exclusive of 3 but **4** save **6** except, saving **7** barring, besides **9** excepting, excluding, other than

excommunicate 3 ban **4** oust **5** eject, expel **6** banish, remove **8** unchurch **12** anathematize

excommunication 3 ban **6** ouster **8** anathema **10** banishment **12** proscription

excoriate 4 flay **5** curse **6** berate, revile **7** censure **8** denounce, execrate **9** skin alive

excrescence 4 bump, hump, knob, knot, lump **5** bulge, gnarl **6** nodule **8** swelling **10** protrusion **12** protuberance

excrete 4 void **5** expel **8** evacuate **9** discharge, eliminate

excruciating 5 acute **6** fierce, severe **7** cutting, extreme, intense, racking, violent **9** agonizing, exquisite, torturous **10** lacerating, tormenting, unbearable **11** unendurable **12** insufferable

exculpate 5 clear **6** acquit, excuse, pardon **7** absolve **9** exonerate, let one off, vindicate

excursion 4 hike, ride, tour, trek, trip, walk **5** drive, jaunt, sally, tramp **6** cruise, flight, junket, outing, ramble, sortie, stroll, voyage **10** expedition **12** pleasure trip

excusatory 9 defensive **10** apologetic **11** extenuatory, vindicatory **13** justificatory

excuse 4 free **5** alibi, clear, spare **6** acquit, defend, exempt, let off, pardon, reason **7** absolve, condone, defense, explain, forgive, indulge, justify, release **8** argument, bear with, mitigate, overlook, palliate, pass over **9** disregard, exculpate, exemption, exonerate, extenuate, gloss over, let one off, relieve of, vindicate, whitewash **10** absolution **11** exoneration, vindication **12** apologize for **13** justification **16** make allowance for **17** accept one's apology

execrable 4 vile **5** awful **8** dreadful, terrible **9** atrocious, revolting **10** abominable

execrate 4 hate **5** abhor **6** detest, loathe **7** despise **9** abominate, can't stand, excoriate **10** shrink from **11** can't stomach **12** be revolted by **13** be nauseated by, find repulsive **15** be disgusted with **20** regard with repugnance

execration 4 hate **6** hating **7** disgust **8** loathing **9** despising, repulsion, revulsion **10** repugnance **11** abomination, detestation

execute 2 do **3** act **4** kill, play, slay **5** enact **6** effect, murder, render **7** achieve, enforce, fulfill, perform, realize, sustain **8** carry out, complete, massacre **9** discharge **10** accomplish, administer, consummate, effectuate, perpetrate, put to death **11** assassinate **12** carry through **13** put into effect

execution 5 doing **7** killing, slaying **9** discharge, effecting, rendition **10** completion **11** achievement, carrying out, fulfillment, performance, realization, transaction **14** accomplishment, administration, implementation, interpretation, putting to death

executioner 6 hit man, killer, slayer **7** butcher, hangman **8** assassin, murderer

Executioner's Song, The
author: **12** Norman Mailer
subject: **11** Gary Gilmore

executive 3 CEO, CFO **4** suit **7** manager **8** chairman, director, overseer **9** president **10** leadership, managerial, supervisor **11** directorial, supervisory **13** administrator **14** administrative, superintendent

executives 5 suits **7** leaders **8** managers, officers **9** directors **13** governing body **14** administration

executor 4 doer **5** agent **9** performer **13** administrator

exegesis 10 exposition **11** explanation **14** interpretation **18** explication de texte

exemplar 5 ideal, model **7** example, pattern **8** original, specimen, standard **9** archetype, prototype

exemplary 5 ideal, model **6** sample **7** typical **8** laudable, sterling **9** admirable, emulative, estimable, nonpareil **10** noteworthy **11** commendable, meritorious **12** illustrative, praiseworthy **14** characteristic, representative

exemplification 7 epitome, essence, example **8** citation, evidence **10** embodiment **11** case in point **12** illustration **13** documentation **14** representation **15** personification

exemplify 6 depict, embody, typify **8** instance **9** epitomize, personify, represent **10** illustrate **11** demonstrate **12** characterize

exempli gratia 6 such as **10** for example **19** for the sake of example
abbreviation: **2** eg

exempt 4 free **5** clear, freed, spare **6** except, excuse, immune, pardon, spared **7** absolve, cleared, excused, release, relieve **8** absolved, excepted, relieved **9** not liable, privilege **10** privileged

exemption 6 excuse **7** expense, freedom, release **8** immunity **9** allowance, deduction, exception **10** absolution **12** dispensation

exercise 3 use **4** show **5** apply, drill, exert, teach, train, tutor, wield **6** employ, school, warm-up **7** break in, develop, display, execute, exhibit, perform, prepare, program, utilize, workout **8** accustom, aerobics, carry

out, ceremony, movement, practice, training **9** discharge, inculcate, schooling **10** daily dozen, discipline, employment, gymnastics, isometrics **11** application, demonstrate, give lessons, performance, utilization **12** calisthenics **14** do calisthenics

exert 3 use **5** apply, wield **6** employ, expend **7** utilize **8** exercise, put forth, resort to **9** discharge, make use of **11** put in action, set in motion

exertion 4 toil, work **5** labor, pains **6** effort, energy **7** travail, trouble **8** activity, endeavor, industry, strength, struggle **11** application, elbow grease

ex facie 9 on the face **10** apparently **11** from the face

ex facto 8 actually **15** according to fact

exhalation 4 puff **6** breath, wheeze, whoosh **10** expiration **12** breathing out

exhale 4 huff, pant, puff **6** expire **7** breathe, respire **10** breathe out

exhaust 3 fag, tax **4** bush, poop, tire **5** drain, empty, spend, use up **6** expend, finish, strain, weaken **7** consume, deplete, disable, draw off, draw out, fatigue, wear out **8** enervate, overtire **9** dissipate **10** debilitate, devitalize, run through **13** sap one's energy

exhausted 4 beat, gone **5** all in, spent **6** bushed, done in, pooped, used up **7** drained, emptied, wearied, worn out **8** bankrupt, consumed, depleted, expended, fatigued, finished, tired out **9** dead tired, enervated, played out **11** devitalized **12** impoverished

exhausting 5 tough **6** tiring, uphill **7** arduous **8** toilsome **9** difficult, fatiguing, Herculean, laborious, Sisyphean, wearisome **10** burdensome

exhaustion 7 fatigue, using up **8** draining, spending **9** depletion, tiredness, weariness **10** enervation **11** consumption

exhaustive 6 all-out **7** in-depth **8** complete, profound, sweeping, thorough **9** intensive **12** all-embracing, all-inclusive **13** comprehensive

exhibit 3 air **4** show **6** flaunt, parade, reveal, unveil **7** display **8** brandish **9** put on view **10** exhibition, exposition, make public **11** demonstrate **12** bring to light **13** public showing

exhibition 4 show **5** array **7** display, exhibit, showing **9** unveiling **10** exposition **13** demonstration, public showing

exhibitionist 7 flasher, show-off **15** attention-seeker

exhilarate 4 lift **5** cheer, elate **6** excite, perk up **7** animate, delight, enliven, gladden, hearten, quicken **9** stimulate **10** invigorate

exhilaration 6 gaiety **7** delight, elation **8** gladness, vivacity **9** animation **10** exaltation, excitement, joyousness, liveliness **11** high spirits **16** lightheartedness

exhort 3 bid **4** goad, prod, spur, urge **5** egg on, press **6** advise, enjoin **7** beseech, implore **8** admonish, advocate, appeal to, persuade **9** encourage, plead with, recommend **14** give a pep talk to

exhortation 6 sermon, urging **7** bidding, lecture, pep talk **8** dictates, harangue, prodding **9** prompting

exhumation 9 digging up **12** disinterment **13** disentombment

exhume 5 dig up **8** disinter

exigency 3 fix, jam **5** needs, pinch **6** crisis, pickle, plight, scrape, strait **7** demands **8** hardship, quandary **9** emergency, extremity, urgencies **10** difficulty **11** constraints, contingency, necessities, predicament **12** circumstance, requirements

exigent 5 vital **6** urgent **8** critical, exacting, pressing **9** demanding, difficult, necessary

exile 2 DP **4** oust **5** eject, expel **6** banish, deport, emigre, pariah **7** outcast, refugee **8** drive out, expellee **9** expulsion **10** banishment, expatriate

Exile, The
author: **9** Pearl Buck

exiled person 5 exile **6** emigre **7** outcast **8** expellee **10** expatriate

exist 4 last, live, stay **5** abide, ensue, occur **6** endure, happen, obtain, remain **7** breathe, prevail, survive

existence 4 life **5** being **7** reality **8** presence, survival **9** actuality, animation, endurance **11** continuance, materiality, subsistence, tangibility

existent 4 real **5** alive **6** actual, extant, living **7** present **8** existing, tangible **9** surviving, to be found **11** in existence

existing 4 real **5** being **6** actual, extant, living **7** ongoing, present **9** existence, surviving, to be found **10** continuing, prevailing **11** established, in existence **12** accomplished

exit 4 blow **5** go out, leave, split **6** cut out, depart, egress, escape, exodus, way out **7** retreat **8** withdraw **9** departure **10** withdrawal **11** take a powder

ex libris 15 out of the books of **16** from the library of

ex nihilo nihil fit 25 out of nothing nothing is made **27** nothing is created from nothing

exocuticle
consists of: **9** sclerotin

exodus 4 exit **5** exile **6** flight, hegira **9** departure, migration **10** emigration, going forth

Exodus
  author: **8** Leon Uris
  story of founding of: **6** Israel
exonerate 4 free **5** clear **6** acquit **7** absolve, forgive **9** exculpate, vindicate **12** find innocent
exoneration 8 clearing **10** absolution **11** exculpation, vindication
exorbitant 4 dear **5** undue **6** costly **7** extreme **8** enormous **9** egregious, excessive, expensive, out-of-line **10** high-priced, inordinate, oppressive, outrageous, overpriced **11** extravagant **12** extortionate, preposterous, unreasonable
exorcise 5 expel **7** cast out **8** get rid of
Exorcist, The
  author: **18** William Peter Blatty
  director: **15** William Friedkin
  cast: **8** Lee J Cobb **10** Linda Blair **11** Jason Miller, Max von Sydow **12** Ellen Burstyn
  Oscar for: **10** screenplay
exoskeleton
  of insect: **5** shell **8** body wall
  part: **10** epicuticle, exocuticle **11** endocuticle
exoteric 4 open **6** public, simple **7** popular **8** exterior, external, outsider
exotic 5 alien **6** quaint, unique **7** foreign, strange, unusual **8** colorful, peculiar, striking **9** different, not native **10** from abroad, intriguing, outlandish, unfamiliar **11** exceptional **13** not indigenous
expand 4 grow, open **5** swell, widen **6** dilate, evolve, extend, fatten, spread, unfold, unfurl, unroll **7** amplify, augment, develop, distend, enlarge, inflate, magnify, stretch, unravel **8** heighten, increase, multiply **9** outspread, spread out **10** aggrandize
expanded 4 grew **5** grown **7** dilated, swelled, swollen, widened **8** enlarged, extended, unfolded, unfurled, unrolled **9** augmented, broadened, increased, outspread, spread out, stretched **10** heightened **11** aggrandized
expanse 4 area **5** field, range, reach, space, sweep **6** extent **7** breadth, compass, stretch **9** magnitude
expansion 6 growth **8** dilation, increase, swelling, widening **9** enlarging, extension, spreading **10** amplifying, distention, magnifying, stretching **11** development, enlargement, lengthening, multiplying **12** augmentation **13** amplification
expansive 4 free, open, vast, wide **5** broad **6** genial **7** affable, amiable, general, liberal **8** effusive, generous, outgoing **9** bounteous, bountiful, capacious, extensive, exuberant **10** voluminous **11** extroverted, far-reaching, uninhibited, unrepressed, wideranging **12** unrestrained **13** comprehensive

expatiate 6 expand **7** amplify, enlarge, expound **9** discourse, elaborate
expatriate 2 DP **5** exile **6** emigre, pariah **7** outcast, refugee **15** displaced person
expatriation 5 exile **9** expulsion **10** banishment
expect 5 guess, trust **6** assume, demand, plan on, reckon **7** believe, count on, foresee, hope for, imagine, look for, presume, require, suppose, surmise **8** envision, reckon on, rely upon **9** calculate **10** anticipate, bargain for, conjecture, reckon upon **11** contemplate **13** look forward to
expectancy 11 expectation **12** anticipation
expectant 4 agog **5** eager, ready **7** anxious, hopeful, waiting **9** expecting **10** looking for, optimistic **12** anticipating, apprehensive
expectation 4 hope **5** trust **6** belief, chance **8** prospect, reliance **9** assurance **10** confidence, expectancy, likelihood **11** presumption **12** anticipation **13** contemplation
expedient 4 help, wise **5** means **6** resort, tactic, useful **7** benefit, helpful, measure, politic, selfish, stopgap **9** advantage, advisable, conniving, desirable, effective, judicious, makeshift, opportune, practical, strategem **10** beneficial, instrument, profitable, worthwhile **11** calculating, selfseeking, self-serving **12** advantageous
expedite 4 rush **5** hurry **6** hasten **7** advance, forward, further, promote, quicken, speed up **8** dispatch **10** accelerate, facilitate **11** precipitate, push through
expedition 4 trek **6** voyage **7** journey, mission **8** campaign, voyagers **9** explorers, travelers, wayfarers **10** enterprise **11** adventurers, exploration
expeditious 4 fast **5** alert, awake, hasty, quick, rapid, ready, swift **6** prompt, snappy, speedy **7** instant **8** punctual **9** effective, immediate **10** bright-eyed **11** efficacious
expel 4 fire, oust, sack, spew, void **5** eject, evict, exile **6** banish, bounce, remove **7** cashier, cast out, dismiss, drum out, excrete **8** dislodge, drive out, evacuate, force out, throw out **9** discharge, eliminate
expellee 2 DP **5** exile **14** banished person **15** displaced person
expend 3 pay **4** give **5** drain, empty, spend, use up **6** donate, lay out, pay out **7** consume, exhaust, fork out, wear out **8** disburse, dispense, shell out, squander **9** dissipate, go through **10** contribute
expendable 7 payable **9** available, forgoable, spendable **10** consumable, extraneous **11** disbursable, dispensable,

replaceable, superfluous **12** nonessential **14** relinquishable
expended 5 spent **6** used up **7** drained, emptied, paid out **8** consumed **9** disbursed, exhausted **10** dissipated
expenditure 3 use **4** cost **5** price **6** charge, outlay, output **7** payment **8** exertion, expenses, spending **9** expending, paying out **10** employment, money spent **11** application, consumption **12** disbursement
expense 4 cost, rate **5** drain, price **6** amount, charge, figure, outlay **9** depletion, quotation
expensive 4 dear **6** costly **9** excessive **10** exorbitant, high-priced, immoderate, overpriced **11** extravagant **12** uneconomical, unreasonable **15** beyond one's means
experience 3 see **4** bear, feel, know, meet, view **5** doing, event, sense **6** affair, behold, endure, suffer **7** episode, observe, sustain, undergo **8** exposure, incident, perceive, practice, training **9** adventure, encounter, go through, happening, seasoning, withstand **10** occurrence **11** familiarity, live through, observation **17** personal knowledge **18** firsthand knowledge
experienced 4 able, wise **6** expert, master **7** capable, knowing, skilled, trained, veteran **8** seasoned **9** competent, efficient, practical, qualified **10** well-versed **11** worldly-wise **12** accomplished **13** sophisticated
experiential 9 empirical, firsthand, practical
experiment 4 test **5** assay, flier, trial **6** feeler, try out **7** analyze, examine, explore, venture **8** analysis, research **11** examination, investigate **12** seek proof for, verification **13** investigation **14** mess around with
experimental 3 new **4** test **5** fresh, rough, trial **7** radical **9** tentative **10** conceptual, first-draft **11** conjectural, speculative **13** developmental, trial-and-error
experimentation 7 testing **8** analysis, research **10** experiment **11** examination, exploration **13** investigation, trial and error
experimenter 6 tester **10** researcher **15** experimentalist
expert 3 ace, apt, pro, wiz **4** able, deft, whiz **5** adept, crack, doyen, maven, mavin, shark **6** adroit, artist, facile, master, wizard **7** artiste, capable, perfect, skilled, trained, veteran **8** masterly, skillful, virtuoso **9** authority, competent, masterful, practiced, qualified **10** first-class, past-master, proficient, specialist **11** connoisseur, crackerjack, experienced **12** accomplished, professional **13** knowledgeable
  French: **6** au fait

expertise 5 savvy, skill 7 know-how 10 expertness 12 special skill 14 specialization 15 professionalism

expertness 5 savvy, skill 7 ability, know-how 8 training 9 expertise 10 capability, competence, experience 11 proficiency 12 special skill 13 qualification 14 accomplishment, specialization 15 professionalism

expiate 7 appease 8 atone for 13 make amends for 16 pay the penalty for

expiation 6 amends, shrift 7 penance 9 atonement 11 appeasement 16 paying the penalty

expiration 3 end 5 death, dying 6 demise, ending, finish 7 passing, closing 8 decrease, exhaling 10 conclusion 11 termination 12 breathing out

expire 3 die, end 5 cease, lapse 6 finish, perish, run out 7 decease, kick off, succumb 8 conclude, pass away 9 terminate 11 come to an end, discontinue 13 kick the bucket 14 give up the ghost

expired 4 dead, died 6 lapsed, ran out, run out 7 defunct, laspsed 8 deceased, lifeless, perished 10 passed away 11 came to an end, come to an end 14 gave up the ghost

explain 6 fathom 7 clarify, clear up, justify, resolve 8 describe, spell out 9 elucidate, explicate, interpret, make clear, make plain 10 account for, illuminate, illustrate 11 demonstrate, rationalize 14 give a reason for 20 give an explanation for

explainer 6 critic 7 analyst 8 reviewer 10 translator 11 commentator, interpreter

explanation
French: 15 eclaircissement

explicate 7 analyze, clarify, develop, explain 8 annotate 9 elucidate, interpret 10 elucidated, illuminate, illustrate

explication 8 analysis 10 commentary 11 elucidation, explanation 12 illumination 13 clarification 14 interpretation

explication de texte 8 exegesis 11 explanation 14 interpretation 17 literary criticism

explicit 5 blunt, clear, exact, frank, plain 6 candid, direct 7 certain, express, pointed, precise 8 absolute, definite, distinct, specific 9 outspoken 10 unreserved 11 categorical, unequivocal, unqualified 15 straightforward 16 clearly expressed

explicitness 7 clarity 9 clearness, precision 11 unambiguity

explode 5 belie, blast, burst, erupt, go off 6 blow up, expose, refute, set off 7 destroy 8 detonate, disprove 9 discredit, repudiate 10 invalidate, prove

false, prove wrong 11 burst loudly 12 utter noisily 14 burst violently, express noisily 18 discharge violently 19 burst out emotionally

exploit 4 feat 5 abuse 6 misuse 7 utilize 8 profit by, put to use 9 adventure, brave deed, heroic act, make use of 10 daring deed 11 achievement 12 capitalize on 14 accomplishment, use to advantage 15 take advantage of

exploited 6 abused 7 ill-used, misused 11 downtrodden 15 took advantage of 16 taken advantage of

exploration 5 probe 7 inquiry 8 scrutiny 9 discovery 10 expedition, experiment 11 examination 12 scouting trip 13 investigation

explore 3 try 5 plumb, probe, scout 6 survey, try out 7 analyze, examine, feel out, pry into 8 look into, research, traverse 9 delve into, penetrate, range over 10 scrutinize, search into, travel over 11 inquire into, investigate, reconnoiter 14 experiment with

explorer
American: 4 Byrd, Pike 5 Boone, Clark, Lewis, Peary, Perry
Australian: 4 Hume 5 Sturt 6 Stuart 8 Mitchell
British: 4 Bell, Cook, Park 5 Baker, Bligh, Bruce, Cabot, Davis, Drake, Grant, Puget, Scott, Smith, Speke 6 Baffin, Burton, Hudson, Lander 7 Raleigh, Stanley 8 Franklin 9 Frobisher, MacKenzie, Vancouver 10 Shackleton 11 Livingstone
Danish: 6 Bering 7 Niebuhr
Dutch: 6 Tasman 7 Barents, Le Maire 8 Schouten 10 Linschoten
French: 6 Joliet 7 Cartier, Jolliet, La Salle 9 Champlain, Marquette 12 Bougainville
Italian: 8 Columbus 9 Marco Polo, Verrazano 15 Amerigo Vespucci
Moslem: 10 Ibn Battuta
Norwegian: 8 Amundsen
Portuguese: 3 Cam, Cao 4 Dias, Diaz 6 Cabral, Da Gama 7 Almeida 8 Covilhao, Magellan 11 Albuquerque 23 Prince Henry the Navigator
Russian: 10 Middendorf 11 Przhevalsky
Spanish: 6 Balboa, Cortes, De Soto 7 Pizarro 8 Coronado, Orellana, Valdivia 11 Ponce de Leon
Swedish: 12 Nordenskjold
Viking: 10 Eric the Red 11 Leif Ericson

explosion 3 fit 4 clap 5 blast, burst, crack 6 report 7 tantrum 8 eruption, outbreak, outburst, paroxysm 9 blowing up, discharge 10 detonation 11 fulmination

explosive 3 TNT 5 shaky, tense 6 touchy 7 cordite, keyed up 8 critical, dynamite, perilous, strained, ticklish,

unstable, volatile 9 dangerous, emotional, gelignite 10 ammunition, precarious 12 pyrotechnics 13 nitroglycerin

exponent 6 backer 8 advocate, champion, defender, promoter 9 expounder, proponent, spokesman, supporter 12 propagandist

export 7 send out 8 dispatch 10 sell abroad 11 foreign sale 12 ship overseas

expose 4 bare, risk, show 5 brand, offer, strip 6 betray, denude, divest, hazard, let out, reveal, submit 7 display, divulge, exhibit, imperil, let slip, subject, uncover, unearth 8 denounce, disclose, endanger 10 jeopardize, reveal to be 12 acquaint with, bring to light 16 leave unprotected

exposé 6 baring 8 exposure 10 divulgence, revelation

exposed 4 open 5 bared 8 divulged, laid open, revealed, unmasked 9 denounced, disclosed, displayed, uncovered, unearthed 11 unprotected, unsheltered

exposition 4 expo, fair, mart, show 6 bazaar, market 7 account, display, exhibit, picture 8 exegesis 9 trade fair, trade show 10 commentary, exhibition, world's fair 11 description, elucidation, explanation, explication 12 illustration, presentation 13 clarification, demonstration 14 interpretation

expostulate 5 argue 6 enjoin, exhort, object, reason 7 caution, counsel, protest 8 forewarn 9 plead with 11 remonstrate 13 cry out against, reason against 14 inveigh against

exposure 4 view 5 vista 6 expose 7 outlook 8 frontage, prospect 9 divulging, unmasking 10 disclosure, divulgence, laying bare, laying open, revelation, subjection, submission, uncovering 11 perspective 12 public notice 15 bringing to light

expound 6 defend, uphold 7 explain 8 describe 9 elucidate, explicate, hold forth, make clear

express 3 say 4 fast, show, word 5 clear, couch, exact, lucid, plain, quick, rapid, speak, state, swift, utter, vivid, voice 6 convey, direct, evince, phrase, relate, reveal 7 certain, declare, divulge, exhibit, nonstop, precise 8 definite, describe, disclose, evidence, explicit, forceful, specific, vocalize 9 high-speed, make known, verbalize 10 articulate, particular 11 categorical, communicate, unequivocal 12 put into words

expression 4 look, mien, term, tone, word 5 idiom, style 6 airing, aspect, phrase, saying 7 emotion, meaning, stating, telling, venting, voicing, wording 8 language, locution, phrasing, relating, speaking, uttering **9** assertion, eloquence **10** appearance, modulation **11** countenance, declaration, enunciation, phraseology **12** articulation, setting forth, turn of phrase **13** communication

expressionless 5 blank, empty **6** vacant **7** deadpan **12** inexpressive

expressive 5 vivid **6** moving **7** telling **8** eloquent, forceful, poignant, powerful, striking **9** effective **10** compelling, indicative, meaningful, thoughtful **11** significant **14** characteristic

expressly 7 clearly, plainly **9** decidedly, pointedly, precisely, specially **10** definitely, distinctly, explicitly **12** particularly, specifically **13** categorically, unequivocally **18** in no uncertain terms

express sorrow 3 cry **4** weep **6** grieve, lament **7** condole, console **10** sympathize **11** commiserate

expropriate 4 take **5** seize **8** take over **10** commandeer, confiscate **11** appropriate

expropriation 7 seizure **10** arrogation, taking over **12** confiscation **13** commandeering

expulsion 5 exile **6** ouster **7** ousting, removal **8** ejection, eviction **9** debarment, discharge, dismissal, exclusion, expelling **10** banishment **11** elimination, prohibition, throwing out **12** proscription

expunge 5 erase **6** delete, efface, rub out **7** blot out, destroy, wipe out **9** eradicate, strike out **10** obliterate

expurgate 3 cut **4** blip, edit **5** bleep, purge **6** censor, cut out, delete, excise, remove **8** bleep out **10** bluepencil, bowdlerize

exquisite 4 fine **5** dainty **6** choice, lovely, superb **7** elegant, perfect **8** delicate, flawless, peerless, precious, splendid **9** admirable, excellent, faultless, matchless **10** consummate, fastidious, impeccable, meticulous **11** superlative **12** incomparable **14** discriminating

exquisiteness 6 beauty **8** delicacy, elegance, fineness **10** loveliness, perfection **12** flawlessness

extant 6 living **7** present **8** existent, existing **9** surviving, to be found **11** in existence

Extasie, The
   author: **9** John Donne

extemporaneous 5 ad-lib **7** offhand **9** extempore, impromptu **10** improvised, off the cuff, unprepared **11** extemporary, spontaneous, unrehearsed **12** without notes **13** without notice **14** unpremeditated **15** spur-of-the-moment **19** off the top of one's head

extemporary 5 ad-lib **9** extempore, impromptu **10** improvised, off the

cuff, unprepared **14** extemporaneous **19** off the top of one's head

extempore 5 ad-lib **7** offhand **9** impromptu **10** improvised, off the cuff, unprepared **11** extemporary, unrehearsed **12** without notes **14** extemporaneous, unpremeditated **15** spur-of-the-moment **19** off the top of one's head

extemporize 5 ad-lib **6** make up **9** improvise **14** speak impromptu **15** speak off the cuff

extend 4 give **5** grant, offer, widen **6** bestow, expand, impart, put out, spread, submit **7** advance, amplify, augment, broaden, draw out, enlarge, hold out, proffer, prolong, stretch **8** continue, elongate, increase, lengthen, protract, reach out **10** make longer, stretch out **12** stretch forth

extended 4 long **7** widened **8** drawn out, enlarged, expanded, thorough, unfolded, unfurled **9** broadened, continued, extensive, prolonged, spread out **10** lengthened, protracted, widespread **12** stretched out **13** comprehensive

extending 8 full form **9** expansion **10** drawing out, elongation, proffering, stretching **11** enlargement, lengthening **12** putting forth

extension 3 arm, ell **4** wing **5** annex, delay **6** branch, length, outlay **7** adjunct **8** addition, appendix, increase **9** appendage, expansion, outgrowth **10** drawing out, proffering **11** enlargement, lengthening **12** continuation, postponement, prolongation

extensive 4 huge, long, vast, wide **5** broad, great, large **7** lengthy **8** enormous, extended, far-flung, thorough **9** capacious, universal **10** protracted, voluminous **12** all-inclusive, considerable **13** comprehensive

extensiveness 4 span **5** range, reach, scope **6** extent, spread **7** breadth, compass, expanse, stretch

extent 4 area, size, time **5** range, reach, scope, sweep **6** amount, degree, length **7** breadth, compass, expanse, stretch **8** duration **9** amplitude, magnitude **10** dimensions

extenuate 6 excuse, temper **7** explain, justify, qualify **8** mitigate, moderate

extenuating 9 lessening, tempering **10** mitigating, moderating, qualifying **11** attenuating, diminishing, explanatory, justifiable

exterior 4 face, skin **5** alien, outer, shell **6** exotic, facade, finish, manner **7** bearing, coating, foreign, outside, outward, surface **8** covering, demeanor, external **9** extrinsic, outer side, outermost **10** extraneous **11** superficial

exterminate 3 zap **4** kill **5** erase, waste **7** abolish, destroy, expunge,

root out, wipe out **8** demolish, massacre **9** eliminate, eradicate, slaughter **10** annihilate, extinguish

external 5 alien, outer **7** foreign, outside, outward, surface **8** exterior **9** extrinsic, outermost **10** extraneous **11** superficial

extinct 4 dead, gone, lost **6** put out **7** defunct, died out, gone out **8** quenched, vanished **12** extinguished

extinction 5 death **7** eclipse **9** wiping out **11** destruction, eradication **13** disappearance

extinguish 3 end, zap **4** dash, do in, kill **5** crush, douse, quash **6** cancel, dispel, put out, quench, stifle **7** abolish, blow out, destroy, smother, wipe out **8** demolish, snuff out **9** eliminate, eradicate, suffocate

extinguished 6 put out **7** gone out **8** quenched **15** no longer burning

extirpate 5 erase **7** abolish, destroy, extract, pull out, root out, wipe out **8** demolish **9** eradicate **10** annihilate, extinguish, obliterate **11** exterminate

extol 4 laud **6** praise **7** acclaim, applaud, commend, glorify **8** eulogize **9** celebrate **10** compliment **16** sing the praises of

extort 5 educe, exact **6** coerce, elicit **7** extract **9** shake down

extortion 5 force, graft **6** payola, ransom **7** threats, tribute **8** coercion **9** blackmail, hush money, shakedown **14** forced payments

extortionate 5 undue **7** extreme **9** excessive, out-of-line **10** exorbitant, inordinate **12** unreasonable

extra 4 more **5** spare **7** adjunct, further, surplus **9** accessory, auxiliary, redundant, unusually **10** additional, attachment, complement, especially, remarkably, uncommonly **11** superfluous, unnecessary **12** additionally, appurtenance, particularly, supplemental **13** exceptionally **15** extraordinarily

extract 3 get **4** cite, cull **5** educe, evoke, exact, gleen, juice, quote, wrest **6** choose, deduce, derive, elicit, obtain, pry out, remove, select **7** copy out, distill, draw out, essence, excerpt, passage, pull out, root out, take out **8** abstract, bring out, citation, pluck out, press out, separate **9** extirpate, extricate, quotation, selection **10** distillate, squeeze out **11** concentrate

extraction 5 stock **7** descent, removal **8** ancestry **10** derivation, drawing out, pulling out

extraneous 5 alien **6** exotic **7** foreign, strange **9** extrinsic, unrelated **10** immaterial, incidental, irrelevant, not germane **11** superfluous **12** adventitious, inadmissible, nonessential, not pertinent **13** inappropriate

extraordinary 3 odd **4** rare **5** queer

6 unique **7** amazing, notable, strange, unusual **8** uncommon **9** fantastic, monstrous, unheard of **10** incredible, phenomenal, remarkable **11** exceptional **12** unbelievable **13** inconceivable

extraterrestrial 2 ET **3** Alf **6** cosmic **10** outer-space **12** interstellar, otherworldly **14** interplanetary

extravagance 5 folly, waste **6** excess **7** caprice **9** absurdity **10** profligacy **11** prodigality, squandering, unrestraint **12** immoderation, improvidence, overspending, recklessness, wastefulness **13** excessiveness **14** capriciousness **16** inordinate outlay, unreasonableness

extravagant 4 wild **6** absurd, costly, unreal **7** foolish **8** fabulous, lavishly, prodigal, spending, wasteful **9** excessive, expensive, fantastic, high-flown, imprudent **10** exorbitant, high-priced, immoderate, inordinate, openhanded, outlandish, outrageous, overpriced, profligate **11** improvident, spendthrift, squandering **12** overspending, preposterous, unreasonable, unrestrained

extravaganza 4 fair **5** opera **6** ballet **7** pageant **8** carnival, operetta **9** spectacle, stage show **10** exposition, vaudeville **11** opera bouffe, spectacular **12** Broadway show, opera comique, son et lumiere, wild west show **14** phantasmagoria **17** sound and light show

extreme 3 end **5** depth **6** excess, height, severe **7** intense, radical, unusual **8** advanced, boundary, farthest, uncommon **9** excessive, extremity, nth degree, outermost, very great **10** avant-garde, immoderate, inordinate, outrageous **11** exaggerated, extravagant, most distant **13** extraordinary

extremely 4 very **5** quite **7** awfully **8** terribly **9** curiously, intensely, unusually **10** abnormally, especially, freakishly, peculiarly, remarkably, singularly, uncommonly **11** exceedingly, excessively, unnaturally **12** immoderately, surprisingly **13** exceptionally **15** extraordinarily

extremely painful 7 racking **9** agonizing, torturous **10** tormenting, un-

bearable **11** intolerable, unendurable **12** excruciating, insufferable

extremity 3 arm, end, leg, tip, toe **4** edge, foot, hand, limb **5** bound, brink, limit, reach **6** border, finger, margin **7** confine, extreme **8** boundary, terminus **9** outer edge, periphery

extricate 4 free **5** loose **6** get out, rescue **7** deliver, release **8** liberate, untangle **9** disengage **11** disencumber, disentangle **12** wriggle out of

extrication 6 escape **7** loosing, release **10** liberation **11** deliverance **13** disengagement **15** disentanglement

extrinsic 5 alien **7** foreign **9** accessory **10** accidental, extraneous, incidental **11** dispensable **12** nonessential

extrovert 7 show-off **13** exhibitionist **14** life of the party **17** hail-fellow-well-met

extroverted 8 outgoing, sociable **9** expansive **10** gregarious **12** unrestrained

extrude 4 spew **5** eject, expel **7** project, push out **8** force out, protrude, stickout **9** thrust out

exuberance 3 zip **4** elan, life, zeal **5** vigor **6** energy, spirit **8** buoyancy, vitality, vivacity **9** animation, eagerness **10** enthusiasm, excitement, liveliness **13** effervescence, sprightliness

exuberant 4 lush, rich **5** eager **6** lavish, lively **7** copious, excited, profuse, zealous **8** abundant, animated, spirited, vigorous **9** bounteous, energetic, luxuriant, plenteous, plentiful, sprightly **12** enthusiastic **13** superabundant

exudation 3 sap, tar **4** ooze **5** pitch, sweat **7** leakage, seepage **8** bleeding, drainage **9** discharge, excretion

exude 4 drip, emit, ooze **5** sweat **7** secrete **9** discharge

exult 4 crow **5** gloat, glory **7** rejoice **8** be elated **10** be jubilant, jump for joy **11** be delighted **13** be exhilarated **15** be in high spirits

exultant 5 happy **6** elated, joyful **7** crowing **8** boasting, ecstatic, euphoric, gloating, jubilant **9** rapturous, rejoicing **10** triumphant

exultation 3 joy **7** elation, ovation,

rapture, triumph **9** rejoicing **10** jubilation

Eyck, Jan van
  born: **8** Flanders, Maaseyck **10** Maastricht
  artwork: **9** Timotheos **15** Ghent Altarpiece **18** Adoration of the Lamb, The Man in a Red Turban, The Virgin in a Church **20** The Arnolfini Marriage **24** Arnolfini Wedding Portrait **29** The Madonna with Chancellor Rolin **30** The Madonna with Canon van der Paele

eye 3 orb **4** scan, view **5** sight, study, taste, watch **6** behold, gaze at, look at, peeper, regard, survey, take in, vision **7** inspect, observe, stare at **8** eyesight, glance at **10** perception, scrutinize **14** discrimination
  part: **4** iris, lens, rods **5** cones, nerve, pupil **6** cornea, muscle, retina **11** blood vessel

eyeful 4 doll **5** beaut, peach, Venus **6** beauty **7** stunner **8** knockout **10** good-looker **13** beautiful girl **14** beautiful woman

eyeglass, eyeglasses 4 lens **5** specs **6** eyecup, lenses **7** goggles, monocle **8** bifocals, cheaters, contacts, pince-nez **9** lorgnette **10** spectacles

Eye of the Needle
  author: **10** Ken Follett

eyesight 4 eyes **5** sight **6** vision

Eyes Wide Shut
  director: **14** Stanley Kubrick
  cast: **9** Sky Dumont (Sandor Szavost), Todd Field (Nick Nightingale), Tom Cruise (Bill Harford) **12** Nicole Kidman (Alice Harford) **13** Sydney Pollack (Victor Ziegler) **15** Marie Richardson (Marion)

eyewitness 5 gaper, gazer **6** gawker, viewer **7** witness **8** attester, attestor, beholder, informer, looker-on, observer, onlooker, passerby **9** bystander, spectator, testifier **10** rubberneck

eyre 4 lake, tour **7** circuit

Ezekiel
  father: **4** Buzi

Ezra
  father: **7** Seraiah

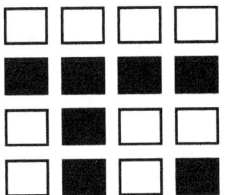
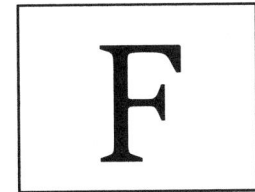
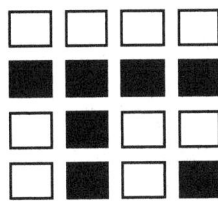

Fabares, Ruby Bernadette Nanette
  real name of: 13 Nanette Fabray
  aunt of: 14 Shelley Fabares

fable 3 fib, lie **4** hoax, myth, tale, yarn
  6 legend **7** fiction, leg-pull, parable,
  romance, untruth, whopper **8** allegory
  9 fairy tale, falsehood, invention, tall
  story **11** fabrication

fabled 6 unreal **7** storied **8** fabulous,
  fanciful, mythical **9** imaginary, legendary **10** fictitious **12** mythological

Fables
  author: 5 Aesop **16** Jean de La Fontaine
  ends with: 5 moral
  feature: 4 hare **8** tortoise **10** sour
  grapes

Fabray, Nanette
  real name: 28 Ruby Bernadette
  Nanette Fabares
  partner: 9 Sid Caesar
  born: 10 San Diego CA
  roles: 7 Baby Nan **12** The Band
  Wagon **13** Sid Caesar Hour **15** High
  Button Shoes, Our Gang comedies

fabric 5 cloth, frame, stuff **6** makeup **7**
  textile, texture **8** dry goods, material **9**
  framework, structure, substance, yard
  goods **10** foundation **12** organization,
  substructure **14** infrastructure, super-
  structure
  cotton: 4 duck **5** denim, drill, scrim,
  terry **6** burlap, calico, canvas, chintz,
  dimity, madras, muslin, oxford, poplin **7** batiste, buckram, flannel, gingham, organdy, percale, ticking **8**
  chambray **9** crinoline, sailcloth **10**
  broadcloth, printcloth, seersucker **11**
  cheesecloth, dotted Swiss
  linen: 4 canvas, damask **7** butcher,
  cambric **8** birds-eye **9** huckaback
  natural: 4 jute, silk, wool **5** linen **6**
  cotton **8** asbestos
  silk: 3 raw **4** tram **7** organza **8** organzie **9** organzine
  synthetic: 5 nylon, orlon, rayon **6**
  olefin **7** acetate, acrylic **9** polyester
  type: 4 felt, lace, lame **5** crepe,
  gauze, moire, serge, voile **6** damask,
  faille, jersey, melton, velour, velvet **7**
  brocade, chiffon, flannel, foulard,
  gingham, taffeta **8** chenille, cordu-
  roy, tapestry **9** gabardine, velveteen
  wool: 4 felt **5** crepe, serge, tweed,
  twill **6** boucle, covert, faille, melton,
  woolen **7** challis, doeskin, Donegal,

worsted **8** homespun, Shetland **9** Astrakhan, gabardine, sharkskin **10**
hopsacking **11** Harris tweed, herringbone
  from goats: 8 cashmere
  sheep: 5 Iraqi **6** Hirrik, merino,
  Romney, Somali **7** Lincoln **8** Cotswold, Tatarian **9** Hampshire,
  Southdown **10** Corriedale, Dorset
  Down, Dorset Horn, Shropshire,
  Sikkim Bera **13** Hampshire Down
  other wool-bearing animals:
  5 camel, llama **6** alpaca, vicuna

fabricate 4 fake, form, make **5** build,
  erect, feign, forge, frame, hatch, shape
  6 design, devise, invent, make up **7**
  compose, concoct, falsify, fashion,
  produce, trump up **8** assemble, contrive, simulate **9** construct, embroider,
  formulate **11** counterfeit, manufacture

fabrication 3 fib, lie **4** myth, yarn **5**
  fable **6** makeup **7** fiction, forgery, untruth **8** building, creation, erection **9**
  fairy tale, falsehood, invention **10** assemblage, concoction, fashioning, production **11** composition, manufacture
  12 constructing, construction **13** prevarication **16** cock-and-bull story

Fabritius, Carel
  real name: 13 Carel Pietersz
  born: 14 Midden-Beemster, The Netherlands
  artwork: 11 View of Delft **12** The
  Goldfinch **19** The Raising of Lazarus

fabulous 5 great **6** fabled, superb **7**
  amazing, storied **8** fanciful, invented,
  mythical, smashing **9** fantastic, imaginary, legendary, marvelous, wonderful
  10 apocryphal, astounding, fictitious,
  incredible, stupendous **11** astonishing,
  spectacular **12** mythological, unbelievable **13** extraordinary

facade 4 face, mask **6** veneer **8** frontage, pretense **9** front view **10** false
  front **13** building front

face 3 air, mug, pan **4** coat, gall, grit,
  look, pout, puss, sand **5** brass, cheek,
  cover, front, image, nerve, pluck,
  spunk **6** aspect, daring, facade, kisser,
  mettle, repute, visage **7** bravado, dignity, front on, grimace, obverse, overlay, surface **8** boldness, confront,
  features, forepart, frontage, good
  name, overlook, prestige **9** encounter,
  hardihood, impudence, semblance **10**
  appearance, confidence, effrontery, ex-

pression, give toward, look toward,
reputation, turn toward **11** countenance, physiognomy, self-respect

Face
  character in: 12 The Alchemist
  author: 6 Jonson

facet 3 cut **4** part, side **5** angle, phase,
  plane **6** aspect **7** surface

facetious 5 comic, droll, funny, witty
  6 clever, jocose, joking, jovial **7**
  amusing, comical, jesting, jocular,
  playful **8** humorous **12** wisecracking

face-to-face 6 direct **8** one-on-one,
  personal **9** firsthand

facile 3 apt **4** glib **5** adept, handy,
  quick, slick **6** adroit, artful, casual,
  clever, fluent, smooth **7** cursory, shallow **8** careless, skillful **10** effortless,
  proficient **11** superficial

facilitate 3 aid **4** ease **6** foster, help
  in, smooth **7** advance, forward, further, lighten, promote, speed up **8** expedite, simplify **10** accelerate, make
  easier

facility 3 aid **4** bent, ease **5** knack,
  means, skill **7** aptness, fluency **8** deftness, easiness, resource **9** advantage,
  appliance, dexterity, readiness **10**
  adroitness, capability, competence, efficiency, expertness, smoothness **11**
  convenience, proficiency **14** effortlessness, practicability

facsimile 3 fax **4** copy **5** clone, Xerox
  7 replica, reprint **8** likeness **9** duplicate, imitation, photostat **10** transcript
  12 reproduction

fact 3 act **4** deed **5** event, truth **6** verity **7** reality **8** incident, specific **9** actuality, certainty, happening, thing
  done **10** occurrence, particular **12** circumstance

faction 3 set **4** bloc, gang, ring, sect,
  side, unit **5** cabal, clash, group, split
  6 breach, circle, clique, schism, strife
  7 combine, coterie, discord, rupture,
  section **8** conflict, division, minority,
  sedition **9** rebellion **10** contention,
  disruption, dissension, dissidence, insurgency, quarreling **11** subdivision
  12 disagreement **13** splinter group **15**
  incompatibility

factious 7 warring **8** divisive, fighting,
  mutinous **9** alienated, bickering, combative, estranged **10** contending, rebellious **11** belligerent, contentious,

disaffected, disagreeing, dissentious, quarrelsome **12** disputatious **13** at loggerheads, insubordinate **15** insurrectionary **16** at sixes and sevens

factitious 4 sham **5** phony **9** pretended, synthetic, unnatural **10** artificial **12** manufactured

factor 4 part **5** agent, cause **6** reason **7** element **9** component, influence **11** constituent **12** circumstance **13** consideration

factory 4 mill, shop **5** plant, works **8** workshop **11** manufactory

factotum 4 aide **6** Figaro **8** handyman **9** gal Friday, guy Friday, man Friday **10** girl Friday **12** right-hand man **15** jack-of-all-trades

factual 4 real, true **5** exact, plain **6** actual **7** certain, correct, genuine, literal **8** accurate, concrete, definite, faithful **9** authentic, unadorned **10** scrupulous, verifiable

faculty, faculties 4 bent, gift, wits **5** flair, knack, power, skill **6** genius, reason, talent **7** quality **8** aptitude, capacity, function, penchant, teachers **9** adeptness, endowment **10** capability, professors **12** mental powers, skillfulness **13** teaching staff

fad 4 mode, rage, whim **5** craze, fancy, mania, vogue **6** whimsy **7** fashion **10** dernier cri, latest word **11** latest thing

faddish 2 in **6** trendy **10** innovative **11** fashionable

fade 3 die, dim, ebb **4** blur, dull, fail, flag, pale, wane **5** droop, taper **6** bleach, lessen, recede, whiten, wither **7** crumble, decline, dwindle, fall off, grow dim, shrivel **8** diminish, dissolve, evanesce, languish, make pale, melt away, pass away **9** disappear, dissipate, evaporate, lose color

fade away 3 die, ebb **6** recede **7** subside **8** diminish

faded 4 drab, dull, pale **5** dingy **6** grayed **7** died out **8** bleached, dwindled, whitened, withered **9** colorless, shriveled, washed out

Faerie Queene, The
   author: 13 Edmund Spenser
   character: 3 Una **5** Guyon **6** Duessa **8** Artegall, Gloriana (the Faerie Queen) **9** Archimago, Britomart **12** Prince Arthur **14** Red Cross Knight

Fafnir
   origin: 12 Scandinavian
   form: 6 dragon
   father: 8 Hreidmar
   brother: 5 Otter, Regin
   killed: 8 Hreidmar
   killed by: 6 Sigurd

fag 4 bush, butt, poop, tire, weed **5** weary **6** tucker **7** exhaust **9** cigarette

Fagin
   character in: 11 Oliver Twist
   author: 7 Dickens

Fahrenheit
   abbreviation: 1 F

Fahrenheit 451
   author: 11 Ray Bradbury

Fahrenheit, Gabriel Daniel
   field: 7 physics
   nationality: 6 German
   invented: 16 thermometer scale **18** alcohol thermometer, mercury thermometer

fail 3 die, ebb **4** bomb, flag, flop, fold, wane **5** abort, crash, droop, flunk **6** desert, slip up **7** decline, dwindle, forsake, founder, give out, go under, let down, misfire **8** be in vain, collapse, fade away, languish, lay an egg, miscarry **9** disappear, fall short, fizzle out **10** end in smoke, go bankrupt, not succeed, run aground **11** be still-born, come to grief, deteriorate, fall through, go up in smoke, miss the mark **12** come to naught, turn out badly **13** come to nothing **15** go out of business **16** meet one's Waterloo, meet with disaster

fail at 11 fall short of **12** be defeated in, not succeed at **16** be unsuccessful at

failed
   French: 6 manque

failing 4 weak **5** fault, shaky **6** defect, ebbing, foible, waning **7** folding, frailty **8** drooping, flagging, giving up, slipping, weakness **9** deficient, dwindling, giving out, weakening, weak point **10** deficiency, going under **11** shortcoming **12** unsuccessful **13** insufficiency

fail to include 4 drop, omit **5** elide **8** leave out, pass over

failure 3 dud **4** bomb, flop, mess, ruin **5** botch, crash, loser **6** fizzle, mishap, muddle, turkey **7** decline, default, failing, folding, misfire, washout **8** collapse, downfall **9** breakdown, ruination **10** bankruptcy, ne'er-do-well

faint 3 dim, low **4** pale, soft, thin, weak **5** dizzy, faded, frail, giddy, muted, small, swoon, timid **6** dulcet, feeble, little, meager, remote, slight, subtle, torpid **7** fearful, fragile, languid, muffled, obscure, pass out, worn out **8** black out, collapse, cowardly, delicate, drooping, fatigued, timorous **9** exhausted, inaudible, lethargic, whispered **10** indistinct **11** lightheaded, lily-livered, vertiginous **13** inconspicuous **17** lose consciousness

fainthearted 4 weak **5** timid **6** feeble **8** cowardly **10** irresolute **11** halfhearted, indifferent, lily-livered

faintheartedness 9 cowardice **12** cowardliness, yellow streak **13** pusillanimity, yellow feather **17** pusillanimousness **18** chickenheartedness

fair 4 fine, just, pale, so-so **5** blond,

bonny, sunny **6** blonde, bright, comely, creamy, decent, honest, justly, kosher, lovely, medium, pretty, proper, square **7** average, cricket, legally, not dark, upright **8** adequate, candidly, carnival, honestly, mediocre, middling, moderate, ordinary, passable, pleasant, rainless, squarely, sunshiny, unbiased **9** beautiful, cloudless, equitable, ethically, honorable, honorably, impartial, justified, objective, tolerable, unclouded **10** aboveboard, attractive, evenhanded, exhibition, legitimate, pretty good, reasonable, truthfully **11** indifferent, respectable **12** forthrightly, light-colored, light-skinned, on the up-and-up, run-of-the-mill, satisfactory, unprejudiced **13** disinterested, dispassionate **19** according to the rules

Fair, A A
   pseudonym of: 18 Erle Stanley Gardner

Fairbanks, Douglas
   real name: 17 Douglas Elton Ulman
   wife: 12 Mary Pickford
   son: 18 Douglas Fairbanks Jr
   born: 8 Denver CO
   roles: 9 Robin Hood **11** The Iron Mask **14** The Black Pirate, The Mark of Zorro **16** The Thief of Bagdad **18** The Three Musketeers **23** The Private Life of Don Juan

Fairbanks, Douglas Jr
   father: 16 Douglas Fairbanks
   wife: 12 Joan Crawford
   born: 9 New York NY
   roles: 8 Gunga Din **12** Little Caesar **15** Sinbad the Sailor **16** That Lady in Ermine **17** Catherine the Great **18** The Prisoner of Zenda **19** The Corsican Brothers

fair dealing 7 honesty **8** fairness **15** trustworthiness

Fairfax, Gwendolen
   character in: 27 The Importance of Being Earnest
   author: 5 Wilde

Fairfax, Jane
   character in: 4 Emma
   author: 6 Austen

Fairfax, Mrs
   character in: 8 Jane Eyre
   author: 15 Charlotte Bronte

fairly 5 fully **6** justly, rather, really **7** rightly **8** actually, honestly, passably, properly, somewhat, squarely **9** equitably, honorably, so to speak, tolerably **10** absolutely, completely, moderately, positively, reasonably **11** impartially, objectively **12** evenhandedly, legitimately **15** dispassionately **19** in a manner of speaking
   Latin: 9 pari passu

fairness 7 balance, honesty, justice **8** equality, fair play **11** objectivity **12**

impartiality **14** even-handedness **16** equal opportunity

fair play 7 cricket, justice **8** equality, fairness **12** impartiality **16** equal opportunity

fair-skinned 4 pale **5** blond, light **6** blonde **17** light-complexioned

fairy 3 elf **5** pixie **6** sprite **10** leprechaun

fairy tale 3 fib **4** myth **5** fable **6** legend **7** fantasy, fiction **8** tall tale **9** invention **11** fabrication **16** cock-and-bull story, Mother Goose story
German: **7** Marchen

fait accompli 16 accomplished fact, thing already done

faith 4 sect **5** creed, trust **6** belief, church, fealty **7** loyalty, promise **8** credence, fidelity, reliance, religion, security **9** assurance, certainty, certitude, constancy **10** confidence, conviction, obligation, persuasion

faithful 4 true **5** close, exact, loyal, tried **6** honest, strict, trusty **7** devoted, factual, precise, similar, staunch, upright **8** accurate, constant, lifelike, reliable, resolute, truthful **9** steadfast **10** dependable, scrupulous, true-to-life, unswerving, unwavering, verifiable **11** trustworthy **13** conscientious, incorruptible

faithfulness 6 fealty **7** loyalty **8** devotion, fidelity **9** constancy **10** allegiance **11** reliability **13** steadfastness

faithless 5 false **6** fickle **8** disloyal **10** inconstant, perfidious, unreliable **11** treacherous **13** untrustworthy

faithlessness 7 doubt **7** perfidy **9** disbelief, falseness, treachery **10** disloyalty, fickleness, infidelity, skepticism **11** inconstancy **13** unreliability **14** perfidiousness, unfaithfulness

fake 4 hoax, ruse, sham **5** bogus, dodge, dummy, faker, false, feign, forge, fraud, phony, put-on, quack, trick **6** deceit, forged, humbug, poseur, pseudo **7** falsify, forgery, not real, pretend, trump up **8** artifice, contrive, deceiver, delusion, imposter, invented, simulate, specious, spurious **9** charlatan, concocted, contrived, deception, dissemble, fabricate, imitation, imposture, pretender, simulated **10** artificial, fabricated, fictitious **11** contrivance, counterfeit, dissimulate, fabrication, make-believe

faker 5 fraud, phony **6** humbug **8** imposter **9** charlatan, pretender

fakir 5 Hindu **6** Muslim **7** ascetic, dervish

falcon 4 eyas **5** hobby, saker **6** desert, lanner, merlin **7** goshawk, kestrel, prairie, shaheen, tiercel **8** caracara, falconet **9** gyrfalcon, peregrine
cover eyes: **4** seel

Falcon and the Snowman, The
author: **13** Robert Lindsey
director: **15** John Schlesinger
cast: **8** Sean Penn (Andrew Daulton Lee, the Snowman) **13** Timothy Hutton (Christopher John Boyce, the Falcon)

Falconer
author: **11** John Cheever

Falconet, Etienne-Maurice
born: **5** Paris **6** France
artwork: **9** The Bather **12** Bathing Nymph **13** Milo of Crotona, Peter the Great **19** Pygmalion and Galatea

falconry 7 hawking
equipment: **4** lure **5** cadge **6** jesses **7** creance

Falk, Lee
creator/artist of: **10** The Phantom **19** Mandrake the Magician

Falk, Peter
born: **9** New York NY
roles: **7** Columbo **9** Murder Inc **12** The Great Race **13** Murder by Death, Wings of Desire **17** The Cheap Detective **19** Pocketful of Miracles **21** It's a Mad Mad Mad Mad World, Robin and the Seven Hoods

fall, falls 3 die, ebb, err, sin **4** drop, plop, ruin, slip, wane **5** droop, lapse, occur, slope, slump, spill **6** autumn, crop up, defeat, happen, perish, plunge, topple, tumble **7** be slain, be taken, capture, cascade, cheapen, come off, crumple, decline, descend, descent, falling, plummet, sinking, succumb **8** cataract, collapse, come down, decrease, diminish, disgrace, downfall, drop down, dropping, go astray, hang down, lowering **9** crash down, overthrow, reduction, surrender, take place, waterfall **10** capitulate, come to pass, corruption, debasement, depreciate, diminution, subsidence, subversion, transgress **11** be destroyed, harvest time **12** capitulation, depreciation, Indian summer **15** loss of innocence

Fall, The
author: **11** Albert Camus

Falla, Manuel de
born: **5** Cadiz, Spain
composer of: **11** El Amor Brujo, La Atlantida, La Vida Breve, Life Is Short **14** Fantasia Betica **15** Love the Magician **19** The Three-Cornered Hat **21** El sombrero de tres picos **25** Nights in the Gardens of Spain

fallacious 5 false, wrong **6** faulty, flawed, untrue **8** delusive, mistaken **9** deceptive, erroneous, illogical, incorrect **10** inaccurate, misleading, untruthful

fallacy 4 flaw **5** catch, error, fault **7** mistake, pitfall **8** delusion, illusion **9** misbelief **10** faultiness **11** false belief, false notion **13** inconsistency, misconception **15** misapprehension

fall apart 5 decay **7** break up, crumble, shatter **8** fragment, splinter **10** go to pieces **11** fragmentize **12** disintegrate

fall away 4 fade, wane **5** abate **7** drop off, slacken, subside **8** mitigate, taper off

fall back 6 recede **7** back off, retreat

fallen 4 dead **5** loose, slain **6** ousted, ruined, sinful **7** debased, deposed, dropped, immoral, spilled, toppled, tumbled **8** sprawled **9** butchered, disgraced, massacred, turned out **10** discharged, overthrown **11** slaughtered

fallen short
French: **6** manque

fall for 7 believe, swallow

fall guy 4 dupe, pawn, tool **5** patsy **7** cat's-paw

fallible 5 frail, human **6** faulty, mortal, unsure **9** imperfect **10** unreliable

fall in drops 4 drip, rain **7** dribble, drizzle **8** sprinkle

falling apart 6 ruined, shabby **7** rickety, run-down **8** decaying, decrepit **9** crumbling **10** broken-down, collapsing, ramshackle, tumbledown **11** dilapidated **13** deteriorating

falling into decay 6 ruined, shabby **7** rotting, run-down **8** decrepit **9** crumbling, moldering **10** broken-down, tumbledown **11** dilapidated, in disrepair **13** deteriorating

falling off 3 ebb **4** fall, wane **7** decline **8** decrease **9** dwindling, lessening, reduction **10** diminution **13** deterioration

falling out 4 spat **7** dispute, quarrel **8** argument, squabble **10** difference **12** disagreement

fall in with 6 concur **7** conform **8** accede to **9** acquiesce **11** go along with

fall off 4 drop, wane **6** lessen, plunge, reduce, topple **7** decline, drop off, plummet, slacken, subside **8** decrease, diminish, moderate, peter out

Fall of the House of Usher, The
author: **13** Edgar Allan Poe
character: **8** Narrator **13** Madeline Usher, Roderick Usher

fallow 4 arid, idle **5** inert **6** barren, unused **7** dormant, unsowed, worn out **8** depleted, inactive, untilled **9** exhausted, unplanted **10** unfruitful **12** uncultivated, unproductive

fall short 6 be less, fail at, give up **9** be lacking, lag behind **10** have too few **11** fail to reach, miss the mark **12** be inadequate **14** be insufficient

fall to one's lot 4 fall **5** occur **6** befall, chance, happen **7** turn out **9** come about **10** come to pass

fall upon 5 fly at **6** assail, attack, dive at **7** embrace, lunge at, set upon **8** thrust at, tuck into

false 4 fake, sham **5** bogus, phony,

wrong **6** ersatz, faulty, forged, pseudo, tricky, unreal, untrue **7** devious, feigned, inexact, invalid, unsound **8** delusive, disloyal, mistaken, spurious, two-faced **9** deceitful, deceiving, deceptive, dishonest, erroneous, faithless, imitation, incorrect, unfounded **10** apocryphal, artificial, factitious, fallacious, inaccurate, inconstant, misleading, not correct, perfidious, traitorous, unfaithful, untruthful **11** counterfeit, make-believe, treacherous **12** hypocritical **13** double-dealing

false front 4 mask, sham, show **6** facade, screen, veneer **8** pretense

false-hearted 8 two-faced **9** deceitful, deceiving, faithless **10** perfidious **13** double-dealing, untrustworthy

falsehood 3 fib, lie **5** lying, story **6** canard, deceit **7** fiction, figment, perfidy, perjury, untruth, whopper **8** bad faith, white lie **9** deception, duplicity, hypocrisy, invention, mendacity **10** dishonesty, distortion, inaccuracy **11** dissembling, fabrication, insincerity **12** misstatement, two-facedness **13** deceptiveness, dissimulation, double-dealing, falsification **17** misrepresentation

falseness 5 fraud **6** deceit **7** perfidy **9** duplicity, treachery **10** dishonesty **12** spuriousness **13** deceitfulness, double-dealing, faithlessness **14** untruthfulness

falsified 5 false, phony **6** forged, made-up **7** assumed **10** fictitious

falsify 4 fake **5** belie, rebut **6** doctor, misuse, refute **7** confute, distort, pervert **8** disprove **10** tamper with **12** misrepresent

Falstaff
  opera by: 5 Verdi
  character: 4 Anne **6** Fenton, Pistol **7** Dr Caius **8** Bardolph **11** Dame Quickly **12** Mistress Ford, Mistress Page **15** Mistress Quickly, Sir John Falstaff

Falstaff, Sir John
  character in: 12 Henry IV Part I **13** Henry IV Part II **22** The Merry Wives of Windsor
  author: 11 Shakespeare

falter 3 lag **4** halt, reel **5** demur, waver **6** dodder, mumble, shrink, teeter, totter **7** shamble, shuffle, stagger, stammer, stumble, stutter **8** hesitate **9** fluctuate, vacillate **10** dillydally **11** be undecided **12** be irresolute, show weakness **14** blow hot and cold

fame 4 note **5** eclat, glory **6** renown, repute **7** laurels **8** eminence, prestige **9** celebrity, notoriety **10** notability, popularity, prominence, reputation **11** distinction, preeminence **15** illustriousness

famed 5 noted **6** famous **7** notable **8**

renowned **9** prominent, well-known **10** celebrated

familiar 3 pal **4** bold, chum, cozy, free, snug **5** buddy, close, crony, known, stock, usual **6** chummy, common, friend **7** forward, general **8** accepted, amicable, at home in, everyday, frequent, friendly, habitual, informal, intimate, ordinary, seasoned, versed in **9** abreast of, brotherly, confidant, customary, fraternal, gemutlich, intrusive, simpatico, skilled in, well-known **10** accessible, accustomed, acquainted, apprised of, conversant, proverbial, unreserved **11** cognizant of, commonplace, impertinent, traditional **12** confidential, conventional, hand and glove, no stranger to, proficient at **13** boon companion, companionable, disrespectful **15** taking liberties

familiarity 4 ease **5** amity, skill **7** know-how, mastery **8** coziness, intimacy **9** closeness, impudence, indecorum, knowledge, unreserve **10** casualness, chumminess, cognizance, disrespect, experience, fellowship, fraternity, friendship **11** association, brotherhood, conversance, forwardness, impropriety, informality, naturalness, presumption, proficiency **12** acquaintance, impertinence, unconstraint, undue liberty, unseemliness **13** brotherliness, comprehension, intrusiveness, understanding

familiarize 5 edify, teach, tutor **6** inform, orient (oneself), school, season **7** educate **8** accustom, acquaint, instruct **9** enlighten, habituate, inculcate **11** acclimatize

family 3 kin, set **4** clan, kind, line, race, sept **5** blood, breed, brood, class, group, house, issue, order, stock, tribe **7** dynasty, kinfolk, kinsmen, lineage, progeny **8** ancestry, category, division, kinsfolk **9** forebears, genealogy, offspring, parentage, relations, relatives **10** extraction, kith and kin **11** forefathers **14** classification
  goddess of: 6 Cardea

Family Affair
  character: 4 Jody **5** Buffy, Cissy **8** Mr (Giles) French **9** Bill Davis
  cast: 10 Brian Keith **11** Anissa Jones, Kathy Garver **14** Sebastian Cabot **15** Johnnie Whitaker

family line 4 tree **7** lineage **8** ancestry **9** blood line, genealogy, parentage

Family Moskat, The
  author: 19 Isaac Bashevis Singer

Family Reunion, The
  author: 7 T S Eliot

Family Ties
  character: 4 Nick **5** Ellen **6** Skippy **10** Alex Keaton **11** Elyse Keaton **12** Andrew Keaton, Steven Keaton **13** Mal-

lory Keaton **14** Jennifer Keaton
  cast: 9 Marc Price **11** Michael J Fox, Tina Yothers **12** Michael Gross **14** Justine Bateman **20** Meredith Baxter-Birney

family tree 7 lineage **8** ancestry, pedigree **9** blood line, genealogy

famine 4 lack, want **6** dearth, hunger **7** paucity, poverty **8** scarcity **9** depletion **10** deficiency, exhaustion, famishment, meagerness, scantiness, starvation **11** destitution, half rations, short supply **13** acute shortage, extreme hunger, insufficiency

famished 6 hungry **7** starved

famous 5 noted **7** eminent, notable **8** far-famed, renowned, well-known **9** notorious, prominent **10** celebrated **11** conspicuous, illustrious **13** distinguished

famous person 4 name, star **7** notable **8** luminary, somebody **9** celebrity, personage, superstar **11** personality

fan 3 bug, nut **4** buff **5** fiend, freak **6** addict, rooter, zealot **7** booster, fanatic **8** follower, partisan

fanatic 5 crazy **6** maniac, zealot **7** hothead, radical **8** activist, militant **9** extremist **10** enthusiast **24** member of the lunatic fringe

fanaticism 6 fervor **8** activism, zealotry **9** dogmatism, extremism, monomania, obsession **10** enthusiasm, radicalism **11** extreme zeal, militantism **12** intemperance **13** ruling passion **15** opinionatedness

fancied 5 liked **6** dreamt, took to, unreal **7** assumed, desired, dreamed, thought **8** imagined, supposed **9** conceived, imaginary, preferred

fanciful 3 odd **6** unreal **7** bizarre, curious, flighty, unusual **8** fabulous, humorous, illusory, mythical, quixotic, romantic **9** eccentric, fantastic, imaginary, invective, legendary, visionary, whimsical **10** apocryphal, capricious, chimerical, fictitious **11** imaginative

fanciful talk 7 blarney **9** hyperbole, tall tales **11** fish stories **12** exaggeration

fancy 3 yen **4** fine, idea, like, want **5** crave, dream, enjoy, favor, opine, showy, taste, think **6** assume, custom, deluxe, desire, florid, liking, notion, ornate, relish, rococo, take it, take to, vagary, vision, whimsy **7** baroque, caprice, conceit, dream of, elegant, fantasy, figment, gourmet, imagine, leaning, longing, long for, picture, presume, reverie, special, suppose, surmise, suspect, unusual **8** be fond of, crotchet, daydream, fondness, illusion, not plain, penchant, superior, weakness, yearn for **9** elaborate, epicurean, expensive, hankering, superfine **10** be bent upon, conceive of, conjecture, decorative, high-priced, ornamental, partiality **11** distinctive, exceptional, extravagant, gingerbread, hanker after, have a mind to, imagination, inclination **12** have an eye for, predilection **13** be pleased with, take a liking to

fancy house 4 stew **5** house **6** bagnio **7** brothel **8** bordello, cathouse **10** bawdy house, whorehouse **13** sporting house **14** house of ill fame **16** house of ill repute **19** house of prostitution

fang 4 claw, nail, root, take, tang, tusk **5** prong, seize, tooth **6** obtain **7** capture, procure **8** eyetooth **9** chelicera

fanny 3 bum **4** buns, rump, seat, tush **6** behind, bottom **8** backside, buttocks, derriere **9** fundament

Fanny
  author: 9 Erica Jong

Fanny
  character in: 9 Fanny Hill **13** Joseph Andrews
  author: 7 Cleland **8** Fielding

fan out 7 scatter **8** disperse **9** spread out

fantasize 5 dream, fancy **7** imagine **8** daydream

fantastic 3 mad, odd **4** huge, wild **5** antic, crazy, great, queer, weird **6** absurd, superb **7** amazing, bizarre, extreme, strange **8** enormous, fabulous, fanciful, freakish, illusory, quixotic, romantic, terrific **9** grotesque, imaginary, marvelous, visionary, wonderful **10** chimerical, far-fetched, incredible, irrational, outlandish, ridiculous, tremendous **11** extravagant, implausible, sensational **12** preposterous, unbelievable

fantasy 4 mind **5** dream, fancy **6** mirage, notion, vision, whimsy **7** caprice, chimera, fiction, figment, phantom, reverie **8** daydream, illusion, phantasm **9** imagining, invention, nightmare, unreality **10** apparition **11** fabrication, imagination, make-believe, supposition **13** hallucination, realm of dreams, visionary idea

Fantasy Island
  character: 6 Tattoo **8** Mr Roarke
  cast: 16 Herve Villechaize, Ricardo Montalban

far 4 afar, much **6** deeply, remote, way-off, yonder **7** distant, greatly **11** beyond range, out-of-the-way **12** considerably, immeasurably, incomparably

Faraday, Michael
  field: 7 physics **9** chemistry
  worked in: 11 electricity
  developed: 9 generator **12** electrolysis
  liquified: 8 chlorine
  discovered: 6 carbon **7** benzene **24** electromagnetic induction
  named for him: 5 farad

far and near 10 every place, everywhere, far and wide **11** in all places

far and wide 10 every place, everywhere, far and near **11** in all places

Far Away and Long Ago
  author: 8 W H Hudson

farce 4 sham **6** parody **7** mockery **8** drollery, nonsense, pretense, travesty **9** absurdity, burlesque, horseplay, low comedy **10** buffoonery, tomfoolery **11** broad comedy, make-believe **12** harlequinade **14** ridiculousness

farceur 3 wag **5** joker

farcical 5 droll, funny, silly **6** absurd, stupid **7** asinine, comical, foolish **8** humorous **9** laughable, ludicrous, senseless **10** irrational, ridiculous

fare 2 do **3** fee **4** diet, food, menu **5** board, get on, rider, table **6** charge, client, manage **7** make out, perform, regimen, turn out **8** customer, get along, victuals **10** provisions **11** comestibles, ticket price **12** food and drink, passage money **15** paying passenger **20** cost of transportation

Farenheit 9/11
  director: 12 Michael Moore
  cast (as themselves): 6 Al Gore **10** Craig Unger, Neil Cavuto, Tim Russert **11** Colin Powell, George W. Bush, Helen Thomas, John Conyers **12** Jim McDermott, John Ashcroft, Lila Lipscomb **13** Osama bin Laden, Paul Wolfowitz, Saddam Hussein **14** Donald Rumsfeld **15** Condoleezza Rice

farewell 6 so long **7** good-bye, parting **8** Godspeed **9** departing, departure **11** leave-taking, parting wish, valediction **17** parting compliment
  French: 5 adieu **8** au revoir
  German: 14 auf Wiedersehen
  Hawaiian: 5 aloha
  Italian: 4 ciao **5** addio **11** arrivederci
  Japanese: 8 sayonara
  Latin: 4 vale
  Spanish: 5 adios

Farewell to Arms, A
  author: 15 Ernest Hemingway
  character: 13 Frederic Henry **16** Catherine Barkley

far-fetched 7 dubious **8** doubtful, strained, unlikely **10** cockamamie, improbable **11** implausible **12** preposterous, unconvincing

Far from Heaven
  director: 10 Todd Haynes
  cast: 11 Dennis Quaid (Frank Whitaker) **13** Julianne Moore (Cathy Whitaker) **14** Dennis Haysbert (Raymond Deagan) **16** Patricia Clarkson (Eleanor Fine)

Far From the Madding Crowd
  author: 11 Thomas Hardy
  character: 10 Fanny Robin, Gabriel Oak **12** Sergeant Troy **14** Farmer Boldwood **17** Bathsheba Everdene
  setting: 6 Wessex

Fargo
  director: 8 Joel Coen **9** Ethan Coen
  cast: 9 Steve Park (Mike Yanagita) **10** Tony Denman (Scotty Lundegaard) **12** Steve Buscemi (Carl Showalter), William H. Macy (Jerry Lundegaard) **13** Harve Presnell (Wade Gustafson), Kristin Rudrud (Jean Lundegaard), Peter Stormare (Gaear Grimsrud) **16** Frances McDormand (Marge Gunderson), John Carroll Lynch (Norm Gunderson)

farina 4 meal, mush **5** flour **6** cereal, pollen, starch **8** semolina

farm 3 sow **4** plow, reap **5** plant, ranch, tract **6** grange, spread **7** harvest **9** cultivate **10** plantation **11** till the soil **12** country place

farmable 6 arable **7** friable **8** plowable, tillable **10** cultivable

farm animal 2 ox **3** cow, ewe, hen, hog, pig, ram, sow **4** bull, goat **5** beast, brute, horse, sheep **7** chicken, rooster

farm boundaries
  god of: 8 Silvanus, Sylvanus

farmer 6 grower, raiser, reaper **7** granger, planter, rancher **8** agrarian **9** harvester **10** agronomist, husbandman **12** sharecropper **13** agriculturist, truck gardener **15** tiller of the soil

farming
  god of: 4 Thor

far-off 6 remote **7** distant, far-away **11** unreachable **12** inaccessible **13** unforeseeable

farouche 3 shy **6** fierce, sullen **10** unsociable

far-out 3 mad **4** wild **5** crazy, weird **7** bizarre, strange **10** outlandish **14** fantastic

Far Pavilions, The
  author: 6 M M Kaye

Farragut, David
  served in: 8 Civil War **10** Mexican War **19** War of Eighteen-Twelve
  captured: 9 Mobile Bay **10** New Orleans
  saying: 30 Damn the torpedoes, full speed ahead

far-reaching 4 wide **5** broad **8** sweeping **9** expansive, extensive, universal, unlimited **11** wide-ranging

Farrell, James T
  author of: 11 Judgment Day **12** Studs Lonigan, Young Lonigan **29** The Young Manhood of Studs Lonigan

far-removed 6 far-off, remote **7** distant, faraway

farrow 6 barren **7** piglets, sterile **9** infertile **10** unpregnant

Farrow, Mia
  real name: 27 Maria de Lourdes Villier Farrow

father: 10 John Farrow
mother: 16 Maureen O'Sullivan
husband: 11 Andre Previn 12 Frank Sinatra
companion: 10 Woody Allen
daughter: 12 Soon-Yi Previn
born: 12 Los Angeles CA
roles: 5 Zelig 11 John and Mary, Peyton Place 12 Angela Mooney, The Hurricane 13 Rosemary's Baby 14 The Great Gatsby 16 Allison MacKenzie 19 Hannah and Her Sisters 20 The Purple Rose of Cairo

far side 4 back 7 reverse 8 back side

Far Side, The
creator/artist: 10 Gary Larson

farsighted 4 wise 5 acute 6 shrewd 7 prudent 9 farseeing, hyperopic, judicious, prescient, provident 10 forehanded, foreseeing 11 clairvoyant, levelheaded

farther 6 beyond, deeper, longer 7 further, remoter 9 lengthier 10 more remote 11 more distant, more removed

farthermost 7 extreme 8 farthest, furthest 11 furthermost, most distant

farthest 3 end 4 most 7 extreme, longest 8 furthest, remotest, ultimate 9 uttermost 11 farthermost, furthermost

fascia 4 band, sash 5 board, strip 6 fillet, girdle, ribbon, tissue 7 bandage 8 membrane 9 dashboard

fascinate 5 charm, rivet 6 absorb, allure 7 beguile, bewitch, delight, enchant, engross 8 enravish, enthrall, entrance, transfix 9 captivate, enrapture, overpower, spellbind 14 hold spellbound

fascinating 8 alluring, charming, gripping, riveting 9 absorbing, beguiling 10 bewitching, delightful, enchanting, engrossing, entrancing 11 captivating, enthralling, interesting 12 overpowering, spellbinding

fascination 4 draw, lure 5 charm 6 allure 9 magnetism 10 attraction 11 captivation

fascism 6 Nazism 9 autocracy, oligarchy 10 plutocracy 11 corporatism, police state 13 corporativism 14 corporate state 15 totalitarianism 17 national socialism 21 right-wing dictatorship

fascist 8 dictator 9 Mussolini, rightwing 10 black shirt, brown shirt, repressive, tyrannical 11 dictatorial, doctrinaire 12 storm trooper

fashion 3 air, fad, hew, way 4 form, make, mode, mold, rage 5 carve, craze, forge, frame, habit, shape, style, tenor, trend, usage, vogue 6 create, custom, design, devise, manner 7 compose, pattern, produce 8 attitude, behavior, contrive, demeanor 9 construct, fabricate 10 convention 11 manufacture

fashionable 2 in 3 hip 4 chic 5 smart 6 modish, with-it 7 current, in style, in vogue, popular, stylish, voguish 9 in fashion 10 all the rage, prevailing
French: 9 de rigueur

fashionable world
French: 10 grand monde

fashion designer 4 (Christian) Dior 5 Kenzo, (Jean) Patou, Prada 6 Adolfo, (Georgio) Armani, Lanvin, Poiret, (Coco) Chanel 7 Galanos, (Gianni) Versace, Halston, Missoni, (Pierre) Balmain 8 Givenchy 9 Courreges, Mary Quant, Valentino 10 Balenciaga, Donna Karan, Mainbocher, Perry Ellis 11 Calvin Klein, Emilio Pucci, Ralph Lauren 12 Liz Claiborne, Lucien Lelong, Norman Norell, Pierre Cardin, Schiaparelli 13 Karl Lagerfeld, Rudi Gernreich 14 Pauline Trigere 15 Claire McCardell 16 Gloria Vanderbilt, Yves Saint-Laurent
Empress Eugenie's: 5 (Charles Frederick) Worth
Marie Antoinette's: 10 Rose Bertin
Empress Josephine's: 19 Louis Hippolyte Leroy

fashioned 4 made 5 built 6 formed, framed, molded, shaped, styled 7 adapted, crafted, created, devised, managed, modeled 9 contrived, patterned 11 constructed 12 accommodated

fashion plate 4 dude 5 dandy 12 Beau Brummell, clotheshorse, man of fashion, sharp dresser 14 woman of fashion

fast 4 firm, taut, true, wild 5 ahead, brisk, fleet, fully, hasty, loose, loyal, quick, rapid, rigid, swift, tight 6 famish, firmly, flying, rakish, secure, speedy, stable, starve, steady, wanton, winged 7 abiding, devoted, durable, fasting, fast day, fixedly, hastily, hurried, immoral, lasting, lustful, quickly, rapidly, solidly, soundly, staunch, swiftly, tightly 8 constant, enduring, faithful, fastened, go hungry, immodest, reckless, resolute, securely, speedily, unfading 9 debauched, dissolute, hurriedly, immovable, immovably, in advance, permanent, resistant, steadfast 10 completely, dissipated, firmly tied, lascivious, licentious, profligate, starvation, stationary, unswerving, unwavering 11 accelerated, expeditious, extravagant, intemperate, pleasure-mad, tenaciously 12 hunger strike, ineradicable, lickety-split

Fast, Howard
author of: 9 Spartacus 11 Freedom Road 13 The Immigrants 15 Citizen Tom Paine

fasten 3 bar, fix, pin, tie, wed 4 bind, bolt, clip, fuse, hold, hook, join, lash, link, lock, moor, snap, weld, yoke 5 affix, clamp, clasp, dowel, focus, hitch, close, latch, rivet, screw, stick, truss, unite 6 adhere, anchor, attach, button, cement, couple, direct, pinion, secure, solder, tether 7 connect 8 dovetail 11 put together

fastener 3 peg, pin, tie 4 clip, glue, grip, hook, line, nail, snap, tack 5 catch, clamp, clasp, cleat, latch, screw, strap, truss 6 buckle, button, cement, staple, thread, zipper 7 bracket 8 barrette 9 fastening, safety pin, thumbtack 10 clothespin, connection, hook and eye

fastening 4 snap 5 clasp 8 coupling 9 attaching 10 attachment, connection

fasten together 3 tie 4 dock, join 6 couple, hook up, link up

fastidious 5 fussy, picky 6 choosy, dainty, proper, queasy 7 finicky 8 exacting, precious 9 difficult, squeamish 10 meticulous, particular 11 overprecise, overrefined, persnickety 12 hard to please, overdelicate 13 hypercritical

Fastidious Brisk
character in: 22 Every Man out of His Humour
author: 6 Jonson

fastidiousness 4 care 12 exactingness 14 discrimination 15 persnicketiness

fat 4 full, oily 5 beefy, fatty, flush, heavy, obese, palmy, plump, pudgy, stout, suety 6 chubby, fleshy, grease, greasy, portly, rotund 7 copious, fertile, lumpish, paunchy, replete, stuffed 8 abundant, blubbery, chockful, fruitful, thickset, unctuous 9 animal fat, corpulent, fortunate, lucrative, plenteous, plentiful, rewarding 10 overweight, potbellied, productive 11 well-stocked 12 remunerative

fatal 6 deadly, lethal, mortal 7 ruinous 8 terminal, virulent 10 calamitous, disastrous 11 destructive 12 catastrophic, causing death

fatalism 8 stoicism 11 resignation 12 acquiescence, helplessness 13 powerlessness 14 predestination

fatality 5 death 8 casualty 9 lethality, mortality 10 deadliness, malignancy 11 banefulness

fatal woman see 11 femme fatale

fate 3 lot 4 doom 5 karma, moira 6 effect, future, kismet, upshot 7 chances, destiny, fortune, outcome, portion 8 prospect 10 providence 11 consequence 12 will of heaven 14 predestination

fated 4 sure 5 bound, meant 6 doomed 7 certain 8 destined

fateful 5 fatal 7 crucial, ominous 8 critical, decisive 9 momentous 10 disastrous, portentous 11 significant

Fates
also: 5 Morae 6 Moerae, Moirai, Parcae
named: 6 Clotho 7 Atropos 8 Lachesis

goddesses of: 7 destiny
number of goddesses: 5 three
called: 12 weird sisters
parents: 4 Zeus 5 Night 6 Themis
father 3 dad, pop 4 abbe, cure, papa, sire 5 beget, begin, daddy, found, hatch, maker, padre, pater 6 author, create, design, old man, parson, pastor, priest 7 creator, founder 8 ancestor, begetter, designer, engender, forebear, inventor, preacher 9 architect, confessor, originate, procreate 10 forefather, male parent, originator, progenitor
French: 4 pere
Father 4 Abba
Father, The
author: 16 August Strindberg
Father Knows Best
character: 11 Jim Anderson 13 Betty Anderson (Princess), Kathy Anderson (Kitten) 15 James Anderson Jr (Bud) 16 Margaret Anderson
cast: 9 Billy Gray, Jane Wyatt 11 Robert Young 12 Lauren Chapin 13 Elinor Donahue
fatherland 6 Heimat, patria, patrie 8 homeland 10 birthplace, motherland, native land, native soil 13 mother country, native country
fatherly 6 benign, kindly, tender 8 parental, paternal 9 indulgent 10 beneficent, benevolent
father of his country
Latin: 12 Pater Patriae
father of stars/wind 8 Astraeus
Father of the Bride
director: 16 Vincente Minnelli
cast: 11 Billie Burke, Joan Bennett, Leo G Carroll 12 Spencer Tracy 15 Elizabeth Taylor
sequel: 21 Father's Little Dividend
father of the family
Latin: 13 paterfamilias
Father of the Rivers see 4 Nile
Fathers and Sons
author: 12 Ivan Turgenev
character: 5 Katya, Pavel 6 Arkady, Vasily 8 Bazaroff, Fenichka 9 Kirsanoff 15 Madame Odintzoff
fathom 5 probe 6 divine, follow 7 hunt out, root out, uncover, unravel 8 discover 9 ferret out, figure out, penetrate 10 comprehend, understand 16 get to the bottom of
fathom
abbreviation: 4 fath
fatigue 3 fag 4 bush, tire 5 drain, weary 6 tedium, tucker, weaken 7 exhaust, languor, wear out 8 enervate, overtire 9 heaviness, lassitude, tiredness, weariness 10 debilitate, drowsiness, enervation, exhaustion 12 debilitation, listlessness 13 overtiredness
fatigued 4 beat 5 all in, jaded, spent, tired, weary 6 bushed, done in,

fagged, pooped 7 worn out 8 dog-tired, weakened 9 dead tired, enervated, exhausted, overtaxed 10 overworked 11 debilitated, tuckered out
fatiguing 6 tiring 7 arduous, tedious 8 tiresome 9 wearisome 10 exhausting
Fatima
character in: 9 Bluebeard
fatti maschii, parole femine 29
deeds are manly words are womanish
motto of: 8 Maryland
fatty 4 oily 5 lardy, suety 6 greasy 7 buttery 8 blubbery 9 shortened
fatuous 5 inane, silly, vapid 6 obtuse, simple, stupid 7 asinine, foolish, idiotic, moronic, puerile, vacuous, witless 8 besotted, imbecile 9 brainless, senseless 10 ridiculous
faucet 3 tap 4 cock 5 spout, valve 6 nozzle, outlet, spigot 7 bibcock
Faulkland
character in: 9 The Rivals
author: 8 Sheridan
Faulkner, William
author of: 7 The Bear 8 Sartoris 9 Sanctuary, The Hamlet 10 The Reivers 11 As I Lay Dying 13 Light in August 15 Absalom Absalom! 17 Intruder in the Dust 18 The Sound and the Fury
fictional county: 13 Yoknapatawpha
award: 5 Nobel 10 literature
fault 3 bug, sin 4 flaw, slip, snag 5 blame, crime, error, guilt, stain, taint, wrong 6 defect, foible, glitch, impugn 7 blemish, blunder, censure, failing, frailty, misdeed, mistake, offense, reprove 8 drawback, weakness 9 criticize, infirmity, oversight, weak point 10 deficiency, impediment, negligence, peccadillo, wrongdoing 11 culpability, dereliction, misdemeanor, shortcoming 12 imperfection, indiscretion 13 answerability, transgression 14 accountability, responsibility
faultfind 3 nag 4 beef, carp, kick 5 cavil, gripe, knock 6 deride, squawk 7 nitpick 8 complain 9 criticize
faultfinder 3 nag 4 bear, crab 5 crank 6 carper, censor, critic, grouch 7 caviler, grouser 8 quibbler, sorehead 9 derogator, detractor, Mrs Grundy, nitpicker 10 bellyacher, complainer, curmudgeon, fuddy-duddy, fussbudget
faultfinding 4 beef, kick 5 gripe 6 squawk 7 beefing, carping, griping, kicking, nagging 9 complaint, criticism, squawking 10 nitpicking 11 complaining, criticizing
faultless 5 ideal 7 correct, perfect 8 accurate, flawless 9 exemplary 10 immaculate, impeccable 11 unblemished 13 unimpeachable 14 irreproachable, without blemish
faulty 3 bad 4 awry 5 amiss, false, wrong 7 injured, unsound 8 impaired, inferior, mistaken 9 defective, defi-

cient, erroneous, imperfect, incorrect 10 inadequate, out of order, unreliable 14 unsatisfactory
faun
form: 5 deity, satyr 7 goat-man
location: 5 rural
Fauna see 7 Bona Dea
Faunus
origin: 5 Roman
form: 5 deity
location: 5 woods
also called: 5 Inuus 6 Fatuus
king of: 6 Latium
father: 5 Picus
son: 7 Latinus
corresponds to: 3 Pan
Faure, Gabriel Urbain
born: 6 France 7 Pamiers
composer of: 5 Dolly 6 Pavane 7 Ballade, Mirages, Requiem, Shylock 8 Penelope 9 Fantaisie, Promethee 12 Le Jardin Clos 13 La Chanson d'Eve 14 La Bonne Chanson 18 L'Horizon Chimerique, Pelleas et Melisande 21 Masques et Bergamasques
Faust
author: 12 Johann Goethe
character: 6 Wagner 8 Gretchen 10 Homunculus 11 Helen of Troy 14 Mephistopheles
Faust
opera by: 6 Gounod
character: 6 Siebel 8 Valentin 10 Marguerite 14 Mephistopheles
Faustulus
vocation: 8 herdsman, shepherd
raised: 5 Remus 7 Romulus
faute de mieux 24 for lack of something better
faux pas 4 goof 5 boner, error, gaffe, lapse 6 boo-boo, howler, slip-up 7 blooper, blunder, mistake 9 false step 11 impropriety 12 indiscretion
favela 4 slum 10 shanty town
Favonius
origin: 5 Roman
personifies: 8 west wind
favor 3 aid 4 abet, back, gift, help, like 5 be for, fancy, humor 6 assist, esteem, foster, oblige, pamper, prefer, succor, uphold 7 approve, commend, endorse, go in for, indulge, kind act, memento, present, service, support 8 advocacy, approval, courtesy, espousal, good deed, good turn, goodwill, largesse, look like, resemble, sanction, side with, souvenir 9 encourage, patronage, patronize, smile upon, take after, use gently 10 act of grace, use lightly 11 accommodate, approbation, be partial to, benefaction, countenance, good opinion 12 be the image of, championship, kindly regard 13 accommodation, goodwill token

favorable 4 fair, good, kind **6** benign, timely **7** helpful, hopeful **8** amicable, friendly, salutary **9** approving, conducive, opportune, promising **10** auspicious, beneficial, convenient, propitious **11** predisposed, serviceable, sympathetic **12** advantageous, commendatory, well-disposed

favorable opinion 6 esteem, regard **7** respect **8** approval **10** admiration **12** appreciation

favorably disposed 7 willing **8** amenable, inclined, obliging **9** agreeable **11** sympathetic

favorite 3 pet **5** fancy, jewel **6** choice **7** darling, special **9** best-liked, preferred **11** front-runner, most popular **13** fair-haired one **14** apple of one's eye

favoritism 4 bias **10** partiality **12** one-sidedness, partisanship

Fawkes, Guy 11 conspirator
  associated with: 13 Gunpowder Plot
  target: 9 King James **10** Parliament

fawn 5 toady **6** pander **7** flatter, truckle **8** pay court **9** be servile, seek favor **12** be obsequious, bow and scrape

fawning 7 servile **8** flattery, toadying **9** adulating, adulation, truckling **10** flattering, obsequious **11** sycophantic **12** ingratiating **14** obsequiousness

fax 4 send **8** transmit **9** facsimile

faze 4 fret **5** abash, daunt, upset, worry **6** bother, flurry, rattle **7** disturb, fluster, perturb **8** confound **9** discomfit, embarrass **10** discompose, disconcert

fazed 5 upset **7** abashed, ruffled **8** agitated, bothered, confused **9** chagrined, unsettled **10** confounded, distracted, nonplussed **11** embarrassed **12** disconcerted

FBI, The
  character: 10 Arthur Ward **21** Inspector Lewis Erskine
  cast: 12 Philip Abbott **16** Efrem Zimbalist Jr

fealty 7 loyalty **8** devotion, fidelity **9** adherence, constancy **10** allegiance, attachment **12** faithfulness

fear 3 awe **4** care **5** alarm, bogey, dread, panic, qualm, worry **6** dismay, esteem, fright, horror, phobia, revere, terror, threat, wonder **7** anxiety, bugaboo, bugbear, concern, quaking, specter **8** affright, venerate **9** cowardice, nightmare, reverence, shudder at, tremble at **10** be afraid of, be scared of, feel awe for, foreboding, take fright, veneration **11** trepidation **12** apprehension, perturbation **13** consternation **14** be frightened of

Fear Factor
  network: 3 NBC
  host: 8 Joe Rogan

fearful 4 dire **5** awful, dread, eerie, lurid, timid **6** afraid, aghast, horrid, scared, uneasy **7** alarmed, anxious, ghastly, macabre, nervous, ominous, panicky, worried **8** alarming, dreadful, horrible, shocking, sinister, skittish, terrible, timorous **9** appalling, concerned, diffident, frightful, tremulous **10** formidable, frightened, portentous, terrifying **11** distressing, frightening, intimidated **12** apprehensive, faint-hearted **13** panic-stricken **14** chicken-hearted

fearfulness fear **5** alarm, dread, panic **6** fright, terror **7** anguish, anxiety **8** timidity **11** trepidation **12** apprehension

fearless 4 bold **5** brave **6** daring, gritty, heroic, plucky **7** doughty, gallant, valiant **8** intrepid, unafraid, valorous **9** audacious, confident, dauntless, unabashed, undaunted **10** courageous, undismayed **11** adventurous, indomitable, lionhearted, unflinching, unshrinking, venturesome, without fear **12** stout-hearted

fearlessness 4 grit **5** pluck, valor **7** bravery, courage **8** boldness **10** confidence **13** dauntlessness

Fear of Flying
  author: 9 Erica Jong

feasible 6 doable, viable **7** fitting, politic **8** possible, suitable, workable **9** advisable, desirable **10** achievable, attainable, reasonable **11** appropriate, conceivable, practicable

feast 4 dine, fete **5** festa, gorge **6** bounty **7** banquet, holiday, jubilee, surplus **8** feast day, festival **9** bacchanal, saint's day **10** gluttonize, gormandize, have a feast, rich supply **11** celebration, eat one's fill, elegant meal, wine and dine

feat 3 act **4** deed, task **6** action, stroke **7** exploit, triumph **8** maneuver **9** adventure **10** attainment, enterprise **11** achievement, performance, tour de force **14** accomplishment

feather 4 down, kind, sort **5** adorn, eider, pinna, plume, quill **7** bristle, plumage, variety **9** character, turn an oar

featherbrained 4 dumb **5** silly **6** simple, stupid **7** foolish, witless **9** brainless **12** muddleheaded, simple-minded **13** rattle-brained **14** scatterbrained

feather in one's cap 5 honor **6** credit **11** distinction

feather one's nest 6 enrich **15** fill one's pockets

feature, features 3 see **4** mark, star **5** fancy, trait **6** aspect, play up, visage **7** display, earmark, imagine, picture, present, quality **8** envision, hallmark, headline, main item, property **9** attribute, character, highlight, specialty, spotlight **10** conceive of, lineaments **14** characteristic

February
  event: 4 Lent **5** Purim **8** Leap year **9** Mardi Gras **12** Ash Wednesday, Groundhog Day (2)
  flower: 6 violet **8** primrose
  French: 7 Fevrier
  gem: 8 amethyst
  German: 7 Februar
  holiday: 9 Candlemas (2) **13** President's Day Valentine's Day (14) **14** Chinese New Year **16** Lincoln's Birthday (12) **19** Washington's Birthday (22)
  Italian: 8 Febbraio
  Latin: 6 Februa
  number of days: 10 twenty-nine (every 4 years) **11** twenty-eight
  origin of name: 7 Februus
    Roman god of: 12 purification
  place in year:
    Gregorian: 6 second
    Roman: 7 twelfth
  Spanish: 7 Febrero
  Zodiac signs: 6 Pisces **8** Aquarius

Fechner, Gustav Theodore
  nationality: 6 German
  founder of: 22 experimental psychology

fecit 6 he made (it) **7** she made (it)

feckless 3 lax **5** slack **6** remiss **8** careless, heedless **9** negligent, worthless **10** neglectful **11** thoughtless **13** irresponsible

Fecundity
  goddess of: 5 Freia, Freya

Fed
  Federal Reserve System: 6 the Fed
  FBI agent: 4 G-man **6** feebie, fibbie
  Treasury agent: 4 T-man
  head: 12 Alan Greenspan

Federalist Party
  president belonging to: 5 Adams **10** Washington

federate 5 unite **7** combine **12** join together

federation 5 union **6** league **7** combine **8** alliance **9** coalition, syndicate **10** sisterhood **11** association, brotherhood, confederacy **12** amalgamation **13** confederation

fee 4 fare, hire, toll, wage **5** price **6** charge, salary, tariff **7** payment, stipend **9** emolument **10** commission, honorarium **12** compensation, remuneration **13** consideration

feeble 4 flat, lame, poor, puny, tame, thin, weak **5** faint, frail, vapid **6** ailing, flabby, flimsy, infirm, meager, paltry, senile, sickly, slight **7** fragile, insipid **8** decrepit, delicate, disabled, impotent, weakened **9** colorless, declining, doddering, enervated, enfeebled, forceless, not strong, powerless **10** inadequate, spiritless, wishy-washy **11** debilitated, ineffective, ineffectual

feeble-minded 4 dull, dumb **6** senile, stupid **7** moronic **8** backward, childish, retarded **9** imbecilic, senseless, subnormal **10** half-witted, weak-minded **12** mentally slow

feeble-mindedness 6 dotage, idiocy **8** dullness, senility, slowness **9** denseness, stupidity **11** retardation

feed 3 eat **4** fare, fuel, mash **5** cater, feast, graze **6** devour, fodder, forage, foster, viands **7** augment, bolster, consume, gratify, nourish, nurture, pasture, satisfy, support, sustain **8** maintain, take food, victuals **9** encourage, foodstuff, provender **10** minister to, provisions, strengthen **11** comestibles, nourishment, wine and dine

feeder 6 branch **7** channel **9** tributary

feel 3 paw, see **4** know **5** grope, press, probe, reach, sense, think, touch **6** finger, fumble, handle, makeup, notice **7** believe, discern, feeling, observe, palpate, texture **8** perceive **9** be aware of, be moved by, character, sensation **10** comprehend, experience, manipulate, suffer from, understand **11** be convinced, be stirred by, be touched by, composition

feel aversion toward 4 hate **5** abhor **6** detest **7** despise **8** abominate, can't abide, can't stand **11** can't stomach **12** be revolted by **13** find repugnant, find repulsive **14** view with horror

feeler 7 antenna **8** proposal, tentacle **10** experiment **12** trial balloon

feel indebted 10 appreciate, be beholden, be grateful **13** feel obligated

feeling 4 aura, pity, view, zeal **5** ardor, gusto, sense, verve **6** fervor, spirit, thrill, warmth **7** concern, emotion, opinion, passion **8** attitude, instinct, reaction, response, sympathy **9** affection, awareness, intuition, sensation, sentiment, vehemence **10** atmosphere, compassion, enthusiasm, impression **11** earnestness, inclination, point of view, sensibility, sensitivity

feeling life is wearisome
  Latin: 12 taedium vitae

feelings 3 ego **5** pride **8** emotions, passions **10** self-esteem **13** sensibilities, sensitivities **16** susceptibilities

feel pain 4 ache, hurt **5** smart **6** suffer **7** agonize **9** be in agony **11** be tormented **12** be in distress

feet 4 dogs, pads, paws **5** hoofs **6** hooves **8** gunboats, tootsies

feign 4 fake, sham **5** forge, put on **6** affect, assume, cook up, invent, make up **7** concoct, pretend **8** simulate **9** fabricate **11** counterfeit, make a show of, make believe

feigned 4 fake, sham **5** bogus, phony **6** ersatz **8** spurious **9** imitation, insincere, pretended, simulated **10** artificial **11** counterfeit, make-believe

feint 4 hoax, mask, move, pass, ploy, ruse, wile **5** blind, bluff, dodge, trick

6 gambit **7** pretext **8** artifice, maneuver, pretense **9** stratagem **10** subterfuge **13** feigned attack

Feldman, Marty
  born: 6 London **7** England
  roles: 11 Silent Movie **17** Young Frankenstein **24** The Last Remake of Beau Geste

feldspar
  varieties: 8 sunstone **9** amazonite, moonstone

felicitate 4 hail **6** salute **10** wish one joy **11** rejoice with **12** congratulate **18** give one's best wishes **28** wish many happy returns of the day

felicitations 3 joy **6** cheers **9** blessings, greetings **10** best wishes, good wishes **11** compliments, salutations **12** pat on the back **15** congratulations **24** many happy returns of the day

felicitous 3 apt **5** happy **6** joyful, joyous **7** fitting, germane, well-put **8** inspired, pleasing, relevant, suitable, well-said **9** effective, fortunate, pertinent **10** propitious, well-chosen **11** appropriate

felicity 5 bliss, charm, grace, knack, skill **6** heaven, nicety **7** aptness, delight, ecstasy, fitness **8** paradise **9** beatitude, happiness **12** blissfulness **13** effectiveness **15** appropriateness

Felix the Cat
  creator: 11 Pat Sullivan

fell 4 raze **5** level **7** cut down, destroy, hew down **8** demolish **9** knock down, prostrate

Feller, Bob (Robert)
  nickname: 11 Rapid Robert
  sport: 8 baseball
  position: 7 pitcher
  team: 16 Cleveland Indians

Fellini, Federico
  director of: 8 Amarcord, Casanova, La Strada **11** La Dolce Vita **15** Nights of Cabiria **18** Juliet of the Spirits

fellow 3 boy, guy, mac, man, pal **4** chap, chum, dude, gent, mate, peer **5** equal **6** friend **7** comrade, consort **8** coworker **9** associate, colleague, companion **10** compatriot

fellow conspirator 4 ally **6** cohort **7** abettor **8** henchman **9** accessory **11** confederate **12** collaborator

fellow creature 5 human **6** mortal, person **10** individual

fellow feeling 6 regard **7** empathy, kinship **8** affinity, fondness **10** attraction, partiality

fellowship 5 amity **7** society **8** intimacy **10** affability, cordiality, fraternity, friendship **11** amicability, association, brotherhood, comradeship, familiarity, sociability **12** friendliness **13** companionship

felon 5 crook, cruel, thief **6** fierce, out-

law, wicked **7** convict, illegal, villain, whitlow **8** criminal, gangster, jailbird, murderer **10** law-breaker, malefactor **11** public enemy **12** inflammation

felony 5 arson, crime **6** murder **7** assault, misdeed, offense, robbery **8** burglary **9** blackmail **10** kidnapping, wrongdoing **12** capital offense

female 3 cow, dam, hen, sow **4** girl, mare **5** bitch, tabby, woman **6** heifer **7** distaff, womanly **8** feminine, ladylike **9** womanlike

feminine 4 soft **5** woman **6** dainty, female, gentle **7** distaff, girlish, womanly **8** delicate, ladylike **10** femalelike, like a woman **14** of the female sex

femininity 8 softness **10** femaleness, gentleness **11** girlishness, womanliness **12** feminineness **13** female quality

femme 4 wife **5** woman

femme de chambre 9 lady's maid **11** chambermaid

femme fatale 4 vamp **5** siren **7** charmer **10** fatal woman, seductress **11** enchantress

femur
  bone of: 5 thigh **8** upper leg

fen 3 bog **4** moor, sump **5** marsh, swale, swamp **6** bottom, morass, slough **7** lowland, wetland **8** quagmire

fence 3 pen **4** coop, duel, gird, rail **5** hedge, hem in **6** corral, secure, wall in **7** barrier, confine, palings **8** encircle, palisade, stockade, surround **9** barricade, encompass **11** cross swords

fencing
  equipment: 4 epee, foil, mask **5** saber, sword **8** plastron
  part of weapon: 5 blade, forte, guard **6** foible, handle, medium, pommel
  term: 3 hit **5** prime, sixte, touch **6** octave, quarte, quinte, tierce **7** en garde, on guard, seconde, septime
  deceptive move: 5 feint
  movement: 4 beat **5** lunge, parry **6** double, fleche, thrust **7** advance, cutover, recover, retreat, riposte **9** disengage **11** froissement

fend 2 do **5** avert, avoid, parry, repel, shift **6** manage **7** keep off, make out, provide, repulse, support, survive, ward off **8** push away

fender 3 pad **4** curb **5** guard **6** buffer, bumper, shield, sluice **7** cushion, railing **9** fireguard, protector **10** cowcatcher, fire screen, protection, wheel guard

fend off 5 avert, dodge, evade, parry, repel **6** escape **7** ward off **8** sidestep, stave off

fennel
  botanical name: 17 Foeniculum vulgare

family: 7 parsley
varieties: 3 dog **4** wild **5** giant **8** Florence **9** common dog **11** common giant
mythical aid to: 9 fortifier **11** aphrodisiac, slenderizer **12** rejuvenation, stops hiccups **16** restores eyesight
use: 4 duck, fish **5** bread, rolls **7** chicken **8** apple pie **16** seafood casserole

Fenrir
also: 6 Fenris
origin: 12 Scandinavian
form: 4 wolf **7** monster
father: 4 Loki
mother: 9 Angerboda, Angrbodha, Angurboda
sister: 3 Hel
brother: 11 Iormungandr, Jormungandr **14** Midgard Serpent
ate: 4 Odin **5** Othin
killed by: 5 Vidar

Fenris *see* **6** Fenrir

Fenton
character in: 22 The Merry Wives of Windsor
author: 11 Shakespeare

feral 4 wild **6** brutal, deadly, ferine, fierce, savage **7** bestial, untamed, vicious **9** ferocious **12** uncultivated **14** undomesticated

Ferber, Edna
author of: 5 Giant, So Big **8** Cimarron, Show Boat **9** Ice Palace, Stage Door (with George S Kaufman) **13** Dinner at Eight (with George S Kaufman), Saratoga Trunk **14** The Royal Family (with George S Kaufman)

Ferdinand
king of: 5 Spain
wife: 8 Isabella
patron of: 8 Columbus

Ferdinand
character in: 10 The Tempest
author: 11 Shakespeare

Ferdinand
character in: 16 Love's Labour's Lost
author: 11 Shakespeare

Ferdinand the Bull
author: 9 Munro Leaf
disliked: 12 bullfighting

Ferd'nand
creator: 3 Mik **13** Dahl Mikkelsen

Feria
origin: 5 Roman
form: 7 holiday

Fermat, Pierre de
field: 11 mathematics
nationality: 6 French
discovered: 16 analytic geometry

ferment 4 foam, mold, sour, turn **5** froth, yeast **6** enzyme, fester, leaven, seethe, tumult, unrest, uproar **7** agitate, inflame, smolder, turmoil **8** bubble up, disquiet **9** agitation, commotion, leavening **10** disruption,

effervesce, turbulence **11** be turbulent, fomentation

fermented 6 soured, worked **7** seethed **8** agitated

Fermi, Enrico
field: 7 physics
nationality: 7 Italian
developed: 10 atomic bomb **20** uranium fission theory
awarded: 10 Nobel Prize

fern
varieties: 3 air, cup, lip, man, oak, saw **4** ball, blue, claw, deer, dish, felt, fire, gold, hand, iron, king, lace, lady, male, moss, nest, pine, sago, tara, tree, wall, wart, wood **5** beard, beech, chain, cloak, fancy, glade, glory, grape, grass, hedge, holly, marsh, plume, royal, strap, swamp, sweet, sword, table, water, whisk **6** adder's, bamboo, basket, Boston, button, carrot, coffee, cotton, cuplet, dagger, ladder, meadow, mother, ribbon, shield, silver, tongue, turnip, winter **7** bladder, bottle, brittle, bulblet, crested, emerald, feather, Fee's lip, fragile, Goldie's, hacksaw, Halberd, hammock, leather, New York, ostrich, parsley, peacock, rainbow, walking **8** bear-foot, bear's-paw, cinnamon, climbing, elk's-horn, fishtail, floating, florist's, fragrant, hairy lip, Hartford, licorice, mosquito, Nebraska, Savannah, snuffbox, soft tree, staghorn **9** asparagus, bird's-nest, black tree, blond tree, Christmas, common cup, deer's-foot, downy wood, flowering, glossy cup, hare's foot, long beech, sensitive, vegetable, Venus hair, viscid lip, wavy cloak, woolly lip **10** Alabama lip, Boott's wood, broad beech, deer-tongue, Duff's sword, erect sword, five-finger, hay-scented, lady ground, maidenhair, scented oak, shoestring, silver tree, silver-back, silver-lace, silver-leaf, slender lip, strawberry, upside-down, woolly tree **11** Braun's holly, coastal wood, Coville's lip, crested felt, crested wood, dwarf Boston, elephant-ear, Fendler's lip, hart's-tongue, interrupted, Jamaica gold, leatherleaf, leatherwood, narrow beech, netted chain, Northern oak, Parry's cloak, Pursh's holly, rabbit's-foot, rattlesnake, Sierra water, walking leaf **12** Adder's-tongue, American wall, berry bladder, Clinton's wood, Dudley's holly, Eaton's shield, English hedge, Hawaiian tree, Java staghorn, limestone oak, mountain wood, Northern lady, resurrection, Southern lady, squirrel-foot, toothed sword, Western holly, Western sword **13** California lip, Cleveland's lip, Dudley's shield, European chain, fan maidenhair, Fendler's cloak, Florida ribbon, leathery grape,

Malay climbing, mountain holly, Northern holly, prickly shield, Prince-of-Wales, spinulose wood, Tasmanian tree, triangle water, Virginia chain, wild bird's nest **14** Anderson's holly, Australian tree, bulblet bladder, California gold, common staghorn, dissected grape, dwarf asparagus, hen-and-chickens, imbricate sword, silver-king tree, West Indian tree **15** American parsley, California cloak, California holly, Delta maidenhair, East Indian holly, European parsley, mountain bladder, mountain parsley **16** black-stemmed tree, daisy-leaved grape, Farley maidenhair, Tassel maidenhair, Tracy's maidenhair **17** Bermuda maidenhair, brittle maidenhair, climbing bird's nest, walking maidenhair **18** Aleutian maidenhair, American maidenhair, Barbados maidenhair, Northern maidenhair, Trailing maidenhair, Triangular staghorn **20** Australian maidenhair, California maidenhair

fernet-branca
type: 8 aperitif
origin: 5 Italy
flavor: 4 herb

Fern Hill
author: 11 Dylan Thomas

ferocious 6 brutal, deadly, fierce, savage **7** bestial, brutish, enraged, violent **8** fiendish, maddened, ravening, ruthless **9** atrocious, barbarous, merciless, murderous, predatory, rapacious **10** relentless **11** cold-blooded **12** bloodthirsty

ferocity 7 cruelty **8** savagery **9** barbarity, brutality, harshness **10** fierceness, inhumanity, savageness **11** brutishness, viciousness **12** ruthlessness

Ferrer, Jose
real name: 33 Jose Vincente Ferrer de Otero y Cintron
wife: 8 Uta Hagen **15** Rosemary Clooney
son: 6 Miguel
born: 8 Santurce **10** Puerto Rico
roles: 7 I Accuse **9** Joan of Arc **11** Moulin Rouge, Ship of Fools **14** The Caine Mutiny **16** Cyrano de Bergerac (Oscar), Lawrence of Arabia **24** The Greatest Story Ever Told

ferret out 5 dig up **6** detect **7** find out, root out, uncover, unearth **8** discover **9** ascertain

fertile 4 rich **5** loamy **6** fecund **8** creative, fruitful, original, prolific **9** fructuous, ingenious, inventive, luxuriant, plenteous **10** fecundated, fertilized, fructified, generative, productive, vegetative **11** imaginative, resourceful **12** reproductive

Fertility
god of: 7 Bacchus, Mutinus **8** Lupercus, Picumnus

goddess of: 4 Isis **5** Fauna **6** Athena, Athene, Brigit, Libera, Pallas, Saitis, Tellus **7** Astarte, Berchta, Bona Dea, Demeter, Perchta **11** Tritogeneia **12** Pallas Athena **16** Alalcomean Athena

fertilize 6 enrich, manure **8** fructify **9** fecundate, pollinate **10** impregnate, inseminate

fertilizer 4 dung, muck **5** guano, niter **6** manure, potash **7** compost **8** bonemeal, dressing **10** enrichener **14** superphosphate

fervent 4 keen **5** eager, fiery **6** ardent, devout, fervid, fierce, hearty, heated **7** burning, earnest, intense, zealous **8** spirited, vehement **9** heartfelt **10** passionate **11** impassioned, warmhearted **12** enthusiastic, wholehearted

fervid 5 eager **6** ardent, raging **7** burning, earnest, fanatic, fervent, intense, zealous **8** spirited **10** passionate **11** impassioned **12** all-consuming

fervor 4 fire, zeal, zest **5** ardor, gusto, piety, verve **6** warmth **7** passion **9** animation, eagerness, intensity, vehemence **10** devoutness, enthusiasm, heartiness **11** earnestness, seriousness **14** purposefulness

Feste
clown in: 12 Twelfth Night
author: 11 Shakespeare

Fester *see* **12** Addams Family

fester 3 rot, vex **4** fret, gall, grow, rile **5** chafe, pique **6** nettle, plague, rankle **7** blister, form pus, inflame, putrefy, smolder, torment **8** irritate, ulcerate **9** intensify, suppurate

festering 6 putrid **7** rotting **8** infected, inflamed, rankling **10** putrefying **11** suppurating

festina lente 15 make haste slowly

festival 4 fete, gala **5** feast **6** fiesta **7** gala day, holiday, jubilee **8** carnival, jamboree **11** celebration, festivities

Festival of
Adonis: 6 Adonia
Apollo: 5 Delia **8** Didymaea **9** Delphinia **12** Daphnephoria
Athena: 6 Lenaea **8** Diipolia **9** Pyanepsia **11** Oschophoria
Attica: 13 Rural Dionysia **14** Lesser Dionysia
Bacchus: 11 Bacchanalia
Boeotians: 7 Daedala **13** Little Doedala
Demeter: 5 Haloa
Dionysus: 5 Haloa **8** Dionysia
flowers: 11 Anthesteria
Greeks: 6 Heraea **9** Pyanepsia **11** Scirophoria, Skirophoria **13** Thesmorphoria
Persephone: 5 Haloa
Roman: 8 Floralia, Matralia **9** Lemuralia, Liberalia **10** Larentalia, Lupercalia, Matronalia, Parentalia, Saturnalia
spring: 11 Anthesteria

wine: 11 Anthesteria
Zeus: 6 Diasia **8** Didymaea

festive 3 gay **4** gala **5** jolly, merry **6** festal, joyous **7** larkish, playful **8** sportive **9** convivial **10** frolicsome **11** celebratory **12** lighthearted

festivity 3 joy **4** fete, gala **5** feast, mirth **6** fiesta, gaiety, levity **7** fanfare, jollity, jubilee, revelry **8** festival, jamboree **9** merriment, rejoicing **11** celebration, merrymaking

festoon 3 lei **4** swag **5** chain, curve **6** wreath **7** garland, hanging **8** decorate

fetch 3 get **4** cost **5** bring, go for, yield **6** afford, obtain **7** procure, realize, sell for **8** amount to, retrieve

fetching 6 divine, lovely **8** adorable, becoming, charming, engaging, pleasing **9** appealing **10** attractive, delightful **11** captivating

fete 4 gala **5** feast, party, treat **6** regale **7** banquet, holiday **8** carnival, festival **9** bal masque **11** celebration, garden party, wine and dine **13** fete champetre

fete champetre 11 garden party **15** outdoor festival

fetid 4 foul, gamy, rank **5** fusty, moldy, musty, nasty **6** putrid, rancid, rotten **7** noisome, stenchy, tainted **8** mephitic, stifling, stinking **9** stenchful **10** malodorous **11** ill-smelling, suffocating

fetish 4 idol, joss **5** charm, craze, image, mania, totem **6** amulet, scarab **7** passion **8** idee fixe, talisman **9** obsession **10** golden calf, phylactery **11** magic object **12** superstition **13** preoccupation

fetter 4 bind, bond, cage, curb, yoke **5** chain, tie up **6** duress, hamper, hinder, hobble, impede, shut in, tether **7** confine, durance, manacle, pin down, shackle, tie down, trammel, truss up **8** bracelet, encumber, handcuff, hold back, restrain **9** hindrance, restraint **13** put into bilbos **15** bind hand and foot

feud 3 row **4** fuss, spat, tiff **5** argue, brawl, clash, set-to **6** affray, bicker, breach, enmity, fracas, schism, strife **7** discord, dispute, faction, ill will, quarrel, rupture, wrangle **8** argument, bad blood, be at odds, clashing, conflict, disagree, squabble, vendetta **9** animosity, bickering, hostility **10** falling out **11** altercation, controversy **12** disagreement, hard feelings
famous: 6 McCoys **9** Hatfields

feudal lord
Japanese: 6 daimyo

Feuerbach, Anselm
born: 6 Speyer **7** Germany
artwork: 9 Iphigenia **15** Judgment of Paris, Plato's Symposium **18** The Fall of the Titans

fever 4 fire, heat **5** ardor, craze, flush,

furor **6** desire, frenzy, warmth **7** ferment, illness, pyrexia **8** delirium, sickness **9** agitation **10** enthusiasm, excitement **11** temperature **12** restlessness

feverish 3 hot **5** fiery **6** ardent, red-hot **7** burning, excited, fanatic, febrile, fervent, fevered, flushed, parched, pyretic, zealous **8** frenzied, inflamed, restless **9** impatient, overeager, wrought-up **10** high-strung, passionate **11** impassioned

few 4 rare, some, thin **5** scant **6** meager, paltry, scanty, scarce, skimpy, sparse, unique **7** handful, limited, not many, several, unusual **8** exiguous, piddling, sporadic, uncommon **9** hardly any **10** infrequent, occasional **11** scarcely any, small number **13** infinitesimal, insignificant **14** inconsiderable

Fezziwig
character in: 15 A Christmas Carol
author: 7 Dickens

fiance, fiancee 6 future **7** engaged, pledge **8** intended, promised **9** affianced, betrothed, bride-to-be, groom-to-be **10** bride-elect, groom-elect

fiasco 4 bomb, flop **5** botch **6** fizzle **7** debacle, washout **8** disaster **10** nonsuccess

fiat 3 act, law **4** rule **5** edict, order, ukase **6** decree, dictum, ruling **7** command, mandate **11** commandment

fiat lux 15 let there be light

fib 3 lie **5** hedge **7** fiction, untruth **8** white lie **9** half-truth, invention **10** equivocate **11** fabrication, harmless lie, prevaricate **13** falsification, prevarication, tell a white lie **15** stretch the truth **17** misrepresentation

fiber 4 hemp, jute, silk **5** fibre, linen, nylon, rayon, shred, sinew, sisal **6** cotton, dacron, manila, nature, strand, thread **7** quality, texture **8** filament **9** character, polyester, structure

fibrolite
source: 5 Burma, Mogok

fibula
bone of: 8 lower leg

fickle 5 giddy **6** fitful **7** erratic, flighty **8** shifting, unstable, unsteady, variable, volatile, wavering **9** frivolous, mercurial, spasmodic, whimsical **10** capricious, changeable, inconstant, irresolute, unreliable **11** fluctuating, light-headed, vacillating **12** inconsistent **13** feather-headed, unpredictable, untrustworthy **14** feather-brained

fiction 3 fib, lie **4** play, tale, yarn **5** fable, novel **7** fantasy, forgery, novella, romance, whopper **8** tall tale **9** falsehood, invention, narrative **10** concoction, short novel, short story **11** fabrication, imagination, made-up story **12** storytelling **13** prevarication **16** cock-and-bull story

fictional 6 made-up 8 invented, literary, mythical 9 storybook 10 fictitious 11 theoretical 12 hypothetical

fictitious 4 fake, sham 5 bogus, false, phony 6 forged, made-up, unreal, untrue 7 assumed, feigned 8 fanciful, invented, mythical, spurious 9 imaginary, legendary, simulated, trumped-up, unfounded 10 apocryphal, artificial, fabricated, fraudulent, not genuine 11 counterfeit 14 supposititious

fiddle 3 bow, saw, toy 4 fool 5 cheat, dally, fraud 6 dawdle, monkey, potter, putter, tamper, trifle, violin 7 falsify, finagle, fritter, swindle 9 deception 10 fool around, mess around 12 monkey around

Fidei Defensor 18 Defender of the Faith
title of: 17 English sovereigns

Fidelio
opera by: 9 Beethoven
character: 5 Rocco 7 Leonora (Fidelio), Pizarro 8 Fernando 9 Florestan

fidelity 5 honor 6 fealty 7 honesty, loyalty, probity 8 accuracy, devotion 9 adherence, closeness, constancy, exactness, good faith, integrity, precision, sincerity 10 allegiance, exactitude 11 earnestness, reliability, staunchness 12 faithfulness, truthfulness 14 correspondency 15 trueheartedness, trustworthiness

Fides
origin: 5 Roman
personifies: 9 good faith

fidget 4 fret, fuss, jerk, stew, toss 5 chafe, worry 6 jiggle, squirm, twitch, wiggle, writhe 7 twiddle, wriggle

fidgety 5 antsy, fussy, jerky, jumpy 6 uneasy 7 jittery, nervous, restive, squirmy, twitchy, unquiet 8 restless 9 impatient, irritable, tremulous 12 apprehensive

fief 4 land 6 domain, estate 9 territory

field 3 lea 4 area, grab, lawn, line, mead, turf, yard 5 arena, catch, court, front, glove, green, heath, lists, orbit, range, reach, realm, scope, sward, sweep 6 circle, common, course, domain, extent, meadow, pick up, region, sphere 7 acreage, calling, diamond, expanse, pasture, run down, stretch 8 clearing, province, retrieve, spectrum 9 bailiwick, grassland, territory 10 department, occupation, profession 12 battleground

Field, Sally
born: 10 Pasadena CA
roles: 5 Sybil 6 Gidget 8 Norma Rae (Oscar) 9 Punchline, Surrender 11 Forrest Gump 12 The Flying Nun 14 Murphy's Romance, Steel Magnolias 15 Absence of Malice 16 Legally

Blonde Two, Places in the Heart (Oscar) 18 Smokey and the Bandit

Fielding, Cecil
character in: 15 A Passage to India
author: 7 Forster

Fielding, Henry
author of: 6 Amelia 7 Shamela 8 Tom Jones, Tom Thumb 12 Jonathan Wild 13 Joseph Andrews

Field of Blood 8 Aceldama

Fields, W C
real name: 23 William Claude Dukenfield
born: 14 Philadelphia PA
roles: 5 Poppy 8 Micawber 11 The Bank Dick 16 David Copperfield 17 My Little Chickadee 27 Never Give a Sucker an Even Break

Fields of Mourning
location: 10 underworld
inhabited by: 14 shades of lovers
lovers who died by: 7 suicide

fiend 5 beast, brute, demon, devil, Satan 6 dybbuk 7 incubus, monster, villain 8 succubus 9 barbarian, hellhound, scoundrel 10 evil spirit 12 wicked person 14 devil incarnate 16 prince of darkness

fiendish 4 evil, foul 5 cruel 6 wicked 7 demonic, heinous, impious, satanic, vicious 8 barbaric, demoniac, devilish 9 monstrous, nefarious 10 demoniacal, diabolical, villainous

fierce 4 fell, wild 5 cruel, feral, fiery 6 brutal, fervid, raging, savage, strong 7 enraged, extreme, fearful, fervent, furious, intense, leonine, untamed, violent 8 horrible, menacing, powerful, ravening, ravenous, terrible, tigerish, uncurbed, vehement 9 barbarous, bellicose, ferocious, impetuous, merciless, truculent, unbridled, voracious 10 immoderate, inordinate, passionate 11 threatening 12 bloodthirsty, overpowering, overwhelming, unrestrained
French: 8 farouche

fierceness 4 zeal 7 passion 8 ferocity, wildness 9 pugnacity, vehemence 10 savageness

fiery 5 afire, angry, irate 6 ablaze, alight, ardent, fervid, fierce, red-hot, torrid 7 blazing, burning, febrile, fervent, fevered, flaming, glaring, glowing, peppery, pyretic, violent, zealous 8 choleric, feverish, flashing, headlong, inflamed, spirited, vehement, wrathful 9 excitable, hotheaded, impetuous, impulsive, irascible, irritable 10 full of fire, high-strung, mettlesome, passionate, sweltering 11 hot-tempered, impassioned, precipitate 12 enthusiastic

fiesta 4 fete, gala 5 feast, party 6 picnic 7 funfair 8 carnival, feast day, festival, jamboree 9 saint's day 10 block party, observance, street fair 11 cele-

bration 13 commemoration 15 festive occasion

fig 5 Ficus
varieties: 3 keg, sea 4 bush, cape, Java, Zulu 5 cedar, clown, Congo, rusty 6 common, Devil's, exotic, golden, Indian, Kaffir, Mysore, sacred 7 Barbary, cluster, oak-leaf, spotted, weeping 8 climbing, creeping, Dracaena, mulberry, sycamore 9 Hottentot, mistletoe, strangler 10 East Indian, fiddle-leaf, glossy-leaf, little-leaf, Moreton Bay, Philippine 11 Port Jackson 16 West Indian laurel

Figaro
character in: 18 The Barber of Seville 19 The Marriage of Figaro
author: 12 Beaumarchais

fight 3 box, row, war 4 bout, duel, feud, fray, grit, spar, spat, tiff, tilt, wage 5 argue, brawl, brush, clash, event, joust, match, melee, pluck, round, scrap, set-to 6 battle, bicker, combat, engage, fracas, mettle, oppose, resist, spirit, strife, tussle 7 carry on, conduct, contend, contest, discord, dispute, go to war, quarrel, repulse, scuffle, tourney, wage war, wrangle 8 confront, dogfight, gameness, skirmish, squabble, struggle 9 bickering, encounter, pugnacity, scrimmage, toughness, wrangling 10 contention, difference, dissension, prizefight, strive with, tournament 11 altercation, armed action, battle royal, bellicosity, clash of arms, controversy 12 belligerency, do battle with, rise up in arms, struggle with 13 armed conflict, combativeness, confrontation, exchange blows, pitched battle

fight back 7 counter, get even, hit back, pay back 9 retaliate 10 strike back 13 counterattack

Fight Club
director: 12 David Fincher
cast: 8 Brad Pitt (Tyler Durden), Meat Loaf (Bob Paulson) 11 Zach Grenier (Richard Chesler) 12 Edward Norton (narrator) 18 Helena Bonham Carter (Marla Singer)

fighter 5 boxer 7 soldier, sparrer, warrior 8 pugilist, scrapper 9 combatant 10 militarist 11 belligerent

fighting 3 war 4 fray 5 brawl, melee 6 action, battle, bicker, combat, rumpus, tumult, tussle 7 contest, dispute, quarrel, warfare 8 battling, brawling, conflict, skirmish, squabble 9 bickering, disputing 10 engagement, quarreling, squabbling 11 clash of arms, controversy, hostilities

Fighting Marine
nickname of: 10 Gene Tunney

fighting men 4 army 6 legion, troops 7 legions, militia 8 military, soldiers, soldiery **13** military force **15** military machine

fighting spirit 9 animosity, hostility, pugnacity **10** antagonism **11** bellicosity **12** belligerence **14** aggressiveness

fight shy of 5 avoid, dodge, elude, evade, skirt **6** escape **8** sidestep

figment 5 fable, fancy, story **6** canard **7** fantasy, fiction, product **8** creation **9** falsehood, invention **10** concoction **11** fabrication

figuration 4 form **7** outline **9** formation, structure **12** constitution

figurative 6 florid, ironic, ornate **7** flowery **8** humorous, symbolic **9** satirical **10** not literal **11** allegorical **12** hyperbolical, metaphorical

figure, figures 3 cut, man, sum **4** body, cast, cost, foot, form, mark, plan, rate, sign, sums **5** add up, adorn, build, count, digit, force, frame, guess, judge, motif, price, shape, think, total, tot up, value, woman **6** amount, appear, assess, cipher, design, device, emblem, factor, leader, number, person, reckon, schema, symbol **7** anatomy, believe, compute, contour, count up, diagram, drawing, imagine, notable, numeral, outline, pattern, presume, suppose **8** appraise, be placed, eminence, estimate, ornament, physique, presence **9** calculate, character, diversify, embellish, have a part, personage, play a part, quotation, variegate **10** arithmetic, conjecture, shine forth, silhouette **11** be mentioned, be prominent **12** calculations, computations, illustration

figurehead 4 tool **5** dummy, front, token **6** cipher, puppet **8** ornament **9** nonentity

figure out 6 reckon **7** compute, find out, work out **8** discover **9** ascertain, calculate, determine

figure roughly 5 guess **6** reckon **8** estimate **11** approximate, make a stab at

figure up 3 add **5** add up, total, tot up **6** reckon **7** compute, count up **9** calculate

figurine 7 bibelot **8** ornament **9** statuette

Fiji
capital/largest city: 4 Suva
others: 3 Mba **4** Mbua **5** Navua **6** Labasa **7** Lautoka, Nausori, Vaileka, Vunisea **8** Korolevu, Savusavu **9** Singatoka
school: 12 South Pacific
head of state: 14 British monarch **15** governor general
monetary unit: 6 dollar
island: 4 Ngau **6** Ovalau, Rotuma, Yasawa **7** Kandavu, Taveuni **8** Viti Levu **9** Vanua Levu
highest point: 8 Victoria **9** Tomanivi
river: 4 Rewa **8** Ndreketi

sea: 4 Koro **7** Pacific
people: 6 Fijian, Indian **7** Chinese **10** Melanesian, Polynesian **11** Micronesian
language: 5 Hindi **6** Fijian **7** English
religion: 5 Hindu, Islam **9** Methodist **13** Roman Catholic
feature:
    cluster houses: 5 mbure

filament 4 hair, line, wire **5** fiber, fibre **6** cilium, ribbon, strand, string, thread

filbert 7 Corylus
varieties: 3 red **4** cork, Momi, plum **5** azure, China, giant, Greek, joint, Nikko, noble, white **6** alpine, balsam, Fraser, Korean, needle, Scotch, silver, summer **7** cascade, Douglas, lowland, Spanish **8** Algerian, Japanese, Sakhalin, Southern **9** Himalayan, Shasta Red **10** dwarf Nikko, Santa Lucia **11** bristlecone **13** Pacific silver **14** Southern balsam

filch 3 cop, rob **4** copy, crib, hook, lift **5** boost, heist, steal, swipe **6** pilfer, pirate **7** purloin **8** arrogate **10** plagiarize **11** appropriate, expropriate

file 3 row **4** data, line, list, rank, tier **5** apply, chain, index, put in, queue, store **6** drawer, folder, record, stacks, string **7** catalog, dossier, put away, records, request **8** archives, classify, petition **9** catalogue, chronicle
type: 4 mill, nail, rasp, wood **5** round **9** half-round **13** three-cornered

filial 7 dutiful, sonlike **10** daughterly, respectful

fill 3 act **4** cram, glut, lade, load, meet, pack, puff, sate **5** crowd, gorge, lay by, lay in, serve, stock, store **6** answer, assign, blow up, charge, dilate, do duty, expand, infuse, make up, occupy, outfit, supply, take up **7** distend, execute, furnish, inflate, pervade, preside, provide, satiate, satisfy, suffuse, surfeit **8** carry out, function, permeate, saturate **9** discharge, provision, replenish **10** full amount, impregnate, overspread

filled in 7 stood in **9** completed, **11** substituted

filled out 6 marked **7** matured **9** completed

fillet 4 band **5** slice, strip **6** ribbon **7** bandeau, circlet

fillip 3 tap **4** flip, snap, toss **5** flick, tonic **6** buffet **8** stimulus

Fillmore, Millard
presidential rank: 10 thirteenth
party: 4 Whig
state represented: 2 NY
defeated: 5 no one
    succeeded upon death of: 6 Taylor
cabinet:
    State: 7 (Daniel) Webster, (Edward) Everett

    Treasury: 6 (Thomas) Corwin
War: 6 (Charles Magill) Conrad
Attorney General: 10 (John Jordan) Crittenden
Navy: 6 (William Alexander) Graham **7** (John Pendleton) Kennedy
Postmaster General: 4 (Nathan Kelsey) Hall **7** (Samuel Dickinson) Hubbard
Interior: 6 (Alexander Hugh Holmes) Stuart
born: 7 Locke NY
died/buried: 9 Buffalo NY
education:
    studied: 3 law
religion: 9 Unitarian
interests: 5 civic
    first chancellor of University of: 7 Buffalo
    founder: 22 Buffalo General Hospital **24** Buffalo Historical Society
political career: 13 state assembly, Vice President **24** US House of Representatives
civilian career: 6 lawyer (New York Supreme Court) **7** teacher **10** wool carder **12** cloth dresser
notable events of lifetime/term: 25 Compromise of Eighteen-Fifty
    act: 13 Fugitive Slave
father: 9 Nathaniel
mother: 6 Phoebe (Millard)
siblings: 5 Cyrus, Julia **11** Phoebe Maria **12** Almon Hopkins, Calvin Turner **13** Charles DeWitt **14** Darius Ingraham, Olive Armstrong
wife: 7 Abigail (Powers) **8** Caroline (Carmichael McIntosh)
children: 11 Mary Abigail **13** Millard Powers

fill with air 5 bloat **6** billow, blow up, expand **7** balloon, distend, inflate, puff out **8** swell out

fill with dread 5 alarm, panic **6** dismay **7** perturb, terrify, unnerve **8** disquiet, frighten

fill with gloom 6 darken, sadden **8** dispirit

fill with wonder 3 awe **5** amaze **7** astound **8** astonish **9** fascinate

film, films 4 cine, coat, haze, mist, skin, veil **5** cloud, flick, movie, sheet, shoot **6** cinema, flicks, movies, screen **7** coating **8** membrane

filmy 3 dim **4** fine, hazy, thin **5** gauzy, misty, sheer, wispy **8** cobwebby, finespun, gossamer **10** diaphanous, seethrough

fils 3 son

filter 4 leak, ooze, seep **5** drain, exude, sieve **6** effuse, purify, refine, screen, strain **7** clarify, cleanse, dribble, trickle, well out **8** filtrate, strainer

filth 3 mud **4** dirt, dung, mire, muck, porn, slop, smut **5** offal, slime, slush, trash **6** manure, ordure, refuse, sewage, sludge **7** carrion, excreta, garbage, squalor **8** impurity, lewdness, ribaldry, vileness **9** excrement, grossness, indecency, nastiness, obscenity, pollution **10** corruption, defilement, immorality, indelicacy, putridness **11** pornography, squalidness **13** contamination **14** suggestiveness

filthy 4 foul, vile **5** black, dirty, grimy, gross, messy, nasty **6** grubby, impure, odious, soiled **7** defiled, dirtied, obscene, smirchy, squalid, unclean **8** befouled, slovenly, unwashed **9** repulsive **10** besmirched, disgusting **12** contaminated

finagle 3 con, gyp **4** plot, rook **5** cheat, mulct, trick **6** chisel, fleece, scheme, wangle **7** defraud, swindle **8** engineer, intrigue, maneuver

final 4 last, rear **6** ending, latest **7** closing, extreme **8** complete, decisive, finished, hindmost, rearmost, terminal, thorough, ultimate **10** concluding, conclusive, definitive, exhaustive, hindermost **11** irrevocable, terminating **12** unappealable, unchangeable **13** determinative
French: 7 dernier

finale 3 end **5** close, finis **6** finish, windup **7** curtain **8** epilogue, last part, swan song **10** conclusion **11** culmination, termination

final limit
Latin: 14 terminus ad quem

finally 6 lastly **10** eventually, inexorably, ultimately **11** inescapably **12** conclusively, definitively, in conclusion **16** incontrovertibly
French: 5 enfin
Latin: 10 ad extremum

final section 4 coda **5** rider **6** ending **7** last act **8** addendum, epilogue **9** afterword **10** conclusion

final settlement 8 solution **11** disposition

finance 6 pay for **7** banking **8** accounts **9** economics **10** underwrite

financial backer 5 angel **6** patron **7** sponsor **9** supporter **10** benefactor

financial support 7 backing, subsidy **10** assistance **12** contribution

financier 5 angel **6** backer, banker, broker **7** rich man **10** capitalist **11** millionaire, underwriter

Financier, The
author: 15 Theodore Dreiser
character: 12 Aileen Butler, Edward Butler **15** Henry Cowperwood **16** Frank A Cowperwood **23** Lillian Semple Cowperwood

Finch, Peter
real name: 15 Peter Ingle-Finch
born: 6 London **7** England
roles: 7 Network (Oscar) **11** Lost Horizon **12** The Nun's Story **15** The Pumpkin Eater **18** Sunday Bloody Sunday

Finchley, Sondra
character in: 17 An American Tragedy
author: 7 Dreiser

find 3 get, see, win **4** earn, espy, gain, meet, rule, spot **5** award, catch, dig up, judge, learn **6** attain, come by, decide, decree, detect, expose, locate, regain **7** achieve, acquire, adjudge, bargain, bonanza, discern, get back, godsend, good buy, hit upon, procure, recover, uncover, unearth **8** bump into, come upon, discover, disinter, lucky hit, meet with, retrieve, windfall **9** ascertain, determine, discovery, encounter, pronounce, repossess **10** adjudicate **11** acquisition

fin de siecle 8 decadent **15** end of the century

find fault 3 nag **4** beef, carp **5** blame, cavil, gribe **6** grouse, squawk **7** nitpick **8** complain **9** bellyache, criticize, disparage **10** disapprove

find guilty 5 blame **6** indict **7** condemn, convict **8** sentence **9** implicate

finding 6 decree, ruling **7** verdict **8** decision

Finding Neverland
director: 11 Marc Forster
cast: 7 Ian Hart (Sir Arthur Conan Doyle) **8** Nick Roud (George Llewelyn-Davies) **9** Luke Spill (Michael Llewelyn-Davies) **10** Johnny Depp (Sir James Matthew Barrie) **11** Joe Prospero (Jack Llewelyn-Davies), Kate Winslet (Sylvia Llewelyn-Davies) **13** Dustin Hoffman (Charles Frohman), Julie Christie (Emma du Maurier), Radha Mitchell (Mary Ansell Barrie) **14** Kelly MacDonald (Peter Pan) **15** Freddie Highmore (Peter Llewelyn-Davies)

find innocent 5 clear **6** acquit **9** exonerate

find out 5 learn **6** detect, locate **7** uncover, unearth **8** discover **9** ascertain, determine, establish

find repulsive 4 hate **5** abhor **6** detest, loathe **7** despise **8** execrate, recoil at **9** abominate

fine 4 airy, chic, fair, keen, neat, nice, rare, thin **5** bonny, clear, dandy, gauzy, mulct, nifty, sharp, sheer, silky, small, smart, sunny, swell **6** assess, bonnie, bright, charge, choice, comely, dainty, flimsy, ground, lovely, minute, modish, pretty, silken, slight, spiffy, subtle, superb **7** damages, elegant, forfeit, fragile, penalty, perfect, powdery, precise, refined, slender, stylish, tenuous **8** cobwebby, delicate, ethereal, flawless, gossamer, handsome, penalize, pleasant, polished, powdered, rainless, skillful, splendid, superior, tasteful **9** admirable, beautiful, brilliant, cloudless, excellent, exquisite **10** assessment, attractive, con-

summate, diaphanous, fastidious, pulverized, swimmingly **11** excellently, exceptional, lightweight, magnificent, transparent, well-favored **12** accomplished **13** hairsplitting, unsubstantial
music: 3 end

fine clothes 8 glad rags **10** Sunday best **16** best bib and tucker

fine-looking 4 fair **5** bonny **6** bonnie, comely, lovely, pretty, seemly **8** gorgeous, handsome **9** beauteous, beautiful, exquisite, ravishing **10** attractive **11** resplendent **15** pulchritudinous

fineness 6 beauty **8** delicacy, elegance, thinness **10** perfection, smoothness **12** flawlessness **13** exquisiteness

fine points 3 art **7** finesse, nuances **8** niceties **10** subtleties **11** refinements **12** distinctions

finer 6 better **8** superior

finery 6 frills, tinsel **7** baubles, gaudery, gewgaws **8** frippery, spangles, trinkets **9** trappings, trimmings **13** paraphernalia

finesse 4 ruse, tact, wile **5** craft, dodge, guile, savvy **7** cunning **8** artifice, delicacy, intrigue, trickery **9** deception, stratagem **10** artfulness, discretion, subterfuge
French: 11 savoir-faire

fine workmanship 8 delicacy **9** precision **13** craftsmanship

finger 3 paw **4** feel, poke, ring **5** digit, index, punch, thumb, touch **6** caress, feeler, handle, middle, pinkie, pollex **7** pointer, squeeze, toy with, twiddle **8** identify, play with **10** manipulate

finicky 5 fussy, picky **6** choosy **8** niggling **10** fastidious, meticulous, nitpicking, overprecise, particular, pernickety **11** persnickety **14** discriminating, overparticular

finish 3 end **4** coat, face, gild, goal, kill, last, seal, stop **5** cease, close, glaze, use up **6** clinch, defeat, devour, ending, finale, settle, veneer, wind up **7** achieve, coating, consume, curtain, destroy, fulfill, get done, lacquer, realize, surface, varnish **8** carry out, complete, conclude, dispatch, epilogue, exterior, get rid of, knock off, make good **9** discharge, eradicate, objective, polishing, terminate **10** accomplish, completion, conclusion, consummate, denouement **11** discontinue, exterminate, termination

finished 4 full **5** ended, final, ideal, whole **6** entire, urbane **7** classic, elegant, perfect, refined, shapely, skilled, trained, well-set **8** complete, flawless, polished, well-bred **9** beautiful, completed, concluded, exquisite, faultless **10** consummate, cultivated, impeccable **11** consummated **12** accomplished

finishing stroke 9 death blow
French: 11 coup de grace

finish off 4 kill, slay **7** destroy, execute, wipe out **8** complete, dispatch **9** eradicate, polish off **10** annihilate **11** exterminate

finite 7 bounded, limited **8** confined, temporal **9** countable **10** measurable, restricted, short-lived, terminable **13** circumscribed

Finland
  other name: 5 Suomi **15** Suomen Tasavalta
  capital/largest city: 8 Helsinki **11** Helsingfors
  others: 3 Aba, Abo, Kem **4** Kemi, Ouli, Oulu, Ouou, Pori, Vasa **5** Enare, Espoo, Kotka, Lahti, Rauma, Turku, Vaasa **6** Imatra, Kuopio **7** Joensuu, Kajaani, Kokkola, Mikkeli, Tampere, Tapiola **9** Jyvaskyla, Mariehamn, Rovaniemi **12** Lappeenranta
  measure: 5 kannu, verst **6** fathom, kannor **8** otlinger, skalpund, tunnland
  monetary unit: 4 mark **5** penni **6** markka
  island: 5 Aland, Karlo **6** Aaland **7** Hailuto **9** Vallgrund **10** Ahvenanmaa
  lake: 3 Juo, Muo **4** Kemi, Kiui, Nasi, Oulu, Puru, Pyha, Simo **5** Enara, Enare, Hauki, Inari, Kalla, Lappa, Lesti, Puula, Saima **6** Ladoya, Lentua, Saimaa, Sounne, Syvari **7** Koitere, Nilakka, Pielien **9** Kallavesi, Pielavesi
  mountain: 7 Laltiva **10** Saari Selka
  highest point: 6 Haltia **11** Haldetsokka
  river: 4 Kala, Kemi, Kymi, Oulu, Pats, Simo, Teno **5** Ivalo, Lotta, Ounas, Siika, Torne **6** Iijoki, Lapuan, Muonio, Pasvik, Tornoi, Vuoski **7** Kitinen **8** Kokemaki
  sea: 6 Baltic **8** Atlantic
  physical feature:
    gulf: 7 Bothnia, Finland
    isthmus: 7 Karelia
    peninsula: 13 Fennoscandian
  people: 3 Jew, Vod, Vot, Yak **4** Avar, Finn, Hame, Lapp, Turk, Veps **5** Fioun, Gypsy, Ijore, Inger, Suomi, Vepse **6** Magyar, Ostiak, Ostyak, Tarast, Tavast, Ugrian, Zyrian **7** Lappish, Mordvin, Permiak, Samoyed, Uralian **8** Cheremis, Estonian, Karelian, Livonian, Swekoman **9** Tavastian **11** Karjalaiset, Suomalaiset
    athlete: 10 Paavo Nurmi
    composer: 8 Sibelius
    designer: 9 Marimekko
  language: 4 Avar, Lapp **5** Karel, Ugric, Vogul **6** Magyar, Ostyak, Tarast **7** Finnish, Olonets, Samoyed, Swedish **8** Estonian **10** Olonetsian
  religion: 19 Evangelical Lutheran
  place:
    canal: 6 Saimaa
    castle: 10 Saint Olaf's **11** Olavinlinna
    fortress: 8 Sveaborg **11** Suomen-

linna
    memorial: 8 Sibelius
    pine ridge: 10 Punkaharju
  feature:
    game: 9 pesapallo
  food:
    dish: 11 Karelian pie
    fruit: 16 yellow cloudberry
    liqueur: 9 Mesimarja

Finn
  also: 5 Fionn **13** Fionn MacCumal
  origin: 5 Irish
  king of: 4 gods **14** Tuatha De Danann
  son: 6 Ossian
  father: 5 Cumal **6** Comhal

Finnegans Wake
  author: 10 James Joyce
  family: 9 Earwicker

Finney, Albert
  wife: 10 Anouk Aimee
  born: 7 England, Salford
  roles: 5 Annie **7** Big Fish, Scrooge **8** Tom Jones **10** The Dresser **12** Shoot the Moon **13** Two for the Road **14** Erin Brockovich **17** Under the Volcano **29** Saturday Night and Sunday Morning

Finnish Mythology *see* **21** Scandinavian Mythology

Finno-Ugric
  language family: 6 Uralic
  Finnic group: 4 Lapp **6** Votyak, Zyryan **7** Finnish, Mordvin, Permian **8** Estonian **9** Cheremiss
  Ugric group: 5 Vogul **6** Ostyak **7** Ob-Ugric **9** Hungarian

Fionn, Fionn MacCumal *see* **4** Finn

fiord, fjord 5 firth, inlet **7** estuary
  location: 6 Norway

fir 4 pine **5** cedar, larch **6** alpine, balsam, linden, spruce **7** conifer, cypress, douglas **9** evergreen

Firbolg
  origin: 5 Greek, Irish
  defeated by: 9 Fomorians
  ousted by: 4 gods **14** Tuatha De Danann

fire 3 can, vim **4** bake, boot, burn, cook, dash, dump, elan, hurl, oust, sack, stir **5** ardor, blaze, eject, flame, flare, flash, force, gusto, let go, light, power, punch, rouse, salvo, shell, shoot, spark, verve, vigor **6** arouse, bounce, depose, excite, fervor, foment, genius, ignite, incite, kindle, luster, spirit, stir up, vivify, volley **7** animate, bombard, bonfire, cashier, dismiss, inferno, inflame, inspire, project, quicken, sniping, trigger **8** enfilade, fervency, inspirit, radiance, splendor, vivacity **9** broadside, cannonade, discharge, eagerness, fusillade, galvanize, holocaust, instigate, intensity, stimulate, vehemence **10** brilliance, effulgence, enthusiasm **11** bombardment, earnestness, inspiration

13 conflagration, sharpshooting **15** imaginativeness
  god of: 4 Loki **5** Ishum **6** Vulcan **10** Hephaestus, Hephaistos
  goddess of: 6 Brigit

Fire and Ice
  author: 11 Robert Frost

firearm 3 gun, rod **5** piece, rifle **6** pistol **7** shotgun **8** revolver **10** machine gun **12** shooting iron **13** submachine gun **20** Saturday-night special

firefight 5 clash **6** battle, combat **8** skirmish

firefly 8 glowworm, lampyrid **9** candlefly **12** lightning bug

Fire Next Time, The
  author: 12 James Baldwin

fire off 5 eject, shoot **6** launch **8** detonate **9** discharge

Fireside Theatre
  host: 9 Jane Wyman **11** Frank Wisbar, Gene Raymond

Firestarter
  author: 11 Stephen King

fire up 4 fuel, rile **5** anger, light, rouse **6** arouse, excite, ignite, incite, kindle **7** animate, enthuse, inspire **8** activate, energize, irritate, vitalize **9** galvanize, stimulate

firm 4 bent, fast, grim, hard, taut **5** close, dense, fixed, house, rigid, rocky, solid, stiff, stony, tight, tough **6** dogged, flinty, intent, moored, rooted, secure, stable, steady, steely **7** compact, company, dead set, decided, earnest, serious, settled, staunch **8** anchored, business, constant, definite, fearless, obdurate, resolute, resolved, unshaken **9** confirmed, hard-nosed, immovable, obstinate, steadfast, tenacious, unbending **10** adamantine, compressed, determined, inexorable, inflexible, invincible, persistent, unwavering, unyielding **11** corporation, established, partnership, unalterable, unfaltering, unflinching **12** conglomerate, indissoluble, organization **13** establishment

firmament 3 air, sky **5** ether, space, vault **6** canopy, welkin **7** heavens, the blue, the void **10** outer space

firmness 8 tenacity **9** obstinacy **10** resolution **11** persistence, staunchness **12** resoluteness **13** determination, inflexibility, steadfastness

first 4 head, main **5** basic, prime, start, vital **6** before, eldest, maiden, outset, primal, rather, sooner **7** highest, leading, premier, primary, ranking, supreme **8** earliest, foremost, original, primeval, superior **9** beginning, essential, inception, initially, paramount, primitive, principal **10** aboriginal, elementary, preeminent, preferably, primordial **11** fundamental, rudimentary **12** commencement, introduction, introductory

first among equals
Latin: **16** primus inter pares
first appearance 4 dawn **5** debut **9** beginning **12** introduction
firstborn 5 elder, older **6** eldest, oldest
First Circle
author: **23** Aleksandr Solzhenitsyn Jr
first god *see* **8** god, first
firsthand 6 direct **8** personal **9** empirical **10** unmediated **12** experimental
First Lady of the Theater
nickname of: **10** Helen Hayes **16** Katherine Cornell
first-line 4 main **5** chief **7** primary **8** foremost
first moving thing
Latin: **12** primum mobile
first-rate 3 ace **4** A-one, best, fine, tops **5** crack, elite, great, prime **6** choice, finest, select **7** top-hole **8** splendid, superior, top-notch, very good **9** admirable, estimable, excellent, exclusive, nonpareil, top drawer, topflight, wonderful **10** noteworthy, stupendous **11** commendable, outstanding **12** above-average, incomparable **13** distinguished
First State
nickname of: **8** Delaware
first step 5 start **9** beginning **12** commencement
firth 5 fjord, inlet **7** estuary
fiscal 8 economic, monetary **9** budgetary, financial, pecuniary
fish 3 net **4** cast, hook, hunt **5** angle, grope, seine, trawl, troll **6** ferret, search **7** rummage
fish
class: **7** Agnatha **12** Osteichthyes **14** Chondrichthyes
fin: **4** anal, tail **6** caudal, dorsal, median, paired, pelvic **7** adipose, ventral **8** pectoral
kind: **3** cod, eel, gar, ray **4** bass, carp, hake, opah, pike, tuna **5** brill, perch, shark, skate, sword, trout **6** bichir, blenny, marlin, minnow, mullet, salmon, tarpon **7** anchovy, catfish, dogfish, dolphin, hagfish, herring, lamprey, piranha, sunfish **8** bluefish, cavefish, crayfish, flounder, goldfish, lungfish, mackerel, menhaden, moray eel, pilchard, sea horse, squirrel, sturgeon **9** killifish, pygmy goby, swordfish **10** coelacanth, flying fish, paddlefish, rabbit fish, rocksucker, whale shark **11** anemonefish, electric eel, electric ray, lanternfish, longnose gar **13** butterflyfish **14** largemouth bass
part: **3** fin **4** gill **5** scale **6** cirrhi **10** gas bladder **11** swim bladder **12** rete mirabile
shellfish:
crustacean: **4** crab **6** shrimp **7** lobster **8** blue crab, king crab, snow crab **9** langouste **11** langoustine **13** Dungeness crab, horseshoe crab
mollusk: **4** clam **6** mussel, oyster, quahog **8** surf clam **9** horse clam, razor clam **11** geoduck clam
young: **3** fry **10** fingerling
Fisher, Bud
creator/artist of: **11** Mutt and Jeff
Fisher, Carrie
father: **11** Eddie Fisher
mother: **13** Debbie Reynolds
husband: **9** Paul Simon
role: **12** Princess Leia
films: **7** Shampoo **8** Soap Dish, Star Wars **12** This Is My Life **16** The Blues Brothers **17** When Harry Met Sally **18** The Return of the Jedi **19** The Empire Strikes Back, Hannah and Her Sisters
author: **16** Surrender the Pink **18** Delusions of Grandma **20** Postcards from the Edge
Fisher, Ham
creator/artist of: **10** Joe Palooka
Fisher, Vardis
author of: **10** The Mothers **13** Children of God **17** The Testament of Man
fisherman 5 eeler **6** angler, caster, jacker, netter, seiner **7** trawler, troller **8** piscator **9** flycaster, Waltonian **17** the compleat angler
Fishermen
goddess of: **11** Britomartis
Fishes
constellation of: **6** Pisces
fish story 3 fib, lie **7** fiction, whopper **9** falsehood, tall story **16** cock-and-bull story
fishy 3 odd **4** dull **5** blank, queer, shady, weird **6** vacant **7** dubious, strange, suspect **8** doubtful, peculiar, slippery **9** dishonest **10** farfetched, glassy-eyed, improbable, suspicious, unreliable **11** exaggerated, extravagant **12** questionable, unscrupulous **14** expressionless
fission 7 atomize **8** breaking, cleavage, scission **9** severance, splitting **10** breaking up, sunderance **12** disseverance, reproduction
fissure 3 gap **4** rift, slit **5** chink, cleft, crack, gully, split **6** breach, cranny, groove, hiatus **8** aperture, cleavage
fit 4 able, good, hale, meet, ripe, suit, well, whim **5** adapt, agree, alter, burst, equal, equip, hardy, match, ready, right, shape, sound, spasm, spell, train **6** access, accord, adjust, become, concur, enable, in trim, mature, primed, proper, robust, seemly, strong, timely, worthy **7** adapted, apropos, capable, caprice, conform, correct, empower, fashion, healthy, prepare, qualify, rectify, seizure, toned up, trained **8** apposite, becoming, co-

incide, crotchet, decorous, eligible, graduate, grand mal, outbreak, outburst, paroxysm, petit mal, prepared, relevant, suitable **9** calibrate, competent, consonant, deserving, efficient, explosion, harmonize, initiated, opportune, pertinent, qualified **10** acceptable, applicable, capacitate, convenient, convulsion, correspond, seasonable **11** appropriate, capacitated
fitful 4 weak **6** broken, random, uneven **7** erratic **8** listless, off-and-on, periodic, sporadic, unsteady, variable **9** irregular, spasmodic **10** capricious, changeable, convulsive **11** fluctuating **12** disconnected, intermittent
fitness
Hebrew: **7** kashrut **8** kashruth
fit out 4 robe **5** array, dress, equip **6** attire, clothe, supply **7** appoint, deck out, prepare
fitting 3 apt **4** meet **6** proper, seemly **8** decorous, suitable **9** congruous **11** appropriate
French: **11** comme il faut
fit to be eaten 6 edible **9** palatable **10** comestible, consumable, digestible
fit together 4 join **5** hinge, unite **6** hook up **7** connect **8** dovetail **9** interlock **10** articulate
Fitzgerald, Barry
real name: **20** William Joseph Shields
born: **6** Dublin **7** Ireland
roles: **10** Going My Way **11** The Quiet Man **19** How Green Was My Valley
FitzGerald, Edward
author of: **24** The Rubaiyat of Omar Khayyam (translation)
Fitzgerald, F Scott
wife: **10** Zelda Sayre
author of: **10** The Crack-Up **13** The Last Tycoon **14** The Great Gatsby **16** Tender Is the Night **18** This Side of Paradise **24** The Beautiful and the Damned
coined term: **7** Jazz Age
Fitzgerald, George Francis
field: **7** physics
nationality: **5** Irish
theory of: **24** electromagnetic radiation
Fitzgerald, Geraldine
born: **6** Dublin **7** Ireland
roles: **11** Dark Victory **12** Ah Wilderness, Rachel Rachel **15** Watch on the Rhine **16** Wuthering Heights **24** Long Day's Journey into Night
Fitzsimmons, Bob (Robert Prometheus)
sport: **6** boxing
Fitzsimmons, Maureen
real name of: **12** Maureen O'Hara
Five, The
group of: **16** Russian composers
member: **3** Cui **7** Borodin **9** Balakirev **10** Mussorgsky **14** Rimsky-Korsakov

Five Easy Pieces
  director: **11** Bob Rafelson
  cast: **10** Karen Black **11** Fannie Flagg **12** Susan Anspach **13** Jack Nicholson **14** Billy Breen Bush, Sally Struthers

five-o'clock shadow 5 beard **7** stubble **8** bristles, whiskers

fix 3 jam, put, set **4** bind, make, mend, mess, moor, spot **5** place, rivet **6** adjust, anchor, attach, decide, fasten, harden, impose, muddle, pickle, plight, repair, scrape, secure, settle **7** congeal, connect, correct, dilemma, impasse, implant, patch up, prepare, rebuild **8** assemble, hot water, make fast, make firm, quandary, regulate, renovate, set right, solidify **9** establish, prescribe, retaliate, stabilize **10** difficulty **11** consolidate, involvement, predicament **12** entanglement

fixation 5 quirk **6** fetish **7** complex **8** crotchet, delusion **9** monomania, obsession **13** preoccupation

fixed 3 set **4** fast, firm **5** rigid, still **6** intent, rooted, stable, steady **8** constant, fastened, resolute, unpliant **9** immovable, unbending **10** determined, inflexible, motionless, persistent, stationary, unwavering

fixed idea 4 bias **5** slant **9** obsession **13** preconception
  French: **8** idee fixe

fixedness 8 firmness **9** constancy, stability **10** immobility **12** immutability **16** unchangeableness

fixed regard 7 staring **9** diligence **10** absorption, intentness **11** engrossment **13** concentration

Fixer, The
  author: **14** Bernard Malamud

fixing 6 repair **7** mending, mooring, placing, putting, setting **8** deciding, imposing, righting, riveting, settling, trimming **9** adjusting, anchoring, attaching, fastening, hardening, preparing, repairing **10** adjustment, assembling, congealing, connecting, correcting, implanting, rectifying, regulating, regulation **11** determining, prescribing, solidifying, stabilizing **12** establishing **13** consolidating

fixture 6 addict **7** devotee, habitue, regular **8** equipage **9** apparatus, appendage, appliance, equipment **10** attachment **11** appointment **12** appurtenance **13** paraphernalia

fix up 4 plan **6** design, devise **7** arrange, prepare **8** renovate, schedule

fix upon 4 pick **6** choose, opt for, select **7** call out, extract, pick out

fizz 4 foam **5** froth **7** bubbles **11** carbonation **13** effervescence

fizziness 9 foaminess **10** bubbliness, frothiness **13** effervescence

fizzing 6 bubbly **7** foaming **8** bubbling **9** sparkling **12** effervescent, effervescing

fizzle 3 dog, dud **4** bomb, fail, flop, hiss, mess **5** abort, botch **6** bubble, fiasco, gurgle, muddle, turkey **7** failure, founder, misfire, sputter, washout **8** collapse, disaster, miscarry

fizzy 6 bubbly **8** bubbling **9** sparkling **12** effervescent

flabbergast 4 stun **5** amaze, shock **6** puzzle **7** astound, stagger, stupefy **8** astonish, bewilder, bowl over, confound, overcome **9** dumbfound

flabbergasted 5 agape **6** amazed, gaping **9** awestruck, stupefied **10** astonished, dumbstruck, spellbound **11** dumbfounded **12** hornswoggled **13** thunderstruck

flabby 4 lame, limp, soft, weak **5** baggy, slack **6** doughy, effete, feeble, flimsy, floppy, spongy **7** flaccid **8** impotent, listless, yielding **9** enervated, inelastic **10** out of shape, spiritless **11** adulterated, emasculated

flag 3 ebb, sag **4** fade, fail, pall, sink, tire, wane, warn, wave, wilt **5** abate, faint, slump **6** banner, colors, dodder, emblem, ensign, signal, totter **7** decline, give way, pennant, subside, succumb **8** grow weak, languish, Old Glory, standard, streamer **9** grow weary, Union Jack **12** Stars and Bars **15** Stars and Stripes

flagellant 7 ascetic **8** penitent **13** self-mortifier

flagon 3 gun, jug, mug **4** ewer **5** flask, stein **6** bottle, carafe, vessel **7** canteen **8** schooner

flagrant 5 gross, sheer **6** arrant, brazen, crying **7** blatant, glaring, heinous, obvious **8** immodest **9** audacious, barefaced, flaunting, monstrous, notorious, shameless **10** outrageous, scandalous **11** conspicuous

Flaherty, Margaret (Pegeen)
  character in: **24** Playboy of the Western World
  author: **5** Synge

flail 4 beat, lash, whip **5** swing **6** thresh **7** scourge

flair 4 bent, dash, feel, gift **5** knack, style, taste, touch, verve **6** genius, talent **7** faculty, feeling, panache **8** aptitude, capacity **9** ingenuity **11** discernment

flake 3 bit **4** chip, peel **5** fleck, layer, patch, scale, sheet, strip **7** chip off, crumble, peel off, shaving **8** scale off

flaky 4 bats, gaga, nuts **5** balmy, batty, crisp, daffy, dotty, goofy, loony, nutty, scaly, short, wacky **6** scabby, screwy, scurfy **8** scabious, squamous **9** eccentric **10** flocculent

flamboyant 4 wild **5** gaudy, jazzy, showy **6** flashy, florid, garish, ornate, rococo **7** baroque, dashing **8** colorful, exciting **10** theatrical **11** sensational **12** ostentatious

flame 4 beau, fire, glow **5** ardor, blaze, blush, flare, flash, flush, glare, gleam, light, lover, spark, swain **6** fervor, ignite, kin-dle, redden, warmth **7** passion **8** fervency **9** affection, boyfriend, intensity **10** enthusiasm, excitement, girlfriend, sweetheart **13** conflagration

flaming 5 afire, fiery **6** ablaze, alight, ardent, bright, fervid, stormy **7** blazing, burning, fervent, glaring, glowing, igneous, intense, shining, violent **8** flagrant, vehement **9** brilliant, egregious **10** passionate, smoldering **11** conspicuous, inflammable

flammable 7 igneous **10** combustive, incendiary **11** combustible, inflammable

flan 3 pie **4** gust, puff, tart **6** expand, pastry **7** custard, dessert **12** creme caramel

flanerie 8 dawdling, idleness

flaneur 5 idler **6** loafer **7** dawdler

flank 3 hip **4** edge, line, loin, side, wing **5** cover, skirt **6** border, fringe, haunch, screen, shield

Flannagan, John Bernard
  born: **7** Fargo ND
  artwork: **6** New One, Not Yet **9** Beginning **11** Dragon Motif **15** Triumph of the Egg **16** Jonah and the Whale

flap 3 bat, fly, tab **4** bang, beat, flop **5** apron, shake, skirt **6** lappet **7** agitate, banging, flutter, vibrate **9** oscillate

flare 4 burn, glow **5** blaze, erupt, flame, flash, glare, gleam, taper, torch, widen **6** blow up, dilate, expand, ignite, signal, spread **7** bell out, broaden, distend, explode, stretch **8** boil over, break out **9** coruscate **10** incandesce

flash 4 glow, wink **5** blaze, blink, burst, flame, flare, glare, gleam, jiffy, shake, shine, spark, touch, trice **6** minute, moment, second, streak **7** flicker, glimmer, glisten, glitter, instant, sparkle **8** instance, outburst, radiance **9** coruscate **10** occurrence **11** coruscation, fulmination, scintillate **13** incandescence

Flash Gordon
  creator: **8** Dan Berry **11** Alex Raymond **12** Austin Briggs
  character: **11** Emperor Ming **12** Princess Aura
  companion: **4** Dale
  portrayed by: **12** Buster Crabbe

flashy 4 loud **5** gaudy, jazzy, showy, smart **6** garish, sporty, tawdry, tinsel, vulgar **7** raffish **8** dazzling **9** bedizened **10** flamboyant, tricked out **11** pretentious **12** ostentatious

flask 6 bottle **7** canteen **9** container

flat, flats 3 low **4** dead, dull **5** clear, equal, flush, level, marsh, plain, plane, prone, shoal, shoes, stale, total, vapid **6** direct, planar, smooth, supine **7** blowout, exactly, insipid, laid low, leveled, levelly, loafers, prairie, regular, shallow **8** absolute, complete, definite, lowlands, positive, puncture, thorough, unbroken **9** apartment, downright, precisely, prostrate, reclining, recumbent, tasteless **10** flavorless, horizontal, peremptory **11** unequivocal, unpalatable, unqualified **12** deflated tire, horizontally, unmistakable

flatfish 3 ray **4** sole **5** brill, fluke **6** turbot **7** halibut, sand dab, sunfish, teleost **8** flounder

Flathead *see* **5** Salis **7** Chinook

flatness 8 dullness **9** levelness, staleness **10** insipidity **13** tastelessness **14** flavorlessness

flatten 4 deck, even, fell **5** crush, floor, level, plane **6** defeat, ground, smooth **7** deflate **8** compress, overcome **9** overwhelm, prostrate

flatter 4 fool, laud **5** court, extol, honor, toady **6** become, cajole, delude **7** adulate, beguile, deceive, mislead, wheedle **8** blandish, bootlick, butter up, eulogize, soft-soap **9** brown-nose, sweet-talk, truckle to **10** compliment, overpraise, panegyrize

flatterer 5 toady **6** fawner, yes man **8** eulogist, truckler, wheedler **9** sycophant **10** bootlicker **11** lickspittle **13** apple-polisher

flattering 7 lauding **8** praising **9** extolling, favorable, laudatory **10** gratifying **13** complimentary

flattering attention 5 court **7** fawning

flattery 6 eulogy **7** blarney, fawning, snow job **8** cajolery, encomium, jollying, soft soap, toadying, toadyism **9** adulation, panegyric, servility, truckling, wheedling **10** sycophancy **12** blandishment **14** obsequiousness

Flaubert, Gustave
   author of: 8 Salammbo **12** Madame Bovary **21** A Sentimental Education **24** The Temptation of St Anthony

flaunt 3 air **4** brag, wave **5** boast, sport, strut, vaunt **6** blazon, dangle, parade **7** exhibit, show off **8** brandish, flourish **9** advertise, broadcast

flavor 4 aura, lace, soul, tang, tone **5** gusto, imbue, savor, spice, style, tenor **6** aspect, infuse, lacing, relish, season, spirit **7** essence, instill **8** ambience, piquancy **9** attribute, seasoning

flavorful 4 rich **5** nutty, sapid, spicy, tangy, tasty, zesty **6** savory **7** peppery, piquant **8** aromatic **9** palatable, toothsome **10** appetizing

flavoring 4 herb, salt **5** spice **6** pepper **7** essence, extract, vanilla **8** additive, seasoner **9** chocolate, condiment, seasoning

flavorless 4 dull, flat, thin, weak **5** bland, stale, vapid **6** watery **7** insipid **9** tasteless

flaw 3 mar **4** blot, harm, spot, vice **5** error, fault, speck, stain **6** blotch, deface, defect, foible, impair, injure, injury, smudge, weaken **7** blemish, failing, fallacy, frailty, mistake **8** weak spot, weakness **9** deformity, disfigure **10** compromise, defacement **11** shortcoming **12** imperfection **13** disfigurement

flawed 6 faulty **8** impaired **9** defective, imperfect

flawless 5 sound **7** perfect **9** errorless, faultless **10** immaculate, impeccable

flawlessness 8 accuracy **10** perfection **11** correctness **14** immaculateness

flay 4 bark, pare, peel, skin **5** scalp, scold, strip **6** assail, fleece, punish, rebuke **7** plunder, upbraid **9** castigate, excoriate **11** decorticate

flea
   varieties: 3 bat, dog, rat **5** mouse **6** rodent **9** carnivore **10** sticktight

fleck 3 dot, jot **4** drop, mark, mole, spot **5** flake, speck **6** bespot, dapple, mottle, streak, tittle **7** blemish, freckle, spatter, speckle, stipple **8** particle, small bit **9** bespeckle **10** besprinkle

Fledermaus, Die
   also: 6 The Bat
   operetta by: 7 (Johann) Strauss
   character: 5 Adele, Falke, Frank **6** Alfred **9** Rosalinda **14** Prince Orlofsky **18** Baron von Eisenstein

fledgling 4 tyro **6** novice **8** beginner, freshman **9** greenhorn **10** apprentice, tenderfoot

flee 4 shun, skip **5** avoid, dodge, elude, evade, split **6** decamp, desert, vanish **7** abscond, fly away, make off **8** speed off **9** cut and run, disappear **10** fly the coop

fleece 3 gyp **4** bilk, dupe, gull, rook, wool **5** cheat, cozen, trick **7** deceive, defraud, swindle **9** bamboozle, victimize

fleet 3 run **4** band, fade, fast, flow, navy, skim, spry, swim, unit **5** agile, array, brief, creek, drift, float, hasty, inlet, light, quick, rapid, shift, ships, short, swift **6** abound, active, armada, nimble, number, speedy, sudden, vanish **7** caravan, cursory, hurried **8** flotilla, squadron **9** disappear, momentary, transient **10** evanescent, transitory **11** expeditious **13** instantaneous

fleeting 5 brief, quick **7** passing **8** flitting, fugitive, temporal **9** ephemeral, fugacious, momentary, temporary, transient **10** evanescent, perishable, transitory **11** impermanent, precarious, unenduring

Fleming, Alexander
   field: 12 bacteriology
   nationality: 7 British
   discovered: 10 penicillin
   awarded: 10 Nobel Prize

Fleming, Henry
   character in: 20 The Red Badge of Courage
   author: 5 Crane

Fleming, Ian
   author of: 4 Dr No **9** Moonraker **10** Goldfinger **11** Thunderball **12** Casino Royale **13** Live and Let Die **15** For Your Eyes Only **16** The Spy Who Loved Me, You Only Live Twice **18** From Russia with Love **20** Chitty Chitty Bang Bang
   character: 1 M, Q **6** Oddjob **7** Blofeld, SPECTRE (organization) **9** James Bond **14** Miss Moneypenny **15** Auric Goldfinger

Fleming, Victor
   director of: 13 The Wizard of Oz **14** Treasure Island **15** Gone With the Wind (Oscar) **18** Captains Courageous

flesh 3 fat, man **4** body, meat, pulp **5** brawn, power, vigor **6** embody, fatten, people **7** fatness, fill out, mankind, realize **8** humanity, physique, strength **9** carnality, substance **10** sensuality **11** materiality **13** individualize, particularize

flesh and blood 3 kin **4** real **5** a body, child **6** family **7** kindred **8** children **9** corporeal, offspring, relations, relatives **10** kith and kin **11** substantial

flesh-eating 9 predatory **10** predaceous **11** carnivorous

fleshy 3 fat **5** beefy, obese, plump, stout, tubby **6** chubby, portly, rotund, stocky **7** paunchy **8** roly-poly, thickset **9** corpulent, succulent **10** overweight, potbellied

Fletcher, Louise
   born: 12 Birmingham AL
   roles: 17 The Cheap Detective **25** One Flew Over the Cuckoo's Nest (Oscar)

Fletcher, Susannah Yolande
   real name of: 12 Susannah York

flex 4 bend **5** curve

flexible 4 mild, soft **5** lithe **6** docile, genial, gentle, limber, pliant, supple **7** amiable, ductile, elastic, plastic, pliable, springy **8** bendable, yielding **9** adaptable, compliant, malleable, resilient, tractable **10** changeable, extensible, manageable, responsive, submissive **11** complaisant

Flibbertigibbet
   character in: 10 Kenilworth
   author: 5 Scott

flick 4 film **5** brush, graze, movie, sweep, whisk

Flicka
   nickname of: 17 Frederica Von Stade

Flicka 5 horse
in: **14** My Friend Flicka

flicker 4 flit, glow, sway **5** blaze, flame, flare, flash, gleam, glint, shake, spark, throb, trace, waver **6** quaver, quiver, waggle **7** flutter, glimmer, glisten, glitter, modicum, pulsate, shimmer, sparkle, tremble, vestige, vibrate, wriggle **8** undulate **9** coruscate, fluctuate, oscillate, scintilla, vacillate

Flickertail State
nickname of: **11** North Dakota

flicks 5 films **6** cinema, grazes, movies, sweeps, whisks **7** brushes

flier 4 bill **5** pilot **6** notice **7** aviator, leaflet, venture **8** brochure, bulletin, circular, handbill **10** experiment **12** announcement **13** advertisement

flight 4 rout, rush, wing **5** flock **6** escape, exodus, flying, hegira **7** fleeing, retreat, soaring, winging **8** squadron **10** withdrawal **11** aeronautics

flighty 5 dizzy, giddy **6** fickle **8** quixotic, reckless, unstable, volatile **9** frivolous, mercurial, whimsical **10** capricious, changeable, inconstant, indecisive, irresolute **11** harebrained, impractical, light-headed, thoughtless **13** irresponsible **14** scatterbrained

flimsy 4 poor, thin, weak **5** cheap, filmy, frail, gauzy, petty, sheer **6** feeble, shabby, shoddy, sleazy, slight, trashy **7** foolish, fragile, ill-made, shallow, trivial **8** cobwebby, delicate, gossamer, trifling **9** frivolous, worthless **10** diaphanous, inadequate, jerry-built, ramshackle **11** dilapidated, superficial **13** unsubstantial

flinch 3 fly, shy **4** jerk **5** cower, quail, quake, start, wince **6** blench, cringe, falter, quaver, quiver, recoil, shiver, shrink **7** contort, grimace, retreat, shudder

fling 2 go **3** try **4** ball, bash, cast, dash, emit, hurl, lark, toss **5** eject, expel, heave, pitch, sling, spree, trial **6** let fly, propel **7** attempt **8** bit of fun **11** precipitate

Flintstones, The
character: **7** Pebbles **8** Bamm Bamm **11** Betty Rubble **12** Barney Rubble **14** Fred Flintstone **15** Dino the Dinosaur, Wilma Flintstone
voice: **8** Alan Reed, Mel Blanc **10** Don Messick **12** Bea Benaderet, Gerry Johnson **13** Jean Vander Pyl
city: **7** Bedrock
creator: **12** Hanna-Barbera

flinty 4 cold, hard **5** cruel, harsh, stern, stony **6** inured, steely **7** callous **8** hardened **10** unyielding **11** hard-hearted, insensitive

flip 3 tap **4** bold, pert, spin, toss, turn **5** brash, flick, fresh, throw, thumb **6** cheeky, fillip **8** impudent, insolent, turn over **9** unabashed

flippant 4 glib, pert, rude **5** brash,

lippy, saucy **6** cheeky, nimble **7** voluble **8** impudent, insolent, trifling **9** bumptious, frivolous, talkative **11** impertinent **12** presumptuous **13** disrespectful

Flipper
character: **8** Bud Ricks **10** Sandy Ricks **11** Porter Ricks
cast: **10** Brian Kelly, Luke Halpin **11** Tommy Norden
Flipper played by: **4** Suzy

flirt 3 toy **4** play, vamp **5** dally, tease **6** trifle **8** coquette **12** heartbreaker

flit 4 dart, scud, skim, wing **5** speed **6** hasten, scurry **7** flicker, flutter

Flite, Miss
character in: **10** Bleak House
author: **7** Dickens

flivver 3 car **4** auto, heap **5** motor **6** jalopy, wheels **7** machine, vehicle **8** motorcar **9** tin lizzie **10** automobile

float 3 bob **4** waft **5** drift, hover, slide **6** bear up, buoy up, hold up, launch **8** levitate

floating 4 free **5** awash, loose **6** adrift, afloat, errant **7** buoyant, wafting **8** drifting **9** fluctuant, wandering **10** unattached

flock 2 go **3** mob, run **4** band, bevy, gang, herd, mass, pack, rush **5** bunch, crowd, crush, drove, group, surge, troop **6** clique, gather, huddle, muster, stream, throng **7** cluster, company, coterie **8** converge **9** gathering, multitude **10** assemblage, collection, congregate **11** aggregation **12** congregation
of fish: **6** school
of game birds: **5** covey
of geese: **6** gaggle
of insects: **5** swarm
of lions: **5** pride
of seals or whales: **3** pod
of young birds: **5** brood

flocks
god of: **3** Pan

flock together 6 gather, mingle **7** convene **8** assemble **9** associate **10** congregate

flog 4 beat, cane, club, cuff, drub, hide, lash, maul, whip **5** birch, flail, smite, strap **6** cudgel, paddle, strike, switch, thrash **7** scourge **8** lambaste **9** horsewhip **10** flagellate

flood 4 flow, glut, gush, tide **6** deluge, drench, shower, stream **7** cascade, current, torrent **8** downpour, flow over, inundate, overflow, saturate, submerge, wash over **9** overwhelm **10** cloudburst, inundation, outpouring, oversupply
period before: **12** antediluvian

Flood
author: **16** Robert Penn Warren

flooded 6 flowed, surged **7** deluged, glutted, overran, swamped **8** drenched, engulfed **9** inundated, out-

poured, washed out **10** downpoured, overflowed

floor 2 KO **4** base, deck, fell, kayo, tier **5** level, stage, story **6** bottom, ground **7** minimum, parquet **8** base rate, flooring, pavement **9** prostrate

flop 4 bomb, bust, drop, fail, fold, plop **5** close **6** fiasco, fizzle, topple, tumble, turkey **7** failure, go under, shutter, washout **8** disaster, lay an egg **14** disappointment

Flora
origin: **5** Roman
goddess of: **7** flowers

floral 6 bloomy **7** verdant **8** blossomy **9** botanical **10** herbaceous

Floralia
origin: **5** Roman
form: **8** festival

Florence
artist: **6** Giotto **7** Cimabue **8** Ghiberti **9** Donatello **10** Michelozzi **11** della Robbia **12** Brunelleschi, Michelangelo
capital of: **7** Tuscany **15** Firenze province
cathedral/church: **10** San Lorenzo, San Miniato, Santa Croce **18** Santa Maria del Fiore
Italian: **7** Firenze
landmark: **5** David, Pieta **6** Uffizi **8** Bargello **11** Pitti Palace **12** Ponte Vecchio **13** Boboli Gardens **14** Loggia dei Lanzi, Palazzo Vecchio **19** Piazza della Signoria **22** Baptistry of San Giovanni, Ospedale degli Innocenti
mountain: **9** Apennines
religious reformer: **10** Savonarola
river: **4** Arno
ruler: **5** Goths **6** Medici, Romans **8** Lombards **9** Etruscans **15** Byzantine Empire
tomb of: **7** Galileo, Rossini **11** Machiavelli **12** Michelangelo **15** Lorenzo de Medici

florescence 5 bloom **9** flowerage **10** blossoming

florid 4 rosy **5** gaudy, ruddy, showy **6** blowsy, hectic, ornate, rococo **7** baroque, flowery, flushed, reddish **8** inflamed, red-faced, rubicund, sanguine **9** elaborate **10** flamboyant, ornamented **12** ostentatious **13** grandiloquent

Florida
abbreviation: **2** FL **3** Fla
nickname: **6** Flower **8** Sunshine **10** Peninsular
capital: **11** Tallahassee
largest city: **12** Jacksonville
others: **4** Tice **5** Cocoa, Miami, Ocala, Tampa **7** Hialeah, Orlando, Palatka, Sebring **8** Sarasota **9** Bradenton, Palm Beach, Pensacola **10** Clearwater **11** Brooksville, Coral Gables, Gainesville, St Augustine **12** Daytona

Beach, Ft Lauderdale, St Petersburg
college: 4 Nova **5** Barry, Miami, Tampa **6** Eckerd **7** Rollins, Stetson
explorer: 11 Ponce de Leon
feature:
  amusement park: 5 Epcot **10** Marineland **11** Disney World
  canal: 5 Miami **7** Tamiami
  museum: 8 Ringling
  national park: 10 Everglades
professional sports teams:
  baseball: 7 Marlins **9** Devil Rays
  basketball: 4 Heat **5** Magic
  football: 7 Jaguars **8** Dolphins **10** Buccaneers
  hockey: 8 Panthers **9** Lightning
tribe: 3 Ais **5** Ocale, Utina **6** Calusa, Chatot, Potano **7** Timucua **8** Seminole
people: 5 conch **7** cracker, Osceola
island: 7 Bahamas, Sanibel **8** Biscayne
  key: 4 Long, Vaca, West **5** Largo **7** Big Pine **8** Biscayne **9** Sugarloaf
lake: 4 Dora **6** Apopka, Harney, Jessup, Newnan **7** Ledwith **8** Arbuckle **9** Kissimmee **10** Okeechobee
land rank: 12 twenty-second
physical feature:
  bay: 8 Biscayne **9** Apalachee **10** Waccasassa
  cape: 5 Sable **7** Kennedy **9** Canaveral
  gulf: 6 Mexico
  sea: 8 Atlantic
  springs: 6 Silver **7** Rainbow
  swamp: 10 Everglades, Okefenokee
river: 6 Banana, Indian **7** Aucilla, Manatee, Scambia, St Johns, Suwanee **9** Ochlawaha **12** Apalachicola
state admission: 13 twenty-seventh
state bird: 13 mockingbird
state fish: 16 Atlantic sailfish
state mammal: 7 dolphin
state flower: 13 orange blossom
state motto: 12 In God We Trust
state song: 11 Swanee River **14** Old Folks at Home
state tree: 13 sabal palmetto **15** cabbage palmetto
florilegium 7 garland **8** chapbook, treasury **9** anthology
Florizel
  character in: 14 The Winter's Tale
  author: 11 Shakespeare
floruit 12 he flourished **13** she flourished
flotilla 5 fleet **6** armada
Flotow, Friedrich von
  born: 7 Germany **11** Mecklenburg
  composer of: 6 Martha **11** Die Matrosen **19** Alessandro Stradella
flotsam 4 junk **6** debris, refuse **7** garbage **8** castoffs
flounce 3 hem **4** edge, leap, skip, trim, trip **5** bound, caper, frill, stamp, stomp, storm, strut **6** bounce, edging,

fringe, gambol, prance, ruffle, sashay, spring **7** valance **8** furbelow, ornament, skirting, trimming
flounder 4 fish, flop, halt, limp **5** lurch, waver **6** falter, hobble, muddle, totter, tumble, wallow, welter **7** blunder, shamble, stagger, stumble **8** flatfish, hesitate, struggle
Flounder, The
  author: 11 Gunter Grass
flourish 4 curl, dash, grow, pomp, rant, show, turn **5** bloom, bluff, get on, shake, strut, sweep, swing, swish, twirl, twist, wield **6** flaunt, flower, hot air, parade, splash, thrive, waving **7** blossom, bravado, burgeon, cadenza, fanfare, fustian, glitter, prosper, shaking, succeed, swagger **8** boasting, brandish, curlicue, fare well, get ahead, swinging, vaunting, wielding **9** agitation, grace note, thrashing **10** decoration **11** braggadocio, brandishing, fanfaronade, ostentation **12** appoggiatura **13** embellishment, magniloquence, swashbuckling **14** grandiloquence
flourishing 8 swinging, swishing, thriving, wielding **9** flaunting **10** prospering, successful **11** brandishing
flout 3 rag **4** defy, mock, twit **5** chaff, scorn, spurn, taunt **6** gibe at, insult
flow 3 jet, run **4** flux, gush, pass, pour, rush, seep, tide **5** drain, drift, float, flood, glide, issue, spout, spurt, surge, sweep, swirl, train **6** abound, course, deluge, efflux, effuse, filter, plenty, rapids, stream **7** cascade, current, debouch, torrent, well out **8** effusion, millrace, plethora, sequence **9** abundance, discharge, effluence, emanation **10** outpouring, succession **11** debouchment, progression
flower 3 bud **4** best, blow, open, pick, posy **5** bloom, cream, elite, ripen **6** mature **7** blossom, bouquet, burgeon, develop, nosegay, prosper **8** flourish **11** aristocracy
flower arranging, art of
  Japanese: 7 ikebana
Flower Fables
  author: 15 Louisa May Alcott
flowering 4 peak **5** bloom **6** height, heyday **8** blooming, maturing **10** blossoming, developing, prospering **11** flourishing
flowers
  goddess of: 5 Flora
Flowers of Evil
  author: 17 Charles Baudelaire
  French title: 14 Les Fleurs du Mal
Flower State
  nickname of: 7 Florida
flowery 5 fancy **6** floral, florid, ornate **8** blooming **10** blossoming, burgeoning, euphuistic, figurative, florescent, ornamental, rhetorical **11** embellished

12 efflorescent, magniloquent **13** grandiloquent
Flowery Kingdom *see* **5** China
flowing 4 flux **5** fluid **6** ebbing, fluent, smooth **7** current, copious, gliding, running **8** abundant **9** liquefied, plentiful **10** continuity, pouring out, proceeding
fluctuate 4 sway, vary, veer **5** shift, swing, waver **6** dawdle, falter, wobble **8** hesitate, undulate **9** alternate, oscillate, vacillate **10** dillydally
fluctuation 5 shift **6** change **7** veering **8** shifting, swinging **9** deviation, variation **11** alternation, oscillation, vacillation
flue 3 net **4** barb, down, pipe, tube, vent **5** fluff, fluke, shaft **6** funnel **7** channel, chimney, passage **9** smokejack
fluent 4 glib **5** vocal **6** facile **7** voluble **8** effusive, eloquent **9** garrulous, talkative **10** articulate, effortless
fluff 3 err, nap **4** down, flub, fuzz, lint, miss, puff, slip, soft **5** botch, floss, froth, primp **6** forget **7** blunder **8** feathers
fluffy 5 downy, fuzzy, nappy, wooly **6** fleecy, woolly **8** feathery
fluid 6 liquid, watery **7** unfixed **8** flexible, floating, shifting, solution, unstable **9** adaptable, liquefied, unsettled **10** adjustable, changeable, indefinite
fluid ounce
  abbreviation: 4 fl oz
fluke 3 hap **5** freak **6** chance **7** miracle **8** accident, windfall **9** mischance **11** vicissitude **12** stroke of luck
flummery 7 dessert, pudding **9** gibberish **10** doubletalk, mumbo jumbo **11** obfuscation
flunky 6 lackey, menial, minion **7** servant **9** attendant, underling
fluorine
  chemical symbol: 1 F
flurry 3 ado **4** fuss, gust, heat, puff, stir **5** alarm, fever, flush, haste, panic **6** breeze, bustle, pother, rattle, shower, squall, tumult **7** agitate, confuse, disturb, fidgets, fluster, flutter, perturb **8** confound, disquiet **9** agitation, commotion, confusion **10** discompose, disconcert, turbulence **11** disturbance, hurry-scurry, trepidation **12** discomposure, perturbation, restlessness
flush 4 even, glow, swab, tint, wash **5** bloom, blush, color, elate, flood, level, rinse, scour, scrub, shock, spray **6** access, dampen, deluge, douche, drench, excite, puff up, quiver, redden, sponge, thrill, tremor **7** animate, flutter, glowing, impulse, moisten, redness, wash out **8** rosiness, rosy glow, squarely, strength **9** freshness,

make proud, ruddiness **10** exultation, jubilation

flushed 3 hot, red **4** rosy, ruby **5** aglow, **6** florid, torrid **7** crimson, excited, scarlet **8** blushing, feverish **10** prosperous

flushed with success 5 proud **6** elated

fluster 4 daze **5** shake, upset **6** dither, flurry, hubbub, muddle, ruffle **7** agitate, confuse, disturb, flutter, perplex, perturb, startle, turmoil **8** befuddle, bewilder **9** agitation, commotion, confusion, discomfit **10** discompose, disconcert **12** bewilderment, discomfiture, discomposure **14** discombobulate

flute 4 fife, fold, pipe, roll, tube, wind **5** crimp **6** furrow, groove **7** piccolo, whistle **8** recorder **9** wine glass **14** champagne glass

flutter 3 bob **4** flap, flit, soar, stir, wave, wing **5** hurry, shake, throb **6** flurry, quiver, ripple, thrill, tremor, wobble **7** beating, flitter, fluster, pulsate, tremble, twitter **8** flapping, tingling **9** agitation, commotion, confusion, palpitate, sensation, vibration **12** perturbation

fluvial 7 aquatic

fluviatile 7 aquatic

flux 4 flow, tide **5** flood **6** course, motion, stream, unrest **7** current **8** mutation, shifting **10** alteration, transition **11** fluctuation **12** modification **14** transformation

fly 4 flap, flee, sail, skip, soar, wave, wing **5** coast, float, glide, hover, hurry, split, swoop **6** hasten, hustle **7** flutter, run away, take off, vibrate **8** take wing, undulate

fly
varieties: 3 bat, bot **4** blow, deer, dung, gnat, horn, moth, rust, sand **5** beach, black, crane, dance, drone, flesh, fruit, horse, house, march, marsh, midge, mydas, punky **6** bee fly, cactus, maggot, pomace, robber, stable, tsetse, warble, window **7** chalcid, seaweed, skipper, soldier, tachima **8** lousefly, mosquito, stiletto **9** leaf miner **10** flat-footed, fungus gnat, humpbacked **11** thickheaded **14** black scavenger

fly apart 5 burst **6** blow up **7** explode, shatter **8** detonate, fragment

fly at 6 assail, attack

fly-by-night 5 shady **6** shifty **7** crooked **8** unstable, untrusty **9** dishonest **10** unreliable **12** disreputable, undependable **13** irresponsible, untrustworthy

Flying Dutchman, The
opera by: 6 Wagner
character: 4 Erik **5** Senta **6** Daland **11** The Dutchman

Flying Fish
constellation of: 6 Volans

Flying Nun, The
character: 9 Sister Ana **11** Sister Sixto **13** Carlos Ramirez **14** Mother Superior **15** Sister Bertrille **16** Sister Jacqueline
cast: 10 Sally Field **12** Alejandro Rey, Linda Dangcil, Marge Redmond **14** Shelly Morrison **17** Madeleine Sherwood

fly in the ointment 5 hitch **7** problem, trouble **8** drawback, nuisance **9** hindrance **10** impediment **12** disadvantage

Flynn, Errol
real name: 17 Leslie Thomas Flynn
born: 6 Hobart **8** Tasmania **9** Australia
roles: 10 The Sea Hawk **12** Captain Blood **14** Too Much Too Soon **15** The Sun Also Rises **24** The Adventures of Robin Hood **26** The Charge of the Light Brigade

fly off the handle 6 see red

fly the coop 4 bolt, flee **6** escape, run off **7** abscond, get away, make off, run away, skip out, take off

foal 4 cade, colt **5** filly, young **9** fledgling

foam 4 fizz, head, scum, suds **5** froth, spume **6** lather **7** sparkle **8** bubbling **13** effervescence

foaming 5 sudsy **6** bubbly, frothy **7** lathery **8** bubbling, frothing

foamy 5 fizzy **6** frothy **7** lathery **8** bubbling **9** sparkling **12** effervescent

fob 5 chain, medal, strap **6** ribbon **8** ornament **9** medallion

focal 3 key **4** main **5** chief **7** central, pivotal **8** foremost **9** principal

Foch, Ferdinand
served in: 3 WWI
nationality: 6 French
rank: 7 marshal **16** commander-in-chief
battle: 5 Marne, Somme

Foch, Nina
real name: 20 Nina Consuelo Maud Fock
born: 6 Leyden **11** Netherlands
roles: 9 Spartacus **14** Executive Suite, Song to Remember **17** An American in Paris, My Name Is Julia Ross **18** The Ten Commandments

Fock, Nina Consuelo Maud
real name of: 8 Nina Foch

focus 3 aim, fix, hub **4** core **5** haunt, heart **6** adjust, center, direct, middle, resort **7** nucleus, retreat **8** converge **9** limelight, spotlight **10** rendezvous **11** concentrate **12** headquarters

focusing 6 aiming **9** adjusting, centering, directing **10** adjustment, converging **11** pinpointing **13** concentrating

fodder 4 feed, food **6** forage, silage **7** rations **9** provender

foe 5 enemy, rival **8** attacker, opponent **9** adversary, assailant, combatant, contender, disputant **10** antagonist, competitor

fog 3 dim **4** daze, haze, smog, soup **5** brume, cloud **6** darken, muddle, stupor, trance **7** confuse, obscure, pea soup, perplex **8** bewilder **9** murkiness **10** cloudiness **12** bewilderment

Fogg, Phileas
character in: 26 Around the World in Eighty Days
author: 10 Jules Verne
valet: 12 Passepartout

foggy 3 dim **4** dark, hazy **5** dusky, filmy, fuzzy, misty, murky, musty, soupy, vague **6** cloudy, smoggy, spacey **7** brumous, clouded, obscure, shadowy, unclear **8** confused, nebulous, overcast, vaporous **9** beclouded **10** indistinct

foible 4 kink **5** quirk **6** defect, whimsy **7** failing, frailty **8** crotchet, weak side, weakness **9** infirmity **10** deficiency **11** shortcoming **12** imperfection

Foible
character in: 16 The Way of the World
author: 8 Congreve

foil 3 nip **4** balk, film, leaf **5** check, flake, match, sheet, wafer **6** hinder, lamina, set off, thwart **7** enhance, prevent **8** backdrop, contrast **9** frustrate **10** antithesis, complement, supplement **11** correlative, counterpart

foist 6 impose, unload **7** palm off, pass off

fold 3 hug, lap, pen, sty **4** bend, curl, sect, tuck, wrap, yard **5** clasp, close, crimp, flock, group, layer, pleat **6** corral, crease, dog-ear, double, encase, enfold, furrow, gather, parish, pucker, ruffle, rumple, wrap up **7** crinkle, crumple, embosom, embrace, entwine, envelop, flounce, overlap, wrinkle **8** barnyard, compound, doubling, stockade **9** community, corrugate, enclosure **12** congregation

folder 7 booklet, leaflet **8** brochure, circular, pamphlet **9** portfolio

foliage 6 leaves **7** leafage, verdure

folklore 5 myths **6** fables **7** legends **10** traditions

folks 3 kin **6** family, people **7** kinsmen, parents **8** everyone **9** relatives **10** kith and kin

folksy 6 casual, chatty **8** familiar, friendly, homespun, informal, sociable **10** neighborly **14** conversational **15** unsophisticated

folk tale
German: 7 Marchen

Follett, Ken
author of: 8 Jackdaws, Whiteout **12**

Hornet Flight **14** Eye of the Needle, Night Over Water **15** On Wings of Eagles, The Hammer of Eden, The Key to Rebecca **22** The Man from St Petersburg

follow 3 dog **4** copy, heed, hunt, mind, note, obey, tail **5** aim at, chase, grasp, hound, stalk, trace, track, trail, watch **6** attend, notice, pursue, regard, shadow, take up **7** cherish, emulate, imitate, observe, replace, succeed **8** practice, supplant **9** accompany, cultivate, prosecute **10** comprehend, understand

follower 3 fan **4** tail **5** pupil, toady **6** chaser, hunter, shadow, stooge **7** admirer, apostle, convert, devotee, protege, pursuer, servant, stalker **8** adherent, advocate, disciple, hanger-on, henchman, parasite, partisan, retainer, servitor **9** accessory, attendant, dependent, proselyte, satellite, supporter, sycophant

following 4 next **5** below, suite, train **6** public **7** ensuing, retinue **8** audience **9** adherents, clientele, entourage, partisans, patronage **10** attendance, consequent, sequential, subsequent, succeeding, successive **11** consecutive

Follow the Fleet
  director: 12 Mark Sandrich
  cast: 11 Fred Astaire **12** Ginger Rogers **13** Randolph Scott **21** Harriet Hilliard Nelson
  song: 11 We Saw the Sea **13** Let Yourself Go **24** Let's Face the Music and Dance

follow-up 7 ensuing **8** sequence **9** aftermath **10** subsequent

folly 6 idiocy, levity **7** inanity, mistake **8** nonsense, trifling **9** absurdity, asininity, frivolity, giddiness, silliness **10** imbecility, imprudence, tomfoolery **11** doltishness, fatuousness, foolishness **12** indiscretion **13** brainlessness, irrationality, senselessness

foment 4 goad, spur, urge **5** rouse **6** arouse, excite, foster, incite, kindle, stir up **7** agitate, inflame, promote, provoke, quicken **8** irritate **9** aggravate, galvanize, instigate, stimulate **10** exacerbate

fond 5 naive **6** ardent, doting, loving, tender **7** amorous, devoted **8** desirous, enamored, harbored, held dear **9** cherished, indulgent, preserved, sustained **10** infatuated, passionate **11** impassioned, sentimental **12** affectionate **16** overaffectionate

Fonda, Henry
  wife: 16 Margaret Sullavan
  son: 5 Peter
  daughter: 4 Jane
  born: 13 Grand Island NE
  roles: 7 Jezebel, Warlock **8** Fail Safe **10** Fort Apache, In Harm's Way, The Best Man, The Lady Eve **12** On

Golden Pond (Oscar) **13** Mister Roberts, Ox-Bow Incident, The Longest Day **14** Twelve Angry Men, Young Mr Lincoln **16** Advise and Consent, Battle of the Bulge, How the West Was Won, The Grapes of Wrath **18** The Boston Strangler **19** My Darling Clementine, The Immortal Sergeant **21** Sometimes a Great Notion

Fonda, Jane
  father: 5 Henry
  brother: 5 Peter
  husband: 9 Ted Turner, Tom Hayden **10** Roger Vadim
  born: 9 New York NY
  roles: 5 Julia, Klute (Oscar) **10** Barbarella, Coming Home (Oscar) **11** A Doll's House **12** Any Wednesday, On Golden Pond **13** China Syndrome **17** Barefoot in the Park **23** They Shoot Horses Don't They?

Fonda, Peter
  father: 5 Henry
  sister: 4 Jane
  daughter: 7 Bridget
  born: 9 New York NY
  roles: 7 The Trip **9** Easy Rider, Ulee's Gold **13** The Wild Angels

fondle 3 hug, neck, pet **4** neck **5** spoon **6** caress, cuddle, nestle, nuzzle, smooch, stroke **7** embrace, make out **8** canoodle **10** bill and coo

fondness 4 bent, care, love **5** ardor, fancy **6** desire, liking **7** passion **8** devotion, penchant, weakness **9** affection **10** attachment, partiality, preference, propensity, tenderness **11** amorousness, inclination **12** predilection **14** susceptibility

fond utterance 9 sweet talk **10** endearment **12** sweet nothing

Fons
  origin: 5 Roman
  god of: 7 springs

fons et origo 15 source and origin

Fontaine, Joan
  real name: 25 Joan de Beauvoir de Havilland
  sister: 17 Olivia de Havilland
  husband: 11 Brian Aherne
  born: 5 Japan, Tokyo
  roles: 3 Ivy **7** Ivanhoe, Rebecca **8** Casanova, Gunga Din, Jane Eyre, The Women **9** Suspicion (Oscar) **12** The Devil's Own **15** Frenchman's Creek, September Affair **16** Tender Is the Night, The Constant Nymph

Fontanne, Lynn
  husband: 10 Alfred Lunt
  born: 6 London **7** England
  roles: 8 The Visit **9** Quadrille, The Pirate **10** The Sea Gull **13** O Mistress Mine **15** Design for Living **18** The Great Sebastians **19** The Taming of the Shrew

food 4 chow, feed, grub **5** board **6** fodder, forage, silage, viands **7** edibles,

nurture, pasture, rations **8** eatables, victuals **9** nutrition, pasturage, provender **10** provisions, sustenance **11** comestibles, nourishment, subsistence

food, miraculous 5 manna

fool 3 ass, con, oaf **4** bilk, clod, dolt, dupe, gull, hoax, jest, joke **5** cheat, chump, clown, cozen, cut up, dummy, dunce, feign, goose, idiot, klutz, moron, ninny, tease, trick **6** diddle, fleece, frolic, humbug, jester, nitwit, rip off, stooge **7** beguile, buffoon, deceive, defraud, half-wit, Pierrot, pretend **8** bonehead, dummkopf, flimflam, hoodwink, imbecile, lunkhead, meathead, numskull **9** bamboozle, blockhead, harlequin, ignoramus, numbskull, simpleton **10** dunderhead, nincompoop, scaramouch **11** Punchinello

fool around 3 toy **4** idle **5** clown, dally **6** dawdle, loiter, trifle

foolhardy 4 rash **5** brash, hasty **6** madcap **8** careless, heedless, reckless **9** daredevil, hotheaded, impetuous, imprudent, impulsive **10** headstrong, incautious **11** harebrained, thoughtless

foolish 5 inane, silly **6** absurd, stupid, unwise **7** asinine, fatuous, idiotic, moronic, witless **9** brainless, imbecilic, imprudent, ludicrous, senseless **10** boneheaded, incautious, indiscreet, ridiculous **12** preposterous **13** irresponsible, unintelligent

foolishness 5 folly **6** idiocy, lunacy **8** unwisdom **9** absurdity, asininity, puerility, silliness, stupidity **10** imbecility, imprudence **11** fatuousness, witlessness **12** childishness, extravagance, indiscretion **13** brainlessness, senselessness **14** ridiculousness **15** injudiciousness **16** irresponsibility, preposterousness

foot 3 dog, pad, paw **4** base, hoof **6** bottom, tootsy **7** trotter **8** infantry **10** foundation
  abbreviation: 2 ft

football
  term: 3 end **4** bomb, down, draw, flat, punt, sack **5** blitz, guard, zebra **6** center, fumble, option, pocket, safety, tackle **7** audible, bootleg, flanker, holding, kickoff, lateral, offside, platoon, reverse, rollout, shotgun **8** clipping, gridiron, halfback, turnover **9** crackback, field goal, nose guard, scrimmage, touchback **10** conversion, cornerback, linebacker, nose tackle **11** quarterback **12** encroachment

Hall of Fame:
  location: 4 Ohio **6** Canton
  1963: 4 Bell (Bert), Carr (Joe), Hein (Mel), Mara (Tim) **5** Baugh (Sammy), Clark (Dutch), Halas (George), Henry (Pete) **6** Hutson

(Don), Nevers (Ernie), Thorpe (Jim) **7** Hubbard (Cal), Lambeau (Curly), McNally (John Blood) **8** Nagurski (Bronko), Marshall (George P)
1964: 5 Lyman (Link) **6** Healey (Ed), Hinkle (Clarke), Rooney (Art) **7** Trafton (George) **9** Conzelman (Jimmy), Michalske (Mike)
1965: 6 Graham (Otto), Grange (Red) **7** Luckman (Sid) **8** Driscoll (Paddy), Fortmann (Daniel J), Van Buren (Steve) **10** Chamberlin (Guy), Waterfield (Bob)
1966: 3 Ray (Hugh "Shorty") **5** Guyon (Joe), Owens (Steve) **6** Dudley (Bill), Herber (Arnie), McAfee (George), Turner (Clyde "Bulldog") **8** Kiesling (Walt)
1967: 5 Brown (Paul E), Layne (Bobby) **6** Reeves (Dan), Strong (Ken) **7** Bidwill (Charles W), Tunnell (Emlen) **8** Bednarik (Chuck), Stydahar (Joe)
1968: 6 Hirsch (Elroy), Motley (Marion), Trippi (Charley) **7** Battles (Cliff), Donovan (Art), Millner (Wayne) **13** Wojciechowicz (Alex)
1969: 5 Neale (Earle "Greasy"), Perry (Joe) **7** Edwards (Albert Glen "Turk") **8** Stautner (Ernie) **9** Nomellini (Leo)
1970: 5 Fears (Tom), Pihos (Pete) **9** McElhenny (Hugh) **12** Christiansen (Jack)
1971: 5 Brown (Jim) **6** Hewitt (Bill), Kinard (Frank "Bruiser"), Tittle (Y A) **8** Lombardi (Vince) **10** Robustelli (Andy) **11** Van Brocklin (Norm)
1972: 4 Hunt (Lamar) **6** Matson (Ollie), Parker (Ace) **9** Marchetti (Gino)
1973: 5 Berry (Raymond) **6** Parker (Jim) **7** Schmidt (Joe)
1974: 4 Lane (Dick "Night Train") **5** Groza (Lou "The Toe") **6** George (Bill) **7** Canadeo (Tony)
1975: 5 Brown (Roosevelt), Moore (Lenny) **6** Connor (George) **7** Lavelli (Dante)
1976: 4 Ford (Len) **6** Taylor (Jim) **8** Flaherty (Ray)
1977: 5 Gregg (Forrest), Starr (Bart) **6** Sayers (Gale), Willis (Bill) **7** Gifford (Frank)
1978: 6 Ewbank (Weeb), Wilson (Larry) **7** Alworth (Lance), Leemans (Tuffy) **8** Nitschke (Ray)
1979: 3 Mix (Ron) **4** Lary (Yale) **6** Butkus (Dick), Unitas (Johnny)
1980: 4 Otto (Jim) **5** Jones (David "Deacon"), Lilly (Bob) **8** Adderley (Herb)
1981: 5 Davis (Willie), Ringo (Jim) **6** Badgro (Morris "Red"), Blanda (George)
1982: 4 Huff (Sam) **5** Musso (George), Olsen (Merlin) **6** Atkins (Doug)
1983: 4 Bell (Bobby) **6** Gilman (Sid)

8 Mitchell (Bobby), Warfield (Paul) **9** Jurgensen (Sonny)
1984: 5 Brown (Willie) **6** Taylor (Charley) **9** McCormack (Mike) **11** Weinmeister (Arnie)
1985: 6 Gatski (Frank), Namath (Joe) **7** Rozelle (Pete), Simpson (OJ) **8** Staubach (Roger)
1986: 6 Lanier (Willie), Walker (Doak) **7** Hornung (Paul), Houston (Ken) **9** Tarkenton (Fran)
1987: 6 Csonka (Larry), Dawson (Len), Greene (Joe), Langer (Jim), Upshaw (Gene) **7** Johnson (John Henry), Maynard (Don)
1988: 3 Ham (Jack) **4** Page (Alan) **5** Ditka (Mike) **11** Biletnikoff (Fred)
1989: 4 Wood (Willie) **5** Shell (Art) **6** Blount (Mel) **8** Bradshaw (Terry)
1990: 6 Griese (Bob), Harris (Franco), Landry (Tom) **7** Lambert (Jack), St Clair (Bob) **8** Buchanan (Buck) **9** Hendricks (Ted)
1991: 5 Jones (Stan) **6** Hannah (John) **7** Schramm (Tex) **8** Campbell (Earl), Stenerud (Jan)
1992: 5 Davis (Al) **6** Barney (Lem), Mackey (John) **7** Riggins (John)
1993: 4 Noll (Chuck) **5** Fouts (Dan), Walsh (Bill) **6** Little (Larry), Payton (Walter)
1994: 5 Grant (Bud), Kelly (Leroy), Smith (Jackie), White (Randy) **7** Dorsett (Tony), Johnson (Jimmy)
1995: 5 Finks (Jim) **6** Jordan (Henry), Selmon (Lee Roy) **7** Largent (Steve), Winslow (Kellen)
1996: 5 Gibbs (Joe) **6** Joiner (Charlie), Renfro (Mel) **8** Creekmur (Lou), Dierdorf (Dan)
1997: 4 Mara (Wellington) **5** Shula (Don) **6** Haynes (Mike) **7** Webster (Mike)
1998: 5 Munoz (Anthony) **6** Krause (Paul) **8** McDonald (Tommy) **10** Singletary (Mike), Stephenson (Dwight)
1999: 4 Mack (Tom), Shaw (Billy) **6** Taylor (Lawrence) **7** Newsome (Ozzie) **9** Dickerson (Eric)
2000: 4 Long (Howie), Lott (Ronnie) **6** Rooney (Dan), Wilcox (Dave) **7** Montana (Joe)
2001: 4 Levy (Mary), Yary (Ron) **5** Swann (Lynn) **6** Slater (Jackie) **7** Munchak (Mike) **10** Buoniconti (Nick), Youngblood (Jack)
2002: 4 Allen (George), Kelly (Jim) **6** Casper (Dave) **7** Hampton (Dan) **10** Stallworth (John)
2003: 5 Allen (Marcus), Stram (Hank) **6** Bethea (Elvin), Lofton (James) **13** DeLamielleure (Joe)
2004: 5 Brown (Bob), Eller (Carl), Elway (John) **7** Sanders (Barry)
2005: 5 Young (Steve) **6** Marino (Dan) **7** Pollard (Fritz) **8** Friedman (Benny)

other player/coach: 8 Kyle Rote, Ray Lewis, Tom Brady **9** Amos Stagg, Earl Blaik, Jerry Rice, Lou Little, **10** Bear Bryant, Brett Favre, Bruce Smith, Bubba Smith, Joe Paterno, Ken Stabler, Larry Brown, Tiki Barber, Troy Aikman, Walter Camp, Warren Moon, Warren Sapp **11** Ahmad Rashad, Craig Morton, Deion Sanders, Earl Morrall, Floyd Little, Jim Plunkett, Knute Rockne, Michael Vick, Reggie White **12** Bud Wilkinson, Curtis Martin, Joe Thiesmann, Roman Gabriel, William Perry **13** Ara Parseghian, Donovan McNabb, Peyton Manning **14** Lydell Mitchell, Michael Strahan

football bowl games 3 Sun **4** Rose **5** Gator, Peach, Sugar, Super **6** Citrus, Cotton, Fiesta, Orange **7** Holiday, Liberty, Outback

football leagues

National Football League (NFL): 11 New York Jets **12** Buffalo Bills, Chicago Bears, Detroit Lions **13** Dallas Cowboys, Denver Broncos, Miami Dolphins, New York Giants **14** Atlanta Falcons, Los Angeles Rams **15** Baltimore Ravens, Cleveland Browns, Green Bay Packers, Seattle Seahawks, Tennessee Oilers (formerly Houston) **16** Kansas City Chiefs, Minnesota Vikings, New Orleans Saints, Phoenix Cardinals (formerly St Louis), San Diego Chargers **17** Cincinnati Bengals, Indianapolis Colts (formerly Baltimore), Los Angeles Raiders (formerly Oakland) **18** New England Patriots, Philadelphia Eagles, Pittsburgh Steelers, Tampa Bay Buccaneers, Washington Redskins **23** San Francisco Forty-Niners

United States Football League (USFL): 10 Denver Gold **12** Chicago Blitz **14** Baltimore Stars, Boston Breakers **15** Houston Gamblers, Oakland Invaders, Oklahoma Outlaws, Tampa Bay Bandits **16** Arizona Wranglers, Memphis Showboats, Michigan Panthers, Orlando Renegades, Portland Breakers **17** Jacksonville Bulls, Los Angeles Express, New Jersey Generals, Philadelphia Stars **18** Washington Federals **19** Birmingham Stallions **21** San Antonio Gunslingers

football team (NFC)
Atlanta: 7 Falcons
   stadium: 11 Georgia Dome
Arizona: 9 Cardinals
   stadium: 8 Sun Devil
   formerly in: 7 St. Louis
Carolina: 8 Panthers
   stadium: 13 Bank of America
Chicago: 5 Bears
   stadium: 12 Soldier Field
Dallas: 7 Cowboys
   stadium: 5 Texas

Detroit: 5 Lions
   stadium: 9 Ford Field
Green Bay: 7 Packers
   stadium: 9 Milwaukee **12** Lambeau Field
Minnesota: 7 Vikings
   stadium: 9 Metrodome
New Orleans: 6 Saints
   stadium: 18 Louisiana Superdome
New York: 6 Giants
   stadium: 6 Giants
Philadelphia: 6 Eagles
   stadium: 16 Lincoln Financial
Saint Louis: 4 Rams
   stadium: 15 Edward Jones Dome
   formerly in: 10 Los Angeles
San Francisco: 11 Forty-Niners
   stadium: 11 Monster Park
Seattle: 8 Seahawks
   stadium: 10 Qwest Field
Tampa Bay: 10 Buccaneers
   stadium: 12 Raymond James
Washington: 8 Redskins
   stadium: 10 FedEx Field

football team (AFC)
Baltimore: 6 Ravens
   stadium: 9 M and T Bank
   formerly in: 9 Cleveland
Buffalo: 5 Bills
   stadium: 11 Ralph Wilson
Cincinnati: 7 Bengals
   stadium: 9 Paul Brown
Cleveland: 6 Browns
   stadium: 6 Browns
Denver: 7 Broncos
   stadium: 8 Mile High
Houston: 6 Texans
   stadium: 7 Reliant
Indianapolis: 5 Colts
   stadium: 7 RCA Dome
   formerly in: 9 Baltimore
Jacksonville: 7 Jaguars
   stadium: 6 Alltel
Kansas City: 6 Chiefs
   stadium: 9 Arrowhead
Los Angeles: 7 Raiders
   stadium: 16 Memorial Coliseum
   formerly in: 7 Oakland
Miami: 8 Dolphins
   stadium: 8 Dolphins
New England: 8 Patriots
   stadium: 8 Gillette
New York: 4 Jets
   stadium: 6 Giants
Oakland: 7 Raiders
   stadium: 14 McAfee Coliseum
   formerly in: 10 Los Angeles
Pittsburgh: 8 Steelers
   stadium: 10 Heinz Field
San Diego: 8 Chargers
   stadium: 8 San Diego
Tennessee: 6 Titans
   stadium: 11 The Coliseum
footfall 3 pad **4** pace, step **5** tread **8** footstep
foothold 4 grip, hold **7** support **8** purchase
footloose 4 free **8** carefree **9** fancy-free **10** unattached **11** uncommitted **12** unencumbered
footnote 5 gloss **9** reference **10** annotation **11** explanation **12** afterthought
footnote abbreviations 2 ca, ms, nd, qv **3** mss **4** et al, ibid **5** et seq, infra, op cit, pseud, supra **6** loc cit
footpad 5 thief **6** bandit, mugger, outlaw, robber **10** highwayman
footpath 4 lane, ramp **5** jetty, trail **8** sidewalk
foot soldiers 8 infantry **10** fusilliers, musketeers
footstool 6 buffet **7** hassock, ottoman **8** footrest
footwear
   French: 9 chaussure
fop 4 beau, dude **5** dandy, swell **7** coxcomb **8** popinjay **9** prettyboy **11** Beau Brummel
foppish 4 vain **5** gaudy, showy **6** ornate **7** finical **8** affected, dandyish **9** dandified **12** ostentatious **13** overelaborate
forage 4 feed, food, hunt, raid, seek **6** fodder, ravage, search, silage **7** despoil, explore, pasture, plunder, rummage **8** scavenge, scrounge **9** pasturage, provender **10** provisions
foray 4 raid **5** sally **6** attack, inroad, invade, ravage, thrust **7** pillage, plunder, venture **8** invasion **9** incursion **10** expedition **11** depredation
forbear 4 quit, stop **5** cease, forgo **6** desist, endure, eschew, forego, give up, suffer **7** abstain, refrain **8** abnegate, renounce, tolerate
forbearance 4 pity **5** mercy **6** pardon **8** clemency, eschewal, leniency, meekness, mildness, patience **9** endurance, tolerance **10** abstention, abstinence, continence, indulgence, moderation, submission, temperance **11** longanimity, resignation **12** mercifulness
forbearing 6 denial **7** lenient, refusal **8** eschewal, tolerant **9** indulgent **10** abnegation, abstention, abstinence, permissive, refraining **13** nonindulgence **16** nonparticipation
forbid 3 ban, bar **4** veto **5** taboo **6** enjoin, hinder, impede, oppose, refuse, reject **7** exclude, gainsay, inhibit, obviate, prevent **8** disallow, obstruct, preclude, prohibit, restrain **9** interdict, proscribe
forbiddance 3 ban **4** no-no **5** taboo **7** barring, embargo **9** exclusion, interdict **11** prohibition **12** interdiction, proscription
forbidden 4 no-no, tabu **5** taboo **6** banned **8** debarred **10** prohibited, proscribed
   German: 8 verboten
forbidden fruit
   type: 6 brandy **7** liqueur
   origin: 7 America
   flavor: 5 honey **6** orange **10** grapefruit
forbidding 4 dour, grim, ugly **6** odious **7** hideous, ominous **8** horrible, sinister **9** abhorrent, offensive, repellent, repulsive **10** unfriendly, unpleasant **11** prohibitive, prohibitory, threatening **12** disagreeable, inhospitable **14** unapproachable
force 3 pry, vim **4** army, body, coax, crew, drag, gang, make, pull, push, team, unit, urge **5** break, clout, corps, drive, group, impel, might, power, press, squad, value, vigor, wrest **6** coerce, compel, duress, effect, elicit, energy, enjoin, extort, impact, import, impose, induce, oblige, propel, stress, thrust, weight, wrench **7** cogency, intrude, meaning, obtrude, potency, require, squeeze, stamina **8** charisma, coercion, division, efficacy, emphasis, momentum, persuade, pressure, squadron, strength, validity, violence, vitality **9** animation, battalion, constrain, magnetism, overpower, puissance **10** attraction, compulsion, constraint, detachment **11** necessitate, weightiness **12** significance **13** effectiveness
   Latin: 3 vis
forced 5 slave **7** binding, coerced, labored, obliged **8** affected, enslaved, grudging, mannered, required, strained **9** compelled, impressed, insincere, mandatory, unwilling **10** artificial, compulsory, obligatory **11** constrained, involuntary
forceful 5 pithy, valid, vivid **6** cogent, potent, robust, strong, virile **7** dynamic, intense **8** emphatic, powerful, puissant, vigorous **9** effective, energetic **10** impressive
forceless 4 weak **8** impotent
force measurement 4 dyne **6** newton **7** poundal
Force of Destiny, The
   also: 17 La Forza del Destino
   opera by: 5 Verdi
   character: 7 Leonora **8** Don Carlo **9** Don Alvaro
forcible 8 coercive **10** compulsory
ford 3 car **4** span, wade **5** cross, shoal **6** bridge, stream **7** passage **8** crossing, tin lizzy
Ford, Gerald Rudolph
   born: 17 Leslie Lynch King Jr
   adopted by/named after: 10 step father
   nickname: 5 Jerry **7** Mr Clean
   presidential rank: 12 thirty-eighth
   party: 10 Republican
   state represented: 2 MI
   elected to neither: 10 presidency **14** vice presidency
   vice president: 11 (Nelson A) Rockefeller

cabinet:
  state: 9 (Henry A) Kissinger
  treasury: 5 (William E) Simon
  defense: 8 (Donald H) Rumsfeld
    11 (James) Schlesinger
  attorney general: 4 (Edward H)
    Levi **5** (William B) Saxbe
  interior: 6 (Rogers Clark Ballard)
    Morton, (Thomas S) Kleppe **8**
    (Stanley K) Hathaway
  agriculture: 4 (Earl Lauer) Butz **6**
    (John A) Knebel
  commerce: 4 (Frederick B) Dent **6**
    (Rogers Clark Ballard) Morton **10**
    (Elliot L) Richardson
  labor: 5 (W J) Usery (Jr) **6** (John
    T) Dunlop **7** (Peter J) Brennan
  HEW: 7 (F David) Mathews **10**
    (Caspar W) Weinberger
  HUD: 4 (James T) Lynn **5** (Carla
    Anderson) Hills
  transportation: 7 (William T) Cole-
    man (Jr) **8** (Claude S) Brinegar
born: 7 Omaha NE
education:
  University: 8 Michigan
  Law School: 4 Yale
religion: 12 Episcopalian
interests: 4 golf **6** boxing, skiing **8**
  football, swimming
vacation spot: 2 CO **4** Vail
author: 27 A Time To Heal: An Autobiography
political career: 13 vice president **19**
  House minority leader **24** US House
  of Representatives
civilian career: 6 lawyer
  assistant football coach at: 4 Yale
military service: 6 US Navy **10** lieutenant, World War II
notable events of lifetime/term: 9
  recession **12** Bicentennial
  assassination attempts on: 4 Ford
  clemency for: 12 draft dodgers,
    draft evaders
  kidnapping/trial/conviction of: 11
    Patty Hearst
  scandal: 8 Lockheed **10** Hays Affair
  talks: 4 SALT
quotes: 19 I am a Ford not a Lincoln
father:
  natural: 15 Leslie Lynch King
  adoptive: 17 Gerald Rudolph Ford
mother: 7 Dorothy (Gardner King
  Ford)
siblings:
  half-brothers: 12 James Francis **13**
    Thomas Gardner **14** Richard Addi-
    son
  wife: 9 Elizabeth (Bloomer Warren)
    nickname: 5 Betty
  children: 4 John **5** Susan **6** Steven **7**
    Michael
Ford, Glenn
  real name: 11 Gwyllyn Ford
  wife: 13 Eleanor Powell
  born: 6 Canada, Quebec
  roles: 4 Rage **5** Gilda, Jubal **6** Santee

8 Cimarron **11** The Rounders **14** Is
Paris Burning? **17** Interrupted Melody **18** Don't Go Near the Water **19**
The Blackboard Jungle **23** Teahouse
of the August Moon
Ford, Harrison
  nickname: 5 Harry
  born: 9 Chicago IL
  companion: 16 Calista Flockhart
  roles: 7 Frantic, Witness **8** Star Wars
    11 Blade Runner, The Fugitive **12**
    Patriot Games **15** Return of the Jedi
    16 American Graffiti, Presumed Inno-
    cent **19** Raiders of the Lost Ark **20**
    The Empire Strikes Back **21** Clear
    and Present Danger **30** Indiana Jones
    and the Temple of Doom
Ford, John
  author of: 13 Perkin Warbeck **17** 'Tis
    Pity She's a Whore **19** The Lover's
    Melancholy
Ford, John
  director of: 10 Stagecoach **11** The In-
    former (Oscar), The Quiet Man (Os-
    car) **12** The Hurricane, The Search-
    ers **13** Grapes of Wrath (Oscar),
    Mister Roberts (with Mervyn LeRoy),
    The Lost Patrol **17** The Long Voyage
    Home **19** How Green Was My Valley
    (Oscar), My Darling Clementine **27**
    The Man Who Shot Liberty Valence
Ford, Thelma Booth
  real name of: 12 Shirley Booth
Ford and Mistress Ford
  characters in: 22 The Merry Wives
    of Windsor
  author: 11 Shakespeare
fore 5 front **7** frontal **8** anterior, headmost
forearm 4 ulna **5** prime, ready **7** prepare
forebear 8 ancestor, begetter **10** antecedent, procreator, progenitor
foreboding 4 omen **5** dread **6** augury,
  boding **7** portent **9** intuition, misgiving **10** prescience, prognostic **11** premonition **12** apprehension, presentiment
forecast 5 augur **6** augury, divine, expect **7** outlook, portend, predict, presage, project **8** envisage, envision,
  prophesy **9** calculate, prevision, prog-
  nosis **10** anticipate, conjecture, prediction, prescience, projection **11** extrapolate **12** anticipation, precognition,
  presentiment **13** prognosticate **15**
  prognostication
forefather 6 author **8** ancestor, begetter **9** patriarch, precursor **10** antecedent, originator, procreator, progenitor
  12 primogenitor
forefront 4 fame, head, lead **8** vanguard **9** celebrity
foreign 5 alien **6** exotic, remote **7** distant, strange, unknown, unusual **8**
  imported **9** barbarous, extrinsic, irregular, unrelated **10** extraneous, hea-

thenish, introduced, irrelevant, outlandish, unfamiliar **11** incongruous,
inconsonant, unconnected **12** antipathetic, inadmissible, inapplicable, incompatible, inconsistent **13** inappropriate **16** uncharacteristic
Foreign Correspondent
  director: 15 Alfred Hitchcock
  cast: 10 Joel McCrea, Laraine Day **13**
    George Sanders **14** Robert Benchley
    15 Albert Basserman, Herbert Mar-
    shall
foreigner 5 alien, pagan **6** emigre **8**
  newcomer, outsider, stranger **9** barbarian, immigrant, nonnative, outlander
  German: 9 Auslander
foreign officer 6 consul **8** diplomat,
  minister **10** ambassador **14** representative **15** charge d'affaires
foreknowledge 9 intuition, prevision
  10 prescience **11** premonition **12** anticipation, apprehension, clairvoyance,
  precognition, presentiment
foreman 4 boss **7** manager **8** chairman, overseer **9** president, spokesman
  10 supervisor **11** coordinator **14** superintendent
foremost 4 head, main **5** chief, vital **7**
  capital, leading, supreme **8** cardinal
  9 essential, paramount, principal **10**
  preeminent
forerunner 4 omen, sign **5** token **6**
  augury, herald **7** portent, presage **8**
  ancestor **9** harbinger, precursor, prototype **10** progenitor, prognostic **11**
  predecessor, premonition
foresee 5 augur **6** divine, expect **7**
  predict, presage **8** envision, prophesy
  10 anticipate **13** prognosticate
foreshadow 5 augur **7** presage, promise **9** prefigure
foresight 6 wisdom **8** planning, prudence, sagacity **9** prevision **10** discretion, precaution, prescience, providence, shrewdness **12** anticipation,
  clairvoyance, perspicacity, precognition, preparedness **13** premeditation
  14 farsightedness
forest 4 bush, wood **5** copse, grove,
  stand, woods **6** jungle **7** thicket **8**
  wildwood, woodland **10** timberland,
  wilderness
forestall 5 avert, avoid, block, deter **6**
  thwart **7** head off, obviate, prevent,
  ward off **8** preclude **10** anticipate, circumvent, counteract
Forester, C S (Cecil Scott)
  author of: 6 The Gun **14** A Ship of
    the Line **15** Payment Deferred, The
    African Queen **24** Captain Horatio
    Hornblower
forests
  god of: 3 Pan **7** Silenus, Virbius
  pertaining to: 6 silvan, sylvan
  nymph: 5 dryad

foretell 5 augur 6 divine 7 portend, predict, presage 8 prophesy, soothsay 9 apprehend 13 prognosticate

forethought 4 heed 7 caution 8 prudence, sagacity, wariness 10 discretion, precaution, providence, shrewdness 11 carefulness 12 anticipation, deliberation 13 consideration, premeditation 14 circumspection, farsightedness

forever 6 always 9 eternally, undyingly 10 constantly 11 ceaselessly, continually, incessantly, perpetually, unceasingly 12 interminably 13 everlastingly, unremittingly
Latin: 11 in perpetuum

forewarn 4 bode 5 alert 6 advise, notify, signal, tip off 7 caution, portend, presage, prewarn 8 cry havoc

foreword 7 preface, prelude 8 preamble, prologue 12 introduction

for example
Latin: 2 eg 13 exempli gratia

forfeit 4 fine, miss 5 waive, waste, yield 6 waiver 7 damages, default, let slip, penalty 8 squander 9 surrender 10 assessment

forge 4 copy, form, make 5 clone, shape 6 devise, hearth, smithy 7 falsify, fashion, furnace, imitate, produce, turn out 8 contrive, simulate 9 fabricate, ironworks 11 counterfeit, manufacture

forgery 4 copy, fake, hoax, sham 5 clone, fraud 7 cloning 9 deception, imitation 11 counterfeit, fraudulence 13 falsification 14 counterfeiting

forget 6 slight 7 neglect 8 overlook, pass over 9 disregard

forgetful 6 remiss 7 out of it 8 amnesiac, careless, heedless, mindless 9 negligent, oblivious, unmindful 10 neglectful 11 inattentive

forget-me-not 8 Myosotis
varieties: 5 white 6 alpine, garden 7 Chinese 8 creeping

forgive 5 clear 6 acquit, excuse, pardon 7 absolve, condone, release, set free 8 overlook, reprieve 9 discharge, exculpate, exonerate

forgiveness 6 pardon 7 amnesty 9 remission 10 absolution

forgiving 6 benign, kindly 8 excusing 9 benignant, pardoning 11 kindhearted

forgo 4 skip 5 waive, yield 6 eschew, give up 8 abnegate, renounce 9 sacrifice, surrender 10 relinquish

fork 4 bend, stab 5 angle, elbow, split 6 branch, crotch, divide, impale, pierce, ramify, skewer 7 diverge, trident 8 division 9 bifurcate, pitchfork 10 divergence, separation 11 bifurcation 12 intersection

forked 5 cleft, tined 6 horned, zigzag 7 angular, divided, pronged 8

branched 9 ambiguous, deceitful, equivocal 10 bifurcated

fork out 5 spend 6 expend 8 disburse, dispense

for lack of something better
French: 12 faute de mieux

forlorn 4 lone 6 abject, bereft, dismal, dreary, lonely 7 unhappy 8 bereaved, dejected, deserted, desolate, forsaken, helpless, hopeless, lonesome, pathetic, pitiable, solitary, wretched 9 abandoned, depressed, desperate, destitute, forgotten, miserable, woebegone 10 despairing, despondent, dispirited, friendless 11 comfortless 12 disconsolate, inconsolable 13 brokenhearted

form 3 cut, hew, way 4 body, cast, kind, make, mode, mold, plan, rite, rule, sort, trim, type 5 being, brand, build, carve, class, forge, found, frame, genre, genus, guise, habit, image, model, order, phase, set up, shape, stamp, style, usage 6 aspect, chisel, create, custom, design, devise, fettle, figure, manner, matrix, person, ritual, sculpt, system 7 acquire, anatomy, compose, conduct, contour, decorum, develop, fashion, fitness, harmony, liturgy, manners, outline, pattern, produce, species, variety 8 ceremony, comprise, contract, likeness, physique, practice, presence, rough-hew, symmetry 9 character, construct, establish, etiquette, fabricate, framework, propriety, sculpture, semblance, structure 10 appearance, constitute, deportment, figuration, proceeding, proportion, regularity 11 arrangement, description, incarnation, manufacture, orderliness, shapeliness 12 denomination 13 configuration, manifestation 15 conventionality

formal 4 cool, prim 5 aloof, fancy, fixed, grand, legal, rigid, smart, stiff 6 dressy, lawful, proper, solemn, strict 7 distant, outward, pompous, prudish, regular, settled, stilted, stylish 8 decorous, definite, explicit, external, official, positive, reserved, starched 9 customary 10 ceremonial, inflexible, prescribed 11 ceremonious, highfalutin, perfunctory, punctilious, ritualistic, standoffish, straitlaced 12 conventional 13 authoritative 14 uncompromising

formal discussion 6 debate, parley 8 dialogue 10 conference

formality 4 rite 6 custom, motion, ritual 7 decorum, reserve 8 ceremony, coolness 9 etiquette, propriety, punctilio 10 ceremonial, convention 15 conventionality

Forman, Milos
director of: 7 Amadeus (Oscar), Ragtime 12 Man on the Moon 21 The People vs Larry Flynt 25 One Flew Over the Cuckoo's Nest (Oscar)

formation 3 set 6 makeup 7 genesis 8 building, creation 9 structure 10 generation, production 11 arrangement, composition, development, fabrication, manufacture 12 organization 13 configuration, constellation, establishment

formative 7 plastic, shaping 9 sensitive 10 accessible 11 susceptible 13 determinative 14 impressionable

former 2 ex 4 gone, past 5 olden, prior 6 bygone, gone by, lapsed, of yore, whilom 7 ancient, earlier, elapsed, old-time, quondam 8 anterior, previous 9 aforesaid, erstwhile, preceding 10 antecedent, first-named 14 aforementioned
French: 8 ci-devant

formerly 4 once 5 of old 6 ere now, lately, of yore, whilom 7 long ago 8 hitherto 9 anciently 10 originally, previously

former student 6 alumna 7 alumnus, dropout 8 graduate

formidable 6 taxing 7 awesome, fearful, mammoth, onerous 8 alarming, dreadful, imposing, menacing, terrific 9 dangerous, demanding, difficult 10 forbidding, impressive, portentous, terrifying 11 threatening 12 overpowering, overwhelming

formless 5 vague 9 amorphous, shapeless

Formosa see 6 Taiwan

formula 4 cant, plan, rule 5 chant 6 cliche, recipe, saying, slogan 7 precept 9 blueprint, guideline, platitude, principle, rigmarole 10 pleasantry 11 incantation 12 prescription

formulate 5 draft, frame, state 6 define, devise, invent 7 compose, itemize, specify 11 systematize 13 particularize

Fornax
origin: 5 Roman
goddess of: 6 baking

fornication 8 adultery

for one's country
Latin: 9 pro patria

Forrest, Nathan Bedford
served in: 8 Civil War
side: 11 Confederate
known for: 12 cavalry raids

Forrest Gump
director: 14 Robert Zemeckis
cast: 8 Tom Hanks (Forrest Gump) 10 Gary Sinise (Dan Taylor), Sally Field (Mrs. Gump) 11 Robin Wright (Jenny Curran) 17 Mykelti Williamson (Bubba Blue)

forsake 4 deny, drop, flee, quit 5 leave, spurn, waive, yield 6 abjure, depart, desert, give up, reject, resign, vacate 7 abandon, cast off, disavow, discard, lay down 8 abdicate, disclaim, go back on, jettison, part with, renounce **9** repudiate, surrender **10** relinquish

forsaken 4 bare **5** empty **8** deserted, desolate, rejected **9** abandoned, discarded, neglected **11** uninhabited

Forsete *see* **7** Forseti

Forseti
also: 7 Forsete
origin: 12 Scandinavian
god of: 7 justice
father: 5 Baldr **6** Balder, Baldur
mother: 5 Nanna
dwelling place: 7 Glitnir

Forster, E M (Edward Morgan)
author of: 7 Maurice **10** Howards End **14** A Room with a View **15** A Passage to India **17** The Longest Journey **22** Where Angels Fear to Tread
member of: 15 Bloomsbury Group

forswear 4 deny **5** spurn **6** abjure, disown, eschew, give up, recant, reject, revoke **7** disavow, gainsay, retract **8** abdicate, disclaim, renounce, take back **9** disaffirm, repudiate **10** contravene

Forsyte Saga, The
author: 14 John Galsworthy
trilogy including: 9 To Let **10** In Chancery **16** The Man of Property
character: 3 Jon **4** June **5** Fleur **6** Dartie **7** Annette **8** Winifred **9** Old Jolyon **11** Young Jolyon **12** Irene Forsyte **13** Soames Forsyte **14** Philip Bosinney

Forsythe, John
real name: 17 John Lincoln Freund
born: 12 Penn's Grove NJ
roles: 5 Topaz **7** Dynasty, Madame X **11** In Cold Blood **14** Bachelor Father, Charlie's Angels **15** Blake Carrington **16** And Justice for All **19** The Trouble with Harry **23** Teahouse of the August Moon

fort 4 base, camp **6** castle **7** bastion, bulwark, citadel, station **8** fastness, garrison **10** stronghold

forte 4 bent **5** knack, skill **6** talent **8** strength **9** specialty **11** proficiency
music: 4 loud
abbreviation: 1 f

forth 5 ahead **6** onward **7** outward

forthcoming 5 handy, on tap **6** at hand **7** helpful **8** imminent **9** available, impending **10** accessible, obtainable, openhanded **11** approaching, cooperative, prospective

for the greater glory of God
Latin: 19 ad majorem Dei gloriam

for the public good
Latin: 14 pro bono publico

for the time being
Latin: 10 pro tempore

For the Time Being
author: 7 W H Auden

for this purpose only
Latin: 5 ad hoc

forthright 4 open **5** blunt, frank **6** candid, direct, openly **7** bluntly, frankly, up-front **8** candidly, directly, straight **9** outspoken **10** truthfully **11** outspokenly, plain-spoken **15** straightforward **17** straightforwardly

forthrightness 6 candor **7** honesty **8** openness **9** frankness, sincerity **19** straightforwardness

forthwith 4 ASAP, stat **6** at once, pronto **7** quickly **8** directly, in a jiffy, promptly, right off **9** instantly **11** immediately **12** straightaway

fortification 5 tower **7** bastion, bulwark, citadel, rampart **8** fortress, garrison **9** earthwork **10** breastwork, stronghold

fortify 4 lace **5** boost, brace, cheer **6** buoy up, enrich, harden, secure, shield, urge on **7** build up, bulwark, hearten, protect, shore up, stiffen, support, sustain **8** buttress, embolden, garrison, reassure **9** encourage, reinforce, stimulate **10** invigorate, strengthen

fortissimo
music: 8 very loud
abbreviation: 2 ff

fortitude 4 dash, grit, guts, sand **5** nerve, pluck, spunk, valor **6** daring, mettle, spirit **7** bravery, courage, heroism, prowess **8** backbone, boldness, firmness, tenacity **9** endurance, hardihood **10** resolution **11** intrepidity **12** fearlessness, resoluteness **13** dauntlessness, determination

Fort-Lamy
former name of: 8 N'Djamena
capital of: 4 Chad

fortress 7 bastion, bulwark, citadel, rampart **8** buttress acropolis **10** stronghold

fortuitous 5 happy, lucky, stray **6** casual, chance, random **9** haphazard, hit-or-miss **10** accidental, incidental, undesigned, unexpected, unintended, unpurposed **11** inadvertent **12** adventitious **13** serendipitous, unintentional **14** unpremeditated

fortuity 6 chance **8** accident **12** happenstance

Fortuna
origin: 5 Roman
goddess of: 7 fortune
corresponds to: 5 Tyche

fortunate 4 fair, rich, rosy **5** happy, lucky, palmy **6** benign, bright, timely **7** blessed, booming, favored, halcyon, well-off **8** well-to-do **9** favorable, opportune, promising **10** auspicious, convenient, felicitous, profitable, propitious, prosperous, successful **11** encouraging, flourishing **12** advantageous, providential

Fortunate Isles *see* **13** Canary Islands

Fortunato
character in: 20 The Cask of Amontillado
author: 3 Poe

fortune, fortunes 3 lot **4** doom, fate, luck, mint, pile, star **5** karma, means **6** chance, estate, income, kismet, riches, wealth **7** bonanza, capital, destiny, godsend, portion, revenue **8** accident, fatality, gold mine, good luck, lady luck, opulence, property, treasure, windfall **9** affluence, haphazard, substance **10** prosperity, providence **11** dame fortune **12** circumstance **13** circumstances
goddess of: 5 Tyche **7** Fortuna

Fortunes of Nigel, The
author: 14 Sir Walter Scott

fortuneteller 4 seer **5** augur, Gypsy, sibyl **6** medium, oracle **7** palmist, prophet **8** magician **10** soothsayer **11** chiromancer, clairvoyant **12** crystal gazer

for two
French: 5 a deux

Forty Days of Musa Dagh, The
author: 11 Franz Werfel

42nd Parallel, The
author: 13 John Dos Passos

Forty-Second Street
director: 10 Lloyd Bacon
cast: 9 Guy Kibbee, Una Merkel **10** Dick Powell, Ruby Keeler **11** Bebe Daniels, George Brent **12** Ginger Rogers, Warner Baxter
choreographer: 13 Busby Berkeley
song: 15 Young and Healthy **17** Forty-Second Street **19** Shuffle Off to Buffalo **28** You're Getting to Be a Habit with Me

Forty Thieves, The
story in: 13 Arabian Nights
character: 7 Ali Baba
code word: 10 Open Sesame

forty winks 3 nap **4** doze **6** catnap, snooze

forum 6 medium, outlet **7** rostrum, seminar **8** platform **9** symposium **10** colloquium

forward, forwards 3 out **4** back, bold **5** ahead, brash, fresh, relay, sassy **6** assist, brazen, cheeky, hasten, onward, pass on, send on, spread **7** advance, frontal, further, go-ahead, promote, quicken, re-route **8** anterior, champion, immodest, impudent, insolent, up-to-date **9** advancing, barefaced, intrusive, offensive, presuming, readdress, shameless **10** accelerate, unmannerly **11** impertinent, progressive **12** enterprising, presumptuous **13** overconfident
French: 7 en avant

forwardness 4 gall **5** brass, cheek **8** audacity, boldness **10** brazenness, effrontery **11** presumption **13** bumptiousness, obtrusiveness

for what use
Latin: **7** cui bono

For Whom the Bell Tolls
author: **15** Ernest Hemingway
director: **7** Sam Wood
character: **5** Maria, Pablo, Pilar **6** Andres, Rafael **7** Anselmo, El Sordo **8** Augustin, Fernando **12** Robert Jordan
cast: **10** Gary Cooper **12** Akim Tamiroff **13** Ingrid Bergman, Joseph Calleia, Katina Paxinou **15** Arturo de Cordova
score: **11** Victor Young
Oscar for: **17** supporting actress (Paxinou)

for whose benefit
Latin: **7** cui bono

For Your Eyes Only
author: **10** Ian Fleming

Forza del Destino, La *see* **17** Force of Destiny, The

Fosse, Bob
director of: **5** Lenny **7** Cabaret (Oscar) **11** All That Jazz

fossil 4 fogy, rock **5** fogey, oldie, relic, stone **7** imprint, antique **9** remainder **13** petrification

foster 3 aid **4** back, feed, rear, tend **5** favor, nurse, raise **6** foment, harbor, mother, rear up, take in **7** advance, bring up, care for, cherish, forward, further, nourish, nurture, promote, protect, support, sustain **8** advocate, befriend, hold dear, sanction, side with, treasure **9** encourage, patronize, stimulate **11** accommodate, countenance

Foster, Alicia Christian
real name of: **11** Jodie Foster

Foster, Harold
creator/artist of: **6** Tarzan **13** Prince Valiant

Foster, Jodie
real name: **21** Alicia Christian Foster
born: **7** Bronx NY
roles: **7** Contact **8** Maverick **9** Tom Sawyer **10** Taxi Driver, The Accused (Oscar) **11** Bugsy Malone **13** Little Man Tate **20** The Silence of the Lambs (Oscar) **28** The Dangerous Lives of Altar Boys

Foster, Stephen Collins
born: **15** Lawrenceville PA
composer of: **11** Swanee River **13** Camptown Races **16** Beautiful Dreamer **17** My Old Kentucky Home, The Old Folks at Home **27** Jeanie with the Light Brown Hair

Foucault, Jean Bernard Leon
field: **7** physics
nationality: **6** French
proved: **19** Earth spins on its axis
measured: **15** velocity of light
named for him: **8** pendulum **16** Foucault currents

Foucault's Pendulum
author: **10** Umberto Eco

foul 3 wet **4** base, clog, evil, lewd, soil, vile **5** dirty, foggy, grimy, gross, gusty, misty, muddy, murky, nasty, rainy, sully, taint **6** choked, cloudy, coarse, defile, filthy, grubby, odious, putrid, risque, scurvy, smelly, smutty, soiled, sordid, stormy, tangle, turbid, vulgar, wicked **7** abusive, begrime, drizzly, ensnare, hateful, heinous, impeded, obscene, pollute, profane, smeared, squalid, squally, stained, sullied, tangled, unclean **8** begrimed, besmirch, blustery, ensnared, entangle, immodest, indecent, infamous, stinking, unseemly **9** atrocious, besmeared, entangled, insulting, loathsome, monstrous, nefarious, notorious, obnoxious, repulsive, revolting **10** abominable, bedraggled, detestable, disgusting, encumbered, flagitious, indelicate, malodorous, putrescent, scurrilous, villainous **11** blasphemous, disgraceful **12** contemptible

foul play 5 crime **6** murder **8** violence **9** treachery

foul-smelling 4 rank **5** acrid, fetid, musty **6** putrid, smelly **7** noisome, reeking **8** stinking **10** malodorous

foul up 3 mar **4** goof, muff, ruin **5** botch, mix up, spoil **6** bungle, mess up, muddle **7** blunder, butcher, confuse, louse up, screw up **9** mismanage

found 4 base, rear, rest **5** build, erect, raise, set up, start **6** create, ground, locate, settle **7** develop, sustain **8** colonize, organize **9** construct, establish, institute, originate

foundation 3 bed **4** base, foot, fund, rock, root **5** basis, cause **6** bottom, cellar, ground, motive, origin, reason, source **7** charity, premise, purpose, support **8** basement, creation, pedestal **9** endowment, rationale **10** assumption, groundwork, settlement **11** benefaction, institution **12** commencement, installation, philanthropy, substructure, underpinning **13** establishment, justification **14** infrastructure, understructure

foundational 3 key **4** base, core **5** basic, prime **7** primary **9** essential **10** elementary

foundation garment 6 corset, girdle **8** corselet

founder 4 fall, limp, reel, sink, trip **5** abort, drown, lurch, swamp **6** author, father, go down, go lame, hobble, perish, plunge, sprawl, topple, tumble **7** break up, builder, capsize, creator, go under, planner, stagger, stumble, succumb **8** collapse, miscarry **9** architect, organizer, shipwreck **10** originator, strategist **12** disintegrate

foundered 4 sank **6** failed **7** beached,

swamped **8** capsized, went down **9** collapsed

founding 5 birth **8** creation, settling **9** beginning **11** institution, origination **12** introduction, organization **13** establishment

found on 6 base on **7** model on **8** stem from **10** derive from **11** establish on

fountain 3 jet **4** flow, gush, well **5** birth, cause, spout **6** cradle, feeder, origin, reason, source, spring **7** genesis **8** purveyor, supplier **9** beginning, reservoir, upswelling **10** derivation, wellspring

fountainhead 4 font **6** origin, source, spring **9** beginning **10** wellspring

Fountainhead, The
author: **7** Ayn Rand
character: **11** Howard Roark
profession: **9** architect

fourgon 3 van **7** tumbril

Four Horsemen of the Apocalypse, The
author: **19** Vicente Blasco Ibanez
based on: **10** Revelation
horsemen: **3** War **5** Death **6** Famine **10** Pestilence

400 Blows, The
director: **16** Francois Truffaut
cast: **10** Albert Remy **13** Claire Maurier **14** Patrick Auffray **15** Jean-Pierre Leaud

Four Quartets
author: **7** T S Eliot

fourth dimension 4 time

fourth estate 5 press **10** journalism

fowl 3 hen **4** cock, duck, game **5** banty, capon, chick, goose, quail **6** bantam, grouse, pigeon, turkey **7** chicken, cornish, leghorn, poultry **8** duckling

Fowles, John
author of: **7** A Maggot **8** Mantissa, The Magus **9** Wormholes **10** The Aristos **12** Daniel Martin, The Collector **13** The Ebony Tower **25** The French Lieutenant's Woman

fox 9 scavenger
young: **3** kit, pup
group of: **5** leash, skulk

Fox (Mesquakie, Red Earth People)
language family: **9** Algonkian **10** Algonquian
location: **4** Iowa **9** Wisconsin
allied with: **4** Sauk **8** Kickapoo

Fox, Fontaine
creator/artist of: **16** Toonerville Folks **18** Toonerville Trolley

foxglove 9 digitalis
varieties: **5** false, rusty **6** common, yellow **7** Grecian, Mexican **10** downy false **12** willow-leaved

foxiness 5 guile **7** cunning, slyness **8**

artifice, trickery, wiliness **10** crafti-ness, shrewdness

fox-trot 5 dance **13** ballroom dance

Foxx, Jimmy (James Emory)
  nickname: 7 Double X
  sport: 8 baseball
  team: 12 Boston Red Sox **21** Philadel-phia Athletics

Foxx, Redd
  real name: 16 John Elroy Sanford
  born: 9 St Louis MO
  roles: 13 Sanford and Son **19** Cotton Comes to Harlem

foxy 3 sly **4** wily **5** canny, sharp, slick **6** artful, astute, clever, crafty, shifty, shrewd, sneaky, tricky **7** cunning, de-vious, oblique **8** guileful, scheming, stealthy **9** conniving, deceitful, decep-tive, designing, insidious, underhand **10** intriguing

foyer 4 hall **5** lobby **6** loggia **8** ante-room **9** vestibule **11** antechamber

fracas 3 row **4** fray, to-do **5** brawl, broil, clash, fight, melee, scrap **6** bat-tle, ruckus, rumpus, strife, uproar **7** scuffle **9** imbroglio **10** donnybrook, free-for-all **11** altercation, embroilment

fraction 3 bit, few **4** chip **5** crumb, piece, ratio, scrap **6** morsel, trifle **7** cutting, portion, section, segment, shaving **8** fragment, particle, quotient **10** proportion **11** subdivision

fractious 5 cross, huffy **6** shirty, touchy, unruly **7** fretful, grouchy, pee-vish, pettish, waspish, wayward, will-ful **8** contrary, perverse, petulant, shrewish, snappish **9** irascible, irrita-ble, querulous **10** rebellious, refrac-tory **11** quarrelsome **12** disputatious, recalcitrant, unmanageable

fracture 4 rend, rift **5** break, crack, fault, sever, split **6** breach, cleave **7** disrupt, rupture, shatter **8** cleavage, division **9** severance **10** separation

Fra Diavolo, ou L'Hotellerie de Terracine
  also: 31 Brother Devil or The Inn at Terracina
  comic opera by: 5 Auber
  character: 7 Lorenzo, Zerlina **11** Lady Allcash, Lord Allcash **17** Marquis di San Marco

fragile 4 soft, weak **5** crisp, frail **6** dainty, feeble, flimsy, infirm, sleazy, slight, tender **7** brittle, crumbly, fria-ble, rickety, shivery **8** decrepit, deli-cate **9** breakable, ephemeral, frangi-ble, splintery **10** evanescent, tumbledown **11** dilapidated **13** unsub-stantial

fragility 7 frailty **8** delicacy, weakness **9** frailness **10** feebleness **11** brittle-ness **12** frangibility

fragment 3 bit **4** chip, snip **5** crumb, cut up, piece, scrap, shard, shred, trace **6** chop up, divide, morsel **7** break up, crumble, portion, remnant,

section, segment, shatter, vestige **8** disunite, fraction, separate, splinter, survival **12** disintegrate

fragmentary 6 broken, choppy **7** scrappy **8** detached **9** piecemeal, scat-tered, segmented **10** disjointed, frac-tional, incomplete, unfinished **12** dis-connected

Fragonard, Jean-Honore
  born: 6 France, Grasse
  artwork: 8 The Swing **10** Stolen Kiss, The Bathers, The Warrior **12** Le Bil-let Doux **14** Progress of Love **16** La Chemise Enlevee **18** Storming the Citadel **40** Coresus Sacrificing Him-self to Save Callirhoe

fragrance 4 aura, balm **5** aroma, scent **7** bouquet, incense, perfume **9** redo-lence, sweetness

fragrant 5 balmy, spicy **7** odorous **8** aromatic, perfumed, redolent **11** odor-iferous

Fragrant Harbor see **8** Hong Kong

frail 4 puny, weak **6** feeble, flimsy, in-firm, sleazy, slight, weakly **7** brittle, crumbly, fragile, rickety, shivery **8** de-crepit, delicate, fallible **9** breakable, frangible, splintery **10** perishable, vul-nerable **11** dilapidated **13** unsubstan-tial

frailness 8 delicacy, weakness **9** fragil-ity **11** unsoundness

frailty 3 sin **4** flaw, vice **5** fault **6** de-fect, foible **7** blemish, failing **11** falli-bility **12** imperfection **14** susceptibility

frame 3 rim, set **4** body, case, cast, form, make, mold, mood, plan **5** build, draft, hatch, humor, set up, shape, state **6** border, casing, design, devise, edging, figure, indite, invent, map out, nature, scheme, sketch, sys-tem, temper **7** anatomy, backing, chassis, concoct, contour, housing, outline, setting **8** attitude, conceive, contrive, mounting, organize, phy-sique, skeleton **9** formulate, structure **11** disposition, scaffolding, systema-tize, temperament **12** constitution, construction

frame of mind 4 mood **7** climate **8** attitude **10** atmosphere **11** disposition

framer 6 author, shaper **7** creator, planner **10** formulator

framework 5 shell, truss **7** carcass **8** skeleton, template **9** structure **10** foundation **11** scaffolding **14** infra-structure

Framley Parsonage
  author: 15 Anthony Trollope

France
  other name: 4 Gaul
  anthem: 14 La Marseillaise
  capital/largest city: 5 Paris
  others: 4 Nice, St. Lo **5** Brest, Lille, Lyons, Rouen, Vichy **6** Amiens, Cal-ais, Cannes, Carnac, Cognac, Dieppe, Grasse, Nantes, Prades, Rheims **7**

Antibes, Avignon, Bayonne, Dunkirk, Le Havre, Les Baux **8** Bordeaux, Boulogne, Chartres, Grenoble, Poi-tiers, Toulouse **9** Cherbourg, Roque-fort **10** La Rochelle, Marseilles, Saint-Denis, Strasbourg **12** Saint-Nazaire **13** Aix-en-Provence, Fon-tainebleau
  school: 8 Grenoble, Saint Cyr, Sor-bonne **10** Montpelier
  division: 5 Anjou, Bearn, Berry, Maine, Savoy **6** Alsace, Artois, Mar-che, Poitou **7** Gascony, Guienne, Pic-ardy **8** Auvergne, Bordeaux, Brittany, Burgundy, Dauphine, Flanders, Lor-raine, Lyonnais, Normandy, Pro-vence, Touraine **9** Aquitaine, Cham-pagne, Languedoc **11** Ile de France **12** Bourbonnaise, Franche-Comte
  measure: 3 pot, sac **4** aune, mine, muid, pied, velt **5** arpen, carat, ligne, minot, pinte, point, pouce, velte **6** arpent, hemine, league, quarte, setier
  monetary unit: 5 franc **7** centime
  weight: 3 sol **4** gros, kilo, once **5** carat, livre, pound, tonne **6** gramme **7** tonneau **8** esterlin **9** esterling
  island: 2 Re **3** Yeu **4** Cite **5** Groix, Hyere **6** Comoro, Oleron, Tahiti, Ushant **7** Corsica, Leeward, Reunion **8** Windward **10** Guadeloupe, Marti-nique **12** New Caledonia
  lake: 6 Annecy, Cazaux, Geneva
  mountain: 4 Jura **5** Pelat **6** Vosges **8** Ardennes, Pyrenees **10** French Alps **11** Pic Montcalm
  highest point: 5 Blanc **9** Mont Blanc
  river: 3 Lys **4** Oise, Yser **5** Aisne, Eiser, Isere, Loire, Meuse, Rhine, Rhone, Saone, Seine **7** Garonne, Gi-ronde
  sea: 5 North **8** Atlantic **13** Mediterra-nean
  physical feature:
    bay: 6 Biscay **7** Arachon
    beach: 4 Utah **5** Omaha
    cape: 5 Hague, Talma
    channel: 7 English **8** La Manche
    gulf: 4 Lion
  people: 6 Franks
    artist: 5 Corot, David, Degas, Ma-net, Monet **6** Braque, Ingres, Mil-let, Renoir, Seurat **7** Cezanne, Daumier, Gauguin, Matisse, Utrillo **8** Pissarro **9** Delacroix, Fragonard, Gericault
    author: 4 Gide, Hugo, Zola **5** Ca-mus, Dumas **6** France, Proust, Ra-cine, Sartre, Villon **7** Moliere **8** Rabelais, Rousseau, Voltaire **9** Corneille, Descartes, Giraudoux, Montaigne **10** Baudelaire
    composer: 5 Bizet, Ravel, Satie **6** Franck, Gounod **7** Berlioz, De-bussy, Poulenc
    king: 5 Henri, Louis **6** Clovis, Philip **7** Charles **9** Hugh Capet **11** Charlemagne **13** Louis Philippe **14**

Henry of Navarre

leader: 6 Chirac, Danton, Petain **7** Colbert, Mazarin **8** de Gaulle, D'Estaing, Pompidou **9** Joan of Arc, Richelieu **10** Mitterrand **11** Robespierre **17** Napoleon Bonaparte

queen: 7 Eugenie **9** Josephine **13** Marie de Medici **15** Marie Antoinette

language: 6 French

expressions: 6 deja vu **7** apropos, detente, en masse, faux pas, vis-a-vis **8** de riguer **9** bete noire, c'est la vie, coup d'etat **10** bon appetit **11** coup de grace, joie de vivre, raison d'etre, savoir faire, tour de force **12** carte blanche, cause celebre, je ne sais quoi, nouveau riche, fait accompli **14** creme de la creme, noblesse oblige

religion: 5 Islam **7** Judaism **8** Huguenot **10** Protestant **13** Roman Catholic

place:
cathedral: 6 Rheims **8** Chartres **9** Madeleine, Notre Dame **10** Sacre-Coeur **14** Sainte-Chapelle **15** Mont-Saint-Michel
chapel: 8 Ronchamp
gardens: 9 Tuileries
hall of mirrors: 16 Galerie des Glaces
museum: 6 Louvre **14** Pompidou Center
palace: 6 Elysee **10** Luxembourg, Versailles **12** Grand Trianon, Petit Trianon, **13** Fontainebleau
prison: 8 Bastille
racetrack: 6 Le Mans **7** Auteuil **10** Longchamps
resort: 3 Pau **5** Vichy **6** Cannes, Menton **7** Antibes, Mentone, Riviera **8** Biarritz, Chamonix, Grenoble **9** Cote d'Azur **11** Aix-les-Bains
section of Paris: 8 Left Bank **9** Right Bank **10** Montmartre, Rive Droite, Rive Gauche **12** Latin Quarter
street: 13 Champs-Elysees **17** Place de la Concorde
woods: 14 Bois de Boulogne **15** Bois de Vincennes

possession: 12 French Guiana
island: 6 Futuna, Hoorne, Wallis **7** Reunion **8** Miquelon **10** Guadeloupe, Martinique **11** Saint Pierre **12** New Caledonia **15** French Polynesia

feature:
airport: 4 Orly **9** Le Bourget **15** Charles de Gaulle
bicycle race: 12 Tour de France
dance: 5 gavot **6** branle, canary, cancan **7** boutade, gavotte
fortification: 11 Maginot Line
holiday: 11 Bastille Day
monument: 13 Arc de Triomphe **14** Tomb of Napoleon

national theater: 16 Comedie Francaise
sightseeing boat: 12 bateau mouche
tower: 6 Eiffel

food:
cheese: 4 bleu, Brie **6** Bonbel **7** Boursin **8** Muenster **9** Camembert, Marcillat, Port-Salut, Roquefort **11** Coulommiers
dessert: 6 mousse
dish: 4 pate **5** crepe **6** canape, quiche **7** souffle **8** escargot, piperade, pot au feu **9** cassoulet, tournedos **14** pate de foie gras
drink: 6 cognac **8** bordeaux, burgundy **9** champagne
french fries: 12 pommes frites
pastry: 7 brioche **8** napoleon **9** croissant
soup: 8 a l'oignon **13** bouillabaisse
steak: 7 bifteck

France, Anatole
real name: 30 Jacques Anatole Francois Thibault
author of: 5 Thais **12** Golden Verses **13** My Friend's Book, Penguin Island **17** The Gods Are Athirst **20** The Revolt of the Angels **25** Le Crime de Sylvestre Bonnard **27** At the Sign of the Reine Pedauque

franchise 5 grant, right **6** ballot **7** charter, freedom, license **8** immunity, suffrage **9** privilege **10** permission **11** prerogative **13** authorization

Franciosa, Anthony
real name: 14 Anthony Papales
born: 9 New York NY
wife: 14 Shelley Winters
roles: 12 The Naked Maja **13** A Hatful of Rain, Long Hot Summer, Name of the Game, Wild Is the Wind **15** Assault on a Queen

Francis, Dick
author of: 4 Bolt, Risk **5** Nerve, Proof **6** Banker, Reflex **7** Break In, Enquiry, Forfeit, Rat Race **8** Dead Cert, For Kicks, Slayride, Trial Run, Twice Shy, Whip Hand **9** Bonecrack, The Danger, Knockdown, Shattered **10** Blood Sport, High Stakes, In the Frame, Second Wind **11** Come to Grief, Smokescreen **12** Flying Finish

Franck, Cesar
born: 5 Liege **7** Belgium
composer of: 4 Ruth **5** Hulda **6** Psyche **7** Rebecca **8** Ghiselle **9** Les Djinns **10** Les Eolides, Redemption **13** La Tour de Babel, Les Beatitudes, The Beatitudes **16** Le Chasseur Maudit **17** The Accursed Hunter

Franco, Francisco
dictator of: 5 Spain
title: 10 el caudillo
party: 7 falange, fascist
followers: 11 fifth column

Franglais 13 French-English **14** French-American

frank 4 bold, free, open **5** clear, plain, round **6** candid, direct, honest, patent **7** artless, evident, genuine, natural, sincere, up-front **8** apparent, distinct, explicit, manifest **9** downright, ingenuous, outspoken **10** aboveboard, forthright, unreserved **11** plainspoken, transparent, unambiguous, undisguised, unequivocal **12** unmistakable **15** straightforward

Frank, Anne
author of: 19 The Diary of Anne Frank

Frankenstein
author: 17 Mary Godwin Shelley
character: 7 Clerval, Justine, William **9** Elizabeth **10** The Monster **12** Robert Walton **18** Victor Frankenstein

Franklin, Benjamin
author of: 20 Poor Richard's Almanack
inventor of: 12 lightning rod **13** bifocal lenses, Franklin stove

frankness 6 candor **7** honesty **8** openness **9** bluntness, sincerity **10** directness **11** artlessness **13** guilelessness **14** forthrightness **19** straightforwardness

frantic 3 mad **4** wild **5** crazy, rabid **6** hectic, insane, raging, raving **7** berserk, excited, furious, nervous, violent **8** agitated, deranged, frenetic, frenzied **9** delirious **10** distracted, distraught, infuriated **11** impassioned, overwrought **12** ungovernable

fraternal 6 hearty, loving, social **7** devoted, kindred, related **8** amicable, friendly **9** brotherly **11** warmhearted **12** affectionate **14** consanguineous

fraternity 4 clan, club **5** union **6** circle, clique, league **7** company, coterie, kinship, society **8** alliance **9** coalition **10** federation **11** association, brotherhood, confederacy, propinquity **13** brotherliness, consanguinity, interrelation

fraternize 3 mix **5** unite **6** concur, hobnob, mingle **7** combine, consort **8** coalesce **9** associate, cooperate, harmonize, pal around, socialize **10** sympathize **11** confederate

Fratres Arvales see **5** Arval

frau 4 lady, wife **12** married woman

fraud 4 fake, hoax, hype, ruse, sham **5** cheat, craft, guile, knave, quack, rogue, trick **6** deceit, humbug, rascal **7** swindle **8** artifice, cheating, cozenage, impostor, swindler, trickery **9** charlatan, chicanery, con artist, deception, duplicity, imposture, pretender, stratagem, swindling, treachery **10** dishonesty, mountebank, subterfuge **11** counterfeit, four-flusher, machination **13** dissimulation

fraudulence 6 deceit **8** trickery **9** deception **13** deceitfulness, deceptiveness **17** misrepresentation

fraudulent 4 sham, wily **5** bogus, false **6** crafty, tricky **7** crooked, cunning, knavish **8** cheating, guileful, spurious **9** deceitful, deceptive, dishonest **11** counterfeit, treacherous, underhanded **12** dishonorable, unprincipled

fraught 4 full **5** heavy, laden **6** filled, loaded **7** charged, replete, teeming **8** attended, pregnant **9** abounding **11** accompanied

fraulein 4 miss **9** young lady **14** unmarried woman

Fraunhofer, Joseph von
  field: 7 physics
  nationality: 6 German
  established: 12 spectroscopy

fray 3 rub **4** fret, fuss, riot, spat, tiff **5** brawl, chafe, fight, melee, ravel, set-to **6** battle, combat, fracas, rumble, rumpus, strain, tatter, tumult, tussle **7** contest, dispute, frazzle, quarrel, scuffle, warfare, wear out, wrangle **8** conflict, skirmish, squabble **9** bickering, commotion **10** contention, dissension, engagement **11** altercation, controversy **12** disagreement

Frazer, Sir James G
  author of: 14 The Golden Bough

freak 3 fad, odd **4** kink, turn, whim **5** craze, fancy, humor, queer, quirk, sport, twist **6** marvel, oddity, vagary, whimsy, wonder **7** anomaly, bizarre, caprice, erratic, monster, strange, unusual **8** crotchet, mutation, peculiar **9** curiosity, deviation **10** aberration **11** abnormality, monstrosity

freakish 3 odd **5** queer, weird **7** bizarre, strange, unusual **8** peculiar, singular, uncommon **9** eccentric, fantastic **10** outlandish **13** extraordinary

Frederick
  character in: 11 As You Like It
  author: 11 Shakespeare

Frederick I
  nickname: 10 Barbarossa
  position: 16 Holy Roman Emperor
  dynasty: 12 Hohenstaufen
  wife: 7 Beatrix
  battle: 7 Legnano

Frederick II
  position: 12 king of Sicily **13** king of Germany **16** Holy Roman Emperor
  battle: 8 Bouvines

Frederick the Great
  nickname: 8 Old Fritz
  position: 13 King of Prussia
  invaded: 7 Silesia
  war: 13 Seven Years' War **18** Austrian Succession

free 3 big, lax **4** able, bold, easy, idle, idly, open, save **5** clear, extra, let go, loose, rid of, spare **6** daring, devoid, exempt, giving, gratis, lavish, parole, ransom, redeem, unbond, uncage,

wanton **7** allowed, assured, forward, liberal, loosely, manumit, release, unchain, unleash **8** at no cost, careless, costless, devoid of, familiar, fearless, generous, handsome, immune to, informal, let loose, liberate, prodigal, released, unfasten **9** abandoned, audacious, available, boundless, bounteous, bountiful, confident, delivered, discharge, disengage, dissolute, expansive, extricate, footloose, lacking in, leisurely, liberated, permitted, unblocked, unbridled, unchained, unclogged, unimpeded, unmuzzled, unshackle **10** autonomous, bighearted, carelessly, chargeless, emancipate, gratuitous, licentious, manumitted, munificent, openhanded, unattached, unconfined, unfettered, unhampered, unoccupied, unreserved, unshackled **11** emancipated, enfranchise, independent, uncluttered, uncommitted, uninhibited, unrepressed **12** enfranchised, overfamiliar, uncontrolled, unencumbered, unobstructed, unrestrained **13** complimentary, unceremonious, unconstrained

free-and-easy 6 breezy, casual, jaunty **7** buoyant, relaxed **8** debonair, informal **12** lighthearted, presumptuous, unrestrained **13** unconstrained

freed 6 exempt, loosed, spared **7** cleared, excused **8** absolved, let loose, released, relieved **11** emancipated

freedom 4 play **5** range, scope, sweep, swing **6** candor, margin **7** abandon, license, release **8** autonomy, boldness, latitude, openness, rudeness **9** bluntness, frankness, impudence, indecorum **10** directness, disrespect, liberation **11** abandonment, forwardness, impropriety, inormality, manumission, naturalness, sovereignty, unrestraint **12** emancipation, impertinence, unconstraint **13** downrightness **14** unreservedness **15** enfranchisement

free-flowing 7 copious, gushing, profuse **8** effusive

free-for-all 3 row **4** fray **5** brawl, fight, melee, scrap **6** affray, fracas, ruckus, tussle **7** rhubarb, ruction, wrangle **9** brannigan **10** donnybrook

free from bias 7 neutral **9** impartial, unbigoted **12** unprejudiced **13** disinterested

free from moisture 3 dry **4** arid, sere **5** parch **6** dry out **7** parched **8** dried out, rainless **9** dehydrate **10** dehydrated, desertlike, desiccated

free hand 12 carte blanche, open sanction **13** full authority

free rein 12 carte blanche, open sanction **13** full authority

free-spoken 6 chatty **7** voluble **9** talkative **10** loquacious, unreserved **13** communicative

Free State
  nickname of: 8 Maryland

Freestone State
  nickname of: 11 Connecticut

Freetown
  capital of: 11 Sierra Leone

freeze 3 nip **4** bite, cool, halt, stop **5** chill, frost, sting **6** arrest, benumb, harden, pierce **7** ceiling, congeal, terrify **8** glaciate, solidify **11** anesthetize, refrigerate, restriction

freezing 3 icy **6** arctic, frigid **7** glacial

Frege, Gottlieb
  field: 11 mathematics
  nationality: 6 German
  founded: 13 symbolic logic

Freia *see* **5** Freya

freight 4 haul, lade, load, ship **5** cargo, carry, goods **6** burden, charge, convey, lading **7** baggage, cartage, luggage, portage **8** transmit, truckage **9** transport **10** conveyance **13** transshipment

Freischutz, Der
  also: 11 The Marksman
  opera by: 5 Weber
  character: 3 Max **6** Agathe, Caspar, Samiel

Freki
  origin: 12 Scandinavian
  form: 4 wolf
  owner: 4 Odin **5** Othin
  received: 4 food
  exception: 4 meat
  fellow wolf: 4 Geri

French, Daniel Chester
  born: 8 Exeter NH
  artwork: 7 (seated) Lincoln (at Lincoln Memorial) **21** The Minute Man of Concord

French-American
  French: 9 Franglais

French civil code 12 Code Napoleon

French Connection, The
  director: 15 William Friedkin
  cast: 11 Fernando Rey, Gene Hackman (Popeye Doyle), Roy Scheider
  Oscar for: 5 actor (Hackman) **7** editing, picture **8** director **10** screenplay
  sequel: 21 The French Connection II

French-English
  French: 9 Franglais

French Guinea *see* **6** Guinea

French Indonesia *see* **7** Vietnam

French is spoken here
  French: 18 ici on parle francais

French Lieutenant's Woman, The
  director: 10 Karel Reisz
  author: 10 John Fowles
  cast: 9 Leo McKern **11** Hilton McRae, Jeremy Irons, Meryl Streep
  script: 12 Harold Pinter

French national anthem 12 Marseillaise

French national theater 16 Comedie Francaise

French parliament
　formal sessions: **12** lit de justice

French Somaliland see **8** Djibouti

French Sudan, Soudan see **4** Mali

French Togoland see **4** Togo

frenzied 3 mad **4** wild **7** excited, frantic, furious **8** agitated, ecstatic **9** delirious

frenzy 3 fit **4** fury **5** craze, furor, mania, state **6** access **7** mad rush, madness, seizure, turmoil **8** delirium, hysteria, outburst **9** obsession, transport **11** distraction

Frenzy
　director: **15** Alfred Hitchcock
　cast: **8** Jon Finch **10** Anna Massey **11** Barry Foster **16** Barbara Leigh-Hunt

frequency 9 iteration **10** recurrence, regularity, repetition **11** persistence, reiteration

frequent 5 daily, haunt, usual **6** common, wonted **7** regular **8** constant, everyday, familiar, habitual, numerous, ordinary, resort to **9** continual, customary, incessant, perpetual, recurrent **10** accustomed **11** reiterative

frequently 5 often **7** usually **8** ofttimes **9** generally **10** constantly, habitually, ordinarily, repeatedly **11** continually, customarily, incessantly, perpetually, recurrently

frere 4 monk **5** friar **7** brother

Frescobaldi, Girolamo
　born: **5** Italy **7** Ferrara
　composer of: **13** Fiori Musicali **14** Musical Flowers

fresh 3 fit, hot, new **4** bold, cool, fair, keen, late, pert, pure, rare, rosy, rude **5** alert, brisk, chill, clear, green, nervy, novel, ready, ruddy, sassy, saucy, stiff, sweet **6** active, biting, brassy, brazen, bright, cheeky, lively, modern, recent, rested, snotty, unique, unused, unworn **7** bracing, cutting, forward, glowing, just out, nipping, strange, uncured, undried, unfaded, untried, unusual **8** assuming, blooming, brand-new, creative, flippant, gleaming, impudent, insolent, original, stinging, unabated, undimmed, unsalted, unsmoked, unwilted, up-to-date **9** energetic, inventive, obtrusive, refreshed, sparkling, undecayed, unpickled, unspoiled, unwearied, wholesome **10** meddlesome, new-fangled, refreshing, unfamiliar, unimpaired, unwithered **11** flourishing, invigorated, modernistic, smartalecky, untarnished **12** presumptuous, unaccustomed

freshen 4 wash **5** brace, calve, clean, groom, renew **6** air out, breeze, desalt, revive **7** cool off, sweeten **8** renovate, spruce up **9** deodorize

freshet 5 crest, flood **11** overflowing

Freshman, The

director: 9 Sam Taylor **12** Fred Newmeyer

cast: 11 Harold Lloyd **13** Jobyna Ralston **14** Brooks Benedict

Fresnel, Augustin Jean
　field: **7** physics
　nationality: **6** French
　worked in: **6** optics

fret 3 eat, rub, vex **4** fray, fume, gall, gnaw, mope, pine, pout, stew, sulk **5** brood, chafe, erode, sulks, worry **6** abrade, lament, ruffle, tatter **7** agonize, corrode, fidgets **8** disquiet, distress, irritate, vexation, wear away **9** annoyance, excoriate **10** irritation **11** displeasure, peevishness **12** discomposure

fretful 5 cross, huffy, sulky, tense **6** cranky, shirty, touchy **7** grouchy, nervous, peevish, pettish, waspish **8** contrary, petulant, snappish **9** crotchety, irritable, querulous **11** complaining **12** cantankerous

fretfulness 5 worry **6** unease **7** anxiety **10** crankiness **11** peevishness **12** irritability

Freud, Sigmund
　lived in: **6** Vienna
　collaborator: **6** Breuer
　disciple: **4** Jung **5** Adler
　daughter: **4** Anna
　method: **15** free association **19** dream interpretation
　coined: **2** id **8** superego **14** psychoanalysis
　author of: **13** Totem and Taboo **22** Interpretation of Dreams **37** Group Psychology and the Analysis of the Ego, Jokes and Their Relation to the Unconscious

Freund, John Lincoln
　real name of: **12** John Forsythe

Frey
　also: **5** Freyr
　origin: **12** Scandinavian
　god of: **5** peace **8** marriage **10** prosperity
　race: **5** Vanir
　father: **5** Niord, Njord
　home: **7** Alfheim

Freya
　also: **5** Freia
　origin: **8** Teutonic
　goddess of: **4** love **6** beauty **9** fecundity
　race: **5** Vanir
　leader of: **9** Valkyries
　father: **5** Niord, Njord

Fri see **5** Frigg

friable 7 crumbly **9** breakable, frangible

friar
　French: **5** frere

Friar Lawrence
　character in: **14** Romeo and Juliet
　author: **11** Shakespeare

Friar Tuck
　character in: **9** Robin Hood

friary 5 abbey **6** priory **8** cloister **9** hermitage, monastery

friction 6 strife **7** chafing, discord, grating, quarrel, rubbing **8** abrasion, bad blood, conflict, fretting **9** animosity, attrition, hostility **10** antagonism, contention, dissension, dissidence, opposition, resentment, resistance **12** disagreement **13** counteraction

Friday
　character in: **14** Robinson Crusoe
　author: **5** Defoe

Friday
　from: **5** Freya, Frigg
　heavenly body: **5** Venus
　French: **8** vendredi
　Italian: **7** venerdi
　Spanish: **7** viernes
　German: **7** freitag

Friedan, Betty
　author of: **14** The Second Stage **19** The Feminine Mystique
　co-founder of: **3** NOW **28** National Organization for Women

Friedkin, William
　director of: **11** The Exorcist **19** The French Connection (Oscar)

Friedman, Milton
　author of: **12** Free to Choose (with Rose Friedman) **20** Capitalism and Freedom

Friedrich, Caspar David
　born: **7** Germany **10** Greifswald
　artwork: **22** The Cross on the Mountains **26** Man and Woman Gazing at the Moon, The Ruined Monastery of Eldena, Two Men Contemplating the Moon

friend 3 pal **4** ally, beau, chum, date, mate **5** amigo, buddy, crony, lover **6** backer, cohort, escort, fellow, intime, minion, patron **7** brother, comrade, consort, partner **8** adherent, advocate, confrere, coworker, defender, favorite, follower, henchman, intimate, mistress, myrmidon, paramour, partisan, playmate, retainer, sidekick, soulmate **9** associate, bedfellow, colleague, companion, confidant, copartner, supporter **10** benefactor, encourager, playfellow, well-wisher **12** acquaintance
　French: **3** ami **4** amie **9** bonne amie
　Spanish: **5** amiga, amigo

friendliness 5 amity **8** bonhomie, good will **9** geniality **10** affability, amiability, cordiality, fraternity **11** amicability, camaraderie, sociability **14** neighborliness **16** companionability

friendly 4 kind **6** allied, ardent, benign, chummy, clubby, genial, kindly, loving, social **7** affable, amiable, cordial, devoted, helpful **8** amicable, familiar, generous, gracious, intimate, salutary **9** brotherly, convivial, favorable, fortunate, fraternal, opportune **10** accessible, auspicious, beneficial, hospitable, neighborly, not hostile, propitious **11** kindhearted, sympathetic, warmhearted **12** advantageous, affectionate **13** companionable

Friendly, Fred W
 president of: **7** CBS News
 collaborator: **13** Edward R. Murrow
 show: **8** See It Now

Friendly Fire
 author: **8** C D B Bryan

Friendly Islands *see* **5** Tongo

Friendly Persuasion
 director: **12** William Wyler
 author: **12** Jessamyn West
 cast: **10** Gary Cooper **11** Richard Eyer **12** Marjorie Main **14** Anthony Perkins, Dorothy McGuire
 score: **14** Dimitri Tiomkin

friendly understanding
 French: **15** entente cordiale

friend of the court
 Latin: **12** amicus curiae

friendship 5 amity **6** accord, comity **7** concord, harmony **8** close tie, goodwill, intimacy, sympathy **10** consonance, cordiality, fellowship, fraternity **11** brotherhood, comradeship, familiarity **12** amicableness **13** companionship, understanding **14** neighborliness **16** acquaintanceship

Friesen, Samille Diane
 real name of: **10** Dyan Cannon

Frigg
 also: **3** Fri **5** Frija **6** Frigga
 origin: **8** Teutonic
 goddess of: **3** sky **6** clouds **8** marriage
 husband: **4** Odin **5** Othin
 race: **4** Asar **5** Aesir

Frigga *see* **5** Frigg

fright 4 fear, funk **5** alarm, dread, panic, scare **6** dismay, horror, terror, tremor **7** anxiety, concern, flutter, quaking **8** cold feet **9** misgiving, quivering, the creeps **10** the jitters, the willies **11** disquietude, palpitation, trepidation **12** apprehension, intimidation, perturbation **13** consternation

frighten 5 alarm, daunt, scare, shock **6** affray, excite **7** agitate, horrify, petrify, startle, terrify **8** disquiet **9** terrorize **10** intimidate

frightened 6 afraid, scared **7** alarmed, panicky **9** horrified, petrified, terrified **10** terrorized

frightening 5 awful, dread **7** fearful **8** alarming, dreadful **10** horrifying, terrifying **11** hair-raising

frightful 5 awful, lurid, nasty **6** grisly, horrid **7** baleful, extreme, fearful, ghastly, hideous, macabre, ogreish **8** alarming, dreadful, fearsome, freakish, gruesome, horrible, horrific, shocking, sinister, terrible, terrific **9** appalling,

loathsome, monstrous, offensive, repellent, repulsive, revolting **10** abominable, detestable, disgusting, horrendous **12** insufferable

frigid 3 icy, raw **4** cold, cool, prim **5** aloof, bleak, gelid, stiff **6** biting, bitter, chilly, formal, frosty **7** austere, cutting, distant, glacial, nipping **8** freezing, piercing **10** forbidding **11** straitlaced **12** unresponsive

frigidity 7 iciness **8** coldness **9** aloofness **10** frostiness **16** unresponsiveness

Frija *see* **5** Frigg

frill 3 air **5** extra **6** edging, fringe, ruffle **7** flounce **8** falderal, frippery, furbelow, ornament **9** gathering, mannerism **10** decoration **11** affectation, superfluity **13** embellishment

fringe 3 hem, rim **4** edge, mane **5** limit, skirt **6** border, edging, margin, tassel **7** enclose, outline, selvage **8** decorate, frontier, skirting, surround, trimming **9** embellish, periphery

frisk 3 hop **4** jump, lark, leap, romp, skip, trip **5** bound, caper, cut up, dance, sport **6** bounce, cavort, frolic, gambol, prance, search, spring **7** disport, examine, inspect, ransack **8** look over

frisky 4 spry **5** agile, peppy **6** active, lively, nimble **7** jocular, playful, waggish **8** animated, mirthful, prankish, spirited, sportive **9** vivacious **10** frolicsome, rollicking

fritter 4 blow **5** use up, waste **7** deplete, pancake **8** fool away, idle away, squander **9** dissipate

fritter away 4 blow **5** waste **6** misuse **8** misspend, squander **9** dissipate

fritter away time 4 idle **6** dawdle **10** dillydally

Fritzi Ritz
 aunt to: **5** Nancy
 creator: **15** Ernie Bushmiller **16** Larry Whittington
 character: **4** Phil **5** Nancy, Rollo **6** Sluggo

frivolity 3 fun **4** jest, play **5** folly, sport **6** levity, whimsy **7** abandon **8** airiness, dallying, frippery **9** emptiness, flippancy, giddiness, lightness **10** fickleness, triviality, wantonness **11** flightiness **15** thoughtlessness

frivolous 4 airy, vain **5** barmy, dizzy, empty, inane, light, minor, petty, silly **6** flimsy, frothy, paltry, slight, stupid **7** fatuous, flighty, foolish, trivial, witless **8** careless, flippant, heedless, niggling, piddling, trifling **9** brainless, imprudent, pointless, senseless, unserious, worthless **10** insouciant **11** extravagant, harebrained, impractical, improvident, nonsensical, superficial, unimportant **13** insignificant, rattlebrained **14** shallowbrained

frizzle 4 curl **5** crimp

frock 4 coat, gown, robe, suit **5** cloak, dress, smock **6** blouse **7** cassock, soutane **8** chasuble, surplice, vestment **9** clericals **10** canonicals

frog 3 pad, pod **4** knot, wood **5** frosh, hitch, track **6** holder, peeper, toggle **7** crawler, croaker, cushion, leopard, tadpole **8** bullfrog, fastener, pickerel, pollywog **9** amphibian, plow frame **12** flower holder

Frogs, The
 author: **12** Aristophanes
 character: **5** Pluto **6** Charon **7** Bacchus **8** Dionysus, Hercules, Xanthias **9** Aeschylus, Euripides

Froissart, Jean
 author of: **8** Meliador **10** Chronicles

frolic 3 fun **4** lark, play, romp, skip **5** act up, antic, caper, frisk, mirth, prank, sport, spree **6** cavort, gaiety, gambol **7** disport, jollity, make hay **8** escapade **9** amusement, festivity, joviality, merriment **10** buffoonery, pleasantry, recreation, skylarking, tomfoolery **11** merrymaking **13** entertainment

frolicsome 5 antic, jolly, merry **6** cheery, jaunty, lively **7** playful **8** cheerful, mirthful, prankish **9** sprightly **12** lighthearted

Frollo, Claude
 character in: **23** The Hunchback of Notre Dame
 author: **4** Hugo

from 2 de, ex, of **3** for, fro **5** off of, out of **7** against **8** starting **9** beginning

from abroad 5 alien **6** exotic **7** foreign **8** imported

fromage 6 cheese

from behind
 Latin: **6** a tergo

From Here to Eternity
 director: **13** Fred Zinnemann
 author: **10** James Jones
 cast: **9** Donna Reed **11** Deborah Kerr **12** Frank Sinatra, George Reeves **13** Burt Lancaster **14** Ernest Borgnine **15** Montgomery Clift
 setting: **11** Pearl Harbor
 Oscar for: **7** picture **8** director **12** screenwriter **15** supporting actor (Sinatra) **17** supporting actress (Reed)

from inside
 Latin: **7** ab intra

from outside
 Latin: **7** ab extra

From Russia With Love
 author: **10** Ian Fleming

from scratch 4 anew **14** from ground zero **16** from the beginning **20** from fresh ingredients

from side to side 4 over, sway **5** cross **7** athwart, swaying, zigzag **12** back and forth

from the beginning
 Latin: **5** ab ovo **6** de novo **8** ab initio

from the chair
Latin: **10** ex cathedra
from the depths
Latin: **11** de profundis
from the face
Latin: **7** ex facie
from the fact
Latin: **7** de facto
from the founding of the city
Latin: **13** ab urbe condita
from the library of
Latin: **8** ex libris
from the seat of authority
Latin: **10** ex cathedra
front 3 air, top **4** face, fore, head, lead, mask, mien **5** first **6** facade, give on, regard **7** bearing, initial, look out **8** anterior, carriage, demeanor, presence, pretense, trenches, vanguard **9** beginning, semblance
Front, The
director: **10** Martin Ritt
cast: **10** Lloyd Gough, Woody Allen, Zero Mostel **13** Joshua Shelley, Michael Murphy **16** Herschel Bernardi
frontage 7 outlook **8** exposure, prospect
frontier 4 edge **5** march, verge **6** border, limits **7** extreme, marches **8** boundary, confines, outposts **9** backlands, backwoods, outskirts, perimeter **10** hinterland **11** territories
front matter 8 foreword **9** title page **12** introduction **15** table of contents **20** introductory material
Front Page, The
author: **8** Ben Hecht **16** Charles MacArthur
director: **11** Billy Wilder **14** Lewis Milestone
actor: **9** Mae Clarke, Mary Brian, Pat O'Brien **10** David Wayne, Jack Lemmon **12** Carol Burnett, George E Stone **13** Adolphe Menjou, Allen Garfield, Susan Sarandon, Walter Catlett, Walter Matthau **14** Charles Durning **15** Andrew Pendleton, Vincent Gardenia **19** Edward Everett Horton
character: **4** Earl **5** Burns, Grant, Hildy, Peggy **6** Walter **7** Hartman, Johnson **8** Williams
frost 4 rime **5** chill **7** iciness **8** coolness, distance **9** aloofness, cold spell, frigidity **10** chilliness, glaciality **13** inhospitality **14** unfriendliness
Frost, Robert
author of: **7** Birches **10** Fire and Ice, Home Burial **11** Mending Wall **13** Brown's Descent **15** The Road Not Taken **17** After Apple-Picking **21** The Death of the Hired Man **30** Stopping by Woods on a Snowy Evening
frostiness 3 nip **4** bite **5** chill **7** iciness **8** coldness, coolness **9** crispness,

frigidity, hoariness, sharpness **10** chilliness, wintriness
frosting 3 mat **4** trim **5** glass, icing **7** cooling, topping **8** chilling, divinity, freezing, trimming **13** embellishment, ornamentation
frosty 3 icy **4** cold, cool **5** bleak, chill, hoary **6** frigid, wintry **8** freezing
froth 4 bosh, fizz, foam, fume, head, scum, suds, surf **5** spume, trash, yeast **6** lather, trivia **7** bubbles, rubbish **8** flummery, frippery, nonsense, trumpery, whitecap **9** frivolity **10** balderdash, triviality **12** fiddle-faddle
frothy 5 fizzy, foamy, light **6** bubbly **7** trivial **9** frivolous **15** inconsequential
froward 5 balky **6** unruly **7** wayward, willful **8** contrary, perverse, stubborn **9** difficult, fractious, obstinate **10** headstrong, refractory **11** disagreeing, intractable **12** recalcitrant **13** contradictory **15** unaccommodating
frown 4 fret, mope, muse, pout, sulk **5** glare, scowl **6** glower, ponder **14** discountenance
frowning 4 dark **5** angry **6** gloomy, somber, sullen **8** scowling **9** glowering
frown upon 7 condemn, dislike **8** object to **14** discountenance
frowsy, frowzy 5 fusty, musty, stale **6** sloppy, untidy **7** tousled, unkempt **8** slovenly
frozen 3 icy **4** cold, iced, numb **5** chill, gelid, polar **6** arctic, chilly, cooled, wintry **7** chilled, clogged, glacial, stymied **8** benumbed, hibernal, icebound **10** obstructed, stalemated **11** frostbitten, immobilized **12** refrigerated
fructify 5 bloom **6** sprout, thrive **7** blossom, prosper, succeed **8** flourish
frugal 4 slim **5** scant, tight **6** skimpy, stingy **7** ascetic, sparing, thrifty **9** niggardly, penny-wise **10** abstemious, economical, unwasteful **12** parsimonious
frugality 6 thrift **7** economy **8** prudence, stinting **9** parsimony **10** scantiness, stinginess **11** thriftiness **12** cheeseparing **13** niggardliness, pennypinching **16** parsimoniousness
fruit 4 crop **5** award, issue, yield, young **6** effect, profit, result, return, reward, upshot **7** benefit, harvest, outcome, produce, product, progeny, revenue **8** earnings **9** advantage, emolument, offspring, outgrowth **10** production **11** consequence **12** remuneration
fruitful 6 fecund **7** fertile **8** blooming, prolific, yielding **9** effective **10** productive, profitable, successful **11** efficacious **12** advantageous, fructiferous
fruition 8 maturity, ripeness **10** attainment **11** achievement, fulfillment, realization **12** consummation, satisfac-

tion **13** actualization, gratification **15** materialization
fruitless 4 arid, vain **5** empty, inept **6** barren, futile, hollow **7** sterile, useless **8** abortive, bootless, nugatory **9** infertile, pointless, worthless **10** profitless, unavailing, unprolific **11** incompetent, ineffective, ineffectual, inoperative, purposeless, unrewarding **12** unproductive, unprofitable, unsuccessful **13** inefficacious
fruit trees
goddess of: **6** Pomona
frumpy 4 drab **5** dowdy **8** slovenly **10** slatternly **12** unattractive
frustrate 3 bar **4** balk, foil **5** block, check, upset **6** baffle, cancel, defeat, hinder, impede, thwart **7** counter, cripple, fluster, inhibit, nullify, prevent **8** dispirit, obstruct, prohibit, suppress **9** forestall, hamstring, undermine **10** circumvent, disappoint, disconcert, discourage, dishearten
frustration 6 defeat **7** balking, chagrin, failure, foiling, letdown **8** futility **9** hindrance, thwarting **10** bafflement, inhibition, nonsuccess **11** obstruction **12** discomfiture, interference **13** contravention, counteraction **14** disappointment, nonfulfillment **15** dissatisfaction
fry 4 cook **5** brown, grill, saute **7** frizzle **9** fricassee
fry 4 fish **5** child, young **8** children, small fry
Fry, Christopher
author of: **9** Yard of Sun **12** The Firstborn **13** Venus Observed **20** The Dark Is Light Enough **21** The Lady's Not for Burning
frying pan 3 wok **6** frypan **7** browner, griddle, skillet
fuchsia
varieties: **4** cape, tree **5** hardy **10** California **11** honeysuckle
fuddled 5 bosky, dopey, drunk, tipsy **6** boozed, groggy **7** maudlin, muddled, sozzled, tippled **8** confused **9** stupefied **10** inebriated **11** intoxicated
fudge 3 lie **4** bosh, fake **5** candy, cheat, evade, hedge, hunch, patch, welch **7** falsify, penuche **8** divinity
fuel 3 fan, gas, oil **4** coal, feed, fire, wood **5** light, means, stoke **6** charge, fill up, fodder, ignite, incite, kindle **7** impetus, inflame, sustain **8** activate, energize, gasoline, material, recharge, stimulus **9** petroleum, stimulate **10** ammunition, motivation, sustenance **11** inspiration, wherewithal
fugitive 4 hobo **5** brief, exile, hasty, nomad, rover, short, tramp **6** errant, fading, flying, loafer, outlaw **7** cursory, elusive, erratic, escaped, escapee, fleeing, hurried, passing, refugee, runaway, summary, vagrant **8** apostate, deserter, escaping, fleeting,

BORDERS

**BORDERS
BOOKS MUSIC AND CAFE**
4600 Sheblyville Road
Louisville, KY 40207
(502) 893-0133

STORE: 0616   REG: 09/26   TRAN#: 5626
SALE   10/25/2009   EMP: 00838

R .I WEBSTERS CROSSWORD PUZ DI
   8295382   QP T   18.95

         Subtotal   18.95
BR: 8260521656   S

         Subtotal   18.95
         KENTUCKY 6%   1.14
1 Item Total   20.09
         AMEX   20.09
ACCT # /S XXXXXXXXXXX3004
         AUTH: 519268
NAME: JOHNSON/A

10/25/2009 03:37PM

Shop online
24 hours a day
at Borders.com

Bob Saget (Danny Tanner) **10**
[S]tamos (Jesse Katsopolis) **11**
Olsen (Michelle Tanner),
[C]oulier (Joey Gladstone) **12**
Barber (Kimmy Gibbler), Jo-
[W]eetin (Stephanie Tanner), Lori
[L]n (Becky Donaldson Kat-
[sopolis] **13** Mary-Kate Olsen (Mi-
[chelle T]anner) **14** Candace Cameron
[(DJ T]anner)

[p]**ure 6** enough, plenty **9**
[suffi]ce, plenitude **10** competence
[suffic]iency

[?]
11 P G Wodehouse
satiety **8** richness **9** ampli-
[rou]ndness, satiation **12** com-
14 voluminousness

[?]e **7** rousing **8** electric, excit-
[t]ed **9** thrilling **11** galvanizing,
[?]g **12** electrifying, soul-

[?] **5** vital **8** animated, spirited,
9 ebullient, energetic, exu-
[?]vacious

[?] **5** vital **6** lively **8** animated
[?]n and vigor 5 peppy **6**
[in]invigorated

[?] the open **8** daylight, open-

[?]ly, quite **6** richly, wholly **7**
[ut]terly **8** entirely **9** copiously,
10 abundantly, altogether,
[?]y, positively, throughout
[ful]lly **12** sufficiently **13** sub-

[?]ed **7** perfect **8** achieved,
[?]executed, finished **9** com-
[?]fected, performed **11** con-
12 accomplished

[?] **4** boil, rage, rant **7** explode
[?]e

[?] **against 5** roast **6** berate **7**
[?] call down, chastise **9** casti-

[?]n **7** violent **8** bursting,
[?] discharge, explosion

---

full-bodied 3 fat **4** rich **5** ample, lofty
6 hearty, mature, robust **9** flavorful
10 meaningful

Fuller, R Buckminster
architect of: **10** US Pavilion (Expo '67
Montreal) **13** Dymaxion House
form: **12** geodesic dome

full-fledged 5 adept **6** expert, mature
7 skilled, trained **8** complete, masterly, schooled **9** qualified, topflight
10 proficient **11** experienced **13** authoritative

full form 9 extension **10** elongation **11**
enlargement **12** augmentation **13** amplification

full-grown 4 ripe **5** adult, manly, of
age, matured, womanly **9** developed

Full House
network: **3** ABC

fulsome 3 fat **4** foul **5** suave **6** lavish,
odious **7** cloying, lustful, noisome, obscene **8** overdone, unctuous **9** excessive, obnoxious, offensive, repulsive,
tasteless **10** disgusting, obsequious

Fulton, Robert
nationality: **8** American
inventor of: **9** steamboat (Clermont),
submarine **12** Fulton's folly **13** marine torpedo

fumble 3 err, mar **4** blow, muff **5**
grope, spoil **6** bobble, boggle, bollix,
bungle, goof up, mess up, muddle **7**
butcher, louse up, screw up **9** mishandle

fume 3 gas **4** boil, burn, emit, foam,
haze, puff, rage, rant, rave, reek, waft
5 exude, scent, smell, smoke, stink,
vapor **6** billow, exhale, miasma,

---

seethe, stench **7** carry on, explode,
flame up, flare up, smolder **10** exhalation

fun 3 gas **4** ball, game, jest, lark, play,
romp, trip **5** antic, blast, cheer, mirth,
prank, sport, spree **6** frolic, gaiety,
joking **7** jollity, revelry, whoopee **8**
escapade, good time, pleasure **9**
amusement, diversion, enjoyment,
horseplay, joviality, merriment **10**
buffoonery, recreation, relaxation, skylarking, tomfoolery **11** distraction,
playfulness, waggishness **13** entertainment

Funafuti
capital of: **6** Tuvalu

function 3 act, job **4** duty, fete, gala,
help, role, task, work **5** feast, field,
niche, party, place, power, range,
scope, serve **6** affair, behave, do duty,
office, soiree, sphere **7** banquet, benefit, concern, faculty, operate, perform,
purpose **8** activity, business, capacity,
ceremony, occasion, province **9** festivity, objective, operation, reception **13**
entertainment

functional 6 useful **7** working **8** oper-
able **9** operative, practical **11** serviceable, utilitarian

functionary 8 employee, official **10**
bureaucrat **13** administrator

functioning 5 in use **6** active, at
work, usable **7** working **9** effectual,
operating, operative

fund 3 pot **4** bank, foot, lode, mine,
pool, vein, well **5** endow, float, fount,
hoard, kitty, stock, store **6** pay for,
spring, supply **7** finance, nest egg, reserve, savings, support **8** treasure **9**
endowment, patronize, reservoir **10**
foundation, investment, repository,
storehouse, underwrite **12** accumulation

fundament 3 can **4** buns, rump, seat
5 fanny **6** behind, bottom **8** backside,
buttocks, haunches **9** posterior **12**
hindquarters

fundamental 3 key **4** ABC's, base,
main **5** axiom, basic, basis, chief,
first, major, vital **7** central, crucial, element, primary **8** cardinal, integral **9**
component, essential, necessary, principal, principle, requisite **10** elementary, foundation, groundwork, underlying **11** cornerstone **13** indispensable

funds 4 cash, jack, pelf **5** bread,
dough, lucre, means, money, moola **6**
assets, income, wampum, wealth **7**
capital, scratch **8** finances, property **9**
resources **11** wherewithal

funeral 4 wake **5** rites **6** burial **7** requiem **9** cremation, interment, obse-
quies **10** entombment, inhumation

funeral song 5 dirge, elegy **6** lament
7 requiem **8** threnody **11** lamentation

funereal 3 sad **4** grim **5** weepy **6** dismal, dreary, gloomy, solemn, somber,

woeful **7** doleful **8** desolate, dirgeful, grieving, mournful **9** cheerless, woebegone **10** depressing, lachrymose, lugubrious **13** brokenhearted

fun-filled 5 happy **6** joyful, joyous **8** pleasant, pleasing **9** enjoyable **10** delightful **11** pleasurable

Fungoso
    character in: **22** Every Man Out of His Humour
    author: **6** Jonson

fungus, fungi 4 mold, myco, rust, smut **5** ergot, yeast **6** mildew **7** truffle **8** mushroom **9** toadstool **11** thallophyte

fun-loving 5 jolly, merry **6** genial, jovial **7** affable **8** sociable **9** convivial **10** gregarious

funnel 4 cone, duct, flue, pipe, pour **5** focus, shaft **6** direct, filter, siphon **7** channel, chimney, conduit **9** stovepipe **10** smokestack, ventilator **11** concentrate

funny 3 odd **5** antic, comic, droll, merry, queer, weird, witty **6** absurd, jocose **7** amusing, bizarre, comical, curious, jesting, jocular, offbeat, strange, unusual, waggish **8** farcical, humorous, mirthful, peculiar, sporting, uncommon **9** diverting, facetious, hilarious, laughable, ludicrous **10** outlandish, ridiculous

Funny Girl
    director: **12** William Wyler
    cast: **8** Lee Allen **10** Kay Medford, Omar Sharif **11** Anne Francis **13** Walter Pidgeon **15** Barbra Streisand (Fanny Brice)
    score: **9** Jule Styne **10** Bob Merrill
    sequel: **9** Funny Lady
    song: **6** People **18** Don't Rain on My Parade

funnyman 3 wag, wit **4** card, fool, mime, zany **5** clown, comic, joker **6** jester, madcap **7** buffoon **8** comedian, humorist, jokester **9** harlequin

fuoco, con
    music: **8** with fire

fur 3 fox **4** down, hair, lamb, mink, pelt, seal **5** coney, lapin, otter, sable **6** beaver, fleece, jaguar, kit fox, nutria, rabbit, red fox **7** blue fox, cheetah, leopard, muskrat, opossum, raccoon **8** black fox, cross fox, squirrel, white fox **9** silver fox **10** animal skin, chinchilla **11** karakul lamb, Persian lamb **13** broadtail lamb **14** mouton-dyed lamb

furbelow 5 frill **6** fringe **7** falbala, flounce **8** trimming

furbish 4 buff **5** renew, shine **6** polish **7** burnish **8** renovate

Furiae *see* **6** Furies

Furies
    5 Dirae **6** Erinys, Furiae, Semnai **7** Allecto, Erinyes, Megaera **9** Eumenides, Tisiphone

    form: **7** spirits
    sex: **6** female
    mother: **4** Gaea
    father: **6** Uranus
    born of the blood of: **6** Uranus
    Greek name: **6** Erinys **7** Erinyes **9** Eumenides
    Roman name: **5** Dirae **6** Furiae

furious 3 mad **4** wild **5** angry, fiery, irate, rabid **6** enrage, fierce, fuming, raging, savage, stormy **7** intense, rampant, violent **8** frenetic, frenzied, heedless, maddened, provoked, reckless, up in arms, vehement, wrathful **9** fanatical, irascible, turbulent **10** infuriated, passionate, tumultuous, unbalanced **11** tempestuous **12** ungovernable, unrestrained

furl 4 coil, curl, fold, roll, wrap **5** truss **6** curl up, fold up, furdle, roll up, spiral

furlong
    abbreviation: **3** fur

furnace 4 kiln, oven **5** forge, stove **6** boiler, heater **11** incinerator

Furnace
    constellation of: **6** Fornax

furnish 3 arm, rig **4** gird, give, vest **5** array, dress, endow, equip, favor, fit up, grant, stock **6** fit out, outfit, purvey, render, supply **7** appoint, indulge, prepare, provide **8** accoutre, bestow on, decorate **9** provision **11** accommodate

furnishings 5 decor **9** equipment **11** accessories **12** haberdashery

furnish room for 5 lodge, put up **6** billet **7** shelter **11** accommodate

furniture 7 effects **8** chattels, movables, property **11** possessions **12** appointments

furor 3 fad **4** flap, rage, to-do, word **5** craze, mania, noise, thing, vogue **6** fervor, frenzy, hoopla, lunacy, raving, uproar **7** fashion, madness, passion **8** brouhaha, insanity, reaction **9** agitation, commotion, obsession, transport **10** dernier cri, enthusiasm, excitement, fanaticism

furrow 3 cut, dig, rut **4** knit, line, plow, rift, seam **5** cleft, crack, ditch, ridge, track **6** crease, groove, pucker, trench, trough **7** channel, crevice, fissure, wrinkle **10** depression **11** corrugation

furry 4 soft **5** downy, hairy, scary **6** cuddly, fleecy, pelted, shaggy **8** fearsome, horrible **11** hair-raising

further 3 aid, new, too, yet **4** also, back, help, more **5** again, extra, favor, fresh, other, spare, speed **6** abroad, assist, back up, beyond, foster, hasten, oblige, to boot, yonder **7** advance, afar off, besides, farther, forward, promote, quicken, stand by, work for **8** champion, expedite, likewise, moreover **9** accessory, ancillary,

auxiliary, encourage, propagate **10** accelerate, additional, strengthen **11** accommodate **12** additionally, contributory, supplemental **13** supplementary

furtherance 3 aid **4** help, lift **5** favor **6** succor **7** advance, defense, support **8** advocacy, interest **9** patronage, promotion **10** assistance **11** advancement, cooperation, countenance **12** championship

furthering 3 aid **6** aiding, growth **8** abetting, advocacy, espousal **9** assisting, fostering, promoting, promotion **10** assistance, supporting **11** advancement, encouraging, propagating, propagation **12** accelerating, acceleration, encouragement **13** strengthening

furthermore 3 too **4** also **6** as well, to boot **7** besides **8** likewise, moreover **10** in addition **12** additionally

furthermost 7 extreme **8** farthest **11** farthermost

furtive 3 sly **4** wily **5** shady **6** covert, crafty, hidden, masked, secret, shifty, sneaky, unseen, veiled **7** cloaked, elusive, evasive, private **8** secluded, shrouded, skulking, sneaking, stealthy **9** collusive, secretive, underhand **10** mysterious, undercover, unrevealed **11** clandestine **12** confidential **13** surreptitious **14** conspiratorial

fury 3 fit, hag, ire, pet **4** gall, huff, rage, snit **5** force, might, shrew, vixen, wrath **6** attack, choler, frenzy, spleen, virago **7** assault, bluster, dudgeon, hellcat, tantrum **8** acerbity, acrimony, ferocity, outburst, severity, she-devil, spitfire, violence **9** intensity, termagant, vehemence, virulence **10** excitement, fierceness, turbulence **11** impetuosity

fuse 4 join, link, meld, melt, weld, wick **5** blend, merge, smelt, torch **6** league, mingle, solder **7** combine **8** coalesce, federate, ignition, solidify **9** associate, detonator **10** amalgamate, assimilate **11** confederate, consolidate, incorporate, intermingler

fusillade 4 hail, rain **5** salvo, spray **6** volley **7** barrage, battery **8** drumfire, enfilade **9** broadside, cannonade **11** bombardment

fusion 5 blend, union **6** league **7** combine, melding, melting, merging **8** alliance, blending, compound, smelting **9** coalition, synthesis **10** commixture, dissolving, federation **11** association, coalescence, combination, commingling, confederacy, unification **12** amalgamation, intermixture, liquefaction **13** agglomeration, confederation

fuss 3 ado, nag **4** carp, fool, fret, fume, pomp, spat, stew, stir, tiff, to-do **5** annoy, cavil, labor, set-to, worry **6** bother, bustle, excite, fidget, flurry, hubbub, hustle, niggle, pester, pother, potter, putter, rattle, scurry, tinker **7**

agitate, confuse, dispute, fluster, flutter, nitpick, quarrel, quibble, perturb, trouble, turmoil **8** ceremony **9** agitation, commotion, confusion **10** disconcert, hurly-burly, turbulence **11** disturbance, superfluity **12** perturbation **15** ceremoniousness
Yiddish: 7 tzimmes

fuss over 6 dote on

fussy 4 busy **6** ornate **7** finical, finicky, nervous **8** bustling, critical, exacting **9** assiduous, cluttered, crotchety, demanding, squeamish **10** compulsive, fastidious, meticulous, nitpicking, old-maidish, particular, scrupulous **11** painstaking, persnickety

fusty 5 moldy, musty, stale **6** foisty, rancid, stuffy **8** obsolete **9** out of date **10** malodorous **12** old-fashioned

Futabatei, Shimei
  author of: 16 The Drifting (Floating) Cloud
futile 4 idle, vain **5** empty, petty **7** trivial, useless **8** abortive, bootless, nugatory, trifling **9** frivolous, fruitless, valueless, worthless **10** profitless, unavailing **11** ineffective, ineffectual, unimportant **12** unprofitable, unsuccessful **13** insignificant
future 4 hope **5** after, later **6** coming, latter, morrow, offing, to come **7** by-and-by, ensuing, outlook **8** eventual,

prospect, tomorrow, ultimate **9** following, hereafter, impending, projected **10** in prospect, subsequent, succeeding **11** anticipated, expectation, opportunity, prospective **12** anticipation
  Spanish: 6 manana
Future Shock
  author: 12 Alvin Toffler
fuzz 4 down, lint **5** fluff **6** police
fuzzy 3 dim **4** hazy **5** downy, foggy, linty, misty, murky, vague, wooly **6** fluffy, frizzy, woolly **7** blurred, obscure, shadowy, unclear **8** confused **9** pubescent **10** indefinite, indistinct

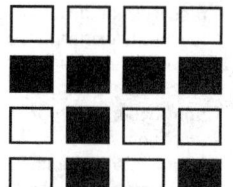 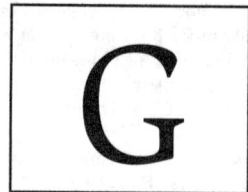 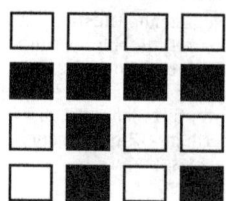

gab 3 jaw, rap, yak **4** blab, chat **5** prate **6** babble, gibber, gossip, jabber, patter **7** baloney, blarney, blather, chatter, prattle **8** chitchat, idle talk, talk idly **10** balderdash **12** conversation

gabble 3 rap **4** blab **5** prate **6** babble, drivel, gossip, jabber **7** blather, chatter, prattle, twaddle **8** babbling, chitchat, idle talk **9** gibbering, jabbering **10** blathering, chattering **14** chitterchatter

gabfest 3 rap **4** chat, talk **7** palaver **8** chitchat **10** discussion **12** conversation **13** confabulation

gable 4 edge, peak, roof, wall **6** detail, dormer, pinion **7** aileron **8** pediment, triangle

Gable, Clark
real name: 17 William Clark Gable
wife: 13 Carole Lombard
nickname: 7 The King
born: 7 Cadiz OH
roles: 7 Red Dust **8** Saratoga **10** The Misfits **11** Rhett Butler **15** Gone With the Wind **18** It Happened One Night (Oscar)

Gabo, Naum
real name: 17 Naum Neemia Pevsner
born: 6 Russia **7** Brainsk
founder: 14 Constructivism
artwork: 6 Column **11** Spiral Theme **16** Sculptural Models **19** Kinetic Construction **24** Variations of Spheric Theme

Gabon Republic
capital/largest city: 10 Libreville
others: 4 Oyem **5** Bongo, Kango **6** Mitzic, Moanda, Mouila, Omvane **7** Makokou, Mounana **9** Lambarene **10** Port-Gentil **11** Franceville
monetary unit: 5 franc **7** centime
lake: 7 Anengue, Azinguo
mountain: 5 Mpele **7** Chaillu, Cristal, Mikongo **8** Balaquri, Birougou
highest point: 8 Iboundji
river: 4 Como **6** Abanga, Ivindo, Ogooue **7** Ngounie
sea: 8 Atlantic
physical feature:
  cape: 5 Lopez
people: 4 Fang **6** Adouma, Bakota, Bateke, Echira, Okande, Omyene **7** Eshiras **8** Bandjabi, Bapounou
  leader: 3 Mba **5** Bongo
  philanthropist: 16 Albert

Schweitzer
language: 6 French
religion: 5 Islam **7** animism **10** Protestant **13** Roman Catholic
feature:
  tree: 6 okoume
food: 6 manioc **9** Dika bread
Gabor, Eva
mother: 5 Jolie
sister: 5 Magda **6** Zsa Zsa
born: 7 Hungary **8** Budapest
roles: 4 Gigi **10** Green Acres **12** My Man Godfrey **13** A Royal Scandal, Forced Landing **15** Youngblood Hawke **18** The Truth About Women **20** The Last Time I Saw Paris
Gabor, Zsa Zsa
real name: 9 Sari Gabor
mother: 5 Jolie
sister: 3 Eva **5** Magda
husband: 10 Nick Hilton **13** George Sanders
born: 7 Hungary **8** Budapest
roles: 4 Lili **11** Moulin Rouge **14** Lovely To Look At **20** The Story of Three Loves
Gaborone, Gaberones
capital of: 8 Botswana
Gabriel 9 archangel
means: 8 man of God **11** God is strong
spoke to: 4 Mary **9** Zacharias, Zechariah
Gad
father: 5 Jacob
mother: 6 Zilpah
brother: 3 Dan **4** Levi **5** Asher, Judah **6** Joseph, Reuben, Simeon **7** Zebulun **8** Benjamin, Issachar, Naphtali
sister: 5 Dinah
descendant of: 6 Gadite
gadget 4 tool **6** device, doodad, jigger **7** gimmick, novelty **9** accessory, doohickey **10** attachment **11** contraption, contrivance, thingamabob, thingamajig
Gaea
also: 2 Ge **4** Gaia
origin: 5 Greek
goddess of: 5 earth
husband: 6 Uranus
children: 6 Pontus, Titans, Uranus **7** Cyclops, Erinyes **9** mountains **13** Hecatonchires
son: 6 Nereus **7** Iapetus, Oceanus
daughter: 4 Rhea **5** Theia **6** Phoebe,

Tethys, Themis **9** Mnemosyne
corresponds to: 6 Tellus
Gaelic
language family: 12 Indo-European
branch: 4 Erse **6** Celtic
subgroup: 4 Manx **5** Irish **8** Scottish
gaffe 4 goof **5** boner **6** boo-boo **7** blunder **11** impropriety **12** indiscretion
French: 7 faux pas **9** gaucherie
gag 4 hoax, hush, jest, joke, stop **5** block, choke, heave, retch **6** muffle, muzzle, stifle **7** cloture, foolery, silence, smother **8** stoppage, suppress **9** horseplay, restraint **13** facetiousness
Gaia see **4** Gaea
gaiety, gayety 3 fun **4** show **5** mirth **6** frolic, tinsel **7** elation, glitter, jollity, spirits **8** airiness, frippery, trumpery, vivacity **9** amusement, animation, brummagem, gaudiness, merriment, showiness **10** brightness, brilliance, garishness, jauntiness, joyousness, liveliness **11** celebration, merrymaking **12** cheerfulness, colorfulness, exhilaration, sportiveness **13** effervescence, sprightliness
gain, gains 3 add, bag, get, hit, net, win **4** jump, leap, plus, reap **5** bloom, bonus, fetch, glean, put on, reach, wages, yield **6** attain, come to, gather, income, obtain, pick up, profit, return, salary, secure, thrive **7** achieve, acquire, blossom, capture, collect, improve, procure, produce, prosper, recover, revenue **8** addition, arrive at, black ink, dividend, earnings, flourish, increase, overtake, proceeds, winnings **9** accretion, advantage, increment **10** attainment **11** improvement **12** accumulation, compensation, remuneration
Gaines, Ernest J
author of: 16 In My Father's House **18** A Gathering of Old Men, A Lesson Before Dying **33** The Autobiography of Miss Jane Pittman
gainful 4 rich **6** paying **9** lucrative **10** productive, profitable **12** remunerative
gainfully 8 usefully **10** profitably **11** lucratively **12** productively **14** remuneratively
gain recognition 9 establish
gainsay 4 deny **6** abjure, oppose, refute **7** disavow, dispute **9** repudiate **10** contradict, controvert

Gainsborough, Thomas
born: **7** England, Sudbury
artwork: **10** The Blue Boy **14** The Morning Walk **15** Mr and Mrs Andrews, The Hon Mrs Graham **16** Viscount Ligonier **26** Peasant Girl Gathering Sticks

gait 4 pace, step, walk **5** tread **6** stride **7** bearing **8** carriage **10** deportment
French: **8** demarche

gaiter 4 boot, shoe, spat, vamp **5** chaps, strad **6** gaskin, hugger, puttee **7** legging **8** cuttikin, overshoe

gala 3 gay **5** grand, party **7** benefit, festive, opulent **8** festival, majestic, splendid **9** festivity, glamorous, sumptuous **10** ceremonial, fancy-dress, glittering **11** celebration, celebratory, magnificent, spectacular, star-studded
French: **4** fete

Galahad
character in: **16** Arthurian romance
father: **8** Lancelot
mother: **6** Elaine
quest: **9** Holy Grail
symbol of: **6** purity **8** nobility

Galatea
form: **6** maiden, statue **8** sea nymph
father: **6** Nereus
mother: **5** Doris
courted by: **10** Polyphemus
lover: **4** Acis
killed: **4** Acis
statue carved by: **9** Pygmalion
brought to life by: **9** Aphrodite
son: **6** Paphos

gale 3 fit **4** blow, gust, stir **6** flurry, squall, tumult, uproar **7** cyclone, tempest **8** eruption, outbreak, outburst **9** agitation, commotion, windstorm

Galileo Galilei
nationality: **7** Italian
birthplace: **4** Pisa
inventor of: **6** sector **11** thermometer
studied: **6** motion **8** pendulum
discovered: **18** Jupiter's satellites
constructed: **9** telescope
formulated: **18** law of falling bodies
author of: **8** Dialogue **10** Discourses **18** The Starry Messenger
condemned for: **6** heresy

gall 3 bug, irk, vex **4** bile, flay, fret, miff, rile **5** anger, annoy, brass, chafe, cheek, gripe, nerve, score, sting, venom **6** abrade, bruise, enrage, harass, injure, nettle, offend, rancor, ruffle, spleen **7** affront, incense, provoke, rub sore **8** acrimony, audacity, boldness, irritate, rudeness, temerity **9** animosity, assurance, displease, excoriate, impudence, insolence, malignity, sauciness, virulence **10** bitterness, brazenness, effrontery, exacerbate, exasperate **11** presumption

gallant 4 bold, dude, game, stud **5** blood, brave, dandy, gutsy, noble, suave, swell **6** daring, heroic, kindly, plucky, polite, urbane **7** courtly, dashing, valiant **8** cavalier, fearless, gay blade, intrepid, mannerly, obliging, resolute, stalwart, valorous, well-bred **9** attentive, courteous, dauntless **10** chivalrous, courageous, thoughtful **11** considerate, gentlemanly, lionhearted **12** stouthearted

gallantries 10 attentions **11** compliments **12** pleasantries

gallantry 4 grit, sand **5** nerve, pluck, valor **6** daring, mettle, spirit **7** bravery, courage, dashing, heroism, prowess, suavity **8** chivalry, courtesy, urbanity **9** derring-do, fortitude, gentility **10** politeness **11** courtliness, intrepidity **12** fearlessness, resoluteness **13** attentiveness, dauntlessness, determination **14** courageousness

gallery 4 stoa **5** salon **6** arcade, loggia, piazza **7** balcony, passage, portico **8** cloister, corridor **9** bleachers, colonnade, mezzanine, triforium **10** ambulatory, grandstand, passageway

Gallia Belgica *see* **7** Belgium

galliano
type: **7** liqueur
origin: **5** Italy
flavor: **5** herbs, spice
color: **6** yellow
with creme de cacao: **14** Golden Cadillac
with rum: **9** Bossa Nova
with vodka: **16** Harvey Wallbanger

gallinule 3 hen **4** coot, fowl, rail, sora **7** moorhen **8** dabchick, hyacinth, rallidae, ricebird, swamphen

Gallipoli
director: **9** Peter Weir
cast: **7** Mark Lee **8** Bill Kerr **9** Mel Gibson **11** Robert Grubb

gallivant, galavant 3 gad **4** kite, roam, rove **5** jaunt, range, stray **6** ramble, travel, wander **7** gallant, meander, traipse, **8** gad about **9** philander

gallon
abbreviation: **3** gal

gallop 3 fly, hie, jog, run **4** bolt, dart, dash, flit, race, rush, scud, skim, trot, whiz **5** bound, hurry, scoot, shoot, speed, whisk **6** hasten, scurry, spring, sprint **7** mad dash, scamper, scuttle, tear out **8** fast clip, fast gait **9** skedaddle

Galloping Ghost
nickname of: **9** Red Grange

gallows 4 rope **5** noose **6** gibbet, halter **8** scaffold

galore 7 aplenty, to spare

galosh, galoche 4 boot, clog, shoe **6** arctic, patten, rubber **8** overshoe

Galsworthy, John
author of: **5** To Let **6** Strife **7** Justice **9** Loyalties **10** In Chancery **11** The Skin Game **13** A Modern Comedy **14** The Forsyte Saga **15** End of the Chapter **16** The Man of Property **22** Indian Summer of a Forsyte

Galt, John
character in: **13** Atlas Shrugged
author: **7** Ayn Rand

galvanize 4 fire, move, stir, wake **5** rally, rouse, treat **6** arouse, awaken, charge, excite, foment, spur on, thrill **7** inspire, provoke, quicken **8** activate, energize, vitalize **9** electrify, stimulate

galvanizing 7 rousing **8** electric, exciting, spirited **9** inspiring, thrilling **11** stimulating **12** electrifying, soul-stirring

Galveston Giant
nickname of: **11** Jack Johnson

Gamaliel
father: **6** Simeon **8** Pedahzur
grandfather: **6** Hillel
taught: **4** Paul

Gambia
capital/largest city: **6** Banjul **8** Bathurst
others: **5** Bakau, Basse, Mansa **7** Bintang, Brikama, Kuntaur **10** Georgetown
monetary unit: **5** butut, pound **6** dalasi
island: **7** Ft James, St Mary's **8** Elephant
river: **3** Bao **6** Gambia **7** Bintang, Nianija **9** Sandougou
sea: **8** Atlantic
people: **4** Fula, Jola **5** Foula, Wolof **6** Fulani **8** Mandingo, Serahuli **9** Seranuleh
language: **4** Fula **5** Wolof **6** Fulani **7** English, Malinke **8** Mandingo
religion: **5** Islam **10** Protestant **13** Roman Catholic

gambit 4 ploy, ruse **5** feint, trick **6** scheme **8** artifice, maneuver **9** stratagem

gamble 3 bet **4** back, risk **5** flyer, wager **6** chance, hazard, toss-up **7** trust in, venture **9** speculate **11** speculation, uncertainty

gambler 5 dicer, shark, sharp, sport **6** banker, bettor, bookie, dealer, player **7** hustler **8** gamester, hazarder **10** speculator

Gambler, The
author: **16** Fyodor Dostoevsky
character: **6** Astley, Polina **10** The General **11** Mlle Blanche **15** Marquis de Grieux **16** Alexey Ivanovitch **22** Antonida Tarasyevitchev

gambol 3 hop **4** leap **5** bound, caper, frisk, sport, vault **6** bounce, cavort, frolic, prance, spring **7** disport, rollick

game 3 bad, fun **4** golf, halt, lame, lark, play, polo, pool, prey, romp **5** antic, brave, cocky, darts, gimpy, jacks, match, rugby, sport, spree **6** boccie, boxing, daring, frolic, gaiety, gambol, heroic, plucky, quarry, soccer, spunky, squash, tennis **7** archery, bowling, contest, crooked, croquet, curling, fencing, frisbee, gallant, hawking, hunting, hurling, jai alai, limping, pastime, tourney, valiant, willing **8** baseball, crippled, deformed, disabled, fearless, football, handball, hobbling, intrepid, lacrosse, ping pong, resolute, skittles, spirited, valorous, wild fowl **9** amusement, badminton, billiards, dauntless, diversion, festivity, merriment, wrestling **10** basketball, courageous, determined, horseshoes, ice-skating, lawn tennis, recreation, tournament, volleyball **11** competition, distraction, merrymaking, racquetball, table tennis, unflinching **12** shuffleboard **13** entertainment, incapacitated, roller-skating

board game: 4 Clue, Life, ludo **5** chess **7** Othello **8** checkers, cribbage, dominoes, draughts, fanorona, Monopoly, Scrabble **10** backgammon **14** Trivial Pursuit

Chinese: 6 Ma-jong, wei-ch'i **7** mahjong **8** Mah-jongg

Egyptian: 5 Senat

Indian: 7 pachisi **8** parchesi, shatranj **9** ashtapada, parcheesi **10** shaturanga

Japanese: 2 Go **3** I-go **5** Sho-gi

Korean: 5 Nyout, Pa-tok

Swedish: 5 tablut

card game: 3 loo, war **4** brag, fish, skat, vint **5** ombre, poker, rummy, tarot, whist **6** boston, bridge, casino, chemmy, ecarte, euchre, go fish, hearts, memory, piquet, pocher **7** bezique, canasta, cooncan, old maid, plafond, primero **8** baccarat, conquian, cribbage, gin rummy, napoleon, patience, pinochle, slapjack **9** blackjack, pelmanism, solitaire, spoil five, twenty-one **11** chemin de fer, crazy eights **13** concentration **14** contract bridge **16** beggar-my-neighbor, trente et quarante

gamete 3 egg **4** ovum **5** sperm **6** oocyte, zygote **8** germ cell, oosphere **12** spermatozoan, spermatozoon

Gamow, George
field: 7 physics **9** cosmology
proponent of: 13 big bang theory
deciphered: 11 genetic code
proposed: 13 quantum theory
established: 17 Gamow-Teller theory

Gamp, Sarah
character in: 16 Martin Chuzzlewit
author: 7 Dickens

gamut 3 ken **5** reach, scope, sweep **6** extent **7** compass, purview

Gandhi
director: 19 Richard Attenborough
cast: 11 Ben Kingsley **13** Candice Bergen
Oscar for: 5 actor (Kingsley) **7** picture

gang 3 mob **4** band, body, crew, pack,

pals, ring, team **5** chums, crowd, flock, group, party, relay, shift, squad, troop **6** clique, outfit **7** buddies, company, coterie, cronies, friends, phalanx **8** comrades **9** coworkers, neighbors **10** associates, classmates, companions, contingent, detachment **11** schoolmates

gangster 4 goon, hood, thug **5** crook, felon, tough **6** bandit, gunman **7** hoodlum, mafioso, mobster, ruffian **8** criminal, hooligan **9** racketeer •

Gant, Eugene
character in: 17 Look Homeward Angel, Of Time and the River
author: 5 Wolfe

Ganymede
also: 9 Catamitus
cupbearer of: 4 gods

gap 3 cut **4** gash, hole, rent, rift, slit, slot, void **5** abyss, break, chasm, chink, cleft, crack, gulch, gully, notch, pause **6** breach, canyon, cavity, divide, hiatus, lacuna, ravine, recess, vacuum, valley **7** crevice, fissure, interim, opening **8** aperture, crevasse, fracture, interval, puncture **9** disparity, interlude **10** difference, divergence **12** intermission, interruption

gape 4 gasp, gawk, gaze, ogle, part, peer, yawn **5** split, stare **6** cleave, expand **7** fly open **8** wide open, separate **10** rubberneck

gaping 6 astare **7** gawking, staring, yawning **13** rubbernecking

garb 3 rig **4** gear, gown, robe, suit, togs **5** dress, getup, habit **6** attire, finery, livery, outfit **7** apparel, clothes, costume, raiment, uniform, vesture **8** clothing, garments, vestment, wardrobe **9** trappings **11** habiliments

garbage 4 dirt, junk **5** offal, swill, trash, waste **6** debris, litter, refuse **7** carrion, rubbish **9** sweepings

garbage in, garbage out 4 GIGO
term in: 9 computers

garble 5 mix up **6** jumble **7** confuse, distort **8** fragment

Garbo, Greta
real name: 21 Greta Louisa Gustaffson
born: 6 Sweden **9** Stockholm
roles: 4 Love **7** Camille **8** Conquest, Mata Hari **9** Ninotchka **10** Grand Hotel **12** Anna Christie, Anna Karenina **13** Queen Cristina, Two-Faced Woman **14** The Painted Veil **16** Flesh and the Devil

Garcia Lorca, Federico
author of: 5 Yerma **12** Blood Wedding, Gypsy Ballads **19** House of Bernarda Alba

Garcia Marquez, Gabriel
author of: 9 Leaf Storm **22** Love in the Time of Cholera **23** The Autumn of the Patriarch **24** The General in his Labyrinth **25** Chronicle of a

Death Foretold, One Hundred Years of Solitude
award: 5 Nobel **10** Literature

garcon 3 boy **6** waiter **7** servant

garden 4 Eden, lawn, plot, yard **7** Arcadia **8** paradise **10** Gethsemane
type: 4 herb, rock, rose **5** truck **6** flower, formal **7** kitchen **9** botanical, vegetable

gardenia
varieties: 5 crape **9** butterfly

Garden of the Finzi Continis, The
director: 14 Vittorio De Sica
author: 14 Giorgio Bassani
cast: 10 Fabio Testi **11** Romolo Valli **12** Helmut Berger **14** Dominique Sanda **15** Lino Capolicchio
Oscar: 11 foreign film

Garden of the West
nickname of: 6 Kansas

garden party
French: 13 fete champetre

gardens
god of: 9 Vertumnus
goddess of: 5 Venus

Garden State
nickname of: 9 New Jersey

garden variety 5 plain **6** common, simple **7** regular **8** everyday, familiar, ordinary **11** commonplace

Gardner, Ava
husband: 9 Artie Shaw **12** Frank Sinatra, Mickey Rooney
born: 12 Smithfield NC
roles: 7 Mogambo **8** Show Boat **9** Mayerling, Naked Maja **10** On the Beach **15** The Sun Also Rises **18** Snows of Kilimanjaro **19** The Barefoot Contessa, The Night of the Iguana

Gardner, Erle Stanley
character: 9 Paul Drake **10** Perry Mason **11** Della Street **14** Hamilton Burger
also wrote as: 6 A A Fair

Gardner, John
author of: 7 Grendel **12** October Light **14** Nickel Mountain, The Art of Living, The King's Indian **17** Michelsson's Ghosts **20** The Sunlight Dialogues, The Wreckage of Agathon

Gareth
character in: 16 Arthurian romance

Garfield, James Abram
presidential rank: 9 twentieth
party: 10 Republican
state represented: 2 OH
defeated: 3 (Neal) Dow **6** (James Baird) Weaver, (John Wolcott) Phelps **7** (Winfield Scott) Hancock
vice president: 6 (Chester Alan) Arthur
cabinet:
state: 6 (James Gillespie) Blaine
treasury: 6 (William) Windom
war: 7 (Robert Todd) Lincoln
attorney general: 8 (Isaac Wayne)

MacVeagh
navy: 4 (William Henry) Hunt
postmaster general: 5 (Thomas Lemuel) James
interior: 8 (Samuel Jordan) Kirkwood
born: 2 OH **6** Orange **8** log cabin
died: 9 Elberon NJ
died by: 13 assassination
buried: 11 Cleveland OH
education:
  seminary: 6 Geauga
  college: 5 Hiram (Eclectic Institute) **8** Williams
  studied: 3 law
religion: 17 Disciples of Christ
political career: 8 US Senate (declined seat) **11** state Senate **24** US House of Representatives
civilian career: 6 lawyer **7** teacher **11** lay preacher
military service: 6 US Army **8** Civil War **12** major general
notable events of lifetime/term:
  exposure of: 15 Star Route frauds
father: 7 Abraham
mother: 5 Eliza (Ballou)
siblings: 4 Mary **5** James **6** Thomas **9** Mehitabel
wife: 8 Lucretia (Rudolph)
  nickname: 5 Crete
children: 4 Mary **5** Abram, Eliza **6** Edward **12** James Rudolph **13** Harry Augustus, Irvin McDowell

Garfield, John
real name: 15 Julius Garfinkle
born: 9 New York NY
roles: 6 Juarez **10** Humoresque **11** Body and Soul **26** The Postman Always Rings Twice

Gargamelle
character in: 22 Gargantua and Pantagruel
author: 8 Rabelais

Gargantua and Pantagruel
author: 16 Francois Rabelais
character: 7 Panurge **10** Gargamelle, Grangosier, Picrochole **23** Frere Jean des Entommeures

gargantuan 4 huge, vast **5** great **7** hulking, immense, mammoth, massive, titanic **8** colossal, enormous, gigantic, lubberly, towering **9** herculean, monstrous, overgrown **10** prodigious, stupendous, tremendous **11** elephantine **13** amplitudinous

Gargery, Joe
character in: 17 Great Expectations
author: 7 Dickens

garish 4 loud **5** cheap, gaudy, showy **6** brassy, bright, flashy, tawdry, tinsel, vulgar **7** blatant, glaring **9** flaunting, obtrusive **11** pretentious **12** ostentatious **13** overelaborate

garland 3 bay, lei **4** halo **5** crown **6** corona, diadem, fillet, laurel, wreath **7** chaplet, circlet, coronet, festoon **8** chapbook, headband, treasury **9** anthology **10** collection **11** florilegium

Garland, Hamlin
author of: 18 Main-Travelled Roads **20** Rose of Dutcher's Coolly

Garland, Judy
real name: 11 Frances Gumm
husband: 7 Sid Luft **16** Vincente Minnelli
daughter: 9 Lorna Luft **12** Liza Minnelli
costar: 12 Mickey Rooney
born: 13 Grand Rapids MN
roles: 7 Dorothy **11** A Star Is Born, Babes in Arms **12** Easter Parade **13** The Wizard of Oz **14** The Harvey Girls **15** A Child Is Waiting, Meet Me in St Louis

garlic
botanical name: 13 Allium sativum
origin: 4 Asia **13** Mediterranean
charm against: 7 poverty, witches **13** whooping cough
use: 4 fish, fowl, meat **5** salad **10** vegetables **13** Italian dishes, salad dressing
varieties: 4 crow, hog's, wild **5** bear's, false, field, giant, grace, mouse, stag's, sweet **6** levant **7** serpent, society, Spanish, striped **8** daffodil, oriental **11** great-headed, round-headed **16** fragrant-flowered

Garm
origin: 12 Scandinavian
form: 8 watchdog
watches over: 3 Hel
location: 8 Niflheim

garment, garments 4 garb, gear, togs **5** dress, habit **6** attire, outfit **7** apparel, clothes, costume, raiment **8** clothing, vestment **10** habiliment

garner 4 reap **5** amass, hoard **6** gather, heap up **7** acquire, collect **8** assemble **10** accumulate

Garner, James
real name: 15 James Baumgarner
born: 8 Norman OK
roles: 8 Maverick, Sayonara **11** Jim Rockford **12** Bret Maverick, Hour of the Gun, Space Cowboys **13** Darby's Rangers, Rockford Files **14** Murphy's Romance, The Great Escape, Victor Victoria **23** Support Your Local Sheriff **25** The Americanization of Emily

garnet
varieties: 6 syrope **9** almandite, demantoid, hessonite, rhodolite **12** grossularite
month: 7 January

garnish 4 deck, gild, trim **5** adorn, array **6** bedeck, doll up, set off **7** festoon, furbish, smarten **8** beautify, decorate, emblazon, ornament, spruce up, trimming **9** adornment, embellish, embroider **10** decoration **13** embellishment

garret 4 loft **5** attic

garrison 4 fort **5** guard **6** patrol, secure **7** battery, bivouac, brigade, platoon, station **8** division, regiment, squadron **10** detachment, escadrille **13** fortification

garrulity 8 verbiage **9** loquacity, prosiness, verbosity, wordiness **13** talkativeness

garrulous 5 gabby, windy, wordy **6** chatty **7** gossipy, prating, verbose, voluble **8** babbling, chattery, effusive **9** prattling, talkative **10** loquacious

Garry Moore Show, The
cast: 9 Allen Funt, Denise Lor, John Byner, Ken Carson **11** Chuck McCann, Marion Lorne **12** Carol Burnett, Durward Kirby, Jackie Vernon, Pete Barbutti **13** Dorothy Loudon

Garson, Greer
born: 7 Ireland **10** County Down
roles: 10 Mrs Miniver (Oscar) **11** Madame Curie **12** Her Twelve Men **13** Mrs Parkington, Random Harvest **14** Goodbye Mr Chips **16** That Forsyte Woman **17** Pride and Prejudice **19** Sunrise at Campobello

gas 4 fuel, fume **5** vapor **6** petrol **7** essence

gascon 7 boaster, bragger, egotist **8** blowhard, braggart **9** swaggerer **11** braggadocio

gasconade 4 brag, crow **5** boast **7** bravado **8** boasting **11** braggadocio

gash 4 hack, rend, rent, slit, tear **5** carve, cleft, crack, lance, slash, slice, split, wound **6** cleave, incise, pierce **7** dissect, fissure, quarter **8** incision, lacerate

Gaskell, Elizabeth
author of: 4 Ruth **8** Cranford **10** Mary Barton **13** North and South **24** The Life of Charlotte Bronte

Gaslight
director: 11 George Cukor
cast: 10 Terry Moore **12** Charles Boyer **13** Dame May Whitty, Ingrid Bergman **14** Angela Lansbury **15** Halliwell Hobbes

Gasoline Alley
creator: 9 Bill Perry, Frank King **10** Dick Moores
character: 3 Eve **4** Adam, Hope **6** Clovia, Gideon, Nubbin **7** Chipper, Gabriel **10** Walt Wallet
wife: 14 Phyllis Blossom
children: 4 Judy **5** Corky **7** Skeezix
daughter-in-law: 9 Nina Clock
dog: 5 Punky

gasp 4 gulp, pant, puff **5** blurt **6** suck in, wheeze **10** vociferate

gastronome 7 epicure, gourmet **9** bon vivant

gastronomy 9 epicurism

gastropod, gasteropod 4 slug **5** cowry, snail, whelk **6** cowrie, limpet, nerite **7** abalone, mollusk **8** univalve

gate 3 tap 5 crowd, house, valve 6 portal, sluice, spigot 7 doorway 8 audience, hatchway 9 turnstile 10 attendance

gateau 4 cake 7 dessert

gatekeeper 5 guard 6 porter 7 St. Peter 8 watchman

Gates, Horatio
served in: 16 Revolutionary War 18 French and Indian War
battle: 6 Camden 8 Saratoga
defeated: 8 Burgoyne
defeated by: 10 Cornwallis

gateway 4 adit 5 entry 6 access, portal 7 doorway, opening 8 entrance, entryway 10 passageway

Gath 14 Philistine city

gather 4 fold, mass 5 amass, group, infer, learn, pleat, shirr, stack 6 assume, deduce, heap up, muster, pile up, pucker, ruffle 7 cluster, collect, convene, marshal, observe 8 assemble, conclude 9 stockpile 10 accumulate, congregate, understand 11 concentrate

gathering 3 mob 4 gang, pack 5 bunch, crowd, crush, drove, flock, horde, party, press 6 throng 7 company, meeting, roundup, turnout 8 assembly, conclave 9 concourse, multitude 10 assemblage, collection, conference, convention 11 aggregation, convergence, convocation 12 accumulation, congregation 13 concentration

gather together 4 herd 5 amass, hoard, rally 6 muster 7 collate, collect, compile, marshal, round up, sweep up 8 assemble, shepherd 9 aggregate, stockpile 10 accumulate, congregate

Gatling, Richard Jordan
nationality: 8 American
inventor of: 10 machine gun 16 steam-powered plow

gatophobia
fear of: 4 cats

gauche 5 inept 6 clumsy, oafish 7 awkward, boorish, ill-bred, uncouth 8 bungling, plebeian, tactless 9 inelegant, maladroit, tasteless, unrefined 10 blundering, uncultured, ungraceful, unmannerly, unpolished 11 proletarian 13 ungentlemanly

gaucherie 5 gaffe 7 blunder, faux pas 11 impropriety 12 indiscretion

Gaudeamus igitur 22 Let us therefore be joyful

gaudy 4 loud, sham 5 cheap, showy, vivid 6 flashy, flimsy, garish, tawdry, tinsel, vulgar 7 glaring, intense 8 colorful, dazzling, lustrous, striking 9 brilliant, sparkling, tasteless, worthless 10 bespangled, glittering 11 pretentious 12 ostentatious

gauge, gage 4 rate, size 5 guess, judge, meter 6 assess 7 adjudge, measure 8 appraise, estimate, evaluate, standard 9 ascertain, calculate, criterion, yardstick 11 measurement
type: 4 ring 5 bevel

Gauguin, Paul Eugene Henri
born: 5 Paris 6 France
artwork: 9 Nevermore 12 The Tahitians 13 The White Horse 15 The Yellow Christ 18 Horsemen on the Beach 23 The Vision after the Sermon (Jacob Wrestling with the Angel) 25 Be in Love and You Will Be Happy 26 The Spirit of the Dead Watching 36 Where Do We Come From? Who Are We? Where Do We Go?
book: 6 Noa Noa

Gaul see 6 France

gaunt 4 bony, grim, lank, lean, slim, thin 5 bleak, lanky, spare 6 barren, meager, skinny, wasted 7 haggard, pinched, scraggy, scrawny, slender, spindly, starved 8 deserted, desolate, forsaken, raw-boned, skeletal, withered 9 emaciated, shriveled 10 cadaverous, forbidding 14 spindle-shanked

Gauss, Carl Friedrich
field: 7 physics 9 astronomy 11 mathematics
nationality: 6 German
worked in: 9 magnetism 11 electricity 12 number theory
named for him: 9 Gauss's Law

Gautier, Marguerite
character in: 7 Camille
author: 5 Dumas (fils)

Gautier, Theophile
author of: 6 La Peri 7 Giselle 8 Albertus 11 Young France 13 Emaux et Camees 16 Enamels and Cameos 20 Mademoiselle de Maupin, The Romance of the Mummy
doctrine: 14 Art for art's sake

gauzy 5 filmy, sheer 6 flimsy, sleazy 10 diaphanous 11 translucent, transparent

gave up 4 quit 5 ceded 7 dropped, forsook, yielded 8 forswore, resigned 9 abandoned, abdicated, forfeited, renounced 11 surrendered 12 discontinued, relinquished

Gawain
character in: 16 Arthurian romance
opponent: 11 Green Knight

gawk 4 gape, gaze, peer 10 rubberneck

gawky 6 clumsy, klutzy 7 awkward, lumpish 8 bungling, fumbling, lubberly, ungainly, unwieldy 9 all thumbs, graceless, ham-fisted, ham-handed, maladroit 10 blundering, ungraceful

gay 3 fun 4 airy, glad 5 happy, jolly, merry, showy, sunny, vivid 6 blithe, bright, cheery, elated, frisky, genial, jaunty, jocose, jovial, joyful, joyous, lively, social 7 buoyant, chipper, colt-ish, dashing, festive, gleeful, glowing, intense, jocular, playful, smiling, waggish 8 animated, cheerful, colorful, exultant, gladsome, humorous, jubilant, lustrous, skittish, spirited, splendid, sportive, volatile 9 brilliant, convivial, frivolous, hilarious, rejoicing, sparkling, sprightly, sumptuous, vivacious 10 flamboyant, frolicsome, glittering, homosexual, insouciant, theatrical, variegated 12 effervescent, lighthearted, multicolored

Gay, John
author of dialogue/lyrics for: 15 The Beggar's Opera

Gay, Walter
character in: 12 Dombey and Son
author: 7 Dickens

gay blade 3 fop 4 beau 5 blade, dandy 7 playboy 8 cavalier 9 ladies' man 12 boulevardier, man-about-town

Gay Divorcee, The
director: 12 Mark Sandrich
cast: 10 Alice Brady, Erik Rhodes 11 Betty Grable, Fred Astaire 12 Ginger Rogers 19 Edward Everett Horton
song: 11 Continental, Night and Day

Gay-Lussac, Joseph
field: 7 physics 9 chemistry
nationality: 6 French
discovered: 24 law of combining gas volumes
invented: 10 hydrometer

Gaynor, Mitzi
real name: 20 Franceska Mitzi Gerber
husband: 8 Jack Bean
born: 9 Chicago IL
roles: 8 Les Girls 10 Golden Girl 12 Anything Goes, South Pacific 14 The Joker Is Wild 32 There's No Business Like Show Business

gaze 3 eye 4 gape, ogle, peek, peer, scan 5 glare, lower, stare, study, watch 6 behold, glance, glower, peruse, regard, survey 7 examine, inspect, observe, witness 8 look long, pore over, scrutiny 10 rubberneck, scrutinize 11 contemplate

gaze at 4 view 5 watch 6 behold, look at 7 stare at 8 look upon 11 contemplate

gazpacho 4 soup
ingredients: 6 onions 7 peppers 8 tomatoes 9 cucumbers

Gazza Ladra, La
also: 17 The Thieving Magpie
opera by: 7 Rossini

Ge see 4 Gaea

gear 3 cam, rig 4 duds, garb, togs 5 dress, tools 6 attire, outfit, tackle, things 7 apparel, clothes, rigging 8 clothing, cogwheel, flywheel, garments, material, property 9 apparatus, equipment, trappings 10 belongings, implements 11 accessories, instruments 12 contrivances 13 accoutrements, paraphernalia

Geb
  also: 3 Keb
  origin: 8 Egyptian
  god of: 5 earth
  daughter: 4 Isis
  son: 6 Osiris
  sister: 3 Nut

Geer, Will
  born: 11 Frankfort IN
  roles: 7 Grandpa 10 The Waltons
  11 In Cold Blood

Gehenna 4 hell

Gehrig, Lou (Henry Louis)
  nickname: 9 Iron Horse
  sport: 8 baseball
  position: 9 first base
  team: 14 New York Yankees

Geist 4 mind 6 spirit

gelatin 4 agar, glue 5 aspic, gelee, jelly 6 glutin, pectin 7 protein, sericin

gelatinize 3 set 4 jell 7 congeal, stiffen, thicken 9 coagulate

gelatinous 7 colloid, viscous 8 mucu-lent 9 jelly-like

geld 5 alter 8 castrate 10 emasculate

gelid 3 icy 6 frigid, frozen 8 freezing

gem 4 dear, doll, rock 5 beaut, bijou, jewel, peach, prize 6 marvel, wonder 8 treasure
  type: 4 jade, opal, ruby, sard 5 agate, amber, beryl, coral, pearl, topaz 6 garnet, pyrope, quartz, spinel, zircon 7 apatite, cat's-eye, citrine, diamond, emerald, jadeite, kunzite, olivine, peridot 8 amethyst, corundum, feld-spar, hematite, lazurite, nephrite, sapphire, steatite, sunstone 9 alman-dite, amazonite, carnelian, deman-toid, enstatite, fibrolite, malachite, moonstone, morganite, rhodolite, scapolite, spodumene, tiger's-eye, turquoise 10 aquamarine, blood-stone, chalcedony, hessionite, rose quartz, tourmaline 11 alexandrite, chrysoberyl, chrysocolla, chryso-prase, lapis lazuli, rock crystal, topaz quartz 12 grossularite

Gemini
  symbol: 5 twins
  planet: 7 Mercury
  rules: 14 communications
  born: 3 May 4 June
  twins: 6 Castor, Pollux

Gem State
  nickname of: 5 Idaho

gemutlich 4 easy 9 agreeable, congen-ial, simpatico 11 comfortable

gendarme 9 policeman

gender 3 sex 4 kind, male, sort, type 5 class 6 female, neuter 8 feminine 9 masculine

genealogy 4 line 5 birth, house, stock 7 lineage 8 ancestry, pedigree 9 par-entage 10 derivation, extraction

Gene Autry Show, The
  cast: 10 Pat Buttram

horse: 8 Champion
theme song: 20 Back in the Saddle Again

general 5 basic, broad, usual, vague 6 common, normal, public, wonted 7 blanket, current, generic, inexact, nat-ural, overall, popular, regular, typical 8 everyday, frequent, habitual, ordi-nary, pandemic, sweeping 9 custom-ary, extensive, imprecise, panoramic, prevalent, universal, worldwide 10 ac-customed, collective, ecumenical, pre-vailing, widespread 11 unspecified 12 conventional, nonexclusive, nontech-nical 13 comprehensive, miscellane-ous

General Electric Theater
  host: 12 Ronald Reagan

general idea 4 gist 5 drift, tenor 6 ef-fect, import 7 purport 10 impression 11 implication

generality 6 cliche, truism 9 platitude 12 universality 14 collectiveness 17 miscellaneousness 18 indiscriminate-ness

generalization 3 law 5 axiom 7 bro-mide 9 inference, statement

generalize 5 infer, judge 8 conclude

generally 5 often 6 always, mainly, mostly 7 as a rule, chiefly, largely, usually 9 currently, typically 10 fre-quently, habitually, ordinarily, repeat-edly 11 extensively, principally, uni-versally

general/military leader
  American:
    Revolutionary War: 3 (Light Horse Harry) Lee 5 Allen, Barry, Gates, Jones, Wayne 6 Arnold, Greene, Marion, Morgan 10 Washington
    War of 1812: 4 Hull 5 Perry, Scott 7 Decatur
    Mexican War: 5 Scott 6 Kearny
    Civil War: 3 Lee 5 Early, Grant, Meade 6 Thomas, (JEB) Stuart 7 Forrest, Pickett, Sherman, (Stone-wall) Jackson 8 Farragut, Sheridan 9 McClellan 10 Beauregard, Long-street
    Indian Wars: 6 Custer 7 Houston 10 Crazy Horse
    WWI: 4 Sims 8 Mitchell, Pershing
    WWII: 4 King 5 Clark 6 Arnold, Halsey, Nimitz, Patton 7 Bradley, Merrill 8 Marshall, Stilwell 9 Chennault, Doolittle, MacArthur 10 Eisenhower, Wainwright
    Korean War: 7 Ridgway 9 Mac-Arthur
    Vietnam War: 6 Abrams 12 West-moreland
    Gulf War: 6 Powell 11 Schwarz-kopf
    Iraq War: 6 Franks 7 Abizaid
  British: 4 Byng, Haig, Howe, Slim 5 Wolfe 6 French, Gordon, Harris, Nel-son, Wavell 7 Allenby, Clinton,

Dowding, Wingate 8 Braddock, Bur-goyne, Cromwell, Jellicoe, Lawrence 9 Alexander, Kitchener 10 Cornwal-lis, Montgomery, Wellington 11 Marlborough, Mountbatten

Carthagenian: 8 Hannibal 13 Hamil-car Barca

French: 3 Ney 4 Foch 5 Murat 6 Gi-raud, Joffre, Petain, Roland 7 Nivelle 8 De Gaulle, Montcalm, Napoleon 9 Lafayette 10 Bernadotte

German: 5 Kluck 6 Moltke, Paulus, Rommel, Scheer 7 Blucher, Goering, Tirpitz 8 Bismarck, Goebbels, Guderian 9 Rundstedt 10 Falken-hayn, Hindenburg, Kesselring, Lu-dendorff, Schlieffen 17 Frederick the Great

Israeli: 5 Dayan

Japanese: 10 Tojo Hideki 15 Yama-moto Isoroku

Macedonian: 7 Ptolemy 8 Philip II 9 Alexander (the Great)

Norman: 7 William (the Conqueror)

Roman: 5 Sulla 6 Brutus, Pompey, Seneca, Trajan 7 Crassus, Hadrian, Lepidus 8 Gracchus, Octavian (Cae-sar Augustus), Tiberius 9 Vespasian 10 Flamininus, Mark Antony 11 Ga-ius Marius 12 Julius Caesar 15 Cas-sius Longinus, Scipio Africanus 18 Tarquinius Superbus

Russian: 6 Zhukov 7 Kutuzov, Voronov 8 Brusilov, Kerensky, Kornilov, Samsonov 9 Bagration 10 Timoshenko, Vasilevsky

generate 4 bear, coin, form, make, sire 5 beget, breed, cause, frame, spawn, yield 6 create, evolve, father, induce, invent 7 develop, fashion, produce 8 contrive, engender, fructify, occasion 9 construct, fabricate, fecun-date, fertilize, institute, originate, pro-create, propagate, reproduce 10 effec-tuate, impregnate 11 proliferate

generation 3 kin 4 clan, line, race 5 breed, house, issue, stock, tribe 6 family, growth, strain 7 genesis, line-age, progeny 8 breeding, creation 9 begetting, causation, evolution, forma-tion, offspring 10 production 11 de-velopment, engendering, origination, procreation, propagation 12 impregna-tion, reproduction 13 fertilization, proliferation

generic 6 common 7 general 8 sweep-ing 9 universal 10 collective 11 gen-eralized, unspecified 12 nonexclusive 13 comprehensive 14 nonrestrictive

generosity 6 bounty 7 charity 8 altru-ism, courtesy, kindness, largesse 9 abundance, nobleness 10 liberality 11 benevolence, hospitality, magnanimity

generous 5 ample, large, lofty, noble 6 humane, lavish 7 copious, liberal 8 abundant, effusive, obliging, princely, prodigal 9 bounteous, bountiful, hon-orable, plenteous, plentiful, plethoric, unselfish, unstinted **10** altruistic, beneficent, benevolent, bighearted, charitable, freehanded, free-giving, highminded, hospitable, munificent, openhanded, ungrudging, unstinting **11** considerate, extravagant, magnanimous, overflowing **12** humanitarian, largehearted, unrestricted **13** accommodating, philanthropic

genesis 4 rise, root **5** birth **6** origin **8** creation **9** begetting, beginning, inception **10** generation **11** engendering **12** commencement

geneticist
American: 5 Temin **6** Morgan, Muller

genetics
science of: 8 heredity
researcher: 6 Mendel

Genghis Khan
also: 11 Jenghiz Khan
name means: 14 universal ruler
position: 13 Mongol emperor
defeated: 6 Russia **10** Chin empire
occupied: 6 Peking

genial 3 gay **4** glad, kind, warm **5** civil, happy, jolly, merry, sunny **6** bright, cheery, hearty, jaunty, jocund, jovial, joyful, joyous, kindly, lively, social **7** affable, amiable, chipper, cordial, festive **8** cheerful, friendly, gracious, mirthful, pleasant, sociable **9** agreeable, congenial, convivial, courteous, expansive, sparkling, vivacious **10** neighborly **12** lighthearted **13** companionable

geniality 10 affability, cordiality **11** sociability **12** conviviality, friendliness **13** expansiveness

genius 3 ace, wit **4** bent, gift, mind, whiz **5** brain, flair, knack **6** expert, master, wisdom **7** faculty, insight, prodigy **8** aptitude, judgment, penchant, sagacity, wizardry **9** ingenuity, intuition, invention **10** mastermind, perception, proclivity, propensity **11** imagination, percipience **12** intelligence, predilection **13** understanding

Genius, The
author: 15 Theodore Dreiser

genius loci 16 guardian of a place

genre 4 kind, sort, type **5** breed, class, genus, group, order, style **6** school **7** fashion, species, variety **8** category, division **11** description **14** classification

genteel 4 tony **5** civil, elite, ritzy, swank, swell **6** modish, poised, polite, urbane **7** courtly, elegant, high-hat, refined, stylish **8** cultured, decorous, ladylike, mannerly, polished, wellbred **9** courteous, high-class, hightoned, patrician **10** cultivated, wellspoken **11** fashionable, gentlemanly, highfalutin, over-refined, pretentious **12** aristocratic, silk-stocking, thoroughbred

gentian 8 Gentiana

varieties: 5 blind, green, horse **6** alpine, bottle, closed, Sierra, yellow **7** crested, fringed, prairie, spurred **8** Catesby's, soapwort, stemless **9** Mendocino **10** pine barren

gentil 4 kind **5** noble **6** gentle

gentile
Yiddish: 3 goy
man: 7 shegetz
woman: 6 shiksa

gentility 6 polish **7** decorum, suavity **8** breeding, chivalry, civility, courtesy, urbanity **9** gallantry, propriety, punctilio **10** refinement **11** cultivation, savoir-faire **12** mannerliness

gentle 3 low **4** calm, easy, kind, meek, mild, soft, tame **5** balmy, bland, light, quiet **6** benign, broken, docile, kindly, placid, serene, slight, smooth, tender **7** lenient, pacific, subdued **8** harmless, merciful, moderate, peaceful, tolerant, tranquil **9** indulgent, temperate, tractable **10** manageable, thoughtful, untroubled **11** considerate, sympathetic **12** domesticated **13** compassionate, tenderhearted
French: 6 gentil

gentleman 3 don, guy, man, one **4** chap, gent **5** swell **6** fellow, person, squire **7** esquire, hidalgo **8** cavalier **9** caballero, chevalier, patrician **10** aristocrat, individual

Gentleman Jim
nickname of: 12 James Corbett

gentlemanly 6 polite **7** courtly, gallant, refined **8** cultured, decorous, mannerly, polished, well-bred **9** courteous, dignified **10** cultivated

Gentleman's Agreement
director: 9 Elia Kazan
based on novel by: 12 Laura Z Hobson
cast: 10 Anne Revere **11** Celeste Holm, Gregory Peck **12** John Garfield **14** Dorothy McGuire
Oscar for: 7 picture **17** supporting actress (Holm)

Gentlemen Prefer Blondes
author: 9 Anita Loos

gentleness 8 calmness, docility, mildness, serenity, tameness **10** compassion, tenderness **12** mercifulness, peacefulness, tractability

gentle wind 4 waft **6** breath, breeze, zephyr

gently 6 easily, kindly, meekly, mildly, softly, tamely **7** amiably, lightly **8** benignly, placidly, smoothly, tenderly **9** gradually **10** delicately, moderately, pleasantly, soothingly **15** compassionately, sympathetically

gentry 5 elite **7** society **8** nobility **10** blue bloods, gentlefolk **11** aristocracy, aristocrats

genuflect 4 bend **6** kowtow

genuine 4 open, pure, real, true **5** frank, naive, plain, solid **6** actual, candid, honest, proven, simple **7** artless, earnest, natural, sincere **8** bona fide, sterling, true-blue **9** authentic, guileless, heartfelt, ingenuous, simonpure, unalloyed, veritable **10** legitimate, unaffected **13** unadulterated **15** straightforward, unsophisticated

genuineness 7 honesty **9** frankness, sincerity **10** candidness, simplicity **11** artlessness **13** guilelessness **14** unaffectedness **19** straightforwardness

genus 4 kind, sort, type **5** class, group **7** variety **8** category, division **14** classification

geologist
British: 4 Hall
German: 6 Werner
Scottish: 6 Hutton

geoponics 7 tillage **8** agronomy **9** husbandry **10** agronomics **11** agriculture, cultivation

George Burns and Gracie Allen Show, The
character: 9 Mr Beasley (Mailman) **11** Harry Morton **13** Blanche Morton
theme song: 8 Love Nest

Georgetown
capital of: 6 Guyana

Georgia (former Soviet Union)
capital/largest city: 7 Tbilisi
others: 6 Batumi **7** Kutaisi, Rustavi, Sukhumi
division: 7 Ossetia **8** Abkhazia, Adzharia
head of state: 9 president
government: 8 republic
monetary unit: 5 ruble
mountain: 8 Caucasus
river: 4 Kura **5** Rioni
sea: 5 Black
people: 5 Azeri **7** Russian **8** Armenian, Georgian, Ossetian **9** Abkhazian
language: 8 Georgian
religion: 14 Georgian Church **15** Russian Orthodox

Georgia (US)
abbreviation: 2 GA
nickname: 5 Peach **7** Cracker **21** Empire State of the South
capital/largest city: 7 Atlanta
others: 4 Rome **5** Jesup, Macon **6** Albany, Athens, Dalton, Plains, Sparta **7** Augusta, Conyers, Cordele, Decatur, Griffen, Vidalia **8** Columbus, LaGrange, Marietta, Moultrie, Savannah, Valdosta, Waycross **9** Brunswick **11** College Park, Gainesville, Thomasville **13** Andersonville
college: 4 Tift **5** Clark, Emory, Paine **6** Mercer **7** Atlanta, Spelman **8** Wesleyan **9** Morehouse **10** Agnes Scott **11** Georgia Tech
explorer: 15 James Oglethorpe
feature: 16 Little White House
amusement park: 19 Six Flags

Over Georgia
national cemetery: 13 Anderson-ville
national monument: 8 Ocmulgee **11** Fort Pulaski **13** Fort Frederica
tribe: 5 Creek, Guale, Yuchi **6** Chiaha, Oconee, Uchean **7** Yamasee **8** Hitchiti
people: 6 Ty Cobb **7** cracker **10** Bobby Jones **11** Juliette Low **15** Erskine Caldwell **16** Margaret Mitchell **18** Joel Chandler Harris
island: 3 Sea **6** Jekyll, Sapelo **7** Ossabaw **10** Cumberland
lake: 6 Lanier, Martin **7** Harding, Nottely **8** Bankhead, Hartwell, Sinclair
land rank: 11 twenty-first
mountain: 5 Stone **7** Lookout **8** Kennesaw **9** Blue Ridge **11** Alleghenies **13** High Point Peak
  highest point: 17 Brasstown Bald Peak
physical feature:
  sea: 8 Atlantic
  springs: 4 Warm
  swamp: 10 Okefenokee
president: 11 Jimmy Carter
river: 3 Pea **5** Flint **6** Etowah, Oconee, Pigeon **7** Conecuh, Satilla, St Mary's, Tugaloo **8** Altamaha, Ocmulgee, Ogeechee, Savannah, Suwannee **9** Chattooga **13** Chattahoochie
state admission: 6 fourth
state bird: 13 brown thrasher
state fish: 14 largemouth bass
state flower: 12 Cherokee rose
state motto: 6 Wisdom **20** Justice and Moderation
state song: 7 Georgia
state tree: 7 live oak
Georgia Peach
  nickname of: 6 Ty Cobb
Georgics, The
  author: 6 Vergil, Virgil
  called: 17 agricultural poems
gephyrophobia
  fear of: 7 bridges
Geraint
  character in: 16 Arthurian romance
  wife: 4 Enid
geranium 11 Pelargonium
  varieties: 3 ivy **4** fish, lime, mint, pine, rock, rose, show, wild **5** apple, fancy, house, lemon, regal, zonal **6** almond, alpine, cactus, jungle, nutmeg, orange **7** apricot, bedding, coconut, feather, hanging, knotted, polecat **8** crowfoot, fern-leaf, horsehoe **9** beefsteak, oak-leaved **10** California, gooseberry, peppermint, strawberry, sweetheart, village-oak **11** grape-leaved, herb-scented, maple-leaved, rose-scented **12** silver-leaved, southernwood, sweet-scented **13** black-flowered, pansy-flowered, pheasant's-foot **14** Lady Washington, little-leaf rose **15** mint-scented rose

16 Martha Washington **17** English finger-bowl
Gerber, Franceska Mitzi
  real name of: 11 Mitzi Gaynor
Gerd, Gerda
  origin: 12 Scandinavian
  husband: 4 Frey **5** Freyr
Gere, Richard
  roles: 5 Yanks **7** Chicago **9** The Jackal **10** Breathless, Cotton Club, Unfaithful **11** Pretty Woman **12** Days of Heaven, Runaway Bride **14** American Gigolo **19** Looking for Mr Goodbar **22** An Officer and a Gentleman
  former wife: 13 Cindy Crawford
  cause: 5 Tibet
germ 3 bud, bug, egg **4** ovum, root, seed **5** ovule, spark, spore, virus **6** embryo, origin, source, sprout **7** microbe, nucleus, seed bud **8** bacillus, offshoot, rudiment **9** bacterium, beginning **12** fountainhead **13** microorganism
German 3 Hun **4** balt, Goth **5** boche, heine, jerry, kraut, Saxon **6** Teuton **7** tedesco **8** Prussian, Teutonic **9** deutscher
  article: 3 das, dem, den, der, des, die, ein **4** eine, eins
  empire: 5 reich
  pronoun: 3 ich, mir, sie, uns
  man: 4 herr
  storm and stress: 13 sturm und drang
  thank you: 5 danke **10** danke schon
  toast: 6 prosit **10** gesundheit
  woman: 4 frau **8** fraulein
German-Dutch
  language family: 12 Indo-European
  branch: 8 Germanic
  group: 15 Western Germanic
  language: 9 Low German **10** High German
germane 3 apt, fit **6** native, proper **7** apropos, fitting, related **8** material, relative, relevant, suitable **9** connected, intrinsic, pertinent **10** applicable **11** appropriate **12** appertaining
germaneness 9 relevance **10** pertinence **13** applicability **15** appropriateness
Germanic
  language family: 12 Indo-European
  group: 6 Gothic **15** Western Germanic
Germanic Mythology
  chief of gods: 5 Wotan
    corresponds to Scandinavian: 4 Odin
  dwarf: 15 Rumpelstiltskin
  dwarves: 8 Niblungs **9** Nibelungs
  emperor: 15 Dietrich von Bern
  epic: 14 Nibelungenlied
  goddess of clouds/sky/marriage: 3 Fri **5** Frigg, Frija **6** Frigga
  goddess of death/fertility: 7 Berchta, Perchta

goddess of love/ beauty/fecundity: 5 Freya
goddess of moon/ witch: 5 Holle
god of thunder: 5 Donar
god of winter sports: 4 Ullr **5** Uller
hero: 6 Sigurd **9** Siegfried
heroine: 6 Gudrun, Kudrun **7** Guthrun **8** Brunhild **9** Kriemhild
king: 7 Siggeir
king of dwarves: 8 Alberich
knight of the holy grail: 9 Lohengrin
magic cloak: 9 Tarnkappe
maidens: 9 Valkyries
nature spirit: 7 Eriking
nymph: 7 Lorelei, Lurelei
water spirit: 3 Nix
German is spoken here
  German: 25 hier wird Deutsch gesprochen
German literary movement (18th cent) 13 sturm und drang
Germany
  capital: 6 Berlin
  government leader: 10 chancellor, Helmut Kohl
  monetary unit: 12 Deutsche mark
  people: 3 Hun **4** Slav, Sorb, Wend **5** Saxon
    artist: 4 Marc **5** Durer **7** Barlach, Cranach, Gropius, Holbein **9** Grunewald **14** Mies van der Rohe
    author: 4 Mann, Marx **5** Grass **6** Brecht, Elsner, Goethe **7** Johnson, Lessing **8** Hochhuth
    composer: 4 Bach **5** Weill **6** Brahms, Handel, Wagner **7** Strauss **8** Schumann **9** Beethoven, Hindemith **11** Mendelssohn
    conductor: 5 Henze **6** Walter **9** Klemperer **11** Furtwangler, Stockhausen
    historical leader: 6 Hitler, Kaiser **8** Bismarck **10** Barbarossa
    Prussian noble: 6 Junker
    religious leader: 6 Luther
  language: 6 German **10** High German **11** Hochdeutsch
  religion: 8 Lutheran **10** Protestant **13** Roman Catholic **17** Evangelical Church
  food:
    bread: 12 pumpernickel
    dish: 9 lebkuchen
    dumpling: 6 knodel
    frankfurter: 15 wiener wurstchen
    fruit bread: 7 stollen
    ham: 11 Westphalian
    potato salad: 14 kartoffelsalat
    pot roast: 11 sauerbraten
    sausage: 5 wurst **9** blutwurst, bratwurst **10** brockwurst, knackwurst, leberwurst
    sole: 8 seezunge
Germany, East
  capital/largest city: 10 East Berlin
  others: 4 Jena **5** Halle, Waren **6** Erfurt, Weimar **7** Cottbus, Dresden, Leipzig, Meissen, Potsdam, Rostock,

Schwedt, Wannsee, Zwickau **9** Frankfurt, Magdeburg **10** Angermunde, Warnemunde, Wittenberg **11** Neustrelitz **13** Karl-Marx-Stadt (Chemnitz)

school: 8 Humboldt

division: 6 Saxony **9** Thuringia **11** Brandenburg, Mecklenburg **12** Saxony-Anhalt

government: 11 Volkskammer (Peoples' Chamber)

monetary unit: 4 mark **7** Ostmark, pfennig

lake: 6 Muritz

mountain: 3 Ore **4** Harz **10** Erzgebirge

highest point: 11 Fichtelberg

river: 4 Elbe, Oder **5** Havel, Saale, Spree **6** Neisse, Warnow

sea: 6 Baltic

physical feature:
  forest: 10 Thuringian
  place: 10 Berlin Wall **17** Checkpoint Charlie
  castle: 9 Sans Souci
  church: 8 St Thomas **12** Thomaskirche
  city center: 13 Karl Marx Platz **14** Alexanderplatz, Neubrandenberg
  comic opera: 12 Komische Oper
  gate: 11 Brandenburg
  museum: 7 Zwinger **8** Pergamon **10** Goethe Haus
  opera house: 18 Deutsche Staatsoper

feature:
  china: 7 Dresden
  fair: 7 Leipzig
  theater company: 16 Berliner Ensemble

Germany, West
capital: 4 Bonn
largest city: 10 West Berlin
others: 4 Kiel **5** Essen, Mainz, Trier **6** Aachen, Bochum, Bremen, Kassel, Lubeck, Minden, Munden, Munich **7** Cologne, Hamburg, Hanover, Krefeld, Munster **8** Augsburg, Biberach, Dortmund, Duisberg, Duisburg, Freiburg, Mannheim, Solingen **9** Darmstadt, Karlsruhe, Nuremberg, Oldenburg, Stuttgart, Wiesbaden, Wuppertal **10** Dusseldorf, Heidelberg, Steingaden **11** Saarbrucken **12** Oberammergau **13** Gelsenkirchen **15** Frankfurt am Main **16** Mulheim an der Ruhr

school: 4 Bonn **7** Hamburg **10** Heidelberg **16** Ludwig-Maximilian

division: 4 Saar **5** Baden, Hesse **6** Bremen **7** Bavaria **9** Rhineland **10** Palatinate, Westphalia **11** Lower Saxony, Wurttemberg **17** Schleswig-Holstein

head of government: 10 chancellor

monetary unit: 4 mark **7** pfennig **12** Deutsche mark

island: 11 East Frisian **12** North Frisian

lake: 9 Constance **11** Inner Alster, Outer Alster

mountain: 4 Harz **8** Feldberg **11** Black Forest **12** Bavarian Alps

highest point: 9 Zugspitze

river: 3 Ems **4** Elbe, Main, Nahe, Ruhr, Saar, Wese **5** Donau, Rhine, Weser **6** Danube, Neckar **7** Moselle, Pegnitz

sea: 5 North **6** Baltic

physical feature:
  canal: 4 Kiel **10** Mittelland
  forest: 5 Black **7** Bohemia **9** Teu Toburg
  place: 17 Checkpoint Charlie
  botanical garden: 18 Pflantzen und Blumen
  boulevard: 14 Kurfurstendamm
  church: 12 Frauenkirche (Cathedral of Our Lady) **13** Kaiser Wilhelm **16** Gadachtniskirche
  city center: 11 Marienplatz
  fortress: 9 Marksburg
  fountain: 14 Schoner Brunnen
  garden: 10 Englischer
  hall: 9 Beethoven
  museum: 8 Residenz **9** Durer Haus **12** Schatzkammer **14** Alte Pinakothek
  opera house: 18 Deutsches Opern Haus
  park/zoo: 18 Hagenbecks Tierpark
  residential district: 11 Hansa Vierte **12** Hanse Viertel
  resort (on Baltic): 10 Travemunde
  theater: 9 Cuvillies

feature:
  beer cellar: 11 bierkellern
  beer garden: 10 biergarten
  beer hall: 10 bierhallen
  beer room: 10 bierstuben
  cars: 3 BMW **4** Opel **7** Porsche **10** Volkswagen **12** Mercedes-Benz
  children: 6 kinder
  city hall: 5 Romer **7** Rathaus
  festival: 11 Oktoberfest
  folk songs: 11 volkslieder
  kitchen: 5 kuche
  old city: 8 Altstadt
  pre-Lent carnival: 8 Fasching
  secondary school: 9 gymnasium
  states: 6 lander
  wine street: 11 Weinstrasse

germicide 11 bactericide **12** disinfectant

Germinal
  author: 9 Emile Zola

germinate 3 bud **4** blow, open **5** bloom, shoot **6** flower, push up, sprout **7** blossom, burgeon, develop **8** generate, spring up, vegetate

germination 9 sprouting **11** propagation

Gershom
  means: 13 stranger there
  father: 5 Moses
  mother: 8 Zipporah
  brother: 12 Eliezar

Gershwin, George
  born: 10 Brooklyn NY
  partner/lyricist: 11 Ira Gershwin
  composer of: 9 Funny Face **11** Of Thee I Sing **12** Porgy and Bess **13** Cuban Overture **14** Rhapsody in Blue **15** Strike Up the Band **17** An American in Paris

Gertrude
  character in: 6 Hamlet (mother)
  author: 11 Shakespeare
  husband: 8 Claudius
  widow of: 6 Hamlet

Gervin, George
  nickname: 6 Iceman
  sport: 10 basketball
  team: 15 San Antonio Spurs

Gesta Romanorum
  author: 7 unknown

gestation 9 evolution, pregnancy **10** epigenesis, generation, incubation, maturation **11** development, propagation

gesticulate 3 nod **4** wink **5** nudge, shrug **6** beckon, motion, signal **8** indicate **9** pantomime

gesture 3 nod **4** sign, wave, wink **5** nudge, shrug, touch **6** beckon, motion, signal **8** courtesy, dumb show, flourish, high sign **9** formality, pantomime **13** demonstration

get 3 bag, fix, net, wax, win **4** beat, coax, earn, gain, grab, grip, grow, have, hear, move, reap, sway, take, turn **5** annoy, catch, fetch, glean, grasp, learn, reach, seize, sense, upset **6** arrive, attain, baffle, become, collar, come by, come to, enlist, entrap, fathom, follow, induce, obtain, pick up, pocket, prompt, puzzle, secure, snatch, suborn, take in, turn to **7** achieve, acquire, capture, confuse, contact, dispose, ensnare, go after, incline, inherit, mystify, perplex, prepare, procure, realize, receive, wheedle, win over **8** bewilder, confound, contract, irritate, perceive, persuade **9** influence, transport **10** comprehend, disconcert, predispose, understand

get a kick out of 4 like **5** eat up, enjoy, fancy, savor **6** relish **10** appreciate

getaway 6 escape, exodus, flight **10** decampment

get done 2 do **6** finish **8** complete **10** accomplish

get even 6 avenge **7** counter, hit back, pay back, revenge **9** retaliate

Gethsemane 6 garden

get into 3 don **5** enter, put on

get in touch with 5 reach **7** contact

get lost 4 scat, shoo **5** be off, leave, scram **6** beat it, begone, depart, go away **7** vamoose

get one's dander up 4 gall, rile **5**

anger **6** enrage, madden, nettle, ruffle **7** incense, inflame, outrage **9** infuriate

get out of bed 4 rise **5** arise **12** rise and shine

get rid of 4 drop, dump, junk, shed **5** ditch, scrap **6** banish, cut out, delete, remove, unload **7** abolish, discard, weed out **8** jettison, stamp out, throw out **9** eliminate, eradicate **10** annihilate **11** exterminate

Get Smart
  character: **5** Hymie (CONTROL robot) **7** Agent 99, Carlson, Starker **8** Larrabee, The Chief (Thaddeus) **12** Maxwell Smart (Agent 86) **15** Conrad Siegfried
  cast: **8** Don Adams **9** King Moody **10** Stacy Keach **11** Dave Ketchum, Dick Gautier, Edward Platt **12** Bernie Kopell **13** Barbara Feldon **14** Robert Karvelas
  Max worked for: **7** CONTROL
  foe: **4** KAOS

get the better of 4 foil, rout **5** crush, quell **6** baffle, defeat, thwart **7** conquer **8** confound, overcome **9** frustrate, overthrow

get the upper hand of 5 quell **6** master **7** conquer **8** dominate, overcome, surmount

get the worst of 4 fail, fall, lose

Getting Even
  author: **10** Woody Allen

get to 5 reach **8** approach

get-together 2 do **3** bee **4** meet **5** agree, party, visit **6** affair, gather, hobnob **7** meeting **8** assemble, assembly **9** gathering

getup 3 rig **6** attire, outfit **7** costume **8** disguise, ensemble

get up 4 find, rise **5** arise, rouse, stand **8** assemble

get used to 5 adapt, inure **6** adjust **8** accustom **9** acclimate, habituate

gewgaws 7 baubles, doodads, trifles **8** trinkets **9** bric-a-brac, gimcracks, kickshaws, ornaments **11** knickknacks

Ghana
  other name: **9** Gold Coast
  capital/largest city: **5** Accra, Akkra
  others: **3** Oda **4** Axim, Fian, Keta, Tala, Tema **5** Bawku, Enchi, Lawra, Legon, Sampa, Yapei **6** Dunkwa, Karaga, Kpandu, Kumasi, Nsawam, Obuasi, Swedru, Tamale, Tarkwa, Wasipe **7** Antubia, Damongo, Mampong, Prestea, Sekondi, Sunyani, Winneba **8** Akosombo, Kintampo, Takoradi **9** Cape Coast **15** Sekondi-Takoradi
  school: **6** Kumasi **9** Cape Coast
  monetary unit: **4** cedi **5** ackey
  lake: **5** Volta **8** Bosumtwi
  mountain: **12** Akwapim Hills
  highest point: **8** Afadjato
  river: **3** Oti, Pra **4** Daka, Tano **5** Afram, Volta **7** Ankobra, Kulpawn

10 Black Volta, White Volta
  sea: **8** Atlantic
  physical feature:
    gulf: **6** Guinea
  people: **2** Ga **3** Ewe **4** Akan, Akim, Akra, Aksa **5** Ahafo, Brong, Inkra **7** Akwapim, Ashanti, Dagomba **8** Mamprusi **9** Mole-Dagbani
  language: **2** Ga **3** Ewe, Gur, Kwa, Twi **5** Fanti, Hausa **7** Dagomba, English
  religion: **5** Islam **7** animism **13** Roman Catholic
  feature:
    castle: **14** Christiansborg
    dam: **8** Akosombo
    national dress: **5** kente
    UN leader: **9** Kofi Annan

ghastly 3 wan **4** grim, ugly **5** ashen, pasty, weird **6** dismal, glassy, grisly, horrid, odious, pallid **7** fearful, ghostly, haggard, hideous, uncanny **8** blanched, dreadful, gruesome, horrible, shocking, spectral, terrible **9** appalling, colorless, deathlike, frightful, ghostlike, loathsome, repellent, repulsive, revolting **10** cadaverous, corpselike, forbidding, horrendous, lackluster, terrifying

Ghiberti, Lorenzo
  born: **5** Italy **8** Florence
  artwork: **9** St Matthew, St Stephen **15** Gates of Paradise (baptistry doors) **16** St John the Baptist **19** The Sacrifice of Isaac

ghost 4 hint **5** demon, shade, spook, trace **6** goblin, shadow, sprite, wraith **7** banshee, chimera, phantom, specter **8** phantasm **9** hobgoblin, phantasma, semblance **10** apparition, suggestion **12** Doppelganger **13** manifestation **15** materialization

Ghost and Mrs Muir, The
  character: **11** Candice Muir, Martha Grant **12** Jonathan Muir **13** Claymore Gregg **14** Mrs Carolyn Muir **18** Captain Daniel Gregg
  TV cast: **8** Reta Shaw **9** Hope Lange **13** Edward Mulhare **14** Harlen Carraher, Kellie Flanagan **19** Charles Nelson Reilly
  setting: **11** Gull Cottage
  director: **17** Joseph L Mankiewicz
  movie cast: **8** Edna Best **11** Gene Tierney, Rex Harrison **13** George Sanders

Ghostbusters
  director: **11** Ivan Reitman
  screenplay: **10** Dan Aykroyd **11** Harold Ramis
  cast: **10** Bill Murray, Dan Aykroyd **11** Harold Ramis **15** Sigourney Weaver

ghostly 4 pale **5** eerie, weird **6** spooky, unreal **7** ghastly, phantom, shadowy, uncanny **8** illusive, spectral **9** unearthly **10** phantasmal, wraithlike **11** phantomlike **12** supernatural

ghostly double
  German: **12** Doppelganger

Ghosts
  author: **11** Henrik Ibsen
  character: **7** Manders **12** Oswald Alving **14** Jacob Engstrand, Mrs Helen Alving **15** Regina Engstrand

ghoulish 5 eerie, scary, weird **7** demonic, hellish, macabre, ogreish, satanic **8** diabolic, fiendish, gruesome, infernal, sinister **9** monstrous **10** horrifying, zombielike **11** hair-raising, necrophilic

Giacometti, Alberto
  born: **11** Switzerland **12** Stampa-Tessin
  artwork: **3** Dog **7** The Cage **8** Caroline **10** City Square **11** Head of Diego, Man Pointing **14** Reclining Woman **17** The Palace at Four Am **19** Hands Holding the Void

Gianni Schicchi
  opera by: **7** Puccini
  character: **11** Buoso Donati

giant 3 big **4** huge **5** titan **7** Goliath, spanker, thumper, whopper **8** behemoth, colossus, strapper **9** Gargantua **14** Brobdingnagian

Giant
  director: **13** George Stevens
  author: **10** Edna Ferber
  cast: **9** James Dean **10** Chill Wills, Rock Hudson **11** Jane Withers **12** Carroll Baker **15** Elizabeth Taylor
  setting: **5** Texas
  Oscar for: **8** director

Giant see **8** Gigantes

giant people 6 Anakim

Giants in the Earth
  author: **9** O E Rolvaag
  character: **3** Ole **5** Beret **8** Per Hanea **9** Anna Marie **12** Hans Kristian **15** Peder Victorious

gibber 3 gab **4** blab **5** prate **6** babble, gabble, jabber **7** blabber, blather, chatter, prattle **8** chitchat

gibberish 4 blab, bosh **6** babble, drivel, gabble **7** blather, twaddle **8** nonsense **10** balderdash, double-talk, flapdoodle, hocus-pocus, mumbo-jumbo **12** gobbledegook

Gibbon, Edward
  author of: **33** The (History of the) Decline and Fall of the Roman Empire

gibbous 6 convex, curved, humped **7** bulging, rounded, swollen **8** swelling **10** humpbacked, protuberant

Gibbs family
  characters in: **7** Our Town
  member: **6** George **7** Rebecca
  author: **6** Wilder

gibe, jibe 3 rag **4** jeer, mock, quip, razz, twit **5** chaff, flout, knock, toast, scoff, sneer, taunt **6** deride, needle, rail at **7** mockery, poke fun, sarcasm

8 brickbat, derision, ridicule, taunting **9** criticism, wisecrack

Gibraltar
other name: 11 rock of Tarik **13** Djebel al-Tarik **15** rock of Gibraltar
largest city: 9 Gibraltar
government: 18 British crown colony
head of government: 15 governor general
mountain: 6 Misery
sea: 13 Mediterranean
physical feature:
   bay: 5 Ceuta, Rosia, Sandy **6** Catlan **9** Algeciras
   cliffs: 17 Pillars of Hercules
people: 6 Jewish **7** British, Maltese, Spanish **8** Italians **10** Portuguese
language: 7 English, Spanish
feature: 12 King's Bastion
   gardens: 7 Alameda **11** Barbary apes

Gibson, Mel
roles: 6 Mad Max **8** Maverick **9** Gallipoli, The Bounty **10** Braveheart, The Patriot **12** Lethal Weapon **14** The Road Warrior, We Were Soldiers **26** The Year of Living Dangerously
director: 10 Braveheart (Oscar) **21** The Passion of the Christ

Giddens, Regina
character in: 14 The Little Foxes
author: 7 Hellman

giddy 5 dizzy, faint, silly **6** fickle, fitful **7** awesome, erratic, flighty, muddled, reeling **8** careless, dizzying, fainting, fanciful, reckless, swimming, unsteady, volatile, whirling **9** befuddled, frivolous, impulsive, mercurial, whimsical **10** capricious, changeable, inconstant **11** hare-brained, harum-scarum, lightheaded, thoughtless, vacillating, vertiginous **12** inconsistent, overpowering **13** irresponsible, rattlebrained

Gide, Andre
author of: 13 The Immoralist **15** Strait Is the Gate **17** The Counterfeiters **18** Lafcadio's Adventure (The Vatican Swindle) **19** The Pastoral Symphony

Gideon 11 Hebrew judge
father: 5 Joash, Ophra
son: 9 Abimelech
also called: 9 Jerubbaal

Gidget
character: 5 Larue **10** Anne Cooper, John Cooper **16** Francine (Gidget) Lawrence **21** Professor Russ Lawrence
cast: 9 Don Porter **10** Peter Deuel, Sally Field **11** Betty Conner **13** Lynette Winter
film role: 9 Sandra Dee

Gielgud, Sir John
born: 6 London **7** England
roles: 6 Arthur, Becket, Hamlet **7** Macbeth **9** Saint Joan **26** The Barretts of Wimpole Street **27** The Importance of Being Earnest

gift 3 aid, dot, fee, sop, tip **4** alms, bent, boon, dole, help, turn **5** award, bonus, bribe, craft, dower, dowry, favor, flair, forte, graft, grant, knack, power, prize, skill **6** genius, legacy, talent, virtue **7** aptness, bequest, faculty, handout, largess, premium, present, quality, tribute **8** aptitude, capacity, donation, facility, gratuity, offering, property **9** attribute, endowment, expertise, ingenuity **10** adroitness, capability, competency **11** benefaction, proficiency **12** contribution **13** consideration, qualification

gifted 4 able, deft **5** adept, crack, handy, quick, slick **6** adroit, bright, clever, expert, facile, master, wizard **7** capable, skilled **8** finished, masterly, polished, superior, talented **9** brilliant, ingenious, inventive, practiced, qualified **10** proficient **11** crackerjack, experienced, resourceful **12** accomplished

Gift From the Sea, The
author: 19 Anne Morrow Lindbergh

gig 3 job **4** trap **5** stint **6** chaise **7** dogcart **8** carriage, curricle **10** engagement

Gigantes
single member: 5 giant
father: 6 Uranus
mother: 4 Gaea
heads of: 3 men
bodies of: 8 serpents
attacked: 4 gods

gigantic 4 huge, vast **5** bulky, jumbo **6** mighty **7** hulking, immense, lumpish, mammoth, massive, titanic **8** colossal, enormous, lubberly, towering, unwieldy **9** herculean, monstrous, ponderous, strapping **10** gargantuan, prodigious, stupendous, tremendous, voluminous **11** elephantine

giggle 6 cackle, hee-hee, simper, tee-hee, titter **7** chuckle, snicker, snigger, twitter

Gigi
director: 16 Vincente Minnelli
based on story by: 7 Colette
cast: 8 Eva Gabor **11** Leslie Caron **12** Louis Jourdan **15** Hermione Gingold, Jacques Bergerac **16** Maurice Chevalier
score: 14 Lerner and Loewe
Oscar for: 7 picture **8** director
song: 4 Gigi **15** I Remember It Well **25** Thank Heaven for Little Girls **29** The Night They Invented Champagne

Gilbert, Cass
architect of: 14 US Customs House (NYC) **17** Woolworth Building (NYC) **20** Supreme Court Building (Washington DC) **21** Minnesota State Capitol (St Paul) **22** George Washington Bridge

Gilbert, John
real name: 11 John Pringle
wife: 9 Ina Claire **11** Leatrice Joy **13** Virginia Bruce
born: 7 Logan UT
roles: 4 Love **12** The Big Parade **13** The Merry Widow **15** A Woman of Affairs **16** Flesh and the Devil

Gilbert, William
field: 7 physics
nationality: 7 British
father of: 11 electricity
named for him: 27 CGS unit of magnetomotive force

Gilbert, W S, and Sullivan, Arthur Seymour
composers of: 7 Ivanhoe **8** Iolanthe, Patience **9** Ruddigore, The Mikado **11** H M S Pinafore, Princess Ida, The Sorcerer, Trial by Jury **12** The Grand Duke **13** The Gondoliers, Utopia Limited **19** The Yeoman of the Guard **20** The Pirates of Penzance **24** Thespis or The Gods Grown Old
produced by: 10 D'Oyly Carte
devotees: 9 Savoyards

Gilbert Islands see **8** Kiribati

Gil Blas (of Santillane)
author: 11 Alain LeSage
character: 6 Scipio **11** Don Alphonso

Gilbreth, Frank B, Jr
author of: 17 Cheaper by the Dozen (with Ernestine Gilbreth Carey)

gild 4 bend **5** slant, twist **7** cover up, stretch, touch up **10** exaggerate

Gilded Age, The
authors: 9 Mark Twain **19** Charles Dudley Warner

gilded youth
French: 13 jeunesse doree

Gileadite password 10 Shibboleth

Giles Goat-Boy
author: 9 John Barth

Gilgal 5 wheel **6** circle

Gilgamesh
origin: 8 Sumerian
king of: 4 Uruk **5** Erech
servant: 6 Enkidu
event: 5 flood

gill
abbreviation: 2 gi

Gilligan's Island
character: 7 Skipper (Jonas Grumby) **8** Gilligan **9** Mrs Howell (Lovey), Professor (Roy Hinkley) **11** Ginger Grant **14** Mary Ann Summers **17** Thurston Howell III
cast: 9 Bob Denver, Dawn Wells, Jim Backus **10** Alan Hale Jr, Tina Louise **14** Natalie Schafer, Russell Johnson
ship: 6 Minnow

Gills, Solomon
character in: 12 Dombey and Son
author: 7 Dickens

Gilmore Girls
network: 2 WB

creator: 19 Amy Sherman-Palladino
cast: 8 Liza Weil (Paris Geller), Sean Gunn (Kirk Gleason) **10** Keiko Agena (Lane Kim) **11** Kelly Bishop (Emily Gilmore) **12** Alexis Bledel (Rory Gilmore), Lauren Graham (Lorelai Gilmore) **14** Edward Herrmann (Richard Gilmore), Jared Padalecki (Dean Forester), Scott Patterson (Luke Danes), Yanic Truesdale (Michel Gerard) **15** Melissa McCarthy (Sookie St. James), Milo Ventimiglia (Jess Mariano)
gimcrack 5 bijou, curio **6** bauble, gewgaw, trifle **7** trinket, whatnot **8** kickshaw, ornament **9** bagatelle, plaything **10** knickknack **11** contrivance, thingamabob, thingamajig
gimmick 4 plan, ploy, ruse, wile **5** angle, dodge, stunt **6** design, device, gadget, scheme **7** wrinkle **9** stratagem **10** subterfuge **11** contrivance
gin
origin: 11 Netherlands
ingredient: 4 sloe **6** grains **12** juniper berry
type: 6 Geneva **8** Plymouth **9** London dry
drink: 5 Allen **6** Gibson, gimlet **7** Belmont, Bennett, gin Fizz, swizzle **8** Pink Lady **9** Gin Rickey **10** Tom Collins **11** Alabama Fizz, gin and tonic **12** Grand Passion **14** Casino Cocktail
with anisette: 8 Snowball **11** Bachio Punch
with apricot brandy: 14 Boston Cocktail
with brandy: 15 Bermuda Highball
with Chartreuse: 5 Bijou **9** Green Lady
with cherry brandy: 14 Singapore Sling
with Cointreau: 7 Florida **9** White Lady **13** Sweet Patootie **14** Flying Dutchman
with creme de cacao: 9 Alexander
with creme de cassis: 8 Parisian
with creme de menthe: 6 Caruso, Virgin
with creme Yvette: 9 Union Jack
with Curacao: 8 Blue Moon, Napoleon **9** Blue Devil **14** Flying Dutchman
with Dubonnet: 3 BVD **8** Napoleon
with Grand Marnier: 7 Red Lion
with grapefruit juice: 8 Salty Dog
with kirsch, kirschwasser: 7 Florida **10** Lady Finger
with onions: 6 Gibson
with orange juice: 5 Abbey **13** Orange Blossom
with Pernod: 7 Dubarry
with rum: 3 BVD
with scotch: 12 Barbary Coast
with sherry: 11 Renaissance
with strawberries: 10 Bloodhound
with Swedish Punch: 5 Biffy
with vermouth: 5 Bijou, Bronx,

Tango **6** Caruso **7** Bermuda, Cabaret, Martini **10** Bloodhound
with vodka: 15 Russian Cocktail
ginger 3 pep, tan **5** brown, spice **6** energy
varieties: 3 red **4** wild **5** crape, crepe, shell, torch, white **6** canton, common, Kahili, orchid, spiral, yellow **9** butterfly **10** small shell, variegated
botanical name: 8 Zingiber **12** Z officinales
Sanskrit: 9 singabera
origin: 4 Asia **5** China, India **7** Jamaica
use: 6 tongue **7** vinegar **9** beef stock **11** baked dishes, gingerbread **12** chicken stock
gingerly 6 warily **7** charily, timidly **8** daintily **9** carefully, finically, guardedly, heedfully, mincingly, prudently **10** cautiously, delicately, discreetly, hesitantly, vigilantly, watchfully **11** squeamishly **12** fastidiously, suspiciously **13** circumspectly
gingham 5 cloth **6** cotton, fabric, striped **8** chambray **9** checkered
gin mill 3 bar **4** dive **6** saloon, tavern **9** honky-tonk, roadhouse
Ginnungagap
origin: 12 Scandinavian
void filled with: 4 mist
between: 9 Nifelheim **10** Muspelheim
Ginsberg, Allen
author of: 4 Howl **7** Kaddish **10** Planet News **11** Mind Breaths **16** The Fall of America **20** Reality and Sandwiches
Giordano, Umberto
born: 5 Italy **6** Foggia
composer of: 6 Fedora **8** Mala Vita **13** Andrea Chenier **14** Madame Sans-Gene
Giorgione da Castelfranco
born: 5 Italy **12** Castelfranco
artwork: 10 The Tempest **13** Ordeal of Moses, Sleeping Venus **17** Judgment of Solomon **19** The Concert Champetre (disputed) **20** The Three Philosophers **23** Adoration of the Shepherds
Giotto di Bondone
born: 5 Italy **8** (near) Florence
artwork attributed: 17 Ognissanti Madonna **31** Presentation of Christ in the Temple **32** St Francis Surrounded by his Brothers
Giovanelli
character in: 11 Daisy Miller
author: 5 James
Giovanni's Room
author: 12 James Baldwin
giraffe
constellation of: 14 Camelopardalis
kin: 5 okapi
other name: 10 camelopard
girandole 11 candelabrum, candlestick **12** candleholder

Girardon, Francois
born: 6 France, Troyes
artwork: 13 Bathing Nymphs **14** Galley of Apollo, Virgin of Troyes **16** Rape of Persephone **17** (tomb for) Cardinal Richelieu **23** Apollo Tended by the Nymphs
Giraudoux, Jean
author of: 5 Bella **6** Judith, Ondine, Racine **7** Electra **12** Amphitryon 38 **15** Tiger at the Gates **18** Madwoman of Chaillot **20** My Friend from Limousin
gird 3 pen, tie **4** belt, girt, loop, ring **5** brace, hem in, hitch, steel, strap, truss **6** circle, fasten, girdle, harden, secure, wall in **7** besiege, confine, enclose, fortify, hedge in, prepare, stiffen, sustain, tighten **8** blockade, buttress, encircle, lay siege, surround **9** encompass **10** strengthen **12** circumscribe
girder 4 beam **5** brace, truss **6** binder, rafter **7** support, tie-beam
girdle 3 hem **4** band, belt, ring, sash **5** girth, hedge, stays **6** bodice, circle, corset **7** baldric, circlet, contour **8** boundary, cincture, corselet **9** surcingle, waistband **10** cummerbund **12** waist cincher **17** foundation garment
girl 4 bird, cook, help, lass, maid, minx, miss **5** angel, chick, nymph, wench **6** damsel, kitten, lassie, maiden, pigeon, virgin **7** baggage, colleen, darling, fiancee, ingenue, nymphet **8** daughter, domestic, handmaid, lady love, mistress, scullion **9** affianced, betrothed, inamorata, lady's maid, soubrette **10** sweetheart **11** maidservant
French: 10 demoiselle, jeune fille
girl Friday 4 aide **6** helper **9** assistant, secretary **10** amanuensis **12** office worker **23** administrative assistant
girlfriend 6 steady **7** beloved, sweetie **8** best girl **10** one and only, sweetheart
Girl in a Swing
author: 12 Richard Adams
girlish 8 girl-like, maidenly, youthful **10** maidenlike
Girl of the Golden West, The
opera by: 7 Puccini
setting: 8 Gold Rush **10** California
character: 6 Minnie **7** Johnson, Sheriff
Girl Scouts
founded by: 11 Juliette Low
abbr: 5 GSUSA
rank: 7 brownie **10** tenderfoot
girt 4 belt, bind, gird, ring **5** bound, girth **6** belted, circle, girdle, ringed **7** circled, girdled **9** encircled
girth 5 cinch **9** perimeter **10** saddle band **13** circumference
Giselle
ballet by: 4 (Adolphe Charles) Adam

Gish, Lillian
   real name: 12 Lillian Gishi **15** Lillian de Guiche
   born: 13 Springfield OH
   roles: 8 La Boheme **10** Enoch Arden **11** Annie Laurie, Intolerance, Way Down East **12** Duel in the Sun **13** Scarlet Letter **14** Broken Blossoms **16** Portrait of Jennie **17** Orphans of the Storm, The Birth of a Nation

Gissing, George
   author of: 5 Demos **13** New Grub Street **14** The Nether World

gist 3 nut **4** core, crux, meat, pith **5** drift, force, heart, sense, tenor, theme **6** burden, center, effect, import, kernel, marrow, spirit **7** essence, purport **8** main idea **9** main point, substance **11** implication **12** significance

give 3 buy, pay, tip **4** bend, ease, emit, hire, lend, show, sink **5** admit, allot, allow, apply, award, bribe, deign, endow, grant, issue, leave, offer, relax, utter, voice, yield **6** accord, addict, afford, assign, attach, bestow, bounce, commit, confer, convey, devote, donate, enable, enrich, hand to, impart, loosen, notify, open on, permit, recede, relent, render, shrink, supply, tender, unbend, vest in **7** concede, consign, deliver, entrust, fork out, furnish, hand out, let know, present, proffer, provide, requite, retreat, slacken, announce, bequeath, collapse, dispense, exchange, fork over, hand over, lead on to, make over, move back, put forth, shell out **9** apportion, break down, dispose of, equip with, favor with, look out on, present to, pronounce, subscribe, surrender, vouchsafe **10** articulate, become soft, compensate, contribute, deliquesce, distribute, recompense, remunerate, resilience, supply with **11** communicate, flexibility, provide with, springiness

give aid to 4 help **6** assist, succor **7** help out **8** befriend **9** look after **10** minister to

give a leg up 3 aid **4** help, lift **5** boost, hoist, raise **6** assist **7** elevate

give and take 8 exchange **10** compromise **11** interchange, reciprocity

give a pep talk to 4 goad, prod, spur **5** press **6** exhort **9** encourage

give a reason for 7 clarify, clear up, explain, justify **9** elucidate **10** account for

give as security 4 pawn **6** pledge **7** deposit, pay down, put down

give away 6 bestow, betray, donate, reveal **7** hand out

give birth 4 bear **5** hatch **6** create, invent **7** deliver, develop **9** originate **10** bring forth

give confidence to 7 inspire **8** embolden, inspirit **9** encourage

give courage 5 brace **6** buck up **7** hearten **8** inspirit, motivate

give energy to 7 animate, enliven **8** activate, energize, vitalize **9** stimulate **10** invigorate

give enjoyment 5 amuse, charm **6** divert, please **7** beguile, delight **8** enthrall **9** entertain

give forth 4 emit, gush **5** exude, issue **7** send out **8** throw off, transmit **9** discharge

give full attention 7 pay heed **8** fasten on **11** concentrate

give in 5 defer, yield **6** accede, cave in, submit **7** succumb **9** surrender **10** capitulate **12** knuckle under

give in to 7 yield to **9** indulge in, partake of **16** abandon oneself to

give leave 3 let **5** allow **6** permit **8** sanction **9** authorize **14** give permission

give moral support to 3 aid **4** abet, back, help **6** assist, uphold **7** support, sustain **8** sanction **9** encourage

given 3 apt **4** wont **5** prone **6** likely, wonted **7** awarded, donated, granted, offered **8** accorded, bestowed **9** committed, conferred, entrusted, presented **10** accustomed, handed over, in the habit **11** contributed **13** furnished with, made a donation, presented with **17** made a contribution

give new life to 3 fan **4** fire **6** awaken, revive **8** revivify **10** rejuvenate **11** reincarnate

give oneself to 8 dedicate **10** buckle down, consecrate

give one's word 3 vow **5** swear **6** assure, pledge **7** certify, promise, warrant **9** guarantee

give one walking papers 3 axe, can **4** fire, oust, sack **5** let go **6** bounce, lay off **7** cashier, dismiss, release **8** get rid of **9** discharge, terminate **11** give the gate, send packing

give out 4 quit, tell, tire **6** assign, inform, reveal, run out **7** divulge, dole out, mete out **8** allocate, announce, disclose, dispense, proclaim **9** apportion, broadcast, parcel out **10** distribute, make public, portion out **11** disseminate

give over 4 cede **5** yield **9** surrender **10** relinquish

give permission 3 let **5** allow **6** accede, permit **7** approve **8** sanction **9** acquiesce, authorize, give leave

give rise to 4 sire **5** breed, cause **6** lead to **7** produce **8** engender, generate, occasion **9** call forth **10** bring about

give support to 3 aid **4** abet **5** serve **6** defend, prop up, second **7** bolster, comfort, sustain **8** buttress, champion **10** contribute, minister to, provide for, stick up for

give the go-ahead 4 okay **5** order **6** direct **7** appoint, charter, empower **8** contract **9** authorize **10** commission

give the lie to 5 belie **8** disprove **9** repudiate **10** contradict, controvert

give the raspberry 3 boo, pan **4** razz **6** deride, hoot at **8** ridicule **11** give the bird **17** give the Bronx cheer

give the right to 5 allow **6** permit **7** entitle, qualify **9** authorize

give the slip 4 duck **5** avoid, dodge, elude, evade

give up 4 cede, drop, lose, quit, skip **5** forgo, let go, waive, yield **6** eschew, resign **7** abandon, forfeit, forsake **8** abdicate, forswear, renounce **9** sacrifice, surrender **10** relinquish **11** discontinue

give up the ghost 3 die **6** expire, pass on, perish **7** decease **8** pass away **15** breathe one's last

give vent 4 free **5** let go **7** release **8** let loose, liberate **12** give free rein

give way 4 fall **6** buckle, cave in **7** crumple **8** collapse **10** break apart

giving birth 7 bearing **8** creating, creation, delivery, hatching **9** inventing, invention **10** childbirth, delivering **11** originating, origination, parturition

giving up 7 refusal **8** dropping, quitting, yielding **9** resigning **10** abandoning, abdicating, abdication, abstinence, continence, forbearing, forfeiting, forfeiture, self-denial **11** abandonment, forswearing, resignation **12** renunciation, surrendering **14** relinquishment

gizmo 4 tool **6** device, doodad, gadget **7** whatsis **9** apparatus, implement, invention, mechanism **10** instrument **11** contraption, contrivance, thingamabob, thingamajig

glacial 3 icy, raw **4** cold **5** chill, gelid, polar **6** arctic, biting, bitter, frigid, frosty, frozen, wintry **7** hostile **8** freezing, inimical, piercing **9** congealed **10** disdainful, unfriendly **12** antagonistic, bone-chilling, contemptuous

Glackens, William James
   born: 14 Philadelphia PA
   artwork: 9 Promenade **11** Chez Mouquin **15** Nude with an Apple **16** Washington Square (A Holiday in the Park) **17** Luxembourg Gardens

glad 5 happy **6** elated, joyful, joyous **7** elating, gleeful, pleased, tickled **8** blissful, cheerful, cheering, pleasing, rejoiced **9** contented, delighted, joygiving **10** delightful, entrancing, gratifying **11** exhilarated, tickled pink **12** exhilarating

gladden 5 cheer, elate **6** please **7** animate, cheer up, delight, enliven, gratify, hearten, rejoice **8** inspirit, pleasure **9** make happy **10** exhilarate

gladdened 5 happy **6** joyful, joyous **8** cheerful

glade 4 dell, glen, lawn, vale, wood **5** grove, marsh, vista **6** canada, hollow, valley **7** opening **8** clearing

Gladiator
director: **11** Ridley Scott
cast: **10** Oliver Reed (Proximo) **11** Derek Jacobi (Gracchus) **12** Russell Crowe (Maximus) **13** Connie Nielson (Lucilla), Djimon Hounsou (Juba), Richard Harris (Marcus Aurelius) **14** Joaquin Phoenix (Commodus)

gladness 3 joy **4** glee **5** bliss, cheer, mirth **7** delight, gaiety, jollity **8** pleasure **9** happiness **10** joyfulness **11** contentment **12** cheerfulness

glad rags 5 array **6** attire, finery **10** Sunday best

Gladsheim
origin: **12** Scandinavian
palace of: **4** Odin **5** Othin
location: **8** Valhalla

gladsome 3 gay **5** happy, merry **6** cheery, joyful, joyous **8** cheerful **12** lighthearted

glamor, glamour 5 charm, magic **6** allure **7** glitter, romance **8** illusion **9** adventure, challenge, magnetism **10** excitement **11** enchantment, fascination **14** attractiveness

glamorous, glamourous 8 alluring, charming, dazzling, exciting, magnetic **10** attractive, bewitching, enchanting **11** captivating, charismatic, fascinating

glance 4 kiss, peek, peep, scan, skim, slip **5** brush, graze, shave, touch **6** bounce, careen, squint **7** glimpse, rebound **8** ricochet **9** brief look, quick look, quick view
French: **6** apercu

glance through 4 scan, skim **6** browse, peruse **7** dip into **8** look over **9** check over

gland
part of: **15** endocrine system
type: **4** duct **8** ductless
kind: **3** oil **5** sweat **7** adrenal, thyroid **8** pancreas **9** pituitary **11** parathyroid
ductless gland secretes: **8** hormones

glare 4 glow **5** blaze, flame, flare, flash, gleam, glint, gloss, lower, scowl, sheen **6** dazzle, glower **7** flicker, glimmer, glisten, glitter, radiate, shimmer, sparkle, twinkle **8** radiance **9** angry look, black look, dirty look **10** brightness, harsh light, luminosity **12** resplendence

glaring 4 rank **5** gross, harsh, vivid **6** arrant, bright, strong **7** blatant, flaring, intense, obvious **8** blinding, dazzling, flagrant, piercing **9** audacious, brilliant, egregious **10** glittering, outrageous, shimmering **11** conspicuous,

penetrating, resplendent, unconcealed, undisguised **12** unmistakable

Glasgow, Ellen
author of: **10** Vein of Iron **12** Barren Ground **13** In This Our Life, Sheltered Life **18** They Stooped to Folly **20** The Romantic Comedians

glass 6 beaker, goblet **7** chalice, tumbler **10** tumblerful
type of: **4** fizz, sour **5** flute, tulip **6** jigger, sherry **7** balloon, collins, cordial, red wine, snifter **8** cocktail, highball **9** champagne, white wine **10** hollow-stem, pousse cafe **12** old-fashioned

glasshouse 7 nursery **8** hothouse **10** greenhouse **12** conservatory

glassiness 7 clarity **8** dullness, flatness **9** shininess **10** brilliance, luminosity **12** lifelessness, transparency

Glass Key, The
author: **15** Dashiell Hammett
character: **9** Shad O'Rory **10** Janet Henry, Opal Madvig, Paul Madvig **11** Ned Beaumont **12** Senator Henry **13** Bernie Despain

Glass Menagerie, The
director: **12** Irving Rapper
author: **17** Tennessee Williams
character: **5** Laura **6** Amanda **12** Tom Wingfield
cast: **9** Jane Wyman **11** Kirk Douglas **13** Arthur Kennedy **16** Gertrude Lawrence

glassware 5 agata **6** aurene **7** crystal, favrile, steuben, vitrics **8** amerina, stemware
worker: **7** glazier

glassy 4 dull **5** clear, shiny **6** glazed, smooth **8** lifeless **10** glittering **11** transparent

Glauber, Johann Rudolf
field: **9** chemistry
nationality: **6** German
prepared: **12** tartar emetic **13** sodium sulfate (Glauber's salt) **16** hydrochloric acid

Glaucus
god of: **3** sea
father: **5** Minos
ally of: **7** Trojans
loved by: **5** Circe **6** Scylla **10** Amphitrite

glaze 4 blur **5** gloss **6** enamel, finish **7** grow dim, varnish **8** film over **9** glass over

glazed 4 iced **5** filmy **6** coated, glassy, shined, smooth **7** glossed, sugared **8** enameled, lustrous, polished **9** burnished, varnished

Glazunoff, Alex K (Glazunov, Alexander Konstantinovich)
born: **6** Russia **12** St Petersburg
composer of: **10** Chopiniana, The Seasons **11** Stenka Razin **13** Hymn to Pushkin **15** Memorial Cantata

gleam 3 bit, jot, ray **4** beam, drop,

glow, hint, iota **5** blink, flare, flash, glare, glint, gloss, grain, sheen, shine, spark, speck, trace **6** luster, streak **7** flicker, glimmer, glimpse, glisten, glitter, inkling, shimmer, sparkle, tiny bit, twinkle **8** least bit, radiance **9** coruscate **10** brightness, brilliance, effulgence **11** coruscation, scintillate

gleaming 5 clear, shiny **6** bright, flashy, glossy **7** shining, radiant **8** dazzling, glinting, luminous, lustrous, polished, splendid **9** brilliant, burnished, sparkling **10** glistening

glean 4 cull **5** amass **6** gather, pick up **7** harvest **10** accumulate **13** piece together **14** scrape together

gleanings 8 analects, extracts **10** miscellany, selections **11** collectanea, miscellanea **15** commonplace book

Gleason, Jackie
real name: **18** Herbert John Gleason
nickname: **15** Mr Saturday Night
born: **10** Brooklyn NY
roles: **5** Gigot **6** The Toy **10** The Hustler **11** Life of Riley, The Poor Soul **12** Ralph Kramden **13** Joe the Bartender, The Honeymooners **17** Don't Drink the Water, Jackie Gleason Show, The Time of Your Life **18** Smokey and the Bandit **22** Requiem for a Heavyweight **24** Reggie Van Gleason the Third

glebe 3 sod **4** clod, land, plot, soil **5** earth, field **6** termon **8** kirktown **10** church land

glee 3 joy **5** mirth, verve **6** gaiety **7** delight, ecstasy, jollity, rapture **8** gladness, hilarity, laughter **9** joviality, merriment **10** exultation, jocularity, joyfulness, joyousness, liveliness **11** playfulness **12** cheerfulness, exhilaration, sportiveness **13** jollification, sprightliness

glee club 6 chorus **12** singing group **13** choral society

gleeful 3 gay **4** glad **5** happy, jolly, merry **6** elated, jocund, jovial, joyful, joyous, lively **7** festive **8** blissful, cheerful, exultant, mirthful **9** delighted **11** exhilarated **12** lighthearted

Gleipnir
origin: **12** Scandinavian
chain that bound: **6** Fenrir, Fenris

glen 4 dale, dell, vale **6** bottom, hollow

Glencaire Cycle
author: **12** Eugene O'Neill

Glengarry Glenn Ross
director: **10** James Foley
author: **10** David Mamet
cast: **8** Al Pacino (Ricky Roma), Ed Harris (Dave Moss) **9** Alan Arkin (George Aaronow) **10** Jack Lemmon (Shelley Levene) **11** Alec Baldwin (Blake), Kevin Spacey (John Williamson) **13** Jonathan Pryce (James Lingk)

glib 4 oily **5** gabby, quick, ready, suave

6 facile, fluent, smooth **7** devious, voluble **8** flippant, slippery, unctuous **9** insincere, talkative

glide 3 run **4** flow, roll, sail, skim, slip, soar **5** coast, drift, float, issue, skate, slide, steal **6** elapse, stream **7** proceed **8** glissade

glider 5 swing **7** aviator **9** sailplane **10** hydroplane

glimmer 3 bit, ray **4** beam, drop, glow, hint **5** blink, flare, flash, glare, gleam, grain, shine, speck, trace **7** flicker, glimpse, glisten, glitter, shimmer, sparkle, twinkle **9** coruscate, scintilla **10** flickering, intimation **11** scintillate

glimpse 3 see, spy **4** espy, peek, peep, spot **6** glance, peek at, peep at, squint **9** brief look, quick look, quick view **12** catch sight of, fleeting look
French: 6 apercu

Glinka, Mikhail Ivanovich
    born: 6 Russia **8** Smolensk
    composer of: 12 Ivan Sussanin, Karaminskaya **13** Jota Aragonesa **18** Russlan and Ludmilla

glint 4 gaze, look, peep **5** flash, gleam, sheen, shine, stare **6** glance **7** appear, glimmer, glimpse, glisten, glitter, shimmer, sparkle, twinkle **9** coruscate **11** scintillate

glissade 5 coast, glide, slide

glissando
    music: 7 sliding

glisten 4 glow **5** flash, gleam, glint, shine **7** flicker, glimmer, glister, glitter, radiate, shimmer, sparkle, twinkle **9** coruscate **11** scintillate

glitter 4 fire, glow, pomp, show **5** flare, flash, gleam, glint, sheen, shine **6** luster, thrill, tinsel **7** beaming, display, glamour, glimmer, glisten, radiate, sparkle, twinkle **8** grandeur, radiance, splendor **9** pageantry, showiness **10** brilliance, excitement, refulgence **11** electricity

glittering 6 bright **7** radiant, shining **8** luminous, lustrous **9** brilliant, sparkling **11** coruscating

gloaming 4 dusk **7** evening **8** twilight

gloat 4 bask, brag **5** exult, strut, vaunt **7** revel in, swagger, triumph **8** crow over **9** glory over

global 5 world **6** all-out **7** general **9** planetary, unbounded, universal, unlimited, worldwide **10** widespread **13** comprehensive, international **16** intercontinental

globe 3 orb **4** ball **5** Earth, world **6** planet, sphere **7** globule **8** spheroid, spherule **9** biosphere

globule 4 ball, bead, bleb, blob, drop **5** globe **6** bubble, pellet, sphere **7** blister, droplet **8** particle, spheroid

glogg

type: 5 punch
origin: 6 Sweden

gloom 3 woe **4** dark, dusk, murk **5** blues, dolor, grief, shade **6** misery, sorrow **7** despair, dimness, sadness, shadows **8** darkness, distress, doldrums **9** blackness, dejection, dinginess, duskiness, murkiness, obscurity **10** cloudiness, depression, gloominess, low spirits, melancholy, mopishness, moroseness, oppression **11** despondency, forlornness, unhappiness **12** hopelessness **13** cheerlessness **16** disconsolateness, heavy-heartedness

gloomy 3 dim, sad **4** dark, dour, down, dull, glum, grim, mopy, sour **5** dusky, moody, mopey, murky, shady **6** cloudy, dismal, dreary, morbid, morose, shaded, somber **7** doleful, forlorn, shadowy, sunless, unhappy **8** dejected, desolate, downcast, frowning, funereal, overcast **9** cheerless, depressed, heartsick, miserable, sorrowful, woebegone **10** chapfallen, despondent, dispirited, ill-humored, melancholy **11** comfortless, crestfallen, discouraged, downhearted, low-spirited, pessimistic **12** disconsolate, disheartened, heavy-hearted **13** in the doldrums **14** down in the dumps, down in the mouth

Gloria in Excelsis Deo 22 Glory in the highest to God

Gloriana
    character in: 15 The Faerie Queene
    author: 7 Spenser

Gloriana
    opera by: 7 Britten
    character: 10 Elizabeth I **11** Earl of Essex

glorification 7 worship **8** devotion **9** adoration, adulation **10** exaltation, veneration **13** magnification

glorify 4 laud **5** adore, deify, exalt, extol, honor **6** praise, revere **7** beatify, dignify, elevate, ennoble, idolize, worship **8** canonize, enshrine, sanctify, venerate **9** celebrate, glamorize **10** consecrate **11** apotheosize, immortalize, romanticize

glorious 4 fine **5** grand, great, noble, noted **6** august, divine, famous, superb **7** eminent, glowing, honored, notable, radiant, shining, stately, sublime, supreme **8** dazzling, gorgeous, imposing, lustrous, majestic, renowned, splendid **9** beautiful, brilliant, dignified, excellent, marvelous, sparkling, wonderful **10** celebrated, delightful, impressive, preeminent **11** illustrious, magnificent, resplendent **12** praiseworthy **13** distinguished

glory 4 fame, mark, name **5** boast, honor, revel, vaunt **6** esteem, homage, praise, renown, repute **7** dignity, majesty, worship **8** blessing, eminence, grandeur, nobility, prestige,

splendor **9** adoration, celebrity, gratitude, solemnity, sublimity **10** admiration, excellence, notability, veneration **11** benediction, distinction, preeminence, stateliness **12** magnificence, resplendence, thanksgiving **14** impressiveness **15** illustriousness

Glory in the highest to God
    Latin: 19 Gloria in Excelsis Deo

gloss 4 glow, mask, veil **5** cloak, color, glaze, gleam, japan, sheen, shine **6** enamel, excuse, luster, polish, veneer **7** cover up, lacquer, shimmer, varnish **8** annotate, disguise, mitigate, radiance **9** whitewash **10** annotation, brightness, brilliance, commentary, smooth over **11** explain away, explanation, rationalize **12** luminousness, treat lightly **14** interpretation

gloss over 4 hide, mask, veil **7** conceal, cover up **9** dissemble, whitewash **12** misrepresent

glossy 5 photo, shiny, showy, silky, sleek, slick **6** bright, satiny, smooth **7** picture, shining **8** gleaming, lustrous, magazine, polished **9** burnished

glove 3 kid **4** cuff, mitt **5** catch, thumb **6** gusset, mitten, muffle **7** chevron **8** gauntlet

glow 4 fill, heat **5** ardor, bloom, blush, color, flush, gleam, gusto, shine **6** fervor, thrill, tingle, warmth **7** flicker, glimmer, glisten, glitter, radiate, shimmer, smolder, twinkle **8** radiance **9** eagerness, intensity, radiation, reddening, vividness **10** brightness, enthusiasm **11** earnestness

glower 4 pout, sulk **5** frown, glare, lower, scowl, stare

glowing 3 hot, red **4** rave **5** ruddy, vivid **6** ardent, bright, florid, raving **7** fervent, flaming, flushed **8** ecstatic, exciting **9** rhapsodic, thrilling **10** passionate **11** luminescent, sensational, stimulating **12** enthusiastic

Glubbdubdrib
    fictional land in: 16 Gulliver's Travels
    author: 5 Swift

Gluck, Christoph Willibald (von)
    born: 7 Bavaria **8** Neumarkt
    composer of: 5 Orfeo **6** Armide **7** Alceste **13** Paride ed Elena **14** Echo et Narcisse **17** Iphigenie en Aulide **18** Iphigenie en Tauride

glue 3 fix, gum **5** affix, epoxy, paste, putty, stick **6** adhere, cement, fasten, mortar **7** plaster, stickum **8** adherent, adhesive, concrete, fixative, mucilage **11** agglutinate

gluey 5 gooey, gummy, mucid, ropey, slimy, tacky, thick, **6** sticky, viscid **7** stringy, viscous **8** adhesive **12** mucilaginous

glum 6 gloomy, morose **8** dejected **9** cheerless **10** melancholy **14** down in the mouth

glut 4 bolt, clog, cram, drug, fill, gulp, jade, load, sate **5** choke, flood, gorge, stuff **6** burden, deluge, devour, excess, gobble **7** congest, overeat, satiate, surfeit, surplus **8** gobble up, obstruct, overdose, overfeed, overload, plethora, saturate **10** gormandize, oversupply, saturation **11** obstruction, superfluity **13** overabundance, supersaturate **14** superabundance **15** supersaturation

glutinous 5 gluey, bummy, mucid, ropey, slimy, tacky, thick **6** sticky, viscid **7** viscous **8** adhesive **10** gelatinous **12** musilaginous

glutton 3 hog, pig **6** gorger **7** stuffer **8** gourmand **9** chowhound, overeater **10** belly-slave **11** gormandizer, trencherman

gluttonous 6 greedy **7** hoggish, piggish, swinish **8** edacious, grasping, ravening, ravenous **9** excessive, voracious **10** insatiable, omnivorous **11** intemperate

gluttony 8 rapacity, voracity **10** overeating **11** gourmandism, hoggishness, piggishness **12** gormandizing, intemperance, ravenousness **13** voraciousness

gnarled 6 knotty, rugged, snaggy **7** crooked, knotted, nodular, twisted **8** leathery, wrinkled **9** contorted, distorted **11** full of knots **13** weatherbeaten

gnash 4 gnaw **5** chomp

gnat 7 no-see-um
　group of: 5 cloud, horde

gnaw 4 bite, chew, fret, gall **5** chafe, chomp, eat at, grate, graze, munch, worry **6** browse, crunch, harrow, nibble, rankle **7** torment, trouble **8** distress, nibble at, ruminate **9** eat away at, masticate

gnome 3 elf **4** pixy **5** dwarf, troll **6** goblin, sprite **10** leprechaun

gnostic 4 sage, wise **6** clever, shrewd **7** knowing **8** mandaean, simonian **10** insightful

gnothi seauton 11 know thyself

gnu 7 brindle **8** antelope **10** wildebeest
　type: 5 C gnou **9** C taurinus **12** Connochaetes

go 3 act, end, fit, fly, pep, run, try, vim **4** blow, dash, elan, fare, flee, flow, jibe, lead, life, pass, quit, stir, turn, wend, work **5** agree, begin, be off, blend, drive, force, get on, lapse, leave, reach, scram, slide, split, steam, tally, trial, verve, vigor, whirl **6** accord, beat it, be used, belong, chance, decamp, depart, effort, elapse, energy, expire, extend, mettle, pass by, repair, result, retire, spirit **7** advance, attempt, be given, be known, comport, fall out, glide by, move out, operate, perform, proceed, slip off, take off, turn out, vamoose, work out

8 ambition, endeavor, function, move away, progress, slip away, sneak off, spread to, start for, steal off, vitality, vivacity, withdraw **9** animation, harmonize, terminate, transpire **10** enterprise, experiment, initiative

goad 4 move, prod, push, spur, urge, whet **5** drive, egg on, impel, press, prick, set on **6** arouse, exhort, fillip, incite, motive, propel, stir up **8** pressure, stimulus **9** constrain, incentive, stimulant, stimulate **10** cattle prod, inducement **11** instigation

goal 3 aim, end **4** home, mark, wire **5** point, score, tally **6** design, intent, object, target **7** end line, purpose **8** ambition, goal line, terminus **9** intention, objective **10** finish line

go along with 5 usher **6** assent, convoy, escort **8** accede to, shepherd **9** accompany, agree with, chaperone, consent to **10** comply with

go ashore 4 land **6** debark **9** disembark

go astray 3 err, sin **6** wander **7** deviate, do wrong **9** misbehave **10** transgress **13** fall from grace

goat 3 kid **4** buck, butt **5** billy, nanny **6** victim **7** fall guy **9** scapegoat **11** whipping boy **13** laughingstock
　breed: 6 Angora, Chamal, Nubian, Saanen **7** Granada **8** La Mancha **10** Toggenburg **11** Anglo-Nubian **12** French Alpine **13** British Alpine
　combining form: 4 aego **5** capri
　family: 7 Bovidae
　female: 3 doe **5** capra, nanny **7** doeling
　genus: 5 Capra
　goat-boy: 5 Giles
　goat-milk cheese: 7 chevret
　goat-man: 5 satyr
　god: 3 Pan **5** satyr **7** Aegipan
　group of: 4 herd **5** tribe
　hair: 5 kasha, tibet
　hair of Angora goat: 6 mohair
　male: 4 buck **5** billy
　meat: 7 cabrito
　star: 7 capella
　young: 3 kid

Goat, Horned Goat
　constellation of: 11 Capricornus

goat god 3 Pan **5** satyr

go away 3 ebb **4** fade, scat, wane **5** abate, leave, scram **6** depart, lessen, retire **8** withdraw **9** disappear

gob 3 dab, tar **4** clot, glob, lump, mass **6** sailor **7** Jack Tar

go back 6 return **7** retreat

gobble 3 caw **4** bolt, gulp, wolf **5** raven, stuff **6** cackle, devour, gabble, gaggle **8** bolt down, cram down, gulp down

gobbledygook 4 bosh, bunk, cant, tosh **6** jargon **7** rubbish, twaddle **8** buncombe, nonsense, tommyrot **9** gibberish, moonshine **10** balderdash,

double-talk, hocus-pocus, mumbo jumbo **11** foolishness **12** fiddle-faddle

gobble up 6 devour **8** bolt down, gulp down, wolf down

go before 7 precede, predate **8** antecede, antedate **9** come first, go ahead of **10** anticipate

go-between 5 agent, envoy, fixer, proxy **6** deputy, second **7** arbiter **8** delegate, emissary, mediator **9** messenger, middleman, moderator **10** arbitrator, interceder, negotiator **12** intermediary **13** intermediator **14** representative

goblet 3 cup **5** glass **6** vessel **7** chalice

goblin 4 ogre **5** bogey, demon, troll **7** gremlin **8** bogeyman

go by 4 pass **6** elapse, pass by, roll by, rush by, slip by **7** glide by, slide by **8** slip away

go by car 4 ride **5** drive, motor

go-cart 4 cart **5** buggy **6** barrow **8** carriage, handcart, pushcart, stroller **11** wheelbarrow

go crimson 4 burn, glow **5** blush, color, flame, flush **6** redden

God, god 4 Lord **5** Allah, deity **6** Elohim, Jahveh, Yahweh **7** Holy One, Jehovah, Skaddai **8** divinity, the Deity **9** Our Father **10** the Creator, the Godhead **11** divine being, God Almighty, the Almighty **13** the Omnipotent, the Omniscient **14** the All-Merciful, the Man Upstairs **15** the Supreme Being
　Hebrew: 6 Adonai
　Latin: 7 Dominus

god, first
　origin: 12 Scandinavian
　known as: 7 Forsete, Forseti

God and Man at Yale
　author: 17 William F Buckley Jr

God and my right
　French: 14 Dieu et mon droit
　motto of: 18 royal arms of England

God be with us
　German: 10 Gott mit uns

God be with you
　Latin: 12 Deus vobiscum

Godbole, Professor
　character in: 15 A Passage to India
　author: 7 Forster

Goddard, Jean-Luc
　director of: 10 Breathless

Goddard, Paulette
　real name: 10 Marion Levy
　husband: 14 Charlie Chaplin **15** Burgess Meredith **18** Erich Maria Remarque
　born: 11 Great Neck NY
　roles: 11 Modern Times, Unconquered **15** So Proudly We Hail **16** Standing Room Only, The Great Dictator **19** Diary of a Chambermaid

Goddard, Robert Hutchings
　nationality: 8 American

inventor of: 12 rocket engine **22** liquid propellant rocket

Godden, Rumer
 author of: 8 The River **14** Black Narcissus, Kitchen Madonna **16** The Peacock Spring **18** In This House of Brede, The Greengage Summer **19** An Episode of Sparrows **23** The Battle of Villa Fiorita

God enriches
 Latin: 9 ditat Deus
 motto of: 7 Arizona

Godfather, The
 author: 9 Mario Puzo
 family: 8 Corleone
 director: 18 Francis Ford Coppola
 cast: 8 Al Pacino (Michael) **9** James Caan (Sonny) **10** John Cazale (Fredo), John Marley, Talia Shire **11** Diane Keaton **12** Marlon Brando (Don Vito Corleone), Richard Conte, Robert Duvall **14** Sterling Hayden **17** Richard Castellano
 Oscar for: 5 actor (Brando) **7** picture **10** screenplay
 sequel: 18 The Godfather Part II

Godfather, The, Part II
 director: 18 Francis Ford Coppola
 cast: 8 Al Pacino **10** John Cazale, Talia Shire **11** Diane Keaton **12** Lee Strasberg, Robert DeNiro, Robert Duvall
 Oscar for: 7 picture **10** screenplay **15** supporting actor (DeNiro)
 sequel to: 12 The Godfather

godforsaken 5 bleak **6** lonely, remote **8** deserted, desolate, wretched **9** abandoned, neglected

god from a machine
 Latin: 13 deux ex machina

God is with us
 German: 10 Gott mit uns

godless 4 evil **6** wicked **7** heathen, impious, profane, ungodly **8** agnostic, depraved **9** atheistic **10** unhallowed **11** blasphemous, irreligious, unrepentant, unrighteous **12** sacrilegious, unsanctified

godlessness 7 atheism **8** apostasy, unbelief **9** disbelief **10** irreligion

godlike 4 holy **5** godly, pious **6** deific, divine, sacred **8** immortal, olympian

godliness 5 piety **8** devotion, holiness **9** reverence **10** devoutness **12** spirituality

godly 4 good, holy **5** moral, pious **6** devout, divine, sacred **7** devoted, saintly **8** faithful, hallowed, reverent **9** believing, God-loving, pietistic, religious, righteous, spiritual **10** God-fearing, sanctified **11** consecrated, pure in heart, reverential

go down 3 ebb **4** drop, fade, wane **5** abate, lower, slide **6** lessen, plunge, reduce, weaken **7** descend, plummet, slacken, subside **8** decrease, diminish, moderate

God's Grace
 author: 14 Bernard Malamud

God's Little Acre
 author: 15 Erskine Caldwell

Godthaab
 capital of: 9 Greenland

God willing
 Latin: 10 Deo volente

God wills it
 Latin: 8 Deus vult
 cry of: 9 Crusaders

Goes, Hugo van der
 born: 5 Ghent **8** Flanders
 artwork: 7 The Fall **14** The Lamentation **19** The Death of the Virgin **21** The Adoration of the Magi **22** The Adoration of the Child **26** The Adoration of the Shepherds

Goethe, Johann
 author of: 5 Faust **6** Egmont **24** The Sorrows of Young Werther **29** Wilhelm Meister's Apprenticeship

go-getter 4 doer **7** hustler **8** achiever, live wire

go-getting 7 driving, dynamic **8** forceful, hustling **9** ambitious, assertive, energetic **10** aggressive **11** harddriving, hard-working, industrious

Gogol, Nikolai
 author of: 7 The Nose **9** Dead Souls **10** Taras Bulba **11** The Overcoat **19** The Inspector-General

go hand in hand 5 match, tally **6** concur, square **7** coexist **9** accompany

go hungry 4 fast **6** famish, starve **7** abstain

Going My Way
 director: 10 Leo McCarey
 cast: 10 Bing Crosby (Father O'Malley) **12** Gene Lockhart **15** Barry Fitzgerald
 Oscar for: 4 song **5** actor (Crosby) **7** picture **8** director **15** supporting actor (Fitzgerald)
 song: 15 Swinging on a Star

gold 3 bar **4** gilt **5** aurum, ingot **6** beauty, nugget, purity, yellow **7** bullion **8** goodness, goodwill, humanity, kindness **11** beneficence
 chemical symbol: 2 Au

gold and silver
 Spanish: 9 oro y plata
 motto of: 7 Montana

Gold Bug, The
 author: 13 Edgar Allan Poe

Gold Coast *see* **5** Ghana **11** Sierra Leone

golden 4 best, gilt, rosy **5** blest, blond, great, happy, palmy **6** bright, gilded, joyous, timely **7** aureate, halcyon, richest, shining **8** beatific, glorious, happiest, splendid **9** favorable, opportune, priceless, promising **10** auspicious, delightful, propitious, seasonable **11** exceptional, flourishing,

resplendent **12** advantageous, bright-yellow **13** extraordinary

Golden Age
 first age of: 3 man
 world ruled by: 6 Cronus, Saturn

Golden Ass, The
 author: 14 Lucius Apuleius
 character: 4 Milo **5** Fotis **6** Lucius **8** Charites, Pamphile **9** Lepolemus **10** Thrasillus

Goldenberg, Emmanuel
 real name of: 15 Edward G Robinson

Golden Bough, The
 branch of: 9 mistletoe
 sacred to: 10 Proserpina
 used by: 6 Aeneas
 at shrine of: 5 Diana **7** Virbius
 author: 15 Sir James G Frazer

Golden Bowl, The
 author: 10 Henry James
 character: 8 Mr Verver **12** Maggie Verver, Mrs Assingham **13** Prince Amerigo **14** Charlotte Stant

Golden Boy
 nickname of: 11 Paul Hornung

golden brown 3 tan **5** tawny, toast **6** sienna **7** tobacco **8** chestnut

Golden Cockerel, The
 also: 8 Le Coq d'Or **15** Zolotoy Petushok
 opera by: 14 Rimsky-Korsakov
 character: 9 King Dodon **14** Queen of Shemaka

golden egg-layer
 form: 5 goose
 made of: 4 gold

Golden Fleece
 made of: 4 gold
 kept at: 7 Colchis
 kept by: 10 King Aeetes
 stolen by: 5 Jason **9** Argonauts
 accomplice: 5 Medea

Golden Girls, The
 network: 3 NBC
 cast: 10 Betty White (Rose Martin Lindstrom Nylund) **11** Herb Edelman (Stan Zbornak) **12** Estelle Getty (Sophia Spirelli Petrillo Weinstock) **13** Rue McClanahan (Blanche Elizabeth Hollingsworth Devereaux) **14** Beatrice Arthur (Dorothy Petrillo Zbornak Hollingsworth)

Golden Legend
 author: 13 William Caxton

goldenrod 8 Solidago
 varieties: 5 sweet, white **6** Wreath **7** seaside **8** bluestem, European **10** California

Golden State
 nickname of: 10 California

golden youth
 French: 13 jeunesse doree

goldfinch
 group of: 5 charm

Goldfinger
 director: 11 Guy Hamilton

author: 10 Ian Fleming
cast: 9 Gert Frobe (Auric Goldfinger)
10 Bernard Lee (M) **11** Lois Maxwell
(Miss Moneypenny) **12** Harold
Sakata (Oddjob), Shirley Eaton **13**
Honor Blackman (Pussy Galore),
Sean Connery (James Bond, 007)

Golding, William
author of: 8 Free Fall **13** A Moving
Target **14** Lord of the Flies, Rites of
Passage **15** Darkness Visible

gold mine 7 bonanza **10** mother lode

Gold Rush, The
director: 14 Charlie Chaplin
cast: 9 Mack Swain, Tom Murray **11**
Georgia Hale **14** Charlie Chaplin (Little Tramp)
setting: 5 Yukon

Goldsmith, Oliver
author of: 18 She Stoops to Conquer,
The Deserted Village **19** The Vicar of
Wakefield

goldwasser
form: 7 liquor
origin: 6 France **7** Germany
flavor: 4 herb **5** spice **7** caraway
flecked with: 8 gold leaf

golf
**average number strokes to com-
plete a hole: 3** par
ball in another's path: 6 stymie
championship: 3 PGA **6** US Open **9**
Grand Slam **11** British Open **17** Masters' Tournament
club: 4 iron, wood **6** driver, putter **7**
brassie **8** long iron **9** sand wedge,
short iron **10** middle iron **13** pitching wedge
club carrier: 6 caddie
course also called: 5 links
golf ball formerly called: 6 guttie
8 feathery
hole scored in one stroke: 3 ace **9**
hole-in-one
one stroke less than par: 6 birdie
one stroke more than par: 5 bogey
part of the course: 3 cup, tee **4** hole
5 apron, green, rough **6** bunker, hazard **7** fairway **8** sand trap
position: 3 lie
stance: 4 open **6** closed, square **7** address
two strokes less than par: 5 eagle
type of competition: 5 match, skins
6 stroke
uprooted turf: 5 divot
warning cry: 4 fore
golfer 8 Ben Hogan, Ernie Els, Lee Elder, Sam Snead **9** Carol Mann, Hale
Irwin, Patty Berg, Tom Watson **10**
Betsy Rawls, Bobby Jones, Deane Be-
man, Gary Player, Hubie Green, Jim
Demaret, Judy Rankin, Kerrie Webb,
Lee Trevino, Nancy Lopez, Tiger
Woods, Vijay Singh **11** Ben Cren-
shaw, Billy Casper, Byron Nelson,
Calvin Peete, Donna Caponi, Gene

Sarazen, Julius Boros, Tom Weiskopf,
Walter Hagen **12** Arnold Palmer, Jack
Nicklaus, Joanne Carner, Johnny
Miller, Mickey Wright, Retief Goosen,
Sandra Haynie, Sergio Garcia **13** Phil
Mickelson **14** Cary Middlecoff, Kathy
Whitworth **15** Annika Sorenstam **16**
Roberto DeVicenzo **19** Susie Maxwell
Berning **20** Severiano Ballesteros **21**
Babe Didrikson Zaharias

Golgotha 7 Calvary
means: 10 skull place

Goliath 5 giant
home: 4 Gath **9** Philistia
slain by: 5 David
weapon: 9 slingshot

golliwogg 3 toy **4** doll **9** plaything

Gomer Pyle USMC
character: 5 Bunny **7** Frankie **9** Corp
Boyle **11** Duke Slayter, (Sgt) Vince
Carter
cast: 9 Jim Nabors, Roy Stuart **10** Ted
Bessell **11** Frank Sutton **12** Ronnie
Schell **13** Barbara Stuart

Gomorrah
destroyed with: 5 Sodom **6** Zeboim
10 Admah

Gondoliers, The
operetta by: 18 Gilbert and Sullivan
character: 4 Luiz **5** Tessa **7** Casilda **8**
Gianetta **13** Marco Palmieri **15** Duke
of Plaza-Toro **16** Giuseppe Palmieri

gone 3 ago, out **4** away, dead, left,
lost, past **6** absent, ruined, used up **7**
defunct, died out, extinct, missing **8**
departed, finished, hopeless, vanished
11 disappeared

Goneril
character in: 8 King Lear
author: 11 Shakespeare

Gone With the Wind
author: 16 Margaret Mitchell
character: 5 Mammy **6** Big Sam,
Prissy **7** Dr Meade **10** Ellen (Robil-
lard) O'Hara **11** Gerald O'Hara,
Honey Wilkes, India Wilkes **12** Ashley Wilkes, Aunt Pittypat, Belle Watling **13** Scarlett O'Hara, Tarleton
twins **15** Mrs Merriweather **21** Melanie Hamilton Wilkes
Scarlett's husband: 11 Rhett Butler
12 Frank Kennedy **15** Charles Hamilton
Scarlett's children: 4 Emma, Wade **6**
Bonnie
Scarlett's sister: 7 Carreen, Suellen
director: 13 Victor Fleming
cast: 9 Ona Munson **10** Clark Gable
(Rhett Butler) **11** Evelyn Keyes, Vivien Leigh (Scarlett O'Hara) **12** Leslie
Howard (Ashley Wilkes) **13** Ann
Rutherford **14** Hattie McDaniel
(Mammy), Thomas Mitchell (Gerald
O'Hara) **16** Butterfly McQueen
(Prissy) **17** Olivia de Havilland (Mel-
anie Hamilton Wilkes)
score: 10 Max Steiner

Oscar for: 7 actress (Leigh), picture **8**
director **12** screenwriter **17** supporting actress (McDaniel)
producer: 14 David O Selznick

good 3 ace, fit, new **4** best, boon, fine,
full, gain, kind, pure, real **5** ample,
crack, favor, great, large, merit,
moral, pious, prize, right, solid,
sound, sunny, valid, value, worth **6**
adroit, choice, devout, entire, genial,
honest, humane, kindly, lively, new-
est, profit, proper, seemly, select, tip-
top, useful, virtue, wealth, worthy **7**
adapted, benefit, capable, capital, dutiful, fitting, genuine, godsend,
healthy, orderly, service, sizable,
skilled, success, upright, welfare **8** adequate, becoming, blessing, bonafide,
cheerful, complete, decorous, gracious, innocent, interest, kindness,
obedient, obliging, pleasant, precious,
reliable, salutary, skillful, smartest, sociable, splendid, suitable, thorough,
topnotch, valuable, virtuous, windfall
9 admirable, advantage, agreeable, authentic, convivial, deserving, efficient,
enjoyable, enjoyment, excellent, exemplary, expensive, favorable, first-
rate, happiness, healthful, honorable,
priceless, qualified, religious, righteous, unsullied, untainted, wholesome, wonderful **10** altruistic, beneficent, beneficial, benevolent,
excellence, first-class, legitimate, proficient, prosperity, sufficient, worthwhile **11** appropriate, commendable,
considerate, improvement, kindhearted, substantial, sympathetic,
well-behaved **12** advantageous, considerable, praiseworthy, satisfactory
13 companionable, conscientious,
righteousness
French: 3 bon **4** bien
Spanish: 5 bueno
German: 3 gut

Good as Gold
author: 12 Joseph Heller

Good Book 5 Bible

good breeding 5 grace **6** polish
7 manners **9** gentility **10** refinement
11 cultivation

good buy 4 deal **5** steal **7** bargain

goodby, goodbye 3 bye **6** bye-bye,
bye now, so long **7** parting, send-off **8**
farewell, Godspeed **9** departure **10**
separation **11** be seeing you, leave-
taking, see you later **12** God be with
you **15** till we meet again
French: 5 adieu **8** au revoir
German: 14 auf Wiedersehen
Hawaiian: 5 aloha
Italian: 4 ciao **5** addio **11** arrivederci
Japanese: 8 sayonara
Latin: 4 vale
Spanish: 5 adios **12** hasta la vista

Goodbye, Mr Chips
director: 7 Sam Wood

Goodbye Girl, The
author: **11** James Hilton
cast: **11** Greer Garson, Paul Henreid (von Henreid), Robert Donat
Oscar for: **5** actor (Donat)
character: **7** Mr Chips **10** Mrs Wickett **12** Kathy Bridges
school: **10** Brookfield

Goodbye Girl, The
director: **11** Herbert Ross
based on play by: **9** Neil Simon
cast: **11** Marsha Mason **12** Quinn Cummings **15** Richard Dreyfuss
Oscar for: **5** actor (Dreyfuss)

good counsel
god of: **6** Consus

good day
French: **7** bonjour
German: **8** guten tag
Spanish: **10** buenos dias
Italian: **10** buon giorno

good deal 3 buy **5** steal **7** bargain

good deed 8 kindness **11** benefaction **12** philanthropy
Hebrew: **7** mitsvah, mitzvah

Good Earth, The
author: **10** Pearl S Buck
character: **4** O-Lan **6** Nung En **7** Nung Wen, The Fool **8** Wang Lung **11** Pear Blossom **12** Lotus Blossom
director: **14** Sidney Franklin
cast: **8** Keye Luke, Paul Muni **10** Tilly Losch **11** Jessie Ralph, Luise Rainer **14** Walter Connolly **15** Charley Grapewin
Oscar for: **7** actress (Rainer)

good feelings 3 era **8** good will **11** benevolence **12** friendliness

Goodfellas
author: **15** Nicholas Pileggi
director: **14** Martin Scorsese
cast: **8** Joe Pesci (Tommy DeVito) **9** Ray Liotta (Henry Hill) **10** Tony Darrow (Sonny Bunz) **11** Frank Sivero (Frankie Carbone), Paul Sorvino (Paul Cicero) **12** Robert De Niro (Jimmy Conway) **14** Lorraine Bracco (Karen Hill)

good form 9 etiquette, good taste **10** politeness **11** good manners

good-for-nothing 5 idler **6** loafer **7** useless **9** no-account, shiftless, worthless

good fortune 4 luck **7** bonanza **8** fortuity, lady luck, windfall **9** blessings **10** lucky break

good friend
French: **6** bon ami **9** bonne amie

good health 5 vigor **7** fitness **8** vitality **10** robustness

Goodhue, Bertram Grosvenor
architect of: **13** St Bartholomew (NYC) **14** St Thomas Church (NYC) **25** Chapel at US Military Academy (West Point), National Academy of Sciences (Washington DC) **28** Nebraska State Capitol Building (Lincoln)

style: **13** Gothic Revival **15** Spanish Colonial

good humor 10 affability, amiability, cheeriness, kindliness, mellowness **12** cheerfulness, complaisance, pleasantness **15** kindheartedness

good-humored 4 mild, warm **6** cheery, genial, gentle, kindly, mellow **7** affable, amiable **8** cheerful, pleasant **9** congenial, easygoing **11** complaisant

good-looker 3 fox **4** doll, hunk **5** beaut, Venus **6** Adonis, beauty, eyeful **7** stunner **8** knockout **11** handsome Dan

good-looking 4 fair, foxy, sexy **5** bonny **6** comely, lovely, pretty **8** alluring, clean-cut, gorgeous, handsome, stunning **9** beauteous, beautiful, exquisite, ravishing **10** attractive, bewitching, enchanting **11** captivating, eye-catching, well-favored **15** pulchritudinous

good looks 6 beauty **10** comeliness, loveliness **11** pulchritude **12** handsomeness **14** attractiveness

good luck
Yiddish: **8** mazel tov

goodly 4 tidy **5** ample, large **7** sizable **11** substantial **12** considerable

good manners 8 courtesy **9** amenities, etiquette, gentility **10** politeness, refinement

good name 4 face **5** image **10** reputation **11** self-respect

good nature 6 warmth **9** geniality, good humor **10** affability, amiability, cordiality, likability **12** complaisance, pleasantness **13** agreeableness

good-natured 4 warm **5** sunny **6** genial, kindly **7** affable, amiable **8** cheerful, friendly, obliging, pleasant **9** agreeable, congenial, easygoing **11** complaisant, good-humored, warmhearted **13** accommodating

goodness 3 boy, gee, hey, say, wow **5** favor, honor, mercy, merit, piety, value, worth, wowee **6** profit, purity, virtue **7** benefit, decorum, gee whiz, heavens, honesty, probity, service **8** boy-oh-boy, devotion, gracious, kindness, morality **9** advantage, innocence, integrity, land alive, landsakes, nutrition, propriety, rectitude **10** generosity, kindliness, sakes alive, usefulness **11** benevolence, nourishment **12** virtuousness **13** righteousness, wholesomeness **14** heavens to Betsy

good night
French: **7** bon soir **9** bonne nuit
German: **9** gute nacht
Spanish: **12** buenas noches
Italian: **10** buona notte

good opinion 6 esteem, regard **7** respect **8** approval **10** admiration

good person 4 dear, love **5** angel **7** darling **10** sweetheart

goods 4 gear **5** cloth, stock, wares **6** fabric, things **7** effects, fabrics **8** chattels, material, movables, property, textiles **9** inventory, trappings **11** commodities, furnishings, merchandise, possessions **13** appurtenances, paraphernalia

good sense 6 brains, wisdom **8** judgment **12** intelligence

good taste 10 refinement **11** cultivation, discernment **14** discrimination

good-tempered 5 sunny **7** amiable, smiling **8** cheerful **12** sweet-natured

good time 3 fun **9** amusement, diversion, enjoyment **13** entertainment

good times 4 boom **8** fat years

good turn 5 favor **7** service **8** good deed

goodwill 5 amity **8** kindness **9** benignity **10** cordiality, kindliness **11** amicability, benevolence **12** friendliness **15** kindheartedness

Good Will Hunting
authors: **9** Matt Damon **10** Ben Affleck
director: **10** Gus Van Sant
cast: **9** Matt Damon (Will Hunting) **10** Ben Affleck (Chuckie Sullivan), Cole Hauser (Billy McBride) **12** Casey Affleck (Morgan O'Mally), Minnie Driver (Skylar) **13** Robin Williams (Sean Maguire) **16** Stellan Skarsgard (Gerald Lambeau)

good wishes 4 best **5** favor **6** regard **7** consent, regards **8** approval, blessing, respects, sanction **11** compliments

good word 6 praise **10** compliment **11** approbation **12** commendation **14** congratulation

Goodyear, Charles
nationality: **8** American
developed: **16** vulcanized rubber

goof 3 err **4** boob, flub, fool, mess **5** botch, error, gum up **6** bollix, booboo, bungle, fumble, slip up **7** blunder, mistake **10** oversight

Goolagong Cawley, Evonne
sport: **6** tennis
heritage: **19** Australian Aborigine

go on all fours 5 crawl, creep

goose
young: **7** gosling
group of: **5** flock, skein **6** gaggle

goose egg 3 nil, zip **4** zero **5** aught **6** cipher, naught **7** nothing **11** horse collar

go over 5 audit, check **6** review **7** examine, inspect **10** scrutinize **11** investigate

Gopher State
nickname of: **9** Minnesota

Gorbachev, Mikhail Sergeyevich
party: **9** Communist
country: **4** USSR **6** Russia **31** Union of Soviet Socialist Republics

born: 9 Stavropol 10 Privolnoye 16 Krasnogvardeisky

education: 21 Moscow State University

political career: 9 Politburo 16 General Secretary 20 Agriculture Secretary 23 Stavropol Communist Party 35 Deputy Supreme Soviet Central Committee

policy: 8 glasnost 11 perestroika

distinguishing characteristic: 19 strawberry birthmark (head)

wife: 15 Raisa Maksimovna
  occupation: 7 teacher

daughter: 5 Irisa
  occupation: 6 doctor 9 physician

grandchild: 6 Oksana

Gorcey, Leo
born: 9 New York NY
roles: 4 Spit 10 Bowery Boys 11 Dead End Kids

Gordimer, Nadine
author of: 8 Get A Life 9 The Pickup 11 July's People 12 The Lying Days 13 A Guest of Honor 15 Burger's Daughter 16 A Soldier's Embrace 17 None to Accompany Me 21 The Late Bourgeois World
award: 10 Nobel Prize

Gordon, Ruth
real name: 15 Ruth Gordon Jones
husband: 11 Garson Kanin
born: 11 Wollaston MA
roles: 11 Where's Poppa? 13 Rosemary's Baby 14 Harold and Maude 17 Inside Daisy Clover 20 Abe Lincoln in Illinois

gore 5 blood 7 carnage 8 butchery 9 bloodshed, slaughter

Gore, Albert
born: 10 Washington (DC)
father was: 7 senator
wife: 6 Tipper 13 Mary Elizabeth
children: 5 Sarah 6 Albert 7 Karenna, Kristin
education: 7 Harvard 10 Vanderbilt
profession: 10 journalist
author of: 17 Earth in the Balance
political career: 6 Senate 13 vice president 22 House of Representatives
ran for: 9 president
party: 8 Democrat 10 Democratic

Gorgas, William Crawford
field: 8 medicine
position: 18 army surgeon general
conquered: 7 malaria 11 yellow fever
location: 11 Panama Canal

gorge 3 gap, ire 4 bolt, cram, craw, dale, dell, fill, glen, glut, gulp, pass, sate, vale 5 abyss, anger, blood, chasm, cleft, gulch, gully, mouth, stuff, wrath 6 canyon, defile, devour, gobble, gullet, hatred, hollow, muzzle, nausea, ravine, throat 7 disgust, indulge, overeat, satiate 8 crevasse 9 animosity, esophagus, repulsion, re-

vulsion 10 gluttonize, gormandize, repugnance 11 overindulge

gorgeous 4 fine, rich 5 grand 6 bright, costly, lovely 7 elegant, opulent, shining 8 dazzling, glorious, imposing, splendid, stunning 9 beautiful, brilliant, exquisite, luxurious, ravishing, sumptuous 10 attractive, glittering, impressive 11 good-looking, magnificent, resplendent, splendorous 13 splendiferous

Gorgons
form: 7 maidens 8 monsters
names: 6 Medusa, Stheno 7 Euryale, Sthenno
father: 7 Phorcys
mother: 4 Ceto
protectress: 6 Graeae, Graiae
hair of: 6 snakes
hands of: 5 brass
turned viewers to: 5 stone

Gorgosaurus
type: 8 dinosaur, theropod
location: 7 Alberta 12 North America
period: 10 Cretaceous

gorilla
group of: 4 band
studied by: 10 Dian Fossey

Gorky, Arshile
real name: 21 Vosdanig Manoog Adokian
born: 7 Armenia 11 Khorkomvari
artwork: 5 Agony 15 Diary of a Seducer 17 Making the Calendar 21 The Artist and his Mother, Water of the Flowery Hill 22 The Liver is the Cock's Comb

Gorky, Maxim (Maksim)
real name: 25 Alekseimaksimovich Peshkov
author of: 7 V I Lenin 11 My Childhood 14 The Lower Depths 18 The Small Town Okurov 20 City of the Yellow Devil, Twenty-six Men and a Girl 27 The Life of Matthew Kozhemyakin

gormandize 5 feast, raven 6 devour

gory 5 scary 6 bloody, creepy 9 murderous 10 horrifying, sanguinary, terrifying 11 bloodsoaked, ensanguined, frightening 12 bloodstained, bloodthirsty 13 bloodcurdling

gospel, Gospel 5 credo, creed 8 doctrine 11 the good news, the last word 12 the final word 13 the whole truth, ultimate truth
  the first four books of the New Testament: 4 Luke, John, Mark 7 Matthew

Gospel writers 4 John, Luke, Mark 7 Matthew 9 synoptist

gospodin (Russian) 2 Mr 6 Mister

gossamer 5 filmy, gauzy, sheer 8 cobwebby 10 diaphanous 13 insubstantial

gossip 4 news 6 babble, report, tattle 7 comment, hearsay, prattle, scandal,

twaddle 8 idle talk 10 backbiting 12 tittle-tattle 13 newsmongering

gossiper 3 pry 4 blab 5 prate, snoop, yenta 6 gabble, magpie, meddle, tattle 7 babbler, meddler, prattle, snooper, tattler 8 busybody 9 chatterer 10 chatterbox, newsmonger, talebearer, tattletale 11 rumormonger 12 blabbermouth, gossipmonger 13 scandalmonger

Go Tell It on the Mountain
author: 12 James Baldwin

Gothic
language family: 12 Indo-European

go through 4 bear 6 endure, suffer 7 sustain, undergo 9 encounter, withstand 10 experience

go to 3 see 5 visit 6 attend 8 appear at, frequent

go to bed 6 retire, turn in 7 lie down, sack out 8 flake out 9 hit the hay 10 call it a day, hit the sack 11 catch some z's

go to pieces 5 break, crack 7 break up, crack up, crumble, give way, shatter 8 splinter 9 break down, fall apart 11 lose control 12 disintegrate

go to work on 6 attack, tackle 8 set about 9 undertake

go to wrack and ruin 5 decay 7 crumble 9 fall apart 12 disintegrate

Gotterdammerung 17 Twilight of the Gods
see: 8 Ragnarok

Gott mit uns 11 God be with us, God is with us

gouge 5 carve, drill, scoop 6 chisel, extort 10 overcharge

gouge out 5 drill 6 hollow 8 carve out, scoop out 9 chisel out, hollow out 10 whittle out

Gould, Chester
creator/artist of: 9 Dick Tracy

Gould, Elliott
real name: 16 Elliott Goldstein
wife: 15 Barbra Streisand
born: 10 Brooklyn NY
roles: 4 MASH 12 Ocean's Eleven 13 Little Murders 14 The Long Goodbye 15 California Split, Getting Straight 19 Bob & Carol & Ted & Alice

Goulding, Edmund
director of: 10 Grand Hotel 11 Dark Victory 13 The Dawn Patrol

go under 4 fail, fall, sink 9 go belly up 10 go bankrupt

Gounod, Charles Francois
born: 5 Paris 6 France
composer of: 5 Faust 6 Gallia, Sappho, Te Deum 8 Cinq-Mars, Mireille 9 La Colombe, Polyeucte 10 Mors et Vita 11 Marie Stuart, Stabat Mater 13 La Reine de Saba 14 Romeo and Juliet 16 La Nonne Sanglante, Philemon et Baucis 17 La Tribute de Zamora 18 Le Medecin Malgre Lui

gourd 4 pepo 9 Cucurbita
varieties: 3 ash, ivy, rag, wax 4 club 5 snake, white 6 bitter, bottle, dipper, sponge, teasel, viper's 7 fig-leaf, Malabar, serpent, trumpet 8 calabash, hedgehog, Missouri 9 dishcloth 10 goareberry, gooseberry, knobkerrie, silver-seed 11 sugar-trough 12 Hercules'-club 14 scarlet-fruited

gourmand 7 glutton 8 big eater 9 bon vivant, chowhound 11 gormandizer, trencherman

gourmet 7 epicure 9 bon vivant 10 gastronome 11 connoisseur, gastronomer 12 gastronomist

gourmet cooking
French: 12 haute cuisine

gout 5 style, taste 10 preference

govern 3 run 4 boss, curb, form, head, lead, rule, sway, tame 5 check, guide, pilot, steer 6 bridle, direct, manage 7 command, control, incline, inhibit, oversee 8 dominate, restrain 9 influence, supervise 10 administer, discipline, hold in hand 11 hold in check, superintend 13 be at the helm of 14 pull the strings 16 keep under control 17 exercise authority 18 be in the driver's seat

governed 3 led 5 ruled 6 guided 7 steered, subject 8 directed 9 dependent 10 controlled, supervised 12 administered 13 superintended

governing 6 ruling 7 curbing, guiding, heading, leading, swaying 8 bridling, checking, managing, piloting, reigning, steering 9 directing, inclining 10 inhibiting, management, overseeing 11 controlling, influencing, restraining, supervision 13 administering 14 administrating, administration, superintending

governing body 10 government, management, parliament 12 powers that be 14 administration 16 board of directors, board of governors 18 executive committee

government 3 law 4 rule 5 state 6 regime 7 command, control 8 dominion, guidance 9 authority, direction 10 domination, management, regulation 11 supervision 13 governing body, statesmanship 14 administration
absence of: 7 anarchy
absolute: 7 czarism, tsarism, tyranny 9 autocracy, despotism
by the best: 11 aristocracy
by church: 9 theocracy
by elders: 12 gerontocracy
by technologists: 11 technocracy
by few: 9 oligarchy
by mob: 10 ochlocracy
by people: 9 democracy
by rich: 10 plutocracy
by three: 8 triarchy 11 triumvirate
by two: 7 biarchy 10 duumvirate

by women: 8 gynarchy 10 matriarchy

governor
Turkish: 3 bey
Barbary States: 3 dey

Gowan
character in: 12 Little Dorrit
author: 7 Dickens

go with 6 convey, convoy, escort 7 conduct 9 accompany

gown 4 robe 5 dress, frock 10 nightdress

goy 6 non-Jew 7 Gentile

Goya (y Lucientes, Francisco Jose de)
born: 5 Spain 13 Fuente de todos
artwork: 8 Proverbs 10 Disparates 11 Tauromaquia 12 Los Caprichos, The Naked Maja 15 Majas on a Balcony 17 The Disasters of War 21 Charles IV and his Family

grab 3 bag, nab 4 grip, hold, pass 5 catch, clasp, grasp, lunge, pluck, seize 6 clutch, collar, snatch 7 capture

grace 4 deck, love, tact, trim 5 adorn, charm, endow, exalt, favor, honor, mercy, merit, piety, skill, taste 6 beauty, bedeck, enrich, pardon, polish, set off, virtue 7 charity, culture, decorum, dignify, dress up, elevate, enhance, garnish, glorify, manners, smarten, suavity 8 beautify, clemency, decorate, elegance, felicity, fluidity, God's love, holiness, lenience, ornament, reprieve, sanctity, spruce up, urbanity 9 embellish, endowment, etiquette, exemption, extra time, God's favor, good looks, propriety 10 aggrandize, comeliness, devoutness, excellence, indulgence, refinement 11 cultivation, forgiveness, lissomeness, pulchritude, saintliness, willowiness 12 dispensation, gracefulness, mannerliness, mercifulness 14 accomplishment, divine goodness
French: 11 savoir faire

graceful 5 lithe 6 comely, limber, lovely 7 elegant, lissome, shapely, sinuous, willowy 8 delicate 9 beautiful, lithesome, sylphlike 10 attractive 11 light-footed

gracefulness 8 delicacy, fluidity 10 suppleness 11 lissomeness

graceless 5 gawky, inept 6 clumsy 7 awkward 10 ungraceful 11 heavy-handed

Graces
also: 7 Gratiae 9 Charities
goddesses of: 6 beauty
father: 4 Zeus
mother: 8 Eurynome
names: 4 Auxo 5 Cleta 6 Aglaia, Thalia 7 Phaenna 8 Hegemone 10 Euphrosyne

Grace Under Fire
network: 3 ABC
cast: 10 Dave Thomas (Russell Nor-

ton), Julie White (Nadine Swoboda) 11 Brett Butler (Grace Kelly), Casey Sander (Wade Swoboda), Cole Sprouse (Patrick Kelly) 12 Dylan Sprouse (Patrick Kelly) 13 Jon Paul Steuer (Quentin Kelly), Kaitlin Cullum (Libby Kelly)

gracious 2 my 3 boy, gee, wow 4 kind 5 civil, mercy, oh boy 6 benign, humane, kindly, polite, tender, ye gods 7 affable, amiable, clement, cordial, courtly, gee whiz, lenient, my stars 8 friendly, goodness, merciful, obliging, pleasant 9 benignant, courteous, landsakes 10 benevolent, charitable, chivalrous, hospitable 11 good heavens, good natured, kindhearted 13 compassionate 14 heavens to Betsy

gradation 4 step 5 stage 6 degree 7 shading 8 grouping, ordering 9 arranging 11 arrangement 12 organization 14 classification

grade 4 bank, even, hill, mark, ramp, rank, rate, sort, step 5 brand, caste, class, level, order, pitch, place, slope, stage, value 6 degree, estate, rating, smooth, sphere, status 7 flatten, incline, quality, station 8 classify, gradient, position, standing 9 acclivity, condition, declivity, intensity

grade-A 2 A-1 4 aces, a-one, fine, tops 5 grade, great, prime, super 6 choice, superb, tip-top 7 capital 8 peerless, sterling, superior, top-notch 9 excellent, first-rate, matchless, superfine 10 first-class, preeminent, tremendous 11 outstanding, superlative

gradient 4 ramp, tilt 5 pitch, slant, slope 6 ascent 7 incline, leaning 9 steepness 11 inclination

gradual 4 slow 6 gentle, steady 7 regular 8 measured 9 graduated, piecemeal 10 continuous, deliberate, drop-by-drop, inch-by-inch, step-by-step, successive 11 incremental, progressive 13 imperceptible, slow-but-steady 14 little-by-little

graduate 5 grade 6 alumna 7 alumnus, mark off 9 calibrate 10 measure out 14 grant a degree to, receive a degree

Graduate, The
director: 11 Mike Nichols
cast: 12 Anne Bancroft (Mrs Robinson) 13 Dustin Hoffman, Katharine Ross 14 Murray Hamilton, William Daniels
score: 17 Simon and Garfunkel
Oscar for: 8 director

Graeae
also: 6 Graiae
goddesses of: 3 sea
number: 5 three
names: 4 Enyo 5 Deino 9 Pemphredo
father: 7 Phorcys
mother: 4 Ceto
sisters: 7 Gorgons

protectresses of: 7 Gorgons
personified: 6 old age
three shared: 6 one eye **8** one tooth
eye stolen by: 7 Perseus
corresponds to: 4 Enyo

Graf 5 count

graffito, graffiti 4 name **6** slogan **7** drawing, scratch **8** scribble **10** defacement

graft 3 bud **4** join, last, slip, swag **5** booty, infix, inset, plant, scion **6** bribes, payola, splice, spoils, sprout **7** bribery, implant, ingraft, payoffs, plunder, rake-off **8** kickback **9** hush money **10** corruption, transplant **12** implantation **13** inserted shoot

Graham, Bruce
architect of: 17 John Hancock Center (Chicago)

Grahame, Kenneth
author of: 19 The Wind in the Willows

Graiae *see* **6** Graeae

grain 3 bit, dot, jot, rye **4** atom, corn, dash, iota, mite, oats, seed, whit **5** crumb, grist, maize, ovule, pinch, spark, speck, touch, trace, wheat **6** barley, cereal, kernel, millet, morsel, pellet, tittle, trifle **7** granule, modicum **8** fragment, molecule, particle **9** scintilla
abbreviation: 2 gr
god of: 7 Robigus
goddess of: 6 Ribigo

Grain Coast *see* **11** Sierra Leone

Grainger, Percy Aldridge
born: 9 Australia, Melbourne
composer of: 14 Country Gardens **17** Handel in the Strand **19** Rosenkavalier Ramble

gram
abbreviation of: 1 g

Gram
origin: 12 Scandinavian
mentioned in: 8 Volsunga
form: 5 sword
owned by: 7 Sigmund
used by: 6 Sigurd
killed: 6 Fafnir

grand 2 A-1 **3** big **4** fine, full, good, head, huge, keen, main **5** chief, fancy, great, large, lofty, noble, regal, royal, showy, super, swell **6** august, choice, groovy, kingly, lordly, superb **7** dashing, elegant, exalted, haughty, mammoth, opulent, pompous, queenly, stately, sublime, supreme **8** arrogant, complete, elevated, fabulous, glorious, imperial, imposing, majestic, palatial, princely, real cool, real gone, smashing, splendid, striking, terrific **9** admirable, dignified, excellent, first-rate, grandiose, luxurious, marvelous, principal, sumptuous, wonderful **10** impressive, monumental, out-of-sight **11** highfalutin, magnificent, preten-

tious, sensational **12** ostentatious **13** comprehensive, distinguished

Grand Canyon State
nickname of: 7 Arizona

grande dame 9 great lady

grandee 5 noble **8** nobleman **9** blue blood **10** aristocrat

Grandees
author: 17 Stephen Birmingham

grandeur 4 fame, pomp **5** glory, state **6** luster **7** dignity, majesty **8** eminence, nobility, splendor **9** celebrity, loftiness, solemnity, sublimity **10** augustness, excellence, importance **11** distinction, stateliness **12** magnificence, resplendence **14** impressiveness

Grand Hotel
author: 9 Vicki Baum
character: 9 Miss Flamm **12** Baron Gaigern **14** Dr Otternschlag, Otto Kringelein **27** Herr Generaldirektor Preysing **32** Elisaveta Alexandrovna Grusinskaya
director: 14 Edmund Goulding
cast: 10 Greta Garbo **12** Joan Crawford, Wallace Beery **13** John Barrymore **15** Lionel Barrymore
setting: 6 Berlin

Grand Illusion
director: 9 Jean Renoir
cast: 5 Dalio **7** Carette **9** Dita Parlo, Jean Gabin **13** Pierre Fresnay **16** Erich von Stroheim

grandiloquent 5 lofty **6** florid, turgid **7** flowery, pompous, stilted, swollen **8** inflated **9** bombastic, grandiose, highflown **10** rhetorical **11** highfalutin, pretentious **12** high-sounding, magniloquent

grandiose 5 grand **7** pompous, splashy **8** affected **9** high-flown **10** flamboyant, theatrical **11** extravagant, highfalutin, pretentious

Grand Marnier
type: 6 brandy, cognac **7** liqueur
origin: 6 France
flavor: 6 orange
with gin: 7 Red Lion

grand monde 10 great world **11** best society **16** fashionable world

grand prix 10 grand prize

grand prize
French: 9 grand prix

Grange, Red (Harold)
nickname: 14 Galloping Ghost
sport: 8 football
team: 11 U of Illinois **12** Chicago Bears

Granger, Edith
character in: 12 Dombey and Son
author: 7 Dickens

Grangosier
character in: 22 Gargantua and Pantagruel
author: 8 Rabelais

Granite State
nickname of: 12 New Hampshire

grant 4 boon, cede, gift, give **5** admit, allot, allow, award, endow, favor, yield **6** accord, assign, bestow, confer, donate, permit **7** agree to, bequest, concede, consent, deal out, largess, present, subsidy, tribute **8** accede to, allocate, bestowal, dispense, donation, gratuity, offering **9** allotment, allowance, apportion, consent to, endowment, vouchsafe **10** assignment, concession, indulgence **11** benefaction **12** contribution, presentation **13** appropriation

Grant, Cary
real name: 23 Archibald Alexander Leach
wife: 10 Dyan Cannon **13** Barbara Hutton
born: 7 England **8** Bristol
roles: 6 Topper **9** Dream Wife, Houseboat **10** Indiscreet **11** Blonde Venus, Father Goose **13** To Catch a Thief **14** Bringing Up Baby, Monkey Business, The Bishop's Wife **15** She Done Him Wrong **16** North by Northwest **17** Arsenic and Old Lace, I Was a Male War Bride **18** Operation Petticoat **20** The Philadelphia Story **21** None But the Lonely Heart

Grant, Lee
real name: 21 Lyova Haskell Rosenthal
born: 9 New York NY
roles: 7 Shampoo **10** Plaza Suite **11** Peyton Place, The Landlord **14** Detective Story **19** In the Heat of the Night **20** Divorce American Style

Grant, Ulysses Simpson
real name: 17 Hiram Ulysses Grant
nickname: 3 Sam **4** Lyss **27** Unconditional Surrender Grant
presidential rank: 10 eighteenth
party: 10 Republican
state represented: 2 IL
defeated: 5 (David) Davis, (James) Black **6** (Charles) O'Conor **7** (Horace) Greeley, (Horatio) Seymour **9** (William Slocomb) Groesbeck
vice president: 5 (Thomas W) Ferry (acting) **6** (Henry) Wilson (died in office 1875), (Schuyler) Colfax
cabinet:
state: 4 (Hamilton) Fish **9** (Elihu Benjamin) Washburne
treasury: 7 (Alexander Turney) Stewart, (Benjamin Helm) Bristow, (Lot Myrick) Morrill **8** (George Sewall) Boutwell **10** (William Adams) Richardson
war: 2 (Alphonso) Taft **7** (James Donald) Cameron, (John Aaron) Rawlins, (William Worth) Belknap
attorney general: 4 (Alphonso) Taft, (Ebenezer Rockwood) Hoar **7** (Amos Tappan) Akerman **8** (George Henry) Williams **10** (Ed-

wards) Pierrepont
navy: 5 (Adolph Edward) Borie 7 (George Maxwell) Robeson
postmaster general: 5 (James Noble) Tyner 6 (Marshall) Jewell 8 (James William) Marshall, (John Angel James) Creswell
interior: 3 (Jacob Dolson) Cox 6 (Columbus) Delano 8 (Zachariah) Chandler
born: 15 Point Pleasant OH
died: 15 Mount McGregor NY
buried: 9 New York NY
education: 9 West Point 17 US Military Academy
religion: 9 Methodist
author: 24 Personal Memoirs of US Grant 30 Around the World with General Grant
political career:
secretary of: 3 War (interim appointment)
civilian career: 6 farmer
military service: 6 US Army 8 Civil War 10 Mexican War 18 Illinois Volunteers 20 Commander of Union Army
notable events of lifetime/career: 5 Panic (of 1873) 8 Civil War 11 Black Friday (gold panic) 16 Custer's Last Stand
Act: 10 Salary Grab
conspiracy: 11 Whiskey Ring
scandal: 14 Credit Mobilier
quote: 60 "No terms except unconditional and immediate surrender can be accepted"
father: 9 Jesse Root
mother: 6 Hannah (Simpson)
siblings: 5 Clare 10 Orvil Lynch 11 Mary Frances 13 Samuel Simpson, Virginia Paine
wife: 5 Julia (Boggs Dent)
children: 5 Ellen 9 Jesse Root 13 Frederick Dent 14 Ulysses Simpson

granted
French: 7 d'accord

grantee 8 receiver 9 recipient 11 beneficiary

grant immunity to 4 free 5 clear, spare 6 except, excuse, exempt 7 absolve, release, relieve 9 privilege

grantor 5 giver 8 bestower 10 benefactor

granulate 5 crush 6 powder 9 pulverize 11 crystallize

granulated 6 ground 7 crushed 8 powdered 10 pulverized 12 crystallized

granule 5 grain 7 crystal 8 particle

grape 5 Vitis 13 Vitis vinifera
varieties: 3 cat, red, sea 4 amur, blue, bush, cape, rock, sand, tail 5 bear's, bunch, frost, Javan, sugar, veldt 6 canyon, Damson, Miller, Oregon, pigeon, possum, summer, winter 7 African, Bullace, catbird,

chicken, Concord, Spanish 8 European, mountain 9 evergreen, panhandle, river-bank 10 silver-leaf 11 southern fox 13 sweet mountain
wine: 5 Gamay 6 Cayuga, Duriff, Merlot, Muscat, Shiraz 7 Barbera, Catawba 8 Baco Noir, Dolcetto, Labrusca, Nebbiolo, Verduzzo 9 Aglianico, Fume Blanc, Huxelrebe, Pinot Noir, Primitivo, Trebbiano, Zinfandel 10 Chardonnay, Sangiovese 11 Chenin Blanc, Petite Sirah, Pinot Bianco, Seyval Blanc 13 Cabernet Franc, Montepulciano 14 Sauvignon Blanc 15 Gewurztraminer 17 Cabernet Sauvignon 20 Johannisberg Riesling

Grapes of Wrath, The
author: 13 John Steinbeck
character: 4 Noah 6 Connie, Ma Joad, Pa Joad 7 Jim Casy, Tom Joad 12 Rose of Sharon
director: 8 John Ford
cast: 10 Henry Fonda 11 Jane Darwell 12 Dorris Bowden 13 John Carradine 15 Charley Grapewin
Oscar for: 17 supporting actress (Darwell)

graphic 4 seen 5 clear, drawn, lucid, vivid 6 visual 7 painted, printed, visible, written 8 distinct, explicit, forcible, lifelike, pictured, striking 9 pictorial, realistic, trenchant 10 expressive 11 descriptive, picturesque 12 illustrative

grappa
type: 6 brandy 7 liqueur
origin: 5 Italy
made from: 9 grape pulp

grapple 4 face, grip, hold, meet 5 catch, clasp, fight, grasp, seize 6 breast, clutch, combat, engage, fasten, tackle, take on 7 contend, grapnel, wrestle 8 confront, deal with, do battle, make fast, struggle 9 encounter, large hook, lay hold of 11 hold tightly

grasp 3 get, ken 4 grab, grip, hold, sway, take 5 catch, clasp, infer, power, range, reach, savvy, scope, seize, sense, skill, sweep 6 clinch, clutch, deduce, fathom, follow, master, snatch, take in, talent 7 catch at, compass, control, embrace, grapple, mastery, seizing, seizure 8 clutches, gripping, perceive 9 handclasp, knowledge, seize upon 10 comprehend, perception, understand 13 comprehension, understanding

grasping 5 venal 6 greedy 7 hoggish, miserly, selfish, wolfish 8 covetous 9 mercenary, predatory, rapacious 10 avaricious 11 acquisitive

graspingness 5 greed 7 avarice 8 rapacity, venality 10 greediness 12 covetousness

grass
varieties: 3 cup, cut, dog, eel, elk,

mat, nut, oat, oil, pin, rib, rye, Uva 4 barn, bear, bent, blue, chee, cord, crab, deer, fish, hair, lace, love, Lyme, moor, Nard, palm, Para, rice, rush, silk, star, tape, worm, yard 5 arrow, Bahia, beach, beard, Brome, Carib, China, cloud, curly, Ditch, fever, goose, lemon, Means, Melic, Mondo, natal, quack, sedge, shave, shore, Smilo, spike, squaw, Sudan, sword, Vasey, wheat, white, witch, zebra 6 Aleppo, alkali, basket, Bengal, Buffel, Canary, carpet, Dallis, Dudder, finger, gallow, Guinea, Indian, Korean, Manila, Napier, orange, orchid, Pampas, Rescue, Rhodes, ribbon, ripple, scurvy, signal, starry, switch, Tobosa, velvet, vernal, viper's, Zoysia 7 Bermuda, Brahman, Bristle, Buffalo, Esparto, Harding, Johnson, Kleberg, Pangola, poverty, pudding, quaking, Ravenna, sea lyme, serpent, tall oat, Wallaby, Widgeon 8 Angleton, blue-eyed, blue love, Boer love, elephant, fountain, hairy cup, lazy man's, molasses, Ree wheat, sand love, scorpion, tuber oat 9 blue conch, centipede, common rye, hairy crab, hare's-tail, Hungarian, Malojilla, Mascarene, Oregon rye, rancheria, tall wheat, water star, yellow nut 10 Amur silver, beavertail, big quaking, blue finger, citronella, English rye, false wheat, golden-eyed, Indian rice, Italian rye, Korean lawn, Kuma bamboo, purple-eyed, rabbit-foot, rabbit-tail, reed canary, tufted hair, Washington, western rye, yellow-eyed 11 annual beard, branched cup, desert wheat, domestic rye, dwarf meadow, feather love, giant finger, green needle, Lehmann love, Nepal silver, Pentz finger, prairie cord, ringed beard, St Augustine, sweet vernal, Texas needle, Texas winter, weeping love 12 Common carpet, crested wheat, crinkled hair, European dune, Indian basket, Japanese lawn, Japanese love, Korean velvet, perennial rye, slender wheat, squirreltail, western wheat 13 American beach, Australian rye, billion-dollar, European beach, Himalaya fairy, Japanese sedge, little quaking, Paraguay Bahia, plains bristle, Siberian wheat 14 African Bermuda, bluebunch wheat, Japanese carpet, Pensacola Bahia, perennial veldt, pubescent wheat, Saint Augustine, stiff-hair wheat 15 European feather, Wilmington Bahia 16 creeping windmill, Pacey's English rye 17 Australian feather, intermediate wheat, Mediterranean salt, Transvaal dog-tooth 18 Australian windmill, California blue-eyed, Mexican everlasting 19 Fairway crested wheat 20 standard crested wheat

Grass, Gunter
author of: **6** Floods, The Rat **8** Crab Walk, Dog Years **10** The Tin Drum **11** Cat and Mouse, The Flounder **12** Too Far Afield **16** Local Anaesthetic, The Call of the Toad **18** The Meeting at Telgte **20** From the Diary of a Snail **33** Headbirths or The Germans Are Dying Out

grasshopper
variety: **5** pygmy **6** meadow, monkey **7** katydid **10** band winged, cone headed, long-horned, slant-faced **11** bush katydid, leaf-rolling, short-horned **12** shield-backed, spur-throated

grassland 3 lea **4** farm, vale, veld **5** field, pampa, plain, range, veldt **6** meadow **7** pasture, prairie, savanna **8** farmland, flatland, savannah **10** plantation

grate 3 irk, jar, rub, vex **4** bars, burr, buzz, gall, rasp **5** annoy, chafe, clack, grill, grind, mince, shred **6** abrade, gnaw at, hearth, jangle, rankle, scrape, scream, screen **7** firebed, firebox, grating, lattice, scratch, screech **8** irritate **9** fireplace, pulverize **10** exasperate, firebasket **11** latticework

grateful 7 obliged **8** beholden, indebted, thankful **9** gratified, obligated **12** appreciative

Grateful Dead
members: **7** Bob Weir **8** Phil Lesh **10** Mickey Hart **11** Jerry Garcia **12** Brent Mydland, Vince Welnick **13** Keith Godchaux, Tom Constanten **14** Bill Kreutzmann **17** Donna Jean Godchaux, Ron "Pigpen" McKernan
lyricist: **12** Robert Hunter
fans: **9** Deadheads
songs: **6** Althea, Iko Iko, Ripple **7** Cassidy, Sugaree, Truckin', US Blues **8** Big River, The Wheel, Wharf Rat **9** Alligator, Box of Rain, Good Lovin', Jack Straw, St Stephen **10** Casey Jones, Stagger Lee, Stella Blue **11** Maggie's Farm, Picasso Moon, Ship of Fools, The Other One, Touch of Grey **12** Don't Ease Me In, Tennessee Jed **13** Blues for Allah, Cosmic Charlie, Hell in a Bucket, I Know You Rider, I Need a Miracle, Sugar Magnolia **14** Alabama Getaway, Franklin's Tower, Throwing Stones, Uncle John's Band, West LA Fadeaway **15** Brokedown Palace, Cold Rain and Snow, Cumberland Blues, Scarlet Begonias, Shakedown Street, Terrapin Station **16** Estimated Prophet, Friend of the Devil **17** China Cat Sunflower, Feel Like a Stranger, Fire on the Mountain, New Speedway Boogie **18** New Minglewood Blues **20** Man Smart Woman Smarter **22** It Must Have Been the Roses

gratefulness 6 thanks **9** gratitude **12** appreciation, thankfulness

Gratiae see **6** Graces

Gratiano
character in: **19** The Merchant of Venice
author: **11** Shakespeare

gratification 3 joy **4** glee, kick **5** bliss **6** relish, solace, thrill **7** comfort, delight, ecstasy, elation, rapture **8** gladness, humoring, pleasing, pleasure, soothing **9** enjoyment, happiness, transport **10** indulgence, jubilation, satisfying **11** contentment, enchantment **12** exhilaration, satisfaction

gratified 5 happy **7** content, pleased **9** satisfied **11** comfortable

gratify 4 suit **5** amuse, favor, humor **6** coddle, divert, pamper, please, regale, soothe, thrill, tickle **7** appease, delight, enchant, flatter, gladden, indulge, refresh, satisfy **8** enthrall, entrance, interest, recreate **9** enrapture, entertain, transport **10** compliment, exhilarate

gratifying 8 humoring, pleasant, pleasing, soothing **9** agreeable, enjoyable, indulging, pampering, rewarding **10** delightful, satisfying **11** pleasurable

grating 4 bars, fret, grid **5** grate, harsh, raspy **6** creaky, grille, shrill **7** jarring, lattice, rasping, raucous, squeaky, tracery, trellis **8** abrasive, annoying, filigree, fretwork, gridiron, jangling, piercing, scraping, strident **9** offensive, vexatious **10** discordant, gate of bard, irritating, unpleasant **11** cacophonous, displeasing, high-pitched **12** disagreeable, exacerbating, exasperating

grating noise 7 discord, rasping **8** grinding **9** cacophony, harshness **10** disharmony, dissonance

gratis 4 free **10** gratuitous, on the house **13** complimentary, without charge

gratitude 6 thanks **10** obligation **11** recognition **12** appreciation, beholdenness, gratefulness, thankfulness, thanksgiving **14** acknowledgment

gratuitous 4 free **6** gratis, wanton **7** donated, willing **8** baseless, unproven **9** unfounded, voluntary **10** free of cost, groundless, irrelevant, unasked for, unprovoked **11** conjectural, impertinent, presumptive, spontaneous, uncalled for, unjustified, unwarranted **13** complimentary, unrecompensed

gratuity 3 tip **4** gift **8** donation
French: **7** douceur **9** pourboire

Graustark
author: **20** George Barr McCutcheon

grave 4 dour, sage, tomb **5** acute, crypt, mound, quiet, sober, staid, vault, vital **6** gloomy, sedate, solemn, somber, urgent **7** crucial, earnest, ossuary, serious, subdued, weighty **8**

catacomb, cenotaph, critical, frowning, pressing **9** dignified, important, long-faced, mausoleum, momentous, sepulcher **10** thoughtful **11** burial ground, grim visaged, significant **13** consequential, philosophical **16** last resting place, place of interment
music: **6** solemn **7** serious

Graves, Robert
author of: **9** I Claudius, King Jesus **14** Claudius the God **15** The White Goddess **16** Goodbye to All That

graveyard 7 charnel, ossuary **8** boneyard, boot hill, cemetery **10** churchyard, necropolis **12** memorial park, potter's field **13** burying ground

gravitate 4 fall, head, move, sink, tend **6** settle **7** be drawn, descend, incline **8** converge, zero in on **9** be prone to **10** lean toward

gravity 4 pull **6** danger, import, moment **7** concern, dignity, urgency **8** calmness, enormity, grimness, serenity, sobriety **9** emergency, magnitude, solemnity, staidness **10** attraction, gloominess, importance, sedateness, solemnness, somberness **11** consequence, earnestness, gravitation, seriousness **12** significance, tranquillity **13** consideration, crucial nature **14** critical nature, pull of the earth, thoughtfulness **16** mutual attraction

gray, grey 3 dun **4** ashy, dark, drab, pale **5** ashen, foggy, hoary, misty, murky, slate **6** cloudy, dismal, gloomy, silver, somber **7** clouded, grayish, grizzly, neutral, silvery, sunless **8** overcast **9** cheerless, pearl-gray **10** depressing, gray-haired, grayheaded **11** dove-colored, hoaryheaded **12** mouse-colored, silverhaired **13** salt and pepper

Gray, Harold
creator/artist of: **17** Little Orphan Annie

Gray, Thomas
author of: **32** Elegy Written in a Country Churchyard

grayness 4 murk **6** pallor **8** drabness **9** bleakness **10** somberness

Grayson, Kathryn
real name: **19** Zelma Kathryn Hedrick
born: **14** Winston-Salem NC
roles: **8** Show Boat **10** Kiss Me Kate **13** Anchors Aweigh, The Desert Song **15** The Vagabond King

graze 3 rub **4** crop, rasp, skim, skin **5** brush, grind, swipe **6** abrade, browse, bruise, glance, scrape **7** pasture, scratch **8** abrasion, eat grass **16** turn out to pasture

Grease
director: **13** Randal Kleiser
cast: **8** Didi Conn (Frenchy), Eve Arden (Principal McGee) **9** Edd Byrnes (Vince Fontaine), Kelly Ward (Putzie), Sid Caesar (Coach Calhoun) **10**

Barry Pearl (Doody) **11** Jeff Conaway (Kenickie) **12** Joan Blondell (Vi), John Travolta (Danny Zuko), Michael Tucci (Sonny) **13** Frankie Avalon (The Teen Angel) **16** Olivia Newton-John (Sandy Olsson), Stockard Channing (Betty Rizzo)

grease 3 fat, oil **4** balm, lard **5** salve **6** anoint, tallow **7** unguent **8** ointment **9** drippings, lubricant, lubricate

grease the palm 3 tip **5** bribe **6** buy off, pay off

greasy 3 fat **4** oily, waxy **5** fatty, lardy, slick **7** buttery **8** slippery, slithery **10** lardaceous, oleaginous

great 3 apt, big **4** able, a-one, cool, fine, good, high, huge, kind, many, phat, vast, well **5** chief, crack, grand, grave, gross, heavy, large, noble, noted, super, swell **6** adroit, choice, expert, famous, groovy, humane, loving, strong, superb **7** awesome, crucial, decided, eminent, extreme, grandly, immense, leading, mammoth, notable, serious, titanic, weighty **8** abundant, colossal, critical, enormous, esteemed, fabulous, generous, gigantic, glorious, gracious, manifold, renowned, skillful, smashing, splendid, superbly, superior, terrific, very well **9** boundless, countless, cyclopean, excellent, fantastic, first-rate, important, marvelous, momentous, monstrous, prominent, unlimited, wonderful **10** altruistic, celebrated, gargantuan, high-minded, inordinate, out-of-sight, prodigious, proficient, pronounced, remarkable, splendidly, stupendous, tremendous, voluminous **11** crackerjack, excellently, extravagant, illustrious, magnanimous, magnificent, outstanding, sensational, significant, superlative, wonderfully **12** considerable **13** consequential, distinguished, inexhaustible, magnificently, multitudinous **14** out of this world

Great Ajax
origin: **5** Greek
hero of: **9** Trojan War

greater 4 more **5** finer **6** better, bigger, larger **8** superior

Great Escape, The
director: **11** John Sturges
cast: **11** James Coburn, James Garner **12** Steve McQueen **13** David McCallum **14** Charles Bronson **15** Donald Pleasance **19** Richard Attenborough
setting: **7** Germany, POW camp

greatest 4 best, most **5** ultra **6** picked, select, utmost **7** extreme, highest, maximal, maximum, noblest, supreme **8** champion **9** first-rate **11** superlative, unsurpassed

Greatest Show on Earth, The
director: **13** Cecil B DeMille
cast: **11** Betty Hutton, Cornel Wilde **12** James Stewart **13** Dorothy La-

mour, Gloria Grahame **14** Charlton Heston
Oscar for: **7** picture

Great Expectations
author: **14** Charles Dickens
character: **3** Pip **7** Estella **9** Compeyson, Mr Jaggers **10** Joe Gargery **12** Abel Magwitch, Miss Havisham **13** Herbert Pocket
director: **9** David Lean
cast: **9** John Mills **11** Martita Hunt **12** Alec Guinness, Bernard Mills **13** Valerie Hobson **16** Francis L Sullivan

Great Gatsby, The
author: **16** F Scott Fitzgerald
character: **9** Jay Gatsby **11** Tom Buchanan **12** Myrtle Wilson, Nick Carraway **13** Daisy Buchanan

Great God Brown, The
author: **12** Eugene O'Neill

great lady
French: **10** grande dame

Great Lake 4 Erie **5** Huron **7** Ontario **8** Michigan, Superior

Great Land
nickname of: **6** Alaska

greatly 6 vastly **7** largely, notably **8** markedly, mightily, very much **9** immensely **10** abundantly, enormously, infinitely, powerfully, remarkably **12** considerably, immeasurably, tremendously

great mishap 5 wreck **6** blight, fiasco **7** tragedy **8** calamity, disaster **9** cataclysm, ruination **11** catastrophe

greatness 8 eminence, nobility **9** loftiness **10** excellence, importance, notability, prominence **11** preeminence, superiority **12** magnificence **15** illustriousness

Great Profile
nickname of: **13** John Barrymore

Great Railway Bazaar, The
author: **11** Paul Theroux

great world
French: **10** grand monde

Great Ziegfeld, The
director: **14** Robert Z Leonard
cast: **8** Myrna Loy **10** Fanny Brice **11** Frank Morgan, Luise Rainer (Anna Held) **13** Virginia Bruce, William Powell
Oscar for: **7** actress (Rainer), picture

grebe 4 bird, fowl, loon **5** diver **6** dipper **7** henbill **8** dabchick **9** hell-diver **10** water witch

Grecco, Al
character in: **20** Appointment in Samarra
author: **5** O'Hara

Greco, El Greco
real name: **23** Domenikos Theotokopoulos
born: **5** Crete **6** Candia
artwork: **7** Espolio (Disrobing of Christ), Laocoon **12** View of Toledo

19 Cleaning of the Temple **20** Healing of the Blind Man **21** Burial of the Count Orgaz **27** Christ Stripped of His Garments **28** San Ildefonso at his Writing Desk **29** Cardinal Fernando Nino de Guevara **42** Christ Driving the Money-Changers from the Temple

Greece
other name: **5** Ellas **16** Hellenic Republic
capital/largest city: **6** Athens
others: **4** Enor **5** Canea, Corfu, Pylos, Volos **6** Delphi, Patras, Sparta **7** Chalcis, Corinth, Olympia, Piraeus **8** Salonika, Thessaly **9** Epidaurus, Gallipoli **10** Herakleion **11** Hermoupolis
school: **5** Crete **6** Athens, Patras, Thrace **8** Ioannina, Salonika
division: **6** Attica, Epirus, Thrace **7** Boeotia **8** Thessaly **9** Macedonia
measure: **3** pik **4** bema, piki, pous **5** baril, chous, cubit, diote, doron, maris, pekhe, podos, pygon, xylon **6** acaena, bacile, barile, cotula, dichas, gramme, hemina, koilon, lichas, milion, orgyia, palame, pechys, schene, xestes **7** amphora, bacvhel, chenica, choenix, cyathos, diaulos, metreta, stadium, stremma **8** condylos, daktylos, dekapode, dolichos, medimnos, medimnus, metretes, palaiste, plethron, plethrum, stathmos **9** hemiekton, oxybaphon
monetary unit: **5** lepta **7** drachma
weight: **3** mna, oke **4** mina, obol **5** livre, pound **6** diobol, kantar, obolos, obolus, talent **7** chalcon, drachma **8** diobolon
island: **3** Ios **5** Chios, Corfu, Crete, Delos, Melos, Naxos, Paros, Samos, Syros, Tenos, Thera, Zante **6** Andros, Euboea, Ionian, Ithaca, Lemnos, Lesbos, Patmos, Rhodes, Skyros, Thasos **7** Mykonos **8** Cyclades, Mytilene, Skiathos, Skopelos **9** Alonnisos **10** Cephalonia, Dodecanese, Samothrace **16** Northern Sporades
lake: **5** Karla, Volve **6** Copais, Kopais, Prespa, Voweis **8** Ioannina, Koroneia, Vistonis **9** Trichonis, Vegoritis
mountain: **3** Ida **4** Idhi, Oeta, Oite, Ossa **5** Athos **6** Ithome, Peleon, Pelion, Pindus **7** Grammos, Helicon, Rhodope **8** Hymettos, Smolikas, Taygetos, Taygetus **9** Parnassus **10** Hagion Oros, Lycabettus, Pentelicus
highest point: **7** Olympus
river: **4** Arta **6** Peneus, Struma, Vardar **7** Hellada, Maritsa **8** Achelous, Aliakmon
sea: **5** Crete **6** Aegean, Ionian **7** Mirtoon **13** Mediterranean
physical feature:
gulf: **7** Corinth, Saronic
peninsula: **6** Balkan **10** Chalcidice **12** Peloponnesus

plain: 7 Boeotia **8** Thessaly
plateau: 7 Arcadia
valley: 5 Nemea
people: 5 Greek **6** Achean, Dorian, Ionian **7** Aeolian, Hellene
artist: 7 El Greco
author: 5 Homer **6** Hesiod, Pindar **8** Menander **9** Aeschylus, Euripides, Sophocles **11** Kazantzakis **12** Aristophanes
god: 4 Ares, Hera, Leto, Zeus **5** Cupid **6** Apollo, Cronus, Hermes, Hestia **7** Artemis, Demeter **8** Dionysus, Poseidon **9** Aphrodite **10** Hephaestus, Persephone **12** Pallas Athena **13** Phoebus Apollo
historian: 9 Herodotus **10** Thucydides
king: 11 Constantine
lawmaker: 5 Draco, Solon **8** Lycurgus, Pericles
leader: 10 Papandreou
mathematician: 6 Euclid **10** Archimedes, Pythagoras
mythological: 5 Atlas, Helen, Jason, Medea, Paris **6** Hector, Medusa **7** Ariadne, Chimera, Pandora, Pegasus, Perseus, Theseus **8** Achilles, Heracles, Minotaur, Odysseus **9** Agamemnon, Andromeda, Iphigenia, King Minos **10** Prometheus **11** Bellerophon
orator: 11 Demosthenes
philosopher: 5 Plato **8** Socrates **9** Aristotle
physician: 11 Hippocrates
sculptor: 5 Myron **7** Phidias **10** Praxiteles
tycoon: 7 Onassis
language: 5 Greek
religion: 14 Greek Orthodoxy
place:
  ruins: 5 Delos, Pella, Pylos, Samos **6** Delphi, Sparta, Thebes, Tiryns **7** Corinth, Eleusis, Elevsis, Knossos, Mycenae, Olympia **9** Acropolis, Epidaurus, Parthenon **13** Palace of Minos
  feature: 8 Olympics **12** Olympic Games
  coffeeshop: 7 kaphene
  marketplace: 5 agora
  port: 7 Piraeus
  presidential guard: 7 Evzones
  village square: 7 plateia
  food:
    dish: 4 gyro **7** baklava, mousaka **8** moussaka, souvlaki, dolmades **10** shish kabob
    liquor: 4 ouzo
    wine: 7 retsina
greed 7 avarice, avidity, craving **8** cupidity, rapacity **11** itching palm, money-hunger, piggishness, selfishness **12** covetousness **13** rapaciousness **14** avariciousness
greediness 7 avarice **8** gluttony, ra-

pacity, voracity **12** covetousness, graspingness **15** acquisitiveness
greedy 4 avid **5** eager **6** ardent, hungry **7** anxious, burning, craving, fervent, hoggish, piggish, selfish, swinish, wolfish **8** covetous, famished, grasping, ravenous **9** devouring, impatient, mercenary, predatory, rapacious, thirsting, voracious **10** avaricious, gluttonous, insatiable **11** acquisitive, money-hungry **12** gormandizing
Greek
language family: 12 Indo-European
ancient branch: 5 Attic, Doric, Ionic **6** Aeolic
Greek alphabet 5 alpha **4** beta **5** gamma **5** delta **7** epsilon **4** zeta **3** eta **5** theta **4** iota **5** kappa **6** lambda **2** mu **2** nu **2** xi **7** omicron **2** pi **3** rho **5** sigma **3** tau **7** upsilon **3** phi **3** chi **3** psi **5** omega
Greek Anthology, The
author: 8 Cephalas, Meleager
Greek measure 4 mina **5** cubit **6** obolos, talent **7** drachma, stadion
Greek Mythology
afterworld of the blessed: 7 Elysium
amber islands: 10 Electrides
architect of labyrinth: 8 Daedalus
blood-sucking monster: 5 Lamia
cupbearer to the gods: 8 Ganymede **9** Catamitus
dragon: 8 basilisk
drink of the gods: 6 nectar
eagle/lion monster: 7 griffin, griffon, gryphon
enchantress: 5 Circe
female warrior: 6 Amazon
fire-breathing monster: 7 Chimera
first man: 12 Alalcomeneus
food/drink/perfume of the gods: 8 ambrosia
the Furies: 5 Dirae **6** Erinys, Furiae, Semnai **7** Erinyes **9** Eumenides
  names: 7 Allecto, Megaera **9** Tisiphone
goat god: 7 Aegipan
goddess of beauty: 6 Graces **7** Gratiae **9** Charities
  names: 4 Auxo **5** Cleta **6** Aglaia, Thalia **7** Phaenna **8** Hegemone **10** Euphrosyne
goddess of childbirth: 8 Ilithyia **10** Eileithyia
  corresponds to Roman: 6 Lucina
goddess of the dawn: 3 Eos
  corresponds to Roman: 6 Aurora
goddesses of destiny: 5 Fates, Morae **6** Moerae, Moirai
  names: 5 Moira **6** Clotho **8** Lachesis
  corresponds to Roman: 6 Parcae
goddess of discord: 4 Eris
  corresponds to Roman: 9 Discordia
goddess of divine punishment/ recklessness: 3 Ate
goddess of divine retribution: 8 Ad-

rastea
goddess of the earth: 2 Ge **4** Gaea, Gaia
  corresponds to Roman: 6 Tellus
goddess of earth/fertility: 7 Demeter
  corresponds to Roman: 5 Ceres
goddess of earth/Hades: 5 Brimo **6** Hecate, Hekate
goddess of fortune: 5 Tyche
  corresponds to Roman: 7 Fortuna
goddess of healing: 4 Iaso
goddess of health: 6 Hygeia
  corresponds to Roman: 5 Salus
goddess of the hearth: 6 Hestia
  corresponds to Roman: 5 Vesta
goddess of justice: 4 Dice, Dike **6** Astrea **7** Astraea
goddesses of literature/the arts: 5 Muses **7** the Nine **8** Pierides **10** Castalides
  names: 4 Clio **5** Aoede, Erato, Mneme **6** Melete, Thalia, Urania **7** Euterpe **8** Calliope **9** Melpomene **10** Polyhymnia **11** Terpsichore
  corresponds to Roman: 7 Camenae
muse of astronomy: 6 Urania
muse of dancing/choral song: 11 Terpsichore
muse of history: 4 Clio
muse of idyllic poetry/comedy: 6 Thalia
muse of love poetry: 5 Erato
muse of meditation: 6 Melete
muse of memory: 5 Mneme
muse of music/lyric poetry: 7 Euterpe
muse of poetry/epic: 8 Calliope
muse of sacred music/dance: 10 Polyhymnia
muse of song: 5 Aoede
muse of tragedy: 9 Melpomene
goddess of love/beauty: 6 Urania **7** Cyprian, Paphian **8** Cytherea **9** Aphrodite **10** Anadyomene
  corresponds to Roman: 5 Venus
goddess of memory: 9 Mnemosyne
goddess of the night: 3 Nyx
goddess of peace: 5 Irene
  corresponds to Roman: 3 Pax
goddess of the rainbow: 4 Iris
goddess of sailors: 5 Brizo
goddess of the sea: 10 Amphitrite
goddesses of the sea: 6 Graeae, Graiae
  names: 4 Enyo **5** Deino **9** Pemphredo
goddesses of seasons/growth/ decay/social order: 4 Hour **5** Horae
  names: 4 Dice, Dike **5** Carpo, Irene **6** Thallo **7** Eunomia
goddess of spring flowers: 6 Thallo
goddess of summer fruit: 5 Carpo
goddess of victory: 4 Nike
  corresponds to Roman: 6 Athena **8** Victoria
goddess of war: 4 Enyo
  corresponds to Roman: 7 Bellona

**goddess of wisdom/fertility/arts/
warfare: 6** Athena, Athene, Pallas,
Saitis **11** Tritogeneia **12** Pallas
Athena **18** Alalcomenean Athena
  corresponds to Roman: 7 Minerva
goddess of youth/spring: 4 Hebe
**god of beekeeping/winemaking/
husbandry: 9** Aristaeus
god of censure/ridicule: 5 Momos,
Momus
god of dreams: 6 Icelus, Oniros **7**
Oneiros **8** Morpheus
god of earth: 10 Trophonius
god of Eleusinian mysteries: 7 Bacchus
god of erotic desire: 7 Himeros
**god of fire/metalworking/
handicrafts: 10** Hephaestus,
Hephaistos
  corresponds to Roman: 6 Vulcan
god of the heavens: 4 Zeus
  corresponds to Roman: 4 Jove **7**
    Jupiter
  corresponds to Egyptian: 4 Amen,
    Amon **5** Ammon **6** Amen Ra,
    Amon Ra
**god of light/healing/music/poetry/
prophecy/beauty: 6** Apollo
god of love: 4 Eros
  corresponds to Roman: 4 Amor **5**
    Cupid
god of male power/procreation: 7
Priapus
  corresponds to Roman: 7 Mutinus
god of marriage: 5 Hymen **9** Hymenaeus
  corresponds to Roman: 8 Talassio
god of medicine/healing: 9 Asclepius
  corresponds to Roman: 11 Aescu-
    lapius
god of oaths: 6 Horcus
god of recovery from illness: 11 Te-
lesphorus
god of sea/caused earthquakes: 8
Poseidon
  corresponds to Roman: 7 Neptune
**god of shepherds/flocks/pastures/
forests: 3** Pan **7** Sinoeis
god of sleep: 6 Hypnos, Hypnus
  corresponds to Roman: 6 Somnus
god of the sun: 6 Helios **8** Hyperion
  corresponds to Roman: 3 Sol
god of the underworld: 6 Infiri
god of war: 4 Ares **8** Theritas
  corresponds to Roman: 4 Mars
god of wine/fertility/drama: 5 Evius
7 Bacchus **8** Dionysus
Gorgon monster: 6 Medusa
hundred-headed monster: 5 Ladon **8**
Typhoeus
islands of the blessed: 10 Hesperides
man/horse monster: 7 centaur
**messenger of gods/god of roads/
commerce/invention/cunning/
thieves: 6** Hermes
  corresponds to Roman: 7 Mercury
monster that asked riddles: 6

Sphinx
**monsters that turn people to stone:
7** Gorgons
moon goddess/huntress/virgin: 6
Phoebe, Selene **7** Artemis
  corresponds to Roman: 5 Diana
  corresponds to Cretan: 11 Brito-
    martis
nine-headed water serpent: 5 Hydra
nymph: 7 Calypso
one-eyed giant: 7 Cyclops
oracle of Apollo: 13 Delphic oracle
personification of death: 4 Mors **8**
Thanatos
**personification of punishment/
revenge: 5** Poena, Poine
personification of soul: 6 Psyche
physician to gods of Olympia: 5
Paeon
prophetess: 9 Alexandra, Cassandra
queen of heaven: 4 Hera, Here
  corresponds to Roman: 4 Juno
race of gods: 6 Titans
  names: 4 Rhea, Thia **5** Coeus,
    Crius **6** Cronus, Phoebe, Tethys,
    Themis **7** Iapetus, Oceanus **8** Hy-
    perion **9** Mnemosyne
river god: 6 Asopus, Peneus, Simois
7 Inachus, Pelegon **8** Achelous
river in Hades: 4 Styx **5** Lethe **7** Acheron, Cocytus
  ferryman: 6 Charon
  river of forgetfulness: 5 Lethe
ruler of the winds: 6 Aeolus
satyr/god of the forest: 7 Silenus
sea god: 6 Nereus, Triton **7** Glaucus,
Phorcys, Proteus
sea monster: 6 Scylla
seer: 6 Mopsus **8** Tiresias
serpent: 6 dipsas
serpent of darkness: 5 Apepi **7** Apophis
seven against Thebes: 6 Tydeus **8**
Adrastus, Capaneus **9** Polynices **10**
Amphiaraus, Hippomedon **13** Parthenopaeus
seven sisters: 8 Pleiades
  names: 4 Maia **6** Merope **7** Alcy-
    one, Celaeno, Electra, Sterope,
    Taygete
sorceress: 5 Medea
**spirits of disease/evil/old age/death:
5** Keres
**three-headed dog that guards un-
derworld: 8** Cerberus
twins: 8 Dioscuri **15** Castor and Pollux
two-headed serpent: 11 Amphisbaena
underworld: 5 Hades,
  corresponds to Roman: 3 Dis **5**
    Orcus, Pluto **8** Dis Pater
underworld darkness: 6 Erebus
underworld spirit: 6 Chthonian
virgin huntress: 8 Atalanta, Atalante
whirlpool: 9 Charybdis
winged horse: 5 Arion **7** Pegasus
woman/beast monster: 6 Python **8**

Delphyne
woman/bird monster: 5 Harpy
woman/serpent monster: 7 Echidna
wood nymph: 5 dryad
Greek uncial codex 4 Syri **6** Regius **8**
Ephraemi **9** Laudianus, Vaticanus **10**
Sinaiticus **11** Basiliensis **12** Alexandri-
nus, Sangallensis **13** Koridethianus
green 3 raw **4** jade, lawn, lime, turf **5**
crude, heath, olive, rough, sward,
young **6** callow, campus, common,
tender, unripe **7** awkward, emerald,
verdant, verdure **8** greenish, gullible,
ignorant, immature, inexpert, not
cured, not dried, pea-green, sea-green,
unsmoked, untanned, unversed **9**
blue-green, credulous, grassplot, lime-
green, unfledged, unskilled, untrained
10 aquamarine, chartreuse, golf
course, grass-green, greensward, kelly-
green, olive green, uninformed, unmellowed, unpolished, unseasoned **11**
cobalt green, forest green,
undeveloped, yellow-green **12** easily
fooled, green-colored, not fully aged,
putting green, village green **13** inexperienced, undisciplined **14** underdeveloped **15** unsophisticated
Green Acres
  character: 7 Mr Haney **8** Eb Dawson
    10 Fred Ziffel, Sam Drucker **11** Doris
    Ziffel, Hank Kimball, Lisa Douglas
    20 Oliver Wendell Douglas
  cast: 8 Eva Gabor, Fran Ryan **9** Alvy
    Moore, Frank Cady, Tom Lester **10**
    Pat Buttram **11** Eddie Albert **13** Bar-
    bara Pepper, Hank Patterson
  pig: 6 Arnold
  town: 11 Hooterville
green at the gills 6 queasy, sickly **7**
bilious **8** nauseous **9** nauseated, sickening
greenback 4 bill **8** banknote **12** treasury note **15** legal-tender note **17** silver
certificate
Green Bay
  football team: 7 Packers
Greene, Graham
  author of: 11 The Third Man **12**
    Brighton Rock, Ways of Escape **14**
    The Human Factor **16** Monsignor
    Quixote **17** The End of the Affair,
    The Ministry of Fear, Travels with
    My Aunt **19** The Heart of the Matter,
    The Power and the Glory
Greene, Lorne
  born: 6 Canada, Ottawa **7** Ontario
  roles: 5 Adama **7** Bonanza **11** Peyton
    Place **12** Autumn Leaves, The Bucca-
    neer **13** Ben Cartwright **16** The Sil-
    ver Chalice **19** Battlestar Galactica
Greene, Nathanael
  served in: 16 Revolutionary War
  rank: 16 brigadier general **20** quarter-
    master general
  battle: 7 Cowpens, Trenton **12** Eutaw

Springs, Hobkirk's Hill **18** Guilford Court House

green-eyed monster 4 envy **8** jealousy **12** covetousness

Green for Danger
    director: **13** Sidney Gilliat
    cast: **7** Leo Genn **9** Sally Gray **11** Alastair Sim **12** Rosamund John, Trevor Howard

greenhorn 4 rube, tyro **6** novice, rookie **7** learner **8** beginner, neophyte, newcomer **9** fledgling **10** apprentice, tenderfoot **14** babe in the woods

Green Hornet, The
    character: **4** Kato **9** Britt Reid (The Green Hornet)
    cast: **8** Bruce Lee **11** Van Williams
    car: **11** Black Beauty
    creator: **11** Bert Whitman
    sidekick: **4** Kato

Green House, The
    author: **16** Mario Vargas Llosa

Greening of America, The
    author: **12** Charles Reich

greenish 6 sickly **7** bilious

Greenland
    alternate name: **14** Kalaalit Nunaat
    capital/largest city: **3** Nuk **8** Godthaab, The Point
    others: **4** Etah, Nord **5** Thule **6** Ivigut, Umanak **7** Godhavn, Ivigtut **10** Nanortalik **11** Julianehaab **12** Angmagssalik, Sukkertoppen **14** Christianshaab
    government: **20** home rule under Denmark
    monetary unit: **3** ore **5** krone
    island: **5** Disko
    mountain: **5** Forel, Payer **7** Khardyu **8** Peterman **15** Petermannsbjerg
    highest point: **9** Gunnbjorn **16** Gunnbjornsfjaeld
    sea: **6** Arctic **9** Greenland
    physical feature: **9** Inland Ice
        bay: **5** Disko **6** Baffin **8** Melville
        cape: **4** Jaal **6** Grivel, Walker **8** Bismarck, Brewster, Farewell, Lowenorn **11** Morris Jesup
        glacier: **10** Jacobshavn
        strait: **5** Davis **7** Denmark
    people: **3** Ita **6** Eskimo **8** European
    explorer: **10** Eric the Red
    language: **6** Danish, Eskimo **11** Greenlandic
    religion: **19** Evangelical Lutheran
    feature:
        airbase: **4** Etah **5** Thule
        animal: **7** caribou

Green Mansions
    author: **8** W H Hudson
    character: **4** Rima **5** Nuflo **6** Mr Abel

Greenmantle
    author: **10** John Buchan

Green Mile, The
    author: **11** Stephen King
    director: **13** Frank Darabont
    cast: **8** Tom Hanks (Paul Edgecomb) **10** Bonnie Hunt (Jan Edgecomb), David Morse (Brutus Howell) **12** Graham Greene (Arlen Bitterbuck), Michael Jeter (Eduard Delacroix) **13** James Cromwell (Hal Moores) **19** Michael Clarke Duncan (John Coffey)

Green Mountain State
    nickname of: **7** Vermont

Greenough, Horatio
    born: **8** Boston MA
    artwork: **16** George Washington **18** The Chanting Cherubs

Green Pastures, The
    author: **12** Marc Connelly

Greenstreet, Sydney
    born: **7** England **8** Sandwich
    roles: **9** The Fat Man **10** Casablanca **16** The Maltese Falcon **19** Passage to Marseilles

green with envy 7 envious, jealous **8** covetous

greet 4 hail, meet **5** admit **6** accept, accost, salute **7** receive, speak to, welcome **9** smile upon, recognize **10** bid welcome

greeting 6 salute **7** welcome **8** saluting **9** reception, welcoming **10** salutation **12** introduction, presentation

greetings 4 best **5** hello **7** regards **8** respects **10** best wishes, good wishes, salutation **11** compliments, remembrance, well-wishing **13** felicitations
    Latin: **5** salve

gregarious 6 genial, lively, social **7** affable **8** friendly, outgoing, sociable **9** convivial, talkative, vivacious **11** extroverted **13** companionable

gremlin 3 imp **5** demon, gnome **6** goblin

Grenada
    other name: **11** Isle of Spice
    capital/largest city: **9** St Georges
    others: **8** Sauteurs
    head of state: **14** British monarch **15** governor general
    island: **8** Windward **9** Carriacou **10** Grenadines
    lake: **10** Grand Etang
    highest point: **11** St Catherine
    sea: **9** Caribbean
    physical feature:
        bay: **9** St Georges'
    people: **5** Black, Negro **6** Indian
    discoverer: **8** Columbus
    language: **7** English
    religion: **8** Anglican **10** Protestant **13** Roman Catholic
    food:
        spice: **4** mace **6** nutmeg

grenade 7 missile **9** pineapple

Grendel
    character in: **7** Beowulf
    author: **11** John Gardner

Grewgious, Mr
    character in: **22** The Mystery of Edwin Drood
    author: **7** Dickens

Grey, Joel
    real name: **8** Joel Katz
    born: **13** Cleveland Ohio
    daughter: **12** Jennifer Grey
    roles: **7** Cabaret, George M **13** Come September **14** The Fantasticks **23** The Seven Percent Solution

Grey, Zane
    author of: **18** Valley of Wild Horses **20** The Spirit of the Border **21** Riders of the Purple Sage, The Last of the Plainsmen

greyhound
    group of: **5** leash

Greystoke, Lord
    real identity of: **6** Tarzan

griddle cake 6 blintz, waffle **7** crumpet, hot cake, pancake **8** corncake, flapcake, flapjack **10** battercake **11** flannel cake **13** buckwheat cake
    French: **5** crepe **12** crepe suzette
    German: **11** pfannkuchen
    Hungarian: **10** palacsinta
    Indian: **8** chapatty

Gride, Arthur
    character in: **16** Nicholas Nickleby
    author: **7** Dickens

grief 3 woe **4** care **5** agony, worry **6** burden, misery, ordeal, sorrow **7** anguish, anxiety, concern, despair, remorse, sadness, trouble **8** distress, grieving, hardship, nuisance, vexation **9** grievance, heartache, suffering **10** affliction, desolation, discomfort, heartbreak **11** despondency, tribulation **12** wretchedness **13** inconvenience

griefstricken 7 joyless, unhappy **8** saddened, wretched **9** sorrowful **13** brokenhearted

Grieg, Edvard Hagerup
    born: **6** Bergen, Norway
    composer of: **5** I Host **8** Bergljot, In Autumn, Peer Gynt **11** Lyric Pieces **12** Landjaenning **14** Fra Holbergs Tid, Lyriske Stykker **15** Sigurd Jorsalfar **16** From Holberg's Time **17** Recognition of Land **18** Foran Sydens Kloster **22** At a Southern Convent Gate

grievance 4 beef, hurt **5** wrong **6** injury **7** outrage **8** hardship, iniquity **9** complaint, injustice **10** affliction, bone to pick, disserve

grieve 3 cry, rue, sob **4** moan, pain, wail, weep **5** be sad, mourn **6** bemoan, deject, harass, lament, sadden, sorrow **7** afflict, agonize, depress, oppress, torture **8** disquiet, distress **10** discomfort **11** be anguished

grieve over 5 mourn **6** bemoan, bewail, lament **7** cry over **8** moan over, weep over

grievous 3 sad **5** acute, grave, harsh, heavy **6** severe, tragic, woeful **7** crucial, glaring, harmful, heinous, painful, serious, very bad **8** critical, shameful, shocking **9** agonizing, appalling, atrocious, monstrous, nefarious, sorrowful **10** burdensome, calamitous, deplorable, iniquitous, lamentable, outrageous, unbearable **11** destructive, distressing, intolerable, significant **12** insufferable **13** heartbreaking

griffin
also: 7 griffon, gryphon
form: 7 monster
head of: 5 eagle
wings of: 5 eagle
body of: 4 lion
guards of: 4 gold
location: 7 Scythia

Griffith, Andy
real name: 20 Andrew Samuel Griffith
born: 8 Mt Airy NC
roles: 7 Matlock **13** Will Stockdale **15** A Face in the Crowd, Angel in My Pocket **18** No Time for Sergeants **19** The Andy Griffith Show

Griffith, D W
director of: 11 Intolerance **14** Broken Blossoms **17** Orphans of the Storm, The Birth of a Nation

Griffith, Hugh
born: 5 Wales **8** Anglesey **10** Marian Glas
roles: 6 Ben-Hur **8** Lucky Jim, Tom Jones

griffon *see* **7** griffin

grill 3 fry **4** cook, grid, pump, quiz, sear **5** broil, query **7** broiler, grating, griddle **8** gridiron, question **9** crossbars **11** interrogate **12** cross-examine

grim 4 foul, hard, ugly **5** cruel, harsh, lurid, stern, sulky **6** brutal, fierce, gloomy, grisly, grumpy, horrid, morose, odious, severe, somber, sullen **7** austere, ghastly, hideous, inhuman, macabre, squalid, vicious **8** dreadful, fiendish, gruesome, horrible, resolute, scowling, shocking, sinister **9** appalling, ferocious, frightful, heartless, loathsome, merciless, obstinate, repellent, repugnant, repulsive, revolting **10** determined, forbidding, implacable, inexorable, relentless, unyielding

grimace 4 face **5** scowl, smirk, sneer **6** glower **7** wry face
French: 4 moue

grime 4 dirt, dust, smut, soil, soot **5** filth **6** smudge

Grimhild
origin: 12 Scandinavian
mentioned in: 8 Volsunga
form: 9 sorceress
husband: 5 Giuki, Gjuki
daughter: 6 Gudrun, Kudrun **7** Guthrun
son: 6 Gunnar
tricked Sigurd to marry: 6 Gudrun, Kudrun **7** Guthrun

Grimm Brothers (Jakob and Wil-

helm)
editors of: 15 Hansel and Gretel **16** Grimm's Fairy Tales

grim reaper 5 death **12** angel of death

grim-visaged 8 frowning, scowling **9** long-faced **10** stern-faced

grin 4 beam **5** smile, smirk **6** rictus, simper **11** crack a smile

grind 4 file, grit, mill, rasp, whet **5** chore, crush, gnash, grate **6** abrade, drudge, polish, powder, scrape **7** crammer, hard job, plodder, sharpen, slavery **8** bookworm, drudgery **9** granulate, pulverize, triturate

Gringoire
character in: 23 The Hunchback of Notre Dame
author: 4 Hugo

grip 3 bag **4** grab, hilt, hold **5** clasp, grasp, rivet, seize **6** clench, clutch, handle, retain, snatch, valise **7** attract, control, impress, mastery, satchel **8** clutches, hold fast, suitcase **9** gladstone, handclasp, handshake, retention, spellbind **10** domination, perception

gripe, gripes 4 beef, carp, fret, kick, pain, pang, rail **5** cavil, colic, spasm, whine **6** cramps, grouch, grouse, kvetch, mutter, squawk, twinge, twitch **7** grumble, protest, whining **8** complain, distress, grousing, bellyache, complaint, find fault, grievance, grumbling **10** affliction

Grisham, John
author of: 7 The Firm **9** Bleachers, The Broker, The Client **10** The Chamber, The Partner, The Summons **11** A Time to Kill, The Brethren **12** The Last Juror, The Rainmaker, The Testament **13** A Painted House **14** The King of Torts, The Runaway Jury **15** The Pelican Brief, The Street Lawyer

grisly 4 foul, gory, grim **5** lurid **6** horrid, odious **7** ghastly, hideous, macabre **8** dreadful, gruesome, horrible, shocking, sinister **9** abhorrent, appalling, frightful, loathsome, repellent, repugnant, repulsive, revolting **10** abominable, forbidding, horrendous

grit 3 rub **4** dirt, dust, guts, muck, rasp, sand, soot **5** filth, gnash, grate, nerve, pluck, spunk **6** crunch, mettle, scrape **7** courage, stamina **8** backbone, tenacity **9** fortitude **10** doggedness, resolution **12** perseverance **13** determination, grind together

Grizzly Bear State 10 California

groan 4 howl, moan, roar, wail **5** bleat, crack, creak, whine **6** bellow, bemoan, lament, murmur, squeak **7** grumble, screech, whimper **8** complain

grocery store
Spanish: 6 bodega

groggy 5 dazed, dizzy, dopey, shaky,

woozy **6** addled, punchy **7** muddled, reeling, stunned **8** confused, sluggish, unsteady **9** befuddled, lethargic, perplexed, stupefied **10** bewildered, punch-drunk, staggering

groom 4 comb, wash **5** boots, brush, curry, dress, drill, green, prime, primp, train, valet **6** flunky, lackey, spouse **7** clean up, consort, develop, educate, footman, freshen, hostler, husband, prepare, refresh, rub down, servant **8** exercise, initiate, make neat, make tidy, practice, spruce up **9** currycomb, make ready, stableboy **10** bridegroom, manservant **12** indoctrinate **13** livery servant

groove 3 cut, rut, use **4** rule **5** flute, habit, score, usage **6** custom, furrow, gutter, hollow, trench **7** channel, cutting, scoring **8** practice **9** procedure **10** beaten path, convention **11** corrugation **12** fixed routine, second nature

grope 3 paw **5** probe **6** finger, fumble **7** fish for, venture **9** feel about **11** feel one's way, move blindly, try one's luck **13** search blindly

Gropius, Walter
architect of: 5 Fagus (factory) **7** Bauhaus (Dessau) **13** Pan Am Building (NYC) **31** Harvard University Graduate Center

gross 3 bag, big, fat **4** bulk, earn, huge, lewd, mass, rank, reap, vast **5** bulky, crude, great, heavy, large, obese, plain, sheer, total, utter, whole **6** carnal, coarse, earthy, entire, pick up, ribald, smutty, sordid, take in, vulgar **7** glaring, heinous, immense, lump sum, massive, obscene, obvious, titanic, uncouth **8** colossal, complete, enormous, flagrant, gigantic, improper, indecent, manifest, unseemly, unwieldy **9** aggregate, downright, egregious, lecherous, monstrous, offensive, unrefined **10** gargantuan, indelicate, lascivious, licentious, outrageous, overweight, prodigious, stupendous **11** unequivocal, unmitigated, unqualified

grossness 7 obesity **8** hugeness, lewdness, ribaldry **9** crudeness, heaviness, indecency, obscenity, roughness, vulgarity **10** coarseness, indelicacy, inelegance **14** lasciviousness

grossularite
species: 6 garnet

grotesque 3 odd **4** wild **5** antic, weird **6** absurd, exotic, far-out, rococo, way-out **7** baroque, bizarre, strange **8** deformed, fanciful, peculiar **9** contorted, distorted, eccentric, fantastic, misshapen, odd-shaped, unnatural **10** outlandish **11** extravagant, incongruous **12** preposterous

grotto 4 cave **6** burrow, cavern, hollow, recess, tunnel **8** catacomb

grouch 3 cry **4** beef, carp, crab, fret,

kick, mope, pout, rail, sulk **5** cavil, crank, gripe, growl, moper, whine **6** grouse, mutter, pouter **7** grumble, kill-joy, protest **8** complain, grumbler **9** bellyache, find fault **10** complainer, curmudgeon, spoilsport, wet blanket

grouchy 5 cross, testy **6** crabby, cranky, grumpy, touchy **8** snappish **10** ill-humored, out of sorts **11** ill-tempered **12** cantankerous **13** short-tempered

ground, grounds 3 set, sod **4** area, base, call, dirt, farm, land, loam, soil, turf, yard **5** acres, basis, beach, cause, dregs, drill, earth, field, found, lawns, realm, teach, train **6** campus, domain, estate, excuse, inform, motive, object, reason, region, secure, settle, sphere, strand **7** account, confirm, deposit, dry land, educate, founder, gardens, habitat, prepare, purpose, support, terrain **8** district, exercise, firm land, initiate, instruct, occasion, organize, practice, premises, property, province, sediment, the earth **9** arguments, bailiwick, establish, fix firmly, institute, principle, rationale, settlings, territory **10** discipline, inducement, real estate, terra firma **11** pros and cons **12** indoctrinate **14** considerations

grounded 5 based **6** kept in, taught **7** aground, beached, bounded, drilled, founded, secured, trained **8** informed, prepared, stranded **9** foundered, initiated **10** kept at home, instructed, restricted **11** disciplined, established **12** washed ashore **13** indoctrinated

grounding 8 training **9** education **10** background, experience **11** preparation **14** indoctrination **15** familiarization

groundless 4 idle **5** empty, false **6** faulty, flimsy, unreal, untrue **8** baseless, needless, unproved **9** erroneous, illogical, imaginary, unfounded **10** chimerical, fallacious, gratuitous **11** uncalled for, unjustified, unsupported, unwarranted **13** unjustifiable, without reason

groundwork 4 base, root **5** basis **6** cradle, ground, origin, source, spring **7** bedrock, footing, grounds, taproot **8** keystone, learning, planning, practice, training **9** spadework **10** foundation **11** cornerstone, fundamental, preparation **12** fundamentals, underpinning **14** apprenticeship, indoctrination

group 3 set **4** band, clan, file, gang, herd, pack, sift, size, sort **5** align, bunch, class, crowd, flock, grade, hoard, index, party, place, range, swarm, tribe, troop **6** assign, branch, circle, clique, family, hobnob, league, line up, mingle, throng **7** arrange, catalog, cluster, combine, company, consort, coterie, faction, marshal, section, species, variety **8** classify, division,

graduate, organize, register **9** associate, gathering **10** assemblage, collection, coordinate, detachment, fraternity, fraternize **11** aggregation, alphabetize, association, brotherhood, subdivision **12** congregation **14** classification, representation

Group, The
    author: 12 Mary McCarthy
grouping 7 sorting **8** arraying, ordering **10** assemblage, assortment **11** arrangement, disposition **12** distribution, organization
group of performers 6 troupe **7** company **8** ensemble
Group Portrait of a Lady
    author: 12 Heinrich Boll
grouse 4 beef, crab, fret, fume, fuss, kick **5** gripe **6** grouch, mutter, squawk, take on **7** carry on, grumble **8** complain, gamebird **9** bellyache
grove 4 bosk **5** brake, copse **6** forest, pinery, timber **7** coppice, orchard, thicket, wood lot **8** wildwood, woodland **9** shrubbery **10** plantation
grovel 4 fawn **5** cower, crawl, stoop, toady **6** cringe, kowtow, snivel **7** flatter, truckle **12** bow and scrape **13** demean oneself, humble oneself **14** lick the boots of
groveling 6 abject **7** fawning, servile **8** cowering, crawling, cringing, toadying **9** kowtowing, truckling **11** bootlicking **17** bowing and scraping
grow 3 bud, sow, wax **4** boom, farm, rise, till **5** bloom, breed, plant, raise, ripen, surge, swell, widen **6** become, expand, extend, flower, garden, mature, spread, sprout, thrive **7** advance, amplify, blossom, develop, enlarge, fill out, get to be, improve, magnify, produce, prosper, shoot up, stretch, succeed **8** come to be, flourish, fructify, increase, mushroom, progress, spring up, vegetate **9** cultivate, germinate, propagate, skyrocket **10** aggrandize
Growing Up in New Guinea
    author: 12 Margaret Mead
growl 4 fret, snap **5** croak, grind, gripe, groan, grunt, snarl, whine **6** grouse, murmur, mutter, rumble **7** grumble **8** complain, talk back
grown-up 3 big, man **4** lady, ripe **5** adult, of age, woman **6** mature, senior **7** worldly **9** full-blown, full-grown, gentleman **11** full-fledged **13** sophisticated
growth 4 crop, hump, lump, rise **5** gnarl, prime, surge, swell, tumor **6** sowing, spread **7** advance, harvest, produce, success **8** increase, maturity, planting, progress **9** expansion, extension, flowering, increment **10** burgeoning, matureness, production, prospering **11** advancement, cultivation, development, enlargement, ex-

crescence, flourishing, improvement, propagation **12** augmentation, mass of tissue **13** amplification
    goddess of: 4 Hour **5** Horae
Groza, Lou
    nickname: 6 The Toe
    sport: 8 football
    team: 15 Cleveland Browns
grub 3 bum, dig **4** food, toil, worm **5** cadge, dig up, larva, mooch, slave **6** drudge, sponge **7** rummage
grubber 5 slave **6** drudge, toiler **7** laborer
grubby 4 foul **5** dirty, grimy, messy, muddy, nasty, seedy, tacky **6** beat-up, filthy, frowzy, frumpy, shabby, shoddy, sloppy, smudgy, soiled, sordid **7** squalid, unclean, unkempt **8** begrimed, slovenly, unwashed **9** besmeared **10** bedraggled
grudge 4 envy **5** pique, spite **6** animus, hatred, malice, rancor, resent **7** dislike, ill will **8** aversion, begrudge **9** animosity **10** resentment **11** malevolence **12** hard feelings
grudging 7 envious **8** hesitant, spiteful **9** reluctant, resentful, unwilling **10** ungenerous **13** penny-pinching
grueling 4 hard **6** brutal, tiring **7** racking **9** fatiguing, punishing, torturous **10** exhausting
gruesome 4 gory, grim **5** awful **6** grisly, horrid **7** fearful, ghastly, hideous, macabre **8** horrible, shocking, terrible **9** frightful, loathsome, repellent, repulsive, revolting **10** forbidding, horrendous, horrifying **13** blood-curdling, spine-chilling
gruff 4 curt, rude, sour, tart **5** bluff, blunt, harsh, husky, raspy, rough, sharp, short, stern, sulky, surly **6** abrupt, croaky, crusty, grumpy, hoarse, ragged, sullen **7** bearish, brusque, caustic, crabbed, cracked, grouchy, peevish, throaty, uncivil, waspish **8** churlish, guttural, impolite, snarling, strident **9** bristling, insulting **10** ill-humored, ill-natured, ungracious **11** ill-tempered **12** discourteous
grumble 4 fret **5** chafe, gripe, growl **6** grouch, grouse, mutter **8** complain **9** find-fault
grump 4 crab **5** crank **6** grouch **8** grumbler, sourball **10** curmudgeon
grumpy 4 sour **5** moody, sulky, surly, testy **6** crabby, cranky, crusty, sullen **7** grouchy, peevish, pettish **8** churlish **9** irritable, splenetic **10** ill-humored, out of humor, out of sorts **11** disgruntled, ill-disposed, ill-tempered **12** cantankerous
grunt 3 cry **4** bark, call, gasp, howl **5** burro, croak, groan, snort, utter **6** bellow, grouch, mumble, murmur, mutter, shriek **7** howling, whisper **8** complain **9** ululation **11** foot soldier, infantryman

Grunwald, Matthais (Grunewald, Mathis)
real name: 23 Mathis Gothardt Neithardt
born: 7 Germany **8** Wurzburg
artwork: 14 The Crucifixion **15** The Resurrection **20** Altarpiece at Isenheim

Grushenka
character in: 20 The Brothers Karamazov
author: 11 Dostoyevsky

Gryce, Percy
character in: 15 The House of Mirth
author: 7 Wharton

gryphon see **7** griffin

Guam
capital: 5 Agana
largest city: 8 Tamuning
others: 4 Agat, Apra, Toto, Yigo **5** Magua **6** Dededo, Merizo **8** Inarajan, Mangilao, Mongmong, Sinajana, Talofofo, Tamuning **9** Barrigada, Finegayan, Santa Rita
member of: 7 Mariana (islands)
mountain: 5 Tenjo
highest point: 6 Lamlam
sea: 7 Pacific **9** Philippine
people: 7 Spanish **8** American, Chamorro, Filipino **11** Micronesian
  explorer: 8 Magellan
  ruler: 5 Japan, Spain **12** United States
language: 7 English **8** Chamorro
religion: 16 Roman Catholicism
feature: 7 typhoon **9** coral reef
Air Force base: 8 Andersen
product: 5 copra **6** banana, papaya

guarantee, guaranty 4 avow, bail, bond, pawn, word **5** swear **6** affirm, allege, assure, attest, avowal, insure, pledge, surety **7** deposit, endorse, promise, sponsor, testify, voucher, warrant **8** contract, covenant, security, vouch for, warranty **9** agreement, answer for, assurance, insurance, testimony **10** collateral, underwrite **11** affirmation, endorsement, word of honor **12** give one's word

guard 4 mind, save, tend **5** watch **6** attend, convoy, defend, escort, patrol, picket, screen, secure, sentry, shield, warder **7** conduct, defense, protect, shelter **8** defender, garrison, guardian, keep safe, preserve, security, sentinel, watchdog, watchman **9** bodyguard, concierge, custodian, guardsman, protector, safeguard, watch over **10** doorkeeper, gatekeeper, protection **12** preservation **13** keep watch over

guard against 6 beware **10** look out for **11** take warning, watch out for

guarded 4 wary **5** cagey, chary, leery **7** careful, heedful, mindful, prudent **8** cautious, discreet, hesitant **9** in custody, protected, tentative **10** re-

strained, suspicious, under guard **11** circumspect, on one's guard

guardian 5 guard **6** convoy, escort, keeper, patrol, patron, picket, sentry, warden, warder **7** curator, trustee **8** advocate, champion, defender, sentinel, shepherd, wardsman, watchdog **9** attendant, bodyguard, caretaker, conductor, custodian, preserver, protector, safeguard, vigilante **10** benefactor **11** conservator **13** friend at court, guardian angel **14** legal custodian

guardian of a place
Latin: 10 genius loci

guardianship 4 care **6** charge **7** custody, keeping **10** protection **11** safekeeping, supervision, trusteeship

Guatemala
capital/largest city: 13 Guatemala City
others: 4 Ocos **5** Coban, Vieja **6** Chahal, Chisec, Cuilco, Flores, Iztapa, Jalapa, Salama, Solola, Tacana, Tecpan, Yaloch, Zacapa **7** Antigua, Cuilapa, Jutiapa, San Jose **8** Progreso **9** Escuintla, Tiquisate **10** Livingston **11** Totonicapan **13** Puerto Barrios, Quezaltenango **14** San Pedro Carcha **16** Chichicastenango
school: 9 San Carlos
measure: 4 vara **6** cuarta, tercia **7** cajuela, manzana **10** caballeria
monetary unit: 4 peso **7** centavo, quetzal
weight: 4 caja **5** libra
lake: 5 Dulce, Guija, Peten **6** Izabal **7** Atitlan **9** Amatitlan, Peten Itza
mountain: 4 Agua, Mico **5** Fuego, Madre **6** Pacaya, Tacana **7** Atitlan, Toliman **8** La Candon, Las Minas **10** Acatenango, Santa Maria **12** Cuchumatanes
highest point: 8 Tajumuko **9** Tajamulco
river: 4 Azul **5** Bravo, Dulce, Lapaz **6** Belize, Chixoy, Negino, Pasion, Samala **7** Chiapas, Motagua, Sarstun, Sastoon **8** Polochic, Rio Dulce, Sarstoon **10** Usumacinta
sea: 7 Pacific **8** Atlantic **9** Caribbean
physical feature:
  bay: 8 Amatique
  gulf: 8 Honduras
people: 3 Mam **4** Chol, Itza, Ixil, Maya **5** Xinca **6** Caribe, Quiche **7** ladinos, mestizo, Pocomam **13** Guatemaltecos
language: 6 Quiche **7** Spanish
religion: 13 Roman Catholic
place:
  church: 10 Santo Tomas
  ruins: 5 Mayan, Tikal **8** Uaxactun
feature:
  bird: 7 quetzal
  clarinet: 8 chirimta
  dance: 5 elson **8** guarimba
  flute: 3 xul
  military dictator: 8 Caudillo

food:
  dish: 6 pepian **10** enchiladas **13** gallo en chicha
  fruit: 4 anay

guava 7 Psidium **16** Psidium guineense
varieties: 5 apple **6** common, purple, yellow **7** Cattley, Chilean **9** pineapple **10** Costa Rican, strawberry **13** yellow cattley **16** purple strawberry, yellow strawberry

Gudrun
also: 6 Kudrun **7** Guthrun
origin: 12 Scandinavian
mentioned in: 8 Volsunga
father: 5 Giuki, Gjuki **6** Hertel
mother: 8 Grimhild
brother: 6 Gunnar
husband: 4 Atli **6** Herwig, Sigurd
killed: 4 Atli
corresponds to: 9 Kriemhild

guess 4 deem, view **5** fancy, judge, opine, think **6** assume, belief, deduce, divine, gather, reckon, regard, theory **7** believe, daresay, feeling, imagine, opinion, predict, suppose, surmise, suspect, venture **8** conclude, estimate, theorize **9** postulate, speculate, suspicion **10** assumption, conjecture, divination, hypothesis, prediction **11** hypothesize, make a stab at, postulation, presumption, speculation, supposition

guesswork 7 surmise **10** conjecture, hypothesis **11** supposition **13** shot in the dark

guest 5 diner **6** caller, client, friend, inmate, lodger, patron, roomer **7** boarder, company, habitue, invitee, patient, visitor **8** customer **9** sojourner **10** frequenter **14** paying customer

Guest, Judith
author of: 14 Ordinary People

Guevara 3 Che **7** Ernesto
born: 9 Argentina
active in: 15 Cuban Revolution
friend: 6 Castro
role in: 5 Evita
killed in: 7 Bolivia

guffaw 4 howl **6** scream **10** belly laugh, horse laugh

guidance 3 tip **4** clue, help, hint, lead **6** advice, escort **7** conduct, counsel, pointer **8** auspices **9** direction **10** leadership, management, protection, suggestion **11** information, instruction, supervision **12** intelligence **13** enlightenment

guide 4 lead, rule **5** model, pilot, steer, usher **6** beacon, convoy, direct, escort, govern, handle, leader, manage, marker, master, mentor **7** adviser, command, conduct, control, example, marshal, monitor, oversee, pattern, steerer, teacher **8** chaperon, cicerone, director, engineer, helmsman, landmark, lodestar, maneuver, polestar, regulate, shepherd, signpost **9** accompany, attendant, conductor, counselor **10** manipulate

guidebook **5** bible **6** manual **8** Baedeker, handbook **13** reference book

Guidry, Ron (Ronald Ames)
nickname: **18** Louisiana Lightning
sport: **8** baseball
position: **7** pitcher
team: **14** New York Yankees

guild **5** hansa, hanse, order, union **6** league **7** company, society **8** alliance **9** coalition **10** craft union, federation, fraternity, labor union, sisterhood, trade union **11** association, brotherhood, confederacy, corporation

Guildenstern
character in: **6** Hamlet
associated with: **11** Rosencrantz
author: **11** Shakespeare

guile **5** craft, fraud **6** deceit, tricks **7** cunning, slyness **8** artifice, strategy, trickery, wiliness **9** chicanery, deception, duplicity, treachery **10** artfulness, craftiness, dishonesty, hankypanky, stratagems, trickiness **11** fraudulence **13** sharp practice

guileless **4** open **5** frank, naive **6** candid, honest, simple **7** artless, natural, sincere **8** harmless, innocent, truthful **9** ingenuous, innocuous **10** aboveboard, unaffected **11** undesigning, unoffending **15** straightforward, unselfconscious, unsophisticated

guilelessness **6** candor **9** innocence, sincerity **10** candidness, directness **11** artlessness **13** ingenuousness

guilt **3** sin **4** blot, vice **5** shame, wrong **6** infamy, stigma **7** misdeed **8** disgrace, dishonor, misdoing, trespass **9** black mark, turpitude **10** guiltiness, misconduct, sinfulness, wrongdoing **11** criminality, culpability, degradation, delinquency, dereliction, humiliation, misbehavior, self-disgust **13** transgression

guiltless **4** good, pure **5** clean **6** chaste **7** angelic, sinless **8** innocent, unfallen, virtuous **9** blameless, childlike, faultless **10** immaculate, inculpable, unblamable **11** uncorrupted
French: **12** sans reproche

guilt-stricken **7** ashamed **18** conscience-stricken

guilty **5** sorry, wrong **6** erring, sinful **7** ashamed, corrupt, hangdog, immoral **8** blamable, contrite, criminal, culpable, penitent, sheepish **9** offensive, regretful, repentant **11** blameworthy **18** conscience-stricken

Guinea
other name: **12** French Guinea **13** Rivieres du Sud
capital/largest city: **7** Conakry
others: **4** Boke, Fria, Labe **5** Beyla **6** Dabola, Kankan, Kindia **7** Dubreka, Siguiri **8** Kerouane **9** Kouroussa, Nzerekore

measure: **7** jacktan
monetary unit: **4** iliy, syli **5** franc **6** cauris
weight: **4** akey, piso, uzan **5** benda, seron **6** quinto **8** aguirage
island: **3** Los **5** Tombo **7** Tristao
mountain: **4** Loma **6** Tamgue **11** Fouta Djalon
highest point: **5** Nimba
river: **4** Milo **5** Kogon, Niger **6** Bafing, Faleme, Gambia **7** Kolente, Senegal **8** Konkoure, Tinkisso **13** Great Scarcies
sea: **8** Atlantic
physical feature:
  cape: **5** Verga
people: **4** Koma, Loma, Nalu, Susu, Toma **5** Kissi, Manon **6** Fulani, Guerzi **7** Landoma, Malinke **8** Kouranke, Landuman **11** Kissi-Sherbo **12** Guerze-Kpelle
language: **5** Fulbe, Mande **6** Arabic, French, Fulani **7** English
religion: **5** Islam **7** animism
feature:
  plant: **11** globeflower
  tree: **4** akee **5** dalli

Guinea-Bissau
other name: **16** Portuguese Guinea
capital/largest city: **6** Bissau
others: **4** Buba **5** Catio, Farim **6** Bafata, Bolama, Cacheu, Cacine, Dandum, Mansoa **7** Bissora, Bubaque, San Joav **9** Fulacunda **10** Nova Lamego **11** Madina do Boe, Madine do Boe, Sao Domingos
monetary unit: **4** peso **6** escudo **8** centavos
island: **4** Roxa **6** Orango **7** Bijagos, Formosa
river: **4** Geba **6** Cacheu, Mansoa **7** Corubal
sea: **8** Atlantic
people: **6** Fulani **7** Balanta, Balante, mulatto **8** Mandingo, Mandyako
language: **5** Fulah **7** Balante, Crioulo **8** Mandingo **10** Portuguese **21** Cape Verde-Guinea Creole
religion: **5** Islam **7** animism **12** Christianity

Guinevere
character in: **16** Arthurian romance
husband: **6** Arthur
lover: **8** Lancelot

Guinness, Sir Alec
born: **6** London **7** England
roles: **8** Star Wars **11** Oliver Twist **13** Doctor Zhivago **14** Our Man in Havana, The Ladykillers **15** A Passage to India, Ben Obi Wan Kenobi, Lavender Hill Mob **16** Lawrence of Arabia **17** Great Expectations **21** Kind Hearts and Coronets **22** Tinker Tailor Soldier Spy **23** The Bridge on the River Kwai (Oscar)

guise **4** garb, mode **5** dress, habit **6** attire **7** apparel, clothes, costume, fash-

ion **8** clothing, disguise, pretense **10** masquerade

Gulag Archipelago, The
author: **23** Aleksandr Solzhenitsyn Jr

gulch **3** gap **4** rift **5** abyss, chasm, cleft, crack, gorge, gully, split **6** arroyo, breach, divide, ravine **8** crevasse

gulf **4** cove, rent, rift **5** abyss, chasm, cleft, firth, fjord, gully, inlet, split **6** canyon, lagoon **7** estuary, opening **8** crevasse **10** separation

gull **3** gyp **4** dupe, rook **5** cozen, trick **7** deceive, defraud, sea gull, sea bird, swindle **9** bamboozle, victimize

gullet **3** maw **4** craw, crop **5** belly, gorge, tummy **6** dewlap, throat **7** abdomen, channel, stomach, weasand **9** beer belly, esophagus

gullible **5** green, naive **6** simple **8** innocent, trustful, trusting **9** credulous **11** easily duped **12** easily fooled, overtrusting, unsuspicious **13** easily cheated, inexperienced **14** easily deceived **15** unsophisticated

Gulliver's Travels
author: **13** Jonathan Swift
character: **14** Lemuel Gulliver
visited: **6** Laputa, Yahoos **8** Blefuscu, Lilliput, Luggnagg **9** Balnibari **10** Houyhnhnms **11** Brobdingnag **12** Glubbdubdrib

gully **3** gap **5** ditch, gorge, gulch **6** defile, furrow, gutter, ravine, trench **7** channel **11** small canyon, small valley, watercourse **13** drainage ditch

gulp **4** bolt, swig, wolf **5** quaff, swill **6** devour, guzzle **7** swallow, toss off **8** mouthful

gulp down **4** bolt **6** devour, gobble **7** swallow **8** gobble up, wolf down

gum **3** wax **5** latex, resin **6** chicle **8** mucilage **10** Eucalyptus
varieties: **3** cup, red **4** blue, cape, gray, rose, snow, sour **5** apple, black, cider, coral, giant, gully, Karri, Manna, sugar, swamp, sweet **6** cotton, Deane's, desert, gimlet, salmon, snappy, Tupelo **7** Barbary, cabbage, Fuchsia, maiden's, Morocco, scarlet, spotted **8** Formosan, Lehmann's, mountain, scribbly, spinning **9** forest red, Murray red, steedman's **10** Australian, candle-bark, red-spotted, Sydney blue, Timor mine, tumble-down, urn-fruited **11** Blakely's red, blue weeping, salmon white, small-leaved, strickland's **12** lemon-scented, red-flowering, silver-dollar **13** American sweet, Oriental sweet, Tasmanian blue, Tasmanian snow **14** yellow-flowered **15** Omeo round-leaved, round-leaved snow **16** rough-barked manna, scarlet-flowering **17** heart-leaved silver **20** silver-leaved mountain

gummed 5 glued, gummy, stuck **6** sticky **8** adhering, adhesive

gummy 5 gluey, gooey, gunky **6** gloppy, sticky, viscid **7** rubbery, viscous **8** adhesive **10** gelatinous **12** mucilaginous

gumption 3 zip **4** dash, push **5** drive, spunk, verve **6** energy, hustle, pizazz, spirit **7** courage **10** enterprise, get-up-and-go, initiative **12** forcefulness **14** aggressiveness **15** resourcefulness

gumshoe 3 tec **4** dick **6** shamus **9** detective **10** private eye **12** investigator

gun 3 aim, gat, rod, try **4** Colt, hunt, iron **5** piece, rifle, shoot **6** cannon, Magnum, mortar, musket, pistol **7** attempt, carbine, firearm, Gatling, go after, Long Tom, shotgun **8** howitzer, ordnance, revolver **9** automatic, Big Bertha, derringer, equalizer, flintlock, forty-five, twenty-two, Remington **10** fieldpiece, machine gun, six-shooter, three-fifty, Walther PPK, Winchester **11** blunderbuss, thirty-eight, trusty-rusty **12** fowling piece, muzzle loader, shooting iron **13** Kentucky rifle **14** artillery piece, Smith and Wesson
   invented by:
     breechloader: 8 Thornton
     magazine: 9 Hotchkiss
     silencer: 5 Maxim

Gunga Din
   story in: 18 Barrack-Room Ballads
   author: 14 Rudyard Kipling
   director: 13 George Stevens
   cast: 8 Sam Jaffe **9** Cary Grant **12** Joan Fontaine **14** Victor McLaglen **18** Douglas Fairbanks Jr
   setting: 5 India
   remade as: 13 Soldiers Three **14** Sergeants Three

gunman 6 bandit, outlaw, robber, sniper **7** hoodlum **9** assailant, desperado, holdup man

Gunnar
   origin: 12 Scandinavian
   father: 5 Giuki, Gjuki
   mother: 8 Grimhild
   sister: 6 Gudrun, Kudrun **7** Guthrun
   wife: 8 Brynhild
   Brynhild won by: 6 Sigurd

Gunsmoke
   character: 3 Sam (the bartender) **8** Doc (Dr Galen) Adams **10** Quint Asper **11** Newly O'Brien **12** Chester Goode, Festus Haggen, Kitty Russell (Miss Kitty) **18** Marshall Matt Dillon **24** Clayton Thaddeus (Thad) Greenwood
   cast: 9 Ken Curtis **10** Buck Taylor, Roger Ewing **11** Amanda Blake, James Arness **12** Burt Reynolds, Dennis Weaver, Glenn Strange, Milburn Stone
   setting: 9 Dodge City
   saloon: 10 Longbranch

Guns of August, The
   author: 15 Barbara W Tuchman

Guns of Navarone, The
   director: 12 J Lee Thompson
   based on novel by: 15 Alistair MacLean
   cast: 10 David Niven **11** Gregory Peck, James Darren **12** Anthony Quinn, Stanley Baker **13** Anthony Quayle

Gunther
   origin: 8 Germanic
   mentioned in: 14 Nibelungenlied
   king of: 8 Burgundy
   wife: 8 Brunhild
   sister: 9 Kriemhild
   killed by: 9 Kriemhild

gurgle 5 plash **6** babble, bubble, burble, murmur, ripple **7** sputter **8** bubbling, gurgling

guru 5 guide **6** leader, master **7** teacher **9** preceptor **10** instructor

gush 3 gab, gas, jet, run **4** blab, bull, rush, well **5** issue, prate, spout, spurt **6** babble, burble, drivel, hot air, splash, squirt, stream **7** baloney, blabber, blather, chatter, pour out, prattle, rubbish, torrent, twaddle **8** nonsense, outburst, rattle on **10** outpouring **11** mawkishness **12** emotionalism **14** sentimentalism, talk effusively **16** run off at the mouth

gushiness 12 effusiveness, emotionalism **17** demonstrativeness

gushing 6 lavish **7** pouring, profuse **8** effusive, spurting **10** flattering **11** free-flowing **12** demonstative, unrestrained **16** overenthusiastic

gushy 8 effusive **12** unrestrained **13** demonstrative **16** overenthusiastic

gussy up 5 adorn **7** dress up, enhance **8** beautify, decorate, ornament **9** embellish

gust 3 fit **4** blow, puff, wind **5** blast, burst, draft **6** breeze, flurry, squall, zephyr **8** outbreak, outburst, paroxysm **9** explosion

Guster
   character in: 10 Bleak House
   author: 7 Dickens

gusto 3 joy **4** zeal, zest **5** savor **6** fervor, relish **7** delight **8** appetite, pleasure **10** enthusiasm **12** appreciation, exhilaration, satisfaction

gusto, con
   music: 9 with style, with taste

gusty 5 blowy, windy **6** breezy **7** squally **8** blustery

gut 4 raze **5** belly, clean, level, tummy **6** bowels, paunch, ravage **7** abdomen, consume, midriff, stomach, viscera **8** entrails, lay waste **9** bay window, beer belly, spare tire **10** disembowel, eviscerate, intestines, midsection **11** breadbasket

guten abend 11 good evening

Gutenberg
   nationality: 6 German
   inventor of: 11 movable type
   printer of: 14 Gutenberg Bible

guten morgen 11 good morning

guten tag 7 good day

Guthrie, A B Jr
   author of: 6 Arfive **9** The Big Sky **10** The Way West **13** The Last Valley **16** Fair Land Fair Land, The Blue Hen's Chick, The Thousand Hills

Guthrun *see* **6** Gudrun

Gutman, Casper
   character in: 16 The Maltese Falcon
   author: 7 Hammett

guts 4 dash, grit **5** nerve, pluck, spunk **6** bowels, daring, mettle, spirit, vitals **7** bravado, bravery, courage, gizzard, innards, insides, viscera **8** audacity, backbone, boldness **9** fortitude **10** intestines **11** intrepidity

gutsy 4 game **5** brave **6** heroic, plucky **7** doughty, valiant **8** fearless, intrepid, stalwart, unafraid, valorous **9** dauntless, undaunted **10** courageous **11** lionhearted, unflinching **12** stouthearted

guttural 3 low **4** deep **5** gruff, harsh, husky, raspy, thick **6** hoarse **7** throaty **8** croaking **12** inarticulate

guy 3 boy, joe, kid, man **4** body, chap, dude, gent, rope **5** bloke, human, joker **6** fellow, hombre, person **8** blighter, up-holder **9** supporter **10** individual

Guyana
   name means: 12 land of waters
   other name: 13 British Guiana
   capital/largest city: 10 Georgetown
   others: 7 Charity **8** Hyde Park, Rosignol **9** Jonestown, Mackenzie
   island: 6 Leguan **9** Wakenaam
   mountain: 5 Amuku, Ariwa, Kamoa **6** Akarai, Kanuku **7** Caburai **9** Pacaraima
   highest point: 7 Roraima
   river: 5 Waini **6** Barama **7** Amakura, Baruima, Berbice **8** Demerara, Mazaruni, Rupununi **9** Essequibo **10** Burro-Burro
   ocean: 8 Atlantic
   physical feature:
     falls: 5 Great, Tiger **7** Kamaria **8** Kaieteur **9** Serikoeng **10** Surwakwima **15** Fredrik Willem IV
   people: 6 Akawai, Arawak, Creole, Taruma **7** African, Chinese, mulatto **10** Portuguese
   language: 5 Hindi **7** English
   religion: 5 Hindu, Islam **8** Anglican **13** Roman Catholic

Guy Fawkes
   author: 16 William Ainsworth

Guy Mannering
   author: 14 Sir Walter Scott

Guyon
   character in: 15 The Faerie Queene
   author: 7 Spenser
Guys and Dolls
   director: 17 Joseph L Mankiewicz
   based on story by: 11 Damon Runyon
   cast: 10 Stubby Kaye **11** Jean Simmons **12** Frank Sinatra, Marlon Brando, Vivian Blaine
   setting: 11 New York City
   score: 12 Frank Loesser
   song: 11 Luck Be a Lady **12** Guys and Dolls **26** Sit Down You're Rocking the Boat
guzzle 4 bolt, swig **5** quaff, swill **6** devour, imbibe, tipple **7** toss off **8** gulp down
guzzler 5 drunk **6** boozer **7** imbiber, tippler **8** devourer, drunkard **9** alcoholic
Gwawl

   origin: 5 Welsh
   mentioned in: 10 Mabinogion
   rival of: 5 Pwyll
   sought hand of: 8 Rhiannon
Gwydion
   origin: 5 Welsh
   son: 14 Llew Llaw Gyffes
   sister: 9 Arianhrod
   lover: 9 Arianhrod
Gwyn
   origin: 7 British
   god of: 7 rebirth **9** afterlife
Gyas
   companion of: 6 Aeneas
Gyes see **5** Gyges
Gygaea, Gyge
   form: 5 nymph
   location: 4 lake
Gyges
   also: 4 Gyes
   member of: 13 Hecatonchires

gymnasium 5 arena **6** circus **7** stadium **10** hippodrome
gymnast 10 Olga Korbut **13** Mary Lou Retton, Nadia Comaneci
gymnastics 9 exercises **10** acrobatics **11** contortions **16** physical training
Gynaecothoenas
   epithet of: 4 Ares
   means: 17 feasted by the women
gynophobia
   fear of: 5 women
gyp 3 con **4** bilk, burn, fake, hoax, rook, scam, soak **5** cheat, cozen, fraud, phony, trick **6** diddle, fleece, humbug, ripoff **7** con game, defraud, swindle **8** flimflam, hoodwink **9** bamboozle, deception
gypsy
   Italian: 7 zingara, zingaro
gyrate 5 swirl, twirl, wheel, whirl **6** circle, rotate, spiral **7** revolve **9** pirouette **10** spin around

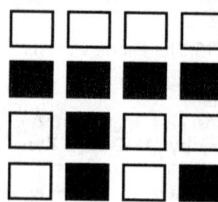

habeas corpus 11 have the body **23** produce the person in court
legal writ guards against: 19 illegal imprisonment

habiliments 4 garb, wear **5** dress **6** attire, outfit **7** clothes, costume, raiment, regalia **8** clothing, wardrobe **9** vestments

habit 3 rut, way **4** garb, gear, robe, rule, wont **5** dress, trait, usage **6** attire, custom, groove, livery, manner, outfit **7** apparel, clothes, costume, garment, leaning, raiment, routine, uniform, vesture **8** clothing, fondness, habitude, nun's wear, practice **9** mannerism, trappings **10** beaten path, convention, observance, partiality, proclivity, propensity **11** habiliments, inclination, peculiarity **12** predilection, second nature **13** accoutrements, fixed practice **14** matter of course, predisposition **15** behavior pattern

habitat 3 pad **4** digs, home, spot, zone **5** abode, haunt, place, range, realm, roost **6** domain, locale, milieu, region **7** housing, lodging, setting, terrain **8** domicile, dwelling, home base, lodgment, precinct, quarters **9** territory **10** habitation **11** environment, natural home **12** place of abode **13** dwelling place **14** stamping ground **15** natural locality **17** native environment

habitation 3 pad **4** digs, home **5** abode, haunt, house, roost **6** colony **7** habitat, housing, lodging, shelter, tenancy **8** domicile, dwelling, lodgment, quarters **9** community, occupancy, residence **10** occupation, settlement **12** place of abode **13** dwelling place, temporary stay **16** place of residence

Habit of Being, The
author: 15 Flannery O'Connor

habitual 5 fixed, usual **6** common, normal, wonted **7** chronic, natural, regular, routine, typical **8** addicted, constant, expected, familiar, frequent, periodic, repeated **9** confirmed, continual, customary, incessant, ingrained, perpetual, recurrent **10** accustomed, deep-rooted, deep-seated, inveterate, methodical, systematic **11** established, traditional **12** conventional, second nature **14** by force of habit

habitual practice 4 wont **5** habit **6** custom

habituate 5 adapt, drill, imbue, inure, train **6** harden, school, season **7** break in, instill **8** accustom, initiate **9** inculcate **10** discipline, make used to **12** indoctrinate

habitue 7 regular **10** frequenter **13** regular patron **15** frequent visitor **16** constant customer

hacek 13 inverted caret **15** diacritical mark

hack 3 cab, cut, hew, nag **4** bark, chip, chop, gash, plug, rasp, slit, taxi **5** coach, cut up, notch, slash, slice, whack **6** cleave, mangle **7** hackney, taxicab **8** lacerate, mutilate **9** cart horse, dray horse, scribbler, workhorse **10** cough drily, cut roughly, draft horse, hired horse, shaft horse **11** common horse, penny-a-liner **12** hackney coach, worn-out horse **13** carriage horse **16** grubstreet writer **18** horse-drawn carriage

hackle 3 peg **4** card, comb, hack, hook, ruff **5** curry, plume, quill **6** heckle, mangle **7** bristle, feather, plumage

Hackman, Gene
born: 15 San Bernardino CA
roommate: 13 Dustin Hoffman
roles: 8 Superman **10** Unforgiven **11** Popeye Doyle, Runaway Jury **13** Absolute Power **14** Bonnie and Clyde **15** The Conversation **18** Welcome to Mooseport **19** The French Connection (Oscar) **20** The Poseidon Adventure

hackneyed 4 dull, worn **5** banal, inane, stale, stock, trite, vapid **6** common, jejune **7** cliched, humdrum, insipid, routine, worn-out **8** bromidic, ordinary, shopworn, well-worn **9** moth-eaten **10** pedestrian, threadbare, uninspired **11** commonplace, stereotyped **12** conventional **13** platitudinous, unimaginative

Hadassah 6 Esther

Hades 4 hell
also: 3 Dis **5** Pluto **10** lower world, Underworld
corresponds to: 5 Orcus
god of: 5 Orcus, Pluto
goddess of: 6 Hecate, Hekate

Haenigsen, Harry
creator/artist of: 5 Penny **7** Our Bill

hafnium
chemical symbol: 2 Hf

hag 3 bat, nag **4** drab, fury **5** biddy, crone, frump, harpy, shrew, vixen, witch **6** beldam, gorgon, ogress, virago **7** hellcat **8** battle-ax, harridan **9** termagant

Hagar
servant of: 5 Sarah
husband: 7 Abraham
son: 7 Ishmael

Hagar the Horrible
creator: 9 Dik Browne

Hagen
origin: 8 Germanic
mentioned in: 14 Nibelungenlied
killed by: 9 Kriemhild
killed: 9 Siegfried

Haggadah 7 parable **8** anecdote
source: 6 Talmud
read at: 5 seder **8** Passover

haggard 4 beat, wild, worn **5** gaunt, spent, tired, upset, weary **6** bushed, fagged, pooped, raging, wasted **7** ranting **8** careworn, drooping, fatigued, flagging, frenzied, harassed, harrowed, overcome, toilworn, wild-eyed **9** exhausted, woebegone **10** hollow-eyed **11** debilitated, overwearied, overwrought, tuckered out, wild-looking **12** tired-looking

Haggard, H Rider
author of: 3 She **17** King Solomon's Mines
noted phrase: 18 She who must be obeyed

haggle 6 barter, bicker, dicker, higgle **7** bargain, dispute, quarrel, quibble, wrangle **8** beat down, squabble

Hagiographa
Hebrew: 7 Ketubim

hagiographer 19 writer of saints' lives

Hagman, Larry
mother: 10 Mary Martin
born: 13 Weatherford TX
roles: 6 Dallas **7** J R Ewing **15** I Dream of Jeannie

Hahn, Otto
field: 9 chemistry
nationality: 6 German
discovered: 13 protoactinium **14** nuclear isomers
awarded: 10 Nobel Prize

Haida
language family: 6 Masset, Na-Dene **10** Skidegatta

tribe: 7 Kaigani
location: 6 Alaska **15** British Columbia **21** Queen Charlotte Islands
related to: 7 Tlingit **9** Tsimshian
associated with: 9 totem pole **13** wood sculpture

hail 3 ave **4** call **5** cheer, exalt, extol, greet, hello, honor, shout **6** accost, call to, esteem, salute **7** acclaim, address, applaud, commend, glorify, receive, shout at, usher in, welcome **8** cry out to, eulogize, greeting **9** accosting **10** calling out, compliment, panegyrize, salutation **11** make welcome
German: 4 heil
Latin: 3 ave **5** salve

Hailey, Arthur
author of: 5 Hotel **6** Wheels **7** Airport **12** In High Places **14** Final Diagnosis **16** The Moneychangers

hail-fellow-well-met 8 familiar, friendly, intimate, outgoing, sociable **9** extrovert **10** gregarious

Hail Mary
Latin: 8 Ave Maria **12** rosary prayer

Hail the Conquering Hero
director: 14 Preston Sturges
cast: 10 Ella Raines **12** Eddie Bracken **14** Raymond Walburn **15** William Demarest **16** Franklin Pangborn

hail to victory
German: 8 sieg heil

Hair
writers: 9 James Rado **11** Gerome Ragni
composer: 13 Galt MacDermot
character: 3 Hud **4** Woof **6** Berger, Claude, Crissy, Dionne, Jeanie, Sheila
songs: 4 3500 **8** Aquarius **9** Ain't Got No **12** Colored Spade **17** Manchester England

hair 3 fur, mop **4** coat, down, iota, mane, pelt, wool **5** bangs, curls, locks **6** fleece **7** tresses **8** ringlets **12** narrow margin
loss: 8 alopecia, baldness

haircut, hairdo 3 bob, bun, cut **4** Afro, clip, crop, fade, perm, shag, trim, updo **5** bangs, braid, butch, swirl **6** boogie, mohawk **7** beehive, buzzcut, chignon, cornrow, crewcut, flattop, fuzz cut, natural, pachuco, page boy, pigtail, shingle, tonsure, upsweep **8** bouffant, brushcut, coiffure, ducktail, ponytail, razorcut **9** barbering, hairstyle, permanent, pompadour **10** feathercut, french knot

haircutter 6 barber **11** hairdresser, hair stylist

hairdresser 8 coiffeur **9** coiffeuse **10** beautician, haircutter **11** beauty salon **12** beauty parlor
French: 8 coiffeur

hair-raising 5 eerie **7** bristle **8** exciting **9** thrilling **10** terrifying **11** astonishing

12 breathtaking, electrifying **13** horripilation, spine-tingling

hairsplitting 4 fine **6** minute, subtle **7** carping **8** caviling, delicate, hairline, niggling **9** minuscule, quibbling **10** nitpicking, unapparent **12** faultfinding, overcritical **13** imperceptible, inappreciable, infinitesimal **15** inconsequential

hairy 5 bushy, furry, wooly **6** fleecy, pilose, shaggy, woolly **7** hirsute

Hairy Ape, The
author: 12 Eugene O'Neill

Haiti
name means: 15 mountainous land
other name: 12 Santo Domingo
capital/largest city: 12 Port-au-Prince
others: 5 Aquin, Furcy, Limbe **6** Hinche, Jacmel, St Marc **7** Jeremie, Leogane, Saltrou **8** Gonaives, Kenscoff, Les Cayes **10** Cap-Haitien
monetary unit: 6 gourde **8** centimes
island: 5 Vache **6** Gonave, Tortue **7** Navassa, Tortuga **8** Caymites **10** Hispaniola **14** Grande Cayemite **15** Greater Antilles
lake: 8 Saumatre
mountain: 4 Nord **5** Cahos **6** Macaya, Noires **7** Lahotte **8** Troudeau
highest point: 7 La Selle, Laselle
river: 9 Guayamoul **10** Artibonite
sea: 8 Atlantic **9** Caribbean
physical feature:
gulf: 6 Gonave
passage: 8 Windward
people: 5 Taino **7** African, mulatto
discoverer: 8 Columbus
liberator: 19 Toussaint Louverture
ruler: 7 Papa Doc **8** Duvalier
language: 6 Creole, French, patois
religion: 6 voodoo **13** Roman Catholic
feature:
dance: 5 mambo
festival: 9 Mardi Gras
fortress: 10 La Ferriere **24** Citadelle du Roi Christophe
security force: 8 bogeymen **15** Tontons Macoutes
food:
sweet potato: 6 batata

Hakenkreuz 11 hooked cross **12** Nazi swastika

HAL
character in: 14 Two Thousand One (2001)
author: 6 Clarke

Halas, George
nickname: 8 Papa Bear
sport: 8 football
position: 5 coach, owner
team: 12 Chicago Bears

halcyon 4 calm, fair **5** happy, quiet, sunny **6** blithe, golden, hushed, joyous, placid, serene **7** pacific **8** carefree, cheerful, peaceful, tranquil **9** cloudless, contented, reposeful, un-

clouded, unruffled **10** unagitated, untroubled

hale 3 fit **4** well **5** hardy, sound **6** hearty, robust, rugged, sturdy **7** healthy, in shape **8** vigorous **9** energetic, in the pink, strapping **10** ablebodied, robustious **12** in fine fettle

Hale, Edward Everett
author of: 21 The Man Without a Country
hero: 11 Phillip Nolan

Hale, George Ellery
field: 9 astronomy
initiated: 20 Mt Palomar Observatory
invented: 17 spectroheliograph

Hale, Nathan, 7 patriot
hanged as a: 3 spy

Hale-Bopp 5 comet

Haley, Alex
author of: 5 Roots **26** The Autobiography of Malcolm X

Haley, Jack
born: 8 Boston MA
roles: 6 Tin Man **13** The Wizard of Oz

half 4 part, some **6** all but, barely, fairly, feebly, halved, in part, meager, partly, rather, scanty, skimpy, slight, weakly **7** divided, faintly, limited, partial, portion, section **8** fraction, middling, moderate, passable, passably, slightly **9** deficient, imperfect, partially, tolerable, tolerably **10** fractional, inadequate, incomplete, moderately, relatively **12** fifty percent, inadequately, insufficient, pretty nearly **13** after a fashion, comparatively **14** insufficiently

half-asleep 6 drowsy, groggy, unwary **7** out-of-it, unaware **8** sluggish **9** not-with-it, oblivious

half-hearted 4 cold, cool, tame **5** blase, faint **7** languid, passive **8** listless, lukewarm **9** apathetic, lethargic **10** ambivalent, irresolute, lackluster, phlegmatic, spiritless, unaspiring **11** indifferent, perfunctory **13** lackadaisical **14** unenthusiastic

half homer 15 Biblical measure

half-moon 3 arc, bow **4** arch **5** curve **8** crescent

Half Moon 4 ship
of: 11 Henry Hudson

halfway 6 almost, in part, medial, medium, middle, midway, nearly, partly, rather **7** midmost **8** somewhat **9** partially, to a degree **10** middlemost, moderately **11** equidistant, in the middle **12** intermediate, pretty nearly, to some extent **13** in some measure **18** between two extremes

half-wit 4 dolt, dope, fool **5** dummy, dunce, idiot, moron, ninny **6** dimwit, nitwit **7** dullard **8** dumb-dumb, imbecile, numskull **9** blockhead, numbskull, simpleton **10** nincompoop **15** mental defective, mental deficient

half-witted 4 dumb **5** silly **6** stupid **7** asinine, foolish, idiotic, moronic **9** dimwitted, imbecilic, senseless **11** lamebrained **12** feeble-minded, simple-minded

hall 5 entry, foyer, lobby **6** arcade **7** chamber, gallery, hallway, passage **8** anteroom, club room, corridor, entrance **9** vestibule **10** auditorium, dining hall, passageway **11** antechamber, banquet hall, concert hall, waiting room **12** amphitheater, assembly room, meeting place **13** reception room

Hall, Diane
real name of: **11** Diane Keaton

Hall, James
field: **7** geology **9** chemistry
nationality: **7** British
founded: **12** geochemistry **19** experimental geology

Hall, James Norman
author of: **17** Mutiny on the Bounty
co-author: **15** Charles Nordhoff

Hallel 6 praise **16** liturgical prayer

Haller, Albrecht von
field: **7** biology
nationality: **5** Swiss
founded: **15** modern neurology

Haller, Harry
character in: **11** Steppenwolf
author: **5** Hesse

Halley, Edmund
field: **9** astronomy
nationality: **7** British
discovered: **12** Halley's Comet

hallmark 4 sign **5** badge, stamp **6** device, emblem, symbol **14** characteristic

halloo 3 cry **4** call, hail, yell **5** shout **6** cry out, holler

hallow 5 bless **7** respect **8** dedicate, sanctify, venerate **10** consecrate

hallowed 4 holy **6** sacred **7** blessed, honored **9** beatified, dedicated **10** sacrosanct, sanctified **11** consecrated

Halloween
date: **7** October (31)
also called: **13** All Hallows Eve
symbol: **7** pumpkin **12** jack-o-lantern
saying: **12** trick or treat

hallucination 5 dream **6** mirage, vision **7** chimera, fantasy, figment **8** delusion, illusion **9** nightmare **10** aberration, apparition **14** phantasmagoria

hallway 4 hall **5** entry, foyer **7** passage **8** corridor, entryway **10** passageway

halo 6 aurora, corona, luster, nimbus **7** aureole, dignity, majesty **8** grandeur, holiness, radiance, sanctity, splendor **9** solemnity, sublimity **11** ring of light **12** chromosphere, luminousness, magnificence, resplendence **13** spiritual aura **15** illustriousness

Hals, Franz
born: **7** Antwerp, Holland
artwork: **9** Gypsy Girl **10** Hille Bobbe (The Witch of Haarlem) **13** The Jolly Toper **14** Jacobus Zaffius **15** The Merry Company **19** The Laughing Cavalier **22** Portrait of a Standing Man **24** The Regents of the Almshouse **26** Yonker Ramp and his Sweetheart **28** The Regentesses of the Almshouse **33** The Banquet of the St George Civic Guard

Halsey, William F
served in: **3** WWI **4** WWII
rank: **12** fleet admiral
battle: **9** Leyte Gulf **11** Philippines **14** Solomon Islands

halt 3 end **4** balk, curb, foil, quit, rest, rout, stay, stem, stop, wait, whoa **5** abate, block, brake, break, cease, check, close, crush, delay, pause, quash, quell, stall, tarry **6** bridle, cut off, defeat, draw up, hamper, hinder, impede, linger, pull up, recess, rein in, scotch, subdue, thwart, wind up **7** heave to, inhibit, prevent, put down, repress, respite, squelch, suspend, time out **8** break off, breather, choke off, don't move, hang fire, interval, knock off, leave off, overturn, prohibit, restrain, restrict, shut down, suppress, vanquish **9** cessation, frustrate, interlude, interrupt, overthrow, terminate **10** call it a day, extinguish, shut up shop, standstill, suspension **11** come to a halt, come to a stop, discontinue, hold in check, termination **12** intermission, interruption, throttle down **13** spike one's guns **14** breathing spell, discontinuance

halting 6 ending **7** curbing **8** episodic, hesitant, stopping **9** faltering, stumbling **10** calling off, discursive, suspending **11** restraining, terminating **13** discontinuous **14** calling a halt to, putting a stop to

halting place
Spanish: **6** posada

halutz 7 pioneer **26** person who emigrates to Israel

halve 6 bisect **9** cut in half **10** split in two **13** divide equally

ham, 6 emoter **9** overactor **20** amateur radio operator

Ham
character in: **16** David Copperfield
author: **7** Dickens

Ham
father: **4** Noah
brother: **4** Shem **7** Japheth
son: **3** Put **4** Cush **6** Canaan **7** Misraim
descendant of: **6** Hamite

Hamadryad
form: **5** dryad
spirit of: **4** tree

Haman
served: **9** Ahasuerus also see **6** Esther

Hamill, Mark
born: **9** Oakland CA
roles: **8** Star Wars **10** Reeseville **13** Luke Skywalker **15** Return of the Jedi **20** The Empire Strikes Back

Hamilton
capital of: **7** Bermuda

Hamilton, Alexander
1st Secretary: **8** Treasury
slain by: **9** Aaron Burr
in: **4** duel

Hamilton, Charles
character in: **15** Gone With the Wind
author: **8** Mitchell

Hamilton, Iain
composer of: **6** Aurora **7** Alastor **8** Sinfonia **9** Pharsalia **11** The Bermudas **18** Threnos In Time of War **20** The Royal Hunt of the Sun **21** The Catiline Conspiracy

Hamilton, Margaret
real name: **23** Margaret Hamilton Meserve
born: **11** Cleveland OH
roles: **4** Cora **13** The Wizard of Oz **23** The Wicked Witch of the West
commercial: **12** Maxwell House

Hamito-Semitic
language also known as: **11** Afro-Asiatic
branch: **6** Berber, Chadic **7** Semitic **8** Cushitic, Egyptian

hamlet 4 burg **7** village **8** hick town, tank town **10** crossroads **11** whistle stop **12** one-horse town, small village **13** jerkwater town

Hamlet
author: **18** William Shakespeare
character: **7** Horatio, Laertes, Ophelia **8** Claudius, Gertrude, Polonius, The Ghost **11** Rosencrantz **12** Guildenstern
soliloquy: **13** To be or not to be
skull: **6** Yorick
castle: **8** Elsinore
setting: **7** Denmark
director: **15** Laurence Olivier
cast: **11** Basil Sydney, Felix Aylmer, Jean Simmons **12** Eileen Herlie **15** Laurence Olivier
Oscar for: **5** actor (Olivier) **7** picture

Hamlet, The
author: **15** William Faulkner
character: **4** Eula, Jody **6** Labove **8** Ab Snopes **9** V K Ratliff **10** Flem Snopes, Mink Snopes, Will Varner **11** Isaac Snopes **12** Henry Armstid

Hamlin, Vincent T
creator/artist of: **8** Alley Oop

Hammarskjold, Dag 7 Swedish **13** United Nations **16** secretary-general

hammer 3 hit, tap **4** bang, form, make, nail **5** drive, forge, knock, pound, punch, shape, whack **6** pummel, rammer, strike **7** beat out, fash-

ion
type: 4 claw, jack, tack **5** gavel, steam **6** mallet, sledge **8** ballpeen **10** pile driver **12** upholsterers

Hammer, Mike
detective created by: 14 Mickey Spillane

hammered 5 drunk **6** banged, beaten, shaped **7** knocked, pounded, whipped, wrought **8** battered, repeated **10** terrorized

Hammett, Dashiell
author of: 10 Red Harvest, The Thin Man **11** The Glass Key **12** The Dain Curse **16** The Maltese Falcon
character: 4 Asta (dog) **8** Sam Spade **11** Miles Archer, Nick Charles, Nora Charles **13** Continental Op

hamper 3 gag **4** balk, curb, stem **5** block, check, stall **6** fetter, hinder, hog-tie, hold up, impede, muzzle, retard, thwart **7** inhibit, prevent, shackle **8** encumber, handicap, obstruct, restrain, restrict **9** frustrate **13** interfere with

Hampton, Hope
nickname: 22 The Duchess of Park Avenue
born: 14 Philadelphia PA
roles: 8 Star Dust **13** Lawful Larceny, The Road to Reno **16** The Price of a Party

hamstring 6 impair, muscle, tendon **7** cripple, disable **8** handicap **10** debilitate

Hamsun, Knut
author of: 3 Pan **6** August, Hunger **8** Victoria **9** Mysteries, Vagabonds **16** Children of the Age **18** The Growth of the Soil

Hananiah *see* **8** Shadrach

hand, hands 3 aid, man, paw **4** care, fist, give, help, hold, lift, mitt, palm, pass **5** guide, power, reach **6** assist, charge, convey, helper, menial, script, worker **7** command, control, custody, deliver, keeping, laborer, ovation, present, support, workman **8** auspices, dominion, employee, guidance, handyman, hired man, longhand, meat-hook **9** assistant, associate, authority, hired hand **10** assistance, domination, management, minister to, penmanship, possession, turn over to, workingman **11** calligraphy, furnish with, handwriting, supervision **12** jurisdiction **13** member of a crew **15** burst of applause, manual extremity, round of applause

handbag 3 bag **4** grip **5** purse **6** clutch, valise **7** satchel **8** moneybag, reticule **10** pocketbook, portmanteau

handbill 5 flier, tract **6** notice **7** leaflet **8** bulletin, circular **12** announcement **13** advertisement

handbook 5 bible **6** manual **8** baede-

ker **9** guidebook, vade mecum **13** reference book

handcart 4 cart **6** barrow **8** pushcart **10** handbarrow **11** wheelbarrow

handcuffs 5 cuffs, irons **6** chains **7** fetters **8** manacles, shackles **9** bracelets

hand down 4 will **5** leave **6** hand on, pass on **8** bequeath

Handel, George Frederick (Georg Friedrich)
born: 5 Halle **7** Germany
lived in: 7 England
composer of: 4 Nero, Saul **5** Serse, Silla, Siroe, Teseo **6** Admeto, Alcina, Almira, Esther, Flavio, Jeptha, Joseph, Ottone, Samson, Semele, Xerxes **7** Amadigi, Athalia, Deborah, Lotario, Messiah, Rinaldo, Rodrigo, Solomon, Tolomeo **8** Atalanta, Berenice, Hercules, Scipione, Theodora **9** Agrippina, Radamisto, Rodelinda, Tamerlano **10** Alessandro, Belshazzar, Floridante, Water Music **12** Giulio Cesare, Il Pastor Fido, Muzio Scevola **13** Israel in Egypt, Riccardo Primo **14** Acis and Galatea, Fireworks Music **15** Alexander's Feast, Judas Maccabaeus **16** Hornpipe Concerto **19** Julius Caesar in Egypt, Ode for St Cecilia's Day **22** The Royal Fireworks Music **23** Hallelujah Organ Concerto, The Harmonious Blacksmith **24** The Triumph of Time and Truth

handful 7 minimum, modicum **10** scattering, smattering, sprinkling, thimbleful, tiny amount **11** scant amount, small number **13** small quantity

handgun 3 rod **5** piece, rifle **6** pistol, weapon **7** firearm, shotgun **8** revolver **9** automatic, twenty-two **12** shooting iron **20** Saturday night special

handicap 4 curb **5** limit **6** burden, defect, hamper, hinder, impede, retard, thwart **7** barrier, inhibit, repress, shackle **8** deafness, drawback, encumber, hold back, lameness, obstacle, restrain, restrict, suppress **9** blindness, detriment **10** difficulty, impediment, inhibition, limitation **11** encumbrance, restriction, shortcoming **12** disadvantage **13** inconvenience **14** stumbling block

handicapped 7 limited **8** burdened, disabled, held back, hindered, impaired, retarded **10** encumbered, restrained, restricted **13** disadvantaged

handicrafts
god of: 10 Hephaestus, Hephaistos

handicraftsman 7 artisan **10** handworker **12** handicrafter

handiness 7 utility **8** deftness **9** dexterity **10** adroitness, usefulness **11** convenience **12** availability **13** accessibility

hand in glove 5 as one **10** side by side **13** close together

handle 3 paw, ply, run, tag, use **4** feel, grip, hilt, hold, knob, name, poke, pull, sell, work **5** carry, grasp, guide, knead, pilot, pinch, shaft, shank, steer, swing, touch, treat **6** caress, CB name, deal in, employ, finger, fondle, manage, market, pick up, stroke **7** care for, command, conduct, control, massage, moniker, operate, paw over, trade in, utilize **8** cognomen, deal with, maneuver **9** traffic in **10** manipulate, take care of **11** appellation, merchandise **12** offer for sale **13** bring into play

handout 4 alms, dole **7** freebie **19** something for nothing

hand out 4 deal, give **5** grant **6** bestow, confer, donate **7** dole out, mete out, present **8** dispense **9** apportion **10** contribute, distribute

hand over 4 cede **5** grant, yield **6** give up, tender **7** abandon, release **8** transfer **9** deliver up, surrender **10** relinquish

handsome 4 fair **5** ample, bonny, noble **6** benign, comely, lovely, pretty **7** elegant, liberal, sightly, sizable, stately **8** abundant, generous, gracious, imposing, merciful, princely, splendid, stunning, tasteful **9** beauteous, beautiful, bountiful, exquisite, unselfish **10** attractive, benevolent, big-hearted, impressive, sufficient, well-formed **11** fine-looking, good-looking, magnanimous **12** considerable, easy to look at, humanitarian **13** compassionate, easy on the eyes **16** well-proportioned

hand to hand
Spanish: 9 mano a mano

handy 4 deft, near, nigh **5** adept, on tap **6** adroit, at hand, clever, expert, on call, on hand, useful, wieldy **7** capable, helpful, skilled **8** skillful **9** available, competent, dexterous, easy to use, efficient, practical **10** accessible, convenient, manageable, obtainable, proficient **11** at one's elbow, close at hand, in readiness, ready to hand, serviceable **12** accomplished **14** nimble-fingered **15** within easy reach **16** easily accessible **17** at one's beck and call

hang 3 bow, sag **4** drop, gist, rest **5** affix, hinge, knack, lie in, lower, lynch, point, trail **6** append, attach, dangle, depend **7** incline, meaning, suspend, thought **8** lean over, let droop, repose in, string up, turn upon **9** be pendant, be pendent **11** be dependent, be subject to, bend forward, swing freely **12** be contingent, bend downward **13** revolve around **15** die on the gallows, fasten from above **16** execute by hanging, send to the gallows

hangdog 6 abject **7** ashamed **8** defeated, degraded, hopeless, resigned, wretched **9** miserable **10** browbeaten, chapfallen, humiliated, shamefaced **11** crestfallen, embarrassed, intimidated **13** guilty-looking

hang down 3 sag **5** droop

hanger-on 7 admirer, groupie **8** follower **9** sycophant

hanging object
 Japanese: **8** kakemono

hang loosely 3 bag, sag **5** droop

hangout 3 den **5** haunt

hang out 3 mix **4** live **5** dwell **6** hobnob, loiter, mingle, reside **7** consort **9** associate, be friends, pal around, run around **10** fraternize, hang around **11** keep company

hanker after 4 want **5** covet, crave, fancy **6** desire **7** long for, pine for **8** aspire to, yearn for **9** lust after **11** have a yen for, have an eye on, hunger after, thirst after

hankering 3 yen **4** itch, urge **6** aching, desire, hunger, pining, thirst **7** craving, longing **8** yearning

Hanna-Barbera
 creators of: **6** Top Cat **7** Jetsons **8** Yogi Bear **11** Tom and Jerry **15** Quickdraw McGraw **16** Huckleberry Hound **14** The Flintstones

Hannah
 husband: **7** Elkanah
 son: **6** Samuel

Hanoi
 capital of: **7** Vietnam **12** North Vietnam
 river: **3** Red **4** Yuan **7** Song Koi
 delta: **6** Tonkin
 airport: **6** Gia Lam

Hans Brinker
 author: **5** (Mary Elizabeth Mapes) Dodge
 character: **4** Raff **5** Gleck, Hilda **6** Gretel **7** Boekman, Mevrouw
 feature: **12** silver skates

Hansel and Gretel
 author: **13** Grimm Brothers (Jakob and Wilhelm)
 opera by: **11** Humperdinck
 character: **5** Witch
 feature **4** oven **16** gingerbread house

Hans Kristian
 character in: **16** Giants of the Earth
 author: **7** Rolvaag

Hanson, Howard
 born: **7** Wahoo NE
 composer of: **5** Sacra (symphony No 5) **6** Nordic (symphony No 1) **7** Requiem (symphony No 4) **8** Romantic (symphony No 2) **10** Merry-Mount

haphazard 6 casual, chance, fitful, random **7** aimless, chaotic **8** careless, on-and-off, slapdash, sporadic **9** arbitrary, hit-or-miss **10** accidental, disordered, disorderly, fortuitous, undesigned, undirected, unthinking **11**

purposeless, unorganized **12** disorganized, unmethodical, unsystematic **14** indiscriminate, unpremeditated **15** catch-as-catch-can

hapless 6 cursed, jinxed, no-good, rotten, woeful **7** forlorn, unhappy, unlucky **8** accursed, hopeless, ill-fated, luckless, wretched **9** miserable **10** ill-starred **11** star-crossed, unfortunate

happen 5 arise, ensue, occur **6** appear, befall, betide, crop up, result **7** turn out **8** become of, spring up **9** be borne by, be the case, come about, eventuate, take place, transpire **10** be one's fate, come to pass **11** be endured by **12** be suffered by **13** be one's fortune, fall to one's lot, present itself

happening 4 case **5** event **6** advent, affair, matter **7** episode **8** accident, incident, occasion **9** adventure, incidence **10** experience, occurrence, proceeding **11** vicissitude **12** circumstance, happenstance **20** just one of those things

happenstance 4 luck **6** chance **8** accident, fortuity

happiness 3 joy **4** glee **5** bliss, cheer, mirth **6** gaiety **7** comfort, content, delight, ecstasy, elation, jollity, rapture **8** blessing, felicity, gladness, pleasure **9** beatitude, enjoyment, merriment, rejoicing, transport **10** cheeriness, exuberance, exultation, jubilation **11** blessedness, contentment, high spirits **12** cheerfulness, satisfaction **13** gratification **16** lightheartedness, sense of well-being

happy 3 fit, gay **4** glad, meet **5** lucky **6** elated, joyful, joyous, timely **7** content, fitting, gleeful, pleased, tickled **8** blissful, cheerful, cheering, ecstatic, exultant, jubilant, pleasant, pleasing **9** agreeable, contented, delighted, exuberant, favorable, fortunate, gratified, opportune, overjoyed, rapturous, rhapsodic **10** auspicious, convenient, delightful, felicitous, gratifying, propitious, seasonable **11** exhilarated, tickled pink, transported **12** advantageous **13** in high spirits **15** in seventh heaven

Happy Days
 character: **6** Arnold, Fonzie **10** Ralph Malph **11** Potsie Weber **12** Chachi Arcola **14** Pinky Tuscadero **15** Chuck Cunningham **16** Alfred Delvecchio, Arthur Fonzarelli, Howard Cunningham, Joanie Cunningham, Leather Tuscadero, Marion Cunningham, Richie Cunningham
 cast: **8** Roz Kelly **9** Donny Most, Erin Moran, Pat Morita, Ron Howard, Scott Baio, Tom Bosley **10** Al Molinaro, Marion Ross, Suzi Quatro **12** Henry Winkler **13** Anson Williams,

Gavan O'Herlihy **15** Randolph Roberts

happy-go-lucky 6 blithe **7** buoyant, flighty, relaxed **8** carefree, careless, feckless, heedless, skittish **9** easygoing, unworried **10** insouciant, nonchalant, optimistic, untroubled **11** free-and-easy, unconcerned **12** devil-may-care, light-hearted **13** irresponsible **14** scatterbrained **23** without a worry in the world

harangue 6 speech, tirade **7** lecture, oration **8** diatribe, scolding **9** contumely, sermonize **12** denunciation, vituperation

Harare
 capital of: **8** Zimbabwe

harass 3 cow, irk, vex **4** bait, ride **5** annoy, beset, bully, harry, hound, tease, worry **6** attack, badger, bother, heckle, hector, pester, plague **7** assault, bedevil, besiege, disturb, torment **8** browbeat, distress, irritate **9** persecute **10** discommode, exasperate, intimidate **14** raid frequently

harbinger 4 clue, omen **5** token **6** herald, symbol **7** portent **8** signaler **9** announcer, first sign, precursor **10** forerunner, indication, proclaimer

Harbonna 6 eunuch

harbor 3 bay **4** cove, dock, feel, goal, hide, hold, keep, pier, port, quay **5** basin, haven, house, inlet, lodge, wharf **6** asylum, billet, foster, lagoon, refuge, retain, shield, take in **7** care for, cling to, conceal, nurture, protect, quarter, retreat, shelter **8** hideaway, keep safe, maintain, muse over, terminus **9** brood over, sanctuary **11** concealment, destination, hiding place **12** give refuge to **13** bear in the mind, terminal point **18** protected anchorage

Harcorates *see* **5** Horus

hard 3 sad **4** cold, firm, mean, ugly **5** cruel, eager, harsh, heavy, rigid, rough, solid, stern, stiff, stony, tight, tough **6** bitter, brutal, fierce, firmly, keenly, knotty, severe, steely, strict, strong, sullen, thorny, unkind **7** angrily, arduous, callous, closely, complex, cryptic, eagerly, earnest, harmful, heavily, hostile, hurtful, inhuman, intense, onerous, sharply, solidly, tightly, to heart, vicious, violent, willing, zealous **8** animated, baffling, critical, diligent, exacting, fiercely, forceful, forcibly, hardened, intently, involved, pitiless, powerful, puzzling, rocklike, ruthless, severely, spirited, spiteful, steadily, strongly, stubborn, untiring, venomous, vigorous **9** arduously, assiduous, bellicose, confusing, difficult, earnestly, energetic, furiously, herculean, insulting, intensely, intricate, laborious, malicious, merciless, painfully, rancorous, seriously, strenuous, stringent, unbending, unpliable, unsparing, violently, wearisome **10** burdensome, diligently, forcefully, formidable, impervious, implacable, inexorable, inflexible, lamentable, melancholy, oppressive, perplexing, persistent, powerfully, relentless, resolutely, rigorously, tormenting, unbearable, unflagging, unfriendly, unpleasant, untiringly, unyielding, vigorously, vindictive **11** acrimonious, agonizingly, assiduously, belligerent, bewildering, complicated, distressing, emotionally, hardhearted, industrious, insensitive, intolerable, laboriously, persevering, troublesome, unceasingly, unmalleable, unrelenting, unremitting, unsparingly **12** antagonistic, cantankerous, determinedly, disagreeable, enterprising, impenetrable, persistently, relentlessly, thick-skinned, unfathomable, unflaggingly **13** conscientious, disheartening, distressfully, energetically, indefatigable, industriously, with much anger **14** uncompromising, with much sorrow **15** conscientiously **16** with all one's might **18** with strong feelings

hard-and-fast 3 set **6** strict **7** binding **8** exacting, rigorous **9** mandatory, unbending **10** compelling, compulsory, inflexible, obligatory, undeniable, unyielding **11** irrevocable, unalterable, unremitting **12** indisputable **13** incontestable **14** uncompromising

Hardcastle family
   characters in: 18 She Stoops to Conquer
   author: 9 Goldsmith

hard drinker 3 sot **4** lush, soak, wino **5** drunk, rummy, souse, toper **6** barfly, boozer **7** guzzler, imbiber, tippler **8** drunkard **9** alcoholic **11** dipsomaniac **14** problem drinker **16** two-fisted drinker

harden 3 dry, gel, set **4** cake, fire, firm **5** adapt, adjust, blunt, enure, inure, steel **6** anneal, freeze, season, temper **7** calcify, callous, congeal, fortify, petrify, stiffen, thicken, toughen **8** accustom, solidify **9** fossilize, make tough, reinforce **10** discipline, invigorate, strengthen **11** crystallize, turn to stone **12** restrengthen **13** make unfeeling

hard feelings 5 anger **6** grudge, hatred, rancor **7** ill will **8** acrimony **9** animosity, hostility **10** antagonism, bitterness **12** spitefulness

hardheaded 4 cool **5** balky **6** astute, mulish, poised, shrewd **7** willful **8** contrary, sensible, stubborn **9** immovable, objective, obstinate, pigheaded, practical, pragmatic, realistic, unbending, unfeeling **10** coolheaded, impersonal, inflexible, refractory, self-willed, unyielding **11** down-to-earth, intractable, tough-minded, unemotional, unflappable **14** self-controlled

hardhearted 4 cold, hard, mean **5** cruel, stony **6** brutal, Hannah **7** callous, inhuman **8** pitiless, ruthless, uncaring **9** heartless, merciless, unfeeling, unpitying, unsparing **11** coldblooded, indifferent, insensitive, remorseless, unforgiving **12** cruelhearted, thick-skinned **13** unsympathetic

hardihood 4 grit **5** pluck, spunk **6** mettle **7** courage **8** strength **9** endurance, fortitude **10** resolution **12** resoluteness

Harding, Warren Gamaliel
   presidential rank: 11 twenty-ninth
   party: 10 Republican
   state represented: 2 OH
   defeated: 3 (James Middleton) Cox, (William Wesley) Cox **4** (Eugene Victor) Debs **7** (Aaron Sherman) Watkins **8** (Robert Charles) Macauley **11** (Parley Parker) Christensen
   vice president: 8 (Calvin) Coolidge
   cabinet:
      state: 6 (Charles Evans) Hughes
      treasury: 6 (Andrew William) Mellon
      war: 5 (John Wingate) Weeks
      attorney general: 9 (Harry Micajah) Daugherty
      navy: 5 (Edwin) Denby
      postmaster general: 3 (Harry Stewart) New **4** (Hubert) Work, (William Harrison) Hays
      interior: 4 (Albert Bacon) Fall, (Hubert) Work
      agriculture: 7 (Henry Cantwell) Wallace
      commerce: 6 (Herbert Clark) Hoover
      labor: 5 (James John) Davis
   born: 9 Corsica OH (now Blooming Grove)
   died: 2 CA (while in office) **12** San Francisco
   buried: 8 Marion OH
   education:
      College: 11 Ohio Central
   religion: 7 Baptist
   interests: 5 poker
      played musical instrument: 6 cornet **7** helicon
   political career: 8 US Senate **15** Ohio State Senate
      lieutenant governor of: 4 Ohio
   civilian career: 9 publisher **13** schoolteacher **15** newspaper editor **17** insurance salesman
   notable events of lifetime/term:
      Act: 21 Fordney-McCumber Tariff
      peace treaty with: 7 Austria, Germany, Hungary
      scandal: 10 Teapot Dome (oil)
      Treaty: 9 Five-Power, Nine-Power **16** Four-Power Pacific
   father: 11 George Tryon
   mother: 6 Phoebe (Elizabeth Dickerson)

stepmother: 4 Mary (Alice Severns) **6** Eudora (Kelley Luvisi)
   siblings: 11 George Tryon **12** Mary Clarissa **14** Charity Malvina, Phoebe Caroline **15** Abigail Victoria **16** Charles Alexander, Eleanor Priscilla
   wife: 8 Florence (Kling DeWolfe)
   children:
      illegitimate daughter: 21 Elizabeth Ann Christian (by mistress Nan Britton)

hardly 4 just, only **6** barely, rarely **7** faintly, in no way **8** not often, not quite, scarcely **9** almost not, by no means **10** in no manner, uncommonly **12** certainly not, infrequently **13** not by any means **15** not by a great deal

hardnosed 4 hard **5** harsh, rigid, stern, tough **6** severe, shrewd, strict **8** critical, hard-line, exacting, stubborn **9** demanding, unbending, unsparing **10** hardheaded, inflexible, nonsense, unyielding **11** calculating, intractable **12** unsentimental **14** uncompromising

Hardouin-Mansart, Jules
   architect of: 8 Orangery (Versailles) **12** Chateau du Val (St Germain-en-Laye), Grand Trianon (Versailles), Place Vendome (Paris) **15** Chateau de Clagny (Versailles) **16** Galerie des Glaces (Hall of Mirrors at Versailles), Les Invalides (Church of the Dome, Paris)

hard-pressed 7 harried, put-upon **9** embattled **10** overworked

hardship 3 woe **4** load **5** agony, grief **6** burden, misery, ordeal, sorrow **7** problem, travail, trouble **8** handicap **9** adversity, privation, suffering **10** affliction, difficulty, misfortune **11** cross to bear, encumbrance, tribulation, unhappiness **12** wretchedness

hard sledding 8 tough job **10** difficulty, tough going, uphill work **11** arduousness **13** laboriousness

hard times 4 bust **5** slump **8** bad times **9** recession **10** depression

Hard Times
   author: 11 Studs Terkel

Hard Times
   author: 14 Charles Dickens
   character: 9 Sissy Jupe **10** Mrs Sparsit **11** Mr Bounderby **12** Tom Gradgrind **14** James Harthouse **15** Louisa Gradgrind, Thomas Gradgrind **16** Stephen Blackpool

hard to catch 3 sly **4** foxy, wily **6** crafty, shifty, tricky **7** elusive, evasive **8** slippery

hard to grasp 6 arcane **7** complex, elusive **8** abstruse, baffling, puzzling, slippery **9** difficult, enigmatic **10** perplexing **16** incomprehensible

hard to manage 6 unruly **7** froward, willful **8** perverse, stubborn **9** difficult, fractious, obstinate **10** inflexible, refractory, unyielding **11** intractable **12** obstreperous, unmanageable

hard to please 5 fussy, picky **7** exigent, finicky **8** critical **10** fastidious, meticulous, particular

Hardwick, Elizabeth
  author of: 11 Simple Truth **12** A View of My Own **15** Sleepless Nights **20** Seduction and Betrayal

Hardwicke, Sir Cedric
  born: 3 Lye **7** England
  roles: 14 On Borrowed Time **21** Livingstone and Stanley **36** A Connecticut Yankee in King Arthur's Court

hardwood 4 wood **8** leadwood
  kind: 3 ash, elm, oak **4** teak **5** beech, birch, maple **6** cherry, linden, walnut **7** hickory **8** mahogany, rosewood, sycamore

hardworking 8 diligent, sedulous **9** assiduous **11** industrious, persevering **12** enterprising **13** conscientious

hardy 3 fit **4** hale **5** tough **6** hearty, mighty, robust, rugged, strong, sturdy **7** healthy **8** stalwart, vigorous **9** strapping **10** able-bodied **12** in fine fettle **13** physically fit **15** in good condition

Hardy, Oliver
  partner: 10 Stan Laurel
  born: 8 Harlem GA
  roles: 8 Pardon Us **9** Saps at Sea **10** Way Out West

Hardy, Thomas
  author of: 10 The Dynasts **14** Jude the Obscure **20** The Return of the Native **21** Tess of the D'Urbervilles **22** Far from the Madding Crowd, The Mayor of Casterbridge
  mythical county: 6 Wessex
  represents: 11 Dorsetshire

hare
  constellation of: 5 Lepus
  group of: 4 down, husk

harebrained 5 silly, wacko, wacky **7** asinine, flighty, foolish **8** skittish **9** dimwitted, senseless **10** half-witted **11** empty-headed **12** simple-minded **13** rattlebrained **14** featherbrained, scatterbrained

harem 5 serai, wives **6** purdah, serail, senana, zenana **8** love nest, seraglio **10** concubines
  room: 3 oda
  guard 6 eunuch

Hargreaves, James
  nationality: 7 English
  inventor of: 13 spinning jenny

Harker, Jonathan
  character in: 7 Dracula
  author: 6 Stoker

harlot 3 pro **4** bawd, doxy, jade, pros, slut, tart **5** whore **6** chippy, wanton **7** jezebel, trollop **8** call girl, mistress, strumpet **9** courtesan, kept woman **10** prostitute **11** fallen woman **12** painted woman, scarlet woman, streetwalker

Harlow, Jean
  real name: 16 Harlean Carpenter
  nickname: 15 Blonde Bombshell
  born: 12 Kansas City MO
  roles: 7 Red Dust **8** Riffraff, Saratoga **9** Bombshell, China Seas **11** Hell's Angels, Libeled Lady **13** Dinner at Eight

harm 3 ill, mar, sin **4** evil, hurt, maim, pain, ruin, vice **5** abuse, agony, havoc, spoil, wound, wrong **6** damage, debase, deface, ill-use, impair, injure, injury, malice, misuse, trauma **7** blemish, cripple, degrade, scourge **8** aggrieve, calamity, hardship, iniquity, maltreat, mischief, villainy **9** adversity, detriment, disfigure, suffering, undermine **10** defacement, immorality, impairment, misfortune, sinfulness, wickedness **11** destruction, devastation, malevolence **12** do violence to **13** deterioration, maliciousness

harmful 3 bad **7** adverse, baneful, hurtful, ruinous **8** damaging **9** dangerous, injurious, unhealthy **10** pernicious **11** deleterious, destructive, detrimental, unhealthful, unwholesome **17** counterproductive

harmless 4 mild, safe **6** benign, gentle **7** sinless **8** innocent, nontoxic **9** blameless, guiltless, incorrupt, innocuous, peaceable **10** not hurtful **11** inoffensive **12** not dangerous **15** unobjectionable

harmlessness 6 safety **9** innocence **10** gentleness **11** nontoxicity **12** nonvirulence **13** innocuousness **15** inoffensiveness

Harmon, Young John
  character in: 15 Our Mutual Friend
  author: 7 Dickens

Harmonia
  father: 4 Ares
  mother: 9 Aphrodite
  husband: 6 Cadmus
  daughter: 3 Ino

harmonious 5 sweet **6** dulcet **7** amiable, cordial, unified **8** amicable, friendly, in accord, matching **9** agreeable, congenial, in harmony, melodious **10** compatible, consistent, euphonious, likeminded **11** coordinated, harmonizing, in agreement, mellifluous, sympathetic **12** synchronized **13** sweet-sounding **17** agreeably combined

harmonium 9 reed organ

harmonize 3 fit **4** jibe, mesh **5** agree, blend, chime, tally **6** accord, adjust, attune **7** conform **8** be in tune **9** reconcile **10** complement, correspond, go together **13** sing in harmony

harmony 5 amity, order, peace, unity **6** accord **7** balance, concord **8** matching, symmetry, sympathy **9** agreement, unanimity **10** conformity, fellowship, friendship, proportion **11** amicability, cooperation, correlation, parallelism **12** congeniality, coordination, mutual regard **13** compatibility, mutual fitness **14** like-mindedness **15** organic totality **17** good understanding **19** harmonious relations, pleasing consistency **21** concurrence in opinions

Harmony
  goddess of: 9 Concordia

harness 4 curb, rein, tugs, yoke **5** lines, reins, rig up **6** bridle, collar, employ, halter, muzzle, straps, tackle, traces **7** exploit, hitch up, utilize **8** restrain **9** caparison, trappings **12** put in harness, render useful **13** control and use, turn to account **14** make productive **22** direct to a useful purpose

Harper, Joe
  character in: 9 Tom Sawyer
  author: 5 Twain

harp on 7 dwell on **9** reiterate **18** repeat persistently

Harpy
  form: 7 monster
  head of: 5 woman
  body of: 4 bird
  father: 7 Thaumas
  mother: 7 Electra
  names: 5 Aello **7** Celaeno, Ocypete, Podarge

harridan 3 hag **5** crone, shrew, witch **6** virago **8** battle-ax, old crone **12** mean old woman

harried 5 upset **7** worried **8** harassed, troubled **10** distraught

Harris, Joel Chandler
  author of: 18 Uncle Remus (His Songs and Sayings)
  character: 7 Brer Fox, tar baby **8** Brer Bear **10** Brer Rabbit

Harris, Julie
  real name: 14 Julia Ann Harris
  born: 18 Grosse Pointe Park MI
  roles: 6 Harper **10** East of Eden, I Am a Camera **11** The Haunting **14** A Shot in the Dark, The Hiding Place **19** The Last of Mrs Lincoln **21** The Member of the Wedding **22** Requiem for a Heavyweight **27** And Miss Reardon Drinks a Little

Harris, Richard
  born: 7 Ireland **8** Limerick
  roles: 7 Camelot **8** Cromwell, The Field **9** Gladiator **15** A Man Called Horse **16** The Molly Maguires, This Sporting Life **17** Mutiny on the Bounty, The Guns of Navarone **20** The Cassandra Crossing **26** The Return of a Man Called Horse **31** Harry Potter and the Sorcerer's Stone **33** Harry Potter and the Chamber of Secrets

Harris, Roy
  composer of: 16 Folksong Symphony **17** American Portraits **27** When

Johnny Comes Marching Home
(overture)

Harrison, Benjamin
nickname: **3** Ben **9** Little Ben
presidential rank: **11** twenty-third
party: **10** Republican
state represented: **2** IN
defeated: **4** (Clinton Bowen) Fisk **6**
(James Langdon) Curtis **7** (Robert
Hall) Cowdrey **8** (Albert) Redstone,
(Alson Jenness) Streeter, (Belva Ann
Bennett) Lockwood **9** (Grover)
Cleveland
vice president: **6** (Levi Parsons) Morton
cabinet:
   state: **6** (James Gillespie) Blaine,
   (John Watson) Foster
   treasury: **6** (Charles) Foster, (William) Windom
   war: **6** (Stephen Benton) Elkins **7**
   (Redfield) Proctor
   attorney general: **6** (William
   Henry Harrison) Miller
   navy: **5** (Benjamin Franklin) Tracy
   postmaster general: **9** (John)
   Wanamaker
   interior: **5** (John Willock) Noble
   agriculture: **4** (Jeremiah McLain)
   Rusk
born: **11** North Bend OH
died/buried: **14** Indianapolis IN
education:
   prep school: **14** Farmer's College
   University: **21** Miami University of
   Ohio
   later studied: **3** law
religion: **12** Presbyterian
interests: **7** fishing, hunting **8** swimming
political career: **8** US Senate
   city attorney: **12** Indianapolis
   reporter of: **19** Indiana supreme
   court
   secretary of: **31** Republican state
   central committee
civilian career: **6** lawyer **12** law professor
military service: **8** Civil War **16** brigadier general
notable events of lifetime/term:
   Act: **16** Dependent Pension, Sherman Anti-Trust **21** Sherman Silver
   Purchase
   Tariff: **8** McKinley
father: **9** John Scott
mother: **9** Elizabeth (Ramsey Irwin)
siblings: **8** Mary Jane **9** John Irwin,
John Scott **10** Anna Symmes, James
Irwin **12** James Findlay **13** Carter
Bassett **14** Archibald Irwin
   half sisters: **9** Elizabeth **13** Sarah
   Lucretia
wife: **4** Mary (Scott Lord Dimmick) **8**
Caroline (Lavinia Scott)
children: **9** Elizabeth, Mary Scott **15**
Russell Benjamin

Harrison, Lou

born: **10** Portland OR
composer of: **8** Rapunzel, Solstice **13**
Changing World **15** Four Strict
Songs, Johnny Appleseed **17** The
Perilous Chapel **19** Almanac of the
Seasons **22** At the Tomb of Charles
Ives

Harrison, Peter
architect of: **11** Brick Market (Newport RI), King's Chapel (Boston) **14**
Redwood Library (Newport RI),
Touro Synagogue (Newport RI)

Harrison, Rex
real name: **21** Reginald Carey Harrison
nickname: **8** Sexy Rexy
wife: **10** Kay Kendall **11** Lilli Palmer
13 Rachel Roberts
born: **6** Huyton **7** England
roles: **9** Cleopatra **10** My Fair Lady
(Oscar) **12** Blithe Spirit, Henry Higgins **14** Doctor Dolittle **16** The Foxes
of Harrow **17** Unfaithfully Yours **18**
The Ghost and Mrs Muir **20** Anna
and the King of Siam

Harrison, Wallace K
architect of: **13** Lincoln Center (NYC)
14 Socony Building (NYC) **17** Rockefeller Center (NYC) **22** Metropolitan
Opera House (NYC) **25** United Nations Headquarters (NYC) **34** Nelson
A Rockefeller Empire State Plaza (Albany NY), ALCOA Building (Pittsburgh, with Max Abramovitz)

Harrison, William Henry
nickname: **6** Old Tip **22** The Washington of the West
presidential rank: **5** ninth
party: **4** Whig
state represented: **2** OH
defeated: **6** (James G) Birney **8** (Martin) Van Buren
vice president: **5** (John) Tyler
cabinet:
   state: **7** (Daniel) Webster
   treasury: **5** (Thomas) Ewing
   war: **4** (John) Bell
   attorney general: **10** (John Jordan)
   Crittenden
   navy: **6** (George Edmund) Badger
   postmaster general: **7** (Francis)
   Granger
born: **2** VA **17** Charles City County
18 Berkeley plantation
died: **12** Washington DC
buried: **11** North Bend OH
education: **16** privately tutored (at
home)
   College: **13** Hampden-Sydney (did
   not graduate)
   later studied: **8** medicine
religion: **12** Episcopalian
political career: **8** US Senate **11** state
Senate **24** US House of Representatives
   governor of: **16** Indiana Territory
   minister: **8** Colombia
civilian career: **6** farmer **7** soldier

military service: **6** US Army **12** major
general **19** War of Eighteen Twelve
   battle: **6** (the) Thames **8** Lake Erie
   10 Tippecanoe
notable events of lifetime/term: **24**
Land Act of Eighteen Hundred
   campaign slogan: **21** Tippecanoe
   and Tyler too
   treaty of: **10** Greenville
father: **8** Benjamin
mother: **9** Elizabeth (Bassett)
siblings: **3** Ann **4** Lucy **5** Sarah **8**
Benjamin **9** Elizabeth **13** Carter Bassett
wife: **4** Anna (Tuthill Symmes)
children: **8** Benjamin **9** John Scott **10**
Mary Symmes **11** Anna Tuthill **12**
James Findlay, William Henry **13**
Carter Bassett, Lucy Singleton **16**
Elizabeth Bassett, John Cleves Symmes

Harrow 10 prep school
rival: **4** Eton

harrowing 7 fearful, painful **8** alarming, chilling **9** traumatic, upsetting **10**
disturbing, terrifying, tormenting **11**
distressing, frightening **13** bloodcurdling

harry 3 irk, vex **4** bait, gall, raid, ride,
sack **5** annoy, beset, bully, haunt,
hound, tease, worry **6** badger, bother,
harass, heckle, hector, pester, plague
7 disturb, pillage, plunder, torment,
trouble **8** distract, distress, irritate **9**
terrorize **10** exasperate, intimidate **16**
attack repeatedly

**Harry Potter and the Chamber of
Secrets**
author: **9** J K Rowling
director: **13** Chris Columbus
cast: **9** Tom Felton (Draco Malfoy) **10**
Emma Watson (Hermione Granger),
John Cleese (Nearly Headless Nick)
11 Alan Rickman (Severus Snape),
Jason Isaacs (Lucius Malfoy), Maggie
Smith (Minerva McGonagall), Rupert
Grint (Ron Weasley) **12** Matthew
Lewis (Neville Longbottom) **13** Rich-
ard Harris (Albus Dumbledore) **14**
Kenneth Branagh (Gilderoy Lock-
hart), Robbie Coltrane (Rubeus Ha-
grid) **15** Daniel Radcliffe (Harry Potter) **16** Shirley Henderson (Moaning
Myrtle)

**Harry Potter and the Goblet of
Fire**
author: **9** J K Rowling
director: **10** Mike Newell
cast: **9** Tom Felton (Draco Malfoy) **10**
Emma Watson (Hermione Granger),
Gary Oldman (Sirius Black), John
Cleese (Nearly Headless Nick), Katie
Leung (Cho Chang) **11** Alan Rick-
man (Severus Snape), Jason Isaacs
(Lucius Malfoy), Maggie Smith (Mi-
nerva McGonagall), Rupert Grint
(Ron Weasley) **12** Matthew Lewis
(Neville Longbottom), Ralph Fiennes

(Lord Voldemort), Timothy Spall (Peter Pettigrew) **13** Clemence Poesy (Fleur Delacour), Michael Gambon (Albus Dumbledore) **14** Brendan Gleeson (Alastor "Mad-Eye" Moody), Robbie Coltrane (Rubeus Hagrid) **15** Daniel Radcliffe (Harry Potter) **16** Shirley Henderson (Moaning Myrtle) **17** Miranda Richardson (Rita Skeeter)
tournament: 10 Triwizards

Harry Potter and the Prisoner of Azkaban
author: 9 J K Rowling
director: 13 Alfonso Cuaron
cast: 9 Tom Felton (Draco Malfoy) **10** Emma Watson (Hermione Granger), Gary Oldman (Sirius Black), John Cleese (Nearly Headless Nick) **11** Alan Rickman (Severus Snape), Maggie Smith (Minerva McGonagall), Rupert Grint (Ron Weasley) **12** David Thewlis (Professor Lupin), Emma Thompson (Sybil Trelawney), Matthew Lewis (Neville Longbottom), Timothy Spall (Peter Pettigrew) **13** Michael Gambon (Albus Dumbledore) **14** Robbie Coltrane (Rubeus Hagrid) **15** Daniel Radcliffe (Harry Potter)

Harry Potter and the Sorcerer's Stone
British title: 34 Harry Potter and the Philosopher's Stone
author: 9 J K Rowling
director: 13 Chris Columbus
cast: 9 Tom Felton (Draco Malfoy) **10** Emma Watson (Hermione Granger), John Cleese (Nearly Headless Nick) **11** Alan Rickman (Severus Snape), Maggie Smith (Minerva McGonagall), Rupert Grint (Ron Weasley) **12** Matthew Lewis (Neville Longbottom) **13** Richard Harris (Albus Dumbledore) **14** Robbie Coltrane (Rubeus Hagrid) **15** Daniel Radcliffe (Harry Potter)
non-magical people: 7 Muggles
school: 8 Hogwarts
shopping: 11 Diagon Alley

harsh 4 hard, mean **5** cruel, raspy, rough, sharp, stern **6** bitter, brutal, hoarse, severe, shrill, unkind **7** abusive, caustic, glaring, grating, jarring, rasping, raucous, squawky **8** piercing, pitiless, ruthless, scratchy, strident, ungentle **9** Draconian, heartless, merciless, too bright, unmusical, unsparing **10** discordant, overbright, unpleasant, vindictive **11** cacophonous, hardhearted **12** uncharitable, unharmonious

harshness 5 rigor **7** cruelty, discord **9** brutality, cacophony, raspiness, roughness, sternness, stridency **10** dissonance, shrillness, unkindness **12** ungentleness **13** heartlessness **14** unpleasantness **15** hardheartedness

Hart, Johnny
creator/artist of: 2 B C **13** The Wizard of Id

Hart, Moss
author of: 15 Once in a Lifetime **20** You Can't Take It with You (with George S Kaufman) **21** The Man Who Came to Dinner (with George S Kaufman)

Harte, Bret
author of: 20 The Luck of Roaring Camp **22** The Outcasts of Poker Flat

Hartford
hockey team: 7 Whalers

Hartley, Vivian Mary
real name of: 11 Vivien Leigh

harum-scarum 5 giddy **6** wildly **7** erratic, flighty, foolish **8** careless, confused **9** aimlessly, haphazard, impetuous, impulsive, unplanned, unsettled **10** bewildered, recklessly, unreliable **11** haphazardly, harebrained, impulsively **12** absent-minded, capriciously, disorganized, inconsistent, undependable **13** rattlebrained **14** featherbrained, scatterbrained

Harun ar-Rashid 6 caliph **7** Baghdad **13** Arabian Nights

harvest 3 cut, mow **4** crop, gain, pick, reap **5** amass, fruit, pluck, yield **6** gather, haying, mowing, output, result, return, reward **7** benefit, collect, cutting, picking, produce, product, reaping **8** fruition, gleaning, proceeds **9** aftermath, amassment, gathering, outgrowth **10** accumulate, collection, harvesting **12** accumulation **13** season's growth

harvest time 4 fall **6** autumn **8** maturity **12** Indian summer

Harvey
director: 11 Henry Koster
based on play by: 9 Mary Chase
cast: 6 rabbit **8** Peggy Dow **9** James Stewart (Elwood P Dowd) **13** Cecil Kellaway, Josephine Hull
Oscar for: 17 supporting actress (Hull)

Harvey, Laurence
real name of: 19 Larushka Misch Skikne
wife: 16 Margaret Leighton
born: 9 Lithuania, Yomishkis
roles: 7 Darling **12** Life at the Top, Room at the Top **14** Of Human Bondage, Summer and Smoke **16** Butterfield Eight **17** Walk on the Wild Side

Harvey, William
field: 7 anatomy
nationality: 7 British
discovered: 18 circulation of blood

Hasen, Irwin
creator/artist of: 5 Dondi **9** Goldbergs **11** Wonder Woman **12** Green Lantern

hash out 6 review **7** discuss **8** consider, talk over

hasp 4 lock **5** catch, clasp, latch **7** closure **8** fastener

Hassam, (Frederick) Childe
born: 12 Dorchester MA
artwork: 13 Southwest Wind **14** Summer Sunlight, Washington Arch **15** Against the Light **23** Boston Commons at Twilight

hassle 3 bug, row, vex **5** annoy, fight, harry, hound, scrap, set-to **6** badger, battle, bother, harass, tussle **7** contest, dispute, quarrel **8** argument, conflict, squabble, struggle **9** persecute

hassock 4 boss, pess, seat, tuft, wedge **5** bunch, chair, group, trush **6** buffet, plants, tuffet **7** ottoman, tussock **9** footstool, vegetable

hasta la vista 6 good-by, so long **7** goodbye **12** until I see you **16** until we meet again

hasta manana 13 until tomorrow **14** see you tomorrow

haste 4 rush **5** hurry, speed **8** celerity, dispatch, rapidity, rashness **9** fleetness, quickness, swiftness **10** expedition, speediness, undue speed **11** hurriedness **12** recklessness **13** careless hurry, impetuousness, impulsiveness, precipitation

hasten 3 fly, run **4** bolt, dart, dash, flit, jump, race, rush **5** egg on, hurry, impel, speed, whisk **6** hustle, incite, scurry, sprint, urge on **7** advance, drive on, hurry on, hurry up, promote, quicken, scamper, scuttle, speed up **8** expedite, make time **10** accelerate, lose no time **11** go full blast, precipitate, push forward **12** step on the gas **13** go on the double **14** step right along **15** go like lightning, make short work of, work against time **20** go hell-bent for leather

hastily 4 fast **5** apace **6** pronto, rashly **7** quickly **8** promptly, speedily **9** hurriedly, like a shot, posthaste, summarily **10** carelessly, heedlessly, recklessly, too quickly **11** impetuously, impulsively, on the double **12** lickety-split, straightaway **13** precipitately, thoughtlessly **18** hell-bent for leather **20** like greased lightning, on the spur of the moment

hasty 4 fast, rash **5** brief, fleet, quick, rapid, swift **6** abrupt, prompt, rushed, speedy **7** cursory, hurried, passing **8** fleeting, headlong, heedless, reckless **9** impetuous, impulsive, momentary **10** breathless **11** precipitate, superficial, unduly quick **12** quick as a wink **19** without deliberation

hat
French: 7 chapeau

hatch 4 plan, plot **5** frame **6** cook up, create, design, devise, evolve, invent, make up **7** concoct, dream up, fashion, produce, think up **8** conceive, contrive **9** construct, fabricate, formulate, improvise, originate **10** bring forth **11** give birth to, manufacture

hatchlings 5 brood, young **6** chicks **9** offspring

hate 5 abhor, dread, venom **6** animus, detest, enmity, hatred, loathe, malice, rancor **7** be sorry, despise, dislike, wince at **8** acrimony, aversion, be sick of, distaste, execrate, loathing **9** abominate, animosity, antipathy, be tired of, disliking, hostility, not care to **10** abhorrence, be averse to, feel sick at, recoil from, repugnance, resentment, shrink from **11** abomination, be hostile to, be reluctant, be unwilling, detestation, malevolence, wish to avoid **12** be repelled by **14** have no taste for, hold in contempt, revengefulness, vindictiveness **16** bear malice toward, have no stomach for **17** feel disinclined to, not have the heart to **19** regard as distasteful

hateful 4 evil, foul, mean, ugly, vile **5** nasty **6** odious, sinful, wicked **7** heinous **8** infamous, scornful **9** abhorrent, atrocious, loathsome, monstrous, obnoxious, offensive, repellent, repugnant, revolting, sickening **10** abominable, deplorable, despicable, detestable, disdainful, disgusting, forbidding, full of hate, irritating, unbearable, unpleasant, villainous **11** distasteful, intolerable, unendurable **12** contemptible, contemptuous, insufferable **13** objectionable

Hathaway, Anne
husband: 11 Shakespeare

Hathor
origin: 8 Egyptian
goddess of: 3 joy **4** love
symbol: 4 ears, head **5** horns
patron of: 5 dance, music
personifies: 3 sky

hatred 4 hate **5** venom **6** animus, enmity, malice, rancor **7** disgust, dislike, ill will **8** acrimony, aversion, bad blood, distaste, loathing **9** animosity, antipathy, hostility, revulsion **10** abhorrence, antagonism, bitterness, repugnance, resentment **11** abomination, detestation, malevolence **14** revengefulness, vindictiveness

haughtiness 4 airs **5** pride **7** conceit, hauteur **8** snobbery **9** arrogance **10** snootiness **13** condescension **14** disdainfulness, high-handedness **16** superciliousness

haughty 5 aloof **6** lordly, snooty, uppish, uppity **7** high-hat, stuck-up **8** arrogant, scornful, snobbish **9** conceited, officious **10** disdainful, highhanded, hoity-toity **11** highfalutin, overbearing, overly proud, patronizing, swell-headed **12** contemptuous **13** condescending, high and mighty

haul 3 bag, lug, tow, tug **4** cart, drag, draw, gain, jerk, move, pull, swag,

take, tote, yank **5** booty, bring, carry, catch, fetch, heave, truck, yield **6** convey, profit, remove, reward, spoils, wrench **7** capture, takings **9** transport

haunches 4 buns, rear, rump, seat **5** nates **7** rear end **8** buttocks **9** fundament, posterior **12** hindquarters

haunt 3 vex **5** beset, worry **6** live in, obsess, plague, prey on **7** disturb, terrify, torment, trouble, weigh on **8** distress, frequent, frighten **9** hang out at, preoccupy, terrorize **10** hang around, hover about, loiter near, visit often **11** beat a path to **12** linger around

haunts 3 den **4** cave, hole, lair, nest **6** burrow **7** hangout **8** hideaway **9** waterhole **10** rendezvous **12** meeting place **14** gathering place **15** stamping grounds

haute couture 11 high fashion

haute cuisine 11 fine cooking **14** gourmet cooking

hauteur 5 swank **7** conceit, disdain **8** snobbery **9** arrogance, loftiness **10** snootiness **11** haughtiness **12** affectedness, snobbishness **13** condescension **14** disdainfulness, highhandedness **16** superciliousness **19** patronizing attitude

haut monde 5 elite **10** blue bloods, upper class, upper crust **11** aristocracy, high society **14** creme de la creme

Havana
capital of: 4 Cuba
gulf: 6 Mexico
landmark: 15 Cabaret Parisien **16** Castillo del Morro **17** Castillode la Punta, Jose Marti Monument **18** Castillo de la Atares, Castillo de la Fuerza, Garcia Lorca Theater **19** Maximo Gomez Monument **21** Latinamericano Stadium **22** Academy of Science of Cuba
river: 10 (Rio) Almendares
Spanish: 8 La Habana

Havasupai, Supai
location: 7 Arizona **11** Grand Canyon
related to: 7 Yavapai **8** Hualapai

have 3 buy, eat, get, own, use **4** bear, fool, gain, gull, hold, host, keep, make, must **5** beget, carry, cheat, drink, enjoy, force, grasp, ought, smoke, trick **6** accept, affirm, compel, harbor, obtain, outwit, permit, retain, suffer **7** achieve, acquire, defraud, exhibit, possess, realize, receive, swindle **8** comprise, maintain, manifest, outsmart, perceive, tolerate **9** encompass, encounter, partake of, recognize, victimize **10** comprehend, experience, understand

have a go at 3 try **6** hazard, tackle **7** attempt **8** give a try **9** undertake **10** give a whirl **12** take a crack at, take a whack at

have a good opinion of 5 favor **6**

admire, revere **7** approve, respect **9** believe in **10** appreciate

have a hand in 7 advance, forward **9** influence **10** take part in **12** contribute to **13** be conducive to, participate in **14** help bring about

have an eye on 4 want **5** covet, crave, fancy **6** desire **7** long for, pine for **8** aspire to, yearn for **9** lust after **11** have a yen for

have a yen for 4 want **5** covet, crave **6** desire **7** long for, wish for **8** yearn for **9** lust after **11** hanker after **13** have a fancy for

have bearing on 5 apply, refer **6** relate **7** concern, pertain **9** appertain, touch upon **13** be pertinent to, have respect to

have done with 4 drop, junk, shed **7** abandon, discard **9** dispose of **10** relinquish **12** dispense with

have faith in 5 trust **6** rely on **9** believe in **16** have confidence in

have guests 8 play host **9** entertain **10** give a party **13** keep open house **16** offer hospitality

Have Gun Will Travel
character: 6 Hey Boy **7** Hey Girl, Paladin
cast: 6 Lisa Lu **7** Kam Tong **12** Richard Boone
setting: 12 San Francisco **13** Hotel Carleton

have in mind 4 mean, want, wish **6** desire, intend **10** think about

haven 4 port **5** cover **6** asylum, harbor, refuge **7** hideout, retreat, shelter **8** hideaway **9** sanctuary

have no hope 6 give up **7** despair **11** be desperate

have plenty 6 abound, be rich **8** flourish, overflow **10** be numerous, have enough **11** be plentiful **14** be well supplied **18** have more than enough

have the body
Latin: 12 habeas corpus
legal writ guards against: 19 illegal imprisonment

have too few 4 lack, want **7** be scant **9** fall short **13** be deficient in, have a dearth of **14** have a paucity of **15** be in short supply, have a scarcity of, not have enough of

having life 5 alive, vital **6** living, viable **7** animate

having the means 3 fit **4** able **6** fitted **7** capable, equal to **8** adequate **9** qualified **12** being solvent **20** having the wherewithal

Havisham, Miss
character in: 17 Great Expectations
author: 7 Dickens

havoc 4 ruin **5** chaos **8** calamity, disaster, disorder, upheaval **9** cataclysm, ruination **11** catastrophe, destruction, devastation **12** wrack and ruin **16** widespread damage

Havoc, June 7 actress
- **sister: 12** Gypsy Rose Lee
- **dramatized as: 5** Gypsy
- **billed as: 8** Baby June

Hawaii
- **abbreviation: 2** HI
- **nickname: 5** Aloha **15** Sandwich Islands **20** Paradise of the Pacific
- **capital/largest city: 8** Honolulu
- **others: 3** Ewa **4** Aiea, Hana, Hilo, Laie, Paia **5** Kapaa, Kapaa, Lihue, Maili **6** Kailua, Kekaha **7** Kahului, Kaneohe, Lanikae, Wahiawa, Waianae, Wailuku
- **college: 9** Chaminade, Hawaii Loa **12** Brigham Young **13** Hawaii Pacific
- **dance: 4** hula
- **explorer: 4** Cook **7** Gaetano
- **feature:**
  - **district: 7** Lahaina
  - **national park: 9** Haleakala **15** Hawaii Volcanoes
- **festivity: 4** luau
- **food: 3** poi **4** taro
- **foreigner: 5** haole
- **gift: 3** lei
- **greeting: 5** aloha
- **goddess: 4** Pele
- **king: 10** Kamehameha
- **medicine man: 6** Kahuna
- **musical instrument: 3** uke **7** ukulele, ukelele
- **native woman: 6** wahine
- **people: 5** Don Ho **9** Hiram Fong **10** Polynesian **11** Sanford Dole, Bette Midler **12** Daniel Inouye, Father Damien
- **porch: 5** lanai
- **queen: 12** Liliuokalani
- **island name: 4** Kure **9** Kahoolawe
  - **big isle: 6** Hawaii
  - **friendly isle: 7** Molokai
  - **garden isle: 5** Kauai
  - **gathering place: 4** Oahu
  - **house of the sun: 9** Haleakala
  - **mystery isle: 6** Niihau
  - **pineapple isle: 5** Lanai
  - **valley isle: 4** Maui
- **lake: 5** Waiau
- **land rank: 12** forty-seventh
- **mountain: 3** Kea, Loa **5** Kaala **6** Kohala, Kohala, Koolau **7** Kamakou, Waianae **8** Maunaloa **9** Lanaihale
  - **highest point: 8** Maunakea
- **physical feature:**
  - **bay: 5** Pohue **6** Halawa, Kiholo, Mamala **7** Kamohio, Kaneohe, Waiagua **8** Kawaihae, Maunalua
  - **beach: 7** Waikiki
  - **canyon: 6** Waimea
  - **channel: 3** Aua **5** Kaiwi **6** Kalohi **7** Pailolo
  - **crater: 7** Kilauea **9** Punchbowl
  - **desert: 3** Kau
  - **harbor: 5** Pearl
  - **promontory: 11** Diamond Head
  - **valley: 3** Iao **5** Manoa
  - **volcano: 7** Kilauea **8** Maunakea, Maunaloa **9** Haleakala
- **state admission: 8** Fiftieth
- **state bird: 4** nene **13** Hawaiian goose
- **state flower: 5** lehua **11** red hibiscus **15** scarlet hibiscus
- **state motto: 44** The Life of the Land is Perpetuated in Righteousness
- **state song: 11** Hawaii Ponoi **12** Our Own Hawaii
- **state tree: 5** kukui **9** candlenut

Hawaii
- **author: 13** James Michener

Hawaiian swimmer 14 Duke Kahanamoku

Hawaii Five-O
- **character: 4** Kono **5** Wo Fat **8** Ben Kokua **11** Chin Ho Kelly **13** Danny Williams **14** Steve McGarrett
- **cast: 4** Zulu **7** Kam Fong **8** Jack Lord **11** Khigh Dhiegh **12** Al Harrington **14** James MacArthur

hawk 4 bird, sell, vend **6** falcon, peddle **8** militant **9** accipiter, warmonger
- **young: 4** eyas
- **group of: 4** cast

Hawk, Sir Mulberry
- **character in: 16** Nicholas Nickleby
- **author: 7** Dickens

Hawkes, John
- **author of: 10** Second Skin **11** The Cannibal, The Lime Twig **12** The Beetle Leg **15** The Blood Oranges

Hawkeye 11 Natty Bumppo
- **author: 6** Cooper

Hawkeye Pierce 4 Mash **8** Alan Alda

Hawkeye State
- **nickname of: 4** Iowa

Hawkins, Jim
- **character in: 14** Treasure Island
- **author: 9** Stevenson

Hawkline Monster, The
- **author: 16** Richard Brautigan

Hawks, Howard
- **director of: 8** Red River, Rio Bravo, Scarface **11** The Big Sleep **12** Sergeant York **13** His Girl Friday **14** Bringing Up Baby **16** To Have and Have Not, Twentieth Century

Hawn, Goldie
- **husband: 10** Bill Hudson **12** Gus Trinkonis
- **companion: 11** Kurt Russell
- **born: 12** Washington DC
- **children: 10** Kate Hudson **12** Oliver Hudson
- **roles: 7** Laugh-In, Shampoo **8** Foul Play **9** Overboard **12** Cactus Flower **15** Private Benjamin, The Out-of-Towners **17** The First Wives Club **18** Butterflies Are Free

hawser 4 line, rope **5** cable **7** mooring

hawthorn 9 Crataegus
- **varieties: 5** water, yeddo **6** Indian **7** English

Hawthorne, Nathaniel
- **author of: 13** The Marble Faun **14** Twice-told Tales **16** The Scarlet Letter **20** Mosses from an Old Manse **24** The House of the Seven Gables

Haydee
- **character in: 21** The Count of Monte Cristo
- **author: 5** Dumas (pere)

Haydn, Franz Joseph
- **born: 6** Rohrau **7** Austria
- **called: 9** Papa Haydn
- **composer of: 7** The Bird, The Joke **10** Gypsy Rondo, The Seasons **11** The Creation **12** Emperor's Hymn, Wild Band Mass **13** The Apothecary **14** Lord Nelson Mass, Theresienmesse **15** Mass in Time of War **16** Il Mondo della Luna, Mariazellermesse **17** The World of the Moon **38** The Seven Last Words of Our Savior on the Cross
  - **quartet: 3** Sun **4** Bird, Frog, Lark, Tost **5** Dream, Razor, Witch **6** Fifths, Maiden **7** Emperor, Erdoedy, Russian, Sunrise, The Bell, The Hunt **8** Farmyard, Horseman, The Jokes **9** The Donkey **14** The House on Fire, The Row in Vienna
  - **symphony: 4** Fire **5** Paris **6** Le Midi, Le Soir, Loudon, Merkur, Oxford, The Hen **7** Evening, Le Matin, Mercury, Morning, Salomon, The Bear, The Hunt **8** Abschied, Alleluia, Drum Roll, Farewell, Military, Mourning, Surprise, The Clock, The Queen, The Storm **9** Children's, Christmas **10** La Passione, La Tempesta, The Miracle, The Passion **11** The Imperial **12** Der Philosoph, Maria Theresa, The Afternoon **13** Auf dem Anstand **14** The Philosopher **15** The Schoolmaster, Trauersymphonie, With the Horn Call **17** At the Hunting Place **18** Mit dem Hornersignal

Hayes, Elvin
- **nickname: 4** Big E
- **sport: 10** basketball
- **team: 8** San Diego **14** Houston Rockets

Hayes, Helen
- **real name: 15** Helen Hayes Brown
- **nickname: 29** First Lady of the American Theater
- **son: 14** James MacArthur
- **roles: 7** Airport **9** Anastasia **22** The Sin of Madelon Claudet (Oscar)

Hayes, Rutherford B (Birchard)
- **nickname: 8** Rud Hayes
- **presidential rank: 10** nineteenth
- **party: 10** Republican
- **state represented: 2** OH
- **defeated: 5** (Green Clay) Smith **6** (James B) Walker, (Peter) Cooper, (Samuel Jones) Tilden
- **vice president: 7** (William Almon) Wheeler

cabinet:
  state: 6 (William Maxwell) Evarts
  treasury: 7 (John) Sherman
  war: 6 (Alexander) Ramsey **7**
    (George Washington) McCrary
  attorney general: 6 (Charles) Devens
  navy: 4 (Nathan) Goff (Jr) **8** (Richard Wigginton) Thompson
  postmaster general: 3 (David McKendree) Key **7** (Horace) Maynard
  interior: 6 (Carl) Schurz
born: 10 Delaware OH
died/buried: 9 Fremont OH
education:
  preparatory school: 4 Webb
  College: 6 Kenyon
  Law School: 7 Harvard
religion: 9 Methodist
political career: 24 US House of Representatives
  city solicitor of: 10 Cincinnati
  governor of: 4 Ohio
civilian career: 6 farmer, lawyer
military service: 6 US Army **8** Civil War **12** Ohio infantry **18** brevet major general
notable events of lifetime/term: 10 Depression (of 1873) **15** railroad strikes (of 1877) **18** civil service reform **24** specie payments resumption **Act: 26** Bland-Allison Silver Purchase
father: 10 Rutherford
mother: 6 Sophia (Birchard)
siblings: 7 Lorenzo **11** Sarah Sophia **13** Fanny Arabella
wife: 4 Lucy (Ware Webb)
children: 5 Fanny **8** James Webb (renamed Webb Cook) **11** George Crook **12** Manning Force, Scott Russell **14** Joseph Thompson, Sardis Birchard (renamed Birchard Austin) **15** Rutherford Platt

hayseed 4 hick, rube **5** yokel **6** rustic **7** bumpkin, peasant **10** clodhopper

Hayward, Susan
  real name: 14 Edythe Marrener
  husband: 10 Jess Barker
  born: 10 Brooklyn NY
  roles: 11 I Want to Live (Oscar) **14** I'll Cry Tomorrow, My Foolish Heart **18** With a Song in My Heart **23** Smash Up The Story of a Woman

Hayworth, Rita
  real name: 22 Margarita Carmen Cansino
  husband: 7 Aly Khan **10** Dick Haymes **11** Orson Welles
  born: 10 Brooklyn NY
  roles: 5 Gilda **9** Cover Girl **14** Separate Tables **17** Miss Sadie Thompson, You'll Never Get Rich

hazan 18 cantor of a synagogue

hazard 3 bet **4** dare, luck, risk **5** fluke, guess, offer, peril, stake, wager **6** chance, danger, expose, gamble, menace, mishap, submit, threat **7** advance, daresay, imperil, pitfall, presume, proffer, suppose, venture **8** accident, chance it, endanger, jeopardy, theorize, threaten, throw out **9** mischance, speculate, tempt fate, volunteer **10** conjecture, jeopardize, misfortune **11** coincidence, hypothesize, imperilment, take a chance, trust to luck **12** endangerment, happenstance, stroke of luck

hazardous 4 iffy **5** risky, shaky **6** chancy, unsafe, unsure **7** dubious, unsound **8** doubtful, insecure, perilous, unstable **9** dangerous, uncertain **10** precarious, unreliable **11** speculative, threatening **13** untrustworthy

haze 3 fog **4** daze, film, mist, pall, veil **5** cloak, cloud, smoke, vapor **6** mantle, muddle, screen **9** fogginess **12** befuddlement, bewilderment **16** state of confusion

hazel 3 nut **4** tree **5** brown, shrub, tawny **8** brownish **14** yellowish-brown
  varieties: 4 tree **5** Chile, witch **6** winter **7** Chinese, Turkish **8** American, European, Japanese **11** spike winter **12** Chinese witch **13** Japanese witch **15** buttercup winter

Hazel
  character: 12 George Baxter, Harold Baxter **13** Dorothy Baxter
  cast: 9 Don DeFore **12** Shirley Booth, Whitney Blake **13** Bobby Buntrock
  creator: 6 Ted Key

hazelnut 7 Corylus
  varieties: 6 beaked **7** Chinese, Turkish **8** American, European, Japanese

Hazlitt, William
  author of: 6 essays **17** The Spirit of the Age **32** The Characters of Shakespeare's Plays

hazy 3 dim **5** dusky, faint, filmy, foggy, misty, murky, smoky, vague **6** bleary, blurry, cloudy, smoggy, veiled **7** bleared, general, muddled, obscure, unclear **8** confused, nebulous, overcast **9** ambiguous, uncertain **10** ill-defined, indefinite

head 2 go, IQ **3** aim, CEO, end, hie, tip, top **4** acme, apex, bent, boss, czar, duce, font, fore, gift, jefe, king, lead, main, mind, peak, rise, rule, tsar, turn, well **5** begin, brain, chief, crest, crown, drive, first, front, guide, pilot, prime, queen, ruler, start, steer **6** climax, crisis, direct, genius, govern, honcho, launch, leader, manage, origin, ruling, source, spring, summit, talent, vertex, zenith **7** ability, admiral, captain, command, conduct, control, foreman, general, go first, highest, leading, make for, manager, marshal, monarch, precede, premier, primary, proceed, ranking, supreme, topmost **8** aptitude, be head of, big

wheel, capacity, chairman, dictator, director, dominant, foremost, fountain, fruition, headmost, initiate, judgment, managing, pinnacle, start off, superior, suzerain, upper end **9** acuteness, beginning, commander, commodore, extremity, forefront, front rank, governing, intellect, introduce, mentality, paramount, potentate, president, principal, sovereign, supervise, uppermost **10** administer, be master of, birthplace, cleverness, commandant, commanding, conclusion, first place, gray matter, inaugurate, lead the way, move toward, perception, preeminent, supervisor, wellspring **11** be at the helm, controlling, culmination, discernment, forward part, highest rank, officiate at, preside over, superintend, take the lead, termination **12** apprehension, field marshal, fountainhead, guiding light, place of honor, take charge of, take the reins, turning point, utmost extent **13** administrator, go at the head of, most prominent, prime minister, understanding **14** chief executive, highest ranking, superintendent **15** be in the vanguard, make a beeline for, quickness of mind **16** commander-in-chief, direct one's course, inevitable result **17** commanding general, have authority over **18** be in the driver's seat, chairman of the board, go in the direction of

head
  contains: 4 eyes **5** brain, mouth, skull **9** braincase **10** optic nerve **12** ocular muscle **13** cranial cavity, lacrimal organ, orbital cavity **14** buccaval cavity

headache 5 trial **6** strain, stress **7** problem, trouble **8** migraine, nuisance **10** affliction, difficulty **13** inconvenience, pain in the neck

headdress 3 cap, hat **6** bonnet **7** chapeau **12** headcovering

headgear 3 cap, fez, hat, tam **4** cowl, hood, kepi, topi, veil **5** beret, busby, crown, derby, miter, mitre, opera, shako, shawl, snood, straw, terai, tiari, topee, toque **6** beanie, boater, bonnet, bowler, cloche, fedora, helmet, mobcap, panama, sailor, trilby, turban **7** bicorne, biretta, chapeau, hardhat, homberg, pillbox, porkpie, stetson, **8** babushka, kerchief, mantilla, nightcap, skullcap, snap-brim, sombrero, tarboosh, tricorne, yarmulke **9** stovepipe, sunbonnet, ten-gallon **10** pith helmet **11** deerstalker, dolly varden

headland 4 bank, crag **5** bluff, cliff **8** palisade **9** precipice **10** promontory

headlong 6 abrupt **8** abruptly, heedless, pell-mell, reckless **9** headfirst, impetuous **10** heedlessly, recklessly **11** impetuously, precipitate, precipitous **13** head over heels, precipitously

headman 5 chief 6 leader 7 foreman 8 alderman, princeps 9 commander 10 councilman, supervisor 14 public official, superintendent

head-on 6 direct 7 frontal 10 face-to-face

headshrinker 6 shrink 7 analyst 12 psychiatrist 13 psychoanalyst

headstrong 4 rash 6 dogged, mulish, unruly 7 defiant, froward, willful 8 contrary, obdurate, reckless, stubborn 9 hotheaded, imprudent, impulsive, obstinate, pigheaded 10 bullheaded, incautious, refractory 11 intractable 12 incorrigible, recalcitrant, ungovernable, unmanageable 14 uncontrollable 22 bent on having one's own way

heady 4 hard 6 potent, strong 8 alluring, exciting, inviting, stirring, tempting 9 seductive, thrilling 10 high-octane 11 high-voltage, tantalizing 12 exhilarating, intoxicating

heal 4 cure, knit, mend 5 right, salve, treat 6 heal up, remedy, settle, soothe 7 compose, get well, improve, recover, rectify, relieve 8 heal over, make well 9 alleviate, make whole, reconcile 10 conciliate, convalesce, recuperate 11 set to rights 14 make harmonious, return to health 20 restore good relations

healed 4 knit 5 cured 6 mended 7 got well 8 relieved

healing 6 curing 7 mending 8 knitting, soothing 9 emollient, improving, restoring 10 making well 11 restorative 13 strengthening
  god of: 6 Apollo 7 Phoebus, Pythius 9 Asclepius, Musagetes 11 Aesculapius
  goddess of: 4 Iaso

health 5 vigor 7 fitness, stamina 8 strength, vitality 9 hardihood, hardiness, well-being 10 robustness 16 general condition 17 physical condition
  goddess of: 6 Hygeia

healthful 7 healthy 8 hygienic, salutary 9 wholesome 10 beneficial, nourishing, nutritious, salubrious 12 healthgiving, invigorating

healthiness 6 health 9 good shape, soundness 10 good health, robustness 12 salutariness 13 good condition, healthfulness, wholesomeness 14 salubriousness

healthy 3 fit 4 hale 5 hardy, sound 6 hearty, robust, strong, sturdy 8 vigorous 9 in the pink 10 able-bodied 12 in fine fettle 18 sound of mind and limb

heap 3 gob, lot 4 fill, gobs, hunk, load, lots, lump, mass, mess, pack, pile, slew 5 amass, award, batch, bunch, flood, group, mound, ocean, slews, stack, store, world 6 accord, assign, bundle, deluge, engulf, gather, jum-

ble, load up, oceans, oodles, pile up, plenty, worlds 7 barrels, cluster, collect, mete out, present 8 good deal, inundate, pour upon 9 abundance, gathering, great deal, multitude, profusion 10 assemblage, collection, shower upon 11 aggregation, concentrate 12 accumulation

heap up 5 amass 6 pile up 7 stack up 10 accumulate

hear 4 heed 5 admit, favor, grant, judge, learn 6 attend, be told, gather, look on 7 approve, concede, examine, find out, receive, witness 8 accede to, appear at, discover, hear tell, hold with, listen to 9 acquiesce, ascertain, hearken to 10 understand 11 acknowledge

hear!
  French: 4 oyez
  cry used by: 10 court crier
  precedes: 5 trial 12 proclamation

hearing 5 probe, sound 6 review 7 council, earshot, inquiry 8 audience 9 interview 10 conference 11 examination, questioning 12 consultation 13 interrogation, investigation

hearken to 4 heed, mark, mind 6 attend 8 listen to 11 take to heart 14 pay attention to

hearsay 4 talk 5 rumor 6 gossip, report 8 idle talk 9 grapevine 11 scuttlebutt

heart 3 hub, nub 4 base, core, crux, guts, love, meat, mood, pith, root, soul 5 humor, pluck, spunk, valor 6 center, daring, desire, kernel, middle, nature, source, spirit 7 bravery, charity, courage, emotion, essence, nucleus, stomach 8 audacity, backbone, boldness, clemency, feelings, firmness, fondness, gameness, interior, main part, sympathy 9 affection, fortitude, gallantry, inner part, rudiments, sentiment, tolerance 10 brass tacks, compassion, enthusiasm, essentials, foundation, gentleness, indulgence, manfulness, principles, resolution, tenderness, true nature 11 busiest part, central part, disposition, forgiveness, nitty-gritty, temperament 12 fearlessness, fundamentals, quintessence, resoluteness 13 audaciousness
  part: 5 aorta, valve 6 atrium 7 chamber 9 ventricle
  pumps: 5 blood

heartache 3 woe 4 pain 5 grief 6 misery, sorrow 7 anguish, sadness, torment, trouble 8 distress 9 suffering 11 tribulation, unhappiness

heartbreaker 4 vamp 5 flirt, tease 8 coquette

Heartbreak House
  author: 17 George Bernard Shaw

hearten 4 abet 5 cheer 6 assure, solace 7 animate, cheer up, comfort, console, enliven, gladden 8 brighten,

embolden, energize, inspirit, reassure 9 encourage 10 invigorate

heartening 7 hopeful 9 favorable 10 auspicious, reassuring 11 encouraging

heartfelt 4 deep, full 5 total 6 ardent, devout, entire, honest 7 earnest, fervent, genuine, intense, sincere 8 complete, profound, thorough 10 keenly felt 12 all-inclusive, wholehearted

hearth 4 home 5 abode, house 8 fireside 9 fireplace, household 10 family life 12 family circle 13 chimney corner
  goddess of: 4 Caca 5 Salus, Vesta 6 Hestia

Heart Is a Lonely Hunter, The
  author: 15 Carson McCullers
  character: 8 Mr Singer 9 Mick Kelly 10 Dr Copeland, Jake Blount 11 Biff Brannon

heartless 4 cold, mean 5 cruel 6 brutal, savage, unkind 7 callous, inhuman, unmoved 8 pitiless, ruthless, uncaring 9 unfeeling, unpitying, unstirred 10 unmerciful 11 coldhearted, cold-blooded, hardhearted, insensitive 12 cruelhearted, unresponsive 13 unsympathetic

Heart of Darkness
  author: 12 Joseph Conrad
  character: 5 Kurtz 7 Marlowe

Heart of Dixie
  nickname of: 7 Alabama

Heart of Juliet Jones, The
  creator: 9 Stan Drake
  character: 3 Eve

Heart of Midlothian, The
  author: 14 Sir Walter Scott

Heart of the Matter, The
  author: 12 Graham Greene
  character: 5 Yusef 6 Wilson 7 Mrs Rolt 9 Mrs Scobie 11 Major Scobie

heart-stopper 5 belle 6 beauty 7 charmer, stunner 8 knockout 10 good-looker 13 beautiful girl 14 beautiful woman

hearty 4 hale, warm, well 5 ample, hardy, sound 6 lively, robust, strong 7 cordial, genuine, healthy, profuse, sincere, zestful 8 complete, effusive, generous, thorough, vigorous 9 heartfelt, unbounded 10 unreserved 12 enthusiastic, unrestrained, wholehearted 13 physically fit

hearty appetite
  French: 10 bon appetit

Heaslop, Ronald
  character in: 15 A Passage to India
  author: 7 Forster

Heat
  director: 11 Michael Mann
  cast: 8 Al Pacino (Vincent Hanna) 9 Jon Voight (Nate), Val Kilmer (Chris Shiherlis) 10 Ashley Judd (Charlene Shiherlis) 11 Diane Venora (Justine Hanna), Tom Sizemore (Michael

Cheritto) **12** Amy Brenneman (Eady), Robert De Niro (Neil McCauley) **17** Mykelti Williamson (Sergeant Drucker)

heat 3 fry **4** bake, boil, cook, sear, stew, warm, zeal **5** ardor, broil, roast, steam **6** braise, climax, fervor, height, simmer, stress, thrill, warmth, warm up **7** hotness, make hot, passion, rapture, swelter **8** fervency, hot spell, warmness **9** eagerness, intensity, transport **10** enthusiasm, excitement **12** bring to a boil

heated 3 hot **5** angry, fiery, irate **6** bitter, fierce, raging, stormy **7** excited, fervent, furious, intense, violent **8** frenzied, inflamed, vehement **9** emotional **10** infuriated, passionate **11** impassioned, tempestuous

heated discussion 7 dispute **8** argument **10** war of words **11** controversy **12** disagreement

heath 5 Erica
　varieties: 4 Tree **5** Berry, Besom, Irish, Otago, Spike **6** Dorset, Scotch, Spring **7** Cornish, Fringed, Spanish, Twisted **9** Cranberry **11** Cross-leaved

Heathcliff
　character in: 16 Wuthering Heights
　loved: 5 Cathy
　author: 6 Bronte

heathen 3 goy **4** boor **5** pagan **6** savage **7** atheist, gentile, infidel **8** agnostic, idolator **9** barbarian, ignoramus **10** polytheist, troglodyte, unbeliever **11** non-believer **17** uncivilized native

heather 7 Calluna
　varieties: 3 Bog, Red **4** Bell, Snow **5** Beach, False, White **6** French, Golden, Scotch **8** Corsican, Mountain **9** Christmas **11** White winter **13** Mediterranean **18** Everblooming French

heat up 3 fan, zap **4** goad, nuke, warm, whet **6** arouse **7** enhance, sharpen **8** increase **9** aggravate, intensify **10** strengthen

heave 3 peg, pry, sob **4** arch, blow, cast, emit, fire, hurl, lift, moan, pant, puff, puke, toss **5** boost, bulge, chuck, eject, fling, groan, hoist, lever, pitch, raise, retch, sling, surge, swell, throw, vomit **6** dilate, drag up, draw up, exhale, expand, haul up, launch, let fly, propel, pull up, tilt up, yank up **7** elevate **8** thrust up **9** discharge, palpitate **11** regurgitate

heaven, Heaven, the Heavens 3 wow **4** Zion **5** bliss, glory, mercy, space **6** my oh my, utopia **7** delight, ecstasy, Elysium, my stars, nirvana, Olympus, rapture **8** boy oh boy, goodness, land sake, paradise, Valhalla **9** afterlife, dreamland, next world, Shangri-la **10** afterworld, Beulah Land, life beyond, outer space, perfection, sheer bliss **11** enchantment, the Holy City,

world beyond, world to come **12** eternal bliss, good gracious, New Jerusalem, the City of God, the firmament **13** Abraham's bosom, Elysian fields, seventh heaven **14** heavens to Betsy, our eternal home **15** life everlasting, our Father's house, the heavenly city **16** goodness gracious, Isle of the Blessed, supreme happiness, the abode of saints, the Celestial City, the vault of heaven **17** complete happiness, the wild blue yonder **18** Island of the Blessed, the celestial sphere, the heavenly kingdom, the kingdom of Heaven **19** the celestial expanse **21** the happy hunting ground
　god of: 2 An **3** Anu **4** Jove, Zeus **7** Jupiter

Heaven Can Wait (1943)
　director: 13 Ernst Lubitsch
　cast: 9 Don Ameche **11** Gene Tierney **12** Marjorie Main **13** Charles Coburn

Heaven Can Wait (1978)
　director: 9 Buck Henry **12** Warren Beatty
　cast: 10 Dyan Cannon, Jack Warden **12** Warren Beatty **13** Julie Christie
　remake of: 17 Here Comes Mr Jordan

heavenly 6 divine **7** angelic, blessed, saintly, sublime **8** beatific, blissful

Heavens and Earth
　author: 19 Stephen Vincent Benet

Heaven's My Destination
　author: 14 Thornton Wilder

heavy 3 big, fat, sad **4** deep, dull, full, hard, lazy, slow **5** broad, bulky, dense, grave, gross, harsh, hefty, large, obese, plump, rough, stout, thick **6** clumsy, coarse, deadly, dreary, fierce, gloomy, leaden, pained, portly, raging, rugged, savage, solemn, strong, sturdy, torpid, woeful **7** awesome, complex, copious, doleful, forlorn, furious, intense, joyless, languid, lumpish, massive, notable, onerous, profuse, roaring, ruinous, serious, tearful, tedious, violent, weighty **8** abundant, agonized, burdened, crushing, cumbrous, damaging, dejected, desolate, downcast, forceful, grieving, grievous, imposing, lifeless, listless, mournful, pedantic, profound, seething, sluggish, stricken, tiresome, unwieldy **9** apathetic, cheerless, corpulent, depressed, difficult, excessive, extensive, harrowing, important, injurious, laborious, lethargic, lumbering, miserable, momentous, ponderous, rampaging, sorrowful, turbulent, wearisome **10** burdensome, calamitous, cumbersome, distressed, full of care, immoderate, impressive, inordinate, melancholy, monotonous, noteworthy, oppressive, overweight, pernicious, phlegmatic, unbearable, unstinting **11** crestfallen, deleterious, destructive, detrimental, distressing, extravagant, intemperate, intolerable, significant,

tempestuous, unendurable, unrelenting, unremitting **12** considerable, disconsolate, hard to endure, overwhelming, unrestrained **13** consequential, grief-stricken, of great import **16** laden with sorrows **18** of great consequence

heavy-handed 5 harsh **6** clumsy **7** awkward **8** bungling **9** graceless, maladroit **10** blundering, oppressive, ungraceful

heavyhearted 3 sad **4** glum **6** dismal, gloomy, morose **7** doleful, forlorn, joyless, unhappy **8** dejected, downcast **9** cheerless, depressed, sorrowful **10** despondent, melancholy **11** downhearted **14** down in the dumps, down in the mouth

Hebe
　goddess of: 5 youth **6** spring
　father: 4 Zeus
　mother: 4 Hera
　brother: 4 Ares
　husband: 8 Hercules
　handmaiden to: 4 gods
　corresponds to: 8 Juventas

Hebrew alphabet
　or: 5 aleph
　b/v: 4 beth
　g: 5 gimel
　d: 6 daleth
　h: 2 he **5** cheth
　v/w: 3 vav
　z: 5 zayin
　y/j/i: 3 yod
　k/kh: 4 kaph
　l: 5 lamed
　m: 3 men
　n: 3 nun
　`: 4 ayin
　p/f: 2 pe
　k: 4 koph
　r: 4 resh
　sh/s: 4 shin
　s: 3 sin **4** sadi **6** samekh
　t: 3 tav **4** teth

Hebrew Judge 4 Ehud, Elon, Jair, Tola **5** Abdon, Ibzan **6** Gideon, Samson, Samuel **7** Deborah, Othniel, Shamgar **8** Jephthah

Hebrew months
　first: 4 Ahib, Nisn **6** Ehanim, Tishri
　second: 3 Bul, Civ **4** Iyar **7** Heshvan
　third: 5 Sivan **6** Kislev
　fourth: 5 Tebet **6** Tammuz, Tebeth
　fifth: 2 Ab **7** Shelbat
　sixth: 4 Adar, Elul **6** Veadar
　seventh: 4 Abib **5** Nisan **6** Tishri **7** Ethanim
　eighth: 3 Zif **4** Iyer **11** Marcheshvan
　ninth: 5 Sivan **7** Chislev
　tenth: 6 Tabeth, Tammuz
　eleventh: 2 Ab **6** Shebat
　twelfth: 4 Adar, Elul

he carved it
　Latin: 8 sculpsit

Hecate
 also: **6** Hekate
 goddess of: **5** earth, Hades
 associated with: **6** hounds **7** sorcery **10** crossroads
 corresponds to: **5** Brimo

heckle 3 boo **4** bait, hiss, hoot, mock, razz, ride, twit **5** annoy, bully, chivy, harry, hound, taunt **6** badger, harass, harrow, hector, jeer at, molest, needle **7** provoke **9** shout down

Heckle and Jeckle 7 magpies **8** cartoons

hectare
 abbreviation of: **2** ha

hectic 3 mad **4** wild **6** stormy **7** chaotic, frantic, furious **8** feverish, frenetic, frenzied, headlong **9** breakneck, turbulent **10** tumultuous

hectoliter
 abbreviation of: **2** hl

hectometer
 abbreviation of: **2** hm

hector 4 bait, ride **5** bully, harry, hound, tease, worry **6** badger, harass, needle, plague **7** torment, swagger **8** browbeat

Hector
 father: **5** Priam
 mother: **6** Hecuba
 brother: **5** Paris
 sister: **9** Cassandra
 wife: **10** Andromache
 son: **8** Astyanax
 hero of: **9** Trojan War
 killed by: **8** Achilles

Hecuba
 also: **5** Maera **6** Hecabe
 father: **5** Atlas
 husband: **5** Priam **8** Tegeates
 son: **5** Paris **6** Hector **7** Helenus, Polites, Troilus **9** Deiphobus, Polydorus
 daughter: **6** Creusa **7** Laodice **8** Polyxena **9** Cassandra
 changed into: **3** dog **5** bitch
 hound of: **7** Icarius

Hecuba
 author: **9** Euripides
 character: **8** Odysseus, Polyxena **9** Agamemnon, Polydorus **10** Polymestor

Hedda Gabler
 author: **11** Henrik Ibsen
 character: **10** Judge Brack **11** Hedda Tesman, Thea Elvsted **12** George Tesman **13** Eilert Lovberg **17** Miss Juliana Tesman

heder 12 Jewish school

hedge 3 hem **4** duck, edge, ring, wall **5** bound, dodge, evade, fence, guard, hem in, limit **6** border, margin, shut in, waffle **7** barrier, enclose, mark off, outline **8** encircle, hedgerow, surround **9** be evasive, delineate, demarcate, insurance, pussyfoot, temporize **10** equivocate, protection **11** delineation, row of bushes **12** compensation

13 circumference, fence of shrubs **14** beg the question, counterbalance **17** beat around the bush

he died
 Latin: **5** obiit

he does not pursue
 Latin: **14** non prosequitur

hedonist 8 Sybarite **9** debauchee, libertine **10** dissipater, profligate, sensualist, voluptuary **14** pleasure seeker

hedonistic 7 sensual **9** epicurean, libertine, sybaritic **10** voluptuous **11** intemperate **13** self-indulgent **15** pleasure-seeking

he drew this
 Latin: **10** delineavit

heed 4 care, mind, obey **5** bow to, pains, study **6** concur, follow, hold to, notice, regard **7** defer to, observe, perusal, respect, yield to **8** accede to, consider, listen to, prudence, scrutiny, submit to **9** attention, be ruled by, give ear to **10** bear in mind comply with, precaution, take note of **11** carefulness, examination, heedfulness, mindfulness, observation, take to heart **12** take notice of **13** attentiveness **14** fastidiousness, meticulousness, pay attention to, scrupulousness **17** conscientiousness

heedful 4 wary **5** alert, aware, cagey, chary **7** alive to, careful, mindful, prudent **8** cautious, discreet, vigilant, watchful **9** attentive, concerned, conscious

heedless 3 lax **4** rash **5** slack **6** remiss, unwary **7** foolish, unaware, witless **8** careless, mindless, reckless, uncaring **9** foolhardy, frivolous, impetuous, imprudent, negligent, oblivious, unheeding, unmindful **10** incautious, neglectful, unthinking, unwatchful **11** harebrained, improvident, inattentive, thoughtless, unconcerned, unobservant, unobserving **12** happy-go-lucky **14** scatterbrained

heedlessly 5 blind **6** rashly **8** headlong **9** foolishly, witlessly **10** carelessly, mindlessly, recklessly **11** frivolously, impetuously, impulsively, negligently, unmindfully **12** neglectfully, unthinkingly **13** inattentively, thoughtlessly, unconcernedly **15** inconsiderately, uncooperatively

heedlessness 8 rashness **9** unconcern **10** negligence **11** inattention, unawareness **12** carelessness, indiscretion, mindlessness, recklessness **13** unmindfulness **15** thoughtlessness **16** irresponsibility

heel 3 cad, cur, end, rat **4** list, rind, tilt **5** churl, crust, louse **6** rotter **7** bounder, caitiff, dastard

he engraved it
 Latin: **8** sculpsit

Heep, Uriah

character in: **16** David Copperfield
 author: **7** Dickens

he flourished
 Latin: **7** floruit

hefty 3 big **5** beefy, bulky, burly, heavy, husky, large, stout **6** brawny, hearty, mighty, robust, rugged, strong, sturdy **7** hulking, massive, sizable, weighty, well-fed **8** muscular, powerful, stalwart, thickset **9** corpulent, strapping **11** substantial

hegemony 7 control **9** authority, dominance, influence, supremacy

Heggen, Thomas
 author of: **9** Mr Roberts

hegira 6 exodus, flight **7** journey

he himself said it
 Latin: **9** ipse dixit

Heidi 4 girl
 location: **9** Swiss Alps
 author **12** Johanna Spyri
 friend: **5** Peter

Heifetz, Jascha
 born: **6** Russia
 instrument: **6** violin

height 4 acme, apex, hill, peak, rise **5** bluff, cliff, crest, knoll, limit, mound, tower **6** apogee, heyday, summit, zenith **7** hilltop, maximum, plateau **8** altitude, eminence, highland, highness, mountain, palisade, pinnacle, tallness, ultimate **9** elevation, extremity, flowering, high point, loftiness, supremacy **10** perfection, promontory **11** culmination **12** consummation, upward extent, utmost degree, vantage point

heighten 5 raise **7** elevate **8** increase **9** aggravate, intensify

heil 4 hail

Heimberger, Eddie Albert
 real name of: **11** Eddie Albert

Heine, Heinrich
 author of: **9** Atta Troll **11** Book of Songs **19** Germany A Winter's Tale

Heinlein, Robert
 author of: **10** Double Star **16** Starship Troopers **20** The Green Hills of Earth **22** Stranger in a Strange Land **23** The Moon Is a Harsh Mistress

heinous 4 evil, foul, vile **5** gross, nasty **6** grisly, horrid, odious, sinful, wicked **7** beastly, ghastly, hideous, inhuman, vicious **8** infamous, shocking, terrible **9** abhorrent, atrocious, loathsome, monstrous, nefarious, offensive, repugnant, repulsive, revolting, sickening **10** abominable, deplorable, despicable, detestable, disgusting, iniquitous, outrageous, scandalous, villainous **11** disgraceful, distasteful **12** contemptible **13** objectionable, reprehensible

heinousness 4 evil **7** outrage **8** atrocity, baseness, enormity, foulness, savagery, vileness, villainy **9** barbarity, depravity, malignity **10** inhumanity

13 loathsomeness, monstrousness **14** outrageousness

heir, heiress 7 legatee **9** inheritor **10** inheritrix **11** beneficiary, inheritress **12** heir apparent **15** heir presumptive

Heiress, The
director: **12** William Wyler
based on novel by: **10** Henry James
  film title: **16** Washington Square
cast: **13** Miriam Hopkins **15** Montgomery Clift, Ralph Richardson **17** Olivia de Havilland
score: **12** Aaron Copland
Oscar for: **7** actress (de Havilland)

Hekate see **6** Hecate

Hel
origin: **12** Scandinavian
goddess of: **5** death
rules: **8** Niflheim **10** underworld
father: **4** Loki
mother: **9** Angerboda, Angrbodha, Angurboda
brother: **6** Fenrir, Fenris **11** Iormungandr, Jormungandr **14** Midgard Serpent
color of body: **4** blue **5** flesh
home of: **4** dead

Helen
father: **4** Zeus
mother: **4** Leda
brother: **6** Castor, Pollux
sister: **8** Timandra **12** Clytemnestra
husband: **8** Menelaus
abducted by: **5** Paris
carried off to: **4** Troy
abduction caused: **9** Trojan War
quote: **33** the face that launched a thousand ships

Helena
character in: **20** All's Well That Ends Well **21** A Midsummer Night's Dream
author: **11** Shakespeare

helicopter
invented by: **8** Sikorsky
also: **8** autogyro **9** eggbeater

Helios
origin: **5** Greek
god of: **3** sun
father: **8** Hyperion
mother: **4** Thia
children: **5** Circe **6** Aeetes **8** Phaethon
corresponds to: **3** Sol

heliotrope 12 Heliotropium
varieties: **6** garden, winter, yellow **7** seaside

helium
chemical symbol: **2** He

hell, Hell 5 agony, grief, Hades **6** misery, the pit **7** Abaddon, anguish, despair, Gehenna, inferno, remorse, torment **8** Appolyons, hell fire, the abyss **9** martyrdom, perdition, suffering **10** lake of fire **12** hopelessness, wretchedness **13** bottomless pit, Satan's kingdom, the lower world, the underworld **14** place of the lost, the Devil's

house, the nether world, the shades below **15** everlasting fire, home of lost souls, infernal regions **16** abode of the damned

Hellen
king of: **8** Thessaly
father: **9** Deucalion
mother: **6** Pyrrha
wife: **6** Orseis
son: **5** Dorus **6** Aeolus, Xuthus
ancestor of: **8** Hellenes

Hellenic Republic see **6** Greece

Heller, Joseph
author of: **7** Catch-22 **8** God Knows **10** Good as Gold, Now and Then **11** Closing Time, Picture This **16** No Laughing Matter **17** Something Happened

hellion 5 devil, rogue, scamp **9** scoundrel **13** mischief-maker

hellish 4 foul, vile **5** awful **6** brutal **7** hateful **8** accursed, damnable, dreadful, horrible, infernal **9** atrocious, revolting **10** abominable, disgusting

Hellman, Lillian
author of: **5** Maybe **10** Pentimento **13** Scoundrel Time **14** The Little Foxes, Toys in the Attic **15** Watch on the Rhine **16** The Children's Hour **17** An Unfinished Woman **22** Another Part of the Forest

hello
French: **7** bonjour
German: **8** guten tag
Spanish: **10** buenos dias
Hebrew **6** shalom
Italian: **4** ciao **10** buon giorno
Latin: **3** ave

Hello-Central
character in: **36** A Connecticut Yankee in King Arthur's Court
author: **5** Twain

help 3 aid **4** back, balm, calm, care, crew, cure, ease, gift, lift, save **5** allay, emend, force, guide, hands, salve, serve, staff **6** advice, advise, assist, give to, menial, relief, remedy, rescue, soothe, succor, uphold **7** advance, backing, console, correct, endorse, further, helpers, improve, nurture, promote, rectify, relieve, servant, service, stand by, support, welfare, workers, workmen **8** advocate, befriend, champion, domestic, factotum, farmhand, guidance, laborers, maintain, mitigate, retainer, retrieve, side with **9** alleviate, chip in for, employees, encourage, extricate, lend a hand, make whole, promotion, put at ease, underling, workhands, work force **10** ameliorate, apprentice, assistance, assistants, bring round, corrective, friendship, go to bat for, hired hands, kind regard, minister to, preventive, protection, stick up for **11** advancement, benevolence, cooperation, endorsement, furtherance, good offices,

helping hand, make healthy, restorative **12** bring through, contribute to, contribution, hired helpers, intercede for **13** collaboration, cooperate with, encouragement, take the part of

helper 3 aid **4** aide **5** angel **6** backer, deputy, patron, second **7** adjunct, partner, servant **8** adjutant, advocate, champion, confrere, co-worker, employee, retainer **9** assistant, associate, auxiliary, colleague, man Friday, right hand, supporter **10** accomplice, aide-de-camp, apprentice, benefactor, girl Friday **11** confederate, helping hand, subordinate **12** collaborator, right-hand man **13** good samaritan **14** fairy godmother

helpful 4 fine, good, kind, nice **6** usable, useful **8** obliging, splendid, valuable **9** excellent, favorable, practical **10** beneficial, profitable, supportive **11** considerate, cooperative, serviceable **12** advantageous, constructive **13** accommodating

helping hand 3 aid **4** aide, hand **5** boost **6** assist, hand up, helper, succor **7** abettor, support **9** assistant **10** assistance

helplessness 8 weakness **9** impotence, inability, infirmity **10** dependence, feebleness, ineptitude **12** incapability, incompetence, inefficiency **13** powerlessness, vulnerability

Helsinki
capital of: **7** Finland

hem 3 box, rim **4** bind, brim, edge, welt **5** bound, brink, skirt, verge **6** border, edging, fringe, impede, margin, turn up **7** confine, enclose, stammer, stutter, turning **8** compress, encircle, restrain, surround

he made it
Latin: **5** fecit

hem in 4 best **5** fence **7** besiege, confine, enclose **8** encircle, surround

Hemingway, Ernest
author of: **9** In Our Time **14** A Moveable Feast **15** A Farewell to Arms, The Sun Also Rises **16** To Have and Have Not **18** Islands in the Stream, The Old Man and the Sea **19** For Whom the Bell Tolls **21** The Snows of Kilimanjaro **34** The Short Happy Life of Francis Macomber

hemlock 5 Tsuga **15** Conium maculatum
varieties: **5** Dwarf, Water **6** Canada, Ground, Poison **7** Siebold, Spotted, Western **8** Carolina, Japanese, Mountain

hemp 14 Cannabis sativa
varieties: **3** Bog **5** Cuban, Sisal **6** Deccan, Indian, Manila **7** African **8** Deckaner **9** Bowstring, Mauritius **10** New Zealand **13** Colorado River **15** Ceylon bowstring, Indian bowstring **16** African bowstring

hen
young: **6** pullet **7** lobster

henchman 4 goon, thug **6** flunky, lackey, minion, stooge, yes-man **7** gorilla **8** hanger-on, hireling, retainer **9** attendant, bodyguard **10** hatchet man, lieutenant **12** right-hand man, strong-arm man

Henderson, Marge
creator/artist of: **10** Little Lulu

henna 3 dye **5** rinse **6** auburn, russet **8** cinnamon **11** rust-colored **12** reddish-brown **13** copper-colored

henpecked 4 meek **5** timid **6** docile **8** obedient **10** browbeaten, submissive, wife-ridden **11** unassertive

Henry, Frederic
character in: **15** A Farewell to Arms
author: **9** Hemingway

Henry Esmond
author: **16** William Thackeray
character: **5** Frank **7** Beatrix **9** Lord Mohun **10** Father Holt **11** James Stuart **12** Rachel Esmond **13** Francis Esmond

Henry IV
author: **18** William Shakespeare
character: **7** Hotspur **11** Prince Henry, Thomas Percy **14** Edmund Mortimer, Sir Walter Blunt **15** John of Lancaster, Mistress Quickly, Sir John Falstaff **18** Earl of Westmoreland, King Henry the Fourth

Henry V
author: **18** William Shakespeare
character: **7** Dauphin, Montjoy **15** Charles the Sixth (King of France) **17** Princess Katharine
director: **15** Laurence Olivier
cast: **11** Leslie Banks **12** Robert Newton **13** Renee Asherson **15** Laurence Olivier

Henry VI
author: **18** William Shakespeare
character: **6** Edward (Prince of Wales) **7** Charles (Dauphin of France), Eleanor, Louis XI (King of France) **8** Lady Bona, Lady Grey **9** Joan of Arc **10** Lord Talbot **11** Bolingbroke **12** John Beaufort, Lord Clifford, Lord Hastings **13** Henry Beaufort, Joan La Pucelle **15** Margaret of Anjou, Margery Jourdain **16** Bastard of Orleans, Cardinal Beaufort
  duke: **4** York (Richard Plantagenet) **7** Bedford, Suffolk **8** Somerset **10** Gloucester
  earl: **7** Suffolk, Warwick **9** Salisbury
  Richard Plantagenet's son: **6** Edmund, Edward, George **7** Richard

Henry VIII
author: **18** William Shakespeare
character: **7** Cranmer **8** Gardiner **10** Anne Boleyn **12** Thomas Wolsey **14** Queen Katharine, Thomas Cromwell **16** Cardinal Campeius

  duke: **7** Norfolk, Suffolk **10** Buckingham

Henze, Hans Werner
born: **7** Germany **10** Westphalia
composer of: **6** Ariosi, Ondine **8** King Stag **10** El Cimarron **11** Konig Hirsch **12** The Bassarids, The Young Lord **14** Being Beauteous **15** The Runaway Slave **17** Boulevard Solitude **18** Der Prinz von Homburg, The Raft of the Medusa **19** Elegy for Young Lovers **48** The Long and Weary Journey to the Flat of Natasha Ungeheur

Heorot
great hall in: **7** Beowulf

he painted it
Latin: **6** pinxit

Hepburn, Audrey
real name: **19** Audrey Hepburn-Ruston
husband: **9** Mel Ferrer
born: **7** Belgium **8** Brussels
roles: **6** Ondine **7** Charade, Sabrina **9** Bloodline, Funny Face **10** My Fair Lady **11** War and Peace **12** Roman Holiday (Oscar), The Nun's Story **13** Green Mansions, Wait Until Dark **18** Love in the Afternoon **19** Breakfast at Tiffany's

Hepburn, Katharine
co-star: **12** Spencer Tracy
born: **10** Hartford CT
roles: **7** Desk Set, Holiday **8** Adam's Rib **10** Alice Adams, Pat and Mike, Summertime **12** Morning Glory (Oscar), On Golden Pond (Oscar), The Rainmaker **14** Woman of the Year **15** The African Queen, The Lion in Winter (Oscar) **18** Suddenly Last Summer **20** The Philadelphia Story **23** Guess Who's Coming to Dinner (Oscar) **24** Long Day's Journey into Night

Hephaestus
also: **10** Hephaistos
father: **4** Zeus
mother: **4** Hera
god of: **4** fire **11** handicrafts **12** metalworking
vocation: **5** smith
wife: **9** Aphrodite
corresponds to: **6** Vulcan

Hephzibah
husband: **8** Hezekiah
son: **8** Manasseh

Hepzibah *see* **9** Hephzibah

Hera
also: **4** Here
origin: **5** Greek
queen of: **6** Heaven
father: **6** Cronos, Cronus, Kronos
mother: **4** Rhea
brother: **4** Zeus
husband: **4** Zeus
son: **4** Ares
daughter: **9** Eilithyia **10** Hephaestus

birthplace: **5** Samos
festival: **7** Daedala
counterfeit: **7** Nephele
corresponds to: **4** Juno
epithet: **6** Anthea, Bunaea **8** Henioche **9** Prodromia

Heracles *see* **8** Hercules

Heracles, Children of
author: **9** Euripides
character: **6** Hyllus, Iolaus **7** Alcmene, Macaria **8** Demophon **10** Eurystheus

Heracles, Madness of
author: **9** Euripides
character: **4** Hera **5** Lycus **6** Megara **7** Theseus **8** Heracles **10** Amphitryon

Herakles *see* **8** Hercules

herald 4 clue, omen, sign **5** crier, envoy, token, usher **6** augury, inform, report, reveal, symbol **7** courier, divulge, portent, presage, publish, usher in, warning **8** announce, forecast, foregoer, foretell, proclaim **9** advertise, harbinger, indicator, make known, messenger, precursor, prefigure, publicize **10** forerunner, indication, proclaimer **11** bruit abroad, communicate, give voice to, predecessor **13** give tidings of

heraldic emblem 4 arms **5** crest **8** blazonry, insignia **10** coat of arms

heraldry
also called: **4** arms **10** coat of arms
band: **3** bar **4** bend, fess, orle
black: **5** sable
blue: **5** azure
border: **4** orle
bottom: **4** base
center: **5** fesse
coat of arms of cities/countries/colleges: **14** impersonal arms
coat of arms on shield/crest/helmet/motto: **19** armorial achievement
colors: **8** tincture
concerns family's: **8** heritage **9** genealogy
described as: **9** blazoning
divided diagonally: **7** per bend
divided vertically and horizontally: **9** quartered
expert: **8** armorist
for holding shield: **10** supporters
fur: **4** vair **6** ermine
gold/yellow: **2** or
green: **4** vert
helmet top: **5** crest
horizontal band: **4** fess
illegitimacy mark: **5** baton **6** baston **11** bar sinister **12** bend sinister
intrafamily distinctions: **12** differencing
  daughter: **7** lozenge
  eldest son: **5** label
  younger son: **7** cadency
left part: **8** sinister
main figure: **6** charge **8** ordinary **14** heraldic device

metal: 2 or **6** argent
motto in: 6 scroll
orange: 5 tenne
placed on lord's: 6 banner, shield **8** garments **14** horse trappings
portrayed as: 6 emblem, symbol
position: 7 courant, dormant, passant, rampant, salient **8** couchant, trippant
purple: 7 purpure
red: 5 gules
red-purple: 8 sanguine
right part: 6 dexter
shield: 10 escutcheon
sunshade: 8 mantling
  held by: 6 wreath
  made of: 4 silk
surface/background: 5 field
top: 5 chief
two or more colors: 16 lines of partition
vertical band: 4 pale
wavy: 4 ente, onde, unde
when worn by followers: 5 badge **6** livery
white/silver: 6 argent

herb 4 drug **5** plant, spice **6** annual, physic **7** herbage, perfume **8** aromatic, biennial, medicine **9** flavoring, perennial, seasoning, succulent
  kind: 3 bay, rue **4** corn, dill, hemp, mint, rose, sage **5** anise, basil, curry, chili, grass, onion, peony, thyme, wheat **6** catnip, celery, chives, clover, fennel, garlic, pepper, sesame **7** boneset, caraway, ginseng, lavender, mustard, oregano, parsley **8** camomile, licorice, rosemary, tarragon **9** buttercup, marijuana, spearmint **10** peppermint **11** wintergreen

Herbert, George
  author of: 9 The Temple
Herbert, Victor
  born: 6 Dublin **7** Ireland
  composer of: 14 Babes in Toyland, Hero and Leander **15** Naughty Marietta
herbivorous 10 vegetarian **11** planteating **14** noncarnivorous
Herceius
  epithet of: 4 Zeus
  means: 14 of the courtyard
herculean, Herculean 4 hard **5** burly, hefty, tough **6** brawny, mighty, robust, rugged, strong, sturdy **7** arduous, onerous **8** muscular, powerful, toilsome, wearying **9** difficult, fatiguing, laborious, strapping, strenuous **10** burdensome, exhausting, formidable, prodigious **12** backbreaking
Hercules
  also: 7 Alcides **8** Heracles, Herakles **9** Carnopian
  father: 4 Zeus
  mother: 7 Alcmene
  cousin: 10 Eurystheus
  wife: 4 Hebe **6** Megara **8** Deianira

son: 5 Lamus **6** Hyllus **8** Telephus **11** Therimachus
daughter: 7 Macaria
teacher: 6 Chiron
gift: 8 strength
performed: 6 labors
number of labors: 6 twelve
epithet: 7 Charops **8** Buphagus **9** Ipoctonus
corresponds to: 6 Sancus **10** Semo Sancus
Hercyna
  form: 5 nymph
  location: 8 fountain
  playmate: 10 Persephone
herd 3 lot, mob **4** army, band, body, gang, goad, host, lead, mass, pack, spur **5** array, bunch, crowd, drive, drove, flock, force, group, guide, horde, party, press, rally, swarm, tribe, troop **6** gather, huddle, legion, muster, number, throng **7** cluster, collect, company, convene, round up **8** assemble, assembly, conclave **9** gathering, multitude **10** assemblage, collection **11** convocation **12** congregation
Herds
  god of: 8 Silvanus, Sylvanus
herdsman 6 cowboy, driver, drover **7** cowpoke **8** shepherd
Herdsman
  constellation of: 6 Bootes
herd together 5 flock, group **6** gather **7** cluster, collect **10** congregate **12** band together
hereafter 5 limbo **6** heaven **8** paradise **9** afterlife, from now on, next world, Purgatory **10** afterworld, future life, henceforth, life beyond, ultimately **11** in the future, world to come **12** at a later date, at a later time, henceforward, subsequently **14** life after death **15** heavenly kingdom
here and there 6 around **11** at intervals **18** in this place and that
  Latin: 6 passim
Here Comes Mr Jordan
  director: 13 Alexander Hall
  cast: 11 Claude Rains, Evelyn Keyes, Rita Johnson **16** Robert Montgomery
  remade as: 13 Heaven Can Wait
hereditary 6 inborn, inbred **7** genetic **9** ancestral, heritable, inherited **10** congenital, handed-down **11** established, inheritable, traditional
here lies
  Latin: 8 hic jacet
heresy 7 dissent, fallacy **8** apostasy **10** dissension, heterodoxy, iconoclasm, irreligion **11** unorthodoxy **13** nonconformity **15** unsound doctrine
heretic 7 skeptic **8** apostate, recreant, recusant, renegade **9** dissenter **10** backslider **11** freethinker, misbeliever **12** deviationist **13** nonconformist
heretical 7 radical **9** dissident **10** un-

orthodox **12** iconoclastic **13** nonconforming, nonconformist **14** unconventional
heretofore
  French: 8 ci-devant
Hereward the Wake
  author: 15 Charles Kingsley
Hergesheimer, Joseph
  author of: 8 Java Head **19** The Three Black Pennys
heritage 6 estate, legacy **7** portion **9** patrimony, tradition **10** birthright **11** inheritance **16** family possession
Hermaphroditus
  father: 6 Hermes
  mother: 9 Aphrodite
  loved by: 8 Salmacis
  joined with: 8 Salmacis
  became: 8 bisexual
Hermes
  origin: 5 Greek
  occupation: 6 herald
  messenger of: 4 gods
  father: 4 Zeus
  mother: 4 Maia
  son: 3 Pan **6** Prylis **7** Abderus, Daphnis **14** Hermaphroditus
  birthplace: 7 Arcadia
  god of: 4 luck **5** roads, sleep **6** dreams, wealth **7** cunning, thieves **8** commerce **9** fertility, invention, merchants
  invented: 4 lyre
  sandals had: 5 wings
  epithet: 6 Dolius **8** Agoraeus **9** Spelaites **10** Criophorus **11** Argiphontes **12** Argeiphontes, Psychopompus
  corresponds to: 5 Thoth **7** Mercury
hermetic 6 mystic, occult **7** obscure **8** abstruse, airtight, esoteric, mystical **9** recondite
Hermia
  character in: 21 A Midsummer Night's Dream
  author: 11 Shakespeare
hermine, L'
  author: 11 Jean Anouilh
Hermione
  character in: 14 The Winter's Tale
  author: 11 Shakespeare
Hermione
  father: 8 Menelaus
  mother: 5 Helen
  husband: 7 Orestes
  son: 9 Tisamenus
hermit 7 eremite, recluse **8** cenobite, monastic, solitary **9** anchorite **11** desert saint **14** solitudinarian **16** religious recluse
hermitage 5 abbey **6** friary, priory **7** convent, retreat **8** cloister **9** monastery
hero, heroine 4 idol, star **7** gallant **8** brave man, champion, great man, male lead, male star, noble man **9** daredevil, daring man, main actor **10** adventurer, leading man **11** protago-

nist, valorous man **12** man of courage, man of the hour **13** chivalrous man, popular figure **15** fearless fighter, idealized person, intrepid warrior, legendary person

Hero
character in: **19** Much Ado About Nothing
author: **11** Shakespeare

Hero
vocation: **9** priestess
priestess of: **9** Aphrodite
lover: **7** Leander
death by: **7** suicide **8** drowning

Herod Antipas
father: **13** Herod the great
mother: **8** Malthace
grandfather: **9** Antipater
wife: **8** Herodias
half brother: **6** Philip
beheaded: **14** John the Baptist

Herodias
husband: **6** Philip **12** Herod Antipas
daughter: **6** Salome

Herodotus
called: **15** Father of History
wrote history of: **11** Persian Wars

Herod Philip
daughter: **6** Salome

heroic 4 bold, epic **5** brave, grand, noble **6** daring **7** classic, exalted, gallant, Homeric, valiant **8** elevated, fearless, highbrow, inflated, intrepid, mythical, resolute, valorous **9** bombastic, dauntless, dignified, grandiose, high-flown, legendary, undaunted **10** chivalrous, courageous **11** exaggerated, extravagant, lionhearted, pretentious, unflinching **12** mythological, ostentatious, stouthearted

heroic act 4 feat **7** exploit **9** brave deed

heroism 5 valor **6** daring **7** bravery, courage, prowess **8** boldness, chivalry, nobility **9** fortitude, gallantry **11** intrepidity **12** fearlessness **13** dauntlessness **14** courageousness **15** lionheartedness

Herophilus
field: **7** anatomy
nationality: **5** Greek
experimented with: **15** post-mortem exams

Heros
author: **8** Menander

herpetophobia
fear of: **8** reptiles

Herrenvolk 10 master race

Herrick, Robert
author of: **10** Hesperides **20** Corinna's Going A Maying **26** Gather ye rosebuds while ye may

Herriman, George
creator/artist of: **8** Krazy Kat

Herschel, William
field: **9** astronomy

nationality: **7** British
discovered: **6** Uranus

Hersey, John
author of: **7** The Wall **9** Hiroshima **13** A Bell for Adano, The Conspiracy **22** My Petition for More Space

Hertz, Heinrich
field: **7** physics
nationality: **6** German
discovered: **13** electric waves **18** wireless telegraphy
named for him: **13** hertzian waves
unit of: **9** frequency

Herzog
author: **10** Saul Bellow

he sculptured it
Latin: **8** sculpsit

Hesiod
author of: **8** Theogony **12** Works and Days

hesitancy 10 indecision, reluctance, unsureness **11** uncertainty, vacillation **12** irresolution

hesitant 5 loath **6** unsure **7** halting **8** doubtful, wavering **9** diffident, faltering, reluctant, tentative, uncertain, undecided **10** hesitating, indecisive, irresolute **11** halfhearted, hanging back, vacillating **15** shilly-shallying **17** lacking confidence, sitting on the fence

hesitate 4 balk, halt **5** delay, pause, shy at, waver **6** falter **7** scruple, stick at **8** be unsure, hang back **9** stickle at, vacillate **10** dillydally, shrink from, think twice **11** be reluctant, be uncertain, be undecided, be unwilling, stop briefly **12** be irresolute, shilly-shally **16** straddle the fence

hesitating 8 doubtful, hesitant **10** indecisive, irresolute, on the fence

he speaks
Latin: **8** loquitur

Hesperia
also: **5** Italy **16** Iberian Peninsula

Hesperides
author: **13** Robert Herrick

Hesperides
form: **6** nymphs
guarded: **12** golden apples
guarded with: **5** Ladon **6** dragon
names: **5** Aegle **6** Hestia **7** Erythea, Hespera **8** Arethusa **9** Hespereia, Hesperusa
islands of the: **7** blessed
form of: **6** heaven

Hess, Victor Francis
field: **7** physics
discovered: **10** cosmic rays
awarded: **10** Nobel Prize

Hesse, Hermann
author of: **6** Demian **9** Rosshalde **10** Siddhartha **11** Steppenwolf **12** Magister Ludi **14** Peter Camenzind **15** Beneath the Wheel **16** Death and the Lover, Journey to the East, The Glass Bead Game

Hesselberg, Melvyn Edouard
real name of: **13** Melvyn Douglas

Hessian
native of: **5** Hesse **7** Germany
soldier: **9** mercenary
aided: **7** British
in: **16** Revolutionary War

Hestia
origin: **5** Greek
goddess of the: **6** hearth
father: **6** Cronos, Cronus, Kronos
mother: **4** Rhea
corresponds to: **5** Vesta

Heston, Charlton
real name: **13** Charles Carter
born: **10** Evanston IL
roles: **5** El Cid, Moses **6** Ben-Hur (Oscar) **15** Planet of the Apes **18** The Ten Commandments **21** The Agony and the Ecstasy **22** The Greatest Show on Earth
organization: **3** NRA **24** National Rifle Association

heterogeneous 5 mixed **6** motley, unlike, varied **7** diverse, jumbled **8** assorted **9** composite, disparate, divergent, unrelated **10** dissimilar, variegated **11** diversified **13** miscellaneous

hew 2 ax **3** cut, lop **4** chop, form, hack, mold **5** carve, model, prune, sever, shape **6** chisel, cut out, devise **7** cut down, fashion, whittle **8** chop down **9** sculpture

he wrote it
Latin: **8** scripsit

hex 4 harm, jinx, sign **5** curse, spell, witch **6** hoodoo, voodoo, whammy **7** bewitch, enchant, evil eye, ill wind, possess **8** sorcerer **9** sorceress **11** malediction

Hexateuch 27 first six books of Old Testament
see also **7** Books of **12** Old Testament

heyday 4 acme **5** bloom, crest, flush, prime, vigor **6** zenith **9** flowering, salad days

Heyerdahl, Thor
author of: **7** Kon-Tiki **16** The Ra Expeditions

Hi and Lois
creator: **9** Dik Browne **10** Mort Walker
character:
brother: **12** Beetle Bailey
children: **3** Dot **4** Chip **5** Ditto **6** Trixie
dog: **4** Dawg
friend: **7** Thirsty

hiatus 3 gap **4** void **5** blank, break, lapse, space **6** lacuna, vacuum **7** interim **8** interval **10** disruption **12** interruption

Hiawatha, The Song of
author: **24** Henry Wadsworth Longfellow
character: **5** Nahma **7** Kwasind, Nokomis, Wenonah **8** Mondamin **9** Chi-

biabos, Minnehaha **11** Mudjekeewis **12** Pau-Puk-Keewis, Pearl-Feather

hibernate 5 sleep **6** retire **8** withdraw **13** become dormant

hibernating 6 asleep **7** dormant **8** inactive, sleeping **9** quiescent

Hibernia *see* **7** Ireland

hibiscus
varieties: **7** Chinese **8** Hawaiian, Japanese

hic jacet 8 here lies

hick 4 boor, rube **5** yokel **6** rustic **7** hayseed

Hickock, James B 5 scout **7** marshal
called: **8** Wild Bill

hickory 5 Carya
varieties: **4** Pale, Sand **5** Broom, Swamp, Water **6** Pignut **7** Chinese **8** Mountain, Shagbark **9** Mockernut, Shellbark **10** White-heart **12** Small-fruited

Hicks, Edward
born: **11** Attleboro PA
artwork: **19** The Peaceable Kingdom

hidden away 6 buried, cached **7** stashed **8** closeted, pocketed, secluded, secreted **9** concealed **10** out of sight **11** stashed away **12** inaccessible, undiscovered

hidden meaning 6 enigma, puzzle, riddle, secret **7** mystery

hidden motive
French: **13** arriere pensee

hide 4 mask, pelt, skin, veil **5** cache, cloak, cloud, cover **6** lie low, screen, shroud **7** conceal, curtain, leather, obscure, repress, seclude, secrete **8** disguise, suppress

hideaway 7 hideout, retreat **11** hiding place, secret place

hideous 4 grim, ugly, vile **5** awful **6** horrid, odious **7** ghastly, macabre **8** dreadful, gruesome, horrible, shocking **9** abhorrent, appalling, frightful, grotesque, loathsome, monstrous, repellent, repugnant, repulsive, revolting, sickening **10** abominable, detestable, disgusting, horrendous

hiding place 5 cache **8** hideaway **9** hidey hole **10** repository **11** secret place

Hieronimo
character in: **17** The Spanish Tragedy
author: **3** Kyd

hier wird Deutsch gesprochen 18 German is spoken here

Higgins, Henry
character in: **9** Pygmalion **10** My Fair Lady
author: **4** Shaw

Higgs
character in: **7** Erewhon
author: **6** Butler

high 3 gay, top **4** main, tall **5** aloft, chief, far up, grand, great, jolly, lofty, merry, noble, prime, sharp, undue,
way up **6** alpine, august, elated, jovial, joyful, joyous, shrill **7** capital, eminent, exalted, excited, extreme, gleeful, leading, notable, playful, primary, serious, soaring, soprano **8** cheerful, elevated, exultant, foremost, imposing, jubilant, mirthful, peerless, piercing, strident, superior, towering, uncurbed **9** ascendant, excellent, excessive, exuberant, important, overjoyed, principal, prominent, unbridled, uppermost **10** exorbitant, immoderate, inordinate, preeminent **11** cloud-capped, exaggerated, exhilarated, extravagant, high-pitched, illustrious, intemperate, predominant, significant, skyscraping **12** earsplitting, high-reaching, lighthearted, unreasonable, unrestrained **13** consequential, distinguished

high-and-mighty 5 lofty **6** lordly **7** haughty **8** arrogant **9** imperious **11** overbearing

highborn 5 noble **8** highbred, wellborn **9** patrician **10** of high rank, upper-class **12** aristocratic, of high degree, silk-stocking **13** of gentle blood

highbred 5 noble, regal **6** lordly **7** refined **8** highborn, wellborn **9** patrician **11** aristocracy, blue-blooded

highbrow 4 snob **5** brain **7** bookish, Brahmin, egghead, elitist, erudite, scholar, thinker **8** cultured, mandarin, snobbish **9** scholarly **10** cultivated, double-dome, mastermind **12** intellectual **13** knowledgeable

highest good
Latin: **11** summum bonum

highest point
Latin: **11** ne plus ultra

high fashion
French: **12** haute couture

high-flown 4 wild **5** lofty, proud **6** absurd, florid, lordly, turgid, unreal **7** flowery, orotund, pompous **8** elevated, fabulous, inflated **9** bombastic, excessive, fantastic, grandiose **10** flamboyant, immoderate, inordinate, outrageous **11** exaggerated, extravagant, highfalutin, pretentious, sententious **12** magniloquent, preposterous, presumptuous, unreasonable, unrestrained **13** grandiloquent, self-important

High German
language family: **12** Indo-European
branch: **8** Germanic
group: **15** Western Germanic
subgroup: **11** German-Dutch
division: **6** German **7** Yiddish

high-hat 5 aloof **6** formal, la-di-da, snooty **7** haughty **8** snobbish **12** supercilious

highjinks, hijinks 6 antics, capers, pranks, stunts **11** shenanigans **12** monkeyshines

highland, Highlands 4 rise **7** heights,
plateau, uplands **8** headland **9** tableland **10** promontory **11** hill country **17** mountainous region
refers especially to: **8** Scotland
dance: **5** fling

highlight 4 peak **6** accent, climax, stress **7** feature, point up **9** emphasize, high point, underline **10** accentuate, focal point, make bright

highly qualified 3 fit **4** able **7** trained **8** eligible, prepared, skillful **9** practiced **10** proficient **11** experienced **12** accomplished

highly regarded 6 prized **7** admired, revered **8** esteemed **9** respected, treasured **13** well thought of

highly valued 4 dear **5** loved **6** adored **7** beloved, revered **8** esteemed, precious **9** cherished, treasured

highly visible 7 glaring, obvious **8** distinct **9** prominent **11** conspicuous, outstanding

high-minded 4 fair, just **5** lofty, moral, noble **6** honest, worthy **7** ethical, sincere, upright **8** truthful, virtuous **9** exemplary, honorable, reputable, righteous, uncorrupt **10** chivalrous, idealistic, principled, scrupulous **13** conscientious, square-dealing

High Noon
director: **13** Fred Zinnemann
cast: **10** Gary Cooper (Will Kane), Grace Kelly **12** Lloyd Bridges **14** Thomas Mitchell
score: **14** Dimitri Tiomkin
Oscar for: **5** actor (Cooper)

high old time 4 ball, lark **5** fling, revel, spree **8** escapade

high-pitched 5 acute, sharp **6** shrill **7** clarion, squeaky **8** piercing

high place 3 tor **4** hill, peak, rise **5** aerie, bluff, cliff, knoll, ridge **6** height, summit, upland **7** hillock, hummock, plateau **8** eminence, mountain **9** elevation **10** prominence, promontory

high point, highest point 3 cap, top **4** acme, apex, peak **5** crest, crown **6** apogee, climax, height, heyday, summit, tiptop, vertex, zenith **8** eminence, pinnacle **9** flowering **10** prominence **11** culmination

high position 4 note **8** eminence, high rank, standing **9** supremacy **10** ascendancy, importance, notability, prominence **11** distinction, preeminence

high-powered 7 driving, dynamic **8** forceful **9** ambitious, assertive, energetic, go-getting **10** aggressive **11** hard-driving

high praise 5 kudos, paean **6** eulogy **7** hosanna, plaudit **8** encomium **9** laudation, panegyric **11** acclamation

high-priced 4 dear, high **6** costly,

pricey 9 expensive 10 exorbitant, overpriced 11 extravagant

high-principled 5 moral, noble 6 chaste, honest, worthy 7 ethical, upright 9 honorable, reputable 10 idealistic 11 responsible, trustworthy 13 conscientious

high quality 5 merit 7 quality 9 greatness 10 excellence, perfection 11 distinction, superiority

high-ranking 3 top 5 grand, great, lofty, regal, royal 6 august 7 eminent, exalted, supreme 8 elevated, esteemed, imposing 9 important, paramount, venerable 10 preeminent 11 illustrious 13 distinguished

High Sierra
director: 10 Raoul Walsh
cast: 9 Ida Lupino 10 Alan Curtis, Joan Leslie 13 Arthur Kennedy 14 Humphrey Bogart (Mad Dog Earle)
remade as: 17 Colorado Territory 19 I Died a Thousand Times

high society 5 elite 6 jet set 9 haut monde, top drawer 11 aristocracy 14 creme de la creme
French: 9 haut monde

High Society
director: 14 Charles Walters
cast: 10 Bing Crosby, Grace Kelly 11 Celeste Holm 12 Frank Sinatra, Louis Calhern 14 Louis Armstrong
score: 10 Cole Porter
remake of: 20 The Philadelphia Story
song: 8 True Love 10 Did You Evah? 16 You're Sensational

high-speed 4 fast 5 quick, rapid, swift 6 speedy 7 express

high-spirited 5 vital 6 lively 8 animated 9 exuberant, vivacious 12 effervescent, enthusiastic

high spirits 5 vigor 6 gaiety 7 delight, elation 8 gladness, vitality, vivacity 9 animation 10 enthusiasm, exaltation, excitement, joyousness, liveliness 12 exhilaration 16 lightheartedness

high-strung 4 edgy 5 jumpy, moody, tense 6 uneasy 7 jittery, nervous, uptight 8 neurotic, restless, skittish 9 emotional, excitable, impatient, wrought-up 10 hysterical 13 oversensitive, temperamental 14 easily agitated, hypersensitive

High Tor
author: 15 Maxwell Anderson

highway 7 freeway, parkway, thruway 8 hard road, highroad, main road, speedway, turnpike 9 paved road 10 expressway, interstate, main artery 12 four-lane road, thoroughfare
British: 9 coach road, royal road 12 King's highway 13 Queen's highway

highwayman 5 crook, thief 6 bandit, outlaw, robber 7 brigand, footpad

hike 4 rise, roam, rove, trek, walk 5 leg it, march, raise, tramp 6 draw up, hoof it, jerk up, pull up, ramble,

trudge, wander 7 hitch up, raise up 8 addition, increase 9 expansion 10 escalation 12 augmentation 13 journey on foot 14 go by shank's mare

hilarious 3 gay 5 jolly, merry, noisy 6 jocund, jovial, joyful, joyous, lively 7 comical, gleeful, riotous 8 jubilant, mirthful 9 exuberant, laughable, very funny 10 boisterous, hysterical, rollicking, uproarious, vociferous 11 exhilarated 12 high-spirited 13 highly amusing 14 laugh-provoking

hilarity 3 fun, gig, joy 4 glee, riot 5 laugh, mirth, noisy 6 comedy, gaiety, giggle, levity 7 chortle, chuckle, jollity 8 hysteria, laughter 9 amusement, funniness, joviality, jubilance, merriment 10 exuberance 12 exhilaration, humorousness 14 uproariousness

Hilbert, David
field: 8 geometry 11 mathematics
nationality: 6 German
formulated: 12 modern axioms

hill 4 bank, dune, heap, pile, ramp, rise 5 bluff, butte, cliff, climb, grade, knoll, mound, mount, slope 6 height 7 hillock, hilltop, hummock, incline, upgrade 8 eminence, foothill, highland, hillside 9 acclivity, declivity, downgrade, elevation 10 prominence, promontory

Hill, Arthur
born: 6 Canada 7 Melfort 12 Saskatchewan
roles: 13 All the Way Home 15 The Ugly American 17 Look Homeward Angel 25 Who's Afraid of Virginia Woolf?

Hill, George Roy
director of: 6 Hawaii 8 The Sting (Oscar) 20 The Little Drummer Girl 23 The World According to Garp 29 Butch Cassidy and the Sundance Kid

Hillary, Edmund
born: 10 New Zealand
climbed: 9 Mt. Everest
explored: 9 South Pole

Hiller, Arthur
director of: 25 The Americanization of Emily

hillock 4 hill, rise 5 knoll, mound 7 hummock 8 eminence

Hill Street Blues
character: 5 LaRue, Renko 9 Bobby Hill, Jablonski, Joe Coffey, Lucy Bates 10 Fay Furillo, Mick Belker, Washington 11 (Lt) Norman Buntz 12 Howard Hunter, (Captain) Frank Furillo 13 Henry Goldblum 14 Joyce Davenport
cast: 8 Joe Spano 10 Bruce Weitz, Ed Marinaro, Kiel Martin 11 Betty Thomas, Charles Haid, Dennis Franz 12 Robert Prosky 13 James B Sikking, Michael Warren, Veronica Hamel 14 Taurean Blacque 15 Daniel J Travanti

Hilton, James
author of: 11 Lost Horizon 14 Good-Bye Mr Chips

Hilton, Paris
great-grandfather: 12 Conrad Hilton
sister: 5 Nicky
co-star: 12 Nicole Richie
roles: 8 The Hillz 9 Bottom's Up 10 House of Wax, Pledge This! 12 Raising Helen 13 The Simple Life

Himalayas 9 mountains
countries 5 India, Nepal, Tibet, 6 Bhutan 8 Pakistan
peak: 7 Everest 9 Annapurna
native: 6 sherpa
Climber: 7 Hillary 13 Tenzing Norkay
legendary creature: 4 yeti 17 Abominable Snowman

Hind see 5 India

Hindemith, Paul
born: 5 Hanau 7 Germany
composer of: 8 The Demon 9 Cardillac 10 Heriodiade 12 Ludus Tonalis, Neues vom Tage, News of the Day 13 Sancta Susanna 14 Cupid and Psyche, Mathis Der Maler 15 In Praise of Music 17 Murder Hope of Women 18 Die Harmonie der Welt, Nobilissima Visione 19 The Four Temperaments 23 Morder Hoffnung der Frauen

hinder 3 bar 4 curb, foil, stay, stop 5 block, check, delay, deter, spike, stall 6 arrest, detain, fetter, hamper, hobble, hog-tie, hold up, impede, retard, stifle, stymie, thwart 7 inhibit 8 encumber, handicap, hold back, obstruct, restrain, slow down 9 frustrate, hamstring 13 interfere with

Hindi
language family: 12 Indo-European
branch: 11 Indo-Iranian
group: 5 Indic
official language of: 5 India

hindmost 4 last, rear 7 tail end 12 farthest back

hindpart 4 tail 6 far end 7 rear end 8 backside, buttocks, haunches 9 afterpart, posterior

hindquarters 4 rear, rump 7 rear end, tail end 8 back legs, backside, buttocks, haunches 9 posterior

hindrance 3 bar 4 clog, curb, snag 5 catch 6 fetter 7 barrier, shackle 8 blockade, blockage, handicap, obstacle 9 barricade, restraint, retardant 10 constraint, difficulty, impediment, limitation 11 encumbrance, obstruction, restriction 12 interference 14 stumbling block

hinge 4 hang, rest, turn 5 pivot, swing 6 depend 7 be due to 9 arise from 10 result from 11 be subject to, emanate from 13 revolve around

hint 3 bit, jot, tip 4 clue, idea, iota 5 grain, imply, pinch, tinge, touch, trace, whiff 6 little, notion, tip off 7 inkling, pointer, signify, soupcon, suggest, whisper **8** allusion, indicate, innuendo, intimate **9** insinuate, suspicion **10** impression, indication, intimation, smattering, suggestion **11** implication, indirection, insinuation **12** flea in the ear, slight amount **13** word to the wise

hinted 7 implied, oblique **8** implicit, indirect **9** suggested

hinterland 6 sticks **7** boonies, country **8** interior, midlands **9** backwater, backwoods, boondocks, rural area **11** countryside

Hippalectryon
form: **7** monster
head and forelegs of: **5** horse
legs, tail and body of: **4** cock

Hippocampus
form: **7** monster
body of: **5** horse
tail of: **4** fish

Hippocrene
form: **6** spring
location: **12** Mount Helicon

hippodrome 5 arena **6** circus **7** stadium **8** coliseum

Hippogriff
form: **7** monster
combined: **5** horse **7** griffin

Hippolyte
also: **7** Antiope **9** Hippolyta
queen of: **7** Amazons
husband: **7** Theseus
son: **10** Hippolytus
Hercules stole her: **6** girdle

Hippolytus
author: **9** Euripides
character: **7** Artemis, Phaedra, Theseus **9** Aphrodite

Hippolytus
father: **7** Theseus
mother: **9** Hippolyta
stepmother: **7** Phaedra
loved by: **7** Phaedra
killed by: **8** Poseidon

hire 3 fee, get, let, pay **4** cost, gain, rent **5** lease, wages **6** charge, employ, engage, income, obtain, profit, retain, reward, salary, secure, take on **7** appoint, charter, payment, procure, stipend **8** earnings, receipts **9** emolument **10** recompense **12** compensation, remuneration

hireling 4 goon, thug **6** flunky, lackey, menial, minion, stooge **7** gorilla **8** henchman, retainer **9** strong-arm **10** hatchet man

Hiroshima
author: **10** John Hersey

hirsute 5 bushy, downy, hairy, nappy, wooly **6** shaggy, woolly **7** bearded, bristly, prickly, unshorn **8** bristled, unshaven **9** whiskered **11** bewhiskered

His Girl Friday
director: **11** Howard Hawks
cast: **9** Cary Grant **12** Gene Lockhart, Ralph Bellamy **15** Rosalind Russell
remake of: **12** The Front Page

Hispania see **5** Spain

hiss 3 boo **4** mock, razz **6** deride, heckle, hoot at, jeer at, revile **7** catcall, scoff at, sneer at **9** shout down **10** Bronx cheer **16** give the raspberry

histology
study of: **6** tissue

historian
American: **4** Webb **5** Adams **6** Brooks, De Voto, Durant, Fisher, Miller, Nevins, Sparks, Turner **7** Morison, Parkman, Taussig, Tuchman **8** Bancroft, Channing, Prescott, Robinson **10** Hofstadter, McCullough **11** Schlesinger
British: **4** Bede (the Venerable) **6** Gibbon, Turner **7** Toynbee **8** Macaulay **9** Trevelyan
Chinese: **10** Ssu-ma Ch'ien, Ssu-Ma Kuang
French: **5** Bayle, Blanc, Bloch, Taine **7** Braudel **8** Mabillon, Michelet, Voltaire **11** Tocqueville
German: **5** Ranke **7** Mommsen **8** Spengler **10** Burckhardt, Treitschke
Greek: **8** Polybius **9** Herodotus **10** Thucydides
Islamic: **8** al Tabari **10** Ibn Khaldun
Italian: **4** Polo, Vico **5** Croce **11** Machiavelli **12** Guicciardini
Latin: **4** Livy **7** Sallust, Tacitus
Scottish: **7** Carlyle

historic 5 famed **7** notable **8** renowned **9** memorable, well-known **10** celebrated **11** outstanding

historical 4 past, real, true **6** actual, bygone, former **7** ancient, factual **8** attested, recorded **9** authentic **10** chronicled, documented

historical period 3 age, era **4** date, time **5** epoch, stage

history 4 epic, saga, tale **5** story **6** annals, change, growth, record, resume, review **7** account, the past **8** old times **9** chronicle, days of old, narration, narrative, portrayal, tradition, yesterday **10** bygone days, days of yore, olden times, the old days, yesteryear **11** bygone times, development, former times, local events, major events, world events **12** actual events **13** an unusual past, human progress **14** military action, national events, recapitulation **15** political change

History of Mr Polly, The
author: **7** H G Wells
character: **6** Miriam **8** Uncle Jim **13** The Plump Woman

History of the English-Speaking Peoples, A
author: **17** Winston S Churchill

histrionics 4 fuss **6** acting, tirade **7**

bluster, bombast **8** outburst **9** dramatics, hamminess, staginess, theatrics **10** dramaturgy, playacting **11** performance, rodomontade **13** melodramatics, temper tantrum, theatricality **16** ranting and raving

hit 3 bat, jab, lob, rap, tap **4** bang, bash, beat, belt, blow, boon, bump, butt, clip, club, coup, cuff, damn, drub, find, flog, hurt, move, pelt, poke, slam, slap, slug, sock, stir, swat **5** abash, baste, clout, crack, crush, flail, knock, paste, pound, punch, reach, rouse, smack, smash, smite, thump, touch, upset, whack **6** affect, arouse, assail, attack, attain, batter, cudgel, effect, impact, incite, pommel, revile, strike, thrash, thwack, wallop, winner **7** achieve, assault, censure, clobber, condemn, execute, godsend, impress, inflame, provoke, quicken, realize, shatter, success, triumph, trounce, victory **8** arrive at, bang into, blessing, bring off, denounce, lambaste, overcome, reproach **9** criticize, deal a blow, devastate, lash out at, overwhelm, sensation, smash into **11** collide with, connect with, deal a stroke, strike out at **12** go straight to **13** make a bull's-eye, send to the mark **14** popular success, strike together **16** mount an offensive

hit back 7 counter, get even, pay back **9** fight back, retaliate **10** strike back

hitch 3 tie, tug **4** curb, draw, halt, haul, hike, jerk, knot, loop, pull, snag, stop, yank, yoke **5** catch, check, clamp, delay, raise, tying **6** attach, couple, fasten, mishap, secure, tether **7** bracket, connect, harness, joining, mistake, problem, trouble **8** coupling, handicap, make fast, obstacle **9** attaching, fastening, hindrance, mischance, restraint **10** connection, difficulty, impediment, limitation **11** restriction **12** complication, interruption, loop together, put in harness **14** stumbling block

Hitchcock, Alfred
director of: **6** Frenzy, Marnie, Psycho **7** Rebecca, Vertigo **8** Lifeboat, The Birds **9** Notorious, Suspicion **10** Family Plot, Rear Window, Spellbound **13** To Catch a Thief **14** Dial M for Murder, Shadow of a Doubt **15** The Lady Vanishes **16** North by Northwest **17** Strangers on a Train **18** The Thirty-Nine Steps **19** The Trouble with Harry **20** Foreign Correspondent

hither 2 on **4** here, near **5** close **6** closer, nearby, nearer, onward **7** close by, forward **8** over here **11** to this place **12** to the speaker

hitherto 6 ere now, hereto **7** thus far, till now, up to now **8** until now **10** before this, heretofore

Hitler, Adolf
author of: **9** Mein Kampf

hit man 6 killer, slayer **8** assassin, hired gun, murderer **11** executioner **12** exterminator

hit-or-miss 3 lax **6** casual, fitful **7** aimless, cursory **8** slapdash **9** haphazard **10** incomplete **11** purposeless, superficial, unorganized **12** unsystematic **15** catch-as-catch-can

hive 3 hub **5** heart **6** center, colony **7** cluster **9** busy place **11** swarm of bees

H M S Pinafore
subtitle: **23** The Lass That Loved a Sailor
operetta by: **18** Gilbert and Sullivan
character: **11** Dick Deadeye **14** Ralph Rackstraw **15** Captain Corcoran, Little Buttercup, Sir Joseph Porter **17** Josephine Corcoran

Hoagland, Edward
author of: **15** African Calliope **17** The Tugman's Passage

hoar 3 old **4** aged, rime **5** frost, moldy, mushy, passe, stale, white **6** old hat **7** ancient, antique, elderly, grayish **8** grizzled **9** out of date

hoard 4 fund, heap, mass, pile **5** amass, buy up, cache, lay up, store **6** save up, supply **7** acquire, collect, lay away, reserve **8** quantity **9** amassment, gathering, stockpile, store away **10** accumulate, collection **12** accumulation

hoarse 5 gruff, harsh, husky, raspy, rough **6** croaky **7** cracked, rasping, raucous, throaty **8** gravelly, guttural, scratchy

hoary 3 old **4** aged, gray, hoar **5** dated, passe, white **6** grayed, old hat **7** ancient, antique, grizzly **8** grizzled, whitened **9** out-of-date **11** gray with age **12** white with age

hoax 3 gyp **4** bilk, dupe, fake, fool, gull, yarn **5** bluff, cheat, cozen, fraud, prank, spoof, trick **6** canard, delude, humbug, take in **7** deceive, defraud, fiction, mislead, swindle **8** hoodwink **9** bamboozle, chicanery, deception, fish story, victimize **10** hocus-pocus

Hoban, James
architect of: **13** The White House, Great Hotel (Washington, DC)

Hobbes, Thomas
author of: **9** Leviathan

Hobbit, The
prelude to: **14** Lord of the Rings
author: **10** J R R Tolkien
character: **5** Bilbo **7** Baggins
wizard: **7** Gandalf

hobble 4 bind, gimp, halt, limp **5** block, check, cramp **6** fetter, hamper, hinder, hog-tie, impede, lumber, stymie, thwart, toddle **7** inhibit, manacle, shackle, shamble, shuffle, stagger, stumble **8** encumber, handicap, hold

back, lame gait, obstruct, restrain, restrict **9** constrain, frustrate, hamstring **10** uneven gait, walk lamely **13** interfere with

hobby 7 pastime, pursuit **8** sideline **9** amusement, avocation, diversion **10** relaxation **13** entertainment **14** divertissement

hobbyhorse 5 hobby **7** pastime **8** interest, toy horse **9** diversion **10** enthusiasm **11** distraction **12** rocking horse

hobgoblin 3 imp **4** ogre **5** bogey **6** goblin **7** bugaboo, bugbear **9** bete-noire

hobnob 3 mix **4** club **6** mingle **7** consort, hang out **9** associate, rub elbows **10** fraternize

hobo 3 beg, bum **5** stiff, tramp **6** beggar, cadger, loafer **7** drifter, migrant, moocher, vagrant **8** derelict, vagabond, wanderer **9** scrounger **11** beachcomber

hoc est 6 this is

Ho Chi Minh City
formerly: **6** Saigon
river: **6** Saigon
delta: **6** Mekong
former capital of: **9** Indochina **11** Cochin China **12** South Vietnam

hockey
athlete: **8** Bobby Orr, Brad Park **9** Bobby Hull, Brett Hull, Ken Dryden, Mike Bossy, Pavel Bure **10** Doug Harvey, Eddie Shore, Ed Giacomin, Gordie Howe, Guy Lafleur, Patrick Roy, Ray Bourque, Rod Gilbert, Stan Mikita **11** Bobby Clarke, Brian Leetch, Denis Potvin, Eric Lindros, Jaromir Jagr, Jean Ratelle, Mark Messier, Mike Richter **12** Chris Chelios, Jean Beliveau, Marcel Dionne, Mario Lemieux, Phil Esposito, Wayne Gretzky **13** Bernard Parent, Dominick Hasek, Jacques Plante, Larry Robinson, Martin Brodeur, Pat La Fontaine **14** Alex Delvecchio, Maurice Richard, Peter Forsbergl **15** Bernie Geoffrion

hockey team
Anaheim: **11** Mighty Ducks
Atlanta: **9** Thrashers
Boston: **6** Bruins
Buffalo: **6** Sabres
Calgary: **7** Flames
Carolina: **10** Hurricanes
Chicago: **11** Black Hawks
Colorado: **9** Avalanche
Columbus: **11** Blue Jackets
Dallas: **5** Stars
Detroit: **8** Red Wings
Edmonton: **6** Oilers
Florida: **8** Panthers
Los Angeles: **5** Kings
Minnesota: **4** Wild
Montreal: **9** Canadiens
Nashville: **9** Predators
New Jersey: **6** Devils

New York: **7** Rangers **9** Islanders
Ottawa: **8** Senators
Philadelphia: **6** Flyers
Phoenix: **7** Coyotes
Pittsburgh: **8** Penguins
St Louis: **5** Blues
San Jose: **6** Sharks
Tampa Bay: **9** Lightning
Toronto: **10** Maple Leafs
Vancouver: **7** Canucks
Washington: **8** Capitals
Winnipeg: **4** Jets

hocus-pocus 4 bosh, bull, hoax, sham **5** chant, charm, cheat, magic, spell **6** bunkum, deceit, fakery, humbug **7** con game, hogwash, rubbish, swindle **8** delusion, flimflam, tommyrot, trickery **9** deception, moonshine, poppycock **10** dishonesty, flapdoodle, hanky-panky, magic spell, magic words, mumbo jumbo, subterfuge **11** bewitchment, incantation, legerdemain, magic tricks **12** fiddle-faddle, magic formula **13** sleight of hand

Hoder
also: **5** Hodur
origin: **12** Scandinavian
brother: **5** Baldr **6** Balder, Baldur
father: **4** Odin **5** Othin
killed: **5** Baldr **6** Balder, Baldur

hodgepodge, hotchpotch 3 mix **4** hash, mess, olio **6** jumble, medley, muddle **7** melange, mixture **8** mishmash **9** composite, confusion, patchwork, potpourri **10** miscellany

Hoff, Jacobus Hendricus van't
field: **9** chemistry
nationality: **5** Dutch
researched: **7** gas laws **10** carbon atom **14** thermodynamics
awarded: **10** Nobel Prize

Hoffman, Dustin
born: **12** Los Angeles CA
roommates: **11** Gene Hackman **12** Robert Duvall
roles: **4** Hook **5** Lenny **6** Ishtar **7** Rainman, Tootsie **8** Papillon **9** Wag the Dog **10** Ratso Rizzo **11** Runaway Jury, The Graduate, The Lost City **12** Little Big Man **14** Kramer vs Kramer (Oscar), Midnight Cowboy **19** All the President's Men

Hofmann, Hans
born: **7** Germany **11** Weissenberg
artwork: **6** Spring **7** The Gate **13** Effervescence **14** Fantasia in Blue, Magenta and Blue **16** Sanctum Sanctorum

Hofstadter, Richard
author of: **14** The Age of Reform

hog 3 pig, sow **4** arch, boar, trim **5** broom, sheep, swine **6** gorger, porker **7** baconer, glutton, take all **9** razorback **10** locomotive

Hogan, Paul
country: **9** Australia
wife: **14** Linda Koslowski

roles: 10 Mick Dundee **15** Crocodile Dundee **17** Strange Bedfellows
commercial: 6 Subaru

Hogan's Heroes
character: 7 (Peter) Newkirk **8** Lt Carter **10** Sgt (Hans) Schultz **11** Louis LeBeau **14** Col Robert Hogan **15** Col Wilhelm Klink
cast: 8 Bob Crane **10** John Banner, Larry Hovis **11** Robert Clary **13** Richard Dawson **15** Werner Klemperer

Hogarth, William
born: 6 London **7** England
artwork: 12 Captain Coram **14** A Rake's Progress **15** Marriage a la Mode, The Beggar's Opera **16** A Harlot's Progress **19** Garrick as Richard III

hogshead 3 keg, tun, vat **4** butt, cask, drum **6** barrel

hogwash 3 rot **4** bull, bunk **5** hokum, hooey, stuff **6** bunkum, drivel, hot air, humbug **7** baloney, blather, spinach, twaddle **8** claptrap, nonsense, tommyrot **9** poppycock **10** applesauce **11** foolishness **13** horsefeathers **16** stuff and nonsense

hoi polloi 6 rabble, the mob **7** the herd **8** canaille, populace, riffraff, the crowd, the plebs **9** the masses, the proles, the vulgar **10** commonalty **12** the multitude **14** the lower orders, the proletariat, the rank and file **15** the common people, the lower classes, the working class

hoist 4 lift **5** heave, raise, run up **6** bear up, pull up, take up, uplift **7** elevate, raise up, upraise **9** bear aloft

Hokusai, Katsushika
born: 3 Edo **5** Japan, Tokyo
artwork: 5 Crabs, Manga **10** Waterfalls **11** Chushingura **25** Thirty-six Views of Mount Fuji

Holabird, William
partner: 11 Martin Roche
architect of: 12 Gage Building **13** Cable Building, Crerar Library (City Hall, Chicago) **14** Tacoma Building **15** McClurg Building **17** Marquette Building

Holbein, Hans (the Elder)
born: 7 Germany **8** Augsburg
son: 11 Hans Holbein (the Younger)
artwork: 11 St Sebastian **14** Fountain of Life **18** Kaisheim Altarpiece **31** Presentation of Christ in the Temple

Holbein, Hans (the Younger)
born: 7 Germany **8** Augsburg
father: 11 Hans Holbein (the Elder)
artwork: 7 Erasmus **9** Henry VIII **11** Jane Seymour **12** Dance of Death **13** The Dead Christ

hold 4 bear, bind, bond, curb, deem, grip, halt, have, hilt, keep, knob, lock, prop, rule, stay, sway, take, urge **5** block, brace, carry, check, clasp, cling, count, defer, grasp, guard, limit, offer, power, shaft, shore, stall, stand, stick, strap, think, unite, watch **6** adhere, affirm, assert, assume, cleave, clinch, clutch, deduct, detain, direct, enfold, handle, hinder, hold up, join in, manage, occupy, reckon, regard, retain, submit, take in, tender, thwart, uphold **7** advance, believe, carry on, command, conduct, confine, contain, control, declare, embrace, enclose, enforce, execute, hold off, include, inhibit, mastery, possess, present, presume, prevent, profess, propose, protect, repress, reserve, support, suppose, surmise, suspend, toehold, venture **8** advocate, conceive, conclude, consider, engage in, foothold, handhold, hold back, hold down, leverage, maintain, obligate, postpone, purchase, put forth, restrain, restrict, set aside, suppress, withhold **9** advantage, anchorage, authority, be in force, dominance, forestall, frustrate, influence, keep valid, ownership, stay fixed, stick fast **10** ascendancy, attachment, desist from, domination, possession, put forward, understand **11** accommodate, preside over

hold a candle to 5 equal, match **6** be up to **7** compare **8** approach **10** be as good as **11** come close to, compete with **12** be comparable **14** bear comparison

hold against 6 resent **8** begrudge

hold back 3 lag **4** curb, deny, keep, slow **5** check, dally, limit, stall **6** arrest, bridle, falter, refuse **7** contain, inhibit, keep out, reserve, retrain **8** hesitate, keep back, maintain, restrain, withhold **9** constrain

hold close 3 hug **5** clasp **6** cuddle, harbor **7** cherish, embrace, snuggle

Holden, William
real name: 23 William Franklin Beedle Jr
nickname: 4 Bill
born: 9 O'Fallon IL
roles: 6 Picnic **7** Network, Sabrina **9** Golden Boy **13** Born Yesterday **14** The Country Girl **15** Stalag Seventeen (Oscar), Sunset Boulevard **23** The Bridge on the River Kwai

hold fast 4 fuse, hold **5** cling, stick **6** adhere

hold firmly 4 grip **5** clasp, grasp **6** clench, clinch, clutch **10** grab hold of

hold forth 5 orate **7** expound **9** discourse, expatiate, speechify

hold in abeyance 5 table **6** recess, shelve **7** suspend **8** lay aside, postpone

hold in bondage 7 control, enchain, enslave, entrall **8** dominate **9** subjugate **12** make a slave of

holdings 6 assets **8** property **10** securities **11** commodities

hold in high regard 5 honor, prize, value **6** admire, esteem, revere **7** cherish, respect **8** look up to, treasure, venerate **10** rate highly, set store by **13** think highly of **18** attach importance to

hold one's own 4 cope **6** manage **7** contend **11** be a match for **20** maintain one's position **22** keep one's head above water

hold rapt 5 charm **7** beguile, bewitch, enchant **8** enthrall, entrance **9** captivate, enrapture, fascinate, spellbind, transport

hold to 4 bind **8** obligate

hold together 4 bind, fuse, glue, hold, join **5** cling, stick, unite **6** cement, cohere **7** combine **11** consolidate

holdup 3 rob **4** bear, halt, stay, stop **5** delay, heist, steal, theft **6** hijack, retain, uphold **7** robbery, stickup, support, sustain **8** stoppage **9** hindrance **12** interruption

hold up 4 prop, slow **5** block, brace, check, delay **6** bear up, detain, endure, hinder, impede, manage **7** bolster, present, stand up, support, sustain **8** keep back, obstruct **13** rob at gunpoint

hold up under 4 bear **6** endure, manage **8** tolerate

hold warmly 3 hug **5** clasp **6** cuddle **7** embrace, snuggle

hole 3 den, gap, pit **4** brig, cage, cave, flaw, keep, lair, rent, slit, slot **5** break, crack, fault, shaft **6** breach, burrow, cavern, cavity, crater, defect, dugout, lockup, pocket, prison, tunnel **7** dungeon, fallacy, opening, orifice, slammer **8** aperture, dark cell, puncture **9** concavity, open space **10** depression, excavation **11** discrepancy, hollow place, indentation, perforation **13** inconsistency

Holgrave, Mr
character in: 24 The House of the Seven Gables
author: 9 Hawthorne

holiday 3 gay **4** fete, gala **5** feria **6** cheery, fiesta, joyful, joyous, junket, outing **7** festive, holy day, jubilee **8** cheerful, feast day, festival, vacation **11** celebrating, celebration, merrymaking
American: 6 Easter **7** Kwanzaa **8** Arbor Day, Labor Day **9** Christmas (Dec 25), Halloween (Oct 31) **10** Father's Day, Good Friday, Mother's Day **11** Columbus Day, Election Day, Memorial Day, New Year's Day (Jan 1), Veterans' Day (Nov 11) **12** Children's Day, Thanksgiving **15** Independence Day (July 4), St Valentine's Day (Feb 14) **23** National Grandparents' Day
birthday: 8 Lincoln's **11** Robert E Lee's (Jan 19), Washington's **17**

Martin Luther King's (Jan 15)
Hawaiian: 13 Kamehameha Day (June 11)
British: 8 Hogmanay (Dec 31) **9** Boxing Day (Dec 26) **11** Harvest Home **12** Guy Fawkes Day (Nov 5), Twelfth Night (Jan 5) **14** Queen's Birthday (June) **15** Commonwealth Day (May 24), Mothering Sunday **19** Feast of Saint Swithin (July 15)
Canadian: 11 Victoria Day **14** Queen's Birthday, Remembrance Day
Chinese: 7 New Year **15** Lantern Festival **17** Confucius' Birthday (Sept 28) **18** Dragon Boat Festival
French: 11 Bastille Day (May 14)
German: 11 Oktoberfest
Greek: 7 Genesia **11** Feast of Pots
Indian: 4 Holi **6** Basant, Diwali (New Year) **17** Hindu fire festival **22** Mahatma Gandhi's Birthday (Oct 2)
Irish: 16 Saint Patrick's Day (March 17)
Italian: 13 Liberation Day (April 25)
Japanese: 11 Hina-Matsuri **12** Children's Day (May 5), Feast of Dolls (March 3) **15** Constitution Day (May 3) **17** Girls' Doll Festival
Jewish: 6 Purim **6** Sukkot **7** Shavuot, Sukkoth **8** Hanukkah, Passover **9** Yom Kippur **12** Rosh Hashanah **20** Hamishah Assar B'Shevat, The New Year of the Trees **21** Feast of the Tabernacles
Korean: 6 Ch'usok
Latin American: 12 Day of the Race
Moslem: 7 Mouloud **8** Id-al-Adha, Id-al-Fitr **12** Maulid-an-Nabi **14** month of Ramadan
religious: 6 Advent **7** Lady Day (Mar 25) **8** Epiphany, Shabuoth **9** Candlemas, Mardi Gras, Martinmas (Nov 11), Pentecost **10** Whitsunday **11** All Souls' Day (Nov 2) **12** Ascension Day, Ash Wednesday, Feast of Weeks **13** Shrove Tuesday, Trinity Sunday **15** Annunciation Day (Mar 25) **16** Feast of All Saints **20** Feast of Corpus Christi **23** Day of Our Lady of Guadalupe (Dec 12) **27** Purification of the Virgin Mary **30** Feast of the Immaculate Conception (Dec 8)
Roman: 7 Feralia **10** Saturnalia
Scottish: 8 Hogmanay **12** Candlemas Day **19** Festival of the Virgin
South American: 21 Simon Bolivar's Birthday (July 24)
Sri Lankan: 5 Wesak
Soviet Union: 6 May Day (May 1) **14** Lenin's Birthday (April 22) **39** Day of the Great October Socialist Revolution (Nov 7)
Swedish: 13 Santa Lucia Day (Dec 13)
Thai: 11 Visakha Puja
Vietnamese: 3 Tet
holiness 8 sanctity **9** godliness **10** sacredness **11** blessedness, saintliness

Holland *see* **11** Netherlands
holler 4 bark, roar, yell **5** gripe, shout **6** bellow, cry out, grouse **8** complain **9** hue and cry
Holliday, Judy
real name: 11 Judith Tuvim
born: 9 New York NY
roles: 8 Adam's Rib **13** Born Yesterday (Oscar) **15** Bells Are Ringing
Hollinshed, Raphael
author of: 37 Chronicles of England Scotland and Ireland
hollow 3 dip, low, rut **4** cave, dale, deep, dell, dent, dull, glen, hole, sink, vain, vale, void **5** ditch, empty, false, muted **6** cavern, cavity, crater, dig out, dimple, furrow, futile, groove, pocket, sunken, vacant, vacuum, valley **7** channel, concave, useless **8** crevasse, empty out, excavate, gouge out, indented, not solid, nugatory, rumbling, scoop out, specious, unfilled **9** cavernous, concavity, deceptive, depressed, fruitless, pointless, valueless, worthless **10** depression, profitless, sepulchral, unavailing, unresonant **11** indentation, meaningless, nonresonant **12** unprofitable **13** curving inward, disappointing, reverberating **14** expressionless, unsatisfactory **15** inconsequential
Holloway, Stanley
born: 6 London **7** England
roles: 10 My Fair Lady **15** Alfred Doolittle **18** The Lavender Hill Mob
Hollow Men
author: 7 T S Eliot
hollowness 4 void **6** vacuum **7** vacancy **9** emptiness
hollow out 4 bore **5** drill **6** dig out **8** carve out, gouge out, scoop out **9** chisel out **13** tunnel through
holly 4 Ilex
varieties: 3 box, sea **4** dune **5** Cuban, Dutch, dwarf, false, Furin, Kashi, swamp, Tsuru **6** desert, horned, Oregon, Sarvis, Soyogo, summer **7** African, Chinese, English, Georgia, Madeira **8** American, European, hedgehog, Japanese, Kurogane, mountain **9** box-leaved, Highclere, miniature, moonlight, porcupine, Singapore **10** Costa Rican, luster-leaf, West Indian **11** large-leaved, Puerto Rican, screw-leaved **12** Canary Island, gold hedgehog, myrtle-leaved, smooth-leaved **14** silver hedgehog
hollyhock 6 mallow **7** Antwerp, figleaf **8** biennial **9** ficifolia, Malvaceae **10** alcea rosea
Hollywood's Mermaid
nickname of: 14 Esther Williams
Hollywood Squares
host: 9 Jon Bauman **12** John Davidson **13** Peter Marshall
regular: 8 Wally Cox **9** Paul Lynde **10** Joan Rivers **11** George Gobel **13**

Cliff Arquette (Charley Weaver), Shadoe Stevens **14** Whoopi Goldberg
Holmes, Oliver Wendell
author of: 12 Old Ironsides **30** The Autocrat of the Breakfast Table
Holmes, Sherlock
address: 11 (221B) Baker Street
appears in: 13 The Sign of Four **14** The Naval Treaty **15** A Study in Scarlet, The Speckled Band **16** Scandal in Bohemia, The Blue Carbuncle, The Copper Beeches **18** The Red-Headed League, The Solitary Cyclist **22** Hound of the Baskervilles
assistants: 21 Baker Street Irregulars
author: 16 (Sir) Arthur Conan Doyle
brother: 7 Mycroft
femme fatale: 10 Irene Adler
foe: 17 Professor Moriarty
hat: 11 deerstalker
hobby: 6 violin
housekeeper/landlady: 9 Mrs Hudson
keeps tobacco in: 7 slipper **14** Turkish slipper
police: 17 Inspector Lestrade
sidekick: 12 Dr John Watson
holocaust 4 ruin **5** havoc **6** ravage **7** bonfire, carnage, inferno, killing **8** butchery, genocide, massacre **10** deadly fire, mass murder **11** devastation **12** annihilation **13** conflagration
Holofernes
character in: 16 Love's Labour's Lost
author: 11 Shakespeare
Holofernes
general of: 14 Nebuchadnezzar
killed by: 6 Judith
Holst, Gustav Theodore
born: 7 England **10** Cheltenham
composer of: 7 Savitri **10** Egdon Heath, Ode to Death, The Planets **11** Hammersmith **12** St Paul's Suite **13** Fugal Concerto **14** The Hymn of Jesus, The Perfect Fool **16** Somerset Rhapsody **17** The Cloud Messenger **19** Hymns from the Rig-Veda
holy 4 pure **5** godly, moral, pious **6** adored, devout, divine, sacred, solemn **7** angelic, blessed, from God, revered, saintly, sinless **8** faithful, hallowed, heavenly, reverent, virtuous **9** from above, guileless, religious, righteous, spiritual, undefiled, unspotted, unstained, unworldly, venerated, worshiped **10** heaven-sent, immaculate, inviolable, sacrosanct, sanctified, worshipped **11** consecrated, pure in heart, uncorrupted
Latin: 7 sanctus
Holy Ark
Hebrew: 10 Aron Kodesh
holy of holies
Latin: 16 sanctum sanctorum
Holy one *see* **5** Jesus
Holy Spirit, Holy Ghost 9 Paraclete **13** presence of God **23** third person of

the Trinity
Latin: 15 Spiritus Sanctus
Greek: 12 Hagion Pneuma

holy war
Arabic: 5 jehad, jihad

Homadus
form: 7 centaur
killed by: 8 Hercules

homage 5 honor **6** esteem, praise, regard **7** respect, tribute, worship **8** devotion **9** adoration, adulation, deference, obeisance, reverence **10** exaltation, veneration **13** glorification

Homagyrius
epithet of: 4 Zeus
means: 9 assembler

hombre 3 man

home 5 abode, haunt, haven, house **6** asylum, cradle, refuge **7** habitat, hangout **8** domicile, dwelling, hospital **9** orphanage, poorhouse, residence **10** habitation, native land, sanatorium **11** institution **12** fountainhead **13** dwelling place, home sweet home **14** stamping ground **16** place of residence **18** natural environment **25** place where one hangs one's hat

Home Burial
author: 11 Robert Frost

homegrown 5 local **6** native **8** domestic **10** indigenous

Home Improvement
network: 3 ABC
cast: 8 Tim Allen (Tim Taylor) **11** Earl Hindman (Wilson Wilson, Jr.), Richard Karn (Al Borland) **12** Debbe Dunning (Heidi Keppert) **14** Taran Noah Smith (Mark Taylor), Zachery Ty Bryan (Brad Taylor) **18** Patricia Richardson (Jill Taylor) **20** Jonathan Taylor Thomas (Randy Taylor)
show within the show: 8 Tool Time

Home Is the Sailor
author: 10 Jorge Amado

homelike 4 cozy **5** comfy, homey **6** simple **8** cheerful, domestic, familiar, informal, inviting **11** comfortable

homely 4 cozy, drab, snug **5** comfy, homey, plain **6** modest, rustic, simple **7** artless, natural **8** everyday, familiar, homelike, homespun, ordinary, uncomely **9** graceless **10** ill-favored, provincial, unaffected, unassuming, ungraceful, unhandsome **11** comfortable **12** plain-looking, unattractive **13** unpretentious

Homer
author of: 5 Iliad **7** Odyssey

Homer, Winslow
born: 8 Boston MA
painter of: 9 seascapes
artwork: 9 High Cliff **10** Breezing Up, Eight Bells **11** Marine Coast, Northeaster, The Life Line **13** The Fog Warning, The Gulf Stream **21** Inside the Bar Tynemouth, Prisoners from the Front

home rule 8 autonomy **11** sovereignty **12** independence **14** self-government

homespun 5 plain **6** folksy, homely, modest, native, simple **7** artless, natural **8** down-home, homemade **9** handwoven **10** hand-loomed, unaffected **11** hand-crafted, hand-wrought **13** unpretentious

homey 4 cozy **6** casual, folksy **8** down-home, homelike, homespun, informal **15** unsophisticated

homicide 6 killer, murder, slayer **7** slaying **8** foul play, murderer, regicide, vaticide **9** bloodshed, man killer, manslayer, matricide, parricide, patricide, uxoricide **10** fratricide **11** infanticide **12** manslaughter

Homicide: Life on the Streets
network: 3 NBC
cast: 9 Jon Polito (Steve Crosetti), Kyle Secor (Tim Bayliss), Ned Beatty (Stan Bolander) **10** Melissa Leo (Kay Howard) **11** Reed Diamond (Mike Kellerman), Yaphet Kotto (Al Giardello) **12** Clark Johnson (Meldrick Lewis) **13** Andre Braugher (Frank Pembleton), Daniel Baldwin (Beau Felton), Richard Belzer (John Munch) **14** Isabella Hofman (Megan Russert)

homiletic 7 preachy **8** didactic **10** moralizing

homily 6 sermon **7** lecture **10** preachment **11** exhortation

homogeneous 4 akin, pure **7** kindred, similar, uniform, unmixed **8** all alike, constant, of a piece **9** identical, unvarying **10** consistent **13** of the same kind, unadulterated

homology 7 analogy **8** likeness, relation **10** similarity **12** relationship **14** correspondence

Honduras
name means: 6 depths
capital/largest city: 11 Tegucigalpa
others: 4 Tela, Yoro **5** Copan, Danli, Lapaz **6** Roatan **7** Gracias, La Ceiba **8** Trujillo, Yuscaran **9** Choluteca, Juticalpa **10** El Progreso **11** Comayaguela **12** Puerto Cortes, San Pedro Sula
measure: 4 vara **5** milla **6** mecate **7** cajuela
monetary unit: 4 peso **7** centavo, lempira
island: 3 Bay **5** Bahia, Utila **6** Roatan **7** Bonacca, Guanaja
lake: 5 Criba, Yojoa **6** Brewer
mountain: 4 Pija **6** Agalta **7** Celaque **9** Esperanza
highest point: 8 Las Minas
river: 4 Coco, Sico, Ulua **5** Aguan, Lempa, Negro, Tinto, Wanks **6** Patuca, Sulaco **7** Olancho, Paulaya, Segovia **8** Guiavope, Santiago **9** Choluteca **10** Chamelecon
sea: 7 Pacific **8** Atlantic **9** Caribbean

physical feature:
coast: 5 North **8** Mosquito **10** Costa Norte
gulf: 7 Fonseca **8** Honduras
port: 7 Laceiba **8** Trujillo
people: 4 Maya, Paya, Sumo, Ulva **5** Carib, Lenca, Pipil **6** Tauira **7** Jicaque, mestizo, Miskito **8** Mosquito
discoverer: 8 Columbus
farmer: 9 campesino
language: 7 English, Spanish
religion: 13 Roman Catholic
place:
ruins: 5 Copan **8** Tenampua
feature:
bird: 9 zenzontle
dance: 5 sique **7** mascaro
estate: 10 latifundia
farm: 6 milpas **10** minifundia
musical instrument: 7 caramba, marimba
tree: 8 cockspur
food:
beans: 8 frijoles
beef dish: 6 tapado
corn: 5 maize
stuffed corn cake: 10 naca tamale
tripe stew: 10 mondongo

hone 4 long, moan, pine, tool, whet **5** stroke, strope, whine, yearn **6** hanker, grumble, mutter, sharpen **9** whetstone

Honegger, Arthur
born: 5 Havre **6** France
nationality: 5 Swiss
member of: 6 Les Six, The Six
composer of: 5 Rugby **6** Judith **7** L'Aiglon **8** Antigone **9** The Eaglet **10** Le Roi David **13** Pastorale d'ete **18** Jeanne d'Arc au Bucher, Liturgical Symphony **19** Pacific Two-Thirty-One

honest 4 fair, just, open, real, true **5** blunt, frank, legal, plain, solid, valid **6** candid, decent, lawful, proper, square **7** artless, ethical, genuine, sincere, upright **8** bona fide, clear-cut, faithful, innocent, reliable, straight, true-blue, truthful, virtuous **9** authentic, blameless, guileless, honorable, ingenuous, reputable, righteous **10** aboveboard, dependable, forthright, law-abiding, legitimate, on the level, principled, reasonable, scrupulous, unaffected, unreserved **11** plainspoken, trustworthy, undisguised **12** on the up-and-up, tried and true **13** conscientious, fair and square **15** straightforward, unsophisticated **16** as good as one's word, straight-shooting **17** open and aboveboard
honest man: 10 Abe Lincoln
Searcher: 8 Diogenes

honesty 4 word **5** honor **7** probity **8** fairness, good name, morality, scruples, veracity **9** innocence, integrity, rectitude, sincerity **10** principles **11** just dealing, uprightness **12** faithfulness, reputability, truthfulness **13**

guiltlessness, square dealing **15** trustworthiness **16** incorruptibility, straight shooting

honeybee
   classification: **6** social
   live in: **4** hive **6** colony
   headed by: **5** queen
   male: **5** drone
   laborer: **6** worker
   food-gatherer: **7** forager
   gather: **6** nectar, pollen
   produce: **5** honey
   queen's food: **10** royal jelly
   pertaining to: **5** apian
   keeper: **8** apiarist

honeyed 4 kind **5** sweet **6** sugary **7** cloying, fawning **10** flattering, saccharine **12** ingratiating **13** complimentary

honeyed words 4 line **7** blarney **8** cajolery, flattery, soft soap **9** sweet talk

Honey in the Horn
   author: **7** H L Davis

Honeymooners, The
   character: **8** Ed Norton **12** Alice Kramden, Ralph Kramden, Trixie Norton
   cast: **8** Jane Kean **9** Art Carney **12** Sheila MacRae **13** Audrey Meadows, Jackie Gleason, Joyce Randolph
   Ralph's job: **9** bus driver
   Ed's job: **5** sewer
   lodge: **8** Raccoons
   Saying: **16** You're the greatest **38** One of these days Alice, pow, right in the kisser

honeysuckle 8 Lonicera **19** Aquilegia canadensis, Justicia californica **24** Rhododendron prinophyllum
   varieties: **3** fly **4** bush, cape **5** coral, giant, grape, hairy, swamp **6** desert, French, purple, yellow **7** Arizona, Jamaica, trumpet **8** Himalaya, Japanese, swamp fly, Tatarian **9** chaparral, Tartarian **10** yellow cape **11** European fly **12** giant Burmese, long-flowered, South African **13** Hall's Japanese

Hong Kong
   part of: **5** China
   name means: **13** incense harbor **14** fragrant harbor
   capital: **8** Victoria
   largest city:
      section: **7** Kowloon **8** Hong Kong, Victoria
      others: **4** Tai O **5** Tai Po **8** Aberdeen, Pingshan, Yuenlong **9** Shataukok **10** Sheungshui
   division: **7** Kowloon **8** Hong Kong **14** New Territories
   former government: **18** British crown colony
   head of state: **14** British monarch **15** governor general
   island: **5** Lamma **6** Lan Tao, Lantau, Middle, Poi Toi **8** Hong Kong **9** Ap

Lei Chau **11** Stonecutter
   mountain: **6** Castle **8** Victoria
   highest point: **9** Tai Mo Shan
   river: **5** Pearl **6** Canton **8** Sham Chun
   sea: **10** South China
   physical feature:
      bay: **4** Mirs **6** Quarry **7** Kowloon, Repulse **9** Deep Water
      harbor: **4** Tolo **8** Aberdeen, Hong Kong, Victoria
      peak: **8** Victoria
      peninsula: **7** Kowloon
   people: **5** Hakka, Haklo, Punti, Tanka **7** British, Chinese **8** American, Japanese **9** Cantonese **10** Portuguese
   language: **7** Chinese, English **9** Cantonese
   religion: **5** Hindu, Islam **6** Taoism **8** Buddhism **12** Christianity
   feature:
      airport: **6** Kai Tak
      clothing: **6** samfoo **9** cheongsam
      houseboat: **6** sampan
      rock: **5** Amahs **6** Sha Tin
      temple: **18** Ten Thousand Buddhas

Honiara
   capital of: **14** Solomon Islands

honi soit qui mal y pense 31 shamed be the one who thinks evil of it
   motto of: **16** Order of the Garter

honk 4 toot **5** blare, blast **7** trumpet

honky-tonk 4 dive **7** gin mill **9** roadhouse, nightclub

honor 3 pay **4** cash, fame, laud, note, take **5** adore, exalt, extol, favor, glory, grant, leave, power, right, truth, value **6** accept, admire, credit, esteem, homage, praise, redeem, regard, renown, repute, revere, virtue **7** acclaim, commend, decency, dignify, glorify, honesty, liberty, probity, respect, tribute, worship **8** eminence, fairness, good name, goodness, justness, look up to, make good, pleasure, prestige, sanction, venerate, veracity **9** adoration, celebrity, constancy, deference, greatness, integrity, principle, privilege, rectitude, reverence, sincerity **10** admiration, compliment, exaltation, good report, importance, notability, permission, prominence, veneration **11** acknowledge, approbation, distinction, pay homage to, recognition, think much of, uprightness **12** commendation, faithfulness, high standing, pay tribute to, truthfulness **13** authorization, bow down before, glorification, have regard for, honorableness, make payment on **14** high-mindedness, scrupulousness **15** illustriousness, trustworthiness **17** a feather in one's cap, conscientiousness

honorable 4 good **5** noble, title **6** decent, honest, lordly, square **7** upright **9** elevated, reputable, respected **10** creditable **11** distinctive, illustrious,

respectable, trustworthy **12** considerable **13** distinguished

hood 4 cowl, lout, punk **5** bully, rowdy, scarf, tough **6** vandal **7** hoodlum, ruffian **8** hooligan **9** barbarian, roughneck **10** delinquent **12** headcovering, neighborhood

Hood, Raymond
   architect of: **11** RCA Building (Rockefeller Center) **17** Daily News Building (NYC) **18** McGraw-Hill Building (NYC) **22** Chicago Tribune Building **24** American Radiator Building
   style: **13** International

hoodlum 4 hood, punk, thug **5** crook, rowdy, tough **6** gunman **7** bruiser, gorilla, mobster, ruffian **8** criminal, gangster, hooligan, plug-ugly **9** desperado, strong arm **10** delinquent

hoodwink 3 gyp **4** dupe, fool, gull, hoax, rook **5** cheat, cozen, trick **7** deceive, defraud, mislead, swindle **8** inveigle **9** bamboozle, victimize

hook 3 arc, bag, bow, nab, net **4** arch, bend, bill, curl, gaff, grab, loop, take, trap, wind **5** angle, catch, crook, curve, elbow, fluke, hitch, latch, seize, snare **6** buckle, collar, fasten, peavey, secure **7** capture, crampon, ensnare, grapnel, grapple, pothook **8** crescent, make fast **9** horseshoe

Hooke, Robert
   field: **7** physics **9** astronomy
   nationality: **7** British
   discovered: **9** Orion star **15** Jupiter rotation **20** moon's center of gravity **21** earth's center of gravity
   invented: **10** microscope
   named for him: **15** law of elasticity

hooked 8 addicted **9** compelled, obsessive **10** compulsive, habituated **14** uncontrollable

hooked cross
   German: **10** Hakenkreuz

hook up 4 ally, dock, join **5** hinge **6** couple, link up **7** connect **8** assemble **10** articulate **11** fit together **14** fasten together

hooligan 4 hood, lout, punk **5** bully, rowdy, tough **6** vandal **7** hoodlum, ruffian **9** barbarian, roughneck **10** delinquent

hoopla 4 hype **8** ballyhoo **9** promotion, publicity **10** hullabaloo, propaganda **11** advertising **15** public relations

Hoosier Schoolmaster, The
   author: **15** Edward Eggleston

Hoosier State
   nickname of: **7** Indiana

hoot 3 boo, din **4** bawl, blow, hiss, honk, howl, jeer, moan, mock, razz, roar, wail, yelp, yowl **5** shout, sneer, taunt, whoop **6** bellow, chorus, cry out, deride, outcry, racket, scream, shriek, shrill, tumult, uproar **7** catcall, cry down, scoff at, screech, sing out, sneer at, snicker, ululate, wailing, whistle **8** proclaim, shouting **9** caterwaul, commotion, raspberry, screaming, snicker at **10** Bronx cheer, screeching

Hoover, Herbert Clark
nickname: 13 Great Engineer **14** Great Secretary **17** Great Humanitarian **18** Great Public Servant
presidential rank: 11 thirty-first
party: 10 Republican
state represented: 2 CA
defeated: 5 (Alfred Emanuel) Smith **6** (George William) Norris, (Norman) Thomas, (William Frederick) Varney, (William Zebulon) Foster **8** (Verne L) Reynolds
vice president: 6 (Charles) Curtis
cabinet:
  state: 7 (Henry Lewis) Stimson
  treasury: 5 (Ogden Livingston) Mills **6** (Andrew William) Mellon
  war: 4 (James William) Good **6** (Patrick Jay) Hurley
  attorney general: 8 (William DeWitt) Mitchell
  navy: 5 (Charles Francis) Adams
  postmaster general: 5 (Walter Folger) Brown
  interior: 6 (Ray Lyman) Wilbur
  agriculture: 4 (Arthur Mastick) Hyde
  commerce: 6 (Robert Patterson) Lamont, (Roy Dikeman) Chapin
  labor: 4 (William Nuckles) Doak **5** (James John) Davis
born: 12 West Branch IA
died: 13 New York City NY
buried: 12 West Branch IA
education:
  University: 8 Stanford
religion: 5 Quaker **16** Society of Friends
interests: 7 fishing
vacation spot: 10 Camp Hoover **11** Rapidan Camp **22** Shenandoah National Park
author: 7 Memoirs **11** On Growing Up **14** An American Epic **16** Years of Adventure **18** Principles of Mining, The Great Depression **20** America's First Crusade **21** American Individualism, The Challenge to Liberty
political career: 19 US Food Administrator
  head of: 23 American Relief Committee **28** Commission for Relief in Belgium
director: 38 General Relief and Reconstruction of Europe
  member/chairman: 22 Supreme Economic Council
  secretary of: 8 Commerce
  chairman of: 17 Hoover Commissions
civilian career: 6 author **14** mining engineer **18** consulting engineer
notable events of lifetime/term: 15

Great Depression
  conference: 11 London Naval
  crash of: 11 stock market
  Tariff: 11 Hawley-Smoot
named for him: 11 Hoover apron, Hoover plate (clean plate), Hooverville (shantytown)
father: 10 Jesse Clark
mother: 6 Huldah (Randall Minthorn)
siblings: 3 May **13** Theodore Jesse
wife: 3 Lou (Henry)
children: 10 Allan Henry **12** Herbert Clark
first lady:
  vice president of: 10 Girl Scouts

hop 3 bob **4** ball, jump, leap, prom, romp, skip, step, trip **5** bound, caper, dance, frisk, mixer, vault **6** bounce, gambol, prance, soiree, spring **7** Humulus
varieties: 4 Wild **5** False **6** Common **8** European, Japanese

hope 3 yen **4** help, wish **5** crave, dream, faith, fancy, trust **6** aspire, belief, chance, desire, expect, hunger, rescue, yen for **7** believe, count on, craving, dream of, longing, long for **8** ambition, daydream, feel sure, optimism, prospect, reckon on, reliance, yearn for, yearning **9** assurance, hankering, have faith, hunger for, salvation, take heart **10** anticipate, aspiration, assumption, be bent upon, confidence, conviction, expectancy **11** be confident, contemplate, expectation, have an eye to, possibility, presumption, reassurance, saving grace **12** anticipation, be optimistic, heart's desire **13** encouragement, have a fancy for, look forward to **14** have a hankering **17** great expectations **18** have one's heart set on **19** look on the bright side

Hope, Anthony
real name: 21 Sir Anthony Hope Hawkins
author of: 15 Rupert of Hentzau **18** The Prisoner of Zenda
Hope, Bob
real name: 16 Leslie Townes Hope
co-star: 10 Bing Crosby **13** Dorothy Lamour
born: 6 Eltham **7** England
roles:
  Road to: 3 Rio **4** Bali **6** Utopia **7** Morocco **8** Hong Kong, Zanzibar **9** Singapore
performed for: 3 USO

hopeful 7 assured, in hopes **8** cheering, sanguine, trusting **9** confident, expectant, favorable, fortunate, promising **10** auspicious, heartening, of good omen, optimistic, propitious, reassuring **11** encouraging **12** anticipative
hopeless 3 sad **4** lost, vain **6** abject, futile **7** forlorn, useless **8** dejected, downcast **9** depressed, incurable,

pointless **10** beyond help, despairing, despondent, impossible, melancholy, past remedy **11** downhearted, heartbroken, irreparable, irrevocable, pessimistic, sick at heart **12** beyond recall, disconsolate, heavyhearted, irredeemable, irreversible **13** grief-stricken, irretrievable **14** down in the mouth, sorrow-stricken

hopelessness 7 despair **8** futility **9** pessimism **11** uselessness

Hopi (Hopitu, Moki)
language family: 10 Shoshonean
location: 7 Arizona
adapted culture of: 6 Pueblo
ceremony: 10 snake dance

Hopkins, Anthony
born: 5 Wales **10** Port Talbot
roles: 5 Nixon, Proof **7** Dracula **8** Hannibal **9** Alexander, Red Dragon **10** Audrey Rose **11** A Doll's House **12** Meet Joe Black, Young Winston **14** The Elephant Man **15** The Lion in Winter **20** The Silence of the Lambs

Hopper, Edward
born: 7 Nyack NY
artwork: 10 Nighthawks **18** Early Sunday Morning, House by the Railroad **19** Second Story Sunlight **20** Sunlight in a Cafeteria **21** Lighthouse at Two Lights

Horae
also: 5 Hours
goddesses of: 5 decay **6** growth **7** seasons **11** social order
names: 4 Dice, Dike **5** Irene **7** Eunomia

Horatio
character in: 6 Hamlet
author: 11 Shakespeare
Horatio
character in: 17 The Spanish Tragedy
author: 3 Kyd
Horatius
origin: 5 Roman
defended: 6 bridge
  over: 5 Tiber
  against: 9 Etruscans

horde 3 mob **4** band, gang, host, pack **5** bunch, crowd, crush, drove, party, swarm, tribe, troop **6** legion, throng **7** company **8** assembly **9** gathering, multitude **10** assemblage **12** congregation

Horgan, Paul
author of: 10 Whitewater **13** Lamy of Santa Fe **18** The Thin Mountain Air

horizon 4 area **5** field, range, realm, scope, vista, world **6** bounds, domain, sphere **7** compass, expanse, outlook, purview, stretch **8** frontier, prospect **11** perspective

horizontal 4 even, flat **5** flush, level, plane, plumb, prone **6** supine **8** parallel (to something) **9** lying down, prostrate, reclining, recumbent **14** flat on one's back

horizontal support 3 tie 4 beam 5 brace, joist 6 girder, header, lintel 8 crossbar

hormone 4 ACTH 5 auxin 6 cortin 7 estrone, insulin, steroid 8 endocrin, estrogen, galactin, lactogen, secretin 9 adrenalin, cortisone 12 progesterone, testosterone

horn 4 tusk 5 cornu, point, spike 6 antler 11 excrescence
　brass instrument: 4 oboe, tuba 5 bugle 6 cornet 7 bassoon, trumpet 8 alto horn, baritone, clarinet, trombone 9 euphonium, saxophone 10 French horn, mellophone, sousaphone 11 English horn

Horn of Africa *see* 7 Somalia

Hornung, Paul
　nickname: 9 Golden Boy
　sport: 8 football
　position: 6 runner 11 placekicker
　team: 15 Green Bay Packers

horny 4 hard 5 tough 7 callous, lustful 8 callused, hardened 12 thick-skinned 14 pachydermatous

horologe 5 clock 9 timepiece 11 chronometer

horoscope *see* 9 astrology

horrendous 4 gory 5 awful 6 horrid 7 ghastly, hideous 8 dreadful, horrible, shocking, terrible 9 appalling, frightful, repellent, repulsive, revolting 10 horrifying

horrible 3 bad 4 foul, rank, vile 5 awful, nasty 6 grisly, horrid, odious 7 ghastly, hideous 8 dreadful, gruesome, shocking, terrible, unsavory 9 abhorrent, appalling, atrocious, frightful, harrowing, loathsome, monstrous, obnoxious, repellent, repulsive, revolting, sickening 10 abominable, despicable, detestable, disgusting, forbidding, nauseating, unbearable, unpleasant 11 disquieting, distasteful, unspeakable 12 disagreeable, insufferable

horrid 3 bad 4 foul, grim, ugly 5 awful, nasty, rough 6 bratty, horror, shaggy, wicked 7 fearful, hideous 8 dreadful, gruesome, horrible, shocking, terrible 9 bristling, frightful, offensive, revolting, vexatious 10 abominable, detestable, unpleasant 11 troublesome 12 disagreeable

horrific 4 dire 5 awful 7 fearful, ghastly 8 dreadful, horrible, shocking, terrible 9 appalling

horrified 6 aghast 8 appalled 9 petrified, terrified 10 frightened 13 thunderstruck 14 terror-stricken

horrify 5 daunt, repel, shock 6 appall, dismay, revolt, sicken 7 disgust, petrify, terrify 8 affright, disquiet, frighten, nauseate 10 disconcert, dishearten 11 make one sick 15 make one turn pale 18 make one's flesh

creep 22 make one's hair stand on end

horrifying 5 awful, dread 8 alarming, dreadful 10 terrifying 11 frightening, hair-raising

horror 3 woe 4 fear 5 alarm, crime, dread, panic 6 dismay, hatred, misery, terror 7 anguish, cruelty, disgust, dislike, outrage, torment 8 atrocity, aversion, distaste, distress, hardship, loathing 9 antipathy, awfulness, privation, repulsion, revulsion, suffering 10 abhorrence, affliction, discomfort, inhumanity, repugnance 11 abomination, detestation, hideousness, trepidation 12 apprehension, terribleness, wretchedness

horror-struck 6 aghast 7 fearful 8 appalled 9 horrified, terrified 10 frightened 13 scared to death

hors de combat 8 disabled 13 out of the fight

hors d'oeuvre 3 dip 6 canape, relish, tidbit 9 antipasto, appetizer 10 finger food

horse 4 colt, foal, hack, jade, mare, plug, pony, sire, stud 5 bronc, filly, mount, pacer, pinto, steed 6 bronco, dobbin, equine, nellie 7 cavalry, charger, cow pony, gelding, hackney, hussars, lancers, mustang, palfrey, trotter 8 cossacks, dragoons, galloper, stallion, troopers, yearling 9 broodmare, racehorse 10 cavalrymen, draft horse 12 horse cavalry, horse marines, quarter horse, thoroughbred 13 horse soldiers, mounted troops 15 mounted troopers, mounted warriors
　Achilles': 7 Xanthus
　Alexander the Great's: 10 Bucephalus
　anatomy: 4 hock, hoof, loin, mane, tail 5 croup, flank, shank 6 cannon, gaskin, haunch, stifle 7 coronet, crupper, fetlock, gambrel, nostril, pastern, withers 11 throatlatch
　Australian: 5 myall 8 warragal, warrigal, yarraman
　breed: 6 Morgan, Nubian, Tarpan 7 Arabian, Belgian, mustang 8 Galloway, Shetland 9 Appaloosa, Percheron 10 Clydesdale, Lippizaner 12 Narragansett, Standardbred, Thoroughbred 15 Tennessee-Walker
　Bellerophon's: 7 Pegasus
　Caligula's: 9 Incitatus (made a senator)
　castrated: 7 gelding
　color: 3 bay, dun 4 gray, pied, roan, zain 5 morel, pinto 6 calico, dapple, sorrel 7 piebald 8 chestnut, palomino, schimmel (gray)
　combining form: 4 eque, equi 5 hippo
　Dick Turpin's: 9 Black Bess
　Don Quixote's: 9 Rosinante
　family: 7 Equidae 9 Miohippus, Orohippus

female: 3 dam 4 mare 5 filly
French: 6 cheval
gear: 3 bit 4 rein, tack 6 saddle 7 blinder, harness, snaffle 9 surcingle 11 saddlecloth
Gen Custer's: 8 Comanche
Gene Autry's: 8 Champion
Gen Grant's: 10 Cincinnati
Gen Robert E Lee's: 9 Traveller
Gen Sherman's: 6 Rienzi
genus: 5 equus
Gulliver's Travels: 9 Houyhnhnm
kind: 3 cob 4 race 6 bronco, hunter, jumper 7 charger, mustang, palfrey, quarter, trotter 8 destrier
legendary: 6 Trojan
Lone Ranger's: 6 Silver
male: 4 colt 8 stallion
measure: 4 hand
Mohammed's: 7 Alborak
movie/story: 6 Flicka 8 Champion 10 Seabiscuit 11 Black Beauty 14 National Velvet 16 The Black Stallion
Napoleon's: 7 Marengo
Odin's: 8 Sleipnir
Orlando's: 11 Vegliantino
pace: 4 lope, trot 5 amble 6 canter, gallop
pair of: 4 span, team 6 tandem
race: 5 derby, plate 6 exacta 7 pick six 8 claiming, handicap 9 allowance 11 daily double, sweepstakes 12 steeplechase, weight-for-age
riding show: 8 gymkhana
riding sport: 4 polo
Rinaldo's: 6 Bayard
Roy Rogers': 7 Trigger
Siegfried's: 5 Grani
small: 4 pony
Stonewall Jackson's: 12 Little Sorrel
Tom Mix's: 4 Tony
Tonto's: 5 Scout
television: 4 Mr. Ed
three: 6 random, troika 7 unicorn
Wellington's (at Waterloo): 10 Copenhagen
wild: 5 fuzzy 6 bramby, kumrah, outlaw, tarpan 7 jughead 8 bangtail, fuzztail, warragal, warrigal
Will Rogers': 8 Soapsuds 10 Bootlegger
winged: 7 Pegasus
young: 4 colt, foal 5 filly 8 yearling

horseback riding
　athlete: 11 Frank Chapot 17 William Steinkraus

horse collar 3 zip 4 zero 5 aught, zilch 6 cipher, naught 8 goose egg

Horse Knows the Way, The
　author: 9 John O'Hara

horseman 5 groom, rider 6 hussar, jockey, lancer, ostler 7 cossack, dragoon, hostler, trainer, trooper 9 postilion, stableboy, stableman 10 cavalryman, equestrian, roughrider 11 horse marine, stable owner 12 equestrienne, horse breeder, horse soldier, stable

keeper 14 cavalry soldier, horseback rider, mounted trooper

horseplay 6 pranks **7** foolery **9** cutting up **10** buffoonery, tomfoolery **13** fooling around, horsing around

horse racing
god of: 6 Consus
jockey: 8 Del Insko **11** Bill Hartack, Eddie Arcaro **12** Angel Cordero, Bill Haughton, Laffit Pincay, Steve Cauthen **13** Johnny Longden, Stanley Dancer **15** Willie Shoemaker
Triple Crown: 7 Belmont **9** Preakness **13** Kentucky Derby

horse soldier 6 hussar, lancer **7** dragoon, trooper **8** cavalier, horseman **10** cavalryman

horse trooper 6 hussar, lancer **7** dragoon, Mountie **8** cavalier, horseman **10** cavalryman **12** horse soldier **14** mounted soldier **16** mounted policeman

Horton, Edward Everett
sidekick of: 11 Fred Astaire
born: 10 Brooklyn NY
roles: 15 Cinderella Jones, Her Primitive Man **18** Springtime for Henry

Horus
origin: 8 Egyptian
god of: 3 sun
Greek name: 10 Harcorates
symbol: 6 falcon
mother: 4 Isis
father: 6 Osiris
enemy: 3 Set **4** Seth

hosannas 4 yeas **5** kudos **6** bravos, cheers, paeans **7** acclaim, hurrahs, huzzahs, yippees **8** applause **10** hallelujas **11** halleluiahs

hose, hosiery 5 socks **6** nylons, tights **7** anklets, argyles, hosiery **9** knee-highs, pantyhose, stockings **10** bobby-socks

Hosea
father: 5 Beeri

hospitable 4 open, warm **6** genial **7** cordial **8** amenable, amicable, friendly, gracious, sociable, tolerant **9** agreeable, convivial, receptive, welcoming **10** accessible, gregarious, neighborly, openhanded, open-minded, responsive **12** approachable

hospital 4 home **6** asylum, clinic **7** sick bay **8** pavilion, rest home **9** infirmary **10** polyclinic, sanatorium **11** nursing home **13** medical center
French: 9 hotel Dieu

hospital, private
French: 13 maison de sante

hospitality 5 cheer **6** warmth **7** welcome **8** openness **9** geniality **10** cordiality, heartiness, kindliness **11** amicability, sociability **12** congeniality, conviviality, friendliness **13** Gemutlichkeit **14** hospitableness, neighborliness **15** warmheartedness

god of: 6 Sancus **10** Dius Fidius, Semo Sancus

host, hostess 3 lot, mob **4** army, band, body, crew, gang, mess **5** array, crowd, drove, emcee, group, horde, party, swarm, troop **6** legion, throng **7** company, maitre d', meeting **8** conclave, congress, hosteler, hotelier, landlord, welcomer **9** gathering, innkeeper, multitude **10** confluence, convention, headwaiter, party giver, proprietor **11** convocation, hotel keeper **12** congregation, head waitress, hotel manager, proprietress, receptionist **17** restaurant manager **18** master of ceremonies **20** mistress of ceremonies

hostage 6 pledge **7** captive **8** prisoner

Hostage, The
author: 12 Brendan Behan

hostel 3 inn **4** hall **5** hotel, lodge **7** hospice, lodging, shelter **8** hospital, hostelry

hostile 3 icy **4** cold, mean, ugly **5** angry, at war, enemy, testy **6** at odds, at outs, bitter, chilly, cranky, malign, touchy, unkind **7** opposed, vicious, warring **8** battling, clashing, contrary, fighting, opposing, snappish, spiteful, venomous **9** bellicose, bristling, dissident, malicious, malignant, truculent **10** contending, ill-natured, malevolent, on bad terms, unfriendly **11** belligerent, contentious, disagreeing, ill-disposed, quarrelsome **12** antagonistic, cantankerous, disagreeable, disputatious, incompatible **13** argumentative, at loggerheads, unsympathetic

hostile act 4 raid **6** strike, threat **7** assault, offense **8** act of war, invasion **9** hostility, incursion **10** aggression

hostile nation 3 foe **5** enemy **7** invader

hostility 3 war **4** duel, feud, fray, hate **5** anger, clash, fight, venom **6** battle, combat, enmity, fracas, hatred, malice, rancor, spleen **7** contest, dispute, ill will, scuffle, warfare, warring **8** act of war, argument, battling, conflict, fighting **9** animosity, antipathy, bickering **10** antagonism, bitterness, contention, dissidence, opposition, state of war **11** altercation, malevolence, viciousness **12** belligerence, contrariness, disagreement **14** unfriendliness, vindictiveness

hot 3 new, top **4** good, late, live, near, warm **5** fiery, fresh, nippy, sharp **6** ardent, baking, biting, fervid, fierce, heated, hectic, latest, molten, raging, recent, red-hot, stormy, sultry, torrid **7** boiling, burning, earnest, excited, furious, intense, melting, peppery, piquant, popular, pungent, searing, violent **8** agitated, animated, broiling, feverish, frenzied, roasting, scalding, sizzling, steaming, vehement, very

warm **9** emotional, excellent, scorching, simmering, very close, wrought-up **10** attractive, blistering, passionate, smoldering, successful, sweltering **11** electrified, fast-selling, most popular, radioactive, sought after, tempestuous **12** incandescent **14** fast and furious, highly seasoned, in close pursuit

hot air 7 bombast **8** rhetoric **9** hyperbole **12** exaggeration **13** overstatement

hotel de ville 9 a city hall
literally: 16 mansion of the city

hotel Dieu 9 a hospital **12** mansion of God

Hotel New Hampshire, The
author: 10 John Irving

Hotel Rwanda
director: 11 Terry George
cast: 9 Nick Nolte (Colonel Oliver) **10** Don Cheadle (Paul Rusesabagina) **11** Desmond Dube (Dube), Tony Kgoroge (Gregoire) **12** Neil McCarthy (Jean Jacques) **13** Sophie Okonedo (Tatiana Rusesabagina) **14** Hakeem Kae-Kazim (George Rutaganda), Joaquin Phoenix (Jack Daglish)

hothouse 6 tender **7** fragile, nursery **8** delicate **10** glasshouse, greenhouse **12** conservatory **13** over-protected

hot temper 4 fire **5** anger **6** pepper **8** acrimony **9** short fuse

hot-tempered 7 peppery **9** emotional, excitable **13** easily ruffled, quick-tempered

hot water 3 jam **4** mess **6** pickle **7** trouble **10** difficulty **11** predicament

Houghston, Walter
real name of: 12 Walter Huston

hound 3 dog, fan, nag, nut, pup **4** bait, buff, hunt, mutt, tail **5** annoy, chase, doggy, freak, harry, lover, pooch, puppy, stalk, track, trail, whelp, worry **6** addict, badger, canine, follow, harass, hector, keep at, needle, pester, pursue **7** bedevil, poochie **9** keep after **10** aficionado, hunting dog **11** afficionado
dog breed: 6 beagle, borzoi, saluki **7** basenji, harrier, whippet **9** dachshund, greyhound **10** bloodhound, otter hound **11** Afghan hound, basset hound, Ibizan hound **12** pharaoh hound **14** Irish wolfhound **15** English foxhound **16** American foxhound **17** Norwegian elkhound, Scottish deerhound **18** Rhodesian ridgeback **20** black and tan coonhound
group of: 3 cry **4** mute, pack

Hound of the Baskervilles, The
author: 19 Sir Arthur Conan Doyle
character: 8 Dr Watson **14** Sherlock Holmes **19** Sir Henry Baskerville

hour 3 day **4** span, time **5** space **6** period **8** interval
abbreviation: 2 hr

Hour *see* **5** Horae

House, M.D.
    network: 3 FOX
    creator: 10 David Shore
    cast: 8 Omar Epps (Eric Foreman), Sela Ward (Stacy Warner) **10** Chi McBride (Edward Vogler), Hugh Laurie (Gregory House) **12** Jesse Spencer (Robert Chase) **13** Lisa Edelstein (Lisa Cuddy) **16** Jennifer Morrison (Allison Cameron) **17** Robert Sean Leonard (James Wilson)

house, House 4 clan, firm, hall, home, keep, line, shop **5** abode, board, lodge, put up, store **6** billet, church, family, garage, harbor, strain, temple **7** Commons, company, concern, contain, council, descent, dynasty, lineage, quarter, shelter, theater **8** ancestry, assembly, audience, building, business, congress, domicile, dwelling **9** ancestors, household, residence **10** auditorium, family tree, habitation, hippodrome, opera house, spectators **11** accommodate, concert hall, corporation, legislature, noble family, partnership, royal family **12** business firm, lower chamber, meeting place, organization **13** dwelling place, establishment
    god of: 8 Silvanus, Sylvanus

housebreaker 5 thief **6** robber **7** burglar **8** pilferer **9** purloiner **10** cat burglar **14** second-story man

housebreaking 5 theft **7** break-in, robbery **8** burglary, stealing **12** burglarizing **19** breaking and entering

House Divided, A
    author: 9 Pearl Buck

household 4 home **5** house **6** family, hearth, menage **8** of a house **9** for a house **10** for a family, for home use **12** family circle
    goddess of: 6 Brigit

household gods 5 lares, Roman **7** penates

household help 4 cook, maid **7** footman, steward **8** domestic, gardener, handyman, houseboy **9** charwoman, chauffeur, domestics, majordomo, nursemaid **11** housekeeper

household of three
    French: 12 menage a trois

House of Atreus, The
    author: 9 Aeschylus
    character: 7 Electra, Orestes **9** Aegisthus, Agamemnon, Cassandra **12** Clytemnestra

house of health
    French: 13 maison de sante

House of Mirth, The
    author: 12 Edith Wharton
    character: 8 Lily Bart, Mr Selden **9** Gus Trenor **10** Judy Trenor, Mr Rosedale, Percy Gryce **12** Bertha Dorset, George Dorset

House of the Seven Gables, The

    author: 18 Nathaniel Hawthorne
    character: 10 Mr Holgrave **14** Phoebe Pyncheon **16** Clifford Pyncheon **20** Judge Jaffrey Pyncheon, Miss Hepzibah Pyncheon

house of worship 6 chapel, church, mosque, temple **8** basilica **9** cathedral, synagogue **10** house of God, Lord's house, tabernacle

housewife 4 wife **8** hausfrau **9** homemaker **11** housekeeper

housing 4 case, home **5** abode, house **6** casing, jacket, sheath, shield **7** lodging, shelter **8** covering, domicile, dwelling, envelope, lodgment, quarters **9** enclosure, residence **10** habitation **14** accommodations

Housman, A E
    author of: 14 A Shropshire Lad

Houston
    baseball team: 6 Astros
    basketball team: 6 Comets **7** Rockets
    canal: 11 Houston Ship
    channel: 12 Buffalo Bayou
    football team: 6 Oilers, Texans **8** Gamblers
    landmark: 4 NASA **12** Alley Theater **14** Jesse Jones Hall **22** Manned Spacecraft Center **29** San Jacinto Battlefield Monument
        battleship: 5 Texas
    named after: 10 Sam Houston
    planned by: 7 A C Allen, J K Allen
    stadium: 9 Astrodome
    street: 15 Old Spanish Trail
    university: 4 Rice **12** Texas Medical **13** Texas Southern

Houston, Sam
    position: 9 US Senator
    governor of: 5 Texas **9** Tennessee
    president of: 15 Republic of Texas
    served in: 9 Creek Wars **15** Texas Revolution
    battle: 10 San Jacinto
    defeated: 9 Santa Anna

Houston, Whitney
    husband: 10 Bobby Brown
    roles: 10 Cinderella **12** The Bodyguard **15** Waiting to Exhale **16** The Preacher's Wife
    songs: 6 Exhale **9** Count on Me **11** So Emotional **12** How Will I Know, I Have Nothing, I'm Every Woman **14** When You Believe **15** One Moment in Time, You Give Good Love **16** My Love Is Your Love **17** I'm Your Baby Tonight **18** All the Man That I Need, I Believe in You and Me, I Will Always Love You **20** The Greatest Love of All **21** Saving All My Love for You, Where Do Broken Hearts Go **22** Didn't We Almost Have It All **23** I Wanna Dance with Somebody

Houyhnhnms
    race of horses in: 16 Gulliver's Travels
    author: 5 Swift

hovel 3 hut **4** dump, hole **5** cabin, shack **6** shanty

hover 4 flit, hang **5** float, haunt, pause, poise, waver **6** attend, falter, seesaw **7** flitter, flutter **9** fluctuate, hang about, vacillate

Hovhaness, Alan
    born: 12 Somerville MA
    composer of: 10 Magnificat

how
    Latin: 7 quo modo

Howard, Catherine
    husband: 9 Henry VIII
    number: 5 fifth
    fate: 8 beheaded

Howard, Ron
    born: 2 OK **6** Duncan
    roles: 4 Opie **9** Happy Days **11** The Shootist **16** American Graffiti, Richie Cunningham **19** The Andy Griffith Show
    director of: 6 Cocoon, Gung Ho, Splash, Willow **8** Apollo 13 **9** Backdraft **13** Cinderella Man **14** A Beautiful Mind, Grand Theft Auto

Howard, Sidney
    author of: 13 The Silver Cord **22** They Knew What They Wanted

Howard, Trevor
    born: 7 England **12** Cliftonville
    roles: 6 The Key **13** Ryan's Daughter, Sons and Lovers **14** Brief Encounter **23** The Invincible Mr Disraeli

Howards End
    author: 9 E M Forster
    character: 9 Jacky Bast **10** Paul Wilcox, Ruth Wilcox **11** Henry Wilcox, Leonard Bast **13** Charles Wilcox, Helen Schlegel **16** Margaret Schlegel, Theobald Schlegel

how are you
    German: 8 wie geht's **9** wie geht es

Howe, Elias
    nationality: 8 American
    invented: 13 sewing machine

Howells, William Dean
    author of: 12 Indian Summer **15** A Modern Instance **20** A Hazard of New Fortunes, The Rise of Silas Lapham

How Green Was My Valley
    author: 16 Richard Llewellyn
    director: 8 John Ford
    character: 6 Marged **7** Bronwen **10** Beth Morgan **11** Iestyn Evans **12** Gwilym Morgan
        Morgan children: 4 Davy, Huur, Ivor, Owen **5** Ianto **6** Gwilym **8** Angharad
    cast: 7 Anna Lee **9** John Loder **11** Donald Crisp **12** Maureen O'Hara **13** Roddy McDowall, Walter Pidgeon
    Oscar for: 7 picture **8** director **15** supporting actor (Crisp)

howl 3 bay, cry **4** bark, hoot, roar, wail, yell, yelp, yowl **5** groan, shout,

whine 6 bellow, clamor, cry out, outcry, scream, shriek, uproar **7** ululate

howler 4 goof **5** error **6** boo-boo **7** blooper, blunder, mistake

How To Win Friends and Influence People
author: **12** Dale Carnegie

hoyden 3 imp **4** brat, chit **6** tomboy

Hoyle, Edmund
rules for: **5** cards **9** card games
saying: **16** according to Hoyle

Hoyle, Fred
field: **9** astronomy
nationality: **7** British
developed: **17** steady-state theory

Hoyt, Rosemary
character in: **16** Tender Is the Night
author: **10** Fitzgerald

Hsitsang see **5** Tibet

Hualapai
language family: **5** Yuman
location: **7** Arizona
related to: **7** Yavapai **9** Havasupai

hub 3 nub **4** axis, core **5** focus, heart, pivot **6** center, middle **10** focal point

Hubble, Edwin Powell
field: **9** astronomy
studied: **15** galactic nebulae
named for him: **14** Hubble constant, space telescope

hubbub 3 din **4** fuss, stir, to-do **5** noise **6** babble, bedlam, bustle, clamor, pother, racket, ruckus, tumult, uproar **7** ferment, turmoil **8** disorder **9** agitation, commotion, confusion, hue and cry **10** hullabaloo, hurly-burly **11** disturbance, pandemonium **12** perturbation

Hubert
creator: **11** Dick Wingert

huckleberry 9 Vaccinium **11** Gaylussacia
varieties: **2** He **3** Box, Red **4** Blue, Shot **5** Black, Dwarf, Hairy, Squaw, Sugar **6** Garden **8** Thin-leaf **9** Evergreen **10** California, Little-leaf

Huckleberry Finn (The Adventures of)
author: **9** Mark Twain
character: **3** Jim **9** Tom Sawyer **12** Widow Douglas **13** Judge Thatcher

huckster 5 adman **6** badger, hawker, kidder, seller, vendor **7** haggler, peddler

Hud
director: **10** Martin Ritt
cast: **10** John Ashley, Paul Newman **12** Patricia Neal **13** Melvyn Douglas **14** Brandon de Wilde
Oscar for: **7** actress (Neal) **15** supporting actor (Douglas)

huddle 4 heap, herd, mass, mess **5** bunch, crowd, group **6** cuddle, curl up, jumble, medley, muddle, nestle, throng **7** cluster, collect, meeting, snuggle **8** converge, disarray, disorder

9 confusion, gathering **10** conference, discussion, hodge-podge **12** think session

Hudibras
author: **12** Samuel Butler
character: **6** Ralpho **8** Crowders **9** Sidrophel

Hudson, Rock
real name: **12** Roy Scherer Jr
co-star: **8** Doris Day
born: **10** Winnetka IL
roles: **5** Giant **10** Pillow Talk **15** A Farewell to Arms, McMillan and Wife **20** Magnificent Obsession

Hudson, W H
author of: **13** Green Mansions, The Purple Land **17** Far Away and Long Ago
bird-girl: **4** Rima

hue 4 cast, tint, tone **5** color, shade, tinge **8** tincture **10** coloration

hue and cry 4 call, howl, roar, yell, yowl **5** alarm, alert, shout, storm **6** bellow, clamor, hubbub, outcry, shriek, uproar **7** thunder **10** cry of alarm, hullabaloo

huff 3 pet **4** fury, rage, snit **7** bad mood, dudgeon, outrage **8** ill humor, vexation **9** annoyance, petulance **10** fit of anger, fit of pique, resentment

huffy 4 curt, hurt **5** angry, cross, irate, moody, sulky, surly, testy **6** cranky, grumpy, moping, morose, shirty, sullen, touchy **7** in a snit, peevish, waspish, wounded **8** churlish, offended, petulant, snappish **9** glowering, in a lather, in a pucker, irritable, querulous, rancorous, resentful, sensitive **10** ill-humored, out of sorts **11** disgruntled, quarrelsome, thin-skinned **12** discontented **14** easily offended, hard to live with, hypersensitive

hug 4 hold **5** clasp **6** clutch, cuddle, nestle **7** cling to, embrace, snuggle, squeeze **9** hold close, hover near **11** keep close to **13** cling together, follow closely **15** parallel closely, press to the bosom

huge 4 vast **5** giant, great, jumbo **6** mighty **7** immense, mammoth, massive, titanic **8** colossal, enormous, gigantic, imposing **9** cyclopean, extensive, herculean, leviathan, monstrous **10** gargantuan, monumental, prodigious, staggering, stupendous **11** elephantine, extravagant, spectacular **12** overwhelming **14** Brobdingnagian

hugeness 4 bulk **8** enormity, vastness **9** great size, immensity, largeness, magnitude **11** massiveness

Huggins, Charles Brenton
field: **10** physiology
researched: **6** cancer **12** chemotherapy
awarded: **10** Nobel Prize

Hughes, Langston
author of: **9** The Big Sea **12** One-

Way Ticket **13** The Weary Blues **19** Shakespeare in Harlem **20** The Panther and the Lash

Hughes, Richard
author of: **18** A High Wind in Jamaica

Hughes, Thomas
author of: **19** Tom Brown's Schooldays

Hugh the Drover
opera by: **15** Vaughan Williams
character: **4** Mary **12** The Constable **14** John the Butcher

Hugin
origin: **12** Scandinavian
form: **5** raven
owned by: **4** Odin **5** Othin
personifies: **7** thought
duty: **10** newsbearer
other raven: **5** Munin

Hugo, Victor
author of: **7** Ruy Blas **13** Les Miserables **16** Notre Dame de Paris **23** The Hunchback of Notre Dame
character: **6** Javert **9** Esmeralda, Quasimodo **11** Jean Valjean

hulk 4 ship **5** giant, wreck **8** behemoth

hulking 3 big **5** bulky, heavy, husky **7** massive **8** powerful, unwieldy **9** oversized, ponderous **10** cumbersome

hull 3 pod **4** case, husk, peel, rind, skin **5** shell, shuck **7** coating **8** carapace **9** epidermis, tegmentum **10** integument

Hull, Isaac
served in: **19** War of Eighteen-Twelve
sunk ship: **9** Guerriere (British)
commander of ship: **12** Constitution

hullabaloo 3 din **4** stir **5** babel **6** bedlam, clamor, hubbub, ruckus, tumult, uproar **9** confusion **11** pandemonium
Yiddish: **7** tzimmes

hum 4 buzz, purr, whir **5** croon, drone, thrum **6** be busy, bustle, intone, murmur, thrive **7** buzzing, droning, purring, vibrate **8** be active, whirring **9** vibration **10** faint sound **13** be in full swing

human 3 man **5** of man, of men **6** gentle, humane, kindly, mortal, person **7** hominid, like man, manlike **8** merciful, personal **10** anthropoid, individual **11** Homo sapiens, sympathetic

Human Comedy, The
author: **14** Honore de Balzac, William Saroyan

humane 4 kind **5** human **6** kindly, tender **7** pitying **8** merciful **9** unselfish **10** benevolent, bighearted, charitable, goodwilled **11** magnanimous, sympathetic, warmhearted **12** humanitarian **13** compassionate, philanthropic

humanitarian 4 kind **6** humane **8** generous **10** altruistic, benevolent, charitable **11** kind-hearted **12** large-hearted **13** compassionate, philanthropic **14** philanthropist

humanity 3 man **4** love **5** mercy **6** people **7** charity, mankind, mortals **8** goodwill, kindness, sympathy **9** humankind, humanness, mortality **10** compassion, gentleness, humaneness, kindliness, tenderness **11** benevolence, Homo sapiens, human beings, human nature, magnanimity **12** the human race **13** brotherly love, fellow feeling **15** warmheartedness **16** fraternal feeling

humanum est errare 12 to err is human

Humbert Humbert
character in: **6** Lolita
author: **7** Nabokov

humble 3 low **4** meek, poor **5** abase, abash, crush, lower, lowly, plain, shame **6** common, debase, demean, demure, gentle, modest, shabby, simple, subdue **7** chasten, conquer, degrade, mortify, obscure, put down **8** bring low, derogate, disgrace, dishonor, inferior, ordinary, plebeian, pull down, wretched **9** bring down, embarrass, humiliate, make lowly, miserable **10** inglorious, low-ranking, make humble, obsequious, put to shame, respectful, unassuming **11** deferential, subservient, unimportant, unpresuming **12** self-effacing, take down a peg **13** insignificant, unpretentious **14** unostentatious **15** inconsequential, undistinguished

humbled 5 cowed **7** abashed, debased, subdued **9** conquered, disgraced **10** brought low, humiliated

Humboldt, Alexander von
nationality: **6** German
originator of: **7** ecology **10** geophysics

Humboldt's Gift
author: **10** Saul Bellow

humbug 3 fib, gyp, lie **4** bull, bunk, dupe, fake, fool, gull, hoax, liar, lies, sham **5** cheat, cozen, dodge, faker, fraud, hokum, lying, quack, spoof, trick **6** bunkum, con man, deceit, fibber, phooey, take in **7** beguile, blather, cheater, deceive, falsify, fiction, forgery, mislead, rubbish, sharper, swindle **8** artifice, claptrap, flimflam, flummery, hoodwink, impostor, nonsense, perjurer, pretense, swindler, trickery **9** bamboozle, charlatan, deception, fabricate, falsehood, hypocrisy, hypocrite, imposture, mendacity, poppycock, trickster **10** balderdash, hocus-pocus, mountebank, pretension **11** counterfeit, make-believe **12** equivocation, misrepresent **13** confidence man, double-dealing, falsification **15** pretentiousness

humdinger 4 lulu, oner **5** dandy,

doozy **6** beauty, hummer, marvel **8** Jim dandy, superior **10** ripsnorter **12** lollapalooza **13** extraordinary

humdrum 4 blah, dull, dumb, flat **5** banal, trite **6** boring, common, dreary **7** insipid, mundane, routine, tedious, trivial **8** everyday, lifeless, mediocre, ordinary, tiresome, wearying **9** hackneyed, unvarying, wearisome **10** monotonous, pedestrian, uneventful, unexciting, uninspired **11** commonplace, indifferent, uninspiring **12** conventional, run-of-the-mill **13** unexceptional, uninteresting

humerus
bone of: **8** upper arm

humid 4 damp, dank **5** moist, muggy, soppy **6** clammy, steamy, sticky, sultry

humidity 4 smog **8** dampness, moisture **9** mugginess **10** stickiness

humiliate 5 abash, crush, shame **6** debase, humble, subdue **7** chagrin, chasten, degrade, mortify, put down **8** belittle, bring low, disgrace, dishonor **9** discomfit, embarrass **11** make ashamed **13** bring down a peg

humiliated 7 abashed, crushed, debased, humbled **8** degraded **9** chagrined, disgraced, mortified

humiliation 5 shame **7** chagrin **8** disgrace, dishonor **9** abasement **10** debasement **11** degradation **12** discomfiture **13** embarrassment, mortification

humility 7 modesty, shyness **8** meekness, timidity **9** lowliness **10** demureness, diffidence, humbleness **11** bashfulness **13** self-abasement **17** unpretentiousness

hummock 4 hill, rise **5** knoll, mound **7** hillock, tussock

Humologumena 17 New Testament books

humor 3 wit **4** baby, gags, mood, puns **5** farce, jests, jokes, spoil **6** cajole, comedy, joking, pamper, parody, satire, soothe, suffer, temper, whimsy **7** appease, flatter, foolery, fooling, indulge, jesting, mollify, placate, spirits, waggery **8** drollery, give in to, jocosity, low humor, nonsense, raillery, ridicule, tolerate, travesty, wordplay **9** burlesque, funniness, low comedy, put up with, slapstick, wittiness **10** buffoonery, caricature, comicality, comply with, high comedy, jocoseness, jocularity, tomfoolery, wisecracks, witticisms **11** broad comedy, disposition, foolishness, frame of mind, go along with **12** monkeyshines **13** ludicrousness **14** ridiculousness

humorist 3 wag, wit **4** card **5** comic **8** comedian

humorous 5 comic, droll, funny, witty **6** jocose **7** amusing, comical, jocular, waggish **8** farcical, mirthful, sportive **9** facetious, laughable, ludicrous, satir-

ical, whimsical **10** ridiculous **11** nonsensical, rib-tickling **13** sidesplitting

hump 4 arch, bend, bump, knob, lift, lump, rise **5** bulge, hunch, knurl, mound, put up, tense **8** swelling **9** convexity **10** projection, prominence **11** excrescence

Humperdinck, Engelbert
born: **4** Bonn **7** Germany
composer of: **10** The Miracle **15** Hansel and Gretel

Humphry Clinker
author: **19** Tobias George Smollet
character: **10** Mr Dennison **12** Jerry Melford, Lydia Melford **14** George Dennison, Matthew Bramble **15** Winifred Jenkins **18** Miss Tabitha Bramble **26** Lieutenant Obadiah Lismahago

Humpty Dumpty
character in: **12** nursery rhyme **22** Through the Looking Glass
author: **7** Carroll

hunch 4 arch, bend, clue, hump, idea **5** tense **7** feeling, glimmer, inkling **8** good idea **9** intuition, suspicion **10** foreboding **11** premonition **12** presentiment

Hunchback of Notre Dame, The
author: **10** Victor Hugo
character: **9** Esmeralda, Gringoire, Quasimodo **12** Claude Frollo **20** Phoebus de Chateaupers

hunched 4 bent **7** crooked, slumped, stooped **9** contorted

hundredweight
abbreviation: **3** cwt

Hungary
capital/largest city: **8** Budapest
others: **4** Gyor, Pecs **5** Harta **6** Mohacs, Sopron, Szeged **7** Komarom, Miskolc, Szentes **8** Dubrecen, Kaposuar, Szegedin **9** Kecskemet **10** Albertirsa **11** Nagykanizsa, Szombathely
measure: **3** ako **4** hold, yoke **5** itcze, marok, metze **7** huvelyk
monetary unit: **4** gara **5** balas, krone, pengo **6** filler, forint, gulden, korona, ongara, ungara
weight: **7** vamfont **8** vammazsa
island: **8** Margaret
lake: **5** Ferto **7** Balaton, Velence **9** Blatensee **10** Neusiedler, Plattensee
mountain: **4** Alps, Bukk **5** Matra, Tatra **6** Bakony, Mecsek, Vertes **7** Cserhat, Gerecse **8** Borzsony, Zempleni **9** Korishegy **10** Carpathian
highest point: **5** Kekes
river: **3** Mur, Sio **4** Duna, Raab, Raba, Sajo, Zala **5** Bodva, Drava, Drave, Ipoly, Kapos, Koros, Maros, Tarna, Tisza **6** Danube, Henrad, Poprad, Szamos, Theiss, Zagyva **7** Vistula **8** Berretyo
physical feature:
canal: **3** Sio **6** Sarviz
forest: **6** Bakony

plain: 6 Puszta
port: 5 Fiume
people: 3 Hun **4** Serb **5** Croat, Gypsy **6** Cigany, Magyar, Slovak, Ugrian
composer: 5 Lehar, Liszt **6** Bartok, Kodaly
national hero: 5 Arpad
playwright: 6 Molnar
language: 6 German, Magyar, Slovak **8** Croatian **9** Hungarian **10** Finno-Ugric
religion: 8 Lutheran **9** Calvinism **13** Roman Catholic **16** Eastern Orthodoxy
place:
church: 32 Gothic Coronation Church of Matthias
ruins: 8 Aquincum
square: 6 Heroes
tomb: 14 Turbe of Gul Baba **16** Father of the Roses
feature:
dance: 3 kos **7** czardas **10** varsoviana
dog: 4 puli
musical instrument: 8 taragata **9** czimbalom
food:
dish: 6 gulyas **7** goulash **15** chicken paprikas
pastry: 4 rete **5** torte
wine: 5 Tokay **10** Bulls Blood

hunger 3 yen **4** itch, love, lust, want, wish **5** crave, greed **6** desire, famine, hanker, liking, relish, thirst **7** burn for, craving, itch for, long for, pant for **8** appetite, fondness, voracity, yearn for, yearning **9** hankering, lust after **10** greediness, starvation **11** have a yen for, thirst after **12** malnutrition, ravenousness

hungry 5 eager **6** greedy **7** starved **8** ravenous, starving **9** voracious

hunk 3 gob, wad **4** clod, glob, lump, mass **5** block, chunk, piece **6** gobbet **7** portion **8** quantity

hunt 4 seek **5** chase, probe, shoot, stalk, trace, track, trail **6** course, follow, pursue **7** explore, go after, look for **8** coursing, drive out **9** ferret out, search for, try to find **11** go in quest of, inquire into **14** riding to hounds **20** leave no stone unturned

Hunt, Richard Morris
architect of: 8 Biltmore (Asheville NC) **11** Marble House (Newport RI), The Breakers (Newport RI) **12** Lenox Library (NYC) **14** Studio Building (NYC) **19** National Observatory (Washington DC) **22** William Vanderbilt House (NYC) **23** Metropolitan Museum of Art (NYC)

hunter
constellation of: 5 Orion
French: 8 chasseur

Hunter, Jim
nickname: 7 Catfish

sport: 8 baseball
position: 7 pitcher
team: 14 New York Yankees **16** Oakland Athletics

Hunter, Kim
real name: 8 Jane Cole
born: 9 Detroit MI
roles: 16 Stairway to Heaven, The Seventh Victim **21** A Streetcar Named Desire

Hunting
god of: 7 Verbius
goddess of: 5 Diana **7** Artemis

Hunting Dogs
constellation of: 13 Canes Venatici

hurdle 4 jump, leap, snag, wall **5** bound, clear, fence, hedge, vault **6** hazard **7** barrier **8** obstacle, surmount **9** hindrance, roadblock **10** difficulty, impediment, spring over **11** obstruction **12** interference **14** stumbling block

hurl 4 cast, toss **5** chuck, fling, heave, pitch, sling, throw **6** launch, let fly, propel **7** fire off, project **9** discharge

hurly-burly 4 stir **5** furor **6** action, bustle, hubbub, hustle, uproar **8** activity **9** commotion **10** hullabaloo

hurrah, hurray 4 fine, good **5** bravo, cheer, great, huzza **6** huzzah, salute **7** acclaim, hosanna **9** excellent, halleluia, wonderful **10** exaltation, hallelujah

hurricane 7 cyclone, monsoon, tempest, typhoon **9** windstorm

Hurricane, The
director: 8 John Ford
cast: 7 Jon Hall **9** Mary Astor **12** C Aubrey Smith **13** Dorothy Lamour, Raymond Massey
setting: 9 Manikoora

hurried 4 fast **5** hasty **6** hectic, rushed, speedy **7** cursory, frantic **8** careless, feverish, frenetic, headlong, slapdash, slipshod **9** breakneck, haphazard, impulsive **11** precipitate, superficial

hurry 3 ado, zip **4** bolt, dart, dash, fuss, goad, prod, rush, stew, whiz **5** egg on, haste, speed **6** flurry, hasten, hustle, push on, scurry, tumult, urge on **7** drive on, flutter, press on, scuttle, speed up, turmoil **8** make time, move fast, pressure, scramble, step on it **9** commotion, go quickly, make haste, step along **10** accelerate, get a move on, get hopping, lose no time, make tracks **11** come quickly, get cracking, go like a shot, go like sixty **12** step on the gas **13** go like the wind **14** cover the ground **15** hustle and bustle

hurt 3 cut, mar **4** ache, balk, burn, foil, harm, lame, maim, mark, maul, pain, pang, scar **5** agony, block, check, grief, limit, lower, pique, smart, spike, sting, stung **6** aching, bruise, damage, deface, dismay, grieve, hamper, hin-

der, impair, impede, injure, lessen, mangle, marked, miffed, misery, morose, narrow, offend, oppose, pained, piqued, reduce, retard, thwart, weaken **7** agonize, bruised, chagrin, cripple, crushed, damaged, disable, exclude, inhibit, injured, mangled, painful, scarred, scratch, torment, torture, trouble, wounded **8** aggrieve, crippled, decrease, dejected, diminish, disabled, dismayed, distress, encumber, hold back, minimize, mutilate, obstruct, offended, preclude, restrain, smarting, soreness, wretched **9** aggrieved, annoyance, chagrined, dejection, disfigure, forestall, frustrate, heartsick, indignant, miserable, mortified, mutilated, resentful, scratched, suffering **10** discomfort, distressed, heartbreak, melancholy, resentment **11** aggravation, crestfallen, heartbroken **12** disheartened, wretchedness **13** embarrassment, mortification

Hurt, John
born: 7 England **22** Chesterfield Derbyshire
roles: 5 Alien **6** Rob Roy **8** Partners **9** I Claudius (TV; Caligula), You're Dead **14** The Elephant Man **15** Midnight Express **18** Crime and Punishment **31** Harry Potter and the Sorcerer's Stone

Hurt, William
roles: 5 Smoke **8** Body Heat, Dark City **9** Gorky Park **10** Eyewitness **11** The Big Chill, Trial by Jury **13** Broadcast News **16** The Blue Butterfly **20** Kiss of the Spider Woman, Children of a Lesser God

hurtful 5 cruel **6** deadly **7** abusive, baleful, harmful **8** crushing, improper, stinging, wounding **9** injurious

hurtle 3 fly, hie, run, zip **4** bolt, dart, dash, race, rush, tear, whiz **5** bound, lunge, scoot, shoot, speed, spurt, whisk **6** charge, gallop, plunge, scurry **7** scamper, scuttle **11** go like a shot **13** go like the wind **14** go lickety-split

husband 3 man **4** keep, mate, save **5** amass, groom, hoard, hubby, store **6** old man, retain, save up, spouse **7** consort **8** conserve, maintain, preserve, set aside **10** accumulate, bridegroom, married man

husbandry 7 farming **9** geoponics **11** agriculture, crop-raising **12** conservation
god of: 9 Aristaeus

hush 4 calm **5** quell, quiet, shush, still **6** shut up, soothe **7** be quiet, be still, keep mum, mollify, silence **8** be silent, pipe down, quietude **9** quiet down, quietness, stillness **10** knock it off **11** tranquility **12** peacefulness, tranquillity

hushed 4 calm **5** quiet, still **6** calmed, gentle, lulled, silent **7** allayed, quieted, soothed, stifled **8** pacified, silenced, tranquil **12** tranquilized **13** tranquillized

hush money 5 bribe **6** payoff, payola **7** tribute **9** blackmail, extortion

huskiness 5 brawn **9** beefiness **10** hoarseness, robustness, ruggedness, sturdiness **11** muscularity

husky 3 big **5** beefy, burly, gruff, harsh, hefty, plump, rough, solid, stout, thick **6** brawny, coarse, hoarse, robust, stocky, strong, sturdy **7** cracked, grating, rasping, raucous, throaty **8** athletic, croaking, guttural, muscular, powerful, thickset **9** strapping **10** overweight **12** strong as an ox **15** broad-shouldered

husky, **8** Siberian
   work: 7 sled dog

hussar 8 cavalier, horseman **10** cavalryman **12** horse soldier, horse trooper **14** mounted soldier

hussy 4 bawd, jade, minx, slut, tart **5** wench, whore **6** harlot, wanton **7** baggage, trollop **8** strumpet **9** brash girl, lewd woman, saucy miss **10** adulteress, loose woman, prostitute **11** brazen woman, fallen woman **12** scarlet woman **17** woman of easy virtue

hustle 3 ado, fly **4** bolt, dart, dash, fuss, prod, push, rush, stir, toss **5** elbow, hurry, nudge, scoot, shove, throw **6** bounce, bustle, flurry, hasten, hubbub, jostle, scurry, tumult **7** flutter, scuttle, speed up, turmoil **8** make time, scramble, shoulder, step on it **9** commotion, make haste, step along **10** lose no time **11** hurry-scurry, move quickly **12** be aggressive

hustler 4 doer **6** con man, dynamo, hooker **8** go-getter, live-wire, swindler **10** prostitute **12** streetwalker

Hustler, The
   director: 12 Robert Rossen
   cast: 10 Paul Newman **11** Piper Laurie **12** George C Scott **13** Jackie Gleason (Minnesota Fats)

Huston, John
   director of: 8 Key Largo **10** The Misfits **11** Moulin Rouge **12** Prizzi's Honor **13** Asphalt Jungle **15** The African Queen **16** The Maltese Falcon **19** The Night of the Iguana **27** The Treasure of the Sierra Madre (Oscar)
   father: 12 Walter Huston
   wife: 11 Evelyn Keyes
   born: 8 Nevada MO
   daughter: 8 Anjelica
   roles: 9 Chinatown **11** Winter Kills

Huston, Walter
   real name: 15 Walter Houghston
   son: 10 John Huston
   born: 6 Canada **7** Toronto
   roles: 9 Dodsworth **18** All That Money Can Buy **27** The Treasure of the Sierra Madre

hut 4 shed **5** cabin, hutch, shack **6** lean-to, shanty **7** cottage, shelter

hutch 3 pen, sty **4** cage, coop, cote, crib, shed **5** stall **9** enclosure

Hutchinson, A S M
   author of: 13 If Winter Comes

Hutton, Betty
   real name: 18 Betty June Thornburg
   born: 13 Battle Creek MI
   roles: 15 Annie Get Your Gun **19** Greatest Show on Earth

Hutton, James
   field: 7 geology
   nationality: 8 Scottish
   founder of: 7 geology

Hutton, Timothy
   father: 9 Jim Hutton
   wife: 11 Debra Winger **21** Aurore Giscard d'Estaing
   son: 10 Milo Hutton, Noah Hutton
   roles: 4 Taps **6** Daniel, Kinsey **10** Playing God **14** Ordinary People **22** The Falcon and the Snowman

Huxley, Aldous
   author of: 11 Crome Yellow **13** Brave New World **17** Point Counter Point
   brother: 6 Julian

Huxley, Julian
   field: 7 biology
   nationality: 7 British
   promoted theory of: 9 evolution

Huygens, Christiaan
   nationality: 5 Dutch
   invented: 13 pendulum clock
   discovered: 12 Saturn's rings
   formulated: 17 wave theory of light

hyacinth 10 Hyacinthus **20** Hyacinthus orientalis
   varieties: 4 musk, pine, star, wild, wood **5** Dutch, grape, Roman, water **6** common, garden, meadow, nutmeg, starry, summer, Tassel **7** feather, peacock **11** common grape

Hyacinthus
   father: 7 Amyclas
   daughter: 7 Orthaea
   loved by: 6 Apollo **8** Zephyrus
   killed by: 5 quoit **6** discus
   from his blood sprang: 6 flower
      petals marked: 4 AI-AI
      means: 4 alas

Hyades
   also: 5 Hyads **10** Palilicium
   form: 6 nymphs
   father: 5 Atlas **7** Oceanus
   mother: 6 Tethys **7** Pleione
   sisters: 8 Pleiades
   nurtured: 8 Dionysus
   placed among: 5 stars

hybrid 5 cross **7** amalgam, mixture **9** composite, half-breed **10** crossbreed

hybridize 5 cross **14** cross-fertilize, cross-pollinate

Hydra
   form: 12 water serpent
   number of heads: 4 nine
   killed by: 8 Hercules

hydrangea
   varieties: 4 Wild **6** French, Peegee **8** Climbing

hydrogen
   chemical symbol: 1 H

hydrophobia 6 rabies
   fear of: 5 water

Hygeia
   father: 9 Asclepius
   goddess of: 6 health
   corresponds to: 5 Salus

hygienic 4 pure **5** clean **7** aseptic, healthy, sterile **8** germ-free, harmless, salutary, sanitary **9** healthful, wholesome **10** salubrious, unpolluted **11** disease-free, disinfected, uninjurious **12** prophylactic **14** uncontaminated

Hylaeus
   form: 7 centaur
   born on: 5 cloud

Hymen
   also: 9 Hymenaeus
   god of: 8 marriage
   holds: 5 torch
   corresponds to: 8 Talassio

hymenoptera
   class: 8 hexapoda
   phylum: 10 arthropoda
   group: 3 ant, bee **4** wasp **6** chacid, sawfly **12** ichneumon fly

hymn 5 paean, psalm **6** anthem **12** song of praise **14** devotional song **17** song in praise of God

Hymn to Proserpine
   author: 24 Algernon Charles Swinburne

Hypatia
   author: 15 Charles Kingsley

hyper 7 keyed-up **10** high-strung, overactive

hyperbole 8 metaphor **11** enlargement **12** exaggeration **13** magnification, overstatement **14** figure of speech

hyperbolize 6 overdo **7** amplify, magnify, stretch **9** embroider, overstate **10** exaggerate

hyperborean 6 arctic **8** freezing, northern **13** septentrional

Hyperborean
   inhabitant of: 8 Paradise

Hyperion
   also: 6 Helios
   form: 5 Titan
   father: 6 Uranus
   mother: 4 Gaea
   sister: 5 Theia
   son: 6 Helios
   daughter: 3 Eos **6** Selene
   corresponds to: 6 Apollo

Hyperion
   author: **9** John Keats **24** Henry Wadsworth Longfellow
hypersensitive 6 touchy **9** emotional **13** temperamental
Hypnos
   also: **6** Hypnus
   god of: **5** sleep
   father: **6** Erebus
   mother: **3** Nyx
   brother: **8** Thanatos
   corresponds to: **6** Somnus
hypnotic 9 soporific **11** mesmerizing **12** spellbinding
hypnotize 7 control **9** mesmerize, spellbind
hypocrisy 6 deceit, fakery **7** falsity **9** duplicity, mendacity, phoniness **10** dishonesty **11** dissembling, insincerity **12** two-facedness
hypocrite 5 phony **8** deceiver **9** pretender **10** dissembler
Hypocrite 15 whited sepulcher
hypocritical 5 false, phony **7** feigned **8** feigning, two-faced **9** deceitful, deceptive, dishonest, insincere, truthless **11** counterfeit
hyporchema
   form: **9** choral ode
   origin: **5** Greek
   honored: **6** Apollo **8** Dionysus
hypothalamus
   regulates: **15** body temperature
   located in: **5** brain
hypothesis 6 theory, thesis **7** premise, theorem **8** proposal **9** assertion, postulate **10** assumption, conclusion, conjecture **11** explanation, guesstimate, presumption, proposition, speculation, supposition
hypothesize 5 infer **6** assume **7** imagine, presume, suppose **8** theorize **9** postulate, speculate **10** conjecture
hypothetical 7 assumed, dubious **8** possible, supposed **9** imaginary, uncertain **10** contingent, postulated **11** conditional, conjectural, presumptive, speculative, theoretical **12** questionable **13** suppositional
Hypselosaurus
   type: **8** dinosaur, sauropod
   location: **6** France **8** Mongolia
   period: **10** Cretaceous
Hypsilophodon
   type: **8** dinosaur **10** ornithopod
   location: **7** England
   period: **10** Cretaceous
Hyrie
   transformed into: **4** swan
hyssop 8 Hyssopus **18** Hyssopus officialis
   varieties: **5** anise, giant, water **9** blue giant **10** nettle-leaf **11** fennel giant, purple giant, yellow giant **12** Mexican giant **13** fragrant giant, wrinkled giant
Hyssop 13 Biblical plant
hysteria 3 fit **5** panic **6** frenzy **8** delirium
hysterical 5 crazy, droll **6** absurd, crazed, raving **7** amusing, comical **8** farcical, frenzied, worked-up **9** laughable, ludicrous, wrought-up **10** distracted, distraught, ridiculous, uproarious **11** carried away, overwrought, wildly funny **13** beside oneself, out of one's wits **14** uncontrollable
hysterics 3 fit **12** emotionalism

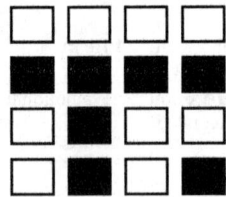

I, Claudius
author: **12** Robert Graves
story of: **36** Tiberius Claudius Drusus Nero Germanicus (Emperor of Rome) (on Masterpiece Theater) actors: **8** John Hurt **11** Derek Jacobi, Sheila White **12** Brian Blessed, Sian Phillips **14** Patrick Stewart, Margaret Tyzack

I, the Jury
author: **14** Mickey Spillane
hero: **10** Mike Hammer

I Am a Fugitive from a Chain Gang
director: **11** Mervyn LeRoy
cast: **8** Paul Muni **11** Helen Vinson **13** Glenda Farrell, Preston Foster

I am unwilling to contend
Latin: **14** nolo contendere

Ibanez, Vicente Blasco
author of: **30** The Four Horsemen of the Apocalypse

Iberian Peninsula
also: **8** Hesperia
comprising: **5** Spain **8** Portugal

Ibsen, Henrik
author of: **6** Ghosts **8** Peer Gynt **11** A Doll's House, Hedda Gabler, Rosmersholm, The Wild Duck **16** The Master Builder **18** An Enemy of the People, John Gabriel Borkman

I came, I saw, I conquered
Latin: **12** veni vidi vici
author: **12** Julius Caesar

Icarus
father: **8** Daedalus
built: **5** wings
flew too near: **3** sun
death by: **8** drowning

ICC 28 Interstate Commerce Commission

ice 3 gem **4** berg, floe, gems, rime **5** chill, frost, glace **6** freeze, icicle, jewels **7** crystal, dessert, glacier, jewelry, sherbet **8** diamonds **11** refrigerant, refrigerate

ice-cold 3 icy **4** cold **5** gelid, polar **6** arctic, bitter, frigid, frosty, wintry **7** chilled, frosted, glacial, subzero **8** chilling, freezing, Siberian, unheated, unwarmed **9** stone-cold, supercold **11** hyperborean, supercooled **12** bone-chilling

ice cream 7 dessert, sherbet **4** soda **5** glace **6** frappe, sundae **7** dessert, parfait, sherbet, spumoni, tortoni

ice hockey *see* **6** hockey

Iceland
other name: **15** Lydveldid Island
capital/largest city: **9** Reykjavik
others: **3** Hof **6** Geysir **7** Akranes, Husavik **8** Akureyri, Keflavik, Kopasker **9** Kopavogur **10** Hveragerdi, Isafjordur **12** Siglufjordur **13** Hafnarfjordur, Neskaupstadur, Seydisfjordur
government:
general assembly: **7** Althing
measure: **3** set **4** alin **5** almud **6** almenn, ferfet, pattur **7** fathmur, fermila, oltunna
monetary unit: **5** aurar, eyrir, krona
weight: **4** pund **5** pound, tunna **6** smjors
island: **7** Heimaey, Surtsey, Westman
lake: **6** Myvatn **10** Thorisvatn **14** Thingvallavatn
mountain: **5** Jokul **10** Orafajokul
volcano: **4** Laki **5** Askja, Hekla, Katla **7** Surtsey
highest point: **17** Hvannadalshnjukur
river: **5** Hvita **7** Fnjoska, Thjorsa **15** Jokulsa a Fjollum
sea: **9** Greenland **13** North Atlantic
physical feature:
fjord: **4** Eyja
geyser: **5** gryla **6** geysir **11** Great Gusher
glacier: **6** Jokull **11** Orafajokull, Vatnajokull
plain: **15** Skeidharasandur
waterfall: **9** Godafoss, Gullfoss **9** Dettifoss
people: **6** Celtic, Viking **8** Norseman **9** Norwegian
first settler: **8** Arnarson
hero: **4** Bele, Eric, Leif **10** Sigurdsson
language: **5** Norse **9** Icelandic
religion: **19** Evangelical Lutheran
place:
national shrine: **11** Thingvellir
feature:
airport: **9** Kopavogur
bird: **4** gull **6** falcon **9** gyrfalcon
literary genre: **4** saga
wrestling: **5** glima
food:
dish: **4** skyr, svio **7** bloomor **8** harofisk

Iceman
nickname of: **12** George Gervin

Iceman Cometh, The
author: **12** Eugene O'Neill
role: **6** Hickey

Ice Palace
author: **10** Edna Ferber

ice skating
athlete: **9** Apolo Ohno, Janet Lynn, John Curry **10** Carol Heiss, Dick Button, Eric Heiden, Sonja Henie **11** Elvis Stojko, Oksana Baiul, Sarah Hughes, Sheila Young **12** Brian Boitano, Katarina Witt, Michelle Kwan, Peggy Fleming, Tara Lipinski **13** Dorothy Hamill, Nancy Kerrigan, Scott Hamilton **14** Linda Fratianne **15** Kristi Yamaguchi

ich dien 6 I serve
motto of: **13** Prince of Wales

I Ching 30 ancient Chinese book of divination

ichor
form: **5** fluid
in veins of: **4** gods

Ichthyocentaur
form: **8** creature
location: **3** sea
head/torso: **5** human
legs: **5** horse
tail: **4** fish

iciness 4 cold **5** chill **9** frigidity **10** chilliness, frostiness, wintriness **12** slipperiness

ici on parle francais 18 French is spoken here **19** here one speaks French

icky 5 gluey, gooey, gross, gucky, gummy, mushy, nasty, tacky, weepy **6** sticky, syrupy, viscid **7** maudlin, viscous **8** bathetic **9** glutinous, offensive, repulsive, revolting **10** disgusting **12** mucilaginous

icon, ikon 4 idol **5** image **6** effigy, figure, statue **7** picture **8** likeness **11** sacred image

iconoclast 5 rebel **7** radical, upstart **9** dissenter **13** nonconformist, revolutionary

icy 3 raw **4** cold, cool **5** aloof, gelid **6** arctic, chilly, frigid, frosty, frozen, glazed, sleety, wintry **7** distant, glacial, haughty, hostile **8** chilling, freezing, slippery **9** impassive **10** forbidding, unfriendly **11** coldhearted, unemotional

Ida
form: **5** nymph

watched over: 4 Zeus
mount: 5 Crete **7** Phrygia

Idaea
form: 5 nymph
domain: 8 Mount Ida
husband: 7 Phineus **9** Scamander
son: 6 Teucer

Idaho
abbreviation: 2 ID **3** Ida
nickname: 3 Gem
capital/largest city: 5 Boise
others: 4 Buhl **5** Malad, Nampa **6**
Moscow **7** Orofino, Rexburg **8** Caldwell, Lewiston **9** Pocatello, Twin
Falls **10** Idaho Falls **11** Coeur
d'Alene
college: 17 Northwest Nazarene
explorer: 13 Lewis and Clark
feature: 9 Sun Valley **17** Continental
Divide
dam: 5 Oxbow **8** Brownlee
national monument: 16 Craters of
the Moon
tribe: 5 Banak, Shake **6** Cayuse, Paiute, Spokan **7** Bannock, Kutenai,
Spokane **8** Kalispel, Nez Perce, Sahaptin, Shoshone, Shoshoni **9** Shos-
honee **11** Coeur d'Alene
people: 9 Ezra Pound, Sacagawea **11**
Chief Joseph **17** William Edgar Borah
lake: 4 Bear **5** Grey's **6** Priest **11**
Coeur d'Alene, Pend Oreille **22**
American Falls Reservoir
land rank: 10 thirteenth
mountain: 4 Ryan **5** Rocky **6** Rhodes,
Taylor, Tetons **7** Cabinet **8** Ban-
nocks, Big Baldy, Bluenose, Saw-
tooth **9** Wasatches **10** Clearwater **11**
Beaverheads, Bitterroots **13** Selkirk
Ranges
highest point: 5 Borah
physical feature:
falls: 5 Moyie **8** Shoshone **9** Upper
Mesa
springs: 4 Soda **6** Hooper **7** Lava-
hot
river: 4 Bear **5** Boise, Snake, St Joe **6**
Locksa, Salmon **7** Payette, Spokane
8 Kootenai **11** Coeur d'Alene, Pend
Oreille
state admission: 10 forty-third
state bird: 16 mountain bluebird
state flower: 7 syringa
state motto: 13 It Is Perpetual **16** Let
It Be Perpetual
state song: 15 Here We Have Idaho
state tree: 16 western white pine

Idas
father: 8 Aphareus
mother: 5 Arene
brother: 7 Lynceus
wife: 8 Marpessa
daughter: 9 Cleopatra

idea 4 clue, hint, view **6** belief, notion
7 concept, feeling, inkling, insight,
opinion, outlook, thought **8** approach,
proposal, solution **9** sentiment **10**
conception, conclusion, conviction,
impression, indication, intimation,
suggestion **12** apperception, appreciation **13** approximation, mental picture, understanding **14** interpretation,
recommendation

ideal 3 aim **4** hero, idol **5** dream,
model **7** epitome, optimal, pattern,
perfect **8** exemplar, last word, paradigm, standard, ultimate **9** archetype,
criterion, excellent, exemplary, faultless, matchless, objective **10** impeccable **11** inspiration

idealism 8 optimism **9** meliorism **10**
utopianism **11** romanticism

idealist 7 dreamer, utopian **8** romantic
9 Pollyanna, stargazer, visionary **11**
romanticist **13** perfectionist

idealized 6 dreamy **7** utopian, wishful
8 fanciful, illusory, romantic **10** optimistic **11** pie-in-the-sky, unrealistic **13**
insubstantial

idea man 7 advisor **8** inventor **9** innovator **10** consultant **12** entrepreneur

idee fixe 9 fixed idea, obsession
music: 14 recurring motif

idem 24 the same as previously given
28 the same as previously mentioned

identical 4 twin **7** uniform **8** selfsame, very same **9** duplicate **15** interchangeable **17** indistinguishable

identification 2 ID **5** badge, label **6**
dogtag **7** license **8** passport **9** detection **10** connection, revelation **11** affiliation, association, credentials, pinpointing, recognition **12** confirmation,
verification **13** ascertainment

identify 4 know **5** place **6** finger, verify **7** combine, pick out, specify **9** associate, designate, determine, recognize, single out **11** distinguish

identifying device 4 logo, mark, sign
5 badge **6** emblem, ensign, symbol **8**
insignia, logotype

identity 4 name, self **6** accord **7** harmony, oneness, rapport **9** unanimity
11 delineation, duplication, personality **13** individuality **15** differentiation,
distinctiveness

ideology 5 dogma, ethos **6** ideals, theory **7** program **8** doctrine **9** rationale
10 principles

Ides of March, The
author: 14 Thornton Wilder

id est 6 that is
abbreviation: 2 ie

idiocy 5 folly **6** lunacy **7** fatuity, inanity, madness, suicide **8** insanity **9** absurdity, asininity, cretinism, mongol-
ism, stupidity **11** foolishness **13**
foolhardiness, senselessness

idiom 5 argot, lingo, slang **6** brogue,
jargon, patois, phrase, speech **7** dialect **8** language, localism, parlance **10**
vernacular **13** colloquialism

idiomatic 6 common **8** informal, ordinary **10** vernacular **14** conversational

idiosyncrasy 3 tic **5** quirk **6** oddity **7**
anomaly **9** mannerism **11** distinction,
peculiarity **12** eccentricity

idiot 3 ass **4** boob, dolt, dope, fool,
jerk **5** cluck, dummy, dunce, moron,
ninny **6** cretin, dimwit, nitwit **7** half-
wit **8** dumbbell, numskull **9** blockhead, numbskull, simpleton **10** nincompoop

Idiot, The
author: 16 Fyodor Dostoevsky
character: 7 Myshkin **11** Mme
Epanchin **14** Aglaya Epanchin, Par-
fen Rogozhin **16** Natasya Filipovna
19 Ganya Ardalionovitch **22** Prince
Lef Nicolaievitch

idiotic 5 crazy, dopey, nutty **6** absurd,
addled, stupid **7** asinine, doltish, foolish, moronic **9** foolhardy, imbecilic,
senseless **10** half-witted, irrational, ridiculous **12** feebleminded **13** rattlebrained

I direct
Latin: 6 dirigo
motto of: 5 Maine

idle 4 laze, lazy, loaf, vain **5** empty, inert, petty, vapid, waste, while **6**
drowsy, fallow, futile, otiose, putter,
torpid, unused **7** aimless, fritter, jobless, languid, trivial, useless, wait out
8 baseless, bootless, fool away, inactive, indolent, listless, slothful, sluggish, trifling **9** at leisure, enervated,
fruitless, lethargic, out of work, pointless, somnolent, valueless, worthless
10 not working, unemployed, unoccupied **11** unimportant **12** unproductive
15 unsubstantiated

idleness 5 sloth **7** inertia **8** laziness,
lethargy **9** indolence **10** inactivity **11**
joblessness, languidness **12** sluggishness, unemployment
French: 8 flanerie

idler 3 bum **6** loafer **7** drifter, vagrant
10 ne'er-do-well
French: 7 flaneur

idol 4 hero, icon **5** relic **6** effigy, statue
7 darling **8** artifact **9** superstar **10**
simulacrum, golden calf **11** graven
image, inspiration

idolatry 5 mania **7** madness, passion,
worship **8** devotion **9** adoration, obsession **10** veneration **11** idolization,
infatuation **12** image worship **13** preoccupation

idolization 7 worship **9** adulation, reverence **10** exaltation, veneration

idolize 5 adore, deify, honor, prize **6**
admire, revere **7** worship **8** treasure,
venerate **9** reverence **11** apotheosize

Idomeneo, re di Creta
also: 20 Idomeneus King of Crete
opera by: 6 Mozart
character: 4 Ilia **7** Electra **8** Ida-
mante, Poseidon

Idomeneus
 king of: 5 Crete
 father: 9 Deucalion
I don't know what
 French: 12 je ne sais quoi
I Dream of Jeannie
 character: 7 Jeannie 9 Dr Bellows 10 (Captain) Tony Nelson 11 Gen Peterson, (Captain) Roger Healey 13 Amanda Bellows
 cast: 9 Bill Daily 11 Barbara Eden, Hayden Rorke, Larry Hagman 13 Barton MacLane, Emmaline Henry
 Tony's job: 9 astronaut
idyllic 6 rustic, sylvan 7 bucolic 8 arcadian, pastoral, peaceful, romantic 9 unspoiled
Idylls of the King, The
 author: 18 Alfred Lord Tennyson
 based on story of: 10 King Arthur
if 2 an 6 though 7 whether 8 although, provided 9 condition, supposing 10 even though 11 stipulation, supposition
iffy 4 moot 5 risky 6 chancy, unsure 7 dubious, erratic 8 arguable, doubtful 9 debatable, uncertain, undecided, unsettled, whimsical 10 capricious, disputable, unresolved 11 conjectural, speculative 12 questionable 13 problematical, unpredictable
if you please
 French: 12 s'il vous plait
ignitable 8 burnable 9 flammable 10 combustive, incendiary 11 combustible, inflammable 13 conflagrative
ignite 4 burn, fire 5 blaze, flame, light 6 blow up, kindle 7 explode, inflame 8 catch fire, touch off 9 catch fire, set fire to, set on fire 11 catch on fire
ignoble 3 low 4 base, foul, mean, vile 6 craven 7 debased, heinous 8 cowardly, degraded, depraved, indecent, infamous, inferior, shameful, unworthy 9 dastardly, nefarious 10 degenerate, despicable 11 disgraceful 12 contemptible, dishonorable 13 discreditable, pusillanimous 14 unconscionable
ignominious 3 low 5 sorry 6 abject 8 grievous, shameful, wretched 9 degrading 10 despicable, inglorious, unbearable 11 disgraceful, humiliating 12 dishonorable, disreputable 13 discreditable
ignominy 5 shame 6 infamy 8 contempt, disgrace, dishonor 11 degradation, humiliation
ignoramus 4 fool 5 dunce 6 nitwit 7 low-brow 8 numskull 9 numbskull, simpleton 10 illiterate 11 know-nothing
ignorance 9 confusion 10 illiteracy 11 unawareness 12 backwardness 13 obliviousness, unfamiliarity 15 unenlightenment

ignorant 4 dumb 5 naive 6 stupid 7 asinine, blind to, fatuous, shallow, unaware 8 innocent, untaught 9 in the dark, unknowing, unlearned, untrained, untutored, unworldly 10 illiterate, uneducated, uninformed, unlettered, unschooled 11 insensitive, uncognizant 12 unperceptive 13 irresponsible, unenlightened, unintelligent 15 unknowledgeable
ignore 4 omit, skip, snub 5 scorn 6 eschew, slight 7 neglect 8 overlook, pass over 9 disregard
Igraine
 character in: 16 Arthurian romance
 son: 6 Arthur
 by: 14 Uther Pendragon
Iguanodon
 type: 8 dinosaur 10 ornithopod
 means: 11 iguana tooth
 found by: 13 Gideon Mantell
 location: 6 Africa, Europe, Sussex 7 Belgium, England
 period: 10 Cretaceous
 characteristic: 10 duck-billed
ikebana
 Japanese: 21 art of arranging flowers
Ile de France see 9 Mauritius
Ilha Formosa see 6 Taiwan
Iliad, The
 author: 5 Homer
 character: 5 Paris, Priam 6 Hector 8 Achilles, Menelaus 9 Agamemnon, Patroclus 11 Helen of Troy
 subject: 9 Trojan War
Iliniwek see 8 Illinois
Ilion
 Greek name for: 11 ancient Troy
Ilium
 Latin name for: 11 ancient Troy
ill, ills 3 woe 4 evil, foul, harm, sick, vile 5 abuse, cross, no way, surly, trial 6 ailing, damage, hardly, injury, laid up, malady, malice, nowise, plague, poorly, sickly, sorrow, unkind, unwell, wicked 7 ailment, cruelty, disease, failing, harmful, invalid, not well, ominous, outrage, peevish, trouble, unlucky, unsound 8 diseased, mischief, scarcely, sinister, vengeful 9 afflicted, complaint, infirmity, malicious, unhealthy 10 affliction, disturbing, foreboding, indisposed, misfortune, wickedness 11 abomination, acrimonious, malefaction, threatening, unfavorable 12 inauspicious, unpropitious 15 under the weather
ill-advised 4 dumb, rash 5 hasty, silly 6 myopic, stupid, unwise 7 foolish 9 foolhardy, ill-judged, impolitic, imprudent, misguided, senseless 10 indiscreet, unthinking 11 injudicious 12 shortsighted 13 ill-considered, irresponsible
ill-at-ease 3 shy 4 edgy 6 on edge, uneasy 7 abashed, fidgety, nervous 8 bothered, troubled 9 disturbed, non-

plused, perturbed 10 disquieted, nonplussed 11 discomfited, discomposed, embarrassed 12 disconcerted 13 self-conscious, uncomfortable 15 discountenanced
ill-boding 4 dire 7 ominous 9 ill-omened 11 apocalyptic 12 inauspicious
ill-bred 4 rude 5 crude 7 boorish, uncivil, uncouth 8 churlish, impolite 10 unmannerly 11 ill-mannered 12 discourteous
ill-defined 3 dim 4 hazy 5 faint, murky 6 blurry 7 blurred, clouded, shadowy 8 nebulous, obscured 10 indistinct
illegal 5 wrong 6 banned 7 illicit 8 criminal, not legal, outlawed, unlawful 9 felonious, forbidden 10 actionable, prohibited, proscribed 12 illegitimate, unauthorized, unsanctioned 13 against the law
illegible 7 unclear 8 obscured 9 scribbled 10 unreadable 14 indecipherable, undecipherable, unintelligible
illegitimate 7 bastard, illegal, illicit, lawless, natural 8 baseborn, improper, unlawful 10 prohibited 11 misbegotten, unwarranted 12 unauthorized, unsanctioned
ill-fated 6 doomed, jinxed 7 hapless, unlucky 8 blighted, luckless 9 ill-omened 10 ill-starred
ill-favored 4 ugly 5 plain 6 homely 8 unlovely 9 repulsive, unsightly 12 disagreeable, unattractive
ill-fortune 6 mishap 7 bad luck 8 calamity, disaster, hardship 9 adversity 10 misfortune 11 catastrophe
ill health 6 malady 7 ailment, disease, illness 8 sickness 9 infirmity
ill-humored 5 sulky, testy 6 crabby, grumpy, sullen 7 grouchy 10 in a bad mood, unfriendly, unsociable
illiberal 5 petty, small 6 biased, narrow 7 bigoted 9 hidebound 10 brassbound, intolerant, prejudiced, ungenerous 11 opinionated, small-minded 12 narrow-minded, short-sighted
illicit 7 illegal, lawless 8 criminal, improper, not legal, unlawful 9 felonious 10 prohibited 11 black-market, clandestine 12 illegitimate, not permitted, unauthorized 13 against the law, impermissible 15 under-the-counter
Illinois
 abbreviation: 2 IL 3 Ill
 nickname: 4 Tall 6 Sucker 7 Prairie 13 Land of Lincoln
 capital: 11 Springfield
 largest city: 7 Chicago
 others: 4 Pana 5 Alton, Cairo, Elgin, Flora, Olney, Pekin 6 Albion, Berwyn, Canton, Herrin, Joliet, Peoria, Skokie 7 Batavia, Decatur, Genesco, Mendota, Nokomis 8 Evanston, Rockford, Waukegan 9 Centralia 10

Barrington **11** Bloomington
college: 4 Knox **5** Barat **6** Aurora, DePaul, Eureka, Loyola, Olivet, Quincy, Shimer **7** Bradley, Chicago, Wheaton **8** Millikin **9** Augustana **12** Northwestern **16** Illinois Wesleyan **23** Illinois Institute of Tech
explorer: 6 Joliet **7** Jolliet **9** Marquette
feature: 10 stockyards
  airport: 5 O'Hare **6** Midway
  museum: 18 Science and Industry
  seaway: 10 St Lawrence
  trail: 7 Lincoln
tribe: 3 Fox **4** Sauk **9** Kaskaskia
people: 9 Black Hawk, Jack Benny **10** Casey Jones, Jane Addams, Walt Disney **12** Carl Sandburg, William Daley **14** Adlai Stevenson **15** Ernest Hemingway **20** William Jennings Bryan
lake: 3 Fox **5** Grass **7** Calumet **8** Michigan, Pistakee
land rank: 12 twenty-fourth
mountain: 6 Ozarks
  highest point: 12 Charles Mound
physical feature:
  hills: 7 Shawnee
president: 14 Abraham Lincoln
river: 4 Ohio, Rock **5** Spoon **6** Wabash **7** Chicago, Elkhorn **8** Big Muddy, Illinois, Mackinaw, Sangamon **9** Kaskaskia **10** Des Plaines **11** Mississippi
state admission: 11 twenty-first
state bird: 8 cardinal
state flower: 6 violet
state motto: 29 State Sovereignty, National Union
state song: 8 Illinois
state tree: 7 burl oak **8** white oak
Illinois (Iliniwek)
  language family: 9 Algonkian **10** Algonquian
  tribe: 6 Peoria **7** Cahokia, Tamaroa **9** Kaskaskia, Moingwena **10** Michigamea
  location: 4 Iowa, Ohio **7** Indiana **8** Illinois, Michigan, Missouri **9** Wisconsin
  built: 12 Cahokia Mound
  murdered: 7 Pontiac
  related to: 5 Miami **6** Ojibwa **7** Ojibway
illiterate 7 witless **8** childish, ignorant, unversed **9** unlearned, untutored **10** amateurish, incoherent, uneducated, uninformed, unlettered, unreliable, unschooled **11** not educated, uninitiated, unscholarly **12** uninstructed **13** unenlightened, ungrammatical **15** unknowledgeable
ill-made 6 shoddy **7** awkward **8** deformed, inferior **9** makeshift, malformed **10** jerry-built, jury-rigged **15** misproportioned
ill-mannered 4 rude **5** crude **6** coarse **7** boorish, ill-bred, loutish, uncivil **8**

impolite **9** offensive, ungallant **10** ill-behaved, ungracious **12** discourteous **13** disrespectful
ill-natured 4 sour **5** cross, nasty, surly **6** bitter, cranky, malign **7** caustic, grouchy, peevish **8** captious, churlish, spiteful, venomous **9** crotchety, irascible, irritable, malignant, rancorous, splenetic **10** ill-humored, unfriendly **11** acrimonious, contentious, quarrelsome **12** antagonistic, cantankerous
illness 6 malady **7** ailment, disease **8** disorder, sickness **9** complaint, ill health, infirmity **10** affliction, disability, poor health **11** malfunction **13** indisposition
illogical 4 wild **5** crazy, dopey, nutty, silly, wacky **6** absurd, far-out, screwy **7** asinine, offbeat, unsound **9** erroneous, senseless **10** fallacious, irrational, off-the-wall, ridiculous **11** incongruent, incongruous, nonsensical, unreasoning **12** inconsistent, preposterous, unreasonable **13** contradictory
ill-omened 4 dire **7** adverse, ominous **9** ill-boding **11** apocalyptic, unfavorable **12** inauspicious, unpropitious
ill-smelling 4 foul, high, olid, rank **5** fetid, fusty **6** putrid, rancid, smelly, stinky, strong **7** reeking **8** stinking **10** malodorous
ill-starred 4 dire **5** fatal **6** tragic **7** adverse **8** ill-fated **10** calamitous, disastrous **11** unfortunate **12** catastrophic, inauspicious
ill-suited 5 inapt **8** mismated, unsuited **9** misjoined, unfitting **10** ill-adapted, ill-matched, malapropos, mismatched, unbecoming, unsuitable **11** incongruous, unbefitting, uncongenial **12** incompatible, inconsistent **13** inappropriate
ill-tempered 4 mean, rude, sour **5** angry, cross, harsh, nasty, testy **6** bitter, cranky, shirty **7** acerbic, furious, grouchy, peevish, waspish **8** choleric, churlish, petulant **9** crotchety, irascible, irritable **10** bad-natured, ill-humored, ill-natured, in a bad mood, unpleasant **11** acrimonious **12** cantankerous
ill-treatment 4 harm **5** abuse **6** ill-use, injury, misuse **7** cruelty **13** mortification
illuminate 5 edify, light **7** clarify, enhance, explain, light up **8** brighten, illumine, instruct, spell out **9** elucidate, enlighten, exemplify, irradiate, make clear **12** throw light on **13** cast light upon
illuminated 3 lit **5** lit up **6** bright **7** lighted **9** clarified, decorated, illumined **10** brightened, elucidated, irradiated
illumination 6 lights, wisdom **7** insight **8** lighting **9** education, knowledge **10** illumining, lighting up, per-

ception, revelation **11** edification, information, instruction, irradiation **13** comprehension, enlightenment
Illuminations, Les
  author: 13 Arthur Rimbaud
illumined 3 lit **7** lighted **8** luminous **11** illuminated
ill-use 4 harm, hurt **5** abuse **6** injure, misuse **7** assault, cruelty, harming **8** maltreat, mistreat **10** bodily harm **12** maltreatment, mistreatment
illusion 5 error, fancy **6** mirage, vagary, vision **7** caprice, chimera, fallacy **8** delusion, phantasm **9** deception, false idea, misbelief, semblance, unreality **10** apparition, false image, hocus-pocus, humbuggery, impression **11** false belief, fata morgana **13** hallucination, misconception, misimpression **15** misapprehension
illusive 5 false **6** unreal **7** phantom, seeming **8** apparent, chimeric, fanciful, fantastic, illusory **9** deceptive **10** ostensible **11** illusionary
illusory 4 sham **5** false **6** unreal **7** seeming **8** apparent, delusive, fanciful, illusive, spurious **9** deceptive, erroneous, imaginary **10** fallacious, misleading, ostensible **11** counterfeit, unrealistic **13** hallucinatory
illustrate 4 show **6** define **7** clarify, explain, picture, point up, portray **8** decorate, ornament **9** bring home, delineate, elucidate, emphasize, make clear, represent **10** illuminate **11** demonstrate **12** pictorialize, throw light on **16** make intelligible
illustration 5 image, plate **6** figure **7** drawing, example, picture **8** instance, specimen **9** portrayal **10** photograph **14** representation **15** exemplification
illustrious 5 famed, great, noted **6** famous **7** eminent, honored, notable **8** glorious, lustrous, peerless, renowned, splendid **9** acclaimed, brilliant, exemplary, matchless, prominent **10** celebrated **11** magnificent **13** distinguished
illustriousness 8 grandeur **9** greatness **11** distinction **12** magnificence
ill will 4 gall **5** anger, spite **6** animus, enmity, hatred, malice, rancor, spleen **7** dislike **8** acrimony, aversion, bad blood, loathing **9** animosity, antipathy, hostility **10** abhorrence, antagonism, bitterness, contention **11** malevolence **12** hard feelings, spitefulness
ill wind 7 bad luck **8** bad break, hard luck **9** adversity, mischance **10** misfortune
Illyrius
  father: 6 Cadmus
Ilmarinen
  origin: 7 Finnish
  form: 10 blacksmith
  hero in: 8 Kalevala

forged: 5 Sampo
Sampo's owner: 5 Louhi

I Love Lucy
  character: 9 Fred Mertz **10** Ethel
    Mertz **11** Little Ricky, Lucy Ricardo
    12 Ricky Ricardo
  cast: 9 Desi Arnaz **11** Lucille Ball,
    Vivian Vance **14** William Frawley
  Ricky's club: 7 Babaloo **9** Tropicana

Il Penseroso
  author: 10 John Milton
  companion piece: 8 L'Allegro

image 4 copy, icon, idea, idol **6** double, effigy, fetish, figure, memory, simile, statue, symbol, visage **7** concept, picture, replica **8** likeness, metaphor, portrait **9** depiction, duplicate, facsimile, mirroring, semblance **10** photograph, reflection, simulacrum **11** countenance, delineation, incarnation **12** recollection, reproduction **13** mental picture **14** figure of speech, representation

imaginable 8 feasible **9** thinkable **11** conceivable

imaginary 4 sham **5** fancy, phony **6** made-up, unreal **7** fancied, fiction, figment **8** delusion, fabulous, fanciful, illusion, illusory, invented, mythical, romantic **9** fantastic, figmental, legendary **10** factitious, fictitious **11** counterfeit, make-believe

imagination 5 fancy **7** cunning, thought **9** ingenuity, invention **10** astuteness, creativity, enterprise **12** creativeness **13** inventiveness **14** thoughtfulness **15** creative thought, resourcefulness

imaginative 6 clever **7** unusual **8** creative, inspired, original **9** ingenious, inventive **10** innovative **11** resourceful **12** enterprising **16** off the beaten path, out of the ordinary

imagine 5 fancy, guess, infer, judge **6** assume, gather **7** believe, dream up, picture, presume, pretend, project, suppose, surmise, suspect **8** conceive, envisage, envision **9** fantasize, visualize **10** conjecture

imbecile 3 ass **4** dolt, dope, fool, jerk **5** dummy, dunce, idiot, moron, ninny **6** nitwit **7** dingbat **8** dumbbell **9** blockhead, simpleton **10** nincompoop

imbecilic 4 dumb **5** inane, silly **6** absurd, stupid **7** asinine, foolish **8** careless, mindless **11** thoughtless

imbecility 6 idiocy **8** dullness, dumbness **9** asininity, stupidity, thickness **16** simplemindedness

imbibe 4 swig, tope **5** drink, quaff **6** guzzle, ingest, tipple **7** consume, partake, swallow **8** chugalug, toss down, wash down

imbiber 3 sot **4** wino **5** drunk, toper **7** drinker, tippler **8** consumer, drunkard, ingester

imbroglio 3 row **4** fray **5** brawl, broil,

clash, fight, melee, scrap **6** fracas, ruckus, rumpus, uproar **7** scuffle **8** argument **9** confusion **11** altercation, embroilment **12** entanglement **13** embarrassment

imbue 4 fill, fire, tint **5** bathe, color, endow, steep, tinge **6** arouse, infuse **7** animate, impress, ingrain, inspire, instill, pervade, suffuse **8** permeate, tincture **9** inculcate

Imhotep
  father: 4 Ptah
  mother: 7 Sekhmet
  position: 6 scribe, vizier, writer **9** architect, physician
  architect of pyramid: 8 Sakkarah

imitate 3 ape **4** copy, mime **5** mimic **6** mirror, parody, parrot **7** emulate, pass for **8** look like, simulate **9** duplicate, represent **10** caricature **11** counterfeit, impersonate

imitation 4 fake, mock, sham **5** aping, phony **6** ersatz, parody **7** man-made, mimicry, takeoff **8** travesty **9** burlesque, facsimile, semblance, simulated, synthetic **10** adaptation, artificial, caricature, impression, similarity, simulation **11** counterfeit, duplication, make-believe **12** reproduction **13** impersonation **14** representation

Imitation of Christ, The
  author: 13 Thomas a Kempis

immaculate 4 pure **5** clean, ideal **6** chaste, intact, virgin **7** perfect, saintly, sinless **8** flawless, innocent, spotless, unsoiled, virginal, virtuous **9** faultless, guiltless, shipshape, stainless, unstained, unsullied **11** spic and span, untarnished **13** above reproach, unimpeachable **14** irreproachable **15** unexceptionable

immanent 6 inborn, inbred, innate **7** natural **8** inherent **9** ingrained, intrinsic **10** congenital, deep-rooted, deepseated, indigenous, indwelling **11** instinctive, instinctual

Immanuel 7 Messiah **11** Jesus Christ
  means: 9 God with us

immaterial 7 ghostly, shadowy, trivial **8** bodiless, ethereal, mystical, noumenal, spectral, trifling, unbodied **9** spiritual, unearthly **10** evanescent, extraneous, impalpable, intangible, irrelevant, of no moment **11** disembodied, incorporeal, not relevant, unimportant **12** extramundane, extrasensory **13** insignificant, insubstantial, unsubstantial **14** of no importance **15** inconsequential, of little account

immature 5 green, young **6** callow, unripe **7** babyish, kiddish, puerile **8** childish, juvenile, unformed, youthful **9** embryonic, half-grown, infantile, not mature, pubescent **10** unfinished, unmellowed **11** out of season, rudimentary, undeveloped **16** wet behind the ears

immeasurable 7 endless, immense **8** infinite **9** boundless, limitless, unbounded, unlimited **10** fathomless **11** illimitable, inestimable, measureless, never-ending **12** incalculable, interminable, unfathomable **13** inexhaustible

immediate 4 near, next, nigh **5** close, hasty, local, swift **6** abrupt, nearby, prompt, recent, speedy, sudden **7** express, instant, nearest **8** adjacent, punctual **9** proximate, undelayed **10** contiguous **13** instantaneous

immediately 3 now **4** ASAP, stat **9** instantly, right away **10** this minute **12** without delay
  French: 11 tout de suite

immemorial 5 olden **7** ageless, ancient **8** dateless, hallowed, timeless **9** ancestral, legendary, venerable **11** time-honored **12** long-standing, mythological **15** long-established

immense 4 huge, vast **5** great **7** mammoth, massive **8** colossal, enormous, gigantic **9** extensive, monstrous **10** prodigious, stupendous, tremendous **11** measureless **14** Brobdingnagian

immensity 8 enormity, hugeness, vastness **9** largeness **12** enormousness

immerse 3 dip **4** duck, dunk, sink, soak **5** bathe, douse, lower, steep **6** absorb, drench, engage, occupy, plunge **7** engross **8** submerge

immerse briefly 3 dip **4** dunk

immersion 7 bathing, dunking **8** drowning **10** absorption, submersion **11** engrossment, involvement, submergence **13** concentration, preoccupation

immigrant 5 alien **7** migrant, settler **8** colonist, newcomer **9** foreigner, nonnative

immigrate 6 move to, settle **7** migrate **8** colonize

imminent 4 near **7** looming **8** menacing, perilous **9** immediate, impending **10** near at hand **11** approaching, close at hand, threatening

immobile 4 fast **5** fixed, quiet, rigid, stiff, still **6** at rest, laid up, rooted, secure, stable, static **7** riveted **9** immovable, not moving, quiescent, steadfast **10** motionless, stationary, stock-still **11** unbudgeable **13** incapacitated

immobilize 3 fix, set **4** stud **6** disarm, freeze, splint **7** disable **8** paralyze, transfix **12** incapacitate

immoderate 5 undue **7** extreme **8** whopping **9** excessive, unbridled **10** exorbitant, gargantuan, inordinate, prodigious **11** extravagant, intemperate, uncalled-for **12** unreasonable, unrestrained **14** unconscionable

immoderation 6 excess **10** debauchery **11** dissipation, prodigality, unrestraint **12** extravagance, intemperance, recklessness **13** excessiveness **14** prodigiousness

immodest 4 lewd, vain **5** gross, loose **6** brazen, coarse, risque, wanton **7** pompous **8** boastful, braggart, indecent, inflated, unchaste **9** bombastic, conceited, shameless **10** indecorous, indelicate, peacockish, suggestive **11** exaggerated, pretentious **12** self-centered

immoral 4 evil, lewd **5** dirty, wrong **6** sinful, wicked **7** corrupt, heinous, obscene, raunchy, vicious **8** depraved, indecent, infamous, prurient **9** debauched, dissolute, nefarious, salacious, unethical **10** dissipated, iniquitous, licentious, profligate **12** pornographic, unprincipled

Immoralist, The
   author: **9** Andre Gide

immorality 3 sin **4** evil **9** decadence, depravity, indecency, obscenity, prurience **10** corruption, debasement, degeneracy, sinfulness **13** salaciousness

immortal 3 god **6** divine **7** abiding, eternal, undying **8** enduring **9** deathless **11** everlasting **12** imperishable

Immortals 6 giants, greats, titans **7** the gods **8** demigods **13** all-time greats
   Greek/Roman: **8** pantheon

immovable 3 icy, set **4** cold, fast **5** fixed **6** dogged, secure, steely, stolid **7** adamant, settled **8** detached, fastened, immobile, obdurate, resolute, stubborn **9** heartless, impassive, unfeeling **10** inexorable, inflexible, stationary, unbendable **11** coldhearted, unbudgeable **12** unchangeable **13** unimpressible, unsympathetic **16** unimpressionable

immune 4 free, safe **5** clear **6** exempt **9** protected, resistant **12** invulnerable **13** unsusceptible

immunity 7 freedom **9** exemption **10** resistance **16** unsusceptibility

immure 3 hem, pen **4** cage, coop, jail, wall **6** entomb, intern, wall in, wall up **7** confine, enclose, seclude **8** cloister, imprison **11** incarcerate

immutability 9 endurance, stability **14** changelessness

immutable 4 firm **5** fixed, solid **6** stable **7** lasting **8** constant, enduring **9** permanent, unaltered, unvarying **10** changeless, inflexible, unchanging **11** unalterable **12** unchangeable, unmodifiable **14** intransmutable **16** incontrovertible

Imogen
   character in: **9** Cymbeline
   author: **11** Shakespeare

imp 3 elf **4** brat **5** demon, devil, gnome, pixie, scamp **6** goblin, hoyden, rascal, sprite, urchin **7** upstart **9** hobgoblin **10** evil spirit, leprechaun

impact 4 jolt **5** brunt, crash, force, shock, smash **6** burden, effect, thrust **7** contact **9** collision, influence **10** concussion **11** implication **12** repercussion

impair 3 mar **4** harm, hurt **6** damage, hinder, injure, lessen, reduce, weaken, worsen **7** cripple, subvert, vitiate **8** decrease, enervate, enfeeble, undercut **10** debilitate **11** detract from

impaired 6 broken, faulty, flawed **7** damaged **9** defective, deficient, imperfect

impairment 4 flaw, harm **5** fault **6** damage, defect, injury, malady **7** ailment, illness **8** debility, disorder, handicap, sickness, weakness **9** detriment, hindrance, infirmity **10** disability, impediment, inadequacy **12** debilitation

impale 3 fix, pin **4** gore, stab, tack **5** affix, stick **8** transfix **10** run through

impart 4 give, lend, tell **5** grant, offer, share **6** accord, afford, pass on, relate, render, report, reveal **7** confide, consign, deliver, divulge, mention **8** bestow on, confer on, disclose, dispense **9** make known **10** contribute **11** communicate

impartial 4 fair, just **7** neutral **8** detached, unbiased **9** equitable, objective **10** evenhanded, fair-minded, open-minded **11** nonpartisan **12** unprejudiced **13** disinterested, dispassionate

impartiality 7 justice **8** equality, fair play, fairness **10** detachment, neutrality **17** objectivity

impasse 4 snag **7** dead end, dilemma **8** cul-de-sac, deadlock, quandary, standoff **9** stalemate **10** blind alley, bottleneck, standstill **11** predicament

impassioned 5 eager, fiery **6** ardent, heated **7** earnest, excited, fervent, intense, rousing, zealous **8** animated, forceful, inspired, stirring

impassive 4 calm, cool **5** aloof, stony **6** sedate, stolid **7** stoical, unmoved **8** reserved **9** apathetic, untouched **10** impervious, insensible, phlegmatic **11** emotionless, indifferent, inscrutable, unemotional, unperturbed **13** dispassionate, imperturbable, unimpressible **16** unimpressionable

impassiveness 8 coldness **9** aloofness, stolidity **12** indifference **15** emotionlessness

impassivity 6 apathy **8** coolness, stoicism **9** aloofness, stolidity **10** dispassion **15** emotionlessness **16** imperturbability

impatient 4 edgy **5** fussy, hasty, itchy, rabid, tense, testy **6** ardent, touchy **7** annoyed, anxious, brusque, hurried, nervous, peevish, restive **8** agitated, feverish, restless **9** excitable, irascible,

irritable, irritated **10** high-strung, intolerant, passionate **12** enthusiastic

impeach 4 slur **6** accuse, assail, attack, charge, impugn, indict **7** arraign, slander **8** badmouth, belittle, question **9** challenge, discredit, disparage, inculpate **11** incriminate **16** call into question

impeccable 7 perfect **8** flawless **9** blameless, excellent, faultless **10** immaculate **11** unblemished **12** irreprovable, unassailable **13** unimpeachable **14** irreproachable **15** unexceptionable

impecunious 4 poor **5** broke, needy **6** hard-up **7** pinched **8** bankrupt, indigent **9** destitute, insolvent, penniless **10** down-and-out, straitened **12** impoverished **15** poverty-stricken

impede 5 block, check, delay, deter, stall **6** arrest, halter, hamper, hinder, retard, stymie, thwart **7** disrupt, inhibit **8** hold back, obstruct, slow down **9** frustrate, interrupt, sidetrack **13** interfere with

impediment 4 flaw **5** block, delay **6** defect **7** barrier **8** blockage, drawback, handicap, obstacle **9** deformity, hindrance **10** detraction **11** obstruction **12** interference **14** stumbling block

impedimenta 4 gear **7** baggage **9** equipment **13** accoutrements, paraphernalia

impel 4 goad, prod, push, spur, urge **5** drive, force **6** compel, incite, induce, prompt **7** require **8** motivate **9** constrain, stimulate **11** necessitate

impend 4 brew, hang, loom **5** hover, lower **6** menace **8** approach, draw near, overhang, threaten

impending 4 near **6** coming **7** brewing, looming **8** imminent, menacing, oncoming **9** immediate **11** approaching, forthcoming, threatening

impenetrable 5 dense, solid, thick **6** sealed **7** elusive, obscure **8** puzzling **9** insoluble **10** impassable, impervious, insensible, inviolable, mysterious, unpalpable **11** inscrutable, unenterable **12** inaccessible, inexplicable, invulnerable, unfathomable **16** incomprehensible

impenitent 4 lost **6** inured **7** callous, defiant **8** hardened, obdurate **9** unashamed **10** uncontrite **11** remorseless, unrepentant, unrepenting **12** incorrigible, unapologetic **13** irreclaimable

imperative 6 urgent **7** crucial, needful **8** critical, pressing **9** essential, mandatory, necessary, requisite **10** compulsory, obligatory **11** unavoidable

imperceptible 5 minor, scant, small **6** hidden, minute, slight, subtle **7** minimal **8** academic **10** indistinct **12** undetectable, unnoticeable **13** infinitesimal, insignificant, unappreciable, unperceivable **14** inconsiderable

imperceptive 5 blind 9 unfeeling 11 insensitive, unobservant 12 inpercipient, unperceptive 13 unsympathetic

imperfect 6 faulty, flawed 8 deformed, fallible, impaired 9 blemished, defective

imperfection 4 flaw 5 fault 6 defect 7 blemish 8 weakness 9 deformity 10 faultiness, impairment, inadequacy 11 fallibility, shortcoming 13 insufficiency 14 incompleteness

imperial 5 bossy 6 feudal, lordly 8 despotic 9 arbitrary, imperious 10 autocratic, high-handed, peremptory, repressive, tyrannical 11 dictatorial, domineering, magisterial, overbearing 13 authoritarian

Imperial Presidency, The
author: 20 Arthur M Schlesinger Jr

imperil 4 risk 6 chance, expose, gamble, hazard 8 endanger 10 compromise, jeopardize 13 put in jeopardy

imperious 5 bossy, lofty 6 lordly 7 haughty 8 arrogant, despotic, imperial 10 autocratic, commanding, peremptory, tyrannical 11 dictatorial, domineering, overbearing 13 high-and-mighty

imperiousness 9 arrogance, loftiness 11 haughtiness

imperishable 6 stable 7 durable, lasting 14 indestructible

imperium 4 rule 5 realm 6 domain, empire 8 dominion 11 sovereignty

impermanent 7 passing 8 fleeting, fugitive, not fixed, unstable 9 ephemeral, temporary, transient 10 evanescent, transitory, unenduring

impermeable 5 dense, solid, tight 6 opaque 9 nonporous 10 impervious, waterproof

impersonal 4 dead 6 remote 7 general, inhuman, neutral 8 detached, lifeless, soulless 9 impartial, impassive, inanimate, inorganic, objective 10 spiritless 11 perfunctory 13 disinterested, dispassionate

impersonate 3 ape 4 copy, mime 5 mimic 6 pose as 7 imitate, portray 9 personify, represent 11 pretend to be 12 masquerade as

impertinence 4 sass 5 cheek, sauce 7 affront 8 audacity, boldness, rudeness 9 freshness, impudence, insolence, sauciness 10 cheekiness, disrespect, effrontery, incivility 11 irrelevance 17 disrespectfulness, inappropriateness

impertinent 4 rude 5 fresh, surly 6 brassy, brazen, smarty 7 uncivil 8 arrogant, impudent, insolent 9 extrinsic, insulting, unrelated 10 extraneous, immaterial, irrelevant, not germane, peremptory, unmannerly 11 unimportant 12 discourteous, presumptuous 13 disrespectful, inappropriate 14 beside the point

imperturbability 5 poise 6 aplomb 8 calmness, coolness 9 composure, sangfroid 10 equanimity, steadiness 11 self-control, tranquility 12 tranquillity 14 presence of mind, self-possession

imperturbable 4 calm, cool 6 sedate, serene 8 composed 9 collected, impassive, unanxious, unfazable, unruffled 10 impervious 11 levelheaded, undisturbed, unexcitable, unflappable, unflustered 13 dispassionate, unsusceptible

impervious 6 closed 8 immune to 11 impermeable 12 impenetrable, inaccessible, invulnerable 14 unapproachable

impetuosity 8 rashness 11 spontaneity, unrestraint 12 recklessness 13 impulsiveness 14 capriciousness

impetuous 4 rash 5 hasty 6 abrupt, stormy 7 rampant, violent 8 forcible, headlong, vehement 9 impulsive 10 capricious, inexorable, relentless, unexpected 11 precipitate 14 unpremeditated

impetus 4 prod, push, spur 5 boost, drive, force, start 6 motive 7 impulse 8 momentum, stimulus 9 impulsion, incentive 10 motivation, propulsion 11 moving force, stimulation

impiety 9 blasphemy, sacrilege 10 disrespect, irreligion 11 irreverence, ungodliness

impinge 7 intrude, obtrude, violate 8 encroach, infringe, trespass 10 transgress

impious 7 godless, immoral, profane, ungodly 8 apostate, renegade 9 perverted 10 iniquitous, irreverent 11 blasphemous, irreligious 12 iconoclastic, sacrilegious 13 disrespectful

impiousness 7 impiety 9 blasphemy, sacrilege 10 disrespect 11 irreverence, ungodliness

impish 5 elfin 7 implike, puckish, roguish 8 prankish, rascally, sportive 11 mischievous

implacable 10 inexorable, inflexible, relentless, unamenable 11 intractable, unrelenting 12 unappeasable, unpacifiable 14 irreconcilable, uncompromising

implant 3 fix, set, sow 4 root 5 embed, graft, imbed, inlay, teach 6 infuse, insert 7 impress, instill 8 entrench 9 establish, inculcate 10 impregnate

implausible 8 doubtful, unlikely 9 illogical, senseless 10 far-fetched, improbable, incredible, outrageous, ridiculous 12 preposterous, unbelievable, unreasonable 13 inconceivable

implement 4 tool 5 begin, enact, piece, start 6 device 7 achieve, article, fulfill, realize, utensil 8 activate, carry out 9 apparatus, appliance, equip-

ment, materials 10 accomplish, bring about, instrument 11 set in motion 13 put into effect

implicate 7 connect, embroil, ensnare, involve 8 entangle 9 associate, inculpate 11 incriminate

implication 6 effect 7 outcome 8 innuendo, overtone 9 inference 10 connection, intimation, suggestion 11 association, connotation, consequence, insinuation, involvement 12 entanglement, ramification, significance

implicit 5 total 6 hinted, innate 7 certain, implied, staunch 8 absolute, complete, inferred, inherent, profound, resolute 9 deducible, steadfast, suggested 10 understood, unreserved, unshakable 13 unquestioning

implied 5 tacit 7 oblique 8 indirect 9 implicity, indicated

implode 11 burst inward 17 compress violently

implore 3 beg 4 urge 6 obtest 7 beseech, entreat 9 importune, plead with 10 supplicate

imply 4 hint, mean 6 denote 7 bespeak, betoken, connote, presume, signify, suggest 8 evidence, indicate, intimate 9 insinuate 10 presuppose

impolite 4 rude 7 ill-bred, uncivil 9 impolitic, unfitting, ungenteel, unrefined 10 undecorous, unmannerly 12 discourteous 13 disrespectful, inconsiderate

impoliteness 8 rudeness 10 bad manners, incivility 11 boorishness, discourtesy

import 6 burden, moment, thrust 7 meaning 9 overtones 10 importance 11 connotation, implication 12 ramification, significance

importance 4 rank 5 value, worth 6 esteem, import, moment, repute, weight 7 stature 8 eminence, position 9 influence, relevance 11 consequence, seriousness, weightiness 12 significance 13 essentialness, momentousness

Importance of Being Earnest, The
author: 10 Oscar Wilde
character: 12 Cecily Cardew, Jack Worthing, Letitia Prism 16 Gwendolen Fairfax 17 Algernon Moncrieff (Algy) 20 Lady Augusta Bracknell 21 Reverend Canon Chasuble

important 5 great, major 7 leading, notable, seminal, serious, weighty 8 creative, esteemed, foremost, original 9 momentous, prominent 10 imperative, meaningful, preeminent, remarkable 11 distinctive, influential, significant 13 consequential

imported 5 alien 6 exotic 7 foreign 9 not native

importunate 7 begging 8 pleading 9

imploring **10** entreating, persistent **11** troublesome **12** supplicating

importune 3 beg, sue **4** pray **5** plead **6** adjure, exhort **7** beseech, entreat, implore **8** appeal to, petition **10** supplicate

importunity 4 plea **6** appeal **7** request **8** entreaty, petition **12** supplication

impose 3 set **4** levy **5** apply, enact, foist, force, lay on **6** peddle, slap on **7** command, dictate, inflict, palm off, place on **9** establish, institute, introduce, prescribe **10** thrust upon

impose upon 5 annoy **6** bother, illuse **8** ill-treat, maltreat, mistreat **15** take advantage of

imposing 5 grand, lofty **7** massive, stately **8** majestic, striking, towering **10** commanding, impressive, monumental **11** outstanding **12** aweinspiring

imposition 5 abuse **6** burden, ill use **8** foisting **10** obligation **15** taking advantage

impossible 8 stubborn **9** insoluble **10** unbearable, unsolvable, unyielding **11** intolerable, intractable, not possible **12** insufferable, intransigent, unachievable, unanswerable, unattainable, unimaginable, unmanageable **13** inconceivable **16** out of the question

impost 3 fee, tax **4** duty, fine, toll **6** charge, excise, tariff **10** assessment

impostor 4 sham **5** cheat, duper, fraud, phony, quack **6** con man **7** bluffer, shammer **8** deceiver **9** charlatan, defrauder, pretender, trickster **10** dissembler, mountebank **11** counterfeit, flimflam man, masquerader, pettifogger **12** impersonator

imposture 4 fake, hoax, play, ruse, sham **5** cheat, fraud, trick **6** deceit, humbug **7** forgery, swindle **8** artifice, delusion, pretense, quackery **9** deception, falsehood, imitation **10** pretension **11** charlatanry, counterfeit, fraudulence **12** charlatanism **13** impersonation, mountebankery

impotence 8 weakness **9** paralysis **10** disability, incapacity, inefficacy **12** helplessness **13** powerlessness **14** ineffectuality **15** ineffectiveness

impotent 4 weak **5** frail **6** feeble **7** hapless **8** disabled, feckless, helpless **9** paralyzed, powerless **11** ineffective

impound 3 pen **4** cage **5** pen in, seize **6** coop up, encage, lock up, shut in **7** confine **13** hold in custody

impoverish 4 bust, ruin **5** break, drain **6** beggar, pauper, reduce **7** deplete, exhaust **8** bankrupt, make poor **9** pauperize **18** send to the poorhouse

impoverished 4 poor **6** abject, barren, bereft, effete, used up **7** drained, sterile, wanting, worn out **8** depleted, indigent, wiped out **9** destitute, ex-

hausted **10** down-and-out, pauperized **11** impecunious **12** unproductive, without means

impractical 6 sloppy, unwise **8** careless, quixotic, romantic **10** looseended, starry-eyed **11** unrealistic **12** disorganized **13** helter-skelter, unintelligent

imprecation 5 curse **8** anathema **11** malediction

impregnable 6 mighty, potent, strong, sturdy **8** powerful **10** invincible **12** invulnerable, unassailable, unattackable **13** unconquerable

impregnate 3 wet **4** soak **5** steep **6** dampen, drench, imbrue, infuse **7** moisten, suffuse **8** fructify, inundate, permeate, saturate **9** fecundate, fertilize **10** inseminate

impresario 7 manager, sponsor **8** director **9** conductor, organizer **12** entrepreneur

impress 4 grab, move, stir, sway **5** reach, touch **6** affect, excite, sink in, strike **8** bedazzle **9** electrify, influence, overpower, overwhelm

impression 4 idea, mark, mold, view **5** hunch, stamp, trace, track **6** belief, effect, impact, notion **7** contour, feeling, impress, imprint, opinion, outline, surmise **9** influence, reception, sensation **10** conviction **11** indentation **13** understanding

impressionable 8 gullible, passible, sentient **9** affective, receptive **10** vulnerable **11** suggestible

impressive 5 grand **6** august, moving **8** exciting, imposing, majestic, striking **9** memorable, thrilling **11** magnificent, outstanding **12** awe-inspiring, overpowering, soul-stirring **13** unforgettable

imprimis 15 in the first place

imprint 3 fix **4** etch, mark, sign **5** infix, press, stamp, title **6** indent **7** engrave, impress **8** inscribe **9** engraving **10** depression, impression **11** indentation

imprison 3 pen **4** jail **6** coop up, engage, entomb, immure, lock up **7** confine, fence in, impound, shackle **8** restrain **9** constrain **11** hold captive, incarcerate

improbable 8 doubtful, unlikely **9** illogical **11** implausible **12** unreasonable **13** unforeseeable

improbable solution in a play's plot
Latin: **13** deus ex machina

impromptu 6 sudden **7** offhand **9** impulsive, makeshift, on the spot **10** improvised, off the cuff, unexpected, unprepared **11** spontaneous, unrehearsed **14** extemporaneous, unpremeditated, without warning **15** spur-of-the-moment **16** extemporane-

ously, on a moment's notice **19** off the top of one's head

improper 4 lewd **5** inapt, unfit **8** indecent, off-color, unseemly **9** ill-suited, irregular **10** indecorous, malapropos, out of place, suggestive, unbecoming, unsuitable **12** inharmonious **13** inappropriate, unconformable
French: 5 outre

impropriety 5 gaffe **7** blunder, faux pas **9** gaucherie, indecorum, vulgarity **10** bad manners **11** boorishness **12** impoliteness, indiscretion

improve 4 help **5** rally **6** better, enrich, repair **7** correct, develop, enhance **9** cultivate **10** ameliorate, recuperate

improvement 4 gain **6** reform, repair **7** advance, upswing **8** additive, progress **9** amendment **10** betterment, emendation, refinement **11** advancement, enhancement, reclamation **12** amelioration **14** reconstruction

improvidence 10 imprudence **11** prodigality **12** extravagance, wastefulness **13** shiftlessness **16** shortsightedness

improvident 6 lavish **8** prodigal, reckless, wasteful **9** imprudent, negligent, unthrifty **10** thriftless **11** extravagant, spendthrift **12** shortsighted **14** unparsimonious

improvise 5 ad-lib **6** make up, wing it **11** extemporize

improvised 5 ad-lib **7** devised, offhand **8** invented **9** concocted, contrived, dreamed-up, extempore, hatched-up, impromptu, makeshift **10** off-the-cuff, originated, unprepared **11** extemporary, spontaneous, unrehearsed **12** extemporized **14** extemporaneous, unpremeditated **15** improvisational, spur-of-the-moment

imprudent 4 rash **5** crazy, dopey **6** unwise **7** foolish **8** heedless, mindless, untoward **9** foolhardy **10** ill-advised, incautious, indiscreet, unthinking **11** inadvisable, injudicious, thoughtless **13** ill-considered

impudence
Yiddish: **7** chutzpa **8** chutzpah

impudent 4 bold, rude **5** brash, fresh, nervy, saucy **6** brazen, cheeky **7** forward, upstart **8** impolite, insolent **9** bumptious, shameless **11** impertinent, smart-alecky, wiseacreish **12** discourteous **13** disrespectful

impugn 4 deny **5** knock, libel **6** assail, attack, berate, negate, oppose **7** asperse, slander **8** denounce, question **9** challenge, criticize **10** contradict **14** call in question, cast aspersions **16** call into question

impugnment 7 slander **10** aspersions

impulse 4 bent, goad, push, spur, urge, whim **5** drive, fancy, force **6** desire, motive, notion, thrust, whimsy **7**

caprice, impetus, whimsey **8** instinct, momentum, movement, stimulus, stirring **9** incentive **10** incitement, motivation **11** inclination, inspiration, instigation

impulsive 4 rash **7** driving, offhand **8** forceful, forcible, notional **9** impelling, impetuous, impromptu, unplanned, whimsical **10** capricious, incautious, propellant, propelling **11** involuntary, spontaneous **12** devil-may-care **13** unpredictable **14** extemporaneous, unpremeditated **15** spur-of-themoment

impulsiveness 8 rashness **11** impetuosity, spontaneity, unrestraint **12** recklessness, whimsicality **14** capriciousness

impunity 8 immunity **9** clearance, exemption, privilege **10** absolution **11** prerogative **12** dispensation

impure 4 foul, lewd **5** dirty **6** coarse, filthy, smutty **7** debased, defiled, immoral, lustful, noisome, noxious, obscene, sullied, tainted, unclean **8** degraded, devalued, immodest, improper, indecent, polluted, prurient, unchaste, vitiated **9** lecherous, salacious, unrefined **10** indecorous, indelicate, libidinous, licentious **11** adulterated, depreciated, unwholesome **12** contaminated

impurity 5 alloy, dross, filth, taint **8** foulness **9** dirtiness, pollutant, pollution **10** adulterant, corruption, defilement **11** contaminant, taintedness, uncleanness **12** adulteration **13** contamination, foreign matter **15** unwholesomeness

imputation 6 charge **10** accusation, allegation, ascription **11** attribution

impute 5 refer **6** assign, charge, credit, relate **7** ascribe **9** attribute

inability 10 inaptitude, incapacity, ineptitude **12** helplessness, incapability, incompetence **13** maladroitness, powerlessness

in absence
Latin: **10** in absentia

in absentia 9 in absence

inaccessible 9 not at hand **11** unreachable **12** unattainable, unobtainable **14** unapproachable

in accord 9 agreeable, approving, in harmony, of one mind **10** concurring, consenting **11** in agreement
French: **9** en rapport

inaccuracy 4 goof, slip **5** error, fault, wrong **6** boo-boo **7** blunder, erratum, fallacy, mistake **9** unclarity **10** faultiness **11** imprecision, inexactness **13** incorrectness, unreliability **14** fallaciousness

inaccurate 3 off **5** false, wrong **6** faulty **7** inexact **8** mistaken **9** erroneous, imprecise, incorrect, off target **10** fallacious, unreliable **11** not on target, off the track **13** wide of the mark

inaction 8 abeyance, deferral, dormancy, dullness, idleness **9** cessation, indolence **10** inactivity, quiescence, somnolence, suspension **11** complacency

inactive 4 dull, idle, lazy **5** inert, quiet, still **6** low-key, otiose, static, torpid, unused **7** dormant, languid **8** indolent, slothful, sluggish **9** do-nothing, easygoing, leisurely, sedentary, somnolent **10** on the shelf **11** inoperative **12** out of service

inactivity 4 rest **5** quiet **6** disuse **7** inertia **8** dormancy, idleness, inaction **9** stillness **10** quiescence

in actuality
Latin: **6** in esse

in addition 3 and, too **4** also, more, plus, then **5** above, added, again, extra **6** as well, beyond **7** besides, further **8** moreover **10** additional **12** additionally, supplemental

inadequacy 4 lack **7** failing **10** deficiency, impairment **11** shortcoming **13** insufficiency

inadequate 5 inept, short, unfit **6** meager, scanty, too raw **7** lacking, not up to, wanting **8** below par, unfitted **9** deficient, imperfect, incapable **11** incompetent, unqualified **12** insufficient

inadmissible 10 disallowed, extraneous **11** intolerable **12** not permitted, unacceptable **14** nonpermissible

in advance 6 before, in time, sooner **7** earlier **9** before now **10** beforehand **11** ahead of time **13** before the fact

inadvertent 7 unmeant **10** accidental, fortuitous, unintended, unthinking **11** involuntary **13** unintentional **14** unpremeditated

inadvisable 5 risky **6** chancy, unwise **9** impolitic, imprudent **10** ill-advised **11** inexpedient, injudicious, inopportune

in aeternum 7 forever

in agreement
French: **9** en rapport

inalienable 6 sacred **8** absolute, defended, inherent **9** protected **10** inviolable, sacrosanct **12** unassailable **13** unforfeitable, unimpeachable

in all
Latin: **6** in toto

in all places 10 every place, everywhere, far and near, far and wide

in a low voice
Latin: **9** sotto voce

inamorata 4 lady, love **5** lover **7** beloved, darling **8** ladylove, mistress, paramour, truelove **10** sweetheart

inane 4 dumb **5** dopey, empty, silly, vapid **6** absurd, jejune, stupid **7** asinine, fatuous, foolish, idiotic, insipid, shallow, vacuous **9** pointless, senseless **10** ridiculous, unthinking **11**

meaningless, nonsensical **13** unintelligent

inanimate 4 cold, dead, dull **5** inert **6** asleep, stolid **8** lifeless, soulless **9** inorganic, insensate, nonliving, senseless, unfeeling **10** insensible, insentient **11** unconscious

inanity 6 drivel **7** hogwash, vacuity **8** nonsense, vapidity **9** absurdity, asininity, silliness **11** foolishness **13** pointlessness, senselessness **14** ridiculousness

Inanna
origin: **8** Sumerian
goddess of: **3** war **4** love
sister: **10** Ereshkigal
realm: **6** heaven
corresponds to: **6** Ishtar **7** Astarte, Mylitta **9** Ashtoreth

in any case 6 anyhow, anyway **9** at any rate **10** in any event

inapplicable 5 unfit **6** not apt **8** unsuited **10** inapposite, irrelevant, not germane, unsuitable **12** incompatible, not pertinent **13** inappropriate

inappropriate 5 inapt **8** ill-timed, improper, unsuited **9** unfitting **10** indecorous, in bad taste, out of place, unbecoming, unsuitable **11** incongruous **12** incompatible, infelicitous
French: **10** mal a propos

inapt 8 improper, unseemly, unsuited **9** ill-suited, incorrect, unfitting **11** incongruous **13** inappropriate

inaptness 9 inability, ineptness **10** clumsiness, inaptitude, ineptitude **12** incompetence **13** maladroitness **14** unskillfulness

in arrears 4 late **7** overdue **10** delinquent

inarticulate 4 dumb, mute **7** babbled, blurred, garbled, mumbled **8** confused, wordless **9** paralyzed **10** incoherent, indistinct, speechless, tongue-tied **12** inexpressive **14** unintelligible **15** uncommunicative

inartistic 9 graceless, inelegant, tasteless **10** ungraceful **11** unaesthetic **12** unattractive

in a series
French: **7** en suite

in a set
French: **7** en suite

in attendance 4 here **7** present, serving **9** appearing, caring for, on the spot, waiting on **12** accompanying, looking after, taking care of

inattention 6 apathy **10** negligence **12** carelessness **14** lack of interest **16** absentmindedness, unresponsiveness

inattentive 7 unaware **8** careless, heedless **9** forgetful, negligent, unmindful **10** distracted **11** daydreaming, thoughtless, unobservant **12** absentminded

inaugurate 5 set up, start **6** induct,

launch **7** instate, kick off, usher in **8** initiate **9** institute, undertake **10** embark upon **11** set in action

inauguration 5 start **9** beginning, induction **10** dedication **11** origination **12** commencement

inaugurator 6 author, father **7** creator, founder, starter **9** initiator, organizer **10** originator, prime mover

inauspicious 7 unlucky **9** ill-chosen, ill-omened **10** badly timed, disastrous **11** unfavorable, unfortunate, unpromising **12** infelicitous, unpropitious

in a vacuum
Latin: **7** in vacuo

in bad faith
Latin: **8** mala fide

in being
Latin: **6** in esse

inborn 5 basic **6** inbred, innate, native **7** natural **8** inherent **9** inherited, intrinsic, intuitive **10** congenital **11** fundamental, instinctive **14** constitutional

inbred 6 inborn, innate, primal **7** natural **8** inherent **9** ingrained, inherited, intrinsic, intuitive **10** congenital, deep-rooted, deep-seated, hereditary, indwelling **11** instinctive, instinctual **12** deeply rooted **14** constitutional

Inca
language family: **7** Quechua
location: **4** Peru **5** Chili **7** Bolivia, Ecuador **9** Argentina **12** South America
leader: **7** Huascar **8** Topa Inca **9** Atahualpa, Pachacuti **10** Manco Capac **11** Huayna Capac
conquered by: **7** Pizarro
ruins: **11** Machu Picchu, Sacsahuaman, Tambo Machay

incalculable 7 dubious **8** infinite **9** countless, uncertain **11** inestimable, innumerable, measureless, uncountable **12** immeasurable, incomputable **13** unforeseeable, unpredictable

incandesce 4 burn, glow **5** flare, flash

incandescent 7 dynamic, glowing, radiant **8** electric, galvanic, magnetic, white-hot **9** brilliant **11** high-powered **12** electrifying **13** scintillating

incantation 3 hex **4** jinx **5** chant, charm, magic, spell **6** voodoo **7** sorcery **8** wizardry **10** black magic, hocus-pocus, invocation, mumbo-jumbo, necromancy, witchcraft **11** abracadabra, conjuration

incapable 5 inept, unfit **6** unable **8** helpless, impotent, inferior **9** powerless, unskilled, untrained **10** inadequate **11** incompetent, ineffective, inefficient, unqualified

incapacitate 4 maim, undo **5** lay up **7** cripple, disable **8** enfeeble, handicap, paralyze, sideline **9** make unfit **10** disqualify **13** make powerless **14** put out of action **15** render incapable

incapacitated 6 laid up **8** crippled,

disabled, disarmed, helpless, stricken **9** hamstrung, paralyzed, sidelined **10** on the shelf, prostrated **11** immobilized, out of action **12** hors de combat **14** flat on one's back

incapacity 7 illness **8** sickness **9** crippling **10** deficiency, disability **12** incapability

incarcerate 3 pen **4** jail **6** commit, coop up, immure, intern, lock up **7** confine, impound **8** imprison, restrain

incarceration 9 detention **10** commitment, internment **11** confinement, durance vile **12** imprisonment **18** institutionalizing

incarnate 8 embodied, manifest **9** personify **10** actualized, in the flesh **11** objectified, personified

Incarnations
author: **16** Robert Penn Warren

incautious 4 rash **5** brash **6** unwary **8** careless, heedless, reckless **9** hotheaded, impetuous, imprudent, impulsive, overhasty **10** headstrong, indiscreet, unthinking **11** injudicious, thoughtless

incendiary 8 agitator, arsonist **12** inflammatory

incense 3 ire **5** anger **6** burn up, enrage, madden **7** inflame, provoke **9** infuriate, make angry **13** make indignant
spice: **6** stacte

incensed 3 mad **5** angry, irate **6** fuming, raging **7** enraged, furious **8** burned up, inflamed, outraged, provoked **9** affronted, indignant **10** infuriated

incentive 4 lure, spur **6** come-on, motive **8** stimulus **10** enticement, inducement, motivation **11** inspiration **13** encouragement

inception 5 birth, debut, onset, start **6** origin, outset **7** arrival **9** beginning **12** commencement, inauguration

incessant 8 constant, unbroken, unending **9** ceaseless, continual, perpetual, unceasing **10** continuous, persistent **11** everlasting, unrelenting, unremitting **12** interminable **13** uninterrupted

inch
abbreviation: **2** in

In Chancery
author: **14** John Galsworthy
part of trilogy: **11** Forsyte Saga

inchoate 7 budding, nascent **8** formless, unformed, unshaped **9** amorphous, beginning, embryonic, incipient, shapeless **10** commencing, disjointed, uncohesive **11** unorganized **12** disconnected

incidence 4 rate **5** range, scope **6** extent **8** occasion **9** frequency, happening **10** commonness, occurrence, phenomenon **11** routineness

incident 5 clash, event, scene **6** affair **7** episode, related **8** occasion **9** happening **10** incidental, occurrence **11** contretemps, disturbance

incidental 5 minor **9** accessory, secondary **10** extraneous, unexpected **11** subordinate, unlooked-for

incidentally 7 apropos, by the by **8** by the way **9** in passing **14** speaking of that **15** parenthetically **21** while we're on the subject

incidentals 6 extras **8** minutiae **10** minor items **11** accessories, odds and ends **13** appurtenances

incinerate 4 burn **7** consume, cremate **9** carbonize **13** reduce to ashes

incineration 6 firing **7** burning, flaming **8** ignition, kindling **9** cremation **10** combustion **13** carbonization

incinerator 4 oven **6** burner **7** furnace

incipient 7 budding, nascent **8** inchoate **9** beginning, embryonic, fledgling, promising **10** developing, half-formed **11** rudimentary

in circulation 4 rife **6** abroad, around **7** at large **9** all around **11** going around **12** spread around **14** around and about **15** making the rounds

incise 4 etch **5** carve **7** cut into, engrave

incision 3 cut **4** scar, gash, nick, slit **5** cleft, notch, score, slash, slice, wound **6** furrow

incisive 4 curt, keen **5** acute, brisk, crisp, sharp **6** biting, shrewd **7** cutting, express, mordant, precise, probing, summary **8** analytic, piercing **9** trenchant, well-aimed **10** perceptive **11** intelligent, penetrating

incite 4 goad, prod, stir **5** drive, egg on, impel, rouse **6** arouse, excite, fire up, foment, induce, prompt, stir up, urge on **7** actuate, agitate, inflame, provoke **8** activate **9** instigate, stimulate

incitement 6 urging **7** arousal, driving, goading **8** egging on, exciting, firing up, stirring **9** agitating, fomenting, inflaming, prompting, provoking **10** activation, stirring up **11** provocation, stimulation

incivility 8 rudeness **9** barbarism, impudence, indecorum, surliness, vulgarity **10** bad manners, coarseness, disrespect **11** boorishness, discourtesy, misbehavior, uncouthness **12** impoliteness, tactlessness **14** unpleasantness

inclement 3 raw **4** foul **5** harsh, nasty, rough **6** bitter, severe, stormy **7** violent **11** tempestuous

inclination 3 bow, dip, nod **4** bend, bent, hill, rake, rise **5** grade, pitch, slant, slope **6** liking **7** bending, leaning, sloping **8** fondness, lowering, penchant, tendency **9** acclivity, inclining, proneness **10** preference, procliv-ity, propensity **11** disposition **12** pre-dilection **14** predisposition

incline 3 bow **4** bend, cant, hill, lean, like, rake, seem, tend, tilt, wont **5** be apt, enjoy, pitch, slant, slope **6** prefer **7** decline **8** be likely, gradient **9** ac-clivity **10** lean toward **11** bend for-ward, have a mind to

inclined 3 apt **5** prove **6** liable, likely **7** given to **10** disposed to **11** predis-posed

incline downward 3 dip, sag **4** sink **5** droop, slant, slope

inclined to delay 4 slow **5** tardy **6** remiss **8** dawdling, dilatory, sluggish **9** reluctant **10** foot-dragging **13** dilly-dallying **15** procrastinating

include 5 cover **6** enfold, entail, take in **7** contain, embrace, involve, sub-sume **8** comprise **9** encompass **10** comprehend **11** incorporate

inclusive 7 general, overall **8** sweep-ing, taking in **9** embracing, including **10** comprising, encircling **11** sur-rounding **12** encyclopedic **13** compre-hending, comprehensive, incorporat-ing **15** all-encompassing

incognito 7 unknown, unnamed **8** nameless **9** concealed, disguised, pro-tected **10** in disguise, uncredited, un-dercover, unrevealed **11** undisclosed **12** unidentified **14** unacknowledged, unrecognizable

incognizant 6 obtuse **7** unaware **8** ig-norant, unseeing **9** unknowing **13** un-conscious of **15** uncomprehending

incoherent 7 muddled, unclear **8** con-fused, rambling **9** illogical **10** dis-jointed, irrational **11** bewildering, nonsensical **12** inconsistent **14** unin-telligible

In Cold Blood
author: **12** Truman Capote
director: **13** Richard Brooks
cast: **11** Paul Stewart, Robert Blake, Scott Wilson **12** John Forsythe

income 5 means, wages **6** salary **7** rev-enue **8** earnings **9** emolument **10** live-lihood

income, annual
French: **5** rente

incomparable 8 peerless **9** matchless, unequaled, unrivaled **10** inimitable **11** ne plus ultra, superlative **12** tran-scendent **13** beyond compare **14** un-approachable

incompatibility 6 strife **7** discord **8** friction, variance **9** disaccord, wran-gling **10** antagonism **11** being at odds, discordance **13** lack of harmony

incompatible 6 at odds, jarring **8** clashing, contrary, unsuited **10** at var-iance, discordant, mismatched **11** dis-agreeing, incongruous, uncongenial **12**

antagonistic, inconsistent, inharmoni-ous **13** contradictory, inappropriate

incompetency 9 inability, unfitness **10** ineptitude **11** lack of skill **12** inef-ficiency **15** ineffectiveness

incompetent 5 inept, unfit **8** inexpert **9** incapable, unskilled, untrained **11** ineffective, ineffectual, inefficient, un-qualified **14** lacking ability

incomplete 6 broken **7** partial, want-ing **9** defective, deficient **10** unfin-ished **11** fragmentary

incompleteness 8 omission **10** defi-ciency **11** shortcoming **15** unfinished state

incomprehensible 7 obscure **8** ab-struse, baffling **9** confusing **10** befud-dling **11** bewildering, inscrutable, un-graspable **12** impenetrable, unfathomable **14** unintelligible **19** be-yond comprehension, beyond under-standing

incomprehension 10 bafflement, puz-zlement **12** bewilderment **19** failure to understand

inconceivable 7 strange **8** unlikely **10** improbable, incredible **11** unthinkable **12** beyond belief, unbelievable, uni-maginable **14** highly unlikely

in conclusion
French: **5** enfin

inconclusive 4 open **9** unsettled **10** indecisive, indefinite, unresolved, up in the air **11** not definite **12** uncon-vincing, undetermined **13** indetermi-nate

incongruity 8 variance **9** disparity **10** aberration, disharmony, divergence **11** abnormality, discrepancy **13** dissimi-larity, inconsistency, unsuitability **17** inappropriateness

incongruous 3 odd **6** far-out **8** con-trary **10** at variance, discrepant, out of place, outlandish, unsuitable **11** conflicting, disagreeing **12** incompati-ble, inconsistent, out of keeping **13** contradictory, inappropriate **14** irrec-oncilable

inconsequential 5 petty **6** slight **7** trivial **8** nugatory, picayune, piddling, trifling **9** valueless **10** negligible, of no moment **11** meaningless, unimpor-tant **13** insignificant **15** of no conse-quence

inconsiderable 5 light, minor, petty, small **6** little, modest, paltry, slight **7** minimal, trivial **8** picayune, trifling **9** no big deal **10** negligible **11** unimpor-tant **13** insignificant, no great shakes **15** inconsequential

inconsiderate 4 rash, rude **6** remiss, unkind **7** uncivil **8** careless, impolite, tactless, uncaring **9** negligent **10** un-gracious, unthinking **11** insensitive, thoughtless **12** disregardful, uncharita-ble

inconsistency 8 variance **9** disparity **10** difference, divergence **11** discrep-ancy, incongruity **12** disagreement **13** dissimilarity

inconsistent 6 fickle **7** erratic, way-ward **8** contrary, notional, unstable, variable **9** changeful, dissonant **10** changeable, discrepant, inconstant, ir-resolute **11** inaccordant, incongruous, inconsonant, vacillating **12** incompati-ble, inharmonious **13** contradictory, unpredictable **14** irreconcilable

inconsolable 7 crushed **8** dejected, desolate, wretched **9** miserable **10** de-spondent **12** disconsolate **13** broken-hearted

inconsonant 10 discordant **12** out of keeping, unharmonious

inconspicuous 3 dim **5** faint, muted **6** modest **9** unnoticed **10** unapparent, unassuming **11** unobtrusive **12** not egregious, unnoticeable **14** unostenta-tious

inconstancy 10 fickleness, infidelity **11** instability **14** capriciousness, changeableness, unfaithfulness

inconstant 6 fickle, untrue **7** erratic **8** cavalier, disloyal, unstable **9** mercu-rial **10** capricious, changeable, un-faithful **11** interrupted, uncommitted, undedicated, unsteadfast

incontinence 8 rashness **12** reckless-ness **13** lack of control **16** irresponsi-bility

incontinent 8 unchaste **12** unre-strained

incontrovertibility 8 sureness **9** cer-tainty **12** absoluteness, definiteness **13** undeniability **14** irrefutability, con-clusiveness **15** indisputability **16** in-contestability **17** unquestionability

incontrovertible 9 apodictic **10** unar-guable, undeniable **11** established, ir-refutable **12** indisputable **14** beyond question, unquestionable

inconvenience 6 bother, put out **7** trouble **8** hardship, headache, nui-sance **9** annoyance, disoblige, put one out **10** discomfort **13** be a nuisance to, pain in the neck

inconvenient 7 awkward, unhandy **8** annoying, tiresome, untimely **10** both-ersome, burdensome **11** distressing, inopportune, troublesome

Incoronazione di Poppea, L'
also: **22** The Coronation of Poppaea
opera by: **10** Monteverdi
character: **4** Nero **6** Ottone **7** Ottavia

incorporate 4 fuse **6** embody, work in **7** include **10** amalgamate, assimilate **11** consolidate

incorporated 6 united **8** embodied, included **11** amalgamated, assimilated **12** consolidated

incorporeal 6 occult, unreal **7** ghostly, phantom **8** bodiless **9** spiritual, unearthly, unfleshly, unworldly **10** immaterial, intangible **11** disembodied **12** supernatural **13** insubstantial

incorrect 5 false, wrong **6** untrue **7** inexact **8** mistaken **9** erroneous **10** fallacious, inaccurate

incorrectness 5 error **9** wrongness **10** inaccuracy **12** carelessness, slovenliness

incorrigible 6 unruly **8** hardened, hard-core, hopeless **10** beyond help, delinquent **11** intractable **12** beyond saving, past changing, unmanageable **14** uncontrollable

incorrigible child
French: **14** enfant terrible

incorruptible 4 pure **6** honest **7** upright **8** reliable **9** faultless, righteous **10** unbribable **11** trustworthy **14** irreproachable

increase 3 wax **4** grow **5** add to, swell **6** enrich, expand **7** advance, augment, burgeon, enhance, enlarge **8** multiply **12** become larger

increasing 7 growing **9** enlarging, expansion, extending, extension **10** drawing out **11** enlargement **12** augmentation

incredible 6 absurd **7** amazing, awesome **10** astounding, farfetched, remarkable **11** astonishing **12** preposterous, unbelievable, unimaginable **13** extraordinary, inconceivable

Incredible Hulk, The
character: **9** Jack McGee **11** David Banner
cast: **9** Bill Bixby **10** Jack Colvin **11** Lou Ferrigno

incredulous 7 dubious **8** doubtful **9** skeptical **10** suspicious **11** distrustful **12** disbelieving

increment 4 gain, rise **5** raise **6** growth, profit **7** benefit **8** addition, increase **9** accretion **10** supplement **11** enlargement **12** accumulation, appreciation, augmentation **13** proliferation

incriminate 5 blame **6** accuse, charge, indict

incrimination 5 blame **7** charges **10** accusation, indictment

incubate 3 set, sit **4** plot **5** breed, brood, clock, cover, hatch **6** scheme **7** develop, gestate, sit upon **8** generate

incubus 5 demon **8** bad dream **9** nightmare

inculcate 5 drill, imbue, infix, teach, train **6** impart, infuse **7** implant, impress, instill **8** instruct **9** brainwash, condition, enlighten **12** indoctrinate

inculpable 5 clear **8** innocent **9** blameless, guiltless, not guilty **10** not at fault, unblamable **14** not responsible

incur 6 arouse, assume, incite, stir up **7** acquire, bring on, involve, provoke **8** bring out, contract, fall into

incurable 8 cureless, hopeless **9** ceaseless **10** beyond cure, inveterate, relentless, unflagging **12** incorrigible, irremediable **13** dyed-in-the-wool, uncorrectable

incursion 4 push, raid **5** foray **6** attack, inroad, sortie **7** assault **8** invasion **11** advance into, impingement **12** encroachment, infiltration

indebted 5 bound **7** bounden **8** beholden, grateful, thankful **9** obligated **10** chargeable **11** accountable **15** under obligation

indebtedness 4 debt **5** debit **7** arrears **9** liability **10** balance due, obligation **11** liabilities

indecency 10 immorality **12** unseemliness **13** offensiveness, salaciousness **14** indecorousness

indecent 4 blue, lewd, rude **5** bawdy, dirty **6** filthy, smutty, vulgar **7** ignoble, ill-bred, immoral, obscene, uncivil **8** immodest, improper, prurient, unseemly **9** offensive, salacious **10** in bad taste, indecorous, indiscreet, licentious, unbecoming **11** unwholesome **12** pornographic

indecipherable 7 cryptic **9** enigmatic, illegible **10** unreadable **11** inscrutable

indecision 5 doubt **6** acrisy **7** dilemma, swither **8** wavering **10** hesitation **11** fluctuation, vacillating, vacillation, uncertainty **12** irresolution

indecisive 4 weak **7** dubious, unclear **8** doubtful, hesitant, wavering **9** confusing, debatable, mercurial, uncertain, unsettled **10** disputable, hesitating, irresolute, wishy-washy **11** halfhearted, vacillating **12** inconclusive **13** indeterminate **17** blowing hot and cold

indecorous 5 gross **6** sinful, wicked **7** ill-bred **8** immodest, improper, lowclass, unseemly **9** unfitting **10** unbecoming, unsuitable **11** blameworthy **13** inappropriate, reprehensible

indecorum 8 bad taste **9** immodesty, indecency, vulgarity **11** impropriety **12** impoliteness, unseemliness

indeed 5 truly **6** in fact, really **7** for sure, in truth **8** actually, to be sure **9** certainly, in reality, veritably **10** positively, to be honest, undeniably **11** joking apart **13** in point of fact, with certainty **14** to tell the truth **15** as a matter of fact, without question **16** strictly speaking

indefatigable 6 dogged **7** staunch **8** diligent, sedulous, tireless, untiring **9** energetic **10** persistent, unflagging, unwearying **11** persevering, unfaltering **13** inexhaustible

indefensible 8 improper, vincible **9** pregnable, untenable **10** vulnerable **11** defenseless, inexcusable, unprotected, unspeakable **12** open to attack, unpardonable **13** unjustifiable

indefinite 3 dim **5** vague **6** unsure **7** inexact, obscure, unknown **8** doubtful **9** ambiguous, amorphous, limitless, tentative, uncertain, unsettled **10** illdefined, indecisive, indistinct, inexplicit **11** illimitable, measureless, unspecified **12** undetermined **13** indeterminate

indefiniteness 6 vagary **9** ambiguity, vagueness **10** indecision **11** uncertainty **12** equivocation

indelible 4 fast **5** fixed, vivid **7** lasting **8** deep-dyed **9** ingrained, memorable, permanent **10** unerasable **11** unremovable **12** ineradicable **13** unforgettable

indelicate 4 lewd, rude **5** broad, crude, gross **6** clumsy, coarse, risque, vulgar **7** awkward, obscene **8** immodest, improper, indecent, off-color, unseemly **9** offensive, unrefined **10** indecorous, indiscreet, suggestive, unbecoming

in demand 7 popular **9** desirable **11** sought after

indemnification 7 payment **10** recompense, reparation **12** compensation

indemnify 3 pay **5** atone, cover, repay **6** insure, secure **7** pay back, protect, rectify, requite, satisfy **8** make good **9** make right, make up for, reimburse **10** compensate, make amends, recompense, remunerate **15** make restitution

indemnity 7 redress **8** coverage, security **9** insurance, repayment **10** protection **11** restitution **12** compensation **15** indemnification

indent 5 notch, set in **6** recess **7** set back

indentation 3 bay, cut, pit **4** dent, nick **5** gouge, inset, niche, notch, score **6** cavity, furrow, pocket, recess **8** incision **9** concavity **10** depression

indented 6 hollow, sunken, zigzag **7** concave, notched **9** depressed

indenture 4 bind **8** contract **10** apprentice

indentured 5 bound **10** contracted **11** apprenticed

independence 7 freedom, liberty **8** autonomy **10** liberation **11** sovereignty **12** emancipation, self-reliance **14** self-government **17** selfdetermination

independent 4 free **7** solvent, well-off **8** affluent, separate, unallied, wellto-do **9** apart from, exclusive, on one's own, sovereign, uncoerced, well-fixed **10** autonomous, well-heeled **11** self-reliant, unconnected **12** unassociated, uncontrolled **13** selfdirecting, self-governing, unconstrained **15** individualistic, selfdetermining

indescribable 9 ineffable **11** beyond words, indefinable, unutterable **12**

overwhelming **13** inexpressible **17** beyond description **20** beggaring description

indestructible 8 enduring **9** permanent **11** everlasting, infrangible, unbreakable **12** imperishable

indeterminate 5 vague **7** obscure, unclear **8** not clear **9** ambiguous, uncertain, undefined **10** indefinite, perplexing, unresolved **11** problematic, unspecified **12** undetermined, unstipulated

index 4 clue, mark, sign **5** proof, token **7** catalog, symptom **8** evidence, glossary, register **9** catalogue, indicator **10** indication **13** manifestation **16** alphabetical list

Index Librorum Prohibitorum 22 index of prohibited books

index of prohibited books
   Latin: 25 Index Librorum Prohibitorum

India
   other name: 4 Hind **6** Bharat **12** Bharat Varsha
   capital: 8 New Delhi
   largest city: 8 Calcutta
   others: 4 Agra, Gaya, Pune **5** Poona, Surat **6** Bombay (Mumbai), Jaipur, Kanpur, Lahore, Madras, Madura, Mumbai (Bombay), Mysore, Nagpur **7** Banaras **8** Kolhapur, Mandalay, Mirzapur, Shahpura, Srinagar **9** Ahmedabad, Bangalore, Hyderabad **10** Darjeeling
   division: 3 Goa **5** Assam, Bihar, Jammu **6** Kerala, Orissa, Punjab, Sikkim **7** Gujarat, Haryana, Kashmir, Manipur, Mizoram, Tripura **8** Nagaland **9** Jharkhand, Karnataka, Meghalaya, Rajasthan, Tamil Nadu **10** Chandigarh, West Bengal **11** Chattisgarh, Daman and Diu, Lakshadweep, Maharashtra, Pondicherry, Uttaranchal **12** Uttar Pradesh **13** Andhra Pradesh, Madhya Pradesh **15** Arunchal Pradesh, Himachal Pradesh **17** Andaman and Nicobar **19** Dadra and Nagar Haveli
   measure: 3 ady, gaz, gez, jow, lan **4** byee, coss, depa, doph, hath, koss, kunk, raik, rati, seit, taun, tola **5** bigha, covid, crosa, denda, depoh, drona, erosa, garce, hasta, krosa, parah, ratti, salay, yojan **6** adhaka, amunam, covido, cudava, dumbha, geerah, moolum, mushti, ouroub, palgat, parran, prasha, ropani, tipree, unglee, yojana **7** dhanush, gavyuti, khahoon, niranga, prastha **8** okthabah
   monetary unit: 3 lac, pie **4** lakh, pice **5** abidi, rupee
   weight: 3 mod, pai, vis **4** drum, hoen, kona, pala, pank, pice, ruay, tael, tali, tola, wang, yava **5** adpad, candy, hubba, maund, tical **6** karsha **8** mangelin

island: 6 Agatti, Chilka **7** Andaman, Minicoy, Nicobar **8** Amindivi **9** Laccadive **11** Lakshadweep
lake: 5 Jheel, Lonar, Wular **6** Chilka, Colair, Dhebar, Kolair **7** Kolleru, Pulicat, Pushkar, Sambahr
mountain: 8 Aravalli **9** Broad Peak, Distaghil, Himalayas, Karakoram, Nanda Devi, Rakaposhi **10** Gasherbrum, Masherbrum **11** Nanga Parbat **12** Eastern Ghats, Kanchenjunga, Western Ghats
   hills: 4 Chin, Naga **5** Khasi **6** Lushai **7** Nilgiri
highest point: 12 Godwin Austen
river: 3 Son **4** Beas, Kosi, Tapi **5** Gogra, Indus, Jumna, Tapti **6** Gandak, Ganges, Jhelum, Kaveri, Kistna, Sutlej, Yamuna **7** Cauveri, Cauvery, Chambal, Damodar, Hooghly, Krishna, Narbada, Narmada **8** Godavari, Mahanadi **10** Bhagirathi **11** Brahmaputra
sea: 6 Indian **7** Arabian
physical feature:
   bay: 6 Bengal
   cape: 7 Comorin
   desert: 4 Thar **9** Rajasthan
   forest: 3 Gir
   gulf: 5 Kutch **6** Cambay, Mannar
   pass: 9 Karakoram
   plain: 12 Indo-Gangetic
   plateau: 6 Deccan **7** Shillon **11** Chota Nagpur
   rains: 7 monsoon
   strait: 4 Palk
   swamp: 9 Sundarban **11** Rann of Kutch
   valley: 13 Vale of Kashmir
people: 2 Ao **3** Gor **4** Bhil **5** Aryan **6** Badaga, Pathan **7** Sherani **9** Dravidian **10** Andamanese
   caste: 3 Jat **5** Sudra **6** Rajput, Shudra **7** Brahman, Brahmin, Harijan, Maratha, Vaishya **9** Kshatriya **11** Untouchable
   dynasty: 5 Gupta, Mogul **6** Maurya, Rajput **8** Marathas **14** Delhi Sultanate
   god: 4 Kali, Rama, Siva **5** Durga, Laxmi, Shiva **6** Brahma, Kumara, Vishnu **7** Ganesha, Hanuman, Krishna, Lakshmi **9** Kartikeya **10** Subramanya
   ruler: 5 Akbar, Asoka, Babur, Timur **7** Humayun **8** Hyder Ali, Jahangir **9** Aurangzeb, Shah Jahan **11** Rajiv Gandhi, Tippu Sultan **12** Indira Gandhi **13** Queen Victoria **15** Jawaharlal Nehru, Mohandas K (Mahatma) Gandhi **18** Chandragupta Maurya
language: 4 Urdu **5** Hindi, Oriya, Tamil **6** Sindhi, Telugu **7** Bengali, English, Kannada, Malayam, Marathi, Punjabi **8** Assamese, Gujarati, Kashmiri, Sanskrit **9** Malayalam
religion: 4 Sikh **5** Hindu, Islam, Parsi

7 Jainist, Judaism **8** Buddhism **11** Zoroastrian **12** Christianity
place:
   cathedral: 10 Saint Thome
   fortress: 3 Red **11** Saint George
   mausoleum: 8 Taj Mahal
   minaret: 9 Qutb Minar
   mosque: 10 Jama Masjid
   park: 6 Maidan
   president's residence: 17 Rashtrapati Bhavan
   railway station: 8 Victoria
   shrine: 7 Raj Ghat
   street: 7 Raj Path **11** Chowringhee, Marine Drive **12** Chandni Chauk **14** Connaught Place
   temple: 5 Birla **6** Ellora, Golden **7** Kailasa **10** Ajanta Cave
feature:
   dance: 6 nautch **7** cantico
   religious text: 7 Rig Veda
   shrine: 5 stupa
food:
   beer: 5 apong
   bread: 7 chapati
   liquor: 4 soma, sura **5** shrab
   tea: 5 assam

Indian
   constellation: 5 Indus

Indiana
   abbreviation: 2 IN **3** Ind
   nickname: 7 Hoosier
   capital/largest city: 12 Indianapolis
   others: 4 Gary, Peru **6** Brazil, Goshen, Hobart, Jasper, Kokomo, Marion, Muncie, Wabash **7** Elkhart, Ft Wayne, Hammond, LaPorte, Whiting **8** Columbus, Richmond **9** Lafayette, Mishawaka, South Bend, Vincennes **10** Evansville, Huntington, Logansport, Terre Haute **11** Bloomington, East Chicago **12** Connorsville, Michigan City
   college: 4 Ball **6** Bethel, Butler, DePauw, Goshen, Marion, Purdue, Wabash **9** Notre Dame **10** Evansville, Valparaiso
   professional sports teams:
      basketball: 6 Pacers
      football: 5 Colts
   explorer: 7 La Salle
   feature: 10 New Harmony **12** Indian mounds
      national memorial: 14 Lincoln boyhood
   tribe: 3 Wea **5** Miami **7** Shawnee
   people: 7 Hoosier **10** Cole Porter, Eugene Debs, Gus Grissom, Red Skelton **12** Wilbur Wright **15** Booth Tarkington, Theodore Dreiser **18** James Whitcomb Riley
   lake: 5 Clear, James **6** Monroe **7** Manitou, Wawasee **8** Michigan **9** Mansfield **11** Maxinkuckee
   land rank: 12 thirty-eighth
   mountain: 13 Greensfort Top
   physical feature:
      cave: 9 Wyandotte

river: 4 Ohio **5** White **6** Maumee, Wabash **8** Kankakee **10** Tippecanoe, Whitewater
state admission: 10 nineteenth
state bird: 8 cardinal
state flower: 5 peony **6** zinnia
state motto: 19 Crossroads of America
state song: 28 On the Banks of the Wabash Far Away
state tree: 5 tulip **11** tulip poplar

Indiana
author: 10 George Sand
character: 4 Noun **7** Delmare **13** Rodolphe Brown **15** Raymon de Ramiere

Indianapolis
features: 8 Speedway **20** Indianapolis Speedway **21** Rock and Roll Hall of Fame
football team: 5 Colts

Indic
language family: 12 Indo-European
branch: 11 Indo-Iranian
subgroup: 5 Hindi, Oriya **6** Nepali, Sindhi **7** Bengali, Marathi, Pakrits, Panjabi **8** Assamese, Gujarati, Kashmiri **9** Sinhalese

indicate 4 mean, show, tell **5** imply **6** denote, evince, record, reveal **7** bespeak, point to, signify, specify, suggest **8** point out, register, stand for **9** be a sign of, designate, establish, make known, represent, symbolize

indication 4 clue, hint, mark, omen, sign **5** token **6** augury, boding, signal **7** gesture, mention, portent, presage, showing, symptom, telling, warning **8** evidence, pointing **9** foretoken **10** foreboding, indicating, intimation, signifying, suggestion **11** designation, premonition **13** demonstration, manifestation

indicative 8 symbolic **10** denotative, emblematic, evidential, expressive, indicatory, suggestive **11** connotative, designative, significant, symptomatic **13** symptomatical **14** characteristic, representative

indicator 4 clue **5** guide **7** pointer **10** indication

indict 4 cite **6** accuse, charge, have up, impute, pull up **7** arraign, bring up, impeach **9** criminate, inculpate, prosecute **11** incriminate **13** prefer charges

indifference 6 apathy **7** disdain, neglect **8** coldness, no import **9** aloofness, unconcern **10** negligence, paltriness, triviality **11** disinterest, impassivity, inattention, insouciance, nonchalance **12** carelessness, unimportance **13** impassiveness, insensibility, insensitivity **14** insignificance, lack of interest

indifferent 4 cool, fair, rote, so-so **5** aloof **6** medium, modest **7** average, unmoved **8** detached, mediocre, mid-

dling, moderate, ordinary, passable **9** apathetic, impassive, not caring, unmindful **10** impervious, insensible, insouciant, nonchalant, second-rate, uninspired **11** commonplace, perfunctory, unconcerned **12** uninterested **13** insusceptible **15** undistinguished **17** betwixt and between, neither good nor bad

indigence 4 need, want **6** penury **7** begarry, poverty **9** pauperism, privation **11** destitution, dire straits **13** pennilessness

indigenous 6 native **7** endemic **8** domestic, homebred **9** home-grown **10** aboriginal **13** autochthonous, originating in

indigent 4 poor **5** needy **6** hard-up, in need, in want **7** pinched **8** badly off **9** destitute, moneyless, penniless **12** impoverished **15** poverty-stricken

indiges
title in: 4 Rome
suggests: 11 deification
for service to: 7 country

indigestible 4 rich **13** unassimilable

indignant 3 mad **4** sore **5** angry, huffy, irate, riled **6** fuming, miffed, peeved, piqued, put off, put out **8** incensed, offended, provoked, steaming, worked up, wrathful **9** resentful, wrought up **10** displeased, infuriated **15** on one's high horse

indignation 3 ire **4** fury, huff, rage **5** pique, wrath **6** animus, choler, dismay, uproar **7** umbrage **8** vexation **9** annoyance **10** irritation, resentment **11** displeasure

indignity 4 slur **5** abuse **6** insult, slight **7** affront, offense, outrage **8** dishonor, rudeness **9** injustice **11** discourtesy, humiliation **12** mistreatment **13** slap in the face

indigo 3 dye **4** blue **8** dark blue, deep blue, navy blue **10** Indigofera
varieties: 4 wild **5** false **7** bastard **8** wild blue **9** blue false **10** plains wild, white false **12** prairie false **13** fragrant false

indirect 5 vague **6** remote, zigzag **7** crooked, devious, distant, evasive, hedging, oblique, winding **8** rambling, tortuous **9** ancillary, secondary **10** circuitous, derivative, digressive, discursive, incidental, meandering, roundabout, unintended **13** unintentional

indirection 8 rambling **10** digression, meandering, zigzagging **14** circuitousness, circumlocution, roundaboutness

indiscernible 6 hidden **9** invisible **10** indistinct **12** undetectable, unnoticeable **13** imperceptible

indiscreet 6 unwise **7** foolish **8** careless, tactless, unseemly **9** foolhardy, ill-judged, impolitic, imprudent, tasteless, untactful **10** incautious **11** improvident, injudicious, thoughtless,

unbefitting, uncalled-for **12** undiplomatic **13** inconsiderate, uncircumspect

indiscretion 8 rashness **10** imprudence **12** carelessness, heedlessness, recklessness, tactlessness **13** foolhardiness, insensitivity **15** thoughtlessness **16** irresponsibility

indiscriminate 6 motley, random **7** aimless, chaotic, jumbled, mongrel **8** confused, slapdash, unchoosy **9** haphazard, hit-or-miss **10** hodgepodge **11** promiscuous, unselective **12** disorganized, unsystematic **16** higgledy-piggledy, undistinguishing

in disorder 5 messy **6** blowsy, frowsy, mussed, sloppy, untidy **7** ruffled, rumpled, tousled, unkempt **8** uncombed **10** disarrayed, disheveled, disordered, disorderly **11** disarranged

indispensable 5 basic, vital **6** needed **7** crucial, needful **8** required **9** essential, mandatory, necessary, requisite **10** compulsory, imperative, obligatory **11** fundamental

indispensable condition
Latin: 10 sine qua non

indispensable element 9 basic need, essential, necessity, requisite **10** sine qua non **11** requirement

indisposed 3 ill **5** loath **6** ailing, averse, laid up, sickly, unwell **7** opposed **8** hesitant, taken ill **9** bedridden, reluctant, unwilling **10** not oneself **11** disinclined **15** under the weather

indisposition 5 upset **6** malady **7** ailment, illness **8** sickness **9** complaint, ill health

indisputable 4 sure **7** assured, certain, decided, evident, obvious **8** absolute, apparent, clear-cut, definite, positive **10** conclusive, unarguable, undeniable **11** indubitable, irrefutable **12** unassailable, unmistakable **13** incontestable **14** unquestionable **16** incontrovertible **20** beyond a shadow of doubt

indissoluble 5 fixed **7** abiding, lasting **8** constant, enduring **9** immutable, indelible, permanent, perpetual **11** everlasting **12** imperishable, ineradicable

indistinct 3 dim **4** weak **5** faint, muddy, murky, vague **6** cloudy, hidden **7** blurred, clouded, muffled, obscure, shadowy, unclear **8** confused, nebulous, puzzling **9** ambiguous, enigmatic, illegible, inaudible, uncertain **10** ill-defined, incoherent, indefinite, mysterious, out of focus **11** not distinct **13** indeterminate **14** indecipherable, unintelligible **16** incomprehensible

indistinguishable 7 obscure, unclear **9** invisible **10** indistinct, unapparent **12** unnoticeable, unobservable **13** a carbon copy of, identical with, imperceptible, inconspicuous, indiscernible

individual 6 person, unique 7 one's own, private, special, unusual 8 distinct, especial, original, personal, separate, singular, somebody, specific, uncommon 9 different, exclusive 10 particular 11 distinctive, independent 12 personalized 14 characteristic, unconventional

individuality 6 cachet 10 uniqueness 11 distinction, singularity, specialness 13 particularity 15 distinctiveness

individually 4 each 5 apart 6 apiece, singly 8 a la carte, uniquely 10 one at a time, peculiarly, personally, separately 12 respectively 13 distinctively 18 characteristically

Indochina 9 peninsula
  includes: 4 Laos 6 Malaya 7 Myanmar, Vietnam 8 Cambodia, Thailand

indoctrinate 5 brief, drill, teach, train, tutor 6 infuse, school 7 educate, implant, instill 8 initiate 9 brainwash, inculcate 12 propagandize

indoctrination 5 drill 8 drilling, teaching, training 9 education, schooling 10 initiation, instilling 11 inculcation, instruction

Indo-European
  language branch: 5 Greek 6 Celtic, Italic 7 Romance 8 Albanian, Armenian, Germanic 9 Anatolian, Tocharian 11 Balto-Slavic, Indo-Iranian

Indo-Iranian
  language family: 12 Indo-European
  ancient: 7 Avestan 8 Sanskrit 10 Old Persian
  modern Iranian: 5 Indic, Tajik 6 Pashto 7 Baluchi, Kurdish, Persian
  modern Indic: 4 Pali 5 Hindi, Oriya 6 Nepali, Sindhi 7 Bengali, Marathi, Panjabi 8 Assamese, Gujarati, Kashmiri 9 Sinhalese

indolence 5 sloth 7 inertia, languor, laxness 8 idleness, laziness 10 inactivity

indolent 4 lazy 5 inert, slack 7 lumpish 8 dawdling, dilatory, inactive, listless, slothful, sluggish 9 do-nothing, easygoing, lethargic, shiftless 13 lackadaisical

indomitable 6 dogged 7 doughty, staunch, valiant 8 cast-iron, fearless, intrepid, resolute, stalwart, stubborn 9 dauntless, steadfast, undaunted 10 courageous, formidable, invincible, unwavering, unyielding 11 insuperable, persevering, unflinching, unshrinking 12 invulnerable, unassailable 13 indefatigable, irrepressible, unconquerable

Indonesia
  other name: 9 Nusantara 12 Tanah Airkita 21 Netherlands East Indies
  capital/largest city: 7 Jakarta 8 Djakarta
  others: 5 Bogor, Medan 6 Malang, Manado 7 Bandung 8 Macassar, Semarang, Surabaya 9 Hollandia, Palembang, Surakarta 10 Jogjakarta, Yogyakarta 11 Banjarmasin
  measure: 5 depah, depoh
  monetary unit: 3 sen 6 rupiah
  weight: 5 catty, ounce, thail 6 soekoe
  island: 3 Aru 4 Bali, Buru, Java 5 Ambon, Ceram, Seram, Spice, Sumba, Timor 6 Bangka, Borneo, Flores, Lombok, Madura, Tidore 7 Belawan, Celebes, Morotai, Sumatra, Sumbawa, Ternate 8 Belitung, Moluccas, Sulawesi 9 Halmahera, New Guinea 10 Kalimantan 11 Lesser Sunda 12 Greater Sunda
  lake: 4 Toba 5 Ranau 6 Towuti
  river: 4 Hari, Musi, Solo 5 Rokan 6 Asahan, Barito, Kampar 7 Brantas, Kaptuas 9 Indrogiri, Mamberamo, Martapura
  sea: 4 Java, Savu 5 Banda, Ceram, Timor 6 Flores, Indian 7 Arafura, Celebes, Molucca, Pacific 10 Philippine, South China
  physical feature:
    strait: 5 Sunda 7 Makasar, Malacca 8 Makassar
    volcano: 6 Slamet 8 Krakatoa
  people: 5 Batak, Dayak, Dyaks, Malay 6 Papuan, Toraja 7 Battaks, Chinese, Igorots 8 Acehnese, Achinese, Balinese, Javanese, Madurese, Sudanese 11 Minang Kabau
    leader: 7 Suharto, Sukarno
  language: 5 Tetum 6 Bahasa, Igorot 7 English, Gyarung, Malayan 8 Balinese, Chamorro, Javanese, Madurese, Sudanese 10 Indonesian, Polynesian
  religion: 5 Hindu, Islam 7 animism 8 Buddhism 12 Christianity, Confucianism
  place:
    palace: 6 Kraton
    pyramid: 5 Stupa 9 Borobudur
    shrine: 6 Dagoba, Kraton
  feature:
    cap: 5 pitji
    cloth: 5 batik
    jacket: 6 kebaja
    lizard: 12 Komodo dragon
    scarf: 9 selendang
    shadow play: 6 wajang, wayang
    skirt: 4 kain 6 sarong
    tree: 4 supa
  food:
    ceremonial dinner: 9 selamatan

indoors 6 at home, inside, shut in, shut up, within 10 in the house 11 sequestered

Indo-Pacific
  language subgroup: 4 Kate 5 Kiwai 7 Andaman, Merauke 8 Highland, Tasmania 9 Ekari-Moni, Hollandia, Timor-Alor 10 New Britain 12 Astrolabe Bay, Bougainville 14 Vogelkop-Kamoro 16 Eastern New Guinea, Northern Salomons 17 Northern Halmahera

indorse *see* 7 endorse

In Dubious Battle
  author: 13 John Steinbeck

indubitable 4 sure 7 certain 9 undoubted 10 conclusive 11 irrefutable, unequivocal 12 indisputable, unmistakable 14 unquestionable 16 incontrovertible

indubitably 6 surely 7 for sure 8 of course 9 certainly, doubtless 10 for certain 11 undoubtedly 12 without doubt 14 unquestionably, with no question

induce 3 get 4 coax, spur, sway 5 cause, impel 6 arouse, effect, incite, lead to, prompt 7 actuate, bring on, dispose, incline, inspire, produce, provoke, win over 8 activate, motivate, occasion, persuade 9 encourage, influence, instigate, prevail on 10 bring about, bring round, give rise to 11 prevail upon, set in motion

inducement 4 bait, goad, spur 5 cause 6 ground, motive, reason 8 stimulus 9 incentive 10 allurement, attraction, enticement, incitement, persuasion, temptation 11 inspiration, instigation, provocation

induct 5 crown, draft, frock 6 enlist, invest, lead in, ordain, sign up 7 bring in, install, instate, usher in 8 enthrone, initiate, register 9 conscript, establish, introduce 10 consecrate, inaugurate

in due course 4 then 6 thence 10 eventually 11 accordingly 15 at the proper time 19 in the fullness of time

indulge 4 baby 5 favor, humor, serve, spoil, treat 6 coddle, cosset, oblige 7 appease, cater to, gratify, yield to 8 pander to 9 give way to 11 accommodate, go along with, mollycoddle

indulgence 6 excess, luxury 8 kindness, lenience, patience 9 allowance, benignity, tolerance 10 compassion, debauchery, profligacy, sufferance 11 dissipation, forbearance, forgiveness 12 extravagance, graciousness, immoderation, intemperance 13 understanding 14 permissiveness

indulgent 4 kind 6 benign, tender 7 clement, lenient, patient, sparing 8 humoring, obliging, tolerant, yielding 9 easygoing, forgiving, pampering 10 forbearing, permissive 11 complaisant, forebearing 12 conciliatory 13 understanding

Indus
  constellation near: 4 Grus, Pavo
  river in: 4 Asia 5 India, Tibet 8 Pakistan
  into: 10 Arabian Sea

industrious 4 busy 6 active 7 zealous 8 diligent, occupied, sedulous, tireless 9 assiduous, energetic 10 productive, purposeful, unflagging **11** hardworking, painstaking, persevering, unremitting **12** businesslike, enterprising **13** indefatigable

industry 2 go **4** toil, zeal **5** field, labor, trade **6** bustle, energy, hustle **8** activity, business, commerce, hard work **9** assiduity, diligence **10** enterprise **11** application, manufacture **12** perseverance, sedulousness **13** assiduousness **15** industriousness **16** indefatigability

inebriate 3 sot **4** lush, soak, wino **5** drunk, rummy, souse, toper **6** barfly, boozer **7** tippler **8** drunkard **9** alcoholic **11** dipsomaniac

inebriated 4 high **5** drunk, oiled, tight, tipsy **6** bombed, loaded, potted, stoned, tanked, zonked **7** drunken, smashed, sozzled, wrecked **8** besotted **9** befuddled, plastered **10** in one's cups **11** intoxicated **12** drunk as a lord **17** under the influence **20** three sheets to the wind

ineffable 5 ideal **6** divine, sacred **9** spiritual **10** indefinite, untellable **11** indefinable, unspeakable, unutterable **12** transcendent **13** indescribable, inexpressible **14** incommunicable, transcendental

in effect 6 active **8** a reality **9** activated, effective, operative **11** in operation

ineffective 4 vain, weak **6** futile **7** useless **8** impotent **9** fruitless, incapable, powerless, worthless **10** inadequate **11** inefficient, inoperative, not much good, of little use **12** unproductive

ineffectual 4 lame, vain, weak **5** inept **6** feeble, futile **7** hapless, useless **8** impotent **10** inadequate, not up to par, profitless, unavailing **11** incompetent, ineffective, inefficient **12** unproductive, unprofitable, unsuccessful **13** inefficacious **14** unsatisfactory

inefficient 5 inept, slack **6** futile **8** slipshod **9** pointless, unskilled **10** inadequate **11** incompetent, indifferent, ineffective, ineffectual **12** not efficient, unproductive **13** inefficacious **14** good-for-nothing

inelegance 9 crudeness, grossness, roughness, vulgarity **10** coarseness **13** tastelessness

inelegant 4 ugly **6** coarse, common **8** inferior **9** tasteless, unrefined **10** ungraceful

ineligible 5 unfit **10** unentitled, unsuitable **11** not eligible, unqualified **12** disqualified, unacceptable

ineluctable 4 sure **5** fated **7** certain **10** ineludible, inevasible, inevitable, inexorable, sure as fate, unevadable **11** inescapable, irrevocable, unavoidable, unstoppable **13** unpreventable

inept 5 empty, inane, silly, unapt **6**

clumsy **7** asinine, awkward, fatuous, foolish **8** bungling **9** maladroit, pointless, senseless, unfitting, unskilled, untrained **10** out of place, unsuitable **11** incompetent, ineffective, ineffectual, inefficient, nonsensical, unqualified **13** inappropriate, inefficacious

ineptitude 9 inability **10** clumsiness, inadequacy **11** awkwardness **12** incompetence **14** ineffectuality **15** ineffectiveness

inequality 8 imparity, inequity **9** disparity, diversity, prejudice **10** difference, divergence, favoritism, unfairness, unlikeness **11** inconstancy, unequalness **12** irregularity, variableness **13** disproportion, dissimilarity, dissimilitude

inequity 4 bias **9** injustice, prejudice **10** favoritism, inequality, unfairness **14** discrimination

ineradicable 7 lasting **9** indelible, permanent **10** inerasable **12** ineffaceable **14** indestructible

inert 4 dull, numb **5** slack, still **6** leaden, static, supine, torpid **7** languid, passive **8** immobile, inactive, listless, sluggish **9** impassive, inanimate, quiescent **10** motionless, phlegmatic, stationary

inertia 6 apathy, stupor, torpor **7** languor **8** dullness, inaction, laziness, lethargy **9** indolence, inertness, lassitude, passivity, torpidity, weariness **10** inactivity, supineness **11** passiveness **12** listlessness, sluggishness

inertness 6 apathy **8** lethargy **9** passivity **10** quiescence **12** sluggishness **14** motionlessness

inescapable 4 sure **7** certain, evident **8** manifest, positive **10** inevitable **11** ineluctable, predestined, unavoidable

in esse 7 in being **11** in actuality **16** actually existing

inestimable 7 sumless **8** precious **9** priceless **10** invaluable **11** beyond price, measureless **12** immeasurable, incalculable, unmeasurable

inevitable 4 sure **5** fated **7** certain **8** destined **10** ineludible **11** ineluctable, inescapable, predestined, unavoidable **13** predetermined, unpreventable

inexact 3 off **6** faulty, sloppy **8** careless, slovenly **9** defective, imperfect, imprecise **10** inaccurate, unspecific **11** approximate

in exactly the same words
Latin: **19** verbatim et literatim

inexcusable 10 unbearable **11** intolerable, unallowable **12** indefensible, unforgivable, unpardonable **13** unjustifiable

inexhaustible 7 endless **8** infinite, tireless, unending **9** boundless **13** indefatigable **15** measurelessness

in existence 5 alive **6** extant, living **8**

existent, existing **9** surviving, to be found

inexorable 4 firm **5** cruel, stiff **6** dogged **7** adamant **8** obdurate, pitiless, ruthless **9** immovable, merciless, unbending **10** adamantive, determined, inflexible, relentless, unyielding **11** inescapable, intractable **12** irresistible **14** uncompromising

inexpedient 6 futile, unwise **7** useless **11** detrimental, impractical, inadvisable, injudicious, undesirable **13** not worthwhile **15** disadvantageous

inexpensive 5 cheap **8** moderate **9** low-priced **10** economical, reasonable **13** nominal-priced, popular-priced

inexpensive table wine
French: **12** vin ordinaire

inexperienced 5 fresh, green, naive **6** callow **7** untried **8** inexpert, unversed **9** unfledged, unskilled, untrained, untutored **10** unfamiliar, unschooled, unseasoned **11** uninitiated, unpracticed **12** unaccustomed, unacquainted, unconversant **15** unsophisticated

inexpert 5 inept **6** clumsy, gauche **7** awkward **8** bungling **9** incapable, maladroit **10** amateurish, unpolished, unskillful **11** incompetent, ineffective, inefficient, unqualified **14** unaccomplished

inexplicable 8 abstruse, baffling, puzzling **9** insoluble **10** insolvable, mysterious, mystifying, perplexing **11** enigmatical, inscrutable **12** unfathomable **13** unaccountable, unexplainable **14** undecipherable **16** incomprehensible

inexpressive 5 blank, empty **6** vacant **14** expressionless

in extenso 12 at full length

in extremis 9 near death **11** in extremity **15** on the outer edges **19** at the uttermost limit

in extremity
Latin: **10** in extremis

in fact
Latin: **7** de facto

infallible 4 sure **7** assured, certain, perfect **8** flawless, inerrant, positive, reliable, surefire, unerring **9** apodictic, faultless, foolproof, unfailing **10** dependable, impeccable **11** irrefutable **13** unimpeachable **16** incontrovertible

infamous 3 low **4** base, evil, foul, vile **6** odious, sinful, sordid, wicked **7** corrupt, heinous, ignoble, immoral, knavish **8** damnable, recreant, shameful **9** abhorrent, monstrous, nefarious, notorious **10** abominable, detestable, iniquitous, of evil fame, outrageous, perfidious, profligate, scandalous, scurrilous, villainous **11** disgraceful, of ill repute, opprobrious, treacherous **12** dishonorable, disreputable

infamy 4 evil **5** odium, shame **7** scandal **8** contempt, disgrace, dishonor, ignominy, villainy **9** discredit, disesteem, disrepute, notoriety **10** corruption, opprobrium, wickedness **11** abomination **13** despicability, notoriousness

infancy 6 cradle, nonage **8** babyhood, minority **9** beginning, childhood, inception **10** immaturity

infant 3 kid **4** babe, baby **5** child **7** neonate, newborn, preemie, toddler **8** nursling, suckling

infantile 7 babyish **8** childish, juvenile **9** childlike, infantine **10** infantlike, sophomoric

infantryman 6 Zouave **7** dogface, dragoon **8** chasseur, doughboy, sorefoot **11** foot soldier

infatuated 7 charmed, smitten **8** beguiled, enamored, inflamed, obsessed **9** bewitched, enchanted, entranced **10** captivated, enraptured, enthralled, spellbound **11** carried away, intoxicated **12** having a crush

infatuation 4 rave **5** craze, crush, folly, mania **6** desire **7** passion **9** obsession, puppy love **10** enthusiasm **11** fascination, foolishness **12** passing fancy

infect 4 ruin **5** spoil, taint, touch **6** blight, damage, poison **7** afflict, corrupt **9** indispose, influence **11** contaminate

infected 6 impure, morbid, septic **7** corrupt, tainted **8** cankered, diseased, poisoned **12** contaminated

infection 6 blight **7** disease **9** contagion, virulence **11** suppuration

infectious 8 catching, epidemic, virulent **9** catchable, infective, spreading **10** compelling, contagious, inoculable **11** captivating **12** communicable, irresistible

infecund 6 barren, farrow **7** sterile **9** infertile **12** unproductive

infer 4 deem **5** glean, guess, judge, opine **6** deduce, gather, reason, reckon **7** presume, suppose, surmise **8** conclude **9** speculate **10** conjecture

inference 4 clue **10** intimation, suggestion **11** insinuation

inferior 4 poor **6** junior **8** low-grade, mediocre **9** secondary **10** low-quality, second-rate, subsidiary **11** indifferent, subordinate, subservient, substandard **12** not up to snuff

infernal 4 vile **5** awful, black, lower **6** cursed, Hadean, nether **7** heinous, hellish, Stygian, vicious **8** accursed, damnable, devilish, fiendish, horrible, terrible **9** atrocious, execrable, malicious, monstrous, nefarious, Plutonian **10** abominable, demoniacal, diabolical, flagitious, horrendous, iniquitous
also: 9 Tartarean
refers to: 10 underworld

inferno 4 hell, oven **5** abyss, Hades **6** hotbox, the pit, Tophet **7** furnace, roaster, sizzler **8** hellfire, hellhole, scorcher **9** perdition **10** lower world, underworld **11** netherworld **12** fiery furnace **13** nether regions **15** infernal regions **16** fire and brimstone, the bottomless pit

Inferno
part I of: 12 Divine Comedy
author: 14 Dante Alighieri

infertile 4 arid, bare **6** barren, effete, fallow **7** drained, sterile **8** depleted, desolate, impotent, infecund **9** exhausted, fruitless **10** unfruitful, unprolific **12** unproductive **13** nonproductive

infest 4 team **5** beset, crawl, creep, swarm **6** abound, infect, plague, ravage **7** overrun, torment **9** crawl with, swarm with

infestation 6 plague, ravage **9** lousiness, pervasion **11** overrunning **12** overswarming

in few words
Latin: 12 paucis verbis

infidel 5 pagan **6** savage **7** atheist, heathen, heretic, skeptic **8** agnostic, apostate, idolater **9** barbarian **10** unbeliever **11** nonbeliever

infidelity 6 breach **7** falsity, perfidy **8** adultery, betrayal **9** disregard, violation **10** disloyalty, infraction **12** nonadherence **13** nonobservance, transgression **14** unfaithfulness

infiltrate 4 leak, seep **5** imbue, steep **6** absorb, seep in **7** pervade **8** colonize, permeate **9** insinuate, penetrate

infinite 4 vast **5** great **7** endless, immense **8** enormous **9** boundless, limitless, unbounded, unlimited **10** tremendous, without end **11** illimitable, measureless **12** immeasurable, incalculable, interminable **13** inexhaustible **15** uncircumscribed

infinitesimal 3 wee **4** puny, tiny **6** minute **7** diminutive, negligible **11** microscopic **13** imperceptible, inappreciable, insignificant, undiscernible **14** extremely small, inconsiderable

infinity 7 forever **8** eternity **10** infinitude, perpetuity **11** endlessness, eternal time **12** sempiternity **13** boundlessness, limitlessness **14** illimitability **15** everlastingness, immeasurability, incalculability, measurelessness **16** inexhaustibility **19** incomprehensibility

Infiri
gods of: 10 underworld

infirm 3 ill **4** weak, worn **5** anile, frail, shaky **6** ailing, feeble, poorly, sickly **7** failing, fragile, unsound **8** decrepit, disabled, helpless, unstable, weakened **9** doddering, emaciated, enervated, enfeebled, powerless **11** debilitated **12** strengthless

infirmary 6 clinic **7** sick bay **8** hospital

infirmity 4 flaw **5** fault **6** defect, malady **7** ailment, failing, frailty, illness **8** debility, disorder, handicap, sickness **9** fragility, frailness **10** deficiency, disability, infirmness **11** instability **12** debilitation, imperfection, unstableness **13** indisposition, vulnerability

in flagrante delicto 8 in the act **9** red-handed

inflame 4 fire, rile **5** craze, rouse **6** arouse, enrage, excite, heat up, ignite, incite, kindle, madden, stir up, work up **7** agitate, incense, provoke **8** enkindle **9** electrify, stimulate **10** intoxicate

inflamed 3 mad **5** angry, irate, riled **6** crazed, fuming, roused **7** aroused, enraged, excited, fired up, furious, incited **8** agitated, incensed, provoked, reddened **9** steamed up, stirred up **10** infuriated **11** intensified

inflame with love 6 enamor **9** enrapture, impassion, infatuate

inflammable 5 fiery **8** choleric, volatile **9** excitable, flammable, ignitable, impetuous, overhasty, sensitive **10** high-strung, incendiary **11** combustible, precipitate **12** inflammatory

inflammation 4 acne, fire, gout, sore **6** canker, firing **7** arousal, chafing **8** bursitis, ignition, kindling, soreness, sore spot, swelling **9** agitation **10** incitement, irritation **13** conflagration, rabblerousing
suffix: 4 itis

inflammatory 5 fiery, rabid **8** arousing, enraging, inciting, mutinous, volcanic **9** demagogic, explosive, insurgent **10** incendiary, rebellious **11** combustible, fulminating, inflammable, intemperate, provocative **13** rabble-rousing, revolutionary

inflate 5 bloat, swell **6** blow up, dilate, expand, fill up, pump up **7** distend, improve, puff out **10** appreciate **11** rise in value

inflated 5 blown, gassy, tumid, wordy **6** blew up, turgid **7** bloated, blown up, dilated, flowery, pompous, swollen, verbose **8** boastful, enlarged, expanded **9** bombastic, distended, overblown, swelled up **10** rhetorical, swelled out **11** exaggerated, pretentious

inflection 4 tone **5** tenor **6** accent **10** modulation **11** enunciation, tone of voice **12** articulation **13** pronunciation

inflexible 4 firm, hard, taut **5** fixed, rigid, solid, stiff **6** dogged, mulish **7** adamant **8** obdurate, resolute, stubborn **9** hidebound, immovable, immutable, ironbound, obstinate, pigheaded, stringent, tenacious, unbending, unplastic **10** adamantine, determined, headstrong, impervious, implacable, inexorable, unwavering, unyielding **11** hard and fast, intractable, not flexible, unmalleable **12** unchangeable **14** uncompromising

inflict 4 dump **5** lay on, wreak **6** impose, unload **7** put upon **9** visit upon **10** administer, perpetrate **11** bring to bear

inflorescence 5 bloom **6** flower **7** blossom, cluster **8** blooming **9** flowering **10** blossoming

> **type: 4** cyme **5** spike, umbel **6** corymb, raceme, spadix **7** panicle **9** capitulum **14** verticillaster

influence 4 hold, move, pull, stir, sway **5** clout, guide, impel, power **6** arouse, effect, incite, induce, prompt, weight **7** act upon, actuate, control, dispose, incline, inspire, mastery, potency, provoke **8** dominion, leverage, persuade, pressure, prestige **9** advantage, authority **10** ascendancy, domination, predispose

influential 6 moving, potent, strong **7** leading, weighty **8** forceful, powerful, puissant **9** effective, effectual, important, inspiring, momentous **10** activating **11** efficacious, significant **12** instrumental **13** consequential

influx 5 entry **6** inflow **7** arrival, indraft, ingress **9** flowing in, incursion, inpouring **10** converging, inundation **12** infiltration

in force 6 extant **7** en masse **8** in effect **9** effective, operative **11** in existence, in operation, operational **14** in large numbers

inform 3 rat **4** fink, tell **5** edify **6** advise, clue in, notify, snitch, squeal, tattle, tell on, tip off **7** apprise, let know **8** acquaint, denounce, forewarn, report to **9** declare to, enlighten **11** communicate, familiarize, serve notice **14** blow the whistle

inform against 5 rat on **6** betray, fink on, tell on **7** sell out **8** denounce, squeal on **11** double-cross **16** blow the whistle on

informal 4 easy **6** casual, simple **7** natural, offhand **8** familiar **9** easygoing, not formal **10** unofficial **11** spontaneous **12** come-as-you-are **13** unceremonious, unconstrained **14** unconventional

informal preliminary conference
> **French: 10** pourparler

informant 6 source **7** adviser, tipster **8** appriser, informer, notifier, reporter **9** announcer, spokesman **10** respondent **11** enlightener, horse's mouth, spokeswoman

information 4 data, news **5** facts, notes **6** notice, papers, report **7** account, tidings **8** briefing, bulletin, evidence, material **9** documents, knowledge, materials **10** communique **11**

fact-finding **12** announcement, intelligence, notification **13** enlightenment

informed 4 told, up on, wise **5** aware, posted, talked, taught, warned **7** abreast, advised, knowing, learned, tattled **8** apprised, betrayed, educated, notified, reported, snitched, up to date **9** au courant, permeated **10** acquainted, instructed **11** enlightened, intelligent **13** knowledgeable

informer 3 rat **4** fink **5** Judas **6** canary **7** blabber, stoolie, tattler, traitor **8** betrayer, mouchard, snitcher, squealer **11** stool pigeon

Informer, The
> **author: 13** Liam O'Flaherty
> **director: 8** John Ford
> **cast: 10** Una O'Connor **11** Wallace Ford **12** Heather Angel **13** Margot Grahame, Preston Foster **14** Victor McLaglen
> **score: 10** Max Steiner
> **remade as: 7** Up Tight

infraction 6 breach **8** trespass **9** violation **10** peccadillo **11** lawbreaking **12** disobedience, encroachment, infringement, unobservance **13** nonobservance, transgression

infrastructure 4 base, root **5** basis **6** bottom, fabric, ground **7** bedrock, footing, support **9** framework, substrate **10** foundation, groundwork, substratum **12** substructure, underpinning **14** understructure

infrequent 3 few **4** rare **6** fitful, seldom, unique **7** unusual **8** sporadic, uncommon **9** spasmodic **10** occasional **16** few and far between

infringe 5 break **6** butt in, invade **7** disobey, impinge, infract, intrude, violate **8** encroach, overstep, trespass **10** contravene, transgress

in front 5 ahead, first **6** before **7** forward

in full possession of one's faculties
> **Latin: 12** compos mentis

infuriate 3 vex **4** gall, rile **5** anger, chafe **6** enrage, madden, offend **7** incense, inflame, outrage, provoke **8** irritate **9** aggravate, burn one up, make angry **10** exasperate **15** raise one's dander

infuriating 7 irksome **8** annoying, enraging **9** maddening, provoking **10** irritating **11** aggravating **12** exasperating, inflammatory

infuse 5 imbue **7** fortify, implant, inspire, instill **8** impart to, pour into **9** inculcate, insinuate, introject

in futuro 11 in the future

Inge, William
> **author of: 6** Picnic **7** Bus Stop **19** Come Back Little Sheba **26** The Dark at the Top of the Stairs

in general 7 as a rule, usually **10** by and large, on the whole

ingenious 4 deft **6** adroit, artful, clever, crafty, expert, shrewd **7** cunning **8** masterly, original, skillful, stunning **9** brilliant, dexterous, inventive, masterful **11** resourceful

ingenuity 5 flair, skill **7** cunning, know-how, mastery **8** aptitude, deftness, facility **9** adeptness, dexterity, expertise, sharpness **10** adroitness, astuteness, brilliance, cleverness, shrewdness **11** imagination **12** good thinking, skillfulness **13** ingeniousness, inventiveness **15** imaginativeness, quick-wittedness, resourcefulness

ingenuous 4 open **5** frank, naive **6** direct, honest **7** artless, genuine, natural, up front **8** trusting **9** guileless **10** unaffected **11** openhearted **13** simplehearted **15** straightforward, unsophisticated **16** straight-shooting

ingenuousness 7 naivete **8** openness **9** frankness **11** artlessness

ingest 3 eat **4** gulp, take **5** drink **6** absorb, devour, imbibe, take in **7** consume, swallow **8** gulp down

inglorious 3 low **4** base, evil, mean, vile **6** odious **7** corrupt, heinous, ignoble **8** depraved, flagrant, infamous, shameful, shocking **9** atrocious, degrading, nefarious **10** despicable, detestable, outrageous, scandalous **11** disgraceful, ignominious, opprobrious **12** contemptible, dishonorable

in good condition
> **French: 10** embonpoint

in good health 2 OK **4** fine, hale, well **6** hearty, robust, tiptop **7** healthy **8** all right, blooming, vigorous **9** full of pep, in the pink **17** full of vim and vigor

in good time 5 early **7** betimes **11** ahead of time

ingot 3 bar **5** block

ingrained 4 deep, firm **5** fixed **6** inborn, inbred, innate, rooted **8** inherent, thorough **9** confirmed, implanted, indelible, intrinsic **10** deep-rooted, deep-seated, inveterate **14** constitutional

Ingram, Blanche
> **character in: 8** Jane Eyre
> **author: 6** Bronte

ingratiating 4 oily **5** sweet **6** genial, smarmy **7** affable, amiable, cordial, fulsome, gushing, likable, lovable, winning, winsome **8** charming, engaging, friendly, gracious, magnetic, pleasing, unctuous **9** appealing, congenial **10** attractive, enchanting, obsequious, oleaginous, personable, persuasive **11** captivating, good-humored, self-serving **12** presumptuous

ingratiation 7 blarney **8** flattery **9**

sweet talk **12** inveiglement **13** blandishments

ingratitude 14 ungratefulness **18** lack of appreciation

ingredient 4 part **6** aspect, factor **7** element, feature **9** component, essential, principle **11** constituent, contributor **12** integral part

Ingres, Jean-Auguste-Dominique
born: 6 France **9** Montauban
artwork: 9 Odalisque, The Source **13** Mme Moitessier **14** The Turkish Bath **15** Valpincon Bather **16** Roger and Angelica **17** The Vow of Louis XIII **21** Comtesse d'Haussonville **25** The Ambassadors of Agamemnon **26** The Vow of Louis the Thirteenth

ingress 5 entry, way in **6** access **8** entrance

inhabit 5 lodge **6** live in, occupy, people, settle, tenant **7** dwell in **8** populate, reside in

inhabitant 6 inmate, lessee, lodger, native, renter, tenant **7** boarder, citizen, denizen, dweller, settler **8** occupant, occupier, resident, villager **9** inhabiter

inhalation 4 gasp **5** sniff **6** breath **11** breathing in

inhale 5 sniff, snuff **6** suck in **7** inspire, respire **9** breathe in, inbreathe

inherent 6 inborn, inbred, innate, native **7** natural **9** essential, ingrained, intrinsic **10** deep-rooted, hereditary, inveterate **11** inalienable, inseparable **14** constitutional

inherit 3 get **6** be left, come by **7** acquire **8** come into **9** come in for **10** fall heir to

inheritance 6 devise, estate, legacy **7** bequest **8** bestowal, heritage **9** endowment, patrimony **10** bequeathal, birthright

inherited 8 came into, heirloom, unearned **10** handed down

inheritor 4 heir **7** legatee **11** beneficiary

Inherit the Wind
director: 13 Stanley Kramer
based on play by: 10 Robert E Lee **14** Jerome Lawrence
cast: 8 Dick York **9** Gene Kelly **10** Elliot Reid **11** Harry Morgan **12** Spencer Tracy (Clarence Darrow) **13** Frederic March (William Jennings Bryan) **16** Florence Eldridge

inhibit 3 bar, gag **4** curb, stop **5** block, check **6** arrest, enjoin, forbid, hinder, impede, muzzle **7** control, harness, prevent, repress, smother **8** hold back, obstruct, prohibit, restrain, restrict, suppress **9** constrain **11** hold in leash

inhibited 4 cold **6** barred, curbed, frigid **7** bridled, checked, guarded **8** hindered, reserved **9** repressed **10** controlled, obstructed, restrained **11** constrained, discouraged, held in check **12** unresponsive **14** under restraint

inhibition, inhibitions 5 check **7** reserve **8** blockage **9** misgiving, restraint, stricture **10** constraint, impediment **11** guardedness, mental block, obstruction, restriction **12** constriction **17** self-consciousness

in high spirits 2 up **3** gay **5** happy, merry **6** elated, jaunty, joyful, joyous **7** buoyant **8** carefree, ecstatic, exultant, jubilant **9** overjoyed **11** exhilarated, on cloud nine **13** up in the clouds **15** on top of the world

in hoc signo vinces 26 in this sign shalt thou conquer
motto of: 19 Constantine the Great
from vision of: 5 cross

inhospitable 4 cold, cool, rude **5** aloof **6** unkind **7** distant, hostile **8** impolite **10** unfriendly, ungracious, unobliging, unsociable **11** standoffish, uncongenial, unreceptive, unwelcoming **12** discourteous, unneighborly **13** inconsiderate **14** unapproachable **15** unaccommodating

inhuman 5 cruel **6** brutal, savage **7** brutish, satanic, vicious **8** barbaric, demoniac, fiendish, pitiless, ruthless, venomous **9** barbarous, heartless, malignant, merciless, monstrous, unfeeling **10** diabolical, malevolent **11** coldhearted, cold-blooded, hardhearted

inhumane 6 brutal, savage **7** inhuman **8** fiendish, pitiless, ruthless **9** barbarous, heartless, merciless, unfeeling, unpitying **10** unmerciful **11** coldblooded, hardhearted **12** bloodthirsty **13** unsympathetic

inhumanity 6 sadism **7** cruelty **8** atrocity, savagery **9** barbarism, barbarity, brutality **11** brutishness, heinousness, malevolence, viciousness **12** fiendishness, ruthlessness **13** heartlessness, mercilessness **15** coldbloodedness **16** bloodthirstiness

inhumation 6 burial **9** interment **10** entombment

inimical 5 toxic **6** at odds **7** harmful, hateful, hostile, hurtful, ruinous **8** venomous, virulent **9** dangerous, illwilled, injurious, on the outs, poisonous, rancorous **10** unfriendly **11** acrimonious, deleterious, destructive, detrimental, ill-disposed **12** antagonistic, antipathetic, disputatious **13** at loggerheads, at sword's point

inimitable 4 rare **6** unique **7** supreme **8** peerless **9** matchless, nonpareil, unequaled, unmatched, unrivaled **10** consummate, preeminent, unexcelled **11** superlative, unsurpassed **12** incomparable, unparalleled **13** beyond compare

iniquitous 4 base, evil, vile **6** sinful,

wicked **7** corrupt, debased, immoral, vicious **8** depraved, infamous **9** nefarious **10** evil-minded **12** blackhearted **13** reprehensible

iniquity 3 sin **4** evil, vice **5** wrong **6** infamy **7** knavery, outrage, roguery **8** inequity, villainy **9** depravity, evildoing, flagrancy, turpitude **10** corruption, dishonesty, immorality, miscreancy, profligacy, sinfulness, unfairness, unjustness, wickedness, wrongdoing **11** abomination **13** transgression **14** gross injustice **15** unrighteousness

in isolation
Latin: 7 in vacuo

initial 5 first **6** maiden, primal **7** opening, primary **8** germinal, original, starting **9** beginning, inaugural, incipient **10** commencing, initiatory **12** introductory

initiate 4 haze, open **5** begin, found, set up, start **6** induct, invest, launch, take in **7** bring in, install, kick off, receive, usher in **8** be opened, commence, get going, set afoot, set going **9** enter upon, establish, institute, introduce, originate **10** inaugurate, lead the way **11** break ground, get under way, take the lead **12** acquaint with **13** blaze the trail **15** familiarize with **16** lay the first stone, lay the foundation **19** start the ball rolling

initiation 5 onset, start **6** outset **7** genesis, opening **8** entrance, guidance, outbreak, starting **9** beginning, inception, induction **10** admittance, initiating, ushering in **11** inculcation **12** commencement, inauguration, introduction **14** indoctrination **15** formal admission

initiative 4 lead **8** dynamism **9** first move, first step **10** creativity, enterprise, get-up-and-go, leadership **11** originality **12** forcefulness **14** aggressiveness

in its original place
Latin: 6 in situ

inject 3 put **4** pump **5** force, imbue, infix **6** infuse, insert **7** instill, throw in **8** intromit **9** interject, introduce **11** interpolate

injection 4 hypo, shot **7** booster, vaccine **9** antitoxin, insertion **10** hypodermic **11** inoculation, vaccination **12** shot in the arm

injudicious 4 dumb, wild **5** crazy **6** stupid, unwise **7** foolish, unsound **8** heedless, reckless **9** audacious, foolhardy, hotheaded, imprudent, senseless **10** self-willed, unsuitable **11** inadvisable

injunction 4 writ **5** edict, order **7** command **10** admonition, court order

Injun Joe
character in: 9 Tom Sawyer
author: 9 Mark Twain

injure 3 mar **4** harm, hurt, lame, maim **5** abuse, spoil, stain, sting, sully, wound, wrong **6** bruise, damage, debase, deface, deform, impair, malign, mangle, misuse, offend, scathe **7** afflict, affront, blemish, violate, vitiate **8** do harm to, ill-treat, lacerate, maltreat, mutilate **9** disfigure

injured 4 hurt, lame **6** abused, harmed, maimed, marred, piqued **7** bruised, damaged, defaced, grieved, scathed, wounded, wronged **8** crippled, deformed, impaired, insulted, offended **9** afflicted, affronted, aggrieved **10** disfigured

injurious 7 abusive, adverse, harmful, hurtful, noxious, ruinous **8** damaging, inimical **9** corrosive **10** calamitous, disastrous, pernicious **11** deleterious, destructive, detrimental

injury 3 cut **4** blow, gash, harm, hurt, stab **5** abuse, wound **6** bruise, damage, lesion **7** affront, outrage, scratch **9** aspersion, contusion, indignity, injustice **10** affliction, defamation, detraction, disservice, impairment, laceration, mutilation **12** vilification

injustice 3 sin **4** bias, evil **5** wrong **6** injury **7** bigotry, offense, tyranny **8** foul play, inequity, iniquity **9** prejudice, unjust act **10** disservice, favoritism, inequality, infraction, partiality, unfairness, unjustness, wrongdoing **11** malpractice, persecution **12** encroachment, infringement, partisanship **13** transgression

in keeping 6 normal **7** natural **8** becoming **9** congruous, consonant **10** consistent **11** appropriate, in agreement **12** in compliance, in conformity

inkling 3 cue, tip **4** clue, hint, idea **6** notion **7** glimmer, whisper **8** innuendo **9** suspicion, vague idea **10** conception, glimmering, indication, intimation, suggestion **11** insinuation, supposition

inky 3 jet **4** dark **5** black, raven, sable **7** stygian **9** coal-black

inlet 3 bay **4** cove, gulf **5** bight, fiord, firth, fjord **6** harbor, strait **7** estuary, narrows **8** waterway

in line 4 even **6** in a row **7** aligned, in order **8** queued up, straight **12** under control

in loco 7 in place **16** in the proper place

in loco parentis 16 replacing a parent **19** in the place of a parent

inmate 3 con **5** felon **6** lodger, tenant **7** convict, denizen **8** prisoner, resident **10** inhabitant

in medias res 19 in the middle of things **21** in the middle of the story

in memoriam 10 in memory of **13** as a memorial to, to the memory of

In Memoriam A H H
author: **18** Alfred Lord Tennyson

in memory of
Latin: **10** in memoriam

In Memory of W B Yeats
author: **7** W H Auden

inmost 5 inner **6** inside **7** central **8** interior **9** innermost

in motion 5 afoot, astir **6** active, moving **7** on the go, working **8** under way **9** on the move, operating, operative **10** responsive

inn 5 hotel, lodge, motel, serai **6** hostel, imaret, tavern **7** hospice, pension **8** hostelry **9** roadhouse **11** caravansary, public house
French: **7** auberge
Spanish: **6** posada

innards 4 guts **6** bowels, vitals **7** gizzard, insides, viscera **10** intestines **14** liver and lights

innate 6 inborn, inbred, native **7** natural **8** inherent **9** essential, ingrained, inherited, intrinsic, intuitive **10** congenital, hereditary, indigenous **11** instinctive **14** constitutional

inner 6 hidden, inside, inward, mental, middle **7** central, private, psychic **8** esoteric, interior, internal, personal **9** concealed, emotional, spiritual, unobvious **10** more secret **12** more intimate **13** psychological

inner circle 4 core **5** bosom, cadre, heart **6** center **7** nucleus

inner city 8 core city, downtown **9** urban area **10** city limits, metropolis **11** central city **16** metropolitan area

Inner Mongolia
other name: **9** Neimenggu, Neimengku
part of: **5** China
capital: **6** Hohhot **7** Huhehot
desert: **4** Gobi
tent: **4** yurt

innermost 6 inmost, secret **7** deepest **10** deep-rooted, deep-seated **11** most private **12** most intimate, most personal

innermost part 4 core, crux, pith, soul **6** center, kernel **7** essence, nucleus

Inness, George
born: **10** Newburgh NY
artwork: **7** The Monk **14** Home of the Heron, Peace and Plenty **16** Delaware Water Gap **17** The Delaware Valley **19** The Lackawanna Valley

Innisfail see **7** Ireland

innkeeper 4 host, oste **6** tapper, venter **7** padrone **8** boniface, hosteler, hotelier, landlord, publican **10** proprietor **12** maitre d'hotel, restaurateur

innocence 6 purity **7** naivete **8** chastity **9** freshness **10** clean hands, simplicity **11** artlessness, sinlessness **12** incorruption, spotlessness **13** blame-

lessness, guilelessness, guiltlessness, impeccability, inculpability, ingenuousness, stainlessness **14** immaculateness

innocent 3 tot **4** baby, naif, open, pure, tyro **5** clean, naive **6** chaste, honest, novice, simple **7** artless, ingenue, sinless, upright **8** harmless, pristine, spotless, virginal, virtuous **9** blameless, childlike, faultless, greenhorn, guileless, guiltless, ingenuous, innocuous, little one, stainless, uncorrupt, undefiled, unstained, unsullied, unworldly, well-meant **10** artless one, immaculate, impeccable, inculpable, tenderfoot, young child **11** inoffensive, unblemished, uncorrupted, unmalicious, unoffending **12** unsuspicious **13** meaning no harm, unimpeachable **14** above suspicion, irreproachable **15** unsophisticated
Latin: **12** integer vitae

Innocents, The
director: **11** Jack Clayton
based on story by: **10** Henry James (The Turn of the Screw)
cast: **11** Deborah Kerr, Megs Jenkins **13** Peter Wyngarde **15** Michael Redgrave
script: **12** Truman Capote **16** William Archibald

Innocents Abroad, The
author: **9** Mark Twain (Samuel Clemens)

innocuous 4 dull, mild **5** banal, empty, trite, vapid **6** barren **7** insipid **8** harmless, innocent, painless **9** pointless **11** commonplace, inoffensive, meaningless

innocuousness 6 safety **9** blandness, innocence **12** harmlessness **15** inoffensiveness

in no uncertain terms 7 clearly, plainly **9** expressly **10** definitely, distinctly **13** categorically, unequivocally

innovation 5 shift **7** novelty **8** updating **10** alteration, dernier cri, new measure, remodeling, renovation **11** institution, latest thing **12** commencement, inauguration, introduction, streamlining **13** modernization

innovator 7 deviser, planner **9** contriver **10** instigator, originator **11** inaugurator

Inns of Court 8 Gray's Inn **11** Inner Temple, Lincoln's Inn **12** Middle Temple **14** legal societies
in: **6** London
member: **9** barrister

innuendo 4 hint **7** whisper **8** overtone **9** inference **10** imputation, intimation **11** implication, insinuation

innumerable 6 myriad **8** numerous **9** countless **10** numberless, unnumbered **12** incalculable **13** multitudinous

Ino
also: **9** Leucothea

goddess of: 3 sea
father: 6 Cadmus
mother: 8 Harmonia
sister: 5 Hgave **6** Semele **7** Autonoe
husband: 7 Athamas
son: 8 Learchus **10** Melicertes
stepson: 7 Phrixus
stepdaughter: 5 Helle
saved: 8 Odysseus
cared for infant: 8 Dionysus
changed into: 10 sea goddess

inoculate 5 imbue, shoot **6** infuse, inject, insert **7** implant, instill **8** immunize **9** inculcate, vaccinate

inoculation 4 shot **6** needle **7** booster **9** injection **10** hypodermic **11** vaccination **12** immunization

inoffensive 4 mild, safe **5** bland **7** neutral **8** harmless, innocent **9** endurable, innocuous, tolerable **10** sufferable **11** unoffending **15** unobjectionable

inoffensiveness 6 safety **9** innocence **10** neutrality **12** harmlessness **13** innocuousness

in one's debt 7 obliged **8** beholden, indebted **9** obligated **15** under obligation

in one's own person
Latin: **16** in propria persona

in one's own place
Latin: **7** suo loco

in one's own right
Latin: **7** suo jure

in one's rightful place
Latin: **7** suo loco

inoperable 6 broken **10** broken down, unworkable **11** ineffective

in operation 5 in use **7** in force, working **8** in effect **9** operating, operative

inoperative 4 dead, down **8** inactive **10** not working, out of order

inopportune 7 awkward **8** ill-timed, untimely **10** badly timed, ill-advised, unsuitable **11** troublesome, undesirable, unfavorable, unfortunate **12** inauspicious, incommodious, inconvenient, unpropitious, unseasonable **13** inappropriate **15** disadvantageous

in order 2 OK **4** neat, tidy **6** proper **7** correct, perfect **8** all right

inordinate 5 undue **6** lavish, wanton **7** extreme, profuse, surplus **8** needless, overmuch, shocking **9** excessive **10** deplorable, exorbitant, immoderate, irrational, outrageous, scandalous **11** disgraceful, extravagant, intemperate, overflowing, superfluous, uncalled-for, unnecessary **12** unreasonable, unrestrained **13** superabundant **14** super-saturated, unconscionable **16** disproportionate

inordinately 6 overly, unduly **9** extremely **11** excessively **12** immoderately, outrageously, prodigiously **13** extravagantly, intemperately, superfluously, unnecessarily

inorganic 4 dead **7** mineral **8** lifeless **9** inanimate, nonliving **10** artificial

in passing
French: **9** en passant

in perpetuum 7 forever

in petto 11 in the breast **12** not disclosed

in pieces 6 broken **7** asunder, smashed **8** in shreds, sundered **9** torn apart **13** in smithereens

in place
Latin: **6** in loco, in situ

in plain sight 7 exposed, obvious **10** in full view, noticeable **12** out in the open **17** in front of one's nose

in posse 11 potentially **13** in possibility

in possibility
Latin: **7** in posse

in propria persona 15 in one's own person

inquest 5 probe **7** autopsy, delving, hearing, inquiry, probing **8** necropsy **10** postmortem **11** inquisition **13** investigation

inquire 3 ask **5** probe, query, study **6** search **7** examine, explore, inspect **8** check out, look into, look over, question **9** track down **10** look deeper, scrutinize **11** investigate

inquirer 5 asker, snoop **6** seeker **7** auditor, querier, quizzer, student **8** pollster, searcher **9** catechist **10** inquisitor, questioner **12** interlocutor, interrogator, investigator

inquiry, enquiry 4 hunt, quiz **5** probe, query, quest, study **6** search, survey **7** inquest **8** analysis, question, research, scrutiny **9** interview **10** inspection **11** examination, exploration, inquisition, questioning **13** interrogation, investigation

inquisitive 4 nosy **6** prying, snoopy **8** meddling, snooping **9** inquiring, intrusive, searching **10** meddlesome, too curious **11** interfering, overcurious, questioning

in re 13 in the matter of

in reality
Latin: **7** de facto

in rem 15 against the thing
of a legal proceeding: 18 against the property

in rerum natura 19 in the nature of things

in retreat 10 backing off, retreating **11** withdrawing, backing away

in reverse 8 backward **9** backing up **22** in the opposite direction

insalubrious 7 harmful, noisome, noxious **8** inimical, virulent **9** injurious, unhealthy **10** pernicious **11** deleterious, detrimental, unhealthful, unwholesome

insane 3 mad **4** bats, daft, dumb, loco, nuts, wild, zany **5** balmy, batty, crazy, loony, manic, nutty, potty **6** absurd, crazed, raving **7** berserk, bizarre, bonkers, cracked, foolish, idiotic, lunatic, tetched, touched, unsound **8** demented, frenzied, maniacal, unhinged **9** eccentric, imbecilic, imprudent, insensate, paranoiac, psychotic, senseless **10** ridiculous, unbalanced **11** injudicious **12** mad as a hatter, off one's chump, round the bend, unreasonable **13** off one's rocker, out of one's head, out of one's mind, out of one's wits, schizophrenic **15** bats in the belfry, mad as a March hare, stark staring mad **17** nutty as a fruitcake

insanity 5 folly, mania **6** idiocy, lunacy, raving **7** madness **8** dementia, paranoia **9** aberrance, absurdity, craziness, monomania, psychosis, stupidity **10** aberration **11** derangement, foolishness, unsoundness **12** loss of reason **13** hallucination, mental illness, schizophrenia, senselessness

insatiable 8 ravenous **9** insatiate, limitless, voracious **10** bottomless, gluttonous, implacable, omnivorous **12** unappeasable, unquenchable

inscribe 3 pen **4** etch, mark, seal, sign **5** blaze, brand, carve, write **6** chisel, incise, letter, scrawl **7** engrave, impress, imprint **9** scribble autograph

inscription 5 motto, title **6** legend, rubric **7** address, caption, epigram, epitaph, heading, titulus, writing **8** colophon, epigraph, graffiti **9** engraving, lettering **10** dedication

inscrutable 6 arcane, hidden, masked, veiled **7** deadpan, elusive **8** baffling, puzzling **9** concealed, enigmatic **10** mysterious, mystifying, perplexing, poker-faced, unknowable, unreadable, unrevealed **12** inexplicable, unfathomable, unsearchable **14** indecipherable, unintelligible **16** incomprehensible

insect 3 ant, bee, bug, fly **4** flea, gnat, moth, pest, wasp **5** aphid, imago **6** bedbug, beetle, cicada, earwig, hornet, mantis, mayfly, vermin **7** chigger, cricket, firefly, katydid, ladybug, termite **8** horsefly, housefly, lacewing, mosquito **9** arthropod, butterfly, cockroach, dragonfly **10** silverfish **11** grasshopper
study of: 10 entomology
young: 4 grub, pupa **5** larva, nymph **6** larvae, maggot **9** chrysalis **11** caterpillar
anatomy: 4 palp **5** cerci, notum **6** cercus, feeler, labium, labrum, ocelli, thorax **7** antenna, maxilla, ocellus **8** antennae, mandible, maxillae **9** pro-

boscis, spiracles **10** ovipositor **11** exoskeleton

insectivore 4 mole **5** shrew **6** desman, tenrec **7** moon rat **8** alamiqui, anteater, hedgehog **9** solenodon

insecure 4 weak **5** frail, risky, shaky **6** infirm, unsafe, unsure, wobbly **7** dubious, exposed, not firm, not sure, rickety, unsound **8** critical, doubtful, in danger, perilous, unstable, unsteady **9** dangerous, diffident, hazardous, in a bad way, tottering, unassured, uncertain, under fire **10** endangered, precarious, ramshackle, unreliable, unshielded, vulnerable **11** defenseless, dilapidated, unprotected, unsheltered

insecurities 4 risk **5** peril **6** danger, hazard **7** pitfall **8** jeopardy **11** contingency

insecurity 5 doubt **9** self-doubt, shakiness **10** diffidence, unsafeness **11** dubiousness, incertitude, instability, uncertainty **12** doubtfulness, endangerment, insecureness, unsteadiness **13** vulnerability **14** precariousness **15** defenselessness, lack of assurance **16** apprehensiveness

insensate 4 cold **5** cruel **6** brutal **8** inhumane **9** heartless, unfeeling **11** unconscious

insensibility 4 coma **5** swoon **6** apathy, torpor, trance **8** blackout, dullness, lethargy, numbness, obduracy, oblivion, stoicism **9** analgesia, catalepsy **10** anesthesia, obtuseness **12** incognizance, indifference, mindlessness **13** insensitivity, unfeelingness **15** unconsciousness

insensible 4 cold **9** insensate, senseless **11** unconscious

insensitive 4 cold, dead, numb **5** blase **7** callous **8** hardened **9** apathetic, impassive, insensate, unaware of, unfeeling **10** impervious, insensible **11** indifferent, unconcerned **12** thick-skinned **15** uncompassionate

insensitiveness 8 rudeness **10** coarseness, indelicacy **12** tactlessness **13** insensibility, insensitivity **17** inconsiderateness

inseparable 8 attached **11** indivisible, unseverable **12** indissoluble

insert 3 add **5** embed, enter, imbed, infix, inlay, inset, pop in, put in, set in **6** infuse, inject, push in, tuck in **7** drive in, implant, intrude, place in, press in, slide in, stick in, stuff in, wedge in **8** thrust in **9** interject, interlard, interpose, introduce **10** put between **11** interpolate, intersperse

insertion 2 ad **5** entry, graft, inlay, inset **7** implant **11** insinuation, parenthesis **12** interjection **13** advertisement

inset 4 gore **5** embed, godet, imbed, inlay, panel **6** insert **9** insertion

in seventh heaven 6 elated, joyful, joyous **8** ecstatic, euphoric **9** exuberant, rapturous **11** on cloud nine **13** up in the clouds

inside 2 in **5** inner **6** inmost, inward, secret **7** private **8** cliquish, esoteric, interior, internal, intimate **9** inner part, inner side, innermost **12** confidential

inside information 3 tip **10** inside dope

inside out 9 backwards **10** in disorder, topsy turvy **11** wrong side to

Insider, The
director: **11** Michael Mann
cast: **8** Al Pacino (Lowell Bergman) **9** Debi Mazar (Debbie De Luca) **11** Diane Venora (Liane Wigand) **12** Russell Crowe (Jeffrey Wigand) **13** Lindsay Crouse (Sharon Tiller) **15** Philip Baker Hall (Don Hewitt) **18** Christopher Plummer (Mike Wallace)

insides 4 guts **6** bowels, vitals **7** gizzard, innards, viscera **10** intestines

insidious 3 sly **4** foxy, wily **5** shady **6** artful, covert, crafty, sneaky, subtle, tricky **7** crooked, cunning, devious, furtive **8** guileful, slippery, sneaking, stealthy **9** concealed, deceitful, designing, disguised, secretive, underhand **10** contriving, perfidious, pernicious, undercover, undetected **11** clandestine, deleterious, treacherous, underhanded **12** disingenuous, falsehearted **13** Machiavellian, surreptitious

insight 6 acumen **9** intuition **10** perception **11** discernment, penetration **12** apprehension, perceptivity, perspicacity **13** comprehension, intuitiveness **14** perceptiveness
French: **6** apercu

insignia 3 bar **4** mark, sign, star **5** badge, medal, patch **6** emblem, stripe, symbol **7** chevron, epaulet, oak leaf **10** decoration **13** badge of office

insignificance 8 puniness **9** pettiness, smallness **10** meagerness, triviality **11** irrelevance **12** unimportance

insignificant 4 puny **5** petty, small **6** flimsy, meager, minute, paltry **7** trivial **8** niggling, not vital, nugatory, picayune, piddling, trifling **9** minuscule, worthless **10** immaterial, irrelevant, negligible, of no moment, second-rate **11** indifferent, meaningless, unimportant **12** nonessential **13** small potatoes **14** inconsiderable **15** inconsequential, of little account, of no consequence **18** not worth mentioning

insincere 5 false, lying **6** untrue **7** devious, evasive **8** guileful, two-faced, uncandid **9** deceitful, dishonest, equivocal **10** fraudulent, perfidious, untruthful **11** dissembling **12** disingenuous, hypocritical, mealymouthed **13** dissimulating, double-dealing

insincerity 4 sham **6** deceit **8** pre-

tense, uncandor **9** deception, falseness, hypocrisy, mendacity **11** affectation, shallowness, unfrankness **12** uncandidness **13** artificiality **16** disingenuousness

insinuate 5 imply **6** inject, insert **7** asperse, let fall, suggest, wheedle, whisper **8** intimate **10** ingratiate **11** worm one's way

insinuation 4 hint **8** allusion, infusion, innuendo **9** aspersion, insertion, intrusion **10** allegation, imputation, intimation, suggestion **11** implication, penetration **12** ingratiation, interjection

insipid 4 arid, blah, drab, dull, flat, lean **5** banal, bland, empty, inane, stale, trite, vapid **6** barren, boring, jejune, stupid **7** prosaic **8** lifeless, zestless **9** pointless, savorless, tasteless, wearisome **10** monotonous, nambypamby, wishy-washy **11** commonplace **12** unappetizing **13** characterless, uninteresting

insist 4 aver, hold, urge, warn **5** claim, vouch **6** assert, demand, exhort, repeat, stress **7** caution, command, contend, persist, protest, require **8** admonish, maintain **9** reiterate **10** asseverate **13** lay down the law **14** take a firm stand **15** stand one's ground

insistence 6 demand, urging **7** urgency **8** exigency, pressure **9** clamoring **11** persistence **12** perseverance **14** imperativeness

insistent 4 firm **7** adamant **8** emphatic, repeated, stubborn **9** assertive, demanding **10** determined, unyielding **11** unrelenting

in situ 7 in place **18** in its original place

insolence 4 gall **7** disdain, hauteur **8** audacity **9** arrogance, impudence **10** brazenness, disrespect, effrontery, incivility, lordliness **11** haughtiness, presumption **12** disobedience, impertinence, impoliteness **13** bumptiousness, imperiousness **14** unmannerliness **16** superciliousness

insolent 4 rude **5** fresh, nervy **6** brazen, cheeky **7** defiant, galling, haughty **8** arrogant, impolite, impudent **9** audacious, bumptious, insulting **10** disdainful, outrageous, unmannerly **11** impertinent, overbearing **12** contemptuous, discourteous, presumptuous, supercilious **13** disrespectful

insoluble 12 inexplicable, unanswerable **13** undissolvable, unexplainable **14** undecipherable **16** incomprehensible

insolvent 5 broke **6** ruined **8** bankrupt, wiped out **9** destitute, moneyless, penniless **10** down-and-out, out of money **11** impecunious **12** impoverished, overextended

insomnia 11 nuit blanche, pervigilium, wakefulness 12 insomnolence 13 sleeplessness

insouciant 4 airy 5 perky 6 breezy, casual, jaunty 7 buoyant, offhand 8 carefree, debonair, flippant 9 easygoing, mercurial, unruffled, sans souci, whimsical 10 capricious, nonchalant, untroubled 11 free and easy, indifferent, unconcerned 12 devil-may-care, happy-go-lucky, lighthearted

inspect 3 eye 4 scan 5 probe, study 6 peer at, peruse, review, survey 7 examine, explore, observe 8 pore over 10 scrutinize 11 contemplate, investigate, reconnoiter

inspection 4 scan 5 audit, check, probe, study 6 review, survey 7 perusal 8 checking, scrutiny 9 appraisal, oversight 11 examination

inspector 7 analyst, auditor 8 analyzer, examiner, overseer, reviewer 9 appraiser, detective 11 scrutinizer 12 investigator
　　famous: 3 Fix, Fox 4 Japp 5 Queen 6 Alleyn, Bucket, Gerard, Gideon, Javert 7 Maigret 8 Clouseau, Lestrade 9 Dalgliesh

Inspector-General, The
　　author: 12 Nikolai Gogol
　　character: 4 Anna, Osip 5 Maria 26 Ivan Alexandrovich Hlestakov 35 Anton Antonovich Skvoznik-Dmukhanovsky

inspiration 4 idea, spur 5 fancy, flash 6 motive 7 impulse 8 afflatus, stimulus 9 incentive, influence, prompting 10 compulsion, incitement, motivation, revelation 13 encouragement

inspire 4 fire, stir 5 cause, exalt, impel, rouse 6 arouse, excite, induce, prompt, vivify 7 animate, enliven, hearten, produce, promote, provoke, quicken 8 embolden, engender, enkindle, illumine, inspirit, motivate, occasion 9 encourage, galvanize, influence, stimulate 10 give rise to, illuminate

inspired 3 apt 5 fired, moved 6 elated 7 elegant, exalted, excited, incited, touched, well-put 8 creative, original, prompted 9 impressed, ingenious, inventive, motivated 10 encouraged, felicitous, influenced, stimulated, well-chosen 11 exhilarated, imaginative 13 well-expressed

inspiring 5 grand 6 moving 7 awesome 8 eloquent, stirring 9 affecting, brilliant 10 impressive 11 encouraging, magnificent, stimulating

inspirit 5 boost, cheer, rouse 6 buoy up, uplift 7 animate, comfort, enliven, hearten, inspire 9 encourage, give a lift

in spite of himself
　　French: 9 malgre lui

instability 8 wavering, weakness 9

hesitancy 10 fitfulness, hesitation, indecision, insecurity 11 flightiness, fluctuation, inconstancy, vacillation 12 irresolution, unstableness, unsteadiness 13 changeability, inconsistency, mercurialness, vulnerability 14 capriciousness, changeableness

install, instal 3 lay 4 seat 5 crown, embed, imbed, lodge, plant 6 induct, invest, locate, move in, ordain 7 arrange, emplace, instate, receive, situate, station, usher in 8 coronate, initiate, position 10 establish, inaugurate, set in place

installation 5 plant 6 agency 8 facility 9 formation, induction 10 foundation, initiation, ordination 11 appointment, institution, investiture 12 inauguration, military base, organization 13 establishment

installment 4 part, unit 5 issue 6 laying 7 chapter, payment, section, segment 8 division, fragment, locating

instance 4 case, time 6 sample 7 example 8 occasion, specimen 9 precedent, prototype 10 antecedent 11 case in point 12 circumstance, illustration

instant 5 flash, jiffy, quick, trice 6 abrupt, minute, moment, prompt, second, sudden 8 premixed 9 immediate, on the spot, precooked, twinkling 10 ready-to-use 11 split second 12 unhesitating

instantaneous 5 rapid, swift 6 abrupt, direct, prompt, speedy, sudden 9 immediate 13 quick as a flash

instantaneously 6 at once 7 quickly, rapidly 8 in a flash, in no time, instanter, right now 9 on the spot, right away 11 immediately 21 in the twinkling of an eye

instantly 6 at once 7 quickly 8 directly, in a flash, promptly, right now 9 instanter, on the spot 10 here and now 11 immediately 12 quick as a wink, without delay 15 instantaneously 17 without hesitation

instar
　　insect period between: 5 molts 7 molting

in statu quo 17 in the state in which (something is or was)

instead 6 in lieu, rather 10 in its place

instigate 4 goad, spur, urge 5 begin, rouse, start 6 foment, incite, kindle, prompt, stir up 7 provoke 8 initiate 9 stimulate 10 bring about 11 set in motion

instigator 6 shaper 7 inciter 9 architect, innovator 10 prime mover, ringleader

instill, instil 4 pour 5 mix in, teach 6 impart, induce 7 implant, inspire 8 engender 9 inculcate

instinct 4 gift 5 knack 6 genius, nature 7 faculty 8 aptitude, capacity, ten-

dency 9 intuition, mother wit 10 proclivity

instinctive 6 inborn, inbred, innate, native 7 natural 8 inherent, inspired 9 automatic, impulsive, intuitive, unlearned 10 deep-seated, unacquired 11 instinctual, involuntary, spontaneous

institute 4 pass 5 begin, enact, found, set up, start 6 ordain, school 7 academy, college, society 8 commence, get going, initiate, organize 9 establish, introduce, originate, prescribe, undertake 10 constitute, foundation, inaugurate 11 association, get under way 13 put into effect 14 bring into being

institution 4 rite 5 habit, usage 6 custom, prison, ritual, school 7 academy, college, company, fixture 8 bughouse, madhouse, nuthouse, seminary 9 institute 10 convention, crazy house, foundation, university 11 association 12 organization 13 establishment

institutionalize 6 commit, detain 7 confine, put away 8 imprison 11 incarcerate

in strict confidence 7 sub rosa 9 between us, entre nous, privately 14 confidentially 15 between you and me 16 between me and thee, between ourselves

instruct 3 bid 5 brief, coach, drill, guide, order, teach, train, tutor 6 advise, direct, inform, notify, school 7 apprise, command, educate 8 acquaint 9 catechize, enlighten 12 indoctrinate

instruction 8 coaching, guidance, pedagogy, teaching, training, tutelage, tutoring 9 education 11 instructing 14 indoctrination

instructions 4 rule 5 maxim, moral, motto 6 advice, homily, lesson 7 precept 9 direction, guideline 11 explanation, information 12 prescription 13 specification 14 recommendation

instructive 8 didactic, edifying 11 educational 12 enlightening

instructor 3 don 4 guru 5 coach, guide, tutor 6 mentor 7 counsel, maestro, teacher, trainer 8 educator, lecturer 9 governess, pedagogue, preceptor, professor 10 schoolmarm 12 schoolmaster 13 schoolteacher 14 schoolmistress

instrument 4 deed, tool 5 agent, grant, means, paper 6 agency, device, gadget, medium 7 charter, machine, utensil, vehicle 8 contract 9 apparatus, appliance, equipment, expedient, implement, mechanism 11 contrivance

instrumental 5 vital 6 active, useful 7 crucial, helpful 8 a means to, decisive, valuable 9 assisting, conducive, effective, effectual, essential 10 functional 12 contributory

instrumentality 5 force, means 6

agency, charge **9** influence, mediation **12** intervention

insubordinate 6 unruly **7** defiant **8** insolent, mutinous **9** fractious **10** disorderly, rebellious, refractory **11** disobedient, intractable, uncompliant **12** recalcitrant, ungovernable, unsubmissive

insubordination 6 mutiny, revolt **7** anarchy **8** sedition **9** rebellion **10** dissention, insurgence, unruliness **12** disobedience, insurrection **13** noncompliance **14** refractoriness

insubstantial 4 airy, weak **5** frail, shaky, small **6** flimsy, modest, paltry, slight, unreal **7** fragile, trivial, unsound **8** baseless, bodiless, delicate, ethereal, gossamer, piddling, trifling, unstable **9** imaginary, visionary **10** groundless, immaterial, impalpable, intangible **12** apparitional **14** inconsiderable

in succession
French: **7** en suite

insufferable 7 hateful **8** dreadful **10** abominable, detestable, disgusting, outrageous, unbearable **11** intolerable, unendurable, unspeakable **13** insupportable

insufficiency 4 lack, need, want **6** dearth **7** drought, paucity **8** scarcity, shortage **10** deficiency, inadequacy, meagerness, scantiness **11** undersupply

insufficient 6 scanty, skimpy, sparse **7** lacking, wanting **8** impotent **9** deficient, not enough **10** inadequate **11** incompetent **14** unsatisfactory

insular 5 petty **6** biased, narrow **7** bigoted, limited, isolated **9** illiberal, insulated, parochial **10** intolerant, prejudiced, provincial **12** narrow-minded

insulate 5 cover **6** cut off, detach, enisle, shield **7** cushion, isolate, protect, seclude **8** separate **9** segregate, sequester **10** disconnect

insult 3 cut **4** slap **5** abuse, cheek, scorn **6** deride, offend, slight **7** affront, offense, outrage **8** be rude to, belittle, rudeness **9** disparage, impudence, indignity **11** discourtesy, lese majesty

insulting 4 rude **5** nasty **7** abusive, uncivil, vicious **8** impolite, insolent **9** invidious, offensive **10** defamatory, derogatory **11** disparaging **12** discourteous **13** disrespectful

insuperable 8 crushing **9** defeating **10** impassable, impossible, invincible, unbeatable, unyielding **12** inexpugnable, overpowering, overwhelming **13** overmastering, unconquerable **14** insurmountable

insurance 6 policy **8** coverage, security, warranty **9** assurance, guarantee, indemnity

insure 6 secure **10** underwrite

insurgent 5 rebel **7** lawless **8** mutineer, mutinous, partisan, renegade, resister, revolter **9** breakaway, dissident, guerrilla **10** disorderly, rebellious **11** disobedient **13** insubordinate, revolutionary, revolutionist **15** insurrectionist

insurmountable 8 hopeless, too great **10** unbeatable **11** beyond reach, insuperable **13** unconquerable

insurrection 4 riot **6** mutiny, revolt, rising **8** outbreak, uprising **9** rebellion **10** insurgence, revolution

intact 4 safe **5** sound, whole **6** unhurt **7** perfect **8** complete, integral, unbroken, unharmed **9** undamaged, uninjured, untouched **10** in one piece, unimpaired **11** in good shape **15** without a scratch

intangible 5 vague **7** elusive, shadowy **8** abstract, ethereal, fleeting, fugitive **9** transient **10** accidental, evanescent, immaterial, impalpable **11** abstraction, untouchable **12** imponderable **13** imperceptible, insubstantial

integer 5 digit, whole **6** entity, figure, number **7** numeral **11** whole number

integer vitae 8 innocent **15** blameless in life

integral 4 full **5** basic, total, whole **6** entire, intact **7** perfect, rounded **8** complete, finished, inherent **9** component, essential, fulfilled, necessary, requisite **10** fulfilling **11** constituent, well-rounded **13** indispensable

integrate 3 mix **4** fuse **5** blend, merge, unify, unite **6** mingle **7** combine **8** intermix **10** amalgamate **11** desegregate **13** bring together

integrated 6 entire, joined, linked, united **7** blended, merged, unified, unitary **8** combined **9** composite, undivided **10** harmonized, reconciled **11** coordinated, synthesized **12** desegregated, unsegregated

integration 5 union **6** fusion, mixing **8** blending **9** combining, synthesis **11** combination **12** assimilation **13** desegregation

integrity 5 unity **6** purity, virtue **7** decency, honesty, probity **8** cohesion, morality, strength **9** character, coherence, principle, rectitude, wholeness **11** reliability, self-respect, uprightness **12** completeness

integument 4 coat, hide, husk, rind, skin **5** shell, **7** coating, cuticle, epiderm, exoderm **8** covering, envelope, membrane

integumentary system
component: **4** hair, skin **5** nails

intellect 3 wit **4** mind **5** brain, sense **6** brains, wisdom **7** thinker **9** cognition, mentality **10** perception **11** mental power, rationality **12** intellectual, intelligence **13** consciousness, understanding

intellectual 4 sage **5** brain **6** brainy, mental, pundit, savant **7** bookish, egghead, scholar, thinker **8** abstract, academic, cerebral, highbrow, longhair, mandarin, rational, studious **9** intellect, of the mind, reasoning, scholarly **10** thoughtful **11** intelligent
French: **9** bel-esprit

intelligence 4 dope, news **6** acumen, advice, brains, notice, report, wisdom **7** tidings **8** sagacity **9** intellect, knowledge **10** advisement, shrewdness **11** information **12** notification, perspicacity **13** comprehension, understanding

intelligent 4 keen, sage, wise **5** alert, canny, quick, sharp, smart **6** astute, brainy, bright, clever, shrewd **7** knowing, prudent **8** informed, sensible, thinking **9** brilliant, sagacious **10** perceptive, thoughtful **11** clearheaded, quick-witted, sharp-witted **12** well-informed **13** perspicacious

intelligentsia 5 mensa **7** academe **8** thinkers **10** ivory tower **13** intellectuals

intelligible 5 clear, lucid **7** evident, obvious **8** apparent, clear-cut, coherent, definite, distinct **11** unambiguous, well-defined **12** unmistakable **14** comprehensible, understandable

intemperance 10 alcoholism, insobriety **11** dissipation, drunkenness, inebriation **12** immoderation, recklessness **13** excessiveness **16** irresponsibility

intemperate 5 harsh **6** brutal, rugged, severe **7** extreme, violent **8** bibulous, uncurbed **9** dissolute, excessive, inclement **10** dissipated, gluttonous, immoderate, inordinate **11** extravagant, inabstinent, incontinent **12** unrestrained **13** overindulgent

intend 3 aim **4** mean, plan, wish **6** aspire, design, expect **7** project, propose, resolve **9** calculate, determine **10** have in mind **11** contemplate

intended 5 meant **6** fiance, future **7** engaged, fiancee, implied, willful **8** proposed, purposed **9** affianced, betrothed, bride-to-be, groom-to-be, voluntary **10** calculated, deliberate **11** intentional

intense 4 deep, keen **5** acute, sharp **6** ardent, potent, strong **7** burning, earnest, extreme, fervent, violent **8** emphatic, forceful, forcible, powerful, vehement **10** passionate **12** concentrated, considerable

intensely 4 very **5** hotly **6** deeply, keenly **7** acutely, eagerly, vividly **8** ardently, heatedly, terribly **9** extremely, fervently, seriously, violently, zealously **10** forcefully, powerfully, profoundly, vehemently, vigorously **11** excessively, exquisitely, strenuously **12** considerably, passionately **13** energetically

intensify 5 boost **6** deepen, worsen **7** magnify, quicken, sharpen **8** escalate, heighten, increase, redouble **9** aggravate, reinforce **10** accelerate, strengthen

intensifying 9 worsening **10** increasing, magnifying, redoubling, sharpening **11** aggravating, heightening, reinforcing **12** exacerbating **13** strengthening

intensity 4 zeal **5** ardor, depth, force, power, vigor **6** energy, fervor **7** emotion, passion, potency **8** severity, strength **9** magnitude, vehemence **11** earnestness **12** forcefulness

intensive 6 all-out **7** growing, radical **8** complete, sweeping, thorough **10** exhaustive, increasing **11** comprehensive **12** concentrated **13** thoroughgoing

intent 3 aim, end, set **4** bent, gist, plan **5** drift, fixed **6** burden, design, import, steady **7** earnest, intense, meaning, purport, purpose **8** absorbed, piercing, resolved **9** engrossed, insistent, intention, steadfast, substance, tenacious, unbending **10** determined, unwavering **11** preoccupied **12** concentrated, significance, undistracted **13** determination, premeditation

intention 3 aim, end **4** goal, plan **6** design, intent, object, target **7** purpose, resolve **10** objective **10** resolution **13** determination

intentional 6 willed **7** planned **8** designed, intended **9** voluntary **10** calculated, deliberate, purposeful **12** contemplated, premeditated **13** done on purpose

intently 6 deeply, raptly **9** fervently, zealously **10** absorbedly **11** attentively **12** passionately **18** without distraction **22** with undivided attention

intentness 10 absorption **11** engrossment **13** concentration

inter 4 bury **5** inurn **6** entomb, inhume **7** inearth, lay away **9** lay to rest **11** ensepulcher

interact 4 join, mesh **5** coact, unite **6** engage **7** combine, conjoin **8** dovetail **9** cooperate, interlace, intermesh, interplay, interwork **10** coordinate, interreact

inter alia 16 among other things

inter alios 17 among other persons

interbreed 3 mix **5** cross **8** intermix **10** crossbreed

intercede 5 plead **6** step in **7** mediate, speak up **9** arbitrate, interpose, intervene, offer help **12** offer support **14** put in a good word **16** lend a helping hand

intercept 3 nab **4** grab, stay, stop, take **5** catch, seize **6** ambush, arrest, cut off, detain **7** deflect, reroute

intercessor 5 agent **6** bishop, broker **8** advocate, mediator **9** go-between, middleman **12** intermediary, spokesperson

interchange 5 shift **6** switch **7** trading **8** exchange, junction, swapping, transfer **9** alternate, crossover **10** substitute **11** give and take, reciprocity

interchangeable 8 parallel, tradable **9** analogous **10** equivalent, switchable, synonymous **12** exchangeable, transposable **13** corresponding

interconnected 8 adjacent **10** contiguous, juxtaposed **12** conterminous, labyrinthine

intercourse 4 talk **5** trade **6** coitus, parley **7** pairing, traffic **8** colloquy, commerce, congress, coupling, dealings, exchange **9** communion, discourse, relations **10** connection, copulation **12** conversation **14** communications, correspondence

interdict 3 ban, bar **5** taboo **6** enjoin, forbid **7** barring, censure **8** prohibit, restrain, restrict **9** proscribe **11** forbiddance, prohibition **12** proscription

interdiction 3 ban **7** barring **11** forbiddance, prohibition **12** proscription

interest, interests 4 gain, good, part, weal **5** bonus, hobby, share, stake, touch, yield **6** absorb, affect, behalf, divert, engage, notice, profit, regard **7** attract, benefit, concern, holding, involve, pastime, portion, pursuit, service **8** dividend **9** advantage, attention, avocation, curiosity, preoccupy, suspicion **10** absorption, investment **11** engrossment **13** preoccupation

interested 6 active **7** engaged **8** diverted **9** committed, concerned **10** fascinated, responsive

interesting 7 curious **8** engaging, magnetic, pleasing, riveting, striking **9** absorbing, appealing, arresting **10** attractive, suspicious **11** fascinating, stimulating **12** entertaining

interfere 3 jar, mix **6** butt in, horn in, meddle, rush in, step in **7** counter, intrude **8** conflict **9** frustrate, intercede, interpose, intervene **11** get in the way **14** be a hindrance to, be an obstacle to, be inconsistent, stick in one's oar

interference 3 bar **6** static **8** clashing, conflict, friction, invasion, meddling **9** collision, hindrance, intrusion **12** interception, interruption, intervention

interfere with 6 hinder, impede, thwart **7** disrupt **9** interrupt

interim 7 stopgap **8** interval, meantime, temporal **9** interlude, temporary, tentative **10** pro tempore **11** provisional

interior 4 bush **5** inner **6** inmost, inside, inward **8** internal **9** backwoods, heartland, innermost, upcountry **10** hinterland

Interiors

director: **10** Woody Allen

cast: **10** E G Marshall **11** Diane Keaton **12** Marybeth Hurt **13** Geraldine Page **15** Kristin Griffith **16** Maureen Stapleton

screenplay: **10** Woody Allen

interject 5 put in **6** inject, insert, slip in **7** force in, sneak in, throw in **9** interpose, introduce **11** interpolate

interjection 2 ah, er, lo, oh, ow, um **3** aha, cry, fie, hey, huh, ugh, wow **4** ahem, alas, darn, dear, drat, egad, gosh, heck, jeez, oops, ouch, phew, rats **5** aside, golly, zowie **6** eureka, hooray, hurrah, hurray **7** gee-whiz, jeepers **9** insertion **11** ejaculation, exclamation **13** interpolation, interposition

interlace 3 mix **4** knit, link **5** braid, plait, twine, twist, weave **7** wreathe **9** alternate **10** intertwine, interweave **11** intersperse

interlaced 5 woven **6** linked, twined **7** braided, knitted, plaited, twisted **8** entwined, latticed, wreathed **9** interknit **10** interwoven **11** intertwined **12** interspersed

interlocutor 8 minstrel **9** converser, dialogist **12** interrogator **14** man in the middle

interlope 6 invade, meddle **7** intrude, obtrude **8** encroach, infringe, trespass **9** interfere

interloper 7 invader, meddler **8** intruder, outsider **10** interferer, trespasser **11** gatecrasher **15** persona non grata

interlude 5 break, event, letup, pause **6** recess **7** episode, respite **8** incident, interval **12** intermission **14** breathing spell

intermediary 6 midway, umpire **7** referee **8** bridging, mediator **9** go-between, in-between, mediating, middleman **10** arbitrator **11** adjudicator, arbitrating

intermediate 3 mid **4** fair, mean, so-so **6** median, medium, middle, midway **7** average, halfway, mediate, midmost **8** mediocre, middling, moderate **11** intervening

interment 6 burial **7** funeral **10** entombment, inhumation

Intermezzo

director: **13** Gregory Ratoff

cast: **8** Edna Best **12** Leslie Howard **13** Cecil Kellaway, Ingrid Bergman

interminable 6 prolix **7** endless **8** infinite, unending **9** boundless, ceaseless, incessant, limitless, perpetual, unlimited **10** continuous, long-winded **11** illimitable **12** long-drawn-out

intermingle 3 mix **4** fuse **5** blend, merge, mix up, unite **6** commix **7** combine **8** emulsify, intermix **9** commingle, interfuse, interlace **10** amalgamate, homogenize, interblend **12** conglomerate

intermission 3 gap **4** halt, rest, stop **5** break, pause **6** hiatus, recess **7** interim **8** interval, stoppage **9** interlude **10** suspension

intermittent 6 fitful **8** on and off, periodic, sporadic **9** irregular, recurrent, spasmodic **10** occasional **13** discontinuous **15** on-again-off-again

intermix 3 mix **5** blend, cross, mix in **6** mingle **10** crossbreed, interbreed **11** intermingle, intersperse

intern 6 commit, detain **7** confine, impound **8** imprison, restrain

internal 5 inner, state **6** inmost **8** domestic, interior **9** executive, political, sovereign **12** governmental **14** administrative

international 9 worldwide **12** cosmopolitan

international affairs
  god of: 6 Sancus **10** Dius Fidius, Semo Sancus

Internet
  terms: 3 AOL, DSL, FAQ, FTP, GIF, ISP, net, PDF, RDF, URL, USI, web, WWW **4** baud, blog, chat, host, HTML, Java, link, MIME, post, SMTP, spam, wi-fi, worm, VOIP **5** ASCII, cyber, e-mail, flame, Lycos, TCP/IP, virus, Yahoo **6** applet, cookie, dial-up, domain, Google, Gopher, online, server, Usenet, web log **7** browser, netizen, spiders, spyware, Website **8** bookmark, download, firewall, Username **9** AltaVista, hypertext, newsgroup, webmaster **10** cyberspace, netiquette **11** blogosphere, interactive, trojan horse **12** search engine, World Wide Web
  based on: 7 ARPAnet

internment 9 detention **10** commitment, impounding **11** confinement **12** imprisonment

inter nos 16 between ourselves

interpolate 3 add **5** put in **6** inject, insert, work in **7** implant, intrude, stick in, throw in, wedge in **8** sandwich **9** insinuate, interject, interlard, interline, intervene, introduce **11** intercalate, intersperse

interpose 6 butt in, impose, inject, insert, meddle, step in **7** intrude, mediate, obtrude **9** arbitrate, insinuate, intercede, interfere, interject, interrupt, intervene, negotiate **11** come between, interpolate

interpret 3 see **4** read, take **6** accept, define, render, reword **7** clarify, explain, make out, restate, unravel **8** construe, decipher **9** elucidate, explicate, figure out, make clear, puzzle out, translate **10** account for, paraphrase, understand

interpretation 7 reading, version **8** analysis **9** rendition **10** commentary **11** explanation **12** construction

interpreter 7 analyst **9** explainer **10** translator **11** commentator

interrelated 9 companion, connected **10** compatible, correlated **13** complementary, correspondent, corresponding

interrelation 10 connection **11** association, correlation **12** relationship

interrogate 3 ask **4** test **5** grill, probe, query **7** examine **8** question **9** catechize **11** investigate **12** cross-examine **18** give the third degree

interrogation 4 quiz **5** probe, query **7** inquiry **8** grilling, querying, question, quizzing **9** catechism, inquiring **11** examination, inquisition, questioning

interrupt 4 stop **5** sever **7** cut in on, disjoin, disturb **8** break off **9** break in on, intersect, punctuate **10** disconnect **11** discontinue **13** interfere with

interrupted 6 broken, cut off, halted **7** checked, stalled, stopped **8** arrested, broke off, deferred **9** broken off, disturbed, suspended **11** broke in upon, intercepted **12** discontinued

interruption 3 gap **4** halt, rift, stop **5** break, pause **6** hiatus, lacuna **9** hindrance, interlude **11** obstruction **12** interference, intermission **13** disconnection, discontinuity

inter se 15 among themselves **17** between themselves

intersect 4 meet **5** cross **6** bisect, divide **7** overlap **8** crosscut, transect, traverse **9** cut across **10** crisscross

intersection 6 corner **8** crossing, junction **10** crossroads **11** interchange

intersperse 3 dot, mix **5** strew **6** mingle, pepper **7** bestrew, scatter, wedge in **8** disperse, intermix, sprinkle **9** broadcast, interfuse, interject, interlard, interpose **11** intercalate, interpolate

interstice 4 slit, slot **5** crack, space **7** opening, orifice **8** aperture, interval

intertwine 4 lace **5** braid, plait, twine, twist, weave **7** entwine **8** entangle **9** interlace

interval 3 gap **4** gulf, rest, rift **5** break, cleft, pause, space, spell **6** breach, hiatus, recess, season **7** interim, opening **9** interlude **10** interspace, separation **12** intermission, interruption

intervene 4 pass **6** befall, butt in, step in **7** break in, intrude, mediate **9** arbitrate, intercede, interfere, interpose, interrupt, take place **10** come to pass **11** come between

intervention 9 butting in, intrusion, mediation **10** breaking in, stepping in **11** arbitration **12** intercession, interference **13** interposition **14** intermediation

interview 4 chat, talk **6** parley **7** meeting **8** audience **10** conference, evaluation, round table **11** questioning **12** consultation, conversation

interweave 3 mix **4** fuse, join, knit, lace, link **5** blend, braid, plait, twine, twist **6** splice **7** wreathe **9** interlace, interknit **10** intertwine **11** intersperse

intestinal 5 inner **7** enteric **8** internal, visceral

intestines 4 guts **6** bowels **7** insides, viscera **8** entrails

in the air 2 up **5** above, aloft **7** skyward **8** all about, in the sky, overhead **10** everywhere **11** in the clouds

in the doghouse 9 in bad odor **10** in disfavor, in disgrace, in ill favor **11** in disrepute

in the end 6 one day **7** finally **8** sometime **10** eventually, ultimately **13** sooner or later **17** in the course of time
  French: 5 enfin

in the family
  French: 9 en famille

in the first place
  Latin: 8 imprimis

in the future
  Latin: 8 in futuro
  Spanish: 6 manana

In the Heat of the Night
  director: 13 Norman Jewison
  cast: 8 Lee Grant **10** Rod Steiger **11** Warren Oates **13** Sidney Poitier (Virgil Tibbs)
  score: 11 Quincy Jones
  Oscar for: 5 actor (Steiger) **7** picture **10** screenplay

in the know 9 cognizant **11** on the inside **13** fully informed, knowledgeable **23** having inside information

in the manner of
  French: 3 a la

in the matter of
  Latin: 4 in re

in the meantime
  Latin: 9 ad interim

in the middle of things
  Latin: 11 in medias res

in the midst of 5 among **7** amongst **12** surrounded by **13** in the middle of

in the nature of things
  Latin: 13 in rerum natura

in the neighborhood of 6 almost, around, nearly **7** close to **9** generally, just about **10** more or less, not far from **13** approximately **15** in the vicinity of

in the place cited
  Latin: 6 loc cit **10** loco citato

in the place of a parent
  Latin: 14 in loco parentis

in the same manner that
  Latin: 7 quo modo

in the same place
  Latin: 4 ibid **6** ibidem

in the state in which
Latin: **10** in statu quo

in the style of
French: **7** a la mode

in the very act of committing the crime
Latin: **18** in flagrante delicto

in the vicinity of 4 near **6** almost, around, nearly **7** close to **9** just about **10** more or less, not far from **13** approximately **19** in the neighborhood of

in the way
French: **6** de trop

in the whole
Latin: **6** in toto

in the work cited
Latin: **5** op cit **11** opere citato

in the year of the reign
Latin: **9** anno regni

in the year of the world
Latin: **9** anno mundi

In This House of Brede
author: **11** Rumer Godden

in this sign shalt thou conquer
Latin: **16** in hoc signo vinces
motto of: **19** Constantine the Great
from vision of: **5** cross

intimacy 5 amity **6** caring, warmth **8** dearness, fondness **9** affection, closeness **10** chumminess, endearment, fraternity, lovemaking, tenderness **11** brotherhood, camaraderie, familiarity **12** friendliness

intimate 3 pal **4** chum, dear, deep, hint **5** bosom, buddy, close, crony, imply, rumor **6** allude, direct **7** guarded, private, special, suggest **8** detailed, familiar, indicate, personal, profound, thorough **9** cherished, confidant, first-hand, innermost, insinuate **12** confidential
French: **6** intime

intimately 7 closely **8** secretly, very well **9** privately **10** familiarly, personally **11** essentially **13** intrinsically **14** confidentially

intimation 4 clue, hint, sign **5** rumor **7** inkling, portent **8** allusion, innuendo **10** indication, suggestion **11** insinuation **13** veiled comment

Intimations of Immortality
author: **17** William Wordsworth

intime 4 cozy **8** intimate

in time 6 before, sooner **7** earlier **9** before now, in advance **10** beforehand, eventually **11** ahead of time **13** before the fact, sooner or later

intimidate 3 cow **5** alarm, bully, daunt, scare **6** coerce, menace, subdue **7** buffalo, terrify **8** browbeat, frighten **9** terrorize

intimidated 5 cowed, fazed **6** scared **7** crushed, daunted, subdued **10** browbeaten, frightened, terrorized

intimidation 7 tyranny **8** bullying, coercion **9** despotism **11** browbeating, terrorizing, tyrannizing **12** scare tactics

intimidator 5 bully **6** despot **7** coercer **9** oppressor, tormenter, tormentor **10** browbeater

into 2 in, to **5** among **6** inside, toward, within **7** against

intolerable 7 hateful, racking **9** abhorrent, agonizing, excessive, loathsome, torturous **10** abominable, outrageous, unbearable **11** unendurable **12** excruciating, insufferable, unreasonable **13** insupportable

intolerance 4 bias **6** racism **7** bigotry **8** weak spot **9** no stomach, prejudice **10** chauvinism, xenophobia **12** low tolerance **16** hypersensitivity, narrowmindedness

Intolerance
director: **10** D W Griffith
cast: **8** Mae Marsh **11** Lillian Gish **12** Robert Harron **17** Constance Talmadge

intolerant 7 bigoted, hostile, jealous **9** fanatical, parochial, resentful, sectarian **10** prejudiced, xenophobic **11** mistrustful **12** chauvinistic, closed-minded, narrow-minded

intonation 4 tone **5** pitch **6** accent **8** chanting **10** modulation, inflection

intone 3 hum, say **4** song **5** chant, croon, drawl, mouth, speak, utter, voice **6** murmur, recite **8** intonate, modulate, singsong, vocalize **9** enunciate, pronounce **10** articulate

in toto 5 in all, uncut **6** entire, wholly **7** totally **8** as a whole, entirely, outright **10** completely, in the whole, unabridged **11** all together, uncondensed

intoxicant 3 gin, rum **4** beer, grog, wine **5** booze, drink **6** liquor, tipple, whisky **7** alcohol, spirits, whiskey **8** cocktail, highball **9** inebriant

intoxicated 4 high, rapt **5** drunk, oiled, tight, tipsy **6** bombed, elated, loaded, stewed, stinko, stoned, zonked **7** drunken, exalted, smashed, wrecked **9** delighted, enchanted, entranced, plastered **10** enthralled, inebriated, infatuated, in one's cups **11** exhilarated, transported

intoxicating 4 hard **5** heady **6** potent **7** elating **9** alcoholic, spiritous **11** inebriating **12** exhilarating

intoxication 3 joy **5** bliss **7** elation, rapture **8** euphoria **9** poisoning, tipsiness **10** excitement, insobriety **11** drunkenness, inebriation **12** befuddlement, stupefaction

intractable 6 mulish, ornery, unruly **7** froward, willful **8** obdurate, perverse, stubborn **9** fractious, obstinate **10** headstrong, inflexible, refractory **11** unmalleable **12** contumacious, incorrigible, ungovernable, unmanageable **14** hard to cope with, uncontrollable

intransigent 7 diehard **8** obdurate, stubborn **9** steadfast, unmovable **10** inflexible, iron-willed, unyielding **11** intractable, unbudgeable **14** uncompromising

intrepid 4 bold **5** brave **6** daring, heroic **7** doughty, valiant **8** fearless, resolute, valorous **9** audacious, dauntless **10** courageous, undismayed **11** adventurous

intrepidity 4 guts **5** spunk, valor **6** mettle **7** bravery, courage **8** backbone **9** fortitude, sangfroid **12** fearlessness **13** dauntlessness

intricacy 10 complexity **11** involvement **12** complication, entanglement **15** complicatedness

intricate 6 knotty, tricky **7** complex, devious, tangled **8** involved **9** entangled **11** complicated

intrigue 3 spy **4** fire, plot **5** amour **6** absorb, arrest, scheme **7** attract, collude, knavery, romance **8** conspire, enthrall, scheming **9** fascinate, machinate, titillate **10** conspiracy, love affair **11** machination **13** double-dealing **15** interest greatly, tickle one's fancy

intriguer 7 cheater, plotter, schemer **8** conniver, finagler **9** trickster **10** machinator, wirepuller **11** conspirator, Machiavelli, manipulator

intriguing 8 engaging, exciting **9** absorbing, beguiling **11** captivating, enthralling, fascinating, interesting

intrinsic 5 basic, per se **6** inborn, inbred, innate, native **7** natural **8** inherent **9** essential, ingrained **10** indigenous, underlying **11** fundamental

introduce 3 add **4** show, urge **5** begin, offer, put in, start **6** create, expose, import, inform, infuse, insert **7** advance, bring in, kick off, lead off, present, propose, sponsor, throw in **8** acquaint, initiate, lead into **9** establish, institute, interject, interpose, make known, originate, recommend **10** put forward **11** familiarize, interpolate

introduction 6 change **7** novelty, opening, preface, prelude **8** foreword, preamble, prologue **9** insertion, precursor **10** bringing in, conducting, innovation, ushering in **11** instituting, institution

introductory 7 initial **9** beginning, prefatory **10** initiatory, precursory **11** acquainting, preliminary **13** getacquainted

introspection 8 brooding **10** meditation, reflection, rumination **12** deliberation, self-analysis, self-scrutiny **13** contemplation, soul-searching **15** self-examination, self-observation, self-questioning

introspective 7 pensive **10** reflective **13** contemplative, lost in thought

introversion 7 reserve **8** brooding **10**

constraint, diffidence, withdrawal **13** introspection

introvert 5 loner **7** brooder, thinker **13** contemplative, private person

introverted 3 shy **5** stiff **8** reserved **9** inhibited, repressed, withdrawn **10** antisocial, restrained **13** inner-directed, introspective

intrude 4 push **6** butt in, impose, meddle, thrust **7** obtrude **8** encroach, trespass **9** interfere, interlope, interpose, intervene

intruder 10 encroacher, interferer, interloper, intervener, trespasser **11** gate-crasher

Intruder in the Dust
    author: **15** William Faulkner

intrusive 4 nosy **5** pushy **6** prying, snoopy **8** in the way, invasive **9** hindering, obtrusive, officious, unwelcome **10** meddlesome **11** impertinent, interfering, interruptive

intuition 5 flash, hunch **7** insight, surmise **8** instinct **9** guesswork, telepathy **10** sixth sense **11** second sight **12** clairvoyance, precognition

intuitive 6 inborn, inbred, innate, native **7** natural, psychic **10** telepathic **11** clairvoyant, instinctive, intuitional, nonrational **12** extrasensory

Inuit *see* **6** Eskimo

inundate 4 glut **5** drown, flood, swamp **6** deluge, drench, engulf **8** load down, overcome, overflow, saturate, submerge **9** overwhelm **10** overburden, overspread

inundation 4 glut **5** flood **6** deluge **9** avalanche

in unison 5 as one **8** in chorus **9** all at once **11** all together

inure 5 adapt, steel, train **6** adjust, custom, harden, season, temper **7** toughen **8** accustom **9** acclimate, get used to, habituate **10** discipline, naturalize, strengthen **11** acclimatize, desensitize, familiarize **12** become used to **15** learn to live with **16** become hardened to

in use 8 employed **9** operating **11** functioning, operational

in vacuo 9 in a vacuum **11** in isolation

invade 5 flood, limit **6** assail, attack, engulf, infect, infest **7** assault, overrun, violate **8** permeate, restrict, strike at, trespass **9** intrude on, march into, penetrate

invader 6 raider **8** attacker, intruder, marauder **9** aggressor, assailant **10** trespasser

invalid 4 null, sick, void, weak **5** false **6** ailing, infirm, sickly, unwell **7** amputee, cripple, unsound, useless **8** disabled, not valid, nugatory, weakened **9** enfeebled, forceless, illogical, paralytic, powerless, worthless **10** dead letter, fallacious, paraplegic **11** debili-

tated, ineffective, inoperative, unsupported **12** unconvincing **13** incapacitated, unsupportable **14** good-for-nothing, valetudinarian

invalidate 5 annul **6** cancel, refute, repeal, weaken **7** nullify, vitiate **8** abrogate, make void, undercut **9** discredit, undermine **11** countermand

invalidation 7 voiding **9** annulment **10** abrogation **12** cancellation **13** nullification

invaluable 4 rare **6** choice **9** priceless **11** beyond price, inestimable

invariable 7 uniform **8** constant **9** immutable, unfailing, unvarying **10** changeless, consistent, unchanging, unwavering **11** unalterable, undeviating **12** unchangeable

invariably 4 ever **6** always **7** forever **9** every time, uniformly **10** all the time, constantly **11** perpetually, universally **15** in every instance **16** without exception

invasion 4 raid **5** foray **6** attack, breach, inroad, sortie **7** assault **8** trespass **9** incursion, intrusion, onslaught **10** aggression, juggernaut, usurpation **11** penetration **12** encroachment, infiltration, infringement, overstepping

Invasion of the Body Snatchers
    director:
       1956 version: **9** Don Siegel
       1978 version: **13** Philip Kaufman
    cast:
       1956 version: **10** Dana Wynter, Larry Gates **11** King Donovan **13** Kevin McCarthy
       1978 version: **11** Brooke Adams **12** Jeff Goldblum, Leonard Nimoy **16** Donald Sutherland

invective 4 rant **5** venom **6** insult **7** censure, railing, sarcasm **8** diatribe **9** contumely **10** execration, harsh words, revilement **11** verbal abuse **12** billingsgate, denunciation, vilification, vituperation

inveigh 4 rail, slam **5** abuse, knock, scold **6** rebuke, revile **7** censure, put down, run down, upbraid **8** belittle, denounce, harangue, reproach **9** castigate, criticize, dress down **10** vituperate

inveigh against 5 abuse **6** defame, rail at, revile **7** protest **8** denounce **9** castigate

inveigle 4 coax, lure **5** tempt, trick **6** allure, cajole, entice, rope in, seduce, suck in **7** beguile, ensnare, flatter, mislead, wheedle **8** persuade, softsoap **9** bamboozle, sweet-talk

inveiglement 7 coaxing **8** cajolery, flattery **9** wheedling **10** enticement, persuasion **13** blandishments

invent 4 coin **6** cook up, create, devise, make up **7** concoct, develop, fashion, think up, trump up **8** conceive, contrive **9** conjure up, fabri-

cate, formulate, originate **10** come up with **11** put together

invented 6 fabled, made up **8** fabulous, fanciful, mythical **9** fantastic, imaginary, legendary **10** apocryphal, fictitious

invention 3 lie **4** fake, sham **6** design, device, gadget **7** fiction, forgery, machine **8** creation, trumpery **9** apparatus, discovery, fertility, implement, ingenuity, inventing **10** concoction, creativity, production **11** contraption, contrivance, development, fabrication, imagination, originality, origination **13** dissimulation, inventiveness, prevarication **15** resourcefulness

invention
    god of: **6** Hermes

inventive 6 bright, clever **9** ingenious **11** resourceful

inventiveness 9 ingenuity **10** cleverness, creativity **11** imagination, originality **15** imaginativeness

inventor 5 maker **6** author **7** creator, deviser **8** engineer, producer, tinkerer **9** architect, generator, innovator **10** discoverer, originator
    of air brake: **12** Westinghouse
    of automobile: **7** Daimler
    of barometer: **10** Torricelli
    of camera: **7** Eastman
    of cotton gin: **7** Whitney
    of cylinder lock: **4** Yale
    of dynamite: **5** Nobel
    of elevator: **4** Otis
    of gyrocompass: **6** Sperry
    of helicopter: **8** Sikorsky
    of linotype: **12** Mergenthaler
    of machine gun: **7** Gatling
    of movable type: **9** Gutenberg
    of phonograph, incandescent lamp, mimeograph, dictating machine, fluoroscope: **6** Edison
    of photography: **6** Niepce, Talbot **8** Daguerre
    of Polaroid: **4** Land
    of quick-freezing: **8** Birdseye
    of reaper: **9** McCormick
    of radio: **7** Marconi
    of revolver: **4** Colt
    of rocket engine: **7** Goddard
    of sewing machine: **4** Howe
    of sleeping car: **7** Pullman
    of steamboat: **6** Fulton
    of steam engine: **4** Watt
    of steam locomotive: **10** Stephenson
    of telegraph: **5** Morse
    of telephone: **4** Bell
    of transistor: **7** Bardeen **8** Brattain, Shockley
    of wireless telegraph: **7** Marconi
    of vulcanized rubber: **8** Goodyear

inventory 4 roll **5** goods, index, stock **6** roster, supply **7** catalog **8** register, schedule **9** stock list **10** accounting **11** merchandise, stock-taking

inverse 8 backward, contrary, converse, indirect, inverted, opposite, reversed **11** back to front, bottom-to-top, right-to-left

inversion 7 turning **8** reversal **9** ectropion, turnabout **10** transposal **12** resupination **13** transposition

inverted 7 inverse **8** bottom up **10** upside-down

invest 4 fill, garb, give **5** adorn, allot, array, color, cover, dress, endow, imbue **6** clothe, devote, enable, enrich, infuse, supply **7** appoint, license **8** set aside **9** apportion

investigate 4 sift **5** probe, query, study **6** survey **7** analyze, dissect, explore, inspect **8** ask about, look into, pore over, question, research **9** anatomize, delve into **10** scrutinize

investigation 5 probe, study **6** review, search, survey **7** anatomy, inquiry **8** analysis, research, scrutiny **10** dissection, inspection **11** fact-finding

investigator 6 shamus **7** analyst, gumshoe **8** examiner, inquirer, observer **9** detective **10** private eye, researcher

investment 4 ante, risk **5** share, stake **7** venture **8** offering

inveterate 6 inured **7** adamant, chronic, diehard **8** constant, habitual, hardened **9** confirmed, incurable, ingrained, recurrent, steadfast **10** continuous, deep-rooted, deep-seated **11** established **12** long-standing, unregenerate **15** unreconstructed

invidious 7 vicious **8** spiteful **9** insulting, malicious, offensive, rancorous, resentful, slighting **10** malevolent

invigorate 4 stir **5** brace, cheer, liven, pep up, renew, rouse, zip up **6** jazz up, vivify **7** animate, enliven, fortify, refresh, restore **8** energize, vitalize **9** stimulate **10** exhilarate, rejuvenate, strengthen

invigorated 6 braced **7** revived **8** animated, restored, vivified **9** energized, full of pep, quickened, refreshed **10** stimulated **11** rejuvenated **12** strengthened **17** full of vim and vigor

invigorating 7 bracing **9** animating, healthful **10** energizing, enlivening, quickening, refreshing, vitalizing **11** restorative, stimulating **12** rejuvenating **13** strengthening

invincible 10 unbeatable **11** impregnable, indomitable, insuperable **12** invulnerable, undefeatable **13** irrepressible, unconquerable **14** insurmountable

in vino veritas 18 in wine there is truth

inviolable 4 holy, pure **6** chaste, divine, sacred, secret **7** blessed **8** hallowed **9** dedicated, inviolate, undefiled **10** sacrosanct **11** consecrated, impregnable, trustworthy **12** impenetrable, invulnerable, unassailable **13** incorruptible

inviolate 4 pure **6** intact, sacred, secret **8** hallowed **9** unaltered, unchanged, undefiled, unstained **10** inviolable, sacrosanct

invisible 6 covert, hidden, unseen, veiled **7** obscure **9** concealed, unseeable **10** unapparent **13** imperceptible, undiscernible

Invisible Man
   author: **12** Ralph Ellison

Invisible Man, The
   author: **7** H G Wells
   character: **4** Hall **6** Dr Kemp, Marvel **7** Griffin **11** Colonel Ayde

invitation 3 bid **4** call, lure **5** offer **7** bidding, summons **8** open door **9** challenge **10** allurement, enticement, inducement, temptation **12** solicitation

invite 3 bid **4** call, lure, urge **5** tempt **6** entice, induce **7** attract, solicit, welcome **9** encourage

inviting 4 warm **8** alluring, charming, engaging, enticing, magnetic, tempting **9** appealing, welcoming **10** attractive, intriguing

invocation 4 plea **6** appeal, orison, prayer **8** petition **9** summoning **12** supplication

in vogue 2 in **6** modish **7** a la mode, current, in style, stylish **9** in fashion **11** fashionable **12** le dernier cri

invoke 3 beg, use **5** apply **6** ask for, employ **7** beseech, conjure, entreat, implore, pray for **8** call upon, petition, resort to **9** appeal for, call forth, implement, importune, introduce **10** supplicate

involuntary 6 forced, reflex **7** coerced **8** unchosen, unwilled **9** automatic, reluctant, unwilling **10** compulsory **11** inadvertent, instinctive, spontaneous, unconscious **13** unintentional **15** against one's will

involve 5 imply, mix up **6** commit, engage, entail, wrap up **7** contain, embroil, include **8** comprise, depend on, entangle **9** implicate, preoccupy

involved 7 complex, engaged, mixed up, wound up **8** absorbed, immersed **9** committed, elaborate, embroiled, engrossed, entangled, intricate, wrapped up **10** implicated **11** complicated, preoccupied

involve deeply 5 mix up **6** absorb, commit, wrap up **7** embroil, engross, immerse **8** entangle **9** implicate, preoccupy

invulnerable 10 formidable, invincible, unbeatable **11** impregnable, indomitable, insuperable **12** imperishable, inexpungable, unassailable, undefeatable **13** unconquerable, undestroyable

inward, inwards 5 inner **6** mental, toward **7** going in, ingoing, private **8** incoming, interior, inwardly, personal **9** spiritual, the inside **10** interiorly

in what way
   Latin: **7** quo modo

in which case 4 then, when **6** thence **9** whereupon **11** accordingly **12** at which point

In Which We Serve
   director: **9** David Lean **10** Noel Coward
   script: **10** Noel Coward
   cast: **9** John Mills **10** Noel Coward **12** Bernard Miles, Celia Johnson

in wine there is truth
   Latin: **13** in vino veritas

Io
   father: **7** Inachus
   husband: **9** Telegonus
   loved by: **4** Zeus
   son: **7** Epaphus
   changed into: **6** heifer
   color of heifer: **5** white
   guarded by: **5** Argus
   pursecuted by: **6** gadfly
   sent by: **4** Hera
   corresponds to: **4** Isis

iodine
   chemical symbol: **1** I

Iolanthe
   author: **9** W S Gilbert

Iole
   father: **7** Eurytus
   loved by: **8** Heracles
   captive of: **8** Heracles, Hercules

Ion
   author: **9** Euripides
   character: **6** Apollo, Athene, Crensa, Xuthus

ion 15 charged particle
   part of: **8** molecule
   charge: **8** negative, positive
   loses or gains: **8** electron
   called: **5** anion **6** cation **12** dissociation

Ionesco, Eugene
   born: **7** Romania, Slatina
   author of: **7** MacBett **9** The Chairs, The Killer, The Lesson **10** Rhinoceros **11** Exit the King **14** The Bald Soprano

iota 3 bit, jot **4** atom, spot, whit **5** shred, spark, speck **7** smidgin **8** particle **9** scintilla **11** faint degree, small amount **15** tiniest quantity

IOU 4 chit, debt, note **6** marker **10** obligation **12** promise to pay **14** promissory note

Iowa
   abbreviation: **2** IA
   nickname: **7** Hawkeye
   capital/largest city: **9** Des Moines
   others: **4** Ames **5** Amana, Mason, Perry **6** Algona, Keokuk, Le Mars, Marion, Newton **7** Anamosa, Clinton, Dubuque, Ft Dodge, Ottumwa **8** Waterloo **9** Davenport, Ft Madison,

Marquette, Mason City, Sioux City **10** Burlington, Cedar Falls, West Branch **11** Cedar Rapids **12** Marshalltown **13** Council Bluffs

college: 3 Coe **5** Corot, Drake, Loras **7** Cornell, Parsons **8** Grinnell, Wartburg **12** Iowa Wesleyan

explorer: 6 Joliet **7** Jolliet **9** Marquette **13** Lewis and Clark

feature: 13 Amana Colonies **17** first apple orchard

church: 11 Little Brown

national historical site: 13 Herbert Hoover

national monument: 12 Effigy Mounds

state fair: 4 Iowa

tribe: 3 Fox **4** Sauc **5** Ioway, Omaha **9** Muscoutin, Winnebago

people: 7 Hawkeye **9** Grant Wood **10** John L Lewis **11** Billy Sunday **15** Buffalo Bill Cody, Charles Ringling

lake: 5 Clear, Storm **6** Spirit **7** Rathbun **11** East Okoboji, West Okoboji

land rank: 11 twenty-fifth

president: 13 Herbert Hoover

river: 4 Iowa **5** Cedar, Floyd, Skunk **8** Big Sioux, Missouri **9** Des Moines **11** Mississippi, Nishnabotna **12** Wapsipinicon

state admission: 11 twenty-ninth

state bird: 16 eastern goldfinch

state flower: 8 wild rose

state motto: 45 Our Liberties We Prize and Our Rights We Will Maintain

state song: 13 The Song of Iowa

state tree: 3 oak

Iowa, Ioway

language family: 6 Siouan

location: 4 Iowa

related to: 3 Oto **8** Missouri

Iphigenia

father: 9 Agamemnon

mother: 12 Clytemnestra

brother: 7 Orestes

sister: 7 Electra **12** Chrysothemis

saved by: 7 Artemis

Iphigenia in Aulis

author: 9 Euripides

character: 8 Achilles, Menelaus **9** Agamemnon **12** Clytemnestra

Iphigenia in Tauris

author: 9 Euripides

character: 5 Thoas **6** Athena **7** Orestes, Pylades

Iphigenie en Aulide

also: 16 Iphigenia in Aulis

opera by: 5 Gluck

character: 7 Artemis, Calchas **8** Achilles **9** Agamemnon **12** Clytemnestra

Iphigenie en Tauride

also: 17 Iphigenia in Tauris

opera by: 5 Gluck

character: 5 Diana, Thoas (King of Scythia) **7** Orestes, Pylades **9** the Furies

ipse dixit 15 he himself said it **21** assertion without proof

ipsissima verba 8 verbatim **12** the very words

ipso facto 15 by the fact itself **24** by the very nature of the deed

ipso jure 14 by the law itself **16** by operation of law

IRA 19 Irish Republican Army **27** Individual Retirement Account

Iraklion

capital of: 5 Crete

Iran

name means: 15 land of the Aryans

earlier name: 5 Media **6** Persia

capital/largest city: 6 Tehran **7** Teheran

others: 3 Qum **4** Shah **5** Ahwaz, Urmia **6** Abadan, Bandar, Kashan, Meshed, Shiraz, Tabriz **7** Birjand, Hamadan, Isfahan, Mashhad, Zahidan **11** Bandar Abbas

supreme head of state: 5 faghi **17** religious guardian

measure: 3 gaz, zar, zer **4** cane **5** gareh, kafiz, makuk, qasab **6** charac, chebel, ghalva **7** capicha, chenica, farsakh, mansion, mishara **8** parasang, piamaneh, stathmos

monetary unit: 3 pul **4** asar, gran, rial **5** bisti, daric, dinar, larin, shahi, toman **6** stater **7** ashrafi, pahlavi

weight: 3 ser **4** dung, rotl, seer **5** abbas, artel, pinar, ratel **6** batman, dirhem, karwar, miscal, nimman **7** abbassi **8** tcheirek

lake: 5 Niris, Tasht, Tuzlu, Urmia **6** Sahweh, Sistan **7** Maharlu **8** Nemekser, Urumiyeh

mountain: 6 Elburz, Zagros

highest point: 8 Demavend

river: 4 Aras **5** Araks, Atrak, Atrek, Karun, Safid, Sefid **6** Gargan

sea: 7 Arabian, Caspian

physical feature:

desert: 9 Dasht-i-Lut **11** Dasht-i-Kavir

gulf: 4 Oman **7** Persian

strait: 6 Hormuz

people: 3 Lur, Tat **4** Arab, Kurd, Turk **5** Medes **6** Galcha, Gilani, Jewish, Shugni **7** Baluchi, Persian **8** Armenian, Bactrian, Bartangi, Parthian, Scythian **9** Bakhtiari **11** Azerbaijani, Mazandarani

mister: 4 agha

dynasty: 5 Qajar **7** Arsacid, Pahlavi, Safavid **8** Parthian, Seleucid **9** Sassanian **10** Achaemenid

statesman, mathematician, poet: 11 Omar Khayyam

ruler: 5 Abbas, Cyrus **6** Darius, Xerxes **10** Rafsanjani **23** Shah Mohammed Reza (Riza) Pahlavi **25** Ayatollah Ruhollah Khomeini

religious leader: 6 mullah **9** ayatollah

language: 4 Luri, Zend **5** Farsi, Turki **6** Arabic **7** Baluchi, Kurdish, Persian **8** Armenian **11** Azerbaijani

religion: 5 Baha'i, Islam **7** Judaism **9** Shia Islam **11** Zoroastrian **12** Christianity

place:

dam: 5 Karaj

mosque: 4 Shad **5** Royal **12** Masjidi-i-Shah **18** Madreseh Chahar Bagh

ruins: 4 Susa **10** Persepolis

feature: 13 Peacock Throne

head cloth: 6 chador **7** chawdar

parliament: 6 majlis

underground water channel: 5 qanat

food: 5 kabob

soured milk: 4 mast

stuffed vegetables/leaves: 5 dolma **6** dolmeh

Iraq

capital/largest city: 7 Baghdad

others: 2 Ur **3** Kut **5** Al Faw, Amara, Ashur, Basra, Erbil, Mosul, Najaf, Qurna **6** Hillah, Kirkuk, Tikrit **7** Karbala, Mandali, Samarra, Umm Qasr **8** Al Zubair

division:

ancient: 5 Akkad, Sumer **7** Assyria **9** Babylonia **11** Mesopotamia

monetary unit: 4 fils **5** dinar

lake: 6 al-Milh **7** Sanniya **8** al-Hammar

mountain: 6 Qalate, Zagros **7** Qaarade **9** Kurdistan

highest point: 7 Halgurd

river: 6 Diyala, Hawran, Tigris **8** Great Zab **9** al-Ubayyid, Euphrates, Little Zab **11** Shatt-al-Arab

physical feature:

desert: 6 Syrian **8** al-Hajava

gulf: 7 Persian

people: 4 Arab, Kurd **5** Sunni **6** Shiite **7** Bedouin

leader: 6 Faisal, Sargon **7** Abbasid, Hussein, Ottoman **9** Hammurabi **13** Harun al-Rashid, Saddam Hussein **14** Nebuchadnezzar **16** Abbasid Caliphate

language: 5 Farsi **6** Arabic **7** Kurdish, Persian, Turkish

religion: 5 Islam **12** Christianity

place:

ancient: 14 Hanging Gardens

arch: 9 Ctesiphon

mosque: 5 Great **9** Kadhimain

ruins: 2 Ur **7** Babylon, Nineveh, Samarra

Sumerian temple tower: 8 Ziggurat

feature:

marketplace: 4 souk

war: 4 Gulf, Iraq **11** Desert Storm **12** Desert Shield

irascibility 8 acerbity **9** bad temper, crossness, testiness **10** crabbiness, crankiness **11** peevishness, waspishness **12** irritability **16** cantankerousness

irascible 5 cross, testy 6 cranky, grumpy, ornery, touchy 7 grouchy, peevish, waspish 8 choleric 9 irritable, splenetic 10 ill-humored 11 bad-tempered, hot-tempered, intractable 12 cantankerous

irate 3 mad 5 angry, livid, rabid, riled, vexed 6 galled 7 angered, annoyed, enraged, furious 8 burned up 9 indignant, irritated 10 infuriated

ire 4 fury, rage 5 anger, wrath 6 choler 7 outrage, umbrage 8 vexation 10 resentment 11 indignation

Ireland
 other name: 4 Eire, Erin 5 Ierne 8 Hibernia 9 Innisfail 11 Emerald Isle
 capital/largest city: 6 Dublin
 others: 4 Cobh, Cork, Erne, Suir, Tara 5 Adare, Ennis, Sligo 6 Bangor, Galway, Lurgan, Mallow, Tralee, Ulster 7 Athlone, Belfast, Donegal, Dundalk, Kildare, Wexford 8 Drogheda, Kilkenny, Limerick 9 Craigavon, Tipperary, Waterford 10 Queenstown 11 Londonderry
 school: 7 Trinity
 division: 4 Cork, Down, Mayo 5 Clare, Kerry, Meath 6 Antrim, Armagh, Galway, Tyrone, Ulster 7 Donegal, Kildare, Wexford, Wicklow 8 Kilkenny, Limerick 9 Fermanagh, Killarney, Tipperary, Waterford 11 Londonderry
  ancient: 6 Ulster 7 Munster 8 Connacht, Leinster
 head of government: 9 taoiseach (prime minister)
 measure: 4 mile 6 bandle 8 crannock
 monetary unit: 3 rap 4 real 5 pence, pound 6 turney 8 shilling
 island: 3 Man 4 Aran, Bear, Holy, Tory 5 Clare, Clear, Magee 6 Achill, Saltee, Whiddy 7 Blasket, Gorumna, Rathlin 8 Aranmore, Inisheer 9 Inishmore 10 Inishbofin
 lake: 3 Doo, Key, Ree, Tay 4 Conn, Derg, Erne, Mask 5 Allen, Barra, Capra, Gowna, Leane, Lough, Neagh 6 Boderg, Cooter, Corrib, Ennell 7 Dromore, Gougane, Oughter, Sheelin 9 Killarney
 mountain: 5 Galty 6 Croagh, Mourne 7 Errigal, Muckish, Patrick, Wicklow 8 Comeragh 10 Benna Beola, Twelve Bens, Twelve Pins 13 Knockmealdown 19 Macgillycuddy's Reeks
 highest point: 13 Carrantuohill
 river: 3 Lee, May 4 Bann, Deel, Erne, Nore, Suir 5 Boyne, Clare, Feale, Flesk, Foyle, Laune 6 Bandon, Barrow, Corrib, Liffey, Slaney 7 Kenmare, Munster, Shannon 10 Blackwater
 sea: 5 Irish 8 Atlantic
 physical feature:
  bay: 4 Clew 5 Sligo 6 Bantry, Dingle, Galway, Tralee 7 Donegal, Dundalk

  cape: 5 Clear
  channel: 5 North 9 St George's
  cliffs: 5 Moher
  point: 6 Cahore 8 Carnsore
 people: 4 Celt, Erse, Gael 6 Celtic 9 Hibernian
  author: 4 Shaw 5 Behan, Burke, Joyce, Swift, Synge, Wilde, Yeats 6 O'Casey, Steele 7 Beckett, O'Connor 8 O'Faolain, Sheridan, Stephens 9 Goldsmith, O'Flaherty 13 St John Gogarty
  leader: 4 Tone 5 Ahern 6 Devlin, Valera 7 Grattan, Parnell, Redmond 8 O'Connell 9 Brian Boru 12 Saint Patrick
  legend: 9 Cuchulain 11 Finn Mac-Cool
 language: 4 Erse 5 Irish 6 Gaelic 7 English
 religion: 8 Anglican 13 Roman Catholic
 feature:
  airport: 7 Shannon
  castle: 4 Tara 7 Blarney
  crystal: 9 Waterford
  dance: 3 jig 4 reel
  game: 7 hurling
  lottery: 16 Irish Sweepstakes
  manuscript: 11 Book of Kells
  museum: 10 James Joyce
  political movement: 8 Sinn Fein
  race: 10 Irish Derby
  relic: 13 Ardagh Chalice
  revolutionary society: 6 Fenian
  stone: 7 Blarney
  street: 8 O'Connell
  theater: 5 Abbey
 food:
  beer: 5 stout

Ireland forever
 Gaelic: 11 Erin go bragh

I Remember Mama
 director: 13 George Stevens
 based on play by: 13 John Van Druten
 cast: 10 Ellen Corby, Irene Dunne, Philip Dorn 12 Oscar Homolka 16 Barbara Bel Geddes
 setting: 12 San Francisco

Irene
 member of: 5 Horae, Hours
 personifies: 5 peace
 corresponds to: 3 Pax

iridescence 7 glitter 11 opalescence, pearliness 12 nacreousness, play of colors

iridescent 5 shiny 7 glowing 8 colorful, nacreous 9 prismatic 10 changeable, opalescent 11 rainbowlike

iris
 varieties: 3 fan, red 4 roof, wall, wild 5 Dutch, dwarf, house 6 copper, German, orchid, Sierra, Spuria, violet, yellow 7 African, bearded, crested, English, Evansia, Lamance, peacock, Persian, Prairie, Spanish, walking 8 Japanese, mourning, Sibe-

rian, stinking 9 beachhead, beardless, butterfly, Palestine 10 snake's-head

Iris
 goddess of: 7 rainbow
 messenger of: 4 gods
 father: 7 Thaumas
 mother: 7 Electra
 sisters: 7 Harpies
 husband: 8 Zephyrus

Irish 4 Erse 4 Celtic, dander, Gaelic, temper
 accent: 6 brogue
 death spirit: 7 banshee
 flower: 8 shamrock
 girl: 7 colleen
 king: 9 Brian Boru
 legislature: 4 Dail
 saint: 7 Patrick
 society: 8 Sinn Fein
 theater: 5 Abbey

Irish gods 14 Tuatha De Danann

Irishman 4 Celt, Gael, Kelt, Mick 5 Paddy 7 Irisher 9 Hibernian, orangeman 10 bogtrotter

Irish Mythology
 cats: 8 Kilkenny
 fairies: 4 Side
 god of love/beauty/youth: 7 Angus Og
 god of poetry/eloquence: 4 Ogma
 god of sea: 8 Manannan
 gods: 14 Tuatha De Danann
 hero: 10 Cuchulainn
 invaders/ancestors: 9 Milesians
 king: 4 Bres 5 Ronan 9 Conchabar 10 Matholwych
 king of gods: 4 Finn 5 Fionn
 pirate/demon: 8 Fomorian
 sea goddess: 3 Ler, Lir
 spirit: 4 Puca 5 Pooka
  corresponds to British: 4 Puck

irk 3 bug, vex 4 gall 5 annoy 6 bother, pester, ruffle 7 provoke 8 irritate

irksome 5 pesky 6 plaguy, vexing 7 plaguey, tedious 8 annoying, tiresome, wearying 9 difficult, provoking, vexatious, wearisome 10 bothersome, irritating, nettlesome 11 troublesome

iron
 chemical symbol: 2 Fe

Iron Age
 period of: 4 time
 followed age of: 6 Bronze

ironclad 5 fixed 6 strict 9 immutable, permanent 10 inexorable, inflexible, rigoristic, unchanging 11 irrevocable, unalterable 12 irreversible, unchangeable, unmodifiable

Iron Horse
 nickname of: 9 Lou Gehrig

ironic, ironical 3 odd 5 funny, weird 6 biting 7 abusive, caustic, curious, cutting, mocking, strange 8 derisive, sardonic, sneering, stinging 9 facetious, insincere, pretended, sarcastic 10 surprising, unexpected 11 implausible, incongruous **12** inconsistent **13** contradictory

irons 5 bonds **6** chains **7** fetters, presses, smooths **8** manacles, shackles **9** golf clubs, handcuffs **10** restraints

Ironside
character: 7 (Det Sgt) Ed Brown **10** Mark Sanger **11** Fran Belding **12** Eve Whitfield **14** Robert Ironside
cast: 11 Don Galloway, Don Mitchell, Raymond Burr **13** Elizabeth Baur **15** Barbara Anderson

irony 7 mockery, sarcasm **9** absurdity **11** incongruity, indirection **12** contrariness **13** facetiousness **14** implausibility

Iroquoian
tribe: 6 Cayuga, Mohawk, Oneida, Seneca **8** Cherokee, Iroquois, Onandaga **9** Tuscarora **12** Kaniengehaga

Iroquois
language family: 9 Iroquoian
tribe: 6 Cayuga, Mohawk, Oneida, Seneca **8** Onondaga **9** Tuscarora
location: 6 Canada **7** New York **11** Connecticut **13** Massachusetts
leader: 11 Cornplanter, Joseph Brant
formed: 10 Six Nations **19** League of the Iroquois
supernatural force: 6 Orenda
prophet: 10 Ganiodaiyo

irrational 6 absurd **7** foolish, unsound **8** baseless **9** illogical, unfounded **10** ill-advised, unthinking **11** nonsensical, unreasoning **12** unreasonable

irreclaimable 4 lost **6** wicked **7** corrupt, debased **9** abandoned, reprobate **12** disreputable, irredeemable, irreformable **16** beyond redemption

irreconcilable 7 opposed **12** incompatible, inconsistent, intransigent, unadjustable, unappeasable, unbridgeable

irreformable 6 wicked **7** corrupt **9** abandoned, reprobate, shameless **11** unrepentant **12** disreputable **13** irreclaimable

irrefutable 10 undeniable **12** indisputable, not refutable **13** proof positive **14** unquestionable **16** incontrovertible

irrefutably 6 surely **10** definitely, positively, undeniably **12** conclusively, indisputably **13** incontestably **14** unquestionably **16** incontrovertibly

irregular 3 odd **5** bumpy, queer, rough **6** broken, uneven **7** crooked, unusual **8** aberrant, abnormal, improper, peculiar, singular **9** anomalous, desultory, eccentric, haphazard, not smooth, out of line, unaligned, unfitting **10** indecorous, unexpected, unsuitable **12** asymmetrical, unmethodical, unsystematic **13** inappropriate, nonconforming **14** unconventional **16** uncharacteristic

irregularity 7 anomaly **9** asymmetry, deviation **10** aberration, divergence,

unevenness **11** abnormality, peculiarity **12** constipation, eccentricity

irrelevant 5 inapt **7** foreign, off base **9** unfitting, unrelated **10** extraneous, immaterial, malapropos, not apropos, not germane **11** impertinent, unconnected **12** nonpertinent **14** beside the point

irreligion 7 atheism **8** apostasy, unbelief **9** disbelief **11** godlessness

irreligious 6 unholy **7** godless, impious, profane, ungodly **8** agnostic **9** atheistic **10** irreverent **11** unbelieving **12** not religious, sacrilegious

irremediable 8 hopeless **9** incurable **11** irreparable **12** beyond remedy

irreparable 9 unfixable **10** remediless **12** irremediable, irreversible **13** beyond redress, uncompensable, uncorrectable

irreplaceable 6 unique **9** essential **13** indispensable

irrepressible 7 vibrant **8** bubbling, galvanic, undamped **9** ebullient **10** boisterous, full of life **11** tempestuous **12** unquenchable **13** unsquelchable **14** uncontrollable, unrestrainable

irreproachable 8 flawless **9** blameless, faultless, stainless, unspotted **10** impeccable, inculpable **11** unblemished **12** above reproof, without fault **13** unimpeachable

irresistible 8 alluring, enticing **9** beckoning, seductive **10** enchanting, superhuman **11** tantalizing **12** overpowering, overwhelming

irresolute 4 weak **6** fickle, unsure **8** doubtful, hesitant, unsteady, wavering **9** faltering, uncertain, undecided, unsettled **10** changeable, hesitating, indecisive, unresolved **11** vacillating

irresolution 5 doubt **9** hesitancy **10** hesitation, indecision

irresponsibility 8 rashness **10** immaturity, imprudence **11** foolishness **12** carelessness, heedlessness, indifference, indiscretion, recklessness **13** unreliability **15** thoughtlessness, undependability **17** untrustworthiness

irresponsible 4 rash **7** foolish **8** careless, immature, reckless **9** imprudent, overhasty **10** capricious, incautious, unreliable **11** harebrained, indifferent, injudicious, thoughtless **12** undependable **13** ill-considered, untrustworthy **14** not responsible, scatterbrained

irresponsible person
French: 14 enfant terrible

irreverence 7 impiety **9** blasphemy, sacrilege **10** irreligion

irreverent 5 saucy **6** brazen **7** impious, profane **8** critical, impudent, sneering **9** debunking, shameless, skeptical, slighting **11** blasphemous, disparaging, irreligious **12** nosethumbing **13** disrespectful

irrevocable 5 final **10** conclusive **11** unalterable **12** irreversible, unchangeable

irritability 6 spleen **8** acerbity, edginess **9** crossness, huffiness, petulance, testiness **10** crabbiness, crankiness, impatience **11** fretfulness, peevishness, short temper, waspishness **12** irascibility

irritable 5 testy **6** grumpy, touchy **7** fretful, grouchy, peevish, pettish, waspish **8** snappish **9** impatient, irascible **10** ill-humored **11** easily vexed, ill-tempered

irritate 3 irk, vex **5** anger, annoy, chafe, peeve **6** nettle, worsen **7** inflame, provoke **8** make sore **9** aggravate, make angry **10** exasperate

irritated 3 mad, raw **4** sore **5** cross, irked, irate, testy, vexed **6** chafed, crabby, galled, miffed, peeved, piqued, put out **7** annoyed, burning, nettled, peevish **8** burned up, choleric, incensed, inflamed, provoked **9** impatient, irascible **10** aggravated **11** exasperated

irritating 5 acrid, harsh, rough **7** caustic, chafing, galling, irksome, rasping **8** abrasive, annoying **9** provoking, vexatious **10** bothersome **11** infuriating, troublesome **12** exasperating

irritation 6 bother **7** chafing **8** distress, vexation **9** annoyance **10** discomfort **11** irksomeness

irruption 4 raid **5** break, foray **6** inroad **7** upsurge **8** bursting, invasion **9** incursion, intrusion

Irving, John
author of: 13 The Fourth Hand, Until I Find You **16** A Widow for One Year **18** The Cider-House Rules **19** A Prayer for Owen Meany **20** The Hotel New Hampshire **23** The World According to Garp

Irving, Washington
author of: 10 Salmagundi **12** Rip Van Winkle **13** The Sketch Book **23** The Legend of Sleepy Hollow

Isaac
father: 7 Abraham
mother: 5 Sarah
brother: 7 Ishmael
wife: 7 Rebekah
son: 4 Esau **5** Jacob
birthplace: 5 Gerar
burial place: 9 Machpelah
blessed: 5 Jacob
sacrificed at: 6 Moriah

Isaac of York
character in: 7 Ivanhoe
author: 5 Scott

Isabella
character in: 17 Measure for Measure
author: 11 Shakespeare

Isaiah
means: 12 Jehovah saves
father: 4 Amoz

son: 11 Shearzashub **18** Maharshalal-hashbaz

Iscariot *see* **5** Judas

Isenstein
origin: **12** Scandinavian
home of: **8** Brunhild
location: **8** Isenland

I serve
German: **7** ich dien
motto of: **13** Prince of Wales

Iseult, Isolde, Isolt
character in: **16** Arthurian romance
lover: **7** Tristan **8** Tristram
betrothed to: **8** King Mark

I shall rise again
Latin: **8** resurgam

Isherwood, Christopher
author of: **10** I Am a Camera **13** Berlin Stories **17** Down There on a Visit
character: **11** Sally Bowles

Ishmael
narrator in: **8** Moby Dick
author: **8** Melville

Ishmael
father: **7** Abraham
mother: **5** Hagar
means: **11** God will hear
brother: **5** Isaac
son: **5** Kedar **7** Kedemah
descendant of: **10** Ishmaelite

Ishtar
also: **7** Mylitta
origin: **8** Assyrian **10** Babylonian
goddess of: **3** war **4** love
queen of: **6** heaven
corresponds to: **6** Inanna **7** Astarte **9** Ashtoreth

Isis
origin: **8** Egyptian
goddess of: **9** fertility
hieroglyphic symbol: **6** throne
husband: **6** Osiris
brother: **6** Osiris
son: **5** Horus
father: **3** Geb, Keb
mother: **3** Nut
horns of: **3** cow
headdress: **9** solar disk
corresponds to: **2** Io

Islam
adherent: **4** Sufi **5** Shiah **6** Moslem, Muslim, Shiite, Wahabi **7** Sunnite **8** Islamite **9** Mussulman **10** Mohammedan
crusade: **5** Jahad, Jihad
deity: **5** Allah
fasting month: **7** Ramadan
flight from Mecca: **6** hegira
founder/prophet: **8** Mohammed, Muhammad
holy city: **5** Mecca **6** Medina
house of worship: **6** mosque
Islamic school: **8** madrassa, madressa
legal verdict: **5** fatwa
other names: **9** Moslemism **13** Mohammedanism
pilgrimage to Mecca: **4** hadj, hajj

holy building: **5** Kaaba
religious leader: **4** imam
scripture: **5** Koran

Islamabad
capital of: **8** Pakistan

Islamic 6 Moslem, Muslim **10** Mohammedan

island 4 isle **5** atoll, haven, islet, oasis **6** refuge **7** enclave, retreat, shelter **9** sanctuary

Islands of the Blessed *see* **10** Hesperides

isle, islet 3 ait, cay, key **4** holm **5** atoll, islet **6** island

Isle of Cloves *see* **8** Tanzania

Isle of Spice *see* **7** Grenada

Isleta (Tuei)
language family: **6** Pueblo, Tanoan
location: **9** New Mexico, Rio Grande

isn't that so?
French: **9** n'est-ce pas?
German: **9** nicht wahr?

isolate 6 banish, detach, enisle **7** seclude **8** insulate, separate, set apart **9** segregate, sequester **10** disconnect, place apart, quarantine

isolated 4 lone, solo **5** alone, apart **6** cut off, lonely, remote, unique **7** insular, removed **8** detached, secluded, set apart, solitary **9** separated, unrelated **10** segregated **11** out-of-the-way, quarantined, sequestered

isolation 7 privacy **8** solitude **9** aloneness, apartness, hermitism, seclusion **10** desolation, detachment, insularity, insulation, quarantine, separation **11** confinement, segregation **12** separateness

isoptera
class: **8** hexapoda
phylum: **10** arthropoda
group: **7** termite **8** white ant

Ispahan
also: **7** Isfahan **8** Aspadana
location: **4** Iran
capital of: **6** Persia
river: **8** Zayandeh

I Spy
character: **13** Kelly Robinson **14** Alexander Scott
cast: **9** Bill Cosby **10** Robert Culp
Kelly's cover: **9** tennis bum

Israel
former name: **5** Jacob
means: **12** soldier of God
wrestled with: **5** angel

Israel
other name: **4** Zion **6** Canaan, Yishuv **9** Palestine **12** Promised Land
capital: **9** Jerusalem
largest city: **12** Tel Aviv-Jaffa
others: **4** Acre, Elat, Gaza **5** Eilat, Elath, Haifa, Holon, Jaffa, Jenin **6** Ashdod, Bat Yam, Dimona, Hebron, Nablus **7** Netanya, Rehovot, Tel Aviv

8 Nazareth, Ramallah, Ramat Gan **9** Beersheba, Bene Beraq, Bethlehem
school: **6** Hebrew **14** Technion-Israel **26** Weizmann Institute of Science
division: **5** Judea, Negev, Sinai **7** Galilee **8** West Bank **9** Gaza Strip **12** Golan Heights
government:
legislature: **7** Knesset
political parties: **5** Labor, Likud, Mapam
measure: **3** cab, car, hin, kab, kor **4** bath, ezba, omer, reed **5** cubit, donum, dunam, ephah, ganeh, homer, kaneh
monetary unit: **3** mil **5** agora, agura, pound, pruta **6** agorot, shekel
lake: **5** Huleh **7** Dead Sea **8** Kinneret, Tiberias **12** Sea of Galilee
mountain: **4** Nafh, Sagi **5** Harif, Ramon, Tabor **6** Atzmon, Carmel, Hatira
highest point: **5** Meron **6** Meiron
river: **4** Qarn **5** Faria, Malik, Sareq **6** Hadera, Jordan, Kishon, Qishon, Sarida, Yarkon, Yarmuk **7** Lakhish
sea: **3** Red **4** Dead **7** Galilee **13** Mediterranean
airline: **4** El Al
physical feature:
bay: **5** Haifa
desert: **5** Negev, Sinai
gulf: **5** Aqaba
plain: **5** Judea **6** Sharon **7** Zebulun **9** Esdraelon
people: **3** Jew **4** Arab **5** Druze **10** Circassian **11** Palestinian
ancient: **6** Hebrew
immigrant: **4** olim
Jew born in Israel: **5** sabra
leader: **4** Eban, Meir **5** Begin, Dayan, Herzl, Peres, Rabin **6** Ben-Zvi, Eshkol, Sharon **7** Sharett **8** Weizmann **9** Ben-Gurion
language: **6** Arabic, French, Hebrew **7** English, Yiddish
religion: **5** Baha'i, Islam **7** Judaism **12** Christianity
place:
church: **13** Holy Sepulcher
gates to Old Jerusalem: **3** New **4** Dung, Zion **5** Jaffa **6** Herod's **8** Damascus **10** St Stephen's
mosque: **13** Dome of the Rock
mount: **4** Zion **6** Olives, Scopus
shrine: **3** Bab **4** Book **11** Wailing Wall, Western Wall **18** Garden of Gethsemane
tomb: **9** Sanhedrin **10** King David's
way of sorrows: **11** Via Dolorosa
feature: **14** Dead Sea Scrolls
collective village: **7** kibbutz **9** kibbutzim
cooperative village: **6** moshav **8** moshavim
dance: **4** hora
movement: **7** Zionism
Palestinian uprising: **8** intifada

peace agreement: 16 Camp David Accords
tree: 5 judas
wave of immigration: 5 aliya **6** aliyot
food:
  dish: 4 pita **6** hummus **7** falafel
Israel, tribes of 3 Dan, Gad **4** Levi **5** Asher, Judah **6** Joseph, Reuben, Simeon **7** Zebulun **8** Benjamin, Issachar, Naphtali
Israel-born
  Hebrew: 5 sabra
Israelite 3 Jew **6** Hebrew, Jewish, Semite **7** Judaist **8** Hebraist
  descended from: 5 Jacob
  king: 4 Ahab, Elah, Jehu, Omri, Saul **5** David, Hosea, Nadab, Zimri
Issachar
  father: 5 Jacob
  mother: 4 Leah
  brother: 3 Dan, Gad **4** Levi **5** Asher, Judah **6** Joseph, Reuben, Simeon **7** Zebulun **8** Benjamin, Naphtali
  sister: 5 Dinah
  descendant: 11 Issacharite
Is Sex Necessary?
  author: 7 E B White **12** James Thurber
issuance 8 emission **9** allotment, discharge, emanation **12** dispensation, distribution
issue 4 gush, rise, stem **5** allot, arise, ensue, erupt, go out, heirs, spout, yield **6** emerge, follow, number, result, spring **7** dispute, emanate, flow out, give out, outcome, outflow, pass out, problem, proceed, product, progeny **8** children, dispense, drainage, eruption, granting, heritors, issuance, question **9** circulate, discharge, effluence, grow out of, offspring, posterity, pour forth **10** distribute, outpouring **11** consequence, descendants, publication **12** dispensation, distributing
Istanbul
  area: 7 Beyoglu **8** Stamboul
  capital of: 6 Turkey
  formerly: 9 Byzantium **14** Constantinople
  landmark: 10 Hippodrome **11** Hagia Sophia **12** Galata Bridge **14** Bosporus Bridge **26** Palais de la Culture d'Istanbul
  mosque: 3 New **8** Mihrimah **9** Yeni Camii **11** Suleymaniye
  museum: 13 Topkapi Palace **14** Archaeological **20** Turkish and Islamic Art
  rulers: 4 Rome **6** Athens, Darius, Rhodes, Sparta **8** Persians, Suleiman **9** Macedonia **11** Latin Empire **12** Ottoman Turks **15** Byzantine Empire, Turkish Republic **19** Constantine the Great
  sea: 5 Black **7** Marmara **8** Bosporus **10** Golden Horn

isthmus 4 neck, spit **5** point, strip **6** narrow, strait, tongue **7** narrows
  name: 4 Suez **6** Panama **7** Corinth
I sustain the wings
  Latin: 12 sustineo alas
  motto of: 10 US Air Force
Italic
  language family: 12 Indo-European
  branch: 5 Latin, Oscan **7** Umbrian
italics 11 slanted type
Italy
  also: 8 Hesperia
  capital/largest city: 4 Roma, Rome
  others: 4 Pisa **5** Genoa, Milan, Padua, Turin, Udine **6** Amalfi, Ancona, Assisi, Naples, Rimini, Savona, Venice, Verona **7** Bologna, Bolzano, Brescia, Catania, Messina, Palermo, Ravenna, Taranto, Trieste **8** Florence
  division: 6 Apulia, Latium, Marche, Molise, Umbria, Veneto **7** Abruzzi, Liguria, Tuscany **8** Calabria, Campania, Lombardy, Piedmont **10** Basilicata **12** Valle d'Agosta **13** Emilia-Romagna **17** Trentino-Alto Adige **19** Friuli-Venezia Giulia
    independent enclave: 9 San Marino **11** Vatican City
  measure: 3 pie **4** orna **5** palma, palmo, punto, salma, stero **6** barile, miglie, moggio, rubbio, tomolo **7** braccio, secchio **8** giornata, quadrato
  monetary unit: 4 lira, lire, tara **5** grano, paolo, soldo **6** danaro, denaro, ducato **7** testone **8** zecchino **9** centesini
  weight: 5 carat, libra, oncia, pound **6** denaro, libbra
  island: 4 Elba **5** Capri, Egadi, Eolie **6** Ischia, Istria, Linosa, Lipari, Sicily, Ustica **7** Aeolian, Trieste, Vulcano **8** Lampione, Sardinia **9** Borromean, Lampedusa, Stromboli **10** Isola Bella **11** Pantelleria
  lake: 4 Como, Iseo, Nemi **5** Garda **6** Albano, Lesina, Lugano, Varano **7** Bolsena, Perugia **8** Maggiore **9** Bracciano, Trasimeno
  mountain: 4 Alps, Etna, Visa **5** Amaro, Blanc, Corno, Somma **6** Cimone, Ortles **9** Apennines, Dolomites, Maritimes **11** Gennargentu **12** Gran Paradiso **16** Abruzzi Apennines
    Alps: 6 Apuane, Carnic, Julian, Otztal **7** Bernina **8** Ligurian **9** Lepontine
  volcano: 4 Etna **7** Vulcano **8** Vesuvius **9** Stromboli
  highest point: 4 Rosa
  river: 2 Po **4** Adda, Agri, Arno, Liri, Nera, Reno, Sele, Taro **5** Adige, Crati, Mannu, Oglio, Parma, Piave, Salso, Stura, Tiber, Tirso **6** Aniene, Belice, Isonzo, Mincio, Ofanto, Panaro, Rapido, Sangro, Simeto, Tanaro, Tevere, Ticino **7** Biferno, Bradano, Chienti, Metauro, Montone, Ombrone, Pescara, Rubicon, Secchia,

Trebbia **8** Volturno
  sea: 6 Ionian **8** Adriatic, Ligurian **10** Tyrrhenian **13** Mediterranean
  physical feature:
    bay: 6 Naples
    channel: 5 Malta
    grotto: 4 Blue
    gulf: 5 Gaeta, Genoa **6** Venice **7** Salerno, Taranto **11** Manfredonia
    hills of Rome: 7 Caelian, Viminal **8** Aventine, Palatine, Quirinal **9** Esquiline **10** Capitoline
    lagoon: 6 Venice
    pass: 5 Resia **6** Maloja **7** Bernina, Brenner, Simplon **9** Mont Cenis **13** Saint Gotthard **17** Great Saint Bernard
    resort: 14 Italian Riviera
    strait: 6 Sicily **7** Messina, Otranto **9** Bonifacio
  people: 7 Italian
    ancient: 5 Latin, Remus **6** Sabine **7** Lombard, plebian, Romulus **8** Etruscan **9** patrician
    architect: 5 Nervi, Ponti, Salvi **6** Vasari **7** Alberti, Guarini, Juvarra, Vignola **8** Ammanati, Bramante, Palladio **9** Borromini, De Sanctis **12** Brunelleschi, Michelangelo
    artist: 5 Balla, Carra **6** Batoni, Gaulli, Guardi, Titian **7** Bellini, Chirico, Cimabue, Cortona, Da Vinci, Raphael, Tiepolo, Uccello **8** Carracci, Mantegna, Masaccio, Severini **9** Benvenuti, Canoletto, Giorgione **10** Botticelli, Caravaggio, Modigliani, Tintoretto **11** Buoninsegna, Fra Angelico **12** Michelangelo **13** Giotto Bondone **14** della Francesca
    composer: 5 Verdi **7** Bellini, Cavalli, Corelli, Puccini, Rossini, Vivaldi **8** Mascagni, Piccinni **9** Donizetti, Scarlatti **10** Monteverdi, Palestrina **11** Leoncavallo
    emperor: 4 Nero, Otho **5** Galba, Nerva, Titus **6** Trajan **7** Hadrian **8** Caligula, Claudius, Commodus, Domitian, Octavian, Tiberius **9** Caracalla, Vespasian, Vitellius **10** Diocletian **11** Constantine **13** Antoninus Dius **14** Caesar Augustus, Marcus Aurelius
    film director: 6 de Sica **7** Fellini **8** Visconti **9** Antonioni **10** Bertolucci, Rossellini, Wertmuller, Zeffirelli
    god: 4 Juno, Mars **5** Ceres, Diana, Janus, Lares, Venus **6** Apollo, Vulcan **7** Bacchus, Jupiter, Minerva, Neptune, Penates **8** Quirinus
  Italian author: 3 Eco **4** Levi **5** Bembo, Bruno, Pulci, Tasso **6** Aretino, Vasari **7** Ariosto, Bassani, Deledda, Moravia **8** Bandello, Petrarch **9** Boccaccio, D'Annunzio, Sannazaro **10** Cavalcanti, Guinicelli, Metastasio, Pirandello, Stra-

parola **11** Castiglione, Machiavelli **12** Guicciardini, Michelangelo **14** Dante Alighieri

Latin author: 4 Cato, Livy, Ovid **5** Pliny, Varro **6** Cicero, Gallus, Horace, Seneca, Vergil, Virgil **7** Donatus, Juvenal, Martial, Plautus, Sallust, Tacitus, Terence **8** Boethius, Catullus, Lucilius, St Jerome **9** St Ambrose, Suetonius **11** St Augustine

ruler: 4 Moro **6** Cavour, Enrico **7** Mazzini **9** Mussolini **10** Berlinguer **14** Victor Emmanuel **15** Alcide de Gasperi

ruler/military leader: 5 Sulla **6** Brutus, Pompey, Seneca **7** Crassus, Lepidus **8** Gracchus **10** Mark Antony **12** Gaius Marious, Julius Caesar **15** Cassius Longinus, Scipio Africanus **18** Tarquinius Superbus

old ruling family: 4 Este **6** Borgia, Medici, Sforza **8** Visconti

sculptor: 6 Canova, Marini, Pisano **7** Bernini, Bologna, Cellini **8** Antelami, Boccioni, Ghiberti **9** Donatello, Sansovino **10** Giacometti, Pollaiuolo, Verrocchio **11** Della Robbia **12** Michelangelo

wife: 7 Poppaea **9** Agrippina, Messalina **13** Livia Drusilla

language: 5 Ladin, Latin **6** French, German **7** Italian, Slovene **8** Friulian **9** Sardinian

expressions: 4 ciao **5** bella **10** primadonna

religion: 13 Roman Catholic

place:

arch: 11 Constantine

baths: 9 Caracalla

bridge: 5 Sighs **12** Ponte Vecchio

cathedral/church: 5 Siena **7** St Mark's, Vatican **8** San Marco, St Peter's **13** Sistine Chapel

fountain: 5 Trevi

museum: 5 Duomo **6** Uffizi **8** Bargello, National **10** Capitoline **11** Pitti Palace, Villa Giulia **16** Gallerio Borghese

opera house: 7 La Scala

palace: 5 Doges

road: 9 Appian Way

ruins: 5 Forum **7** Capitol, Pompeii **8** Pantheon **9** Catacombs, Colosseum **11** Herculaneum **13** Circus Maximus

steps: 7 Spanish

tower: 18 Leaning Tower of Pisa

feature:

unification movement: 12 Risorgimento

food:

cheese: 6 romano **7** fontina, ricotta **8** parmesan

dish: 5 pizza **6** scampi **7** gnocchi, lasagna, lasagne, polenta, ravioli, risotto **9** antipasti, antipasto **17**

chicken cacciatora, cacciatore

ice cream: 6 gelato **7** spumoni

meat: 6 salami **9** pepperoni **10** mortadella, prosciutto

soup: 8 caciucco **10** minestrone

wine: 7 Chianti

itch 3 yen **4** ache, long, pine **5** crave, crawl, creep, yearn **6** desire, hanker, hunger, thirst, tickle **7** craving, prickle **8** appetite, have a yen, pruritis, tingling, yearning **9** hankering

it does not follow

Latin: 11 non sequitur

item 4 unit **5** entry, piece, point, story, thing **6** detail, matter, notice, report **7** account, article, feature, subject **8** dispatch, notation **9** paragraph **10** particular **11** news article

itemization 4 list **7** listing **11** enumeration

itemize 6 detail **7** specify **8** spell out **9** enumerate

items of business 4 list **6** agenda, docket **7** program **8** schedule

iterate 6 repeat **7** restate **9** reiterate

It Girl

nickname of: 8 Clara Bow

it grows as it goes

Latin: 12 crescit eundo

motto of: 9 New Mexico

Ithaca

ancient home of: 8 Odysseus, Penelope

modern home of: 7 Cornell (University)

It Happened One Night

director: 10 Frank Capra

cast: 8 Alan Hale, Ward Bond **10** Clark Gable **11** Roscoe Karns **14** Walter Connolly **16** Claudette Colbert

Oscar for: 5 actor (Gable) **7** actress (Colbert), picture **8** director

remade as: 16 Eve Knew Her Apples **20** You Can't Run Away from It

I think therefore I am

Latin: 13 cogito ergo sum

said by: 9 Descartes

itinerant 5 nomad, rover **6** roamer, roving **7** migrant, nomadic, roaming, vagrant **8** vagabond, wanderer, wayfarer **9** footloose, transient, traveling, wandering, wayfaring **11** peripatetic

itinerary 3 log **5** diary, route **6** course **7** account, circuit, day book, journal **8** schedule **9** timetable **10** travel plan

it is not clear; it is not evident

Latin: 9 non liquet

it is not lawful; it is not permitted

Latin: 8 non licet

it is sweet to do nothing

Italian: 14 dolce far niente

It's a Gift

director: 13 Norman Z McLeod

cast: 8 W C Fields **9** Baby LeRoy, Tommy Bupp **10** T Roy Barnes **13**

Charles Sellon, Morgan Wallace **14** Kathleen Howard

remake of: 17 It's the Old Army Game

It's a Wonderful Life

director: 10 Frank Capra

cast: 9 Donna Reed **11** Beulah Bondi **12** Henry Travers, James Stewart **13** Gloria Grahame **15** Lionel Barrymore

remade as: 22 It Happened One Christmas

itsy-bitsy 3 wee **4** tiny **5** dwarf, pygmy, small, teeny **6** bantam, little, minute, petite **9** miniature, miniscule **10** diminutive, teeny-weeny **11** microscopic, pocket-sized

It Takes a Thief

character: 8 Noah Bain **12** Alister Mundy, Wallie Powers **14** Alexander Mundy

cast: 11 Edward Binns, Fred Astaire **12** Robert Wagner **13** Malachi Throne

Itza

language family: 6 Toltec

location: 6 Mexico **7** Chichen, Yucatan **14** Central America

Iulus *see* **8** Ascanius

Ivan 4 czar, tsar **8** the Great **11** the Terrible **18** grand duke of Muscovy **English equivalent: 4** John **personifies: 6** Russia

Ivanhoe

author: 14 Sir Walter Scott

character: 7 Rebecca **8** Guilbert **9** Robin Hood **10** Lady Rowena **11** Isaac of York **12** King Richard I **14** Cedric the Saxon, Sir Brian de Bois **16** Wilfred of Ivanhoe **19** King Richard the First

Ivanhoe, Burle Icle

real name of: 8 Burl Ives

I've Got a Secret

host: 10 Bill Cullen, Garry Moore, Steve Allen

Ives, Burl

real name: 16 Burle Icle Ivanhoe

nickname: 17 Wayfaring Stranger

born: 6 Hunt IL

roles: 8 Big Daddy **10** East of Eden **13** The Big Country **14** Our Man in Havana **16** Cat on a Hot Tin Roof **18** Desire Under the Elms

Ives, Charles

born: 9 Danbury CT

composer of: 11 Putnam's Camp **13** Concord Sonata **19** Washington's Birthday **20** Central Park in the Dark **21** The Unanswered Question **23** Three Places in New England

ivory 4 tusk **6** dentin

source: 6 walrus **8** elephant

used for: 4 dice **9** piano keys **13** billiard balls

color: 5 cream **8** off-white

Ivory Coast

French name: 11 Cote d'Ivoire

capital/largest city: 7 Abidjan
  new capital: 12 Yamoussoukro
others: 3 Man **4** Divo **5** Daloa, Tabou
6 Adzobe, Bonoua, Bouake, Danane,
Gagnoa **7** Korhogo, Odienne, Seguela
8 Dimbokro **9** Agboville, Bondoukou,
Sassandra **10** Abengourou **11** Grand
Bassam **14** Ferkessedougou
monetary unit: 5 franc **7** centime
highest point: 5 Nimba
river: 3 Bia **5** Comoe, Komoe **7** Bandama, Cavally **9** Sassandra
ocean: 8 Atlantic
physical feature:
  cape: 6 Palmas
  gulf: 6 Guinea
  lagoon: 3 Aby **5** Ebrie
  wind: 9 harmattan
people: 3 Abe, Dan, Kru, Kwa **4**
Akan, Bete, Dida, Guro, Koua, Lobi,
Wobe **5** Abron, Abure, Attie, Baule,
Guere, Mande, Mossi **6** Baoule, Lagoon, Senufo, Senufu **7** Dan Guro,
Kroumen, Malinke, Voltaic **10** Anyi-
Baoule **11** Lobi-Kulango **12** Agnis-
Ashanti
language: 4 Akan **6** Dioula, French
religion: 5 Islam **7** animism **13** Roman Catholic
place:
  canal: 5 Vridi

  dam: 7 Bandama
  game reserve: 9 Sassandra
  feature: 7 kola nut
Ivory Coast *see* **11** Sierra Leone
ivory-towered 6 remote **8** academic,
romantic **11** conjectural, impractical,
theoretical, unrealistic **12** hypothetical
ivy 6 Cissus, Hedera **15** Kalmia latifolia
  varieties: 3 fan, red **4** baby, tree **5**
grape, Irish, Nepal, water **6** aralia,
Baltic, Boston, canary, devil's, German, ground, marine, parlor, poison,
spider, switch **7** colchis, English,
Italian, Madeira, Mexican, parsley,
Persian, Swedish **8** Algerian, American, coliseum, fragrant, Japanese,
red-flame **9** bird's-foot, ghost-tree,
heart-leaf **10** five-leaved, Kenilworth,
variegated **12** Hagenburger's **13** Solomon Island **14** miniature grape **15**
Gloire-de-Marengo
Ivy League colleges 4 Yale **5** Brown
7 Cornell, Harvard **8** Columbia **9**
Dartmouth, Princeton **12** Pennsylvania
(Penn)
I Want to Live!
  director: 10 Robert Wise
  cast: 12 Simon Oakland, Susan Hayward (Barbara Graham) **13** Theodore
Bikel **15** Virginia Vincent

  score: 12 Johnny Mandel
  Oscar for: 7 actress (Hayward)
I will defend
  Latin: 6 tuebor
IWW 8 Wobblies **10** labor union **27** Industrial Workers of the World
  leader: 4 Debs **6** DeLeon **7** Haywood
  members: 6 miners **9** lumbermen **16**
migratory workers
Ixion
  king of: 8 Lapithae
  wife: 3 Dia
  son: 9 Pirithous
  children: 8 centaurs
  loved: 4 Hera
  punished by: 4 Zeus
  bound to: 5 wheel
Iyar 17 second Hebrew month
Iynx
  father: 3 Pan
  mother: 4 Echo
Izmir
  formerly: 6 Smyrna
  location: 6 Turkey **9** Aegean Sea
11 Gulf of Izmir
  settle by: 7 Ionians **8** Aeolians
  ruled by: 13 Ottoman Empire
izzard 3 zed, zee

 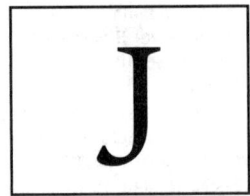 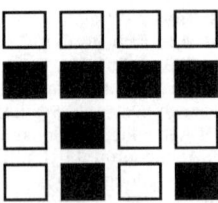

ja 3 yes

jab 3 cut, dig, hit, rap, tap **4** belt, blow, bump, clip, goad, lick, pelt, plug, poke, poke, prod, sock, stab, swat **5** elbow, nudge, paste, swing **6** strike, stroke

jabber 3 gab, gas **4** blab **5** clack, prate **6** babble, cackle, drivel, gibber, gossip, hot air, patter, ramble, rattle, raving **7** blabber, blather, chatter, gushing, maunder, palaver, prating, prattle, ranting, twaddle, twattle **8** chitchat, idle talk, nonsense, talk idly **9** gibberish **10** maundering **14** chitterchatter

jack 4 flag **5** knave, money **6** ensign, sailor

jackass 3 ass **4** fool, mule **5** burro, dummy, idiot **6** donkey

Jack Benny Show, The
  cast: 8 Mel Blanc **9** Dennis Day, Don Wilson **11** Frank Nelson **13** Artie Auerbach, Eddie (Rochester) Anderson **14** Mary Livingston
  Jack's car: 7 Maxwell
  Jack played: 6 violin

jacket 4 case, coat **5** cover **6** blazer, casing, folder, sheath **7** wrapper **8** envelope, mackinaw, wrapping **9** container, enclosure, short coat, sport coat **10** dinner coat **11** windbreaker

Jackson, Andrew
  nickname: 10 Old Hickory
  presidential rank: 7 seventh
  party: 10 Democratic
  state represented: 2 TN **9** Tennessee
  defeated: 4 (Henry) Clay **5** (John Quincy) Adams
  vice president: 7 (John Caldwell) Calhoun **8** (Martin) Van Buren
  cabinet:
    state: 6 (Louis) McLane **7** (John) Forsyth **8** (Martin) Van Buren **10** (Edward) Livingston
    treasury: 5 (William John) Duane **6** (Louis) McLane, (Samuel Dulucenna) Ingham **8** (Levi) Woodbury
    war: 4 (Lewis) Cass **5** (John Henry) Eaton
    attorney general: 5 (Roger Brooke) Taney **6** (Benjamin Franklin) Butler **7** (John McPherson) Berrien
    navy: 6 (John) Branch **8** (Levi) Woodbury **9** (Mahlon) Dickerson
    postmaster general: 5 (William Taylor) Barry **7** (Amos) Kendall

  born: 8 Waxhaw SC
  died/buried: 11 Nashville TN
  education:
    college: 4 none
    studied: 3 law
    admitted to: 3 bar
  religion: 12 Presbyterian
  political career: 8 US Senate **24** US House of Representatives
    judge: 22 Tennessee Superior Court
  civilian career: 6 lawyer
  military service: 12 major general **16** brigadier general
    defeated: 6 Creeks **9** Cherokees
    captured: 9 Pensacola
    military governor of: 7 Florida
  notable events of lifetime/term:
    battle: 5 Alamo **10** New Orleans
    fought: 5 duels
    scandal/wife suspected of: 6 bigamy
    war: 8 Creek War **13** Revolutionary **16** First Seminole War **19** War of Eighteen Twelve
  father: 6 Andrew
  mother: 9 Elizabeth (Hutchinson)
  siblings: 4 Hugh **6** Robert
  wife: 6 Rachel (Donelson Robards)
  children:
    adopted: 11 wife's nephew **15** Andrew Jackson Jr

Jackson, Anne
  husband: 10 Eli Wallach
  born: 10 Millvale PA
  roles: 3 Luv **10** The Typists

Jackson, Charles
  author of: 14 The Lost Weekend

Jackson 5 4 Tito **6** Jackie, Marlon **7** Michael **8** Jermaine
  songs: 3 ABC **10** I'll Be There **12** I Want You Back **14** The Love You Save

Jackson, Glenda
  born: 7 England **10** Birkenhead
  roles: 10 Elizabeth R, The Rainbow **11** Women in Love (Oscar) **13** A Touch of Class (Oscar) **14** The Music Lovers **16** Mary Queen of Scots **18** Sunday Bloody Sunday
  politics: 10 Parliament **11** Labour Party **14** House of Commons **18** Member of Parliament

Jackson, Jesse Louis
  title: 8 Reverend
  party: 10 Democratic
  born: 12 Greenville SC

  education: 20 University of Illinois **26** Chicago Theological Seminary **49** North Carolina Agricultural and Technical State College
  religion: 7 Baptist
  civilian career: 4 SCLC **9** PUSH Excel **13** Operation PUSH **17** Democratic primary **20** Operation Breadbasket **24** National Rainbow Coalition **37** Southern Christian Leadership Conference

Jackson, Michael
  born: 2 IN **4** Gary
  father: 6 Joseph
  mother: 9 Katherine
  siblings: 4 Tito **5** Janet, Randy **6** Jackie, La Toya, Marlon **7** Maureen **8** Jermaine
  wife: 16 Lisa Marie Presley
  ranch: 9 Neverland
  trademark: 5 glove **8** moonwalk
  recordings: 3 Bad **7** HIStory, Triumph, Victory **8** Thriller **9** Dangerous **10** Off the Wall **27** HIStory Past, Present, and Future
  film: 6 The Wiz
  group: 8 Jacksons **11** Jackson Five

Jackson, Reggie
  nickname: 13 Mister October
  sport: 8 baseball
  position: 8 outfield
  known for: 7 hitting
  team: 9 Oakland A's **14** New York Yankees **16** California Angels

Jackson, Shirley
  author of: 10 The Lottery **28** We Have Always Lived in the Castle

Jackson, Stonewall (Thomas)
  served in: 8 Civil War **10** Mexican War
  side: 11 Confederate
  battle: 7 Bull Run **8** Antietam, Richmond **9** Seven Days **14** Fredericksburg **16** Chancellorsville, Shenandoah Valley

Jacksonville
  football team: 7 Jaguars

Jacob
  father: 5 Isaac
  mother: 7 Rebekah
  brother: 4 Esau
  wives: 4 Leah **6** Rachel
  concubines: 5 Bilah **6** Zilpah
  son: 3 Dan, Gad **4** Levi **5** Asher, Judah **6** Joseph, Reuben, Simeon **7** Zebulun **8** Benjamin, Issachar, Naph-

tali
daughter: 5 Dinah
dream of: 6 ladder
wrestled with: 5 angel
name changed to: 6 Israel
burial place: 9 Machpelah

Jacob, Francois
field: 7 biology
nationality: 6 French
discovered: 3 RNA
awarded: 10 Nobel Prize

jacuzzi 4 bath **9** whirlpool

jade
species: 7 jadeite **8** nephrite
source: 5 Burma, China **6** Mexico **7** Mogaung **10** New Zealand **12** United States

jaded 5 blase, bored, sated, spent, stale, tired, weary **6** cloyed, dulled, fagged **7** glutted, satiate, spoiled, wearied, worn-out **8** dog-tired, fatigued, overused, satiated, shopworn, tired out **9** exhausted, played out, surfeited **11** overwearied **12** overindulged

jadeite
variety: 4 jade

JAG
network: 3 CBS
creator: 17 Donald P. Bellisario
cast: 11 Karri Turner (Harriet Sims Roberts) **12** John M. Jackson (Admiral Chegwidden) **13** Catherine Bell (Sarah MacKenzie) **17** David James Elliott (Harmon Rabb) **18** Patrick Labyorteaux (Bud Roberts)

jagged 5 jaggy, rough, spiny **6** barbed, broken, craggy, nicked, ridged, rugged, snaggy, spiked, thorny, uneven, zigzag **7** angular, bristly, cragged, notched, pointed, spinous, studded **8** indented, serrated **9** irregular, knifelike **10** crenulated, saw-toothed **12** sharp-toothed

Jagger, Mick
born: 12 Dartford, Kent (UK)
musician for: 13 Rolling Stones
songs: 8 Star, Star, Lady Jane **9** Start Me Up **10** Brown Sugar, The Citadel, She's So Cold, Wild Horses **11** Ruby Tuesday **12** Paint It Black **13** Get Off My Cloud **14** Honky Tonk Woman **15** Jumpin' Jack Flash
body feature: 4 lips
wife: 6 Bianca
companion: 9 Jerri Hall

jaguar 3 cat **5** tiger **6** feline **7** panther **8** uturuncu

jail 3 bag, can, jug, nab, pen **4** book, brig, bust, cell, keep, stir **5** clink, pinch, pound, run in, seize **6** arrest, collar, cooler, lockup, prison, take in **7** arraign, bring in, capture, confine, dungeon, slammer **8** bastille, big house, hoosegow, imprison, stockade **9** apprehend, black hole, calaboose, guardroom, workhouse **10** guardhouse **11** incarcerate, reformatory **12** half-

way house, penitentiary, reform school, station house **13** hold in custody, police station **14** detention house **16** penal institution **17** house of correction

jailbird 3 con **5** felon, lifer **7** convict **8** prisoner

jailer 5 guard, screw **6** gaoler, keeper, warden **7** turnkey **9** custodian

Jair 11 Hebrew judge

Jakarta, Djakarta
capital of: 9 Indonesia

Jake's Thing
author: 12 Kingsley Amis

jalopy 3 car **4** auto, heap **5** motor **6** wheels **7** flivver, machine, vehicle **8** motorcar **9** tin lizzie **10** automobile

jam 3 fix, mob, ram, sea **4** army, cram, herd, host, mess, pack, push, stop **5** block, cease, crowd, crush, drove, flock, horde, pinch, press, shove, stall, stick, stuff, swarm, tie-up, wedge **6** arrest, edge in, pickle, plight, scrape, strait, throng, thrust, work in, worm in **7** congest, dilemma, foist in, force in, squeeze, suspend, trouble **8** hot water, obstruct, quandary, sandwich **9** interrupt, multitude, overcrowd **11** malfunction, predicament **13** agglomeration

Jamaica
name means: 18 land of wood and water
capital/largest city: 8 Kingston
others: 6 May Pen **8** Ocho Rios **9** Morant Bay, Port Maria, Port Royal **10** Mandeville, Montego Bay **11** Port Antonio, Spanish Town **12** Saint Ann's Bay, Savanna-la-Mar
head of state: 14 British monarch **15** governor general
monetary unit: 7 quattie
island: 4 Navy **15** Greater Antilles
mountain: 8 Sir John's
highest point: 4 Blue
river: 5 Black, Cobre, Great, Minho, White **9** Rio Grande
sea: 8 Atlantic **9** Caribbean
physical feature: 13 Portland Bight
  area: 14 Cockpit Country
  bay: 4 Buff, Hope, Long **6** Morant **9** Discovery **10** Black River, Bluefield's, Old Harbour
  point: 6 Galina **8** Portland **9** North East, North West, South East **11** North Negril, South Negril
people: 7 African, Chinese **10** East Indian
  ancient: 6 Arawak **7** Ciboney
  discoverer: 8 Columbus
  leader: 5 Seaga **6** Garvey, Manley **10** Bustamante
language: 6 Creole **7** English
religion: 7 Baptist **8** Anglican **9** Methodist **11** Church of God, Rastafarian **13** Roman Catholic
place:

beach: 11 Doctor's Cave
botanical garden: 4 Hope
racetrack: 12 Caymanas Park
feature:
  evil spirits: 7 duppies
  guerrilla fighters: 7 Maroons
  tree: 4 poui **5** cedar, ceiba, mahoe, saman **6** cassia, guango **7** logwood **8** mahogany **9** casuarina, poinciana **10** silkcotton **11** lignum vitae
  witch doctor: 8 obeah man
food:
  coffee: 12 Blue Mountain
  drink: 3 rum **4** jake **8** tia maria
  fruit: 5 guava, mango **6** pawpaw
  spicy soup: 9 pepper pot

jamboree 2 do **4** bash, gala **5** party, revel, spree **6** fiesta, frolic **7** blowout, jubilee, shindig **8** carnival, carousal, festival **9** festivity **11** celebration
French: 4 fete **13** fete champetre

James 7 apostle
also called: 12 James the Less
father: 7 Zebedee **8** Alphaeus
brother: 4 John, Levi **5** Judas
disciple of: 5 Jesus
killed by: 12 Herod Agrippa
with John called: 13 sons of thunder

James, Henry
author of: 11 Daisy Miller, The American **13** The Bostonians, The Golden Bowl **14** Roderick Hudson, The Ambassadors **15** The Aspern Papers **16** Washington Square **17** The Turn of the Screw, The Wings of the Dove **18** The Portrait of a Lady **19** Princess Casamassima

James, P D
author of: 12 Cover Her Face **13** Innocent Blood, The Murder Room **15** A Certain Justice, Unnatural Causes **17** Death in Holy Orders, Devices and Desires **21** Shroud for a Nightingale **22** Death of an Expert Witness, The Skull Beneath the Skin
character: 12 Cornelia Gray **13** Adam Dalgliesh

James the Less *see* **5** James

jammed 4 full **5** stuck **6** filled, loaded, massed, packed, rammed, wedged **7** blocked, crammed, crowded, crushed, pressed, stuffed **8** overfull, squeezed **10** obstructed, sandwiched **11** overcrowded

Janacek, Leos
born: 8 Hukvaldy **14** Czechoslovakia
composer of: 5 Mladi, Youth **6** Jenufa **8** In the Mist **10** Taras Bulba **13** Katya Kabanova **14** Glagolitic Mass **17** On an Overgrown Path **18** The Makropoulos Case **21** From the House of the Dead, The Cunning Little Vixen **24** The Diary of One Who Vanished, The Excursions of Mr Broucek

Jane
 character in: **6** Tarzan
 author: **9** Burroughs
Jane Eyre
 author: **15** Charlotte Bronte
 character: **5** Mason **7** Mrs Reed **10** Grace Poole, Mary Rivers, Mrs Fairfax **11** Adele Varens, Bertha Mason, Diana Rivers **12** Bessie Leaven, St John Rivers **13** Blanche Ingram **15** Edward Rochester
 school: **6** Lowood
 house: **10** Thornfield
 director: **15** Robert Stevenson
 cast: **11** Orson Welles **12** Joan Fontaine **14** Margaret O'Brien
jangle 3 din, jar **4** ring **5** annoy, chime, clang, clank, clash, crash, upset **6** jingle, racket, rattle **7** clangor, clatter, grate on **8** irritate **9** cacophony **11** reverberate **13** reverberation **14** tintinnabulate
janitor: 6 super **6** porter **8** handyman **9** caretaker, custodian, janitress **11** cleaning man **12** cleaning lady **13** cleaning woman **14** maintenance man, superintendent
Janssen, David
 real name: **16** David Harold Meyer
 born: **9** Naponee NE
 roles: **6** Harry O **11** The Fugitive **14** Richard Diamond **15** Dr Richard Kimble
January
 event: **15** Inauguration Day (every 4 years)
 flower: **8** snowdrop **9** carnation
 French: **7** Janvier
 gem: **6** garnet
 German: **6** Januar
 holiday: **7** Kwanzaa (1, last day) **8** Epiphany (6) **11** New Year's Day (1) **12** Twelfth Night (5) **19** Martin Luther King Day
 Italian: **7** Gennaio
 number of days: **9** thirty-one
 origin of name: **5** Janus
  Roman god of: **5** doors **8** doorways **10** beginnings
 place in year:
  Gregorian: **5** first
  Julian/Roman: **8** eleventh
 Spanish: **5** Enero
 Zodiac sign: **8** Aquarius **9** Capricorn
Janus
 origin: **5** Roman
 god of: **8** doorways **9** rising sun **10** beginnings, setting sun
Japan
 other name: **5** Nihon **6** Nippon
 name means: **18** Land of the Rising Sun
 capital/largest city: **3** Edo **5** Tokyo
 others: **4** Kobe, Naha **5** Kyoto, Osaka **6** Nagoya, Sendai **7** Fukuoka, Niigata, Sapporo **8** Kanazawa, Kawasaki, Nagasaki, Yokohama **9** Hiro-

shima, Kagoshima **10** Kitakyushu
 school: **4** Chuo, Keio **5** Hosei, Kyoto, Nihon, Tokyo **6** Sophia, Waseda **7** Fukuoka **8** Doshisha
 head of state: **7** emperor
 measure: **2** go **3** boo, cho, djo, fun, inc, ken, kin, kon, rin, shi, sho, sun, tan **4** hiro, isse, kati, koku, niyo, shoo **5** carat, catty, issho, ittan, momme, picul, shaku **6** kwamme **8** hiyak-kin **9** hiyak-hiro **11** komma-ichida, kujira-shaku
 monetary unit: **2** bu **3** mon, rin, rio, sen, shu, yen **4** cash, mibu, oban **5** koban, obang, tempo **6** cobang, ichebu, ichibu, itzebu, kobang **7** itzeboo, itziboo
 weight: **2** mo **3** fun, kon, rin **4** kati, kwan **5** carat, catty, momme **8** hiyakkin
 island: **3** Iki, Izu, Oki, Tsu **4** Oita, Sado, Yaku **5** Amami, Awaji, Bonin, Hondo, Kuril, Rebun, Sikok **6** Honshu, Kiushu, Kyushu, Loochu, Marcus, Riukiu, Tanega, Tyukyu **7** Cipango, Hachijo, Iwo Jima, Okinawa, Rishiri, Shikoko, Shikoku, Volcano **8** Hokkaido, Miyajima, Okigunto, Okushiri, Tsushima, Yakujima
 lake: **4** Biwa, Suwa, Toya **6** Towada **8** Kutchawa, Shikotsu
 mountain: **3** Uso, Zao **5** Asahi, Asama, Hondo, Yesso **6** Asosan, Enasan, Hiuchi, Kiusiu, Yariga **7** Hakusan, Kujusan, Tokachi **8** Fujiyama **9** Japan Alps
 highest point: **4** Fuji **7** Fujisan
 river: **4** Tone, Yalu **8** Ishikari, Tonegawa **11** Shinano-gawa
 sea: **3** Suo **5** Japan **6** Inland **7** Amakusa, Okhotsk, Pacific **8** Tsushima
 physical feature:
  bay: **3** Ise **4** Miku, Tosa, Yedo **5** Amori, Mutsu, Osaka, Otaru, Tokyo **6** Ariake, Atsumi, Sendai, Suruga, Toyama, Wakasa **7** Uchiura
  cape: **3** Iro, Oki, Oma, Toi **4** Daio, Esan, Jizo, Mela, Mino, Noma, Nomo, Sada, Sawa, Shio, Soya, Suzu **5** Erimo, Kyoga, Rurui **6** Todoga **7** Shiriya **8** Ashizuri, Shakotan **12** Muroto Nojima
  channel: **3** Kii **5** Bungo
  current: **5** Japan **7** Okhotsk **8** Kuro Shio
  divine wind: **8** kamikaze
  gulf: **6** Sagami
  plain: **4** Nobi **5** Kanto
  strait: **4** Soya **5** Korea, Osumi **6** Nemuro, Tanega, Tokara **7** Tsugaru **8** Tsushima **9** La Perouse
 people: **3** Eta **6** Korean **8** Japanese, Okinawan **10** Buramkumin
  ancient: **4** Ainu **5** Jomon, Yayoi
 artist: **4** Okyo **5** Buson, Jocho, Korin, Taiga, Unkei **6** Buncho, Eitoku, Kenzan, Koetsu, Reisai, Ses-

shu, Sesson, Shubun **7** Baiitsu, Choshun, Foujita, Gyokudo, Hokusai, Josetsu, Sanraku, Sharaku, Sotatsu, Utamaro **8** Harunobu, Kiyonaga, Motonobu **9** Hiroshige, Mitsunobu
 author: **5** Basho **7** Abe Kobo **8** Mori Ogai **11** Ueda Akinari **12** Ihara Saikaku, Mishima Yukio, Sakyo Komatsu **13** Natsume Soseki, Zeami Motokiyo **14** Shimazaki Toson, Tsubouchi Shoyo **15** Motoori Norinaga, Murasaki Shikibu **16** Fujiwara Nokisaki, Kawabata Yasunari **17** Tanizaki Junichiro **19** Chikamatsu Monzaemon
 dynasty: **5** Meiji, Taira **6** Yamato **8** Fujiwara, Minamoto
 leader: **4** Hojo **5** Kammu, Meiji **6** Go-Toba, Ieyasu **7** Akihito, Go-Daigo **8** Hirohito, Nobunaga, Yoritomo **9** Hideyoshi, Yoshimasa **10** Tojo Hideki, Yoshimitsu **11** Hara Takashi, Ito Hirobumi **12** Tanaka Kakuei **13** Konoe Fumimaro, Shotoku Taishi **14** Yoshida Shigeru **15** Ashikaga Takauji **18** Matsukata Mayayoshi
 legendary ruler: **5** Jimmu, Jingo **7** Izanagi
 shogunate: **8** Ashikaga, Kamakura, Tokugawa
 language: **8** Japanese
  alphabet/characters: **4** kana **5** kanji **8** hiragana, katakana
  dialect: **5** Kanto
 religion: **6** Tendai **7** Shingon **8** Buddhism **9** Shintoism **12** Confucianism
 place:
  castle: **4** Nijo
  hall: **5** Hoodo **7** Phoenix **12** Golden Buddha
  mausoleum: **4** Ojin **7** Nintoku
  palace: **7** Akasaka, Katsura
  shrine: **5** Heian **11** Itsukushima **16** Grand Shrine of Ise
  temple: **6** Kotoku **7** Byodoin, Horyuji, Ryoanji, Senso-ji, Todaiji **8** Enkakuji, Kenchoji, Kofukuji **9** Kinkakuji **13** Asakusa Kannon
 feature:
  abacus: **7** soroban
  bed: **5** futon
  clothing: **6** kimono
  festival: **13** Cherry Blossom
  firm: **4** Sony **5** Honda **6** Mitsui, Nissan, Toyota, Yasuda **7** Iwasaki **8** Sumitomo **10** Mitsubishi
  flower arranging: **7** ikebana
  painting style: **4** kano, tosa **5** nanga, nisee, onnae, rarae, rimpa, shijo **6** chinso, otokoe, sesshu, ukiyoe **7** konpeki, nihonga, yamatoe
  paper folding art: **7** origami
  poem: **4** waka **5** haiku, tanka
  puppet theater: **7** bunraku
  rush floor covering: **6** tatami

sport: 4 judo **6** karate **13** sumo wrestling
statue: 8 Daibutsu **11** Great Buddha
tea ceremony: 7 chanoyu
theater: 2 no **3** noh **6** kabuki
the way of the warrior/code of honor: 7 bushido
tree: 6 bonsai
wood block print: 6 ukiyoe
food:
  beverage: 4 sake **8** green tea
  dish: 5 sushi **7** sashimi, tempura **8** sukiyaki, teriyaki, yakitori
  noodle: 4 soba

Japanese
independent language of: 5 Japan **13** Ryukyu Islands

jape 4 gibe, joke **5** antic, caper, prank **7** mockery

Japheth
father: 4 Noah
brother: 3 Ham **4** Shem

Jaques
character in: 11 As You Like It
author: 11 Shakespeare

jar 3 din, jug, pot, urn **4** bong, bray, buzz, daze, faze, jolt, rock, stir, stun **5** blare, blast, brawl, clang, clank, crash, crock, flask, floor, quake, shake, shock, throw, upset **6** beaker, bottle, impact, jangle, jiggle, joggle, racket, rattle, vessel **7** agitate, astound, clangor, clatter, confuse, disturb, fluster, perturb, shake up, startle, stupefy, trouble, upheave, vibrate **8** befuddle, bewilder, bleating, canister, clashing, convulse, decanter, demijohn, disquiet, distract, unsettle **9** agitation, cacophony, container **10** concussion, discompose, disconcert, receptacle **11** discordance
Spanish: 4 olla

jargon 4 bosh, bull, bunk, cant **5** argot, fudge, hooey, idiom, lingo, prate, usage **6** babble, brogue, drivel, patois, pidgin, piffle **7** baloney, blabber, blather, dialect, fustian, hogwash, prattle, rubbish, twaddle **8** folderol, malarkey, nonsense, parlance, tommyrot, verbiage **9** gibberish, moonshine, poppycock, rigmarole **10** balderdash, flapdoodle, hocus-pocus, rigamarole, vernacular, vocabulary **11** abracadabra, jabberwocky, phraseology, shibboleths **12** gobbledygook, lingua franca **14** grandiloquence

Jarndyce, John
character in: 10 Bleak House
author: 7 Dickens

jarring 4 rude **5** harsh, rough **6** jangly **7** grating, jolting, rasping, shaking **8** clashing, grinding, jangling, rattling, strident **9** dissonant, wrenching **10** discordant **12** nerve-racking **13** nerve-wracking

Jarry, Alfred

author of: 7 King Ubu **11** Ubu in Chains **13** Ubu the Cuckold

jasmine 8 Jasminum
varieties: 4 blue, cape, rock, star **5** crape, night, royal **6** orange, yellow **7** Arabian, Chilean, Italian, Spanish **8** Carolina, cinnamon, Japanese, Paraguay, pinwheel, primrose, windmill **9** angel-wing **10** Catalonian, Madagascar **11** Confederate

Jason
leader of: 9 Argonauts
father: 5 Aeson
mother: 8 Alcimede, Polymede
half-brother: 6 Pelias
son: 5 Thoas **6** Euneus, Pheres **7** Medeius **8** Mermerus, Tisander **9** Alcimenes, Thessalus
daughter: 7 Eriopis
teacher: 6 Chiron **7** centaur, Cheiron
retrieved: 12 Golden Fleece
ship: 4 Argo
loved by: 5 Medea
loved: 6 Glauce

Jasper, John
character in: 22 The Mystery of Edwin Drood
author: 7 Dickens

jaundiced 5 blase, bored **6** bitter **7** cynical, envious, hostile, jealous **8** covetous, doubting, satiated **9** green-eyed, resentful, skeptical **10** embittered, suspicious **11** mistrustful

jaunt 4 spin, tour, trip **6** airing, flight, junket, outing, ramble, stroll **9** adventure, excursion, promenade, short trip **10** expedition

jaunty 4 airy, neat, trim **5** natty, perky **6** blithe, bouncy, breezy, dapper, lively, sporty, spruce **7** buoyant **8** carefree, debonair **9** sprightly, vivacious **12** lighthearted, high-stepping, high-spirited

Java
other name: 5 Djawa
capital/largest city: 7 Jakarta **8** Djakarta
others: 5 Bogor, Dessa **6** Kediri, Malang **7** Bandung, Batavia **8** Semarang, Surabaja, Surabaya **9** Surakarta **11** Djokjakarta **13** Pelabuhanratu
government: 9 Indonesia
measure: 3 kan **4** paal, rand **5** palen
weight: 4 amat, pond, tali **5** pound **6** soekel
island: 4 Bali **5** Sunda **6** Lombok, Madura
mountain: 4 Amat, Gede **5** Lawoe, Murjo, Prahu **6** Raoeng, Slamet **8** Soembing
highest point: 6 Semuru **7** Semeroe
river: 4 Solo **7** Brantas
sea: 4 Java **6** Indian **7** Pacific
physical feature:
  plateau: 4 Ijen
  strait: 5 Sunda
people: 5 Krama, Kromo **6** Kalang **8**

Javanese, Madurese **9** Sundanese
dynasty: 7 Mataram **9** Majapahit, Srivijaya
language: 4 Kavi, Kawi **5** Malay **6** Sassak **8** Balinese, Madurese, Sudanese **16** Bahasa Indonesian
religion: 5 Hindu, Islam **7** animism **8** Buddhism
place:
  temple: 6 Chandi, Thandi **9** Borobudur, Prambanan
feature:
  cloth: 3 kat **5** batik, kapok
  dance: 7 seri mpi
  dancer: 6 bedoyo
  fishing boat: 4 prau
  ornamental dagger: 4 kris
  puppet play: 6 wajang, wayang
food:
  fruit: 6 durian, lomboy, nangca **7** gondang

javelin 4 dart **5** lance, shaft, spear **10** projectile

jaw 3 gab, rap **4** chat, chin, talk **7** jawbone, palaver **8** chitchat, converse, mandible **10** chew the fat, chew the rag **11** confabulate

Jaws
author: 13 Peter Benchley
director: 15 Steven Spielberg
cast: 10 Robert Shaw **11** Roy Scheider **12** Lorraine Gary **15** Richard Dreyfuss
score: 12 John Williams
Oscar for: 5 score

Jayhawker State
nickname of: 6 Kansas

jazz musician 8 Art Tatum **9** Bud Powell **10** Miles Davis **11** Lester Young **12** Benny Goodman, John Coltrane **13** Charles Mingus, Charlie Parker, Duke Ellington, Thelonius Monk **14** Dizzy Gillespie, Louis Armstrong, Ornette Coleman, Wynton Marsalis

jealous 4 wary **7** anxious, envious, mindful **8** covetous, grudging, watchful **9** concerned, green-eyed, regardful, resentful **10** possessive, protective, suspicious **11** mistrustful, mistrusting **12** apprehensive

jealousy 4 envy **8** distrust, jaundice, mistrust **9** suspicion **10** resentment **12** covetousness **14** possessiveness **16** green-eyed monster
color: 5 green

Jebus
city captured by: 5 David
renamed: 9 Jerusalem
inhabitant: 8 Jebusite

jeer 3 boo, bug, dig, rap **4** barb, hiss, hoot, mock, razz, slam, slur **5** abuse, flout, hound, knock, scoff, scorn, sneer, taunt, whoop **6** deride, harass, heckle, hector, insult, revile **7** catcall, laugh at, mockery, obloquy **8** derision, ridicule, scoffing **9** aspersion, contumely, poke fun at, whistle at

Jeffers, Robinson
author of: **5** Medea, Tamar **6** Cawdor **8** Solstice **9** Dear Judas **12** Roan Stallion **14** Thurso's Landing **18** The Women at Point Sur **21** The Tower Beyond Tragedy

Jefferson, Thomas
nickname: **16** Sage of Monticello
presidential rank: **5** third
party: **20** Democratic-Republican
state represented: **2** VA
defeated: **5** (John) Adams **8** (Charles Cotesworth) Pinckney
vice president: **4** (Aaron) Burr **7** (George) Clinton
cabinet:
  state: **7** (James) Madison
  treasury: **6** (Samuel) Dexter **8** (Albert) Gallatin
  war: **8** (Henry) Dearborn
  attorney general: **6** (Caesar Augustus) Rodney **7** (Levi) Lincoln **12** (John) Breckenridge
  navy: **5** (Robert) Smith
born: **2** VA **14** Shadwell estate **15** Goochland (Albemarle) County
died/buried: **10** Monticello
education: **14** William and Mary
interests: **6** violin **7** writing **11** agriculture **12** architecture
favorite foods: **10** French food **11** French wines
vacation: **12** Poplar Forest
author: **25** Declaration of Independence, Notes on the State of Virginia
political career: **8** governor **16** House of Burgesses **19** Virginia legislature **25** Declaration of Independence, Second Continental Congress
  secretary of: **5** state
  minister to: **6** France
civilian career: **6** farmer, lawyer
notable events of lifetime/term:
  expedition: **13** Lewis and Clark
  prohibition of: **19** importation of slaves
  purchase: **9** Louisiana
father: **5** Peter
mother: **4** Jane (Randolph)
siblings: **4** Jane, Lucy, Mary **6** Martha **8** Randolph **9** Anna Scott, Elizabeth **10** Peter Field
wife: **6** Martha (Wayles Skelton)
children: **4** Mary **6** Martha
associated with: **12** Sally Hemings

Jeffersons, The
character: **8** Florence **9** Tom Willis **11** Helen Willis **12** Harry Bentley **15** George Jefferson, Lionel Jefferson, Louise Jefferson, Ralph the Doorman **20** Jenny Willis Jefferson
cast: **9** Mike Evans **10** Damon Evans, Marla Gibbs, Roxie Roker **11** Ned Wertimer **12** Paul Benedict **13** Franklin Cover, Isabel Sanford **14** Sherman Hemsley **15** Berlinda Tol-

bert
George's business: **11** dry cleaning
spinoff from: **14** All in the Family

Jeffreys, Harold
field: **7** physics **9** astronomy
nationality: **7** British
explained: **7** weather
studied: **10** Earth's core **11** solar system

Jeffries, James Jackson
nickname: **14** The Boilermaker
sport: **6** boxing
class: **11** heavyweight

jehad see **5** jihad

Jehioada
father: **7** Paseach
son: **7** Benaiah
means: **12** Jehovah knows

Jehoshaphat
father: **3** Asa **6** Ahitub, Nimshi, Parnah
mother: **8** Jehorani
means: **13** Jehovah judges

Jehovah **3** god **4** YHWH **5** diety

Jehu
father: **6** Hanani **11** Jehoshaphat **14** reckless driver

jejune **4** dull **5** banal, inane, stale, trite, vapid **7** humdrum, insipid, puerile **8** ordinary **9** hackneyed **10** pedestrian, unexciting, unoriginal, wishy-washy **11** commonplace **12** conventional **13** uninteresting

jell **3** gel, jam, set **4** clot, firm **5** jelly **7** congeal, thicken **9** coagulate **10** gelatinize

jellyfish **5** hydra, polyp, softy **6** coward, medusa, nettle **7** sunfish **8** weakling **10** ctenophore, pantywaist **11** milquetoast, mollycoddle **12** coelenterate, invertebrate, siphonophore **18** Portuguese man-of-war

je ne sais quoi **13** I don't know what **18** indefinable quality

Jenner, Bruce
sport: **13** track and field
known for: **9** decathlon
won: **8** Olympics

Jenner, Edward
nationality: **7** British
discovered: **11** vaccination **19** smallpox inoculation

Jenney, William Le Baron
architect of: **21** Home Insurance Building (Chicago)

jeopardize **4** risk **6** expose, hazard **7** imperil **8** endanger **10** compromise **11** put into danger

jeopardy **4** risk **5** peril **6** danger, hazard **8** exposure, unsafety **9** liability **10** insecurity **11** imperilment **12** endangerment **13** vulnerability **14** precariousness

Jephthah **11** Hebrew judge
father: **6** Gilead

Jeremiah

father: **7** Hilkiah **10** Habazaniah
daughter: **7** Mamutal
grandson: **7** Jehohaz
friend, scribe: **6** Baruch

jerk **3** ass, tic, tug **4** dope, dupe, fool, pull, snap, yank **5** dummy, dunce, idiot, klutz, pluck, shake, spasm, start, twist **6** quiver, reflex, thrust, twitch, wrench **7** tremble **8** convulse **9** trembling

jerky **4** beef, meat **5** jolty, jumpy **6** choppy, elboic, jouncy **7** biltong, charqui, fidgety, twitchy **9** dried beef, spasmodic, twitching

Jeroboam
father: **5** Joash, Nebat
successor: **9** Zachariah

Jerry
(British): **6** German

jerry-built **4** weak **5** frail, run-up, shaky, tacky **6** faulty, flimsy, shoddy, sleazy **7** rickety, unsound **8** gimcrack, slipshod, thrown-up, unstable **9** cheap-jack, defective **10** ramshackle **13** unsubstantial **14** thrown-together

jersey **3** cow **5** maillot, shirt **6** tricot **7** sweater **8** camisole, guernsey, pullover **10** undershirt

Jersey Joe
nickname of: **10** Joe Walcott

Jerusalem
author: **12** William Blake

Jerusalem
former name: **5** Jebus
pool of: **6** Siloam **8** Bethesda

Jerusalem
Arabic: **14** Bayt al-Muqaddas
capital of: **6** Israel
Hebrew: **12** Yerushalayim
hills: **7** Judaean
landmark: **6** al-Aqsa **11** Wailing Wall, Western Wall **12** Israel Museum **13** Dome of the Rock **14** Dead Sea Scrolls **15** Shrine of the Book **17** Rockefeller Museum **24** Church of the Holy Sepulcher
mount: **6** Olives, Scopus
river: **6** Kidron
ruler: **5** Arabs, David, Herod **6** Persia, Romans **7** British, Saladin, Seljuks, Solomon **8** Ayyubids, Fatimids, Ptolemy I **9** Crusaders, Maccabees, Mamelukes **10** Canaanites **12** Antiochus III **13** Pontius Pilate **15** Byzantine Empire **17** Alexander the Great, Antiochus the Third
street: **11** Via Dolorosa

Jerusalem Delivered
author: **13** Torquato Tasso

Jervis, Mrs
character in: **6** Pamela
author: **10** Richardson

jessamine **8** Jasminum
varieties: **3** day **5** night, poet's **6** orange, yellow **12** willow-leaved **13** night-blooming **14** Carolina yellow

Jesse
father: **4** Obed
grandfather: **4** Boaz
grandmother: **4** Ruth
great-grandfather: **5** Rahab
son: **5** David, Eliab **7** Shammah **8** Abinadab

jest 3 gag, pun **4** fool, game, gibe, jape, joke, josh, quip **5** act up, crack, laugh, prank, tease, trick **6** banter, bon mot **9** wisecrack, witticism **10** crack jokes, pleasantry **11** horse around

jester 3 wag, wit **4** card, fool, mime, zany **5** clown, comic, joker, mimer, mimic **6** madcap, mummer **7** buffoon **8** comedian, funnyman, humorist, quipster **9** harlequin **10** motley fool **11** merry-andrew, pantomimist, punchinello

jesting 6 joking **7** teasing **8** sportive **9** bantering, unserious **12** wisecracking

Jesus
also called: **7** Holy One, Messiah **8** Nazarene, Son of God **9** the Christ **12** Man of Sorrows **13** Prince of Peace **14** Savior Anointed
mother: **4** Mary
stepfather: **6** Joseph
birthplace: **9** Bethlehem
lived in: **8** Nazareth
death place: **9** Jerusalem
buried by: **17** Joseph of Arimathea
disciples: **4** John, Jude **5** James, Peter, Simon **6** Andrew, Philip, Thomas **7** Matthew **12** James the Less **13** Judas Iscariot **20** Bartholomew Nathanael
secret follower: **9** Nicodemus
famous discourse: **16** Sermon on the Mount

jet 4 gush **5** flush, issue, shoot, spout, spray, spurt, surge, swash **6** effuse, nozzle, rush up, squirt, stream **7** sparger, sprayer, Spritze, syringe **8** atomizer, fountain, shoot out, Spritzer **9** discharge, sprinkler

Jethro
daughter: **8** Zipporah
son-in-law: **5** Moses

Jetsons, The
character: **5** Astro **10** Jane Jetson, Judy Jetson **11** Elroy Jetson **12** George Jetson **13** Cosmo G Spacely
voices: **8** Mel Blanc **10** Daws Butler, Don Messick, Janet Waldo **13** George O'Hanlon **14** Penny Singleton

jettison 4 dump **5** eject, scrap **6** unload **7** cast off, discard **8** throw out **9** discharge, eliminate, pitch over, throw over **13** toss overboard

jetty 4 dike, dock, mole, pier, quay, slip **5** black, ebony, groin, levee, raven, slide, wharf **6** bridge **7** sea wall **8** buttress **10** breakwater

jeu de mots 3 pun **11** play on words

jeu d'esprit 9 witticism **17** witty literary work

literally: **12** play of spirit

jeune fille 4 girl **9** young girl **13** unmarried girl

jeunesse doree 11 gilded youth, golden youth

Jew 6 Essene, Hebrew, Judean, Semite **7** Edomite, Judaist, Moabite **8** Hebraist, Sephardi **9** Israelite

jewel 3 ace, gem, pip **4** bead, dear, find, ring, whiz **5** honey, pearl, prize, stone, tiara **6** bangle, bauble, brooch, locket, winner **7** earring, pendant, trinket **8** bracelet, knockout, necklace, ornament, pure gold, treasure **9** humdinger, lavaliere **10** topnotcher **11** crackerjack, masterpiece

jewelry 4 gems, gold **6** silver **7** bangles, gewgaws, regalia **8** trinkets **10** adornments **14** precious stones

Jewett, Sarah Orne
author of: **26** The Country of the Pointed Firs

Jewish 6 Hebrew, Judaic **7** Hebraic, Semitic
bread: **5** matzo **6** matzoh **7** challah
candelabrum: **7** menorah
ceremonial robe: **5** kitel
color: **5** white
coming of age: **10** bar mitzvah, bat mitzvah
dietary laws: **7** kashrut **8** kashruth
fit to eat: **6** kosher
not fit to eat: **4** tref
group: **8** Hadassah **9** B'nai B'rith
holy day/festival: **5** Purim, seder **6** Sukkot **7** Shavuot **8** Chanukah, Hanukkah, Passover **9** Yom Kippur **12** Rosh Hashanah
law/scripture: **5** Torah **6** Gemara, Talmud, Tanach **7** Mishnah
liturgical prayer: **6** Yigdal **8** Kol Nidre
recited on eve of: **9** Yom Kippur
marriage canopy: **6** chupah
months:
1st: **6** Tishri
2nd: **7** Heshvan
3rd: **6** Kislev
4th: **5** Tevet
5th: **6** Shevat
6th: **4** Adar
7th: **5** Nisan
8th: **4** Iyar
9th: **5** Sivan
10th: **6** Tammuz
11th: **2** Av
12th: **4** Elul
prayerbook: **6** mahzor, siddur **7** machzor
quarter: **6** ghetto, mellah
school: **5** heder **6** cheder
skullcap: **5** kipah **8** yarmulka
service to commemorate the dead: **6** Yizkor
synagogue: **4** shul **5** schul
toast: **8** mazel tov

Jewkes, Mrs
character in: **6** Pamela
author: **10** Richardson

Jew of Malta, The
author: **18** Christopher Marlowe
character: **7** Abigail, Barabas **8** Ithamore **15** Governor of Malta

Jezebel
director: **12** William Wyler
cast: **10** Bette Davis, Fay Bainter, Henry Fonda **11** Donald Crisp, George Brent **15** Margaret Lindsay
Oscar for: **7** actress (Davis) **17** supporting actress (Bainter)

Jezebel
father: **7** Ethbaal
husband: **8** King Ahab
daughter: **8** Athaliah
opposed: **6** Elijah
killed: **6** Naboth
father-in-law: **4** Omri

JFK
director: **11** Oliver Stone
cast: **8** Joe Pesci (David Ferrie) **9** John Candy (Dean Andrews), Ray LaPere (Abraham Zapruder) **10** Gary Oldman (Lee Harvey Oswald), Jack Lemmon (Jack Martin), Kevin Bacon (Willie O'Keefe) **11** Edward Asner (Guy Bannister), Sissy Spacek (Liz Garrison) **12** Kevin Costner (Jim Garrison) **13** Sally Kirkland (Rose Cheramie), Tommy Lee Jones (Clay Shaw/Clay Bertrand), Walter Matthau (Senator Long) **15** Vincent D'Onofrio (Bill Newman) **16** Brian Doyle-Murray (Jack Ruby)

jib 3 arm, shy **4** balk, boom, sail, tack **5** demur, gigue, stick **6** recoil **7** scruple

jibe 2 go **3** fit **4** mesh, tack **5** agree, fit in, match, shift, tally **6** accord, concur, square **7** conform **8** coincide, dovetail **9** harmonize **10** correspond, go together **11** fit together

jiffy 3 sec **4** jiff **5** flash, shake, trice **6** minute, moment, second **7** half a mo, instant **9** twinkling **10** nanosecond **11** microsecond, millisecond, split second

jigger 4 dram, shot **5** glass **6** device, doodad, gadget, object **7** bicycle, gimmick, measure **9** doohickey, shot glass **10** boneshaker **11** contraption, thingumabob

jiggle 4 jerk **5** shake **6** bounce, fidget, joggle, jostle, twitch, wiggle **7** agitate, wriggle

jihad 6 strife **7** holy war **8** struggle

jilt 5 leave **6** betray, desert **7** forsake, let down **12** break off with **17** break an engagement

Jim
character in: **15** (The Adventures of) Huckleberry Finn
author: **5** Twain

jimmy 3 bar, pry **5** force, lever **7** crowbar

jingle 4 ring **5** clang, clank, clink, ditty **6** jangle, tinkle **7** clatter, ringing **8** doggerel, facetiae, limerick **10** catchy poem, catchy song **12** product theme **13** reverberation **14** commercial tune **16** tintinnabulation

jingoism 10 chauvinism, flag-waving, patriotics **11** nationalism **14** over-patriotism, spread-eagleism **15** super-patriotism **16** ultranationalism

jinn 3 imp **5** afrit, demon, genie, jinni **6** afreet, spirit **8** jinniyeh

jinx 3 hex **5** curse **6** plague, whammy **7** bugaboo, bugbear, evil eye, ill wind, nemesis **9** evil spell
French: **9** bete noire

jitney 3 bus, cab

jitterbug 5 dance, lindy **8** lindy hop **12** boogie-woogie

jitters 6 shakes **7** anxiety, fidgets, jim-jams, shivers, willies **9** jumpiness, quivering, shakiness, tenseness, the creeps, whim-whams **10** uneasiness **11** butterflies, fidgetiness, nervousness **12** skittishness **13** heebie-jeebies **16** screaming-meemies

jittery 5 jumpy **6** uneasy **7** anxious, nervous

Jivaro, Shuara, Jibaro
tribe: **6** Achual, Antipa **8** Aguaruna, Huambiza
location: **4** Peru **7** Ecuador **12** South America
noted for: **7** tsantsa (shrunken heads)

Joab
mother: **7** Zeruiah
brother: **6** Asahel **7** Abishai
commanded: **10** David's army
killed: **5** Abner, Amasa **7** Absalom
killed by: **7** Benaiah
conspired to overthrow: **5** David

Joad family
characters in: **16** The Grapes of Wrath
members: **2** Ma, Pa **3** Tom **4** Noah **6** Connie **12** Rose of Sharon
author: **9** Steinbeck

Joan of Arcadia
network: **3** CBS
cast: **11** Jason Ritter (Kevin Girardi), Joe Mantegna (Will Girardi) **12** Amber Tamblyn (Joan Girardi), Michael Welch (Luke Girardi) **14** Becky Wahlstrom (Grace Polk) **15** Mary Steenburgen (Helen Girardi) **20** Christopher Marquette (Adam Rove)

job 3 lot **4** care, duty, part, role, spot, task, work **5** chore, craft, field, place, quota, share, stint, trade, trust **6** affair, career, charge, errand, living, metier, office, output **7** calling, concern, mission, opening, portion, product, pursuit **8** activity, business, capacity, contract, exercise, function, position, province, vocation **9** allotment, piecework, situation **10** assignment, com-mission, engagement, enterprise, live-lihood, occupation, profession **11** achievement, appointment, perfor-mance, undertaking **14** accomplish-ment, responsibility

Job 8 sufferer
father: **8** Issachar
friend: **5** Elihu **6** Bildad, Zophar **7** Eliphaz

job holder 6 worker **8** employee, hireling

job seeker 7 hopeful **8** aspirant **9** applicant, candidate

Jocasta
also: **8** Epicaste
queen of: **6** Thebes
father: **9** Menoeceus
brother: **5** Creon
husband: **5** Laius **7** Oedipus
son: **7** Oedipus **8** Eteocles **9** Polynices
daughter: **6** Ismene **8** Antigone
death by: **7** hanging, suicide

Jochebed
father: **4** Levi
husband: **5** Amram
nephew: **5** Amram
son: **5** Aaron, Moses

jockey 5 Baeza, Krone **6** Arcaro, Pincay **7** Cauthen, Cordero, Cruguet, Hartack **8** McCarron, McHargue, Turcotte **9** Shoemaker, Velasquez

jocose 3 fun **4** arch **5** comic, droll, funny, jolly, merry, witty **6** joking, jovial **7** amusing, comical, jesting, jocular, playful, roguish, teasing, waggish **8** humorous, mirthful, prankish, sportive **9** facetious

jocular 3 gay **5** droll, funny, jolly, merry, witty **6** jocose, jocund, joking, jovial **7** amusing, jesting, playful, roguish, rompish, waggish **8** humorous, mirthful, prankish, sportive **9** facetious **10** frolicsome **12** entertaining, lighthearted

jocund 5 jolly, merry **6** breezy, cheery, elated, jovial, lively **8** cheerful, debonair, pleasant **9** easygoing **10** untroubled **12** happy-go-lucky, lighthearted

Joel
means: **12** Jehovah is God
father: **4** Nebo **6** Samuel **7** Azariah, Pedaiah, Pethuel
brother: **6** Nathan

Joe Palooka
creator: **9** Ham Fisher **11** Tony DiPreta
character:
children: **3** Joe **5** Buddy **7** Joannie
friend: **9** Little Max **10** Jerry Leemy
manager: **11** Knobby Walsh
valet: **6** Smokey
wife: **8** Anne Howe
profession: **5** boxer

jog 3 bob, jar, tug **4** jerk, pull, rock, stir, trot, yank **5** nudge, shake, twist **6** bounce, jiggle, jostle, jounce, prompt, twitch, wrench **7** actuate, animate **8** activate, energize **9** stimulate

jogger 4 memo **6** layboy, runner **7** trotter **8** reminder **10** memorandum

Johannesburg
airport: **8** Jan Smuts
area: **4** Rand **9** Transvaal
capital of: **11** South Africa
landmark: **13** Carlton Centre **14** Africana Museum **16** Union Observatory **17** Zoological Gardens **20** Melrose Bird Sanctuary
township: **6** Soweto **7** Lenasia **10** Nancefield
university: **13** Rand Afrikaans, Witwatersrand

John
father: **7** Zebedee
brother: **5** James
son: **5** Peter
called, with brother: **9** Boanerges **13** sons of thunder
pertaining to John or his writings: **9** Johannine

John Barleycorn
personification of: **6** liquor **7** whiskey

John Brown's Body
author: **19** Stephen Vincent Benet

John Bull
personification of: **7** England **10** Englishman

John Mark *see* **4** Mark

Johnny Belinda
director: **13** Jean Negulesco
cast: **8** Lew Ayres **9** Jane Wyman **15** Charles Bickford
Oscar for: **7** actress (Wyman)

Johnny Cash Show, The
cast: **9** Jim Varney **10** Howard Mann **11** Carl Perkins, Steve Martin **14** June Carter Cash, Tennessee Three **15** Statler Brothers **32** Mother Maybelle and the Carter Family

Johnny-come-lately 8 newcomer **9** latecomer **10** new arrival **11** late arrival

Johnny U
nickname of: **12** Johnny Unitas

Johns, Glynis
born: **8** Pretoria **11** South Africa
roles: **11** Mary Poppins **13** The Sundowners, Under Milk Wood **17** A Little Night Music **26** Around the World in Eighty Days

Johns, Jasper
born: **9** Augusta GA
artwork: **4** Flag **6** Studio, Target **8** Watchman **10** Fool's House **12** Device Circle **13** Painted Bronze (Beer Cans) **14** The Barber's Tree **19** Target with Four Faces **22** Target with Plaster Casts

Johnson, Andrew
presidential rank: **11** seventeenth
party: **8** Democrat
state represented: **2** TN

defeated: 5 no one
succeeded upon death of: 7 Lincoln
cabinet:
  state: 6 (William Henry) Seward
  treasury: 9 (Hugh) McCulloch
  war: 7 (Edwin McMasters) Stanton **9** (John McAllister) Schofield
  attorney general: 5 (James) Speed **6** (William Maxwell) Evarts **8** (Henry) Stanbery
  navy: 6 (Gideon) Welles
  postmaster general: 7 (Alexander Williams) Randall **8** (William) Dennison
  interior: 5 (John Palmer) Usher **6** (James) Harlan **8** (Orville Hickman) Browning
born: 9 Raleigh NC
died: 16 Carter's Station TN
buried: 13 Greeneville TN
education: 9 no college **12** self-educated
political career: 8 US Senate **13** vice president **22** House of Representatives
  first president to be: 9 impeached (1868)
  found: 9 not guilty
  mayor of: 11 Greeneville (TN)
  governor of: 9 Tennessee
civilian career: 6 tailor
military service: 8 Civil War **12** US Volunteers **16** brigadier general
military governor of: 9 Tennessee
notable events of lifetime/term: 14 Reconstruction
  Purchase: 6 Alaska
father: 5 Jacob
mother: 4 Mary (McDonough)
  stepfather: 15 Turner Dougherty
sibling: 7 William
wife: 5 Eliza (McCardle)
children: 4 Mary **6** Andrew, Martha, Robert **7** Charles

Johnson, Don
born: 10 Flatt Creek (MO)
roles: 6 Tin Cup **7** Melanie **8** Dead-Bang, Paradise **9** Cease Fire, Just Legal, Miami Vice **11** Guilty as Sin, Nash Bridges **13** Born Yesterday **16** In Pursuit of Honor, The Long Hot Summer
wife: 15 Melanie Griffith

Johnson, Earvin
nickname: 5 Magic
sport: 10 basketball
position: 5 guard
team: 16 Los Angeles Lakers

Johnson, Jack (John Arthur)
nickname: 11 Little Artha **14** Galveston Giant
sport: 6 boxing
class: 11 heavyweight

Johnson, Lyndon Baines
nickname: 3 LBJ **15** Landslide Lyndon
presidential rank: 11 thirty-sixth

party: 10 Democratic
state represented: 2 TX
succeeded upon death of: 7 Kennedy
defeated: 4 (Earle Harold) Munn, (Eric) Hass **6** (John) Kasper **7** (Clifton) DeBerry **9** (Barry Morris) Goldwater
vice president: 4 none (first term) **8** (Hubert Horatio) Humphrey
cabinet:
  state: 4 (David Dean) Rusk
  treasury: 4 (Joseph William) Barr **6** (Clarence Douglas) Dillon, (Henry Hamill) Fowler
  defense: 8 (Clark McAdams) Clifford, (Robert Strange) McNamara
  attorney general: 5 (William Ramsey) Clark **7** (Robert Francis) Kennedy **10** (Nicholas deBelleville) Katzenbach
  postmaster general: 6 (Lawrence Francis) O'Brien, (William Marvin) Watson **9** (John Austin) Gronouski
  interior: 5 (Stewart Lee) Udall
  agriculture: 7 (Orville Lothrop) Freeman
  commerce: 5 (Cyrus Rowlett) Smith **9** (John Thomas) Connor, (Luther Hartwell) Hodges **10** (Alexander Buel) Trowbridge
  labor: 5 (William Willard) Wirtz
  HEW: 5 (Wilbur Joseph) Cohen **7** (John William) Gardner **10** (Anthony Joseph) Celebrezze
  HUD: 4 (Robert Colwell) Wood **6** (Robert Clifton) Weaver
  transportation: 4 (Alan Stevenson) Boyd
born: 11 (near) Stonewall TX
died/buried: 13 (near) Johnson City TX
education:
  teachers' college: 19 Southwest Texas State
  law school: 10 Georgetown
religion: 17 Disciples of Christ
vacation spot: 8 LBJ Ranch
author: 15 The Vantage Point
political career: 8 US Senate **13** vice president **24** US House of Representatives
civilian career: 7 teacher
military service: 6 US Navy **10** World War II **11** World War Two
notable events of lifetime/term: 9 race riots **10** Vietnam War **12** Great Society
  act: 11 Civil Rights **12** Voting Rights **19** Economic Opportunity
  assassination of: 14 Robert F Kennedy **18** Martin Luther King Jr
  capture of: 6 Pueblo
  Pueblo captured by: 10 North Korea
  treaty: 23 Nuclear Non-Proliferation
  war: 7 Vietnam **11** Arab-Israeli

father: 7 Sam Ealy
mother: 7 Rebekah (Baines)
siblings: 10 Sam Houston **12** Lucia Huffman **13** Josefa Hermine, Rebekah Luruth
wife: 7 Claudia (Alta Taylor)
  nickname: 8 Lady Bird
children: 9 Lynda Bird **10** Luci Baines
First Lady:
  responsible for: 24 Highway Beautification Act
  author: 16 A White House Diary

Johnson, Philip Cortelyou
architect of: 10 Glass House (New Canaan CT), Wiley House (New Canaan CT) **12** Hodgson House (New Canaan CT) **13** Pennzoil Place (Houston TX) **14** Bolssonas House (New Canaan CT) **16** Amon Carter Museum (Ft Worth TX) **17** Sheldon Art Gallery (Lincoln NE) **18** A T and T Headquarters (NYC), Kline Science Center (Yale) **19** New York State Theater (Lincoln Center)

Johnson, Samuel
author of: 8 Rasselas, The Idler **18** The Lives of the Poets **22** The Vanity of Human Wishes **30** Dictionary of the English Language

Johnson, Walter
nickname: 8 Big Train
sport: 8 baseball
position: 7 pitcher
team: 18 Washington Senators

John the Baptist
father: 9 Zechariah
mother: 9 Elizabeth
descendant of: 5 Aaron
precurser of: 5 Jesus **10** the Messiah

joie de vivre 11 joy of living **19** delight in being alive

join 3 hug, mix **4** abut, ally, band, bind, fuse, glue, link, meet, pool **5** affix, brush, chain, enter, graze, marry, merge, paste, reach, skirt, stick, touch, unify, unite **6** adjoin, attach, bridge, cement, cohere, couple, fasten, scrape, solder, splice **7** combine, connect, verge on **8** border on, enlist in, enroll in, federate, hold fast **9** associate, cooperate, syndicate **10** amalgamate, fraternize **11** confederate, consolidate **12** conglomerate

joined 3 met, wed **4** tied **5** bound, fused, glued, mated, yoked **6** allied, bonded, linked, merged, paired, seamed, united, welded **7** coupled, married, related, spliced **8** attached, cemented, combined, enlisted, fastened **9** bracketed, connected **10** associated, hand-in-hand, integrated **11** hand-in-glove

join forces 4 ally **5** merge, unite **6** league, team up **7** combine **8** coalesce **9** affiliate, cooperate **11** consolidate **12** band together

joint 4 hock, knee, knot, link **5** elbow,

hinge, nexus **6** allied, common, mutual, shared, united **7** knuckle, unified **8** combined, communal, coupling, junction, juncture **9** associate, community, conjoined, corporate, unanimous **10** associated, collective, connection, hand-in-hand, like-minded **11** coalitional, conjunctive, cooperative **12** articulation, consolidated **13** collaborative

kind:
ball and socket: 3 hip **8** shoulder
fused: 5 skull **11** base of spine
hinged: 4 knee **5** elbow
unfused: 3 hip, jaw **4** knee **5** elbow **8** shoulder

joint action 7 concert **8** teamwork **11** cooperating, cooperation, give-and-take **13** collaboration, participation

joint effort 7 concert **8** teamwork **11** cooperation **13** collaboration

jointly 8 arm in arm, in common, in unison, mutually, together, unitedly **10** conjointly, hand-in-hand, side by side **12** collectively **13** in association, in conjunction

join together 3 wed **4** fuse, weld **5** marry, unify, unite **6** solder **9** integrate **10** amalgamate **11** consolidate, incorporate

join up 6 enlist, enroll, sign up **9** volunteer

joist 4 beam **5** brace **6** timber **7** support

joke 3 gag, pun, wit **4** butt, dupe, fool, gibe, goof, gull, jape, jest, josh, lark, mock, quip **5** antic, caper, cinch, clown, farce, prank, put-on, roast, tease, trick **6** banter, bon mot, deride, frolic, gambol, gibe at, jeer at, parody, satire, take in, target, trifle, whimsy **7** buffoon, bumpkin, chortle, lampoon, laugh at, nothing, scoff at, smile at, snicker **8** anecdote, badinage, poohpooh, pushover, repartee, ridicule, town fool, travesty **9** burlesque, diversion, horseplay, simpleton, wisecrack, witticism **10** pleasantry **11** horse around, monkeyshine **13** facetiousness, laughingstock

joker 3 wag, wit **4** snag, trap, zany **5** catch, clown, hitch, mimic, rider, snare, trick **6** jester, madcap **7** codicil, pitfall, punster **8** addendum, comedian, funnyman, humorist **10** subterfuge, supplement **11** wisecracker
French: 7 farceur

jokester 3 wag **5** comic, cutup, joker **8** comedian **9** prankster

Joliba *see* **5** Niger

Joliot-Curie, Frederic
field: 9 chemistry
nationality: 6 French
discovered: 23 artificial radioisotopes
awarded: 10 Nobel Prize
wife: 16 Irene Joliot-Curie

Joliot-Curie, Irene

field: 7 physics
nationality: 6 French
discovered: 23 artificial radioisotopes
awarded: 10 Nobel Prize
husband: 14 Frederic Joliot
father: 11 Pierre Curie
mother: 10 Marie Curie

jollity 3 fun **4** glee, play, romp **5** cheer, mirth, revel, sport **6** frolic, gaiety **7** revelry, whoopee **8** hilarity **9** amusement, festivity, jocundity, joviality, merriment, pleasure **10** jocularity **11** merrymaking **12** conviviality

jolly 3 gay **5** droll, funny, happy, merry **6** jocund, jovial **7** gleeful, jocular, playful **8** cheerful, mirthful, sportive **9** fun-loving **10** delightful, rollicking **12** high-spirited

Jolly Roger 11 pirate's flag **18** skull and crossbones

jolt 3 bob, jar, jog **4** bump, jerk, jump, stun **5** lurch, quake, shake, shock, start, throw, upset **6** bobble, bounce, jiggle, joggle, jostle, jounce, quiver, trauma, twitch **7** disturb, perturb, setback, shake up, shaking, startle **8** convulse, reversal **9** agitation, take aback **11** thunderbolt

Joltin' Joe
nickname of: 11 Joe DiMaggio

Jonah
father: 7 Amittai
swallowed by: 9 large fish
preached in: 7 Nineveh
hometown: 10 Gathhepher

Jonathan
means: 11 Jehovah gave
father: 4 Jada, Saul **6** Joiada, Kereah **8** Abiathar
friend: 5 David
son: 9 Meribkaal **12** Mephibosheth

Jonathan Livingston Seagull
author: 11 Richard Bach

Jonathan Wild
author: 13 Henry Fielding

Jones, Inigo
architect of: 11 Queen's House (Greenwich) **14** Banqueting Hall (Whitehall Palace, London)
restoration: 16 St Paul's Cathedral

Jones, James
author of: 7 Whistle **14** The Thin Red Line **15** Some Came Running **18** From Here to Eternity

Jones, James Earl
birth name: 9 Todd Jones
born: 11 Arkabutla MS
roles: 6 The Man **7** Othello **8** Star Wars **12** Patriot Games **13** Field of Dreams **15** The Emperor Jones **17** The Great White Hope **20** The Hunt for Red October **21** Clear and Present Danger
voice of: 10 Darth Vader

Jones, John Paul
served in: 11 Russian navy **16** Revolutionary War **21** British merchant

marine
commander of ship: 6 Ranger **10** Providence **15** Bonhomme Richard
defeated ship: 7 Serapis
saying: 23 "I have not yet begun to fight"

Jones, Shirley
husband: 11 Jack Cassidy, Marty Ingels
born: 10 Smithton PA
roles: 8 Carousel, Oklahoma **11** Elmer Gantry, The Music Man **18** The Partridge Family

Jones, Tom
born: 5 Wales **10** Pontypridd
songs: 7 Delilah **9** She's a Lady **11** Thunderball **13** Love Me Tonight **15** Letter to Lucille **16** What's New Pussycat **21** Green Green Grass of Home

Jong, Erica
author of: 5 Fanny **11** Sappho's Leap **12** Fear of Flying **15** Inventing Memory **18** At the Edge of the Body **20** How to Save Your Own Life

jonquil 4 bulb, lily **8** daffodil **9** narcissus

Jonson, Ben
author of: 6 The Fox **7** Sejanus, Volpone **11** A Tale of a Tub **12** The Alchemist **15** Bartholomew Fair **18** Every Man in His Humo(u)r **21** Every Man out of His Humo(u)r **23** Epicene or the Silent Woman

Jordan
other name: 24 Hashemite Kingdom of Jordan
capital/largest city: 5 Amman
ancient name: 12 Philadelphia
others: 4 Krak, Ma'an, Salt **5** Aqaba, Ariha, Irbid, Jenin, Karak, Kerak, Sarga, Zarga, Zerke **6** Bethel, Hebron, Jarash, Jerash, Madaba, Nablus, Ramtha **7** Al-Aqaba, Bethany, El-Kerak, El Zerga, Jericho, Kirmoab, Nabulus, Samaria **8** Al-Khalil, Ram Allah **9** Bethlehem, Jerusalem
school: 7 yarmouk
division: 8 East Bank, West Bank **11** Transjordan
ancient state: 4 Edom, Moab **5** Ammon, Judah **6** Gilead
head of state: 4 King **8** Abdullah **11** King Hussein
wife: 5 Rania
father: 7 Hussein
monetary unit: 4 fils **5** dinar
mountain: 3 Hor **4** Nebo **5** Bukka, Dabab **6** Ataiba, Gilead, Mubrak
highest point: 9 Jabal Ramm, Jebel Ramm
river: 6 Jordan, Yarmuk **11** Nahr-az-Zarga
sea: 3 Red **4** Dead **7** Galilee **13** Mediterranean
physical feature:
desert: 6 Syria
gulf: 5 Aqaba

plateau: 11 Transjordan
valley: 4 Ghor 9 Great Rift
wind: 7 Khamsin
people: 4 Arab, Kurd 7 Bedouin, Checher 8 Armenian, Assyrian 10 Circassian 11 Palestinian
ancient: 8 Armonite 9 Nabataean
ruler: 5 Talal 6 Faisal, Greeks, Romans 7 Hussein 8 Abdullah, Selucidas 9 Crusaders 10 Ibn Hussein, Nabataeans 12 Ottoman Turks 18 Abdullah Ibn Hussein
tribe: 5 Qaysi 6 Yamani
language: 6 Arabic
religion: 5 Islam 13 Greek Orthodox
place:
canal: 8 East Gher
ruins: 5 Ajlun, Petra 6 Jarash 7 Al Karak
feature:
headdress: 8 kaffiyeh
village headman: 7 mukhtar
village square: 5 sahah
food:
dessert: 7 baklava
pastry: 7 katayif
Jordan, Robert
character in: 19 For Whom the Bell Tolls
author: 9 Hemingway
Jormungandr
also: 10 Jormungand 11 Iormungandr 14 Midgard Serpent
origin: 12 Scandinavian
form: 7 serpent
father: 4 Loki
mother: 9 Angerboda, Angrbodha, Angurboda
brother: 6 Fenrir, Fenris
sister: 3 Hel
wrapped around: 5 world
killed by: 4 Thor
death place: 6 Vigrid
killed: 4 Thor
Jo's Boys
author: 15 Louisa May Alcott
sequel to: 11 Little Women
Joseph
father: 4 Bani 5 Aseph, Jacob 10 Mattathias
mother: 6 Rachel
brother: 3 Dan, Gad 4 Levi 5 Asher, Judah 6 Reuben, Simeon 7 Zebulun 8 Benjamin, Issachar, Naphtali
wife: 4 Mary 7 Asenath
stepson: 5 Jesus
also called: 20 Barsabbas of Arimathea 21 Barsabbas of Arimathaea
buried: 5 Jesus
slave of: 8 Potiphar
Joseph Andrews
author: 13 Henry Fielding
character: 5 Fanny 9 Lady Booby 11 Mrs Slipslop, Parson Adams, Peter Pounce 13 Pamela Andrews
josh 3 guy, kid, rag, rib 4 dish, haze, jape, jest, jive, joke, quiz, razz, ride,

twit 5 chaff, jolly, put on, roast, tease 6 banter, needle 8 ridicule
Joshua
means: 18 Jehovah is salvation
father: 3 Nun
succeeded: 5 Moses
captured: 7 Jericho, Lachish
hid spies: 5 Rahab
jostle 3 jab 4 bump, butt, poke, prod, push 5 crowd, elbow, shove 7 collide 8 shoulder 10 hit against, run against 12 knock against
jot 3 bit, dot 4 iota, list, mite, note, snip, whit 5 enter, speck, trace 6 record, trifle 7 modicum, one iota, put down, set down, smidgen, snippet 8 flyspeck, particle, register, scribble, take down 9 scintilla
jotting 4 memo, note 6 doodle 8 scribble 10 memorandum, scribbling
Jotun
origin: 12 Scandinavian
form: 5 giant
conflicts with: 4 gods
enemy: 4 Asar 5 Aesir
Joule, James Prescott
field: 7 physics
nationality: 7 British
established law of: 20 conservation of energy
named for him: 10 unit of work
jounce 3 bob 6 bounce 7 rebound 8 ricochet
Jourdain, Monsieur
character in: 21 The Bourgeois Gentleman 22 Le Bourgeois Gentilhomme
author: 7 Moliere
Jourdan, Louis
real name: 11 Louis Gendre
born: 6 France 9 Marseille
roles: 4 Gigi 6 Can Can 9 Octopussy 15 The Paradine Case 23 Three Coins in the Fountain 24 Letter from an Unknown Woman
journal 3 log 5 album, daily, diary, paper, sheet 6 annual, ledger, memoir, record, weekly 7 almanac, daybook, gazette, history, logbook, monthly, tabloid 8 calendar, magazine, notebook, register, yearbook 9 chronicle, newspaper, quarterly, scrapbook 10 chronology, confession, memorandum, memory book, periodical, record book 11 account book, daily record, publication 13 autobiography
journalism 15 the fourth estate
journalist 6 author, editor, writer 7 byliner, diarist, newsman 8 reporter 9 columnist, newswoman 12 newspaperman 13 correspondent 14 newspaperwoman
Journal of the Plague Year, A
author: 11 Daniel Defoe
journey 3 fly, way 4 roam, rove, sail, tour, trek, trip, wend 5 jaunt, quest, route, tramp 6 course, cruise, flight,

junket, outing, ramble, roving, travel, voyage, wander 7 circuit, meander, odyssey, passage, transit 8 divagate, navigate, sightsee, vagabond 9 excursion, itinerary, take a trip, wandering 10 divagation, expedition, pilgrimage 11 peregrinate 13 peregrination
journey's end 4 goal 9 objective 11 destination
joust 4 tilt 5 combat, jostle 7 contend, contest, tourney 8 run a tilt 10 contention, tournament
Jove *see* 7 Jupiter
jovial 3 gay 5 jolly, merry, sunny 6 blithe, cheery, hearty, jocose, jocund 7 buoyant, gleeful, jocular, playful, zestful 8 cheerful, humorous, laughing, mirthful, sportive 9 convivial, fun-loving, hilarious 10 delightful, frolicsome, rollicking
joviality 3 fun 4 glee 5 cheer, gaity, mirth 7 delight, jollity, revelry 8 buoyancy 9 jocundity, merriment 10 joyfulness, liveliness 11 high spirits
jowl 3 jaw 5 cheek, chops 6 muzzle 8 mandible
joy 3 gem 4 glee 5 jewel, pride, prize 6 gaiety 7 delight, ecstasy, elation, rapture 8 gladness, pleasure, treasure 9 enjoyment, happiness 10 excitement, exultation, jubilation 11 contentment, delectation 12 cheerfulness, exhilaration, satisfaction
goddess of: 6 Hathor
Joyce, James
author of: 7 Ulysses 9 Dubliners 13 Finnegans Wake 31 A Portrait of the Artist as a Young Man
joyful 4 glad, rosy 5 happy 6 bright, elated 7 blessed, pleased 8 cheerful, ecstatic, exultant, gladsome, jubilant, pleasing 9 delighted, full of joy, overjoyed 10 delightful, enraptured, gratifying, heartening 11 pleasurable, transported 12 heartwarming
joyless 3 sad 4 glum, grim 5 black 6 dismal, gloomy, morbid, woeful 7 doleful, forlorn, unhappy 8 dejected, desolate, dolorous, downcast, mournful 9 cheerless, depressed, sorrowful, woebegone 10 despondent, in the dumps, lugubrious, melancholy 11 downhearted, pessimistic 12 disconsolate, heavyhearted 14 down in the mouth
joy of living
French: 11 joie de vivre
Joy of Sex, The
author: 11 Alex Comfort
joyous 3 gay 4 glad 5 happy, merry 7 festive, gleeful 8 cheerful, gladsome, mirthful 9 rapturous, wonderful 10 delightful, gratifying, heartening 11 pleasurable 12 heartwarming, lighthearted
joyousness 4 glee 8 gladness 9 happiness, merriment 10 blitheness, exu-

berance **11** high spirits **16** lightheart-edness

jubilant 3 gay **4** glad **5** happy, jolly, merry **6** blithe, cheery, elated, enrapt, joyful, joyous **7** buoyant, charmed, gleeful, pleased, radiant, smiling **8** cheerful, ecstatic, exultant, gladsome, laughing, mirthful **9** delighted, delirious, exuberant, gladdened, gratified, overjoyed, rapturous, rejoicing, rhapsodic **10** blithesome, captivated, enraptured **11** exhilarated, intoxicated, tickled pink **12** happy as a lark, lighthearted **13** in high spirits

jubilation 5 bliss **9** rejoicing **11** celebration **12** exhilaration

jubilee 2 do **4** bash, fete, gala **5** blast, party **6** frolic, revels **7** blowout, holiday, revelry, shindig **8** festival, wingding **9** festivity **10** jubilation, observance **11** anniversary, celebration, merrymaking **12** conviviality **13** commemoration

Judah
father: 5 Jacob
mother: 4 Leah
brother: 3 Dan, Gad **4** Levi **5** Asher, Judah **6** Joseph, Reuben, Simeon **8** Benjamin, Issachar, Naphtali
sister: 5 Dinah
wife: 5 Shuah
son: 2 Er **4** Onan **5** Perez, Zerah **6** Baruch, Shelah
daughter-in-law: 5 Tamar
last king of: 8 Zedekiah
descendant of: 8 Judahite

Judah, tribes of *see* **14** Israel, tribes of

Judas
brother: 5 James
also called: 8 Thaddeus
disciple of: 5 Jesus

Judas Iscariot 8 betrayer
disciple of: 5 Jesus
betrayed: 5 Jesus
replaced by: 8 Matthias

Jude 7 apostle
brother: 5 James

Jude the Obscure
author: 11 Thomas Hardy
character: 10 Jude Fawley **12** Arabella Donn, Sue Bridehead **14** Drusilla Fawley **16** Little Father Time **17** Richard Phillotson

judge 3 try **4** deem, find, hear, rank, rate **5** fancy, gauge, guess, infer, juror, value, weigh **6** assess, assume, censor, critic, decide, deduce, expert, reckon, regard, review, rule on, settle, size up, umpire **7** adjudge, analyze, arbiter, believe, conduct, discern, imagine, justice, referee, resolve, suppose, surmise **8** appraise, assessor, conclude, consider, estimate, official, reviewer **9** appraiser, arbitrate, ascertain, authority, determine, evaluator, moderator **10** adjudicate, arbitrator,

conjecture, magistrate **11** adjudicator, connoisseur, distinguish **12** pass sentence

Judging Amy
network: 3 CBS
cast: 8 Tyne Daly (Maxine Gray) **11** Jessica Tuck (Gillian Gray), Karle Warren (Lauren Cassidy) **12** Amy Brenneman (Amy Madison Gray), Dan Futterman (Vincent Gray) **13** Richard T. Jones (Bruce Van Exel) **14** Marcus Giamatti (Peter Gray) **16** Jillian Armenante (Donna Kozlowski)

judgment, judgement 4 view **5** sense, taste **6** acumen, belief, decree, ruling **7** finding, opinion, verdict **8** decision, estimate, sentence **9** appraisal, deduction, valuation **10** assessment, conclusion, conviction, discretion, perception, persuasion, shrewdness **11** arbitration, discernment, percipience **14** discrimination, perceptiveness

Judgment at Nuremberg
director: 13 Stanley Kramer
cast: 11 Judy Garland **12** Spencer Tracy **13** Burt Lancaster **14** Richard Widmark, William Shatner **15** Marlene Dietrich, Montgomery Clift **16** Maximilian Schell (Oscar)

Judgment Day 8 doomsday **13** end of the world **14** day of reckoning **15** the Last Judgment

Judgment Day
author: 13 James T Farrell

Judgment of Paris *see* **5** Paris

judicial 5 legal **8** imposing, juristic, majestic, official **9** magistral **11** magisterial **13** distinguished

judiciary 5 bench, court **11** court system

judicious 4 just, sage, wise **5** acute, sober, sound **6** astute, shrewd **7** knowing, politic, prudent, tactful **8** sensible **9** sagacious **10** diplomatic, discerning, percipient, reasonable, reflective, thoughtful **11** levelheaded **13** perspicacious **14** discriminating

judiciousness 4 tact **6** acumen, wisdom **8** prudence, sagacity **9** good sense **10** discretion **11** discernment, percipience **12** perspicacity **14** discrimination

Judique, Mrs Tanis
character in: 7 Babbitt
author: 5 Lewis

Judith
husband: 4 Esau
killed: 10 Holofernes

jug 3 jar, urn **4** ewer **5** crock, stein **6** bottle, carafe, flagon, vessel **7** pitcher, tankard **8** decanter, demijohn **9** container

juggle 4 redo **5** alter **6** modify **7** falsify **8** disguise, fool with **9** keep aloft **10** manipulate, meddle with, reorganize,

tamper with, tinker with **12** misrepresent

juggler 5 cheat **6** jester **8** conjuror, deceiver, jongleur, magician, shuffler **15** prestidigitator

Juice
nickname of: 9 O J Simpson

juicy 3 wet **4** lush, racy **5** fluid, lurid, moist, pulpy, runny, sappy, spicy, vivid **6** fluent, liquid, risque, watery **7** flowing, graphic **8** colorful, dripping, exciting, luscious **9** succulent, thrilling **10** intriguing **11** captivating, fascinating, picturesque, provocative, sensational, tantalizing

Jules and Jim
director: 16 Francois Truffaut
cast: 10 Henri Serre **11** Marie Dubois, Oskar Werner **12** Jeanne Moreau

Julia
character in: 20 Two Gentlemen of Verona
author: 11 Shakespeare

Julia
character: 10 Corey Baker, Eddie Edson, Julia Baker **11** Hannah Yarby **14** Earl J Waggedorn, Marie Waggedorn **15** Dr Morton Chegley
cast: 10 Lloyd Nolan, Marc Copage **11** Betty Beaird, Michael Link **12** Eddie Quillan, Lurene Tuttle, Paul Winfield **14** Diahann Carroll

Julia
director: 13 Fred Zinnemann
based on story by: 14 Lillian Hellman (Pentimento)
cast: 9 Jane Fonda (Lillian Hellman) **11** Hal Holbrook **12** Jason Robards (Dashiell Hammett) **15** Vanessa Redgrave (Julia) **16** Maximilian Schell
Oscar for: 12 screenwriter **15** supporting actor (Robards) **17** supporting actress (Redgrave)

Julius Caesar
author: 18 William Shakespeare
character: 6 Brutus (Marcus Brutus), Portia **7** Cassius (Gaius Cassius) **9** Calpurnia **10** Mark Antony (Marcus Antonius)
director: 17 Joseph L Mankiewicz
cast: 10 James Mason **11** Deborah Kerr, Greer Garson, John Gielgud **12** Edmond O'Brien, Louis Calhern, Marlon Brando

July
flower: 8 larkspur **9** water lily
French: 7 Juillet
holiday: 11 Bastille Day (14), Dominion Day (1) **15** Independence Day (4) **16** Saint Swithin's Day (15)
gem: 4 ruby
German: 4 Juli
Italian: 6 Luglio
number of days: 9 thirty-one
origin of name: 12 Julius Caesar
place in year:
  Gregorian: 7 seventh

Roman: 5 fifth
Spanish: 5 Julio
Zodiac sign: 3 Leo **6** Cancer

jumble 3 mix **4** heap, mess, olio, stew **5** bunch, chaos, mix up, pitch, snarl **6** ball up, medley, muddle, pile up, tangle, tumble **7** clutter, farrago, melange, mixture, scatter **8** disarray, mishmash **9** aggregate, confusion, patchwork, potpourri **10** hodgepodge, miscellany, salmagundi **11** gallimaufry **12** accumulation **14** conglomeration

jumbled 5 messy **7** chaotic, mixed up, snarled, tangled **8** confused **9** cluttered, illogical **10** disjointed, incoherent **11** disarranged **12** disconnected, disorganized

jumbo 4 huge, vast **5** giant **6** mighty **7** immense, mammoth, titanic **8** colossal, enormous, gigantic, towering **9** cyclopean, monstrous, oversized **10** monumental, stupendous **11** elephantine, mountainous

jump 3 hop **4** buck, leap, pass, skip **5** boost, bound, pitch, start, surge, vault, wince **6** ambush, attack, blench, bounce, flinch, gambol, go over, hurdle, prance, recoil, spring, switch, upturn, zoom up **7** advance, barrier, digress, maunder, overrun, upsurge **8** fall upon, obstacle **9** barricade, increment, skyrocket **10** impediment **11** obstruction **12** augmentation

jumper 4 frog, sled, toad **5** dress, horse, shirt, smock **6** blouse, hopper, jacket, leaper **7** overall **8** coverall, kangaroo

jump for joy 5 exult **7** rejoice

jumpy 5 nervy, shaky **6** goosey, uneasy **7** alarmed, anxious, fidgety, fretful, jittery, nervous, panicky, twitchy, uptight **8** aflutter, agitated, fluttery, skittish **9** trembling, twitching **10** frightened **12** apprehensive

junction 6 linkup **7** conflux, joining **10** confluence, crossroads **11** concurrence, convergence, interchange **12** intersection

juncture 4 pass, seam **5** joint **6** crisis, linkup, moment **7** closure, joining, meeting **8** interval, occasion **10** confluence, connection **11** convergence, point in time **12** intersection **13** critical point

June
characteristic: 8 weddings
event: 12 Midsummer Day (24), Midsummer Eve (23) **14** summer solstice (21)
flower: 4 rose
French: 4 Juin
gem: 5 pearl **9** moonstone **11** alexandrite
German: 4 Juni
holiday: 7 Flag Day (14) **10** Father's Day (third Sunday) **13** Kamehameha Day (11) **22** Jefferson Davis' birth-

day (3)
Italian: 6 Giugno
number of days: 6 thirty
origin of name: 4 Juno (Roman goddess) **6** Junius (Roman clan) **8** juniores (youths)
place in year:
  Gregorian: 5 sixth
  Roman: 6 fourth
saying: 24 What is so rare as a day in June
Spanish: 5 Junio
Zodiac sign: 6 Cancer, Gemini

jungle 4 bush, wild **5** woods **10** rain forest, wilderness **11** undergrowth **12** swampy forest, virgin forest

Jungle, The
author: 13 Upton Sinclair
character: 3 Ona **5** Jonas **6** Marija **8** Elzbieta **12** Jurgis Rudkus **13** Antanas Rudkus
criticism of: 19 meat-packing industry

Jungle Books, The
author: 14 Rudyard Kipling
character: 3 Kaa **5** Akela, Baloo, Hathi **6** Buldeo, Messau, Mowgli **8** Bagheera **9** Shere Khan **11** Gray Brother

Jungle Jim
creator: 11 Alex Raymond
character: 4 Joan, Kolu

junior 5 later, lower, minor, newer **6** lesser **7** younger **8** inferior **9** secondary **11** subordinate

juniper 9 Juniperus
varieties: 4 ashe, plum **5** Greek, Irish, shore **6** common, ground, needle, Polish, Sierra, Syrian **7** African, incense, prickly, Sargent **8** creeping, drooping, mountain, red-berry, Waukegan **9** alligator, blue-spire, Himalayan, prostrate **10** California **11** cherrystone **12** Canary Island, sweetfruited **13** Rocky Mountain

junk 4 dump **5** scrap, trash, waste **6** debris, litter, refuse **7** clutter, discard, garbage, rubbish, rummage **8** castoffs, oddments, throw out **9** dispose of, throw away **11** odds and ends

junket 4 tour, trip **7** journey **9** excursion

Juno
origin: 5 Roman
queen of: 6 heaven
father: 6 Saturn
brother: 7 Jupiter
husband: 7 Jupiter
son: 4 Mars
protectress of: 5 women **8** marriage
epithet: 6 Lucina, Moneta **7** Curitis, Pronuba, Sospita
festival: 10 Matronalia
corresponds to: 4 Hera, Here

Juno and the Paycock
author: 10 Sean O'Casey

junta 5 cabal **7** council **9** committee **18** military government

Jupiter
also: 4 Jove
god of: 5 light **7** heavens, weather **9** lightning **11** thunderbolt
epithet: 5 Ultor **7** Elicius, Pluvius
corresponds to: 4 Zeus

Jupiter
position: 5 fifth
satellite: 2 Io **6** Europa **8** Amalthea, Callisto, Ganymede
characteristic: 7 red spot

Jura 11 Swiss canton **13** mountain range

Jurassic period
dinosaur from: 10 Diplodocus **11** Apatosaurus, Stegosaurus **12** Brontosaurus, Camarasaurus, Camptosaurus, Ceratosaurus, Megalosaurus **13** Brachiosaurus, Compsognathus, Ornitholestes

Jurgens, Curt
also: 11 Curd Jurgens
born: 6 Munich **7** Germany
roles: 6 Lord Jim **12** The Blue Angel **13** The Enemy Below, The Longest Day **16** The Spy Who Loved Me **25** The Inn of the Sixth Happiness

jurisdiction 3 say **4** area, beat, rule, sway, zone **5** field, range, reach, scope **6** bounds, domain, sphere **7** circuit, command, compass, control, quarter **8** district, dominion, hegemony, latitude, precinct, province **9** authority, bailiwick **10** legal right **11** prerogative

jurist 5 judge **6** lawyer **7** counsel, justice **8** advocate, attorney **9** barrister, counselor, solicitor **10** magistrate **12** legal adviser **13** attorney-at-law

jury 5 panel, peers **6** assize, twelve **9** committee, makeshift, veniremen

jury-rigged 9 improvised, makeshift, temporary

jus 3 law **5** right
jus civile 8 civil law
jus gentium 12 law of nations
jus naturale 11 law of nature
jus sanguinis 12 right of blood
(law) citizenship of child is same as: 7 parents
jus soli 11 right of land, right of soil
(law) citizenship of child based on place of: 5 birth

just 3 but, due **4** fair, firm, good, only, sane **5** fully, moral, quite, solid, sound **6** at most, barely, decent, hardly, honest, lately, merely, proper, simply, strong, worthy **7** condign, ethical, exactly, fitting, logical, merited, only now, upright **8** adequate, balanced, deserved, entirely, narrowly, recently, scarcely, sensible, suitable, unbiased **9** befitting, blameless, equitable, honorable, impartial, justified, objective, perfectly, precisely, reputable, righteous, unbigoted, uncorrupt

10 aboveboard, absolutely, acceptable, completely, evenhanded, fair-minded, high-minded, no more than, nothing but, not long ago, principled, reasonable, scrupulous, upstanding **11** appropriate, justifiable, trustworthy, well-founded **12** conscionable, open to reason, unprejudiced, well-grounded **13** conscientious, disinterested, dispassionate

just about 6 almost, around, barely, nearly **7** close to **10** not far from **12** on the point of **13** approximately

Just Above My Head
author: **12** James Baldwin

just a moment ago
French: **11** tout a l'heure

justice 5 honor, right, truth **6** amends, equity, the law, virtue **7** honesty, payment, penalty, probity, redress **8** fair play, fairness, goodness, legality **9** atonement, integrity, rightness **10** correction, lawfulness, legitimacy, reparation **11** just desserts, proper cause, uprightness **12** chastisement, compensation, equitability, remuneration, satisfaction **13** due punishment, equitableness, justification, righteousness **17** constitutionality
god of: **7** Forsete, Forseti

goddess of: **4** Dice, Dike **6** Astrea **7** Astraea

Justice
author: **14** John Galsworthy

Justice Clement
character in: **19** Every Man in His Humour
author: **6** Jonson

justice to all
Latin: **15** justitia omnibus
motto of: **18** District of Columbia

justifiable 9 excusable **10** defensible **11** explanatory, extenuating, supportable

justification 5 alibi **6** excuse **7** apology, defense, pretext, support **8** sanction **10** accounting, adjustment, validation **11** explanation, vindication **12** confirmation **13** rectification **14** reconciliation

justification for existence
French: **11** raison d'etre

justify 6 back up, defend, excuse, uphold **7** bear out, confirm, explain, support, sustain, warrant **8** sanction, validate **9** vindicate **10** account for, prove right

justitia omnibus 12 justice to all
motto of: **18** District of Columbia

just now
French: **11** tout a l'heure

Just Shoot Me!
network: **3** NBC
cast: **10** David Spade (Dennis Finch) **11** George Segal (Jack Gallo) **12** Wendie Malick (Nina Van Horn) **15** Enrico Colantoni (Elliot DiMauro), Laura San Giacomo (Maya Gallo)

just the same 6 anyhow, anyway **12** nevertheless

just the thing 7 apropos **8** suitable **11** appropriate **12** exactly right

Justus *see* **5** Titus

jut 5 bulge **6** beetle, extend **7** poke out, project **8** overhang, protrude, shoot out, stand out, stick out **13** thrust forward

jute 19 Corchorus capsularis
varieties: **5** Bimli, China, Tossa, white **7** bastard **10** Bimlipatum

juvenile 5 child, minor, young, youth **6** boyish, callow, infant, junior **7** girlish **8** childish, immature, teenager, youthful **9** childlike, pubescent, stripling, youngster **10** adolescent, sophomoric **15** unsophisticated

juxtaposed 6 next to **8** adjacent, touching **9** proximate **10** contiguous, side by side **12** conterminous

juxtaposition 5 touch **7** balance, contact **8** contrast, nearness **9** adjacency, proximity **10** apposition, contiguity

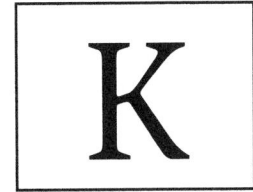
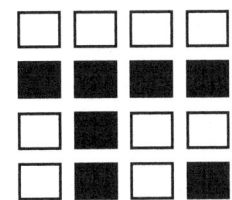

K
character in: **9** The Castle
author: **5** Kafka

Ka
origin: **8** Egyptian
form: **6** spirit
trait: **11** immortality

kabob 5 cabab, cabob, kabab, kebab, kebob **7** shaslik **8** shashlik **9** shashlick

Kabul
capital of: **11** Afghanistan

Kafka, Franz
author of: **7** Amerika **8** The Trial **9** The Castle **16** The Metamorphosis

kahlua
type: **6** brandy
origin: **6** Mexico
flavor: **6** coffee
with rum: **10** Black Maria
with tequila: **9** Brave Bull
with vodka: **12** Black Russian

Kahn, Albert
architect of: **15** River Rouge Plant **17** Highland Park Plant **20** Athletic Club Building (Detroit) **21** General Motors Building (Detroit)

Kahn, Louis Isadore
architect of: **16** Kimbell Art Museum (Ft Worth TX) **23** Yale Center for British Art **24** Yale University Art Gallery **28** Phillips Exeter Academy Library (NH) **31** Richards Medical Research Building (U of PA) **33** Salk Institute for Biological Studies (La Jolla CA)

Kahn, Madeline
born: **8** Boston MA
roles: **5** Cosby **9** Paper Moon **10** What's Up Doc? **14** Blazing Saddles **17** Young Frankenstein

kaiser 5 ruler **7** emperor, Wilhelm **8** autocrat

kakemono 6 scroll **13** hanging object

kale 16 Brassica oleracea (Acephala Group)
varieties: **3** sea **4** Ruvo, tall, tree **6** Indian, Scotch **7** cabbage, Chinese, Italian, kitchen **8** Siberian **9** flowering, Tronchuda **10** decorative, ornamental, Portuguese **13** dwarf Siberian **16** ornamental-leaved

kaleidoscopic 6 mobile, motley **7** protean **8** shifting, unstable, variable **9** checkered **10** changeable, variegated **11** fluctuating, many colored, rainbowlike, vacillating **12** ever-changing

Kaleva 8 folk hero
origin: **7** Finnish **8** Estonian

Kali
also: **3** Uma **5** Durga **7** Parvati
husband: **4** Siva **5** Shiva
festival: **6** dewali
goddess of: **5** death **7** disease

Kalimantan see **6** Borneo

Kampala
capital of: **6** Uganda

Kampuchea see **8** Cambodia

Kandinsky, Wassily (Vasily)
born: **6** Moscow, Russia
artwork: **7** Striped **8** Twilight **10** Black Lines **11** Impressions **12** Blue Mountain (no 84), Compositions, Violet Orange **13** Black Relation **14** Improvisations **15** Capricious Forms **17** Bavarian Mountains, The Street in Murnau **23** Painting with White Border

Kanga
character in: **13** Winnie the Pooh
author: **5** Milne
child: **3** Roo

kangaroo
young: **4** joey
group of: **3** mob **5** troop

Kaniengehaga see **6** Mohawk

Kansas
abbreviation: **2** KS **4** Kans
nickname: **5** Wheat **9** Jayhawker, Sunflower **15** Garden of the West
capital: **6** Topeka
largest city: **7** Wichita
others: **4** Hays, Iola **5** Colby, Dodge **6** Salina **7** Abilene, Chanute, Emporia, Liberal **8** Atchison, Lawrence **9** Great Bend **10** Belleville, Hutchinson, Kansas City **11** Coffeeville, Leavenworth **12** Junction City
college: **5** Baker, Tabor **7** Bethany **8** Sterling, Washburn
explorer: **8** Coronado
feature: **16** Eisenhower Center
  fort: **5** Riley, Scott
  Indian training school: 16 Haskell Institute
  penitentiary: **11** Leavenworth
  reservoir: **11** Tuttle Creek
tribe: **3** Kaw **4** Pani **5** Kansa, Kiowa, Osage **6** Pawnee **7** Arapaho, Wichita **8** Cheyenne, Comanche, Kickapoo
people: **7** Jayhawk **9** Alf Landon **10** Robert Dole **11** Damon Runyon **13** Amelia Earhart, Karl Menninger **14** Walter Chrysler **15** Edgar Lee Masters
lake: **6** Cheney, Kerwin, Neosho **7** Milford
land rank: **10** fourteenth
mountain:
  highest point: **9** Sunflower
physical feature:
  plains: **5** Great, Osage
president: **17** Dwight D Eisenhower
river: **3** Kaw **6** Kansas **8** Arkansas, Cimarron, Missouri **9** Smoky Hill **10** Republican
state admission: **12** thirty-fourth
state bird: **17** western meadowlark
state flower: **9** sunflower
state motto: **29** To the Stars Through Difficulties
state song: **14** Home on the Range
state tree: **10** cottonwood

Kansas City
baseball team: **6** Royals
football team: **6** Chiefs
landmark: **12** Union Station **22** Nelson-Atkins Art Gallery
river: **6** Kansas **8** Missouri

Kant, Immanuel
author of: **20** Critique of Pure Reason

Kantor, MacKinlay
author of: **13** Andersonville

Karloff, Boris
real name: **17** William Henry Pratt
born: **7** Dulwich, England
roles: **12** Frankenstein

karma 3 act **4** aura, deed, duty, fate, rite **5** force, power **6** action, kismet, spirit **7** destiny **9** vibration

Kasdan, Lawrence
director of: **11** The Big Chill

Kashmiri
language family: **12** Indo-European
branch: **11** Indo-Iranian
group: **5** Indic
spoken in: **5** (northern) India

kashruth, kashrut 7 fitness **17** Jewish dietary laws

Katharina
character in: **19** The Taming of the Shrew
author: **11** Shakespeare

Katmandu, Kathmandu
capital of: **5** Nepal

Katzenjammer Kids
also: 17 Captain and the Kids
creator: 12 Rudolph Dirks
character: 4 Hans **5** Fritz, Momma **10** der Captain **12** der Inspector

Kaufman, George S
author of:
    with Edna Ferber: 9 Stage Door **13** Dinner at Eight **14** The Royal Family
    with Moss Hart: 15 Once in a Lifetime **20** You Can't Take It with You **21** The Man Who Came to Dinner

Kay (Sir Kay)
character in: 16 Arthurian romance
foster brother: 6 Arthur

Kaye, Danny
real name: 19 David Daniel Kaminski
born: 10 Brooklyn NY
wife: 10 Sylvia Fine
roles: 14 The Court Jester **19** The Inspector General **21** Hans Christian Andersen **26** The Secret Life of Walter Mitty

Kaye, M M
author of: 9 Trade Wind **12** Death in Kenya **15** Death in Zanzibar, Shadow of the Moon, The Far Pavilions

Kazakhstan
capital/largest city: 7 Alma-Ata
others: 9 Karaganda **13** Petropavlovsk, Semipalatinsk
head of state: 9 president
government: 8 republic
monetary unit: 5 ruble
sea: 4 Aral **7** Caspian
physical feature: 7 steppes **12** Lake Balkhash
people: 6 Kazakh
language: 6 Kazakh

Kazan, Elia
director of: 10 East of Eden, Viva Zapata **15** On the Waterfront (Oscar) **18** Splendor in the Grass **19** Gentleman's Agreement (Oscar) **20** A Tree Grows in Brooklyn **21** A Streetcar Named Desire

Kazantzakis, Nikos
author of: 13 Zorba the Greek **14** Freedom or Death, The Greek Passion **25** The Last Temptation of Christ

kazoo 5 bazoo, zarah **6** hewgag **11** eunuch flute
French: 8 mirliton

Keach, Stacy
real name: 18 Walter Stacy Keach Jr
born: 10 Savannah GA
brother: 5 James
roles: 3 Doc **6** Luther **10** Mike Hammer **13** False Identity **16** American History X **24** Twinkle Twinkle Killer Kane

Kearny, Stephen Watts
served in: 10 California, Mexican War
commander of: 13 Army of the West
occupied: 9 New Mexico
battle: 10 San Gabriel, San Pasqual

Keaton, Buster
real name: 19 Joseph Francis Keaton
born: 7 Piqua KS
roles: 6 Go West **7** College **10** The General **12** The Cameraman

Keaton, Diane
real name: 9 Diane Hall
born: 12 Los Angeles CA
roles: 4 Reds **7** Sleeper **8** Baby Boom **9** Annie Hall (Oscar) **12** Shoot the Moon, The Godfather **13** The Good Mother **14** Play It Again Sam **17** The First Wives Club **19** Looking for Mr Goodbar, Something's Gotta Give **20** The Little Drummer Girl

Keats, John
author of: 5 Lamia **8** Endymion, Hyperion, Isabella **11** Ode to Autumn, Ode to Psyche **14** Ode on Indolence **15** Ode on Melancholy, The Eve of St Agnes **16** Ode on a Grecian Urn **17** Ode to a Nightingale **20** La Belle Dame Sans Merci **31** On First Looking into Chapman's Homer

Kedemah
also called: 5 Kedar
father: 7 Ishmael
mother: 5 Hagar
descendant of: 8 Kedarite

Keel (of Argo)
constellation of: 6 Carina

Keel, Howard
real name: 17 Harry Clifford Leek
costar: 14 Kathryn Grayson
born: 11 Gillespie IL
roles: 6 Dallas, Kismet **8** Show Boat **10** Kiss Me Kate **13** Clayton Farlow **15** Annie Get Your Gun **27** Seven Brides for Seven Brothers

Keeler, Ruby
husband: 8 Al Jolson
costar: 10 Dick Powell
born: 6 Canada **7** Halifax
roles: 15 Footlight Parade **17** Forty-Second Street **32** Gold Diggers of Nineteen Thirty-Three

keel over 5 faint, swoon, upset **7** capsize, tip over **8** collapse, fall down, fall flat, flip over, overturn, turn over **10** turn turtle

keen 4 avid, fine **5** acute, alert, eager, sharp **6** ardent, astute, clever, fervid, fierce, shrewd **7** earnest, excited, fervent, intense, zealous **8** incisive **9** impatient, paper thin, razorlike **10** discerning **11** finely honed, impassioned, penetrating, quick-witted **12** enthusiastic **13** perspicacious **14** discriminating

Keene, Carolyn
created: 18 Nancy Drew mysteries
father: 17 Edward Stratemeyer

keen-eyed 5 alert **8** vigilant, watchful **9** attentive, eagle-eyed, observant, sharp-eyed, wide-awake

keen-minded 5 acute, sharp, smart **6** astute, clever, shrewd **10** perceptive **11** penetrating

keenness 4 zeal, zest **5** ardor **6** acumen, fervor **7** passion **9** acuteness, eagerness, sharpness **10** astuteness, cleverness, enthusiasm, excitement, shrewdness **11** discernment **12** anticipation, intelligence, perspicacity

keen-sighted 4 sage, wise **5** acute, sharp **6** astute, shrewd **8** piercing **9** eagle-eyed, judicious, sagacious, sharp-eyed **10** discerning **11** intelligent, penetrating **12** clear-sighted, sharp-sighted **13** perspicacious

keep 3 bar **4** clog, fort, have, heap, hold, mind, pile, stay **5** abide, block, carry, cramp, delay, deter, guard, honor, lay in, place, stack, stall, stand, stick, stock, store, tie up, tower **6** arrest, castle, detain, donjon, endure, hamper, hinder, hobble, hold up, impede, living, pay for, remain, retain, retard **7** care for, carry on, citadel, deposit, furnish, inhibit, observe, possess, prevent, shackle, support, sustain **8** conserve, continue, encumber, fortress, hang on to, hold back, maintain, obstruct, preserve, restrain **9** celebrate, constrain, hamstring, persevere, persist in, ritualize, safeguard, solemnize, watch over **10** accumulate, daily bread, livelihood, provide for, stronghold, sustenance **11** commemorate, maintenance, memorialize, subsistence **12** room and board **13** fortification

keep an eye on 5 watch **7** oversee **9** chaperone, look after, watch over

keep apart 7 isolate **8** separate **9** segregate

keep at bay 7 beat off, fend off, ward off **8** stave off

keep back 5 check, delay **6** detain, hold up, retain **8** withhold

keep busy 3 use **6** employ, engage, occupy **7** utilize

keep clear of 4 shun **5** avoid, dodge, elude, evade, skirt **6** escape

keep company 4 date **5** court **7** consort, hang out **8** go around, go steady **9** accompany, associate **10** fraternize, go together

keeper 5 guard, nurse **6** duenna, escort, jailer, sentry, warden **7** curator **8** chaperon, guardian, retainer, sentinel, wet nurse **9** attendant, bodyguard, caretaker, chaperone, custodian, governess, nursemaid, protecter, protector **11** conservator, nurserymaid **13** guardian angel

keep in mind 8 consider, remember **10** think about

keep mum 13 button one's lip

keep off 7 fend off, stay off, ward off 8 stave off

keep one's counsel 12 remain silent 13 button one's lip

keep open 8 hold open 16 leave unscheduled

keep out 6 reject 8 prohibit 9 blackball, blacklist

keep out of sight 4 hide 5 cover 6 lay low, lie low 7 conceal, cover up, secrete 10 camouflage

keep private 4 hide 7 conceal, reserve 8 withhold

keepsake 5 relic, token 6 emblem, memory, symbol 7 memento 8 memorial, reminder, souvenir 11 remembrance 18 token of remembrance

keep secret 4 hide 6 hush up 7 conceal, cover up 8 suppress, withhold

keep silent 10 remain dumb 15 not breathe a word

keep steady 5 poise 7 balance 9 stabilize

keep to 5 cling, stick 6 adhere, be true, cleave, hold to 7 be loyal, stand by 8 maintain

keg 3 tub, tun, vat 4 butt, cask, drum, tank 6 barrel 7 rundlet 8 hogshead, puncheon 9 container, kilderkin

Keller, Helen
in childhood: 4 deaf 5 blind
teacher: 12 Anne Sullivan
play and film: 16 The Miracle Worker
author: 13 William Gibson
actors: 9 Patty Duke 12 Anne Bancroft
both won: 6 Oscars

Kellerman, Sally
born: 11 Long Beach CA
roles: 4 MASH 15 Hot Lips Houlihan

Kelly, Gene
real name: 17 Eugene Curran Kelly
born: 12 Pittsburgh PA
roles: 7 Pal Joey 9 Brigadoon, On the Town 13 Anchors Aweigh 15 Singin' in the Rain 17 An American in Paris 18 The Three Musketeers

Kelly, Grace
husband: 21 Prince Rainier Grimaldi
nickname: 11 Ice Princess
born: 14 Philadelphia PA
princess of: 6 Monaco
roles: 7 Mogambo 8 High Noon 10 Rear Window 11 High Society 13 To Catch a Thief 14 Dial M for Murder, The Country Girl (Oscar)

Kelly, Walt
creator/artist of: 4 Pogo

kelp 3 ash 4 agar, alga, leag 5 varec, varic, wrack 7 seaweed
source of: 4 soda 6 iodine 9 potassium

Kelpie
origin: 8 Scottish
form: 5 horse 6 spirit

habitat: 4 lake 5 river
causes: 8 drowning
warns of: 8 drowning

Kelvin
abbreviation: 1 K

Kelvin, William Thomson
field: 7 physics 11 mathematics
nationality: 7 British
worked on: 4 heat 11 electricity
invented: 12 electrometer, galvanometer 13 tide predictor
named for him: 22 Kelvin temperature scale

Kempis, Thomas a
author of: 20 The Imitation of Christ

Keneally, Thomas
author of: 10 A River Town 12 Confederates 13 The Great Shame 14 Schindler's List 15 The Tyrant's Novel 17 Office of Innocence

Kenilworth
author: 14 Sir Walter Scott
character: 6 Alasco, Dudley (Earl of Leicester) 10 Amy Robsart 12 Wayland Smith 13 Richard Varney 14 Queen Elizabeth 15 Flibbertigibbet 16 Edmund Tressilian

Kennedy, Arthur
real name: 17 John Arthur Kennedy
born: 11 Worcester MA
roles: 6 Becket 9 All My Sons 11 Peyton Place 12 Blind Victory 16 Death of a Salesman

Kennedy, Frank
character in: 15 Gone With the Wind
author: 8 Mitchell

Kennedy, John Fitzgerald
nickname: 3 JFK 4 Jack
presidential rank: 11 thirty-fifth
party: 10 Democratic
state represented: 2 MA
defeated: 5 (Richard Milhous) Nixon
vice president: 7 (Lyndon Baines) Johnson
cabinet:
  state: 4 (David Dean) Rusk
  treasury: 6 (Clarence Douglas) Dillon
  defense: 8 (Robert Strange) McNamara
  attorney general: 7 (Robert Francis) Kennedy
  postmaster general: 3 (James Edward) Day 9 (John Austin) Gronouski
  interior: 5 (Stewart Lee) Udall
  agriculture: 7 (Orville Lothrop) Freeman
  commerce: 6 (Luther Hartwell) Hodges
  labor: 5 (William Willard) Wirtz 8 (Arthur J) Goldberg
  HEW: 8 (Abraham Alexander) Ribicoff 10 (Anthony Joseph) Celebrezze
born: 11 Brookline MA
died: 8 Dallas TX

died by: 13 assassination
assassinated by: 6 (Lee Harvey) Oswald
buried: 25 Arlington National Cemetery
education:
  prep school: 6 Choate
  University: 7 Harvard 9 Princeton 23 London School of Economics
religion: 13 Roman Catholic
interests: 7 sailing 8 football 13 touch football
vacation spot: 9 Cape Cod MA 13 Hyannis Port MA
author: 15 Strategy of Peace, Why England Slept 17 Profiles in Courage (Pulitzer Prize)
political career: 9 US Senator 24 US House of Representatives
civilian career: 17 newspaper reporter
military service: 6 US Navy 10 lieutenant 11 World War Two
  commander of: 6 PT boat
notable events of lifetime/term: 9 Bay of Pigs 10 Berlin Wall, Peace Corps 18 Cuban missile crisis
  march: 11 Civil Rights
  treaty: 14 Nuclear Test-Ban
quote: 17 Ich bin ein Berliner (I am a Berliner) 35 We stand today on the edge of a New Frontier 61 Ask not what your country can do for you ask what you can do for your country
father: 13 Joseph Patrick
mother: 4 Rose (Fitzgerald)
siblings: 4 Jean 6 Eunice, Joseph 8 Kathleen, Patricia, Rosemary 11 Edward Moore 13 Robert Francis
wife: 10 Jacqueline (Lee Bouvier)
  nickname: 6 Jackie
  second marriage to: 7 Onassis
children: 14 John Fitzgerald (John-John, JFK Jr.), Patrick Bouvier (died in infancy) 15 Caroline Bouvier

Kennicott, Dr Will and Carol
characters in: 10 Main Street
author: 5 Lewis

Kentucky
abbreviation: 2 KY
nickname: 9 Bluegrass 11 Corncracker
capital: 9 Frankfort
largest city: 10 Louisville
others: 5 Berea 6 Corbin, Hazard 7 Ashland, Glasgow, Newport, Paducah, Shively 8 Danville 9 Covington, Henderson, Lexington, Owensboro 12 Bowling Green, Hopkinsville, Madisonville
college: 5 Berea 6 Centre 7 Ashbury, Brescia 8 Ursuline 12 Transylvania
explorer: 11 Daniel Boone
feature: 9 Obelisk
  birthplace: 14 Abraham Lincoln
  fort: 4 Knox
  national park: 11 Mammoth Cave
  race: 13 Kentucky Derby

racetrack: **14** Churchill Downs
trail: **10** Wilderness
tribe: **7** Shawnee **8** Cherokee, Iroquois
people: **11** corncracker, John M Harlan **13** Louis Brandeis **16** Frederick M Vinson, Robert Penn Warren
lake: **8** Kentucky **10** Cumberland
land rank: **13** thirty-seventh
mountain: **4** Pine **10** Cumberland
  highest point: **5** Black **8** Big Black
physical feature:
  basin: **9** Bluegrass
  cave: **7** Mammoth
  gap: **10** Cumberland
  plain: **7** Coastal
  plateau: **10** Cumberland
president: **14** Abraham Lincoln
  Confederate president: **14** Jefferson Davis
river: **3** Dix **4** Ohio, Salt **5** Green **6** Barren **7** Licking **8** Big Sandy, Kentucky **9** Tennessee **10** Cumberland **11** Mississippi
state admission: **9** fifteenth
state bird: **8** cardinal
state flower: **9** goldenrod
state motto: **26** United We Stand Divided We Fall
state song: **17** My Old Kentucky Home
state tree: **10** coffee tree **11** tulip poplar **12** yellow poplar

Kenya
capital/largest city: **7** Nairobi
others: **5** Nyeri, Thika, Wajir **6** Kisumu, Kitale, Lodwar, Moyale, Nakuru, Webuye **7** Eldoret, Kericho, Malindi, Mandera, Mombasa, Nanyuki **9** Lokitaung
measure: **4** wari
monetary unit: **4** cent **5** pound **8** shilling
island: **5** Manda, Patta
lake: **6** Magadi, Nakuru, Natron, Rudolf **7** Turkana **8** Naivasha, Victoria
mountain: **5** Elgon, Kulai, Nyira, Nyiru **6** Matian **7** Logonot **8** Aberdare
highest point: **5** Kenya **6** Kinyaa **9** Kirinyaga
river: **3** Lak **4** Athi, Dawa, Kuja, Tana **5** Nzoia **6** Galana **8** Turkwell
sea: **6** Indian
physical feature:
  bay: **7** Formosa
  desert: **6** Chalbi
  escarpment: **3** Mau
  gulf: **9** Kavirondo
  highlands: **5** Kenya, Kisii, Luyla **7** Kericho
  plain: **4** Kano
  plateau: **5** Nandi, Yatta **6** Elgeyo
  valley: **9** Great Rift
people: **3** Luo **4** Arab, Meru **5** Bantu, Elgey, Galla, Kamba, Kisii, Luhya, Masai, Nandi, Tugen **6** Kikuyu, Ogaden, Somali **7** Baluhya, Hamitic, Hilotic, Kipsigi, Swahili, Turkana **8**

Kalenjin, Marakwet
  god: **4** Ngai
  leader: **5** Mboya **12** Jomo Kenyatta **13** Daniel Arap Moi
language: **3** Luo **5** Bantu, Luhya, Masai **6** Kikuyu **7** English, Swahili **8** Guyerati **10** Hindustani
religion: **5** Islam **7** animism **8** Anglican **13** Roman Catholic
place:
  archeological excavation: **11** Gamble's Cave
  mosque: **5** Khoja
  museum: **9** Fort Jesus
  national park/wildlife preserve: **4** Meru **5** Nyeri, Tsavo **6** Arusha **7** Manyara, Nairobi, Samburu **8** Aberdare, Amboseli **10** Lake Nakuru, Mount Kenya, Rift Valley
  ruins: **4** Gedi
feature:
  garment: **5** kanga **7** kitenge
  round house: **6** shamba
  secret organization: **6** Mau Mau
  tree: **6** ayieke, baobab
food:
  fish: **7** tilapia
  wine: **5** tembo

Kepler, Johannes
nationality: **6** German
invented: **14** convex eyepiece **21** astronomical telescope
formulated:
  three laws of planetary motion (Kepler's Laws): **10** law of areas **11** harmonic law **24** elliptical orbit of planets
author of: **14** Astronomia nova, Harmonice mundi **16** Rudolphine Tables **23** Mysterium cosmographicum **30** Epitome astronomiae Copernicanae

kerchief 5 cloth, scarf **7** muffler **8** babushka, bandanna, kaffiyah, neckwear **9** headpiece, neckcloth **11** neckerchief **12** handkerchief

Keres
origin: **5** Greek
spirits of: **4** evil **5** death **6** old age **7** disease

Keres-Siouan
language branch: **5** Keres **7** Caddoan **9** Iroquoian **11** Siouan-Yuchi

kernel 3 nub, nut, pip, pit **4** core, germ, gist, pith, seed **5** grain, stone **6** center, marrow **7** nucleus **12** quintessence

Kerouac, Jack
author of: **6** Big Sur **9** On the Road **13** The Dharma Bums **16** Lonesome Traveler

Kerr, Deborah
real name: **22** Deborah Jane Kerr-Trimmer
born: **8** Scotland **11** Helensburgh
roles: **11** Edward My Son, The King and I **12** The Hucksters **13** The Sundowners **14** Separate Tables, The

Chalk Garden **18** From Here to Eternity **19** The Night of the Iguana **20** Heaven Knows Mr Allison

Kesey, Ken
author of: **10** Sailor Song **21** Sometimes a Great Notion **25** One Flew Over the Cuckoo's Nest
group: **15** Merry Pranksters

Ketcham, Hank
creator/artist of: **15** Dennis the Menace

kettle 3 pan, pot, tub, vat **6** boiler, teapot, tureen **8** cauldron, crucible, saucepan

Ketubim 8 writings **11** Hagiographa

Keturah
husband: **7** Abraham

kewpie 4 doll
originator: **9** Rose O'Neil **13** carnival prize

key 3 cue, fit **4** clue, gear, mode, suit **5** adapt, light, point, scale **6** adjust, answer, direct, opener **7** address, finding, meaning, pointer **8** indicant, solution, tonality **9** indicator **10** exposition, indication, resolution **11** elucidation, explanation, explication, translation **14** interpretation

Key, Ted
creator/artist of: **5** Hazel

keyboard instrument 5 organ, piano **6** spinet **8** psaltery, virginal **9** harmonium **10** clavichord, pianoforte **11** harpsichord

keyed up 5 tense **7** excited, nervous **8** volatile **9** emotional, explosive

key element 9 essential, vital part **18** primary constituent **20** indispensable element

Key Largo
director: **10** John Huston
based on story by: **15** Maxwell Anderson
cast: **12** Claire Trevor, Lauren Bacall **14** Humphrey Bogart **15** Edward G Robinson, Lionel Barrymore
Oscar for: **17** supporting actress (Trevor)

Keynes, John Maynard
author of: **44** The General Theory of Employment Interest and Money

keynote 3 nub **4** core, gist, pith **5** heart, theme **6** marrow **7** essence, nucleus, pattern **8** main idea, quiddity **9** substance **11** nitty-gritty, salient idea **12** central point

keystone 4 base, crux, root **5** basis **8** gravamen, linchpin **9** principle **10** foundation, mainspring

Keystone State
nickname of: **12** Pennsylvania

KGB 4 USSR **14** security police **18** intelligence agency

Khachaturian, Aram Ilich
born: **6** Tiflis **7** (Soviet) Georgia

composer of: 6 Gayane **9** Spartacus **12** Song of Stalin

khaki 5 cloth **6** fabric **7** uniform **9** olive-drab **14** yellowish-brown

khan, kahn 3 inn **4** lord **5** chief, ruler **6** prince **7** emperor **9** chieftain, sovereign **11** caravansary
famous: 3 Aga, Ali **4** Yuan **6** Kublai **7** Genghis **8** Ghenghis

Khartoum
capital of: 5 Sudan

Khayyam, Omar
born: 6 Persia
famous as: 4 poet **9** statesman **13** mathematician
name means: 9 tentmaker
author of: 11 The Rubaiyat

Khoisan
language spoken by: 3 San **7** Bushmen **9** Khoikhoin **10** Hottentots
includes: 5 Hatsa **7** Sandawe
distinguishing sound: 5 click

Khomeini, Ruholla
title: 9 ayatollah
ruled: 4 Iran

Khruschev, Nikita
premier of: 4 USSR
followed: 8 Bulganin
preceded: 7 Kosygin

Khyber Pass
between: 8 Pakistan and **11** Afghanistan
range: 9 Hindu Kush

kibbutz 10 collective **11** Israeli Farm

kibitzer 3 pry **5** prier, snoop **6** butt-in **7** advisor, meddler, snooper, watcher **8** busybody, onlooker **9** buttinsky

kick 3 fun, hit, out, pep, vim **4** beef, boot, dash, fret, fume, fuss, life, punt, snap, tang, zest **5** eject, force, gripe, growl, power, punch, verve, vigor **6** flavor, grouch, grouse, object, recoil, remove, return, strike, stroke, thrill **7** boot out, cast out, grumble, fly back, protest, rebound, sparkle, turn out **8** backlash, complain, jump back, piquancy, pleasure, pungency, reaction, throw out, vitality **9** amusement, animation, complaint, enjoyment, find fault, grievance, intensity, make a fuss, objection **10** excitement, spring back **11** give the gate, remonstrate, send packing, show the door **12** protestation **13** gratification, remonstration

Kickapoo
language family: 9 Algonkian **10** Algonquian
location: 5 Texas **6** Kansas, Mexico **9** Chihuahua, Wisconsin
related to: 3 Fox, Sac **4** Sauk

kickback 3 cut **5** bribe, graft, share **6** boodle, payoff, payola **9** hush money **10** commission, percentage, protection, recompense **12** compensation, remuneration **15** protection money

kick downstairs 4 bust **6** demote **7** degrade

kickoff 5 start **7** opening **9** beginning, inception, launching **12** inauguration

kick out 4 oust **5** eject, evict, expel **8** throw out **9** discharge

kicks 3 fun **7** thrills **8** pleasure **10** excitement **11** stimulation

kick upstairs 5 boost **7** advance, elevate, promote

kid 3 rag, rib, tot **4** baby, fool, gull, jest, joke, josh, mock, ride, tyke **5** bluff, child, cozen, harry, put on, tease, trick, youth **6** delude, infant, moppet, plague, shaver, squirt **7** beguile, deceive, laugh at, mislead **8** goat hide, goatskin, hoodwink, juvenile, ridicule, teenager, yearling **9** bamboozle, billy goat, little one, make fun of, nanny goat, offspring, young goat, youngster **10** adolescent **11** goat leather, young person **12** little shaver

Kid, The
nickname of: 11 Ted Williams **13** William Bonney (Billy)

kid around 5 clown, cut up **10** fool around, play around **11** clown around

Kidd, William 13 pirate captain
born: 8 Scotland
end: 6 hanged

Kidder, Margot
born: 6 Canada **11** Yellow Knife
roles: 7 Sisters **8** Lois Lane, Superman **11** The Last Sign, Tribulation **12** Silent Cradle **14** Some Kind of Hero **19** The Amityville Horror

Kiddush 6 prayer **8** blessing **14** sanctification

Kidman, Nicole
born: 6 Hawaii **8** Honolulu
nationality: 10 Australian
spouse: 9 Tom Cruise
children: 12 Connor Antony, Isabella Jane
roles: 8 The Hours, To Die For **9** Bewitched **11** Moulin Rouge **12** Cold Mountain, Eyes Wide Shut **13** Batman Forever, Days of Thunder **14** The Interpreter **18** The Portrait of a Lady

kidnap 5 seize, steal **6** abduct, hijack, snatch **7** bear off, capture, impress, skyjack **8** bear away, carry off, shanghai **10** run off with **11** make off with **13** hold for ransom

Kidnapped
author: 20 Robert Louis Stevenson
character: 9 Alan Breck **10** Rankeillor **12** David Balfour **15** Ebenezer Balfour

Kigali
capital of: 6 Rwanda

Kiley, Richard
born: 9 Chicago IL
roles: 7 Redhead **13** Man of La Mancha **16** Advise and Consent

Kilimanjaro, Mount
in: 6 Africa **8** Tanzania
feature: 15 highest in Africa
see also **9** Hemingway

Kilkenny Cats
origin: 5 Irish
form: 4 cats
number: 3 two
left after fight: 5 tails

kill 4 beat, do in, halt, hang, ruin, slay, stay **5** break, check, drown, erase, lynch, quell, shoot, waste **6** behead, defeat, murder, poison, rub out, stifle **7** bump off, butcher, cut down, destroy, execute, garrote, silence, smother, squelch, wipe out **8** blow away, dispatch, get rid of, knock off, massacre, strangle, string up **9** dismember, finish off, shoot down, slaughter, suffocate **10** asphyxiate, decapitate, disembowel, extinguish, guillotine, put a stop to, put an end to, put to death **11** assassinate, burn to death, electrocute, exterminate **13** mortally wound

killer 6 hit man, slayer **7** butcher **8** assassin, murderer **11** executioner **12** exterminator

Killers, The
director: 13 Robert Siodmak
based on story by: 15 Ernest Hemingway
cast: 10 Ava Gardner **12** Edmond O'Brien **13** Burt Lancaster

killer whale 4 orca **7** grampus **11** Orcinus orca

killing 4 coup **5** fatal **6** big hit, deadly, lethal, mortal, murder **7** bonanza, cleanup, deathly, hanging, slaying, success, suicide **8** butchery, fatality, homicide, lynching, massacre, regicide, shooting, smash hit, stabbing, windfall **9** bloodshed, execution, garroting, martyrdom, matricide, murderous, patricide, poisoning, slaughter, uxoricide **10** cleaning up, decimation, fratricide, immolation, impalement, sororicide, strangling **11** crucifixion, devastating, elimination, infanticide **12** annihilation, death-dealing, decapitation, excruciating, guillotining, manslaughter, master stroke, stroke of luck, violent death **13** electrocution, extermination, strangulation **17** capital punishment

Killing Fields
director: 11 Roland Joffe
based on article by: 15 Sydney Schanberg (The Death and Life of Dith Pran)
cast: 10 Haing S Ngor **12** Sam Waterston
setting: 8 Cambodia
Oscar for: 15 supporting actor (Ngor)

Killing Time
author: 12 Thomas Berger

killjoy 6 grouch **8** grumbler, sourball,

sourpuss 9 Cassandra, gloomy Gus, worrywart **10** complainer, malcontent, spoilsport, wet blanket **11** crapehanger, party-pooper

kill time 4 idle **6** dawdle **9** waste time **10** fool around

Kilmer, Joyce
author of: **5** Trees

kiln 3 ost **4** bake, burn, fire, oast, oven **5** drier, glaze, stove, tiler **7** furnace **8** calciner, limekiln **9** oasthouse

kiloliter
abbreviation: **2** kL

kilometer
abbreviation: **2** km

Kim
author: **14** Rudyard Kipling
character: **9** Mahbub Ali **11** Tibetan Lama **12** Kimball O'Hara **16** Colonel Creighton **22** Hurree Chunder Mookerjee

kimono 4 gown, robe
traditional costume of: **5** Japan
sash: **3** obi
ornament: **7** netsuke

kin 4 akin, clan, kith, race **5** folks, tribe **6** family, people **7** kinfolk, kinsmen, related **8** clansmen, kinfolks **9** next of kin, relations, relatives, tribesmen **10** kith and kin **11** connections, consanguine, distaff side, spindle side **13** flesh and blood **14** kissing cousins

kind 3 ilk **4** cast, make, mold, sort, type **5** brand, breed, caste, civil, class, genre, genus, style **6** benign, gentle, kidney, kindly, nature, polite, strain, tender **7** amiable, cordial, variety **8** amicable, friendly, generous, gracious, merciful, obliging **9** courteous **10** bighearted, charitable, neighborly, thoughtful **11** considerate, description, designation, good-hearted, goodhumored, good-natured, softhearted, sympathetic, warmhearted, wellmeaning **12** affectionate, welldisposed **13** accommodating, compassionate, tenderhearted, understanding
French: **6** gentil

kindhearted 4 good, warm **6** benign, gentle, humane, kindly, loving **7** helpful **8** amicable, generous, gracious, merciful **10** altruistic, charitable, thoughtful **11** considerate, goodhearted, good-natured, softhearted, sympathetic, warmhearted, wellmeaning **12** affectionate, humanitarian **13** accommodating, compassionate, philanthropic, tenderhearted, understanding

kindheartedness 5 mercy **8** altruism, goodness, goodwill, humanity, sympathy **10** compassion, humaneness, tenderness **11** benefaction, benevolence, magnanimity **12** graciousness, philanthropy **13** consideration, understanding, unselfishness **14** charitableness **15** humanitarianism

kindle 4 fire, goad, prod, stir, urge, whet **5** awake, light, rouse, waken **6** arouse, excite, foment, ignite, incite, induce, stir up **7** agitate, animate, inflame, inspire, provoke, quicken, sharpen **8** enkindle **9** call forth, intensify, set fire to, set on fire, stimulate **10** invigorate

kindling 4 fuel **5** brush, paper, twigs **6** firing, tinder **7** burning, flaming **8** firewood, igniting, ignition, lighting, shavings **9** brushwood **10** combustion, enkindling

kindly 4 good, warm **6** benign, gentle, gently, humane, tender, warmly **7** amiable, amiably, civilly, cordial, devoted, patient **8** amicable, amicably, benignly, friendly, generous, gracious, humanely, merciful, tenderly **9** cordially, courteous **10** benevolent, bighearted, charitable, charitably, generously, graciously, mercifully, neighborly **11** considerate, goodhumored, good-natured, magnanimous, softhearted, sympathetic, warmhearted, well-meaning **12** affectionate, benevolently, bigheartedly, humanitarian **13** compassionate, considerately, good-humoredly, goodnaturedly, magnanimously, philanthropic, softheartedly, tenderhearted, understanding, warmheartedly, wellmeaningly **14** affectionately, wellmanneredly **15** compassionately, sympathetically, tenderheartedly, understandingly **17** philanthropically

kindness 3 aid **4** gift, help **5** favor, grace, mercy **6** bounty **7** charity **8** good deed, good turn, goodness, goodwill, humanity, patience, sympathy **9** tolerance **10** act of grace, assistance, compassion, generosity, humaneness, kind office, toleration **11** benefaction, beneficence, benevolence, magnanimity **12** act of charity, graciousness, philanthropy **13** consideration, understanding, unselfishness **14** charitableness **15** humanitarianism

kindred 4 akin, like **5** alike **6** allied, united **7** related, similar **8** agreeing, familial, matching **9** accordant, analogous, congenial, simpatico **10** harmonious, resembling **11** consanguine, sympathetic **13** corresponding

kine 4 cows, oxen **6** cattle **9** livestock

kinfolk 3 kin **6** family **7** kinsmen **8** clansmen **9** relations, relatives **10** kith and kin

King, Stephen
author of: **2** It **4** Cujo **6** Carrie, Misery **8** The Stand **9** Christine, Salem's Lot **10** Bag of Bones, Black House, Night Shift, Rose Madder, The Shining **11** Firestarter, Pet Sematary, The Dead Zone **12** Dreamcatcher, Skeleton Crew, The Dark Tower **16** Different Seasons, The Tommyknockers

king 3 HRH **5** liege, ruler **7** monarch **8** suzerain **9** potentate, protector, sovereign **10** His Majesty **11** crowned head, royal person, the anointed **18** defender of the faith
Latin: **3** rex

king/emperor/dynasty
of Afghanistan: **8** Barakzai
of Albania: **3** Zog **9** Ahmet Zogu
of Algeria: **3** bey, dey **6** disawa **8** Jugurtha **9** bevlerbay, Masinissa
of Austria: **7** Charles, Francis **9** Ferdinand, Habsburgs **10** Franz Josef
of Bahrain: **9** al-Khalifa
of Belgium: **7** Leopold **8** Baudouin
of China: **3** Han, Sui **4** Chou, Ch'in, Ming, Sung, T'ang **5** Ch'ing, Shang **6** Manchu
of Crete: **5** Minos
of Denmark: **4** Hans, Knud **6** Canute **8** Frederik **9** Christian **10** Gorm the Old **15** Harold Bluetooth
of Egypt: **5** Khufu, Menes, Zoser **6** Farouk, Khafre, Ptulol, Ramses **7** Saladin **8** Horemheb, Menkaure **9** Akhenaten, Amenemhet, Amenhotep **10** Mentuhotep **11** Tutankhamen
of England: **3** Hal **4** Cnut, John, Lear **5** Henry, James **6** Alfred, Arthur, Canute, Edmund, Edward, Egbert, George, Harold **7** Charles, Richard, Stephen, William **9** Cymbeline **18** Richard Coeur de Lion **19** Richard the Lionheart **21** Richard the Lionhearted
of France: **5** Henri, Louis **6** Clovis, Philip **7** Charles **8** Napoleon **9** Hugh Capet **11** Charlemagne **21** Richard the Lionhearted **13** Louis Philippe **14** Henry of Navarre
of Germany: **6** Kaiser **7** Wilhelm **9** Frederick **10** Barbarossa
of Greece: **5** Creon **6** Atreus **7** Theseus **8** Menelaus **10** Agammemnon **11** Constantine
of India: **5** Akbar, Asoka, Babur, Gupta, Mogul, Timur **6** Maurya, Rajput **7** Humayun **8** Hyder Ali, Jahangir, Marathas **9** Aurangzeb, Shah Jahan **11** Tippu Sultan **14** Delhi Sultanate **18** Chandragupta Maurya
of Iran: **5** Abbas, Cyrus, Qajar **6** Darius, Xerxes **7** Arsacid, Pahlavi, Safavid **8** Parthian, Seleucid **9** Sassanian **10** Achaemenid **15** Shah Reza Pahlavi
of Iraq: **6** Faisal, Sargon **7** Hussein **9** Hammurabi **13** Harun al-Rashid **14** Nebuchadnezzar
of Ireland: **9** Brian Boru
of Italy/Rome: **4** Nero, Otho **5** Galba, Nerva, Titus **6** Trajan **7** Hadrian **8** Caligula, Claudius, Commodus, Domitian, Octavian, Tiberius **9** Caracalla, Vespasian, Vitellius **10** Diocletian **11** Constantine **13** Antoninus Dius **14** Caesar Augustus, Marcus Aurelius, Victor Emmanuel

of Japan: 5 Jimmu, Jingo, Meiji, Taira **6** Yamato **7** Akihito, Izanagi **8** Ashikaga, Fujiwara, Hirohito, Kamakura, Minamoto, Tokugawa
of Java: 7 Mataram **9** Majapahit, Srivijaya
of Jordan: 5 Talal **6** Faisal **7** Hussein **8** Abdullah, Selucidas **10** Ibn Hussein, Nabataeans
of Korea: 2 Yi **4** Choe **5** Ki-tse, Koryo **6** Chi-tsi, Chi-tzu, Tangun
of Kuwait: 5 Ahmad, Sabah, Salem **7** Mubarak **12** Jaber al-Ahmed, Sabah al-Salim **15** Abdullah al-Salim
of Liechtenstein: 7 Florian **13** Francis Joseph **16** von Liechtenstein
of Luxembourg: 8 Sigefroi, Wencelas **12** Jean l'Aveugle **21** House of Nassau-Weilburg
of Madagascar: 6 Merina
of Malawi: 6 Maravi
of Maldives: 4 Didi
of Mexico: 10 Maximilian
of Monaco: 5 Louis **6** Albert, Honore **7** Antoine, Charles, Rainier **9** Florestan
of Mongolia: 8 Jahangir, Jehangir **10** Kublai Khan, Tsendenbal **11** Genghis Khan
of Morocco: 6 Hassan **7** Alawite, Almohad **8** Mohammed **9** Almoravid
of Nepal: 8 Mahendra **9** Tribhuwan **10** Birenda Bir **12** Bikram Sha Dev **17** Prithwi Narayan Sha
of the Netherlands: 7 Beatrix, Juliana, William **10** Wilhelmina
of Nigeria: 3 Ife, Nok, Oyo **5** Benin **6** Fulani **10** Kanem-Borno
of Norway: 4 Olaf, Olav **5** Olave, Oscar **6** Haakon, Harold, Magnus, Sverre
of Peru: 7 Huascar **9** Atahualpa **10** Manco Capac
of Poland: 5 Piast **7** Casimir, Jagello **8** Augustus
of Portugal: 6 Manuel, Philip, Sancho **7** Alfonso **9** Ferdinand, Sebastian **23** Prince Henry the Navigator
of Qatar: 18 Ahmad bin Ali al-Thani **22** Khalifa bin Hamad al-Thani
of Rumania: 5 Carol **7** Michael
of Russia: 4 Ivan, Paul **5** Peter **6** Alexis **7** Michael **8** Nicholas **9** Alexander **12** Boris Godunov
of Sardinia: 12 Charles Felix **13** Charles Albert **14** Victor Emmanuel
of Saudi Arabia: 4 Fahd, Saud **6** Faisal, Khalid **7** Ibn Saud **9** Abdul Aziz
of Scotland: 5 David, James **6** Duncan **7** Kenneth, Macbeth, Malcolm, Stuarts, William **9** Alexander **14** Robert the Bruce **19** Bonnie Prince Charlie
of Sicily: 4 Eryx **5** Bomba, Henry, Peter, Roger **7** Charles, Cocalus, Leontes **9** Ferdinand, Frederick
of Spain: 6 Pelayo, Philip, Ramiro, Sancho, Witiza **7** Alfonso, Almohad,

Charles, Umayyad **8** al-Mansur, Reccared, Roderick **9** Almoravid, Ferdinand, Leovigild **10** Juan Carlos **11** Abd al-Rahman, Reccosvinth
of Swaziland: 3 Kbe **5** Nyama **6** Mswati, Sozisa **7** Sobhuza
of Sweden: 4 Vosa, Wasa **5** Oscar **6** Gustav **8** Gustavus **10** Carl Gustav **12** Gustav Adolph **13** Charles Gustav **22** Jean Baptiste Bernadotte
of Syria: 5 Rezin **6** Faisal, Hazael **8** Benhadad **9** Antiochus
of Thailand: 4 Rama **7** Chakkri, Mongkut **10** Chao Phraya **12** Prahjadhipok **13** Chulalongkorn **17** Bhumibol Adulyadej
of Tongo: 11 George Tupou **14** Taufaahau Tupou
of Tunisia: 6 Hafsid **7** Fatimid **8** Aghlabid, Almohade **10** Husseinite
of Turkey: 8 Mausolus
of Uganda: 6 Mutesa, Mwanga **8** Kabarega
of Upper Volta: 4 Naba **5** Mogho
of Zimbabwe: 9 Lobengula, Mzilikaze
King, Frank
    creator/artist of: 13 Gasoline Alley
King, Martin Luther
    born: 7 Atlanta, Georgia
    died: 7 Memphis **9** Tennessee
    wife: 12 Coretta Scott
    career: 8 minister (Southern Baptist), activist
    notable moments: 17 "I Have A Dream" speech **26** march from Selma to Montgomery
    award: 5 Nobel, Peace
King and I, The
    director: 10 Walter Lang
    cast: 10 Rita Moreno, Yul Brynner **11** Deborah Kerr **12** Martin Benson
    score: 21 Rodgers and Hammerstein
    from the book: 20 Anna and the King of Siam
    song: 12 Shall We Dance? **16** Getting to Know You, Hello Young Lovers **18** Something Wonderful
King Arthur
    opera by: 7 Purcell
    character: 6 Merlin, Osmond, Oswald **8** Emmeline, Philadel **14** Duke of Cornwall
kingdom 4 land **5** duchy, field, realm, state **6** domain, empire, nation, sphere **7** country, dukedom **8** dominion, monarchy **9** territory **12** principality
King John
    author: 18 William Shakespeare
    character: 6 Elinor **9** Constance **11** Prince Henry **13** Hubert de Burgh **15** Blanch of Castile, Lewis the Dauphin **16** Arthur of Bretagne Cardinal Pandulph, William Longsword, William Mareshall **19** Philip Faulconbridge, Robert Faulconbridge
King Kong

director:
    1933: 13 Merian C Cooper **17** Ernest B Schoedsack
    1976: 14 John Guillermin
    cast:
    1933: 7 Fay Wray **10** Bruce Cabot **11** James Flavin **12** Noble Johnson **15** Robert Armstrong
    1976: 11 Jeff Bridges **12** Jessica Lange, John Randolph **13** Charles Grodin
    setting (final scene): 19 Empire State Building
    score: 10 Max Steiner
King Lear
    author: 18 William Shakespeare
    character: 5 Edgar, Regan **6** Edmund **7** Goneril **8** Cordelia **10** Earl of Kent **12** Duke of Albany, King of France **14** Duke of Cornwall **16** Earl of Gloucester
kingly 5 grand, noble, regal, royal **6** august, lordly, mighty **7** queenly, stately **8** absolute, despotic, glorious, kinglike, imperial, majestic, princely, splendid **9** imperious, monarchal, patrician, sovereign **10** autocratic, commanding, tyrannical **11** magnificent **12** awe-inspiring
king of gods 4 Amen, Amon, Finn, Zeus **5** Ammon, Enlil, Fionn, Wotan **6** Marduk **7** Jupiter **8** Merodach **12** Baal Merodach **13** Fionn MacCumal
King of Hearts
    character in: 28 Alice's Adventures in Wonderland
    author: 7 Carroll
King of Queens, The
    network: 3 CBS
    cast: 10 Kevin James (Doug Heffernan), Leah Remini (Carrie Spooner Heffernan) **12** Jerry Stiller (Arthur Spooner), Patton Oswalt (Spence Olchin) **13** Gary Valentine (Danny Heffernan) **14** Victor Williams (Deacon Palmer)
King of Righteousness 11 Melchizedek
Kingsley, Ben
    real name: 13 Krishna Bhanji
    roles: 5 Bugsy **6** Gandhi (Oscar) **8** Betrayal **11** Oliver Twist **14** Schindler's List **17** Rules of Engagement
    award: 10 Knighthood
Kingsley, Charles
    author of: 7 Hypatia **10** Alton Locke **11** Westward Ho! **14** The Water Babies **15** Hereward the Wake
King Solomon's Mines
    author: 13 H Rider Haggard
    character: 5 Twala **6** Gagool, Umbopa **14** Sir Henry Curtis **15** Allan Quatermain, Captain John Good
King's Row
    author: 14 Henry Bellamann
    director: 7 Sam Wood

cast: 10 Betty Field **11** Ann Sheridan, Claude Rains **12** Ronald Reagan **13** Charles Coburn **14** Judith Anderson, Robert Cummings
score: 21 Erich Wolfgard Korngold
character: 11 Drake McHugh, Elise Sandor **13** Randy Monaghan **14** Cassandra Tower, Parris Mitchell

Kingston
capital of: 7 Jamaica

kink 4 coil, flaw, knot, pang **5** cramp, crick, crimp, frizz, gnarl, hitch, quirk, snarl, spasm, twist **6** defect, foible, glitch, oddity, tangle, twinge, vagary **7** crinkle, frizzle **8** crotchet **9** queerness, stiffness, weirdness **10** difficulty **11** peculiarity, singularity **12** charley horse, complication, eccentricity, freakishness, idiosyncrasy, imperfection

kinky 3 odd **4** sick, wiry **5** kooky, queer **6** frizzy, matted, quirky, twisty **7** bizarre, deviant, frizzly, knotted, strange, tangled, twisted, unusual **8** aberrant, abnormal, crinkled, freakish, frizzled, peculiar, perverse **9** eccentric, unnatural **10** unorthodox **13** idiosyncratic

Kinshasa
capital of: 5 Congo

kinsman 3 sib, son **4** aunt, heir **5** child, uncle **6** cousin, father, mother, parent, sister **7** brother **8** daughter, landsman, relation, relative **9** offspring **10** countryman **11** grandfather, grandmother **13** blood relation, blood relative

Kiowa
language family: 6 Tanoan
location: 6 Plains **7** Montana **8** Colorado, Oklahoma
allied with: 7 Arapaho **8** Comanche **11** Kiowa Apache
deity: 5 Taime

Kiowa Apache
language family: 12 Shapwailutan
location: 6 Plains

Kipling, Rudyard
author of: 3 Kim **8** Gunga Din, Mandalay **11** Danny Deaver **12** The Seven Seas **13** Just So Stories, The Jungle Book **18** Barrack-Room Ballads, Captains Courageous

Kirchhoff, Gustav Robert
field: 7 physics
nationality: 6 German
discovered: 6 cesium **8** rubidium
developed: 12 spectroscope
named for him: 19 electric circuit laws

Kirchner, Ernst Ludwig
born: 7 Germany **13** Aschaffenburg
artwork: 11 Street Scene **12** Street Berlin **13** Moonlit Winter **21** Self-portrait with Model

Kirghiz *see* **10** Kyrgyzstan

Kiribati

other name: 14 Gilbert Islands
capital/largest city: 6 Tarawa
others: 5 Betio **7** Bairiki, Bonriki **9** Bikenibeu
school: 12 South Pacific
monetary unit: 4 cent **6** dollar
island: 5 Flint, Ocean **6** Banaba, Canton, Malden, Tarawa **7** Abemama, Fanning, Gilbert, Marakei, Nonouti, Phoenix, Vostock **8** Caroline, Starbuck **9** Christmas, Enderbury, Tabiteuea **10** Butaritari, Equatorial, Washington **12** Northern Line, Southern Line
sea: 7 Pacific
people: 8 Banabans **10** Polynesian **11** Micronesian
language: 6 Samoan **7** English **10** Gilbertese
religion: 5 Baha'i **8** Anglican **9** Methodist **11** Church of God **13** Roman Catholic **19** Seventh Day Adventist

kirsch, kirschwasser
type: 6 brandy **7** liqueur
origin: 6 France **7** Germany **11** Switzerland
flavor: 6 cherry
with gin: 7 Florida **10** Lady Finger
with vodka: 12 Volga Boatman

kismet 3 end, lot **4** doom, fate **5** karma, moira **7** destiny, fortune, portion **8** God's will **10** Providence **11** will of Allah **12** circumstance **13** inevitability **14** predestination

kiss 4 buss, neck **6** smooch, salute **8** osculate

Kissinger, Henry
born: 6 Fuerth **7** Germany
career: 9 statesman **11** businessman **16** Secretary of State
author: 9 Diplomacy **15** Years of Upheaval **18** The White House Years
award: 10 Nobel Prize

kit 3 rig **4** gear **5** tools **6** outfit, tackle, things **7** devices **8** supplies, utensils **9** equipment, trappings **10** implements, provisions **11** furnishings, impediments, instruments, necessaries **13** accoutrements, paraphernalia

Kitasato, Shibasaburo
field: 12 bacteriology
nationality: 8 Japanese
isolated: 7 anthrax, tetanus **9** dysentery **13** bubonic plague
developed: 19 diphtheria antitoxin

kitchen 6 bakery, cocina, galley **7** cuisine **8** cookroom, scullery **9** bakehouse, cookhouse

Kitchener, Horatio Herbert
also: 18 first Earl Kitchener
nationality: 7 British
served in: 7 Boer War **15** South African War
battle: 8 Khartoum, Omdurman
governor of: 8 the Sudan
commander in chief of: 5 India **12**

Egyptian army
consul general of: 5 Egypt

kitel 20 Jewish ceremonial robe
color: 5 white

Kitely
character in: 19 Every Man in His Humour
author: 6 Jonson

kittenish 3 coy **7** playful **10** coquettish

Klamath
language family: 8 Penutian
location: 6 Oregon **10** California
related to: 5 Modoc **6** Cayuse, Molala

Klee, Paul
born: 11 Switzerland **14** Munchenbuchsee
artwork: 9 Locksmith **11** Ad Parnassum **18** Barbarian Sacrifice, Demon above the Ships **20** The Twittering Machine **22** Revolution of the Viaduct **23** Dance-Play of the Red Skirts **24** Dance Monster to my Soft Song **35** The Vocal Fabric of the Singer Rosa Silber

Kleist, Heinrich von
author of: 11 Penthesilea **14** The Marquise of O **16** The Broken Pitcher **18** The Prince of Homburg

Kline, Kevin
roles: 4 Dave **8** De-Lovely, In and Out **11** The Big Chill **13** Sophie's Choice **15** The Emperor's Club **16** A Fish Called Wanda **17** Pirates of Penzance

Klugman, Jack
born: 14 Philadelphia PA
roles: 6 Quincy **12** Oscar Madison, The Odd Couple

klutz 5 dummy **9** blockhead **11** satchelfoot **13** fumblefingers

klutzy 4 dumb **6** clumsy, stupid **7** awkward **9** graceless

knack 4 bent, gift, turn **5** flair, forte, skill **6** genius, talent **7** ability, faculty, finesse **8** aptitude, capacity, facility **9** dexterity, expertise, ingenuity, quickness, readiness **10** adroitness, capability, cleverness, competence, efficiency, propensity **11** inclination, proficiency **13** dexterousness

knave 3 cad, cur, dog, rat **4** jack (cards) **5** phony, rogue, scamp **6** con man, rascal, rotter, varlet, wretch **7** bounder, culprit **8** scalawag, swindler **9** charlatan, con artist, reprobate, scoundrel **10** blackguard **11** rapscallion **14** good for nothing

knee breeches 8 breeches, jodhpurs, knickers **9** plus fours **14** knickerbockers

kneel 3 bow **6** curtsy, kowtow, salaam **7** bow down **9** genuflect **13** make obeisance **16** prostrate oneself

knell 4 peal, ring, toll **5** chime, sound **6** stroke **7** pealing, ringing, tolling

Knickerbocker Holiday
  author: **15** Maxwell Anderson

knickknack, nicknack 3 toy **6** bauble, gewgaw, trifle **7** bibelot, trinket **8** frippery, gimcrack **9** bagatelle, bric-a-brac, plaything **11** thingamajig

knife 3 cut **4** dirk, shiv, stab **5** blade, slash, wound **6** cutter, pierce **7** cut down, cutlery **8** cut apart, lacerate, mutilate
  type: **3** pen **4** jack **5** bowie, bread, putty, table **6** dagger, paring, pocket **7** butcher, carving, hunting, machete, palette, pruning, scalpel **8** skinning, stiletto, surgical **11** switchblade

knight 4 hero **7** fighter, gallant, paladin, soldier, Templar, warrior **8** cavalier, champion, defender, guardian, horseman, Lancelot **9** gentleman, man-at-arms, protecter, protector **10** equestrian, vindicator

Knight
  character in: **18** The Canterbury Tales
  author: **7** Chaucer

Knightley, George
  character in: **4** Emma
  author: **6** Austen

Knights, The
  author: **12** Aristophanes
  character: **5** Demus **6** Nicias **11** Demosthenes **20** Cleon the Paphlagonian

knit 3 tat **4** ally, bind, draw, join, knot, link **5** braid, plait, twist, unify, unite, weave **6** attach, crease, fasten, furrow, stitch **7** connect, crochet, wrinkle **10** intertwine, interweave **12** draw together

knob 3 nub **4** bulb, bump, grip, hold, hump, knot, knur, lump, node, snag **5** bulge, gnarl, knurl, latch, lever, swell **6** handle, nubbin **8** handhold, swelling, tubercle **9** convexity **10** projection, prominence, protrusion **12** protuberance, protuberosity

knock 3 bat, hit, pat, rap, tap **4** bang, beat, belt, blow, bomb, bump, clip, cuff, dash, kick, lick, push, slam, slap, sock, swat, thud **5** abuse, cavil, clout, crack, crash, decry, pound, punch, smack, smash, smite, thump, whack **6** batter, carp at, defeat, hammer, jostle, murder, peck at, pummel, strike, stroke, thwack, wallop **7** censure, condemn, failure, setback **8** belittle, lambaste **9** criticism, criticize, deprecate, disparage, reprehend **12** condemnation, faultfinding, reprehension

knock down 4 deck, down, drop, fell **5** floor **7** flatten **8** bowl over, discount **9** take apart **11** disassemble

knock off balance 6 rattle **7** shake up **8** unsettle **9** take aback **11** disorganize

knockout 2 KO **4** doll **5** beaut, Venus **6** beauty, eyeful **7** stunner

knock out of shape 4 maul **5** crush **6** batter, beat up, mangle

knoll 4 hill, rise **5** mound

knot 3 bun **4** bump, frog, heap, hump, loop, lump, mass, pack, pile, star, tuft **5** braid, bunch, clump, group, hitch, knurl, plait, twist **6** bundle, circle **7** cat's-paw, chignon, cluster, epaulet, rosette **8** ornament **9** gathering **10** assemblage, collection, intertwist **13** interlacement
  type: **3** bow, top **4** flat, slip **5** slide **6** double, single, square **7** running **8** hangman's, overhand, shoulder, surgeon's **9** half-hitch **11** figure-eight, midshipman's

Knots Landing
  character: **9** Abby Ewing, Gary Ewing **10** Greg Sumner **11** Valene Ewing **12** Mac Mackenzie **14** Karen Mackenzie, Paige Forrester
  cast: **10** Donna Mills, Joan Van Ark **11** Julie Harris, Kevin Dobson, Michelle Lee **13** William Devane **14** Douglas Sheehan, Ted Shackelford **17** Nicolette Sheridan

knotty 4 hard **5** bumpy, rough, tough **6** coarse, flawed, knobby, knurly, rugged, snaggy, thorny, tricky, uneven **7** complex, gnarled, knurled, nodular **8** baffling, involved, puzzling, ticklish, unsmooth **9** blemished, difficult, intricate **10** perplexing **11** complicated, troublesome **12** rough-grained **13** coarse-grained, problematical

know 3 see **6** be sure, be wise, notice **7** be smart, discern, make out, realize **8** identify, perceive **9** apprehend, be assured, be aware of, be certain, be close to, get wise to, recognize **10** be informed, be positive, understand **11** be confident, be sagacious, be thick with, distinguish, feel certain, have down pat, have no doubt **12** discriminate, have down cold, have the ear of **13** be cognizant of, be intelligent, have knowledge, rub elbows with **14** be familiar with

knowable 9 thinkable **11** conceivable, discernible, perceivable **14** understandable

know for sure 9 be certain **10** be positive

know-how 3 art **4** bent, gift **5** craft, flair, knack, savvy, skill **6** talent **7** ability, mastery **8** aptitude, capacity, deftness **9** adeptness, expertise, knowledge, technique **10** adroitness, capability, competence, experience, expertness **11** proficiency **12** skillfulness **15** professionalism
  French: **11** savoir-faire

knowing 4 deep, wise **5** aware, canny, sharp, smart, sound **6** astute, brainy, bright, clever, shrewd **7** erudite, fraught, learned, sapient **8** academic, educated, eloquent, highbrow, literary,

profound, schooled, sensible **9** conscious, judicious, revealing, sagacious **10** discerning, expressive, meaningful, perceptive, percipient, scholastic, widely read **11** enlightened, intelligent, significant **12** intellectual, well-informed **13** comprehending, knowledgeable, perspicacious, philosophical, sophisticated, understanding

knowing how to live
  French: **11** savoir-vivre

knowing just what to do
  French: **11** savoir-faire

know-it-all 5 brash **13** overconfident

knowledge 3 ken, tip **4** data, hint, lore, news **5** sense **6** memory, notice, report, wisdom **7** inkling, mention, tidings **8** learning **9** awareness, education, erudition, schooling, statement **10** cognizance, intimation, perception **11** cultivation, declaration, familiarity, information, realization, recognition, revelation, scholarship **12** announcement, book learning, intelligence, notification **13** communication, comprehension, consciousness, enlightenment, pronouncement
  god of: **4** Odin **5** Othin

knowledgeable 3 hip **4** up on **8** at home in, versed in **12** familiar with, well-informed **14** acquainted with, conversant with
  French: **9** au courant

knowledge of the world
  French: **11** savoir-vivre

known 5 noted, plain **6** common, famous, patent **7** evident, obvious, popular **8** apparent, definite, distinct, familiar, manifest, palpable **9** notorious, prominent **10** celebrated, recognized **11** self-evident

know thyself
  Greek: **13** gnothi seauton

knuckle under 5 yield **6** give in, submit **7** bow down **9** surrender **10** capitulate

knurled 5 bumpy, lumpy **6** gnarly, knobby, knotty, knurly, nubbly, ridged **7** bulging, gnarled, knotted, nodular

koala
  family: **9** marsupial
  habitat: **9** Australia
  food: **10** eucalyptus
  resembles: **9** small bear
  kin of: **6** wombat

Koch, Robert
  field: **12** bacteriology
  nationality: **6** German
  isolated: **2** TB **12** tuberculosis
  awarded: **10** Nobel Prize

Kodaly, Zoltan
  born: **7** Hungary **9** Kecskemet
  composer of: **9** Hary Janos **11** Czinka Panna, Missa Brevis, Szekely Fono **14** Budavari Te Deum **15** Dances of Galanta **17** Dances of Marosszek,

Peacock Variations, Psalmus Hungaricus **28** The Spinning Room of the Szekelys

Koestler, Arthur
author of: **14** Darkness at Noon **15** The Sleepwalkers

Kohinoor, Koh-i-noor 7 diamond **6** (106) carats
from: **5** India
part of: **18** British Crown Jewels

kohoutek 5 comet
named for: **15** Czech astronomer

Kojak
character: **5** (Det) Rizzo **7** (Det) Stavros **9** (Lt) Theo Kojak **10** (Det) Saperstein **11** Frank McNeil **12** (Lt) Bobby Crocker
cast: **9** Dan Frazer **10** Vince Conti **11** Kevin Dobson, Mark Russell **12** Telly Savalas **13** George Savalas (Demosthenes)
trademark: **8** lollipop
phrase: **14** Who loves ya baby?

Kollwitz, Kathe
real name: **12** Kathe Schmidt
born: **10** Konigsberg **11** East Prussia
artwork: **3** War **5** Death, Pieta **11** Proletariat **13** Weavers' Revolt (Weaver's Rebellion) **14** Mother and Child, The Peasants' War **18** Death Seizing a Woman

Kol Nidre 4 vows **8** promises **22** Jewish liturgical prayer
recited on eve of: **9** Yom Kippur

Kong
nickname of: **11** Dave Kingman

Kon-Tiki
author: **13** Thor Heyerdahl
name of: **4** raft

kook 3 nut **5** crazy, flake, loony, wacko **6** cuckoo, weirdo **7** dingbat **8** crackpot **9** ding-a-ling, eccentric, fruitcake, harebrain, screwball **10** crackbrain

Koran 5 Islam, Quran **9** Word of God **10** Sacred book
revelations to: **8** Mohammed
division: **4** sura
dictated by: **7** Gabriel **9** archangel

Korea
other name: **6** Chosen **17** land of morning calm
capital:
North Korea: **9** Pyongyang
South Korea: **5** Seoul
largest city: **5** Seoul
others: **5** Masan, Mokpo, Pusan, Sinpo, Suwon, Taegu, Wonju **6** Chonju, Inchon, Kangso, Kunsan, Taejon, Wonsan **7** Hanyang, Hungnam, Kaesong, Kangson, Kwangju **8** Chongjin, Chunchon, Kimchaek
school: **5** Busan **6** Yonsei **7** Hanyang **8** Kim Chaek, Kyung Hee **9** Kim Il Sung
division:
ancient: **5** Silla **6** Chosen **7** Ko-

guryo, Paekche
monetary unit: **3** woh, won **4** chun, hwan, kwan
weight: **3** won
island: **4** Chin, Koje **5** Cheju, Sinmi **6** Anmyon, Huksan, Namhae **7** Tokchok **8** Quelpart **10** Paengnyong
mountain: **4** Wang **5** Chiri, Halla **6** Kwanmo, Sobaek **7** Diamond, Kyebang, Nangnim, Taebaek **8** Changpai, Hamgyong, Myohyang **9** Paektu-san **10** Kumgang-san
highest point: **6** Paektu **9** Paektu-san
river: **3** Han, Kin, Kum, Kun, Nam **4** Lobk, Yalu **5** Amnok, Imjin, Tumen **6** Namhan, Pukhan, Somjin, Soyang, Yesong **7** Naktong, Taedong **8** Changjin, Youngsan **9** Chongchon
sea: **5** Japan **6** Yellow **9** East China
physical feature:
bay: **5** Korea **6** Yongil **7** Kanghwa, Kyonggi **9** Tongjoson
cape: **4** Musu
point: **7** Changgi **8** Changsan
strait: **5** Korea
valley: **7** Naktong
people: **6** Korean
artist: **8** Chong Son **10** Kimtlong-do
dynasty: **2** Yi **4** Choe **5** Koryo
leader: **6** Sejong **8** Yi Sung-gy **9** Kim Il Sung, Kim Jong Il **11** Chun Doo Hwan, Syngman Rhee **12** Park Chung Hee
legendary leader: **5** Ki-tse **6** Chi-tse, Chi-tzu, Tangun
poet: **10** Hwang Chini
Unification Church Leader **12** Sun Myung Moon
language: **6** Korean
alphabet: **6** hangul
religion: **6** Taoism **7** animism **8** Buddhism **9** Chondogyo **12** Christianity, Confucianism
place:
palace: **8** Kyongbok
temple: **7** Haein-sa **17** Hall of Eternal Life
tomb: **14** Dancing Figures
feature:
clothing: **5** chima
game: **3** yut **5** akoan **6** ho-hpai **7** kol-ye-si **9** ryong-hpai, sang-ryouk **10** ke-pouk-hpai, sin-syo-tyen **12** tjak-ma-tchi-ki **15** kko-ri-pouk-tchi-ki
martial art: **9** tae-kwon-do
musical instrument: **6** chaing **7** kayagum, komungo
porcelain: **7** Celadon
porch: **4** maru
pottery: **8** pun-chong
food:
bean curd: **4** tubu
hot pickle: **6** kimchi
meat-filled dumpling: **5** mandu
noodle: **5** kuksu

Korman, Harvey
born: **9** Chicago IL

roles: **11** High Anxiety **13** Danny Kaye Show **14** Blazing Saddles **16** Carol Burnett Show

Kornberg, Arthur
field: **12** biochemistry
sythesized: **3** DNA, RNA **15** ribonucleic acid **20** deoxyribonucleic acid
awarded: **10** Nobel Prize

kosher 5 right **6** proper **7** ethical **8** fit to eat **10** aboveboard **12** on the up and up

Kosinski, Jerzy
author of: **5** Steps **7** Cockpit **9** Blind Date **10** Being There **11** Passion Play **12** The Devil Tree **14** The Painted Bird

Kowalski, Stanley
character in: **21** A Streetcar Named Desire
wife: **6** Stella
sister-in-law: **7** Blanche
author: **8** Williams

kowtow 4 bend, fawn **5** cower, stoop, toady **6** bow low, cringe, curtsy, grovel, salaam **7** truckle **8** bootlick, butter up, softsoap **9** genuflect **11** apple-polish **12** bow and scrape **16** prostrate oneself

kowtowing 7 fawning, servile **8** toadying **9** groveling **10** obsequious

Kraken
origin: **9** Norwegian
form: **7** monster
habitat: **3** sea
caused: **10** whirlpools

Kramer, Stanley
director of: **10** On the Beach **11** Ship of Fools **14** Inherit the Wind, The Defiant Ones **19** Judgment at Nuremberg

Kramer vs Kramer
director: **12** Robert Benton
based on novel by: **11** Avery Corman
cast: **10** Howard Duff **11** Justin Henry, Meryl Streep **13** Dustin Hoffman, Jane Alexander
Oscar for: **5** actor (Hoffman) **7** picture **8** director **10** screenplay **17** supporting actress (Streep)

Krantz, Judith
author of: **8** Scruples **13** Princess Daisy **16** I'll Take Manhattan, Mistral's Daughter

Krazy Kat
creator: **14** George Herriman
character:
cop: **12** Offissa B Pupp
mouse: **6** Ignatz
prop: **5** brick
place: **4** jail **14** Coconino County **24** Kelly's Exclusive Brick Yard

Krebs, Hans Adolf
field: **9** chemistry
nationality: **6** German
discovered: **15** citric acid cycle
awarded: **10** Nobel Prize

Kreisler, Fritz
born: **6** Vienna **7** Austria
composer of: **7** Allegro **10** Pr-
aeludium **15** Caprice Viennois **16**
Tambourin Chinois

Kreutzer, Rodolphe
born: **6** France **10** Versailles
composer of: **16** Etudes ou Caprices

Kreutzer Sonata, The
author: **10** Leo Tolstoy
character: **13** Mme Pozdnishef,
Trukhashevsky **16** Vasyla Pozdnishef

Krieg 3 war

Kriemhild
origin: **8** Germanic
mentioned in: **14** Nibelungenlied
brother: **7** Gunther
husband: **9** Siegfried
slew: **5** Hagan **7** Gunther
avenged: **6** murder **9** Siegfried
corresponds to: **6** Gudrun, Kudrun **7**
Guthrun

Kristin Lavransdatter
author: **12** Sigrid Undset

Kronos see **6** Cronus

Kropp, Albert
character in: **25** All Quiet on the
Western Front
author: **8** Remarque

krypton
chemical symbol: **2** Kr

Kuala Lumpur
capital of: **8** Malaysia

Kubla Khan
author: **15** Samuel Coleridge
city: **6** Xanadu
river: **4** Alph

Kubrick, Stanley
director of: **6** Lolita **9** Spartacus **11**
Barry Lyndon **12** Eyes Wide Shut,
Paths of Glory **13** Dr Strangelove (or
How I Learned to Stop Worrying and
Love the Bomb) **15** Full Metal Jacket
16 A Clockwork Orange **30** Two
Thousand and One A Space Odyssey

kudos 4 fame **5** award, glory, honor,
prize **6** esteem, praise, renown, repute
7 acclaim, plaudit **8** citation, prestige
9 celebrity, laudation **10** admiration,
decoration **12** commendation **14** cele-
bratedness

Kudrun see **6** Gudrun

Kukla, Fran & Ollie
hostess: **11** Fran Allison

puppet: **5** Kukla, Ollie (Oliver J
Dragon) **8** Mercedes **9** Cecil Bill **10**
Col Crackie **11** Beulah Witch **12**
Olivia Dragon **13** Delores Dragon **14**
Fletcher Rabbit **18** Mme Ophelia
Oglepuss

kummel
origin: **7** Germany
flavor: **7** caraway

kumquat 10 Fortunella
varieties: **4** oval **5** round **6** Marumi,
Nagami **16** Australian desert

Kung Fu
character: **8** Master Po **9** Master Kan
14 Kwai Chang Caine
cast: **8** Keye Luke **9** Philip Ahn **11**
Radames Pera **14** David Carradine
Caine raised in: **13** Shaolin Temple

kunzite
species: **9** spodumene

Kupka, Frank (Frantisek)
born: **6** Opocno **7** Bohemia **14** Czechoslovakia
artwork: **12** Black Accents, The Cathedral **16** Etude pour la Fugue **17**
Fugue in Red and Blue **23** Fugue in
Two Colors Amorpha **25** Philosophical Architecture

Kuprin, Aleksandr
author of: **7** The Duel **10** Yama the
Pit

Kurosawa, Akira
director of: **3** Ran **8** Rashomon **12**
Seven Samurai

Kurtz
character in: **15** Heart of Darkness
author: **6** Conrad

Kuwait
name means: **9** small fort
capital/largest city: **10** Kuwait City
others: **6** Ahmadi **7** Hawalli **8** Abdullah, al-Jahrah, Fahaheel, Shuwaykh
9 al-Shuayba **12** Mena al-Ahmadi,
Mina Abd Allah, Mina al-Ahmadi
head of state: **4** emir
monetary unit: **4** fils **5** dinar
island: **5** Warba **7** Bubiyan, Failaka
physical feature:
bay: **6** Kuwait **12** Khor Abdullah
duststorm: **4** kaus
gulf: **7** Persian
oasis: **6** Jahrah
people: **4** Arab **5** Iraqi, Saudi **6** Indian **7** Bedouin **8** Egyptian **9** Pakistani **11** Palestinian

ruling family: **5** Sabah
sheikh (Sabah family): **5** Ahmad,
Salem **7** Mubarak **12** Jaber al-
Ahmed, Sabah al-Salim **15** Abdullah al-Salim
religion: **5** Islam
war: **4** Gulf **11** Desert Storm, Persian
Gulf **12** Desert Shield
enemy: **4** Iraq **13** Saddam Hussein

Kwa
language family: **16** Niger-
Kordofanian
group: **10** Niger-Congo
includes: **3** Ewe, Ibo, Twi **4** Bini,
Nupe, Togo **6** Yoruba **7** Dahomey

Kwakiutl
language family: **8** Wakashan
location: **6** Canada **15** British Columbia, Vancouver Island **20** Queen
Charlotte Island
related to: **10** Nootka **10** Bellabella
noted for: **10** totem poles **15** Cannibal Society, wooden sculpture
called: **14** potlatch people

Kwanzaa
alternate form: **6** Kwanza
word origin: **7** Swahili (first fruits)
celebrated in: **7** January **8** December
celebrated by: **16** African Americans
originator: **7** Karenga **10** Ron
Karenga **14** Maulana Karenga
guiding principles: **5** faith (imani),
unity (umoja) **7** purpose (nia) **10**
creativity (kuumba) **17** self-
determination (kujichagulia) **20** cooperative economics (ujamaa) **31**
collective work and responsibility
(ujima)

Kyd, Thomas
author of: **17** The Spanish Tragedy

Kyrgyzstan
formerly: **10** Kirghiz SSR
capital/largest city: **6** Frunze **7** Bishkek
head of state: **9** president
government: **8** republic
monetary unit: **3** som
mountain: **8** Tian Shan
people: **5** Uzbek **6** Kyrgyz **7** Kirghiz,
Russian
language: **6** Turkic **7** Kirghiz, Russian
religion: **6** Muslim **10** Sunni Islam

Kyrie eleison 13 Lord have mercy

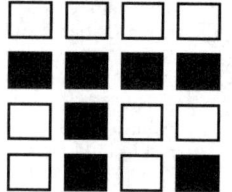 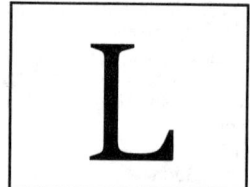 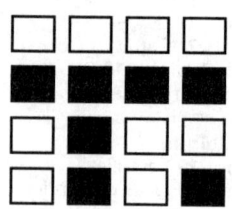

Laban
father: 7 Bethuel
grandfather: 5 Nahor
daughter: 4 Leah 6 Rachel
sister: 7 Rebekah
son-in-law: 5 Jacob

label 3 tag 4 mark, name, note, seal, sign, slip 5 brand, stamp, tally, title 6 define, docket, ticket 7 earmark, mark off, sticker 8 classify, describe 9 designate 10 denominate, put a mark on 11 appellation, designation, inscription 12 characterize 13 specification 14 classification, identification 16 characterization

labor, labour 4 plod, toil, work 5 slave, sweat 6 drudge, effort, suffer 7 agonize, travail, workers, workmen 8 drudgery, exertion, laborers, manpower, plodding, plug away, struggle 9 employees, grind away, work force 10 birth pangs, childbirth, menial work, smart under 11 birth throes, manual labor, parturition 12 accouchement, be affected by, be burdened by, be troubled by 13 be the victim of 14 employ one's time, work like a slave

labored 5 heavy, stiff 6 clumsy, forced, wooden 7 awkward, cramped, halting, studied 8 drawnout, overdone, strained 9 contrived, difficult, laborious, maladroit, ponderous, unnatural 13 self-conscious, unspontaneous

laborer 4 esne, hand, peon, serf 6 coolie, drudge, menial, toiler, worker 7 plodder, workman 8 handyman, hired man, hireling, workhand 9 hired hand 10 roustabout, wage earner, workingman 11 proletarian 12 manual worker 16 blue-collar worker

laborious 4 hard 6 brutal, severe, uphill 7 arduous, irksome, labored, onerous, wearing 8 rigorous, tiresome, toilsome, wearying 9 demanding, difficult, effortful, fatiguing, herculean, strenuous, wearisome 10 burdensome, oppressive, struggling 11 troublesome

laboriously 4 hard 9 arduously 14 with difficulty 15 with great effort

laboriousness 5 trial 8 tough job 10 difficulty, rough going, uphill work 11 arduousness 12 hard sledding 15 troublesomeness

labor omnia vincit 15 work conquers all
motto of: 8 Oklahoma

Labors of Hercules *see* 8 Hercules

labyrinth 3 web 4 knot, maze 5 snarl 6 jungle, morass, riddle, tangle 7 complex, network 9 intricacy, mare's nest 10 complexity, perplexity, wilderness 11 convolution

Labyrinth
form: 4 maze
location: 5 Crete
built by: 8 Daedalus
for: 9 King Minos
challenged by: 7 Theseus
he was aided by: 7 Ariadne
with: 6 thread
housed: 8 Minotaur

Lacaille, Nicholas Louis de
field: 9 astronomy
nationality: 6 French
mapped: 14 constellations

lace 3 tie 4 beat, bind, cane, dope, lash, whip 5 braid, cinch, close, flail, spank, spike, strap, tie up, truss 6 dope up, fasten, flavor, infuse, punish, secure, switch, tether, thrash 7 fortify, spice up, suffuse, tighten 8 chastise, make fast, make taut 10 strengthen 11 add liquor to 12 add spirits to, draw together, give a beating

Lacedaemon
founder of: 6 Sparta
father: 4 Zeus
mother: 7 Taygete
wife: 6 Sparta
son: 7 Amyclas
daughter: 8 Eurydice
descendants: 5 Helen 6 Castor, Pollux 8 Dioscuri 9 Hippocoon, Tyndarius 12 Clytemnestra

lacerate 3 cut, rip 4 gash, hurt, pain, scar, stab, tear 5 lance, sever, slash, slice, wound 6 deface 7 agonize, scratch, torment, torture 8 distress, give pain, puncture 10 excruciate 11 inflict pain

lacerating 5 acute 6 fierce, severe 7 cutting, extreme, intense, violent 12 excruciating

laceration 3 cut, rip 4 tear 5 wound 10 mutilation

Lachaise, Gaston
born: 5 Paris 6 France
artwork: 12 Standing Nude 13 Standing Woman 14 Floating Figure

Lachesis
form: 4 Fate
holds: 12 thread of life
determines: 6 length 7 destiny

lachrymose 3 sad 5 teary, weepy 6 crying 7 maudlin, tearful, weeping 8 mournful 10 melancholy

lack 4 miss, need, want 6 dearth 7 absence 8 omission, scarcity, shortage 9 be missing, be short of, depletion, neediness, privation, scantness 10 deficiency, exhaustion 11 deprivation, fall short of 12 be inadequate 13 be caught short, be deficient in 14 be found wanting, be insufficient

lackadaisical 4 idle 7 languid, loafing 8 lifeless, listless, mindless 9 apathetic, lethargic, unexcited 10 inanimated, phlegmatic, spiritless, unaspiring, uninspired 11 indifferent, languishing, unambitious, unconcerned, unexcitable, unmotivated 12 uninterested 13 dillydallying

lackey 4 page 5 slave, toady, usher, valet 6 butler, flunky, helper, menial, minion, squire, waiter 7 servant, steward 8 employee, follower, hanger-on, hireling, inferior, retainer 9 assistant, attendant, cupbearer, mercenary, underling

lacking 7 needing, wanting 9 deficient 10 inadequate 12 falling short, insufficient
French: 6 manque

lackluster 4 blah, dead, drab, dull 5 bland, muted 6 boring, dreary, leaden, pallid, somber 7 humdrum, nothing, prosaic, subdued 8 lifeless, mediocre, ordinary 9 colorless 10 lusterless 11 commonplace 12 run-of-the-mill 13 uninteresting

lack of conviction 5 doubt 8 question 9 misgiving 10 hesitation, indecision 11 uncertainty
trait of: 14 Doubting Thomas

lack of faith 5 doubt 7 atheism 8 distrust, mistrust 9 disbelief, suspicion

lack of feeling 6 apathy 8 coldness, numbness 11 impassivity 15 emotionlessness, hardheartedness, passionlessness

lack of interest 5 ennui 6 apathy 7 boredom 9 unconcern 12 indifference

lack of respect 8 contempt, rudeness

9 disregard **10** disrespect **11** discourtesy, irreverence **12** impoliteness

lack of skill 9 inability **10** clumsiness, ineptitude **11** awkwardness **12** incompetency

Laclos, Pierre Choderlos de
　author of: **22** Les Liaisons Dangereuses

Lacombe, Lucien
　director: **10** Louis Malle
　cast: **12** Pierre Blaise **13** Aurore Clement **16** Holger Lowenadler

LA Confidential
　director: **12** Curtis Hanson
　cast: **9** Guy Pearce (Edmund Exley), Ron Rifkin (Ellis Loew) **11** Danny DeVito (Sid Hudgens), Kevin Spacey (Jack Vincennes), Kim Basinger (Lynn Bracken) **12** Russell Crowe (Bud White) **13** James Cromwell (Dudley Smith) **15** David Strathairn (Pierce Patchett)

laconic 4 curt **5** blunt, brief, pithy, short, terse **7** compact, concise, pointed, spartan, summary **8** succinct **9** condensed **10** to the point **12** concentrated **14** sparing of words

lacquer 4 coat **5** glaze **7** coating, shellac, varnish

lacrimoso
　music: **7** tearful

lacrosse
　Indian name: **9** bagataway
　circle around goal: **6** crease
　played with: **5** stick **6** crosse **14** pouched racquet
　players/team: **3** ten
　position: **6** goalie **9** attackman **10** defenseman, midfielder
　term: **6** riding **8** clearing

lacuna 3 gap, pit **4** gulf, hole, void **5** blank, break, crack, ditch, pause, space **6** breach, cavity, hiatus **7** caesura, fissure, interim, opening, vacancy **8** interval, omission **10** interstice, suspension **12** interruption **13** discontinuity

lacustrine 7 aquatic **8** riparian **11** lake-growing **12** lake-dwelling

lacy 4 fine **5** filmy, gauzy, meshy, netty, sheer, webby **6** barred, frilly, netted, porous, webbed **7** gridded, netlike **8** cobwebby, delicate, filigree, gossamer, lacelike, retiform **9** filigreed **10** diaphanous, reticulate **11** latticelike, transparent

lad 3 boy, kid **5** sprig, youth **6** shaver, sprout **8** juvenile, young man **9** schoolboy, stripling, young chap, youngster **11** young fellow

Ladd, Alan
　son: **5** David **6** Alan Jr
　co-star: **12** Veronica Lake
　born: **12** Hot Springs AR
　roles: **5** Shane **13** The Blue Dahlia **14** The Great Gatsby, This Gun for Hire

ladies' man 4 beau, stud **5** spark **6**

escort, gigolo **7** playboy **8** cavalier, gay blade

Ladino
　also: **7** Judezmo **12** Judeo-Spanish
　spoken by: **9** Sephardim
　based on: **10** Old Spanish
　script: **6** Hebrew **7** mestizo

Ladoga, Lake
　largest in: **6** Europe
　located in: **6** Russia

La Dolce Vita
　director: **15** Federico Fellini
　cast: **9** Lex Barker, Nadia Gray **10** Anouk Aimee **11** Anita Ekberg **19** Marcello Mastroianni

ladrone 5 thief **6** bandit, outlaw

lady 4 wife **5** woman **6** female, matron, spouse **7** duchess, peeress **8** baroness, countess **10** aristocrat, noblewoman **11** gentlewoman, marchioness, viscountess, woman of rank **13** well-bred woman
　German: **4** frau
　Italian: **5** donna
　Spanish/Portuguese: **4** dona

Lady Chatterley's Lover
　author: **10** D H Lawrence
　character: **7** Mellors **19** Constance Chatterley

Lady Eve, The
　director: **14** Preston Sturges
　cast: **10** Henry Fonda **13** Charles Coburn **14** Eugene Pallette **15** Barbara Stanwyck, William Demarest

Lady for a Day
　director: **10** Frank Capra
　based on story by: **11** Damon Runyon
　cast: **9** Guy Kibbee, May Robson **13** Warren William
　remade as: **19** Pocketful of Miracles

Lady from the Sea, The
　author: **11** Henrik Ibsen

Lady in Chair
　constellation of: **10** Cassiopeia

ladylike 5 civil **6** modest, polite, proper **7** courtly, elegant, genteel, refined **8** cultured, decorous, mannerly, polished, well-bred **9** courteous, dignified **10** cultivated **11** respectable **12** well mannered **13** well brought up

Lady of the Camellias, The *see* **7** Camille

Lady of the Lake, The
　author: **14** Sir Walter Scott
　character: **9** Allan Bane **11** Roderick Dhu **12** Ellen Douglas **13** Malcolm Graeme **14** James Fitz-James, James of Douglas

Lady Oracle
　author: **14** Margaret Atwood

lady's maid
　French: **14** femme de chambre

Lady's Not for Burning, The
　author: **14** Christopher Fry

lady's-slipper, lady-slipper

varieties: **4** pink **5** showy **6** orchid **8** mountain, ram's-head **9** two-leaved **10** small white **11** large yellow, small yellow

Lady Vanishes, The
　director: **15** Alfred Hitchcock
　cast: **9** Paul Lukas **13** Dame May Whitty **15** Michael Redgrave **16** Margaret Lockwood

Lady Windermere's Fan
　author: **10** Oscar Wilde
　character: **10** Mrs Erlynne **14** Lord Darlington, Lord Windermere **18** Lord Augustus Lorton

Laertes
　son: **8** Odysseus

Laertes
　character in: **6** Hamlet
　sister: **7** Ophelia
　father: **8** Polonius
　author: **11** Shakespeare

La Farge, John
　born: **9** New York NY
　artwork: **14** Maua Our Boatman **17** The Muse of Painting **18** Red and White Peonies

La Fayette, Comtesse de
　author of: **19** La Princesse de Cleves

Lafayette, Marquis de
　also: **38** Marie Joseph Paul Yves Roch Gilbert du Motier
　nationality: **6** French
　served in: **14** July Revolution **16** French Revolution **18** American Revolution
　battle: **8** Yorktown **10** Brandywine

Lafcadio's Adventures (The Vatican Swindle)
　author: **9** Andre Gide

La Fontaine, Jean de
　author of: **6** Fables

lag 4 drag, halt, inch, limp, snag **5** dally, delay, hitch, tarry, trail **6** be idle, be late, be slow, dawdle, falter, hold up, linger, loiter, trudge **7** be tardy, setback, slacken, stagger **8** be behind, hang back, slowdown **9** be overdue, inch along **10** drag behind, slackening **11** slowing down **12** bide one's time, take one's time **13** falling behind, procrastinate

laggard 4 mope, poke, slow, slug **5** idler, snail, tardy **6** loafer, remiss **7** dallier, dawdler, lounger **8** lingerer, loiterer, potterer, putterer, slowfoot, slowpoke, sluggard, sluggish **9** donothing, straggler **12** dilly-dallier **13** stick-in-the-mud

lagniappe, lagnappe 3 tip **4** gift, perk **5** bonus, favor, prize **7** largess, memento, present **8** gratuity, largesse **9** pourboire

Lagos
　former capital of: **7** Nigeria

Lahr, Bert
　real name: **14** Irving Lahrheim
　born: **9** New York NY

roles: 12 Cowardly Lion **13** The Wizard of Oz

laic 3 lay **5** civil **6** laical **7** amateur, popular, profane, secular, worldly **8** temporal **11** nonclerical, nonpastoral **12** secularistic **13** inexperienced **15** nonprofessional **17** nonecclesiastical

lair 3 den, lie, mew **4** hole, nest **5** cover, haunt **6** burrow, cavern, covert **7** hideout, retreat **8** hideaway **9** sanctuary **12** resting place

laissez-faire, laisser-faire 8 hands off **9** let them be, unconcern **12** indifference **14** let-alone policy, live and let live **15** noninterference, nonintervention

laissez-passer 4 pass **6** permit **11** allow to pass

Laius
   king of: 6 Thebes
   father: 8 Labdacus
   great-grandfather: 6 Cadmus
   wife: 7 Jocasta
   son: 7 Oedipus
   killed by: 7 Oedipus

Lajeunesse, Gabriel
   character in: 10 Evangeline
   author: 10 Longfellow

lake
   of Afghanistan: 7 Helmand **13** Hamud-i-Helmand
   of Albania: 4 Ulze **5** Matia, Ohrid **6** Prespa **7** Ochrida, Scutari, Shkoder **8** Ohridsko
   of Algeria: 5 Hodna **6** Sabkha **7** Cherqui, Fedjadj, Meirhir **10** Azzel Matti, Meherrhane
   of Andorra: 11 Engolasters
   of Argentina: 6 Viedma **7** Cardiel, Fagnano, Musters **11** Buenos Aires, Mar Chiquita, Nahuel Huapi
   of Armenia: 3 Van **5** Sevan, Urmia **8** Urumiyah
   of Australia: 4 Eyre **5** Carey, Cowan, Frome, Moore, Wells **6** Austin, Barlee, Bulloo, Dundas, Harris, Mackay **7** Amadeus, Blanche, Everard, Torrens **8** Carnegie, Gairdner **9** MacDonald **10** Yammayamma **14** Disappointment
   of Austria: 6 Almsee **7** Fertoto, Mondsee **8** Bodensee, Traunsee **9** Constance **10** Neusiedler
   of Benin: 5 Aheme **6** Nokoue
   of Bolivia: 5 Poopo **7** Allagas, Coipasa, Rogagua **8** Titicaca **10** Desaguader
   of Botswana: 3 Dow, Xau **5** Ngami
   of Brazil: 4 Aima, Feia **5** Mirim **13** Logo dos Platos
   of Burundi: 7 Rugwero **8** Tshohoha **10** Tanganyika
   of Cambodia: 8 Tonle Sap
   of Cameroon: 4 Chad
   of Canada: 4 Cree, Erie, Gras, Seul **5** Garry, Huron, Rainy **6** Louise, St John **7** Abitibi, Dubawnt, Nipigon, Ontario, Testlin **8** Kootenay, Manitoba, Okanagan, Reindeer, Superior, Winnipeg **9** Athabaska, Great Bear, Nipissing **10** Great Slave, Mistassini **12** Winnipegosis
   of Central African Republic: 4 Assa
   of Chad: 4 Chad
   of Chile: 5 Ranco **6** Yelcho **7** Puyehue, Rupanco **8** Cochrane **10** General Paz, Llanquihue **11** Buenos Aires
   of China: 3 Tai **4** Chao, Na-mu **5** Kaoyu, Oling, Telli **6** Bamtso, Bornor, Ebinor, Erhhai, Khanka, Lopnor, Namtso, Poyang **7** Chaling, Hungtse, Karanor, Kokonor **8** Hulunnor, Montcalm, Taroktso, Tellinor, Tienchih, Tsinghai, Tungting
   of Colombia: 4 Tota
   of the Democratic Republic of the Congo: 4 Kivu **5** Mweru, Tumba **6** Albert, Edward, Upemba **9** Mai-Ndombe **10** Tanganyika
   of the Republic of the Congo: 5 Mweru, Tumba **6** Albert, Nyanza, Upemba **7** Leopold **11** Stanley Pool
   of Costa Rica: 6 Arenal
   of Denmark: 6 Arreso
   of Djibouti: 4 Abbe **5** Assal
   of Dominican Republic: 10 Enriquillo
   of Egypt: 4 Edku, Idku **5** Qarun **6** Maryut, Moeris, Nasser **7** Manzala **8** Burullus, Mareotis
   of El Salvador: 5 Guiha, Guija **8** Ilopango **10** Coatepeque
   of England: 8 Grasmere **9** Ennerdale, Ullswater, Wastwater **10** Buttermere, Windermere **12** Derwentwater **13** Coniston Water
   of Estonia: 5 Pskov **6** Peipus **9** Vortsjarv
   of Ethiopia: 3 Abe **4** Tana **5** Abaya, Shola, Tanna, Tsana, Tzana, Zeway **6** Dambea, Dembea, Rudolf **8** Blue Nile, Stefanie
   of Finland: 3 Juo, Muo **4** Kemi, Kiui, Nasi, Oulu, Puru, Pyha, Simo **5** Enara, Enare, Hauki, Inari, Kalla, Lappa, Lesti, Puula, Saima **6** Ladoya, Lentua, Saimaa, Sounne, Syvari **7** Koitere, Nilakka **8** Pielinen **9** Kalvesi, Pielavesi
   of France: 6 Annecy, Cazaux, Geneva
   of Gabon Republic: 7 Anengue, Azinguo
   of Germany: 6 Muritz **9** Constance **11** Inner Alster, Outer Alster
   of Ghana: 5 Volta **8** Bosumtwi
   of Greece: 5 Karla, Volve **6** Copais, Kopais, Prespa, Voweis **8** Ioannina, Koroneia, Vistonis **9** Trichonis, Vegoritis
   of Grenada: 10 Grand Etang
   of Guatemala: 5 Dulce, Guija, Peten **6** Izabal **7** Atitlan **8** Amatitlan, Peten Itza
   of Haiti: 8 Saumatre
   of Honduras: 5 Criba, Yojoa **6** Brewer
   of Hungary: 5 Ferto **7** Balaton, Velence **9** Blatensee **10** Neusiedler, Plattensee
   of Iceland: 6 Myvatn **10** Thorisvatn **14** Thingvallavatn
   of India: 5 Jheel, Lonar, Wular **6** Chilka, Colair, Dhebar, Kolair **7** Kolleru, Pulicat, Pushkar, Sambahr
   of Indonesia: 4 Toba **5** Ranau **6** Towuti
   of Iran: 5 Niris, Tasht, Tuzlu, Urmia **6** Sahweh, Sistan **7** Maharlu **8** Nemekser, Urumiyeh
   of Iraq: 6 al-Milh **7** Sanniya **8** al-Hammar
   of Ireland: 3 Doo, Key, Ree, Tay **4** Conn, Derg, Erne, Mask **5** Allen, Barra, Carra, Gowna, Leane, Lough, Neagh **6** Boderg, Cooter, Corrib, Ennell **7** Dromore, Gougane, Oughter, Sheelin **9** Killarney
   of Israel: 5 Huleh **7** Dead Sea **8** Kinneret, Tiberias **12** Sea of Galilee
   of Italy: 4 Como, Iseo, Nemi **5** Garda **6** Albano, Lesina, Lugano, Varano **7** Bolsena, Perugia **8** Maggiore **9** Bracciano, Trasimeno
   of Japan: 4 Biwa, Suwa, Toya **6** Towada **8** Kutchawa, Shikotsu
   of Kazakhstan: 8 Balkhash
   of Kenya: 6 Magadi, Nakuru, Natron, Rudolf **7** Turkana **8** Naivasha, Victoria
   of Lebanon: 5 Quran **6** Qirawn
   of Lithuania: 5 Dysna
   of Luxembourg: 8 Haut Sure
   of Macedonia: 5 Ohrid **6** Prespa **7** Ochrida
   of Madagascar: 5 Itasy **7** Alaotra, Kinkony
   of Malawi: 5 Nyasa **6** Chilwa, Malawi
   of Mali: 2 Do **4** Debo **5** Garou **7** Korarou **9** Faguibine
   of Mexico: 7 Chapala, Texcoco **9** Patzcuaro
   of Mongolia: 3 Uvs **5** Har Us **6** Bor Nor **7** Ghirgis, Ubsa Nor **8** Airik Nor, Durga Nor, Hobsogol, Khara Usu **9** Khubsugul, Khukhu-Nur **10** Khirgis Nor
   of Montenegro: 7 Scutari, Shkoder
   of Mozambique: 5 Nyasa **6** Chuali, Nyassa **8** Nhavarre
   of Myanmar: 4 Inle
   of Nauru: 11 Buada Lagoon
   of the Netherlands: 7 Haarlem **10** Ijsselmeer **11** Grevelingen, Hazinguliet
   of New Zealand: 3 Ada **4** Gunn, Ohau **5** Hawea, Taupo **6** Pukaki, Pupuke, Te Anau, Tekapo, Wanaka **7** Brunner, Diamond, Kanieri, Okareka, Rotorua **8** Okataina, Paradise, Rotoaira, Wakatipi **9** Manapouri
   of Nicaragua: 7 Managua **9** Nicaragua

of Niger: 4 Chad
of Nigeria: 4 Chad
of the Nile: 4 Tana **5** Kyoga, Tsana **6** Albert, Edward, Nasser **8** Victoria
of Norway: 4 Alte **5** Ister, Mjosa, Snasa **6** Femund **7** Rostavn, Tunnsjo
of Panama: 5 Gatun
of Paraguay: 4 Vera, Ypoa **8** Ypacarai
of Peru: 8 Titicaca
of Poland: 5 Goplo, Mamry **8** Niegocin, Sniardwy **13** Stettin Lagoon
of Puerto Rico: 5 Loiza **6** Carite **8** Dos Bocas **9** Caonillas, Guatajaca
of Romania: 5 Sinoe **6** Snagov
of Russia: 3 Seg **4** Azov, Kola, Neva **5** Byelo, Chany, Elton, Erara, Ilmen, Lacha, Onega, Vozhe **6** Baikal, Ladoga **10** Caspian Sea
of Rwanda: 4 Kivu **5** Ihema **6** Bufera, Bulera, Mohasi **7** Rugwero, Ruhnodo **8** Mugesera, Tshohoha
of Sardinia: 6 Omodeo
of Scotland: 3 Awe, Dee, Lin, Tay **4** Earn, Fyne, Gair, Gare, Linn, Ness, Oich, Ryan, Sloy **5** Duich, Leven, Lochy, Lough, Morar, Maree, Nevis **6** Laggan, Linnhe, Lomond **7** Katrine, Rannoch, St Marys
of Senegal: 6 Guiers
of Sicily: 7 Pergusa **8** Camarina
of Slovenia: 4 Bled
of Spain: 4 Lago **9** Albrifera
of the Sudan: 2 No **4** Chad, Toad **6** Nasser
of Sweden: 4 Ster **5** Asnen, Malar, Silja, Vaner **6** Vanern, Vatter, Wennen **7** Hielmar, Malaren, Vattern **8** Dalalven **9** Hjalmaren
of Switzerland: 3 Uri, Zug **4** Biel, Thon, Thun **5** Ageri, Leman, Morat **6** Bienne, Brienz, Geneva, Lugano, Sarnen, Wallen, Zurich **7** Hallwil, Lucerne, Lungern **8** Maggiore, Vierwald **9** Bielersee, Constance, Neuchatel, Sarnersee, Thunersee
of Syria: 5 Merom **7** Djeboid **8** Tiberias
of Tanzania: 5 Eyasi, Nyasa, Rukwa **6** Malawi, Natron, Nyassa **7** Manyara **8** Victoria **10** Tanganyika
of Thailand: 9 Nong Lahan
of Tibet: 3 Aru, Bam, Bum, Nam **4** Mema, Tosu **5** Jagok, Tabia **6** Dagtse, Garhur, Kashun, Nam Iso, Seling, Tangra, Yamdok **7** Kyaring, Terinam, Tsaring, Zilling **8** Jiggitai **9** Tengrinor **11** Manasarowar
of Tunisia: 6 Achkel, Djerid **7** Bizerte
of Turkey: 3 Tuz, Van **7** Egridir **8** Beysehir
of Uganda: 5 Kioga, Kyoga **6** Albert, Edward, George **8** Victoria
of the United States: 4 Erie, Mead **5** Huron, Tahoe **6** Cayuga, Finger, George, Itasca, Oneida, Seneca **7** Iliamma, Ontario **8** Michigan, Superior **9** Champlain, Great Salt, Salton Sea, Teshekpuk, Winnebago **10** Okeechobee **11** Yellowstone **13** Pontchartrain, Wallenpaupack, Winnipesaukee **14** Lake of the Woods
of Uruguay: 5 Merin, Mirim **18** Embalse del Rio Negro
of Venezuela: 9 Maracaibo, Tacarigua
of Wales: 4 Bala **6** Vyrnwy
of Yugoslavia: 7 Scutari
of Zambia: 5 Mweru **6** Kariba **9** Bangweulu **10** Tanganyika
of Zimbabwe: 4 Kyle **6** Kariba

Lake, Veronica
real name: 29 Constance Frances Marie Ockelman
co-star: 8 Alan Ladd
born: 10 Brooklyn NY
roles: 13 The Blue Dahlia **14** I Married a Witch, This Gun for Hire **16** Sullivan's Travels

Lake Isle of Innisfree, The
author: 7 W B Yeats

L'Allegro
author: 10 John Milton
companion piece: 11 Il Penseroso

Lalo, (Victor Antoine) Edouard
born: 5 Lille **6** France
composer of: 7 Namouna **8** Le Roi d'Ys **11** The King of Ys **15** Spanish Symphony **18** Symphonie Espagnole

lama 4 monk **6** priest
in: 7 Lamaism
high priest: 9 Dalai Lama
locale: 5 Tibet

Lamarck, Jean B
field: 7 biology
forerunner of theory of: 9 evolution
author of: 21 Philosophie Zoologique

Lamarr, Hedy
real name: 21 Hedwig Eva Maria Kiesler
born: 6 Vienna **7** Austria
roles: 7 Ecstasy **16** Samson and Delilah

Lamas, Fernando
wife: 10 Arlene Dahl **14** Esther Williams
son: 7 Lorenzo
born: 9 Argentina **11** Buenos Aires
roles: 13 The Merry Widow **16** Dangerous When Wet **23** The Girl Who Had Everything

Lamb, Charles
author of: 12 Essays of Elia **13** Dream Children **20** Tales From Shakespeare **25** A Dissertation upon Roast Pig **31** Specimens of English Dramatic Poets
pseudonym: 4 Elia
sister: 4 Mary

lambaste 4 beat, drub, lick, pelt, whip **5** scold, smear **6** berate, defeat, pummel, rebuke, subdue, thrash, wallop **7** bawl out, censure, chew out, clobber, cuss out, shellac, trounce **8** bludgeon, denounce, vanquish **9** castigate, dress down, light into, overwhelm, reprimand

lambent 6 bright **7** radiant, shining **8** luminous, lustrous **10** flickering, shimmering

Lambert, Constant
born: 6 London **7** England
composer of: 9 Horoscope, Rio Grande **14** Romeo and Juliet **17** Music for Orchestra **27** Summer's Last Will and Testament

lame 4 game, halt, weak **5** sorry **6** clumsy, feeble, flimsy, infirm, maimed; uncool **7** failing, halting, hobbled, limping, unsound, wanting **8** crippled, deformed, disabled **9** deficient, faltering **10** inadequate **11** ineffectual **12** insufficient, unconvincing, unpersuasive **14** unsatisfactory

lamebrain 3 ass, sap **4** fool **5** booby, dunce, idiot, moron, ninny **6** dimwit, nitwit **7** fathead, half-wit **8** bonehead, dumb-dumb, imbecile, lunkhead, numskull **9** blockhead, numbskull **10** dunderhead, nincompoop **11** chowderhead

lamebrained 4 dumb **6** stupid **7** asinine, foolish, idiotic, moronic **8** crackpot **9** dimwitted, imbecilic **10** halfwitted **12** feeble-minded, simpleminded

Lamech
father: 9 Methusael **10** Methuselah
wives: 4 Adah **6** Zillah
son: 5 Jabal, Jubal **9** Tubalcain
daughter: 6 Naamah

lament 3 cry, sob **4** moan, wail, weep **5** dirge, mourn **6** bewail, outcry, plaint, regret **7** deplore, keening, requiem, whimper **8** mourning **9** death song **11** condole with, lamentation **12** funeral music **13** complain about **14** express pity for, show concern for, sympathize with **15** commiserate with

lamentable 4 dire **6** woeful **7** piteous **8** dreadful, grievous, pathetic, pitiable, shameful, terrible, wretched **9** miserable **10** deplorable **11** distressing, regrettable, unfortunate **13** disheartening, heartbreaking

Lamia
author: 9 John Keats

Lamia
form: 7 monster
characteristic: 12 blood-sucking

La Motta, Jake (Jacob)
nickname: 9 Bronx Bull
sport: 6 boxing
class: 12 middleweight
movie biography: 10 Raging Bull

Lamour, Dorothy
real name: 23 Mary Leta Dorothy Kaumeyer
trademark: 6 sarong
co-star: 7 Bob Hope **10** Bing Crosby
born: 12 New Orleans LA
roles:

Road to: 3 Rio 4 Bali 6 Utopia 7 Morocco 8 Hong Kong, Zanzibar 9 Singapore

L'Amour, Louis
author of: 5 Hondo, Lando 7 Sackett, Shalako 8 Conagher 10 Key-Lock Man, Rivers West 14 The Californios, The Daybreakers 15 Westward the Tide 16 How the West Was Won, Over on the Dry Side 21 The Man from Broken Hills, To the Far Blue Mountains

lamp 4 bulb 5 light, torch 6 beacon 7 blinker, lantern 9 headlight, spotlight 10 chandelier, floodlight, Kleig light, night light 11 searchlight 12 ceiling light, reading light 14 ceiling fixture
invented by:
　arc: 6 Staite
　incandescent: 6 Edison
　incandescent frosted: 6 Pipkin
　incandescent gas: 8 Langmuir
　Kleig: 7 Kleigel
　mercury vapor: 6 Hewitt
　miner's safety: 4 Davy
　neon: 6 Claude

Lampedusa, Giuseppe di
author of: 10 The Leopard

lampoon 5 farce, put-on, spoof, squib 6 parody, satire, send up 7 mockery, takeoff 8 diatribe, ridicule, satirize, travesty 9 broadside, burlesque 10 caricature, pasquinade 11 make light of

Lamus
father: 8 Hercules
mother: 7 Omphale
attacked: 5 ships

lanai 4 deck 5 porch 7 terrace, veranda

Lancaster 17 English royal house
faction in: 13 War of the Roses
founder: 11 John of Gaunt
symbol: 7 red rose

Lancaster, Burt
real name: 22 Burton Stephen Lancaster
born: 9 New York NY
roles: 5 Moses 9 All My Sons, Local Hero 11 Elmer Gantry (Oscar) 12 Atlantic City, The Rainmaker 13 Field of Dreams, The Rose Tattoo 14 Seven Days in May 16 Sorry Wrong Number 17 Birdman of Alcatraz 18 From Here to Eternity 19 Come Back Little Sheba, Sweet Smell of Success

lance 4 gaff, pike 5 shaft, spear 7 assegai, halberd, harpoon, javelin

Lancelot, Launcelot
character in: 16 Arthurian romance
also called: 13 Lancelot du Lac
father: 3 Ban
son: 7 Galahad
lover: 6 Elaine 9 Guinevere
home: 10 Joyous Gard

lancer 8 cavalier, horseman 10 cavalryman 12 horse soldier, horse trooper 14 mounted soldier

Lanchester, Elsa
real name: 17 Elizabeth Sullivan
husband: 15 Charles Laughton
born: 7 England 8 Lewisham
roles: 15 Come to the Stable 22 The Bride of Frankenstein 24 Witness for the Prosecution 25 The Private Life of Henry VIII 31 The Private Life of Henry the Eighth

land 3 get, lea, nab, net 4 area, dirt, dock, gain, grab, lawn, loam, moor, park, soil, take, ward, zone 5 acres, catch, earth, grass, green, humus, light, put in, realm, seize, shire, snare, state, tie up, tract 6 alight, anchor, canton, clinch, colony, county, debark, domain, empire, fields, ground, meadow, nation, parish, realty, region, secure 7 acreage, capture, country, descend, dry land, grounds, kingdom, pasture, section, set down, subsoil, terrain, win over 8 come down, district, dominion, farmland, homeland, location, mainland, make land, make port, precinct, property, province, republic, vicinity 9 cornfield, disembark, grassland, lay anchor, lay hold of, lead one to, reach land, territory 10 bring one to, carry one to, come to land, drop anchor, fatherland, motherland, native land, native soil, real estate, settle down, settlement, terra firma, wheat field 11 countryside, put into port 12 commonwealth, put into shore, real property, village green 13 the old country

Landau, Lev Davidovitch
field: 7 physics
nationality: 7 Russian
discovered: 12 liquid helium 14 ferromagnetism
awarded: 10 Nobel Prize

landed property 5 manor 6 estate 8 compound 12 countryplace

land force 4 army 6 legion, troops 7 legions 8 infantry, soldiers, soldiery 9 artillery

Landless, Neville and Helena
characters in: 22 The Mystery of Edwin Drood
author: 7 Dickens

landlord 5 owner 6 holder, squire 8 landlady 9 landowner, possessor 10 freeholder, landholder, proprietor 13 property owner 14 lord of the manor

landmark 8 keystone, monument, signpost 9 benchmark, guidepost, highlight, high point, milestone, watershed 11 cornerstone 12 turning point 16 historic building

Landmarks
god of: 8 Terminus

Land of Enchantment
nickname of: 9 New Mexico

Land of Lincoln
nickname of: 8 Illinois

Land of Opportunity
nickname of: 8 Arkansas

Land of Sky-blue Waters
nickname of: 9 Minnesota

Land of Steady Habits
nickname of: 11 Connecticut

Land of Ten Thousand Lakes
nickname of: 9 Minnesota

Land of the Dakotas
nickname of: 11 North Dakota

Land of the Midnight Sun
nickname of: 6 Alaska

Landon, Michael
real name: 20 Eugene Maurice Orowitz
born: 13 Forest Hills NY
roles: 7 Bonanza, Sam's Son 15 Highway to Heaven 19 Little Joe Cartwright 20 I Was a Teenage Werewolf 23 Little House on the Prairie

landscape 4 view 5 scene, sight, vista 6 aspect 7 scenery 8 panorama, prospect 9 spectacle 10 rural scene, scenic view 14 natural scenery

landscape architect 7 Le Notre, Olmsted

landsman 10 countryman 13 fellow citizen

Landsteiner, Karl
field: 8 medicine 9 pathology
distinguished: 7 blood types
identified: 8 RH factor
awarded: 10 Nobel Prize

lane 3 way 4 pass, path, road 5 alley, byway, drive, route, track, trail 6 access, avenue, bypath, course 7 passage, roadway 8 alleyway, approach, footpath 10 passageway

Lang, Walter
director of: 7 Desk Set 11 The King and I

Lange, Jessica
born: 9 Cloquet MN
roles: 7 Country, Frances, Tootsie 8 Cape Fear, King Kong 11 All That Jazz 16 Crimes of the Heart 26 The Postman Always Rings Twice

Langella, Frank
born: 9 Bayonne NJ
roles: 7 Dracula 23 The Diary of a Mad Housewife

Langland, William
author of: 12 Piers Plowman

Langmuir, Irving
field: 9 chemistry
invented: 15 atomic blowtorch 17 gas-tungsten lights
awarded: 10 Nobel Prize

language 4 cant, jive 5 argot, idiom, lingo, prose, slang, words 6 jargon, patois, speech, tongue 7 cursing, cussing, dialect, diction, wording 8 parlance, rhetoric, swearing, verbiage 9 discourse, elocution, profanity 10 expression, use of words, vernacular, vocabulary 11 imprecation, phraseology, profane talk **12** mother tongue, native tongue **13** colloquialism **14** public speaking, self-expression **16** manner of speaking, mode of expression **17** oral communication, reading and writing, verbal intercourse

of Afghanistan: 4 Dari **5** Farsi **6** Afghan, Pashto, Pushtu **7** Balochi, Baluchi, Persian

of Albania: 3 Geg **4** Cham, Gheg, Hish, Tosk **5** Greek **8** Albanian

of Algeria: 6 Arabic, Berber, French, Zenata **7** Senhaja

of Andorra: 6 French **7** Catalan, Spanish

of Angola: 5 Bantu **8** Kimbundu, Oumbundu **9** Ovimbundu **10** Portuguese

of Antigua and Barbuda: 7 English

of Argentina: 7 Spanish

of Armenia: 7 Russian **8** Armenian

of Australia: 6 Yabber **7** English **9** aborigine (dialects)

of Austria: 5 Czech **6** German, Magyar **8** Croatian **9** Slovenian

of Azerbaijan: 6 Turkic

of the Bahamas: 6 Creole **7** English

of Bahrain: 4 Urdu **5** Farsi **6** Arabic **7** English, Persian

of Bangladesh: 6 Bihari **7** Bengali, English

of Barbados: 7 English

of Belgium: 5 Dutch **6** French, German **7** Flemish

of Benin: 3 Fon **5** Dendi **6** Bariba, French, Fulani, Yoruba

of Bermuda: 7 English

of Bhutan: 5 Hindi, Lhoke **7** Tibetan **8** Dzongkha, Nepalese

of Bolivia: 6 Aymara **7** Quechua, Spanish

of Borneo: 5 Malay **7** Chinese, English

of Bosnia-Herzegovina: 13 Serbo Croatian

of Botswana: 5 Bantu, Click **6** Tswana **7** English, Khoisan **8** Setswana

of Brazil: 10 Portuguese

of Brunei: 4 Iban **5** Malay **7** Chinese, English

of Bulgaria: 9 Bulgarian

of Burkina Faso: 4 Bobo, Lobi, More, Samo **5** Dyula, Mande, Mossi **6** French

of Burundi: 6 French **7** Kirundi, Swahili

of Cambodia: 5 Khmer **6** French

of Cameroon: 4 Bulu **5** Bantu, Bassa, Hausa **6** Douala, Ewondo, French, Fulani **7** English **8** Bamileke, Fulfulde

of Canada: 6 Eskimo, French **7** English

of Canary Islands: 7 Spanish

of Cape Verde: 7 Crioulo **10** Portuguese **13** Verdean Creole

of Central African Republic: 5 Sango,

Zande **6** French

of Chad: 4 Sara **5** Turku **6** Arabic, French

of Chile: 7 Spanish

of China: 7 Chinese **8** Mandarin, Shanghai **9** Cantonese

of Colombia: 7 Spanish

of Comoros: 6 Arabic, French **7** Swahili **8** Malagasy

of the Democratic Republic of the Congo: 5 Bantu **6** French **7** Chiluba, Kikongo, Lingala, Swahili **8** Sudanese, Tshiluba

of the Republic of the Congo: 4 Susu **5** Bantu, Fiote **6** French, Kituba **7** Bangala, Lingala

of Costa Rica: 7 Spanish

of Crete: 5 Greek **6** Minoan **7** Linear A, Linear B

of Croatia: 8 Croatian **10** Serbo Croat

of Cuba: 7 Spanish

of Cyprus: 5 Greek **7** Turkish **8** Armenian

of Czechoslovakia/Czech Republic: 5 Czech **6** German, Magyar, Slovak **7** Russian **9** Hungarian

of Denmark: 4 Odan **6** Danish **8** Faeroese **11** Greenlander

of Djibouti: 4 Afar **6** Arabic, French, Somali

of Dominican Republic: 6 French **7** English, Spanish

of Ecuador: 6 Jibaro **7** Quechua, Spanish

of Egypt: 6 Arabic, Coptic, French **7** English

of El Salvador: 7 Spanish

of England: 7 English

of Equatorial Guinea: 4 Bubi, Fang **6** pidgin **7** Spanish

of Eritrea: 7 Amharic

of Estonia: 5 Tartu **10** Finno-Ugric

of Ethiopia: 3 Giz **4** Afar, Agow, Geez, Saho **5** Geeze, Ghese, Smali, Tigre **6** Arabic, Harari **7** Amharic, English, Italian, Russian **8** Gallinya, Irob-Saho, Tigrinya

of Fiji: 5 Hindi **6** Fijian **7** English

of Finland: 4 Avar, Lapp **5** Karen, Ugric, Vogul **6** Magyar, Ostyak, Tarast **7** Finnish, Olonets, Samoyed, Swedish **8** Estonian **10** Olenetsian

of France: 6 French

of Gabon Republic: 6 French

of the Gambia: 4 Fula **5** Wolof **6** Fulani **7** English, Malinke **8** Mandingo

of Georgia: 8 Georgian

of Germany: 6 German **10** High German **11** Hochdeutsch

of Ghana: 2 Ga **3** Ewe, Gur, Kwa, Twi **5** Fanti, Hausa **7** Dagomba, English

of Gibraltar: 7 English, Spanish

of Greece: 5 Greek

of Greenland: 6 Danish, Eskimo **11** Greenlandic

of Grenada: 7 English

of Guatemala: 6 Quiche **7** Spanish

of Guinea: 5 Fulbe, Mande **6** Arabic, French, Fulani **7** English

of Guinea-Bissau: 5 Fulah **7** Balante, Crioulo **8** Mandingo **10** Portuguese **21** Cape Verde–Guinea Creole

of Guyana: 5 Hindi **7** English

of Haiti: 6 Creole, French, patois

of Honduras: 7 English, Spanish

of Hong Kong: 7 Chinese, English **9** Cantonese

of Hungary: 6 German, Magyar, Slovak **8** Croatian **9** Hungarian **10** Finno-Ugric

of Iceland: 5 Norse **9** Icelandic

of India: 4 Urdu **5** Hindi, Oriya, Tamil **6** Sindhi, Telugu **7** Bengali, English, Kannada, Malayam, Marathi, Punjabi **8** Assamese, Gujarati, Kashmiri, Sanskrit **9** Malayalam

of Indonesia: 5 Tetum **6** Bahasa, Igorot **7** English, Gyarung, Malayan **8** Balinese, Chamorro, Javanese, Madurese, Sudanese **10** Indonesian, Polynesian

of Iran: 4 Luri, Zend **5** Farsi, Turki **6** Arabic **7** Baluchi, Kurdish, Persian **8** Armenian **11** Azerbaijani

of Iraq: 5 Farsi **6** Arabic **7** Kurdish, Persian, Turkish

of Ireland: 4 Erse **5** Irish **6** Gaelic **7** English

of Israel: 6 Arabic, French, Hebrew **7** English

of Italy: 5 Ladin, Latin **6** French, German **7** Italian, Slovene **8** Friulian **9** Sardinian

of Ivory Coast: 4 Akan **6** Dioula, French

of Jamaica: 6 Creole **7** English

of Japan: 5 Kanto **8** Japanese

of Java: 4 Kavi, Kawi **5** Malay **6** Sassak **8** Balinese, Madurese, Sudanese **16** Bahasa Indonesian

of Jordan: 6 Arabic

of Kazakhstan: 6 Kazakh

of Kenya: 3 Luo **5** Bantu, Luhya, Masai **6** Kikuyu **7** English, Swahili **8** Buyerati **10** Hindustani

of Kiribati: 6 Samoan **7** English **10** Gilbertese

of Korea: 6 Korean

of Kuwait: 6 Arabic

of Kyrgyzstan: 6 Turkic **7** Kirghiz

of Laos: 3 Lao, Man, Meo **6** French **7** English

of Latvia: 7 Lettish

of Lebanon: 6 Arabic, French, Syriac **7** English, Turkish **8** Armenian

of Lesotho: 5 Sotho **7** English, Sesotho

of Liberia: 3 Kru, Kwa **5** Mande **7** English

of Libya: 6 Arabic, Berber **7** English, Italian

of Liechtenstein: 6 German **10** Alemannish

of Lithuania: 5 Zmudz **6** Baltic **10** Lithuanian

of Luxembourg: 6 French, German **7** English **13** Letzeburgesch

of Macao: 7 Chinese, English **9** Cantonese **10** Portuguese

of Macedonia: 10 Macedonian

of Madagascar/Malagasy Republic: 6 French **8** Malagasy, Malgache

of Malawi: 3 Yao **4** Cewa **5** Bantu, Ngoni, Tonga **6** Nyanja **7** English, Tumbuka **8** Chichewa **10** Chitumbuka

of Malaysia: 4 Bugi, Dyak **5** Malay, Tamil **6** Battok, Rejang **7** Chinese, English, Lampong, Niasese **8** Achinese, Javanese, Makassar **14** Bahasa Malaysia

of Maldives: 6 Arabic, Divehi

of Mali: 5 Dogon, Dyula, Feulh, Mande, Marka **6** Berber, French, Fulani **7** Bambara, Malinke, Senoufo, Songhai

of Malta: 7 English, Italian, Maltese

of Mauritania: 4 Fula **5** Wolof **6** Arabic, French **7** Phoolor, Tukulor **8** Fulfulde, Mandingo **9** Sarakolle **10** Hassaniyya

of Mauritius: 4 Urdu **5** Hindi, Tamil **6** Creole, French **7** English

of Mexico: 5 Mayan, Otomi **6** Mixtec **7** Mazahua, Mazatec, Nahuatl, Spanish, Totonac, Zapotec **8** Tarascan

of Moldova: 8 Romanian **9** Moldovian

of Monaco: 6 French **7** English, Italian **10** Monegasque

of Mongolia: 6 Kazakh **16** Khalkha Mongolian

of Montenegro: 13 Serbo-Croatian

of Morocco: 6 Arabic, Berber, French **7** Spanish

of Mozambique: 3 Yao **5** Makua **6** Nyanji, Thonga **7** Swahili **10** Portuguese

of Myanmar: 3 Lai **4** Chin, Kuki, Pegu, Shan **5** Karen **6** Kachin **7** Burmese

of Namibia: 5 Bantu **6** German **7** English, Khoisan **9** Afrikaans

of Nauru: 7 English, Nauruan

of Nepal: 6 Nepali, Newari **7** English

of the Netherlands: 5 Dutch **7** English, Frisian

of New Guinea: 4 Motu **7** English **16** Melanesian Pidgin

of New Zealand: 5 Maori **7** English

of Nicaragua: 7 English, Spanish

of Niger: 5 Hausa, Mande **6** Djerma, French, Fulani, Tuareg **8** Mandingo, Tamashek

of Nigeria: 3 Ibo **4** Efik, Igbo **5** Hausa **6** Yoruba **7** English

of Norway: 4 Lapp **5** Norse **6** Bokmal **7** Nynorsk, Riksmal **8** Landsmal, Samnorsk **9** Landsmaal, Norwegian

of Oman: 4 Urdu **5** Hindi **6** Arabic **7** Baluchi

of Pakistan: 4 Urdu **6** Pushtu, Sindhi **7** Baluchi, Bengali, English, Punjabi

of Panama: 7 English, Spanish

of Paraguay: 6 German **7** Guarani, Spanish

of Peru: 6 Aymara **7** English, Quechua, Spanish

of the Philippines: 4 Moro **5** Bicol, Bikol **6** Ibanag **7** Cebuano, English, Ilocano, Spanish, Tagalog, Visayan **8** Filipino **9** Pampangan, Philipino **10** Samar-Leyte **13** Bamboo-English **14** Panay-Hiligayon

of Poland: 6 Kaszub, Polish **10** Pomeranian

of Polynesia: 4 Niue, Uvea **5** Maori **6** Samoan, Tongan **7** Austral, Tagalog, Tokelau **8** Hawaiian, Tahitian **9** Marquesan, Tuamatuan **10** Mangarevan

of Portugal: 10 Portuguese

of Qatar: 6 Arabic

of Romania: 6 French, Magyar **7** Russian **8** Romanian, Rumanian **9** Hungarian

of Russia: 5 Evenk **6** Buriat, Kalmyk **7** Finnish, Russian **8** Ossetian

of Rwanda: 6 French **7** Swahili **11** Kinyarwanda

of Samoa: 6 Samoan **7** English

of San Marino: 7 Italian

of Sao Tome and Principe: 10 Portuguese

of Sardinia: 7 Italian

of Saudi Arabia: 6 Arabic

of Scotland: 4 Erse **6** Celtic, Gaelic, Keltic, Lallan **7** English, Lalland

of Senegal: 5 Wolof **6** French

of the Seychelles: 6 Creole, French **7** English

of Sierra Leone: 4 Krio **5** Limba, Mende, Mendi, Temne **6** Creole **7** English

of Singapore: 5 Malay, Tamil **7** Chinese, English **8** Mandarin

of Slovakia: 6 Slovik Slovak

of Slovenia: 7 Slovene

of the Solomon Islands: 7 English **13** Pidgin English **16** Melanesian Pidgin

of Somalia: 6 Arabic, Somali **7** English, Italian

of South Africa: 4 Taal, Zulu **5** Bantu, Hindi, Nguni, Sotho, Swazi, Tamil, Venda, Xhosa **6** Telegu, Thonga **7** English, Khoisan, Ndebele, Sesotho **8** Bujarati, Fanakalo **9** Afrikaans **13** Kitchen-Kaffir

of Spain: 6 Basque **7** Catalan, Spanish **8** Balearic, Galician **9** Castilian, Valencian

of Sri Lanka: 4 Pali **5** Tamil **7** English **9** Sinhalese

of Sudan: 2 Ga **3** Efe, Ewe, Ibo, Kru, Vak, Vei **4** Efik, Mole, Tshi **6** Arabic, Nubian, Yoruba **7** English **8** Mandango, Mandingo **9** Ta Bedawie

of Suriname: 5 Carib, Dutch, Hindi **6** Arawak **7** English **8** Javanese, Taki-Taki **10** Hindustani **11** Sranan Tongo **12** Sranang Tongo

of Swaziland: 5 Ngumi **7** English,

Siswati **9** Afrikaans **10** Portuguese

of Sweden: 4 Lapp **7** Swedish

of Switzerland: 5 Ladin **6** French, German **7** Italian **8** Romansch **14** Switzerdeutsch

of Syria: 6 Arabic, French, Syriac **7** Aramaic, English, Kurdish, Turkish **8** Armenian

of Taiwan: 4 Amon, Amoy **5** Hakka, Kuo Yu **6** Minnan **9** Taiwanese **15** Mandarin Chinese

of Tajikistan: 5 Tajik **7** Tadzhik

of Tanzania: 5 Bantu **6** Arabic **7** English, Khoisan, Nilotic, Swahili **8** Cushitic, Gujarati

of Thailand: 3 Lao, Tai **4** Ahom, Shan, Thai **5** Kadai **7** Bangkok, English **9** Krung Thep **12** Chinese Malay

of Tibet: 5 Balti **6** Ladkhi **7** Bhutani, Bodskad **8** Sanskrit **9** Bhutanese

of Togo: 3 Ana, Ewe, Twi **4** Mina **5** Hausa **6** French, Kabrai, Kabrie **7** Bassari, Dagomba, Quatchi **8** Kotokoli, Lotocoli

of Tonga: 6 Tongan **7** English

of Trinidad and Tobago: 6 French **7** Chinese, English, Spanish **10** Portuguese **12** French Patois

of Tunisia: 6 Arabic, Berber, French

of Turkey: 6 Arabic **7** Kurdish, Turkish

of Turkmenistan: 6 Turkic **10** West Turkic

of Tuvalu: 6 Samoan **7** English **8** Tuvaluan **10** Polynesian

of Uganda: 5 Ateso, Ganda **7** English, Luganda, Swahili

of Ukraine: 9 Ukrainian

of United Arab Emirates: 5 Farsi **6** Arabic **7** English, Persian

of Uruguay: 7 Italian, Spanish

of Uzbekistan: 5 Uzbek

of Vanuatu: 6 French **7** Bislama, English **16** Melanesian Pidgin

of Venezuela: 4 Pume **7** Spanish

of Vietnam: 3 Yue **4** Cham **5** Khmer, Rhade **6** French **7** Chinese, English **9** Cantonese **10** Vietnamese

of Wales: 5 Welsh **6** Celtic, Cymric, Keltic, Kymric **7** Cymraeg, English

of Western Sahara: 16 Hassaniyya Arabic

of Western Samoa: 6 Samoan **7** English

of Yemen: 6 Arabic

of Yugoslavia: 8 Albanian, Croatian **9** Hungarian **11** Montenegrin **13** Herzegovinian, Serbo-Croatian

of Zambia: 4 Lozi **5** Bemba, Lunda, Tonga **6** Luvale, Nyanja **7** English **9** Afrikaans

of Zimbabwe: 3 Ila **5** Bantu, Shona **7** English, Ndebele

language, artificial

of James Cooke Brown: 6 Loglan

of Hans Freudenthal: 6 Lincos **13** Lingua Cosmica

of Alexander Gode: 11 Interlingua

of C K Ogden: 12 Basic English
of J M Schleyer: 7 Volapuk
of Jean Francois Sudre: 8 Solresol
of L L Zamehof: 9 Esperanto
language, extinct 6 Dacian, Hattic, Lycian, Lydian, Palaic **7** Cornish, Elamite, Hittite, Hurrian **8** Etruscan, Illyrian, Phrygian, Sumerian, Thracian, Urartian **9** Dalmatian **15** Cuneiform Luwian **18** Hieroglyphic Luwian
languid 4 dull, slow, weak **5** faint, heavy, inert, shaky, spent, weary **6** feeble, infirm, leaden, sickly, supine, torpid **7** rickety, unsound, worn-out **8** drooping, fatigued, inactive, lifeless, listless, sluggish, unstable **9** apathetic, declining, doddering, enervated, exhausted, inanimate, lethargic, trembling, unhealthy **10** indisposed, spiritless **11** debilitated **12** on the decline **13** lackadaisical
languidness 6 apathy, torpor **7** inertia **8** lethargy **12** listlessness, sluggishness **13** indisposition
languish 3 ebb **4** fade, fail, flag, wane, wilt **5** covet, droop, faint **6** desire, hunger, sicken, thirst, wither **7** dwindle, long for, pine for, sigh for **8** diminish, give away, take sick, yearn for **9** become ill, break down, hanker for, hunger for, thirst for, waste away **10** go downhill **11** deteriorate, have a yen for, hunger after **12** be desirous of **13** go into decline
languor 5 ennui **6** torpor **7** inertia **8** dullness, hebetude, lethargy **9** indolence, lassitude, torpidity, weariness **10** dispassion, dreaminess **11** languidness, leisureness **12** lifelessness, listlessness, sluggishness
lank 4 bony, lean, limp, thin **5** gaunt, spare **6** skinny, slight **7** angular, scrawny **8** straight
lanky 4 bony, lean **5** gaunt, gawky, rangy, spare, weedy **6** skinny **7** angular, scrawny **8** gangling, rawboned **11** tall and thin
Lansbury, Angela
  born: 6 London **7** England
  roles: 4 Mame **8** Gaslight **10** JB Fletcher **11** Sweeney Todd **14** Murder She Wrote **15** Jessica Fletcher **22** The Manchurian Candidate
Laocoon
  vocation: 6 priest
  father: 5 Priam
  mother: 6 Hecuba
  sons: 3 two (unnamed)
  warned: 7 Trojans
  warned of: 11 Trojan horse
  killed by: 11 sea serpents
Laomedon
  king of: 4 Troy
  father: 4 Ilus
  wife: 6 Strymo
  son: 5 Priam **6** Lampus **7** Clytius **8** Hicetaon, Tithonus
  daughter: 7 Hesione **8** Themiste
Laos
  other name: 7 Lan Xang **23** land of a million elephants
  capital/largest city: 9 Viengchan, Vientiane
  others: 4 Nape **5** Pakse, Xieng **6** Paklay **7** Thakhek **11** Savannakhet, Xiang Khoang **12** Luang Prabang **14** Louangphrabang
  school: 12 Sisavangvong
  measure: 3 bak
  monetary unit: 2 at **3** att, kip
  mountain: 3 Lai, Loi, San **4** Copi, Khat **5** Atwat **6** Khoung, Tiubia **15** Annam Cordillera
  highest point: 3 Bia **7** Phou Bia
  river: 3 Noi **4** Done **5** Khong **6** Mekong, Sebang
  physical feature:
    plain: 4 Jars
    plateau: 8 Bolovens
  people: 2 Lu **3** Kha, Lao, Man, Meo, Tai, Yao, Yun **4** Miao, Thai **5** Hmong **8** Lao Teung **10** Phoutheung
  leader: 7 Fa Ngoun **8** Souphanouvong **14** Souligna Vongsa, Souvanna Phouma
  language: 3 Lao, Man, Meo **6** French **7** English
  religion: 7 animism **8** Buddhism **17** Theravada Buddhism
  feature:
    Buddhist priest: 5 bonze
    Communist guerrilla group: 9 Pathet Lao
    musical instrument: 5 khene
    temple: 3 wat
    trail: 9 Ho Chi Minh
Laothoe
  concubine of: 5 Priam
  son: 6 Lycaon **9** Polydorus
Lao-tzu, Lao-tze, Lao-Tse, Lao-tsze
  author of: 10 Tao Te Ching
  founder of: 6 Taoism
lap 3 sip **4** lick, wash **5** awash, drink, plash, slosh **6** babble, bubble, gurgle, lick up, murmur, ripple, splash, tongue
La Paz
  administrative capital of: 7 Bolivia
Laphria
  epithet of: 7 Artemis
Laphystius
  epithet of: 4 Zeus
lapidary 11 stonecutter
  expert in: 4 gems
lapis lazuli 9 azure-blue **17** semiprecious stone
  species: 8 lazurite
  source: 10 Badakhshan **11** Afghanistan
Laplace, Pierre S
  field: 7 physics **9** astronomy
  nationality: 6 French
  hypothesis of: 18 nebular solar system
Lapland
  region of: 6 Norway, Sweden **7** Finland
  peninsula: 4 Kola
  native: 4 Lapp
  herders of: 8 reindeer
lapse 3 gap, sag **4** drop, fall, flaw, go by, loss, sink, slip, stop, wane **5** boner, break, cease, droop, error, fault, pause, slump **6** breach, elapse, expire, hiatus, laxity, pass by, period, recede, recess, run out, slip by, wither, worsen **7** blunder, decline, descent, failing, failure, faux pas, interim, passage, relapse, respite, subside **8** collapse, downfall, elapsing, interval, omission, slip away **9** backslide, disregard, interlude, oversight, slump down, terminate **10** degenerate, falling off, forfeiture, infraction, negligence, peccadillo, regression **11** backsliding, delinquency, dereliction, deteriorate, shortcoming **12** degeneration, intermission, interruption, lose validity **13** deterioration, process of time, slight mistake **14** become obsolete, fall into disuse
lapsus linguae 16 a slip of the tongue
Laputa 12 Flying Island
  inhabitants: 11 visionaries
  in: Gulliver's Travels
lar *see* **5** lares
Lara
  character in: 9 Dr Zhivago
  author: 9 Pasternak
larboard 8 left side
  same as: 4 port
larceny 5 fraud, theft **7** bilking, forgery, looting, robbery, sacking **8** burglary, cheating, fleecing, stealing **9** extortion, pilferage, pilfering, swindling **10** absconding, peculation, plagiarism, purloining **11** defalcation, depredation **12** embezzlement, grand larceny, petit larceny, petty larceny, safecracking **13** appropriation, housebreaking **16** misappropriation
larder 5 cuddy **6** pantry, spence **7** buttery **8** food room **9** stillroom, storeroom **10** supply room **11** storage room
Lardner, Ring
  author of: 11 The Love Nest, You Know Me Al **12** Treat Em Rough **16** Gullible's Travels
Larentalia
  origin: 5 Roman
  event: 8 festival
lares
  form: 7 spirits
  watched over: 5 house **6** hearth **9** community **10** crossroads
  single member: 3 lar
  companions: 7 penates
  correspond to: 8 Dioscuri

large 3 big, fat **4** high, huge, vast, wide **5** ample, broad, grand, great, heavy, hulky, obese, plump, roomy **6** goodly, mighty, portly, rotund **7** copious, immense, liberal, massive, sizable **8** colossal, enormous, gigantic, imposing, man-sized, outsized, spacious, sweeping, towering **9** boundless, capacious, expansive, extensive, giant-like, kingsized, limitless, monstrous, overgrown, ponderous, strapping, unlimited, unstinted **10** exorbitant, gargantuan, stupendous **11** extravagant, far-reaching, magnificent, substantial **12** considerable **13** comprehensive **14** Brobdingnagian

large-hearted 8 generous **10** altruistic, benevolent, charitable **12** humanitarian **13** philanthropic

largely 6 mainly, mostly, widely **7** chiefly, greatly **9** generally, primarily **10** on the whole **11** extensively, principally **12** considerably **13** predominantly, substantially **14** for the most part, to a great extent

large-scale 3 big **4** epic, huge, vast, wide **5** broad, great **6** all-out, heroic, mighty **8** colossal, far-flung, gigantic **9** extensive, monstrous **10** gargantuan, stupendous, tremendous **11** far-reaching, wide-ranging **15** all-encompassing

largess, largesse 3 aid **4** boon, gift, help **5** favor, mercy **6** bounty, reward **7** charity, payment **8** bestowal, donation, gratuity, kindness, offering **9** benignity **10** assistance, generosity **11** benefaction, benevolence **12** philanthropy, remuneration

large store 8 emporium **11** supermarket **15** department store

largo
　music: **4** slow **14** dignified tempo

lark 3 gag **4** game, jape, romp, whim **5** antic, caper, fling, prank, spree, trick **6** frolic, gambol **7** caprice **8** escapade **11** high old time **12** sportiveness
　group of: **10** exaltation

larkspur 9 Consolida **10** Delphinium
　varieties: **4** Tall **5** Dwarf **6** Rocket

La Rochefoucauld, Francois
　author of: **6** Maxims **7** Maximes

larva
　insect stage after: **3** egg
　insect stage before: **4** pupa
　legless: **6** maggot

lascivious 4 foul, lewd **5** bawdy, dirty, gross, lurid **6** coarse, filthy, impure, ribald, sordid, vulgar, wanton **7** immoral, lustful, obscene, ruttish, squalid **8** depraved, immodest, improper, indecent, prurient **9** lecherous, salacious, shameless **10** indelicate, licentious, unblushing **11** dirty-minded, unwholesome

lash 3 fix, hit, tie **4** beat, bind, blow, flog, moor, rope, whip **5** brace, curse, flail, hitch, knock, leash, pound, scold, smack, strap, thong, tie up, truss **6** attach, berate, buffet, fasten, hammer, pinion, revile, secure, strike, stroke, tether, thrash, whip up **7** lecture, scourge, upbraid **8** lambaste, make fast **9** castigate, horsewhip **10** take to task, tongue-lash **11** rail against **13** cat-o'-nine-tails

lashed together 4 tied **5** bound **6** tied up **7** secured, trussed **8** fastened

lash out at 5 fly at **6** assail, attack, strike **8** fall upon

Las Palmas
　capital of: **13** Canary Islands

lass 4 girl, maid, miss **5** wench **6** damsel, female, lassie, lovely, maiden, pretty, virgin **7** colleen **10** schoolgirl, young woman

Lasser, Louise
　father: **8** S J Lasser
　husband: **10** Woody Allen
　born: **9** New York NY
　roles: **7** Bananas **11** Ladykillers **22** Mary Hartman Mary Hartman

lassie 4 girl, lass, maid **6** maiden **7** colleen **10** young woman

Lassie
　character: **5** Timmy **9** Doc Weaver **10** Jeff Miller, Paul Martin, Ruth Martin **11** Corey Stuart, Ellen Miller **12** Gramps Miller **17** Sylvester (Porky) Brockway
　cast: **10** Jan Clayton, Jon Provost, Jon Shepodd, Robert Bray **11** Arthur Space, Tommy Rettig **12** Donald Keeler, June Lockhart **14** Cloris Leachman, George Chandler **15** George Cleveland
　type of dog: **6** collie

lassitude 5 ennui **6** apathy, torpor **7** boredom, fatigue, inertia, languor, malaise **8** debility, doldrums, dullness, lethargy, weakness **9** faintness, indolence, tiredness, torpidity, weariness **10** droopiness, drowsiness, enervation, exhaustion, feebleness, supineness **11** languidness, prostration **12** indifference, lack of energy, listlessness, sluggishness

lasso 4 lash, rope **5** catch, noose, reata, riata, thong **6** lariat

last 3 end **4** go on, keep, live, stay, wear **5** abide, after, exist, final, stand **6** behind, ending, endure, extend, finale, finish, hold on, hold up, remain, utmost **7** carry on, closing, extreme, finally, hold out, outlive, outwear, persist, stand up, subsist, survive, tailing **8** at the end, continue, doomsday, farthest, final one, furthest, hindmost, hold good, in back of, maintain, rearmost, terminal, terminus, trailing, ultimate **9** in the rear, persevere **10** Armageddon, concluding, conclusion, conclusive, eventually, terminally, ultimately **11** crack of doom, crucial time **12** in conclusion, tagging along **13** Day of Judgment
　French: **7** dernier

Last Analysis, The
　author: **10** Saul Bellow

Last Days of Pompeii, The
　author: **18** Edward Bulwer-Lytton
　character: **4** Ione **5** Nydia **7** Arbaces, Glaucus **9** Apaecides

Last Frontier
　nickname of: **6** Alaska

lasting 4 firm **5** fixed, solid **7** abiding, chronic, durable, eternal **8** constant, enduring, immortal, lifelong, long-term **9** incessant, lingering, long-lived, permanent, perpetual, steadfast, unceasing **10** continuing, deep-rooted, deep-seated, perdurable, persistent, protracted **11** established, never-ending **12** indissoluble **14** indestructible, of long duration **17** firmly established

Last Lion, The
　author: **17** William Manchester

lastly 6 at last **7** finally, to sum up **8** after all, in the end **10** on the whole **12** in conclusion **19** all things considered **33** taking everything into consideration

Last of the Mohicans, The
　author: **19** James Fenimore Cooper
　character: **5** Magua, Uncas **9** Cora Munro **10** Alice Munro **11** Natty Bumppo **12** Chingachgook **18** Major Duncan Heyward

last part 3 end **6** ending, finale, finish **8** third act **10** denouement **12** final chapter

Last Picture Show, The
　director: **16** Peter Bogdanovich
　based on story by: **13** Larry McMurtry
　cast: **10** Ben Johnson **11** Jeff Bridges **12** Ellen Burstyn **13** Eileen Brennan **14** Cloris Leachman, Cybill Shepherd, Timothy Bottoms
　Oscar for: **15** supporting actor (Johnson) **17** supporting actress (Leachman)

Last Puritan, The
　author: **15** George Santayana

La Strada
　director: **15** Federico Fellini
　cast: **11** Aldo Silvana **12** Anthony Quinn **15** Giulietta Masina, Richard Basehart
　score: **8** Nino Rota
　Oscar for: **11** foreign film

last resort
　French: **8** pis aller

Last Samurai, The
　director: **11** Edward Zwick
　cast: **6** Koyuki (Taka) **9** Togo Igawa (General Hasegawa), Tom Cruise (Nathan Algren) **11** Ken Watanabe (Katsumoto), Tony Goldwyn (Colonel Bagley) **12** Masato Harada (Omura),

Timothy Spall (Simon Graham) **13**
Billy Connolly (Zebulon Gant) **15**
William Atherton (Winchester Rep)
20 Shichinosuke Nakamura (Emperor Meiji)

Last Tango in Paris
> director: **18** Bernardo Bertolucci
> cast: **12** Marlon Brando **14** Maria Schneider

Last Waltz, The
> director: **14** Martin Scorsese
> cast: **7** The Band **8** Bob Dylan **9** Neil Young **10** The Staples **11** Eric Clapton, Muddy Waters, Neil Diamond, Van Morrison **12** Joni Mitchell **13** Emmylou Harris

last word
> French: **10** dernier cri

latch 3 bar **4** bolt, clip, hasp, hook, lock, loop, shut, snap **5** catch, clamp, close **6** buckle, button, clinch, fasten, secure **8** make fast **9** fastening

late 3 new **4** dead, gone, slow **5** fresh, tardy **6** held up, put off, recent **7** delayed, newborn, overdue, tardily **8** departed, detained, dilatory, passed on **9** after time, postponed **10** behindhand, behind time, dilatorily, unpunctual **16** recently deceased

late arrival 7 laggard **8** lateness, newcomer **9** immigrant, latecomer, tardiness **16** Johnny-come-lately

Late George Apley, The
> author: **10** J P Marquand

lately 6 of late **7** just now **8** latterly, recently, right now **9** currently, presently, yesterday **10** not long ago **13** a short time ago

Late Mattia Pascal, The
> author: **15** Luigi Pirandello

latency 8 abeyance, deferral, dormancy, inaction **10** quiescence, suspension

latent 6 covert, hidden **7** abeyant, dormant, lurking, passive **8** inactive, sleeping **9** concealed, potential, quiescent, suspended, unaroused, unexposed **10** in abeyance, intangible, unapparent, unrealized **11** not manifest, undeveloped, unexpressed **13** inconspicuous

later 4 next **5** since **6** behind, in time, mature **7** ensuing, tardily **8** in a while, in sequel **9** afterward, following, presently, thereupon **10** consequent, more recent, most recent, subsequent, succeeding, successive, thereafter **11** after a while, consecutive **12** subsequently, successively, toward the end

lateral 4 side **5** sided **7** flanked, oblique, sloping **8** edgeways, edgewise, flanking, sidelong, sideward, sideways, sidewise, skirting, slanting

Late Show with David Letterman
> feature: **11** Ask Mr Melman **15** Stupid Pet Tricks **18** Brush with Greatness, Stupid People Tricks
> bandleader: **10** Paul Shafer
> city: **7** New York

latest fashion
> French: **10** dernier cri

lather 4 foam, head, scum, soap, suds **5** froth, spume, sweat **6** soap up **8** make foam, soapsuds **9** make froth **11** shaving foam

Latin
> language family: **12** Indo-European
> branch: **6** Italic
> group: **7** Romance
> subgroup: **6** French **7** Catalan, Italian, Romansh, Spanish **8** Romanian **9** Provencal **10** Portuguese **13** Rhaeto-Romanic

Latino, Latina 8 Hispanic **13** Latin American

Latinus
> king of: **6** Latium
> father: **6** Faunus
> mother: **6** Marica
> wife: **5** Amata
> daughter: **7** Lavinia

latitude 5 range, scope, sweep **6** leeway, margin **7** license **8** free play **9** amplitude, elbowroom, full swing **10** indulgence, liberality **11** opportunity, unrestraint **12** independence **15** freedom of action, freedom of choice **16** unrestrictedness

Latona *see* **4** Leto

La Tour, Georges de
> born: **3** Vic **6** France **8** Lorraine
> artwork: **7** Peasant **10** The New Born **12** Peasant's Wife, The Card Cheat **15** St Peter Penitent **16** The Fortune Teller **18** The Denial of St Peter **23** The Education of the Virgin **31** St Sebastian Tended by the Holy Women

Latrobe, Benjamin Henry
> architect of: **9** US Capitol **15** Sedgeley Mansion (PA) **18** Baltimore Cathedral **22** Philadelphia Waterworks
> style: **12** Greek Revival, Neoclassical **13** Gothic Revival

latter 3 end **4** last **5** final, later **6** ending, latest, modern **7** ensuing **8** terminal **10** most recent, subsequent, succeeding, successive **13** last-mentioned **15** second-mentioned

lattice 4 fret, grid **5** frame, grate **6** grille, screen **7** framing, grating, network, trellis, webwork **8** fretwork, openwork **9** framework, reticulum **11** trelliswork **12** reticulation

Latvia
> former name: **30** Latvian Soviet Socialist Republic
> capital/largest city: **4** Riga
> others: **5** Cesis, Libau **6** Dvinsk, Libava, Tukums **7** Jelgava, Jurmala, Liepaja, Rezekne **8** Dunaberg, Dunaburg, Valmiera **9** Ventspils **10** Daugavpils
> government: **8** republic
> measure: **3** let **4** stof **5** stoff, verst **6** arshin, kulmet **7** verchoc, verchok **8** krouchka, pourvete **9** deciatine, lofstelle, pourvette **10** tonnseteel
> monetary unit: **3** lat **4** latu **6** rublis, santim **7** kapeika, santima
> weight: **9** liespfund
> lake: **7** Aluksne
> river: **4** Ogre **5** Gauja, Venta **6** Salaca **7** Daugava, Lielupe **12** Western Dvina
> sea: **6** Baltic
> physical feature:
>> cape: **8** Domesnes
>> gulf: **4** Riga
>> strait: **4** Irbe
> people: **3** Kur, Liv **4** Balt, Cour, Lett **7** Latgale, Latvian, Russian, Zemgale
>> former ruler: **15** Teutonic Knights
> language: **7** Lettish
> religion: **8** Lutheran **13** Roman Catholic

laud 5 extol, honor **6** praise **7** acclaim, commend, glorify

laudable 5 model, noble **8** sterling **9** admirable, estimable, excellent, exemplary **10** creditable **11** commendable, meritorious **12** praiseworthy **13** unimpeachable **17** deserving of esteem **18** worthy of admiration

laudation 6 praise **7** acclaim **8** applause, approval **11** approbation **12** commendation

laudatory 8 admiring, honoring, praising **9** adulatory, approving, extolling, favorable **10** eulogistic, eulogizing, flattering, glorifying **11** acclamatory, approbatory, celebratory, encomiastic, panegyrical **12** commendatory **13** complimentary

laugh 4 glee, ha-ha, ho-ho, howl, roar **5** mirth **6** cackle, giggle, guffaw, titter **7** break up, chortle, chuckle, snicker, snigger **10** bellylaugh, horselaugh **12** express mirth **14** roll in the aisle, split one's sides

laughable 5 comic, dopey, droll, funny, inane, merry, silly, witty **6** absurd, stupid **7** amusing, asinine, comical, foolish, risible **8** farcical, tickling **9** diverting, grotesque, hilarious, ludicrous **10** outlandish, outrageous, ridiculous **11** rib-tickling **12** preposterous **13** sidesplitting

Laugh-In, Rowan & Martin's
> regular: **8** Dan Rowan **9** Gary Owens, Judy Carne, Ruth Buzzi **10** Dick Martin, Goldie Hawn, Larry Hovis, Lily Tomlin **11** Arte Johnson, Henry Gibson **12** Jo Anne Worley **13** Eileen Brennan
> saying: **10** Sock it to me **15** Here come de judge, You bet your bippy **24** Beautiful downtown Burbank **31** Look that up in your Funk and Wagnalls

laughingstock 3 ass 4 butt, dupe, fool, joke 8 fair game 11 figure of fun

laugh off 6 deride 7 dismiss, put down 8 belittle, ridicule 9 disparage

laughter 3 joy 4 glee 5 mirth 6 gaiety 7 jollity, revelry 8 hilarity 9 joviality, merriment 11 merrymaking 12 conviviality, exhilaration

Laughton, Charles
  wife: 14 Elsa Lanchester
  born: 7 England 11 Scarborough
  roles: 9 Rembrandt 10 Jamaica Inn 13 Les Miserables 15 Ruggles of Red Gap, The Paradine Case 16 Advise and Consent 17 Mutiny on the Bounty 23 Barretts of Wimpole Street, The Hunchback of Notre Dame 24 Witness for the Prosecution 25 The Private Life of Henry VIII (Oscar)

launch 4 fire, hurl 5 begin, eject, float, found, impel, shoot, start, throw 6 let fly, propel, unveil 7 fire off, project, send off 8 catapult, initiate, premiere, put to sea 9 cast forth, discharge, establish, institute, introduce, set afloat 10 embark upon, inaugurate, set forth on 11 set in motion, venture upon 13 thrust forward 15 set into the water

launder 4 soak, wash 5 clean, rinse, scour, scrub 7 cleanse, wash out 11 wash and iron

Launfal
  knight of: 10 round table

Laura
  director: 13 Otto Preminger
  cast: 11 Clifton Webb, Dana Andrews, Gene Tierney 12 Vincent Price 14 Judith Anderson

laurel 6 Kalmia, Laurus 13 Laurus nobilis 14 Ficus benjamina 15 Cordia alliodora
  varieties: 3 bog, pig 4 pale 5 black, dwarf, great, sheep 6 Alpine, cherry, ground, Indian, purple, Sierra, spurge, tropic 7 Chinese, English, red-twig, weeping, western 8 American, drooping, Himalaya, Japanese, mountain, Portugal 9 Tasmanian 10 Australian, California, variegated 11 Alexandrian

Laurel, Stan
  real name: 22 Arthur Stanley Jefferson
  partner: 11 Oliver Hardy
  born: 7 England 9 Ulverston
  roles: 8 Pardon Us 9 Saps at Sea 10 Way Out West

laurels 4 fame 5 award, glory, honor, kudos, prize 6 credit, praise, renown, reward 7 acclaim, tribute 8 accolade, applause, citation 9 celebrity 10 decoration, popularity 11 acclamation, distinction, recognition 12 commendation 15 illustriousness

Laurie
  also: 16 Theodore Laurence

character in: 11 Little Women
  author: 6 Alcott

laus Deo 11 praise to God 13 praise be to God

lavation 7 bathing, washing 8 ablution, cleaning 9 cleansing

lavender 4 herb, mint 5 aspic, behen, lilac, spick, spike 6 purple 7 inkroot 8 amethyst, stichado 9 lavendula
  represents: 6 purity
  uses: 6 sachet 7 perfume 8 medicine 9 cosmetics

laver 11 footed basin

Laverne and Shirley
  character: 12 Frank De Fazio 13 Carmine Ragusa, Lenny Kolowski, Mrs Edna Babish, Shirley Feeney 14 Laverne De Fazio 15 Andrew (Squiggy) Squiggman
  cast: 10 Eddie Mekka, Phil Foster 12 Betty Garrett, David L Lander 13 Cindy Williams, Michael McKean, Penny Marshall
  girls worked in: 12 Shotz Brewery
  theme song: 23 Making Our Dreams Come True
  spinoff from: 9 Happy Days

Lavinia
  father: 7 Latinus
  mother: 5 Amata
  husband: 6 Aeneas

lavish 4 free, lush, wild 5 plush, waste 6 shower 7 copious, opulent, pour out, profuse 8 abundant, effusive, generous, prodigal, squander 9 bounteous, bountiful, dissipate, excessive, exuberant, impetuous, luxuriant, plenteous, plentiful, sumptuous, unsparing 10 immoderate, munificent, profligate, unstinting 11 extravagant, fritter away, intemperate, overindulge, overliberal, spend freely 12 give overmuch, greathearted, overwhelming, unrestrained, without limit

lavishness 6 bounty 8 lushness, opulence 9 profusion 10 luxuriance 11 munificence, prodigality 12 extravagance, immoderation 13 bountifulness, plenteousness, sumptuousness

Lavoisier, Antoine
  field: 9 chemistry
  nationality: 6 French
  founder: 15 modern chemistry
  named: 6 oxygen 8 hydrogen

law 3 act 4 bill, code, fuzz, rule, writ 5 axiom, bylaw, canon, dogma, edict, model, truth 6 decree, police 7 justice, mandate, precept, statute, theorem 8 absolute, legality, standard 9 criterion, enactment, gendarmes, legal form, ordinance, postulate, principle 10 civil peace, convention, due process, invariable, regulation 11 commandment, formulation, fundamental, orderliness, working rule 13 jurisprudence, standing order 14 generalization, rules of conduct 15 legal profes-

sion
  Latin: 3 jus
  goddess of: 4 Maat

law-abiding 6 honest 7 upright 9 honorable 10 aboveboard, principled

Law and Order
  network: 3 NBC
  creator: 8 Dick Wolf
  cast: 9 Chris Noth (Mike Logan) 10 Dann Florek (Donald Cragen), Steven Hill (Adam Schiff) 11 Angie Harmon (Abbie Carmichael), Carey Lowell (Jamie Ross), Dianne Weist (Nora Lewin), Jerry Orbach (Lennie Briscoe), Paul Sorvino (Phil Cerreta) 12 Annie Parisse (Alexandra Borgia), Dennis Farina (Joe Fontana), Jesse L Martin (Ed Green), Jill Hennessy (Claire Kincaid), Sam Waterston (Jack McCoy) 13 Benjamin Bratt (Reynaldo Curtis), Elisabeth Rohm (Serena Southerlyn), George Dzundza (Max Greevey), Richard Brooks (Paul Robinette) 15 Michael Moriarty (Benjamin Stone) 16 Michael Imperioli (Nick Falco), S Epatha Merkerson (Anita Van Buren) 18 Fred Dalton Thompson (Arthur Branch)

Law and Order: Criminal Intent
  network: 3 NBC
  creator: 8 Dick Wolf
  cast: 9 Chris Noth (Mike Logan) 11 Kathryn Erbe (Alexander Eames) 13 Jamey Sheridan (James Deakins) 14 Courtney B Vance (Ron Carver) 15 Anabella Sciorra (Carolyn Barak), Vincent D'Onofrio (Robert Goren)

Law and Order: Special Victims Unit
  network: 3 NBC
  creator: 8 Dick Wolf
  cast: 4 Ice-T (Fin Tutuola) 6 B D Wong (George Huang) 9 Diane Neal (Casey Novak) 10 Dann Florek (Donald Cragen) 11 Dean Winters (Brian Cassidy) 12 Michelle Hurd (Monique Jefferies) 13 Richard Belzer (John Munch) 14 Stephanie March (Alexandra Cabot) 15 Mariska Hargitay (Olivia Benson) 17 Christopher Meloni (Elliot Stabler)

lawbreaker 3 con 4 hood, thug 5 crook, felon 6 outlaw 7 convict, culprit 8 criminal, jailbird, offender, scofflaw 9 miscreant, wrongdoer 10 delinquent, malefactor, recidivist 11 perpetrator 12 transgressor

lawful 3 due 5 legal, licit 6 proper, titled 7 allowed, granted 8 rightful 9 legalized, statutory, warranted 10 authorized, legitimate, prescribed 11 legitimized, permissible 15 legally entitled 16 legally permitted

lawless 6 unruly, wanton 7 chaotic, defiant, illegal, riotous, wayward 8 anarchic, mutinous, unlawful, wide open 9 insurgent, out of hand, unbridled **10** disorderly, licentious, rebellious, refractory, ungoverned **11** disobedient, lawbreaking, terroristic **12** disorganized, freewheeling, illegitimate, noncompliant, unrestrained **13** insubordinate, transgressive **14** uncontrollable

lawlessness 5 chaos **7** anarchy **8** disorder

lawn 4 park, turf, yard **5** glade, grass, sward **7** grounds, terrace **10** grassy plot, green field, greensward, meadowland **12** grassy ground

law of a place
  Latin: **7** lex loci

Law of Moses 5 Torah **10** Pentateuch **15** Ten Commandments

law of nations
  Latin: **10** jus gentium

law of nature
  Latin: **11** jus naturale

Lawrence, Carol
  real name: **16** Carol Maria Laraia
  husband: **12** Robert Goulet
  born: **13** Melrose Park IL
  roles: **5** Maria **13** West Side Story

Lawrence, D H
  author of: **10** The Rainbow **11** Women in Love **13** Sons and Lovers **20** Lady Chatterley's Lover

Lawrence, Ernest Orlando
  field: **7** physics
  invented: **9** cyclotron
  awarded: **10** Nobel Prize

Lawrence, Gertrude
  real name: **29** Alexandra Dagmar Lawrence Klasen
  born: **6** London **7** England
  roles: **9** Pygmalion **11** The King and I **17** The Glass Menagerie

Lawrence, T E
  also: **18** Lawrence of Arabia
  served in: **3** WWI **10** Arab Revolt
  advisor to: **6** Faisal **12** Husayn Ibn Ali
  fought against: **5** Turks **8** Ottomans
  author of: **20** Seven Pillars of Wisdom

Lawrence of Arabia
  director: **9** David Lean
  cast: **10** Jose Ferrer, Omar Sharif **11** Claude Rains, Jack Hawkins, Peter O'Toole (T E Lawrence) **12** Alec Guinness, Anthony Quinn **13** Anthony Quayle
  Oscar for: **7** picture **8** director **14** cinematography

Lawrence Welk Show, The
  champagne lady: **8** Alice Lon **11** Norma Zimmer
  cast: **7** Aladdin **11** Larry Hooper, Myron Floren **12** Bobby Burgess **13** Barbara Boylan, Lennon Sisters
  Welk played: **9** accordion

lawyer 6 jurist, legist **7** counsel, shyster **8** advocate, attorney **9** barrister, counselor, counsel **10** mouthpiece,

prosecutor **11** pettifogger **12** legal advisor **14** special pleader **15** ambulance chaser

lax 4 hazy, limp, weak **5** agape, loose, slack, vague **6** casual, flabby, floppy, remiss **7** cryptic, flaccid, inexact, lenient, not firm, relaxed **8** careless, derelict, drooping, heedless, nebulous, slipshod, uncaring, yielding **9** confusing, imprecise, negligent, oblivious, undutiful, unheeding, unmindful **10** ill-defined, incoherent, neglectful, permissive **11** hanging open, indifferent, thoughtless, unconcerned **12** loose-muscled, unstructured **13** irresponsible **15** unconscientious

laxness 7 neglect **9** looseness, slackness **10** negligence **11** imprecision **12** carelessness, indifference

Laxness, Halldor Kiljan
  author of: **12** Iceland's Bell **14** The Atom Station **17** Independent People **25** The Great Weaver from Kashmir
  won: **10** Nobel Prize

lay 3 air, bet, put, set **4** bear, fell, fine, form, give, laic, lend, levy, make, plan, poem, raze, rest, seat, song, tune **5** align, allot, apply, ditty, exact, floor, hatch, level, offer, place, stage, wager **6** assess, assign, ballad, charge, demand, depict, devise, gamble, ground, hazard, impose, impute, laical, layout, locate, melody, repose, strain **7** amateur, arrange, concoct, contour, deposit, dispose, forward, present, produce, profane, proffer, refrain, secular, set down, situate, station **8** allocate, assemble, beat down, give odds, inexpert, organize, oviposit, position **9** attribute, elucidate, enunciate, formulate, knock down, knock over, prostrate, roundelay, situation **10** cause to lie, topography **11** arrangement, disposition, nonclerical, orientation, put together **12** conformation **13** configuration, inexperienced, nonspecialist **14** partly informed, unprofessional **15** nonprofessional **17** nonecclesiastical

lay at the door of 6 assign **7** ascribe **8** charge to **9** attribute

lay bare 4 bare, show **6** expose, reveal, unmask, unveil, unwrap **7** divulge, exhibit, publish, uncover **8** disclose **9** broadcast, make known **10** make public **11** communicate

lay down arms 5 yield **6** give up **7** succumb **8** cry quits **9** surrender **10** capitulate **11** come to terms, sue for peace **13** declare a truce **17** acknowledge defeat

layer 3 bed, lap, ply **4** coat, fold, leaf, seam, slab, tier, zone **5** level, plate, scale, sheet, stage, story **6** lamina **7** stratum **9** thickness

layman 4 laic **6** sister **7** amateur, brother **8** outsider **9** churchman **10**

catechumen **11** churchwoman, communicant, parishioner **16** nonprofessional **16** member of the flock

layoff 4 fire **6** firing, idling, ouster, the axe **7** dismiss, release, sacking, the boot, the gate, the sack **8** pink slip, shutdown **9** closedown, discharge, dismissal, hard times, the bounce **10** cashiering, depression, the heave-ho **11** furloughing, termination **12** unemployment **13** disemployment, walking papers **20** discharge temporarily

lay off 7 dismiss, forfeit, release, set free **8** get rid of, liberate **9** discharge, terminate **11** give the gate, send packing

Lay of the Last Minstrel, The
  author: **14** Sir Walter Scott
  character: **8** Margaret, The Dwarf **13** Lady Buccleuch, Lord Cranstoun **17** Master of Buccleuch **19** Ghost of Michael Scott **21** Sir William of Deloraine

lay on 6 bestow, confer, supply **7** present, provide

lay open 4 open **6** expose, open up **7** clarify **9** make plain **18** make understandable

layout 4 form, plan **5** chart, draft, dummy, model, motif, spend **6** design, expend, pay out, sketch, spread **7** diagram, drawing, fork out, outline, pattern **8** disburse, shell out **9** blueprint, delineate, placement, spread out, structure **11** arrangement, composition

lay waste 4 ruin **5** level, wreck **6** ravage **7** despoil, destroy, wipe out **8** demolish, desolate **9** devastate, eradicate **10** annihilate, obliterate

Lazarus 6 beggar
  means: **8** God helps
  sister: **4** Mary **6** Martha
  hometown: **7** Bethany
  resurrected by: **5** Jesus

Lazarus
  author: **14** Leonid Andreyev

Lazarus, Mell
  creator/artist: **5** Momma **9** Miss Peach

lazurite
  variety: **11** lapis lazuli

lazy 3 lax **4** idle, slow **5** inert, slack **6** drowsy, sleepy, torpid **7** laggard, languid **8** inactive, indolent, listless, slothful, sluggish **9** apathetic, easygoing, lethargic, shiftless **10** languorous, slow-moving **13** unindustrious **15** unwilling to work

lazy person 5 drone, idler **6** loafer **14** good-for-nothing

l'chaim, l'chayim 5 toast **6** Hebrew, to life

Leachman, Cloris
  born: **11** Des Moines IA
  roles: **7** Phyllis **9** Spanglish **11** High

Anxiety **12** Kiss Me Deadly **17** Young Frankenstein **18** Mary Tyler Moore Show, The Last Picture Show

lead 2 go **3** aim, top **4** clue, draw, edge, have, head, hero, hint, live, lure, pass **5** charm, excel, guide, model, outdo, pilot, steer, tempt **6** allure, convey, direct, entice, extend, induce, manage, margin, pursue, seduce **7** advance, attract, bring on, command, conduct, control, example, go first, incline, issue in, marshal, pioneer, precede, proceed, produce, stretch, surpass, undergo **8** domineer, go before, guidance, moderate, outstrip, persuade, priority, result in, shepherd, star part **9** advantage, come first, direction, go through, headliner, influence, plurality, rank first **10** branch into, experience, first place, indication, precedence, precedency, set the pace, show the way, tend toward **11** antecedence, be in advance, leading role, preside over, protagonist

lead
  chemical symbol: 2 Pb
  mineral: 10 fiedlerite
  ore: 6 galena, pyrite

lead astray 4 dupe, lure **6** delude **7** beguile, deceive, ensnare, mislead **19** lead up the garden path

leaden 4 dark, dull, glum, gray **5** inert, murky **6** dreary, gloomy, numbed, somber, torpid **7** grayish, languid **8** burdened, careworn, darkened, deadened, listless, sluggish, unwieldy **9** depressed, inanimate **10** cumbersome, hard to move

leader 4 boss, guru, head **5** chief, guide, mogul **6** bigwig, honcho, master, mentor, tycoon **7** captain, foreman, kingpin, magnate, manager, pioneer, prophet **8** director, superior **9** chieftain, commander, conductor, godfather, pacemaker, patriarch **10** forerunner, pacesetter, pathfinder, supervisor **11** frontrunner, torchbearer, trailblazer

leadership 4 helm, lead, sway **5** reins, wheel **7** command, primacy **8** charisma, guidance, headship, hegemony **9** captaincy, supremacy **10** domination, mastership **11** managership, preeminence, stewardship **12** directorship, governorship, guardianship, self-reliance **13** ability to lead, self-assurance **14** administration **15** managerial skill, superintendency **17** authoritativeness

leading 3 top **4** head, main **5** basic, chief, first, great, prime **6** ruling **7** advance, guiding, initial, leadoff, notable, primary, ranking, stellar, supreme, topmost **8** advanced, dominant, foremost **9** directing, essential, governing, nonpareil, paramount, principal, prominent, sovereign, unri-

valed **10** motivating, preeminent, underlying **11** controlling, outstanding, pacesetting **12** unchallenged, unparalleled **13** most important **14** quintessential **15** most influential, most significant

lead on 4 goad **5** egg on **6** entice **7** mislead, support **9** encourage **19** lead up the garden path

lead the way 4 lead, show, take **5** guide **6** escort **7** conduct

leaf 4 flip, foil, page, skim **5** blade, bract, folio, frond, green, inset, petal, sheet, thumb **6** browse, glance, insert, needle **7** foliole, lamella, leaflet **9** cotyledon, extension, turn green **10** lamination **12** sheet of metal
  edge: 5 erose **7** crenate, dentate
  angle: 4 axil
  aperture: 7 stoma
  kind: 5 calyx, petal, sepal **7** corolla

leaflet 2 ad **4** bill **5** flier, flyer, tract **6** folder, notice **7** booklet, handout **8** brochure, bulletin, circular, handbill, pamphlet **9** broadside, throwaway **10** broadsheet **12** announcement **13** advertisement

league 4 ally, band **5** cabal, group, guild, merge, union **6** cartel **7** combine, compact, company, network, society **8** alliance **9** coalition **10** conspiracy, federation, fraternity, join forces **11** association, confederacy, confederate, consolidate, cooperative, partnership **13** collaboration, confederation, confraternity

Leah
  means: 7 wild cow
  father: 5 Laban
  husband: 5 Jacob
  sister: 6 Rachel
  slave: 6 Zilpah
  son: 4 Levi **5** Judah **6** Reuben, Simeon **7** Zebulun **8** Issachar
  daughter: 5 Dinah
  burial place: 9 Machpelah

leak 3 ebb, rip **4** blab, gash, hole, ooze, rent, rift, seep, vent **5** break, chink, cleft, crack, drain, exude, fault, spill **6** breach, efflux, escape, filter, let out, reveal, take in **7** confide, crevice, divulge, dribble, fissure, let slip, opening, outflow, rupture, seepage **8** aperture, disclose, draining, give away, puncture **9** discharge, percolate **10** interstice, make public **11** be permeable, perforation **12** admit leakage **16** let enter or escape

leakage 5 issue **7** outflow, seepage **9** discharge

Leakey, Louis S Bazett
  field: 12 anthropology
  discovered: 8 early man
  worked at: 8 Tanzania **12** Olduvai Gorge
  wife: 4 Mary
  son: 7 Richard

lean 3 aim, bow, tip **4** bend, cant, lank, list, poor, rely, rest, slim, tend, thin, tilt **5** gaunt, lanky, lurch, scant, slant, slope, small, spare, weedy **6** barren, depend, meager, modest, nonfat, prefer, scanty, skinny, sparse, svelte **7** angular, count on, incline, recline, scraggy, scrawny, slender, spindly, trust in, willowy **8** exiguous, rawboned, resort to, skeletal **9** emaciated **10** inadequate, set store by **11** be partial to, have faith in, prop oneself **12** insufficient, seek solace in **14** rest one's weight, support oneself

Lean, David
  director of: 10 Summertime **11** Oliver Twist **13** Doctor Zhivago, Ryan's Daughter **15** A Passage to India **16** Lawrence of Arabia (Oscar) **17** Great Expectations **23** The Bridge on the River Kwai (Oscar)

Leander
  loved: 4 Hero
  swam nightly: 10 Hellespont
  death by: 8 drowning

leaning 4 bent, turn **5** slant **7** relying **8** affinity, tendency **9** proneness **10** dependence, partiality, preference, proclivity, propensity **11** inclination **14** predisposition

leap 3 hop **4** jete, jump, romp, rush, skip **5** bound, caper, frisk, vault **6** bounce, cavort, frolic, gambol, hasten, hurtle, prance, spring **7** hop over **8** jump over **9** bound over, saltation **10** hurtle over, jump across, spring over

Lear, Norman
  TV producer of: 5 Maude **13** The Jeffersons **14** All in the Family

Learchus
  father: 7 Athamas
  mother: 3 Ino
  killed by: 7 Athamas

learn 3 con **4** hear **6** detect, master, pick up **7** find out, uncover, unearth **8** discover, memorize **9** ascertain, determine, ferret out **10** become able **12** find out about

learned 4 deep, wise **7** erudite **8** cultured, educated, informed, lettered, literate, profound, schooled, well-read **9** scholarly **10** cultivated **12** accomplished, intellectual, well-educated **13** knowledgeable

Learned, Michael
  roles: 5 Nurse **10** The Waltons

learner 4 tyro **5** pupil, tutee **6** novice, rookie **7** draftee, recruit, scholar, student, trainee **8** beginner, disciple, enlistee, follower, freshman, neophyte **9** fledgling, greenhorn, novitiate, proselyte, schoolboy **10** apprentice, schoolgirl, tenderfoot **11** schoolchild

learning 4 lore **5** study **6** wisdom **7** culture **8** teaching **9** education, erudition, knowledge, schooling **11** cultivation, edification, information, instruction, scholarship **13** comprehension, enlightenment, understanding

Learning
  god of: **5** Thoth

Leary, Timothy
  phrase: **19** Tune in, turn on, drop out

leash 4 curb, lead, line, rein, ruin **5** strap, thong **6** bridle, choker, fasten, hold in, stifle, string, tether **7** contain, control, harness **8** restrain, suppress

leatherneck 6 gyrene, marine

Leather-Stocking Tales
  author: **19** James Fenimore Cooper
  includes: **10** The Prairie **11** The Pioneers **13** The Deerslayer, The Pathfinder **20** The Last of the Mohicans
  hero of: **7** Hawkeye **10** Pathfinder, The Trapper **11** Natty Bumppo **13** The Deerslayer **15** Leather-stocking **16** Le Longue Carabine

leave 2 go **3** fly **4** cede, exit, flee, jilt, keep, quit, will **5** allot, be off, cause, endow, forgo, going, split, waive, yield **6** assign, bug out, commit, decamp, depart, desert, eschew, forego, give up, legate, move on, recess, resign, retain, set out **7** abandon, abscond, bequest, consent, consign, deposit, entrust, forsake, holiday, let stay, liberty, parting, produce, push off, release, respite, retreat, sustain, take off, time off **8** approval, bequeath, farewell, furlough, generate, give over, maintain, result in, sanction, shove off, vacation **9** allowance, apportion, departure, hotfoot it, let remain, surrender, tolerance **10** concession, depart from, embark from, go away from, indulgence, permission, relinquish, retire from, sabbatical, sufferance, withdrawal **11** bid farewell, endorsement **13** absent oneself, understanding

leave a ship 4 land **6** debark **8** go ashore **9** disembark **11** abandon ship

leave behind 4 jilt **6** desert, vacate **7** abandon, discard, forsake **8** evacuate **9** cast aside **10** relinquish **11** outdistance

leave cold 4 bore **12** leave unmoved **15** leave unaffected

Leave It To Beaver
  character: **11** June Cleaver, Ward Cleaver **12** Eddie Haskell, Wally Cleaver **13** Beaver (Theodore) Cleaver
  cast: **7** Tony Dow **9** Ken Osmond **12** Hugh Beaumont, Jerry Mathers **18** Barbara Billingsley

leave off 3 end **4** halt, quit, stop **5** cease **6** desist, finish **7** suspend **8** conclude **11** discontinue, refrain from

leave out 4 drop, omit **6** except, reject **7** exclude

Leaves of Grass
  author: **11** Walt Whitman

leave suddenly 3 fly **4** flee **6** cut out,

decamp, run off **7** abscond, make off, run away, rush off, take off **11** take a powder **15** be off and running

leave-taking 4 exit **5** adieu **7** goodbye, leaving, parting, send-off **8** au revoir, farewell **9** departure **10** withdrawal

leave undone 4 quit **6** give up **7** abandon, forsake, neglect **8** give up on

Lebanon
  ancient name: **9** Phoenicia
  capital/largest city: **6** Beirut **8** Beyrouth
  others: **3** Sur **4** Arca, Tyre **5** Ehden, Halba, Hamat, Sahle, Saida, Sayda, Sidon, Sofar, Zahla, Zahle **6** Byblos, Ghazir, Juniye, Tibnin **7** Baalbek, Batroun, Bsherri, Rachaya, Tripoli, Zgharta **8** Djezzine, El Hermel, Hasbaiya, Merjuyun **9** Broummana, Marjayoun **10** Beited Dine, Heliopolis
    ancient city: **8** Carthage
  school: **4** Arab **8** American, Lebanese **11** Saint Joseph
  division:
    ancient: **4** Tyre **5** Arwad, Sidon **6** Byblos, Jubayl
  monetary unit: **5** livre, pound **7** piastre
  lake: **5** Quran **6** Qirawn
  mountain: **4** Mzar **5** Aruba **6** Hermon **7** Lebanon, Sannine **8** Kadischa, Kenisseh **9** Kennisseh **10** al-Mukammal **11** Anti-Lebanon
  highest point: **7** es Sauda **13** Qurnat al-Sawda
  river: **3** Dog, Joz **5** Barid, Kebir, Lycos **6** Auwali, Barada, Damour, Litani **7** Hasbani, Leontes, Orontes **8** Kasemieh
  sea: **13** Mediterranean
  physical feature:
    cape: **10** Pigeon Rock **11** Ras esh Shiqa **12** Qadisha Gorge
    plain: **4** Bika **5** Bekaa
    valley: **5** Beqaa **6** al-Biqa **9** Great Rift
    wind: **7** khamsin
  people: **4** Arab **11** Palestinian
    ancient: **9** Canaanite **10** Phoenician
    leader: **6** Bashir, Sarkis **7** Chamoun **8** Franjieh **9** al-Din Maan **11** Amin Gemayel **13** Bashir Gemayel
    poet: **11** Kahlil Gibran
    rulers: **5** Arabs **6** French, Greeks, Romans **7** Syrians **8** Hittites, Ottomans, Persians **9** Assyrians, Crusaders, Egyptians, Mamelukes **11** Babylonians
  language: **6** Arabic, French, Syriac **7** English, Turkish **8** Armenian
  religion: **5** Druse, Druze, Islam **8** Maronite, Melchite **10** Protestant **11** Monophysite **12** Christianity **13** Greek Catholic **14** Greek Orthodoxy **17** Armenian Orthodoxy
  place:

  dam: **5** Qarun
  ruins: **7** Baalbek **15** Temple of Bacchus, Temple of Jupiter
  feature:
    Christian group: **10** Phalangist
    dance: **6** dabkeh, dabkey
    tree: **5** cedar
  food:
    dish: **6** kibbeh **8** tabouleh
    drink: **4** arak **6** arrack

Le Bel, Joseph Achille
  field: **9** chemistry
  nationality: **6** French
  founded: **15** stereochemistry

Le Bourgeois Gentilhomme
  author: **7** Moliere
  character: **7** Cleonte, Dorante **9** M Jourdain **16** Monsieur Jourdain

Le Carre, John
  real name: **13** David Cornwell
  author of: **11** A Perfect Spy **13** Smiley's People **15** Absolute Friends, The Night Manager **17** The Tailor of Panama **18** The Looking Glass War **19** A Small Town in Germany **20** The Little Drummer Girl **21** The Honorable Schoolboy **22** Tinker Tailor Soldier Spy **26** The Spy Who Came in from the Cold

lechayim, lehayim 6 to life

lecherous 4 lewd **5** randy **6** carnal **7** goatish, lustful, ruttish **8** prurient **9** salacious, satyrlike **10** lascivious, libidinous, licentious, lubricious

lechery 4 lust **8** lewdness **9** carnality, prurience **10** satyriasis **11** lustfulness, nymphomania **13** salaciousness **14** lasciviousness

Le Cid
  author: **9** Corneille
  composer: **21** Leconte Dehisle, Charles **13** Jules Massenet

Leconte de Lisle, Charles
  author of: **14** Poemes Antiques, Poemes Barbares

Le Corbusier
  real name: **23** Charles Edouard Jeanneret
  architect of: **10** La Tourette (monastery) **15** Notre Dame du Haut (Ronchamp France) **16** Unite d'Habitation (Marseilles)
  planned city of: **10** Chandi garh (capital of the Punjab)
  style: **6** Purism **12** New Brutalism

lecture 4 talk **5** chide, scold, speak **6** homily, preach, rail at, rebuke, sermon, speech **7** address, censure, chiding, expound, oration, reading, re proof, reprove, upbraid, warning **8** admonish, call down, harangue, moralize, reproach **9** discourse, hold forth, reprimand, sermonize, talking-to **10** preachment, take to task **12** chastisement, disquisition, remonstrance

lecture hall 9 classroom **10** auditorium **12** amphitheater, assembly hall

lecturelike **7** donnish, preachy **8** academic, didactic, pedantic **9** homiletic **10** moralizing

LED **18** light emitting diode **19** alphanumeric display

Leda
father: **8** Thestius
husband: **9** Tyndareus
lover: **4** swan, Zeus
son: **6** Castor, Pollux **8** Dioscuri **10** Polydeuces
daughter: **5** Helen **6** Phoebe **8** Philonoe, Timandra **12** Clytemnestra

Leda and the Swan
author: **7** W B Yeats

ledge **4** sill, step **5** ridge, shelf **6** mantel, offset **8** foothold, shoulder **10** projection **11** mantelpiece, mantelshelf, outcropping

Lee, Bruce
born: **12** San Francisco
son: **7** Brandon
roles: **7** Marlowe **11** Fists of Fury, Game of Death **14** The Green Hornet, Enter the Dragon **17** Return of the Dragon, Chinese Connection **24** Bruce Lee: Curse of the Dragon

Lee, Christopher
born: **6** London
roles: **5** Jocks **6** Albino, Serial **7** The Girl **8** Caravans **9** Shaka Zulu, The Keeper, The Gorgon **10** Dark Places **11** Eye for an Eye, Horror Hotel, Moulin Rouge, Killer Force **12** Count Dracula, The Wicker Man, The Oblong Box, Scream of Fear **13** The Death Train **14** Treasure Island **15** Journey of Horror **16** Castle of Fu Manchu, The Creeping Flesh, A Tale of Two Cities **17** The Four Musketeers **23** Return from Witch Mountain **25** The Hound of the Baskervilles **30** The Private Life of Sherlock Holmes

Lee, Gypsy Rose
born: **7** Seattle
author of: **5** Gypsy **8** Doll Face **15** Lady of Burlesque
roles: **11** The Stripper, My Lucky Star **13** Screaming Mimi

Lee, Harper
author of: **18** To Kill a Mockingbird

Lee, Henry
nickname: **15** Light Horse Harry
served in: **16** Revolutionary War
member of: **10** US Congress **19** Continental Congress
governor of: **8** Virginia
suppressed: **16** Whiskey Rebellion
son: **7** Robert E

Lee, Peggy
born: **9** Jamestown (ND)
roles: **7** Mr. Music **13** The Jazz Singer **15** Pete Kelly's Blues **18** Ladies Sing the Blues

Lee, Robert E
father: **5** Henry **15** Light Horse Harry
born: **11** Stratford VA **18** Westmore-

land County
wife: **21** Mary Ann Randolph Custis
served in: **8** Civil War **10** Mexican War
commander of: **22** Army of Northern Virginia
suppressed raid: **9** John Brown **12** Harper's Ferry
battle: **7** Bull Run **8** Antie tam **10** Gettysburg **14** Fredericksburg **16** Chancellorsville, Seven Days' Battles
surrendered at: **20** Appomattox Court House
president of: **17** Washington College

Lee, Spike
original name: **17** Sheldon Jackson Lee
born: **2** GA **7** Atlanta
wife: **17** Tonya Linette Lewis
films: **8** Clockers, Malcolm X **9** He Got Game, She Hate Me **10** School Daze **11** Jungle Fever **15** Do the Right Thing, She's Gotta Have It
company: **18** Forty Acres and A Mule
ads for: **4** Nike

Lee, Stan **10** cartoonist
of: **9** Spider-Man

leek **18** Allium ampeloprasum
emblem of: **5** Wales
varieties: **4** lily, rose, sand, wild **5** lady's **6** meadow

leer **4** ogle **5** fleer, smirk **6** goggle

leery **4** wary **5** cagey, chary **6** unsure **7** guarded **8** cautious, doubtful, hesitant **9** skeptical, undecided **10** suspicious **11** circumspect, distrustful, mistrustful

Leeuwenhoek, Anton van
field: **10** microscopy
father of: **12** microbiology
discovered: **13** red blood cells

leeway **4** play **5** scope, slack **6** margin **7** cushion, headway, reserve **8** headroom, latitude **9** allowance, clearance, elbow room, extra time, tolerance **11** flexibility **13** room for choice **14** margin for error **15** maneuverability

left behind **7** vacated **8** deserted, forsaken, forsook **9** abandoned, discarded, evacuated **12** relinquished

leftover **6** excess, legacy, unused **7** overage, residue, surplus, uneaten **8** leavings, oddments, residual, survivor **9** carry-over, remainder, remaining

left-wing **7** leftist, liberal, radical **9** socialist **11** progressive

left-winger **7** leftist, liberal, radical **9** socialist **11** progressive

Lefty
nickname of: **5** Gomez **12** Steve Carlton

leg **3** gam, lap, pin **4** limb, part, post, prop **5** brace, femur, shank, stage, stump, tibia **6** column, fibula, member, pillar **7** portion, section, segment, stretch, support, upright

legacy **4** gift **6** devise, estate **7** be-

quest, vestige **8** heirloom, heritage, leftover, survivor **9** carry-over, throwback, tradition **10** birthright, hand-me-down **11** inheritance

legal **4** fair **5** licit, of law, valid **6** kosher, lawful **7** cricket **8** forensic, judicial, juristic, rightful **9** courtroom, juridical **10** legitimate, sanctioned **11** permissible

legal advisor **6** lawyer **7** counsel **8** advocate, attorney **9** barrister, counselor, so licitor **13** attorney-at-law **14** counselor-at-law

legal form **4** writ **8** document **10** instrument

legality **8** validity **9** licitness **10** lawfulness, legitimacy **17** constitutionality

legalization **8** sanction **9** enactment **10** permission, validation **13** authorization **14** legitimization

legalize **5** enact **6** permit **8** sanction, validate **9** authorize **10** legitimize

legal residence **4** home **8** domicile, dwelling

legal tender **4** cash **5** money **8** currency

legate **5** agent, envoy **6** deputy **8** emissary **14** representative

legatee **4** heir **7** heiress **9** inheritor **11** beneficiary

legation **7** embassy, mission **8** ministry **9** consulate **10** delegation **11** chancellery

legend **3** key **4** edda, lore, myth, saga, tale **5** fable, motto, story, title **7** caption, fiction, proverb **8** folklore **11** inscription

legendary **5** famed **6** fabled, famous, mythic **7** storied **8** fabulous, fanciful, mythical **9** imaginary **10** apocryphal, celebrated, fictitious, proverbial

Legend of Good Women, The
author: **15** Geoffrey Chaucer
character: **4** Dido **5** Medea **6** Thisbe **7** Alceste, Ariadne, Lucrece, Phyllis **9** Cleopatra, Hypsipyle, Philomela **12** Hypermnestra

Legend of Sleepy Hollow, The
author: **16** Washington Irving
character: **12** Brom Van Brunt (Brom Bones), Ichabod Crane **16** headless horseman, Katrina Van Tassel

Leger, Fernand
born: **6** France **8** Argentan
artwork: **8** Bargeman **10** Adam and Eve, The Wedding, Three Women **11** The Builders, The Cyclists, The Mechanic, The Stairway **14** The Great Parade **15** Le Grand Dejeuner **16** Contrasting Forms, Nudes in the Forest **21** Butterflies and Flowers

legerdemain **7** cunning **8** deftness, jugglery, juggling, trickery **9** deception **10** adroitness, artfulness **11** maneuvering **13** sleight of hand **16** prestidigitation

legible 4 neat 5 clear, plain 7 visible 8 clear-cut, distinct, readable 12 decipherable 14 comprehensible, understandable

legion 3 mob, sea 4 army, host, mass 5 corps, drove, horde, spate, swarm 6 myriad, throng, troops 7 brigade 8 division 9 multitude

leg irons 5 bonds, irons 6 chains 7 fetters 8 shackles

legislation 3 act 4 bill 6 ruling 7 measure, statute 9 amendment, enactment, law making, ordinance

legislator 7 senator 8 alder man, delegate, lawgiver, lawmaker 10 councilman 11 assemblyman, congressman 13 congresswoman 14 representative 15 parliamentarian

legislature 4 diet 5 house 6 senate 7 chamber, council 8 assembly, congress 10 parliament

legitimacy 8 legality, validity 10 lawfulness 11 correctness, genuineness 12 authenticity, rightfulness 15 appropriateness

legitimate 4 fair, just, true 5 legal, licit, sound, valid 6 lawful, proper 7 correct, genuine, logical, tenable 8 rightful 9 authentic, justified, plausible 10 believable, reasonable 11 appropriate, well-founded

leg-pull 4 hoax 9 deception 13 practical joke

Legree, Simon 13 cruel overseer
  character in: 14 Uncle Tom's Cabin
  author: 5 Stowe

LeGuin, Ursula K
  author of: 5 Gifts 13 Lathe of Heaven 14 Rocannon's World 15 The Dispossessed 16 Always Coming Home 17 Tales from EarthSea 21 The Left Hand of Darkness

Lehar, Franz (Ferencz)
  born: 7 Komarno (then Hungary, now Czechoslovakia)
  composer of: 9 Gipsy Love 13 The Merry Widow 20 The Count of Luxembourg

Lehmbruck, Wilhelm
  born: 7 Germany 9 Meiderich
  artwork: 11 Rising Youth 12 Man Flung Down, Praying Woman, Seating Youth 13 Kneeling Woman, Standing Woman, Standing Youth

Leigh, Janet
  husband: 10 Tony Curtis
  daughter: 14 Jamie Lee Curtis
  born: 8 Merced CA
  roles: 6 Psycho, The Fog 10 The Vikings 11 Little Women, Touch of Evil

Leigh, Vivien
  real name: 17 Vivian Mary Hartley
  husband: 15 Laurence Olivier
  born: 5 India 10 Darjeeling
  roles: 11 Ship of Fools 12 Anna Karenina 13 Blanche du Bois, Scar-

lett O'Hara 14 Waterloo Bridge 15 Gone With the Wind (Oscar) 17 That Hamilton Woman 21 A Streetcar Named Desire (Oscar), Roman Spring of Mrs Stone

Leighton, Margaret
  husband: 12 Max Reinhardt 14 Laurence Harvey, Michael Wilding
  born: 7 England 10 Barnt Green 14 Worcestershire
  roles: 12 The Go-Between 13 The Winslow Boy 14 Separate Tables 19 The Night of the Iguana

leisure 4 ease, rest 6 recess, repose 7 holiday, respite, time off 8 free time, vacation 9 diversion, idle hours, spare time 10 recreation, relaxation

leisurely 4 idle, slow 6 casual, slowly 7 languid, relaxed, restful 9 unhurried 10 slow-moving 11 lingeringly, unhurriedly 12 without haste 13 lackadaisical

Lemmon, Jack
  real name: 18 Jack Uhler Lemmon III
  wife: 11 Felicia Farr
  born: 8 Boston MA
  roles: 7 Missing 8 Out to Sea 10 April Fools 12 Grumpy Old Men, Save the Tiger (Oscar), The Apartment, The Great Race, The Odd Couple 13 China Syndrome, Mister Roberts, Some Like It Hot 18 Days of Wine and Roses, Under the Yum-Yum Tree 19 How to Murder Your Wife
  co-star: 13 Walter Matthau
  character: 10 Felix Ungar

lemon 11 Citrus limon
  varieties: 4 wild 5 dwarf, giant, Meyer, water 6 garden, wonder 9 wild water 12 Chinese dwarf 14 American wonder
  slang for: 3 dud 9 defective

lemures
  form: 6 ghosts
  characteristic: 10 maleficent 11 troublesome

lend 4 give, loan 6 impart, in vest, supply 7 advance, furnish 10 contribute

lend a hand 3 aid 6 assist 7 help out

lend assistance 3 aid 4 abet, help 6 succor 7 relieve 16 give a helping hand

lend one's name to 7 endorse, support 9 recommend

length 3 run 4 span, term, time 5 piece, range, reach 6 extent, period 7 compass, measure, portion, section, segment, stretch 8 distance, duration, end to end 9 longitude, magnitude 11 elapsed time, measurement

lengthen 3 pad 5 add to 6 expand, extend, let out, pad out 7 augment, drag out, draw out, fill out, prolong, spin out, stretch 8 elongate, flesh out, increase, protract 9 attenuate, string out

lengthening 8 full form 9 extending, extension 10 elongation, stretching 11 extenuation, protraction 12 prolongation

lengthy 5 windy, wordy 6 padded, prolix 7 endless 8 drawn out, extended, overlong, rambling 9 elongated, extensive, garrulous, longdrawn, prolonged 10 digressive, discursive, long-winded, protracted 12 interminable

leniency 5 mercy 7 charity 8 clemency 9 tolerance 10 compassion 11 forbearance, magnanimity 12 mercifulness 13 forgivingness

lenient 4 kind, mild, soft 6 gentle 7 clement, liberal, patient, sparing 8 merciful, moderate, tolerant 9 easygoing, forgiving, indulgent 10 benevolent, charitable, forbearing, permissive 11 kindhearted, soft-hearted, sympathetic 13 compassionate, tenderhearted

Lenin, Vladimir Illyich
  surname: 7 Ulyanov
  also called: 7 Nikolai
  founder of: 10 Bolshevism
  leader of: 17 Russian Revolution
  premier of: 4 USSR

Lenni-Lenape *see* 8 Delaware

Lennon, John
  born: 9 Liverpool (UK)
  wife: 7 Cynthia, Yoko Ono
  sons: 4 Sean 6 Julian
  songs: 5 Woman 6 Mother 7 Imagine 9 Stand By Me 10 Jealous Guy 12 Instant Karma
  killed: 11 New York City
  killer: 11 Mark Chapman
  see also 7 Beatles

Lenny
  director: 8 Bob Fosse
  cast: 8 Jan Miner 11 Stanley Beck 13 Dustin Hoffman (Lenny Bruce) 14 Valerie Perrine (Honey Harlowe)

Leno, Jay
  host of: 14 The Tonight Show
  author of: 9 Headlines (Books I-IV) 17 Leading with My Chin

Le Notre, Andre
  landscape architect of: 6 Clagny 9 Tuileries 10 Versailles 12 Saint Germain 13 Fontainebleau 22 Chateau de Vaux-le-Vicomte

lens
  invented by:
    achromatic: 7 Dollond
    bifocal: 8 Franklin
    fused bifocal: 6 Borsch

Lenya, Lotte
  real name: 16 Karoline Blamauer
  husband: 9 Kurt Weill
  born: 7 Austria, Hitzing
  roles: 5 Jenny 18 From Russia with Love, The Seven Deadly Sins, The Three-Penny Opera

Leo
symbol: **4** lion
planet: **3** Sun
rules: **7** romance **10** creativity
born: **4** July **6** August

Leonard, Elmore
author of: **4** Swag **5** Glitz, Stick **6** Be
Cool, Hombre **7** La Brava **9** Cat
Chaser, Gold Coast, Gunsights, The
Hot Kid, The Hunted **10** Mr Majes-
tyk, Mr Paradise **11** Pagan Babies **12**
The Big Bounce **14** Fifty-Two
Pick-Up, Valdez Is Coming **16** Dou-
ble Dutch Treat, The Bounty Hunters
18 Forty Lashes Less One

Leonato
character in: **19** Much Ado About
Nothing
author: **11** Shakespeare

Leoncavallo, Ruggiero
born: **5** Italy **6** Naples
composer of: **8** Serafita **10** I Pagliacci

Leontes
character in: **14** The Winter's Tale
author: **11** Shakespeare

Leonteus
leader of: **6** Greeks
leader at: **4** Troy
suitor of: **5** Helen

leopard 3 cat **7** panther **10** spotted cat
group of: **4** leap

Leo the Lip
nickname of: **11** Leo Durocher

lepidoptera
class: **8** hexapoda
phylum: **10** arthropoda
group: **4** moth **9** butterfly

leprechaun 3 elf, imp **5** dwarf, gnome
6 sprite **12** little person

Ler
also: **3** Lir
origin: **5** Irish
personifies: **3** sea
son: **8** Manannan
corresponds to: **4** Llyr

Lerner, Alan J.
born: **7** New York
author of: **4** Gigi **7** Camelot **9** Brigadoon **10** My Fair Lady **17** An American in Paris
composer of: **7** Tribute **15** The Little
Prince
producer of: **14** Paint Your Wagon

Lesage, Le Sage, Alain
author of: **7** Gil Blas **8** Turcaret

Lesbos
island in: **6** Aegean
home of: **6** Sappho

Lescaze, William
architect of: **18** Borg-Warner Building
(Chicago) **38** Philadelphia Savings
Fund Society Building

Lescot, Pierre
architect of: **10** Cour Carree **20** Fontaine des Innocents
rebuilding of: **6** Louvre

lese-majeste, lese majesty 5 crime
7 treason
against: **12** king's dignity

Lesotho
other name: **10** Basutoland
capital/largest city: **6** Maseru
others: **4** Roma **5** Joels **6** Leribe,
Morija **7** Quthing, Sekakes **8** Mafe-
teng, Matsieng **9** Marakabei, Qachas
Nek, Semonkong **10** Butha Buthe,
Mokhotlong, Thaba Bosiu **11** Mo-
hales Hoek **12** Sehlabathebe, Teyate-
yaneng
head of state: **4** king
monetary unit: **4** cent, rand
mountain: **6** Maloti, Maluti **7** Central
8 Injasuti, Machache **10** Ben Macdhui **11** Drakensberg, Thaba Putsoa
highest point: **16** Thabana Ntlenyana
river: **5** Senqu **6** Orange, Tugela **7**
Caledon **9** Makhaleng
physical feature:
gorge: **5** Oxbow
people: **4** Zulu **5** Bantu, Tembu **6** Basuto **7** Basotho
leader: **7** Moshesh **9** Mosheshwe
10 Moshoeshoe **14** Leabua Jonathan
language: **5** Sotho **7** English, Sesotho
religion: **7** animism **13** Roman Catholic **18** Lesotho Evangelical
feature:
blanket: **4** kobo
house: **8** rondavel
water project: **11** Malibamatso

less 5 fewer **6** barely, little **7** smaller **8**
meagerly, slighter **10** not as great **11**
more limited

lessen 3 ebb **4** ease, sink, thin, wane **5**
abate, lower **6** dilute, reduce, shrink **7**
abridge, decline, dwindle, lighten,
slacken, subside **8** contract, decrease,
diminish, mitigate, wind down **9** alleviate **10** depreciate

lessening 6 waning **8** decrease, dilution **9** abatement, deduction, dwindling, reduction, shrinkage **10** diminution, lightening, mitigation,
shortening, slackening **11** abridgement, alleviation, contraction, diminishing, slacking off **12** abbreviation,
condensation, depreciation

Lesseps, Ferdinand 8 engineer **9**
Suez Canal

lesser 4 less **5** minor **7** humbler, smaller **8** inferior, slighter **9** secondary **11**
secondarily

Lessing, Doris
author of: **8** Shikasta **11** Mara and
Dann **13** The Fifth Child **16** The
Four-Gated City, The Good Terrorist
17 The Golden Notebook **20** The
Sirian Experiments **21** The Story of
General Dann **37** Marriages Between
Zones Three Four and Five
series: **14** Canopus in Argus **18** Chil-
dren of Violence

lesson 5 class, drill, guide, model,
moral, study **6** caveat, notice, rebuke
7 caution, example, message, reading,
segment, warning **8** exemplar, exercise, homework **9** deterrent **10** admonition, advisement, assignment, punishment, recitation, Scriptures **11**
instruction **12** remonstrance

Lestrade, Inspector
character in: **14** (The Adventures of)
Sherlock Holmes
author: **10** Conan Doyle

let 4 make, rent **5** admit, allow, cause,
grant, lease, leave **6** enable, permit,
sublet, suffer **7** approve, charter, concede, empower, endorse, hire out, license, warrant **8** sanction, sublease,
tolerate **9** authorize

let
term in: **6** tennis
serve touches: **3** net

let down 4 drop **5** lower **6** betray **8**
push down **10** disappoint **11** disillusion

letdown 3 rue **4** balk, blow **6** fizzle,
regret **7** chagrin, set back **8** comedown **10** anticlimax, bafflement, bitter
pill, dashed hope, discontent **11** frustration **12** blighted hope, discomfiture
13 mortification **14** disappointment,
disenchantment, disgruntlement **15**
disillusionment, dissatisfaction

let fall 4 drop **5** let go **7** release

let fly 4 cast, hurl **5** eject, fling, heave,
sling, throw **6** launch, propel

let go 3 axe, can **4** fire, free, lose,
oust, sack **6** bounce, give up

lethal 5 fatal, toxic **6** deadly, mortal **7**
baneful, killing **8** venomous, virulent
9 dangerous, malignant, poisonous
11 destructive **13** mortally toxic

lethargic 4 dull, idle, lazy **5** inert **6**
drowsy, sleepy, torpid **7** languid, passive **8** comatose, indolent, listless,
slothful, sluggish **9** apathetic, enervated, somnolent, soporific **10** dispirited, lackluster, unspirited **11** debilitated, indifferent

lethargy 5 sloth **6** apathy, stupor, torpor **7** inertia, languor **8** dullness, laziness **9** indolence, lassitude, torpidity
10 drowsiness, inactivity **12** indifference, listlessness, slothfulness, sluggishness

Lethe
form: **5** river
location: **5** Hades
caused: **13** forgetfulness

let in 5 admit **7** receive **12** allow to enter

let loose 4 free **5** let go **6** let fly **7** release, set free, unleash **8** give vent,
liberate **12** give free rein

Leto
also: **6** Latona
father: **5** Coeus

mother: 6 Phoebe
son: 6 Apollo
consort: 4 Zeus
daughter: 5 Diana **7** Artemis

let off 5 let go **6** acquit, excuse, exempt **7** release, set free **8** liberate **9** discharge

let slip 6 betray, expose, reveal **7** divulge, uncover **8** blurt out, disclose, give away

Let's Make a Deal
host: 9 Monty Hall
announcer: 10 Jay Stewart

letter 4 note **7** epistle, message, missive **8** dispatch, document **9** substance **10** billet-doux

Letter, The
director: 12 William Wyler
based on story by: 15 Somerset Maugham
cast: 10 Bette Davis **14** Frieda Inescort **15** Gale Sondergaard, Herbert Marshall, James Stephenson
setting: 6 Malaya

Letterman, David
Host of: 26 Late Show with David Letterman

letter ordering imprisonment
French: 14 lettre de cachet
carried seal of: 4 king **9** sovereign

letters 8 learning **9** erudition **10** literature **13** belles lettres

Letters from the Underground
author: 16 Fyodor Dostoevsky

Letter to Three Wives, A
director: 17 Joseph L Mankiewicz
cast: 10 Ann Sothern **11** Jeanne Crain, Jeffrey Lynn, Kirk Douglas, Paul Douglas **12** Linda Darnell, Thelma Ritter
Oscar for: 6 script **8** director

let the buyer beware
Latin: 12 caveat emptor

let the people rule
Latin: 13 regnat populus
motto of: 8 Arkansas

let there be light
Latin: 7 fiat lux

lettre de cachet 26 letter ordering imprisonment **28** letter under the sovereign's seal

lettuce 7 Lactuca
varieties: 3 cos **5** chalk, frog's, lamb's, water **6** Boston, garden, miner's **7** iceberg, prickly, romaine **8** escarole **9** asparagus **11** common lamb's

letup 4 lull **5** pause **6** relief **7** respite **8** decrease, interval, slowdown, stopping, surcease, vacation **9** abatement, cessation, interlude, lessening, remission **10** slackening **11** retardation

Let Us Now Praise Famous Men
author: 9 James Agee

Let us therefore be joyful
Latin: 15 Gaudeamus igitur

Le Vau, Louis
architect of: 6 Louvre **10** Versailles **12** Hotel Lambert **22** Chateau de Vaux-le-Vicomte **24** College des Quatres Nations

levee 3 dam **4** bank, dike, pier, quay, wall **5** ditch, jetty, ridge, wharf **6** durbar **9** reception **10** embankment

level 3 aim, bed **4** even, flat, rank, raze, tied, vein, zone **5** align, floor, flush, grade, layer, plane, point, stage, story, wreck **6** direct, height, lay low, reduce, smooth, topple **7** aligned, even out, flatten, landing, on a line, station, stratum, uniform **8** equalize, make even, position, tear down, together **9** devastate, elevation, knock down **10** consistent, horizontal, on a par with, unwrinkled **11** achievement, neck and neck **12** on an even keel

level-headed 4 sage **5** sound **6** poised, stable, steady **7** prudent **8** balanced, cautious, composed, sensible **9** collected, judicious, practical, unruffled **10** cool-headed, dependable, thoughtful **11** circumspect **12** eventempered **13** dispassionate **14** selfcontrolled

levelheadedness 6 aplomb **9** good sense, soundness, stability **10** equanimity **11** common sense **13** judiciousness

Levene, Sam
real name: 12 Samuel Levine
born: 6 Russia
roles: 12 Guys and Dolls **13** Nathan Detroit **15** The Sunshine Boys

lever 3 bar, pry **5** jimmy, raise **7** crowbar

Lever, Charles
author of: 14 Charles O'Malley

Leverrier, Urbain Jean Joseph
field: 9 astronomy
nationality: 6 French
co-discovered: 7 Neptune
worked with: 14 John Couch Adams

Levi
father: 5 Jacob **6** Melchi, Symeon
mother: 4 Leah
son: 6 Kohath, Merari **7** Gershom
brother: 3 Dan, Gad **5** Asher, Judah **6** Joseph, Reuben, Simeon **7** Zebulun **8** Benjamin, Issachar, Naphtali
sister: 5 Dinah
violated: 5 Dinah
also called: 7 Matthew
descendant of: 6 Levite

Leviathan 6 dragon **10** sea monster
means: 13 spirally bound
represents: 14 terrible powers

Leviathan
author: 12 Thomas Hobbes

Levin, Ira
author of: 6 Sliver **13** Rosemary's Baby **16** The Stepford Wives

Levin, Konstantin
character in: 12 Anna Karenina
author: 7 Tolstoy

Levi-Strauss, Claude
method: 13 structuralism
author of: 13 Mythologiques, The Savage Mind **16** Tristes Tropiques **22** Structural Anthropology **29** Elementary Structures of Kinship

Levitch, Joseph
real name of: 10 Jerry Lewis

levity 3 fun **5** mirth **6** joking, whimsy **8** hilarity, trifling **9** flippancy, frivolity, lightness, silliness **10** jocularity, pleasantry, triviality **11** flightiness, foolishness **16** lightheartedness

levy 3 fee, tax **4** duty, make, toll, wage **5** draft, exact, start **6** assess, call up, charge, demand, enlist, excise, impose, muster, pursue, tariff **7** carry on, collect **9** calling up, conscript, prosecute **10** assess ment, imposition **12** conscription

Levy, Marion
real name of: 15 Paulette Goddard

Lew Archer, Private Detective
author: 13 Ross MacDonald

lewd 5 bawdy **6** ribald, risque, vulgar, wanton **7** goatish, immoral, lustful, obscene **8** indecent, prurient **9** lecherous, libertine, salacious **10** lascivious, libidinous, licentious, lubricious **11** Rabelaisian **12** pornographic

Lewis, C S
author of: 10 Perelandra **13** Prince Caspian, The Last Battle **14** Surprised by Joy, The Silver Chair, Til We Have Faces **17** The Horse and His Boy **18** The Magician's Nephew **19** The Screwtape Letters **20** Out of the Silent Planet **21** The Chronicles of Narnia **25** The Voyage of the Dawn Treader **29** The Lion the Witch and the Wardrobe

Lewis, Jerry
real name: 13 Joseph Levitch
partner: 10 Dean Martin
born: 8 Newark NJ
roles: 8 The Caddy **10** The Bellboy, The Sad Sack **11** Cinderfella **12** The Geisha Boy **16** Artists and Models **17** The Nutty Professor **20** The Disorderly Orderly

Lewis, Sinclair
author of: 7 Babbitt **9** Dodsworth **10** Arrowsmith, Main Street **11** Elmer Gantry **14** Cass Timberlane

lexicon 5 gloss, index **8** code book, glossary, synonymy, wordbook, wordlist **9** thesaurus, wordstock **10** dictionary, vocabulary **11** concordance, onomasticon

lex loci 11 law of a place

lex non scripta 9 common law **12** unwritten law

lex scripta 10 statute law, written law

Leyden, Lucas (Lukas) van
  born: 6 Leiden, Leyden 14 The Netherlands
  artwork: 12 Last Judgment 14 The Card Players, The Game of Chess 26 Mohammed and the Murdered Monk

Lhasa
  capital of: 5 Tibet

liability 4 debt, drag, duty, onus 5 debit, minus 6 arrear, burden 8 drawback, handicap, obstacle 9 hindrance 10 impediment, obligation 11 encumbrance, shortcoming 12 disadvantage, indebtedness 13 inconvenience 14 responsibility, stumbling block

liable 3 apt 4 open 5 prone 6 likely 7 exposed, ripe for, subject 8 disposed, inclined 9 obligated, sensitive 10 answerable, chargeable, vulnerable 11 accountable, responsible, susceptible

liaison 4 bond, link 5 amour, union 7 contact 8 alliance, intrigue, mediator 9 adventure, dalliance, go-between 10 connection, flirtation, love affair 11 association, cooperation, interchange 12 coordination, entanglement 13 communication

liar 6 fibber 8 perjurer 9 falsifier 10 fabricator 11 story teller 12 prevaricator

libation 4 wine 5 drink, water 6 liquid 8 ambrosia, beverage, offering, potation 9 sacrifice

libel 4 slur 5 smear 6 defame, malign, revile, vilify 7 asperse, blacken, calumny, obloquy, slander 8 derogate 9 aspersion, discredit, disparage 10 calumniate, defamation 12 vilification

Libeled Lady
  director: 10 Jack Conway
  cast: 8 Myrna Loy 10 Jean Harlow 12 Spencer Tracy 13 William Powell 14 Walter Connolly
  remade as: 9 Easy to Wed

Libera
  origin: 7 Italian
  goddess of: 4 wine 9 fertility, vineyards
  husband: 5 Liber
  corresponds to: 10 Persephone

liberal 5 ample, broad 6 casual, lavish 7 leftist, lenient 8 abundant, advanced, flexible, generous, handsome, left-wing, prodigal, reformer, tolerant, unbiased 9 bounteous, bountiful, impartial, not strict, plenteous, reformist, unbigoted, unsparing 10 fair-minded, forbearing, left-winger, munificent, not literal, openhanded, open-minded, unrigorous, unstinting 11 broadminded, enlightened, extravagant, libertarian, magnanimous, progressive 12 freethinking, humanitarian, open to reason, unprejudiced 14 latitudinarian

liberal arts
  7 trivium: 5 logic 7 grammar 8 rhetoric
  10 quadrivium: 5 music 8 geometry 9 astronomy 10 arithmetic

liberality 10 generosity 11 benevolence, munificence 12 philanthropy 13 bountifulness 14 openhandedness

liberate 5 let go 6 let out, redeem, rescue, spring 7 absolve, deliver, manumit, release, set free 8 let loose 9 discharge, disengage, extricate, unshackle 10 emancipate 11 disencumber

liberated 5 freed, let go 7 rescued, set free 8 let loose, released 10 discharged, extricated 11 emancipated

liberation 6 escape, rescue 7 freedom, freeing, release 8 delivery 9 letting go, releasing 11 manumission 12 emancipation

Liberia
  capital/largest city: 8 Monrovia
  others: 4 Sino 5 Gribo, Rebbo 6 Bopora, Gbanga, Harper, Kakata 7 Bgarnga, Kolahun, Nanakru, Tappita, Vonjama 8 Buchanan, Garraway, Marshall, Nanakaru, Sass Town 9 Grand Cess, River Cess, Roysville 10 Careysburg, Greenville, Sanoquelli 11 Robertsport 12 Sanniquellie
  school: 7 Liberia 10 Cuttington 15 Our Lady of Fatima 16 Booker Washington
    religious school/secret society: 4 poro 5 sande
  measure: 4 kuba
  monetary unit: 4 cent 6 dollar
  mountain: 3 Uni 4 Bong, Putu 5 Niete, Nimba 9 Bomi Hills
  highest point: 6 Wutivi
  river: 4 Cess, Lofa, Mano 5 Duobe, Lotta, Manna, Morro, Sinoe 6 Cestos, Douobe 7 Cavalla, Cavally 8 San Pedro 9 Saint John, Saint Paul, Sehnkwehn
  sea: 8 Atlantic
  physical feature:
    wind: 9 harmattan
  people: 2 Gi 3 Gio, Kra, Kru, Kwa, Vai, Vei 4 Gola, Kroo, Krou, Loma, Mano, Toma 5 Bassa, Gibbi, Gissi, Grebo 6 Gbande, Kpelle, Kpuesi, Krooby, Kruman 7 Krooboy, Krooman 8 Mandingo 15 Americo-Liberian
    leader: 3 Doe 6 Tubman 7 Roberts, Tolbert
  language: 3 Kru, Kwa 5 Mande 7 English
  religion: 5 Islam 7 animism 10 Protestant 12 Christianity
  feature:
    clothing: 5 lappa
    rubber plantation: 9 Firestone

Libertas
  origin: 5 Roman
  personifies: 7 liberty

liberte egalite fraternite 25 liberty

equality fraternity
  motto of: 16 French Revolution

liberties 6 misuse 7 license 9 violation 10 distortion 11 familiarity, impropriety 13 falsification

libertine 4 goat, lewd, rake, roue 5 loose, satyr 6 lecher, wanton 7 immoral, lustful, seducer 8 unchaste 9 debauchee, dissolute, lecherous, reprobate, womanizer 10 immoralist, lascivious, libidinous, licentious, profligate, sensualist, voluptuary

liberty 5 leave, right 7 freedom, license 8 autonomy, delivery, free time, furlough, sanction, vacation 9 privilege 10 liberation, permission, shore leave 11 citizenship, manumission 12 carte blanche, dispensation, emancipation, independence 15 enfranchisement 17 self-determination

liberty equality fraternity
  French: 24 liberte egalite fraternite
  motto of: 16 French Revolution

Libra
  symbol: 6 scales 7 balance
  planet: 5 Venus
  rules: 8 marriage
  born: 7 October 9 September

Libreville
  capital of: 13 Gabon Republic

Libya
  capital/largest city: 7 Tripoli
    summer capital: 8 Benghazi
  others: 4 Homs, Marj, Surt 5 Beida, Darna, Derna, Khums, Kufra, Sebha, Sidri, Zawia 6 Garian, Murzuq, Tobruk 7 Es Sidar, Gharyan, Misrata 8 Ajdabiya, Misurata, Rashanuf 12 Marsa el Brega
  school: 7 Alfateh 9 Garyounis
  division: 6 Fezzan 9 Cyrenaica 12 Tripolitania
  measure: 3 dra, pik, saa 4 kele 5 bozze, donum, jabia, teman, uckia 6 barile, gorraf, misura 7 mattaro, termino 8 kharouba
  weight: 4 kele 6 gorraf 8 kharouba
  monetary unit: 5 dinar
  mountain: 5 Green 13 Jabal al Akhdar, Tibesti Massif
  highest point: 9 Bette Peak
  sea: 13 Mediterranean
  physical feature:
    desert: 6 Libyan, Sahara 9 Calanscio
    gulf: 5 Bomba, Sidra, Sirte
    oasis: 4 Ghat 5 Kufra, Sebha 7 Tazerbo 8 Al-Kufrah, Ghudamis
    plain: 6 al Marj, Gefara 7 Jaffara
    plateau: 12 Gebel Nefuisa, Jabal Nafusah
    wind: 6 ghibli
  people: 4 Arab, Tebu 6 Berber, Tuareg 7 Gaetuli 8 Getulans, Harratin
    leader: 6 Battus 7 Jalloud, Qadhafi 8 Aegyptus 9 al-Qaddafi, Karamanli 13 Idris al-Senusi

religious leader: 8 al-Senusi
ruler: 4 Rome **5** Italy **6** Greece **9** Phoenicia **12** Ottoman Turks
language: 6 Arabic, Berber **7** English, Italian
  alphabet: 8 tifinagh
religion: 5 Islam
feature: 14 Tropic of Cancer
  clothing: 5 lanaf **9** barracano
  festival: 3 Mez **7** Fantasi
  Islamic law: 6 sharia
  leader: 6 sheikh
  ruins: 11 Leptis Magna
food:
  dish: 5 bazin **8** couscous
  red pepper: 6 filfil

license 3 let **4** pass, visa **5** allow, grant, leave, right **6** enable, laxity, permit **7** anarchy, approve, certify, charter, empower, endorse, freedom, liberty, warrant **8** accredit, audacity, disorder, latitude, passport, sanction, temerity **9** admission, allowance, authorize, franchise, looseness, privilege, slackness **10** brazenness, commission, debauchery, unruliness **11** certificate, free passage, lawlessness, libertinism, presumption, safe-conduct **12** carte blanche, dispensation, recklessness

licentious 4 lewd **5** dirty, loose **6** amoral, sleazy, wanton **7** brutish, goatish, immoral, lawless, lustful, raunchy, ruttish **8** depraved, prodigal **9** abandoned, debauched, dissolute, excessive, lecherous, libertine, salacious **10** dissipated, lascivious, libidinous, lubricious, profligate, ungoverned **11** promiscuous **12** unprincipled, unrestrained, unscrupulous **13** irresponsible, unconstrained

licentiousness 7 abandon **8** lewdness **10** immorality, wantonness

licit 5 legal, legit, valid **6** kosher, lawful **9** allowable, statutory **10** acceptable, admissible, authorized, legitimate, sanctioned **11** permissible **12** authorizable, sanctionable **14** constitutional

lick 3 bit, dab, hit, jot, lap **4** beat, blow, drub, fire, hint, iota, rout, slap, snip, sock, suck, whip **5** crack, punch, sally, shred, spank, speck, taste, touch, trace **6** defeat, ignite, kindle, master, sample, stroke, subdue, thrash, tongue, wallop **7** clobber, conquer, modicum, smidgen, trounce **8** outmatch, overcome, particle, vanquish **9** overpower, overthrow, scintilla, subjugate **10** smattering **12** denunciation

lid 3 cap, top **4** cork, curb, plug **5** cover, limit **7** ceiling, maximum, stopper, stopple **9** operculum, restraint

lie 3 fib **4** loll, rest, stay **5** abide, exist, range, story **6** belong, deceit, extend, inhere, lounge, obtain, remain, repose, sprawl **7** falsify, fiction, perjury, recline, romance, untruth **8** misstate,

tall tale 9 deception, embellish, embroider, fabricate, falsehood, invention **10** equivocate **11** fabrication, prevaricate **12** equivocation **13** falsification, prevarication **17** misrepresentation

Liechtenstein
capital/largest city: 5 Vaduz
others: 4 Haag **6** Balzer, Eschen, Iradug, Schaan **7** Balzers, Bendern, Nendeln, Planken, Triesen **12** Schellenberg
division:
  ancient province: 6 Rhaeti **7** Rhaetia
government:
  legislature: 7 Landtag
monetary unit: 6 rappen **7** franken
mountain: 4 Alps **8** Naafkopf, Rhatikon **12** Three Sisters
highest point: 15 Vorder-Grauspitz
river: 5 Rhine
physical feature:
  valley: 6 Lavena, Samina
people: 8 Alemanni
  leader: 7 Florian **8** Hans Adam **15** Francis Joseph II **16** von Liechtenstein
language: 6 German **10** Alemannish
religion: 13 Roman Catholic
place:
  castle: 9 Gutemburg, Gutenberg
feature:
  legendary dwarf: 10 wildmannli
  wine: 7 Vaduzer

lie down 6 retire **7** go to bed, recline **8** take a nap **11** take a snooze **15** catch forty winks

life 4 path, soul, zest **5** being, human, plant, story, verve, vigor **6** animal, career, course, energy, memoir, person, spirit **8** creature, duration, life span, lifetime, lifework, organism, survival, vitality, vivacity **9** animation, biography, existence, life story, longevity **11** subsistence **13** autobiography
French: 3 vie

Life Before Man
author: 14 Margaret Atwood

Lifeboat
director: 15 Alfred Hitchcock
cast: 10 John Hodiak **12** Mary Anderson **13** William Bendix **16** Tallulah Bankhead

life-giving 5 vital **9** vivifying **12** invigorating

Life Is Beautiful
Italian title: 12 La Vita e bella
director: 14 Roberto Benigni
cast: 12 Lidia Alfonsi (Guicciardini) **13** Sergio Bustric (Ferruccio Papini) **14** Giustino Durano (Eliseo Orefice), Roberto Benigni (Guido Orefice) **16** Nicoletta Braschi (Dora)

life jacket 7 Mae West

lifeless 4 dead, dull, flat, late **5** inert, stiff, vapid **6** boring, hollow, static, torpid, wooden **7** defunct **8** deceased,

departed, inactive, lifeless, sluggish **9** colorless, inanimate **10** lackluster, spiritless

lifelessness 5 death **7** inertia **8** dullness, limpness, vapidity **9** blandness **10** flaccidity, inactivity **13** colorlessness

Life Magazine
founder: 9 Henry Luce

Life of Dante
author: 17 Giovanni Boccaccio

Life of Emile Zola
director: 15 William Dieterle
cast: 8 Paul Muni **11** Donald Crisp **12** Gloria Holden **15** Gale Sondergaard **17** Joseph Schildkraut (Dreyfus)
Oscar for: 7 picture

Life of Riley, The
character: 4 Babs **6** Dangle, Junior **8** Peg Riley **9** Jim Gillis **10** Cunningham, Digby (Digger) O'Dell **11** Waldo Binney **13** Chester A Riley **14** Honeybee Gillis
cast: 9 John Brown, Lanny Rees, Sid Tomack **10** Tom D'Andrea **12** Emory Parnell, Wesley Morgan **13** Gloria Winters, Jackie Gleason, Lugene Sanders, Robert Sweeney, William Bendix **14** Gloria Blondell, Rosemary DeCamp **16** Douglas Dumbrille, Marjorie Reynolds, Sterling Holloway

Life of Samuel Johnson, The
author: 12 James Boswell

life of the party 7 show-off **9** extrovert **13** exhibitionist **17** hail-fellow-well-met

Life on the Mississippi
author: 9 Mark Twain

life span 4 life **8** lifetime **14** life expectancy

Life With Father
author: 13 Clarence Day Jr
director: 13 Michael Curtiz
cast: 9 ZaSu Pitts **10** Irene Dunne **11** Edmund Gwenn **13** William Powell **15** Elizabeth Taylor
setting: 11 New York City

lifework 6 career **7** calling **8** vocation **10** livelihood, occupation, profession

lift 4 high, palm, pick, rear, rise, soar, take **5** boost, climb, exalt, filch, heave, hoist, pinch, raise, steal, swipe **6** ascend, ascent, banish, cancel, pilfer, pirate, pocket, remove, revoke, snatch, thieve, uplift, vanish **7** elation, elevate, purloin, raise up, raising, rescind, scatter, upraise **8** disperse **9** disappear, dissipate, float away **10** ascendance, move upward, plagiarize, put an end to **11** appropriate, countermand, inspiration, make off with, reassurance **12** give a boost to, shot in the arm **13** encouragement, enheartenment

ligament
holds: 5 bones

Ligeia
  author: 13 Edgar Allan Poe
  character: 19 Lady Rowena Trevanion
light 3 gay **4** airy, beam, easy, fair, fall, find, fire, glow, lamp, land, pale, puny, side, soft, stop **5** aglow, angle, blaze, blond, faint, flame, funny, glare, guide, happy, jolly, match, model, perch, petty, put on, roost, shine, slant, small, spare, spark, sunny, torch **6** alight, aspect, beacon, blithe, bright, candle, chance, frugal, gentle, get off, ignite, jaunty, kindle, luster, meager, paltry, scanty, settle, simple, slight, turn on **7** amusing, buoyant, chipper, clarify, come off, descend, get down, gleeful, insight, lantern, lighten, lighter, lucifer, not dark, not rich, paragon, radiant, radiate, sparkle, sunbeam, trivial **8** approach, attitude, bleached, blondish, brighten, carefree, cheerful, come upon, discover, dismount, ethereal, exemplar, gossamer, graceful, illumine, jubilant, luminous, meet with, moderate, moonbeam, not heavy, paradigm, radiance, sportive, step down, switch on, trifling, untaxing **9** brilliant, catch fire, direction, encounter, frivolous, irradiate, light-hued, set fire to, sprightly, stumble on, sylphlike, viewpoint **10** abstemious, brightness, brilliance, burdenless, come across, come to rest, effortless, effulgence, floodlight, happen upon, illuminate, light-toned, luminosity, manageable, restricted, set burning, weightless **11** conflagrate, elucidation, illuminated, information, make radiant, superficial, undemanding, underweight **15** inconsequential
  god of: 6 Apollo **7** Mithras, Phoebus, Pythius **8** Heimdall **9** Musagetes
  Latin: 3 lux
  measurement: 7 candela **11** candlepower
light-colored 4 pale **5** beige, blond **6** blonde, flaxen, pastel **7** neutral, whitish **9** yellowish
light-complexioned 4 fair, pale **12** white-skinned
lighten 4 buoy, ease, lift **5** abate, allay, blaze, elate, flare, flash, gleam, shine **6** buoy up, lessen, reduce, revive, temper, unload, uplift **7** assuage, enliven, gladden, inspire, light up, relieve **8** brighten, mitigate, moderate, unburden **9** alleviate, coruscate, disburden, irradiate **10** illuminate, make bright **11** become light, disencumber, make lighter, scintillate
light-filled 5 sunny **6** bright **7** well-lit **11** illuminated
lighthearted 3 gay **4** airy, glad **5** jolly, merry, sunny **6** blithe, cheery, joyful, joyous, lively **7** buoyant, cheered, chipper **8** carefree, cheerful, sanguine **9** sprightly **10** insouciant,

untroubled **11** free and easy **12** effervescent
lightheartedness 3 joy **4** glee **5** mirth **8** gladness **9** happiness, merriment **10** blitheness, exuberance, joyfulness, joyousness **11** high spirits
Light in August
  author: 15 William Faulkner
  character: 8 Doc Hines, Joe Brown **9** Lena Grove, McEachern **10** Byron Bunch **12** Joanna Burden, Joe Christmas
lightless 4 dark **5** black, murky **7** stygian **9** unlighted **13** unilluminated
lightly 6 airily, easily, gently, nimbly, softly, thinly, weakly **7** blandly, faintly, quickly, readily, swiftly, timidly **8** blithely, facilely, gingerly, meagerly, slightly, sparsely **9** buoyantly, sparingly **10** carelessly, flippantly, hesitantly, moderately **11** frivolously, slightingly **13** indifferently, thoughtlessly, unconcernedly, without effort **14** without concern
lightness 8 airiness, radiance **10** brightness, fluffiness, luminosity **12** illumination, luminousness
lightning rod
  invented by: 8 Franklin
light of day 8 daylight, sunlight, sunshine
light sleep 3 nap **4** doze **6** catnap, snooze **10** forty winks
light wind 4 waft **6** breeze, zephyr **10** gentle wind **11** breath of air
lignum vitae 10 wood of life
  tree species: 8 Guaiacum
likable, likeable 4 nice **6** genial **7** amiable, lovable, winsome **8** charming, engaging, loveable, pleasant, pleasing **9** agreeable, appealing, simpatico **10** attractive **11** complaisant, sympathetic
like 4 akin, care, dote, same, wish **5** enjoy, equal, fancy, favor, savor **6** admire, allied, choose, esteem, relish **7** approve, cognate, endorse, matched, related, similar, support, uniform **8** be fond of, parallel, selfsame, think fit **9** analogous, congruent, have a mind, identical **10** comparable, equivalent, homologous, resembling **11** be partial to, much the same **12** feel inclined, have a crush on, take a shine to **13** corresponding, find agreeable **14** take pleasure in
likelihood 8 prospect **10** good chance **11** possibility, probability **12** potentiality
likely 3 apt, fit **4** able **6** liable, proper **8** credible, destined, inclined, probable, probably, rational, reliable, suitable **9** befitting, plausible, promising, qualified **10** believable, presumably, reasonable **11** appropriate, verisimilar **16** in all probability

like-mindedness 6 accord **7** concord, harmony, rapport **8** affinity **9** agreement **12** congeniality **13** compatibility
likeness 5 image, model, study **6** effigy **7** analogy, picture, replica **8** affinity, portrait **9** agreement, depiction, facsimile, portrayal, rendition, semblance **10** similarity, similitude **11** delineation, resemblance **14** correspondence, representation
likes 9 favorites **10** prejudices **11** preferences **12** inclinations, partialities
likewise 3 and, eke, too **4** also **5** ditto **6** as well **7** be sides, equally, the same **8** moreover **9** similarity **10** in addition
liking 4 bent **5** fancy, taste **7** leaning **8** affinity, appetite, fondness, penchant, soft spot, weakness **9** affection **10** partiality, preference, proclivity, propensity **11** inclination **12** predilection
Li'l Abner
  creator: 6 Al Capp
  character: 5 Pappy **7** Salomey (pig), Wolf Gal **10** Joe Btfsplk, Mammy Yokum, Marryin' Sam **11** Adam Lazonga, Hairless Joe **12** Lena the Hyena, Tobacco Rhoda **13** Joanie Phoanie **14** Daisy Mae Scragg, Evil-Eye Fleegle, Stupefyin' Jones **15** Fearless Fosdick, Henry Cabbage Cod, Lonesome Polecat, Moonbeam McSwine **16** General Bullmoose, Sir Cecil Cesspool **17** Sen Jack S Phogbound **18** J Roaringham Fatback **21** Appassionata von Climax
  brewery: 23 Big Barnsmell's Skonk Works
  event: 15 Sadie Hawkins Day
  juice: 16 Kickapoo Joy Juice
  kingdom: 14 Lower Slobbovia
  mountain: 11 Onnecessary
  animal: 6 Schmoo
  people: 7 kygmies
  place: 8 Dogpatch
  railroad: 11 West Po'k Chop
  ruler: 14 King Nogoodnick
lilac 7 Syringa
  varieties: 4 late, vine, wild **6** common, Indian, summer **7** Chinese, cutleaf, Persian **9** Himalayan, Hungarian **12** Japanese tree **16** Catalina mountain
Lili
  director: 14 Charles Walters
  cast: 9 Mel Ferrer **11** Leslie Caron, Zsa Zsa Gabor **16** Jean-Pierre Aumont
Lilies of the Field
  director: 11 Ralph Nelson
  cast: 8 Lisa Mann **10** Lilia Skala **13** Sidney Poitier
  Oscar for: 5 actor (Poitier)
Liliom
  author: 12 Ferenc Molnar
  source for: 8 Carousel
lillet

type: 8 aperitif
origin: 6 France
flavor: 6 orange
color: 3 red **5** white

Lilliput
fictional land in: 16 Gulliver's
Travels
inhabitants: 10 tiny people
author: 5 Swift

lilliputian 3 wee **4** tiny **5** dwarf, short,
small, teeny, weeny **6** little, midget,
minute, petite **9** miniature **10** diminutive, teeny-weeny **11** pocket-sized

Lilongwe
capital of: 6 Malawi

lily 6 Lilium
varieties: 3 Alp, cow, day, pig **4**
Arum, bell, boat, corn, fawn, fire,
flax, herb, palm, pine, pond, rain,
roan, rock, sand, Sego, star, toad,
wood **5** adobe, Aztec, blood, bugle,
calla, coast, cobra, crane, Cuban,
fairy, globe, glory, Gray's, Ifafa,
lemon, magic, natal, queen, regal,
royal, showy, snake, spear, swamp,
sword, tiger, torch, trout, water,
wheel **6** Alpine, Amazon, Canada,
Crinum, desert, Easter, eureka, ginger, hidden, Kaffir, Marhan,
meadow, one-day, orange, Oregon,
shasta, Sierra, spider, sunset, tartar,
turban, voodoo, yellow, Zephyr **7** African, Bermuda, chamise, checker,
garland, leopard, madonna, Nan-
keen, panther, redwood, thimble,
toad-cup, triplet, trumpet, western **8**
Atamasco, Barbados, bluebead, Carolina, climbing, Columbia, flamingo,
gloriosa, Guernsey, Humboldt, Jaco-
bean, Japanese, long's red, Mariposa,
Martagon, Michigan, mountain, paradise, Peruvian, plantain, Siberian,
Solomon's, St Bruno's, St James's,
turk's cap **9** alligator, avalanche,
butterfly, caucasian, celestial, chaparral, checkered, Eucharist, Kamchatka, naked-lady, orange-cup, pineapple, pinewoods, pot-of-gold, red
ginger, red spider, St Joseph's **10**
belladonna, blackberry, blue funnel,
fairy water, giant water, globe spear,
gold-banded, Josephine's, orange-
bell, pink Easter, pygmy water, royal
water, small tiger, St Bernard's,
Washington, white water, wild yellow, yellow-bell, yellow pond **11** African corn, Amazon water, blue African, candlestick, dwarf ginger,
golden-rayed, milk-and-wine, Palmer
spear, Scarborough, southern red,
yellow water **12** African blood, Chinese white, golden spider, prickly
water, resurrection, speckled wood,
white trumpet **13** Bermuda Easter,
cape blue water, Chinese sacred,
Egyptian water, fragrant water, India
red water, lavender globe, magnolia
water, minor Turk's-cap, perfumed

fairy, pink porcelain, scarlet ginger,
showy Japanese, tuberous water,
wild orange-red **14** Chinese-lantern,
lesser Turk's cap, little Turk's-cap,
Santa Cruz water, yellow Turk's-cap
15 Australian water, backhouse hybrid, golden hurricane, scarlet
Turk's-cap **16** American Turk's cap,
Bellingham hybrid, Cape Cod pink
water, fragrant plantain, Japanese
Turk's-cap, western orange-cup **17**
midsummer plantain **18** European
white water, seersucker plantain **20**
narrow-leaved plantain

lily-livered 6 afraid, craven, scared,
yellow **7** chicken, fearful, gutless **8**
cowardly **9** dastardly **12** fainthearted
13 pusillanimous, yellow-bellied **14**
chicken-hearted, chicken-livered **22**
showing the white feather

lily-white 4 good, pure **6** biased, decent, proper, racist **7** bigoted, upright
8 all-white, innocent, virtuous **9**
blameless, exclusive, exemplary, faultless, guiltless, honorable, righteous **10**
impeccable, inculpable, prejudiced,
segregated, upstanding **11** uncorrupted **12** unintegrated **13** unimpeachable **14** discriminatory, irreproachable

Lima
capital of: 4 Peru
foothills of: 5 Andes
founder: 7 Pizarro
nickname: 11 city of kings
ocean: 7 Pacific
port: 6 Callao
river: 5 Rimac
square: 12 Plaza de Armas

limb 3 arm, gam, leg, pin **4** part, spur,
twig, wing **5** bough, shoot, sprig **6**
branch, member **9** appendage, extension, outgrowth **10** projection, pros-
thesis

limber 5 agile, lithe, relax **6** loosen,
pliant, supple **7** bending, elastic, lissome, pliable **8** flexible **9** lithesome,
malleable

lime 18 Citrus aurantifolia
varieties: 3 key **4** wild **7** Mexican,
Persian, Rangpur, Spanish **8** Mandarin **10** West Indian **14** Australian
wild **15** Australian round **16** Australian desert, Australian finger

Limenia
epithet of: 9 Aphrodite
means: 11 of the harbor

Limerick
county in: 7 Ireland
gave name to: 12 nonsense poem
rhyme scheme: 5 aabba
popularized by: 10 Edward Lear

limit 3 end **4** curb **8** boundary, end
point, restrain, ultimate **13** breaking
point

limitation 4 curb **5** quota **8** boundary,
decrease **9** lessening, reduction, re-

straint **10** shortening **11** abridgement,
restriction, shortcoming **13** qualification, specification

limited 5 fixed **6** finite, narrow **7**
bounded, cramped, defined, minimal,
special **8** confined **9** delimited, specified **10** controlled, restrained, restricted **13** circumscribed

limitless 7 endless, eternal, unbound **8**
infinite, unending **9** boundless, unlimited **11** measureless **12** immeasurable

limits 3 rim, top **4** curb, edge **5** bound,
check, quota **6** border, define, fringe,
margin, narrow **7** ceiling, confine, delimit, inhibit, maximum, qualify **8**
confines, frontier, restrain, restrict **9**
perimeter, periphery, prescribe, restraint **10** boundaries **11** limitations
12 restrictions

limn 4 draw **6** sketch **7** picture **9** delineate

Limnaea
epithet of: 7 Artemis
means: 9 of the lake

limp 3 lax **4** gimp, halt, soft, weak **5**
crawl, loose, skulk, slack **6** droopy,
falter, flabby, floppy, hobble **7** flaccid
8 drooping, lameness, yielding **9** dead
tired, enervated, exhausted

limpid 4 pure **5** clear, lucid **8** clear-cut,
pellucid, vitreous **11** crystalline, per-
spicuous, translucent, transparent, unambiguous **15** straightforward

Lincoln, Abraham
nickname: 9 Honest Abe **20** Illinois
Rail Splitter
presidential rank: 9 sixteenth
party: 4 Whig **10** Republican
state represented: 2 IL
defeated: 4 (John) Bell **7** (John
Charles) Fremont, (Stephen Arnold)
Douglas **9** (George Brinton) McClellan **12** (John Cabell) Breckinridge
vice president: 6 (Hannibal) Hamlin
7 (Andrew) Johnson
cabinet:
state: 6 (William Henry) Seward
treasury: 5 (Salmon Portland)
Chase **9** (Hugh) McCulloch, (William Pitt) Fessenden
war: 7 (Edwin McMasters) Stanton,
(Simon) Cameron
attorney general: 5 (Edward)
Bates, (James) Speed
navy: 6 (Gideon) Welles
postmaster general: 5 (Montgomery) Blair **8** (William) Dennison
interior: 5 (Caleb Blood) Smith,
(John Palmer) Usher
born: 2 KY **8** log cabin **11** Larue
County **17** Sinking Spring farm
died: 12 Washington DC, Fords Theater
died by: 13 assassination
assassinated by: 15 John Wilkes
Booth
buried: 13 Springfield IL

education:
  studied: **3** law
interests: **7** theater
  received patent for: **25** adjustable buoyant chambers (for lifting boats)
political career: **16** state legislature **24** US House of Representatives
civilian career: **6** lawyer **8** surveyor **10** postmaster
military service:
  War: **9** Black Hawk
  US Army: **7** private
  captain of company of: **10** volunteers
notable events of lifetime/term: **8** Civil War **24** Emancipation Proclamation
  Act: **9** Homestead, Income Tax, Judiciary **12** Conscription
  debates: **14** Lincoln-Douglas
  speech: **17** Gettysburg Address
father: **6** Thomas
mother: **5** Nancy (Hanks)
  stepmother: **5** Sarah (Bush Johnston)
siblings: **5** Sarah **6** Thomas
  stepbrother: **4** John
  stepsister: **7** Matilda **9** Elizabeth
wife: **4** Mary (Ann Todd)
children: **6** Thomas **10** Robert Todd **11** Edward Baker **14** William Wallace

Lind, James
field: **8** medicine
nationality: **8** Scottish
eliminated: **6** scurvy

Lindbergh, Anne Morrow
author of: **14** Gift from the Sea **15** Bring Me a Unicorn **16** North to the Orient **19** War Within and Without

linden **5** Tilia
varieties: **6** Indoor **7** Crimean **8** American, Japanese **9** Mongolian **10** Manchurian **11** Large-leaved **13** Pendent silver **19** Small-leaved European

lindy **5** dance **8** lindy hop **9** jitterbug
nickname for: **16** Charles Lindbergh

line, lines **4** card, cord, dash, draw, file, idea, mark, note, part, race, rank, rope, rule, tier, word **5** align, array, breed, cable, craft, front, house, model, queue, range, score, slash, stock, trade **6** belief, border, column, crease, family, furrow, letter, method, metier, policy, report, scheme, series, stance, strain, strand, streak, stripe, system, thread **7** calling, circuit, conduit, contour, cordage, example, lineage, marshal, outline, pattern, purpose, pursuit, queue up, routine, towline, wrinkle **8** ancestry, business, dialogue, doctrine, fishline, ideology, inscribe, position, postcard, trenches, vanguard, vocation **9** conductor, crow's foot, direction, frontline, genealogy, intention, principle **10** barri-

cades, convention, firing line, livelihood, long stroke, occupation, procession, profession, underscore **11** demarcation

lineage **4** line **5** blood, stock **7** descent **8** ancestry, heredity, pedigree **9** genealogy, parentage **10** derivation, extraction

linen
fabric: **6** canvas, damask **7** butcher, cambric **8** birds-eye **9** huckaback
plant: **4** flax
finest from: **7** Belgium, Ireland
processing term: **6** shives, sliver **7** carding, hackled, retting **8** beetling, breaking, rippling, spinning **9** scutching

line of march **4** path **5** route, track **11** parade route

line of reasoning **4** case **7** premise **8** argument **10** hypothesis

line up **4** book **5** align **6** engage, even up **7** arrange, procure, program, queue up **8** schedule **9** form a line, put in a row **10** arrange for

line-up **5** slate **6** roster **8** schedule

linger **4** lag **4** idle, last, stay, wait **5** dally, delay, tarry, trail **6** dawdle, hang on, loiter, remain **7** persist, survive **9** die slowly **10** dillydally, hang around

lingering **4** slow **7** abiding, chronic, delayed, lagging, lasting, staying, waiting **8** dawdling, delaying, dragging, drawn out, dwelling, enduring, hovering, tarrying **9** loitering, remaining **10** protracted, sauntering **15** procrastinating

lingo **4** cant, talk **5** argot, idiom, slang **6** jargon, patois, tongue **7** dialect **8** language, parlance **10** vernacular

linguist **8** polyglot **10** grammarian, translator **11** etymologist, interpreter, philologist, phonetician, phonologist, semanticist **12** morphologist **13** lexicographer

liniment **4** balm **5** salve **7** unguent **8** ointment **9** emollient

link **3** tie **4** bind, bond, fuse, loop, ring **5** group, joint, tie in, unite **6** couple, relate, splice **7** bracket, combine, conjoin, connect, involve, liaison **8** junction, relation **9** associate, implicate **10** connection, connective **11** association **12** interconnect, relationship

linkage **3** tie **4** bond **6** hookup **10** connection **11** affiliation, association, correlation

link up **4** dock, join **6** couple, hook up **7** connect **9** affiliate **14** fasten together

Linnaeus, Carolus
field: **6** botany
nationality: **7** Swedish
developed: **8** taxonomy **18** nomenclature system

linotype
invented by: **12** Mergenthaler

Linus
vocation: **4** poet **8** musician
father: **6** Apollo
mother: **8** Psamathe
inventor of: **6** melody, rhythm
identified with: **5** crops **9** withering **10** harvesting
student: **8** Hercules
killed by: **8** Hercules

lion **3** cat **6** cougar **7** wildcat **9** celebrity **12** man of the hour **15** king of the jungle
group of: **5** pride
constellation of: **3** Leo

lionhearted **4** bold **5** brave **6** heroic **7** valiant **8** fearless, intrepid, stalwart, unafraid, valorous **9** audacious, dauntless **10** courageous **11** indomitable **12** stouthearted
see **8** Richard I

Lion in Winter, The
director: **13** Anthony Harvey
cast: **10** Jane Merrow **11** Peter O'Toole (Henry II) **13** Timothy Dalton **14** Anthony Hopkins **16** Katharine Hepburn (Eleanor of Aquitaine)
Oscar for: **7** actress (Hepburn)

lionize **5** exalt **6** admire, praise, revere **7** acclaim, adulate, ennoble, flatter, glorify **8** enshrine, eulogize **9** celebrate, glamorize **10** aggrandize **11** immortalize

lion's share **4** bulk, most **8** majority **9** major part **11** greater part **13** preponderance

lip **3** lap, rim **4** brim, edge, kiss, lick, wash **5** apron, mouth, spout, utter **6** labial, labium, margin **8** backtalk, labellum **9** insincere **10** embouchure, mouthpiece **11** superficial

Lipchitz, Jacques
real name: **17** Chaim Yakob Lipchiz
born: **9** Lithuania **11** Druskieniki **12** Druskininkai
artwork: **4** Head **6** Bather, Figure **7** Harpist **9** Sacrifice **10** Prometheus **11** Benediction, Joie de Vivre **12** Peace on Earth **14** Man with a Guitar **15** Acrobats on a Ball, Man with Mandolin, Song of the Vowels **17** Notre Dame de Liesse, Sailor with a Guitar **19** Pierrot with Clarinet, Return of the Prodigal **24** Virgin of the Inverted Heart

Lipizzaner **11** stocky horse
bred in: **7** Austria
color: **5** white
used in: **8** dressage **18** jumping exhibitions

Lipmann, Fritz Albert
field: **12** biochemistry
discovered: **9** Coenzyme A
awarded: **10** Nobel Prize

Lippi, Filippino
born: **5** Italy, Prato

father: 15 Fra Filippo Lippi
artwork: 20 The Vision of St Bernard 24 The Life of St Thomas Aquinas 26 The Lives of Sts Philip and John

Lippi, Fra Filippo
born: 5 Italy 8 Florence
son: 9 Filippino
artwork: 15 Madonna and Child, The Feast of Herod 19 The Tarquinia Madonna 21 Coronation of the Virgin 25 The Madonna Adoring Her Child

liqueur 5 booze, drink, hooch 7 alcohol, potable, spirits 8 beverage, potation 9 aqua vitae, drinkable, inebriant, moonshine 10 intoxicant
almond: 8 amaretto
anise: 8 absinthe
apple: 8 calvados
apricot: 10 abricotine
caraway: 6 kummel 7 aquavit
chocolate: 12 creme de cacao
citrus: 10 goldwasser, liquor d'or
coffee: 6 Kahlua
grape: 6 Metaxa
herb: 6 pernod 7 raspail 10 vielle cure 11 fiori alpini
honey: 8 Drambuie
medicinal: 11 Benedictine
mint: 13 creme de menthe
orange: 6 strega 7 curacao 9 cointreau 12 Grand Marnier
raspberry: 9 framboise

liquid 5 drink, fluid 6 melted, molten, thawed 7 potable 8 beverage, solution

liquidate 3 hit, pay 4 kill 5 clear, erase, waste 6 cancel, murder, pay off, rub out, settle, wind up 7 abolish, break up, destroy, wipe out 8 close out, conclude, demolish 9 discharge, dispose of, eradicate, put to rest, terminate 10 account for, do away with 11 assassinate

liquor 3 gin, rum, rye 5 booze, broth, hooch, juice, sauce, vodka 6 brandy, liquid, redeye, rotgut, Scotch 7 bourbon, extract, spirits, whiskey 9 drippings, moonshine 10 inebriants 11 intoxicants
measure: 4 pint, pony, shot 5 fifth, quart 6 jigger, magnum
symbol: 14 John Barleycorn

Lir *see* 3 Ler

Lisbon
capital of: 8 Portugal
landmark:
castle: 11 Saint George
monastery: 9 Jeronimos
square: 10 Black Horse
tower: 5 Belem
Moorish name: 7 Lixbuna
ocean: 8 Atlantic
Portuguese: 6 Lisboa
river: 5 Tagus
Roman name: 14 Felicitas Julia
rulers: 5 Moors 6 French, Romans 7 British, Germans, Spanish 11 Phoenicians

lissome 5 agile, lithe, quick 6 limber, lively, nimble, pliant, supple 7 slender 8 flexible, graceful 9 lithesome, sprightly 11 light-footed

list 3 tip 4 bend, heel, lean, roll, tilt 5 index, slant, slate, slope, table 6 careen, muster, record, roster 7 catalog, in cline, leaning 8 register, schedule, tabulate 9 catalogue, inventory

listen 4 hark, hear, heed, list 6 attend 7 give ear, hearken 8 give heed, listen in, overhear 9 be all ears, bend an ear, eavesdrop 10 take notice 12 pay attention

listener 3 ear 6 hearer 7 auditor 10 overhearer 12 eavesdropper

Lister, Joseph
field: 7 surgeon 8 medicine
nationality: 7 British
pioneer of: 17 antiseptic surgery

listless 4 down, dull, lazy 6 dreamy, drowsy, leaden, mopish, torpid 7 languid 8 in active, indolent, lifeless, sluggish 9 apathetic, enervated, lethargic, soporific 10 phlegmatic, spiritless 11 indifferent, unconcerned 12 uninterested 13 lackadaisical

Liston, Charles
nickname: 5 Sonny
sport: 6 boxing
class: 11 heavyweight

Liszt, Franz (Ferencz)
born: 7 Hungary, Raiding
teacher: 6 Czerny
daughter: 6 Cosima
son-in-law: 6 Wagner
composer of: 5 Dante (symphony), Faust (symphony) 8 Christus 9 Psalm XIII 10 Nuages gris 13 Psalm Thirteen 17 Years of Pilgrimage 18 Annees de Pelerinage 19 Hungarian Rhapsodies 22 The Legend of St Elizabeth

litany 4 list 7 account, catalog, recital 9 catalogue, narration, rendition 10 recitation, repetition 11 description, enumeration

literacy 7 culture 8 learning 9 erudition 11 edification, eruditeness, learnedness, scholarship 12 intelligence 13 enlightenment

literal 4 real, true 5 exact 6 actual, direct, honest, strict 7 correct, factual, precise, prosaic 8 accurate, faithful, reliable, truthful, verbatim 9 authentic 10 adlitteram, dependable, meticulous, scrupulous, undisputed 11 trustworthy, undeviating, word-for-word 12 matter-of-fact 13 authoritative, conscientious, unimaginative, unimpeachable

literary 6 poetic 7 bookish, of books 8 artistic, lettered, literate 12 intellectual

literate 7 learned 8 cultured, educated, lettered, literary, schooled, well-read 12 well-informed 13 knowledgeable

literati 9 highbrows 12 connoisseurs 13 intellectuals 14 intelligentsia

literature 4 lore 5 books, works 6 papers, theses 7 letters 8 classics, writings 9 treatises 11 scholarship 12 publications 13 belles lettres, dissertations

lithe 5 agile 6 limber, nimble, pliant, supple 7 lissome, pliable 8 bendable, flexible, graceful

Lithgow, John
roles: 9 Footloose 17 Terms of Endearment 19 Third Rock from the Sun 21 Harry and the Hendersons 23 The World According to Garp 29 The Adventures of Buckaroo Banzai

lithium
chemical symbol: 2 Li

Lithuania
other/former name: 5 Litva 7 Lietuva 33 Lithuanian Soviet Socialist Republic
capital/largest city: 5 Vilna 6 Kaunas 7 Vilnius
others: 4 Balt, Lett 5 Aesti, Kouno, Memel 6 Kovnac 7 Jel gava, Palanga, Telsiai 8 Ignalina, Kapsukas, Klaipeda, Siauliai 9 Panevezys 10 Elektrenai
government: 8 republic
monetary unit: 3 lit 5 marka 6 centas 7 ostmark, skatiku 8 auksinas
lake: 5 Dysna
mountain: 15 Samogitian Hills
highest point: 9 Juozapine
river: 5 Neman, Neris, Rusne 6 Dubysa, Nieman, Viliya 7 Nemunas, Nevezis, Nevezys 8 Pregolya
sea: 6 Baltic
physical feature:
lagoon: 8 Courland, Kuronian
people: 4 Balt, Lett 5 Zhmud 6 Jewish, Litvak, Polish 7 Aistian, Russian, Yatvyag 10 Lithuanian, Samogitian 11 Belorussian
language: 5 Zmudz 6 Baltic 10 Lithuanian
religion: 8 Lutheran 13 Roman Catholic

litigation 4 suit 7 contest, dispute, lawsuit 10 contention, day in court 11 controversy, disputation, legal action, prosecution

litter 3 bed 4 heap, junk, lair, mess, nest, pile 5 issue, strew, trash, young 6 debris, jumble, pallet, refuse 7 bedding, clutter, kittens, progeny, puppies, rubbish, scatter 8 leavings 9 offspring, stretcher

little 3 bit, dot, jot, wee 4 dash, drop, hint, iota, mean, mild, tiny, whit 5 brief, crumb, elfin, faint, fleet, hasty, never, petty, pinch, pygmy, quick, scant, short, small, speck, trace 6 bantam, hardly, meager, minute, narrow, paltry, petite, rarely, seldom, skimpy, slight, trifle 7 minimum, modicum, not much, passing, stunted, trivial **8** dwarfish, fragment, inferior, mediocre, not at all, not often, particle, piddling, pittance, scarcely, slightly, some what, trifling, unworthy **9** by no means, deficient, hardly any, itsy-bitsy, itty-bitty, miniature, momentary, pint-sized, third-rate, worthless **10** diminutive, inflexible, negligible, short-lived, suggestion, undersized **11** commonplace, Lilliputian, microscopic, of no account, opinionated, pocket-sized, scarcely any, small amount, unimportant **12** insufficient, run-of-the-mill, short-sighted **13** infinitesimal, insignificant, next to nothing

Little America
on: **10** Antarctica **12** Ross Ice Shelf
bases established by: **11** Admiral Byrd

Little Annie Rooney
creator: **14** Darrell McClure

Little Artha
nickname of: **11** Jack Johnson

Little Bighorn 5 river **7** Wyoming
battle site of: **5** Sioux **6** Custer, Dakota **8** Cheyenne
called: **16** Custer's last stand
see also **13** Custer, George A.

Little Big Man
author: **12** Thomas Berger
director: **10** Arthur Penn
cast: **11** Faye Dunaway **12** Martin Balsam **13** Dustin Hoffman (Jack Crabb) **14** Chief Dan George **15** Richard Mulligan

little by little
French: **7** peu a peu
Spanish: **9** poco a poco

Little Caesar
director: **11** Mervyn LeRoy
cast: **13** Glenda Farrell **15** Edward G Robinson (Rico) (Caesar Enrico Bandello) **18** Douglas Fairbanks Jr

Little Corporal 8 Napoleon

Little Dipper 11 star cluster
in: **9** Ursa Minor **10** Little Bear

Little Dorrit
author: **14** Charles Dickens
character: **3** Amy (Little Dorrit), Tip **4** Rugg **5** Casby, Fanny, Flora, Gowan **6** Affery, Merdle, Pancks, Rigaud (Blandois) **7** Meagles **8** Mr F's Aunt **9** Mrs Merdle **10** Flintwinch **13** Arthur Clennam, William Dorrit **16** Monsieur Blandois, Young John Chivery

Little Fox
constellation of: **9** Vulpecula

Little Foxes, The
author: **14** Lillian Hellman
character: **13** Regina Giddens
director: **12** William Wyler
cast: **10** Bette Davis (Regina) **12** Teresa Wright **14** Richard Carlson **15** Herbert Marshall

prequel: **22** Another Part of the Forest

Little House on the Prairie
author: **18** Laura Ingalls Wilder
character: **6** Albert **7** Dr Baker **8** Rev Alden **9** Mr Edwards **10** Andy Garvey, Lars Hanson, Nels Oleson **11** Adam Kendall, Alice Garvey, Mary Ingalls **12** Grace Ingalls, Laura Ingalls, Nellie Oleson, Willie Oleson **13** Carrie Ingalls, Harriet Oleson **14** Charles Ingalls, Eva Beadle Simms, Jonathan Garvey **15** Caroline Ingalls
cast: **10** Dabbs Greer, Kevin Hagen **11** Karl Swenson, Merlin Olsen, Richard Bull **12** Hersha Parady, Karen Grassle, Victor French **13** Alison Arngrim, Linwood Boomer, Michael Landon **14** Melissa Gilbert **15** Jonathon Gilbert, Sidney Greenbush, Wendy Turnbeaugh **16** Brenda Turnbeaugh, Charlotte Gilbert, Lindsay Greenbush **17** Katherine McGregor, Matthew Laborteaux, Patrick Laborteaux **18** Melissa Sue Anderson
setting: **6** Winoka **9** Minnesota, Plum Creek **11** Walnut Grove

Little John
character in: **9** Robin Hood

Little King, The
creator: **10** Otto Soglow
technique: **9** pantomine

little-known 6 unsung **7** obscure, unnoted **10** unrenowned

Little Lord Fauntleroy
author: **15** Frances H Burnett

Little Lulu
creator: **14** Marge Henderson

Little Match Girl, The
author: **21** Hans Christian Andersen

Little Men
author: **15** Louisa May Alcott

Little Mermaid, The
author: **21** Hans Christian Andersen

Little Mo
nickname of: **15** Maureen Connolly

Little Nemo in Slumberland
creator: **11** Winsor McCay
character: **6** Dr Pill **8** cannibal, princess
clown: **4** Flip
dog: **6** Blutch

little one 3 tot **4** babe, baby, tyke **5** child **6** infant, wee one **7** toddler

Little Orphan Annie
creator: **10** Harold Gray
character:
foster father: **13** Daddy Warbucks
dog: **5** Sandy
saying: **13** Leapin' Lizards

little people 5 elves **6** dwarfs **7** fairies, midgets **11** leprechauns

Little Prince, The
author: **21** Antoine de Saint-Exupery

Little Rhody
nickname of: **11** Rhode Island

Little Tramp
nickname of: **14** Charlie Chaplin

Little Women
author: **15** Louisa May Alcott
character: **6** Laurie (Theodore Laurence), Marmee **10** John Brooke **14** Professor Bhaer
March sisters: **2** Jo **3** Amy, Meg **4** Beth
director:
1933 version: **11** George Cukor
1949 version: **11** Mervyn LeRoy
cast (1933): **9** Paul Lukas **10** Frances Dee, Jean Parker **11** Joan Bennett **16** Katharine Hepburn (Jo)
cast (1949): **9** Mary Astor **10** Janet Leigh **11** June Allyson **12** Peter Lawford **14** Margaret O'Brien **15** Elizabeth Taylor

liturgical 6 ritual **10** ceremonial **11** ceremonious, sacramental

liturgy 4 mass, rite **6** ritual **7** service, worship **8** ceremony, services **9** communion, sacrament

lituus
form: **5** staff
shape: **7** crooked

Lityerses
father: **9** King Midas
held: **15** reaping contests
killed: **6** losers

livable, liveable 4 cozy, snug **5** comfy, homey **8** bearable, passable, pleasant, suitable **9** agreeable, endurable, enjoyable, habitable, tolerable **10** acceptable, convenient, gratifying, satisfying, worthwhile **11** comfortable

live 2 be **3** hot **4** bunk, feed, stay **5** abide, afire, aglow, alive, dwell, exist, fiery, lodge, quick, stand, vital **6** ablaze, active, aflame, alight, at hand, billet, bodily, endure, hold on, living, obtain, occupy, red-hot, remain, reside, settle, thrive **7** animate, at issue, be alive, blazing, breathe, burning, current, flaming, fleshly, going on, ignited, persist, prevail, subsist, survive **8** existent, flourish, get ahead, get along, have life, increase, multiply, physical, pressing, take root, up-to-date, white-hot **9** breathing, corporeal **10** draw breath

live and keep well
Latin: **11** vive valeque

Live and Let Die
author: **10** Ian Fleming

live dissolutely 7 carouse, debauch **9** dissipate **11** overindulge

livelihood 3 job **5** trade **6** career, living, metier **7** calling, support, venture **8** business, position, vocation **9** situation **10** enterprise, line of work, occupation, profession, sustenance **11** maintenance, subsistence, undertaking

liveliness 3 pep, zip **4** brio, elan **5** vigor **7** agility **8** alacrity, vitality, vivacity **9** animation, briskness, eagerness **10** ebullience, nimbleness **13** sprightliness

lively 5 alert, brisk, eager, peppy, perky, vivid **6** active, ardent, bouncy **7** buoyant, excited, fervent, intense **8** animated, spirited, vigorous **9** energetic, excitable, sprightly, vivacious **12** enthusiastic

liven 4 buoy **5** cheer, elate, pep up **6** perk up, vivify **7** animate, delight, enliven, fortify, gladden, hearten, punch up, quicken **8** brighten, embolden, energize, inspirit **10** exhilarate, invigorate, strengthen

liver
　stores: 8 glycogen
　color: 3 red **5** brown
　produces: 4 bile **10** blood cells

Livermore Larruper
　nickname of: 7 Max Baer

livery 4 garb, suit **5** dress **6** attire **7** costume, raiment, regalia, uniform **8** clothing **9** vestments

Lives of a Bengal Lancer
　director: 13 Henry Hathaway
　cast: 10 Gary Cooper **12** Franchot Tone **14** Sir Guy Standing **15** Richard Cromwell

Lives of the Poets, The
　author: 13 Samuel Johnson

live through 4 know **7** survive, undergo **9** go through **10** experience

livid 3 mad **4** pale **5** angry, irate, riled, vexed **6** fuming, galled, purple, raging **7** bruised, enraged, furious **8** contused, incensed, inflamed, outraged, provoked, wrathful **9** indignant, steamed up, ticked off **10** discolored, infuriated **11** exasperated **12** black-and-blue

living 3 job **4** life, live, work **5** alive, being, quick, trade **6** active, bodily, career, extant, income **7** animate, calling, fleshly, going on, organic, venture **8** business, embodied, enduring, existent, existing, material, up-to-date, vocation **9** animation, breathing, corporeal, existence, incarnate, lifestyle, operative, permanent, remaining, surviving, way of life **10** employment, enterprise, having life, in the flesh, line of work, livelihood, occupation, persisting, prevailing, profession, subsisting, sustenance **11** maintenance, subsistence **13** drawing breath

living being 8 creature, organism

living conditions 10 atmosphere **11** environment **13** circumstances

living picture
　French: 13 tableau vivant

living quarters 4 home **5** abode, house **6** billet **7** housing, lodging, shelter **8** domicile, dwelling, quarters **9** apartment, residence **10** habitation **13** dwelling place

Livy

also: 11 Titus Livius
author of: 13 Ab urbe condita **26** From the Foundation of the City

lizard 3 dab, eft, uma **4** adda, gila, newt, seps, tegu, uran **5** agama, anole, anoli, gecko, idler, shrink **6** aguana, dragon, iguana, komodo, moloch **7** lounger, monitor, reptile, saurian **8** dinosaur, lacerata, scorpion **9** alligator, blind worm, chameleon, crocodile, galliwasp **10** chuckwalla, glass snake, horned toad, salamander **11** gila monster **12** Komodo dragon
　characteristic: 6 scales **7** molting **9** oviparous **11** cold-blooded **12** regeneration
　constellation of: 7 Lacerta

llama 6 alpaca, kechua, mammal, vicuna **7** guanaco **8** ungulate **13** Peruvian sheep

llano 11 grassy plain
　in: 12 South America

Llewellyn, Richard
　author of: 19 How Green Was My Valley

Llew Llaw Gyffes
　origin: 5 Welsh
　father: 7 Gwydion
　mother: 9 Arianhrod
　wife: 10 Blodenwedd
　curses bestowed by: 9 Arianhrod

Lloyd
　origin: 5 Welsh
　form: 8 magician
　cast spells upon: 7 Pryderi

Lloyd, Harold
　born: 10 Burchard NE
　roles: 9 Feet First **10** Safety Last **11** The Freshman **13** The Kid Brother

Lloyd Webber, Andrew
　born: 6 London
　composer of: 4 Cats **5** Evita **6** Jeeves **12** Bombay Dreams, Song and Dance **13** Aspects of Love **15** Sunset Boulevard, Tell Me on a Sunday **16** Starlight Express **20** Jesus Christ Superstar, The Phantom of the Opera **39** Joseph and the Amazing Technicolor Dreamcoat
　awards: 7 peerage **10** Knighthood

Llud
　also: 4 Ludd, Nudd
　origin: 5 Welsh
　king of: 7 Britain
　rid kingdom of: 6 plague
　famous for: 10 generosity

Llyr
　origin: 5 Welsh
　son: 10 Manawyddan
　corresponds to: 3 Ler, Lir

load 3 try, vex **4** care, fill, haul, heap, lade, pack, pile **5** cargo, crush, stack, stuff, worry **6** burden, hamper, hinder, lading, misery, strain, weight **7** afflict, carload, freight, oppress, trouble **8** capacity, contents, encumber, handicap, pressure, shipload, ship-

ment **9** overwhelm, plane load, truckload, wagonload, weigh down **10** affliction, deadweight, depression, misfortune, oppression **11** encumbrance

loads 4 lots, much **5** heaps, piles, scads **6** oodles, plenty **14** more than enough

loaf 4 idle, loll **5** dally **6** be lazy **7** goof off **8** kill time, malinger **9** do nothing, gold brick, laze about, waste time **10** take it easy **12** lounge around

loafer 3 bum **4** shoe **5** idler **6** no-good **7** laggard, shirker, sponger, wastrel **8** deadbeat, loiterer, sluggard **9** goldbrick, lazybones **10** lazy person, malingerer, ne'er-do-well **11** couch potato **12** lounge lizard **15** drugstore cowboy
　French: 7 flaneur

loan 4 lend **5** allow **6** credit **7** advance, lending **8** mortgage **9** advancing

loath 4 loth **6** averse **7** against, counter, hostile, opposed **8** inimical **9** reluctant, resisting, unwilling **10** indisposed, set against **11** disinclined

loathe 4 hate **5** abhor, scorn **6** detest, eschew **7** deplore, despise, disdain, dislike **9** abominate **10** blench from, flinch from, recoil from, shrink from **11** keep clear of, shy away from **12** draw back from **14** be unable to bear, find disgusting, view with horror **16** have no stomach for

loathing 4 hate **5** odium **6** hatred **7** disgust, dislike **8** aversion, distaste **9** antipathy, repulsion, revulsion **10** abhorrence, repugnance **11** abomination, detestation

loathsome 4 foul, mean, rank, vile **5** nasty **6** odious **7** hateful **9** abhorrent, invidious, obnoxious, offensive, repugnant, repulsive, revolting, sickening **10** abominable, despicable, detestable, disgusting, nauseating, unbearable **11** distasteful

lobby 5 foyer **8** anteroom, politick **9** vestibule **11** antechamber, pull strings, waiting room **12** entrance hall

lobscouse 4 meat **8** hardtack **10** vegetables **11** sailor's stew

local 6 narrow, native, nearby **7** insular, limited **8** citywide, confined, regional **9** adjoining, homegrown, parochial, sectional **10** provincial **11** territorial **12** neighborhood **13** circumscribed

locale 4 area, site, spot, zone **6** region **7** quarter, section, setting **8** locality, location, precinct, province, vicinity **12** neighborhood

locality 4 area, site, spot, zone **5** place **6** locale, region **7** quarter, section **8** district, location, precinct, province, vicinity **9** territory **12** neighborhood

locate 3 fix, put **4** find, live, post, seat, stay **5** dwell, place **6** detect, move to, reside, settle **7** deposit, discern, hit upon, set down, situate, station, uncover, unearth **8** come upon, meet with, pinpoint **9** establish, ferret out, light upon, search out, stumble on, track down **10** settle down **12** put down roots

location 4 site, spot **5** place **6** locale **8** district, position **9** situation **11** whereabouts **12** neighborhood

Lochinvar
character in: **7** Marmion
bride: **5** Ellen
author: **5** Scott

Loch Ness
in: **8** Scotland
home of: **6** Nessie **7** monster

lock 3 bar, dam, pen **4** bang, bolt, cage, coil, curl, grab, grip, hank, hold, hook, jail, join, link, tuft **5** catch, clamp, clasp, grasp, latch, seize, skein, tress, unite **6** clinch, coop up, fasten, lock up, secure, shut in **7** confine, embrace, entwine, grapple, impound, padlock, ringlet **8** dock gate, imprison **9** canal gate, fastening, floodgate, interlink **10** intertwine, sluice gate **11** incarcerate

lock, cylinder
invented by: **4** Yale

Lockhart, Gene
daughter: **12** June Lockhart
granddaughter: **11** Ann Lockhart
born: **6** Canada, London **7** Ontario
roles: **12** Madame Bovary **16** Death of a Salesman **19** The Inspector General **20** Abe Lincoln in Illinois

lock horns 4 feud, tiff **5** argue, brawl, clash, fight **7** dispute, quarrel, wrangle **8** squabble **9** altercate

Lockit 4 Lucy
character in: **12** Beggar's Opera
author: **3** Gay

lockup 3 jug, pen **4** jail, stir **5** clink, pokey **6** cooler, prison **7** slammer **8** big house, hoosegow **11** reformatory **12** penitentiary

lock up 3 pen **4** cage, jail **6** coop up, secure **7** confine, impound **8** imprison, restrain, restrict **11** incarcerate

Lockyer, Joseph Norman
field: **9** astronomy
nationality: **7** British
discovered: **6** helium

loco citato 15 in the place cited
abbreviation: **6** loc cit

locomotive
invented by:
electric: **4** Vail
experimental: **6** Fenton, Hedley **10** Stephenson, Trevithick
first US: **6** Cooper
practical: **10** Stephenson

locust 7 Robinia
varieties: **4** moss **5** black, honey, mossy, swamp, sweet, water **6** clammy, yellow **7** African, bristly **8**

ship-mast **10** West Indian **13** Allegheny moss, South American

locution 4 term **5** idiom, trope, usage **6** phrase, saying **7** wording **8** idiolect, phrasing **9** set phrase, utterance, verbalism **10** expression **11** phraseology, regionalism **12** turn of phrase **14** figure of speech

lode 3 bed **4** seam **7** deposit

lodge 3 bed, hut **4** camp, file, room, stay **5** cabin, catch, hotel, house, motel, put up **6** billet, harbor, resort, submit **7** cottage, quarter, shelter, sojourn **8** register

lodging 4 room **8** quarters **13** accommodation

Loewe, Frederick
born: **6** Vienna
Composer of: **4** Gigi **7** Camelot **8** Galateya **9** Brigadoon **10** My Fair Lady **14** Paint Your Wagon **15** The Little Prince

loft 3 lob **5** attic, pop up **6** belfry, garret **7** balcony, gallery, hit high, mansard **8** top floor **9** attic room, throw high **10** clerestory

loftiness 5 pride **9** arrogance **11** haughtiness **13** imperiousness **16** superciliousness

Lofting, Hugh
author of: **10** Dr Dolittle

lofty 4 cold, high, tall **5** aloof, grand, great, noble, proud **6** lordly, mighty, remote, snooty **7** distant, eminent, exalted, haughty, leading, soaring, stately, stuck-up, sublime **8** arrogant, elevated, glorious, imposing, insolent, majestic, puffed-up, scornful, snobbish, superior, towering **9** conceited, dignified, imperious, important **10** disdainful, hoity-toity, preeminent **11** high ranking, illustrious, patronizing **12** high-reaching **13** condescending, distinguished, high-and-mighty, self-important

lofty bearing 7 dignity, majesty **10** augustness **11** stateliness

log 5 block, diary, stump **6** docket, lumber, record, timber **7** account, daybook, journal, logbook **8** calendar, schedule

Logan, Mount
in: **5** Yukon **12** St. Elias range
highest mt. in: **6** Canada

loges 5 boxes **7** balcony **9** mezzanine

loggia 5 lanai, porch **6** arcade, piazza **7** balcony, gallery

logic 5 sense **6** reason **7** cogency **8** analysis, argument **9** coherence, deduction, good sense, induction **10** dialectics

logical 5 clear, sound, valid **6** cogent, likely **7** germane **8** coherent, rational, relevant, sensible **9** deducible, pertinent, plausible **10** analytical, consistent, most likely, reasonable **11** en-

lightened, intelligent **13** well-organized

logos 4 word **5** ratio **6** saying, speech **7** thought **9** discourse, reckoning **10** proportion

logy 4 dull **5** inert, tired, weary **6** drowsy, groggy, sleepy, torpid **8** comatose, lifeless, listless, sluggish **9** enervated, inanimate, lethargic **10** phlegmatic **12** hebetudinous

Lohengrin
opera by: **6** Wagner
character: **4** Elsa **6** Ortrud **9** Gottfried (Duke of Brabant) **25** Count Frederick of Telramund

Lohengrin
origin: **8** Germanic
knight of: **9** Holy Grail
father: **8** Parsifal, Parzival

loiter 4 idle, laze, loaf, loll, lurk **5** dally, skulk, slink, tarry **6** dawdle **10** dillydally, hang around **11** hover around **12** shilly-shally

Loki
origin: **12** Scandinavian
mentioned in: **9** Lokasenna
god of: **4** fire
son: **6** Fenrir, Fenris
daughter: **3** Hel
fathered: **10** Jormungand **11** lormungandr, Jormungandr **14** Midgard Serpent
mother of his children: **9** Angerboda, Angrbodha, Angurboda
caused death of: **5** Baldr **6** Balder, Baldur
form: **5** giant
extorted treasure from: **7** Andvari
function: **4** evil **6** strife **7** discord **8** mischief

Lolita
author: **15** Vladimir Nabokov
character: **6** Lolita **14** Humbert Humbert
director: **14** Stanley Kubrick
based on novel by: **15** Vladimir Nabokov
cast: **7** Sue Lyon (Lolita) **10** James Mason (Humbert Humbert) **12** Peter Sellers **14** Shelley Winters

loll 3 sag **4** drag, drop, flap, flop, idle, lean, loaf **5** droop, relax, slump **6** dangle, dawdle, lounge, repose, slouch, sprawl **7** goof off, recline **8** flop over, languish

Lollobrigida, Gina
born: **5** Italy **7** Subiaco
roles: **7** Trapeze **14** Anne of Brooklyn, The Wayward Wife **15** Solomon and Sheba **20** Buona Sera Mrs Campbell **27** The World's Most Beautiful Woman

Loman, Willy
character in: **16** Death of a Salesman
author: **6** Miller
epitome of: **8** salesman

Lombard, Carole

real name: 15 Jane Alice Peters
husband: 10 Clark Gable
born: 11 Fort Wayne IN
roles: 12 My Man Godfrey **13** Nothing Sacred, To Be Or Not To Be **16** Twentieth Century

Lome
  capital of: 4 Togo

London
  airport: 7 Gatwick **8** Heathrow, Stansted
  architect: 4 Wren
  area: 4 Soho **6** Camden **7** Brixton, Chelsea, Holborn, Pimlico **8** Vauxhall **9** Bayswater, Belgravia, Islington, Southwark **10** Bloomsbury, Kensington, Paddington, Shoreditch **11** Notting Hill, St John's Wood **13** Knightsbridge
  capital of: 7 England **12** Great Britain **13** United Kingdom
  landmark: 6 Big Ben **8** Hyde Park **9** Whitehall, Wimbledon **11** Regent's Park, Saint James's, Tate Gallery, Tower Bridge **12** Covent Garden, London Bridge **13** British Museum, Tower of London **14** British Library, Speaker's Corner **15** National Gallery, Trafalgar Square **16** Buckingham Palace, Piccadilly Circus, Westminster Abbey **17** Kensington Gardens, Royal Festival Hall, Westminster Palace **18** Houses of Parliament **19** Saint Paul's Cathedral **23** Victoria and Albert Museum
  police: 7 bobbies
    established by: 13 Sir Robert Peel
  prime minister's residence: 16 Ten Downing Street
  river: 6 Thames
  Roman name: 9 Londinium
  subway: 11 Underground

London, Jack
  author of: 9 White Fang **10** The Sea Wolf **16** The Call of the Wild

lone 4 only, sole **5** alone **6** single, unique **8** isolated, singular, solitary, unpaired **9** unabetted **10** individual, unattended, unescorted **13** companionless, unaccompanied

loneliness 9 isolation, seclusion **12** lonesomeness, solitariness **14** friendlessness

Loneliness of the Long Distance Runner, The
  author: 12 Alan Sillitoe
  director: 14 Tony Richardson
  cast: 11 Avis Bunnage, Peter Madden **12** Tom Courtenay **15** Michael Redgrave

lonely 6 remote **7** forlorn **8** deserted, desolate, forsaken, hermitic, isolated, lonesome, secluded, solitary, unsocial **9** by oneself, reclusive, withdrawn **10** friendless, unattended **11** uninhabited, unpopulated **12** unfrequented **13** companionless, unaccompanied

Lone Ranger, The
  character: 5 Tonto
  cast: 8 John Hart **12** Clayton Moore **14** Jay Silverheels
  horse: 5 Scout **6** Silver
  saying: 8 kemo sabe
  Lone Ranger used: 13 silver bullets
  theme: 19 William Tell Overture

lonesome 5 alone, aloof **6** lonely **7** forlorn, insular **8** desolate, detached, forsaken **9** alienated, withdrawn **10** friendless, unfriended **13** companionless

Lone Star State
  nickname of: 5 Texas

long 4 hope, lust, pine, sigh, want, wish **5** covet, crave, yearn **6** aspire, hanker, hunger, thirst **7** lengthy, spun out **8** drawn-out, extended, have a yen, in length, unending **9** elongated, extensive, prolonged **10** be bent on, protracted **11** far-reaching, have a desire **12** from end to end, interminable, outstretched

Long, Crawford Williamson
  field: 8 medicine
  first used: 5 ether

Long Day's Journey into Night
  author: 12 Eugene O'Neill
  director: 11 Sidney Lumet
  cast: 13 Dean Stockwell **14** Jason Robards Jr **15** Ralph Richardson **16** Katharine Hepburn

Longest Day, The
  director: 10 Ken Annakin **12** Andrew Marton, Bernard Wicki
  cast: 9 John Wayne, Mel Ferrer **10** Henry Fonda, Red Buttons, Robert Ryan, Rod Steiger **12** Peter Lawford
  setting: 4 D-Day **8** Normandy (Allied invasion)

long-faced 4 glum **6** dismal, gloomy **7** doleful, unhappy **8** dejected, mournful **10** lugubrious **14** down in the mouth

Longfellow, Henry Wadsworth
  author of: 8 Hyperion, (The Song of) Hiawatha **10** Evangeline **15** Paul Revere's Ride **18** Tales of a Wayside Inn **21** The Wreck of the Hesperus **27** The Courtship of Miles Standish

longing 3 yen **4** wish **6** ardent, pining, thirst **7** craving, wishful **8** desirous, yearning **9** hankering, hungering **10** aspiration **11** languishing

long-lasting 7 chronic, lengthy, tedious **8** enduring, extended **9** prolonged **10** continuing, protracted

long live
  French: 4 vive

long past 3 old **5** olden **6** gone by, of yore **7** ancient, long ago **8** long gone

long-standing 4 long **5** hardy, hoary **6** rooted **7** abiding, ancient, chronic, durable, lasting **8** enduring, habitual,

hallowed, unfading **9** confirmed, continual, long-lived, perennial, perpetual, venerable **10** continuous, deep-rooted, deep-seated, inveterate, persistent, persisting **11** long-lasting, time-honored **15** long-established

Longstreet, James
  served in: 8 Civil War
  side: 11 Confederate
  battle: 7 Bull Run **10** Gettysburg **11** Chickamauga **14** Fredericksburg **18** Wilderness Campaign
  after war joined: 11 Republicans
  US minister to: 6 Turkey

Long Voyage Home, The
  director: 8 John Ford
  based on play by: 12 Eugene O'Neill
  cast: 9 Ian Hunter, John Wayne **13** Wilfrid Lawson **14** Thomas Mitchell **15** Barry Fitzgerald

long-wearing 5 tough **6** strong, sturdy **7** durable, lasting **8** enduring **11** substantial

long-winded 5 wordy **6** prolix **7** lengthy, tedious, verbose **8** rambling **9** garrulous **10** digressive, discursive

long-windedness 8 rambling **9** garrulity, prolixity, verbosity, wordiness **14** discursiveness

look 3 air, see **4** cast, face, gape, gaze, mien, ogle, peek, peep, scan, seem, show, view **5** front, glare, guise, sight, stare, study, watch **6** appear, behold, glance, regard, survey **7** bearing, examine, exhibit, glimpse **8** demeanor, manifest, once-over, presence, scrutiny **10** appearance, be directed, cut a figure, expression, scrutinize **11** contemplate, countenance, observation

look after 4 help **6** assist, defend **7** help out, protect **10** minister to **11** watch out for **17** take under one's wing

look askance at 7 condemn **8** object to **9** frown upon **10** disapprove **14** discountenance **15** take exception to **16** find unacceptable, view with disfavor

look at 3 see **4** view **6** behold, notice, regard **7** examine, inspect, witness **10** scrutinize

Look Back in Anger
  director: 14 Tony Richardson
  based on play by: 11 John Osborne
  cast: 7 Mary Ure **10** Edith Evans **11** Claire Bloom **13** Richard Burton **15** Donald Pleasance

look down on 7 despise, disdain **9** frown upon, patronize **10** condescend **13** put on airs with **14** hold in contempt

looker-on 6 viewer **7** watcher, witness **8** beholder, observer, onlooker **9** bystander, spectator

look for 4 seek 5 await 6 expect, pursue 7 hunt for 9 search for 10 anticipate

look for the woman
French: 15 cherchez la femme

look forward to 5 await 6 expect 7 long for, wait for 9 pin hope on 10 anticipate 17 count the days until

Look Homeward, Angel
author: 11 Thomas Wolfe
character: 7 Ben Gant 9 Eliza Gant 10 Eugene Gant, Laura James, Oliver Gant 15 Margaret Leonard

look in the eye 4 defy, face 5 brave 8 confront 9 challenge

look into 5 probe 7 examine, explore 10 scrutinize 11 inquire into, investigate

lookout 4 heed 5 guard, scout, vigil 6 patrol, sentry 7 spotter 8 observer, sentinel, watchdog, watchman 9 alertness, attention, awareness, readiness, vigilance 10 precaution 11 guardedness, mindfulness, watchkeeper 12 surveillance, watchfulness

look out 4 mind 6 beware 8 take care, watch out 9 be careful, be on guard 11 take warning 12 be on the alert

look over 4 scan, skim 5 judge 6 assess, peruse, survey 7 dip into 8 appraise, evaluate 13 browse through, glance through

look through 4 scan, skim 6 browse, peruse 7 dip into 8 look over 9 check over 13 glance through

look toward 7 count on 10 anticipate 13 look forward to

look upon 3 see 4 view 6 be hold, gaze at, look at 7 observe, stare at

look upon as 4 deem, hold 5 count, judge, think 6 regard, view as 7 account, believe 8 consider, take to be

look up to 5 honor 6 admire, esteem, revere 7 respect 8 venerate

loom 4 hulk, rise, soar 5 tower 6 appear, ascend, emerge 8 stand out 9 take shape

loom, power
invented by: 10 Cartwright

loop 3 eye 4 bend, coil, curl, furl, ring, roll, turn 5 braid, curve, noose, plait, twirl, twist, whorl 6 circle, eyelet, spiral 7 opening, ringlet 8 aperture, encircle, loophole 10 wind around 11 convolution, curve around

Loos, Anita
author of: 22 Gentlemen Prefer Blondes

loose 4 fast, free, lewd, undo, wild 5 freed, let go, slack, untie, vague 6 freely, loosen, unbind, undone, untied, wanton 7 immoral, inexact, loosely, release, set free, slacken, unbound, uncaged, unchain, unleash, unloose, unyoked 8 careless, heedless, liberate, not tight, rakehell, unbridle, unchaste, unfasten, unjoined, untether 9 abandoned, debauched, dissolute, imprecise, liberated, libertine, unbridled, unchained, unleashed, unmanacle, unshackle 10 dissipated, inaccurate, licentious, not binding, profligate, unattached, unexacting, unfastened, unfettered, unhandcuff, untethered 11 not fastened, unconnected 12 unimprisoned 13 unconstrained

loose-fitting 4 limp 5 baggy, loose, slack 6 draped, droopy 7 sagging 9 overlarge, oversized

loosely connected 5 jerky 6 fitful 8 episodic, rambling 9 spasmodic, wandering 10 digressive, discursive, meandering

loosen 3 lax 4 ease, free, undo 5 break, relax, untie 6 limber, unbend, unbind 7 release, relieve, slacken, unchain, unscrew 8 liberate, unbuckle, unfasten, work free 10 emancipate

looseness 8 fastness, lewdness, wildness 9 slackness, vagueness 10 debauchery, immorality, inaccuracy, profligacy, wantonness 11 dissipation, dissolution, imprecision 12 carelessness, heedlessness, inexactitude 14 licentiousness

loot 3 rob 4 haul, raid, sack, swag, take 5 booty, prize, strip 6 boodle, fleece, pilfer, ravage, spoils 7 pillage, plunder, ransack 11 stolen goods

looter 5 thief 6 robber, vandal 7 brigand 8 pillager 9 despoiler, plunderer

lop 3 cut 4 chip, chop, crop, dock, flop, sned, snip, trim 5 droop, prune, sever 6 cut off, deduct, detach, remove, slouch 7 cut back 8 amputate, truncate

Lopez, Nancy
sport: 4 golf
husband: 9 Ray Knight
  sport: 8 baseball

lopsided 4 awry 5 askew 6 aslant, tipped, uneven 7 crooked, leaning, listing, slanted, tilting, unequal 8 cockeyed, inclined, slanting 9 irregular 10 asymmetric, off-balance, unbalanced 15 disproportional 16 disproportionate

loquacious 5 gabby, talky, windy, wordy 6 blabby, chatty, prolix 7 prating, verbose, voluble 8 babbling, chattery 9 garrulous, prattling, talkative 10 chattering, long-winded

loquitur 8 he speaks 9 she speaks

lord 4 king 5 chief, crown, ruler 6 leader, master 7 monarch 8 overlord, seignior, superior 9 commander, landowner, sovereign 10 landholder, proprietor

Japanese: 6 daimyo
Turkish: 3 beg, bey

Lord
Latin: 7 Dominus

Lord be with you, the
Latin: 15 Dominus vobiscum

Lord have mercy
Greek: 12 Kyrie eleison

Lord Jim
author: 12 Joseph Conrad
character: 5 Stein 6 Marlow 9 Dain Waris 14 Gentleman Brown

lordliness 7 disdain 8 contempt 9 arrogance, insolence, loftiness 11 haughtiness 13 imperiousness 16 superciliousness

lordly 4 cold 5 aloof, bossy, grand, lofty, noble, proud, regal 6 august, remote, snooty 7 distant, elegant, eminent, exalted, haughty, stately, stuck-up 8 arrogant, despotic, imposing, majestic, princely, puffed-up, scornful, snobbish 9 conceited, dignified, imperious, sumptuous 10 disdainful, hoity-toity, tyrannical 11 dictatorial, domineering, magisterial, magnificent, patronizing 13 condescending, high-and-mighty, self-important

Lord of the Flies
author: 14 William Golding

Lord of the Rings, The
author: 10 J R R Tolkien
creatures: 3 elf, ent, orc 5 dwarf 6 hobbit

Lord of the Rings, The: The Fellowship of the Rings
author: 10 J R R Tolkien
director: 12 Peter Jackson
cast: 7 Ian Holm (Bilbo Baggins) 8 Liv Tyler (Arwen), Sean Bean (Boromir) 9 Billy Boyd (Pippin), Sala Baker (Sauron), Sean Astin (Sam Gamgee) 10 Andy Serkis (Gollum), Elijah Wood (Frodo Baggins) 11 Craig Parker (Haldir), Ian McKellen (Gandalf), Noel Appleby (Everard Proudfoot) 12 Orlando Bloom (Legolas Greenleaf) 13 Cate Blanchett (Galadriel) 14 Christopher Lee (Saruman), John Rhys-Davies (Gimli), Viggo Mortensen (Aragorn) 15 Dominic Monaghan (Merry)

Lord of the Rings, The: The Return of the King
author: 10 J R R Tolkien
director: 12 Peter Jackson
cast: 7 Ian Holm (Bilbo Baggins) 8 Liv Tyler (Arwen), Sean Bean (Boromir) 9 Billy Boyd (Pippin), Ian Hughes (Irolas), John Noble (Denethor), Peter Tait (Shagrat), Sala Baker (Sauron), Sean Astin (Sam Gamgee) 10 Andy Serkis (Gollum), Elijah

Wood (Frodo Baggins), Paul Norell (King of the Dead) **11** Bernard Hill (Theoden), Ian McKellen (Gandalf), Miranda Otto (Eowyn), Noel Appleby (Everard Proudfoot) **12** Bruce Hopkins (Gamling), Orlando Bloom (Legolas Greenleaf), Thomas Robins (Deagol) **13** Bruce Phillips (Grimbold), Cate Blanchett (Galadriel) **14** Alexandra Astin (Elanor Gamgee), John Rhys-Davies (Gimli), Viggo Mortensen (Aragorn) **15** Dominic Monaghan (Merry), Lawrence Makoare (Witch King/Gothmog)

Lord of the Rings, The: The Two Towers
   author: 10 J R R Tolkien
   director: 12 Peter Jackson
   cast: 8 John Bach (Madril), Liv Tyler (Arwen) **9** Billy Boyd (Pippin), Jed Brophy (Sharku/Snaga), Karl Urban (Eomer), Sean Astin (Sam Gamgee) **10** Andy Serkis (Gollum), Brad Dourif (Grima Wormtongue), Elijah Wood (Frodo Baggins) **11** Bernard Hill (Theoden), Craig Parker (Haldir), David Wenham (Faramir), Hugo Weaving (Elrond), Ian McKellen (Gandalf), Miranda Otto (Eowyn) **12** Bruce Hopkins (Gamling), Orlando Bloom (Legolas Greenleaf) **13** Cate Blanchett (Galadriel) **14** Christopher Lee (Saruman), John Rhys-Davies (Gimli), Viggo Mortensen (Aragorn) **15** Dominic Monaghan (Merry)

Lord Weary's Castle
   author: 12 Robert Lowell
lore 7 beliefs, legends **10** traditions
Lorelei
   also: 7 Lurelei
   origin: 8 Germanic
   form: 5 nymph
   dwelling place: 5 cliff, Rhine
   lured: 7 boatmen
   caused shipwrecks by: 7 singing
Lorelei Lee
   role in: 22 Gentlemen Prefer Blondes
   played by: 6 Monroe **8** Channing
   song: 27 Diamonds Are a Girl's Best Friend
Loren, Sophia
   real name: 14 Sofia Scicolone
   husband: 10 Carlo Ponti
   born: 4 Rome **5** Italy
   roles: 5 El Cid **6** Soleil **8** Two Women (Oscar) **9** Arabesque, Houseboat **11** Pret a Porter **13** Man of La Mancha **14** Grumpier Old Men, The Black Orchid **16** Between Strangers **18** Desire Under the Elms **20** Marriage Italian Style **21** A Countess from Hong Kong, The Pride and the Passion

Lorentz, Hendrik Anton
   field: 7 physics
   nationality: 5 Dutch
   discovered: 17 special relativity
   named for him: 21 Lorentz transformation **34** Lorentz-Fitzgerald Length Contraction
   awarded: 10 Nobel Prize
Loring, Eugene
   choreographer of: 11 Billy the Kid
Lorna Doone
   author: 11 R D Blackmore
   character: 8 John Ridd **9** Tom Faggus **11** Carver Doone **13** Sir Ensor Doone **14** Jeremy Stickles **15** Reuben Huckaback
Lorre, Peter
   real name: 16 Laszlo Lowenstein
   born: 7 Hungary **9** Rosenberg
   roles: 1 M **6** Mr. Moto **7** Mad Love **9** Joel Cairo **10** Casablanca, The Verdict **12** The Big Circus **14** Three Strangers **16** The Maltese Falcon **18** Crime and Punishment, The Mask of Dimitrios
Los Angeles
   airport: 3 LAX **7** Burbank **23** Los Angeles International
   area: 5 Watts **6** Bel Air, Downey, Venice **7** Anaheim, Compton, Norwalk **8** Mar Vista, Pasadena, Torrance, Westwood **9** Brentwood, Hollywood, Inglewood, Long Beach **10** Culver City **11** Century City, Garden Grove, Palos Verdes, Santa Monica **12** Beverly Hills, Marina del Rey **16** Pacific Palisades
      San Fernando Valley: 6 Encino **7** Tarzana, Van Nuys, Ventura **10** Northridge **11** Sherman Oaks
   baseball team: 7 Dodgers
   basketball team: 6 Lakers, Sparks **8** Clippers
   hockey team: 5 Kings
   landmark: 5 Forum **10** Disneyland **11** Civic Center, Getty Museum, Watts Towers **12** Griffith Park **13** Farmers' Market, Hollywood Bowl, Hollywood Park, La Brea Tar Pits, Magic Mountain **15** Knott's Berry Farm **16** Bonaventure Hotel **17** Norton Simon Museum **22** Grauman's Chinese Theater **23** Griffith Park Observatory
   mountains: 10 San Gabriel **11** Santa Monica
   nickname: 15 City of the Angels
   street: 4 Vine **10** Rodeo Drive **12** Olvera Street **15** Mulholland Drive **16** Van Nuys Boulevard **17** Wilshire Boulevard **18** Hollywood Boulevard **20** Santa Monica Boulevard
   university: 3 USC **4** UCLA **7** Caltech **10** Pepperdine **17** Occidental College **31** California Institute of Technology

lose 4 fail, miss **6** forget, ignore, mislay **7** confuse, forfeit **8** misplace **9** fail to win, stray from **10** be the loser, fail to heed **11** be thrown off **12** be defeated in, be deprived of, suffer loss of, take a licking
lose control 5 break, crack **7** crack up **9** fall apart **10** go to pieces **15** go off the deep end
lose faith 6 give up **7** despair **9** lose heart **10** have no hope **18** become disenchanted
lose force 3 die **7** run down **9** lose power
lose heart 6 give up **7** de spair **17** become discouraged
lose one's cool 12 fly into a rage **13** become enraged, throw a tantrum **14** lose one's temper **15** fly off the handle
loser 4 flop **7** failure **8** defeated **9** conquered **10** vanquished
lose track of 4 lose **9** let escape **11** lose sight of
lose vigor 4 flag **5** droop **6** sicken, weaken, wither **7** decline
loss 4 ruin **5** wreck **6** defeat, losing **7** licking, removal, undoing **8** overturn, riddance, wrecking **9** abolition, mislaying, privation **10** amount lost, demolition, extinction, forfeiture, misplacing, number lost **11** bereavement, deprivation, destruction, dissolution, eradication, expenditure, extirpation
loss of life 5 death **8** fatality **9** mortality
Lost
   network: 3 ABC
   cast: 9 Yungin Kim (Sun Paik-Kwon) **10** Matthew Fox (Jack Shephard), Mira Furlan (Danielle Rousseau) **11** Jorge Garcia (Hugo "Hurley" Reyes), Maggie Grace (Shannon Rutherford), Terry O'Quinn (John Locke) **12** Daniel Dae Kim (Jin-Soo Kwon), Josh Holloway (James "Sawyer" Ford) **13** Emilie de Ravin (Claire Littleton), Naveen Andrews (Sayid Jarrah) **14** Ian Somerhalder (Boone Carlyle) **15** Dominic Monaghan (Charlie Pace), Evangeline Lilly (Kate Austin), Harold Perrineau (Michael Dawson) **18** Malcolm David Kelley (Walt Lloyd)
lost 5 stray **6** absent, astray, killed, ruined, wasted **7** lacking, mislaid, missing, misused, strayed, wrecked **8** absorbed, murdered, perished, vanished, wiped out **9** abolished, destroyed, engrossed, misplaced, off-course **10** demolished, eradicated, extirpated, gone astray, misapplied, squandered **11** annihilated, misdirected, obliterated, preoccupied **12** exterminated

Lost Horizon
author: **11** James Hilton
character: **10** Hugh Conway, Rutherford **12** Henry Barnard, Miss Brinklow **14** Father Perrault **20** Captain Mallison Chang
director: **10** Frank Capra
cast: **5** Margo **8** H B Warner, Sam Jaffe **9** Jane Wyatt **10** John Howard **12** Isabel Jewell, Ronald Colman **14** Thomas Mitchell **19** Edward Everett Horton
setting: **5** Tibet

Lost in America
director: **12** Albert Brooks
cast: **12** Albert Brooks, Julie Hagerty

Lost in Space
character: **5** Robot **7** Don West **12** Judy Robinson, Will Robinson **13** Penny Robinson **14** Dr Zachary Smith **15** Maureen Robinson **16** Prof John Robinson
cast: **9** Billy Mumy **11** Guy Williams, Mark Goddard **12** June Lockhart, Marta Kristen **14** Jonathan Harris **16** Angela Cartwright
ship: **9** Jupiter II

lost in thought 7 pensive **8** absorbed **9** engrossed, wrapped up **13** contemplative, in a brown study, introspective

Lost Patrol, The
director: **8** John Ford
cast: **8** Alan Hale **11** Wallace Ford **12** Boris Karloff **14** Victor McLaglen
score: **10** Max Steiner

Lost Weekend, The
author: **14** Charles Jackson
director: **11** Billy Wilder
cast: **9** Jane Wyman, Mary Young **10** Frank Falen, Ray Milland **11** Philip Terry **12** Doris Dowling **13** Howard da Silva
Oscar for: **5** actor (Milland) **7** picture **8** director **10** screenplay

lot 4 fate, lots, many, much, plot **5** field, patch, quota, share, straw, tract **6** oceans, oodles, ration **7** counter, measure **8** beaucoup, property **9** allotment, allowance, great deal

Lot
grandfather: **5** Terah
father: **5** Haran
uncle: **7** Abraham
son: **5** Ammon
hometown: **5** Sodom
rescued by: **6** angels
fled to: **4** Zoar

lothario 3 rip **4** rake, roue, wolf **5** lover, Romeo, sheik **6** lecher **7** Don Juan, seducer, swinger **8** Casanova, loverboy **9** debauchee, debaucher, libertine, womanizer **10** lady-killer, profligate, sensualist **11** philanderer, skirtchaser

Lothario
character in: **15** The Fair Penitent
author: **4** Rowe

Loti, Pierre
author of: **18** An Iceland Fisherman
pseudonym of: **5** Viaud

lotion 4 balm, wash **5** salve **6** liquid **7** unction, unguent **8** cosmetic, liniment, ointment, solution **9** demulcent, emollient, freshener, skin cream **10** after-shave, astringent **11** conditioner, embrocation, moisturizer

Lotis
form: **5** nymph
changed into: **4** tree **5** lotus

lotophagi
means: **11** lotus-eaters

lots 4 much **5** heaps, loads, plots, scads **10** quantities

lotus 7 Nelumbo **13** Nymphaea lotus
varieties: **4** blue **5** water, white **6** sacred **8** American, Egyptian **10** East Indian

lotus-eaters 9 lotophagi
appear in: **7** Odyssey

loud 5 gaudy, noisy, showy, vivid **6** bright, flashy, garish **7** blatant, booming, intense, splashy **8** colorful, sonorous **9** clamorous, deafening **10** resounding, stentorian, thundering, vociferous **11** ear-piercing, loud-mouthed **12** earsplitting, ostentatious

loud sound 4 bang, boom, clap, honk, howl, peal, roar, slam, toot **5** blare, blast, burst, crash **6** bellow, report, scream, shriek **7** clatter, thunder **9** explosion **10** detonation

Lou Grant
character: **6** Animal **8** Joe Rossi **10** Art Donovan **11** Charlie Hume **12** Billie Newman **15** Margaret Pynchon
cast: **10** Jack Bannon, Mason Adams **11** Edward Asner, Linda Kelsey **12** Robert Walden **13** Nancy Marchand **14** Darryl Anderson
paper: **17** Los Angeles Tribune
spinoff of: **18** Mary Tyler Moore Show

Louis, Joe
real name: **14** Joe Louis Barrow
nickname: **11** Brown Bomber
sport: **6** boxing
class: **11** heavyweight

Louis, Morris
born: **11** Baltimore MD
artwork: **4** Veil **5** Signa **7** Stripes **8** Unfurled **15** Mountains and Sea

Louise
opera by: **11** Charpentier
character: **6** Julian

Louisiana
abbreviation: **2** LA
nickname: **5** Bayou, Sugar **6** Creole **7** Pelican
capital: **10** Baton Rouge
largest city: **10** New Orleans
others: **5** Houma **6** Bunkie, Gretna, Kenner, Minden, Monroe, Ruston **7** Bastrop **8** Bogalusa **9** Lafayette, Opelousas **10** Alexandria, Shreveport **11** Lake Charles
college: **3** LSU **6** Loyola, Tulane **7** Dillard, Newcomb **9** Grambling
explorer: **7** La Salle **9** Iberville **13** Pierre Lemoyne
feature:
area: **5** bayou **13** French Quarter
festival: **9** Mardi Gras
music: **4** jazz
stadium: **9** Superdome
street: **7** Bourbon
tribe: **4** Adai, Ioni, Rees, Waco **5** Caddo, Haini, Washa **6** Eyeish, Pawnee **7** Andarko, Arikara, Atakapa **8** Ovachita **9** Bayogoula, Nachitoch
people: **5** Cajun **6** Creole **7** Acadian, pelican **8** Huey Long **14** Lillian Hellman, Louis Armstrong
island: **5** Avery
lake: **3** Iat **4** Iatt **5** Caddo, Clear, Cross, Larto, White **6** Borgne, Saline **8** Darbonne, Maurepas **9** Bistineau, Calcasieu, Catahoula **10** False River **13** Pontchartrain
land rank: **11** thirty-first
mountain:
highest point: **8** Driskill
physical feature: **15** Head of the Passes **17** coastal marshlands
delta: **11** Mississippi
gulf: **6** Mexico
salt domes: **11** Five Islands
river: **3** Red **5** Amite, Bayou, Pearl **6** Tensas **8** Ouachita **11** Mississippi
state admission: **10** eighteenth
state bird: **19** eastern brown pelican
state flower: **8** magnolia
state motto: **5** Union **7** Justice **10** Confidence
state song: **15** Give Me Louisiana **16** You Are My Sunshine
state tree: **11** bald cypress

Louisiana Lightning
nickname of: **9** Ron Guidry

lounge 4 flop, idle, laze, loaf, loll, rest, sofa **5** couch, dally, divan, lobby, relax, sleep, slump **6** dawdle, daybed, repose, slouch, sprawl **7** recline, slumber **8** kill time, languish **9** davenport, do nothing, lie around, vestibule **10** dillydally, stretch out, take it easy **12** chaise longue

lourd
music: **5** heavy

Lourenco Marques
capital of: **10** Mozambique

louse 3 cad, rat **4** heel **5** churl, knave **6** rascal, rotter, vermin **8** parasite **9** scoundrel

louse up 3 mar 4 goof, muff, ruin 5 botch, spoil 6 bungle, foul up, mess up 7 butcher, do badly, screw up 9 mismanage 11 make a mess of

lousy 3 bad 4 mean 5 awful, nasty 6 crummy, rotten, shabby, unkind 7 hateful, vicious 8 dreadful, inferior, infested, terrible 9 unethical, worthless 10 pediculous, second-rate, unpleasant 12 contemptible

lout 3 ape, oaf 4 boor, clod 5 booby, churl, clown, dummy, dunce, klutz, yokel 6 lummox, rustic 7 bumpkin, dullard

loutish 4 rude 5 crude 6 coarse, gauche, oafish, vulgar 7 boorish, uncouth 9 unrefined 10 unpolished 11 peasantlike

lovable, loveable 4 cute 5 sweet 6 cuddly, lovely, taking 7 darling, winning, winsome 8 adorable, charming, engaging, fetching 9 endearing 10 enchanting 11 captivating

love 3 man 4 beau, bent, dear, girl, mind, turn 5 adore, amity, amour, angel, ardor, enjoy, fancy, flame, honey, lover, savor, taste, woman 6 admire, bask in, choice, esteem, fellow, relish 7 beloved, charity, cherish, concord, darling, dearest, emotion, leaning, passion, rapture, revel in, sweetie 8 affinity, be fond of, devotion, fondness, goodwill, hold dear, loved one, mistress, paramour, penchant, precious, sympathy, treasure, truelove, weakness 9 adoration, affection, boyfriend, delight in, inamorata, rejoice in, sentiment 10 admiration, appreciate, attachment, cordiality, friendship, girlfriend, partiality, proclivity, solicitude, sweetheart, sweetie pie, tenderness 11 amorousness, benevolence, brotherhood, inclination, infatuation 12 be enamored of, congeniality, predilection

   god of: 4 Amor, Eros 5 Cupid 7 Angus Og

   goddess of: 5 Freia, Freya, Venus 6 Hathor, Inanna, Ishtar 7 Astarte, Mylitta 9 Aphrodite

Love, the Magician
   also: 11 El Amor Brujo
   ballet by: 5 Falla

Love Actually
   director: 13 Richard Curtis
   cast: 9 Bill Nighy (Billy Mack), Hugh Grant (the Prime Minister) 10 Colin Firth (Jamie), Joanna Page (Judy), Liam Neeson (Daniel), Lucia Moniz (Aurelia) 11 Alan Rickman (Harry), Laura Linney (Sarah), Nina Sosanya (Annie) 12 Emma Thompson (Karen), Gregor Fisher (Joe), Kris Marshall (Colin) 13 Andrew Lincoln

(Mark), Keira Knightly (Juliet), Martin Freeman (John), Rowan Atkinson (Rufus) 14 Rodrigo Santoro (Karl), Thomas Sangster (Sam) 15 Chiwetel Ejiofor (Peter) 17 Martine McCutcheon (Natalie)

love affair 5 amour 7 liaison, romance 14 affaire de coeur

Love Boat, The
   character: 3 Ace 10 (Cruise Director) Julie McCoy 11 (Dr) Adam Bricker, (Purser Burl) Gopher Smith 14 (Captain) Merrill Stubing 15 (Bartender) Isaac Washington
   cast: 8 Ted Lange 10 Fred Grandy 11 Lauren Tewes 12 Bernie Kopell, Gavin MacLeod
   ship: 15 Pacific Princess

love child 7 bastard 12 natural child 17 illegitimate child

love conquers all
   Latin: 15 omnia vincit amor

loved one 4 love, wife 5 lover 6 fiance, spouse 7 be loved, dearest, fiancee, husband 9 boyfriend 10 girlfriend, sweetheart 12 family member

Love for Three Oranges, The
   opera by: 9 Prokofiev

Love in the Afternoon
   director: 11 Billy Wilder
   cast: 10 Gary Cooper 13 Audrey Hepburn 16 Maurice Chevalier
   setting: 5 Paris

Lovelace, Richard
   author of: 18 To Althea from Prison 23 To Lucasta Going to the Wars

loveliness 6 beauty 9 good looks 11 pulchritude 14 attractiveness

lovely 4 cute, fine, good 5 sweet 6 comely 7 elegant, lovable, winning, winsome 8 adorable, alluring, charming, engaging, fetching, handsome, pleasant, pleasing 9 agreeable, beautiful, endearing, enjoyable, exquisite 10 attractive, delightful, enchanting 11 captivating, fascinating 12 irresistible

Love Me Tonight
   director: 15 Rouben Mamoulian
   cast: 8 Myrna Loy 14 Charlie Ruggles 16 Maurice Chevalier 17 Jeanette MacDonald
   score: 14 Rodgers and Hart
   song: 4 Mimi 5 Lover 14 Isn't It Romantic

love of country
   Latin: 11 amor patriae

lover 3 fan, man, nut 4 beau, buff, dear, girl, love 5 flame, freak, honey, Romeo, swain, woman, wooer 6 fellow, suitor 7 admirer, beloved, darling, devotee, Don Juan, fanatic, sweetie 8 Casanova, follower, Lothario, loved one, lover boy, mistress,

paramour, truelove 9 boyfriend, inamorata 10 aficionado, enthusiast, girlfriend, sweetheart 11 afficionado
   French: 6 bon ami 9 bonne amie
   Italian: 8 cicisbeo

Lovers and Other Strangers
   director: 8 Cy Howard
   cast: 8 Gig Young 9 Anne Meara, Bea Arthur 11 Anne Jackson 13 Bonnie Bedelia, Harry Guardino 14 Cloris Leachman, Michael Brandon 17 Richard Castellano

love seat 4 sofa 5 couch 6 settee 13 courting chair

lovesick 7 amorous 8 yearning 10 moonstruck

Love's Labour's Lost
   author: 18 William Shakespeare
   character: 4 Dull 7 Maria 7 Berowne, Costard, Dumaine 8 Rosaline 9 Ferdinand, Katherine 10 Holofernes, Jaquenetta, Longaville 16 Princess of France 18 Don Adriano de Armado

Love Song of J Alfred Prufrock, The
   author: 7 T S Eliot

Love Story
   author: 10 Erich Segal

loving 4 fond, kind, warm 6 ardent, caring, doting, erotic, tender 7 amatory, amorous, devoted 8 enamored, friendly 10 benevolent, passionate, solicitous 11 sympathetic, warm hearted 12 affectionate

loving word 9 sweet talk 10 endearment 12 sweet nothing

low 4 base, blue, deep, down, evil, glum, mean, soft, vile 5 awful, cruel, dirty, dumpy, faint, gross, lower, lowly, muted, prone, quiet, short, small, squat 6 brutal, coarse, common, cruddy, crummy, feeble, gentle, gloomy, humble, hushed, little, paltry, scurvy, softly, sordid, stubby, stumpy, sunken, vulgar, wicked 7 coastal, concave, corrupt, doleful, heinous, muffled, obscene, quietly, snubbed, squalid, subdued, unhappy 8 cowardly, degraded, dejected, depraved, downcast, inferior, low-lying, low-slung, mediocre, murmured, sawed-off, soothing, terrible, trifling, undersea, unworthy 9 dastardly, depressed, lethargic, nefarious, prostrate, repugnant, repulsive, submarine, submerged, truncated, unethical, whispered 10 abominable, despicable, despondent, dispirited, melancholy, outrageous, scandalous 11 ignominious, scoundrelly, underground, unimportant 12 contemptible, disheartened, dishonorable 14 down in the mouth

Low, Juliette
   founder of: 10 Girl Scouts

lowbred 4 non-U **6** coarse, common, vulgar **7** lowbrow, peasant **10** lower-class, uncultured

low-down 4 base, mean **5** dirty **10** despicable **12** contemptible **13** reprehensible

Lowell, James Russell
author of: 12 The Cathedral **15** The Biglow Papers **16** A Fable for Critics **21** The Vision of Sir Launfal

Lowell, Robert
author of: 8 Day by Day **9** Skunk Hour **10** The Dolphin **11** Life Studies **15** For the Union Dead **16** Lord Weary's Castle

lower 3 cut, dim **4** damp, drop, duck, mute, pare, sink, sulk **5** frown, glare, pared, prune, scowl **6** deduct, glower, lop off, muffle, reduce, soften, subdue **7** curtail, depress, immerse, let down, put down, reduced, repress, shorten **8** decrease, diminish, grow dark, lessened, make less, pare down, pull down, submerge, take down, tone down **9** curtailed, decreased, make lower, pared down **10** abbreviate, diminished

lower-case letter 9 minuscule **11** small letter

lower-class 4 poor **6** common **7** lowbred, lowbrow, peasant **9** unrefined **10** blue-collar **12** working-class

lower classes 6 proles, rabble **8** canaille, riffraff **9** hoi polloi, peasantry **11** proletariat **13** the common herd, working people **16** the great unwashed

lower depths 4 pits, scum **5** dregs **6** rabble **8** canaille, riffraff **14** scum of the earth

Lower Depths, The
also called: 11 At the Bottom **14** A Night's Lodging
author: 10 Maxim Gorky

lower in rank 4 bust **6** demote **7** degrade

lower in spirits 6 deject, sadden **7** depress **8** dispirit **10** dishearten

low-key 4 soft **5** loose, muted **6** gentle, subtle **7** muffled, relaxed, subdued **8** laid-back, softened, soft-sell **9** modulated, toned-down **10** low-pitched, restrained **11** low-pressure, understated, unobtrusive **14** unostentatious

lowliness 8 baseness **9** obscurity **10** humbleness

lowly 3 low **6** humble, modest, simple, softly **7** ignoble, low born, lowbred, obscure **8** baseborn, plebeian **10** unassuming **11** proletarian **13** unpretentious

low-minded 4 lewd, vile **5** crude, gross **6** coarse, smutty, vulgar **7** obscene, uncouth **9** obnoxious, offensive **11** disgraceful **12** contemptible

low point, lowest point 4 base, foot, zero **5** depth, nadir, worst **6** bottom **7** perigee **10** rock bottom

low-priced 5 cheap, token **6** budget, modest **7** bargain, cut-rate, low-cost, nominal, reduced **8** closeout, moderate **9** dirt-cheap **10** discounted, economical, marked-down, reasonable **11** inexpensive **15** bargain-basement

low-ranking 5 minor, petty **11** subordinate, unimportant

low-spirited 3 low, sad **4** blue, down, glum **6** gloomy, morose, woeful **7** doleful, forlorn, unhappy **8** dejected, desolate, downcast **9** depressed, heart sore, sorrowful, woebegone **10** despondent, dispirited, melancholy **11** crestfallen, discouraged, downhearted **12** disconsolate, disheartened **14** down-in-the-mouth

low spirits 4 funk **5** gloom **6** dismay, sorrow **7** despair **8** dejected **9** pessimism **10** depression, desolation, melancholy, moroseness **11** despondency **12** hopelessness **14** discouragement **15** downheartedness

Loy, Myrna
real name: 13 Myrna Williams
co-star: 13 William Powell
born: 13 Raidersburg MT
roles: 10 The Thin Man **11** Nora Charles **17** Cheaper by the Dozen **22** The Best Years of Our Lives

loyal 4 firm, true **6** trusty **7** devoted, dutiful, staunch **8** constant, faithful, reliable, resolute, true-blue **9** steadfast **10** dependable, scrupulous, unswerving, unwavering **11** trustworthy **12** tried and true

loyalist 4 tory **12** conservative

loyalty 6 fealty **8** devotion, fidelity, firmness **9** adherence, constancy **10** allegiance **11** reliability, staunchness **12** faithfulness **13** dependability, steadfastness **15** trustworthiness

lozenge 4 drop, pill **6** tablet, troche **8** pastille **9** cough drop

Luanda
capital of: 6 Angola

Lubitsch, Ernst
director of: 9 Ninotchka **13** Heaven Can Wait, To Be or Not To Be

Lucas, Charlotte
character in: 17 Pride and Prejudice
author: 6 Austen

Lucas, George
home: 14 Skywalker Ranch
director of: 8 Star Wars **16** American Graffiti
producer: 6 Tucker, Willow **8** Star Wars (series) **12** Indiana Jones (series)
company: 3 ILM **23** Industrial Light and Magic

Lucentio
character in: 19 The Taming of the Shrew
author: 11 Shakespeare

Lucerne
German: 6 Luzern
river: 5 Reuss
landmark: 9 Hofkirche **11** Am Rhyn House **15** Mariahilf Church

Lucia di Lammermoor
opera by: 9 Donizetti
based on novel by: 14 Sir Walter Scott
called: 20 The Bride of Lammermoor

Luciana
character in: 17 The Comedy of Errors
author: 11 Shakespeare

Luciani, Albino 13 Pope John Paul I **20** Pope John Paul the First

lucid 5 clear **6** bright, direct, normal **7** certain, precise, radiant, shining **8** accurate, apposite, dazzling, luminous, lustrous, pellucid, positive, rational, specific **9** brilliant, sparkling **10** articulate, perceptive, responsive, to the point **11** clearheaded, crystalline, illuminated, resplendent, transparent **12** crystal clear, intelligible **13** clear thinking, scintillating, well-organized **14** comprehensible, understandable **15** straightforward

Lucifer
means: 5 Satan **11** fallen angel, light bearer **13** friction match

Lucina
origin: 5 Roman
goddess of: 10 childbirth
corresponds to: 4 Juno **8** Ilithyia **10** Eileithyia

Lucio
character in: 17 Measure for Measure
author: 11 Shakespeare

luck 3 lot **4** fate **6** chance, kismet **7** destiny, fortune, success, triumph, victory **8** accident, fortuity, good luck, Lady Luck **11** good fortune, piece of luck **12** happenstance
god of: 12 Bonus Eventus

lucky 4 good **5** happy **6** in luck, timely **7** blessed, favored **9** favorable, fortunate, opportune, promising **10** auspicious, beneficial, felicitous, of good omen, propitious **12** providential

Lucky Jim
author: 12 Kingsley Amis

lucky piece 4 tiki **5** charm **6** amulet, grigri **8** shamrock, talisman **10** lucky charm **11** rabbit's foot

lucrative 7 gainful **8** fruitful **10** beneficial, high-income, high-paying, profitable **11** moneymaking **12** remunerative

Lucretia
husband: 26 Lucius Tarquinius Collatinus
raped by: 16 Sextus Tarquinius
death by: 7 suicide

Lucretius
   author of: **13** De rerum natura **19** On the nature of things

Lucullan 4 rich **6** lavish **7** gourmet **9** epicurean, luxurious

Lucy Show, The
   also: **9** Here's Lucy
   character: **9** Kim Carter **10** Lucy Carter **11** Craig Carter **12** Harry Conners, Vivian Bagley **13** Mary Jane Lewis, Sherman Bagley **14** Lucy Carmichael **15** Chris Carmichael, Harrison Cheever, Jerry Carmichael, Theodore J Mooney **18** Harrison Otis Carter
   cast: **9** Ralph Hart **10** Candy Moore, Dick Martin, Gale Gordon, Lucie Arnaz, Roy Roberts **11** Desi Arnaz Jr, Lucille Ball, Vivian Vance **12** Jimmy Garrett **13** Mary Jane Croft

ludicrous 4 wild **5** comic, crazy, funny **6** absurd, far-out **7** amusing, comical **8** farcical **9** laughable **10** outlandish, ridiculous **11** nonsensical **12** preposterous

Ludlum, Robert
   author of: **15** The Matlock Paper **17** The Bourne Identity, The Parsifal Mosaic, The Road to Gandolfo **18** The Bourne Supremacy, The Bourne Ultimatum, The Osterman Weekend **19** The Gemini Contenders **20** The Matarese Countdown, The Rhinemann Exchange **23** The Chancellor Manuscript, The Scarlatti Inheritance

Luftwaffe 9 air weapon **18** German Nazi air force

lug 3 tow, tug **4** bear, drag, draw, haul, pull, tote **5** carry, heave **9** transport

luggage 4 bags, gear **6** trunks **7** baggage, effects, valises **9** suitcases **13** accouterments

Luggnagg
   fictional land in: **16** Gulliver's Travels
   author: **5** Swift

Lugnasad
   origin: **5** Irish
   feast date: **11** August first

Lugosi, Bela
   real name: **10** Bela Blasko
   born: **5** Lugos **7** Hungary
   roles: **7** Dracula **21** Murders in the Rue Morgue

lugubrious 4 dour, glum **6** gloomy, morose, rueful, somber, woeful **7** doleful, elegiac **8** dolorous, downcast, funereal, mournful **9** miserable, sorrowful, woebegone **10** depressing, melancholy

Luke
   birthplace: **7** Antioch
   companion: **4** Paul
   occupation: **9** physician
   wrote: **6** Gospel

lukewarm 4 cool, mild, warm **5** aloof, tepid **8** detached, uncaring **9** apa-

thetic, temperate **11** halfhearted, indifferent, perfunctory, unconcerned **12** uninterested **13** lackadaisical **14** unenthusiastic **15** body-temperature, room-temperature

lull 3 gap **4** calm, ease, halt, hush **5** break, pause, quell, quiet, still **6** hiatus, lacuna, pacify, recess, soothe, subdue **7** assuage, caesura, compose, mollify, respite **8** breather, calmness **9** interlude **12** brief silence, interruption

Lully, Jean-Baptiste
   born: **5** Italy **8** Florence
   composer of: **4** Atys, Isis **6** Persee, Psyche, Roland, Thesee **7** Alceste, Phaeton **10** Le Sicilien, Proserpine **11** Bellerophon **13** Acis et Galatee, Amadis de Gaule, L'Amour medecin **14** Acis and Galatea, Armide et Renaud, Le mariage force **16** Cadmus et Hermione **17** Achille et Polyxene, Cadmus and Hermione **19** Achilles and Polyxene **20** Les Amants magnifiques **22** Le Bourgeois Gentilhomme, Monsieur de Pourceaugnac

lulu 3 pip **4** oner **5** dandy, doozy **8** Jim Dandy **9** allowance, humdinger, wonderful **10** remarkable

lumber 3 log **4** plod, wood **5** barge, clump, stamp **6** boards, planks, trudge, waddle **7** shamble, shuffle **8** flounder **9** fell trees

Lumber State
   nickname of: **5** Maine

Lumet, Sidney
   director of: **7** Network, Serpico **13** The Pawnbroker **14** Twelve Angry Men **15** Dog Day Afternoon **24** Long Day's Journey Into Night

luminary 3 VIP **5** light, wheel **6** bigwig **7** big shot, notable **8** somebody **9** celebrity, dignitary, personage **10** luminosity **11** illuminator

luminescent 5 aglow **7** glowing **8** gleaming, luminous **9** twinkling **10** flickering, glimmering, glistening, shimmering **11** fluorescent **14** phosphorescent

luminosity 4 glow **5** gleam, sheen, shine **6** luster **8** radiance **10** brightness, brilliance

luminous 6 bright **7** glowing, radiant, shining **8** lustrous **9** brilliant **10** irradiated **11** illuminated, luminescent **15** reflecting light

lump 3 gob, mix **4** bump, cake, clod, fuse, heap, hunk, knob, knot, mass, node, pile, pool **5** amass, batch, blend, bunch, chunk, clump, group, knurl, merge, tumor, unite **6** gather, growth, nodule **7** collect, combine, compile **8** assemble, swelling **9** aggregate **10** protrusion, tumescence **11** excrescence **12** protuberance

lumpish 4 dull, slow **5** bulky, dumpy, heavy, lumpy **6** clumsy **7** awkward **8**

clod dish, ungainly, unwieldy **9** corpulent **10** cumbersome, overweight

Lumpkin, Tony
   character in: **18** She Stoops to Conquer
   author: **9** Goldsmith

lump together 4 fuse, pool **7** combine **10** amalgamate **11** consolidate, incorporate

Luna
   personifies: **4** moon
   Greek: **6** Selene

lunacy 5 folly, mania **6** idiocy **7** madness **8** dementia, insanity **9** absurdity, asininity, craziness, silliness, stupidity **10** imbecility, imprudence, insaneness **11** foolishness **13** foolhardiness, senselessness

lunatic 3 mad, nut **4** daft, loco **5** batty, crazy, loony, nutty, potty **6** cuckoo, insane, madman, maniac, screwy **7** bonkers, cracked, touched **8** crackers, demented, demoniac, deranged, maniacal, unhinged **9** psychotic, senseless **10** irrational, psychopath, reasonless, unbalanced **11** crazy person, mentally ill, not all there **12** crackbrained, insane person, psychopathic, round the bend **13** off one's rocker, of unsound mind, out of one's mind

lunch
   French: **8** dejeuner

luncheonette 4 cafe **5** diner **7** beanery **8** snack bar **9** hash house, lunchroom **10** coffee shop **11** eating house **12** lunch counter, sandwich shop

lunchroom 4 cafe **5** diner, grill **8** snack bar **9** cafeteria **12** luncheonette

lunge 3 cut, jab **4** dash, dive, pass, rush, stab **5** hit at, lurch, swing, swipe **6** attack, charge, plunge, pounce, thrust **7** set upon **8** fall upon, strike at **9** make a pass

lunkhead 3 ass **4** dope, fool **5** booby, dunce, idiot, moron, ninny **6** dimwit, nitwit **7** fat head, halfwit **8** bonehead, dumb-dumb, imbecile, numskull **9** blockhead, lamebrain, numbskull **10** dunderhead, nincompoop **11** chowderhead

Lunt, Alfred
   wife: **12** Lynn Fontanne
   born: **11** Milwaukee WI
   roles: **12** The Guardsman **13** The Ragged Edge

Lupercalia
   origin: **5** Roman
   event: **8** festival
   honoring: **6** Faunus **8** Lupercus
   to procure: **9** fertility

Lupercus
   origin: **5** Roman
   god of: **9** fertility
   corresponds to: **3** Pan **6** Faunus

Lupino, Ida 7 actress **8** director
husband: 10 Howard Duff **12** Collier Young, Louis Hayward
born: 6 London **7** England
roles: 8 Devotion **10** The Hard Way **12** Junior Bonner, Women's Prison **13** Escape Me Never **15** Strange Intruder **17** On Dangerous Ground **18** The Light That Failed, While the City Sleeps

lurch 4 cant, keel, list, reel, roll, sway, tilt, toss **5** lunge, pitch, slant **6** careen, plunge, swerve, teeter, totter **7** incline, stagger, stumble

Lurch 6 butler
on: 15 The Addams Family

lure 4 bait, coax, trap **5** bribe, decoy, snare, tempt **6** allure, cajole, come-on, entice, induce, seduce **7** attract, beguile **8** cajolery, persuade **9** fascinate, tantalize **10** allurement, attraction, enticement, inducement, temptation **11** drawing card **12** blandishment

Lurelei *see* **7** Lorelei

lurid 4 gory, grim **5** eerie, fiery, vivid **6** bloody **7** carmine, flaming, ghastly, glaring, glowing, graphic, scarlet, shining **8** dramatic, rubicund, sanguine, shocking **9** appalling, bright-red **11** sensational **12** melodramatic **13** bloodcurdling

lurk 4 hide **5** prowl, skulk, slink, sneak **9** lie in wait

Lusaka
capital of: 6 Zambia

luscious 5 tasty **6** savory **7** scented **8** aromatic, fragrant, perfumed **9** delicious, flavorful, succulent, toothsome **10** appetizing, delectable **13** mouthwatering

lush 4 posh, rich **5** dense, fancy, grand **6** ornate **7** elegant, profuse **8** abundant, prolific, splendid **9** elaborate, luxuriant, luxurious, sumptuous **11** flourishing, magnificent

lust 5 covet, crave **6** be lewd **7** craving, lechery, passion **8** lewdness **9** carnality, hunger for, sexuality **10** satyriasis **14** lasciviousness, libidinousness

lust after 4 want **5** covet, crave **6** desire **11** have a yen for, have an eye on, hunger after, thirst after

luster 4 fame, glow **5** gleam, glory, gloss, honor, merit, sheen, shine **6** dazzle **7** burnish, glimmer, glitter, sparkle **8** prestige, radiance **9** radiation **10** brightness, brilliance, luminosity, notability, refulgence **11** distinction **12** luminousness, resplendence **15** illustriousness

lusterless 3 dim, wan **4** dead, drab, dull, flat **5** faded, matte, muted **7** prosaic **9** colorless, tarnished

Lust for Life
author: 11 Irving Stone
director: 16 Vincente Minnelli
based on story by: 11 Irving Stone
cast: 11 James Donald, Kirk Douglas (Vincent Van Gogh), Pamela Brown **12** Anthony Quinn (Gaugin)
Oscar for: 15 supporting actor (Quinn)

lustful 4 lewd **6** carnal **8** prurient **9** lecherous, salacious **10** lascivious, libidinous

lustrous 6 bright, glossy **7** glowing, radiant, shining **8** dazzling, gleaming, luminous, polished **9** burnished, effulgent **10** glistening **11** coruscating, illuminated **12** incandescent

lusty 4 hale **5** husky, sound **6** brawny, hearty, robust, rugged, sturdy, virile **7** healthy **8** vigorous **9** exuberant, strapping **10** full of life **11** uninhibited **12** unrestrained, wholehearted **13** irrepressible

Lutetia
Latin: 5 Paris

Luther, Martin
born: 7 Germany **8** Eisleben
author: 16 Ninety-Five Theses **27** On the Freedom of a Christian Man **46** Address to the Christian Nobility of the German Nation **51** A Prelude Concerning the Babylonian Captivity of the Church
excommunicated by: 8 Pope Leo X **15** Pope Leo the Tenth
summoned before: 11 Diet of Worms
founded: 11 Lutheranism, Reformation **13** Protestantism

lux 5 light

Luxembourg
other name: 9 Luxemburg **13** Lucilinburhuc
name means: 10 little fort
capital/largest city: 10 Luxembourg
others: 4 Hamm **5** Roodt, Wiltz **6** Mersch, Remich **7** Kopstal, Lintgen, Petange, Redange, Vianden **8** Capellen, Clervaux, Diekirch, Frisange **9** Dudelange **10** Echternach, Ettelbruck, Hesperange, Larochette **11** Differdange, Wormeldange **12** Grevenmacher, Troisvierges, Wasserbillig **14** Esch-sur-Alzette
division: 6 Esleck **7** Bon Pays, Gutland, Oesling
measure: 5 fuder
monetary unit: 5 franc **7** centime
lake: 8 Haut Sure
mountain: 8 Ardennes
highest point: 8 Huldange **9** Burgplatz **11** Wemperhardt
river: 3 Our **4** Sure, Syre **5** Alert, Clerf, Eisch, Mosel, Sauer, Wiltz **6** Chiers **7** Alzette, Moselle **8** Petrusse **11** Ernz Blanche

physical feature:
plateau: 4 Bock **8** Ardennes, Lorraine
valley: 7 Moselle
people: 6 French, German **12** Luxembourger
ruler: 8 Sigefroi, Wencelas **12** Jean l'Aveugle **21** House of Nassau-Weilburg
saint: 10 Willibrord
language: 6 French, German **7** English **13** Letzeburgesch
religion: 13 Roman Catholic
food:
pastry: 20 les pensees brouilles

luxuriant 4 lush, rank **5** dense, fancy, grand **6** florid, ornate **7** elegant, flowery, profuse, teeming **8** abundant, splendid **9** elaborate, exuberant, luxurious, overgrown, sumptuous **10** flamboyant **11** extravagant, flourishing, magnificent

luxuriate 4 bask **6** relish **7** delight **8** wallow in **9** indulge in

luxurious 4 rich **5** grand **6** costly, effete **7** elegant, wealthy **8** decadent, pampered **9** enjoyable, expensive, indulgent, sumptuous **10** gratifying **11** comfortable, pleasurable

luxuriousness 4 ease **6** luxury **7** comfort **8** richness **10** costliness **13** sumptuousness

luxury 5 bliss **6** heaven, riches, wealth **7** delight **8** paradise, pleasure **9** enjoyment **10** high living, indulgence **12** extravagance, nonessential, nonnecessity, satisfaction **13** gratification

LXX *see* **15** Septuagint

Lycaon
king of: 7 Arcadia
father: 8 Pelasgus
son: 8 Maenalus, Tegeates
tested: 4 Zeus
turned into: 4 wolf

Lycidas
author: 10 John Milton
elegy for: 10 Edward King

Lycus
king of: 6 Thebes **7** Cilicia
father: 7 Pandion **9** Chthonius
mother: 5 Pylia
brother: 7 Nycteus
wife: 5 Dirce
niece: 7 Antiope
son: 5 Lycus
succeeded: 8 Sarpedon
killed by: 6 Zethus **7** Amphion **12** Antiope's sons

Lydia
kingdom in: 9 Asia Minor
king: 7 Croesus
queen: 7 Omphale
capital: 6 Sardis
conquered by: 8 Persians

lying down 5 in bed, prone **6** supine **7** napping, resting **8** snoozing **9** reclining, recumbent **10** taking a nap **13** taking a snooze

Lyle, Albert Walter
  nickname: **6** Sparky
  sport: **8** baseball
  author of: **11** The Bronx Zoo

Lyly, John
  author of: **20** Euphues and His England **22** Euphues the Anatomy of Wit

lynch 4 hang **6** gibbet **8** string up

Lynde, Paul
  born: **13** Mount Vernon OH
  roles: **12** Bye Bye Birdie **16** Holly-

wood Squares **17** Beach Blanket Bingo **18** Under the Yum-Yum Tree

lynx 3 cat **6** bobcat **7** wildcat

Lyonnesse
  place: **12** near Cornwall **16** Arthurian romance
  birthplace of: **8** Tristram
  fate: **11** sunk into sea

Lyre
  constellation of: **4** Harp, Lyra
  star: **4** Vega

lyric, lyrical 6 poetic **7** lilting, melodic, musical, singing, tuneful **8** songlike **9** melodious **10** euphonious

11 mellifluent, mellifluous **13** sweet-sounding

Lyrical Ballads
  author: **17** William Wordsworth **21** Samuel Taylor Coleridge

lyrics 4 poem **5** words

Lysander
  character in: **21** A Midsummer Night's Dream
  author: **11** Shakespeare

Lysistrata
  author: **12** Aristophanes
  character: **7** Lampito **8** Cinesias, Cleonice, Myrrhine **10** Magistrate **14** Old Men of Athens (Chorus)

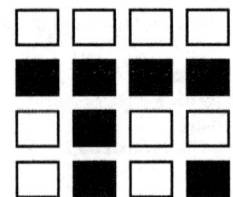

M
   director: **9** Fritz Lang
   cast: **10** Peter Lorre **11** Inge Landgut
   12 Ellen Widmann **15** Gustav Grundgens
   setting: **6** Berlin
Mabinogian
   origin: **5** Welsh
   tales of: **7** romance
macabre 4 grim **5** eerie, weird **6**
   grisly, horrid **7** ghastly, ghostly **8**
   dreadful, gruesome, horrible, horrific
   9 frightful, ghostlike, unearthly **11**
   frightening
Macao
   other name: **5** Aomen, Macau
   part of: **5** China
   former territory of: **8** Portugal
   former monetary unit: **3** avo **6** pataca, pataco
   island: **5** Taipa **7** Coloane
   highest point: **5** Hag-Sa
   river: **5** Pearl **6** Canton
   sea: **10** South China
   people: **7** Chinese, Macaoan **10** Portuguese
   language: **7** Chinese, English **9** Cantonese **10** Portuguese
   religion: **6** Taoism **8** Buddhism **13**
      Roman Catholic
   place:
      street: **11** Praia Grande
   feature:
      houseboat: **6** sampan
Macareus
   father: **6** Aeolus
   mother: **7** Encrete
   sister: **6** Canace
MacArthur, Douglas
   served in: **3** WWI **4** WWII **9** Korean
      War, World War I **10** World War II
      11 World War One, World War Two
   commander of: **15** Rainbow (42nd)
      Division **19** United Nations forces **24**
      US Army forces in the Pacific
   rank: **15** five-star general **16** army
      chief of staff
   battle: **5** Luzon, Pusan **6** Inchon **9**
      New Guinea **11** Leyte Island, Philippines **14** Bismark Islands, Solomon
      Islands **15** Bataan Peninsula **16** Admiralty Islands, Corregidor Island
   accepted surrender of: **5** Japan
      surrender occurred aboard: **8** Missouri
   chairman of: **13** Remington Rand

   author of: **13** Reminiscences
   smoked: **11** corncob pipe
   saying: **12** "I shall return"
Macbeth
   author: **18** William Shakespeare
   character: **6** Banquo, Duncan (King of
      Scotland) **7** MacDuff, Malcolm **11**
      Lady Macbeth **12** Three Witches
   title: **5** thane
   domain: **6** Glamis
   director: **13** Roman Polanski
   cast: **8** Jon Finch **10** Martin Shaw **13**
      Nicholas Selby **14** Francesca Annis
Maccabees
   title of: **5** Judas
   patriarch: **10** Mattathias
   means: **8** hammerer
   holiday: **8** Hanukkah
MacDonald, John D
   author of: **11** Condominium
   character: **11** Travis McGee
MacDonald, Ross
   real name: **13** Kenneth Millar
   author of: **8** The Chill **10** Black
      Money **13** The Blue Hammer **14** The
      Goodbye Look
   character: **9** Lew Archer
MacDowell, Edward Alexander
   born: **9** New York NY
   composer of: **9** Sea Pieces **11** To a
      Wild Rose **13** Fireside Tales **15** Poems after Heine **16** Hamlet and
      Ophelia, New England Idylls, Woodland Sketches **17** Idylls after Goethe
MacDuff
   character in: **7** Macbeth
   author: **11** Shakespeare
mace
   origin: **9** Indonesia
   from same tree as: **6** nutmeg
   tree: **17** Myristica fragrans
   use: **4** fish **7** seafood **9** cherry pie,
      pound cake **16** chicken fricassee
Macedonia
   formerly part of: **10** Yugoslavia
   capital/largest city: **6** Skopje
   head of state: **9** president
   government: **8** republic
   monetary unit: **5** denar
   river: **6** Struma, Vardar
   people: **4** Turk **9** Albanian **10** Macedonian
   language: **10** Macedonian
   religion: **27** Macedonian Orthodox
      Christian
macerate 4 fade, mash, pulp, soak **5**

   souse, steep **6** shrink, soften, squash,
   wither **7** decline, liquefy, shrivel
   8 dissolve, emaciate, fluidize, permeate, saturate **9** liquidize, waste away
   10 lose weight
MacGraw, Ali
   real name: **12** Alice MacGraw
   husband: **8** Bob Evans **12** Steve McQueen
   born: **12** Pound Ridge NY
   roles: **7** Dynasty **9** Love Story **10** The
      Getaway **13** The Winds of War **15**
      Goodbye Columbus
Macheath, Captain
   character in: **12** Beggar's Opera
   author: **3** Gay
   see Threepenny Opera
ma chere 6 my dear
Machiavelli, Niccolo
   author of: **9** The Prince **11** The Art
      of War **16** Discourses on Livy
   home: **8** Florence
   The "Prince": **12** Cesare Borgia
Machiavellian 6 amoral, crafty **7** cunning, devious **8** scheming **9** deceitful,
   designing **10** perfidious **11** self-
   serving, treacherous, underhanded **12**
   falsehearted, unscrupulous
machination 4 plot, rule, ruse **5**
   dodge **6** design, device, scheme **8** artifice, intrigue, maneuver **9** stratagem
   10 conspiracy **11** contrivance
machine 3 set **4** army, body, camp,
   club, gang, pool, ring **5** corps, crowd,
   force, group, setup, trust, union **6** device, system **7** combine, coterie, faction, society **9** apparatus, appliance,
   machinery, mechanism, structure **11**
   association **12** organization **13** establishment
machine gun
   invented by: **7** Gatling
   improved by: **5** Maxim **9** Hotchkiss
machinery 4 gear **5** setup, tools **6**
   agency, makeup, system, tackle,
   wheels **9** apparatus, mechanism,
   resources, structure **12** contrivances,
   organization
macho 5 he-man, manly **6** strong, virile
Machpelah
   location: **6** Hebron
   burial place of: **4** Leah **5** Isaac, Jacob, Sarah **7** Abraham, Rebekah
Machu Picchu 5 ruins

of: 5 Incas
in: 4 Peru

Macilente
character in: 22 Every Man out of His Humour
author: 6 Jonson

MacInnes, Helen
author of: 13 North from Rome 14 Above Suspicion 16 Decision at Delphi 17 The Venetian Affair 21 The Salzburg Connection

macintosh, mackintosh 7 slicker 8 raincoat 10 waterproof

Mack, Connie
real name: 30 Cornelius Alexander McGillicuddy
sport: 8 baseball
position: 7 manager
team: 21 Philadelphia Athletics

MacKellar
character in: 21 The Master of Ballantrae
author: 9 Stevenson

mackerel
young: 5 spike 6 tinker 7 blinker

mackinaw 4 coat 6 jacket 8 overcoat

Mack the Knife see 15 Three Penny Opera

MacLaine, Shirley
real name: 19 Shirley MacLean Beaty
brother: 12 Warren Beatty
born: 10 Richmond VA
roles: 6 Can Can 9 Bewitched 10 Being There 11 Irma La Douce 12 Guarding Tess, Sweet Charity, The Apartment 14 Steel Magnolias 15 Some Came Running, The Turning Point, Two for the Seesaw 16 The Children's Hour 17 Terms of Endearment (Oscar) 19 The Trouble with Harry 20 The Bliss of Mrs Blossom

MacMurray, Fred
wife: 9 June Haver
born: 10 Kankakee IL
roles: 11 My Three Sons 12 The Apartment 14 Above Suspicion, The Caine Mutiny 15 Double Indemnity 20 The Miracle of the Bells

macrocosm 6 cosmos, nature 7 heavens 8 creation, universe 9 firmament

mad 4 avid, daft, loco, nuts, wild 5 angry, balmy, crazy, irate, nutty 6 ardent, crazed, cuckoo, fuming, insane, miffed, screwy, ticked 7 cracked, enraged, excited, fanatic, furious, in a huff, lunatic, riled up, teed off, touched 8 crackers, demented, deranged, frenzied, incensed, maniacal, provoked, unhinged, up in arms, worked up, wrathful 9 devoted to, non compos, seeing red, ticked off, wrought up 10 distracted, distraught, infatuated, infuriated, in love with, irrational, unbalanced 11 boiling over, exasperated, impassioned, not all there 12 enthusiastic, round the bend

13 beside oneself, in high dudgeon, not quite right, off one's rocker, out of one's mind

Mad About You
network: 3 NBC
cast: 9 Helen Hunt (Jamie Stemple Buchman) 10 Anne Ramsay (Lisa Stemple), John Pankow (Ira Buchman), Lisa Kudrow (Ursula Buffay), Paul Reiser (Paul Buchman) 11 Louis Zorich (Burt Buchman) 12 Tommy Hinkley (Jay Selby) 13 Cynthia Harris (Sylvia Buchman)

Madagascar
other name: 16 Malagasy Republic
capital/largest city: 10 Tananarive 12 Antananarivo
others: 6 Tulear 7 Majanga, Nossibe, Toliary 8 Manakara, Tamatave 9 Faradofay, Mananjory, Toamasina 10 Antisirabe 11 Antsiranana, Diego-Suarez, Fort Dauphin
measure: 7 gantang
monetary unit: 5 franc 7 centime
island: 6 Barren, Radama 7 Nossi-Be 11 Sainte-Marie 12 Chesterfield
lake: 5 Itasy 7 Alaotra, Kinkony
mountain: 4 Boby 9 Ankaratra 12 High Plateaus, Tsiafajavona 17 Tsaratanana Massif
highest point: 11 Maromokotro
river: 5 Ikopa, Mania, Sofia 7 Mangoky, Mangoro, Onilahy 8 Ivoloina, Manambao, Mananara 9 Betsiboka, Manambolo 10 Manarandra 11 Tsiribihina
ocean: 6 Indian
physical feature:
  bay: 6 Radama 8 Antongil 9 Mahajamba 10 Sahamalaza
  cape: 5 Saint-Andre 11 Sainte-Marie 14 Saint-Sebastien
  channel: 10 Mozambique
  lagoon: 9 pangalane
  plateau: 9 Ankaizina
people: 4 Arab, Bara, Hova 5 Malay 6 Merina, Tanala 7 African 8 Betsileo, Mahafaly, Malagasy, Sakalava 9 Antaimoro, Antaisaka, Antandroy, Tsimihety 10 Indonesian, Polynesian 13 Betsimisaraka
  dynasty: 6 Merina
  leader: 9 Ratsiraka, Tsiranana 11 Ranamantsoa
language: 6 French 8 Malagasy, Malgache
religion: 5 Islam 7 animism 10 Protestant 13 Roman Catholic
place:
  market: 4 Zoma
  royal estate: 4 Rova
feature:
  animal: 4 zebu 5 lemur 6 foussa
  musical instrument: 11 jego vaotavo
  proverb: 8 hainteny
  shawl: 5 lamba

food:
  vegetable: 7 brettes
madam, madame 3 Mrs 4 dame, lady 6 matron 7 dowager 8 mistress
  German: 4 Frau
  Spanish: 6 senora
  Italian: 5 donna 7 signora
  Spanish/Portuguese: 4 dona
Madame Bovary
  author: 15 Gustave Flaubert
  character: 10 Emma Bovary, Leon Dupuis 13 Charles Bovary 17 Rodolphe Boulanger
Madame Butterfly
  also: 15 Madama Butterfly
  opera by: 7 Puccini
  character: 5 Bonze 6 Suzuki 9 Cho-Cho-San, Cio-Cio-San, Sharpless 14 Prince Yamadori 19 Lieutenant Pinkerton
  aria: 7 Un bel di
mad as a hatter 3 mad 4 daft, nuts 5 crazy, nutty 6 insane 7 cracked, touched 8 demented, deranged, unhinged 10 unbalanced 13 off one's rocker, out of one's head 14 off one's trolley 15 mad as a March hare 17 nutty as a fruitcake
mad as a March hare 3 mad 4 daft, nuts 5 crazy, nutty 6 insane 7 cracked, touched 8 demented, deranged, unhinged 10 unbalanced 12 mad as a hatter 13 out of one's head 14 off one's trolley 17 nutty as a fruitcake
madcap 4 rash, wild, zany 5 brash, clown, giddy, joker 6 unruly 7 erratic, flighty, foolish 8 reckless 9 hotheaded, impetuous, impulsive, senseless 10 incautious 11 impractical, thoughtless 12 unconsidered 13 inconsiderate, undisciplined
madden 3 vex 4 gall 5 anger, craze, pique, upset 6 enrage, frenzy 7 derange, incense, inflame, outrage, provoke, torment, unhinge 9 aggravate, infuriate, unbalance 10 exasperate
made 5 built 6 formed 7 created 8 composed, produced 9 assembled, developed 10 fabricated 11 constructed 12 manufactured
madeira
  type: 4 wine 6 brandy 7 liqueur 8 aperitif
  origin: 7 Madeira
Madeira Islands
  capital: 7 Funchal
  city: 5 Monte
  island: 6 Grande 7 Dezerte, Madeira 8 Desertas 9 Selvagens 10 Porto Santo
  ocean: 8 Atlantic
  owned by: 8 Portugal
  stone aqueduct: 7 levadas
  wine: 4 Bual 5 Tinta, Tinto 6 Canary, Gomera 7 Malmsey, Marsala, Sercial 8 Verdelho

made-up 5 false 7 assumed, created 8 fanciful, invented 9 fictional, imaginary, pretended, thought-up 10 fictitious 11 make-believe, theoretical 12 hypothetical

Mad Hatter
  character in: 28 Alice's Adventures in Wonderland
  author: 7 Carroll

madhouse 6 asylum, bedlam, uproar 7 turmoil 8 loony bin, nuthouse

Madison, James
  nickname: 23 Father of the Constitution
  presidential rank: 6 fourth
  party: 20 Democratic-Republican
  state represented: 2 VA
  defeated: 7 (DeWitt) Clinton 8 (Charles Cotesworth) Pinckney
  vice president: 5 (Elbridge) Gerry 7 (George) Clinton
  cabinet:
    state: 5 (Robert) Smith 6 (James) Monroe
    treasury: 6 (Alexander James) Dallas 8 (Abraham Alfonse Albert) Gallatin, (George Washington) Campbell, (William Harris) Crawford
    war: 6 (James) Monroe, (William) Eustis 8 (William Harris) Crawford 9 (John) Armstrong
    attorney general: 4 (Richard) Rush 6 (Caesar Augustus) Rodney 7 (William) Pinkney
    navy: 5 (William) Jones 8 (Paul) Hamilton 13 (Benjamin Williams) Crowninshield
  born: 12 Port Conway VA 16 King George County
  died/buried: 2 VA 12 Orange County 16 Montpelier estate
  education:
    tutored at home by: 15 Rev Thomas Martin
    school: 15 Donald Robertson
    college of: 9 New Jersey (now Princeton University)
  religion: 12 Episcopalian
  interests: 3 law 11 agriculture 14 natural history
  author: 16 Federalist Papers (with Hamilton and Jay)
  political career: 24 US House of Representatives 25 Second Continental Congress
    secretary of: 5 state
    signed: 12 Constitution
  civilian career: 6 farmer 7 planter
  military service:
    colonel of: 19 Orange County militia
  notable events of lifetime/term: 19 War of Eighteen Twelve
    battle of: 10 New Orleans
    treaty of: 5 Ghent
    Washington DC burned by: 7 British

father: 5 James
mother: 7 Eleanor (Rose Conway)
siblings: 5 Sarah 6 Reuben 7 Ambrose, Catlett, Francis, William 9 Elizabeth 11 Nelly Conway 13 Frances Taylor
wife: 8 Dorothea (Payne Todd)
  nickname: 6 Dolley
first lady:
  saved: 11 state papers 25 George Washington's portrait

madman 3 nut 5 loony 6 maniac 7 lunatic 8 demoniac 9 psychotic 10 psychopath

Mad Max
  director: 12 George Miller
  cast: 9 Mel Gibson
  sequel: 14 The Road Warrior 17 Beyond Thunderdome (with Tina Turner)

madness 6 lunacy, oddity 8 delusion, dementia, illusion, insanity 9 craziness 11 derangement

Madonna
  nickname: 15 The Material Girl
  husband: 8 Sean Penn 10 Guy Ritchie
  children: 5 Rocco 7 Lourdes
  recordings: 5 Evita, Music 7 Erotica, Madonna 8 True Blue 10 Ray of Light 11 Like a Prayer, Like a Virgin 12 American Life
  films: 5 Evita 9 Dick Tracy, Swept Away 11 Truth or Dare 12 Who's That Girl 14 Body of Evidence 16 Shanghai Surprise 17 A League of Their Own 23 Desperately Seeking Susan
  tour: 6 Girlie 13 Blond Ambition
  books: 3 Sex

Madrid
  area: 9 Salamanca 19 Ciudad Universitaria
  capital of: 5 Spain
  landmark: 14 National Palace 18 Biblioteca Nacional
    bull ring: 22 Plaza de Toros Monumental
    museum: 5 Prado
  mountain: 18 Sierra de Guadaramma
  river: 10 Manzanares
  square: 10 Plaza Mayor 11 Plaza del Sol 13 Plaza de Espana
  street: 13 Paseo del Prado

Madwoman of Chaillot
  author: 13 Jean Giraudoux

maelstrom 4 eddy 5 shoot, swirl 6 bedlam, rapids, tumult, uproar, vortex 7 riptide, torrent 8 disorder, madhouse, undertow, upheaval 9 confusion, whirlpool 10 white water 11 pandemonium
  location: 6 Norway

maenad, menad 5 lenae 7 bacchae, bassara 8 clodones, thyiades 9 bacchante 10 mimallones
  companion of: 7 Bacchus 8 Dionysus

Maeterlinck, Maurice
  author of: 8 The Blind 11 The Blue Bird, The Intruder 19 Pelleas and Melisande

ma foi 6 my word, really 7 my faith

magazine 6 weekly 7 arsenal, journal, monthly 9 quarterly 10 periodical, powder room 13 military depot, munitions room

Magdalene see 4 Mary

magenta 6 maroon 7 carmine, crimson, fuchsia 9 vermilion 12 purplish rose 13 reddish purple

Maggie: A Girl of the Streets
  author: 12 Stephen Crane

maggot 4 grub, worm 5 larva 8 mealworm

Magi
  also called: 7 wise men 11 astrologers
  followed: 15 Star of Bethlehem
  visited: 5 Jesus
  gifts: 4 gold 5 myrrh 12 frankincense
  singular: 5 magus

magic 4 lure 5 charm, spell 6 hoodoo, voodoo 7 sorcery 8 charisma, jugglery, witchery, wizardry 9 occultism, voodooism 10 allurement, black magic, demonology, divination, hocus-pocus, witchcraft 11 captivation, conjuration, enchantment, fascination, legerdemain, the black art 12 entrancement 13 sleight of hand 16 prestidigitation
  god of: 5 Thoth

Magic
  nickname of: 13 Earvin Johnson

Magic Flute, The
  also: 14 Die Zauberflote
  opera: 6 Mozart
  character: 6 Pamina, Tamino 8 Papagena, Papageno, Sarastro 10 Monostatos 12 Queen of Night

magician 5 magus 6 shaman, wizard 7 juggler, warlock 8 conjurer, sorcerer 9 alchemist 11 illusionist, medicine man, necromancer, witch doctor 12 escape artist 15 prestidigitator

Magic Mountain, The
  author: 10 Thomas Mann
  character: 6 Naphta 7 Clavdia 11 Hans Castorp, Settembrini 15 Joachim Ziemssen

magisterial 9 imperious 10 autocratic, peremptory 11 dictatorial, domineering, overbearing 13 condescending

Magister Ludi: The Glass Bead Game
  author: 12 Hermann Hesse

magistrate 2 JP 5 judge 7 prefect 17 justice of the peace

Magna Carta 7 charter
  forced by: 6 barons
  upon: 8 King John
  at: 9 Runnymede
  guaranteeing: 14 civil liberties

magna cum laude 15 with great praise

Magna Graecia 27 ancient Greek colonies in Italy

Magna Mater 3 Ops **4** Rhea **6** Cybele

Magnani, Anna
nickname: **10** Nannerella
roles: **8** Open City **13** The Rose Tattoo (Oscar) **15** The Fugitive Kind **21** Secret of Santa Vittoria

magnanimous 7 liberal **8** generous, princely **9** forgiving, unselfish **10** altruistic, beneficent, charitable **12** largehearted **13** philanthropic

magnate 3 VIP **5** giant, mogul, nabob **6** big gun, bigwig, leader, tycoon **7** big shot, notable **8** big wheel, great man **9** celebrity **13** empire builder, industrialist

magnesium
chemical symbol: **2** Mg

magnetic 8 alluring, charming, inviting **9** of a magnet, seductive **10** attractive, enchanting, entrancing, persuasive **11** captivating, charismatic, fascinating **12** irresistible

magnetism 4 lure **5** charm **6** allure **8** charisma **9** mesmerism, seduction **10** allurement, attraction, enticement **11** captivation, enchantment, fascination

magnification 5 honor **7** worship **9** adoration, blowing up, expansion, inflation, reverence **11** acclamation, enlargement, idolization **12** exaggeration **13** amplification, glorification, overstatement

magnificence 4 pomp **5** glory, state **6** luxury **7** glitter, majesty, royalty **8** grandeur, richness, splendor **10** brilliance **13** sumptuousness

magnificent 4 fine **5** grand, noble **6** august, superb **7** elegant, exalted, stately, sublime **8** glorious, imposing, majestic, splendid **9** brilliant, exquisite, wonderful **10** commanding, impressive **11** resplendent **12** transcendent **13** extraordinary

Magnificent Ambersons, The
director: **11** Orson Welles
based on novel by: **15** Booth Tarkington
cast: **7** Tim Holt **10** Anne Baxter **12** Joseph Cotten **14** Agnes Moorehead **15** Dolores Costello

Magnificent Obsession, The
author: **13** Lloyd C Douglas

Magnificent Seven, The
director: **11** John Sturges
cast: **10** Brad Dexter, Eli Wallach, Yul Brynner **11** James Coburn **12** Robert Vaughn, Steve McQueen **13** Horst Buchholz **14** Charles Bronson
setting: **6** Mexico
score: **14** Elmer Bernstein
remake of: **12** Seven Samurai
sequel: **16** Return of the Seven **20** Magnificent Seven Ride

magnify 4 laud **5** adore, boost, exalt, extol **6** blow up, double, expand, praise, puff up, revere **7** acclaim, amplify, enlarge, glorify, greaten, inflate, stretch, worship **8** heighten, maximize, overrate **9** embroider, overstate, reverence **10** exaggerate

magniloquence 7 bombast, fustian **8** euphuism, tumidity **9** pomposity, turgidity **10** orotundity **11** fanfaronade, grandiosity **14** grandiloquence **15** pretentiousness

magniloquent 5 tumid, windy, wordy **6** turgid **7** pompous, verbose **8** inflated **9** bombastic **13** grandiloquent

magnitude 4 bulk, fame, mass, size **6** extent, renown, repute, volume **7** bigness, expanse, measure **8** eminence, enormity, hugeness, vastness

Magnolia
director: **18** Paul Thomas Anderson
cast: **8** Pat Healy (Sir Edmund Godfrey) **9** Neil Flynn (Daniel Hill), Tom Cruise (Frank T J Mackey) **12** Jason Robards (Earl Partridge), William H Macy (Donnie Smith) **13** Julianne Moore (Linda Partridge), Mark Flannagan (Joseph Green) **14** Genevieve Zweig (Mrs Godfrey), Jeremy Blackman (Stanley Spector) **15** Philip Baker Hall (Jimmy Gator) **20** Philip Seymour Hoffman (Phil Parma)

magnolia
varieties: **4** ashe, star **6** saucer **7** Chinese **8** southern, umbrella **11** greatleaved

Magnum, P. I.
character: **2** TC **4** Rick **7** Higgins **12** Thomas Magnum
cast: **10** Tom Selleck **12** Roger E Mosley **13** John Hillerman
setting: **6** Hawaii

Magog
father: **7** Japheth

Magritte, Rene Francois Ghislain
born: **7** Belgium **8** Lessines
artwork: **14** La Belle Captive, The False Mirror, The Key of Dreams **15** Memory of a Voyage **18** L'Empire des Lumieres (The Empire of Light), The Menaced Assassin

Magua
character in: **20** The Last of the Mohicans
author: **6** Cooper

Magus *see* **4** Magi

Magyar 9 Hungarian

Mahican *see* **7** Mohican

mah-jongg 4 game
origin: **7** Chinese
play piece: **4** tile
suit: **3** bam, dot **5** crack, winds
dragon: **3** red **5** white
term: **4** kong, pung **6** flower

Mahler, Gustav
born: **7** Austria, Bohemia
composer of: **12** Resurrection (sym-

phony No 2) **15** Das Klagenlied **16** Songs of a Wayfarer **17** Das Lied von der Erde, Kindertotenlieder, The Song of the Earth **19** Des Knaben Wunderhorn **28** Lieder eines fahrenden Gesellen

mahogany 4 tree, wood **5** brown **8** hardwood **9** Swietenia **12** reddishbrown
varieties: **3** red **5** swamp, white **7** African, big-leaf, Florida, Senegal, Spanish **8** Honduras, mountain **9** Nyasaland, Venezulan **10** West Indian

mahzor, machzor 16 Jewish prayer book

Maia
member of: **8** Pleiades
place in group: **6** eldest
father: **5** Atlas
mother: **7** Pleione
son: **6** Hermes

maid 6 tweeny **7** servant **8** domestic **9** hired girl, housemaid, lady's maid, nursemaid **10** parlor maid **11** maidservant **12** upstairs maid **13** female servant
French: **6** au pair

maiden, maidenly 4 girl, lass, maid, miss **5** chick, first **6** chaste, damsel, lassie, virgin **7** colleen, girlish, ingenue, initial, untried **8** original, virginal, youthful **9** inaugural, soubrette, unmarried **10** demoiselle, initiatory **12** introductory

Maid Marian
beloved of: **9** Robin Hood

maidservant 4 amah, ayah, char, lass, maid **5** bonne **6** au pair, tweeny **7** abigail **8** charlady, domestic **9** hired girl, lady's maid, tirewoman **10** handmaiden, parlormaid

Maidu
language family: **8** Penutian
location: **10** California
noted for: **8** basketry

mail 4 arms, post **5** armor **6** get out **7** airmail, harness, letters, panoply **8** dispatch, packages **9** postcards **10** send by mail, send by post, suit of mail **11** surface mail **12** mail delivery, put in the mail **13** postal service **14** defensive armor, drop in a mailbox **17** post-office service

Mailer, Norman
author of: **7** Marilyn **11** The Deer Park **12** Harlot's Ghost **15** An American Dream **16** Armies of the Night **18** The Naked and the Dead **19** The Executioner's Song

Maillol, Aristide
born: **6** France **13** Banyuls-sur-mer
artwork: **5** Night, Torso **7** Le Desir (Desire) **11** Ile de France **12** Young Cyclist **14** Action in Chains, The Three Nymphs **16** The Mediterranean (Seated Woman) **17** Monument

to Cezanne, Monument to Debussy
18 Venus with a Necklace

maim 3 cut, rip **4** gash, lame, maul, rend, tear **5** slash, wound **6** deface, hobble, injure, mangle, savage **7** cripple, disable **8** lacerate, mutilate **9** disfigure, dismember, hamstring **12** incapacitate

main 4 head **5** chief, prime, vital **6** urgent **7** capital, central, crucial, leading, primary, special, supreme **8** critical, foremost, pressing **9** essential, important, necessary, paramount, principal, requisite **10** particular, preeminent **11** outstanding, predominant **13** consequential, indispensable

Main, Marjorie
   real name: 13 Mary Tomlinson
   partner: 12 Wallace Beery **13** Percy Kilbride
   born: 7 Acton IN
   roles: 7 Dead End **8** Ma Kettle

Maine
   abbreviation: 2 ME
   nickname: 6 Lumber **8** Pine Tree **10** Wonderland
   capital: 7 Augusta
   largest city: 8 Portland
   others: 4 Bath, Saco **5** Hiram, Orono **6** Auburn, Bangor **7** Kittery **8** Boothbay, Lewiston, Ogunquit **9** Bar Harbor, Biddeford, Brunswick, Skowhegan **10** Waterville **11** Millinocket, Presque Isle
   college: 5 Bates, Colby **7** Bowdoin
   explorer: 6 Cabots **8** Norsemen
   feature: 8 lobsters **19** West Quoddy Headlight
      beach: 10 Old Orchard
      national park: 6 Acadia
      waterway: 18 Allagash Wilderness
   tribe: 6 Abnaki **7** Wewenoc
   people: 10 downeaster **11** Dorothea Dix, Stephen King **19** Edna St Vincent Millay **24** Henry Wadsworth Longfellow
   island: 4 Orrs **8** Mt Desert **10** Campobello
   lake: 5 Sebec, Wyman **6** Sebago **8** Rangeley, Schoodic **9** Flagstaff, Moosehead **10** Chesuncook
   land rank: 11 thirty-ninth
   mountain: 5 Kineo, White **7** Bigelow **8** Cadillac
      highest point: 8 Katahdin
   physical feature:
      bay: 5 Casco **9** Penobscot **12** Merrymeeting **13** Passamaquoddy
      sand dunes: 13 Desert of Maine
   river: 4 Saco **6** St John **7** St Croix **8** Allagash, Kennebec **9** Aroostook, Kennebago, Penobscot **12** Androscoggin
   state admission: 11 twenty-third
   state bird: 9 chickadee
   state fish: 16 land-locked salmon
   state flower: 7 thistle **8** pine cone **22** white pine cone and tassel

   state motto: 7 I Direct
   state song: 16 State of Maine Song
   state tree: 16 eastern white pine

mainly 6 mostly **7** chiefly **8** above all **9** in the main, most of all, primarily **10** on the whole **11** principally **13** predominantly **14** for the most part, in great measure **16** first and foremost

main point 3 nut **4** core, crux, gist, meat **5** basis, heart, theme **6** kernel **7** essence **10** brass tacks **11** nitty-gritty **15** sum and substance

mainspring 5 agent, cause **6** motive **9** incentive **10** motivation

mainstay 4 prop **6** anchor, pillar **7** bulwark **8** backbone, buttress **16** pillar of strength

Main Street
   author: 13 Sinclair Lewis
   character: 14 Carol Kennicott **15** Dr Will Kennicott

maintain 4 aver, avow, hold, keep **5** claim, state, swear **6** affirm, allege, assert, defend, insist, keep up, uphold **7** care for, contend, declare, finance, profess, stand by, support, sustain **8** conserve, continue, preserve **9** keep alive, keep going **10** provide for, take care of

maintenance 4 keep **6** living, repair, upkeep **7** keeping, support **10** livelihood, protection, sustenance **11** safekeeping, subsistence, sustainment **12** conservation, preservation, safeguarding

maison de sante 10 sanitarium **13** house of health

maize 4 corn, milo **5** grain **6** cereal, silage, yellow **7** zea mays **10** Indian corn

majestic, majestical 5 grand, lofty, noble, regal, royal **6** august, famous, superb **7** elegant, eminent, stately, sublime **8** esteemed, glorious, imperial, imposing, princely, renowned, splendid **10** impressive **11** illustrious, magnificent **13** distinguished

majesty 4 pomp **5** glory **6** luster **7** dignity **8** elegance, eminence, grandeur, mobility, splendor **9** elevation, loftiness, solemnity, sublimity **10** augustness **11** distinction, stateliness **12** gloriousness, magnificence **14** impressiveness

major 4 main **5** chief, prime, vital **6** larger, urgent **7** capital, crucial, greater, leading, primary, ranking, serious, supreme **8** critical, foremost, pressing **9** essential, important, necessary, paramount, principal, requisite **10** preeminent **11** outstanding, predominant, significant **13** consequential, indispensable

Major Barbara
   director: 13 Gabriel Pascal
   based on play by: 17 George Bernard Shaw

cast: 11 Deborah Kerr, Rex Harrison, Wendy Hiller **12** Robert Morley, Robert Newton **14** Sybil Thorndike

majority 4 bulk, mass **8** best part, legal age, maturity **9** adulthood, seniority, womanhood **10** lion's share **13** preponderance

major key (in music)
   German: 3 dur

Major prophets see **8** prophets

majuscule 7 capital **11** large letter **13** capital letter **15** uppercase letter

make 3 fix **4** form, kind, mark, meet, pass **5** beget, brand, build, catch, cause, enact, erect, force, frame, impel, press, reach, shape, speak, utter **6** attain, compel, create, devise, draw up, effect, foment, makeup, oblige, render **7** appoint, compose, deliver, dragoon, fashion, produce, require **8** arrive at, assemble, construct, establish, fabricate, formation, legislate, pronounce, structure **10** bring about, fashioning **11** composition, manufacture

make a bet 3 bet **4** risk **5** stake, wager **6** chance, gamble, hazard, plunge **7** venture

make a clean breast of 7 confess, lay bare, own up to **8** blurt out **14** come clean about

make a dash 3 fly, run **4** flee **6** escape **7** get away **8** make a run **10** make a break, take flight **12** make a getaway

make a deal 5 agree **6** settle **10** compromise **11** come to terms, meet halfway **14** strike a bargain

make advances 8 approach, come on to, sound out **11** proposition **13** make overtures, put the moves on

make a fuss over 6 dote on **7** protest **8** crow over

make again 4 copy **6** remake, repeat **9** duplicate **11** reconstruct

make a getaway 4 bolt, flee, skip **6** escape **7** get away, make off, run away **8** make a run, slip away **9** break free, cut and run, make a dash **10** break loose, fly the coop, take flight

make a gift of 4 give **6** donate **7** present **8** bequeath **10** contribute

make allowance for 6 excuse, pardon **7** forgive, indulge **8** bear with, pass over

make amends 5 atone **6** make up, square **7** expiate **9** do penance **10** compensate

make a mess of 3 mar **4** goof, muff, ruin **5** botch, spoil **6** bungle, foul up, mess up **7** butcher, do badly, louse up, screw up **9** mismanage

make a mistake 3 err **4** goof **6** mess up, slip up **12** miscalculate

make an effort 3 try 5 essay 6 strive, work at 7 attempt 8 endeavor

make appear 5 evoke 6 elicit 7 produce 9 conjure up 10 bring forth

make a racket 3 cry 4 howl, yell 5 shout 6 bellow, clamor, holler, scream 7 bluster 8 make a din 10 vociferate 12 raise a rumpus

make a stab at 3 try 5 essay, guess 6 reckon, take on 7 attempt, surmise, venture 8 estimate, give a try 9 undertake 10 conjecture 11 approximate 12 take a crack at, take a fling at

make a stand 9 stand fast 13 refuse to yield 17 fight to the last man

make a statement 6 remark 7 clarify, comment, discuss, explain, expound 9 elucidate, talk about

make aware 4 tell 5 edify 6 advise, inform, notify, reveal 7 apprise 8 acquaint, disclose 9 divulge to, enlighten, introduce 11 familiarize 16 bring to (one's) attention

make away with 3 eat 4 kill, take 5 spend, steal 6 kidnap, murder 7 abolish, consume, destroy 8 carry off, embezzle, get rid of 9 dissipate

make-believe 4 fake, sham 5 false, phony 6 made-up, make-up, unreal 7 assumed, charade, fantasy, feigned, fiction 8 creation, imagined, invented, pretense, spurious 9 fantastic, imaginary, invention, pretended, simulated 10 artificial, fictitious 11 counterfeit, fabrication 13 falsification

make certain of 6 assure, clinch, ensure 8 be sure of 10 make sure of

make damp 5 bedew 6 dampen 7 moisten 8 sprinkle

make dark 3 dim 6 darken 7 blacken, obscure

make different 4 vary 5 alter, amend 6 change, modify, mutate 7 convert, remodel 9 transform, transmute 12 metamorphose

make distinctive 8 set apart 9 single out 11 distinguish 12 characterize 13 differentiate

make easy 4 ease 6 smooth 7 explain, lighten 8 simplify 10 clear a path, facilitate

make eligible 5 allow 6 permit 7 entitle, qualify 9 authorize

make evident 4 show 5 prove 6 reveal 7 exhibit 8 manifest 9 establish, make clear, make plain 11 demonstrate

make fast 3 fix 4 moor 5 affix, tie up 6 attach, fasten, secure 7 connect

make feeble 6 weaken 7 wear out 8 enervate 10 debilitate, devitalize

make furious 5 anger 6 enrage, madden 7 incense, inflame 9 infuriate

make giddy 5 dizzy 12 make unsteady 15 make lightheaded

make good 5 repay 6 arrive, make it

7 fulfill, succeed 11 reach the top 15 make restitution

make happy 5 amuse, cheer, elate 6 please 7 delight, gratify 9 entertain

make haste slowly
Latin: 12 festina lente

make hostile 5 repel 6 offend 7 provoke 8 alienate 10 antagonize

make ill 5 repel 6 infect, revolt, sicken 7 afflict, disgust, repulse 8 disagree, distress, make sick, nauseate 9 discomfit 14 turn the stomach

make ill at ease 5 upset 6 rattle 7 fluster 8 distress 9 discomfit, embarrass 10 disconcert

make impure 4 foul, soil 5 dirty, spoil, taint 6 befoul, blight, defile, infect, poison 7 corrupt, pollute 10 adulterate 11 contaminate

make inroads 6 invade 7 impinge, intrude 8 encroach, infringe, trespass 9 penetrate

make known 4 tell 6 advise, impart, inform, notify, report, reveal, unveil 7 apprise, divulge, lay bare, publish, uncover 8 disclose 9 broadcast 10 give notice, make public 11 communicate

make less forceful 6 soften, weaken 9 undermine 10 devitalize, emasculate

make light of 8 belittle, minimize, pooh-pooh, sneeze at 9 deprecate, disparage, underrate 10 depreciate, undervalue 13 underestimate

make merry 5 revel 7 carouse, roister 9 celebrate, have a ball 15 paint the town red

make much of 5 honor 6 praise 7 acclaim, applaud, commend, flatter 8 fuss over

make nervous 5 annoy, upset 7 agitate, disturb, perturb, trouble, unnerve 10 disconcert

make off with 4 lift 5 boost, steal, swipe 6 abduct, kidnap, snatch 7 bear off 8 carry off 10 run off with 11 get away with

make one's blood boil 5 anger 6 enrage, madden 7 incense, inflame 9 infuriate

make one's eyes pop 4 stun 5 amaze, shock 6 dazzle 7 stagger, startle 8 astonish 9 electrify 11 flabbergast

make out 3 see 4 espy 6 behold, descry, detect, fill in, notice 7 discern, observe, pick out 8 get along, perceive, write out 12 catch sight of

make plain 7 clarify, clear up, explain, lay open 9 elucidate, explicate, make clear 10 illuminate 11 disentangle, shed light on 12 bring to light

make possible for 5 allow 6 enable, permit 7 empower, qualify 10 capacitate

make public 3 air 4 tell, vent 5 print, utter, voice 6 expose, inform, reveal,

spread 7 declare, display, divulge, exhibit, express, give out, publish 8 announce, disclose, proclaim, televise 9 broadcast, circulate, publicize

maker, Maker 3 god 4 poet 5 smith 6 author, forger 7 builder, creator, founder 8 declarer, inventor, producer 9 architect, generator 10 originator 12 manufacturer

make ready 5 prime 7 arrange, forearm, prepare

make reparation for 5 atone, repay 6 pay for 10 compensate, recompense, remunerate

make restitution 5 repay 7 pay back 9 reimburse 10 compensate, recompense

make right 3 fix 5 amend, emend 6 remedy, repair 7 correct, improve, rectify

make self-conscious 5 abash 6 rattle 7 chagrin, fluster 9 discomfit, embarrass 10 disconcert

makeshift 6 make-do 7 standby, stopgap 8 slapdash 9 alternate, expedient, temporary, tentative 10 substitute 11 provisional

make sick 6 revolt 7 disgust 8 nauseate

make smaller 6 lessen, reduce, shrink, take in 8 decrease, diminish

make sure 5 cinch 6 assure, clinch, decide, ensure, secure, settle 9 ascertain 11 double-check

make thinner 4 thin 6 dilute 9 water down 10 adulterate

make tracks 2 go 4 scat, shoo 5 be off, leave, scram 6 beat it, cut out, depart, go away 8 withdraw 10 hit the road

make uncomfortable 3 try 7 agitate, perturb 8 disquiet, distress 9 discomfit, embarrass 10 discompose

make uneasy 6 rattle 7 disturb, perturb, trouble, unnerve 8 disquiet, distress 9 discomfit, embarrass 10 discomfort, discompose, disconcert

make uniform 4 even 5 equal 6 smooth 7 balance 8 equalize 10 straighten

makeup 5 frame 9 character, cosmetics, framework, structure 11 composition, personality 12 constitution, organization

make up 4 form 5 cover 6 invent 7 arrange, concoct 8 assemble 9 improvise, reconcile 10 compensate, constitute 11 put together

make up for 5 atone 7 expiate 8 make good 10 make amends 13 compensate for

make up one's mind 6 decide 7 resolve 9 determine

make use of 3 use 5 apply 6 employ, engage, occupy 7 exploit, utilize 8 keep busy, put to use **13** turn to account

make weary 4 do in, poop, tire **7** exhaust, wear out **8** enervate

makeweight 6 weight **7** ballast

make well 4 cure, heal

make wider 5 widen **6** dilate, expand **7** broaden, stretch **9** spread out

make worse 6 worsen **8** heighten, increase **9** aggravate, intensify **10** exacerbate

making excuses 8 alibiing **9** defending **10** justifying **11** apologizing

Making of the President, The (series)
  author: **14** Theodore H White

making the rounds 5 about **6** abroad **11** circulating, going around **13** going the route

Malachi
  means: **11** my messenger
  identified with: **4** Ezra **8** Mordecai, Nehemiah **10** Zerubbabel

maladroit 5 inept **6** clumsy, gauche **7** awkward, unhandy **8** bumbling, bungling, tactless **9** impolitic, unskilled **10** blundering, left-handed, ungraceful

maladroitness 9 gaucherie, inability **10** clumsiness, ineptitude **11** awkwardness, unhandiness **12** incompetence

malady 7 ailment, disease, illness **8** disorder, sickness **9** affection, complaint, infirmity **10** affliction, disability

mala fide 10 in bad faith, not genuine

malaise 4 pang **5** throb **6** twinge **7** anxiety **8** disquiet **9** lassitude **10** uneasiness, discomfort **11** nervousness

Malamud, Bernard
  author of: **8** The Fixer **9** God's Grace **10** The Natural, The Tenants **11** Dubin's Lives **12** The Assistant

Malaprop, Mrs
  character in: **9** The Rivals
  author: **8** Sheridan

Malawi
  other name: **9** Nyasaland
  capital: **8** Lilongwe
  largest city: **8** Blantyre
  others: **4** Bana **5** Dedza, Limbe, Mzuzu, Zomba **6** Kasese, Mzimba, Salima **7** Chipoka, Chiromo, Deep Bay, Karonga, Katumbi **8** Chikwawa, Chilumbe, Kota Kota, Nkata Bay **9** Monkey Bay **10** Port Herald **12** Fort Johnston, Livingstonia
  monetary unit: **6** kwacha **7** tambala
  lake: **5** Nyasa **6** Chilwa, Malawi
  mountain: **11** Livingstone
  highest point: **6** Mlanje **7** Mulanje
  river: **3** Bua **5** Shire **7** Dwangwa **11** South Rukuru
  physical feature:
    highlands: **5** Shire
    plateau: **5** Nyika

    valley: **5** Shire **9** Great Rift
  people: **3** Yao **4** Sena **5** Bantu, Lomwe, Ngoni **6** Cheiva, Maravi, Ngonde, Nyanja **7** Tumbuka
    dynasty: **6** Maravi
    explorer: **16** David Livingstone
    leader: **5** Banda
  language: **3** Yao **4** Cewa **5** Bantu, Ngoni, Tonga **6** Nyanja **7** English, Tumbuka **8** Chichewa **10** Chitumbuka
  religion: **5** Islam **7** animism **10** Protestant **12** Presbyterian **13** Roman Catholic
  feature:
    village: **5** mudzi

Malaysia
  capital/largest city: **11** Kuala Lumpur
  others: **4** Ipoh, Sibu **5** Anson, Davao, Telok **6** Iloilo, Johore, Kupang, Manado, Penang, Pinang **7** Bintulu, Kuantan, Kuching, Melalap **8** Port Weld, Sandakan **10** Georgetown, Kota Baharu **11** Johor Baharu, Port Dickson **12** Kota Kinabulu **14** Port Swettenham
  division: **5** Sabah **6** Malaya **7** Malacca, Sarawak
  head of state:
    supreme head of state: **18** yang di-pertuan agong
  measure: **3** pau, tun **4** para, pipe, tael, wang **5** parah **6** chupak, parrah **7** gantang
  monetary unit: **3** sen, tra **4** taro, trah **7** ringgit, tampang
  weight: **4** chee, mace, tael, wang **7** tampang
  island: **6** Banggi, Borneo, Labuan, Penang, Pinang, Tioman **7** Pangkor, Sebatik **8** Langkawi **10** Perhentian **11** Balambangan
  mountain: **4** Bulu, Hose, Iban, Iran, Main, Mulu, Niut, Raja **5** Murjo, Niapa, Ophir **6** Blumut, Kapuas, Leuser, Slamet **7** Binaija, Brassey, Crocker **8** Rindjani **11** Gunong Korbu, Gunong Tahan
  highest point: **8** Kinabalu
  river: **5** Klang, Kutai, Perak **6** Barito, Pahang, Rajang, Rejang **7** Sarawak **12** Kinabatangan
  sea: **4** Sulu **7** Celebes **10** South China
  physical feature:
    bay: **5** Labuk
    cape: **5** Sirik
    highlands: **7** Cameron
    passage: **6** Sibutu
    peninsula: **5** Malay
    point: **13** Tanjong Gelang
    strait: **6** Johore **7** Balabac, Malacca
  people: **4** Iban **5** Dayak, Malay **6** Indian **7** Chinese, Kadazan **9** Pakistani, Sri Lankan **10** Bangladesh, Indonesian
  language: **4** Bugi, Dyak **5** Malay, Tamil **6** Battok, Rejang **7** Chinese, English, Lampong, Niasese **8** Achi-

nese, Javanese, Makassar **14** Bahasa Malaysia
    alphabet: **5** tagal
  religion: **5** Hindu, Islam **6** Taoism **7** animism **8** Buddhism **12** Christianity, Confucianism
  place:
    mosque: **8** National
  feature:
    cap: **7** songkok
    cloth: **4** tapa **5** batik
    clothing: **4** baju, malo, sari **5** badju, pareu **6** cabaya, kebaya, sam-foo, sarong **9** cheongsam
    dance: **4** haka, hula **5** joget
    game: **9** sepakraga
    hamlet: **7** kampong
    parish: **5** mukim
    rice paddy: **4** padi
    scarf: **9** selendang
    self-defense: **5** silat
    shadow play: **6** menora
    spirit: **5** hantu
  food:
    drink: **4** kava
    fruit: **6** durian **8** rambutan **10** mangosteen

Malcolm
  character in: **7** Macbeth
  author: **11** Shakespeare

Malcolm in the Middle
  network: **3** FOX
  cast: **12** Frankie Muniz (Malcolm) **13** Bryan Cranston (Hal), Jane Kaczmarek (Lois) **14** Justin Berfield (Reese) **15** Erik Per Sullivan (Dewey) **17** Craig Lamar Traylor (Stevie Kenarban) **20** Christopher Masterson (Francis)

Malcolm X
  director: **8** Spike Lee
  author: **8** Malcolm X **9** Alex Haley
  cast: **8** Spike Lee (Shorty) **10** Albert Hall (Baines) **11** Al Freeman Jr (Elijah Muhammad), Delroy Lindo (Archie) **13** Angela Bassett (Betty Shabazz), James McDaniel (Brother Earl), Theresa Randle (Laura) **16** Denzel Washington (Malcolm X)

Malcolm X
  original name: **13** Malcolm Little
  born: **7** Omaha NE
  religion: **5** Islam **11** Black Muslim **13** Nation of Islam
  assassinated in: **6** Harlem **11** New York City
  book about: **26** The Autobiography of Malcolm X
    author: **9** Alex Haley
  film about: **8** Malcolm X
    director: **8** Spike Lee

malcontent 4 glum, sour **5** rebel **6** grouch, grumpy, morose, sullen, uneasy **7** grouchy, growler, repiner, restive **8** dejected, downcast, grumbler, restless **9** insurgent, irritable **10** complainer, despondent **11** faultfinder **12**

discontented, dissatisfied, faultfinding, hard to please

mal de mer 11 seasickness

Malden, Karl
real name: 16 Mladen Sekulovich
born: 6 Gary IL
roles: 6 Patton 8 Baby Doll 15 On the Waterfront 21 A Streetcar Named Desire 24 The Streets of San Francisco

Maldives
capital/largest city: 4 Male
government:
legislature: 6 Majlis
monetary unit: 5 laree, rupee
island: 3 Ari, Gan 4 Addu, Male 5 Rasdu 6 Felidu, Hulele, Mulaku 7 Malcolm, Minicoy, Nilandu 8 Maldives, Suvadiva 9 Fadiffolu, Wilingili 10 Haddummati, Kolumadulu 11 Tiladummati 13 Ihavandiffulu, Miladummadulu 16 North Malosmadulu, South Malosmadulu
sea: 6 Indian 7 Arabian 9 Laccadive
physical feature:
channel: 4 Wadu 7 Kardiva 8 Veimandu 10 Equatorial 11 Eight Degree 17 One and a Half Degree
people: 4 Arab 6 Indian 9 Sinhalese 10 Singhalese
ruling family/sultans: 4 Didi
language: 6 Arabic, Divehi
religion: 5 Islam
feature:
coconut fiber: 4 coir
dried coconut: 5 copra

male 3 boy, man, ram, tom 4 bull 5 manly, youth 6 tomcat 7 manlike, rooster 8 stallion 9 billy goat, masculine

Male
capital of: 8 Maldives

male bird 4 cock 5 drake 6 gander 7 rooster

maledict 4 damn 5 curse 8 denounce 9 proscribe 12 anathematize

malediction 5 curse 8 anathema, diatribe 9 damnation, evil spell 10 execration 11 fulmination, imprecation 12 denunciation, proscription

malefactor 5 felon, knave, rogue 6 sinner 7 culprit 8 criminal, evildoer, offender 9 miscreant, scoundrel, wrongdoer 10 malfeasant

male hairdresser
French: 8 coiffeur

malentendu 7 mistake 16 misunderstanding

male power
god of: 7 Priapus

Malevich, Kasimir Severinovich
born: 4 Kiev 6 Russia
artwork: 11 Black Square 15 The Knife Grinder 18 Eight Red Rectangles 19 Woman with Water Pails 34 Suprematist Composition White on White

malevolence 4 evil, hate 5 spite 6 enmity, grudge, hatred, malice, rancor, spleen 7 despite, ill will 9 hostility, malignity 10 antagonism, malignance, malignancy 12 spitefulness 13 maliciousness

malevolent 5 surly 6 malign, sullen 7 baleful, vicious 8 sinister, spiteful, venomous 9 invidious, malicious, malignant, rancorous, resentful 10 illnatured, pernicious, revengeful 11 acrimonious, ill-disposed 14 illintentioned

malfeasance 5 crime 8 misdeeds 10 misconduct, wrongdoing

malformation 9 deformity 10 aberration, distortion 11 abnormality, monstrosity, peculiarity 12 grotesquerie, irregularity 13 disfigurement

malformed 7 twisted 8 deformed 9 contorted, distorted, grotesque, irregular, misshapen

malfunction 6 glitch, malady 7 problem 9 complaint

malgre lui 16 in spite of himself

Mali
other name: 11 French Sudan 12 French Soudan 16 Sudanese Republic
capital/largest city: 6 Bamako
others: 3 Gao 5 Kayes, Mopti, Segou 6 Djenne 7 Sikasso 8 Taoudeni, Timbuktu 10 Tombouctou
division: 5 Sahel 7 Azaouad
monetary unit: 5 franc 7 centime
lake: 2 Do 4 Debo 5 Garou 7 Korarou 9 Faguibine
mountain: 4 Mina 6 Iforas 7 Manding
highest point: 12 Hombori Tondo
river: 4 Bani 5 Bagoe, Bakoy, Diaka, Niger 6 Bafing, Bakoye, Baoule, Faleme 7 Azaouak, Senegal
physical feature:
desert: 6 Sahara 8 Chech Erg 10 Sekkane Erg 13 Haricha Hamada
plateau: 14 Adrar des Iforas
valley: 5 Niger 7 Tilemsi
people: 3 Bwa 4 Fula, Kyan, Moor, Peul 5 Dogon, Dyula, Fulbe, Marka 6 Berber, Dognon, Fulani, Senufo, Tuareg 7 Bambara, Fellata, Malinke, Miniaka, Songhai, Soninke 8 Khasonke, Mandingo, Senoulfo
leader: 4 Umar 5 Keita 6 Traore 9 Mansa Musa
language: 5 Dogon, Dyula, Feulh, Mande, Marka 6 Berber, French, Fulani 7 Bambara, Malinke, Senoufo, Songhai
religion: 5 Islam 7 animism
place:
ruins: 8 Terhazza
feature:
empire: 4 Mali 5 Ghana 7 Bambara, Songhai

malice 4 hate 5 spite, venom 6 enmity,

grudge, hatred, rancor 7 ill will 8 acrimony 9 animosity, malignity 10 antagonism, bitterness, evil intent, resentment 11 malevolence 12 spitefulness

malice aforethought
legal term: 51 planning to commit a crime without just cause or provocation

malicious 7 baleful, harmful, hateful, vicious 8 spiteful 9 invidious, malignant, rancorous, resentful 10 malevolent, revengeful, vindictive 11 acrimonious, ill-disposed

malign 3 bad 4 evil 5 abuse, black 6 defame, revile, vilify 7 baneful, harmful, hateful, noxious, ominous, put down, run down, slander 8 backbite, bad mouth, belittle, derogate, menacing, sinister 9 denigrate, deprecate, disparage, injurious, malicious, malignant 10 malevolent, pernicious, speak ill of 11 deleterious, detrimental, threatening 14 inveigh against

malignancy 5 spite, tumor 6 cancer, malice, rancor 7 ill will, sarcoma 8 acrimony, neoplasm, toxicity 9 carcinoma, hostility, virulence 10 bitterness 11 malevolence, viciousness 12 hard feelings, spitefulness, vengefulness 13 poisonousness

malignant 4 evil 5 fatal, toxic 6 bitter, deadly 7 hateful, hostile, vicious 8 fiendish, spiteful, venomous, virulent 9 invidious, malicious, poisonous, rancorous, resentful 10 diabolical, evil-minded, malevolent, pernicious, revengeful, vindictive 11 acrimonious, ill-disposed

malignant spirit 3 imp 5 demon, devil 7 gremlin

malignity 4 evil 5 spite, venom 6 animus, rancor, spleen 7 ill will 8 acrimony 9 animosity 12 hard feelings, spitefulness, venomousness

malinger 4 loaf 5 dodge, evade, shirk, slack 7 goof off 9 goldbrick

mall 4 yard 5 court, plaza 6 arcade, circus, piazza, square 8 cloister 9 colonnade, esplanade, promenade 10 quadrangle 12 parade ground

Mallarme, Stephane
author of: 8 Herodias 18 L'Apres Midi d'un faune 19 The Afternoon of a Faun

Malle, Louis
director of: 10 Pretty Baby 12 Atlantic City 13 Lacombe Lucien 16 Murmur of the Heart
wife: 13 Candice Bergen

malleable 6 docile, pliant 7 ductile, plastic, pliable 8 flexible, moldable, workable 9 adaptable, compliant, teachable, tractable 10 governable, manageable 12 easily shaped 13 easily wrought 14 impressionable

mallet
  type: 6 rubber, wooden 12 plastic-faced
malnutrition 10 emaciation, starvation 16 undernourishment
malodorous 4 rank 5 acrid, fetid, musty 6 putrid, smelly 7 noisome, reeking 8 stinking 12 foul-smelling
Malone, Dorothy
  real name: 20 Dorothy Eloise Maloney
  husband: 15 Jacques Bergerac
  born: 9 Chicago IL
  roles: 11 Peyton Place 14 Too Much Too Soon 16 Written on the Wind
Malory, Sir Thomas
  author of: 14 Le Morte d'Arthur
Malpighi, Marcello
  field: 10 physiology
  nationality: 7 Italian
  founded: 18 microscopic anatomy
malpractice 10 negligence
Malraux, Andre
  author of: 8 Man's Fate 11 Anti-Memoirs, Days of Wrath, The Royal Way 13 The Conquerors 18 The Voices of Silence
Malta
  capital: 8 Valletta
  largest city: 6 Sliema
  others: 5 Marfa, Mdina, Mgarr, Mosta, Nadut, Paola, Rabat 6 Zejtun 7 Senglea, Zeibrun 8 Cospicua, Floriana, Mellieha, Victoria 10 Birkirkara, Birzebbuga, Vittoriosa
  measure: 4 rotl 5 artal, canna, parto, ratel, salma 6 kantar 7 caffiso
  monetary unit: 4 cent 5 grain, grano, pound
  island: 4 Gozo 5 Malta 6 Comino, Filfla 7 Filfola 9 Cominotto 10 Comminotto
  highest point: 12 Dingli Cliffs
  sea: 13 Mediterranean
  physical feature:
    bay: 7 St Paul's 8 Mellieha 10 Marsaxlokk
    channel: 11 North Comino, South Comino
    harbor: 5 Grand 10 Marsamxett
  people: 7 Maltese
    leader: 7 Mintoff 9 Buttigieo 18 Parisot de La Valette
    ruler: 5 Arabs 6 Romans 7 British 8 Napoleon 10 Byzantines 11 Hospitalers, Phoenicians 13 Carthaginians 15 Holy Roman Empire, Knights of St John
  language: 7 English, Italian, Maltese
  religion: 13 Roman Catholic
  feature:
    gondola boat: 7 dghaisa
Maltese Falcon, The
  author: 15 Dashiell Hammett
  director: 9 John Huston
  cast: 9 Mary Astor (Brigid O'Shaughnessy) 10 Peter Lorre (Joel Cairo) 12 Elisha Cook Jr (Wilmer), Gladys George 14 Humphrey Bogart (Sam Spade) 17 Sydney Greenstreet (the Fat Man)
  character: 6 Wilmer 8 Sam Spade 9 Joel Cairo 11 Miles Archer 12 Casper Gutman, Floyd Thursby 18 Brigid O'Shaughnessy
  remade as: 13 Satan Met a Lady
malt liquor 3 ale 4 beer, bock, brew 5 stout 6 porter
maltreat 4 harm, hurt 5 abuse 6 ill-use, injure 8 mistreat
maltreatment 5 abuse 6 ill-use, injury 7 assault, cruelty 10 bodily harm, oppression 11 manhandling, molestation, persecution 12 mistreatment
Malvolio
  character in: 12 Twelfth Night
  author: 11 Shakespeare
Mama
  character: 4 Nels 6 Dagmar, Katrin, TR Ryan 9 Aunt Jenny 10 (Papa) Lars Hansen 11 (Mama) Marta Hansen
  cast: 8 Iris Mann 9 Peggy Wood, Ruth Gates 11 Judson Laire, Robin Morgan 12 Rosemary Rice 13 Dick Van Patten, Kevin Coughlin
  dog: 6 Willie
  based on book: 16 Mama's Bank Account
  author: 13 Kathryn Forbes
  setting: 12 San Francisco
  theme: 12 Holverg Suite 13 The Last Spring
mamma, mama 2 ma 3 mam, mom, mum 4 wife 5 madre, mammy, mater, mommy, mummy, mumsy, woman 6 mother, parent
mammal
  bat (chiroptera): 4 tomb 5 fruit, naked, smoky 7 mastiff, vampire 9 fisherman, horseshoe, leaf-nosed, sac-winged, slit-faced, thumbless 10 disk-winged, free-tailed, moustached 11 funnel-eared, hollow-faced, mouse-tailed 12 false vampire, sheath-tailed, sucker-footed, yellow-winged 14 vespertilionid 21 New Zealand short-tailed
  carnivore: 3 cat, dog, fox 4 bear, lion, lynx, mink, puma, wolf 5 civet, dingo, fossa, hyena, otter, panda, skunk, tayra, tiger 6 badger, bobcat, coyote, ferret, grison, hyaena, jackal, jaguar, marten, olingo, weasel 7 polecat, raccoon 8 aardwolf, kinkajou, mongoose, suricate 9 wolverine 10 cacomistle, coatimundi
  cetacea: 4 gray 5 pilot, right, whale 6 beluga, killer 7 dolphin, rorqual 8 humpback, narwhale, porpoise 10 sperm whale 11 beaked whale 16 bottle-nosed whale
  edentata: 5 sloth 8 anteater 9 armadillo, tree sloth
  egg-laying: 7 echidna 13 spiny anteater 18 duck-billed platypus
  even-toed ungulate: 2 ox 3 elk, hog, pig 4 deer, goat, oxen 5 bison, camel, llama, moose, okapi, sheep 6 alpaca, cattle, duiker, vicuna 7 buffalo, caribou, gazelle, giraffe, guanaco, muntjak, peccary 8 antelope 9 mouse deer 10 chevrotain 12 hippopotamus
  hyracoidea: 5 hyrax
  insect-eating: 4 mole 5 shrew 6 desman, tenrec 7 gymnure, moon rat 8 hedgehog 9 shrew-mole, solenodon 10 golden mole, otter shrew, water shrew 13 elephant shrew
  lagomorpha: 4 hare, pika 6 rabbit
  marsupials/pouched: 5 koala 6 cuscus, numbat, possum, wombat 7 opossum, wallaby 8 kangaroo 9 bandicoot, phalanger 14 Tasmanian devil
  odd-toed ungulate: 3 ass 5 horse, kiang, tapir, zebra 6 onager, quagga 10 rhinoceros
  pinnipedia: 4 seal 6 walrus 7 sea lion
  primate: 5 lemur, loris, potto 6 avahis, aye-aye, baboon, galago, gibbon, indris, monkey, people 7 gorilla, tamarin, tarsier 8 marmoset, simpoona 9 orangutan, tree shrew 10 chimpanzee
  proboscidea: 8 elephant
  rodent: 4 cavy, vole 5 coypu, gundi, hutia, mouse 6 agouti, beaver, coruro, gerbil, gopher, jerboa, nutria 7 blesmol, cane rat, hamster, lemming, mole-rat, rock rat 8 capybara, chipmunk, dormouse, sewellel, spiny rat, squirrel, tucu-tuco, viscacha 9 chozchori, false paca, pacaranas, porcupine, woodchuck 10 chinchilla, prairie dog, springhare 11 kangaroo rat, pocket mouse, viscacha rat 13 kangaroo mouse 16 Speke's pectinator
  sirenia: 6 dugong, sea cow 7 manatee
  tubulidentata: 8 aardvark
mammon, Mammon 4 gain, gold 5 money 6 profit, riches, wealth 9 affluence 11 possessions 13 material goods, the god of money
Mammon, Sir Epicure
  character in: 12 The Alchemist
  author: 6 Jonson
mammoth 4 huge 5 great 6 mighty 7 immense, massive 8 colossal, enormous, gigantic, whopping 9 cyclopean, herculean, monstrous, ponderous, very large 10 gargantuan, monumental, prodigious, stupendous, tremendous 11 elephantine, mountainous
Mammy
  character in: 15 Gone With the Wind
  author: 8 Mitchell

Mamoulian, Rouben
  director of: **13** Love Me Tonight, Silk Stockings **14** Queen Christina, The Mark of Zorro

man 3 boy, guy, one **4** chap, gent, hand, male, soul **5** equip, hubby, human, staff **6** anyone, attend, butler, fellow, fit out, helper, outfit, people, person, spouse, waiter, worker **7** footman, husband, laborer, mankind, someone, subject, workman **8** employee, garrison, handyman, henchman, humanity, liegeman, somebody **9** assistant, gentleman, hired hand, humankind **11** Homo sapiens
  Spanish: **6** hombre

Man, first 4 Adam **12** Alalcomeneus
  Nordic: **3** Ask

Man, Isle of
  capital: **7** Douglas
  location: **8** Irish Sea
  native: **4** Manx **7** Manxman
  Manx cat lacks: **4** tail

man about town 5 blade **7** playboy **8** cavalier, gay blade **12** boulevardier

manacle, manacles 3 ply, run, use **4** cope, fare, head, rule, work **5** bonds, get on, guide, irons, order, pilot, shift, steer, wield **6** chains, direct, fetter, govern, handle, make go **7** command, conduct, control, operate, oversee, shackle, succeed, survive, work out **8** cope with, deal with, dominate, get along, handcuff, maneuver, shackles **9** bracelets, handcuffs, look after, supervise, watch over **10** accomplish, administer, bring about, manipulate, put in irons, take care of **11** be at the helm, hand fetters, preside over, put in chains, superintend **12** have charge of, hold the reins

manage 4 care, rule **6** bosses, charge, wheels **7** bigwigs, command, conduct, control, dealing, running, tactics **8** big shots, guidance, handling, ordering, planning, strategy, top brass **9** direction, directors, operation **10** conducting, executives, overseeing, regulation **11** generalship, negotiation, supervision, supervisors, transaction **12** manipulation, organization **14** administration, administrators **15** superintendence

manageable 4 easy **6** docile, pliant, wieldy **8** amenable, flexible **9** compliant, tractable **10** governable, submissive **12** controllable

management 4 boss, head **5** agent, chief **7** foreman, planner **8** overseer **9** budgeteer, majordomo, organizer, tactician **10** impresario, negotiator, supervisor **11** manipulator **13** administrator **14** superintendent

manager 4 boss, head **5** agent, chief **7** foreman, planner **8** overseer **9** budgeteer, majordomo, organizer, tactician **10** impresario, negotiator, supervisor

11 manipulator **13** administrator **14** superintendent

managerial 9 executive **10** management **11** supervisory **14** administrative, organizational

Managua
  capital of: **9** Nicaragua

Manala see **7** Tuonela

Manama
  capital of: **7** Bahrain

manana 6 future **8** tomorrow **11** in the future

Man and Superman
  author: **17** George Bernard Shaw

Manassa Mauler
  nickname of: **11** Jack Dempsey

Manasseh
  father: **6** Joseph
  mother: **7** Asenath
  great uncle: **4** Esau
  grandfather: **5** Jacob
  descendant of: **9** Manassite

man-at-arms 7 fighter, soldier, warrior **9** combatant **10** cavalryman

Manchester, William
  author of: **11** The Last Lion **14** American Caesar **15** Goodbye Darkness **19** The Glory and the Dream **20** The Death of a President

Manchuria
  also: **7** Manchow
  city: **5** Aigun, Hulan, Kirin, Peian, Penki **6** Anshan, Antung, Dairen, Fu-Shun, Hailar, Harbin, Hokang, Mukden, Penchi, Yenchi **7** Hulutao, Ikuliho, Ssuping, Tantung **8** Chinchao, Paicheng, Shenyang **9** Changchun, Chiamussu, Manchouli, Miuchwang **10** Port Arthur **11** Chichihaerh, Mutanchiang
  peninsula: **8** Liaotung
  province: **5** Jehol, Jilin, Kirin **8** Liaoning **12** Heilongjiang, Heilungkiang
  river: **4** Amur, Liao, Yalu **5** Argun, Mutan, Nonni, Tumen **6** Ussuri **7** Sungari
  tribe: **5** Tungu **6** Manchu, Mongol

Mandalay
  found in: **18** Barrack-Room Ballads
  author: **14** Rudyard Kipling

mandamus
  legal term: **48** writ from a superior court commanding that a thing be done
  literally: **9** we command

Mandan
  language family: **6** Siouan
  location: **11** North Dakota
  ceremony: **5** Okipa

Mandarins, The
  author: **16** Simone de Beauvoir

mandate 5 edict, order **6** behest, charge, decree **7** bidding, command, dictate **8** approval, sanction **9** authority, direction, directive **10** commission, dependency **11** instruction, req-

uisition **12** protectorate **13** authorization

mandatory 7 binding, exigent, needful **8** required **9** called for, essential, necessary, requisite **10** compulsory, imperative, obligatory, peremptory

Manderley
  house in: **7** Rebecca
  author: **9** Du Maurier

mandible 3 jaw **4** beak, bill, jowl **7** maxilla **8** lower jaw
  part: **4** mala **5** angle, molar, ramus **6** corpus

Mandrake the Magician
  creator: **7** Lee Falk **9** Phil Davis
  character: **5** Narda **6** Lothar

Manes
  spirits or souls of: **4** dead

Manet, Edouard
  born: **5** Paris **6** France
  artwork: **7** Olympia **8** The Fifer **9** Emile Zola **10** Argenteuil **12** The Guitarist **19** Le Dejeuner sur l'Herbe (Luncheon on the Grass) **25** The Bar at the Folies-Bergeres **31** Execution of the Emperor Maximilian

Manette, Dr and Lucie
  characters in: **16** A Tale of Two Cities
  author: **7** Dickens

maneuver 4 move, plot, ploy **5** dodge, guide, pilot, steer, trick **6** deploy, device, gambit, scheme, tactic **7** finagle **8** artifice, contrive, intrigue **9** stratagem **10** manipulate **11** contrivance, machination, pull strings

Man for All Seasons, A
  director: **13** Fred Zinnemann
  based on play by: **10** Robert Bolt
  cast: **9** Leo McKern **10** Robert Shaw **11** Orson Welles, Wendy Hiller **12** Paul Scofield (Sir Thomas More), Susannah York **14** Nigel Davenport **15** Vanessa Redgrave
  Oscar for: **5** actor (Scofield) **7** picture **8** director

man Friday 4 aide **8** adjutant, employee **9** assistant **10** aide de camp **12** right-hand man
  source: **14** Robinson Crusoe

Man from UNCLE, The
  character: **9** Mr Waverly **12** Napoleon Solo **13** Illya Kuryakin
  cast: **11** Leo G Carroll **12** Robert Vaughn **13** David McCallum
  foe: **6** THRUSH

manful 5 brave **8** resolute **10** courageous

manganese
  chemical symbol: **2** Mn

mangle 3 cut **4** harm, hurt, lame, maim, maul, ruin, tear **5** crush, press, slash **6** damage, impair, injure **7** flatten **8** lacerate, mutilate **9** disfigure

manhandle 4 maul **5** abuse **6** batter **7** rough up **8** maltreat, mistreat **9** pull about, push about **10** knock about, slap around

Manhattan
director: **10** Woody Allen
cast: **9** Anne Byrne **10** Woody Allen **11** Diane Keaton, Meryl Streep **13** Michael Murphy **15** Mariel Hemingway

Manhattan Transfer
author: **13** John Dos Passos

manhood 5 prime **8** legal age, machismo, majority, maleness, maturity, virility **9** adulthood, manliness, mature age **10** manfulness **11** masculinity

mania 4 rage **5** craze **6** frenzy, lunacy, raving **7** craving, madness, passion **8** delirium, delusion, dementia, fixation, hysteria, insanity **9** monomania, obsession **10** aberration, compulsion, enthusiasm, fanaticism **11** fascination, infatuation

maniac 3 ass, nut **4** fool **5** loony **6** cuckoo, madman, nitwit **7** half-wit, lunatic **9** psychotic, screwball, simpleton **10** crackbrain, psychopath

manic 2 up **4** high **7** excited, frantic, hyped up **8** agitated, frenzied, worked up **9** wrought up **10** freaked out, switched on **11** hyperactive

manifest 4 bare, open, show **5** clear, frank, plain **6** candid, evince, expose, patent, reveal, unveil **7** display, divulge, evident, exhibit, express, obvious, uncover, visible **8** apparent, disclose, evidence, indicate, palpable **9** make known **10** noticeable **11** demonstrate, make visible, self-evident, transparent, unconcealed, undisguised

manifestation 4 show **7** display, example, symptom **8** evidence, instance **10** exhibition, expression, indication, revelation **12** illustration, presentation, proclamation, public notice **13** demonstration

manifesto 4 bull **5** edict, ukase **6** notice **9** broadside, statement **10** communique, encyclical **11** declaration **12** announcement, annunciation, notification, proclamation, public notice **13** position paper, pronouncement **14** pronunciamento

manifold 4 many **6** myriad, varied **7** complex, diverse **8** multiple, numerous **9** many-sided, multiform **10** variegated **11** diversified, innumerable **12** multifarious **13** multitudinous

Manila
capital of: **11** Philippines
former name: **8** Maynilad
island: **5** Luzon
landmark: **9** Rizal Park **16** San Agustin Church
river: **5** Pasig
section: **10** Quezon City
university: **10** Santo Tomas

Man in the Gray Flannel Suit, The
author: **11** Sloan Wilson

manipulate 3 pat, ply, use **4** feel, work **5** drive, pinch, wield **6** employ, finger, handle, manage, stroke **7** control, deceive, defraud, massage, operate, squeeze

Manitoba
bay: **6** Hudson
capital: **8** Winnipeg
city: **6** Carman, The Pas **7** Brandon, Caribou, Dauphin, Selkirk **8** Flin Flon, Lynn Lake, Wabowden, Winnipeg **9** Churchill, Killarney, Sherridon, Swan River **10** St Boniface **11** Norway House, York Factory **16** Portage La Prairie
flower: **11** windflower **13** prairie crocus
Indian tribe: **4** Cree **6** Eskimo, Ojibwa **8** Chippewa **10** Assiniboin
lake: **4** God's, Swan **5** Cedar, Moose **6** Island **7** Dauphin, Red Deer **8** Manitoba, Reindeer, St Martin, Waterhen, Winnipeg **9** Granville
mountain: **4** Hart **5** Baldy
name means: **16** lake of the prairies **18** Great Spirit's strait **19** Great Spirit's narrows
nickname: **15** Prairie Province **16** Keystone Province
province of: **6** Canada
river: **3** Red **4** Seal, Swan **5** Hayes **6** Nelson, Roseau, Souris **7** Pembina **8** Winnipeg **9** Churchill **11** Assiniboine **12** Saskatchewan
university: **7** Brandon **10** St Boniface

Mankiewicz, Joseph L
director of: **6** Sleuth **9** Cleopatra **11** All About Eve (Oscar) **12** Guys and Dolls, Julius Caesar **18** The Ghost and Mrs Muir **19** A Letter to Three Wives (Oscar)

mankind 3 man **6** people **7** mortals, persons, society **8** humanity **9** humankind **11** Homo sapiens

manlike 5 macho, manly **6** virile **8** hominoid **9** masculine

manly 4 bold, male **5** brave, hardy, husky, noble **6** brawny, daring, heroic, manful, plucky, robust, strong, sturdy, virile **7** gallant, staunch, valiant **8** athletic, fearless, malelike, muscular, powerful, resolute, stalwart, vigorous **9** masculine, strapping **10** chivalrous, courageous **11** gentlemanly, indomitable, self-reliant **12** stouthearted
Spanish: **5** macho

man-made 4 mock, sham **6** formed **7** crafted, created **8** produced **9** fashioned, ready made, simulated, synthetic **10** artificial, fabricated, factitious, originated **11** constructed, handcrafted **12** manufactured

Mann, Delbert

director of: **5** Marty (Oscar) **14** Separate Tables

Mann, Thomas
author of: **12** Buddenbrooks **13** Death in Venice, Doctor Faustus **16** The Magic Mountain

manna 4 boon **5** award **6** reward **7** bonanza **16** divine sustenance

mannequin 4 form **5** dummy, model **6** figure

manner 3 air, way **4** form, kind, make, mode, mold, race, rank, sort, type **5** brand, breed, caste, genre, grade, guise, habit, stamp, style **6** aspect, custom, method, strain **7** bearing, conduct, fashion, species, variety **8** behavior, carriage, category, demeanor, practice, presence **9** character **10** appearance, deportment **14** classification

mannered 6 formal **7** stilted, studied **8** affected **9** contrived, unnatural **10** artificial **11** ceremonious

mannerism 4 airs, pose **5** habit **8** pretense **10** pretension **11** affectation, singularity **12** eccentricity, idiosyncrasy

mannerly 5 civil **6** polite **7** courtly, gallant, genteel, refined **8** well-bred **9** courteous **10** chivalrous **11** gentlemanly, well-behaved

manner of living
Latin: **12** modus vivendi

manner of looking at the world
German: **14** Weltanschauung

manner of speaking 7 diction **9** elocution **10** intonation **13** pronunciation

manners 6 polish **7** decorum **8** behavior, breeding, courtesy **9** amenities, deference, etiquette, gallantry, gentility, politesse, propriety **10** deportment, politeness, refinement **11** courtliness

Mannix
character: **9** Joe Mannix, Peggy Fair **10** (Lt) Adam Tobias **13** Lou Wickersham
cast: **10** Gail Fisher, Robert Reed **11** Mike Connors **16** Joseph Campanella

Mannon family
members: **4** Ezra, Orin **7** Lavinia **9** Christine
characters in: **22** Mourning Becomes Electra
author: **6** O'Neill

Manoah
son: **6** Samson

mano a mano 5 alone **8** conflict **13** confrontation, in a small group
literally: **10** hand to hand

Man of a Thousand Faces
nickname of: **9** Lon Chaney

Man of Nazareth
author: **14** Anthony Burgess

Man of Property, The
author: **14** John Galsworthy

Man of Sorrows *see* **5** Jesus

Manolin
character in: **18** The Old Man and the Sea
author: **9** Hemingway

Manon Lescaut
author: **11** Abbe Prevost

manor house 6 estate, manoir **7** chateau, mansion **11** stately home

manpower 4 help **5** brawn, labor **9** work force, employees

manque 6 failed, missed **7** lacking **11** fallen short, unfulfilled

Mansart, Francois
architect of: **14** Chateau de Berny **18** Hotel de la Vrilliere **33** Church of Sainte Marie de la Visitation
feature: **11** mansard roof

manservant 5 groom, valet **6** butler **7** footman **8** factotum **9** chauffeur

Man's Fate
author: **12** Andre Malraux

Mansfield, Jayne
real name: **14** Vera Jane Palmer
husband: **14** Mickey Hargitay
born: **10** Bryn Mawr PA
roles: **15** Hell on Frisco Bay **26** Will Success Spoil Rock Hunter

Mansfield, Katherine
author of: **5** Bliss **12** The Dove's Nest **14** The Garden Party

Mansfield Park
author: **10** Jane Austen
character: **5** Yates **8** Mrs Grant **9** Mrs Norris, Rushworth **10** Fanny Price **11** Lady Bertram **12** Mary Crawford **13** Henry Crawford **16** Sir Thomas Bertram
  Bertram children: **3** Tom **5** Julia, Maria **6** Edmund

mansion 5 manor, villa **6** castle, estate, palace **7** chateau **10** manor house

manslaughter 6 murder **7** killing **8** homicide

manta 3 ray **4** cape **5** cloak, shawl **9** devilfish

Mantegna, Andrea
born: **5** Italy **14** Isola di Carturo
artwork: **9** Parnassus **16** Camera degli Sposi (Bridal Chamber) **18** The Triumph of Caesar, The Triumph of Virtue **20** Madonna della Vittoria

Mantius
father: **8** Melampus
son: **6** Clitus

mantle 4 cape, film, mask, pall, veil **5** cloak, cloud, cover, scarf, tunic **6** canopy, screen, shroud **7** blanket, curtain, wrapper **8** covering, envelope, mantilla

Mantle, Mickey (Charles)
sport: **8** baseball
position: **8** outfield
team: **14** New York Yankees

manual 6 primer **8** handbook, physi-cal, textbook, workbook **9** guidebook **10** done by hand **12** hand-operated, nonautomatic **15** instruction book

manual skill 8 deftness **9** dexterity, handiness **10** adroitness **12** coordination

manufacture 4 form, make, mold **5** build, frame **6** cook up, create, devise, invent, make up **7** concoct, fashion, produce, think up, trump up **8** assemble **9** construct, fabricate **11** mass produce, put together

manufacturing 8 devising **9** inventing, producing **10** industrial **11** fabricating, nonagrarian

manumission 7 freeing **10** liberation **11** setting free **12** emancipation

manumit 4 free **7** set free **8** liberate **10** emancipate

manure 4 dung **5** feces **6** ordure **7** compost, excreta **8** dressing **10** fertilizer

manuscript 6 script **10** typescript **14** shooting script **15** written document

Manvah
son: **6** Samson

Man Who Came to Dinner, The
director: **15** William Keighley
based on play by: **8** Moss Hart **14** George S Kaufman
cast: **10** Bette Davis **11** Ann Sheridan, Billie Burke **12** Monty Woolley **13** Richard Travis

Man Who Fell to Earth, The
director: **12** Nicholas Roeg
cast: **7** Rip Torn **9** Buck Henry **10** Candy Clark, David Bowie

Man Who Shot Liberty Valence, The
director: **8** John Ford
cast: **9** John Wayne, Lee Marvin, Vera Miles **12** Edmund O'Brien, James Stewart

Man Without a Country, The
author: **17** Edward Everett Hale
character: **11** Philip Nolan

Manx 3 cat **8** Goidelic
spoken on: **10** Isle of Man
manx cat lacks: **4** tail

many 4 a lot, lots **5** a heap, heaps, piles **6** divers, dozens, myriad, scores, sundry **7** numbers, several, various **8** numerous **9** countless **10** a profusion, numberless **11** an abundance, innumerable **13** multitudinous

manzanita 14 Arctostaphylos
varieties: **4** dune, Ione, Otay **5** hairy, hoary, Morro, Parry, Pecho **6** island, Sonoma, woolly **7** Mexican, Pajarro, pine-mat **8** big-berry, Del Norte, Eastwood, Mariposa, Monterey, shagbark, Stanford **9** Fort Bragg, greenleaf, heart-leaf, little Sur, white-leaf **10** serpentine, silver-leaf **11** brittleleaf, pink-bracted

Maori
native of: **10** New Zealand

Mao Zedong
also: **10** Mao Tse-Tung
born: **5** China
leader of: **10** communists
title: **8** Chairman
led: **9** Long March
book: **16** The Little Red Book

map 4 plan, plot **5** chart, graph, ready **6** design, devise, lay out **7** arrange, diagram, prepare, project **8** contrive, organize **9** elevation **10** make a map of, projection **14** representation **18** topographical chart

maple 4 Acer
varieties: **3** red **4** Amur, hard, rock, soft, vine **5** black, chalk, field, hedge, Nikko, river, sugar, swamp, white **6** Balkan, canyon, Norway, Oregon, parlor, sierra, silver, Triden **7** big-leaf, Florida, Persian, scarlet, striped **8** big-tooth, Drummond, fullmoon, Hawthorn, Hornbeam, Japanese, mountain, Shantung, Sycamore, Tatarian **9** ash-leaved, eagleclaw, flowering, paperbark, Schwedler, Tartarian **11** Montpellier **12** Pennsylvania **13** Rocky Mountain, Southern sugar **18** Rocky Mountain sugar

map out 3 map **5** chart, draft **6** devise, lay out **7** diagram, outline **8** block out **9** delineate, formulate

Maputo
capital of: **10** Mozambique

mar 4 hurt, maim, mark, nick, ruin, scar **5** botch, spoil, stain, taint **6** blight, damage, deface, defile, impair **7** blemish, destroy, scratch **8** diminish, mutilate **9** disfigure

Marabar Caves
setting in: **15** A Passage to India
author: **7** Forster

Maranatha
means: **9** O Lord come

maraschino
type: **7** liqueur
origin: **5** Italy
flavor: **6** cherry
color: **3** red **5** white

Marathi
language family: **12** Indo-European
branch: **11** Indo-Iranian
group: **5** Indic
spoken in: **5** (northern) India

Marathonian bull *see* **10** Cretan bull

marauder 6 looter, pirate, ranger **7** corsair, ravager, spoiler **8** pillager **9** buccaneer, despoiler, guerrilla, plunderer, privateer **10** depradator, freebooter

marble 3 jet **4** vein **5** agate **6** basalt, blotch, mottle, streak **7** calcite **8** dolomite **9** limestone **10** serpentine, travertine **12** anthraconite
quarry: **7** Carrara

Marble Faun, The
 author: **18** Nathaniel Hawthorne
 character: **5** Hilda **6** Kenyon, Miriam
  9 Donatello

marbles
 type: **3** mib, taw **4** aggy, duck, immy,
  migg **5** agate, monny, scrap **6** com-
  mie, glassy, hoodle, marine **7** cat's
  eye, rainbow, shooter **9** carnelian **16**
  peppermint stripe
 term: **3** hit **4** shot **6** edgers, ringer **7**
  bowling, for fair, histing, lagging, lag
  line, lofting **8** circling, for keeps,
  hunching **9** pitch line **10** roundsters
  11 knuckle down **13** knuckling down

Marc, Franz
 born: **6** Munich **7** Germany
 artwork: **10** Blue Horses **12** Yellow
  Horses **13** Fighting Forms

Marceline
 character in: **19** The Marriage of Figaro
 author: **12** Beaumarchais

march **2** go **4** hike, rise, step, trek,
 walk **5** tramp **6** file by, growth, parade **7** advance, proceed **8** progress **9**
 group walk **10** go directly, procession,
 walk in step **11** advancement, development, progression **12** martial music

March
 event: **9** Mardi Gras **11** Ides of March
  (15) **12** Ash Wednesday **13** vernal
  equinox (21)
 flower: **7** jonquil **8** daffodil
 French: **4** Mars
 gem: **10** aquamarine, bloodstone
 German: **4** Marz
 holiday: **12** St Joseph's Day (19) **13**
  St Patrick's Day (17)
 Italian: **5** Marzo
 number of days: **9** thirty-one
 origin of name: **4** Mars
  Roman god of: **3** war
 place in year:
  Gregorian: **5** third
  Roman: **5** first
 saying: **20** Beware the Ides of March
  40 March comes in like a lion and
  goes out like a lamb
 Spanish: **6** Marcha
 Zodiac sign: **5** Aries **6** Pisces

March, Fredric
 real name: **29** Ernest Frederick McIntyre Bickel
 born: **8** Racine WI
 roles: **11** A Star Is Born **12** Anna
  Karenina, The Buccaneer **13** Les Miserables **14** Anthony Adverse, Inherit
  the Wind, Mary of Scotland, Seven
  Days in May **16** Death of a Salesman
  17 Alexander the Great, Dr Jekyll
  and Mr Hyde (Oscar), The Desperate
  Hours **18** Death Takes a Holiday **19**
  The Affairs of Cellini **22** The Best
  Years of Our Lives (Oscar) **23** Barretts of Wimpole Street

Marchen **8** folk tale **9** fairy tale

March family
 members: **2** Jo **3** Amy, Meg **4** Beth **6**
  Marmee
 characters in: **11** Little Women
 author: **6** Alcott

March Hare
 character in: **28** Alice's Adventures in
  Wonderland
 author: **7** Carroll

Marchmain family
 characters in: **19** Brideshead Revisited
 author: **5** Waugh

Marciano, Rocky
 real name: **23** Rocco Francis Marche-
  giano
 nickname: **19** Brockton Blockbuster
 sport: **6** boxing
 class: **11** heavyweight

Marconi, Guglielmo
 nationality: **7** Italian
 nickname: **16** father of wireless
 invented/discovered: **5** radio **12** radio signals **16** magnetic detector **30**
  wireless high frequency telegraph
 shared (1919): **20** Nobel Prize for
  physics

Marcus Welby MD
 character: **11** (Dr) Steven Kiley **13**
  Consuelo Lopez
 cast: **11** James Brolin, Robert Young
  12 Elena Verdugo

Mardi (and a Voyage Thither)
 author: **14** Herman Melville
 character: **4** Alma, Jarl, Mohi, Taji **5**
  Media, Samoa, Yoomy **6** Yillah **7**
  Annatoo **10** Babbalanja, Braidbeard
  11 Queen Hautia

Mardi Gras **7** holiday **8** carnival, festival, jamboree **10** fat Tuesday **13**
 Shrove Tuesday
 king: **3** rex
 social club: **5** krewe

Marduk
 also: **8** Merodach **12** Baal Merodach
 origin: **10** Babylonian
 chief of: **4** gods

mare **3** sea **9** brood mare **11** female
 horse

mare nostrum **6** our sea
 ancient Roman name for: **13** Mediterranean

margin **3** hem, rim **4** edge, side **5**
 bound, skirt, verge **6** border, fringe,
 leeway **7** confine **8** boundary **9** allowance, extra room, safeguard

marginal **9** on the edge **11** in the margin **12** barely useful

mariage de convenance **21** marriage
 of convenience

marigold **7** Tagetes
 varieties: **3** big, bur, fig, pot **4** cape,
  corn, wild **5** Aztec, fetid, field,
  marsh, water **6** desert, French, signet
  7 African **12** sweet-scented

marijuana, marihuana **3** boo, kif,

pot, tea **4** hash, hemp, herb, weed **5**
bhang, blunt, dagga, ganja, grass,
joint **6** buddha, moocah, reefer **7**
chronic, hashish **8** cannabis, loco-
weed, mary jane

Marin, John Cheri (3rd)
 born: **12** Rutherford NJ
 artwork: **8** Sea Piece **12** Maine Islands **13** Tunk Mountains **16** Beach
  Flint Island **19** Movement Fifth Avenue **21** Seaside Interpretation **26**
  Camden Mountain Across the Bay

marine **3** sea **5** naval **6** gyrene **7**
 aquatic, oceanic, of ships, pelagic **8**
 maritime, nautical, of the sea, seagoing **9** salt-water, seafaring **10** ocean-
 going **11** leatherneck **13** oceano-
 graphic

mariner **3** gob, tar **4** salt **5** pilot **6**
 sailor, sea dog, seaman **7** boatman **8**
 deck hand, helmsman, seafarer **9** navigator, yachtsman **10** bluejacket **12**
 seafaring man **16** able-bodied seaman

Marion, Francis
 nickname: **8** Swamp Fox
 served in: **16** Revolutionary War
 type of warfare: **9** guerrilla
 area fought in: **13** South Carolina
 battle: **12** Eutaw Springs

marionette **6** puppet **10** fantoccino
 famous: **4** Judy **5** Punch **9** Pinocchio
 dummy: **13** Mortimer Snerd **15** Charlie McCarthy
 maker: **4** Sarg

marital **6** wedded, wifely **7** married,
 nuptial, spousal **8** conjugal **9** connubial, husbandly **10** of marriage **11**
 matrimonial

maritime **5** naval **6** marine **7** aquatic,
 coastal, oceanic, of ships **8** nautical,
 of the sea, seagoing **9** seafaring

marjoram
 botanical name: **8** Majorana, O vulgare, Origanum **16** M hortensis
  moench
 origin: **4** Asia **13** Mediterranean
 family: **4** mint
 symbol of: **5** honor **9** happiness
 charm against: **10** witchcraft
 used as: **12** air sweetener
 use: **4** eggs, fish, meat **5** salad **8**
  stuffing **9** vegetable

Marjorie Morningstar
 author: **10** Herman Wouk

mark **3** cut, mar, pit **4** dent, goal,
 harm, heed, line, mind, nick, note,
 pock, rate, scar, show, sign, spot **5**
 badge, brand, grade, judge, label,
 notch, point, proof, score, stain,
 stamp, token, track **6** attend, bruise,
 deface, denote, emblem, evince, injure, intent, rating, regard, reveal,
 streak, symbol, target, typify **7** betoken, blemish, correct, imprint, measure, scratch, signify, suggest, symptom, write in, write on **8** bull's-eye,
 colophon, disclose, evidence, hall-

mark, indicate, manifest, point out, standard, stand for **9** be a sign of, criterion, designate, disfigure, objective, symbolize, yardstick **10** impression, indication, touchstone **11** distinguish **12** characterize **13** differentiate

Mark
  also: **8** John Mark
  mother: **4** Mary
  cousin: **8** Barnabas
  wrote: **11** Gospel

Mark (King Mark)
  character in: **16** Arthurian romance

Mark Antony
  also: **14** Marcus Antonius
  character in: **12** Julius Caesar
  author: **11** Shakespeare

mark down 4 note **5** enter, lower **6** record, reduce **7** put down **9** write down

marked 5 clear, great, noted, plain **6** dotted, scored, severe, showed, spotty, tabbed, tagged, traced **7** branded, labeled, pointed, specked, spotted, stained, tracked **8** destined, speckled, striking, targeted **9** indicated, prominent **10** emphasized, identified, made note of, noticeable, remarkable, singled out **11** conspicuous, distinctive, outstanding **12** considerable **13** distinguished

marker 3 IOU, peg, run, tab **4** chip, flag, sign **5** score **6** etcher, scorer, tablet, ticket **7** counter **8** bookmark, memorial, monument, recorder

market 4 hawk, sell, vend **5** stand **6** bourse, peddle, retail **7** grocery **9** dispose of **10** curb market, meat market **11** butcher shop, grocer's shop, marketplace

marketplace 4 mart **5** agora, arena, plaza **6** bazaar, market, square **8** exchange

Mark of Zorro, The
  director: **15** Rouben Mamoulian
  cast: **11** Tyrone Power **12** Linda Darnell **13** Basil Rathbone **15** Gale Sondergaard
  score: **12** Alfred Newman

mark out 8 describe **9** delineate

marksman 8 dead shot, good shot, sure shot **9** crack shot **12** sharpshooter

marksmanship 3 aim **5** skill **8** accuracy **13** sharpshooting

Marley's Ghost
  character in: **15** A Christmas Carol
  author: **7** Dickens

Marlow
  character in: **7** Lord Jim
  author: **6** Conrad

Marlowe
  character in: **15** Heart of Darkness
  author: **6** Conrad

Marlowe, Christopher
  author of: **8** Edward II **13** Doctor Faustus, The Jew of Malta **14** Hero and Leander **15** Edward the Second **19** Tamburlaine the Great

Marmion
  author: **14** Sir Walter Scott
  character: **11** Lord Marmion **13** Ralph de Wilton **14** Clara Fitz-Clare **16** Archibald Douglas **19** Constance de Beverley

Marnie
  director: **15** Alfred Hitchcock
  cast: **10** Diane Baker **11** Sean Connery, Tippi Hedren

maroon 4 plum, wine **6** desert, strand **7** abandon, forsake, magenta **8** cast away, jettison **9** put ashore **10** cast ashore, terra cotta **11** brownish-red, leave behind **15** leave high and dry

Marple, Miss Jane
  detective created by: **14** Agatha Christie

Marquand, J P
  author of: **13** Wickford Point **18** The Late George Apley
  character: **6** Mr Moto

marquee 4 tent **6** awning, canopy **8** marquise

marred 6 ruined **7** damaged, injured, spoiled **8** impaired **9** blemished, destroyed **10** disfigured

marriage 7 wedding, wedlock **8** nuptials **9** matrimony
  god of: **4** Frey **5** Freyr, Hymen **9** Hymenaeus
  goddess of: **3** Fri **5** Frigg, Frija **6** Frigga, Tellus

marriage broker
  Yiddish: **8** shadchan **9** schatchen

marriage of convenience
  French: **19** mariage de convenance

Marriage of Figaro, The
  also: **15** Le Nozze di Figaro
  opera: **6** Mozart
  character: **7** Susanna **8** Countess **9** Cherubino, Dr Bartolo **10** Marcellina **13** Count Almaviva

Marriage of Figaro, The
  author: **12** Beaumarchais
  character: **6** Figaro **7** Suzanne **8** Cherubin **9** Marceline **10** Dr Bartholo **13** Count Almaviva **16** Countess Almaviva

married 3 wed **5** mated **6** joined, united, wedded **7** hitched, marital **8** combined, espoused **9** connubial **11** matrimonial, tied the knot

married woman
  German: **4** frau

marry 3 wed **7** espouse, make one **10** get spliced, tie the knot **13** join in wedlock **14** join in marriage, lead to the altar, take in marriage

Marryat, Frederick
  author of: **11** Peter Simple **16** Mr Midshipman Easy

Mars
  also: **6** Mamers, Mavors
  origin: **5** Roman
  god of: **3** war
  mother: **4** Juno
  wife: **5** Nerio
  epithet: **5** Ultor **8** Gradivus
  corresponds to: **4** Ares

Mars
  position: **6** fourth
  nickname: **9** Red Planet
  satellite: **6** Deimos, Phobos

Marseillaise 20 French national anthem

marsh 3 bog, fen **5** swamp **6** morass, slough **7** bottoms, wetland **8** quagmire **9** everglade, marshland, quicksand

Marsh, Dame Ngaio
  author of: **9** Dead Water **12** Final Curtain **13** Death at the Bar **14** Enter a Murderer **19** Singing in the Shrouds
  character: **10** Troy Alleyn **14** Roderick Alleyn

Marsh, Reginald
  born: **5** Paris **6** France
  artwork: **9** The Bowery **10** Pip and Flip **14** Why Not Use the El? **16** Tattoo and Haircut **17** Twenty-Cent Haircut

marshal 5 align, array, chief, group, order **6** deploy, draw up, gather, leader, line up, muster **7** arrange, collect, manager, sheriff **8** assemble, director, marechal, mobilize, organize **9** fire chief **10** law officer, supervisor **11** police chief **12** chief officer, field marshal **13** generalissimo

Marshall, George C
  served in: **3** WWI **4** WWII **9** Korean War, World War I **10** World War II **11** World War One, World War Two
  rank: **12** chief of staff **16** general of the army
  author of: **12** Marshall Plan
  secretary of: **5** state **7** defense
  winner of: **15** Nobel Peace Prize (1953)

Marshall, Penny
  husband: **9** Rob Reiner
  brother: **13** Garry Marshall
  born: **7** Bronx NY
  roles: **5** Myrna **12** The Odd Couple **14** Laverne DeFazio **17** Laverne and Shirley
  director: **3** Big **17** A League of Their Own **20** Riding in Cars with Boys

marshy 3 wet **4** miry **5** boggy, fenny, muddy **6** swampy **7** paludal, paludic **11** waterlogged

marsupial 5 koala **6** numbat, possum, wombat **7** cuscuse, opossum, wallaby **8** kangaroo **9** bandicoot, phalanger **14** Tasmanian devil

mart 4 show **6** market **8** exchange **9** trade fair, trade show **10** exposition

Martha
  sister: **4** Mary
  brother: **7** Lazarus
  home: **7** Bethany
martial 7 hostile, Spartan, warlike **8**
  militant, military **9** bellicose, combative, soldierly **10** pugnacious **11** belligerent, contentious
Martian Chronicles, The
  author: **11** Ray Bradbury
Martin, Dean
  real name: **16** Dino Paul Crocetti
  partner: **10** Jerry Lewis
  born: **14** Steubenville OH
  roles: **8** Matt Helm, Rio Bravo, The
  Caddy **9** The Stooge **10** Living It Up
  12 Four for Texas, Sailor Beware **14**
  Toys in the Attic **15** Some Came
  Running **16** Artists and Models
Martin, Mary
  son: **11** Larry Hagman
  born: **13** Weatherford TX
  roles: **6** I Do I Do **8** Peter Pan **12**
  Sound of Music, South Pacific
Martin, Steve
  born: **6** Waco TX
  roles: **7** The Jerk **8** Shopgirl **9** Bow-
  finger **11** Three Amigos **15** The Out-
  of-Towners **16** Father of the Bride **17**
  Cheaper by the Dozen, Pennies From
  Heaven, Saturday Night Live **19** The
  Man with Two Brains **20** Dead Men
  Don't Wear Plaid **26** Planes Trains
  and Automobiles
  author: **8** Shopgirl **10** Cruel Shoes,
  Pure Drivel **22** The Pleasure of My
  Company
Martin Chuzzlewit
  author: **14** Charles Dickens
  character: **5** Mercy **7** Charity **8** Tom
  Pinch **9** Pecksniff, Ruth Pinch, Sarah
  Gamp **10** Mark Tapley, Mary Graham **15** Jonas Chuzzlewit **17** Anthony Chuzzlewit
martinet 6 despot, tyrant **8** dictator **10**
  hard master, taskmaster **11** drillmas-
  ter, Simon Legree **12** little Caesar **13**
  authoritarian, drill-sergeant
Marty
  director: **11** Delbert Mann
  cast: **10** Betsy Blair **11** Joe De Santis
  14 Ernest Borgnine **15** Esther Minci-
  otti
  Oscar for: **5** actor (Borgnine) **7** picture
  script: **14** Paddy Chayefsky
martyr 5 saint **8** sufferer
martyrdom 5 agony **6** ordeal **7** anguish, torment, torture **9** bitter cup,
  suffering **10** affliction **11** cup of sorrow **13** crown of thorns
marvel 4 gape **6** be awed, rarity, wonder **7** miracle **8** be amazed **9** spectacle **10** phenomenon
Marvell, Andrew
  author of: **9** The Garden **16** To His
  Coy Mistress

marvelous, marvellous 4 A-one, fine
  5 grand, great, super **6** divine, lovely,
  superb **7** amazing **8** colossal, fabulous, heavenly, smashing, splendid **9**
  fantastic, first-rate, wonderful **10** phenomenal, remarkable, stupendous **11**
  astonishing, magnificent, outstanding,
  sensational **13** extraordinary
marvelous to relate
  Latin: **13** mirabile dictu
Marx, Bernard
  character in: **13** Brave New World
  author: **6** Huxley
Marx, Karl
  author of: **10** Das Kapital **18** Communist Manifesto (with Friedrich
  Engels)
Marx Brothers 5 Chico (Leonard),
  Gummo (Milton), Harpo (Adolph, Arthur) Zeppo (Herbert) **7** Groucho (Julius)
  costar: **14** Margaret Dumont
  born: **9** New York NY
  roles: **8** Coconuts, Duck Soup **11** The
  Big Store **13** Horse Feathers **14** A
  Day at the Races, Animal Crackers,
  Monkey Business **16** A Night at the
  Opera
  Groucho's TV show: **14** You Bet Your
  Life
Mary 6 Virgin **7** Madonna **8** Holy Mary
  9 Magdalene, of Cleopas **10** Virgin
  Mary **11** Mother of God, Regina Coeli
  13 Queen of Heaven **15** Mother of
  Sorrows **17** Mother of the Church
  mother: **4** Anna, Anne
  husband: **6** Joseph **7** Alpheus, Cleopas
  son: **4** Jude, Mark **5** Jesus, Moses, Simon **12** James the Less
  sister: **6** Martha
  brother: **7** Lazarus **8** Barnabas
  cousin: **9** Elizabeth
  home: **8** Nazareth
  visitor: **7** Gabriel
  flower: **4** lily **8** marigold
Mary
  author: **10** Sholem Asch
Maryland
  abbreviation: **2** MD
  nickname: **4** Free **7** Cockade **12** Old
  Line State
  capital: **9** Annapolis
  largest city: **9** Baltimore
  others: **5** Essex **6** Easton, Laurel,
  Towson **8** Aberdeen, Bethesda, Poco-
  moke **9** Frederick, Ocean City, Rock-
  ville **10** Cumberland, Hagerstown,
  Pikesville **11** Catonsville, College
  Park
  college: **4** Hood **7** Goucher, St John's
  9 Annapolis **10** Washington **11** Towson State **12** Johns Hopkins, Naval
  Academy
  feature:
    fort: **7** McHenry
    national battlesite: **8** Antietam

  presidential retreat: **9** Camp David
  race: **9** Preakness **12** Steeplechase
  racetrack: **5** Bowie **6** Butler, Laurel
    7 Pimlico
  tribe: **5** Conoy **9** Nanticoke
  people: **6** Wesort **8** Terrapin **10** Spiro
    Agnew **11** crawthumper **14** Sargent
    Shriver **15** Francis Scott Key
    explorer: **7** Calvert
  lake: **8** Patapsco **9** Deep Creek, Loch
    Raven, Pretty Boy **10** Rocky Gorge
    11 Triadelphia
  land rank: **11** forty-second
  mountain: **4** Dans **8** Piedmont **9** Blue
    Ridge **11** Appalachian
    highest point: **8** Backbone
  physical feature:
    bay: **10** Chesapeake
    sea: **8** Atlantic
    swamp: **7** Pocoson
    valley: **5** Great **10** Hagerstown
  river: **3** Elk **7** Chester, Potomac **8**
    Choptank, Patapsco, Patuxent, Poco-
    moke **11** Susquehanna
  state admission: **7** seventh
  state bird: **15** Baltimore oriole
  state fish: **11** striped bass
  state flower: **14** black-eyed Susan
  state motto: **22** Manly Deeds Wom-
    anly Words **43** Thou Hast Crowned
    Us With the Shield of Thy Good Will
  state song: **18** Maryland My Mary-
    land
  state tree: **8** white oak
Mary Poppins
  director: **15** Robert Stevenson
  based on story by: **9** P L Travers
  cast: **6** Ed Wynn **11** Dick Van Dyke
    (Bert), Glynis Johns **12** Julie An-
    drews **14** David Tomlinson **16** Her-
    mione Baddeley
  score: **13** Robert Sherman **14** Richard
    Sherman
  Oscar for: **4** song **5** score **7** actress
    (Andrews) **13** visual effects
  song: **14** Chim-chim-cheree
Mary Queen of Scots
  director: **14** Charles Jarrott
  cast: **12** Trevor Howard **13** Glenda
    Jackson (Elizabeth I), Timothy Dal-
    ton **14** Nigel Davenport **15** Patrick
    McGoohan, Vanessa Redgrave (Mary
    of Scotland)
Mary Tyler Moore Show, The
  character: **8** Lou Grant **9** Ted Baxter
    12 Gordon (Gordy) Howard, Mary
    Richards, Sue Ann Nivens **13** Bess
    Lindstrom **14** Marie Slaughter **15**
    Murray Slaughter **16** Phyllis Linds-
    trom, Rhoda Morgenstern **23** Geor-
    gette Franklin Baxter
  cast: **8** John Amos **9** Ted Knight **10**
    Betty White **11** Edward Asner **12**
    Gavin MacLeod, Georgia Engel **13**
    Joyce Bulifant, Lisa Gerritsen, Valerie
    Harper **14** Cloris Leachman
  setting: **11** Minneapolis
Mary Worth

creator: 8 Carey Orr **9** Dale Allen **10** Dale Connor **13** Allen Saunders
character: 4 Bill, Slim

Masaccio
real name: 26 Tommaso di Ser Giovanni di Mone
born: 5 Italy **27** Castel San Giovanni di Valdarno
artwork: 14 The Holy Trinity **15** The Tribute Money **24** The Expulsion from Paradise

Mascagni, Pietro
born: 5 Italy **7** Leghorn
composer of: 4 Iris **6** Nerone **7** Isabeau **10** Le Maschere **11** L'Amico Fritz **14** Il Piccolo Marat **19** Cavalleria Rusticana

masculine 4 bold, male **5** brave, hardy, husky, macho, manly **6** brawny, daring, manful, plucky, robust, strong, sturdy, virile **7** staunch, valiant **8** athletic, fearless, forceful, intrepid, muscular, powerful, resolute, vigorous **9** strapping **10** courageous **11** indomitable, self-reliant **12** stouthearted

Masefield, John
author of: 7 Cargoes **8** Sea Fever **16** Salt Water Ballads

Maseru
capital of: 7 Lesotho

mash 4 mush **5** crush, paste, puree, smash **6** squash **8** mishmash **9** pulverize

M*A*S*H (TV Series)
character: 10 (Capt) BJ Hunnicut, (Lt Col) Henry Blake, (Maj) Frank Burns **12** (Corp) Radar O'Reilly **13** Father (John) Mulcahy, (Capt Benjamin Franklin) Hawkeye Pierce, (Col) Sherman Potter **14** (Corp) Maxwell Klinger **15** (Maj Margaret) Hot Lips Houlihan **19** (Capt) Trapper John McIntyre **24** (Maj) Charles Emerson Winchester
cast: 8 Alan Alda **9** Jamie Farr **11** Harry Morgan, Loretta Swit, Mike Farrell, Wayne Rogers **12** Gary Burghoff **13** Larry Linville **15** McLean Stevenson **16** David Ogden Stiers **18** William Christopher
war: 6 Korean
MASH stands for: 26 Mobile Army Surgical Hospital
tent: 5 Swamp
theme: 17 Suicide Is Painless

M*A*S*H (Film)
director: 12 Robert Altman
cast: 10 Jo Ann Pflug **11** Elliot Gould (Trapper John McIntyre), Tom Skerritt (B J Hunnicut) **12** Gary Burghoff (Radar O'Reilly), Robert Duvall (Frank Burns) **14** Sally Kellerman (Margaret Hot Lips Houlihan) **16** Donald Sutherland (Hawkeye Pierce)

masjid 6 mosque

mask 4 hide, veil **5** blind, cloak, cover

6 domino, screen, shroud **7** conceal, cover-up, curtain, obscure **8** disguise **9** face guard, false face **10** camouflage, keep secret

Mask
director: 16 Peter Bogdanovich
cast: 4 Cher **10** Eric Stoltz (Rocky Dennis), Sam Elliott

masked 9 concealed, covered up, disguised **10** in disguise, masquerade

Masked Ball, A
also: 17 Un Ballo in Maschera
opera by: 5 Verdi
character:
first version: 9 Count Horn **10** King Gustav **12** Count Ribbing
second version: 3 Sam, Tom **13** Count Riccardo

masking 6 hiding **7** veiling **8** covering **9** eclipsing, obscuring **10** concealing, covering up

Mason, Bertha
character in: 8 Jane Eyre
author: 6 Bronte

Mason, James
wife: 6 Pamela
born: 7 England **12** Huddersfield
roles: 6 Lolita **7** Lord Jim **9** Bloodline **10** Georgy Girl, The Verdict **13** Heaven Can Wait **14** Humbert Humbert, Murder by Decree, The Seventh Veil **15** Prisoner of Zenda **16** North by Northwest **17** The Boys from Brazil

Mason, Marsha
husband: 9 Neil Simon
born: 9 St Louis MO
roles: 10 Chapter Two **11** Blume in Love **14** The Goodbye Girl **15** Max Dugan Returns **17** Cinderella Liberty

Masque of the Red Death, The
author: 13 Edgar Allan Poe

masquerade 4 mask, ruse, veil **5** cloak, cover, guise, trick **6** masque, pose as, screen, shroud **7** cover-up, pretext **8** artifice, pretense **9** bal masque **10** camouflage, masked ball, subterfuge **11** impersonate **12** harlequinade

Masquerade Party
host: 9 Bert Parks **10** Bud Collier **11** Peter Donald **12** Eddie Bracken, Robert Q Lewis **14** Douglas Edwards

mass, Mass 3 jam, lot, mob **4** body, bulk, cake, clot, heap, host, hunk, knot, lump, pack, pile **5** amass, batch, block, bunch, chunk, clump, corps, crowd, crush, group, horde, press, stack, troop **6** bundle, gather, matter, throng, weight **7** collect, pyramid **8** assemble, best part, main body, majority, material **9** aggregate, Eucharist, gathering, plurality **10** accumulate, assemblage, assortment, collection, concretion, congregate, cumulation, lion's share **11** aggregation, consolidate, greater part **12** accumulation, congre-

gation **13** Holy Communion, holy sacrament, preponderance **14** conglomeration

Massachusetts
abbreviation: 2 MA **4** Mass
nickname: 3 Bay **7** Puritan **9** Baked Bean, Old Colony
capital/largest city: 6 Boston
others: 4 Ayer, Lynn, Otis **5** Athol, Barre, Lenox, Salem **6** Agawam, Dedham, Groton, Nahant, Natick, Revere, Saugus, Woburn **7** Belmont, Beverly, Concord, Danvers, Everett, Holyoke, Ipswich, Medford, Peabody, Taunton, Waltham **8** Brockton, Chicopee, Cohasset, Plymouth, Scituate, Yarmouth **9** Arlington, Attleboro, Braintree, Brookline, Cambridge, Lexbridge, Lexington, Worcester **10** Gloucester, New Bedford, Pittsfield **11** Springfield **12** Provincetown, Williamstown
college: 3 MIT **5** Clark, Curry, Smith, Tufts **6** Babson **7** Amherst, Harvard, Simmons, Wheaton **8** Brandeis, Williams **9** Hampshire, Holy Cross, Merrimack, Radcliffe, Wellesley **11** Springfield **12** Mount Holyoke, Northeastern **13** Boston College
feature: 10 Walden Pond **12** Plymouth Rock
national seashore: 7 Cape Cod
village: 13 Old Sturbridge
tribe: 6 Nauset **8** Pocomtuc **10** Wampanoags
people: 8 Pilgrims **9** Amy Lowell, Elias Howe, John Kerry **10** Cyrus Field, Eli Whitney **11** Clara Barton, John Hancock, Samuel Adams, Samuel Morse **12** Henry Thoreau, Robert Lowell, Winslow Homer **13** James Whistler, Joseph Kennedy, Robert Kennedy **14** Emily Dickinson **15** Henry Cabot Lodge **16** Benjamin Franklin, Edward "Ted" Kennedy **17** Ralph Waldo Emerson **18** Bartholomew Gosnold, James Russell Lowell, Nathanial Hawthorne **19** Oliver Wendell Holmes, William Cullen Bryant **21** John Greenleaf Whittier
explorer: 8 Norsemen
island: 5 Duke's **9** Nantucket **13** Chappaquidick **15** Martha's Vineyard
lake: 5 Onota **7** Quabbin, Rohunta, Webster **8** Long Pond **11** Watuppa Pond **16** Assawompsett Pond **17** Chaubunagungamaug
land rank: 10 forty-fifth
mountain: 3 Tom **6** Brodie, Potter **7** Alander, Everett, Taconic **10** Berkshires
highest point: 8 Greylock
physical feature:
bay: 8 Buzzard's
cape: 3 Ann, Cod
sea: 8 Atlantic
president: 9 John Adams **14** Calvin Coolidge **15** John Quincy Adams **21**

John Fitzgerald Kennedy
river: 6 Nashua 7 Charles, Concord, Quaboag, Taunton 8 Chicopee 9 Deerfield, Merrimack 10 Blackstone, Housatonic 11 Connecticut
state admission: 5 sixth
state bird: 9 chickadee
state flower: 9 mayflower 15 trailing arbutus
state motto: 37 With the Sword She Seeks Peace Under Liberty 45 By the Sword We Seek Peace But Peace Only Under Liberty
state song: 22 All Hail to Massachusetts
state tree: 11 American elm

massacre 7 butcher, carnage 8 butchery, decimate 9 bloodbath, slaughter 10 mass murder 12 bloodletting

massage 3 rub 4 flex 5 chafe, knead 6 finger, handle, stroke 7 rubbing, rub down, stretch 8 kneading, stroking 10 manipulate 12 manipulation

Massasoit *see* 10 Wampanoags

Massenet, Jules Emile Frederic
born: 6 France 9 St Etienne
composer of: 5 Le Cid, Manon, Thais 7 Werther 9 Herodiade 11 David Rizzio 12 Don Quichotte 13 Le Roi de Lahore 21 Le Jongleur de Notre-Dame

masses 6 plebes, proles, rabble, the mob 7 the many 8 the crowd 9 hoi polloi, plebeians 11 the populace, the riffraff 12 the multitude 13 the common herd 14 the proletariat, the rank and file 15 the common people, the lower classes, the working class 16 the great unwashed

massive 4 huge, vast 5 ample, bulky, great, heavy, hefty, massy, solid 7 hulking, immense, mammoth, titanic, weighty 8 colossal, enormous, gigantic, imposing, towering, whopping 9 cyclopean, extensive, monstrous, ponderous 10 gargantuan, impressive, monumental, stupendous 11 elephantine, substantial

massiveness 4 bulk, size 6 volume, weight 7 bigness 8 enormity, hugeness, vastness 9 amplitude, bulkiness, greatness, immensity, largeness, magnitude

mast 4 main, nuts, pole, post, spar 5 spirit, staff, stick, stuff 6 acorns, pillar 9 beechnuts, chestnuts
type: 4 fore, main 6 jigger, mizzen
support: 4 bibb

master 3 ace 4 able, A-one, best, boss, curb, deft, head, lord, main, tame, whiz 5 check, chief, crack, grasp, owner, prime, ruler 6 bridle, choice, expert, genius, gifted, govern, leader, manage, subdue, wizard 7 conquer, control, excel at, head man, manager, primary, skilled, skipper, supreme 8 director, dominate, finished, governor,

masterly, overcome, overlord, overseer, regulate, suppress, talented, virtuoso 9 authority, conqueror, craftsman, first-rate, paramount, practiced, principal 10 controller, proficient, supervisor 12 get the hang of, ship's captain

Master and Commander: The Far Side of the World
author: 13 Patrick O'Brian
director: 9 Peter Weir
cast: 9 Billy Boyd (Barrett Bonden) 10 James D'Arcy (Tom Pullings) 11 Chris Larkin (Captain Howard), Paul Bettany (Stephen Maturin) 12 Russell Crowe (Jack Aubrey) 13 Edward Woodall (William Mowett)

Master Builder, The
author: 11 Henrik Ibsen
character: 5 Hilda 7 Solness

master craftsman 7 artisan 12 masterworker 13 skilled worker

masterful 4 able, deft 5 bossy 6 expert, superb 7 dynamic, skilled 8 finished, forceful, masterly, resolute, skillful, virtuoso 9 excellent 10 commanding 11 domineering, self-reliant 12 accomplished, strong-willed 13 authoritarian, self-confident

masterfulness 6 genius 10 capability, competence, excellence 11 proficiency

Master Melvin
nickname of: 6 Mel Ott

mastermind 4 plan, sage 6 direct, expert, genius, master, pundit, wizard 7 old hand, planner 8 conceive, director, engineer, organize, virtuoso 9 authority, initiator, organizer 10 specialist 11 moving force

Master of Ballantrae, The
author: 20 Robert Louis Stevenson
character: 4 Chew 5 Teach 9 MacKellar 11 Henry Durrie, James Durrie 12 Alison Graeme, Francis Burke, Secundra Dass

master of ceremonies 4 host 5 emcee 11 toastmaster

master of the family
Latin: 13 paterfamilias

masterpiece 5 jewel, prize 7 classic, paragon 8 monument, treasure 9 nonpareil 10 brainchild 11 chef d'oeuvre, ne plus ultra, prizewinner

Masterpiece Theater
host: 13 Alistair Cooke

master race
German: 10 Herrenvolk

Masters, Edgar Lee
author of: 19 Spoon River Anthology

Mastersingers of Nuremberg, The
also: 27 Die Meistersinger von Nurnberg
opera by: 6 Wagner
character: 9 Eva Pogner, Hans Sachs 10 Beckmesser 18 Walther von Stolzing

mastery 4 rule, sway 5 grasp 7 ability, command, control 8 deftness, whip hand 9 dominance, supremacy, upper hand 10 adroitness, attainment, domination, leadership 11 achievement, acquirement, proficiency, superiority 14 accomplishment

masticate 4 chew, gnaw 5 chomp, munch 6 nibble

Mastroianni, Marcello
born: 5 Italy 11 Fontana Liri
roles: 13 Eight and a Half 7 La Notte 11 La Dolce Vita, The Stranger, White Nights 19 Divorce Italian Style

mat 3 dim, pad, rug 4 dead, dull, flat 5 doily, muted 6 carpet, matrix, tangle 7 bedding, bolster, coaster, cushion, support 8 entangle 10 lackluster, lusterless
Japanese: 6 tatami

Mata Hari
real name: 21 Gertrud Margarete Zelle
worked as: 3 spy 6 dancer
worked for: 7 Germans
executed by: 6 French

match 3 fit 4 game, join, mate, meet, pair, peer, suit, twin, yoke 5 adapt, agree, equal, event, unite 6 couple, double, oppose 7 be alike, be equal, combine, connect, contend, contest, vie with 8 parallel 9 companion, duplicate, harmonize 10 correspond, equivalent, tournament 11 competition, counterpart

matched 5 equal 8 of a piece 9 identical 11 coordinated

matching 4 twin 5 equal 6 paired 10 equivalent 11 harmonizing 13 corresponding

matchless 4 rare 7 supreme 8 crowning, foremost, peerless, sterling, superior 9 exemplary, first rate, priceless, paramount, unequaled, unmatched, unrivaled 10 invaluable, preeminent, unbeatable, unexcelled 11 inestimable, superlative, unsurpassed 12 incomparable, unparalleled

matchmaker
Yiddish: 8 shadchan 9 schatchen

mate 3 pal 4 chum, twin, wife 5 buddy, crony, hubby, match 6 couple, friend, spouse 7 cohabit, comrade, consort, husband, pair off, partner 8 copulate, coworker, sidekick 9 associate, colleague, companion, duplicate 10 better half, equivalent 11 confederate, counterpart 12 fellow worker, ship's officer

materfamilias 15 mother of a family

material 5 stuff 6 matter 8 elements 9 substance 12 constituents

materialism 5 greed 12 covetousness 15 acquisitiveness

materialistic 6 greedy 8 covetous, grasping 11 acquisitive, unspiritual

materiality 9 existence 11 tangibility

materialization 5 ghost, shade 6 coming, wraith 7 phantom, specter 9 emergence 10 apparition, appearance 13 manifestation

materialize 4 loom, rise, show 5 bob up, issue, pop up 6 appear, crop up, emerge, turn up 9 come forth 10 burst forth 11 come to light, spring forth 12 come into view

materially 7 vitally 8 palpably, tangibly 9 in the main, seriously 10 monetarily 11 corporeally, essentially, financially, in substance 12 considerably, emphatically 13 significantly, substantially 14 for the most part

material possessions 6 assets, estate, wealth 7 fortune 8 property 10 belongings 12 worldly goods

material proof 8 evidence 13 documentation

materials 4 data 5 cloth, facts, notes, tools 6 stocks, stores, timber 7 fabrics, figures 8 concrete, dry goods, supplies, textiles 9 citations, equipment, machinery, yard goods 10 essentials, piece goods, quotations, references 11 impressions 12 observations 15 bricks and mortar

materiel 4 gear 6 stores 8 supplies 9 equipment, materials 10 provisions 16 military supplies

Mater Matuta *see* 6 Matuta

maternal 4 fond 6 doting 8 motherly 9 of a mother, shielding 10 motherlike, protective, sheltering

maternity 5 labor 8 delivery 9 pregnancy 10 childbirth, motherhood 11 parturition 12 accouchement, childbearing

mathematical, mathematic 5 exact, rigid 6 strict 7 precise 8 accurate, rigorous, unerring 10 meticulous, scientific, scrupulous 11 punctilious, well-defined 13 computational

mathematician
 American: 5 Aiken 6 Wiener
 British: 6 Newton 7 Babbage
 French: 6 Fermat 9 D'Alembert, Descartes
 German: 5 Frege, Gauss 6 Bessel 7 Hilbert
 Greek: 6 Euclid, Thales 11 Anaximander
 Norwegian: 4 Abel
 Swiss: 5 Euler 9 Bernoulli

Mathewson, Christy
 nickname: 5 Matty 6 Big Six
 sport: 8 baseball
 position: 7 pitcher
 team: 13 New York Giants

Matholwych
 king of: 7 Ireland
 wife: 7 Branwen

matinee 9 early show 16 early performance 20 afternoon performance

Matisse, Henri Emile Benoit
 born: 6 France 16 Chateau Cambresis (Le Cateau)
 artwork: 5 Dance, Music 8 The Slave 10 Odalisques 11 Joie de Vivre 12 Harmony in Red, La Serpentine 13 Head with Tiara, The Open Window 15 Bathers by a River, Memory of Oceanie, Woman with the Hat 16 Heads of Jeannette 19 Torso with Arms Raised 20 Goldfish and Sculpture

matriarch 7 dowager 10 female head, grande dame 11 female ruler 12 female leader 13 materfamilias

matriculate 4 join 5 enter 6 enlist, enroll, sign up 7 check in 8 register

matriculation 9 signing up 10 enrollment 12 registration

matrimonial 6 bridal, wedded, wifely 7 marital, married, nuptial, spousal 8 conjugal, hymeneal 9 affianced, connubial, husbandly 11 epithalamic

matrimony 7 wedlock 8 marriage 11 holy wedlock

Matrix, The
 director: 13 Andy Wachowski 14 Larry Wachowski
 cast: 11 Hugo Weaving (Agent Smith), Keanu Reeves (Neo) 12 Gloria Foster (Oracle) 13 Joe Pantoliano (Cypher) 14 Carrie-Anne Moss (Trinity) 17 Laurence Fishburne (Morpheus)

matrix 3 die 4 cast, form, mold 5 frame, punch, stamp

Matrix Reloaded, The
 director: 13 Andy Wachowski 14 Larry Wachowski
 cast: 8 Ian Bliss (Bane), Nona Gaye (Zee) 10 Collin Chou (Seraph), Paul Cotter (Corrupt) 11 Anthony Wong (Ghost), Harry Lennix (Lock), Hugo Weaving (Agent Smith), Keanu Reeves (Neo) 12 Gloria Foster (Oracle) 13 Joe Pantoliano (Cypher), Lambert Wilson (Merovingian), Randall Duk Kim (Keymaker) 14 Carrie-Anne Moss (Trinity), Helmut Bakaitis (the Architect), Monica Bellucci (Persephone) 15 Harold Perrineau (Link) 16 Jada Pinkett Smith 17 Laurence Fishburne (Morpheus)

Matrix Revolutions, The
 director: 13 Andy Wachowski 14 Larry Wachowski
 cast: 8 Ian Bliss (Bane), Nona Gaye (Zee) 9 Mary Alice (Oracle) 10 Collin Chou (Seraph), Paul Cotter (Corrupt) 11 Anthony Wong (Ghost), Harry Lennix (Lock), Hugo Weaving (Agent Smith), Keanu Reeves (Neo) 13 Joe Pantoliano (Cypher), Lambert Wilson (Merovingian), Nathaniel Lees (Mifune), Randall Duk Kim

(Keymaker), Tanveer K Atwal (Sati) 14 Carrie-Anne Moss (Trinity), Helmut Bakaitis (the Architect), Monica Bellucci (Persephone) 15 Harold Perrineau (Link), Henry Blasingame (Deux Ex Machina) 16 Jada Pinkett Smith (Niobe) 17 Laurence Fishburne (Morpheus)

matron 4 dame 5 madam 7 dowager 8 forelady, mistress, overseer 9 forewoman 10 directress 11 housekeeper 12 married woman 14 superintendent

matter 3 fix 4 gist, snag, text 5 count, drift, event, sense, stuff, theme, thing, topic 6 affair, crisis, import, moment, object, scrape, strait, thesis 7 content, dilemma, episode, essence, purport, signify, subject, trouble 8 argument, business, elements, exigency, material, obstacle, quandary 9 adventure, emergency, happening, situation, substance 10 difference, difficulty, experience, impediment, importance, occurrence, perplexity, proceeding 11 carry weight, consequence, predicament, transaction 12 circumstance, significance

matter-of-course 5 usual 6 common 7 routine 8 everyday, ordinary, standard 9 customary 11 commonplace, established

matter-of-fact 4 real 5 blunt, frank 6 candid, direct 7 factual, literal, mundane, natural, prosaic 8 ordinary, sensible 9 outspoken, practical, pragmatic, realistic 10 hardheaded, nononsense, unaffected, uninspired, unromantic 11 commonplace, common-sense, down-to-earth, straight-out 13 unimaginative, unsentimental 15 straightforward

matter-of-factness 10 detachment 11 impassivity 12 practicality 13 impassiveness 17 unimaginativeness

Matthau, Walter
 real name: 13 Walter Matthow 23 Walter Matuschanskavasky
 born: 9 New York NY
 roles: 5 Kotch 8 A New Leaf, Out to Sea 9 Hanging Up 10 Plaza Suite 11 Pete n Tillie 12 Bad News Bears, Ensign Pulver, Grumpy Old Men, The Front Page, The Odd Couple 14 Grumpier Old Men 15 California Suite, The Sunshine Boys 16 The Fortune Cookie 22 A Guide for the Married Man
 co-star: 10 Jack Lemmon
 character: 12 Oscar Madison

Matthew 7 apostle
 father: 7 Alpheus
 also called: 4 Levi
 wrote: 6 Gospel

Matthiessen, Peter
 author of: 10 Sand Rivers 14 The Snow Leopard

maturation 6 growth **8** fruition, ripening **9** growing up

mature 4 ripe **5** adult, bloom, grown, manly, of age, ready, ripen **6** flower, grow up, mellow, nubile, virile **7** blossom, develop, grown-up, matured, womanly **8** finished, maturate, seasoned **9** come of age, completed, full-blown, full-grown, perfected, practiced **10** middle-aged **11** become adult, experienced, full-fledged, in one's prime **12** marriageable

Mature, Victor
  born: 12 Louisville KY
  roles: 7 The Robe **11** After the Fox, Kiss of Death **12** Cry of the City, One Million BC **16** Samson and Delilah **19** Androcles and the Lion

matured 3 big **4** aged, ripe **5** adult, grown **6** formed **7** ripened **8** flowered, mellowed, seasoned **9** blossomed, developed, full-blown, full-grown **11** full-fledged

maturity 7 manhood **8** legal age, majority, practice, ripeness **9** adulthood, composure, full bloom, readiness, seasoning, womanhood **10** completion, experience, full growth, maturation, matureness, perfection **11** culmination, fulfillment **12** age of consent

Matuta
  origin: 5 Roman
  goddess of: 3 sea **4** dawn **7** harbors **10** childbirth
  called: 11 Mater Matuta

Maude
  character: 5 Carol **7** Phillip **10** Henry Evans **12** Florida Evans, Maude Findlay, Mrs Naugatuck **13** Walter Findlay **14** Dr Arthur Harmon **20** Vivian Cavender Harmon
  cast: 8 Bill Macy, John Amos **10** Conrad Bain **11** Esther Rolle **13** Brian Morrison, Rue McClanahan **14** Beatrice Arthur, Kraig Metzinger **15** Adrienne Barbeau **16** Hermione Baddeley
  spinoff from: 14 All in the Family
  spinoff: 9 Good Times

maudlin 5 gushy, mushy, teary **6** slushy **7** gushing, mawkish, tearful **8** bathetic **9** emotional **10** lachrymose **11** sentimental **13** overemotional

maudlinism 6 bathos **11** mawkishness **14** sentimentalism, sentimentality

Maugham, W Somerset
  author of: 9 The Circle **10** Our Betters **11** Cakes and Ale **12** Miss Thompson **13** The Razor's Edge **14** Of Human Bondage **15** The Constant Wife **18** The Moon and Sixpence **21** Lady Frederick Ashenden

maul 4 beat **5** stomp **6** batter, beat up, bruise, mangle, pummel, thrash **7** rough up **9** manhandle **10** knock about

Mauldin, Bill
  creator/artist of: 7 Up Front **12** Willie and Joe

Mau Mau 13 secret society
  of: 6 Kikuyu
  in: 5 Kenya

maunder 4 loaf **5** drift, run on, stray **6** babble, dawdle, gabble, gibber, ramble, wander **7** blather, meander, prattle, saunter **8** flounder, ramble on, straggle **9** go on and on, hem and haw **10** dillydally

maundering 7 diffuse **8** rambling **9** wandering **10** digressive, disjointed, roundabout **14** drift, run on, stray **6** babble, dawdle, gabble, gibber, ramble, wander **7** blather, meander, prattle, saunter **8** flounder, ramble on, straggle **9** go on and on, hem and haw **10** dillydally

Maupassant, Guy de
  author of: 6 Belami **9** Ball of Fat, Mont-Oriol **11** A Woman's Life, The Necklace **12** Ball of Tallow **16** Mademoiselle Fifi

Mauriac, Francois
  author of: 8 Genitrix **10** The Egoists **12** Viper's Tangle **15** A Kiss to the Leper, The Desert of Love **20** A Woman of the Pharisees

Mauritania
  capital/largest city: 10 Nouakchott
  others: 4 Atar **5** Kaedi, Rosso **6** Fderik **7** Akjoujt **10** Nouadhibou
  division: 5 Sahel **7** Chemama
  monetary unit: 5 khoum **7** ouguiya
  highest point: 11 Kediat Idjil
  river: 7 Senegal
  sea: 8 Atlantic
  physical feature:
    desert: 6 Sahara
    valley: 7 Chemama **12** Senegal River
  people: 4 Arab, Fula, Moor **5** Black, Fulbe, Wolof **6** Bafour, Berber, Fulani **7** African, Soninke, Tukulor **8** Sarakole **9** Sarakolle **10** Toucouleur **12** Halphoolaren
    leader: 4 Luly **5** Salek **6** Daddah **8** Haidalla
    ruler: 6 France **9** Almoravid **14** Kingdom of Ghana
  language: 4 Fula **5** Wolof **6** Arabic, French **7** Phoolor, Tukulor **8** Fulfulde, Mandingo **9** Sarakolle, Hassaniya
  religion: 5 Islam
  place:
    mosque: 5 Grand
  feature:
    beehive hut: 4 ruga
    priest-teacher: 8 marabout
    waterskin: 6 guerba
  food:
    dish: 7 meshuri
    tea: 5 attay

Mauritius
  other name: 11 Ile de France
  capital/largest city: 9 Port Louis
  others: 6 Reduit **8** Curepipe **9** Mahebourg **13** Quartre Bornes **19** Grande Riviere Sud-Est
  head of state: 14 British monarch **15** governor general
  monetary unit: 4 cent **5** rupee
  island: 3 Est **4** Flat **5** Ambre, Cerf's, Morne, Round **7** Agalega, Serpent **9** Mauritius, Rodrigues, Rodriguez, St Brandon **9** Gunner's Quoin **15** Cargados Carajos
  highest point: 27 Piton de la Petite Riviere Noire
  sea: 6 Indian
  people: 6 Creole, French, Indian **7** African, Chinese **8** European **13** Indo-Mauritian
    leader: 8 Jugnauth **9** Ramgoolam
    ruler: 5 Dutch **6** French **7** English
  language: 4 Urdu **5** Hindi, Tamil **6** Creole, French

mausoleum 10 family tomb **11** stately tomb **18** sepulchral monument

mauve 4 plum, puce **5** lilac **6** violet **8** lavender **11** light purple **12** bluish purple

maverick 5 loner **8** yearling **9** dissenter, dissident, eccentric **11** independent **13** individualist, noncomformist

Maverick
  character: 12 Bart Maverick, Bret Maverick **13** Brent Maverick **16** Samantha Crawford **24** Cousin Beauregard Maverick
  cast: 9 Jack Kelly **10** Roger Moore **11** James Garner **13** Diane Brewster, Robert Colbert

maw 4 craw, crop, jaws **5** mouth **6** gullet, muzzle, throat

mawkish 7 gushy, mushy, teary **7** maudlin, tearful **9** emotional, nostalgic, schmaltzy **10** lachrymose **11** sentimental **15** oversentimental

mawkishness 4 mush **5** slush **6** bathos **9** mushiness, soppiness **10** maudlinism, slushiness **14** sentimentalism, sentimentality

maxim 3 saw **4** rule **5** adage, axiom, motto **6** old saw, saying, truism **7** proverb **8** aphorism, apothegm **9** platitude

Maximes
  author: 23 Francois La Rochefoucauld

Maxims of the Law
  author: 12 Francis Bacon

maximum 3 top **4** most **6** utmost **7** highest, largest, maximal, optimum, supreme **8** foremost, greatest **9** paramount **11** unsurpassed

Maxwell, Elsa 6 author **7** hostess **9** socialite **10** party-giver **23** "The hostess with the mostes'"

May
  characteristic: 7 Maypole **13** queen of the May

flower: 8 hawthorn 15 lily of the valley
French: 3 Mai
gem: 7 emerald
German: 3 Mai
holiday: 6 May Day (1) 10 Mother's Day (2nd Sunday) 11 Memorial Day (last Monday) 14 Armed Forces Day (3rd Saturday)
Italian: 6 Maggio
number of days: 9 thirty-one
origin of name: 4 Maia
  Roman goddess of: 6 spring
place in year:
  Gregorian: 5 fifth
  Roman: 5 third
saying: 27 April showers bring May flowers
Spanish: 4 Mayo
Zodiac sign: 6 Gemini, Taurus
May, Elaine
real name: 12 Elaine Berlin
partner: 11 Mike Nichols
born: 14 Philadelphia PA
roles: 8 A New Leaf 15 California Suite
director of: 16 The Heartbreak Kid
writer/director of: 8 A New Leaf
Maya
city: 4 Coba 5 Tulum, Uxmal 6 Akumal, Cuello, Izamal 8 Calakmul, Palenque 11 Chichen Itza
conqueror: 8 Alvarado
day: 5 uayeb
language family: 5 Mayan 10 Maya-Quiche
location: 5 Tikal 6 Belize, Mexico 7 Chiapas, Mayapan, Tabasco, Yucatan 8 Honduras 9 Guatemala 11 Chichen Itza 14 Central America
month: 5 uinal 6 uninal
noted for: 9 astronomy 12 architecture 19 hieroglyphic writing
rain god: 4 Chac 5 Chaac 7 Chac Mol 8 Chac Mool
ruins: 9 Yaxchilan 20 Temple of Inscriptions
underworld: 7 Xibalba
year: 4 haab
maybe 6 mayhap 7 perhaps 8 feasibly, possibly 9 perchance 10 God willing, imaginably 11 conceivably 12 peradventure
Maybe
author: 14 Lillian Hellman
Mayberry RFD
character: 5 Alice 7 Aunt Bee 8 Sam Jones 9 Mike Jones 10 Goober Pyle 11 Emmett Clark 13 Howard Sprague, Millie Swanson
cast: 8 Ken Berry 10 Jack Dodson 11 Buddy Foster, Paul Hartman 13 Alice Ghostley, Arlene Golonka, Frances Bavier, George Lindsey
mayfly
varieties: 5 small 6 stream 9 burrowing

mayhem 4 maim 6 felony 7 battery, cripple 8 mutilate, violence 9 crippling, dismember 10 mutilation 13 disfigurement
may he rest in peace
Latin: 16 requiescat in pace
may it do good
Latin: 6 prosit
Mayo, Virginia
real name: 13 Virginia Jones
husband: 12 Michael O'Shea
born: 9 St Louis MO
roles: 17 The West Point Story 22 The Best Years of Our Lives 26 The Secret Life of Walter Mitty
Mayor of Casterbridge, The
author: 11 Thomas Hardy
character: 13 Donald Farfrae, Richard Newson 14 Lucetta Le Sueur 15 Michael Henchard 19 Elizabeth Jane Newson, Susan Henchard-Newson
Mays, Willie
nickname: 9 Say Hey Kid
sport: 8 baseball
position: 11 center field
team: 11 New York Mets 13 New York Giants 18 San Francisco Giants
may she live forever
Latin: 12 esto perpetua
motto of: 5 Idaho
may she rest in peace
Latin: 16 requiescat in pace
maze 5 snarl 6 jungle, tangle 7 complex, meander, network 9 labyrinth 11 convolution
mazel tov 8 good luck
Mbabane
capital of: 9 Swaziland
McBeal, Ally *see* 10 Ally McBeal
McCambridge, Mercedes
real name: 32 Carlotta Mercedes Agnes McCambridge
born: 8 Joliet IL
roles: 5 Giant 8 Cimarron 11 Touch of Evil 14 All the King's Men 15 A Farewell to Arms 18 Suddenly Last Summer
McCarey, Leo
director of: 8 Duck Soup 10 Going My Way (Oscar) 13 The Awful Truth (Oscar) 15 Ruggles of Red Gap 17 The Bells of St Mary's
McCarthy, Mary
author of: 8 The Group
sister of: 5 Kevin
McCay, Winsor
creator/artist of: 23 Little Nemo in Slumberland
McClellan, George B
nickname: 9 Little Mac 16 The Young Napoleon
served in: 8 Civil War 10 Mexican War
side: 5 Union
commander of: 16 Army of the Potomac

battle: 8 Antietam 18 Peninsular campaign
governor of: 9 New Jersey
McCloud
character: 10 Sam McCloud 13 Chris Coughlin, (Sgt) Joe Broadhurst 14 Peter B Clifford
cast: 8 JD Cannon 11 Terry Carter 12 Dennis Weaver, Diana Muldaur
McClure, Darrell
creator/artist of: 17 Little Annie Rooney
McCrea, Joel
wife: 10 Frances Dee
born: 12 Los Angeles CA
roles: 11 Buffalo Bill 14 Palm Beach Story 16 Sullivan's Travels, The Great Man's Lady 17 Reaching for the Sun, The More the Merrier 20 Foreign Correspondent
McCreary, Fainy (Mac)
character in: 3 USA
author: 9 Dos Passos
McCullers, Carson
author of: 17 The Mortgaged Heart 18 Member of the Wedding 21 The Ballad of the Sad Cafe 23 Reflections in a Golden Eye, The Heart Is a Lonely Hunter
McCullough, Colleen
author of: 3 Tim 8 The Touch 10 Morgan's Run 13 Master's of Rome (series), The Thornbirds 15 The October Horse 19 An Indecent Obsession
McCutcheon, George Barr
author of: 9 Graustark
McEvoy, JP
creator/artist of: 10 Dixie Dugan
McGinley, Phyllis
author of: 12 Three Decades 15 A Pocketful of Wry 24 The Horse Who Lived Upstairs
McHale's Navy
character: 7 Christy 9 Willy Moss 11 Fuji Kobiaji, Happy Haines 12 Harrison (Tinker) Bell, Lester Gruber 13 Virgil Farrell, (Ensign) Charles Parker, (Lt Cdr) Quinton McHale 14 (Lt) Elroy Carpenter 18 (Capt) Wallace B Binghamton
cast: 8 Joe Flynn 9 Tim Conway 10 Billy Sands, Gary Vinson, John Wright, Yoshio Yoda 11 Bob Hastings, Edson Stroll 12 Gavin MacLeod 14 Carl Ballantine, Ernest Borgnine
McKenna, Siobhan
born: 7 Belfast, Ireland
roles: 11 King of Kings 13 Doctor Zhivago 14 Of Human Bondage 24 Playboy of the Western World
McKim, Charles M
architect of: 27 Lutheran Church of the Redeemer (Houston)
McKim, Mead, and White
partners: 13 Stanford White 18

Charles Follen McKim **21** William Rutherford Mead
architects of: 11 Century Club **14** University Club, Washington Arch **17** Vanderbilt Mansion **18** Columbia University (NYC) **19** Boston Public Library, Pennsylvania Station (NYC), (first) Madison Square Garden (NYC) **21** New York Herald Building, Pierpont Morgan Library (NYC) **31** Madison Square Presbyterian Church
style: 7 Shingle **18** Italian Renaissance

McKinley, William
nickname: 13 Major McKinley
presidential rank: 11 twenty-fifth
party: 10 Republican
state represented: 2 OH
defeated: 4 (Eugene Victor) Debs **5** (Seth Hockett) Ellis, (William Jennings) Bryan **6** (John McCauley) Palmer, (Wharton) Barker **7** (Charles Eugene) Bentley, (John Granville) Woolley, (Jonah Fitz Randolph) Leonard **8** (Charles Horatio) Matchett, (Joseph Francis) Malloney, (Joshua) Levering
vice president: 6 (Garret Augustus) Hobart **9** (Theodore) Roosevelt
cabinet:
　state: 3 (John Milton) Hay, (William Rufus) Day **7** (John) Sherman
　treasury: 4 (Lyman Judson) Gage
　war: 4 (Elihu) Root **5** (Russell Alexander) Alger
　attorney general: 4 (Philander Chase) Knox **6** (John William) Griggs **7** (Joseph) McKenna
　navy: 4 (John Davis) Long
　postmaster general: 4 (James Albert) Gary **5** (Charles Emory) Smith
　interior: 5 (Cornelius Newton) Bliss **9** (Ethan Allen) Hitchcock
　agriculture: 6 (James) Wilson
born: 7 Niles OH
died: 9 Buffalo NY
　died by: 13 assassination
buried: 8 Canton OH
education:
　college: 10 Allegheny
　law school: 6 Albany
religion: 9 Methodist
political career: 24 US House of Representatives
　governor of: 4 Ohio
civilian career: 6 lawyer
military service: 7 captain **8** Civil War **11** brevet major
notable events of lifetime/term:
　Act: 13 Dingley Tariff
　Peace Conference: 5 Hague
　Treaty of: 5 Paris
　war with: 5 Spain
father: 7 William
mother: 5 Nancy (Campbell Allison)
siblings: 4 Anna, Mary **5** Abner, Helen, James **10** Abbie Celia **12** Da-

vid Allison **14** Sarah Elizabeth
wife: 3 Ida (Saxton)
children: 3 Ida **9** Katherine

McManus, George
creator/artist of: 12 The Newlyweds **16** Bringing Up Father

McMillan, Edwin Mattison
field: 7 physics **9** chemistry
developed: 16 synchrocyclotron
awarded: 10 Nobel Prize

McMillan and Wife
character: 7 Mildred **13** Sally McMillan **14** (Sgt) Charles Enright **15** (Commissioner) Stewart McMillan
cast: 10 John Schuck, Rock Hudson **11** Nancy Walker **15** Susan Saint James

McMurtry, Larry
author of: 10 Boone's Lick, Texasville **12** Buffalo Girls, Cadillac Jack, Comanche Moon, Dead Man's Walk, Lonesome Dove **14** Horseman Pass By **15** Leaving Cheyenne, Streets of Laredo **17** Terms of Endearment **18** The Last Picture Show

McPhee, John
author of: 15 The Founding Fish **16** In Suspect Terrain **20** Coming into the Country **23** The Curve of Binding Energy **26** Encounters with the Archdruid

McQueen, Steve
real name: 21 Terrence Steven McQueen
wife: 10 Ali MacGraw
born: 8 Slater MO **14** Indianapolis IN
roles: 7 Bullitt, The Blob **8** Papillon **14** The Great Escape, The Sand Pebbles **16** The Cincinnati Kid **17** Thomas Crown Affair, Wanted Dead or Alive **19** The Magnificent Seven

McTeague
author: 11 Frank Norris

mea culpa 7 my fault **14** through my fault

Mead, Margaret
author of: 14 My Earlier Years **16** Blackberry Winter **18** Coming of Age in Samoa **20** Growing Up in New Guinea **42** Sex and Temperament in Three Primitive Societies
husband: 14 Gregory Bateson

Meade, George Gordon
served in: 8 Civil War **10** Mexican War
side: 5 Union
battle: 7 Bull Run **8** Antietam **10** Gettysburg **13** South Mountain **14** Fredericksburg **16** Chancellorsville **18** Peninsular campaign
commander of: 16 Army of the Potomac

meadow 3 lea **4** mead, park **5** field, green **6** forage **7** herbage, pasture, savanna **9** grassland, pasturage

meager 4 bare, lean, slim, thin **5** scant, short, spare, token **6** little, pal-

try, scanty, scarce, skimpy, slight, sparse **7** scrimpy, slender, stinted, wanting **9** deficient **10** inadequate **12** insufficient **13** insubstantial

meagerness 8 sparsity **9** smallness **10** inadequacy, measliness, scantiness, skimpiness, sparseness **13** insufficiency **14** insignificance

meal 4 bran, chow, diet, eats, fare, food, grub, menu **5** feast, flour, grits **6** farina, groats, repast, spread **7** banquet, cooking, cuisine, oatmeal **8** cornmeal, victuals **10** bill of fare **11** nourishment, refreshment

mealymouthed 6 unsure **7** devious **8** hesitant **9** deceptive, insincere

mean 3 low, par, say **4** base, evil, norm, plan, poor, rude, rule, vile, want, wish **5** aim at, cheap, close, cruel, imply, nasty, petty, small, tight, venal **6** denote, flimsy, greedy, hint at, intend, malign, medium, menial, normal, paltry, sleazy, sordid, stingy, tell off, trashy, unfair **7** average, balance, betoken, dream of, drive at, express, hoggish, inhuman, miserly, point to, propose, purpose, regular, resolve, selfish, signify, squalid, suggest, think of, trivial, vicious **8** aspire to, gimcrack, grasping, indicate, inferior, inhumane, intimate, low-grade, picayune, piddling, pitiless, rubbishy, say truly, shameful, standard, stand for, trifling, uncaring, wretched **9** illiberal, low-paying, malicious, mercenary, merciless, miserable, niggardly, penurious, symbolize, unfeeling **10** avaricious, compromise, despicable, have in mind, have in view, jerrybuilt, low-ranking, malevolent, pinchpenny, second-rate, ungenerous, villainous **11** closefisted, commonplace, disgraceful, happy medium, hardhearted, self-seeking, small-minded, tightfisted, unimportant **12** contemptible, disagreeable, dishonorable **13** insignificant, unsympathetic **15** inconsequential

meander 4 loop, rove, wind **5** snake, stray, twist **6** circle, ramble, spiral, wander, zigzag **8** undulate **9** convolute, corkscrew

meandering 7 devious, sinuous, turning, winding **8** indirect, rambling, tortuous, twisting **9** wandering **10** circuitous, roundabout, serpentine

meaning 3 aim, end **4** gist, goal, hint, meat, pith, plan, view **5** drift, force, point, sense, value, worth **6** burden, design, intent, object, scheme, thrust, upshot **7** content, essence, pointer, purport, purpose **9** intention, substance **10** denotation, indication, intimation, suggestion **11** implication **12** significance **15** sum and substance

meaningful 4 deep **5** meaty, pithy **6** useful **7** pointed, serious **8** eloquent, explicit, pregnant **9** designing, important **10** expressive, gratifying, portentous, purposeful, suggestive, worthwhile **11** significant, substantial **13** consequential

meaningless 5 trite **6** absurd, paltry, stupid **7** aimless, fatuous, foolish, idiotic, shallow, trivial, useless **8** baffling, piddling, puzzling **9** enigmatic, facetious, frivolous, illegible, senseless, valueless, worthless **10** incoherent, mystifying, perplexing **11** bewildering, inscrutable, nonsensical, purposeless, unessential, unimportant **12** impenetrable, inexplicable, inexpressive, preposterous **13** insignificant, unsubstantial **14** undecipherable

Mean Joe
   nickname of: 9 Joe Greene

means 3 way **4** jack, mode **5** bread, dough, funds, money **6** avenue, course, income, method, resort, riches, wealth **7** capital, dollars, measure, process, revenue **8** property **9** affluence, long green, resources, substance **11** alternative, wherewithal

mean-spirited 3 low **4** base, poor, vile **5** cheap, nasty, petty, small, snide, sorry, tight, venal **6** abject, measly, paltry, scurvy, shabby, sordid, stingy **7** ignoble, miserly, selfish, vicious **8** tightwad, wretched **9** miserable, penurious **10** ungenerous **12** parsimonious

Mean Streets
   director: 14 Martin Scorsese
   cast: 11 Amy Robinson, David Proval **12** Harvey Keitel, Robert DeNiro

meantime 7 interim **8** interval **9** meanwhile

meanwhile 8 meantime **12** concurrently, in the interim **13** at the same time **14** simultaneously

measurable 10 assessable, computable, mensurable, reckonable **11** appraisable **12** determinable

measure 3 act, law **4** bill, plan, rule, size, step, time **5** bound, clock, gauge, judge, limit, means, plumb, quota, range, scale, scope, share, sound, value **6** amount, assess, course, degree, design, extent, method, resort, scheme, survey **7** portion, project **8** appraise, evaluate, proposal, quantity **9** allotment, allowance, enactment, procedure, restraint, yardstick **10** limitation, moderation, proceeding, temperance

measure, unit of
   of Afghanistan: 3 paw, sir **5** jerib, karoh **6** khurds **7** kharwar
   of Algeria: 3 pik **5** rebis, tarri **6** termin
   of Argentina: 4 sino **5** legua **6** cuadra, lastre **7** manzana
   of Australia: 4 arna, naut, saum
   of Austria: 4 fass, fuss, joch, mass,

muth, yoke **5** halbe, linie, meile, metze, pfiff, punkt **6** achtel, becher, leipoa, seidel **7** klafter, viertel **8** dreiling **12** futtermassel
   of Belgium: 3 vat **4** aune, pied **5** carat **6** perche **8** boisseau
   of Bolivia: 6 league **7** celemin
   of Borneo: 7 gantang
   of Brazil: 2 pe **4** moio, sack, vara **5** braca, legoa, milha, tonel **6** canada, cuarto, quarto, tarefa **7** garrafa **8** alqueire
   of Bulgaria: 3 oka, oke **5** krine, lekhe, likhe
   of Canada: 3 ton **5** minot, perch, point **6** arpent **7** chainon
   of the Canary Islands: 8 fanegada
   of Chile: 4 vara **5** legua, linea **6** cuadra **7** fanega
   of China: 3 cho, fan, fen, pau, tou, tun, yan, yin **4** chek, chih, fang, kish, papa, quei, shih, teke, tsan, tsun **5** catty, chang, ching, sheng, shing **6** chupak, gungli, kungho, kungmu, tching **7** kungfen, kungyin **8** kungchih, kungshih **9** kungching
   of Colombia: 4 vara **7** azumbre, celemin
   of Costa Rica: 4 vara **5** cafiz, cahiz **6** fanega, tercia **7** cajuela, cantaro, manzana **8** caballeria
   of Cuba: 4 vara **5** bocoy, cocoy, tarea **6** cordel, fanega **10** caballeria
   of former Czechoslovakia: 3 lan **4** mira **5** korec, liket, stopa **6** merice, strych
   of Denmark: 3 ell, fod, mil, pot **4** alen **5** album, anker, kande, linje, paegl **7** landmil, oltonde, ortonde, skieppe, viertel **8** fjerding **9** ottingkar **10** korntonde
   of the Dominican Republic: 3 ona **5** tarea **6** fanega
   of Ecuador: 5 libra **6** cuadra, fanega
   of Egypt: 3 apt, dra, hen, rob **4** arab, dira, draa, khet, nief, ocha, roub, theb, wudu **5** abdat, ardab, cubit, farde, fedan, keleh, kerat, kilah, sahme **6** artaba, aurure, baladi, kantar, keddah, robhah, schene **7** choryos, daribah, malouah, roubouh, toumnah **8** kassabah, kharouba **10** diramimari, diribaladi
   of El Salvador: 4 vara **5** cafiz, cahiz **6** fanega **7** batella, botella, cantara, manzana
   of England: 3 cut, ell, lea, pin, rod, ton, tun, vat **4** acre, bind, butt, comb, coom, cran, foot, gill, goad, hand, hank, heer, hide, inch, last, line, mile, nail, pace, palm, peck, pint, pipe, pole, pool, rood, rope, sack, seam, span, trug, typp, wist, yard, yoke **5** bodge, chain, cubit, digit, float, floor, fluid, hutch, jugum, minim, ounce, perch, point, prime, quart, skein, stack, truss **6** barrel, bovate, bushel, cranne,

fathom, firkin, gallon, hobbet, hobbit, league, manent, oxgang, pottle, runlet, square, strike, sulung, thread, tierce **7** auchlet, furlong, kenning, quarter, rundlet, seamile, spindle, tertian, virgate **8** carucate, chaldron, hogshead, landyard, puncheon, quadrant, standard
   of Estonia: 3 tun **4** elle, liin, sund, toll, toop **5** verst **6** sagene, versta **7** kulimet **8** tonnland
   of Ethiopia: 3 tat **4** cubi, kuba **5** derah, messe **6** cabaho, sinjer, sinzer, tanica **7** entelam, farsakh, farsang, ghebeta
   of Finland: 5 kannu, verst **6** fathom, kannor **8** ottinger, skalpund, tunnland
   of France: 3 pot, sac **4** aune, mine, pied, velt **5** arpen, carat, ligne, minot, pinte, point, pouce, velte **6** arpent, hemine, league, quarte, setier
   of Germany: 3 gon, lot, ohm **4** elle, fuss, gran, joch, last, rute, skot, unze, zoll **5** fuder, halbe, linie, meile, pfund, werst **6** schock, seidel **7** juchart, juchert, klafter, skrupul, stadion, zentner **8** schainos, scheffel, schoppen, seemeile **9** rheinfuss, wegstunde **11** reichsmeile **12** pferdestarke
   of Greece: 3 pik **4** bema, piki, pous **5** baril, chous, cubit, diote, doron, maris, pekhe, podos, pygon, xylon **6** acaena, bacile, barile, cotula, dichas, gramme, hemina, koilon, lichas, milion, orgyia, palame, pechys, schene, xestes **7** bacvhel, chenica, choenix, cyathos, diaulos, metreta, stadium, stremma **8** condylos, daktylos, dekapode, dolichos, medimnos, medimnys, metretes, palaiste, plethron, plethrum, stathmos **9** hemiekton, oxybaphon
   of Guatemala: 4 vara **6** cuarta, tercia **7** cajuela, manzana **10** caballeria
   of Guinea: 7 jacktan
   of Honduras: 4 vara **5** milla **6** mecate **7** cajuela
   of Hungary: 3 ako **4** hold, yoke **5** itcze, marok, metze **7** huvelyk
   of Iceland: 3 set **4** alin **5** almud **6** almenn, ferfet, pottur **7** fathmur, fermila, oltunna
   of India: 3 ady, gaz, gez, jow, lan **4** byee, coss, depa, doph, hath, koss, kunk, raik, rati, seit, taun, tola **5** bigha, covid, crosa, danda, depoh, drona, erosa, garce, hasta, krosa, parah, ratti, salay, yojan **6** adhaka, amunam, covido, cudava, cumbha, geerah, moolum, mushti, ouroub, palgat, parran, prasha, ropani, tipree, unglee, yojana **7** dhanush, gavyuti, khahoon, niranga, prastha **8** okthabah
   of Indonesia: 5 depah, depoh
   of Iran: 3 gaz, zar, zer **4** cane **5**

gareh, kafiz, makuk, qasab **6** charac, chebel, ghalva **7** capicha, chenica, farsakh, mansion, mishara **8** parasang, piamaneh, stathmos
of Ireland: 4 mile **6** bandle **8** crannock
of Israel: 3 cab, car, hin, kab, kor **4** bath, ezba, omer, reed **5** cubit, donum, dunam, ephah, ganeh, homer, kaneh
of Italy: 3 pie **4** orna **5** palma, palmo, punto, salma, stero **6** barile, miglie, moggio, rubbio, tomolo **7** braccio, secchio **8** giornata, quadrato
of Japan: 2 go **3** boo, cho, djo, fun, inc, ken, kin, kon, rin, shi, sho, sun, tan **4** hiro, isse, kati, koku, niyo, shoo **5** carat, catty, issho, ittan, momme, picul, shaku **6** kwamme **8** hiyak-kin **9** hiyak-hiro **11** komma-ichida, kujira-shaku
of Java: 3 kan **4** paal, rand **5** palen
of Kenya: 4 wari
of Korea: 2 ri **3** ch'i, kan, kun, mal **4** dwei, geun, sodu **5** daedu, pyong **6** chngbo **7** soseung **8** daeseung
of Laos: 3 bak
of Latvia: 3 let **4** stof **5** stoff, verst **6** arshin, kulmet **7** verchoc, verchok **8** krouchka, pourvete **9** deciatine, lofstelle, pourvete **10** tonnseteel
of Liberia: 4 kuba
of Libya: 3 dra, pik, saa **4** kele **5** bozze, donum, jabia, teman, uckia **6** barile, gorrah, misura **7** mattaro, termino **8** kharouba
of Luxembourg: 5 fuder
of Madagascar: 7 gantang
of Malaysia: 3 pau, tun **4** para, pipe, tael, wang **5** parah **6** chupak, parrah **7** gantang
of Malta: 4 rotl **5** artal, canna, parto, ratel, salma **6** kantar **7** caffiso
of Mexico: 3 bag, pie **4** alma, onza, vara **5** almud, baril, carga, jarra, labor, legua, libra, linea, marco, sitio **6** adarme, almude, arroba, carega, fanega, ochaua, terceo **7** pulgada, quintal **9** cuarteron, cuartillo **10** caballeria
of Morocco: 4 kala, muhd, rotl, saah, sahh, ueba **5** artal, cadee, gerbe, ratel **6** covado, dirhem, fanega, izenbi, kintar, tangin, tomini **8** quintral
of Myanmar: 2 ly **3** dha, gon, mau, sao, tao, tat **4** byee, phan, seit, taun, that **5** shita, thuoc **6** lamany, palgat **7** chaivai **8** okthabah
of the Netherlands: 2 el **3** aam, ahm, ell, kan, vat **4** duim, mijl, rood, rope **5** anker, roede, wisse **6** bunder, legger, maatje, mutsje, streep **7** schepel **8** mimgelen, steekkan
of Nicaragua: 4 vara **5** cahiz **6** suerte **7** cajuela, manzana **10** cabelleria
of Norway: 3 fot, mal **4** alen **5** kande **6** fathom **7** skieppe **9** korntonde

of Pakistan: 5 kanal, marla, masha, maund
of Panama: 7 celemin
of Paraguay: 3 pie **4** lino, lira, lire, vara **5** legua **6** cuadra, fanega
of Peru: 4 topo **5** galon **7** celemin **8** fanegada
of the Philippines: 4 loan **5** braza, catty, cavan, chupa, fardo, ganta, picul, punto **6** apatan, balita, lachsa, quinon **7** quilate **8** chinanta
of Poland: 3 cal **4** mila, pret **5** morga, sazen, vloka, wloka **6** cwierc, cwierk, kwarta, lokiec **7** garniec **9** kwarterka
of Portugal: 2 pe **4** bota, moio, vara **5** almud, fanga, geira, linha, milha **6** almude, covado **7** alquier, ferrado, selamin **8** alqueire
of Puerto Rico: 6 cuerda **10** cabelleria
of Rumania: 7 faltche
of Russia: 3 fut, lof **4** duim, fass, loof, pood, quar, stof **5** duime, foute, korec, korek, ligne, osmin, pajak, stoff, stoof, vedro, verst **6** charka, liniya, osmina, paletz, sagene, stekar, tchast, tsarki, versta, verste **7** archine, arsheen, botchka, chkalik, garnetz, verchoc, verchok **8** boutylka, chetvert, krouchka, kroushka **9** chetverik **10** dessiatine **11** polugarnetz
of Saudi Arabia: 4 rotl **5** kerat, koddi, mahnd **6** artaba, covido, qintar, rizmah **7** farsakh, quintal **8** farasang
of Scotland: 3 cop **4** boll, cran, fall, mile, peck, pint, rood, rope, span **5** crane, lippy **6** audlet, davach, firlot, lippie, noggin **7** chalder, choppin **8** mutchkin, stimpart, stimpert **9** particate, shaftment, shathmont
of Sicily: 5 salma **7** caffiso
of Sierra Leone: 4 load **6** kettle
of Somalia: 3 top **4** caba **5** chela, darat, tabla **6** cubito **8** parsalah
of South Africa: 4 vara
of Spain: 3 pie **4** codo, dedo, paso, vara **5** braza, cahiz, carga, legua, medio, palmo, sesma **6** cordel, cuarta, fanega, racion, yugada **7** azumbre, celemin, estadel, pulgada **8** fanegada
of Sri Lanka: 4 para, seer **5** parah **6** amunam, parrah
of Sudan: 2 ud
of Suriname: 7 ketting
of Sweden: 3 aln, fot, ref, tum **4** alar, amar, famn, kapp, last, stop **5** carat, foder, kanna, linje, nymil, spann **6** fathom, jumfru **7** oxhuvud, tunland **8** fjarding, koltunna, tunnland
of Switzerland: 3 imi, pot **4** aune, fuss, muid, pied, zoll **5** lieue, linie, maass, pouce, staab, toise **6** perche, strich **7** klafter, viertel **9** quarteron **10** holzlafter **11** holzklafter

of Syria: 5 makuk **6** garava
of Thailand: 2 wa **3** can, ken, niv, rai, sat, sok, wah **4** cohi, keup, niou, tang **5** kwien, leeng, sesti, vouah **6** kabiet, kanahn **7** chaimeu **8** changawn **9** anukabiet
of Tunisia: 3 saa **4** saah **5** cafiz **6** mettar **8** milerole
of Turkey: 3 dra, oka, pik **4** draa, khat, kile, zira **5** berri, kileh, zirai **6** arshin, chinik, fortin, halebi **7** nocktat
of Uruguay: 4 vara **6** cuadra, suerte
of Venezuela: 5 galon, milla **6** fanega **7** estadel
of Vietnam: 4 gang, phan, thon
of Wales: 5 cover **7** cantred, crannoc, listred
of Yugoslavia: 3 oka, rif **4** akov, ralo **5** donum, khvat, lanaz, plaze, stopa **6** motyka, ralico **9** danoranja
measured 5 equal, exact **6** steady **7** precise, regular, studied, uniform **8** verified **10** calculated, deliberate **11** cold-blooded, intentional, well-planned **12** premeditated **13** predetermined
Measure for Measure
author: 18 William Shakespeare
character: 5 Lucio **6** Angelo, Juliet **7** Claudio, Escalus, Mariana **8** Isabella **9** Vincentio
measureless 7 endless **8** infinite **9** boundless, unlimited **12** immeasurable
measurement 4 area, mass, size **5** depth, width **6** extent, height, length, volume, weight **7** breadth, content, gauging **8** capacity, plumbing, sounding **9** amplitude, appraisal, dimension, magnitude, measuring, reckoning, surveying **10** assessment, estimation, evaluation **11** mensuration
Biblical: 4 omer **5** cubit, ephah **6** shekel
champagne: 6 magnum **8** jeroboam, rehoboam **9** balthazar **10** methuselah, salmanazar **14** Nebuchadnezzar
cloth: 4 bolt
cotton: 4 bale
electricity: 3 ohm **4** volt, watt **5** joule **6** ampere **10** horsepower
energy: 3 BTU **5** joule **7** calorie **11** kilocalorie **18** British thermal unit
firewood: 4 cord
force: 4 dyne **6** newton **7** poundal
gold/jewelry: 5 carat, karat, point
Greek: 4 mina **5** cubit **6** obolos, talent **7** drachma, stadion
gun: 5 gauge **7** caliber
light: 7 candela **11** candlepower
liquor/spirits: 4 pint, pony, shot **5** fifth, quart **6** jigger, magnum
metric system: 5 liter, meter **9** deciliter, decimeter, dekaliter, dekameter, kiloliter, kilometer, nanometer **10** centiliter, centimeter, cubic meter, hectoliter, hectometer, milliliter, millimeter **11** square meter **14** cubic

dekameter **15** cubic centimeter, cubic millimeter, square decimeter, square dekameter, square kilometer **16** square centimeter, square hectometer, square millimeter
metric weight: 3 ton **4** gram **5** tonne **7** quintal **8** dekagram, kilogram **9** centigram, hectogram, microgram, milligram
paper: 4 ream **5** quire
pressure: 6 pascal **10** atmosphere
Roman: 2 as **5** cubit, libra **6** pondus **7** stadium
sound: 7 decibel
temperature: 6 degree, Kelvin **7** Celsius **10** Fahrenheit
time: 3 day **4** hour, week, year **5** month, score **6** decade, minute, second **7** century **10** millennium, nanosecond **11** microsecond, millisecond
typography: 2 em, en **4** pica **5** point
unit: 3 cup, rod **4** acre, dram, foot, gill, inch, link, mile, peck, pint, yard **5** chain, minim, ounce, quart **6** barrel, bushel, circle, degree, fathom, gallon **7** furlong, hectare **8** angstrom, hogshead, teaspoon **9** cubic foot, cubic inch, cubic yard, square rod **10** fluid ounce, right angle, square foot, square inch, square mile, square yard, tablespoon **25** international nautical mile
weight: 3 ton **4** dram **5** grain, ounce, pound **7** scruple **8** short ton **9** ounce troy, pound troy **11** pennyweight **13** hundredweight
measure out 6 ration **7** dole out, mete out **9** apportion
meat 3 nut **4** core, fare, food, gist, grub **5** heart, point **6** kernel **7** edibles, essence, nucleus **8** victuals **9** provender, substance **10** provisions, sustenance **11** comestibles, nourishment
mechanic 6 joiner **7** artisan **9** automatic, craftsman, machinist **11** uninspired **12** grease monkey
mechanical 4 cold **7** routine **9** automatic, unfeeling **10** impersonal, self-acting, unthinking **11** instinctive, involuntary, machinelike, perfunctory, unconscious **13** machine-driven
mechanism 4 tool **5** motor, works **7** machine, utensil **9** apparatus, appliance, implement, machinery **10** instrument **11** contrivance
medal 5 award, honor, prize **6** laurel, reward, ribbon, trophy **8** citation **9** medallion **10** decoration
Medawar, Peter Brian
field: 7 biology
nationality: 7 British
discovered: 23 acquired immune tolerance
awarded: 10 Nobel Prize
meddle 5 mix in **6** butt in, horn in, kibitz **7** intrude, pry into **9** interfere, interlope, intervene **10** tamper with

meddler 3 pry **5** snoop **7** Paul Pry **8** busybody **10** interferer, Nosy Parker
meddlesome 4 nosy **5** pushy **6** prying, snoopy **7** pushing **8** meddling, snooping **9** intrusive, obtrusive, officious **11** impertinent, interfering **12** presumptuous
Medea
author: 9 Euripides
character: 5 Creon, Jason **6** Aegeus, Glauce
Medea
form: 9 sorceress
father: 6 Aeetes
mother: 5 Idyia
aunt: 5 Circe
brother: 8 Apsyrtus
sister: 9 Chalciope
lover: 5 Jason
son: 6 Medeus, Pheres **8** Mermerus, Tisander **9** Alcimenes, Thessalus
killed: 7 her sons
escaped to: 6 Athens
Medeus
father: 6 Aegeus
mother: 5 Medea
Media 14 ancient kingdom
present day: 4 Iran
capital: 8 Ecbatana
King: 6 Darius, Xerxes **9** Ahasueras
inhabitant: 4 Mede **5** Aryan **7** Persian **8** Parthian
media 5 press, radio **9** magazines **10** billboards, journalism, newspapers, television **11** journalists
singular: 6 medium
medial 4 mean **6** median **7** average
median 3 mid, par **4** mean, norm **5** mesne **6** center, medial, medium, middle **7** average, central, halfway **8** middling, midpoint, moderate **12** intermediate
mediate 6 pacify, step in, umpire **7** referee **8** moderate **9** arbitrate, intercede, interpose, intervene, negotiate, reconcile **10** conciliate, propitiate
mediation 6 parley **10** adjustment, compromise, discussion **11** arbitration, give-and-take, negotiation, peacemaking **12** conciliation, intercession, intervention, pacification **14** reconciliation
mediator 6 umpire **7** referee **9** go-between, moderator **10** arbitrator, negotiator, peacemaker, reconciler **12** intermediary
medical 7 healing **8** curative, remedial, salutary, sanative **9** medicinal **10** medicative **11** restorative, therapeutic
medical abbreviation
a c: 11 before meals
ad lib: 8 as needed **9** as desired
agit: 5 shake
aq: 5 water
b i d: 9 twice a day
cap: 4 take **7** capsule
coch: 8 spoonful

dil: 6 dilute **8** dissolve
fldxt: 12 fluid extract
ft: 4 make
ft mist: 12 make a mixture
ft pulv: 11 make a powder
gr: 5 grain
gt: 4 drop
gtt: 5 drops
h s: 9 at bedtime
in d: 5 daily
lot: 6 lotion
mod praesc: 21 in the manner prescribed
O: 4 pint
O D: 8 right eye
O S: 7 left eye
O U: 9 in each eye
ol: 3 oil
p c: 9 after food **10** after meals
p o: 7 by mouth
p r n: 25 as circumstances may require
pil: 3 pill
pulv: 6 powder
q i d: 14 four times daily
rep: 6 repeat
s o s: 11 if necessary
ss: 7 one half
tab: 6 tablet
t i d: 15 three times daily
ut dict: 10 as directed
Medical Center
character: 9 (Dr) Joe Gannon **11** Nurse Wilcox, (Dr) Paul Lochner **13** Nurse Chambers **14** Nurse Courtland, (Dr) Jeanne Bartlett
cast: 9 James Daly **11** Chad Everett, Chris Hutson **12** Audrey Totter, Jayne Meadows **14** Corinne Camacho
medical practitioner 6 doctor, medico **9** physician
medication 4 balm **5** tonic **6** elixir, remedy **7** nostrum, panacea **8** medicine **10** medicament, palliative **11** restorative
Medici, Giovanni de' 8 Pope Leo X **15** Pope Leo the Tenth
Medici, Giulio 14 Pope Clement VII **21** Pope Clement the Seventh
medicine 4 balm, drug, pill **5** salve, tonic **6** remedy **7** nostrum **10** healing art, medication **11** restorative **12** therapeutics **13** materia medica
god of: 9 Asclepius **11** Aesculapius
medieval 8 Dark Ages **10** antiquated, Middle Ages **12** old-fashioned **14** pre-Renaissance
mediocre 4 so-so **5** petty **6** common, meager, medium, normal, paltry, slight **7** average **8** inferior, ordinary, passable, trifling **9** tolerable **10** negligible, pedestrian, second-rate **11** commonplace, indifferent, unimportant **12** run-of-the-mill **13** inappreciable, insignificant **14** fair-to-middling, inconsiderable **15** inconsequential, undistinguished

mediocrity 8 poorness **9** pettiness **10** low-quality, meagerness, paltriness, triviality **11** inferiority **12** indifference, ordinariness, unimportance **14** insignificance **15** commonplaceness

meditate 4 muse, plan **5** aim at, study, think **6** devise, ponder **7** concoct, dream of, propose, reflect **8** cogitate, consider, contrive, mull over, ruminate **9** dwell upon **10** deliberate **11** contemplate

meditation 4 yoga **5** study **6** musing, poring **7** mulling, reverie, thought **8** brooding **9** discourse, pondering **10** cogitation, reflection, rumination **12** deliberation **13** consideration, contemplation

Mediterranean
called by ancient Romans: 11 mare nostrum
coast: 7 Riviera
gulf: 5 Lions, Sidra, Tunis **7** Antalya, Catania, Taranto **8** Hammamet **9** Iskenderon
island: 4 Elba **5** Capri, Corfu, Crete, Ibiza, Malta **6** Cyprus, Euboea, Lesbos, Rhodes, Sicily **7** Corsica, Majorca, Minorca **8** Balearic, Sardinia
resort: 4 Nice **5** Capri **6** Cannes **7** Riviera **9** Cote d'Azur **10** Costa Brava
river into: 2 Po **4** Ebro, Nile **5** Rhone
sea: 5 Black **6** Aegean, Ionian **8** Adriatic, Ligurian **10** Tyrrhenian
strait: 8 Bosporus **9** Bosphorus, Gibraltar **11** Dardanelles
wind: 7 mistral, sirocco

medium 3 way **4** form, mean, mode, tool **5** means, organ **6** agency, avenue, common, milieu, normal **7** average, balance, channel, diviner, psychic, setting, vehicle **8** middling, moderate, ordinary **9** go-between, middle way, mid-course **10** atmosphere, compromise, golden mean, instrument, moderation **11** clairvoyant, environment, happy medium **12** crystal-gazer, intermediary, intermediate, middle ground, spiritualist, surroundings **13** fortuneteller **15** instrumentality

medley 4 hash, mess, olio **6** jumble, mosaic **7** farrago, melange, mixture **8** mishmash, pastiche **9** patchwork, potpourri **10** assortment, hodgepodge, miscellany **11** gallimaufry

Medon
mentioned in: 5 Iliad **7** Odyssey
father: 6 Oileus
mother: 5 Rhene
position: 6 herald
friend of: 8 Penelope
killed by: 6 Aeneas

medulla
part of: 5 brain
controls: 6 glands **7** muscles

Medusa

form: 6 Gorgon
father: 7 Phorcys
mother: 4 Ceto
sisters: 6 Graiae
loved by: 8 Poseidon
children: 7 Pegasus **8** Chrysaor
sight of her caused people to turn to: 5 stone
killed by: 7 Perseus

meek 4 mild **6** docile, gentle, humble, modest **8** lamblike, retiring, tolerant, yielding **9** compliant, spineless, tractable, weak-kneed **10** spiritless, submissive, unassuming **11** acquiescent, complaisant, deferential, unassertive, unresisting **13** long-suffering, tenderhearted, unpretentious

meekness 7 pliancy, shyness **8** docility, humility **9** passivity **10** diffidence, humbleness **11** bashfulness **13** nonresistance **14** self-effacement

meet 3 apt, fit **4** abut, face, good, heed, obey **5** cross, equal, greet, match, rally, right **6** adjoin, answer, border, follow, gather, muster, proper, seemly **7** abide by, collect, convene, execute, fitting, fulfill, observe, perform, respect, run into, satisfy, welcome **8** assemble, becoming, bump into, confront, converge, decorous, opposite, relevant, suitable **9** agreeable, allowable, befitting, congruous, discharge, encounter, intersect, permitted, pertinent **10** admissable, comply with, congregate, felicitous **11** acknowledge, appropriate, permissible **12** come together

meet eye to eye 4 face **8** confront, face up to **11** meet vis-a-vis

meet halfway 6 settle **9** make a deal **10** compromise **11** come to terms **14** strike a bargain **18** split the difference

meet head on 4 face **5** crash **6** oppose **7** collide, crack up **8** confront, face up to **9** challenge, encounter

meeting 4 date **5** group, tryst **6** caucus **7** council **8** assembly, conclave, congress **9** encounter, gathering **10** conference, convention, engagement, rendezvous **11** assignation, convocation, get-together **12** introduction, presentation **13** confrontation

Meeting at Telgte
author: 11 Gunter Grass

meeting of the minds 7 concert, concord, harmony **9** agreement **11** concordance **13** understanding

meeting place 5 mecca **10** focal point, rendezvous

Meet Me in St Louis
director: 16 Vincente Minnelli
cast: 8 Leon Ames, Tom Drake **9** Mary Astor **11** Judy Garland **12** June Lockhart, Marjorie Main **13** Lucille Bremer **14** Margaret O'Brien
song: 11 Trolley Song **14** The Boy

Next Door **33** Have Yourself a Merry Little Christmas

Meet the Press
moderator: 9 Ned Brooks **10** Bill Monroe, Tim Russert **11** Edwin Newman **14** Lawrence Spivak, Martha Rountree

meet with 4 meet **6** endure **7** undergo **8** come upon **9** encounter **10** come across, experience

Mefitis
also: 8 Mephitis
prevented: 5 winds
kind of winds: 7 harmful

Megaera
member of: 6 Furies

Megamede
husband: 12 King Thespius
number of daughters: 5 fifty

Megara
father: 5 Creon
husband: 8 Hercules
son: 11 Therimachus

Mehuman 6 eunuch

Mein Kampf
author: 11 Adolf Hitler
means: 7 my fight **8** my battle

Meitner, Lise
field: 7 physics
nationality: 8 Austrian
collaborator: 8 Otto Hahn
contributed to: 21 atomic bomb development
discovered: 12 protactinium **16** fission of uranium

Melaenis
epithet of: 9 Aphrodite
means: 5 black

melancholia 7 despair **10** depression, desolation, melancholy **11** despondency

melancholy 4 blue, glum **5** blues, dumps, gloom, moody **6** dismal, dreary, gloomy, mopish, morose, somber **7** despair, doleful, forlorn, joyless, unhappy **8** dejected, desolate, doldrums, dolorous, downcast, funereal, mournful **9** cheerless, dejection, depressed, heartsick, moodiness, plaintive **10** calamitous, depressing, depression, despondent, dispirited, gloominess, low spirits **11** despondency, discouraged, downhearted, forlornness, languishing, melancholia, sick at heart, unfortunate **12** disconsolate, heavyhearted **14** down in the dumps, down in the mouth **16** disconsolateness
French: 6 triste **9** tristesse

melange 3 mix **4** olio **6** jumble, medley **7** mixture **8** compound, mishmash, pastiche **9** pasticcio, patchwork, potpourri **10** assemblage, assortment, hodgepodge, miscellany **11** gallimaufry

Melanippe
form: 4 foal

foal born to: 6 Euippe
transformed into: 4 Arne, girl
father: 4 Ares
queen of: 7 Amazons

Melanosaurus
type: 8 dinosaur
period: 8 Triassic

Melba, Nellie
title: 4 dame
born: 9 Australia
voice: 7 soprano
named for her: 10 Melba toast, Peach melba

Melbourne
bay: 7 Hobson's **11** Port Phillip
landmark: 20 Flemington Racecourse
river: 5 Yarra **6** Plenty **9** Mary Creek, Patterson **11** Maribyrnong **12** Diamond Creek **13** Kororoit Creek **14** Dandenong Creek, Gardiner's Creek **16** Moonee Ponds Creek
state: 8 Victoria
university: 6 Monash **7** La Trobe

Melchizedek
means: 19 king of righteousness
hometown: 5 Salem
contemporary: 7 Abraham

meld 3 mix **4** fuse, join **5** blend, merge, unite **6** jumble, mingle **7** combine **8** coalesce, intermix, scramble **9** commingle **10** amalgamate, intertwine, interweave **11** consolidate, incorporate, intermingle

Meleager
father: 4 Ares **6** Oeneus
mother: 7 Althaea
uncle: 9 Plexippus
slew: 14 Calydonian boar
loved: 8 Atalanta
killed: 15 mother's brothers
sisters: 11 Meleagrides

melee 3 row **4** fray, riot **5** brawl, scrap, set-to **6** fracas, rumpus, tussle **7** scuffle **8** disorder, dogfight **9** commotion, fistfight **10** free-for-all **11** altercation, pandemonium

Meliad
form: 5 nymph
nymph of: 6 flocks **10** fruit trees

mellifluous 4 soft **5** sweet **6** dulcet, mellow, smooth **7** musical **8** resonant **9** full-toned, melodious **10** euphonious, harmonious, sweet-toned **13** sweet-sounding

Mellors
character in: 20 Lady Chatterley's Lover
author: 8 Lawrence

mellow 4 rich, ripe, soft **5** drunk, sweet **6** mature, season, soften **7** matured, relaxed **8** luscious, tolerant **9** delicious **10** full-bodied **11** sympathetic **12** full-flavored **13** compassionate, understanding

mellowness 8 full body, fullness, maturity, richness, ripeness, softness **9**

tolerance **10** compassion, smoothness **12** lusciousness, pleasantness

melodic 5 lyric **7** tuneful

melodious 4 rich, soft **5** clear, lyric, sweet **6** dulcet, mellow, smooth **7** melodic, musical, ringing, tuneful **8** resonant **9** full-toned **10** euphonious, sweet-toned **11** mellifluent, mellifluous

melodrama 9 theatrics **12** emotionalism **13** theatricality

melodramatic 5 corny, hammy, hokey, stagy **7** maudlin, mawkish **8** cornball, frenzied **10** flamboyant, histrionic **11** exaggerated, overwrought, sensational, sentimental, spectacular **13** overemotional

melody 3 air **4** aria, song, tune **5** ditty, theme **6** ballad, strain, timbre **7** concord, euphony **10** musicality **11** tunefulness **12** mellifluence **13** melodiousness **14** harmoniousness **15** mellifluousness

melon
varieties: 4 pear **5** mango, snake, stink **6** casaba, citron, Dudaim, netted, nutmeg, orange, winter **7** Persian, serpent **8** honeydew **10** cantaloupe, preserving, watermelon **11** pomegranate **16** Oriental pickling, Queen Anne's pocket **17** Chinese preserving

Melpomene
member of: 5 Muses
personifies: 7 tragedy

melt 4 fade, fuse, pass, thaw **5** blend, merge, shade, touch **6** affect, disarm, dispel, soften, vanish **7** appease, dwindle, liquefy, mollify, scatter **8** dissolve **9** disappear, dissipate, evaporate, waste away **10** arouse pity, conciliate, propitiate

melt away 5 dry up **8** vaporize **9** evaporate

Melville, Herman
author of: 4 Omoo **5** Mardi, Typee **7** Redburn **8** Moby Dick **9** Billy Budd **12** Benito Cereno **16** The Confidence Man **20** Bartleby the Scrivener

Melvin and Howard
director: 9 Jonathan Demme
cast: 9 Paul LeMat **12** Jason Robards **15** Mary Steenburgen
Oscar for: 6 script **17** supporting actress (Steenburgen)

member 3 arm, leg, toe **4** foot, hand, limb, part, tail, wing **5** bough, digit, organ, piece, shoot **6** branch, finger, pinion **7** element, portion, section, segment **8** fragment **9** appendage, component, extremity **10** ingredient **11** constituent

member
of the bar: 4 beak **7** counsel **8** advocate, attorney **9** barrister, counselor **10** mouthpiece **12** legal advisor **13** attorney-at-law

of a crew: 4 hand, mate **6** ensign, ganger, gunner, purser, yeoman **7** bowsman, oarsman, steward, swabbie **8** cabin boy, coxswain, deckhand, helmsman **9** first mate, navigator

of faculty: 3 don, PhD **4** prof **5** tutor **6** doctor, master **7** teacher **8** lecturer **9** professor **10** instructor

of family: 3 son **4** aunt **5** niece, uncle **6** cousin, father, mother, nephew, sister **7** brother **8** daughter, grandson **11** grandfather, grandmother **13** granddaughter

of legislature: 4 whip **6** deputy **7** senator, speaker **8** delegate, lawmaker **10** legislator, politician **11** congressman **12** congresswoman **14** representative

of religious order: 3 nun **4** dame, monk **5** Clare, friar, priest **6** father, hermit, Jesuit, sister **7** Alexian, ascetic, brother, Cluniac, Templar **8** Capuchin, cenobite, minister, Trappist **9** Carmelite, Dominican **10** Carthusian, Cistercian, Franciscan **11** Augustinian, Benedictine **14** mother superior

Member of the Wedding, The
author: 15 Carson McCullers
character: 6 Jarvis **11** Janice Evans **13** Frankie Addams, John Henry West **16** Honey Camden Brown **18** Berenice Sadie Brown

membership 4 club **6** league, roster **7** company, society **9** community, personnel **10** connection, fellowship, fraternity **11** affiliation, association, brotherhood

membrane 3 web **4** film, skin **6** lining, sheath **7** coating **8** envelope, pellicle **9** thin sheet **10** integument

memento 5 favor, relic, token **6** record, trophy **8** keepsake, memorial, reminder, souvenir **11** memorabilia, remembrance **12** remembrancer **13** commemoration

memento mori 23 remember that thou must die **31** object serving as a reminder of death

Memnon
origin: 8 Oriental **9** Ethiopian
father: 8 Tithonus
mother: 3 Eos **4** Dawn
brother: 8 Emathion
companions: 10 Memnonides
fought with: 7 Trojans
killed by: 8 Achilles
made immortal by: 4 Zeus
commemorated with: 11 giant statue
at: 6 Thebes

Memnonides see **6** Memnon

memo
French: 11 aide memoire

memoir 4 life **5** diary **7** journal **9** biography, life story **10** adventures **11** confessions, experiences, reflections

13 autobiography, recollections, reminiscences

Memoirs of a Dutiful Daughter
author: **16** Simone de Beauvoir

memorabilia 6 papers **7** records **8** archives **9** documents

memorable 6 famous **7** eminent, notable, salient **8** historic, stirring, striking **9** important, momentous, prominent, red-letter **10** celebrated, impressive, noteworthy, remarkable **11** illustrious, outstanding, significant **13** distinguished, extraordinary, unforgettable

memorandum 4 memo, note **5** brief **6** agenda, minute, record **7** jotting **8** reminder **11** brief report, list of items

memorial 6 homage **7** tribute **8** monument **10** monumental **11** testimonial **13** commemorative

memorialization 11 celebration **13** commemoration

memorialize 4 mark **5** honor **9** celebrate **11** commemorate, pay homage to **12** pay tribute to

memory 4 fame, mark, name, note **5** glory, honor, token **6** esteem, recall, regard, renown, repute **7** memento, respect **8** eminence, keepsake, memorial, prestige, reminder, souvenir **10** estimation, reputation **11** distinction, remembering, remembrance, testimonial **12** recollection, remembrancer, reminiscence **13** commemoration
goddess of: **9** Mnemosyne

Memphis
basketball team: **9** Grizzlies
feature:
    home: **5** Elvis **9** Graceland
    hotel: **7** Peabody
    noted for: **12** ducks in lobby
river: **11** Mississippi

menace 3 cow **4** risk **5** bully, daunt, peril **6** danger, hazard, threat **7** imperil, pitfall, portend, presage, terrify **8** browbeat, endanger, forebode, jeopardy, threaten **9** terrorize **10** intimidate, jeopardize **11** be a hazard to, imperilment **12** endangerment

menacing 7 hostile **9** dangerous **11** belligerent, threatening, treacherous **12** antagonistic

menage a trois 9 threesome **16** household of three

Menander
author of: **5** Heros **13** Perikeiromene **14** The Arbitration, The Misanthrope **16** The Rape of the Lock

Men at Arms
author: **11** Evelyn Waugh

Mencken, H L
author of: **10** Prejudices **19** The American Language
editor of: **10** The Mercury **11** The Smart Set
coined word: **9** booboisie, eclysiast

mend 3 fix **4** cure, darn, heal, knit **5** amend, emend, patch **6** better, reform, remedy, repair, revise **7** correct, improve, rectify, restore, retouch, touch up **8** overhaul, renovate **9** meliorate **10** ameliorate **11** recondition

mendacious 5 false, lying **8** spurious **9** deceptive **10** misleading, untruthful

mendacity 5 fraud, lying **6** deceit **7** falsity, perfidy **9** chicanery, deception, duplicity, falsehood, hypocrisy **10** dishonesty **11** insincerity **13** double-dealing, falsification, prevarication **14** untruthfulness **17** misrepresentation

Mendel, Gregor Johann
field: **6** botany
nationality: **8** Austrian
discovered: **14** laws of heredity
founded: **8** genetics

Mendeleyev (Mendeleev), Dimitri Ivanovich
field: **9** chemistry
nationality: **7** Russian
devised: **11** periodic law **13** periodic table

Mendelssohn, (Jakob Ludwig) Felix
born: **7** Germany, Hamburg
composer of: **6** Elijah, St Paul **7** Athalie, Italian (symphony No 4), Lorelei, Ruy Blas **8** Antigone, Scottish (symphony No 3) **11** Reformation (symphony No 5), The Hebrides **12** Hymn of Praise (symphony No 2) **17** Songs without Words **21** A Midsummer Night's Dream

mendicant 6 beggar **10** alms-seeker, panhandler

Mending Wall
author: **11** Robert Frost

Menelaus
king of: **6** Sparta
father: **6** Atreus
mother: **6** Aerope
brother: **9** Agamemnon
wife: **5** Helen
son: **11** Megapenthes, Nicostratus
daughter: **8** Hermione

mene mene tekel upharsin 20 handwriting on the wall **30** numbered numbered weighed divided
foretells destruction of: **10** Belshazzar
from Biblical book of: **6** Daniel

menhaden 4 pogy **5** pogie **6** bunker **7** alewife, bugfish, ellfish, fatback, herring, oldwife, sardine **8** bonyfish, hardhead, ladyfish **10** mossbunker

menial 3 low **4** mean **5** drone, lowly, slave, toady **6** abject, drudge, flunky, helper, humble, lackey **7** fawning, ignoble, servant, servile, slavish **8** cringing, employee **9** degrading, groveling, sycophant, truckling, underling **10** apprentice, obsequious **11** bootlicking, subordinate, subservient, sycophantic

menial labor 4 toil **5** grind **8** drudgery

Men in Black
director: **15** Barry Sonnenfeld
cast: **7** Rip Torn (Chief Zed) **9** Will Smith (Agent Jay) **12** Tony Shalhoub (Jack Jeebs) **13** Siobhan Fallon (Beatrice), Tommy Lee Jones (Agent Kay) **15** Linda Fiorentino (Agent L), Vincent D'Onofrio (Edgar)

Men in Black II
director: **15** Barry Sonnenfeld
cast: **7** Rip Torn (Chief Zed) **9** Will Smith (Agent Jay) **12** Tony Shalhoub (Jack Jeebs) **13** Rosario Dawson (Laura Vasquez), Tommy Lee Jones (Agent Kay) **14** Lara Flynn Boyle (Serleena) **15** Johnny Knoxville (Scrad/Charlie) **16** Patrick Warburton (Agent Tee)

Menjou, Adolphe
born: **12** Pittsburgh PA
roles: **9** Golden Boy, Pollyanna **11** A Star Is Born **12** The Front Page **13** A Woman of Paris **15** A Farewell to Arms, State of the Union **16** Little Miss Marker **18** A Bill of Divorcement

Mennonite 4 sect
oppose: **15** military service
favor: **10** plain dress
kin to: **5** Amish

meno
music: **4** less

Menominee, Menomini, Menomonie
language family: **9** Algonkian **10** Algonquian
location: **4** Ohio **7** Indiana **8** Illinois, Michigan **9** Wisconsin

menorah 11 candelabrum, candlestick **12** candleholder
number of candles: **5** seven

Menotti, Gian-Carlo
born: **5** Italy **10** Cadigliano
composer of: **9** The Consul, The Medium **12** The Island God, The Telephone **19** Amelia Goes to the Ball **24** Amahl and the Night Visitors

mens sana in corpore sano 22 a sound mind in a sound body

mental 5 crazy, nutty **6** insane, psycho **7** cracked, lunatic, psychic **8** abstract, cerebral, neurotic, rational **9** disturbed, in the mind, of the mind, psychotic **10** disordered, subjective, unbalanced **11** intelligent, mentally ill **12** intellectual, metaphysical **13** psychological

mental application 9 diligence **10** absorption, intentness **11** deep thought, engrossment, fixed regard **13** concentration **14** close attention

mental disorder 5 quirk **6** lunacy, oddity **7** madness **8** delusion, insanity, neurosis **9** craziness, psychosis **10** aberration **11** abnormality, derangement, mental lapse, peculiarity, strangeness **12** eccentricity, idiosyncrasy **13** schizophrenia **15** manic depression

mental hospital 6 asylum **8** madhouse **11** institution

mental institution 6 asylum **8** madhouse **11** funny farm **12** insane asylum

mentality 4 mind **6** acumen, brains, wisdom **8** judgment, sagacity **9** intellect **10** gray matter, perception **11** discernment **12** intelligence, perspicacity

mental lapse 5 quirk **6** lunacy, oddity **7** madness **8** rambling, straying **9** wandering **10** aberration **11** derangement, peculiarity **12** eccentricity **13** forgetfulness

mentally incapable
    Latin: 15 non compos mentis

mentally sound
    Latin: 12 compos mentis

mention 3 say **4** cite, hint, name, tell **5** imply, state **6** hint at, notice, remark, report, tell of **7** comment, divulge, inkling, narrate, observe, recount, refer to, specify **8** allude to, allusion, disclose, intimate **9** insinuate, make known, reference, statement, touch upon, utterance **10** advisement, indication, suggestion **11** designation, insinuation, observation **12** acquaintance, announcement, notification **13** communication, enlightenment, specification

mentor 4 guru **5** guide, tutor **6** master **7** adviser, monitor, proctor, teacher **9** counselor, preceptor, professor **10** instructor

Mentor
    advisor of: 8 Odysseus
    educated: 10 Telemachus

Mephibosheth
    father: 8 Jonathan
    also called: 9 Meribbaal
    grandfather: 4 Saul
    son: 5 Micha

Mephistopheles
    character in: 5 Faust
    author: 6 Goethe

Mephitis see **7** Mefitis

mer 3 sea

Merab
    father: 4 Saul
    sister: 6 Michal
    brother-in-law: 5 David

mercantile 5 trade **8** business **10** commercial **16** buying-and-selling

mercantilism 5 trade **8** business, commerce, exchange **13** commercialism

Mercedes
    character in: 21 The Count of Monte Cristo
    author: 5 Dumas (pere)

mercenary 5 venal **6** for pay, greedy **7** for gain, selfish **8** covetous, grasping, hireling, monetary **10** avaricious **11**

acquisitive, paid soldier **12** hired soldier

merchandise 4 sell **5** goods, stock, trade, wares **6** deal in, market **7** effects, staples **8** huckster **9** advertise, publicize, traffic in **10** belongings, buy and sell, distribute **11** commodities **12** stock in trade

merchant 6 broker, dealer, hawker, jobber, monger, trader, vendor **7** peddler **8** chandler, retailer, salesman **9** purchaser, tradesman **10** saleswoman, shopkeeper, wholesaler **11** storekeeper, tradeswoman

Merchant of Venice, The
    author: 18 William Shakespeare
    character: 6 Portia **7** Antonio, Jessica, Lorenzo, Nerissa, Shylock **8** Bassanio, Gratiano

merci 8 thank you

merci beaucoup 16 thank you very much

merciful 4 kind **6** benign, humane, tender **7** clement, feeling, lenient, pitying, sparing **8** gracious **9** forgiving **10** beneficent **11** kindhearted, softhearted, sympathetic **13** compassionate, understanding

merciless 4 fell **5** cruel, harsh **6** fierce, severe **7** callous, inhuman **8** inhumane, pitiless, ruthless **9** ferocious, heartless, unpitying, unsparing **10** relentless, unmerciful **11** cold-blooded, hardhearted, remorseless, unrelenting

Mercouri, Melina
    husband: 11 Jules Dassin
    born: 6 Athens, Greece
    roles: 7 Topkapi **10** Gaily Gaily **13** Never on Sunday **15** Once Is Not Enough

mercurial 6 fickle, lively, mobile **7** erratic, flighty, kinetic, protean **8** electric, spirited, unstable, variable, volatile **9** impetuous, impulsive **10** capricious, changeable, inconstant **11** fluctuating **13** irrepressible, unpredictable

mercury
    chemical symbol: 2 Hg

Mercury
    origin: 5 Roman
    messenger of: 4 gods
    god of: 7 science, thieves **8** commerce **9** eloquence
    corresponds to: 6 Hermes, Ogmios

Mercutio
    character in: 14 Romeo and Juliet
    author: 11 Shakespeare

mercy 4 pity **5** grace **6** lenity **7** charity **8** blessing, clemency, humanity, kindness, lenience, leniency, sympathy **9** good thing, tolerance **10** compassion, humaneness, lucky break **11** benevolence, forbearance, forgiveness, piece of luck **13** commiseration, fellow feeling **15** softheartedness **17** tenderheart-

edness
    Latin: 12 misericordia

Mercy seat see **16** Ark of the Covenant

mere 4 bald, bare, sole **5** plain, scant, sheer, utter **6** common, paltry **7** mundane **8** nugatory, ordinary, trifling **10** negligible, uneventful **11** commonplace, unmitigated **13** insignificant, unappreciable **14** inconsiderable

mere 6 mother

Meredith, Burgess
    wife: 15 Paulette Goddard
    born: 11 Cleveland OH
    roles: 5 Magic, Rocky **6** Batman (the Penguin) **7** Madame X **8** Foul Play **12** Grumpy Old Men, Hurry Sundown, Of Mice and Men **14** Grumpier Old Men **15** Magnificent Doll, Such Good Friends **16** Advise and Consent

Meredith, George
    author of: 9 The Egoist **10** Modern Love **14** Evan Harrington **16** Beauchamp's Career **19** Diana of the Crossways **25** The Ordeal of Richard Feverel

merely 3 but **4** just, only **5** quite **6** barely, in part, purely, simply, solely **7** utterly **8** scarcely, wholly **10** absolutely

meretricious 4 mock, sham **5** bogus, false, phony **6** pseudo, shoddy, tawdry **8** delusive, specious, spurious **9** deceptive **10** fraudulent, misleading **11** counterfeit

merge 4 fuse, join, weld **5** blend, unify, unite **6** link up **7** combine **8** coalesce, converge, intermix **9** associate, become one, integrate, interfuse, interlock **10** amalgamate, synthesize **11** confederate, consolidate **12** band together, interconnect

mergence 3 mix **5** blend **7** merging, mixture **8** mingling **10** concoction **11** combination

Mergenthaler, Ottmar
    nationality: 8 American
    invented: 8 linotype

merger 5 union **7** wedding **8** marriage **9** coalition **12** amalgamation **13** confederation, consolidation

meridian 3 tip, top **4** acme, apex, brow, peak **5** crest, crown, point, ridge **6** apogee, climax, summit, vertex, zenith **7** heights **8** pinnacle **11** culmination

Merimee, Prosper
    author of: 6 Carmen **7** Colomba

merit 4 earn, rate **5** value, worth **6** credit, desert, invite, prompt, talent, virtue **7** ability, benefit, deserve, quality, stature, warrant **8** efficacy **9** advantage **10** be worthy of, excellence, worthiness **11** distinction **12** be entitled to **13** justification

merited 3 due **5** rated **6** earned **8** deserved, rightful

meritorious 4 fine **6** worthy **8** laudable **9** admirable, estimable, excellent, exemplary **10** creditable, noteworthy **11** commendable, exceptional **12** praiseworthy

Mermaid Tycoon
nickname of: **14** Esther Williams

Merman, Ethel
real name: **20** Ethel Agnes Zimmermann
husband: **14** Ernest Borgnine
born: **9** Astoria NY
autobiography: **6** Merman
roles: **11** Call Me Madam **12** Anything Goes, Panama Hattie **15** Annie Get Your Gun **16** Stage Door Canteen **21** Alexander's Ragtime Band

Mermerus
father: **5** Jason
mother: **5** Medea

Merope
member of: **8** Pleiades
father: **5** Atlas **8** Oenopion
husband: **7** Polybus **8** Sisyphus **11** Cresphontes, Polyphontes
son: **7** Aepytus
raped by: **5** Orion
raised: **7** Oedipus

merrily 5 gaily **6** gladly **7** briskly, happily, lightly, lustick, quickly **8** blithely, jocundly, jovially, joyfully, joyously **9** festively, gleefully **10** cheerfully, laughingly, mirthfully **11** hilariously, vivaciously **14** lightheartedly

Merrimac *see* **9** Pennacook

merriment 3 fun **4** glee **5** cheer, mirth **6** frolic, gaiety, hoopla, levity **7** good fun, jollity, revelry, whoopee **8** hilarity, laughter **9** amusement, festivity, good humor, jocundity, joviality **10** jocularity, jubilation, liveliness, skylarking **11** celebration, gleefulness, good spirits, merrymaking **12** conviviality, exhilaration, sportiveness **16** lightheartedness

merry 3 gay **5** happy, jolly **6** blithe, cheery, jocund, jovial, joyous, lively **7** festive, gleeful, jocular **8** animated, carefree, cheerful, gladsome, laughing, mirthful, partying, reveling, sportive **9** convivial, fun-loving, sprightly, vivacious **10** frolicsome, rollicking, skylarking **12** high-spirited, lighthearted

merrymaking 5 sport **6** frolic, gaiety, hoopla, revels **7** jollity, revelry, whoopee **8** carousal **9** festivity, funmaking, high jinks, merriment, rejoicing, whoop-de-do **10** saturnalia **11** bacchanalia, celebration, festivities **12** conviviality

Merry Wives of Windsor, The
author: **18** William Shakespeare
character: **4** Ford, Page **5** Caius **6** Doctor, Fenton **7** Slender **8** Anne Page **12** Mistress Ford, Mistress Page **15** Mistress Quickly, Sir John Falstaff

mesa 4 hill, peak **5** bench, butte, table **7** plateau, terrace **9** cartouche, tableland

Mescalero
language family: **6** Apache
location: **6** Mexico **9** New Mexico
related to: **5** Lipan **10** Chiricahua

mesh 3 fib, net, web **4** grid, jibe **5** agree, sieve, tally **6** engage, enmesh, grille, plexus, screen **7** connect, engaged, netting, network, webbing, webwork **8** dovetail, interact, lacework, meshwork, openwork **9** grillwork, interlock, intermesh **10** coordinate, correspond, interweave, wickerwork **11** fit together, latticework **12** reticulation

Meshach
former name: **7** Mishael
companion: **6** Daniel
friend: **8** Abednego, Shadrach

Mesmer, Franz (Friedrich) Anton
nationality: **6** German
developed: **8** hypnosis

mesmerize 4 charm **7** bewitch **8** enthrall, entrance **9** fascinate, hypnotize, magnetize, spellbind, transport

Mesopotamian mythology
god of agriculture/earth: **5** Dagan
corresponds to Phoenician: **5** Dagon

Mesquakie *see* **3** Fox

mess 3 fix **4** hash, stew **5** mix-up, pinch **6** crisis, jumble, litter, muddle, pickle, plight, scrape, strait **7** clutter, dilemma, trouble **8** disarray, disorder, hot water, mess hall, mishmash, quandary **9** cafeteria, confusion, imbroglio, refectory, situation **10** commissary, difficulty, dining hall, dining room, hodgepodge **11** predicament **14** conglomeration

message 4 news, note, word **5** moral, point, theme **6** letter, notice, report **7** meaning, missive, purport, tidings **8** bulletin, dispatch **9** statement **10** communique, memorandum **12** intelligence **13** communication

mess around with 4 test **6** try out **8** fool with, play with **10** tinker with **14** experiment with

messenger 5 envoy **6** bearer, runner **7** carrier, courier **8** delegate, emissary **9** deliverer, go-between **11** delivery boy, delivery man **12** intermediary

messenger of gods 4 Iris **6** Hermes **7** Mercury

Messiaen, Olivier Eugene Prosper Charles
born: **6** France **7** Avignon
composer of: **11** Exotic Birds, Turangalila **13** Chronochromie **20** Le Nativite du Seigneur **22** Quartet for the End of Time **27** Vingt Regards sur l'Enfant Jesus **33** Et exspecto resur-rectionem mortuorum **41** Transfiguration de Notre Seigneur Jesus Christ

Messiah
means: **11** anointed one
see also **10** Jesus

Messick, Dale
creator/artist of: **19** Brenda Starr Reporter

messiness 5 chaos, mix-up, upset **6** jumble **7** clutter **8** disarray, disorder, scramble, shambles **9** confusion **10** disharmony, sloppiness, untidiness **12** dishevelment **14** disarrangement **15** disorganization

mess up 3 mar **4** goof, muff, ruin **5** botch, spoil **6** bungle, foul up, jumble **7** blunder, butcher, disturb, do badly, louse up, screw up **9** mismanage **10** disarrange **11** disorganize, make a mess of, make an error **12** make a mistake

messy 4 ugly **6** blowsy, frowsy, grubby, sloppy, untidy **7** awkward, chaotic, jumbled, tangled, unkempt **8** confused, littered **9** cluttered, difficult **10** bedraggled, disheveled, disordered, slatternly, topsy-turvy, unenviable, unpleasant **11** disarranged **12** embarrassing, inextricable **13** uncomfortable

mesto
music: **8** mournful

metal
alloy: **5** brass, monel **6** bronze, nickel, niello, pewter, solder
bar: **3** gad **4** risp **5** ingot
bolt: **5** rivet
box: **8** canister
casting: **3** peg
classification: **5** light, noble **6** alkali, common **7** coinage **8** platinum, precious **9** rare earth **10** low-melting, refractory, transition **11** high-melting **14** semiconductors
clippings: **7** scissel
coarse: **5** matte
corrosion: **4** rust
crude: **3** ore **4** slug
cymbals: **3** tal
deposit: **4** lode, vein
design: **7** chasing
disk or plate: **4** shim **5** medal, paten **6** platen, sequin
eyelet: **7** grommet
filings: **5** lemel
god of: **6** Vulcan **10** Hephaestus
heaviest: **6** osmium
kind: **3** tin **4** gold, iron, lead, zinc **6** barium, cerium, cesium, copper, erbium, nickel, osmium, radium, silver, sodium **7** arsenic, bismuth, calcium, holmium, iridium, lithium, rhodium, silicon, terbium, thulium **8** actinium, aluminum, antimony, europium, lutetium, platinum, rubidium, samarium, selenium, titanium, tungsten **9** beryllium, magnesium, palla-

dium, potassium, ruthenium, strontium **10** molybdenum, phosphorus
layer: 7 plating
leaf: 4 foil
lightest: 7 lithium
liquid: 7 mercury
mass: 3 pid **5** ingot **7** bullion
piece: 4 jack, slug
refuse: 4 slag **5** dross
shaper: 5 swage
suit: 4 mail **5** armor **6** armour
thread: 4 lame, wire
trademark: 5 monel
ware: 4 tole **6** Revere
worker: 5 smith **6** forger, welder **7** armorer, riveter **8** armourer **9** goldsmith, ironsmith **10** blacksmith **11** coppersmith, silversmith **12** metallurgist

Metalious, Grace
  author of: 11 Peyton Place
metalworking
  god of: 6 Vulcan **10** Hephaestus, Hephaistos
metamorphose 6 change, mutate **7** convert **9** transform **11** transfigure
Metamorphoses
  author: 4 Ovid
metamorphosis 8 mutation **10** alteration, conversion **11** permutation **12** change of form, modification **13** radical change, transmutation **14** transformation **15** series of changes, startling change, transfiguration **18** transmogrification
Metamorphosis, The
  author: 10 Franz Kafka
metaphor 5 image, trope **6** simile **7** analogy **8** metonymy, parallel **11** equivalence **14** figure of speech, representation
metaphysical 5 basic, lofty, vague **6** far-out **7** eternal **8** abstract, abstruse, esoteric, mystical, ultimate **9** essential, high-flown, recondite, universal **10** impalpable, intangible, jesuitical, oversubtle **11** existential, fundamental, ontological, speculative **12** cosmological, intellectual, unanswerable **13** philosophical **15** epistemological
Metaphysics
  author: 9 Aristotle
metaxa
  type: 6 brandy **7** liqueur
  origin: 6 Greece
mete, mete out 5 allot **6** assign, divide **7** deal out, dole out **8** allocate, disburse, dispense **9** apportion, parcel out **10** administer, distribute, measure out
meteoric 4 fast **5** fiery, rapid, swift **6** speedy, sudden **7** blazing, flaming, instant **8** flashing, unabated **10** inexorable **11** ineluctable, unstoppable
meter
  abbreviation: 1 m

method 3 way **4** form, mode, plan, tack **5** means, order, style, usage **6** course, design, manner, scheme, system **7** fashion, formula, process, program, purpose, routine **8** approach, efficacy **9** procedure, technique, viability **13** modus operandi
methodical, methodic 4 neat, tidy **5** exact **7** careful, logical, orderly, precise, regular, uniform **10** analytical, deliberate, meticulous, systematic **12** businesslike **13** well-regulated
methodization 5 order **11** arrangement **12** organization **14** categorization, classification **15** systematization
methodize 5 order **7** arrange **8** classify, organize **11** systematize
Methuselah
  father: 5 Enoch
  son: 6 Lamech
  years lived: 23 nine hundred and sixty-nine
  known as: 9 oldest man
meticulous 4 nice **5** exact, fussy **7** finical, finicky, precise **8** exacting, sedulous **10** fastidious, particular, scrupulous **11** painstaking, punctilious **13** conscientious, perfectionist
meticulousness 4 care **5** pains **12** sedulousness, thoroughness **14** fastidiousness, scrupulousness **17** conscientiousness
metier 3 job **4** area, line, work **5** craft, field, forte, trade **7** calling, pursuit **8** activity, business, lifework, province, vocation **9** specialty **10** employment, livelihood, occupation, profession
meting out 8 alloting **9** bestowing, doling out **10** allocating, conferring, consigning, dealing out, dispensing **11** designating **12** apportioning, distributing, measuring out
Metis
  member of: 6 Titans
  father: 7 Oceanus
  mother: 6 Tethys
  consort of: 4 Zeus
  daughter: 6 Athena
Metropolis
  director: 9 Fritz Lang
  cast: 10 Alfred Abel **12** Brigitte Helm
metropolitan area 4 city **8** core city, downtown, environs **9** inner city, precincts, urban area **10** city limits, metropolis **11** central city **16** business district
mettle 3 vim **4** grit, guts **5** nerve, pluck, spunk, valor, vigor **6** spirit **7** bravery, courage, heroism **8** audacity, backbone, boldness, gameness, temerity **9** derring-do, fortitude, gallantry, manliness **10** enthusiasm, resolution **11** intrepidity **12** fearlessness **13** determination
mettlesome 4 bold, edgy **5** brave, fiery **6** ardent, plucky, spunky **7** gingery, peppery **8** restless, skittish, spir-

ited **9** excitable, impatient **10** courageous, high-strung **12** high-spirited
Mexica see **5** Aztec
Mexico
  other name: 8 New Spain
  capital/largest city: 10 Mexico City
  others: 4 Leon **5** La Paz, Taxco **6** Cancun, Celaya, Merida, Oaxaca, Puebla, Toluca **7** Durango, Guaymas, Tampico, Tijuana, Torreon **8** Acapulco, Culiacan, Ensenada, Irapuato, Mazatlan, Mexicali, Saltillo, Veracruz **9** Chihuahua, Matamoros, Monterrey, Queretaro, Salamanca, Zacatecas **10** Hermosillo **11** Guadalajara, Nuevo Laredo **12** Ciudad Juarez, Villahermosa **13** Coatzacoalcos, Piedras Negras, San Luis Potosi **14** Puerto Vallarta **15** Netzahualcoyotl
    ancient city: 4 Tula **7** Texcoco **8** Tlacopan **10** Monte Alban **11** Teotihuacan **12** Tenochtitlan **13** Tula de Allende
  division: 6 Colima, Oaxaca, Puebla, Sonora **7** Chiapas, Durango, Hidalgo, Jalisco, Sinaloa, Tabasco, Yucatan **8** Campeche, Coahuila, Tlaxcala, Veracruz **9** Chihuahua, Michoacan, Nuevo Leon, Zacatecas **13** San Luis Potosi **14** Baja California
  measure: 3 bag, pie **4** alma, onza, vara **5** almud, baril, carga, jarra, labor, legua, libra, linea, marco, sitio **6** adarme, almude, arroba, carega, fanega, ochaua, terceo **7** pulgada, quintal **9** cuarteron, cuartillo **10** caballeria
  monetary unit: 4 onza, peso **5** adobe, claco, tlaco **6** azteca, cuarto, dinero **7** centavo, piaster
  weight: 3 bag **4** onza **5** libra, marco **6** arroba, tercio **7** quintal
  island: 6 Carmen, Cedros **7** San Jose, Tiburon **8** Cerralvo **10** Tres Marias **13** Espiritu Santo **14** Santa Magdelena, Santa Margarita **15** Angel de la Guarda
  lake: 7 Chapala, Texcoco **9** Patzcuaro
  mountain: 6 Colima, Tacana, Toluca **9** Paricutin **11** Ixtacihuatl, Sierra Madre **12** Popocatepetl **14** Sierra Zacateca **16** Chiapas Highlands **24** Transverse Volcanic Sierra
  highest point: 7 Orizaba **12** Citlaltepetl
  river: 4 Mayo **5** Yaqui **6** Balsas, Fuerte, Grande, Panuco **8** Colorado, Grijalva **10** Papaloapan, Usumacinta **13** Bravo del Norte, Coatzacoalcos, Lerma-Santiago
  sea: 7 Pacific **8** Atlantic **9** Caribbean
  physical feature:
    bay: 8 Campeche **9** Olas Atlas
    cape: 10 Corrientes
    desert: 6 Sonora
    gulf: 6 Mexico **8** Campeche **10** California **11** Tehuantepec
    isthmus: 11 Tehuantepec

peninsula: 7 Yucatan **14** Baja California

plain: 7 Tabasco

plateau: 7 Mexican

valley: 7 Chiapas

people: 6 Indian **7** Mestizo, Spanish

architect: 7 O'Gorman

artist: 6 Orozco, Rivera, Tamayo **9** Siqueiros

composer: 6 Chavez

emperor: 10 Maximilian

explorer: 6 Cortes, Cortez **7** Cordoba **8** Alvarado, Grijalva

god: 6 Tlaloc **12** Quetzalcoatl **14** Huitzilopochtl

leader: 3 Fox, Gil **4** Diaz **5** Lopez, Rubio, Villa **6** Calles, Huerta, Juarez, Madero, Valdes, Zapata **7** Obregon **8** Carranza, Iturbide, Portillo, Santa Ana **9** Diaz Ordaz, Montezuma, Rodriguez **13** Madrid Hurtado **16** Salinas de Gortari

revolutionary/priest: 13 Morelos y Pavon **16** Hidalgo y Costilla

soldier/explorer: 12 conquistador

viceroy: 7 Mendoza

writer: 3 Paz **5** Nervo, Reyes, Yanez **6** Azuela, Guzman, Najera **7** Fuentes

language: 5 Mayan, Otomi **6** Mixtec **7** Mazahua, Mazatec, Nahuatl, Spanish, Totonac, Zapotec **8** Tarascan

religion: 13 Roman Catholic

place:

cathedral: 10 Assumption

center of Mexico City: 6 Zocalo **21** Plaza de la Constitucion

floating gardens: 10 Xochimilco

museum: 28 Shrine of the Virgin of Guadalupe

park: 7 Alameda **11** Chapultepec

ruins: 5 Mitla, Uxmal **8** Palenque **10** Monte Alban **11** Chichen Itza, Teotihuacan **20** Temple of Quetzalcoatl

street: 13 Avenida Juarez **16** Paseo de la Reforma

temple/pyramid: 7 Cholula **8** Castillo

feature:

agreement: 5 NAFTA

Christmas tradition: 6 pinata

coffee plantation: 5 finca

empire: 4 Maya **5** Aztec, Olmec **6** Mixtec, Toltec **7** Zapotec

large estate: 8 hacienda

musician: 8 mariachi

small farm/commune: 6 ejidos

sport: 7 jai alai **12** bullfighting

tree: 9 sapodilla **11** chicozapote

food:

corn cake: 8 tortilla

dish: 4 mole, taco **5** huevo, pollo **6** tamale **7** burrito, chorizo, taquito, tostada **8** empanada **9** enchilada, guacamole, sopadilla **10** chili verde, quesadilla **11** chimichanga **12** chili relleno

drink: 6 pulque **7** tequila

Mexico City

Aztec name: 12 Tenochtitlan

capital of: 6 Mexico

landmark: 13 Mercado Merced **15** Chapultepec Park **19** Basilica of Guadalupe

bull ring: 11 Plaza Mexico

floating gardens: 10 Xochimilco

pyramids: 11 Teotihuacan

square: 6 Zocalo **22** Plaza de las Tres Culturas

street: 16 Paseo de la Reforma

Meyerbeer, Giacomo

real name: 17 Jacob Liebmann Beer

born: 6 Berlin **7** Germany

composer of: 7 Dinorah **10** Le Prophete, The African, The Prophet **12** Les Huguenots, The Huguenots, The North Star **14** Robert le Diable, Robert the Devil

mezza voce

music: 9 half voice **10** half volume

mezzo

music: 4 half

Miami

bay: 8 Biscayne

county: 4 Dade

developer: 7 Flagler

museum: 4 Lowe **12** Villa Viscaya

ocean: 8 Atlantic

people: 5 Cuban **8** Hispanic

professional sports teams:

baseball: 7 Marlins **14** Florida Marlins

basketball: 4 Heat **9** Miami Heat

football: 8 Dolphins **13** Miami Dolphins

section: 7 Hialeah **10** Bal Harbour **11** Coral Gables

stadium: 10 Orange Bowl

tropical garden: 9 Fairchild

university: 5 Barry **8** St Thomas

zoo: 11 Crandon Park

Miami (Twightwee)

language family: 9 Algonkian **10** Algonquian

tribe: 3 Wea **5** Miami **10** Piankashaw

location: 4 Ohio **7** Indiana **8** Illinois, Michigan **9** Wisconsin

leader: 12 Little Turtle

allied with: 6 Peoria

Miami Vice

character: 4 Gina **5** Trudy **8** (Capt) Castillo **13** Riccardo Tubbs, Sonny Crockett

cast: 10 Don Johnson **11** Olivia Brown **15** Saundra Santiago **16** Edward James Olmos **20** Phillip Michael Thomas

Micah Clarke

author: 19 Sir Arthur Conan Doyle

Micawber, Mr

character in: 16 David Copperfield

author: 7 Dickens

Michael

author: 17 William Wordsworth

Michael

means: 12 Who is like God

father: 8 Izrahiah **11** Jehoshaphat

son: 4 Omri **8** Zabadiah

also: 9 archangel

Michel

father: 4 Saul

husband: 5 David, Palti

sister: 5 Merab

Michelangelo Buonarotti (Simoni)

architect of: 11 Campidoglio (Capitoline Hill) **12** Medici Chapel (Florence) **13** Farnese Palace **21** Palazzo Medici-Riccardi (Florence) **22** Palazzo dei Conservatori (Capitoline Hill) **24** Convent of San Marco Library

born: 5 Italy **7** Caprese

patron: 12 Pope Julius II **14** Lorenzo d'Medici **19** Pope Julius the Second **21** Lorenzo the Magnificent

artwork: 5 David, Moses, Pieta **6** Brutus, Slaves **7** Bacchus **9** The Victor **10** Holy Family **12** Madonna Pitti **15** The Last Judgment **18** Conversion of St Paul **20** Madonna Seated on a Step, Sistine Chapel Ceiling **21** The Flight of the Lapites, The Martyrdom of St Peter

Michelozzo

architect of: 21 Palazzo Medici-Riccardi (Florence) **24** Convent of San Marco Library

Michelson, Albert A

field: 7 physics

established: 12 speed of light **15** velocity of Earth

awarded: 10 Nobel Prize

Michener, James A

author of: 5 Space **6** Alaska, Hawaii, Iberia, Legacy, Poland **8** Caravans, Sayonara **9** The Source **10** Centennial, Chesapeake **11** The Covenant, The Drifters **16** The Fires of Spring **18** The Bridges at Toko-ri **22** Tales of the South Pacific

Michigan

abbreviation: 2 MI **4** Mich

nickname: 4 Lake **9** Wolverine **10** Automobile **15** Water Wonderland **16** Winter Wonderland

capital: 7 Lansing

largest city: 7 Detroit

others: 4 Caro, Troy **5** Flint, Niles, Wayne **6** Adrien, Alpena, Bad Axe, Monroe, Owosso, Warren, Wassar **7** Bay City, Holland, Jackson, Livonia, Midland, Pontiac, Saginaw, Trenton, Wyoming **8** Ann Arbor, Cadillac, Dearborn, Escanaba, Ironwood, Manistee, Muskegon, Petoskey, Royal Oak **9** Cheboygan, Hillsdale, Kalamazoo, Marquette, Port Huron, Roseville, Wyandotte **10** Birmingham, River Rouge **11** Battle Creek, Grand

Rapids **12** Benton Harbor, Traverse City **13** Sault Ste Marie, St Clair Shores
  college: 4 Alma, Hope **5** Wayne **6** Adrian, Albion, Calvin, Olivet, Owosso **7** Detroit, Oakland **9** Hillsdale, Kalamazoo, Marygrove
  feature:
    bridge: 8 Mackinac
    canal: 3 Soo **12** Sault St Marie
    festival: 12 Holland Tulip
    national park: 10 Isle Royale
    village: 10 Greenfield
  tribe: 6 Ojibwa, Ottawa **8** Chippewa **10** Potawatomi
  people: 9 Henry Ford, wolverine **11** Bruce Catton, Edgar A Guest, Julie Harris, Ralph Bunche, Ring Lardner **16** Charles Lindburgh
    explorer: 6 Joliet **7** La Salle, Nicolet **9** Marquette **12** Etienne Brule, Sault St Marie
  island: 8 Mackinaw
  lake: 4 Burt, Erie **5** Clear, Huron, Round, Torch **6** Austin, Devils, Moline **7** Bawbees, St Clair **8** Houghton, Michigan, Superior
  land rank: 11 twenty-third
  mountain: 6 Copper **7** Gogebic **9** Menominee, Porcupine
    highest point: 12 Mount Curwood
  physical feature:
    bay: 7 Saginaw, Thunder **8** Keweenaw, Sturgeon
    straits: 8 Mackinac
  president: 10 Gerald Ford
  river: 4 Cass **5** Grand, Huron **6** Raisin **7** Detroit, Saginaw, St Clair, St Mary's **8** Escanaba, Muskegon **9** Menominee
  state admission: 11 twenty-sixth
  state bird: 5 robin
  state fish: 5 trout
  state flower: 12 apple blossom
  state motto: 11 I Will Defend **39** If You Seek a Pleasant Peninsula Look About You
  state song: 18 Michigan My Michigan
  state tree: 16 eastern white pine

Mickey Mouse
  creator: 10 Walt Disney
  character: 5 Morty **6** Ferdie **11** Minnie Mouse
  cow: 10 Clarabelle

Micklewhite, Maurice Joseph
  real name of: 12 Michael Caine

Micmac
  language family: 9 Algonkian **10** Algonquian
  location: 6 Canada **10** Nova Scotia **12** Newfoundland, New Brunswick **14** Gaspe Peninsula **16** Cape Breton Island **18** Prince Edward Island

microbe 4 germ **5** virus **6** gamete, zygote **8** bacillus, parasite **9** bacterium **10** spirochete **13** microorganism, streptococcus **14** staphylococcus

microbiologist

American: 7 Waksman **9** Baltimore
Dutch: 11 (van) Leeuwenhoek

Micronesia
  part of: 7 Oceania
  island: 3 Nui **4** Guam, Rota, Truk, Wake **5** Makin, Nauru, Wotho **6** Bikini, Ellice, Majuro, Ponape **7** Gilbert, Mariana **8** Caroline, Kiribati, Marshall

microorganism 3 bug **4** germ **5** virus **7** microbe **8** bacillus, pathogen **9** bacterium

microphobia
  fear of: 12 small objects

microscope
  invented by:
    compound: 7 Janssen
    electronic: 5 Knoll, Ruska
    field ion: 7 Mueller
  single lens model improved by: 11 (van) Leeuwenhoek
  first observed: 8 protozoa **13** red blood cells **19** single-celled animals

microscopic, microscopical 4 tiny **5** teeny **6** atomic, minute **9** invisible **10** diminutive, very little **13** imperceptible, infinitesimal

microscopy
  founder: 11 Robert Hooke **13** Jan Swammerdam **16** Marcello Malpighi **19** Anton van Leeuwenhoek

Midas
  king of: 7 Phrygia
  father: 7 Gordius
  gift: 11 golden touch
  gift from: 7 Silenus
  ears changed to those of: 3 ass
  changed by: 6 Apollo

midday 4 noon **7** noonday **8** meridian, noontide, noontime

middle 3 act, gut, hub, mid **4** core, main **5** belly, heart, midst, waist **6** center, course, medial, median, midway, throes **7** central, halfway, midmost, midriff, nucleus, process, stomach **8** midpoint **9** heartland **10** midsection **12** intermediate

Middle Ages
  French: 8 moyen age

middle-class 4 mass **8** ordinary **9** bourgeois **10** mainstream, middlebrow

middle Europe
  German: 12 Mitteleuropa

middle ground 4 mean **7** balance **8** midpoint **11** equilibrium **12** common ground

Middle Kingdom *see* **5** China

middleman 5 agent **6** broker, dealer, jobber **7** liaison **8** mediator **9** gobetween **10** wholesaler **11** distributor, intercessor **12** entrepreneur, intermediary

Middlemarch
  author: 11 George Eliot
  character: 5 Celia **12** Will Ladislaw

13 Rosamond Viney **14** Dorothea Brooke, Edward Casaubon, Tertius Lydgate **15** Sir James Chettam

middlemost 4 mean **5** inner **6** inmost, median **7** central, midmost **8** interior

middle-of-the-road 8 moderate **10** mainstream

middle-of-the-roader 8 moderate **12** mainstreamer

middle way
  Latin: 8 via media

middling 4 fair, so-so **6** medium **7** average, fairish, minimal **8** mediocre, moderate, ordinary, passable **9** tolerable **10** pretty good, second-rate **11** indifferent **12** run-of-the-mill, unremarkable

Midgard
  also: 10 Mithgarthr
  origin: 12 Scandinavian
  means: 10 abode of man
  located between: 8 Niflheim **10** Muspelheim
  connected to Asgard by: 7 bifrost **13** rainbow bridge
  formed from brow of: 4 Ymir

midget 4 doll, runt **5** dwarf, pygmy **6** peewee, puppet, shrimp, squirt **7** manikin **8** half-pint, munchkin, small fry, Tom Thumb **9** pipsqueak **10** fingerling, homunculus **11** hop-o'-my-thumb, lilliputian

Midi 5 skirt **16** the south of France

midlands 8 interior **10** hinterland **13** central region

midmost 5 inner **6** inmost, middle **7** central, pivotal **8** interior **10** middlemost

Midnight Cowboy
  director: 15 John Schlesinger
  cast: 9 Jon Voight **11** John McGiver, Sylvia Miles **13** Brenda Vaccaro, Dustin Hoffman (Ratso Rizzo)
  Oscar for: 7 picture

Midnight Express
  director: 10 Alan Parker
  cast: 8 John Hurt **9** Bo Hopkins, Brad Davis (Billy Hayes) **10** Randy Quaid **12** Irene Miracle
  setting: 13 Turkish prison
  score: 14 Giorgio Moroder
  Oscar for: 5 score **6** script

midori
  type: 7 liqueur
  origin: 5 Japan
  flavor: 5 melon

midpoint 4 core, mean **5** focus **6** center, middle **15** point of no return

midriff 3 gut **4** guts **5** belly, tummy **6** paunch **7** abdomen, stomach **9** diaphragm **10** midsection **11** breadbasket

midst 3 eye, hub **4** core **5** bosom, heart, thick **6** center, depths, middle **7** nucleus **8** interior

Midsummer Night's Dream, A
  author: 18 William Shakespeare

character: 4 Puck (Robin Goodfellow) **6** Bottom, Helena, Hermia, Oberon **7** Theseus, Titania **8** Lysander **9** Demetrius, Hippolyta

midterm 4 exam, test **6** review **11** examination

midwife
French: 11 accoucheuse

mien 3 air **4** look **5** guise, style **6** aspect, manner, visage **7** bearing, feature **8** attitude, behavior, carriage, demeanor, presence **9** semblance **10** appearance, deportment, expression **11** countenance

Mies van der Rohe, Ludwig
architect of: 14 German Pavilion (1929 International Exposition, Barcelona), Lake Shore Drive (apartment towers, Chicago), Tugendhat House (Brno Czechoslovakia) **15** National Gallery (West Berlin), Seagram Building (NYC)
style: 13 International
principle: 10 less is more

miff 3 irk, vex **4** rile **5** anger, annoy, chafe, pique **6** nettle, offend, rankle **7** affront, provoke **8** irritate **9** put one off **10** exasperate **11** make one sore **14** rub the wrong way **15** raise one's dander

Mifune, Toshiro
born: 5 China **8** Tsingtao
roles: 6 Midway, Shogun **8** Rashomon **12** Seven Samurai **13** Throne of Blood

Miggs, Miss
character in: 12 Barnaby Rudge
author: 7 Dickens

might 3 may **5** brawn, clout, force, power, vigor **6** energy, muscle **7** potency, prowess **8** strength **9** influence, lustihood, puissance, toughness **10** capability, competence, durability, robustness, sturdiness **11** capableness **12** forcefulness

mighty 4 able, bold, huge, vast, very **5** brave, hardy, husky, lusty, stout, truly **6** brawny, manful, potent, really, robust, strong, sturdy **7** immense, massive, titanic, valiant **8** colossal, enormous, forceful, gigantic, imposing, majestic, powerful, puissant, stalwart, towering, valorous, vigorous **9** monstrous, strapping **10** courageous, gargantuan, invincible, monolithic, monumental, prodigious, stupendous **11** elephantine, exceedingly, indomitable, of great size **12** overpowering, particularly **13** exceptionally **14** Brobdingnagian

migrate 4 move, trek **6** travel **7** journey **8** emigrate, relocate, resettle **9** immigrate

migration 4 trek **6** exodus, flight, moving **7** passage **8** diaspora, movement

mikado 5 ruler **7** emperor, monarch **9** sovereign **10** locomotive **15** Japanese emperor

Mikado, The
subtitle: 15 The Town of Titipu
operetta by: 18 Gilbert and Sullivan
character: 4 Ko-Ko **6** Mikado, Peep-Bo, Yum-Yum **7** Katisha, Pooh-Bah **8** Nanki-Poo, Pish-Tush **9** Pitti-Sing

Mikkelsen, Dahl
also: 3 Mik
creator/artist of: 8 Ferd'nand

mikrophobia
fear of: 5 germs

mikvah 16 public ritual bath
used by: 12 Orthodox Jews

mild 4 calm, easy, soft, warm **5** balmy, bland **6** docile, gentle, placid, serene, smooth **7** pacific, summery **8** delicate, moderate, not sharp, pleasant, soothing, tranquil **9** easygoing, emollient, not severe, not strong, temperate **10** forbearing, not extreme, springlike **11** complaisant, uninjurious **12** good-tempered

mildew 4 mold **6** blight, fungus

mildewed 5 fusty, moldy **10** discolored

mildness 8 calmness, delicacy, serenity, softness **9** placidity **10** gentleness, good temper

Mildred Pierce
director: 13 Michael Curtiz
based on novel by: 10 James M Cain
cast: 8 Ann Blyth, Eve Arden **10** Jack Carson **12** Bruce Bennett, Joan Crawford, Zachary Scott
Oscar for: 7 actress (Crawford)

mild-tempered 7 equable, patient **9** easygoing **11** good-natured, unflappable

mile
abbreviation: 2 mi

Miles, Sarah
brother: 11 Christopher
husband: 10 Robert Bolt
born: 7 England **11** Ingatestone
roles: 6 Blow-Up **10** The Servant **11** The Hireling **12** Hope and Glory **13** Ryan's Daughter, White Mischief **16** Lady Caroline Lamb

miles gloriosus 15 boastful soldier

Miles Gloriosus
author: 7 Plautus

Milesian
origin: 5 Irish
invaders from: 5 Spain
invaded: 7 Ireland
defeated: 14 Tuatha De Danann
ancestors of: 5 Irish

milestone 7 jubilee **8** milepost, signpost **10** road marker **11** anniversary **12** red-letter day, turning point

Milestone, Lewis
director of: 12 Of Mice and Men, The Front Page **13** A Walk in the Sun **17** Mutiny on the Bounty **25** All Quiet on the Western Front (Oscar)

Milestones
author: 13 Arnold Bennett

milieu 5 scene **7** culture, element, setting **8** ambience, backdrop **10** background **11** environment, mise-en-scene **12** surroundings

militant 7 defiant, extreme, martial, warlike, warring **8** fighting, military **9** assertive, bellicose, combatant, combative **10** aggressive, pugnacious **11** belligerent, contentious **12** disputatious, paramilitary, warmongering **14** uncompromising

military 4 army **5** armed, crisp **6** strict, troops **7** martial, militia, Spartan, warlike **8** generals, soldiers **9** combative, defensive, regulated, soldierly, warmaking **10** regimented **11** armed forces, belligerent, soldierlike

military force 4 army, navy **6** legion, troops **7** legions, militia **8** military, regiment, soldiers, soldiery **9** battalion **11** fighting men **13** fighting force

military machine 4 army **6** legion, troops **11** armed forces **13** fighting force

military rank abbreviation
admiral: 3 adm
brigadier general: 2 bg **7** brig gen
captain: 3 cpt **4** capt
chief petty officer: 3 CPO
colonel: 3 col
commander: 5 comdr
corporal: 3 cpl
ensign: 3 ens
general: 3 gen
lieutenant: 2 lt **5** lieut
lieutenant colonel: 3 ltc **5** lt col
lieutenant general: 3 ltg **5** lt gen **8** lieut gen
major: 3 maj
major general: 2 mg **6** maj gen
master sergeant: 4 msgt
non-commissioned officer: 3 nco
private: 3 pvt
private first class: 3 pfc
sergeant: 3 sgt
sergeant first class: 3 sfc
sergeant major: 4 smaj **6** sgt maj
specialist: 4 spec
staff sergeant: 4 ssgt

military storehouse 6 armory **7** arsenal **8** magazine **9** arms depot **13** ordnance depot **14** ammunition dump

military stores 7 arsenal, weapons **8** ordnance **9** munitions **10** ammunition

military unit 4 army, crew, unit **5** corps, force, squad **6** legion, outfit **7** brigade, company **8** regiment, squadron **9** battalion, task force **10** contingent, detachment

milksop 4 baby, wimp **5** mouse, pansy, sissy, softy **6** coward **7** crybaby, nebbish **8** mama's boy, poltroon, weakling **9** fraidy-cat **10** namby-pamby, pantywaist, scaredy-cat, weak sister **11** milquetoast, mollycoddle

mill 4 roam, teem **5** crush, grind, shape, swarm, works **6** finish, groove **7** factory, meander **8** converge **9** granulate, pulverize

Mill, John Stuart
author of: **9** On Liberty **14** Utilitarianism **20** The Subjection of Women **28** Principles of Political Economy

Millais, Sir John Everett
born: **7** England **12** Southampton
artwork: **7** Bubbles **9** Blind Girl **12** Autumn Leaves, Chill October **13** My First Sermon **18** Lorenzo and Isabella **25** Christ in the Carpenter's Shop **36** Young Men of Benjamin Seizing Their Brides

Millament, Mrs
character in: **16** The Way of the World
author: **8** Congreve

Milland, Ray
real name: **21** Reginald Truscott-Jones
born: **5** Neath, Wales
roles: **9** Beau Geste **11** Blonde Crazy **14** Dial M for Murder, The Lost Weekend (Oscar) **22** Bulldog Drummond Escapes

Millay, Edna St Vincent
author of: **11** Second April **13** The Harp Weaver **19** Make Bright the Arrows **20** A Few Figs from Thistles

millennium 13 thousand years **9** age of gold **21** one-thousandth anniversary

Miller
character in: **18** The Canterbury Tales
author: **7** Chaucer

Miller, Ann
real name: **17** Lucille Ann Collier
autobiography: **15** Miller's High Life
born: **9** Chireno TX
roles: **9** On the Town, Stage Door **10** Hit the Deck, Kiss Me Kate **11** Sugar Babies **16** The Kissing Bandit

Miller, Arthur
wife: **13** Marilyn Monroe
author of: **8** The Price **11** The Crucible **12** After the Fall **16** Death of a Salesman **17** Resurrection Blues **18** A View from the Bridge **19** Finishing the Picture

Miller, Henry
author of: **5** Nexus, Sexus **6** Plexus **14** Tropic of Cancer **17** Tropic of Capricorn **18** The Rosy Crucifixion **21** The Colossus of Maroussi

Milles, Carl
real name: **23** Wilhelm Carl Emil Andersen
born: **5** Lagga **6** Sweden
artwork: **5** Diana, Jonah **6** Europa **12** Man and Nature, Playing Bears **13** Peace Monument **15** Orpheus Foun-

tain **18** Meeting of the Waters, Saltsjobaden Church (bronze doors)

millet 16 Panicum miliaceum
varieties: **3** hog **5** pearl, Sanwa **6** finger, Indian **7** African, foxtail, Italian **8** barnyard, browntop, Japanese **16** Japanese barnyard

Millet, Jean-Francois
born: **6** France, Gruchy
artwork: **5** Sower **7** Angelus **11** The Gleaners, The Winnower **14** Potato Planters, The Man with a Hoe **23** Oedipus Taken from the Tree

Millett, Kate
author of: **6** Flying **14** Sexual Politics

milligram
abbreviation: **2** mg

milliliter
abbreviation: **2** mL

millimeter
abbreviation: **2** mm

Millionaire, The
character: **14** Michael Anthony
cast: **12** Marvin Miller

Million Dollar Baby
director: **13** Clint Eastwood
cast: **11** Brian O'Byrne (Father Horvak), Hilary Swank (Maggie Fitzgerald) **13** Clint Eastwood (Frankie Dunn), Morgan Freeman (Eddie Dupris) **15** Margo Martindale (Earline Fitzgerald)

Mill on the Floss, The
author: **11** George Eliot
character: **8** Bob Jakin, Mrs Glegg **9** Lucy Deane, Mrs Pullet **11** Philip Wakem, Tom Tulliver **12** Stephen Guest **14** Maggie Tulliver

Mills, Hayley
real name: **15** Rose Vivian Mills
father: **4** John
sister: **6** Juliet
husband: **11** Ray Boulting
born: **6** London **7** England
roles: **8** Stricken, Tiger Bay **9** Pollyanna **11** Summer Magic **13** The Parent Trap **14** The Chalk Garden **15** The Moon-Spinners **19** In Search of Castaways **20** The Trouble with Angels

Mills, John
daughter: **6** Hayley, Juliet
born: **7** England **10** Felixstowe
roles: **12** Tunes of Glory **13** Ryan's Daughter **14** The Chalk Garden **17** Great Expectations **19** Swiss Family Robinson

Mills, Robert
architect of: **10** Post Office (Washington DC) **12** Patent Office (Washington DC) **14** Circular Church (Charleston) **15** Unitarian Church (Philadelphia) **16** Treasury Building (Washington DC) **18** Washington Monument **25** Sansom Street Baptist Church (Philadelphia) **29** Egyptian Revival Monument Church (Rich-

mond VA)
style: **12** Greek Revival

millstream 3 run **4** race **5** brook, canal, creek, river **6** branch

Milne, A A
author of: **13** Winnie-the-Pooh **20** The House at Pooh Corner
character: **3** Roo **4** Pooh **5** Kanga **6** Eeyore, Piglet, Tigger **16** Christopher Robin

Milo, Milos
island of: **6** Greece **8** Cyclades **9** Aegean Sea
found: **5** Venus **6** statue
missing: **4** arms

Milosz, Czeslaw
author of: **11** Native Realm, The Usurpers **13** Bells in Winter **14** Seizure of Power, The Captive Mind

milquetoast 4 wimp **7** milksop, nebbish **11** mollycoddle

Milton
author: **12** William Blake

Milton, George
character in: **12** Of Mice and Men
author: **9** Steinbeck

Milton, John
author of: **7** Lycidas **8** L'Allegro **11** Il Penseroso **12** Areopagitica, Paradise Lost **15** Samson Agonistes **16** Paradise Regained **29** On the Morning of Christ's Nativity

Milton Berle Show, The
host: **11** Milton Berle
regulars: **10** Fatso Marco **11** Arnold Stang, Jack Collins, Milton Frome, Ruth Gilbert **12** Irving Benson **13** Bobby Sherwood
announcer: **8** Sid Stone **11** Jimmy Nelson **13** Jack Lescoulie
orchestra: **8** Alan Roth, Billy May **11** Victor Young
theme: **7** Near You
Milton Berle's nickname: **12** Mr Television
sponsor: **5** Buick **6** Texaco

Milwaukee
baseball team: **7** Brewers
basketball team: **5** Bucks
Indian name: **16** Mahn-a-waukee Seepe
lake: **8** Michigan
river: **9** Milwaukee, Menomonee, **12** Kinnickinnic
university: **9** Marquette

mimic 3 ape **4** aper, copy, echo, mime **6** mirror, parrot **7** copycat, copyist, feigner, imitate, take off **8** imitator, simulate **9** reproduce **10** burlesquer **11** counterfeit, impersonate **13** impressionist

Mimir
origin: **12** Scandinavian
god of: **3** sea
decapitated by: **5** Vanir
head sent to: **4** Odin **5** Othin
oracle for: **4** Asar **5** Aesir

mimosa 14 Acacia dealbata **18** Albizia Julibrissin
  varieties: 5 Texas **6** golden **7** prairie **8** Egyptian
  cocktail contains: 9 champagne **10** orange juice

mince 4 dice, pose **5** grate, shred **6** refine, soften **7** posture, qualify **8** chop fine, hold back, mitigate, moderate, palliate **9** gloss over, put on airs, whitewash **12** attitudinize **14** affect delicacy, affect primness **15** give oneself airs **16** affect daintiness, soften one's speech **18** cut into small pieces **19** be mealymouthed about **20** cut into tiny particles

mince words 5 dodge, hedge, stall **10** equivocate **11** be ambiguous **13** avoid the issue **17** beat around the bush

mind 4 hate, heed, note, obey, tend, will, wits **5** abhor, bow to, brain, focus, sense, watch **6** brains, choice, detest, eschew, follow, intent, liking, memory, notice, notion, reason, recall, regard, resent, sanity **7** dislike, marbles, observe, opinion, outlook, thought **8** adhere to, attend to, be wary of, judgment, object to, reaction, response, submit to, take care, thinking **9** attention, awareness, be careful, cognition, faculties, intellect, intention, look after, sentiment **10** be cautious, comply with, conception, conclusion, gray matter, impression, perception, propensity, recoil from, reflection, shrink from, take care of **11** acquiesce to, be wary about, inclination, percipience, point of view, rationality, remembrance **12** apprehension, disapprove of, intelligence, recollection, reminiscence, take charge of, take notice of **13** be conscious of, comprehension, concentration, consciousness, consideration, contemplation, look askance at, preoccupation, ratiocination, retrospection, understanding **14** pay attention to
  German: 5 Geist

mindful 4 wary **5** aware **7** alert to, alive to, careful, heedful **8** cautious, sensible, watchful **9** cognizant, conscious, observant, regardful **10** absorbed in, open-eyed to, thoughtful **11** attentive to, engrossed in, taken up with **12** occupied with **15** preoccupied with

mindfulness 9 alertness, awareness **10** perception **12** acquaintance **13** attentiveness, consciousness, understanding

mindless 6 insane, obtuse, stupid **7** asinine, doltish, idiotic, unaware, witless **8** careless, heedless **9** apathetic, cretinous, imbecilic, oblivious, unattuned, unheeding **10** neglectful, regardless, sophomoric, unthinking **11** inattentive, indifferent, nonsensical, thoughtless, unobservant, unreasoning

12 disregardful, simple-minded **13** inconsiderate, unintelligent **14** indiscriminate

mine 3 pit **4** fund **5** cache, hoard, shaft, stock, store **6** dig for, quarry, supply, tunnel, wealth **7** extract, reserve **8** dig under, excavate, treasure **9** abundance, booby-trap **10** excavation **12** accumulation

Mineo, Sal
  real name: 14 Salvatore Mineo
  born: 7 Bronx NY
  roles: 5 Giant, Tonka **6** Exodus **18** Rebel Without a Cause, Who Killed Teddy Bear?

mineral 3 jet, ore **4** coal, gold, iron, mica, opal, spar, talc **5** beryl, topaz **6** augite, barite, blende, cerine, copper, galena, garnet, iolite, pinite, rutile, sandix, silver, sphene, spinel, sulfur **7** amesite, apatite, azurite, biotite, bornite, calcite, citrine, coesite, crystal, cuprite, cyanite, element, gahnite, helvite, jadeite, kernite, kunzite, niobite, olivine, prasine, zeolite, zircon **8** asbestos, borocite, chlorite, cinnabar, corundum, dolomite, epsomite, fayalite, feldspar, fluorite, graphite, hematite, lazulite, siderite, sodalite, stibnite, triplite, wellsite **9** aragonite, argentite, carnelian, celestite, cerussite, danburite, fosterite, kaolinite, lawsonite, magnetite, malachite, muscovite, petroleum, phenakite, scapolite, tridymite, turquoise, wulfenite **10** calaverite, chalcedony, orthoclase, pyrrhotite, sphalerite, tourmaline, wolfachite **11** alexandrite, chrysoberyl, melanterite **12** brazilianite, chalcopyrite, fincalconite, fluorapatite **13** rhodochrosite

Minerva
  origin: 5 Roman
  goddess of: 3 war **4** arts **6** wisdom **11** handicrafts
  corresponds to: 6 Athena

mingle 3 mix **4** fuse, join **5** blend, merge, unite **6** hobnob **7** combine, consort **8** coalesce, intermix **9** associate, circulate, commingle, interfuse, interlard, socialize **10** amalgamate, fraternize, intertwine, interweave **11** intermingle, intersperse **12** rub shoulders

miniature 3 wee **4** tiny **5** elfin, pygmy **6** bantam, little, petite **9** minuscule **10** diminutive, pocket-size, small-scale **11** lilliputian, microcosmic, microscopic

minim
  abbreviation: 3 min

minimal 5 token **7** minimum, nominal **13** least possible, unappreciable

minimize 5 dwarf **6** reduce, shrink **8** belittle, mitigate **9** underrate **10** depreciate, undervalue

minimum 4 base **5** basic, least **7** modicum **8** smallest

minister 4 abbe, tend **5** padre, rabbi, serve, vicar **6** answer, cleric, father, oblige, parson, pastor, priest **7** care for, cater to **8** attend to, chaplain, pander to, preacher, reverend **9** clergyman, secretary **10** evangelist, revivalist, take care of **11** accommodate **12** ecclesiastic **13** cabinet member

ministerial 6 cleric **8** churchly, clerical, pastoral, priestly **14** ecclesiastical

ministration 3 aid **4** care **6** charge **7** comfort **9** attention **10** protection **11** supervision

Minnehaha
  character in: 8 Hiawatha
  author: 10 Longfellow

Minnelli, Liza
  father: 8 Vincente
  mother: 11 Judy Garland
  born: 12 Los Angeles CA
  roles: 6 Arthur **7** Cabaret (Oscar) **11** Stepping Out **14** New York New York **16** The Sterile Cuckoo **17** Flora the Red Menace

Minnelli, Vincente
  director of: 4 Gigi (Oscar) **9** Brigadoon **11** Lust for Life **15** Bells Are Ringing, Meet Me in St Louis **16** Father of the Bride **17** An American in Paris

Minnesota
  abbreviation: 2 MN **4** Minn
  nickname: 6 Gopher **9** North Star **19** Land of Sky-blue Waters **22** Land of Ten Thousand Lakes
  capital: 6 St Paul
  largest city: 11 Minneapolis
  others: 3 Ada, Ely **4** Mora **5** Edina **6** Austin, Duluth, Newulm, Winona **7** Babbitt, Bemidji, Fosston, Hibbing, Mankato, Red Wing, St Cloud **8** Brainerd, Moorhead **9** Albertlea, Blue Earth, Richfield, Rochester, Roseville **10** Minnetonka, Robinsdale **11** Bloomington, St Louis Park **14** Brooklyn Center **18** International Falls
  college: 6 Bethel, St Olaf, Winona **7** Bemidji, Hamline **8** Adolphus, Augsburg, Carleton, St Thomas **10** Macalester
  feature:
    monument: 10 Paul Bunyan
    national monument: 9 Pipestone **12** Grand Portage
    national park: 9 Voyageurs'
    Norse artifact: 19 Kensington Rune Stone
  tribe: 5 Sioux **6** Dakota, Ojibwa, Santee **8** Chippewa **9** Menominee
  people: 11 Judy Garland **12** Mayo brothers **13** Harold Stassen, Lauris Norstad, Sinclair Lewis **16** F Scott Fitzgerald
    explorer: 8 Hennepin, Norsemen, Radisson **9** Greysolon **12** Groseilliers **19** Sieur Duluth of du Lhut
  lakes: 3 Red **5** Leech, Rainy **6** Itasca **7** Bemidji **8** Superior **9** Mille Lacs **10**

Minnewaska **14** Lake of the Woods, Winnibigoshish
land rank: 7 twelfth
mountain: 6 Cuyuna, Mesabi **7** Misquah **9** Vermilion
  highest point: 5 Eagle
physical feature: 6 Big Bog **14** Northwest Angle
  falls: 9 Minnehaha
river: 3 Red **5** Rainy **6** Pigeon **7** St Croix, St Louis **9** Des Moines, Minnesota **10** St Lawrence **11** Mississippi
state admission: 12 thirty-second
state bird: 10 common loon
state fish: 7 walleye
state flower: 14 moccasin flower **24** pink and white lady's slipper
state motto: 17 The Star of the North
state song: 13 Hail Minnesota
state tree: 13 Norway red pine
baseball team: 5 Twins
basketball team: 4 Lynx **12** Timberwolves
football team: 7 Vikings
hockey team: 4 Wild

Minni *see* **7** Armenia
minor 5 child, light, petty, small, youth **6** infant, lesser, paltry, slight **7** trivial **8** nugatory, picayune, piddling, teenager, trifling **9** secondary, youngster **10** adolescent **11** subordinate, unimportant **13** insignificant **14** inconsiderable **15** inconsequential
minority 4 less **5** youth **6** lesser, nonage **7** boyhood, infancy **8** girlhood **9** childhood, juniority **10** immaturity **11** adolescence
minor-league 4 punk **5** dinky, seedy, tacky **6** cheesy, common, lesser, shabby **8** inferior, small-fry **9** secondary, small-time **10** bush-league, second-rate **13** insignificant

Minos
king of: 5 Crete
father: 4 Zeus
mother: 6 Europa
brother: 8 Sarpedon **12** Rhadamanthys
wife: 8 Pasiphae
daughter: 7 Ariadne, Phaedra
ordered: 9 Labryinth
became: 5 judge
  in: 5 Hades

Minotaur
form: 7 monster
combined: 3 man **4** bull
father: 10 Cretan bull
mother: 8 Pasiphae
home: 9 Labryinth
ate flesh of: 6 humans
killed by: 7 Theseus

minstrel 4 bard, poet **6** dancer, end man, lyrist, player, singer **8** comedian, songster **9** blackface, poetaster, serenader, versifier **10** troubadour **11**

entertainer **12** interlocutor, vaudevillian **15** song-and-dance man

mint
varieties: 3 dog, red **4** wood **5** apple, field, lemon, stone, water **6** coyote, dotted, orange, Scotch **7** Meehan's **8** bergamot, Corsican, creeping, Japanese, mountain **9** pineapple
flavor: 7 menthol **9** spearmint **10** peppermint
liqueur: 13 creme de menthe
botanical name: 6 Mentha **8** Labiatae, M spicata **9** M piperita
origin: 13 Mediterranean
related herb: 7 oregano **8** marjoram, rosemary
symbol of: 11 hospitality
mythical nymph: 6 Mintha
  beloved of: 5 Pluto
  Mintha trod underfoot by: 10 Persephone
cure for: 7 hiccups
antidote for: 16 sea serpent stings
use: 4 lamb **5** salad **6** fruits

Minthe
form: 5 nymph
changed into: 9 mint plant
changed by: 10 Persephone

minuscule 3 wee **4** tiny **5** small **6** minute **10** teeny-weeny **11** small letter **13** infinitesimal **15** lowercase letter

minute 3 wee **4** fine, puny, tiny, wink **5** close, exact, flash, jiffy, petty, scant, shake, teeny, trice **6** breath, little, moment, petite, second, slight, strict **7** careful, instant, minikin, precise **8** detailed, itemized, trifling **9** miniature, twinkling **10** a short time, diminutive, exhaustive, meticulous, negligible, scrupulous **11** lilliputian, microscopic **12** sixty seconds **13** conscientious, imperceptible, inappreciable, infinitesimal, insignificant **14** extremely small, inconsiderable
abbreviation: 3 min

minute portion 3 bit, sip **4** bite **5** crumb, grain, scrap, shred, speck **6** morsel, sliver **7** swallow **8** fragment, mouthful, particle
minutiae 6 trivia **7** trifles **8** niceties **10** bagatelles, pedantries, subtleties **11** odds and ends, particulars **12** minor details, trivialities **15** particularities
minx 4 jade, slut **5** hussy, huzzy, wench **7** baggage **10** prostitute

Minyades
daughters of: 6 Minyas

Miolnir
hammer of: 4 Thor
mir 5 peace, world **21** Russian village commune
mirabile dictu 12 strange to say **17** marvelous to relate
miracle 4 omen, sign **6** marvel, wonder **7** mystery, portent, prodigy **9** di-

vine act, sensation, spectacle **10** phenomenon **11** masterpiece

Miracle of Morgan's Creek, The
director: 14 Preston Sturges
cast: 9 Diana Lynn **11** Betty Hutton **12** Brian Donlevy, Eddie Bracken **15** William Demarest

Miracle on 34th Street
director: 12 George Seaton
based on story by: 15 Valentine Davies
cast: 9 John Payne **11** Edmund Gwenn (Kris Kringle), Natalie Wood **12** Gene Lockhart, Maureen O'Hara, Thelma Ritter
Oscar for: 12 screenwriter **15** supporting actor (Gwenn)

Miracle Worker, The
director: 10 Arthur Penn
cast: 9 Patty Duke (Helen Keller) **10** Victor Jory **11** Inga Swenson **12** Anne Bancroft (Anne Sullivan)
Oscar for: 7 actress (Bancroft) **17** supporting actress (Duke)

miraculous 6 divine **7** amazing, magical **9** marvelous, visionary, wonderful **10** incredible, mysterious, phenomenal, prodigious, remarkable **11** astonishing, astounding, exceptional, spectacular, supernormal **13** extraordinary, preternatural, wonderworking **14** thaumaturgical
miraculous food 5 manna
Miraculous writing
also: 4 mene **5** perez, tekel **8** upharsin
means: 7 divided, weighed **8** numbered
interpreted by: 6 Daniel
mirage 5 fancy **7** fantasy **8** delusion, illusion, phantasm **9** unreality **12** will-o'-the-wisp **13** hallucinations, misconception **14** castle in the air **15** optical illusion

Miranda
character in: 10 The Tempest
author: 11 Shakespeare
Miranda, Carmen
real name: 26 Maria do Carmo Miranda da Cunha
nickname: 18 Brazilian Bombshell
born: 8 Portugal **16** Marco de Canavezes
roles: 10 Copacabana **14** That Night in Rio **15** Weekend in Havana **16** Down Argentine Way **22** Springtime in the Rockies

mire 3 bog, fen, mud **4** cake, muck, ooze, soil **5** marsh, muddy, slime, slush, smear **6** enmesh, sludge **7** begrime, bog down, ensnare, spatter **8** besmirch, entangle, quagmire

Miriam
father: 5 Amram
mother: 8 Jochebed
brother: 5 Aaron, Moses
Miro, Joan

born: 5 Spain 8 Montroig 9 Barcelona
artwork: 9 Help Spain, The Reaper 13 Dutch Interior 14 Constellations 16 Catalan Landscape 19 Dog Barking at the Moon 20 Still Life with Old Shoe 26 Woman and Bird in the Moonlight

mirror 4 copy, show 5 glass, image, model 7 epitome, example, paragon, reflect 8 exemplar, manifest, paradigm, standard 10 reflection 11 cheval glass 12 looking glass

mirth 4 glee 6 gaiety, levity 7 jollity 8 drollery, hilarity, laughter 9 amusement, festivity, happiness, jocundity, joviality, merriment 10 jocularity 11 good spirits, merrymaking, playfulness 12 cheerfulness

mirthful 3 gay 4 glad 5 happy, jolly, merry 6 blithe, jocose, jovial, joyful, joyous 7 gleeful, jocular, risible

mirthless 3 sad 4 dour, glum 6 gloomy, morose 7 joyless, unhappy 8 dejected 9 cheerless, sorrowful 10 in the dumps, melancholy 14 down in the mouth

miry 3 wet 4 oozy 5 boggy, mucky, muddy, slimy, slushy, soggy 6 claggy, swampy 7 sloughy

misadventure 3 ill 4 slip 6 mishap 7 debacle, failure, reverse, setback 8 bad break, calamity, casualty, disaster 9 adversity, mischance 10 infelicity, misfortune 11 catastrophe, contretemps

misanthrope 5 cynic 7 skeptic 9 pessimist 10 misogynist

Misanthrope, Le
    author: 7 Moliere
    character: 7 Alceste, Arsinoe, Eliante 8 Celimene, Philinte

misanthropic 4 cold 5 surly 6 morose 7 cynical, distant 10 antisocial, unfriendly, unsociable 11 distrustful 12 discourteous, inhospitable, unneighborly, unpersonable, unresponsive 14 unapproachable 15 unaccommodating

misapply 5 abuse 6 misuse 9 misemploy 13 use improperly

misapprehension 5 mixup 7 mistake 11 misjudgment 13 misconception 14 miscalculation 15 false impression, misconstruction 16 misunderstanding 17 misinterpretation

misappropriate 4 bilk 5 abuse, cheat, mulct, steal 6 misuse 7 defraud, purloin, swindle 8 embezzle, misapply, peculate 9 defalcate, misemploy

misappropriation 6 misuse, taking 11 defalcation 12 embezzlement

misbehave 5 act up 7 disobey, do wrong 10 transgress 15 get into mischief

misbehavior 5 lapse 7 misdeed, offense 8 acting up, trespass 9 impudence 10 bad conduct, bad manners,

disrespect, misconduct 11 delinquency, dereliction, impropriety, misdemeanor 12 indiscretion 13 transgression 16 obstreperousness, unmanageableness

miscalculate 3 err 8 misjudge 10 guess wrong 11 misestimate

miscalculation 5 error 10 inaccuracy 13 misestimation

miscarriage 4 slip 5 botch 6 fizzle 7 default, failing, failure, misfire, undoing, washout 8 casualty, collapse

miscarry 4 fail 5 abort, botch 6 fizzle, go awry 9 terminate 12 come to naught

miscellanea 8 analects 9 anthology, gleanings, scrapbook 10 collection, miscellany, selections 11 collectanea

miscellaneous 5 mixed 6 divers, motley, sundry, varied 7 diverse, mingled, various 8 assorted, manifold 9 different 11 diversified 13 heterogeneous

miscellaneous collection
    Latin/pseudo Latin: 14 omniumgatherum

miscellany 5 blend 6 jumble, medley 7 melange, mixture, variety 8 analects, extracts, mishmash, pastiche 9 anthology, gleanings, potpourri 10 assortment, collection, hodgepodge, salmagundi, selections 11 collectanea, compilation, gallimaufry, miscellanea 14 conglomeration, omnium-gatherum

mischance 6 ill lot, mishap 7 bad luck, ill luck, ill wind 8 accident 9 adversity 10 infelicity, misfortune 12 misadventure

mischief 4 evil 5 wrong 6 injury, malice 7 devilry, knavery, roguery 8 deviltry, foul play, plotting, scheming, villainy 9 depravity, devilment, rascality 10 orneriness, wrongdoing 11 naughtiness, playfulness, roguishness, shenanigans, willfulness 12 prankishness, sportiveness 14 capriciousness

mischief-maker 3 imp 5 demon, devil, scamp 7 gremlin, hellion 9 scoundrel 10 hell-raiser

mischievous 3 sly 5 elfin 6 elfish, impish, malign, vexing, wicked 7 harmful, naughty, noxious, playful, roguish, teasing, vicious, waggish 8 annoying, devilish, prankish, spiteful, sportive 9 injurious, malicious, malignant, uninvited 10 frolicsome, gratuitous, pernicious 11 deleterious, destructive, detrimental, uncalled for 12 exacerbating

misconceive 3 err 4 lose, miss 8 misjudge 12 misinterpret 13 misunderstand

misconception 5 error 8 delusion 11 misjudgment 13 erroneous idea 14 misinformation 15 misapprehension, misconstruction 16 misunderstanding 17 misinterpretation, misrepresentation

misconduct 7 misdeed, misstep 10 misprision, peccadillo, wrongdoing 11 delinquency, dereliction, impropriety, malefaction, malfeasance, misbehavior, misdemeanor 13 transgression

misconstrue 7 distort, mistake 8 misjudge 9 misreckon, misrender 12 misapprehend, miscalculate, misinterpret, mistranslate 13 misunderstand

miscreant 3 bum 4 heel 5 knave, scamp 6 bad egg, rascal, sinner, wretch 7 villain 8 evildoer, lost soul, scalawag 9 reprobate, scoundrel 10 blackguard, black sheep, malefactor

misdeed 3 sin 4 slip 5 crime, lapse, wrong 6 felony 7 faux pas, offense, outrage 8 atrocity, trespass 9 violation 10 misconduct, peccadillo 11 malfeasance, misbehavior, misdemeanor 12 indiscretion, infringement 13 transgression

misdemeanor 3 sin 5 crime, fault 7 offense, misdeed 8 disorder 10 peccadillo 11 misbehavior 13 transgression

misdoer 5 crook 8 criminal 9 miscreant, wrongdoer 10 delinquent

mise en scene 6 milieu 7 setting 8 ambience 10 atmosphere, background 11 environment 12 stage setting, surroundings

miser 5 piker 7 hoarder, niggard, Scrooge, skimper 8 tightwad 9 skinflint 10 cheapskate, pinchpenny 12 pennypincher, stingy person

Miser, The
    also: 6 L'Avare
    author: 7 Moliere
    character: 5 Elise 6 Valere 7 Anselme, Cleante, Mariane 8 Harpagon

miserable 3 sad 4 mean 5 inept, needy, sorry 6 abject, scurvy, shabby, sordid, woeful 7 abysmal, crushed, doleful, forlorn, grieved, hapless, unhappy 8 beggarly, degraded, dejected, desolate, dolorous, feckless, inferior, mournful, pathetic, pitiable, rubbishy, very poor, wretched 9 appalling, atrocious, cheerless, depressed, desperate, heartsick, sorrowful, woebegone 10 chapfallen, deplorable, despicable, despondent, heavy-laden, lamentable, second-rate, unbearable 11 crestfallen, heartbroken, unfortunate 12 contemptible, disconsolate, impoverished 13 brokenhearted 14 down in the mouth

Miserables, Les
    author: 10 Victor Hugo
    character: 6 Javert 7 Cosette, Fantine 10 Thenardier 11 Jean Valjean 15 Father Madeleine, Marius Pontmercy 17 Eponine Thenardier

misericordia 5 mercy 10 compassion

miserliness 6 penury 9 frugality, parsimony 10 stinginess 13 niggardliness, penny-pinching 15 tight-fistedness

miserly 4 mean, near 5 cheap, tight 6

frugal, greedy, meager, stingy **7** selfish **8** grasping, grudging, pinching **9** illiberal, niggardly, penurious, scrimping **10** avaricious, ungenerous **11** closefisted, closehanded, tight-fisted **12** parsimonious **13** penny-pinching

misery 3 woe **4** blow **5** agony, curse, grief, trial **6** ordeal, regret, sorrow **7** anguish, bad deal, bad news, chagrin, despair, sadness, torment, trouble **8** bad scene, calamity, disaster, distress, exaction, hardship **9** dejection, heartache, privation, suffering **10** affliction, bitter pill, depression, desolation, melancholy, misfortune **11** catastrophe, despondency, tribulation **12** wretchedness

Misfits, The
　director: **10** John Huston
　based on story by: **12** Arthur Miller
　cast: **10** Clark Gable, Eli Wallach **12** Thelma Ritter **13** Marilyn Monroe **15** Montgomery Clift

misfortune 4 blow, loss **6** misery, mishap **7** bad luck, reverse, setback, tragedy, trouble **8** calamity, casualty, disaster, downfall, hard luck, hardship **9** adversity, hard times, ruination **10** affliction, ill fortune **11** catastrophe, tribulation **12** misadventure

misgiving, misgivings 4 fear **5** alarm, doubt, dread, qualm, worry **7** anxiety, dubiety **8** disquiet, mistrust **9** suspicion **10** foreboding, skepticism **11** dubiousness, uncertainty **12** apprehension, doubtfulness, presentiment, reservations **14** second thoughts

misguided 5 at sea **6** adrift, faulty, misled, unwise **7** in error **8** mistaken **9** erroneous, imprudent, led astray, off course **10** ill-advised, indiscreet, misadvised **11** injudicious, misdirected, misinformed

mishap 4 slip, snag **5** botch **6** fiasco, slipup **7** reverse, setback **8** casualty, disaster **9** mischance **10** difficulty, misfortune **11** miscarriage **12** misadventure

mishmash 3 mix **4** hash, stew **5** salad **6** jumble, medley, muddle **7** melange **8** mixed bag, pastiche, scramble **9** patchwork **10** assemblage, crazy quilt, hodgepodge, miscellany, salmagundi **14** conglomeration, omnium-gatherum

misinform 7 deceive, mislead **8** misguide **9** misdirect **10** lead astray **12** misrepresent

misinterpret 11 misconstrue **12** misapprehend **13** misunderstand

misinterpretation 13 misconception **16** misunderstanding **17** misrepresentation

misjudge 3 err **7** mistake **10** exaggerate, understate **11** misconceive, misconstrue **12** misapprehend, miscalculate, misinterpret, overestimate **13** misunderstand, underestimate

mislay 4 lose, miss **8** displace, misplace

mislead 4 dupe, fool, gull **6** betray, delude, entice, seduce, take in **7** beguile, deceive **8** hoodwink, inveigle, misguide **9** bamboozle, misdirect, misinform, play false, victimize **10** lead astray **11** double-cross, string along

misleading 6 luring **8** deluding **9** deceiving **10** misguiding **11** hoodwinking

mismanage 3 mar **4** flub, muff, ruin **5** botch, spoil **6** bollix, bungle, foul up, mess up **7** louse up, screw up **9** mishandle **11** make a hash of, make a mess of

misnomer 8 misusage, solecism **9** barbarism, misnaming **11** malapropism

misogynic 7 cynical **11** woman-hating **12** misanthropic

misogynist 5 cynic **10** woman-hater **11** misanthrope

misplace 4 lose **5** abuse **6** mislay **11** lose track of

misreckon 8 misjudge **10** guess wrong, miscompute **11** misestimate **12** miscalculate

misrepresent 7 falsify, mislead **8** disguise

misrepresentation 7 mockery **8** altering, travesty, twisting **9** burlesque, doctoring **10** caricature, distortion, falsifying **12** adulteration, exaggeration, misstatement **13** falsification

miss 4 blow, girl, lack, lady, lass, lose, loss, maid, muff, skip, slip, want **5** avert, avoid, error, forgo, let go, woman **6** bypass, damsel, escape, forego, lassie, maiden, miscue, pass by **7** blunder, colleen, default, failure, fly wide, let pass, let slip, long for, mistake, neglect, old maid, overrun **8** leave out, omission, overlook, pass over, senorita, slip up on, spinster, yearn for **9** disregard, fall short, false step, gloss over, go without, overshoot, oversight, surrender, young lady **10** demoiselle, schoolgirl **12** be absent from **13** feel the loss of, mademoiselle

missal 10 prayer book

missed
　French: **6** manque

misshapen 7 twisted **8** deformed **9** contorted, distorted

missile 4 ball, dart **5** arrow, lance, shaft, shell, spear, stone **6** bullet, rocket **7** harpoon, javelin **10** projectile

missing 4 AWOL, gone, lost **6** absent **7** lacking, left out, not here **8** avoiding, skipping **10** longing for, not present **11** overlooking, yearning for **12** disregarding

Missing
　director: **22** Constantine Costa-Gavras

cast: **8** John Shea **10** Jack Lemmon **11** Sissy Spacek **13** Melanie Mayron

mission 3 end, job **4** task **5** quest **6** charge **7** calling, mandate, pursuit **8** legation, ministry **9** objective **10** assignment, commission, delegation, enterprise **11** raison d'etre, undertaking

Mission
　tribe: **7** Chumash, Juaneno, Luiseno **8** Diegueno, Costanoan **10** Gabrielino **11** Fernandario
　location: **10** California

Mission: Impossible
　character: **5** Casey, Paris **10** Rollin Hand **11** Dana Lambert, James Phelps **12** Daniel Briggs **13** Barney Collier **14** Cinnamon Carter, Willie Armitage
　cast: **10** Greg Morris, Peter Lupus, Steven Hill **11** Barbara Bain, Peter Graves **12** Leonard Nimoy, Martin Landau **14** Lynda Day George **15** Lesley Ann Warren

Mississippi
　abbreviation: **2** MS **4** Miss
　nickname: **5** Bayou **6** Mudcat **8** Magnolia
　capital/largest city: **7** Jackson
　others: **6** Biloxi, Helena, Laurel, Tupelo, Winona **7** Belzoni, Corinth, Grenada, Natchez **8** Bogalusa, Columbus, Gulfport, Meridian **9** Kosciusko, Vicksburg **10** Clarksdale, Pascagoula **11** Hattiesburg **13** Pass Christian
　college: **4** Rust **6** Alcorn **7** Jackson **8** Belhaven, Millsaps, Tougaloo **11** Mississippi **12** Blue Mountain, William Carey
　feature: **12** Natchez Trace
　　national military park: **9** Vicksburg
　　national seashore: **11** Gulf Islands
　tribe: **3** Sac **5** Tious **6** Biloxi, Mandan, Tunica **7** Choctaw, Natchez, Tonikan **8** Chicksaw
　people: **11** Eudora Welty **15** William Faulkner **17** Tennessee Williams
　　explorer: **6** DeSoto, Joliet **9** Iberville, Marquette
　island: **3** Cat **4** Horn, Ship **9** Petit Bois
　lake: **4** Enid **6** Sardis **7** Barnett, Grenada **8** Pickwick **9** Arkabutla, Okatibbee
　land rank: **12** thirty-second
　highest point: **7** Woodall
　physical feature:
　　delta: **10** Yazoo Basin
　　hills: **8** Fall Line **9** Tennessee **11** Loess Bluffs
　　prairie: **5** Black **7** Jackson
　　sound: **11** Mississippi
　river: **4** Leaf **5** Pearl, Yazoo **8** Big Black **9** Tombigbee, Yalobusha **10** Homochitto, Pascagoula **11** Mississippi **12** Tallahatchie
　state admission: **9** twentieth
　state bird: **11** mockingbird

state flower: 8 magnolia
state motto: 14 By Valor and Arms
state song: 13 Go Mississippi
state tree: 8 magnolia
missive 4 note **6** billet, letter **7** epistle, message **13** communication **14** correspondence

Miss Lonelyhearts
author: 13 Nathanael West

Missouri
abbreviation: 2 MO
nickname: 5 Ozark **6** Show-Me **7** Bullion **15** Mother of the West
capital: 13 Jefferson City
largest city: 7 St Louis
others: 5 Eldon, Hayti, Lamar, Macon, Rolla **6** Butler, Joplin, Mexico **7** Bethany, Bolivar, Cameron, Clayton, Lebanon, Moberly, Sedalia **8** Berkeley, Columbia, Hannibal, Kirkwood, Sikeston, St Joseph **10** Bonne Terre, Kansas City **11** Springfield, Warrensburg **12** Independence **13** Cape Girardeau, Webster Groves
college: 5 Avila, Drury **6** Tarkio **7** Lincoln, St Louis, Webster **8** Stephens **10** Washington **11** Westminster
feature:
  dam: 5 Osage
  tribe: 3 Fox, Sac **4** Sauk **5** Osage **7** Shawnee **8** Cherokee, Missouri
  people: 7 TS Eliot **9** Mark Twain **10** Jesse James **11** Omar Bradley **12** Helen Traubel, Sara Teasdale **13** John J Pershing, Marianne Moore, Samuel Clemens **15** Reinhold Niebuhr **22** George Washington Carver
  explorer: 6 Joliet **7** La Salle **9** Marquette
lake: 7 Norfolk **9** Tablerock, Taneycomo **10** Bull Shoals **14** Kaysinger Bluff **15** Lake of the Ozarks
land rank: 10 nineteenth
mountain: 6 Ozarks **10** St Francois
  highest point: 8 Taumsauk
physical feature: 8 Bootheel **9** Big Spring
  plains: 4 Till **5** Osage
  plateau: 5 Ozark
president: 12 Harry S Truman
river: 4 Salt **5** Grand, Osage, White **6** Platte **7** Current, Meramec **8** Big Muddy, Chariton, Missouri **9** Des Moines, Gasconade, St Francis **11** Mississippi
state admission: 12 twenty-fourth
state bird: 8 bluebird
state flower: 8 hawthorn
state motto: 41 The Welfare of the People Shall Be the Supreme Law
state song: 13 Missouri Waltz
state tree: 7 dogwood

Miss Peach
creator: 11 Mell Lazarus
character: 3 Ira **6** Arthur, Lester, Marcia **8** Francine
place: 9 Kamp Kelly **11** Kelly School

misspend 5 waste **8** squander **9** dissipate, throw away **11** fritter away
misspent 6 wasted **8** depraved **9** debauched, dissolute, idled away **10** misapplied, profitless, squandered, thrown away
misstate 5 alter **6** bollix, garble **7** confuse, distort, falsify, pervert **8** misquote **9** misreport **12** misrepresent
misstatement 3 fib, lie **4** tale **5** error **7** falsity, untruth **9** falsehood **13** prevarication **17** misrepresentation
misstep 3 sin **4** goof, slip, vice **5** boner, error, fault, gaffe, lapse **6** booboo, defect, foul-up **7** blooper, faux pas, offense, screw-up **11** delinquency, dereliction, shortcoming **12** indiscretion **13** transgression
miss the mark 4 fail **9** fall short **11** come up short
miss the point 7 mistake **11** fail to catch, misconceive **12** misapprehend **13** misunderstand
mist 3 fog **4** haze, murk, smog **5** steam, vapor **7** drizzle
mistake 4 slip **5** boner, error, gaffe, mix-up **6** slipup **7** blooper, blunder, confuse, faux pas, misstep **8** confound, misjudge **9** misreckon, oversight **11** misconstrue, misidentify **12** misapprehend, miscalculate, misinterpret **13** misunderstand **14** miscalculation
French: 10 malentendu
mistaken 5 at sea, false, wrong **6** faulty, untrue **7** at fault, in error, unsound **8** deceived **9** erroneous, illogical, incorrect, off course, unfounded **10** fallacious, groundless, inaccurate, ungrounded **11** unjustified
Mister 3 aga, dom, don, pan, reb, sir **4** agha, babu, herr **5** sahib, senor **6** senhor, signor **7** mynheer **8** monsieur

Mister Roberts
author: 12 Thomas Heggen
director: 8 John Ford **11** Mervyn LeRoy
cast: 8 Ward Bond **10** Henry Fonda, Jack Lemmon (Ensign Pulver) **11** Betsy Palmer, James Cagney **13** William Powell
Oscar for: 15 supporting actor (Lemmon)

Mister Saturday Night
nickname of: 13 Jackie Gleason
mistreat 4 harm **5** abuse, bully, hound, wrong **6** harass, ill-use, injure, misuse, molest **7** assault, oppress, outrage, pervert, torment, violate **8** ill-treat, maltreat **9** brutalize, manhandle, mishandle, persecute
mistreatment 5 abuse **6** ill-use, injury **7** assault, cruelty, harming **10** bodily harm, oppression **11** manhandling, molestation, persecution **12** maltreatment

mistress 3 Mrs **4** doxy, lady, Miss **5** lover, Madam **6** matron **8** ladylove, paramour **9** concubine, headwoman, housewife, inamorata, kept woman **10** chatelaine, girlfriend, sweetheart
mistrust 5 doubt, qualm **7** anxiety, dubiety, suspect **8** distrust, question, wariness **9** challenge, chariness, leeriness, misgiving, suspicion **10** disbelieve, skepticism
misty 4 dewy, hazy **5** filmy, foggy, murky **6** cloudy, opaque, steamy **8** nebulous, overcast, vaporous **10** indistinct
misunderstand 7 confuse, misread, mistake **8** misjudge **9** misreckon **11** misconceive, misconstrue **12** misapprehend, miscalculate, misinterpret, miss the point
misunderstanding 4 rift, spat **5** set-to **7** discord, dispute, quarrel, wrangle **8** conflict, squabble **10** difference, dissension, misreading **11** altercation, contretemps, misjudgment **12** disagreement **13** misconception **15** false impression, misapprehension **16** miscomprehension **17** misinterpretation
French: 10 malentendu
misuse 4 harm, hurt **5** abuse, waste, wrong **6** debase, injure **7** corrupt, exploit, outrage, pervert, profane **8** illtreat, maltreat, misapply, mistreat, wrong use **9** misemploy **10** corruption, perversion, prostitute **11** desecration, profanation, squandering **12** ill treatment, maltreatment, mistreatment, prostitution **13** misemployment **14** misapplication **15** take advantage of

Mitchell, Billy (William Lendrum)
advocate of: 8 air power
court-martialed for: 15 insubordination
served in: 3 WWI
rank: 16 brigadier general
commander of: 15 US army air forces

Mitchell, Margaret
author of: 15 Gone With the Wind

Mitchell, Silas Weir
author of: 9 Hugh Wynne (Free Quaker) **11** Roland Blake

Mitchell, Thomas
born: 11 Elizabeth NJ
roles: 7 Our Town **8** Doc Boone **9** The Outlaw **10** Stagecoach **11** Gerald O'Hara, Lost Horizon **15** Gone With the Wind **19** Only Angels Have Wings

Mitchum, Robert
born: 12 Bridgeport CT
roles: 6 Midway **10** Winds of War **11** Thunder Road **13** Ryan's Daughter, The Longest Day, The Sundowners **15** The Story of G I Joe **16** Farewell My Lovely **20** Heaven Knows Mr Allison

mite 3 bit, jot 4 atom, iota, whit 5 scrap, speck 6 spider 7 smidgen 8 arachnid, particle

Mitford, Jessica
  author of: 21 The American Way of Death 22 Kind and Usual Punishment

Mitford, Nancy
  author of: 14 Noblesse Oblige 16 The Pursuit of Love 18 Love in a Cold Climate
  coined term: 1 U 4 non-U

Mithgarthr *see* 7 Midgard

Mithras
  origin: 7 Persian
  god of: 5 light, truth
  corresponds to: 3 Sol

mitigate 4 ease 5 allay, blunt 6 lessen, reduce, soften, soothe, temper, weaken 7 assuage, lighten, mollify, placate, relieve 8 diminish, moderate, palliate 9 alleviate, extenuate 10 ameliorate

mitigating 6 easing 8 allaying, blunting, reducing 9 assuaging, lessening, relieving, softening, tempering 10 lightening, moderating, palliating, palliative 11 diminishing, extenuating 12 ameliorating

Mitteleuropa 12 middle Europe

mitzvah, mitsvah 8 good deed 11 commandment

mix 3 add 4 beat, club, fold, fuse, join, stir, whip 5 admix, alloy, blend, merge, put in, unite 6 commix, fusion, hobnob, mingle 7 combine, consort, include, mixture 8 assembly, coalesce, compound, intermix, mingling 9 associate, commingle, interfuse, interlard, introduce, socialize 10 amalgamate, fraternize, intertwine, interweave 11 incorporate, intermingle, intersperse, put together

mixed 4 coed 5 fused 6 hybrid, motley 7 alloyed, blended, inmixed, mingled, mongrel, not pure 8 combined 9 composite, uncertain 10 ambivalent, indecisive, interwoven, variegated 11 adulterated, diversified, half and half, put together 12 conglomerate, inconclusive 13 heterogeneous, male-and-female, miscellaneous

mixed-up 6 addled 7 chaotic, jumbled, muddled, tangled 8 confused, rambling 9 befuddled, illogical, nonplused, perplexed 10 bewildered, disjointed, incoherent, irrational, nonplussed 12 disconnected, disorganized 13 disharmonious, heterogeneous

Mixtec
  tribe: 7 Zapotec

mixture 3 mix 4 hash, stew 5 alloy, blend, union 6 fusion, jumble, medley 7 amalgam, melange 8 compound, mishmash, pastiche 9 admixture, composite, potpourri 10 commixture, hodgepodge, salmagundi 11 association, combination 12 adulteration, amalgamation, intermixture

mixup 4 mess, riot 5 fight, melee, snafu 6 fracas, muddle, tangle 7 mistake 8 disorder 9 confusion, imbroglio 11 misjudgment 14 miscalculation 16 miscomprehension, misunderstanding

mix up 5 addle 6 mess up, muddle 7 confuse, nonplus, perplex 8 befuddle, bewilder 10 disarrange

Mneme
  member of: 5 Muses
  personifies: 6 memory

Mnemosyne
  origin: 5 Greek
  member of: 6 Titans
  goddess of: 6 memory
  father: 6 Uranus
  mother: 4 Gaea
  daughters: 5 Muses

Moab
  son of: 3 Lot
  land near: 7 Dead Sea
  home of: 4 Ruth 5 Naomi

Moabite god 7 Chemosh

moan 3 sob 4 keen, wail 5 groan 6 bemoan, bewail, lament, plaint 7 grumble 11 lamentation

moan over 5 mourn 6 bemoan, bewail, lament 7 cry over 8 weep over 10 grieve over

moat 4 foss 5 ditch, fosse, graff 6 gutter, rundel, trench

mob 4 gang, herd 5 crowd, crush, horde, Mafia, swarm 6 masses, rabble, throng 7 flock to 8 assembly, populace, surround 9 gathering, hoi polloi, multitude, plebeians, syndicate 10 converge on 11 proletariat, rank and file 14 organized crime

mobile 6 active, motile 7 kinetic, movable, nomadic 8 portable, rootless 9 footloose, traveling, wandering 10 ambulatory, locomotive

mobilize 6 call up, muster, summon 7 marshal 8 activate, organize 10 call to arms 11 put in motion

mobster 4 hood 6 hitman 7 hoodlum, Mafioso 8 gangster 10 gang member

Moby Dick
  author: 14 Herman Melville
  character: 4 Ahab 5 Stubb 7 Ishmael 8 Fedallah, Queequeg, Starbuck

mock 3 ape 4 copy 5 belie, mimic, scorn, spurn, taunt 6 deride, insult, jeer at, parody, revile, show up 7 imitate, laugh at, let down, profane, scoff at, sneer at 8 ridicule 9 burlesque, frustrate, make fun of, poke fun at 10 caricature, disappoint, make game of 11 make sport of

mockery 4 joke, sham 5 farce, scorn 7 jeering, mimicry, sarcasm 8 derision, raillery, ridicule, scoffing, travesty 9 burlesque, contumely 10 disrespect, ridiculing 13 laughingstock

Mock Turtle
  character in: 28 Alice's Adventures in Wonderland
  author: 7 Carroll

mode 3 cut, fad, way 4 form, rage, rule 5 craze, means, style, taste, trend, vogue 6 course, custom, manner, method, system 7 fashion, process 8 approach, practice 9 condition, procedure, technique 10 appearance

model 4 cast, copy, form, mold, show, type 5 build, dummy, ideal, shape, sport, style 6 design, mirror, mock-up 7 display, example, fashion, outline, paragon, pattern, perfect, replica, subject, variety, version 8 exemplar, paradigm, peerless, standard 9 archetype, criterion, exemplary, facsimile, mannequin, prototype, simulated 10 simulacrum 14 representation, representative

model on 6 base on 7 found on 10 derive from

mode of operating
  Latin: 2 mo 13 modus operandi

moderate 4 calm, cool, curb, fair, hush, mild, tame 5 abate, chair, sober 6 direct, gentle, lessen, manage, medium, modest, soften, subdue, temper 7 average, careful, conduct, control, oversee 8 diminish, measured, mediocre, middling, ordinary, passable, rational, regulate, restrain, tone down 9 judicious, peaceable, temperate, unruffled 10 not violent, reasonable 11 inexpensive, preside over 12 mainstreamer, medium-priced

moderation 7 abating, economy 8 allaying 9 abatement, frugality, lessening, remission, restraint 10 continence, diminution, mitigation, palliation, relaxation, temperance 11 alleviation, forbearance, self-control 12 moderateness 13 temperateness 14 abstemiousness 19 avoidance of extremes

moderator 8 chairman, mediator 10 chairwoman, negotiator

modern 3 new 6 modish, recent 7 current, in vogue 8 up-to-date 10 present-day 11 fashionable, streamlined 12 contemporary 15 contemporaneous 16 twentieth-century

modernistic 3 neo 6 modern 7 moderne 10 new-fangled 12 contemporary

modernity 5 vogue 7 fashion, new look, novelty, the rage 8 last word 14 newfangledness 15 contemporaneity 16 new fashionedness

modernize 4 redo 5 renew 6 do over, revamp, update 7 restore 8 redesign, renovate 9 refurbish 10 regenerate, rejuvenate, streamline 11 recondition

13 bring up to date **16** move with the times

modern times 5 today **8** nowadays **10** the present **13** the here and now

Modern Times
director: **14** Charles Chaplin
cast: **12** Henry Bergman **14** Charlie Chaplin, Chester Conklin **15** Paulette Goddard **19** Stanley "Tiny" Sandford

modest 3 coy, shy **4** meek, prim **5** plain, quiet, timid **6** demure, humble, proper, simple **7** bashful, limited, nominal, prudish, unshowy **8** blushing, discreet, moderate, reserved, timorous **9** diffident, shrinking **10** unassuming **11** circumspect, constrained, inexpensive, puritanical, straitlaced, unassertive, unobtrusive **12** medium-priced, not excessive, self-effacing, unpretending **13** unpretentious **14** unostentatious

modesty 7 coyness, prudery, reserve, shyness **8** humility, plainess, timidity **9** propriety, restraint, reticence **10** constraint, demureness, diffidence, humbleness, simplicity **11** bashfulness, naturalness **12** timorousness **14** reasonableness, self-effacement **15** inexpensiveness

modicum 3 bit, dab, jot **4** atom, dash, drop, inch, iota, mite, whit **5** crumb, grain, pinch, scrap, speck, tinge, touch **6** morsel, sliver, snatch, trifle **7** handful, minimum, smidgen **8** fraction, fragment, particle **9** little bit **10** sprinkling **11** small amount **13** small quantity

modification 6 change **8** revision **9** variation **10** adjustment, alteration, conversion, emendation, regulation **14** transformation **15** differentiation

modify 4 redo, vary **5** adapt, alter, limit, lower, remit **6** adjust, change, narrow, reduce, remold, revise, rework, soften, temper **7** control, convert, qualify, remodel, reshape **8** moderate, modulate, restrain, restrict, tone down **9** condition, refashion, transform, transmute **10** reorganize **12** transmogrify

Modigliani, Amedeo
born: **5** Italy **7** Leghorn, Livorno
artwork: **10** Seated Nude **13** Reclining Nude, Yellow Sweater **15** Jeanne Hebuterne

modish 2 in **3** now **4** chic **5** natty, nifty, sharp, smart, today **6** dapper, snazzy, spiffy, trendy, with it **7** a la mode, current, faddish, in style, in vogue, stylish, voguish **9** high-style **11** fashionable **13** up-to-the-minute

Modoc
language family: **12** Shapwailutan
division: **10** Lutuamnian
location: **6** Oregon **10** California
leader: **14** Chief Kintpuash (Captain Jack)
related to: **7** Klamath

Modred
character in: **16** Arthurian romance

Mod Squad, The
character: **9** Linc Hayes, (Capt) Adam Greer **11** Julie Barnes, Pete Cochran
cast: **11** Michael Cole, Peggy Lipton, Tige Andrews **19** Clarence Williams III

modulate 4 pass **5** lower **6** accord, attune, change, reduce, soften, temper **8** moderate, progress, regulate, tone down, turn down **9** harmonize

modulation 4 tone **5** pitch **6** accent **9** reduction **10** expression, regulation, transition

modus operandi 15 mode of operating
abbreviation: **2** mo

modus vivendi 14 manner of living

Mogadishu, Mogadiscio
capital of: **7** Somalia

mogul 3 VIP **4** czar, lord **5** baron, power, wheel **6** bigwig, tycoon **7** big shot, magnate, notable **8** big wheel **9** personage, potentate

Mohammed
also: **7** Mahomet, Prophet **8** Muhammad
born: **5** Mecca
clan: **6** Hashim
daughter: **6** Fatima
deity: **5** Allah
died: **6** Medina
father: **6** Abdallah, Abdullah
father-in-law: **7** Abu Bakr, Abubekr
flight: **4** hadj **6** hegira, hejira
follower: **6** Moslem, Muslim, Wahbi **10** Mohammedan
grandfather: **13** Abd al-Muttalib
horse: **5** Buraq **7** Alborrak
mother: **5** Amina
religion: **5** Islam
shrine: **5** Kaaba
son: **7** Ibrahim
adopted: **3** Ali
successor: **4** imam **5** calif **6** caliph **7** Abu Bakr
tribe: **7** Koreish, Quraysh
uncle: **5** Abbas **8** Abu Talib
wife: **5** Aisha **6** Ayesha, Safiya **7** Khadija **8** Khadidja, Kadijah

Mohammedan 4 Sufi **6** Moslem, Muslim, Shiite **7** Islamic, Moorish, Sunnite **10** Mahometan, Muhammadan, Muhammedan

Mohave, Mojave
language family: **5** Yuman
location: **7** Arizona **10** California

Mohawk (Kaniengehaga)
language family: **9** Iroquoian
location: **6** Canada, Quebec **7** New York **11** Lake Ontario
leader: **8** Hiawatha **11** Joseph Brant
member of: **19** League of the Iroquois

Mohegan, Mohican, Mahican
language family: **9** Algonkian **10** Algonquian
location: **7** New York **9** Wisconsin **11** Connecticut **12** Hudson Valley
leader: **5** Occom, Uncas **12** Chingachgook
allied with: **6** Pequot
with Delaware: **11** Loup Indians, Wolf Indians
subject of novel: **20** The Last of the Mohicans
author: **19** James Fenimore Cooper

Moira
personifies: **4** fate

moist 3 wet **4** damp, dank, dewy **5** humid, misty, muggy, rainy **6** clammy, drippy, watery **7** aqueous, drizzly, tearful, wettish, wet-eyed **8** dripping, vaporous **10** lachrymose

moisten 3 dew, wet **4** damp, hose, mist, soak **5** spray, water **6** dampen, douche, splash, sponge **8** humidify, irrigate, saturate, vaporize **10** moisturize

moisture 3 dew, wet **4** damp, mist **5** sweat, vapor **7** drizzle, exudate, wetness **8** dampness, dankness, humidity **9** moistness, mugginess **10** wateriness **11** evaporation **12** perspiration

Mojave see **6** Mohave

Moki see **4** Hopi

mold 3 cut, die, ilk **4** cast, form, kind, line, make, rust, sort, turn, type **5** brand, frame, knead, model, shape, stamp, train **6** blight, create, figure, fungus, kidney, lichen, matrix, mildew, render, sculpt, shaper **7** contour, convert, develop, fashion, outline, pattern, quality, remodel **9** character, construct, formation, structure, transform

molding 4 cyma, dado, gula, ogee **5** ovolo

Moldova
other name: **8** Moldavia
capital/largest city: **8** Chisinau, Kishinev
head of state: **9** president
government: **8** republic
monetary unit: **5** ruble
river: **8** Dniester
people: **7** Gagauzi **8** Moldovan **9** Moldavian
language: **8** Romanian **9** Moldavian
religion: **15** Russian Orthodox

moldy 5 fusty, hoary, musty, stale **7** spoiled **8** mildewed

molest 3 irk, vex **4** fret, harm, hurt **5** abuse, annoy, beset, harry, worry **6** attack, bother, harass, hector, injure, pester, plague **7** assault, disturb, torment, trouble **8** maltreat

Moliere (Jean-Baptiste Poquelin)
author of: **6** Scapin **8** Tartuffe, The Miser **10** Amphitryon **13** Le Misanthrope **17** The School for Wives **19**

The Imaginary Invalid **20** The School for Husbands **22** Le Bourgeois Gentilhomme

Moll Flanders
   author: 11 Daniel Defoe
   character: 5 Robin **6** Jemmy E **10** Sea Captain

mollification 8 soothing **9** placation **11** appeasement, assuagement **12** conciliation

mollify 4 calm, curb, dull, ease, lull **5** abate, allay, blunt, check, quell, quiet, still **6** lessen, pacify, reduce, soften, soothe, temper **7** appease, assuage, lighten, placate **8** decrease, mitigate, moderate, palliate **9** tone down

mollusk 4 clam, slug **5** conch, cowry, murex, snail, squid, whelk **6** chiton, cockle, cowrie, limpet, mussel, oyster, teredo, triton **7** abalone, bivalve, geoduck, octopus, scallop **8** argonaut, nautilus, shipworm **9** shellfish **10** cuttlefish, nudibranch, periwinkle

mollycoddle 3 pet **4** baby, wimp **5** sissy, spoil **6** cosset, coward, pamper **7** cater to, crybaby, indulge, milksop **8** give in to, mama's boy, weakling **9** cream puff **11** milquetoast, overindulge

Molnar, Ferenc
   author of: 6 Liliom **7** The Swan **12** The Guardsman

Moloch 3 god **5** diety
   also: 6 Molech
   worshiped by: 9 Ammonites

molt 4 cast, shed, slip **6** change, slough **7** castoff, discard, ecdysis **8** exuviate

molten 6 melted, red-hot **7** fusible, igneous, smelted **8** magmatic **9** liquefied

molto
   music: 4 very

Moly
   form: 4 herb
   given to: 8 Odysseus
   given by: 6 Hermes
   to counteract spells of: 5 Circe

moment 5 flash, jiffy, trice, value, worth **6** import, minute, second, weight **7** concern, gravity, instant **8** interest, juncture **9** twinkling **10** importance **11** consequence, weightiness **12** significance

momentary 5 brief, hasty, quick, short **6** sudden **7** instant, passing **8** flashing, fleeting, fugitive, imminent **9** ephemeral, immediate, temporary, transient **10** short-lived, transitory **13** instantaneous

momentous 5 grave **7** crucial, fateful, salient, serious, weighty **8** critical, decisive, eventful **9** essential, important, ponderous **11** far-reaching, influential, significant, substantial **12** earthshaking **13** consequential

momentous occurrence 5 event **8** occasion **9** milestone **12** red-letter day, turning point

momentum 2 go **4** dash, push **5** drive, force, speed, vigor **6** energy, moment, thrust **7** headway, impetus, impulse **8** velocity **10** propulsion

Mommsen, Theodor
   author of: 16 The History of Rome

Momus
   also: 5 Momos
   god of: 7 censure **8** ridicule

Monaco
   capital: 11 Monaco-Ville
   largest city: 10 Monte Carlo
   others: 9 Fontville
   division: 9 Fontville **10** Monte Carlo **11** La Condamine, Monaco-Ville
   head of government: 15 minister of state
   head of state: 6 prince
   monetary unit: 5 franc **7** centime
   river: 7 Vesubie
   sea: 13 Mediterranean
   physical feature: 9 Cote d'Azur
   people: 6 French **7** Italian **10** Monegasque
      oceanographer: 15 Jacques Cousteau
      prince: 5 Louis **6** Albert, Honore **7** Antoine, Charles, Rainier **9** Florestan
      princess: 5 Grace **8** Caroline **9** Stephanie **10** Grace Kelly
      ruler: 4 Rome **5** Genoa **6** Greece **8** Grimaldi, Saracens **9** Phoenicia
   language: 6 French **7** English, Italian **10** Monegasque
   religion: 13 Roman Catholic
   place:
      beach: 8 Larvotto
      casino: 10 Monte Carlo
      gardens: 6 Exotic
      museum: 12 Oceanography
      park: 18 Princess Antoinette
   feature:
      auto race: 15 Monaco Grand Prix

Monaco-Ville
   capital of: 6 Monaco

Mona Lisa
   also called: 10 La Gioconda
   artist: 15 Leonardo da Vinci
   noted for: 5 smile
   museum: 6 Louvre

monarch 3 HRH **4** czar, doge, emir, khan, king, rani, shah, tsar **5** rajah, ruler, queen **6** caesar, kaiser, prince **7** czarina, emperor, empress, majesty, pharaoh **8** kaiserin, princess **9** chieftain, potentate

monarchical 9 czaristic **10** autocratic **11** dictatorial

monastery 5 abbey **6** friary, priory **7** convent, nunnery, retreat **8** cloister

monastic 7 ascetic, monkish, recluse **8** celibate, hermitic, secluded, solitary **9** cloistral, reclusive, unworldly **10** cloistered, hermitlike **11** sequestered **13** contemplative

mon cher 6 my dear

Moncrieff, Algernon (Algy)
   character in: 27 The Importance of Being Earnest
   author: 5 Wilde

Mond, Mustapha
   character in: 13 Brave New World
   author: 6 Huxley

Monday
   French: 5 lundi
   German: 6 montag
   heavenly body: 4 moon
   Italian: 6 lunedi
   means: 12 day of the moon
   Spanish: 5 lunes

Mondrian, Piet
   real name: 23 Pieter Cornelis Mondriaan
   born: 10 Amersfoort **14** The Netherlands
   artwork: 5 Trees **10** The Red Tree **12** Ocean and Pier **17** Evening Landscapes **18** Landscape with a Mill **20** Broadway Boogie-Woogie **29** Composition in Red Yellow and Blue

Monet, Claude Oscar
   born: 5 Paris **6** France
   artwork: 7 Poplars **9** Haystacks, The Thames **11** Water Lilies **14** Rouen Cathedral **16** Women in the Garden **17** Impression Sunrise **18** Mornings on the Seine **21** The Bridge at Argenteuil

monetary 6 fiscal **9** budgetary, financial, pecuniary, sumptuary

money 4 cash, coin **5** bread, bucks, dough, funds **6** assets, riches, specie, wealth **7** capital, coinage, payment, revenue, scratch **8** currency, hard cash, proceeds **9** affluence, long green **10** collateral, greenbacks **11** wherewithal

money-carrier
   French: 12 porte-monnaie

moneyed, monied 4 rich **5** flush, swell **6** flashy, loaded **7** elegant, opulent, solvent, wealthy **8** affluent **10** prosperous

money-grubbing 5 venal **6** greedy **8** covetous, grasping **9** mercenary **10** avaricious

money lender 6 banker, lender, usurer **7** lombard, shylock **9** loanshark **10** pawnbroker

money saved 7 nest egg, savings **10** investment

money spent 6 outlay **7** payment **8** expenses **11** expenditure

Mongolia
   other name: 13 Outer Mongolia
   capital/largest city: 9 Ulan Bator
   others: 5 Kobdo **6** Darhan **10** Choibalsan, Sukhe Bator, Tsetserlik, Uliassutai

ancient capital: 9 Karakoram
government:
  legislature: 17 People's Great Hural
  18 People's Great Khural
monetary unit: 5 mongo, mungo **6** tugrik **7** tughrik
weight: 3 lan
lake: 3 Uvs **5** Har Us **6** Bor Nor **7** Ghirgis, Ubsa Nor **8** Airik Nor, Durga Nor, Hobsogol, Khara Usu **9** Khubsugul, Khukhu-Nur **10** Khirgis Nor
mountain: 4 Cast, Orog **5** Altai **6** Kentei, Sevrej **7** Ich Ovoo, Khangai, Khentei **8** Tannu-Ola **9** Edrengijn **10** Cagaan Bogd **11** Munky Sardyk **14** Hangayn-Hentiyn, Monch Chajrchan
highest point: 10 Tabun Bogdo
river: 3 Tes **4** Egin, Onon, Tuul, Uldz **5** Kobdo, Tesin **6** Orkhon **7** Kerulen, Selenga, Selenge **8** Dzabkhan, Dzavchan
physical feature:
  desert: 4 Gobi **5** Ordos, Shamo
  plateau: 8 Mongolia
  region: 10 Great Lakes
people: 5 Oirat, Tungu **6** Buryat, Darbet, Khoton, Mongol **7** Kazakhs, Khalkha **8** Tuvinian **9** Dariganga
  leader: 8 Jahangir, Jehangir **10** Kublai Khan, Tsendenbal **11** Genghis Khan
  ruler: 4 Huns **5** Ching **6** Manchu **7** Kirghiz, Uighurs **8** Hsiung-nu
  spiritual/secular ruler: 12 Living Buddha **21** Jebtsun Damba Khutu Khtu
language: 6 Kazakh **16** Khalkha Mongolian
religion: 7 Lamaism **9** Shamanism **15** Tibetan Buddhism
place:
  monastery: 6 Gandun
  feature:
    felt tent: 4 yurt
    nomadic herder: 4 arat
  food:
    fermented mare's milk: 5 airag

Mongolian
language family: 6 Altaic
group: 6 Buryat **7** Khalkha

Mongoose, The
nickname of: 11 Archie Moore

mongrel 3 cur **4** mutt **5** mixed **6** hybrid **7** bastard **8** offshoot **9** anomalous, crossbred **10** crossbreed

moniker 3 tag **4** name **5** label, title **6** eponym, handle **7** epithet, surname **8** cognomen, nickname, taxonomy **9** sobriquet **11** appellation, designation **12** denomination

monitor 2 TV **4** tend **5** guide, teach **6** censor, direct, pickup, police, screen, sensor **7** oversee, proctor, scanner **8** overseer, watchdog **9** supervise **14** disciplinarian

Monk
network: 3 USA
cast: 9 Ted Levine (Leland Stot-

tlemeyer) **11** Bitty Schram (Sharona Fleming) **12** Stanley Kamel (Dr. Kroger), Tony Shalhoub (Adrian Monk) **13** Traylor Howard (Natalie Teeger) **17** Jason Gray-Stanford (Randall Disher)

Monkees, The
cast/musician: 9 Davy Jones, Peter Tork **10** David Jones **11** Micky Dolenz, Mike Nesmith

monkey 3 ape, ass, toy **4** butt, dupe, fool, jerk **5** clown, jimmy **6** baboon, fiddle, meddle, simian, tamper, tinker, trifle **7** buffoon, primate **13** laughingstock
group of: 5 troop
god: 7 Hanuman
kind: 3 owl **4** saki, titi **5** aotus, lemur, titis **6** baboon, guenon, howler, langur, rhesus, spider **7** colobus, Goeldi's, guereza, macaque, tamarin, tarsier, uakaris **8** capuchin, mandrill, marmoset, squirrel, talapoin **11** douroucouli

monkey business 6 capers **9** highjinks **11** shenanigans

monkeyshines 6 antics, capers, pranks **7** hijinks **10** buffoonery, tomfoolery **11** foolishness

monocle 4 quiz **5** glass **7** lorgnon **8** eyeglass

Monoclonius
type: 8 dinosaur **10** ceratopsid
location: 12 North America
characteristic: 6 horned

Monod, Jacques
field: 7 biology
nationality: 6 French
researched: 3 RNA **8** genetics
awarded: 10 Nobel Prize

monograph 8 tractate, treatise **9** discourse **12** disquisition, dissertation

monolith 5 stone **6** column, menhir, pillar, statue **7** obelisk **8** memorial, monument

monologue, monolog 6 screed, sermon, speech **7** address, lecture, oration **9** discourse, soliloquy **11** expatiation **12** disquisition

monopolize 3 own **6** absorb, corner, manage, take up **7** consume, control, preempt **8** arrogate, dominate, regulate, take over **9** cartelize **11** appropriate

monopoly 4 bloc **5** trust **6** cartel, corner **7** combine, control **8** dominion **9** copyright, ownership, syndicate **10** consortium, domination **11** sovereignty **12** jurisdiction **14** proprietorship

Monopoly 9 board game
invented by: 6 Darrow
places: 2 go, RR **4** jail **6** chance **9** Boardwalk, Park Place
piece: 5 hotel, house

monotonous 3 dry **4** dull, flat **5** banal **6** boring, dreary, jejune, stodgy, torpid

7 droning, humdrum, insipid, mundane, prosaic, routine, tedious **8** plodding, singsong, tiresome, toneless, unvaried **9** colorless, soporific, wearisome **10** pedestrian **11** repetitious, somniferous **13** uninteresting

monotony 3 rut **5** ennui **6** tedium **7** boredom, humdrum **8** dullness, flatness, prosaism, sameness **9** iteration **10** dreariness, redundancy, uniformity **11** reiteration, tediousness **13** wearisomeness **14** predictability

Monroe, Earl
nickname: 12 Earl the Pearl
sport: 10 basketball
position: 5 guard

Monroe, James
presidential rank: 5 fifth
party: 20 Democratic-Republican
state represented: 2 VA
defeated: 4 (Rufus) King **5** (John Quincy) Adams
vice president: 8 (Daniel D) Tompkins
cabinet:
  state: 5 (John Quincy) Adams
  treasury: 8 (William Harris) Crawford
  war: 7 (John Caldwell) Calhoun
  attorney general: 4 (Richard) Rush, (William) Wirt
  navy: 8 (Samuel Lewis) Southard, (Smith) Thompson **13** (Benjamin Williams) Crowninshield
born: 2 VA **18** Westmoreland County
died: 13 New York City NY
buried: 10 Richmond VA
education: 14 William and Mary (did not graduate)
religion: 12 Episcopalian
political career: 8 US Senate
  governor of: 8 Virginia
  minister: 5 Spain **6** France **12** Great Britain
  secretary of: 3 war **5** state
civilian career: 6 lawyer
military service: 5 major **7** captain **10** lieutenant **16** Revolutionary War **17** lieutenant colonel
  wounded in Battle of: 7 Trenton
notable events of lifetime/term: 5 Panic (of 1819) **14** Monroe Doctrine
  Agreement: 9 Rush-Bagot
  Compromise: 8 Missouri
  war: 8 Seminole
father: 6 Spence
mother: 9 Elizabeth (Jones)
siblings: 6 Andrew, Spence **9** Elizabeth **11** Joseph Jones
wife: 9 Elizabeth (Kortright)
  nickname: 5 Eliza
children: 11 Maria Hester **14** Eliza Kortright

Monroe, Marilyn
real name: 23 Norma Jean Mortenson Baker
husband: 11 Joe DiMaggio **12** Arthur Miller

born: 12 Los Angeles CA
roles: 7 Bus Stop, Niagara **10** The Misfits **13** Some Like It Hot **16** The Seven-Year Itch **22** Gentlemen Prefer Blondes, How To Marry a Millionaire **23** The Prince and the Showgirl

Monrovia
capital of: 7 Liberia

monseigneur 6 my lord

monsieur 2 Mr **3** sir **6** mister, my lord

Monsignor Quixote
author: 12 Graham Greene

monster 4 Fury, gila, ogre, yeti **5** argus, beast, brute, demon, devil, fiend, freak, ghoul, giant, golem, harpy, hydra, lamia, satyr, titan **6** dragon, gorgon, marvel, oddity, savage, threat, wonder, wretch, zombie **7** anomaly, caitiff, centaur, chimera, deviant, grendel, incubus, mammoth, mermaid, vampire, variant, villain **8** bogeyman, colossus, gargoyle, Loch Ness, succubus, werewolf **9** barbarian, curiosity, cutthroat, scoundrel **10** blackguard, phenomenon **11** abnormality, miscreation **12** Frankenstein, lusus naturae

monstrous 4 bald, evil, huge **5** cruel, giant **6** grisly, mighty, odious **7** ghastly, harried, heinous, hideous, hulking, immense, mammoth, obscene, obvious, satanic, titanic, vicious **8** colossal, enormous, fiendish, flagrant, gigantic, gruesome, horrible, outright, shocking **9** atrocious, egregious, nefarious, revolting **10** diabolical, gargantuan, outrageous, prodigious, scandalous, stupendous, tremendous, villainous **14** Brobdingnagian

monstrousness 8 baseness, enormity, evilness, vileness, villainy **9** barbarity, depravity, malignity **10** inhumanity, wickedness **11** heinousness, viciousness **13** atrociousness, offensiveness **14** outrageousness

Montague family
characters in: 14 Romeo and Juliet
author: 11 Shakespeare
member: 5 Romeo

Montaigne, Michel de
author of: 6 Essais, Essays

Montalban, Ricardo
born: 6 Mexico **10** Mexico City
roles: 4 Khan **8** Mr Roarke **9** The Colbys **13** Fantasy Island **24** Star Trek II: The Wrath of Khan

Montalvo, Garcia de
author of: 12 Amadis of Gaul

Montana
abbreviation: 2 MT **4** Mont
nickname: 6 Big Sky **7** Bonanza, Stubtoe **8** Mountain, Treasure
capital: 6 Helena
largest city: 8 Billings
others: 4 Kipp **5** Butte, Havre, Malta **6** Hardin **7** Bozeman, Chinook, Choteau, Forsyth, Glasgow, Roundup **8** Anaconda, Missoula **9** Kalispell **10** Great Falls
college: 7 Carroll **10** Great Falls **13** Rocky Mountain
feature: 17 Continental Divide
   cemetery: 6 Custer
   national park: 7 Glacier **11** Yellowstone
tribe: 4 Cree, Crow, Hohe **5** Sioux **6** Atsina, Atsina, Salish **7** Arapaho, Bannock, Kutenai, Siksika **8** Cheyenne, Chippewa, Flatfoot, Flathead, Shoshone **9** Blackfeet **11** Assiniboine
people: 8 Myrna Loy **9** Will James **10** Gary Cooper **14** Charles Russell **15** Jeannette Rankin
   explorer: 13 Lewis and Clark **16** Pierre Jean de Smet
lake: 5 Tiber **6** Hebgen **8** Flathead, Fort Peck, Medicine **10** Yellowtail **11** Canyon Ferry, Hungry Horse
land rank: 6 fourth
mountain: 4 Ajax **5** Baldy, Cowan, Crazy, Lewis **6** Sphinx, Torrey **7** Bighorn, Big Belt, Hilgard, Purcell, Rockies, Trapper **8** Absaroka, Gallatin, Pentagon, Snowshoe
   highest point: 11 Granite Peak
physical feature: 10 Great Falls
river: 3 Sun **4** Milk **5** Clark, Teton **6** Marias, Powder, Tongue, Willow **7** Madison, Shields **8** Columbia, Kootenai, Missouri **9** Blackfoot **10** Bitterroot **11** Musselshell, Yellowstone
state admission: 10 forty-first
state bird: 17 western meadowlark
state fish: 26 black-spotted cutthroat trout
state flower: 10 bitterroot
state motto: 13 Gold and Silver
state song: 7 Montana
state tree: 13 Ponderosa pine

Montana, Bob
creator/artist of: 6 Archie

Montand, Yves
real name: 7 Ivo Livi
wife: 14 Simone Signoret
born: 5 Italy **14** Monsummano Alto
roles: 1 Z **12** Let's Make Love **14** Is Paris Burning?

montani semper liberi 28 mountaineers are always free men
motto of: 12 West Virginia

Montcalm, Louis Joseph
also: 17 Marquis de Montcalm
nationality: 6 French
served in: 18 French and Indian War
battle: 6 Oswego, Quebec (siege) **8** Carillon **11** Ticonderoga **16** Fort William Henry
killed in battle at: 6 Quebec **15** Plains of Abraham

mont-de-piete 10 pawnbroker
literally: 8 bank of pity

Montenegro
name means: 13 black mountain
other name: 4 Zeta **8** Crna Gora
capital: 7 Cetinje **8** Titograd **9** Podgorica
cities: 3 Bar **5** Kotor, Tivat **6** Niksic, Ulcinj **8** Antivari, Dulcigno, Ivangrad, Pljevlja **10** Hercegnovi **11** Sveti Stefan
division:
   Roman province: 7 Illyria
governed by: 10 Yugoslavia
monetary unit: 4 para **6** florin **7** perpera
lake: 7 Scutari, Shkoder
mountain: 8 Durmitor **11** Dinaric Alps
river: 3 Lim **4** Piva, Tara, Zeta **6** Moraca **7** Ceotina
sea: 8 Adriatic
physical feature:
   gulf: 5 Kotor
people: 4 Serb, Slav **11** Montenegrin
   former ruler (Orthodox bishop): 7 vladike **8** vladika
language: 13 Serbo-Croatian
religion: 16 Serbian Orthodoxy

Monteverdi, Claudio
born: 5 Italy **7** Cremona
composer of: 5 Adone, Orfeo **7** Arianna **14** La Favola d'Orfeo **17** The Fable of Orpheus **21** The Coronation of Poppea **22** L'incoronazione di Poppea **24** Il Ritorno d'Ulisse in patria **34** Il Combattimento di Tancredi e Clorinda

Montevideo
capital of: 7 Uruguay

Montezuma
emperor of: 6 Aztecs
in: 6 Mexico
conquered by: 6 Cortez

Montgomery, Bernard Law
also: 27 (first) Viscount Montgomery of Alamein
author of: 7 Memoirs **17** A History of Warfare
battle: 9 El Alamein
chief: 19 British general staff
commander of: 17 British Eighth Army **32** British occupation forces in Germany
commando raid: 6 Dieppe
deputy supreme commander: 4 NATO
Eighth Army called: 10 Desert Rats
evacuation of: 7 Dunkirk
fought against: 6 Rommel **11** Africa Corps, Afrika Korps
invasion: 6 Sicily **8** Normandy
member: 12 House of Lords
nationality: 7 British
nickname: 5 Monty
served in: 3 WWI **4** WWII

Montgomery, Robert
real name: 17 Henry Montgomery Jr
daughter: 9 Elizabeth
born: 8 Beacon NY
roles: 11 The Big House **13** Night Must Fall **17** Here Comes Mr Jordan

month

1st day: 7 calends
13th or 15th: 4 ides
9th before ides: 5 nones
half: 9 fortnight
next: 7 proximo
preceding: 3 ult(imo)
present: 4 inst(ant)
Month in the Country, A
author: 12 Ivan Turgenev
Mont-Oriol
author: 15 Guy de Maupassant
Montreal
airport: 6 Dorval **8** St Hubert **12** Cartierville
former baseball team: 5 Expos
founder: 11 Maisonneuve
hill: 10 Mount Royal
hockey team: 9 Canadiens
island: 5 Jesus **6** Bizard, Perrot **8** Montreal **9** des Soeurs **14** de Boucherville
lake: 7 St Louis
landmark: 12 Place des Arts **13** Molson Stadium **16** Chateau de Ramezay **17** Church of Notre Dame, St Sulpice Seminary **21** Man and His World Exhibit
original name: 10 Ville-Marie
province: 6 Quebec
river: 6 Ottawa **10** St Lawrence **11** des Prairies **14** des Milles Isles
subway: 5 Metro
university: 6 McGill
Montresor
character in: 20 The Cask of Amontillado
author: 3 Poe
Mont Saint Michel and Chartres
author: 10 Henry Adams
Monty
nickname of: 15 Montgomery Clift **17** (General) Bernard Montgomery
monument 4 slab **5** token **6** shrine **7** memento, obelisk, witness **8** cenotaph, memorial, monolith, reminder **9** testament, tombstone **10** gravestone **11** remembrance, testimonial **13** commemoration
monumental 4 huge **5** fatal, heavy **7** awesome, classic, epochal, immense, lasting, massive **8** colossal, decisive, enduring, gigantic, historic, immortal, statuary **9** cyclopean, egregious, memorable **10** horrendous, monolithic, shattering, stupendous **11** inestimable **12** catastrophic **13** unprecedented
mooch 3 beg, bum **5** cadge **6** hustle, sponge **7** solicit **8** freeload
mood 5 blues, dumps, humor **6** spirit, temper **7** feeling **8** doldrums, vexation **9** condition **10** depression, gloominess, melancholy **11** disposition, melancholia, temperament **14** predisposition **16** hypersensitivity
moody 4 mean **5** sulky, surly, testy **6** crabby, dismal, fickle, gloomy, mopish, morbid, morose, sullen **7** erratic,

flighty, peevish, unhappy **8** brooding, dejected, notional, variable, volatile **9** impetuous, impulsive, irascible, irritable, mercurial, saturnine, whimsical **10** capricious, changeable, despondent, inconstant, lugbrious, melancholy **11** pessimistic **12** inconsistent **13** temperamental, unpredictable
Mookerjee, Hurree Chunder
character in: 3 Kim
author: 7 Kipling
moon 4 gape, lamp, luna, roam **5** dream, month, stare **6** dawdle, wander **8** daydream **9** satellite
god of: 3 Sin **5** Nanna **6** Meztli
goddess of: 4 Luna **5** Diana, Holle, Tanit **6** Hecate, Hekate, Phoebe, Selena, Selene, Tanith **7** Artemis, Astarte, Cynthia
full: 9 plenilune
new: 5 prime
waning: 7 waiand
Moon and Sixpence, The
author: 16 W Somerset Maugham
moonless 4 dark **5** black, murky **7** stygian **9** lightless, unlighted **13** unilluminated
Moonlighting
character: 11 Maddie Hayes **12** Agnes Dipesto, David Addison
cast: 11 Bruce Willis **13** Allyce Beasley **14** Cybill Shepherd
detective agency: 8 Blue Moon
Moon Mullins
creator: 12 Frank Willard
character: 4 Kayo **5** Mamie **9** Mushmouth **11** Uncle Willie **15** Lady Plushbottom, Lord Plushbottom **16** Moonshine Mullins
moonshine 5 hokum **6** bunkum, humbug **7** bootleg **8** clockade, homebrew, malarky, nonsense **10** balderdash, bathtub gin **11** mountain dew
moonstone
species: 8 feldspar
source: 5 Burma, Mogok
Moonstone, The
author: 13 Wilkie Collins
character: 7 Dr Candy **12** Lady Verinder, Sergeant Cuff **13** Franklin Blake **14** John Herncastle, Rachel Verinder **15** Rosanna Spearman **16** Godfrey Ablewhite
moor 3 fen **4** dock, down, fell, lash, wold **5** affix, berth, chain, heath, marsh, tie up **6** anchor, attach, fasten, secure, steppe, tether, tundra, upland **7** savanna, tie down **8** make fast **9** wasteland
Moore, Archie
nickname: 11 The Mongoose
real name: 18 Archibald Lee Wright
sport: 6 boxing
class: 16 light-heavyweight
Moore, Clement C
author of: 23 A Visit from Saint Nicholas

Moore, Dick
creator/artist of: 13 Gasoline Alley
Moore, Dudley
nickname: 12 Cuddly Dudley
wife: 11 Suzy Kendall, Tuesday Weld
born: 5 Essex **7** England **8** Dagenham
roles: 3 Ten **6** Arthur **8** Lovesick, Six Weeks **9** Bedazzled **13** Micki and Maude **16** Arthur on the Rocks **17** Like Father Like Son
plays: 5 piano
Moore, George
author of: 12 Esther Waters **15** Hail and Farewell
Moore, Henry
born: 7 England **10** Castleford
artwork: 4 Mask **8** Two Forms **9** North Wind **10** Bird Basket **11** Family Group, Head of a Girl **12** Locking Piece **13** Nuclear Energy **15** Reclining Figure **20** Four-Piece Composition
Moore, Marianne
author of: 12 Like a Bulwark, Nevertheless, O To Be a Dragon, Tell Me Tell Me
Moore, Mary Tyler
husband: 11 Grant Tinker
born: 10 Brooklyn NY
roles: 4 Mary **12** Mary Richards **14** Ordinary People **18** The Dick Van Dyke Show **21** The Mary Tyler Moore Show
Moore, Mrs
character in: 15 A Passage to India
author: 7 Forster
Moore, Roger
born: 6 London **7** England
roles: 8 Bullseye, The Saint **12** Simon Templar
as James Bond: 9 Moonraker, Octopussy **12** A View to a Kill **13** Live and Let Die **15** For Your Eyes Only **16** The Spy Who Loved Me **22** The Man with the Golden Gun
Moorehead, Agnes
born: 9 Clinton MA
roles: 6 Endora **9** Bewitched **11** Citizen Kane **13** Johnny Belinda **15** Dear Dead Delilah **20** Magnificent Obsession **23** The Magnificent Ambersons
mooring 4 hook, line, rope **5** cable, chain **6** anchor, hawser
moot 4 open **7** eristic **8** arguable, disputed **9** debatable, undecided, unsettled **10** disputable, unresolved **11** conjectural **12** questionable **13** controversial, problematical **14** controvertible
mope 4 fret, pine, pout, sulk **5** brood, worry **6** grieve, grouse, lament, repine **7** grumble **8** languish
Mopsus
occupation: 4 seer
mother: 5 Manto
grandfather: 8 Tiresias

member of: 9 Argonauts
founded: 6 oracle
location: 6 Mallus **7** Cilicia
cofounder: 11 Amphilochus
epithet: 9 Ampycides

moral 3 tag **4** fair, just, pure **5** adage, maxim, motto, noble, right **6** honest, lesson, proper, saying **7** epigram, ethical, message, proverb, saintly **8** aphorism, didactic, personal, virtuous **9** estimable, homiletic, honorable, preaching **10** aboveboard, highminded, principled **11** meritorious, sermonizing, tendentious **12** conscionable

moral code 5 ethos **6** ethics **9** integrity, standards **10** principles

morale 4 mood **6** spirit, temper **10** confidence, resolution **11** disposition
French: 13 esprit de corps

morality 5 honor **6** ethics, habits, tastes, virtue **7** modesty, probity **8** fairness, goodness **9** integrity, rectitude **10** chasteness **11** uprightness **13** righteousness

moralize 6 preach **7** lecture

moralizing 7 preachy **8** didactic **9** homiletic

morally corrupt 6 effete **8** decadent, depraved **10** degenerate

moral sense 9 integrity **10** conscience

morass 3 bog, fen **4** mire **5** marsh, swamp **6** slough **8** quagmire, wetlands **9** quicksand

morbid 3 sad **4** dour, glum, grim **5** moody **6** gloomy, morose, somber **8** brooding **9** depressed, saturnine **10** despondent, lugubrious **11** melancholic, pessimistic, unwholesome

morbid condition 6 malady **7** ailment, disease, illness **8** sickness **9** infirmity

Morcerf, Comte de (Fernand)
character in: 21 The Count of Monte Cristo
author: 5 Dumas (pere)

mordant 6 biting, bitter **7** acerbic, caustic, cutting, waspish **8** incisive, piercing, scathing, scornful, stinging, venomous, virulent **9** acidulous, malicious, sarcastic, trenchant **11** acrimonious

Mordecai
cousin: 6 Esther
served: 15 Ahasuerus Xerxes
enemy: 5 Haman

more 5 added, extra, other, spare **6** longer **7** further, reserve **10** additional **12** additionally, supplemental **13** supplementary

More, Thomas
author of: 6 Utopia

Moreau, Frederic
character in: 21 A Sentimental Education
author: 8 Flaubert

Moreau, Gustave
born: 5 Paris **6** France
artwork: 7 Orpheus **13** Dance of Salome (Salome Dancing), The Apparition **16** Hesiod and the Muse **18** The Poet and the Siren **19** Oedipus and the Sphinx **27** Diomedes Devoured by His Horses

Morel, Paul
character in: 13 Sons and Lovers
author: 8 Lawrence

Moreno, Rita
real name: 20 Rosita Dolores Alverio
born: 7 Humacao **10** Puerto Rico
roles: 8 Blue Moon **13** Pagan Love Song, The Deerslayer, West Side Story **14** The Four Seasons **15** Singin' in the Rain

more or less 5 about **6** around **8** somewhat **9** generally, just about **13** approximately

moreover 3 too **4** also **7** besides, further **11** furthermore **12** more than that

mores 4 code **5** ethos, forms, rules **6** usages **7** customs, rituals **9** etiquette, practices, standards **10** traditions **11** conventions, observances, proprieties

more than enough 5 ample **6** excess, plenty **7** copious, profuse **8** plethora **9** abundance, amplitude, bountiful, excessive, profusion **10** oversupply

Morgan, Daniel
served in: 16 Revolutionary War
commander of: 8 riflemen **13** sharpshooters
battle: 7 Cowpens **8** Saratoga **12** Bemis Heights, Freeman's Farm
helped suppress: 16 Whiskey Rebellion

Morgan, Thomas Hunt
founder of: 8 genetics
awarded: 10 Nobel Prize

Morgan family
characters in: 19 How Green Was My Valley
members: 4 Beth, Davy, Huur, Ivor, Owen **5** Ianto **6** Gwilym **8** Angharad
author: 9 Llewellyn

morganite
color: 4 pink **5** peach

Morgan le Fay
character in: 16 Arthurian romance

Moriarty, Professor
villain in: 14 (The Adventures of) Sherlock Holmes
author: 10 Conan Doyle

moribund 5 dying **6** doomed, waning **10** stagnating

Morier, James
author of: 18 Hajji Baba of Ispahan

morituri te salutamus 28 we who are about to die salute thee
said by: 15 Roman gladiators
said to: 13 Roman emperors

Mork & Mindy
character: 4 Mork **6** Eugene **10** Cora Hudson **13** Mindy McConnel **17** Frederick McConnel
cast: 9 Pam Dawber **11** Conrad Janis **13** Elizabeth Kerr, Robin Williams **14** Jeffrey Jacquet
Mork's planet: 3 Ork
phrase: 8 nanu nanu
spinoff from: 9 Happy Days

Morland, Catherine
character in: 15 Northanger Abbey
author: 6 Austen

Morley, Robert
born: 6 Semley **7** England
roles: 5 Melba **10** Oscar Wilde **11** Beau Brummel, Edward My Son **12** Major Barbara **15** Marie Antoinette, The African Queen **21** The Man Who Came to Dinner

Mormon State
nickname of: 4 Utah

morning 4 dawn **5** early, sunup **7** sunrise **8** daybreak, daylight, forenoon **9** matutinal

morning-glory 7 Ipomoea **10** Calystegia **11** Convolvulus
varieties: 3 red **4** wild **5** beach, dwarf **6** Ceylon, common, silver, woolly, yellow **9** Brazilian **16** Imperial Japanese

Morocco
other name: 7 Barbary **8** Maroquin **9** Al Maghrib **13** Maghrib el Aksa **19** Mauretania Tingitana
capital: 5 Rabat **6** Rabbat
largest city: 10 Casablanca
others: 3 Fes, Fez, Sla **4** Ifni, Safi, Sale, Sali, Taza **5** Ceuta, Oujda, Porte, Saffi **6** Agadir, Meknes, Semara, Tetuan **7** Elarish, Kenitra, Larache, Mazagan, Mililla, Mogador, Tangier, Tetouan **8** Kouribga, Tinerhir **9** Marrakech, Marrakesh **10** Youssoufia **11** Port-Lyautey
division:
  disputed territory: 13 Western Sahara
head of state: 4 king
measure: 4 kala, muhd, rotl, saah, sahh, ueba **5** artal, cadee, gerbe, ratel **6** covado, dirhem, fanega, izenbi, kintar, tangin, tomini **8** quintral
monetary unit: 4 flue, okia, rial **5** floos, franc, okieh, ounce **6** dirham, miskal **8** mouzouna
weight: 4 rotl **5** artel, ratel **6** dirhem, kintar **7** quintal
island: 7 Madeira
mountain: 3 Rif **4** Bani **5** Abyla, Atlas, Sarro **8** Tidiguin **9** Anti-Atlas, High Atlas, Jebel-Musa **11** Middle Atlas
highest point: 12 Jebel Toubkal **13** Djebel Toubkal
river: 3 Dra, Ziz **4** Sous **5** Sebou **6** Gheris **7** Tensift **8** Moulouya **9** Oum er Rbia

sea: 8 Atlantic **13** Mediterranean
physical feature:
    cape: 3 Nun, Sim **4** Juby, Noun, Rhir **6** Cantin
    desert: 6 Sahara
    oasis: 8 Tafilelt
    plain: 5 Rharb
    strait: 9 Gibraltar
    valley: 7 Ouergha
    wind: 5 leste **7** charqui
people: 4 Arab, Moor **6** Berber, French **7** Spanish
    dynasty: 7 Alawite, Almohad **9** Almoravid
    leader: 5 Idris **7** Lyautey **8** Hassan II, Mohammed **9** Abd el-Krim
    philosopher: 8 Averroes
language: 6 Arabic, Berber, French **7** Spanish
religion: 5 Islam
place:
    ruins: 9 Volubilis
    feature:
        clothing: 4 haik **7** jellaba
        hat: 3 fez
        Islamic holy war: 5 jehad, jihad
        shanty town: 10 bidonville
    food:
        dish: 8 couscous
moron 3 ass, nut, oaf, sap **4** boob, dolt, dope, fool **5** dummy, dunce, idiot, loony, ninny **6** dimwit, nitwit **7** half-wit, jackass **8** bonehead, dumbbell, dumbhead, imbecile, numskull **9** blockhead, numbskull, simpleton **10** muttonhead, nincompoop

Moroni
    capital of: 7 Comoros

Moros
    mother: 3 Nyx
    personifies: 4 fate

morose 3 low, sad **4** blue, dour, glum, sour **5** cross, moody, sulky, surly, testy **6** cranky, gloomy, grumpy, mopish, solemn, sullen **7** waspish **8** churlish, downcast, mournful **9** depressed, irascible, saturnine **10** despondent, melancholy **11** crestfallen

moroseness 5 gloom **8** glumness **9** pessimism, sulkiness, surliness **10** sullenness

Morpheus
    god of: 6 dreams
    father: 6 Hypnos

morphology
    study of: 9 structure

Morris, Willie
    author of: 5 Yazoo **10** Good Old Boy **15** North Toward Home

Morris, Wright
    author of: 8 Will's Boy **10** Plain's Song **13** Field of Vision, My Uncle Dudley

Morrison, Toni
    real name: 19 Chloe Anthony Wofford
    author of: 4 Jazz, Love, Sula **7** Beloved, Tar Baby **8** Paradise **12** The Bluest Eye **13** Song of Solomon
    honor: 10 Nobel Prize **13** Pulitzer Prize

Morrow, Vic
    born: 7 Bronx NY
    roles: 6 Combat **8** Cimarron **14** God's Little Acre **15** The Twilight Zone **18** Portrait of a Mobster **19** The Blackboard Jungle
    daughter: 18 Jennifer Jason Leigh

Morse, Samuel F B
    nationality: 8 American
    invented: 9 Morse code **17** electric telegraph **24** electromagnetic telegraph

morsel 3 bit, nip, sip **4** bite, drop, iota, whit **5** crumb, grain, piece, scrap, snack, speck, taste, touch, trace **6** dollop, nibble, sliver, tidbit **7** modicum, segment, swallow **8** fraction, fragment, mouthful, particle **9** scintilla

mortal 4 deep, type **5** fatal, grave, human **6** deadly, lethal, living, person, severe **7** earthly, extreme, intense, mundane **8** creature, enormous, fleeting, temporal **9** character, corporeal, ephemeral **10** individual, transitory **12** unimaginable

mortality 7 carnage **8** fatality **9** bloodshed, ephemeral, slaughter **10** transience **11** evanescence **12** impermanence **13** extermination **14** transitoriness

mortar 6 cannon, cement, vessel **7** plaster **8** adhesive

Morte d'Arthur, Le
    author: 12 Thomas Malory

mortification 3 rot **5** decay, shame **7** chagrin, penance **8** ignominy **11** humiliation **12** putrefaction **13** embarrassment

mortified 6 rotted **7** abashed, ashamed, debased **8** dismayed, festered, tortured **9** chagrined, putrefied **11** discomfited, embarrassed

mortify 3 rot **4** deny, fast **5** abash, decay, shame **6** appall, fester **7** chagrin, horrify, putrefy **9** discomfit, embarrass **10** discipline, disconcert

Mosaic law 10 Pentateuch **15** Ten Commandments

Moscow
    airport: 12 Sheremetyevo
    canal: 11 Moscow-Volga
    capital of: 4 USSR **6** Russia **11** Soviet Union
    hills: 5 Lenin
    landmark: 7 Kremlin **8** Lubyanka (prison) **9** Gorky Park, Red Square **12** Lenin Library **13** Izmailovo Park, Sokolniki Park **14** Bolshoi Theater **16** Moscow Art Theater **21** Luzhniki Sports Complex
    museum: 6 Armory **7** Pushkin **10** Historical **16** Tretyakov Gallery **28** Central Museum of the Soviet Army
    river: 5 Setun, Volga, Yauza **6** Moscow
    Russian: 6 Moskva

Moses
    father: 5 Amram
    mother: 8 Jochebed
    sister: 6 Miriam
    brother: 5 Aaron
    wife: 8 Zipporah
    son: 7 Eliezar, Gershom
    father-in-law: 6 Jethro
    received: 15 Ten Commandments
    patriarch of: 10 Israelites
    saw: 11 burning bush
    successor: 6 Joshua
    pertaining to: 6 Mosaic

Moses, Grandma
    real name: 17 Anna Mary Robertson, Mary Anne Robertson
    born: 11 Greenwich NY
    artwork: 23 Out for the Christmas Trees

mosey 4 poke **5** amble **6** stroll **7** saunter, shuffle

Moslem 4 Moor **5** Islam, Sunni **6** Muslim, Shiite **7** Islamic **10** Mohammadan, Muhammadan

mosque 6 temple
    Arabic: 6 masjid, musjid

Mosquito Coast, The
    author: 11 Paul Theroux
    director: 9 Peter Weir
    cast: 11 Helen Mirren **12** Harrison Ford, River Phoenix

Mosquito State
    nickname of: 9 New Jersey

moss
    varieties: 4 ball, club, gold, rose **5** broom, bunch, coral, fairy, Irish, spike, water **6** Scotch, spring **7** cushion, haircap, peacock, Spanish **8** floating, fountain, Japanese, mat spike **9** dwarf club, flowering **10** little club, pincushion **11** basket spike, meadow spike, shining club **12** treelet spike **13** Douglas's spike

Mossbauer, Rudolph Ludwig
    field: 7 physics
    nationality: 6 German
    discovered: 15 Mossbauer effect **28** recoil-free gamma ray absorption
    awarded: 10 Nobel Prize

most 4 best, very **6** degree **7** maximum **9** extremely

most distant point 5 limit, reach **8** boundary **9** extremity **11** ultima Thule

Mostel, Zero
    real name: 16 Samuel Joel Mostel
    born: 10 Brooklyn NY
    roles: 8 The Front **10** Rhinoceros **11** The Enforcer **12** The Producers **15** Du Barry Was a Lady **16** Fiddler on the Roof **17** Panic in the Streets

most important 3 key, top **4** head, main **5** chief **7** central, highest, leading **8** cardinal, dominant, foremost, greatest **9** paramount, principal, uppermost **10** preeminent **11** outstanding, predominant

mostly 6 mainly **7** as a rule, chiefly, greatly, largely **8** above all **9** generally, primarily, specially **10** especially **11** principally **12** particularly **13** predominantly

most prominent 7 leading **8** dominant **10** preeminent **11** outstanding

most successful 6 banner, record **7** winning **10** triumphant **11** outstanding

mote 3 dot **4** iota **5** speck **8** particle **9** scintilla

moth
    varieties: **4** hawk, luna, tent **5** ghost, gypsy, plume, royal, swift, yucca **6** hornet, lappet, miller, urania **7** clothes, emperor, flannel, hook tip, leopard, tussock **8** army worm, forester, imperial, polka dot **9** carpenter, clearwing **10** forest tent **11** pseudosphex **12** African peach **13** American tiger, giant Hercules **14** tropical sphinx **15** Chinese silkworm, glover's silkworm **20** striped morning sphinx

moth-eaten 5 holey **6** old-hat **7** worn-out **8** outmoded **10** antiquated, threadbare **11** dilapidated

mother 3 mom, mum **4** bear, mama, mind, mums, rear, tend **5** beget, breed, mammy, mater, momma, mommy, mummy, nurse, raise **6** origin, source **7** care for, indulge, nurture, old lady, produce, protect **8** conceive, stimulus **10** wellspring **11** inspiration
    French: **4** mere **5** maman
    Spanish: **5** madre
    Italian: **5** mamma
    of wind: **3** Eos
    of stars: **3** Eos
    of gods: **5** Nammu

mother country 8 homeland **10** fatherland, native land, native soil, old country **13** native country

Mother Goose in Prose
    author: **14** Lyman Frank Baum

motherly 4 kind **6** gentle, loving, tender **7** devoted **8** maternal, parental **9** indulgent **10** protective, sheltering

mother of a family
    Latin: **13** materfamilias

Mother of the West
    nickname of: **8** Missouri

mother's helper
    French: **6** au pair

motif 4 form, idea **5** shape, style, theme, topic **6** design, figure, thread **7** pattern, refrain, subject **9** treatment

motion 3 cue, nod **4** flow, flux, move, sign, stir **5** drift **6** action, beckon, signal, stream **7** gesture, kinesis, passage, request **8** mobility, movement, progress **10** indication, suggestion **11**

gesticulate, proposition **13** gesticulation **14** recommendation

motionless 4 calm, dead, idle **5** fixed, inert, still **6** at rest, frozen, stable, static **8** immobile, inactive, lifeless, tranquil, unmoving **9** immovable, quiescent **10** stationary, transfixed **11** immobilized **12** unresponsive

motion picture 3 pic **4** cine, film, show **5** flick, movie **6** cinema, talkie **8** flickers **10** photodrama **11** picture show **13** moving picture

motivate 4 goad, move, stir **5** egg on, impel **6** arouse, induce, prompt, stir up, turn on **7** actuate, provoke **8** activate, persuade **9** influence, stimulate

motivation 5 cause **6** reason **7** impetus, impulse **9** causation, impulsion **11** provocation

motive 3 aim, end **4** goal, spur **5** cause **6** design, object, reason **7** grounds, purpose **8** occasion, stimulus, thinking **9** incentive, intention, prompting, rationale **10** enticement, incitement, inducement **11** inspiration, instigation, provocation

motley 4 pied **5** mixed, tabby **6** hybrid, sundry, unlike, varied **7** dappled, piebald, watered **8** assorted, brindled, speckled **9** checkered, composite, different, disparate, divergent, harlequin, patchwork **10** dissimilar, iridescent, polychrome, variegated **11** diversified, incongruous, varicolored **12** multicolored **13** heterogeneous, kaleidoscopic, miscellaneous

motor 3 car **4** auto, ride, tour **5** drive, pilot, wheel **6** engine, turbine **7** machine **8** efferent **10** automobile

motorcar 4 auto, heap **6** jalopy, wheels **7** flivver, machine, vehicle **9** tin lizzie **10** automobile

motor vehicle 3 bus, cab, car, van **4** auto, heap, jeep, limo, taxi **5** motor, sedan, truck, wagon **6** jalopy, jitney, pickup, wheels **7** flivver, hardtop, machine, omnibus, town car, vehicle **9** limousine, tin lizzie **10** automobile **11** convertible

mottled 4 pied **5** tabby **7** blotchy, flecked, piebald, specked **8** brindled, speckled, stippled **10** iridescent, multicolor, variegated **11** varicolored **12** parti-colored **13** kaleidoscopic, polychromatic

motto 3 saw **4** rule **5** adage, axiom, maxim **6** byword, dictum, saying, slogan, truism **7** epigram, precept, proverb **8** aphorism **9** catchword, principle, watchword

moue 4 pout **7** grimace

Moulin Rouge
    1952:
        director: **10** John Huston
        cast: **10** Jose Ferrer (Toulouse-Lautrec) **11** Suzanne Flon, Zsa Zsa

Gabor **12** Eric Pohlmann
    setting: **5** Paris **10** Montmartre

Moulin Rouge
    2001:
        director: **11** Baz Luhrmann
        cast: **12** Ewan McGregor (Christian), Jim Broadbent (Harold Zidler), Nicole Kidman (Satine) **13** John Leguizamo (Toulouse-Lautrec) **15** Richard Roxburgh (the Duke)

mound 4 bump, dune, heap, hill, pile, rick **5** knoll, mogul, ridge, stack **7** bulwark, hillock, hummock, rampart **9** earthwork **10** embankment **12** entrenchment

Mound Builders
    location: **15** Ohio River Valley **22** Mississippi River Valley
    known for: **13** earthen mounds

mount 3 fit, fix, rig, set, wax **4** go up, grow, pony, rise, soar **5** affix, camel, climb, equip, frame, horse, scale, steed, surge, swell **6** ascend, fit out, outfit, set off **7** augment, charger, climb up, get over, get upon, install, set into **8** elephant, increase, multiply, straddle **9** intensify

mountain 3 alp **4** peak **5** bluff, butte, range, ridge **6** height, massif **7** volcano **8** eminence, highland **9** elevation
    of Afghanistan: **3** Koh **5** Safeo **6** Chagai, Pamirs **7** Nowshak **8** Koh-i-Baba, Safed Koh, Sulaiman **9** Himalayas, Hindu Kush, Istoro Nal **11** Khwaja Amran, Paropamisus
    of Albania: **5** Shala **6** Pindus **8** Koritnjk **10** Mount Korab **12** Albanian Alps
    of Algeria: **5** Aissa, Atlas, Aures, Dahra, Tahat **6** Chelia **7** Ahaggar, Kabylia, Mouydir **8** Djurjura **9** Djurdjura, Tell Atlas **12** Saharan Atlas
    of Andorra: **6** d'Etats **8** l'Estanyo **8** Pyrenees **10** Cataperdis **11** Como Pedrosa
    of Angola: **4** Moco **5** Chela **6** Loviti **16** Humpata Highlands
    of Antigua and Barbuda: **9** Boggy Peak
    of Argentina: **4** Toro **5** Andes, Chato, Laudo, Potro **6** Conico, Pissis, Rincon **8** Famatina, Murallon, Olivares, Tronador, Zapaleri **9** Aconcagua, Tupungato **10** Cordillera **13** Ojos del Salado **15** Cerro Mercedario, Sierra de Cordoba
    of Armenia: **6** Ararat, Taurus **8** Karabekh **7** Aladagh **12** Mount Aragats
    of Australia: **3** Ise **4** Blue, Olga, Ossa, Zeil **5** Bruce, Snowy **6** Cradle, Doreen, Garnet, Gawler, Magnet, Morgan **7** Bongong, Gregory **8** Augustus, Brockman, Cuthbert, Herbert, Jusgrave, Mulligan, Surprise **9** Murchison, Kosciusko, Woodroffe **14** Australian Alps **15** New England

Range **18** Great Dividing Range

of Austria: 4 Alps **6** Tirols, Tyrols, Stubai **8** Eisenerz, Rhatikon **9** Dolomites, Kitzbuhel **10** Hohe Tauern **13** Grossglockner **14** Silvretta Group

of Azerbaijan: 8 Caucasus

of Bangladesh: 10 Keokradong **15** Chittagong Hills

of Barbados: 6 Chalky **7** Hillaby

of Belgium: 8 Ardennes **16** Signal de Botrange

of Benin: 7 Atakora

of Bhutan: 5 Black **9** Himalayas **10** Chomo Lhari, Kula Kangri

of Bolivia: 4 Jara **5** Andes, Cusco, Cuzco **6** Sajama, Sorata, Sunsas **7** Illampu **8** Ancohuma, Illimani, Mururata, Sansimon, Santiago, Zapaleri **12** Eastern Range, Western Range **18** Cordillera Oriental **20** Cordillera Occidental

of Borneo: 4 Iran, Raja **5** Saran **6** Kapuas, Muller, Nijaan, Tebang **8** Kinabalu, Kinibalu, Schwaner

of Bosnia-Herzegovina: 11 Dinaric Alps

of Brazil: 3 Mar **5** Geral, Organ, Piaui **6** Acarai, Gurupi, Parima, Urucum **7** Amambai, Carajas, Gradaus, Neblina, Oragaos, Roraima **8** Bandeira, Itatiaia, Roncador, Tombador **9** Pacaraima, Sugar Loaf **10** Tumuc-Humac

of Brunei: 6 Teraja **9** Ulu Tutong **10** Pagon Priok

of Bulgaria: 3 Kom **5** Botev, Pirin, Sapka **6** Balkan, Musala, Sredna **7** Vikhren **8** Musallah **11** Rila-Rhodope

of Burkina Faso: 4 Tema **8** Nakourou **10** Tenakourou, Tenekourou

of Burundi: 8 Nyarwana **9** Nyamisana

of Cambodia: 3 Pan **7** Dangrek, Dong Rek **8** Cardamom, Elephant **10** Phnom Aoral, Phnom Aural

of Cameroon: 5 Mbabo **7** Bambuto, Kapsiki, Mandara **8** Batandji, Cameroon **9** Atlantika

of Canada: 5 Coast, Logan, Royal **6** Robson, Skeena **7** Cariboo, Cascade, Purcell, Rockies, Selkirk, Stelias, St Elias **8** Columbia, Hazelton, Monashee **9** Mackenzie, Notre Dame, Tremblant **10** Laurentian, Richardson, Shickshock **14** Jacques Cartier

of Canary Islands: 5 Teide, Teyde **6** La Cruz **8** El Cumbre, Tenerife

of Cape Verde: 4 Cano, Fogo **10** Pico de Cano

of Central African Republic: 5 Karre, Tinga **6** Mongos **9** Dar Challa **11** Kayagangiri

of Chad: 7 Tibesti, Touside **9** Emi Koussi

of Chile: 4 Maca, Toro **5** Chato, Maipo, Maipu, Paine, Potro, Pular, Torre, Yogan **6** Apiwan, Burney,

Conico, Jervis, Poquis, Rincon **7** Chaltel, Copiapo, Fitzroy, Palpana, Velluda **8** Cochrane, Tronador, Yanteles **9** Tupungato **13** Ojos del Salado

of Colombia: 5 Abibe, Andes, Baudo, Chita, Cocuy, Huila, Pasto **6** Ayapel, Perija, Purace, Tolima, Tunahi **7** Chamusa, del Ruiz **8** Oriengal **10** Santa Marta **14** Cristobal Colon **17** Central Cordillera, Eastern Cordillera, Western Cordillera

of Costa Rica: 4 Poas **5** Barba, Irazu **6** Blanco **7** Central, Gongora **9** Talamanca, Turrialba **10** Guanacaste **14** Chirripo Grande

of Crete: 3 Ida **5** Dikte, Phino **6** Juktas **7** Lasithi, Madaras **8** Leuka Ori, Theodore, Thriphte **9** Psiloriti

of Croatia: 10 Julian Alps **11** Dinaric Alps, Styrian Alps

of Cuba: 6 Copper **7** Cristal, Maestra, Organos **8** Camaguey, Trinidad, Turquino **9** Las Villas **11** Pinar del rio **12** Guaniguanico **14** Sancti-Spiritus

of Czech Republic: 3 Ore **5** Grant, Tatra **6** Sumava **7** Gerlach, Sudeten **8** Krkonose **9** High Tatra **10** Carpathian **11** Gerlachovka

of Denmark: 12 Ejer Bavnehoj, Yding Skovhoj **14** Himmelbjaerget

of Djibouti: 5 Gouda **9** Moussa Ali

of Dominican Republic: 4 Tina **5** Gallo, Neiba **6** Duarte **7** Baoruco, Central **8** Bahoruco, Oriental **13** Septentrional

of Ecuador: 5 Andes **6** Condor, Sangay **7** Cayambe **8** Antisana, Cotopaxi **9** Cotacachi, Pichincha **10** Chimborazo

of Egypt: 5 Sinai, Uekia **6** Gharib **8** Katerina **9** Katherina **13** Shayib al-Banat

of El Salvador: 6 Izalco **8** Santa Ana

of England: 5 Black **7** Pennine, Snowdon **8** Cambrian, Cumbrian **11** Scafell Pike

of Equatorial Guinea: 5 Mitra **11** Santa Isabel

of Ethiopia: 4 Amba, Batu, Guge, Guna, Talo **5** Ahmar, Choke **9** Rasdashan, Ras Deshen

of Finland: 6 Haltia **7** Laltiva **10** Saari Selka **11** Haldetsokka

of France: 4 Alps, Jura **5** Blanc, Pelat **6** Vosges **8** Ardennes, Pyrenees **9** Mont Blanc **10** French Alps **11** Pic Montcalm

of Gabon Republic: 5 Mpele **7** Chaillu, Cristal, Mikongo **8** Balaquri, Birougou, Iboundji

of Georgia: 8 Caucasus

of Germany: 3 Ore **4** Harz **8** Feldberg **9** Zugspitze **10** Erzgebirge **11** Black Forest, Fichtelberg **12** Bavarian Alps

of Ghana: 8 Afadjato **12** Akwapim Hills

of Gibraltar: 6 Misery

of Greece: 3 Ida **4** Idhi, Oeta, Oite, Ossa **5** Athos **6** Ithome, Peleon, Pelion, Pindus **7** Grammos, Helicon, Olympus, Rhodope **8** Hymettos, Smolikas, Targetos, Taygetus **9** Parnassus **10** Hagion Oros, Lycabettus, Pentelicus

of Greenland: 5 Forel, Payer **7** Khardyu **8** Peterman **9** Gunnbjorn **15** Petermannsbjerg **16** Gunnbjornsfjaeld

of Guatemala: 4 Agua, Mico **5** Fuego, Madre **6** Pacaya, Tacana **7** Atitlan, Toliman **8** La Candon, Las Minas, Tajumuko **9** Tajamulco **10** Acatenango, Santa Maria **12** Cuchumatanes

of Guinea: 4 Loma **5** Nimba **6** Tamgue **11** Fouta Djalon

of Guyana: 5 Amuku, Ariwa, Kamoa **6** Akarai, Kanuku **7** Caburai **9** Pacaraima

of Haiti: 4 Nord **5** Cahos **6** Macaya, Noires **7** Lahotte, Laselle **8** Troudeau

of Honduras: 4 Pija **6** Agalta **7** Celaque **8** Las Minas **9** Esperanza **25** Central American Cordillera

of Hong Kong: 6 Castle **8** Victoria **9** Tai Mo Shan

of Hungary: 4 Alps, Bukk **5** Kekes, Matra, Tatra, Vetes **6** Bakony, Mecsek **7** Cserhat, Gerecse **8** Borzsony, Zempleni **9** Korishegy **10** Carpathian

of Iceland: 4 Laki **5** Askja, Hekla, Jokul, Katla **7** Surtsey **10** Orafajokul **16** Hvannadalshnukur

of India: 8 Aravalli **9** Broad Peak, Distaghil, Himalayas, Karakoram, Nanda Devi, Rakaposhi **10** Gasherbrum, Masherbrum **11** Nanga Parbat **12** Eastern Ghats, Godwin Austen, Kanchenjunga, Western Ghats

of Iran: 6 Elburz, Zagros **8** Demavend

of Iraq: 6 Qalate, Zagros **7** Halgurd, Qaarade **9** Kurdistan

of Ireland: 5 Galty **6** Croagh, Mourne **7** Errigal, Muckish, Patrick, Wicklow **8** Comeragh **10** Benna Beola, Twelve Bens, Twelve Pins **13** Carrantuohill, Knockmealdown **19** Macgillycuddy's Reeks

of Israel: 4 Nafh, Sagi **5** Harif, Meron, Ramon, Tabor **8** Atzmon, Carmel, Hatira, Meiron

of Italy: 4 Alps, Etna, Rosa, Viso **5** Amaro, Blanc, Corno, Somma **6** Cimone, Ortles **7** Vulcano **8** Vesuvius **9** Apennines, Dolomites, Maritimes, Stromboli **10** Apuane Alps, Carnic Alps, Julian Alps, Otztal Alps **11** Bernina Alps, Gennargentu **12** Gran Paradiso, Ligurian Alps **13** Lepontine Alps **16** Abruzzi Apennines

of Jamaica: 4 Blue **8** Sir Johns

of Japan: 3 Uso, Zao **4** Fuji **5** Asahi, Asama, Hondo, Yesso **6** Asosan, Enasan, Hiuchi, Kiusiu, Yariga **7** Fujisan, Hakusan, Kujusan, Tokachi **8**

Fujiyama **9** Japan Alps
of Java: 4 Amat, Gede **5** Lawoe, Murjo, Prahu **6** Raoeng, Semuru, Slamet **7** Semeroe **8** Soembing
of Jordan: 9 Jabal Ramm, Jebel Ramm
of Kenya: 5 Elgon, Kenya, Kulai, Nyira, Nyiru **6** Kinyaa, Matian **7** Logonot **8** Aberdare **9** Kirinyaga
of Korea: 4 Wang **5** Chiri, Halla **6** Kwanmo, Paektu, Sobaek **7** Diamond, Kyebang, Nangnim, Taebaek **8** Chang-pai, Hamgyong, Myohyang **9** Paektu-san **10** Kumgang-san
of Kyrgyzstan: 8 Tian Shan
of Laos: 3 Bia, Lai, Loi, San **4** Copi, Khat **5** Atwat **6** Khoung, Tiubia **7** Phou Bia **15** Annam Cordillera
of Lebanon: 4 Mzar **5** Aruba **6** Hermon **7** es Sauda, Lebanon, Sannine **8** Kadischa, Kenisseh **9** Kennisseh **10** al-Mukammal **11** Anti-Lebanon **13** Qurnat al-Sawda
of Lesotho: 6 Maloti, Maluti **7** Central **8** Injasuti, Machache **10** Ben Macdhui **11** Drakensberg, Thaba Putsoa **16** Thabana Ntlenyana
of Liberia: 3 Uni **4** Bong, Putu **5** Niete, Nimba **6** Wutivi **9** Bomi Hills
of Libya: 5 Green **9** Bette Peak **13** Jabal al Akhdar, Tibesti Massif
of Liechtenstein: 4 Alps **8** Naafkopf, Rhatikon **12** Three Sisters **15** Vorder-Grauspitz
of Lithuania: 9 Juozapine **15** Samogitian Hills
of Luxembourg: 8 Ardennes, Huldange **9** Burgplatz **11** Wemperhardt
of Macedonia: 3 Sar **5** Korab, Kosuf, Nidze **9** Osogovski **10** Malesevski
of Madagascar: 4 Boby **9** Ankaratra **11** Maromokotro **12** High Plateaus, Tsiafajavona **17** Tsaratanana Massif
of Malawi: 6 Mlanje **7** Mulanje **11** Livingstone
of Malaysia: 4 Bulu, Hose, Iban, Iran, Main, Mulu, Niut, Raja **5** Murjo, Niapa, Ophir **6** Blumut, Kapuas, Leuser, Slamet **7** Binaija, Brassey, Crocker **8** Kinabalu, Rindjani **11** Gunong Korbu, Gunong Tahan
of Mali: 4 Mina **6** Iforas **7** Manding **12** Hombori Tondo
of Mexico: 6 Colima, Tacana, Toluca **7** Orizaba **9** Paricutin **11** Ixtacihuatl, Sierra Madre **12** Citlaltepetl, Popocatepetl **14** Sierra Zacateca **16** Chiapas Highlands **24** Transverse Volcanic Sierra
of Mongolia: 4 Cast, Orog **5** Altai **6** Kentei, Sevrej **7** Ich Ovoo, Khangai, Khentei **8** Tannu-Ola **9** Edrengijn **10** Cagaan Bogd, Tabun Bogdo **11** Munky Sardyk **14** Hangayn-Hentiyn, Monch Chajrchan
of Montenegro: 8 Durmitor **11** Dinaric Alps
of Morocco: 3 Rif **4** Bani **5** Abyla,

Atlas, Sarro **8** Tidiguin **9** Anti-Atlas, High Atlas, Jebel-Musa **11** Middle Atlas **12** Jebel Toubkal **13** Djebel Toubkal
of Mozambique: 5 Binga **7** Lebombo
of Myanmar: 4 Chin, Naga, Pegu, Popa **5** Dawna **6** Arakan, Kachin, Lushai, Patkai **7** Karenni **8** Nattaung, Peguyoma, Saramati, Victoria **10** Tenasserim **11** Hkakabo Razi, Manipur Hill **12** Tanen Taunggi
of Namibia: 9 Brandberg **14** Khomas Highland, Koakoveld Hills
of Nepal: 6 Cho Oyu, Churia, Makalu **7** Everest, Lhotse I, Manaslu, Siwalik **8** Lhotse II **9** Annapurna, Himalayas **10** Dhaulagiri, Gosainthan, Himalchuli **11** Ganesh Himal **12** Kanchenjunga **14** Mahabharat Lekh
of New Guinea: 4 Snow **6** Orange **7** Bismark, Wilhelm **8** Victoria **9** Carstensz **10** Puncak Jaya **11** Owen Stanley **12** Albert Edward
of New Zealand: 4 Cook, Eden, Flat, Owen **5** Allen, Chope, Lyall, Mitre, Ohope, Otari, Young **6** Egmont, Stokes, Tasman **7** Aorangi, Cameron, Coronet, Ernslaw, Huiarau, Pihanga, Ruahine, Ruapehu, Tauhera, Tutamee, Tyndall **8** Aspiring, Richmond, Tauranga **9** Messenger, Murchison, Ngauruhoe, Raukumara, Tongariro **11** Remarkables **12** Southern Alps
of Nicaragua: 4 Leon **5** Negro, Viejo **6** Madera, Telica **7** Managua, Mogoton, Saslaya **9** Momotombo
of Niger: 7 Bagzane, Greboun **9** Air Massif
of Norway: 5 Sogne **6** Kjolen **7** Numedal **8** Blodfjel, Snohetta, Telemark, Ustetind **9** Harteigen, Jotunheim, Langfjell, Ramnanosi **10** Dovrefjell, Galdhoepig, Glitretind, Vibmesnosi **11** Myrdalfjell **12** Galdhopiggen **13** Glittertinden **14** Aardangerjokul, Hallingskarvet, Skagastolstind
of Oman: 4 Qara **5** Green, Hafit, Harim, Nakhl, Tayin **6** al-Sham **8** el-Akhdar **11** Jabal Akhdar **13** Green Mountain
of Pakistan: 3 Pab, Pub **4** Salt **6** Makran **7** Kirthar **8** Himalaya, Safed Koh, Sulaiman **9** Hindu Kush, Karakoram, Tirich Mir **11** Makran Coast **12** Godwin Austin **13** Central Makran **11** Takht-i-Sulaiman
of Panama: 4 Baru, Maje **5** Chico, Gandi **6** Darien **7** Columan, San Blas, Veragua **8** Chiriqui, Santiago, Tabasara **10** Costa Rican **14** Serrania de Sapo **17** Aspave Highlands **17** Cordillera Central
of Peru: 5 Andes **7** El Misti, Huamina **8** Coropuna **9** Huascaran
of Philippines: 3 Apo, Iba **4** Mayo, Taal **5** Albay, Askja, Hibok, Mayon,

Pulog **6** Pagsan **7** Banahao, Canlaon
of Poland: 4 Rysy **5** Tatra **6** Beskid **7** Pieniny, Sudeten **9** Beshchady, High Tatra, Holy Cross **10** Carpathian
of Portugal: 4 Acor, Lapa **5** Gerez, Marao, Mousa **6** Bornes, Peneda **7** Larouco **8** Caramulo **9** Caldeirao, Monchique **11** Pico da Serra **14** Serra da Estrela
of Puerto Rico: 4 Toro **5** Cayey, Punta **6** Yunque **8** Guilarte, Luquilla **10** Torrecilla **17** Cordillera Central
of Romania: 5 Banat, Bihor, Negoi **6** Codrul, Rodnei **7** Apuseni, Balkans, Caliman, Fagaras **8** Pietrosu **9** Moldavian **10** Carpathian, Moldoveanu **17** Transylvanian Alps
of Russia: 5 Altai, Lenin, Sayan, Urals **6** Anadyr, Elbrus, Koryak, Pamirs, Pobedy **7** Belukha, Crimean, Khibiny, Stanovi, Zhiguli **8** Caucasus, Dzhughur, Stanavoi, Tien Shan **9** Kopet Dagh, Narodnaya, Pamir-Alai, Yablonovy **11** Sikhote-Alin, Verkhoyansk
of Rwanda: 7 Mitumba, Virunga **8** Muhavura **9** Karisimbi
of Samoa: 4 Fito, Vaea **5** Alava **6** Savaii **7** Matafao **8** Silisili **9** Rainmaker
of San Marino: 6 Titano **9** Apennines
of Sardinia: 4 Rasu **5** Ferry, Linas **7** Gallura, Limbara **8** Marghine, Serpeddi, Vittoria **11** Gennargentu
of Saudi Arabia: 5 Razih **6** Tuwayq **10** Jebal Sawda
of Scotland: 5 Attow, Ochil **6** Sidlaw **7** Cheviot **8** Ben Nevis, Grampian **9** Ben Lomond, Highlands, Trossachs
of Senegal: 6 Gounou **12** Fouta Djallon
of Sicily: 4 Erei, Etna, Moro, Sori **5** Aetna, Atlas, Erici, Hybla, Iblei, Ibrei **7** Nebrodi, Vulcano **9** Apennines, Le Madonie, Stromboli **10** Peloritani
of Sierra Leone: 4 Loma **9** Bintimani **10** Tingi Hills
of Sikkim: 7 Dongkya, Donkhya **9** Himalayas, Singalili **10** Darjeeling **12** Kanchenjunga
of Singapore: 6 Mandai **7** Panjang **10** Bukit Timah
of Slovakia: 7 Sudetes **8** Low Tatra **9** High Tatra, Slovak Ore **10** Carpathian, Nizke Tatry **11** Visoke Tatry **15** White Carpathian
of Slovenia: 4 Kras **7** Triglav **10** Carnic Alps, Julian Alps, Karawanken **11** Dinaric Alps
of the Solomon Islands: 5 Balbi **11** Popomanasiu
of Somalia: 5 Guban **7** Surud Ad **11** Migiurtinia, Ogo Highland
of South Africa: 3 Aux, Kop **5** Table **7** Kathkin **8** Injasuti **9** Stormberg **10** Devil's Peak, Sneeuwberg **11** Drakensberg **12** Giant's Castle **13** Witwatersrand **14** Mont-aux-Sources **15** Great Escarpment

of Spain: 4 Gata **5** Aneto, Rouch, Teide **6** Cuenca, Estats, Europa, Gredos, Magina, Morena, Nethou, Nevada, Teleno, Toledo **7** Alcaraz, Banuelo, Catalan, Cerredo, Demanda, Iberian, La Sagra, Moncayo, Perdido **8** Almanzor, Asturias, Galician, Maladeta, Monegros, Montseny, Mulhacen, Penalara, Pyrenees **10** Albarracin, Cantabrian, Guadarrama, Torrecilla

of Sri Lanka: 5 Pedro **7** Sri Pada **9** Adams Peak **14** Pidurutalagala

of Sudan: 4 Nuba **6** Red Sea **7** Imatong, Kinyeti **9** Dongotona **10** Jabal Marra, Jebel Marra **18** Ethiopian Highlands

of Surinam: 4 Emma **6** Kayser, Oranje **10** Julianatop, Tumuc-Humac, Wilhelmina **13** Eilert's Il Haan, Van Ach Van Wyck **15** Guiana Highlands

of Swaziland: 7 Emlembe **8** Highveld **11** Drakensberg

of Sweden: 4 Sarv **5** Ammar, Kebne **6** Helags, Kjolen, Ovniks, Sarjek **7** Kjollen **10** Kebnekaise

of Switzerland: 3 Dom **4** Alps, Jura, Rigi, Rosa, Todi **5** Adula, Blanc, Cenis, Eiger, Genis, Karpf, Righi **6** Linard, Pizela, Sentis **7** Bernina, Beverin, Grimsel, Pilatus, Rotondo **8** Balmhorn, Jungfrau **9** Weisshorn **10** Diablerets, Matterhorn, St Gotthard, Wetterhorn **11** Burgenstock **12** Dufourspitze **13** Rheinwaldhorn **14** Finsteraarhorn

of Syria: 6 Carmel, Hermon **7** Alawite, Libanus **10** Nusairiyya **11** Anti-Lebanon

of Taiwan: 5 Tatun **6** Tzukao, Yu Shan **7** Taitung **8** Morrison **10** Sinkao Shan **11** Hsin-Kao Shan **15** Chungyang Shanmo

of Tajikistan: 13 Communism Peak

of Tanzania: 4 Kibo, Mero **8** Usambara **11** Kilimanjaro

of Thailand: 5 Dawna, Khieo **6** Phanom **8** Dang Raek, Inthanon, Kao Prawa, Maelamun **9** Khao Luang **11** Bilauktaung, Doi Inthanon

of Tibet: 5 Kamet, Sajum **6** Kailas, Kunlun **7** Bandala, Everest **9** Himalayas, Karakoram

of Togo: 4 Togo **7** Atakora, Baumann, Koronga

of Tunisia: 5 Atlas **6** Chambi, Mrhila **7** Tebessa **8** High Tell, Zaghouan **12** Northern Tell **18** Dorsale Tunnisienne

of Turkey: 2 Ak **3** Ala **4** Alai, Dagh, Kara **5** Hasan, Hinis, Honaz, Murat, Murit **6** Ala Dag, Ararat, Bingol, Bolgar, Pontic, Suphan, Taurus **7** Aladagh, Erciyas **8** Karacali **10** Kackar Dagi

of Uganda: 4 Oboa **5** Elgon **7** Virunga **9** Mufumbiro, Ruwenzori **10**

Margherita **18** Mountains of the Moon

of Ukraine: 7 Crimean **10** Carpathian

of United States: 4 Hood **5** Coast, Green, Kenai, Ozark, Rocky, White **6** Alaska, Brooks, DeLong, Elbert, Helena, Mesabi, Pocono, Shasta **7** Cascade, Chugach, Foraker, Harvard, Kilauea, Massive, Olympic, Olympus, Rainier, St Elias, Whitney **8** Catskill, Davidson, Endicott, Katahdin, Mauna Loa, McKinley, Mitchell, Ouachita, St Helens, Wrangell **9** Allegheny, Blue Ridge, Kuskokwim, North Peak, Pike's Peak **10** Black Hills, Blanca Peak, Grand Teton, Washington, Williamson **11** Appalachian, Santa Monica **12** Sierra Nevada **14** Berkshire Hills

of Uruguay: 6 Animas **10** Grand Hills **14** Cuchilla Grande **15** Mirador Nacional

of Vanuatu: 6 Lopevi **11** Tabwemasana

of Venezuela: 3 Pao **4** Pava, Yair **5** Andes, Duida, Icutu **6** Concha, Cuneva, Merida, Parima, Sierra, Yumari **7** Bolivar, Imutaca, Masaiti, Roraima **8** Gurupira **9** Pacaraima **10** Auyan-Tepui **11** Turimiquire **18** Cordillera del Norte

of Vietnam: 6 Badinh, Badink **7** Nindhoa, Ninhhoa **8** Fansipan, Knontran, Ngoklinh, Ngoklink, Tchepone, Tclepore **18** Annamese Cordilera

of Wales: 6 Berwyn **7** Snowdon **8** Cambrian **9** Prescelly **13** Brecon Beacons

of Western Samoa: 4 Fito, Vaea **13** Mauga Silisili

of Yemen: 6 Shuayb, Thamir **7** Djehaff

of Yugoslavia: 6 Balkan **8** Durmitor **11** Dinaric Alps

of Zaire: 7 Crystal, Mitumba, Virunga **9** Ruwenzori **10** Margherita, Nyaragongo **18** Mountains of the Moon

of Zambia: 8 Muchinga **12** Mafinga Hills

of Zimbabwe: 5 Vumba **6** Manica **7** Inyanga **9** Inyangani **11** Chimanimani, Matopo Hills

Mountain
  constellation of: 5 Mensa

mountaineers are always free men
  Latin: 19 montani semper liberi
  motto of: 12 West Virginia

Mountain State
  nickname of: 7 Montana **12** West Virginia

Mountbatten, Louis
  also: 27 first Earl Mountbatten of Burma
  nationality: 7 British
  position: 12 first sea lord
  supreme allied commander of: 13

Southeast Asia
  chief of: 25 British combined operations
  viceroy of: 5 India
  served in: 3 WWI **4** WWII
  directed invasion of: 10 Madagascar
  recaptured: 5 Burma

mountebank 5 cheat, fraud, phony, quack **6** con man, humbug **7** hustler, sharper **8** huckster, operator, swindler **9** charlatan, con artist **11** quacksalver

mounted soldier 6 hussar, lancer **7** dragoon **8** cavalier, horseman **10** cavalryman

mourn 3 cry, rue, sob **4** keen, pine, wail, weep **6** bemoan, bewail, grieve, lament, regret, sorrow **7** deplore, despair **8** languish, weep over

mournful 3 sad **5** black, sorry, weepy **6** dismal, rueful, somber, triste, woeful **7** doleful, joyless, unhappy **8** dejected, dirgeful, dolorous, funereal, grievous, saddened **9** depressed, plaintive, sorrowful **10** depressing, dispirited, lamentable, lugubrious, melancholy **11** distressing, melancholic **12** heavy hearted

mourning 3 woe **5** black, crape, dolor, grief, weeds **6** sorrow **7** anguish, despair **8** grieving **9** lamenting, sorrowing **11** bereavement, lamentation

Mourning Becomes Electra
  author: 12 Eugene O'Neill
  character: 4 Seth **10** Hazel Niles, Peter Niles **16** Captain Adam Brant
    Mannon family: 4 Ezra, Orin **7** Lavinia **9** Christine

mourning period
  Hebrew: 6 shibah, shivah

mouser 3 cat **4** puss **5** kitty, pussy **6** feline **8** pussycat

Mousetrap, The
  author: 14 Agatha Christie

mousseline 6 muslin

mousy 3 shy **4** drab, dull **5** timid, wimpy **7** bashful, fearful **8** timorous **9** colorless, unnoticed, withdrawn **11** unobtrusive **13** inconspicuous

mouth 3 bay, say **4** bell, jaws, lips **5** inlet, speak, voice **6** outlet, portal **7** declare, estuary, opening **8** aperture, propound **9** pronounce

mouthful 3 dab **4** bite **5** taste **6** morsel, nibble

mouthpiece 4 reed **6** lawyer **7** counsel **8** advocate, attorney **9** counselor

mouth-watering 8 inviting, tempting **9** appealing **10** appetizing **11** tantalizing

movable, moveable 4 free **5** loose **6** mobile, motile, moving **8** portable **10** changeable

movables 4 gear **5** goods **7** baggage, effects, luggage **9** equipment **10** belongings **11** impedimenta, possessions **13** accoutrements, paraphernalia

move 2 go **3** act, ask, get **4** bear, deed, fire, lead, pass, ploy, step, stir, sway, turn, urge **5** begin, budge, carry, cause, drive, impel, plead, rouse, shift, touch **6** action, affect, arouse, attack, convey, excite, exhort, incite, induce, motion, prompt, strike, stroke, switch **7** advance, budging, gesture, go ahead, impress, inspire, measure, operate, proceed, propose, provoke, request, suggest **8** function, interest, locomote, maneuver, motivate, persuade, relocate, start off, stirring, transfer, transmit **9** impassion, influence, recommend, stimulate, transport, transpose **10** transplant **11** opportunity

move downward 3 dip **4** dive, drop, fall, sink **6** plunge, tumble **7** decline, descend, plummet **8** decrease

movement 4 part **5** drive, steps, works **6** action, effort, motion **7** crusade, measure, program, section **8** activity, division, gestures, maneuver, progress, stirring **9** agitation, execution, mechanism, operation **10** locomotion **11** undertaking

move out 5 leave **6** depart, vacate **8** evacuate

move quickly 3 fly, run **4** bolt, dash, race, rush, tear **5** hurry **6** hasten, sprint

move sideways 4 edge **5** sidle **8** sidestep

move slyly 4 edge, lurk **5** sidle, skulk, slink, sneak, steal

move up 5 boost, climb, heave, hoist, raise, scale **6** ascend, uplift **7** advance, elevate, promote, upraise

move upward 4 rise, soar **5** climb, mount **6** ascend **7** take off

movie 4 film, show **5** flick **6** cinema **7** feature, picture, showing **9** screening
  invented by:
    machine: 7 Jenkins
    panoramic: 6 Waller
    projector: 6 Edison
    talking: 14 Warner Brothers

moving 5 motor **6** mobile, motile **8** exciting, poignant, spurring, stirring, touching **9** affecting, inspiring **10** impressive, locomotive, motivating **11** interacting, stimulating

moving about 5 astir **6** active **7** on the go

Mowgli
  character in: 14 The Jungle Books
  author: 7 Kipling

moxie 4 grit, guts, sand **5** nerve, pluck, spunk **6** mettle, spirit **7** courage, stamina **8** audacity, backbone **9** hardihood, toughness **10** pluckiness **13** dauntlessness

moyen age 10 Middle Ages

Mozambique
  capital/largest city: 6 Maputo **15** Lourenco Marques
  others: 4 Tete **5** Beira, Pemba, Zumbo **6** Chemba, Nacala, Pafuri, Sofala **7** Nampula **8** Mutarara **9** Inhambane, Quelimane **11** Porto Amelia
  school: 15 Eduardo Mondlane
  monetary unit: 6 escudo **7** centavo, metical
  island: 6 Inhaca **7** Angoche **8** Bazanuto **9** Benguerua
  lake: 5 Nyasa **6** Chuali, Nyassa **8** Nhavarre
  mountain: 7 Lebombo
    highlands: 6 Namuli **9** Gorongosa
  highest point: 5 Binga
  river: 4 Buzi, Save **5** Lurio, Msalu **6** Rovuma, Ruvuma **7** Ligonha, Limpopo, Lugenda, Messaio, Zambezi **8** Changane
  ocean: 6 Indian
  physical feature:
    cape: 7 Delgado
    channel: 10 Mozambique
  people: 3 Yao **5** Bantu, Chopi, Lomue, Lomwe, Macua, Makua, Ngoni, Nguni, Shona **6** Maravi, Thouga **7** Maconde, Makonde **10** Portuguese
    explorer: 11 Vasco de Gama
    leader: 8 Chissano **9** Dos Santos **12** Samora Machel **15** Eduardo Mondlane
  language: 3 Yao **5** Makua **6** Nyanji, Thonga **7** Swahili **10** Portuguese
  religion: 5 Islam **7** animism **13** Roman Catholic
  place:
    game reserve: 8 Marromeu **9** Gorongosa, Gorongoza **18** Maputo Elephant Park
    reservoir: 11 Cabora Bassa
  feature:
    bride price: 6 lobolo

Mozart, Wolfgang Amadeus
  born: 7 Austria **8** Salzburg
  cataloguer: 6 Kochel
  composer of: 4 Linz (symphony No 36) **5** Paris (symphony No 31) **6** Prague (symphony No 38) **7** Don Juan, Haffner (symphony No 35), Jupiter (symphony No 41), Requiem, Turkish (concerto) **8** Idomeneo **9** Credo Mass, Mitridate **10** Lucio Silla **11** Don Giovanni, Hunt Quartet, Il Re Pastore, Sparrow Mass **12** A Musical Joke, Cosi Fan Tutte (So Do They All or Women Are Like That), Haydn Quartet, Spatzenmesse **13** The Magic Flute, Trumpet Sonata, Turkish Sonata **14** Coronation Mass, Stadler Quintet, Die Zauberflote **15** Haffner Serenade, La Finta Semplice, Prussian Quartet **16** Dissonant Quartet, La Clemenza di Tito, Posthorn Serenade, Serenata Notturna **17** A Little Night Music **18** Jeunehomme Concerto, La Finta Giardiniera, The Clemency of Tito **19** Bastien und Bastienne, The Marriage of Figaro **20** Eine Kleine Nachtmusik, The Pretender Gardener **21** Der Schauspieldirektor, Ein Musikalischer Spass **22** The Pretending Simpleton **25** Die Entfuhrung aus dem Serail **27** The Abduction from the Seraglio

Mr, Mister
  Russian: 8 gospodin
  French: 8 monsieur
  Yiddish: 3 Reb

Mr Basketball
  nickname of: 8 Bob Cousy

Mr Cub
  nickname of: 10 Ernie Banks

Mr Deeds Goes to Town
  director: 10 Frank Capra
  cast: 10 Gary Cooper (Longfellow Deeds), Jean Arthur **14** George Bancroft

Mr Ed
  character: 9 Carol Post **10** Kay Addison, Wilbur Post **12** Roger Addison **14** Gordon Kirkwood, Winnie Kirkwood
  cast: 8 Leon Ames **9** Alan Young **11** Connie Hines, Edna Skinner **12** Larry Keating **18** Florence MacMichael
  Mr Ed was: 12 talking horse

Mr Midnight
  nickname of: 10 Steve Allen

Mr Peepers
  character: 9 Mrs Gurney **11** Marge Weskit, Mr Remington **12** Harvey Weskit **14** Nancy Remington **15** Robinson Peepers **20** Superintendent Bascom
  cast: 8 Wally Cox **9** Gage Clark **11** Ernest Truex, Marion Lorne, Tony Randall **14** Patricia Benoit **16** Georgiann Johnson
  Mr Peepers taught: 7 science
  school: 13 Jefferson High

Mr Sammler's Planet
  author: 10 Saul Bellow

Mrs Dalloway
  author: 13 Virginia Woolf
  character: 10 Miss Kilman, Peter Walsh, Sally Seton **15** Richard Dalloway **16** Clarissa Dalloway **17** Elizabeth Dalloway

Mrs Miniver
  director: 12 William Wyler
  cast: 11 Greer Garson **12** Teresa Wright **13** Dame May Whitty, Walter Pidgeon
  Oscar for: 7 actress (Garson), picture **8** director **17** supporting actress (Wright)

Mr Smith Goes to Washington
  director: 10 Frank Capra
  cast: 9 Guy Kibbee **10** Jean Arthur **11** Claude Rains **12** Edward Arnold, James Stewart **14** Thomas Mitchell

Mrs Warren's Profession
 author: **17** George Bernard Shaw
Mr Television
 nickname of: **11** Milton Berle
much 3 far **4** a lot, lots **5** about, ample, heaps, loads, often **6** almost, indeed, nearly, overly, rather, scores **7** copious, greatly **8** abundant, good deal, plenty of, quantity, somewhat, striking **9** decidedly, important, plenteous, plentiful, regularly **10** frequently, impressive, noteworthy, oftentimes, satisfying, sufficient, worthwhile **11** appreciable, exceedingly, excessively, sufficiency **12** considerable **13** approximately, consequential

Much Ado About Nothing
 author: **18** William Shakespeare
 character: **4** Hero **7** Claudio, Don John, Leonato **8** Beatrice, Benedick, Dogberry, Don Pedro
much in little
 Latin: **13** multum in parvo
much loved 4 dear **7** beloved, darling, dearest **8** precious **9** cherished, treasured
mucilage 3 gum **4** glue **5** paste **6** cement **8** adhesive
mucilaginous 5 gluey, gummy, gunky **6** gloppy, sticky **8** adhesive
muck 3 mud **4** dirt, dung, gunk, mire, ooze, slop **5** filth, slime **6** sewage, sludge **7** compost, garbage
muck up 4 soil **5** dirty, muddy **7** pollute
mud 4 dirt, muck, soil, wire
Mudcat State
 nickname of: **11** Mississippi
muddied 5 dirty, grimy **6** grubby, soiled **7** stained **8** begrimed, confused
muddle 3 fog **4** blow, daze, haze, mess, muff, ruin **5** botch, chaos, mix up, spoil, throw **6** boggle, bungle, fumble, goof up, jumble, mess up, pother, rattle **7** blunder, clutter, confuse, nonplus, stupefy **8** bewilder, confound, disarray, disorder **13** disconcertion **14** disarrangement
muddlebrained 5 inept **7** witless **8** confused **11** lamebrained
muddled 5 fuzzy **7** bemused **8** confused **10** bewildered
muddy 4 dull **5** dirty, grimy, vague **6** filthy, grubby **7** obscure **8** begrimed, confused
muff 5 botch, spoil **6** bungle **10** handwarmer
muffle 3 gag **4** dull, hush, mask, mute, veil, wrap **5** cloak, cover, quell, quiet, still **6** dampen, deaden, shroud, soften, stifle, swathe **7** conceal, enclose, envelop, silence, swaddle
muffled 3 low **4** dull, soft **5** faint, muted **6** dulled, feeble, hushed, veiled **7** cloaked, covered, quelled, quieted,

stilled, subdued, swathed, wrapped **8** deadened, shrouded, silenced, softened, swaddled **9** concealed, enveloped, inaudible **10** indistinct, suppressed
mug 3 cup **4** face, puss, toby **5** stein, stoup **6** beaker, flagon, goblet, kisser, visage **7** chalice, tankard, toby jug, tumbler **11** countenance
mugger 8 assailer, attacker **9** assailant, assaulter
mugginess 4 damp **8** dampness, dankness, humidity **9** humidness **10** sultriness **14** oppressiveness
muggy 5 close, humid **6** clammy, steamy, sticky, stuffy, sultry, sweaty **8** steaming, vaporous **10** oppressive, sweltering
mulberry 5 Morus
 varieties: **3** red **4** Aino **5** black, paper, white **6** French, Indian **7** Russian **8** American, silkworm
mulct 4 bilk **6** extort **7** defraud, swindle
mule 3 ass **5** burro **6** donkey **7** jackass
 group of: **4** span
mulish 5 balky **6** ornery **8** perverse, stubborn **9** fractious, obstinate **10** refractory **11** intractable **12** recalcitrant
mull, mull over 5 study, weigh **7** ponder **8** consider, meditate, pore over, ruminate **10** deliberate
Muller
 character in: **25** All Quiet on the Western Front
 author: **8** Remarque
Muller, Hermann Joseph
 field: **8** genetics
 researched: **5** X-rays **8** mutation
 awarded: **10** Nobel Prize
Muller, Paul
 field: **9** chemistry
 nationality: **5** Swiss
 established: **16** DDT as insecticide
 awarded: **10** Nobel Prize
Mulligan, Buck
 character in: **7** Ulysses
 author: **5** Joyce
multicolored 10 variegated
multifarious 4 many **5** mixed **6** divers, motley, sundry, varied **7** diverse, protean, several, various **8** manifold, numerous **9** different, multiplex **10** variegated **11** diversified **13** heterogeneous, miscellaneous
multiple 4 many **7** various **8** manifold
multiply 5 add to, beget, breed, raise **6** extend, spread **7** augment, enhance, enlarge, magnify **8** generate, heighten, increase **9** intensify, procreate, propagate, reproduce **11** proliferate
multitude 3 mob **4** army, herd, host, mass, pack, slew **5** array, crowd, crush, drove, flock, flood, horde, troop **6** legion, myriad, scores, throng **7** conflux

multum in parvo 12 much in little **23** a great deal in a small space
mum 4 mute **5** quiet, still, tacit **6** silent **8** taciturn, wordless **9** secretive **12** closemouthed **15** uncommunicative
mumble 5 growl, grunt, mouth **6** murmur, mutter, rumble **7** stammer **9** hem and haw
mumbo jumbo 3 rot **4** blah, bosh, cant, tosh **5** bilge, hokum, hooey, tripe **6** hot air, humbug **7** baloney **8** flummery **9** gibberish, sophistry **10** double talk, hocus pocus **11** doublespeak, jabberwocky, obfuscation **12** fiddle-faddle, gobbledygook, obscurantism
Mummy, The
 director: **10** Karl Freund
 cast: **10** Zita Johann **12** Boris Karloff, David Manners **16** Bramwell Fletcher
munch 4 chew, gnaw **5** champ, chomp, crush, grind **9** masticate
Munch, Edvard
 born: **5** Loten **6** Norway **10** Hedemarken
 artwork: **6** The Cry **7** Puberty, The Kiss **9** The Scream **11** Dance of Life **12** Frieze of Life **21** Death in the Sick Chamber
Munchausen, Baron 4 liar **7** solider **10** adventurer **11** exaggerator
Munchkins
 characters in: **13** The Wizard of Oz
 author: **4** Baum
mundane 5 petty **7** earthly, humdrum, prosaic, routine, worldly **8** day-to-day, everyday, ordinary **9** practical **10** pedestrian **11** commonplace, down-to-earth, terrestrial
Muni, Paul
 real name: **16** Muni Weisenfreund
 born: **7** Austria, Lemberg (now Lvov Ukraine)
 roles: **6** Juarez **8** Scarface **10** The Valiant **12** The Good Earth **14** Clarence Darrow, Inherit the Wind **15** The Last Angry Man **18** The Life of Emile Zola **22** The Story of Louis Pasteur (Oscar) **26** I Am a Fugitive from a Chain Gang
municipal 4 city **5** civic **6** public **9** community **14** administrative
municipality 4 city, town **6** parish **7** village **8** township **9** bailiwick
munificence 6 bounty **7** charity **8** largesse **9** patronage **10** generosity, liberality **11** benefaction, beneficence, benevolence **12** philanthropy **13** bounteousness, bountifulness **14** charitableness **15** humanitarianism
munificent 4 free **6** kindly, lavish **7** liberal, profuse **8** generous, princely **9** bounteous, bountiful **10** altruistic, beneficent, benevolent, charitable, freehanded, open-handed **11** extravagant, magnanimous **12** eleemosynary, humanitarian **13** philanthropic

Munin
origin: **12** Scandinavian
form: **5** raven
owned by: **4** Odin **5** Othin
personifies: **6** memory
duty: **10** newsbearer
other raven: **5** Hugin

Munsters, The
character: **11** Lily Munster **12** Eddie
(Edward Wolfgang) Munster **13** Herman Munster **14** Grandpa Munster,
Marilyn Munster
cast: **7** Al Lewis **9** Pat Priest **10** Fred
Gwynne **11** Beverly Owen **12** Butch
Patrick **13** Yvonne DeCarlo

Muppet Show, The
character: **4** Rolf **5** Gonzo **6** Animal,
Beaker **7** Scooter **9** Miss Piggy **10**
Fozzie Bear **13** Kermit the Frog (Kermie)

Murasaki, Lady
author of: **14** The Tale of Genji

murder 4 kill, slay **5** abuse, waste **6**
mangle, misuse **7** butcher, corrupt,
cut down, killing **8** homicide, knock
off **9** agonizing, slaughter **10** bastardize, formidable, impossible, oppressive, unbearable **11** assassinate, intolerable **12** manslaughter **13**
assassination, very difficult **14** commit
homicide, use incorrectly

Murder, She Wrote
character: **15** Jessica (JB) Fletcher
cast: **14** Angela Lansbury
setting: **9** Cabot Cove

murderer 4 Cain **6** killer, slayer
7 butcher **8** assassin, Barabbas, homicide **9** cutthroat

Murder in the Cathedral
author: **7** T S Eliot

Murder of Roger Ackroyd, The
author: **14** Agatha Christie

Murder on the Orient Express
author: **14** Agatha Christie
detective: **13** Hercule Poirot

murderous 4 gory **5** cruel, rough **6**
bloody, brutal, deadly, savage, trying
7 killing **9** dangerous, difficult, ferocious **11** devastating **12** bloodthirsty,
disagreeable

Murdoch, Iris
author of: **7** The Bell **11** Under the
Net **12** A Severed Head, The Sea the
Sea **14** The Black Prince, The Green
Knight **15** Jackson's Dilemma, Nuns
and Soldiers **17** The Good Apprentice, The Nice and the Good **20** The
Philosopher's Pupil **24** The Book and
The Brotherhood **30** The Sacred and
Profane Love Machine

Murdstone, Mr
character in: **16** David Copperfield
author: **7** Dickens

**Murillo, Bartolome (Bartolomeo)
Esteban**
born: **5** Spain **7** Seville
artwork: **13** Angels' Kitchen **14**

Death of St Clare **15** The Two Trinities **17** Vision of St Anthony **23** The
Immaculate Conception **24** Dream of
the Roman Patrician

murk 3 fog **4** haze, mist **5** gloom **6** miasma **7** pea soup **8** darkness

murky 3 dim **4** dark, gray, hazy **5**
dusky, foggy, misty **6** cloudy, dismal,
dreary, gloomy, somber **7** obscure,
sunless **8** lowering, overcast, vaporous **9** cheerless

murmur 3 hum **4** buzz, purl, purr,
sigh **5** drone, sough, swish **6** lament,
mumble, mutter, rumble, rustle **7**
grumble, lapping, whimper, whisper **8**
low sound, susurrus **9** complaint, undertone

murophobia
fear of: **4** mice

Murphy, Eddie
roles: **3** Raw **4** I Spy **5** Shrek **13**
Trading Places **14** The Golden Child
15 Coming to America, Doctor Doolittle, Forty-Eight Hours **16** Beverly
Hills Cop **17** Saturday Night Live,
The Nutty Professor **19** Beverly Hills
Cop Two

Murphy Brown
network: **3** CBS
cast: **9** Faith Ford (Corky Sherwood),
Pat Corley (Phil) **10** Grant Shaud
(Miles Silverberg), Jane Leeves (Audrey Cohen) **12** Joe Regalbuto
(Frank Fontana) **13** Candice Bergen
(Murphy Brown) **16** Charles Kimbrough (Jim Dial), Robert Pastorelli
(Eldin)

Murray, Bill
roles: **7** Stripes **9** Meatballs **10** Caddyshack **12** Ghostbusters, Groundhog
Day, What About Bob **13** Broken
Flowers, The Razor's Edge **17** Lost
in Translation, Saturday Night Live
27 Not Ready for Prime Time Players

Murray, Don
wife: **9** Hope Lange
born: **11** Hollywood CA
roles: **7** Bus Stop **13** A Hatful of Rain
16 The Bachelor Party, The Hoodlum
Priest

Murray, Jeanne
real name of: **13** Jean Stapleton

Murray, Mina
character in: **7** Dracula
author: **6** Stoker

Musaeus
occupation: **4** poet, seer

Musagetes see **6** Apollo

Muscat, Masqat
capital of: **4** Oman

muscle 4 grit, thew **5** bicep, brawn,
force, might, power, sinew, vigor **6**
energy, flexor, tendon **7** potency,
prowess, stamina **8** virility **9** puissance **10** sturdiness **16** muscular
strength
kind: **4** limb **5** axial **6** smooth **7** dy-

namic, flexors, special, striped **8** postural, striated **9** abductors, extensors,
voluntary **11** involuntary
fuel: **4** food
action: **4** pull
specific: **6** rectus **7** deltoid, oblique **8**
omohyoid **9** abdominal, abdominis,
sartorius **10** pectoralis **11** intercostal,
sternohyoid **13** biceps brachii, rectus
femoris **14** vastus medialis **15**
brachioradialis, vastus lateralis **16**
serratus anterior, tensor fascia lata
17 quadriceps femoris **18** transverse
thoracic **19** sternocleidomastoid **20**
transversus abdominis
supplementary structure: **6** sheath
10 deep fascia, retinacula **14** synovial bursae, synovial sheath

muscular 3 fit **5** burly, husky, tough **6**
brawny, sinewy, strong **8** athletic,
powerful **9** strapping

muscular contraction 3 tic **5** cramp,
crick, spasm **6** stitch **12** charley horse

musculoskeletal system
component: **4** bone **6** muscle, tendon
8 ligament

muse 4 mull **6** ponder, review **7** reflect
8 cogitate, consider, meditate, ruminate **9** speculate **10** deliberate **11** contemplate

Musee des Beaux Arts
author: **7** W H Auden

Muses
also: **7** the Nine **8** Pierides **10** Castalides
form: **9** goddesses
names: **4** Clio (history) **5** Erato (love
poetry) **6** Thalia (comedy), Urania
(astronomy) **7** Euterpe (music, lyric
poetry) **8** Calliope (epic poetry) **9**
Melpomene (tragedy) **10** Polyhymnia
(sacred poetry) **11** Terpsichore
(dance)
father: **4** Zeus
mother: **9** Mnemosyne
corresponds to: **7** Camenae

Musgrave, Thea
born: **8** Scotland **9** Edinburgh
composer of: **11** The Decision **16**
The Five Ages of Man **17** Beauty and
the Beast, The Voice of Ariadne

mush 5 slush **6** drivel **8** porridge **14**
sentimentalism, sentimentality

mushiness 5 slush **6** bathos **10** sponginess **11** mawkishness **14** sentimentalism, sentimentality

mushroom 4 grow **5** burst, fungi **6**
blow up, expand, fungus, spread,
sprout **7** burgeon, explode, shoot up
8 flourish, increase, spring up **9** toadstool **11** proliferate
part: **3** cap **4** veil **5** gills, stalk, tubes,
volva **6** button, hyphae, spores **7** annulus, basidia **10** rhizomorph
non-poisonous: **5** field, honey, morel,
table **6** oyster **7** inky cap, parasol **8**
puffball, shiitake **9** fairy-ring, mor-

chella, shaggy cap, stinkhorn **10** champignon **11** chanterelle **12** edible bolete, slippery jack **16** old man of the woods

poisonous: 7 amanita **8** death cap, sickener **9** fly agaric **12** jack-o-lantern **13** devil's boletus **15** destroying angel

study of: 8 mycology

mushy 4 soft **5** foggy, misty, pappy, pulpy, vague **6** cloudy, quaggy, spongy **7** maudlin, mawkish, squashy, squishy **8** effusive, romantic, squelchy **10** lovey-dovey **11** sentimental, tear-jerking **12** affectionate

Musial, Stan
nickname: 10 Stan the Man
sport: 8 baseball
team: 16 St Louis Cardinals

music 4 song, tune **5** score **6** melody **7** euphony, harmony **8** lyricism **10** minstrelsy **11** tunefulness **13** melodiousness

god of: 5 Brage, Bragi **6** Apollo **7** Phoebus, Pythius **9** Musagetes

musical 5 lyric, sweet **6** dulcet **7** lilting, lyrical, melodic, tuneful **9** melodious **10** euphonious, harmonious **11** mellifluent

musical instrument 3 lur, sax, saz **4** bass, bell, drum, fife, gong, harp, horn, lute, lyre, oboe, outi, pipe, tuba, viol **5** argul, banjo, bugle, cello, cobza, flute, kazoo, organ, piano, guena, rabob, sansa, shawm, sheng, sitar, viola **6** bagana, chimes, cornet, cymbal, fiddle, guitar, spinet, treble, violin, zither **7** bagpipe, bassoon, cittern, clavier, kithara, marimba, panpipe, pibcorn, piccolo, samisen, strings, tambura, theorbo, timpani, trumpet, ukulele **8** autoharp, bass drum, calliope, clarinet, dulcimer, Jew's harp, mandolin, psaltery, recorder, talharpa, triangle, trombone, virginal **9** accordion, balalaika, castanets, harmonica, harmonium, krummhorn, rommelpot, saxophone, snare drum, xylophone **10** bongo drums, clavichord, concertina, flugelhorn, French horn, kettledrum, sousaphone, tambourine, vibraphone **11** English horn, harpsichord **12** jouhikantele

classification: 4 horn, reed, wind **5** brass **6** string **8** keyboard, woodwind **10** electronic, percussion

musical terms
agitated: 7 agitato
all players/singers together: 5 tutti
becoming quicker: 11 accelerando
continue without a break: 5 segue
disconnected/each note separate: 8 staccato
end: 4 fine
expressively: 10 espressivo
abbreviation: 5 espr
fast: 6 veloce **7** allegro
gentle: 5 soave

gently: 9 doucement
getting slower: 10 allargando
getting weaker and slower: 7 calando
gradually getting louder: 9 crescendo
abbreviation: 5 cresc
gradually getting softer: 10 diminuendo **11** decrescendo
abbreviation: 3 dim **4** decr
gradually slowing: 11 rallentando
abbreviation: 4 rall
half: 5 mezzo
half voice/half volume: 9 mezza voce
heavy: 5 lourd
in an undertone/in a low voice: 9 sotto voce
leisurely: 6 comodo
less: 4 meno
light: 8 leggiero
little: 4 poco
lively: 3 vif
loud: 5 forte
abbreviation: 1 f
moderately slow and even: 7 andante
more: 3 piu
mournful: 5 mesto
not too much: 9 non troppo
plucked instead of bowed: 9 pizzicato
abbreviation: 4 pizz
quick/vivacious: 6 vivace
repeat from beginning: 6 da capo
abbreviation: 2 D C
shaking and quavering/rapid alternation of notes: 5 trill
silent: 4 tace
singing/songlike/flowing: 9 cantabile
sliding: 9 glissando
slow: 5 lento **6** adagio
slow dignified tempo: 5 largo
slow down: 5 cedez
smooth/connected: 6 legato
soft: 5 piano
abbreviation: 1 p
solemn/serious: 5 grave
sorrowful: 7 dolente
strict time: 10 tempo gusto
sudden accent: 9 sforzando
abbreviation: 2 sf
sweetly: 5 dolce
tearful: 9 lacrimoso
tenderly: 10 affettuoso
trembling vibrating effect/rapid reiteration of a single pitch: 7 tremolo
very: 5 molto
very loud: 10 fortissimo
abbreviation: 2 ff
very soft: 10 pianissimo
abbreviation: 2 pp
with fire: 8 con fuoco
with spirit/vigor: 7 con brio
with style/taste: 8 con gusto
with the mute: 10 con sordino

musician 4 bard **5** piper **6** artist, player, singer, violer **7** bandman, cellist, drummer, pianist, twanger **8** minstrel, organist, virtuoso **9** performer, trumpeter, violinist **11** saxophonist

Music Man, The
director: 13 Morton Da Costa
cast: 12 Buddy Hackett, Shirley Jones (Marian the librarian) **13** Robert Preston (Professor Harold Hill) **15** Hermione Gingold
setting: 9 River City
score: 15 Meredith Willson
song: 15 Till There Was You **19** Seventy-Six Trombones

music school 12 conservatory
French: 13 conservatoire

musing 6 absent, dreamy **7** mulling **8** absorbed **9** pondering **10** meditating, meditative, reflecting, reflective

musjid 6 mosque

Muskogean, Muskhogean
tribe: 4 Cree **7** Alabama, Alibamu, Choctaw, Natchez **8** Seminole **9** Chickasaw

Muslim see **6** Moslem

muslin
French: 10 mousseline

muss 4 mess **6** foul up, jumble, ruffle, rumple, tangle, tousle **7** crumple, disturb **8** dishevel, disorder **9** bedraggle **10** disarrange

mussed 5 messy **6** frowzy, untidy **7** ruffled, rumpled, tousled, unkempt **8** uncombed **10** disarrayed, disheveled, disordered, disorderly **11** disarranged

Mussorgsky (Moussorgsky), Modest Petrovich
born: 5 Pskov **6** Russia
member of: 7 The Five
composer of: 7 Sunless **10** The Nursery **12** Boris Godunov **13** Khovanshchina **19** Night on Bald Mountain **21** Songs and Dances of Death **22** Pictures at an Exhibition

mustard
botanical name: 5 B alba **6** B hirta, B nigra **7** B juncea **8** Brassica
also called: 7 sinapis
origin: 4 Asia **5** China
use: 6 hotdog, sauces **7** egg roll **9** hamburger **13** salad dressing

muster 4 call **5** amass, raise, rally **6** gather, line up, summon **7** collect, company, convene, convoke, marshal, meeting, round up, turnout **8** assemble, assembly, mobilize **9** convocate, gathering **10** assemblage, confluence, congregate, inspection **11** aggregation **12** accumulation **13** agglomeration

musty 3 old **4** damp, dank, worn **5** banal, dirty, dusty, moldy, stale, tired, trite **6** frousy, frouzy, frowsy, frowzy, old hat, stuffy **7** worn-out **8** familiar, mildewed **9** hackneyed **10** antiquated, threadbare **11** commonplace

mutable 6 fickle **7** pliable **8** flexible, variable **9** adaptable, alterable, mercurial, versatile **10** adjustable, changeable, inconstant, modifiable, permutable **11** convertible, metamorphic **13** transformable

mutate 4 turn **5** alter **6** change **7** convert **9** transform

mutation 6 change **7** anomaly **9** deviation, variation **10** alteration **12** modification **13** metamorphosis **14** transformation **15** transfiguration **18** transmogrification

mutatis mutandis 30 necessary changes having been made

mute 3 mum **4** dumb **5** quiet, tacit **6** silent **8** aphasiac, nonvocal, reserved, reticent **9** unsounded, unuttered, voiceless **10** speechless **12** inarticulate, noncommittal, unpronounced **13** unarticulated **15** uncommunicative

muted 3 dim, low **4** dull, soft, weak **5** quiet **6** dulled, feeble **7** muffled **8** deadened, softened **10** indistinct, lackluster

mutilate 4 lame, maim **6** cut off, deform, excise, mangle **7** butcher, cripple **8** amputate, lacerate, truncate **9** disfigure, dismember

mutineer 5 rebel **9** dissident, insurgent **10** malcontent **15** insurrectionist

mutinous 6 unruly **10** dissenting, rebellious **13** revolutionary

Mutinus
   origin: 5 Roman **7** Italian
   god of: 9 fertility
   fertility in: 8 marriage
   corresponds to: 7 Priapus

mutiny 4 coup **5** rebel **6** revolt, rise up **8** takeover, upheaval, uprising **9** overthrow, rebellion **10** insurgency **12** insurrection

Mutiny on the Bounty
   author: 15 Charles Nordhoff, James Norman Hall
   character: 6 Tehani **9** Roger Byam **12** William Bligh (Captain Bligh) **13** George Stewart **17** Fletcher Christian
   director: 10 Frank Lloyd
   cast: 10 Clark Gable (Fletcher Christian) **12** Eddie Quillan, Franchot Tone **13** Herbert Mundin **15** Charles Laughton (Captain Bligh)
   Oscar for: 7 picture

mutt 3 cur, dog, pup **5** puppy **7** mongrel

Mutt and Jeff
   creator: 7 Al Smith **9** Bud Fisher
   character: 5 A Mutt **6** Cicero **7** Mrs Mutt

mutter 4 carp **5** gripe, growl, grunt **6** grouch, grouse, kvetch, mumble, murmur, rumble **7** grumble, whisper **8** complain

mutual 5 joint **6** common, shared **7** related **8** communal, returned **10** coincident, reciprocal **11** correlative, interactive

mutual understanding 6 accord **9** agreement

muzzle 3 gag **4** bind, curb **5** check, quiet, still **6** bridle, rein in, stifle **7** harness, silence **8** strangle, suppress, throttle

Myanmar
   former name: 5 Burma
   other name: 16 Land of the Pagodas
   capital and largest city: 6 Yangon **7** Rangoon
      ancient capital: 3 Ava **4** Pegu **8** Mandalay
      others: 2 Ye **3** Ava **4** Pegu **5** Akyab, Bhamo, Katha, Minbu, Namtu, Papun, Prome, Tavoy **6** Hsenwi, Hsipaw, Lashio, Maymyo, Monywa, Shwebo **7** Bassein, Henzada, Pakokku, Toungoo **8** Moulmein, Myingyan
   measure: 2 ly **3** dha, gon, mau, sao, tao, tat **4** byee, phan, seit, taun, that **5** shita, thuoc **6** lamany, palgat **7** chaivai **8** okthabah
   monetary unit: 3 pya **4** kyat
   weight: 2 ta **3** can, pai, vis **4** binh, kyat, ruay, viss **5** behar, candy, ticul **6** abucco **7** peiktha
   lake: 4 Inle
   mountain: 4 Chin, Naga, Pegu, Popa **5** Davna **6** Arakan, Kachin, Lushai, Patkai **7** Karenni **8** Nattaung, Peguyoma, Saramati, Victoria **10** Tenasserim **11** Manipur Hill **12** Tanen Taunggi
   highest point: 11 Hkakabo Razi
   river: 3 Hka **6** Salwin, Sutang **7** Irawadi, Kaladan, Myitnge, Salween, Schweli, Sittang **8** Chindwin, Indawgyi **9** Irrawaddy
   sea: 7 Andaman
   physical feature:
      bay: 4 Siam **6** Bengal, Hunter **7** Heanzay **8** Thailand
      gulf: 8 Martaban
      plateau: 4 Shan
      port: 5 Akyab **7** Bassein, Henzada **8** Moulmein
   people: 2 Ao, Vu, Wa **3** Kaw, Lai, Lao, Mon, Pyu, Tai, Was **4** Akha, Chin, Juki, Kadu, Laos, Lolo, Miao, Naga, Sema, Shan, Thai, Tsin **5** Karen, Lhota **6** Birman, Burman, Kachin, Peguan, Rengma **7** Akhlame, Burmese, Kakhyen, Palauna, Palaung, Siamese **8** Mon-Khmer **9** Arakanese **12** Tibeto-Berman
   leaders: 3 U Nu **5** Ne Win **6** Suu Kyi, U Thant **7** Aung San
   language: 3 Lai **4** Chin, Kuki, Pegu, Shan **5** Karen **6** Kachin **7** Burmese, English
   religion: 5 Hindu, Islam **8** Buddhism **12** Christianity
   place:
      mines: 6 Mawchi **7** Bawdwin
      pagoda: 9 Shwe Dagon
      road: 4 Ledo **5** Burma **9** Stillwell
   feature:
      ball game: 7 chin-lon
      festival: 5 Water **6** Lights **10** Thadin-gyut
      silk headband: 10 gaungbaung
      skirt: 6 longyi
      traveling theatrical group: 4 Pwes

My Antonia
   author: 11 Willa Cather
   character: 9 Jim Burden **15** Antonia Shimerda

My Darling Clementine
   director: 8 John Ford
   cast: 7 Tim Holt **8** Ward Bond **10** Henry Fonda (Wyatt Earp) **12** Linda Darnell, Victor Mature (Doc Holliday) **13** Walter Brennan

my dear
   French: 7 ma chere, mon cher

My Fair Lady
   director: 11 George Cukor
   based on play by: 17 George Bernard Shaw (Pygmalion)
   cast: 11 Rex Harrison (Professor Henry Higgins) **13** Audrey Hepburn (Eliza Doolittle) **15** Stanley Holloway **16** Wilfrid Hyde-White
   score: 14 Lerner and Loewe
   Oscar for: 7 picture
   song: 14 The Rain in Spain **24** I Could Have Danced All Night

my faith
   French: 5 ma foi

my fault
   Latin: 8 mea culpa

My Favorite Martian
   character: 8 Tim O'Hara **11** Uncle Martin **15** Mrs Lorelei Brown
   cast: 9 Bill Bixby **10** Ray Walston **13** Pamela Britton

Myles
   king of: 7 Laconia
   invented: 9 grain mill

My Little Margie
   character: 7 Charlie **9** Mrs Odetts **11** Mr Honeywell **13** Freddie Wilson **14** Margie Albright, Vernon Albright **15** Roberta Townsend
   cast: 9 Don Hayden, Gale Storm **10** Willie Best **12** Clarence Kolb **13** Hillary Brooke **14** Charles Farrell **15** Gertrude Hoffman

my lord
   French: 8 monsieur **11** monseigneur
   Italian: 9 monsignor **10** monsignore

My Man Godfrey
   director: 13 Gregory La Cava
   cast: 10 Alice Brady, Mischa Auer **11** Gail Patrick **13** Carole Lombard, William Powell

myriad 6 untold **7** endless **8** infinite, manifold **9** boundless, countless, limitless, uncounted **11** innumerable, measureless **12** immeasurable, incalculable **13** multitudinous

Myrina
   husband: 8 Dardanus

myrmidon 6 cohort 8 follower, henchman

Myrmidons
  people of: 6 Aegina 8 Thessaly
  created by: 4 Zeus
  created from: 4 ants
  characteristic: 7 warlike
  leader: 6 Peleus 8 Achilles

Myrrha
  also: 6 Smyrna
  father: 11 King Cinyras
  loved: 7 Cinyras
  crime: 6 incest
  son: 6 Adonis
  changed into: 6 myrtle 9 myrrh tree

Myrtilus
  charioteer of: 8 Oenomaus

myrtle 6 Myrtus 10 Vinca minor 14 Myrtus communis 18 Cyrilla racemiflora 23 Umbellularia californica
  varieties: 3 bog, gum, sea, wax 4 cape, Jew's, sand 5 crape, crepe, downy, dwarf, Greek, honey, scent 6 German, Oregon, Polish, willow 7 box sand, classic, running, Swedish 10 Western tea 11 candleberry, Queen's crape, sandverbena 13 Allegheny sand, bracelet honey, California wax 16 Australian willow

Mysia
  epithet of: 7 Demeter

mysophobia
  fear of: 4 dirt

mysterious 4 dark 6 cloudy, covert, hidden, secret 7 cryptic, obscure, strange, unknown 8 baffling, puzzling 9 enigmatic, secretive 10 perplexing, sphinxlike, undercover 11 clandestine, inscrutable 12 impenetrable, inexplicable, supernatural, unfathomable 13 surreptitious 14 undecipherable

Mysterious Stranger, The
  author: 9 Mark Twain

mystery 6 enigma, occult, puzzle, riddle, secret 7 problem, secrecy 9 conundrum, obscurity, symbolism, vagueness 11 ambivalence, elusiveness 12 ineffability, quizzicality 13 ineffableness, mystification

Mystery of Edwin Drood, The see 10 Edwin Drood

mystical, mystic 5 inner 6 hidden, occult 7 cryptic, obscure 8 abstruse, esoteric, ethereal, symbolic 9 enigmatic, secretive 10 cabalistic, symbolical, unknowable 11 inscrutable, nonrational 12 metaphysical, otherworldly 14 transcendental

Mystic River
  author: 12 Dennis Lehane
  director: 13 Clint Eastwood
  cast: 8 Sean Penn (Jimmy Markum) 10 Emmy Rossum (Katie Markum), Kevin Bacon (Sean Devine), Tim Robbins (Dave Boyle) 11 Laura Linney (Annabeth Markum), Thomas Guiry (Brendan Harris) 12 Kevin Chapman (Val Savage) 15 Marcia Gay Harden (Celeste Boyle) 17 Laurence Fishburne (Whitey Powers)

mystification 9 confusion 10 bafflement, perplexity, puzzlement 12 bewilderment

mystify 4 fool 5 elude 6 baffle, puzzle 7 confuse, deceive, mislead, perplex 8 bewilder, confound 9 bamboozle

myth 3 fib, lie 4 tale, yarn 5 error, fable, story 6 canard, legend 7 fantasy, fiction, hearsay, parable 8 allegory, delusion, illusion, tall tale 9 fairy tale, falsehood 10 shibboleth 13 prevarication

mythical, mythic 6 fabled, unreal 8 illusory 9 imaginary, legendary, pretended 10 conjured-up, fabricated, fantasized, fictitious 13 unsubstantial

mythological, mythologic 6 unreal 8 fabulous, illusory, imagined 9 fantastic, imaginary, legendary, unfactual 10 fictitious

My Three Sons
  character: 11 Chip Douglas, Mike Douglas 12 Steve Douglas 13 Robbie Douglas 18 Katie Miller Douglas, Uncle Charley O'Casey 20 Ernie Thompson Douglas, Michael Francis (Bub) O'Casey
  cast: 8 Don Grady, Tina Cole 12 Tim Considine 13 Fred MacMurray 14 William Frawley 15 Barry Livingston, William Demarest 17 Stanley Livingston
  dog: 5 Tramp

my word
  French: 5 ma foi

nab **4** bust, grab, nail, snag **5** catch, pinch, seize, snare **6** arrest, collar, detain, haul in, pick up, pull in, snatch **7** capture **9** apprehend

nabob **3** VIP **4** lord **5** mogul, nawab **6** deputy, tycoon **7** magnate **8** governor **9** plutocrat **10** capitalist **11** billionaire, millionaire

Nabokov, Vladimir
    author of: **3** Ada **4** Mary, Pnin **6** Lolita **8** Pale Fire

nadir **4** base, zero **5** floor **6** apogee, bottom **7** nothing **8** low point **10** rock bottom **11** lowest point

Nadja
    author: **11** Andre Breton

nag **4** fury, goad, harp **5** annoy, devil, harpy, scold, shrew, vixen **6** badger, bicker, harass, hassle, heckle, hector, nettle, peck at, pester, pick at, pick on, plague, rail at, tartar, virago **7** bedevil, upbraid **8** battle-ax, irritate **9** importune, termagant, Xanthippe

Nahua *see* Aztec

Nahuatl *see* Uto-Aztecan

Naiad
    form: **5** nymph
    location: **5** water

nail **3** fix, pin **4** brad, claw, spad **5** talon **6** fasten, hammer, secure
    part: **3** bed **4** root

Naipaul, V S
    author of: **10** Guerrillas **15** A Bend in the River **17** A House for Mr Biswas **19** The Return of Eva Peron, The Suffrage of Elvira

Nairobi
    capital of: **5** Kenya

naive **4** open **5** green, plain **6** candid, simple, unwary, unwise **7** artless, foolish, natural, unjaded **8** gullible, immature, innocent **9** childlike, credulous, guileless, ingenuous, unspoiled, unworldly **10** unaffected, unassuming **11** susceptible **12** unsuspecting, unsuspicious **15** unsophisticated

naivete, naiveté **6** candor **7** modesty **8** openness **9** credulity, frankness, greenness, innocence, sincerity **10** callowness, simplicity **11** artlessness, foolishness, naturalness **12** childishness, inexperience **13** ingenuousness **14** unaffectedness **16** simplemindedness

naked **4** bald, bare, nude, pure **5** bared, frank, plain, sheer **6** patent, simple, unclad **7** blatant, exposed **8** disrobed, laid bare, manifest, palpable, undraped, wide-open **9** in the buff, unclothed, uncovered, undressed **11** perceptible, unappareled, unqualified, unvarnished **15** in the altogether

Naked and the Dead, The
    author: **12** Norman Mailer

Naked City
    character: **5** Libby **9** (Det) Adam Flint **10** (Det Lt) Dan Muldoon, (Lt) Mike Parker **11** (Det) Jim Halloran, (Sgt) Frank Arcaro **13** Janet Halloran
    cast: **9** Paul Burke **11** Nancy Malone **12** John McIntire **13** Harry Bellaver, Horace McMahon, Suzanne Storrs **15** James Franciscus
    setting: **11** New York City
    theme: **19** Somewhere in the Night

Namath, Joe (Joseph William)
    nickname: **11** Broadway Joe
    sport: **8** football
    position: **11** quarterback
    team: **11** New York Jets

namby-pamby **3** coy **4** dull, prim, weak **5** banal, inane, vapid **6** prissy **7** insipid, mincing, sapless **9** colorless, innocuous, simpering **10** indecisive, wishy-washy **13** characterless

name **3** dub, tag **4** call, term **5** label, title **6** choose, ordain, select **7** appoint, baptize, epithet, specify **8** christen, cognomen, delegate, deputize, nominate, taxonomy **9** authorize, designate, signature, sobriquet **10** commission **11** appellation, designation **12** denomination, nomenclature

nameless **5** minor **7** obscure, unknown, unnamed **8** untitled **9** anonymous, unheard-of, unhonored **12** undesignated

namely
    Latin: **3** viz **9** videlicet

Name of the Game
    character: **8** Andy Hill **9** Joe Sample, Ross Craig **10** Dan Farrell, Jeff Dillon **11** Glenn Howard **12** Peggy Maxwell
    cast: **9** Ben Murphy, Gene Barry **10** Mark Miller **11** Cliff Potter, Robert Stack **13** Tony Franciosa **15** Susan Saint James
    business: **8** magazine **10** publishing

Name of the Rose, The
    author: **10** Umberto Eco

Name That Tune

    host: **9** Red Benson **10** Bill Cullen **12** George de Witt
    orchestra: **11** Harry Salter

Namibia
    former name: **15** South West Africa
    capital/largest city: **8** Windhoek
    others: **6** Tsumeb **8** Luderitz **9** Walvis Bay **10** Oranjemund, Swakopmund **12** Keetmanshoop
    monetary unit: **4** cent, rand
    mountain: **14** Khomas Highland, Koakoveld Hills
    highest point: **9** Brandberg
    river: **4** Fish **6** Cunene, Orange **7** Zambezi **8** Okavango
    sea: **8** Atlantic
    physical feature:
        bay: **6** Walvis
        desert: **5** Namib **8** Kalahari
        region: **12** Caprivi Strip
    people: **4** Nama **5** Bantu **6** Damara, Herero, Ovambo, Tswara **7** Bushman, colored **8** Okavango **9** Hottentot
    language: **5** Bantu **6** German **7** English, Khoisan **9** Afrikaans
    religion: **7** animism **8** Lutheran
    feature:
        homeland: **9** bantustan

Nammu
    origin: **8** Sumerian
    mother of: **4** gods
    personifies: **3** sea

Namtar
    origin: **8** Akkadian, Sumerian
    form: **5** demon
    personifies: **5** death

Nana
    author: **9** Emile Zola

Nana (Nurse) (dog)
    character in: **8** Peter Pan
    author: **6** Barrie

Nancy
    character in: **11** Oliver Twist
    author: **7** Dickens

Nancy
    creator: **15** Ernie Bushmiller
    character: **5** Rollo **6** Sluggo **10** Aunt Fritzi

Nanna
    origin: **12** Scandinavian
    husband: **5** Baldr **6** Balder, Baldur
    habitat: **4** moon

Nannerella
    nickname of: **11** Anna Magnani

Nanny, The
network: **3** CBS
cast: **10** Lauren Lane (C C Babcock) **11** Daniel Davis (Niles), Nicholle Tom (Maggie Sheffield), Renee Taylor (Sylvia Fine) **12** Fran Drescher (Fran Fine), Madeline Zima (Grace Sheffield) **17** Benjamin Salisbury (Brighton Sheffield) **18** Charles Shaughnessy (Maxwell Sheffield)

nanometer
abbreviation: **2** nm

Naoise
origin: **5** Irish
wife: **7** Deirdre
uncle: **9** Conchobar
killed by: **9** Conchobar
father: **6** Usnach, Usnech

Naomi
husband: **9** Elimelech
daughter-in-law: **4** Ruth
son: **6** Mahlon **7** Chilion

nap 3 nod **4** doze, rest **6** cat nap, drowse, siesta, snooze **7** doze off, drop off, goof off, shut-eye, slumber **8** drift off **10** forty winks

napery 5 doily **6** linens, napkin **10** tablecloth

Naphtali
father: **5** Jacob
mother: **6** Bilkah
brother: **3** Dan, Gad **4** Levi **5** Asher, Judah **6** Joseph, Reuben, Simeon **7** Zebulun **8** Benjamin, Issachar
sister: **5** Dinah
descendant of: **10** Naphtalite

Napoleon Bonaparte
also: **9** Napoleon I **18** Emperor of the French
battle: **3** Ulm **5** Eylau **6** Lutzen, Moscow, Toulon (siege), Wagram **7** Bautzen, Dresden, Leipzig, Marengo, Mondovi **8** Borodino, Waterloo **9** Friedland **10** Austerlitz **13** Aspern-Essling, Jena-Auerstadt, Peninsular War **22** War of the Fifth Coalition
born: **7** Corsica
exile to: **4** Elba **11** Saint Helena
fought against: **7** Kutuzov **10** von Blucher, Wellington **14** Barclay de Tolly
French fleet destroyed at: **9** Trafalgar
  destroyed by: **6** Nelson
laws: **14** Napoleonic Code
marshal/general under: **3** Ney **5** Murat **7** Massena **10** Bernadotte
position: **7** emperor **11** first consul **13** consul for life
tomb: **5** Paris **9** Invalides
wife: **9** Josephine **20** Marie-Louise of Austria

narcissism 6 egoism, vanity **7** conceit **8** self-love **11** egocentrism **16** selfcenteredness

narcissist 6 egoist **7** egotist **11** egocentrist **12** self-absorbed, self-admiring

narcissistic 4 smug, vain **6** vanity **7** conceit, selfish **8** egotistic, puffed-up **9** conceited **10** egocentric, egoistical **11** egomaniacal, egotistical

narcissus
varieties: **5** poet's **6** poetaz **7** leedsii, trumpet **10** paper-white, polyanthus **16** primrose peerless

Narcissus
father: **8** Cephisus
mother: **8** Leiriope
loved: **7** himself
loved by: **4** Echo
punished by: **9** Aphrodite
changed into: **6** flower

narcotic 4 drug, morphine **5** opium **6** herion, opiate **8** medicine, sedative **9** soporific **10** medicament, medication, painkiller **12** tranquilizer **14** pharmaceutical

Narragansett
language family: **9** Algonkian **10** Algonquian
location: **11** Connecticut, Rhode Island
related to: **7** Niantic
involved in: **9** Pequot War **14** King Philip's War **15** Great Swamp Fight

narrate 6 detail, recite, relate, render, repeat, retell **7** portray, recount **8** describe, set forth **9** chronicle **10** tell a story **15** give an account of

narration 7 recital, telling **8** relating, speaking **9** voice-over **10** recitation, recounting **11** chronicling, description **12** storytelling

narrative 4 tale **5** story **6** report **7** account, recital **8** dialogue, episodic **9** anecdotal, chronicle, statement **10** historical **12** storytelling

narrow 3 set **4** fine, slim **5** close, scant, small, tight **6** biased, scanty **7** bigoted, cramped, pinched, shallow, slender, tapered **8** confined, dogmatic, isolated, squeezed **9** hidebound, illiberal, parochial **10** attenuated, compressed, intolerant, provincial, restricted **11** constricted, incapacious, opinionated, reactionary **12** conservative

narrowing 5 taper **8** tapering **9** squeezing **11** compressing **12** constricting

narrow-minded 5 petty **7** bigoted, prudish **8** one-sided **9** hidebound, parochial, unworldly **10** provincial **11** opinionated, reactionary, straitlaced **12** conservative **15** unsophisticated

narrow-mindedness 4 bias **7** bigotry **9** prejudice **10** unfairness **11** intolerance

narrows 4 neck, pass **5** canal **6** ravine, strait **7** channel, isthmus, passage

Nasca see **5** Nazca

Nascimento, Edson Arantes do
real name of: **4** Pele

Nash, Ogden
author of: **6** Versus **9** Hard Lines **20** The Private Dining Room **21** I'm a Stranger Here Myself

Nashville
director: **12** Robert Altman
cast: **10** Karen Black, Lily Tomlin **11** Henry Gibson **12** Ronee Blakley **13** Barbara Harris, Michael Murphy **14** Keith Carradine **16** Geraldine Chaplin
Oscar for: **4** song
song: **6** I'm Easy

Nassau
capital of: **7** Bahamas

Nasser, Gamal Abdel
president of: **5** Egypt **18** United Arab Republic

nasty 4 foul, mean, vile **5** awful **6** odious **7** beastly, hateful, vicious **8** horrible **9** repellent, revolting **10** abominable, disgusting, nauseating, unpleasant **11** distasteful **12** disagreeable

Natchez
language family: **10** Muskhogean
tribe: **6** Avoyel, Taensa
location: **11** Mississippi **13** South Carolina
allied with: **7** Choctaw
practiced: **14** head flattening

nates 4 buns, rear, rump, seat **7** rear end **8** buttocks, haunches **9** fundament, posterior **12** hindquarters

Nathan
father: **5** Attai
served: **5** David **7** Solomon

Nathanael, Nathaniel see **5** Jesus **8** Apostles **11** Bartholomew

nation 4 host, race **5** realm, state, tribe **6** empire, people **7** country, kingdom **8** republic **9** community **11** sovereignty **12** commonwealth

national park, Canada
Alberta: **5** Banff **6** Jasper **9** Elk Island **11** Wood Buffalo **13** Waterton Lakes
British Columbia: **4** Yoho **7** Glacier **8** Kootenay **10** Pacific Rim **11** Gulf Islands, Gwaii Haanas **15** Mount Revelstoke
Manitoba: **6** Wapusk **14** Riding Mountain
New Brunswick: **5** Fundy **13** Kouchibouguac
Newfoundland and Labrador: **9** Gros Morne, Terra Nova
Northwest Territories: **7** Aulavik, Nahanni **11** Wood Buffalo **12** Tuktut Nogait
Nova Scotia: **10** Kejimkujik **19** Cape Breton Highlands
Nunavut: **8** Sirmilik **9** Auyuittuq **12** Quttinirpaaq, Ukkusiksalik
Ontario: **8** Pukaskwa **10** Point Pelee **14** Bruce Peninsula **17** St Lawrence Islands **18** Georgian Bay Islands
Prince Edward Island: **18** Prince Edward Island
Quebec: **8** Forillon **10** La Mauricie **17**

Mingan Archipelago

Saskatchewan: 10 Grasslands **12** Prince Albert

Yukon: 6 Kluane, Vuntut **7** Ivvavik

national park, U.S.

Alaska: 6 Denali, Katmai **9** Lake Clark **10** Glacier Bay **11** Kenai Fjords, Kobuk Valley **15** Wrangell-St Elias **16** Gates of the Arctic

Arizona: 7 Saguaro **11** Grand Canyon **15** Petrified Forest

Arkansas: 10 Hot Springs

California: 7 Redwood, Sequoia **8** Yosemite **10** Joshua Tree **11** Death Valley, Kings Canyon **14** Channel Islands, Lassen Volcanic

Canada: 4 Yoho **5** Banff, Fundy **6** Jasper, Kluane **8** Kootenay **9** Auyuittuq **13** Waterton Lakes

Colorado: 9 Mesa Verde **13** Rocky Mountain **14** Great Sand Dunes **24** Black Canyon of the Gunnison

Florida: 8 Biscayne **10** Everglades **11** Dry Tortugas

Hawaii: 9 Haleakala **15** Hawaii Volcanoes

Kentucky: 11 Mammoth Cave

Maine: 6 Acadia

Michigan: 10 Isle Royale

Minnesota: 9 Voyageurs

Montana: 7 Glacier **11** Yellowstone

Nevada: 10 Great Basin **11** Death Valley

New Mexico: 15 Carlsbad Caverns

North Carolina: 19 Great Smoky Mountains (with Tennessee)

North Dakota: 17 Theodore Roosevelt

Ohio: 14 Cuyahoga Valley

Oregon: 10 Crater Lake

South Carolina: 8 Congaree

South Dakota: 8 Badlands, Wind Cave

Tennessee: 19 Great Smoky Mountains (with North Carolina)

Texas: 7 Big Bend **18** Guadalupe Mountains

Utah: 4 Zion **6** Arches **11** Bryce Canyon, Canyonlands, Capital Reef

Virginia: 10 Shenandoah

Washington: 7 Olympic **12** Mount Rainier **13** North Cascades

Wyoming: 10 Grand Teton **11** Yellowstone

National Velvet

director: 13 Clarence Brown

cast: 10 Anne Revere **11** Donald Crisp **12** Mickey Rooney **14** Angela Lansbury **15** Elizabeth Taylor

horse: 6 The Pie

Oscar for: 17 supporting actress (Revere)

sequel: 19 International Velvet

native 4 home **5** basic, local, natal **6** inborn, inbred, innate, savage **7** citizen, endemic, natural **8** domestic, inherent, national, paternal **9** aborigine, elemental, homegrown, ingrained, in-

herited, intrinsic, primitive **10** congenital, countryman, hereditary, indigenous **11** instinctive **12** countrywoman **13** autochthonous

Native Americans

major tribes: 3 Ute **4** Crow, Hopi, Iowa, Pima **5** Creek, Aleut, Haida, Kiowa, Lummi, Omaha, Osage, Sioux **6** Apache, Eskimo, Lumbee, Mandan, Mohawk, Navajo, Oneida, Ottawa, Paiute, Pequot, Pueblo, Seneca **7** Bannock, Catawba, Choctaw, Tlingit **8** Arapahoe, Cherokee, Chippewa, Comanche, Kickapoo, Nez Perce, Onondaga, Seminole, Shoshone **9** Blackfoot, Chickasaw, Penobscot, Sac and Fox, Wampanoag, Winnebago **10** Athabascan, Potawatomi **11** Assiniboine **12** Narragansett **13** Passamaquoddy

see also Individual Entries

native country 7 country **8** homeland **10** fatherland **13** mother country

native-grown 5 local **8** domestic **9** homegrown **10** indigenous

native land 8 homeland **10** birthplace, fatherland, native soil **13** mother country, native country

native of Israel

Hebrew: 5 sabra

native soil 8 homeland **10** fatherland, native land **13** mother country, native country

Native Son

author: 13 Richard Wright

NATO

members: 5 Italy, Spain **6** Canada, France, Greece, Latvia, Norway, Poland, Turkey **7** Belgium, Denmark, Estonia, Germany, Hungary, Iceland, Romania **8** Bulgaria, Portugal, Slovakia, Slovenia **9** Lithuania **10** Luxembourg **11** Netherlands **12** United States **13** Czech Republic, United Kingdom

natty 4 chic, neat, posh, tidy, trim **5** smart **6** dapper, jaunty, snappy, spruce **7** dashing, modish, stylish **11** fashionable

Natty Bumppo

also: 7 Hawkeye **10** Pathfinder, The Trapper **13** The Deerslayer **15** Leatherstocking **16** Le Longue Carabine

character in: 23 The Leatherstocking Tales

friend: 5 Uncas **12** Chingachgook

author: 6 Cooper

natural 5 plain **6** inborn, native, normal **7** earthly, genuine, regular **8** God-given, inherent **9** essential, intuitive, unstudied **10** unaffected, unmannered **11** instinctive, spontaneous, terrestrial **13** unpretentious **14** characteristic **15** straightforward

in craps: 5 seven **6** eleven

Natural, The

director: 13 Barry Levinson

based on story by: 14 Bernard Malamud

character: 7 Roy Hobbs

cast: 10 Glenn Close **12** Robert Duvall **13** Robert Redford

Natural Born Killers

director: 11 Oliver Stone

cast: 7 Ed White (Pinball Cowboy) **9** O-Lan Jones (Mabel), Sean Stone (Kevin) **11** Tom Sizemore (Jack Scagnetti) **12** Steven Wright (Emil Reingold) **13** Juliette Lewis (Mallory Knox), Lanny Flaherty (Earl), Tommy Lee Jones (Dwight McClusky) **14** Robert Downey Jr (Wayne Gale), Woody Harrelson (Mickey Knox) **15** Richard Lineback (Sonny)

natural child 7 bastard **9** love child **17** illegitimate child

natural gift 5 flair **6** talent **7** ability, faculty **8** aptitude **9** attribute, endowment

natural habitat 5 range **6** domain, milieu **7** element **9** territory **11** environment

naturalize 5 adapt, adopt **6** adjust **8** accustom **9** acclimate **11** domesticate, familiarize

naturalness 4 ease **9** sincerity **10** simplicity **11** artlessness, genuineness **12** unconstraint **14** unaffectedness

nature 4 bent, kind, mood, sort, type **5** birth, earth, globe, humor, stamp, style, trait **6** cosmos, spirit **7** essence, feature, variety **8** category, creation, instinct, property, universe **9** character **11** disposition, peculiarity **12** constitution **13** particularity **14** characteristic

goddess of: 6 Cybele **9** Dindymene **10** Berecyntia

Nature

author: 17 Ralph Waldo Emerson

naught 3 nil **4** zero **5** nihil, zilch **6** cipher **7** nothing, useless **9** worthless

naughty 3 bad **4** blue **5** bawdy, dirty **6** ribald, risque, vulgar **7** wayward, willful **8** devilish, off-color, perverse **9** fractious, obstinate **11** disobedient, misbehaving, mischievous **12** pornographic, recalcitrant, unmanageable **13** disrespectful

Nauru

other name: 14 Pleasant Island

capital: 13 Yaren District

cities: 3 Boe, Ewa **4** Aiwo, Ijuw **5** Baiti, Buada, Nibok, Uaboe, Yaren **6** Anabar, Anetan, Meneng **7** Anibare **10** Denigomodu

monetary unit: 4 cent **6** dollar

lake: 11 Buada Lagoon

sea: 7 Pacific

physical feature:

bay: 7 Anibare

lagoon: 5 Buada

point: 4 Anna **6** Meneng

people: 7 Chinese **10** Melanesian, Polynesian **11** Micronesian
  explorer: 9 John Fearn
language: 7 English, Nauruan
religion: 10 Protestant **13** Roman Catholic
feature: 9 phosphate

nausea 7 disgust, heaving **8** contempt, loathing, retching, sickness, vomiting **9** repulsion, revulsion **10** queasiness **11** airsickness, biliousness, car sickness, seasickness **12** upset stomach **14** motion sickness, travel sickness

Nausea, Nausee
  author: 14 Jean-Paul Sartre

nauseate 5 repel, upset **6** offend, revolt, sicken **7** disgust, repulse **8** make sick **15** turn one's stomach

nauseated 3 ill **4** sick **5** upset **6** queasy **8** repelled, revolted **9** disgusted

nauseating 9 offensive, repellent, repulsive, revolting, sickening **10** disgusting

nauseous 4 sick **5** upset **6** queasy **9** abhorrent, nauseated, offensive, repellent, repulsive, revolting, sickening, upsetting **10** disgusting, nauseating **12** unappetizing

Nausicaa
  father: 8 Alcinous
  position: 8 princess
  aided: 8 Odysseus

Nausithous
  father: 8 Poseidon
  mother: 8 Periboea
  occupation: 8 helmsman
  employer: 7 Theseus
  became: 4 king
  realm: 8 Phaeacia

nautical 5 naval **6** marine **7** aquatic, boating, oceanic **8** maritime, of the sea, seagoing, yachting

nautical mile
  abbreviation: 3 nmi

Nautilus
  submarine in: 32 Twenty Thousand Leagues Under the Sea
  skipper: 11 Captain Nemo
  author: 5 Verne

Navajo, Navaho (Dine)
  language family: 10 Athapascan, Athapaskan
  location: 4 Utah **7** Arizona **9** New Mexico
  noted for: 7 weaving **14** silversmithing
  dwelling: 5 hogan

navigate 3 fly **4** ride, sail, ship **5** cross, steer **6** cruise, voyage **8** maneuver, sail over **11** plot a course **12** chart a course

navigation 7 boating, sailing **8** cruising, piloting, voyaging **9** traveling **10** seamanship
  god of: 5 Niord, Njord

Navigators Islands *see* **12** Western Samoa

navy 5 fleet **6** armada, convoy **8** flotilla, warships

navy-blue 6 indigo **8** dark blue, deep blue

nay 4 also, deny, vote **5** never **6** denial, refuse **7** against, but also, refusal **8** negative

Nazarene *see* **5** Jesus

Nazarene, The
  author: 10 Sholem Asch

Nazca, Nasca
  location: 4 Peru **12** South America
  noted for: 8 ceramics, textiles **10** Nazca lines (sketches on plain)

Nazi 7 facost
  air force: 9 Luftwaffe
  swastika: 10 Hakenkreuz
  collaborator: 8 quisling
  elite guard: 13 schutzstaffel
  leader: 4 Hess **6** Hitler **7** Himmler **8** Goebbels
  police: 7 gestapo
  trials: Nuremberg

N'Djamena
  capital of: 4 Chad

Neal, Patricia
  husband: 9 Roald Dahl
  born: 9 Packard KY
  roles: 3 Hud (Oscar) **15** A Face in the Crowd, The Fountainhead **18** The Subject Was Roses

near 4 nigh **5** about, close **6** all but, almost **7** close by, close to, looming **8** approach, come up to, imminent, next door **9** alongside, close with, impending **10** hereabouts **11** approaching, practically, proximately, threatening **13** approximately ·

nearby 5 close, handy **6** at hand **7** close by **8** next door **9** adjoining **10** accessible, hereabouts

near death
  Latin: 10 in extremis

near home 5 close **7** close by **10** hereabouts

nearly 4 nigh **5** about **6** all but, almost **7** close to, roughly **11** practically **13** approximately

nearly equal 5 close **7** similar **10** nip-and-tuck **11** approaching

nearly even 5 close **10** head to head, nip-and-tuck **11** neck and neck

nearness 8 intimacy, vicinity **9** adjacency, closeness, handiness, immediacy, proximity **10** contiguity **11** propinquity **12** availability, neighborhood **13** accessibility, approximation

nearsighted 6 myopic
  opposite: 9 hyperopic **10** presbyopic

neat 4 tidy **5** clean, great **6** groovy **7** concise, correct, orderly **8** accurate, exciting, original, straight, striking, succinct **9** competent, dexterous, efficient, ingenious, organized, purposive,

shipshape **10** controlled, immaculate, methodical, systematic **11** imaginative, intelligent, uncluttered

neatness 5 order **8** tidiness **11** orderliness **12** organization

Nebraska
  abbreviation: 2 NE **4** Nebr
  nickname: 4 Beef **8** Antelope **10** Blackwater, Cornhusker **12** Tree-planter's
  capital: 7 Lincoln
  largest city: 5 Omaha
  others: 5 Cozad **6** Gering **7** Kearney **8** Beatrice, Hastings **9** Broken Bow **11** Grand Island, North Platte, Scottsbluff
  college: 4 Dana **5** Doane **8** Duchesne, Hastings **9** Creighton **15** Midland Lutheran
  feature: 8 Boys' Town
    national monument: 11 Scott's Bluff **15** Agate Fossil Beds
  tribe: 3 Oto **4** Otoe **5** Kiowa, Omaha, Ponca, Sioux **6** Pawnee
  people: 10 Henry Fonda **11** Fred Astaire, Roscoe Pound
  lake: 7 Merritt, Sherman, Swanson **10** McConaughy **13** Lewis and Clark
  land rank: 9 fifteenth
  physical feature: 8 Badlands
    hills: 4 Sand **5** Drift, Loess
    plains: 5 Great
  river: 4 Loup **5** Logan **6** Dismal, Nemaha, Platte **7** Big Blue, Elkhorn **8** Missouri, Niobrara **10** Little Blue, Republican **12** Harlan County
  state admission: 13 thirty-seventh
  state bird: 17 western meadowlark
  state flower: 9 goldenrod
  state motto: 20 Equality Before the Law
  state song: 17 Beautiful Nebraska
  state tree: 3 elm **10** cottonwood

nebris
  skin of: 4 fawn

Nebrophonus *see* **5** Thoon

Nebuchadnezzar
  father: 12 Nabopolassar
  son: 10 Bel shazzar **12** Evilmerodach
  same as: 7 Nabucco **14** Nebuchadrezzar
  king of: 7 Babylon
  conquered: 9 Jerusalem
  destroyed: 6 temple
  deported: 4 Jews
  into: 7 slavery
  general: 11 Holophernes

nebula 4 Crab, Ring, Veil **5** Great **6** Lagoon **7** Rosette **9** Horsehead

nebulous 3 dim **4** dark, hazy **5** murky, vague **6** cloudy **7** obscure, unclear **8** confused **9** ambiguous, uncertain **10** impalpable, indefinite, indistinct, intangible **13** indeterminate

necessarily 8 perforce **9** naturally **10** inevitably, inexorably **11** accordingly **12** compulsorily **13** automatically, axiomatically, unqualifiedly **16** incontrovertibly

necessary 6 needed, urgent, wanted **7** crucial, desired, exigent, fitting, needful **8** required **9** called for, essential, requisite **10** compulsory, imperative, obligatory **13** indispensable

necessary changes having been made
Latin: 15 mutatis mutandis

necessitate 5 cause, force, impel **6** compel, demand, oblige **7** call for, enforce, require **9** constrain, prescribe

necessitation 5 cause, force **6** demand, duress **8** coercion, pressure **10** compulsion, constraint, obligation **11** enforcement, requirement

necessity, necessities 4 must, need **6** demand, needed **7** urgency **8** exigency, pressure **9** essential, requisite **10** sine qua non **11** requirement **13** indispensable
Latin: 10 sine qua non

neck 3 pet **4** kiss, nape, pass **6** caress, cervix, cuddle, fondle, smooth, strait **7** channel, isthmus, make out **9** narrowing

neckerchief 5 scarf **8** bandanna, kerchief

necklace 3 tie **5** beads, chain, noose **6** choker, collar, locket, pearls, string **7** jewelry, pendant **8** ornament **9** lavaliere

necktie 3 bow **4** band **5** ascot, black, scarf **6** cravat, string **7** Windsor **10** four in hand **11** half Windsor **12** hangman's rope

necromancer 5 hexer, magus, witch **6** wizard **7** charmer, warlock **8** conjurer, exorcist, magician, sorcerer **9** enchanter, occultist, voodooist **10** soothsayer **13** black magician, thaumaturgist

necromancy 5 magic, spell **7** sorcery **8** black art **10** witchcraft **11** enchantment, foretelling

necrophobia
fear of: 5 death **10** dead bodies

necropolis 8 cemetery **9** graveyard **12** burial ground **13** burying ground

nectar
drink of: 4 gods
gives: 4 life

nee 4 born **11** maiden-named

need 4 lack, want, wish **5** crave, exact **6** demand, penury **7** call for, longing, poverty, require, straits **8** distress, exigency, yearn for **9** essential, extremity, indigence, necessity, requisite **10** bankruptcy, insolvency **11** desideratum, destitution, necessitate, requirement **13** impecuniosity, pennilessness

needed 5 vital **7** crucial **9** essential, necessary, requisite **13** indispensable

needful 7 wishful **8** required **9** essen-

tial, necessary, requisite **10** imperative **13** indispensable

needle 3 vex **4** josh, leaf, ride, twit **5** annoy, chaff, harry, taunt, tease **6** badger, harass, hector **7** torment **9** indicator
prefix: 3 acu

needle-shaped 5 sharp **6** peaked, spiked **7** pointed **8** piercing **10** bodkin-like

needless 7 useless **9** excessive, pointless, redundant **10** gratuitous, pleonastic, unavailing **11** dispensable, purposeless, superfluous, uncalled-for, unessential, unnecessary **12** overabundant

needlework 6 sewing **7** basting, brocade, darning, tacking, tatting **8** applique, knitting, quilting **9** stitching **10** embroidery **11** cross-stitch, needlepoint

needy 4 poor **5** broke **6** hard-up, in want **8** indigent, strapped **9** destitute, money less, penniless **10** down-and-out **12** impoverished **15** poverty-stricken

ne'er-do-well 3 bum **5** idler, loser **6** loafer, no-good **7** goof-off, sad sack, wastrel **8** layabout **9** do-nothing, no-account **10** black sheep **14** good-for-nothing

nefarious 3 bad, low **4** base, evil, foul, vile **6** odious, wicked **7** beastly, ghastly, heinous, hellish, ungodly, vicious **8** depraved, devilish, infamous, infernal, shameful **9** atrocious, execrable **10** abominable, despicable, detestable, iniquitous, scandalous, villainous **11** disgraceful, opprobrious, unspeakable **12** dishonorable **13** unmentionable

Nefertem
origin: 8 Egyptian
personifies: 5 lotus
true identity: 4 Ptah

Nefertiti
queen: 5 Egypt
husband: 8 Ikhnaton **9** Amenhotep
nephew: 11 Tutankhamen

negate 4 deny, veto, void **5** quash, quell, rebut **6** defeat, disown, refute, repeal, revoke, squash **7** blot out, destroy, disavow, gainsay, nullify, retract, reverse, squelch, wipe out **8** abrogate, disallow, disclaim, set aside, vanquish **9** overthrow, overwhelm, repudiate **10** contradict, invalidate

negating 7 denying, voiding **8** refuting, revoking **9** reversing **10** cancelling, nullifying **11** disallowing **12** invalidating, setting aside **13** contradicting

negation 6 denial **7** counter **8** reversal **9** rejection **10** abrogation, disclaimer, refutation **11** confutation, repudiation **12** invalidation **13** contradiction, nullification

negative 4 blue, dark **5** bleak **6** at odds, gloomy **7** dubious, opposed **8** contrary, doubtful, downbeat, inimical, opposing, refusing **9** declining, demurring, dissident, jaundiced, objecting, rejecting, reluctant, skeptical, unwilling **10** dissenting, fatalistic **11** disagreeing, pessimistic **12** antagonistic, disapproving **13** uncooperative **14** unenthusiastic

neglect 4 fail, omit **5** let go, shirk **6** forget, ignore, laxity, pass by, pass up, slight **7** abandon, default, laxness, let pass, let ride, let slip **8** be remiss, idleness, let slide, omission, overlook, pass over, shake off **9** disregard, oversight, passivity, slackness **10** inaccuracy, negligence, remissness **11** dereliction, inattention, inexactness **12** carelessness, fecklessness, indifference, slovenliness **13** noncompliance, unfulfillment **14** nonpreparation **16** underachievement

neglected 7 dropped, ignored, omitted, shirked, unkempt **8** forsaken, untended **9** abandoned, cast aside, forgotten **10** overlooked, uncared for **11** disregarded

neglectful 4 lazy **5** slack **6** remiss, untrue **8** careless, derelict, heedless **9** forgetful, negligent, oblivious, unheeding, unmindful **10** inconstant, thriftless, unfaithful, unthinking, unwatchful **11** improvident, inattentive, indifferent, respectless, thoughtless, unobservant **12** devil-may-care, disregardant, disregardful, happy-go-lucky **15** procrastinating

negligee, neglige 4 robe **6** kimono **7** wrapper **8** bathrobe, peignoir **9** housecoat **12** dressing gown

negligence 6 laxity **7** neglect **11** disregarded **12** carelessness

negligent 3 lax **5** slack **6** remiss, untidy **8** careless, heedless, slovenly **9** forgetful, unheeding, unmindful **10** neglectful, unthinking, unwatchful **11** inattentive, indifferent, thoughtless, unobservant **13** inconsiderate

negligible 5 minor, petty, small **6** minute, paltry, slight **7** trivial **8** piddling, trifling **11** unimportant **13** insignificant **15** inconsequential

negotiate 4 cash, make, pass **6** barter, cash in, convey, dicker, haggle, handle, manage, redeem, settle **7** arrange, consign, deliver, discuss, get over **8** contract, cope with, deal with, hand over, make over, pass over, sign over, transact, transfer, transmit, turn over **10** bargain for **11** come to terms, meet halfway

negotiation 4 deal **6** treaty **8** argument, haggling **9** dickering **10** bargaining **11** arbitration, arrangement **12** compromising

negotiator 7 arbiter **8** mediator **9** go-between **10** arbitrator **12** intermediary

Nehemiah
father: **5** Azbuk **14** Hachaliah

neigh 5 hinny **6** nicker, whinny

neighbor 4 abut, meet **5** touch **6** adjoin, be near, border, friend **7** conjoin **8** borderer, border on **9** associate **12** acquaintance

neighborhood 4 area, part, side, ward **5** place, range **6** locale, parish, region, sphere **7** quarter, section **8** confines, district, environs, precinct, purlieus, vicinity **9** community

neighboring 4 near, next **5** close **6** at hand, nearby **7** close by **8** abutting, adjacent **9** adjoining, bordering **10** contiguous **11** surrounding **12** circumjacent

neighborly 4 kind **5** civil **6** chummy, kindly, polite **7** affable, amiable, cordial, helpful **8** amicable, friendly, gracious, obliging **9** courteous **10** hospitable **11** considerate, warmhearted **12** well-disposed

Neighbors
author: **12** Thomas Berger

Neith
origin: **8** Egyptian
personifies: **10** femininity
son: **2** Ra
corresponds to: **6** Athena

Nekhbet
origin: **8** Egyptian
form: **7** vulture
guardian of: **5** Egypt **10** Upper Egypt

Nelson, Harriet Hilliard
real name: **14** Peggy Lou Snyder
husband: **5** Ozzie
son: **4** Rick **5** David
born: **11** Des Moines IA
roles: **30** The Adventures of Ozzie and Harriet

Nelson, Horatio
also: **14** Viscount Nelson
nationality: **7** British
battle: **9** Trafalgar **11** Bay of Abukir **15** Battle of the Nile **16** Cape Saint Vincent **18** Battle of Copenhagen
defeated: **5** Danes **6** French **7** Spanish
flagship: **7** Victory
killed at: **9** Trafalgar
lover: **16** Emma Lady Hamilton

Nelson, Ozzie
real name: **18** Oswald George Nelson
wife: **15** Harriet Hilliard
son: **4** Rick **5** David
born: **12** Jersey City NJ
roles: **30** The Adventures of Ozzie and Harriet

Nemean
epithet of: **4** Zeus **5** games
precursor of: **8** Olympics

Nemean lion
strangled by: **8** Hercules

nemesis 4 ruin **5** match, **6** rival **7** avenger, goddess, justice, revenge, undoing **8** downfall, punisher, Waterloo **9** overthrow, vengeance **10** punishment **11** destruction, retaliation, retribution **16** instrument of fate

nemine contradicente 11 unanimously **18** no one contradicting

nemine dissentiente 11 unanimously **15** no one dissenting

Nemo
character in: **10** Bleak House
author: **7** Dickens

Nemo, Captain
character in: **32** Twenty Thousand Leagues Under the Sea
author: **5** Verne
submarine: **8** Nautilus

nene 13 Hawaiian goose

neologism, neology 7 coinage **9** nonce word

neon
chemical symbol: **2** Ne

neonate 4 baby **6** infant **7** newborn

neophyte 4 tyro **5** pupil **6** novice, rookie **7** amateur, convert, entrant, learner, recruit, student, trainee **8** beginner, disciple, newcomer **9** greenhorn, novitiate, proselyte **10** apprentice, tenderfoot **11** probationer

neoplasm 5 tumor **6** cancer, growth **7** sarcoma **9** carcinoma **10** malignancy **14** carcinosarcoma

Nepal
other name: **9** Shangri-La
capital/largest city: **8** Katmandu **9** Kathmandu
others: **5** Patan, Patna **6** Gurkha **7** Birganj **8** Bhadgaon, Lalitpur **9** Bhaktapur **10** Biratnagar
university: **9** Tribhuvan
division: **5** Terai **13** High Himalayas
monetary unit: **4** anna, pice **5** mohar, paisa, rupee
mountain: **6** Cho Oyu, Churia, Lhotse, Makalu **7** Manaslu, Siwalik **9** Annapurna, Himalayas **10** Dhaulagiri, Gosainthan, Himalchuli **11** Ganesh Himal **12** Kanchenjunga **14** Mahabharat hekh
highest point: **9** Mt Everest
river: **4** Kali, Kosi, Mugu, Seti **5** Babai, Bheri, Rapti, Sarda, Tamur **6** Gandak **7** Karnali **8** Narayani
physical feature:
  plain: **5** Terai
  valley: **5** Nepal **8** Katmandu
people: **3** Rai **4** Aoul **5** Bhote, Limbu, Magar, Murmi, Newar, Tharu **6** Bhutia, Gurkha, Gurung, Nepali, Sherpa, Tamang **7** Kiranti, Tibetan **8** Gorkhali, Nepalese
  birthplace of: **6** Buddha **13** Gautama Buddha **17** Siddhartha Gautama
  king: **8** Mahendra **9** Tribhuwan **18** Prithwi Narayan Shah **23** Birenda

Bir Bikram Shah Dev
  ruler: **4** Rana **5** Malla **6** Rajput
language: **6** Nepali, Newari
religion: **8** Buddhism, Hinduism
place:
  dam: **6** Gandak
  shrine: **9** Swayambhu **10** Gorakhnath
  feature:
    animal: **3** dzo, yak **7** dzopkyo
    arch: **6** Juddha
    god/goddess: **5** Indra **6** Kumari
    legend: **4** Yeti **17** abominable snowman
    soldiers: **6** Gurkha

Nepali
language family: **12** Indo-European
branch: **11** Indo-Iranian
group: **5** Indic
spoken in: **5** Nepal

nepenthe 4 drug **5** drink, opium **6** heroin, opiate **7** hashish **8** narcotic

nephrite
variety: **4** jade

ne plus ultra 4 acme **6** finest **8** ultimate **12** highest point

nepotism 10 favoritism
patron of: **9** relatives

Neptune
origin: **5** Roman
god of: **3** sea
corresponds to: **8** Poseidon

Neptune
position: **6** eighth
satellite: **6** Nereid, Triton
color: **4** blue
studied by: **7** Voyager (2)

Nereid
form: **5** nymph
location: **3** sea
father: **6** Nereus

Nereus
god of: **3** sea
father: **6** Pontus
mother: **4** Gaea
father of: **7** Nereids
number of Nereids: **5** fifty
son: **7** Nerites

Nerissa
character in: **19** The Merchant of Venice
author: **11** Shakespeare

neritic 7 aquatic, coastal **8** offshore

Nero
name: **18** Nero Claudius Caesar
emperor of: **4** Rome
mother: **9** Agrippina
father: **19** Domitius Ahenobarbus
stepfather: **8** Claudius
tutor: **6** Seneca
son: **11** Britannicus
wife: **7** Octavia **13** Poppaea Sabina
successor: **5** Galba

nerve 4 dash, gall, grit, guts, sass **5** brass, cheek, crust, pluck, spunk, valor **6** mettle, spirit **7** bravery, courage **8** backbone, boldness, coolness, gameness, strength, tenacity **9** arrogance, assurance, derring-do, endurance, flippancy, fortitude, gallantry, hardihood, hardiness, impudence, insolence, sauciness **10** assumption, brazenness, confidence, effrontery, steadiness **11** intrepidity, presumption **12** fearlessness, impertinence, resoluteness **13** determination **16** stoutheartedness

nerveless 4 calm, dead, weak **5** brave, frail, inert **6** feeble, flabby **7** flaccid **8** cowardly **9** powerless **10** courageous **12** fainthearted

nervous 4 wild **5** jumpy, shaky, tense **6** touchy, uneasy **7** alarmed, anxious, excited, fearful, fidgety, jittery, peevish, ruffled **8** feverish, neurotic, skittish, startled, timorous, unstrung **9** delirious, disturbed, excitable, impatient, irritable, sensitive, trembling, tremulous, unsettled **10** high-strung, hysterical **12** apprehensive

nervousness 6 tremor **7** anxiety, flutter, shaking, tension **8** hysteria, timidity **9** agitation, quivering, the creeps, the shakes, trembling, twitching **10** the fidgets, touchiness **11** disturbance, fidgetiness, stage fright **12** apprehension, excitability, irascibility, irritability, perturbation, timorousness **16** hypersensitivity

nervous system
  component: 3 CNS **4** ears, eyes **5** brain, taste, touch **7** ganglia **8** nerve end **10** nerve fiber, spinal cord

nervy 4 bold, firm, rude **5** brash, gutty, gutsy, sassy **6** brassy, brazen, cheeky, gritty, plucky, strong **7** assured, nervous **10** courageous, determined **12** stouthearted

Nesbitt, Cathleen
  born: 7 England **8** Cheshire
  roles: 10 My Fair Lady **18** Upstairs Downstairs **23** Three Coins in the Fountain

Nessus
  form: 7 centaur
  shot by: 8 Hercules
  caused death of: 8 Hercules

n'est-ce pas? 10 isn't that so?

nestle 3 lie, pet **4** live, snug, stay **5** clasp, dwell, lodge **6** bundle, caress, coddle, cosset, cuddle, enfold, fondle, huddle, nuzzle, occupy, remain, settle **7** embrace, inhabit, lie snug, snuggle **8** lie close **10** settle down

Nestor
  origin: 5 Greek
  attributes: 6 oldest, wisest
  father: 6 Neleus
  son: 10 Thasymedes **11** Pisistratus
  epithet: 7 Nelides

net 3 web **4** earn, gain, grab, grid, grip, mesh, snag, take, trap **5** catch, clasp, grate, seize, snare **6** clutch, enmesh, gather, grille, obtain, pick up, screen,

snap up, take in **7** acquire, bring in, capture, collect, ensnare, grating, lattice **8** entangle, gather in, gridiron, Internet, meshwork **9** apprehend, grillwork, lay hold of, screening **10** accumulate **11** latticework

constellation of: 9 Reticulum

nether 5 basal, below, lower, under **6** bottom, lowest **8** downward, inferior **9** subjacent **10** bottommost

Netherlands
  other name: 7 Holland **12** Low Countries
  capital/largest city: 9 Amsterdam
  others: 3 Urk **5** Delft, Lisse **6** Almelo, Arnhem, Leiden, Velsen **7** Haarlem, Helmond, Hengelo, Limburg, Tilberg, Tilburg, Utrecht **8** Aalsmeer, Enschede, Ijmuiden, Nijmegen, The Hague **9** Apeldoorn, Dordrecht, Eindhoven, Groningen, Rotterdam **12** Scheveningen
  division: 6 Twente **7** Drenthe, Limburg, Utrecht, Zeeland **9** Friesland, Groningen **10** Gelderland, Overijssel **12** North Brabant, North Holland, South Holland **19** Netherlands Antilles
  government:
    legislature: 4 Raad **11** Eerste Kamer, Tweede Kamer
  head of state: 4 king **5** queen **7** monarch
  measure: 2 el **3** aam, ahm, ell, kan, vat **4** duim, mijl, rood, rope **5** anker, roede, wisse **6** bunder, legger, maatje, mutsje, streep **7** schepel **8** mimgelen, steekkan
  monetary unit: 4 doit, oord, raps **5** crown, daler, rider, ryder **6** florin, gulden, stiver, suskin **7** daalder, ducaton, escalan, escalin, guilder, stooter, stuiver **8** albertin, ducatoon **9** dubbeltje **12** rijksdaalder **13** albertustaler
  weight: 3 ons **4** last, pond **5** bahar **6** korrel **7** wichtje
  island: 5 Texel **7** Ameland, Frisian **8** Antilles, Vlieland
  lake: 7 Haarlem **10** Ijsselmeer **11** Grevelingen, Havingvliet
  highest point: 11 Vaalserberg
  river: 3 Eem, Lek **4** Leck, Maas, Waal, Ysel **5** Donge, Hunse, Meuse, Rhine, Schie, Yssel **6** Dintel, Dommel, Ijssel, Kromme **7** Scheldt
  sea: 5 North
  physical feature:
    canal: 6 Oranje **7** Juliana, Merwede **8** Drentsch, North Sea **10** Wilhelmina **11** New Waterway
    former bay: 9 Zuider Zee
    port: 9 Europoort
  people: 5 Dutch **7** Frisian **9** Hollander **10** Surinamese **12** Netherlander **13** South Moluccan
    artist: 4 Eyck, Hals **5** Appel, Bosch **7** Van Gogh, Vermeer **8** Mondrian,

Ruisdael **9** Rembrandt
    author: 6 Vondel **7** Erasmus, Grotius, Spinoza **8** Vestdijk **9** Anne Frank
    explorer: 6 Tasman
    king: 7 William
    queen: 7 Beatrix, Juliana **10** Wilhelmina
    ruler: 5 Spain **13** House of Orange **15** Holy Roman Empire
    scientist: 7 Huygens **11** Leeuwenhoek
  language: 5 Dutch **7** English, Frisian
  religion: 13 Dutch Reformed, Protestantism **16** Roman Catholicism
  place:
    airport: 8 Schiphol
    bird sanctuary: 9 Waddenzee
    miniature town: 9 Madurodam
    museum: 9 Frans Hals, Stedelijk **11** Mauritshuis, Rijksmuseum **14** Vincent Van Gogh **19** Boymans-van Beuningen
    seat of government: 7 Den Haag **8** The Hague **11** 'sGravenhage
    tower: 14 Schreierstoren
  feature:
    cheese market: 9 kaasmarkt
    earth mounds: 6 terpen
    flower: 5 tulip
    flower parade: 12 Bloemencorso
    pottery: 5 Delft
    reclaimed land: 6 polder
    wooden shoes: 7 klompen
  food:
    cheese: 4 Edam **5** Gouda **6** Leyden **7** cottage
    dish: 10 nasi goreng, rijsttafel
    drink: 3 gin **8** anisette, schnapps
    pea soup: 10 erwtensoep

Netherlands East Indies see **9** Indonesia

netherworld 4 hell **5** Hades **10** underworld **14** infernal region

nettle 3 vex **4** bait, gall, miff, rile **5** annoy, beset, chafe, harry, pique, sting **6** bother, harass, ruffle **7** perturb, prickle, provoke **8** irritate **9** displease **10** exasperate

nettle 6 Urtica
  varieties: 4 dead, dumb, hemp, rock **5** false, flame, hedge, horse, Roman **6** spurge **7** painted **8** stinging **9** white dead **11** spotted dead **12** western horse

network 3 web **4** grid, mesh, trap **5** grate, group, snare **6** grille, scheme, system **7** complex, netting, station

Network
  director: 11 Sidney Lumet
  based on story by: 14 Paddy Chayefsky
  cast: 9 Ned Beatty **10** Peter Finch, Wesley Addy **11** Faye Dunaway **12** Robert Duvall **13** William Holden **16** Beatrice Straight
  Oscar for: 5 actor (Finch) **7** actress

(Dunaway) **17** supporting actress (Straight)

networks *see* **18** Television Networks

neuroptera
  class: 8 hexapoda
  phylum: 10 arthropoda
  group: 7 ant lion, fishfly **8** alderfly, lacewing, snakefly

neurotic 4 sick **7** anxious, intense, nervous **8** abnormal, unstable **9** disturbed, obsessive, unhealthy **10** distraught, immoderate **11** overwrought

neuter 5 fixed **6** barren, fallow, gelded, spayed **7** asexual, sexless, sterile **8** impotent **9** infertile

Neutra, Richard J
  architect of: 15 Mathematics Park (Princeton) **16** Lovell Heath House (Los Angeles CA) **17** von Sternberg House (Northridge CA) **22** Orange County Courthouse (Santa Ana CA)

neutral 4 mean **5** aloof **6** medium, middle, normal, remote **7** average **8** pacifist, peaceful, unbiased **9** impartial, in-between, peaceable, withdrawn **10** achromatic, indefinite, of two minds, unaffected, uninvolved **11** half-and-half, indifferent, nonpartisan, unconcerned **12** fence sitting, intermediate, noncombatant **13** disinterested, dispassionate **14** nonbelligerent, noninterfering **16** nonparticipating **18** noninterventionist

neutralize 4 halt, stop **5** annul, block, check **6** cancel, defeat, impede, negate, offset, stymie **7** balance, disable, nullify, prevent **8** overcome, suppress **9** frustrate, overpower **10** counteract **12** counterpoise, incapacitate **14** counterbalance

neutralizer 7 blocker **9** nullifier **12** counteractor, counteragent **15** counterbalancer

Neuvillette, Christian de
  character in: 16 Cyrano de Bergerac
  author: 7 Rostand

Nevada
  abbreviation: 2 NV **3** Nev
  nickname: 6 Silver **9** Sagebrush
  capital: 10 Carson City
  largest city: 8 Las Vegas
  others: 3 Ely, Nye **4** Elko, Reno **6** Fallon, Nellis, Sparks, Storey, Washoe **7** Boulder, Gerlach **9** Hawthorne, Henderson **11** Weed Heights **12** Virginia City
  college: 4 UNLV
  explorer: 7 Fremont **13** Jedediah Smith
  feature: 12 Comstock Lode
    dam: 5 Davis **6** Hoover
    hot springs: 4 Tule **9** Punch Bowl, Steam Boat
    national monument: 11 Death Valley
  tribe: 5 Modoc, Washo **6** Digger, Mohave, Paiute **7** Klamath **8** Acho-

mawi, Atsugewi, Shoshone
  lake: 4 Mead, Ruby **5** Tahoe, Weber **6** Mohave, Walker **7** Pyramid **8** Lahontan, Rye Patch **9** Wild Horse
  land rank: 7 seventh
  mountain: 4 East, Pine, Ruby **5** White **7** Rockies, Toiyabe, Wasatch **13** Sierra Nevadas
    highest point: 12 Boundary Peak
  physical feature: 7 geysers **10** hot springs
    basin: 5 Great
    cave: 6 Gypsum
    desert: 7 Sonoran
    plateau: 8 Columbia
  river: 5 Reese **6** Carson, Walker **7** Truckee **8** Colorado, Humboldt
  state admission: 11 thirty-sixth
  state bird: 7 sagehen **16** mountain bluebird
  state flower: 9 sagebrush
  state motto: 16 All for Our Country
  state song: 15 Home Means Nevada
  state tree: 9 pinon pine **15** single-leaf pinon

never 4 ne'er **7** not ever **8** at no time, not at all

never-ending 6 steady **7** abiding, eternal, lasting, nonstop **8** constant, enduring, immortal, infinite, repeated, unbroken **9** ceaseless, continual, incessant, perennial, perpetual, recurring, unceasing **10** continuous, persistent, relentless **11** everlasting, unremitting **12** interminable, undiminished **13** uninterrupted

never-failing 4 firm, sure **6** proven, trusty **7** abiding **8** enduring, reliable **9** steadfast **10** dependable **11** trustworthy, undeviating, unfaltering **12** unhesitating, tried-and-true

nevermore 6 no more **10** never again

Never on Sunday
  director: 11 Jules Dassin
  cast: 11 Jules Dassin, Titos Vandis **14** Georges Foundas, Melina Mercouri
  setting: 6 Greece

nevertheless 3 but, yet **6** anyhow, anyway, even so, though **7** however **8** after all, although **10** contrarily, in any event, regardless **12** contrariwise **15** notwithstanding

new 4 late **5** fixed, fresh, green, novel **6** modern, reborn, recent, remote, unused **7** altered, changed, current, just out, rebuilt, resumed, untried **8** original, reopened, repaired, restored, up-to-date **9** recreated, refreshed, remodeled, renovated, uncharted, unessayed, untouched **10** revivified, unexplored, unfamiliar, ungathered, unseasoned, unventured **11** regenerated, uncollected, unexercised **12** unaccustomed **13** reconstructed, reinvigorated

New Atlantis
  author: 12 Francis Bacon

New Brunswick
  abbreviation: 2 NB
  bay: 5 Fundy, Maces **7** Shepody **9** Chignecto, Miramichi **13** Passamaquoddy
  channel: 5 Minas **10** Grand Manan
  city: 7 Moncton **8** Bathurst **9** Riverview **10** Edmundston, Saint John **11** Fredericton
  island: 4 Deer **6** Miscou **7** Machias **10** Campobello, Grand Manan
  known as: 16 Atlantic province, maritime province
  lake: 5 Grand **8** Oromocto **12** Magagudavic **14** Chiputneticook
  people: 5 Irish **6** French **7** Acadian, English **8** American, Scottish **9** Algonkian **10** Anglo Saxon
  religion: 6 Canaan **7** Baptist **8** Anglican **10** Protestant **12** Presbyterian, United Church **13** Roman Catholic
  river: 5 Cains, Green **6** Renous, Salmon **7** Tobique **8** Kedgwick, Nashwak, Oromocto **9** Miramichi, Patapedia, Saint John **10** Nepisiguit, Richibucto, Saint Croix **11** Petitcodiac, Restigouche, Upsalguitch **12** Kennebecasis

newcomer 4 tyro **5** alien **6** novice **7** entrant **8** intruder, neophyte, outsider, stranger **9** foreigner, immigrant, outlander **10** interloper, trespasser

New Deal Agency 3 AAA, CCC, CWA, FCA, FHA, FSA, NRA, NYA, PWA, REA, SEC, SSB, TVA, WPA **4** FCIC, FDIC, FERA, HOLC, NLRD, USHA

New Delhi
  capital of: 5 India
  designed by: 7 Lutyens
  earlier city: 5 Dilli **8** Dhillika, Din Panah, Kilookai **9** Firozabad **11** Tughlukabad **12** Indraprastha **13** Shah Jahanabad
  invader: 5 Timur **6** Abdali **7** British, Rohilas **8** Marathas **9** Nadir Shah
  landmark: 7 Red Fort **9** India Gate, Qutb Minar **10** Iron Pillar, Jama Masjid **12** Humayun's Tomb **14** Connaught Place **15** Rajghat Memorial **17** Rashtrapati Bhavan (Presidential Palace) **23** Jantar Mantar Observatory **30** Gandhi National Museum and Library
  river: 6 Yamuna
  street: 7 Raj Path (Kingsway)
  university: 15 Jawaharlal Nehru

New England
  capital: 6 Boston **7** Augusta, Concord **8** Hartford **10** Montpelier, Providence
  city: 4 Lynn **5** Barre **6** Bangor, Lowell, Nashua **7** Hyannis, Rutland, Warwick **8** Brockton, Cranston, Lawrence, Lewiston, New Haven, Portland, Stamford **9** Cambridge, Fall River, New London, Pawtucket, Waterbury, Worcester **10** Bridgeport, Burlington, Manchester, Pittsfield,

Portsmouth, Woonsocket **11** Brattle-boro, Springfield
football team: 8 Patriots
Indians: 6 Abnaki, Pequot **7** Mahican, Mohegan, Niantic, Nipmuck, Wangunk **8** Algonkin, Iroquois **9** Algonquin, Pennacook **10** Quinnipiac **12** Narragansett
lake: 6 Sebago, Tiogue **7** Sunapee **9** Champlain, Moosehead **10** Candlewood **11** Pemaduncook **13** Winnipesaukee
mountain: 5 Green, White **8** Greylock, Katahdin **9** Berkshire, Mansfield **10** Washington **11** Appalachian
river: 5 Otter **6** Thames **7** Charles **8** Kennebec, Pawtucket, Winooski **9** Merrimack, Missiquoi, Naugatuck, Pawcatuck, Penobscot, Saint John **10** Housatonic, Providence, Quinnipiac **11** Connecticut **12** Androscoggin
state: 5 Maine **7** Vermont **11** Connecticut, Rhode Island **12** New Hampshire **13** Massachusetts
newfangled 5 novel **6** modern, modish **7** stylish
new-fashioned 6 modern, modish **7** stylish **8** up-to-date
Newfoundland
abbreviation: 4 Nfld
capital: 10 Saint Johns
city: 19 Happy Valley Goose Bay
lake: 7 Jeddore, Melville **8** Meelpaeg **10** Michikamau
mountain: 9 Long Range
river: 5 Eagle **6** Fraser, Gander **8** Exploits, Naskaupi **9** Churchill
section: 8 Labrador
New Granada *see* **8** Colombia
New Guinea
capital/largest city: 11 Port Moresby
others: 3 Lae, Wau **4** Daru **5** Soron, Wewak **6** Aitape, Kikori, Medang, Rabaul **7** Gorolka, Kitbadi
division:
 western half of island: 9 Indonesia, Irian Jaya
 eastern half of island: 14 Papua New Guinea
monetary unit: 4 kina, toea
island: 3 Aru **4** Aroe, Buka **5** Arroe, Ceram, Japen, Jobie, Manus **6** Cretin, Mussau, Ninigo, Waigeu **7** Sainson, Solomon **8** Bismarck, Kiriwina, Schouten, Woodlark **9** Admiralty, Trobriant **10** Louisiande, New Britain, New Ireland **12** Bougainville **14** D'Entrecasteaux
mountain: 4 Snow **6** Orange **8** Bismarck, Victoria **9** Carstensz **11** Owen Stanley **12** Albert Edward
highest point:
 Irian Jaya: 9 Carstensz **10** Puncak Jaya
 Papua New Guinea: 7 Wilhelm
river: 3 Fly **4** Hamu, Hany, Ramu **5** Degul, Sepik **6** Kikori, Purari **7** Amberno, Markham

sea: 5 Ceram, Coral, Sepik **6** Indian **7** Arafura, Pacific, Solomon **8** Bismarck
physical feature:
 bay: 3 Oro **5** Milne **8** Geelvink
 gulf: 4 Huon **5** Papua
 strait: 6 Torres, Vitiaz
people: 5 Pygmy **6** Papuan **7** Negrito **10** Melanesian
 explorer: 15 Jorge de Menesses
 ruler: 7 Germany **9** Australia **11** Netherlands **12** Great Britain
language: 4 Motu **7** English **16** Melanesian Pidjin
religion: 5 Islam **7** animism **10** Protestant **13** Roman Catholic
feature:
 bird: 7 mudlark **9** cassowary
food:
 dried coconut meat: 5 copra
New Hampshire
abbreviation: 2 NH
nickname: 7 Granite
capital: 7 Concord
largest city: 10 Manchester
others: 5 Dover, Keene **6** Berlin, Durham, Exeter, Nashua **7** Hanover, Laconia **8** Sandwich **9** Claremont, Rochester **10** Portsmouth **12** Bretton Woods
college: 5 Keene **6** Rivier **9** Dartmouth, St Anselms **10** New England
feature: 14 Great Stone Face
 notch: 7 Kinsman, Pinkham **8** Crawford **9** Franconia
tribe: 6 Abnaki **9** Pennacook
people: 11 Robert Frost **12** Daniel French **13** Daniel Webster, Horace Greeley, Mary Baker Eddy
 explorer: 9 Champlain **16** Captain John Smith
island: 4 Star **5** White **6** Shoals **7** Lunging
lake: 5 Squam **7** Ossipee, Sunapee, Umbagog **8** Newfound **10** Winnisquam **13** Winnipesaukee
land rank: 11 forty-fourth
mountain: 5 Flume, White **6** Moriah, Paugus **7** Waumbek **8** Chocorua, Sandwich **9** Franconia, Monadnock **11** Profile Peak **12** Presidential
 highest point: 10 Washington
physical feature:
 bay: 5 Great
president: 14 Franklin Pierce
river: 4 Saco **6** Israel **7** Bellamy **8** Souhegan **9** Merrimack **10** Piscataqua **11** Connecticut, Salmon Falls **12** Androscoggin
state admission: 5 ninth
state bird: 11 purple finch
state flower: 11 purple lilac
state motto: 13 Live Free Or Die
state song: 15 Old New Hampshire **26** New Hampshire My New Hampshire
state tree: 10 paper birch, white birch
Newhart

character: 4 Dick **6** Joanna **7** Michael **9** Stephanie
cast: 9 Mary Frann **10** Bob Newhart, Julia Duffy **12** Peter Scolari
Newhart, Bob
born: 9 Chicago IL
roles: 3 Bob **7** Newhart **10** Cold Turkey **12** George and Leo **17** The Bob Newhart Show
films: 3 Elf **7** Catch-22 **8** In and Out
New Hebrides *see* **7** Vanuatu
New Jersey
abbreviation: 2 NJ
nickname: 6 Garden **8** Mosquito
capital: 7 Trenton
largest city: 6 Newark
others: 4 Lodi **5** Ewing, Ft Lee **6** Camden, Dumont, Haddon, Kearny, Linden, Nutley, Orange, Rahway, Totowa **7** Bayonne, Cape May, Clifton, Hoboken, Hohokus, Keyport, Madison, Matawan, Netcong, Oradell, Paramus, Passaic, Raritan, Teaneck, Tenafly, Wyckoff **8** Carteret, Cranford, Freehold, Garfield, Hillside, Metuchen, Paterson, Secaucus, Watchung **9** Bridgeton, Elizabeth, Engle wood, Hawthorne, Irvington, Maplewood, Montclair, Ocean City, Princeton **10** Asbury Park, Belleville, Ft Monmouth, Hackensack, Jersey City, Livingston, Long Branch, Morristown, Perth Amboy **11** Bergenfield **12** Atlantic City, Collingswood, New Brunswick
colleges: 4 Drew **5** Rider **6** Upsala **7** Rutgers **8** Caldwell, Monmouth, St Peter's **9** Princeton, Seton Hall **10** Bloomfield **18** Fairleigh-Dickinson
feature: 9 Boardwalk **16** Delaware Water Gap
tribe: 8 Delaware **11** Lenni-Lanape
people: 9 Aaron Burr **11** Joyce Kilmer, Paul Robeson **12** Stephen Crane, Thomas Edison **13** James Lawrence **19** James Fenimore Cooper **21** William Carlos Williams
 explorer: 6 Hudson **9** Verrazano
lake: 6 Mohawk **9** Greenwood, Hopatcong
land rank: 10 forty-sixth
mountain: 8 Piedmont **10** Kittatinny **13** First Watchung **14** Second Watchung
 highest point: 9 High Point
physical feature: 9 Palisades, Sandy Hook
 bay: 8 Delaware
 cape: 3 May
 ocean: 8 Atlantic
president: 15 Grover Cleveland
river: 4 Toms **6** Dennis, Haynes, Hudson, Mantua, Ramapo **7** Mullica, Passaic, Raritan **8** Cohansey, Delaware, Tuckahoe **10** Hackensack
state admission: 5 third
state bird: 16 eastern goldfinch
state flower: 6 violet

state motto: 20 Liberty and Prosperity
state tree: 6 red oak
basketball team: 4 Nets
football team: 8 Generals
hockey team: 6 Devils

Newley, Anthony
wife: 11 Joan Collins
born: 6 London **7** England
roles: 11 Oliver Twist **15** Doctor Doolittle **25** Stop the World I Want to Get Off **41** The Roar of the Greasepaint The Smell of the Crowd

newly 4 anew **6** afresh, lately, of late **7** freshly, just now **8** recently

newly rich person
French: 12 nouveau riche

Newlywed Game, The
host: 10 Bob Eubanks
executive producer: 11 Chuck Barris

Newlyweds, The
creator: 13 George McManus
character: 12 Baby Snookums

Newman, Barnett
born: 9 New York NY
artwork: 7 Abraham, The Wild **8** Onement I **18** Stations of the Cross **19** Vir Heroicus Sublimis

Newman, John Henry (Cardinal)
author of: 18 Apologia pro Vita Sua

Newman, Paul
wife: 14 Joanne Woodward
born: 11 Cleveland OH
company: 10 Newman's Own
roles: 3 Hud **6** Harper, Picnic **8** The Sting, Twilight **10** The Hustler, The Verdict **11** Nobody's Fool **12** Cool Hand Luke **15** Absence of Malice, The Color of Money, Where the Money Is **16** Cat on a Hot Tin Roof, Message in a Bottle, The Left-Handed Gun, The Long Hot Summer, The Silver Chalice **17** The Hudsucker Proxy **29** Butch Cassidy and the Sundance Kid

New Mexico
abbreviation: 2 NM **4** N Mex
nickname: 8 Sunshine **17** Land of Enchantment
capital: 7 Santa Fe
largest city: 11 Albuquerque
others: 3 Jal **4** Taos **5** Aztec, Belen, Hobbs, Raton **6** Clovis, Deming, Gallup, Grants **7** Artesia, Bananea, Roswell, Socorro, Torreon **8** Carlsbad **9** Las Cruces, Los Alamos **10** Alamogordo **13** Piedras Negras
college: 7 Sante Fe **11** Albuquerque
feature: 11 Four Corners
dam: 5 Butte **8** Elephant
labs: 6 Sandia **17** Los Alamos National
national monument: 10 Aztec Ruins, White Sands **11** Chaco Canyon **17** Gila Cliff Dwelling
national park: 15 Carlsbad Caverns

observatory: 14 Sacramento Peak
tribe: 3 Sia **4** Hano, Piro, Tano, Taos, Tewa, Tiwa, Zuni **5** Acoma, Jemez, Kares, Manso, Pecos, Tiqua, Tonoa **6** Apache, Isleta, Laguna, Navaho, Navajo, Pueblo **7** Anasazi, Picuris **8** Santa Ana **9** Mescalero **12** Santo Domingo
people: 9 Kit Carson, Peter Hurd **11** Bill Mauldin
explorer: 5 Onate **6** de Niza, de Vaca **8** Coronado
lake: 6 El Vado, Navajo, Sumner **7** Conchas **8** McMillan **10** Alamogordo **13** Elephant Butte
land rank: 5 fifth
mountain: 5 Jemez **6** Sandia **7** Manzano, Mimbres, Rockies, Truchas **8** Mogollon **9** Guadalupe, San Andres **10** Nacimiento, Sacramento **11** Mount Taylor **15** Sangre de Christo
highest point: 11 Wheeler Peak
physical feature:
basin: 8 Tularosa
desert: 15 Jornada de Muerto
plains: 5 Great
river: 3 Ute **4** Gila **5** Pecos **7** San Jose, San Juan **8** Canadian **9** Rio Grande
state admission: 12 forty-seventh
state bird: 10 roadrunner
state fish: 14 cutthroat trout
state flower: 5 yucca
state motto: 15 It Grows as It Goes
state song: 14 O Fair New Mexico **16** Asi es Nuevo Mexico
state tree: 5 pinon **8** tarantah **15** velvet ash pinyon

New Orleans
basketball team: 7 Hornets
event: 9 Mardi Gras, Sugar Bowl **25** International Jazz Festival
football team: 6 Saints
landmark: 7 Cabildo **9** Old Square, Superdome **10** Vieux Carre **12** Pirate's Alley **13** French Quarter
noted for: 4 jazz
people: 5 Cajun **6** Creole **7** Acadian
river: 11 Mississippi
street: 5 Royal **7** Bourbon
university: 6 Loyola, Tulane

news 4 dirt, dope, talk, word **5** flash, libel, piece, rumor, story **6** babble, expose, gossip, report **7** account, article, chatter, hearsay, lowdown, mention, message, release, scandal, slander, tidings **8** bulletin, dispatch, exposure **9** statement **10** communique, disclosure, divulgence, revelation **11** information **12** announcement, intelligence

news account 4 item **5** story **6** report **7** release **8** bulletin, dispatch **10** communique

newsmonger 6 gossip **8** busybody, reporter

News of the Day
also: 12 Neues vom Tage

opera by: 9 Hindemith
character: 5 Laura **7** Eduoard

New Spain see **6** Mexico

newspaper 3 rag **5** daily, paper, sheet **6** herald, weekly **7** courant, gazette, journal, tabloid, tribune **10** periodical **11** publication

New Testament
books of: 4 Acts, John, Jude, Luke, Mark **5** James, Peter, Titus **6** Romans **7** Hebrews, Matthew, Timothy **8** Philemon **9** Ephesians, Galatians **10** Colossians, Revelation **11** Corinthians, Philippians **13** Thessalonians
books: 12 Humologumena

Newton, Isaac
field: 11 mathematics
nationality: 7 English
discovered laws of: 6 motion **7** gravity **8** calculus
discovered: 13 color spectrum **15** binomial theorem **16** method of fluxions
invented: 21 infinitesimal calculus

New York
abbreviation: 2 NY
nickname: 6 Empire **9** Excelsior
capital: 6 Albany
largest city: 7 New York
others: 3 Rye **4** Rome, Troy **5** Ilion, Islip, Nyack, Olean, Owego, Utica **6** Attica, Auburn, Cohoes, Elmira, Goshen, Ithaca, Oneida, Oswego, Tappan **7** Ardsley, Babylon, Batavia, Buffalo, Congers, Endwell, Geneseo, Hewlett, Mahopac, Merrick, Messena, Mineola, Montauk, Oneonta, Pennyan, Suffern, Syosset, Wantagh, Yaphank, Yonkers **8** Bethpage, Catskill, Endicott, Herkimer, Kingston, Ossining, Pottsdam, Saratoga, Tuckahoe **9** Rochester, Scarsdale **10** Binghamton, Bronxville, Mamaroneck **11** Cooperstown, New Rochelle, Schenectady, White Plains **12** Poughkeepsie
college: 4 Bard, CUNY, Iona, Pace, SUNY **5** Finch, Keuka **6** Hobart, Hunter, Vassar **7** Adelphi, Barnard, Colgate, Cornell, Fordham, St John's **8** Columbia, Skidmore, Syracuse **9** Juilliard, Rochester, West Point **13** Sarah Lawrence **30** Rensselaer Polytechnic Institute
feature:
prison: 6 Attica **8** SingSing
tribe: 4 Erie **6** Cayuga, Mohawk, Oneida, Seneca **7** Mohican, Montauk **8** Iroquois, Onondaga **9** Manhattan,
people: 7 John Jay **8** Walloons **9** Jonas Salk **10** Henry James **11** Rockefeller, Walt Whitman **12** Eugene O'Neill **13** DeWitt Clinton, John Burroughs **14** Herman Melville **15** Peter Stuyvesant **16** Eleanor Roosevelt, Washington Irving **17** Fiorello La Guardia
explorer: 6 Hudson **9** Champlain,

Verrazano **16** Dutch West India Co
island: 4 Fire, Long **5** Ellis **6** Staten **7**
Bedloe's, Fisher's, Liberty, Shelter,
Welfare **8** Thousand **9** Governors,
Manhattan
lake: 4 Erie **6** Cayuga, Finger, George,
Oneida, Otisco, Otsego, Owasco,
Placid, Seneca **7** Conesus, Ontario,
Saranac, Schroon **8** Saratoga **9**
Champlain
land rank: 9 thirtieth
mountain: 4 Bear **5** Slide **7** Taconic **9**
Catskills **11** Adirondacks
   highest point: 5 Marcy
physical feature:
   bay: 7 Jamaica, Peconic **8** Moriches
   canal: 4 Erie **7** Gowanus
   falls: 7 Niagara
   valley: 6 Mohawk
president: 14 Martin Van Buren **14**
   Teddy Roosevelt **15** Millard Fillmore
   17 Theodore Roosevelt **23** Franklin
   Delano Roosevelt
river: 4 East **5** Black, Tioga **6** Harlem,
   Hoosic, Hudson, Mohawk, Oswego **7**
   Ausable, Genesee, Niagara **10** St
   Lawrence **11** Susquehanna
state bird: 8 bluebird
state fish: 10 brook trout
state flower: 4 rose
state motto: 9 Excelsior (Ever upward, still higher)
state tree: 10 sugar maple

New York City
nickname: 6 Gotham **8** Big Apple
airport: 3 JFK **6** Newark **9** La
   Guardia **12** John F Kennedy
area: 4 Soho **6** Harlem **7** Chelsea,
   Midtown, Tribeca **8** Broadway **9** Chinatown, Manhattan **10** Stuyvesant
   11 Bensonhurst, Brownsville, Little
   Italy **12** Hell's Kitchen **13** Spanish
   Harlem **16** Greenwich Village **17**
   Bedford-Stuyvesant
baseball team: 4 Mets **7** Yankees
basketball team: 6 Knicks **7** Liberty
   14 Knickerbockers
borough: 5 Bronx **6** Queens **8** Brooklyn, Richmond **9** Manhattan **12** Staten Island
early governor: 10 Stuyvesant
feature:
   building: 11 Empire State
   hall of fame: 8 baseball
   park: 7 Central
   square: 5 Times, Union **6** Herald
   statue: 7 Liberty
   street/avenue: 4 Park, Wall **5** Fifth
      7 Madison **8** Broadway
   tomb: 6 Grant's
football team: 4 Jets **6** Giants
former name: 12 New Amsterdam
hockey team: 7 Rangers
island: 4 City, Long **5** Ellis, Ward's **6**
   Riker's, Staten **7** Liberty **8** Randall's
   9 Governor's, Manhattan, Roosevelt
landmark: 5 Macy's **8** Aqueduct,
   Bronx Zoo **9** Unisphere **10** Jones

Beach **11** Battery Park, Central Park,
   Coney Island, Penn Station, Shea Sta-
   dium, Times Square **12** Carnegie
   Hall **13** Gracie Mansion, Lincoln
   Center, Port Authority, Rockaway
   Beach, Trinity Church, United Na-
   tions, Yankee Stadium **14** Waldorf-
   Astoria **15** NY Public Library, NY
   Stock Exchange, Seagram Building,
   Statue of Liberty **16** Chrysler Build-
   ing, World Trade Center **17** Arthur
   Ashe Stadium, Hayden Planetarium,
   Rockefeller Center, Woolworth Build-
   ing **18** Astoria Film Studios, Radio
   City Music Hall **19** Empire State
   Building, Grand Central Station,
   Madison Square Garden, St Patrick's
   Cathedral **22** Metropolitan Opera
   House **29** Cathedral of Saint John
   the Divine
mayor: 4 Koch **6** Walker **7** Dinkins **8**
   Bloomberg, Giuliani **9** La Guardia
museum: 6 Jewish **7** Whitney **9**
   Cloisters **10** Guggenheim **12** Cooper-
   Hewitt, Metropolitan **15** Frick Collection **17** Museum of Modern Art
   (MoMA) **30** American Museum of
   Natural History
river: 4 East **6** Harlem, Hudson
street: 6 Bowery **8** Broadway **9** Lexington **10** Park Avenue, Wall Street
   11 Central Park, Fifth Avenue, Sutton Place **13** Madison Avenue **17**
   Forty-Second Street
university: 3 NYU **6** Queens **7** Barnard, Fordham, Yeshiva **8** Brooklyn,
   Columbia **13** Hunter College **22** Juilliard School of Music **23** City University of New York

New Zealand
native's nickname: 4 Kiwi
other name: 8 Aotearoa **12** Nieuw
   Zeeland **23** Land of the Long White
   Cloud
capital: 10 Wellington
largest city: 8 Auckland
others: 5 Leuin, Oreti, Otaki, Taupo **6**
   Clutha, Foxton, Oamaru, Picton,
   Timaru **7** Dunedin, Manu Kau, Rae-
   tihi, Rotorua **8** Hamilton, Kawakawa,
   Touranga **9** Lyttelton **10** Queenstown
   12 Christchurch, Invercargill, Port
   Chalmers **13** Port Nicholson **14** Na-
   pier-Hastings **15** Palmerston North
school: 5 Otago **6** Massey **7** Waikato
   8 Auckland, Victoria **10** Canterbury
division: 11 North Island, South Island
head of state: 14 British monarch **15**
   governor general
monetary unit: 4 cent **6** dollar
island: 4 Cook, Niue, Otea **5** North,
   South **6** Bounty, Chatam, Snares **7**
   Stewart, Tokelau **8** Auckland, Campbell, Kermadec, Puketutu **9** Antipo-
   des **10** Resolution, Three Kings **12**
   Great Barrier
lake: 3 Ada **4** Gunn, Ohau **5** Hawea,

Taupo **6** Pukaki, Pupuke, Te Anau,
   Tekapo, Wanaka **7** Brunner, Diamond, Kanieri, Okareka, Rotorua **8**
   Okataina, Paradise, Rotoaira, Waka-
   tipu **9** Manapouri
mountain: 4 Eden, Flat, Owen **5** Allen, Chope, Lyall, Mitre, Ohope,
   Otari, Young **6** Egmont, Stokes, Tasman **7** Cameron, Coronet, Ernslaw,
   Huiarau, Pihanga, Ruahine,
   Ruapehu, Tauhera, Tutamoe, Tyndall
   8 Aspiring, Richmond, Tauranga **9**
   Messenger, Murchison, Ngauruhoe,
   Raukumara, Tongariro **11** Remarkables **12** Southern Alps
highest point: 4 Cook **7** Aorangi
river: 4 Avon **5** Mokau, Waipa **6** Clutha, Rakaia, Tamaki, Waihou,
   Wairau, Wairoa **7** Waikato, Waitaki
   8 Clarence, Manawatu, Wanganui **10**
   Rangitikei
sea: 6 Tasman **12** South Pacific
physical feature:
   bay: 4 Ohua **5** Evans, Hawke, Lyall
      6 Awarua, Cloudy, Golden, Plenty,
      Tasman **7** Fitzroy, Pegasus, Pov-
      erty **8** Halfmoon, Rangaunu
   bight: 7 Karamea **10** Canterbury **13**
      North Taranaki, South Taranaki
   cape: 4 East, West **5** North **6** Eg-
      mont **8** Farewell, Foulwind, Pal-
      liser **9** Southwest
   channel: 8 Colville
   falls: 10 Sutherland
   glacier: 3 Fox **6** Tasman **11** Franz
      Joseph
   gulf: 7 Hauraki
   harbor: 7 Kaipara, Manukau **9**
      Waitemata
   peninsula: 5 Mahia, Otago
   plains: 10 Canterbury
   sound: 8 Doubtful
   strait: 4 Cook **7** Foveaux
people: 3 Ati **5** Arawa, Dutch, Maori
   7 British, Ringatu **10** Polynesian
   author: 5 Frame **9** Mansfield **10**
      Ngaio Marsh **12** Ashton-Warner
   explorer: 4 Cook **6** Tasman
   mountain climber: 7 Hillary
language: 5 Maori **7** English
religion: 8 Anglican **9** Methodist **10**
   Protestant **12** Presbyterian **13** Roman
   Catholic
place:
   national park: 9 Fiordland, Fjord-
      land, Tongariro
feature:
   animal: 7 tuatara
   bird: 3 kea, tui **4** kiwi, weka **6** ta-
      kahe **7** apteryx **8** bellbird
   tree: 4 rimu, tawa **5** kauri, matai **6**
      totara
food:
   fish: 4 mako
   fruit: 4 kiwi **9** tamarillo **17** Chinese
      gooseberry
next-door 8 adjacent **9** adjoining **10**

connecting, contiguous, juxtaposed, side-by-side, **12** conterminous

next to 6 beside **8** abutting, adjacent **9** adjoining, bordering **10** contiguous, juxtaposed **12** conterminous

next world, the 6 Heaven **8** eternity, paradise **12** the hereafter **14** the world to come

Nez Perce (Numipu)
language family: 10 Shahaptian
location: 5 Idaho **6** Oregon **10** Washington
leader: 11 Chief Joseph

Niamey
capital of: 5 Niger

nib 3 end, tip, top **4** apex, peak **5** point **6** height, tiptop, vertex **7** extreme **8** pinnacle **9** extremity

nibble 3 nip **4** bite, chew, gnaw, peck **5** crumb, munch, speck, taste **6** crunch, morsel, peck at, tidbit **8** fragment, particle

Nibelung, ring of
origin: 8 Germanic
mentioned in: 14 Nibelungenlied
stolen by: 8 Alberich

Nibelungenlied
origin: 8 Germanic
form: 4 epic
date written: 17 thirteenth century
related to: 8 Volsunga
author: 7 unknown
character: 5 Etzel (Attila), Hagen **6** Gernot **7** Gunther **8** Brunhild, Dankwart, Giselher **9** Kriemhild, Siegfried
inspired: 6 Wagner

Nibelungs, Niblungs
origin: 8 Germanic, Teutonic
followers of: 9 Siegfried
race: 6 dwarfs
possessed: 8 treasure
captured by: 9 Siegfried
family of: 7 Gunther

Nicaragua
capital/largest city: 7 Managua
others: 4 Leon, Rama **6** Masaya **7** Corinto, Granada **8** Jinotega **9** Matagalpa **10** Bluefields, Chinandega
division: 13 Mosquito Coast
measure: 4 vara **5** cahiz **6** suerte **7** cajuela, manzana **10** cabelleria
monetary unit: 4 peso **7** centavo, cordoba
weight: 3 bag **4** caha, caja **8** tonelada
island: 7 Ometepe
lake: 7 Managua **9** Nicaragua
mountain: 4 Leon **5** Negro, Viejo **6** Madera, Telica **7** Managua, Saslaya **9** Momotombo
highest point: 7 Mogoton
river: 4 Coco, Tuma **5** Wanks **6** Grande, Poteca **7** San Juan **8** Tipitapa **9** Escondido
sea: 7 Pacific **9** Caribbean
physical feature:
gulf: 7 Fonseca

people: 4 Mico, Mixe, Rama, Smoo, Ulva **5** Cukra, Diria, Lenca, Sambo, Toaca **6** Mangue **7** mestizo, Miskito **8** Mosquito **9** Matagalpa
author: 5 Dario
explorer: 6 Davila **7** Cordoba **8** Columbus
group: 6 Contra **10** Sandinista
leader: 6 Somoza, Walker, Zelaya **7** Nicardo **8** Chamorro
language: 7 English, Spanish
religion: 13 Roman Catholic
place:
cathedral: 12 Metropolitan
feature:
dance: 5 sones **10** zapateados, zarabandas
food:
beans: 8 frijoles
dish: 10 naca tamale
drink: 5 tiste **9** pinolillo
fruit: 6 zapote

nice 4 deft, fine, good, kind **5** dandy, exact, fussy, great, swell **6** divine, genial, lovely, proper, seemly, strict, subtle **7** amiable, amusing, careful, cordial, correct, finicky, genteel, likable, precise, refined, winning **8** accurate, charming, cheerful, delicate, friendly, gracious, jim-dandy, ladylike, pleasant, pleasing, rigorous, skillful, unerring, virtuous, well-bred **9** agreeable, congenial, excellent, fantastic, marvelous, sensitive, wonderful **10** attractive, delightful, enchanting, entrancing, fastidious, methodical, meticulous, scrupulous **11** interesting, painstaking, pleasurable, punctilious, respectable, sympathetic, warmhearted **13** compassionate, understanding, well brought up **17** overconscientious

nicely 6 neatly **7** exactly, fussily, happily **9** carefully, precisely **10** accurately, critically, pleasantly, unerringly **11** faultlessly, fortunately, opportunely **12** attractively, fastidiously

nicety 4 care, tact **5** flair, grace **6** acumen, polish **7** culture, finesse, insight **8** accuracy, delicacy, elegance, subtlety **9** attention, exactness, precision **10** refinement **11** cultivation, penetration, preciseness, sensitivity **12** perspicacity, subtle detail, tastefulness **13** elaborateness, particularity **14** discrimination, fastidiousness, meticulousness

niche 4 cove, nook, slot **5** berth, trade **6** alcove, cavity, corner, cranny, dugout, hollow, metier, recess **7** calling **8** position, vocation **9** cubby hole **10** depression, pigeon hole **11** proper place **13** hole in the wall

Nicholas Nickleby
author: 14 Charles Dickens
character: 5 Smike **11** Arthur Gride, Newman Noggs **12** Kate Nickleby, Madeline Bray **13** Lord Verisopht,

Ralph Nickleby **14** Frank Cheeryble **15** Sir Mulberry Hawk, Vincent Crummles, Wackford Squeers **17** Cheeryble Brothers

Nichols, Mike
Wife: 11 Diane Sawyer
director of: 6 Closer **7** Catch-22 **11** The Birdcage, The Graduate (Oscar) **13** Primary Colors **14** Regarding Henry **15** Carnal Knowledge **25** Who's Afraid of Virginia Woolf?
partner: 9 Elaine May

Nicholson, Ben
born: 6 Denham **7** England
artwork: 9 Fireworks **11** White Relief **12** Tuscan Relief **13** Painted Relief **14** At the Chat Botte

Nicholson, Jack
born: 9 Neptune NJ
roles: 4 Wolf **5** Hoffa **6** Batman **8** Ironweed **9** Chinatown, Easy Rider **10** The Shining **11** A Few Good Men, Mars Attacks, The Two Jakes **12** Prizzi's Honor, The Passenger **13** The Last Detail **14** As Good As It Gets (Oscar), Five Easy Pieces **15** Carnal Knowledge **17** Terms of Endearment **20** The Witches of Eastwick **22** The King of Marvin Gardens **25** One Flew Over the Cuckoo's Nest (Oscar) **26** The Postman Always Rings Twice

nicht wahr? 10 isn't that so?

nick 3 cut, jag, mar **4** chip, dent, gash, mark, scar **5** cleft, gouge, notch, score, wound **6** damage, deface, indent, injure, injury **7** marking, scarify, scoring, scratch **8** incision, lacerate **10** depression **11** indentation

nickel
chemical symbol: 2 Ni

Nickel Mountain
author: 11 John Gardner

nickname 6 handle **7** agnomen, epithet, moniker, pet name **8** baby name, cognomen **9** pseudonym, sobriquet **10** diminutive **11** appellation, designation

Nicomachean Ethics
author: 9 Aristotle

Nidhogg
origin: 12 Scandinavian
form: 7 serpent
domain: 8 Niflheim
gnaws on lowest root of: 9 Iggdrasil, Yggdrasil

niello 5 alloy
of: 6 sulfur
with: 4 lead **6** copper, silver
used as: 5 inlay

Nielsen, Carl August
born: 6 Odense **7** Denmark
composer of: 9 Maskarade **12** Saul and David **16** Inextinguishable (symphony No 4)

Nietzsche, Friedrich
author of: 14 The Will to Power **17**

Beyond Good and Evil, The Birth of Tragedy **20** Thus Spake Zarathustra

Niflheim
origin: 12 Scandinavian
ruler of: 3 Hel
purpose: 10 punish dead
climate: 3 fog **4** cold **8** darkness

nifty 4 chic, fine, neat, posh **5** natty, smart **6** clever, dapper **7** dashing, stylish **8** splendid **10** attractive **11** fashionable

Niger
other name: 6 Joliba, Kworra, Ramtil
capital/largest city: 6 Niamey
others: 5 Goure **6** Agadex, Agadez, Maradi, Tahoua, Zinder
division:
  region: 3 Air **5** Arlit, Sahel
monetary unit: 5 franc **7** centime
lake: 4 Chad
mountain: 7 Bagzane **9** Air Massif
highest point: 7 Greboun
river: 5 Niger **6** Dillia
physical feature:
  desert: 6 Sahara
  oasis: 6 Kaouar
  plateau: 5 Djado **6** Tegama **7** Tchigai **8** Mengueni **11** Adar Doutchi, Djerma Ganda
people: 4 Daza, Idjo, Idyo, Idzo, Peul, Teda **5** Hausa, Warri **6** Djerma, Fulani, Kanuri, Songha, Toubou, Tuareg **13** Djerma-Songhai
  conqueror: 13 Usman Dan Fodio
  leader: 5 Diori **6** Saibou **7** Ousmane **8** Kountche
language: 5 Hausa, Mande **6** Djerma, French, Fulani, Tuareg **8** Mandingo, Tamashek
religion: 5 Islam **7** animism **12** Christianity
place:
  ruins: 6 Agadez
feature:
  cavalry: 5 Dosso
  empire: 4 Mali **6** Fulani **7** Songhai **10** Kanem-Borno
  tree: 6 acacia, baobab

Nigeria
capital: 5 Abuja
largest city: 5 Lagos
new capital: 5 Abuja
others: 3 Aba, Ado, Ede, Isa, Iwo, Jos, Oyo **4** Bida, Bidi, Buea, Kano, Offa, Yola **5** Benin, Bonny, Enugu, Warri, Zaria **6** Burutu, Ibadan, Ilesha, Ilorin, Kachia, Kaduna, Kadune, Kokoto, Mushin, Takoba **7** Calabar, Onitsha, Oshogbo **8** Abeokuta **9** Maiduguri, Ogbomosho **12** Port Harcourt
division: 3 Air, Isa, Oyo **4** Kano, Nupe, Ondo **5** Asben, Benin, Bornu, Ijebu, Ogoja, Warri **6** Biafra, Degema, Owerri, Sokoto **7** Adamawa
monetary unit: 4 kobo **5** naira
lake: 4 Chad
highest point: 7 Dimlang
river: 3 Oli **4** Gana, Yobe **5** Benin,

Benue, Cross, Niger **6** Kaduna, Sokoto **7** Calabar, Gongola **8** Komadugu **9** Sambreiro
sea: 8 Atlantic
physical feature:
  bight: 5 Benin, Bonny **6** Biafra
  delta: 5 Niger
  gulf: 6 Guinea
  plains: 5 Bornu **9** Hausaland
  plateau: 3 Jos, Udi **6** Bauchi
  port: 5 Lagos **7** Calabar **8** Harcourt
people: 3 Abo, Aro, Djo, Ebo, Edo, Ibo, Ijo, Tiv, Vai **4** Beni, Bini, Eboe, Efik, Egba, Ejam, Ekoi, Idyo, Igbo, Ijaw, Nupe **5** Angas, Benin, Gwari, Hausa **6** Chamba, Fulani, Ibibio, Kanuri, Yoruba **11** Hausa-Fulani
  author: 6 Achebe
  British colonial ruler: 6 Goldie, Lugard
  kingdom: 3 Ife, Nok, Oyo **5** Benin **6** Fulani **10** Kanem-Borno
  leader: 5 Gowon **6** Balewa, Ojukwu, Schick **7** Awolowo, Azikine, Azikiwe, Shagari **8** Obasanjo **9** Babangida **13** Usman dan Fodio
language: 3 Ibo **4** Efik, Igbo **5** Hausa **6** Yoruba **7** English
religion: 5 Islam **7** animism **12** Christianity
place:
  dam: 6 Kainji
  mosque/walled city: 4 Kano
feature:
  dress: 4 riga **7** agbados
  tree: 5 abura, afara **6** obeche **10** terminalia
  war: 7 Biafran

niggard 4 mean **5** cheap, miser, tight **6** stingy **7** miserly **8** scrimper **9** skinflint **10** ungenerous **12** parsimonious

niggardliness 6 penury **8** meanness **9** closeness, parsimony **10** stinginess **11** miserliness **13** penny-pinching **15** tight-fistedness

niggardly 4 mean, poor **5** cheap, close, sorry, tight **6** flimsy, frugal, meager, measly, paltry, saving, scanty, shabby, stingy, tawdry **7** miserly, scrubby, sparing, thrifty **8** beggarly, grubbing, grudging, stinting, wretched **9** illiberal, mercenary, miserable, penurious **10** hardfisted, second-rate, ungenerous **11** closefisted **12** contemptible, insufficient, parsimonious

niggling 5 fussy, minor, petty, small **7** finicky **8** caviling, nugatory, picayune, piddling, trifling **9** quibbling **10** negligible, nit-picking **12** pettifogging **13** insignificant **15** inconsequential

nigh 4 near **5** close, handy **6** almost, at hand, nearly **7** close by **8** adjacent **9** bordering **11** neighboring, practically

night 4 dark, dusk **7** bedtime, evening, sundown **8** darkness, eventide **9** murkiness, obscurity **13** tenebrous-

ness
goddess of: 3 Nox

nightclub
French: 5 boite **11** boite de nuit

nightfall 4 dark, dusk **6** sunset **7** evening, sundown **8** darkness, eventide, gloaming, moonrise, twilight
French: 10 crepuscule

Night Gallery
host: 10 Rod Serling

Nightingale, Florence
birthplace: 7 England
worked in: 10 Crimean War
founded: 13 modern nursing
nickname: 18 The Lady with the Lamp
first woman to receive: 12 Order of Merit

nightingale
group of: 5 watch

Nightline
host: 9 Ted Koppel

nightly 4 dark **7** evening, obscure **9** nocturnal **11** nocturnally

nightmare 7 incubus **8** bad dream, succubus **13** hallucination

Night of the Iguana, The
director: 10 John Huston
based on play by: 17 Tennessee Williams
cast: 7 Sue Lyon **8** Skip Ward **10** Ava Gardner **11** Deborah Kerr **13** Richard Burton
setting: 6 Mexico

nightshade 16 Solanum dulcamara
varieties: 4 ball **5** black **6** common, deadly, sticky **7** Malabar **8** stinking **9** melon-leaf, poisonous, soda-apple **10** enchanter's

Nights of Cabiria
director: 15 Federico Fellini
cast: 13 Amedeo Nazzari **14** Francois Perier **15** Giulietta Masina
remade as: 12 Sweet Charity

nightstick 3 rod **4** mace, wand **5** baton, staff **6** cudgel **7** scepter **8** bludgeon **9** billy club, truncheon **10** shillelagh

nighttime 4 late **5** night **9** late-night, nighttide, nocturnal

Night to Remember, A
director: 8 Roy Baker
based on story by: 10 Walter Lord
cast: 9 Jill Dixon **11** Kenneth More **13** David McCallum **16** Laurence Naismith
setting: 7 Titanic

nihil 7 nothing

nihilism 5 chaos **6** anomie **7** license **9** amorality, anarchism, emptiness, terrorism **10** alienation, iconoclasm, radicalism, skepticism **11** agnosticism, lawlessness, nothingness **12** nonexistence **16** irresponsibility

nihilist 5 rebel **9** anarchist, terrorist **13** revolutionary

Nihon *see* 5 Japan

Nike
origin: 5 Greek
goddess of: 7 victory
father: 11 Titan Pallas
mother: 4 Styx
brother: 5 Zelos
corresponds to: 6 Athena 8 Victoria

nil 4 none, null, zero 6 cipher, naught 7 nothing, nullity 11 nonexistent

Nile
boat: 5 baris 6 cangia, nuggar, sandal 7 felucca, gaiassa 8 dahabeah
cities: 3 Qus 4 Abri, Argo, Idfu, Isna, Juba, Qina 5 Aswan, Asyut, Cairo, Kokka, Kusti, Luxor, Meroe, Minya, Rejaf, Saite, Tanis, Tanta 6 Atbara, Faiyum 7 Malakel, Mansura, Rosetta 8 Khartoum, Omdurman, Rusayris 9 Was Madani 10 Alexandria
dam: 6 Sannar 9 Aswan High, White Nile
desert bordering: 6 Libyan, Nubian 7 Arabian
falls: 5 Ripon 8 Kabalega 9 Murchison
feature: 6 Sphinx
  pyramid: 4 Giza
  temple: 8 Ramses II 9 Abu Simbel 11 Deir el-Bahri, Medinet Habu
flows into: 13 Mediterranean
flows through: 5 Egypt, Kenya, Sudan, Zaire 6 Rwanda, Uganda 7 Burundi 8 Ethiopia, Tanzania
island: 4 Roda 6 Philae
lake: 4 Tana 5 Kyoga, Tsana 6 Albert, Edward, Nasser 8 Victoria
other name: 4 Hapi 20 The Father of the Rivers
people: 3 Jur, Luo, Lwo, Nuo, Suk 4 Bari, Beja, Golo, Luoh, Madi 5 Nilot 7 Shilluk
plain: 6 Gezira
plant: 4 sudd 5 lotus
starting point: 5 Tsana 8 Victoria
swamp: 4 Sudd
tributary: 4 Arab 5 Rahad, Sobat 6 Atbara, Ghazai, Kagera 7 Rosetta 8 Blue Nile, Damietta 9 Bahr Jebel, White Nile

Niles, Hazel and Peter
characters in: 22 Mourning Becomes Electra
author: 6 O'Neill

nil nisi bonum 21 nothing unless it is good

nil sine numine 27 nothing without the divine will
motto of: 8 Colorado

nimble 4 deft, spry 5 agile, fleet, light, quick, rapid, ready, swift 6 active, expert, lively, prompt, speedy, supple 8 animated, skillful, spirited 9 dexterous, mercurial, sprightly 10 proficient

nimbleness 7 agility 8 alacrity, spryness 9 dexterity, quickness 10 limberness, suppleness

nimble-witted 5 droll, witty 6 clever 11 resourceful

nimbus 4 aura, disk, halo 5 cloud, vapor 7 aureole 8 radiance

Nimitz, Chester
served in: 3 WWI 4 WWII
commander of: 12 Pacific fleet
rank: 12 fleet (five-star) admiral 22 chief of naval operations
battle: 6 Midway 9 Leyte Gulf 13 Philippine Sea

Nimoy, Leonard
born: 8 Boston MA
films: 7 Mr Spock 8 Star Trek 14 Funny About Love 16 Three men and a Baby 17 Mission: Impossible 21 Star Trek: The Voyage Home 22 Star Trek: The Wrath of Khan 24 Star Trek: The Final Frontier 25 Star Trek: The Search for Spock

Nimrod
father: 4 Cush
grandfather: 3 Ham
great grandfather: 4 Noah
founded: 5 Accad, Calah, Resen 7 Nineveh 8 Rehoboth
famed as: 6 hunter

nincompoop 4 boob, dolt, dope, fool, jerk 5 dummy, dunce, idiot, klutz, moron, ninny 6 dimwit, lummox, nitwit 7 half-wit, jackass 8 bonehead, dummkopf, imbecile, lunkhead, numskull 9 blockhead, dumb bunny, harebrain, numbskull, simpleton 10 dunderhead, dunderpate, muddlehead, noodlehead 11 knucklehead, rattlebrain 12 featherbrain, scatterbrain

Nine, the *see* 5 Muses

Nineteen Eighty-Four
author: 12 George Orwell
character: 4 Syme 5 Julia 6 O'Brien 11 Charrington 12 Winston Smith

1919
author: 13 John Dos Passos

Ninety-Five Theses
author: 12 Martin Luther

Nineveh
founder: 6 Nimrod

Nine worthies
mentioned in: 16 medieval romances
three each of: 4 Jews 6 Pagans 10 Christians
names: 5 David 6 Arthur, Hector, Joshua 11 Charlemagne 12 Julius Caesar 15 Judas Maccabaeus 17 Alexander the Great 18 Godefroy de Bouillon

ninny 3 ass, sap 4 fool, simp 5 booby, dunce, idiot, moron 6 dimwit, nitwit 7 fathead, half-wit 8 bonehead, dumbdumb, imbecile, lunkhead, numskull 9 blockhead, dumb bunny, lamebrain, numbskull 10 dunderhead, nincompoop 11 chowderhead

Ninotchka
director: 13 Ernst Lubitsch
cast: 9 Ina Claire 10 Bela Lugosi, Greta Garbo 13 Melvyn Douglas
setting: 5 Paris
remade as: 13 Silk Stockings

Ninurta
also: 5 Ninib
origin: 8 Sumerian 10 Babylonian
type of god: 4 hero
personifies: 4 wind 9 south wind
father: 5 Enlil
avenger of: 5 Enlil

Ninus
wife: 9 Semiramis
founder of: 7 Nineveh

Niobe
father: 8 Tantalus
mother: 5 Dione
brother: 6 Pelops
husband: 7 Amphion
children: 9 seven sons 14 seven daughters
children called: 6 Niobid
taunted: 4 Leto
children killed by: 6 Apollo 7 Artemis
changed into: 5 stone
changed by: 4 Zeus

Niord
also: 5 Njord
origin: 12 Scandinavian
god of: 4 wind 10 navigation, prosperity
king of: 5 Vanir
son: 4 Frey 5 Freyr
daughter: 5 Freia, Freya

nip 3 cut, lop 4 bite, clip, crop, dock, grab, grip, ruin, snag, snap, snip 5 blast, check, chill, clamp, clasp, crack, crush, frost, grasp, pinch, quash, seize, sever, shear, snare, tweak 6 benumb, clutch, cut off, freeze, pierce, snatch, sunder, thwart 7 curtail, destroy, shorten, squeeze 8 compress, cut short, demolish 9 frustrate 10 abbreviate

nip-and-tuck 5 close

nip in the bud 7 prevent 8 preclude 9 forestall, frustrate

Nippon *see* 5 Japan

nippy 3 raw 5 brisk, chill, crisp, sharp 6 biting, chilly 7 cutting

Nip/Tuck
network: 2 FX
cast: 10 Dylan Walsh (Sean McNamara), Linda Klein (Nurse Linda) 11 John Hensley (Matt McNamara), Valerie Cruz (Grace Santiago) 12 Famke Janssen (Ava Moore) 13 Julian McMahon (Christian Troy) 14 Jessalyn Gilsig (Gina Russo) 15 Joely Richardson (Julia McNamara), Vanessa Redgrave (Erica Noughton)

nit-pick 4 carp, pick 5 cavil 9 criticize

nitrate 4 salt 5 ester 6 sodium 9 potassium 10 fertilizer

nitrogen
chemical symbol: 1 N

nitty-gritty 4 core, crux, gist, meat, pith **5** heart **7** essence **9** substance

nitwit 3 ass **4** clod, dolt, fool **5** booby, dummy, dunce, idiot, klutz, moron, ninny **7** fathead, pinhead **8** bonehead, dumb-dumb, imbecile, lunkhead, meathead, numskull, peabrain **9** birdbrain, blockhead, lamebrain, numbskull **10** dunderhead, nincompoop, noodlehead **11** chowderhead

Niven, David
  real name: 21 James David Graham Niven
  autobiography: 16 The Moon's a Balloon **21** Bring on the Empty Horses
  born: 8 Scotland **10** Kirriemuir
  roles: 11 Phileas Fogg **12** Casino Royale, My Man Godfrey **14** The Pink Panther, Separate Tables (Oscar) **16** Stairway to Heaven, Wuthering Heights **18** The Prisoner of Zenda **26** Around the World in Eighty Days

Nix, nixie
  origin: 8 Germanic
  form: 6 spirit
  habitat: 5 water

Nixon
  director: 11 Oliver Stone
  cast: 7 J T Walsh (John Ehrlichman) **8** Ed Harris (E Howard Hunt) **9** Joan Allen (Pat Nixon) **10** Bob Hoskins (J Edgar Hoover), E G Marshall (John Mitchell), James Woods (H R Haldeman) **11** David Paymer (Ron Ziegler), Paul Sorvino (Henry Kissinger) **12** Annabeth Gish (Julie Nixon Eisenhower), Madeline Kahn (Martha Mitchell), Powers Boothe (Alexander Haig) **14** Anthony Hopkins (Nixon) **15** David Hyde Pierce (John Dean), Mary Steenburgen (Hannah Nixon)

Nixon, Richard Milhous
  presidential rank: 13 thirty-seventh
  party: 10 Republican
  state represented: 2 CA
  defeated: 7 (George Corley) Wallace **8** (Hubert Horatio) Humphrey
  vice president: 4 (Gerald Rudolph) Ford **5** (Spiro Theodore) Agnew
  cabinet:
    state: 6 (William Pierce) Rogers **9** (Henry A) Kissinger
    treasury: 5 (William E) Simon **6** (George P) Shultz **7** (David Matthew) Kennedy **8** (John Bowden) Connally
    defense: 5 (Melvin Robert) Laird **10** (Elliot L) Richardson **11** (James R) Schlesinger
    attorney general: 5 (William B) Saxbe **8** (John Newton) Mitchell **10** (Elliot L) Richardson **11** (Richard G) Kleindienst
    postmaster general: 6 (Winton Malcolm) Blount
    interior: 6 (Rogers Clark Ballard) Morton, (Walter Joseph) Hinkel
    agriculture: 4 (Earl Lauer) Butz **6**

(Clifford Morris) Hardin
    commerce: 4 (Frederick B) Dent **5** (Maurice Hubert) Stans
    labor: 6 (George Pratt) Shultz **7** (James Day) Hodgson, (Peter J) Brennan
    HEW: 5 (Robert Hutchinson) Finch **10** (Caspar W) Weinberger, (Elliot Lee) Richardson
    HUD: 4 (James T) Lynn **6** (George Wilcken) Romney
    transportation: 5 (John Anthony) Volpe **8** (Claude S) Brinegar
  born: 2 CA **10** Yorba Linda
  died: 7 New York **11** New York City
  education:
    college: 8 Whittier
    law school: 14 Duke University
  religion: 6 Quaker **16** Society of Friends
  interests: 8 football
  vacation spot: 11 Key Biscayne (FL), San Clemente (CA)
  dog: 8 Checkers **11** King Timahoe
  author: 9 Six Crises **10** The Real War **11** Beyond Peace **27** RN: The Memoirs of Richard Nixon
  political career: 8 US Senate **13** Vice President **24** US House of Representatives
  civilian career: 6 lawyer
  military service: 6 US Navy **10** lieutenant, World War II
  notable events of lifetime/term:
    Calley court martialed for: 13 Mylai Massacre
    court martial of: 6 Calley
    creation of: 10 Bangladesh
    crisis: 3 oil **6** energy
    embargo on: 3 oil
    first men on: 4 moon
    incident: 11 Wounded Knee
    pardon of Nixon by: 4 Ford
    publication of: 14 Pentagon Papers
    resignation of: 5 Agnew, Nixon
    scandal: 9 Watergate
    student deaths at: 9 Kent State
    treaty: 10 Seabed Arms **32** Nonproliferation of Nuclear Weapons
    trip to: 5 China
    war: 7 Vietnam **10** Middle East **12** East Pakistan
  quotes: 31 A respectable Republican cloth coat **35** You won't have Nixon to kick around any more
  father: 14 Francis Anthony
  mother: 6 Hannah (Milhous)
  siblings: 11 Arthur Burdg **12** Harold Samuel **13** Edward Calvert, Francis Donald
  wife: 8 (Thelma Catherine) Patricia (Ryan)
    nickname: 3 Pat
  children: 5 Julie **8** Patricia
    Julie married: 15 David Eisenhower
    Patricia married: 9 Edward Cox
    Patricia's nickname: 6 Tricia

Njord *see* **5** Niord

no 3 nay, nix, not **4** none, veto
  French: 3 non
  German: 4 nein
  Spanish: 2 no
  Italian: 2 no
  Russian: 4 nyet

Noah
  father: 6 Lamech
  grandfather: 10 Methuselah
  son: 3 Ham **4** Shem **7** Japheth
  grandson: 3 Put **4** Cush **6** Canaan **7** Misraim
  great grandson: 6 Nimrod
  built: 3 ark
  collected: 5 pairs **7** animals
  survived: 5 flood
  pertaining to: 8 Noachian

Noah's Ark
  made of: 10 gopherwood
  landfall: 6 Ararat

nob 4 peer, toff **5** swell **9** patrician **10** aristocrat

Nobel, Alfred
  nationality: 7 Swedish
  invented: 8 dynamite
  originated: 10 Nobel Prize

Nobel Prizes
  Literature:
    1901: 20 Rene F A Sully-Prudhomme
    1902: 14 Theodor Mommsen
    1903: 20 Bjornstjerne Bjornson
    1904: 13 Jose Echegaray **15** Frederic Mistral
    1905: 17 Henryk Sienkiewicz
    1906: 14 Giosue Carducci
    1907: 14 Rudyard Kipling
    1908: 13 Rudolf C Eucken
    1909: 13 Selma Lagerlof
    1910: 12 Paul von Heyse
    1911: 18 Maurice Maeterlinck
    1912: 16 Gerhart Hauptmann
    1913: 21 Sir Rabindranath Tagore
    1915: 13 Romain Rolland
    1916: 19 Verner von Heidenstam
    1917: 11 K A Gjellerup **17** Henrik Pontoppidan
    1919: 15 Carl F G Spitteler
    1920: 13 Knut Hamsun
    1921: 13 Anatole France
    1922: 25 Jacinto Benavente y Martinez
    1923: 18 William Butler Yeats
    1924: 17 Wladyslaw S Reymont
    1925: 17 George Bernard Shaw
    1926: 13 Grazia Deledda
    1927: 12 Henri Bergson
    1928: 12 Sigrid Undset
    1929: 10 Thomas Mann
    1930: 13 Sinclair Lewis
    1931: 14 Erik A Karlfeldt
    1932: 14 John Galsworthy
    1933: 10 Ivan A Bunin
    1934: 15 Luigi Pirandello
    1936: 12 Eugene O'Neill
    1937: 17 Roger Martin du Gard
    1938: 10 Pearl S Buck

1939: **15** Frans E Sillanpaa
1944: **15** Johannes V Jensen
1945: **15** Gabriela Mistral
1946: **12** Hermann Hesse
1947: **9** Andre Gide
1948: **7** T S Eliot
1949: **15** William Faulkner
1950: **15** Bertrand Russell (Earl Russell)
1951: **14** Par F Lagerkvist
1952: **15** Francois Mauriac
1953: **21** Sir Winston L S Churchill
1954: **15** Ernest Hemingway
1955: **15** Halldor K Laxness
1956: **16** Juan Ramon Jimenez
1957: **11** Albert Camus
1958: **15** Boris L Pasternak
1959: **18** Salvatore Quasimodo
1960: **14** Saint-John Perse
1961: **9** Ivo Andric
1962: **13** John Steinbeck
1963: **13** George Seferis
1964: **14** Jean Paul Sartre
1965: **17** Mikhail A Sholokhov
1966: **10** Nelly Sachs **17** Samuel Joseph (Shmuel Y) Agnon
1967: **19** Miguel Angel Asturias
1968: **16** Yasunari Kawabata
1969: **13** Samuel Beckett
1970: **22** Aleksandr I Solzhenitsyn
1971: **11** Pablo Neruda
1972: **12** Heinrich Boll
1973: **12** Patrick White
1974: **13** Eyvind Johnson **14** Harry Martinson
1975: **14** Eugenio Montale
1976: **10** Saul Bellow
1977: **17** Vicente Aleixandre
1978: **19** Isaac Bashevis Singer
1979: **14** Odysseus Elytis
1980: **13** Czeslaw Milosz
1981: **12** Elias Canetti
1982: **20** Gabriel Garcia Marquez
1983: **14** William Golding
1984: **15** Jaroslav Seifert
1985: **11** Claude Simon
1986: **11** Wole Soyinka
1987: **13** Joseph Brodsky
1988: **13** Naguib Mahfouz
1989: **10** Camilo Cela
1990: **10** Octavio Paz
1991: **14** Nadine Gordimer
1992: **12** Derek Walcott
1993: **12** Toni Morrison
1994: **12** Kenzaburo Oe
1995: **12** Seamus Heaney
1996: **17** Wislawa Szymborska
1997: **7** Dario Fo
1998: **12** Jose Saramago
1999: **11** Gunter Grass
2000: **15** Gao Xingjian
2001: **9** VS Naipaul
2002: **11** Imre Kertesz
2003: **9** JM Coetzee
2004: **15** Elfriede Jelinek
2005: **12** Harold Pinter

Physiology/Medicine:
1901: **15** Emil A von Behring

1902: **13** Sir Ronald Ross
1903: **12** Niels R Finsen
1904: **11** Ivan P Pavlov
1905: **10** Robert Koch
1906: **12** Camillo Golgi **19** Santiago Ramon y Cajal
1907: **16** Charles L A Laveran
1908: **11** Paul Ehrlich **15** Elie Metchnikoff
1909: **11** Emil T Kocher
1910: **14** Albrecht Kossel
1911: **16** Allvar Gullstrand
1912: **14** Alexis Carrel
1913: **14** Charles R Richet
1914: **12** Robert Barany
1919: **11** Jules Bordet
1920: **12** Shack A S Krogh
1922: **12** Otto Meyerhof **14** Archibald V Hill
1923: **13** John J R Macleod **20** Sir Frederick G Banting
1924: **15** Willem Einthoven
1926: **15** Johannes Fibiger
1927: **19** Julius Wagner-Jauregg
1928: **16** Charles J H Nicolle
1929: **17** Christiaan Eijkman **20** Sir Frederick G Hopkins
1930: **15** Karl Landsteiner
1931: **12** Otto H Warburg
1932: **12** Edgar D Adrian **21** Sir Charles Sherrington
1933: **13** Thomas H Morgan
1934: **12** George R Minot **14** George H Whipple, William P Murphy
1935: **11** Hans Spemann
1936: **9** Otto Loewi **13** Sir Henry H Dale
1937: **31** Albert Szent-Gyorgyi von Nagyrapolt
1938: **16** Corneille Heymans
1939: **13** Gerhard Domagk
1943: **9** Henrik Dam **12** Edward A Doisy
1944: **14** Herbert S Gasser, Joseph Erlanger
1945: **11** Ernst B Chain **16** Sir Howard W Florey **19** Sir Alexander Fleming
1946: **14** Hermann J Muller
1947: **9** Carl F Cori **10** Gerty T Cori **16** Bernardo A Houssay
1948: **11** Paul H Muller
1949: **11** Walter R Hess **21** Antonio C de A F Egas Moniz
1950: **12** Philip S Hench **14** Edward C Kendall **16** Tadeus Reichstein
1951: **10** Max Theiler
1952: **14** Selman A Waksman
1953: **11** Fritz A Lipmann, Sir Hans A Krebs
1954: **11** John F Enders **13** Thomas H Weller **17** Frederick C Robbins
1955: **14** Axel H T Theorell
1956: **13** Andre Cournand **15** Werner Forssmann **20** Dickenson W Richards Jr
1957: **11** Daniel Bovet

1958: **12** Edward L Tatum **13** George W Beadle **15** Joshua Lederberg
1959: **11** Severo Ochoa **14** Arthur Kornberg
1960: **13** Peter B Medawar **15** Sir Frank M Burnet
1961: **14** Georg von Bekesy
1962: **12** James D Watson **14** Francis H C Crick **16** Maurice H F Wilkins
1963: **16** Alan Lloyd Hodgkin **18** Sir John Carew Eccles **20** Andrew Fielding Huxley
1964: **11** Feodor Lynen **12** Konrad E Bloch
1965: **10** Andre Lwoff **12** Jacques Monod **13** Francois Jacob
1966: **17** Francis Peyton Rous **21** Charles Brenton Huggins
1967: **10** George Wald **12** Ragnar Granit **20** Haldan Keffer Hartline
1968: **13** Robert W Holley **14** H Gobind Khorana **18** Marshall W Nirenberg
1969: **11** Max Delbruck **14** Alfred D Hershey, Salvador E Luria
1970: **11** Ulf von Euler **13** Julius Axelrod **14** Sir Bernard Katz
1971: **17** Earl W Sutherland Jr
1972: **13** Rodney R Porter **14** Gerald M Edelman
1973: **12** Konrad Lorenz **13** Karl von Frisch **17** Nikolaas Tinbergen
1974: **12** Albert Claude **15** Christian de Duve **16** George Emil-Palade
1975: **12** Howard M Temin **14** David Baltimore, Renato Dulbecco
1976: **15** Baruch S Blumberg **22** Daniel Carleton Gajdusek
1977: **13** Andrew Schally, Rosalyn S Yalow **14** Roger Guillemin
1978: **11** Werner Arber **13** Daniel Nathans, Hamilton Smith
1979: **13** Allan M Cormack **17** Godfrey Hounsfield
1980: **11** Jean Dausset **12** George D Snell **15** Baruj Benacerraf
1981: **11** David H Hubel **12** Roger W Sperry **14** Torsten N Wiesel
1982: **9** John R Vane **15** Bengt Samuelsson **17** Sune Karl Bergstrom
1983: **17** Barbara McClintock
1984: **11** Niels K Jerne **13** Cesar Milstein **16** Georges J F Koehler
1985: **13** Michael S Brown **16** Joseph L Goldstein
1986: **12** Stanley Cohen **18** Rita Levi-Montalcini
1987: **14** Susumu Tonegawa
1988: **10** James Black **14** Gertrube B Elion **16** George H Hitchings
1989: **12** Harold Varmas **14** J Michael Bishop
1990: **12** Joseph Murray **14** E Donnall Thomas

1991: 10 Edwin Neher 11 Bert Sakmann
1992: 10 Edwin Krebs 12 Edmond Fisher
1993: 12 Phillip Sharp 14 Richard Roberts
1994: 12 Alfred Gilman 13 Martin Rodbell
1995: 12 Edward B Lewis 14 Eric F Wieschaus
1996: 13 Peter C Doherty 16 Rolf M Ziwkernagel
1997: 16 Stanley B. Prusiner
1998: 10 Ferid Murad 12 Louis Ignarro 15 Robert Furchgott
1999: 12 Gunter Blobel
2000: 10 Eric Kandel 13 Arvid Carlsson, Paul Greengard
2001: 7 Tim Hunt 9 Paul Nurse 14 Leland Hartwell
2002: 11 John Sulston 13 Sydney Brenner 14 H Robert Horvitz
2003: 13 Paul Lauterbur 14 Peter Mansfield
2004: 9 Linda Buck 11 Richard Axel
2005: 12 J. Robin Warren 14 Barry J. Marshall

Chemistry:
1901: 16 Jacobus H van't Hoff
1902: 11 Emil Fischer
1903: 16 Svante A Arrhenius
1904: 16 Sir William Ramsay
1905: 17 J F W Adolf von Baeyer
1906: 12 Henri Moissan
1907: 13 Eduard Buchner
1908: 19 Sir Ernest Rutherford
1909: 14 Wilhelm Ostwald
1910: 11 Otto Wallach
1911: 11 Marie S Curie
1912: 12 Paul Sabatier 14 Victor Grignard
1913: 12 Alfred Werner
1914: 17 Theodore W Richards
1915: 18 Richard Willstatter
1918: 10 Fritz Haber
1920: 13 Walther Nernst
1921: 14 Frederick Soddy
1922: 13 Francis W Aston
1923: 10 Fritz Pregl
1925: 16 Richard Zsigmondy
1926: 15 Theodor Svedberg
1927: 15 Heinrich Wieland
1928: 12 Adolf Windaus
1929: 15 Sir Arthur Harden 19 Hans von Euler-Chelpin
1930: 11 Hans Fischer
1931: 9 Carl Bosch 16 Friedrich Bergius
1932: 14 Irving Langmuir
1934: 11 Harold C Urey
1935: 16 Irene Joliot-Curie 19 Frederic Joliot-Curie
1936: 12 Peter J W Debye
1937: 10 Paul Karrer 17 Sir Walter N Haworth
1938: 11 Richard Kuhn
1939: 14 Adolf Butenandt, Leopold Ruzicka

1943: 14 Georg von Hevesy
1944: 8 Otto Hahn
1945: 16 Artturi I Virtanen
1946: 12 James B Sumner 13 John H Northrop 15 Wendell M Stanley
1947: 17 Sir Robert Robinson
1948: 12 Arne Tiselius
1949: 15 William F Giauque
1950: 9 Kurt Alder, Otto Diels
1951: 13 Glenn T Seaborg 14 Edwin M McMillan
1952: 14 Archer J P Martin, Richard L M Synge
1953: 17 Hermann Staudinger
1954: 13 Linus C Pauling
1955: 17 Vincent du Vigneaud
1956: 15 Nikolai N Semenov 20 Sir Cyril N Hinshelwood
1957: 17 Sir Alexander R Todd (Baron Todd)
1958: 15 Frederick Sanger
1959: 17 Jaroslav Heyrovsky
1960: 13 Willard F Libby
1961: 12 Melvin Calvin
1962: 10 Max F Perutz 12 John C Kendrew
1963: 11 Giulio Natta, Karl Ziegler
1964: 26 Dorothy Mary Crowfoot Hodgkin
1965: 19 Robert Burns Woodward
1966: 15 Robert S Mulliken
1967: 12 Manfred Eigen 15 Sir George Porter 27 Ronald George Wreyford Norrish
1968: 11 Lars Onsager
1969: 9 Odd Hassel 13 Derek H R Barton
1970: 18 Luis Federico Leloir
1971: 15 Gerhard Herzberg
1972: 13 Stanford Moore 18 Christian B Anfinsen, William Howard Stein
1973: 16 Ernst Otto Fischer 17 Geoffrey Wilkinson
1974: 10 Paul J Flory
1975: 14 John W Cornforth, Vladimir Prelog
1976: 16 William N Lipscomb
1977: 13 Ilya Prigogine
1978: 13 Peter Mitchell
1979: 11 Georg Wittig 13 Herbert C Brown
1980: 8 Paul Berg 13 Walter Gilbert 15 Frederick Sanger
1981: 12 Kenichi Fukui 13 Roald Hoffmann
1982: 9 Aaron Klug
1983: 10 Henry Taube
1984: 21 Robert Bruce Merrifield
1985: 11 Jerome Karle 16 Herbert A Hauptman
1986: 8 Yuan T Lee 12 John C Polanyi 16 Dudley Herschbach
1987: 11 Donald J Cram 16 Charles J Pederson
1988: 11 Robert Huber 13 Hartmut Michel 17 Johann Deisenhofer

1989: 10 Thomas Cich 12 Sidney Altman
1990: 10 Elias Corey
1991: 12 Richard Ernst
1992: 13 Rudolph Marcus
1993: 10 Kary Mullis 12 Michael Smith
1994: 10 George Olah
1995: 11 Paul Crutzen, Mario Molina 16 F Sherwood Rowland
1996: 11 Robert F Curl 15 Richard E Smalley, Sir Harold W Kroto
1997: 9 Jens C Skou 10 Paul D Boyer 11 John E Walker
1998: 9 John Pople 10 Walter Kohn
1999: 11 Ahmed Zewail
2000: 10 Alan Heeger 14 Alan MacDiarmid 15 Hideki Shirakawa
2001: 11 Ryoji Noyori 14 William Knowles 16 K Barry Sharpless
2002: 8 John Fenn 11 Koichi Tanaka 12 Kurt Wuthrich
2003: 9 Peter Agre 17 Roderick MacKinnon
2004: 9 Irwin Rose 12 Avram Hershko 16 Aaron Ciechanover
2005: 11 Yves Chauvin 13 Robert H. Grubbs 15 Richard R. Schrock

Physics:
1901: 16 Wilhelm K Roentgen
1902: 12 Pieter Zeeman 15 Hendrik A Lorentz
1903: 11 Marie S Curie, Pierre Curie 15 A Henri Becquerel
1904: 11 John W Strutt (Lord Rayleigh)
1905: 13 Philipp Lenard
1906: 16 Sir Joseph Thomson
1907: 16 Albert A Michelson
1908: 15 Gabriel Lippmann
1909: 10 Karl F Braun 16 Guglielmo Marconi
1910: 20 Johannes D van der Waals
1911: 11 Wilhelm Wien
1912: 10 Nils G Dalen
1913: 20 Heike Kamerlingh Onnes
1914: 10 Max von Laue
1915: 16 Sir William H Bragg, Sir William L Bragg
1917: 14 Charles B Barkla
1918: 9 Max Planck
1919: 13 Johannes Stark
1920: 14 Charles E Guillaume
1921: 14 Albert Einstein
1922: 10 Nils H D Bohr
1923: 15 Robert A Millikan
1924: 14 Karl M G Siegbahn
1925: 11 Gustav Hertz, James Franck
1926: 11 Jean B Perrin
1927: 14 Arthur H Compton 15 Charles T R Wilson
1928: 18 Sir Owen W Richardson
1929: 15 Louis V de Broglie
1930: 23 Sir Chandrasekhara V Raman
1932: 16 Werner Heisenberg

1933: 11 Paul A M Dirac **16** Erwin Schrodinger
1935: 16 Sir James Chadwick
1936: 11 Victor F Hess **13** Carl D Anderson
1937: 16 Clinton J Davisson **17** Sir George P Thomson
1938: 11 Enrico Fermi
1939: 15 Ernest O Lawrence
1943: 9 Otto Stern
1944: 11 Isidor I Rabi
1945: 13 Wolfgang Pauli
1946: 14 Percy W Bridgman
1947: 18 Sir Edward V Appleton
1948: 17 Patrick M S Blackett
1949: 12 Hideki Yukawa
1950: 12 Cecil F Powell
1951: 14 Ernest T S Walton **17** Sir John D Cockcroft
1952: 10 Felix Bloch **14** Edward M Purcell
1953: 12 Frits Zernike
1954: 7 Max Born **12** Walther Bothe
1955: 13 Polykarp Kusch, Willis E Lamb Jr
1956: 11 John Bardeen **15** Walter H Brattain **16** William B Shockley
1957: 11 Tsung Dao Lee **12** Chen Ning Yang
1958: 9 Igor Y Tamm **10** Ilya M Frank **15** Pavel A Cherenkov
1959: 11 Emilio Segre **15** Owen Chamberlain
1960: 13 Donald A Glaser
1961: 11 Robert Hofstadter, Rudolf L Mossbauer
1962: 10 Lev D Landau
1963: 11 J Hans Jensen **16** Eugene Paul Wigner **18** Maria Goeppert Mayer
1964: 17 Charles Hard Townes **25** Nikolai Gennadiyevich Basov **30** Aleksandr Mikhailovich Prokhorov
1965: 18 Shinichiro Tomonaga **22** Julian Seymour Schwinger, Richard Phillips Feynman
1966: 13 Alfred Kastler
1967: 17 Hans Albrecht Bethe
1968: 12 Luis W Alvarez
1969: 14 Murray Gell-Mann
1970: 12 Hannes Alfven **15** Louis Eugene Neel
1971: 11 Dennis Gabor
1972: 11 John Bardeen, Leon N Cooper **20** John Robert Schreiffer
1973: 8 Leo Esaki **11** Ivar Giaever **15** Brian D Josephson
1974: 12 Antony Hewish **13** Sir Martin Ryle
1975: 8 Aage Bohr **13** Ben R Mottelson **15** L James Rainwater
1976: 12 Samuel C C Ting **13** Burton Richter
1977: 13 John H Van Vleck, Sir Nevill Mott **15** Philip W Anderson
1978: 12 Arno A Penzias, Peter Kapitza (Pyotr Kapitza) **13** Robert

W Wilson
1979: 10 Abdus Salam **14** Sheldon Glashow, Steven Weinberg
1980: 9 Val L Fitch **12** James W Cronin
1981: 12 Kai M Siegbahn **14** Arthur Schawlow **19** Nicolaas Bloembergen
1982: 14 Kenneth G Wilson
1983: 14 William A Fowler **25** Subrahmanyan Chandrasekhar
1984: 11 Carlo Rubbia **15** Simon van der Meer
1985: 16 Klaus von Klitzing
1986: 10 Ernst Ruska, Gerd Binner **14** Heinrich Rohrer
1987: 12 K Alex Mueller **13** J Georg Bednorz
1988: 12 Leon M Lederman **14** Melvin Schwartz **15** Jack Steinberger
1989: 11 Hans Dehmelt **12** Norman Ramsey, Wolfgang Paul
1990: 12 Henry Kendall **13** Richard Taylor **14** Jerome Friedman
1991: 12 Pierre Gennes
1992: 13 George Charpak
1993: 12 Joseph Taylor, Russell Hulse
1994: 13 Clifford Shull **17** Bertram Brockhouse
1995: 11 Martin l Perl **15** Frederick Reines
1996: 9 David M Lee **16** Douglas D Osheroff **17** Robert C Richardson
1997: 9 Steven Chu **16** William D Phillips **20** Claude Cohen-Tannoudji
1998: 10 Daniel Tsui **12** Horst Stormer **14** Robert Laughlin
1999: 14 Geradus 't Hooft **15** Martinus Veitman
2000: 9 Jack Kilby **13** Zhores Alferov **14** Herbert Kroemer
2001: 10 Carl Wieman **11** Eric Cornell **16** Wolfgang Ketterie
2002: 14 Raymond Davis Jr **16** Masatoshi Koshiba, Riccardo Giacconi
2003: 14 Anthony Leggett, Vitaly Ginzburg **15** Alexei Abrikosov
2004: 10 David Gross **12** Frank Wilczek **14** David Politzer
2005: 9 John L. Hall **11** Roy J. Glauber **14** Theodor W. Hänsch

Peace:
1901: 13 Frederic Passy **15** Jean Henri Dunant
1902: 12 Elie Ducommun **18** Charles Albert Gobat
1903: 17 Sir William R Cremer
1904: 27 Institute of International Law
1905: 24 Baroness Bertha von Suttner
1906: 17 Theodore Roosevelt
1907: 12 Louis Renault **14** Ernesto T Moneta
1908: 12 Fredrik Bajer **14** Klas P

Arnoldson
1909: 16 Auguste Beernaert **35** Paul H Balluat d'Estournelles de Constant
1910: 24 International Peace Bureau
1911: 12 Alfred H Fried **13** Tobias M C Asser
1912: 9 Elihu Root
1913: 15 Henri La Fontaine
1917: 30 International Red Cross Committee
1919: 13 Woodrow Wilson
1920: 13 Leon Bourgeois
1921: 15 Christian L Lange **19** Karl Hjalmar Branting
1922: 14 Fridtjof Nansen
1925: 13 Charles G Dawes **26** Sir Joseph Austen Chamberlain
1926: 14 Aristide Briand **16** Gustav Stresemann
1927: 12 Ludwig Quidde **17** Ferdinand E Buisson
1929: 13 Frank B Kellogg
1930: 15 (Lars Olof Jonathan) Nathan Soderblom
1931: 10 Jane Addams **20** Nicholas Murray Butler
1933: 15 Sir Norman Angell
1934: 15 Arthur Henderson
1935: 16 Carl von Ossietzky
1936: 19 Carlos Saavedra Lamas
1937: 13 E A Robert Cecil (Viscount Cecil)
1938: 36 Nansen International Office for Refugees
1944: 30 International Red Cross Committee
1945: 11 Cordell Hull
1946: 9 John R Mott **11** Emily G Balch
1947: 21 Friends Service Council **31** American Friends Service Committee
1949: 11 John Boyd Orr (Baron Orr)
1950: 12 Ralph J Bunche
1951: 11 Leon Jouhaux
1952: 16 Albert Schweitzer
1953: 15 George C Marshall
1954: 51 Office of the United Nations High Commissioner for Refugees
1957: 14 Lester B Pearson
1958: 28 Rev Dominique Georges Henri Pire
1959: 16 Philip J Noel-Baker
1960: 14 Albert J Luthuli
1961: 15 Dag Hammarskjold
1962: 13 Linus C Pauling
1963: 25 League of Red Cross Societies **30** International Red Cross Committee
1964: 18 Martin Luther King Jr
1965: 26 United Nations Children's Fund (UNICEF)
1968: 10 Rene Cassin
1969: 30 International Labor Organ-

ization (ILO)

1970: 14 Norman E Borlaug

1971: 11 Willy Brandt

1973: 8 Le Duc Tho **15** Henry A Kissinger

1974: 10 Eisaku Sato **12** Sean Mac-Bride

1975: 15 Andrei D Sakharov

1976: 13 Betty Williams **15** Mairead Corrigan

1977: 20 Amnesty International

1978: 10 Anwar Sadat **13** Menachem Begin

1979: 12 Mother Teresa

1980: 19 Adolfo Perez Esquivel

1981: 51 Office of the United Nations High Commissioner for Refugees

1982: 10 Alva Myrdal **19** Alfonso Garcia Robles

1983: 10 Lech Walesa

1984: 17 Bishop Desmond Tutu

1985: 51 International Physicians for the Prevention of Nuclear War

1986: 10 Elie Wiesel

1987: 17 Oscar Arias Sanchez

1988: 31 United Nations peacekeeping troops

1989: 9 Dalai Lama

1990: 16 Mikhail Gorbachev

1991: 13 Aung San Suu Kyi

1992: 15 Rigoberta Menchu

1993: 9 F W de Klerk **13** Nelson Mandela

1994: 11 Yasir Arafat, Shimon Peres **12** Yitzhak Rabin

1995: 13 Joseph Rotblat

1996: 14 Jose Ramos Horta **23** Carlos Filepe, Ximenes Belo

1997: 12 Jody Williams

1998: 8 John Hume **12** David Trimble

1999: 22 Medecins Sans Frontieres (20 Doctors Without Borders)

2000: 10 Kim Dae-jung

2001: 9 Kofi Annan **13** United Nations

2002: 11 Jimmy Carter

2003: 11 Shirin Ebadi

2004: 14 Wangari Maathai

2005: 4 IAEA (International Atomic Energy Agency) **16** Mohamed El-Baradei

Economics:

1969: 12 Jan Tinbergen, Ragnar Frisch

1970: 14 Paul A Samuelson

1971: 13 Simon S Kuznets

1972: 13 Kenneth J Arrow, Sir John R Hicks

1973: 15 Wassily Leontief

1974: 12 Gunnar Myrdal **18** Friedrich A von Hayek

1975: 17 Tjalling C Koopmans **18** Leonid V Kantorovich

1976: 14 Milton Friedman

1977: 11 Bertil Ohlin, James E Meade

1978: 13 Herbert A Simon

1979: 14 Sir Arthur Lewis **15** Theodore Schultz

1980: 14 Lawrence R Klein

1981: 10 James Tobin

1982: 10 George J Stigler

1983: 12 Gerard Debreu

1984: 15 Sir Richard Stone

1985: 16 Franco Modigliani

1986: 19 James McGill Buchanan

1987: 12 Robert M Solow

1988: 13 Maurice Allais

1989: 14 Trygve Haavelmo

1990: 12 Merton Miller **13** William Sharpe **14** Harry Markowitz

1991: 11 Ronald Coase

1992: 10 Gary Becker

1993: 11 Robert Fogel **12** Douglas North

1994: 8 John Nash **12** John Harsanyi **14** Reinhard Selten

1995: 14 Robert E Lucas Jr.

1996: 14 James A Mirrlees **15** William S Vickrey

1997: 13 Myron S Scholes, Robert C Merton

1998: 10 Amartya Sen

1999: 12 Robert Mundell

2000: 12 James Heckman **14** Daniel McFadden

2001: 13 George Akerlof **14** A Michael Spence, Joseph Stiglitz

2002: 11 Vernon Smith **14** Daniel Kahneman

2003: 11 Robert Engle **12** Clive Granger

2004: 11 Finn Kydland **14** Edward Prescott

2005: 13 Robert J. Aumann **16** Thomas C. Schelling

nobility 5 elite, lords **7** dignity, majesty, peerage, primacy, royalty **8** breeding, eminence, grandeur, high rank, prestige, splendor **9** gentility, grandness, greatness, loftiness, sublimity, supremacy **10** blue bloods, mightiness, patricians, patriciate, upper crust **11** aristocracy, distinction, exaltedness, preeminence, stateliness, superiority **12** magnificence

nobility obliges
    French: 14 noblesse oblige

noble 3 don **4** high, just, lord, peer **5** famed, grand, great, lofty, moral, regal, royal **6** famous, gentle, honest, knight, lordly, squire, superb, worthy **7** awesome, courtly, eminent, ethical, exalted, grandee, stately, sublime, supreme, upright **8** baronial, cavalier, elevated, glorious, handsome, highborn, imperial, imposing, lordlike, majestic, princely, renowned, selfless, splendid, superior, virtuous **9** chevalier, dignified, estimable, excellent, exemplary, gentleman, honorable, patrician, personage, reputable **10** aristocrat, impressive, preeminent **11** magnanimous, magnificent, meritori-

ous, pureblooded, trustworthy **12** aristocratic, thoroughbred **13** distinguished, incorruptible
    French: 6 gentil

Noble House
    author: 12 James Clavell

nobleman 4 lord, peer **7** grandee **9** patrician **10** aristocrat

noblesse oblige 15 nobility obliges

noblewoman 4 dame, lady, rani **5** begum, queen **6** milady **7** czarina, duchess, empress, peeress, sultana **8** baroness, contessa, countess, maharani, princess **11** marchioness

Nobody Knows My Name
    author: 12 James Baldwin

Nobody's Fool
    author: 12 Richard Russo
    director: 12 Robert Benton
    cast: 8 Gene Saks (Wirf Wirfley) **10** Dylan Walsh (Peter Sullivan), Paul Newman (Sully Sullivan) **11** Bruce Willis (Carl Roebuck), Josef Sommer (Clive Peoples Jr) **12** Jessica Tandy (Beryl Peoples) **15** Melanie Griffith (Toby Roebuck) **17** Pruitt Taylor Vince (Rub Squeers) **20** Philip Seymour Hoffman (Officer Raymer)

nock 5 notch
    in: 5 arrow

nocturnal 4 dark **5** night **7** nightly, obscure **8** darkling **9** nighttime

nod 3 bob **4** doze, hail, show, sign **5** agree, greet, lapse, let up **6** assent, beckon, concur, drowse, motion, reveal, salute, signal **7** consent, drop off, fall off, gesture, signify **9** recognize

node 3 bud **4** bump, burl, hump, knob, knot, lump **5** bulge, joint **6** button **8** swelling **10** prominence, tumescence **11** excrescence **12** protuberance

nodule 3 sac, wen **4** bump, cyst, knob, knot, lump, stud **5** bulge **6** growth **8** swelling **9** outgrowth **10** projection, prominence, protrusion, tumescence **11** excrescence **12** protuberance

noel, Noel 4 yule **5** carol **8** yuletide **9** Christmas **13** Christmastide

No Exit
    author: 14 Jean-Paul Sartre

noggin 3 cup, mug **4** bean, head, pate **5** gourd **6** noodle

Noguchi, Hideyo
    field: 12 bacteriology
    nationality: 8 Japanese
    isolated: 8 syphilis

noise 3 ado, din **4** bang, blab, boom, echo, pass, roar, stir, wail **5** babel, blare, blast, bruit, rumor, sound, voice **6** bedlam, clamor, hubbub, racket, repeat, report, rumble, tumult, uproar **7** barrage, bluster, clatter, thunder **8** brawling, gabbling, rumbling, shouting **9** cacophony, cannonade, circulate, commotion, discharge

10 dissonance, hullabaloo **11** pandemonium **12** caterwauling, vociferation **13** reverberation

noiseless 5 quiet, still, tacit **6** hushed, silent **9** soundless, voiceless

noisemaker 4 bell, horn **5** siren **6** rattle **7** clacker, clapper, snapper, whistle

noisome 4 foul, rank **5** acrid, fetid, toxic **6** putrid, rotten, smelly **7** baneful, harmful, hurtful, noxious, reeking **8** mephitic, stinking **9** injurious, offensive, poisonous, unhealthy **10** malodorous, nauseating, pernicious **11** deleterious, detrimental **12** evil-smelling

noisy 4 loud **5** alive **6** lively, raging, shrill, stormy **7** blaring, blatant, furious, grating, jarring, rackety **8** animated, piercing, strident **9** clamorous, deafening, dissonant, turbulent **10** boisterous, clangorous, discordant, rampageous, resounding, thundering, thunderous, tumultuous, uproarious **11** cacophonous, tempestuous **12** earsplitting

Nolan, Lloyd
   born: 14 San Francisco CA
   roles: 7 Airport **12** Captain Queeg **22** Queeg **26** The Caine Mutiny Court Martial

Nolde, Emil
   real name: 10 Emil Hansen
   born: 5 Nolde **7** Germany
   artwork: 7 Prophet **10** Papua Youth **11** Tropical Sun **12** The Magicians, The Pentecost **13** The Last Supper, Three Russians **14** Doubting Thomas **20** Life of Maria Aegyptica **22** Christ Among the Children, Christ and the Adùlteress

nolens volens 10 willy-nilly **19** whether willing or not

noli me tangere 10 touch me not

nolle prosequi 14 do not prosecute **19** be unwilling to pursue

nolo contendere 21 I am unwilling to contend

no longer able to fight
   French: 12 hors de combat

no longer in existence 4 dead, gone, lost **7** defunct, died out, extinct **8** vanished

Nolte, Nick
   born: 7 Omaha NE
   roles: 4 Hulk **5** U-Turn, Weeds **7** The Deep, Cape Fear **10** Cannery Row **11** Lorenzo's Oil, Mother Night **12** I Love Trouble **13** Prince of Tides **14** Rich Man Poor Man **15** Forty-Eight Hours **16** North Dallas Forty **20** Breakfast of Champions

nomad 4 arab, hobo, okie **5** gypsy, mover, rover, stray, tramp **6** roamer **7** migrant, rambler, refugee, runaway, strayer, tuareg, vagrant **8** bohemian, emigrant, migrator, renegade, traveler, vagabond, wanderer **9** immigrant, itinerant, straggler

nomadic 6 roving **7** migrant, roaming, vagrant **8** drifting, vagabond **9** footloose, itinerant, migratory, strolling, traveling, wandering

nom de guerre 5 alias **7** war name **9** pseudonym **11** assumed name

nom de plume 5 alias **7** pen name **9** false name, pseudonym **11** assumed name, writing name

nomenclature 5 lingo, terms **6** jargon, naming **8** glossary, language, taxonomy **10** nomination, vocabulary

nominal 3 low **5** cheap, small **6** puppet **7** minimum, titular, trivial **8** baseless, moderate, official, so-called, trifling **9** pretended, professed, purported, suggested **10** groundless, ostensible, reasonable

nominate 3 tag **4** call, name, pick, term **5** elect, label, style **6** choose, invest, select **7** elevate, install, propose, suggest **9** authorize, recommend

nomination 8 election **9** accession, selection **10** suggestion

nominee 7 hopeful **8** aspirant, eligible **9** applicant, candidate **10** competitor, contestant

nonadjustable 5 fixed, rigid **9** immovable **10** inflexible

nonalcoholic 4 soft **15** nonintoxicating

nonattendance 3 cut **7** absence, truancy **11** absenteeism

nonbeliever 5 cynic, pagan **7** atheist, doubter, heathen, infidel, skeptic **8** agnostic, apostate **10** backslider, empiricist, questioner, unbeliever **11** disbeliever, freethinker **14** doubting Thomas

nonbinding 8 optional **9** voluntary **12** unimperative **13** discretionary

nonce 6 pro tem **7** present **9** time being

nonchalance 9 composure, unconcern **13** offhandedness
   French: 11 insouciance

nonchalant 3 lax **4** cool, idle, lazy **5** blase, slack **6** casual **7** languid, offhand, unmoved **8** careless, heedless, indolent, listless **9** apathetic, collected, easygoing, lethargic, unexcited, unheeding, unmindful, unruffled, unstirred, withdrawn **10** insensible, insouciant, phlegmatic, unaffected

noncombatant 7 neutral **8** civilian

noncommittal 3 mum **4** cool, mute, safe, wary **5** vague **7** careful, evasive, guarded, neutral, politic, prudent **8** cautious, discreet, reserved **9** ambiguous, equivocal, tentative **10** indecisive, indefinite, unspeaking **11** circumspect, temporizing

noncompliance 6 breach **7** failure, neglect **9** disregard **10** resistance **11** dereliction

noncompliant 6 unruly **7** defiant, froward, naughty, wayward **8** contrary, mutinous, perverse, stubborn **9** differing, dissident, fractious, objecting, obstinate, resistant, resistive, undutiful **10** disorderly, dissenting, rebellious, refractory, unorthodox, unyielding

non compos mentis 14 not of sound mind **17** mentally incapable

nonconfirming 7 denying **8** negating, refuting **9** rejecting **10** disavowing **11** disclaiming, repudiating

nonconformist 3 nut **4** beat, card **5** freak, hippy, loner, rebel **6** oddity, weirdo **7** heretic, oddball, radical **8** bohemian, crackpot, deserter, maverick, original, reformer, renegade, vagabond **9** character, dissenter, dissident, eccentric, exception, insurgent, protester, screwball **10** dissenting, iconoclast, rebellious, schismatic **13** individualist, revolutionary

nonconformity 5 quirk **6** oddity **7** anomaly **9** deviation, rebellion **10** aberration, divergence, resistance

noncongenial 6 unlike **8** opposite **9** different, disparate, ill-suited, unrelated **10** dissimilar **11** disagreeing **12** disagreeable, incompatible **13** unsympathetic

nondescript 5 usual, vague **8** ordinary **9** amorphous, colorless **11** stereotyped **12** unimpressive **13** characterless, undistinctive, unexceptional **15** undistinguished

nonentity 4 zero **6** cipher, nobody **7** nothing, no-count, nullity **8** small-fry, unperson **10** mediocrity

nonessential 5 frill **6** luxury, trivia **7** trivial **9** extrinsic, secondary, trimmings **10** accidental, extraneous, incidental, irrelevant, peripheral, subsidiary

nonexclusive 4 open **6** public, shared **7** divided **12** unrestricted

nonexistence 4 lack, void **7** absence **8** oblivion **11** nothingness

nonexistent 4 gone **5** short **6** absent **7** lacking, missing, wanting **11** unavailable **12** insufficient

nonindulgence 7 refusal **8** eschewal, forgoing **9** avoidance, eschewing **10** abstaining, abstention, refraining **11** forbearance **16** nonparticipation

nonirritating 4 calm **5** bland **6** benign **7** calming **8** soothing, tranquil **9** temperate

non licet 13 it is not lawful **16** it is not permitted

non liquet 12 it is not clear **14** it is not evident

nonmaterialistic 9 spiritual **10** idealistic **12** intellectual

nonmember 5 guest 7 outcast, visitor 8 outsider

nonnatural 7 manmade 9 synthetic 10 artificial, fabricated, factitious 12 manufactured

nonobservance 6 breach 7 failure, neglect 9 disregard 11 dereliction 13 noncompliance

non obstante 15 notwithstanding

no-nonsense 4 grim, hard 5 grave, harsh, rigid, sober, stern 6 ardent, intent, severe, solemn, strict 7 earnest, serious 8 critical, diligent, exacting, resolute 9 committed, dedicated, demanding, hardnosed, practical, pragmatic, unbending, unsparing 10 determined, hardheaded, purposeful, sobersided 12 businesslike

nonpareil 5 elite, ideal, model, super 6 symbol, unique 7 epitome, paragon, pattern, supreme 8 exemplar 9 unequaled, unmatched, unrivaled 10 apotheosis 11 exceptional, unsurpassed 13 extraordinary 14 representative
French: 11 ne plus ultra 14 creme de la creme

nonparticipation 7 refusal 8 eschewal, forgoing 9 avoidance, eschewing 10 abstaining, abstention, refraining, sitting out 11 forbearance

nonpartisan 4 fair, just 8 unbiased, unswayed 9 equitable, impartial, objective, unbigoted 10 impersonal, uninvolved 12 freethinking, unaffiliated, unimplicated, uninfluenced, unprejudiced 13 disinterested

nonpermissible 9 forbidden 10 disallowed 11 intolerable 12 inadmissible, unacceptable

nonplus 4 balk, faze, foil, halt, stop 5 abash, stump, upset 6 baffle, bother, dismay, muddle, puzzle, stymie 7 astound, confuse, disturb, mystify, perplex 8 astonish, bewilder, confound, deadlock 9 dumbfound, embarrass 10 disconcert 11 flabbergast 14 discountenance

nonplussed, nonplused 5 at sea, fazed 7 at a loss, baffled, floored, mixed-up, muddled, puzzled, stumped 8 confused 9 befuddled, mystified, unsettled 10 bewildered, confounded 12 disconcerted

nonpoisonous 4 safe 8 nontoxic 11 nonvenomous, nonvirulent

non possumus 8 we cannot

nonpresence 3 cut 7 absence, truancy 11 absenteeism

nonprofessional 3 lay 4 laic 7 dabbler
French: 7 amateur 10 dilettante

non prosequitur 15 he does not pursue

non repetatur 11 do not repeat

nonresident 7 tourist, visitor 9 transient 11 out-of-towner

nonresistance 6 assent 7 pliancy 8 docility, giving in, meekness, yielding 9 deference, obedience, passivity 10 compliance, conforming, conformity, pliability, submission 12 acquiescence, complaisance

nonresistant 4 meek 6 docile, pliant 7 passive, pliable 8 deferent, obedient, yielding 9 compliant 10 conforming, submissive 11 acquiescent, complaisant, deferential

nonscholarly 8 untaught 9 unlearned 10 uneducated, unlettered, unpedantic, unschooled

nonsectarian 10 ecumenical 11 interchurch 16 undenominational 17 nondenominational 19 interdenominational

nonsense 3 rot 4 bosh, bunk 5 folly, trash 6 antics, babble, drivel, joking, piffle 7 baloney, blather, bombast, chatter, fooling, garbage, hogwash, inanity, prattle, rubbish, trifles, twaddle 8 claptrap, flummery 9 absurdity, frivolity, gibberish, high jinks, horseplay, moonshine, silliness, stupidity 10 balderdash, flapdoodle, tomfoolery, triviality 11 foolishness, shenanigans 12 childishness, extravagance 13 facetiousness, ludicrousness, senselessness 14 ridiculousness 15 meaninglessness

nonsensical 4 wild 5 crazy, funny, inane, silly 6 absurd, stupid 7 asinine, comical, foolish 8 farcical 9 facetious, laughable, ludicrous 10 irrational, ridiculous

non sequitur 15 it does not follow

nonspecialized 11 generalized

nonspecific 4 hazy 5 vague 7 general, inexact 9 imprecise, uncertain 10 indefinite, undetailed 11 approximate, generalized

nonspiritual 7 earthly, profane, secular, worldly 8 material, temporal 13 materialistic

nonstop 7 endless, express 8 constant, unbroken 9 incessant 10 continuous, unrelieved 11 unremitting 12 interminable

nonstudious 9 unlearned 10 uneducated, unlettered, unpedantic, unschooled

nontaxable 9 sheltered 10 deductible

nontechnical 6 simple 8 academic 13 uncomplicated

nontypical 7 unusual 8 abnormal, uncommon 9 anomalous, irregular 16 unrepresentative

non-U see 12 Mitford, Nancy

nonuniform 5 mixed 6 unlike 7 altered, changed, erratic, unalike 8 changing, variable 9 deviating, different, irregular, multiform 10 dissimilar

11 fluctuating, nonstandard 12 inconsistent

nonvital 9 accessory, extrinsic 10 disposable, expendable, incidental 11 dispensable, superfluous, unessential, unimportant, unnecessary

nonvocational 8 academic

nonvolitional 6 reflex 8 unwilled 9 automatic 11 instinctive, involuntary, spontaneous 12 uncontrolled

noodle 4 bean, head, pate 5 gourd, pasta 6 noggin 8 practice 9 improvise

nook 3 den 4 cove, lair 5 haven, niche 6 alcove, cavity, corner, cranny, dugout, recess, refuge 7 retreat, shelter 8 hideaway 9 cubbyhole 10 depression 11 hiding place

noon 6 midday, zenith 8 high noon, meridian

no one contradicting
Latin: 19 nemine contradicente

no one dissenting
Latin: 18 nemine dissentiente

noose 3 tie 4 bond, hang, loop 5 catch, hitch, lasso, snare 6 choker, entrap, halter, lariat, tether

Nootka
language family: 8 Wakashan
tribe: 5 Makah 6 Hoiath, Ozette 7 Ahosath, Nitinat 8 Machlath, Otsosath, Tokwaath 9 Ihatisath, Mowachath, Nochalath, Qayokwath, Tsishaath, Yoloilath 10 Hishkwiath, Hochoqtlis, Manohisath, Tlaokwiath 11 Chiqtlisath, Hopachasath, Qiltsamaath
location: 10 Washington 15 Vancouver Island
leader: 8 Maquinna 10 Wikaninish
related to: 5 Makah
noted for: 7 whaling

Nordhoff, Charles
author of: 17 Mutiny on the Bounty (with James Norman Hall)

Nordic Mythology see 21 Scandinavian Mythology

Norge see 6 Norway

noria 10 water wheel

norm 3 par 4 rule, type 5 gauge, model 7 average, measure, pattern 8 standard 9 barometer, criterion, yardstick 12 measuring rod

normal 3 fit, par 4 sane 5 sound, usual 6 steady 7 average, healthy, natural, regular, typical, uniform 8 constant, expected, mediocre, middling, ordinary, rational, reliable, standard 9 incessant, steadfast, unceasing 10 conforming, consistent, continuous, dependable, reasonable, unchanging 11 conformable, rightminded, unremitting 12 conventional 13 uninterrupted 14 representative

Normandy, Normandie
beach: 4 Gold, Juno, Utah 5 Omaha, Sword

borders: 7 Picardy **8** Brittany **14** English Channel
church/shrine: 12 Saint Etienne **15** Mont Saint Michel
city: 4 Caen, St. Lo **5** Rouen **7** Le Havre **9** Cherbourg
event: 4 D Day **17** Operation Overlord
region of: 6 France
river: 5 Seine

Norma Rae
director: 10 Martin Ritt
cast: 9 Pat Hingle **10** Ron Liebman, Sally Field **11** Beau Bridges
Oscar for: 4 song **7** actress (Field)
song: 16 It Goes Like It Goes

Norn
origin: 12 Scandinavian
form: 6 virgin **7** goddess
personifies: 4 fate
original Norn: 5 Urdar
the three: 3 Urd **5** Skuld **8** Verdandi
known as: 12 weird sisters

Norris, Frank
author of: 6 The Pit **8** McTeague **10** The Octopus

Norse Mythology
abode of man: 7 Midgard **10** Mithgarthr
afterworld: 6 Manala **7** Tuonela
began race of giants: 4 Ymir
blacksmith/hero: 9 Ilmarinen
boar: 10 Saehrimnir
bridge of gods: 7 Bifrost
dragon: 6 Fafnir
dwarf: 5 Skuld **7** Andvari
earth is made from: 4 Ymir
elf: 4 Norn **8** Verdandi
epic: 8 Kaleva
final battle: 15 Gotterdammerung **17** Twilight of the Gods
first god: 4 Buri **7** Forsete, Forseti
first man: 3 Ask
first woman: 5 Embla
folk hero: 8 Kalevala
giant: 4 Loki **5** Jotun, Thrym **6** Thiazi, Thjazi **7** Skrymir
giantess: 3 Urd **5** Thokk **9** Angerboda, Angrbodha, Angurboda
giant's realm: 9 Jotunheim
goat: 7 Heidrun
goddesses: 7 Asynjur
goddess of death: 3 Hel
goddess of forbidden marriages: 4 Lofn
goddess of marriage: 4 Frey **5** Freyr
goddess of peace: 4 Frey **5** Freyr
goddess of prosperity: 4 Frey **5** Freyr
goddess of spring: 4 Idun **5** Iduna, Ithun **6** Ithunn
goddess of the sea: 3 Ran
god of beauty/radiance: 5 Baldr **6** Balder, Baldur
god of dawn: 8 Heimdall
god of farming: 4 Thor
god of fire: 4 Loki
god of knowledge: 4 Odin **5** Othin

corresponds to Germanic: 5 Wotan
god of justice: 7 Forseti
god of light: 8 Heimdall
god of music: 5 Bragi
god of navigation: 5 Niord, Njord
god of poetry: 4 Odin **5** Bragi, Othin
corresponds to Germanic: 5 Wotan
god of prosperity: 5 Niord, Njord
god of rain: 4 Thor
god of sea: 5 Aegir, Mimir
god of thunder: 4 Thor
god of underworld: 8 Niflheim
god of victory: 3 Tyr
god of war: 4 Odin **5** Othin
corresponds to Germanic: 5 Wotan
god of wind: 5 Niord, Njord
god of wisdom: 4 Odin **5** Othin
corresponds to Germanic: 5 Wotan
hero: 11 Vainamoinen **12** Lemminkainen
home of dead: 3 Hel
king: 5 Gjuki
magician: 11 Joukahainen
magic necklace: 11 Brisingamen
misty void: 11 Ginnungagap
mountain: 11 Hindarfjall
nature spirit: 7 Eriking
oak tree: 9 Barnstock, Branstock
Odin's court/hall: 8 Valhalla
Odin's father: 3 Bor
Odin's horse: 8 Sleipnir
Odin's magic ring: 8 Draupnir
Odin's palace: 9 Gladsheim
Odin's raven: 5 Hugin, Munin
Odin's spear: 6 Gungni
Odin's throne: 10 Hlidskjalf
Odin's wolf: 4 Geri **5** Freki
race of gods: 5 Vanir
saga: 8 Vulsunga
sea monster: 6 Kraken
serpent: 7 Nidhogg **11** Jormungandr
Sigmund's sword: 4 Gram
slave: 8 Kullervo
sorceress: 5 Louhi **8** Grimhild
Thor's hammer: 7 Miolnir
Thor's servant: 7 Thialfi
tree with three roots: 9 Iggdrasil, Yggdrasil
Valkyrie: 8 Brynhild **9** Brunhilde, Sigrdrifa **11** Brunnehilde
virgin goddess: 3 Urd **4** Norn **5** Skuld, Urdar **8** Verdandi
warrior: 8 Baresark **9** Berserker
watchdog: 4 Garm
wolf monster: 6 Fenrir, Fenris
north 5 polar, upper **6** arctic

North America
nation: 4 Cuba **5** Haiti **6** Belize, Canada, Mexico, Panama **7** Bahamas, Jamaica **8** Barbados, Honduras **9** Costa Rica, Guatemala, Nicaragua **10** El Salvador, Puerto Rico, Saint Lucia **12** Saint Vincent, United States **17** Dominican Republic, Trinidad and

Tobago **28** Saint Vincent and the Grenadines
desert: 6 Mojave **7** Painted, Sonoran **11** Death Valley
island: 4 Long **6** Baffin, Cayman, Kodiak **7** Antigua, Bermuda, Iceland **8** Aleutian, Catalina, Thousand **9** Antilles, Greenland, Nantucket, Vancouver **10** Cape Breton **12** Newfoundland, Prince Edward **14** Queen Charlotte
ocean/sea/bay: 6 Arctic, Baffin, Bering, Hudson, Mexico **7** Chukchi, Lincoln, Pacific **8** Amundsen, Atlantic, Beaufort, Labrador **9** Caribbean, Greenland **10** California, Chesapeake, St Lawrence
river: 3 Red **4** Ohio **5** Peace, Snake, Yukon **6** Hudson **8** Arkansas, Colorado, Columbia, Missouri **9** Churchill, Mackenzie, Rio Grande **10** St Lawrence **11** Mississippi **12** Saskatchewan
lake: 4 Erie **5** Huron **7** Ontario **8** Michigan, Superior, Winnipeg **9** Great Bear, Nicaragua **10** Great Lakes, Great Slave
mountain range: 5 Ozark, Rocky **6** Alaska **7** Cascade **9** Blue Ridge **10** Laurentian **11** Appalachian, Sierra Madre **12** Sierra Nevada
highest point: 6 Denali **13** Mount McKinley
lowest point: 11 Death Valley
city: 4 Nome **5** Miami **6** Boston, Dallas, Denver, Havana, Ottawa, Quebec **7** Atlanta, Calgary, Chicago, Detroit, Houston, Memphis, New York, Phoenix, Seattle, Toronto **8** Montreal, Portland, San Diego **9** Anchorage, Milwaukee, Reykjavik, Vancouver **10** Kansas City, Los Angeles, Mexico City, New Orleans, Washington **11** Philadelphia, San Antonio, San Francisco
mineral: 3 oil, tin **4** coal, gold, lead, salt, zinc **6** cobalt, copper, nickel, quartz, silver **7** iron ore, mercury, sulphur, uranium **8** aluminum, antimony, asbestos, chromium, platinum, titanium, tungsten **9** magnesium, manganese, petroleum **10** molybdenum, natural gas

Northanger Abbey
author: 10 Jane Austen
character: 8 Mrs Allen **10** John Thorpe **12** James Morland **14** Isabella Thorpe **16** Catherine Morland
Tilney family: 5 Henry **7** Captain, Eleanor, General

North by Northwest
director: 15 Alfred Hitchcock
cast: 9 Cary Grant **10** James Mason **11** Leo G Carroll **12** Martin Landau **13** Eva Marie Saint **17** Jessie Royce Landis
setting (climax): 13 Mount Rushmore
score: 15 Bernard Herrmann

North Carolina
 abbreviation: **2** NC **4** N Car
 nickname: **7** Tar Heel **8** Old North **10**
  Turpentine
 capital: **7** Raleigh
 largest city: **9** Charlotte
 others: **4** Bath **6** Durham, Lenoir,
  Shelby, Wilson **7** Edenton, Hickory,
  Kinston, New Bern, Roxboro, Tar-
  boro **8** Gastonia **9** Albemarle, Asheville, Goldsboro, Henderson, Kitty
  Hawk, Lumberton **10** Chapel Hill,
  Greensboro, Greenville, Kannapolis,
  Wilmington **11** Statesville, Thomasville, Williamston **12** Fayetteville,
  Jacksonville, Winston-Salem
 college: **4** Duke, Elon **7** Catawba **8**
  Davidson **10** Wake Forest
 feature:
  battle site: **18** Guilford Courthouse
  national park: **19** Great Smoky
   Mountains (with Tennessee)
  national seashore: **11** Cape Lookout **12** Cape Hatteras
 tribe: **3** Eno **5** Coree **6** Cheraw **7** Buffalo, Moratok, Pamlico **8** Chowanoc,
  Hatteras **9** Tuscarora
 people: **6** O Henry (William Sidney
  Porter) **7** tarheel **11** Billy Graham,
  John Edwards, Thomas Wolfe **13**
  Dolley (Dolly) Madison, Edward R
  Murrow, Michael Jordan **14** Richard
  Gatling
  explorer: **6** de Soto **8** de Ayllon **9**
   Verrazano
 island: **7** Roanoke
 lake: **6** Norman, Phelps **7** Fontana **8**
  Waccamaw **12** Mattamuskeet
 land rank: **12** twenty-eighth
 mountain: **5** Black, Unaka **6** Harris **9**
  Blue Ridge **10** Great Smoky **13**
  Clingman's Dome
  highest point: **8** Mitchell
 physical feature: **10** Outer Banks **11**
  French Broad **15** Little Tennessee
  cape: **4** Fear **7** Lookout **8** Hatteras
  plateau: **8** Piedmont
  sea: **8** Atlantic
  sound: **4** Core **5** Bogue **7** Croatan,
   Pamlico
  swamp: **6** Dismal
 president: **9** James Polk **13** Andrew
  Johnson
 river: **3** Haw, Tar **4** Fear **5** Neuse **6**
  Chowan, Lumber, Peedee, Yadkin **7**
  Roanoke, Wateree
 state admission: **7** twelfth
 state bird: **8** cardinal
 state fish: **11** channel bass
 state flower: **7** dogwood **9** goldenrod
 state motto: **20** To Be Rather Than
  To Seem
 state song: **16** The Old North State
 state tree: **4** pine
 state dance: **4** shag
North Dakota
 abbreviation: **2** ND **4** N Dak
 nickname: **5** Sioux **11** Flickertail **16**
  Land of the Dakotas
 capital: **8** Bismarck
 largest city: **5** Fargo
 others: **5** Minot **9** Bottineau, Jamestown, Williston **10** Grand Forks
 college: **4** Mary **9** Jamestown
 feature:
  dam: **4** Oahe **8** Garrison
  garden: **18** International Peace
  national park: **17** Theodore Roosevelt
  tribe: **5** Sioux **6** Mandan **7** Arikara,
   Hidatsa **8** Chippewa
 people: **12** Eric Sevareid
  explorer: **6** Carver **8** Thompson,
   Varennes **13** Lewis and Clark
 lake: **5** Stump **6** Devils **9** Sakakawea
 land rank: **11** seventeenth
 mountain: **6** Turtle **8** Killdeer **10**
  Black Butte
  highest point: **10** White Butte
 physical feature:
  basin: **9** Williston
  plain: **8** The Slope
  valley: **8** Red River
 river: **3** Red **4** Park, Rush **5** Cedar,
  Goose, Heart, James, Knife, Mouse **6**
  Souris **7** Deslacs, Pembina **8** Missouri, Cheyenne, Wild Rice **9** Otter
  Tail **10** Cannonball **11** Yellowstone
  12 Boise de Sioux **14** Little Missouri
  18 Red River of the North
 state admission: **8** fortieth **11** thirty-
  ninth (with South Dakota)
 state bird: **17** western meadowlark
 state fish: **12** northern pike
 state flower: **15** wild prairie rose
 state motto: **45** Liberty and Union
  Now and Forever One and Inseparable
 state song: **15** North Dakota Hymn
 state tree: **11** American elm
North Dallas Forty
 director: **11** Ted Kotcheff
 based on story by: **9** Peter Gent
 cast: **8** Mac Davis **9** Nick Nolte **11**
  Dayle Haddon **14** Charles Durning
Northern Crown
 constellation of: **14** Corona Borealis
Northern Exposure
 network: **3** CBS
 creator: **10** John Falsey **11** Joshua
  Brand
 cast: **9** Rob Morrow (Joel Fleischman)
  10 John Collum (Holling Vincoeur)
  11 Barry Corbin (Maurice Minni-
  field), Elaine Miles (Marilyn Whirlwind), John Corbett (Chris Stevens),
  Peg Phillips (Ruth-Anne Miller) **12**
  Cynthia Geary (Shelly Tambo Vin-
  coeur), Janine Turner (Maggie
  O'Connell) **14** Darren E Burrows (Ed
  Chigliak)
Northern Rhodesia see **6** Zambia
North Korea see **5** Korea
North Star State
 nickname of: **9** Minnesota

North Vietnam see **7** Vietnam
Northwest Passage
 director: **9** King Vidor
 author: **14** Kenneth Roberts
 cast: **10** Ruth Hussey **11** Robert
  Young **12** Spencer Tracy **13** Walter
  Brennan
Northwest Territories
 abbreviation: **3** NWT
 borders: **7** Alberta **11** Arctic Ocean,
  Beaufort Sea **12** Saskatchewan **15**
  British Columbia
 city: **6** Inuvik **8** Hay River **9** Fort
  Smith **11** Yellowknife **12** Frobisher
  Bay
 country: **6** Canada
 island: **5** Banks **7** Melville **8** Bathurst
  Somerset, Victoria **13** Prince Patrick
 lake: **9** Great Bear **10** Great Slave
 mineral: **3** oil **4** gold, lead, zinc **6** silver **8** tungsten **9** petroleum
 native: **5** Inuit **6** Eskimo
North wind
 associated with: **6** Boreas
Norway
 other name: **5** Norge **20** Land of the
  Midnight Sun
 capital: **4** Oslo **11** Christiania
 largest city: **4** Oslo
 others: **3** Gol, Nes **4** Bodo, Moss,
  Odda, Rena, Voss **5** Bjort, Floro, Ha-
  mar, Molde, Skien, Skjak, Vadso **6**
  Bergen, Horton, Larvik, Narvik,
  Tromso **7** Alesund, Arendal, Dram-
  men, Harstad, Sandnes **8** Aalesund,
  Kirkenes **9** Stavanger, Trondheim **10**
  Hammerfest **12** Kristiansand
 division: **3** Amt **4** Oslo **5** Fylke,
  Troms **6** Bergen, Opland, Tromso **7**
  Finmark, Hedmark, Ostfold **8** Lete-
  mark, Nordland, Rogaland, Vestfold
  9 Ostlandet
  former: **11** Kalmar Union
  province called: **6** fylker
 government:
  legislature: **8** Storting
 head of state: **4** king
 measure: **3** fot, mal **4** alen **5** kande **6**
  fathom **7** skieppe **9** korntonde
 monetary unit: **3** ore **5** krone
 weight: **3** lod **4** mark, pund **10**
  bismerpund
 island: **4** Vega **5** Bomlo, Donna,
  Froya, Hitra, Hopen, Senja, Smola,
  Soroy **6** Alsten, Averoy, Bouvet, Hin-
  noy, Karmoy, Kvaloy, Solund, Van-
  noy **7** Gurskoy, Lofoten, Mageroy,
  Seiland **8** Jan Mayen, Svalbard
 lake: **4** Alte **5** Ister, Mjosa, Snasa **6**
  Femund **7** Rostavn, Tunnsjo
 mountain: **5** Sogne **6** Kjolen **7**
  Numedal **8** Blodfjel, Snohetta, Telemark, Ustetind **9** Harteigen, Jotunheim, Langfjell, Ramnanosi
  10 Dovrefjell, Galdhoepig, Glitretind,
  Vibmesnosi **11** Myrdalfjell **14** Aardangerjokul, Hallingskarvet, Skagastolstind

highest point: 12 Galdhopiggen **13** Glittertinden

river: 3 Ena **4** Alta, Klar, Otra, Rana, Tana, Teno **5** Bardu, Begna, Glama, Lagen, Orkla, Otter, Rauma, Reisa **6** Glomma, Lougen, Namsen, Pasvik

sea: 5 North **6** Arctic **7** Barents **8** Atlantic **9** Norwegian, Skagerrak

physical feature:
  cape: 4 Naze **7** Nordkyn **8** Nordkapp **9** Lindesnes
  fjord: 4 Oslo **5** Sogne
  glacier: 12 Jostedalsbre
  inlet: 2 Is **3** Kob, Ran **4** Alst, Ands, Bokn, Nord, Ofot, Salt, Sunn, Tyri, Vest **5** fiord, fjord, Folda, Lakse, Sogne **6** Bjorna, Hadsel **7** Hortens **9** Trondheim
  plateau: 5 Doure, Dovre, Fjeld **9** Hardanger

people: 4 Lapp **5** Samme **6** Nordic, Viking
  artist: 5 Munch
  author: 5 Ibsen **6** Hamsun, Undset **7** Holberg **8** Bjornson **9** Wergeland
  composer: 5 Grieg **7** Sinding **8** Svendsen
  explorer: 4 Eric, Leif, Mohn, Sars **6** Nansen **8** Amundsen
  explorer/statesman: 6 Nansen **8** Amundsen **9** Heyerdahl
  king: 4 Olaf, Olav **5** Olave, Oscar **6** Haakon, Harold, Magnus, Sverre
  mathematics: 4 Abel
  Nazi collaborator: 8 Quisling
  Norse god/goddess: 3 Sif, Tyr **4** Frey, Idun, Loki, Odin, Thor **5** Bragi, Freya, Hoder, Woden **6** Balder, Eostre, Frigga, Hermod
  sculptor: 8 Vigeland

language: 4 Lapp **5** Norse **6** Bokmal **7** Nynorsk, Riksmal **8** Landsmal, Samnorsk **9** Landsmaal, Norwegian

religion: 19 Evangelical Lutheran **22** National Church of Norway

place:
  castle: 8 Akershus
  cathedral: 7 Nidaras
  museum: 7 Kon Tiki **10** Viking Ship **15** Polar Expedition
  park: 7 Frogner

former colony: 7 Vinland

feature:
  dance: 6 gangar **7** halling **8** springar **9** spingleik
  literature form: 4 edda, saga

food:
  bread: 8 flat brod
  cheese: 3 Ost **7** gjetost **9** gammelost, Jarlsberg
  drink: 7 aquavit

Norwegian Mythology *see* **21** Scandinavian Mythology

nose
  sense of: 5 smell
  part: 7 nostril **14** olfactory patch

nosegay 4 posy **7** bouquet **10** tussymussy

nosiness 6 prying **9** curiosity **15** inquisitiveness

nostalgia 6 pining, regret **7** longing **11** remembrance **12** homesickness **13** regretfulness

Nostradamus
  name: 7 Michael **17** Michelde Notredame
  occupation: 7 prophet **9** physician **10** astrologer **13** metaphysicist
  wrote: 9 Centuries

Nostromo
  author: 12 Joseph Conrad

nostrum 4 balm, cure, dose, drug **5** draft **6** elixir, physic, potion, remedy **7** cure-all, formula, panacea **8** medicine **9** treatment **10** medicament **12** prescription

nosy, nosey 6 prying, snoopy **7** all ears, curious **8** snooping **9** intrusive **11** inquisitive, overcurious **13** eavesdropping

nota bene 8 note well **10** take notice

notability 4 fame **6** import, moment, renown **8** eminence **9** celebrity **10** importance, prominence **11** consequence, distinction, preeminence **12** significance

notable 3 VIP **4** name **5** famed, wheel **6** biggie, bigwig, famous, marked **7** eminent, salient **8** luminary, renowned, striking **9** celebrity, dignitary, personage, prominent, reputable **10** celebrated, pronounced, remarkable **11** conspicuous, outstanding, personality **13** distinguished

notably 7 visibly **8** markedly **10** distinctly, strikingly **11** prominently **12** unmistakably **13** conspicuously, outstandingly

not alike 8 distinct **9** different, differing, disparate, divergent **10** dissimilar **11** contrasting

notation 5 entry **10** memorandum

not bright 3 dim **4** dark, dull **5** dense, dusky, murky **6** cloudy, stupid **7** clouded **8** obscured **13** unilluminated

notch 3 cut **4** dent, mark, nick, nock **5** grade, level, score **6** degree **7** scoring, scratch **11** indentation

not disclosed
  Italian: 7 in petto

note 4 bill, fame, line, mark **5** bread, draft, enter, green, money, write **6** regard, renown **7** epistle, jot down, lettuce, message, missive, put down, scratch, set down, voucher **8** currency, dispatch, eminence, mark down, perceive **9** bank draft, celebrity, greenback **10** communique, importance, memorandum, prominence, reputation **11** certificate, consequence, distinction

notebook 3 log **5** diary **6** record **7** journal **9** looseleaf
  French: 6 cahier

noted 6 famous **7** eminent **8** renowned **9** prominent, reputable **10** celebrated, remarkable **11** illustrious, outstanding **13** distinguished

Notes from the Underground
  author: 16 Fyodor Dostoevsky

note well
  Latin: 8 nota bene

noteworthy 7 unusual **8** singular **9** important **10** remarkable **11** outstanding, significant, substantial **12** considerable **13** distinguished, exceptionable

not far from 4 near **6** all but, almost, nearly **7** close to **8** not quite **13** approximately

not genuine 4 fake, sham **5** bogus, false, phony **6** ersatz, unreal **7** feigned **8** spurious **9** imitation, insincere, pretended, synthetic **10** artificial, fraudulent **11** counterfeit **12** hypocritical
  Latin: 8 mala fide

not germane 9 extrinsic, unrelated **10** extraneous, immaterial, irrelevant **11** incongruous, inconsonant, unconnected **12** incompatible, nonessential **13** inappropriate

not guilty 5 clear **8** innocent **9** blameless **10** inculpable, unblamable

nothing 3 air, nix, zip **4** none, zero **5** stuff, trash, zilch **6** bauble, bubble, cipher, gewgaw, naught, trifle, trivia **7** duck egg, nullity, rubbish, trinket **8** goose egg **9** bagatelle, obscurity **14** insignificance **16** inconsequentials
  Latin: 5 nihil

nothing is created from nothing
  Latin: 16 ex nihilo nihil fit

nothingness 4 void **5** death **8** oblivion **9** emptiness **10** triviality **12** nonexistence **14** insignificance

Nothing Sacred
  director: 14 William Wellman
  cast: 13 Carole Lombard, Frederic March **14** Walter Connolly
  score: 11 Oscar Levant
  remade as: 10 Living It Up
  script: 8 Ben Hecht

nothing unless it is good
  Latin: 12 nil nisi bonum

nothing without the divine will
  Latin: 13 nil sine numine
  motto of: 8 Colorado

notice 3 eye, see **4** dope, heed, info, mark **5** goods **6** poster, rating, regard, review, take in **7** leaflet, mention, observe, warning **8** brochure, circular, critique, handbill, pamphlet **9** appraisal, attention, knowledge, statement **10** advisement, cognizance, disclosure **11** declaration, information **12** announcement, intelligence **13** advertisement, communication, specification

noticeable 5 clear, plain **7** evident, obvious **8** definite, distinct, manifest, palpable, striking **10** observable **11** appreciable, conspicuous, perceivable, perceptible **12** unmistakable

notification 4 news, word **6** advice, report **7** message, release **8** bulletin, dispatch **9** statement **10** communique **11** information **12** announcement, intelligence **13** communication

notify 4 tell, warn **6** advise, inform **7** apprise, let know **8** acquaint, send word **9** enlighten

not indigenous 5 alien **6** exotic **7** foreign **8** imported **9** nonnative **10** extraneous **11** naturalized

notion 4 idea, view, whim **5** fancy, humor, quirk **6** belief, vagary, whimsy **7** caprice, conceit, concept, opinion **8** crotchet **9** suspicion **10** conception, intimation **12** eccentricity

not native 5 alien **6** exotic **7** foreign **8** imported **10** extraneous **11** naturalized

not of sound mind
  Latin: **15** non compos mentis

not ordinary 4 rare **6** exotic, unique **7** bizarre, foreign, strange, unusual **8** peculiar, singular, uncommon **9** anomalous, different, fantastic **11** distinctive, outstanding **14** unconventional

notoriety 4 blot **5** shame, stain **6** infamy, stigma **7** scandal **8** disgrace, dishonor, ignominy **9** discredit, disrepute **11** degradation

notorious 6 arrant **7** blatant, glaring **8** infamous, renowned **9** egregious **10** celebrated, outrageous **11** outstanding

Notorious
  director: **15** Alfred Hitchcock
  cast: **9** Cary Grant **11** Claude Rains **12** Louis Calhern **13** Ingrid Bergman

not pertinent 9 unrelated **10** extraneous, immaterial, irrelevant **11** incongruous, unconnected **13** inappropriate

not quite 6 all but, almost, nearly

Notre Dame 9 cathedral
  style: **6** Gothic
  location: **5** Paris
  setting for: **20** Hunchback of Notre Dame
  feature: **7** statues **9** gargoyles

not required 8 elective, optional **9** voluntary

not too seriously
  Latin: **13** cum grano salis

Notus
  origin: **5** Greek
  personifies: **9** south wind

not wanted
  French: **6** de trop

notwithstanding
  Latin: **11** non obstante

not working 4 dead **8** inactive **10** unemployed **11** inoperative **12** unresponsive

Nouakchott
  capital of: **10** Mauritania

Noumea
  capital of: **12** New Caledonia

nourish 4 feed **5** nurse **6** suckle **7** nurture, sustain

nourishing 4 rich **6** hearty **7** healthy **9** fostering, nurturing, wholesome **10** nutritious, sustaining **11** maintaining **12** invigorating **13** strengthening

nourishment 4 chow, eats, food, grub, meat **5** bread **6** viands **8** victuals **9** nutriment, nutrition **10** sustenance **11** comestibles

nouveau riche 9 newly rich (person)

Novak, Kim
  real name: **19** Marilyn Pauline Novak
  born: **9** Chicago IL
  roles: **6** Picnic **7** Pal Joey, Vertigo **14** Of Human Bondage **17** Bell Book and Candle **20** The Jeanne Eagels Story **22** The Man with the Golden Arm **31** Amorous Adventures of Moll Flanders

Nova Scotia
  borders: **10** Bay of Fundy **12** New Brunswick **13** Atlantic Ocean **16** Gulf of St Lawrence **20** Northumberland Strait
  city: **5** Truro **6** Sydney **7** Amherst, Halifax **8** Glace Bay, Yarmouth **9** Dartmouth **10** New Glasgow
  country: **6** Canada
  island: **10** Cape Breton
  means: **11** New Scotland
  mineral: **3** oil **4** lead, salt, sand, zinc **6** barite, gravel, gypsum, silver **9** celestite, petroleum **10** natural gas
  mountain: **5** North **8** Cobequid
  part of: **6** Acadia **12** Appalachians **17** Maritime Provinces **18** Atlantic Provinces
  river: **4** Avon **5** Clyde **6** LaHave, Medway, Mersey **7** St Mary's **12** Shubenacadie

novel 3 new **6** unique **7** unusual **8** original, singular, uncommon **9** different **10** innovative, unorthodox **14** unconventional
  French: **5** roman

novelty 5 token **6** bauble, change, gewgaw **7** memento, newness, trinket **8** gimcrack, souvenir, surprise **9** bagatelle, variation **10** innovation, knick-knack, uniqueness **11** originality

November
  event: **11** Election Day
  flower: **13** chrysanthemum
  French: **8** Novembre
  gem: **5** topaz
  German: **8** November
  holiday: **11** All Souls' Day (2), Veterans Day (11) **12** All Saints' Day (1), Guy Fawkes Day (5), Thanksgiving (4th Thursday)
  Italian: **8** Novembre
  number of days: **6** thirty

  origin of name: **5** novem (Latin meaning nine)
  place in year:
    Gregorian: **8** eleventh
    Roman: **5** ninth
  Spanish: **9** Noviembre
  Zodiac sign: **7** Scorpio **11** Sagittarius

novice 4 tyro **5** pupil **7** amateur, learner, student **8** beginner, disciple, newcomer **9** greenhorn **10** apprentice, tenderfoot

Novum Organum
  author: **12** Francis Bacon

novus ordo seclorum 24 a new order of the ages is born
  author: **6** Vergil, Virgil
  work: **8** Eclogues
  motto of: **11** US Great Seal

Now, Voyager
  director: **12** Irving Rapper
  cast: **10** Bette Davis **11** Claude Rains, Janis Wilson, Paul Henreid **12** Gladys Cooper
  score: **10** Max Steiner

now and then 8 on-and-off, periodic, sometime, sporadic **9** irregular, sometimes, temporary **10** infrequent, occasional **11** irregularly **12** infrequently, occasionally, periodically, sporadically

Nox, Nyx
  goddess of: **5** night

noxious 4 foul **6** deadly, lethal, putrid **7** baneful, beastly, harmful, hurtful, noisome **8** damaging, virulent **9** injurious, loathsome, poisonous, revolting **10** abominable, disgusting, pernicious, putrescent **11** deleterious **12** foul-smelling

nth degree 5 limit **6** utmost **7** extreme

nuance 5 shade, touch **6** nicety **7** finesse **8** delicacy, fineness, keenness, subtlety **9** sharpness, variation **10** modulation, refinement **11** discernment

nub 4 core, crux, gist, hump, knob, knot, lump, node **5** bulge, heart **6** kernel **7** essence **8** swelling **10** projection, prominence, tumescence **11** nitty-gritty **12** protuberance

nubbin 3 ear **4** corn, lump, stub **5** bulge, fruit, piece, stump **10** diminutive

nubbly 5 lumpy, rough **6** coarse, knobby, pebbly

nucleus 3 nub **4** core, pith, seed **5** heart **6** center, kernel

nude 3 raw **4** bare **5** bared, naked **6** unclad **7** exposed **8** in the raw, stripped **9** unadorned, unarrayed, unclothed, uncovered, undressed
  French: **9** au naturel

nudge 3 jab, jog, nod **4** bump, jolt, poke, prod, push **5** elbow, press, punch, shove, touch **6** jostle, motion, signal **8** indicate

nugatory 4 idle **5** empty **6** hollow, otiose, paltry **7** trivial, useless **8** piddling, trifling **9** meritless, valueless, worthless **10** profitless **11** ineffectual **12** functionless **15** inconsequential

nugget 4 hunk, lump **5** chunk, piece

nuisance 4 bore, fret, hurt, pain, pest **5** curse, thorn, worry **6** blight, bother, burden, plague **7** scourge, torment, trouble **8** handicap, vexation **9** annoyance, grievance **10** affliction, irritation, misfortune, pestilence **11** aggravation, botheration **13** inconvenience

Nuk
  capital of: 9 Greenland

Nukualofa
  capital of: 5 Tonga

null 2 NG **4** void **6** no good **7** invalid **9** valueless, worthless **10** immaterial **11** inoperative, nonexistent, unimportant **13** insignificant

nullification 6 repeal **7** voiding **8** recision **9** abolition, annulment **10** abrogation, rescinding **11** abolishment **12** cancellation, invalidation

nullify 4 veto, void **5** annul **6** cancel, repeal, revoke **7** abolish, rescind, retract **8** abrogate, make void, override, set aside **10** invalidate

nullity 6 cipher, naught **7** nothing **9** nonentity

numb 4 dead **6** frozen **8** deadened **9** insensate, unfeeling **10** insensible, narcotized **12** anesthetized

number 3 mob, sum, tot **4** army, bevy, book, herd, host, mass, part **5** array, bunch, count, crowd, digit, group, issue, swarm, tally, total **6** amount, cipher, figure, reckon, scores, symbol **7** chapter, company, compute, edition, foliate, integer, numeral, passage, section **8** division, estimate, magazine, numerate, paginate, quantity **9** abundance, aggregate, calculate, character, enumerate, multitude, paragraph, quarterly **10** assemblage, quantities **13** preponderance

numbered numbered weighed divided
  Aramaic: 21 mene mene tekel upharsin
  called: 16 writing on the wall
  foretells destruction of: 10 Belshazzar
  Biblical book of: 6 Daniel

numberless 6 myriad **7** copious, umpteen **8** unending, zillions **9** countless, plenteous, unbounded, uncounted **11** illimitable, uncountable **12** immeasurable **13** multitudinous

numbness 8 deadness **11** insentience

numeral 5 digit **6** cipher, figure, letter, number, symbol **7** integer **9** character

numerate 3 add **5** count, tally, total **6** number, reckon **7** compute, tick off **9** calculate

numerophobia
  fear of: 7 numbers

numerous 4 many **6** myriad **7** copious, profuse **8** abundant **9** plentiful **13** multitudinous

Numidia *see* **7** Algeria

Numipu *see* **8** Nez Perce

Numitor
  king of: 9 Alba Longa
  father: 5 Proca
  brother: 7 Amulius
  daughter: 10 Rhea Silvia
  grandson: 5 Remus **7** Romulus

numskull, numbskull 3 sap **4** dolt, dope, fool, jerk **5** dummy, dunce, idiot, klutz, ninny **6** dimwit, nitwit **7** dullard, half-wit **8** bonehead, dummkopf, imbecile, lunkhead, silly ass **9** blockhead, simpleton **10** dunderhead, muttonhead, nincompoop, noodlehead **11** chowderhead, knucklehead **12** scatterbrain

Nun *see* **4** Nunu

Nunavut
  name means: 7 our land
  abbreviation: 2 NU
  borders: 8 Manitoba **9** Baffin Bay, Hudson Bay **11** Arctic Ocean, Labrador Sea **20** Northwest Territories
  capital/largest city: 7 Iqaluit
  country: 6 Canada
  island: 6 Devon **7** Baffin **8** Victoria **9** Elizabeth, Ellesmere **11** King William **13** Prince of Wales
  mineral: 4 gold, zinc **9** petroleum
  people: 5 Inuit

nuncio 5 envoy **6** legate **8** diplomat, minister **9** messenger **10** ambassador **11** papallegate **14** representative

nunnery 5 abbey, order **6** priory **7** cenacle, convent **8** cloister **9** hermitage, monastery **10** sisterhood

Nun's Story, The
  director: 12 Fred Zinneman
  based on story by: 12 Kathryn Hulme
  cast: 10 Dean Jagger, Edith Evans, Peter Finch **13** Audrey Hepburn, Peggy Ashcroft **15** Colleen Dewhurst

Nunu
  also: 3 Nun
  origin: 8 Egyptian
  god of: 5 ocean
  personifies: 5 chaos

nuptial 7 marital **8** conjugal, hymeneal **9** connubial **11** matrimonial

nuptials 7 wedding **8** marriage **9** espousals, hymeneals **12** matrimonials

Nurmi, Paavo
  nickname: 13 The Flying Finn
  sport: 5 track
  won: 8 Olympics

nurse 4 feed **5** nanny, treat **6** attend, doctor, foster, harbor, remedy, sister, succor, suckle **7** care for, nourish, nurture, promote **8** attend to, guard-

ian **9** attendant, cultivate, encourage, governess
  Hindi/Indian: 4 ayah
  Orient: 4 amah
  famous: 11 Edith Cavell, Sister Kenny **19** Florence Nightingale

nursery 6 hotbed **9** incubator, preschool **10** greenhouse, schoolroom **12** conservatory, kindergarten

nursery rhyme character 3 Tom **4** Jack, Jill, Mary **5** Peter, Polly **6** Bo-Peep **8** King Cole **9** Jack Sprat **10** Jack Horner, Miss Muffet **11** Mother Goose **12** Humpty Dumpty **13** Little Boy Blue, Mother Hubbard

nurture 4 feed, mess, rear, tend **5** breed, raise, teach, train, tutor **6** foster, school **7** bring up, develop, educate, nourish, prepare, sustain, victual **8** instruct, maintain **9** cultivate, provision **10** discipline, strengthen

Nusantara *see* **9** Indonesia

nut 3 fan, pit **4** buff, seed **5** freak, idiot, loony, stone **6** madman, maniac, zealot **7** devotee, fanatic, lunatic, oddball **8** crackpot **9** eccentric, screwball **10** aficionado, enthusiast, psychopath **11** afficionado

Nut
  origin: 8 Egyptian
  goddess of: 3 sky

nut-brown 5 tawny **6** auburn, brunet **8** brunette, cinnamon

Nutcracker, The
  also: 13 Shchelkunchik
  ballet by: 11 Tchaikovsky
  based on fairy tale by: 11 ETA Hoffmann
  contains: 17 Waltz of the Flowers **24** Dance of the Sugarplum Fairy
  characters: 4 mice **5** Clara, Fritz **6** prince **10** nutcracker **11** toy soldiers **12** Drosselmeyer **14** Sugarplum Fairy

nutmeg
  botanical name: 17 Myristica fragrans
  from same plant as: 4 mace
  origin: 9 Indonesia
  use: 5 punch **6** eggnog **8** desserts **10** vegetables **11** baked dishes

Nutmeg State
  nickname of: 11 Connecticut

nutriment 4 chow, eats, fare, feed, food, meat, mess **5** board **6** fodder, forage **7** aliment, edibles **8** eatables, victuals **9** foodstuff, groceries, provender **10** provisions, sustenance **11** nourishment, subsistence

nutrition 4 chow, feed, food, grub **6** fodder, forage, silage **7** edibles, rations **8** eatables **9** groceries, pasturage, provender **10** foodstuffs, provisions, sustenance **11** nourishment, subsistence

nutritious 9 wholesome **10** nourishing, sustaining

nuts 3 mad **4** bats, daft **5** balmy,

crazy, dotty, loony, potty, wacko, wacky **6** insane **7** bananas, bonkers, cracked, touched **8** demented, deranged, unhinged **10** unbalanced

nutty 3 mad **4** daft **5** balmy, crazy, dippy, dotty, goofy, inane, loony, silly, wacko, wacky **6** cuckoo, insane, screwy, weirdo **7** bonkers, cracked, foolish, lunatic, meshuga, touched **8** bughouse, demented **9** senseless **10** addlepated, squirrelly **11** harebrained **12** crackbrained

nuzzle 3 pat, pet **4** buss, kiss **5** smack **6** caress, coddle, cosset, cuddle, fondle, nestle **7** embrace, snuggle

Nyasaland *see* **6** Malawi

nyctophobia
    fear of: **8** darkness **14** the dark of night

nyet
    Russian: **2** no

nymph 5 belle, dryad, houri, naiad, nixie, oread, sylph **6** beauty, daphne, kelpie, maenad, nereid, ondine, sprite, undine **7** charmer, galatea **8** Eurydice **9** hamadryad

Nymphaea
    epithet of: **9** Aphrodite
    means: **6** bridal

NYPD Blue
    network: **3** ABC
    creator: **12** Steven Bochco
    cast: **10** Gail O'Grady (Donna Abandando), Jimmy Smits (Bobby Simone), Kim Delaney (Diane Russell) **11** David Caruso (John Kelly), Dennis Franz (Andy Sipowicz), Esai Morales (Tony Rodriguez), Gordon Clapp (Greg Medavoy) **12** Amy Breneman (Janice Licalsi), Henry Simmons (Baldwin Jones), Rick Schroder (Danny Sorenson) **13** Bill Brochtrup (John Irvin), Charlotte Ross (Connie McDowell Sipowicz), James McDaniel (Arthur Fancy) **14** Andrea Thompson (Jill Kirkendall), Sharon Lawrence (Sylvia Costas Sipowicz) **16** Nicholas Turturro (James Martinez) **17** Mark-Paul Gosselaar (John Clark) **18** Jacqueline Obradors (Rita Ortiz) **21** Garcelle Beauvais-Nilon (Valerie Heywood)

Nyx, Nox
    form: **7** goddess
    personifies: **5** night
    originated from: **5** Chaos
    children: **3** Ker **4** Eris **5** Fates, Geras, Momus, Moros, Oizys **6** Aether, Hemera, Hypnos, Somnus **7** Nemesis, Oneiroi **8** Thanatos

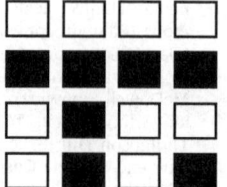
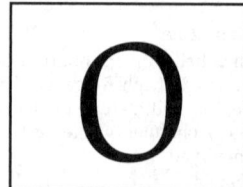
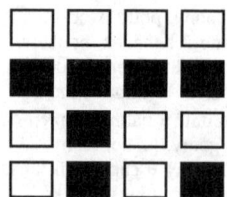

oaf **3** sap **4** boob, boor, clod, dolt, dope, fool, jerk, lout **5** booby, dummy, dunce, idiot, klutz, moron, ninny **6** lummox, nitwit **7** dullard, half-wit **8** bonehead, imbecile, numskull **9** blockhead, ignoramus, numbskull, simpleton **10** dunderhead, nincompoop

oafish **4** rude **5** crude **6** coarse, gauche, vulgar **7** boorish, doltish, loutish, uncouth **9** unrefined **10** unpolished

oak **7** Quercus
varieties: **3** bur, cow, pin, red, she **4** bear, blue, cork, deer, Holm, jack, live, maul, post, silk **5** black, Emory, holly, scrub, ubame, water, white **6** basket, Belote, canyon, Ceylon, Daimyo, gambel, gander, Havard, Indian, island, Kermes, Konara, laurel, Oregon, poison, possum, Turkey, Turner, valley, willow, yellow **7** Ballota, Bartram, Belloot, Catesby, Durmast, English, Georgia, Italian, Kellogg, leather, Lebanon, overcup, scarlet, shingle, Spanish, tanbark, truffle, western **8** Arkansas, bluejack, chestnut, McDonald, mossy-cup, shinnery, Texas red **9** blackjack, Engelmann, flowering, Jerusalem, Mongolian, pubescent, swamp post **10** Chinquapin, Darlington, ring-cupped, Spanish red, swamp white **11** huckleberry, Japanese red, northern pin, northern red, Shumard's red **12** interior live, laurel-leaved, rock chestnut, southern live, yellow-barked **13** dwarf chestnut, oriental white, swamp chestnut **14** Austrian turkey, California live, yellow chestnut **15** California black, California field, California scrub, California white **16** high-ground willow **17** Japanese evergreen **18** Rocky Mountain scrub
venerated by: **6** Druids

Oakie, Jack
real name: **19** Lewis Delaney Offield
born: **9** Sedalia (Sadalia) MO
roles: **16** The Great Dictator **17** Alice in Wonderland

Oakland
baseball team: **2** A's **9** Athletics
football team: **7** Raiders

oar **3** row **4** pole **5** blade, rower, scull **6** paddle, propel **9** propeller
blade: **4** palm, peel

fulcrum: **5** thole **7** oarlock, rowlock
part: **4** loom **5** shaft **6** collar

oarsman **5** pilot, rower **6** bowman **7** mariner, sculler **8** helmsman **9** gondolier, propeller

oasis **5** haven **6** asylum, harbor, refuge **7** retreat, sanctum, shelter **9** green spot, sanctuary, water hole **11** fertile area **13** watering place

oast **4** kiln, oven

oat, oats **5** Avena **11** Avena sativa
varieties: **3** sea **4** wild **6** potato **8** animated **9** Tartarian **11** slender wild

Oates, Joyce Carol
author of: **4** Them **6** Blonde **8** The Falls **9** Childwold, Middle Age **10** Bellefleur, The Barrens, Wonderland **11** Unholy Loves, Wheel of Love **15** I'll Take You There, The Tattooed Girl **18** A Bloodsmoor Romance **19** Do With Me What You Will

oath **3** vow **5** curse **6** avowal, pledge **8** cuss word, swearing **9** affidavit, blasphemy, expletive, obscenity, profanity **10** adjuration, deposition **11** affirmation, attestation, declaration, imprecation, malediction

oaths
god of: **6** Horcus, Sancus **10** Dius Fidius, Semo Sancus

oatmeal **6** cereal **7** pottage **8** drammock, porridge

Obadiah **4** Obad **7** prophet **12** minor prophet
father: **4** Azel **6** Jehiel **8** Izrahiah, Shemaiah
son: **8** Ishmaiah
predicted fall of: **4** Edom

Obata, Gyo
architect of: **20** Dallas–Ft Worth Airport **25** National Air and Space Museum (Smithsonian Institution)

obdurate **5** cruel, harsh **6** mulish **7** adamant, callous, unmoved, willful **8** hardened, pitiless, stubborn, uncaring **9** immovable, merciless, obstinate, pigheaded, unfeeling, unpitying, unsparing, untouched **10** bullheaded, headstrong, inflexible, unmerciful, unyielding **11** cold-blooded, hardhearted, intractable **12** ungovernable, unmanageable **13** unsympathetic **14** uncontrollable **15** uncompassionate

obeah **5** charm, magic **6** fetish, voodoo

7 sorcery **10** witchcraft
practiced in: **6** Guiana **10** West Indies

obedience **8** docility, yielding **9** deference, ductility, obeisance **10** accordance, allegiance, compliance, subjection, submission **11** conformance, dutifulness, willingness **12** acquiescence, subservience, tractability **14** conformability, submissiveness

obedient **5** loyal **6** docile **7** devoted, dutiful **8** amenable, faithful, obeisant, yielding **9** compliant, tractable **10** governable, law-abiding, respectful, submissive **11** acquiescent, deferential, subservient

obeisance **3** bow **5** honor **6** curtsy, esteem, fealty, homage, regard **7** loyalty, respect **8** courtesy, fidelity, humility, kneeling **9** deference, obedience, reverence **10** allegiance, humbleness, subjection, submission, veneration **11** prostration **12** genuflection **13** self-abasement

obelisk **5** pylon, shaft, tower **6** column, dagger, needle, pillar **8** memorial, monolith, monument

Oberon
character in: **21** A Midsummer Night's Dream
author: **11** Shakespeare
consort: **7** Titania

Oberon
opera by: **5** Weber
character: **5** Reiza
setting: **18** court of Charlemagne **21** court of Haroun al Rashid

Oberon, Merle
real name: **26** Estelle Merle O'Brien Thompson
husband: **14** Alexander Korda
born: **8** Tasmania
roles: **5** Hotel **7** Desiree **15** A Song to Remember **16** Wuthering Heights **19** The Scarlet Pimpernel **25** The Private Life of Henry VIII **30** The Private Life of Henry the Eighth

obese **3** fat **5** gross, heavy, plump, porky, pudgy, stout, tubby **6** chubby, fleshy, portly, rotund **7** paunchy **9** corpulent **10** overweight, potbellied

obesity **3** fat **7** fatness, liposis **8** adiposis, enormity **9** heaviness, plumpness, stoutness **10** corpulence, overweight

obey **4** heed, mind **5** bow to, serve **6** assent, concur **7** abide by, observe, respect, yield to **8** accede to, submit to **9** acquiesce, conform to, succumb to **10** comply with, toe the line **12** follow orders

obfuscate 4 blur **5** befog **6** garble, mess up, muddle **7** becloud, confuse, distort, fluster, obscure, stupefy **8** confound, scramble **10** complicate

obfuscation 8 flummery **9** confusion **10** doubletalk, mumbo jumbo

obi 4 sash **5** obeah **6** girdle

obiit 6 he died **7** she died

obiter dictum 9 diversion **10** digression, divagation, side remark

object 3 aim, end, use **4** body, butt, dupe, form, gist, goal, pith, prey **5** abhor, basis, cause, knock, point, sense, thing **6** balk at, carp at, design, device, dingus, gadget, intent, loathe, motive, oppose, quarry, reason, target, victim **7** article, cavil at, condemn, dislike, essence, frown on, meaning, mission, protest, purpose, subject **8** be averse, cynosure, denounce **9** abominate, criticize, doohickey, incentive, intention, objective, principle, recipient, substance **10** inducement, phenomenon **11** contrivance, explanation, thingamabob, thingamajig **12** be at odds with, disapprove of, significance **13** find fault with, take exception **18** remonstrate against

objection 4 beef, kick **5** cavil **7** protest **8** demurral, rebuttal **9** challenge, complaint, criticism, exception **10** dissension, opposition **11** disapproval, reservation **12** disagreement **13** contradiction **14** disapprobation, opposing reason **15** counter argument

objectionable 4 foul, vile **5** nasty **6** odious **8** unseemly **9** abhorrent, loathsome, obnoxious, offensive, revolting **10** abominable, despicable, disgusting, unbearable, unpleasant **11** displeasing, distasteful, intolerable, unendurable **12** disagreeable, unacceptable **13** inappropriate

objective 3 aim, end **4** fair, goal, just, mark, real **6** actual, design, intent, target **7** mission, purpose **8** detached, unbiased, unswayed **9** impartial, intention, uncolored **10** impersonal, open-minded **11** destination **12** uninfluenced, unprejudiced **13** disinterested, dispassionate

objectivity 8 fairness **10** detachment, neutrality **12** impartiality

object to 7 condemn, dislike **9** frown upon **12** disapprove of **14** discountenance **15** take exception to **16** find unacceptable

objet d'art 5 bijou, curio **7** bibelot, trinket **9** art object

oblation 4 gift **8** offering **9** offertory **10** collection

obligated 5 bound **6** forced, liable **7** pledged **8** beholden, indebted **9** committed **11** constrained

obligation 4 bond, care, debt, duty, oath, onus, word **6** charge, pledge **7** compact, promise **8** contract, guaranty, warranty **9** agreement, guarantee, liability **10** a favor owed, commitment, constraint **12** indebtedness **13** answerability, understanding **14** accountability, responsibility

obligatory 7 binding **8** coercive, enforced, required **9** mandatory, necessary, requisite **10** compulsory, imperative, peremptory **11** unavoidable

oblige 3 aid **4** bind, help, make **5** favor, force, impel, serve **6** assist, coerce, compel **7** require, support **8** obligate **9** constrain **11** accommodate, do a favor for, necessitate **13** do a service for, to be duty bound

obliged 5 bound **7** favored, pleased **8** assisted, beholden, indebted, required, thankful **9** compelled **12** accommodated

obliging 4 kind **6** polite **7** amiable, helpful **8** cheerful, friendly, gracious **9** agreeable, courteous **10** solicitous **11** complaisant, considerate, cooperative, good-natured, sympathetic **12** well-disposed **13** accommodating

oblique 3 sly **4** awry **5** askew **6** aslant, covert, hinted, masked, tilted, veiled **7** cloaked, devious, furtive, implied, slanted, sloping **8** allusive, diagonal, inclined, indirect, slanting, sneaking **9** suggested, underhand

obliterate 4 raze **5** erase, level **6** cancel, delete, efface, remove, rub out **7** abolish, blot out, destroy, expunge, wipe out **9** eradicate, write over **10** annihilate, strike over

obliteration 8 deletion **9** abolition, expunging, wiping out **11** blotting out, destruction, eradication **12** annihilation

oblivion 5 limbo **7** the void **9** blankness, disregard, obscurity, unconcern **11** blotting out, nothingness **12** nonexistence **13** forgetfulness, insensibility, obliviousness **14** insignificance **15** unconsciousness

oblivious 8 careless **9** forgetful, unaware of, unmindful **10** heedless of, insensible **11** inattentive, unconcerned, unobservant **12** disregardful, undiscerning **13** unconscious of

Oblonsky, Prince Stepan
   character in: 12 Anna Karenina
   author: 7 Tolstoy

obloquy 5 abuse, odium, shame **6** infamy, rebuke **7** calumny, censure, railing **8** contempt, disfavor, disgrace, ignominy, reviling **9** discredit, invective **10** defamation, opprobrium, scurrility **11** degradation, humiliation, verbal abuse **12** billingsgate, condemnation, denunciation, dressing-down, vilification

obnoxious 4 foul, vile **5** nasty **6** odi-

ous **7** hateful **8** unseemly **9** abhorrent, loathsome, offensive, repellent, repugnant, revolting **10** abominable, despicable, detestable, disgusting, nauseating, unbearable, unpleasant **11** displeasing, intolerable, unendurable **12** disagreeable, insufferable **13** inappropriate, objectionable

oboe family
   instruments: 5 shawm **6** curtal, pommer, racket **7** bassoon, bombard, curtall, hautboy **8** crumhorn, schalmey, tenoroon **10** Cor Anglais, oboe d'Amore **11** English horn, heckelphone, sarusophone **12** oboe da caccia, sarrusophone **13** contra bassoon, double bassoon

O'Brien, Hugh
   real name: 11 Hugh J Krampe
   born: 11 Rochester NY
   roles: 9 Wyatt Earp **27** The Life and Legend of Wyatt Earp

O'Brien, Edna
   author of: 5 Night **11** A Pagan Place, In the Forest **13** The Lonely Girl **14** Down by the River, The Country Girl **20** August Is a Wicked Month **24** Girls in Their Married Bliss, House of Splendid Isolation

O'Brien, Margaret
   real name: 18 Angela Maxine O'Brien
   born: 12 Los Angeles CA
   roles: 8 Jane Eyre **11** Little Women **15** Meet Me in St Louis **24** Our Vines Have Tender Grapes

O'Brien, Pat
   real name: 26 William Joseph Patrick O'Brien
   born: 11 Milwaukee WI
   roles: 12 Hildy Johnson, The Front Page **13** Some Like It Hot, The Last Hurrah **20** Angels with Dirty Faces **22** Knute Rockne All American
   autobiography: 12 Wind on My Back

obscene 4 blue, foul, lewd **5** bawdy, dirty **6** filthy, smutty, vulgar, x-rated **8** indecent, prurient **9** salacious **10** lascivious, lubricious **12** pornographic, scatological **16** morally offensive

obscenity 8 cuss word, lewdness **9** dirtiness, indecency, profanity, prurience, swear word, taboo word, vulgarity **10** filthiness, smuttiness **11** pornography **13** salaciousness **14** four-letter word, lasciviousness

obscuration 7 eclipse, masking, veiling **8** cloaking, clouding, covering **9** darkening, shadowing **10** concealing **11** concealment

obscure 3 dim, fog **4** blur, dark, hide, mask, veil **5** bedim, befog, block, cloak, cloud, cover, dingy, dusky, faint, murky, vague **6** cloudy, darken, hidden, muddle, screen, shadow, shroud, somber, unsung **7** becloud, conceal, confuse, cryptic, curtain, eclipse, shadowy, unclear, unknown, unnoted **8** befuddle, confused, disguise, nameless, puzzling **9** confusing, enigmatic, forgotten, lightless, obfuscate, uncertain, unheard of, unlighted **10** indefinite, indistinct, overshadow, perplexing, unrenowned **11** indefinable, inscrutable, little known, out-of-the-way, unimportant **12** unfathomable **13** inconspicuous, insignificant, unilluminated **15** inconsequential

obscurity 3 fog **4** mist **5** cloud, shade **6** shadow **7** dimness, mystery, opacity, privacy **8** darkness **9** ambiguity, seclusion, vagueness **10** cloudiness

obsequies 5 rites **6** burial **7** funeral **15** memorial service

obsequious 6 menial **7** fawning, servile, slavish **8** cowering, cringing, toadying **9** kowtowing, truckling **11** bootlicking, deferential, subservient, sycophantic **12** ingratiating, mealy-mouthed **14** apple-polishing

observance 4 rite **6** custom, regard, ritual **7** heeding, keeping, obeying **8** ceremony, practice **9** adherence, attending, attention, following, formality, solemnity **10** ceremonial, compliance **11** celebration, observation **13** commemoration **15** memorialization

observant 5 alert, awake, aware **7** careful, heedful, mindful **8** vigilant, watchful **9** attentive, conscious, regardful, wide-awake **10** perceptive **12** on the lookout

observation 4 heed, idea, view **5** probe **6** eyeing, notice, remark, search, seeing, survey, theory **7** comment, finding, opinion, viewing **8** interest, judgment, scrutiny, spotting, watching **9** assertion, attention, beholding, detection, diagnosis, discovery, glimpsing, observing, statement **10** cognizance, commentary, inspection, reflection **11** description, examination, heedfulness **12** surveillance, watchfulness **13** pronouncement **20** firsthand information

observatory 5 tower **7** lookout **9** satellite **11** planetarium
   name: 4 Hale, Lick **6** Yerkes **7** Palomar, Whipple **8** Kitt Peak, Mt Wilson **11** Las Campanas, Mount Wilson **12** Big Bear Solar **14** Royal Greenwich

observe 3 eye, say, see **4** espy, heed, keep, mark, note, obey, ogle, spot, view **5** honor, opine, state, watch **6** assert, behold, detect, follow, notice, peer at, regard, remark, size up, survey **7** abide by, comment, declare, defer to, execute, fulfill, glimpse, inspect, make out, mention, perform, reflect, respect, stare at **8** adhere to, announce, carry out, discover, perceive, sanctify, theorize **9** celebrate, recognize, solemnize **10** be guided by, comply with, consecrate **11** acknowl-

edge, acquiesce to, commemorate, take stock of **12** catch sight of **14** pay attention to

observer 6 viewer **7** watcher **8** onlooker **12** investigator

obsessed 5 beset **7** haunted **8** hung up on, maniacal **9** dominated, possessed **10** controlled **15** having a fixation

obsession 5 craze, mania, quirk **6** phobia **8** fixation **9** fixed idea, monomania **11** infatuation **13** preoccupation **16** overwhelming fear **18** neurotic conviction

obsolescent 8 dying out **9** declining **11** on the way out **12** disappearing **16** becoming obsolete **17** becoming out-of-date

obsolete 3 out **5** dated, passe **6** bygone **7** antique, archaic, extinct **8** outdated, out of use, outmoded **9** out-of-date **10** antiquated **12** old-fashioned, out of fashion

obstacle 3 bar **4** curb, snag **5** block, catch, check **6** hurdle **7** barrier, problem **8** blockade, stoppage **9** barricade, hindrance, roadblock **10** difficulty, impediment, limitation **11** obstruction, restriction **12** interference **14** stumbling block

obstetrician
   French: 10 accoucheur

obstinacy 8 rigidity **10** mulishness, resistance **11** willfulness **12** stubbornness **13** inflexibility, intransigence, pigheadedness

obstinate 6 dogged, mulish **7** staunch, willful **8** obdurate, resolute, stubborn **9** pigheaded, steadfast, tenacious, unbending **10** headstrong, inflexible, refractory, self-willed, unyielding **11** intractable **12** recalcitrant, ungovernable, unmanageable **14** uncontrollable **20** unreasonably stubborn

obstreperous 4 loud **5** noisy **6** unruly **8** perverse **9** clamorous, rampaging **10** boisterous, disorderly, refractory, roistering, uproarious, vociferous **11** disobedient **12** uncontrolled, ungovernable, unmanageable, unrestrained **14** uncontrollable

obstruct 3 bar **4** curb, halt, hide, mask, stop **5** block, check, cloak, close, cover, dam up, debar, delay, limit, stall **6** arrest, hinder, hobble, impede, plug up, retard, shroud, stifle, thwart **7** eclipse, inhibit, shut off **8** blockade, choke off, close off, restrict, suppress, throttle **9** barricade, frustrate **18** bring to a standstill

obstruction 3 bar **4** curb, snag, stop **5** block, check, hitch **6** hurdle **7** barrier **8** blockage, obstacle, stoppage **9** barricade, hindrance **10** bottleneck, impediment **11** encumbrance

obtain 3 get **4** earn, gain, hold, take **5** exist, glean, stand **6** attain, come

by, gather, pick up, secure **7** achieve, acquire, prevail, procure, receive **9** get hold of **14** get one's hands on **16** gain possession of

obtainment 11 achievement, acquirement, acquisition, procurement

obtrude 5 eject, expel, force **6** butt in, impose, meddle, thrust **7** presume, project **9** interfere

obtrusive 4 nosy **5** brash **6** prying, snoopy **7** bulging, forward, salient **8** familiar, meddling **9** intruding, intrusive, prominent **10** aggressive, jutting out, meddlesome, projecting, protruding **11** conspicuous, impertinent, interfering, outstanding, protuberant, sticking out, trespassing **12** interrupting, presumptuous

obtuse 4 dull, slow **5** blunt, dense, thick **6** simple, stupid **7** blunted **8** ignorant, not sharp **9** unpointed **10** insensible, not pointed, slow-witted **11** insensitive, unsharpened **12** imperceptive, thick-skinned **15** uncomprehending

obtuseness 8 dullness **9** denseness, ignorance, stupidity **13** insensitivity **14** slow-wittedness **15** thick-headedness **16** lack of perception, simplemindedness **19** lack of comprehension

obverse 4 face **5** front **10** complement **11** counterpart
   of coin: 4 head

obviate 5 avert, avoid, parry **6** divert, remove **7** fend off, prevent, ward off **8** preclude, stave off **9** forestall, sidetrack, turn aside **10** circumvent, do away with **11** nip in the bud

obvious 5 clear, plain **6** patent **7** evident, glaring, visible **8** apparent, distinct, manifest, palpable, striking, unhidden, unmasked, unveiled **10** undeniable **11** conspicuous, discernible, perceptible, self-evident, unconcealed, undisguised **12** in plain sight, unmistakable **24** plain as the nose on your face

O.C., The
   network: 3 FOX
   cast: 8 Alan Dale (Caleb Nichol) **9** Adam Brody (Seth Cohen) **10** Kelly Rowan (Kirsten Cohen) **11** Tate Donovan (Jimmy Cooper) **12** Mischa Barton (Marissa Cooper), Rachel Bilson (Summer Roberts) **13** Melinda Clarke (Julie Cooper-Nichol) **14** Peter Gallagher (Sandy Cohen) **16** Benjamin McKenzie (Ryan Atwood)
   setting: 12 Orange County

ocarina 11 sweet potato **14** wind instrument

O'Casey, Sean
   author of: 10 Purple Dust **12** The Green Crow **17** Juno and the Paycock **18** The Shadow of a Gunman **20** The Plough and the Stars

occasion 4 base, time **5** basis, cause, event **6** advent, affair, chance, elicit, ground, lead to, motive, prompt, reason **7** episode, grounds, inspire, opening, provoke, venture **8** incident, instance **9** adventure, happening, rationale, situation **10** bring about, experience, motivation, occurrence **11** celebration, explanation, opportunity, provocation **12** circumstance, special event, suitable time **13** justification, opportune time **14** convenient time, important event, particular time

occasional 4 rare **6** fitful, random **8** sporadic, uncommon **9** irregular, recurring, scattered, spasmodic, uncertain **10** incidental, infrequent, now and then, unreliable **12** intermittent

occasionally 6 rarely, seldom **7** at times **8** fitfully **9** sometimes **10** now and then **11** irregularly **12** infrequently, once in a while, periodically, sporadically **14** from time to time, intermittently **15** every now and then, once in a blue moon

occidental 7 Western **8** American, European **9** Hesperian, Westerner

occlude 4 clog, plug **5** block, choke, close **6** shut up, stop up **7** congest, shut off, stopper **8** choke off, obstruct **9** barricade, constrict **11** strangulate

occult 4 dark **5** magic **6** arcane, hidden, mystic, secret, veiled **7** obscure, private **8** esoteric, mystical, shrouded **9** concealed **10** cabalistic, mysterious, unrevealed **11** undisclosed **12** supernatural

occupancy 3 use **6** tenure **7** tenancy **8** lodgment **9** enjoyment, habitancy **10** engagement, habitation, occupation, possession **11** inhabitancy

occupant 5 owner **6** lessee, lodger, native, renter, roomer, tenant **7** dweller, settler **8** colonist, occupier, resident **9** addressee **10** inhabitant **11** householder

occupation 3 job **4** line, work **5** craft, forte, trade **6** career, living, metier, sphere **7** calling, control, pursuit, seizure **8** activity, business, capacity, conquest, lifework, vocation **9** specialty **10** employment, line of work, livelihood, possession, profession, subjection **11** foreign rule, subjugation **14** specialization **15** military control **18** military occupation

occupied 5 in use **6** amused, took up, used up **7** dwelt in, engaged, lived in, overran, overrun, taken up **8** absorbed, tenanted **9** concerned, conquered, inhabited, resided in **12** had control of, held in thrall **13** was situated in **16** took possession of

occupy 3 use **4** be in, be on, busy, fill, hold **5** amuse, sit in **6** absorb, employ, engage, fill up, room in, take up **7** concern, conquer, dwell in, engross,

enslave, inhabit, lodge in, overrun, pervade, possess **8** permeate, reside in, saturate **9** entertain, subjugate **10** monopolize **11** have control **12** be situated in, hold in thrall **14** be the tenants of **16** take possession of

occur 3 hit **4** rise **5** arise, ensue **6** appear, befall, crop up, emerge, happen, result, strike, turn up **7** be found, come off, develop **8** spring up **9** come about, eventuate, take place, transpire **10** come to pass **11** materialize **13** cross one's mind, enter one's mind

occurrence 5 event **6** affair **7** episode, venture **8** business, incident, instance, occasion **9** adventure, emergence, happening, situation, unfolding **10** appearance, experience, proceeding **11** development, transaction **12** circumstance **13** manifestation **15** materialization

ocean 3 sea **4** deep, main, pond **5** flood, water **7** big pond, high sea **9** briny deep
 god of: 3 Nun **4** Nanu **7** Neptune, Oceanus **8** Poseidon

Oceania, Oceanica 9 Melanesia, Polynesia **10** Micronesia **11** Australia
 ocean: 12 South Pacific
 island: 4 Cook, Guam, Fiji, Maui, Niue, Wake **5** Aunuu, Bonin, Kauai, Lanai, Tonga **6** Bikini, Futuna, Hawaii, Marcus, Midway, Rurutu, Tahiti, Tubuai, Tuvalu, Wallis **7** Gambier, Gilbert, Iwo Jima, Leeward, Mariana, Molokai, Phoenix, Solomon, Tokelau, Tuamotu, Tutuila, Vanuatu, Volcano **8** Aitu taki, Bismarck, Bora-Bora, Johnston, Kiribati, Marshall, Pitcairn, Windward **9** Australia, Christmas, Marquesas, Trobriand **10** New Zealand **12** New Caledonia, Western Samoa **14** Papua New Guinea **15** French Polynesia

oceanic 6 marine **7** aquatic, pelagic **8** seagoing **9** thalassic

Oceanid
 form: 5 nymph
 location: 3 sea
 father: 7 Oceanus
 mother: 6 Tethys

Ocean's Eleven
 director: 1960 version: 14 Lewis Milestone
 2001 version: 16 Steven Soderbergh
 cast: 1960 version: 10 Dean Martin (Sam Harmon), Joey Bishop (Mushy O'Connors) **11** Cesar Romero (Duke Santos) **12** Akim Tamiroff (Spyros Acebos), Frank Sinatra (Danny Ocean), Peter Lawford (Jimmy Foster), Richard Conte (Tony Bergdorf), Sammy Davis Jr (Josh Howard) **13** Patrice Wymore (Adele Ekstrom) **14** Angie Dickinson (Beatrice Ocean)
 2001 version: 8 Brad Pitt (Rusty Ryan) **9** Bernie Mac (Frank Catton),

Matt Damon (Linus), Scott Caan (Turk Malloy), Shaobo Qin (Yen) **10** Andy Garcia (Terry Benedict), Carl Reiner (Saul Bloom) **12** Casey Affleck (Virgil Malloy), Eddie Jemison (Livingston Dell), Elliott Gould (Reuben Tishkoff), Julia Roberts (Tess Ocean) **13** George Clooney (Danny Ocean)

Oceanus
 member of: 6 Titans
 father: 6 Uranus
 mother: 4 Gaea
 consort of: 6 Tethys
 father of: 8 Oceanids **9** river gods
 son: 7 Proteus
 daughter: 5 Doris, Persa **7** Philyra
 form: 6 stream

ocelot 3 cat **7** wildcat

ochlophobia
 fear of: 6 crowds

Ochoa, Severo
 born: 5 Spain
 profession: 10 biochemist

Ockelman, Constance Frances Marie
 real name of: 12 Veronica Lake

O'Connor, Carroll
 born: 7 Bronx NY
 roles: 6 Gideon **10** Return to Me **12** Archie Bunker, Archie's Place **14** All in the Family **19** In the Heat of the Night
 restaurant: 12 The Ginger Man

O'Connor, Donald
 born: 9 Chicago IL
 roles: 9 Beau Geste **15** Singin' in the Rain **18** Tom Sawyer Detective **21** Francis the Talking Mule

O'Connor, Flannery
 author of: 9 Wise Blood **15** The Habit of Being **17** Mystery and Manners **20** A Good Man Is Hard to Find, The Violent Bear It Away

Octavia
 brother: 8 Augustus
 husband: 4 Nero **10** Mark Antony
 grandson: 8 Caligula

October
 flower: 6 cosmos **9** calendula
 French: 7 Octobre
 gem: 4 opal **10** tourmaline
 German: 7 Oktober
 holiday: 9 Halloween (31) **11** Columbus Day (12) **16** United Nations Day (24)
 Italian: 7 Ottobre
 number of days: 9 thirty-one
 origin of name: 4 octo (Latin meaning eight)
 place in year:
  Gregorian: 5 tenth
  Roman: 6 eighth
 Spanish: 7 Octubre
 Zodiac sign: 5 Libra **7** Scorpio

Octopus, The
 author: 11 Frank Norris

odd 4 rare **5** extra, funny, queer, spare, weird **6** casual, far-out, quaint, single, sundry, unique **7** bizarre, curious, not even, strange, surplus, unusual, various **8** freakish, left over, peculiar, periodic, singular, sporadic, uncommon **9** irregular, remaining, spasmodic, unmatched **10** occasional, outlandish **13** miscellaneous **15** being one of a pair **16** out of the ordinary **17** not divisible by two

oddball 3 nut **4** kook **5** freak **6** weirdo **8** crackpot, original **9** character, eccentric, screwball **10** one-of-a-kind

Odd Couple, The
  character: 3 Roy **5** Myrna, Roger, Speed **6** Miriam, Murray, Vinnie **10** Felix Unger **11** Gloria Unger **12** Cecily Pigeon, Oscar Madison **14** Blanche Madison **15** Gwendolyn Pigeon, (Dr) Nancy Cunningham
  cast: 10 Al Molinaro, Archie Hahn **11** Brett Somers, Carol Shelly, Jack Klugman, Larry Gelman, Monica Evans, Tony Randall **12** Garry Walberg, Janice Hansen, Ryan McDonald **13** Elinor Donahue, Joan Hotchkiss, Penny Marshall
  setting: 11 New York City
  Felix's job: 12 photographer
  Oscar's job: 12 sportswriter
  based on play by: 9 Neil Simon

Odd Couple, The
  director: 8 Gene Saks
  based on play by: 9 Neil Simon
  cast: 10 Jack Lemmon (Felix Unger) **11** Herb Edelman, John Fiedler **13** Walter Matthau (Oscar Madison)

oddity 5 freak, sight **6** marvel, rarity, wonder **9** curiosity, queerness **10** phenomenon, uniqueness **11** abnormality, bizarreness, peculiarity, singularity, strangeness, unusualness **12** eccentricity, freakishness **13** individuality, unnaturalness **14** outlandishness
  Latin: 8 rara avis

oddly amusing 5 droll, kooky **9** laughable, whimsical **10** ridiculous

odd person 3 nut **4** kook **5** flake, freak **6** looney, weirdo **7** oddball **8** crackpot **9** character, eccentric, screwball

odds and ends 4 olio **6** scraps **8** remnants **9** leftovers **10** hodgepodge, miscellany **11** this and that **13** bits and pieces **18** miscellaneous items

ode 4 epic, hymn, poem **5** lyric, paean, psalm, verse **6** ballad **8** canticle
  type: 8 Horatian, Pindaric

Ode on a Grecian Urn
  author: 9 John Keats

Ode on Indolence
  author: 9 John Keats

Ode on Melancholy
  author: 9 John Keats

Ode to a Nightingale
  author: 9 John Keats

Ode to Autumn
  author: 9 John Keats

Ode to Duty
  author: 17 William Wordsworth

Ode to Psyche
  author: 9 John Keats

Ode to the West Wind
  author: 18 Percy Bysshe Shelley

Odets, Clifford
  author of: 9 Golden Boy **12** Awake and Sing **14** The Country Girl **15** Waiting for Lefty **17** The Flowering Peach

Odin
  also: 5 Othin
  brother: 2 Ve **4** Vili
  children: 4 Hodr, Thor **5** Baldr **6** Balder, Baldur
  counterpart: 5 Woden, Wotan
  court: 8 Valhalla
  father: 3 Bor
  god of: 3 war **6** poetry, wisdom **9** knowledge
  grandson: 7 Volsung
  home: 9 Gladsheim
  horse: 8 Sleipnir
  magic ring: 8 Draupnir
  Norse myth: 10 chief deity
  origin: 12 Scandinavian
  raven: 5 Hugin, Munin
  remaining eye: 3 sun
  ruler of: 5 Aexir
  spear: 7 Gungnir
  throne: 10 Hlidskjalf
  wife: 3 Fri **5** Frigg, Frija **6** Frigga
  wolf: 4 Geri **5** Freki

odious 4 evil, foul, vile **5** hated, nasty **6** rotten **7** hateful, heinous, hideous **8** infamous **9** invidious, loathsome, monstrous, obnoxious, offensive, repugnant, repulsive, revolting, sickening **10** abominable, despicable, detestable, disgusting, nauseating, unbearable **11** intolerable, unendurable **12** contemptible **13** objectionable

odium 5 shame **6** hatred, infamy **7** disgust **8** contempt, disfavor, disgrace, dishonor, ignominy **9** antipathy, discredit, disesteem, disrepute **10** abhorrence, disrespect, opprobrium, repugnance **11** detestation, disapproval **14** disapprobation

odonata
  class: 8 hexapoda
  phylum: 10 arthropoda
  group: 9 damselfly, dragonfly

odor 4 aura **5** aroma, scent, smell, stink **6** flavor, stench **7** bouquet, essence, perfume **9** effluvium, fragrance **10** atmosphere

odoriferous 4 rank **5** acrid, fetid **6** putrid, smelly **7** noisome, odorous, pungent, reeking, scented **8** aromatic, fragrant, perfumed, stinking **10** malodorous

odorous 4 rank **5** acrid, fetid **6** smelly **7** noisome, pungent, reeking, scented **8** aromatic, fragrant, perfumed, stinking

Odysseus
  also: 7 Ulysses
  king of: 6 Ithaca
  father: 7 Laertes
  mother: 8 Anticlea
  hero of: 5 Iliad **7** Odyssey
  wife: 8 Penelope **9** Callidice
  son: 9 Telegonus **10** Polypoetes, Telemachus **11** Polyporthis
  seduced by: 5 Circe
  killed by: 9 Telegonus
  epithet: 10 Laertiades

Odyssey
  author: 5 Homer
  character: 4 Zeus **5** Arete, Circe, Helen **6** Athene, Nestor, Scylla, Sirens **7** Calypso, Cyclops **8** Alcinous, Menelaus, Nausicaa, Odysseus, Penelope, Poseidon, Tiresias **9** Charybdis **10** Telemachus **11** Lotus-eaters

Oedipus
  king of: 6 Thebes
  father: 5 Laius
  mother: 7 Jocasta
  foster father: 7 Polybus
  foster mother: 6 Merope **8** Periboea
  wife: 7 Jocasta
  son: 8 Eteocles **9** Polynices
  daughter: 6 Ismene **8** Antigone
  killed: 5 Laius
  defeated: 6 Sphinx

Oedipus at Colonus
  author: 9 Sophocles
  character: 5 Creon **6** Elders, Ismene **7** Theseus **8** Antigone **9** Polynices

Oedipus Rex (Oedipus Tyrannus)
  author: 9 Sophocles
  character: 5 Creon, Laius **7** Jocasta **8** Tiresias

oeil-de-boeuf 16 small round window
  literally: 8 bull's eye

Oeneus
  king of: 7 Calydon
  wife: 7 Althaea
  son: 8 Meleager

oenology
  science of: 5 wines **10** winemaking

Oenone
  form: 5 nymph
  father: 6 Cebren
  husband: 5 Paris

Oersted, Hans Christian
  field: 7 physics
  nationality: 6 Danish
  founded: 16 electromagnetism
  isolated: 16 metallic aluminum
  named for him: 11 oersted unit

oeuvre 4 work **5** works **13** artist's output

O'Faolain, Sean
  author of: 15 The Heat of the Sun **17** A Nest of Simple Folk **22** Midsummer Night's Madness

of a piece 5 alike, equal **7** matched, the same **8** all in one **9** analogous, identical **10** equivalent, homogenous, synonymous **13** evenly matched, one and the same

of bad character 5 shady **8** unsavory **11** of ill repute **12** disreputable, unprincipled

off 2 by **3** bad, far, ill, odd **4** afar, away, down, from, kill, poor, stop **5** amiss, apart, aside, crazy, wrong **6** absent, begone, lessen, remote **7** distant, further, in error, stopped, tainted **8** abnormal, canceled, inferior, mistaken **9** imperfect

offal 4 junk, slag **5** dregs, trash, waste **6** debris, refuse **7** carcass, carrion, garbage, grounds, remains, residue, rubbish **8** leavings

off base 5 amiss, wrong **8** improper, mistaken **10** out of order, unsuitable **13** inappropriate

offbeat 3 odd **7** strange **8** peculiar **9** different, eccentric **14** unconventional

off-center 6 askew **7** strange **9** eccentric **10** imbalanced, nonaligned, unbalanced **12** unreasonable **14** unconventional

off-color 4 blue, lewd, racy, sexy **5** bawdy, dirty, salty, spicy **6** earthy, risque, smutty, wicked **7** naughty, obscene, raunchy **8** improper, indecent, scabrous **9** offensive **10** indelicate, indiscreet, suggestive

off duty 8 inactive **9** at leisure **10** unoccupied **13** on one's own time

Offenbach, Jacques
    born: **7** Cologne, Germany
    composer of: **13** La Belle Helene **15** Tales of Hoffmann, La Vie Parisienne **22** Orpheus in the Underworld

offend 3 err, sin, vex **4** fret, gall, miff, rile **5** anger, annoy, chafe, lapse, pique, wound **6** insult, madden, nettle, rankle **7** affront, disgust, incense, inflame **8** irritate **9** aggravate, displease, misbehave **10** antagonize, disgruntle, exasperate, transgress **13** fall from grace

offender 5 crook, felon **6** sinner **7** culprit **8** criminal, violator **9** wrongdoer **10** malefactor, trespasser

offense 3 sin **4** gibe, harm, slap, slip, snub, twit **5** abuse, crime, lapse, taunt **6** attack, charge, felony, insult **7** affront, assault, misdeed, outrage, umbrage **8** atrocity, enormity, evil deed, rudeness **9** impudence, indignity, insolence, offensive, violation **10** aggression, disrespect, infraction, peccadillo, wickedness **11** delinquency, humiliation, malfeasance, misdemeanor, shortcoming **13** embarrassment, transgression **15** breach of conduct

offensive 4 foul, rank, rude, ugly **5** nasty, onset **6** attack, horrid **7** abusive, assault, hideous, offense, uncivil **8** charging, impudent, insolent, storm-

ing **9** abhorrent, assailing, attacking, insulting, loathsome, obnoxious, onslaught, repugnant, repulsive, revolting, sickening, ungallant **10** abominable, aggression, aggressive, assaulting, bombarding, detestable, disgusting, nauseating, unmannerly, unpleasant **11** belligerent, distasteful, intolerable **12** disagreeable, embarrassing, insufferable **13** disrespectful, objectionable

offensiveness 8 rudeness **9** impudence, insolence, nastiness **10** disrespect, horridness, incivility **13** repulsiveness **14** unpleasantness **15** distastefulness

offer 3 bid **5** put up **6** bestow, extend, render, submit, tender **7** advance, hold out, present, proffer, propose, suggest **8** bestow on, offering, overture, proposal, propound, put forth **9** be willing, volunteer **10** invitation, put forward, submission, suggestion **11** make a motion, proposition **12** bring forward **14** put on the market **19** place at one's disposal

offer hospitality 4 host **7** welcome **8** play host **9** entertain **10** give a party, have guests **13** keep open house

offering 3 bid **4** alms, gift **5** goods, wares **6** course **7** charity, present, tribute **8** anathema, bestowal, donation, oblation **9** sacrifice **11** beneficence **12** contribution
    to God: **6** corban **7** deodate
    to household deities: **4** bali

offertory 4 gift **8** oblation, offering **10** collection

offhand, offhanded 5 ad-lib, hasty **6** casual, chance, random **7** relaxed **8** careless, cavalier, heedless **9** facetious, haphazard, impromptu, unplanned, unstudied **10** improvised, nonchalant, off-the-cuff, unprepared **11** spontaneous, thoughtless, unconcerned, unrehearsed **12** off-the-record **14** extemporaneous, unpremeditated

Office, The
    network: **3** BBC **10** BBC America
    cast: **9** Lucy Davis (Dawn Tinsley) **12** Ricky Gervais (David Brent) **13** Martin Freeman (Tim Canterbury) **14** Mackenzie Crook (Gareth Keenan)

office 3 job **4** post, role **8** capacity, function, position **10** commission, occupation **11** appointment

officer 3 cop **4** head **7** manager **8** director, gendarme, governor **9** constable, detective, executive, patrolman, policeman, president, secretary, treasurer **10** bureaucrat **12** commissioner **13** administrator, vice-president

officers 8 managers **10** executives, management **14** administration

offices 4 duty, help, task **5** favor, trust **6** charge **7** service **8** function, province **10** assistance

office seeker 7 hopeful, nominee **8** aspirant **9** candidate

Office Space
    director: **9** Mike Judge
    cast: **8** Gary Cole (Bill Lumbergh) **9** Ajay Naidu (Samir Nagheenanajar) **11** David Herman (Michael Bolton), Stephen Root (Milton Waddams) **13** Richard Riehle (Tom Smykowski), Ron Livingston (Peter Gibbons) **15** Jennifer Aniston (Joanna)

office worker 5 clerk, steno **6** typist **9** file clerk, secretary **10** bookkeeper, keypuncher **13** data processor **14** clerical worker

official 5 agent **6** formal, vested **7** manager, officer **8** approved, chairman, director, licensed **9** authentic, certified, dignitary, executive, warranted **10** accredited, authorized, sanctioned, supervisor **11** functionary **13** administrator, authoritative **14** administrative **18** administrative head

official communication 5 edict, order, ukase **6** report **7** release **8** bulletin **10** communique **12** proclamation

officialdom 10 government **11** authorities, bureaucracy **14** administration

official paper 4 writ **5** order **8** document **10** instrument

officiate 3 run **4** head, lead **5** chair, emcee **6** direct, handle, manage **7** oversee, preside **8** moderate, regulate **9** supervise **10** administer **11** superintend **12** be in charge of

officious 6 prying **7** pompous **8** meddling **9** intrusive, kibitzing, obtrusive **10** high-handed, meddlesome **11** domineering, interfering, overbearing, patronizing **13** high and mighty, selfassertive, self-important **16** poking one's nose in

Offield, Lewis Delaney
    real name of: **9** Jack Oakie

offset 6 redeem **7** balance, nullify **8** equalize, knock out **9** cancel out, make up for **10** counteract, neutralize **11** countervail **12** compensate for, counterweight **14** counterbalance

offshoot 4 limb **5** scion, shoot **6** branch **7** adjunct **9** aftermath, byproduct, outgrowth **10** descendant

offspring 3 fry **4** heir, seed **5** brood, child, issue, scion, spawn, young **6** family, litter **7** progeny **8** children, increase **9** posterity **10** descendant, succession **11** descendants

off the mark 5 amiss **6** afield, astray **9** off target **16** off the right track

off-the-record 5 privy **6** secret **7** private **11** undisclosed **12** confidential **16** not to be disclosed **17** not for publication

off the top of one's head 5 ad-lib **7** offhand **9** extempore, impromptu **10** improvised, unprepared **11** extemporary, unrehearsed **14** extemporaneous, unpremeditated

of good quality 4 good **6** worthy **8** superior **9** excellent **10** creditable

of high rank 5 noble, regal, royal **6** lordly, titled **7** courtly **11** blue-blooded **12** aristocratic

Of Human Bondage
  author: 16 W Somerset Maugham
  director: 12 John Cromwell
  character: 5 Weeks **7** Hayward **11** Louisa Carey, Philip Carey **12** Sally Athelny, William Carey **13** Mildred Rogers, Miss Wilkinson, Thorpe Athelny
  cast: 10 Bette Davis, Frances Dee, Kay Johnson **12** Leslie Howard

of its own kind
  Latin: 10 sui generis

Of Mice and Men
  author: 13 John Steinbeck
  director: 14 Lewis Milestone
  character: 4 Slim **5** Candy **6** Crooks, Curley **11** Lennie Small **12** George Milton
  cast: 10 Betty Field **11** Lon Chaney Jr (Lenny) **15** Burgess Meredith, Charles Bickford
  score: 12 Aaron Copland

of one's own right
  Latin: 8 sui juris

of poor quality 5 junky **6** flimsy, shoddy, sleazy, trashy **8** inferior **11** substandard

of secondary importance 8 nonvital **9** accessory, extrinsic **10** incidental **11** dispensable, unnecessary **12** nonessential

often 3 oft **4** much **7** usually **8** commonly, ofttimes **9** generally, regularly **10** constantly, frequently, habitually, oftentimes, repeatedly **11** continually, customarily, over and over, recurrently **12** periodically, time and again

of the dead say nothing but good
  Latin: 21 de mortuis nil nisi bonum

of the faith
  Latin: 6 de fide

of their own kind
  Latin: 10 sui generis

of the old school 5 passe **8** outdated, outmoded **9** out-of-date **12** conservative, old-fashioned **18** establishmentarian

Of Time and the River
  author: 11 Thomas Wolfe
  character: 10 Eugene Gant

oft-repeated 5 trite **7** popular **8** constant, familiar, frequent, habitual, well-worn **9** continual, recurring, well-known **10** persistent **11** widely known

of what good
  Latin: 7 cui bono

Ogdoad
  also: 3 Heh

origin: 8 Egyptian
number of gods: 5 eight

ogle 3 eye **6** gape at, gawk at, goggle, leer at **7** stare at **8** goggle at **10** give the eye, scrutinize **15** give the once-over, stare at greedily **16** cast sheep's eyes at, gaze at with desire

Ogma
  origin: 5 Irish
  god of: 6 poetry **9** eloquence
  inventor of: 12 Ogham letters

Ogmios
  origin: 6 Gaelic
  god of: 9 eloquence
  corresponds to: 7 Mercury

ogre, ogress 5 brute, demon, fiend, ghoul, harpy **6** despot, tyrant **7** bugbear, monster **8** bogeyman, dictator, martinet **11** slave driver

Ogygia
  island of: 7 Calypso

Ogygus
  king of: 7 Boeotia
  father: 8 Poseidon

O'Hara, John
  author of: 7 Pal Joey **11** A Rage to Live **13** The Instrument **14** From the Terrace, The Hat on the Bed **16** Butterfield Eight **17** Ten North Frederick **19** The Horse Knows the Way **20** Appointment in Samarra

O'Hara, Maureen
  real name: 18 Maureen Fitzsimmons
  nickname: 18 Queen of Technicolor
  born: 7 Ireland **8** Milltown
  roles: 7 Big Jake **9** McLintock **10** Lady Godiva **11** The Quiet Man **13** North to Alaska, The Parent Trap **16** The Foxes of Harrow **19** How Green Was My Valley **20** Hunchback of Notre Dame **27** Miracle on Thirty-fourth Street

O'Hara, Scarlett
  character in: 15 Gone With the Wind
  family: 6 Gerald **7** Carreen, Suellen
  author: 8 Mitchell

O Henry
  real name: 19 William Sidney Porter
  author of: 11 The Last Leaf **16** Cabbages and Kings, The Gift of the Magi **18** The Cop and the Anthem **19** The Ransom of Red Chief

Ohio
  abbreviation: 2 OH
  nickname: 7 Buckeye
  capital: 8 Columbus
  largest city: 9 Cleveland
  others: 3 Ada **4** Kent, Lima **5** Akron, Berea, Cadiz, Niles, Parma, Piqua, Xenia **6** Athens, Canton, Dayton, Elyria, Lorain, Marion, Newark, Tiffin, Toledo, Warren **7** Ashland, Findlay, Fremont, Norwood, Wooster **8** Alliance, Bluffton, Fostoria, Lakewood, Marietta, Sandusky **9** Ashtabula, Kettering, Lancaster, Massillon, Struthers, Vermilion, Willowick **10**

Cincinnati, Huntington, Portsmouth, Rocky River, Willoughby, Youngstown, Zanesville **11** Painesville, Springfield **12** Steubenville
  college: 4 Kent **5** Akron, Hiram, Miami **6** Dayton, Kenyon, Xavier **7** Antioch, Oberlin, Wooster **8** Defiance, Dennison, Marietta, Ursuline **10** Wittenberg **11** Case Western **12** Bowling Green, Ohio Wesleyan
  feature:
    hall of fame: 11 Pro Football
    race: 12 Soap Box Derby
  tribe: 4 Erie **7** Wyandot **13** Mound Builders
  people: 7 buckeye, Cy Young **8** Zane Grey **10** Clark Gable, T Hart Crane **11** Annie Oakley, Lillian Gish **12** James Thurber, Lowell Thomas, Norman Thomas **13** Neil Armstrong, Orville Wright, Thomas A Edison **14** Barney Oldfield, Clarence Darrow **15** William T Sherman **16** Sherwood Anderson **18** Norman Vincent Peale
    explorer: 7 La Salle
  lake: 4 Erie **5** Grand **6** Berlin, Dillon, Hoover, Indian **8** Delaware **13** Mosquito Creek
  land rank: 35 thirty-fifth
  mountain:
    highest point: 12 Campbell Hill
  physical feature:
    caverns: 4 Ohio, Zane **6** Seneca
    spring: 8 Blue Hole
  president: 13 Ulysses S Grant **14** James A Garfield, Warren G Harding **15** William McKinley **16** Rutherford B Hayes **17** William Howard Taft **20** William Henry Harrison
  river: 5 Grand, Miami **6** Maumee, Scioto, Wabash **7** Hocking **8** Cuyahoga, Sandusky **9** Muskingum, Tennessee **10** Cumberland **11** Monongahela
  state admission: 11 seventeenth
  state bird: 8 cardinal
  state flower: 16 scarlet carnation
  state motto: 27 With God All Things Are Possible
  state song: 13 Beautiful Ohio
  state tree: 7 buckeye

Ohm, Georg Simon
  field: 7 physics
  nationality: 6 German
  discovered: 20 electrical resistance
  named for him: 7 ohm unit

oil 4 balm, lard **5** cream, salve **6** anoint, grease, pomade **7** unguent **8** liniment, ointment **9** lubricant, lubricate, melted fat, petroleum **12** melted grease
  type: 4 corn, fuel, hair **5** crude, motor, olive, whale **6** canola **7** cooking, mineral **9** safflower, vegetable

oily 5 fatty, lardy, slick **6** greasy, smarmy **7** buttery, fawning, servile **8** slippery, slithery, toadying, unctuous **9** groveling, sebaceous **10** lubricious,

oleaginous 11 bootlicking, subservient **12** ingratiating

ointment 4 balm **5** salve **6** lotion, pomade **7** pomatum, unguent **8** liniment **9** emollient, spikenard

Ojibwa, Ojibway *see* **8** Chippawa

OK 4 fine, good **7** approve, endorse **8** all right, approval **9** authorize **11** endorsement **13** authorization
  French: **7** d'accord

O'Keeffe, Georgia
  born: **12** Sun Prairie WI
  artwork: **7** Stables **9** Black Iris **14** Patio with Cloud **15** Lake George Barns **22** Light Coming on the Plains **26** Black Flower and Blue Larkspur
  husband: **15** Alfred Stieglitz

Oklahoma
  abbreviation: **2** OK **4** Okla
  nickname: **6** Boomer, Sooner
  capital/largest city: **12** Oklahoma City
  others: **3** Ada **4** Alva, Enid, Hugo **5** Altus, Miami, Ponca, Tulsa **6** Duncan, El Reno, Guymon, Idabel, Lawton **7** Ardmore, Guthrie, Sapulpa, Shawnee **8** Anadarko, Fort Sill, Muskogee **9** Blackwell, Claremore, McAlester **10** Stillwater **12** Bartlesville
  college: **5** Tulsa **6** Norman **7** Cameron **8** Langston, Phillips **10** Stillwater **11** Oral Roberts **12** Oklahoma City **15** Bethany Nazarene **17** American Christian
  feature:
    hall of fame: **14** American Indian
    national park: **6** Platte
  tribe: **3** Kaw, Oto **4** Iowa, Loup, Otoe, Waco **5** Caddo, Kansa, Osage, Ponca **6** Apache, Ottawa, Pawnee, Quapaw **7** Shawnee, Wichita **8** Arapahoe, Tawakoni
    Five Civilized Tribes: **5** Creek **7** Choctaw **8** Cherokee, Seminole **9** Chickasaw
  people: **4** Okie **6** Sooner **9** Jim Thorpe **10** Will Rogers **12** Mickey Mantle **14** Maria Tallchief
    explorer: **8** Coronado
  lake: **5** Atoka, Grand, Hulah **6** Texoma, Wister **7** Eufaula, Heyburn, Oologah **8** Keystone **9** Pensacola, Tenkiller **10** Fort Gibson **11** Thunderbird **12** Markham Ferry **17** Lake O' The Cherokees
  land rank: **10** eighteenth
  mountain: **6** Ozarks **8** Ouachita
    highest point: **9** Black Mesa
  physical feature: **9** Panhandle
    plains: **5** Great
  river: **3** Red **5** Grand **6** Little, Neosho **7** Washita **8** Arkan sas, Canadian, Cimarron **9** Verdigris **15** Muddy Boggy Creek
  state admission: **10** forty-sixth
  state bird: **23** scissor-tailed flycatcher
  state fish: **9** white bass
  state flower: **9** mistletoe
  state motto: **22** Labor Conquers All Things
  state song: **8** Oklahoma
  state tree: **6** redbud

Oklahoma!
  director: **13** Fred Zinnemann
  cast: **10** Rod Steiger **11** Eddie Albert **12** Gordon MacRae, Shirley Jones **13** Gloria Grahame, James Whitmore **18** Charlotte Greenwood
  score: **21** Rodgers and Hammerstein
  choreographer: **12** Agnes de Mille
  song: **23** People Will Say We're in Love **24** Surrey with the Fringe on Top

Olbers, Heinrich Wilhelm Matthaus
  field: **9** astronomy
  nationality: **6** German
  discovered: **5** Vesta **6** comets, Pellas **9** asteroids

old 4 aged, used **5** hoary, of age **6** beat-up, bygone, of yore **7** ancient, antique, archaic, elderly, outworn, rundown, vintage, wornout **8** battered, decrepit, familiar, grizzled, much-used, obsolete, outdated, timeworn **9** crumbling, hackneyed, out-of-date, venerable, weathered **10** antiquated, broken-down, gray-headed, ramshackle, tumbledown **11** dilapidated, from the past, gray with age, obsolescent, time-honored, traditional **12** deteriorated, old-fashioned, white with age **13** weather-beaten **14** of long standing **15** long established

Old Aches and Pains
  nickname of: **11** Luke Appling

old age 6 dotage **7** ripe age **8** maturity, senility **11** advanced age **15** second childhood

Old Bay State
  nickname of: **13** Massachusetts

Old Bulgarian
  also: **15** Old Church Slavic
  language family: **12** Indo-European
  group: **11** Balto-Slavic
  status: **7** archaic
  used in: **14** Orthodox church

Old Chinook
  nickname of: **10** Washington

Old Colony State
  nickname of: **13** Massachusetts

Old Curiosity Shop, The
  author: **14** Charles Dickens
  character: **5** Quilp **9** Fred Trent, Mrs Jarley **10** Kit Nubbles, Sally Brass **11** Grandfather **12** Sampson Brass **13** Dick Swiveller **15** Little Nell Trent **18** The Single Gentleman

Old Dominion
  nickname of: **8** Virginia

olden 4 past **6** bygone, former, of yore **7** ancient, long-ago **8** departed

Oldest Man 10 Methuselah

old-fashioned 5 corny, dated, passe **7** antique, archaic **8** obsolete, outdated, outmoded **9** out-of-date **10** antiquated, out of style **11** obsolescent, traditional **12** long-standing, out of fashion **13** unfashionable **14** behind the times

Old-Fashioned Girl, An
  author: **15** Louisa May Alcott

old hand 3 pro **6** expert, master **8** virtuoso **9** authority **12** professional

old hat 5 passe, stale **6** demode **7** archaic, outworn **8** obsolete, outdated, outmoded **9** out-of-date **10** antiquated, superseded **11** obsolescent **12** old-fashioned **13** unfashionable **14** behind the times

old-line 11 established, traditional **12** conservative

Old Line State
  nickname of: **8** Maryland

Old Maid, The
  author: **12** Edith Wharton

Old Man and the Sea, The
  author: **15** Ernest Hemingway
  character: **7** Manolin **8** Santiago

Old Mortality
  author: **14** Sir Walter Scott
  character: **5** Edith **11** Henry Morton **12** Basil Olifant, Lord Evandale **19** John Balfour of Burley **21** Lady Margaret Bellenden **27** Colonel Grahame of Claverhouse

Old North
  nickname of: **13** North Carolina

old saw 5 adage, maxim **6** cliche, saying, truism **7** bromide, proverb **9** old saying **10** expression **11** old chestnut

oldster 5 elder **6** codger, old man **7** ancient **8** old woman **13** senior citizen

Old Testament
  first five books: **10** Pentateuch
  first six books: **9** Hexateuch
  first seven books: **10** Heptateuch
  books of: **3** Job **4** Amos, Ezra, Joel, Ruth **5** Hosea, Jonah, Kings, Micah, Nahum, Songs, Tobit **6** Baruch, Daniel, Esther, Exodus, Haggai, Isaiah, Joshua, Judges, Judith, Psalms, Samuel, Sirach, Wisdom **7** Ezekiel, Genesis, Malachi, Numbers, Obadiah **8** Habakkuk, Jeremiah, Macabees, Nehemiah, Proverbs **9** Leviticus, Zechariah, Zephaniah **10** Chronicles **11** Deuteronomy **12** Ecclesiastes **13** Song of Solomon **14** Ecclesiasticus

Oldtown Folks
  author: **19** Harriet Beecher Stowe

old-world 6 formal **7** courtly, gallant, old-line **8** European, orthodox **10** ceremonial, chivalrous, prescribed **11** ceremonious, continental, established, traditional **12** conservative, conventional, old-fashioned

Ole
  character in: 16 Giants of the Earth
  author: 7 Rolvaag
oleoresin 3 gum **5** anime, apiol, elemi **6** balsam **7** solvent **10** turpentine
olio 4 stew **6** jumble, medley **7** melange, mixture **8** mishmash **9** potpourri **10** assortment, collection, hodgepodge, hotchpotch, miscellany
olive 12 Olea europaea
  varieties: 3 tea **4** wild **5** black, false, holly, sweet **6** common, desert, spurge **7** Russian **8** American, fragrant **11** Californian
olive-drab 5 khaki **13** greenish-brown
Oliver
  character in: 11 As You Like It
  author: 11 Shakespeare
Oliver!
  director: 9 Carol Reed
  based on story by: 14 Charles Dickens (Oliver Twist)
  cast: 8 Jack Wild, Ron Moody (Fagin) **10** Mark Lester (Oliver), Oliver Reed **11** Shani Wallis
  Oscar for: 7 picture **8** director
  musical version of: 11 Oliver Twist
  song: 16 Consider Yourself, Food Glorious Food **17** As Long As He Needs Me
Oliver Twist
  author: 14 Charles Dickens
  character: 5 Fagin, Monks (Edward Leeford), Nancy **6** Bumble **9** Bill Sikes, Mrs Maylie **10** Mr Brownlow, Rose Maylie
  director: 9 David Lean
  cast: 8 Kay Walsh **12** Alec Guinness (Fagin), Robert Newton **13** Anthony Newley (Artful Dodger) **16** Francis L Sullivan, John Howard Davies
  remade as: 7 Oliver!
Olivia
  character in: 12 Twelfth Night
  author: 11 Shakespeare
Olivier, Sir Laurence
  born: 7 Dorking, England
  wife: 11 Vivien Leigh **13** Joan Plowright
  roles: 6 Becket, Hamlet (Oscar), Henry V, Sleuth **7** Rebecca **9** The Bounty **11** Marathon Man **16** Wuthering Heights **17** Pride and Prejudice, The Boys from Brazil, The Devil's Disciple **19** Shoes of the Fisherman **23** The Prince and the Showgirl
olivine
  variety: 7 peridot
olla 3 jar, pot **10** earthen pot
Olmsted, Frederick Law
  landscape architect of: 11 Central Park (NYC, with Calvert Vaux) **12** Prospect Park (Brooklyn NY) **13** Fairmount Park (Philadelphia) **14** Biltmore Estate (Asheville NC), Mount Royal Park (Montreal)
Olsen, Merlin (Jay)

  sport: 8 football
  team: 14 Los Angeles Rams
  TV roles: 12 Father Murphy **15** Highway to Heaven **23** Little House on the Prairie
O Lucky Man
  director: 15 Lindsay Anderson
  cast: 9 Alan Price **13** Rachel Roberts **15** Malcolm McDowell, Ralph Richardson
  score: 9 Alan Price
Olwen
  origin: 5 Welsh
  form: 8 princess
  father: 16 Yspadaden Penkawr
Olympic Games
  site:
    1896: 6 Athens
    1900: 5 Paris
    1904: 7 St Louis
    1906: 6 Athens
    1908: 6 London
    1912: 9 Stockholm
    1920: 7 Antwerp
    1924: 5 Paris **8** Chamonix
    1928: 8 St Moritz **9** Amsterdam
    1932: 10 Lake Placid, Los Angeles
    1936: 6 Berlin **21** Garmisch-Partenkirchen
    1948: 6 London **8** St Moritz
    1952: 4 Oslo **8** Helsinki
    1956: 9 Melbourne **15** Cortina d'Ampezzo
    1960: 5 Tokyo **11** Squaw Valley
    1968: 8 Grenoble **10** Mexico City
    1972: 6 Munich **7** Sapporo
    1976: 8 Montreal **9** Innsbruck
    1980: 6 Moscow **10** Lake Placid
    1984: 8 Sarajevo **10** Los Angeles
    1988: 5 Seoul **7** Calgary
    1992: 9 Barcelona **11** Albertville
    1994: 11 Lillehammer
    1996: 7 Atlanta
    1998: 6 Nagano
    2000: 6 Sydney
    2002: 12 Salt Lake City
    2004: 6 Athens
    2006: 5 Turin
    2008: 7 Beijing
    2010: 9 Vancouver
    2012: 6 London
Omaha
  language family: 6 Siouan **7** Dhegiha
  location: 4 Iowa **8** Nebraska, Oklahoma
Oman
  other name: 13 Muscat and Oman
  capital: 6 Masqat, Muscat
  largest city: 5 Matra **6** Matrah
  others: 3 Sur **4** Fida **5** Dubai, Nazwa, Nigwa, Sohar, Wazit **6** Khasab, Marbat, Murbat, Suwaih, Tinouf **7** Khabura, Salalah **8** Ashkhara
  government: 9 Sultanate
  head of state/government: 6 sultan
  monetary unit: 3 gaj, gaz **4** rial **5** baiza, ghazi **7** mahmudi
  island: 6 Masera, Masira **7** Masirah

    10 Kuria Muria
  mountain: 4 Qara **5** Hafit, Harim, Nakhl, Tayin **8** el-Akhdar **11** Jabal Akhdar **13** Green Mountain
  highest point: 6 al-Sham
  sea: 6 Indian **7** Arabian
  physical feature:
    cape: 7 Madraka **9** Ras Al Hadd **13** Ras Dharbat 'Ali
    gulf: 4 Oman
    peninsula: 7 Arabian **8** Musandam
    plain: 6 Dhofar **7** Batinah
    strait: 6 Hormuz
  people: 4 Arab
  ruler: 12 Qabus Bin Said **13** Said Bin Taimur
  language: 4 Urdu **5** Hindi **6** Arabic **7** Baluchi
  religion: 5 Islam
  war: 4 Gulf **11** Desert Storm
omega 3 end **4** last **5** final **6** ending **8** terminus
  opposite: 5 alpha
omen 4 sign **5** token **6** augury, herald **7** auspice, portent, presage, warning **9** foretaste, harbinger, precursor **10** foreboding, indication
ominous 7 unlucky **8** menacing, minatory, monitory, sinister **9** dismaying, ill-omened **10** foreboding, ill-starred, portentous
omission 3 gap **4** hole **7** neglect **9** exception, exclusion, oversight **10** leaving out, negligence **11** delinquency, elimination **12** noninclusion **13** neglected item **16** something omitted
omit 3 cut **4** drop, fail, jump, miss, shun, skip **5** avoid, elide **6** bypass, delete, except, forget, ignore, slight **7** excerpt, exclude, let slip, neglect **8** leave out, overlook, pass over, preclude, set aside **11** forget about
omnia vincit amor 15 love conquers all
Omnibus
  host: 13 Alistair Cooke
omnipotent 6 mighty **7** supreme **8** almighty, powerful, puissant **11** all-powerful
omniscient 7 all-wise, supreme **8** infinite **9** all-seeing **10** all-knowing, pre-eminent
omnium gatherum 23 miscellaneous collection
omnivorous 7 hoggish **8** edacious, ravenous **9** crapulous, rapacious, voracious **10** gluttonous, polyphagic, predacious **12** pantophagous
Omoo
  author: 14 Herman Melville
  character: 10 Captain Bob **15** Doctor Long Ghost
Omphale
  queen of: 5 Lydia
  father: 8 Iardanus
  husband: 6 Tmolus

son: 5 Lamus
served by: 8 Hercules

Omri
father: 6 Becher **7** Michael
son: 4 Ahab
daughter-in-law: 7 Jezebel

on 2 at **4** atop, near, over, upon **5** about, above, ahead, along, anent **7** against, forward, planned **8** abutting, adjacent, attached, intended, touching **9** occurring **10** concerning, juxtaposed

on-and-off 6 spotty **8** episodic **9** irregular, spasmodic, temporary **10** now-and-then, occasional

On Beginning and Perishing
author: 9 Aristotle

once 7 ages ago, long ago, one time **8** formerly, hitherto, years ago **9** at one time **10** heretofore, previously **11** a single time, for the nonce, in times past, some time ago **12** in the old days, some time back **13** once upon a time, on one occasion

once-in-a-lifetime 6 unique **7** special **8** singular **11** one-time-only

once more 4 anew **5** again **9** once again, over again **11** one more time

on cloud nine 6 elated, joyful, joyous **8** ecstatic, euphoric **9** exuberant, rapturous **15** in seventh heaven

oncoming 5 close **7** looming, nearing **8** imminent **9** advancing, impending, onrushing **11** approaching, bearing down

on course 8 on target **15** on the right track

Ondine
author: 13 Jean Giraudoux

one 2 an **3** you **4** a man, lone, only, sole **5** a body, a soul, whole **6** a thing, entire, single, unique **7** a person, someone **8** complete, singular, solitary, somebody **10** individual, unrepeated

One, Two, Three
director: 11 Billy Wilder
cast: 11 James Cagney **12** Pamela Tiffin **13** Arlene Francis, Horst Buchholz
setting: 10 West Berlin
score: 11 Andre Previn

O'Neal, Ryan
real name: 16 Patrick Ryan O'Neal
born: 12 Los Angeles CA
daughter: 10 Tatum O'Neal
roles: 7 The List **8** Faithful **9** Love Story, Paper Moon **10** What's Up Doc **11** Barry Lyndon, People I Knew, Peyton Place **12** Oliver's Story

O'Neal, Tatum
born: 12 Los Angeles CA
father: 9 Ryan O'Neal
roles: 9 Paper Moon **12** Bad News Bears **14** Little Darlings **17** The Scoundrel's Wife **19** International

Velvet
husband: 11 John McEnroe

one and the same 5 equal **7** matched **9** identical

one by one 6 singly **10** one at a time, separately, single file **12** individually

One Day at a Time
character: 9 Ann Romano **11** Julie Cooper **13** Barbara Cooper **15** Dwayne Schneider
cast: 14 Bonnie Franklin **15** Pat Harrington Jr **17** Mackenzie Phillips, Valerie Bertinelli

One Day in the Life of Ivan Denisovich
author: 23 Aleksandr Solzhenitsyn Jr

One Flew Over the Cuckoo's Nest
director: 11 Milos Forman
based on story by: 8 Ken Kesey
cast: 13 Jack Nicholson **14** Louise Fletcher, Michael Beryman **15** William Redfield
Oscar for: 5 actor (Nicholson) **7** actress (Fletcher), picture **8** director **10** screenplay

One Hour with You
director: 11 George Cukor **13** Ernst Lubitsch
cast: 14 Genevieve Tobin **16** Maurice Chevalier **17** Jeanette MacDonald
remake of: 17 The Marriage Circle
song: 14 What Would You Do

one-hundred percent 5 sheer, total, utter, whole **7** supreme **8** absolute, complete **10** consummate **17** through-and-through

O'Neill, Eugene
author of: 8 The Straw **11** The Hairy Ape **12** Ah Wilderness, Anna Christie **13** Marco Millions **14** Glencairn Cycle **15** The Emperor Jones, The Iceman Cometh **16** Beyond the Horizon, Strange Interlude, The Great God Brown **18** Desire Under the Elms **20** The Moon of the Caribees **22** A Moon for the Misbegotten, All God's Chillun Got Wings, Mourning Becomes Electra **24** Long Day's Journey into Night
daughter: 4 Oona
son-in-law: 7 Chaplin

Oneiros
also: 6 Oniros
origin: 5 Greek
god of: 6 dreams

oneness 5 union, unity **7** concord, harmony **8** entirety, identity, sameness, totality **9** agreement, aloneness, integrity, wholeness **10** uniformity, uniqueness **11** singularity **12** completeness **13** individuality

one-of-a-kind 4 rare **6** unique **7** strange, unusual **8** original **9** eccentric

oneology
science of: 5 wines **10** winemaking

onerous 5 heavy **6** taxing **7** arduous, painful, weighty **8** crushing, grievous

9 demanding, wearisome **10** burdensome, exhausting, oppressive **11** distressing **12** hard to endure

one thing in return for another
Latin: 10 quid pro quo

one-time 3 old **4** past **5** early, prior **6** former, recent **7** earlier, quondam **8** previous **9** erstwhile
French: 8 ci-devant

one voice 4 solo **6** unison **7** concert

one who has a fixed income
French: 7 rentier

On First Looking Into Chapman's Homer
author: 9 John Keats

on foot
French: 5 a pied

ongoing 7 endless, lasting **8** enduring, unbroken, unending **10** continuing, proceeding **11** never-ending, unremitting **13** uninterrupted

On Golden Pond
director: 10 Mark Rydell
based on play by: 14 Ernest Thompson
cast: 9 Jane Fonda **10** Doug McKeon, Henry Fonda (Norman Thayer Jr) **16** Katharine Hepburn
setting: 5 Maine
Oscar for: 5 actor (Fonda) **7** actress (Hepburn)

on guard 4 wary **5** alert **7** careful, heedful **8** cautious, vigilant, watchful

on hand 5 handy, on tap **6** at hand **9** available **10** accessible, convenient **14** at one's disposal

on horseback
French: 7 a cheval

onion 6 Allium **10** Allium cepa
varieties: 3 red, sea, top **4** leek, tree, wild **5** green, gypsy, pearl, swamp, Welsh, white **6** German, potato, yellow **7** Bermuda, Danvers, nodding, prairie, shallot, Spanish **8** climbing, Egyptian, false sea, scallion, Valencia **9** Catawissa, ever-ready, flowering, two-bladed **10** multiplier, red-skinned **16** Japanese bunching
origin: 9 Asia Minor
called by Robert Louis Stevenson: 14 rose among roots

Oniros see **7** Oneiros

On Liberty
author: 14 John Stuart Mill

onlooker 5 gazer, ogler **6** viewer **7** watcher, witness **8** beholder, kibitzer, observer **9** bystander, spectator **10** eyewitness, rubberneck

only 4 just, lone, sole **5** alone **6** barely, merely, purely, simply, single, singly, solely, unique **7** at least **8** by itself, singular, solitary **9** by oneself, exclusive, unmatched **10** individual, no more than, nothing but, one and only, unrepeated **11** exclusively **12** individually, unparalleled

on one's uppers 5 broke **9** destitute **10** down and out

On Plants
author: **9** Aristotle

On Revolution
author: **12** Hannah Arendt

onrush 4 flow, flux, gush, tide, wave **5** flood, onset, storm, surge **6** attack, charge, deluge, spring, stream **7** assault, cascade, current, torrent **9** avalanche

onset 4 push, raid **5** birth, sally, start **6** attack, charge, onrush, outset, thrust **7** assault, genesis, infancy, offense **8** founding, invasion, outbreak, storming **9** beginning, inception, incursion, offensive, onslaught **10** incipience, initiation **12** commencement, inauguration

onslaught 4 coup, push, raid **5** blitz, foray, onset, sally **6** attack, charge, putsch, thrust **7** assault, offense **8** invasion **9** incursion, offensive **10** aggression, blitzkrieg

on tap 5 handy **6** at hand, on hand **9** available **10** accessible, convenient

Ontario
bay: **6** Hudson
canal: **5** Trent **6** Rideau
capital: **7** Toronto
city: **3** Emo **4** Galt **6** London, Ottawa **7** Windsor **8** Hamilton, Kingston **9** Kitchener
explored by: **5** French **6** British
industry: **6** mining **11** agriculture **13** manufacturing
lake: **6** Simcoe
province of: **6** Canada
river: **6** Ottawa, Thames **7** Niagara **10** St Lawrence
settled by: **9** Loyalists
university: **4** York **5** Brock, Trent **8** McMaster

on the alert 4 wary **7** careful, mindful, on guard **8** cautious, watchful **9** wide awake **12** on the lookout

On the Beach
author: **10** Nevil Shute
director: **13** Stanley Kramer
cast: **10** Ava Gardner **11** Fred Astaire, Gregory Peck **13** Donna Anderson **14** Anthony Perkins

on the contrary
French: **11** au contraire

on the dot 7 exactly **8** promptly **9** on the nose, precisely **10** punctually

on the face
Latin: **7** ex facie

on the go 4 busy **6** active, mobile **8** in motion **9** energetic, on the move **13** indefatigable

On the Heavens
author: **9** Aristotle

on the move 5 astir **6** active, mobile **7** on the go **8** in motion

on the nose 5 exact **7** exactly, precise

8 accurate, on target **9** precisely **10** accurately, on the money

on the outer edges
Latin: **10** in extremis

on the right track 8 on course, on target

On the Soul
author: **9** Aristotle

On the Town
director: **9** Gene Kelly **12** Stanley Donen
cast: **9** Ann Miller, Gene Kelly, Vera-Ellen **12** Betty Garrett, Frank Sinatra
setting: **11** New York City
score: **11** Adolph Green, Betty Comden **16** Leonard Bernstein
song: **14** New York New York

On the Waterfront
director: **9** Elia Kazan
cast: **8** Lee J Cobb **10** Karl Malden, Pat Henning, Rod Steiger **12** Leif Erickson, Marlon Brando **13** Eva Marie Saint
Oscar for: **5** actor (Brando) **7** picture **8** director **10** screenplay **17** supporting actress (Saint)

on the whole 9 in general **10** by and large **27** considering the circumstances

onto 4 atop, upon **5** aware, privy **6** aboard

onus 4 duty, load **5** cross **6** burden, strain, weight **9** liability **10** obligation **11** encumbrance **13** burden of proof **14** responsibility

onus probandi 13 burden of proof

onward, onwards 5 ahead, along **7** forward, ongoing **9** advancing, frontward **11** moving ahead, progressive
French: **7** en avant, en route

oodles 4 gobs, lots, many **5** heaps, loads, scads **6** plenty

ooze 4 drip, leak, mire, muck, seep, silt **5** bleed, drain, exude, slime, sweat **6** filter, sludge **7** dribble, leakage, seepage, soft mud, trickle **8** alluvium **9** discharge, exudation, percolate, secretion, transpire

oozing 5 leaky, weepy **6** sweaty **7** exuding, seepage, seeping **8** bleeding, sweating

opal
color: **3** red **5** black, white **6** orange **11** transparent
source: **6** Mexico **9** Australia **14** Lightning Ridge
variety: **8** fire opal

opalescent 5 milky **6** pearly **8** irisated, luminous **10** iridescent

opaque 4 dark, dull, hazy **5** muddy, murky **7** clouded, muddied, obscure, unclear **8** abstruse **9** difficult **12** impenetrable, unfathomable **14** nontranslucent, nontransparent, unintelligible **16** incomprehensible

opaqueness 7 opacity **8** dullness **9**

denseness, muddiness, murkiness, obscurity **10** cloudiness **11** unclearness **15** impenetrability **17** unintelligibility **19** incomprehensibility

open 4 ajar, fair, just, wide **5** agape, begin, clear, crack, found, frank, plain, unbar **6** candid, create, direct, expand, gaping, honest, launch, unfold, unlock, unseal, unshut **7** artless, exposed, lay open, natural, not shut, sincere, unblock, unclose, yawning **8** commence, extended, outgoing, unbiased, unclosed, unfasten, unfenced, unfolded, unlocked, unsealed **9** available, coverless, establish, expansive, impartial, institute, not closed, objective, originate, receptive, unbigoted, unbounded, uncovered, uncrowded, undertake, welcoming **10** accessible, forthright, impersonal, inaugurate, responsive, unenclosed, unfastened **11** extroverted, uncluttered, uninhabited **12** permit access, unobstructed, unprejudiced **13** disinterested, doing business **15** straightforward

open-air 7 outdoor, outside **10** unconfined
Italian: **8** al fresco

open and aboveboard 6 candid, honest **7** ethical **10** forthright **12** on the up and up **15** straightforward

Open Boat, The
author: **12** Stephen Crane

Open City
director: **17** Roberto Rossellini
cast: **11** Aldo Fabrizi, Anna Magnani **16** Marcello Pagliero
setting: **4** Rome

open-eyed 5 alert, awake, aware **7** heedful, mindful **8** vigilant, watchful, wide-eyed **9** attentive, wideawake

open-handed 6 lavish **7** liberal **8** generous, prodigal **9** bounteous, bountiful **10** altruistic, beneficent, benevolent, ungrudging, unstinting **11** magnanimous

openhandedness 10 generosity, liberality **11** benevolence, generousity, munificence **12** extravagance

openhearted 7 artless, sincere **8** trusting **9** ingenuous

opening 3 gap, job **4** gash, hole, rent, rift, slit, slot, spot, tear, vent **5** break, chink, cleft, crack, place, space, start **6** breach, chance **7** fissure, kickoff, preface, prelude, send-off, vacancy **8** aperture, occasion, overture, position **9** beginning, first part, launching, situation **10** initiation **11** opportunity, possibility **12** commencement, inauguration, installation, introduction

openly 6 freely **7** frankly **8** directly, honestly, publicly **9** obviously

open-minded 4 fair **7** liberal **8** amenable, flexible, tolerant, unbiased **9** adaptable, impartial, objective, receptive **10** responsive, undogmatic **11** broad-minded **12** unprejudiced **13** disinterested, nonjudgmental

openmouthed 4 agog, awed **5** agape **6** aghast, amazed **8** wide-eyed **9** awestruck, bewitched, marveling, staggered, stupefied, surprised **10** astonished, confounded **10** dumbstruck, enthralled, spellbound **11** dumbfounded **12** wonderstruck **13** flabbergasted, thunderstruck

openness 6 candor **7** honesty **8** daylight **9** frankness, sincerity **11** artlessness **13** guilelessness **14** forthrightness **19** straightforwardness

open sanction 8 free hand, free rein **13** full authority
French: 12 catre blanche

open the eyes of 8 disabuse **11** set straight

open to choice 8 elective, optional **9** voluntary

openwork 3 net **4** lace **6** eyelet **7** lattice, Madeira, tracery **8** filigree

opera 5 score **7** musical **8** libretto **11** composition
by Bellini: 5 Norma
by Bizet: 6 Carmen
by Delibes: 5 Lakme
by Donizetti: 10 La Favorita **11** Don Pasquale **12** Maria Stuarda **13** L'Elisir d'Amore **17** Lucia di Lammermoor **19** La Figlia di Regimente
by Gounod: 5 Faust
by Leoncavallo: 10 I Pagliacci
by Mozart: 8 Idomeneo **10** Magic Flute **11** Don Giovanni **12** Cosi fan tutte **16** Marriage of Figaro
by Offenbach: 15 Tales of Hoffmann
by Ponchielli: 10 La Gioconda
by Puccini: 5 Tosca **8** La Boheme **12** Manon Lescaut **15** Madame Butterfly
by Rossini: 8 Tancredi **11** William Tell **15** The Barber of Seville
by Smetana: 13 The Bartered Bride
by Strauss: 6 Salome **7** Elektra **15** Ariadne auf Naxos **16** Der Rosenkavalier
by Tchaikovsky: 12 Eugene Onegin
by Verdi: 4 Aida **6** Otello **8** Falstaff **9** Rigoletto **10** La Traviata **11** Il Trovatore
by Wagner: 8 Parsifal **9** Lohengrin **10** Tannhauser **16** Tristan and Isolde **17** The Flying Dutchman **21** The Ring of the Nibelungs
comic: 5 buffa **7** comique
glass: 9 lorgnette
hat: 5 crush, gibus
house: 3 Met **6** Sydney **7** La Scala **12** Covent Garden, Metropolitan
singer: 4 bass, diva **5** basso, buffa, buffo, tenor **7** soprano **8** baritone **9** contralto **10** coloratura, prima donna **12** mezzo soprano
singular: 4 opus

solo: 4 aria
text: 8 libretto

operate 2 go **3** run **4** go in, work **6** behave, manage, open up **7** oversee, perform **8** function **11** superintend **14** perform surgery **18** perform an operation

operating 6 active **7** working **8** in motion **9** operative **10** responsive

operation 5 force **6** action, agency, effect **7** conduct, pursuit, running, surgery, working **8** activity, exertion **9** influence, procedure **10** management, overseeing **11** exploratory, performance, supervision **15** instrumentality, superintendence

operative 3 spy **4** dick **5** agent, in use **6** acting, active, shamus, worker **7** in force, working **8** in effect, in motion, workable **9** activated, detective, effective, effectual, operating **10** functional, private eye, responsive **11** efficacious, secret agent

operator 4 doer, user **5** agent, pilot **6** driver, worker **7** manager **9** performer

opere citato 14 in the work cited
abbreviation: 5 op cit

Ophelia
character in: 6 Hamlet
author: 11 Shakespeare

ophidiophobia
fear of: 6 snakes

Ophion
form: 7 serpent
created from: 9 north wind
created by: 8 Eurynome

Ophir
father: 6 Joktan
source of: 4 gold

opiate 4 dope **6** downer **7** anodyne **8** hypnotic, narcotic, nepenthe, sedative **9** analgesic, calmative, soporific, stupefier **10** depressant, painkiller, palliative **12** somnifacient, stupefacient, tranquilizer

opine 3 say **4** deem **5** allow, guess, offer, state, think **6** assume, reckon **7** believe, imagine, presume, suggest, surmise **8** conclude, consider, estimate **9** speculate, volunteer **10** conjecture, have a hunch

opinion 4 idea, view **6** belief, notion, theory **7** surmise **8** estimate, judgment, thinking **9** sentiment, suspicion **10** assessment, assumption, conception, conclusion, conjecture, conviction, estimation, evaluation, impression, persuasion **11** speculation

opinionated 8 dogmatic, obdurate, stubborn **9** obstinate, pigheaded, unbending **10** bullheaded, headstrong, inflexible, unyielding **12** closedminded **14** uncompromising

O Pioneers!
author: 11 Willa Cather

Opis
companion of: 7 Artemis

Opobalsammum 12 Biblical tree

Oppenheimer, Julius Robert
field: 7 physics
directed development of: 10 atomic bomb
location: 9 Los Alamos, New Mexico
chaired: 3 AEC **22** Atomic Energy Commission

Opper, Frederick
creator/artist of: 13 Happy Hooligan **17** Alphonse and Gaston, And Her Name Was Maud

opponent 3 foe **5** enemy, rival **8** resister **9** adversary, assailant, contender, disputant **10** antagonist, challenger, competitor, opposition

opportune 3 apt **5** happy, lucky **6** proper, timely **7** fitting **8** suitable **9** expedient, favorable, fortunate, welltimed **10** auspicious, convenient, felicitous, profitable, propitious, seasonable **11** appropriate **12** advantageous

opportunity 4 time, turn **5** means **6** chance, moment **7** opening **8** occasion **9** situation **10** good chance **11** contingency

oppose 4 buck, defy **5** fight **6** battle, combat, resist, thwart **7** contest **8** obstruct **9** withstand **12** be set against, speak against

opposed 3 con **4** anti **6** averse, pitted **7** adverse, against, counter, hostile **8** contrary, disputed, objected, resisted **9** contested, countered **10** confronted, contrasted, reciprocal **12** contradicted

opposer 5 rival **8** opponent **9** adversary **10** antagonist, competitor

opposite 5 other **6** facing **7** adverse, counter, reverse **8** contrary, converse, opposing **9** differing **11** conflicting **12** antagonistic, antithetical **13** contradictory, counteractive

opposite number 5 equal **8** parallel **10** equivalent **11** correlative, counterpart

opposition 3 foe **5** enemy, rival **6** enmity **8** aversion, defiance, opponent **9** adversary, contender, hostility, other side, rejection **10** antagonism, antagonist, competitor, negativism, resistance **11** contrariety, disapproval **12** disagreement

oppress 3 tax, try, vex **4** pain **5** abuse, worry **6** burden, deject, grieve, sadden, sorrow **7** depress, trouble **8** cast down, dispirit, maltreat **9** despotize, persecute, tyrannize, weigh down **10** discourage, dishearten

oppressed 7 crushed **9** exploited **10** tyrannized **11** downtrodden, subservient

oppressive 5 cruel, harsh **6** brutal, severe, trying, vexing **7** onerous, painful, wearing **8** despotic, grievous, pressing **9** worrisome **10** burdensome, depressing, repressive, tyrannical, unbearable **11** distressing, hardhearted, troublesome **12** discouraging **13** uncomfortable

oppressor 6 despot, tyrant **8** autocrat, dictator

opprobrious 4 base **6** wicked **7** abusive, corrupt, damning **8** infamous, reviling, shameful, shocking **9** malicious, maligning, nefarious, vilifying, vitriolic **10** censorious, deplorable, despicable, malevolent, outrageous, scandalous, scurrilous, unbecoming **11** acrimonious, disgraceful, fulminating **12** condemnatory, denunciatory, dishonorable, disreputable, faultfinding **13** hypercritical, objectionable, reprehensible

opprobrium 5 shame **6** infamy **8** disgrace, dishonor **9** disrepute **12** denunciation

Ops
origin: **5** Roman
goddess of: **6** plenty
husband: **6** Saturn
son: **7** Jupiter
called: **10** Magna Mater
corresponds to: **4** Rhea **6** Cybele **9** Dindymene **10** Berecyntia

opt for 4 pick, take **5** adopt **6** choose, select, take up **7** embrace, espouse, fix upon, pick out **8** decide on, settle on

optimism 10 confidence **11** hopefulness **12** cheerfulness, sanguineness **13** bright outlook, encouragement

optimistic 6 bright **7** hopeful, roseate **8** buoyed up, cheerful, sanguine **9** confident, favorable, heartened, promising **10** auspicious, encouraged, heartening, propitious **11** encouraging, rose-colored **12** enthusiastic

optimum 4 acme, A-one, best, peak **5** crest, ideal, prime **6** choice, height, select, zenith **7** capital, perfect, supreme **8** flawless **9** faultless, first-rate **10** perfection, unexcelled **11** superlative **12** quintessence

option 4 will **5** voice **6** choice, liking **8** decision, election, free will, pleasure **9** franchise, privilege, selection **10** discretion, partiality, preference **11** alternative **12** predilection

optional 4 open **8** elective, unforced **9** allowable, open-ended, voluntary **10** volitional **11** not required **12** discretional **13** discretionary, nonobligatory

opulence 6 bounty, plenty, riches, wealth **7** fortune **8** elegance, luxuries, richness **9** abundance, affluence, amplitude, profusion **10** cornucopia, lavishness, plentitude, prosperity **11** copiousness, great wealth **13** sumptuousness

opus 4 work **5** piece **6** effort **7** attempt, product **8** creation **9** handiwork, invention **10** brainchild, production **11** composition

oracle, Oracle 4 sage, seer **5** augur, sibyl **6** wizard **7** adviser, diviner, prophet **9** predictor, Scripture **10** forecaster, soothsayer **11** clairvoyant

oral 5 vocal **6** spoken, verbal, voiced **7** uttered **8** ingested **9** swallowed **10** of the mouth, verbalized **11** articulated, using speech
Latin: **8** viva voce

orange
varieties: **4** king, mock, sour, wild **5** blood, hardy, natal, navel, Osage, sweet **6** bitter, common, Panama, Temple **7** Florida, Mexican, Satsuma, Seville, Spanish **8** Bergamot, Mandarin, Otaheite, Valencia **9** Tachibana, vegetable **10** Chinese box, trifoliate **13** African cherry, Mediterranean **15** Jamaica mandarin **17** house-blooming mock
liqueur: **7** Curacao

orangutan, orang-outang 3 ape **4** mias **5** satyr **6** primate **10** anthropoid
characteristic: **8** arboreal **11** herbivorous
native land: **6** Borneo **7** Sumatra
species: **13** Pongo pygmaeus

ora pro nobis 9 pray for us

orate 6 recite, speak **7** declaim **11** make a speech

oration 4 talk **5** spiel **6** eulogy, sermon, speech **7** address, lecture, recital **9** discourse, monologue, panegyric **10** peroration **11** declamation **12** disquisition, formal speech

orator 6 talker **7** speaker **8** lecturer, preacher **9** declaimer **10** sermonizer **11** rhetorician, speechmaker, spellbinder **12** elocutionist **13** public speaker

oratory 6 speech **7** bombast **8** delivery, rhetoric **9** elocution, eloquence, preaching **11** declamation **12** speechifying, speechmaking **14** grandiloquence

orb 4 ball, moon **5** globe **6** sphere **7** globule **8** spheroid

orbit 3 way **4** path **5** cycle, route, track **6** circle, course **7** channel, circuit, pathway **10** trajectory **13** revolve around **14** circumnavigate

orchards
god of: **9** Vertumnus

orchestra 3 pit **4** band **6** stalls **7** parquet **8** ensemble, parterre **12** Philharmonic

orchestrate 5 adapt, score **7** arrange, compose

orchestration 5 score **10** adaptation **11** arrangement **12** organization

orchid
varieties: **3** bat, bee, fen, fly, nun, nut **4** baby, blue, dove, moth, nun's, rein, swan **5** black, chain, cigar, cobra, coral, giant, jewel, pansy, Salep, showy, snowy, spice, tiger, water, widow **6** bamboo, bottle, cradle, dollar, Easter, helmet, mirror, monkey, pigeon, ragged, sawfly, shower, spider, stream, virgin **7** Alaskan, cowhorn, fringed, hooker's, jumping, peacock, rainbow, rosebud, scarlet, soldier **8** bee-swarm, Cooktown, cranefly, fried-egg, gold-lace, greenfly, hyacinth, nun's-hood, poorman's, Savannah, scorpion, white nun, windmill, woodland **9** bluntleaf, butterfly, chocolate, Christmas, clam-shell, green rein, green swan, white rein **10** buttonhole, five-leaved, golden swan, hay-scented, late spider, leafy white, Sierra rein, slender bog **11** cockle-shell, crested rein, dancing-doll, dancing-lady, early spider, golden chain, green-winged, one-leaf rein, pink slipper, purple-spire, rattlesnake, round-leaved **12** green fringed, pink scorpion, purple-hooded, Southern rein, tall white bog, white fringed **13** crested yellow, golden fringed, green woodland, Northern green, ragged fringed, yellow fringed **14** crested fringed, large butterfly, little clubspur, white butterfly **15** lesser butterfly, lily-of-the-valley **16** downy rattlesnake, Florida butterfly, Northern small bog, purple fringeless, small round-leaved, white-flowered bog **18** large purple fringed, leafy Northern green, small purple fringed, Southern small white **19** lesser purple fringed **20** greater purple fringed

Orcus
god of: **10** underworld
punishes: **7** perjury
corresponds to: **3** Dis **5** Hades, Pluto **8** Dis Pater

ordain 4 name, rule, will **5** elect, enact, frock **6** decree, invest **7** adjudge, appoint, command, dictate **8** delegate, deputize, instruct **9** determine, legislate, prescribe, pronounce **10** commission, consecrate

ordeal 4 care, pain **5** agony, grief, trial, worry **6** burden, misery, sorrow, strain, stress **7** anguish, concern, torment, tragedy, trouble **8** calamity, distress, pressure, vexation **9** heartache, nightmare, suffering **10** affliction, oppression **11** tribulation, unhappiness **12** wretchedness **16** trying experience

order 3 bid, law **4** body, book, calm, club, fiat, form, kind, rank, rule, sort, type **5** breed, caste, class, grade, group, guild, house, lodge, quiet, ukase **6** adjure, ask for, charge, decree, degree, demand, dictum, direct, engage, enjoin, family, status, stripe, system **7** agree to, bidding, caliber, call for, command, company, control, dictate, harmony, pattern, quality, request, reserve, silence, society, species, station **8** alliance, category, division, grouping, instruct, neatness, position, purchase, sorority, standing, tidiness **9** framework, structure, ultimatum **10** discipline, federation, fraternity, imperative, sisterhood, tabulation **11** arrangement, association, brotherhood, commandment, confederacy, designation, instruction, tranquility **12** codification, organization, peacefulness, tranquillity **13** pronouncement **14** categorization, classification

ordered 4 bade, neat, trim **7** regular, uniform **8** arranged **9** shipshape **10** systematic

orderliness 8 neatness, tidiness **10** discipline **12** organization

orderly 4 neat, tidy **5** civil, quiet **6** proper, spruce **8** peaceful **9** organized, peaceable, shipshape, tractable **10** classified, controlled, methodical, restrained, systematic **11** disciplined, uncluttered, well-behaved

ordinance 3 act, law **4** bull, fiat, rule, writ **5** canon, edict, order **6** decree, dictum, ruling **7** command, mandate, statute **9** enactment **10** regulation **11** commandment

ordinarily 7 as a rule, usually **8** commonly, normally **9** generally, regularly, routinely **10** habitually **11** customarily **12** on the average **14** conventionally

ordinary 4 dull, so-so **5** usual **6** common, normal **7** average, humdrum, routine, trivial, typical **8** everyday, familiar, habitual, mediocre, standard **9** customary **10** pedestrian, uninspired **11** commonplace, indifferent, stereotyped, traditional, unimportant **12** conventional, run-of-the-mill, unimpressive **13** insignificant, unexceptional, unimaginative, uninteresting **15** inconsequential, undistinguished

Ordinary People
   director: 13 Robert Redford
   author: 11 Judith Guest
   cast: 10 Judd Hirsch **13** Timothy Hutton **14** Mary Tyler Moore **16** Donald Sutherland
   Oscar for: 7 picture **8** director **12** screenwriter **15** supporting actor (Hutton)

ordinary wine
   French: 12 vin ordinaire

ordnance 4 arms **6** cannon **9** armaments, artillery, munitions

ordnance depot 6 armory **7** arsenal **18** military storehouse

ore 3 tin **4** gold, iron, lead, paco, rock, zinc **5** metal **6** bronze, copper, galena, sulfur **7** halvans, mineral **8** aluminum, cinnabar, hematite **9** melachite

byproduct: 6 gangue
deposit: 3 bed **4** lode, mine, vein **7** bonanza
layer: 4 seam **5** stope
trough: 6 strake
worthless: 4 slag **5** dross, matte

Oread
   form: 5 nymph
   location: 8 mountain
   companion of: 7 Artemis

oregano
   name means: 16 joy of the mountain
   botanical name: 8 O vulgare, Origanum
   also: 6 organy, origan **8** marjoram **9** pizza herb **11** Mexican sage, winter sweet
   origin: 13 Mediterranean
   family: 4 mint
   cure for: 11 indigestion **14** loss of appetite
   first aid for: 12 spider stings **14** scorpion stings
   use: 5 pizza **6** broths **8** stuffing **12** tomato dishes **13** Italian dishes

Oregon
   abbreviation: 2 OR **4** Oreg
   nickname: 6 Beaver, Sunset **7** Webfoot **13** Sawdust Empire
   capital: 5 Salem
   largest city: 8 Portland
   others: 5 Nyssa **6** Albany, Eugene **7** Ashland, Astoria, Medford **8** Portland, Roseburg **9** Corvallis, Pendleton **10** Grant's Pass, Willamette **12** Klamath Falls
   college: 4 Reed **7** Pacific **8** Linfield, Portland **10** Willamette **13** Lewis and Clark
   feature:
      fort: 5 Boise **6** Casper **7** Kearney, Laramie
      national park: 10 Crater Lake
   tribe: 4 Coos **5** Alsea, Kusan, Modoc, Wasco, Yanan, Yunca **6** Cayuse, Chetco, Chinoo, Kuitsh, Molala, Siletz, Tenino, Umpqua **7** Bannock, Clatsop, Klamath, Sastean, Shastan, Takelma, Walpapi, Yaquina **8** Clackama, Klikitat, Nez Perce, Sahaptin, Umatilla **9** Kalapuyan, Tillamook **10** Kalapooian, Wallawalla
   people: 10 Wayne Morse **12** Linus Pauling **15** Phyllis McGinley
      explorer: 13 Lewis and Clark
   lake: 5 Abert, Waldo **6** Harney, McNary **7** John Day, Klamath, Malheur
      deepest in US: 6 Crater
   land rank: 5 tenth
   mountain: 6 Mazama, Tacoma, Walker, Wilson **7** Elkhorn, Grizzly, Jackass, Rainier, Tidbits, Wallowa **8** Cascades **9** Blue Coast, Marys Peak **10** Strawberry
      highest point: 4 Hood
   physical feature:
      bay: 4 Coos

   caves: 11 Marble Halls
      wind: 7 Chinook
   river: 5 Rogue, Snake **6** Imnaha, Owyhee, Powder, Umpqua **7** Blitzen, John Day, Klamath, Silvie's **8** Columbia **9** Deschutes **10** Willamette
   state admission: 11 thirty-third
   state bird: 17 western meadowlark
   state fish: 13 Chinook salmon
   state flower: 7 mahonia **11** Oregon grape
   state motto: 8 The Union
   state song: 14 Oregon My Oregon
   state tree: 10 Douglas fir

Oregon Trail, The
   author: 14 Francis Parkman

Oresteia
   author: 9 Aeschylus
   trilogy includes: 9 Agamemnon, Eumenides **10** Choephoroe

Orestes
   author: 9 Euripides
   character: 5 Helen **6** Apollo, Furies **7** Electra, Pylades **8** Menelaus

Orestes
   father: 9 Agamemnon
   mother: 12 Clytemnestra
   sister: 7 Electra **9** Iphigenia
   wife: 8 Hermione
   son: 9 Tisamenus
   killed: 9 Aegisthus **12** Clytemnestra
   pursued by: 6 Furies

Orfeo, L'
   also: 17 The Story of Orpheus
   opera by: 10 Monteverdi

Orfeo ed Euridice
   also: 18 Orpheus and Eurydice
   opera by: 5 Gluck
   character: 4 Amor, Zeus **6** Furies

Orff, Carl
   born: 6 Munich **7** Germany
   composer of: 7 Der Mond, The Moon **8** Antigone, Die Kluge **9** Schulwerk **10** Prometheus **13** Carmina Burana, The Clever Girl **14** Catulli Carmina **16** Oedipus der Tyrann, Oedipus the Tyrant

organ 6 agency **7** journal, vehicle **9** harmonium **10** hurdy-gurdy, instrument **11** publication

organic 5 alive, quick **6** living **7** animate, natural, ordered, planned, unified **8** designed, physical **9** patterned **10** anatomical, harmonious, methodical, systematic **12** nonsynthetic **13** physiological **14** constitutional

organism 4 cell **5** plant, whole **6** animal, entity, system **7** complex, network, society **8** creature **9** bacterium **10** federation **11** association, corporation, institution, living thing **13** microorganism

organization 4 club, firm, sect **5** corps, group, order, party, union **6** design, league, making, outfit **7** company, forming, harmony, pattern, society **8** alliance, assembly, business, grouping, ordering **9** arranging, formation **10** federation, fellowship, fraternity **11** arrangement, association, composition, corporation, formulation, structuring **12** constitution, coordination **13** establishment, incorporation

organizational 10 managerial **13** developmental **14** administrative

organize 4 file, form, tidy **5** found, group, index, order, set up **6** codify, create, neaten, tidy up **7** arrange, catalog, develop **8** classify, tabulate **9** establish, formulate, originate **10** categorize, coordinate **11** make orderly, systematize

organized 4 neat, tidy **7** logical, orderly **8** coherent **10** methodical, systematic

orgiastic 4 wild **6** wanton **7** drunken, riotous **9** abandoned, debauched, Dionysian, dissolute, libertine **10** dissipated, licentious **12** bacchanalian, unrestrained **13** overindulgent, undisciplined

orgy 7 debauch, wassail **8** carousal **9** bacchanal **10** saturnalia **11** bacchanalia

orient, the Orient 3 fix, set **4** Asia, find **6** locate, relate, square **7** situate **8** accustom **9** acclimate, reconcile **10** the Far East **11** Eastern Asia, familiarize

oriental 4 Arab, fine, Thai, Turk **5** Asian **6** bright, Indian, Korean **7** Asiatic, Chinese, Eastern, Iranian, shining **8** Japanese, lustrous, precious, superior **10** Vietnamese

animal: 4 zebu **5** rasse
building: 6 pagoda
dish: 5 pilau, pilaw **6** pilaff
drum: 6 tomtom
food fish: 3 tai
garment: 3 aba **6** sarong
inn: 4 Khan **5** serai **6** imaret **11** caravansary
laborer: 6 coolie
market: 3 suk, sug **4** souk **6** bazaar
nurse: 4 amah, ayah
prince: 4 amir, haja
sail: 6 lateen
sash: 3 obi
shrub: 3 tea **5** henna **8** oleander
wagon: 5 araba
weight: 2 mo **4** rotl, tael **5** catty, liang **6** cantar

orientation 8 location **9** alignment, direction, situation **10** adjustment **11** acclimation **15** acclimatization, familiarization

orifice 3 gap, pit **4** hole, slit, slot, vent **5** cleft, inlet, mouth **6** cavity, cranny, hollow, lacuna, pocket, socket **7** crevice, fissure, opening, passage **8** alveolus, aperture, entrance

origami
Japanese art of: 12 paper folding

origin 4 base, line, race, rise, root **5**

agent, basis, birth, breed, cause, house, stock **6** author, family, father, ground, growth, mother, reason, source, spring, strain **7** creator, descent, genesis, lineage, taproot **8** ancestry, nativity, producer **9** beginning, emergence, evolution, generator, inception, parentage, principle **10** derivation, extraction, foundation **12** commencement, fountainhead

original 3 new **4** bold **5** basic, basis, first, fresh, novel **6** daring, primal, unique **7** example, initial, pattern, primary, seminal, strange, unusual **8** atypical, creative, earliest, germinal, primeval, singular, uncommon **9** different, essential, first copy, formative, inaugural, ingenious, inventive, prototype **10** aboriginal, newfangled, primordial, underlying, unfamiliar, unorthodox **11** fundamental, imaginative **12** introductory **13** extraordinary **14** unconventional

Original Amateur Hour, The
host: 7 Ted Mack

originality 6 daring **7** newness, novelty **8** boldness **9** freshness, ingenuity **10** cleverness, creativity, uniqueness **11** imagination, singularity, unorthodoxy **13** individuality, inventiveness **17** unconventionality

originally 7 at first, by birth **8** uniquely **9** initially, unusually **10** creatively **11** differently, inventively **13** imaginatively

originate 4 come, flow, rise, stem **5** arise, begin, draft, found, issue, start **6** create, crop up, derive, design, devise, emerge, evolve, father, invent, sprout **7** develop, emanate, proceed **8** commence, conceive, envision, initiate, organize, spring up **9** establish, fabricate, formulate, germinate **10** inaugurate

origination 5 birth **7** genesis **9** inception, invention **10** conception, initiation **11** germination **12** commencement **13** establishment

Origin of Species, The
author: 13 Charles Darwin

Orion
form: 5 giant
vocation: 6 hunter
pursued: 8 Pleiades
killed by: 7 Artemis
became: 13 constellation

Oriya
language family: 12 Indo-European
branch: 11 Indo-Iranian
group: 5 Indic
spoken in: 5 (northern) India

Orkney Islands
county seat: 8 Kirkwall
country: 8 Scotland
firth: 8 Pentland
island: 3 Hay **6** Rousay, Sanday **7** Westray **8** Stronsay **14** South Ron-

aldsay
largest city: 6 Pomona

Orlando
author: 13 Virginia Woolf
character: 5 Sasha **14** Nicholas Greene **28** Archduchess Harriet of Roumania, Marmaduke Bonthrop Shelmerdine

Orlando
character in: 11 As You Like It
author: 11 Shakespeare
novel by: 13 Virginia Woolf

Orlando Furioso
author: 7 Ariosto
character: 6 Rogero **7** Rinaldo **8** Agramant, Angelica, Rodomont **9** Bradamant **11** Charlemagne

Ormazd 10 Ahura Mazda **12** supreme deity
religion: 14 Zoroastrianism

ormolu 5 alloy, brass, paste **6** bronze **7** gilding **8** ornament
imitation of: 4 gold
used to decorate: 5 clock **9** furniture

ornament 4 deck, gild, trim **5** adorn **6** bedeck, enrich, finery, frills **7** festoon, furbish, garnish **8** beautify, decorate, furbelow, trick out, trimming **9** accessory, adornment, embellish **10** decoration, enrich ment **11** elaboration **13** embellishment **14** beautification

ornamental 4 gilt **5** fancy **6** chichi, rococo **10** decorative
ball: 4 bead **6** pompom
button: 4 stud
grass: 4 neti
loop: 5 picot
metal: 5 niello

ornamentation 7 garnish **8** trimming **9** adornment **10** decoration **13** embellishment

ornate 5 fancy, showy **6** flashy, florid, lavish, rococo **7** adorned, baroque, flowery **9** decorated, elaborate, sumptuous **10** flamboyant **11** embellished, pretentious **12** ostentatious

ornery 4 curt, mean **5** surly, testy **6** crabby, grumpy, shirty **7** grouchy, peevish, waspish **8** snappish **9** dyspeptic, irascible, irritable **10** ill-natured **11** ill-tempered, quarrelsome **12** cantankerous

ornithophobia
fear of: 5 birds

ornithopod
type of: 8 dinosaur
member: 9 Iguanodon **10** Edmontonia, Nodosaurus **11** Anatosaurus, Polacanthus, Saurolophus, Scolosaurus, Stegosaurus **12** Ankylosaurus, Camptosaurus, Lambeosaurus, Pisanosaurus **13** Acanthopolis, Corythosaurus, Hypsilophodon, Palaeoscincus **14** Thescelosaurus **15** Parasaurolophus, Procheneosaurus **17** Heterodontosaurus

orotund 4 full, rich **5** clear **6** strong **7**

pompous, ringing, vibrant **8** resonant, sonorous **9** bombastic **10** resounding, rhetorical, stentorian
Latin: 10 ore rotundo

oro y plata 13 gold and silver
motto of: 7 Montana

Orozco, Jose Clemente
born: 6 Mexico **7** Jalisco (Zapotlan) **12** Ciudad Guzman
artwork: 5 Grief **9** Catharsis **11** Omniscience **12** House of Tears **16** National Allegory, Social Revolution **18** Hidalgo and Castillo

Orphans of the Storm
director: 10 D W Griffith
cast: 11 Dorothy Gish, Lillian Gish **17** Joseph Schildkraut

Orpheus
vocation: 4 poet **8** musician
mother: 8 Calliope
wife: 8 Eurydice
member of: 9 Argonauts
went into: 5 Hades
killed by: 7 Maenads

Orpheus in the Underworld
also: 15 Orphee aux Enfers
operetta by: 9 Offenbach

Orsino
character in: 12 Twelfth Night
author: 11 Shakespeare

ort 3 bit **5** crumb, dregs, scrap **6** morsel, refuse, trifle **7** remnant **8** leavings, leftover

orthodox 5 fixed, pious, usual **6** devout, narrow **7** limited, regular, routine **8** accepted, approved, official, ordinary, standard **9** customary, religious **11** commonplace, conformable, established, traditional **12** conventional **13** authoritative, circumscribed

orthoptera
class: 8 hexapoda
phylum: 10 arthropoda
group: 4 leaf **5** stick **6** locust, mantid **7** cricket **9** cockroach **11** grasshopper

Orwell, George
real name: 15 Eric Arthur Blair
author of: 4 1984 **10** Animal Farm **18** Nineteen Eighty-Four **29** Politics and the English Language

oryx 5 beisa **6** pickax **7** gazelle, gemsbok **8** antelope, leucoryx

Osage (Wazhazhe)
language family: 6 Siouan
location: 6 Kansas **8** Arkansas, Missouri, Oklahoma

Osbournes, The
network: 3 MTV
cast: 12 Jack Osbourne, Melinda Varga, Ozzy Osbourne **13** Kelly Osbourne **14** Sharon Osbourne

Oscan
language family: 12 Indo-European
branch: 6 Italic

Oschophoria
origin: 8 Athenian
event: 8 festival
honoring: 7 vintage **8** Dionysus

oscillate 4 vary **5** pulse, swing, waver **6** change, seesaw **7** librate, pulsate, vibrate **8** hesitate **9** alternate, come and go, fluctuate, hem and haw, vacillate **10** ebb and flow, equivocate **12** shilly-shally **16** move back and forth

osier 3 rod **4** wand **5** salix, withe **6** willow **7** dogwood, wilgers **9** twig-withy
species: 14 Salix viminalis
use: 6 wicker **8** basketry

Osiris
origin: 8 Egyptian
god of: 4 dead, Nile
judge of: 4 dead
king of: 4 dead
wife: 4 Isis
sister: 4 Isis
son: 5 Horus
brother: 3 Set **4** Seth **5** Horus
killed by: 3 Set **4** Seth

Oskar Matzerath
character in: 7 Tin Drum
author: 5 Grass

Oslo
capital of: 6 Norway
former name: 11 Christiania
landmark: 8 Storting (Parliament) **11** Royal Palace
mountain: 12 Holmenkollen
park: 7 Frogner
peninsula: 8 Akershus
street: 14 Karl Johansgate

Ossian
character in: 12 Gaelic poetry

ossify 6 harden **7** stiffen **9** fossilize

ossuary 8 boneyard **10** depository, receptacle

ostensible 6 avowed **7** alleged, assumed, feigned, implied, nominal, outward, seeming, surface, titular, visible **8** apparent, declared, illusory, manifest, specious **9** pretended, professed **10** presumable **11** perceivable

ostentation 4 airs, dash, fuss, pomp, ritz, show **5** glitz, gloss, swank **6** splash **7** display, glitter **8** flourish, pretense **9** pageantry, pomposity, showiness, spectacle
French: 7 etalage

ostentatious 4 loud **5** gaudy, showy **6** flashy, florid, garish **7** pompous **8** affected, immodest, overdone **9** grandiose, obtrusive **10** flamboyant, showing off **11** conspicuous, exaggerated, pretentious **15** flaunting wealth

Osterreich *see* **7** Austria

ostracize 3 cut **4** oust, shun, snub **5** avoid, expel **6** banish, disown, reject **7** exclude, shutout **9** blackball, blacklist

Ostwald, Wilhelm
field: 9 chemistry

nationality: 6 German
founded: 17 physical chemistry

O'Sullivan, Maureen
born: 5 Boyle **7** Ireland **15** County Roscommon
daughter: 9 Mia Farrow
roles: 4 Jane (Tarzan movies) **16** David Copperfield **17** Pride and Prejudice **19** Hannah and Her Sisters

Otello
also: 7 Othello
opera by: 5 Verdi **7** Rossini

O tempora! O mores! 14 O times! O customs!
said by: 6 Cicero

Othello
director: 11 Stuart Burge
author: 18 William Shakespeare
character: 4 Iago **6** Cassio, Emilia **9** Desdemona
cast: 11 Frank Finlay, Joyce Redman, Maggie Smith **15** Laurence Olivier

other 4 more **5** added, extra, spare **6** unlike **7** further, reverse **8** contrary, opposite **9** alternate, auxiliary, different, remaining **10** additional, contrasted, dissimilar **11** contrasting **13** contradictory, supplementary **14** differentiated

Other Gods
author: 9 Pearl Buck

Other Side of Midnight, The
author: 13 Sidney Sheldon

other than 3 but **4** save **6** except, saving **7** barring, besides **9** excepting, excluding

otherwise 5 if not **6** or else **9** inversely **10** contrarily **11** differently **12** contrariwise

otherworldly 7 sublime **8** heavenly **9** celestial **14** transcendental

O times! O customs! 1
Latin: 14 O tempora! O mores!

Otionia
father: 10 Erechtheus
sister: 10 Protogonia
death by: 9 sacrifice
   for victory of: 9 Athenians
   over: 11 Eleusinians

otiose 4 idle, lazy **6** futile **7** laggard, resting, useless, worn-out **8** abortive, impotent, inactive, indolent, listless, slothful, sluggish **9** fruitless, lethargic, powerless, somnolent **10** unavailing **11** incompetent, ineffective, inoperative, unrewarding **12** unproductive

Otomi
tribe: 7 Capotec

O'Toole, Peter
born: 7 Ireland **9** Connemara
roles: 6 Becket **7** Creator, Lord Jim **12** Global Heresy **13** Man of La Mancha **14** Goodbye Mr Chips, My Favorite Year, The Last Emperor **15** The Final Curtain, The Lion in Winter **16** Lawrence of Arabia, What's

New Pussycat **18** How to Steal a Million

O'Trigger, Sir Lucius
  character in: **9** The Rivals
  author: **8** Sheridan

Ott, Mel
  nickname: **9** Boy Wonder **12** Master Melvin
  sport: **8** baseball
  position: **8** outfield
  team: **13** New York Giants

Ottawa
  capital of: **6** Canada
  early name: **6** Bytown
  falls: **6** Rideau **9** Chaudiere
  landmark: **18** National Arts Centre **19** Dominion Observatory, Parliament Buildings
  river: **6** Ottawa, Rideau **8** Gatineau
  university: **8** Carleton

Ottawa
  language family: **9** Algonkian **10** Algonquian
  location: **4** Ohio **6** Canada, Kansas **7** Ontario **12** Lake Michigan
  leader: **7** Pontiac

Otter
  origin: **12** Scandinavian
  mentioned in: **8** Volsunga
  form: **5** otter
  father: **8** Hreidmar
  killed by: **4** Loki

ottoman, Ottoman 4 seat, Turk **5** couch, divan, stool **7** sultane, Turkish **9** footstool
  color: **3** red **9** vermilion
  governor: **3** bey, dey **5** pasha
  ruler: **5** Osman **8** Suleiman
  standard: **4** ale

Ouagadougou
  capital of: **10** Upper Volta **11** Burkina Faso

oui 3 yes

ounce
  abbreviation of: **2** oz

ounce troy
  abbreviation of: **3** oz t

Our Bill
  creator: **14** Harry Haenigsen
  character: **6** Walter

Our Crowd
  author: **17** Stephen Birmingham

Our Miss Brooks
  character: **8** Mrs Davis **12** Connie Brooks, Walter Denton **13** Osgood Conklin, Philip Boynton **14** Harriet Conklin
  cast: **8** Eve Arden **10** Dick Crenna, Gale Gordon, Jane Morgan **14** Gloria McMillan, Robert Rockwell
  Miss Brooks taught: **7** English
  school: **11** Madison High

Our Mutual Friend
  author: **14** Charles Dickens
  character: **4** Wegg **5** Venus **6** Boffin **11** Bella Wilfer **17** Mortimer Lightwood, Young John Harmon (Handford, Rokesmith)

our sea
  Latin: **11** mare nostrum
  ancient Roman name for: **13** Mediterranean

Our Town
  author: **14** Thornton Wilder
  character: **12** Simon Stimson
    Gibbs family: **2** Dr **3** Mrs **6** George **7** Rebecca
    Webb family: **2** Mr **3** Mrs **5** Emily, Wally
  director: **7** Sam Wood
  cast: **10** Fay Bainter **11** Martha Scott **13** William Holden

oust 4 fire, sack **5** eject, evict, expel **6** banish, bounce, put out, remove, unseat **7** boot out, cashier, cast out, dismiss, kick out **8** throw out **9** discharge, give the ax **11** give the gate, send packing

ouster 6 firing **7** removal, sacking **8** bouncing, ejection, eviction **9** discharge, dismissal, expelling, expulsion, overthrow **10** banishment, cashiering **11** dislodgment, drumming out, throwing out **13** dispossession

out 2 ex **4** away **5** aloud, eject, forth, not in, passe **6** absent, begone, excuse, public **7** outside **8** exterior, external, revealed **9** in society, in the open, published **10** extinguish

out-and-out 4 pure, sure **5** sheer, total, utter **6** arrant **7** perfect **8** absolute, complete, hardened, outright, positive, thorough **9** confirmed, downright, unlimited **10** inveterate **11** straight out, unequivocal, unmitigated, unqualified **12** unregenerate, unrestricted **13** dyed-in-the-wool, thoroughgoing, unadulterated, unconditional **14** unquestionable

outbrazen 4 dare, defy, face **8** confront **9** challenge, stand up to

outbreak 5 burst **7** display **8** epidemic, eruption, invasion, outburst **9** explosion **10** outpouring **13** demonstration

outbuilding 4 barn, shed **5** privy **6** garage, stable **7** latrine **8** outhouse, woodshed

outburst 5 blast, burst **7** display, thunder **8** eruption, outbreak **9** explosion **10** outpouring **11** fulmination **13** demonstration

outcast 5 exile, rover **6** ousted, outlaw, pariah, roamer **7** refugee, runaway **8** banished, castaway, deportee, derelict, expelled, fugitive, rejected, vagabond **9** discarded **10** expatriate

Outcault, R F
  creator/artist of: **11** Buster Brown **12** The Yellow Kid

outcome 3 end **5** fruit, issue **6** effect, payoff, result, upshot **9** aftermath, outgrowth **11** aftereffect, consequence

outcry 3 cry **4** howl, roar, yell, yelp, yowl **5** noise, shout, whoop **6** bellow, clamor, hubbub, scream, shriek, uproar **7** clangor, protest, screech **9** commotion, complaint, crying out, hue and cry, objection **10** cry of alarm, hullabaloo **12** caterwauling, remonstrance

outdated 5 passe **7** antique **8** outmoded **9** out-of-date **10** antiquated **12** old-fashioned

outdo 3 top **4** beat, best **5** excel, worst **6** better, defeat, exceed, outfox, outwit **7** eclipse, outplay, outrank, surpass **8** outclass, outshine, outstrip, overcome **9** transcend

outdoor festival
  French: **13** fete champetre

outdoor market 5 agora **6** bazaar **10** flea market **11** marketplace

outer 6 distal, remote **7** extreme, farther, outside, outward, without **8** exterior, external, outlying **9** outermost **10** farther out, peripheral

outer edge 3 lip, rim, tip **5** bound **6** margin **8** boundary **9** extremity

Outer Mongolia see **8** Mongolia

outermost 5 outer **6** utmost **7** extreme, outside, outward, surface **8** exterior, external **11** farthest out, most distant, superficial

outfit 3 fit, rig **4** gear **5** array, dress, equip, getup, habit, rig up **6** clothe, supply **7** appoint, costume, furnish **8** accouter, ensemble, wardrobe **9** equipment, provision, trappings **13** accoutrements, paraphernalia

outflow 5 issue **7** leakage, seepage **8** drainage **9** discharge

outgo 4 beat, cost, exit, pass **5** excel, issue, outdo **6** efflux, egress, outlay, outlet **7** outflow, surpass **8** outstrip **9** departure **11** expenditure

outgoing 4 warm **6** genial, social **7** amiable, cordial, exiting, leaving **8** friendly, going out, outbound, sociable **9** convivial, departing **10** gregarious **11** extroverted, sympathetic, warmhearted

outgoing person 9 extrovert **17** hail-fellow-well-met

outgrowth 3 end **4** knob, knot, node **5** bulge, fruit, issue, shoot **6** result, sequel, sprout, upshot **7** product **8** offshoot **9** aftermath **10** conclusion, projection **11** aftereffect, consequence, culmination, excrescence, outcropping **12** protuberance

outing 4 hike, ride, spin, tour, trip, walk **5** drive, jaunt, tramp **6** airing, junket, ramble **7** holiday **9** excursion **10** expedition

outlander 5 alien, exile **6** emigre **7** invader, settler **8** intruder, newcomer, stranger, wanderer **9** Auslander, barbarian, foreigner, immigrant **10** tramontane **12** ultramontane

outlandish 3 odd **5** kooky, queer, weird **6** far-out **7** bizarre, curious, strange, unusual **8** freakish, peculiar **9** eccentric, fantastic, grotesque, unheard-of **10** incredible, outrageous, ridiculous **12** preposterous, unbelievable, unimaginable, unparalleled **13** inconceivable **14** unconventional

outlast 6 endure, hold on, keep on, remain, stay on **7** carry on, hold out, outstay, outwear, perdure, persist, prevail, survive **8** continue

outlaw 3 ban, bar **4** deny, stop **5** felon **6** bandit, forbid, pariah **7** exclude, outcast **8** criminal, disallow, fugitive, prohibit, suppress **9** desperado, interdict, miscreant, proscribe **10** highwayman

outlay 3 fee **4** cost **5** outgo, price **6** charge **7** expense, payment **8** spending **11** amount spent, expenditure **12** disbursement

outlet 3 way **4** door, duct, exit, gate, path, vent **5** means **6** avenue, egress, escape, portal **7** channel, conduit, gateway, opening, passage

outline 4 plot **5** brief, trace **6** digest, limits, resume, review **7** contour, diagram, profile, summary, tracing **8** abstract, synopsis **9** blueprint, delineate, lineation, perimeter, periphery, sketch out **10** abridgment, silhouette **11** delineation **12** condensation
French: 6 apercu

outlook 4 view **5** scene, sight, vista **6** aspect, chance **7** picture, promise **8** attitude, forecast, panorama, prospect **9** spectacle, viewpoint **10** assumption **11** expectation, frame of mind, perspective, point of view, presumption, probability **12** anticipation

outlying 5 outer, rural **6** far-off, remote **7** distant, exurban **8** exterior, suburban **10** peripheral

outmoded 5 corny, dated, passe, tired **6** demode, old hat **7** antique, archaic, vintage **8** obsolete, old-timey, outdated **9** out-of-date **10** antiquated **12** old-fashioned, out-of-fashion **14** behind the times
French: 6 demode

Out of Africa
director: 13 Sydney Pollack
cast: 11 Meryl Streep (Baroness Karen Blixen, Isak Dinesen) **13** Robert Redford (Denys Finch Hatton) **19** Klaus Maria Brandauer (Baron Bror von Blixen)

out of bed 2 up **5** astir **9** up and at 'em **10** on one's feet, up and about **12** rise and shine

out-of-date 5 dated, passe **8** outmoded **10** antiquated **12** oldfashioned
French: 6 demode

out of doors 3 out **5** forth **6** abroad **7** outside **8** alfresco **12** in the open air

out-of-fashion 5 passe **8** obsolete, outmoded **9** out-of-date **12** oldfashioned
French: 6 demode

out of hand 4 wild **5** rowdy **6** unruly **10** disorderly **12** obstreperous, out of control, unmanageable, unrestrained **14** uncontrollable

out of keeping 8 atypical, peculiar, unseemly **9** anomalous, irregular **11** incongruous **12** inconsistent **13** inappropriate

out of kilter 4 awry **5** askew **6** uneven **7** crooked, oblique

out of line 6 unruly **9** excessive **10** exorbitant **12** presumptuous, unreasonable

out of many one
Latin: 13 e pluribus unum
motto of: 12 United States

out of one's head 3 mad **4** daft, nuts **5** crazy, nutty **6** insane **7** cracked, touched **8** demented, deranged, unhinged **10** unbalanced **12** mad as a hatter, off his rocker **15** mad as a March hare **17** nutty as a fruitcake

out of operation 4 dead, down **8** inactive **10** not working, out of order **11** inoperative

out of order 5 amiss **6** faulty **10** not working **11** inoperative, uncalled-for **13** inappropriate

out of place 3 odd **8** unseemly **10** unsuitable **11** incongruous, inconsonant **13** inappropriate

out of shape 4 bent **5** unfit **6** flabby, warped **7** crooked **8** deformed **9** distorted, untrained

out of sorts 5 cross, huffy, testy **6** crabby, cranky, touchy **7** bearish, grouchy, peevish **8** petulant, snappish **9** crotchety, irritable **10** ill-humored **11** ill-tempered **12** cantankerous **13** short-tempered

out of the books of
Latin: 8 ex libris

out of the fight
French: 12 hors de combat

out of the ordinary 4 rare **6** unique **7** notable, unusual **8** singular, uncommon **10** phenomenal, remarkable **11** exceptional **13** extraordinary

Out of the Past
director: 15 Jacques Tourneur
based on novel by: 13 Geoffrey Homes (Daniel Mainwaring) (Build My Gallows High)
cast: 9 Jane Greer **11** Kirk Douglas, Richard Webb **13** Rhonda Fleming, Robert Mitchum

out of touch 7 mixed-up **8** unstable **11** disoriented **12** out of contact **13** incommunicado

out-of-towner 7 tourist, visitor **9** sojourner, transient **11** nonresident

outpace 4 pass **5** outdo **6** exceed, outrun **8** outstrip

outpouring 6 deluge **7** barrage, gushing, outflow **8** effusion

output 4 crop, gain, take **5** yield **6** profit **7** harvest, produce, product, reaping, turnout **8** gleaning, proceeds **9** gathering **10** production **11** achievement **12** productivity **14** accomplishment

outrage 4 evil, gall, rile **5** anger, shock, wrong **6** arouse, enrage, insult, madden, offend, ruffle **7** affront, incense, provoke, steam up **8** atrocity, disquiet, enormity, iniquity **9** barbarity, indignity, infuriate **10** discompose, disrespect, exasperate, gross crime, scandalize **11** desecration, monstrosity, profanation **13** barbarousness, get one's back up, make one see red, slap in the face, transgression **17** make one's blood boil

outraged 3 mad **5** angry, irate, riled **6** fuming, raging **7** enraged, furious **8** incensed, inflamed, offended **9** affronted, indignant **10** displeased, infuriated

outrageous 4 base, foul, rank, rude, vile **5** gross **6** brutal, odious, wicked **7** abusive, extreme, galling, heinous, immense, inhuman **8** enormous, flagrant, inhumane, insolent, scornful, shocking **9** atrocious, barbarous, excessive, insulting, maddening, monstrous, nefarious, offensive, shameless **10** despicable, exorbitant, horrifying, immoderate, iniquitous, scandalous **11** disgraceful, infuriating, unspeakable, unwarranted **12** contemptible, contemptuous, exasperating, preposterous, unreasonable **13** disrespectful, reprehensible **14** unconscionable

outrageousness 8 enormity **9** immensity **10** wickedness **13** atrociousness, monstrousness, offensiveness **16** preposterousness

outre 8 improper

outreach 6 exceed **7** surpass

outright 4 full **5** sheer, total, utter **6** at once, entire, openly **7** utterly, visibly **8** absolute, complete, entirely, patently, promptly, thorough **9** downright, forthwith, instantly, on the spot, out-and-out **10** absolutely, altogether, completely, manifestly, thoroughly, unreserved **11** immediately, unmitigated, unqualified **12** demonstrably, undiminished **13** thoroughgoing, unconditional

outrival 3 dim **5** excel, outdo **6** exceed **7** eclipse, surpass **8** outshine **9** transcend **10** overshadow, tower above

outrush 4 gust **8** overflow

outset 4 dawn **5** birth, start **7** dawning

9 beginning, departure, threshold **12** commencement

outshine 3 dim **5** excel, outdo **6** exceed **7** eclipse, surpass **9** transcend **10** overshadow

outside 4 case, face, skin **5** alien, faint, outer **6** facade, remote, sheath, slight **7** coating, distant, foreign, obscure, outdoor, outward, strange, surface **8** covering, exterior, external, outdoors **9** nonnative, outer side, outermost **10** extraneous, out-of-doors, unfamiliar

outsider 5 alien **7** outcast **8** onlooker, stranger **9** bystander, foreigner, nonmember **14** nonparticipant

outskirts 3 rim **4** edge **6** limits, verges **7** borders, fringes, margins, suburbs **8** environs **9** periphery, precincts **10** perimeters **11** extremities

outspoken 5 blunt, frank **6** candid, direct, honest **7** artless **9** guileless, ingenuous, unsparing **10** forthright, unreserved **11** opinionated, plainspoken **13** undissembling **15** straightforward, undissimulating

outspread 5 broad **6** opened, spread **7** laid out **8** expanded, extended, unfolded, unfurled, unrolled **9** spread out, stretched **12** outstretched

outstanding 3 due **5** famed, great, owing **6** famous, unpaid **7** eminent, notable, payable **8** foremost, renowned, striking **9** best known, exemplary, in arrears, marvelous, memorable, prominent, unsettled **10** celebrated, noteworthy, phenomenal, remarkable **11** exceptional, magnificent, uncollected **13** distinguished, extraordinary, unforgettable

outstrip 4 pass **6** exceed, outrun **7** outpace, surpass **11** leave behind

outward 5 outer **7** evident, outside, surface, visible **8** apparent, exterior, external, manifest **10** observable, ostensible **11** perceivable, perceptible, superficial

outward appearance 4 mien **6** aspect, facade, manner **7** bearing **8** demeanor, exterior

Outward Bound
author: **10** Sutton Vane

outwardly 7 clearly, visibly **9** evidently, seemingly **10** apparently, manifestly, ostensibly **13** on the face of it **16** to all appearances

outwards 3 out **4** away

outweigh 6 exceed **7** eclipse, surpass **8** override **9** rise above **10** overshadow **11** predominate, prevail over **13** be heavier than, weigh more than

outwit 4 dupe, foil, fool, trap **5** trick **6** baffle, outfox, take in, thwart **7** ensnare **8** outsmart **9** get around **10** circumvent **11** outmaneuver

outworn 5 dated, passe **6** bygone **7** defunct, disused, extinct **8** obsolete, rejected **9** abandoned, discarded, forgotten, out-of-date **10** antiquated, superseded **12** old-fashioned **13** unfashionable

ouzo
type: **7** liqueur
origin: **6** Greece
flavor: **5** anise
substitute for: **8** absinthe

oval 5 ovate, ovoid **6** curved, ovular **7** obovate, oviform, rounded **9** egg-shaped **10** elliptical **11** ellipsoidal

ovation 6 cheers, homage, hurrah, hurray, huzzah **7** acclaim, fanfare, tribute **8** applause, cheering **9** adulation **11** acclamation

oven 3 umu **4** kiln, oast **5** baker, range, stove **6** hearth **7** broiler, chamber, kitchen, roaster
clay: **7** tandoor
fork: **7** fruggan, fruggin
mop: **6** scovel

over 3 too **4** also, anew, done, else, gone, past **5** above, again, ended, extra, often **6** afresh, bygone, lapsed, no more, to boot **7** at an end, elapsed, expired, settled, surplus **8** finished, in excess, once more, too great **9** completed, concluded, excessive, remaining **10** additional, all through, in addition, passed away, repeatedly, terminated **11** a second time, superfluous

overabundance 4 glut **6** excess **7** surfeit, surplus **8** plethora **9** abundance, profusion **10** oversupply **11** superfluity **14** superabundance **15** supersaturation **21** embarrassment of riches
French: **19** embarras de richesses

over again 4 anew **5** again **7** all over **8** once more **9** once again

overall 5 total **6** entire **7** general **8** complete, long-term, sweeping **9** extensive, long-range, panoramic **10** exhaustive, widespread **12** all-embracing, all-inclusive **13** comprehensive, thoroughgoing

over-and-above 5 added, extra **7** added on, besides **10** additional, in addition **13** supplementary

overawe 6 dazzle **9** overpower, overwhelm **10** intimidate

overbalance 5 upset **6** topple **8** outweigh

overbearing 5 cocky **6** lordly, snooty **7** haughty, high-hat, pompous, stuck-up **8** arrogant, despotic, egoistic **9** conceited, imperious, know-it-all **10** autocratic, disdainful, egoistical, high-handed, tyrannical **11** dictatorial, domineering, egotistical **13** high-and-mighty, self-assertive, self-important

overburden 3 tax **4** load, task, tire **5** whelm **7** exhaust, wear out **8** encumber, overwork, surcharge **9** overwhelm

overcast 4 dark, dull, gray, hazy **5** foggy, misty, murky **6** cloudy, dreary, gloomy, leaden **7** sunless **8** lowering **11** overclouded, threatening

overcharge 3 gyp, pad **4** rook, skin, soak **5** bleed, cheat, gouge, stick, sting, usury **6** extort, fleece **7** exploit **10** exaggerate

overcoat 3 mac **5** parka **6** duster, poncho, raglan, tabard, ulster **7** oilskin, paletot, topcoat **8** burberry, mackinaw **9** greatcoat, inverness, pea jacket **10** mackintosh, trenchcoat **12** chesterfield, Prince Albert

Overcoat, The
author: **12** Nikolai Gogol
character: **9** Petrovich **26** A Certain Important Personage **28** Akakii Akakiievich Bashmachkin

overcome 4 beat, best, lick **5** crush, quell **6** defeat, master, subdue **7** conquer, put down, survive, win over **8** suppress, surmount, vanquish **9** overpower, overthrow, overwhelm, transcend **11** prevail over, triumph over **14** get the better of

overconfident 5 brash **6** cheeky **8** arrogant, cocksure, egoistic, immodest, impudent **9** conceited **10** egoistical **11** egotistical, self-assured **12** presumptuous

overcrowd 3 jam **4** cram, fill, pack **5** stuff **7** congest

overcrowded 6 filled, jammed, packed **7** crammed, stuffed **9** congested, jampacked

overdecorated 5 gaudy, showy **6** flashy, garish **9** unsightly **12** ostentatious

overdelicacy 11 genteelness, prudishness **12** priggishness **14** overrefinement

overdo 4 gild **6** expand **7** amplify, ham it up, magnify, overact **8** overplay **9** embroider, overstate **10** do to excess, exaggerate **11** carry too far, hyperbolize **12** lay it on thick **13** stretch a point

overdue 4 late, slow **5** tardy **7** belated, delayed, past due **8** dilatory **10** behindhand, behind time, unpunctual **11** long delayed

overdue debt 7 arrears **10** balance due **18** balance outstanding

overflow 4 glut **5** flood **6** excess **7** run over, surplus **8** flow over, inundate, plethora, slop over **9** overspill, profusion **10** overspread, oversupply **11** copiousness, superfluity **13** overabundance **14** superabundance

overflowing 4 full **5** flush **7** replete, swamped **8** abundant, flooding **9** abounding, inundated **11** running over

overgarment 4 cape, coat, robe **5** cloak, habit, parka, shawl, smock **6**

blazer, blouse, duster, jacket, kimono, mantle, poncho **7** sweater, topcoat, wrapper **8** cardigan, raincoat **9** gaberdine, housecoat

overgrown 4 rank **5** giant **7** blown-up **8** colossal, enlarged, forested, gigantic **9** luxuriant, oversized

overhang 3 jut **4** eave **5** bulge, drape, eaves, jetty **6** beetle, impend, sadden, shelve **7** project, suspend **8** protrude, threaten **9** projection

overhaul 4 beat, pass **5** catch **6** revamp **7** rebuild, remodel, restore, service **8** overtake, renovate **11** catch up with, recondition, reconstruct

overhead 3 nut **4** atop, roof **5** above, aloft, on top, upper **6** upward **7** ceiling, topmost, up above **8** superior **9** overlying, uppermost **11** overhanging

overindulge 4 baby **5** spoil, stuff **6** overdo, pamper, pig out **7** carouse, overeat **9** dissipate **11** mollycoddle

overjoyed 6 elated, joyous **8** ecstatic, euphoric, exultant, jubilant, thrilled **9** delighted, enchanted, exuberant, gratified **10** enraptured, enthralled **11** carried away, tickled pink, transported **12** happy as a lark

overlay 4 coat **5** cover, layer **6** carpet, veneer **7** blanket, coating **8** covering **11** superimpose

overload 3 tax **4** glut **5** flood, whelm **6** deluge, excess **7** burnout, surfeit **8** encumber **9** innundate, surcharge

overlook 4 miss, omit, skip **6** excuse, forget, give on, ignore, pass up, slight, survey, wink at **7** blink at, command, forgive, let ride, neglect **8** leave out, look over, pass over, shrug off **9** disregard, look out on **10** tower above **11** forget about, have a view of, leave undone

overlord 4 czar, tsar **7** emperor, monarch **8** autocrat **12** supreme ruler **13** absolute ruler

overly 3 too **4** very **6** highly, unduly **7** acutely, too much **8** overmuch, severely, to a fault, unfairly **9** extremely, intensely **10** needlessly **11** exceedingly, excessively **12** exorbitantly, immoderately, inordinately, unreasonably **18** disproportionately

overly trusting 5 naive **8** gullible **9** credulous **12** unsuspicious

overmodest 3 coy **4** prim **7** prudish **8** priggish **11** puritanical

overmuch 3 too **6** excess **7** surplus **8** plethora **9** profusion

overpass 4 span **6** bridge **9** crossover

overpower 4 beat, best, move, sway **5** crush, quell, worst **6** defeat, master, subdue **7** conquer **8** overcome, vanquish **9** influence, overwhelm

overpowering 6 mighty, strong **8** crushing **10** astounding **12** overwhelming

overpraise 4 line **7** blarney, fawning **8** flattery **11** fulsomeness

overpriced 6 costly **7** too high **9** expensive **10** exorbitant

overproud 4 vain **8** arrogant, egoistic **9** conceited **10** egoistical **11** egotistical, swell-headed **13** self-important

overrate 9 overprize, overvalue **10** overesteem, overpraise **12** overestimate **13** make too much of

overrefined 7 genteel, prudish **8** priggish **12** overdelicate

override 5 crush, quash **7** reverse **8** set aside **10** commission **11** countermand

overrule 4 deny, veto **5** annul, eject, repel, waive **6** cancel, refuse, reject, revoke **7** dismiss, nullify, outvote **8** disallow, outweigh, override, overturn, preclude, set aside, throw out **9** repudiate **10** invalidate **11** countermand

overrun 4 loot, raid, sack **5** choke **6** deluge, engulf, infest, invade **7** despoil, pillage, plunder, surplus **8** inundate, overgrow, pour in on, rove over **9** overwhelm, surge over, swarm over

overseas, oversea 5 alien **6** abroad, exotic **7** foreign **8** external **11** ultramarine **12** transoceanic **14** in foreign lands

oversee 3 run **4** boss, rule **5** guide, pilot, see to, steer, watch **6** direct, govern, handle, manage **7** carry on, command **8** attend to, overlook, regulate **9** supervise **10** administer **11** keep an eye on, preside over, superintend **12** have charge of

overseeing 7 bossing, guiding, running **8** guidance, handling, managing **10** leadership, management **11** attending to, supervising, supervision **13** administering **14** administrating, administration, superintending **15** superintendence

overseer 4 boss, head **5** chief **7** captain, foreman, manager **8** director, governor **10** supervisor, taskmaster **11** slave driver **13** administrator **14** superintendent

overshadow 3 fog **4** hide, mask, veil **5** cover, dwarf, shade **6** darken, screen, shroud **7** conceal, eclipse, obscure **8** outshine **9** tower over

overshadowing 7 eclipse, masking, shading, veiling **8** cloaking **9** darkening, eclipsing, obscuring **10** concealing, surpassing **11** concealment, obscuration **12** towering over

overshoe 3 gum **4** boot **6** arctic, gaiter, galosh, patten, rubber **7** galoshe

overshoot 4 pass **6** exceed, go over **8** go beyond

oversight 6 laxity, slight **7** blunder, mistake, neglect **8** omission **9** disre-

gard **10** negligence **11** inattention **12** carelessness, heedlessness, inadvertence **13** careless error **14** neglectfulness **15** thoughtlessness

oversized 4 huge, vast **7** immense, mammoth **8** colossal, enormous, gigantic **10** monumental **14** Brobdingnagian

overspending 12 extravagance, throwing away

overspread 3 fog **4** coat, fill, pave **5** bathe, cloud, cover, paint, plate, smear **6** clothe, infest **7** blanket, diffuse, overlay, overrun, pervade, suffuse **8** disperse **9** whitewash

overstate 6 overdo, play up **7** enlarge, inflate, lay it on, magnify, stretch, touch up **8** increase, overdraw, oversell **9** embellish, embroider, enlarge on, overpaint **10** exaggerate, overstress **15** spread it on thick

overstep 6 exceed **7** violate **10** transgress

oversupply 4 glut **6** excess **7** surfeit, surplus, too much **8** plethora **11** undue amount **13** overabundance **14** superabundance

overt 4 open **5** plain **6** public **7** evident, obvious, visible **8** apparent, manifest, palpable, revealed **10** easily seen, noticeable, observable, ostensible **11** perceivable, perceptible, unconcealed, undisguised

overtake 4 go by, pass **5** catch, reach **6** befall, gain on **7** run down **8** approach, overhaul **11** catch up with

overtax 4 tire **5** abuse, hoist **6** burden, exceed, strain, stress **7** exhaust **8** overload, overwork **9** misemploy **10** overburden

over the hill 3 old **4** aged **5** aging **7** elderly **11** past the peak **13** past one's prime

overthrow 4 undo **5** crush **6** defeat, mutiny, topple **7** abolish, undoing **8** downfall, overcome, overturn, toppling **9** abolition, bring down, overpower, rebellion **10** do away with, revolution

overtire 3 fag **4** bush, do in, poop **5** drain **7** exhaust, fatigue, wear out **8** enervate

overtone 3 hue **4** hint **5** drift **8** coloring, innuendo **10** intimation, suggestion **11** connotation, implication, insinuation

overtrustful 8 gullible **9** credulous **12** unsuspecting, unsuspicious **13** unquestioning

overture 3 bid **6** motion, signal, tender **7** advance, gesture, preface, prelude **8** approach, foreword, offering, preamble, prologue, proposal **9** beginning **10** invitation, suggestion **11** opening move, proposition **12** introduction

overturn 4 beat, oust **5** crush, upend, upset **6** defeat, depose, thrash, topple **7** capsize, conquer, turn out **8** overcome, push over, vanquish **9** knock down, knock over, overpower, overthrow, overwhelm **14** turn topsy-turvy, turn upside down

overturning
　French: **14** bouleversement

overweening 5 bossy, cocky, pushy **6** brassy **7** haughty, pompous **8** arrogant, egoistic **9** bigheaded, imperious **10** disdainful, egoistical, high-handed, immoderate **11** domineering, egotistical, overbearing, patronizing **12** presumptuous **13** high-and-mighty, overconfident, self-important

overweight 3 fat **5** dumpy, fatty, gross, hefty, obese, piggy, plump, pudgy, stout, tubby **6** chubby, chunky, fleshy, portly, rotund **7** fattish, well-fed **8** roly-poly **9** corpulent **10** potbellied, well-padded **11** beer-bellied, overstuffed **15** well-upholstered

overwhelm 4 beat, bury **5** crush, quash, quell, swamp **6** defeat, engulf **7** conquer, overrun, stagger **8** bowl over, confound, inundate, overcome, vanquish **9** devastate, overpower, overthrow, subjugate

overwhelming 8 crushing **10** staggering **11** astonishing, devastating **12** overpowering

overwork 3 tax **4** task, tire, toil **5** labor **6** burden, strain **7** exhaust, overtax, wear out **9** misemploy **10** overburden

overwrought 4 wild **5** riled **6** touchy, uneasy **7** excited, nervous, ruffled **8** agitated, frenzied, inflamed, wild-eyed, worked up **9** perturbed, wrought up **10** distracted, high-strung **11** carried away, overexcited

Ovid
　author of: **6** Amores **7** Tristia **8** Heroides **11** Ars Amatoria **12** The Art of Love **13** Metamorphoses

ovule 3 egg, nit **4** germ, ovum **6** embryo **7** seedlet

ovum 3 egg **4** cell, germ, seed **5** spore **6** gamete **8** oosphere

owe 8 be in debt **11** be obligated **12** be beholden to, be indebted to

owed 3 due **5** owing **6** unpaid **9** in arrears **11** outstanding

Owen Marshall, Counselor at Law
　character: **11** Jess Brandon **12** Frieda Krause **15** Melissa Marshall
　cast: **9** Lee Majors **10** Arthur Hill **11** Joan Darling **17** Christine Matchett

owing 3 due **4** owed **6** unpaid **9** in arrears **11** outstanding

own 4 avow, have, hold, keep, tell **5** admit, allow, grant, yield **6** assent, concur, retain **7** concede, possess, private **8** disclose, maintain, personal **9** acquiesce, confess to, consent to, recognize **10** individual, particular **11** acknowledge

owner 6 holder, master **7** partner **8** landlady, landlord, mistress **9** copartner, landowner, possessor **10** landholder, proprietor **11** householder, titleholder **12** proprietress

own up to 5 admit **6** accept **7** confess **8** blurt out **9** recognize **11** acknowledge **14** come clean about

ox 3 oaf **4** bull, clod, musk, urus, zebu **5** aiver, beast, bison, gayal, steer **6** auroch, bantin, bovine **7** banteng, buffalo **10** clodhopper
　Cambodian: **7** Kouprey, Kouproh
　Celebesian: **3** goa, noa **4** anoa
　extinct: **4** urus **7** aurochs
　family: **7** bovidae
　genus: **3** bos
　horned: **4** reem
　hornless: **4** moil
　Indian: **4** gaur
　Paul Bunyan's: **4** Babe
　　color: **4** blue
　stall: **4** crib
　team: **4** yoke
　Tibetan: **3** yak
　wild: **3** ure **4** anoa
　young: **4** stot **5** stirk

Ox-Bow Incident, The
　author: **21** Walter Van Tilburg Clark
　character: **5** Canby, Croft **6** Davies, Gerald, Martin, Tetley **9** Gil Carter
　director: **14** William Wellman
　cast: **10** Henry Fonda **11** Dana Andrews **12** Anthony Quinn **13** William Blythe **14** Mary Beth Hughes

oxen
　group of: **4** yoke

oxide 8 compound
　afterburn: **4** calx
　calcium: **4** calx, lime
　cobalt: **6** zaffer, zaffre
　element: **6** oxygen
　iron: **4** rust **8** hematite, limonite **9** colcothar, magnetite
　make by heat: **7** calcine
　sodium: **4** soda
　zinc: **6** cadmia

oxidize 4 burn, char, rust **7** corrode

Oxyderces
　epithet of: **6** Athena
　means: **10** bright-eyed

oxygen
　chemical symbol: **1** O

Oxylus
　origin: **8** Aetolian
　punishment: **5** exile
　chosen leader of: **10** Heraclidae
　led invasion of: **12** Peloponnesus

oyez 4 hear **6** attend
　cry used by: **10** court crier
　preceded: **12** proclamation

Oz *see* Wizard of Oz

Ozark Jubilee
　host: **8** Red Foley **10** Webb Pierce
　theme: **12** Sugarfoot Rag

Ozark State
　nickname of: **8** Missouri

Ozick, Cynthia
　author of: **8** The Shawl **10** Levitation **13** The Pagan Rabbi **17** The Cannibal Galaxy **21** The Messiah of Stockholm, The Puttermesser Papers **24** Heir to the Glimmering World

Ozzie and Harriet, The Adventures of
　cast: **11** David Nelson, Ozzie Nelson, Ricky (Eric) Nelson **13** Harriet Nelson

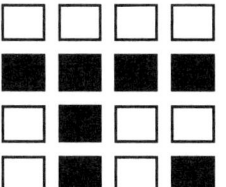 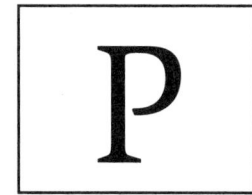 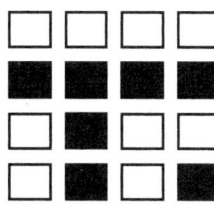

pa 3 dad, paw, pop 4 papa 5 daddy, pater 6 father
  mate: 2 ma

pace 4 clip, flow, gait, rate, step, walk 5 amble, speed, tread 6 motion, stride, stroll 7 saunter 8 momentum, slow gait, velocity

Pacelli, Eugenio Maria Giuseppe Giovanni 11 Pope Pius XII

pachyderm 5 hippo, rhino 8 elephant, ungulate 10 rhinoceros 12 hippopotamus
  characteristic: 4 tusk 5 ivory, trunk 12 thick-skinned
  prehistoric: 7 mammoth 8 mastodon

pachydermatous 4 hard 5 horny, tough 7 callous 8 callused, hardened, leathery 12 thick-skinned 13 elephant-hided

pacific 4 calm 5 quiet, still 6 gentle, placid, serene, smooth 7 halcyon, restful 8 dovelike, peaceful, tranquil 9 pacifying, peaceable, reposeful, unruffled 10 harmonious, untroubled 11 inoffensive, undisturbed 12 conciliatory

pacification 8 soothing 11 appeasement, peacemaking 12 conciliation, nonagression 14 reconciliation

Pacific island 3 Aru, Yap 4 Bali, Fiji, Guam, Maui, Oahu, Rapa, Truk, Wake 5 Mauru, Papua, Samoa 6 Hawaii, Kodiak, Midway, Ryukyu, Tahiti, Taiwan 7 Okinawa 8 Borabora, Eniwetok, Pitcairn, Tasmania 9 New Guinea 12 Bougainville

pacify 4 calm 5 allay, quiet 6 soothe 7 appease, assuage, compose, mollify, placate 9 reconcile 10 conciliate, propitiate

Pacino, Al
  real name: 13 Alberto Pacino
  born: 9 New York NY
  roles: 7 Serpico 8 Scarface 10 The Insider 11 Carlito's Way, People I Know 12 Donnie Brasco, The Godfather 13 Scent of a Woman (Oscar) 14 Any Given Sunday 15 Dog Day Afternoon 16 And Justice for All 17 Glengarry Glen Ross 19 The Merchant of Venice 22 Does a Tiger wear a Necktie (Tony)

pack 3 box, jam, kit, lot, mob, set, tie 4 bevy, bind, cram, fill, heap, herd, load, mass 5 batch, bunch, clump, covey, crowd, drove, flock, group, horde, stuff, swarm, truss 6 bundle, gaggle, gather, packet, parcel, passel, throng 7 cluster, package 8 assemble 9 container, multitude 10 assortment, collection, miscellany 12 accumulation

package 3 box, kit 4 case, pack, wrap 6 bundle, carton, encase, packet, parcel, wrap up 9 container, wrappings

pack closely 4 cram, pack 5 press, stuff 7 compact 8 compress

packed 4 full 6 filled, jammed, loaded, massed, rammed, wedged 7 crammed, crowded, crushed, pressed, stuffed 8 overfull, squeezed 10 sandwiched 11 overcrowded

packet 3 bag, box 4 bale, pack, roll 5 pouch, sheaf 6 bundle, parcel, quiver 7 package

pact 4 bond 6 treaty 7 compact 8 alliance, contract, covenant 9 agreement, concordat 10 convention 11 concordance 13 understanding

pad 3 mat 4 fill 5 stuff 6 blow up, fatten, tablet 7 bolster, cushion, inflate, protect, puff out 8 mattress, notebook 9 upholster 10 cushioning, stretch out

padding 6 filler, lining 7 filling, packing, surfeit, surplus, wadding 8 stuffing, verbiage, wrapping 9 prolixity, verbosity, wordiness 10 redundancy 11 verboseness 12 extravagance 14 superabundance

Paderewski, Ignace (Ignacy Jan)
  born: 6 Poland 9 Kurilowka
  composer of: 5 Manru 9 Minuet in G

pad out 5 add to 6 expand, extend 7 amplify, augment, enlarge, stretch 8 elongate, increase, lengthen

padre 6 cleric, father, priest 8 chaplain 9 clergyman

paean 6 anthem, eulogy 7 hosanna 9 laudation, panegyric 10 hallelujah 11 acclamation 12 hymn of praise
  form: 4 hymn, song
  characteristic: 6 joyful 12 thanksgiving

Paeon
  form: 3 god
  position: 9 physician
  served gods of: 7 Olympia
  corresponds to: 6 Apollo

Paezan
  language family: 13 Macro-Chibchan
  group: 4 Paez 5 Choco 6 Warrau 8 Colorado

pagan 7 atheist, heathen, infidel 8 idolator 9 barbarian 10 heathenish, idolatrous, polytheist, unbeliever 11 nonbeliever 12 polytheistic

Paganini, Niccolo
  born: 5 Genoa, Italy
  played: 6 violin
  composer of: 19 The Carnival of Venice

page 3 boy, lad 4 beep, call, girl, leaf 5 folio, groom, sheet, youth 6 knight, number, summon 7 callboy, contact 8 announce, attendant, messenger 10 apprentice, manservant
  blank: 7 flyleaf
  left-hand: 5 verso
  right-hand: 5 recto

Page, Geraldine
  born: 12 Kirksville MO
  husband: 7 Rip Torn
  roles: 5 Hondo 9 Interiors 11 Pete-n-Tillie 14 Summer and Smoke 16 A Trip to Bountiful (Oscar), Sweet Bird of Youth

Page and Mistress Page
  characters in: 22 The Merry Wives of Windsor
  author: 11 Shakespeare

pageant 4 pomp, rite, show 6 parade, ritual 7 display 8 ceremony 9 spectacle 10 exhibition, procession 12 extravaganza

pageantry 4 pomp, rite, show 5 drama, flair 6 ritual, splash 7 display, glitter, pageant 8 ceremony, grandeur, splendor 9 showiness, spectacle, theatrics 10 flashiness 11 ostentation 12 extravagance, magnificence

Paget, James
  field: 7 surgery 8 medicine
  nationality: 7 British
  founder of: 9 pathology

Pagliacci, I
  also: 9 The Clowns
  opera by: 11 Leoncavallo
  character: 5 Canio, Nedda, Tonio 6 Silvio

Pagnol, Marcel
  author of: 5 Cesar, Fanny 6 Marius, Topaze

Pago Pago
  capital of: 13 American Samoa

Pahlavi *see* 4 Iran

Paige, Leroy
  nickname: 7 Satchel

sport: 8 baseball
position: 7 pitcher

pain 3 vex, woe **4** ache, gall, hell, hurt, pang, rile **5** agony, annoy, chafe, grief, pinch, pique, smart, sting, throb, worry **6** aching, grieve, harass, misery, ordeal, sadden, sorrow, stitch, twinge **7** agonize, anguish, disturb, hurting, malaise, sadness, torment, torture, trouble **8** distress, smarting, soreness **9** displease, heartache, suffering **10** affliction, discomfort, exasperate, heartbreak **11** unhappiness **12** wretchedness

Paine, Thomas
author of: 9 The Crisis **11** Common Sense **14** The Rights of Man

painful 3 sad **4** dire **5** sharp **6** aching, dismal, dreary, trying **7** arduous, hurtful, racking **8** grievous, grueling, pathetic, piercing, smarting, stinging, very sore **9** agonizing, difficult, sorrowful, throbbing, torturous **10** afflictive, disturbing, lamentable, unpleasant **11** disquieting, distasteful, distressful, distressing **12** disagreeable, excruciating

pain in the neck 4 bane **6** bother **7** torment **8** headache, nuisance **9** annoyance **10** affliction

painstaking 5 fussy **7** careful, earnest, finicky, precise **8** diligent, exacting, thorough **9** assiduous, energetic, strenuous **10** meticulous, scrupulous **11** industrious, persevering, punctilious **13** conscientious, thoroughgoing

paint 4 coat, daub, draw, limn, swab, tint **5** adorn, brush, color, cover, horse, rouge, shade, stain **6** depict, enamel, makeup, opaque, sketch **7** pigment, portray, stipple, touch up **8** cosmetic, decorate, describe, variegate **9** delineate, represent

painter 6 artist, drawer **8** sketcher **9** old master **10** delineator **11** illustrator, landscapist, miniaturist **13** watercolorist

Painter, Painter's Easel
constellation of: 6 Pictor

painting 3 art, oil **5** draft, mural, piece **6** canvas, design, tablet **7** cartoon, daubing, drawing, graphic, picture, tableau **8** panorama, portrait, seascape **9** depiction, landscape, still life **10** cerography, watercolor **11** perspective **12** illustration
colloidal: 7 tempera
method: 9 encaustic
on plaster: 5 secco **6** fresco
one-color: 8 monotint **10** monochrome
opaque: 7 gouache
religious: 5 Pieta
style: 5 genre
tool: 5 brush, easel, knife **6** canvas, roller, sponge **7** palette **8** spraygun

pair 3 duo **4** dyad, mate, span, team,

yoke **5** brace, match, unite **6** couple **7** combine, doublet, match up, pair off, twosome

pair off 10 go two by two **11** form couples

Paiute
language family: 10 Shoshonean
tribe: 12 Mono-Paviosto, Snake Indians **13** Digger Indians **14** Northern Paiute, Southern Paiute
location: 4 Utah **5** Idaho **6** Nevada, Oregon **7** Arizona **10** California

Pakistan
name means: 13 Land of the Holy, Land of the Pure
capital: 9 Islamabad
largest city: 7 Karachi
others: 3 Dir, Sui **4** Mari, Sidi **5** Dacca, Qasim, Ralat **6** Chalna, Khulna, Lahore, Multan, Quetta **7** Larkana, Sialkot **8** Jamalpur, Lyallpur, Peshawar, Sargodha **9** Hyderabad **10** Gujranwala, Rawalpindi
school: 9 U of Punjab **10** U of Karachi **12** U of Hyderabad **16** Allama Iqbal Open U **22** Pakistan U of Agriculture **39** Pakistan Institute of International Affairs
division: 3 Dir **4** Sind, Swat **5** Hunza, Kalat **6** Bengal, Kharan, Punjab **7** Chitral **8** Khairpur, Peshawar **10** Bahawalpur, Waziristan **11** Baluchistan
empire: 5 Gupta, Mogul **6** Kushan, Maurya **7** British, Magadha
seceded state: 10 Bangladesh
monetary unit: 4 anna, pice **5** paisa, rupee
weight: 4 seer, tola **5** maund
mountain: 3 Pab, Pub **4** Salt **6** Makran **7** Kirthar **8** Himalaya, Safed Koh, Sulaiman **9** Hindu Kush, Karakoram **11** Makran Coast **13** Central Makran **14** Takht-i-Sulaiman
highest point: 9 Tirich Mir **12** Godwin Austin
river: 3 Nal **4** Bado, Beas, Ravi, Swat, Zhob **5** Dasht, Indus, Kabul **6** Chenab, Ganges, Jamuna, Jhelum, Kundar, Porali, Sutlej **7** Jamunna
sea: 7 Arabian
physical feature:
bay: 8 Soymiani
canal: 4 Nara **5** Rohri
cape: 5 Fasta, Jaddi **6** Jiwani
delta: 6 Ganges **11** Char-Manpura
desert: 4 Sind, Thal, Thar
mountain pass: 5 Bolan **6** Khyber
plateau: 11 Baluchistan
valley: 5 Kohat
people: 5 Sindi, Wazir **6** Afridi, Bengal, Mahsud, Pathan, Sindhi **7** Baluchi, Brahuis, Puktuns, Punjabi, Sherani **8** Khattack, Pushtuns, Shinwari, Yusefazi **11** Mohammedzai
leader: 6 Jinnah **7** Aly Khan **8** Ayub Khan, Zia Ul-Haq **9** Ali Bhutto, Yahya Khan **13** Benazir Bhutto, Mujibur Rahman **15** Mah-

mud of Ghaznbi, Pervez Musharraf
poet: 5 Iqbal, Iqbal
language: 4 Urdu **6** Pushtu, Sindhi **7** Baluchi, Bengali, English, Punjabi
religion: 5 Hindu, Islam **8** Buddhism **12** Christianity
place:
dam: 6 Mangla **7** Tarbela
gardens: 8 Shalamar
mosque: 8 Badshahi
tomb: 15 Emperor Jahangir
feature:
clothing: 5 kurta, pugri, qamis **6** jinnah **7** dupatta, shalwar **8** sherwani **9** churidars
food:
bread: 8 chappati
dish: 5 kebab, pilaf **6** qormas, salans, sautes **10** vermicelli
yogurt: 4 dahi

Pakula, Alan
director of: 5 Klute **13** Sophie's Choice **15** The Pelican Brief **16** Presumed Innocent **19** All the President's Men

pal 4 chum, mate, pard **5** buddy, crony **6** cohort, friend **7** comrade, partner **8** alter ego, intimate, sidekick **9** associate, colleague, companion, confidant **10** accomplice, bosom buddy **13** boon companion

palace 5 villa **6** castle **7** chateau, mansion **8** hacienda
French: 6 palais
Italian: 7 palazzo

palais 6 palace **17** municipal building **18** government building

Palamedes
lieutenant of: 9 Agamemnon

pal around 7 consort, hang out **9** associate, be friends, run around **10** fraternize

palatable 5 tasty **6** savory **8** pleasant **9** agreeable, toothsome **10** appetizing

palatial 4 posh, rich **5** grand, noble, plush, regal, ritzy, showy **6** swanky **7** elegant, opulent, stately **8** imposing, splendid **9** grandiose, luxurious, sumptuous **10** monumental **11** magnificent

palaver 3 gab **4** chat, talk **5** prate **6** confer, gossip, parley **7** consult, discuss, prattle **8** chitchat, idle talk **10** chew the fat, chew the rag, conference, discussion

palazzo 6 palace

pale 3 pen, wan **4** fold, post **5** ashen, close, light, pasty, stake, white **6** anemic, blanch, paling, pallid, picket, sallow, whiten **7** closure, confine, deathly, ghastly, upright, whitish **8** bleached, palisade **9** bloodless, colorless, deathlike, enclosure, ghostlike **10** ash-colored, cadaverous, light-toned

Pale Horse, Pale Rider
author: 19 Katherine Anne Porter

paleness 6 pallor 7 wanness 8 dullness 9 whiteness 13 colorlessness

paleontology
study of: 18 correlation of parts
founder: 13 Georges Cuvier

Palermo
capital of: 6 Sicily

Palestine *see* 6 Israel

Palestrina, Giovanni Pierluigi da
born: 5 Italy 10 Palestrina
composer of: 11 Stabat Mater 18 Missa Papae Marcelli

Paley, Grace
author of: 15 Later the Same Day 26 The Little Disturbances of Man 30 Enormous Changes at the Last Minute

Palici
origin: 5 Roman
form: 4 gods 5 twins
gods of: 14 sulphur springs

paling 4 pale, rail 5 fence, stake 6 picket

Palinurus
steersman of: 6 Aeneas

palisade 5 close, fence 7 bulwark, rampart 8 stockade 9 enclosure

palisades 4 crag 5 ledge 6 bluffs, cliffs 10 escarpment, promontory

pall 4 cloy, haze, sate 5 gloom, weary 6 shadow, sicken 7 dimness, satiate 8 darkness 10 become dull, be tiresome, depression, desolation, melancholy, moroseness, oppression

Palladio, Andrea
real name: 26 Andrea di Pietro della Gondola
architect of: 12 Villa Rotunda (Vicenza Italy) 14 Teatro Olimpico (Vicenza) 19 Church of Il Redentore (Venice) 26 Church of San Giorgio Maggiore (Venice)
style: 9 Palladian

Pallas *see* 6 Athena

Pallas Athena *see* 6 Athena

pallet 3 bed, cot 4 bunk, tick 5 berth 8 mattress, platform

palliate 4 calm, curb, ease, hush, lull, tame 5 abate, allay, check, quiet, sooth, still 6 lessen, modify, reduce, soften, subdue, temper 7 assuage, comfort, cushion, lighten, relieve 8 decrease, diminish, minimize, mitigate, moderate 9 alleviate 10 ameliorate

palliative 4 balm 6 solace 7 anodyne, comfort 10 comforting

pallid 3 wan 4 ashy, blah, dull, pale 5 ashen, bland, pasty, vapid, waxen 6 boring, chalky, peaked, sallow 7 ghostly, humdrum, insipid, tedious 8 blanched, lifeless 9 bloodless, colorless 10 monotonous 13 anemic looking, unimaginative, uninteresting

pallor 7 wanness 8 paleness 9 pastiness, whiteness 10 ashen color, pallidness 11 ghostliness 13 bloodlessness, colorlessness

palm
varieties: 3 Fan, Ita, Key, Nut, Oil, Wax 4 Cane, Date, Doom, Doub, Doum, Fern, Hair, Hemp, King, Lady, Nipa, Nypa, Rock, Sago, Step, Tala, Wine 5 Areca, Areng, Assai, Betel, Black, Bread, Broom, Curly, Grass, Honey, Inaga, Ivory, Jelly, Latan, Manac, Nikau, Peach, Queen, Royal, Snake, Spine, Sugar, Syrup, Toddy, Yatay, Zombi 6 Bamboo, Barbel, Barrel, Bottle, Cherry, Cohune, Coyoli, Gebang, Gomuti, Gru-gru, Hesper, Kentia, Licuri, Manila, Mazari, Needle, Nibung, Parlor, Pignut, Raffia, Rattan, Ruffle, Sagisi, Sentry, Silver, Thatch, Thread, Yellow 7 Arikury, Cabbage, Calappa, Coconut, Coquito, Feather, Fiji fan, Funeral, Jaggery, Leopard, Mexican, Moriche, Overtop, Palmyra, Prickly, Spindle, Talipot, Weddell 8 Betel nut, Carnauba, Cucurite, Dwarf fan, Fishtail, Good luck, Ivory-nut, Mangrove, Pandanus, Peaberry, Princess, Roebelin, Umbrella, Wild date, Windmill 9 Alexander, Alexandra, Butterfly, Christmas, Desert fan, Gippsland, Guadalupe, Hurricane, India date, Macarthur, Ouricouri, Panama-hat, Petticoat, Piccabeen, Porcupine, Pygmy date, Silver saw, Solitaire, Spiny-club, Traveler's 10 African oil, Black-fiber, Canary date, Chinese fan, Cuban belly, Cuban royal, Everglades, Franceschi, Saw cabbage, Sealing-wax, Thatch-leaf, Washington 11 American oil, Chilean wine, European fan, Gingerbread, Mexican blue, Morass royal, Senegal date, Slender lady, Woolly butia 12 Caribee royal, Egyptian doum, Florida royal, Miniature fan, Walking-stick 13 Australian fan, Australian ivy, Australian nut, Belmore sentry, Feather-duster, Florida silver, Florida thatch, Forster sentry, Golden feather, Miniature date, San Jose hesper 14 Common princess, East Indian wine, Puerto Rican hat, Tufted fish tail, Yellow princess 15 Burmese fishtail, Chinese fountain, Chinese windmill, Yellow butterfly 16 Hispaniolan royal, Northern bangalow, Puerto Rican royal 17 Australian cabbage, Clustered fishtail, Mexican Washington, Piccabeen bangalow 18 South American royal

Palm Beach Story, The
director: 14 Preston Sturges
cast: 9 Mary Astor 10 Joel McCrea, Rudy Vallee 15 William Demarest 16 Claudette Colbert

Palmer, Arnold
sport: 4 golf
noted for: 10 Arnie's Army

Palmer, Lilli
real name: 17 Lillie Marie (Maria Lilli) Peiser
born: 5 Posen 7 Germany
husband: 11 Rex Harrison 14 Carlos Thompson
roles: 11 Body and Soul
autobiography: 22 Change Lobsters and Dance

Palmetto State
nickname of: 13 South Carolina

Palm Sunday
author: 12 Kurt Vonnegut

palmy 4 rosy 5 balmy, sunny 6 golden 7 booming, halcyon 8 blooming, pleasant, thriving 9 agreeable, bounteous, congenial 10 prosperous, successful 11 flourishing, pleasurable

Palmyra
Biblical name: 6 Tadmor

palpable 5 clear, plain 7 evident, obvious, tactile, visible 8 apparent, definite, distinct, feelable, manifest, tangible 9 touchable 10 noticeable 11 discernible, perceivable, perceptible 12 recognizable, unmistakable

palpitate 4 beat 5 pound, shake, throb 6 quaver, quiver, shiver 7 flutter, tremble, vibrate 9 go pit-a-pat

palsied 7 quaking, shaking, spastic 9 trembling

palsy-walsy 5 close, palsy, thick 6 chummy 8 friendly, intimate 10 buddy-buddy 14 thick as thieves

paltriness 10 triviality 12 unimportance 14 insignificance 18 inconsequentiality

Paltrow, Gwyneth
mother: 12 Blythe Danner
father: 12 Bruce Paltrow
husband: 11 Chris Martin
husband's band: 8 Coldplay
daughter: 5 Apple
roles: 4 Emma, Hook, Hush 5 Duets, Proof, Seven (Se7en) 6 Bounce, Malice, Sylvia 10 Possession, Shallow Hal 12 Sliding Doors 14 A Perfect Murder, View from the Top 16 Jefferson in Paris 17 Great Expectations, Shakespeare in Love 18 The Royal Tenenbaums 19 The Talented Mr Ripley 21 Moonlight and Valentino 28 Mrs Parker and the Vicious Circle

paltry 4 poor, puny 5 petty, sorry 6 measly, shabby 7 scrubby, trivial 8 inferior, picayune, piddling, trifling, wretched 11 unimportant 13 insignificant, of little value 14 inconsiderable 15 inconsequential

Pamela
author: 16 Samuel Richardson
character: 3 Mr B 9 Mrs Jervis, Mrs Jewkes 10 Lady Davers 13 Pamela Andrews

pamper 5 humor, spoil 6 coddle, cosset 7 cater to, indulge 8 give in to 11 mollycoddle

pampered 7 coddled, humored **8** indulged **9** catered to, cossetted

pamphlet 5 tract **6** folder **7** booklet, leaflet **8** brochure, bulletin, circular **9** monograph, throwaway

pan 3 boo, map, mug, pot **4** face, hiss **6** kisser **8** ridicule, saucepot **9** criticize

Pan
  also: **7** Sinoeis
  origin: **5** Greek
  form combined: **3** man **4** goat
  god of: **6** flocks **7** forests **8** pastures **9** shepherds
  father: **4** Zeus **6** Hermes
  loved: **4** Echo **5** Pitys **6** Syrinx
  invented: **5** pipes **6** syrinx
  corresponds to: **6** Faunus

panacea 6 elixir **7** cure-all, nostrum **13** universal cure

panache 4 dash, elan, tuft **5** flair, plume, style, verve **11** flamboyance

Panama
  capital/largest city: **10** Panama City
  others: **4** Daid **5** Ancon, Colon **6** Azuero, Balboa, Gamboa **8** Dos Bocas, Penonome, Santiago **9** Cristobal **10** Portobello
  division: **5** Cocle, Colon **6** Darien, Panama **7** Herrera **8** Chiriqui, Veraguas **9** Los Santos **12** Bocas del Toro
  measure: **7** celemin
  monetary unit: **4** cent **6** balboa **10** centesimos
  island: **5** Coiba, Pearl **6** Cebaco, Multas, Taboga **7** San Blas **10** Isla Del Rey **12** Bocas del Toro, Juan Gallegos **13** Barro Colorado
  lake: **5** Gatun
  mountain: **4** Baru, Maje **5** Chico, Gandi **6** Darien **7** Columan, San Blas, Veragua **8** Santiago, Tabasara **10** Costa Rican **14** Serrania de Sapo **15** Aspave Highlands **17** Cordillera Central
  highest point: **8** Chiriqui
  river: **5** Chepo, Sambu, Tuira **6** Bayano, Panugo **7** Chagres
  sea: **7** Pacific **9** Caribbean
  physical feature:
    bay: **5** Limon **6** Panama
    dam: **5** Gatun
    gulf: **6** Darien, Panama, Parita **7** Montijo, San Blas **8** Chiriqui **9** Mosquitos, San Miguel
    isthmus: **6** Darien, Panama **7** San Blas
    lagoon: **8** Chiriqui
    peninsula: **6** Azuero **8** Valjente
  people: **4** Cuna **5** Choco **6** Guaymi **7** mestizo
    canal builder: **7** Lesseps
    explorer: **6** Balboa **8** Bastidas, Columbus
    leader: **4** Royo **5** Arias **7** Noriega **8** Guerrero, Torrijos **9** Espriella **12** Simon Bolivar
  poet: **4** Miro **5** Korsi, Sinan
  language: **7** English, Spanish
  religion: **13** Roman Catholic
  place:
    church: **7** San Jose **15** Virgen del Carmen
    plaza: **13** Independencia
    ruins: **9** Old Panama
  feature:
    clothing: **7** montuno, pollera
    dance: **4** caja **7** pujador **9** tamborito
    tree: **4** yaya **5** maria, quira **6** alfaje, cativo
    US operation: **9** Just Cause
  food:
    meat: **6** tazajo
    soup: **8** sancocho

Panama City
  capital of: **6** Panama

pancake 4 blin **5** blini, crepe, kisra, latke, lefse **6** blintz, makeup **7** fritter, hotcake **8** flapjack, slapjack **11** griddlecake **12** silverdollar
  day: **13** Shrove Tuesday

Pancks
  character in: **12** Little Dorrit
  author: **7** Dickens

pancreas
  produces: **7** insulin

Pandareus
  father: **6** Lycaon, Merops
  daughter: **5** Aedon **6** Merope **9** Cleothera
  wounded: **8** Menelaus
  stole: **9** golden dog
  turned to: **5** stone
  killed by: **8** Diomedes

Pandarus
  character in: **18** Troilus and Cressida, Troilus and Criseyde
  author: **7** Chaucer **11** Shakespeare

Pandarus
  son: **7** Alcanor
  companion of: **6** Aeneas

pandemic 4 rife **7** rampant **8** epidemic **10** prevailing, widespread **21** dangerously contagious

pandemonium 3 din **5** chaos **6** bedlam, clamor, hubbub, racket, rumpus, tumult, uproar **7** turmoil **8** disorder **9** commotion **10** hullabaloo **11** disturbance

Pandemos
  epithet of: **9** Aphrodite

pander, panderer 4 mack, pimp **5** cadet **7** hustler **8** procurer **9** maquereau, souteneur **12** fleshpeddler

Pandion the Younger
  king of: **6** Athens
  later reigned in: **6** Megara

Pandora
  form: **10** first woman
  created by: **10** Hephaestus
  presented to: **10** Epimetheus
  daughter: **6** Pyrrha
  given by gods: **3** box
    box contained: **4** hope **5** evils

Pandrosos
  position: **9** priestess
  first priestess of: **6** Athena
  father: **7** Cecrops
  mother: **8** Agraulos

panegyric 6 eulogy, homage, praise **7** tribute **8** citation, encomium, good word **9** extolment, laudation **10** compliment **11** testimonial **12** commendation

panegyrize 4 laud **5** extol **6** praise **8** eulogize

panel 4 jury, pane **5** board, group, piece **6** insert **7** divider **8** bulkhead **9** committee, partition **10** round table **11** compartment, expert group, select group **13** advisory group

pang 4 ache, pain **5** agony, pinch, smart, stick, sting, throb **6** stitch, twinge **7** anguish **8** distress **9** suffering **10** discomfort

Pangloss
  character in: **7** Candide
  author: **8** Voltaire
  characteristic: **8** optimism

pang of conscience 5 demur, qualm **6** unease **7** remorse, scruple **9** misgiving **10** uneasiness **11** compunction

panhandle 3 beg, bum **5** cadge, mooch **6** hustle **7** solicit **9** importune

Panhandle State
  nickname of: **12** West Virginia

Panhellenius
  epithet of: **4** Zeus
  means: **14** god of all Greeks

panic 5 alarm, dread, go ape, scare **6** fright, horror, terror **7** scare **8** affright, hysteria **9** cold sweat, confusion, fall apart **10** go to pieces **11** nervousness, trepidation **12** apprehension, perturbation **13** consternation

panicky 6 scared **7** alarmed, anxious **9** terrified **10** frightened **13** panic-stricken, scared to death **14** terror-stricken

panic-stricken 6 afraid, scared **7** alarmed, anxious, fearful, panicky **9** terrified **13** scared to death **14** terror-stricken

Panjabi
  language family: **12** Indo-European
  branch: **11** Indo-Iranian
  group: **5** Indic
  spoken in: **5** (northern) India

Pankrits
  language family: **12** Indo-European
  branch: **11** Indo-Iranian
  form of: **5** Indic
  followed use of: **8** Sanskrit

pannier 3 bag **4** hoop **6** basket, dossel, pantry **7** corbeil, drapery **9** framework, overskirt
  literally: **11** breadbasket

Panoptes
  epithet of: **5** Argus
  means: **7** all eyes

panorama 5 scene, vista **6** survey **7** diorama, picture, scenery, tableau **8** long view, overview, prospect **10** scenic view **11** perspective **12** bird's-eye view

panoramic 3 ide **7** overall **8** bird's-eye, extended, sweeping **9** extensive **10** far-ranging **11** far-reaching **12** all-embracing, all-inclusive **15** all-encompassing

pansy 5 Viola
  varieties: **4** Wild **5** Field **6** Garden, Orchid **8** Japanese **9** Miniature **11** Monkey-faced **12** European wild

pant 4 blow, gasp, huff, puff **6** wheeze

pant after 4 seek **5** covet, crave **6** desire, pursue **7** hope for, long for, lust for, wish for **8** yearn for **9** hanker for, hunger for, lust after **11** thirst after, have a yen for **14** set one's heart on

Pantagruel see **22** Gargantua and Pantagruel

panther 3 cat **6** cougar **7** leopard

Pantomime Quiz
  host: **10** Mike Stokey **15** Pat Harrington Jr

pantry 5 ambry, store **6** closet, galley, larder **7** butlery, buttery, pannier, spicery **8** cupboard, scullery

pants 5 jeans **6** denims, shorts, slacks **7** drawers, panties **8** breeches, britches, knickers, trousers **9** bluejeans, dungarees **10** underpants **11** undershorts **12** underdrawers

pantywaist 4 wimp **5** sissy, softy **7** crybaby, milksop **8** mama's boy, weakling **10** namby-pamby, sissypants, weak sister **11** Milquetoast, mollycoddle **13** sissy-britches

Panurge
  character in: **22** Gargantua and Pantagruel
  author: **8** Rabelais

Panza, Sancho
  character in: **10** Don Quixote
  author: **9** Cervantes

pap 3 rot **4** bosh, junk, mash, mush, pulp, tosh **5** gruel, paste **6** cereal, drivel, Pablum, trivia **7** rubbish, twaddle **8** soft food **10** balderdash, flapdoodle, triviality

papa 2 pa **3** dad, doc, paw, pop **5** daddy, poppy **6** father, priest **9** Hemingway
  mate: **4** mama

Papa Bear
  nickname of: **11** George Halas

Papago
  language family: **5** Piman **10** Uto-Aztecan
  location: **6** Mexico **7** Arizona
  related to: **4** Pima

papal 9 apostolic, of the pope **10** pontifical

paper 4 bond, deed, news, opus, pulp, work **5** daily, draft, essay, stock, theme **6** record, report, tissue, weekly **7** article, gazette, journal, monthly, tabloid, writing **8** document, gift wrap **9** cardboard, chronicle, newspaper, newsprint, onionskin **10** instrument, manuscript, paperboard, periodical, stationery, typescript **11** certificate, com position, publication

Paper Chase, The
  character: **10** James T Hart, Willis Bell **13** Asheley Brooks **14** Elizabeth Logan, Jonathan Brooks **15** Franklin Ford III **19** Thomas Craig Anderson **29** Professor Charles W Kingsfield Jr
  cast: **10** James Keane **11** Robert Ginty **12** Deka Beaudine, John Houseman **13** James Stephens, Jonathan Segal **14** Francine Tacker, Tom Fitzsimmons
  subject: **9** law school
  Kingsfield's specialty: **11** contract law

paper measure 4 ream **5** quire

Paper Moon
  director: **16** Peter Bogdanovich
  cast: **9** Ryan O'Neal **10** Tatum O'Neal **12** Madeline Kahn (Trixie Delight) **13** John Hillerman
  Oscar for: **17** supporting actress (O'Neal)

Papua New Guinea
  formerly: **16** British New Guinea
  capital: **11** Port Moresby
  town: **3** Thu, Lae **4** Ioma **6** Kikori, Madang
  monetary unit: **4** kina
  island: **6** Misima **10** New Britain
  archipelago: **8** Bismarck
  lake: **6** Murray
  river: **3** Fly **4** Ramu
  sea: **5** Coral **7** Solomon
  strait: **6** Torres
  people: **4** Hula, Kate **5** Kiwai, Kwoma **6** Banaro **7** Arapesh **10** Melanesian
  language: **7** English

papyrus 4 pith, reed **5** paper, sedge **6** scroll **7** bulrush **8** document **10** manuscript
  accordion pleated: **6** orihon
  genus: **7** Cyperus
  origin: **5** Egypt **9** Nile delta **10** Nile valley
  use: **3** mat **4** rope, shoe, sail **5** paper

par 5 level, usual **6** normal, parity **7** average, balance, the norm **8** equality, evenness, identity, sameness, standard **9** stability **11** equilibrium, equivalency **12** equal footing **13** identicalness

parable 4 myth, tale **5** fable, story **6** homily, legend **8** allegory, apologue, folk tale **9** folk story **12** morality tale

Paracelsus
  author: **14** Robert Browning

parade 4 line, pomp, show **5** array, march, strut, train, vaunt **6** column, defile, flaunt, review, string **7** caravan, cortege, display, show off **8** vaunting **9** cavalcade, flaunting, march past, motorcade, pageantry, put on airs, spectacle **10** exposition, grandstand, procession **11** progression **13** demonstration

paradigm 5 ideal, model **6** matrix, sample **7** example, paragon, pattern **8** exemplar, original, standard **9** archetype, criterion, prototype, yardstick

paradise 3 joy **4** Eden **5** bliss **6** heaven, utopia **7** delight, ecstasy, nirvana, rapture **8** pleasure **9** enjoyment, happiness, Shangri-la, transport **11** happy valley **12** Garden of Eden, satisfaction **13** gratification, seventh heaven **15** Land of Cockaigne

Paradise
  also: **9** Paradisio
  part three of: **12** Divine Comedy
  author: **14** Dante Alighieri

Paradise Lost
  author: **10** John Milton
  character: **3** Eve, God **4** Adam **5** Satan **6** Christ **7** Lucifer

Paradise of the Pacific
  nickname of: **6** Hawaii

Paradise Regained
  author: **10** John Milton

paradisiacal 7 elysian, sublime **8** blissful, empyreal, empyrean, ethereal, heavenly **9** celestial, unearthly **12** otherworldly

paradox 5 poser **6** enigma, oddity, puzzle, riddle **7** anomaly **11** incongruity **13** inconsistency

paradoxical 9 ambiguous, enigmatic, equivocal **13** contradictory

paragon 4 norm **5** ideal, model **6** symbol **7** example, pattern **8** exemplar, paradigm, standard **9** archetype, criterion, prototype, yardstick **10** apotheosis

Paraguay
  capital/largest city: **8** Asuncion
  others: **3** Ita **4** Rica, Yuty **5** Belen, Luque, Pilar, Villa **7** Caacupe **8** Trinidad **9** Paraguari **10** Concepcion, Villarrica **11** Encarnacion **26** Puerto Presidente Stroessner
  division: **6** Guaira, Itapua, Olimpo **7** Caazapa **8** Boqueron **10** Concepcion
  measure: **3** pie **4** lino, lira, lire, vara **5** legua **6** cuadra, fanega
  monetary unit: **4** peso **7** guarani, centimo
  weight: **7** quintal
  island:
    floating island: **8** camalote
  lake: **4** Vera, Ypoa **8** Ypacarai
  river: **3** Apa **5** Guazu, Negro, Plata, Verde, Ypane **6** Acaray, Parana **7**

Aguaray, Confuso **8** Paraguay **9** Aquidaban, Pilcomayo, Tebicuary, Tibiquare **10** Monte Lindo **14** Riacho Gonzales **15** Riacho Mosquitos

physical feature:
  falls: 6 Guaira
  plains: 5 Chaco
  plateau: 6 Parana

people: 6 Abipon, Moskoi **7** Guarani, mestizo **8** Guayaqui
  artist: 7 Bestard
  author: 3 Pla **4** Baez **6** Alcala, Bastos, Correa, O'Leary **7** Cervera **8** Casaccia
  composer: 8 Asuncion
  leader: 5 Lopez **7** Francia **10** Stroessner **16** Antequera y Castro
  sculptor: 8 Guggiari

language: 6 German **7** Guarani, Spanish

religion: 9 Mennonite **13** Roman Catholic

place:
  church: 10 Villarrica **11** Incarnation
  dam: 6 Itaipu
  memorial: 16 Pantheon of Heroes
  museum: 5 Godoi
  palace: 10 Government

feature:
  animal: 4 puma **5** tapir **6** iguana, jaguar **7** peccary
  bird: 6 toucan
  clothing: 5 fajas, typoi **6** poncho **7** rebozos **9** bombachas **10** alpargatas
  communes: 11 reducciones
  dance: 7 Sante Fe **15** Paraguayan polka
  fish: 7 piranha
  lace: 7 nanduti
  music: 8 quarania
  townspeople: 9 comuneros
  tree: 5 ceiba **7** lapacho **9** quebracho

food:
  bread: 5 chipa, mbeyu
  dish: 12 sopa paraguay
  tea: 9 yerba mate
  vegetable: 8 mandioca

parallel 4 akin, like, same, twin **5** alike, equal, match **6** follow **7** abreast, analogy, be alike, similar **8** analogue, likeness, relation **9** alongside, analogous, corollary, duplicate **10** collateral, comparable, comparison, concurrent, connection, equivalent, similarity **11** coextensive, coincidence, comparative, compare with, correlation, correlative, counterpart, equidistant, resemblance **12** correspond to **13** corresponding **14** correspondence

parallelism 8 affinity, likeness, sameness **9** agreement **10** comparison, similarity, similitude **11** resemblance **14** correspondence

parallelogram 5 rhomb **6** square **7** diamond, rhombus **8** rhomboid **9** rectangle **11** plane figure **13** quadrilateral

paralyze 4 stun **6** benumb, deaden, disarm, freeze, weaken **7** cripple, destroy, disable, petrify, stupefy, wipe out **8** demolish, enfeeble **10** debilitate, immobilize, neutralize **12** incapacitate

Paramaribo
  capital of: 8 Suriname

paramount 4 main **5** chief **6** utmost **7** capital, highest, leading, premier, supreme **8** cardinal, dominant, foremost, greatest, peerless, superior **9** essential, principal, unmatched **10** preeminent **11** outstanding, predominant **12** incomparable, preponderant, transcendent

paramour 3 man **4** doxy **5** lover, Romeo **6** gigolo **7** Don Juan **8** Casanova, fancy man, lothario, loverboy, mistress **9** boyfriend, concubine, courtesan, inamorata, inamorato, kept woman **10** girlfriend, lady friend, sugar daddy

paranoid 4 wary **7** deluded **9** paranoiac **11** distrustful **14** oversuspicious

parapet 7 bulwark, rampart **8** abutment, palisade **9** barricade, earthwork **10** battlement, breastwork

paraphernalia 3 rig **4** gear **5** stuff **6** outfit, tackle, things **7** effects, harness, regalia **8** fittings, material, supplies, utensils **9** apparatus, equipment, trappings **10** belongings, implements, properties, provisions **11** accessories, furnishings **13** accoutrements

paraphrase 5 recap **6** rehash, reword **7** restate **8** rephrase **12** recapitulate

parasite 5 leech **6** beggar, cadger, loafer **7** moocher, shirker, slacker, sponger **8** deadbeat **9** goldbrick, scrounger **10** freeloader **11** bloodsucker
  inside host: 12 endoparasite
  outside host: 12 ectoparasite

parasol 5 shade **6** shadow **7** roundel **8** sunshade, umbrella
  mushroom: 7 lepiota

par avion 5 by air

parboil 4 boil **5** scald **6** blanch **7** precook

Parca
  origin: 5 Roman
  member of: 6 Parcae
  goddess of: 7 destiny **10** childbirth

Parcae see **5** Fates

parcel 3 lot **4** bale, pack, part, plot **5** allot, piece, tract **6** bundle, divide, packet **7** carve up, deal out, dole out, package, portion, section, segment, split up **8** allocate, dispense, disperse, division, fraction, fragment, property **9** allotment, allowance, apportion, partition **10** distribute **11** piece of land

parceling out 9 allotment, doling out, meting out **10** allocation, assignment,

dealing out **12** distribution **13** apportionment

parcel out 5 allot **7** dole out, give out, mete out **8** allocate, dispense, divide up **9** apportion **10** distribute, portion out

parch 4 bake, burn, char, sear **5** dry up, singe **6** dry out, scorch, sun-dry, wither **7** blister, shrivel **9** dehydrate, dessicate, evaporate

parched 3 dry **4** arid **6** barren **8** withered **9** shriveled **10** dehydrated, desiccated

parchment 6 scroll, vellum **7** papyrus **8** goatskin **9** sheepskin

pardon 5 grace, mercy **6** excuse, wink at **7** absolve, amnesty, blink at, forbear, forgive, indulge, release, set free **8** overlook, reprieve, shrug off **9** discharge, disregard, exculpate, exonerate, remission, vindicate **10** absolution, indulgence **11** deliverance, exculpation, forbearance, forgiveness **12** grant amnesty **16** forgive and forget

Pardoner
  character in: 18 The Canterbury Tales
  author: 7 Chaucer

pare 3 cut, lop **4** clip, crop, dock, hull, husk, peel, skin, trim **5** lower, prune, shave, shear, shell, shuck, slash, strip **6** lessen, reduce, shrink **7** curtail, cut back **8** decrease, diminish **11** decorticate

pare down 3 cut **4** trim **5** shave **6** reduce **7** abridge, curtail, cut down, shorten **8** condense, cut short, diminish **10** abbreviate

parent 3 dam **4** sire **5** model **6** father, mother **7** creator **8** ancestor, begetter, exemplar, original, producer **9** precursor, prototype **10** antecedent, forerunner, originator, procreator, progenitor **11** predecessor

parentage 5 birth, roots, stock **6** family, origin, strain **7** descent, lineage **8** ancestry, forbears, heredity, pedigree **9** ancestors, genealogy **10** background, derivation, extraction, family tree **11** antecedents

Parentalia
  origin: 5 Roman
  event: 8 festival

parenthetical 5 aside **6** braced, casual **8** inserted **9** bracketed **10** extraneous, immaterial, incidental, interposed, irrelevant **11** impertinent, intervening, superfluous

par excellence 8 superior **10** preeminent

parfait d'amour
  type: 7 liqueur
  flavor: 7 violets
  color: 6 purple

Paria
  form: 5 nymph

loved by: 5 Minos
children: 7 Chryses **9** Eurymedon,
   Nephalion, Philolaus
pariah 5 exile, rover, stray **6** outlaw,
   roamer **7** outcast **8** vagabond, wanderer **10** expatriate **11** undesirable,
   untouchable
paring 4 chip, snip **5** scrap, shred,
   slice **6** sliver **7** cutting, peeling, shaving **8** fragment
pari passu 6 fairly **7** equably **10** side
   by side **13** equal progress **17** without
   partiality

Paris
   airport: 4 Orly **9** Le Bourget **15**
      Charles de Gaulle
   area: 5 Passy **6** Clichy, Marais,
      Ternes, Wagram **7** Auteuil **8** Chail-
      lot, Gobelins, Left Bank, St Honore **9**
      Les Halles, Right Bank, St Germain
      10 Montmartre, Rive Droite, Rive
      Gauche, Val de Grace **11** Ile de la
      Cite **12** Hotel de Ville, Latin Quarter,
      Montparnasse
   capital of: 6 France
   city planner: 9 Haussmann
   island: 10 Ile St Louis **11** Ile de la
      Cite
   landmark: 8 Pantheon **9** Notre Dame
      10 Paris Opera, Sacre Coeur **11** Eiffel
      Tower, La Madeleine, Palais Royal
      12 Elysee Palace, Hotel de Ville,
      Place Vendome **13** Arc de Triomphe,
      Palais Bourbon **14** Bois de Boulogne,
      Place de l'Etoile, Pompidou Center,
      Sainte Chapelle, Tomb of Napoleon
      15 Bois de Vincennes **16** Luxem-
      bourg Palace **17** Hotel des Invalides,
      Place de la Bastille, Place de la Con-
      corde **18** Jardin des Tuileries **20**
      Place Charles de Gaulle
   nickname: 11 city of light
   river: 5 Seine
   street: 9 Haussmann, Invalides **10**
      Grand Armee **11** Saint Michel **12**
      Montparnasse, Saint Germain **13**
      Champs Elysees **15** Charles de
      Gaulle
   subway: 5 Metro
   university: 8 Sorbonne

Paris
   character in: 14 Romeo and Juliet
   author: 11 Shakespeare

Paris
   position: 6 prince
   father: 5 Priam
   mother: 6 Hecuba
   brother: 6 Hector **9** Polydorus
   sister: 9 Cassandra
   wife: 6 Oenone
   abducted: 5 Helen
   judgment of: 14 apple of discord
   awarded apple to: 9 Aphrodite
   killed by: 11 Philoctetes
parish 4 fold **5** flock, shire **6** canton,
   county **7** diocese, section **8** brethren,
   district, precinct, province **9** commu-

nity, pastorate **10** department **11**
archdiocese **12** congregation, neighborhood
parity 7 balance **8** equality, sameness
   10 coequality, uniformity **11** equivalence, equivalency **14** correspondence
park 4 lawn **5** field, green, grove,
   woods **6** common, meadow, square **7**
   grounds, reserve **8** parkland, preserve,
   woodland **9** grassland, sanctuary **10**
   public park, quadrangle
Parker, Dorothy
   author of: 6 Resume **9** Big Blonde **10**
      Enough Rope **13** Death and Taxes
      18 After Such Pleasures **19** Laments
      for the Living
parkway 6 avenue **7** thruway **9** boulevard **12** thoroughfare
parlance 4 talk **5** idiom, lingo **6**
   speech **16** manner of speaking
Parlement of Fowles, The
   author: 15 Geoffrey Chaucer
parley 4 talk **6** confab, powwow, summit **7** council, meeting, palaver **8** conclave **9** discourse, mediation, peace
   talk **10** conference, discussion **11** arbitration, negotiation **12** conversation
parliament 4 diet **5** court, house,
   junta **6** fan-tan, senate, sevens **7** cabinet, council **8** assembly, congress **9**
   high court **11** legislature **12** three estates
   Communist: 6 Soviet **9** politburo, pre-
      sidium
   estate: 12 House of Lords **14** House
      of Commons
   Germanic: 9 Bundesrat, Bundestag,
      Bolksraad **11** Volkshammer
   Greek: 5 Boule
   Icelandic: 7 Althing
   Israeli: 7 Knesset **8** Knesseth
   Scandinavian: 7 Lagting, Riksdag **8**
      Lagthing, Storting **9** Odelsting, Stor-
      thing
   Spanish: 6 Cortes
parlor 5 salon **6** saloon **8** best room **9**
   front room **10** living room **11** drawing
   room, sitting room
Parnopius
   epithet of: 6 Apollo
   means: 9 locust god
parochial 5 local, petty, small **6**
   church, little, narrow, parish **7** insular, limited **8** regional **9** hidebound, illiberal, religious, sectional, small-town
   10 provincial, restricted **11** countrified
   12 narrow-minded
parodos
   from Greek drama: 9 choral ode
parody 5 mimic **6** satire **7** lampoon,
   takeoff **8** satirize, travesty **9** burlesque, take off on **10** caricature
Parolles
   character in: 20 All's Well That Ends
      Well
   author: 11 Shakespeare

paroxysm 3 fit **5** spasm, spell **7** seizure **10** convulsion
parrot 3 ape **4** bird, echo, lory **5** macaw, mimer, mimic **6** chorus, monkey
   7 copycat, imitate **8** cockatoo, imitator, parakeet **9** reiterate
parry 4 duck, shun **5** avert, avoid,
   dodge, elude, repel **7** beat off, fend
   off, repulse, ward off **8** sidestep, stave
   off **10** circumvent, fight shy of
Parsifal
   opera by: 6 Wagner
   character: 6 Kundry **8** Amfortas,
      Klingsor **9** Gurnemanz
parsimonious 5 close, tight **6** frugal,
   saving, stingy **7** miserly, sparing,
   thrifty **9** niggardly, penurious **10** economical, ungenerous **11** closefisted,
   tightfisted **13** money-grubbing, penny-
   pinching
parsimony 6 thrift **7** economy **8**
   meanness **10** stinginess **13** niggardliness **15** tightfistedness
parsley 19 Petroselinum crispum
   varieties: 5 horse **7** Chinese, Italian
      12 turnip-rooted
   related herb: 4 dill **5** cumin **6** fennel
   garland worn by: 8 Hercules
   gives speed to: 6 horses
   use in: 11 fines herbes **12** bouquet
      garni
parson 5 clerk, padre **6** cleric, divine,
   father, pastor, priest, rector **7** dominie
   8 minister, preacher, reverend, shepherd, sky pilot **9** clergyman
   French: 4 abbe, cure
parsonage 5 glebe, manse **7** deanery,
   rectory, Vatican **8** vicarage **9** pastorate
part 2 go **3** bit, job **4** care, chip, duty,
   hunk, item, open, rend, role, slit,
   task, tear, unit **5** break, chore, crumb,
   guise, leave, piece, place, scrap, sever,
   shard, share, sherd, shred, slice, split
   6 branch, charge, cleave, depart, detach, detail, divide, go away, member,
   morsel, region, sector, set out, sliver,
   sunder **7** concern, cutting, disjoin, element, portion, push off, section, segment, snippet **8** breakoff, business,
   capacity, disguise, disunite, division,
   fraction, fragment, function, separate,
   set forth, start out **9** character, component, disengage, go one's way **10**
   assignment, break apart, department,
   disconnect, get up and go, ingredient,
   mosey along, say good-bye **11** be on
   one's way, call it quits, constituent,
   subdivision
partake 5 enjoy, savor, share **6** join in,
   sample **7** share in **8** engage in **11** participate
part from 5 leave **9** break with **12**
   separate from
Parthenia
   epithet of: 6 Athena
   means: 6 virgin

Parthenopaeus
  father: **10** Hippomenes
  mother: **8** Atalanta
  member of: **18** Seven against Thebes

partial 6 biased, unfair, unjust **7** limited, slanted **8** one-sided, partisan **9** factional **10** fractional, incomplete, interested, prejudiced, subjective, unbalanced, unfinished **11** fragmentary, inequitable, predisposed, uncompleted **12** inconclusive, prepossessed

partiality 4 bent, bias, love, tilt **5** fancy, slant, taste **6** choice, liking **7** leaning **8** affinity, fondness, penchant, tendency, weakness **9** prejudice **10** attraction, favoritism, preference, proclivity, propensity **11** inclination **12** one-sidedness, partisanship, predilection **14** predisposition

partially 6 in part, partly **7** partway **8** somewhat **9** piecemeal **12** fractionally, incompletely

participant 4 ally **5** party **6** cohort, fellow, helper, member, player, sharer, worker **7** partner **8** confrere, partaker **9** accessory, associate, colleague, performer **10** accomplice **11** contributor, shareholder **12** collaborator, participator

participate 5 share **6** join in **7** partake, perform **8** engage in, take part **9** play a part

particle 3 bit, jot **4** atom, iota, mite, snip, whit **5** crumb, grain, scrap, shred, speck, trace **6** morsel, tittle, trifle **7** granule, modicum, smidgen, snippet **9** scintilla

parti-colored 4 pied **5** plaid **6** motley **7** checked, dappled, mottled **8** colorful **9** checkered **10** variegated **11** manycolored **12** multicolored

particular 4 sole **5** exact, fixed, fussy, picky **6** single, strict **7** express, finicky, special **8** concrete, critical, definite, detailed, distinct, especial, exacting, explicit, itemized, personal, separate, specific **9** demanding **10** fastidious, individual, meticulous, scrupulous **11** painstaking, persnickety, punctilious, well-defined **12** hard to please

particularize 6 detail **7** itemize, specify **9** enumerate

particularly 6 mainly **7** notably **8** markedly **9** eminently, expressly, specially, supremely, unusually **10** definitely, distinctly, especially, explicitly, strikingly **11** principally, prominently **13** exceptionally **15** extraordinarily

particulars 5 facts, items **6** events **7** details **9** specifics **13** circumstances

parti pris 15 position decided **20** preconceived attitude

partisan 3 fan **4** ally **6** backer, biased, rooter, zealot **7** booster, devotee, partial, slanted **8** adherent, advocate, champion, follower, one-sided, up-

holder **9** guerrilla, insurgent, irregular, jayhawker, supporter **10** bushwacker, enthusiast, prejudiced, subjective, unbalanced **11** sympathizer

partition 4 wall **5** allot, fence, panel **6** assign, divide, screen **7** barrier, deal out, divider, mete out, parting, split up **8** allocate, bulkhead, dispense, disperse, dividing, division, separate **9** allotment, apportion, parcel out, separator, severance, splitting, subdivide **10** allocation, assignment, distribute, separation **11** demarcation, segregation **12** distribution, dividing wall **13** apportionment

partly 6 in part **7** part way **8** somewhat **9** not wholly, partially, to a degree **10** relatively **12** fractionally, incompletely **13** after a fashion, comparatively

partly open 4 ajar **5** agape **6** gaping **7** cracked **8** half-open, unclosed **9** squinting **10** half-closed

partner 3 aid, pal **4** ally, chum, mate, wife **5** aider, buddy **6** fellow, friend, helper, sharer, spouse **7** comrade, co-owner, husband **8** confrere, helpmate, partaker, sidekick, teammate **9** accessory, assistant, associate, colleague, companion, co-partner **10** accomplice, better half, joint owner **11** confederate, participant **12** collaborator

Parton, Dolly
  roles: **10** Nine to Five, Rhinestone **12** Straight Talk **14** Steel Magnolias **30** The Best Little Whorehouse in Texas
  theme park: **9** Dollywood

partridge
  group of: **5** covey

Partridge
  character in: **8** Tom Jones
  author: **8** Fielding

Partridge Family, The
  character: **13** Reuben Kinkaid **14** Danny Partridge, Keith Partridge, Tracy Partridge **15** Connie Partridge, Laurie Partridge **20** Christopher Partridge
  cast: **8** Susan Dey **11** David Madden **12** Brian Forster, David Cassidy, Shirley Jones **13** Danny Bonaduce, Suzanne Crough **14** Jeremy Gelbwaks
  song: **14** I Think I Love You

parturition 5 birth **8** delivery **10** childbirth **11** giving birth **12** childbearing

party 2 do **4** band, bash, body, crew, fete, gang, team, unit, wing **5** corps, force, group, squad **6** affair, at-home, league, soiree **7** accused, blow out, company, coterie, faction **8** alliance, claimant, conclave, litigant, wingding **9** appellant, coalition, defendant, festivity, gathering, plaintiff, reception **10** contestant, federation, petitioner, respondent **11** celebration, confeder-

acy, get-together, participant, paticipator, perpetrator

party-pooper 4 drag **10** spoilsport, wet blanket

parvenu 4 snob **6** nobody **7** upstart **8** arrivist, mushroom **9** arriviste **12** nouveau riche

Pascal, Blaise
  nationality: **6** French
  invented: **7** syringe **13** adding machine **14** hydraulic press
  author of: **7** Pensees **19** Lettres provinciales **20** Essay pour les coniques

Pascin, Julius
  real name: **6** Pincas
  born: **5** Vidin **8** Bulgaria
  artwork: **6** Femmes **12** Les Deux Amies **17** Ginette et Mireille

Pasiphae
  father: **6** Helios
  mother: **7** Perseis
  husband: **5** Minos
  daughter: **7** Ariadne, Phaedra **9** Acacallis
  became enamored of: **10** Cretan bull
  mother of: **8** Minotaur

Pasithea
  member of: **6** Graces

pass 2 go **3** cap, die, end, gap, hit, top, use, way **4** best, busy, fill, flow, give, go by, go on, hand, kick, lane, meet, toss **5** canal, exact, excel, gorge, gulch, leave, outdo, route, spend, throw, trail **6** accept, affirm, avenue, be over, canyon, convey, course, decree, depart, devote, elapse, employ, engage, exceed, expend, expire, finish, go away, go past, occupy, ordain, permit, pickle, plight, ratify, ravine, slip by, strait, take up, vanish **7** achieve, advance, approve, channel, confirm, consume, deliver, die away, eclipse, freebie, glide by, go ahead, let have, narrows, pathway, present, proceed, qualify, satisfy, slide by, surpass **8** blow over, dissolve, exigency, fade away, furlough, go beyond, go onward, hand over, juncture, legalize, melt away, outshine, outstrip, passaway, peter out, progress, quandary, sanction, transfer, transmit, turn over **9** authorize, disappear, evaporate, extremity, hand along, legislate, situation, terminate **10** accomplish, difficulty, free ticket, get through, move onward, over shadow, passageway **11** predicament, proposition **12** complication, run its course, solicitation, stand the test **13** authorization **15** amorous overture
  French: **13** laissez passer

passable 4 fair, open, so-so **5** clear **6** not bad **8** adequate, fordable, mediocre, middling **9** allowable, crossable, navigable, tolerable **10** acceptable, admissible, pretty good **11** presentable, respectable, traversable **12** unobstructed

passage 3 way **4** hall, pass, path, road, tour, trek, trip **5** aisle, canal, piece, route, verse **6** access, clause, column, course, junket, tunnel, voyage **7** channel, chapter, hallway, journey, passing, portion, section, transit **8** approach, approval, corridor, movement, sanction, sentence **9** enactment, excursion, paragraph, selection, ship's fare **10** acceptance, expedition, ordainment **11** affirmation, endorsement, legislation, progression **12** confirmation, legalization, ratification **13** authorization

passage out 4 exit **6** egress, outlet

Passages
  author: **10** Gail Sheehy

Passage to India, A
  author: **9** E M Forster
  character: **6** Dr Aziz **8** Mrs Moore **12** Adela Quested **13** Cecil Fielding, Ronald Heaslop **16** Professor Godbole
  setting: **11** Chandrapore **12** Marabar Caves
  director: **9** David Lean
  cast: **9** Judy Davis **12** Alec Guinness **13** Peggy Ashcroft **15** Victor Bannerjee
  Oscar for: **17** supporting actress (Ashcroft)

passageway 4 exit, hall, lane, path, walk **5** aisle **6** access, arcade, tunnel **7** doorway, gangway, gateway, hallway, passage **8** corridor, entrance, entryway, sidewalk **12** companionway

pass away 3 die **6** depart, expire, pass on, perish **7** decease **8** pass over **13** go to one's glory **14** give up the ghost

pass by 4 go by, pass **5** lapse **6** elapse, roll by, slip by **7** glide by, slide by **8** slip away

passe 4 past **5** faded, hoary, stale **6** demode, lapsed, quaint **7** ancient, antique, archaic, disused, outworn, retired **8** obsolete, outdated, outmoded **9** out-of-date **10** antiquated **11** prehistoric **12** antediluvian, old-fashioned, out of fashion **13** superannuated

passenger 4 fare **5** rider **8** commuter, stowaway, traveler, wayfarer

Passepartout
  character in: **26** Around the World in Eighty Days
  author: **5** Verne

pas seul
  ballet: **9** solo dance
  literally: **8** solo step

passim 12 here and there, repeated item

passing 5 brief, death, dying **6** demise, fickle **7** decease, passage **8** adequate, fleeting **9** enactment, ephemeral, momentary, temporary, transient **10** evanescent, expiration, not failing, short-lived, transitory **11** impermanent, legislating

passing the bounds of propriety
  French: **5** outre

passion 4 fire, idol, love, lust, rage, urge **5** ardor, craze, fancy, flame, gusto, heart, mania **6** desire, fervor, hunger, thirst, warmth **7** beloved, craving, ecstasy, emotion, feeling, rapture **8** loved one **9** carnality, eagerness, inamorata, intensity, obsession, sentiment, transport, vehemence **10** carnal love, enthusiasm **11** amorousness, earnestness, infatuation

passionate 3 hot **4** sexy **5** fiery **6** ardent, carnal, erotic, fervid, fierce, heated, loving, raging **7** amorous, earnest, excited, feeling, fervent, furious, intense, lustful **8** desirous, ecstatic, inflamed, sensuous, vehement **9** emotional, heartfelt, wrought-up **11** tempestuous **12** enthusiastic, intoxicating

passionfruit
  type: **7** liqueur
  origin: **6** Hawaii
  flavor: **5** peach

passionless 4 calm, cold **6** placid, serene **7** passive **8** tranquil **9** apathetic, unfeeling **10** spiritless **11** emotionless, indifferent, unemotional

passive 5 inert **6** docile **7** dormant, patient, pliable **8** enduring, inactive, lifeless, listless, resigned, yielding **9** apathetic, compliant, impassive, quiescent, tractable **10** spiritless, submissive **11** acquiescent, unassertive, unresisting **12** nonresistant

passiveness 6 apathy **7** inertia **8** docility **10** quiescence **11** resignation **12** acquiescence, lifelessness **14** submissiveness **16** unresponsiveness

passivity 6 apathy **7** inertia **8** docility, meekness **11** resignation **12** complaisance, lifelessness **13** nonresistance **14** submissiveness

pass muster 2 do **5** serve **6** answer **8** be enough **10** be adequate **12** be sufficient **14** be satisfactory

pass on 3 die **6** depart, expire **7** decease **8** pass away **13** go to one's glory **14** give up the ghost, leave this world **15** breathe one's last

pass over 6 ignore, slight **7** neglect **8** overlook **10** brush aside

pass up 4 miss **6** ignore, refuse

password 3 key **4** word **6** by word, slogan **7** keyword, tessera **9** catchword, watchword **10** open sesame, secret word, shibboleth **11** countersign, passe-parole

Password
  host: **11** Allen Ludden

past 2 by **4** gone **5** ended, prior **6** beyond, bygone, former, gone by **7** ancient, earlier, elapsed, expired, history, long ago, through **8** departed, finished, previous **9** antiquity, days of old **10** days gone by, days of yore, historical, olden times, passed away, yesteryear **11** dead and gone, former times, times gone by **12** ancient times

pasta 4 orzo, ziti **6** elbows, shells **7** gnocchi, lasagna, pastina, ravioli, rotelli **8** ditalini, linguini, macaroni, rigatoni, tortelli **9** canelloni, cavatelli, fettucine, manicotti, spaghetti **10** tortellini, vermicelli
  ingredient: **3** egg **5** flour

pasta sauce 4 ragu **5** pesto, salsa **6** tomato **7** alfredo **8** mushroom, pomodoro **9** bolognese, carbonara

past due 4 late **5** tardy **7** belated, overdue **9** in arrears **10** behindhand

paste 3 gum, hit **4** glue, seal, sock **5** affix, punch, stick **6** attach, cement **7** stickum **8** adhesive, mucilage

pastel 3 dim **4** pale, soft **5** chalk, faded, faint, light, muted **6** crayon **9** washed-out **13** coloring stick **14** coloring pencil

Pasternak, Boris
  author of: **9** Dr Zhivago
  award: **5** Nobel **10** Literature

Pasteur, Louis
  field: **9** chemistry
  nationality: **6** French
  originated: **14** anti-rabies shot, pasteurization
  founded: **12** microbiology
  disproved: **21** spontaneous generation

pastime 3 fun **4** game, play **5** hobby, sport **9** amusement, avocation, diversion **10** relaxation **11** distraction **13** entertainment **14** divertissement

pastis
  type: **7** liqueur
  flavor: **8** licorice
  substitute for: **8** absinthe

past one's prime 3 old **4** aged **5** aging **7** elderly **9** venerable **11** over the hill **12** in one's dotage

pastor 4 cure, dean **5** padre, vicar **6** cleric, father, parson, priest, rector **8** chaplain, minister, preacher **9** clergyman

pastoral 5 rural **6** rustic **7** bucolic, idyllic **8** arcadian, clerical, priestly **9** episcopal **10** sacerdotal **11** ministerial **14** ecclesiastical

Pastoral Symphony, The
  author: **9** Andre Gide

pastorate 6 clergy **8** ministry, the cloth **10** priesthood

pastures
  god of: **3** Pan **6** Dumuzi

pasty 3 wan **4** ashy, gray, pale **5** ashen, gluey, gooey, gummy, white **6** anemic, chalky, doughy, pallid, peaked, sallow, sticky **7** deathly, starchy **9** bloodless, colorless, ghostlike, glutinous, like paste **12** mucilaginous

pat 3 apt, dab, hit, pet, rap, tap 4 cake, daub, easy, glib, slap 5 exact, ideal, ready, slick, thump 6 caress, facile, fondle, simple, smooth, stroke, thwack 7 apropos, fitting, perfect, precise, reliant 8 flippant, suitable 9 contrived, pertinent, rehearsed

patch 3 fix, lot 4 area, darn, mend, plot, spot, zone 5 field, sew up, tract 6 garden, repair, stitch 7 expanse, stretch 8 clearing, insignia 9 reinforce 13 reinforcement

patchwork 4 hash, mess 6 jumble, medley, muddle, tangle 7 grab bag, melange, mixture 8 mishmash, mixed bag, pastiche, scramble 9 confusion, potpourri 10 hodgepodge, miscellany, salmagundi 11 gallimaufry 14 conglomeration, omnium-gatherum

pate 3 pie 4 brow, head 5 brain, crown, paste, pastry, patty, skull 6 noddle, noggin, noodle 9 meat paste

patella
bone of: 7 kneecap

patent 4 bald, bold, open, rank 5 clear, gross, overt, plain 6 permit 7 decided, evident, express, glaring, license, obvious 8 apparent, distinct, flagrant, manifest, palpable, registry, striking 9 copyright, downright, prominent 10 pronounced, unreserved 11 conspicuous, copyrighted, indubitable, self-evident, trademarked, transparent, unconcealed, undisguised 12 unmistakable 15 nonprescription

paterfamilias 6 father 17 father of the family, master of the family 20 master of the household

paternal 4 kind 6 tender 8 fatherly, parental, vigilant, watchful 9 concerned, indulgent 10 benevolent, fatherlike, interested, solicitous 11 patriarchal

Pater Patriae 18 father of his country

path 3 way 4 lane, plan, road, walk 5 byway, means, orbit, route, track, trail 6 access, by path, course 7 pathway, process, walkway 8 approach, footpath

pathetic 3 sad 6 moving, rueful, woeful 7 doleful, piteous, pitiful 8 dolorous, grievous, pitiable, poignant, touching, wretched 9 affecting, miserable, plaintive, sorrowful 10 deplorable, lamentable, to be pitied 11 distressing

Pathfinder, The
author: 19 James Fenimore Cooper
character: 9 Arrowhead, Dew-of-June 10 Charles Cap 11 Mabel Dunham, Natty Bumppo 12 Chingachgook 13 Jasper Western 14 Sergeant Dunham 18 Lieutenant Davy Muir

Pathfinders, The
author: 10 Gail Sheehy

pathogen 3 bug 4 germ 5 virus 7 microbe 8 bacillus 9 bacterium 13 microorganism

pathophobia
fear of: 7 disease

pathos 3 woe 5 agony 6 misery 7 anguish, feeling, sadness 8 distress 9 heartache, poignancy, sentiment 10 desolation 12 pitiableness 13 plaintiveness

Paths of Glory
director: 14 Stanley Kubrick
cast: 11 Kirk Douglas, Ralph Meeker 13 Adolphe Menjou

pathway 4 lane, path, road 5 alley, route, track 6 course 7 passage, walkway 8 footpath 10 passageway

patience 5 poise 7 stamina 8 industry, tenacity 9 composure, diligence, fortitude, restraint, tolerance 10 equanimity, resolution, sufferance 11 application, forbearance, longanimity, persistence, self-control 12 perseverance, tirelessness

Patience 8 operetta
by: 7 Gilbert, Sullivan

patient 4 case 6 dogged, serene 8 composed, diligent, enduring, resolute, tireless 9 dauntless, tenacious, undaunted 10 determined, forbearing, persistent, sick person, unflagging, unswerving, unwavering 11 industrious, persevering, unfaltering, unperturbed 13 indefatigable, long-suffering, uncomplaining

patio 4 deck 5 lanai, porch 6 piazza 7 terrace, veranda

patois 5 argot, idiom, lingo 6 jargon 7 dialect 10 vernacular

Paton, Alan
author of: 19 Too Late the Phalarope 20 Cry the Beloved Country 24 Ah but Your Land Is Beautiful

pat on the back 6 praise 7 plaudit 10 compliment 12 commendation

patriarch 5 elder, ruler 6 father, leader, old man 8 male head 9 chieftain 13 paterfamilias

patrician 4 lord, peer 5 noble 6 lordly 7 genteel, stately 8 highborn, imposing, noble man, princely, well-bred 9 blueblood, dignified, gentle man 10 aristocrat, upper-class 12 aristocratic, silk-stocking

patrimony 3 lot 5 dower, share 6 devise, estate, legacy 7 portion 8 bestowal, heritage, jointure 9 endowment 10 bequeathal, birthright 11 inheritance 12 hereditament

patriotism
Latin: 11 amor patriae

Patroclus
father: 9 Menoetius
mother: 8 Periapis
friend: 8 Achilles
killed by: 6 Hector

patrol 5 guard, scout, watch 6 ranger, sentry, warden 7 protect 8 sentinel 9 safe guard, walk a beat, watch man, watch over 10 stand watch

patron 5 angel, buyer 6 backer, client, friend, helper 7 habitue, shopper, sponsor, visitor 8 advocate, attender, champion, customer, defender, financer, promoter, upholder 9 protector, spectator, supporter 10 benefactor, encourager, frequenter, wellwisher 11 sympathizer 12 benefactress 14 philanthropist

patronage 3 aid 4 help 5 favor, plums, trade 6 buying, custom, spoils 7 backing, charity, clients, dealing, support 8 advocacy, auspices, business, commerce 9 clientele, customers, fosterage 10 assistance, friendship, pork barrel, protection, purchasing 11 benefaction, sponsorship 12 philanthropy 13 encouragement

patronize 5 humor 6 shop at 7 buy from 8 deal with, frequent 9 trade with 10 condescend

patsy 4 dupe, pawn, tool 7 cat's-paw, fall guy

patter 3 pad, pat, rap, tap 4 beat, drum 5 pound, thrum 6 tattoo 7 rat-a-tat, spatter, tapping 8 drumming, sprinkle

pattern 4 copy, form, mold, plan 5 draft, guide, ideal, mimic, model, motif, shape 6 design, follow, sample 7 emulate, example, fashion, imitate, paragon 8 exemplar, original, paradigm, parallel, simulate, specimen, standard 9 archetype, criterion, duplicate, prototype 10 apotheosis, stereotype 12 illustration

Patton
director: 17 Franklin Schaffner
cast: 10 Karl Malden (Omar Bradley) 12 George C Scott (George Patton), Stephen Young 13 Michael Strong
Oscar for: 5 actor (Scott), story 7 picture 8 director 10 screenplay (Francis Ford Coppola and Edmund H North)

Patton, George S
nickname: 15 Old Blood and Guts
served in: 3 WWI 4 WWII 11 World War One, World War Two
commander of: 9 Third Army
invasion of: 8 Normandy 11 North Africa
capture of: 6 Sicily
battle: 5 Bulge
wore: 21 ivory-handled revolvers
memoirs: 12 War As I Knew It

Patty Duke Show, The
character: 7 Richard 8 Ross Lane 9 Cathy Lane, Patty Lane 10 Martin Lane 14 Natalie Masters
cast: 9 Jean Byron, Patty Duke 10 Paul O'Keefe 14 Eddie Applegate 16 William Schallert

paucis verbis 10 by few words, in few words 12 with few words

paucity 4 lack 6 dearth 7 fewness, poverty 8 exiguity, poorness, puniness, scarcity, shortage, sparsity, thinness 10 deficiency, meagerness, scantiness, scarceness 13 insufficiency

Paul
former name: 4 Saul
birthplace: 6 Tarsus
teacher: 8 Gamaliel
companion: 5 Silas 7 Timothy 8 Barnabas, John Mark 9 Trophimus
cities visited: 4 Rome 5 Derbe, Perga, Troas 6 Lystra, Paphos 7 Antioch, Corinth, Ephesus, Iconium, Miletus, Salamis 8 Caesarea, Damascus, Neapolis, Philippi 9 Macedonia 12 Thessalonica
conversion place: 14 road to Damascus
wrote: 8 epistles

Paul Bunyan
author: 12 James Stevens
character: 9 Shanty Boy 10 Hels Helson 11 King Bourbon 12 Sourdough Sam 13 Babe the Blue Ox 14 Hot Biscuit Slim 16 Johnny Inkslinger

Pauli, Wolfgang
field: 7 physics
researched: 13 quantum theory
established: 14 Pauli principle 18 exclusion principle
awarded: 10 Nobel Prize

Paulina
character in: 14 The Winter's Tale
author: 11 Shakespeare

Pauling, Linus Carl
field: 12 biochemistry
worked on: 8 proteins 18 molecular structure
advocated: 8 Vitamin C
awarded: 10 Nobel Prize
  awarded for: 5 peace 9 chemistry

paunch 3 gut, pot 5 belly, tummy 7 abdomen, stomach 8 potbelly 9 bay window, beer belly, spare tire 10 midsection 11 breadbasket, corporation

pauper 6 beggar 7 almsman 8 bankrupt, indigent 9 insolvent, mendicant 10 poor person, starveling 11 charity case 12 down-and-outer

pause 3 gap 4 halt, rest, stop, wait 5 break, cease, delay, let up 6 hiatus 7 interim, time out 8 break off, hesitate, interval 9 cessation, interlude 10 deliberate, suspension 12 intermission, interruption

pave 3 tar 4 face 6 cement 7 asphalt, surface 8 black top 9 resurface 10 macadamize

pavement 4 slab 5 brick 6 cement, hearth, street, tarmac 7 asphalt, cobbles, macadam 8 concrete, driveway, flagging, sidewalk 9 flagstone

pavilion 4 tent, ward, wing 5 arbor,

kiosk 6 gazebo 7 pergola 9 bandshell 11 summerhouse

Pavlov, Ivan Petrovich
nationality: 7 Russian
researched: 9 digestion
studied: 20 behavior conditioning 21 Pavlovian conditioning
awarded: 10 Nobel Prize

paw 2 pa 3 dad, pop, toe 4 feel, foot, grab, hand, maul, mitt, papa 5 daddy, flail, touch 6 caress, clutch, father, handle, scrape, strike 7 rough up 8 forefoot 9 mishandle
mate: 3 maw

pawn 4 bond, dupe, hock, tool 5 agent, patsy 6 flunky, lackey, pledge, puppet 7 cat's-paw 8 borrow on, creature, guaranty, henchman, hireling, security 9 assurance, guarantee, underling 10 instrument 12 raise money on 14 give as security

pawnbroker
French: 11 mont-de-piete

Pawnbroker, The
director: 11 Sidney Lumet
cast: 10 Rod Steiger (Sol Nazerman) 11 Brock Peters 12 Jaime Sanchez 19 Geraldine Fitzgerald
setting: 6 Harlem

Pawnee (Chahiksichhiks)
language family: 7 Caddoan
location: 5 Texas 8 Nebraska, Oklahoma 9 New Mexico
related to: 7 Arikara
god: 6 Tirawa

Pawtuxet
location: 13 Massachusetts
leader: 7 Squanto

Pax
origin: 5 Roman
goddess of: 5 peace
corresponds to: 5 Irene

pax vobiscum 14 peace be with you

pay 3 fee 4 foot, give, meet 5 grant, honor, remit, repay, serve, wages, yield 6 ante up, chip in, extend, income, profit, render, return, salary, settle 7 benefit, bring in, cough up, payment, present, proffer, stipend 8 be useful, earnings, paycheck, shell out 9 bear fruit, liquidate, reimburse 10 come across, compensate, make good on, recompense 12 compensation 13 reimbursement

payable 3 due 4 owed 5 owing 6 mature, unpaid 8 to be paid 9 in arrears, spendable 10 demandable, expendable, receivable 11 outstanding

pay attention 4 heed, note 6 attend, notice 7 observe

Payaya
language family: 12 Coahuiltecan
location: 5 Texas

pay back 5 repay 7 counter, get even 9 reimburse, retaliate 10 recompense, remunerate 15 make restitution

pay for 6 redeem 7 expiate 8 atone for 9 answer for, suffer for 10 compensate, recompense, remunerate 13 make amends for 17 make reparation for

pay heed 6 notice 8 consider 11 concentrate 12 pay attention 13 put one's mind to

pay homage 5 defer, honor 7 acclaim 10 pay tribute

paying back 9 repayment 11 getting even 12 making good on 13 reimbursement

paymaster 6 bursar, purser 7 cashier 10 cashkeeper

payment 3 fee, pay 4 debt 6 outlay, paying, salary 7 premium 8 defrayal, spending 9 allowance, discharge 10 recompense, remittance, settlement 11 expenditure, installment, liquidation 12 compensation, contribution, disbursement, remuneration 13 reimbursement

pay no heed to 4 defy 6 ignore, slight 7 disobey, neglect, violate 8 overlook, pass over 9 disregard 10 brush aside, infringe on 14 shut one's eyes to 16 pay no attention to 17 transgress against

payoff 3 end 4 soap 5 bribe, graft 6 climax, crunch, finale, finish, grease, payola, result, upshot, windup 7 outcome 8 clincher 9 hush money 10 bottom line, conclusion, denouement, protection, resolution 11 culmination

pay off 5 bribe 6 buy off, suborn 13 grease the palm

payola 5 bribe, graft 6 grease, payoff

pay out 5 spend 6 expend, lay out 7 fork out 8 allocate, disburse, dispense, shell out 10 distribute

pay suit 3 woo 5 court 8 pay court

Payton, Walter
nickname: 9 Sweetness
sport: 8 football
position: 11 running back
team: 12 Chicago Bears

pay tribute to 4 laud, tout 5 boost, toast 6 praise, salute 7 applaud, commend 8 eulogize 10 compliment 16 sing the praises of

pea 5 Pisum 12 Pisum sativum
varieties: 4 Flat, Love, Snow, Wild 5 Beach, Caley, Chick, Congo, Coral, Field, Glory, Green, Heart, Heath, Hoary, No-eye, Rough, Sugar, Sweet 6 Angola, Canada, Desert, Garden, Marble, Pigeon, Rosary, Scurfy, Winged, Winter 7 Catjang, Darling, English, Rabbit's, Seaside 8 Earthnut, Egyptian, Princess, Shamrock 9 Asparagus, Black-eyed, Butterfly, Chaparral, Jerusalem, Partridge, Perennial 10 Australian, Singletary, Wild winter 11 Everlasting, Sturt desert, Two-flowered, Winter sweet 12 Edible-

podded **14** Austrian winter **15** Australian flame

peace 4 calm, ease **5** amity, truce **6** accord, repose **7** concord, content, entente, harmony **8** serenity **9** agreement, armistice, composure, placidity **12** pacification, tranquillity **14** reconciliation
god of: 4 Frey **5** Freyr
goddess of: 3 Pax **9** Concordia
Hebrew: 6 shalom
Russian: 3 mir

peace be with you
Latin: 11 pax vobiscum

peaceful 4 calm **5** quiet, still **6** placid, serene, silent **7** pacific, restful **8** amicable, friendly, tranquil **9** agreeable, peaceable, peacetime **10** harmonious, nonviolent, nonwarring, pacifistic, untroubled **11** undisturbed

peacefulness 4 calm **7** concord, harmony **8** calmness, serenity **9** placidity **11** tranquility

peacemaker 8 diplomat, mediator, placater **9** go-between **10** ambassador, arbitrator, negotiator **11** adjudicator, conciliator, pacificator, peacekeeper, peacemonger **12** intermediary

peacemaking 9 pacifying, placating, placatory **11** reconciling **12** conciliating, conciliatory, pacification

peace offering 6 amends **11** appeasement **12** conciliation

peace of mind 8 security, serenity **11** tranquility **16** freedom from worry

peace to you
Hebrew: 14 shalom aleichem

peach 13 Prunus persica
varieties: 4 Muir, Peak, Sims, Vine, Wild **5** Gaume, Hiley, Pavie **6** Carmen, Crosby, Desert, Foster, J H Hale, Lovell, Orejon, Paloro, Peen-to, Salwey **7** Dixigem, Dixired, Elberta, Persian, Quadong **8** Champion, Crawford, Isabella, Redhaven, Russelet **9** Alexander, Freestone, Halehaven, Rochester, Southland **10** Clingstone, Goldeneast, Heath Cling, Summer Snow **12** Chinese Cling, Iron Mountain, Mountain Rose, Oldmixon Free **13** Golden Jubilee, Old mixon Cling, Phillips Cling **14** Belle of Georgia
peach-like: 7 apricot **9** nectarine

Peach State
nickname of: 7 Georgia

Peachum, Polly
character in: 12 Beggar's Opera
author: 3 Gay

peachy 4 fine, keen **5** dandy, super, swell **9** excellent, marvelous, wonderful

peacock
group of: 6 muster

Peacock
constellation of: 4 Pavo

Peacock, Thomas Love
author of: 12 Headlong Hall **14** Crotchet Castle, Nightmare Abbey

peak 3 tip, top **4** acme, apex **5** crest, crown, flood, prime **6** apogee, climax, summit, zenith **8** pinnacle **9** culminate **11** culmination

peaked 3 ill, wan **4** lean, pale, thin, weak **5** ashen, drawn, gaunt, spare, spiked, spiny, white **6** ailing, infirm, pallid, pointy, sallow, sickly, skinny, spiked **7** haggard, pinched, pointed, scrawny, tapered, wizened **9** emaciated, shriveled **11** debilitated

peal 3 din **4** boom, clap, ring, roar, roll, toll **5** blare, blast, clang, crack, crash, knell **6** rumble **7** clangor, resound, ringing **10** resounding **11** reverberate **13** reverberation **14** tintinnabulate **16** tintinnabulation

Peale, Charles Willson
born: 17 Queen Anne County MD
son: 9 Raphaelle, Rembrandt **12** Titian Ramsay
artwork: 26 The Exhumation of the Mastodon
portrait: 8 Franklin **9** Jefferson, John Adams **10** Washington

Peale, Raphaelle
born: 13 Bucks County PA
father: 14 Charles Willson
brother: 9 Rembrandt **12** Titian Ramsay
artwork: 12 After the Bath

Peale, Rembrandt
born: 13 Bucks County PA
father: 14 Charles Willson
brother: 9 Raphaelle **12** Titian Ramsay
artwork: 15 The Court of Death
portrait: 9 Jefferson **10** Washington

peal of bells 7 clangor, ringing **16** tintinnabulation

peanut 3 pod, tot **4** puny, seed **5** petty, small **6** goober, legume, measly, paltry **8** earthpea **9** little one
species: 15 Arachis hypogaea

Peanuts
creator: 14 Charles Schultz
character: 4 Lucy **5** Linus, Sally, Marcy **6** Pig Pen, Snoopy **9** Schroeder, Woodstock **11** Lucy Van Pelt **12** Linus Van Pelt, Charlie Brown **15** Peppermint Patty **19** Little Red Haired Girl
Halloween figure: 12 Great Pumpkin
Snoopy's plane: 12 Sopwith Camel
Snoopy's foe: 8 Red Baron
saying: 9 Good grief

pear 5 Pyrus **13** Pyrus communis
varieties: 4 Bosc, Sand **5** Anjou, Asian, Blind, Melon, Smith **6** Balsam, Burrel, Butter, Comice, Common, Garber, Garlic, Orient, Seckel, Warden **7** Chinese, Kieffer, Prickly, Vinegar **8** Bartlett, Japanese, Oriental

9 Alligator, Evergreen, Muscadine **10** Beurre Bosc, Brandywine, Chaumontel **11** Birch-leaved, Bon Chretien, Paper-spined, Winter Nelis **12** Beurre d'Anjou, Easter Beurre, Sacred garlic, Willow-leaved **13** Flemish Beauty, Waite Bergamot **15** Doyenne du Comice **18** Duchesse d'Angouleme

pearl
grows in: 6 oyster
genus: 8 Pinctada
source: 6 Red Sea **9** Caribbean **11** Persian Gulf **12** South Pacific **16** Gulf of California
composed of: 5 nacre **9** aragonite **10** conchiolin **13** mother-of-pearl
quality: 6 luster **11** iridescence
color: 4 blue, rose **5** black, brown, cream, green, white **6** yellow
shape: 5 round **7** baroque
type: 8 cultured, Oriental (saltwater) **9** simulated **10** freshwater

Pearl-Fishers, The
also: 19 Les Pecheurs de Perles
opera by: 5 Bizet
setting: 6 Ceylon

Pearl of the Antilles see **4** Cuba

Pearly Gates 7 heaven
mentioned in: 10 Revelation

peasant 4 boor, esne, peon, serf **5** churl, knave, yokel **6** farmer, rustic, worker **7** laborer, lowlife, villein **10** countryman, dirt farmer
Arabic: 6 fellah
Indian: 4 ryot **5** kisan **6** raiyat
Irish: 4 kern
Russian: 5 kulak **6** muzhik
Scottish: 6 cotter

peasantlike 5 crude, rough **6** coarse, oafish, rustic, vulgar **7** boorish, loutish, uncouth **9** unrefined **10** unpolished

peccadillo 4 slip **5** lapse **6** boo-boo **7** blunder, faux pas, misdeed, misstep **8** petty sin, trespass **9** false move, wrong step **10** misconduct, wrongdoing **11** misdemeanor **12** transgression

peck 3 pat, rap, tap **4** buss, gobs, lots, mess **5** a slew, batch, bunch, heaps, scads, smack, snack, stack, thump **6** nibble, oodles, pick at, strike, stroke, worlds **8** light jab **9** abundance, light kiss **11** eight quarts
abbreviation of: 2 pk

Peck, Gregory
real name: 17 Eldred Gregory Peck
born: 9 La Jolla CA
roles: 8 Moby Dick **9** Old Gringo **10** On the Beach, Spellbound **11** The Yearling **12** Duel in the Sun, Roman Holiday **15** The Paradine Case **16** Twelve O'Clock High **17** Other People's Money, The Boys from Brazil, The Guns of Navarone **18** To Kill a Mockingbird (Oscar) **19** Gentleman's Agreement, The Keys of the Kingdom **21** The Snows of Kilimanjaro **26** The

Man in the Gray Flannel Suit
autobiography: 12 An Actor's Life

Peckinpah, Sam
director of: 9 Straw Dogs **10** The
Getaway **12** The Wild Bunch

Pecksniff
character in: 16 Martin Chuzzlewit
author: 7 Dickens

peculiar 3 odd **5** queer, weird **6** far-
out, quaint, unique **7** bizarre, curious,
erratic, private, special, strange, typical, unusual **8** abnormal, distinct,
freakish, personal, singular, specific **9**
eccentric, exclusive, whimsical **10** capricious, individual, outlandish, particular **11** distinctive **13** idiosyncratic **14**
characteristic, distinguishing, representative, unconventional

peculiarity 4 mark **5** badge, stamp,
trait **6** oddity **7** feature, quality **8** odd
trait **9** attribute, queerness, weirdness
10 erraticism, uniqueness **11** abnormality, bizarreness, distinction, singularity, strangeness **12** eccentricity,
freakishness, idiosyncrasy **13** particularity, unnaturalness **14** characteristic
21 distinguishing quality

pecuniary 6 fiscal **8** economic, monetary **9** budgetary, financial

pedagogic 7 bookish, donnish **8** academic, didactic, pedantic, tutorial **9**
scholarly **11** educational **12** professorial **13** instructional

pedagogue, pedagog 5 tutor **7**
teacher **8** academic, educator **9** professor **10** instructor, schoolmarm **12**
educationist, schoolmaster **13** schoolteacher **14** schoolmistress

pedant 6 purist **8** bookworm **9** dogma-
tist **13** methodologist

pedantic 5 fussy **7** bookish, finicky,
pompous, stilted **8** academic, didactic,
dogmatic **10** nitpicking, scholastic **11**
doctrinaire, punctilious **13** hairsplitting **14** overparticular

peddle 4 hawk, sell, vend **6** retail **7**
deal out **8** dispense

Peder Victorious
character in: 16 Giants of the Earth
author: 7 Rolvaag

pedestal 4 base, foot **6** bottom, plinth
10 foundation

pedestrian 6 walker **7** mundane, prosaic, tedious, trekker **8** mediocre, ordinary, stroller **9** itinerant **10** ambulatory, for walking, unexciting **11**
commonplace, peripatetic, unimportant **12** foot-traveler, run-of-the-mill
13 insignificant, perambulating, per-
ambulatory, unimaginative **15** inconsequential

pedigree 4 line **6** family, strain **7** descent, lineage **8** ancestry **9** bloodline,
parentage **10** derivation, extraction,
family tree **13** line of descent

peek 3 pry **4** peep, peer **5** watch **6**
glance **7** glimpse

peel 4 bark, hull, husk, pare, rind,
skin, tear, zest **5** flake, scale, shuck,
spade, strip **6** remove **7** undress **11**
decorticate

peel off 6 remove **7** veer off **8** strip
off

peep 4 peek, peer, skim, word **5**
cheep, chirp, tweet **6** emerge, glance,
murmur, mutter, squeak **7** chirrup,
glimpse, peeping, peer out, twitter,
whimper, whisper **9** come forth, quick
look

peeper 3 eye **4** frog **6** voyeur **10** peeping Tom

peer 4 gape, gaze, look, lord, peek,
peep **5** equal, noble, stare **6** appear,
emerge, squint **7** compeer **8** nobleman **9** blue blood, gentleman, patrician **10** aristocrat

peerage 8 nobility **10** blue bloods, patricians **11** aristocracy

Peer Gynt
author: 11 Henrik Ibsen
character: 3 Ase **6** Anitra **7** Solveig
12 The Great Boyg **16** The Button
Moulder
suite composer: 5 Grieg

peerless 7 supreme **8** flawless **9** faultless, matchless, unequaled, un-
matched, unrivaled **10** consummate,
inimitable, preeminent, surpassing,
unexcelled **11** superlative, unsurpassed **12** incomparable, transcendent

peeve 3 bug, eat, irk, vex **4** fret, gall,
rile **5** annoy, chafe, eat at, frost, gripe
6 gnaw at, nettle **7** dislike, perturb,
provoke **8** irritate, vexation **9** aggravate, annoyance, complaint, grievance
10 exasperate, irritation **11** aggravation, provocation **12** exasperation,
give one a pain **13** pain in the neck
14 thorn in the side

peevish 4 mean **5** cross, huffy, sulky,
surly, testy **6** crabby, cranky, grumpy
7 grouchy, pettish **8** churlish, petulant, snappish **9** fractious, irritable,
querulous, splenetic **10** ill-humored,
ill-natured **11** bad-tempered, ill-
tempered, quarrelsome **12** cantankerous

peewee 4 tiny **5** dwarf, small, teeny **6**
little, midget, minute **9** itsy-bitsy, itty-
bitty, minuscule **10** diminutive, teeny-
weeny **11** Lilliputian

Pee Wee
nickname of: 6 Herman (Paul Reu-
bens) **11** Harold Reese

peg 3 pin **4** nail **5** cleat, dowel, spike,
thole **6** skewer, toggle **8** fastener,
tholepin

Pegasus
form: 5 horse
characteristic: 6 winged
mother: 6 Medusa
ridden by: 11 Bellerophon

Peggotty, Clara
character in: 16 David Copperfield
author: 7 Dickens

Pei, I M (Ieoh Ming)
architect of: 10 Miho Museum
(Kyoto) **12** East Building (National
Gallery of Art), L'Enfant Plaza
(Washington DC) **14** East-West Cen-
ter (U of Hawaii), Mile High Center
(Denver) **15** Place Ville Marie (Mont-
real) **16** John Hancock Tower (Bos-
ton), Pyramide du Louvre (Paris) **18**
Everson Museum of Art (Syracuse
NY) **21** Rock and Roll Hall of Fame
(Cleveland) **22** Kips Bay Plaza
Apartments (NYC) **36** National Cen-
ter for Atmospheric Research (Boul-
der CO)

peignoir 4 gown **6** kimono **8** negligee
9 nightgown **12** dressing gown

pejorative 7 mocking **8** debasing, negative, scornful **9** degrading, demean-
ing, slighting **10** belittling, derogatory,
detracting, disdainful, ridiculing, unpleasant **11** deprecatory, disparaging,
downgrading **12** contemptuous, depre-
ciatory, disapproving **15** uncomplimentary

Peking *see* **7** Beijing

pelagic 6 marine **7** aquatic, oceanic **9**
thalassic **11** sea-dwelling

Pele
real name: 24 Edson Arantes do Nascimento
sport: 6 soccer
team: 13 New York Cosmos
nationality: 9 Brazilian

Peleus
king of: 6 Phthia **9** Myrmidons
father: 6 Aeacus
mother: 6 Endeis
brother: 7 Telamon
half-brother: 6 Phocus
wife: 6 Thetis **8** Antigone
son: 8 Achilles
daughter: 8 Polydora

pelf 4 gain **5** booty, lucre, money **6**
mammon, riches, spoils

Pelican State
nickname of: 9 Louisiana

pelisse 4 cape, coat **5** cloak **6** mantle

Pelleas (King Pelleas)
character in: 16 Arthurian romance
daughter: 6 Elaine

Pelleas and Melisande
also: 18 Pelleas et Melisande
opera by: 7 Debussy
character: 6 Golaud, Yniold
author: 18 Maurice Maeterlinck

pellet 3 pea **4** ball, bead, drop, pill **5**
pearl, stone **6** marble, pebble, sphere
7 globule

pell-mell 6 rashly **7** hastily **8** slapdash
9 hurriedly, post haste **10** at half
cock, carelessly, heedlessly, recklessly
11 hurry-scurry, impetuously, impru-

dently **12** incautiously **13** helter-skelter, precipitately, thoughtlessly

pellucid 5 clear, lucid **10** articulate **11** crystalline, translucent, transparent **12** intelligible **14** understandable

Pelops
 father: **8** Tantalus
 sister: **5** Niobe
 son: **6** Atreus, Sciron **7** Letreus **8** Pittheus, Thyestes **9** Alcathous **10** Chrysippus
 daughter: **7** Nicippe **8** Lysidice **9** Astydamia
 resurrected by: **6** Hermes

pelt 3 fur, hit, rap **4** belt, coat, hide, skin, sock **5** pound, punch, whack **6** batter, buffet, fleece, pepper, pummel, strike, thrash, thwack **7** clobber

pen 3 sty **4** cage, coop, crib, fold **5** draft, hutch, pound, quill, stall, write **6** corral, pencil, scrawl **7** compose, paddock **8** compound, scribble, stockade **9** ballpoint, enclosure

penal 7 of jails **8** punitive **9** punishing **10** corrective, penalizing **11** castigatory, retributive **12** disciplinary

penalty 4 fine **7** forfeit **8** handicap **9** suffering **10** assessment, forfeiture, infliction, punishment **11** retribution **12** disadvantage

penance 9 atonement, expiation, hair shirt, penitence **10** contrition, repentance **12** propitiation **13** mortification

penates
 protectors of: **4** home
 companions: **5** lares

penchant 4 bent, bias, gift, turn **5** fancy, flair, knack, taste **6** liking, relish **7** leaning **8** affinity, fondness, tendency **9** prejudice, proneness, readiness **10** attraction, partiality, preference, proclivity, propensity **11** disposition, inclination **12** predilection **14** predisposition

pendant 3 fob **5** charm **6** locket **15** hanging ornament

Pendennis
 author: **25** William Makepeace Thackeray
 character: **9** Laura Bell **10** Henry Foker **12** Blanche Amory **13** Emily Costigan **14** Helen Pendennis, Major Pendennis **15** Arthur Pendennis

pendent, pendant 7 hanging, jutting, pensile **8** dangling, swinging **9** extending, pendulous, suspended **10** projecting, protruding **11** overhanging, protuberant

pendente lite 16 during litigation **19** with a lawsuit pending

pending 8 imminent **9** undecided, unsettled **10** in suspense, unfinished, unresolved, up in the air **11** in the offing **12** undetermined

pendulous 7 hanging, pendent, pen-sile, sagging **8** dangling, drooping, swinging **9** suspended

pendulum
 invented by: **7** Galileo

Penelope
 father: **7** Icarius
 mother: **8** Periboea
 husband: **8** Odysseus **9** Telegonus
 son: **6** Ifalus **10** Telemachus **11** Polyporthis
 fended off: **7** suitors

penetrate 3 get **4** bore **5** catch, enter, prick **6** decode, fathom, invade, pierce, seep in **7** cut into, discern, pervade, unravel **8** decipher, perceive, permeate, puncture, saturate, traverse **9** figure out, perforate **10** comprehend, cut through, impregnate, infiltrate, see through, understand **11** pass through

penetrating 4 keen **5** acrid, alert, alive, aware, harsh, heady, sharp, smart **6** astute, biting, clever, shrewd, strong **7** caustic, pungent, reeking **8** piercing, redolent, stinging **9** pervading, pervasive, trenchant **10** discerning, perceptive, percipient, permeating, saturating, thoughtful **11** intelligent, sharp-witted **13** perspicacious

penetration 5 foray, grasp **6** access, boring **7** insight, passage **8** infusion, invasion, keenness, piercing **9** intrusion, quickness, sharpness **10** astuteness, cleverness, perception, puncturing, shrewdness **11** discernment, perforation **12** intelligence, perspicacity

penguin 8 great auk

Penguin Island
 author: **13** Anatole France

peninsula 4 cape **5** point **8** headland **10** promontory

Peninsula State
 nickname of: **7** Florida

penitence 6 regret, sorrow **7** penance, remorse **9** atonement, attrition, expiation **10** contrition, repentance **11** compunction, humiliation

penitent 5 sorry **6** rueful **7** atoning, devotee, pilgrim **8** contrite **9** regretful, repentant **10** remorseful

penitentiary 3 can, pen **4** jail, stir **5** joint **6** prison **7** slammer **8** big house

Penn, Arthur
 director of: **12** Little Big Man **14** Bonnie and Clyde **16** The Miracle Worker

Penn, Sean
 father: **7** Leo Penn
 wife: **7** Madonna **11** Robin Wright
 roles: **5** U-Turn **7** Bad Boys, The Game **11** Carlito's Way, Mystic River **12** She's So Lovely **14** Dead Man Walking, The Interpreter, The Thin Red Line **15** Shanghai Express **22**

The Falcon and the Snowman **24** Fast Times at Ridgemont High

Pennacook (Merrimac)
 language family: **9** Algonkian **10** Algonquian
 location: **5** Maine **6** Quebec **7** New York, Vermont **10** New England **12** New Hampshire **13** Massachusetts
 leader: **11** Wannalancet **12** Passaconaway
 related to: **6** Abnaki

pen name
 French: **10** nom de plume

pennant 4 flag, jack **6** banner, burgee, colors, ensign, pennon **7** bunting **8** ensignia, standard, streamer **9** banderole, oriflamme

penniless 4 poor **5** broke, needy **6** busted, ruined **8** bankrupt, indigent, strapped, wiped out **9** destitute, flat broke, insolvent, moneyless **10** down-and-out, pauperized **12** impoverished **15** poverty-stricken

pennon 4 flag, jack **6** banner, colors, ensign **7** pennant **8** standard, streamer

Pennsylvania
 abbreviation: **2** PA **5** Penna
 nickname: **8** Keystone
 capital: **10** Harrisburg
 largest city: **12** Philadelphia
 others: **4** Erie, Etna, Plum, York **5** Avoca, Baden **6** Beaver, Bethel, Butler, Easton, Emmaus, Radnor, Ridley, Sharon **7** Altoona, Baldwin, Bristol, Chester, Ephrata, Hanover, Hershey, Lebanon, Reading **8** Abington, Braddock, Bradford, Bryn Mawr, Carlisle, Clairton, Harrison, Hazelton, Monessen, Scranton, Shamokin **9** Aliquippa, Allentown, Bethlehem, Charleroi, Haverford, Jeannette, Johnstown, Lancaster, Meadville, Mill Creek, Newcastle, Swissvale, Uniontown, Whitehall **10** Carbondale, Gettysburg, McKeesport, Norristown, Pittsburgh **11** Springfield, Wilkes Barre **12** State College, Williamsport
 college: **3** PSU **4** Penn, Pitt **5** Gratz, Thiel **6** Drexel, Lehigh, Temple **7** Juniata, LaSalle, Ursinus **8** Alliance, Bryn Mawr, Bucknell, Duquesne, Lycoming **9** Dickinson, Lafayette, Penn State, St Josephs, Villanova **10** Pittsburgh, Swarthmore **12** Carnegie Tech **17** Pennsylvania State
 feature:
  battle site: **10** Gettysburg
  bell: **7** Liberty
  hall: **12** Independence
  historical site: **11** Valley Forge
 tribe: **6** Seneca **7** Shawnee **8** Delaware **11** Lenni-Lanape **13** Susquehannock
 people: **5** Amish, Dutch **10** Stan Musial **11** Andrew Wyeth, Ethel Waters, Mary Cassatt, Stuart Davis **12** An-

drew Mellon, Anthony Wayne, Margaret Mead, Martha Graham, Samuel Barber, Thomas Eakins **13** Clifford Odets, Gertrude Stein **14** George S Kaufman **15** Maxwell Anderson **19** Stephen Vincent Benet
  explorer: 5 Brule **6** Hudson **11** Hendrickson
  lake: 4 Erie **7** Harveys **8** Conneaut **10** Pymatuning **13** Wallenpaupack
  land rank: 11 thirty-third
  mountain: 5 South **6** Pocono **11** Alleghenies
    highest point: 5 Davis
  physical feature:
    peninsula: 11 Presque Isle
    valley: 5 Great
  president: 13 James Buchanan
  river: 4 Ohio **6** Lehigh **7** Clarion, Genesee, Juniata, Licking, Towanda **8** Caldwell, Delaware, Schrader **9** Allegheny **10** Schuylkill **11** Monongahela, Susquehanna
  state admission: 6 second
  state bird: 12 ruffed grouse
  state fish: 10 brook trout
  state flower: 14 mountain laurel
  state motto: 28 Virtue Liberty and Independence
  state tree: 7 hemlock

penny 3 sum **4** cent **5** cheap, pence **6** copper, stiver **7** trivial

penny-pinching 5 close, tight **6** stingy **7** miserly **8** grudging **9** niggardly, penurious **10** ungenerous **11** tight-fisted **12** parsimonious

Penny Serenade
  director: 13 George Stevens
  cast: 9 Cary Grant **10** Irene Dunne **11** Beulah Bondi **13** Edgar Buchanan

pennyweight
  abbreviation of: 3 dwt

Penobscot
  language family: 9 Algonkian **10** Algonquian
  location: 5 Maine **13** Old Town Island
  members of: 17 Abnaki Confederacy

Penrod
  author: 15 Booth Tarkington
  sequel: 12 Penrod and Sam **13** Penrod Jashber
  character: 6 Herman, Verman **9** Sarah Crim **11** Rupe Collins **13** Marjorie Jones **15** Penrod Schofield
  dog: 4 Duke

pensee 7 thought **10** reflection

Pensees
  author: 12 Blaise Pascal

pension 5 grant **6** income, retire **7** annuity, stipend, subsidy **9** allowance **13** boardinghouse **14** retirement fund

pensive 3 sad **5** grave **6** dreamy, musing, solemn, somber **7** serious, wistful **8** dreaming **10** meditative, melancholy, reflective **11** day dreaming **13**

contemplative, introspective **15** sadly thoughtful

Pentateuch 10 Law of Moses **28** first five books of Old Testament
  see also **7** books of **12** Old Testament

Penthesilea
  queen of: 7 Amazons
  father: 4 Ares
  mother: 6 Otrere
  sister: 9 Hippolyta
  killed by: 8 Achilles

Pentheus
  king of: 6 Thebes
  father: 6 Echion
  mother: 5 Agave
  grandfather: 6 Cadmus

pent-up 7 boxed-up, checked, stifled **8** hedged-in, held back, penned-in, penned-up, reined in, stored-up **9** bottled-up, repressed **10** restrained, suppressed

penurious 5 close **6** frugal, stingy **7** miserly, sparing **8** stinting **9** niggardly **12** parsimonious **13** penny-pinching

penury 4 need, want **7** poverty **9** indigence, privation **10** bankruptcy, insolvency **11** destitution **14** impoverishment

peon 4 pawn, serf **5** slave **6** drudge, menial, worker **7** footman, laborer, orderly, peasant, servant

peony 7 Paeonia
  varieties: 4 tree **7** Chinese, Tibetan **8** Majorcan **11** Chinese tree **12** common garden

people 3 kin **5** folks **6** family, humans, the mob **7** kinfolk, mankind, mortals, the herd **8** citizens, humanity, populace, the crowd **9** ancestors, citizenry, commoners, human kind, relatives, the masses, the public, the rabble **10** population **11** Homo sapiens, human beings, individuals, inhabitants, John Q Public, men and women, the millions

People Are Funny
  host: 13 Art Linkletter

pep 3 vim, zip **4** dash, life, snap **5** gusto, verve, vigor **6** energy, ginger, spirit **8** vitality, vivacity **9** animation **10** enthusiasm, get-up-and-go, liveliness

Pepe Le Moko
  director: 14 Julien Duvivier
  cast: 9 Jean Gabin **13** Gabriel Gabrio, Mireille Balin
  remade as: 6 Casbah **7** Algiers

peperomia
  varieties: 3 Ivy **6** Prayer, Vining **7** Ivy-leaf, Leather, Red-edge **8** Coinleaf, Platinum **9** Flowering **10** Silveredge, Silver-leaf, Watermelon **11** Green-ripple **13** Emerald-ripple, Little fantasy

Pepin
  called: 8 the Short

king of: 6 Franks
son: 11 Charlemagne

Pepita
  character in: 21 The Bridge of San Luis Rey
  author: 6 Wilder

Peppard, George
  born: 9 Detroit MI
  wife: 15 Elizabeth Ashley
  roles: 6 Tobruk **7** Banacek **8** The A-Team **16** The Carpetbaggers **19** Breakfast at Tiffany's

pepper 3 dot **6** shower, strafe **7** bombard **8** sprinkle **9** condiment, vegetable

pepper, peppercorn
  botanical name: 5 Piper **7** Pnigrum **8** Capsicum **10** Piperaceae **11** C frutescens
  color: 3 red **5** black, green, white
  origin: 5 India **6** Brazil, Ceylon **7** Malabar, Sarawak, Sumatra **8** Alleppey, Pandjang, Sri Lanka **11** Tellicherry
  varieties: 3 Red **4** Baby, Bell, Bird, Cone, Long, Wild **5** Betle, Black, Chili, Cubeb, Green, Japan, Sweet, White **6** Cherry **7** Cayenne, Celebes, Cluster, Tabasco **8** Capsicum **9** Mild water **10** Australian, Red cluster **12** Mountain long, Tabasco-sauce
  French: 6 poivre
  German: 7 pfeffer
  Italian: 4 pepe
  Latin: 5 piper
  Persian: 5 biber **6** pilpil
  Spanish: 8 pimienta
  Swedish: 6 peppar
  Sanskrit: 7 pippali

peppermint 6 Mentha
  varieties: 4 Gray **5** Black, River, White **6** Silver, Sydney **9** Blackbutt **10** Robertson's **11** Broad-leaved **15** Mount Wellington **17** Narrow-leaved black **19** Nichol's willow-leaved

peppermint schnapps
  type: 7 liqueur
  flavor: 4 mint

peppery 3 hot **5** fiery, sharp, spicy **7** burning, piquant, pungent **14** highly seasoned

peppy 4 spry **5** brisk, perky **6** active, bouncy, frisky, lively, snappy **7** dynamic **8** animated, spirited, vigorous **9** energetic, full of pep, sparkling, sprightly, vivacious **12** enthusiastic

pep up 4 fire **6** excite, vivify, wake up **7** animate, enliven, quicken **8** vitalize

Pepys, Samuel
  author of: 10 Pepys' Diary

Pepys' Diary
  author: 11 Samuel Pepys

Pequot
  language family: 9 Algonkian **10** Algonquian
  location: 11 Connecticut, Rhode Island

perambulate 4 pace, tour, walk 5 amble, mosey 6 ramble, stroll 7 meander, saunter 9 promenade

perceivable 7 visible 8 apparent, distinct 10 detectable, noticeable, observable 11 discernible, perceptible 13 ascertainable

perceive 3 get, see 4 feel, hear, know, note 5 grasp, savvy, sense, smell, taste 6 deduce, detect, gather, notice 7 discern, make out, observe, realize 8 conclude, discover 9 apprehend, be aware of, recognize 10 comprehend, understand 11 distinguish

perceptible 5 clear, plain 7 evident, notable, obvious, visible 8 apparent, distinct, manifest, palpable, tangible, unhidden 9 prominent 10 detectable, noticeable, observable 11 conspicuous, discernible, perceivable, unconcealed, well-defined 12 discoverable, unmistakable 13 ascertainable

perception 5 grasp, sense 7 faculty 8 judgment 9 awareness, detection 10 cognizance, conception 11 discernment, recognition 12 apprehension 13 comprehension, consciousness, understanding 14 discrimination

perceptive 4 keen 5 acute, aware, quick, sharp 6 astute, shrewd 8 sensible 9 sensitive 10 discerning, insightful, responsive 11 intelligent, penetrating, quick-witted 13 understanding

perch 3 sit 4 land, rest, seat 5 eyrie, light, roost 6 alight, settle

Percival, Perceval
character in: 16 Arthurian romance
see 8 Parsifal

percolate 4 boil, brew 6 bubble, seethe

percussion instrument 4 gong 5 anvil, bells, tabor 6 chimes, rattle 7 celesta, cymbals, marimba, taboret, timpani 8 bass drum, side drum, triangle 9 castanets, dulcitone, snare drum, tenor drum, typophone, xylophone 10 kettledrum, tambourine 12 Glockenspiel, tubular bells

Percy, Walker
author of: 8 Lancelot 12 The Moviegoer 14 Love in the Ruins 15 The Second Coming 16 The Last Gentleman

Perdita
character in: 14 The Winter's Tale
author: 11 Shakespeare

perdition 4 Hell, ruin 8 hellfire 9 damnation, ruination 11 destruction 12 condemnation

Perdix
also: 9 Polycaste
brother: 8 Daedalus
son: 5 Talus
changed into: 9 partridge

pere 6 father, senior

Pere Goriot
author: 14 Honore de Balzac
character: 15 Monsieur Vautrin 17 Eugene de Rastignac, Madame de Beauseant 18 Victorine Taillefer 26 Countess Anastasie de Restaud, Baroness Delphine de Nucingen

peregrination 4 trip 5 jaunt, sally 6 hiking, junket, roving, travel 7 journey, roaming 8 rambling, trekking 9 excursion, wandering 10 expedition

Peregrine Pickle
author: 14 Tobias Smollett

Pereira, William
architect of: 13 Cape Canaveral 20 Transamerica Building (San Francisco)

Perelman, S J
author of: 10 Eastward Ha 15 One Touch of Venus (with Ogden Nash and Kurt Weill) 16 The Road to Miltown 18 Strictly from Hunger 24 Under the Spreading Atrophy

peremptory 5 final 6 biased, lordly 8 absolute, decisive, dogmatic 9 assertive, imperious 10 aggressive, highhanded, imperative, obligatory, undeniable 11 dictatorial, domineering, irrevocable, opinionated, overbearing, unavoidable, unequivocal 12 closedminded, irreversible 13 authoritative 14 unquestionable 16 incontrovertible

perennial 5 fixed 7 durable, lasting, undying 8 constant, enduring, timeless 9 ceaseless, continual, immutable, incessant, long-lived, permanent, perpetual, unceasing, unfailing 10 changeless, continuous, persistent, unchanging 11 everlasting, long-lasting, unremitting 12 imperishable 14 indestructible

Perez, Manuel Benitez
nickname: 10 El Cordobes

perfect 4 pure, true 5 exact, ideal, whole 6 effect, entire, evolve, strict 7 achieve, develop, fulfill, precise, realize, sublime, supreme 8 absolute, accurate, complete, faithful, finished, flawless, peerless, thorough, unbroken, unerring 9 blameless, faultless, matchless, undamaged, unequaled, unrivaled, untainted 10 accomplish, consummate, immaculate, impeccable, scrupulous, unimpaired 11 superlative, unblemished, unmitigated, unqualified

perfection 6 purity 9 achieving, evolution, exactness, precision, sublimity 10 completion, excellence, ideal state 11 development, fulfillment, perfectness, realization, superiority 12 accurateness, consummation, flawlessness 13 faultlessness, impeccability 14 accomplishment

perfectly 5 fully, quite 6 purely, wholly 7 totally, utterly 8 entirely, superbly 9 downright, supremely 10 absolutely, altogether, completely, flaw-

lessly, impeccably, infinitely, positively, thoroughly 11 faultlessly, wonderfully 12 consummately, preeminently, to perfection, without fault 13 without defect 14 to the nth degree, without blemish

Perfect Storm, The
author: 15 Sebastian Junger
director: 16 Wolfgang Petersen
cast: 9 Bob Gunton (Alexander McAnally), Diane Lane (Christina Cotter) 10 Allen Payne (Alfred Pierre), John Hawkes (Mike "Bugsy" Moran), Karen Allen (Melissa Brown) 11 John C Reilly (Dale Murphy) 12 Mark Wahlberg (Bobby Shatford) 13 George Clooney (Billy Tyne) 15 William Fichtner (David Sullivan) 25 Mary Elizabeth Mastrantonio (Linda Greenlaw)
ship: 10 Andrea Gail

perfidious 5 false, lying 6 shifty, sneaky 7 corrupt 8 cheating, disloyal, two-faced 9 deceitful, dishonest, faithless 10 traitorous, treasonous, unfaithful, untruthful 11 treacherous, treasonable 12 dishonorable, undependable, unscrupulous 13 double-dealing, untrustworthy

perfidy 6 deceit 7 treason 8 bad faith, betrayal 9 falseness, recreancy, treachery, two-timing 10 disloyalty, infidelity 11 double-cross, inconstancy 13 breach of faith, deceitfulness, double-dealing, faithlessness 14 unfaithfulness

perforate 4 bore, gash, hole, slit, stab 5 drill, prick, punch, slash, split, stick 6 pierce 8 puncture 9 lancinate, penetrate

perform 2 do 3 act 4 meet, play 5 enact 6 attain, depict, effect, finish, render, troupe 7 achieve, execute, fulfill, portray, present, pull off, realize 8 carry out, knock off 9 discharge, dispose of, polish off, represent 10 accomplish, bring about, consummate, perpetrate, take part in

performance 4 play, show 5 doing, opera 6 ballet 7 concert, conduct, recital 8 ceremony, dispatch, exercise 9 acquittal, discharge, execution, rendering, spectacle 10 attainment, completion, exhibition, performing, production 11 achievement, fulfillment, realization, transaction 12 consummation, effectuation, perpetration, presentation 13 entertainment 14 accomplishment

perfume 4 odor 5 aroma, scent, smell 7 bouquet, cologne, essence, extract, sweeten 9 aromatize, fragrance

perfumed 7 odorous, scented 8 aromatic, fragrant 11 odoriferous 12 sweet-scented 13 sweet-smelling

perfunctory 3 lax 5 hasty 6 casual 7 cursory, offhand, routine 8 careless, listless, lukewarm **9** apathetic, negligent **10** mechanical, spiritless, unthinking **11** halfhearted, inattentive, indifferent, passionless, superficial, unconcerned **13** disinterested

pergola 5 arbor, bower **6** ramada **7** balcony, trellis

Per Hanea
character in: 16 Giants of the Earth
author: 7 Rolvaag

perhaps 5 maybe **6** mayhap **8** peut-etre, possibly **9** perchance **10** God willing, imaginably **11** conceivably **12** peradventure

Periboea
father: 9 Alcathous, Hipponous
husband: 6 Oeneus **7** Polybus
son: 6 Tydeus **7** Olenias, Pelegon **14** Telamonian Ajax
foster son: 7 Oedipus

Perichole, La
character in: 21 The Bridge of San Luis Rey
author: 6 Wilder

Pericles, Prince of Tyre
author: 18 William Shakespeare
character: 5 Cleon **6** Marina, Thaisa **7** Dionyza **9** Antiochus **10** Lysimachus

Periclymenus
father: 6 Neleus **8** Poseidon
grandfather: 8 Poseidon
gift: 13 shape-changing
killed by: 8 Hercules

periderm 4 bark **8** covering **9** sheathing

peridot
species: 7 olivine
source: 5 Burma, Mogok **8** Zebirget
color: 11 yellow-green

perigee 5 depth, nadir **8** low point

Perikeiromene (The Rape of the Ringlets)
author: 8 Menander

peril 4 risk **6** danger, hazard, menace, threat **7** pitfall **8** jeopardy, unsafety **10** insecurity **11** uncertainty **13** cause for alarm, vulnerability

perilous 5 risky, shaky **6** chancy, unsafe, unsure **7** ominous **8** insecure, slippery, ticklish **9** dangerous, hazardous, uncertain **10** precarious, vulnerable **11** threatening, venturesome

perimeter 4 edge **6** border, bounds, margin **8** confines **9** periphery **10** borderline **13** circumference

period 3 age, end, eon, era **4** halt, stop, term, time **5** close, epoch, limit **6** finale, finish, season **7** curtain **8** duration, interval **9** cessation, interlude
French: 6 siecle

periodic, periodical 6 cyclic **7** regular, routine **8** frequent, repeated, seasonal **9** recurrent, recurring **12** intermittent

periodical 5 daily, paper **6** annual, review, weekly **7** journal, monthly **8** bulletin, magazine **9** newspaper, quarterly **10** newsletter **11** publication **12** newsmagazine

periodically 5 often **9** regularly, routinely **10** frequently, repeatedly **12** occasionally

peripatetic 6 roving **7** migrant, nomadic, roaming, walking **8** rambling, tramping **9** itinerant, migratory, traveling, wandering **10** ambulating, ambulatory **12** Aristotelian, gallivanting **13** peregrinating

periphery 4 edge **5** bound **6** border **7** fringes **8** boundary **9** outskirts, perimeter **13** circumference

perish 3 die **5** decay **6** expire, vanish **7** crumble **8** pass away **9** disappear **10** come to ruin, wither away **11** be destroyed

perishable 8 fleeting, unstable **9** ephemeral **10** evanescent, short-lived, transitory **12** decomposable

perished 4 dead, died **7** expired **8** lifeless **10** passed away

periwinkle 5 Vinca **12** Catharanthus
varieties: 4 Rose **6** Common, Lesser **7** Greater **10** Madagascar

perjury 13 false swearing **14** lying under oath **20** giving false testimony

Perkins, Anthony
born: 9 New York NY
roles: 6 Psycho **11** Norman Bates **14** Catch Twenty-Two **17** Look Homeward Angel **18** Desire Under the Elms, Friendly Persuasion

perk up 4 lift **5** cheer, rally, renew **6** buoy up, lift up, revive **7** animate, enliven, gladden **8** brighten, vitalize **9** stimulate **10** rejuvenate

perky 3 gay **4** pert **5** alert, brisk, happy, saucy, sunny **6** jaunty, lively **7** smiling **8** animated, cheerful, spirited **9** sprightly, vivacious **11** free and easy **12** full of spirit, lighthearted

permanent 3 set **4** perm, wave **6** stable **7** abiding, durable, endless, eternal, lasting, undying **8** constant, enduring, immortal, infinite, unending, unfading **9** deathless, immutable, long-lived, perpetual, unfailing **10** changeless, unyielding **11** everlasting, long-lasting, never-ending, unalterable **12** imperishable

permeate 4 fill **5** imbue **6** infuse **7** pervade **8** saturate **9** penetrate **11** pass through, seep through, soak through

per mensem 10 by the month

permissible 5 legal, licit **6** lawful **7** allowed, granted **8** licensed **9** allowable, permitted, tolerated **10** admissible, authorized, legitimate, sanctioned **12** unprohibited

permission 5 grant, leave **6** assent, permit **7** consent, license **8** approval, sanction **9** agreement, allowance **10** compliance, concession, indulgence **11** approbation, endorsement **12** acquiescence, dispensation **13** authorization

permissive 3 lax **7** lenient **8** allowing, granting, tolerant **9** assenting, easygoing, indulgent **10** consenting, forbearing, permitting **11** acquiescent **13** unprohibitive **14** unproscriptive

permit 2 OK **3** let **5** allow **6** endure, suffer **7** agree to, approve, condone, endorse, let pass, license, warrant **8** bear with, sanction, tolerate **9** authority, authorize, consent to, put up with **11** give leave to **12** give assent to **13** authorization
French: 13 laissez passer

permit to leave 4 free **5** let go **6** excuse **7** dismiss, release, set free **8** liberate **9** allow to go, discharge, send forth

pernicious 5 fatal, toxic **6** deadly, lethal, mortal **7** baneful, harmful, noxious, serious **8** damaging, venomous **9** dangerous, injurious, malignant, poisonous **10** disastrous **11** deleterious, destructive, detrimental

pernod
type: 8 aperitif
flavor: 5 anise
substitute for: 8 absinthe
with gin: 7 Dubarry
with orange juice: 9 Tiger Tail
with rum: 8 Shanghai
with rye: 3 TNT

peroration 6 sermon, speech, tirade **7** address, lecture, oration **8** diatribe, harangue, jeremiad **9** discourse, philippic **10** filibuster **11** declamation, exhortation

perpendicular 4 sine **5** erect, plumb, sheer, steep **7** upright **8** vertical **10** right angle

perpetrate 2 do **5** enact **6** commit, pursue **7** execute, inflict, perform, pull off **8** carry out, transact

perpetration 5 doing **9** committal **10** commission, committing, performing **11** carrying out, performance

perpetrator 9 performer **11** participant

perpetual 7 abiding, endless, eternal, lasting **8** constant, enduring, repeated, unending **9** ceaseless, continual, incessant, permanent, sustained, unceasing **10** continuous **11** everlasting, never ending, unremitting **12** interminable **13** inexhaustible, uninterrupted

perpetuate 4 save **7** sustain **8** continue, maintain, make last, preserve **10** eternalize **11** immortalize, memorialize

perpetuity 7 all time, forever **8** eternity, infinity **9** end of time **10** permanence **11** endlessness **12** perpetuation, timelessness **13** perdurability, perennialness

perplex 5 mix up, stump **6** baffle, boggle, muddle, puzzle, rattle **7** confuse, mystify, nonplus **8** befuddle, bewilder, confound **9** dumbfound

perplexed 7 anxious, amazed, baffled, bemused, muddled, puzzled **8** confused, doubtful, involved **9** befuddled, intricate, mystified **10** astonished, bewildered, nonplussed

perplexing 4 hard, mazy **6** thorny **7** complex **10** mysterious
riddle: 9 conundrum

perplexity 9 confusion **10** bafflement, puzzlement **12** bewilderment **13** mystification

perquisite 3 due **4** gift, perk **5** right **6** reward **7** benefit, present **9** advantage, emolument, privilege **10** honorarium, inducement, recompense **13** fringe benefit

Perry, Matthew Calbraith
  served in: 10 Mexican War **19** War of Eighteen-Twelve
  rank: 9 commodore
  helped establish: 7 Liberia
  commander of: 17 US African Squadron
  gained treaty with: 5 Japan

Perry, Oliver Hazard
  nickname: 14 Hero of Lake Erie
  served in: 13 Tripolitan War **19** War of Eighteen-Twelve
  battle: 8 Lake Erie
  commander of ship: 7 Niagara **8** Lawrence
  defeated: 7 British
  saying: 31 We have met the enemy and they are ours

Perry, William
  nickname: 12 Refrigerator
  sport: 8 football
  team: 12 Chicago Bears

Perry Como Show, The
  regulars: 8 Don Adams **9** Jack Duffy, Paul Lynde **10** Pierre Olaf **11** Kaye Ballard **12** Sandy Stewart **14** Fontane Sisters **17** Ray Charles Singers **18** Louis Da Pron Dancers **19** Peter Gennaro Dancers
  announcer: 9 Dick Stark, Ed Herlihy **11** Frank Gallop, Martin Block **12** Durward Kirby
  orchestra: 13 Mitchell Ayres
  theme: 16 Dream Along with Me

Perry Mason
  character: 6 Lt Drum **7** Lt Tragg **9** Paul Drake **10** Lt Anderson **11** Della Street **14** Hamilton Burger
  cast: 9 Wesley Lau **10** Ray Collins **11** Barbara Hale, Raymond Burr **13** William Hopper, William Talman **15** Richard Anderson

persecute 3 vex **4** bait **5** abuse, annoy, bully, harry, hound **6** badger, harass, harrow, hector, plague **7** op-

press, torment **8** maltreat **9** tyrannize, victimize

Persephone
  also: 4 Cora, Kore **10** Perserpina, Proserpine
  queen of: 5 Hades
  father: 4 Zeus
  mother: 7 Demeter
  husband: 5 Hades
  abducted by: 5 Pluto
  ate seeds of: 11 pomegranate
  epithet: 11 Carpophorus
  corresponds to: 5 Brimo **6** Libera **8** Despoena

Persepolis
  capital of: 13 Persian Empire
  near modern-day: 10 Shiraz, Iran

Perseus
  father: 4 Zeus
  mother: 5 Danae
  grandfather: 8 Acrisius
  wife: 9 Andromeda
  son: 6 Mestor, Perses **7** Alcaeus, Heleius **9** Electryon, Sthenelus
  daughter: 10 Gorgophone
  saved: 9 Andromeda
  killed: 6 Gorgon, Medusa

perseverance 8 tenacity **10** doggedness, resolution **11** persistence **12** resoluteness **13** determination, steadfastness

persevere 6 hang on, keep on **7** persist **8** keep at it, plug away, work hard **9** not give up, stick to it **10** be resolute, be resolved, hammer away **11** be obstinate, be steadfast, hang in there

persevering 6 dogged **8** constant, diligent, resolute, sedulous **9** keeping on, steadfast, tenacious **10** determined, persistent, unflagging **11** hardworking, industrious, unremitting

Pershing, John J
  nickname: 9 Black Jack
  served in: 3 WWI **11** Philippines, World War One **18** Spanish-American War
  commander of: 21 Mexican border campaign
  trained: 27 American Expeditionary Forces
  battle: 10 Kettle Hill **11** San Juan Hill
  fought against: 5 Moros **11** Pancho Villa
  rank: 16 brigadier general **18** general of the armies
  memoirs: 26 My Experiences in the World War
    won: 13 Pulitzer Prize (for history)

Persia *see* **4** Iran

Persian Gulf War
  caused by: 4 Iraq **13** Saddam Hussein **14** Kuwait invasion
  took place in: 4 Iraq **6** Kuwait **10** Middle East **11** Saudi Arabia
  leaders:
    Allies: 11 Colin Powell **15** Khalid

bin Sultan **18** H Norman Schwarzkopf
    Iraq: 13 Saddam Hussein
  operations: 11 Desert Storm **12** Desert Shield
  weapons: 4 Scud **5** AWACS **6** Abrams, Apache **7** Bradley, Patriot, Stealth **8** Tomahawk
  battle: 6 Khafji **18** mother of all battles

Persian Mythology
  god of light/truth: 7 Mithras

Persians, The
  author: 9 Aeschylus
  character: 6 Atossa, Xerxes **13** Ghost of Darius

persist 4 go on, last, stay **6** endure, hang on, hold on, remain **7** hold out, survive **8** continue, keep at it, not yield **9** not give up, persevere, stand fast, stick to it **10** be resolute **11** be obstinate, be tenacious, hang in there, never say die

persistence 8 tenacity **9** diligence **11** application **12** perseverance **13** determination

persistent 6 dogged **7** abiding, endless, eternal, lasting **8** constant, enduring, obdurate, resolute, stubborn **9** continual, incessant, obstinate, perpetual, steadfast, sustained, tenacious, unceasing, unfailing **10** continuous, determined, persisting, relentless, unshakable, unswerving **11** persevering, unrelenting, unremitting **12** interminable **13** inexhaustible

persnickety 5 fussy **6** choosy **7** finical, finicky **8** picayune **10** fastidious, fuddy-duddy, meticulous, nitpicking, particular, pernickety **11** overprecise, punctilious **13** overdemanding

person 4 body, soul **5** being, human **6** mortal **8** creature **9** earthling **10** human being, individual, living body, living soul

persona 5 being **6** facade **9** character

personable 4 warm **7** affable, amiable, cordial, likable, tactful **8** amicable, charming, friendly, outgoing, pleasant, sociable **9** agreeable **10** attractive, diplomatic **11** complaisant, sympathetic **12** well-disposed, wellmannered

Personae
  author: 9 Ezra Pound

personage 3 VIP **5** nabob **6** bigwig **7** big name, big shot, notable **8** big wheel, luminary, somebody **9** celebrity, dignitary **11** heavyweight **12** leading light, public figure **13** highmuck-a-muck

persona grata 8 diplomat **16** acceptable person **34** acceptable diplomatic representative

personal 3 own **5** privy **6** bodily, inward, secret **7** private, special **8** intimate, physical **9** corporeal, exclusive

10 individual, particular, subjective **12** confidential

Personal Anthology, A
  author: **15** Jorge Luis Borges
personality 3 ego **4** self **5** charm **6** makeup, nature **8** charisma, identity **9** magnetism **10** affability, amiability **11** disposition, temperament **12** friendliness **13** agreeableness, individuality **15** distinctiveness
persona non grata 15 unwelcome person **18** unacceptable person **33** unwelcome diplomatic representative
Personification of
  aging: **4** Elli
  air: **4** Amen, Amon **5** Ammon **6** Aether
  astronomy: **6** Urania
  breath: **4** Amen, Amon **5** Ammon
  chaos: **4** Nunu
  choral song: **11** Terpsichore
  comedy: **6** Thalia
  confusion: **5** Chaos
  conscience: **5** Aidos
  courage: **5** Arete **6** Virtus
  dance: **8** Polymnia **10** Polyhymnia **11** Terpsichore
  death: **4** Mors **6** Namtar **8** Thanatos
  desert: **3** Set **4** Seth
  desire: **6** Pothos
  divine punishment: **3** Ate **7** Nemesis
  east wind: **5** Eurus **9** Volturnus
  echo: **4** Echo
  emulation: **5** Zelos
  familial affection: **6** Pietas
  fate: **4** Norn **5** Moira, Moras
  fear: **6** Deimos
  femininity: **5** Neith
  fire: **4** Logi
  force: **3** Bia
  good faith: **5** Fides
  grain blight: **7** Robigus
  heaven: **6** Uranus
  hostile nature: **8** Fomorian
  idyllic poetry: **6** Thalia
  liberty: **8** Libertas
  longing: **6** Pothos
  lotus: **8** Nefertem
  meditation: **6** Melete
  memory: **5** Mneme, Munin
  moon: **4** Luna
  nature: **7** Erlking
  night: **3** Nox
  north wind: **6** Boreas
  order: **7** Eunomia
  pain: **5** Oizys
  past: **3** Urd
  peace: **5** Irene
  prayer: **5** Litae
  present: **8** Verdandi
  punishment: **5** Poena, Poine
  recklessness: **3** Ate
  retribution: **7** Nemesis
  revenge: **5** Poena, Poine
  Roman nation: **8** Quirinus
  sacred music: **8** Polymnia **10** Polyhymnia
  sea: **3** Ler, Lir **5** Nammu **6** Pontus **8** Thalassa
  sky: **6** Aether, Hathor
  soul: **6** Psyche
  southeast wind: **5** Eurus **9** Volturnus
  south wind: **5** Notus **7** Ninurta
  strength: **6** Cratus
  sun: **3** Sol
  thought: **5** Hugin
  tragedy: **9** Melpomene
  truth: **7** Alethia
  unavailing effort: **5** Ocnus
  victory: **4** Nike
  wealth: **6** Plutus
  west wind: **8** Favonius, Zephyrus
  wind: **7** Ninurta
  zeal: **5** Zelos
personify 6 embody **7** express **9** exemplify, incarnate, represent, symbolize **11** externalize, incorporate, personalize **12** characterize
personnel 4 crew **5** staff **7** members, workers **8** manpower **9** employees, work force **10** associates
Person to Person
  host: **13** Edward R Murrow **18** Charles Collingwood
perspective 4 view **5** scape, scene, vista **7** outlook **8** overview, prospect **9** broad view, viewpoint **12** bird's-eye view
perspicacious 4 keen **5** acute, alert, awake, sharp **6** astute, shrewd **9** clear-eyed, sagacious **10** discerning, perceptive **11** clearheaded, keen-sighted, penetrating, sharp-witted **12** clear-sighted
perspicacity 6 acumen **8** keenness, sagacity **9** acuteness, alertness, sharpness **10** astuteness, perception, shrewdness **11** discernment **14** discrimination
persuadable 7 willing **8** amenable, obliging **9** malleable, tractable **10** open-minded **16** open to suggestion
persuade 3 get **4** coax, lure, move, sway **5** tempt **6** cajole, entice, induce, prompt **7** wheedle, win over **8** convince, inveigle, motivate, talk into **9** influence
Persuasion
  author: **10** Jane Austen
  character: **7** Mrs Clay **8** Mrs Croft **11** Lady Russell **12** Admiral Croft **25** Captain Frederick Wentworth
    Elliot family: **4** Anne **7** William **9** Elizabeth, Sir Walter
    Musgrove family: **4** Mary **6** Louisa **7** Charles **9** Henrietta
persuasive 6 cogent **7** coaxing, logical, winning **8** alluring, credible, forceful, inviting **9** effective, plausible, seductive **10** believable, compelling, convincing **11** influential
pert 4 flip, spry **5** alert, brash, brisk, fresh, nervy, perky, quick, saucy **6** brassy, brazen, cheeky, lively, nimble **7** chipper **8** flippant, impolite, impu-

dent, insolent **9** audacious, energetic, insulting, sprightly, wide-awake **11** impertinent, smart-alecky **12** discourteous
pertain 2 be **5** apply, touch **6** befall, belong, relate **7** concern, connect
pertinacious 6 dogged **8** stubborn **9** obstinate, tenacious **10** persistent, unyielding **11** persevering
pertinacity 9 obstinacy **10** mulishness **11** persistence, willfulness **12** contrariness, obdurateness, perverseness, stubbornness **13** determination, inflexibility, intransigence, pigheadedness **14** bullheadedness, intractability
pertinence 9 relevance **11** germaneness **12** appositeness **13** applicability
pertinent 3 apt **4** meet **7** apropos, fitting, germane, related **8** apposite, material, relevant, suitable **9** befitting, concerned, congruent, connected **10** applicable, consistent, to the point
  Latin: **5** ad rem
perturb 5 upset, worry **6** bother **7** disturb, fluster, trouble **8** disquiet, distress **10** discompose, disconcert
perturbation 5 alarm, upset, worry **6** dismay **7** anxiety, concern, turmoil **8** distress **9** agitation, commotion **10** excitement **11** disquietude, trepidation **12** apprehension, discomposure **13** consternation
perturbed 5 upset **7** annoyed, worried **8** agitated, troubled **9** disturbed **12** disconcerted
perturbing 6 vexing **7** irksome **8** annoying **9** vexatious **10** bothersome, irritating, unsettling **11** disquieting, distressing, troublesome **13** disconcerting
Peru
  capital/largest city: **4** Lima
    Inca capital: **5** Cuzco
  others: **3** Ica **4** Puno **5** Cuzco, Paita, Pisco, Tacna **6** Callao, Talara **7** Huanuco, Iquitos **8** Arequipa, Castilla, Chiclayo, Chimbote, Mollendo, Pucallpa, Trujillo **9** Cajamarca **10** Yurimaguas
  school: **8** Trujillo **8** San Marcos
  division: **3** Ica **4** Lima, Puno **5** Cusco, Cuzco, Junin, Piura, Tacna **6** Ancash, Loreto, Tumbes
    Inca empire: **13** Tahuantinsuyo
  measure: **4** topo **5** galon **7** celemin
  monetary unit: **3** sol **5** libra **6** dinero, reseta **7** centavo
  weight: **5** libra **7** quintal
  island: **6** Chinca **7** Chincha
  lake: **8** Titicaca
  mountain: **5** Andes **7** El Misti, Huamina **8** Coropuna
  highest point: **9** Huascaran
  river: **3** Ene, Ica, Ilo **4** Napo, Napu **5** Piura, Rimac **6** Amazon, Oroton, Pampas, Yaguas, Yavari **7** Curaray, Mantaro, Maranon, Pastaza, Tapiche, Ucayali **8** Apurimac, Huallaga, Uru-

bamba **11** Madre de Dios, Pau-
cartambo
sea: 7 Pacific
physical feature:
  current: 6 el nino
  desert: 5 Nazca **7** Atacama,
  Sechura
  drizzling rain: 8 ilovizna
  fog: 5 garua
  gulf: 9 Guayaquil
  plateau: 7 Tablazo
people: 4 Ande, Boro, Cana, Inca,
Inka, Lama, Pano, Peba, Piro, Yutu **5**
Campa, Carib, Chana, Colan, Colla,
Jwaro, Moche, Nasca, Senci, Yagua,
Yunca **6** Atalan, Aymara, Canchi,
Chanca, Chanka, Chimer, Cholos,
Cocama, Jibaro, Kechua, Omagua,
Quiche, Quolla, Setibo, Sipibo **7**
Changos, Chincha, Chuncho, Mestizo, Mochica **8** Amahuaca, Criollos,
Mayoruma, Quechuia **9** Callawaya
10 Tiahuanaca, Tiatinagua **11** Chum-
pivilca
  artist: 4 Lazo **7** Montero, Sabogal,
  Szyszlo **8** Codesido
  author: 4 Vega **5** Palma, Prada **8**
  Caviedes **10** Mariategui
  explorer: 7 Pizarro
  Inca leader: 7 Huascar **9** Atahualpa
  10 Manco Capac
  leader: 5 Balta, Pardo, Prado, Torre
  7 Bolivar **8** Castilla, Fujimori **9**
  Santa Cruz **13** Belaunde Terry **15**
  Leguiay y Salcedo, Morales Ber-
  mudez
language: 6 Aymara **7** English,
Quechua, Spanish
religion: 13 Roman Catholic
place:
  bullring: 11 Plaza de Acho
  center of Lima: 12 Plaza de Armas
  church: 10 La Compania
  open market/street: 9 Calle Real
  ruins: 5 Huaco **8** Chan-Chan **9** Cajamarca **11** Machu-Picchu **22** Fortress of Sacsayhuaman
feature:
  animal: 5 llama **6** alpaca, vicuna **7**
  guanaco
  commune: 6 ayllus
  dance: 5 cueca, kaswa **6** cachua
  farmers: 10 campesinos
  priest: 6 villac
  slums: 9 barriadas
  tree: 8 cinchona
food:
  dish: 3 aji, cuy **7** ceviche **10** an-
  ticuchos
  drink: 5 pisco **6** chicha **11** aguar-
  diente
Perugino, Pietro
real name: 14 Pietro Vannucci
also called: 10 Il Perugino **14** Pier
della Pieve
born: 5 Italy **15** Citta della Pieve
artwork: 24 The Crucifixion with
Saints **26** Delivery of the Keys to St

Peter **27** The Giving of the Keys to
St Peter **32** Apparition of the Virgin
to St Bernard, Christ Delivering the
Keys to St Peter

perusal 5 study **6** review **7** reading **8**
scanning, scrutiny **10** inspection, run-
through **11** examination, look-through
12 scrutinizing **13** contemplation
peruse 3 con **4** read, scan **5** study **6**
search, survey **7** examine, inspect **10**
scrutinize
pervade 4 fill **5** imbue **6** infuse **7** suffuse **8** permeate, saturate **9** penetrate
13 spread through **17** diffuse throughout
pervasive 4 rife **7** rampant **8** dominant **9** prevalent **10** ubiquitous **11**
omnipresent, predominant
perverse 5 balky **6** dogged, mulish, ornery **7** wayward, willful **8** contrary,
obdurate, stubborn **9** obstinate, pigheaded **10** hardheaded, headstrong,
inflexible, rebellious **11** disobedient,
intractable, wrongheaded
perversion 9 depravity **10** corruption,
degeneracy, immorality **11** dissipation,
dissolution
pervert 4 warp **5** abuse **6** debase, misuse **7** contort, corrupt, degrade, deprave, distort, falsify, subvert **8** misapply **9** desecrate **12** misrepresent
perverted 5 false **6** faulty, untrue,
warped **7** corrupt, debased, deviant,
twisted, unsound **8** aberrant, abnormal, degraded, depraved **9** contorted,
distorted, erroneous, imperfect, unnatural **10** fallacious, unbalanced **12** mis-
conceived, misconstrued **13** misunder-
stood
pesky 7 chafing, galling, irksome **8** annoying **9** maddening, obnoxious, offensive, vexatious **10** bothersome, disturbing, nettlesome **11** aggravating,
distasteful, infuriating, pestiferous,
troublesome **12** disagreeable, exasperating **13** objectionable
pessimism 5 gloom **7** despair **10**
gloominess **12** hopelessness **13**
gloomy outlook **14** discouragement **15**
downheartedness
pessimist 7 kill-joy **8** sourpuss **9** Cassandra, defeatist, gloomy Gus **10**
spoilsport, wet blanket **11** crepe-
hanger **13** prophet of doom
pessimistic 6 gloomy **8** hopeless **10**
despairing, dispirited **11** discouraged,
downhearted
pest 4 bane **5** curse **6** blight, bother **7**
scourge **8** nuisance, vexation **9** annoyance **10** irritation **13** pain in the
neck
pester 3 irk, nag, vex **4** bait, fret **5** annoy, harry, taunt, worry **6** badger,
bother, harass, hector, nettle, plague
7 disturb, provoke, torment, trouble **8**
irritate

pesticide 3 DDT **7** biocide **8** fumigant
9 fungicide, germacide, vermicide **11**
insecticide
  user: 12 exterminator
pestilence 6 blight, plague **7** disease **8**
epidemic
  god of: 4 Irra
pesto sauce
  ingredients: 5 basil **6** garlic **8** olive
  oil
pet 3 pat **4** baby, dear **6** caress, choice,
fondle, stroke **7** beloved, darling, dearest, favored **8** favorite **9** cherished,
preferred **10** sweetheart **14** apple of
one's eye
pet activity 5 hobby **7** passion **8** interest **10** enthusiasm, hobbyhorse
Petain, Henri Philippe
  rank: 7 general, premier
  nationality: 6 French
  leader of government at: 5 Vichy
  convicted of: 7 treason
Peter 7 apostle
  means: 4 rock
  also called: 5 Simon **6** Cephas
  father: 4 John **5** Jonas
  brother: 6 Andrew
  birthplace: 9 Bethsaida
  hometown: 9 Capernaum
  disciple of: 5 Jesus
  companion: 4 John **5** James
  rebuked: 7 Ananias **8** Sapphira
  secretary: 8 Silvanus
  pertaining to: 7 Petrine
Peter and the Wolf
  composed by: 9 Prokofiev
Peter Grimes
  opera by: 7 Britten
  character: 11 Ellen Orford
Peter Heering, Cherry Heering
  type: 6 brandy **7** liqueur
  origin: 7 Denmark
  flavor: 6 cherry
  color: 3 red
Peter Ibbetson
  author: 15 George Du Maurier
peter out 3 ebb **7** decline, dwindle,
fall off, give out **8** diminish
Peter Pan
  author: 11 James Barrie
  character: 4 John, Smee **7** Michael **9**
  Nurse Nana, Tiger Lily **10** Tinker
  Bell **11** Captain Hook **12** Wendy
  Darling
  locale: 14 Never-never Land
petiole 4 stem **5** spine, stalk, stipe **8**
peduncle **9** leafstalk
petite 3 wee **4** tiny **5** small **6** little **9**
miniature **10** diminutive
petition 3 ask, beg, sue **4** plea, pray,
seek, suit, urge **5** press **6** appeal, invoke, orison, prayer **7** apply to, beseech, entreat **8** appeal to, call upon,
entreaty, proposal **9** imploring, plead
with, request of **10** invocation, suppli-

cate **11** application, beseechment, requisition **12** solicitation, supplication

petitioner 6 suitor **8** claimant **9** solicitor, suppliant **10** supplicant

pet name 8 nickname **9** sobriquet **10** diminutive, endearment

pet phrase 5 maxim, motto **6** saying, slogan **9** catchword

petrified 4 hard **5** dense, solid, stony **6** frozen **8** hardened, rocklike **9** paralyzed **10** solidified **11** hard as a rock, scared stiff **13** turned to stone

Petrified Forest, The
    director: 10 Archie Mayo
    based on play by: 14 Robert Sherwood
    cast: 9 Dick Foran **10** Bette Davis **12** Leslie Howard **14** Humphrey Bogart (Duke Mantee)
    setting: 7 Arizona

Petronius
    author of: 9 Satyricon

Petruchio
    character in: 19 The Taming of the Shrew
    author: 11 Shakespeare

Petticoat Junction
    character: 10 Floyd Smoot, Sam Drucker **11** Homer Bedloe, Kate Bradley **12** Charlie Pratt, Dr Janet Craig, Steve Elliott, Wendell Gibbs **14** Betty Jo Bradley, Uncle Joe Carson **15** Billie Jo Bradley, Bobbie Jo Bradley
    cast: 9 Frank Cady, Linda Kaye, Mike Minor, Rufe Davis **10** Pat Woodell **11** Charles Lane **12** Bea Benaderet, Byron Foulger, June Lockhart, Lori Saunders **13** Edgar Buchanan, Gunilla Hutton, Jeannine Riley **14** Meredith MacRae, Smiley Burnette
    setting: 11 Hooterville **14** Shady Rest Hotel
    train: 10 Cannonball

petto 5 chest **6** breast

petty 4 mean **5** minor, small **6** flimsy, paltry, shabby, slight **7** ignoble, trivial **8** niggling, picayune, piddling, trifling **10** ungenerous **11** small-minded, unimportant **12** narrow-minded **13** insignificant **14** inconsiderable **15** inconsequential

petulance 9 poutiness, sulkiness **11** fretfulness, peevishness **12** irritability

petulant 4 sour **5** cross, gruff, huffy, sulky, surly, testy **6** grumpy, sullen, tetchy, touchy **7** bearish, crabbed, fretful, grouchy, peevish, pettish, uncivil **8** snappish **9** crotchety, fractious, irascible, irritable **10** ill-natured, out of sorts, ungracious **11** complaining, contentious, ill-tempered, quarrelsome, thin-skinned **12** cantankerous, faultfinding

Petulia
    director: 13 Richard Lester
    cast: 10 Arthur Hill, Pippa Scott **12**

George C Scott, Joseph Cotten **13** Julie Christie, Shirley Knight **18** Richard Chamberlain
    setting: 12 San Francisco

petunia
    varieties: 4 Wild **7** Mexican, Seaside **10** Large white **12** Common garden **14** Violet-flowered

peu a peu 14 little by little

peu de chose 14 trifling matter **17** unimportant matter

pew 4 seat **5** bench **6** settle

Peychaud Bitters
    type: 8 aperitif
    origin: 10 New Orleans

Peyton Place
    author: 14 Grace Metalious
    character: 9 Rita Jacks (Harrington) **10** Hannah Cord, Steven Cord **12** Matthew Swain **13** Betty Anderson (Harrington Cord Harrington), Elliott Carson, Julie Anderson **14** Dr Michael Rossi, Dr Robert Morton, George Anderson **16** Allison Mackenzie (Harrington), Leslie Harrington, Norman Harrington, Rodney Harrington **18** Constance Mackenzie (Carson)
    cast (television): 8 Ed Nelson **9** Kent Smith, Mia Farrow, Ryan O'Neal **10** Tim O'Connor **11** Kasey Rogers, Paul Langton, Ruth Warrick **12** Henry Beckman, James Douglas **13** Dorothy Malone **14** Barbara Parkins, Patricia Morrow, Warner Anderson **19** Christopher Connelly
    director (movie): 10 Mark Robson
    cast (movie): 9 Hope Lange **10** Lana Turner, Lloyd Nolan **13** Arthur Kennedy
    score: 11 Franz Waxman

Phaedo
    author: 5 Plato

Phaedra
    father: 5 Minos
    mother: 8 Pasiphae
    sister: 7 Ariadne
    husband: 7 Theseus
    son: 6 Acamas, Demophon
    stepson: 10 Hippolytus
    loved: 10 Hippolytus
    death by: 7 hanging, suicide

Phaenna
    origin: 5 Greek **7** Spartan
    member of: 6 Graces

Phaethon
    father: 6 Helios
    mother: 7 Clymene

phalanx 6 column, parade **9** formation **13** ranks and files

Phallus
    image of: 9 male organ
    symbol of: 9 fertility
    carried in: 6 comedy **9** festivals
    associated with: 3 Pan **6** Hermes **7** Demeter **8** Dionysus

phantasm 5 ghost, shade, spook **6** mi-

rage, spirit, vision **7** fantasy, figment, incubus, phantom, specter **8** delusion, illusion, succubus **10** apparition

Phantasus
    origin: 5 Greek
    god of: 6 dreams

phantom 5 dream, ghost **6** mirage, spirit, vision, wraith **7** chimera, specter **8** illusion, phantasm **10** apparition **13** hallucination

Phantom, The
    creator: 7 Lee Falk **8** Ray Moore
    nickname: 16 The Ghost Who Walks
    mask: 5 black
    costume: 6 purple

Phantom Menace, The see **8** Star Wars

Phantom of the Opera, The
    director:
        1925 version: 12 Rupert Julian
        1943 version: 11 Arthur Lubin
        2004 version: 14 Joel Schumacher
    cast:
        1925 version: 9 Lon Chaney **11** Mary Philbin, Norman Kerry
        1943 version: 10 Hume Cronyn, Jane Farrar, Nelson Eddy **11** Claude Rains **12** Edgar Barrier **13** Susanna Foster
        2004 version: 10 Emmy Rossum **12** Gerard Butler, Minnie Driver **13** Patrick Wilson **17** Miranda Richardson
    setting: 10 Paris Opera

Phaon
    occupation: 7 boatman
    location: 8 Mitylene
    given: 5 youth **6** beauty
    given by: 9 Aphrodite

pharos 5 light **6** beacon, signal **7** seamark **10** lighthouse, watchtower

phase 4 side, step, view **5** angle, facet, guise, level, slant, stage **6** aspect, degree, period **7** feature **8** attitude, juncture **9** condition, viewpoint **10** appearance **11** development **12** circumstance

pheasant
    group of: 4 nest, nide

Phedre, Phaedra
    author: 6 Racine
    character: 6 Aricia **7** Theseus **10** Hippolytus

phenomenal 5 super **6** unique **7** amazing, unusual **8** singular, superior, uncommon **9** fantastic, marvelous, unheard-of **10** incredible, miraculous, prodigious, remarkable, stupendous, surpassing **11** astonishing, exceptional, outstanding, sensational, spectacular **12** overwhelming, unparalleled **13** extraordinary, unprecedented

phenomenon 5 thing **6** marvel, rarity, wonder **7** episode, miracle **8** incident, occasion **9** actuality, curiosity, exception, happening, nonpareil, sensation

10 fact of life, occurrence, proceeding
11 contingency

phial 4 vial **6** bottle, vessel **9** container

Phidias
born: **6** Athens, Greece
artwork: **4** Zeus **6** Amazon **13** Lemnian Athene (Athena Lemnia) **15** Apollo Parnopios, Athena Parthenos, Athena Promachos

Philadelphia
baseball team: **8** Phillies
basketball team: **13** Seventy-Sixers
bay: **8** Delaware
football team: **6** Eagles
founded/planned by: **4** Penn
hockey team: **6** Flyers
landmark: **6** US Mint **8** City Hall **11** Liberty Bell **12** Christ Church, Congress Hall **13** Franklin Field, Roosevelt Park **14** Betsy Ross House, Carpenter's Hall **15** Gloria Dei Church, Veterans Stadium **16** Independence Hall
means: **19** city of brotherly love
museum: **5** Rodin **15** Fels Planetarium **16** Barnes Foundation **17** Franklin Institute
river: **8** Delaware **10** Schuylkill
university: **4** Penn **6** Drexel, Temple **9** Jefferson, St Joseph's **22** Curtis Institute of Music

Philadelphia Story, The
director: **4** George Cukor
based on play by: **11** Philip Barry
cast: **9** Cary Grant **10** Ruth Hussey **12** James Stewart **16** Katharine Hepburn
Oscar for: **5** actor (Stewart)
remade as: **11** High Society

philanderer 3 rip **4** rake, wolf **5** flirt **6** lecher, tomcat, wanton **7** dallier, Don Juan, gallant, swinger, trifler **8** lothario, lover boy, rakehell **9** adulterer, libertine, womanizer **10** ladykiller **11** woman-chaser

philanthropic, philanthropical 7 liberal **8** generous **9** bounteous **10** almsgiving, beneficent, benevolent, charitable, munificent **11** magnanimous **12** eleemosynary, humanitarian

philanthropist 5 donor, giver **8** dogooder **9** almsgiver **11** contributor **12** humanitarian **13** Good Samaritan

philanthropy 6 bounty **7** charity **8** goodness **10** almsgiving, generosity, liberality **11** beneficence, benevolence, munificence **13** unselfishness **14** charitableness, openhandedness **15** humanitarianism **16** largeheartedness **18** public-spiritedness

Philaster
author: **30** Francis Beaumont and John Fletcher

Philemon
friend: **4** Paul
slave: **8** Onesimus
wife: **6** Baucis

entertained: **4** Hera, Zeus
became: **12** temple priest

Philip
hometown: **9** Bethsaida
disciple of: **5** Jesus

Philippines
named for: **15** Philip II of Spain
capital/largest city: **6** Manila
others: **3** Iba **4** Agoa, Bogo, Cebu, Debu, Naga, Palo **5** Albay, Davao, Gapan, Iriga, Lanao, Laoag, Pasay, Vigan **6** Aparri, Baguio, Cavite, Ilagan, Iloilo, Tarlac **7** Bacolod, Basilan, Calapan, Dagupan, Legaspi **8** Batangas, Caloocan, Cotabato, Tacloban **9** Zamboanga **10** Cabanutuan, Dumaguette, Quezon City
school: **10** Santo Tomas **14** Ateneo de Manila
division: **4** Abra, Cebu **5** Aklan, Albay, Bohol, Capiz, Davao, Lanao, Leyte, Rizal, Samar **6** Agusan, Bataan, Cavite, Iloilo, Laguna, Quezon, Tarlac **7** Isabela, Lepanto, Surigao
measure: **4** loan **5** braza, catty, cavan, chupa, fardo, ganta, picul, punto **6** apatan, balita, lachsa, quinon **7** quilate **8** chinanta
monetary unit: **4** peso **6** conant, peseta **7** centavo
weight: **5** catty, picul **6** lachsa **7** quilate **8** chinanta
island: **4** Cebu, Cuyo, Jolo, Poro, Sulu **5** Batan, Bohol, Leyte, Luzon, Panay, Samar, Ticao **6** Culion, Lubang, Negros **7** Babuyan, Batanes, Bisayan, Masbate, Mindoro, Palawan, Paragua, Polillo, Visoyan **8** Mindanao **10** Corregidor, Marinduque
lake: **4** Taal **5** Lanao
mountain: **3** Iba **4** Mayo, Taal **5** Albay, Askja, Hibok, Mayon, Pulog **6** Pagsan **7** Banahao, Canlaon
highest point: **3** Apo
river: **4** Abra, Agno **5** Magat, Pasig **6** Agusan, Laoang **7** Cagayan **8** Mindanao, Pampanga
sea: **4** Sulu **5** Samar **7** Celebes, Pacific, Visayan **10** Philippine, South China
physical feature:
bay: **6** Manila
falls: **9** Pagsanjan **14** Maria Christina
gulf: **4** Moro **5** Albay, Davao, Leyte, Ragay **8** Lingayen
hot springs: **8** Los Banos
national park: **12** Mayon Volcano
ocean trench: **8** Mindanao
peninsula: **6** Bataan
storm: **6** bagyos **7** monsoon, typhoon
volcano: **8** Pinatubo
people: **3** Ati, Eta, Ita, Tao **4** Aeta, Ifil, Moro, Sulu, Tino **5** Abaca, Aripa, Batak, Batan, Bicol, Bikol, Busao, Lutao, Mundo, Sinay, Tagal, Vicol, Yakan **6** Apayao, Baluga, Bilaan,

Biscol, Bontoc, Bontok, Busaos, Ibanag, Ibilao, Ifugao, Igalot, Igorot, Illano, Isinai, Lutayo, Manabo, Manobo, Montes, Sambal, Tagala, Timaua, Timawa, Zambal **7** Bagoboo, Bisayan, Cagayan, Ilocano, Itanega, Malanoa, Mangyan, Naboloi, Negrito, Tagalog, Tirurai, Visayan **8** Arupaata, Babaylan, Bukidono, Filipino, Igorotte, Manguian, Pampanga **9** Arupaatta, Dulangane, Macajambo, Pampangon, Tinguiane **10** Magindanao, Pangasinan **11** Calalangane
author: **5** Rizal
explorer: **7** Legazpe **8** Magellan **10** Villalobos
leader: **5** Ramos **6** Aquino, Marcos, Osmena, Quezon **9** Aguinaldo, Bonifacio, Macapagal, Magsaysay **11** Roxas y Acuna
language: **4** Moro **5** Bicol, Bikol **6** Ibanag **7** Cebuano, English, Ilocano, Spanish, Tagalog, Visayan **8** Filipino, Pilipino **9** Pampangan **10** Samar-Leyte **13** Bamboo-English
religion: **7** animism **9** Aglipayan **10** Protestant **13** Roman Catholic **15** Iglesia ni Kristo
place:
church: **14** Saint Augustine
esplanade: **6** Luneta
fort: **4** Cota, Gota, Kota **5** Lotta **10** Corregidor
president's palace: **10** Malacanang
street: **7** Escolta
US bases: **5** Clark **8** Subic Bay
walled city: **10** Intramuros
feature:
animal: **7** carabao, tamarau, tarsier **9** mouse deer
bird: **7** creeper
clothing: **4** saya **6** camisa **10** balintawak **12** mestiza terno **13** barong tagalog
dance: **9** tinikling
drama: **8** moro-moro
guerrilla fighter: **3** huk
musicians: **12** musikongbuho
naval base: **6** Cavite
song: **8** kundiman
village: **8** barangay
food:
dish: **3** poi **4** baha, sabu, taro **5** balut
drink: **4** beno, vino **5** bubud **6** tampoy **7** pangasi

philistine 5 yahoo **6** savage **7** Babbitt, lowbrow, prosaic **8** ignorant **9** barbarian, bourgeois, unrefined, untutored **10** conformist, uncultured, uneducated, uninformed, unlettered **11** commonplace **12** conventional, uncultivated **13** unenlightened **15** conventionalist **16** anti-intellectual

Philistine city 4 Gath

Philius
epithet of: **4** Zeus
means: **8** friendly

Phillotson, Richard
  character in: **14** Jude the Obscure
  author: **5** Hardy
Philoctetes
  author: **9** Sophocles
  character: **8** Heracles, Odysseus **11**
    Neoptolemus
  inherits arms of: **8** Hercules
  father: **5** Poeas, Poias
  killed: **5** Paris
philodendron
  varieties: **5** Dubia, giant **6** common **7**
    cut-leaf, red-leaf **8** blushing **9** black-
    gold, heart-leaf, horsehead, spade-
    leaf, split-leaf **10** fiddle-leaf, varie-
    gated, velvet-leaf **11** leather-leaf
Philomela
  position: **8** princess
  realm: **6** Athens
  father: **7** Pandion
  sister: **6** Procne
  brother-in-law: **6** Tereus
  raped by: **6** Tereus
  transformed into: **7** swallow **11**
    nightingale
Philomelides
  king of: **6** Lesbos
  defeated by: **8** Odysseus
philosopher/theologian 4 sage **6** sa-
    vant **7** thinker, wise man **8** logician,
    reasoner **9** theorizer **11** rationalist,
    truth seeker **12** dialectician **13** meta-
    physician
  Alsatian: **10** Schweitzer
  American: **4** Eddy **5** Dewey, James,
    Royce, Smith, Young **6** Mather,
    Peirce **7** Edwards, Niebuhr, Russell,
    Tillich **8** Williams **9** McPherson **14**
    Elijah Muhammad
  Austrian: **12** Wittgenstein
  British: **3** Fox **4** Hume, Inge, Knox,
    More, Owen **5** Bacon, Locke,
    Moore **6** Biddle, Cotton, Hobbes,
    Huxley, Newman, Wesley **7** Ben-
    tham, Bradley, Carlyle, Cranmer,
    Russell, Spencer **8** Berkeley, Wycliffe
    9 Whitehead **13** Thomas a Becket **14**
    William of Occam
  Chinese: **6** Lao-tzu **9** Confucius
  Christian: **6** Calvin, Luther, Origen, St
    Paul **7** Abelard **8** St Anselm **9** St Pat-
    rick **10** Duns Scotus, St Benedict **11**
    St Augustine **14** William of Occam
    15 St Thomas Aquinas **16** St Alber-
    tus Magnus
  Czech: **3** Hus
  Danish: **11** Kierkegaard
  Dutch: **7** Erasmus, Spinoza
  El Salvadorian: **9** Masferrer
  French: **5** Comte **6** Calvin, Pascal,
    Sartre **7** Abelard, Bergson, Diderot **8**
    Maritain, Rousseau, Voltaire **9** Des-
    cartes, Levy-Bruhl, Montaigne **11**
    Montesquieu
  German: **4** Kant, Marx **5** Buber, He-
    gel **6** Boehme, Fichte, Herder, Luther
    7 Husserl, Jaspers, Leibniz **9** Heideg-
    ger, Nietzsche, Schelling **10** Muhlen-

berg **11** Melanchthon **12** Schopen-
    hauer **13** Thomas a Kempis **14**
    Schleiermacher
  Greek: **5** Plato **6** St Paul, Thales **8**
    Socrates **9** Aristotle **10** Anaxagoras,
    Anaximenes, Heraclitus, Parmenides,
    Pythagoras **11** Anaximander
  Indian: **6** Buddha **16** Siddharta Gau-
    tama
  Islamic: **7** al Kindi **8** al-Farabi, Aver-
    roes, Avicenna **9** al Ghazali **10** Ibn
    Khaldun
  Italian: **5** Bruno **7** Aquinas, Mazzini
    10 St Benedict, Zeno of Elea **17** St
    Francis of Assisi
  Japanese: **6** Suzuki
  Jewish: **7** Spinoza **10** Maimonides
  Latin: **8** Plotinus **11** St Augustine
  Spanish: **8** Averroes **10** Maimonides
    13 Ortega y Gasset **16** Ignatius of
    Loyola
  Swedish: **10** Swedenborg
  Swiss: **7** Zwingli
philosophic, philosophical 4 calm **5**
    quiet, stoic **6** serene **7** erudite,
    learned, logical, patient, stoical **8** ab-
    stract, composed, rational, resigned,
    tranquil **9** impassive, judicious, saga-
    cious, unexcited, unruffled **10** compla-
    cent, fatalistic, reasonable, theorizing,
    thoughtful **11** imperturbed, theoreti-
    cal, unemotional **14** self-restrained
philosophy 4 calm, view **5** ideas, logic
    6 reason **7** beliefs, opinion, thought **8**
    doctrine, fatalism, patience, serenity,
    stoicism, thinking **9** basic idea, com-
    posure, esthetics, principle, reasoning,
    restraint, viewpoint **10** conception,
    theorizing **11** complacency, convic-
    tions, forbearance, impassivity, meta-
    physics, rationalism, resignation
  means: **12** love of wisdom
  branch: **6** ethics **8** ontology **10** aes-
    thetics **11** metaphysics **12** epistemol-
    ogy
  term: **8** noumenon **9** causality, dialec-
    tic, solipsism
  school of: **7** Sophism **8** idealism, Mi-
    lesian, Stoicism **9** Epicurean, panthe-
    ism, Platonism **10** empiricism, prag-
    matism, Skepticism **11** rationalism
    12 Aristotelian, neoplatonism **13**
    Phenomenology, scholasticism **14** ex-
    istentialism **17** logical positivism
Phil Silvers Show, The
  character: **6** Fender **7** Col Hall, Hen-
    shaw **8** Doberman **9** Sgt Ritzik **12**
    Sgt Joan Hogan **13** Rocco Barbella,
    Sgt Ernie Bilko
  cast: **8** Joe E Ross, Paul Ford **10** Alan
    Melvin, Herbie Faye **13** Harvey Lem-
    beck **15** Elisabeth Fraser, Maurice
    Gosfield
  setting: **6** Kansas **10** Fort Baxter
phlegmatic 4 calm, cool, dull **6** serene
    7 languid, passive, stoical **8** listless,
    sluggish, tranquil **9** apathetic, impas-
    sive, lethargic, unfeeling **10** noncha-

lant, spiritless **11** indifferent, insensi-
    tive, unconcerned, unemotional,
    unexcitable **12** unresponsive **13** im-
    perturbable, unimpassioned **15** unde-
    monstrative
phlox
  varieties: **4** blue, fall, moss, sand,
    star **6** annual, smooth **7** prickly **8**
    creeping, drummond, mountain,
    trailing **9** perennial, sword-leaf,
    thick-leaf **15** summer perennial
Phnom-Penh
  airport: **10** Pochentong
  also: **8** Pnom Penh
  capital of: **8** Cambodia **9** Kampuchea
  pagoda: **12** Preah Morokot
  river: **6** Mekong **8** Tonle Sap
phobia 5 dread **6** horror, terror **7** bug-
    aboo, bugbear **8** aversion, loathing **12**
    apprehension **16** unreasonable fear **19**
    overwhelming anxiety
  fear of animals: **9** zoophobia
  fear of birds: **13** ornithophobia
  fear of blushing: **13** erythrophobia
  fear of bridges: **13** gephyrophobia
  fear of cats: **10** gatophobia **12** aelu-
    rophobia, ailurophobia
  fear of closed/confined spaces: **14**
    claustrophobia
  fear of crowds: **11** ochlophobia
  fear of darkness/the dark of night:
    11 nyctophobia
  fear of death: **13** thanatophobia
  fear of death/dead bodies: **11** nec-
    rophobia
  fear of dirt: **10** mysophobia
  fear of disease: **11** pathophobia
  fear of fire: **10** pyrophobia
  fear of flowers: **11** anthophobia
  fear of flying: **10** aerophobia
  fear of germs: **11** mikrophobia
  fear of hair: **12** trichophobia
  fear of heights: **10** acrophobia
  fear of insanity: **13** dementophobia
  fear of lightning: **11** astraphobia
  fear of men: **11** androphobia
  fear of mice: **10** murophobia
  fear of numbers: **12** numerophobia
  fear of open spaces: **11** agoraphobia
  fear of pain: **10** algophobia
  fear of people: **12** anthrophobia
  fear of reptiles: **13** herpetophobia
  fear of snakes: **13** ophidiophobia
  fear of speaking aloud: **11** pho-
    nophobia
  fear of spiders: **13** arachnophobia
  fear of strangers: **10** xenophobia
  fear of thunder: **12** brontophobia
  fear of the number thirteen: **17** tris-
    kaidekaphobia
  fear of vehicles/driving: **11** amax-
    ophobia
  fear of water: **10** aquaphobia **11** hy-
    drophobia
  fear of women: **10** gynophobia
Phoebe
  member of: **6** Titans
  father: **6** Uranus

mother: 4 Gaea
sister: 6 Themis
daughter: 4 Leto 7 Asteria
identified with: 4 moon
corresponds to: 5 Diana 7 Artemis
Phoebus *see* 6 Apollo
Phoenicia *see* 7 Lebanon
Phoenician Mythology
  god of agriculture/earth: 5 Dagon
    corresponds to Mesopotamian: 5
      Dagan
  bird: 6 Phenix 7 Phoenix
  goddess of fertility/reproduction: 7
    Astarte
Phoenissae (The Phoenician Maidens)
  author: 9 Euripides
  character: 5 Creon 7 Jocasta, Oedipus
    8 Adrastus, Antigone, Eteocles, Tiresias 9 Polynices 10 Menoikieus
Phoenix
  baseball team: 12 Diamondbacks 19
    Arizona Diamondbacks
  basketball team: 4 Suns 7 Mercury
  capital of: 7 Arizona
  event: 5 rodeo
  feature: 10 Papago Park 22 Desert
    Botanical Gardens
  football team: 9 Cardinals
  hockey team: 7 Coyotes
  river: 4 Salt
Phoenix
  also: 6 Phenix
  origin: 10 Phoenician
  form: 4 bird
  gift: 11 immortality
  king of: 9 Dolopians
  father: 7 Amyntor
  mother: 8 Cleobule
  brother: 6 Cadmus
  sister: 6 Europa
  foster son: 8 Achilles
  ancestor of: 11 Phoenicians
Pholus
  form: 7 centaur
  guarded: 4 wine
  wine a gift from: 8 Dionysus
phonograph 4 hi-fi 5 phono 6 stereo
  8 Victrola 9 turntable 10 gramophone
  12 record player
phonophobia
  fear of: 13 speaking aloud
phony, phoney 4 fake, hoax, mock,
  sham 5 bogus, false, fraud, trick 6
  forged, pseudo, unreal, untrue 7 forgery 8 specious, spurious 9 deceptive,
  imitation, pretended, synthetic 10 artificial, fraudulent, not genuine 11
  counterfeit, make-believe, unauthentic
Phorcys
  god of: 3 sea
  sister: 4 Ceto
  children: 5 Ladon 6 Graiae 7
    Echidna, Gorgons 8 Phorcids
  harbor in: 6 Ithaca
phosphorus
  chemical symbol: 1 P

photograph 3 pic 4 film, snap 5 image, print, shoot, still 6 candid, glossy
  7 mugshot, picture, tintype 8 likeness,
  portrait, snapshot 12 daguerrotype
  bath: 5 fixer, toner 7 reducer 9 developer
  book: 5 album
photographer
  American: 4 Haas, Hine, Penn, Riis,
    Rose, Tice 5 (Ansel) Adams, Annan,
    Arbus, Brady, Evans, Hawes, Lange,
    Lynes, Smith, White 6 Avedon, Coburn, Eakins, Man Ray, Strand,
    Turner, Weston 7 Burrows, Eastman,
    Gardner, Jackson, Watkins 8 Bogardus, Davidson, Steichen 9 Muybridge, O'Sullivan, Rothstein, Stieglitz 10 Cunningham, Southworth 11
    Bourke-White, Eisenstaedt, Turberville 13 Watson-Schutze
  British: 5 Evans, Frith 6 Bailey, Beaton, Fenton, Mayall, Talbot 7 Cameron 8 Brewster, Robinson 9 Rejlander 10 MacPherson
  French: 5 Marey, Nadar 6 Baldus, DuCamp, Le Secq, Newton, Niepce 7
    Lumiere 8 Daguerre 12 Sabatier-Blot
    14 Cartier-Bresson
  German: 4 Hoch 5 Ernst 7 Hausman
    8 Stelzner 13 Renger-Patzsch
  Hungarian: 7 Kertesz 10 Moholy-Nagy
  Japanese: 4 Ikko
  Scottish: 4 Hill 7 Adamson
  Spanish: 7 Picabia
photostat 4 copy 7 replica 9 duplicate, facsimile 12 reproduction
phrase 3 put, say 4 word 5 couch, idiom, maxim, state, utter, voice, words
  6 cliche, dictum, impart, remark, saying, truism 7 declare, express, proverb
  8 aphorism, banality, locution 9 enunciate, find words, platitude, utterance,
  verbalize, word group 10 articulate,
  expression 11 communicate
phraseology 5 style 7 diction, wording 13 choice of words 18 manner of
  expression
Phrixus
  father: 7 Athamas
  mother: 7 Nephele
  stepmother: 3 Ino
  sister: 5 Helle
  wife: 9 Chalciope
  son: 5 Argus, Melas 8 Phrontis 10
    Cytissorus
physical 4 real 5 human, solid 6 actual, animal, bodily, carnal, living 7
  fleshly, natural, sensual 8 apparent,
  concrete, corporal, existent, existing,
  external, material, palpable, tangible 9
  corporeal, essential, of the body 11
  substantive
physical checkup 4 exam 8 physical
  11 examination 19 physical examination

physical condition 5 shape 7 fitness,
  stamina 12 constitution
physical disorder 6 malady 7 ailment, disease, illness 8 sickness 9 ill
  health, infirmity
physical training 3 gym 6 sports 8
  exercise 9 athletics, shaping up 10
  gymnastics, working out 12 conditioning
physician 2 GP, MD 3 doc 5 medic 6
  doctor, medico 7 surgeon 8 sawbones
  10 specialist 11 medicine man, pill
  peddler 13 medical doctor
  Alsatian: 10 Schweitzer
  American: 4 Long, Rush, Salk 5 Sabin 6 Dooley, Gorgas 7 Huggins,
    Whipple 8 Williams 9 Blackwell 11
    Landsteiner
  British: 5 Paget 6 Adrian, Harvey,
    Jenner, Lister
  Canadian: 4 Best 7 Banting
  Dutch: 7 Eijkman
  French: 7 Charcot
  German: 6 Mesmer 7 Fechner, Virchow 10 Blumenbach
  Greek: 10 Herophilus 11 Hippocrates
    12 Erasistratus
  Italian: 8 Malpighi
  Russian: 6 Pavlov
  Scottish: 4 Lind
  South African: 7 Barnard
Physician to Olympian gods 5
  Paeon 6 Apollo
physicist
  American: 4 Hess, Rabi 5 Bethe,
    Gamow, Pauli, Yalow 6 Bekesy,
    Teller, Townes, Watson 7 Feynman,
    Richter, Seaborg 8 Einstein, Lawrence, Van Allen 9 Michelson 11
    Chamberlain, Oppenheimer
  Austrian: 7 Doppler, Meitner
  British: 4 Born 5 Bragg, Hooke, Joule
    6 Kelvin 7 Gilbert, Thomson 8 Chadwick, Rayleigh 9 Cockcroft 10 Rutherford
  Danish: 4 Bohr 7 Oersted
  Dutch: 6 Zeeman 7 Lorentz
  French: 6 Ampere 7 Broglie, Coulomb, Fresnel 8 Foucault 9 Becquerel 11 Joliot-Curie
  German: 3 Ohm 5 Hertz, Stark 6
    Planck 7 Rontgen, Wegener 8 Humboldt, Roentgen 9 Kirchhoff, Mossbauer 10 Fahrenheit, Fraunhofer
  Indian: 5 Raman
  Irish: 7 Tyndall 10 Fitzgerald
  Italian: 5 Fermi
  Russian: 6 Landau 8 Cerenkov, Sakharov
  Scottish: 7 Rankine
Physics
  author: 9 Aristotle
physiognomy 4 face 5 shape 6 facade, visage 7 contour, outline, profile
  8 features 10 silhouette 11 countenance

physiology
  founder: 13 William Harvey
  study of: 8 function
  study of nervous sytem: 15 neuro-physiology

pianissimo
  music: 8 very soft
    abbreviation: 2 pp

pianist 4 Hess **5** Liszt, Watts **6** Busoni, Chopin, Gilels, Serkin **7** Cliburn, Hofmann, Richter **8** Backhaus, Horowitz, Schnabel, Schumann, Thalberg, von Bulow **9** Barenboim, Casadesus, Gieseking **10** Gottschalk, Rubinstein **12** Rachmaninoff

piano
  invented by: 10 Cristofori
  player piano: 9 Fourneaux
  forerunner: 6 spinet **10** clavichord **11** harpsichord

piano
  music: 4 soft
    abbreviation: 1 p

piazza 5 patio, porch **6** square **7** gallery, portico, veranda

Piazzi, Giuseppe
  field: 9 astronomy
  nationality: 7 Italian
  discovered: 5 Ceres
  catalogued: 5 stars

picaresque 6 daring **7** raffish, roguish, waggish **8** devilish, prankish, rascally, scampish **9** foolhardy **10** roistering **13** adventuresome **14** mischief-loving

Picasso, Pablo
  born: 5 Spain **6** Malaga
  artwork: 4 Dove **6** Guitar, Jester **7** Ma Jolie, Rooster, She-Goat **8** Guernica **9** Bull's Head, Notre Dame **11** Seated Woman, Woman Diving **12** Head of a Woman **13** Seated Bathers **14** Minotauromachy, Mother and Child, Women of Algiers **15** Ambroise Vollard, Man Holding a Lamb, The Charnel-House, The Large Profile, The Three Dancers **16** Nude in an Armchair **17** Girl Before a Mirror, The Glass of Absinth, The Three Musicians **20** Still Life with a Candle **22** Les Demoiselles d'Avignon **23** Portrait of Gertrude Stein

picayune, picayunish 5 dinky, petty, small **6** flimsy, little, measly, paltry, slight **7** trivial **8** niggling, nugatory, piddling, trifling **11** unimportant **13** insignificant **14** inconsiderable **15** inconsequential

Piccini, Nicola (Piccinni, Niccola)
  born: 4 Bari **5** Italy
  composer of: 5 Didon **6** Roland **11** The Good Girl **15** La buona figliola **18** Iphigenie en Tauride

pick 3 cut **4** crop **5** cream, elect, elite, pluck, prize **6** choice, choose, detach, flower, gather, opt for, select **7** collect, fix upon, harvest, pull off, pull out, the best **9** single out **10** decide

picket 4 pale, post **5** fence, go out, guard, hem in, pen in, stake, watch **6** corral, paling, patrol, sentry, shut in, strike, tether, wall in **7** boycott, enclose, hedge in, lookout, striker, upright, walk out **8** blockade, palisade, restrain, restrict, sentinel **9** blockader, boycotter, protester, restraint, stanchion

picketing 5 march **7** protest **8** marching, on strike, striking **10** protesting **12** protest march **13** demonstrating, demonstration

Pickett, George E
  served in: 8 Civil War **10** Mexican War
  side: 11 Confederate
  battle: 10 Gettysburg
  famous for: 6 charge

Pickford, Mary
  real name: 15 Gladys Mary Smith
  nickname: 18 America's Sweetheart
  born: 6 Canada **7** Toronto
  husband: 16 Douglas Fairbanks **18** Charles Buddy Rogers
  roles: 4 Rags **8** Coquette (Oscar) **9** Pollyanna **19** The Taming of the Shrew **21** The Poor Little Rich Girl **23** Rebecca of Sunnybrook Farm
  home: 8 Pickfair
  memoirs: 17 Sunshine and Shadow
  formed: 13 United Artists
    partners: 10 D W Griffith **14** Charlie Chaplin **16** Douglas Fairbanks

pickings 4 loot **5** booty **6** scraps, spoils **7** plunder, takings **9** leftovers

pickle 3 fix, jam **4** corn, dill, mess, sour **6** crisis, plight, scrape **7** dilemma, gherkin, mustard **8** cucumber, hot water, quandary **9** emergency, extremity, tight spot **10** difficulty, kosher dill, pretty pass **11** predicament **14** bread-and-butter

pickled 5 drunk **6** soused **8** powdered

pick on 5 annoy, bully **6** harass, jibe at **7** torment **8** browbeat

pick out 3 see **4** espy **6** choose, descry, detect, notice, select **7** discern, make out **8** perceive **12** catch sight of

pickup 4 rise **5** boost, truck **7** advance **9** impromptu **11** improvement **12** acceleration

pick up 3 buy, get **6** gather, lift up, look up, obtain, secure **7** acquire, develop, improve, procure **8** contract, retrieve **9** cultivate, get better

Pickwick Papers
  author: 14 Charles Dickens
  character: 6 Perker, Tupman, Wardle, Winkle **9** Sam Weller, Snodgrass **10** Mrs Bardell **11** Emily Wardle **12** Alfred Jingle, Rachel Wardle **13** Arabella Allen

picky 5 fussy **6** choosy **7** finicky **10**
fastidious, particular **11** persnickety **14** discriminating

Picrochole
  character in: 22 Gargantua and Pantagruel
  author: 8 Rabelais

picture 3 see **4** copy, draw, film **5** fancy, flick, image, model, movie, paint, photo, study **6** cinema, depict, double, mirror, sketch **7** believe, drawing, essence, etching, feature, imagine, paragon, portray, tintype **8** envision, likeness, painting, snapshot **9** delineate, duplicate, facsimile, portrayal, represent **10** call to mind, carbon copy, conceive of, dead ringer, embodiment, illustrate, photograph **11** delineation **12** illustration, see in the mind **13** daguerreotype, motion picture, moving picture, spitting image **14** representation **15** exemplification, personification

Picture of Dorian Gray, The
  author: 10 Oscar Wilde
  character: 9 James Vane, Sibyl Vane **13** Basil Hallward **15** Lord Henry Wotton

picturesque 6 exotic, quaint **7** unusual **8** artistic, charming, colorful, striking **9** beautiful, pictorial **10** attractive **11** distinctive, imaginative, interesting

Picus
  origin: 5 Roman **7** Italian
  god of: 11 agriculture
  father: 6 Saturn
  associated with: 10 woodpecker
  loved by: 5 Circe
  changed into: 10 woodpecker
  son: 6 Faunus

piddling 4 puny **5** petty, small **6** flimsy, little, measly, modest, paltry, skimpy, slight **7** trivial **8** picayune, trifling **9** niggardly **11** unimportant **13** insignificant **15** inconsequential

pie 4 tart **6** pastry, quiche **7** cobbler, dessert **8** turnover
  liner: 5 crust, shell
  top: 7 lattice **8** meringue

piebald 6 motley **7** dappled, flecked, mottled, spotted **8** many-hued, speckled **10** variegated **11** many-colored, varicolored **12** multicolored, particolored

piece 3 bit, cut, fix, pat **4** blob, case, hunk, item, lump, mend, part, play, unit, work **5** chunk, drama, essay, patch, scrap, shard, share, shred, slice, story, study, thing **6** amount, entity, length, member, paring, repair, review, sample, sketch, sliver, swatch **7** article, cutting, example, patch up, portion, restore, section, segment **8** creation, division, fraction, fragment, instance, quantity, specimen **9** component, selection **11** composition

piece de resistance 13 principal dish **14** principal event

piece goods 5 cloth, goods **6** fabric **8** dry goods, material **9** yard goods

piecemeal 9 gradually **10** fragmented, one at a time **14** little by little

piece of the action 3 cut, fee **5** piece **7** portion, rake-off **10** commission, percentage

pied 6 motley **7** checked, dappled, mottled, piebald **8** colorful **9** checkered **10** variegated **11** many-colored **12** parti-colored

pied-a-terre 17 temporary dwelling
   literally: 12 foot on ground

Pied Piper
   source: 6 German, legend
   town: 7 Hamelin
   plague: 4 rats
   charmed by: 6 piping
   led away: 4 rats **8** children

Pied Piper of Hamlin, The
   author: 14 Robert Browning

pier 4 anta, dock, mole, quay, slip **5** jetty, levee, wharf **6** pillar **7** landing, support **10** breakwater

pierce 3 cut **4** hurt, pain, stab **5** drill, lance, prick, spear, spike, stick, sting, wound **6** grieve, impale **7** affront **8** distress, puncture **9** penetrate, perforate **10** cut through, run through

Pierce, Franklin
   nickname: 29 Young Hickory of the Granite Hills
   presidential rank: 10 fourteenth
   party: 8 Democrat
   state represented: 2 NH
   defeated: 4 (John Parker) Hale **5** (Winfield) Scott
   vice president: 4 (William Rufus Devane) King (died in office)
   cabinet:
      state: 5 (William Learned) Marcy
      treasury: 7 (James) Guthrie
      war: 5 (Jefferson) Davis
      attorney general: 7 (Caleb) Cushing
      navy: 6 (James Cochran) Dobbin
      postmaster general: 8 (James) Campbell
      interior: 10 (Robert) McClelland
   born: 14 Hillsborough (Hillsboro) NH
   died/buried: 9 Concord NH
   education:
      academy: 7 Hancock **11** Francestown
      college: 7 Bowdoin
      studied: 3 law
   religion: 12 Episcopalian
   political career: 8 US Senate **16** state legislature **24** US House of Representatives
   civilian career: 6 lawyer
   military service: 6 US Army **10** Mexican War **16** brigadier general
   notable events of lifetime/term:
      Act: 6 Tariff (of 1857)
      bill: 14 Kansas-Nebraska
      civil war in: 6 Kansas
      first US: 10 World's Fair
      Manifesto: 6 Ostend
      Purchase: 7 Gadsden
      treaty of: 8 Kanagawa
   father: 8 Benjamin
   mother: 4 Anna (Kendrick)
   siblings: 5 Henry, Nancy **7** Charles, Harriet **9** Charlotte **12** John Sullivan **16** Benjamin Kendrick
      half sister: 9 Elizabeth
   wife: 4 Jane (Means Appleton)
   children: 8 Benjamin, Franklin **11** Frank Robert

piercing 3 raw **4** keen, loud **5** angry, cruel, sharp **6** biting, bitter, fierce, shrill **7** caustic, cutting, furious, grating, hurtful, intense, painful, probing **8** strident **9** agonizing, deafening, searching, shrieking, torturous **10** screeching **11** penetrating **12** earsplitting, excruciating **13** ear-shattering

Pierian
   pertains to: 5 Muses

Pierian Spring
   form: 8 fountain

Pierides *see* **5** Muses

Piero della Francesca (Piero dei Franceschi)
   born: 5 Italy **16** Borgo San Sepolcro
   artwork: 12 Duke of Urbino **15** The Resurrection **18** Federigo and His Wife **19** St John the Evangelist **20** Flagellation of Christ **23** The Compassionate Madonna, The Legend of the True Cross, The Old Age and Death of Adam **24** The History of the True Cross **45** The Madonna and Saints with Frederigo da Montefeltro

Piers Plowman
   author: 15 William Langland

Pietas
   personifies: 17 familial affection

piety 7 loyalty, respect **8** devotion, humility **9** godliness, piousness, reverence **10** devoutness **11** dutifulness, religiosity **13** religiousness

pig 3 hog **5** piggy, porky, swine **6** porker **7** glutton, guzzler **8** gourmand **9** chowhound **11** gormandizer
   male: 4 boar
   female: 3 sow
   young: 5 shoat **6** piglet **11** suckling pig

pigeon
   young: 5 squab **8** squeaker

pigeonhole 4 rank, rate, type **5** brand, cubby, group, label, niche **6** category, classify **9** cubbyhole **10** categorize **11** compartment

pigheaded 6 dogged, mulish **7** willful **8** contrary, obdurate, perverse, stubborn **9** insistent, obstinate, unbending **10** bullheaded, inflexible, refractory, unyielding **11** opinionated, wrongheaded

Piglet
   character in: 13 Winnie-the-Pooh
   author: 5 Milne

pigment 3 dye **4** tint **5** color **8** coloring, dyestuff **14** coloring matter

pigmentation 5 color **9** skin color **10** coloration

pigtail 5 braid, plait, queue **8** ponytail

pike 4 bill **5** lance, spear, spike **6** poleax **7** assegai, freeway, halberd, harpoon, highway, javelin, parkway, thruway **8** autobahn, hard road, speedway, toll road, turnpike **10** expressway, interstate, throughway **12** superhighway
   British: 12 King's Highway **13** Queen's highway
   German: 8 autobahn

piker 5 miser **7** niggard, trifler **8** tightwad **9** skinflint **10** cheapskate, pinchpenny **12** penny pincher

Pilar
   character in: 19 For Whom the Bell Tolls
   author: 9 Hemingway

pilaster 4 pier **6** column, pillar **7** support, upright **8** baluster

pile 3 nap **4** heap, mass, pier, post, shag, warp **5** amass, batch, fluff, grain, hoard, mound, plush, stack, store **6** fleece, gather, piling, pillar **7** collect, pyramid, support, surface, upright **8** assemble, quantity **9** abundance, amassment, profusion, stanchion **10** accumulate, assortment, collection, foundation **11** agglomerate, aggregation, fibrousness **12** accumulation

pile up 4 bank, heap **5** amass, hoard, mound, stack **7** collect **10** accumulate

pile-up 3 jam, mob **4** mass **5** snarl **8** crowding, gridlock **10** bottleneck, congestion **11** obstruction **12** overcrowding

pilfer 3 cop, rob **4** hook, lift **5** boost, filch, heist, pinch, steal, swipe **6** finger, pirate, snitch, thieve **7** purloin **8** shoplift **10** plagiarize

pilferer 5 thief **6** robber **7** burglar **10** shoplifter, sneak thief

pilgrim, Pilgrim 4 haji **5** exile, hadji **6** palmer **7** pioneer, Puritan, settler **8** newcomer, traveler, wanderer, wayfarer **9** foreigner
   father: 5 Alden
   founder: 10 Separatist
   interpreter: 7 Squanto
   leader: 8 Standish
   protector: 7 Templar
   ship: 9 Mayflower, Speedwell

pilgrimage 4 hadj, trek **6** ramble, roving, voyage **7** journey, roaming, sojourn **8** long trip **9** excursion, wandering **13** peregrination
   destination: 5 Mecca **10** Canterbury

Pilgrim's Progress, The
   author: **10** John Bunyan
   character: **7** Despair, Hopeful **8** Apollyon, Faithful **9** Christian, Ignorance **10** Evangelist **14** Worldly Wiseman

pill 3 rob **4** ball, pell **5** bolus **6** bullet, pellet, tablet, pilule **7** capsule **8** medicine **9** cigarette

pillage 3 rob **4** loot, raid, sack **5** booty, rifle, strip **6** fleece, maraud, piracy, ravage, spoils **7** despoil, looting, plunder, robbery **9** filchings **10** plundering

pillager 6 looter, vandal **7** brigand **9** despoiler, plunderer

pillar 3 VIP **4** pile, post, rock **5** shaft, wheel **6** column, piling **7** obelisk, support, upright **8** champion, mainstay, pilaster, somebody **9** colonnade, stanchion

pillow 3 pad **7** bolster, cushion **8** headrest

pilot 4 lead **5** flyer, guide, steer **6** airman, direct, escort, fly-boy, handle, leader, manage **7** aviator, birdman, conduct, control **8** aeronaut, coxswain, helmsman, navigate, wheelman **9** accompany, sky jockey, steersman

Pilot, The
   author: **19** James Fenimore Cooper

Pima (Aatam, Pima Alto)
   language family: **10** Uto-Aztekan
   location: **7** Arizona
   related to: **6** Papago
   descendants of: **7** Hohokam

Pima Alto *see* **4** Pima

pin 4 bind, clip, tine **5** affix, badge, clasp, dowel, medal, prong **6** brooch, fasten, pinion, secure, skewer **8** hold down, hold fast, restrain **10** decoration
   type: **3** hat **4** push **5** stick, thole **6** breast, common, diaper, safety **8** straight

pincer 4 claw **5** chela

pinch 3 bit, cop, jam, jot, nab, nip **4** bust, crib, grab, iota, lift, mite, pain, snip, spot **5** catch, cramp, crimp, crush, filch, run in, speck, steal, swipe, trace, trial, tweak **6** arrest, clutch, collar, crisis, misery, ordeal, pickle, plight, snatch, snitch, strait, tittle **7** capture, purloin, squeeze, tighten **8** compress, exigency, hardship **9** apprehend, emergency **10** affliction, difficulty, discomfort **11** predicament

Pinch, Tom
   character in: **16** Martin Chuzzlewit
   author: **7** Dickens

pinch hitter 5 proxy **7** stand-in **9** alternate **10** substitute

pinchpenny 5 miser **6** frugal, stingy **7** niggard, prudent, thrifty
   Dickensian: **7** Scrooge

Pindar
   author of: **4** Odes **8** Epinicea

pine 3 die, ebb **4** flag, long, sigh, wilt **5** covet, crave, droop, yearn **6** desire, expire, hanker, weaken, wither **7** decline, dwindle, pant for **8** languish **9** hunger for, waste away **11** have a yen for, thirst after **12** fail in health

pine 5 Pinus
   varieties: **3** air, nut, red **4** blue, chir, gray, hoop, Huon, Imou, Jack **5** beach, cedar, Cuban, Emodi, giant, house, Kauri, pitch, Scots, screw, scrub, shore, slash, stone, sugar, white **6** Aleppo, Apache, Bhutan, Bishop, celery, Dammar, digger, ground, Jersey, Korean, limber, Mallee, Norway, Parana, Pinyon, Scotch, spruce, Torrey, Totara, yellow **7** Amboina, Benguet, big-cone, Chilean, Chinese, cluster, Cypress, Formosa, Georgia, Gerard's, hickory, jointed, long-tag, poverty, prickly, prince's, running, Soledad **8** Austrian, Buddhist, cow's-tail, knob-cone, lacebark, Loblolly, longleaf, mahogany, Monterey, mountain, Nepal nut, oldfield, princess, umbrella **9** Brazilian, Calabrian, Chilghoza, Jerusalem, lodgepole, Oyster Bay, shortleaf, white-bark **10** Australian, Bunyabunya, dwarf stone, Macedonian, Moreton Bay, red cypress, Swiss stone, Tenasserim **11** African fern, bristlecone, common screw, Japanese red, Parry pinyon, Port Jackson, thatch screw, twisted-leaf, Veitch screw **12** black cypress, Canary Island, Chinese water, eastern white, frankincense, Italian stone, Mexican stone, Mexican white, two-leaved nut, western white **13** dwarf Siberian, Japanese black, Japanese white, Mexican yellow, New Caledonian, Norfolk Island, Swiss mountain, table mountain **14** Himalayan white, Rottnest Island, southern yellow **15** Mueller's cypress **16** Japanese umbrella, single-leaf pinyon **18** Rough-barked Mexican **19** Rocky Mountain yellow

Pine Tree State
   nickname of: **5** Maine

pin hope on 6 bank on **7** count on, long for, wish for **8** aspire to, yearn for **10** anticipate

pink 8 Dianthus
   varieties: **3** Sea **4** fire, moss, pine, rose, wild **5** cameo, clove, dairy, grass, marsh, swamp **6** button, ground, indian, Kirtle, maiden **7** cheddar, cottage, cushion, Mullein, rainbow **8** Childing, Deptford, election **11** cluster-head **13** fringed indian, spottle kirtle **16** California indian

pinnacle 3 cap, top **4** acme, apex, peak **5** crest, crown, spire, tower **6** belfry, height, summit, tiptop, vertex, zenith **7** steeple **9** bell tower, campanile

pinochle
   also known as: **7** binocle, pinocle **8** penuchle
   derived from: **7** bezique
   points/game: **11** one thousand
   lowest card: **4** nine

pinpoint 3 dot, jot **4** iota, spot **5** speck **6** detail **8** home in on, localize, zero in on **12** characterize

pint
   abbreviation of: **2** pt

pinxit 11 he painted it **12** she painted it

pioneer 5 found, start **6** create, father, herald, invent, leader **7** develop, founder **8** colonist, discover, explorer **9** be a leader, developer, establish, harbinger, innovator, precursor **10** antecedent, forerunner, lead the way, pathfinder, show the way **11** establisher, predecessor, trailblazer **12** first settler, frontiersman **13** blaze the trail **14** early immigrant, founding father
   Hebrew: **6** halutz **7** chalutz

Pioneers, The
   author: **19** James Fenimore Cooper
   character: **10** Indian John **11** Judge Temple, Natty Bumppo **13** Oliver Edwards **14** Hiram Doolittle **15** Elizabeth Temple

pious 4 holy **5** godly **6** devout, divine **7** sainted, saintly **8** faithful, reverent, unctuous **9** dedicated, insincere, pietistic, religious, spiritual **10** worshipful **11** reverential **12** hypocritical **13** rationalizing, sanctimonious, self-righteous **14** holier-than-thou

Pip
   character in: **17** Great Expectations
   author: **7** Dickens

pipe 4 duct, main, peep, sing, tube **5** cheep, chirp, trill, tweet **6** warble **7** conduit, twitter, whistle **8** conveyor **9** conductor **10** play a flute **12** play a bagpipe

piquant 3 hot **4** acid, racy **5** peppy, salty, sharp, spicy, tangy, zesty **6** biting, bitter, bright, clever, lively, savory **7** mordant, peppery, pungent, rousing **8** animated, incisive, piercing, spirited, stinging, vigorous **9** sparkling, trenchant **11** interesting, provacative, stimulating **13** scintillating **14** highly seasoned, strong-flavored

pique 3 ire, irk, vex **4** gall, goad, miff, snit, spur, stir **5** annoy, peeve, rouse, spite **6** arouse, excite, grudge, kindle, malice, nettle, offend **7** affront, incense, perturb, provoke, quicken, umbrage **8** disquiet, irritate, vexation **9** annoyance, displease, stimulate **10** discomfort, exasperate, irritation, resentment **11** displeasure, humiliation, ill feelings, indignation **12** exasperation, hurt feelings **13** embarrassment, mortification, put one's back up **14** vindictiveness

piqued 5 angry, riled, vexed **6** galled, miffed, peeved **7** annoyed, aroused, excited, kindled, nettled, stirred **9** affronted, irritated **10** displeased, stimulated

Pirandello, Luigi
author of: 17 The Old and the Young **18** Tonight We Improvise **19** The Late Mattia Pascal **31** Six Characters in Search of an Author

pirate 3 rob **5** steal **6** raider, robber, sea dog **7** brigand, corsair, plunder **8** marauder **9** buccaneer, privateer **10** freebooter
flag: 9 blackjack **10** Jolly Roger
name: 4 Kidd **6** Morgan **7** Lafitte **10** Blackbeard

Pirate Coast *see* **18** United Arab Emirates

Pirates of Penzance, The
author: 9 W S Gilbert
comic opera by: 18 Gilbert and Sullivan
character: 4 Kate, Ruth **5** Edith, Mabel **6** Isabel **8** Frederic, Sergeant **10** Pirate King **14** General Stanley

pis aller 10 last resort **12** last resource

Pisan Cantos
author: 9 Ezra Pound

Pisanio
character in: 9 Cymbeline
author: 11 Shakespeare

Pisces
symbol: 4 fish
planet: 7 Jupiter, Neptune
rules: 7 secrets
born: 13 February-March

Pisistratus
tyrant of: 6 Athens
father: 11 Hippocrates
son: 7 Hippias **10** Hipparchus

Pissarro, Camille
born: 8 St Thomas **16** Danish West Indies
artwork: 8 Red Roofs **15** Morning Sunlight **21** Lower Norwood Snow Scene **28** Peasant Woman with a Wheelbarrow

pistol (revolver) 3 gat, gun, rod **4** colt, iron **5** luger **6** heater, mauser **7** firearm, sidearm **9** automatic, derringer **20** Saturday night special

pit 3 dip, nut **4** dent, hole, nick, pock, scar, seed **5** gouge, gully, match, notch, stone **6** cavity, crater, dimple, furrow, hollow, indent, kernel, oppose, trough **7** scratch **8** contrast, pockmark **9** concavity, juxtapose **10** depression, set against **11** indentation

Pit, The
author: 11 Frank Norris

Pit and the Pendulum, The
author: 13 Edgar Allan Poe

pitch 3 bob, dip, fix, lob, set, shy, top **4** apex, cant, cast, fall, fire, hurl, jerk, jolt, peak, rock, tone, toss **5** angle, chuck, crown, erect, fling, grade, heave, level, lurch, place, plant, point, raise, set up, shake, slant, sling, slope, sound, throw **6** degree, height, let fly, locate, plunge, propel, settle, summit, topple, tumble, zenith **7** bobbing, incline, rocking, station **8** delivery, harmonic, lurching, pinnacle, undulate **9** declivity, establish, oscillate **10** undulation **11** oscillation **12** fall headlong
speed of: 9 vibration

pitcher 3 jar, jug **4** ewer **6** carafe **8** decanter **9** container **10** spitballer
and catcher: 7 battery
award: 7 Cy Young
brother duo: 4 Dean **5** Perry **6** Niekro
Hall of Famer: 4 Dean, Ford, Wynn **5** Young **6** Hunter, Koufax, Palmer, Willis **7** Carlton, Fingers **8** Drysdale **9** Newhouser
left-hander: 8 southpaw
relief staff: 7 bullpen
reliever: 7 fireman

pitch in 5 begin **7** share in **8** take part **9** cooperate, get to work, join hands **10** act jointly, contribute, get started **11** collaborate, participate **12** make an effort, pull together, work together

pitch into 5 fly at **6** assail, have at **7** assault, set upon

piteous 3 sad **6** moving, woeful **7** pitiful **8** pathetic, pitiable, poignant, touching **9** affecting **10** deplorable **11** distressing **12** heart-rending **13** heartbreaking

pitfall 4 risk, trap **5** peril, snare **6** ambush, danger, hazard **7** springe **8** quagmire **9** booby trap, quicksand **14** stumbling block

pith 4 core, gist, meat **5** heart, point **7** essence, meaning **12** significance

pithy 5 terse **6** cogent **7** concise **8** forceful, succinct **9** effective, trenchant **10** expressive, meaningful, to the point **12** concentrated

pitiful 3 sad **4** poor **5** sorry **6** abject, measly, moving, paltry, shabby **7** doleful, forlorn, piteous **8** dreadful, god-awful, mournful, pathetic, pitiable, poignant, touching, wretched **9** miserable, plaintive, worthless **10** abominable, despicable, lamentable **11** distressing **12** arousing pity, contemptible, heartrending

pitiless 5 cruel **6** brutal **7** inhuman, unmoved **8** ruthless, uncaring **9** heartless, merciless, unpitying, unsparing, untouched **10** implacable, relentless, unmerciful **11** cold-blooded, hardhearted, indifferent, insensitive, unrelenting

pittance 4 mite **5** crumb **6** little, trifle **7** minimum, modicum, smidgen

Pittsburgh
baseball team: 7 Pirates
feature: 14 Fort Pitt Museum **15** Buhl Planetarium
football team: 8 Steelers
formerly: 8 Fort Pitt **12** Fort Duquesne
hockey team: 8 Penguins
noted for: 5 steel
river: 4 Ohio **9** Allegheny **11** Monongahela
university: 8 Duquesne **14** Carnegie-Mellon

Pittypat, Aunt
character in: 15 Gone With the Wind
author: 8 Mitchell

pituitary
located in: 5 brain
known as: 11 master gland

pity 5 mercy, shame **6** lament, lenity, regret **7** charity, feel for, weep for **8** bleed for, clemency, humanity, leniency, sad thing, sympathy **10** compassion, condolence, indulgence, kindliness, tenderness **11** crying shame, forbearance, magnanimity **12** feel sorry for **13** commiseration

piu
music: 4 more

pivot 4 axis, axle, hang, rely, spin, turn **5** focus, hinge, twirl, wheel, whirl **6** center, circle, depend, rotate, swivel **7** fulcrum, hinge on, revolve **9** pirouette

pivotal 5 vital **7** crucial **8** critical, decisive **9** climactic **11** determining

pivotal point 4 axis **12** turning point **13** crucial moment

pixie, pixy 3 elf **5** fairy **6** sprite **10** leprechaun

pizazz 5 flair, vigor, style **6** energy, spirit **8** vitality

pizzicato
music: 21 plucked instead of bowed
abbreviation: 4 pizz

placable 7 lenient **8** flexible, tolerant, yielding **9** indulgent, relenting **10** appeasable, forbearing **12** reconcilable

placard 4 bill, sign **6** notice, poster **8** bulletin **13** advertisement

placate 4 calm, lull **5** quiet **6** pacify, soothe **7** appease, assuage, mollify, win over **9** alleviate **10** conciliate, propitiate

placatory 9 appeasing, pacifying **10** mollifying **12** conciliatory **13** accommodative

place 3 fix, job, put, set **4** area, city, digs, duty, farm, firm, home, land, plot, post, rank, rest, shop, site, spot, town, zone **5** abode, affix, array, berth, house, lodge, niche, plant, point, ranch, space, stand, state, store, venue **6** assign, attach, county, har-

bor, invest, locale, locate, office, region, settle **7** appoint, borough, company, concern, country, deposit, install, quarter, shelter, situate, station, village **8** building, business, classify, district, domicile, dwelling, ensconce, find hire, function, identify, locality, location, lodgings, position, premises, property, province, quarters, remember, standing, township, vicinity **9** recognize, residence, situation, territory **10** commission, get a job for, habitation **11** appointment, find work for, whereabouts **12** neighborhood **13** establishment
Latin: 4 situ

Place in the Sun, A
   director: 13 George Stevens
   based on novel by: 15 Theodore Dreiser (An American Tragedy)
   cast: 14 Keefe Brasselle, Shelley Winters **15** Elizabeth Taylor, Montgomery Clift
   Oscar for: 5 score **9** direction **10** screenplay

placement 8 grouping, location **10** assignment, employment **11** arrangement, disposition, positioning

place of residence 4 home **5** abode, house **7** address, lodging **8** domicile, dwelling **9** residence **10** habitation **14** living quarters

place to stand on
   Greek: 6 pou sto

place upright 5 erect, raise **7** stand up

placid 4 calm, mild **5** quiet **6** gentle, poised, serene, smooth **7** pacific, restful **8** composed, peaceful, tranquil **9** collected, unexcited, unruffled **10** untroubled **11** undisturbed, unexcitable **13** imperturbable, self-possessed **15** undemonstrative

plague 3 irk, vex, woe **4** bane, evil, fret, gall, pain, pest **5** agony, chafe, curse, harry, haunt, peeve, worry **6** badger, blight, bother, burden, cancer, harass, misery, nettle **7** afflict, disturb, perturb, scourge, torment, trouble **8** aggrieve, calamity, disquiet, distress, hardship, pandemic **9** embarrass, persecute, suffering **10** affliction, Black Death, pestilence, visitation
French: 5 peste

Plague, The
   author: 11 Albert Camus
   character: 7 Rambert **10** Jean Tarrou **11** Joseph Grand **14** Father Paneloux, Raymond Cottard **15** Dr Bernard R Rieux

plain 4 bald, bare, open **5** blunt, clear, frank, naked, vivid **6** candid, common, direct, homely, honest, modest, simple **7** average, glaring, legible, obscure, obvious, plateau, prairie, sincere, visible **8** apparent, clear-cut, dis-

tinct, everyday, explicit, manifest, ordinary, palpable, specific, straight, striking, uncomely, unlovely **9** grassland, outspoken, prominent, tableland, unadorned, undiluted **10** forthright, pronounced, unaffected, unassuming, unhandsome, unreserved, well-marked **11** commonplace, conspicuous, discernible, not striking, open country, outstanding, plain-spoken, unambiguous, undecorated, undisguised, unequivocal, ungarnished, unvarnished, well-defined **12** matter-of-fact, not beautiful, unattractive, unmistakable, unornamented **13** unembellished, unpretentious, without frills **14** comprehensible, understandable **15** straightforward, undistinguished

plainly 6 baldly, openly, simply **7** bluntly, clearly, frankly, visibly, vividly **8** candidly, directly, honestly, markedly, modestly **9** doubtless, obviously **10** apparently, definitely, distinctly, explicitly, manifestly, ordinarily, positively, strikingly, undeniably **11** beyond doubt, discernibly, prominently, undoubtedly **12** unaffectedly, unassumingly, unmistakably, without doubt **13** conspicuously, unambiguously, unequivocally **14** comprehensibly, unquestionably

plainness 10 homeliness, simplicity **12** ordinariness

plainspoken 4 open **5** bluff, blunt, frank, plain **6** candid, direct, honest **7** genuine, sincere **8** explicit, straight **9** open-faced, outspoken, unsparing **10** above board, forthright, point-blank **11** straight-out **15** straightforward

plaint 3 cry, sob **4** beef, moan, wail **5** gripe **6** charge, grouse, grudge, lament, regret, squawk **7** grumble, reproof **8** reproach **9** complaint, grievance, objection **10** accusation, resentment **12** remonstrance

plaintive 3 sad **6** rueful **7** doleful, moaning, piteous, pitiful, tearful **8** dolorous, grievous, mournful, pathetic, wretched **9** lamenting, sorrowful, woebegone **10** lugubrious, melancholy **12** heartrending

plait 5 braid, queue, twine, twist, weave **7** pigtail **10** intertwine

plan 3 aim, map, way **4** form, idea, plot **5** frame, shape **6** design, devise, intend, lay out, map out, method, scheme, sketch **7** diagram, outline, prepare, program, project, propose, purpose **8** block out, conceive, contrive, organize, proposal, strategy, think out **9** blueprint, fabricate, procedure, stratagem **10** conception, suggestion **11** proposition
French: 8 demarche

Planchet
   character in: 18 The Three Musket-

eers
   author: 5 Dumas (pere)

Planck, Max
   field: 7 physics
   nationality: 6 German
   developed: 13 quantum theory **15** Planck's constant
   awarded: 10 Nobel Prize

plane 3 jet **4** bird, flat **5** level, plumb **6** degree, status **7** regular, station **8** aircraft, airplane, position, standing **9** condition, elevation
   type: 4 jack **5** block

planet, planets 13 celestial body
   first: 7 Mercury
   second: 5 Venus
   third: 5 Earth
      satellite: 4 Moon
   fourth: 4 Mars
      satellite: 6 Deimos, Phobos
      nickname: 9 Red Planet
   fifth: 7 Jupiter
      satellite: 2 Io **6** Europa **8** Amalthea, Callisto, Ganymede
      characteristic: 7 red spot
   sixth: 6 Saturn
      satellite: 4 Rhea **5** Dione, Janus, Mimas, Titan **6** Phoebe, Tethys **7** Iapetus **8** Hyperion **9** Enceladus
      characteristic: 5 rings
   seventh: 6 Uranus
      satellite: 5 Ariel **6** Oberon **7** Miranda, Titania, Umbriel
      color: 9 blue-green
      characteristic: 5 rings
   eighth: 7 Neptune
      satellite: 6 Nereid, Triton
      color: 5 green
   ninth: 5 Pluto
      satellite: 6 Charon
   asteroid/minor planet/planetoid: 4 Eros, Juno **5** Ceres, Vesta **6** Chiron, Hermes, Icarus, Pallas **7** Astraea, Hidalgo

planetary 6 astral **7** earthly **9** celestial **11** terrestrial **12** astronomical

Planet of the Apes
   director: 18 Franklin J Schaffner
   based on novel by: 12 Pierre Boulle
   cast: 9 Kim Hunter **12** Maurice Evans **13** Roddy McDowall **14** Charlton Heston
   script: 10 Rod Serling

plank 4 deal, deck, slab **5** board, shole, stone **8** platform

planned 7 devised, schemed **8** designed, expected, foreseen, intended, prepared **9** mapped out, organized, projected, rehearsed **10** calculated, purposeful, thought out **11** intentional, prearranged, prepared for **12** premeditated

planner 6 author, framer **7** creator, deviser **8** arranger, designer **9** architect, organizer

plant 4 bush, herb, mill, moss, shop, slip, tree, vine, weed, wort, yard **5** algae, flora, fungi, grass, set in, shrub, works **6** flower, foster, infuse, set out **7** factory, foundry, herbage, implant, inspire, instill, scatter, sow seed **8** business, engender, seedling **9** broadcast, cultivate, establish, inculcate, propagate, vegetable **10** transplant, vegetation **13** establishment, sow the seeds of **14** put in the ground

plaster 4 coat, daub, sand **5** grout, smear **6** bedaub, gypsum, lather, stucco **7** overlay, spackle
mixture of: 4 lime **5** water **6** gypsum

plastered 5 drunk **6** coated, daubed, soused **7** covered, crocked, smeared, swacked **8** mortared, polluted, stuccoed **10** inebriated **11** intoxicated

plastic 4 soft **6** pliant, supple **7** ductile, elastic, pliable **8** flexible, formable, moldable, shapable, yielding **9** malleable, tractable

plate 4 dish **6** saucer **7** helping, platter, portion, serving **10** platterful **11** serving dish

plateau 4 mesa **5** table **6** upland **8** highland **9** tableland

platform 4 dais, goal, plan **5** creed, plank, stage, stand **6** podium, policy, pulpit, tenets **7** program, rostrum

Plath, Sylvia
author of: 5 Ariel **10** The Bell Jar

platinum
chemical symbol: 2 Pt

platitude 3 saw **6** cliche, old saw, truism **7** bromide **8** banality, chestnut **11** commonplace

platitudinous 5 banal, corny, stale, tired, trite, vapid **6** jejune **8** bromidic, ordinary **9** hackneyed **10** pedestrian, unexciting, unoriginal **12** cliche-ridden, conventional **13** unimaginative

Plato
author of: 4 Laws **5** Crito **6** Phaedo **7** Apology, Gorgias, Sophist, Timaeus **8** Philebus, Republic **9** Symposium **10** Parmenides

platoon 4 band, body, crew, team, unit **5** corps, force, group **10** detachment

platter 4 dish, disk, lanx **6** salver **7** record **8** trencher **9** recording

plaudit, plaudits 4 rave **5** cheer, kudos **6** hurrah, huzzah, praise **7** acclaim, bouquet, ovation **8** applause, approval, cheering **10** compliment, hallelujah **11** approbation **12** commendation

plauditory 8 admiring, praising **9** extolling, laudatory, praiseful **12** commendatory **13** complimentary

plausible 5 sound, valid **6** likely **7** logical, tenable **8** credible, feasible, possible, probable, rational, sensible **10** acceptable, believable, convincing, persuasive, reasonable **11** conceivable, justifiable

Plautus
author of: 7 Stichus **8** Mercator **9** Amphitruo, Menaechmi, Pseudolus **10** Amphitryon **14** Miles Gloriosus

play 3 act, fun, toy **4** jest, lark, romp, room, show **5** antic, caper, drama, enact, farce, frisk, revel, space, sport, sweep, swing **6** act out, cavort, comedy, frolic, gambol, leeway, trifle **7** disport, have fun, pageant, perform, skylark, tragedy, vie with **8** pleasure, take part **9** amusement, diversion, elbowroom, enjoyment, make merry, melodrama, perform on, personify, represent, spectacle **10** recreation **11** impersonate, merrymaking

playboy 4 rake, wolf **5** Romeo, sheik **6** lecher **7** Don Juan, swinger **8** Casanova, hedonist, Lothario, party boy **9** jet-setter, ladies' man, partygoer, womanizer **10** lady-killer, profligate **14** pleasure seeker **15** good-time Charlie

Playboy of the Western World, The
author: 19 John Millington Synge
character: 8 Old Mahon **9** Widow Quin **10** Shawn Keogh **16** Christopher Mahon, Margaret Flaherty (Pegeen)

play down 9 underplay **11** de-emphasize

played out 4 beat **5** all in, spent, weary **6** bushed, done in, pooped **7** drained, wearied, worn out **8** depleted, dog tired, fatigued, tired out, unreeled **9** dead tired, exhausted

player 4 jock, mime **5** actor **6** mummer **7** actress, athlete, trouper **8** gamester, opponent, thespian **9** adversary, contender, performer **10** antagonist, competitor, contestant, team member **11** entertainer, participant

play false 4 dupe **5** trick **6** betray **7** deceive, two-time **10** be disloyal **12** be unfaithful **13** be treacherous

playfellow 3 pal **4** chum **5** buddy **6** friend **8** playmate

playful 6 frisky, impish, lively **7** amusing, coltish, jesting, waggish **8** humorous, mirthful, prankish, sportive **9** fun-loving, sprightly **10** capricious, frolicsome, rollicking **12** lighthearted
French: 8 espiegle

play host 4 host **9** entertain **10** give a party, have guests **13** keep open house

playing field 4 bowl **5** arena **7** diamond, stadium **8** gridiron **10** playground **12** amphitheater

playing piece 3 man **4** disk **5** piece **7** counter

play in water 3 dip **4** swim **6** dabble, paddle, splash

play Judas 6 betray **7** sell out, two-time **9** play false **11** double-cross

playmate 3 pal **4** chum **5** buddy **6** friend **10** playfellow

play of spirit
French: 10 jeu d'esprit

play on words
French: 3 pun **9** jeu de mots

plaything 3 toy **4** dupe **5** patsy, sport **6** bauble, trifle **9** diversion

play truant 3 cut **4** skip **8** be absent **9** play hooky

play with 5 bandy **7** torment, toy with **11** have fun with

playwright 6 author, writer **9** dramatist, scenarist **10** dramatizer, dramaturge, librettist, play doctor **12** dramatic poet, dramaturgist, scriptwriter **13** melodramatist

plea 4 suit **5** alibi **6** appeal, excuse, prayer **7** apology, begging, defense, pretext, request **8** argument, entreaty, petition **10** adjuration, beseeching **11** explanation, extenuation, vindication **12** solicitation, supplication **13** justification

plead 3 ask, beg **6** adjure, enjoin **7** beseech, entreat, implore, request, solicit **8** appeal to, petition **9** importune **10** supplicate

pleader 6 beggar **8** advocate, defender, implorer **9** apologist, beseecher **10** importuner, supplicant

plead with 3 beg **4** pray **6** adjure **7** beseech, implore **10** supplicate

pleasant 4 fine, good, mild, nice, soft, warm **6** genial, gentle, lovely, polite **7** affable, amiable, cordial, likable, tactful **8** amicable, charming, cheerful, friendly, inviting, pleasing, sociable **9** agreeable, congenial, enjoyable **10** attractive, felicitous, gratifying, gregarious, satisfying **11** good-humored, good-natured, pleasurable **13** companionable

Pleasant Island see **5** Nauru

pleasantry 4 jape, jest, joke, quip **5** sally **6** bon mot **8** greeting **9** wisecrack, witticism **10** salutation

pleasant-tasting 4 mild **5** sweet, tasty **6** savory **8** luscious **9** delicious, palatable, succulent **10** appetizing, delectable **11** scrumptious **13** mouth-watering

please 3 opt **4** like, suit, want, will, wish **5** amuse, charm, elate, elect **6** choose, desire, divert, prefer, thrill, tickle **7** content, delight, gladden, gratify, satisfy **8** enthrall, entrance **9** enrapture, entertain, fascinate, make happy **10** be inclined **14** give pleasure to
French: 12 s'il vous plait
German: 5 bitte
Spanish: 8 por favor

pleased 4 glad **5** happy, proud **6** elated **8** thrilled **9** delighted, gratified

Pleasence, Donald

born: 7 England, Worksop
roles: 12 The Caretaker **14** The Great Escape **16** You Only Live Twice **17** The Eagle Has Landed **24** The Greatest Story Ever Told

please reply
French: 4 rsvp **20** repondez s'il vous plait

pleasing 6 genial, polite **7** affable, amiable, amusing, likable, winning **8** charming, cheerful, friendly, inviting, mannerly **9** agreeable, congenial, diverting, enjoyable **10** attractive, delightful, gladdening, gratifying, satisfying **11** captivating, fascinating, good-humored, good-natured, pleasurable **12** entertaining, well-mannered

pleasing inactivity
Italian: 14 dolce far niente

pleasurable 8 pleasing **9** agreeable, enjoyable **10** delightful

pleasure 3 fun, joy **4** like, will, wish **5** bliss, cheer, mirth **6** choice, desire, gaiety, option **7** delight, elation, rapture **9** amusement, diversion, enjoyment, festivity, happiness, merriment, selection **10** exultation, jubilation, preference, recreation **11** high spirits, inclination **13** entertainment, gratification **15** beer and skittles **16** lightheartedness
goddess of: 8 Voluptas

pleasure-giving 7 amusing **8** pleasing **9** agreeable, enjoyable **10** delightful **11** pleasurable **12** entertaining

Pleasure of His Company, The
author: 19 Cornelia Otis Skinner

pleasure trip 4 tour **5** jaunt **6** outing **8** vacation **9** excursion

pleat 4 fold **5** crimp, frill **6** crease

pleated 6 fluted, folded **7** creased, crimped **10** corrugated

plebeian 3 low **4** base, mean **5** banal **6** coarse, common, vulgar **7** lowborn, lowbrow, popular **8** commoner, everyman, low-class, ordinary **9** bourgeois, common man, unrefined **10** average man, uncultured **11** bourgeoisie, commonplace, proletarian **12** uncultivated

plebs 5 demos **6** masses **7** commons **8** populace **9** commoners, hoi polloi, plebeians **11** bourgeoisie **12** common people

plecoptera
class: 8 hexapoda
phylum: 10 arthropoda
group: 8 stone fly

pledge 3 vow **4** bail, bond, oath, pact, pawn, word **5** swear, troth **6** assert, avowal, surety **7** compact, promise, warrant **8** contract, covenant, guaranty, security, warranty **9** agreement, assurance, guarantee **10** adjuration, collateral

Pleiades
father: 5 Atlas

mother: 7 Pleione
half-sisters: 6 Hyades
names: 4 Maia **6** Merope **7** Alcyone, Celaeno, Electra, Sterope, Taygete
number of daughters: 5 seven

plenary 4 full **6** entire **7** perfect **8** absolute, complete

plenitude 4 glut, heap, mass **5** flood **6** bounty, plenty, wealth **7** quality, surfeit, surplus **8** fullness, plethora, totality **9** abundance, amplitude, profusion, repletion, wholeness **10** cornucopia, entireness, quantities **11** ample supply, copiousness, full measure, sufficiency **12** completeness **14** more than enough

plenteous 6 lavish **7** copious, profuse **8** abundant **9** bountiful, plentiful

plentiful 4 lush **5** ample, large **6** lavish **7** copious, liberal, profuse **8** abundant, generous, infinite, prolific **9** abounding, bounteous, bountiful, plenteous, unsparing, unstinted **11** overflowing **13** inexhaustible

plenty 4 gobs, lots, slew **5** scads **6** luxury, oceans, oodles, riches, wealth, worlds **8** opulence **9** abundance, affluence, good times, great deal, plenitude, profusion, well-being **10** prosperity **11** ample amount, good fortune, sufficiency **12** a full measure
goddess of: 3 Ops

plethora 4 glut **5** flood **6** excess, wealth **7** overage, surfeit, surplus **8** fullness **9** abundance, amplitude, plenitude, profusion **10** oversupply, redundancy, surplusage **11** superfluity **13** overabundance **14** more than enough, superabundance

pliable 5 lithe **6** limber, pliant, supple **7** elastic, plastic, springy, willing **8** flexible, yielding **9** adaptable, compliant, receptive, resilient, tractable **10** manageable, responsive, submissive **11** acquiescent **13** accommodating **14** easily bendable, impressionable

pliancy 8 docility, meekness, yielding **9** passivity **10** compliance, pliability, submission, suppleness **11** flexibility **12** complaisance

pliant 4 meek **6** supple **7** pliable **8** flexible, yielding **9** compliant **10** submissive **11** deferential

pliers
type: 10 fixed-joint **11** combination, needle-nosed, side-cutting **17** offset combination

plight 3 fix, jam **5** pinch, state, trial **6** crisis, muddle, pickle, scrape **7** dilemma, impasse, straits, trouble **8** distress, exigency **9** condition, emergency, extremity, situation **10** difficulty **11** predicament, tribulation, vicissitude **12** circumstance

Plisthenes
brother/half-brother: 8 Menelaus **9** Agamemnon

father: 6 Atreus
mother: 6 Cleola
sister/half-sister: 8 Anaxibia
sister-in-law: 12 Clytemnestra
uncle: 8 Thyestes

plod 4 drag, grub, moil, plug, slog, toil **5** grind, sweat, tramp **6** drudge, lumber, trudge, waddle **7** peg away, shuffle **8** struggle **9** persevere

plodding 4 dull **6** clumsy **8** trudging **9** laborious **10** pedestrian

plot 3 lot, map **4** area, draw, mark, plan, tale, yarn **5** chart, draft, field, patch, space, story, tract **6** action, design, scheme, sketch **7** collude, compute, diagram, outline, section **8** clearing, conspire, contrive, evil plan, intrigue, maneuver **9** blueprint, calculate, determine, incidents, narrative, story line, stratagem **10** conspiracy, secret plan **11** machination

plotting 4 wily **6** artful, crafty **7** cunning **8** scheming **9** conniving, designing **10** intriguing

Plough and the Stars, The
author: 10 Sean O'Casey

plover
group of: 4 wing **12** congregation

plow, plough 3 cut, dig **4** push, till, work **5** break, dig up, drive, forge, press, shove, spade **6** furrow, harrow, loosen, plunge, turn up **7** break up **8** bulldoze **9** cultivate
invented by:
  cast iron: 7 Ransome
  disc: 5 Hardy

plowable 6 arable **7** friable **8** farmable, tillable **10** cultivable

Plowright, Joan
born: 5 Brigg **7** England
husband: 15 Laurence Olivier
roles: 13 A Taste of Honey, The Dressmaker **14** Enchanted April, The Entertainer, The Summer House

ploy 4 game, ruse, wile **5** trick **6** design, gambit, scheme, tactic **7** gimmick **8** artifice, maneuver, strategy **9** stratagem **10** subterfuge

pluck 4 draw, grab, grit, guts, jerk, pick, sand, yank **5** spunk, valor **6** daring, mettle, pull at, snatch, spirit, uproot **7** bravery, courage, pull off, pull out, resolve **8** boldness, temerity, tenacity **9** extirpate, fortitude **10** doggedness, resolution **11** persistence **12** perseverance **13** determination

pluck out 7 extract, pick out, pull out

plucky 4 bold, game **5** brave, gutsy **6** daring, spunky **7** doughty, valiant **8** fearless, intrepid, spirited, unafraid, valorous **9** audacious, dauntless, undaunted **10** courageous, mettlesome **11** lionhearted, unflinching **12** stouthearted

plug 4 bung, cork **5** close, stuff **6** fill up, stanch, stop up **7** shut off, stopper, stopple

plug up 3 dam 4 clog, plug 5 block, choke, dam up, stuff 6 stop up 7 congest 8 obstruct

plum
> **varieties:** 3 hog 4 Coco, date, Duhr, gage, Java, sand, sloe, wild 5 beach, black, goose, Islay, Jaman, Lansa, Moxie, nanny, Natal, shore, Simon 6 August, Batoko, Canada, Cheney, cherry, common, Damson, ground, Indian, Jambul, Kaffir, Kelsey, Lomboy, Pigeon, Sapote, Sierra, Sisson 7 apricot, Burbank, Cheston, Jambosa, Malabar, Orleans, Pacific, Spanish, Wickson 8 American, Assyrian, Burdekin, European, Hortulan, Jambolan, Japanese, Oklahoma, Prunello, Victoria 9 Allegheny, Chickasaw, Governor's, greengage, marmalade, Myrobalan, wild-goose 10 Madagascar 13 Queensland hog

plumb 4 lead, test, true 5 gauge, level, probe, sheer, sound 6 fathom 7 examine, measure, plummet 8 plumb bob, straight, vertical 9 penetrate

plume 3 pen 4 down 5 egret, pique, preen, pride, prize, quill 7 feather
> **military:** 7 panache

Plumed Serpent, The
> **author:** 10 D H Lawrence

Plummer, Christopher
> **real name:** 28 Arthur Christopher Orme Plummer
> **born:** 6 Canada 7 Toronto
> **wife:** 11 Tammy Grimes 12 Elaine Taylor
> **daughter:** 13 Amanda Plummer
> **roles:** 9 Alexander 14 A Beautiful Mind, Murder by Decree 15 The Sound of Music 16 Nicholas Nickleby 18 Baron Georg von Trapp 20 The Man Who Would Be King 25 The Return of the Pink Panther

plummet 4 dive, fall 6 plunge, tumble 8 nosedive 12 fall headlong

plump 4 drop, firm, flop, plop, sink 5 blunt, buxom, obese, plunk, pudgy, solid, spill, stout 6 abrupt, chubby, direct, fleshy, portly, rotund, sprawl, stocky, tumble 7 rounded 8 collapse, outright 9 corpulent

plumpness
> **French:** 10 embonpoint

plunder 3 rob 4 haul, loot, raid, sack, swag, take 5 booty, rifle, prize, strip 6 fleece, maraud, pilfer, ravage, spoils 7 despoil, pillage, ransack, takings 9 filchings 10 pilferings

plunderer 6 looter, vandal 7 brigand 8 pillager 9 despoiler

plunge 3 dip, fly, run 4 bolt, cast, dart, dash, dive, drop, duck, fall, jerk, roll, jump, leap, push, reel, rock, rush, sink, sway, tear, toss 5 douse, drive, heave, lunge, lurch, pitch, press, shoot, speed, surge, swarm, whisk 6 charge, hasten, hurtle, hustle,

scurry, sprint, streak, thrust, tumble 7 descend, immerse, scuttle 8 scramble, submerge, submerse 12 fall headlong

plunk 4 pick, thud 5 pluck, plumb, strum, twang 6 dollar 7 exactly 8 squarely 9 precisely

plurality 4 bulk, most 8 majority 13 preponderance

plus 5 added, extra, other, spare 6 useful 7 helpful 9 auxiliary, desirable 10 additional, beneficial 12 advantageous, supplemental 13 supplementary

plush 4 lush, posh, rich 5 fancy, grand, ritzy, swank, thick 6 classy, deluxe, lavish, snazzy, swanky 7 elegant, opulent 8 palatial 9 luxurious, sumptuous 11 extravagant

plushy 4 soft 5 cushy, swank 7 opulent, velvety 9 luxurious, sumptuous

Plutarch
> **author of:** 13 Parallel Lives 14 Plutarch's Lives

Pluto
> **also:** 5 Hades
> **god of:** 10 underworld
> **corresponds to:** 3 Dis 5 Orcus 8 Dis Pater

Pluto
> **position:** 5 ninth
> **satellite:** 6 Charon

plutocrat 5 mogul 6 fat cat, tycoon 9 financier 10 capitalist

plutonic 7 abyssal, igneous 9 cimmerian, intrusive, vulcanian

plutonium
> **chemical symbol:** 2 Pu

Plutus
> **author:** 12 Aristophanes
> **character:** 5 Cario 9 Chremylus 11 Blepsidemus
> **god of:** 6 wealth

Plutus
> **personifies:** 6 wealth
> **father:** 6 Iasion
> **mother:** 7 Demeter

Pluvius
> **epithet of:** 7 Jupiter
> **realm:** 4 rain

ply 3 fly, run 4 leaf, sail, work 5 layer, offer, plait, plate, press, sheet, slice, twist, wield 6 employ, follow, handle, lamina, pursue, sheath, strand, supply 7 besiege, carry on, labor at, operate, stratum, utilize 8 exercise, navigate, practice, put to use, urge upon 9 thickness 10 manipulate

poach 3 rob 4 cook 5 shirr, steal 6 plunge, simmer 7 trample 8 encroach, trespass

pocket 3 bag, get, pit 4 gain, lode, sack, vein 5 pouch, purse, pygmy, small, steal, strip, usurp 6 attain, bantam, cavity, come by, hollow, little, obtain, pilfer, strain, streak 7 chamber, compact, handbag, placket, re-

ceive 8 arrogate, envelope, portable 9 miniature 10 diminutive, receptacle 11 appropriate, compartment

pocketbook 3 bag 5 pouch, purse 6 clutch, wallet 7 handbag, satchel 8 moneybag, notecase 9 coin purse 10 money purse 11 shoulder bag
> **French:** 12 porte-monnaie

pocket flask 5 flask 6 bottle 7 canteen

pocket-sized 3 wee 4 tiny 5 dwarf, pygmy, small 6 bantam, little, midget, minute, petite 7 compact 9 miniature 10 diminutive, vest-pocket

poco
> **music:** 6 little

pod 4 case, hull, husk 5 shell 6 jacket, sheath 8 pericarp, seed case 10 seed vessel

Podgorica
> **capital of:** 10 Montenegro
> **once called:** Titograd

podium 4 dais, foot, wall 5 stipe 7 lectern 8 pedestal, platform 9 footstalk

Poe, Edgar Allan
> **author of:** 6 Ligeia 7 Israfel, To Helen 8 The Bells, The Raven 10 Annabel Lee, The Gold Bug 18 The Purloined Letter 20 The Cask of Amontillado, The Pit and the Pendulum 22 The Masque of the Red Death 24 The Fall of the House of Usher, The Murders in the Rue Morgue 29 The Narrative of Arthur Gordon Pym

Poeas
> **also:** 5 Poias
> **lit:** 11 funeral pyre
> > **pyre of:** 8 Hercules
> **son:** 11 Philoctetes

poem 3 lay, ode 4 epic, song 5 elegy, idyll, lyric, rhyme, verse 6 ballad, jingle, sonnet 8 doggerel, limerick, madrigal

poet 4 bard 5 maker 6 lyrist, rhymer, singer 7 reciter 8 lyricist, minstrel, verseman 9 balladeer, balladist, poetaster, rhymester, sonneteer, versifier 10 improviser, librettist, songwriter

poetaster 4 bard, poet 6 rhymer, writer 8 poetizer, rimester 9 rhymester, versifier

poetic, poetical 5 lyric 7 lilting, lyrical, melodic, musical 8 metrical, rhythmic, songlike 9 melodious 11 imaginative

Poetics
> **author:** 9 Aristotle

poetizer 4 bard, poet 6 rhymer, writer 8 rhymster 9 poetaster, versifier

poetry 5 poesy, rhyme, verse 13 versification
> **god of:** 4 Odin, Ogma 5 Brage, Bragi, Othin 6 Apollo 7 Phoebus, Pythius 9 Musagetes

Pogo

creator: 9 Walt Kelly
character: 9 Porkypine, Wiley Catt 10 Boll Weevil 12 PT Bridgeport 13 Deacon Mushrat, Mole MacCarony
  alligator: 6 Albert
  fox: 11 Seminole Sam
  frog: 15 Moonshine Sonata
  hound: 18 Beauregard Bugleboy
  possum: 4 Pogo
  skunk: 16 Ma'm'selle Hepzibah
  snake: 7 Snavely
  sorcerer: 10 Howland Owl
  turtle/pirate captain: 14 Churchy La Femme
  place: 15 Okefenokee Swamp

Pohjola
origin: 7 Finnish
identified with: 7 Lapland
location: 12 North Finland

poignant 3 sad 5 sharp 6 biting, moving, rueful, woeful 7 cutting, doleful, piquant, piteous, pitiful, pungent, tearful 8 grievous, pathetic, piercing, pitiable, touching 9 affecting, sorrowful, trenchant 10 lamentable 11 distressing, penetrating 12 heartrending

poilu
slang: 13 French soldier
in: 9 World War I

point 3 aim, end, hit, nib, run, tip, use 4 apex, bend, bode, core, game, gist, goal, item, mark, meat, pike, pith, spur, time, turn, unit 5 argue, cause, guide, heart, imply, level, limit, place, prong, prove, score, sense, slant, spike, stage, steer, tally, train, value 6 aspect, basket, degree, detail, direct, hint at, kernel, marrow, moment, number, object, reason 7 essence, feature, instant, portend, presage, purpose, quality, signify, suggest, testify 8 indicate, intimate, juncture, main idea, manifest, offshoot, position, sharp end 9 condition, extension, intention, outgrowth 10 foreshadow, particular, projection, prominence, promontory 11 demonstrate 12 protuberance

point-blank 5 blunt 6 direct 10 forthright 11 plainspoken

Point Counter Point
author: 12 Aldous Huxley

point d'appui 4 prop, stay 24 point of battle line support

pointed 5 acute, blunt, sharp 6 biting, direct, peaked, pointy 7 cutting, fitting, hinting, telling 8 accurate, incisive, piercing 9 aciculate, acuminate, cuspidate, pertinent, trenchant 10 emphasized, forthright 11 appropriate, conspicuous, insinuating, penetrating

pointer 3 arm, tip 4 hand, hint 5 arrow, guide, stick 6 needle 7 caution, warning 9 indicator 10 admonition, advisement, suggestion 13 piece of advice 14 recommendation
dog breed: 16 German wirehaired 17

German shorthaired 25 wirehaired pointing griffon

pointless 4 dull 5 blunt 6 absurd, futile, obtuse, stupid 7 aimless, invalid, rounded, unedged, useless 8 bootless, worn down 9 fruitless, illogical, senseless, unpointed, worthless 10 irrational, irrelevant, ridiculous, unavailing 11 ineffectual, meaningless, purposeless, unsharpened 12 inapplicable, preposterous, unproductive, unprofitable, unreasonable

point of view 4 side 5 angle, slant 6 aspect 7 outlook 8 attitude 9 viewpoint 10 standpoint 11 frame of mind, perspective

point the way 5 guide, pilot, usher 6 direct 8 indicate, navigate 14 give directions

point to 5 argue, imply 6 denote 7 express 8 indicate

point up 6 stress 9 emphasize, underline 10 accentuate, underscore

Poirot, Hercule
detective created by: 14 Agatha Christie
nationality: 7 Belgian
famed for: 10 moustaches
phrase: 15 little grey cells
played by: 11 David Suchet (PBS Mystery) 12 Peter Sellers

poise 4 calm 5 raise 6 aplomb 7 balance, elevate 8 presence 9 assurance, composure, hold aloft, sangfroid 10 equanimity 11 savoir faire, self-command, self-control 13 self-assurance 14 presence of mind, self-confidence 15 be in equilibrium

poised 7 assured 8 composed 9 confident 10 controlled 11 self-assured 13 self-possessed

poison 4 bane, evil, harm 5 curse, taint, toxin, venom 6 cancer, canker, debase, defile, impair, infect, plague, weaken 7 corrode, corrupt, degrade, disease, outrage, pollute 8 enormity, make sick 9 malignity 10 adulterate, corruption, debilitate, malignancy, pestilence 11 abomination, contaminate

poisonous 5 fatal, toxic 6 deadly, lethal, mortal 7 baneful, noxious 8 venomous, virulent 10 pernicious 11 deleterious 12 pestilential

Poitier, Sidney
born: 7 Miami FL
wife: 13 Joanna Shimkus
roles: 8 Sneakers 9 The Jackal 11 Virgil Tibbs 12 A Patch of Blue, For Love of Ivy, Porgy and Bess 13 To Sir with Love 14 The Defiant Ones 15 A Raisin in the Sun 16 Lilies of the Field (Oscar) 17 They Call Me Mr Tibbs 19 In the Heat of the Night, The Blackboard Jungle, Uptown Saturday Night 23 Guess Who's Coming to Dinner?

Pokanoket *see* 10 Wampanoags

poke 3 dig, hit, jab 4 butt, drag, gore, idle, jolt, prod, push, stab 5 crawl, dally, delay, mosey, nudge, punch, stick, thump 6 dawdle, fiddle, potter, thrust 7 meander, saunter, shamble, shuffle 8 hang back 10 dillydally 12 shilly-shally

poker
derived from: 5 as nas, gilet 6 brelan 7 primero 11 brouillotte
cards/hand: 4 five 5 seven
bets: 4 ante 5 chips
hand: 4 pair 5 flush 8 straight, two pairs 9 full house 10 royal flush 11 four of a kind 12 three of a kind 13 straight flush
term: 4 ante, call, fold 5 check, raise 6 ante up 7 reraise
variation: 4 draw, stud 5 jacks, Omaha 6 hold em, pai gow 8 jackpots 12 five-card draw 13 seven-card stud

poky, pokey 4 dull, jail, slow 5 dowdy, small 6 dreary, shabby, stodgy, stuffy 7 cramped 8 confined, dawdling, dilatory, frumpish 9 puttering 10 monotonous
creature: 5 sloth, snail 6 turtle 8 slowpoke, tortoise

Poland
other name: 6 Polska 17 the land of the plain
capital/largest city: 6 Warsaw
  medieval capital: 6 Cracow, Krakow
others: 3 Lwo 4 Kodz, Kolo, Lida, Lodz, Lvov, Lyck, Nysa, Oels, Pila 5 Brest, Bytom, Chelm, Dukla, Narev, Opole, Posen, Radom, Sroda, Torun, Vilna 6 Danzig, Elblag, Gdansk, Gdynia, Gnesen, Grodno, Kalisz, Kielce, Kracow, Lublin, Poznan, Tarnow, Zabrze 7 Beuthen, Breslau, Chorzow, Garocin, Gliwice, Litousk, Litovsk, Lyublin, Oleztyn, Stettin, Wroclaw 8 Frombork, Gleiwitz, Katowice, Lidzbark, Liegnitz, Oswiecim, Przemysl, Szczecin, Tarnopol 9 Auschwitz, Bialogard, Bialystok, Bydgoszcz, Sosnowiec, Szcezecin, Walbrzych 11 Czestochowa
school: 6 Warsaw 12 Jagiellonian
division: 7 Galicia, Silesia 8 Podlesia, Volhynia 9 Lithuania, Pomerania
measure: 3 cal 4 mila, pret 5 morga, sazen, vloka, wloka 6 cwierc, cwierk, kwarta, lokiec 7 garniec 9 kwarterka
monetary unit: 4 abia 5 dalar, ducat, grosz, marka, zloty 6 fennig, groszy, gulden, halerz, korona 8 groschen
weight: 3 lut 4 funt 6 kamian 7 skrupul
island: 5 Wolin
lake: 5 Goplo, Mamry 8 Niegocin, Sniardwy 13 Stettin Lagoon
mountain: 5 Tatra 6 Beskid 7

Pieniny, Sudeten **9** Beshchady, High Tatra, Holy Cross **10** Carpathian
highest point: 4 Rysy
river: 3 Bug, San **4** Alle, Brda, Gwda, Lyna, Nysa, Oder, Styr **5** Biala, Drana, Dwina, Narev, Narew, Notec, Podra, Seret, Warta, Wista **6** Neisse, Niemen, Nyeman, Pilica, Pripet, Prosna, Styrpa, Wieprz **7** Nemunas, Vistula, Wistoka **8** Dniester
sea: 6 Baltic
physical feature:
> **forest: 10** Bialowieza
> **gulf: 6** Danzig, Gdansk
> **lagoon: 7** Stettin **12** Frischeshaff
> **plain: 7** Silesia
> **plateau: 6** Lublin
people: 4 Pole, Slav **5** Mazur **8** Silesian
> **astronomer: 10** Copernicus
> **author: 7** Reymont **8** Zeromski **10** Mickiewicz, Wyspianski **11** Sienkiewicz
> **composer: 6** Chopin **10** Paderewski
> **dynasty: 5** Piast **7** Jagello
> **king: 7** Casimir **8** Augustus
> **leader: 5** Kania **6** Gierek **7** Gomulka, Mieszko **8** Boleslaw **9** Pilsudski, Stanislaw **10** Jaruzel ski, Kosciuszko, Lech Walesa
> **pope: 10** John Paul II **20** Cardinal Carol Wojtyla
> **queen: 7** Jadwiga
musician: 7 Kiepura **9** Landowska
scientist: 5 Curie
language: 6 Kaszub, Polish **10** Pomeranian
religion: 13 Roman Catholic
title: 3 pan **4** pani
place:
> **castle: 5** Wawel
> **church: 6** St John **10** Panna Maria
> **monastery: 9** Jasna Gora
> **monument: 17** Heroes of the Ghetto
> **national park: 5** Ojcow **10** Bialowieza
> **palace: 7** Casimir
feature:
> **folk dance: 5** polka **7** mazurka **9** krakowiak, polonaise
> **union: 10** Solidarity
food:
> **dish: 5** bigos **6** pirogi **7** borscht **7** kolduny
> **drink: 5** vodka **7** Krupnik
> **sausage: 8** kielbasa
> **soup: 7** barszca

Polanski, Roman
director of: 4 Tess **7** Macbeth **9** Chinatown **10** The Pianist **11** Oliver Twist **13** Rosemary's Baby **17** Death and the Maiden
polar 3 icy **6** arctic, frigid, wintry **7** glacial, ice-cold **8** freezing **9** antarctic **11** nothernmost **12** southernmost
polaroid 6 camera
> **invented by: 4** Land

pole 3 rod **4** mast, spar **5** shaft, staff, stick **6** tongue **9** pikestaff
> **flax holder: 7** distaff
> **pertaining to: 5** nodal
> **sacred: 7** Asherah
> **Scottish: 5** caber
> **tribal: 5** totem
> **vehicular: 4** neap
police, police officer 4 cops, dick, fuzz, tidy **5** clean, guard **6** neaten, patrol, tidy up **7** clean up, control, marshal, officer, protect, sheriff **8** blue coat, flatfoot, gendarme, regulate, spruce up, troopers **9** gendarmes, men in blue, patrolmen **10** traffic cop **11** arm of the law, keep in order **12** constabulary, cop on the beat
> **French: 8** gendarme
> **Italian: 11** carabiniere
Police Woman
> **character: 9** (Det) Joe Styles, (Lt) Paul Marsh **11** (Det) Pete Royster, (Lt) Bill Crowley **12** (Sgt Suzanne) Pepper Martin
> **cast: 9** Ed Bernard **11** Val Bisoglio **12** Earl Holliman **14** Angie Dickinson, Charles Dierkop
policy 3 way **4** plan, rule **5** habit, style **6** custom, design, method, scheme, system **7** program, routine, tactics **8** behavior, platform, practice, strategy **9** principle, procedure
polish 3 oil, wax **4** buff, sand **5** class, emend, glaze, gloss, grace, rouge, rub up, shine **6** pumice, refine, smooth **7** burnish, correct, culture, enhance, finesse, improve, perfect, sauvity, touch up, varnish **8** abrasive, courtesy, elegance, round out, urbanity **9** gentility, politesse, sandpaper **10** politeness, refinement **11** cultivation, good manners
polished 4 able, deft, fine, oily **5** oiled, suave, waxed **6** buffed, expert, glassy, glazed, glossy, polite, rubbed, sanded, shined, urbane **7** capable, elegant, genteel, refined, skilled **8** cultured, finished, mannerly, masterly, skillful, smoothed **9** brilliant, burnished, courteous, masterful, practiced, varnished **10** cultivated, proficient **11** experienced **12** accomplished
polish off 6 finish **8** complete, get rid of **9** dispose of
polite 4 high **5** civil, elite **6** proper **7** courtly, elegant, gallant, genteel, refined **8** cultured, mannerly, polished, well-bred **9** civilized, courteous, diffident, patrician **10** cultivated, respectful **11** ceremonious, fashionable, gentlemanly, well-behaved **12** well-mannered
politeness 7 decorum **8** courtesy **9** gentility, propriety **10** refinement **11** good manners
Polites
> **character in: 7** Odyssey

brother: 5 Paris **6** Hector
companion: 8 Odysseus
father: 5 Priam
mother: 6 Hecuba
sister: 9 Cassandra
transformed by: 5 Aeaea, Circe
transformed into: 3 hog, pig **5** swine
politic 4 wily, wise **5** chary, suave **6** artful, astute, shrewd, subtle **7** mindful, prudent, tactful **8** cautious, discreet, scheming **9** designing, expedient, judicious, opportune **10** contriving, diplomatic **11** calculating, circumspect, machinating **13** Machiavellian
political party 3 GOP **4** Tory, Whig **5** Labor **7** faction **9** Communist, Greenback, Socialist **10** Democratic, Republican **11** Know-Nothing
political refugee 2 DP **5** exile **6** emigre **10** expatriate **15** displaced person
politician 8 politico **9** incumbent, statesman **10** campaigner, legislator **12** officeholder, office seeker **13** public servant
politics 10 government, statecraft **11** party policy **13** statesmanship **14** affairs of state
Politics
> **author: 9** Aristotle
Polixenes
> **character in: 14** The Winter's Tale
> **author: 11** Shakespeare
Polk, James Knox
> **presidential rank: 8** eleventh
> **party: 8** Democrat
> **state represented: 2** TN
> **defeated: 4** (Henry) Clay **6** (James Gillespie) Birney
> **vice president: 6** (George Mifflin) Dallas
> **cabinet:**
>> **state: 8** (James) Buchanan
>> **treasury: 6** (Robert John) Walker
>> **war: 5** (William Learned) Marcy
>> **attorney general: 5** (John Young) Mason **6** (Isaac) Toucey **8** (Nathan) Clifford
>> **navy: 5** (John Young) Mason **8** (George) Bancroft
>> **postmaster general: 7** (Cave) Johnson
> **born: 2** NC **17** Mecklenburg County
> **died/buried: 2** TN **9** Nashville
> **education: 11** prep schools
>> **university: 13** North Carolina
> **religion: 9** Methodist
> **political career: 2** state legislature **17** Speaker of the House **24** US House of Representatives
>> **governor of: 9** Tennessee
> **civilian career: 6** lawyer
> **notable events of lifetime/term:**
>> **boundary dispute: 9** Northwest
>> **discovery in California of: 4** gold
>> **Proviso: 6** Wilmot
>> **treaty of: 16** Guadalupe Hidalgo

war: 7 Mexican
father: 6 Samuel
mother: 4 Jane
siblings: 7 John Lee **9** Jane Maria, Naomi Tate **10** Lydia Eliza **12** Marshall Tate, Samuel Wilson **14** William Hawkins **15** Franklin Ezekiel, Ophelia Clarissa
wife: 5 Sarah (Childress)

polka 5 dance **10** round dance **13** Bohemian dance

poll 4 head, vote **5** count, tally **6** census, survey, voting **7** canvass, figures, returns **8** register, sampling **9** interview, nose count **10** count noses, voting list **11** voting place

Pollack, Sydney
director of: 11 Out of Africa (Oscar) **12** The Way We Were **15** Absence of Malice **23** They Shoot Horses Don't They?

Pollock, Jackson
born: 6 Cody WY
artwork: 5 Scent **9** Blue Poles **10** The She-Wolf **11** Convergence **12** Autumn Rhythm **13** Eyes in the Heat **17** Easter and the Totem **20** Guardians of the Secret

pollutant 5 fumes, smoke, waste **7** exhaust **8** emission, impurity

pollute 4 foul, soil **5** dirty, sully **6** befoul, debase, defile **7** deprave, profane **9** desecrate **10** adulterate, make filthy **11** contaminate

polluted 4 foul **5** dirty, drunk **6** impure, soiled **7** corrupt, profane, smashed, unclean **9** poisonous **12** contaminated

pollution 7 fouling, soiling **8** defiling, dirtying, foulness, impurity **9** befouling, pollutant **11** uncleanness **12** adulteration **13** contaminating, contamination

Pollux *see* **15** Castor and Pollux

Pollyanna
director: 10 David Swift
based on story by: 13 Eleanor Porter
cast: 9 Jane Wyman **10** Karl Malden **11** Hayley Mills, Richard Egan

polo
equipment: 6 mallet
period of play: 7 chukker
championship: 10 Camacho Cup **13** Coronation Cup **16** Cup of the Americas

Polonius
character in: 6 Hamlet
author: 11 Shakespeare

Polska *see* **6** Poland

poltergeist 5 ghost **6** spirit
literally: 10 noise-ghost
manifestation: 5 knock, noise, prank

Poltergeist
director: 10 Tobe Hooper
cast: 12 Craig T Nelson **14** Jobeth Williams **16** Beatrice Straight

co-writer/producer: 15 Steven Spielberg

poltroon 6 coward, craven **7** caitiff, chicken, dastard **11** yellow-belly

polygon 10 multiangle **11** plane figure
eight-sided: 7 octagon
equal angled: 6 isogon
five-sided: 8 pentagon
four-sided: 6 square **7** rhombus **8** tetragon **9** rectangle, trapezoid
nine-sided: 7 nonagon
seven-sided: 8 heptagon
six-sided: 7 hexagon
ten-sided: 7 decagon
three-sided: 8 triangle
twelve-sided: 9 dodecagon

Polyhymnia
also: 8 Polymnia
member of: 5 Muses
personifies: 5 dance **11** sacred music
mother: 9 Mnemosyne

polymer 5 dimer, nylon **6** hydrol **7** hexamer **8** oligomer

Polynesia
name means: 11 many islands
cities: 4 Apia **7** Papeete **8** Auckland, Pago Pago **9** Nukualofa
island: 4 Cook, Line **5** Samoa, Tonga **6** Easter, Ellice, Hawaii, Midway, Tahiti, Tubuai, Tuvalu **7** Austral, Maupiti, Phoenix, Society, Tokelau, Tuamotu **8** Pitcairn **9** Marquesas **10** New Zealand **15** French Polynesia
sea: 7 Pacific
people: 3 Ati **5** Maori **6** Kanaka, Nivean, Samoan, Tongan **9** Nesogaean **10** Polynesian
explorer: 4 Cook **6** Tasman, Wallis **8** Magellan **9** Roggeveen **12** Bougainville
language: 4 Niue, Uvea **5** Maori **6** Samoan, Tongan **7** Austral, Tagalog, Tokelau **8** Hawaiian, Tahitian **9** Marquesan, Tuamatuan **10** Mangarevan
religion: 12 Christianity
place:
legendary origin: 8 Hawaiiki
feature:
chief: 5 matai
clothing: 5 pareu **6** sarong **8** lava-lava
dance: 4 hula, siva
dwelling: 4 fale
family social unit: 4 aiga
priest: 7 kahunas
supernatural power: 4 mana
food:
dish: 3 kai, poi **4** taro **8** palusami
drink: 3 ava **4** kava, kawa

Polynices
also: 10 Polyneices
father: 7 Oedipus
mother: 7 Jocasta
uncle: 5 Creon
brother: 7 Oedipus **8** Eteocles
sister: 6 Ismene **8** Antigone
killed by: 8 Eteocles

polyp 5 coral, hydra, tumor **6** growth, isopod **7** octopod **10** sea anemone

Polyphemus
form: 7 Cyclops **12** one-eyed giant
father: 6 Elatus **8** Poseidon
mother: 6 Thoosa
joined: 9 Argonauts
killed: 4 Acis
blinded by: 8 Odysseus
loved: 7 Galatea

Polyphides
king of: 6 Sicyon
vocation: 4 seer
protected: 8 Menelaus **9** Agamemnon

polyphony 7 organum **8** faburden **11** fauxbourdon **12** counterpoint

Polypoetes
king of: 10 Thesprotia
father: 6 Apollo **8** Odysseus **9** Pirithous
mother: 6 Phthia **9** Callidice **10** Hippodamia
leader of: 6 Greeks

polysaccharide 6 insulin, starch **7** dextrin **8** galactin, lichenin **9** cellulose **12** carbohydrate

Polyxena
father: 5 Priam
mother: 6 Hecuba
loved by: 8 Achilles

Pomaria *see* **7** Algeria

Pomerania
capital: 7 Stettin
city: 5 Thorn, Torun **6** Anklam
country: 6 Poland **7** Germany
island: 5 Rugen **6** Usedom
province: 7 Pomorze

pommel, pummel 4 beat, hilt, horn, knob, pake **6** finial, strike **9** saddlebow

Pomona
origin: 5 Roman
goddess of: 10 fruit trees

pomp 4 show **5** front, glory, style **7** display **8** ceremony, flourish, grandeur, splendor **9** pageantry, showiness, solemnity, spectacle **10** brilliance **11** affectation, grandiosity, ostentation, pompousness **12** magnificence **14** stately display **15** pretentiousness

pompous 4 vain **5** proud **6** lordly, uppish **7** haughty **8** affected, arrogant, mannered, overdone, puffed-up, snobbish **9** conceited, egotistic, grandiose, imperious **10** blustering, swaggering **11** overbearing, patronizing, pretentious **12** ostentatious, presumptuous, supercilious, vainglorious **13** condescending, high and mighty, self-important

Ponchielli, Amilcare
born: 5 Italy **7** Cremona
composer of: 10 La Gioconda **15** Dance of the Hours

poncho 4 cape **5** cloak, shawl **6** mantle, serape

pond 4 pool, tarn 5 basin 6 lagoon 9 small lake, water hole

ponder 4 muse 5 study 6 wonder 7 examine, reflect 8 cogitate, consider, mull over, ruminate 9 brood over, cerebrate, reflect on, speculate, think over 10 deliberate, meditate on, puzzle over 11 contemplate

ponderous 3 big 4 dull 5 bulky, heavy, hefty, large, wordy 6 boring, bovine, dreary 7 awkward, droning, hulking, labored, lumpish, massive, tedious, weighty 8 cumbrous, enormous, sluggish, unlively, unwieldy 9 corpulent, graceless, lumbering, wearisome 10 burdensome, cumbersome, long-winded, lusterless, monotonous, unexciting, ungraceful 11 heavy-handed

pontiff 4 pope 6 bishop, priest 8 pontifex

pontifical 7 pompous 8 churchly, clerical, dogmatic, priestly 9 apostolic, episcopal, imperious 11 opinionated, overbearing, patronizing, pretentious 13 authoritarian, condescending 14 ecclesiastical

Pontus
personifies: 3 sea
father: 2 Ge
son: 6 Nereus 7 Phorcys

pony 3 nag 4 crib, trot 5 glass, horse, pinto 7 mustang 9 racehorse
breed: 6 Exmoor 8 Shetland

Pooh *See* 13 Winnie-the-Pooh

pooh-pooh 5 knock 7 disdain, put down, run down, sneer at 8 belittle 9 disparage

Pooka *see* 4 Puca

pool 3 pot 4 ally, bank, lake, mere, pond, tarn 5 group, kitty, merge, share, union, unite 6 puddle, splash, stakes 7 combine 8 alliance, fishpond, millpool 9 coalition 10 amalgamate, collective 11 association, consolidate, cooperative 13 confederation

poop 3 fag 4 bush, deck, do in, tire 7 exhaust, fatigue, wear out 8 enervate

pooped 4 beat 5 all in, spent, tired, weary 6 bushed, done in 7 drained, wearied, worn out 8 fatigued, tired out 9 dead tired, exhausted, played out

poor 3 sad 4 bare, dead, vain, worn 5 broke, empty, needy, sorry 6 barren, fallow, faulty, futile, hard up, in need, in want, meager, paltry, wasted 7 forlorn, sterile, unhappy, unlucky, wanting 8 badly off, bankrupt, beggarly, depleted, desolate, devoid of, grieving, indigent, inferior, pathetic, pitiable, strapped, unworthy, wretched 9 defective, deficient, destitute, exhausted, fruitless, imperfect, infertile, insolvent, in straits, miserable, moneyless, penniless, unfertile, worthless 10 distressed, inadequate, pauperized 11

impecunious, unfortunate 12 impoverished, uncultivable, unproductive, unprofitable 15 poverty-stricken

Poor People
author: 16 Fyodor Dostoevsky

Poor Richard's Almanack
author: 16 Benjamin Franklin

pop 4 bang, boom, come, shot, snap, soda 5 arise, blast, burst, crack 6 appear, report 7 explode 8 detonate 9 discharge, explosion, soft drink 10 detonation

pope 3 Leo 4 John, Paul, Pius 5 Peter, Urban 6 Adrian, Eugene, Julius, Martin, Sixtus 7 Clement, Gregory 8 Benedict, Innocent, John Paul, Nicholas 9 Alexander, Callistus
also: 12 Bishop of Rome 13 Vicar of Christ 14 Primate of Italy, Supreme Pontiff 16 Archbishop of Rome 18 Metropolitan of Rome, Patriarch of the West 25 Servant of the Servants of God
office: 6 Papacy 7 Holy See 11 Seat of Peter
elected by: 18 College of Cardinals
elected in: 8 conclave
signal that election is concluded: 10 white smoke
resides: 4 Rome 10 the Vatican 11 Vatican City
former residence: 13 Lateran Palace
summer residence: 14 Castel Gondolfo
papal land holding: 9 patrimony 21 patrimony of Saint Peter
first pope: 10 Saint Peter
pope who crowned Charlemagne: 6 Leo III
pope who excommunicated Luther: 4 Leo X
pope who authorized Michelangelo to paint Sistine Chapel: 8 Julius II
"September Pope": 9 John Paul I
original name of pope:
  Alexander VI: 15 Rodrigo de Borgia
  Callistus III: 15 Alfonso de Borgia
  Clement VII: 14 Giulio de' Medici
  John XXIII: 22 Angelo Giuseppe Roncalli
  John Paul I: 13 Albino Luciani
  John Paul II: 12 Karol Wojtyla 18 Archbishop of Krakow
  Leo X: 16 Giovanni de' Medici
  Pius XI: 12 Achille Ratti
  Pius XII: 35 Eugenio Maria Giuseppe Giovanni Pacelli
popes of Avignon papacy: 6 Urban V 8 Clement V, John XXII 9 Clement VI, Gregory XI, Nicholas V 10 Innocent VI 11 Benedict XII
popes during Great Western Schism:
  Avignon: 10 Clement VII 12 Benedict XIII
  Pisa: 9 John XXIII 10 Alexander V
  Rome: 7 Urban VI 10 Boniface IX, Gregory XII 11 Innocent VII
papal bull/encyclical: 11 Unam sanc-

tam 12 Humanae vitae, Rerum novarum, Vox in excelso 13 Pacem in terris 15 Mater et magistra 19 Populorum progressio 22 Sacerdotalis caelibatus

Pope, Alexander
author of: 10 The Dunciad 12 An Essay on Man 15 Eloisa to Abelard 16 The Rape of the Lock 18 An Essay on Criticism 20 Epistle to Dr Arbuthnot

Pope, John Russell
architect of: 17 Jefferson Memorial 20 National Gallery of Art 23 Temple of the Scottish Rite 24 National Archives Building

Popeye
character in: 9 Sanctuary
author: 8 Faulkner

Popeye
cartoonist: 10 Elzie Segar
character: 5 Bluto, Wimpy 7 Swee' Pea 8 Olive Oyl
food: 7 spinach

popinjay 3 fop 4 beau 5 dandy 7 coxcomb

poplar 7 Populus 22 Liriodendron tulipifera
varieties: 4 gray 5 black, downy, tulip, white 6 balsam, Eugene, yellow 8 Carolina, Lombardy, necklace 10 Queensland 12 Chinese white, silver-leaved 13 Western balsam

poppy 7 Papaver
varieties: 3 sea 4 blue, bush, corn, snow, tree, wind, wood 5 field, opium, plume, satin, tulip, water, Welsh 6 arctic, desert, horned 7 Asiatic, flaming, Iceland, Mexican, prickly, Shirley, Western 8 Flanders, harebell, Matilija, oriental 9 Celandine 10 California, island tree 12 Mexican tulip 13 yellow Chinese 14 California tree
drug: 5 opium 6 heroin 8 morphine

poppycock 3 rot 4 bosh, bunk, jive, tosh 5 froth, fudge, hooey, stuff, trash 6 drivel, humbug 7 baloney, blabber, blather, eyewash, fustian, garbage, hogwash, inanity, prattle, rubbish, twaddle 8 falderal, flummery, nonsense, tommyrot, wish-wash 9 absurdity, gibberish, moonshine, rigmarole 10 applesauce, balderdash, flapdoodle, hocus-pocus, mumbo-jumbo, rigamarole 11 abracadabra, jabberwocky 12 fiddlefaddle, gobbledygook

poppy seed
botanical name: 7 Papaver 11 P somniferum (sleep-bearing poppy)
color: 4 blue 5 white
origin: 4 Asia 6 Europe
guards against: 9 creditors
use: 5 bread, cakes, rolls 6 sweets 10 vegetables 11 butter sauce

populace 4 folk 6 people, public 7 society **9** citizenry, community **10** population

popular 5 cheap, civic, civil, stock **6** famous, public, social **7** admired, current, general, in favor **8** accepted, approved, communal, familiar, favorite, in demand, national, orthodox **9** community, preferred, prevalent, well-known, well-liked **10** affordable, celebrated, democratic **11** established, fashionable, inexpensive, of the people, sought-after

popularity 4 fame, note **5** favor, glory, kudos, vogue **6** esteem, regard, renown, repute **7** acclaim, fashion **8** approval **9** celebrity, notoriety **10** acceptance, admiration, notability, reputation **11** acclamation

popular opinion
  Latin: 9 vox populi

popular whim 3 fad **4** rage **5** craze, mania **7** passion **11** infatuation

populate 6 occupy, people, settle **7** inhabit

populated 5 urban **7** peopled, settled **8** citified, occupied **9** inhabited

population 4 folk **6** people, public **8** citizens, populace **9** citizenry, habitancy, residents **11** body politic, commonality, inhabitants

populous 5 dense **6** jammed **7** crowded, peopled, teeming **8** swarming, thronged

porcelain 5 china **11** ceramic ware

porch 4 stoa **5** lanai, stoop **7** balcony, narthex, portico, veranda **8** solarium, verandah **9** colonnade, vestibule

pore 4 hole, read, scan **5** probe, study **6** outlet, peruse, ponder, review, search, survey **7** dig into, examine, explore, inspect, orifice **8** aperture, consider **9** delve into

Porfiry
  character in: 18 Crime and Punishment
  author: 10 Dostoevsky

Porgy
  author: 13 DuBose Heyward

Porgy and Bess
  opera by: 14 George Gershwin
  character: 4 Bess **5** Clara, Crown, Porgy **6** Serena **11** Sportin' Life
  setting: 10 Catfish Row

pornographic 4 blue, lewd **5** bawdy, dirty, gross **6** coarse, filthy, smutty, vulgar **7** obscene **8** indecent, off-color, prurient **9** salacious **10** lascivious, licentious

porous 4 lacy **6** spongy **7** riddled **8** cellular, pervious **9** absorbent, permeable, sievelike **10** penetrable **11** honeycombed

porpoise 4 leap **5** whale **6** palach, puffer, seahog **7** cowfish, dolphin, surface **8** cetacean
  genus: 8 Phocaena **9** Delphinus

porridge 4 pobs, samp **5** atole, brose, brout, gruel **6** cereal **7** crowdie, oatmeal, polenta **8** flummery

porringer 4 bowl, dish **6** vessel **9** container **10** receptacle

Porsena, Lars
  nationality: 8 Etruscan
  attacked: 4 Rome
  to reinstate: 7 Tarquin

port 4 dock, pier, quay **5** haven, wharf **6** harbor, refuge **7** dry dock, landing, mooring, seaport, shelter **9** anchorage, harborage **11** destination

port
  type: 4 wine **6** brandy
  origin: 8 Portugal
  variety: 4 ruby **5** tawny **7** vintage
  with brandy: 9 Betsy Ross
  with vermouth: 10 Broken Spur

portable 5 handy, light, small **6** bantam, pocket **7** compact, folding, movable **8** cartable, haulable, liftable **9** ready-to-go **10** convenient, conveyable, manageable, vest-pocket **11** pocket-sized

portal, portals 4 adit, arch, door, gate **5** entry **6** wicket **7** doorway, gateway, portico **8** approach, entrance **9** threshold, vestibule **10** portcullis **11** entranceway

Port-au-Prince
  capital of: 5 Haiti

porte-monnaie 5 purse **10** pocketbook **12** money-carrier

portend 4 bode **5** augur **6** denote, herald, warn of **7** bespeak, betoken, point to, predict, presage, signify, suggest **8** forebode, forecast, foretell, forewarn, prophesy **9** foretoken, prefigure **10** foreshadow

portent 4 omen, sign **5** token **6** augury, boding, threat **7** presage, warning **9** harbinger **10** foreboding **11** forewarning

portentous 6 superb **7** amazing, fateful, ominous, pompous **8** alarming, menacing **9** bombastic, grandiose, prophetic **10** foreboding, incredible, prodigious, remarkable, stupendous, surprising **11** astonishing, exceptional, frightening, pretentious, significant, superlative, threatening **12** inauspicious, intimidating, unpropitious

porter 4 brew **5** stout **6** bearer, coolie, redcap, skycap **7** carrier **8** conveyer **9** conductor

Porter, Katherine Anne
  author of: 11 Ship of Fools **12** Old Mortality **14** Flowering Judas **15** The Leaning Tower **18** Pale Horse Pale Rider

Porter, William Sidney
  real name of: 6 O Henry

portfolio 4 case, file **5** album **6** binder, folder **7** dossier **8** envelope **9** scrapbook **10** securities

Porthos
  character in: 18 The Three Musketeers
  author: 5 Dumas (pere)

Portia
  character in: 12 Julius Caesar **19** The Merchant of Venice
  author: 11 Shakespeare

portico 4 stoa **5** lanai **6** piazza **7** balcony, veranda, walkway

portion 3 cut, lot, sum **4** dole, doom, fate, luck, part **5** carve, cut up, moira, piece, sever, share, slice, split **6** amount, divide, kismet, parcel, ration, sector **7** break up, deal out, destiny, fortune, helping, measure, section, segment, serving **8** allocate, disperse, division, fraction, fragment, quantity, separate **9** allotment, allowance, demarcate, partition **10** allocation, distribute, percentage

portion out 5 allot **6** ration **7** dole out, mete out, prorate **8** allocate, dispense, divide up **9** apportion, parcel out **10** distribute, measure out

Portland
  basketball team: 12 Trail Blazers
  football team: 8 Breakers
  river: 8 Columbia **10** Willamette
  university: 4 Reed

Port Louis
  capital of: 9 Mauritius

portly 3 big, fat **4** full **5** beefy, burly, heavy, large, obese, plump, pudgy, round, stout, tubby **6** brawny, chubby, fleshy, rotund, stocky **9** corpulent

portmanteau 3 bag **4** grip **5** cloak **6** mantle, valise **8** suitcase **9** gladstone

Port Moresby
  capital of: 9 New Guinea

Portnoy's Complaint
  author: 10 Philip Roth

Port of Spain
  capital of: 17 Trinidad and Tobago

Porto-Novo
  capital of: 5 Benin

portrait 5 cameo **6** sketch **7** drawing, picture **8** likeness, painting, vignette **9** depiction **10** impression, photograph **11** description

Portrait of a Lady, The
  author: 10 Henry James
  character: 11 Madame Merle, Pansy Osmond **12** Isabel Archer **13** Gilbert Osmond, Lord Warburton, Ralph Touchett **14** Caspar Goodwood **18** Henrietta Stackpole

Portrait of the Artist as a Young Man
  author: 10 James Joyce
  character: 4 Emma **12** Simon Dedalus **14** Stephen Dedalus

portray 3 ape **4** draw, play **5** carve, enact, mimic, model, paint, pose as, sketch **6** depict, detail, figure, pose as, sketch **7** imitate, narrate, picture **8** describe, set forth, simulate **9** delineate, represent, sculpture **10** illustrate, photograph **11** impersonate **12** characterize

portrayal 7 picture **8** portrait **9** picturing **11** delineation, description **14** representation **16** characterization

ports
 god of: 8 Portunus
Portugal
 capital/largest city: 6 Lisbon
 others: 4 Beja, Faro, Ovar **5** Braga, Evora, Olhao, Porto, Viseu **6** Aveiro, Guarda, Leiria, Oporto, Sintra **7** Algarve, Amadora, Bragama, Cascoes, Coimbra, Covilha, Estoril, Funchal, Granada, Setubal **8** Barreiro, Portimao **9** Lusitania **10** Portalegre **14** Vila Nova de Gaia
  Roman city: 10 Portus Cale
 school: 5 Minho **6** Aveiro, Lisbon, Oporto **7** Coimbra
 division: 3 Goa **4** Tejo, Tete **5** Beira, Evora, Macao, Minho, Timor **6** Azores, Loanda **7** Algarve, Madeira **8** Alemteho, Rebatejo **9** Cape Verde **10** Mozambique **11** Estremadura
  Roman district: 9 Lusitania
 measure: 2 pe **4** bota, moio, vara **5** almud, fanga, geira, linha, milha **6** almude, covado **7** alquier, ferrado, selamin **8** alqueire
 monetary unit: 3 avo, rei **4** peca, real **5** conto, crown, dobra, indio, justo, rupia **6** escudo, macuta, octave, pataca, testad, tostao, vintem **7** angalar, centavo, crusado, miereis, testone **8** equipaga, johannes
 weight: 4 onca, once **5** libra, marco **6** arroba **7** arratel **9** excropulo
 island: 6 Azores **7** Madeira **8** Terceira
 mountain: 4 Acor, Lapa **5** Gerez, Marao, Mousa **6** Bornes, Peneda **7** Larouco **8** Caramulo **9** Caldeirao, Monchique **14** Serra da Estrela
 highest point: 11 Pico da Serra
 river: 3 Sor, Tua **4** Lima, Mino, Mira, Sado, Seda, Tago, Tajo, Tejo, Vara **5** Douro, Duero, Le goa, Micha, Minho, Sabar, Tagus, Vouga, Zatas **6** Cavado, Chanca, Quarto, Tamega, Zezere **7** Mondego, Selamin, Sorraia **8** Quadiana, Tonelada
 ocean: 8 Atlantic
 physical feature:
  bay: 7 Setubal
  cape: 4 Roca **7** Mondego **8** Espichel **9** St Vincent
  peninsula: 7 Iberian
  port: 4 Faro **6** Aveiro, Lisbon, Oporto **7** Leixoes
 people: 4 Celt, Moor **7** Iberian **10** Portuguese
  artist: 7 Pereira **9** Goncalves **13** Soares dos Reis
  author: 5 Dinis **6** Camoes, Vieira **7** Garrett, Vicente **9** Deus-Ramos
  explorer: 3 Cam, Cao **4** Dias, Diaz

6 Cabral, Da Gama **7** Almeida **8** Magellan **11** Albuquerque **23** Prince Henry the Navigator
  king: 6 Manuel, Philip, Sancho **7** Alfonso **9** Ferdinand, Sebastian
  leader: 5 Eanes **6** Dombal, Soares **7** Caetano, Carmona, Salazar, Spinola
  queen: 5 Maria **9** Elizabeth
 language: 10 Portuguese
 religion: 13 Roman Catholic
 place:
  church: 5 Jesus **6** Christ **11** Os Jeronimos, Sao Lourenco **12** Old Cathedral **13** Santa Engracia **16** Sao Vicente de Fora
  city square: 15 Praca do Comercio
  dam: 6 Belver, Idanha **13** Castelo do Bode
  fortress-church: 12 Leco do Bailio
  monastery: 8 Alcobaca **12** Hieronymites **20** Santa Maria da Victoria
  monument: 11 Discoveries
  museum: 13 Soares dos Reis
  palace: 6 Cintra
  shrine: 6 Fatima
  former colony: 3 Goa **5** Macad, Macao, Timor **6** Angola **7** Sao Tome **8** Principe, St Thomas **9** Cape Verde **10** Mozambique **12** Guinea Bissau
 feature:
  song: 4 fado
 food:
  dish: 8 bacalhau, bucellas **10** calcavella **11** carcavellos
  sausage: 8 linguica
  wine: 4 port **7** madeira

Portuguese Guinea *see* **12** Guinea-Bissau

Portuguese West Africa *see* **6** Angola

Portunus
 origin: 5 Roman
 god of: 5 ports **7** harbors
posada 3 inn **12** halting place
pose 3 air, set **4** cast, mien **5** group, order, state, style **6** line up, stance, submit **7** advance, arrange, bearing, bring up, posture, present, propose, show off, suggest **8** attitude, carriage, position, propound, set forth, throw out **9** mannerism, postulate **10** put forward

Poseidon
 also: 9 Asphalius
 origin: 5 Greek
 god of: 3 sea
 caused: 11 earthquakes
 father: 6 Cronos
 mother: 4 Rhea
 brother: 4 Zeus
 wife: 10 Amphitrite
 lover: 2 Ge **6** Aethra, Medusa, Thoosa **7** Demeter
 child: 5 Arion **6** Triton **7** Antaeus, Pegasus, Theseus **8** Chrysaor **10** Polyphemus

 symbol: 5 horse **7** trident
 epithet: 11 Ennosigaeus, Hippocurius **12** Prosclystius
 corresponds to: 7 Neptune
poser 5 facer **6** puzzle **7** problem **8** examiner, stickler
posh 4 chic **5** fancy, ritzy, smart, swell **6** chi-chi, classy, deluxe, lavish, swanky **7** elegant, opulent, refined, stylish **9** high-class, luxurious **11** extravagant
position 3 fix, job, put, set **4** duty, pose, post, role, site **5** array, caste, class, locus, lodge, order, place, stand, state **6** career, charge, ground, locate, office, plight, stance, status **7** arrange, deposit, opinion, outlook, posture, situate, station, vantage **8** attitude, capacity, eminence, function, locality, location, prestige, standing **9** condition, elevation, establish, placement, situation, viewpoint **10** assignment, commission, importance, notability, prominence **11** appointment, consequence, disposition, distinction, frame of mind, point of view
position decided upon
 French: 9 parti pris
positive 4 firm, good, real, sure **5** total **6** narrow, useful **7** assured, certain, gainful, helpful **8** absolute, cocksure, complete, decisive, definite, dogmatic, explicit, obdurate, salutary **9** assertive, confident, convinced, effective, immovable, practical, satisfied, veritable **10** applicable, autocratic, beneficial, conclusive, definitive, optimistic, undisputed, undoubting **11** affirmative, cooperative, dead certain, dictatorial, irrefutable, opinionated, overbearing, practicable, progressive, self-assured, serviceable, unequivocal, unqualified **12** confirmatory, constructive, contributory, unchangeable **13** corroborative, thoroughgoing **16** incontrovertible
positively 9 assuredly, certainly, decidedly, literally **10** absolutely, definitely **11** confidently, indubitably **12** emphatically, indisputably, unmistakably, without doubt **13** affirmatively, categorically, unqualifiedly **14** beyond question, unhesitatingly, unquestionably
possess 3 own **4** grab, have, hold **5** boast, enjoy **6** absorb, fixate, obsess, occupy **7** acquire, bedevil, bewitch, command, conquer, consume, control, enchant, overrun **8** dominate, maintain, take over, vanquish **9** fascinate, hypnotize, influence, mesmerize
Possessed, The
 author: 16 Fyodor Dostoevsky
 character: 5 Marya, Pyotr **6** Shatov **7** Nikolay **16** Varvara Stavrogin **17** Stepan Verhovensky
possession 4 hold **5** asset, poise, title

6 effect, owning **7** command, control, control, custody, tenancy **8** calmness, coolness, dominion, province, resource **9** belonging, composure, occupancy, ownership, placidity, sangfroid, territory **10** equanimity, even temper, occupation, possessing **11** equilibrium, self-control **12** accoutrement, protectorate

possibility 4 hope, odds, risk **6** chance, gamble, hazard **7** promise **8** prospect **9** prospects **10** likelihood **11** contingency, eventuality, feasibility, probability, workability **12** potentiality **14** practicability

possible 8 credible, feasible, workable **9** potential, thinkable **10** achievable, admissible, attainable, cognizable, compatible, contingent, imaginable, manageable, obtainable, reasonable **11** conceivable, performable, practicable **12** hypothetical

possibly 5 at all, maybe **6** mayhap **7** could be, perhaps **8** in any way, normally **9** at the most, perchance **10** by any means, God willing **11** conceivably

post 2 PX **3** fix, job, put, set **4** base, beat, camp, pale, part, pile, pole, role, seat, send, spot, work **5** brace, house, lodge, place, put up, round, shaft, stake **6** advise, column, inform, locate, notify, office, picket, report, settle, splint, tack up **7** apprise, declare, install, mission, publish, quarter, routine, situate, station, support, upright **8** acquaint, announce, capacity, disclose, exchange, fasten up, function, instruct, mainstay, position, proclaim **9** advertise, broadcast, circulate, enlighten, establish, make known, situation **10** assignment, settlement

postdate 6 follow **7** succeed **9** come after

poster 4 bill, sign **6** notice **7** placard **8** bulletin **13** advertisement

posterior 3 bum, can **4** back, butt, prat, rear, rump, seat, tail, tush **5** fanny, stern, tushy **6** behind, bottom, caudal, dorsal, hinder **7** keister **8** backside, buttocks, derriere, hindmost, rearward **9** aftermost

posterity 5 heirs, issue, young **6** family **7** descent, history, lineage, progeny **8** children **9** offspring **10** succession, successors **11** descendants

post hoc, ergo propter hoc 29 after this therefore because of it
  describes: 14 logical fallacy

Posthumus, Leonatus
  character in: 9 Cymbeline
  author: 11 Shakespeare

Postman Always Rings Twice, The
  director: 10 Tay Garnett
  based on story by: 10 James M Cain
  cast: 10 Hume Cronym, Lana Turner **12** John Garfield **13** Cecil Kellaway

postpone 4 stay **5** defer, delay, table, waive **6** put off, remand, shelve **7** adjourn, lay over, reserve, suspend

postponement 4 stay **5** delay **6** recess **7** tabling **8** abeyance, deferral **9** deferment, extension **10** suspension

postscript 2 ps **5** rider **7** codicil **8** addendum **10** attachment

postulate 5 axiom, guess **6** assume, hazard, submit, theory **7** premise, presume, propose, surmise, theorem **8** put forth, theorize **9** speculate **10** assumption, conjecture, hypothesis, presuppose **11** hypothesize, presumption

posture 3 air, set **4** case, mien, mood, pose, post, tone **5** phase, place, shape, state, tenor **6** aspect, stance, status **7** bearing, contour, station **8** attitude, carriage, position, standing **9** condition, situation **11** predicament **12** circumstance

Postvorta
  form: 5 nymph
  member of: 7 Camenae
  knowledge of: 4 past

posy 5 bloom, motto **6** flower, phrase **7** blossom, bouquet, corsage, garland, nosegay

pot 3 pan **4** ruin **5** crock, kitty **6** vessel **9** container, marijuana **11** rack and ruin
  Spanish: 4 olla

potable 3 ale **5** clean, drink, water **6** liquor **8** beverage, quencher **9** drinkable

potage 4 soup **9** thick soup

potassium
  chemical symbol: 1 K

potato 16 Solanum tuberosum
  varieties: 3 air, yam **4** duck, swan, wild, Zulu **5** Idaho, Irish, Maine, rural, swamp, sweet, white **6** Russet **7** Burbank, epicure, prairie, Telinga
  dish: 4 chip **5** baked, salad **6** mashed **8** au gratin **9** lyonnaise, scalloped **11** french fries **12** baked stuffed

Potawatomi
  language family: 9 Algonkian **10** Algonquian
  location: 4 Ohio **6** Kansas **7** Indiana **8** Illinois, Michigan, Oklahoma **9** Wisconsin
  leader: 7 Pontiac
  united with: 6 Ojibwa, Ottawa **7** Ojibway

Potemkin
  director: 17 Sergei Eisenstein
  cast: 14 Vladimir Barsky **16** Alexander Antonov **17** Grigori Alexandrov
  famous segment: 11 Odessa Steps

potency 3 vis **5** force, power **6** energy **8** efficacy, strength, virility, vitality

potent 3 solid, tough **6** mighty, strong **7** dynamic **8** forceful, forcible, powerful, vigorous **9** effective, operative **10** compelling, convincing, formidable,

impressive, persuasive **11** efficacious, influential **12** overpowering

potentate 4 lord **5** chief, mogul, ruler **6** prince, satrap, sultan **7** emperor, monarch **8** overlord, suzerain **9** chieftain, sovereign

potential 6 covert, hidden, latent **7** dormant, lurking, passive **8** implicit, possible **9** concealed, quiescent, unexerted **10** unapparent, unrealized **11** conceivable, undisclosed, unexpressed

potentiality 7 ability **10** capability **13** possibilities

potentially
  Latin: 7 in posse

pother 3 ado **4** fuss, stir, to-do **6** bustle, flurry, hustle, tumult **8** activity **9** agitation, commotion

Pothos
  companion of: 9 Aphrodite
  personifies: 6 desire **7** longing

potion 4 brew, dram **5** draft, tonic **6** elixir, mixture, philter **8** libation, potation **10** concoction

Potlatch people see **8** Kwakiutl

Pot of Gold, The
  author: 7 Plautus

Potok, Chaim
  author of: 9 The Chosen **10** The Promise, Wanderings **11** Davita's Harp **15** The Book of Lights **16** My Name Is Asher Lev, Old Men at Midnight

potpourri 4 hash, mess, olio, stew **6** jumble, medley, mosaic, motley **7** farrago, goulash, melange, mixture **8** mishmash, pastiche **9** patchwork **10** hodgepodge, miscellany, salmagundi **11** gallimaufry, olla podrida

pottage 4 soup, stew **6** brewis **8** porridge

Potter, Beatrix
  author of: 11 (The Tale of) Peter Rabbit **21** The Tailor of Gloucester

potter's field 8 boneyard, cemetery **9** graveyard **12** burial ground **13** burying ground

pottery 5 china **8** clayware, crockery **11** ceramic ware, earthenware

pouch 3 bag, kit, sac **4** sack **5** purse **6** pocket, wallet **7** handbag, satchel **8** carryall, ditty bag, reticule, rucksack **9** container **10** pocketbook, receptacle

Poulenc, Francis
  born: 5 Paris **6** France
  member of: 6 Les Six, The Six
  composer of: 9 Les Biches **13** The Carmelites **22** Dialogues des Carmelites

poultice 7 plaster **8** dressing **10** medicament

poultry 3 hen **4** cock, duck, fowl, swan **5** capon, geese, goose, quail **6** grouse, layers, pigeon, turkey **7** chicken, peacock, rooster **8** pheasant **9** partridge **10** guinea fowl

breed: 6 Ancona, Bantam **7** Cornish, Dorking, Leghorn **9** Wyandotte **12** Plymouth Rock **14** Rhode Island Red
disease: 3 pip **4** roup, tick
farm: 7 hennery
house: 4 coop

pounce 4 jump, leap **5** fly at, swoop **6** ambush, dash at, jump at, plunge, snatch, spring **8** downrush, fall upon, surprise

pound 4 bang, beat, drub, drum, maul **5** clomp, clout, crush, grind, march, paste, smack, stomp, throb, thump, tramp **6** batter, bruise, cudgel, hammer, pummel, strike, thrash, thwack, wallop **7** clobber, crumble, pulsate, thunder, trounce **8** lambaste **9** fustigate, palpitate, pulverize **13** sixteen ounces
abbreviation: 2 lb

Pound, Ezra
author of: 6 Cantos **8** Personae **11** Exultations, Pisan Cantos

pound troy
abbreviation: 3 lb t

pour 3 tap **4** drip, drop, flow, gush, ooze, rain, seep, slop **5** drain, flood, issue, spill, spout **6** decant, deluge, drench, effuse, squirt, stream **7** cascade, draw off, dribble, lade out **15** rain cats and dogs **16** come down in sheets **17** come down in buckets

pourboire 3 tip **8** gratuity
literally: 11 for drinking

pourparler 29 informal preliminary conference
literally: 10 for talking

Poussin, Nicholas
born: 6 France **10** Les Andelys
artwork: 10 The Seasons **14** Birth of Bacchus, St John on Patmos **17** Bacchanalian Revel **18** The Burial of Phocion **19** The Poet's Inspiration **20** The Arcadian Shepherds **23** Landscape with Polyphemus, The Holy Family on the Steps **27** The Adoration of the Golden Calf

pou sto 14 place to stand on, where I may stand **16** base of operations

pout 4 crab, fret, fume, mope, sulk **5** brood, frown, lower, scowl **6** glower
French: 4 moue

poverty 4 lack, need, want **6** dearth, penury **7** beggary, deficit, paucity **8** scarcity, shortage **9** indigence, neediness, pauperism, privation **10** bankruptcy, deficiency, insolvency, meagerness, mendicancy **11** destitution **13** insufficiency, pennilessness **14** impoverishment

poverty-stricken 4 poor **5** broke, needy **8** indigent **9** destitute, penniless **10** down and out

powder 4 dust, talc **5** emery **6** pollen, talcum **7** crumble **9** pulverize
antiseptic: 6 formin **7** aristol
applier: 4 puff

cookery: 4 soda
cosmetic: 5 blush, rouge **7** compact
poisonous: 5 robin

powder-blue 5 azure **6** pastel **7** skyblue **8** pale-blue **9** light-blue, robin's egg

powdery 5 dusty, mealy **6** chalky, floury, grated, ground, milled **7** crushed, pestled **8** shredded **10** comminuted, pulverized, triturated

Powell, Dick
real name: 14 Richard E Powell
born: 14 Mountain View AR
wife: 11 June Allyson **12** Joan Blondell
costar: 10 Ruby Keeler
roles: 7 Mrs Mike **8** Cornered **12** Johnny O'Clock **13** Murder My Sweet **15** Footlight Parade **17** Fortysecond Street **32** Gold Diggers of Nineteen Thirty-Three

Powell, Jane
real name: 12 Suzanne Burce
born: 10 Portland OR
roles: 5 Irene **12** Royal Wedding **13** A Date with Judy **27** Seven Brides for Seven Brothers

Powell, Michael
codirector: 17 Emeric Pressburger
director of: 11 The Red Shoes **14** Black Narcissus **16** Stairway to Heaven

Powell, SR
creator/artist of: 22 Sheena Queen of the Jungle

Powell, William
born: 12 Pittsburgh PA
wife: 13 Carole Lombard
costar: 8 Myrna Loy
roles: 10 Philo Vance, The Thin Man **11** Nick Charles **12** My Man Godfrey **13** Mister Roberts **14** Life with Father **16** The Great Ziegfeld **22** How to Marry a Millionaire

power 4 gift, sway **5** brawn, force, might, right, ruler, skill, vigor **6** energy, genius, muscle, status, talent **7** faculty, license, operate, potency, quality **8** activate, aptitude, capacity, energize, iron grip, pressure, prestige, property, strength, vitality **9** attribute, authority, endowment, influence, puissance **10** capability, competence
Latin: 3 vis

Power, Tyrone
born: 12 Cincinnati OH
wife: 9 Annabella **14** Linda Christian
roles: 10 Jesse James **12** Blood and Sand **13** The Razor's Edge **14** Nightmare Alley, The Mark of Zorro **15** The Sun Also Rises **18** Captain from Castile

powerful 5 hardy, husky, stout **6** brawny, cogent, mighty, moving, potent, robust, sturdy **7** intense, rousing **8** athletic, emphatic, exciting, forceful, incisive, muscular, stalwart, vigorous

9 effective, energetic, herculean, strapping **10** able-bodied, commanding, invincible

powerhouse 9 strongman **10** power plant **15** generating plant

powerless 4 weak **6** feeble, infirm **7** unarmed **8** crippled, disabled, feckless, helpless, impotent **9** incapable, pregnable, prostrate **10** impuissant, vulnerable, weaponless **11** debilitated, defenseless, immobilized **13** incapacitated

powerlessness 8 debility, weakness **9** impotence, inability, infirmity **10** enervation, feebleness, inadequacy, incapacity **12** helplessness, incapability, inefficiency **13** vulnerability

powers that be 9 higher-ups **10** government **11** authorities **13** establishment **14** administration

Powhatan
language family: 9 Algonkian **10** Algonquian
tribe: 11 Confederacy
location: 8 Atlantic, Maryland, Virginia
leader: 8 Powhatan **11** Opechancano **13** Wahunsonacock
member: 10 Pocahontas

powwow 4 meet, talk **5** forum **6** caucus, confer, huddle, parley **7** consult, convene, council, discuss, meeting, palaver **8** assembly, colloquy, conclave, congress **9** discourse, interview **10** colloquium, conference, convention, discussion, round table **12** consultation

practicable 6 doable, viable **8** feasible, possible, workable **9** practical **10** achievable, attainable, functional

practical 4 able **5** solid, sound **6** expert, useful, versed **7** skilled, trained, veteran, working **8** seasoned, sensible, skillful **9** efficient, judicious, practiced, pragmatic, qualified, realistic **10** functional, hardheaded, instructed, proficient, systematic, unromantic **11** down-to-earth, experienced, pragmatical, serviceable, utilitarian **12** accomplished, businesslike, matter-of-fact **13** unsentimental

practical joke 4 jape **5** caper, prank, stunt, trick

practically 6 all but, almost, nearly **8** actually, in effect **9** basically, in the main, just about, virtually **11** essentially **13** fundamentally, substantially

practice 2 do **3** use, way **4** deed, mode, play, rule, ruse, ways, wont **5** apply, dodge, drill, habit, train, trick, usage **6** action, custom, device, effect, follow, manner, method, pursue, ritual, work at **7** conduct, fashion, perform, process, qualify, routine, utilize **8** carry out, engage in, exercise, live up to, maneuver, rehearse, tendency, training **9** execution, operation, perform in, procedure, rehearsal, seasoning, set to work, turn to use **10** discipline, observance, prepare for, repetition **11** application, be engaged in, performance, preparation

Practice, The
  network: **3** ABC
  creator: **12** David E Kelley
  cast: **11** James Spader (Alan Shore), Steve Harris (Eugene Young) **13** Camryn Manheim (Ellenor Frutt), Kelli Williams (Lindsay Dole Donnell), Marla Sokoloff (Lucy Hatcher) **14** Dylan McDermott (Bobby Donnell), Lara Flynn Boyle (Helen Gamble), William Shatner (Denny Crane) **15** Lisa Gay Hamilton (Rebecca Washington) **16** Michael Badalucco (Jimmy Berluti)

practiced 4 able, fine **5** adept **6** adroit, expert **7** capable, drilled, pursued, skilled, trained **8** masterly, polished, seasoned, skillful, worked at **9** competent, engaged in, masterful, qualified, rehearsed **10** cultivated, proficient **11** experienced, prepared for **12** accomplished

practice sorcery 5 charm **7** bewitch, conjure, enchant **9** work magic **10** cast a spell

practitioner 6 doctor **7** dentist **9** performer **12** professional

pragmatic 5 sober **8** sensible **9** hardnosed, practical, realistic **10** hardheaded, hard-boiled **11** down-to-earth, utilitarian **12** businesslike, matter-of-fact, unidealistic **13** materialistic, unsentimental

Praia
  capital of: **9** Cape Verde

prairie 3 bay **5** llano, pampa, plain **6** camass, meadow, steppe **7** quamash **9** grassland
  apple: **9** breadroot
  berry: **9** trampillo
  chicken: **6** grouse
  dog: **6** gopher, marmot
  schooner: **12** covered wagon
  state: **8** Illinois
  wolf: **6** coyote

Prairie, The
  author: **19** James Fenimore Cooper
  character: **4** Inez **9** Dr Battius, Ellen Wade, Hard-Heart, Paul Hover **10** Esther Bush **11** Abiram White, Ishmael Bush, Natty Bumppo **16** Captain Middleton

Prairie State
  nickname of: **8** Illinois

praise 4 laud, tout **5** cheer, exalt, extol, honor **6** esteem, eulogy, hurrah, regard, revere **7** acclaim, applaud, approve, build up, commend, glorify, plaudit, respect, root for, tribute, worship **8** accolade, applause, approval, encomium, eulogize, venerate **9** adoration, celebrate, good words, lauda-

tion, panegyric **10** admiration, compliment, panegyrize **11** approbation, compliments, testimonial **12** appreciation, commendation, congratulate **14** congratulation
  Hebrew: **6** hallel

praise be to God
  Latin: **7** laus Deo

praiseful 8 praising **9** extolling, laudatory **10** plauditory **12** commendatory **13** complimentary

praiseworthiness 5 merit **10** excellence **12** admirability, desirability **14** commendability

praiseworthy 4 fine **6** worthy **8** laudable **9** admirable, estimable, excellent, exemplary **11** commendable, meritorious

pram, praam, prahm 4 boat **5** buggy **6** vessel **7** rowboat **8** carriage, stroller **12** perambulator

prance 4 jump, leap, romp, skip **5** bound, caper, dance, frisk, strut, vault **6** bounce, cavort, frolic, gambol, spring **7** swagger

prank 4 joke, lark **5** antic, caper, spoof, stunt, trick **6** gambol **8** escapade, mischief **9** horseplay **10** shenanigan, tomfoolery

prate 3 gab, yak **4** blab, brag, chat, crow, talk **5** boast **6** babble, gabble, jabber **7** blabber, chatter, prattle, twaddle, twattle

Prathet Thai *see* **8** Thailand

prattle 3 gab, yak **4** blab **5** prate **6** babble, gabble, hot air, jabber **7** blather, chatter, twaddle **8** cackling, chitchat, gabbling **9** gibbering, jabbering

Pravda 16 Russian newspaper
  literally: **5** truth

pray 3 beg, bid, sue **4** urge **5** cry to, plead **7** beseech, entreat, implore, request, solicit **8** call upon, invocate, petition **9** importune **10** supplicate

prayer 6 litany, orison, praise **7** worship **9** adoration **12** thanksgiving **13** glorification

prayerful 4 holy **5** godly, pious **6** devout, solemn **8** reverent **9** pietistic, religious, spiritual **10** worshipful **11** reverential

prayers 4 hope, plea, suit **5** dream **6** appeal **7** request **8** entreaty, petition **10** aspiration, invocation **11** beseechment **12** solicitation, supplication

prayer service 9 devotions **13** prayer meeting **14** worship service

pray for us
  Latin: **11** ora pro nobis

pray to 3 beg **5** plead **7** address, entreat, worship **8** call upon, petition, venerate **10** supplicate

preach 4 urge **6** advise, exhort **7** counsel, declare, expound, profess **8** admonish, advocate, homilize, proclaim,

stand for **9** discourse, hold forth, preachify, prescribe, pronounce, propagate, sermonize **10** evangelize, promulgate

preacher 5 vicar **6** curate, parson, pastor **8** chaplain, homilist, minister, reverend, sky pilot **9** churchman, clergyman **10** evangelist, prebendary, sermonizer **12** ecclesiastic **13** man of the cloth

preachy 8 didactic, pedantic **10** moralistic, moralizing

prearranged 7 planned **10** calculated, deliberate, purposeful **11** intentional **12** premeditated

pre-Cambrian 5 Azoic **6** Eozoic **7** primary **10** Archeozoic **11** Proterozoic

precarious 5 risky, shaky **6** chancy, unsafe **7** dubious **8** alarming, critical, doubtful, insecure, perilous, sinister, ticklish, unstable, unsteady **9** hazardous, uncertain **10** touch-and-go, unreliable, vulnerable **12** questionable, uncontrolled, undependable **13** problematical

precaution 4 care **7** caution, defense **8** prudence, security, wariness **9** foresight, provision, safeguard **10** protection **11** carefulness, forethought, heedfulness **12** anticipation **14** circumspection

precede 8 antecede, antedate, go before **9** go ahead of **10** come before

precedence, precedency 8 priority **10** importance, preference, prevalence **11** antecedence, preeminence **12** predominance, preexistence

precedent 5 model **7** example, pattern **8** standard **9** criterion, guideline

preceding 5 prior **6** former **7** earlier **8** anterior, previous **9** aforesaid, foregoing **10** antecedent, first-named, precursory **11** preexistent, preliminary **14** abovementioned, aforementioned, first-mentioned

precept 3 law **4** bull, code, rule **5** axiom, canon, edict, maxim, motto, tenet, truth, ukase **6** byword, decree, dictum **7** dictate, mandate, statute **8** standard, teaching **9** ordinance, principle, yardstick **10** regulation **11** commandment, declaration

preceptor 5 coach, tutor **6** mentor **7** advisor, teacher **8** director **9** admonitor, counselor, principal **10** headmaster **12** headmistress

precincts 7 suburbs **8** environs **9** districts, outskirts **10** boundaries **12** subdivisions **15** surrounding area

precious 4 dear, rare **5** fussy, sweet **6** adored, choice, costly, dainty, prissy, prized, valued **7** beloved, darling, finical, finicky, lovable **8** adorable, affected, uncommon, valuable **9** cherished, expensive, exquisite, priceless, treasured **10** fastidious, high-priced, invaluable, meticulous, particular **11**

beyond price, inestimable, overrefined, pretentious

precipice 4 crag **5** bluff, cliff, ledge **8**
headland, palisade **9** cliff edge, declivity **10** escarpment

precipitate 4 cast, hurl, rash, spur **5**
drive, fling, hasty, throw **6** abrupt,
hasten, launch, let fly, propel, rushed,
speedy, thrust **7** advance, bring on,
hurried, quicken, speed up **8** catapult,
expedite, headlong, reckless **9** discharge, foolhardy, impetuous, imprudent, impulsive **10** accelerate, incautious **11** thoughtless

precipitation 4 hail, rain, rush, snow
5 haste, sleet **8** rainfall, rashness **9**
hastiness **11** impetuously

precipitous 5 hasty, sharp, sheer,
steep **6** abrupt **9** impetuous

precis 5 brief **6** apercu, digest, resume,
sketch **7** epitome, outline, rundown,
summary **8** abstract, synopsis **10**
abridgment, compendium **12** condensation **14** recapitulation

precise 4 true **5** exact, fussy, rigid **6**
strict **7** careful, express, finicky, literal
8 accurate, clear-cut, definite, distinct,
explicit, incisive, specific **9** unbending
10 fastidious, inflexible, meticulous,
particular, to the point **11** painstaking,
unequivocal

precision 5 rigor **8** accuracy, fidelity **9**
attention, exactness **11** factualness,
preciseness **12** authenticity, truthfulness **14** meticulousness

preclude 3 bar, dam **4** balk, curb, foil,
stop **5** avert, avoid, block, check, debar, deter **6** arrest, hamper, hinder,
thwart **7** head off, inhibit, prevent **8**
stave off **9** forestall, frustrate **11** nip
in the bud

preclusion 9 exclusion, restraint **10**
prevention

precocious 3 apt **5** quick, smart **6**
bright, clever, gifted, mature **8** advanced **9** brilliant

preconception 4 bias **6** notion **9** fixed
idea, prejudice **11** prejudgment, presumption **14** predisposition

precursor 4 mark, omen, sign **5** token,
usher **6** herald **7** portent, symptom,
warning **8** vanguard **9** harbinger,
messenger **10** antecedent, forerunner
11 predecessor

precursory 5 prior **8** anterior, previous
9 precedent **10** antecedent **11** preexistent

predaceous, predacious 9 predatory,
rapacious **10** meat-eating **11** carnivorous, flesh-eating

predate 7 precede **8** antecede, antedate, go before

predatory 8 thievish **9** larcenous, marauding, pillaging, piratical, rapacious,
raptorial, vulturine **10** plunderous,
predacious

predecessor 7 forbear **8** ancestor,
forebear, foregoer **10** antecedent, forefather, forerunner

predestination 4 fate **6** kismet **7** destiny, fortune **8** God's will **10** providence **13** inevitability, preordination
16 predetermination

predetermined 5 fated **7** decided,
planned **8** destined **10** calculated, deliberate, preplanned **11** intentional,
prearranged, predestined **12** foreor-
dained, premeditated

predicament 3 fix, jam **4** bind, mess
5 pinch **6** corner, crisis, pickle, plight,
scrape, strait **7** dilemma, trouble
8 hot water, quandary **9** imbroglio,
sad plight **10** difficulty, perplexity

predicate 4 base, real, rest, true **5**
found, imply **6** affirm, assert **7** commend, connote, declare **8** proclaim

predict 4 omen **5** augur **6** divine **7** betoken, foresee, presage **8** envision,
forecast, foretell, prophesy **10** anticipate **13** prognosticate

prediction 6 augury **7** portent **8** forecast, prophecy **10** divination **11** declaration, foretelling, soothsaying **12** announcement, anticipation,
proclamation **13** crystal gazing **15**
prognostication

predilection 4 bent, bias, love **5**
fancy, favor, taste **6** desire, hunger,
liking, relish **7** leaning **8** appetite,
fondness, penchant, tendency **9** prejudice, proneness **10** attraction, partiality, preference, proclivity, propensity
11 inclination **13** prepossession **14**
predisposition

predispose 4 bias, lure, sway, urge **5**
tempt **6** entice, induce, prompt, seduce **7** dispose, incline, win over **8**
persuade **9** encourage, influence, prejudice

predisposed 3 apt **5** given, prone **8**
inclined

predisposition 7 leaning **8** tendency
11 inclination

predominance 7 command, control **8**
currency **9** dominance, supremacy **10**
ascendancy, importance, prevalence
11 preeminence, superiority **12** universality

predominant 4 main **5** chief, major **6**
potent, ruling, strong **7** leading, supreme **8** dominant, forceful, powerful,
reigning, vigorous **9** ascendant, important, paramount, sovereign **11** controlling, influential **13** authoritative

predominate 4 lead **7** prevail **8** dominate

predominating 5 chief **6** ruling **8**
dominant, superior **9** principal **10**
commanding, prevailing **11** controlling, predominant **13** authoritative

preeminence 9 greatness, supremacy
10 ascendancy, importance, leader-

ship, notability, prominence **11** distinction, superiority **12** predominance

preeminent 4 best **5** famed **6** famous
7 eminent, honored, supreme **8** dominant, foremost, greatest, peerless, renowned, superior **9** matchless, paramount, unequaled, unrivaled **10**
celebrated, consummate **11** illustrious,
predominant, unsurpassed **12** incomparable, second to none, unparalleled
13 distinguished
French: **13** par excellence

preempt 4 take **5** seize, usurp **8** arrogate, take over **10** commandeer, confiscate **11** appropriate, expropriate

preen 3 pin **4** perk, trim **5** adorn,
dress, groom, plume, pride, primp,
prink **6** brooch, smooth
wings: **4** whet

preexistent 5 prior **8** anterior, previous **9** precedent **10** antecedent, precursory

preface 4 open **5** begin, proem, start **6**
launch **7** prelude **8** commence, foreword, initiate, lead into, overture, preamble, prologue **9** introduce **12** introduction

prefer 3 opt **4** file **5** adopt, elect, exalt,
fancy, favor, lodge, offer **6** select, take
to, tender **7** dignify, elevate, ennoble,
fix upon, pick out, present, proffer,
promote **8** graduate, set forth **9** single
out

preference 4 bent, bias, pick **5** fancy
6 liking, option **7** leaning **8** favoring,
priority **9** advantage, prejudice, proneness, selection, supremacy **10** ascendancy, partiality, precedence, proclivity,
propensity **11** first choice, inclination
12 predilection **13** predomination **14**
predisposition
French: **4** gout

prefigure 4 hint, type **6** shadow, typify **7** foresee, imagine, presage, suggest **9** adumbrate **10** foreshadow

pregnant 4 full, rich **6** fecund, filled,
gravid **7** copious, fertile, fraught, replete, seminal, teeming, weighty **8**
forceful, fruitful, prolific **9** abounding,
expecting, gestating, important, luxuriant, momentous, plenteous, potential,
with child, with young **10** impressive,
life-giving, meaningful, parturient,
productive, suggestive **11** having a
baby, proliferous, provocative, significant **12** fructiferous, in a family way
French: **8** enceinte

prehistoric 3 old **7** ancient **10** immemorial
continent: **8** Atlantis
epoch: **6** Eocene **7** Miocene **8** Plio-
cene **9** Oligocene, Paleocene **11**
Pleistocene
era: **8** Cenozoic, Mesozoic **9** Paleozoic **10** Archeozoic **11** Proterozoic
implement: **4** celt **6** eolith
period: **7** Neogene, Permian **8** Cam-

brian, Devonian, Jurassic, Silurian, Triassic **9** Paleogene **10** Cretaceous, Ordovician, Quaternary
reptile: 8 dinosaur

prehistoric era 6 Ice Age **8** Cenozoic, Jurassic, Mesozoic, Triassic **9** Paleozoic **10** Cenomanian, Cretaceous **11** Precambrian **15** Upper Cretaceous **16** Pleistocene Epoch

prehistoric man *see* **8** early man

prejudice 3 ill, mar **4** bias, harm, hurt, loss, sway **5** slant, spoil, taint **6** damage, impair, infect, injure, injury, poison **7** bigotry **8** jaundice **9** detriment **10** favoritism, impairment, partiality, predispose, unfairness **11** contaminate, intolerance, prejudgment **12** disadvantage, one-sidedness, predilection **13** preconception **14** discrimination, predisposition

prejudiced 6 biased, unfair, unjust **7** bigoted, slanted **9** arbitrary **10** intolerant **11** close-minded, opinionated **12** narrow-minded

prejudicial 3 bad **6** biased **7** harmful, hurtful **8** damaging, inimical, sinister **9** injurious **11** deleterious, detrimental

prelate 5 abbot **6** bishop, cleric **9** churchman, clergy man **12** ecclesiastic

preliminary 9 prelusive, prelusory **10** initiatory, precursory, prefactory **11** preparative, preparatory **12** introductory

prelude 7 opening, preface **8** overture, preamble, prologue **9** beginning **11** preliminary, preparation **12** introduction

premature 3 raw **5** green, hasty **6** callow, unripe **7** too soon, unready **8** abortive, ill-timed, immature, previous, too early, untimely **9** embryonic, overhasty, unfledged, unhatched, vestigial **10** incomplete, unprepared **11** inopportune, precipitate, rudimentary, undeveloped **12** unseasonable

premeditated 7 planned, plotted, studied, willful **8** intended **9** conscious, contrived, voluntary **10** calculated, considered, deliberate, predevised, purposeful **11** in cold blood, intentional, prearranged, predesigned **13** predetermined **22** with malice aforethought

premeditation 4 plan **6** design **7** purpose **11** calculation, forethought, preplanning **12** deliberation

premier 3 bet **4** head **5** chief, first **6** oldest **7** leading, supreme **8** earliest, foremost **9** principal **13** prime minister

Preminger, Otto
director of: 5 Laura **11** Carmen Jones **16** Anatomy of a Murder

premise 6 theory **8** argument **9** postulate, principle **10** assumption, hypothesis **11** presumption, proposition, supposition **14** presupposition

premises 4 site **8** environs, property, vicinity **9** precincts

premium 4 gain, gift **5** award, bonus, prize **6** bounty, return, reward **7** benefit, payment **8** priority **9** high value, incentive **10** great stock, recompense, reparation **11** overpayment **12** appreciation, compensation, inflated rate, remuneration **13** consideration, encouragement

premonition 4 omen, sign **5** hunch, token **6** augury **7** auspice, feeling, inkling, portent, presage **9** foretoken **10** foreboding, indication, prediction **11** forewarning **12** presentiment

Prendergast, Maurice Brazil
born: 6 Canada **7** St John's **12** Newfoundland
artwork: 6 Dieppe **8** Seashore **11** Picnic Grove **12** The Promenade **16** Ponte della Paglia **17** Along the Boulevard, Four Girls in Meadow **24** Umbrellas in the Rain Venice

Prentice, John
creator/artist of: 8 Rip Kirby

preoccupation 9 immersion, obsession **10** absorption, detachment, dreaminess, employment **11** abstraction, involvement **16** absent-mindedness

preoccupied 6 absent, dreamy **8** absorbed, immersed, involved, obsessed **9** engrossed, wrapped up **10** abstracted, distracted **12** absent-minded

preoccupy 6 absorb, arrest, obsess, take up, wrap up **7** engross, immerse **9** fascinate

preparation 8 prudence, readying **9** foresight, preparing, provision, safeguard **10** precaution **11** expectation, forethought **12** anticipation

preparations 5 plans **7** elixirs **8** guidance, measures, mixtures, training, tutelage **9** dressings, education, seasoning, tinctures **11** concoctions, confections **12** arrangements **13** preliminaries, prepared foods, prescriptions **14** qualifications

prepare 3 fix **5** adapt, prime, ready **7** arrange, be ready, provide **8** get ready **9** make ready, rearrange, take steps

prepared 4 done **5** fixed, ready **6** cooked, primed **7** planned **8** arranged, finished **9** made ready, rehearsed **11** provided for

prepayment 6 credit **7** advance **9** allowance **11** downpayment

preponderance, preponderancy 4 bulk, glut, mass **6** excess **7** surfeit, surplus **8** majority, plethora **9** dominance, plurality, profusion **10** domination, lion's share, oversupply, prevalence, redundancy **12** predominance **14** superabundance

preponderant 3 key **4** main **5** chief, first, major, prime **7** highest, leading, primary, supreme **8** dominant, fore-

most, greatest **9** paramount, principal, uppermost **10** prevailing **11** outstanding, predominant

prepossessing 4 nice **7** winsome **8** alluring, charming, engaging, inviting, pleasant, striking **9** beguiling **10** attractive, bewitching, enchanting, entrancing, personable **11** captivating, fascinating, tantalizing

preposterous 5 inane, outre, silly **6** absurd, stupid **7** asinine, bizarre, fatuous, foolish, idiotic **9** imbecilic, laughable, ludicrous **10** irrational, outrageous, ridiculous **11** nonsensical, unthinkable **12** unreasonable

prerequisite 4 need **6** demand **8** demanded, exigency, required **9** called for, condition, de rigueur, essential, mandatory, necessary, necessity, postulate, requisite **10** imperative, sine qua non **11** requirement, stipulation **13** indispensable, qualification

prerogative 3 due **5** claim, grant, right **6** choice, option **7** freedom, liberty, license, warrant **9** advantage, exemption, franchise, privilege **10** birthright

presage 4 bode, omen, osse, sign **5** augur, token **6** augury, herald **7** betoken, portend, portent, predict **8** forecast, foreshow, foretell, indicate **9** foresight **10** foreboding, foreshadow, indication, prediction, prescience, prognostic **11** premonition **12** presentiment

presbyter 5 elder **13** church officer

prescience 7 presage **9** foresight, prevision **13** foreknowledge

prescribe 3 fix, set **4** rule, urge **5** enact, order **6** assign, decree, demand, direct, enjoin, impose, ordain, settle **7** appoint, command, dictate, require, specify **8** advocate, proclaim **9** authorize, establish, institute, legislate, recommend, stipulate

prescribed 3 set **5** fixed **6** thetic **9** formulary

prescript 3 law **4** rule **5** order **7** precept, statute **10** regulation

prescriptive 7 binding **8** demanded, dictated, didactic, required **9** customary, mandatory, requisite **10** compulsory, imperative, obligatory

presence 3 air **4** life, look, mien **5** being, curse, favor, ghost, group, midst **6** aspect, entity, figure, manner, shadow, spirit, vision, wraith **7** bearing, company, eidolon, phantom, specter **8** carriage, charisma, demeanor, features, phantasm, revenant, vitality **9** character, existence **10** apparition, attendance, deportment, expression, lineaments **11** reification, subsistence **12** neighborhood **13** manifestation

presence of mind 6 aplomb **8** calmness, coolness **9** composure, sangfroid

10 equanimity, steadiness **14** self-possession **16** imperturbability

present 2 in **3** fee, now, tip **4** alms, aver, boon, cite, gift, give, here, near, nigh, read, show, tell **5** about, award, frame, grant, offer, state, today **6** accord, allege, assert, at hand, bestow, bounty, call up, chip in, coeval, confer, donate, hand in, impart, legacy, nearby, on hand, recite, relate, render, rooted, submit, summon, supply, tender, turn in **7** advance, bequest, bring on, current, declare, deliver, display, dole out, exhibit, expound, give out, instant, largess, mete out, not away, produce, profess, proffer, propose, provide, recount, vicinal **8** donation, embedded, existent, existing, give away, give over, gratuity, hand over, nowadays, oblation, offering, propound, put forth **9** apprise of, attending, draw forth, endowment, ensconced, hold forth, immediate, implanted, in the room, introduce, make known, not absent, on-the-spot, prevalent, pronounce, surrender, the moment, unremoved **10** asseverate, come up with, contribute, here and now, liberality, perquisite, put forward **11** benefaction, communicate **12** accounted for, bring forward, contemporary, in attendance

presentable 4 chic, so-so **6** decent, modish, not bad, proper **7** stylish **8** becoming, passable, suitable **9** tolerable **10** acceptable, good enough **11** appropriate, fashionable, fit to be seen, respectable

presentation 3 fee, tip **4** boon, gift, show **5** favor, grant, offer **6** bounty **7** advance, display, exhibit, largess, present, proffer **8** bestowal, exposure, gratuity, oblation, offering, overture, proposal **9** unfolding **10** appearance, compliment, disclosure, exhibition, exposition, liberality, production, proffering, submission, unfoldment **11** benefaction, performance, proposition **13** demonstration

presentiment 7 feeling **10** foreboding **11** forewarning, premonition **12** apprehension

presently 3 now **4** anon, soon **7** shortly **8** directly, in a while, this week, this year **9** at present, currently, forth with **10** any time now, before long, pretty soon **11** after a while, at the moment **12** in a short time

French: 11 tout a l'heure

preservation 6 saving **7** defense **9** salvation **10** protection **11** maintenance, safekeeping **12** conservation, safeguarding

preservative 4 salt **5** brine, spice **8** marinade **12** formaldehyde

preserve, preserves 3 can, dry, jam

4 corn, cure, park, salt, save, seal **5** guard, haven, jelly, nurse, put up, smoke, sweet **6** comfit, defend, embalm, foster, freeze, pickle, refuge, season, secure, shield **7** care for, compote, mummify, protect, reserve, shelter **8** conserve, insulate, keep safe, maintain, marinate **9** dehydrate, keep sound, marmalade, safeguard, sanctuary, sweetmeat, watch over **10** confection, keep intact, perpetuate **11** refrigerate, reservation

preside 4 boss, host, rule **5** chair, watch **6** direct, govern, manage **7** command, conduct, control, hostess, oversee **8** chairman, overlook, regulate **9** keep order, supervise **10** administer **11** superintend **12** administrate, take the chair

president, President 4 head **5** ruler **8** chairman **12** chief officer, chief of state, first citizen **14** chief executive **16** commander in chief, executive officer, head of government

President of the United States
first: 16 George Washington
second: 9 John Adams
third: 15 Thomas Jefferson
fourth: 12 James Madison
fifth: 11 James Monroe
sixth: 15 John Quincy Adams
seventh: 13 Andrew Jackson
eighth: 14 Martin Van Buren
ninth: 20 William Henry Harrison
tenth: 9 John Tyler
eleventh: 10 James K Polk
twelfth: 13 Zachary Taylor
thirteenth: 15 Millard Fillmore
fourteenth: 14 Franklin Pierce
fifteenth: 13 James Buchanan
sixteenth: 14 Abraham Lincoln
seventeenth: 13 Andrew Johnson
eighteenth: 13 Ulysses S Grant
nineteenth: 16 Rutherford B Hayes
twentieth: 14 James A Garfield
twenty-first: 17 Chester Alan Arthur
twenty-second: 15 Grover Cleveland
twenty-third: 16 Benjamin Harrison
twenty-fourth: 15 Grover Cleveland
twenty-fifth: 15 William McKinley
twenty-sixth: 17 Theodore Roosevelt
twenty-seventh: 17 William Howard Taft
twenty-eighth: 13 Woodrow Wilson
twenty-ninth: 14 Warren G Harding
thirtieth: 14 Calvin Coolidge
thirty-first: 13 Herbert Hoover
thirty-second: 18 Franklin D Roosevelt
thirty-third: 12 Harry S Truman
thirty-fourth: 17 Dwight D Eisenhower
thirty-fifth: 12 John F Kennedy
thirty-sixth: 14 Lyndon B Johnson
thirty-seventh: 13 Richard M Nixon
thirty-eighth: 11 Gerald R Ford
thirty-ninth: 11 (James E) Jimmy Carter (Jr)

fortieth: 12 Ronald Reagan
forty-first: 10 George (HW) Bush
forty-second: 11 (William Jefferson) Bill Clinton
forty-third: 10 George (W) Bush

President's Analyst, The
director: 16 Theodore J Flicker
cast: 8 Will Geer **11** James Coburn **12** Severn Darden **16** Godfrey Cambridge

preside over 5 chair, guide **6** direct, govern, manage **7** conduct **8** dominate **9** supervise **10** administer **11** superintend

Presley, Elvis Aron
nickname: 7 The King **14** Elvis the Pelvis **15** King of Rock n Roll
born: 6 Tupelo **11** Mississippi
wife: 9 Priscilla
daughter: 9 Lisa Marie
father: 6 Vernon
mother: 6 Gladys
twin brother: 11 Jessie Garon
manager: 16 Colonel Tom Parker
home: 9 Graceland
location: 7 Memphis **9** Tennessee
song: 8 Hound Dog **10** All Shook Up **11** Don't Be Cruel **12** Love Me Tender **13** Jailhouse Rock **14** Blue Suede Shoes **15** Heartbreak Hotel **17** That's All Right Mama
film: 7 G I Blues **9** Loving You **10** Blue Hawaii, King Creole **12** Love Me Tender, Viva Las Vegas **13** Jailhouse Rock

press 2 TV **3** beg, bug, dun, hit, hug, jam, mob, pet, tap, tax **4** army, body, cram, duty, heap, herd, host, iron, mash, mill, pack, prod, push, rush **5** beset, bunch, clasp, crowd, crush, drove, exact, flick, force, horde, hound, hurry, media, plead, radio, set on, steam, stuff, surge, swarm **6** appeal, bother, burden, caress, compel, duress, enjoin, exhort, extort, fondle, gather, huddle, legion, mangle, push in, reduce, smooth, strain, stress, throng **7** cluster, collect, depress, embrace, entreat, flatten, implore, newsmen, oppress, snuggle, squeeze, trouble **8** assemble, bear down, bear upon, calender, compress, condense, hot-press, insist on, pressure, printing, push down **9** annoyance, be hard put, constrain, constrict, final form, force down, force from, importune, multitude, reporters **10** compulsion, congregate, newspapers, obligation, supplicate, television, thrust down **11** journalists, periodicals, publication **12** bear down upon, broadcasting, come together, news services, newspapermen **14** Fourth Estate

press down 7 compact, depress **8** push down

press forward 5 drive **6** push on **7** advance **10** forge ahead

press home 6 stress **9** emphasize, underline **10** accentuate, underscore

pressing 5 vital **6** crying, needed, urgent **7** crucial, exigent, needful **8** critical **9** clamoring, demanding, essential, important, insistent, necessary **10** imperative **11** importunate **13** indispensable

pressing necessity 6 crisis **7** urgency **8** exigency **9** emergency

press on 9 move ahead, persevere **10** accelerate, forge ahead **11** move forward

pressure 4 bias, care, load, need, pull, sway, want **5** force, hurry, pinch, power, press, trial **6** burden, demand, strain, stress, weight **7** anxiety, density, gravity, potency, squeeze, straits, tension, trouble, urgency **8** coercion, distress, exigency, interest **9** adversity, grievance, heaviness, influence, necessity **10** affliction, compaction, compulsion, difficulty, oppression

pressure measurement 6 pascal **10** atmosphere

prestige 4 fame, mark, note **5** glory, honor **6** esteem, import, regard, renown, report, repute **7** account, respect **8** eminence **9** authority, celebrity **10** importance, notability, prominence, reputation **11** consequence, distinction, preeminence **12** significance

prestigious 5 famed **6** famous **7** eminent, honored, notable **8** esteemed, renowned **9** acclaimed, important, prominent, reputable, respected, well-known **10** celebrated **11** illustrious, outstanding **13** distinguished

Preston, Robert
   real name: 21 Robert Preston Meservey
   born: 17 Newton Highlands MA
   roles: 4 Mame **9** Semi-Tough **11** The Music Man **12** Junior Bonner **14** Victor Victoria **16** How the West Was Won

presumable 6 likely **8** apparent, probable **10** ostensible

presumably 6 likely **8** probably **9** assumably, doubtless **10** apparently, ostensibly **13** presumptively **14** unquestionably **15** in all likelihood **16** in all probability

presume 4 dare **5** fancy, guess, posit **6** assume, deduce, gather, have it, impose, take it **7** believe, imagine, suppose, surmise, suspect, venture **8** be so bold, conceive, make bold, make free **9** postulate, take leave **11** hypothesize, rely too much, think likely **12** take a liberty

presumed 7 assumed, deduced, posited **8** believed, imagined, supposed, surmised **9** suspected **10** postulated **13** took advantage **15** taken for granted

presumption 3 lip **4** gall **5** brass, cheek, guess, nerve, pride **6** belief, daring **7** egotism, premise, surmise **8** audacity, boldness, chutzpah, rudeness **9** arrogance, flippancy, impudence, insolence, postulate **10** assumption, conjecture, effrontery **11** forwardness, haughtiness, prejudgment, speculation, supposition **12** impertinence **13** preconception **14** presupposition

presumptuous 4 bold **5** brash, cocky, fresh, lofty, nervy, proud **6** brassy, brazen, daring, lordly **7** forward, haughty, pompous **8** arrogant, assuming, snobbish **9** audacious, imperious, shameless **10** disdainful **11** dictatorial, domineering, overbearing, patronizing **12** contemptuous, overfamiliar **13** overconfident

presuppose 6 assume **7** presume, suppose **9** speculate **10** conjecture **11** hypothesize

presupposed 7 assumed **8** presumed, supposed **10** speculated **11** conjectured

presupposition 7 premise **10** assumption **11** postulation, presumption

pretend 4 fake, sham **5** claim, fancy, feign, mimic, put on **6** affect, assume **7** imagine, imitate, playact, purport, suppose **8** simulate **9** dissemble **10** masquerade **11** counterfeit, dissimulate, impersonate, make believe

pretended
   French: **9** soi-disant

pretender 5 faker, fraud, phony **8** claimant, imposter

pretense 4 airs, fake, hoax, mask, sham, show **5** cloak, cover, feint, guile, trick, vaunt **6** deceit **7** bluster, bombast, display, pretext **8** boasting, bragging, disguise, trickery **9** deception, false show, imposture, invention, pomposity **10** camouflage, pretension, showing off, subterfuge **11** affectation, counterfeit, fabrication, fanfaronade, make-believe, ostentation **12** affectedness

pretension 4 airs, pomp, show **5** claim, right, title **7** bombast, display **8** ambition, pretense, snobbery **9** hypocrisy, pomposity, showiness **10** aspiration, showing off **11** affectation, ostentation **13** grandioseness **14** self-importance **16** ostentatiousness

pretentious 4 airy, smug **5** gaudy, lofty, showy, stagy **6** flashy, florid, garish, ornate, tawdry **7** blown-up, fatuous, pompous, stuck-up **8** affected, assuming, boastful, inflated, overdone, pedantic, puffed-up, snobbish **9** bombastic, flaunting, insincere, presuming, unnatural **10** hoity-toity, theatrical **11** exaggerated, extravagant, overbearing **12** ostentatious, self-

praising **13** high-and-mighty, self-important

pretentiousness 4 cant **6** humbug **9** hypocrisy **11** insincerity **17** sanctimoniousness

preternatural 5 eerie, weird **6** arcane, occult **7** bizarre, strange, uncanny **8** esoteric, mystical **9** unearthly, unworldly **10** miraculous, mysterious, superhuman **11** hypernormal, preterhuman, supernormal **12** extramundane, metaphysical, supernatural, supranatural **14** transcendental

pretext 5 basis, bluff, feint **6** excuse, ground **8** pretense **9** semblance **10** pretension, subterfuge **11** vindication

pretty 4 fair **5** bonny **6** comely, dainty, fairly, goodly, lovely, rather **7** shapely, sightly, well-set **8** alluring, charming, delicate, engaging, fetching, graceful, handsome, somewhat, well-made **9** beauteous, beautiful **10** adequately, attractive, moderately, reasonably **11** captivating, good-looking, symmetrical, well-favored

pretty child 4 doll **5** cutie **10** living doll

prevail 3 win **4** rule **5** exist, reign **6** abound, obtain, win out **7** conquer, succeed, triumph **8** have sway, hold sway, overcome **9** be a winner, be current **11** be prevalent, be the victor, carry the day, gain the palm, predominate **12** be victorious, be widespread, preponderate

prevailing 3 set **4** main **5** fixed, usual **6** normal **7** current, general, in style, popular **8** definite, dominant **9** customary, prevalent, principal **10** accustomed, widespread **11** established, predominant **12** conventional, preponderant

prevail over 4 beat **5** outdo **6** defeat **7** eclipse, surpass **8** overcome

prevail upon 4 sway **8** convince, persuade **9** influence

prevalent 4 rife **5** usual **6** common, normal **7** general, popular, rampant **8** abundant, everyday, familiar, frequent, habitual, numerous **9** customary, extensive, pervasive, universal **10** prevailing, ubiquitous, widespread **11** commonplace **12** conventional

prevaricate 3 fib, lie **4** fake **6** palter **7** deceive, distort, falsify, mislead, perjure **8** hoodwink, misstate **9** be evasive, dissemble **10** equivocate, tell a story **11** counterfeit **12** be untruthful, misrepresent

prevarication 3 fib, lie **5** fable **7** fiction, untruth, whopper **9** fairy tale, falsehood, fish story, invention **11** fabrication **12** equivocation **16** cock-and-bull story **17** misrepresentation

prevent 3 bar, dam **4** balk, foil, halt, stop, veto **5** avert, avoid, block, deter **6** arrest, forbid, thwart **7** deflect, draw

off, fend off, obviate, rule out, ward off **8** hold back, preclude, prohibit, stave off, turn away **9** forestall, frustrate, intercept, sidetrack, turn aside **10** anticipate, counteract **11** nip in the bud

prevention 6 defeat **8** stoppage **9** avoidance, hindrance, obviation, restraint, thwarting **10** deterrence, inhibition, preclusion **11** elimination, frustration **12** interception **13** forestallment

preview 5 sneak **6** sample, survey **8** futurama **9** foretaste **10** inspection

previous 5 early, prior **6** before, former **7** earlier **8** foregone **9** aforesaid, erstwhile, foregoing, preceding **10** antecedent **14** aforementioned

previously 4 once **6** before **7** earlier, long ago **8** back when, formerly **9** at one time, a while ago, earlier on **10** a while back, heretofore **11** in times past **12** sometime back

Prevost, Abbe
  author of: 12 Manon Lescaut

prey 3 eat **4** dupe, food, game, gull, kill **5** patsy, prize, quest **6** devour, infest, pigeon, quarry, sucker, target, victim **7** cat's-paw, consume, fall guy, live off **8** feed upon **9** feast upon **10** fasten upon, fatten upon, parasitize

Priam
  king of: 4 Troy
  father: 8 Laomedon
  brother: 8 Tithonus
  wife: 6 Hecuba
  son: 5 Paris **6** Hector **9** Polydorus
  daughter: 8 Polyxena **9** Cassandra
  number of sons: 5 fifty
  number of daughters: 5 fifty
  killed by: 11 Neoptolemus

Priamid
  father: 5 Priam

Priapus
  god of: 5 herds **7** gardens **9** fertility, male power **11** procreation
  father: 8 Dionysus
  mother: 9 Aphrodite
  corresponds to: 7 Mutinus

price 3 fee **4** cost, fine, rate **5** value, worth **6** amount, assess, charge, outlay **7** expense, penalty **8** appraise, evaluate, par value **9** face value, list price **10** forfeiture, punishment

Price, Fanny
  character in: 13 Mansfield Park
  author: 6 Austen

Price, Vincent
  born: 9 St Louis MO
  wife: 11 Coral Browne **12** Edith Barrett
  roles: 6 The Fly **8** The Raven **10** House of Wax **13** Tower of London **15** The House of Usher **20** The Pit and the Pendulum **22** The Masque of the Red Death
  expert in: 3 art

Price Is Right, The
  host: 9 Bob Barker **10** Bill Cullen

priceless 4 dear, rare **6** costly, prized, valued **8** peerless, precious, valuable **9** cherished, expensive, treasured **10** high-priced, invaluable **11** beyond price **12** incomparable, without price **13** irreplaceable **17** worth a king's ransom

prick 5 stick **6** pierce **8** puncture

prickle 4 barb, itch **5** point, quill, smart, sting, thorn **6** tingle **7** barbule, bristle, spicule

prickly 5 itchy **6** coarse, thorny **8** scratchy, stinging **9** vexatious

pride 3 joy **4** airs, pomp, show **5** honor **6** egoism, parade, vanity **7** comfort, conceit, delight, dignity, display, egotism, swagger **8** pleasure, self-love, smugness **9** arrogance, be proud of, enjoyment, happiness, immodesty, pomposity, vainglory **10** pretension, self-esteem **11** haughtiness, ostentation, self-respect **14** self-importance

Pride and Prejudice
  author: 10 Jane Austen
  character: 7 Mr Darcy **9** Mr Bingley, Mr Collins, Mr Wickham **14** Charlotte Lucas **15** Caroline Bingley **21** Lady Catherine de Bourgh
    Bennet daughters: 4 Jane, Mary **5** Kitty, Lydia **9** Elizabeth
  director: 14 Robert Z Leonard
  cast: 10 Mary Boland **11** Edmund Gwenn, Greer Garson, Karen Morley **13** Ann Rutherford, Edna May Oliver **15** Laurence Olivier **16** Maureen O'Sullivan

Pride of the Yankees, The
  director: 7 Sam Wood
  cast: 8 Babe Ruth **9** Dan Duryea **10** Gary Cooper (Lou Gehrig) **12** Teresa Wright **13** Walter Brennan

priest 5 padre **6** cleric, father **8** minister, preacher **9** churchman **13** man of the cloth

priesthood 5 cloth **6** clergy **8** ministry, the cloth **9** pastorage

Priestley, J B
  author of: 9 Bright Day **11** Lost Empires **13** Angel Pavement **17** The Good Companions

Priestley, Joseph
  field: 9 chemistry
  nationality: 7 British
  discovered: 6 oxygen **7** ammonia **13** nitrogen oxide
  invented: 11 carbonation

priestly 8 churchly, clerical **10** sacerdotal **14** ecclesiastical

prig 5 bigot, prude **6** pedant **7** puritan **8** bluenose **9** formalist, hypocrite, nitpicker, pretender **10** fuddy-duddy **11** faultfinder **12** bluestocking, precisionist, stuffed shirt **14** attitudinarian

priggish 4 prim, smug **6** stuffy **7** prud-

ish 9 blue-nosed **10** tight-laced **11** puritanical, straitlaced **13** self-righteous, self-satisfied

prim 4 smug, tidy **5** fussy **6** prissy, proper, strict, stuffy **7** haughty, prudish **8** priggish, starched **9** squeamish, unbending **10** fastidious, fuddy-duddy, inflexible, no-nonsense, particular **11** overprecise, puritanical, stiff-necked, straitlaced

prima donna 4 diva, lead, star **6** singer **9** principal
  literally: 9 first lady

primarily 6 mainly, mostly **7** chiefly, largely **9** basically, generally, in the main **11** essentially, principally **13** fundamentally, predominantly **14** for the most part **16** first and foremost

primary 3 key **4** main, star **5** basal, basic, chief, first, prime, vital **6** innate, native, oldest, primal, ruling, utmost **7** highest, initial, leading, nascent, natural **8** cardinal, dominant, earliest, greatest, inherent, original, primeval **9** beginning, elemental, essential, important, necessary, primitive, principal, prominent **10** aboriginal, elementary, indigenous, primordial, rudimental **11** fundamental, predominant, preparatory, rudimentary **12** introductory

primary constituent 5 basic **9** basic need, essential, necessity, requisite **10** sine qua non

primate 3 ape, man **5** avahi, indri, lemur, loris, potto **6** aye-aye, baboon, bishop, galago, gibbon, mammal, monkey **7** gorilla, tamarin, tarsier **8** marmoset, simpoona **9** orangutan, tree shrew **10** archbishop, chimpanzee

prime 2 A1 **3** ace, fit **4** best, main, peak, pink **5** adapt, basal, basic, bloom, breed, brief, chief, coach, early, first, groom, guide, lucky, raise, ready, train, tutor, vital **6** adjust, choice, fill in, flower, Grade A, height, heyday, inform, innate, native, oldest, primal, prompt, ruling, school, seemly, select, timely, utmost, zenith **7** educate, fitting, highest, leading, maximal, natural, prepare, primary, quality, supreme, top-hole **8** best days, cardinal, crowning, earliest, get ready, greatest, inherent, instruct, maturity, original, peerless, suitable, superior **9** befitting, elemental, essential, expedient, important, intrinsic, make ready, matchless, necessary, opportune, paramount, preferred, principal, provident, top-drawer, top-flight, unmatched, well-timed **11** superlative, unsurpassed, without peer **12** unparalleled

prime example 5 model **7** classic **8** exemplar **9** archetype

prime mover 6 author **9** initiator, or-

ganizer **10** originator
Latin: 12 primum mobile

Prime of Miss Jean Brodie, The
   author: 11 Muriel Spark

primer 3 cap **4** book **5** paint **6** manual, reader **8** hornbook, textbook **9** undercoat

primeval 5 early **6** oldest, primal **7** ancient, archaic **8** earliest, original **9** ancestral, legendary, primitive **10** aboriginal, indigenous, primordial **11** fundamental, prehistoric **12** antediluvian, mythological

primitive 4 bare **5** crude, early, first **6** native, simple **7** antique, archaic, artless, ascetic, austere, primary, Spartan **8** backward, earliest, original **9** beginning, unlearned, unrefined, unskilled **10** aboriginal, elementary **11** rudimentary, uncivilized, undeveloped

primordial 5 first **6** primal **7** initial **8** original, primeval **9** beginning, primitive **10** elementary **11** fundamental, prehistoric

primp 5 groom, plume, preen **6** doll up, make up **7** gussy up **8** prettify, spruce up

primrose 7 Primula **15** Primula vulgaris
   varieties: 4 baby, cape, star **5** fairy **6** German, poison **7** Chinese, English, evening **8** bird's-eye **9** buttercup **12** beach evening, white evening **13** desert evening **14** Mexican evening

primum mobile 10 prime mover **16** first moving thing

primus inter pares 16 first among equals

prince
   Italian: 8 principe
   Turkish: 3 beg, bey

Prince
   original name: 18 Prince Rogers Nelson
   alias: 9 The Artist **30** The Artist Formerly Known as Prince
   nickname: 12 Royal Badness
   born: 2 MN **11** Minneapolis
   recording: 6 For You, Parade, Prince **9** Dirty Mind **10** Musicology, Purple Rain **11** Controversy, Crystal Ball **12** Emancipation, New Power Soul **20** Around the World in a Day
   film: 10 Purple Rain **12** 3 Chains o' Gold **13** Sign o' the Times **14** Graffiti Bridge **18** Under the Cherry Moon

Prince, The
   author: 18 Niccolo Machiavelli

Prince and the Pauper, The
   author: 9 Mark Twain
   character: 4 Hugo **8** Tom Canty **9** John Canty **10** Hugh Hendon **11** Miles Hendon **19** Edward Prince of Wales

Prince Edward Island
   abbreviation: 3 PEI
   bay: 5 Rollo **6** Egmont **7** Bedeque **8** Cardigan, Malpeque **9** Cascumpec **12** Hillsborough
   capital: 13 Charlottetown
   gulf: 10 St Lawrence
   people: 4 Scot **5** Irish, Scots **6** French **7** English
      discoverer: 7 Cartier
   province of: 6 Canada
   river: 4 Dunk **5** Eliot, Yorke **12** Hillsborough
   strait: 14 Northumberland

Prince Igor
   also: 9 Kniaz Igor
   opera by: 7 Borodin
   character: 11 Khan Konchak
   contains: 17 Polovetsian dances

princely 3 big **5** noble, royal **8** generous **11** magnificent

prince of darkness 5 Satan **7** Lucifer **8** the Devil **9** Beelzebub

Prince of Peace 5 Jesus **6** Christ

Princess and the Pea, The
   author: 21 Hans Christian Andersen

Princess Casamassima
   author: 10 Henry James

Prince Valiant
   creator: 12 Harold Foster
   character: 5 Ilene **9** Prince Arn **10** King Arthur
      wife: 5 Aleta
   nickname: 3 Val

principal 4 dean, fund, main, star **5** basic, chief, first, money, prime **6** master **7** capital, leading, primary, supreme **8** cardinal, dominant, foremost, greatest, superior, ultimate **9** essential, paramount, preceptor, prominent **10** capital sum, headmaster, leading man, preeminent **11** fundamental, predominant, protagonist **13** most important

principal constituent 4 base **12** chief feature **14** main ingredient

principal dish of a meal
   French: 17 piece de resistance

principal event
   French: 17 piece de resistance

principality 5 angel **9** princedom **14** celestial being, heavenly spirit

principally 6 mainly, mostly **7** chiefly, largely **8** above all **9** basically, primarily **10** especially **12** particularly **13** fundamentally, predominantly **14** for the most part **16** first and foremost

principe 6 prince

principle 3 law **4** code, fact, rule, view **5** axiom, basis, canon, credo, creed, dogma, honor, maxim, tenet, truth **6** belief, dictum, ethics, morals, theory, virtue **7** element, formula, honesty, precept, probity, scruple, theorem **8** attitude, doctrine, goodness, morality, position, rudiment, scruples, teaching **9** direction, integrity, rectitude, standards **10** assumption, regulation **11** fundamental, proposition, uprightness

principled 6 honest **7** upright **9** honorable **10** aboveboard, forthright

Pringle, John
   real name of: 11 John Gilbert

prink 4 deck, fuss **5** adorn, preen, primp **6** spruce

print 3 die **4** copy, text, type **5** issue, plate, press, stamp, write **7** compose, edition, engrave, etching, gravure, impress, picture, publish, woodcut **10** lithograph, silkscreen **11** letterpress

printing press
   invented by:
      rotary: 3 Hoe
      web: 7 Bullock

prior 6 former **7** earlier **8** anterior, previous **9** aforesaid, erstwhile, foregoing, prefatory **10** antecedent, precursory **11** going before, preexistent, preexisting, preparatory **14** aforementioned

Prioress
   character in: 18 The Canterbury Tales
   author: 7 Chaucer

priority 7 urgency **9** immediacy, seniority **10** ascendancy, precedence, precedency, preference **11** antecedence, preeminence, superiority

priory 5 abbey **6** friary **7** convent, nunnery **8** cloister **9** hermitage, monastery

prison 3 can, jug, pen **4** brig, gaol, jail, stir, tank **5** clink, joint, pokey, tower **6** cooler **7** dungeon, slammer **8** bastille, big house **9** calaboose, jailhouse

Prisoner of Zenda
   author: 11 Anthony Hope
   character: 14 Princess Flavia **17** Lady Rose Burlesdon, Rudolph Rassendyll **18** Antoinette de Mauban, Fritz von Tarlenhein **21** Michael Duke of Strelsau **22** Rudolph King of Ruritania
   director: 12 John Cromwell
   cast: 9 Mary Astor **10** David Niven **12** C Aubrey Smith, Ronald Colman (Rudolf Rassendyll) **16** Madeleine Carroll **18** Douglas Fairbanks Jr (Rupert of Hentzau)
   setting: 9 Ruritania

prissy 4 prim **5** fussy **6** proper, stuffy **7** finicky, prudish **8** overnice **9** sissified **10** effeminate **11** strait-laced

Prissy
   character in: 15 Gone With the Wind
   author: 8 Mitchell

pristine 4 pure **8** unmarred, virginal **9** undefiled, unspoiled, unsullied, untouched **10** unpolluted **11** untarnished **14** uncontaminated

Pritchett, V S
   author of: 11 Midnight Oil **16** Collected Stories, The Spanish Temper **19** On the Edge of the Cliff

privacy 6 secret **7** privity, retreat, secrecy **8** security, solitude **9** integrity, isolation, seclusion **10** retirement, withdrawal **11** privateness **12** dissociation, solitariness **13** sequestration

private 4 dark **5** fixed, privy **6** buried, closed, covert, hidden, lonely, remote, secret **7** cryptic, express, limited, obscure, special **8** confined, desolate, esoteric, hush-hush, isolated, lonesome, personal, secluded, solitary **9** concealed, exclusive, inviolate, invisible, nonpublic, not public, reclusive **10** classified, indistinct, mysterious, restricted, undercover, under wraps, unofficial, unrevealed **11** clandestine, nonofficial, sequestered, underground, undisclosed **12** confidential, off-the-record, unfrequented

privateer 6 pirate **7** brigand, corsair **9** buccaneer

private eye 4 dick **6** shamus **7** gumshoe **9** detective **12** investigator

Private Life of Henry VIII, The
director: **14** Alexander Korda
cast: **11** Merle Oberon, Robert Donat **12** Binnie Barnes **14** Elsa Lanchester (Anne of Cleves) **15** Charles Laughton (Henry VIII)

Private Lives
author: **10** Noel Coward
character: **10** Elyot Chase, Sibyl Chase **12** Amanda Prynne, Victor Prynne

Private Lives of Elizabeth and Essex, The
director: **13** Michael Curtiz
cast: **10** Bette Davis (Elizabeth I), Errol Flynn (Essex) **11** Donald Crisp **12** Vincent Price **13** Nanette Fabray **17** Olivia de Havilland
also known as: **17** Elizabeth the Queen

privately 7 sub rosa **8** in secret, secretly **9** between us, entre nous, in private **12** in confidence **14** confidentially **15** between you and me **16** between ourselves **17** behind closed doors

privation 4 lack, need, want **5** pinch **6** misery, penury **7** beggary, poverty, straits **8** distress, exigency, hardship **9** indigence, neediness, pauperism **10** bankruptcy, mendicancy **11** destitution **14** impoverishment **15** impecuniousness

privilege 3 due **4** boon **5** allow, favor, grant, honor, power, right, title **6** patent, permit **7** benefit, charter, empower, entitle, freedom, liberty, license **8** pleasure **9** advantage, authority, franchise **10** birthright **11** entitlement, prerogative **12** prerequisite

privileged 4 free **6** exempt, immune **7** allowed, excused, granted, limited, special **8** entitled, licensed **9** empowered, not liable, permitted, warranted **10** authorized, sanctioned **13** unaccountable

prize 3 cup, gem, pip **4** like, lulu **5** award, catch, crown, dandy, honey, honor, jewel, medal, peach, pearl, value **6** admire, esteem, honors, regard, reward, ribbon, trophy **7** cherish, diamond, guerdon, honored, laurels, premium, respect, winning **8** accolade, champion, citation, hold dear, look up to, pure gold, treasure **9** humdinger, medallion **10** appreciate, blue ribbon, decoration, set store by **11** crackerjack, masterpiece

prized 4 dear **8** esteemed, precious **9** cherished, treasured

prizefight 2 go **4** bout **5** match **6** boxing **7** contest **10** fisticuffs

prizefighter 3 pug **5** boxer **7** slugger **8** pugilist **9** flyweight **11** heavyweight, lightweight **12** bantamweight, middleweight, welterweight **13** featherweight **16** light heavyweight

pro 3 for **5** forth **6** before, expert, master **8** favoring **9** authority **11** affirmative
opposite: **3** con **7** amateur

probability 4 odds **6** chance **10** likelihood

probable 6 likely **7** logical, seeming, tenable **8** apparent, assuring, credible, expected, possible, presumed, supposed **9** plausible, promising, thinkable **10** believable, in the cards, ostensible, presumable, reasonable **11** conceivable, encouraging, presumptive

probably 6 likely **10** most likely, presumably, supposedly **11** as like as not **15** in all likelihood

probe 4 hunt, quiz, seek, test **5** query, study, trial **6** pursue, review, search, survey **7** examine, fish for, inquest, inquire, inquiry, inspect, pry into, rummage **8** analysis, look into, question, scrutinize **11** examination, exploration, interrogate, investigate **13** investigation

probity 5 honor **6** virtue **7** decency, honesty **8** goodness, morality **9** character, integrity, principle **11** uprightness **12** straightness **13** righteousness **14** high-mindedness **15** trustworthiness **16** incorruptibility

problem 5 poser, query **6** puzzle, riddle, unruly **8** question, stubborn **9** conundrum, difficult **10** difficulty **11** intractable **12** disagreement, hard to manage, incorrigible, unmanageable

problematic 7 dubious, unknown **8** doubtful, puzzling **9** difficult, enigmatic, uncertain, unsettled, worrisome **10** perplexing **11** paradoxical, troublesome **12** questionable, undetermined

pro bono publico 16 for the public good

proboscis 4 beak, nose **5** snoot, snout, trunk **6** siphon, sucker, syphon **7** ros-

trum
monkey: **4** kaha **5** kahua

procedure 2 MO **3** way **4** mode **6** course, manner, method **7** process, routine **8** approach, strategy **9** technique **11** methodology **13** modus operandi

proceed 2 go **3** act **4** come, flow, go on, grow, move, stem, work **5** arise, begin, ensue, issue, start **6** derive, follow, move on, push on, result, set out, spring **7** advance, carry on, emanate, go ahead, operate, press on, succeed **8** be caused, commence, continue, function, progress, take rise **9** be derived, go forward, move ahead, originate, undertake

proceedings 4 case, suit **5** cause, trial **6** doings, events, report **7** account, actions, affairs, lawsuit, matters, minutes, records, returns **8** activity, archives, goings on **9** incidents, memoranda **10** happenings, litigation, operations **11** occurrences **12** transactions

proceeds 3 net **4** gain, gate, pelf, take **5** gross, lucre, money, yield **6** assets, income, profit, reward **7** returns, revenue **8** earnings, pickings, receipts, winnings **9** box office

process 3 can, dry **4** fill, flow, flux, mode, plan, ship, step, writ **5** alter, candy, smoke, treat, usage **6** change, course, freeze, handle, manner, method, motion, policy, scheme, system **7** convert, measure, passage, prepare, project, summons **8** deal with, function, movement, practice, preserve, progress, subpoena **9** dehydrate, dispose of, freeze-dry, procedure, transform, unfolding **10** court order, proceeding

procession 4 file, line, rank **5** array, march, train **6** column, course, parade **7** caravan, cortege, pageant, passage **8** progress, sequence **9** cavalcade, motorcade **10** succession **11** progression

Procheneosaurus
type: **8** dinosaur **10** ornithopod
location: **6** Canada
period: **10** Cretaceous

proclaim 3 cry **4** tell **5** blare, state, voice **6** affirm, assert, blazon, herald, report, reveal **7** call out, declare, divulge, give out, profess, publish, release, sing out, trumpet **8** announce, disclose, set forth **9** advertise, broadcast, circulate, enunciate, hawk about, make known, publicize **10** make public, promulgate

proclamation 5 edict, ukase **6** decree **12** announcement **13** pronouncement

proclivity 3 yen **4** bent, bias **5** taste **6** desire, liking **7** impulse, leaning **8** affinity, appetite, penchant, soft spot, tendency **9** affection, prejudice, proneness **10** partiality, propensity **11** disposition, inclination **12** predilection **14** predisposition

procrastinate 3 lag **5** dally, defer, delay, stall, tarry **6** dawdle, linger, loiter **7** adjourn **8** hang back, hesitate, hold back, kill time, postpone, put on ice **9** temporize, waste time **10** be dilatory, dillydally **11** play for time **12** drag one's feet

procrastinating 4 slow **5** tardy **6** remiss **8** dilatory **9** reluctant **12** foot-dragging **13** dillydallying

procreate 3 get **4** bear, sire **5** beget, breed, spawn **6** create, father, mother **7** produce **8** conceive, engender, generate, multiply **9** propagate, reproduce **10** bring forth **11** give birth to, proliferate

procreation
　god of: **7** Priapus

procreator 4 sire **6** father **8** begetter

procrustean 7 drastic **8** ruthless **19** conforming at any cost

Procrustes
　also: **5** giant **8** Damastes **9** Polypemon
　seized: **9** travelers
　killed by: **7** Theseus
　tied them to: **3** bed
　made them fit by: **10** stretching **14** cutting off their feet

procure 3 buy, get, win **4** earn, gain, take **5** evoke, seize **6** attain, come by, effect, elicit, gather, incite, induce, obtain, pick up, secure **7** achieve, acquire, receive **8** contrive, purchase **10** accumulate, bring about, commandeer, lay hands on **11** appropriate

procurement 4 gain **7** seizure **8** purchase **10** attainment, purchasing **11** achievement, acquirement, acquisition **12** accumulation **13** appropriation

prod 3 jab, nag **4** flog, goad, lash, move, poke, push, spur, stir, urge, whip **5** egg on, impel, prick, rouse, shove, speed **6** excite, exhort, incite, needle, prompt, propel, stir up **7** actuate, animate, provoke, quicken **8** motivate, pressure **9** encourage, instigate, stimulate

prodigal 4 lush **5** ample **6** lavish, myriad, wanton **7** copious, profuse, replete, spender, teeming, wastrel **8** abundant, generous, numerous, reckless, swarming, wasteful **9** abounding, bounteous, bountiful, countless, excessive, exuberant, impetuous, luxuriant, plentiful, unthrifty **10** exorbitant, gluttonous, immoderate, inordinate, numberless, profligate, squanderer, thriftless **11** dissipating, extravagant, improvident, innumerable, intemperate, overliberal, precipitate, spendthrift **13** multitudinous

prodigality 10 imprudence, lavishness **12** extravagance, improvidence, overspending, wastefulness

prodigious 3 big **4** huge, rare, vast **5** grand, great, large **6** mighty, unique **7** amazing, immense **8** colossal, enormous, gigantic, renowned, singular, striking, terrific, uncommon, unwonted, wondrous **9** marvelous, monstrous, startling, wonderful **10** astounding, impressive, miraculous, monumental, noteworthy, remarkable, stupendous, surprising, tremendous **11** astonishing, exceptional, farreaching, uncustomary, unthinkable **12** dumbfounding, overwhelming, unimaginable **13** extraordinary, inconceivable, unprecedented

prodigiously 10 enormously, incredibly, remarkably **12** inordinately, tremendously **13** astonishingly, exceptionally, extravagantly, outstandingly, spectacularly **14** overwhelmingly

prodigiousness 6 rarity **8** enormity, hugeness, vastness **10** uniqueness **11** singularity **12** extravagance

prodigy 4 whiz **6** expert, genius, marvel, master, rarity, wizard, wonder **7** stunner, whiz kid **8** rara avis **9** sensation **10** mastermind, phenomenon, wunderkind **11** wonder child

produce 4 bear, form, give, make, show **5** beget, bloom, cause, found, frame, hatch, set up, shape, yield **6** adduce, afford, create, devise, effect, evince, evolve, flower, fruits, greens, invent, reveal, sprout, supply, unmask, unveil **7** achieve, advance, bring in, compose, concoct, develop, display, divulge, exhibit, fashion, furnish, present, provide, staples, turn out, uncover **8** bring off, bring out, conceive, disclose, discover, generate, manifest, set forth **9** bear fruit, construct, fabricate, institute, make plain, originate, procreate, put on view, show forth **10** accomplish, bring about, come up with, effectuate, foodstuffs, give life to, give rise to, put in force, vegetables **11** bring to pass, give birth to, manufacture, materialize **14** bring into being

Producers, The
　film (1968):
　　director: **9** Mel Brooks
　　cast: **9** Dick Shawn **10** Gene Wilder, Zero Mostel **11** Kenneth Mars
　stage musical:
　　director/choreographer: **12** Susan Stroman
　　cast: **10** Nathan Lane **16** Matthew Broderick

production 4 film, play, show **5** drama, movie **6** cinema, circus, making **7** display, exhibit, musical, showing **8** building, carnival, creation **9** execution, formation, producing, stage show **10** appearance, disclosure, revelation **11** fabrication, fulfillment, manufacture, origination, performance **12** construction, effectuation, introduction, presentation **13** demonstration, entertainment, manifestation, manufacturing, motion picture **15** materialization

productive 4 busy, rich **6** active, fecund, paying, useful **7** causing, copious, dynamic, fertile, gainful, teeming **8** creating, creative, fruitful, prolific, valuable, vigorous, yielding **9** effectual, luxuriant, plenteous, plentiful, producing **10** invaluable, profitable, worthwhile **11** efficacious, moneymaking, proliferous **12** contributing, fructiferous, remunerative

profanation 9 sacrilege **10** defilement **11** desecration

profane 3 lay **4** evil, foul, lewd, mock, vile **5** abuse, bawdy, crude, nasty, scorn, waste **6** coarse, debase, filthy, ill-use, impure, misuse, offend, revile, ribald, sinful, unholy, vulgar, wicked **7** abusive, earthly, godless, impious, obscene, outrage, pervert, pollute, satanic, secular, ungodly, violate, worldly **8** agnostic, diabolic, off-color, temporal, unchaste, undevout, unseemly **9** atheistic, blaspheme, desecrate, hellbound, heretical, misemploy, shameless, unsaintly **10** irreverent, prostitute **11** blasphemous, contaminate, irreligious, terrestrial, unbelieving **12** nonreligious, sacrilegious

profanity 5 filth, oaths **7** cursing, cussing, impiety **8** swearing **9** blasphemy, obscenity, scatology **10** dirty words, execration, expletives, scurrility, swearwords **11** irreverence, obscenities, ungodliness **12** billingsgate **15** four-letter words

profess 3 act, own, say **4** aver, avow, fake, sham, tell **5** admit, claim, feign, offer, put on, state, vouch **6** affirm, allege, assert, assume, depose **7** advance, certify, confess, confirm, contend, declare, embrace, pretend, purport **8** announce, lay claim, maintain, practice, proclaim, propound, simulate **9** believe in, dissemble, enunciate, hold forth **10** asseverate, put forward **11** acknowledge, counterfeit, dissimulate

professed 6 avowed **7** alleged **8** admitted **9** confessed, purported **12** acknowledged, self-declared **14** self-proclaimed

profession 3 job, law, vow **4** line, post, word, work **5** claim, craft, field, trade, troth **6** avowal, career, metier, office, pledge, plight, sphere **7** calling, promise, pursuit, service **8** averment, business, endeavor, industry, medicine, position, practice, teaching, vocation **9** assertion, assurance, guarantee, situation, specialty, statement, testimony **10** allegation, confession, deposition, employment, line of work, occupation, walk of life **11** affirmation, attestation, declaration, undertaking, word of honor **12** announcement, confirmation **13** pronouncement **15** acknowledgement

professional 4 paid **5** adept **6** expert **9** authority, competent, practiced **10** specialist **11** experienced

professionalism 5 savvy, skill **7** know-how **9** expertise **10** expertness

professor 3 don **6** regent **7** adjoint, teacher **8** lecturer **10** instructor
retired: **8** emeritus

professorial 6 teachy **7** bookish, donnish, preachy **8** academic, didactic, pedantic, teachery **11** pedagoguish **13** schoolmarmish **15** schoolmasterish **16** schoolteacherish

proffer 5 offer **6** extend, tender **7** advance, hold out, present

proficiency 5 knack, skill **6** acumen **7** ability, know-how **8** aptitude, capacity, deftness, facility **9** adeptness, dexterity, expertise, handiness **10** adroitness, capability, competence **13** qualification **14** accomplishment

proficient 3 apt **4** able, deft, good **5** adept, handy, quick, ready, sharp **6** adroit, clever, expert, gifted **7** capable, skilled, trained **8** masterly, polished, skillful, talented **9** competent, dexterous, effective, efficient, masterful, practiced, qualified, versatile **11** experienced **12** accomplished, professional

profile 4 form, side, tale **5** shape **6** figure, sketch **7** contour, drawing, outline, picture, skyline **8** half face, portrait, side view, vignette **9** biography **10** lineaments, silhouette **11** delineation **13** configuration

Profiles in Courage
author: **12** John F Kennedy

profit 3 pay, use **4** boon, earn, gain, good, help **5** avail, favor, money, serve, value **6** income, return **7** account, benefit, revenue, service, utility, utilize **8** earnings, interest, proceeds, receipts **9** advantage, make money **11** advancement

profitable 6 paying, useful **7** gainful **8** fruitful, salutary, valuable **9** favorable, lucrative, rewarding **10** beneficial, invaluable, productive, well-paying, worthwhile **11** moneymaking, serviceable **12** advantageous, remunerative

profitmaking 8 business **11** moneymaking **13** noncharitable

profits 4 gate, take **5** gains, yield **6** assets, income **7** returns, revenue **8** earnings, receipts

profligacy 10 lavishness **11** dissipation, dissolution, prodigality, unrestraint **12** extravagance, immoderation, improvidence, recklessness, wastefulness **13** excessiveness

profligate 4 evil, fast, rake, roue, wild

5 loose, satyr **6** erotic, lavish, sinful, sinner, wanton, wicked **7** corrupt, immoral, pervert, satyric, wastrel **8** degraded, depraved, prodigal, reckless, wasteful **9** abandoned, debauched, debauchee, dissolute, libertine, reprobate, sybaritic, unbridled, unthrifty, wrongdoer **10** degenerate, dissipated, dissipater, iniquitous, lascivious, licentious **11** extravagant, improvident, promiscuous, spendthrift **12** unprincipled, unrestrained

pro forma 15 according to form, as a matter of form

profound 4 deep, keen, sage, wise **5** acute, sober, utter **6** abject, hearty, moving, severe **7** decided, erudite, extreme, intense, knowing, learned, radical, serious, sincere **8** complete, educated, informed, piercing, positive, thorough **9** heartfelt, out-and-out, recondite, sagacious, scholarly **10** all-knowing, consummate, deep-seated, omniscient, pronounced, reflective, thoughtful **11** enlightened, far-reaching, penetrating **12** intellectual, soul-stirring **13** comprehensive, knowledgeable, philosophical, thoroughgoing

profundity 5 abyss, depth **6** wisdom **8** deepness, sagacity, sapience **9** erudition **11** learnedness, penetration **12** abstractness, abstruseness, profoundness **13** reconditeness, sagaciousness **16** impenetrableness

profuse 4 rich **5** ample, wordy **6** lavish, prolix **7** copious, diffuse, verbose **8** abundant, generous, prodigal, rambling, wasteful **9** bounteous, bountiful, excessive, garrulous, unthrifty **10** digressive, discursive, immoderate, inordinate, long-winded, loquacious, munificent **11** extravagant, improvident, intemperate, spendthrift

profuseness 9 abundance, diffusion, profusion, prolixity, verbosity, wordiness **10** lavishness **11** copiousness, diffuseness

profusion 4 glut **5** waste **6** excess **7** surfeit, surplus **8** plethora **9** abundance, multitude **10** oversupply **11** superfluity **12** extravagance, multiplicity

progenitor 8 ancestor, forebear **10** forefather

progeny 3 kin, son **4** clan, heir, line, race, seed **5** blood, breed, child, heirs, issue, scion, stock, young **6** family **7** kindred, lineage **8** children, offshoot **9** offspring, posterity **10** descendant

prognosticate 7 predict, presage **8** forecast, foretell, prophesy **9** foretoken

prognostication 6 augury **8** forecast, prophecy **10** divination, prediction

prognosticator 4 seer **5** augur **7** prophet **9** predictor **10** forecaster

program 4 bill, book, card, list, plan,

show **5** slate **6** agenda, design, docket, expect, intend, line up, notice, series, sketch **7** arrange, outline **8** bulletin, calendar, playbill, register, schedule, syllabus **9** timetable **10** curriculum, production, prospectus **12** presentation

progress 4 gain, grow, rise **5** climb, get on, mount, ripen **6** action, course, grow up, growth, mature, stride **7** advance, develop, headway, improve, proceed, process, success **8** get ahead, increase, movement **9** get better, go forward, move ahead, promotion, unfolding **10** betterment, enrichment, gain ground **11** achievement, advancement, development, enhancement, furtherance, improvement, make headway, make strides

progression 3 run **5** chain, climb, order **6** ascent, course, series, strain, string **7** advance **8** progress, sequence **10** succession **11** advancement, continuance, furtherance **12** continuation **14** continuousness **15** consecutiveness

progressive 7 dynamic, gradual, liberal, ongoing **8** activist, advanced, populist, up-to-date **9** advancing, enlarging, reformist, spreading, traveling **10** ameliorist **11** incremental **12** enterprising

prohibit 3 ban, bar **4** curb, deny, stay, stop, veto **5** block, check, delay, limit **6** enjoin, forbid, hamper, hinder, impede, negate **7** inhibit, obviate, prevent, repress **8** disallow, obstruct, preclude, restrain, restrict, suppress, withhold **9** proscribe

prohibited
German: **8** verboten

prohibition 3 ban **4** veto **5** edict **7** embargo, sanction **10** temperance **11** forbiddance **12** interdiction

prohibitive, prohibitory 9 enjoining, hindering **10** forbidding, inhibitive, injunction, preventative, repressive **11** disallowing, obstructive, restraining, restrictive, suppressive **12** inadmissible, unacceptable **13** disqualifying **15** circumscriptive

project 3 aim, job **4** cast, emit, fire, goal, plan, send, task, work **5** draft, eject, expel, fling, frame, shoot, throw **6** beetle, design, devise, extend, hurtle, invent, jut out, launch, map out, propel, scheme **7** concoct, outline, propose **8** activity, ambition, bend over, contrive, forecast, overhang, protrude, stand out, stick out, throw out, transmit **9** calculate, discharge, ejaculate, intention, objective, plan ahead **10** assignment **11** extrapolate, undertaking **12** predetermine

projected 6 hurled **7** hurtled, planned **8** extended, forecast, launched, overhung, proposed, stood out, stuck out

9 mapped out, propelled, protruded **10** catapulted **11** conjectural

projectile 4 dart **5** arrow, spear **6** rocket **7** javelin, missile

projecting part 3 arm, ell, leg **4** eave, limb, tail **6** branch, feeler, member **7** antenna **8** tentacle **9** appendage

projection 4 brow, bump, eave **5** bulge, guess, jetty, jutty, ledge, ridge, shelf **8** estimate, forecast, overhang **9** extension, extrusion **10** estimation, prediction, prospectus, protrusion **11** guesstimate **12** protuberance **13** approximation, extrapolation

Prokofiev, Serge
  born: 6 Russia **9** Sontsovka
  composer of: 6 Lt Kije **10** Cinderella, The Gambler **11** War and Peace **13** Scythian Suite, The Fiery Angel **14** Lieutenant Kije, Romeo and Juliet, The Prodigal Son **15** Alexander Nevsky, Peter and the Wolf **17** Classical Symphony **22** The Love for Three Oranges **57** Cantata for the Twentieth Anniversary of the October Revolution

proletarian 6 worker **7** laborer **10** working man

proletariat 5 plebs **6** rabble, the mob **7** populus **8** canaille, laborers, populace **9** commonage, commoners, hoi polloi, the masses **10** commonalty **11** lower orders, rank and file, wage earners **12** lower classes, vulgus mobile, working class **15** the common people **16** the great unwashed

proliferate 4 teem **5** breed, hatch, spawn, swarm **8** increase, multiply **9** procreate, propagate, pullulate **10** regenerate **11** overproduce

prolific 4 lush **6** fecund **7** copious, fertile, profuse **8** abundant, breeding, creative, fruitful, yielding **9** luxuriant **11** germinative, multiplying, procreative, progenitive, proliferous, propagating **12** reproductive

prolix 5 wordy **7** verbose **10** long-winded

prolixity 9 verbosity, wordiness **11** profuseness **14** long-windedness

prologue 7 opening, preface, prelude **8** foreword, overture, preamble **9** beginning **12** introduction

prolong 5 delay **6** extend, retard **7** drag out, draw out, spin out, stretch, sustain **8** continue, elongate, lengthen, maintain, protract **9** attenuate **10** perpetuate

prolongation 5 delay **9** extending, extension **10** drawing out **11** attenuation, dragging out, lengthening, protraction, retardation **12** perpetuation **13** streching out

prolonged 7 lengthy **8** drawn-out, extended **9** continued, long-lived **10** continuing, lengthened, persistent, protracted **11** long-lasting

prom 3 hop **4** ball **5** dance **9** cotillion, promenade

promenade 3 hop **4** ball, prom, walk **5** dance **6** soiree, stroll **9** cotillion

Prometheus
  member of: 6 Titans
  father: 7 Iapetus
  mother: 6 Themis **7** Clymene
  brother: 5 Atlas **10** Epimetheus
  son: 9 Deucalion
  created mankind from: 4 clay
  stole: 4 fire
  punished by: 4 Zeus
  chained to: 4 rock
  released by: 8 Hercules

Prometheus Bound
  author: 9 Aeschylus
  character: 2 Io **3** Bia **6** Hermes, Kratos **7** Oceanus **10** Hephaestus

Prometheus Unbound
  author: 18 Percy Bysshe Shelley
  character: 4 Asia, Ione **5** Earth **7** Jupiter, Mercury, Panthea **8** Hercules **9** Demogoron

prominence 3 tor **4** bump, dune, fame, hill, hump, knob, lump, mark, mesa, name, node, peak, rise, spur **5** bluff, bulge, cliff, crest, honor, jetty, jutty, knoll, knurl, might, mound **6** credit, height, renown, rising, summit, weight **7** dignity, hillock, majesty, process **8** eminence, grandeur, mountain, nobility, outshoot, overhang, pinnacle, prestige, salience, splendor, swelling **9** celebrity, convexity, elevation, extension, extrusion, greatness, influence, notoriety, precipice **10** brilliance, importance, notability, popularity, projection, promontory, protrusion, reputation, tumescence **11** distinction, excrescence, excurvature, preeminence, superiority **12** protuberance, significance

prominent 6 convex, famous **7** bulging, eminent, evident, glaring, honored, jutting, leading, notable, obvious, salient, staring, swollen **8** apparent, definite, excurved, extended, renowned, striking, swelling **9** arresting, important, respected, well-known **10** celebrated, easily seen, jutting out, noticeable, preeminent, projecting, pronounced, protruding, protrusive, remarkable **11** conspicuous, discernible, illustrious, outstanding, prestigious, protuberant **12** recognizable **13** distinguished

promiscuous 3 lax **4** fast, lewd, wild **5** loose, mixed **6** casual, impure, medley, motley, rakish, wanton **7** aimless, chaotic, diverse, immoral, jumbled, mingled, mixed-up, satyric **8** careless, confused, immodest, sweeping, unchaste **9** composite, desultory, dissolute, haphazard, perplexed, scrambled, wholesale **10** commingled, disordered, disorderly, dissipated, in-

termixed, lascivious, licentious, uncritical, undirected, unvirtuous, variegated **11** disarranged, incontinent, indifferent, intemperate, unselective **12** disorganized, of easy virtue, undiscerning **13** helter-skelter, heterogeneous, miscellaneous **14** indiscriminate

promise 3 vow **4** aver, avow, oath, word **5** agree, augur, imply, swear, troth, vouch **6** assure, avowal, hint of, parole, pledge, plight **7** be bound, betoken, suggest, warrant **8** covenant, indicate, warranty **9** agreement, assurance, guarantee, potential, undertake **11** declaration, stipulation, swear an oath, word of honor

Promised Land 6 Canaan
  nickname of: 10 California **6** Israel

promising 4 rosy **5** happy, lucky **6** bright, rising **7** hopeful **8** assuring, cheerful, cheering **9** advancing, favorable, fortunate, looking up **10** auspicious, of good omen, optimistic, propitious, reassuring **11** encouraging, inspiriting, up-and-coming

promissory note 3 IOU **4** bond, chit **6** pledge **7** promise **9** agreement **10** obligation **11** certificate

promontory 4 cape, hill, ness, spur **5** bluff, cliff, jetty, jutty, point **6** height **8** headland, overhang **9** peninsula, precipice **10** embankment, projection

promote 3 aid **4** abet, ease, help, plug, push **5** raise **6** assist, foster, prefer, refine **7** advance, develop, elevate, enhance, forward, further, support, upgrade, work for **8** advocate, expedite, graduate **9** advertise, cultivate, encourage, publicize

promoter 6 backer **8** advocate, champion **9** proponent, supporter

promotion 4 hype **5** raise **7** advance, fanfare, puffery **8** ballyhoo, boosting, progress **9** elevation, publicity, upgrading **10** preferment **11** advancement, advertising, furtherance **12** promulgation **13** advertisement, encouragement

promotive 7 helpful **9** conducive **10** beneficial **12** contributive, contributory, instrumental

prompt 3 cue **4** goad, keen, move, prod, push, spur, stir **5** alert, alive, cause, drive, eager, force, impel, press, quick, ready, sharp **6** active, assist, bright, excite, incite, induce, intent, lively, on time, propel, remind, thrust, timely **7** actuate, animate, dispose, help out, incline, inspire, instant, on guard, provoke, zealous **8** activate, inspirit, motivate, occasion, open-eyed, persuade, punctual, vigilant, watchful **9** attentive, determine, efficient, immediate, influence, instigate, observant, open-eared, stimulate, wide-awake **10** on one's toes **12** jog the memory, unhesitating **13** instantaneous

prompting 6 cueing, urging **7** goading **8** egging on **10** motivation **11** exhortation

promptly 3 pat **4** anon, soon, tite **6** pronto **7** quickly, swiftly **10** punctually **11** immediately

promptness 5 haste **8** alacrity, celerity, dispatch **9** quickness, readiness, swiftness **11** punctuality **15** expeditiousness

promulgate 6 foster **7** explain, expound, present, promote, sponsor **8** instruct, set forth **9** elucidate, enunciate, interpret **11** communicate

promulgation 9 fostering, promotion **11** circulation, instruction, sponsorship **12** distribution, presentation, transmission **13** communication **14** interpretation

prone 3 apt **4** flat **5** level **6** liable, likely **7** subject, tending **8** disposed, face-down, inclined **9** prostrate, reclining, recumbent **10** accustomed, habituated, horizontal **11** predisposed, susceptible

proneness 4 bent, bias, turn **7** leaning **8** penchant, tendency **9** prejudice **10** proclivity, propensity **11** inclination **12** predilection **14** predisposition

prong 4 barb, hook, horn, spur, tine **5** point, spike, tooth **6** branch **10** projection

pronoun 2 he, it, me, my, us, we, ye **3** all, any, few, her, his, one, she, thy, who, you **4** hers, mine, ours, some, thee, them, they, that, this, thou, what, whom **5** no one, their, these, thine, those, which, whose, yours **6** anyone, itself, myself, nobody **7** anybody, herself, himself, nothing, someone, whoever **8** somebody, whomever **9** everybody, something, whosoever **10** everything, themselves
French: 2 il, je, tu **3** ils, lui, mes, moi **4** elle, vous
German: 2 er, es, du **3** ich, mir, sie **4** dein, mein, mich, sich
Italian: 2 io, me, mi, ti, tu, vi **3** cio, lei, lui, mio, tei, voi **4** egli, ella, essa, esse, essi, loro
Spanish: 2 el, la, lo, me, mi, tu, yo **4** ella, ello, suyo, tuyo **5** usted

pronounce 3 say **4** emit, form, rule **5** frame, judge, orate, sound, speak, state, utter, voice **6** decree **7** declare, enounce **8** announce, proclaim, vocalize **9** enunciate **10** articulate

pronounced 4 bold **5** broad, clear, plain, vivid **6** patent **7** decided, evident, obvious, visible **8** apparent, clear-cut, definite, distinct, manifest, positive, unhidden **9** arresting **10** noticeable **11** conspicuous, outstanding, undisguised, well-defined **12** recognizable, unmistakable **14** unquestionable

pronouncement 6 decree **11** declaration **12** announcement, proclamation

pronto 3 now **4** asap, fast, stat **5** quick **7** quickly **8** promptly **11** immediately

Pronuba
epithet of: **4** Juno

pronunciamento 5 edict **12** proclamation **13** pronouncement

pronunciation 6 accent **10** inflection **11** enunciation **12** articulation **16** manner of speaking

proof 4 test **5** essay, proof, sheet, trial **6** galley, ordeal **8** scrutiny, weighing **9** probation **10** assessment **11** attestation, examination **12** confirmation, ratification, verification **13** certification, corroboration, documentation **14** substantiation

proofreader's mark 3 cap, rom **4** dele, ital, stet **5** caret, space

prop 3 set **4** lean, rest, stay **5** brace, stand **6** hold up, pillar **7** bolster, shore up, support **8** buttress, mainstay, shoulder, underpin **9** stanchion, supporter, sustainer **13** reinforcement
French: 11 point d'appui

propaganda 6 hoopla **8** ballyhoo **9** party line, promotion, publicity **10** persuasion **11** advertising

propagandist 8 zealot **9** activist, exponent **9** apologist, proponent, publicist **12** spokesperson

propagate 3 air, sow **4** bear, tell **5** beget, breed, hatch, issue, rumor, spawn, spray **6** blazon, herald, impart, notify, preach, purvey, repeat, report, spread **7** bestrew, give out, implant, instill, publish, scatter, trumpet **8** disperse, engender, generate, increase, multiply, proclaim, put forth **9** broadcast, circulate, enunciate, give birth, inculcate, make known, procreate, publicize, reproduce

propagation 6 laying, siring **7** bearing **8** breeding, hatching, issuance, spawning, yielding **9** begetting, diffusion, gestation, pregnancy, spreading **10** dispersion, generation **11** circulation, engendering, giving birth, procreation, publication **12** distribution, reproduction, transmission **13** dissemination

pro patria 14 for one's country

propel 4 cast, goad, hurl, poke, prod, push, send, toss **5** drive, eject, force, heave, impel, pitch, shoot, shove, sling, start **6** launch, thrust **7** project **8** catapult **9** discharge **11** precipitate, set in motion

propeller, screw
invented by: **7** Stevens **8** Ericsson

propensity 4 bent, bias, turn **5** fancy, favor, taste **6** liking **7** leaning **8** affinity, penchant, pleasure, sympathy, tendency, weakness **9** prejudice **10** at-

traction, partiality, preference, proclivity **11** disposition, inclination **12** predilection **14** predisposition

proper 3 apt, fit, own **4** meet, nice, true **5** per se, right **6** decent, marked, modest, polite, seemly **7** apropos, correct, express, fitting, germane, precise, typical **8** assigned, becoming, decorous, orthodox, peculiar, relevant, specific, suitable **9** befitting, courteous, pertinent **10** acceptable, applicable, individual, particular, respective **11** appropriate, conformable, distinctive **12** conventional **14** characteristic, distinguishing, representative
French: 11 comme il faut

properly 5 aptly, right **7** exactly **8** decently, politely, suitably **9** correctly, perfectly, precisely **10** acceptably, accurately, decorously, tastefully **12** without error **13** appropriately **14** conventionally

property 4 hold, land, mark **5** acres, badge, funds, goods, means, point, stock, title, trait **6** aspect, assets, estate, moneys, realty, wealth **7** acreage, capital, earmark, effects, estates, feature, grounds, quality **8** chattels, holdings, treasure **9** attribute, ownership, resources, territory **10** belongings, real estate **11** investments, peculiarity, possessions, singularity **12** appointments, idiosyncrasy **13** individuality, particularity **14** characteristic, proprietorship

prophecy 6 augury **7** portent **8** forecast **10** divination, prediction, revelation **15** prognostication
god of: **6** Apollo **7** Phoebus, Pythius **9** Musagetes

prophesy 4 warn **5** augur **6** divine **7** forbode, foresee, portend, predict, presage **8** forecast, foretell, forewarn, soothsay **9** apprehend, premonish **13** prognosticate

prophet 4 seer **5** augur, guide, sibyl **6** oracle **7** diviner, palmist, seeress **8** preacher, sorcerer **9** Cassandra, divinator, geomancer, predictor, sorceress **10** evangelist, forecaster, foreteller, prophesier, prophetess, soothsayer **11** clairvoyant, intercessor, interpreter **12** crystal gazer **13** fortune-teller **14** prognosticator

Prophet, major 6 Baruch, Daniel, Elijah, Isaiah **7** Ezekiel **8** Jeremiah

Prophet, minor 3 Gad **4** Amos, Joel **5** Hosea, Jonah, Micah, Nahum **6** Haggai, Nathan **7** Malachi, Obadiah **8** Habakkuk **9** Zechariah, Zephaniah

Prophetess 4 Anna **6** Miriam **7** Deborah **9** Cassandra

prophetic, prophetical 5 vatic **6** mantic **7** fateful, ominous **8** oracular **10** portentous, predictive, presageful

Prophetic Books
author: **12** William Blake

prophylactic 8 hygienic 10 preventive 13 contraceptive

propinquity 7 kinship 8 affinity, nearness, vicinity 9 closeness, proximity 10 similarity

propitiate 4 calm 5 allay 6 pacify, soothe 7 appease, assuage, mollify, placate 10 conciliate 11 accommodate

propitiation 8 soothing 11 appeasement 12 conciliation, pacification

propitious 3 fit 5 bonny, happy, lucky 6 benign, golden 8 suitable 9 agreeable, favorable, fortunate, opportune, promising, well-timed 10 auspicious, beneficial, felicitous 12 advantageous, providential

proponent 6 backer, friend, patron, votary 7 booster 8 advocate, champion, defender, endorser, espouser, exponent, partisan, upholder 9 apologist, spokesman, supporter 10 enthusiast, vindicator 14 representative

proportion 5 ratio 7 balance, harmony 8 evenness, symmetry 9 agreement 11 consistency, correlation, perspective 12 distribution, relationship 14 commensuration, correspondence

proportionate 5 equal 8 balanced 10 comparable, equivalent 12 commensurate 13 commensurable, corresponding

proportions 3 fit, lot 4 area, bulk, form, gear, mass, part, size, span 5 adapt, gauge, grade, match, order, poise, quota, range, ratio, scope, shape, share, width 6 amount, degree, equate, extent, spread, volume 7 balance, breadth, conform, correct, expanse, measure, portion, rectify, segment 8 capacity, division, equalize, fraction, graduate, modulate, regulate 9 amplitude, apportion, greatness, harmonize, magnitude 10 dimensions 12 measurements

proposal 3 bid 4 idea, plan, plot, suit 5 draft, offer 6 appeal, course, design, motion, scheme, sketch, theory 7 outline, proffer, program, project 8 overture, prospect 9 stratagem 10 conception, invitation, nomination, prospectus, resolution, suggestion 11 proposition 12 presentation 14 recommendation

propose 3 aim, woo 4 hope, mean, plan, plot 6 aspire, design, expect, intend, scheme, submit, tender 7 advance, present, proffer, purpose, suggest, venture 8 affiance, propound, put forth, set about, set forth 9 determine, have a mind, introduce, recommend, undertake 10 come up with, have in mind, have in view, put forward 11 contemplate 14 pop the question 21 offer for consideration

proposition 4 deal, pass, plan 5 issue, offer, point, topic 6 matter, scheme 7 advance, bargain, solicit, subject 8

contract, proposal, question 9 agreement, assurance, guarantee 10 resolution, suggestion 11 make a pass at, negotiation, stipulation, undertaking 14 recommendation

propound 4 pose 5 boost 6 assert 7 advance, profess, propose 8 put forth, set forth

proprieties 7 decorum, manners 8 protocol 9 amenities, etiquette 10 civilities 11 conventions

proprietor 5 owner 6 holder, master 7 manager 8 landlord 9 landowner, possessor 10 landholder 11 titleholder 12 proprietress

propriety 7 aptness, decorum, dignity, fitness 8 courtesy 9 etiquette, formality, rightness 10 seemliness 11 correctness, good manners, savoir faire 12 becomingness, decorousness, good behavior, suitableness 13 applicability 14 respectability 15 appropriateness

propulsion 6 launch, thrust 9 launching 10 propelling

prop up 5 brace 7 bolster, support 8 buttress

pro rata 12 in proportion

prorate 6 divide 9 apportion 10 distribute

prosaic 3 dry 4 blah, dull, flat 5 prosy, stale, trite, vapid, wordy 6 common, jejune 7 humdrum, tedious 8 ordinary, plebeian, tiresome 9 hackneyed 10 monotonous, pedestrian, spiritless, unpoetical 12 matter-of-fact 13 platitudinous, unimaginative, uninteresting

Prosclystius
epithet of: 8 Poseidon
means: 7 flooder

proscribe 3 ban 4 damn 5 curse, exile 6 banish, forbid, outlaw 7 boycott, censure, condemn 8 denounce, prohibit 9 interdict, repudiate 10 disapprove 12 anathematize 13 excommunicate

proscription 3 ban 7 barring, censure 8 anathema 9 interdict 11 forbiddance, prohibition 12 condemnation, denunciation, interdiction 15 excommunication

prose 3 dry 4 dull 5 novel 7 fiction, quality, tedious, writing 8 sequence 9 discourse 10 expression 11 commonplace 13 unimaginative

prosecute 3 sue, try 4 wage 6 direct, go with, handle, indict, manage, pursue 7 arraign, carry on, conduct, execute, go to law, perform, prolong, stick to, sustain 8 continue, deal with, follow up, maintain 9 discharge, persist in 10 administer, put on trial, see through 11 take to court 12 bring to trial 14 bring to justice

prosecution 4 suit 6 action 7 conduct, pursuit 11 performance 14 administration

Proserpina *see* 10 Persephone

prosit 11 may it do good
used as: 5 toast

prospect, prospects 4 hope, plan, seek, view 5 scene, vista 6 aspect, design, search, vision 7 chances, explore, go after, look for, outlook, picture, promise, scenery 8 ambition, panorama, proposal 9 candidate, foretaste, intention, landscape, work a mine 10 expectancy, likelihood 11 expectation, possibility, probability 12 anticipation 13 contemplation

prospective 4 to be 6 coming, future, in view, likely, to come 7 looming 8 destined, eventual, expected, foreseen, hoped-for, intended, possible 9 about to be, impending, in the wind, looked-for, potential, promising 10 in prospect 11 approaching, forthcoming, threatening

prosper 4 gain 5 get on 6 flower, thrive 7 advance, succeed 8 fare well, flourish, fructify, get ahead, grow rich, increase, make good, progress 9 bear fruit 15 make one's fortune

prosperity 4 ease, gain 6 luxury, plenty, profit, wealth 7 advance, success, welfare 8 good luck, progress 9 abundance, advantage, affluence, blessings, golden age, good times, palmy days, run of luck, well-being 11 advancement, good fortune
god of: 4 Frey 5 Freyr, Niord, Njord
goddess of: 5 Salus

Prospero
character in: 10 The Tempest
author: 11 Shakespeare

prosperous 4 fair, good, rich, rosy 5 happy, lucky, sunny 6 bright, golden, timely 7 hopeful, moneyed, opulent, smiling, wealthy, well-off 8 affluent, cheering, pleasing, thriving, well-to-do 9 favorable, fortunate, opportune, promising 10 auspicious, heartening, of good omen, propitious, reassuring, successful 11 comfortable, encouraging, flourishing 12 on easy street

prostitute 4 bawd, jade, slut, tart 5 abuse, hussy, lower, spoil, whore 6 chippy, debase, defile, demean, floozy, harlot, hooker, misuse 7 cheapen, corrupt, debauch, degrade, hustler, pervert, profane, sell out, trollop 8 call girl, misapply, strumpet 9 courtesan, desecrate, misdirect, misemploy 12 streetwalker 14 lady of the night

prostrate 4 deck, flat 5 abase, floor, prone, spent 6 fagged, kowtow 7 bow down, flatten, laid out, worn out 8 bowed low, overcome 9 bone weary, crouching, dead tired, exhausted, kneel down, lying flat, overthrow, recumbent 10 beseeching, horizontal 11 on one's knees 12 on bended knee, stretched out, supplicating **13** lying face down **15** fall to one's knees

prostration 3 bow, woe **5** grief **6** misery, sorrow **7** anguish, despair **8** distress, kneeling, weakness **9** abasement, dejection, heartache, impotence, lowliness, paralysis, weariness **10** depression, desolation, enervation, exhaustion, subjection, submission **11** desperation, despondency **12** genuflection, helplessness, wretchedness **13** depth of misery

prosy 4 dull, flat **5** banal, inane **6** stupid **7** humdrum, prosaic, tedious **9** wearisome **11** commonplace **13** uninteresting

protagonist 4 diva, hero, lead, star **7** heroine **9** headliner, principal, superstar, title role **10** leading man, prima donna **11** leading lady **12** danseur noble, jeune premier **13** jeune premiere, main character **14** prima ballerina **16** central character

protect 4 hide, keep, save, tend, veil **5** cover, guard **6** defend, harbor, screen, secure, shield **7** care for, shelter, sustain **8** conserve, maintain, preserve **9** look after, safeguard, watch over **10** take care of

protected 4 safe **5** saved **6** immune, secure **7** guarded, secured **8** anchored, defended, shielded **9** sheltered **10** inviolable **12** invulnerable

protection 3 aid **4** care, keep, wall **5** cover, fence, guard, haven, shade **6** asylum, buffer, charge, harbor, refuge, safety, saving, screen, shield **7** barrier, custody, defense, shelter, support **8** guarding, immunity, preserve, security **9** preserver, safeguard, sanctuary **10** assistance **11** safekeeping **12** championship, conservation, guardianship, preservation

protective 7 careful, heedful **8** fatherly, guarding, maternal, motherly, paternal, sisterly, vigilant, watchful **9** avuncular, brotherly, defensive, shielding **10** preventive, sheltering, solicitous **11** safekeeping **12** bigbrotherly, safeguarding

protective covering 4 coat, husk, mail **5** armor, shell **6** shield **7** coating, plating **8** carapace **10** coat of mail **11** suit of armor **12** armor plating

protectorate 6 colony **7** mandate **8** province, dominion **9** satellite, territory **10** dependency, possession, settlement

protege 4 ward **5** pupil **6** charge **7** student, trainee **9** dependent

pro tempore 9 temporary **11** temporarily **15** for the time being

protest 3 vow **4** aver, avow, beef, deny, kick **5** gripe, march, offer, sit-in, speak, state **6** affirm, allege, assert, assure, attest, avouch, cry out,

insist, object, oppose, strike **7** boycott, contend, declare, dispute, dissent, hold out, profess, testify **8** announce, complain, demurral, disagree, maintain, propound, put forth, set forth **9** enunciate, objection, picketing, pronounce **10** asseverate, contradict, controvert, disapprove, disclaimer, dissidence, opposition, put forward, resistance **11** beg to differ, deprecation **12** disaffection, disagreement, remonstrance, renunciation **13** contradiction, demonstration, remonstration, take exception **14** discountenance

Protestant 5 Amish **6** Mormon, Quaker, Shaker **7** Baptist, Puritan **8** Anglican, Huguenot, Lutheran **9** Adventist, Calvinist, Methodist, Unitarian **12** Episcopalian, Presbyterian **17** Congregationalist **18** Christian Scientist

protest meeting 5 rally, sit-in **13** demonstration

Proteus
  character in: **20** Two Gentlemen of Verona
  author: **11** Shakespeare

Proteus
  god of: **3** sea
  king of: **5** Egypt
  father: **7** Oceanus
  mother: **6** Tethys
  wife: **8** Psamathe
  son: **12** Theoclymenus
  daughter: **7** Theonoe
  gift: **8** prophesy **12** form-changing **13** shape-changing

Prothoenor
  leader of: **9** Boeotians

protocol 5 usage **7** customs, decorum, manners **8** good form **9** amenities, etiquette, formality, standards **11** conventions, proprieties **14** code of behavior, court etiquette, diplomatic code **17** dictates of society

prototypal 5 model **7** classic **9** exemplary **10** archetypal, definitive **12** prototypical

prototype 5 model **7** example **8** original **9** archetype

protozoan 4 cell **5** ameba, cilia **6** amoeba **7** euglena **8** flagella, protista **9** eukaryote, pseudopod **10** paramecium, plasmodium **11** microscopic, unicellular **17** nonphotosynthetic

protract 6 extend, keep up **7** drag out, draw out, prolong, spin out **8** lengthen **9** keep going **10** stretch out

protracted 4 long **7** lengthy **8** drawn-out, extended **9** continued, long-lived, prolonged **10** lengthened, persistent **11** long-lasting

protraction 4 stay **7** lasting **9** extension **10** continuing, drawing out **11** continuance, dragging out, persistence **12** perseverance, prolongation

protrude 5 belly, bulge, swell **6** jut

out **7** project **8** stand out, stick out **11** push forward

protrusion 4 bump, hump **6** hernia **8** swelling **9** extension **10** projection **12** prolongation, protuberance

protuberance 3 bow **4** bump, hump, knob, knot, lump, node, weal, welt **5** bulge, gnarl, ridge **6** rising **8** swelling **9** convexity, elevation, roundness **10** projection, prominence **11** excrescence, excurvature

protura
  class: **8** hexapoda
  phylum: **10** arthropoda
  characteristic: **5** small **6** minute **7** eyeless **8** wingless

proud 4 fine, smug, vain **5** aloof, cocky, grand, great, happy, lofty, noble **6** august, lordly, snooty, snotty, strict, uppish, uppity **7** bloated, exalted, haughty, high-hat, pleased, pompous, revered, stately, storied, stuck-up, swollen **8** affected, arrogant, assuming, boastful, braggart, bragging, elevated, euphoric, glorious, inflated, insolent, majestic, prideful, puffed up, reserved, snobbish **9** admirable, cherished, conceited, contented, delighted, dignified, flaunting, gratified, honorable, imperious, know-it-all, satisfied, venerable **10** complacent, disdainful, high-minded, intolerant, principled, scrupulous **11** egotistical, independent, magnificent, overbearing, patronizing, punctilious **12** contemptuous, self-praising, supercilious, vainglorious **13** condescending, distinguished, high-and-mighty, self- important, self-satisfied **14** self-respecting, self-sufficient

Proust, Marcel
  author of: **23** Remembrance of Things Past **24** A la Recherche du Temps Perdu

prove 3 try **4** test **5** check, end up, probe **6** affirm, attest, result, try out, uphold, verify, wind up **7** analyze, bear out, certify, confirm, examine, justify, support, sustain, warrant, witness **8** document, evidence, look into, make good, manifest, result in, validate **9** ascertain, establish, eventuate, testify to **11** corroborate, demonstrate **12** authenticate, substantiate

proved 5 known **6** proven, upheld **8** affirmed, attested, borne out, verified **9** certified, confirmed, supported, sustained, warranted, witnessed **10** documented **11** established **12** corroborated, demonstrable **13** authenticated, substantiated

prove false 5 belie **6** refute, reject **7** explode **8** disprove **9** discredit **10** invalidate

proven 5 known **6** proved, upheld **8** accepted, affirmed, attested, borne out, verified **9** certified, confirmed, supported, sustained, warranted, witnessed **10** documented, verifiable **11** established **12** corroborated, demonstrable **13** authenticated, substantiated

provender 3 hay **4** chow, corn, eats, feed, food, grub, oats **5** grain **6** fodder, forage, ration, viands **7** nurture **10** provisions **11** subsistence

proverb 3 mot, saw **5** adage, axiom, maxim, moral, motto **6** byword, cliche, dictum, saying, truism **7** bromide, epigram, precept **8** aphorism, apothegm **9** platitude **11** commonplace **13** accepted truth, popular saying

prove wrong 5 belie **6** expose, refute **7** explode **8** disprove **9** discredit

provide 3 arm, fit, pay **4** give, plan **5** allow, award, cater, equip, grant, offer, state, yield **6** accord, afford, bestow, confer, donate, impart, outfit, render, save up, submit, supply, tender **7** arrange, deliver, furnish, prepare, present, produce, require, specify **8** dispense, get ready **9** make plans, postulate, stipulate **10** accumulate, contribute

provide for 7 care for **8** attend to, wait upon **9** look after **10** minister to, take care of

providence 8 prudence **9** foresight, husbandry, provision **11** forethought **14** circumspection, farsightedness, forehandedness

provident 4 wary **5** chary, ready **6** frugal, saving **7** careful, prudent, thrifty **8** cautious, discreet, equipped, vigilant **9** farseeing, judicious **10** discerning, economical, farsighted, forehanded, foreseeing, thoughtful **11** circumspect, foresighted, precautious **12** parsimonious, well-prepared

province 3 job **4** area, duty, part, role, zone **5** field, place, state **6** canton, charge, county, domain, office, region, sphere **7** section, station **8** business, capacity, function **9** authority, bailiwick, territory **10** assignment, department **11** subdivision **12** jurisdiction **13** scope of duties **14** arrondissement, responsibility

provincial 4 rude **5** crude, gawky, local, rough, rural **6** clumsy, gauche, homely, narrow, oafish, rustic **7** awkward, boorish, bucolic, country, hayseed, insular, loutish **8** cloddish, clownish, down-home, homespun, regional, yokelish **9** backwoods, parochial, small-town, unrefined **10** unpolished **11** clodhopping, countrified, territorial **15** unsophisticated

provision 6 giving **8** donation **9** endowment, providing, supplying **10** furnishing

provisional 6 acting, pro tem **7** interim **9** surrogate, temporary, tenta-

tive **10** substitute **11** conditional **12** probationary **15** for the time being

provisions 4 feed, food, term **6** clause, fodder, forage, stores, string, viands **7** article, commons, edibles, proviso **8** eatables, supplies, victuals **9** condition, groceries, provender, readiness, requisite **10** limitation, obligation, precaution, sustenance **11** arrangement, comestibles, forethought, preparation, requirement, reservation, restriction, stipulation, wherewithal **12** anticipation, modification **13** qualification **14** forehandedness, prearrangement

proviso 5 rider **6** clause, string **8** addition **9** amendment, condition **10** limitation **11** requirement, restriction, stipulation **12** modification **13** qualification

provocation 4 goad, spur **5** cause, pique **6** insult, slight **7** affront, offense **8** prodding, stimulus, vexation **9** actuation, annoyance **10** excitation, incitement, irritation, motivation **11** aggravation, fomentation, instigation, stimulation **12** perturbation

provocative 4 sexy **6** vexing **7** irksome **8** alluring, annoying, arousing, exciting, inviting, tempting **9** beguiling, provoking, ravishing, seductive, thrilling, vexatious **10** attractive, bewitching, enchanting, entrancing, intriguing, irritating **11** aggravating, captivating, fascinating, stimulating, tantalizing **12** intoxicating, irresistible

provoke 3 irk, vex **4** fire, gall, move, rile, stir **5** anger, annoy, cause, chafe, evoke, grate, impel, pique, rouse **6** arouse, awaken, compel, create, effect, elicit, enrage, excite, foment, incite, induce, kindle, madden, prompt, put out, stir up **7** actuate, agitate, animate, bring on, incense, inflame, inspire, outrage, produce, quicken **8** generate, get to one, irritate, motivate **9** aggravate, call forth, establish, galvanize, infuriate, instigate, stimulate **10** bring about, exasperate, give rise to **11** get one's goat, put in motion **15** try one's patience **16** get under one's skin

prow 3 bow **4** stem **5** front **10** forward end

prowess 4 grit, guts **5** knack, might, nerve, power, skill, spunk, valor, vigor **6** daring, genius, mettle, spirit, talent **7** ability, bravery, courage, faculty, heroism, know-how, stamina **8** aptitude, boldness, strength **9** adeptness, derring-do, endurance, fortitude, gallantry, hardihood **10** competence, expertness **11** intrepidity, proficiency **12** fearlessness, skillfulness **13** dauntlessness **14** accomplishment

prowl 4 hunt, lurk, roam **5** creep, range, skulk, slink, snack, stalk, steal **6** ramble **8** scavenge

prowler 7 burglar **10** peeping Tom **16** suspicious person

proximate 4 near **5** close **6** beside, nearby, next to **8** adjacent, imminent, next-door **11** forthcoming

proximity 7 presence **8** locality, nearness, vicinity **9** closeness **10** contiguity **11** propinquity **12** togetherness

proximo *see* **5** month

proxy 3 sub **4** vote **5** agent **6** ballot, deputy **7** stand-in **9** alternate **10** substitute

prude 4 prig **6** modest **7** puritan **9** hypocrite **10** goody-goody **13** prim and proper

prudence 4 care, tact **6** thrift, wisdom **7** caution, economy **9** austerity, foresight, frugality, parsimony **10** discretion, precaution **11** calculation, thriftiness **14** thoughtfulness

prudent 4 sage, sane, wary, wise **5** chary **6** frugal, saving, shrewd **7** careful, guarded, heedful, politic, sapient, sparing, thrifty **8** cautious, discreet, prepared, rational, sensible, vigilant **9** expedient, judicious, provident, sagacious, wide-awake **10** discerning, economical, farsighted, prudential, reflecting, thoughtful **11** circumspect, considerate, foresighted, levelheaded, precautious, well-advised **13** self-possessed

Prud'hon, Pierre-Paul
    born: 5 Cluny **6** France
    artwork: 14 Venus and Adonis **15** The Rape of Psyche **16** Empress Josephine **33** Crime Pursued by Vengeance and Justice **38** Justice and Divine Vengeance Pursuing Crime

prudish 3 shy **4** prim, smug **5** timid **6** demure, modest, prissy, queasy, stuffy **7** finical, mincing, precise, stilted **8** pedantic, priggish, skittish, starched **9** squeamish, Victorian **10** fastidious, old-maidish, overmodest, particular **11** punctilious, puritanical, straitlaced **13** sanctimonious, self-righteous

prudishness 8 primness **10** prissiness, puritanism **11** overmodesty **12** overdelicacy, priggishness **14** overrefinement

prudish phrase 9 euphemism **10** bowdlerism

prune 3 cut, lop **4** clip, crop, pull, snip, thin, trim **5** shear **6** reduce **7** abridge, clarify, curtail, shorten, thin out **8** condense, simplify **10** abbreviate

prunelle
    type: 7 liqueur
    origin: 6 France
    flavor: 4 plum

pruning 6 digest **8** clipping, snipping, synopsis, trimming **10** shortening **11** abridgement, cutting back, cut-down form **12** abbreviation, condensation

prurient 4 lewd, sexy 6 carnal 7 fleshy, goatish, immoral, lustful, obscene, priapic, satyric 9 lecherous, salacious 10 hot-blooded, lascivious, libidinous, licentious, lubricious, passionate 12 concupiscent

pry 4 butt, nose, peek, peer, poke, tear, work, worm 5 break, crack, delve, force, jimmy, lever, mix in, prize, probe, smoke, sniff, snoop, wrest, wring 6 butt in, ferret, horn in, meddle, search, winkle, wrench 7 explore, extract, inquire, intrude, squeeze 9 interfere, intervene 15 stick one's nose in

prying 4 busy, nosy 7 peering, raising, seeking 8 levering, snooping 9 searching 10 intrusive, meddling 11 inquisitive

Prynne, Hester
  character in: 16 The Scarlet Letter
  author: 9 Hawthorne

Pryor, Richard
  born: 8 Peoria IL
  roles: 6 The Wiz 9 Stir Crazy 10 Another You 12 Harlem Nights, Silver Streak 17 Lady Sings the Blues 19 Uptown Saturday Night

psalm 3 ode 4 hymn, poem, song 5 canon, chant, verse 6 praise 7 cantata, glorify, introit 8 canticle

Psalter 12 Book of Psalms

Psamathe
  member of: 6 Nereid
  form: 8 princess
  husband: 7 Proteus
  son: 5 Linus 6 Phocus 12 Theoclymenus
  daughter: 7 Theonoe

pseudo 4 fake, mock, sham 5 bogus, false, phony 6 forged 7 feigned 8 spurious 9 pretended, simulated, soi-disant 10 fictitious, fraudulent, self-styled 11 counterfeit, make-believe 13 self-described

pseudonym 5 alias 6 anonym 7 pen name 8 cognomen, nickname 9 false name, sobriquet, stage name 11 assumed name 16 professional name
  French: 10 nom de plume 11 nom de guerre 12 nom de theatre

pseudonymous 7 assumed 10 fictitious 11 pseudonymic

psocoptera
  class: 8 hexapoda
  phylum: 10 arthropoda
  group: 8 booklice

psyche 2 id 3 ego 4 mind, self, soul 5 anima 6 bowels, make up, spirit 8 superego 10 penetralia 11 personality, unconscious 12 subconscious

Psyche
  personifies: 4 soul
  loved by: 4 Eros 5 Cupid
  persecutor: 5 Venus
  immortalized by: 7 Jupiter
  daughter: 8 Voluptas

psychic 5 augur 6 medium, mental, mystic, occult, voyant 7 diviner, prophet, voyante 8 cerebral 9 paragnost, sensitive, spiritual 10 soothsayer, telepathic 11 clairvoyant, telekinetic, telepathist 12 extrasensory, intellectual, spiritualist, supernatural, supersensory 13 preternatural

Psycho
  director: 15 Alfred Hitchcock
  cast: 9 John Gavin, Vera Miles 10 Janet Leigh 12 Martin Balsam 14 Anthony Perkins
  score: 15 Bernard Herrmann
  feature: 10 Bates Motel 11 shower scene

psychoanalysis 7 therapy 8 analysis 14 physchotherapy

psychoanalyst 6 shrink 7 analyst 12 headshrinker

psychologist/psychiatrist
  American: 4 Hall, Hull 5 Dewey, James, Lewin 6 Harlow, Horney, Miller, Rogers, Terman, Tolman, Watson, Witmer 7 Cattell, Chomsky, Erikson, Goddard, Guthrie, Johnson, Masters, Skinner 8 Brothers, Wechsler 9 Thorndike 10 Westheimer
  Austrian: 5 Adler, Freud, Reich
  British: 5 Ellis 7 Eysenck 9 Titchener
  French: 5 Binet
  German: 5 Wundt 6 Koffka, Kohler 7 Fechner 9 Helmholtz, Kraepelin 10 Ebbinghaus, Wertheimer 11 Krafft-Ebing
  Russian: 6 Pavlov
  Swiss: 4 Jung 6 Piaget

psychology 4 head, mind 6 makeup 7 feeling 8 attitude 15 mental processes
  problem/illness: 6 phobia 7 obesity, smoking 8 hysteria, neuroses, paranoia, schizoid 9 drug abuse, obsession, psychoses 10 alcoholism, compulsion, depression 11 sociopathic 13 schizophrenia 14 sexual deviance 15 anxiety reaction 17 passive-aggressive
  term: 2 id 3 ego 6 libido 7 empathy 8 neuroses, superego 9 catatonic, cognition, psychoses 10 inhibition, repression 11 behaviorism, unconscious 12 conditioning, transference 13 actualization, Rorschach test 14 identification, Oedipus complex 19 operant conditioning 20 behavior modification
  type: 6 social 7 Gestalt 8 abnormal, clinical 9 cognitive 10 industrial 11 educational 12 experimental 13 developmental, physiological, psychometrics, psychophysics

psychopomp
  conductor of spirits to: 5 Hades 10 otherworld
  epithet: 12 psychopompus
  epithet of: 6 Charon, Hermes

psychosis 8 dementia, insanity, neurosis, paranoia 9 paranomia, unreality 10 pathomania 12 hallucinosis 13 schizophrenia 14 mental disorder

psychotherapy 7 therapy 8 analysis 14 psychoanalysis

psychotic 3 mad, nut 4 kook, loon 5 crazy, kooky, loony, nutty 6 insane, madman, maniac 7 lunatic 8 demented, deranged 9 disturbed 10 psychopath 12 insane person, psychopathic 15 non compos mentis

Ptah
  origin: 8 Egyptian
  deity of: 17 universal creation
  worshiped at: 7 Memphis

Ptolemy
  author of: 8 Almagest 9 Geography

pub 3 bar, inn 5 local 6 bistro, saloon, lounge, tavern 7 bar room, ginmill, rummery, rum shop, taproom 8 alehouse, grogshop, pothouse 9 road house, speakeasy 10 beer parlor 11 public house

pubescent 7 teenage 8 immature, juvenile 10 adolescent

public 3 mob 4 folk, open 5 civic, civil, frank, overt, plain, state, trade 6 buyers, common, in view, masses, nation, patent, people, shared, social 7 evident, exposed, general, in sight, obvious, outward, patrons, popular, society, visible 8 apparent, audience, communal, divulged, everyone, manifest, national, passable, populace, revealed, societal, unbarred, unfenced 9 available, citizenry, clientele, community, disclosed, followers, following, free to all, hoi polloi, multitude, notorious, political, statewide, unabashed, unashamed, unbounded, used by all 10 accessible, attendance, nationwide, not private, observable, population, purchasers, recognized, supporters, unenclosed 11 body politic, bourgeoisie, commonality, conspicuous, countrywide, discernible, perceivable, proletariat, rank and file, unconcealed, undisguised 12 acknowledged, constituency, unobstructed, unrestricted 14 community-owned

publication 4 book, news 5 issue, paper 6 digest, report 7 edition, gazette, journal, tabloid 8 bulletin, magazine, pamphlet 9 broadcast, newspaper 10 periodical 11 circulation, information 12 announcement, notification

public disturbance 4 riot 6 fracas, ruckus, uproar 7 turmoil 9 commotion

public house 3 bar, pub 5 local 6 saloon, tavern 7 gin mill, taproom 8 alehouse 9 roadhouse

publicity 4 hype, plug, puff 5 blurb, flack 7 build-up, puffery, write-up 8 ballyhoo, currency 9 attention, notoriety, promotion 10 propaganda, publicness 11 advertising, circulation, information **12** promulgation, public notice, salesmanship

publicize 4 hype, plug, puff, push, sell **6** herald **7** acclaim, promote **8** announce, ballyhoo, emblazon, proclaim **9** advertise, broadcast, make known, propagate **10** make public, promulgate **11** circularize **12** propagandize

publicly
　　Latin: 11 coram populo

public matter
　　Latin: 10 res publica

public notice 5 edict, ukase **6** decree **8** bulletin **9** manifesto **12** proclamation **13** pronouncement **14** pronunciamento
　　French: 7 affiche

public speaking 7 oratory **9** lecturing **12** speechmaking

public-spirited 8 generous **10** altruistic, benevolent **12** humanitarian

publish 3 air **4** tell, vent **5** issue, print, utter **6** herald, impart, put out, spread **7** declare, diffuse, divulge, give out, placard, promote, release, trumpet **8** announce, bring out, disclose, proclaim **9** advertise, broadcast, circulate, make known, propagate, publicize **10** make public, promulgate, put to press **11** communicate, disseminate

Puca
　　also: 5 Pooka
　　origin: 5 Irish
　　form: 6 spirit
　　corresponds to: 4 Puck

Puccini, Giacomo
　　born: 5 Italy, Lucca
　　composer of: 5 Tosca **8** La Boheme, Turandot **12** Manon Lescaut **14** Gianni Schicchi, Madam Butterfly **15** Madama Butterfly **18** La Fanciulla del West **22** The Girl of the Golden West

puce 3 red **7** dark red **13** purplish-brown

Puck
　　also: 15 Robin Goodfellow
　　character in: 21 A Midsummer Night's Dream
　　author: 11 Shakespeare
　　form: 6 spirit
　　characteristic: 11 mischievous
　　corresponds to: 4 Puca **5** Pooka

pucker 4 fold, tuck **5** pinch, pleat, purse **6** crease, gather, ruffle, rumple, shrink **7** crinkle, crumble, squeeze, wrinkle **8** compress, contract **12** draw together

puckered 6 pursed, rucked, tucked **7** creased, crinkly, pinched, pleated **8** crinkled, gathered, wrinkled **10** compressed, corrugated

puckish 5 elfin **6** impish **7** playful **8** annoying **9** whimsical **11** mischievous

pudding 5 jello **6** junket **7** custard,

dessert, tapioca **8** pandowdy **9** charlotte, yorkshire **14** floating island

pudgy, podgy 3 fat **5** buxom, dumpy, obese, plump, squat, stout, tubby **6** chubby, chunky, fleshy, rotund, stocky, stubby **7** paunchy **8** roly-poly, thickset

Pueblo (Cliff Dwellers)
　　language family: 4 Tewa, Zuni **6** Queres, Tanoan **10** Shoshonean
　　tribe: 4 Hopi, Tiwa, Towa, Tuei **5** Acoma, Kiowa **6** Isleta
　　location: 4 Utah **7** Arizona **8** Colorado **9** New Mexico
　　noted for: 5 adobe **12** architecture
　　spirit: 7 Kachina **8** Katchina

puerile 3 raw **5** green, inane, petty, silly, vapid **6** callow, simple **7** babyish, foolish, trivial **8** childish, immature, juvenile, piddling **9** childlike, frivolous, infantile, senseless, worthless **10** irrational, ridiculous, sophomoric **11** harebrained, nonsensical

Puerto Rico
　　name means: 8 rich port
　　other name: 9 Borinquen **15** San Juan Bautista
　　capital/largest city: 7 San Juan
　　others: 5 Cayey, Coamo, Lares, Ponce **6** Caguas, Dorado, Manati, Utuado **7** Arecibo, Bayamon, Fajardo, Guanica, Guayama, Humacao **8** Adjuntas, Cabo Rojo, Mayaguez **9** Aquadilla **11** Santa Isabel
　　government: 32 self-governing commonwealth of the U S
　　measure: 6 cuerda **10** caballeria
　　island: 4 Mona **7** Culebra, Vieques **13** Caja de Muertos **15** Greater Antilles
　　lake: 5 Loiza **6** Carite **8** Dos Bocas **9** Caonillas, Guatajaca
　　mountain: 4 Toro **5** Cayey **6** Yunque **8** Guilarte, Luquilla **10** Torrecilla **17** Cordillera Central
　　highest point: 5 Punta
　　river: 5 Camuy, Canas, Loiza, Yauco **6** Anasco, Manati, Tanama **7** Arecibo, Fajardo, La Plata **9** Caonillas
　　sea: 8 Atlantic **9** Caribbean
　　physical feature:
　　　　bay: 5 Sucia **6** Rincon **8** Boqueron **9** Aquadilla **14** Phosphorescent
　　　　sound: 7 Vieques
　　people: 6 gibaro **10** borinqueno
　　　　explorer: 8 Columbus **11** Ponce de Leon
　　　　leader: 10 Munoz Marin
　　language: 7 English, Spanish
　　religion: 10 Protestant **13** Roman Catholic
　　place:
　　　　area of San Juan: 7 Hato Rey **10** Rio Piedras
　　　　beach: 7 Condado
　　　　cathedral: 15 San Juan Bautista
　　　　fortress: 7 El Morro **11** San Jeronimo **12** San Cristobal
　　　　governor's residence: 11 La Forta-

leza
　　　　museum: 14 El Museo de Ponce
　　　　reservoir: 5 Loiza
　　　　tomb: 11 Ponce de Leon
　　feature:
　　　　bird: 4 rola **7** yeguita
　　　　festival: 6 Casals
　　　　housing development: 14 urbanizaciones
　　　　song: 9 aguinaldo
　　　　strolling musicians: 9 parrandas
　　　　tree: 4 mora **5** yafua, yaray **8** emajagua, guayrote **10** guaranguao
　　food:
　　　　dish: 4 sama, sisi **9** moreillas **11** lechon asado
　　　　drink: 3 rum **10** anis-golila

puff 3 bow **4** blow, draw, emit, gasp, hump, node, pant, plug, suck, wisp **5** bloat, blurb, bulge, heave, smoke, swell, whiff **6** blow up, breath, dilate, exhale, expand, extend, flurry, inhale, rising, wheeze **7** bluster, bombast, distend, inflate, puffery, stretch **8** ballyhoo, be winded, dilation, encomium, flattery, flummery, swelling **9** convexity, discharge, elevation, euphemism, extension, inflation, panegyric, publicity, sales talk **10** be inflated, distention, exhalation, overpraise, protrusion, tuberosity **11** be distended, breathe hard, excrescence, excurvature **12** exaggeration, inflammation, protuberance, protuberancy **13** overlaudation

puffed 5 baggy **7** bulbous, swollen **9** ballooned

puffed up 4 vain **5** proud, puffy **7** swollen **8** inflated **9** conceited **11** swell-headed **12** vainglorious **13** self-important

puffery 4 hype **7** big talk, bluster, bombast **9** hyperbole **11** braggadocio

puff out 5 bloat, bulge, swell **6** billow, expand **7** balloon, distend, enlarge, inflate

puffy 3 fat **5** round **6** fleshy **7** bloated, bulging, swollen **8** enlarged, expanded, inflamed, inflated, puffed up **9** corpulent, distended

pugilist 3 pug **5** boxer **7** battler, bruiser, fighter **12** prizefighter

pugnacious 7 defiant, hostile, warlike **8** menacing, militant **9** bellicose, combative, fractious **10** aggressive, unfriendly **11** belligerent, contentious, quarrelsome, threatening **12** antagonistic, disputatious **13** argumentative

pugnacity 9 hostility **10** antagonism **12** belligerence **13** combativeness **14** aggressiveness, fighting spirit **15** contentiousness

puissance 5 force, might, power **6** energy **7** potency, prowess **8** strength

pulchritude 6 beauty **8** fairness **9** bonniness, good looks **10** comeliness, loveliness, prettiness **12** gorgeousness, handsomeness **13** beauteousness, exquisiteness **14** attractiveness, personableness

pulchritudinous 4 fair, fine **5** bonny **6** comely, lovely, pretty **8** gorgeous, handsome **9** beauteous, beautiful, ravishing **10** attractive **11** good-looking

Pulitzer Prize

originator: **14** Joseph Pulitzer

administered by: **18** Columbia University

awarded for: **4** play **5** drama, music, novel **6** poetry **7** cartoon, feature, fiction, history, letters **9** biography, criticism, editorial, reporting **10** commentary, journalism, literature, nonfiction **11** photography **13** autobiography

pull 2 go **3** lug, rip, tow, tug **4** drag, draw, grab, haul, jerk, lure, move, rend, rive, tear, yank **5** drive, sever, shake, split, trawl, troll, twist, wrest, wring **6** allure, appeal, detach, dig out, entice, remove, sprain, strain, uproot, wrench **7** attract, draw out, extract, gravity, stretch, weed out **8** withdraw **9** extirpate, influence, magnetism, take in tow **10** allurement, attraction, enticement **11** fascination **14** attractiveness

pull apart 3 rip, tug **4** drag, rend, tear **6** detach, wrench **7** extract **8** separate **9** criticize, disengage **10** disconnect

pull away 5 wrest **7** remove **8** drawback, withdraw

pull back 7 back off, retreat **8** fall back, withdraw

Pullman, George Mortimer

nationality: **8** American

developed: **9** (railroad) dining car **11** (railroad) sleeping car

pull off 4 pull **6** commit, effect **7** execute, perform **8** carry out **10** perpetuate **13** participate in

pull on 3 don **5** put on **7** get into

pull one's leg 3 kid **4** fool, hoax **5** tease, trick **7** deceive **9** make fun of

pull out 5 leave **7** draw out, extract **8** withdraw

pull over, pullover 4 cite, stop **5** shirt **6** arrest, jersey, slip on, ticket, t-shirt **7** maillot, sweater **8** slip over

pull together 4 join **5** unite **7** pitch in, share in **8** take part **9** cooperate, join hands **10** act jointly, join forces **11** collaborate, participate

pull to pieces 5 shred **4** rend **6** tear up **7** destroy **9** tear apart

pull up 4 halt, rein, stop, weed **5** check, hoist **6** arrest, uplift, uproot **7** extract, reprove

pulp 4 curd, mash, mush, pith **5** crush, flesh, paste, puree, slush, smash **6** squash, tissue **7** journal **8** magazine **9** masticate

Pulp Fiction

director: **16** Quentin Tarantino

cast: **7** Tim Roth (Ringo) **9** Eric Stolz (Lance) **10** Uma Thurman (Mia Wallace), Ving Rhames (Marsellus Wallace) **11** Bruce Willis (Butch Coolidge) **12** John Travolta (Vincent Vega), Steve Buscemi (Buddy Holly) **13** Amanda Plummer (Yolanda) **14** Samuel L Jackson (Jules Winnfield) **15** Rosanna Arquette (Jody) **17** Christopher Walken (Captain Koons)

pulsate 4 beat, tick, wave **5** pound, pulse, shake, throb, thump, waver **6** quaver, quiver, shiver **7** flutter, shudder, tremble, vibrate **8** undulate **9** alternate, come and go, oscillate, palpitate **10** ebb and flow **11** reverberate

pulse 4 beat **5** throb, thump **6** quiver, rhythm, stroke **7** cadence, pulsate, shudder, tremble, vibrate **9** oscillate, palpitate, pulsation, vibration **10** recurrence, undulation **11** oscillation, palpitation

pulverize 4 mash, mill **5** crumb, crush, grind, mince, pound **6** powder **7** atomize, crumble **9** comminate, granulate, triturate **12** reduce to dust

pulverized 6 ground, milled **7** crumbed, crushed, pounded **8** atomized, crumbled, crunched, powdered **10** granulated **12** ground to dust

pummel 4 beat, maul **5** pound **6** batter, thrash **7** trounce

pump 4 quiz, shoe, well **5** grill **7** inflate, slipper **8** question **9** draw water

Pump

constellation of: **6** Antlia

pumpkin 5 fruit, gourd, melon **6** squash **9** vegetable **12** jack o'lantern

pun

French: **9** jeu de mots

punch 3 box, hit, jab **4** beat, blow, chop, clip, conk, cuff, pelt, plug, poke, slam, sock, swat **5** baste, clout, knock, paste, pound, smite, thump, whack **6** pummel, strike, stroke, thrust, thwack, wallop **7** clobber **8** haymaker **10** roundhouse

punchy 3 fat **5** dazed **6** stubby **8** confused, forceful **9** befuddled

punctilious 5 exact, fussy, picky, rigid **6** proper, strict **7** correct, finicky, precise **8** exacting, rigorous **9** demanding **10** meticulous, particular, scrupulous **11** painstaking

punctual 5 early, quick, ready **6** on time, prompt, steady, timely **7** instant, not late, regular **8** constant, on the dot **9** immediate, well-timed **10** in good time, seasonable **11** expeditious **13** instantaneous

punctuate 4 lace **5** break **6** pepper **7** scatter **8** separate, sprinkle **9** interrupt **11** intersperse

punctuation mark 4 dash **5** colon, comma, pause, point, slash **6** accent, ending, hyphen, parens, period, quotes **7** bracket **8** ellipsis **9** semicolon **10** apostrophe **11** parenthesis **12** question mark **13** quotation mark **16** exclamation point

puncture 3 cut **4** bite, hole, nick, pink **5** break, prick, stick, sting, wound **6** pierce **7** deflate, let down, opening, rupture **9** knock down, shoot down **10** depreciate **11** perforation

pundit 4 guru, sage **5** guide **6** critic, expert, master, mentor, savant, wizard **7** thinker **9** authority **13** learned person

pungent 3 hot **4** acid, keen, racy, sour, tart **5** acrid, acute, nippy, salty, sharp, smart, spicy, tangy, tasty, witty **6** biting, bitter, clever, savory, snappy, strong **7** acetous, caustic, cutting, mordent, peppery, piquant, pointed **8** incisive, piercing, poignant, smarting, stinging, stirring, vinegary, wounding **9** brilliant, flavorful, invidious, palatable, sarcastic, sparkling, trenchant **10** astringent, flavorsome, keen-witted **11** acrimonious, penetrating, provocative, stimulating, tantalizing **12** sharp-tasting **13** scintillating, sharp-smelling **14** highly flavored, highly seasoned

punish 4 beat, fine, flog, whip **6** avenge, rebuke **7** chasten, correct, reprove **8** admonish, chastise, imprison, penalize, sentence **9** castigate, dress down, retaliate **10** discipline, take to task **11** get even with, take revenge **14** bring to account **15** take vengeance on

punishing 5 harsh, penal **6** brutal, severe **7** abusive **8** scolding **9** torturing **10** chastizing, tormenting **11** castigating

punishment 4 fine **5** price **7** damages, deserts, flaying, forfeit, hanging, payment, penalty, penance, redress **8** flogging, punition, spanking, whipping **10** chastening, correction, crucifying, discipline, reparation **11** castigation, retribution **12** chastisement, penalization

punk 4 hood, lout, poor **5** bully, lousy, rowdy, tough **6** crummy, rotten **7** hoodlum, ruffian **8** hooligan **9** barbarian, roughneck **10** delinquent

Puntarvolo

character in: **22** Every Man Out of His Humour

author: **6** Jonson

punt e mes

type: **8** aperitif

origin: **5** Italy

flavor: **6** orange

color: **12** reddish-brown

puny 4 poor, thin, tiny, weak **5** frail, light, petty, runty, small **6** bantam, feeble, flimsy, infirm, little, meager, measly, paltry, sickly, slight, weakly **7** fragile, shallow, tenuous, trivial **8** delicate, impotent, picayune, piddling, runtlike, sawed-off, trifling **9** emaciated, miniature, mite-sized, pint-sized, worthless **10** diminutive, inadequate, picayunish, undersized **11** unimportant **12** insufficient **13** insignificant **14** inconsiderable, underdeveloped

pupa 3 egg **5** larva, nymph **6** cocoon **7** wiggler **9** chrysalis **14** transformation

pupil 4 coed, tyro **5** tutee **6** novice **7** learner, scholar, student, trainee **8** beginner, disciple, initiate **9** schoolboy **10** apprentice, schoolgirl **11** probationer **13** undergraduate

puppet 3 toy **4** doll, dupe, pawn, tool **6** flunky, lackey **7** cat's-paw, manikin, servant **8** creature, henchman, hireling **9** jackstraw, lay figure, underling **10** figurehead, instrument, man of straw, marionette **11** subordinate

puppeteer 4 sarg **5** (Bil) Baird **8** Geppetto **9** Jim Henson **10** Shari Lewis

puppy 3 dog, pet, pup **6** canine

Purcell, Henry
born: 6 London **7** England
composer of: 9 Fantasias **10** Bell Anthem, Dioclesian, King Arthur (The British Worthy), The Tempest **12** Golden Sonata **13** Dido and Aeneas **14** The Indian Queen

purchase 3 buy **4** edge, hold **6** buying, pay for, pick up **7** footing, support, toehold **8** foothold, leverage **9** advantage, influence **11** acquirement, acquisition

pure 4 full, mere, neat, true **5** basic, clean, fresh, moral, sheer, stark, utter, whole **6** chaste, decent, entire, higher, virgin **7** angelic, ethical, perfect, sincere, sinless, sterile, unmixed, upright **8** absolute, abstract, complete, flawless, germfree, innocent, positive, purebred, sanitary, spotless, straight, thorough, unmarred, virginal, virtuous **9** blameless, downright, faultless, guileless, guiltless, healthful, inviolate, out-and-out, pedigreed, righteous, unalloyed, undefiled, unmingled, unspoiled, unsullied, untainted, wholesome **10** antiseptic, immaculate, inviolable, sterilized, uninfected, unmodified, unpolluted **11** conjectural, disinfected, fundamental, pure-blooded, speculative, theoretical, unblemished, uncorrupted, unqualified, untarnished **12** full-strength, hypothetical, thoroughbred **13** unadulterated, unimpeachable **14** above suspicion, uncontaminated

puree 4 bisk, pulp, soup **5** paste **6** bisque

purely 4 only **5** fully **6** merely, simply, solely, wholly **7** cleanly, morally, piously, totally **8** chastely, devoutly, entirely, worthily **9** admirably **10** absolutely, completely, flawlessly, in all

honor, innocently, virginally, virtuously **11** essentially, faultlessly **13** incorruptibly

Purgatory, Purgatorio
part II of: 12 Divine Comedy
author: 14 Dante Alighieri

purge 4 kill, oust **5** crush, expel **6** banish, emetic, pardon, physic, purify, remove, up-root **7** clean up, cleanse, cleanup, clyster, dismiss, expiate, purging, rout out, shake up **8** aperient, atone for, clean out, get rid of, laxative, sweep out, wash away **9** cathartic, discharge, eliminate, eradicate, liquidate, purgation, purgative **10** do away with **11** exterminate **12** obtain pardon (from), purification **15** obtain remission (from) **16** obtain absolution (from) **17** obtain forgiveness

purification 7 baptism **9** cleansing **13** sterilization

purify 4 boil **5** clear **6** filter **7** clarify, distill **8** make pure, sanitize **9** disinfect, sterilize **10** chlorinate, pasteurize **13** decontaminate

Purim 11 Feast of Lots
celebrates: 12 deliverance
heroine: 6 Esther
villian: 5 Haman
month: 4 Adar

Puritani, I
also: 11 The Puritans
opera by: 7 Bellini
character: 14 Oliver Cromwell, Queen Henrietta **16** Lord Arthur Talbot

puritanical 4 prim **5** rigid, stiff **6** narrow, prissy, severe, strict, stuffy **7** ascetic, austere, bigoted, prudish, puritan, stilted **8** dogmatic, priggish **9** bluenosed, fanatical **11** stiff-necked, straitlaced **13** sanctimonious

Puritan State
nickname of: 13 Massachusetts

purity 5 honor, piety **6** virtue **7** clarity, decency, honesty, modesty **8** chastity, fineness, holiness, lucidity, morality, pureness, sanctity **9** cleanness, clearness, innocence, integrity, limpidity, plainness, rectitude, virginity **10** brilliance, chasteness, directness, excellence, immaculacy, simplicity, temperance, uniformity **11** cleanliness, homogeneity, saintliness, uprightness **12** virtuousness **13** guilelessness, guiltlessness **14** immaculateness **15** clear conscience **16** incorruptibility

purlieu 4 area **5** haunt, limit **6** border, locale, region, resort **7** district, environ **8** out-skirt **11** surrounding **12** neighborhood

purloin 3 rob **5** steal **6** pilfer **11** appropriate, make off with

Purloined Letter, The
author: 13 Edgar Allan Poe

purloiner 5 thief **6** robber **7** burglar **8** pilferer

purple 4 plum, puce, racy **5** color,

grape, lilac, lurid, mauve, royal **6** florid, orchid, turgid, violet **7** crimson, flowery, furious, fuchsia, magenta **8** amethyst, burgundy, imperial, lavender **9** gastropod

Purple Land *see* **7** Uruguay

Purple Rose of Cairo, The
director: 10 Woody Allen
cast: 9 Mia Farrow **11** Danny Aiello, Jeff Daniels

purport 3 aim, end **4** gist **5** claim, drift, point, sense, tenor, trend **6** allege, burden, design, import, intent, object, reason **7** bearing, meaning, profess, purpose **9** intention, objective, rationale, substance **11** implication **12** significance **13** signification

purpose 3 aim **4** goal, hope, mean, plan, will, wish **5** elect, point, sense **6** aspire, choose, decide, design, desire, intend, intent, motive, object, reason, scheme, target **7** drive at, meaning, mission, persist, project, propose, resolve, think to **8** ambition, conclude, endeavor, function, proposal, set about **9** determine, intention, objective, persevere, rationale, undertake **10** aspiration, motivation, resolution **11** contemplate, disposition, expectation, fixed intent, have a mind to, raison d'etre **13** commit one self, determination

purposeful 7 decided, studied **8** resolute, resolved **9** committed, conscious **10** calculated, considered, deliberate, determined **11** intentional **12** premeditated, strong-willed

purposefulness 7 purpose, resolve **10** resolution **11** decidedness **12** decisiveness, resoluteness **13** determination

purposeless 6 random **7** aimless, useless **8** needless, plotless **9** desultory, driftless, haphazard, irregular, senseless, unplanned **11** meaningless **12** functionless, undetermined, unprofitable

purposely 8 by design **9** advisedly, expressly, knowingly, on purpose, willfully, wittingly **10** designedly, with intent **11** consciously, voluntarily **12** calculatedly, deliberately **13** intentionally

purse 3 bag **4** fold, fund, knit **5** award, bunch, pinch, pleat, pouch, prize, stake **6** clutch, coffer, gather, pucker, wallet **7** handbag, sporran, wrinkle **8** contract, moneybag, proceeds, treasury, winnings **10** pocketbook **11** shoulder bag
French: 12 porte-monnaie

purser 6 bursar **7** cashier **9** paymaster **10** cashkeeper

pursue 4 seek **5** aim at, chase, track, trail **6** aim for, follow, try for **7** be after, carry on, go after, perform **8** aspire to, engage in, labor for, run after

9 race after, strive for **10** chase after, push toward

pursuer 5 pupil **6** seeker **7** devotee, student **8** disciple, follower, searcher **10** aficionado

pursuit 4 hunt **5** chase **6** search **7** pastime **8** activity **9** following **10** occupation

purvey 3 get **4** give, hand **5** cater, equip, yield **6** obtain, outfit, supply **7** deliver, furnish, procure, provide

purveyor 4 pimp **6** seller **8** procurer, provider, supplier

purview 3 ken **4** area **5** field, range, reach, realm, savvy, scope, sweep **6** domain, extent **7** compass, horizon, outlook **8** dominion, overview **9** territory, viewpoint **10** commission, experience **11** mental grasp **13** comprehension, understanding **14** responsibility

push 2 go **3** dun, ram **4** butt, goad, jolt, move, plug, prod, spur, sway, urge, work, worm **5** boost, drive, egg on, elbow, fight, foray, force, forge, harry, hound, impel, nudge, press, rouse, shove, stick, stuff, vigor, wedge **6** arouse, badger, coerce, compel, energy, exhort, harass, heckle, hustle, incite, induce, inroad, jostle, plunge, prompt, propel, thrust, wiggle **7** advance, animate, buffalo, inspire, promote, provoke, squeeze **8** ambition, browbeat, motivate, persuade, shoulder, struggle, vitality **9** advertise, constrain, encourage, importune, incursion, instigate, make known, publicize, stimulate, strong-arm **10** get-up-and-go **11** make one's way, prevail upon, vim and vigor **12** force one's way, propagandize **13** determination

pushcart 5 wagon **6** barrow **8** handcart **10** handbarrow **11** wheelbarrow

push forward 4 goad, prod, spur **5** drive, impel, press **9** urge along

Pushkin, Alexander (Aleksandr) author of: **12** Boris Godunov, Eugene Onegin **16** The Queen of Spades **17** The Bronze Horseman **19** The Captain's Daughter

push through 6 hasten **7** advance, forward **8** dispatch, expedite **10** accelerate, facilitate

pushy 8 forceful **9** assertive, insistent **10** aggressive **11** domineering **12** strong-willed **13** self-assertive

pusillanimous 7 fearful **8** cowardly, timorous **10** spiritless **11** lily-livered **12** apprehensive, fainthearted, meanspirited

pusillanimousness 8 timidity **9** cowardice **12** yellow streak **13** yellow

feather **16** faint heartedness **18** chick-enheartedness

puss 3 cat, mug, pan **4** face **5** kitty **6** feline, kisser, kitten

pussyfoot 5 dodge, evade, hedge, sneak **6** tiptoe, weasel **8** sidestep **13** evade the issue **14** beg the question **15** walk on eggshells **16** straddle the fence

put 3 fix, lay, set **4** cast, pose, rest, word **5** bring, drive, force, heave, offer, pitch, place, state, throw **6** assign, employ, impute, phrase, submit **7** ascribe, deposit, express, present, propose **8** position **9** attribute, enunciate **10** articulate

put a damper on 4 cool, dull **7** depress, squelch **10** discourage, dishearten

put an edge on 4 hone, whet **6** excite **7** sharpen **9** stimulate

put an end to 4 halt, stop **5** annul, quash **6** cancel, finish, repeal, revoke **7** abolish, blot out, rescind, squelch, wipe out **8** abrogate, demolish, dispatch, stamp out **9** eliminate, eradicate, finish off **10** discourage, do away with, put a stop to **12** write finis to

put aside 5 table **6** forget **7** discard, lay away **10** relinquish

put away 3 eat **4** down, stow **5** stash **6** commit **7** confine, consume **9** drink down

put back 4 rout **5** delay **6** defeat, demote, impair, reject, return **7** replace, restore **9** reinstate

put down 4 note, post **5** crush, enter, knock, quash, quell **6** dispel, enlist, record, subdue **7** deposit, disdain, sneer at, squelch **8** belittle, derogate, laugh off, pooh-pooh, suppress **9** denigrate, disparage, humiliate, write down **10** depreciate

put forth 5 offer **6** extend, put out **7** proffer, send out

put forward 4 pose **6** assert **7** advance, profess, propose **8** propound

put in irons 5 chain **6** fetter **7** manacle, shackle **8** handcuff

put in motion 4 move **5** begin, start **6** arouse, launch **8** activate, carry out, commence, initiate **9** instigate, undertake

put in order 5 array **6** neaten, tidy up **7** arrange **8** organize **10** straighten

put in plain sight 4 show **6** set out **7** display, exhibit

put in shackles 6 fetter, hobble **7** enchain, enslave, manacle **8** handcuff, imprison

put into circulation 4 move **5** issue, print **7** publish **10** pass around

put into effect 6 effect **7** achieve, enforce, execute, fulfill, realize **8** carry out, complete **10** accomplish, admin-

ister, consummate, effectuate, perpetrate **12** carry through

put into words 5 voice **7** express **8** describe **9** verbalize **10** articulate **11** communicate

put off 5 delay, repel, stall **6** offend, rebuff, recess **7** adjourn, repulse, set sail, suspend **8** hold back, launched, offended, postpone, rebuffed, repelled, repulsed **9** interrupt **11** discontinue **13** procrastinate

put off guard 4 lull **6** disarm **10** make unwary

put on 3 don **5** affix **6** attach **7** dress in, get into, stick on **8** fasten to

put-on 4 hoax, joke **8** pretense **11** affectation

put on guard 4 warn **5** alert **6** advise, tip off **7** caution **8** forewarn **9** make ready **10** precaution

put out 3 irk **5** annoy, issue **6** quench, retire **7** produce, publish **8** irritate **9** strike out **10** extinguish **11** manufacture **13** leave the shore

put out of order 5 mix up, upset **6** jumble, mess up, muddle **7** confuse, scatter **8** disarray, disorder, displace, put askew, scramble **10** disarrange **11** disorganize

putrefaction 3 rot **5** decay **7** rotting **8** spoilage, spoiling **10** rottenness **12** decompostion

putrefy 3 rot **4** turn **5** decay, spoil, taint **6** molder **8** putresce, stagnate **9** decompose **10** biodegrade **11** deteriorate **12** disintegrate

putrescent 4 foul, rank **5** fetid **6** smelly **7** decaying, spoiling **8** stinking **9** offensive **10** malodorous, putrefying **11** decomposing

putrid 3 bad **4** foul, rank **5** fetid **6** rancid, rotten, spoiled **7** tainted **8** decaying, polluted, purulent, stinking **9** putrefied **10** putrescent **11** decomposing **12** contaminated, putrefactive

putridity 5 decay, filth, taint **8** foulness, impurity **9** dirtiness, pollution, purulence, rancidity **10** rottenness **11** putrescence, uncleanness **13** contamination, decomposition

putsch 6 revolt **8** uprising

putter 4 fool, idle, laze, loaf, loll **5** dally, drift **6** dawdle, diddle, fiddle, loiter, lounge, piddle, potter, tinker **8** golf club, lallygag **10** dillydally

put to death 4 do in, hang, kill, slay **5** slain **6** done in, hanged, killed, murder, poison, rub out **7** bump off, butcher, execute **8** dispatch, executed, massacre, murdered, poisoned, strangle **9** bumped off, butchered, finish off, massacred, strangled, suffocate **11** assassinate, electrocute, exterminate **12** assassinated, electrocuted, exterminated

put to flight 4 rout, shoo **5** chase **6**

dispel **7** cast out, scatter **8** drive off, send away **11** send packing

put together 4 join **5** unite **7** combine **8** assemble

put to shame 6 ashame **7** chagrin, mortify **9** discomfit, embarrass, humiliate

put to sleep 4 lull **5** quiet **6** sedate **8** knock out **9** narcotize **11** anesthetize

put to use 3 use **5** apply **6** employ, engage, occupy **7** exploit, utilize **9** make use of

put under a spell 5 charm **7** bewitch, enchant **8** entrance **9** fascinate, mesmerize, spellbind

put up 3 can **4** hang **5** erect, house, lodge, raise, store **6** billet **7** shelter **8** preserve **11** accommodate **14** furnish room for

put up with 4 bear, take **5** abide, brave, brook, stand **6** endure, suffer **7** stomach, sustain, undergo **8** stand for, submit to, tolerate **9** withstand **11** countenance

Puvis de Chavannes, Pierre Cecile
   born: 5 Lyons **6** France
   artwork: 6 Summer **13** Shepherd's Song **14** Ludus pro patria **16** The Poor Fisherman **17** Life of St Genevieve, The Inspiring Muses **21** Science Arts and Letters

Puzo, Mario
   author of: 6 Omerta **8** Fools Die **10** The Fourth K, The Last Don **12** The Godfather **19** The Fortunate Pilgrim

puzzle 4 foil, mull **5** brood, stump **6** baffle, enigma, outwit, ponder, riddle, wonder **7** confuse, dilemma, mystery, mystify, nonplus, perplex, problem **8** bewilder, confound, hoodwink **9** conundrum **10** bafflement, difficulty, perplexity **12** bewilderment, complication **13** mystification

puzzled 6 amazed **7** baffled **8** befogged, confused, troubled **9** astounded, befuddled, mystified, perplexed **10** bewildered, confounded, nonplussed

puzzling 7 elusive **8** baffling **9** confusing, enigmatic **10** mysterious, mystifying, perplexing **11** bewildering, confounding, enigmatical **12** unfathomable **16** hard to understand, incomprehensible

Pyanepsia
   origin: 5 Greek **8** Athenian
   event: 8 festival
   honoring: 6 Apollo **7** harvest

Pygmalion
   author: 17 George Bernard Shaw
   character: 12 Henry Higgins **14** Eliza Doolittle
   basis for: 10 My Fair Lady
   director: 14 Anthony Asquith
   cast: 11 Wendy Hiller (Eliza Doolittle) **12** Leslie Howard (Professor Henry Higgins) **13** Wilfrid Lawson

Pygmalion
   king of: 6 Cyprus
   avocation: 8 sculptor
   statue named: 7 Galatea
   loved: 7 Galatea
   statue changed to: 5 woman
   wife: 7 Galatea
   daughter: 6 Paphos **8** Metharme

pygmy 3 elf, toy, wee **4** mite, runt, tiny **5** dwarf, elfin, short, small **6** bantam, midget, peewee, shrimp **7** manikin **8** dwarfish, half-pint, Tom Thumb **9** miniature, pipsqueak **10** diminutive, homun culus, undersized **11** Lilliputian

Pyncheon family
   character in: 24 The House of the Seven Gables
   members: 6 Phoebe **8** Clifford, Hepzibah **12** Judge Jaffrey
   author: 9 Hawthorne

Pynchon, Thomas
   author of: 1 V **8** Vineland **13** Mason and Dixon **15** Gravity's Rainbow **23** The Crying of Lot Forty-Nine

Pyongyang
   capital of: 10 North Korea

Pyramus
   form: 5 youth
   location: 7 Babylon
   loved: 6 Thisbe
   died at tomb of: 5 Ninus

pyre 8 woodpile
   rite: 7 funeral
   method: 7 burning

Pyrigenes
   epithet of: 8 Dionysus
   means: 10 born of fire

Pyriphlegethon see **10** Phlegethon

pyromaniac 7 firebug **8** arsonist **10** incendiary **11** firestarter

Pyronia
   epithet of: 7 Artemis
   means: 11 fire goddess

pyrope
   species: 6 garnet
   color: 3 red

pyrophobia
   fear of: 4 fire

pyrotechnics 9 fireworks **16** brilliant display **19** dazzling performance

Pyrrhus
   king of: 6 Epirus
   triumphed over: 5 Romans
   result: 11 heavy losses
   phrase: 14 Pyrrhic victory

Pythagoras
   born: 5 Samos
   vocation: 11 philosopher **13** mathematician
   created: 7 theorem
   of: 13 right triangle

Pythia
   priestess of: 6 Apollo
   location: 6 Delphi
   delivered: 7 oracles

Pythias
   friend: 5 Damon

Pythius see **6** Apollo

  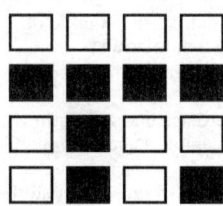

Qatar

capital/largest city: 4 Doha **7** al-Dawha

others: 3 Juh **5** Wagra **6** Dukhan, Umm-Bab **7** al-Khawr, Musayid, Umm Said

government: 7 emirate

head of state/government: 4 emir

monetary unit: 5 riyal **6** dirham

highest point: 13 Aba al-Bawl Hill

physical feature:

  bay: 5 Salwa

  cape: 5 Rakan **6** Laffan **8** Ushayriq **9** al-Matbakh

  gulf: 7 Bahrain, Persian

  people: 4 Arab **6** Pushtu, Yemeni **7** Baluchi, Iranian **9** Pakistani

  rulers: 12 Great Britain, Ottoman Turks

  sheik/sheikh: 18 Ahmad bin Ali al-Thani **22** Khalifa bin Hamad al-Thani

language: 6 Arabic

religion: 5 Islam

  sect: 7 Wahhabi

war: 4 Gulf **11** Desert Storm

QED 21 quod erat demonstrandum

quack 4 fake, sham **5** phony **6** pseudo **9** charlatan, pretender **10** fake doctor, fraudulent **11** counterfeit, quacksalver **15** medical impostor

quackery 5 bluff, guile **6** deceit **7** cunning **9** deception, duplicity **12** charlatanism

Quadrigesima 4 Lent **9** forty days

quaff 4 down, gulp, swig **5** drink, lap up, swill **6** guzzle, imbibe, tipple **7** swallow, toss off **8** belt down, chug-a-lug **9** knock back **11** drink deeply

quagmire 3 bog, fen, fix, jam **4** mess, mire, ooze, quag, sump **5** marsh, pinch, swamp **6** crisis, morass, muddle, pickle, plight, scrape, slough, sludge, strait **7** dilemma **8** hot water, quandary **9** imbroglio, intricacy, quicksand **10** difficulty, perplexity **11** Gordian knot, involvement, predicament **12** entanglement

quail 3 shy **5** cower, quake, shake **6** blanch, flinch, recoil, shrink **7** run away, shudder, tremble **8** fight shy, turn tail **10** lose heart **10** be cowardly, lose spirit, take fright **11** lose courage **12** have cold feet **16** shake in one's boots **17** shiver in one's shoes, show a yellow streak

quail

  group of: 4 bevy **5** covey

quaint 3 odd **4** rare **5** droll, queer **6** unique **7** antique, bizarre, curious, strange, unusual **8** charming, fanciful, old-timey, original, peculiar, singular, uncommon **9** eccentric, whimsical **10** antiquated, outlandish **11** out-of-the-way, picturesque **12** old-fashioned **13** extraordinary **14** unconventional

quake 4 wave **5** quail, shake, spasm, throb **6** blanch, quaver, quiver, ripple, shiver, thrill, tremor **7** shudder, tremble **9** trembling **10** earthquake **18** seismic disturbance

Quaker

  founder: 9 George Fox

  group: 7 friends

  pronoun: 4 thee, thou

qualification 4 gift **5** forte, skill **6** talent **7** ability, faculty, fitness, proviso **8** aptitude, bona fide, capacity, property, standard **9** attribute, condition, endowment, exception, exemption, objection, postulate, provision, requisite **10** capability, competency, credential, limitation **11** achievement, arrangement, eligibility, requirement, reservation, restriction, stipulation **12** escape clause, modification, prerequisite, suitableness **13** certification **14** accomplishment

qualified 3 fit **4** able, meet **5** adept, equal **6** expert, fitted, suited, versed **7** capable, guarded, hedging, knowing, limited, skilled, trained **8** eligible, equipped, licensed, reserved, skillful, talented **9** ambiguous, certified, competent, efficient, equivocal, practiced **10** authorized, indefinite, proficient, restricted **11** conditional, efficacious, experienced, provisional **12** accomplished

qualify 3 fit **4** ease **5** abate, adapt, alter, endow, equip, limit, ready, train **6** adjust, enable, ground, modify, narrow, permit, reduce, soften, temper **7** assuage, certify, empower, entitle, license, make fit, prepare **8** describe, diminish, mitigate, moderate, restrain, restrict, sanction **9** authorize, condition, give power, measure up **10** be accepted, be eligible, commission, legitimate **11** accommodate **12** characterize, circumscribe, make eligible

qualifying 9 tempering **10** mitigating **11** eligibility, extenuating, preparatory

quality 4 mark, rank **5** blood, class, grade, merit, trait, value, worth **6** aspect, family, nature **7** caliber, dignity, faculty, feature **8** capacity, eminence, position, property, standing **9** attribute, character **11** disposition, distinction, high station, temperament **12** constitution, social status **13** qualification **14** characteristic

Quality Street

author: 12 James M Barrie

qualm 4 turn **6** nausea **7** scruple, vertigo **9** faintness, giddiness, misgiving **10** dizzy spell, hesitation, queasiness, reluctance, uneasiness **11** compunction, reservation, sick feeling **13** indisposition, unwillingness **14** disinclination **18** twinge of conscience

quandary 3 fix, jam **4** mire **5** pinch **6** crisis, morass, pickle, plight, scrape, strait **7** dilemma, impasse **8** hot water, quagmire **9** imbroglio **10** difficulty **11** involvement, predicament **12** entanglement, kettle of fish

quantities 4 lots, much **5** heaps, loads **7** amounts

quantity 3 sum **4** area, bulk, dose, mass, size **5** quota, share **6** amount, dosage, extent, length, number, volume **7** expanse, measure, portion **8** vastness **9** abundance, aggregate, allotment, amplitude, extension, greatness, magnitude, multitude **10** proportion **11** measurement **13** apportionment

quarantine 7 confine, isolate **9** isolation, segregate, sequester **13** sequestration **15** cordon sanitaire **18** medical segregation

Quare Fellow, The

author: 12 Brendan Behan

quarrel 3 jar, nag, row **4** carp, feud, fuss, spat, tiff **5** argue, brawl, cavil, clash, fight, scrap **6** bicker, differ, strife **7** contend, discord, dispute, dissent, fall out, wrangle **8** argument, be at odds, conflict, squabble **9** altercate, bickering, complaint, find fault, have words, objection **10** contention, difference, dissension, dissidence, falling out **11** controversy **12** disagreement

13 breach of peace, contradiction, misunderstand **14** apple of discord **15** be at logger heads **16** bone of contention, misunderstanding

quarreling 6 strife **7** discord **8** clashing, conflict, disunity, friction **9** bickering, disputing, scrapping, wrangling **10** contention, dissension, dissidence, squabbling **11** discordance **12** disagreement

quarrelsome 7 peevish **8** captious, churlish, contrary, militant, petulant **9** bellicose, combative, fractious, irascible, querulous, truculent **10** pugnacious **11** belligerent, contentious **12** antagonistic, cantankerous, disagreeable, disputatious **13** argumentative

quarry 3 bed, dig, pit **4** game, lode, mine, prey **5** catch, stone **6** source, victim **8** excavate

quart
abbreviation: **2** qt

quarter, quarters 4 area, part, pity, post, side, spot, zone **5** board, house, lodge, mercy, place, put up, realm, rooms **6** billet, domain, fourth, locale, region, sphere **7** housing, install, lodging, shelter, station, terrain **8** clemency, district, humanity, leniency, locality, location, lodgings, position, precinct, province, sympathy **9** percent, direction, one-fourth, situation, territory **10** compassion, fourth part, indulgence, quadrisect **11** place to live, place to stay, three months **13** quarter dollar, specific place **14** accommodations **15** twenty-five cents

quarterstaff 4 pole **5** staff **6** cudgel

quartz
varieties: **4** sard **5** agate, topaz **8** amethyst **9** carnelian, tiger's-eye **11** rock crystal

quash 4 ruin, stop, undo, void **5** annul, crush, erase, quell, smash, wreck **6** cancel, delete, dispel, efface, quench, recall, revoke, squash, subdue, vacate **7** blot out, destroy, expunge, nullify, put down, repress, rescind, retract, reverse, squelch **8** abrogate, dissolve, override, overrule, overturn, set aside, suppress **9** devastate, eradicate, extirpate, overthrow, overwhelm, repudiate, strike out **10** annihilate, extinguish, invalidate, obliterate, put an end to **11** countermand, exterminate

quasi 4 near, part, semi **6** almost, ersatz **7** halfway, seeming, virtual **8** apparent, somewhat, so-called **9** imitation, synthetic **10** resembling

Quasimodo
character in: **23** The Hunchback of Notre Dame
author: **4** Hugo

Quatermain, Allan
character in: **17** King Solomon's Mines
author: **7** Haggard

quaver 4 beat, sway, wave **5** quake, shake, throb, trill, waver **6** falter, quiver, shiver, teeter, totter, tremor, wobble, writhe **7** pulsate, shudder, tremble, tremolo, vibrate, vibrato, wriggle **9** oscillate, trembling, vibration **14** tremulous shake

quay 4 dock, mole, pier **5** basin, jetty, levee, wharf **6** marina **7** landing **10** waterfront

queasy 5 giddy, upset **6** uneasy **7** bilious, sickish **8** nauseous, qualmish, troubled **9** nauseated, sickening, uncertain **10** nauseating **13** uncomfortable **16** sick to the stomach

Quebec
borders: **7** Ontario **8** Labrador **9** Hudson Bay **12** Newfoundland, United States **13** Atlantic Ocean **16** Gulf of St Lawrence
cape: **5** Gaspe
city: **6** Quebec **8** Montreal **10** Chicoutimi, Sherbrooke **13** Trois Rivieres
highest point: **18** Mont Jacques Cartier
hockey team: **9** Canadiens, Nordiques
island: **9** Anticosti
lake: **5** Gouin **9** Bienville, Eau Claire, Saint Jean **10** Mistassini **11** Manicouagan
mineral: **4** gold, zinc **6** copper **7** iron ore **8** asbestos **9** limestone
mountain: **5** Otish **10** Laurentian, Shickshock **11** Appalachian **12** Monteregians
province of: **6** Canada

Quechua
tribe: **4** Inca

queen 5 ranee **7** czarina, empress **8** princess **13** female monarch
French: **5** reine
German: **7** Konigin
Latin: **6** regina
Spanish: **5** reina

queen/empress/princess
of Egypt: **9** Cleopatra, Nefertari, Nefertiti **10** Hatshepsut, Hetepheres
of England: **3** Mab **4** Anne, Bess, Jane, Mary **7** Eleanor **8** Boadicea, Victoria **9** Catherine, Charlotte, Elizabeth, Guinevere **10** Bloody Mary, Elizabeth I **11** Elizabeth II, Jane Seymour
of France: **7** Eugenie **9** Josephine **11** Marie Louise **14** Marie de Medicis **15** Marie Antoinette
of Italy/Rome: **7** Poppaea **9** Agrippina, Messalina **13** Livia Drusilla
of Monaco: **8** Caroline **9** Stephanie **10** Grace Kelly
of the Netherlands: **7** Beatrix, Juliana **10** Wilhelmina
of Poland: **7** Jadwiga
of Portugal: **5** Maria **9** Elizabeth

of Russia: **9** Alexandra, Catherine **17** Catherine the Great
of Scotland: **4** Mary **13** Saint Margaret **16** Mary Queen of Scots
of Spain: **8** Isabella **16** Elizabeth Farnese
of Sweden: **9** Christina
of Syria: **7** Zenobia
in folklore: **3** Mab **7** Titania

Queen Christina
director: **15** Rouben Mamoulian
cast: **8** Ian Keith **10** Greta Garbo, Lewis Stone **11** John Gilbert **12** C Aubrey Smith

Queen Mab
author: **18** Percy Bysshe Shelley

Queen of Amazons 9 Hippolyta, Hippolyte

Queen of Hearts
character in: **28** Alice's Adventures in Wonderland
author: **7** Carroll

Queen of Heaven 4 Hera, Mary **6** Ishtar **7** Mylitta

Queen of Spades, The
also: **12** Pikovaya Dama
opera by: **11** Tchaikovsky
character: **4** Lisa **6** Herman **8** Countess

Queen of Spades, The
author: **16** Alexander Pushkin

Queen of the Surf
nickname of: **14** Esther Williams

Queen's Necklace, The
author: **14** Alexandre Dumas (pere)
character: **5** Oliva **13** Count de Charny **15** Cardinal de Rohan, Count Cagliostro, Marie Antoinette **16** Andree de Taverney **18** Philippe de Taverney **21** Jeanne de la Motte Valois

Queequeg
character in: **8** Moby Dick
author: **8** Melville

queer 3 gay, odd **4** daft, harm, hurt, rare, ruin **5** crazy, dizzy, droll, faint, fishy, funny, giddy, shady, spoil, weird, woozy, wreck **6** absurd, damage, exotic, impair, injure, quaint, qualmy, queasy, thwart, unique **7** bizarre, comical, curious, disrupt, erratic, reeling, strange, touched, unusual **8** abnormal, bohemian, doubtful, fanciful, freakish, original, peculiar, uncommon, unhinged **9** eccentric, fantastic, grotesque, homosexual, irregular, laughable, ludicrous, unnatural **10** capricious, compromise, farfetched, irrational, outlandish, remarkable, ridiculous, suspicious, unbalanced, unexampled, unorthodox **11** astonishing, exceptional, light-headed, out of the way, slightly ill, vertiginous **12** preposterous, questionable, unparalleled **13** extraordinary, nonconforming, unprecedented **14** unconventional
French: **5** outre

Queer as Folk
network: 8 Showtime
cast: 8 Thea Gill (Lindsay Peterson) 9 Hal Sparks (Michael Novotny-Bruckner) 10 Gale Harold (Brian Kinney), Peter Paige (Emmett Honeycutt) 11 Chris Potter (Dr David Cameron), Harris Allan (Hunter Montgomery), Makyla Smith (Daphne Chanders), Scott Lowell (Ted Schmidt), Sharon Gless (Debbie Novotny) 12 Sherry Miller (Jennifer Taylor) 13 Dean Armstrong (Blake Wyzecki), Jack Wetherall (Vic Grassi), Randy Harrison (Justin Taylor)

Queer Eye for the Straight Guy
network: 5 Bravo
cast: 8 Ted Allen 11 Kyan Douglas, Thom Filicia 12 Jai Rodriguez 14 Carson Kressley

quell 4 calm, dull, ease, hush, lull, rout, ruin, stay, stem 5 abate, allay, blunt, crush, quash, quiet, still, worst, wreck 6 becalm, deaden, defeat, pacify, quench, reduce, soften, soothe, subdue 7 appease, assuage, compose, conquer, destroy, mollify, put down, scatter, silence, squelch 8 beat down, disperse, mitigate, overcome, palliate, stamp out, suppress, vanquish 9 alleviate, overpower, overthrow, overwhelm, subjugate 10 extinguish 11 tranquilize

quench 4 cool, sate 5 allay, crush, douse, quell, slake 6 dampen, put out, stifle 7 appease, blow out, put down, satiate, satisfy, smother 8 stamp out, suppress 10 annihilate, extinguish

Quentin Durward
author: 14 Sir Walter Scott
character: 8 Isabelle 9 Le Balafre 10 Jacqueline 11 King Louis XI 12 Lady Hameline 13 Ludovic Lesley 15 Countess of Croye 16 William de la Marck 18 Hayraddin Maugrabin 20 King Louis the Eleventh 21 Charles Duke of Burgundy 23 Count Philip de Crevecoeur

querulous 4 sour 5 cross, fussy, testy, whiny 6 cranky, touchy 7 crabbed, finical, finicky, fretful, grouchy, peevish, pettish, waspish, whining 8 captious, exacting, petulant, shrewish 9 difficult, grumbling, irascible, irritable, long-faced, obstinate, resentful, splenetic 10 nettlesome 11 complaining, quarrelsome 12 disagreeable, discontented, disputatious, dissatisfied, faultfinding

query 3 ask 4 quiz 5 doubt, issue, quest 6 demand, impugn, search 7 dispute, examine, impeach, inquest,

inquiry, inspect, problem, request, suspect 8 distrust, look into, mistrust, question, sound out 9 catechize, challenge, inquire of 10 controvert 11 examination, inquisition, interrogate, investigate, make inquiry 13 interrogation, investigation

quest 4 hunt, seek 6 pursue, search, voyage 7 crusade, journey, mission, pursuit, seeking 9 adventure 10 enterprise, pilgrimage 11 exploration

Quest for Fire
director: 17 Jean-Jacques Annaud
cast: 10 Ron Perlman 12 Rae Dawn Chong 13 Everett McGill

question 3 ask, rub 4 pump, quiz, test 5 doubt, drill, grill, issue, query 6 impugn, matter, motion, oppose 7 dispute, dubiety, examine, problem, subject, suspect 8 distrust, look into, mistrust, proposal, sound out 9 catechize, challenge, inquire of, misgiving, moot point, objection 10 difficulty, disbelieve 11 controversy, interrogate, investigate, proposition, uncertainty 12 cross-examine 13 consideration

questionable 4 moot 5 fishy, shady 6 unsure 7 dubious, in doubt, suspect 8 arguable, doubtful, puzzling, unproven 9 ambiguous, confusing, debatable, enigmatic, equivocal, in dispute, uncertain, undecided 10 apocryphal, disputable, indefinite, mysterious, mystifying, perplexing, suspicious 12 hypothetical 13 controversial, problematical

queue 3 row 4 file, line, rank 5 chain, train 6 column, string

quibble 3 nag 4 carp, spar 5 argue, cavil, dodge, fence, fudge, shift 6 bicker, haggle, hassle, nicety, niggle, waffle 7 evasion, nitpick, shuffle 8 artifice, pretense, squabble, subtlety, white lie 9 be evasive, duplicity 10 equivocate, pick a fight, subterfuge 11 distraction 12 equivocation 13 dodge the issue, prevarication

quick 3 apt 4 able, deft, fast, keen, spry 5 acute, adept, agile, alert, brief, brisk, eager, fiery, fleet, hasty, rapid, sharp, smart, swift, testy 6 abrupt, active, adroit, astute, brainy, bright, clever, expert, facile, flying, frisky, lively, nimble, prompt, shrewd, speedy, sudden, touchy, winged 7 hurried, peppery, waspish 8 animated, choleric, headlong, petulant, skillful, snappish, spirited, vigilant, vigorous 9 dexterous, energetic, excitable, impatient, impetuous, impulsive, irascible, irritable, sagacious, splenetic, sprightly, vivacious, whirlwind, wideawake 10 discerning, high-strung, hotblooded 11 accelerated, expeditious,

hot-tempered, intelligent, light-footed, penetrating, precipitate 12 nimblefooted 13 perspicacious, temperamental

quicken 4 fire, goad, move, rush, spur, stir, urge 5 drive, egg on, hurry, impel, pique, press, rouse, speed 6 affect, arouse, excite, hasten, hustle, incite, kindle, propel, revive, vivify 7 actuate, advance, animate, enliven, further, hurry on, inspire, provoke, refresh, sharpen 8 activate, dispatch, energize, enkindle, expedite, inspirit, vitalize 9 galvanize, instigate, stimulate 10 accelerate, invigorate 11 precipitate

quick glance
French: 9 coup d'oeil

quickly 4 anon, fast, soon 6 keenly, presto, pronto 7 briefly, hastily, rapidly, swiftly 8 promptly, speedily 9 instantly 11 immediately 12 lickety-split

Quickly, Mistress
character in: 22 The Merry Wives of Windsor
author: 11 Shakespeare

quickness 5 haste, speed 6 acuity 8 alacrity, celerity, keenness, rapidity 9 acuteness, alertness, dexterity, sharpness 10 cleverness, nimbleness, promptness 15 expeditiousness

quick-tempered 5 cross, testy 6 cranky, shirty, touchy 7 grouchy, peevish, waspish 8 choleric, churlish, shrewish, snappish 9 emotional, excitable, irascible, irritable 10 ill-humored 11 bad-tempered, hot-tempered, quarrelsome 12 cantankerous 13 temperamental

quick-witted 4 keen 5 acute, alert, aware, quick, ready, sharp, smart, witty 6 astute, bright, clever, shrewd 8 incisive 9 brilliant, wide-awake 10 discerning, perceptive 11 clearheaded, intelligent, penetrating 13 perspicacious

quid pro quo 4 swap 5 trade 8 exchange 9 tit for tat 21 something for something

quien sabe? 8 who knows?

quiescence 7 latency 8 dormancy, inaction 10 inactivity

quiescent 6 latent 7 dormant 8 inactive 10 in abeyance

quiet 3 low, mum 4 calm, curb, dull, ease, hush, lull, meek, mild, mute, rest, soft, stay, stop 5 abate, allay, blunt, check, fixed, inert, peace, plain, quell, still 6 arrest, at rest, deaden, docile, dozing, gentle, humble, hushed, lessen, mellow, modest, muffle, pacify, placid, repose, sedate, serene, settle, silent, simple, soften, soothe, stable, steady, stifle, subdue, weaken **7** assuage, clement, comfort, compose, dormant, halcyon, mollify, not busy, pacific, passive, patient, relieve, restful, silence, smother, subdued, suspend, unmoved **8** becalmed, calmness, comatose, composed, decrease, immobile, inactive, mitigate, moderate, muteness, not rough, not showy, palliate, peaceful, quietude, reserved, reticent, retiring, serenity, sleeping, stagnant, taciturn, tranquil **9** alleviate, collected, contented, easygoing, immovable, lethargic, makequiet, noiseless, not bright, peaceable, placidity, quietness, set at ease, soundless, stillness, temperate, terminate, unruffled, voiceless **10** coolheaded, gentleness, motionless, phlegmatic, put a stop to, relaxation, slumbering, speechless, stationary, stock-still, unassuming, untroubled **11** discontinue, tranquility, tranquilize, undisturbed, unexcitable, unobtrusive, unperturbed **12** bring to an end, even-tempered, inarticulate, peacefulness, tranquillity **13** at a standstill, dispassionate, imperturbable, noiselessness, soundlessness, unimpassioned, unpretentious **14** unostentatious, unpresumptuous **15** uncommunicative, undemonstrative

quietly 5 coyly **6** calmly, humbly, meekly, mildly, mutely, softly, tamely **8** demurely, modestly, placidly, serenely, silently **9** bashfully, inaudibly, patiently **10** composedly, moderately, peacefully, tranquilly **11** collectedly, contentedly, diffidently, noiselessly, pacifically, soundlessly, temperately, unexcitedly **12** speechlessly, unassumingly, unboastfully **13** unobtrusively, unperturbedly **15** dispassionately, unpretentiously, without ceremony **16** unostentatiously **17** undemonstratively

Quiet Man, The
  director: **8** John Ford
  author: **13** Liam O'Flaherty
  cast: **9** John Wayne **12** Maureen O'Hara **14** Mildred Natwick, Victor McLaglen **15** Barry Fitzgerald
  setting: **7** Ireland
  score: **11** Victor Young
  Oscar for: **8** director

quietness 5 peace, quiet **7** silence **8** softness **9** stillness **12** peacefulness

quietude 4 calm, rest **6** repose **8** easiness **9** composure

quill 3 pen **4** fold, hair, pick, seta, stem, tube **5** pluck, plume, spike, spine, spool **6** bobbin, needle **7** bristle, feather, spindle **9** toothpick

Quilp
  character in: **19** The Old Curiosity Shop
  author: **7** Dickens

quilt 5 cover **6** spread **7** blanket **8** coverlet **9** bedspread, comforter

Quincy, M. E.
  character: **3** Lee **5** Danny, (Sgt) Brill **11** Sam Fujiyama, (Dr) Robert Astin **12** (Lt) Frank Monahan
  cast: **9** Robert Ito **10** John S Ragin **11** Jack Klugman, Joseph Roman, Val Bisoglio **12** Garry Walberg **13** Lynette Mettey
  setting: **10** Los Angeles **11** Danny's Place

Quinn, Anthony
  born: **6** Mexico **9** Chihuahua
  wife: **16** Katherine DeMille
  roles: **7** Oriundi **8** La Strada **10** Viva Zapata **11** Lust for Life **13** Zorba the Greek **17** The Guns of Navarone **22** Requiem for a Heavyweight, The Shoes of the Fisherman
  autobiography: **14** The Original Sin

Quintana and Friends
  author: **16** John Gregory Dunne

quintessence 4 core, gist, pith, soul **5** heart **6** elixir, marrow, nature **7** essence **8** exemplar, quiddity, sum total **9** substance **10** embodiment **12** distillation **15** personification, sum and substance

quip 3 gag, pun **4** barb, gibe, jape, jeer, jest, joke **5** crack, sally, spoof, taunt **6** banter, retort **7** epigram, putdown, riposte, sarcasm **8** badinage, raillery, repartee, wordplay **9** wisecrack, witticism
  French: **6** bon mot **14** double entendre

Quirinus
  origin: **5** Roman
  god of: **3** war
  personifies: **11** Roman nation
  identified with: **7** Romulus

quirk 4 kink, turn, whim **6** fetish, foible, oddity, vagary, whimsy **7** caprice **8** crotchet, odd fancy **9** mannerism **10** aberration **11** abnormality, affectation, peculiarity, sudden twist **12** eccentricity, idiosyncrasy

quisling 6 puppet **7** traitor **12** collaborator **16** collaborationist

quit 3 end, rid **4** free, stop **5** cease, clear, forgo, leave, let go, waive, yield **6** depart, desist, disown, exempt, forego, give up, reject, resign, retire **7** abandon, disavow, drop out, forsake, take off **8** abdicate, absolved, forswear, renounce, withdraw **9** acquitted, foreswear, leave a job, surrender, terminate **10** discharged, exculpated, exonerated, relinquish **11** discontinue

quite 4 very **5** fully, truly **6** highly, hugely, indeed, in fact, in toto, really, surely, vastly, verily, wholly **7** exactly, in truth, totally, utterly **8** actually, entirely, outright **9** assuredly, certainly, extremely, in reality, out-and-out, perfectly, precisely, unusually, veritably **10** absolutely, altogether, completely, enormously, positively, remarkably, throughout **11** exceedingly, excessively **12** considerably **13** exceptionally

Quito
  capital of: **7** Ecuador

quiver 3 tic **4** jerk, jolt, jump, pant **5** quake, shake, spasm, throb **6** quaver, shiver, totter, tremor, twitch, wobble **7** flicker, flutter, pulsate, seizure, shudder, tremble, vibrate, wriggle **8** convulse **9** fluctuate, oscillate, palpitate, pulsation, quivering, twitching, vibration **10** convulsion **11** palpitation

quivering 7 shaking **9** agitating, quavering, shimmying, shivering, trembling, vibrating **10** flittering, fluttering, shuddering, twittering **11** palpitating

qui vive? 12 who goes there?

quixotic 4 wild **6** absurd, dreamy, madcap, poetic **7** utopian **8** fanciful, romantic **9** fantastic, impulsive, visionary, whimsical **10** chimerical, idealistic, ridiculous, starry-eyed **11** impractical, ineffective, sentimental, unrealistic **12** preposterous **13** inefficacious

quiz 3 ask, rib **4** exam, joke, mock, pump, test **5** prank, query, taunt, tease **6** banter **7** examine, inquest, inquiry **8** question, ridicule, sound out **9** catechism, eccentric, inquire of **11** examination, inquisition, interrogate, investigate, questioning **12** cross-examine **13** interrogation, investigation **16** cross-examination

Quiz Kids
  host: **8** Joe Kelly **14** Clifton Fadiman

Quiz Show
  author: **15** Richard N Goodwin
  director: **13** Robert Redford
  cast: **9** Rob Morrow (Dick Goodwin) **10** Hank Azaria (Albert Freedman) **11** David Paymer (Dan Enright), Mira Sorvino (Sandra Goodwin) **12** John Turturro (Herbie Stempel), Paul Scofield (Mark Van Doren), Ralph Fiennes (Charles Van Doren) **15** Elizabeth Wilson (Dorothy Van Doren) **19** Christopher McDonald (Jack Barry)

quizzical 3 coy **4** arch **6** joking **7** baffled, curious, mocking, puzzled, teasing **8** derisive, impudent, insolent **9** bantering, inquiring, perplexed, searching **11** inquisitive, questioning

quoad hoc 12 as much as this, to this extent

quod erat demonstrandum 17 which was to be shown **24** which was to be demonstrated
  abbreviation: **3** QED

quod erat faciendum 16 which was to be done

quod vide 8 which see
  abbreviation: **2** qv

quo jure? 11 by what right?

quo modo 3 how 9 in what way 19 in the same manner that

quondam 4 erst, late, once, past 6 bygone, former 8 formerly, sometime 9 erstwhile

quota 4 part 5 share 6 ration 7 measure, minimum, portion 8 quantity 9 allotment 10 allocation, assignment, percentage, proportion 12 distribution 13 apportionment

quotation 5 quote 7 cutting, excerpt, extract, passage 8 citation, clipping 9 reference, selection 12 illustration

quote 4 cite, name 6 adduce, recall, repeat, retell 7 excerpt, extract, refer to 8 instance 9 exemplify, recollect, reproduce 10 paraphrase

quoted passage 7 excerpt, extract 9 quotation

quotidian 5 daily 6 common 8 everyday, ordinary 11 commonplace

Quo Vadis?
author: 17 Henryk Sienkiewicz
character: 4 Nero 5 Chilo, Lygia, Peter 8 Vinitius 9 Petronius, Tigellius
director: 11 Mervyn LeRoy
cast: 7 Leo Genn 11 Deborah Kerr 12 Peter Ustinov, Robert Taylor
setting: 11 ancient Rome

 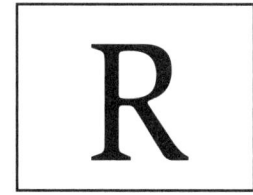 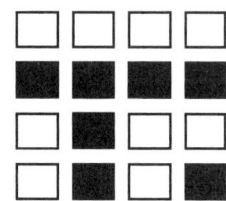

Ra
also: **2** Re
origin: **5** Greek **10** Heliopolis
god of: **3** sun
also worshipped by: **9** Egyptians

Rabat, Rabbat
capital of: **7** Morocco

rabbi 6 master, rabbin **7** scholar, teacher **9** clergyman **15** spiritual leader

rabbinical, rabbinic 8 clerical

Rabbit
series: **9** Rabbit, Run **11** Rabbit Redux **12** Rabbit at Rest, Rabbit Is Rich
author: **10** John Updike

rabbit 4 cony, hare, jack, lure **5** bunny, coney, lapin **6** novice, rodent **8** beginner **10** cottontail, pacesetter

rabble 3 mob **5** swarm **7** the herd **8** populace, riffraff **9** commoners, hoi polloi, the masses **11** proletariat, rank and file **12** lower classes **15** disorderly crowd **16** the great unwashed
French: **8** canaille
German: **17** Lumpenproletariat

Rabelais, Francois
author of: **22** Gargantua and Pantagruel

rabid 4 wild **6** ardent, crazed, raging **7** berserk, fervent, frantic, violent, zealous **8** deranged, frenzied, maniacal, wild-eyed **9** fanatical **11** hydrophobic **17** foaming at the mouth

race 3 fly, run **4** dart, dash, heat, rush **5** hurry **6** hasten, hustle **7** contest, operate **8** campaign **11** competition

racecourse 4 turf **5** track **6** course **9** racetrack

Rachel
father: **5** Laban
husband: **5** Jacob
sister: **4** Leah
son: **6** Joseph **8** Benjamin
slave: **6** Bilhah

Rachmaninov (Rachmaninoff, Rakhmaninov), Sergei
born: **6** Russia **8** Novgorod
composer of: **15** Symphonic Dances **16** The Isle of the Dead **19** Second Piano Concerto **26** Rhapsody on a Theme by (of) Paganini

Racine, Jean Baptiste
author of: **6** Phedre **7** Athalie **8** Berenice **10** Andromache **11** Britannicus

racism 7 bigotry **8** color bar **9** color

line **10** race hatred, racial bias **11** segregation **15** racial prejudice **20** racial discrimination

rack 4 buck, gait, hurt, neck, pace, pain, path **5** agony, cloud, exert, frame, raise, track, trail, worry, wreck, wring **6** canter, holder, strain **7** afflict, agonize, draw off, oppress, stretch, torment, torture **8** distress **9** suffering **10** destruction, excruciate, iron maiden

racked 4 torn **5** paced **6** framed, pained, traced, walked **7** annoyed, tracked, trotted, wronged, worried **8** cantered, suffered, tortured **9** afflicted, anguished, destroyed, oppressed, tormented **10** persecuted

racket 3 din **4** game, line, roar, stir **5** babel **6** clamor, hubbub, rumpus, tumult, uproar **7** clangor, clatter, turmoil **8** business, shouting **9** commotion, loud noise **10** hullabaloo, hurly-burly, occupation, turbulence **11** disturbance, pandemonium **12** caterwauling, vociferation

racketeer 4 hood **5** crook **6** bagman, bandit, extort **7** hoodlum, mafioso, mobster **8** criminal, gangster **12** extortionist

racking 7 painful **9** agonizing, torturous **10** tormenting, unbearable **11** intolerable, unendurable **12** excruciating, insufferable

raconteur 8 fabulist, narrator, romancer **10** anecdotist **11** storyteller **13** teller of tales **14** spinner of yarns

racy 4 keen **5** bawdy, crude, heady, lurid, zesty **6** erotic, lively, ribald, risque, smutty, vulgar **7** buoyant, glowing, obscene, zestful **8** animated, exciting, immodest, indecent, off-color, prurient, spirited, vigorous **9** energetic, fast-paced, salacious, sparkling **10** suggestive **11** stimulating **12** exhilarating, pornographic

radar
invented by: **4** Watt **6** Watson

Radcliffe, Mrs Ann
author of: **10** The Italian **21** The Mysteries of Udolpho

raddle 3 rod **4** reed, scar, twig **5** fence, hedge, rouge, stick, weave **6** branch, ruddle **8** hematite, red ocher, red ochre **10** interweave

radiance, radiancy 3 joy **5** gleam,

gleem, sheen **6** dazzle, luster **7** glitter, rapture, sparkle **8** lambency, splendor **9** animation, happiness **10** brightness, brilliance, brilliancy, effulgence, luminosity, refulgence **11** coruscation, iridescence **12** luminousness, resplendence **13** incandescence
god of: **5** Baldr **6** Balder, Baldur

radiant 5 aglow, happy, sunny **6** bright, elated, joyous **7** beaming, glowing, pleased, shining **8** blissful, dazzling, ecstatic, flashing, gladsome, gleaming, luminous, lustrous **9** brilliant, delighted, effulgent, overjoyed, rapturous, refulgent, sparkling **10** glittering **12** incandescent **13** scintillating

radiate 4 beam, pour, shed **5** carry **6** spread **7** diffuse, diverge, give off, give out, scatter **8** disperse, emit heat, transmit **9** branch out, circulate, emit light, spread out **11** disseminate

radical 4 rash **5** basic, rebel **6** severe **7** drastic, extreme **8** left-wing, militant **9** extremist, firebrand **10** immoderate, inordinate **11** freethinker, fundamental, precipitate **13** revolutionary

radio
invented by: **7** Donovan, Fleming, Marconi **8** De Forest, Nicolson **9** Armstrong, Fessenden **12** Alexanderson

radium
chemical symbol: **2** Ra

radon
chemical symbol: **2** Rn

raffish 3 low **4** fast, wild **5** cheap, rowdy, showy **6** common, flashy, rakish, tawdry, vulgar **7** boorish **8** rakehell **9** worthless **10** dissipated **12** devil-may-care, disreputable

raft 3 lot **4** mass **5** barge, float **6** plenty **7** carrier, pontoon **8** flatboat, platform, quantity **9** abundance, multitude

Raft, George
real name: **11** George Ranft
born: **9** New York NY
roles: **8** Scarface **11** Johnny Angel **12** Guido Rinaldo **13** Some Like It Hot

rag 3 kid, rib **4** scap, song, tune, twit **5** cloth, taunt, taunt, tease **6** harass **7** torment **8** magazine **9** newspaper **11** ragtime tune **14** worn-out garment

ragamuffin 3 bum **4** hobo, waif **5** gamin, tramp **6** beggar, gamine, hoyden, sloven, urchin, wretch **7** vagrant **8** derelict, vagabond **9** itinerant, ragpicker **10** panhandler, street arab **11** guttersnipe **14** tatterdemalion

rage 3 fad, ire **4** boil, fume, fury, mode, rant, rave, roar **5** craze, furor, mania, pique, storm, vogue, wrath **6** blow up, choler, frenzy, seethe, spleen, temper **7** explode, fashion, ferment, flare up, madness, passion, rampage, umbrage **8** paroxysm, the thing **9** animosity, fulminate, raise cain, throw a fit, vehemence **10** bitterness, excitement, irritation, resentment, the "in" thing **11** displeasure, high dudgeon, indignation, the last word **12** current style, le dernier cri, perturbation, violent anger **13** temper tantrum **14** the latest thing **15** fly off the handle, froth at the mouth

ragged 4 rent, torn, worn **5** seedy, tacky **6** beat up, frayed, shabby, shaggy, shoddy **7** patched, run down, worn-out **8** battered, shredded, strained, tattered **9** overtaxed **10** aggravated, threadbare, worn to rags **11** exacerbated

ragging 5 chaff **6** banter **7** kidding, ribbing, teasing **8** chaffing, needling, raillery, taunting, twitting

raging 3 mad **4** wild **5** angry, livid, rabid, rough **6** fierce, raving, stormy **7** fervent, frantic, furious, rampant, violent **8** frenzied, incensed, storming **9** turbulent **10** blustering, ferocious, infuriated **11** tempestuous

Raging Bull
director: 14 Martin Scorsese
cast: 8 Joe Pesci **12** Frank Vincent, Robert De Niro (Jake La Motta) **13** Cathy Moriarty
Oscar for: 5 actor (De Niro)

Ragnarok
also: 15 Gotterdammerung **17** Twilight of the Gods
origin: 12 Scandinavian
event: 11 final battle
battlefield: 6 Vigrid

ragout 4 hash, stew **7** borscht, goulash **9** fricassee

Ragtime
author: 10 E L Doctorow

raid 4 bust **5** foray, onset, sally, storm **6** attack, inroad, invade, razzia, sortie **7** assault, round-up **8** invasion **10** pounce upon **14** surprise attack

Raiders of the Lost Ark
director: 15 Steven Spielberg
cast: 10 Karen Allen, Wolf Kahler **11** Paul Freeman **12** Harrison Ford
sequel: 29 Indiana Jones and the Last Crusade **30** Indiana Jones and the Temple of Doom

rail 3 bar **4** rage, rant **5** scold, fence, train **6** blow up, scream, take on **7** barrier, carry on, declaim, inveigh, railing, railway, the cars **8** banister,

railroad **9** fulminate **10** vituperate, vociferate **11** rant and rave **14** foam at the mouth

rail at 5 scold **6** berate **7** chew out **9** castigate **14** inveigh against

railing 3 bar **5** fence, grate, rails **6** fender **7** barrier, parapet, support **8** banister **9** enclosing **10** balustrade

raillery 5 chaff, sport **6** banter, japing, joking, satire **7** fooling, jesting, joshing, kidding, ragging, razzing, ribbing, teasing **8** badinage, chaffing, roasting, twitting **10** lampoonery, persiflage, pleasantry

railroad sleeping car
French: **8** wagon-lit

railroad station 5 depot **8** terminal, terminus

railway 4 tube **5** track, train **6** cogway, subway **7** cogroad, trolley **8** elevated, monorail, railroad **9** streetcar

raiment 4 duds, togs **5** dress **6** attire **7** apparel, clothes, costume, threads **8** clothing, garments **11** habiliments

rain, rains 4 down, drop, mist, pour **5** spate **6** deluge, lavish, shower, squall **7** drizzle, monsoon, torrent **8** downpour, drencher, plethora, rainfall, send down, sprinkle **9** hurricane, rainstorm **10** cloudburst **13** precipitation, thundershower **15** rain cats and dogs **16** come down in sheets **17** come down in buckets
god of: 4 Thor

Rainbow
goddess of: 4 Iris

Rainbow, The
author: 10 D H Lawrence
character: 10 Anna Lensky **11** Lydia Lensky, Tom Brangwen **12** Will Brangwen **14** Ursula Brangwen **15** Anton Skrebensky

Rainbow Bridge see **7** bifrost

raincoat 3 mac **4** mack **6** poncho, ulster **7** oilskin, slicker **8** burberry **9** tarpaulin **10** mackintosh, trenchcoat, waterproof

rainless 3 dry **4** arid, sere **10** desertlike

Rains, Claude
born: 6 London **7** England
wife: 11 Isabel Jeans
roles: 9 Notorious **10** Casablanca, Now Voyager **13** Mr Skeffington **14** Anthony Adverse **15** The Invisible Man **16** Lawrence of Arabia **17** Here Comes Mr Jordan **20** The Phantom of the Opera **23** Mr Smith Goes to Washington **24** The Adventures of Robin Hood

rain shower 6 shower **7** drizzle **8** sprinkle **12** thunderstorm

rainstorm 6 deluge, shower **8** downfall, downpour **10** cloudburst **12** thunderstorm

rainy 3 wet **4** damp **7** drizzly, showery

11 pouring rain **18** raining cats and dogs

raise 3 end **4** grow, hike, lift, rear, spur, urge **5** amass, boost, breed, build, erect, nurse, pique, put up, rouse, set up, spark **6** arouse, awaken, excite, foster, hike up, jack up, kindle, obtain, stir up **7** advance, bring in, bring up, canvass, collect, develop, elevate, inflame, inflate, inspire, nurture, procure, produce, sharpen, solicit **8** increase, summon up **9** construct, cultivate, elevation, promotion, stimulate, terminate **10** make higher, put forward **11** advancement

raise aloft 5 boost, hoist **6** lift up, uplift **7** elevate, upraise

raised 4 bred, grew **5** anted, built, grown **6** anteed, convex, jacked, lifted, reared, roused **7** aroused, erected, exalted, hoisted, honored, incited **8** elevated, embossed, leavened, mustered **9** brought up, collected **10** cultivated **11** resurrected

Raisin in the Sun, A
director: 12 Daniel Petrie
based on play by: 17 Lorraine Hansberry
cast: 7 Ruby Dee **9** Ivan Dixon **10** Diana Sands **13** Claudia McNeil, Sidney Poitier
setting: 7 Chicago

rake 4 comb, goat, roue **5** rogue, satyr, scour, sport **6** lecher, pepper, rascal **7** Don Juan, playboy, ransack, seducer, swinger **8** Casanova, Lothario, enfilade, prodigal, rakehell **9** debauchee, libertine, womanizer **10** immoralist, profligate, sensualist, voluptuary

rake-off 3 cut, fee **5** piece **10** percentage **16** piece of the action

Rake's Progress, The
etchings by: 7 Hogarth
opera by: 10 Stravinsky
character: 10 Ann Trulove, Nick Shadow **11** Baba the Turk, Mother Goose, Tom Rakewell

rakish 4 airy **6** breezy, dapper, jaunty, sporty **7** dashing, gallant, immoral, lustful **8** cavalier, debonair, depraved, sporting **9** bumptious, debauched, dissolute, lecherous, libertine **10** dissipated, lascivious, profligate, sauntering, swaggering

rally 4 meet, rush **5** score, unite **6** caucus, gather, muster, pick up, powwow, revive **7** catch up, collect, get well, improve, recruit, reunite, revival **8** assemble, assembly, recovery **9** come round, gathering, get better, reconvene **10** assemblage, convalesce, convention, reassemble, recuperate **11** convocation, improvement, mass meeting, pull through, restoration **12** call together, congregation, recuperation **13** convalescence

ram **3** hit, jam **4** beat, bump, butt, dash, goat, slam **5** crash, drive, force, smash **6** batter, hammer, hurtle, strike, thrust **7** run into

Ram
constellation of: **5** Aries

ramble **3** gad **4** hike, roam, rove, wind **5** amble, drift, range, snake, twist **6** stroll, wander, zigzag **7** meander, saunter, traipse **8** gad about, idle walk **9** gallivant **11** perambulate, peregrinate

rambling **6** prolix, uneven **7** diffuse **10** circuitous, digressive, discursive, disjointed

rambunctious **4** wild **5** noisy, rowdy **6** active, unruly **7** raucous, untamed, violent **9** irascible **10** boisterous, pugnacious **11** quarrelsome **14** uncontrollable

Rameau, Jean-Philippe
born: **5** Dijon **6** France
composer of: **6** Platee **8** Dardanus **13** Les Fetes d'Hebe **14** Castor et Pollux **15** Castor and Pollux **16** Les Indes Galantes, The Indigo Suitors **17** Hippolyte et Aricie **20** La Princesse de Navarre

ramification **3** arm **4** part, spur **5** prong **6** branch **8** division, offshoot **9** branching, outgrowth **10** divergence, separation **11** consequence, subdivision

rampage **4** rage **5** storm **7** run amok, run riot

rampant **4** rife **5** erect **6** raging **8** epidemic, pandemic **9** prevalent, unchecked, universal **10** on hind legs, standing up, widespread **12** ungovernable, unrestrained **14** uncontrollable

rampart **7** barrier, bastion, bulwark, parapet **9** barricade, earthwork **10** breastwork **13** defensive wall, fortification **14** protective wall

Ramsay, William
field: **9** chemistry
nationality: **7** British
discovered: **4** neon **5** argon (in air) **6** helium **7** krypton
awarded: **10** Nobel Prize

ramshackle **5** shaky **6** flimsy, shabby **7** rickety, run-down **8** decrepit, unstable, unsteady **9** crumbling, tottering **10** tumbledown **11** dilapidated **13** deteriorating

Ramtil *see* **5** Niger

ranch **4** farm **5** range **6** grange, spread **7** acreage, station **8** hacienda **10** plantation

rancher **6** cowboy, farmer, gaucho **7** cowhand, cowpoke **8** herdsman, sheepman, stockman **9** cattleman **10** cowpuncher

rancid **3** old **4** foul, gamy, high, rank **6** putrid, strong **8** mephitic, stinking **10** malodorous

rancor **4** hate **5** spite **6** animus, enmity, hatred, malice, spleen **7** ill will **8** acrimony **9** animosity, antipathy, hostility **10** antagonism, bitterness, ill feeling, resentment **11** malevolence **12** spitefulness

rancorous **5** nasty **6** bitter **7** hostile **8** churlish, spiteful, vengeful, venomous **9** splenetic **10** ill-natured **11** acrimonious **12** antagonistic

Rand, Ayn
author of: **6** Anthem **13** Atlas Shrugged **15** The Fountainhead **17** Romantic Manifesto
philosophy: **11** objectivism

Randall, Tony
real name: **22** Arthur Leonard Rosenberg
born: **7** Tulsa OK
wife: **13** Heather Harlan
roles: **9** Mr Peepers **10** Felix Unger, Pillow Talk **12** Harvey Weskit, The Odd Couple **13** Fatal Instinct, The Mating Game **20** The Seven Faces of Dr Lao **22** Hitler's SS: Portrait in Evil

random **5** stray **6** casual, chance **7** aimless, offhand **9** haphazard, hit-or-miss, unplanned **10** accidental, fortuitous, occasional, undesigned, unexpected, unintended **12** adventitious **13** unintentional **14** unpremeditated

range **3** run **4** roam, rove **5** field, gamut, limit, orbit, reach, ridge, scope **6** bounds, domain, extend, massif, plains, radius, sierra, sphere, wander **7** explore, pasture, purview, stretch, variety **8** province **9** selection **11** grazing land **16** chain of mountains

Rangoon *see* **6** Yangon

rangy **4** tall **5** broad, lanky **9** expansive, extensive

rank **3** row **4** bald, file, foul, line, lush, rate, sort, tall, type, wild **5** class, crass, dense, grade, gross, level, nasty, order, sheer, stale, stand, total, utter **6** arrant, coarse, column, estate, filthy, jungly, lavish, rancid, status **7** come out, echelon, glaring, profuse, quality, rampant **8** absolute, complete, flagrant, position, standing, tropical **9** atrocious, be classed, come first, downright, have place, luxuriant, monstrous, overgrown **10** outrageous, scurrilous **11** highgrowing, ill smelling, unmitigated **12** over abundant **14** classification, social standing, strong smelling

rank and file **6** troops **17** enlisted personnel, general membership

Rankine, William John Macquorn
field: **7** physics
nationality: **8** Scottish
devised: **12** Rankine Cycle, Rankine Scale **26** Fahrenheit temperature scale
author of: **22** Manual of the Steam Engine

rankle **4** gall, rile **5** chafe, gripe, pique **6** fester **8** irritate **10** not sit well

ransack **3** gut **4** comb, loot, raid, rake, sack **5** rifle, scour, strip **6** ravage, search **7** despoil, pillage, plunder **8** lay waste **9** devastate, vandalize **14** rummage through, turn upside down

ransom **3** buy **4** free, save **5** atone, price **6** redeem, rescue **7** deliver, expiate, reclaim, recover, release **8** liberate, retrieve **10** liberation, redemption

Ransom, John Crowe
member of: **12** the Fugitives
author of: **14** I'll Take My Stand **16** Captain Carpenter **30** Bells for John Whiteside's Daughter

rant **4** fume, rage, rave, yell **5** orate, scold, spout, storm **6** bellow **7** bluster, bombast, bravado, explode **8** harangue **11** declamation **12** exaggeration

rap **3** jaw, pan, tap **4** bang, chat, drum, talk **5** blame, knock, roast, speak, thump **6** dump on **7** clobber **8** converse **9** criticize **10** come down on **11** communicate **14** responsibility, shoot the breeze

rapacious **6** greedy **7** looting, wolfish **8** covetous, grasping, ravenous, thievish **9** marauding, mercenary, pillaging, predatory, voracious **10** avaricious, insatiable, plundering, ransacking

rapacity **5** greed **7** avarice **10** greediness **12** covetousness, graspingness **13** mercenariness

Rape of Lucrece
author: **18** William Shakespeare
character: **7** Tarquin **9** Collatine

Rape of the Lock, The
author: **13** Alexander Pope
character: **5** Ariel **7** Belinda, Umbriel **9** Lord Petre **10** Thalestris

Raphael **9** archangel

Raphael
real name: **14** Raffaello Santi **15** Raffaello Sanzio
born: **5** Italy **6** Urbino
artwork: **7** Disputa **8** Julius II **10** Entombment **14** Sistine Madonna **17** The School of Athens, The Virgin and Child **18** Madonna di Casa Tempi, The Transfiguration **19** The Triumph of Galatea **21** Baldassare Castiglione **22** The Marriage of the Virgin **24** The Expulsion of Heliodorus **28** The Madonna and Child with St John (La Belle Jardiniere)
architect of: **11** Villa Madama (Rome) **16** Pandolfini Palace (Florence) **22** Vidoni-Caffarelli Palace (Rome)

rapid **4** fast **5** brisk, fleet, hasty, quick, swift **6** active, flying, prompt, speedy **7** express, hurried, instant, rushing **8** agitated, feverish **9** galloping, unchecked **11** accelerated, expeditious, precipitate

rapidity 5 haste, speed 8 celerity, velocity 9 fleetness, quickness, swiftness 10 promptness

rapidly 4 fast 5 apace 7 briskly, hastily, quickly, swiftly 8 pell-mell, speedily 9 hurriedly, like a shot, overnight 10 in high gear 11 at full speed 13 expeditiously, helter-skelter

rapids 5 chute 7 current 10 white water

rapport 3 tie 4 link 10 connection, fellowship 11 affiliation, camaraderie 12 relationship 13 understanding 17 interrelationship

rapprochement 6 accord 7 detente, entente 9 agreement 10 adjustment, compromise, settlement 11 appeasement, arrangement 12 conciliation, pacification 13 accommodation, harmonization, reconcilement, understanding 14 reconciliation 16 mutual concession

rapscallion 5 knave, rogue, scamp 6 rascal 7 low-life, villain 8 scalawag 9 scoundrel 10 blackguard, ne'er-do-well, rascallion 14 good-for-nothing

rapt 6 dreamy, enrapt, intent 7 bemused, charmed 8 absorbed, ecstatic 9 attentive, bewitched, delighted, enchanted, engrossed, entranced, rapturous 10 captivated, enraptured, enthralled, fascinated, interested, moonstruck, spellbound 11 transported

rapture 3 joy 5 bliss 6 thrill 7 delight, ecstasy, elation 8 euphoria, felicity 9 beatitude

rapturous 4 rapt 8 beatific, blissful, ecstatic 10 enraptured, enthralled

rare 3 few 6 scarce, unique 7 unusual 8 uncommon 10 hard to find, infrequent 11 exceptional, seldom found 16 few and far between

rarefied 4 thin 6 dilute, purify, rarify, reduce, refine, subtle 7 inflate 8 diminish 9 attenuate, extenuate

rarely 6 hardly, seldom 8 not often 10 hardly ever, uncommonly 12 infrequently, scarcely ever 15 once in a blue moon, on rare occasions 17 once in a great while

raring 4 agog, avid, keen 5 eager 8 desirous 9 impatient 12 enthusiastic

rarity 6 oddity 7 anomaly 8 scarcity 11 unusualness 12 uncommonness 14 remarkableness

rascal 3 cad, imp 4 rake 5 devil, knave, rogue, scamp 7 villain 8 rakehell, scalawag 9 prankster, reprobate, scoundrel, trickster 10 blackguard, delinquent 11 rapscallion

rash 5 brash, hasty 6 abrupt 7 foolish 8 careless, headlong, heedless, reckless 9 foolhardy, impetuous, imprudent, impulsive, premature, unadvised, unchecked 10 incautious,

indiscreet, ungoverned, unthinking 11 adventurous, harebrained, injudicious, precipitate, thoughtless 12 devil-may-care, uncontrolled 13 irresponsible

rashness 8 audacity, boldness 9 riskiness 12 heedlessness, indiscretion, recklessness 13 foolhardiness, impulsiveness 15 precipitousness, thoughtlessness

Rashomon
author: 18 Ryunosuke Akutagawa
director: 13 Akira Kurosawa

Raskolnikov
character in: 18 Crime and Punishment
author: 10 Dostoevsky

rasp 3 irk, nag, rub, vex 4 file 5 chafe, grate, worry 6 abrade, scrape, wheeze 7 grating, scraper, scratch 8 abrasive, irritate 9 huskiness 10 hoarseness

raspberry 11 Rubus idaeus
varieties: 3 red 4 hill 5 black, dwarf 6 Mysore, purple 8 European 9 flowering, Mauritius 11 American red 13 Rocky Mountain 15 Purple-flowering 22 Rocky Mountain flowering
brandy: 9 Framboise

rasping 5 harsh, raspy, rough 6 hoarse 7 chafing, grating, nagging 8 abrading, scraping, worrying 9 offensive 10 irritating

Rasselas
author: 13 Samuel Johnson
character: 5 Imlac 6 Pekuah 7 Nekayah
Rasselas's title: 17 Prince of Abyssinia

rat 3 cad, cur 4 fink, heel 5 churl, knave, louse 6 betray, rascal, rotter, squeal, vermin 7 bounder, villain 8 informer, inform on 9 scoundrel 10 blackguard 11 stool pigeon

rate 3 fee 4 cost, deem, dues, levy, pace, rank, toll 5 class, count, price, speed, tempo 6 charge, figure, look on, regard, tariff 7 expense, measure 8 classify 10 assessment

rate highly 5 prize, value 6 admire, esteem 7 cherish, respect 8 treasure

Rathbone, Basil
real name: 25 Philip St John Basil Rathbone
born: 11 South Africa 12 Johannesburg
roles: 6 Tybalt 7 Karenin 10 Dawn Patrol 11 Mr Murdstone 12 Anna Karenina 14 Romeo and Juliet, Sherlock Holmes, The Mark of Zorro 16 A Tale of Two Cities, David Copperfield 20 The Last Days of Pompeii 24 The Adventures of Robin Hood 25 The Hound of the Baskervilles

rather 4 a bit, very 5 quite 6 fairly, kind of, pretty, sort of 8 slightly, somewhat 10 moderately, more or less, relatively 13 comparatively

rathskeller 6 saloon 8 beer hall

vessel: 4 Toby 5 stein 6 seidel 7 tankard 8 pilsener, schooner

ratification 2 OK 4 okay 7 consent 8 approval, sanction 10 validation 11 affirmation, endorsement 12 confirmation 13 authorization, corroboration 14 seal of approval

ratify 2 OK 4 okay 6 affirm, uphold 7 agree to, approve, certify, confirm, endorse, support 8 accede to, make good, sanction, validate 9 authorize, consent to, make valid 11 acknowledge 12 authenticate

rating 4 mark, rank 5 class, grade, ratio, value 6 degree, rebuke, sailor, seaman 7 ranking 8 standing 9 appraisal 10 assessment, evaluation, percentage 14 classification

ratio 8 equation 10 proportion 11 arrangement 12 distribution 13 apportionment, fixed relation 15 proportionality 17 interrelationship 20 proportional relation

ration, rations 3 due 4 dole, food 5 allot 6 stores 7 measure, mete out 8 allocate 9 allotment, apportion, food share, provender, provision 10 provisions 13 apportionment

rational 4 sage, sane, wise 5 lucid, solid, sound 6 normal 7 logical 8 all there, balanced, credible, feasible 9 advisable, judicious, plausible, sagacious 10 reasonable 11 clearheaded, responsible 12 composmentis 13 perspicacious 15 in one's right mind

rationale 5 basis, logic 6 excuse, reason 7 grounds 9 reasoning 10 key concept, philosophy 11 explanation, foundations 16 underlying reason

rationalize 6 excuse 7 explain, justify 8 palliate 9 whitewash 10 account for 11 explain away 13 put a gloss upon 14 make excuses for 16 make allowance for

ratite 3 em(e)u, moa 4 kiwi, rhea 7 ostrich 9 cassowary

rattan 4 cane, lash, palm, whip 5 thong 6 switch, wicker

Ratti, Achille 10 Pope Pius XI

rattle 3 gab, jar 4 faze 5 clang, clank, clink, prate, shake, throw, upset 6 bounce, flurry, jangle 7 agitate, blather, chatter, clatter, confuse, disturb, fluster, maunder, nonplus, perturb 8 bewilder, clacking, distract 9 discomfit 10 discompose, disconcert 11 roll loosely

rattlebrained 4 dumb 5 silly 6 stupid 7 asinine, doltish, foolish, idiotic, moronic, witless 9 brainless, imbecilic 10 fool-headed, half-witted 11 harebrained, lamebrained

rattled 5 fazed, upset 7 annoyed 9 disturbed, flustered, perturbed, thrown off 10 distracted 11 discomposed 12 disconcerted

rattle on 3 gab **4** blab **5** prate, run on **6** babble, gabble **7** blabber, chatter, prattle **16** run off at the mouth

ratty 4 poor, worn **5** angry, cross, nasty, testy **6** cranky, shabby, touchy **7** tangled, unkempt **8** wretched **9** irascible, motheaten **11** dilapidated

Ratzinger, Joseph 15 Pope Benedict XVI

raucous 4 loud **5** harsh, raspy, rough **6** hoarse, shrill **7** blaring, grating, jarring **8** grinding, jangling, piercing, strident **9** dissonant **10** discordant, stertorous **11** cacophonous **12** ear-splitting, inharmonious

raunchy 4 lewd **5** dirty, gross **6** coarse, smutty, vulgar **8** off-color

Rauschenberg, Robert
born: 12 Port Arthur TX
artwork: 3 Bed **5** Barge **7** Jammers **8** Monogram **11** Retroactive

ravage 3 gut **4** loot, raid, rape, raze, ruin, sack **5** strip, waste, wreck **6** maraud **7** despoil, destroy, overrun, pillage, plunder, ransack, shatter **8** demolish, desolate, lay waste, spoliate **9** devastate **10** lay in ruins

rave 3 wax **4** fume, go on, gush, rage, rant **5** be mad, kudos, storm **6** babble, bubble, ramble **7** be angry, bluster, carry on, explode, flare up, run amok, sputter, thunder **8** flattery **9** be furious, expatiate, go on and on, good press, laudatory **10** effervesce, high praise, rhapsodize **11** blow one's top, compliments

ravel 4 undo **6** unknit **7** unravel, untwine, untwist

Ravel, Maurice
born: 6 France **7** Ciboure
composer of: 6 Bolero **7** La Valse, Mirrors **8** Jeux d'eau **9** Fountains **11** Mother Goose, Sheherazade **14** Daphnis et Chloe **15** Gaspard de la Nuit, L'Heure Espagnole **17** Rapsodie Espagnole, The Tomb of Couperin **20** Pavane for a Dead Infant **21** Don Quichotte a Dulcinee **22** L'Enfant et les Sortileges, Pavane for a Dead Princess **27** Pavane pour une infante de funte, Valses nobles et sentimentales

raven 3 jet **4** crow, dark, inky, rook **5** black, ebony, sable **6** devour **9** coalblack

Raven, The
author: 13 Edgar Allan Poe
woman 6 Lenore
refrain: 9 nevermore

ravenous 6 greedy, hungry **7** piggish, starved **8** covetous, famished, grasping, ravening, starving **9** insatiate, predatory, rapacious, voracious **10** avaricious, gluttonous, insatiable

ravine 3 gap **4** pass, rift, wadi **5** abyss, break, chasm, cleft, crack, gorge, gulch, gully, split **6** arroyo, breach,

canyon, clough, divide, valley **7** fissure **8** crevasse

raving 3 mad **4** wild **6** insane **7** ranting **8** frenzied **9** delirious

ravish 4 rape **5** abuse, charm, cheer **6** defile, snatch, tickle **7** delight, enchant, gladden, outrage, overjoy, violate **8** deflower, enthrall, entrance, knock out **9** captivate, enrapture, fascinate, transport

ravishing 8 alluring, charming, gorgeous, smashing, splendid, striking **9** beautiful **10** bewitching, delightful, enchanting, entrancing **11** captivating, fascinating, sensational

raw 4 bare, cold, damp, rare **5** basic, bleak, crude, frank, fresh, green, harsh, plain, rough, young **6** biting, bitter, brutal, callow, chilly, rookie, unripe **7** cutting, natural, nipping, numbing, unbaked, untried **8** blustery, freezing, ignorant, immature, inexpert, piercing, pinching, uncooked, untaught, untested **9** inclement, underdone, undrilled, unfledged, unrefined, unskilled, untrained, windswept **10** amateurish, unprepared, unseasoned **11** not finished, undercooked, undeveloped, unexercised, uninitiated, unpracticed, unprocessed, unvarnished **13** inexperienced, undisciplined, unembellished **15** not manufactured

rawboned 4 lean **5** gaunt, lanky, spare **7** angular

Rawhide
character: 5 Mushy **8** Gil Favor, Ian Cabot, Wishbone **9** Jim Quince, Pete Nolan **10** Rowdy Yates **11** Joe Scarlett, Solomon King **13** Clay Forrester **14** Hey Soos Patines
cast: 10 Sheb Wooley **11** Charles Gray, David Watson, Eric Fleming, Robert Cabal, Rocky Shahan, Steve Raines **12** James Murdock, Paul Brinegar **13** Clint Eastwood **16** Raymond St Jacques

Rawlings, Marjorie Kinnan
author of: 11 The Yearling

rawness 3 nip **4** bite **5** chill **8** rudeness **9** crudeness, greenness, roughness, sharpness, vulgarity **10** chilliness **12** inexperience

ray 3 arm **4** beam, fish, line **5** gleam, light, manta, shaft, shine, skate, trace **6** branch, streak, stream, stripe **7** radiate **8** particle, plowfish, radiance **9** emanation, radiation

Ray
director: 14 Taylor Hackford
cast: 9 Jamie Foxx (Ray Charles) **10** Larenz Tate (Quincy Jones), Regina King (Margie Hendricks) **11** Harry Lennix (Joe Adams) **12** Sharon Warren (Aretha Robinson) **13** Clifton Powell (Jeff Brown), Richard Schiff (Jerry Wexler) **14** Bokeem Woodbine

(Fathead Newman) **15** Curtis Armstrong (Ahmet Ertegun), Kerry Washington (Della Bea Robinson)

Ray, Man
born: 14 Philadelphia PA
artwork: 4 Gift (Le Cadeau) **7** Manikin **9** The Lovers **13** Observing Time **45** The Rope Dancer Accompanies Herself with Her Shadows

Rayleigh, John William Strutt
field: 7 physics
nationality: 7 British
discovered: 5 argon
awarded: 10 Nobel Prize

rayon
invented by: 4 Swan

raze 4 fell, ruin **5** level, smash, wreck **6** reduce, remove, topple **7** destroy, flatten, wipe out **8** demolish, pull down, tear down **9** break down, dismantle, knock down **10** obliterate

razor
invented by: 6 Schick **8** Gillette

Razorback State
nickname of: 8 Arkansas

Re *see* **2** Ra

reach 3 get, hit **4** find, go to, grab, make, move **5** climb, enter, get to, grasp, seize, touch **6** attain, clutch, come to, extend, grab at, land at, secure, spread **7** contact, stretch **8** amount to, approach, arrive at **9** get hold of, set foot in **10** get as far as, outstretch, stretch out

reachable 6 at hand **8** possible **10** accessible, achievable, attainable, obtainable, procurable

reach the top 6 arrive **7** prosper, succeed **8** make good **13** hit the big time

react 4 work **6** answer, behave, resist, return **7** respond **11** reverberate

reaction 5 reply **6** answer, reflex **8** backlash, response **11** restoration **13** counteraction **14** chemical change **17** counterrevolution, right-wing comeback

reactionary 7 diehard **8** mossback, rightist **9** right-wing **10** regressive **11** right-winger **12** reversionary **17** ultraconservative **20** counterrevolutionary

react to 5 reply **6** answer **7** respond **11** acknowledge

read 2 go **3** say **4** note, scan, show **5** study, utter **6** adduce, peruse, recite **7** analyze, deliver, discern, explain, present **8** construe, decipher, indicate, perceive, pore over **9** apprehend, interpret, translate **10** comprehend, glance over, understand **11** extrapolate

Read, Piers Paul
author of: 5 Alive **6** Ablaze **9** Polonaise **10** Monk Dawson, The Junkers, The Upstart **11** The Templars **12** Alice in Exile **18** Professor's Daughter

Reade, Charles
author of: **13** Peg Woffington **23** The Cloister and the Hearth

readily 6 at once, easily, freely, pronto **7** quickly **8** in no time, promptly, smoothly, speedily **9** expressly, hands down, instantly, willingly **10** graciously **11** immediately, straightway **12** effortlessly, ungrudgingly

readiness 8 alacrity, dispatch **9** alertness **10** promptness **12** preparedness

read the riot act 5 chide, scold **6** berate, rebuke **7** censure, chasten, correct, lecture, reprove **8** admonish **9** dress down, reprimand **10** take to task

ready 3 apt, fit, set **4** deft, keen, ripe, up to **5** acute, alert, eager, equip, handy, on tap, prone, sharp **6** adroit, all set, artful, astute, at hand, bright, clever, expert, facile, fit out, liable, mature, on hand, primed, prompt, shrewd, speedy **7** cunning, equal to, prepare, present, tending, willing **8** disposed, inclined, masterly, punctual, skillful **9** attentive, dexterous, fitted out, furnished, ingenious, in harness, versatile, wide-awake **10** accessible, discerning, perceptive, put in order **11** acquisitive, expeditious, predisposed, quick-witted, resourceful, serviceable

ready for use 5 handy, on tap **6** at hand, on hand **9** available **10** accessible, convenient **11** at one's elbow **14** at one's disposal

ready-made 10 off-the-rack **11** prêt-à-porter, ready-to-wear, store-bought

ready money 4 cash **8** currency **10** cash on hand

ready to go 5 peppy **9** full of pep **10** raring to go **17** full of vim and vigor **24** bright-eyed and bushy-tailed

Reagan, Ronald Wilson
nickname: **5** Dutch **6** Ronnie
presidential rank: **8** fortieth
party:
  current: **10** Republican
  former: **10** Democratic
state represented: **2** CA
defeated: **6** (James Earl) Carter (Jr) **7** (Walter Frederick "Fritz") Mondale **8** (John Bayard) Anderson
vice president: **4** (George Herbert Walker) Bush
cabinet:
  state: **4** (Alexander M) Haig (Jr) **6** (George P) Shultz
  treasury: **5** (Donald T) Regan
  defense: **10** (Caspar W) Weinberger
  attorney general: **5** (William French) Smith
  interior: **4** (James) Watt **5** (William P) Clark
  agriculture: **5** (John R) Block
  commerce: **8** (Malcolm) Baldrige
  labor: **7** (Raymond J) Donovan

health and human services: **7** (Margaret M) Heckler **9** (Richard S) Schweiker
  education: **4** (Terrel H) Bell
  HUD: **6** (Samuel R) Pierce (Jr)
  transportation: **4** (Elizabeth H) Dole **5** (Andrew L) Lewis (Jr)
  energy: **5** (Donald P) Hodel **7** (James B) Edwards
born: **9** Tampico IL
died: **6** Bel-Air **10** California, Los Angeles
buried: **10** California, Simi Valley
college: **6** Eureka
religion: **17** Disciples of Christ
interests: **2** TV **5** track **6** movies **8** football **9** chops wood **10** basketball, jelly beans **13** weightlifting **15** horseback riding
vacation spot: **14** Rancho del Cielo (Santa Barbara CA)
dog: **5** Lucky
author: **18** Where Is the Rest of Me?
political career:
  governor of: **10** California
civilian career: **5** actor **17** radio sportscaster
  host: **15** Death Valley Days **22** General Electric Theater
  president of: **17** Screen Actors Guild
  roles: **8** King's Row **10** Brother Rat **13** John Loves Mary, The Hasty Heart **15** Bedtime for Bonzo **19** The Voice of the Turtle **20** Cattle Queen of Montana **21** The Girl from Jones Beach **22** Knute Rockne All American
military service: **6** US Army **7** captain **10** World War II
notable events of lifetime/term:
  approval of: **10** MX missiles
  assassination attempt on: **6** Reagan **14** Pope John Paul II
  attempted assassination on Reagan by: **15** John W Hinckley Jr
  bombing of: **5** Libya
  hostages freed in: **4** Iran
  invasion of: **7** Grenada
  marines sent to: **7** Lebanon
  nuclear disaster at: **9** Chernobyl
  Russians shot down: **14** Korean airliner
  scandal: **8** Irangate
father: **10** John Edward
  nickname: **4** Jack
mother: **5** Nelle (Wilson)
siblings: **4** (John) Neil
wife: **4** Jane (Wyman) **5** Nancy (Davis)
  Nancy Davis born: **18** Anne Frances Robbins
children: **6** Ronald **7** Maureen, Michael (adopted) **8** Patricia
  Patricia also actress known as: **10** Patti Davis
first lady:
  program: **9** Drug abuse, Just Say

No **12** Alcohol abuse **18** Foster Grandparents

real 4 pure, true **5** solid, valid **6** actual, honest **7** certain, factual, genuine, sincere **8** absolute, bona fide, positive, rightful, tangible, truthful **9** authentic, unalloyed, unfeigned, veracious, veritable **10** legitimate, unaffected **11** not affected, substantial, substantive, unvarnished **12** well-grounded **13** unadulterated **14** unquestionable

realistic 4 real **7** genuine, graphic, natural, precise **8** faithful, lifelike, truthful **9** authentic, depictive, objective, pragmatic **10** true-to-life **11** descriptive, down-to-earth **12** naturalistic **16** representational

reality 4 fact **5** truth **6** verity **9** actuality **11** materiality, tangibility **12** corporeality **14** substantiality **17** physical existence

realization 7 success **8** grasping **10** attainment, perception **11** achievement, culmination, fulfillment **12** appreciation, consummation **13** comprehension, understanding **14** accomplishment

realize 2 do **3** get, net **4** gain **5** clear, grasp **6** absorb, attain, fathom, gather, profit **7** achieve, acquire, cognize, discern, execute, fulfill, imagine, make out, perform, produce **8** carry out, complete, conceive, make good, perceive **9** actualize, apprehend, discharge, make money, penetrate, recognize **10** accomplish, appreciate, bring about, comprehend, consummate, effectuate, understand **11** bring to pass **12** carry through

realized 3 got **6** gained, netted, proved, proven **7** cleared, grasped, made out, saw into **8** absorbed, accepted, effected, executed, existing, fathomed, gathered, imagined, made good, profited **9** completed, conceived, discerned, fulfilled, perceived, performed **10** actualized, penetrated, recognized, understood **11** appreciated, apprehended, consummated, established **12** accomplished, comprehended

really 5 truly **6** indeed, in fact, surely, verily **8** actually **9** certainly, genuinely, literally, veritably **10** absolutely, positively, truthfully **13** categorically **14** unquestionably

realm 4 land **5** field, orbit, state **6** domain, empire, nation, region, sphere **7** country, demesne, kingdom **8** dominion, monarchy, province **11** royal domain

real McCoy, the 4 real **7** genuine **9** authentic **12** the real thing

Realpolitik 10 expediency **13** power politics

Real World, The
network: **3** MTV

location: 5 Miami, Paris **6** Austin, Boston, Hawaii, London **7** Chicago, New York, Seattle **8** Las Vegas, San Diego **10** Los Angeles, New Orleans **12** Philadelphia, San Francisco

reap 3 get, win **4** earn, gain **5** glean, score **6** derive, gather, obtain, profit, secure, take in **7** acquire, bring in, harvest, procure, realize

rear 3 aft, end **4** back, heel **5** after, nurse, raise, stern, train **6** dorsal, foster **7** bring up, care for, cherish, develop, educate, nurture, postern, tail end **8** back part, hind part, hindmost **9** aftermost, after part, at the back, cultivate, in the back, posterior

Rear Window
director: 15 Alfred Hitchcock
based on story by: 15 Cornell Woolrich
cast: 10 Grace Kelly **11** Raymond Burr **12** James Stewart, Thelma Ritter, Wendell Corey

reason 3 wit **4** head **5** cause, logic, sense, solve **6** acumen, brains, figure, motive, sanity **7** grounds, insight **8** lucidity, occasion **9** awareness, faculties, intellect, normality, rationale, reasoning **10** perception **11** common sense, discernment, exhortation, explanation, penetration, rationality **12** apprehension, intelligence, perspicacity, think through **13** argumentation, comprehension, justification, mental balance, understanding **15** clearheadedness

reasonable 4 fair, just, sage, sane, wise **5** sound **6** likely, proper **7** fitting, knowing, lenient, logical, natural, patient, prudent **8** credible, moderate, possible, probable, rational, sensible, suitable, thinking **9** equitable, impartial, judicious, objective, plausible, temperate, tolerable **10** admissible, coolheaded, legitimate, not extreme, reflective, thoughtful **11** circumspect, intelligent, justifiable, level-headed, not unlikely, of good sense, predictable, well-founded **12** not excessive, well-grounded **13** understanding **14** understandable **15** of sound judgment

reasonableness 5 logic **6** sanity, wisdom **8** fairness, prudence **9** good sense **10** moderation **11** credibility, objectivity, rationality **12** good judgment, impartiality, intelligence **13** judiciousness **14** circumspection, thoughtfulness **15** clearheadedness

reasonably 6 almost, fairly **8** passably, somewhat **10** moderately, more or less **13** approximately

reasoning 5 basis, logic **6** ground **7** thought **8** analysis, argument, thinking **9** deduction, inference, rationale **10** cogitation, reflection **11** penetration **13** ratiocination **14** interpretation

reason out 8 mull over **10** deliberate **12** think through

reassure 5 cheer **6** buoy up, uplift **7** bolster, comfort **8** inspirit **9** encourage **13** inspire hope in

reassured 6 buoyed **9** bolstered, comforted, heartened **10** emboldened, encouraged, inspirited

reassuring 7 hopeful **10** auspicious, comforting, heartening **11** encouraging

Reb 2 Mr **5** Rabbi **6** Mister

rebate 6 refund **8** discount **9** abatement

Rebecca
author: 15 Daphne du Maurier
character: 10 Jack Favell, Mrs Danvers (Danny) **12** Frank Crawley **13** Colonel Julyan, Maxim de Winter
house: 9 Manderley
director: 15 Alfred Hitchcock
cast: 10 Nigel Bruce **12** Joan Fontaine **13** George Sanders **14** Judith Anderson (Mrs Danvers) **15** Laurence Olivier (Maxim de Winter)
Oscar for: 7 picture

Rebecca
character in: 7 Ivanhoe
author: 5 Scott

Rebecca see **7** Rebekah

Rebecca of Sunnybrook Farm
author: 17 Kate Douglas Wiggin
character: 4 Cobb **8** Adam Ladd **11** Aunt Miranda **14** Rebecca Randall **15** Emma Jane Perkins

Rebekah
also: 7 Rebecca
father: 7 Bethuel
husband: 5 Isaac
brother: 5 Laban
son: 4 Esau **5** Isaac, Jacob

rebel 3 shy **4** riot **5** avoid, quail, react, wince **6** flinch, mutiny, recoil, revolt, rise up, shrink **7** seceder, traitor, upstart **8** deserter, maverick, resister, turncoat **9** anarchist, dissenter, insurgent **10** iconoclast, malcontent, separatist **12** secessionist **13** nonconformist, revolutionary, revolutionist **15** insurrectionist

rebellion 6 mutiny, putsch, revolt **8** defiance, sedition, upheaval, uprising **9** coup d'etat **10** insurgency, revolution **12** insurrection

rebellious 6 unruly **7** defiant **8** contrary, mutinous, up in arms **9** alienated, fractious, insurgent, seditious, truculent, turbulent **10** disorderly, pugnacious, refractory **11** disobedient, intractable, quarrelsome **12** contumacious, recalcitrant, ungovernable, unmanageable **13** insubordinate, revolutionary **14** uncontrollable **15** insurrectionary

rebelliousness 8 defiance **9** rebellion **12** disobedience

Rebel Without a Cause

director: 11 Nicholas Ray
cast: 8 Sal Mineo **9** James Dean, Jim Backus **11** Natalie Wood

Rebirth
god of: 4 Gwyn

rebound 3 bob **6** bounce, recoil, re-echo **7** flounce **8** recovery, ricochet **10** spring back

rebounding 7 rubbery, springy **9** resilient **11** ricocheting **12** bouncing back

rebuff 4 deny, snub **5** check, repel, spurn **6** ignore, put off, refuse, reject, slight **7** decline, put-down, refusal, repulse **8** turn down **9** disregard, rejection **10** putting off **12** cold shoulder **13** slap in the face **15** keep at a distance

rebuke 5 blame, chide, scold, score **6** berate **7** censure, chew out, chiding, lecture, reproof, reprove, upbraid **8** admonish, berating, call down, reproach, reproval, scolding **9** dress down, reprimand **10** admonition, chewing out, take to task, upbraiding **11** castigation, disapproval **12** admonishment, dressing down, remonstrance, reprehension, take down a peg **13** find fault with, tongue-lashing **15** remonstrate with

rebuttal 5 reply **6** answer, denial, retort **7** defense, riposte **8** disproof, negation, response **9** disproval, rejoinder **10** refutation **11** confutation **12** counterreply, disagreement, surrejoinder **13** contradiction **15** counterargument

recalcitrant 5 balky **6** mulish, unruly **7** willful **8** contrary, stubborn **9** obstinate, pigheaded, unwilling **10** bullheaded, headstrong, refractory **11** disobedient, intractable **12** unsubmissive

recall 5 place **6** memory, revive **8** call back, remember **9** reanimate, recognize, recollect **10** reactivate, remobilize **11** reinstitute, remembrance **12** recollection **17** ability to remember

recant 4 deny **5** unsay **6** abjure, disown, recall, renege, repeal, revoke **7** disavow, rescind, retract **8** disclaim, forswear, renounce, take back, withdraw **9** foreswear, repudiate **10** apostatize **12** eat one's words **14** change one's mind

recantation 6 denial **9** disavowal **10** refutation, retraction, revocation **11** repudiation **12** renunciation

recapitulate 5 recap, sum up **6** relate, repeat, reword **7** recount, restate **8** rephrase **9** epitomize, reiterate, summarize **15** repeat in essence

recapture 6 retake **7** reprise **15** experience again

recede 3 ebb **5** abate **6** back up, go back, retire **7** regress, retreat, subside **10** retrogress

receipt 7 arrival, release, voucher **9** admission, discharge, receiving, reception **10** acceptance, admittance, possession, recipience **11** acquisition, transferral

receipts 3 pay **4** gain, gate, take **5** share, split, wages **6** income, recipe, return **7** formula, payment, profits, returns, revenue **8** earnings, proceeds **9** emolument **10** net profits **12** remuneration **13** reimbursement

receive 3 get **4** meet **5** admit, greet, put up **6** accept, come by, obtain, regard, secure, suffer, take in **7** acquire, adjudge, approve, be given, react to, sustain, undergo, welcome **8** meet with, submit to **9** encounter, entertain **10** experience **11** accommodate

receive willingly 6 accept **10** take gladly **16** accept with thanks **18** accept with open arms

receive with favor 6 praise **7** approve **10** appreciate

receive with open arms 6 invite **7** embrace, welcome **13** accept eagerly **19** roll out the red carpet

recent 3 new **4** late **5** fresh, novel **6** modern **8** up-to-date **9** latter-day **12** contemporary **13** up-to-the-minute

receptacle 3 bag, bin, box, can, jar **4** file, tray **6** basket, bottle, hamper, holder, hopper, vessel **7** carrier **8** receiver **9** container **10** depository, repository **11** compartment

reception 2 do **4** fete **5** party **6** affair, soiree **7** welcome **8** greeting **11** recognition **15** social gathering

receptive 8 amenable, friendly **10** accessible, hospitable, interested, open-minded, responsive **11** susceptible **12** approachable **17** favorably disposed

recess 3 bay, gap **4** bend, cell, cove, fold, gulf, lull, nook, pass, rest, slot **5** break, cleft, gorge, inlet, letup, niche, pause **6** alcove, corner, harbor, hiatus, hollow **7** holiday, interim, respite, time out **8** interval, vacation **9** interlude **10** pigeonhole **11** coffee break, indentation **12** intermission **14** breathing spell

recessed 4 sunk **6** paused, sunken **7** delayed **8** deferred, extended, indented **9** adjourned, dissolved, postponed, prolonged, withdrawn **10** terminated
church wall: 5 ambry
wall: 6 alcove

recesses 6 depths **10** inmost part, penetralia

recession 10 depression **11** recessional **16** economic downturn

recherche 4 rare **5** prize **6** choice, exotic, scarce, select, unique **7** special, unusual **8** original, superior, uncommon, valuable **9** different, priceless **10** one of a kind **11** exceptional

recipe 2 Rx **4** cure, rule **5** axiom **6** elixir, remedy **7** formula, receipt **12** instructions, prescription

recipient 4 heir **5** donee, taker **6** getter **7** legatee **8** accepter, acquirer, obtainer, receiver **9** presentee **11** beneficiary

reciprocal 6 common, linked, mutual, shared **8** returned **9** bilateral, exchanged, one for one **10** equivalent **11** give-and-take **12** interchanged, interrelated **13** complementary, corresponding, given in return **14** interdependent **15** interchangeable

reciprocate 4 feel **6** return **7** requite, respond **9** retaliate **10** make return **11** act likewise, give and take, interchange **12** give in return **19** return the compliment

reciprocity 8 exchange **11** give and take, interchange

recital 4 talk **6** report **7** concert, telling **8** delivery, reciting **9** discourse, narration, narrative, rendition **10** recitation **11** description, particulars, performance **12** dissertation, oral exercise **13** public reading **14** graphic account, recapitulation

recite 4 tell **5** quote, speak **6** relate, repeat **7** declaim, deliver, narrate, perform, recount **10** say by heart **11** communicate

reckless 4 rash, wild **5** giddy, hasty **6** daring, fickle, madcap, unwary **7** flighty, foolish, unaware **8** careless, cavalier, heedless, mindless, unsteady, volatile **9** daredevil, desperate, foolhardy, imprudent, impulsive, negligent, oblivious, unheeding, unmindful **10** incautious, indiscreet, insensible, neglectful, regardless, unthinking, unwatchful **11** harebrained, inattentive, precipitate, thoughtless, unconcerned **12** devil-may-care, unsolicitous **13** inconsiderate, irresponsible, uncircumspect **14** scatterbrained

recklessly 4 fast **5** blind **6** rashly, wildly **7** hastily **8** headlong **9** headfirst **10** carelessly, heedlessly **11** audaciously, desperately, impetuously, impulsively **12** unmindfully **13** irresponsibly, unconcernedly

recklessness 7 abandon **8** rashness **9** disregard, unconcern **10** imprudence, profligacy **11** impetuosity **12** heedlessness, immoderation **13** foolhardiness **15** thoughtlessness **16** irresponsibility

reckon 3 add **4** bank, cope, deal, deem, plan, rank, rate **5** add up, class, count, fancy, guess, judge, tally, think, total, value **6** assess, decide, esteem, expect, figure, handle, regard **7** account, adjudge, balance, bargain, compute, imagine, presume, suppose, surmise **8** appraise, consider, estimate **9** calculate, determine, speculate

reckoning 3 tab **4** bill, doom **5** count, tally, total **6** adding, charge **7** account **8** estimate, judgment **9** appraisal, summation **10** estimation, evaluation **11** calculation, computation **13** final judgment **19** settling of an account

reclaim 6 reform, rescue **7** correct, recover, rectify, restore

reclame 9 notoriety, publicity

recline 4 lean, loll, rest **6** lounge, repose, sprawl **7** lie back, lie down **12** take one's ease

reclining 7 lolling, resting **8** lounging, reposing **9** lying down, recumbent

recluse 3 nun **4** monk **5** crank, loner **6** hermit, hidden, secret **7** ascetic, eremite, erratic, oddball **8** cenobite, crackpot **9** eccentric **10** cloistered **11** sequestered **13** nonconformist

recognition 6 notice **9** discovery **10** acceptance, validation **13** comprehension, understanding **14** acknowledgment, identification **19** diplomatic relations

recognizable 5 clear, plain **8** distinct **10** detectable **11** discernable, perceivable, perceptible **12** identifiable, intelligible **13** ascertainable **14** comprehensible, understandable **15** distinguishable

recognizance 4 bond **6** pledge **10** obligation **11** recognition **15** acknowledgement

recognize 3 see **4** know, spot **5** admit, place, sight **7** discern, make out, pick out, realize, respect, yield to **8** identify, submit to **9** be aware of, concede to **10** appreciate, comprehend, understand **11** acknowledge **14** give the floor to

recognized 5 known **8** accepted, admitted, approved, familiar, realized **9** customary **10** accredited **11** traditional **12** acknowledged, conventional

recoil 4 fail, kick **5** blink, cower, demur, quail, shirk, start, wince **6** blench, cringe, falter, flinch, revolt **7** fly back, rebound, retreat **8** draw back, hang back, jump back **9** bound back **10** shrink back, spring back

recoil at 4 hate **5** abhor **6** detest, eschew, loathe **7** despise **9** abominate, shudder at **10** shrink from **12** be revolted by **14** view with horror

recoiling 7 wincing **9** flinching **10** rebounding **11** drawing back **13** shrinking back, springing back

recollect 5 place **6** recall **8** remember **10** call to mind

recollection 4 mind **6** memoir, memory, recall, record **11** remembrance **12** reminiscence **13** retrospection
French: 8 souvenir

recommend 4 urge **5** favor, order **6** advise **7** counsel, endorse, propose, suggest **8** advocate, vouch for **9** encourage, prescribe **10** put forward **11** speak well of

recommendable 9 advisable, favorable **10** worthwhile

recommendation 4 plug **6** behest, praise **8** approval, good word **9** reference **11** endorsement **12** commendation

recompense 3 pay **5** repay **6** return, reward **7** payment **9** reimburse, repayment **10** compensate, remunerate, reparation **12** compensation, remuneration **15** indemnification

reconcile 5 fix up **6** adjust, make up, resign, settle, square **7** correct, patch up, rectify, reunite, win over **8** persuade **9** harmonize **10** conciliate, propitiate **11** set straight

reconcile oneself 6 submit **9** acquiesce **13** resign oneself

reconciliation 8 fixing up, making up, settling, squaring **10** adjustment, correction, patching up, rectifying **11** resignation, winning over **12** conciliation **13** justification, rectification **15** setting straight

recondite 4 deep **6** arcane, hidden **7** obscure **8** abstruse, esoteric **9** concealed **10** mysterious **16** incomprehensible

reconnaissance 6 survey **7** viewing **8** scouting, scrutiny **10** inspection **11** exploration, observation **12** surveillance **13** investigation **14** reconnoitering

reconnoiter 4 look **5** probe, scout **6** patrol, picket, survey **7** examine **8** remember, traverse

reconsider 5 amend **6** modify, ponder, review, revise **7** correct, rethink, sleep on **8** mull over, reassess **9** reexamine, think over **10** reevaluate **13** think better of **15** think twice about

reconstitute 7 restore **9** recompose **10** add water to **11** reconstruct

reconstruct 7 rebuild **8** make over, recreate **10** reassemble **11** reestablish **12** reconstitute

record 3 log **4** copy, file, list, memo, note, post, show, tape **5** admit, enter **6** annals, career, docket, enroll, report **7** account, archive, catalog, conduct, history, jot down, jotting, journal **8** document, indicate, register, take down **9** chronicle, introduce, write down **10** adventures, background, memorandum, transcribe **11** experiences, make an entry, performance, proceedings **12** unbeaten mark **14** top performance
  French: 11 compte rendu

record, phonograph 2 EP, LP **5** vinyl **7** platter
  invented by: 4 Bell **6** Edison **7** Tainter **8** Berliner **10** Goldenmark

recount 4 tell **6** detail, recite, relate **7** explain, narrate **8** describe **9** count over

recoup 5 atone **6** redeem, regain **7** recover, replace **8** make good, retrieve

9 make up for, reacquire **13** make amends for

recourse 6 choice, option, resort **11** alternative, other choice

recover 4 heal, mend **5** rally **6** offset, pick up, recoup, redeem, regain, retake, revive **7** balance, get back, get well, improve, reclaim, restore, win back **8** make good, retrieve, revivify **9** make up for, reacquire, recapture, reconquer, repossess **10** come around, compensate, convalesce, recuperate, rejuvenate **11** pull through, resuscitate

recovery 4 cure **5** rally **6** recoup, rescue, upturn **7** revival, salvage **8** comeback **9** retrieval **10** betterment, regainment **11** improvement, reclamation, reformation, restoration **12** recuperation **13** business cycle, convalescence

recreancy 8 apostasy **9** cowardice, desertion **10** cravenness, disloyalty, infidelity **13** faithlessness, pusillanimity **14** unfaithfulness

recreant 6 coward, craven, yellow **8** apostate, cowardly, deserter, disloyal, renegade **9** undutiful **10** unfaithful **11** lily-livered **12** dishonorable **13** pusillanimous, yellow-bellied

recreation 4 play **5** hobby, sport **7** pastime **9** amusement, avocation, diversion **10** relaxation **13** entertainment **15** leisure activity

recrimination 5 blame **6** charge **10** accusation **13** countercharge

recruit 4 hire **5** raise, renew **6** employ, enlist, enroll, muster, novice, recoup, revive, rookie **7** draftee, provide, recover, restore **8** beginner, newcomer **9** conscript **10** recuperate

rectangle 3 box **6** oblong, square **7** polygon **10** quadrangle **13** parallelogram, quadrilateral

rectangular 4 long **6** square **7** boxlike **11** right-angled **12** quadrangular **13** quadrilateral

rectification 6 fixing, reform **7** redress **8** righting, squaring **9** remedying, repairing **10** adjustment, correction, regulation **12** setting right **15** putting straight, putting to rights **16** straightening out

rectify 3 fix **4** cure, mend **5** amend, emend, focus, right **6** adjust, attune, reform, remedy, repair, revise, square **7** correct, redress **8** put right, regulate, set right **9** make right **10** straighten

rectitude 5 honor **7** decency, probity **8** morality **9** integrity, principle **11** uprightness **12** virtuousness **13** righteousness **14** high-mindedness **15** trustworthiness **16** incorruptibility **17** irreproachability

rector 6 cleric, parson, pastor, priest **8** minister, preacher **9** churchman, clergyman **12** ecclesiastic

recumbent 4 flat **5** prone **6** supine **7** leaning **8** couchant **9** lying down, prostrate, reclining **10** horizontal **12** stretched out

recuperate 4 heal, mend **7** get well, improve, recover **8** come back **9** get better **10** come around, convalesce **11** be on the mend, pull through **14** return to health **16** regain one's health

recuperation 8 recovery **11** restoration **13** convalescence

recuperative 11 restorative **15** health-restoring

recur 6 repeat, resume, return **7** persist **8** come back, continue, reappear **9** come again **10** occur again

recurrence 5 cycle, round **6** repeat, return **7** relapse, renewal, reprise, routine **8** iterance, rotation **10** continuity, repetition **11** periodicity **12** reappearance

recurrent 7 regular **8** frequent, periodic **9** recurring, repeating **10** repetitive **11** reappearing **12** intermittent **14** appearing again

red 4 pink, rose, rosy, ruby, wine **5** aglow, coral, flame, ruddy **6** auburn, cherry, florid, maroon **7** burning, crimson, flaming, flushed, glowing, scarlet **8** blooming, blushing, cardinal, inflamed, reddened, rubicund **9** rubescent, vermilion **12** blood-colored

Red and the Black, The (Le Rouge et le Noir)
  author: 8 Stendhal
  character: 6 Fouque **8** M de Renal **11** Julien Sorel **16** Mathilde de la Mole

Red Badge of Courage, The
  author: 12 Stephen Crane
  character: 6 Wilson **10** Jim Conklin **12** Henry Fleming

red-blooded 5 lusty, peppy, vital **6** ardent, robust, strong, sturdy **7** dynamic, intense **8** forceful, powerful, spirited, vigorous **9** energetic **10** hot-blooded, passionate

Red Branch
  origin: 5 Irish
  warriors of: 9 Conchobar

Redburn
  author: 14 Herman Melville

red-cheeked 4 rosy **5** ruddy **6** robust **8** blushing **12** apple-cheeked

Red Cross Knight
  character in: 15 The Faerie Queene
  author: 7 Spenser

redden 4 burn, glow **5** blush, color, flame, flush **9** go crimson **12** become florid

reddish 4 rosy, ruby **5** ruddy, rufus **6** flushy, rufous **7** roseate **8** rubicund

reddish-brown 4 rust **5** henna **6** auburn, copper, russet, sienna **8** chestnut, cinnamon

Red Earth People *see* **3** Fox

redeem 4 keep, save **5** cover **6** defray,

ransom, recoup, reform, regain, rescue, settle **7** buy back, convert, fulfill, reclaim, recover, satisfy **8** atone for, make good, retrieve **9** discharge, make up for, repossess **10** evangelize, repurchase

redeemed 5 saved **7** claimed, rescued **8** made good, ransomed, reformed **9** atoned for, delivered, fulfilled, recovered **10** carried out, regenerate **11** repossessed

redemption 6 excuse, pardon, ransom, reform, rescue **7** salvage **8** recovery **9** amendment, atonement, exemption, expiation, salvation **10** conversion **11** deliverance, reformation

Redford, Robert
　real name: 20 Charles Robert Redford
　born: 13 Santa Monica CA
　roles: 5 Aloft **8** The Sting **10** The Natural **11** Legal Eagles, The Clearing **12** The Candidate, The Way We Were **13** Downhill Racer **14** The Great Gatsby **15** Jeremiah Johnson **16** Indecent Proposal **17** Barefoot in the Park, The Horse Whisperer **19** All the President's Men **20** Three Days of the Condor **29** Butch Cassidy and the Sundance Kid
　director: 5 Aloft **8** Quiz Show **14** Ordinary People (Oscar) **17** The Horse Whisperer **19** A River Runs Through It
　film festival: 8 Sundance

Redgrave, Corin
　born: 6 London **7** England
　sisters: 4 Lynn **7** Vanessa
　roles: 8 The Magus **11** To Kill a King **17** A Man for All Seasons **20** In the Name of the Father **23** Four Weddings and a Funeral

Redgrave, Lynn
　born: 6 London **7** England
　father: 18 Sir Michael Redgrave
　siblings: 13 Corin Redgrave **15** Vanessa Redgrave
　roles: 10 Georgy Girl, Howard's End **13** The Bostonians **14** Getting It Right, The Happy Hooker **26** Whatever Happened to Baby Jane
　author of: 7 Vanessa **16** Pussies and Tigers

Redgrave, Sir Michael
　born: 7 Bristol, England
　daughter: 4 Lynn **7** Vanessa
　roles: 11 Dan Peggotty **15** The Lady Vanishes **16** David Copperfield **22** Mourning Becomes Electra **27** The Importance of Being Earnest

Redgrave, Vanessa
　born: 6 London **7** England
　father: 18 Sir Michael Redgrave
　siblings: 12 Lynn Redgrave **13** Corin Redgrave
　husband: 14 Tony Richardson
　roles: 5 Julia, Yanks **6** Agatha,

Blow-Up, Morgan **7** Camelot, Isadora **9** Guinevere **16** Mary Queen of Scots **17** The Lady from the Sea

red-hot 5 aglow, fiery **6** heated, raging **7** blazing, burning, glowing, intense **12** all-consuming

red-letter 5 happy, lucky **6** banner **10** auspicious, felicitous

redness 4 glow **5** blush, flush **8** rosiness **9** ruddiness **10** floridness

redolence 5 aroma, savor **7** bouquet **9** fragrance, good smell **12** pleasant odor

redolent 5 balmy, spicy **6** savory, smelly **7** mindful, odorous, reeking, scented **8** aromatic, fragrant, perfumed, stinking **9** evocative, odiferous **10** expressive, indicative, suggestive **11** odoriferous, reminiscent **13** sweet-smelling

Redon, Odilon
　born: 6 France **8** Bordeaux
　artwork: 10 In the Dream, The Cyclops **11** Le Vieil Ange **13** Flowers of Evil **15** Violette Heymann

redouble 7 augment, magnify **8** heighten, multiply **9** intensify

redoubtable 7 awesome **8** alarming, imposing **10** formidable **11** illustrious **12** awe-inspiring

redound 4 lead, tend **5** cause, surge **6** abound **7** conduce, incline **8** overflow **10** contribute **11** reverberate

redress 4 ease **5** amend, right **6** amends, reform, relief, remedy **7** correct, payment, rectify, relieve **8** easement, set right **9** make up for **10** recompense, reparation **11** restitution **12** compensation, satisfaction **13** compensate for, rectification **15** indemnification **18** make retribution for

Red River
　director: 11 Howard Hawks
　cast: 9 Joanne Dru, John Wayne **11** John Ireland **13** Walter Brennan **15** Montgomery Clift

Reds
　director: 12 Warren Beatty
　cast: 11 Diane Keaton (Louise Bryant), Paul Sorvino **12** Warren Beatty (John Reed) **13** Jack Nicholson, Jerzy Kosinski **14** Edward Herrmann **16** Maureen Stapleton
　Oscar for: 8 director **17** supporting actress (Stapleton)

Red Shoes, The
　author: 21 Hans Christian Andersen
　director: 13 Michael Powell **17** Emeric Pressburger
　cast: 12 Marius Goring, Moira Shearer **13** Anton Walbrook **14** Robert Helpmann

Red Skelton Show, The
　character: 8 Gertrude **10** Heathcliff **13** Mean Widdle Kid **14** San Fernando Red, Sheriff Deadeye, Willie Lump-Lump **16** Bolivar Shagnasty **17**

Cauliflower McPugg **18** Clem Kadiddlehopper **20** Freddie the Freeloader
　saying: 7 I dood it
　closing line: 8 God bless

Red Sky at Morning
　author: 15 Richard Bradford

reduce 3 cut **4** bust, curb, diet, dull, ease, thin **5** abate, blunt, break, check, force, lower, slash, water **6** damage, demote, dilute, lessen, retard, soften, temper, weaken **7** assuage, atrophy, cripple, cut down, leave in **8** diminish, discount, enfeeble, mark down, minimize, mitigate, moderate, modulate, slim down, slow down, tone down, trim down **9** bring down, checkmate, undermine **10** debilitate, devitalize, slenderize **11** lower in rank **12** incapacitate

reduced form 6 digest **7** summary **9** short form **11** abridgement, contraction **12** abbreviation, condensation

reduce speed 4 slow **5** brake **6** rein in **8** slow down **10** decelerate

reduce to nothing 5 erase **7** abolish, destroy, wipe out **8** lay waste **9** eradicate, liquidate **10** annihilate **11** exterminate

reductio ad absurdum 22 reduction to an absurdity

reduction 3 cut **5** break **8** decrease, discount **9** abatement, lessening **10** concession **11** abridgement, subtraction

reduction to an absurdity
　Latin: 18 reductio ad absurdum

redundancy 6 excess **7** surplus **8** verbiage **9** tautology **10** repetition **11** diffuseness, superfluity **13** overabundance **14** circumlocution, repetitiveness

redundant 5 extra **6** excess **7** surplus **10** pleonastic **11** dispensable, inessential, overflowing, repetitious, superfluous, unnecessary **12** tautological **13** superabundant

redwood 19 Adenanthera pavonina, Sequoia sempervirens
　varieties: 4 dawn **5** coast, giant **7** Madeira

reed
　varieties: 3 bur **4** vine **5** Burma, giant **6** common **14** Mauritania vine

reed 9 six cubits

Reed, Sir Carol
　director of: 6 Oliver (Oscar) **11** The Third Man

Reed, Walter S
　field: 12 bacteriology
　discovered cause of: 11 yellow fever

reef 3 bar **4** bank, flat, spit **5** shelf, shoal **7** sandbar, shallow

reek 4 fume **5** smell, smoke, steam, stink **6** stench **7** give off **9** effluvium, emanation

reel 4 rock, roll, spin, sway **5** lurch,

pitch, swirl, waver, whirl **6** rotate, teeter, totter, wobble **7** revolve, stagger, stumble

reeling 5 dizzy, giddy, shaky **6** whirly **8** spinning, unsteady **10** staggering **11** vertiginous

Reese, Harold
    nickname: 6 Pee Wee
    sport: 8 baseball
    position: 9 shortstop
    team: 15 Brooklyn Dodgers

Reeve
    character in: 18 The Canterbury Tales
    author: 7 Chaucer

Reeve, Christopher
    born: 9 New York NY
    author of: 7 Still Me
    roles: 8 Superman **9** Deathtrap **13** The Bostonians **15** Remains of the Day, Somewhere in Time **18** Village of the Damned

refer 2 go **4** cite, send, turn **6** advert, allude, direct, submit **7** consult, deliver, mention **8** hand over, transfer, transmit **9** pass along

referee 5 judge **6** decree, settle, umpire **7** arbiter, mediate **8** judgment, mediator, moderate **9** arbitrate, determine, intercede, intervene, moderator, pronounce **10** adjudicate, arbitrator **11** adjudicator, intercessor **12** intermediary

reference 4 hint **7** inkling, mention **8** allusion, good word, innuendo **10** deposition, intimation, suggestion **11** affirmation, credentials, endorsement, implication, testimonial **13** certification **14** recommendation

reference book 5 atlas, bible **6** manual **9** guidebook **10** dictionary **12** encyclopedia

refine 6 filter, purify, strain **7** cleanse, develop, improve, perfect, process **9** cultivate

refined 5 clean, suave **6** gentle, polite, urbane **7** courtly, elegant, genteel **8** cleansed, cultured, delicate, finished, graceful, ladylike, mannerly, polished, purified, well-bred **9** civilized, clarified, courteous **10** cultivated, fastidious **11** gentlemanly **14** discriminating

refinement 5 grace **6** finish, nicety, polish, step up **7** advance, culture, dignity, finesse, suavity **8** breeding, civility, cleaning, courtesy, delicacy, elegance, fineness, revision, urbanity **9** amendment, cleansing, gentility, propriety **10** betterment, filtration, gentleness, politeness **11** advancement, cultivation, development, discernment, enhancement, good manners, improvement, progression, savoir faire, step forward **12** amelioration, distillation, graciousness, purification, tastefulness **13** courteousness, rectification **14** discrimination, fastidiousness

refitting 8 adapting **10** adaptation, remodeling **11** reequipping, resupplying

reflect 4 cast, copy, muse, show, undo **5** image, study, think, throw **6** betray, evince, expose, mirror, ponder, reason, return, reveal **7** condemn, display, exhibit, express, imitate, present, rebound, uncover **8** cogitate, consider, disclose, give back, indicate, manifest, meditate, mull over, register, ruminate, send back, set forth **9** bring upon, cerebrate, dwell upon, represent, reproduce, speculate, throw back, undermine **10** deliberate **11** concentrate, contemplate, demonstrate

reflection 4 blot, idea, slur, view **5** image, study **6** insult, musing, notion **7** opinion, reproof, thought **8** reproach, thinking **9** attention, pondering, sentiment **10** cogitation, conviction, derogation, impression, imputation, meditation, rumination **11** cerebration, insinuation, mirror image, pensiveness **12** deliberation **13** concentration, consideration, disparagement
    French: 6 pensee

reflective 7 pensive **8** thinking **9** judicious, pondering **10** meditative, ruminative, thoughtful **11** speculative **13** contemplative

reform 4 mend **5** amend, atone, emend **6** better, remedy, repair, repent, revise **7** convert, correct, improve, rebuild, rectify, remodel, restore **8** progress **9** amendment **10** correction **12** mend one's ways, rehabilitate **13** rectification **16** set straight again, turn over a new leaf

reformation 6 change, reform **9** amendment, reforming **10** alteration, conversion **11** improvement **12** modification **14** reorganization

refractory 5 balky **6** mulish, unruly **7** restive, wayward, willful **8** contrary, stubborn **9** fractious, obstinate, pigheaded **10** rebellious **11** disobedient, intractable **12** unmanageable

refrain 5 avoid, forgo **6** desist, eschew, forego, refuse, resist **7** abstain, forbear, hold off **8** leave off, renounce **11** curb oneself, keep oneself **12** stay one's hand **15** restrain oneself

refrain from 5 avoid, forgo **6** desist, eschew, forego **7** abstain, forbear **8** leave off, renounce

refresh 3 jog **4** prod **5** brace, renew, rouse **6** arouse, awaken, prompt, revive, stir up, vivify **7** cool off, freshen, quicken, recruit, restore **8** activate, energize, recreate **9** reanimate, stimulate **10** invigorate, rejuvenate, strengthen

refreshed 7 revived **8** animated, restored, vivified **9** enlivened, freshened **11** invigorated

refreshing 7 bracing **11** revivifying **12**

invigorating **13** strengthening **15** thirst-quenching

refreshment 4 bite, eats **5** drink, snack **6** bracer **7** potable **8** beverage, cocktail, pick-me-up, potation **9** appetizer, drinkable, refresher **10** recreation, relaxation **11** hors d'oeuvre, nourishment, restoration, restorative **12** food and drink, invigoration, rejuvenation **14** reinvigoration, thirst quencher

refrigerate 4 cool **5** chill **6** freeze **7** congeal **8** keep cold, keep cool, put on ice **9** keep on ice

Refrigerator, The
    nickname of: 12 William Perry

refuge 4 home **5** haven **6** asylum, harbor, resort **7** hideout, retreat, shelter **8** safehold **9** anchorage, harborage, sanctuary **10** protection **12** port in a storm **14** help in distress, place of shelter

refugee 2 DP **5** exile **6** bolter, eloper, emigre **7** escapee, evacuee, runaway **8** emigrant, fugitive **9** absconder **10** expatriate **15** displaced person

refulgent 6 bright, lucent **7** glowing, lambent, radiant, shining **8** luminous, relucent **9** brilliant

refund 5 remit, repay **6** rebate, return **7** pay back **9** reimburse, repayment **10** recompense, remittance, remunerate **12** amount repaid **13** give back money, reimbursement **18** make restitution for **19** make compensation for

refurbish 4 mend, redo **5** clean, fix up, renew **6** repair, tidy up **7** freshen, improve, remodel, restore **8** overhaul, renovate, spruce up **11** recondition

refusal 2 no **3** nay **4** veto **6** denial **7** regrets **8** turndown **9** declining, rejection **10** nonconsent **11** declination, disapproval **13** nonacceptance, noncompliance, unwillingness

refuse 2 no **4** deny, junk, veto **5** spurn, trash, waste **6** forbid, litter, reject **7** decline, garbage, rubbish, say no to **8** disallow, prohibit, turn down, withhold

refuse pile 4 dump **6** midden **11** rubbish heap

refuse to submit 4 defy **5** rebel **6** resist **7** disobey, hold out, violate **10** transgress **12** fail to comply

refutation 4 veto **6** denial **7** counter **8** negation, rebuttal **9** disavowal **11** confutation, repudiation **12** invalidation **13** contradiction

refutatory 8 contrary, opposing **10** discrepant **11** conflicting, disagreeing **12** antithetical, inconsistent **13** contradictory **14** countervailing, irreconcilable

refute 4 deny **5** rebut **6** answer **7** confute, counter **8** disprove **9** challenge

10 contradict, invalidate **12** give the lie to

regain 6 recoup, redeem, retake **7** get back, reclaim, recover, win back **8** gain anew, get again, retrieve **9** recapture, repossess

regal 5 grand, noble, proud, royal **6** august, kingly, lordly **7** queenly, stately **8** imposing, kinglike, majestic, princely, splendid **9** queenlike **10** princelike **11** magnificent **13** splendiferous

regale 3 ply **4** fete **5** amuse, feast **6** divert, please **7** banquet, delight, lionize **8** enthrall **9** entertain **10** serve nobly **11** wine and dine **15** feed sumptuously

Regan
character in: **8** King Lear
author: **11** Shakespeare

regard 3 eye, see **4** care, heed, hold, mind, note, rate, scan, view **5** judge, point, think, value, watch **6** accept, admire, aspect, behold, detail, esteem, follow, gaze at, look at, matter, notice, reckon, survey, take in **7** account, believe, concern, put down, respect, set down, subject, thought **8** consider, estimate, listen to, look upon, look up to, note well, relation **9** attention, hearken to, reference **10** admiration, connection, estimation, meditation, reflection, scrutinize **11** contemplate, observation, think well of **12** appreciation **13** cast the eyes on, consideration, think highly of **14** pay attention to

regardful 5 civil **6** polite **7** mindful **8** reverent **9** courteous, observant **10** respectful **11** deferential, reverential

regard highly 6 admire, esteem **7** respect **10** appreciate

regarding 4 in re **5** about, anent **7** apropos **10** concerning, respecting

regardless 6 anyhow, anyway **10** for all that **11** nonetheless **12** nevertheless **15** notwithstanding **19** in spite of everything

regard with repugnance 4 hate **5** abhor **6** detest, loathe **7** despise **8** execrate **9** abominate, can't stand, shudder at **10** recoil from, shrink from **11** can't stomach **12** be revolted by **13** be nauseated by, find repulsive **18** feel aversion toward

regard with suspicion 5 doubt **7** suspect **8** distrust, mistrust, question

regenerate 5 renew **6** redeem, reform, revive, uplift **7** restore **8** inspirit, reawaken, retrieve, revivify **9** enlighten, resurrect **10** rejuvenate **11** resuscitate **12** generate anew **13** give new life to, make a new man of

regent 4 king **5** queen, ruler **8** governor **9** protecter, protector

regime 4 rule **5** power, reign **7** command, control, dynasty **8** dominion **9**

direction **10** government, leadership, management **12** jurisdiction **14** administration

regimen 4 diet, rule **6** system **10** government

regimentation 5 order, rigor **6** method, system **7** control, regimen **9** orthodoxy **10** discipline, regulation, uniformity **12** rigorousness **13** methodization **19** doctrinaire approach

Regin
origin: **12** Scandinavian
mentioned in: **8** Volsunga
brother: **6** Fafnir
raised: **6** Sigurd

region 4 area, land, zone **5** field, range, realm, space, tract **6** domain, sphere **7** country, expanse **8** district, locality, province, vicinity **9** territory **12** neighborhood

regional 5 areal, local, zonal **7** dialect **10** locational, provincial **11** territorial **12** geographical

register 3 log **4** dial, mark, roll, show **5** diary, gauge, meter, range, scale **6** betray, enlist, enroll, heater, ledger, record, sign up **7** betoken, check in, compass, counter, daybook, exhibit, express, logbook, point to, portray, set down **8** disclose, heat duct, heat vent, indicate, manifest, note down, radiator, recorder, registry, take down **9** indicator, write down **10** calculator, heat outlet, hot-air vent, record book **12** put in writing

regnat populus 16 let the people rule
motto of: **8** Arkansas

regress 3 ebb **4** back, exit, fall **6** go back, recede, return, revert **7** relapse, retreat, reverse **8** fall back, pass back, withdraw **9** backslide **10** lose ground, retrogress **11** deteriorate **12** move backward

regressive 8 backward **9** declining, worsening **10** retrograde **13** retrogressive

regret 3 rue, woe **4** moan **5** grief, mourn, qualm **6** bemoan, bewail, lament, repent, sorrow, twinge **7** anguish, apology, deplore, eat crow, remorse, scruple **8** be rueful, grieve at, weep over **9** apologies, grievance, heartache, rue the day **10** be sorry for, contrition, repentance, ruefulness **11** be ashamed of, compunction, lamentation, reservation **12** be remorseful, eat humble pie, eat one's words, self-reproach **13** feel sorrow for, regretfulness, second thought **14** disappointment, feel remorse for, remorsefulness **15** dissatisfaction **16** feel distress over, pang of conscience, self-condemnation

regretful 6 rueful **8** contrite **9** sorrowful **10** apologetic, remorseful **15** self-reproachful

regrettable 6 woeful **7** unhappy **8**

grievous, pitiable **10** calamitous, deplorable, lamentable **11** unfortunate

regular 3 set **4** even, fine, real **5** daily, fixed, plain, usual **6** common, normal, proper, smooth, steady, trusty **7** classic, correct, genuine, habitue, natural, typical, uniform **8** absolute, accepted, complete, constant, everyday, faithful, familiar, frequent, habitual, loyalist, ordinary, orthodox, periodic, stalwart, standard, thorough, true blue **9** customary, recurrent, recurring, unvarying **10** consistent, dependable, invariable, periodical, unchanging **11** commonplace, down-to-earth, established, old reliable, symmetrical, undeviating **12** well-balanced

regulate 3 fix **5** guide **6** adjust, direct, govern, handle, manage **7** balance, control, monitor, oversee, rectify **8** moderate, modulate, organize **9** supervise **10** regularize **11** superintend

regulation 4 rule **5** edict, order **6** decree **7** command, control, dictate, statute **8** handling **9** adjusting, direction, ordinance **10** adjustment **11** commandment **13** standing order

regulator 5 guide **7** manager **8** director, governor, overseer **9** moderator, modulator **10** adjustment, supervisor **14** superintendent **15** adjusting device

regurgitate 4 barf **5** vomit **7** throw up **8** disgorge

rehabilitate 3 fix **4** save **6** redeem, remake **7** restore, salvage **8** make over, readjust, renovate **9** reeducate, refurbish, reinstate **11** recondition, reconstruct, resocialize, set straight **13** straighten out **16** restore to society

rehash 6 repeat, retell, reword **7** restate **8** rephrase **9** iteration, rechauffe

rehearsal 5 drill, recap **6** tryout **7** hearing, reading, test run **8** audition, exercise, practice, trial run **9** polishing **10** perfecting, repetition, run-through **11** preparation, reiteration, walk-through **14** recapitulation

rehearse 5 drill, ready, train **6** go over, polish, recite, relate, repeat, retell **7** narrate, prepare, recount **8** practice **9** reiterate **10** run through **13** read one's lines **14** give a recital of, study one's lines

rehoboam 18 oversize wine bottle
Rehoboth
founder: **6** Nimrod

Reich, Charles
author of: **20** The Greening of America

Reichsfuhrer 11 Reich leader
chief of: **8** SS troops

reign 4 rule **6** govern, regime, regnum, tenure **7** command **8** dominion, hold sway, regnancy, tutelage **9** dominance, influence **10** government, incumbency **11** sovereignty, supervision **12** wear the crown **13** hold authority

14 have royal power, sit on the throne **15** occupy the throne **17** exercise authority **19** exercise sovereignty
Hindu: 3 raj

reign over 4 rule **6** govern **7** command, control **8** dominate

reimburse 5 pay up, remit, repay **6** rebate, refund **7** pay back **8** square up **9** indemnify **10** compensate, recompense, remunerate **15** make restitution

reimbursement 6 refund **9** indemnity, repayment **12** compensation, remuneration

rein, reins 4 curb, hold **5** check, limit, watch **6** bridle **7** control, harness **8** hold back, restrict, suppress **9** restraint **11** keep an eye on

Reiner, Carl
    born: 7 Bronx NY
    son: 9 Rob Reiner
    roles: 15 Your Show of Shows **21** It's a Mad Mad Mad Mad World
    created: 15 Dick Van Dyke Show
    director: 5 Oh God **7** The Jerk **8** The Comic **11** Where's Poppa?
    novel: 13 Enter Laughing

Reiner, Rob
    father: 10 Carl Reiner
    roles: 8 Meathead **10** Mike Stivik **14** All in the Family
    director of: 6 Misery **9** Stand By Me **11** Alex and Emma, A Few Good Men **15** This Is Spinal Tap **16** The Princess Bride **17** When Harry Met Sally **19** Ghosts of Mississippi **20** The American President

reinforce 4 prop **5** steel **7** bolster, brace up, fortify, support **8** buttress **10** strengthen **12** make stronger

reinforcement 4 stay **5** brace, strut **7** bracing, support **10** assistance **11** buttressing **13** strengthening

reinstate 5 renew **6** revive **7** readmit, restore **11** reestablish, reinstitute, reintroduce

reinstatement 7 renewal, revival **11** restoration **13** reinstitution **14** reintroduction **15** reestablishment

reiterate 5 resay **6** hammer, rehash, repeat, retell, reword, stress **7** iterate, reprise, restate **8** rephrase **11** pound away at **12** recapitulate **13** go over and over

reject 4 deny **5** repel, spurn **6** rebuff, refuse **7** castoff, decline, discard, disdain, dismiss, flotsam, repulse, say no to **8** castaway, disallow, shrug off, turn down, turn from **9** repudiate

rejected 6 denied, dumped, jilted **7** cast off, outcast, refused, spurned, unloved **8** disowned, forsaken, lovelorn **9** abandoned, discarded, disproved **10** unaccepted, repudiated **11** invalidated

rejection 6 rebuff **7** disdain, refusal **8** scorning, spurning **9** declining, dismissal, rebuffing, rejecting, ruling out

rejoice 5 exult, glory, revel **6** be glad **7** be happy, delight **8** be elated, jubilate **9** be pleased, celebrate, make merry **10** exhilarate, sing for joy **11** be delighted, be overjoyed **13** be transported

rejoice in 5 eat up, enjoy, savor **6** relish **7** revel in **9** delight in **13** be pleased with, get a kick out of **14** take pleasure in

rejoicing 5 mirth **6** gaiety **7** delight, ecstasy, elation, jollity, jubilee, revelry, triumph **8** cheering, gladness, pleasure, reveling **9** festivity, good cheer, happiness, jubilance, merriment **10** exultation, joyfulness, jubilation, liveliness **11** celebration, merrymaking

rejoin 6 answer, retort **7** respond

rejoinder 5 reply **6** answer, retort, return **7** riposte **8** backtalk, comeback, rebuttal, repartee, response **10** refutation **11** surrebuttal **12** counterblast, remonstrance, surrejoinder **13** countercharge **16** counterstatement

rejuvenate 6 revive **7** restore **8** revivify **9** reanimate **10** revitalize **12** reinvigorate **14** put new life into **17** make youthful again

relapse 4 fall **5** lapse **6** revert, worsen **7** decline, regress, reverse **8** fall back, sink back, slip back, turn back **9** backslide, reversion, worsening **10** degenerate, recurrence, regression, retrogress **11** backsliding, falling back **13** deterioration, retrogression **15** return to illness, turn for the worse

relate 3 say **4** link, tell **5** apply, refer, speak, state, utter **6** attach, belong, convey, detail, impart, recite, report, reveal **7** concern, connect, divulge, narrate, pertain, recount **8** describe, disclose **9** appertain, associate, feel close, make known **10** be relevant **11** communicate, have rapport **12** be responsive, interact well, recapitulate **13** be sympathetic, have reference, particularize **15** feel empathy with, give an account of

related 3 kin **4** akin, said, told **7** kindred, recited **8** narrated, reported **9** recounted **15** of the same family

related by blood 3 kin **4** akin **7** kindred **14** consanguineous, of the same stock **21** having a common ancestor

relation 3 kin, tie **4** bond, link **5** tie-in **6** regard, report **7** account, bearing, concern, kinsman, recital, telling, version **8** relative **9** narrating, narration, narrative, reference, relevance, retelling **10** connection, pertinence, recitation **11** affiliation, application, association, correlation, description **13** applicability, communication **17** interrelationship

relationship 3 kin **5** blood, union **6** affair **7** kindred, kinship, liaison, sibship, society **8** affinity, alliance **10**

connection **11** affiliation, association, correlation **13** consanguinity

relative 3 kin **4** clan, kith **5** blood, folks, tribe **6** allied, cousin, family, people **7** cognate, germane, kinfolk, kinsman, related **8** relation, relevant **9** connected, dependent, kinswoman, pertinent, referable **10** affiliated, applicable, associated, comparable, connection, connective, correlated, kith and kin, pertaining, relational, respective **11** appropriate, comparative, correlative, not absolute **12** interrelated **13** flesh and blood **14** interconnected

relax 4 bend, calm, ease, idle, laze, loaf, rest **5** let up, slack **6** be idle, be lazy, ease up, loosen, soften, soothe, unbend, unwind **7** cool off, holiday, make lax, slacken, take ten **8** decrease, loosen up, take five, vacation **9** lie around **10** take it easy **12** enjoy oneself **13** make less tense **14** make less severe, make less strict

relaxation 3 fun **5** games, hobby, sport **6** repose **7** bending, leisure, pastime **8** pleasure **9** abatement, amusement, avocation, diversion, enjoyment, loosening, remission **10** recreation, slackening **11** refreshment **12** rest from work **13** entertainment

relaxed 3 lax **4** calm, cool, easy, slow, soft **5** loose, slack **6** at ease, casual, gentle, remiss **7** flaccid, lenient **8** informal, laid back, unstrict **9** easygoing, leisurely, negligent, nerveless, unnervous **10** unstrained **11** free and easy, thoughtless
    French: 6 degage

relaxed manner 4 ease **5** poise **6** aplomb **9** composure **10** confidence **11** naturalness **12** unconstraint **14** unaffectedness

relay 3 leg **4** race, tour **5** shift **6** length **8** transfer, transmit **9** conductor, regulator, satellite **10** retransmit
    cylinder: 5 baton
    part: 8 armature, receiver **11** transmitter **13** electromagnet
    race: 6 medley **10** track event

release 4 free **5** let go, loose, untie **6** detach, let out, unbind **7** freeing, present, relieve, set free, unloose **8** liberate, set loose, unfasten **9** circulate, discharge, disengage, dismissal, extricate, letting go, releasing **10** distribute, liberating, liberation **11** circulation, communicate, extrication, publication, setting free **12** distribution, emancipation, set at liberty, setting loose

relegate 3 bar **5** eject, expel **6** assign, banish, charge, commit, demote, reject **7** cast out, consign, discard, dismiss, exclude, keep out, shut out **8** delegate **9** ostracize

relent 4 bend, melt **5** let up, relax, yield **6** give in, soften, unbend, weaken **7** give way **8** have pity **10** be merciful, capitulate, come around **11** give quarter, grow lenient **12** become milder **14** grow less severe

relentless 4 hard **5** harsh, rigid, stern, stiff **6** severe **7** adamant **8** pitiless, rigorous, ruthless **9** merciless **10** implacable, inexorable, inflexible, unyielding **11** remorseless, undeviating, unrelenting **14** uncompromising

relevance 7 aptness, fitness, meaning **9** propriety **10** pertinence **11** materiality, relatedness, suitability **12** significance **13** applicability **15** appropriateness

relevant 3 apt, fit **6** allied, suited, tied in **7** apropos, bearing, cognate, fitting, germane, related **8** apposite, material, suitable **9** connected, intrinsic, pertinent, referring **10** applicable, associated, concerning, to the point **11** appropriate, significant **12** on the subject, to the purpose

reliable 4 true **5** solid, sound **6** trusty **8** faithful **9** unfailing **10** dependable **11** responsible, trustworthy **12** tried and true **13** conscientious

reliance 5 faith, trust **6** belief, credit **8** credence **9** assurance **10** confidence, dependence

relic 5 scrap, token, trace **7** antique, memento, records, remnant, vestige **8** artifact, fragment, heirloom, keepsake, reminder, souvenir **11** remembrance

relief 4 balm, cure, dole, rest **5** break, cheer **6** remedy **7** anodyne, elation, panacea, respite, welfare **8** antidote, easement, lenitive **9** abatement, reduction **10** mitigation, palliation, palliative **11** alleviation, assuagement, peace of mind **12** amelioration **13** encouragement **16** public assistance **17** welfare assistance
Italian: **7** rilievo

relieve 3 aid **4** calm, ease, free, help, mark **5** abate, allay, cheer, spell **6** assist, let out, pacify, remove, set off, solace, soothe, subdue, succor, temper **7** appease, assuage, break up, comfort, console, lighten, mollify, release, replace, support, take out **8** contrast, mitigate, palliate, reassure **9** alleviate, encourage, interrupt, punctuate **12** free from fear

relieved 5 freed **6** calmed, exempt **7** cheered, excused, solaced **8** consoled **9** comforted, reassured **10** encouraged

religion 4 cult, sect **5** canon, creed, dogma, faith, piety **6** belief, church, homage **7** worship **8** devotion, theology **9** adoration, godliness, reverence **10** devoutness, persuasion, veneration **11** affiliation, belief in God **12** belief in gods, denomination, spirituality **13** system of faith **15** system of worship

religionist 8 believer

religiosity 5 piety **8** devotion **10** fanaticism **15** religious fervor

religious 3 nun **4** holy, monk **5** exact, friar, godly, rigid **6** ardent, devout, divine, priest, sacred **7** devoted, staunch **8** constant, faithful, unerring **9** spiritual, steadfast **10** devotional, fastidious, God-fearing, meticulous, scrupulous, unswerving **11** punctilious, theological, undeviating **12** wholehearted **13** conscientious **14** denominational **15** spiritual-minded

religious belief 5 canon, credo, creed, dogma, tenet **8** doctrine

religious fervor 5 piety **7** ecstasy **8** holiness **9** godliness **10** devoutness **12** religiosity, spirituality

religious group 4 sect **12** denomination

religious orders
   Christian: 6 Jesuit **7** Cluniac, Templar **8** Capuchin, Theatine, Trappist, Ursuline **9** Carmelite, Dominican **10** Carthusian, Cistercian, Franciscan **11** Augustinian, Benedictine, Camaldolite **16** Sisters of Charity **20** Order of the Visitation
   non-Christian: 4 Sufi **7** Jainism **8** Dasanami

relinquish 4 cede, deny, drop, quit, shed **5** forgo, leave, let go, waive, yield **6** forego, give up, resign, vacate **7** abandon, cast off, discard, dismiss, forbear, forsake, release **8** abdicate, break off, disclaim, hand over, lay aside, put aside, renounce, sign away **9** deliver up, repudiate, surrender

relinquishable 9 forgoable **10** expendable, foregoable **11** dispensable **12** renounceable

relinquished 5 ceded, let go **6** gave up **7** forgone, given up, yielded **8** cast away, foregone, forsaken **9** abandoned, given away, renounced **10** left behind

relinquishment 7 cession **8** giving up, yielding **9** letting go, rejection, surrender **10** abnegation **11** repudiation **12** renunciation

relish 3 dig **4** like, love, tang, want, wish, zest **5** enjoy, fancy, gusto, savor, spice, taste **6** accent, desire, dote on, flavor, liking, palate **7** delight, longing, stomach **8** appetite, fondness, groove on, penchant, piquancy, pleasure **9** condiment, delight in, enjoyment, hankering, rejoice in **10** appreciate, ebullience, enthusiasm, exuberance, partiality, propensity **11** luxuriate in **12** appreciation, be crazy about, predilection, satisfaction **13** gratification
   type: 4 beef, corn **5** sweet **7** chutney **6** pickle, tomato **10** chili sauce, piccalilli **11** horseradish

reluctance 10 hesitation **13** unwillingness **14** disinclination

reluctant 3 shy **4** slow **5** loath **6** averse **7** laggard **8** hesitant **9** diffident, unwilling **10** indisposed **11** disinclined

rely 3 bet **4** bank, lean, rest **5** count, swear, trust **6** credit, depend, reckon **7** believe **10** feel sure of **11** be dependent **12** give credence

remain 4 go on, last, stay, wait **5** abide, stand **6** be left, endure, hang on, hold up, linger **7** not move, not stir, persist, prevail, stay put, subsist, survive **8** continue, stand pat **10** be left over, stay behind

remainder 4 rest **5** waste **6** excess, refuse **7** balance, overage, remains, remnant, residue, surplus, wastage **8** leavings, residual, residuum **9** leftovers, scourings **10** surplusage **11** superfluity

remains 4 body **5** stiff **6** corpse, scraps **7** cadaver **8** dead body **9** leftovers

remark 3 say, see **4** espy, mark, mind, note, view, word **6** behold, look at, notice, regard, survey **7** comment, mention, observe, pay heed **8** perceive **9** attention **10** commentary, give heed to, make note of, reflection, take note of **11** contemplate, observation **12** fix the mind on, say in passing, take notice of **13** consideration **14** pay attention to

remarkable 6 signal **7** notable, unusual **8** singular, striking **9** memorable **10** impressive, noteworthy, phenomenal **11** conspicuous, exceptional, outstanding **13** distinguished, extraordinary, unforgettable

Remarque, Erich Maria
   author of: 25 All Quiet on the Western Front

Rembrandt (Harmensz) van Rijn
   born: 6 Leiden, Leyden **14** The Netherlands
   artwork: 6 Balaam **9** Bathsheba **13** The Night Watch (The Sortie of the Company of Captain Banning Cocq) **14** The Jewish Bride **15** Old Woman Reading, The Bridal Couple **19** The Blinding of Samson **20** Christ Healing the Sick **21** The Stoning of St Stephen **22** Man with the Golden Helmet, Self-Portrait with Saskia, The Descent from the Cross **24** The Anatomy Lesson of Dr Tulp, The Syndics of the Cloth Hall **36** Aristotle Contemplating the Bust of Homer

remedial 7 healing, helpful, mending **8** curative, salutary, sanative **10** beneficial, corrective **11** meliorative, reformative, restorative, therapeutic **12** advantageous, correctional, prophylactic

remedy 3 aid, fix **4** calm, cure, ease, heal, help, mend **5** amend, emend, right **6** relief, repair, soothe **7** assuage, correct, cure-all, improve, mollify, nostrum, panacea, rectify, redress, relieve, restore **8** make easy, medicine, mitigate, palliate, regulate, set right **9** alleviate, make sound, treatment **10** ameliorate, assistance, corrective, make better, medicament, medication, preventive **13** rectification **15** restore to health

remember 3 tip **6** recall, reward **9** not forget, recognize, recollect **10** appreciate, bear in mind, call to mind, have in mind, keep in mind, take care of, take note of **11** bring to mind **12** bear in memory

remember that thou must die
Latin: **11** memento mori

remembrance 5 favor, relic, token **6** memory, recall **7** memento **8** keepsake, memorial, reminder, souvenir **9** nostalgia **11** recognition, remembering **12** recognizance, recollection, reminiscence **13** commemoration

Remembrance of Things Past
author: **12** Marcel Proust

Remick, Lee
born: **8** Quincy MA
roles: **16** Anatomy of a Murder, The Long Hot Summer **18** Days of Wine and Roses

remind 9 put in mind, suggest to **11** bring back to, bring to mind, put in memory **16** awaken memories of

reminder of death
Latin: **11** memento mori

Remington, Frederic Sackrider
born: **8** Canton NY
artwork: **12** Bronco Buster **23** Roping Horses in the Corral **32** Cavalry Charge on the Southern Plains

reminisce 4 mull, muse **6** ponder **7** reflect **8** hark back, look back, remember **9** recollect, think back **12** tell old tales **16** exchange memories, swap remembrances

reminiscent 9 nostalgic, remindful, similar to **11** analogous to, remembering **12** recollecting **13** retrospective

remiss 3 lax **4** idle, lazy, slow **5** loose, slack **6** sloppy **7** laggard, loafing **8** careless, derelict, dilatory, inactive, indolent, slipshod, slothful, uncaring **9** do-nothing, forgetful, negligent, oblivious, shiftless, undutiful, unmindful **10** delinquent, neglectful, unthinking, unwatchful **11** inattentive, indifferent, thoughtless

remission 4 cure **5** lapse, pause **6** hiatus, pardon **7** respite, retreat **8** decrease **9** abatement, acquittal, cessation, reduction, shrinkage **10** absolution, diminution, hesitation, moderation, modulation, subsidence **11** exoneration, forgiveness, vindication

remit 3 pay **4** free, send, ship **5** clear, let go, relax, slack **6** excuse, let out, pardon, reduce **7** absolve, forgive, for-

ward, release, set free, slacken **8** decrease, diminish, dispatch, liberate, make good, moderate, overlook, pass over, transmit **9** discharge, reimburse **10** compensate **11** put to rights **13** send in payment

remnant 3 bit **5** piece, relic, scrap, shred, token, trace **7** discard, remains, residue, vestige **8** fragment, leavings, leftover, monument, residuum, survival **9** remainder **11** odds and ends

remodel 4 redo **5** adapt, alter, fix up **6** change, modify **7** convert, reshape **8** overhaul, renovate **9** refashion, transform **11** recondition

remodeling 6 change **10** alteration, conversion **12** modification **13** transmutation **14** transformation

remonstrance 6 rebuke **7** censure **8** reproach, scolding **9** criticism, reprimand **10** admonition

remonstrate 5 argue, chide, demur, scold **6** differ, object, rebuke **7** censure, chasten, contend, dispute, dissent, protest, reprove, upbraid **8** admonish, complain, reproach **9** criticize **10** take to task **11** expostulate **13** call to account

remorse 3 rue **4** pang **5** grief, guilt, qualm **6** regret, sorrow **7** anguish **9** penitence **10** contrition, repentance, ruefulness **11** compunction, lamentation, self-reproof **12** self-reproach **13** regretfulness **14** second thoughts

remorseful 8 contrite, penitent **9** chastened, regretful, repentant, sorrowful **10** apologetic **13** grief-stricken **18** conscience-stricken

remote 3 far **4** slim **5** alien, alone, aloof, faint, quiet **6** exotic, far-off, lonely, meager, slight **7** distant, dubious, faraway, foreign, removed, strange **8** detached, doubtful, isolated, secluded, separate, set apart, solitary, unlikely **9** withdrawn **10** far-removed, segregated **11** God-forsaken, implausible, out of the way, sequestered, standoffish

removal 6 moving, ouster **7** doffing **8** deletion, ejection **9** discharge, dismissal, expulsion, taking off, taking out **10** amputation, carting off, cutting away, dislodging, evacuation, lopping off **11** carrying off, chopping off, elimination, transferral **12** cancellation, displacement **14** transportation **15** transplantation

remove 4 doff, drop, fire, move, oust, quit **5** eject, erase, expel, leave, shift **6** cancel, change, cut off, delete, depart, go away, lop off, retire, unseat, vacate **7** blot out, boot out, cart off, chop off, cut away, dismiss, extract, kick out, retreat, take off, take out, wipe out **8** amputate, carry off, dislodge, displace, evacuate, get rid of, sweep out, take away, transfer, with-

draw **9** discharge, eliminate, take leave, transport **10** make an exit, transplant

removed 3 off **4** away, took **5** alone, aloof, apart **6** remote **7** distant, faraway **8** abstract, detached, isolated, reticent, secluded **9** alienated, separate, unrelated, withdrawn **10** segregated, unsociable **11** interspaced, standoffish

remove from office 4 oust **6** depose, unseat **9** discharge

remunerate 3 pay **5** award, grant, repay **6** reward **7** requite, satisfy **9** indemnify, reimburse, vouchsafe **10** compensate, recompense **15** make restitution

remuneration 7 payment **9** repayment **10** recompense, reparation **12** compensation **13** reimbursement **15** indemnification

Remus
father: **4** Mars
mother: **4** Ilia **9** Rea Silvia **10** Rhea Silvia
twin brother: **7** Romulus
raised by: **7** she-wolf

renaissance 7 rebirth, renewal, revival **10** rekindling, renascence, resurgence **11** reawakening, reemergence, restoration **12** regeneration, rejuvenation, resurrection, risorgimento **14** revitalization, revivification **15** reestablishment

rend 3 cut, rip **4** hurt, pain, rive, sear, tear **5** break, crack, sever, split, wound **6** cleave, divide, pierce, sunder **7** afflict, rupture, shatter **8** dissever, fracture, lacerate, polarize, splinter **12** disintegrate, fall to pieces **15** break into pieces

render 2 do **4** cede, give, make, play **5** allot, grant, remit, yield **6** accord, donate, give up, supply, tender **7** deal out, dole out, execute, hand out, pay back, perform, present, requite **8** construe, dispense, fork over, hand over, pay as due, shell out, turn over **9** cause to be, interpret, surrender, translate **10** relinquish **12** give in return, make requital **13** cause to become, make available, make payment of

render impotent 6 defuse, weaken **7** disable, unnerve **8** paralyze **9** undermine **10** devitalize, emasculate

render inoperable 6 damage, impair **7** cripple, disable **12** incapacitate

render null and void 4 void **5** annul **6** cancel, repeal, revoke **7** abolish, nullify, rescind, retract, reverse **8** abrogate, dissolve **10** invalidate

rendezvous 4 date **5** focus, haunt, mecca, tryst **6** gather, muster **7** retreat **8** assemble **9** encounter, tete-a-tete **10** engagement, focal point **11** appointment, assignation, get together **12**

meeting place, watering hole **14** gathering place, stamping ground **15** agreement to meet **17** meet by appointment **18** prearranged meeting

rendition 7 edition, reading, version **9** depiction, portrayal, rendering **11** arrangement, performance, translation **14** interpretation

rend the air 3 cry **4** bawl, howl, wail **6** clamor, scream, shriek, squeal **7** screech **9** caterwaul

renegade 5 rebel **6** outlaw **7** heretic, runaway, slacker, traitor **8** apostate, betrayer, defector, deserter, forsaker, fugitive, mutineer, mutinous, quisling, recreant, turncoat **9** dissenter, insurgent **10** backslider, traitorous, treasonist, unfaithful

renege 7 back out, fink out, pull out **8** back down, fall back, withdraw **9** repudiate, weasel out **11** get cold feet **12** turn one's back **13** break a promise, break one's word **16** go back on one's word

renew 4 save **6** extend, pick up, redeem, resume, retain, revive **7** prolong, refresh, restore, salvage **8** continue, maintain **9** make sound, reinstate, sign again **10** begin again, offer again, regenerate, rejuvenate, revitalize **11** reestablish, take up again **12** reinvigorate **16** put back into shape

renewal 7 revival **9** extension **10** redemption **11** restoration **12** regeneration **13** reinstatement **14** revitalization

Renoir, Pierre-Auguste
 born: **6** France **7** Limoges
 artwork: **4** Lise **6** La Loge **10** The Bathers **12** Margot Berard, The Umbrellas **14** La Grenouillere **19** Le Moulin de la Galette **28** Mme Charpentier and Her Children, The Luncheon of the Boating Party

renounce 4 cede, deny, quit **5** forgo, waive **6** abjure, disown, eschew, forego, give up, recant, reject, resign **7** abandon, cast off, disavow, discard, dismiss **8** abdicate, abnegate, abrogate, disclaim, forswear, lay aside, part with, put aside, turn from, write off **9** cast aside, foreswear, repudiate **10** relinquish **13** give up claim to **15** wash one's hands of

renovate 3 fix **4** mend **6** remake, repair, revamp **7** improve, remodel, restore **8** make over **9** modernize, refurbish **10** redecorate

renown 4 fame, mark, note **6** repute, status **7** acclaim **8** eminence **9** celebrity, notoriety **10** popularity, prominence, reputation **11** distinction

renowned 5 famed, noted **6** famous **7** eminent, notable, popular **9** acclaimed, prominent, well-known **10** celebrated, noteworthy **11** outstanding **13** distinguished

rent 3 fee, gap, let, rip **4** dues, gash, hire, hole, rift, slit, tear **5** break, chasm, chink, cleft, crack, lease, split **6** breach, hiatus, rental, schism, tatter, wrench **7** charter, fissure, opening, payment, rent out, rupture **8** cleavage, crevasse, division, fracture **11** buy the use of sell the use of

rente 6 income **7** revenue **12** annual income

rentier 21 one who has a fixed income

renunciation 6 denial **7** refusal **8** forgoing, spurning **9** disavowal, eschewing, foregoing, rejection, repulsion **10** abjuration, renouncing **11** abandonment, disclaiming, forswearing, repudiation **12** foreswearing **14** relinquishment

Renwick, James, Jr
 architect of: **8** Main Hall (Vassar College) **11** Grace Church (NYC) **15** Corcoran Gallery (now Renwick Gallery, Washington, DC) **19** St Patrick's Cathedral (NYC) **22** Smithsonian Institution (Washington DC)
 style: **13** Gothic Revival

reopen 7 restart **9** begin anew, reconvene, start anew **10** recommence, reinitiate **11** reestablish, reinstitute **12** reinaugurate

repair 2 go **3** fix **4** mend, move **5** amend, emend, patch, renew, shape, state **6** fixing, remedy, remove, retire **7** correct, mending, patch up, rebuild, rectify, redress, restore **8** make good, overhaul, patching, set right, withdraw **9** condition, make up for, refurbish, repairing **10** rebuilding **11** recondition **12** refurbishing **14** reconditioning

reparation 6 amends, return **7** damages, redress **8** requital **9** quittance **10** recompense **11** restitution **12** compensation, satisfaction **13** peace offering

repartee 6 banter, bon mot **7** riposte **8** badinage, chit chat, word play **10** persiflage, witty reply **11** witty retort **12** pleasantries **14** snappy comeback

repast 4 food, meal **5** board, feast, snack, table **6** spread **7** banquet **8** victuals **9** provision **11** nourishment, refreshment

repay 5 match **6** refund, return, reward **7** pay back, requite **9** get back at, indemnify, pay in kind, reimburse **10** recompense, remunerate **11** get even with, reciprocate **12** make requital **14** give in exchange, make a return for **15** make restitution, make retribution **19** return the compliment

repayment 10 paying back, recompense **12** compensation **13** reimbursement **17** making restitution

repeal 4 void **5** annul **6** cancel, revoke **7** abolish, nullify, rescind, voiding **8** abrogate, set aside **9** abolition, annul-

ment **10** abrogation, invalidate, revocation **11** termination **12** cancellation, invalidation **13** nullification **18** declare null and void

repeat 4 echo, redo, tell **5** mimic, quote, rerun **6** pass on, recite, relate, retell **7** imitate, recount, restate, retread, say over **8** say again **9** duplicate, reiterate, reproduce **10** repetition **11** duplication, reiteration **12** perform again

repeated exercises 4 rote **5** drill **8** practice, training

repel 4 foil, rout **5** check **6** dispel, offend, oppose, put off, rebuff, resist, revolt, sicken **7** deflect, disgust, fend off, forfend, hold off, keep off, keep out, repulse, scatter, turn off, ward off **8** alienate, beat back, disperse, nauseate, push back, stave off, throw off **9** chase away, drive away, drive back, force back, frustrate, keep at bay, withstand

repellent 5 proof **9** abhorrent, loathsome, offensive, repelling, repugnant, repulsive, resisting, revolting, sickening **10** disgusting, nauseating **11** distasteful, impermeable

repent 3 rue **6** bemoan, bewail, lament, regret, repine **7** deplore **8** mea culpa, weep over **9** be ashamed **10** be contrite, be penitent **11** be regretful, feel remorse

repentance 5 grief, guilt **6** regret, sorrow **7** remorse **9** penitence **10** contrition **11** compunction **12** self-reproach **16** self-condemnation **17** pangs of conscience

repercussion 4 echo **6** effect, result **8** backlash, reaction **10** concussion, side effect **11** aftereffect, consequence **13** reverberation **15** boomerang effect

repetition 6 repeat **9** iteration, retelling **11** reiteration, restatement **14** recapitulation

repetitious 5 wordy **6** prolix **8** repeated **9** redundant **10** repetitive

Repin, Ilya Efimovich
 born: **6** Russia **8** Chugeyev
 artwork: **15** The Volga Boatmen **18** Zaporozhye Cossacks **19** They Did Not Expect Him **26** Ivan the Terrible Kills His Son

replace 5 spell **6** return **7** put back, restore, succeed **8** supplant **9** supersede

replaceable 10 disposable, expendable **11** dispensable

replenish 5 renew **6** refill, reload **7** refresh, reorder, replace, restock, restore

replenished 7 renewed **8** refilled, replaced, restored **9** restocked

replenishment 7 renewal **9** refilling **10** restocking **11** replacement, restoration

replete 4 full **5** sated **6** gorged, loaded **7** crammed, fraught, stuffed, teeming

8 brimming, satiated **9** abounding, jam-packed, surfeited **11** well-stocked

repletion 4 glut **6** excess **7** surfeit, surplus **9** abundance, plenitude, profusion, satiation **11** sufficiency

replica 4 copy **5** model **6** double **8** likeness **9** duplicate, facsimile, imitation **12** reproduction

reply 5 react **6** answer, rejoin, retort **7** counter, respond **8** reaction, response **9** rejoinder **14** acknowledgment

reply if you please
French: **4** rsvp **20** repondez s'il vous plait

reply to 6 answer **7** counter, react to **8** retort to **9** respond to **11** acknowledge

repondez s'il vous plait 11 please reply **16** reply if you please
abbreviation: 4 rsvp

report 4 bang, boom, note, talk, tell, word **5** crack, noise, rumor, sound, state, story **6** appear, detail, expose, gossip, recite, record, relate, reveal, show up, tell on **7** account, article, check in, divulge, hearsay, message, missive, recount, summary, version, write-up **8** announce, denounce, describe, disclose, dispatch, relation **9** discharge, narration **10** communique, detonation, memorandum **11** communicate, description, information
French: **11** compte rendu

reporter 7 newshen, newsman **8** newshawk **9** anchorman, announcer, columnist, newshound, newswoman **10** journalist, newscaster **11** commentator **12** newspaperman **13** correspondent **14** newspaperwoman

repose 3 lie **4** calm, ease, rest **5** quiet, relax **6** be calm, settle **7** leisure, recline, respite **8** quietude **10** inactivity, quiescence, relaxation **11** tranquility **12** peacefulness, tranquillity

repository 5 depot **8** magazine **9** warehouse **10** storehouse

reprehend 5 decry **7** censure, condemn, reprove **8** denounce, reproach **9** criticize **10** disapprove

reprehensible 3 bad **4** base, evil, foul, vile **6** guilty, wicked **7** heinous, ignoble **8** blamable, culpable, infamous, shameful, unworthy **9** nefarious **10** censurable, despicable, villainous **11** blameworthy, condemnable, disgraceful, inexcusable, opprobrious **12** unpardonable **13** objectionable, unjustifiable

reprehension 6 rebuke **7** censure, reproof **8** reproach **9** criticism **11** disapproval **12** condemnation, denunciation **14** disapprobation

represent 2 be **4** mean, show **5** enact, equal, state **6** denote, depict, pose as, sketch, typify **7** betoken, express, outline, picture, portray, present, serve as **8** appear as, describe, indicate, stand for **9** delineate, designate, symbolize

10 illustrate **11** emblematize, impersonate **12** characterize

representation 5 image **6** effigy, emblem, symbol **7** epitome, essence, picture **8** likeness **9** depiction, portrayal **10** embodiment **12** illustration **15** exemplification **16** characterization

representative 2 MP **3** rep **5** agent, envoy, proxy **6** deputy, varied **7** deputed, elected, proctor, typical **8** balanced, delegate, elective, emissary, symbolic **9** delegated, exemplary, spokesman, surrogate, typifying **10** delegatory, democratic, denotative, emblematic, legislator, mouthpiece, republican, substitute, symbolical **11** assemblyman, congressman, delineative, descriptive **12** exemplifying, illustrative **13** assemblywoman, congresswoman **14** characteristic, cross-sectional

repress 4 curb, hide, mask, veil **5** box up, check, cloak, cover, crush, pen up, quash, quell **6** hold in, muffle, shut up, squash, stifle, subdue **7** conceal, control, inhibit, put down, silence, smother, squelch **8** bottle up, hold back, keep down, restrain, strangle, suppress

repression 8 muffling **9** holding in, restraint, retention **10** inhibition, throttling **11** concealment, holding back, suppression

reprieve 4 lull, stay **5** delay, pause **6** pardon, parole **7** amnesty, respite **8** breather **9** remission **10** moratorium, suspension **11** adjournment **12** postponement **14** breathing spell

reprimand 4 trim **5** chide, scold **6** berate, rail at, rebuff, rebuke, revile **7** censure, chew out, chiding, lecture, obloquy, tell off, upbraid **8** admonish, berating, chastise, denounce, reproach, reproval, scolding, take down, trimming **9** castigate, criticism, criticize, disparage, dispraise, dress down, reprehend, reprobate **10** admonition, chewing out, opprobrium, take to task, upbraiding **11** castigation **12** admonishment, denunciation, dressing down, remonstrance **13** disparagement **16** rap on the knuckles

reprisal 7 redress, revenge **8** requital **9** tit for tat, vengeance **11** counterblow, retaliation, retribution **13** counterattack **16** counteroffensive
Latin: **10** quid pro quo

reproach 4 blot, slur, spot **5** blame, chide, scold, shame, stain, taint **6** charge, insult, malign, rail at, rebuke, revile, stigma, tirade, vilify **7** asperse, blemish, censure, condemn, offense, reproof, reprove, scandal, tarnish, upbraid **8** admonish, denounce, diatribe, disgrace, dishonor, scolding **9** castigate, criticism, criticize, discredit, disparage, indignity, reprimand **10** stig-

matize, take to task, tongue-lash, upbraiding **11** degradation, humiliation **12** remonstrance **13** call to account, embarrassment

reprobate 3 bad, low **4** base, evil, rake, roue, vile **5** scamp **6** pariah, rascal, rotter, sinner, wanton, wicked **7** corrupt, outcast **8** castaway, depraved, derelict, evildoer, prodigal, rakehell **9** abandoned, dissolute, miscreant, shameless, wrongdoer **10** black sheep, degenerate, immoralist, profligate, voluptuary **11** rapscallion, untouchable **12** incorrigible, transgressor, wicked person

reproduce 4 copy, redo, sire **5** beget, breed, match, spawn **6** mirror, repeat, re-echo **7** imitate, reflect **8** generate, multiply **9** duplicate, procreate, propagate, replicate, represent **11** counterfeit, proliferate

reproduction 4 copy **7** replica **8** breeding, likeness **9** duplicate, facsimile, imitation **10** carbon copy, generation, simulation **11** procreation, propagation **13** progeneration, proliferation **14** multiplication, representation
goddess of: 7 Astarte

reproductive system
component: 5 penis **6** testes, uterus, vagina **7** ovaries

reproof 5 blame **6** rebuke **7** censure, chiding **8** reproach, scolding **9** criticism, reprimand **10** admonition **12** condemnation, dressing-down, remonstrance

reprovable 7 at fault **8** blamable, culpable **10** censurable **11** blameworthy **12** reproachable

reprove 5 chide, scold **6** rebuke **7** censure, chasten **8** admonish, reproach **9** castigate, reprimand

reptile 3 asp, eft **4** newt, teju **5** agama, anole, gecko, skink, snake, viper **6** dragon, iguana, lizard, mugger, turtle **7** crawler, creeper, serpent, tuatara **8** basilisk, dinosaur, groveler, terrapin, tortoise **9** alligator, chameleon, crocodile, pterosaur **10** salamander, vertebrate **11** Gila monster, pterodactyl

republic 9 democracy
Latin: 10 res publica

Republic
author: 5 Plato

Republican Party
also called: 3 GOP **13** Grand Old Party
president belonging to: 4 Bush, Ford, Taft **5** Grant, Hayes, Nixon **6** Arthur, Hoover, Reagan **7** Harding, Lincoln, (Andrew) Johnson **8** Coolidge, Garfield, Harrison, McKinley **9** (Theodore) Roosevelt **10** Eisenhower
symbol: 8 elephant

Republic of China see **6** Taiwan

repudiate 4 deny, void **5** annul **6** cancel, desert, disown, reject, repeal, revoke **7** abandon, abolish, cast off, disavow, discard, forsake, nullify, protest, rescind, retract, reverse **8** abrogate, disclaim, dissolve, renounce

repudiation 6 denial **9** disavowal, rejection **10** abrogation, disclaimer, retraction

repugnance 4 hate **5** odium **6** hatred **7** disgust **8** aversion, loathing **9** antipathy, revulsion **10** abhorrence **11** abomination, detestation

repugnant 4 foul, vile **5** nasty **6** odious **7** adverse, counter, hateful, opposed **8** contrary, unsavory **9** abhorrent, loathsome, obnoxious, offensive, repellent, repulsive, revolting, sickening **10** abominable, detestable, disgusting, nauseating, unpleasant **11** distasteful, uncongenial, undesirable, unpalatable **12** antipathetic, disagreeable, insufferable, unacceptable, unappetizing **13** objectionable

repulse 4 shun **5** avoid, repel, spurn **6** ignore, rebuff, refuse, reject **7** refusal **8** shunning, spurning **9** rejection

repulsion 6 hatred **7** disgust, dislike **8** aversion, distaste, loathing **9** antipathy **10** abhorrence, repugnance **11** abomination, detestation **13** indisposition **14** disinclination

repulsive 4 vile **5** nasty **6** odious **7** hateful **9** abhorrent, loathsome, obnoxious, offensive, repellent, repugnant, revolting **10** abominable, detestable, disgusting, nauseating **11** distasteful **12** disagreeable **13** objectionable

repulsiveness 8 ugliness **13** loathsomeness, offensiveness **14** disgustingness, unpleasantness **16** disagreeableness

reputable 7 honored **8** esteemed, reliable **9** respected **10** creditable **11** respectable, trustworthy

reputation 4 name **7** stature **8** standing

repute 3 say **4** deem, fame, hold, view **5** judge, think **6** esteem, reckon, regard, renown **7** account, believe, suppose **8** consider, estimate, standing **9** celebrity, notoriety **10** prominence **14** respectability

request 3 ask **4** seek **6** ask for, bid for, desire, sue for **7** call for, entreat, solicit **8** petition **9** importune **11** application **12** solicitation

requiem 4 dirge **6** lament **8** threnody

requiescat in pace 11 rest in peace **16** may he rest in peace **17** may she rest in peace

require 3 bid **4** lack, miss, need, want **5** crave, imply, order **6** charge, compel, desire, direct, enjoin, entail, oblige **7** command, dictate **9** constrain **11** necessitate

required 6 forced, needed **7** obliged **9** compelled, essential, necessary **10** compulsory, imperative, obligatory

requirement 4 must **8** standard **9** criterion, essential, guideline, requisite **12** prerequisite **13** specification **Latin: 10** sine qua non **11** desideratum

requisite 4 must, need **6** needed **8** required **9** essential, mandatory, necessary, necessity **10** compulsory, imperative, obligatory **11** requirement **12** prerequisite **13** indispensable **Latin: 10** sine qua non **11** desideratum

requisition 4 form **7** request **11** application

requital 7 redress **9** repayment **11** retaliation **12** compensation **15** indemnification

rescind 4 void **5** annul, quash **6** cancel, recall, repeal, revoke **7** abolish, discard, nullify, retract, reverse **8** abrogate, dissolve, override, overrule **10** invalidate **11** countermand **12** counterorder

rescinding 6 recall **7** voiding **8** recision **9** abolition **10** abrogation, retraction, revocation **11** abolishment, dissolution **12** cancellation, invalidation **13** nullification

rescue 4 save **6** ransom, saving **7** deliver, freeing, recover, release, salvage **8** liberate, recovery **9** extricate **10** liberation **11** deliverance, extrication

research 5 probe, study **7** delving, inquiry **8** analysis, scrutiny **10** inspection **11** examination, exploration, factfinding, investigate, scholarship **13** investigation

resemblance 7 analogy **8** affinity, likeness, parallel **10** congruence, similarity, similitude **14** correspondence

resemble 5 favor **6** be like **8** be akin to, look like, parallel **9** take after

resent 3 say **7** dislike

resentful 5 angry **6** bitter **7** annoyed **8** grudging, offended, provoked **10** displeased **12** dissatisfied

resentfulness 5 anger, spite **10** bitterness **15** dissatisfaction

resentment 3 ire **4** huff **5** anger, pique, spite **6** animus, malice, rancor **7** dudgeon, ill will, offense, umbrage **8** acerbity, acrimony, asperity, jealousy, soreness, sourness **9** animosity, crossness **10** bitterness, irritation **11** displeasure, indignation **12** irritability, vengefulness **14** vindictiveness

reservation 4 date **5** doubt **7** booking, proviso, scruple, strings **8** preserve **9** condition, hesitancy, provision **10** encampment, reluctance, settlement **11** appointment, compunction, stipulation, uncertainty **12** installation **13** accommodation, establishment, qualification **14** prearrangement

reserve 4 book, hold, keep, save **5** amass, delay, extra, hoard, lay up, spare, stock, table **6** backup, engage, retain, shelve, unused **7** husband, nest egg, savings **8** conserve, keep back, postpone, preserve, salt away, schedule, withhold **9** aloofness, reticence, stockpile **10** additional, prearrange

reserved 5 aloof, taken **6** booked, formal **7** distant, engaged **8** bespoken, retained, reticent, strained, unsocial **9** inhibited, spoken for **10** restrained, unsociable **11** ceremonious, constrained, standoffish **12** unresponsive **15** uncommunicative, undemonstrative

reservoir 4 fund, pool, tank, well **5** basin, fount, hoard, stock, store **6** supply **7** backlog, cistern **8** millpond **9** container, stockpile **10** depository, receptacle, repository **12** accumulation

Reservoir Dogs
director: 16 Quentin Tarantino **cast: 7** Tim Roth (Mr Orange/Freddy Newandyke) **9** Chris Penn (Eddie Cabot), Kirk Baltz (Marvin Nash) **11** Eddie Bunker (Mr Blue), Randy Brooks (Holdaway) **12** Harvey Keitel (Mr White/Larry Dimmick), Steve Buscemi (Mr Pink) **13** Michael Madsen (Mr Blonde/Vic Vega) **15** Lawrence Tierney (Joe Cabot) **16** Quentin Tarantino (Mr Brown)

res gestae 5 deeds **10** things done **15** accomplishments

reshape 4 redo **5** adapt, alter, block **6** change, modify, reform, remold, rework **7** convert, reframe, remodel **9** refashion, transform

reside 3 lie **4** live, rest, room **5** dwell, exist, lodge **6** belong, occupy **7** inhabit, sojourn **8** domicile

residence 3 pad **4** digs, flat, home, room, stay **5** abode, house, place **7** address, lodging, sojourn **8** domicile, dwelling, quarters **9** apartment, homestead, household **10** habitation **French: 10** pied a terre

resident 5 local **6** lodger, tenant **7** citizen, denizen, dweller **8** occupant, townsman **9** sojourner **10** inhabitant **11** housekeeper

residual 5 extra **7** abiding, lasting, surplus **8** enduring, leftover **9** lingering, remaining **10** continuing **13** supplementary

residue 4 rest **5** dregs **6** scraps **7** balance, remains, remnant **8** leavings **9** remainder

resign 4 quit **5** leave **6** give up, submit **8** abdicate, disclaim, renounce **9** reconcile **10** relinquish

resignation 8 fatalism, patience, quitting, stoicism **9** departure **10** equanimity, retirement, submission, withdrawal **11** passiveness **12**

acquiescence **13** nonresistance **14** submissiveness

resign oneself 5 yield **6** submit **9** acquiesce

resilience 6 recoil **7** rebound **8** buoyancy **10** elasticity **11** flexibility **12** adaptability **13** changeability, nonuniformity **16** lightheartedness

resilient 5 hardy **6** supple **7** buoyant, elastic, rubbery, springy **8** flexible **9** adaptable, expansive, resistant, tenacious **10** rebounding, responsive **13** irrepressible

resin 3 gum, lac, tar **5** amber, copal, elemi, epoxy, jalap, myrrh, pitch, rosin **6** balsam, guaiac, mastic **7** galipot, lacquer, shellac

resist 4 balk, foil, stem, stop **5** fight, repel **6** baffle, combat, oppose, refuse, reject, thwart **7** contest, counter, weather **8** beat back, turn down **9** frustrate, withstand **10** counteract

resistance 6 mutiny, rebuff **7** refusal **8** defiance, struggle **9** obstinacy, rebellion, rejection **10** contention, insurgency, opposition **11** obstruction **12** insurrection **13** intransigence, noncompliance, recalcitrance

resolute 5 stern **6** dogged, steady **7** earnest, staunch, zealous **8** decisive, diligent, intrepid, stubborn, untiring, vigorous **9** assiduous, obstinate, purposive, steadfast, tenacious, unbending **10** deliberate, determined, inflexible, persistent, relentless, unflagging, unswerving, unwavering, unyielding **11** industrious, persevering, undeviating, unfaltering, unflinching **12** pertinacious, strong-minded, strong-willed **13** indefatigable **14** uncompromising

resoluteness 7 purpose, resolve **8** decision, tenacity **11** decidedness, persistence **12** decisiveness, perseverance **13** determination, steadfastness **14** purposefulness

resolution 3 aim **4** goal, plan, zeal **6** design, energy, intent, mettle, motion, object, spirit **7** promise, purpose, resolve **8** ambition, proposal, solution, tenacity **9** constancy, intention, objective, resolving, stability **10** resilience, steadiness **11** earnestness, persistence **12** perseverance, resoluteness **13** determination, steadfastness **14** aggressiveness **16** indefatigability

resolve 4 plan **6** answer, decide, design, intend, set out, settle, vote on **7** adjudge, clear up, explain, purpose **8** decision **9** determine, elucidate **10** commitment, resolution **12** resoluteness **13** determination **14** make up one's mind

resonant 4 full, rich **7** booming, orotund, ringing, vibrant **8** sonorous **9** bellowing **10** resounding, stentorian, thunderous **11** reverberant

resort 3 use **4** hope **5** apply, avail **6** chance, employ, take up **7** utilize **8** exercise, recourse **9** expedient

resound 4 echo, peal, ring **5** clang **6** re-echo **7** vibrate **11** reverberate **14** tintinnabulate

resounding 7 echoing, ringing **9** re-echoing **10** thundering, thunderous **13** reverberating

resource 8 recourse **9** expedient **11** wherewithal

resourceful 4 able **5** ready, sharp, smart **6** adroit, artful, bright, shrewd **7** capable, cunning **8** creative, original, skillful, talented **9** competent, effectual, ingenious, inventive **10** innovative, proficient **11** imaginative **12** enterprising

resourcefulness 9 ingenuity **10** creativity, enterprise **13** inventiveness

resources 5 funds, means, money **6** assets, income **7** capital, effects, revenue **10** belongings, collateral **11** possessions, wherewithal

respect 5 honor, point, sense **6** detail, esteem, matter, notice, praise, regard **7** bearing, feature, viewing **8** approval, courtesy, relation **9** affection, attention, deference, laudation, reference, relevance, reverence **10** admiration, connection, particular, veneration **11** point of view, recognition **12** appreciation, circumstance **13** consideration

respectability 7 decency, decorum **9** gentility, propriety **11** correctness, genteelness

respectable 4 fair **5** ample, civil, noble **6** decent, honest, polite, proper, worthy **7** correct, courtly, passing, refined, upright **8** becoming, decorous, moderate, polished **9** admirable, dignified, estimable, honorable, reputable **10** aboveboard, admissible, sufficient **11** presentable **12** considerable, praiseworthy, satisfactory

respected 6 valued, worthy **7** admired, honored, revered **8** esteemed **9** admirable, venerated

respectful 5 civil **6** formal, genial, polite **7** amiable, winning **8** admiring, decorous, gracious, mannerly, obliging, reverent **9** attentive, courteous, regardful **10** personable, solicitous **11** ceremonious, deferential, reverential **13** accommodating

respects 4 heed, obey **5** honor, prize, value **6** admire, esteem, fealty, follow, regard, revere **7** abide by, cherish, defer to, observe, regards, tribute **8** adhere to, consider, venerate **9** greetings **10** appreciate, understand **11** acknowledge, compliments **12** remembrances **13** consideration

Respighi, Ottorino
    born: 5 Italy **7** Bologna
    composer of: 8 La Fiamma, The Birds **14** The Pines of Rome **18** The

Fountains of Rome **19** La Boutique Fantasque, The Fantastic Toyshop **27** Ancient Airs and Dances for Lute

respiration 9 breathing

respiratory system
    component: 4 lung, nose **6** larynx **7** pharynx, trachea **8** voice box, windpipe **9** bronchius, diaphragm
    action: 9 breathing

respire 7 breathe

respite 4 lull **5** break, delay, letup, pause **6** recess **8** reprieve **9** extension **12** intermission

resplendence 6 dazzle, luster **7** glitter **8** lambency, radiance **10** brilliance, luminosity, refulgence **12** circumstance, magnificence

resplendent 6 bright **7** beaming, blazing, glowing, lambent, radiant **8** dazzling, gleaming, luminous, lustrous, splendid **9** brilliant, refulgent, sparkling **10** glittering **11** coruscating

respond 5 react, reply **6** answer, rejoin **7** speak up **9** recognize **11** acknowledge

respond to 6 answer **7** act upon, react to, reply to **8** thank for **11** acknowledge

response 5 reply **6** answer, retort, return **7** riposte **8** comeback, feedback, reaction, rebuttal **9** rejoinder **10** impression **13** countercharge **14** acknowledgment **16** counterstatement

responsibility 4 duty, task **5** blame, order, trust **6** burden, charge **8** function **9** liability **10** obligation **11** culpability, reliability **13** answerability, dependability **14** accountability **15** trustworthiness

responsible 5 adult, of age **6** guilty, liable, mature **7** at fault, capable **8** culpable, reliable **9** demanding, executive, important **10** answerable, creditable, dependable **11** accountable, challenging, trustworthy **13** conscientious **14** administrative

responsive 5 alive, awake, sharp **8** reactive **9** receptive, sensitive **11** retaliative, retaliatory, susceptible, sympathetic **13** compassionate, understanding **14** impressionable

responsiveness 6 action **7** concern **8** interest **9** attention, awareness **11** sensitivity **13** understanding

res publica 8 republic, the state **12** commonwealth, public matter

rest 2 be **3** end, lay, lie, nap, set **4** base, ease, halt, hang, keep, laze, lean, loaf, loll, lull, prop, rely, stay, stop **5** break, death, exist, hinge, let up, pause, peace, place, quiet, relax, sleep, stand **6** demise, depend, holder, lounge, others, recess, remain, repose, reside, scraps, siesta, snooze, trivet **7** balance, be based, be found, be quiet, decease, deposit, holiday, leisure, lie

down, recline, remains, remnant, residue, respite, set down, slumber, support **8** breather, platform, vacation **9** cessation, departure, leftovers, remainder, stillness **10** complement, quiet spell, relaxation, standstill, suspension **11** hibernation, take time out **12** intermission, interruption **13** take a breather
Latin: **8** residuum

restaurant 5 diner **6** eatery **7** beanery, tearoom **9** cafeteria, chophouse, grillroom, hashhouse, lunchroom **11** coffeehouse **12** luncheonette
French: **4** cafe **6** bistro **9** brasserie
German: **11** rathskeller

restful 4 calm **5** quiet **6** placid, serene **7** pacific, relaxed **8** peaceful, soothing, tranquil **10** unagitated **11** comfortable, undisturbed

restfulness 4 ease **5** quiet **6** repose **8** serenity, softness **10** relaxation **11** tranquility **12** tranquillity

rest in peace
Latin: **16** requiescat in pace

restitution 6 amends **7** redress, replevy **8** replevin, requital, restoral **9** atonement, indemnity, repayment **10** recompense, reparation **11** restoration **12** compensation, remuneration, satisfaction **13** reimbursement, reinstatement **15** indemnification

restive 5 balky **6** mulish, ornery, unruly **7** fidgety, wayward, willful **8** contrary, stubborn **9** fractious, pigheaded **10** rebellious, refractory **11** disobedient, intractable **12** recalcitrant, unmanageable

restless 5 awake, jumpy **6** fitful, uneasy **7** anxious, fidgety, fretful, jittery, nervous, on the go, unquiet, wakeful, worried **8** agitated **9** excitable, impatient, incessant, insomniac, on the move, sleepless, transient, unsettled **10** disquieted, highstrung **11** hyperactive **13** uncomfortable

restoration 7 revival **8** recovery **12** recuperation **13** convalescence, reinstatement **14** rehabilitation, reintroduction, reinvigoration **15** reestablishment

restorative 5 tonic **6** elixir **7** bracing, healing **8** curative **10** beneficial, energizing, fortifying **11** revivifying **12** invigorating, revitalizing **13** strengthening

restore 3 fix **4** cure, dose, heal, mend **5** rally, renew, treat **6** do over, recoup, remedy, repair, rescue, return, revive **7** convert, get back, patch up, put back, rebuild, reclaim, recover, refresh, remodel, retouch, touch up **8** energize, give back, make over, make well, medicate, renovate, retrieve, revivify, recreate **9** reanimate, refurbish, reinstall, reinstate, stimulate **10** exhilarate, revitalize, strengthen **11** recon-

dition, reconstruct, reestablish, reinstitute, resuscitate **12** rehabilitate, reinvigorate

restored 4 kept **5** saved **7** revived **8** replaced **9** conserved, pressured **11** replenished **13** rehabilitated

restrain 3 gag **4** bind, curb, hold, stop **5** check, leash, limit **6** arrest, bridle, fetter, muzzle, pinion, temper, tether **7** chasten, contain, curtail, harness, inhibit, prevent, shackle, trammel **8** handicap, hold back, restrict, suppress, withhold

restrained 4 cool **5** aloof **6** curbed **7** checked, distant **8** held back, reined in, reserved **10** controlled, unfriendly

restraint 4 curb **5** check **7** control **10** limitation

restrict 4 curb, hold **5** check, cramp, crimp, hem in, limit **6** hamper, impede, narrow, thwart **7** confine, inhibit, prevent, squelch **8** hold back, obstruct, straiten, suppress **9** constrain, frustrate **12** circumscribe

restricted 7 cramped, limited **8** confined, hampered, held back **9** exclusive **10** suppressed **13** circumscribed

restriction 4 rule **7** control, curbing, proviso **9** condition, provision **10** limitation, regulation **11** requirement, reservation, stipulation **13** consideration, qualification

restrictive 8 limiting **9** confining, exclusive **12** constraining

result 4 stem **5** arise, end up, ensue, fruit, issue, owe to **6** derive, effect, happen, pan out, report, sequel, spring, upshot, wind up **7** finding, opinion, outcome, product, turn out, verdict **8** decision, judgment, reaction, solution **9** aftermath, culminate, eventuate, originate, outgrowth **10** resolution **11** aftereffect, consequence, development, eventuality **13** determination

resume 2 CV **3** bio **4** go on **5** brief **6** digest **7** epitome, proceed, summary **8** abstract, continue, reembark, synopsis **9** biography, summation **10** abridgment, recommence **11** reestablish **12** condensation
Latin: **15** curriculum vitae
French: **6** precis

resumption 11 recommenced, restoration **12** continuation

resurgam 15 I shall rise again

resurgence 6 return **7** rebirth, renewal, revival **10** renascence **11** reemergence, renaissance **12** rejuvenation **13** recrudescence

ret 4 soak **6** dampen

retailer 5 store **6** dealer, seller, trader **8** merchant, provider, supplier **9** tradesman **10** wholesaler **11** distributor, storekeeper, tradeswoman **12**

merchandiser
French: **9** vivandier **10** vivandiere

retain 4 hold, keep **5** grasp **6** absorb, recall **7** possess **8** hang on to, hold on to, maintain, memorize, remember **9** recollect

retainer 7 servant **8** employee **9** attendant

retainership 4 hire **6** employ **7** service **10** employment

retaliate 5 repay **6** avenge, pay off, return **7** counter, pay back, requite, revenge **11** reciprocate

retaliation 6 talion **7** deserts, revenge **8** reprisal, requital **9** vengeance **10** recompense **11** comeuppance, eye for an eye, interchange, just deserts, lex talionis, retribution **12** compensation **13** reciprocation **14** tooth for a tooth

retard 4 clog, drag **5** block, brake, check, delay **6** arrest, baffle, detain, fetter, hamper, hinder, hold up, impede, slow up **7** draw out, inhibit, prevent, prolong, slacken **8** hold back, obstruct, slow down **10** decelerate

retarded 4 dull, slow **6** simple **7** idiotic, moronic, unsound **8** backward, disabled **9** imbecilic, mongoloid, subnormal **10** slow-witted **11** handicapped **12** simpleminded

reticent 3 shy **5** quiet **6** closed, silent **7** subdued **8** reserved, retiring, taciturn **9** diffident, withdrawn **10** restrained **11** tight-lipped **12** closemouthed **15** uncommunicative

retinue 5 court, staff, suite, train **6** convoy **9** courtiers, employees, entourage, followers, following, personnel, retainers **10** associates, attendance, attendants

retire 6 depart, go away, remove, resign, resort, secede, turn in **7** drop out, retreat **8** abdicate, flake out, withdraw

retired
French: **8** ci-devant

retiring 3 shy **4** meek **5** quiet, timid **6** demure, humble, modest **7** bashful **8** reserved, reticent, sheepish, timorous, unsocial **9** diffident, shrinking, withdrawn **10** unassuming **11** unassertive **12** self-effacing **13** inconspicuous, unpretentious **15** uncommunicative

retort 3 say **4** quip **5** rebut, reply **6** answer, rejoin, return **7** counter, respond, riposte **8** fire back, rebuttal **9** rejoinder

retract 4 deny **6** abjure, disown, draw in, recall, recant, recede, recoil, reel in, repeal, revoke **7** disavow, rescind, retreat, reverse **8** abnegate, abrogate, disclaim, draw back, forswear, peel back, pull back, renounce, take back, withdraw **9** foreswear, repudiate

retraction 6 recall **8** recision **9** disavowal **10** disclaimer, refutation, withdrawal

retreat 2 go **3** den **4** bolt, flee, port **5** haunt, haven, leave **6** asylum, depart, escape, flight, harbor, recoil, refuge, resort, retire, shrink **7** abscond, getaway, privacy, sanctum, shelter, shy away **8** back away, draw back, fall back, hideaway, move back, solitude, turn tail, withdraw **9** departure, isolation, reclusion, sanctuary, seclusion **10** evacuation, immurement, retirement, withdrawal **11** hibernation, rustication

retrench 5 slash **6** reduce, scrape, scrimp **7** curtail, cut back, cut down **8** conserve, cut costs **9** economize **15** tighten one's belt

retribution 6 amends, return, reward **7** justice, nemesis, penalty, redress, revenge **8** reprisal, requital **9** vengeance **10** punishment, recompense, reparation **11** just deserts, restitution, retaliation, vindication **12** satisfaction **13** reciprocation, recrimination

retrieve 4 snag **5** fetch **6** ransom, recoup, redeem, regain, rescue **7** get back, reclaim, recover, salvage **9** recapture, repossess

retriever
  dog breed: 5 Irish **6** golden, Gordon **7** English **8** Labrador **10** flat-coated **11** curly-coated **13** Chesapeake Bay

retrograde 5 worse **6** worsen **7** inverse, retreat, reverse **8** backward **10** regressive **13** retrogressive

retrogress 6 worsen **9** backslide

retrogression 7 decline, setback **9** worsening **11** backsliding

retrogressive 8 backward **9** declining, worsening **11** backsliding

retrospect 6 review **9** flashback, hindsight **11** remembrance **12** afterthought, reminiscence **15** reconsideration

return 3 net **4** earn, gain **5** gross, recur, repay, yield **6** advent, come to, go back, income, profit, render, reseat, reward **7** arrival, benefit, produce, provide, put back, requite, restore, revenue **8** announce, come back, earnings, give back, hand down, interest, proceeds, reappear, recovery, restoral, send back **9** advantage, reinstall, reinstate, retrieval, reversion **10** homecoming, recurrence **11** reciprocate, reestablish, restoration **12** compensation, reappearance **13** reinstatement **15** reestablishment

Return of the Native
  author: 11 Thomas Hardy
  character: 11 Diggory Venn, Eustacia Vye **12** Damon Wildeve **13** Clym Yeobright **17** Thomasin Yeobright

Reuben
  father: 5 Jacob
  mother: 4 Leah

  brother: 3 Dan, Gad **4** Levi **5** Asher, Judah **6** Joseph, Simeon **7** Zebulun **8** Benjamin, Issachar, Naphtali
  sister: 5 Dinah
  descendant of: 9 Reubenite

Reuben sandwich
  ingredient: 3 rye **8** dressing **10** corned beef, sauerkraut **11** Swiss cheese

reunite 5 rewed **7** remarry **9** reconcile

reveal 4 bare, show **6** betray, expose, impart, let out, unfold, unmask, unveil **7** display, divulge, exhibit, give out, lay bare, publish, uncover, unearth **8** disclose, evidence, manifest, point out

revealed 4 open **5** clear, known **7** evident, obvious **8** manifest

revel 4 romp **5** caper, enjoy **6** bask in, frolic, gambol, relish **7** carouse, delight, indulge, rejoice, roister, skylark **8** wallow in **9** celebrate

revelation 6 expose, vision **7** shocker **8** exposure, prophecy **9** admission, bombshell, discovery, eyeopener, unveiling **10** apocalypse, confession, disclosure, divulgence **11** divulgation, divulgement

revelatory 10 expressive **11** informative **13** communicative

reveler 6 barfly, ranter, player **7** drinker **8** bacchant, carouser, drunkard **9** roisterer, rollicker, skylarker **10** merrymaker

revelry 5 spree **7** jollity **8** carnival, carousal, festival, jamboree **9** high jinks, merriment, rejoicing **10** exultation, roistering **11** celebrating, celebration, merrymaking **12** conviviality **13** jollification **14** boisterousness
  god of: 5 Comus

revenge 5 repay **7** pay back, requite **8** reprisal, requital **9** repayment, retaliate, vengeance, vindicate **10** recompense **11** eye for an eye, reciprocate, retaliation, retribution **12** satisfaction

Revenge of the Sith *see* **8** Star Wars

revenue 3 pay **4** take **5** gains, wages, yield **6** income, profit, return, salary **7** annuity, pension, subsidy **8** earnings, interest, pickings, proceeds, receipts **9** allowance, emolument **12** compensation, remuneration

revenue, annual
  French: 5 rente

reverberate 4 boom, echo, ring **5** carry **6** rumble **7** resound, thunder, vibrate

reverberation 4 boom, echo **6** rumble **7** ringing, thunder **8** rumbling **9** vibration **10** resounding, thundering

revere 5 honor **6** esteem **7** defer to, respect **8** venerate

revered 4 adored **7** admired, honored **9** estimable, respected, venerated, worshiped **10** worshipped

reverence 3 awe **4** fear **5** honor, piety **6** esteem, homage, regard **7** respect, worship **8** devotion **9** adoration, deference **10** admiration, devoutness, observance, veneration **11** prostration, religiosity **12** genuflection

reverent 4 pure **5** pious **6** devout, humble, solemn **7** adoring, awesome, devoted **8** faithful **9** religious, spiritual **10** respectful, worshipful

reverential 4 awed **10** respectful, worshipful **11** deferential

reverie 5 dream, fancy **6** musing **7** fantasy **8** daydream **9** dreamland, quixotism **10** brown study, meditation **12** extravagance **13** woolgathering **14** fantasticality

reverse 4 back, rear, tail, undo, void **5** annul, upend, upset **6** cancel, change, defeat, invert, mishap, negate, recall, recant, repeal, revoke, unmake, upturn **7** counter, failure, nullify, rescind, retract, setback, trouble **8** abrogate, backward, contrary, converse, hardship, inverted, opposite, override, overrule, set aside, turn over, withdraw **9** adversity, mischance, posterior, transpose **10** antithesis, invalidate, misfortune **11** countermand, counterpart, frustration **14** disappointment

revert 5 lapse **6** go back, repeat, return **7** regress, relapse **9** backslide **10** recidivate, retrogress

review 4 show **5** study, sum up **6** notice, parade, rehash, survey **7** analyze, journal, retrace, run over **8** critique, evaluate, hash over, magazine, reassess, report on, scrutiny **9** criticism, criticize, reexamine, reiterate, summarize **10** commentary, evaluation, exhibition, exposition, procession, reconsider, reevaluate, reflection, scrutinize **11** examination **12** presentation, reassessment, recapitulate, reevaluation **13** demonstration, retrospection **14** recapitulation **15** reconsideration
  French: 11 compte rendu

revile 4 slur **5** abuse, curse, scold, scorn **6** berate, defame, deride, malign, rebuke, vilify **7** bawl out, chew out, slander, upbraid **8** belittle, denounce, execrate, reproach, sail into **9** blaspheme, castigate, denigrate, disparage **10** vituperate

reviler 6 critic, curser **8** vilifier **9** backbiter, slanderer **10** blasphemer

revise 4 edit, redo **5** alter, amend, emend, fix up **6** change, doctor, modify, recast, redact, revamp, review, update **7** correct, rectify, rewrite **8** emendate, overhaul

revision 6 change **7** edition **9** amendment, recension **10** alteration, correction, emendation **11** improvement **12** modification

revival 7 renewal **11** restoration **13** reinstatement, reinstitution, resuscitation

revive 5 dig up, renew **6** drag up, repeat **7** freshen, refresh, restage **8** reawaken **9** reanimate, reproduce, resurrect **11** resuscitate

revived 7 renewed **8** animated, repeated, restaged **9** enlivened, freshened, refreshed **10** reanimated, reawakened, reproduced **11** invigorated, resurrected **12** resuscitated

revocation 6 repeal **8** recision **9** abolition, annulment **10** abrogation, retraction **11** abolishment, elimination, repudiation **12** cancellation **13** nullification

revoke 4 void **5** annul, erase, quash **6** abjure, cancel, negate, recall, repeal, vacate **7** abolish, dismiss, expunge, nullify, rescind, retract, reverse **8** abrogate, call back, disallow, disclaim, override, overrule, renounce, set aside, take back, withdraw **9** repudiate **10** invalidate **11** countermand

revolt 4 coup, rise **5** rebel, repel, shock **6** appall, mutiny, offend, rise up, sicken **7** disgust, dissent, horrify, repulse **8** disorder, distress, nauseate, sedition, uprising **9** rebellion **10** insurgency, opposition, **12** factiousness, insurrection
German: 6 Putsch

revolting 4 foul, grim, vile **5** nasty **6** horrid, odious **7** hateful, noisome, noxious **8** dreadful, horrible, horrific, shocking, stinking **9** abhorrent, appalling, frightful, invidious, loathsome, obnoxious, offensive, repellent, repugnant, repulsive, sickening **10** abominable, disgusting, malodorous, nauseating **11** distasteful **12** disagreeable **13** objectionable

revolution 6 mutiny, revolt, rising **8** circling, gyration, rotation, uprising **9** rebellion **12** insurrection **14** circumrotation, circumvolution
French: 4 coup **9** coup d'etat
German: 6 Putsch

revolutionary 7 radical **8** mutinous **9** extremist, insurgent, seditious **10** dissenting, rebellious, subversive **13** superadvanced, unprecedented **15** insurrectionary

revolve 4 spin, turn **5** twist, wheel **6** circle, gyrate, rotate **12** circumrotate

revolver 3 gat, gun, rod **4** colt **6** pistol, weapon **7** firearm, handgun, rotator, sidearm **10** six-shooter **20** Saturday night special

revulsion 8 aversion, distaste, loathing **10** abhorrence, repugnance **11** detestation

reward 3 due **5** bonus, prize, repay, wages **6** bounty **7** deserts, guerdon, payment, premium, requite **9** reckoning **10** compensate, recompense, remunerate **12** compensation, remuner-ation **13** consideration
Latin: 10 quid pro quo

rewarding 8 pleasant, valuable **9** enjoyable **10** delightful, gratifying, satisfying **11** pleasurable

rework 4 redo **5** adapt, alter **6** modify **7** remodel, reshape **9** refashion, transform

rex 4 king

Reykjavik
capital of: 7 Iceland

Reynolds, Burt
born: 10 Waycross GA
wife: 9 Judy Carne **12** Loni Anderson
roles: 4 Bean **6** Shamus **9** Cloud Nine, Dan August, Semi-Tough, The Player **10** Striptease **11** Cop-and-a-half, Deliverance **12** Boogie Nights **14** The Longest Yard **17** The Dukes of Hazzard **18** Smokey and the Bandit

Reynolds, Debbie
real name: 19 Mary Frances Reynolds
born: 8 El Paso TX
husband: 11 Eddie Fisher
roles: 6 Mother **13** The Singing Nun, The Tender Trap **15** Singin' in the Rain **19** Tammy and the Bachelor **23** The Unsinkable Molly Brown

Reynolds, Sir Joshua
born: 7 England **8** Plympton
artwork: 14 Lord Heathfield, Miss Jane Bowles **15** Commodore Keppel **18** Mrs Francis Beckford **21** Mrs Abington as Miss Prue **25** Mrs Siddons as the Tragic Muse **38** Lady Sarah Bunbury Sacrificing to the Graces

Rhadamanthus, Rhadamanthys
father: 4 Zeus
mother: 6 Europa
brother: 5 Minos **6** Aeacus **8** Sarpedon
became a judge in: 5 Hades

rhapsodic 6 elated **7** beaming, excited **8** blissful, ecstatic, thrilled **9** delirious, overjoyed, rapturous **11** exhilarated, transported

Rhea
member of: 6 Titans
father: 6 Uranus
mother: 4 Gaea
brother: 6 Cronos, Cronus, Kronos
husband: 6 Cronos, Cronus, Kronos
son: 4 Zeus **5** Hades **8** Poseidon
daughter: 4 Hera **6** Hestia **7** Demeter
called: 10 Magna Mater
corresponds to: 3 Ops **6** Cybele **9** Dindymene **10** Berecyntia
epithet: 6 Antaea

Rhea Silvia
form: 12 vestal virgin
lover: 4 Mars
son: 5 Remus **7** Romulus

Rheingold see **Ring des Nibelungen, Der**

Rhesus
owned: 6 horses

horses captured by: 8 Diomedes, Odysseus

rhetoric 4 bunk, wind **5** hokum, hooey **6** bunkum, hot air **7** fustian, oratory **8** euphuism **9** discourse, elocution, eloquence, hyperbole **10** hocus-pocus **11** flamboyance **13** magniloquence **14** grandiloquence

Rhetoric
author: 9 Aristotle

rhetorical 5 showy, windy **6** florid, ornate, purple, verbal **7** aureate, flowery **8** eloquent, inflated **9** bombastic, grandiose, highflown, stylistic **10** decorative, discursive, euphuistic, expressive, flamboyant, linguistic, oratorical, ornamental **11** disputative, embellished, extravagant **12** disputatious, elocutionary, magniloquent **13** argumentative, grandiloquent

Rhoda
character: 8 Gary Levy **9** Joe Gerard **12** Benny Goodwin **14** Ida Morgenstern, Sally Gallagher **17** Brenda Morgenstern, Martin Morgenstern **22** Rhoda Morgenstern Gerard
cast: 9 Anne Meara, David Groh, Ron Silver **11** Julie Kavner, Nancy Walker **12** Harold J Gould, Ray Buktenica **13** Valerie Harper

Rhode Island
abbreviation: 2 RI
nickname: 11 Little Rhody
capital/largest city: 10 Providence
others: 7 Bristol, Newport **8** Cranston, Kingston, Westerly **9** Pawtucket, Wakefield **10** Woonsocket
college: 3 URI **6** Brown **8** Bryant **9** Pembroke **10** Barrington, Providence **11** Salve Regina **13** Mount St Joseph, Roger Williams **15** Johnson and Wales, Naval War College
feature: 7 Newport
tribe: 7 Niantic **9** Wampanoag **12** Narragansett
people: 8 Puritans **12** George M Cohan **13** Gilbert Stuart, Matthew C Perry, Roger Williams **15** Ambrose Burnside, Nathanael Greene **17** Oliver Hazard Perry
island: 5 Block, Rhode **8** Prudence **9** Aquidneck, Conanicut
lake: 8 Scituate
pond: 7 Wordens **8** Stafford, Watchaug
land rank: 8 fiftieth
mountain: 10 Durfee Hill
highest point: 12 Jerimoth Hill
physical feature:
bay: 12 Narragansett
sea: 8 Atlantic
sound: 11 Block Island
river: 7 Seekonk **8** Pawtuxet **9** Pawcatuck, Pawtucket, Potowomut **10** Blackstone, Providence
state admission: 10 thirteenth
state bird: 14 Rhode Island Red
state flower: 6 violet

state motto: 4 Hope
state song: 11 Rhode Island
state tree: 8 red maple
Rhodesia *see* **8** Zimbabwe
rhodium
  chemical symbol: 2 Rh
rhododendron
  varieties: 4 tree **5** Bluet **6** Indian, Yunnan **7** catawba, fringed, Lapland, silvery, Smirnow **8** Carolina, Chapman's, Fortune's, Fujiyama, piedmont **9** Caucasian, honey-bell, West Coast **11** leather-leaf **12** willow-leaved
rhodolite
  species: 6 garnet
rhubarb 5 Rheum **16** Rheum rhabarbarum
  varieties: 4 wild **5** monk's **6** garden, Sikkim **7** spinach **8** mountain
rhyme 3 pun **4** poem, rune, song **5** chime, clink, meter, poesy, verse **6** jingle, poetry, rhythm **7** measure, poetize, versify **8** assonate, doggerel **10** consonance **12** alliteration
  game: 6 crambo
rhymer, rhymester 4 bard, poet **6** writer **8** minstrel, poetizer **9** poetaster, versifier **10** troubadour
Rhys, Jean
  author of: 7 Quartet **15** Voyage in the Dark, Wide Sargasso Sea
rhythm 4 beat, lilt, time **5** meter, pulse, swing, throb **6** accent, number, stress **7** cadence, measure **8** emphasis, movement **9** pulsation **10** recurrence **11** fluctuation, syncopation **12** accentuation
riant 3 gay **4** airy **5** jolly, merry **6** blithe, bright, jocund, jovial **7** smiling **8** cheerful, laughing, mirthful
rib 3 kid, rag **4** bait, bone, josh **5** chaff, costa, jolly, tease
ribald 4 lewd, racy, rude **5** bawdy, crude, gross **6** coarse, earthy, rakish, risque, vulgar, wanton **7** raffish, uncouth **8** improper, indecent, off-color, prurient, shocking **9** salacious, unrefined **10** lascivious, libidinous, licentious, suggestive
ribbon 3 bow, ray **4** band, sash **5** award, braid, prize, reins, strip **6** cordon, riband **7** binding, rosette **8** memorial, streamer **10** decoration
rice 5 Oryza **11** Oryza sativa
  varieties: 4 wild **6** Indian, pampas **7** basmati **8** mountain **9** Tennessee **10** annual wild
  dish: 5 grits, pilaf, pilau **7** pudding, risotto **8** porridge **9** jambalaya
  liquor: 4 sake
Rice, Anne
  lives: 10 New Orleans
  character: 6 Lestat **8** vampire
  author of: 11 Cry to Heaven **13** Blackwood Farm, Blood Canticle **16**

The Vampire Lestat **17** Vampire Chronicles **19** The Queen of the Damned **23** Interview with the Vampire
Rice, Elmer
  author of: 11 Street Scene **16** The Adding Machine
rich 4 dark, deep, fine, lush **5** flush, heavy, loamy, sweet, vivid **6** bright, costly, fecund, lavish, mellow **7** fertile, filling, intense, moneyed, opulent, wealthy, well-off **8** abundant, affluent, fruitful, in clover, precious, prodigal, resonant, sonorous, splendid, valuable, well-to-do **9** abounding, estimable, expensive, luxuriant, luxurious, priceless, sumptuous **10** euphonious, productive, propertied, prosperous **11** mellifluous **12** on easy street
Richard, Maurice
  nickname: 6 Rocket
  sport: 6 hockey
  team: 17 Montreal Canadiens
Richard Cory
  author: 22 Edwin Arlington Robinson
Richard Diamond, Private Detective
  character: 3 Sam **6** Lt Kile **9** Lt McGough **10** Karen Wells
  cast: 10 Russ Conway **11** Barbara Bain, Regis Toomey **12** David Janssen **13** Roxanne Brooks **14** Mary Tyler Moore
  viewers saw only Sam's: 4 legs
Richard I 11 Coeur de Lion, Lion-Hearted
  father: 7 Henry II
  mother: 7 Eleanor (of Aquitaine)
  brother: 4 John
Richard II
  author: 18 William Shakespeare
  character: 11 John of Gaunt **13** Edmund Langley, Thomas Mowbray **16** Henry Bolingbroke **20** Earl of Northumberland
  Duke of: 4 York **7** Aumerle, Norfolk **8** Hereford **9** Lancaster
Richard III
  author: 18 William Shakespeare
  character: 6 George **7** Richard **8** Edward IV, Lady Anne **10** Henry Tudor (Earl of Richmond) **11** Lord Stanley **12** Lord Hastings **13** Queen Margaret **14** Queen Elizabeth **15** Edward the Fourth **17** Sir William Catesby **19** Edward Prince of Wales
  Duke of: 4 York **8** Clarence **10** Buckingham, Gloucester
Richardson, Joely
  parents: 14 Tony Richardson **15** Vanessa Redgrave
  sister: 7 Natasha
  roles: 9 Maybe Baby **10** The Patriot **12** Event Horizon **13** 101 Dalmatians **14** Shining Through **17** Drowning By Numbers
Richardson, Henry Hobson

architect of: 9 Sever Hall (Harvard) **11** Grace Church (West Medford MA) **13** Trinity Church (Boston) **23** State Asylum for the Insane (Buffalo NY) **27** Marshall Field Wholesale Store (Chicago)
Richardson, Natasha
  parents: 14 Tony Richardson **15** Vanessa Redgrave
  sister: 5 Joely
  roles: 6 Asylum **7** Blow Dry **11** Patty Hearst **12** The Handmaid's Tale **14** Waking Up in Reno **23** Every Picture Tells a Story
Richardson, Samuel
  author of: 6 Pamela (or Virtue Rewarded) **8** Clarissa (Harlowe) **19** Sir Charles Grandison
Richardson, Sir Ralph
  born: 7 England **10** Cheltenham
  roles: 6 Exodus **9** Oscar Wilde, Richard III, The Heiress **11** A Doll's House **12** Anna Karenina **13** Doctor Zhivago **15** Richard the Third **20** Little Lord Fauntleroy **24** Long Day's Journey into Night **26** Greystoke The Legend of Tarzan
Richardson, Tony
  wife: 15 Vanessa Redgrave
  daughter: 5 Joely **7** Natasha
  director of: 7 Blue Sky **8** Tom Jones (Oscar) **14** The Entertainer **15** Look Back in Anger **36** The Loneliness of the Long Distance Runner
riches 4 pelf **5** lucre, means **6** assets, mammon, wealth **7** fortune **8** opulence, treasure **9** resources **10** prosperity **11** possessions
richness 6 wealth **8** fullness, lushness, opulence **9** amplitude, intensity **10** lavishness, mellowness **12** completeness **13** luxuriousness
Richter, Charles Francis
  field: 10 geophysics, seismology
  developed: 12 Richter scale **24** measurement of earthquakes
rickety 4 weak **5** frail, shaky **6** feeble, flimsy, infirm, wasted, weakly, wobbly **7** fragile **8** decrepit, unsteady, withered **9** tottering **10** brokendown, tumbledown **11** debilitated, dilapidated, weakjointed **12** deteriorated
rid 4 free **5** clear, purge **6** remove **8** disabuse, liberate, unburden **9** disburden, eliminate **11** disencumber
Ridd, John
  character in: 10 Lorna Doone
  author: 9 Blackmore
riddance 6 ouster, relief **7** freeing, removal **8** ejection **9** clearance, expulsion **11** deliverance, dislodgment
riddle 5 poser, rebus **6** enigma, puzzle, secret **7** mystery, problem, puzzler, stumper **9** conundrum
ride 4 move **5** annoy, carry, drive, harry, hound **6** badger, handle, harass, hector, manage, needle, travel **7**

control, journey, support **8** progress **9** transport

rider 5 affix **6** suffix **7** adjunct, codicil **8** addendum, addition, appendix **9** amendment, appendage **10** attachment, supplement

ridge 3 bar, rib, rim **4** bank, fret, hill, hump, rise, wale, weal, welt **5** bluff, crest, crimp, knoll, mound, spine **6** ripple **7** crinkle, hillock, wrinkle **10** promontory **11** corrugation

ridicule 3 guy, rib **4** gibe, jeer, josh, mock, razz, ride, twit **5** mimic, scorn, taunt, tease **6** deride, gibe at, parody **7** lampoon, laugh at, mockery, ribbing, sarcasm, scoff at, sneer at, snicker, teasing **8** belittle, derision, sneering, travesty **9** aspersion, burlesque, disparage, humiliate, make fun of, poke fun at **10** caricature, derogation, lampoonery **13** disparagement
god of: 5 Momos, Momus

ridiculous 3 odd **5** crazy, droll, funny, inane, nutty, queer, silly **6** absurd, screwy **7** amusing, asinine, bizarre, comical, fatuous, foolish, idiotic **8** farcical **9** fantastic, frivolous, grotesque, laughable, ludicrous, screwball, senseless **10** hysterical, incredible, irrational, outlandish **11** astonishing, nonsensical **12** preposterous, unreasonable

Rienzi
author: 18 Edward Bulwer-Lytton
composer: 6 Wagner

Riesling, Paul
character in: 7 Babbitt
author: 5 Lewis

rife 5 close, dense, solid, thick **6** common, packed **7** crowded, general, studded, teeming **8** epidemic, pandemic, populous, swarming **9** chockfull, extensive, plumbfull, prevalent, universal **10** prevailing, widespread **11** predominant

riffraff 3 mob **4** herd, scum **5** crowd, dregs, trash **6** masses, proles, rabble, vermin **9** peasantry **10** commonalty **11** proletariat
French: 8 canaille

rifle 3 rob **4** loot, sack **6** ravage **7** despoil, pillage, plunder, ransack **8** spoliate **10** burglarize

rifle, repeating
invented by: 7 Spencer

Rifleman, The
character: 10 Lou Mallory, Mark McCain **11** Lucas McCain **14** Miss Milly Scott **20** Marshal Micah Torrance
cast: 7 Paul Fix **10** Joan Taylor **12** Chuck Connors **13** Patricia Blair **14** Johnny Crawford
setting: 9 New Mexico, North Fork

rift 3 cut, gap **4** gash, gulf, rent, slit **5** abyss, break, chasm, chink, cleft, crack, fault, gorge, gulch, gully, split **6** breach, cranny, ravine **7** breakup,

crevice, fissure, quarrel, rupture **8** aperture, crevasse, division, fracture **12** disagreement **16** misunderstanding

rig 4 gear **5** equip **6** fit out, outfit **8** carriage **9** apparatus, equipment, machinery

Riga *see* **Latvia**

Rigaud
character in: 12 Little Dorrit
author: 7 Dickens

Rigg, Diana
born: 7 England **9** Doncaster
title: 4 Dame
roles: 6 Helena **8** Emma Peel **10** Bleak House **11** Lady Dedlock, The Avengers **12** Julius Caesar **21** A Midsummer Night's Dream **26** On Her Majesty's Secret Service

right 2 OK **3** due **4** deed, fair, good, just, meet, nice, real, sane, true, well **5** amend, emend, exact, grant, honor, ideal, legal, licit, moral, power, solve, sound, valid **6** actual, at once, decent, honest, lawful, morals, normal, proper, remedy, seemly, square, virtue **7** certain, correct, ethical, exactly, factual, fitting, freedom, genuine, liberty, license, perfect, precise, probity, redress, regular, standup, warrant **8** accurate, becoming, clear-cut, definite, directly, goodness, morality, promptly, properly, rational, sanction, straight, suitable, suitably, truthful, virtuous **9** allowable, authentic, authority, correctly, desirable, equitable, exemplary, favorable, favorably, honorable, integrity, nobleness, opportune, ownership, perfectly, precisely, presently, privilege, propriety, rectitude, veracious, veridical, vindicate **10** aboveboard, accurately, admissible, completely, convenient, infallible, legitimate, permission, preferable, reasonable, recompense, scrupulous, undisputed, unmistaken **11** inheritance, immediately, irrefutable, prerogative, punctilious **12** advantageous, jurisdiction, satisfactory **13** appropriately, authorization, incontestable, justification, unimpeachable **14** proprietorship, satisfactorily, unquestionable
Latin: 3 jus

right beside 6 next to **8** abutting, adjacent, touching

righteous 4 fair, good, holy, just **5** godly, moral, pious **6** chaste, devout, honest **7** ethical **8** elevated, innocent, reverent, virtuous **9** blameless, equitable, honorable, incorrupt, religious, spiritual, unsullied

righteousness
goddess of: 4 Maat

righteous person
Hebrew: 6 zaddik

rightful 3 due **4** just, true **5** legal, valid **6** lawful, proper **7** allowed, condign, correct, fitting, merited **8** de-

served **9** deserving, equitable **10** authorized, designated, legitimate, prescribed, sanctioned **11** appropriate, inalienable **14** constitutional

right hand 4 aide, ally **6** helper **7** partner **8** adjutant **9** assistant
French: 10 aide-de-camp

right of blood
Latin: 12 jus sanguinis

right of soil/land
Latin: 7 jus soli

right side up 7 upright **10** on one's feet

Right Stuff, The
director: 13 Philip Kaufman
author: 8 Tom Wolfe
cast: 8 Ed Harris **10** Sam Shepard
Oscar for: 5 score

right-wing 7 old-line **10** nonliberal **11** reactionary **12** conservative **14** nonprogressive

right-winger 8 rightist **11** reactionary **12** conservative

rigid 3 set **4** firm, hard, taut **5** fixed, harsh, sharp, stern, stiff, tense **6** formal, severe, strict, strong, wooden **7** austere **8** exacting, obdurate, rigorous, stubborn, unpliant **9** inelastic, stringent, unbending **10** inflexible, unyielding **11** puritanical, unrelenting **14** uncompromising

Rigoletto
opera by: 5 Verdi
character: 5 Gilda **9** Maddalena **11** Sparafucile **12** Duke of Mantua **15** Countess Ceprano **16** Count of Monterone

rigorous 5 exact, harsh, stern, tough **6** severe, strict, trying **7** austere, correct, precise **8** accurate, exacting **9** demanding, stringent **10** meticulous, scrupulous **11** challenging, punctilious

rig out 4 garb **5** array, dress **6** attire, clothe

rile 3 irk, vex **4** gall, miff, roil **5** anger, annoy, chafe, gripe, peeve, pique **6** bother, enrage, nettle, offend, plague **7** incense, inflame, provoke **8** irritate **9** aggravate, infuriate

Riley, James Whitcomb
called: 11 Hoosier poet
author of: 18 Little Orphant Annie **25** When the Frost Is on the Punkin

rilievo 6 relief

Rilke, Rainer Maria
author of: 11 Book of Hours **12** Duino Elegies, Life and Songs **13** Divine Elegies **16** Sonnets to Orpheus **19** Letters to a Young Poet

rill 5 brook, cleft, creek **6** furrow, groove, runnel, stream **7** channel, rivulet **9** streamlet

rim 3 lip **4** edge, side **5** brink, ledge, verge **6** border, margin **9** outer edge

Rimbaud, Arthur
born: 6 France

author of: 12 Le Bateau Ivre **13** A Season in Hell **14** The Drunken Boat **16** Les Illuminations **17** Sonnet of the Vowels

rime 3 ice **4** hoar **5** chink, cleft, crack, crust, frost **7** crevice, fissure **9** hoar-frost

Rime of the Ancient Mariner, The
    author: 21 Samuel Taylor Coleridge
    character: 6 Hermit **9** Albatross **12** Wedding Guest **14** Ancient Mariner

Rimsky-Korsakov, Nikolai (Nicholas)
    born: 6 Russia **8** Novgorod
    member of: 7 The Five
    composer of: 5 Mlada, Sadko **6** Kitezh **10** Night in May, Snow Maiden, Tzar Saltan **11** Sheherazade **12** Christmas Eve, Scheherazade **16** Spanish Capriccio **17** Capriccio Espagnol, The Golden Cockerel **21** Russian Easter Overture **29** Russian Easter Festival Overture

rind 4 bark, hull, husk, peel, skin **5** crust, shell **6** cortex, fringe **7** epicarp, surface **8** exterior
    pork: 9 crackling

ring 4 aura, band, bloc, buzz, call, echo, gang, hoop, loop, peal, toll, tone **5** cabal, chime, clang, knell, party, sound **6** cartel, circle, cordon, herald, jangle, jingle, league, signal, strike, summon, tinkle **7** besiege, circuit, combine, enclose, quality, resound, seal off, vibrate **8** announce, blockade, encircle, proclaim, striking, surround **9** broadcast, encompass, perimeter, resonance, syndicate, ting-a-ling, vibration **10** federation **11** reverberate **12** circumscribe **13** circumference, reverberation **14** tintinnabulate **16** tintinnabulation

Ring and the Book, The
    author: 14 Robert Browning

Ring des Nibelungen, Der
    also: 12 The Ring Cycle **20** The Ring of the Nibelung(s)
    opera by: 6 Wagner
    part one: 12 Das Rheingold, The Rhine Gold
    part two: 10 Die Walkure **11** The Valkyrie
    part three: 9 Siegfried
    part four: 15 Gotterdammerung **17** Twilight of the Gods
    character: 4 Erda, Mime **5** Freia, Hagen, Wotan **6** Fafner, Fasolt **7** Gunther, Gutrune, Hunding **8** Alberich, Siegmund **9** Siegfried, Sieglinde, Valkyries **10** Brunnhilde

ringleader 5 chief **6** master **10** mastermind

ringlet 4 curl **6** circle

ring-shaped 7 round **8** circular

Rin Tin Tin, The Adventures of
    character: 5 Rusty, (Cpl) Boone **9** (Sgt) Biff O'Hara **10** (Lt) Rip Masters

    cast: 8 Lee Aaker **9** Joe Sawyer **10** James Brown, Rand Brooks

Rio Bravo
    director: 11 Howard Hawks
    cast: 8 Ward Bond **9** John Wayne **10** Dean Martin **11** Ricky Nelson **13** Walter Brennan **14** Angie Dickinson

Rio de Janeiro
    airport: 6 Galeao
    architect: 5 Costa, Reidy **8** Niemeyer
    area: 4 Caju, Lapa **6** Catete, Gamboa, Gloria, Grajau, Tijuca **7** Catumbi, Ipanema **8** Botafogo **10** Copacabana, Vila Isabel **12** Sao Cristovao
    bay: 8 Botafogo, Jurujuba **9** Guanabara
    bridge: 11 Costa e Silva
    celebration: 8 Carnival **9** Mardi Gras
    discovered by: 6 Coelho
    former capital of: 6 Brazil
    island: 10 Governador
    lake: 16 Rodrigo de Freitas
    landmark: 10 Candelaria **14** Mount Corcovado **15** Maracana Stadium **17** Sugarloaf Mountain
      statue of: 17 Christ the Redeemer
    means: 14 river of January
    ocean: 8 Atlantic
    people: 8 Cariocas
    replaced as capital by: 8 Brasilia
    slums: 7 favelas
    suburb: 7 Niteroi

riot 4 rage **5** act up, arise, melee, rebel **6** fracas, mutiny, resist, revolt, rumpus, strife, tumult, uproar **7** rampage, run amok, trouble, turmoil **8** disorder, outburst, uprising, violence **9** commotion, confusion, rebellion **10** Donnybrook, turbulence **11** lawlessness, pandemonium **12** insurrection

rioting 6 tumult, uproar **7** turmoil **8** disorder, outbreak, violence **9** commotion **11** disturbance

riotous 4 loud, wild **5** arroar, noisy, randy **6** stormy, unruly, wanton **7** bacchic, rampant, violent **8** bacchian **9** debauched, dissolute, insurgent, plentiful, tumultuous, turbulent **10** boisterous, dissipated, licentious, rebellious **11** intemperate, overcopious **12** unrestrained **13** superabundant **15** insurrectionary
    party: 4 orgy

rip 3 cut, gap **4** rend, rent, rift, rive, slit, tear **5** burst, sever, shred, slash, split **6** cleave **7** fissure, rupture **8** cleavage, cut apart, fracture, incision, tear open **10** laceration

ripe 3 due, fit **4** come **5** ideal, ready **6** mature, mellow, primed, timely **7** perfect **8** complete, finished, seasoned **9** maturated **10** consummate **12** accomplished

ripen 3 age **4** grow **5** bloom, fruit **6** flower, mature, mellow **7** develop

Rip Kirby

    creator: 11 Alex Raymond **12** John Prentice

Ripley, Robert L
    author of: 14 Believe It or Not

Rip Van Winkle
    author: 16 Washington Irving

rise 4 bank, defy, dune, face, gain, go up, grow, hill, lift, meet, soar **5** climb, get up, knoll, march, mount, rebel, ridge, spire, stand, surge, swell, tower **6** ascend, growth, mutiny, resist, revolt, rocket, strike, thrive **7** advance, balloon, burgeon, disobey, elevate, headway, improve, prosper, stand up, succeed, upswing **8** addition, flourish, increase, progress **9** expansion, extension **10** embankment **11** advancement, enlargement

Rise and Fall of the Third Reich, The
    author: 14 William L Shirer

Rise of Silas Lapham, The
    author: 18 William Dean Howells
    character: 5 Irene **8** Mr Rogers, Penelope, Tom Corey **9** Mrs Lapham

risible 4 rich **5** comic, droll, funny, merry, silly, witty **6** absurd, jocose, jovial **7** amusing, comical, jocular **8** farcical, humorous, mirthful **9** facetious, laughable, ludicrous, whimsical **10** ridiculous **11** nonsensical

rising sun
    god of: 5 Janus

risk 4 dare **5** peril **6** chance, danger, gamble, hazard **7** imperil, venture **8** endanger, jeopardy **9** speculate **10** jeopardize **11** imperilment, speculation, uncertainty **12** endangerment

risky 6 chancy, daring, unsafe **8** insecure, perilous, ticklish **9** dangerous, daredevil, haphazard, hazardous, hit or miss, uncertain **10** precarious **11** adventurous, unprotected, venturesome

risque 4 blue, lewd, racy **5** bawdy, dirty, gross, spicy **6** coarse, daring, ribald, smutty, vulgar **7** immoral, obscene **8** immodest, improper, indecent, off-color **9** offensive, salacious **10** indecorous, indelicate, lascivious, licentious, suggestive **12** pornographic

rite 6 ritual **7** liturgy, service **8** ceremony **9** formality, solemnity **10** ceremonial, observance

rite of passage 6 ritual **7** baptism **8** ceremony, marriage **10** bar mitzvah, bat mitzvah, initiation **11** christening **12** confirmation

Ritt, Martin
    director of: 3 Hud **7** Sounder **8** Norma Rae, The Front **26** The Spy Who Came in From the Cold

Ritter, John
    born: 9 Burbank CA
    father: 9 Tex Ritter
    roles: 9 Hooperman **11** Americathon, Jack Tripper **12** Man of the Year **13**

Three's Company **14** Captain Avenger **16** Eight Simple Rules

Ritter, Thelma
    born: 10 Brooklyn NY
    roles: 10 Pillow Talk, Rear Window, The Misfits **11** All About Eve **15** The Mating Season **17** Birdman of Alcatraz **18** With a Song in My Heart **19** A Letter to Three Wives, Pickup on South Street **21** The Proud and the Profane **27** Miracle on Thirty-Fourth Street

ritual 4 rite **7** service **8** ceremony **10** observance

ritual bathing place
    Jewish Orthodox: 6 mikvah

ritualistic 6 formal, solemn **10** ceremonial **11** ceremonious

ritualize 7 observe **9** celebrate, solemnize **13** ceremonialize

ritzy 4 chic, posh, tony **5** sharp, swank **6** classy, snazzy, spiffy **7** elegant, stylish **9** high-class, high-toned, luxurious, sumptuous

rival 3 foe **5** enemy, equal, excel, fight, match, outdo, touch **6** strive **7** eclipse, surpass **8** approach, opponent, opposing, outshine **9** adversary, competing, contender, disputant **10** antagonist, competitor, contending, contestant

Rivals, The
    author: 23 Richard Brinsley Sheridan
    character: 8 Bob Acres **9** Faulkland **11** Mrs Malaprop **13** Julia Melville, Lydia Languish **17** Sir Lucius O'Trigger **18** Sir Anthony Absolute **19** Captain Jack Absolute (Ensign Beverley)

rive 4 rend **5** crack, split **6** cleave, detach, divide, sunder **7** shatter **8** fracture

riven 4 rent, torn **5** split **7** cleaved, cracked **8** sundered **9** fractured, shattered

River, The
    director: 10 Jean Renoir
    based on novel by: 11 Rumer Godden
    cast: 5 Radha **13** Adrienne Corri, Arthur Shields, Nora Swinburne **15** Patricia Walters
    setting: 5 India **6** Bengal

Rivera, Diego
    born: 6 Mexico **10** Guanajuato
    artwork: 5 Sleep **8** Creation **11** Mother Earth **14** The Fecund Earth **15** Detroit Industry **18** Man at the Crossroads **21** Carnival of Mexican Life **23** Life in Pre-Hispanic Mexico

river mouth 5 delta, firth **7** estuary

rivers
    god of: 6 Peneus, Simois **7** Inachus

Rivers, Reba
    character in: 9 Sanctuary
    author: 8 Faulkner

rivet 3 fix, pin **6** absorb, clinch, engage, fasten, occupy **7** engross **8** fastener **9** fascinate

Rivieres du Sud *see* **6** Guinea

rivulet 3 run **4** rill **5** brook, creek **6** stream **9** streamlet

Riyadh
    capital of: 11 Saudi Arabia

Rizzuto, Phil
    nickname: 7 Scooter
    position: 9 shortstop
    sport: 8 baseball
    team: 14 New York Yankees

road 3 via, way **4** lane, path **5** byway, route, trail **6** avenue, street **7** freeway, highway, parkway **8** turnpike **9** boulevard **10** expressway, throughway **12** thoroughfare

Road Not Taken, The
    author: 11 Robert Frost

roads
    god of: 6 Hermes

road safety
    god of: 6 Sancus **10** Semo Sancus

Road to Perdition, The
    director: 9 Sam Mendes
    cast: 8 Tom Hanks (Michael Sullivan) **9** Liam Aiken (Peter Sullivan) **10** Paul Newman (John Rooney) **11** Ciaran Hinds (Finn McGovern), Daniel Craig (Connor Rooney) **13** Tyler Hoechlin (Michael Sullivan Jr) **18** Jennifer Jason Leigh (Annie Sullivan)

roam 3 gad **4** rove **5** drift, jaunt, prowl, range, stray, tramp **6** ramble, stroll, travel, wander **7** meander, traipse **8** divagate **9** gallivant **11** peregrinate

roan 5 horse **7** grayish, reddish, tannish **8** blackish, brownish

roar 3 bay, cry, din **4** bawl, boom, howl, roll, yell **5** blare, growl, grunt, noise, shout, snort **6** bellow, clamor, guffaw, outcry, racket, rumble, scream, shriek **7** bluster, resound, thunder **8** outburst **10** vociferate

roast 3 pan **4** bake **6** berate **7** scourge **8** barbecue **9** criticize

rob 4 bilk, lift, loot, raid, sack, skin **5** cheat, filch, heist, rifle, seize, steal **6** burgle, fleece, forage, hold up, pilfer, thieve **7** despoil, pillage, plunder, purloin, ransack, stick up, swindle **8** carry off, embezzle **9** bamboozle **10** burglarize **11** appropriate

Robards, Jason
    born: 9 Chicago IL
    wife: 12 Lauren Bacall
    roles: 5 Julia **7** Isadora **9** Dick Diver, Heartwood **10** Ben Bradlee **11** Jamie Tyrone **12** Hour of the Gun **14** A Thousand Acres **15** A Thousand Clowns, Dashiell Hammett, Melvin and Howard, The Disenchanted **16** Tender Is the Night **19** All the Presi-

dent's Men **24** Long Day's Journey into Night

Robbe-Grillet, Alain
    author of: 8 Jealousy **9** The Voyeur **10** The Erasers **14** In the Labyrinth **19** Last Year at Marienbad

robber 4 yegg **5** crook, thief **6** bandit, con man, outlaw, pirate, raider **7** brigand, burglar, forager, rustler, sharper **8** Barabbas, marauder, swindler **9** buccaneer, despoiler, embezzler, larcenist, plunderer **10** highwayman, pickpocket

Robbins, Harold
    original name: 11 Harold Rubin
    author of: 6 Tycoon **8** The Betsy **10** The Raiders **13** The Inheritors **14** Dreams Die First, The Adventurers **16** The Carpetbaggers **17** The Dream Merchants **18** Never Love a Stranger **20** A Stone for Danny Fisher **21** Seventy-Nine Park Avenue

Robbins, Jerome
    choreographer of: 8 Les Noces **9** Fancy Free, Interplay
    director of: 13 West Side Story (with Robert Wise, Oscar)

robe 4 gown **5** dress, habit, smock **6** duster **7** costume, garment **8** bathrobe, vestment **9** housecoat
    French: 8 negligee
    Japanese: 6 kimono

Robe, The
    author: 13 Lloyd C Douglas

robe-de-chambre 12 dressing-gown

Roberts, Kenneth
    author of: 16 Northwest Passage

Roberts, Rachel
    born: 5 Wales **8** Llanelly
    husband: 11 Rex Harrison
    roles: 8 Foul Play **10** Oh Lucky Man **16** This Sporting Life **24** Murder on the Orient Express **29** Saturday Night and Sunday Morning

Robertson, Cliff
    real name: 23 Clifford Parker Robertson
    born: 9 La Jolla CA
    wife: 11 Dina Merrill
    roles: 5 PT-109 **6** Charly (Oscar), JW Coop **9** Obsession **10** Melting Pot **11** Falcon Crest

Robertson, Oscar
    nickname: 7 The Big O
    sport: 10 basketball
    team: 14 Milwaukee Bucks **16** Cincinnati Royals

Robeson, Paul
    born: 11 Princeton NJ
    roles: 7 Othello **8** Show Boat **11** Brutus Jones **15** The Emperor Jones **17** King Solomon's Mines **22** All God's Chillun Got Wings

Robin Hood: Prince of Thieves
    director: 13 Kevin Reynolds
    cast: 11 Alan Rickman (Sheriff of Nottingham), Nick Brimble (Little

John) **12** Brian Blessed (Lord Locksley), Kevin Costner (Robin of Locksley) **13** Morgan Freeman (Azeem) **14** Michael McShane (Friar Tuck), Michael Wincott (Guy of Gisborne) **15** Christian Slater (Will Scarlett), Geraldine McEwan (Mortianna) **25** Mary Elizabeth Mastrantonio (Marian Dubois)

Robin Hood's Adventures
author: **7** unknown
character: **9** Friar Tuck **10** Little John **11** Will Scarlet **14** Band of Merry Men **18** Sir Richard of the Lea **19** Sheriff of Nottingham

robin's-egg-blue 4 aqua **5** azure **7** sky-blue **8** cerulean **9** light blue **10** aquamarine, powder-blue

Robinson, Edward G
real name: **18** Emmanuel Goldenberg
born: **7** Romania **9** Bucharest
roles: **8** Key Largo **12** Little Caesar, Rico Bandello **13** Scarlet Street **15** Double Indemnity, Flesh and Fantasy **16** House of Strangers **19** The Woman in the Window **20** A Dispatch from Reuters **21** Dr Ehrlich's Magic Bullet

Robinson, Edwin Arlington
author of: **6** Merlin **8** Amaranth, Tristram **10** King Jasper **11** Richard Cory **12** Captain Craig **13** Miniver Cheevy, Mr Flood's Party

Robinson, Jackie
sport: **8** baseball
team: **15** Brooklyn Dodgers
first black in: **12** major leagues

Robinson, Sugar Ray
real name: **19** Walker Smith Robinson
sport: **6** boxing
class: **12** middleweight, welterweight

Robinson Crusoe
author: **11** Daniel Defoe
character: **6** Friday

Rob Roy
author: **14** Sir Walter Scott
character: **11** Diana Vernon **18** Sir Frederick Vernon **23** Rob Roy MacGregor Campbell
Osbaldistone family: **5** Frank **7** William **9** Rashleigh **13** Sir Hildebrand

robust 3 fit **4** firm, hale, well, wiry **5** hardy, husky, lusty, sound, stout, tough **6** active, brawny, hearty, mighty, potent, rugged, sinewy, strong, sturdy, virile **7** healthy, staunch **8** athletic, forceful, muscular, powerful, stalwart, vigorous **9** energetic, healthful, strapping, wholesome **10** able-bodied **12** in fine fettle
French: **8** puissant

robustness 5 vigor **8** strength **10** good health, ruggedness, sturdiness **11** healthiness

Roche, Kevin

architect of: **13** Oakland Museum (CA) **14** Fine Arts Center (U of MA), Ford Foundation (NYC) **17** Knights of Columbus (New Haven CT) **21** One United Nations Plaza (NYC) **24** Union Carbide Headquarters (Danbury CT) **31** Power Center for the Performing Arts (U of Michigan)

Rochester, Edward
character in: **8** Jane Eyre
author: **6** Bronte

rock 3 bob, jar **4** crag, reef, roll, stun, sway, toss **5** cliff, flint, pitch, quake, shake, stone, swing, upset **6** gravel, marble, pebble, totter, wobble **7** agitate, bobbing, boulder, disturb, shaking **8** convulse, flounder, undulate, wobbling **9** limestone, oscillate, tottering **10** convulsion, undulation

rock & rye
type: **7** liqueur
flavor: **6** citrus
ingredient: **3** rye **9** rock candy

rock crystal
species: **6** quartz
color: **9** colorless

Rocket
nickname of: **14** Maurice Richard

rocket engine
invented by: **7** Goddard

Rockford Files, The
character: **10** John Cooper **11** Angel Martin, Jim Rockford **12** (Det) Dennis Becker **13** Beth Davenport, (Joseph) Rocky Rockford
cast: **9** Bo Hopkins, Joe Santos, Noah Beery **11** James Garner **14** Stuart Margolin **15** Gretchen Corbett

rock of Tarik see **9** Gibraltar

Rockwell, Norman
born: **9** New York NY
artwork:
covers: **19** Saturday Evening Post
mural: **15** Freedom of Speech

Rocky
director: **13** John G Avildsen
cast: **9** Burt Young **10** Talia Shire **11** Thayer David **12** Carl Weathers **15** Burgess Meredith **17** Sylvester Stallone (Rocky Balboa, the Italian Stallion)
setting: **12** Philadelphia
Oscar for: **7** editing, picture **8** director
sequel: **7** Rocky II, Rocky IV **8** Rocky III, Rocky Two **9** Rocky Four **10** Rocky Three

rod 4 cane, lash, mace, pale, pole, wand, whip **5** baton, birch, crook, staff, stake, stick **6** cudgel, rattan, switch **7** penalty, scepter, scourge **8** caduceus **9** stanchion **10** alpenstock, punishment **11** retribution **12** swagger stick

rod, Aaron's see **9** Aaron's rod

rodent 4 cavy, vole **5** coypu, gundi, hutia, mouse **6** agouti, beaver, cururo,

gerbil, gopher, jerboa, nutria **7** blesmol, cane rat, hamster, lemming, mole-rat, rock rat **8** capybara, chipmunk, dormouse, pacarana, sewellel, spiny rat, squirrel, tucu-tuco, viscacha **9** chozchori, false paca, porcupine, woodchuck **10** chinchilla, prairie dog, springhare **11** kangaroo rat, pocket mouse, viscacha rat **13** kangaroo mouse **16** Speke's pectinator

Roderick Random
author: **14** Tobias Smollett
character: **5** Strap **8** Narcissa **10** Tom Bowling **12** Miss Williams

Rodin, (Francois) Auguste Rene
born: **5** Paris **6** France
artwork: **7** The Kiss **10** Head of Iris, The Thinker, Victor Hugo, Walking Man **14** John the Baptist, The Age of Bronze, The Gates of Hell **16** Monument to Balzac **19** The Burghers of Calais **23** The Man with the Broken Nose

rodomontade 4 rant **5** boast **6** hot air **7** blather, bluster, bombast, fustian **8** bragging, folderol, nonsense, rhetoric **10** balderdash, doubletalk **11** braggadocio **12** boastfulness

roe 3 doe, elk, hen **4** buck, deer, eggs, fawn, fish, hart, hind, milt **5** spawn, sperm **6** caviar **8** fish eggs
of lobster: **5** coral

Roentgen, Rontgen, Wilhelm Konrad
field: **7** physics
nationality: **6** German
discovered: **5** X-rays
awarded: **10** Nobel Prize

Roethke, Theodore
author of: **9** Open House, The Waking **11** The Far Field **15** Straw for the Fire, Words for the Wind

Rogers, Ginger
real name: **23** Virginia Katherine McMath
born: **14** Independence MO
husband: **8** Lew Ayres **15** Jacques Bergerac, William Marshall
partner: **11** Fred Astaire
roles: **6** Top Hat **9** Stage Door **10** Hello Dolly, Kitty Foyle (Oscar) **12** Shall We Dance? **14** The Gay Divorcee **15** Flying Down to Rio, Tom Dick and Harry **17** Forty-Second Street **19** The Major and the Minor **21** The Barkleys of Broadway **30** The Story of Vernon and Irene Castle

Rogers, James Gamble
architect of: **22** Northwestern University (Chicago) **33** Columbia-Presbyterian Medical Center (NYC)

Rogers, Roy
real name: **11** Leonard Slye
born: **12** Cincinnati OH
wife: **9** Dale Evans
sidekick: **10** Gabby Hayes
singing group: **17** Sons of the Pio-

neers
horse: 7 Trigger
roles: 10 Apache Rose 11 Song of Texas 12 My Pal Trigger 13 Song of Arizona, Son of Paleface 17 Heart of the Rockies, Under Western Stars 18 Billy the Kid Returns 19 Tumbling Tumbleweeds 20 The Yellow Rose of Texas 22 Springtime in the Sierras

rogue 3 cur 5 devil, fraud, knave, scamp 6 bad man, rascal, rotter, varlet, wretch 7 bounder, hellion, villain 8 deceiver, evildoer, scalawag 9 miscreant, reprobate, scoundrel 10 blackguard, malefactor, mountebank, scapegrace 11 rapscallion 13 mischiefmaker 14 good-for-nothing 15 snake in the grass

roguish 3 sly 4 arch 5 saucy 8 devilish, rascally 11 mischievous

roil 3 irk, vex 4 mill, rile, stir 5 annoy, muddy 6 ruffle, seethe 7 agitate, disturb, perturb, provoke, turmoil 8 irritate 9 aggravate 10 exasperate

role 3 job 4 duty, part, pose, post, task, work 5 chore, guise 7 posture, service 8 capacity, function 9 character, portrayal 10 assignment 13 impersonation 14 representation 15 personification 16 characterization
Latin: 7 persona

roll 4 boom, coil, curl, echo, flip, flow, furl, knot, list, loop, reel, roar, rock, spin, sway, toss, tube, turn, wind 5 coast, crack, lurch, pitch, sound, spool, surge, swell, swing, swirl, throw, twirl, twist, wheel, whirl 6 billow, gyrate, muster, roster, rotate, rumble, scroll, tumble 7 booming, catalog, entwine, resound, revolve, rocking, thunder, tossing, turning 8 cylinder, drumbeat, drumming, rumbling, schedule, tumbling, undulate 9 inventory 10 undulation 11 reverberate 13 reverberation 15 turn over and over

Rolland, Romain
author of: 14 Jean-Christophe 16 The Soul Enchanted

rollicking 3 gay 5 happy, jolly, merry, sunny 6 bright, hearty, jocund, jovial, joyous, lively 7 gleeful, jocular, playful, romping 8 cheerful, mirthful, spirited 9 exuberant, gamboling, sparkling, sprightly 10 frolicking, frolicsome, hysterical, rip-roaring 12 lighthearted

Rolvaag, Ole Edvart
author of: 15 Peder Victorious, Their Father's God 16 Giants in the Earth

roly-poly 3 fat 5 obese, plump, pudgy, round 6 chubby, rotund 9 corpulent

roman 5 novel 17 metrical narrative

Roman Catholic church
council/synod: 4 Pisa 5 Basel, Trent 6 Nicaea, Vienne, Whitby 7 Ephesus, Pistoia, Sardica 9 Chalcedon, Constance 12 First Vatican 13 Fourth Lateran, Second Vatican 14 Constantinople 15 Ferrara-Florence
official Vatican yearbook: 18 Annuario Pontificio
first Christian emperor: 11 Constantine
gifts of territory/sovereignty to papacy: 15 Donation of Pepin 21 Donation of Constantine

romance 4 bosh, call, pull 5 amour, idyll, novel 6 affair, allure 7 fantasy, fiction 8 illusion 9 courtship, exoticism, fairy tale, fish story, invention, love story, melodrama, moonshine, tall story 10 attachment, concoction, flirtation, love affair 11 fabrication, fascination, imagination 12 exaggeration, relationship, self-delusion 13 flight of fancy, tender passion 16 affair of the heart

Romance language see 5 Latin

Romances sans paroles
author: 12 Paul Verlaine

Romancing the Stone
director: 14 Robert Zemeckis
cast: 11 Danny De Vito 14 Kathleen Turner, Michael Douglas
sequel: 17 The Jewel of the Nile

Roman Holiday
director: 12 William Wyler
cast: 11 Eddie Albert, Gregory Peck 13 Audrey Hepburn
Oscar for: 7 actress (Hepburn)

Romania
other name: 7 Rumania
capital/largest city: 9 Bucharest
others: 4 Aiud, Arad, Cluj, Deva, Iasi 5 Bacau, Balta, Cerna, Jassy, Neamt, Sibiu, Turnu, Yassy 6 Braila, Brasov, Brasso, Eforie, Galatz, Galeti, Lupeni, Mamaia, Oradea, Sighet 7 Bendery, Craiova, Focsani, Giurgiu, Ploesti, Severin 8 Bloiesti, Cernavti, Chisinau, Irongate, Kishenef, Satu-Mare, Temesvar 9 Constanta, Kolozsvar, Timisoara 10 Czernowitz 11 Klausenburg
school: 4 Cuza
division: 4 Alba, Iasi 5 Banat, Bihor, Jassy 6 Ardeal 7 Dobruja 8 Bucovina, Bukovina, Dobrogea, Moldavia, Walachia 9 Maramures 10 Bessarabia 12 Transylvania
  Roman province: 5 Dacia
measure: 7 faltche
monetary unit: 3 ban, lei, leu, lev, ley 4 bani 5 uncia 6 triens
lake: 5 Sinoe 6 Snagov
mountain: 5 Banat, Bihor 6 Codrul, Rodnei 7 Apuseni, Balkans, Caliman, Fagaras 8 Pietrosu 9 Moldavian 10 Carpathian, Moldoveanu 17 Transylvanian Alps
highest point: 11 Moldoveanul
river: 3 Alt, Jui, Olt 4 Prut 5 Aluta, Arges, Buzdu, Moros, Mures, Oltul, Schyl, Siret, Somes, Timis, Vedea 6 Crasna, Danube 7 Argesul 8 Bistrita, Ialomita, Iniester 9 Dimbovita, Jiul Mures
sea: 5 Black
physical feature:
  canal: 4 Bega
  forest: 6 Snagov 7 Baneasa
  gorge: 8 Iron Gate
  peninsula: 6 Balkan
  plain: 5 Banat 9 Moldavian, Walachian 13 Prahova Valley
  plateau: 7 Dobruja
  wind: 6 crivat
people: 6 Dacian 8 Romanian, Rumanian
  artist: 8 Brancusi
  author: 7 Ionesco
  composer: 6 Enesco
  leader: 6 Carol I 7 Michael, Iliescu 8 Ioan Cuza 9 Ceausescu 12 Gheorghiu-Dej, Ion Antonescu
language: 6 French, Magyar 7 Russian 8 Romanian, Rumanian 9 Hungarian
religion: 7 Judaism 8 Lutheran 9 Calvinism, Unitarian 10 Protestant 13 Roman Catholic 16 Romanian Orthodox
place:
  castle: 4 Bran 7 Huniady
  church: 5 Golia 9 Mihaivoda 10 Cretulescu, Patriarchy 11 Curtea Veche, Stavropdeos, Trei Ierarhi
  monastery: 5 Humor 6 Arbore 7 Voronet 8 Sucerita 9 Moldovita
  museum: 11 Peles Castle
  palace: 9 mogosoaia
  park: 7 Baneasa
  resort: 5 Venus 6 Eforie, Mamaia, Neptun 7 Jupiter 10 Costinesti
feature:
  community gathering: 9 sezatoare
  game: 4 oina
food:
  dish: 6 ciorba 7 mititei, sarmala 8 mamaliga 11 imam bayildi
  plum brandy: 5 tuica
Roman measure 2 as 5 cubit, libra 6 pondus 7 stadium

Roman Mythology
collective name for gods: 6 Superi
goddess of anguish: 8 Angerona
goddess of agriculture: 5 Ceres 6 Dea Dia, Vacuna 13 Acca Laurentia
  Ceres corresponds to Greek: 7 Demeter
goddess of the arts: 7 Minerva
  corresponds to Greek: 6 Athena
goddess of baking: 6 Fornax
goddess of chastity: 5 Fauna 7 Bona Dea
goddess of childbirth: 5 Parca 6 Lucina, Matuta, Parcae 11 Mater Matuta
goddess of the dawn: 6 Aurora, Matuta 11 Mater Matuta
  Aurora corresponds to Greek: 3 Eos
goddess of destiny: 5 Parca 6 Parcae

goddess of discord: 9 Discordia
goddess of door hinges: 6 Cardea
goddess of the earth: 6 Tellus
  corresponds to Greek: 4 Gaea
goddess of the family: 6 Cardea
goddess of fertility: 5 Fauna **6** Libera, Tellus **7** Bona Dea
  Libera corresponds to Greek: 10 Persephone
  Tellus corresponds to Greek: 4 Gaea
goddess of flowers: 5 Flora
goddess of fortune: 7 Fortuna
  corresponds to Greek: 5 Tyche
goddess of fruit trees: 6 Pomona
goddess of gardens: 5 Venus
  corresponds to Greek: 9 Aphrodite
goddess of grain/protectress against grain blight: 9 Robigo
goddess of harbors: 6 Matuta **11** Mater Matuta
goddess of harmony: 9 Concordia
goddess of the hearth: 4 Caca **5** Salus, Vesta
  Salus corresponds to Greek: 6 Hygeia
goddess of heaven: 4 Juno
  corresponds to Greek: 4 Hera
goddess of hunting: 5 Diana
  corresponds to Greek: 6 Phoebe **7** Artemis
goddess of longevity: 11 Anna Perenna
goddess of love: 5 Venus
  corresponds to Greek: 9 Aphrodite
goddess of marriage: 4 Juno **6** Tellus
  corresponds to Greek: 4 Gaea, Hera
goddess of marshes: 6 Marica **9** Dea Marica
goddess of the moon: 5 Diana
  corresponds to Greek: 6 Phoebe **7** Artemis
goddess of peace: 3 Pax **9** Concordia
  Pax corresponds to Greek: 5 Irene
goddess of pleasure: 8 Voluptas
goddess of plenty: 3 Ops **10** Magna Mater
goddess of prosperity: 5 Salus
  corresponds to Greek: 6 Hygeia
goddess of the sea: 6 Matuta **11** Mater Matuta
goddess of sleeping infants: 6 Cunina
goddess of the spring: 5 Venus
  corresponds to Greek: 9 Aphrodite
goddess of storms: 11 Tempestates
goddess of victory: 8 Victoria
  corresponds to Greek: 4 Nike
goddess of vineyards: 6 Libera
  corresponds to Greek: 10 Persephone
goddess of war: 7 Bellona
  corresponds to Greek: 5 Enyon
goddess of wine: 6 Libera
  corresponds to Greek: 10 Persephone

goddess of wisdom: 7 Minerva
  corresponds to Greek: 6 Athena
god of agriculture: 5 Picus **6** Saturn **7** Eventus **12** Bonus Eventus
  corresponds to Greek: 6 Cronos, Cronus, Kronos
god of beginnings: 5 Janus
god of boundaries: 8 Terminus
god of commerce: 7 Mercury
  corresponds to Greek: 6 Hermes
god of the dead: 7 Veiovis
god of doorways: 5 Janus
god of drinking/revelry: 5 Comus
god of eloquence: 7 Mercury
  corresponds to Greek: 6 Hermes
god of farm boundaries: 8 Silvanus, Sylvanus
god of fertility: 7 Mutinus, Priapus **8** Lupercus, Picumnus
god of fire/metalworking: 6 Vulcan
  corresponds to Greek: 10 Hephaestus, Hephaistos
god of forest: 7 Virbius
god of gardens: 9 Vertumnus
god of good counsel: 3 Ops **6** Consus
god of grain/protector against grain blight: 7 Robigus
god of healing: 11 Aesculapius
  corresponds to Greek: 9 Asclepius
god of heavens: 4 Jove **7** Jupiter
  corresponds to Greek: 4 Zeus
god of herds: 8 Silvanus, Sylvanus
god of horse racing: 3 Ops **6** Consus
god of hospitality: 6 Sancus **10** Dius Fidius, Semo Sancus
god of the house: 8 Silvanus, Sylvanus
god of hunting: 7 Virbius
god of international affairs: 6 Sancus **10** Dius Fidius, Semo Sancus
god of landmarks: 8 Terminus
god of light: 6 Apollo
god of love: 4 Amor **5** Cupid
  corresponds to Greek: 4 Eros
god of luck: 7 Eventus **12** Bonus Eventus
god of medicine: 11 Aesculapius
  corresponds to Greek: 9 Asclepius
god of music: 6 Apollo
god of oaths: 6 Sancus **10** Dius Fidius, Semo Sancus
god of orchards: 9 Vertumnus
god of ports/harbors: 8 Portunus
god of prosperity: 7 Eventus **12** Bonus Eventus
god of the rising sun: 5 Janus
god of science: 7 Mercury
  corresponds to Greek: 6 Hermes
god of sea: 7 Neptune
  corresponds to Greek: 8 Poseidon
god of seasons: 9 Vertumnus
god of the setting sun: 5 Janus
god of sleep: 6 Somnus
  corresponds to Greek: 6 Hypnos, Hypnus
god of springs: 4 Fons
gods of sulphur springs (twins): 6 Palici

god of the sun: 3 Sol
  corresponds to Greek: 6 Helios **8** Hyperion
god of thievery: 7 Mercury
  corresponds to Greek: 6 Hermes
god of thunder: 7 Taranis
god of thunderstorms: 8 Summanus
god of the Tiber: 9 Tiberinus
god of uncultivated land: 8 Silvanus, Sylvanus
god of underworld: 3 Dis **5** Orcus **8** Dis Pater
  corresponds to Greek: 5 Pluto
god of war: 4 Mars **6** Mamers, Mavors **8** Quirinus
  corresponds to Greek: 4 Ares
god of weather: 4 Jove **7** Jupiter
god of weddings: 8 Talassio
  corresponds to Greek: 5 Hymen **9** Hymenaeus
god of the woods: 6 Faunus **8** Silvanus, Sylvanus
household gods: 5 lares **7** penates
nymphs/deities with gift of prophecy: 7 Camenae
  names: 6 Egeria **8** Carmenta **9** Antevorta, Postvorta
  correspond to Greek: 5 Muses
protectress of childbirth: 8 Carmenta
protectress of cows/oxen: 6 Bubona
protector of flocks/shepherds: 5 Pales
protectress of military age men: 8 Juventas
  corresponds to Greek: 4 Hebe
protectress of women: 5 Diana
  corresponds to Greek: 6 Phoebe **7** Artemis
protectress of women/marriage: 4 Juno
queen of heaven: 4 Juno
  corresponds to Greek: 4 Hera, Here
staff of Mercury: 8 Caduceus
troublesome ghosts: 7 lemures
romantic 4 fond **5** mushy, soppy **6** ardent, dreamy, loving, tender, unreal **7** amorous, devoted, fervent, flighty, idyllic, utopian **8** enamored, fanciful, quixotic **9** fantastic, idealized, imaginary, sensitive, visionary, whimsical **10** idealistic, improbable, passionate **11** extravagant, impassioned, impractical, rhapsodical, sentimental, unrealistic, warmhearted **12** melodramatic, preposterous
romanticize 8 idealize **9** embroider
Rome, ancient
  emperor: 4 Nero, Otho **5** Galba, Nerva, Titus **6** Trajan **7** Hadrian **8** Augustus, Caligula, Claudius, Commodus, Domitian, Tiberius **9** Caracalla, Vespasian, Vitellius **10** Diocletian **11** Constantine, Lucius Verus **13** Antoninus Pius **14** Marcus Aurelius
  emperor's bodyguard: 15 Praetorian Guard

first citizen title: 8 princeps
first triumvirate: 6 Caesar, Pompey 7 Crassus
foe: 4 Gaul 5 Spain 6 Cimbri 7 Perseus, Philip V, Pyrrhus, Teutons 8 Carthage, Hannibal, Iberians, Jugurtha, Samnites, Tarentum, Umbrians 9 Etruscans, Macedonia, Seleucids 11 Latin League 12 Antiochus III 13 Achaean League, Hamilcar Barca
general: 5 Sulla 6 Brutus, Marius, Pompey 7 Crassus 8 Octavian 10 Flamininus, Mark Antony 12 Julius Caesar 14 Caesar Augustus 20 Quintus Fabius Maximus, Scipio Africanus Major, Scipio Africanus Minor
king: 12 Ancus Marcius 13 Numa Pompilius 16 Sextus Tarquinius 17 Tarquinius Priscus (Tarquin the Elder) 18 Tarquinius Superbus (Tarquin the Proud)
reformer: 8 Gracchus
republican ruler: 6 consul 7 senator, tribune 8 plebeian 9 optimates, patrician, populares 10 magistrate
Roman peace: 9 Pax Romana
second triumvirate: 6 Antony 7 Lepidus 8 Octavian (Caesar Augustus)

Rome, Roma
airport: 8 Ciampino 15 Leonardo da Vinci
area: 9 Cinecitta (Cinema City) 10 Trastevere 11 Vatican City
capital of: 5 Italy 6 Latium 11 Papal States, Roman Empire
church: 8 St Peter's 11 San Giovanni 18 Santa Maria Maggiore 19 San Paolo Fuori le Mura
Italian: 4 Roma
landmark: 5 Forum 7 Capitol 8 Pantheon 9 catacombs, Colosseum 12 Palazzo Doria 13 Circus Maximus, Lateran Palace, Sistine Chapel, Vatican Palace, Villa Borghese 14 Palazzo Corsini, Villa Farnesina 16 Baths of Caracalla, Castel Sant'Angelo, Palazzo Barberini 17 Arch of Constantine 19 Saint Peter's Basilica
legendary founders: 5 Remus 6 Aeneas 7 Romulus
nickname: 11 Eternal City
mountain: 8 Apennine
museum: 5 Doria 7 Colonna, Corsini, Vatican 8 Borghese, National 10 Capitoline
river: 5 Tiber
school: 33 Conservatorio di Musica Santa Cecilia
sea: 10 Tyrrhenian
seven hills: 7 Caelian, Viminal 8 Aventine, Palatine, Quirinal 9 Esquiline 10 Capitoline
square/piazza: 6 Popolo, Spagna 7 Colonna, Venezia 9 Quirinale 11 Campidoglio
state within: 11 Vatican City
street: 9 Appian Way, Emmanuele 11

Via del Corso 13 Corso Vittorio
subway: 13 Metropolitana
Romeo 4 beau 5 lover, sheik, swain, wooer 7 Don Juan, gallant 8 Casanova, cavalier, Lothario 9 boyfriend, Lochinvar
French: 8 paramour
Latin: 9 inamorato
Romeo and Juliet
author: 18 William Shakespeare
character: 5 Nurse, Paris 6 Tybalt 8 Benvolio, Mercutio 13 Friar Laurence
family: 7 Capulet 8 Montague
setting: 6 Verona
Romeo and Juliet
director:
   1936 version: 11 George Cukor
   1968 version: 16 Franco Zeffirelli
based on play by: 18 William Shakespeare
cast:
   1936 version: 12 Leslie Howard, Norma Shearer 13 Basil Rathbone, Edna May Oliver, John Barrymore
   1968 version: 9 Milo O'Shea 11 John McEnery, Michael York 12 Olivia Hussey 14 Leonard Whiting
score: 8 Nino Rota
Romeo and Juliet
symphony by: 7 Berlioz
opera by: 6 Gounod
orchestral piece by: 11 Tchaikovsky
ballet by: 9 Prokofiev
Romney, George
born: 7 England 15 Dalton-in-Furness
artwork: 5 Circe 9 Joan of Arc 11 Mrs Robinson, Sensibility 12 Mrs Davenport, Saint Cecilia 19 Mrs Carwardine and Son 22 The Death of General Wolfe 24 The Levenson-Gower Children 26 Sir Christopher and Lady Sykes
Romola
author: 11 George Eliot
character: 5 Bardo, Tessa 10 Tito Melema 15 Baldassarre Calvo
romp 3 hop 4 skip 5 caper, cut up, frisk, sport 6 frolic, gambol 7 disport, rollick
Romulus
father: 4 Mars
mother: 4 Ilia 9 Rea Silvia 10 Rhea Silvia
twin brother: 5 Remus
raised by: 7 she-wolf 9 Faustulus 12 Acca Larentia
first king of: 4 Rome
founder of: 4 Rome
Romus
father: 6 Aeneas 8 Ascanius
possible founder of: 4 Rome
Roncalli, Angelo Giuseppe 13 Pope John XXIII 22 Pope John the Twenty-Third
Ronsard, Pierre de
author of: 17 Sonnets pour Helene
member of: 7 Pleiade

roofing 4 tile, turf 5 slate, terne 6 thatch 7 asphalt, ceiling, pantile, shingle 8 housetop
Roof of the World see 5 Tibet
rook 3 gyp 4 bilk, crow, dupe, gull 5 cheat, cozen, raven, trick 6 castle, fleece 7 deceive, defraud, swindle 8 chessman 9 bamboozle, victimize
rookie 4 tyro 6 novice 8 beginner 9 fledgling, greenhorn 10 apprentice, tenderfoot
Rookies, The
character: 9 Jill Danko, (Officer) Mike Danko 10 (Lt) Eddie Ryker, (Officer) Chris Owens 12 (Officer) Terry Webster, (Officer) Willie Gillis
cast: 11 Kate Jackson, Sam Melville 14 Bruce Fairbairn, Michael Ontkean 16 Gerald S O'Loughlin 18 Georg Stanford Brown
room 4 area 5 range, scope, space 6 chance, extent, leeway, margin, volume 7 chamber, cubicle, expanse, lodging 9 allowance, provision, territory 11 compartment
French: 5 salle
Spanish: 4 sala
Room at the Top
director: 11 Jack Clayton
based on novel by: 10 John Braine
cast: 12 Heather Sears 14 Laurence Harvey, Simone Signoret 16 Hermione Baddeley
Oscar for: 7 actress (Signoret)
sequel: 11 Man at the Top 12 Life at the Top
Room 222
character: 6 Bernie 9 Pete Dixon 11 Liz McIntyre 12 Alice Johnson 14 Seymour Kaufman
cast: 11 Lloyd Haynes 13 David Jolliffe 14 Denise Nicholas, Karen Valentine 18 Michael Constantine
school: 15 Walt Whitman High
roomy 3 big 4 huge, long, vast, wide 5 ample, broad, large 7 immense, lengthy, sizable 8 generous, spacious 9 boundless, capacious, expansive, extensive, unlimited 10 commodious
Rooney, Mickey
real name: 9 Joe Yule Jr
born: 10 Brooklyn NY
wife: 10 Ava Gardner 13 Martha Vickers
co-star: 11 Judy Garland
roles: 4 Puck 8 Boys' Town 9 Andy Hardy 11 Sugar Babies 13 Mickey McGuire 14 Baby Face Nelson, National Velvet, The Human Comedy 21 A Midsummer Night's Dream 30 The Adventures of Huckleberry Finn
Roosevelt, Franklin Delano
presidential rank: 12 thirty-second
party: 10 Democratic
state represented: 2 NY
defeated: 5 (Jacob Sechler) Coxey, (John W) Aiken, (Thomas Edmund)

Dewey, (William) Lemke **6** (Alfred Mossman) Landon, (Claude A) Watson, (David Leigh) Colvin, (Herbert Clark) Hoover, (Norman) Thomas, (Roger Ward) Babson, (William David) Upshaw, (William Hope) Harvey, (William Zebulon) Foster **7** (Earl Russell) Browder, (Wendell Lewis) Willkie **8** (Edward A) Teichert, (Verne L) Reynolds

vice president: 6 (Harry S) Truman, (John Nance) Garner **7** (Henry Agard) Wallace

cabinet:
  state: 4 (Cordell) Hull **10** (Edward Reilly) Stettinius (Jr)
  treasury: 6 (William Hartman) Woodin **10** (Henry) Morgenthau (Jr)
  war: 4 (George Henry) Dern **7** (Henry Lewis) Stimson **8** (Harry Hines) Woodring
  attorney general: 6 (Francis) Biddle, (Frank) Murphy **7** (Robert Houghwout) Jackson **8** (Homer Stille) Cummings
  navy: 4 (Frank) Knox **6** (Charles) Edison **7** (Claude Augustus) Swanson **9** (James Vincent) Forrestal
  postmaster general: 6 (Frank Comerford) Walker, (James Aloysius) Farley
  interior: 5 (Harold LeClaire) Ickes
  agriculture: 7 (Claude Raymond) Wickard, (Henry Agard) Wallace
  commerce: 5 (Daniel Calhoun) Roper, (Jesse Holman) Jones **7** (Henry Agard) Wallace, (Henry Lloyd) Hopkins
  labor: 7 (Frances) Perkins (Wilson)

born: 10 Hyde Park NY
died: 13 Warm Springs GA **16** Little White House
buried: 10 Hyde Park NY
education:
  prep school: 6 Groton
  university: 7 Harvard
  law school: 8 Columbia
religion: 12 Episcopalian
interests: 3 art **4** polo **6** tennis, travel **7** fishing, hunting **8** shooting
vacation spot: 13 Warm Springs GA **16** Campobello Island (Canada)
dog: 4 Fala
author: 27 The Happy Warrior: Alfred E Smith
political career: 12 state senator
  assistant secretary of: 4 Navy
  governor of: 7 New York
civilian career: 6 lawyer **11** bank officer
notable events of lifetime/term: 4 D-Day, WWII **7** New Deal **10** atomic bomb, Depression, World War II **11** World War Two **13** United Nations **15** Atlantic Charter
  act: 9 Lend-Lease
  attack on: 11 Pearl Harbor

  conference: 5 Cairo, Yalta **7** Arcadia, Crimean, Teheran
  scandal: 11 Tammany Hall
quote: 24 A day that will live in infamy **31** Meet every day's troubles as they come **36** The only thing we have to fear is fear itself **50** This generation of Americans has a rendezvous with destiny **53** I pledge you I pledge myself to a new deal for the American people
father: 5 James
mother: 4 Sara (Delano)
siblings:
  half-brother: 5 James
wife: 7 (Anna) Eleanor (Roosevelt)
children: 5 James **7** Elliott **11** Anna Eleanor **13** John Aspinwell **14** Franklin Delano
first lady:
  author: 7 On My Own **13** This I Remember, This Is My Story **34** The Autobiography of Eleanor Roosevelt
  chairwoman: 25 UN Commission on Human Rights
  codirector: 23 Office of Civilian Defense
  member: 35 Democratic National Campaign Committee
  newspaper column: 5 My Day
  US delegate to: 2 UN

Roosevelt, Theodore
nickname: 5 Teddy
presidential rank: 11 twenty-sixth
party: 10 Republican
state represented: 2 NY
succeeded: 8 McKinley
defeated (second term): 4 (Eugene Victor) Debs **6** (Alton Brooks) Parker, (Thomas Edward) Watson **7** (Austin) Holcomb, (Silas Comfort) Swallow **8** (Charles Hunter) Corregan
vice president: 4 none (1st term) **9** (Charles Warren) Fairbanks
cabinet:
  state: 3 (John Milton) Hay **4** (Elihu) Root **5** (Robert) Bacon
  treasury: 4 (Leslie Mortier) Shaw, (Lyman Judson) Gage **9** (George Bruce) Cortelyou
  war: 4 (Elihu) Root, (William Howard) Taft **6** (Luke Edward) Wright
  attorney general: 4 (Philander Chase) Knox **5** (William Henry) Moody **9** (Charles Joseph) Bonaparte
  navy: 4 (John Davis) Long **5** (William Henry) Moody **6** (Paul) Morton **7** (Victor Howard) Metcalf **8** (Truman Handy) Newberry **9** (Charles Joseph) Bonaparte
  postmaster general: 5 (Charles Emory) Smith, (George von Lengerke) Meyer, (Henry Clay) Payne, (Robert John) Wynne **9** (George Bruce) Cortelyou

  interior: 8 (James Rudolph) Garfield **9** (Ethan Allen) Hitchcock
  agriculture: 6 (James) Wilson
  commerce and labor: 6 (Oscar Solomon) Straus **7** (Victor Howard) Metcalf **9** (George Bruce) Cortelyou
born: 13 New York City NY
died/buried: 2 NY **9** Oyster Bay **10** Long Island
education:
  university: 7 Harvard
  law school: 8 Columbia (did not graduate)
religion: 13 Dutch Reformed
interests: 7 hunting (African game), writing **9** exploring (South America) **14** natural history
author: 11 Rough Riders **14** Oliver Cromwell **16** Gouverneur Morris, Thomas Hart Benton **17** African Game Trails, The New Nationalism **19** The Winning of the West **20** Letters to His Children **21** America and the World War
political career: 13 Vice President **15** NY State Assembly **24** US Civil Service Commission
  assistant secretary: 4 Navy
  governor of: 7 New York
  organized party: 9 Bull Moose **11** Progressive
civilian career: 6 author **7** rancher **14** public lecturer
military service: 15 NY National Guard **18** Spanish-American War
  organized cavalry regiment: 11 Rough Riders
  led charge up: 11 San Juan Hill
notable events of lifetime/term: 5 Panic (of 1907) **10** Square Deal **15** Nobel Peace Prize **22** San Francisco earthquake
  Act: 11 Reclamation **14** Meat Inspection **15** Hepburn Railroad, Pure Food and Drug
  bureau of: 12 Corporations **28** Immigration and Naturalization
  first flight by: 14 Wright Brothers
  revolution: 6 Panama
  treaty: 13 Hay-Pauncefote **15** Hay-Bunau-Varilla
quotes: 25 Hasten forward quickly there **28** Speak softly and carry a big stick
father: 8 Theodore
mother: 6 Martha (Bulloch)
siblings: 4 Anna **7** Corinne, Elliott
wife: 5 Alice (Hathaway Lee), Edith (Kermit Carow)
children: 6 Kermit **7** Quentin **8** Alice Lee, Theodore **10** Ethel Carow **16** Archibald Bulloch

rooster
young: 8 cockerel
root 3 fix, set **4** back, base, bind, bulb, clap, hail, nail, rise, stem **5** basis, boost, cheer, fount, radix, start, stick,

tubes **6** bottom, fasten, ground, motive, origin, reason, second, source, spring **7** acclaim, applaud, bolster, cheer on, pull for, radicle, support **8** fountain, occasion, shout for **9** beginning, encourage, establish, inception, rationale **10** derivation, foundation, mainspring **11** fundamental **12** commencement, fountainhead

Root, John Wellborn
partner: **14** Daniel H Burnham
architect of: **10** The Rookery **12** Hotel Statler (Washington DC), Montauk Block **13** Hotel Tamanaco (Caracas) **17** Monadnock Building, Palmolive Building (Chicago) **19** Rand-McNally Building

root for 5 boost **6** urge on **7** cheer on, pull for

root out 5 dig up **6** remove **7** extract, pull out, uncover, unearth **8** discover **9** extirpate, ferret out **12** bring to light

Roots
author: **9** Alex Haley
character: **3** Tom **4** Ames, Bell, Noah **5** Binta, Fanta, Grill, Irene, Kizzy, Lewis, Mingo, Omoro **6** Justin, Martha, Ordell **7** Fiddler, Gardner, Nyo Boto **8** Kintango, Mathilda, Mrs Moore, Tom Moore **9** Evan Brent, Missy Anne **10** Brima Cesay, Capt Davies, Carrington, Jemmy Brent, Kadi Touray, Kunta Kinte, Sam Bennett, Sister Sara **11** Mrs Reynolds, Squire James **12** John Reynolds **13** Chicken George **14** Sir Eric Russell, Stephen Bennett **15** Ol' George Johnson, Third Mate Slater **17** Dr William Reynolds
cast: **8** Burl Ives, John Amos, Ren Woods **9** Ben Vereen, Brad Davis, Moses Gunn, O J Simpson, Vic Morrow **10** Billy Hicks, Ian McShane, John Schuck, Lynne Moody, Olivia Cole, Paul Shenar, Ralph Waite, Robert Reed **11** Beverly Todd, Cicely Tyson, Doug McClure, Edward Asner, Gary Collins, Harry Rhodes, Lane Binkley, LeVar Burton, Lorne Greene, Maya Angelou, Sandy Duncan **12** Carolyn Jones, Chuck Connors, Leslie Uggams, Lloyd Bridges **13** Louis Gosset Jr, Madge Sinclair, William Watson **14** George Hamilton, Lynda Day George, Macdonald Carey **15** Lillian Randolph, Scatman Crothers, Thalmus Rasulala **16** Raymond St Jacques, Richard Roundtree **18** Georg Stanford Brown **20** Lawrence Hilton-Jacobs

rope 3 gad, guy, tie, tow **4** bind, cord, fast, guss, hemp, line, lure, snag, trap, wire, yarn **5** cable, catch, chord, lasso, noose, riata, shank, strap, twine **6** corral, entice, hawser, lariat, seduce, string, tether **7** bobstay, cordage, halyard, lanyard, lashing, painter

8 dragline, restrain
fiber: **5** sisal

Rosaline
character in: **16** Love's Labour's Lost
author: **11** Shakespeare

rose 4 Rosa
varieties: **3** bog, dog, sun, tea, wax **4** baby, gold, moss, musk, rock, rush, sand, wood **5** briar, brier, China, fairy, field, malva, Ophir, pygmy, swamp **6** Alpine, Burnet, copper, cotton, damask, desert, French, ground, Karroo, Lenten, mallow, Nootka, Scotch, velvet **7** baby sun, Banksia, Bourbon, cabbage, cluster, Guelder, Manetti, pasture, prairie, rambler **8** Burgundy, Champney, Cherokee, chestnut, cinnamon, climbing, Japanese, Memorial, mountain, Noisette **9** Christmas, evergreen, hybrid tea, McCartney, Polyantha, Remontant, Turkestan **10** California, Chinquapin, shaggy-rock, underwater **11** confederate, giant velvet, hairy alpine **12** green Mexican, Hawaiian wood, Seven-sisters, white Mexican **13** Himalayan musk, Hybrid Bourbon, Persian yellow, Stuart's desert **15** hybrid perpetual **16** York-and-Lancaster

Rose, Pete (Peter Edward)
nickname: **13** Charlie Hustle
sport: **8** baseball
position: **7** baseman **8** outfield
team: **14** Cincinnati Reds **20** Philadelphia Phillies
scandal: **8** gambling

Roseanne
former name: **4** Barr **6** Arnold
husband: **3** Tom **6** Thomas
television:
show: **8** Roseanne
husband: **3** Dan
children: **2** DJ **5** Becky **7** Darlene
sister: Jackie
town: Lanford

Rosedale, Mr
character in: **15** The House of Mirth
author: **7** Wharton

Rosemary's Baby
director: **13** Roman Polanski
based on novel by: **8** Ira Levin
cast: **9** Mia Farrow **10** Ruth Gordon **14** John Cassavetes, Sidney Blackmer
Oscar for: **17** supporting actress (Gordon)

Rosenberg, Stuart
director of: **12** Cool Hand Luke

Rosenbloom, Maxie
nickname: **12** Slapsie Maxie
sport: **6** boxing
class: **16** light heavyweight

Rosencrantz
character in: **6** Hamlet
associated with: **12** Guildenstern
author: **11** Shakespeare

Rosenkavalier, Der

also: **18** The Knight of the Rose
opera by: **7** (Richard) Strauss
character: **6** Sophie **8** Octavian **9** Baron Ochs **11** Marschallin (Princess von Werderberg)

Rose of Sharon
character in: **16** The Grapes of Wrath
author: **9** Steinbeck

Rose Tattoo, The
director: **10** Daniel Mann
based on play by: **17** Tennessee Williams
cast: **11** Anna Magnani **13** Burt Lancaster
Oscar for: **7** actress (Magnani)

rosiness 5 bloom, blush, flush **7** redness **8** pinkness

Ross, Barney
real name: **14** Barnet Rosofsky
sport: **6** boxing
class: **12** welterweight

Ross, Herbert
director of: **14** The Goodbye Girl **15** The Turning Point

Ross, Katharine
born: **12** Los Angeles CA
aunt: **16** Katharine Hepburn
roles: **9** The Colbys **11** The Graduate **13** Stepford Wives **29** Butch Cassidy and the Sundance Kid

Rossellini, Roberto
director of: **6** Paisan **8** Open City **9** Stromboli **10** The Miracle **15** Germany Year Zero
wife: **13** Ingrid Bergman
daughter: **8** Isabella

Rossen, Robert
director of: **11** Body and Soul **14** All the King's Men

Rossetti, Dante Gabriel
author of: **17** The Blessed Damozel
born: **6** London **7** England
group: **14** Pre-Raphaelites
artwork: **12** Beata Beatrix **15** The Annunciation **17** Ecce Ancilla Domini

Rossini, Gioacchino Antonio
born: **5** Italy **6** Pesaro
composer of: **5** Moise **6** Otello **8** Tancredi **10** Le Comte Ory, Semiramide **11** William Tell **12** Mose in Egitto **13** Guillaume Tell, La Cenerentola **15** Barber of Seville **20** Il Barbiere di Siviglia **22** La Cambiale di Matrimonio

Rossner, Judith
author of: **11** Attachments **14** Ordinary People **19** Looking for Mr Goodbar

Rostand, Edmond
author of: **7** L'Aiglon **10** Chantecler **12** The Romancers **16** Cyrano de Bergerac

roster 4 list, roll **5** cadre, panel, slate **6** agenda, docket, muster, record **7** catalog, listing, posting **8** register, schedule **9** catalogue, directory

rostrum 4 dais **5** stage, stand, stump **6**

podium, pulpit **7** lectern, soapbox **8** platform

Roswell
- **network: 2** WB
- **cast: 9** Jason Behr (Max Evans) **10** Colin Hanks (Alex Whitman) **11** Brendan Fehr (Michael Guerin) **12** Nick Wechsler (Kyle Valenti), Shiri Appleby (Liz Parker) **13** Adam Rodriguez (Jesse Ramirez), Emilie de Ravin (Tess Harding), William Sadler (Jim Valenti) **14** Katherine Heigl (Isabel Evans) **15** Majandra Delfino (Maria DeLuca)

rosy 4 pink **5** ruddy **6** bright, florid **7** flushed, glowing, hopeful, reddish **8** blooming, blushing, cheerful, cheering, flushing, inflamed, rubicund **9** confident, favorable, promising, reddening, rubescent **10** auspicious, felicitous, optimistic, propitious, reassuring **11** encouraging, high-colored, inspiriting **13** full of promise

Roszak, Theodore
- **born: 6** Poland, Poznan
- **artwork: 5** Raven, Surge **7** Anguish **9** Chrysalis, Scavenger, Sea Quarry **11** Sea Sentinel **12** Amorphic Form, Thorn Blossom **18** Specter of Kitty Hawk **20** The Whaler of Nantucket **27** Recollections of the Southwest

rot 3 mar **4** bosh, bull, bunk, harm, hurt, warp **5** decay, go bad, spoil, stain, taint, trash **6** damage, debase, defile, drivel, impair, infect, injure, jabber, molder, poison **7** blather, corrupt, crumble, deprave, inanity, pervert, pollute, putrefy, rubbish, twaddle **8** flummery, folderol, nonsense, putresce **9** absurdity, decompose, gibberish, moonshine, poppycock, purulence, putridity **10** balderdash, corruption, degenerate, flapdoodle **11** contaminate, deteriorate, putrescence **12** disintegrate, fiddle-faddle, gobbledygook, putrefaction **13** contamination, decomposition, deterioration **14** disintegration **16** stuff and nonsense

rotate 4 eddy, reel, roll, spin, turn **5** pivot, swirl, twirl, twist, wheel, whirl **6** change, circle, gyrate, swivel **7** revolve **9** alternate, circulate, pirouette **11** interchange

Roth, Philip
- **author of: 8** The Facts **13** The Human Stain **14** The Dying Animal **15** Goodbye Columbus **16** American Pastoral, Operation Shylock, The Anatomy Lesson, Zuckerman Unbound **17** Portnoy's Complaint **21** The Plot Against America

Rothko, Mark
- **born: 6** Dvinsk, Latvia, Russia **16** Daugavpils Latvia
- **artwork: 5** Light **12** Central Green, Earth and Blue **14** Four Darks in Red

rotten 3 bad **4** base, foul, rank **5** dirty, fetid, nasty, reeky, venal **6** filthy, putrid, rancid, scurvy **7** corrupt, crooked, decayed, devious, immoral, tainted, very bad, vicious **8** criminal, decaying, indecent, purulent, two-faced **9** deceitful, dishonest, dissolute, faithless, insincere, mercenary, moldering, putrefied, worm-eaten **10** decomposed, iniquitous, putrescent, scurrilous, unpleasant, villainous **11** decomposing, disgraceful, treacherous **12** contemptible, dishonorable, unforgivable, unscrupulous **13** double-dealing, untrustworthy

rotter 3 cad, cur, rat **4** heel **5** knave, louse, rogue **6** no-good, rascal **7** bounder, caitiff, villain **9** scoundrel

rotund 3 fat **5** obese, ovate, ovoid, plump, pudgy, round, stout, tubby **6** chubby, curved, fleshy, portly **7** bulbous, lumpish, rounded **8** circular, globular **9** corpulent, egg-shaped, spherical **10** potbellied **11** full-fleshed

Rouault, Georges
- **born: 5** Paris **6** France
- **artwork: 3** Mr X **5** Clown **8** Le Chahut, Miserere, Twilight **9** The Mirror **10** The Old King **11** Fleurs du mal, The Holy Face **12** Head of a Clown **13** Little Olympia **14** The Three Judges **19** Small Family of Clowns **22** Christ Mocked by Soldiers **26** Les Reincarnations du Pere Ubu **28** The Child Jesus among the Doctors

roue 3 cad, rip **4** rake, wolf **6** lecher, wanton **7** bounder, dallier, Don Juan, playboy, seducer, trifler **8** Casanova, debauche, Lothario, rakehell **9** libertine, womanizer **10** profligate **11** philanderer, skirt-chaser

Rouget de Lisle 17 French army officer
- **composer of: 14** La Marseillaise

rough 3 raw **4** beat, hard, rude, wild **5** bluff, blunt, bumpy, crude, cruel, draft, green, gruff, harsh, hasty, husky, quick, raspy, rocky, scaly, sharp, surly, tough, vague **6** abrupt, beat on, broken, brutal, callow, choppy, clumsy, coarse, craggy, crusty, gauche, hoarse, jagged, knotty, ragged, raging, roiled, rugged, savage, severe, stormy, thrash, turbid, uneven, vulgar **7** austere, awkward, bearish, boorish, brusque, chapped, coarsen, drastic, extreme, general, gnarled, grating, ill-bred, inexact, jarring, loutish, outline, rasping, raucous, scraggy, sketchy, stubbly, uncouth, unlevel, untamed, violent **8** agitated, churlish, rigorous, scabrous, scratchy, strident, ungentle, unsmooth **9** brutalize, difficult, ferocious, imperfect, imprecise, inelegant, irregular, manhandle, sketch out, stringent, turbulent, uncourtly, unfeeling, ungenteel, unmusical, unrefined **10** discord-ant, incomplete, indelicate, push around, tumultuous, unfinished, ungracious, unmannerly, unpleasant, unpolished **11** approximate, cacophonous, ill-mannered, preliminary, rudimentary, tempestuous, unluxurious **12** inharmonious **13** inconsiderate, uncomfortable, ungentlemanly

rough going 8 struggle **10** difficulty **11** arduousness **13** laboriousness

Roughing It
- **author: 9** Mark Twain
- **character: 12** Brigham Young, Hank Erickson **16** Slade the Terrible

rough it 4 camp **7** camp out

roughneck 4 hood, lout, punk **5** bully, rowdy, tough **6** vandal **7** hoodlum, ruffian **8** hooligan **9** barbarian **10** delinquent

roughness 7 crudity **8** acrimony, aviation, pungency, violence **9** gruffness, harshness, vulgarity **10** coarseness, inelegance, unevenness, unkindness **11** raucousness **12** irregularity, unsmoothness, unrefinement **13** undevelopment

Rough Riders see Roosevelt, Theodore

rough sketch 5 draft **7** cartoon, outline

rough-textured 5 harsh **6** coarse, nubbly, shaggy, tweedy **7** bristly, prickly **8** scratchy **9** bristling **10** sandpapery

round 3 fat **4** full, oval **5** cycle, obese, orbed, ovate, ovoid, plump, pudgy, stout, total, tubby, whole **6** chubby, circle, curved, entire, fluent, intact, portly, rotund, series, smooth **7** flowing, globoid, perfect, rounded **8** circular, complete, globular, resonant, sonorous, spheroid, thorough, unbroken **9** corpulent, egg-shaped, spherical, undivided **10** ball-shaped, elliptical, harmonious, pear-shaped, procession, succession **11** cylindrical, full-fleshed, mellifluent, progression

roundabout 5 wordy **6** random, zigzag **7** devious, erratic, oblique, sinuous, winding **8** indirect, rambling, tortuous, twisting **9** desultory **10** circuitous, discursive, meandering, serpentine **12** labyrinthine **14** circumlocutory

roundaboutness 9 wandering **10** digression, meandering **11** indirection **14** circuitousness, circumlocution

rounded 6 convex **7** curving **11** protuberant

rounding out 10 developing **12** augmentation **13** amplification

rounding-out 10 complement, completion, perfecting **12** consummation

rounds 4 beat **5** route, skirt, watch **7** circuit

roundup 6 muster, resume **7** meeting,

summary **8** assembly **9** gathering **11** convocation

round up 6 gather, muster, summon **7** collect, convene, convoke, marshal **8** assemble **10** accumulate **12** call together

rouse 4 call, goad, move, prod, spur, stir, wake **5** arise, awake, get up, pique, rally, waken **6** awaken, excite, foment, kindle, incite, stir up, summon, turn on, wake up **7** animate, inflame, inspire, provoke, shake up **8** activate **9** galvanize, instigate, stimulate

roused 2 up **5** astir, awake **7** excited, incited, kindled, rallied, shook up **8** awakened, inflamed, inspired, out of bed, shaken up **9** stirred up **10** up and about

rousing 5 brisk, peppy **6** active, lively **8** animated, exciting, stirring, vigorous **9** awakening, inspiring **10** energizing, refreshing, remarkable **11** provocative, stimulating **12** exhilarating, intoxicating **13** extraordinary

Rousseau, Henri Julien Felix
 nickname: **10** Le Douanier
 born: **5** Laval **6** France
 artwork: **3** War **8** The Dream **12** Child on Rocks, The Waterfall **13** The Hungry Lion **15** Carnival Evening, The Snake Charmer **16** Bouquet of Flowers, The Sleeping Gypsy **17** The Poet and his Muse

Rousseau, Jean Jacques
 author of: **5** Emile **11** Confessions **17** La Nouvelle Heloise, The Social Contract

Rousseau, (Pierre Etienne) Theodore
 born: **5** Paris **6** France
 artwork: **7** Evening **12** After the Rain **15** Edge of the Forest, Under the Birches **18** Descent of the Cattle, Oak Trees at Apremont **19** The Marsh in the Landes **20** The Valley of Tiffauges **21** Meadow Bordered by Trees

roust 4 bust **5** rouse **6** arrest, hassle **7** capture, seizure **12** apprehension

rout 4 beat, drub, lick, ruin, trim **5** chaos, cream, crush, panic, quell, repel, worst **6** defeat, subdue, thrash **7** beating, clobber, conquer, licking, repulse, scatter **8** drive off, drubbing, lambaste, overcome, vanquish **9** chase away, drive away, overpower, overthrow **11** put to flight **15** disorganization **18** throw into confusion

route 3 run **4** beat, pass, path, road, ship, tack **5** remit, round, track **6** artery, course, detour, direct **7** circuit, highway, parkway, passage, roadway **8** dispatch, transmit, turnpike **9** boulevard, itinerary **10** throughway **12** thoroughfare

Route 66
 character: **8** Linc Case **9** Tod Stiles

10 Buz Murdock
 cast: **12** Glenn Corbett, Martin Milner **13** George Maharis
 car: **8** Corvette

routine 4 dull **5** order, usual **6** boring, custom, method, normal, system **7** formula, regular, tedious, typical **8** habitual, ordinary, periodic, practice **9** customary, operation, technique **11** arrangement, predictable **12** conventional, run-of-the-mill **13** unexceptional

rove 4 roam **5** drift, prowl, range **6** ramble, stroll, travel, wander **7** meander, traipse **9** gallivant

roving 6 errant **7** aimless, gadding, migrant, nomadic, roaming, vagrant **8** errantry, rambling, restless **9** desultory, itinerant, traveling, uncertain, wandering **10** changeable, discursive, meandering, inconstant **11** peripatetic **14** discursiveness

row 4 file, line, rank, spat, tier, tiff **5** brawl, chain, melee, queue, range, scrap, set-to, train, swords **6** column, fracas, scrape, series, string **7** echelon, quarrel, wrangle **8** argument, disorder, sequence, squabble **9** imbroglio, wrangling **10** difference, succession **11** altercation, contretemps

rowboat 3 gig **4** bark, dory **5** barge, canoe, dingy, scull, shell, skiff **6** barque, caique, dinghy, wherry
 seat: **4** taft

rowdy 6 unruly **7** lawless, raffish **9** roughneck **10** boisterous, disorderly **11** mischievous **12** obstreperous

Rowena, Lady
 character in: **7** Ivanhoe
 author: **5** Scott

rowing
 athlete: **10** James Dietz **14** Anthony Johnson

Rowlands, Gena
 real name: **23** Virginia Cathryn Rowlands
 born: **9** Cambria WI
 husband: **14** John Cassavetes
 roles: **5** Faces **11** Taking Lives, The Notebook **12** Opening Night **23** A Woman Under the Influence

Rowling, J.K. (Joanne Kathleen)
 born: **7** England **15** Chipping Sodbury
 author of: **17** Harry Potter and the.. **12** Goblet of Fire **14** Sorcerer's Stone **16** Chamber of Secrets, Half-Blood Prince **17** Order of the Phoenix, Prisoner of Azkaban

Roxana
 subtitle: **20** The Fortunate Mistress
 author: **11** Daniel Defoe

Roxane see Cyrano de Bergerac

royal 5 grand, regal **6** august, lavish, superb **7** stately **8** imposing, majestic, splendid **9** monarchal, sovereign **10** munificent **11** fit for a king, magnificent, resplendent

royalty 4 sway **7** command, majesty **8** dominion, hegemony, kingship, regality **9** queenship, supremacy **11** divine right, sovereignty

Royaume de Belgique see **7** Belgium
Roy Rogers Show, The
 regular: **8** Pat Brady **9** Dale Evans
 theme: **16** Happy Trails to You
 horse: **7** Trigger
 dog: **6** Bullet
 jeep: **10** Nellybelle
 ranch: **10** Double R Bar

Ruanda see **6** Rwanda

rub 4 buff, swab, wipe **5** annoy, braze, catch, chafe, clean, hitch, knead, pinch, scour, scrub, smear, thing, touch, trick **6** abrade, finger, handle, polish, secret, smooth, spread, strait, stroke **7** burnish, dilemma, massage, problem, rubdown, setback, slather, trouble **8** handling, hardship, kneading, obstacle, stroking **10** difficulty, impediment, manipulate **12** manipulation

Rubaiyat of Omar Khayyam, The
 author: **11** Omar Khayyam
 translator: **16** Edward FitzGerald

rubber, vulcanized
 invented by: **8** Goodyear

rubber plant 13 Ficus elastica
 varieties: **4** baby **5** dwarf **7** Chinese **8** American, creeping, Japanese **9** mistletoe **11** small-leaved **16** broadleaved India

rubberstamp 6 affirm **7** approve, endorse

rubber tree 10 Schefflera
 varieties: **4** Para **5** India **8** Castilla **11** West African

rubbery 5 tough **6** supple **7** elastic **8** flexible **9** resilient **11** stretchable

rubbing 7 chafing **8** abrading, scraping **12** manipulation

rubbish 3 rot **4** bosh, junk **5** dross, offal, trash, waste **6** babble, debris, drivel, idiocy, jetsam, litter, refuse, rubble **7** blather, garbage, inanity, twaddle **8** folderol, nonsense **9** gibberish, rigmarole, silliness **10** balderdash, flapdoodle, rigamarole

rubbish heap 4 dump **6** midden **10** refuse pile

rubble 4 junk, rock **5** brash, chalk, stent, stone, talus, trash **6** debris, refuse **7** rubbish **8** nonsense **9** fragments **11** foolishness

rube 3 oaf **4** boor, clod, hick **5** yokel **6** rustic **7** bumpkin, hayseed, peasant **10** clodhopper

Rube Goldberg 10 cartoonist
 known for: **23** complicated contraptions

rub elbows 3 mix **4** club **6** hobnob, mingle **7** consort, hang out **9** associate **10** fraternize

Rubens, Peter Paul
born: 6 Siegen 10 Westphalia
artwork: 8 Lion Hunt 10 The Rainbow 15 The Garden of Love 17 Laocoon and his Sons 18 Battle of the Amazons 20 The Raising of the Cross 21 Landscape with Het Steen 22 The Descent from the Cross 23 Altarpiece of St Aldefonso 26 The Adoration of the Shepherds 27 Marchesa Brigida Spinola-Doria, Mystic Marriage of St Catherine 29 Rape of the Daughters of Leucippus 34 Helene Fourment with Two of her Children

rubicund 3 red 4 rosy 5 ruddy 6 florid 7 flushed, reddish

rubidium
chemical symbol: 2 Rb

rub out 4 do in, kill, slay 5 erase 6 efface, murder 7 bump off, destroy, execute, expunge 8 massacre 10 obliterate, put to death 11 assassinate, exterminate

ruby
species: 8 corundum
source: 5 Burma, India, Mogok 7 Bangkok, Kashmir 8 Sri Lanka, Thailand
kind: 4 star
color: 3 red

ruckus 3 row 4 fray, to-do 5 brawl, broil, clash, fight, melee 6 battle, fracas, rumpus, uproar 7 scuffle 9 imbroglio 10 donnybrook, free-for-all 11 embroilment

ruddy 3 red 4 rosy 6 florid 7 flushed, reddish, roseate, scarlet 8 blushing, rubicund, sanguine 11 rosy-cheeked

rude 3 raw 4 wild 5 blunt, crude, fresh, green, gross, gruff, rough, saucy, sulky, surly 6 abrupt, callow, clumsy, coarse, crusty, gauche, homely, rugged, rustic, sullen, uneven, vulgar 7 abusive, artless, awkward, boorish, brusque, brutish, ill-bred, loutish, profane, scraggy, uncivil, uncouth 8 churlish, homebred, ignorant, impolite, impudent, indecent, insolent, slapdash, untaught 9 inelegant, insulting, makeshift, primitive, roughhewn, uncourtly, ungallant, unlearned, unrefined, untrained, untutored 10 illiterate, indecorous, indelicate, peremptory, provincial, uncultured, uneducated, ungraceful, ungracious, unladylike, unmannerly, unpolished 11 bad-mannered, countrified, impertinent, uncivilized, uncourteous, undignified 12 discourteous, roughly built 13 disrespectful, inconsiderate, ungentlemanly

rudeness 9 bluntness, impudence, insolence, sauciness 10 bad manners, coarseness, disrespect, incivility 11 boorishness, discourtesy 12 impertinence, impoliteness 14 ungraciousness 17 inconsiderateness

rudimentary 5 basic 6 simple 7 initial, primary 8 immature 9 elemental, formative, imperfect, premature, primitive, vestigial 10 elementary, incomplete, prototypal 11 undeveloped

rudiments 6 basics 7 essence 8 elements 9 beginning 10 principles 12 fundamentals

Rudolph, Paul
architect of: 16 Jewett Arts Center (Wellesley College) 24 Government Services Center (Boston) 28 School of Architecture Building (Yale)

rue 4 Ruta
varieties: 4 bush, lady, wall 5 goat's 6 common, meadow 10 tall meadow 11 early meadow 12 Alpine meadow

rue 5 mourn 6 bemoan, lament, regret, repent, repine 7 deplore

rueful 3 sad 5 sorry 6 woeful 7 doleful 8 contrite, mournful, dolorous, penitent, repining 9 depressed, plaintive, regretful, sorrowful, sorrowing 10 deplorable, lamentable, melancholy, remorseful, unpleasant

ruff 9 sandpiper
female: 3 ree

ruffian 4 hood, thug 5 brute, bully, crook, knave, rogue, rough, rowdy, tough 6 mugger 7 hoodlum, villain 8 gangster, hooligan 9 cutthroat, roisterer, roughneck, scoundrel 10 blackguard

ruffle 4 fold, muss, wave 5 frill, plait, pleat, ruche, upset 6 edging, excite, muss up, pucker, rimple, ripple, rumple 7 agitate, confuse, crinkle, disturb, flounce, perturb, roughen, trouble, wrinkle 8 disheveln, disorder, disquiet, furbelow, unsettle 9 aggravate, agitation, commotion, corrugate 10 disarrange, discompose, disconcert 11 disturbance

ruffled 5 upset, vexed 7 annoyed, frilled, nettled, pleated 8 agitated, flounced, troubled 9 nonplused, unsettled 10 nonplussed

ruffle one's feathers 3 vex 5 anger, annoy, pique 6 enrage, madden, nettle 7 incense, outrage, provoke 9 displease, infuriate

rugged 4 hale, hard, rude, wiry, worn 5 bumpy, hardy, harsh, husky, lined, rocky, rough, stern, tough 6 brawny, coarse, craggy, jagged, ridged, robust, severe, sinewy, sturdy, taxing, trying, uneven, virile 7 arduous, cragged, onerous, scraggy, uncouth 8 athletic, furrowed, muscular, stalwart, vigorous, wrinkled 9 difficult, graceless, irregular, laborious, masculine, roughhewn, strenuous, unrefined, weathered 12 uncultivated 13 weather-beaten

Ruggles of Red Gap
director: 10 Leo McCarey
cast: 9 ZaSu Pitts 10 Mary Boland 14

Charlie Ruggles 15 Charles Laughton
remade as: 10 Fancy Pants

ruin, ruins 3 gut, pot 4 doom, fall, fell, harm, raze, seed 5 break, crush, decay, level, quash, quell, shell, spoil, upset, wreck 6 beggar, defeat, ravage, squash 7 destroy, failure, remains, shatter, undoing 8 bankrupt, demolish, downfall, lay waste, make poor, overturn, remnants, wreckage 9 breakdown, devastate, disrepair, overthrow, pauperize 10 impoverish 11 destruction, devastation, dissolution 14 disintegration

ruination 4 ruin 5 wreck 6 fiasco 7 trouble 8 disaster 9 adversity, cataclysm 11 destruction, devastation 12 misadventure

ruinous 4 dire 5 fatal 6 deadly 7 adverse, baneful 8 damaging, ravaging 10 calamitous, disastrous, pernicious 11 cataclysmic, deleterious, destructive, devastating 12 catastrophic

Ruisdael, Jacob (Jakob) van
born: 7 Haarlem 14 The Netherlands
uncle: 18 Salomon van Ruysdael
artwork: 5 Dunes 12 The Waterfall 13 View of Haarlem 14 Bentheim Castle 15 Winter Landscape 17 The Jewish Cemetery 28 View on the Amstel near Amsterdam

rule 3 law, run 4 find, form, head, lead, sway 5 adage, axiom, canon, guide, judge, maxim, model, order, reign 6 custom, decide, decree, direct, empire, govern, manage, method, policy, regime, settle, system 7 adjudge, command, control, declare, formula, precept, prevail, resolve, routine 8 conclude, doctrine, dominate, domineer, dominion, pass upon, practice, regnancy, regulate, standard 9 authority, criterion, determine, direction, establish, guideline, influence, ordinance, precedent, principle, pronounce, supremacy 10 adjudicate, administer, convention, domination, government, leadership, regulation, suzerainty 11 predominate, preside over, sovereignty 12 jurisdiction, prescription 14 administration
type: 5 bench 7 folding 9 steel tape
constellation of: 5 Norma

rule out 4 omit 6 delete, except 7 exclude 9 eliminate

ruler 4 boss, czar, emir, head, khan, king, lord, shah, tsar, tzar 5 chief, judge, queen, rajah, sheik 6 dynast, leader, prince, satrap, shogun, sultan 7 arbiter, emperor, manager, measure, monarch, pharaoh, referee, viceroy 8 chairman, director, governor, suzerain 9 chieftain, commander, potentate, president, sovereign, yardstick 10 controller, supervisor 11 coordinator, crowned head, head of state, tape measure **12** straightedge **13** administrator

rules of conduct 6 ethics **9** moral code **10** principles **12** code of ethics

Rules of the Game
  director: **10** Jean Renoir
  cast: **10** Jean Renoir, Mila Parely, Nora Gregor **11** Marcel Dalio

ruling 6 decree **7** regnant **8** decision, dominant, reigning **9** enactment, governing, prescript **10** commanding, widespread **11** controlling, predominant **13** authoritative, predominating

ruling class 11 aristocracy **13** Establishment

Ruling Class, The
  director: **10** Peter Medak
  cast: **10** Arthur Lowe **11** Alastair Sim, Peter O'Toole **12** Harry Andrews

rum
  drink: **4** Bolo, Grog **6** Mojito **7** Gauguin **8** Daiquiri, Navy Grog, Pina Fria **9** Borinquen, Hurricane **10** Pina Colada **12** Boston Cooler **13** Planter's Punch **14** Fish House Punch **15** Bacardi Cocktail **18** Barbados Rum Swizzle
  ingredient: **8** molasses **9** sugar cane
  origin: **10** West Indies
  type: **4** dark **5** light
  with apple brandy: **6** Bolero **8** Apple Pie
  with apricot brandy: **11** Apricot Lady
  with black coffee: **9** Black Rose
  with bouillon: **6** Creole
  with bourbon: **14** Artillery Punch
  with brandy: **15** Quaker's Cocktail
  with Cointreau: **8** Acapulco **10** Casa Blanca **11** Beachcomber **12** Blue Hawaiian
  with cola: **9** Cuba Libre
  with creme de cacao: **6** Panama
  with curacao: **6** Mai-Tai **8** Blue Lady **12** Blue Hawaiian
  with Dubonnet: **3** BVD **10** Bushranger
  with Galliano: **9** Bossa Nova
  with gin: **3** BVD
  with guava: **8** Ocho Rios
  with kahlua: **10** Black Maria
  with milk: **6** Rum Cow **11** Tom-and-Jerry
  with Pernod: **8** Shanghai
  with sloe gin: **11** Shark's Tooth
  with Tia Maria: **10** Black Maria
  with vermouth: **6** Bolero **8** Apple Pie **10** Black Devil **11** Shark's Tooth

rumble 4 bang, boom, clap, roar, roll **7** booming, resound, thunder **8** drumming **9** resonance **11** reverberate **13** reverberation

Rumford, Benjamin Thomson
  invented: **10** photometer **11** calorimeter

Rumina
  protectress of: **14** nursing mothers

ruminant 3 cow, elk, yak **4** deer, oxen **5** bison, camel, llama, moose, sheep **6** alpaca, cattle, vicuna **7** buffalo, giraffe, pensive **8** antelope **10** chevrotain, meditative, thoughtful **13** contemplative

ruminate 4 mull, muse **5** brood, study, think, weigh **6** ponder **7** reflect **8** cogitate, consider, meditate, mull over **9** speculate, think over **10** deliberate, think about **11** contemplate

ruminating 6 musing **7** pensive **8** thinking **10** meditating, meditative, reflecting, reflective, thoughtful **11** chewing over, mulling over, speculative **13** contemplating, contemplative, introspective

rumination 5 study **6** musing **7** mulling, reverie, thought **8** brooding, thinking **9** pondering **10** cogitation, meditation, reflection **11** speculation **12** deliberation **13** consideration, contemplation **15** reconsideration

rummage 4 root **5** probe **7** examine, explore, ransack **10** disarrange, poke around **11** look through

rummy 3 sot **4** lush, soak **5** drunk, souse, toper **6** barfly, boozer **7** tippler **8** card game, drunkard **9** alcoholic **11** dipsomaniac
  also known as: **3** gin, rum **4** rhum **5** romme **8** gin rummy
  derived from: **8** conquien

rumor 4 talk **5** story **6** babble, gossip, report **7** hearsay, whisper **8** innuendo, intimate **9** circulate, insinuate **11** insinuation, scuttlebutt, supposition

rump 4 rear, seat **5** croup, stern **6** behind, bottom, breech, dorsum **7** rear end **8** backside, buttocks, derriere, haunches **9** posterior **12** hindquarters

Rumpelstiltskin
  origin: **8** Germanic
  form: **5** dwarf
  spun: **4** flax
  made: **4** gold

rumple 4 fold, muss **5** crimp, crush **6** crease, pucker, rimple, ruffle, tousle **7** crinkle, crumple, wrinkle **8** dishevel, disorder **9** corrugate **10** disarrange

rumpus 3 ado, row **4** fray, fuss, stir, to-do **5** brawl, melee, noise **6** affray, fracas, hubbub, pother, racket, ruckus, tumult, uproar **7** rhubarb, scuffle, tempest **8** brouhaha, upheaval **9** agitation, commotion, confusion, imbroglio **10** hullabaloo **11** disturbance, embroilment

run 2 be, go **3** fly, get, hie, jog, pen, ply **4** bolt, boss, cost, dart, dash, defy, flee, flow, go by, head, kind, last, meet, melt, pass, pour, push, race, roll, rush, sort, tear, tour, trip, trot, type, vary **5** bleed, bound, class, court, drift, drive, genre, glide, hurry, impel, incur, issue, leave, pilot, print, speed, spell, split, stand, surge, total, while **6** become, canter, course, decamp, direct, elapse, endure, escape, extend, gallop, hasten, hustle, invite, ladder, manage, motion, move on, outing, period, pierce, propel, scurry, series, sprint, streak, stream, thrust, vanish, voyage, wander **7** abscond, add up to, advance, bring on, compete, current, display, freedom, get past, journey, liquefy, meander, operate, oversee, passage, proceed, publish, running, scamper, stretch, take off, vamoose **8** amount to, campaign, continue, dissolve, duration, evanesce, maneuver, meet with, navigate, progress, scramble, separate, tendency **9** direction, disappear, enclosure, encounter, excursion, go quickly, lose color, penetrate, skedaddle, supervise **10** coordinate, pilgrimage **11** continuance **12** beat a retreat, continuation, perpetuation
  baseball: **5** score, tally **17** circuit of the bases

run aground 7 founder **8** collapse

runaround 4 slip **5** dodge **6** bypass **7** evasion **8** shunning, sidestep **9** avoidance **11** elusiveness, evasiveness **12** equivocation

run around 7 consort, hang out **9** associate, pal around **10** fraternize

runaway 4 pure **6** bolter **7** escapee, perfect, refugee **8** absolute, complete, deserter, fugitive **9** out-and-out, unalloyed **10** skedaddler **11** unmitigated, unqualified

run away 3 fly **4** flee **5** elope **6** decamp, escape, run off **7** abscond, make off **8** sneak off **10** fly the coop, make a break, take flight **12** make a getaway

rundown 5 brief **6** digest, precis, resume, review, sketch **7** outline, summary **8** abstract, synopsis **12** capitulation, condensation

run-down 5 frail, seedy, tacky, tired, weary **6** ailing, beat-up, feeble, shabby, sickly **7** rickety, worn out **8** fatigued, tattered **9** crumbling, exhausted **10** broken-down, tumbledown **11** dilapidated **12** deteriorated

run down 4 scan **5** knock **6** slight **7** detract, put down, run over **8** belittle, derogate, ridicule **9** denigrate, deprecate, discredit, disparage, downgrade, enumerate, underrate **10** depreciate, undervalue

run-in 5 brush, set-to **6** battle, fracas **7** scuffle **8** skirmish **9** encounter **10** engagement

run into 4 meet **8** flow into **9** encounter **10** chance upon, meet up with **11** collide with

run off 3 fly **4** flee **5** elope **6** escape **7** abscond, make off, runaway **9** steal away **10** take flight **15** head for the hills

run off at the mouth 3 gab **5** prate

6 babble, gabble **8** rattle on **11** talk too much

run off with 5 seize **6** abduct, kidnap **7** bear off **8** carry off **9** elope with **11** abscond with, make off with

run-of-the-mill 4 dull, so-so **5** banal, stock, usual **6** common, modest **7** average, humdrum, mundane, routine, typical **8** everyday, mediocre, middling, ordinary, passable, standard **10** second-rate **11** commonplace, indifferent, nondescript **12** unimpressive **13** unimaginative **15** undistinguished

runt 3 elf **4** chit **5** dwarf, pygmy **6** midget, peewee, shrimp **8** half-pint, Tom Thumb **11** Lilliputian
  Latin: 10 homunculus

run through 5 spend, waste **6** expend, pierce **7** deplete, exhaust **8** rehearse, squander

runty 5 short **6** bantam **7** dwarfed, squatty, stunted **9** pint-sized

Runyon, Damon
  author of: 12 Guys and Dolls **16** Blue Plate Special

rupture 3 pop **4** part, rent, rift, snap **5** break, burst, clash, cleft, crack, split **6** breach, divide, schism, sunder **7** discord, disrupt, fissure **8** breaking, bursting, cleavage, dissever, disunion, disunite, fracture, friction, puncture **9** severance **10** dissension, falling out, separation **12** disagreement

R U R
  author: 10 Karel Capek **22** Rossum's Universal Robots

rural 4 hick **6** rustic **7** bucolic, country **8** pastoral **10** provincial **11** countrified

rural area 6 sticks **7** boonies, country **8** farmland **9** backwater, backwoods, boondocks **10** hinterland **11** countryside

ruse 4 hoax **5** blind, dodge, feint, shift, trick **6** deceit, device, scheme **8** artifice, maneuver **9** deception, stratagem **10** subterfuge **11** contrivance, machination

rush 3 hie, run **4** dart, dash, goad, leap, push, race, spur, tear, urge, whip **5** drive, haste, hurry, press, speed, storm **6** charge, hasten, hustle, plunge, scurry, sprint, urgent **7** scamper, urgency **8** dispatch, expedite, pressure, scramble **9** emergency **10** accelerate **11** top priority

rush 6 Juncus
  varieties: 3 bog **4** salt, soft, wood **5** spike **6** grassy **8** scouring **9** field wood, flowering **10** common wood, least spike **11** chair-maker's, greater wood, Japanese-mat **12** slender spike **13** dwarf scouring **14** common scouring **18** variegated scouring

Rush, Benjamin
  field: 8 medicine
  established first: 21 free medical dispensary

signer of: 25 Declaration of Independence

Rushdie, Salman
  born: 6 Mumbai **7** Bombay
  author of: 4 Fury **5** Shame **16** Shalimar the Clown, The Moor's Last Sigh, The Satanic Verses **17** Midnight's Children **18** Step Across This Line **23** The Ground Beneath Her Feet **24** Haroun and the Sea of Stories
  edict issued against: 5 fatwa
  issued for: 9 blasphemy
  award: 6 Booker **11** Booker Prize

rush light 3 dip **5** torch **6** candle, tallow

Rushworth
  character in: 13 Mansfield Park
  author: 6 Austen

Ruskin, John
  author of: 13 Fors Clavigera **14** Modern Painters **17** The Stones of Venice **27** The Seven Lamps of Architecture

Russell, Bertrand
  author of: 19 Why I Am Not a Christian **20** Principia Mathematica (with Alfred North)

Russell, Jane
  real name: 29 Ernestine Jane Geraldine Russell
  born: 9 Bemidji MN
  discovered by: 12 Howard Hughes
  roles: 4 Waco **9** The Outlaw **13** The French Line **22** Gentlemen Prefer Blondes, The Revolt of Mamie Stover

Russell, Rosalind
  born: 11 Waterbury CT
  roles: 5 Gypsy **6** Picnic **8** The Women **9** Hired Wife **10** Auntie Mame **11** Sister Kenny **13** His Girl Friday **14** My Sister Eileen **22** Mourning Becomes Electra

russet 5 apple, umber **6** auburn, copper **10** terra-cotta **11** rust-colored **12** reddish-brown

Russia (includes constituent republics of the former USSR)
  other name: 17 Russian Federation
  former name: 4 USSR **11** Soviet Union **31** Union of Soviet Socialist Republics
  member of: 3 CIS **31** Commonwealth of Independent States
  capital/largest city: 6 Moscow
  others: 4 Baku, Eisk, Kiev, Okha, Omsk, Poti, Riga **5** Anapa, Batum, Gorki, Gorky, Memel, Minsk, Sochi, Vilna, Yeisk **6** Batumi, Erevan, Frunze, Odessa, Rostov, Samara, Tiflis **7** Alma-Ata, Derbent, Donetsk, Kharkov, Liepaja, Petsamo, Pivonia, Saratov, Tallinn, Tbilisi, Yerevan **8** Dushanbe, Kishinev, Murmansk, Pechenga, Taganrog, Tashkent **9** Ashkhabad, Astrakhan, Balaklava, Kronstadt, Kuibyshev, Leningrad, Nikolayev, Petrograd, Ulyanovsk,

Volgograd, Yaroslavl **10** Kronshtadt, Sevastopol, Stalingrad, Sverdlovsk **11** Chelyabinsk, Kaliningrad, Makhachkala, Novorossisk, Novosibirsk, Vladivostok **12** St Petersburg, Vladivostok **14** Dnepropetrovsk
  division/country: 6 Latvia **7** Armenia, Belarus, Estonia, Georgia, Moldova, Siberia, Ukraine **8** Moldavia **9** Kirghizia, Lithuania, Turkmenia **10** Azerbaijan, Belorussia, Kazakhstan, Kyrgyzstan, Tajikistan, Uzbekistan **12** Tadzhikistan, Turkmenistan
    former: 4 Kiev **8** Novgorod
  government:
    legislature: 4 Duma, Rada **7** Zemstvo **8** Congress
  measure: 3 fut, lof **4** duim, fass, loof, pood, quar, stof **5** duime, foute, korec, korek, ligne, osmin, pajak, stoff, stoof, vedro, verst **6** charka, liniya, osmina, paletz, sagene, stekar, tchast, tsarki, versta, verste **7** archine, arsheen, botchka, chkalik, garnetz, verchoc, verchok **8** boutylka, chetvert, krouchka, kroushka **9** chetverik **10** dessiatine **11** polugarnetz
  monetary unit: 5 altin, bisti, copec, denga, grosh, kopek, ruble, shaur **6** abassi, copeck, grivna, kopeck, piatak, rouble **7** poltina, valiuta **8** auksinas, deneshka, imperial, polushka **9** poltinnik **10** altininink, chervonets
  weight: 3 lof, lot **4** dola, funt, lana, last, loof, loth, once, pood, poud **5** dolia
  island: 5 Kuril **7** Hiiumaa, Karagin, Shantar, Vaygach, Wrangel **8** Kolguyev, Saaremaa, Sakhalin **9** Andreanof **12** Novaya Zemlya **13** Komandorskiye **14** Franz Josef Land, Novosibirskiye **15** Severnaya Zemlya
  lake: 3 Seg **4** Aral, Azov, Kola, Sego, Topo, Vigo **5** Chany, Elton, Erara, Ilmen, Lacha, Onega, Pskov, Vozhe **6** Baikal, Byeloe, Ladoga, Peipus, Selety, Taymyr, Tengiz, Zaysan **8** Balkhash **10** Caspian Sea
  mountain: 5 Altai, Lenin, Sayan, Urals **6** Anadyr, Elbrus, Koryak, Pamirs, Pobedy **7** Belukha, Crimean, Khibiny, Stanovi, Zhiguli **8** Caucasus, Dzhughur, Stanavoi, Tien Shan **9** Kopet Dagh, Narodnaya, Pamir-Alai, Yablonovy **10** Carpathian **11** Sikhote-Alin, Verkhoyansk
  highest point: 9 Communism
  river: 3 Don, Ili **4** Amur, Lena, Neva, Ural **5** Dvina, Kuban, Neman, Volga **6** Kolyma, Moskva **7** Dnieper, Pechora, Yenisei **8** Amu Darya, Dniester, Ob-Irtysh, Syr Darya **9** Indigirka
  sea: 4 Aral, Azov, Kara **5** Black, Japan, White **7** Arctic, Baltic, Bering, Laptev **8** Barents, Caspian, Chukchi, Okhotsk, Pacific
  physical feature:

gulf: 4 Azov **5** Mezen **9** Kara-Bogaz, Shelikhov
peninsula: 4 Kola **5** Yamal **6** Crimea, Taymyr **7** Chukchi, Karelia **9** Kamchatka **10** Mangyshlak
strait: 5 Tatar **6** Bering **8** Bosporus **11** Dardanelles
people: 3 Jew **4** Slav **5** Ersar, Kulak, Tatar, Uzbec **6** Kazakh, Soviet, Velika **7** Chukchi, Cossack, Kirghiz, Latvian, Russian, Tadzhik, Turkmen **8** Armenian, Estonian, Georgian, Siberian **9** Moldavian, Ukrainian **10** Lithuanian **11** Azerbaijani, Belorussian
  actor: 12 Stanislavsky
  author: 5 Gogol **7** Nabokov, Pushkin, Tolstoy **8** Turgenev **9** Ehrenburg, Pasternak, Sholokhov **10** Dostoevsky **12** Solzhenitsyn
  composer: 6 Glinka **7** Borodin **9** Prokofiev **10** Mussorgsky, Stravinsky **11** Tchaikovsky **12** Rachmaninoff, Shostakovich **14** Rimsky-Korsakov
  cosmonaut: 11 Yuri Gagarin
  czar/tsar/tzar: 4 Ivan, Paul **5** Peter **6** Alexis **7** Michael **8** Nicholas **9** Alexander **12** Boris Godunov
  dancer: 7 Nureyev, Pavlova **8** Danilova, Nijinsky **11** Baryshnikov
  dynasty: 7 Romanov
  early people: 3 Hun **4** Goth **5** Tatar **6** Khazar, Mongol, Tartar **8** Norsemen, Scythian **9** Cimmerian, Sarmatian, Varangian
  empress: 9 Alexandra, Catherine
  hereditary noble: 5 boyar
  leader: 5 Beria, Lenin, Putin **6** Stalin, Suslov **7** Gromyko, Kosygin, Molotov, Trotsky, Yeltsin **8** Andropov, Brezhnev, Bukharin, Bulganin, Kerensky, Malenkov, Podgorny **9** Chernenko, Gorbachev **10** Khrushchev
  monk: 8 Rasputin
  prince: 4 Oleg **5** Rurik **8** Vladimir
  revolutionary: 9 bolshevik **10** Decembrist
  ruler: 5 Tatar **6** Mongol **8** Batu Khan
  scientist: 6 Pavlov **9** Mendeleev **11** Tsiolkovsky
language: 5 Evenk, Tatar, Uzbek **6** Buriat, Kalmyk, Kazakh **7** Finnish, Kirghiz, Latvian, Russian, Tadzhik, Turkmen **8** Armenian, Estonian, Georgian, Ossetian **9** Moldavian, Ukrainian **10** Lithuanian **11** Belorussian
  alphabet: 8 cyrillic
religion: 5 Islam **7** Judaism **8** Buddhism, Lutheran **10** Protestant **13** Roman Catholic **15** Russian Orthodox **16** Armenian Orthodox, Georgian Orthodox
place: 7 Kremlin **9** Red Square
  art gallery: 9 Tretyakov

castle: 8 Starosty
cathedral: 5 Sobor **7** Zagorsk **8** St Basils
cemetery: 11 Piskarevsky
museum: 9 Hermitage **12** Petrodvorets **18** Cathedral of St Isaac
palace: 6 Winter
park: 5 Gorky
ruins: 7 Bukhara **10** Echmiadzin **15** Gediminas Castle
prison: 8 Lubyanka
street: 11 Kreshchatik **14** Nevski Prospekt
theater: 7 Bolshoi
feature:
  collective farm: 7 kolkhoz
  country house: 5 dacha
  dance: 4 kolo **5** gopac, hopak, saber **6** cossac, trepak **7** cosaque, ziganka **8** kozachok **9** tzazatski
  dance company: 5 Kirov **7** Bolshoi
  labor camp: 5 gulag
  musical instrument: 9 balalaika
  secret police: 3 KGB, MGB **4** NKVD, OGPU **5** Cheka
  state farm: 7 sovkhoz
food:
  caviar: 13 ikra zernistia
  cereal: 5 kasha
  sour cream: 7 smetana
  dessert: 8 vareniki
  dish: 4 plov **5** pirau **6** pelemo **8** osetrina, shashlyk **16** kotleta po kievski
  drink: 4 kvas **5** kvass, vodka **6** chacha, kumiss
  filled pastries: 8 piroshki, pirozhki
  soup: 5 shchi **6** borshch **7** borscht, borsch

Russian village commune 3 mir

rust 3 rot **5** decay, stain **6** auburn, blight, russet **7** corrode, crumble, decline, oxidize **9** corrosion, oxidation **11** deteriorate **12** reddish-brown **13** reddish-yellow

rust-colored 5 henna **6** auburn, russet **8** cinnamon **12** reddish-brown

rustic 4 rube, rude **5** crude, plain, rough, rural, yokel **6** coarse, gauche, simple **7** awkward, boorish, bucolic, bumpkin, country, hayseed, loutish, peasant, uncouth **8** agrarian, churlish, cloddish, pastoral **9** inelegant, unrefined **10** clodhopper, countryman, provincial, uncultured, unpolished **11** countrified **13** country person **15** unsophisticated

rustle 3 rub **4** hiss, stir **5** swish, whish **6** riffle

rustler 5 thief **6** bandit, outlaw **7** brigand **9** desperado

rusty 5 moldy, stiff **6** rotten, rusted **7** reddish, tainted **8** corroded, sluggish **11** rust-colored **13** out of practice

rut 3 cut **4** mark **5** ditch, habit, score, tread **6** furrow, groove, gutter, hollow, trench, trough **7** channel, depress, dig into, pattern **8** monotony **9** deep track **10** depression **11** dull routine

Ruth
  husband: 4 Boaz **6** Mahlon
  son: 4 Obed
  father-in-law: 9 Elimelech
  mother-in-law: 5 Naomi
  brother-in-law: 7 Chilion

Ruth, George Herman
  nickname: 4 Babe **12** Sultan of Swat
  sport: 8 baseball
  position: 8 outfield
  team: 14 New York Yankees

Rutherford, Dame Margaret
  born: 6 London **7** England
  roles: 7 The VIPs **10** Jane Marple **12** Blithe Spirit **27** The Importance of Being Earnest

Rutherford, Ernest
  field: 7 physics
  nationality: 7 British
  discovered: 6 proton **13** atomic nucleus, beta radiation **14** alpha radiation, gamma radiation
  awarded: 10 Nobel Prize

ruthless 5 cruel, harsh **6** brutal, deadly, savage **7** bestial, brutish, callous, inhuman, vicious **8** pitiless **9** barbarous, ferocious, heartless, merciless, murderous, unfeeling, unpitying, unsparing **10** relentless, sanguinary, unmerciful **11** cold-blooded, hardhearted, remorseless, unforgiving, unrelenting **12** bloodthirsty

ruthlessness 7 cruelty **9** barbarity, brutality, harshness **10** inhumanity, savageness **11** viciousness

Ruysdael, Salomon van
  born: 7 Naarden **14** The Netherlands
  nephew: 16 Jacob van Ruisdael
  artwork: 9 River Bank **10** River Scene **14** River Landscape **18** River with Ferry Boat

Rwanda
  other name: 6 Ruanda
  capital/largest city: 6 Kigali
  others: 6 Biumba, Butare, Kibuye, Nyanza **7** Astrida, Gisenyi, Kibungu **8** Cyangugu **9** Ruhengeri
  division:
    colonial: 12 Ruanda-Urundi
  monetary unit: 5 franc **7** centime
  lake: 4 Kivu **5** Ihema **6** Bufera, Bulera, Mohasi **7** Rugwero, Ruhnodo **8** Mugesera, Tshohoha
  mountain: 7 Mitumba, Virunga **8** Muhavura
  highest point: 9 Karisimbi
  river: 6 Kagera, Ruzizi **7** Akagera **8** Akanyaru **9** Luvironza **10** Nyawarongo
  physical feature:
    forest: 7 Nyungwe
    valley: 11 Western Rift
  people: 3 Twa **4** Hutu **5** Batwa, Pygmy, Tutsi **6** Bahutu, Watusi **7**

Batutsi
explorer: 5 Speke **6** Gotzen
leader: 9 Kayibanda **11** Habyari-
mana
language: 6 French **7** Swahili **11** Kinyarwanda
religion: 7 animism **13** Roman Catholic
place:
game reserve: 6 Gabiro
park: 6 Albert, Kagera **16** Virunga
Volcanoes
feature:
clothing: 5 pagne
king: 5 mwami
Ryan, Cornelius

author of: 13 A Bridge Too Far, The
Last Battle, The Longest Day
Ryan, Robert
born: 9 Chicago IL
roles: 6 Caught **8** The Set-Up **9** Billy
Budd, Crossfire **12** Clash by Night,
The Wild Bunch **13** Act of Violence,
The Longest Day **14** About Mrs Les-
lie, God's Little Acre **17** Bad Day at
Black Rock **18** The Woman on the
Beach
Ryder, Albert Pinkham
born: 12 New Bedford MA
artwork: 12 The Race Track (Death
on a Pale Horse) **15** Toilers of the

Sea **27** Siegfried and the Rhine Maidens
rye 6 Secale
varieties: 4 wild **5** giant **6** common **8**
Aral wild, blue wild **9** Altai wild, giant wild, Volga wild **10** Canada wild
11 Chinese wild, Russian wild **12** Siberian wild, Virginia wild
type: 6 liquor **7** whiskey
origin: 7 Ireland **8** Scotland
ingredient: 10 mash grains
drink: 9 Cablegram **11** John Collins,
Whiskey Sour
with Cointreau: 10 Temptation
with Pernod: 3 TNT
with vermouth: 8 Brooklyn **9** Algonquin

  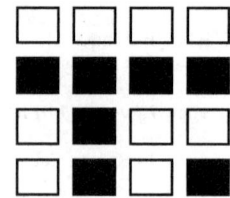

Saarinen, Eero
  father: 5 Eliel
  architect of: 11 St Louis Arch **20** Gateway to the West Arch (St Louis) **26** Trans World Airlines Terminal (NYC) **28** General Motors Technical Center (Warren MI) **39** Columbia Broadcasting Company Headquarters (NYC)
  style: 13 International

Saarinen, Eliel
  son: 4 Eero
  architect of: 16 Cranbrook Academy (Bloomfield Hills MI) **18** Kleinhaus Music Hall (Buffalo) **19** Tanglewood Music Shed (MA) **20** Christ Lutheran Church (Minneapolis MN), First Christian Church (Columbus IN)

Saba *see* **5** Sheba

Sabbath 8 Lord's Day **9** day of rest

Sabbatical: A Romance
  author: 9 John Barth

saber, sabre 3 cut **4** kill, stab **5** blade, sword, wound **6** cutlas, rapier, strike **7** cutlass, soldier **8** scimitar **10** broadsword

Sabin, Albert Bruce
  field: 8 medicine
  developed: 16 oral polio vaccine

sable 3 fur, jet **4** dark, inky **5** black, ebony, raven

sabotage 3 sap **6** retard **7** cripple, destroy, disable, disrupt, subvert **8** paralyze **9** undermine, vandalize **10** subversion **12** incapacitate

sabra 11 Israeli-born **14** native of Israel

Sabra
  type: 7 liqueur
  origin: 6 Israel
  flavor: 6 orange **9** chocolate

Sac *see* **4** Sauk

saccharine 5 gooey, mushy, soppy, sweet **6** sugary, syrupy **7** candied, cloying, honeyed, maudlin, mawkish, sugared **9** offensive, oversweet, revolting, sickening **10** disgusting, nauseating **11** sentimental

sacerdotal 5 papal **8** clerical, pastoral, priestly **9** apostolic, canonical, episcopal **10** pontifical **11** ministerial **12** hierarchical **14** ecclesiastical

Sachs, Hans 13 Meistersinger

sack 3 bag, rob **4** loot, pack, raid **5** pouch, spoil, store, waste **6** duffel, maraud, rapine, ravage, tear up **7** despoil, pillage, plunder, ransack **8** spoliate **9** depredate, duffel bag, gunnysack, haversack, marauding **10** plundering, ravishment **11** depredation, devastation **12** despoliation

sackbut 18 medieval instrument
  resembles: 8 trombone

sacrament 3 vow **4** rite **5** troth **6** pledge, plight, ritual **7** liturgy, promise, service **8** ceremony, contract, covenant **9** solemnity **10** ceremonial, obligation, observance **11** affirmation **12** ministration

sacramental 4 holy **6** ritual **7** blessed **10** ceremonial, liturgical

Sacraments, Seven 7 Baptism, Penance **9** Eucharist, Last Rites, Matrimony **10** Holy Orders **12** Confirmation **13** Holy Communion **14** Extreme Unction, Reconciliation **18** Anointing of the Sick

sacred 4 holy **6** church **7** blessed, revered **8** Biblical, hallowed, hieratic **9** religious, venerable **10** sanctified, scriptural **11** consecrated **14** ecclesiastical

Sacred writings 5 Bible **11** Bibliotheca

sacrifice 4 cede, loss **5** forgo, waive **6** forego, give up, homage **7** cession, forfeit, offer up **8** immolate, oblation, offering, renounce **9** surrender **10** concession, immolation, lustration, relinquish **12** renunciation **14** relinquishment

sacrilege 3 sin **7** impiety, mockery, outrage **8** iniquity **9** blasphemy, profanity, violation **10** irreligion, sinfulness, wickedness **11** desecration, impiousness, irreverence, profanation, profaneness

sacrilegious 7 impious, profane **10** irreverent **11** blasphemous, irreligious

sacrosanct 4 holy **5** godly **6** divine, solemn **8** hallowed, heavenly **9** celestial, inviolate, religious, spiritual **10** inviolable, unexamined **11** consecrated **12** unquestioned

sacrum
  bone of: 11 base of spine

sad 3 low **4** blue, grim, hard, hurt **5** grave **6** dismal, solemn, taxing, tragic, trying, woeful **7** adverse, crushed, doleful, forlorn, grieved, joyless, maudlin, pitiful, serious, unhappy **8** dejected, desolate, downcast, grievous, mournful, pathetic, touching, troubled, wretched **9** cheerless, depressed, difficult, miserable, sorrowful **10** calamitous, chapfallen, despairing, despondent, dispirited, distressed, lachrymose, lamentable, melancholy **11** crestfallen, distressing, pessimistic, troublesome, unfortunate **12** disconsolate, heartrending, heavyhearted, inconsolable **13** brokenhearted, griefstricken, heartbreaking **14** down in the dumps, down in the mouth
  French: 6 triste

Sadat, Anwar el-
  president of: 5 Egypt
  awarded: 15 Nobel Peace Prize
  author of: 18 In Search of Identity

sadden 4 damp, dash **5** crush **6** burden, deject, grieve, sorrow, subdue **7** depress **8** aggrieve, dispirit **10** discourage, dishearten

saddle with 9 stick with **10** burden with **12** encumber with **18** make responsible for

Sade, Marquis de
  author of: 7 Justine **8** Juliette **14** 120 Days of Sodom **26** The Philosopher in the Bedroom

sadistic 6 brutal **7** vicious **8** fiendish, perverse **9** perverted **12** bloodthirsty

sadness
  French: 9 tristesse

sad poem 5 elegy **6** lament

Sad Sack
  creator: 11 George Baker

Saehrimnir
  origin: 12 Scandinavian
  form: 4 boar
  served in: 8 Valhalla
  feat: 12 regeneration

safe 4 firm, sure, wary **5** sound, vault, whole **6** intact, modest, secure, stable, steady, unhurt **7** certain, guarded, prudent **8** cautious, defended, discreet, harmless, reliable, unbroken, unharmed **9** innocuous, protected, undamaged, unexposed, unscathed **10** dependable, protecting **11** circumspect, impregnable, out of danger, trustworthy, unscratched **12** conservative, invulnerable, noncommittal

safeguard 4 ward **5** armor, charm **6** amulet, buffer, defend, harbor, screen, secure, shield **7** bulwark, defense, fortify, protect, shelter **8** conserve, garrison, preserve, security, talisman **10** precaution, protection

safekeeping 4 care **6** charge **7** custody **8** security **9** husbandry **10** protection **12** conservation, guardianship, preservation

Safety Net, The
   author: 12 Heinrich Boll

saffron
   botanical name: 13 Crocus sativus
   also called: 6 Krokus
   Moorish: 6 Zafran
   of all spices most: 6 costly
   color: 6 orange, yellow **12** yellow-orange
   used as: 8 coloring, cosmetic, medicine **9** fabric dye
   origin: 5 Egypt, Syria **8** Holy Land **9** Palestine
   use: 4 rice **5** bread, rolls

sag 3 bow, dip **4** drop, fail, flag, flap, flop, keel, lean, list, sink, sway, tilt, tire **5** droop, pitch, slump, weary **6** billow, plunge, settle, weaken **7** decline, descend, give way **8** diminish

saga 4 epic, myth, tale, yarn **6** legend **7** history, romance **9** adventure, chronicle, narrative
   French: 11 roman-fleuve

sagacious 4 foxy, wise **5** acute, canny, sharp, smart, sound **6** astute, brainy, clever, shrewd **7** cunning, knowing, prudent, sapient, tactful **8** discreet, rational, sensible **9** judicious, practical **10** diplomatic, discerning, perceptive **11** calculating, intelligent **13** perspicacious **14** discriminating

sagacity 6 acumen, brains, smarts, wisdom **8** sapience **9** canniness, smartness **10** astuteness, braininess, cleverness, shrewdness **11** discernment **12** intelligence, perspicacity **13** judiciousness **14** discrimination

Sagan, Carl
   author of: 6 Cosmos **7** Contact **11** Broca's Brain **16** The Dragons of Eden **20** The Demon-Haunted World
   interest: 4 SETI **37** Search for Extra Terrestrial Intelligence

Sagan, Francoise
   real name: 16 Francoise Quoirez
   author of: 13 A Certain Smile **15** Aimez-vous Brahms **16** Bonjour Tristesse

sage 4 guru, wise **5** sound **6** astute, pundit, savant, shrewd **7** egghead, knowing, prudent, sapient, scholar, wise man **8** mandarin, sensible **11** intelligent, philosopher
   French: 6 savant
   Latin: 5 magus, solon

sage 6 Salvia **12** S officinalis
   varieties: 3 bog **4** baby, blue, gray, rose, sand, wood **5** black, lilac, Texas, white **6** autumn, common, desert, garden, purple, silver, yellow

---

7 bladder, gentian, scarlet, Spanish, thistle, Vervain **8** creeping, gray ball, mealy-cup, rose-leaf **9** Bethlehem, Jerusalem **11** Mexican bush **16** pineapple-scented
   means: 6 to heal, to save
   strengthens: 6 memory, wisdom **8** prudence
   makes men: 8 immortal
   origin: 7 Albania **10** Yugoslavia **13** Mediterranean
   use: 4 pork **6** breads, cheese **7** chicken, poultry, seafood **8** stuffing

Sage of Concord
   nickname of: 17 Ralph Waldo Emerson

Sagittarius
   symbol: 6 archer **7** centaur
   planet: 7 Jupiter
   rules: 10 philosophy **15** higher education
   born: 8 November, December

Sagittary
   form: 7 centaur
   carried: 3 bow

said 5 above, quoth **6** quoted, spoken, stated **7** related, uttered **8** repeated

Saigon
   capital of: 7 Vietnam
   now: 13 Ho Chi Minh City

sail 3 fly **4** boat, scud, skim, soar **5** drift, float, glide, steam **6** course, cruise, voyage **8** navigate **9** excursion

sailboat 4 saic, yawl **5** craft, ketch, sloop, yacht **6** vessel **7** sunfish **8** schooner **9** catamaran
   part: 4 boom, mast **6** canvas **7** rigging **8** mainsheet

sailcloth 4 duck **6** canvas

Sailing to Byzantium
   author: 7 W B Yeats

sailor 3 gob, tar **4** salt **6** sea dog, seaman **7** mariner, voyager **8** deckhand, seafarer **9** navigator, yachtsman
   terms: 3 yaw **4** ahoy, alee, conn, draw, fast, furl, heel, list, luff, moor, scud, tack, trim, wake **5** avast, belay, heave, hoist, lie to, pilot, pitch, weigh **6** aweigh **8** aweather, put about

sailors
   patron saint: 4 Elmo

Sails (of Argo)
   constellation of: 4 Vela

saint *see also* under St.:

saint 6 martyr
   Buddhist: 5 arhat **11** bodhisattva
   Chinese: 8 immortal
   Islamic: 3 pir
   lives of the saints: 8 menology **9** hagiology **11** hagiography **13** acta sanctorum
   process of becoming: 12 canonization
   relic box: 6 chasse
   remains: 5 relic
   symbol: 4 halo

Saint, Eva Marie
   born: 8 Newark NJ
   roles: 6 Exodus **15** On the Waterfront **16** North by Northwest

saint, patron
   acolytes: 13 John Berchmans
   actors: 8 Genesius
   artists: 4 Luke
   astronomers: 7 Dominic
   athletes: 9 Sebastian
   authors: 14 Francis de Sales
   aviators: 15 Our Lady of Loreto **16** Therese of Lisieux **17** Joseph of Cupertino
   bakers: 8 Nicholas **18** Elizabeth of Hungary
   bankers: 7 Matthew
   barbers: 5 Louis **6** Cosmas, Damian
   barren women: 9 Felicitas **14** Anthony of Padua
   beggars/cripples: 5 Giles
   blind: 6 Odilia **7** Raphael
   bodily ills: 16 Our Lady of Lourdes
   boy scouts: 6 George
   brides: 14 Nicholas of Myra
   builders: 13 Vincent Ferrer
   butchers: 4 Luke **7** Hadrian **14** Anthony of Egypt
   carpenters: 6 Joseph
   cancer patients: 9 Peregrine
   children: 10 Santa Claus **14** Nicholas of Myra
   comedians: 5 Vitus
   cooks: 6 Martha **8** Lawrence
   deaf: 14 Francis de Sales
   dying: 6 Joseph **8** Barbara
   emigrants: 14 Frances Cabrini
   England: 6 George
   eye sufferers: 4 Lucy
   falsely accused: 15 Raymond Nonnatus
   farmers: 6 George **7** Isidore
   fishermen: 5 Peter **6** Andrew
   foreign missions: 13 Francis Xavier **16** Therese of Lisieux
   foundlings: 13 Holy Innocents
   France: 5 Denis
   gardeners: 6 Fiacre, Phocas **7** Adelard, Dorothy, Tryphon
   heart patients: 9 John of God
   hospitals: 9 John of God **12** Jude Thaddeus **16** Camillus de Lellis
   housewives: 4 Anne
   hunters: 6 Hubert **9** Eustachius
   invalids: 4 Roch
   Ireland: 7 Patrick
   Italy: 7 Anthony
   laborers: 5 James **7** Isidore **9** John Bosco
   lawyers: 3 Ivo **4** Ives **8** Genesius **10** Thomas More
   librarians: 6 Jerome
   lovers: 9 Valentine
   mariners: 4 Elmo **7** Michael **19** Nicholas of Tolentino
   mentally ill: 6 Dympna
   merchants: 14 Nicholas of Myra **15** Francis of Assisi

metalworkers: 7 Eligius
miners: 7 Barbara
mothers: 6 Monica
musicians: 7 Cecilia, Dunstan **15** Gregory the Great
Norway: 4 Olaf, Olav
nurses: 6 Agatha **7** Alexius, Raphael **9** John of God **16** Camillus de Lellis
painters: 4 Luke
philosophers: 6 Justin **21** Catherine of Alexandria
physicians: 4 Luke **6** Cosmas, Damian **7** Raphael **9** Pantaleon
pilgrims: 5 James **7** Alexius
poets: 5 David **7** Cecilia
policemen: 7 Michael
poor souls: 19 Nicholas of Tolentino
postal workers: 7 Gabriel
priests: 19 Jean-Baptiste Vianney
printers: 8 Genesius **9** John of God **16** Augustine of Hippo
prisoners: 6 Dismas **7** Barbara **13** Joseph Cafasso
rheumatism: 15 James the Greater
sailors: 4 Elmo **7** Brendan, Erasmus, Eulalia **8** Cuthbert, Nicholas **11** Christopher **13** Peter Gonzales
scholars: 6 Brigid
scientists: 6 Albert
Scotland: 6 Andrew
sculptors: 6 Claude
seamen: 4 Elmo **14** Francis of Paolo
sick: 7 Michael **9** John of God **16** Camillus de Lellis
singers: 7 Cecilia, Gregory
skiers: 7 Bernard
shoemakers: 7 Crispin
soldiers: 6 George **7** Hadrian **8** Ignatius **9** Joan of Arc, Sebastian **13** Martin of Tours
Spain: 5 James **8** Santiago
students: 13 Thomas Aquinas **21** Catherine of Alexandria
surgeons: 6 Cosmas, Damian
tailors: 9 Homobonus
tax collectors: 7 Matthew
teachers: 15 Gregory the Great **21** Catherine of Alexandria, Jean Baptiste de la Salle
theologians: 9 Augustine **16** Alphonsus Liguori
throat sufferers: 6 Blaise
travelers: 7 Raphael **11** Christopher **14** Anthony of Padua, Nicholas of Myra
Wales: 5 David
winegrowers: 7 Vincent
workingmen: 6 Joseph
writers: 14 Francis de Sales
youth: 13 John Berchmans **15** Aloysius Gonzaga, Gabriel Possenti
Saint, The
   author: 15 Leslie Charteris
   character: 12 Simon Templar **26** Inspector Claude Eustace Teal
   cast: 10 Roger Moore
Saint Anthony's fire 6 herpes **8** ergotism, shingles **10** erysipelas

Saint Elmo's fire 5 flame, hermo **6** castor, corona, furole, helena **9** corposant **12** luminescence
Saint Esprit 9 Holy Ghost **10** Holy Spirit
Saint-Exupery, Antoine de
   author of: 11 Night Flight **12** Southern Mail **15** The Little Prince **16** Wind Sand and Stars
Saint Francis
   born: 6 Assisi
   called: 9 Poverello
Saint-Gaudens, Augustus
   born: 6 Dublin **7** Ireland
   artwork: 7 Puritan **13** Mrs Henry Adams (Grief) **14** General Sherman **15** Admiral Farragut **16** President Lincoln
Saint Joan
   author: 17 George Bernard Shaw
Saint John's bread 5 carob
Saint John's wort 5 amber **6** tutsan **7** ascyrum, cammock **9** androseme, hypericum, rosin-rose **10** broombrush **11** Aaron's-beard
saintliness 6 purity **8** goodness, holiness **9** beatitude, godliness **11** blessedness **12** spirituality
Saint Lucia, St Lucia
   capital: 8 Castries
   highest point: 5 Gimie
   island group: 8 Windward **14** Lesser Antilles
   language: 6 patois
   location: 9 Caribbean
saintly 4 good, holy **5** godly, moral, pious **6** devout **7** angelic, blessed, exalted, sinless, upright **8** beatific, faithful, reverent, virtuous **9** believing, religious, righteous, spiritual **10** benevolent
Saint Paul
   born: 6 Tarsus
   companion: 4 Luke
   epistle: 5 Titus **6** Romans **7** Hebrews, Timothy **8** Philemon **9** Ephesians, Galatians **10** Colossians **11** Corinthians, Philippians **13** Thessalonians
Saint Paul's Cathedral (London)
   architect: 4 Wren
Saint Peter
   called: 4 Rock **5** Simon **6** Cephas
   brother: 6 Andrew
Saint-Saens, (Charles) Camille
   born: 5 Paris **6** France
   composer of: 12 Danse Macabre **14** Samson et Dalila **16** Samson and Delilah **18** La Jeunesse d'Hercule **20** Carnival of the Animals
Saints' lives
   writer of: 12 hagiographer
Saint Vincent, St Vincent
   capital: 9 Kingstown
   highest point: 9 Soufriere
   Indian: 5 Carib **6** Arawak
   island group: 8 Windward **14** Lesser

Antilles
   islands: 10 Grenadines
   language: 6 patois
   location: 9 Caribbean
   volcano: 9 Soufriere
Saint Vitus' dance 6 chorea
sake 3 end **4** care, gain, good **5** cause **6** behalf, object, profit, regard **7** account, benefit, concern, purpose, respect, welfare **8** interest **9** advantage **11** enhancement **13** consideration
sake
   type: 4 wine **6** spirit
   origin: 5 Japan
   ingredient: 4 rice
Sakharov, Andrei Dimitrievich
   field: 7 physics
   nationality: 7 Russian
   researched: 14 nuclear fission
   defended: 12 civil liberty
   exiled to: 5 Gorky
   awarded: 10 Nobel Prize
Saki
   real name: 7 H H Munro
   author of: 8 Reginald **20** Beasts and Super-Beasts **21** The Chronicles of Clovis **23** The Unbearable Bassington
salaam 3 bow **6** homage **9** obeisance
Salacia
   partner of: 7 Neptune
salacious 4 lewd, sexy **7** lustful, obscene **8** indecent **9** lecherous **10** lascivious, libidinous **12** pornographic
salad days 5 prime, youth **6** heyday **9** flowering
salamander 3 eft **4** newt **5** giant, siren, tiger **6** lizard, red eft **7** axolotl, urodela **8** congo eel, mudpuppy **9** amphibian, fire-eater, proteidae **10** hellbender, necturidae **14** red-spotted newt
Salamis
   father: 6 Asopus
   mother: 6 Metope
   son: 8 Cychreus
Salammbo
   author: 15 Gustave Flaubert
   character: 5 Matho **8** Hamilcar, Spendius **9** Narr Havas
   setting: 8 Carthage
salary 3 pay **5** wages **6** income **7** stipend **8** earnings **9** allowance, emolument **10** recompense **12** remuneration
sale 3 cut **7** auction, bargain, selling, special **8** discount, exchange, markdown, transfer **9** reduction
Salem
   suburb of: 6 Boston
   old site of: 11 witch trials
salesperson 5 agent, clerk **6** vendor **8** huckster
salient 6 arrant, marked **7** glaring, notable, obvious **8** flagrant, manifest, palpable, striking **9** egregious, important, prominent **10** noteworthy, noticeable, pronounced, protruding, re-

markable **11** conspicuous, outstanding, substantial **12** considerable

Salii
also: **6** Salian
form: **7** priests
priests of: **4** Mars
guarded: **7** ancilia **13** sacred shields

saline 4 salt **5** briny, salty **8** brackish

Salinger, J D 7 recluse
full name: **19** Jerome David Salinger
author of: **11** Nine Stories **14** Franny and Zooey **18** The Catcher in the Rye **30** Raise High the Roof Beam, Carpenters
character: **4** Esme **10** Buddy Glass **15** Holden Caulfield

Salisbury
capital of: **8** Zimbabwe

Salisbury, Harrison E
author of: **16** American in Russia **19** A Journey for Our Times, Black Night White Snow

Salish (Flatheads)
language family: **8** Salishan
location: **5** Idaho **6** Oregon **7** Montana **10** Washington **15** British Columbia

Salk, Jonas Edward
field: **8** medicine
developed: **12** (inactivated) polio vaccine

salle a manger 10 dining room
literally: **13** hall for eating

sallow 3 wan **4** gray, pale **5** ashen, livid **6** anemic, pallid, sickly, yellow **7** bilious **9** jaundiced, washed-out, yellowish

sallowness 6 pallor **7** wanness **8** paleness **10** sickliness **11** biliousness **13** colorlessness, yellowishness

Sallust
author of: **9** Histories **13** War of Jugurtha **20** Conspiracy of Catiline

sally 3 mot **4** flow, pour, quip, raid, trip **5** erupt, foray, surge **6** attack, banter, charge, outing, retort, sortie, spring, thrust **7** debouch, journey **8** badinage, repartee **9** excursion, wisecrack, witticism **10** expedition **13** counterattack

Salmacis
form: **5** nymph
loved: **14** Hermaphroditus
joined with: **14** Hermaphroditus
became: **13** hermaphrodite **14** bisexual person

Salmagundi
author: **16** Washington Irving

salmon 4 fish, king **5** cohoe **6** silver **7** chinook, Pacific, quinnat, sockeye, spawner **8** Atlantic, humpback
enclosure: **4** yair
female: **4** raun **6** baggit
genus: **12** Oncorhynchus
hatchling: **4** pink **6** alevin

male: **3** gib **4** buck, cock
post-spawning: **4** kelt **7** shedder
pre-spawning: **7** gilling, girling
young: **4** parr **7** essling

Salome
father: **11** Herod Philip
mother: **8** Herodias
husband: **7** Zebedee
opera by: **7** (Richard) Strauss
character: **5** Herod (the Tetrarch) **8** Herodias, Jokanaan (John the Baptist) **9** Narraboth

salon 4 hall **7** gallery **11** drawing room **13** establishment

saloon 3 bar, inn, pub **6** bistro, tavern **7** barroom, ginmill, taproom **8** alehouse **9** roadhouse, speakeasy

salt 3 wit **4** best, corn, cure, pick, save **5** brine, briny, cream, elect, humor, savor, smack, souse, spice **6** choice, flavor, pickle, saline, season, select **8** brackish, marinate, piquancy, pungency **9** seasoning **12** quintessence

Salten, Felix
author of: **5** Bambi

saltwater 3 sea **5** brine, ocean

salty 4 racy **5** briny, funny, spicy, terse, witty **6** corned, ribald, risque, saline **7** pungent, zestful **8** brackish, improper

salubrious 7 bracing, healthy **9** healthful, wholesome **10** beneficial, lifegiving **11** therapeutic **12** invigorating

salubriousness 11 healthiness **13** healthfulness, wholesomeness

Salus
origin: **5** Roman
goddess of: **6** health **10** prosperity
corresponds to: **6** Hygeia

salutary 4 good **6** tonic **6** useful **7** healing, healthy **8** curative, sanitary **9** healthful, wholesome **10** beneficial, profitable **12** advantageous

salutation 3 bow **5** hello, howdy, toast **6** curtsy **7** address, welcome **8** greeting **9** reception
Hawaiian: **5** aloha
Italian: **4** ciao
Latin: **3** ave

salute 3 ave **4** hail, kiss **5** bow to, cheer, greet, honor, nod to, salvo **6** accost, homage, praise, wave to **7** address, applaud, respect, welcome **8** accolade, applause, greeting **9** laudation, reverence **11** acclamation, recognition **12** congratulate

Salvador
author: **10** Joan Didion

salvage 4 junk, save **5** scrap **6** debris, rescue **7** recover, remains, restore **8** recovery, retrieve **9** retrieval **11** reclamation **12** rehabilitate

salvation 4 rock **5** grace **6** rescue, saving **8** election, lifeline, mainstay, recovery, survival **9** retrieval **10** protec-

tion, redemption **11** deliverance, reclamation **12** preservation

salve 4 aloe, balm, calm, ease, hail **5** hello **6** lessen, lotion, pacify, reduce, soothe, temper **7** anodyne, assuage, mollify, relieve, unguent **8** dressing, liniment, mitigate, moderate, ointment **9** alleviate, emollient, greetings **11** alleviative

salver 4 bowl, dish, tray **6** waiter **7** coaster

salvia 4 herb, mint, sage **5** shrub **8** mejorana **9** artemisia

salvo 5 burst **6** volley **7** barrage, battery **8** shelling **9** cannonade, fusillade **11** bombardment

sambuca
type: **7** liqueur
origin: **5** Italy
flavor: **5** anise **10** elderberry

same 4 like, twin, very **5** alike, equal **6** on a par **7** similar, uniform **8** parallel **9** identical, unchanged **10** consistent, equivalent, invariable **13** corresponding

same as previously given
Latin: **4** idem

sameness 6 parity **8** equality, evenness, likeness, monotony **10** similarity, uniformity **11** homogeneity **14** homogenousness

Samoa
capital:
   American Samoa: **8** Pago Pago
   Western Samoa: **4** Apia
studied by: **13** Margaret Mead
cities: **6** Utulei **7** Palauli **8** Fagatogo
division: **12** Western Samoa **13** American Samoa
monetary unit: **4** tala
island: **3** Ofu, Tau **4** Rose **5** Aunuu, Manua, Namua, Upolu **6** Manono, Nuulua, Savaii, Swains **7** Apolima, Nuutele, Olosega, Tutuila **8** Nuusafee
mountain: **4** Vaea **5** Alava **6** Savaii **7** Matafao **9** Rainmaker
highest point: **4** Fito **8** Silisili
sea: **12** South Pacific
physical feature:
   bay: **5** Afono, Leone **6** Fagasa, Falefa, Safata **7** Lafanga, Masefau, Matautu **8** Massacre, Salealua **9** Saluofata
people: **6** Samoan **10** Polynesian
   explorer: **9** Roggeveen **12** Bougainville
language: **6** Samoan **7** English
religion: **6** Mormon **9** Methodist **13** Roman Catholic **15** Latter Day Saints **19** Seventh-Day Adventist **26** Congregational Christianity
feature:
   bird: **3** iao **4** lulu, lupe **6** manuao, manuma, maomao **7** manuali **8** manusina, manutagi
   chief: **5** matai
   chief's daughter: **5** taupo

cloth: 4 para, tapa
clothing: 5 pareu **8** lavalava, puletasi
dance: 4 siva
dwelling: 4 fale
food:
 drink: 3 ava

Samoyed
language family: 6 Uralic
spoken in: 7 Siberia

sample 3 try **4** test **5** model, taste **7** dip into, examine, example, pattern, portion, segment **8** instance, paradigm, specimen **10** experience **12** cross section, illustration **14** representative **15** exemplification

Samson 11 Hebrew judge
father: 6 Manoah
feature: 4 hair **8** strength
weapon: 7 jawbone
mistress/betrayer: 7 Delilah
hometown: 5 Zorah
fate: 7 blinded
brought down: 4 Gaza

Samson Agonistes
author: 10 John Milton

Samuel 11 Hebrew judge
father: 7 Elkanah
mother: 6 Hannah
hometown: 5 Ramah
anointed: 4 Saul **5** David

Sana, Sanaa
capital of: 5 Yemen

San Antonio
basketball team: 5 Spurs
football team: 11 Gunslingers
landmark: 8 The Alamo **9** River Walk

sanctification 8 blessing **9** hallowing **12** consecration
Hebrew: 7 Kiddush

sanctified 4 holy **6** sacred **7** blessed **8** hallowed **11** consecrated

sanctify 5 bless, exalt **6** anoint, hallow, purify, uphold **7** absolve, beatify, cleanse **8** dedicate, enshrine, make holy **10** consecrate, legitimate, legitimize **12** legitimatize

sanctimonious 6 solemn **7** canting, pompous, preachy **8** unctuous **9** overblown, pietistic **11** pharisaical, pretentious **14** holier-than-thou

sanctimoniousness 4 cant, sham **6** humbug **9** hypocrisy **11** insincerity **15** pretentiousness

sanction 5 allow, favor, leave **6** accept, assent, permit, ratify **7** agree to, approve, consent, endorse, liberty, license, penalty, support **8** approval, coercion, pressure **9** authority, authorize **10** legitimate, permission **11** countenance, endorsement **12** commendation, confirmation, ratification **13** authorization

sanctuary 4 park **5** cover, haven **6** asylum, chapel, church, refuge, safety, shrine, temple **7** reserve, retreat, shelter **8** preserve **10** protection

Sanctuary
author: 15 William Faulkner
character: 5 Tommy **6** Popeye **9** Ruby Lamar **10** Lee Goodwin, Reba Rivers **11** Temple Drake **12** Gowan Stevens, Horace Benbow

sanctum sanctorum 12 holy of holies

sanctus 4 holy

Sancus
also: 10 Semo Sancus
origin: 5 Roman
god of: 5 oaths **10** road safety **11** hospitality **20** international affairs
corresponds to: 8 Hercules **10** Dius Fidius

sand 4 grit, guts **5** pluck, spunk **6** mettle **7** bravery, courage, resolve **8** backbone **9** fortitude **10** resolution **12** resoluteness

Sand, George
real name: 14 Aurore Dudevant
protege: 6 Chopin
author of: 5 Lelia **7** Indiana **8** Consuelo **9** Valentine **13** Story of My Life **14** The Country Waif, The Haunted Pool **17** Fanchon the Cricket **19** Les Maitres Sonneurs **23** The Countess of Rudolstadt

sandal 4 clog, flat, shoe, zori **5** scuff, thong **6** loafer **7** slipper **8** flipflop, huarache, moccasin, overshoe **10** espadrille

sandalwood 5 Algum, Almug

sandbank 4 dune, reef **5** shelf, shoal **7** shallow

sandbar 4 bank, flat, reef, spit **5** shelf, shoal **7** shallow

Sandburg, Carl
author of: 3 Fog **7** Chicago **12** Harvest Poems **13** Smoke and Steel **14** Abraham Lincoln, The Cornhuskers **15** Remembrance Rock

Sanders, George
born: 6 Russia **12** St Petersburg
wife: 10 Benita Hume, Magda Gabor **11** Zsa Zsa Gabor
roles: 6 The Fan **7** Ivanhoe, Rebecca **8** The Saint **9** The Falcon **11** All About Eve **12** Forever Amber, The Gay Falcon **18** The Moon and Sixpence **20** Foreign Correspondent **22** The Picture of Dorian Gray **24** The House of the Seven Gables
autobiography: 25 Memoirs of a Professional Cad

San Diego
area: 7 La Jolla, Old Town **8** Coronado **9** Point Loma **10** Balboa Park, Mission Bay **13** Mission Valley **14** Gaslamp Quarter
baseball team: 6 Padres
football team: 8 Chargers
founder: 13 Junipero Serra
landmark: 11 San Diego Zoo **14** Wild Animal Park **30** Scripps Institute of Oceanography

sandpiper 3 ree **4** bird, ruff **5** reeve,

stint, wader **6** common, oxbird, plover **7** fiddler, haybird, spotted, tipbird **8** graybird, sandpeep, shadbird **10** beachrobin

Sands of Iwo Jima
director: 9 Allan Dwan
cast: 8 John Agar **9** Adele Mara, John Wayne **13** Forrest Tucker

sandwich 3 BLT, sub **4** club, deli, hero **5** hogie **6** burger, hoagie, insert **7** grinder, western **8** laminate **9** interpose, submarine **10** lamination **11** combination

sane 5 lucid, sober **7** logical **8** all there, balanced, credible, rational, sensible **9** judicious, plausible, sagacious **10** farsighted, reasonable **11** clearheaded, responsible
Latin: 12 compos mentis

Sanford and Son
character: 5 Bubba **6** Melvin **10** Aunt Esther **11** Donna Harris, Fred Sanford, Grady Wilson, Rollo Larson **12** Julio Fuentes, Officer Smith (Smitty) **13** Lamont Sanford
cast: 8 Redd Foxx **9** Don Bexley **11** Hal Williams, LaWanda Page, Slappy White, Whitman Mayo **12** Demond Wilson, Lynn Hamilton **13** Gregory Sierra **15** Nathaniel Taylor

San Francisco
baseball team: 6 Giants
bay: 12 San Francisco
county: 5 Marin **8** San Mateo **12** San Francisco
football team: 11 Forty-Niners
known as: 12 City by the Bay **19** City by the Golden Gate
landmark: 8 Alcatraz **16** Golden Gate Bridge
noted for: 8 cable car **9** earthquake (1906) **26** crookedest street in the world
street/section: 6 Market **7** Lombard, Nob Hill **8** Presidio **9** Chinatown **10** Montgomery **11** Embarcadero, Russian Hill

sangaree, sangria
flavor: 5 fruit, spice

sangfroid 5 poise **6** aplomb **7** balance **8** coolness **9** composure **10** confidence, equanimity **11** tranquility **12** tranquillity **16** imperturbability

sanguine 3 red **4** rosy **5** happy, ruddy, sunny **6** bright, elated, florid **7** buoyant, crimson, flushed, glowing, hopeful, reddish, scarlet **8** blooming, cheerful, inflamed, rubicund **9** confident **10** optimistic **12** lighthearted

Sanhedrin 7 council

sanitarium, sanitorium 8 hospital **11** institution
French: 13 maison de sante

sanitary 5 clean **7** aseptic, healthy, sterile **8** germ-free, hygienic **9** healthful, wholesome **10** salubrious, sterilized, uninfected, unpolluted **11** disinfected **12** prophylactic

sanitorium *see* **10** sanitarium

sanity 5 sense **6** reason **8** lucidity, saneness **9** coherence, normality **11** rationality **12** sensibleness **14** reasonableness **15** clearheadedness

San Jose
  capital of: **9** Costa Rica

San Juan
  capital of: **10** Puerto Rico

San Juan Bautista *see* **10** Puerto Rico

San Marino
  capital/largest city: **9** San Marino
  enclave in: **5** Italy
  others: **10** Serravalle **13** Borgo Maggiore
  division: **8** Castelli
  government:
    legislature: **22** Great and General Council
  monetary unit: **4** lira, lire **9** centesimi
  mountain: **9** Apennines
  highest point: **6** Titano
  people: **7** Italian **11** San Marinese
    founder: **7** Marinus
  language: **7** Italian
  religion: **13** Roman Catholic
  place: **13** Valloni Palace **17** Palazzo del Governo **19** Basilica of San Marino
  church: **5** Pieve **9** St Francis

San Salvador
  capital of: **10** El Salvador

sans doute 12 without doubt

Sansovino, Andrea
  real name: **14** Andrea Contucci
  born: **5** Italy **14** Monte San Savino
  artwork: **15** Baptism of Christ **20** Virgin Child and St Anne

Sansovino, Il
  real name: **11** Jacopo Tatti
  born: **5** Italy **7** Caprese
  artwork: **4** Mars **7** Bacchus, Logetta, Neptune **10** Old Library **15** Madonna del Parto **16** St John the Baptist

sans pareil 12 without equal

sans peur et sans reproche 29 without fear and without reproach

sans souci 8 carefree **11** without care

Santa Cruz de Tenerife
  capital of: **13** Canary Islands

Santayana, George
  author of: **14** The Last Puritan **16** The Realms of Being, The Sense of Beauty **24** Skepticism and Animal Faith

Santiago
  capital of: **5** Chile

Santiago
  character in: **18** The Old Man and the Sea
  author: **9** Hemingway

Santo Domingo
  capital of: **17** Dominican Republic

Santo Domingo *see* **5** Haiti

Sao Tome
  capital of: **18** Sao Tome and Principe

Sao Tome and Principe
  capital/largest city: **7** Sao Tome
  others: **8** Trindade **11** Porto Alegre **12** Santo Antonio
  monetary unit: **5** dobra **6** escudo **7** centavo
  highest point: **7** Sao Tome
  sea: **8** Atlantic
  physical feature:
    bay: **11** Ana de Chaves
    gulf: **6** Guinea
  people: **7** African **10** Portuguese **11** Cape Verdean
    explorer: **7** Escobar **8** Santarem
  language: **10** Portuguese
  religion: **7** animism **13** Roman Catholic **19** Seventh Day Adventist **21** Evangelical Protestant

sap 3 rob, tax **4** ruin, wear **5** bleed, drain **6** impair, reduce, weaken **7** afflict, cripple, deplete, destroy, disable, exhaust, subvert **8** enervate, enfeeble **9** devastate, undermine **10** debilitate, devitalize

sapient 4 wise **7** knowing **8** profound **9** sagacious **10** discerning, perceptive **11** intelligent **13** knowledgeable

sap one's energy 3 fag **4** bush, poop, tire **5** drain, weary **6** tucker, weaken **7** deplete, exhaust, fatigue, wash out **8** enervate, enfeeble **10** debilitate, devitalize

Sapphira
  husband: **7** Ananias
  lied to: **5** Peter

sapphire 3 gem **4** blue **5** azure, jewel **6** indigo
  species: **8** corundum
  source: **5** Burma, Mogok **6** Ceylon **7** Kashmir **8** Sri Lanka, Thailand **9** Australia
  kind: **4** star

Sappho
  author: **14** Alphonse Daudet

Sarah, Sarai
  father: **5** Asher
  former name: **5** Sarai
  husband: **7** Abraham
  son: **5** Isaac
  slave: **5** Hagar
  burial place: **9** Machpelah

sarcasm 3 rub **4** gibe, jeer, jest **5** irony, scorn, sneer, taunt **7** mockery **8** contempt, derision, ridicule, scoffing **13** disparagement

sarcastic 5 acerb **6** biting, bitter, ironic **7** caustic, cutting, mocking, mordant **8** derisive, piercing, sardonic, scornful, sneering, stinging, taunting **11** disparaging **12** contemptuous

sarcoma 5 tumor **6** cancer, growth **8** neoplasm **10** malignancy

sarcophagus 4 pall **6** coffin

sard
  species: **6** quartz

sardine 4 bang, cram, fish, lile, lour, pack **5** crowd **7** alewife, anchovy, herring **8** pilchard

Sardinia
  other name: **8** Sardegna
  capital: **8** Cagliari
  cities: **4** Bono, Bosa **5** Nuoro, Olbia **7** Alghero, Bonorva, Sassari, Thatari **8** Iglesias, Oristano **11** Porto Torres
  division: **5** Nuoro **7** Arborea, Gallura, Sassari **8** Cagliari, Logudoro
  government: **13** region of Italy
  monetary unit: **7** carline
  island: **7** Caprera **8** Tavolara **9** Maddalena
  lake: **6** Omodeo
  mountain: **4** Rasu **5** Ferry, Linas **7** Gallura, Limbara **8** Marghine, Serpeddi, Vittoria **11** Gennargentu
  river: **5** Mannu, Tirso **6** Lascia **8** Coghinas **10** Flumendosa
  sea: **13** Mediterranean
  physical feature:
    gulf: **6** Orosei, Palmas **7** Asinara **8** Cagliari, Oristano
    plain: **7** Sassari **9** Campidano
    strait: **9** Bonifacio
  people:
    king: **12** Charles Felix **13** Charles Albert **14** Victor Emmanuel
    leader: **6** Cavour
    ruler: **4** Pisa **5** Genoa, Spain **7** Austria, Vandals **9** Byzantium, Phoenicia **12** House of Savoy
  language: **7** Italian
  religion: **13** Roman Catholic
  feature:
    towers: **7** nuraghi
  food:
    cheese: **6** romano **8** pecorino

Sardius 8 gemstone

sardonic 6 biting **7** caustic, cynical, jeering, mocking, mordant, satiric **8** derisive, scornful, sneering, taunting **9** sarcastic **11** disparaging **12** contemptuous

sardonyx 8 gemstone

Sargent, John Singer
  born: **5** Italy **8** Florence
  artwork: **6** Madam X (Madame Gautreau) **7** El Jaleo **17** The Wyndham Sisters **20** Robert Louis Stevenson **21** Carnation Lily Lily Rose **22** Daughters of Edward D Boit **24** Oyster Gatherers of Cancale

Sargon
  captured: **5** Accad
  successor: **11** Sennacherib

Saroyan, William
  author of: **12** My Name Is Aram **14** The Human Comedy **17** The Time of Your Life **22** My Heart's in the Highlands

Sarton, May
  author of: **5** Anger **11** At Eighty-Two,

Kinds of Love **17** Plant Dreaming Deep **20** Faithful Are the Wounds **29** The Education of Harriet Hatfield **33** Mrs Stevens Hears the Mermaids Singing

Sartor Resartus
  author: **13** Thomas Carlyle
Sartre, Jean-Paul
  author of: **6** Nausea, No Exit **8** The Words **17** The Roads to Freedom **19** Being and Nothingness
  philosophy: **14** Existentialism
  quote: **17** Hell is other people
sash 3 tie **4** band, belt **5** frame, scarf, strip **6** casing, corset, girdle, ribbon, window **7** baldric **8** casement **9** doorframe, waistband **10** cummerbund **11** windowframe
  Japanese: **3** obi
  pulley weight: **5** mouse
  window: **5** chess
sashay 4 move, skip **5** glide, mince **6** chasse, travel
sashimi 7 raw fish **12** Japanese dish
Saskatchewan 5 river **8** province
  boundary: **7** Alberta, Montana **8** Manitoba **11** North Dakota **12** Old Northwest **20** Northwest Territories
  capital: **6** Regina
  city: **8** Moose Jaw **9** Saskatoon **12** Prince Albert, Swift Current
  country: **6** Canada
  Indian: **4** Cree **9** Chipewyan **10** Assiniboin
  lake: **8** Reindeer **9** Athabasca, Wollaston
  mountain: **7** Cypress, Pasquia **9** Porcupine **14** Missouri Coteau
  river: **9** Churchill, Frenchman
  river mouth: **12** Lake Winnipeg
Sassoon, Siegfried
  author of: **26** The Memoirs of a Fox-Hunting Man **26** The Memoirs of George Sherston **29** The Memoirs of an Infantry Officer
sassy 4 bark, bold, flip, rude, tree **5** brash, fresh, saucy **6** mouthy, snippy **7** forward **8** impolite, impudent, insolent **12** discourteous **13** disrespectful
Satan 6 Belial, Moloch **7** Lucifer, Old Nick **8** Apollyon, the Devil **9** Beelzebub **10** Old Scratch, the Evil One, the Tempter **11** fallen angel **12** the Foul Fiend **13** the Old Serpent **14** Mephistopheles **19** the Prince of Darkness
satanic 3 bad **4** evil, vile **5** cruel **6** wicked **7** demonic, heinous, hellish, inhuman, vicious **8** devilish, fiendish, infamous, infernal, sadistic **9** malicious, malignant **10** demoniacal, diabolical, malevolent
satchel, Satchel 3 bag **4** case, grip, sack **5** purse **6** valise **7** handbag **8** reticule, suitcase **9** carpetbag, Gladstone, schoolbag
  pitcher, Hall of Famer: **5** Paige

sate 4 cloy, fill, glut **5** gorge, stuff **7** surfeit
satellite 4 moon **5** crony, toady **6** menial, puppet, vassal **7** servant **8** disciple, follower, hanger-on, parasite, retainer **9** assistant, attendant, companion, sycophant, tributary, underling
satellite state 6 colony **8** dominion **10** possession **12** protectorate
satiate 4 bore, cloy, fill, glut, jade **5** slake, stuff, weary **6** overdo, quench, sicken **7** content, disgust, gratify, suffice, surfeit **8** nauseate, overfill, saturate
Satie, Erik
  born: **6** France **8** Honfleur
  composer of: **6** Parade **13** Pieces froides **16** The Three Gymnasts **19** Limp Preludes for a Dog **20** Pieces en forme de poire **23** Pieces in the Shape of a Pear
satiny 4 fine **5** shiny, silky **6** smooth
satire 5 irony **6** banter, parody, send up **7** lampoon, mockery, sarcasm, takeoff **8** acrimony, derision, raillery, ridicule, travesty **9** burlesque **10** caricature, persiflage
satirical 5 comic **6** biting, bitter **7** caustic, mocking, mordant **8** derisive, humorous, ironical, sardonic, scornful, sneering **9** malicious, sarcastic
satirize 4 mock **6** parody **7** lampoon **9** burlesque **10** caricature
satisfaction 5 pride **6** amends **7** comfort, content, damages, deserts, justice, payment, redress **8** pleasure, requital **9** answering, atonement, happiness, quittance, reckoning, repayment **10** correction, recompense, remittance, settlement **11** contentment, fulfillment, restitution **12** compensation, remuneration **13** gratification, rectification, reimbursement
satisfactory 2 OK **4** okay **8** adequate, all right, passable, suitable **9** competent **10** acceptable, sufficient
satisfied 5 happy **7** content, pleased **9** gratified **10** complacent **11** comfortable
satisfy 3 pay **4** fill, meet **5** annul, clear, remit, repay, serve, slake **6** answer, assure, pacify, pay off, please, quench, remove, settle **7** appease, content, delight, fulfill, gratify, mollify, requite, suffice **8** convince, persuade, reassure **9** discharge, reimburse **10** compensate, recompense
satisfying 8 pleasant, pleasing **9** agreeable, enjoyable, rewarding **10** delightful, fulfilling, gratifying **11** pleasurable
satori
  term in: **3** Zen
  means: **13** enlightenment
saturate 4 fill **5** cover, douse, imbue,

souse **6** drench, infuse **7** immerse, pervade, suffuse **8** permeate, submerge **10** impregnate, infiltrate
saturated 3 wet **4** full **5** drunk, soggy, soppy **6** soaked, sodden **8** bursting
Saturday
  day of: **15** Biblical Sabbath
  French: **6** samedi
  from: **8** Saturnus
  German: **7** samstag
  heavenly body: **6** Saturn
  Italian: **6** sabato
  observance: **13** Jewish Sabbath **20** Seventh Day Adventists
  Spanish: **6** sabado
Saturday Night Fever
  director: **10** John Badham
  cast: **11** Barry Miller **12** John Travolta **15** Karen Lynn Gorney
  setting: **8** Brooklyn
  score: **7** Bee Gees
  sequel: **12** Staying Alive
Saturday Night Live, NBC's
  regular: **9** Al Franken, Chris Rock, Mike Myers **10** Bill Murray, Chevy Chase, Dana Carvey, Dan Aykroyd, David Spade, Jane Curtin **11** Adam Sandler, Chris Farley, Eddie Murphy, Gilda Radner, John Belushi, Phil Hartman, Will Ferrel **13** Garrett Morris, Laraine Newman **14** Darrell Hammond **15** Janeane Garofalo
  group: **27** Not Ready For Prime Time Players
  bits: **4** Bees **7** Samurai **9** Coneheads **10** Church Lady **13** Blues Brothers, Weekend Update **16** Pathological Liar **18** Rosanne Rosanna-Dana
Saturn
  origin: **5** Roman
  god of: **11** agriculture
  consort of: **3** Ops
  son: **5** Picus
  corresponds to: **6** Cronos, Cronus, Kronos
Saturn
  position: **5** sixth
  satellite: **4** Rhea **5** Dione, Janus, Mimas, Titan **6** Phoebe, Tethys **7** Iapetus **8** Hyperion **9** Enceladus
  characteristic: **5** rings
saturnalia, Saturnalia 4 orgy **5** revel, spree **7** carouse, debauch, revelry **8** carousal **9** bacchanal **10** debauchery
  origin: **5** Roman
  event: **8** festival
  honoring: **6** Saturn **13** sowing of crops
saturnine 4 dour, glum, grim **5** grave, staid, stern, sulky **6** gloomy, moping, morose, solemn, somber, sullen **7** austere, serious **8** dejected, downcast, reserved, sardonic, taciturn **9** apathetic, cheerless, withdrawn **11** downhearted **15** uncommunicative
satyr
  form: **4** faun **5** deity

location: 8 woodland
part: 3 man **4** goat
attendant of: 7 Bacchus
known for: 7 lechery

Satyricon
  author: 9 Petronius
  character: 4 Gito **8** Ascyltus, Eumolpus **9** Encolpius **10** Trimalchio

sauce 3 dip **4** sass **5** booze, gravy, salsa **6** fillip, flavor **7** alcohol **8** dressing, pertness **9** condiment, flippancy **12** impertinence
  basil: 5 pesto
  fish: 4 alec
  hot: 7 Tabasco
  Indian: 5 curry
  salty: 3 soy

saucy 4 bold, pert, rude, trim **5** brash, cocky, fresh, natty, smart **6** brazen, cheeky, jaunty, lively, spruce **7** forward **8** flippant, impolite, impudent, insolent **9** audacious, barefaced, unabashed **11** impertinent, smart-alecky **12** discourteous **13** disrespectful

Saudi Arabia
  capital/largest city: 6 Riyadh
  others: 4 Abha, Hail, Taif **5** Hofuf, Hufuf, Jedda, Jidda, Yanbu, Yenbo **6** Anaiza, Dammam, Jiddah, Jubail **7** Alhofuf, Buraido, Dhahran **9** Ras Tanura
    holy city: 5 Mecca **6** Medina
  school: 5 Islam **13** King Abd al-Aziz **19** Imam Muhammad bin Saud **20** Petroleum and Minerals
  division: 4 Asir, Nejd **5** Hejaz **6** El Hasa
  government: 8 monarchy
  head of state/government: 4 king
  monetary unit: 5 girsh, gursh, pound, riyal
  weight: 3 oke
  mountain: 6 Tuwayq
    highlands: 4 Asir **5** Hejaz
  highest point: 5 Razih **10** Jebal Sawda
  sea: 3 Red
  natural resource: 3 oil **9** petroleum **10** natural gas
  physical feature:
    desert: 3 Red **5** Dahna, Nafud, Nefud, Nufud **6** al-Dahy, Dahana **10** Rub al Khali
    gulf: 5 Aqaba **7** Persian
    peninsula: 7 Arabian
    plain: 6 Tihama
    plateau: 4 Nejd
  people: 4 Arab **7** Bedouin
    king: 4 Fahd, Saud **6** Faisal, Khalid **7** Ibn Saud **9** Abdul Aziz
    religious leader: 8 Mohammed, Muhammad
  language: 6 Arabic
  religion: 5 Islam
    sect: 5 Sunni **6** Shiite **7** Wahhabi
  place:
    shrine: 5 Kaaba **10** Black Stone
  feature:

annual pilgrimage: 4 hadj, hajj
clothing: 3 aba **4** agal **5** thobe **6** ghutra
kingdom: 5 Hejaz **7** Minaean, Ottoman, Sabaean **9** Himyarite
laws of Islam: 6 sharia
village school: 6 kuttab
war: 4 Gulf **11** Desert Storm **12** Desert Shield

Sauguet, Henri
  born: 6 France **8** Bordeaux
  composer of: 6 La Nuit **10** Les Forains, Les Mirages

Sauk, Sac
  family: 9 Algonkian **10** Algonquian
  tribe: 3 Fox, Sac **8** Kickapoo
  location: 4 Iowa, Ohio **6** Kansas **7** Indiana **8** Illinois, Michigan, Oklahoma **9** Wisconsin
  leader: 9 Blackhawk
  related to: 8 Kickapoo **9** Mesquakie **11** Potawatomie
  involved in: 12 Black Hawk War

Saul
  king of: 4 Edom **6** Israel
  father: 4 Kish
  daughter: 5 Merab **6** Michal
  son: 7 Abinoam **8** Jonathan **10** Ishbosheth
  anointed by: 6 Samuel
  hometown: 6 Gibeah **8** Rehoboth
  successor: 5 David

Saunders, Allen
  creator/artist of: 9 Mary Worth

saunter 4 roam **5** amble, mosey, stray **6** loiter, ramble, stroll, wander **7** meander, traipse **8** straggle **9** promenade

sausage 5 frank, gigot, wurst **6** hotdog, salami, weenie, wiener **7** baloney, bologna **8** kielbasa **9** bratwurst, pepperoni **10** liverwurst **11** frankfurter
  British: 6 banger

sauve qui peut 4 rout **8** stampede **18** every man for himself **23** let him save himself who can

savage 4 boor, wild **5** brute, cruel, feral, fiend, harsh, rough, yahoo **6** animal, bloody, brutal, fierce, maniac, native, rugged, unkind **7** brutish, hoodlum, ruffian, untamed, violent **8** barbaric, hooligan, pitiless, ruthless, sadistic **9** aborigine, barbarian, barbarous, ferocious, merciless, murderous, primitive **10** aboriginal, heathenish, relentless, uncultured, unmerciful **11** uncivilized **12** uncultivated **14** undomesticated

savagery 7 cruelty **8** ferocity **9** barbarism, barbarity, brutality **10** fierceness, inhumanity **12** pitilessness, ruthlessness

savanna, savannah 5 campo, plain **9** grassland

savant 6 genius **7** scholar **13** learned person

save 3 but **4** bank, free, help, hold,

keep **5** amass, guard, hoard, lay by, lay up, put by, spare, stock, store **6** defend, except, garner, heap up, redeem, rescue, shield **7** deliver, deposit, husband, protect, put away, recover, reserve, salvage **8** conserve, preserve, retrench, withhold **9** economize, safeguard **10** accumulate

save up 5 amass, hoard **7** collect, put away **8** salt away, sock away **10** accumulate **12** squirrel away

saving 5 close, tight **6** frugal, stingy **7** careful, miserly, prudent, sparing, thrifty **8** markdown, stinting **9** illiberal, niggardly, provident, redeeming, restoring **10** economical, reclaiming, redemptory, reparative **12** compensating, conservative

savings 3 IRA **5** hoard **7** nest egg, reserve

savior 5 freer **7** rescuer **8** champion, defender, guardian, redeemer **9** deliverer, liberator, preserver, protecter, protector, salvation **11** emancipator

Savior 5 Jesus **6** Christ **8** Redeemer **10** the Messiah **11** Jesus Christ, the Son of God **13** Prince of Peace

Savior anointed 5 Jesus

savoir-faire 4 tact **5** poise **6** aplomb, polish **7** finesse, know-how, suavity **8** presence, urbanity **9** assurance, composure **10** adroitness, discretion, smoothness **11** worldliness **12** complaisance, graciousness **14** self-possession

savoir-vivre 16 knowing how to live **19** knowledge of the world

savor 3 try **4** aura, gist, like, odor, soul, tang, zest **5** aroma, enjoy, scent, smack, smell, spice, taste, trait **6** flavor, nature, relish, sample, season, spirit **7** essence, quality **8** piquancy, property, pungency **9** character, fragrance, substance **10** appreciate, experience **11** peculiarity **13** particularity **14** characteristic

savory 5 tangy, tasty, yummy **6** honest **7** odorous, piquant, pungent **8** alluring, aromatic, charming, edifying, fragrant, luscious, tasteful **9** delicious, flavorous, palatable, reputable, toothsome **10** appetizing, attractive, delectable **11** inoffensive, respectable, scrumptious **13** mouth-watering

savory
  botanical name: 8 Satureia, S montana **10** S hortensis
  origin: 13 Mediterranean
  varieties: 6 summer, winter
  use: 4 eggs, meat **5** beans, salad **6** sauces **8** dressing **11** chicken soup

savvy 5 catch, get it **7** know-how **10** comprehend, understand **13** understanding

saw 3 cut **4** tool **5** adage, maxim, slash **6** saying **7** proverb **8** aphorism
  type: 3 jig, rip **4** back, band, hack **5**

miter **6** coping **7** keyhole **8** circular, crosscut

sawfly
varieties: 4 stem, wood **5** cedar **6** pergid **7** conifer **8** horntail **11** web spinning

saxophone
type: 4 alto **5** tenor

say 2 do **4** hint, hold, read, tell, vote, word **5** bruit, claim, guess, imply, judge, mouth, rumor, speak, state, utter, voice **6** allege, assert, assume, chance, convey, phrase, reason, recite, remark, render, repeat, report, reveal, spread **7** comment, contend, declare, deliver, divulge, express, imagine, mention, perform, suggest, suppose, surmise **8** announce, disclose, intimate, maintain, rehearse, vocalize **9** circulate, franchise, insinuate, pronounce, verbalize **10** articulate, conjecture **11** communicate

Sayers, Dorothy L
author of: 9 Whose Body **12** Strong Poison **14** Have His Carcase, The Nine Tailors, Unnatural Death **15** Clouds of Witness, Five Red Herrings **16** Busman's Honeymoon **19** Murder Must Advertise **30** Unpleasantness at the Bellona Club
character: 6 Bunter **11** Harriet Vane **15** Lord Peter Wimsey

Say Hey Kid
nickname of: 10 Willie Mays

saying 3 saw **5** adage, maxim, moral, motto **6** byword, dictum, truism **7** epigram, precept, proverb **8** aphorism, apothegm **10** expression

Sayonara
director: 11 Joshua Logan
author: 13 James Michener
cast: 9 Miiko Taka **10** Red Buttons **11** James Garner, Martha Scott **12** Marlon Brando, Miyoshi Umeki **16** Ricardo Montalban
score: 12 Irving Berlin
Oscar for: 15 supporting actor (Buttons) **17** supporting actress (Umeki)

scabrous 5 dirty, rough, scaly **7** immoral, leprous **8** indecent, off-color **9** salacious **10** suggestive **12** pornographic

scalding 3 hot **5** harsh **7** boiling, caustic **8** seething, steaming **9** sarcastic

scale, scales 3 key, set **4** chip, film, husk, peel, rise, rule, skin **5** crust, flake, layer, mount, order, plate, range, ratio, scour, shave, shell, weigh **6** adjust, ascend, goupen, ladder, lamina, octave, rub off, scrape, series, spread **7** balance, chip off, clamber, climb up, coating, lamella, measure **8** escalade, membrane, register, regulate, spectrum, surmount **9** continuum, gradation, solfeggio **10** delaminate, graduation, proportion **11**

calibration, progression **14** classification

scale down 4 trim **6** reduce **7** abridge, curtail, shorten **8** compress, condense, decrease, diminish, downsize, moderate **10** abbreviate

scale insects
varieties: 3 lac, pit, wax **5** giant **6** ensign **7** armored **8** mealybug, tortoise **12** ground pearls

scale note 2 do, fa, la, mi, re, so, ti **3** sol
Guido's: 3 ela

scamp 3 imp, rip **5** cut-up, knave, rogue, tease **6** rascal, rotter **7** bounder, villain **8** blighter, scalawag **9** miscreant, prankster, scoundrel **10** scapegrace **11** rapscallion **13** mischief-maker

scamper 3 fly, run, zip **4** dart, dash, flit, race, romp, rush, scud **5** frisk, hurry, scoot **6** frolic, gambol, hasten, scurry, sprint **7** scuttle **8** skedaddle **21** running about playfully

scan 4 skim **5** check, probe, scour, study, sweep **6** peruse, search, size up, survey **7** analyze, examine, explore, inspect **10** scrutinize

scandal 4 blot **5** abuse, libel, odium, shame, stain **6** expose, smirch, stigma **7** calumny, obloquy, outrage, slander **8** disgrace, dishonor, ignominy **9** aspersion, discredit, disesteem, sensation **10** debasement, detraction, opprobrium, revilement **12** vituperation **13** disparagement, embarrassment

scandalize 5 shock **6** appall, defame, insult, offend **7** horrify, outrage **10** calumniate

scandalmonger 6 gossip **8** busybody **10** talebearer, tattletale

scandalous 8 libelous, shameful, shocking **9** gossiping, offensive **10** defamatory, outrageous, scurrilous, slanderous **11** disgraceful **12** disreputable **13** reprehensible

Scandinavia 6 Norway, Sweden **7** Denmark, Faeroes, Iceland

Scandinavian (Norse)
language family: 12 Indo-European
branch: 8 Germanic
group: 15 Western Germanic
language: 6 Danish **7** Faroese, Swedish **9** Icelandic, Norwegian

scant 3 cut **4** bare **5** limit, short, small, stint **6** in need, meager, paltry, reduce, sparse **7** limited **8** exiguous, hold back **9** deficient **10** inadequate, incomplete **12** insufficient

scantiness 10 deficiency, inadequacy, meagerness, skimpiness **13** insufficiency

scanty 4 thin **5** short, small **6** meager, modest, paltry, skimpy, sparse **7** slender, stunted **9** deficient **10** inadequate, undersized **12** insufficient

scapegoat, Scapegoat 4 butt, dupe, gull **5** patsy **6** Azazel, victim **7** fall guy **11** whipping boy **13** laughing-stock

scapolite
source: 5 Burma, Mogok

scapula
bone of: 13 shoulder blade

scar 3 cut, pit **4** dent, flaw, gash, hurt, mark, pock, seam **5** brand, wound **6** affect, bruise, damage, deface, defect, impair, mangle **7** blemish, scratch **8** cicatrix, lacerate, mutilate **9** disfigure, influence

Scaramouch(e) 6 coward, rascal **8** braggart, poltroon

scarce 4 rare **6** scanty, sparse **7** unusual, wanting **8** uncommon **9** deficient

scarcely 4 just **6** at most, barely, hardly **7** but just, faintly **8** slightly

scarcity 4 lack, want **5** stint **6** dearth, rarity **7** fewness, paucity **8** rareness, shortage, sparsity, thinness **10** deficiency, scantiness, sparseness **12** uncommonness **13** insufficiency

scare 4 turn **5** alarm, daunt, panic, shake, shock, start **6** harrow, shiver **7** horrify, jitters, startle, terrify **8** disquiet, frighten **9** terrorize **10** disconcert, dishearten, intimidate **11** nervousness, palpitation **13** consternation

scarecrow 6 effigy **8** straw man

Scarecrow
character in: 13 The Wizard of Oz
author: 4 Baum

scared 5 shaky, timid, upset **6** afraid **7** alarmed, fearful, nervous, spooked **8** startled, timorous **9** diffident, terrified, tremulous **10** frightened **12** apprehensive, fainthearted **13** panic-stricken

scarf 3 boa **4** sash, veil, wrap **5** ascot, shawl, stole **6** choker, cravat, tippet **7** foulard, muffler, overlay **8** babushka, bandanna, mantilla **11** neckerchief

Scarface
director: 11 Howard Hawks
cast: 8 Paul Muni **9** Ann Dvorak **10** George Raft **12** Boris Karloff

scarify 3 cut **6** incise, loosen **7** break up, scratch **8** lacerate **9** cultivate

Scarlatti, Alessandro
born: 6 Sicily **7** Palermo
composer of: 11 Stabat Mater **17** Mitridate Eupatore, The Triumph of Honor **18** Il Trionfo dell Onore **23** Gli equivoci nel sembiante

Scarlatti, Domenico
born: 5 Italy **6** Naples
composer of: 7 Sonatas **9** Cat's Fugue, Essercizi **18** Le Donne di Buon Umore **20** The Good-Humored Ladies **23** Ottavia risituita al trono

scarlet 3 red **6** cherry, claret **7** carmine **8** cardinal

Scarlet Letter, The
author: **18** Nathaniel Hawthorne
character: **5** Pearl **12** Hester Prynne **16** Arthur Dimmesdale **18** Roger Chillingworth

Scarlett *see* **15** Gone With the Wind

scary 3 bad **5** awful, hairy **6** creepy **7** fearful **8** alarming, menacing, shocking **9** difficult **10** disturbing, terrifying **11** frightening, goosepimply, hairraising, threatening **12** discomfiting

scat 3 off, out **4** away, shoo **5** be off, leave, scram **6** beat it, be gone, depart, get out, go away **7** get lost, vamoose

scathing 4 keen, tart **5** sharp **6** biting, brutal, savage **7** caustic, cutting, hostile, mordant, pointed, searing **8** incisive, stinging, virulent **9** ferocious, rancorous, scorching, trenchant, vitriolic, withering **10** lacerating **11** acrimonious, excoriating

scatter 3 sow **4** cast, flee, rout **5** strew, throw **6** dispel **8** disperse, sprinkle **9** broadcast, circulate, dissipate **10** distribute **11** disseminate

scatterbrained 4 rash, wild, zany **5** crazy, dizzy, giddy, nutty, silly **6** madcap, stupid **7** flighty, foolish **8** careless, heedless, reckless, unstable, unsteady **9** foolhardy, forgetful, frivolous, imprudent **11** birdbrained, empty-headed, harebrained **12** absentminded, muddleheaded **13** irresponsible

scattered 6 random, spotty **7** diffuse **9** irregular **10** infrequent, occasional

scattering 6 sowing **7** casting **8** strewing **9** dispersal **10** dispersing, sprinkling **12** broadcasting, distribution **13** dissemination

scavenger 5 hyena **6** magpie **7** vulture **8** salvager **9** collector

scenario 4 book, idea, plan **6** scheme **7** concept, outline, summary **8** abstract, game plan, synopsis, teleplay **10** conception, manuscript, screenplay
French: **6** precis

scene 3 act **4** fuss, part, show, site, spot, to-do, view **5** place, sight, vista **6** locale, region, survey, vision **7** display, episode, picture, scenery, setting **8** backdrop, division, locality, location, panorama, position, prospect, sequence **9** commotion, spectacle **10** background **11** whereabouts

scenery 4 sets, view **5** vista **7** terrain **9** backdrops, landscape, spectacle **11** backgrounds

Scenes from a Marriage
director: **13** Ingmar Bergman
cast: **10** Liv Ullmann **13** Bibi Andersson **15** Erland Josephson

scent 4 odor, path, wake, wind **5** aroma, smell, sniff, spoor, trace, track, trail **6** course, detect, inhale **7** bouquet, breathe, discern, essence,

perfume, pursuit, suspect **9** aromatize, fragrance, get wind of, recognize **11** distinguish

scented 5 spicy **7** odorous, piquant, pungent **8** aromatic, fragrant, perfumed **9** odiferous **13** sweet-smelling

Schaffner, Franklin
director of: **6** Patton (Oscar) **8** Papillon **15** Planet of the Apes **17** The Boys from Brazil **20** Nicholas and Alexandra

schedule 3 fix **4** book, list, plan, roll **5** fit in, slate, table **6** agenda **7** appoint, program, put down, set down **8** calendar **9** inventory, timetable

Scheele, Karl Wilhelm
field: **9** chemistry
nationality: **7** Swedish
discovered: **6** oxygen **8** chlorine **9** glycerine

Scheider, Roy
born: **8** Orange NJ
roles: **4** Jaws **11** All That Jazz, Blue Thunder, The Seven-Ups **14** Chain of Command, Fifty-Two Pickup **15** Still of the Night **19** The French Connection

Schell, Maria
real name: **15** Margarete Schell
born: **6** Vienna **7** Austria
brother: **16** Maximilian Schell
roles: **8** Cimarron, Gervaise **11** End of Desire, White Nights **13** The Last Bridge **20** The Brothers Karamazov

Schell, Maximilian
born: **6** Vienna **7** Austria
sister: **11** Maria Schell
goddaughter: **13** Angelina Jolie
roles: **13** The Young Lions **19** Judgment at Nuremberg (Oscar) **20** Telling Lies in America **21** The Man in the Glass Booth

scheme 3 map, way **4** plan, plot, ruse **5** cabal, chart, frame, means, shift, study **6** course, design, device, devise, layout, method, policy, sketch, system **7** complot, concoct, connive, drawing, network, outline, program, project, tactics **8** conspire, contrive, grouping, intrigue, maneuver, organize, strategy **9** machinate, procedure, stratagem **10** connivance, conspiracy **11** arrangement, contrivance, delineation, disposition, machination **12** organization

scheming 3 sly **4** arch, wily **6** artful, crafty, shrewd, tricky **7** cunning **8** slippery **9** conniving, designing, insidious **10** contriving, intriguing **11** calculating **13** Machiavellian

Schiller, (Johann) Friedrich von
author of: **8** Ode to Joy **9** Don Carlos **11** Maria Stuart, William Tell **17** The Bride of Messina **18** The Maiden of Orleans

Schindler's List
author: **14** Thomas Keneally
director: **15** Steven Spielberg

cast: **10** Liam Neeson (Oskar Schindler) **11** Ben Kingsley (Itzhak Stern) **12** Ralph Fiennes (Amon Goeth) **13** Embeth Davidtz (Helen Hirsch) **15** Caroline Goodall (Emilie Schindler), Jonathan Sagalle (Poldek Pfefferberg)

schism 5 break, split **8** division **10** separation **14** disassociation

Schlegel family
characters in: **10** Howards End
members: **5** Helen **8** Margaret, Theobald
author: **7** Forster

schlepp 3 lug **4** cart, haul, tote **5** carry **6** convey **9** transport

Schlesinger, Arthur M, Jr
author of: **13** A Thousand Days **15** The Age of Jackson **17** The Age of Roosevelt **21** The Imperial Presidency **24** Robert Kennedy and His Times **26** The Cycles of American History

Schlesinger, John
director of: **7** Darling **14** Midnight Cowboy (Oscar) **22** The Falcon and the Snowman

Schlesinger, Leon
creator/artist of: **9** Bugs Bunny

schmaltz 4 corn **14** sentimentalism, sentimentality

Schmeling, Max (Maxmillian Adolph Otto Siegfried)
nickname: **10** Black Uhlan
sport: **6** boxing
class: **11** heavyweight

Schneider, Romy
real name: **20** Rosemarie Albach-Retty
born: **6** Vienna **7** Austria
roles: **8** The Trial **11** The Cardinal **16** Boccaccio Seventy

Schoenberg, Arnold
born: **6** Vienna **7** Austria
composer of: **9** Erwartung **11** De Profundis, Expectation, Gurrelieder **12** The Lucky Hand **13** Moses and Aaron, Ode to Napoleon **14** Verklarte Nacht **16** Die Glucklich Hand, Resplendent Night **17** Transfigured Night **19** A Survivor from Warsaw, Pelleas and Melisande **26** The Book of the Hanging Gardens

Schoenius
father: **7** Athamas
mother: **8** Themisto
wife: **7** Clymene
daughter: **8** Atalanta

scholar 4 coed, sage **5** brain, grind, pupil **6** pundit, savant **7** egghead, learner, student, studier, wise man **8** bookworm, humanist, mandarin **9** collegian, schoolboy **10** schoolgirl **11** matriculant **12** intellectual **13** undergraduate

scholarly 6 humane **7** erudite, learned, liberal **8** academic, educated, informed, lettered, literate, well-read **12** intellectual

scholarship 5 grant **7** stipend **8** learning **9** education, endowment, erudition **12** intelligence, thoroughness **13** enlightenment

scholastic 8 academic, pedantic **9** pedagogic **11** educational **12** professorial **13** instructional

school 3 ism **4** view **5** bunch, crowd, faith, order, style, teach, train **6** belief, lyceum, method, system, theory **7** academy, college, educate, faction, thought **8** doctrine, instruct, seminary **9** institute **10** persuasion, university **12** denomination, kindergarten

schoolbook 3 abc **4** text **5** atlas **6** manual, primer, reader **7** grammar, lessons, speller

School for Scandal, The
   author: 23 Richard Brinsley Sheridan
   character: 5 Maria **6** Rowley **10** Lady Teazle **11** Joseph Surface, Lady Sneerwell **14** Charles Surface, Sir Peter Teazle **16** Sir Oliver Surface

School for Wives, The
   author: 7 Moliere
   character: 5 Agnes **6** Horace, Oronte **7** Enrique **8** Arnolphe **9** Chrysalde

schooling 5 drill **8** drilling, training **9** education **11** instruction, preparation **14** indoctrination

schoolmaster 4 head **5** tutor **7** dominie, pedagog, scholar, teacher **9** pedagogue, principal, professor **10** headmaster, instructor **12** disciplinarian
   fish: 7 snapper
   genus: 8 Lutianus
   species: 6 apodus

Schubert, Franz Peter
   born: 6 Vienna **7** Austria
   composer of: 6 Little (symphony), Tragic (symphony No 4) **8** Sad Waltz **9** Rosamunde **11** Winterreise **12** Trout Quintet **13** Mourning Waltz **17** Die Schone Mullerin **18** Unfinished Symphony (No 8) **24** Death and the Maiden Quartet, Symphony of Heavenly Length

Schulz, Charles
   creator/artist of: 7 Peanuts

Schuman, William
   born: 9 New York NY
   composer of: 8 Undertow **9** Credendum **14** The Mighty Casey **16** American Festival **18** New England Triptych

Schumann, Robert Alexander
   born: 7 Germany, Zwickau
   composer of: 6 Myrten, Spring (symphony No 1) **7** Rhenish (symphony No 3) **8** Arabeske, Carnival **9** Papillons **10** Novelettes **11** Blumenstuck, Butterflies, Nachtstucke, Nightpieces, Novelletten **12** Bunte Blatter, Dichterliebe, Flower Pieces, Kinderscenen, Kreisleriana, Motley Leaves

14 Fantasiestucke **16** David's Band Dances, Symphonic Studies **18** Davidsbundlertanze **19** Frauenliebe und Leben

Schwann, Theodor
   field: 7 biology
   nationality: 6 German
   established: 10 cell theory

Schwarzenegger, Arnold
   roles: 5 Twins **6** Junior **7** Red Heat **8** Commando, Predator, Red Sonja, True Lies **9** End of Days **11** Total Recall **13** The Terminator **15** Kindergarten Cop **16** Collateral Damage **17** Conan the Barbarian, Conan the Destroyer
   wife: 12 Maria Shriver
   politics:
      party: 10 Republican
      governor of: 10 California

Schweitzer, Albert
   field: 8 medicine
   worked in: 5 Gabon **6** Africa
   founded: 17 Lambarene Hospital
   awarded: 15 Nobel Peace Prize

Schwitters, Kurt
   born: 7 Germany **8** Hannover
   artwork: 7 Merzbau
   collages called: 10 Merzbilden

science 3 art **5** skill **6** method **7** finesse **8** aptitude, facility **9** technique **10** discipline **11** acquirement
   god of: 7 Mercury

scintilla 3 dot, jot **4** atom, iota **5** shred, spark, speck, trace **7** glimmer **10** smithereen

scintillate 4 joke, snap **5** amuse, charm, flash, gleam, glint, shine, spark **7** glimmer, glisten, glitter, shimmer, sparkle, twinkle **9** coruscate **10** effervesce

scintillating 5 witty **6** bright, lively **8** animated, charming, dazzling **9** brilliant, ebullient, exuberant, sparkling **10** glittering **11** stimulating **12** effervescent

scion 3 son **4** heir, seed **5** child, issue **7** heiress, progeny **8** daughter, offshoot **9** offspring, posterity, successor **10** descendant **11** progeniture

scissors 5 snips **6** blades, cutter, shears **7** clipper, snipper, trimmer
   French: 8 secateur

scoff 4 jeer, mock, razz **5** flout, knock, taunt **6** deride, rail at, revile **7** condemn, laugh at, put down, run down **8** belittle, ridicule

Scofield, Paul
   real name: 13 David Scofield
   born: 7 England **14** Hurstpierpoint
   roles: 8 King Lear, Quiz Show **11** The Crucible **13** Sir Thomas More **17** A Man for All Seasons (Oscar)

scold 3 nag **5** chide, shrew **6** berate, carp at, nagger, rail at, rebuke, virago **7** censure, reprove, upbraid **9** castigate, criticize, dress down, reprehend,

reprimand, termagant **10** complainer
   Yiddish: 6 kvetch

scolding 7 chiding, reproof **8** berating, rebuking **9** reprimand, talking-to **10** admonition, upbraiding **11** castigation **12** admonishment **13** tongue-lashing

sconce 7 bracket **11** candlestick **12** candleholder

scoop 4 bail, beat **5** clean, clear, gouge, ladle, spoon **6** burrow, dig out, dipper, hollow, shovel, trowel **7** dish out, lade out, lift out **8** excavate

scoop out 3 dig **5** gouge **8** excavate

scoot 3 run **4** dash, rush **6** scurry, sprint

Scooter
   nickname of: 11 Phil Rizzuto

scope 3 aim **4** area, goal, rein, room, span, vent **5** field, force, grasp, range, reach **6** bounds, effect, margin, motive, spread, vision **7** bearing, compass, freedom, liberty, purpose, stretch **8** ambition, confines, latitude **9** extension, influence, intention **10** competence **11** application, destination **13** determination

scorch 3 dry **4** char, sear **5** parch, singe **6** dry out, scathe, wither **7** blacken **8** discolor **9** dehydrate

score, scores 3 cut, mar, run, tab, win **4** bill, debt, gain, gash, goal, lots, make, mark, nick, slit **5** amass, count, facts, grade, hosts, judge, notch, point, slash, tally, truth **6** basket, charge, damage, deface, droves, groove, grudge, masses, pile up, strike, swarms, twenty **7** account, achieve, arrange, legions, reality, scratch, throngs **8** evaluate, incision, register **9** grievance **10** amount owed, difference, multitudes, obligation **11** orchestrate

scoria 4 slag **5** dross **6** cinder, refuse

scorn 5 spurn **6** ignore, rebuff, refuse, reject, slight **7** condemn, despise, disdain, mockery, repulse, sarcasm **8** contempt, derision, ridicule, scoffing, spit upon **9** arrogance, contumely, disregard, ostracize **10** look down on, opprobrium **11** haughtiness

scorned 7 derided, refused **8** despised, rebuffed, rejected, repulsed **9** disdained **10** deprecated, disparaged

scornful 6 lordly **7** cynical **8** arrogant, derisive, insolent, sardonic, scoffing, sneering **9** sarcastic **10** disdainful, ridiculing **11** disparaging **12** contemptuous, supercilious

Scorpio, Scorpius
   symbol: 8 scorpion
   planet: 4 Mars **5** Pluto
   rules: 5 death **7** passion
   born: 7 October **8** November

Scorpion 4 whip **7** scourge
   constellation of: 8 Scorpius

Scorsese, Martin
director of: 6 Casino, Kundun **8** Cape Fear **10** After Hours, Goodfellas, Raging Bull, Taxi Driver, The Aviator **11** Mean Streets **12** The Last Waltz **14** Gangs of New York, Mad Dog and Glory **25** The Last Temptation of Christ

scotch 4 foil, kill, stop **5** crush, quash **6** thwart **7** destroy **8** confound, obstruct, sabotage, suppress **9** undermine **11** nip in the bud

scotch
type: 6 whisky **7** whiskey **10** singlemalt
origin: 8 Scotland
ingredient: 12 cereal grains
drink: 10 Scotch Mist **14** Highland Cooler
with amaretto: 9 Godfather
with cherry brandy: 12 Blood and Sand
with Drambuie: 9 Rusty Nail
with gin: 12 Barbary Coast
with vermouth: 6 Rob Roy **8** Affinity **10** Bobby Burns
brands: 5 J and B **7** Dewars **10** White Horse **11** Chivas Regal, Wild Grouse **12** Johnny Walker

Scotia
poetic: 8 Scotland

Scotland
Roman name: 9 Caledonia
capital: 9 Edinburgh
symbol: 7 thistle
poetic: 6 Scotia
largest city: 7 Glasgow
others: 3 Ayr **4** Duns, Oban **5** Alloa, Banff, Brora, Burgh, Cupar, Ellon, Leith, Perth, Salen, Troon **6** Dundee, Girvan, Hawick **7** Airdrie, Alloway, Dunkeld, Falkirk, Frunock, Mallaig, Paisley, Renfrew **8** Aberdeen, Dumfries, Greenock, Hamilton, Kirkwall, Rothesay, Stirling **9** Clydebank, Dumbarton, Greenlock, Inverness, Kirkcaldy, Peter head, St Andrews **10** Coatbridge, Kilmarnock, Motherwell **11** Dunfermline, Grangemouth
school: 7 Glasgow **8** Aberdeen **9** Edinburgh **12** Saint Andrew's
division: 3 Ayr **4** Bute, Fife, Ross **5** Angus, Banff, Moray, Nairn, Perth **6** Argyll, Lanark, Orkney **7** Berwick, Kinross, Lothian, Peebles, Renfrew, Selkirk, Wigtown **8** Aberdeen, Ayrshire, Cromarty, Dumfries, Roxburgh, Shetland, Stirling **9** Buteshire, Caithness, Dumbarton **10** Kincardine, Midlothian, Sutherland **11** Clackmannan, Kincudbight **12** Renfrewshire **13** Stirlingshire
kingdom: 8 Dalriada **11** Northumbria, Strathclyde
government: 13 United Kingdom
measure: 3 cop **4** boll, cran, fall, mile, peck, pint, rood, rope, span **5**

crane, lippy **6** audlet, davach, firlot, lippie, noggin **7** chalder, choppin **8** mutchkin, stimpart, stimpert **9** particate, shaftment, shathmont
monetary unit: 3 ecu **4** demy, doit, lion, mark, rial, ryal **5** bodle, broad, groat, plack, rider, turne **6** bawbee, folles **7** unicorn **8** atchison, hardhead **9** halfpenny **11** bonnetpiece
weight: 4 boll, drop **5** trone **6** bushel
island: 3 Rum **4** Aran, Bute, Eigg, Fair, Inch, Iona, Jura, Lona, Muck, Mull, Rhum, Skye **5** Arran, Barra, Islay, Lewis **6** Harris, Orkney, Staffa **7** St Kilda **8** Berneray, Cumbraes, Hebrides, Shetland **9** North Uist, South Uist
lake/loch: 3 Awe, Dee, Lin, Tay **4** Earn, Fyne, Gair, Gare, Linn, Ness, Oich, Ryan, Sloy **5** Duich, Leven, Lochy, Lough, Morar, Maree, Nevis **6** Laggan, Linnhe, Lomond **7** Katrine, Rannoch, St Mary's
mountain: 4 Hope **5** Attow, Dearg, Nevis, Tinto, Wyvis **7** Cheviot, Macdhui, Merrick **8** Grampian **9** Ben Lomond, Cairngorm, Highlands, Trossachs
hills: 5 Ochil **6** Calton, Sidlaw **7** Cheviot
highest point: 8 Ben Nevis
river: 3 Ayr, Dee, Don, Esk, Tay **4** Doon, Glen, Nith, Norn, Spey **5** Afton, Annan, Clyde, Forth, Garry, North, Tweed, Ythan **6** Affric, Teviot, Tummel **7** Deveron **8** Findhorn
sea: 5 Irish, North **8** Atlantic, Hebrides
physical feature:
bay: 5 Scapa
canal: 10 Caledonian
channel: 5 Minch, North
firth: 3 Tay **4** Kyle, Lorn **5** Clyde, Forth, Lorne, Moray **6** Linnhe, Solway **7** Comarty, Dornoch **8** Pentland
glen: 8 Glen More **9** Great Glen
hillside: 4 brae
moor: 7 Rannoch
valley: 8 Trossach
people: 4 Gael, Pict, Scot **5** Norse
artist: 7 Raeburn
author: 5 Burns, Scott **6** Barrie, Cronin, Dunbar **7** Barbour, Douglas **8** Henryson **9** Stevenson **10** Conan-Doyle, MacDiarmid, Macpherson
economist: 5 Smith
historian: 7 Carlyle
inventor: 4 Bell
king/leader: 5 David, James **6** Duncan **7** Kenneth, Macbeth, Malcolm, Stuarts, Wallace, William **9** Alexander **14** Robert the Bruce
landowner: 5 laird
philosopher: 4 Hume
prime minister: 9 Macdonald, Mac-

Millan **11** Douglas-Home
prince: 19 Bonnie Prince Charlie
queen: 4 Mary **13** Saint Margaret
religious leader: 8 John Knox
scientist: 7 Fleming
patronymic: 3 Mac
patron saint: 8 Andrew
language: 4 Erse **6** Celtic, Gaelic, Keltic, Lallan **7** English, Lalland
religion: 12 Episcopalian, Presbyterian **13** Roman Catholic
place:
abbey: 5 Kelso **7** Melrose **8** Dryburgh, Jedburgh
castle: 8 Stirling **9** Edinburgh **11** Eilean Donan
church/kirk: 7 St Giles **11** St Cuthbert's
coronation site: 12 Stone of Scone
royal residence: 8 Balmoral
Scott's home: 10 Abbotsford
street: 7 Prince's **9** Royal Mile **11** Sauchiehall
feature:
bird: 3 bae, cae **4** hern, muir, smeu **6** grouse, smeuth, snabby **7** jackdaw **8** throstle **9** swinepipe
clothing: 3 tam **4** kilt **6** tartan **7** filibeg **12** Harris tweeds **13** Shetland knits **15** Fair Isle sweater
dance: 3 bob **4** reel **7** walloch **9** ecossaise **10** petronella **11** strathsprey **12** gilliecallum **13** Highland fling
game: 4 golf **12** caber tossing
holiday: 8 Hogmanay
monster: 6 Nessie **8** Loch Ness
musical instrument: 7 bagpipe
symbol: 7 thistle
food:
bread: 5 scone
cheese: 7 crowdie
dish: 6 haggis **12** finnan haddie **15** kippered herring
drink: 12 Scotch whisky
soup: 11 cock-a-leekie
football team: 6 Oilers

Scott, George C
born: 6 Wise VA
wife: 14 Trish Van Devere **15** Colleen Dewhurst
roles: 4 Rage, Taps **6** Patton (Oscar, refused) **7** Titanic **8** Jane Eyre **13** Dr Strangelove **16** Death of a Salesman, The New Centurions **18** The Day of the Dolphin

Scott, Sir Walter
author of: 6 Rob Roy **7** Ivanhoe, Marmion **8** The Abbot, Waverley **10** Kenilworth **11** The Talisman **12** Guy Mannering, Old Mortality, The Antiquary **14** Quentin Durward **16** The Lady of the Lake **20** The Bride of Lammermoor, The Heart of Midlothian **23** The Lay of the Last Minstrel

Scottish Mythology
spirit/horse: 6 kelpie

scoundrel 3 cad, cur 5 crook, knave, rogue, scamp, thief 6 rascal, rotter, varlet, weasel 7 bounder, ruffian, sharper, varmint, villain 8 scalawag, swindler, turncoat 9 miscreant, trickster 10 blackguard, copperhead, mountebank, ne'er-do-well 11 four-flusher, rapscallion 12 carpetbagger

scoundrelly 3 low 4 mean 7 debased 8 rascally 10 degenerate, despicable, villainous 12 contemptible, disreputable 13 reprehensible

Scoundrel Time
author: 14 Lillian Hellman

scour 4 buff, comb, rake, scan 5 scrub, shine 6 abrade, polish, scrape 7 burnish, cleanse, ransack, rummage 8 brighten, traverse

scourge 3 rod 4 bane, beat, cane, flog, lash, whip 5 birch, blast, curse, flail, strap 6 punish, switch, terror, thrash 7 censure, chasten 8 chastise, scorpion, vexation 9 castigate, excoriate 10 affliction, discipline, flagellate 11 troublement 13 cat-o'-nine-tails

scout 3 spy 4 case 5 guide, pilot 6 escort, spy out, survey 7 lookout, observe 8 outrider, point man, vanguard 9 recruiter 11 reconnoiter 13 reconnoiterer

scowl 4 pout 5 frown, glare, lower 6 glower 7 grimace

scrabble 3 paw 4 claw, rake 5 climb 6 drudge, jostle, scrape, scrawl 7 clamber, grapple, scratch 8 struggle

scram 3 out 4 scat, shoo 5 be off, leave 6 beat it, begone, depart, get out, go away 7 get lost, vamoose 10 make tracks

scramble 3 run, vie 4 race, rush 5 clash, fight, mix up, scrap, upset 6 battle, combat, engage, garble, jostle, jumble, mess up, scurry, strive, tussle 7 collide, confuse, disturb, scatter, scuffle, shuffle 8 disorder, struggle, unsettle 9 scrimmage 10 disarrange, free-for-all 11 competition, disorganize

scramble up 5 climb, mount, scale 7 clamber

scrap 3 bit, dab, jot, row 4 atom, drop, iota, junk, spat 5 brawl, crumb, fight, grain, melee, speck, trace, trash 6 fracas, morsel, refuse, ruckus, sliver 7 abandon, glimmer, minimum, modicum, quarrel, snippet 8 brouhaha, fraction, fragment, jettison, molecule, particle, squabble 10 free-for-all, smattering, sprinkling

scrapbook 5 album 9 portfolio 11 memorabilia, miscellanea

scrape 3 dig 4 buff, gash, mark, rasp, save, skin 5 amass, clean, fight, glean, gouge, grate, graze, grind, plane, run-in, score, scour, scuff, stint 6 abrade, bruise, forage, gather, groove, obtain, pick up, plight, scrimp, secure, smooth, tussle 7 acquire, burnish, dilemma, procure, rub hard, scratch, scuffle, straits 8 abrasion 9 economize, tight spot 10 difficulty 11 predicament 13 confrontation

scratch 3 cut, mar, rub 4 claw, etch, gash, nick, omit, rasp 5 dig at, erase, grate, graze, grind, score 6 cancel, delete, incise, remove, rub out, scrape, scrawl, streak, strike 7 blemish, blot out, exclude, expunge, rule out 8 abrasion, cross out, lacerate, scribble, withdraw 9 eliminate 10 laceration

scratchy 5 rough 6 coarse 7 bristly, prickly 9 irritated 10 irritating

scrawl 4 draw 5 write 6 doodle 7 scratch, writing 8 scrabble, scribble, squiggle 10 penmanship 11 handwriting

scrawniness 8 lankness, leanness, slimness, thinness 10 skinniness, slightness 11 slenderness

scrawny 4 bony, lank, lean, puny 5 drawn, gaunt, lanky, runty, spare 6 sinewy, skinny, wasted 7 angular, scraggy, spindly, stunted 8 rawboned, skeletal 9 emaciated, fleshless 10 attenuated, undersized 11 underweight

screak 4 rasp 5 grate, grind 6 shriek, squeak 7 screech

scream 4 howl, loud, roar, wail, yell, yelp, yowl 5 shout, whine 6 bellow, cry out, holler, outcry, shriek, squawk, squeal 7 screech 11 lamentation

screech 3 cry 4 howl, rasp 6 screak, scream, shriek 9 caterwaul

screen 3 see, web 4 cull, mask, mesh, rate, show, sift, sort, veil, view 5 class, cloak, cover, eject, films, grade, grate, group, guard, order, shade, sieve 6 buffer, cinema, defend, filter, mantle, movies, secure, shield, shroud, sifter, size up, strain, winnow 7 arrange, conceal, curtain, defense, discard, lattice, present, preview, project, protect, secrete, shelter, shutter, weed out 8 colander, coverage, evaluate, jalousie, separate, strainer, withhold 9 eliminate, partition, safeguard 10 protection 11 concealment

screw 4 bolt, join, knot, turn, warp 5 clamp, exact, force, gnarl, rivet, twist, wrest, wring 6 adjust, attach, deform, driver, extort, fasten, garble, wrench 7 contort, distort, pervert, squeeze, tighten 8 fastener, misshape 9 propeller

screwball 3 nut 4 kook 5 flake, freak 6 looney 7 lunatic 8 crackpot 9 character, eccentric

screwdriver
type: 6 rachet 11 spiral-drive 12 Phillips-head

screwy 3 odd 4 daft 5 batty, dotty, flaky, funny, kinky, kooky, nutty, queer, wacky, weird 6 weirdo 7 odd-ball 8 peculiar 9 eccentric 10 unbalanced

Scriabin, Aleksandr (Scriabine, Skryabin)
born: 6 Moscow, Russia
composer of: 7 Mystery 10 Prometheus 12 Vers la flamme 13 Poem of Ecstasy, The Divine Poem, The Poem of Fire

scribble 4 tear 5 squib 6 doodle, scrawl 7 scratch 8 squiggle 9 pull apart
fiber: 4 wool
procedure: 7 carding

scribe, Scribe 3 cut 4 mark, tool 5 clerk, score 6 author, copier, penman, writer 7 copyist, teacher 8 recorder 9 archivist, scrivener, secretary 10 amanuensis, translator 12 newspaperman, stenographer 13 calligraphist
Biblical: 4 Ezra 6 Esdras
French dramatist: 8 Augustin
Palestinian: 5 sofer 6 sopher

scribe of gods 5 Thoth

scrimp 4 save 5 hoard, pinch, skimp, stint 8 begrudge 9 besparing 12 pinch pennies

scrimping 6 frugal 7 sparing 10 economical 11 economizing 12 cheeseparing 15 pinching pennies

scrip 5 paper 8 document 11 certificate

scripsit 7 he wrote 8 she wrote

script 4 book, hand 5 lines, score 6 dialog 7 cursive 8 dialogue, libretto, longhand, scenario 10 manuscript, penmanship 11 calligraphy, chirography, handwriting

Scriptures, the 5 Bible 6 the Law, oracle 8 holy writ, the Bible, the Torah 10 the Gospels 11 The Good Book 12 New Testament, Old Testament, the Word of God 13 the Pentateuch, the Septuagint 14 sacred writings see also 5 Bible

scroll of the Torah
Hebrew: 11 Sepher Torah

Scrooge, Ebenezer
character in: 15 A Christmas Carol
author: 7 Dickens

scrub 4 swab 5 brush, scour 8 scouring 9 brushwood, scrubbing

scrubby 4 base 6 brushy 7 stunted 8 inferior 10 undersized

scrumptious 5 juicy, tasty 6 savory, tender 8 luscious, pleasant, pleasing 9 agreeable, delicious, enjoyable, flavorful, succulent, toothsome 10 appetizing, delectable, delightful, flavorsome 13 mouth-watering

scruple 3 shy 4 balk, care, halt 5 demur, pause, qualm, waver 6 blench, ethics, falter 7 anxiety, concern, refrain 8 hesitate 9 fluctuate, misgiving, principle 10 conscience, hesitation 11 compunction, fearfulness, uncertainty 12 apprehension, doubtfulness, protestation **13** squeamishness **17** conscientiousness

Scruples
  author: **12** Judith Krantz

scrupulous 5 exact **6** honest **7** careful, dutiful, precise, upright **8** cautious, exacting, sedulous **9** honorable **10** deliberate, fastidious, meticulous, principled **11** painstaking, punctilious **13** conscientious

scrupulousness 4 care **5** pains **9** exactness **14** meticulousness **17** conscientiousness

scrutinize 4 scan **5** probe, study **6** peruse, search, survey **7** explore, inspect, observe **11** investigate

scrutiny 5 study, watch **7** inquiry, perusal **9** attention **10** inspection **11** examination **12** surveillance **13** investigation

scuffle 3 row **4** spar **5** brawl, clash, fight, melee, scrap **6** fracas, jostle, rumpus, tussle **8** squabble, struggle **9** commotion, imbroglio **10** donnybrook, free-for-all

sculpsit 10 he carved it **11** she carved it **12** he engraved it **13** she engraved it **14** he sculptured it **15** she sculptured it

sculptor 6 artist, carver, caster, imager, molder **7** marbler, modeler **8** chiseler, engraver
  constellation: **19** Apparatus Sculptoris
  French: **5** Rodin
  Greek: **7** Phidias **10** Praxiteles
  Irish-American: **12** Saint-Gaudens
  Italian: **7** Cellini **12** Michelangelo
  tool: **6** chisel, graver **7** spatula **9** ebauchoir

sculpture 3 cut **4** bust, cast, head, work **5** cameo, carve, erode, model, mould **6** chisel, relief, statue **7** carving, erosion, faience **8** intaglio, statuary **9** cloissone, medallion, statuette
  medium: **4** clay **5** china, stone **6** bronze, enamel, marble **7** ceramic **9** porcelain **10** terra cotta **11** earthenware

scum 4 film, slag **5** crust, dregs, dross, trash **6** rabble, refuse **7** deposit, rubbish, surface **8** riffraff

scurrility 5 abuse **8** rudeness **9** indecency, obscenity, profanity **13** offensiveness, salaciousness

scurrilous 3 low **5** gross **6** coarse, vulgar **7** obscene **8** churlish, derisive, indecent, reviling **9** insulting, offensive, shameless **10** derogatory, detracting, indelicate, slanderous **11** disparaging, foulmouthed **12** contemptuous

scurry 3 hie **4** race, rush, skim **5** haste, hurry, scoot, speed **6** bustle, hasten, hustle, spring **7** rushing, scamper, scuttle **8** hurrying, scooting, scramble **9** confusion, dispersal **10** scattering

scurvy 3 low **4** base, mean, vile **6**

shabby **7** ignoble **9** worthless **10** despicable **12** contemptible, dishonorable

scuttle 4 sink **5** abort, hurry, scrap, speed, wreck **6** hasten, scurry **7** destroy, discard, scamper **8** dispatch, scramble

scuttlebutt 4 talk **5** rumor **6** gossip **7** hearsay, prattle, scandal **8** chitchat

Scylaceus
  origin: **6** Lycian
  ally of: **7** Trojans
  death by: **7** stoning

Scylla
  form: **5** nymph **7** monster
  location: **3** sea **16** Straits of Messina **20** Whirlpool of Charybdis
  father: **7** Phorcys
  mother: **6** Hecate
  loved by: **8** Poseidon
  rival: **10** Amphitrite

Scyphius
  first: **5** horse
  created by: **8** Poseidon

sea 3 bay, ton **4** deep, gulf, host, lake, leap, lots, main, mass, slew, wave **5** bight, flock, flood, ocean, scads, spate, surge, swarm, swell, waves **6** legion, roller, scores, waters **7** breaker **9** abundance, multitude, profusion
  French: **3** mer
  god of: **5** Aegir, Memir **6** Nereus, Triton **7** Glaucus, Neptune, Phorcys, Proteus **8** Poseidon **9** Asphalius
  goddess of: **3** Ino, Ran **6** Graeae, Graiae, Matuta **8** Dictynna, Menannan **9** Leucothea **10** Amphitrite

Sea, the Sea, The
  author: **11** Iris Murdoch

Sea Around Us, The
  author: **13** Rachel L Carson

Seabiscuit
  author: **16** Laura Hillenbrand
  director: **8** Gary Ross
  cast: **11** Chris Cooper (Tom Smith), Gary Stevens (George Woolf), Jeff Bridges (Charles Howard) **12** Tobey Maguire (Red Pollard), William H Macy (Tick Tock McGlaughlin) **14** Elizabeth Banks (Marcela Howard) **15** Valerie Mahaffey (Annie Howard)

seaboard 5 coast **9** shoreline

Seaborg, Glen Theodore
  field: **7** physics
  worked with: **14** actinide series **19** transuranic elements
  headed: **3** AEC **22** Atomic Energy Commission
  awarded: **10** Nobel Prize

seacoast 5 beach, coast, shore **7** seaside **8** littoral **9** coastland, coastline, shoreline, waterside
  French: **4** cote
  Italian: **4** lido **7** riviera

seafarers 4 tars **5** salts **7** sailors, seadogs **8** mariners

Seagull, The
  author: **12** Anton Chekhov

character: **5** Masha **6** Polina **10** Pyotr Sorin **11** Yevgeny Dorn **12** Ilya Shamraev, Irina Arkadin **13** Boris Trigorin, Nina Zaretchyn **16** Semyon Medvedenko **17** Konstantin Treplev

Seah 15 Biblical measure

Sea Hawk, The
  director: **13** Michael Curtiz
  cast: **10** Errol Flynn **11** Claude Rains, Donald Crisp **14** Brenda Marshall
  score: **21** Erich Wolfgang Korngold

seal 2 OK **3** dam, fix **4** cork, lock, mark, plug, shut, stop **5** brand, close, stamp **6** accept, affirm, emblem, fasten, figure, ratify, secure, settle, shut up, signet, stop up, symbol, verify **7** approve, certify, confirm, endorse, imprint **8** colophon, conclude, fastener, hallmark, insignia, sanction, validate **9** determine, establish, trademark **10** impression **12** authenticate
  Latin: **10** imprimatur

seal
  young: **3** pup
  group of: **3** pod

sea lion
  young: **3** pup

seam 3 gap **4** line, lode, mark, scar, vein **5** break, chink, cleft, crack, joint, layer, notch **6** breach, furrow, incise, suture **7** crevice, fissure, joining, opening, rupture, stratum, wrinkle **8** junction, juncture **9** interface

seaman 3 gob, tar **4** hand, mate, salt **5** bosun, middy **6** lubber, merman, sailor, sea dog **7** mariner **9** boatswain **10** bluejacket, midshipman

seamark 5 light **6** beacon, pharos, signal **10** lighthouse, watchtower

sea monster 6 dragon **9** Leviathan

seamstress 10 dressmaker
  French: **9** midinette **10** couturiere

seamy 3 raw **4** dark **5** dirty, nasty, rough **6** coarse, sordid **7** squalid, unclean **10** unpleasant **11** unwholesome **12** disagreeable

sear 4 burn, char, scar **5** blast, singe, steel **6** harden, scorch **7** blister **9** cauterize **10** caseharden

search 4 comb, drag, fish, hunt, look, seek, sift **5** check, frisk, probe, quest, rifle, scour, snoop, study **6** survey, tracer **7** dragnet, examine, explore, inquiry, inspect, pry into, pursuit, ransack, rummage **8** overhaul, scrutiny **10** inspection, scrutinize **11** examination, exploration **13** investigation

Search, The
  director: **13** Fred Zinnemann
  cast: **9** Ivan Jandl **13** Aline MacMahon **14** Jarmila Novotna **15** Montgomery Clift
  setting: **6** Berlin

Searchers, The
  director: **8** John Ford
  cast: **8** Ward Bond **9** John Wayne,

Vera Miles **11** Natalie Wood **13** Jeffrey Hunter

searching 4 dour, keen, nosy **5** sharp **6** prying, shrewd, snoopy **7** curious, groping **8** exacting, piercing, rigorous, thorough **9** observant, quizzical, unsparing **11** inquisitive, penetrating **13** investigative

Seascape
author: **11** Edward Albee

seashore 5 beach, coast

seasick 3 ill **5** barfy, dizzy, faint, giddy, woozy **6** queasy **8** qualmish, vomitous **9** nauseated, squeamish **11** vertiginous

seasickness
French: **8** mal de mer

seaside 5 beach, coast, shore **9** shoreline

season 3 age, dry **4** fall, lace, tame, term **5** adapt, color, drill, inure, prime, ripen, shape, spell, spice, stage, train **6** accent, autumn, finish, flavor, inform, leaven, mature, mellow, period, refine, soften, spring, summer, temper, winter **7** enhance, enliven, prepare, quarter, stretch **8** accustom, duration, heighten, interval, ornament, practice **9** condition, cultivate, embellish **10** discipline

seasoned 6 herbed, inured, salted, spiced **7** veteran **8** flavored, hardened, peppered **9** competent, qualified **10** acclimated, accustomed, habituated **11** experienced **12** familiarized

seasoning 4 dill, herb, mace, sage, salt, zest **5** aging, basil, clove, gusto, onion, spice, thyme **6** drying, garlic, ginger, nutmeg, pepper, relish **7** oregano, paprika, parsley **8** allspice, cinnamon, marjoram, practice, ripening, rosemary, training **9** condiment, flavoring **10** maturation **11** orientation, preparation **15** familiarization

seasons
god of: **9** Vertumnus
goddess of: **5** Horae, Hours

seat 3 box, hub **4** axis, core, home, rump, site, sofa **5** abode, bench, chair, couch, croup, divan, fanny, heart, house, locus, place **6** behind, bottom, center, locale, settle **7** address, capital, cushion, habitat, housing, nucleus, rear end, situate **8** backside, buttocks, derriere, domicile, dwelling, haunches, location, quarters **9** posterior, residence **10** incumbency, membership **12** hindquarters

seat of justice 5 bench, court **8** tribunal **9** judiciary **10** courthouse

Seattle
baseball team: **8** Mariners
basketball team: **11** Supersonics
bay: **7** Elliott
football team: **8** Seahawks
lake: **10** Washington
landmark: **11** Space Needle

site of: **10** World's Fair
sound: **5** Puget

Sea Wolf, The
author: **10** Jack London

Sebastian
character in: **12** Twelfth Night
author: **11** Shakespeare

Seberg, Jean
born: **14** Marshalltown IA
husband: **10** Romain Gary
roles: **6** Lilith **7** Airport **9** Saint Joan **10** Breathless **16** Bonjour Tristesse

Secchi, Angelo
field: **9** astronomy
nationality: **7** Italian
classified: **5** stars

secede 4 quit **5** leave **6** resign, retire **7** forsake **8** withdraw **12** disaffiliate

secession 10 separation, withdrawal **14** disaffiliation

seclude 4 hide **6** retire **7** isolate **8** separate **9** sequester **10** dissociate

secluded 6 covert, cut off, lonely, remote, shut in **7** private **8** closeted, confined, isolated, shut away, solitary **9** reclusive, sheltered, unvisited, withdrawn **10** cloistered **11** out-of-the-way, sequestered **12** unfrequented

seclusion 5 exile **6** asylum, hiding **7** retreat **8** cloister, hideaway, solitude **9** hermitage, isolation, reclusion, sanctuary **10** quarantine, retirement, withdrawal **11** concealment **13** sequestration

second 3 aid **4** abet, back, help, wink **5** agent, favor, flash, jiffy, other, proxy, trice **6** assist, back up, deputy, fill-in, helper, minute, moment, uphold **7** advance, another, endorse, further, instant, one more, outdone, promote, stand by, stand-in, support **8** advocate, delegate, exceeded, inferior **9** alternate, assistant, attendant, encourage, surpassed, twinkling **10** additional, lieutenant, substitute, understudy **11** alternating, subordinate **14** representative
abbreviation: **1** s **3** sec

secondary 5 lower, minor, other **6** backup, lesser **7** smaller **8** inferior, mediocre, middling **9** alternate, ancillary, auxiliary, following, resultant **10** consequent, subsequent, subsidiary **11** subordinate

second childhood 6 dotage **8** senility

secondhand 4 used **8** indirect **10** derivative, hand me down

second-in-command 6 deputy **8** adjutant **9** assistant **10** lieutenant **13** vice president

second-rate 3 bad **4** poor, so-so **5** cheap, tacky **6** shabby **7** average **8** everyday, inferior, mediocre, middling **9** imperfect **10** inadequate, outclassed, pedestrian **11** commonplace, substandard **15** undistinguished

Second Sex, The
author: **16** Simone de Beauvoir

second-story man 5 thief **6** robber **7** burglar **9** cracksman **10** cat burglar

second string 4 subs **5** bench **11** substitutes

second team 5 bench **11** substitutes

secrecy 6 hiding **7** mystery, privacy, private, silence, stealth **8** muteness, solitude **9** closeness, seclusion **10** covertness **11** concealment, furtiveness **13** sequestration **15** clandestineness, confidentiality, underhandedness **17** surreptitiousness **19** uncommunicativeness

secret 3 key, mum **4** dark **6** arcane, covert, enigma, hidden, mystic, occult, puzzle, recipe, unseen **7** formula, furtive, mystery, private, unknown **8** discreet, esoteric, hush-hush, secluded, stealthy **9** concealed, disguised, invisible, secretive **10** confidence, mysterious, undercover, unrevealed **11** camouflaged, clandestine, undisclosed, unpublished **12** confidential, unrevealable **13** surreptitious

Secret Agent
character: **9** John Drake
cast: **15** Patrick McGoohan
theme: **14** Secret Agent Man

secretary 4 aide, desk **5** clerk **6** scribe **7** officer, recorder **10** amanuensis **12** stenographer
French: **10** escritoire

secret council 8 conclave

secrete 4 hide, veil **5** cache, cloak, cover, stash **6** screen, shroud **7** conceal, curtain **8** disguise

secretive 3 mum, sly **4** mute **6** covert, silent **7** cryptic, evasive, furtive, laconic, private **8** discreet, reserved, reticent, stealthy, taciturn **9** enigmatic, withdrawn **10** mysterious **11** tight-lipped, underhanded, unrevealing **13** surreptitious **15** uncommunicative

secretiveness 7 mystery, stealth **9** reticence **11** furtiveness **14** inscrutability, mysteriousness **19** uncommunicativeness

Secret Life of Walter Mitty, The
author: **12** James Thurber
cast: **10** Danny Kaye

sect 4 camp, cult **7** faction **8** division **10** persuasion **11** affiliation **12** denomination

sectarian 6 narrow **7** limited **8** clannish **9** exclusive, parochial **10** provincial, restricted

section 4 area, part, side, unit, ward, zone **5** piece, range, share, slice **6** region, sample, sphere **7** chapter, cutting, measure, passage, portion, segment, terrain **8** district, division, province, specimen, vicinity **9** allotment, increment, territory **10** department, proportion **11** installment **12** neighborhood

sector 4 area, zone **7** theater **8** district

secular 3 lay **4** laic **6** carnal **7** earthly, fleshly, mundane, profane, sensual, worldly **8** material, temporal **9** nonsacred **11** nonclerical **12** nonreligious, nonspiritual **17** nonecclesiastical

secundum 11 according to

secure 3 get, set **4** bind, easy, safe, sure **5** fixed, tight **6** at ease, defend, ensure, fasten, immune, insure, obtain **7** acquire, assured, certain, protect, shelter, tie down **8** absolute, carefree, composed, defended, definite, in the bag, positive, surefire **9** confident, guarantee, protected, reassured, safeguard, sheltered **10** guaranteed **11** impregnable **12** invulnerable, unassailable, unattackable, unthreatened

securities 5 bonds, title **6** stocks **12** certificates

security 4 bond, care, hope, keep **5** faith, trust **6** guards, pledge, police, safety, surety, troops **7** defense, deposit, promise, support **8** reliance, sureness, warranty **9** assurance, certainty, guarantee **10** collateral, confidence, conviction, protection, safeguards **11** maintenance, safekeeping **12** absoluteness, decisiveness, definiteness, positiveness, preservation

sedate 4 calm, cool **5** grave, quiet, sober, staid, still **6** poised, serene, solemn, steady **7** serious, subdued **8** composed, decorous, reserved **9** collected, dignified, impassive, unexcited, unruffled **10** cool-headed **11** levelheaded **13** imperturbable **15** undemonstrative

sedateness 7 decorum, dignity, gravity, reserve **8** calmness **9** composure, soberness, solemnity **11** impassivity, seriousness

sedative 6 easing, opiate **7** anodyne, calming **8** allaying, lenitive, narcotic, relaxing, soothing **9** analgesic, assuasive, calmative, composing, mitigator, soporific **10** comforting, palliative **11** alleviative **12** tranquilizer **13** tranquilizing

sedentary 5 fixed, inert, still **6** seated **7** resting, sitting **8** inactive, unmoving **9** quiescent **10** stationary, unstirring

sedge 4 reed **5** grass **10** marsh grass

sediment 4 lees, scum, slag **5** drègs, dross, waste **6** debris, sludge **7** grounds, remains, residue **8** leavings **9** settlings

sedition 6 mutiny, revolt **7** treason **8** defiance, uprising **9** rebellion **10** disloyalty, insurgency, subversion, unruliness **11** lawlessness **12** disobedience, insurrection **14** rebelliousness, subversiveness

seduce 4 lure, ruin **5** abuse, charm, tempt **6** allure, defile, entice, ravish **7** attract, conquer, corrupt, debauch, deprave, pervert, violate, win over **8** deflower, disgrace, dishonor, persuade **9** captivate

seducer 3 cad **4** wolf **5** letch, Romeo **7** defiler, Don Juan, playboy **8** Casanova, Lothario, lover-boy, ravisher, violater **9** corrupter, debaucher, womanizer **10** deflowerer **11** philanderer **12** heartbreaker
French: 4 roue

seductive 4 sexy **8** alluring, charming, enticing, tempting **9** beguiling, disarming **10** attractive, bewitching, come-hither, enchanting, voluptuous **11** captivating, provocative

seductress 4 vamp **5** siren **7** charmer, Jezebel, Lorelei, mantrap **9** temptress **11** adventuress, enchantress
French: 7 cocotte **11** femme fatale

sedulous 6 dogged **8** diligent, thorough **9** assiduous, steadfast **10** determined, persistent **11** industrious, painstaking, persevering **13** conscientious, indefatigable

sedulousness 4 zeal **8** industry, tenacity **9** assiduity, diligence **11** persistence **12** perseverance

see 3 dig, eye, spy, woo **4** date, espy, know, meet, mind, spot, view **5** court, grasp, sight, visit, watch **6** attend, behold, descry, escort, fathom, notice, regard, survey **7** consult, discern, glimpse, observe, picture, realize, receive, undergo, witness **8** conceive, consider, discover, envision, meditate, perceive, register, ruminate **9** accompany, apprehend, ascertain, determine, encounter, entertain, interview, recognize, visualize **10** appreciate, comprehend, experience, understand **11** contemplate, distinguish
Latin: 4 vide

see above
Latin: 9 vide supra

see after
Latin: 8 vide post

see as above, see as stated above
Latin: 11 vide ut supra

see before
Latin: 8 vide ante

see below
Latin: 9 vide infra

seed 3 pit, sow **4** germ **5** basis, grain, heirs, issue, ovule, plant, stone **6** embryo, origin, source **7** progeny **8** children **9** beginning, offspring, posterity **11** descendants

seedy 4 worn **5** dingy, faded, lousy, mangy, ratty, spent, tacky **6** scuffy, shabby **7** haggard, sickish, squalid **8** slovenly **10** threadbare **11** debilitated

see eye to eye 5 agree **6** concur **11** be of one mind

see fit 5 deign **6** choose, please

see further
Latin: 8 vide post

seek 3 try **4** hunt **5** court, essay, trace **6** demand, invite, pursue **7** attempt, examine, explore, inspect, request, solicit, venture **8** endeavor **9** undertake **10** scrutinize **11** investigate

seek out 4 find **6** pursue **7** embrace, look for, solicit

seek proof 4 test **6** try out **7** analyze, examine **8** research **10** experiment **11** investigate

seem 4 look **6** appear

seeming 7 evident, obvious, surface **8** apparent, presumed, putative, supposed **10** ostensible **11** superficial

seemly 3 due **5** right **6** decent, polite, proper **7** correct, fitting, prudent, refined **8** becoming, decorous, suitable, tasteful, well-bred **9** befitting, courteous **10** acceptable, felicitous **11** appropriate **12** conventional
French: 11 comme il faut

seep 4 drip, leak, ooze, soak **7** diffuse, dribble, suffuse, trickle **8** permeate **9** penetrate

seepage 4 ooze **5** flour, issue **7** leakage, outflow **9** discharge, dribbling, secretion, trickling

seer 4 sage **5** augur **6** medium, oracle **7** diviner, prophet, psychic **8** conjurer, sorcerer **9** sorceress, stargazer **10** astrologer, soothsayer **11** clairvoyant, necromancer **13** fortuneteller **14** prognosticator

seesaw 5 waver **6** teeter **9** alternate, fluctuate, up-and-down, vacillate **12** teeter-totter

seethe 4 boil, brew, cook, fume, rage, rant, rave, roil, stew **5** churn, storm **6** blow up, bubble, simmer **7** bluster, smolder

seething 3 mad **7** boiling **8** agitated, bubbling, frenzied **10** distraught

see through 3 get **6** detect, effect, finish **7** achieve, execute, perform **8** carry out, complete, conclude **9** catch onto, figure out, penetrate **10** comprehend, understand

Segal, Erich
author of: **6** Prizes **8** Only Love **9** Love Story **11** Acts of Faith **12** Oliver's Story **16** Man Woman and Child

Segal, George
born: **9** New York NY
roles: **11** Blume in Love, Where's Poppa? **13** A Touch of Class **18** Fun with Dick and Jane **25** Who's Afraid of Virginia Woolf?

segment 3 leg **4** part **5** cut up, piece, stage **6** cleave **7** disjoin, portion, section, split up **8** disunite, division, separate **9** increment **11** installment

segmented 5 cut up **7** split up **9** sectioned, separated

segregate 6 cut off, detach, divide 7 divorce, isolate, seclude, sort out 8 disunite, insulate, separate 9 sequester 10 disconnect, quarantine

segue
music: 21 continue without a break

seine 3 net 4 drag, fish 5 trawl 7 dragnet

seism 5 quake, shock 6 tremor 8 temblor, upheaval 10 earthquake

seize 3 bag, nab 4 grab, read 5 catch, glean, grasp, pinch, pluck, usurp 6 arrest, clutch, collar, gather, snatch 7 capture, embrace, impound, possess, utilize 8 arrogate 9 apprehend, overpower, overwhelm 10 commandeer, comprehend, confiscate, understand 11 appropriate

seize the day
Latin: 9 carpe diem

seizure 3 fit 5 onset, spell, throe 6 access, arrest, attack, crisis, stroke, taking 7 capture, episode 8 grasping, paroxysm 9 abduction, snatching 10 convulsion, kidnapping, possession, usurpation, visitation 11 impressment 12 apprehension, confiscation 13 appropriation, commandeering

Sekhmet
origin: 8 Egyptian
goddess of: 4 evil

Selden, Mr
character in: 15 The House of Mirth
author: 7 Wharton

seldom 6 rarely 8 scarcely 10 uncommonly 12 infrequently, occasionally, sporadically

select 3 tap 4 A-one, pick, posh 5 elect, elite, fancy 6 choice, choose, chosen, opt for, picked, prefer 8 fourstar, superior, top-notch 9 exclusive, first-rate, preferred 10 first-class, privileged

selection 4 pick 5 range 6 choice, medley, option 7 program, variety 8 choosing, decision 9 potpourri 10 collection, miscellany, preference

selective 5 fussy, picky 6 choosy 7 careful, finicky 8 cautious 10 discerning, fastidious, meticulous, particular 14 discriminating

Selene
goddess of: 4 moon
father: 8 Hyperion
mother: 5 Theia
brother: 6 Helios
sister: 3 Eos
loved: 8 Endymion
daughter: 5 Herse 6 Pandia
corresponds to: 5 Diana 7 Artemis

self 3 ego 6 person, psyche 8 identity 10 individual 11 homogeneity, personality
inner: 5 anima 6 animus
Universal: 5 Atman

self-abnegation 7 modesty 8 humility 10 diffidence 11 bashfulness

self-absorbed 4 vain 8 egoistic 9 egotistic 10 egocentric 11 egotistical 12 narcissistic

self-absorption 6 egoism, vanity 7 conceit 11 egocentrism, selfishness 16 self-centeredness

self-admiration 6 vanity 7 conceit, egotism 8 smugness 9 immodesty, vainglory

self-assertive 4 bold 7 dynamic 8 forceful 9 ambitious, confident 10 aggressive

self-assuming 4 vain 8 arrogant, egoistic 9 conceited 10 egoistical 11 egotistical

self-assurance 6 aplomb 9 brashness 12 cocksureness
French: 9 sangfroid

self-assured 5 brash, cocky 8 cocksure 9 confident

self-centered 4 vain 8 egoistic, immodest 9 conceited, egotistic 10 egocentric 11 egotistical, swellheaded 12 narcissistic

self-centeredness 6 egoism, vanity 7 conceit 10 narcissism 11 egocentrism

self-composure 5 poise 6 aplomb 8 calmness 10 equanimity

self-confidence 5 nerve, pluck 6 mettle, spirit 8 boldness, gameness 9 cockiness 10 resolution 12 cocksureness

self-conscious 7 awkward 8 affected 9 chagrined, ill at ease, unnatural 11 discomposed, embarrassed 12 disconcerted

self-consciousness 7 modesty, reserve, shyness 8 timidity 9 abashment, hesitancy, reticence 10 constraint, demureness, diffidence 11 bashfulness, fearfulness 12 apprehension, sheepishness

self-control 5 poise 6 aplomb 8 firmness, patience, sobriety 9 composure, soberness, soundness, stability, willpower 10 temperance 11 forbearance 14 cool-headedness, unexcitability 15 levelheadedness 16 imperturbability
French: 9 sangfroid 11 savoir-faire

self-critical 6 humble, modest 9 diffident 13 perfectionist

self-criticism 7 modesty 8 humility 10 diffidence 13 perfectionism

self-deception 7 fantasy 8 delusion, illusion 13 hallucination

self-declared 5 sworn 6 avowed 8 admitted 9 confessed, professed 12 acknowledged

self-denial 8 eschewal 10 abnegation, abstention, abstinence, continence 11 forbearance 12 renunciation 14 abstemiousness

self-deprecation

also: 16 self-depreciation 7 modesty 8 humility, meekness 10 humbleness

self-doubt 11 uncertainty

self-effacement 7 modesty, shyness 8 humility, meekness 10 diffidence 11 bashfulness

self-esteem 5 pride 10 confidence

self-evident 5 plain 6 patent 7 glaring, obvious 8 apparent, distinct, explicit, manifest, palpable 10 unarguable, undeniable 11 unambiguous, unequivocal 12 unmistakable 16 incontrovertible

self-explanatory 5 clear, lucid, plain 7 obvious 8 manifest 12 intelligible 15 straightforward

self-governing 4 free 9 sovereign 10 autonomous 11 independent

self-government 8 autonomy, home rule 11 sovereignty 12 independence

self-gratifying 11 intemperate

self-importance 6 egoism, vanity 8 smugness 9 arrogance, immodesty, pomposity, vainglory 11 egocentrism

self-important 4 smug, vain 7 pompous 8 egoistic, immodest 10 egocentric 11 egotistical 12 vainglorious

self-indulgence 12 extravagance, incontinence, intemperance

self-indulgent 9 libertine, sybaritic 10 hedonistic, voluptuous 11 extravagant, incontinent, intemperate

selfish 4 mean 5 tight, venal 6 greedy, stingy 7 miserly 8 covetous, egoistic, grasping, grudging 9 egotistic, illiberal, mercenary, rapacious 10 avaricious, egocentric, ungenerous 11 egotistical 12 parsimonious, uncharitable

self-love 6 egoism, vanity 7 conceit, egotism 9 vainglory 10 narcissism 11 complacency, egocentrism, haughtiness 13 conceitedness 15 swellheadedness
French: 11 amour propre

self-possessed 4 calm, cool 6 poised 7 assured, courtly, refined 8 balanced, composed, polished, resolute 9 collected, confident 12 aristocratic 13 distinguished

self-possession 5 poise 6 aplomb 7 dignity 8 calmness, coolness 9 composure 10 confidence, equanimity, steadiness 16 imperturbability
French: 9 sangfroid

self-praise 6 vanity 7 conceit, egotism 8 bragging, smugness 9 arrogance, immodesty, vainglory 12 boastfulness
Italian: 11 braggadocio

self-propelling 9 automatic

self-questioning 10 uneasiness 13 soul-searching

self-reliance 8 sureness 9 assurance 12 independence

Self-Reliance
author: 17 Ralph Waldo Emerson

self-reliant 5 hardy 6 plucky 7 assured 8 resolute, spirited 10 mettlesome 11 independent 12 enterprising

self-reproachful 8 contrite 9 regretful 10 apologetic, remorseful

self-respecting 5 proud 7 upright 8 decorous 9 dignified, honorable 10 upstanding 11 circumspect 13 distinguished

self-restraint 9 willpower 10 continence 11 forbearance

self-righteous 4 smug 5 pious 7 pompous 9 insincere, pietistic 10 complacent, moralizing 11 pharisaical, pretentious 12 hypocritical, mealy-mouthed 13 sanctimonious 14 holier-than-thou

self-sacrificing 6 heroic 7 gallant 9 unselfish 10 altruistic, martyrlike

self-satisfaction 5 pride 6 vanity 8 smugness 11 complacency

self-satisfied 4 smug, vain 8 cocksure, priggish 9 overproud 10 complacent 11 egotistical 12 narcissistic, vainglorious 13 overconfident

self-secure 4 smug 7 content 9 contented 10 complacent

self-seeking 6 greedy 8 covetous

self-styled
  French: 9 soi-disant

self-willed 8 obdurate, stubborn 9 obstinate, pigheaded 10 headstrong, refractory 11 intractable 12 ungovernable, unmanageable

sell 4 dump, hawk, vend 6 barter, betray, deal in, enlist, handle, market, peddle, unload 7 deceive, trade in, win over 8 convince, dispense

Selleck, Tom
  roles: 8 In and Out, Lassiter, Magnum PI 12 Thomas Magnum 15 High Road to China 16 Quigley Down Under, Three Men and A Baby

seller 6 dealer, jobber, monger, trader, vendor 7 peddler 8 merchant, retailer, salesman 9 middleman, salesgirl, saleslady, tradesman 10 saleswoman, shopkeeper, wholesaler 11 salesperson, storekeeper

Sellers, Peter
  real name: 19 Richard Henry Sellers
  born: 7 England 8 Southsea
  wife: 11 Britt Ekland
  roles: 10 Being There 12 Casino Royale 13 Dr Strangelove, Murder by Death 14 A Shot in the Dark, The Pink Panther 16 What's New Pussycat? 17 Inspector Clouseau 18 The Mouse that Roared 21 The World of Henry Orient

Selli
  priests of: 4 Zeus

sell out 6 betray 11 double-cross

semblance 3 air 4 cast, copy, look, show 5 image 6 aspect 7 bearing, replica 8 likeness, pretense 9 dupli-cate, facsimile 10 simulacrum 11 counterpart 12 reproduction 14 representation
  French: 4 mien

Semele
  also: 6 Thyone
  father: 6 Cadmus
  mother: 8 Harmonia
  loved by: 4 Zeus
  son: 8 Dionysus
  sister: 3 Ino 5 Agave 7 Autonoe

seminal 7 primary 8 creative, fruitful, germinal, original 9 formative 10 generative, productive 11 germinative, originating

Seminole
  language family: 9 Muskogean
  tribe: 8 Cow Creek, Mikasaki
  location: 6 Mexico 7 Florida, Georgia 10 Everglades
  leader: 7 Osceola, Wild Cat 10 Coacoochie

Semiramis
  queen of: 7 Assyria
  husband: 5 Ninus
  founder of: 7 Babylon

Semitic
  language family: 11 Afro-Asiatic 13 Hamito-Semitic
  eastern branch: 8 Akkadian, Assyrian 10 Babylonian
  western branch: 4 Geez 5 Tigre 6 Arabic, Gurage, Harari, Hebrew, Minean, Sabean, Syriac 7 Amharic, Aramaic, Argobba, Moabite 8 Ethiopic, Tigrinya, Ugaritic 9 Canaanite 10 Himyaritic, Phoenician, Qatabanian
  southwest branch: 6 Minean, Sabean 7 Amharic 10 Himyaritic, Qatabanian 11 North Arabic 19 South Arabic-Ethiopic

Semo Sancus *see* 6 Sancus

senatus consultum 17 Roman senate decree

send 4 cast, emit, head, hurl, lead, show, toss 5 drive, fling, guide, refer, relay, shoot, throw 6 convey, direct, launch, propel 7 conduct, deliver, forward, give off, project 8 dispatch, transmit 9 broadcast, cause to go, discharge 11 disseminate

send away 4 oust, rout, shoo 5 chase, evict

send forth 4 emit, gush 5 erupt, expel, issue, let go 7 dismiss, release 8 disgorge, dispatch 9 discharge

send off 4 post 7 forward 8 dispatch, disperse, transmit

send out 4 beam, emit 8 dispatch, transmit 9 discharge

send packing 3 axe, can 4 fire, oust, rout, sack, shoo 5 evict 6 bounce 7 cast out, dismiss

send to Coventry 3 cut 5 eject, expel 6 banish, ignore 7 cast out, exclude 9 ostracize

Seneca
  language family: 9 Iroquoian
  location: 7 New York 15 Canandaigua Lake
  leader: 9 John Abeel, John O'Bail 11 Cornplanter
  member: 19 League of the Iroquois

Senegal
  capital/largest city: 5 Dakar
  others: 5 Bakel, Matam, Thies 7 Bignona, Kaolack, Kaollak 8 Diourbel, Kedougou, Linguere, Rufisque 10 Saint-Louis, Ziguinchor 11 Richard-Toll, Tambacounda
  division: 7 Sudanic 8 Sahelian 9 Casamance
    empire: 4 Mali 5 Jolof 6 Tekrur
  monetary unit: 5 franc 7 centime
  island: 5 Goree
  lake: 6 Guiers
  mountain: 6 Gounou
  highest point: 12 Fouta Djallon
  river: 4 Sine 6 Faleme, Gambia, Saloum 7 Senegal 9 Casamance
  sea: 8 Atlantic
  physical feature:
    desert: 5 Ferlo
    peninsula: 9 Cape Verde
  people: 4 Lebu, Peul, Soce 5 Diola, Dyola, Foula, Laobe, Peulh, Serer, Wolof 6 Fulani, Serere 7 Bambara, Malinke, Tukuler, Tukulor 8 Mandingo
    leader: 7 Senghor
  language: 5 Wolof 6 French
  religion: 5 Islam 7 animism 13 Roman Catholic
  feature:
    musical instrument: 4 kora
    tree: 6 acacia, baobab 7 juniper, oil palm 10 raffia palm

Senhor, Senhora 2 sr 3 man, sra 5 madam (Portuguese)

senile 6 doting, infirm 7 foolish 8 decrepit 9 doddering, senescent 13 superannuated

senior, Senior 4 head, over 5 above, chief, doyen, elder, older 6 better 7 veteran 8 superior

seniority 6 tenure 9 longevity 10 precedence
  French: 4 pere

senor 2 Mr 3 don 5 title 6 mister 8 Spaniard

senora 3 Mrs, sra 4 lady, wife 5 madam, woman 8 mistress

senorita 4 lass, miss
  abbreviation: 4 srta

senorita 6 wrasse
  genus: 8 Oxyjulis
  species: 11 californica

sensation 3 hit 4 stir, to-do 6 thrill, uproar 7 feeling, scandal 9 agitation, awareness, commotion, detection 10 impression, perception

sensational 5 cheap, lurid 6 superb 8 dramatic, exciting, galvanic, shocking, striking **9** emotional, excellent, thrilling **10** electrical, scandalous **11** exaggerated, exceptional, extravagant, outstanding, spectacular **12** meretricious **13** extraordinary **14** heartthrobbing

sensationalism 7 scandal **9** luridness, melodrama **13** grandstanding **15** blood and thunder **16** yellow journalism

sense 3 see, use **4** aura, espy, feel, good, mind, note **5** grasp, guess, point, sight, smell, taste, touch, value, worth **6** descry, detect, divine, reason, regard, take in, wisdom **7** benefit, discern, faculty, feeling, hearing, meaning, purpose, realize, suspect **8** efficacy, function, judgment, perceive, sagacity **9** apprehend, awareness, intuition, recognize **10** atmosphere, comprehend, definition, denotation, impression, understand **11** connotation, premonition, realization, recognition **12** appreciation, intelligence, perspicacity, practicality, presentiment **13** consciousness, signification, understanding **14** reasonableness

Sense and Sensibility
   author: 10 Jane Austen
   character: 10 Lucy Steele **13** Edward Ferrars, Robert Ferrars **14** Colonel Brandon, John Willoughby **16** Sir John Middleton
      Dashwood family: 4 John **5** Fanny **6** Elinor **8** Marianne

senseless 4 dumb, idle, numb **5** crazy, inane, nutty, silly **6** stupid, unwise **7** aimless, foolish, stunned, useless, witless **8** comatose, deadened **9** brainless, foolhardy, illogical, insensate, pointless **10** groundless, ill-advised, insensible, irrational, ridiculous **11** harebrained, meaningless, purposeless, unconscious **12** unreasonable **13** irresponsible

sense of duty 15 moral obligation **21** sense of responsibility

sensibilities 8 feelings, sore spot, thin skin **12** Achilles' heel **14** susceptibility

sensibility 7 feeling **10** perception **11** temperament **14** responsiveness

sensible 4 just, sage, sane, wise **5** aware, plain, sound **7** evident, knowing, logical, obvious, prudent, visible **8** apparent, apprised, credible, discreet, informed, palpable, possible, rational, tangible **9** cognitive, cognizant, conscious, judicious, plausible, sagacious **10** detectable, discerning, farsighted, noticeable, perceiving, perceptive, reasonable, responsive, thoughtful **11** discernible, enlightened, intelligent, perceptible, susceptible **13** perspicacious **14** discriminating

sensitive 4 fine, keen, sore **5** acute, exact **6** tender, touchy **7** painful, precise **8** accurate, delicate, faithful, sentient **10** perceptive, responsive **11**

susceptible, thin-skinned **14** impressionable

sensitiveness 8 delicacy **10** touchiness

sensual 4 lewd, sexy **6** carnal, earthy, erotic **7** fleshly, lustful **9** lecherous **10** hedonistic, licentious, voluptuous

sensualist 8 hedonist, sybarite **9** libertine **10** voluptuary

sensuous 9 delicious, exquisite **10** delightful

sententious 7 orotund, pompous, preachy, stilted **8** didactic, pedantic **9** grandiose, high-flown, pietistic **10** judgmental, moralistic **13** sanctimonious

sentient 5 aware **7** alert to, alive to, awake to, mindful **8** sensible **9** conscious

sentiment, sentiments 4 idea **5** heart **6** notion **7** emotion, feeling, opinion, romance, thought **8** attitude **9** nostalgia, viewpoint **10** tenderness **11** romanticism **12** emotionalism **15** softheartedness

sentimental 5 mushy, weepy **7** maudlin, mawkish, tearful **8** pathetic, romantic **9** emotional, nostalgic **10** lachrymose **12** melodramatic, romanticized

Sentimental Education, A
   author: 15 Gustave Flaubert
   character: 6 Arnoux **9** Dambreuse, Rosanette **11** Des Lauriers, Louise Roque **14** Frederic Moreau

sentimentalism 4 corn, mush **5** slush **6** bathos, pathos **8** schmaltz **9** mushiness, soppiness **10** maudlinism, slushiness **11** mawkishness

sentimentality 4 mush **5** heart **6** bathos, pathos **10** sloppiness **11** mawkishness, temperament **12** emotionalism
   Yiddish: 6 kitsch

Sentimental Journey, A
   author: 14 Laurence Sterne
   character: 5 Maria **6** Yorick **7** La Fleur

sentinel 4 ward **5** guard, scout, watch **6** patrol, picket, ranger **7** lookout **8** guardian, watchman **9** guardsman

sentry 5 guard, watch **7** lookout, vedette, vidette **8** sentinel, watchman
   greeting: 4 halt

Seoul
   capital of: 10 South Korea

separate 3 cut **4** cull, fork, part, sift **5** break, crack, sever, split **6** bisect, detach, divide, ramify, remove, single, spread, sunder **7** crumble, disjoin, diverge, diverse, divorce, isolate, radiate **8** detached, discrete, distinct, disunite **9** bifurcate, break away, come apart, different, disunited, partition, segregate, subdivide **10** autonomous, dis-

connect, dissimilar, divaricate, individual **11** distinguish, independent

separated 6 cut off **7** severed **8** detached **10** disengaged **12** disconnected, disentangled

separate from 5 apart, leave

separately 5 apart **6** singly **7** asunder **9** severally **12** individually

Separate Tables
   director: 11 Delbert Mann
   based on play by: 15 Terence Rattigan
   cast: 10 David Niven **11** Deborah Kerr, Wendy Hiller **12** Rita Hayworth **13** Burt Lancaster
   Oscar for: 5 actor (Niven) **17** supporting actress (Hiller)

separation 3 gap **4** fork **5** break, space, split **6** breach, divide, schism **7** divider, divorce, good-bye, opening, parting, removal, sorting **8** boundary, distance, disunion, division, farewell, interval **9** branching, isolation, partition, severance **10** detachment, divergence **11** bifurcation, disjunction, segregation **12** estrangement **13** disconnection, disengagement **14** disassociation

Sepharvite god 10 Anammelech **11** Adrammelech

Sepher Torah 16 scroll of the Torah
   literally: 9 book of law

September
   characteristic: 11 harvest moon
   event: 14 aurora borealis, Northern lights **15** autumnal equinox
   attack: 9 terrorist (11)
   flower: 5 aster **12** morning glory
   French: 9 Septembre
   gem: 8 sapphire **12** star sapphire
   German: 9 September
   holiday: 8 Labor Day (1st Monday) **10** Michaelmas (29) **15** Grandparents' Day
   Italian: 9 Settembre
   number of days: 6 thirty
   origin of name: 6 septum (Latin meaning seven)
   place in year:
      Gregorian: 5 ninth
      Roman: 7 seventh
   Spanish: 10 Septiembre
   Zodiac sign: 5 Libra, Virgo

septentrional 6 arctic **8** northern **11** hyperborean

Septuagint
   abbreviation: 3 LXX
   author: 10 the Seventy

sepulcher 4 tomb **5** crypt, grave, vault **7** ossuary **8** cenotaph **9** mausoleum, reliquary **10** necropolis

sepulchral 6 hollow **7** charnel **8** funereal, mournful, tomblike **10** lugubrious

sequel 3 end **6** finish, result, upshot **7** outcome, product **8** addendum, epilogue, follow-up, offshoot **9** aftermath,

corollary, outgrowth **10** conclusion, postscript **11** consequence, culmination **12** continuation
French: 10 denouement

sequence 3 run **4** flow **5** chain, cycle, order, round, train **6** course, parade, series, string **7** routine **8** schedule **9** cavalcade **10** procession, succession **11** arrangement, progression **14** successiveness **15** consecutiveness

sequester 6 banish, lock up, retire **7** confine, isolate, seclude **8** separate, withdraw **9** segregate **10** quarantine

sequestered 8 closeted, confined, isolated, secluded **9** insulated, sheltered, withdrawn **10** cloistered **11** dissociated

sequin 4 coin, disk **5** ducat **7** spangle **8** ornament
French: 9 paillette

seraglio 3 oda **5** harem, serai **6** zenana **9** gynaeceum

serape 4 cape **5** shawl **6** mantle, poncho

seraph 5 angel

seraphic 7 angelic **8** beatific, ethereal, heavenly **9** celestial

Seraphim 6 angels

Serapis
origin: **5** Greek **8** Egyptian
form: **5** deity
combination of: **4** Apis, Hapi **6** Osiris

Serbia and Montenegro
other name: **8** Dalmatia **10** Yugoslavia
capital/largest city: **7** Beograd **8** Belgrade
others: **3** Nis **5** Kotor **7** Novisad **8** Pristina, Titograd
division: **6** Kosovo, Serbia **9** Vojvodina, Voyvodina **10** Montenegro
measure: **3** oka, rif **4** akov, ralo **5** donum, khvat, lanaz, plaze, stopa **6** motyka, ralico **9** danoranja
monetary unit: **4** para **5** dinar
weight: **3** oka **5** dramm, tovar, wagon **7** satlijk
lake: **6** Prespa **7** Scutari
mountain: **6** Balkan **8** Crna Cora, Durmitor **9** Sar-Pindus **10** Karawanken
　Alps: **6** Carnic, Julian **7** Dinaric **16** Northern Albanian
river: **4** Sava **5** Drina, Tamis, Timok **6** Danube, Morava **9** Vojvodina
sea: **8** Adriatic
physical feature:
　bay: **5** Kotor
　gulf: **5** Kotor
　peninsula: **6** Balkan
people: **4** Serb, Slav **5** Croat **8** Albanian **10** Macedonian **11** Montenegrin
　author: **6** Andric, Djilas, Krleza **7** Dedijer
　leader: **4** Tito **9** Milosevic, Obrenovic **13** Mikhailovitch
　ruler: **5** Peter **9** Hapsburgs **12** Otto-

man Turks
　sculptor: **9** Mestrovic
language: **7** Bosnian **8** Albanian, Croatian **9** Hungarian **10** Macedonian **11** Montenegrin **13** Serbo-Croatian
　alphabet: **5** Latin **8** Cyrillic
religion: **5** Islam **13** Roman Catholic **15** Eastern Orthodox, Serbian Orthodox
feature:
　coffee house: **7** kafanas
　fields: **5** polje
　military governor: **7** vojvodi
　musical instrument: **5** gusla
　poems: **5** pesme
　slippers: **6** opanki
food:
　dessert: **4** pita
　drink: **5** rakia **6** rakija **7** maraska **9** slivovitz **10** sljivovice **13** Turkish coffee
　meat: **7** shaslik **9** cevapcici **10** culbastija
　soup: **6** corbas

sere 3 dry **4** arid **6** barren **7** parched, wizened **8** droughty, scorched, withered **9** shriveled, unwatered, waterless **10** dehydrated, desiccated **12** dehumidified, moistureless

serene 4 calm, cool, fair **5** clear, quiet, still **6** bright, limpid, placid, poised, sedate, smooth **7** halcyon **8** composed, peaceful, pellucid, tranquil **9** dignified, unruffled **10** nonchalant, unobscured, untroubled **11** undisturbed, unexcitable, unperturbed **13** unimpassioned

serenity 7 dignity **8** calmness, coolness, quietude **9** composure, placidity **10** equanimity, quiescence **11** complacence, nonchalance, tranquility **12** peacefulness, tranquillity **13** collectedness
French: 9 sangfroid

serf 6 cotter, thrall, vassal **7** bondman, peasant, villein

serfdom 4 yoke **6** thrall **7** bondage, slavery **9** servitude, thralldom, vassalage **11** enslavement, subjugation

Sergeant York
director: **11** Howard Hawks
cast: **10** Gary Cooper, Joan Leslie **12** George Tobias **13** Walter Brennan
Oscar for: **5** actor (Cooper)

Sergestus
origin: **6** Trojan
companion to: **6** Aeneas

serial 7 regular **9** continued, piecemeal, recurring **10** continuous, sequential, successive **11** consecutive, incremental

series 3 set **5** chain, cycle, group, order **6** course, number, parade, string **8** sequence **10** procession, succession **11** progression

serious 3 bad, sad **4** grim **5** grave, heavy, sober, staid **6** rueful, sedate,

severe, solemn, somber **7** crucial, decided, earnest, fateful, harmful, pensive, sincere, weighty **8** alarming, critical, dejected, downcast, frowning, perilous, resolute, resolved **9** crippling, dangerous, important, momentous, saturnine **10** determined, portentous, purposeful, thoughtful **13** consequential **14** incapacitating

seriousness 7 gravity **8** severity **9** sincerity, soberness, solemnity **10** importance **11** earnestness

sermon 6 homily, rebuke, tirade **7** lecture, reproof **8** diatribe, harangue **9** preaching **10** admonition, preachment **11** exhortation

serpent, Serpent 3 asp **5** cheat, devil, rogue, Satan, snake, viper **7** reptile, traitor **8** deceiver **9** trickster
constellation of: **7** Serpens

Serpent Holder
constellation of: **9** Ophiuchus

serpentine 4 mazy **6** spiral, zigzag **7** coiling, crooked, devious, sinuous, snaking, winding **8** flexuous, tortuous, twisting **10** circuitous, convoluted, meandering, round about, undulating **12** labyrinthine

Serpico
director: **11** Sidney Lumet
based on story by: **9** Peter Maas
cast: **8** Al Pacino **9** Jack Kehoe **12** John Randolph
setting: **11** New York City

serrate 5 notch **6** jagged, pinked, ridged **7** dentate, grooved, notched, toothed **10** sawtoothed

serration 5 notch, ridge, teeth, tooth **8** notching, sawtooth

servant 3 man **4** cook, girl, help, maid **5** valet **6** butler, flunky, helper, lackey, menial, minion, slavey **7** footman **8** domestic, employee, factotum, henchman, hired man, retainer, scullion **9** attendant, chauffeur, hired girl, hired help, man Friday, underling **10** girl Friday **11** housekeeper

serve 2 do **3** act, aid **4** help, pass, suit, tend, work **5** avail, spend, treat **6** assist, attend, be used, do duty, oblige, supply, wait on **7** content, deliver, further, perform, present, promote, satisfy, suffice, work for **8** carry out, complete, function, hand over, minister **9** officiate **11** fill the bill

service, services 3 aid, use **4** help, mend, rite **5** avail, labor **6** adjust, agency, bureau, effort, employ, profit, repair, ritual, system **7** benefit, support, utility, waiting **8** ceremony, facility, maintain, military **9** advantage, provision, treatment **10** assistance, attendance, ceremonial, department, employment, observance, usefulness **11** celebration, convenience, maintenance **12** ministration **13** accommodation

serviceable 5 tough **6** rugged, strong, sturdy, usable, useful **7** durable, lasting **8** workable **9** effective, operative, practical **10** functional **11** utilitarian

serviceman 6 marine, sailor **7** soldier **9** repairman

servile 4 oily **6** abject, humble, menial **7** fawning, in bonds, slavish **8** cringing, scraping, toadying, unctuous **9** groveling, truckling **10** obsequious, submissive **11** bootlicking, subservient, sycophantic

serving 6 acting **7** dishful, helping, portion, waiting **8** plateful **9** assisting, attending, sufficing **11** ministering

serving counter 3 bar **6** buffet **9** sideboard

servitude 5 bonds **6** chains **7** bondage, fetters, serfdom, slavery **8** shackles **9** thralldom, vassalage **10** oppression **11** enslavement, subjugation **12** enthrallment, imprisonment

Servius Tullius
  also: 7 Tullius
  king of: 4 Rome
  daughter: 6 Tullia
  son-in-law: 7 Tarquin
  killed by: 6 Tullia **7** Tarquin

sesame
  also called: 10 benne seeds
  botanical name: 14 Sesamum indicum
  fairy tale: 10 "open sesame" **25** Ali Baba and the Forty Thieves
  high in: 7 protein
  former/mythical use: 3 oil **8** medicine **10** opens locks **11** lighting oil **16** discovers secrets **21** discovers secret places
  use: 8 bread **6** salads **10** casseroles
  use like: 8 nutmeats **11** chopped nuts

Sesame Street
  character: 4 Bert, Elmo **5** Ernie, Herry, Oscar **6** Snuffy **7** Barkley, Big Bird, Muppets **8** the Count **12** Telly Monster **13** Cookie Monster **15** Mr Snuffleupagus

Sesostris
  king of: 5 Egypt

session 4 bout, term **5** round, synod **6** course, period **7** meeting, quarter, sitting **8** assembly, conclave, semester **10** conference, convention

set 3 cut, fit, fix, gel, kit, lay, put, sic **4** club, drop, firm, line, make, plop, post, rate, sink, stud, suit **5** adapt, align, array, banal, bunch, crowd, embed, fixed, group, imbed, order, place, plunk, ready, rigid, scene, stale, stiff, stock, style, trite, usual **6** adjust, assess, assign, attach, common, confer, create, decree, frozen, harden, line up, locale, locate, ordain, outfit, studio **7** arrange, bearing, complex, congeal, decided, faction, install, jellify, machine, prepare, profile, regular, release, routine, scenery, service, set-

ting, situate, station, thicken, unleash **8** arranged, assembly, backdrop, carriage, definite, estimate, everyday, familiar, firmness, habitual, hardened, location, ornament, position, prepared, regulate, rigidity, solidify, stubborn **9** apparatus, calibrate, customary, determine, establish, hackneyed, immovable, obstinate, prescribe, represent, steadfast **10** accustomed, assortment, collection, inflexible **11** anticipated, commonplace, consolidate, established, prearranged **12** conventional
French: 6 clique **7** coterie

Set
  also: 4 Seth
  origin: 8 Egyptian
  form: 6 animal
  personifies: 6 desert
  brother: 6 Osiris
  killed: 6 Osiris

set about 5 begin **6** assume **9** undertake **10** surrounded

set against 8 alienate, estrange

set apart 5 allot **6** detach, divide **7** earmark, isolate **8** allocate, separate **9** apportion, segregate **11** appropriate

set aside 4 kill **5** allot, annul **6** abjure, cancel, repeal, revoke **7** abandon, abolish, call off, destroy, discard, earmark, nullify, put away, rescind, retract, reverse **8** abrogate, allocate, override, overturn **9** designate, repudiate **10** invalidate **11** discontinue

set at ease 5 cheer **6** please **7** appease, comfort, content, gratify

set at liberty 4 free **5** let go **6** parole **7** manumit, release, unchain **8** liberate, unfetter **9** unshackle **10** emancipate

setback 4 flop, loss, snag **5** hitch, slump **6** defeat, mishap, rebuff **7** failure, relapse, reverse, undoing **8** reversal **9** adversity, mischance, worsening **10** misfortune, regression **13** retrogression **14** disappointment

set down 6 record **7** deposit

set forth 2 go **5** be off, leave **6** assert, avouch, depart **7** advance **8** advocate, propound **10** sally forth

set free 5 let go, loose, untie **6** acquit, loosen, pardon, parole, unbind, uncage, unlock **7** deliver, release **8** liberate, unfetter **9** discharge, disengage, extricate **10** emancipate

Seth *see* **3** Set

Seth
  means: 12 compensation
  father: 4 Adam
  mother: 3 Eve
  son: 4 Enos

set in 5 arise, ensue, occur **6** arrive

set in motion 5 begin, start **6** launch **8** initiate **9** instigate, originate **10** inaugurate

set in order 4 rank, sort **5** align **6** line up **7** arrange, marshal **8** classify, organize **9** methodize **11** systematize

set of beliefs 5 credo, creed, dogma, ethos **6** ethnic, tenets **8** doctrine **10** philosophy, principles **11** convictions

set off 6 depart **7** explode, go forth **8** detonate, start out **10** sally forth

set on fire 4 burn **5** light **6** ignite, kindle

set out 4 pose **5** array, begin, be off, place, range **6** deploy, embark, intend **7** arrange, display **9** undertake

set right 7 correct **8** disabuse

set store by 5 prize, value **6** esteem **7** respect **8** treasure

set straight 5 edify **6** advise, inform **7** educate **8** disabuse **9** enlighten

settee 4 seat, sofa **5** bench

setting 5 scene **6** fixing, locale **7** jelling **8** aligning, ambiance, locating, location, mounting **9** adjusting, arranging, decreeing, hardening, ordaining **10** congealing, regulating, thickening **11** arrangement, determining, environment, prescribing, solidifying **12** establishing, surroundings
French: 6 milieu **11** mise-en-scene

setting sun
  god of: 5 Janus

settle 3 fix, pay, sag **4** calm, drop, land, sink **5** agree, allay, clear, droop, light, lodge, perch, quiet **6** alight, choose, decide, locate, move to, pacify, people, soothe **7** arrange, clarify, clear up, compose, inhabit, rectify, resolve, satisfy, sit down, situate **8** colonize, make good, populate, take root **9** determine, discharge, establish, reconcile **11** precipitate

settled 4 sure **7** certain, decided

settlement 3 sum **4** camp, post **6** amount, colony, hamlet **7** bequest, outpost, payment, village **8** clearing, peopling **9** clearance, discharge **10** adjustment, colonizing, encampment, resolution **11** acquittance, arrangement, liquidation **12** amortization, colonizing, compensation, satisfaction **14** reconciliation

settler 7 pioneer **8** colonist, squatter **9** colonizer, immigrant **11** homesteader **12** frontiersman

settle upon 6 bestow **7** consign **8** bequeath

settlings 4 lees **5** dregs **7** deposit, grounds, remains, residue **8** leavings

set-to 4 spat **5** brush, clash, run-in **6** battle, fracas **7** dispute, quarrel, scuffle **8** argument, skirmish, squabble **10** engagement, falling out **12** disagreement **13** confrontation
French: 11 contretemps

setup 4 plan **6** scheme, system **8** practice **9** apparatus **11** arrangement **12** organization

set up 3 rig 5 erect, found 7 arrange, install 9 construct, establish, institute 10 inaugurate, prearrange

set upon 3 mug 5 beset, fly at 6 assail, attack 7 besiege, lunge at 9 pitch into

Seurat, Georges Pierre
born: 5 Paris 6 France
artwork: 9 The Chahut, The Circus, The Models, The Parade, The Uproar 10 The Bathers 12 Le Grand Jatte, The Yoked Cart 19 Une Baignade Asnieres 23 A Bathing Scene at Asnieres, The Bec du Hoc at Grand champ 40 Sunday Afternoon on the Island of La Grand Jatte

Seuss, Dr
real name: 19 Theodore Seuss Geisel
author of: 12 If I Ran the Zoo 14 The Cat in the Hat 15 Green Eggs and Ham, Horton Hears a Who, If I Ran the Circus 18 Oh the Places You'll Go 19 Horton Hatches the Egg 23 Mister Brown Can Moo Can You? 26 Thidwick The Big-Hearted Moose, How the Grinch Stole Christmas
character: 5 Lorax 6 Grinch, Horton, Yertle 8 Thidwick

Seve
nickname of: 20 Severiano Ballesteros

Seven Against Thebes
author: 9 Aeschylus
character: 6 Ismene 8 Antigone, Eteocles 9 Polynices 11 Theban Women
seven heroes: 6 Tydeus 8 Adrastus, Capaneus 9 Polynices 10 Amphiaraus, Hippomedon 13 Parthenopaeus

Seven Beauties
director: 14 Lina Wertmuller
cast: 11 Fernando Rey 13 Shirley Stoler 17 Giancarlo Giannini

Seven Brides for Seven Brothers
director: 12 Stanley Donen
cast: 9 Tammy Rall 10 Howard Keel, Jane Powell 11 Julie Newmar (Newmeyer), Russ Tamblyn 12 Jeff Richards 14 Virginia Gibson
score: 11 Saul Chaplin 12 Johnny Mercer
choreography: 11 Michael Kidd

Seven Pillars of Wisdom
author: 10 T E Lawrence

Seven Samurai
director: 13 Akira Kurosawa
cast: 11 Yoshio Inaba 13 Toshiro Mifune 14 Takashi Shimura
remade as: 19 The Magnificent Seven

seven seas 6 Arctic, Indian 9 Antarctic 12 North Pacific, South Pacific 13 North Atlantic, South Atlantic

Seven Sisters colleges 5 Smith 6 Vassar 7 Barnard 8 Bryn Mawr 9 Radcliffe, Wellesley 12 Mount Holyoke

Seventeen
author: 15 Booth Tarkington

character: 7 Genesis 9 Miss Pratt, Mrs Baxter 10 Jane Baxter, May Parcher 21 William Sylvanus Baxter

Seventh Heaven (7th Heaven)
network: 2 WB
cast: 11 Barry Watson (Matt Camden), Jessica Biel (Mary Camden) 14 Catherine Hicks (Annie Camden), David Gallagher (Simon Camden), Stephen Collins (Eric Camden) 15 Mackenzie Rosman (Ruthie Camden) 16 Beverley Mitchell (Lucy Camden Kinkirk)

Seventh Seal, The
director: 13 Ingmar Bergman
cast: 9 Nils Poppe 11 Max von Sydow 13 Bibi Andersson 17 Gunnar Bjornstrand

Seventy-Seven Sunset Strip
character: 6 J R Hale, Kookie (Gerald Lloyd Kookson III), Roscoe 7 Suzanne 11 Jeff Spencer, Rex Randolph 12 Stuart Bailey
cast: 9 Edd Byrnes 10 Louis Quinn, Roger Smith 11 Richard Long, Robert Logan 14 Jacqueline Beer 16 Efrem Zimbalist Jr
Kookie's sayings: 10 a dark seven 12 the ginchiest 13 piling up the Z's 14 lend me your comb 15 play like a pigeon 17 headache grapplers 22 keep the eyeballs rolling

seven wonders of the ancient world 8 pyramids (Egypt) 12 Olympian Zeus (sculpted by Phidias) 15 Temple of Artemis (at Ephesus) 16 Colossus of Rhodes 22 Lighthouse (Pharos) at Alexandria 23 hanging gardens of Babylon (of Semiramis) 24 Mausoleum at Halicarnassus

Seven Year Itch, The
director: 11 Billy Wilder
cast: 8 Tom Ewell 10 Sonny Tufts 11 Evelyn Keyes, Victor Moore 13 Marilyn Monroe
setting: 11 New York City

sever 3 saw 4 part, rend, rive, tear 5 slice, split 6 bisect, cleave, cut off, lop off 7 disjoin, rupture, split up 8 amputate, break off, cut in two, dissolve, disunite, separate, truncate 9 dismember, terminate 10 disconnect 11 discontinue

several 3 own 4 a few, some 6 divers, single, sundry 7 certain, diverse, express, private, special 8 assorted, distinct, peculiar, personal, separate, specific 9 different, exclusive 10 individual, particular, respective 11 distinctive, independent

severe 4 cold, dour, grim, wild 5 cruel, grave, harsh, plain, rough, sober, stern, stiff 6 biting, bitter, brutal, chaste, fierce, fuming, raging, savage, sedate, simple, somber, strict, taxing 7 austere, cutting, drastic, extreme, furious, intense, painful, serious, uni-

form, violent 8 piercing, rigorous, ruthless, stinging, vigorous 9 dangerous, demanding, difficult, draconian, merciless, saturnine, turbulent, unadorned, unsparing 10 forbidding, restrained, tumultuous 11 distressing, undecorated, unrelenting 12 conservative

severed 6 cut off 8 detached 9 uncoupled, unhitched 10 unfastened 11 unconnected 12 disconnected

Severini, Gino
born: 5 Italy 7 Cortona
artwork: 9 Harlequin 15 The Armored Train 25 Dancer Sea and Vase of Flowers 32 Dynamic Hieroglyph of the Bal Tabarin

severity 5 rigor 7 cruelty 8 acrimony, violence 9 austerity, gruffness, harshness, sternness 10 asceticism, difficulty, strictness, stringency 11 seriousness 12 grievousness

Seville
former name: 8 Hispalis
landmark: 7 Alcazar, Giralda
plain: 9 Andalusia
river: 12 Guadalquivir
ruler: 5 Moors 6 Romans 7 Vandals 8 Abbasids, Almohads, Iberians 9 Visigoths 10 Almoravids
Spanish: 7 Sevilla

sew 3 hem 4 mend, seam, tack 5 unite 6 fasten, ground, stitch, suture 10 run aground
loosely: 5 baste

sewage 5 waste 6 efflux, refuse 8 effluent 9 effluence

sewing machine
invented by: 4 Howe

sex 4 Eros, love 6 coitus, gender, libido 7 coition 8 maleness 10 copulation, femaleness, femininity, generation, lovemaking 11 masculinity, procreation 12 reproduction

Sex and the City
network: 3 HBO
cast: 9 Chris Noth (Mr Big) 11 Evan Handler (Harry Goldenblatt), John Corbett (Aidan Shaw), Kim Cattrall (Samantha Jones) 12 Cynthia Nixon (Miranda Hobbes), Kristin Davis (Charlotte York), Willie Garson (Stanford Blatch) 14 David Eigenberg (Steve Brady), Kyle MacLachlan (Trey MacDougal) 18 Sarah Jessica Parker (Carrie Bradshaw)

Sexton, Anne
author of: 15 All My Pretty Ones 22 To Bedlam and Part Way Back 23 The Awful Rowing Toward God

sexual 6 coital, erotic 7 amatory, genital, marital, sensual 8 conjugal, intimate, venereal 10 copulatory, generative, libidinous 11 procreative 12 reproductive

sexually stimulating 3 hot 4 sexy 6

erotic, risque **9** salacious **10** suggestive **12** pornographic

sexy 4 lewd **5** bawdy **6** erotic **8** prurient **9** seductive **10** come-hither, coquettish, suggestive, voluptuous **11** flirtatious, provocative

Seychelles
  capital/largest city: 8 Victoria
  monetary unit: 4 cent **5** rupee
  island: 4 Mahe **7** Aldabra, La Digue, Praslin **8** Farquhar **9** Desroches **10** Silhouette
  highest point: 16 Morne Seychellois
  sea: 6 Indian
  people: 5 Asian **6** Creole, French, Indian **7** African, Chinese
    leader: 4 Rene **7** Mancham
  language: 6 Creole, French **7** English
  religion: 8 Anglican **13** Roman Catholic

sforzando
  music: 12 sudden accent

Shabbas 7 Sabbath

shabby 3 low **4** mean, poor, torn, worn **5** cheap, dirty, mangy, raggy, ratty, seedy, sorry, tatty, tight **6** frayed, meager, ragged, sordid, unfair **7** ignoble, rundown, scruffy **8** beggarly, decaying, inferior, slovenly, unworthy, wretched **9** illiberal, miserable, neglected **10** ramshackle, threadbare, tumbledown, ungenerous **11** dilapidated **12** contemptible, deteriorated, dishonorable, impoverished

shabby bar 4 dive **5** joint **7** gin mill **9** honky-tonk

shack 3 hut **5** cabin **6** lean-to, shanty

shackle 3 bar, tie **4** balk, bind, cuff, curb, foil, rein **5** block, bonds, chain, check, cramp, cuffs, deter, irons, limit, stall **6** chains, fetter, hamper, hinder, hobble, hogtie, impede, pinion, retard, secure, tether, thwart **7** inhibit, manacle, prevent **8** encumber, handcuff, restrict **9** forestall, frustrate, hamstring, handcuffs **12** circumscribe

shackled 7 chained, in irons **8** in chains, manacled **10** handcuffed

shadchan, schatchen 10 matchmaker **14** marriage broker

Shaddai 3 God

shade 3 bit, dim, hue, jot **4** atom, cast, hint, hood, iota, tint, tone, veil, whit **5** blind, color, drape, tinge, touch, trace **6** awning, canopy, darken, screen, shadow, shield **7** curtain, modicum, shadows, shutter **8** darkness, particle, semidark **9** scintilla **10** suggestion
  French: 7 soupcon
  form: 6 spirit
  location: 5 Hades

shadow, shadows 3 bit, dog **4** blot, hint, tail **5** cloud, ghost, hound, shade, smear, stain, stalk, taint, tinge, touch, trace, track, trail **6** blight, follow, pursue, smirch, smudge, threat **7**

blemish, specter, whisper **8** penumbra **10** reflection, silhouette, suggestion

Shadow of a Doubt
  director: 15 Alfred Hitchcock
  cast: 10 Hume Cronyn **12** Joseph Cotten, Teresa Wright **14** Macdonald Carey **16** Patricia Collinge
  remade as: 16 Step Down to Terror

shadowy 3 dim **5** shady **6** gloomy, unreal **7** obscure **8** illusory **9** tenebrous **10** indistinct **13** insubstantial

Shadrach
  former name: 8 Hananiah
  friend: 6 Daniel
  companion: 7 Meshach **8** Abednego

shady 5 fishy **7** crooked, devious, dubious, shadowy **9** dishonest, unethical **10** suspicious **11** underhanded **12** disreputable, questionable **13** untrustworthy

shady dealings 5 fraud, graft **7** bribery **10** corruption, dishonesty

shaft 3 cut, pit, ray **4** barb, beam, dart, duct, flue, gibe, hilt, stem, vent, well **5** abyss, arrow, chasm, gleam, lance, patch, pylon, quill, shank, spear, spire, stalk, tower, trunk **6** cavity, column, funnel, handle, insult, pillar, streak, stream **6** affront, chimney, conduit, minaret, obelisk, spindle, steeple **8** brickbat, monolith, pilaster **9** aspersion **10** excavation

shaggy 5 bushy, downy, fuzzy, hairy, nappy, piled, wooly **6** tufted, woolly **7** bearded, hirsute, shagged, unshorn **9** whiskered **11** bewhiskered

shah 4 king **5** ruler **7** emperor, monarch **8** autocrat **9** sovereign

Shahaptian
  tribe: 6 Numipu **8** Nez Perce

Shahn, Ben
  born: 6 Kaunas **9** Lithuania
  artwork: 5 Epoch **8** Handball **12** Seurat's Lunch, The Physicist **16** Pacific Land scape **18** Willis Avenue Bridge **28** The Passion of Sacco and Vanzetti

shake 3 jar, jog, mix **4** jerk, jolt, move, stir, stun, sway, wave **5** elude, quake, swing, touch **6** affect, bounce, jiggle, joggle, jostle, jounce, quaver, quiver, rattle, ruffle, shimmy, shiver, slough, totter, twitch, wobble **7** agitate, disturb, flicker, flutter, perturb, quaking, shudder, stagger, startle, tremble, unnerve, vibrate **8** brandish, disquiet, distress, flourish, frighten, throw off, unsettle, unstring **9** quivering, shivering, trembling **10** discompose, flickering, fluttering

shakedown 6 extort, payoff, search, tryout **7** testing **8** thorough **9** blackmail, extortion, hush money

Shakespeare, William
  also: 10 bard of Avon **12** immortal bard
  author of: 6 Hamlet, Henry V **7**

Henry IV, Henry VI, Macbeth, Othello, Sonnets **8** King John, King Lear, Pericles (Prince of Tyre) **9** Cymbeline, Henry VIII, Richard II **10** Coriolanus, Richard III, The Tempest **11** As You Like It **12** Julius Caesar, Twelfth Night **13** Rape of Lucrece, Timon of Athens **14** Romeo and Juliet, The Winter's Tale, Venus and Adonis **15** Titus Andronicus **16** Love's Labour's Lost **17** Measure for Measure, The Comedy of Errors **18** Antony and Cleopatra, Troilus and Cressida **19** Much Ado About Nothing, The Merchant of Venice, The Taming of the Shrew **20** All's Well That Ends Well **21** A Midsummer Night's Dream **22** The Merry Wives of Windsor **23** The Two Gentlemen of Verona
  birthplace: 15 Stratford-on-Avon
  theater: 4 Swan **5** Globe
  wife: 12 Anne Hathaway

Shakespeare in Love
  director: 10 John Madden
  cast: 9 Judi Dench (Queen Elizabeth) **10** Ben Affleck (Ned Alleyn), Colin Firth (Lord Wessex) **11** Tim McMullen (Frees) **12** Geoffrey Rush (Philip Henslowe), Martin Clunes (Richard Burbage), Tom Wilkinson (Hugh Fennyman) **13** Joseph Fiennes (Will Shakespeare) **14** Gwyneth Paltrow (Viola De Lesseps), Imelda Staunton (Nurse), Steven O'Donnell (Lambert) **17** Nicholas Le Prevost (Sir Robert De Lesseps)

shakeup 5 purge **7** cleanup **8** turnover **10** clean sweep **11** realignment **13** rearrangement, redisposition, restructuring **14** redistribution, reorganization

shake up 3 mix **4** stir **5** churn **7** agitate, disturb

shakiness 6 tremor **10** insecurity **11** instability, uncertainty **12** unsteadiness

shaky 4 weak **5** frail, jumpy **6** flimsy, unsafe, unsure, wobbly **7** dubious, fidgety, fragile, halting, jittery, nervous, teetery **8** hesitant, insecure, unstable, unsteady, wavering **9** faltering, hazardous, quivering, teetering, tottering, trembling, tremulous, uncertain, undecided **10** inconstant, irresolute, precarious, unreliable, unresolved **11** vacillating **12** undependable

shallow 5 shoal **6** frothy, slight **7** surface, trivial **8** knee-deep, skin-deep, trifling **9** frivolous **11** meaningless, superficial, unimportant **13** insubstantial **15** inconsequential

shalom 5 hello, peace **7** goodbye

shalom aleichem 10 peace to you

sham 3 act **4** copy, fake **5** bogus, false, feign, fraud, phony, put on, trick **6** affect, assume, forged **7** feigned, forgery, imitate, pretend **8** pretense, simulate, spurious **9** imitation, pretended, simulated, synthetic **10** artificial, fraudulent **11** counterfeit, make-believe

Shamash
origin: **8** Akkadian
god of: **3** sun

shamble, shambles 4 limp **5** hitch, lurch, stall **6** hobble **7** shuffle **8** butchery **14** slaughterhouse

shame 5 guilt, odium **6** humble, stigma **7** chagrin, mortify, remorse, scandal **8** contempt, disgrace, dishonor, ignominy **9** disrepute, embarrass, humiliate **10** debasement, disrespect **11** degradation, humiliation, self-disgust **12** unworthiness **13** embarrassment, mortification **14** disappointment

shamed be the one who thinks evil of it
French: **20** honi soit qui mal y pense

shamefaced 5 sorry **7** abashed, crushed, humbled, put-down **8** blushing, sheepish **9** chagrined, disgraced, mortified **10** humiliated, remorseful **11** embarrassed

shameful 3 low **4** base, mean, vile **6** odious **7** heinous, ignoble **8** shocking, unworthy **9** dastardly, degrading **10** deplorable, despicable, inglorious, iniquitous, outrageous, villainous **11** disgraceful, ignominious, opprobrious **12** contemptible, dishonorable **13** reprehensible

shameless 4 pert **5** brash, saucy **6** brazen, wanton **7** forward, immoral **8** degraded, flagrant, immodest, impudent, indecent **9** abandoned, audacious, barefaced, boldfaced, dissolute, unabashed **10** indecorous, unblushing, unreserved **11** disgraceful **12** dishonorable

shamelessness 4 gall **5** brass, cheek **8** audacity **10** brazenness, effrontery **11** forwardness, presumption

shamus 3 tec **7** gumshoe **9** detective **10** private eye **12** investigator

Shane
director: **13** George Stevens
cast: **8** Alan Ladd **9** Van Heflin **10** Jean Arthur **11** Jack Palance **12** Elisha Cook Jr **13** Edgar Buchanan **14** Brandon de Wilde

Shanghai
area: **23** International Settlement
landmark: **13** Long Hua Temple **17** People's Opera House **28** Shanghai Industrial Exhibition
river: **6** Wusung **7** Huang-P'u, Yangtze

Shangri-La see **5** Nepal

shanty 3 hut **5** cabin, hovel, shack **6** lean-to

shape 4 form, make, mold, trim **5** array, build, frame, guide, model, order **6** create, fettle, figure, health **7** con-

tour, develop, fashion, outline, profile **8** physique **9** condition, construct, determine **10** silhouette **12** conformation **13** configuration

shapeless 5 baggy **8** formless **9** amorphous, irregular

shapely 3 fit **4** neat, trim **6** comely, gainly **11** symmetrical

shaper 9 architect, innovator **10** instigator, prime mover

Shapley, Howard
field: **9** astronomy
studied: **6** galaxy

Shardik
author: **12** Richard Adams

share 3 cut **4** dole, part **5** allot, cut up, quota, split **6** ration **7** deal out, divvy up, mete out, percent, portion **8** allocate **9** allotment, allowance, apportion **10** percentage **13** apportionment

shared 5 joint **6** common, public **7** general **8** communal **10** collective

share one's sorrow 7 condole **10** sympathize **11** commiserate

Sharif, Omar
real name: **15** Michael Shalhoub
born: **5** Egypt **10** Alexandria
roles: **3** Che **7** Hidalgo **9** Dr Zhivago, Funny Girl, Funny Lady **11** Genghis Khan **12** Nick Arnstein **16** Lawrence of Arabia
expert on: **6** bridge

shark 3 ace **4** fish **5** cheat **6** expert, usurer, wizard **8** predator **9** trickster **12** extortionist

sharp 3 sly **4** acid, curt, fine, foxy, high, keen, sour, tart, wily **5** acrid, acute, alert, angry, awake, blunt, clear, cruel, edged, gruff, harsh, nippy, piked, quick, rapid, salty, sheer, spiny, steep **6** abrupt, artful, astute, barbed, biting, bitter, clever, crafty, crusty, fierce, keenly, marked, pointy, severe, shrewd, shrill, strong, sudden, thorny, tricky, unkind **7** acutely, alertly, angular, bearish, bristly, brusque, caustic, closely, crabbed, cunning, cutting, drastic, exactly, extreme, galling, intense, nipping, piquant, pointed, prickly, quickly, raucous, toothed, violent **8** abruptly, distinct, on the dot, piercing, promptly, scathing, serrated, spiteful, stinging, strident, suddenly, venomous, vertical, vigilant, vinegary **9** conniving, deceptive, excessive, on the nose, precisely, rancorous, unethical, vitriolic **10** contriving, discerning, immoderate, inordinate, perceptive, punctually **11** attentively, calculating, on the button, penetrating, precipitous **12** unprincipled, unscrupulous **13** precipitously
French: **5** juste
Spanish: **7** en punto

Sharp, Becky

character in: **10** Vanity Fair
author: **9** Thackeray

sharp-cornered 6 jagged **7** angular

sharp dresser 3 fop **4** dude **5** dandy **12** Beau Brummell, clotheshorse, fashion plate

sharpen 4 edge, hone, whet **5** grind, strop

sharply pointed 4 keen **5** acute **6** spiked **7** tapered **8** piercing **10** rapierlike **11** needle-nosed

sharpness 3 nip, wit **4** edge, tang **6** acuity, acumen **7** acidity, insight **8** acerbity, acridity, acrimony, keenness, pungency, saliency, tartness **9** acuteness, alertness, quickness **10** causticity, craftiness **12** perspicacity

sharp pain 4 pang, stab **5** cramp **6** twinge

sharpshooter
French: **10** tirailleur

sharp-sighted 5 acute **6** shrewd **8** piercing **9** far-seeing **10** discerning, perceptive **11** penetrating **13** perspicacious

sharp-witted 4 keen **5** acute, alert, canny, quick, smart **6** astute, brainy, clever

Shatner, William
born: **6** Canada **8** Montreal
roles: **8** Star Trek, T J Hooker **17** Captain James T Kirk

shatter 4 rive, ruin **5** break, burst, crack, crash, crush, quash, smash, split, spoil, upset, wreck **6** squash, sunder, topple **7** crumble, destroy, explode, scuttle **8** demolish, fracture, overturn, splinter **9** devastate, pulverize

shattered 6 broken, dashed **7** crushed, smashed **8** crumbled, decrepit **9** flustered **10** demolished, fragmented, splintered, tumbledown **11** crestfallen, demoralized **13** disillusioned, disintegrated

shave 3 cut, lop, mow **4** clip, crop, dock, pare, skin, snip, trim **5** brush, graze, prune, shear **6** barber, cut off, fleece, glance, scrape **7** scissor

Shaw, George Bernard
author of: **7** Candida **9** Pygmalion, Saint Joan **12** Major Barbara **13** Arms and the Man **14** Man and Superman **15** Heartbreak House **16** Back to Methuselah **17** The Devil's Disciple, The Doctor's Dilemma **18** Caesar and Cleopatra **19** Androcles and the Lion **20** Mrs Warren's Profession
member of: **13** Fabian Society

Shaw, Irwin
author of: **12** Top of the Hill **13** The Young Lions **14** Beggarman Thief, Rich Man Poor Man

Shaw, Robert
born: **7** England **12** Westhoughton

wife: 7 Mary Ure
roles: 4 Jaws 7 The Deep 8 The Sting 12 Swashbuckler 13 The Caretakers 17 A Man for All Seasons 20 Force Ten from Navarone 28 The Taking of Pelham One-Two-Three
author of: 14 The Hiding Place 21 The Man in the Glass Booth

Shawabti
origin: 8 Egyptian
form: 8 figurine
where used: 6 burial

shawl 4 wrap 5 scarf 6 mantle 7 paisley 10 fascinator
Mexican: 6 serape
Spanish: 8 mantilla

Shawnee
language family: 9 Algonkian 10 Algonquian
location: 4 Ohio 6 Kansas 8 Missouri, Oklahoma 9 Tennessee 12 Pennsylvania 13 South Carolina
leader: 8 Tecumseh 11 Tenskwatawa
related to: 8 Delaware

Shawshank Redemption, The
author: 11 Stephen King
director: 13 Frank Darabont
cast: 9 Bob Gunton (Warden Norton) 10 Tim Robbins (Andy Dufresne) 11 Clancy Brown (Captain Hadley), Mark Rolston (Bogs Diamond) 13 Morgan Freeman (Ellis Boyd Redding), William Sadler (Heywood)

She
author: 13 H Rider Haggard
character: 6 Ayesha

shear 3 cut, lop 4 clip, crop, snip, trim 5 prune, shave 6 fleece, remove 7 deprive, relieve, scissor

Shearer, Norma
born: 6 Canada 8 Montreal
husband: 7 Irving Thalberg
roles: 8 The Women 9 A Free Soul 11 The Divorcee (Oscar) 14 Romeo and Juliet, Their Own Desire 15 Marie Antoinette 26 The Barretts of Wimpole Street

shears 5 clips, trims 6 prunes 7 pruners 8 clippers, scissors, trimmers

sheath 3 pod 4 case, coat, skin 6 casing, jacket 7 capsule, coating, wrapper 8 covering, envelope, membrane, scabbard, slipcase, wrapping 9 container 10 receptacle

sheathing 6 casing, siding 8 covering

Sheba
also: 4 Saba
visited: 7 Solomon
father: 6 Bichri, Joktan, Raamah 7 Jokshan
grandfather: 4 Cush 7 Keturah
people of: 7 Sabeans

Shebat 19 eleventh Hebrew month

she carved it
Latin: 8 sculpsit

shed 3 hut 4 cast, doff, drop, emit, molt 5 exude, hovel, shack, spill,

strew, throw 6 lean-to, shanty, shower, slough, spread 7 cast off, discard, let fall, let flow, radiate, scatter 8 disperse, lose hair, toolshed 9 broadcast, discharge, tool house 10 distribute 11 disseminate, outbuilding

she died
Latin: 5 obiit

shed light on 7 clarify, explain 9 elucidate, explicate, make clear, make plain 10 illuminate

She Done Him Wrong
director: 7 Lowell Sherman
cast: 7 Mae West (Diamond Lil) 9 Cary Grant, Noah Beery 13 Gilbert Roland

shed tears 3 cry, sob 4 bawl, weep 6 boohoo 7 blubber

Sheehy, Gail
author of: 8 Passages 11 New Passages 14 The Pathfinders 16 The Silent Passage 17 Middletown, America

Sheeler, Charles
born: 14 Philadelphia PA
artwork: 9 Landscape, Upper Deck 11 Incantation 12 City Interior, Rolling Power 15 Bucks County Barn, River Rouge Plant 31 American Landscape Nineteen Thirty

sheen 4 glow 5 glaze, gleam, glint, gloss, shine 6 luster, patina, polish 7 burnish, glister, glitter, shimmer 8 radiance 9 shininess 10 brightness, brilliance, effulgence, glossiness, luminosity, refulgence 12 luminousness, resplendence

Sheen, Martin
real name: 12 Ramon Estevez
born: 8 Dayton OH
son: 12 Charlie Sheen 13 Emilio Estevez
roles: 5 Spawn 8 Badlands 11 The West Wing 12 The Believers 13 Apocalypse Now 14 Catch Twenty-Two 15 Catch Me If You Can 18 The Subject Was Roses 20 The American President 27 The Execution of Private Slovik

Sheena, Queen of the Jungle
creator: 8 SR Powell 13 W Morgan Thomas
character: 3 Bob 4 Chim

she engraved it
Latin: 8 sculpsit

sheep
breed: 5 Iraqi 6 Hirrik, Merino, Panama, Romney, Somali 7 Cheviot, Karakul, Lincoln, Suffolk, Targhee 8 Columbia, Cotswold, Tatarian 9 Montadale, Romeldale, Southdown 10 Corriedale, Dorset Down, Dorset Horn, Shropshire, Sikkim Bera 11 Rambouillet 13 Hampshire Down 15 Border Leicester
female: 3 ewe
family: 7 Bovidae

genus: 4 Ovis
group of: 5 drove, flock 6 cosset
meat: 4 lamb 6 mutton
oil from: 7 lanolin
wild: 5 urial 6 argali 7 bighorn, mouflon
young: 4 lamb 7 lambkin 8 yearling

sheepish 3 shy 4 meek 5 timid 6 docile, guilty, humble 7 abashed, ashamed, bashful, fearful, hangdog, passive, servile 8 blushing, obedient, obeisant, timorous, yielding 9 chagrined, chastened, diffident, mortified, shrinking, tractable 10 shamefaced, submissive 11 embarrassed, subservient, unassertive, unresisting

sheepishness 7 chagrin 8 docility, meekness 10 diffidence 11 bashfulness 12 tractability 13 embarrassment 14 submissiveness 15 unassertiveness

sheer 4 fine, pure, thin 5 bluff, filmy, gauzy, plumb, sharp, steep, total, utter 6 abrupt 7 perfect, unmixed 8 absolute, complete, gossamer, vertical 9 out and out, unalloyed, unbounded, unlimited 10 consummate, diaphanous 11 precipitous, transparent, unmitigated, unqualified 12 unrestrained 13 perpendicular, unadulterated, unconditional

sheet 3 top 4 coat, film, leaf, pane, slab 5 layer, panel, piece, plate 6 sheath, square 7 blanket, coating, overlay 8 bed sheet, covering, membrane 9 rectangle

shegetz 12 non-Jewish boy, non-Jewish man

Sheldon, Sidney
author of: 9 Bloodline 12 Rage of Angels, The Naked Face 15 If Tomorrow Comes 15 The Sky is Falling 17 Windmill of the Gods 19 Nothing Lasts Forever 20 A Stranger in the Mirror 21 Are You Afraid of the Dark 22 The Other Side of Midnight

shelf 4 bank, prop, reef, slab 5 ledge, shoal 6 mantel, mantle 7 bedrock, bracket, stratum 9 supporter 11 mantelpiece, mantlepiece

shell 3 pod 4 bomb, case, hulk, hull, husk, shot 5 pound, round, shuck 6 bullet, fire on, pepper, rocket 7 barrage, bombard, grenade, missile 8 carapace, skeleton 9 cartridge, framework 10 projectile

shellac 4 beat, drub, lick, whip 7 clobber, lacquer, trounce, varnish

Shelley, Mary Wollstonecraft
father: 13 William Godwin
husband: 18 Percy Bysshe Shelley
author of: 12 Frankenstein

Shelley, Percy Bysshe
author of: 7 Adonais, Alastor 8 Queen Mab, The Cenci 10 To a Skylark 16 A Defence of Poetry, Ode to the West Wind 17 Prometheus Unbound

shellfish 4 clam, crab **5** prawn **6** cockle, mussel, oyster, shrimp **7** abalone, lobster, mollusk, scallop **8** barnacle, crawfish, crayfish **9** trunkfish **10** crustacean **13** softshell crab
spawn: 4 spat

shell out 3 pay **6** expend **8** allocate, disburse, dispense **10** contribute

shelter 5 cover, guard, haven, house, lodge **6** asylum, defend, harbor, refuge, safety, shield, take in **7** care for, housing, lodging, protect **8** quarters, security **9** safeguard, sanctuary **10** protection

shelve 5 defer, table **6** put off **7** suspend **8** lay aside, postpone, put aside, put on ice, set aside **10** pigeonhole

Shem
father: **4** Noah
brother: **3** Ham **7** Japheth
son: **8** Arphaxed
descendant of: **6** Semite

shenanigans 5 sport **6** antics, capers, hijinx, pranks, stunts, tricks **8** deviltry, mischief, nonsense **9** highjinks, horseplay, silliness **10** buffoonery, tomfoolery **11** roguishness **12** monkeyshines, sportiveness **14** monkey business **15** mischievousness

she painted it
Latin: **6** pinxit

shepherd 4 herd, lead, show, tend **5** guard, guide, pilot **6** direct, escort, herder, keeper, patron, shield **7** protect, shelter **8** champion, defender, guardian, herdsman, provider **9** custodian, protector, safeguard **10** benefactor

shepherds
god of: **3** Pan **6** Tammuz

sherbet 3 ade, ice **6** sorbet **7** dessert

Shere Khan
character in: **14** The Jungle Books
author: **7** Kipling

Sheridan, Ann
real name: **16** Clara Lou Sheridan
nickname: **9** Oomph Girl
born: **8** Denton TX
husband: **9** Scott McKay **11** George Brent **12** Edward Norris
roles: **8** King's Row **11** Silver River **12** Nora Prentiss **16** Wings for the Eagle **20** Angels with Dirty Faces

Sheridan, Philip H
served in: **8** Civil War **10** Indian Wars
side: **5** Union
commander of: **19** Army of the Shenandoah
rank: **22** general in chief of US army
battle: **9** Five Forks **10** Cedar Creek, Winchester **11** Chattanooga, Chickamauga, Fisher's Hill **12** Sayler's Creek **18** Wilderness Campaign

Sheridan, Richard Brinsley
author of: **9** The Critic, The Duenna,

The Rivals **18** A Trip to Scarborough **19** The School for Scandal

sheriff 7 officer **9** constable
men: **5** posse

Sheriff of Nottingham
character in: **9** Robin Hood

Sherman, William Tecumseh
nickname: **4** Cump
served in: **8** Civil War **10** Mexican War
side: **5** Union
battle: **6** Shiloh **7** Atlanta, Bull Run **8** Savannah **9** Vicksburg **11** Chattanooga **15** Kenesaw Mountain
fought against: **8** Johnston
rank: **20** general in chief of army
famous for: **13** march to the sea (Georgia)
established: **29** Command and General Staff College
saying: **9** War is hell

sherry
type: **4** wine **6** brandy
origin: **5** Jeres, Spain, Xerez
varieties: **4** fino (dry) **5** cream **7** amoroso (sweet), oloroso (medium dry) **10** Manzanilla **11** Amontillado
drink: **6** Adonis, Bamboo **9** Andalusia
with gin: **11** Renaissance
with vermouth: **6** Brazil

Sherwood, Robert E
author of: **13** Idiot's Delight **15** Reunion in Vienna **18** The Petrified Forest **19** Roosevelt and Hopkins, There Shall Be No Night **20** Abe Lincoln in Illinois
screenplay: **22** The Best Years of Our Lives

she sculptured it
Latin: **8** sculpsit

she speaks
Latin: **8** loquitur

She Stoops to Conquer
author: **15** Oliver Goldsmith
character: **6** Marlow **8** Hastings **10** Sir Charles **11** Tony Lumpkin **12** Mr Hardcastle **13** Mrs Hardcastle **14** Kate Hardcastle **16** Constance Neville

she wrote (it)
Latin: **8** scripsit

shibah, shivah 14 mourning period
literally: **9** seven days

shibboleth 6 byword, saying, slogan **8** apothegm **9** catchword

Shibboleth 17 Gileadite password

shield 4 keep, star **5** aegis, badge, cover, guard, house, shade **6** buffer, button, emblem, ensign, fender, harbor, screen, secure **7** buckler, defense, protect, shelter **8** insignia, keep safe, preserve **9** medallion, protecter, protector, safeguard **10** escutcheon, protection

Shield (of Sobieski)
constellation of: **6** Scutum

Shield, The
network: **2** FX
creator: **9** Shawn Ryan
cast: **9** Jay Karnes (Dutch Wagenbach) **10** C C H Pounder (Claudette Wyms), Glenn Close (Monica Rawling) **11** Cathy Cahlin (Corrine Mackey), Michael Jace (Julien Lowe) **13** Catherine Dent (Danielle Sofer), Walton Goggins (Shane Vendrell) **14** Benito Martinez (David Aceveda), Kenneth Johnson (Curtis Lemansky), Michael Chiklis (Vic Mackey)

shielded 6 hidden **7** guarded **9** concealed, protected, sheltered

Shields, Brooke
real name: **20** Christa Brooke Shields
born: **9** New York NY
husband: **11** Andre Agassi, Chris Henchy
roles: **10** Pretty Baby **11** Endless Love **13** The Blue Lagoon, Suddenly Susan
author: **15** Down Came The Rain

shift 2 go **4** move, slip, vary, veer **5** hitch, stint **6** change, swerve, switch **7** chemise, turning, veering **8** exchange, straight, transfer **9** deviation, transpose, variation **10** alteration, assignment, reposition **11** alternating, fluctuation, interchange **12** modification
French: **8** camisole

shiftless 3 lax **4** idle, lazy **8** careless, inactive, indolent, slothful **10** ne'er-do-well **13** lackadaisical **14** good-for-nothing **15** unconscientious

shifty 4 foxy, wily **6** crafty, sneaky, tricky **7** cunning, evasive **8** scheming, slippery **9** conniving, deceitful, dishonest **10** contriving, unreliable **11** maneuvering, treacherous **13** untrustworthy

Shikasta
author: **12** Doris Lessing

shiksa 14 non-Jewish woman

shillelagh 4 club **5** stick **6** cudgel **9** truncheon

shilly-shally 5 stall, waver **6** dawdle, dither, falter, seesaw **8** hesitate **9** fluctuate, hem and haw, oscillate, vacillate

shilly-shallying 8 dawdling, wavering **9** uncertain, undecided **10** indecision, indecisive, irresolute **11** vacillation

Shimazaki Toson
author of: **5** Hakai **20** The Broken Commandment

shimmer 4 beam, glow **5** blink, dance, flash, gleam, quake, shine, waver **6** quiver, shiver **7** flicker, flutter, glisten, sparkle, tremble, twinkle, vibrate **8** blinking **9** coruscate **11** scintillate **12** phosphoresce

shindig 3 hop **4** ball, bash, prom **5** dance, party **6** affair, shindy **7** blowout, revelry **9** barn dance, festivity, record hop **10** masked ball, the dansant

French: 4 fete, gala **6** soiree **9** bal masque **10** bal costume

shine 3 wax **4** beam, buff, glow **5** blink, flash, glare, gleam, glint, gloss, light, rub up, sheen **6** dazzle, luster, polish, waxing **7** buffing, burnish, flicker, glimmer, glisten, glister, glitter, radiate, shimmer, sparkle, twinkle **8** brighten, radiance **9** coruscate, irradiate, polishing **10** brightness, brilliance, burnishing, luminosity **11** scintillate **12** illumination, luminousness **13** incandescence

shininess 5 gleam, glint, gloss, sheen **6** luster, polish **7** shimmer

shining 5 aglow **6** glossy **7** glowing, radiant **8** gleaming, luminous, lustrous **9** brilliant, effulgent **11** illustrious **12** incandescent

Shining, The
  author: 11 Stephen King

shiny 6 bright, glossy **7** glaring, glowing, radiant **8** gleaming, luminous, lustrous, polished **9** brilliant, burnished, effulgent, sparkling **10** glistening, glittering, shimmering **12** incandescent **13** scintillating

ship 4 crew, send **5** craft, liner, route, tramp, yacht **6** packet, tanker, vessel **7** carrier, cruiser, forward, steamer **8** dispatch **9** destroyer, freighter, steamship, transport **10** ocean liner

Ship of Fools
  author: 19 Katherine Anne Porter
  director: 13 Stanley Kramer
  cast: 9 Jose Greco, Lee Marvin **10** Jose Ferrer **11** George Segal, Oscar Werner, Vivien Leigh **14** Simone Signoret **15** Elizabeth Ashley

shipshape 4 neat, snug, taut, tidy, trip, trim **5** tight **6** spruce **7** orderly

Shirer, William L
  author of: 28 The Collapse of the Third Republic **29** The Rise and Fall of the Third Reich

shirk 4 duck, shun **5** avoid, dodge, elude, evade **6** escape, eschew, ignore **7** goof off, neglect **8** malinger, sidestep **9** goldbrick

shirker 5 piker **6** dodger, evader, loafer, rotter, truant **7** deserter, quitter, slacker **9** goldbrick **10** backslider, malingerer

Shirley Temple
  ingredient: 9 ginger ale, grenadine
  also called: 9 Roy Rogers

shirr 5 crimp, smock **6** gather, pucker **8** bake eggs

shirt 3 top **4** sark **5** frock, waist **6** blouse, bodice **10** underwaist

shirty 5 angry, irked, testy, vexed **7** annoyed **9** irritated **11** disgruntled

Shittimwood 12 Biblical tree

shiver 5 quake, shake **6** quaver, shimmy **7** shudder, tremble

shivers 3 bit **5** piece, shard **6** sliver **8** fragment

shivery 3 icy, raw **4** cold, cool **5** brisk, chill, crisp, nippy **6** arctic, biting, bitter, chilly, frigid, frosty, wintry **7** quaking, trembly **8** chilling **9** quivering **11** penetrating

shoal 3 bar **4** bank, flat **5** crowd, shelf **6** school **7** sand bar, shallow **8** sand bank

shock 3 jar, mat, mop **4** blow, bush, cock, crop, daze, jolt, mane, mass, pile, rick, rock, stun, turn **5** scare, shake, sheaf, stack, start, upset **6** appall, bundle, dismay, impact, offend, revolt, thatch, trauma **7** astound, disgust, disturb, horrify, outrage, perturb, stagger, startle, stupefy **8** astonish, bowl over, disquiet, distress, paralyze, surprise, unsettle **9** collision, overwhelm **10** concussion, discompose, disconcert **11** disturbance **13** consternation

shocking 4 foul **5** awful **6** grisly, horrid, odious **7** ghastly, hideous, jarring, jolting **8** gruesome, horrible, indecent, terrible, wretched **9** abhorrent, appalling, frightful, monstrous, offensive, repellent, repugnant, revolting, startling, upsetting **10** abominable, astounding, detestable, disgusting, disturbing, horrifying, outrageous, perturbing, scandalous, staggering, stupefying, surprising, unsettling **11** astonishing, disgraceful, disquieting **12** insufferable, overwhelming **13** disconcerting, reprehensible

shoddy 3 low **4** base, mean, poor **5** dirty, nasty, tacky **6** shabby, sloppy, stingy **7** low-down, miserly **8** careless, inferior, slipshod **9** haphazard, negligent, niggardly **10** second-rate, ungenerous **11** inefficient **12** contemptible **13** inconsiderate, reprehensible

shoe
  French: 9 chaussure

shoemaker 7 cobbler **9** bootmaker

Shoemaker's Holiday, The
  author: 12 Thomas Dekker

Shoes of the Fisherman, The
  author: 11 Morris L West

Shogun
  author: 12 James Clavell

Sholokhov, Mikhail
  author of: 19 And Quiet Flows the Don **21** The Virgin Soul Upturned

shoo 3 out **4** away, oust, rout, scat **5** be off, chase, leave, scram **6** beat it, be gone, depart, get out, go away **7** cast out, get lost, vamoose

shoot 3 bud, fly, hit **4** bolt, cast, dart, dash, drop, fell, fire, hurl, jump, kill, leap, nick, pelt, plug, race, rain, rush, stem, tear, toss, twig, wing **5** eject, fling, go off, hurry, shell, sling, speed, spray, sprig, spurt, sweep, throw, waste **6** charge, launch, let fly, pep-

per, propel, riddle, shower, spring, sprout **7** bombard, explode, pick off, tendril **8** catapult, detonate, open fire **9** discharge

Shootist, The
  director: 9 Don Siegal
  cast: 9 John Wayne, Ron Howard **10** Hugh O'Brien **11** Harry Morgan, Sheree North **12** James Stewart, Lauren Bacall, Richard Boone **13** John Carradine **15** Scatman Crothers

Shoot the Piano Player
  director: 16 Francois Truffaut
  cast: 11 Marie Dubois **12** Nicole Berger **14** Michele Mercier **15** Charles Aznavour
  setting: 5 Paris

shop 3 buy **4** hunt, look, mart, mill **5** plant, store, works **6** browse, market, studio **7** factory **8** emporium, purchase, workshop **9** patronize **10** windowshop **13** establishment

French: 7 atelier **8** boutique

shopkeeper 6 dealer, monger, trader, vendor **8** merchant, purveyor, retailer **9** tradesman

shopworn 5 banal, corny, faded, stale, tired, trite, vapid **6** jejune **10** threadbare

shore 4 bank, hold, land, prop **5** beach, brace, brink, coast **6** hold up, margin, strand **7** bolster, bulwark, seaside, support, sustain **8** buttress, mainstay, seaboard, seacoast, underpin **9** reinforce, riverbank, waterside **10** strengthen

Latin: 10 terra firma

shorebird 3 auk **4** rail, sora **5** snipe, stilt, wader **6** avocet, curlew, plover, puffin **7** lapwing **8** woodcock **9** guillemot, sandpiper **13** oyster catcher

shore up 4 prop **5** brace **6** prop up **7** bolster, support **8** buttress **9** reinforce

short 3 low **4** curt, lean, slim, thin **5** brief, cross, elfin, fleet, gruff, hasty, pygmy, quick, runty, scant, sharp, small, squat, terse, testy, tight **6** abrupt, bantam, little, meager, scanty, scarce, skimpy, slight, sparse, stubby **7** brusque, compact, concise, cursory, lacking, limited, not long, not tall, slender, stunted, summary, wanting **8** abridged, abruptly, dwarfish, fleeting, impolite, snappish, succinct, suddenly, unawares **9** condensed, curtailed, deficient, impatient, momentary, niggardly, pint-sized, truncated **10** by surprise, diminutive, short-lived **11** abbreviated, ill-tempered, Lilliputian, pocket-sized **12** insufficient **13** precipitously **14** without warning

shortage 4 lack, want **6** dearth **7** deficit **8** leanness, scarcity, sparsity **9** shortfall **10** deficiency, inadequacy, scantiness, sparseness **13** insufficiency

shortcoming 4 flaw **5** fault **6** defect, foible **7** blemish, failing, failure, frailty **8** drawback, handicap, weakness **10** deficiency, inadequacy **12** imperfection

shorten 3 cut **4** clip, pare, trim **5** prune, shave, shear **6** lessen, reduce **7** abridge, curtail, cut down **8** condense, contract, cut short, decrease, diminish **10** abridge

shortening 3 fat, oil **4** lard, oleo **6** butter, digest **7** cutting, summary **8** abstract, synopsis, trimming **9** hemming up, margarine, reduction **11** abridgement, compression, contraction, curtailment **12** abbreviation, condensation

short form 6 digest, precis **7** summary **8** abstract, synopsis **11** abridgement, contraction **12** abbreviation, condensation

Short Happy Life of Francis Macomber, The
   author: **15** Ernest Hemingway

short journey 5 jaunt **6** outing **7** day trip **9** excursion

short-lived 5 brief **7** passing **8** fleeting **9** ephemeral, momentary, temporary, transient **10** evanescent, transitory, unenduring **11** impermanent **24** here today and gone tomorrow

shortly 4 anon, soon **7** by and by **8** directly, in a trice, promptly **9** forthwith, presently **10** before long **11** immediately

short narrative 5 essay, story **6** sketch **8** anecdote **10** short story

shortsighted 4 rash **6** myopic **7** foolish **8** careless, heedless, purblind, reckless, weak-eyed **9** amblyopic, imprudent **10** ill-advised, incautious, unthinking **11** improvident, injudicious, nearsighted, thoughtless **12** undiscerning **13** uncircumspect

short-tempered 4 curt **5** cross, huffy, sharp, testy **6** abrupt, cranky, crusty, grumpy, shirty, touchy **7** bearish, grouchy, peevish, waspish **8** choleric, snappish **9** irascible, irritable, splenetic **10** ill-humored, out of sorts, short-fused **11** hot-tempered, ill-tempered **12** cantankerous

Shosha
   author: **19** Isaac Bashevis Singer

Shoshone (Snake)
   language family: **10** Shoshonean
   location: **4** Utah **5** Idaho **6** Nevada **7** Wyoming
   translator: **9** Sacagawea

Shoshonean
   tribe: **4** Hopi, Moki **5** Snake **6** Hopitu, Paiute **7** Bannock **8** Comanche, Shoshoni

Shostakovich, Dmitri (Dimitri)
   born: **6** Russia **12** St Petersburg
   composer of: **7** The Nose **9** Leningrad (symphony No 7) **11** May the First **12** The Golden Age **17** Katerina

Ismailova **19** Lady Macbeth of Mzensk

shot 2 go **3** hit, try **4** dose, move, play, toss **5** balls, blast, crack, drive, essay, guess, salvo, slugs, throw **6** beat-up, archer, bowman, chance, report, ruined, shabby, stroke, volley **7** attempt, bullets, gunfire, shooter, surmise, worn-out **8** decrepit, marksman, rifleman **9** discharge, explosion, fusillade, injection **10** ammunition, conjecture, detonation **11** dilapidated, projectiles **12** falling apart, sharpshooter

shot in the arm 4 lift **5** boost **6** uplift **8** stimulus **13** encouragement

shot in the dark 5 guess **6** notion, theory **9** guesswork, suspicion **10** assumption, conjecture, hypothesis

shoulder 3 rim **4** bank, bear, brow, bump, edge, push, side, take **5** brink, carry, crest, elbow, lunge, shove, skirt, verge **6** assume, border, jostle, margin, take on, thrust, uphold **7** scapula, support, sustain **8** clavicle **9** undertake

shoulder blade 7 scapula **8** omoplate **9** bladebone

shout 3 cry **4** bawl, call, hoot, howl, roar, yell, yelp **5** burst, cheer, hollo, whoop **6** bellow, chorus, clamor, cry out, holler, hurrah, huzzah, outcry, scream, shriek **7** call out, exclaim, screech, thunder **8** outburst **9** hue and cry **10** hullabaloo

shout down 3 boo **4** hiss **6** hoot at, revile **7** catcall, condemn **8** denounce, drown out

shove 4 bump, butt, jolt, prod, push **5** boost, crowd, drive, elbow, force, impel, nudge **6** joggle, jostle, propel, thrust **8** shoulder

show 4 bare, bill, fair, give, lead, mark, play, pomp, pose, sham, sign **5** argue, coach, drama, endow, favor, front, grant, guide, movie, opera, prove, teach, token, tutor, usher **6** appear, attest, ballet, bestow, comedy, direct, effect, evince, expose, hint at, impart, inform, lavish, reveal, school, tender, unveil **7** bear out, bespeak, certify, conduct, confirm, display, exhibit, explain, lay bare, musical, picture, pretext, proffer, program, suggest, uncover **8** ceremony, delusion, disclose, dispense, evidence, illusion, indicate, instruct, intimate, manifest, operetta, point out, pretense, vaunting **9** establish, make clear, make known, represent, spectacle **10** appearance, disclosure, distribute, exhibition, exposition, expression, impression, indication, pretension, production, revelation **11** affectation, attestation, corroborate, counterfeit, demonstrate, performance, testimonial **12** bring to light, substantiate **13** demonstration,

entertainment, manifestation, motion picture

Show Boat
   author: **10** Edna Ferber

showcase 7 cabinet, counter, display, exhibit, vitrine

showdown 3 war **6** battle, climax, combat, crisis **7** face-off **8** clashing, conflict **9** collision, encounter **13** confrontation

shower 3 wet **4** fall, pour, rain, rush **5** flood, salvo, spray, surge **6** deluge, lavish, splash, stream, volley, wealth **7** barrage, bombard, drizzle, torrent **8** downpour, plethora, sprinkle **9** profusion **10** cloudburst, inundation **11** bombardment

showiness 5 eclat **7** glitter **8** splendor **9** jazziness **10** flashiness **11** ostentation **14** grandiloquence

Show-me State
   nickname of: **8** Missouri

show-off 6 egoist **7** boaster, egotist, windbag **8** braggart, fanfaron, flaunter, strutter **9** extrovert, swaggerer **11** braggadocio **13** cock of the walk, exhibitionist **14** life of the party

showpiece 3 gem **5** jewel, pearl, pride, prize **6** rarity, wonder **7** classic, paragon **8** treasure **10** masterwork **11** chef d'oeuvre, masterpiece, prizewinner **17** piece of resistance

show up 4 come **5** outdo **6** appear, arrive, attend, crop up, expose, loom up, reveal, turn up **9** be present **11** come to light, make a fool of **12** come into view **13** become visible

showy 4 loud **5** gaudy, vivid **6** flashy, florid, garish, ornate **7** pompous **8** colorful, gorgeous, imposing, splendid, striking **9** brilliant **11** magnificent, pretentious **12** ostentatious

shred 3 bit, ion, jot, rag **4** atom, band, hair, iota, spot, whit **5** grain, piece, scrap, speck, strip, trace **6** morsel, ribbon, sliver, tatter **7** snippet **8** fragment, molecule, particle **9** scintilla

shrew 3 hag, nag **5** harpy, scold, vixen, yenta **6** kvetch, virago **7** shewolf **8** battle-ax, fishwife, harridan, spitfire **9** termagant, Xanthippe

shrewd 3 sly **4** foxy, keen, wily, wise **5** acute, cagey, canny, quick, sharp, slick, smart **6** artful, astute, clever, crafty, shifty, smooth, tricky **7** careful, cunning, knowing, probing, prudent **8** cautious, crafty, scheming, sensible, slippery **9** designing, farseeing, sagacious **10** contriving, discerning, farsighted, perceptive **11** calculating, circumspect, intelligent, penetrating, quick-witted, self-serving, sharp-witted **12** disingenuous **13** Machiavellian, perspicacious

shrewdness 6 acumen **7** cunning, slyness **8** foxiness, keenness, wiliness **9** acuteness, cageyness, sharpness, slickness, smartness **10** artfulness, astuteness, cleverness, craftiness, smoothness, trickiness **11** carefulness, discernment **12** slipperiness **16** disingenuousness

shriek 3 cry **4** call, hoot, howl, peal, yell, yelp **5** shout, whoop **6** cry out, holler, out-cry, scream, squawk, squeak, squeal **7** screech

shrift 7 penance **9** atonement, expiation **10** confession

shrill 4 high, loud **6** piping **7** blaring, raucous **8** piercing, strident **9** clamorous **10** screeching **11** high-pitched, penetrating

shrimp 5 prawn **6** scampi **8** cocktail

shrine 5 altar **6** chapel, church, temple **7** sanctum **8** monument **9** sanctuary

shrink 3 ebb, shy **4** balk, duck, wane **5** cower, demur, dry up, quail, stick, wince **6** blench, bridle, cringe, flinch, lessen, pucker, recoil, reduce, refuse, retire **7** curtail, decline, deflate, dwindle, retreat, shorten, shrivel, shudder **8** compress, condense, contract, decrease, diminish, draw back, hang back, make less, withdraw **9** constrict **11** make smaller **12** draw together **13** become smaller

shrink from 4 hate, shun **5** abhor, evade **6** balk at, detest, eschew, loathe, resist **7** despise **8** recoil at **9** abominate, shudder at **12** be revolted by **13** find repulsive

shrinking 3 shy **5** timid **6** ebbing, waning **7** bashful **8** reticent, retiring, timorous **9** declining, dwindling **10** decreasing, shriveling **11** contraction, diminishing

shrive 6 pardon **7** absolve, forgive

shrivel 5 dry up, parch, wizen **6** pucker, scorch, shrink, wither **7** wrinkle

Shropshire Lad, A
author: 9 A E Housman

shroud 4 hide, pall, veil, wrap **5** cloak, cloud, cover, sheet **6** clothe, mantle, screen, swathe **7** blanket, conceal, envelop **8** covering **9** cerecloth, cerements **11** burial cloth **12** graveclothes, winding sheet

shrub 4 bush **5** brush **8** beverage **10** fruit drink

shrubbery 4 bush **5** brush **6** bushes, shrubs **9** brushwood **10** underbrush **11** undergrowth

shuck 4 husk, peel, shed **5** chaff, shell, strip

shudder 4 jerk, pang **5** quake, shake, spasm, throb **6** quaver, quiver, shimmy, shiver, tremor, twitch **7** flutter, tremble **8** paroxysm **9** pulsation, trembling **10** convulsion

shudder at 4 hate **5** abhor **6** detest, loathe **8** recoil at **9** abominate, can't stand **10** recoil from, shrink from

shuffle 3 mix **4** drag, gimp, limp, step **5** scuff, slide **6** clumsy, jumble, scrape **7** shamble **8** scramble **9** rearrange **10** disarrange **11** interchange

shul, schul 9 synagogue

shun 5 avoid, dodge, elude, evade, forgo **6** eschew, forego, ignore, refuse, reject **7** boycott, disdain **10** circumvent, fight shy of, shrink from **11** keep clear of, shy away from **12** have no part of, keep away from, steer clear of, turn away from

shut 3 box **4** cage, coop, draw, fold, lock, snap **5** clasp, close, drawn, latch **6** closed, closet, corral, draw to, fasten, intern, locked, lock in, secure **7** confine, drawn to, enclose, fence in, impound, latched, secured **8** cloister, closed up, fastened, imprison **9** barricade, constrain **11** incarcerate

shut down 4 halt, stop **5** cease **7** suspend **9** close down, interrupt **11** discontinue

Shute, Nevil
author of: 10 On the Beach

shut in 4 cage **5** caged, pen in **6** coop up, encage, lock up **7** confine, encaged, enclose **8** confined, cooped up, enclosed, locked up, restrain, restrict **10** restrained, restricted

shut one's eyes to 5 allow **6** ignore, wink at **8** overlook **9** connive in, disregard **11** pay no heed to **14** turn one's back on

shut out 3 bar **5** debar **6** defeat **7** exclude **8** obstruct, prohibit

shutter 5 blind, close, shade **6** screen **7** curtain

shut the door on 3 ban, bar **6** forbid, refuse, reject **7** exclude, keep out, shut out **8** prohibit

shut up 4 cage, coop, hush, lock, pent **5** close, pen in **6** immure **7** be quiet, confine, silence **8** imprison **11** incarcerate

shy 4 balk, meek, wary **5** chary, cower, dodge, leery, minus, scant, short, timid, under, wince **6** blench, demure, flinch, in need, modest, shrink, swerve **7** anxious, bashful, careful, fearful, lacking, needing, nervous, wanting **8** cautious, draw back, jump back, reserved, reticent, skittish, timorous **9** deficient, diffident, shrinking, tremulous **10** suspicious **11** distrustful **12** apprehensive **13** self-conscious

shy away from 4 duck, shun **5** avoid, dodge, spurn **6** balk at, refuse, reject **10** shrink from **12** steer clear of

Shylock
character in: 19 The Merchant of Venice
author: 11 Shakespeare

shyness 8 meekness, timidity **9** reticence **10** diffidence, insecurity **11** bashfulness **12** sheepishness, timor-

ousness **14** self-effacement **15** unassertiveness

shyster 5 rogue **6** lawyer **8** attorney **10** mouthpiece **11** pettifogger **15** ambulance chaser

si 3 yes

Siam see **8** Thailand

Sibelius, Jean
born: 7 Finland **10** Tavastehus
composer of: 6 En Saga **7** Karelia, Legends, Tapiola, The Band **8** Kalevala **9** Finlandia **10** The Tempest **12** The Oceanides, Voces Intimae **14** Ride and Sunrise

Siberia 8 disfavor **10** punishment **14** undesirability
city: 4 Omsk **5** Chita, Tomsk **6** Kurgan **7** Irkutsk, Yakutsk
conqueror: 9 Timafeyev **11** Genghis Khan
continent: 4 Asia
gulf: 2 Ob
inhabitant: 4 Yaku **5** Sagai, Tatar **6** Tartar **7** Yukagir **8** prisoner **17** political prisoner
mountain range: 4 Ural **5** Altai, Altay
river: 2 Ob **3** Ket, Ili, Taz **4** Amga, Amur, Lena, Onon **5** Ishim, Tobol **6** Olekma
sea: 4 Kara **6** Laptev **7** Okhotsk

sibling 6 sister **7** brother
problem: 7 rivalry

sibyl 4 seer **5** augur **6** oracle **7** diviner **9** predictor, sorceress **10** forecaster, prophetess, soothsayer **13** fortune teller **14** prognosticator

Sibyls
form: 10 prophetess
inspired by: 5 deity **6** Apollo
names: 6 Libyan **7** Cumaean **10** Erythraean
prophecies: 14 Sibylline Books

sic 2 so **4** thus

Sicilian Vespers, The
also: 20 Les Vepres Siciliennes
opera by: 5 Verdi
character: 5 Elena **6** Arrigo **7** Procida **8** Monforte

Sicily
other name: 7 Sicilia **9** Trinacria, Triquetra
capital/largest city: 7 Palermo
others: 3 Aci **4** Enna, Noto **6** Ragusa **7** Augusta, Catania, Marsala, Messina, Trapani **8** Syracuse **10** Montelepre
division: 4 Enna **6** Ragusa **7** Catania, Messina, Palermo, Trapani **8** Siracusa, Syracuse **9** Agrigento **13** Caltanissetta
government: 13 region of Italy
measure: 5 salma **7** caffiso
monetary unit: 5 litra, oncia, uncia **6** carlin **7** carline, oncetta
island: 5 Egadi **6** Lipari, Ustica **7** Pelagie **11** Pantelleria

lake: 7 Pergusa **8** Camarina
mountain: 4 Erei, Moro, Sori **5** Atlas, Erici, Hybla, Iblei, Ibrei **7** Nebrodi, Vulcano **9** Apennines, Le Madonie, Stromboli **10** Peloritani
highest point: 4 Etna **5** Aetna
river: 4 Acis **5** Salso, Torto **6** Belice, Simeto **7** Mazzaro, Platani
sea: 6 Ionian **10** Tyrrhenian **13** Mediterranean
physical feature:
  cape: 4 Boeo, Faro **7** Lilibeo, Passaro, Passero, Pelorus
  gulf: 4 Noto **7** Catania
  strait: 7 Messina
  wind: 7 sirocco
people: 5 Elymi, Sican, Sicel **6** Sicani, Siculi
  author: 9 Lampedusa **10** Pirandello
  composer: 7 Bellini
  king: 4 Eryx **5** Bomba, Henry, Peter, Roger **7** Charles, Cocalus, Leontes **9** Ferdinand, Frederick
  ruler: 4 Rome **5** Arabs, Goths, Spain **6** Greeks **7** Germans, Normans, Vandals, Vikings **8** Carthage, Saracens **9** Aragonese, Byzantium, Egyptians, Phoenicia **15** Holy Roman Empire
language: 7 Italian
religion: 13 Roman Catholic
place:
  cathedral: 8 Monreale
  resort: 4 Enna **8** Taormina
  ruins: 14 Villa Imperiale **15** Temple of Concord **18** Valley of the Temples
feature:
  brigands: 5 Mafia
  evening stroll: 11 passeggiata

sick 3 ill **4** weak **5** frail, tired, weary **6** ailing, infirm, laid up, poorly, queasy, sickly, uneasy, unwell **7** crushed, grieved, invalid, unsound **8** delicate, stricken, troubled, wretched **9** afflicted, bored with, disturbed, miserable, nauseated, perturbed, suffering, unhealthy **10** disquieted, distressed, indisposed **11** discomposed, heartbroken **15** under the weather
sicken 5 repel, shock, upset **6** offend, revolt **7** disgust, horrify, make ill, repulse **9** nauseate **14** turn the stomach
sickening 4 foul, vile **5** nasty **7** noisome **8** horrible, unsavory **9** abhorrent, loathsome, offensive, repellent, repugnant, repulsive, revolting **10** disgusting, nauseating **11** distasteful
sickly 3 ill, wan **4** drab, flat, lame, pale, sick, weak **5** ashen, faint, frail, silly **6** ailing, feeble, flimsy, guilty, infirm, leaden, peaked, poorly, sneaky, torpid, unwell **7** insipid, invalid, unsound **8** delicate, smirking **9** afflicted, apathetic, bloodless, simpering, unhealthy **10** cadaverous, lackluster, namby-pamby, snickering, spiritless, uninspired, wishy-washy **11** ineffec-

tive **12** unconvincing **13** self-conscious
sickness 6 malady, nausea **7** ailment, disease, illness **8** debility, disorder, vomiting **9** complaint, frailness, ill health, infirmity **10** affliction, disability, invalidism, poor health, queasiness **11** unsoundness **12** qualmishness **13** indisposition
sic passim 12 so throughout
sic semper tyrannis 19 thus always to tyrants
  motto of: 8 Virginia
sic transit gloria mundi 33 thus passes away the glory of this world
Siddhartha
  author: 12 Hermann Hesse
  story of: 6 Buddha
siddur 16 Jewish prayer book
  literally: 5 order
side 3 hem, rim **4** area, body, brim, edge, half, hand, part, sect, team, view **5** angle, bound, cause, facet, flank, group, house, light, limit, minor, party, phase, skirt, slant, stand, stock **6** allied, aspect, behalf, belief, border, circle, clique, fringe, lesser, margin, region, sector, strain **7** askance, coterie, faction, lateral, lineage, oblique, opinion, postern, quarter, related, section, segment, surface **8** alliance, attitude, boundary, division, indirect, marginal, standing, skirting **9** accessory, bloodline, coalition, on one side, perimeter, periphery, secondary, territory, viewpoint **10** collateral, contingent, federation, incidental, standpoint, subsidiary **11** affiliation, association, unimportant **13** insignificant
Side
  origin: 5 Irish
  form: 7 fairies
  owner: 14 Tuatha De Danann
sideboard 6 buffet **8** credenza
side by side 7 abreast **8** abutting, together **9** adjoining **11** cheek by jowl, in proximity
  Latin: 9 pari passu
sidekick 3 pal **4** aide **5** buddy **6** deputy, friend **9** assistant **10** lieutenant
sideline 5 bench, hobby **8** boundary **9** avocation **14** put out of action
sidestep 4 duck **5** avert, avoid, dodge, elude, evade, skirt **6** bypass, escape **10** circumvent, fight shy of **12** steer clear of
sidestepping 7 dodging, ducking, eluding, evasion **8** skirting **9** avoidance **13** circumvention
sidewalk 4 curb **8** footpath, pavement **9** promenade
sideways, sideway 6 aslant **7** askance, lateral, oblique **8** crabwise, edgeways, edgewise, sidelong, sideward, sidewise **9** crosswise, laterally,

obliquely, to the side **11** from one side
Sideways
  author: 10 Rex Pickett
  director: 14 Alexander Payne
  cast: 8 Sandra Oh (Stephanie) **9** Missy Doty (Cammi) **12** Alysia Reiner (Christine), Jessica Hecht (Victoria), Paul Giamatti (Miles) **13** Duke Mooesekian (Mike Erganian) **14** Virginia Madsen (Maya) **17** Thomas Haden Church (Jack)
side with 5 agree **7** stand by, stick by, support **8** champion **12** take one's part
sidle 4 cant, edge, skew, veer **10** lateralize
Sidney, Sir Philip
  author of: 7 Arcadia **15** Defence of Poesie, Defence of Poetry **18** Apologie for Poetrie, Astrophel and Stella
Sidney, Sylvia
  real name: 11 Sophia Kosow
  born: 7 Bronx NY
  husband: 11 Luther Adler **12** Bennett A Cerf
  roles: 4 Fury **7** Dead End **11** Street Scene **13** Les Miserables **15** Madame Butterfly **17** An American Tragedy **24** Summer Wishes Winter Dreams
Sidrophel
  character in: 8 Hudibras
  author: 6 Butler
siecle 3 age **6** period **7** century
Siegel, Jerry
  creator/artist of: 8 Superman
Siegfried
  origin: 8 Germanic
  mentioned in: 14 Nibelungenlied
  father: 7 Sigmund
  mother: 9 Sieglinde
  wife: 9 Kriemhild
  killed by: 5 Hagen
  same as: 6 Sigurd
  killed: 6 Fafnir
  won for Gunther: 10 Brunnhilde
  stole: 9 Tarnkappe
Sieg Heil 13 hail to victory
  salute used by: 5 Nazis
Sieglinde
  origin: 8 Germanic
  mentioned in: 14 Nibelungenlied
  husband: 7 Sigmund
  son: 9 Siegfried
Sienkiewicz, Henryk
  author of: 8 Quo Vadis?
Sierra Leone
  name means: 12 lion mountain
  other name: 9 Gold Coast **10** Grain Coast, Ivory Coast
  capital/largest city: 8 Freetown
  others: 2 Bo **5** Hepel, Kissi, Lungi, Pepel **6** Bonthe, Kenema, Makeni, Shenge, Sulima
  school: 6 Njaia U **9** Fourah Bay
  measure: 4 load **6** kettle
  monetary unit: 4 cent **5** leone

island: 4 York **6** Banana, Turtle **7** Sherbro
mountain: 4 Loma **10** Tingi Hills
highest point: 9 Bintimani
river: 3 Moa **4** Jong, Mano, Meli, Ribi, Sewa, Taia **5** Bagbe, Mongo, Morro, Rokel **6** Mabole, Rokkel, Scarcy, Waanje **13** Great Scarcies **14** Little Scarcies
sea: 8 Atlantic
physical feature:
  bay: 5 Yawri **7** Sherbro
  cape: 8 Shilling **11** Sierra Leone
  peninsula: 7 Turners **11** Sierra Leone
  wind: 9 harmattan
people: 3 Vai **4** Kono, Loko, Susu **5** Bulom, Kissi, Limba, Mende, Mendi, Temne **6** Creole, Fulani, Syrian **7** Gallina, Koranko, Kuranko, Sherbro, Yalunka **8** Lebanese, Mandingo
  explorer: 6 Cintra
  leader: 6 Margai **7** Stevens
language: 4 Krio **5** Limba, Mende, Mendi, Temne **6** Creole **7** English
religion: 5 Islam **7** animism **12** Christianity
place:
  wharf: 10 King Jimmys
feature:
  cloth: 5 garra
  clothing: 5 lappa **6** caftan
  secret society: 4 poro
food:
  dish: 4 fufu **7** cassava
  sauce: 7 palaver
siesta 3 nap **4** rest **5** break, sleep **6** cat nap, snooze **10** forty winks
sieve 4 sift **6** filter, riddle, screen, sorter, strain **7** tattler **8** colander, strainer **9** separator **12** blabbermouth
sift 4 sort **5** drift, probe, study **6** filter, review, screen, search, winnow **7** analyze, inspect, scatter, sort out **8** separate **10** scrutinize **11** distinguish, investigate **12** discriminate
Siggeir
  origin: 12 Scandinavian
  king of: 5 Goths
  wife: 5 Signy
  causes death of: 7 Volsung
sigh 3 sob **4** hiss, long, moan, pine, weep **5** brood, groan, mourn, whine, yearn **6** grieve, lament, sorrow
sight 3 ken, see, spy **4** bead, espy, gaze, spot, view **5** image, scene, vista **6** behold, seeing, survey, vision **7** display, exhibit, eyeshot, glimpse, observe, pageant, scenery, viewing **8** eyesight, perceive, prospect, scrutiny **9** peepsight, sighthole, spectacle **10** appearance, visibility
sighted 3 saw **4** seen **6** seeing **8** not blind, observed
sightless 5 blind **8** unseeing **9** unsighted
sightly 4 fair **6** lovely, pretty **8** hand-some, pleasing **9** appealing, beautiful **10** attractive
Sigmund
  origin: 8 Germanic **12** Scandinavian
  mentioned in: 8 Volsunga **14** Nibelungenlied
  king of: 11 Netherlands
  father: 7 Volsung
  mother: 4 Liod, Ljod **5** Hliod
  wife: 7 Hiordis, Hjordis **8** Borghild **9** Sieglinde
  sister: 5 Signy
  lover: 5 Signy
  son: 6 Sigurd **9** Siegfried, Sinfiotli
sign 3 nod **4** clue, hint, mark, note, omen, wave **5** badge, brand, index, stamp, token, trait **6** emblem, ensign, figure, herald, motion, signal, symbol **7** earmark, endorse, feature, gesture, go-ahead, placard, portent, presage, symptom, warning **8** evidence, forecast, inscribe, neon sign, road sign, signpost **9** autograph, billboard, guidepost, harbinger, indicator, nameplate, trademark **10** indication, intimation, prognostic, suggestion, underwrite **11** forewarning **13** manifestation **14** characteristic *see also* **6** zodiac
signal 3 cue, nod **4** sign **6** beckon, famous, motion, unique **7** command, eminent, gesture, guiding, honored, notable, warning **8** high sign, password, pointing, renowned, singular, striking **9** arresting, directing, direction, important, indicator, memorable, momentous, prominent, watchword **10** commanding, impressive, indicating, indication, noteworthy, one of-a-kind, remarkable **11** conspicuous, distinctive, exceptional, illustrious, outstanding, significant **12** considerable **13** consequential, distinguished, extraordinary, unforgettable
significance 3 aim **4** note **5** drift, force, merit, sense, value, worth **6** import, intent, moment, object, virtue, weight **7** concern, gravity, meaning, portent, purpose **8** eminence, interest, priority **9** authority, direction, influence, intention, relevance **10** excellence, importance, notability, prominence **11** consequence, distinction, implication
significant 4 main **5** chief, grave, great, major, prime, vital **6** cogent, signal **7** eminent, knowing, notable, serious, telling, weighty **8** critical, distinct, eloquent, eventful, material, pregnant, symbolic **9** important, momentous, paramount, principal, prominent **10** emblematic, expressive, indicative, meaningful, noteworthy, portentous, remarkable, suggestive **11** exceptional, influential, outstanding, substantial, symptomatic **12** considerable **13** consequential, demonstrative **14** representative
signify 4 mean, omen, show, tell **5** ar-gue, augur, imply **6** convey, denote, evince, herald, hint at, import, reveal, typify **7** bespeak, betoken, connote, declare, exhibit, express, portend, predict, presage, promise, suggest **8** announce, disclose, evidence, forebode, foretell, indicate, intimate, manifest, proclaim, set forth, stand for **9** be a sign of, designate, represent, symbolize **10** foreshadow **11** communicate, demonstrate
signing up 7 joining **9** enlisting, enrolling **10** enlistment, enrollment **11** registering **12** registration **13** matriculating, matriculation
Sign of Four, The
  author: 19 Sir Arthur Conan Doyle
  character: 11 Mary Morstan **12** Dr John Watson **13** Jonathan Small **14** Sherlock Holmes, Thaddeus Sholto
Signoret, Simone
  real name: 32 Simone-Henriette-Charlotte Kaminker
  born: 7 Germany **9** Wiesbaden
  husband: 11 Yves Montand **12** Yves Allegret
  roles: 10 Madame Rosa **11** Ship of Fools **12** Room at the Top (Oscar) **14** Is Paris Burning?
  autobiography: 27 Nostalgia Isn't What It Used to Be
sign up 4 join **6** enlist, enroll, join up **8** register **9** volunteer **11** matriculate
Sigurd
  origin: 12 Scandinavian
  mentioned in: 8 Volsunga
  father: 7 Sigmund
  mother: 7 Hiordis, Hjordis
  wife: 6 Gudrun, Kudrun **7** Guthrun
  killed: 6 Fafnir
  acquired treasure of: 8 Andavari
  won for Gunnar: 8 Brynhild
Sigyn
  origin: 12 Scandinavian
  husband: 4 Loki
Sikes, Bill
  character in: 11 Oliver Twist
  author: 7 Dickens
Sikkim
  capital/largest city: 7 Gangtok
  others: 6 Dikchu, Lachen, Namchi, Rangpo, Rumtek **7** Lachung **9** Chungtang
  government: 12 state of India
  mountain: 7 Dongkya, Donkhya **9** Himalayas, Singalili **10** Darjeeling **12** Kanchenjunga
  river: 5 Tista **6** Ranjit **9** Lachen Chu **10** Lachung Chu
  physical feature:
    mountain pass: 6 Natu La **7** Jelep La
    storm: 7 monsoon
  people: 4 Rong **5** Bhote **6** Bhotia, Bhutia, Indian, Lepcha **7** Tibetan **8** Nepalese **9** Mongoloid
    king: 7 chogyal

religion: 5 Hindu **7** Lamaism **15** Tibetan Buddhism

Sikorsky, Igor
  nationality: 7 Russian **8** American
  invented: 10 helicopter

Silas Marner
  author: 11 George Eliot
  profession: 6 weaver
  character: 5 Eppie **11** Dunstan Cass, Godfrey Cass **13** Aaron Winthrop, Nancy Lammeter

silence 3 gag **4** calm, curb, halt, hush, kill, rout, stop **5** allay, check, crush, peace, quash, quell, quiet, still **6** banish, deaden, defeat, muffle, muzzle, repose, squash, stifle, subdue **7** conquer, nullify, put down, quieten, repress, reserve, squelch **8** choke off, dumbness, muteness, overcome, serenity, suppress, vanquish **9** lay to rest, placidity, quietness, reticence, stillness, tongue-tie **10** extinguish, placidness, put an end to, strike dumb **11** taciturnity, tranquility **12** tranquillity **13** noiselessness, secretiveness, soundlessness **14** speechlessness **16** closemouthedness **19** uncommunicativeness

Silence of the Lambs, The
  author: 12 Thomas Harris
  director: 13 Jonathan Demme
  cast: 9 Dan Butler (Roden), Paul Lazar (Pilcher), Ted Levine (Jame Gumb) **10** Scott Glenn (Jack Crawford) **11** Brooke Smith (Catherine Martin), Jodie Foster (Clarice Starling), Kasi Lemmons (Ardelia Mapp) **12** Anthony Heald (Frederick Chilton) **13** Frankie Faison (Barney Matthews) **14** Anthony Hopkins (Hannibal Lecter)

silent 3 mum **4** calm, dumb, idle, mute **5** inert, muted, quiet, still, tacit **6** covert, hidden, hushed, placid, serene, unsaid **7** dormant, implied, muffled **8** discreet, implicit, inactive, inferred, lifeless, peaceful, reserved, reticent, taciturn, tranquil, unspoken, wordless **9** concealed, intimated, noiseless, quiescent, secretive, soundless, suggested, unsounded, unwritten **10** insinuated, mysterious, speechless, tongue-tied, undeclared, understood, unrevealed, unstirring, untalked-of **11** close-lipped, tight-lipped, unexpressed, unmentioned, unpublished, untalkative, unvocalized **12** closemouthed, unpronounced **15** uncommunicative

Silent Spring
  author: 13 Rachel L Carson

Silenus
  god of: 6 forest
  oldest: 5 satyr
  father: 3 Pan **6** Hermes
  foster father of: 8 Dionysus
  teacher of: 8 Dionysus

companion of: 8 Dionysus
  sons: 6 Sileni

silicon
  chemical symbol: 2 Si

silk
  fabric: 4 crin **5** crepe, ninon, satin, surah, tulle **6** faille, pongee, sendal, tussah **7** chiffon, foulard, organza, raw silk, taffeta **8** organzie, paduasoy **10** peau de soie **12** crepe de chine
  lining: 7 sarsnet **8** sarcenet
  measure: 6 denier
  raw silk: 5 grege **6** greige **8** marabout
  source: 6 cocoon **9** silkworms
  waste: 4 noil **5** floss
  watered: 5 moire
  yarn/thread: 4 tram **5** floss

silk-stocking 6 uptown **8** highborn, highbred, wellborn **9** patrician **10** upper-class **11** blue-blooded **12** aristocratic

Silk Stockings
  director: 15 Rouben Mamoulian
  cast: 10 Janis Paige, Peter Lorre **11** Cyd Charisse, Fred Astaire
  setting: 5 Paris
  score: 10 Cole Porter
  remake of: 9 Ninotchka

silky 4 fine, soft **6** satiny, smooth **11** fine-grained

silliness 5 folly **6** drivel, idiocy **7** inanity **9** absurdity, asininity, frivolity **10** buffoonery, tomfoolery **11** foolishness **13** pointlessness **14** playing the fool, ridiculousness

Sillitoe, Alan
  author of: 10 Her Victory **29** Saturday Night and Sunday Morning **36** The Loneliness of the Long-Distance Runner

silly 3 mad **4** dumb **5** crazy, giddy, inane **6** absurd, frothy, insane, stupid, unwary, unwise **7** aimless, asinine, fatuous, foolish, idiotic, shallow, witless **8** childish, farcical **9** brainless, foolhardy, frivolous, laughable, ludicrous, pointless, senseless **10** ill-advised, irrational, ridiculous **11** empty-headed, harebrained, meaningless, nonsensical, purposeless **12** muddleheaded, preposterous, simpleminded, unreasonable **13** inappropriate, irresponsible, muddlebrained, rattlebrained **14** featherbrained **15** inconsequential

Silmarillion, The
  author: 10 J R R Tolkien

silo 3 pit **5** tower
  storage of: 6 fodder **7** missile

Silone, Ignazio
  real name: 17 Secondo Tranquilli
  author of: 9 Fontamara **12** Bread and Wine **26** The Story of a Humble Christian

Silvanus
  also: 8 Sylvanus

god of: 5 herds, house, woods **12** farm boundary **16** uncultivated land

silver 5 coins, plate **6** argent, change **7** jewelry **8** argentum, platinum **9** argentine **10** silverware
  chemical symbol: 2 Ag

Silver
  horse of: 10 Lone Ranger

Silver, Long John
  character in: 14 Treasure Island
  author: 9 Stevenson

Silver, Mattie
  character in: 10 Ethan Frome
  author: 7 Wharton

Silvers, Phil
  real name: 17 Philip Silversmith
  born: 10 Brooklyn NY
  roles: 9 Top Banana **13** Sergeant Bilko **15** High Button Shoes **22** A Guide for the Married Man **37** A Funny Thing Happened on the Way to the Forum
  autobiography: 14 The Laugh Is on Me

s'il vous plaît 6 please **11** if you please

Simenon, Georges
  author of: 8 The Train **12** Act of Passion **14** The Little Saint **15** Maigret's Memoirs **28** The Strange Case of Peter the Lett
  character: 21 Inspector Jules Maigret

Simeon
  father: 5 Jacob
  mother: 4 Leah
  brother: 3 Dan, Gad **4** Levi **5** Asher, Judah **6** Joseph, Reuben **7** Zebulun **8** Benjamin, Issachar, Naphtali
  sister: 5 Dinah
  canticle: 12 nunc dimittis
  descendant of: 9 Simeonite

similar 4 akin, like, twin **5** close **6** allied **7** cognate, kindred **8** agreeing, matching, parallel **9** analogous, duplicate **10** comparable, equivalent, resembling **11** approximate, correlative, much the same, nearly alike **13** correspondent, corresponding

similarity 7 harmony, kinship, oneness **8** affinity, likeness, nearness, sameness **9** agreement, closeness, congruity, semblance **10** congruence, similitude **11** concordance, conformance, equivalence, parallelism, reciprocity, resemblance **13** comparability **14** conformability, correspondence

similarly 4 thus **5** alike **7** equally **8** likewise **11** furthermore, identically **15** correspondingly

similitude 7 analogy **8** likeness, sameness **10** similarity **11** parallelism, resemblance

simmer 4 boil, burn, foam, fume, stew **5** chafe, smart **6** bubble, burble, gurgle, seethe, sizzle

simmer down 7 cool off **8** calm down **14** collect oneself, compose oneself

Simmons, Jean
born: 6 London 7 England
husband: 13 Richard Brooks 14 Stewart Granger
roles: 4 Trio 6 Hamlet 7 Desiree, Ophelia, The Robe 9 Spartacus, Young Bess 11 Elmer Gantry 12 Guys and Dolls 14 The Happy Ending 17 Great Expectations 19 Androcles and the Lion

Simon
also known as: 5 Peter
son: 13 Judas Iscariot
disciple of: 5 Jesus

Simon, Neil
author of: 10 Chapter Two, Plaza Suite 11 Biloxi Blues 12 The Odd Couple 13 Broadway Bound, Lost in Yonkers 15 The Sunshine Boys 16 Come Blow Your Horn 17 Barefoot in the Park 21 Last of the Red Hot Lovers 25 The Prisoner of Second Avenue

Simon & Simon
character: 7 AJ Simon 9 Rick Simon 12 Cecilia Simon 13 Downtown Brown
cast: 7 Tim Reid 10 Mary Carver 13 Gerald McRaney, Jameson Parker
setting: 8 San Diego

Simon Boccanegra
opera by: 5 Verdi
setting: 5 Genoa
character: 5 Maria, Paolo 6 Andrea, Fiesco, Pietro 14 Amelia Grimaldi, Gabriele Adorno

Simon Legree 8 overseer 11 slavedriver
in: 14 Uncle Tom's Cabin

Simonov, Konstantin
author of: 13 Days and Nights

Simon Templar *see* Saint, The

simpatico 7 likable 9 agreeable, congenial, gemutlich

simper 5 smirk 6 giggle, tee-hee, titter 7 snicker, snigger

simple 4 bare, dull, dumb, easy, open, slow, soft, true 5 basic, blunt, dense, frank, green, homey, naive, naked, plain, quiet, sheer, stark, thick 6 callow, candid, common, direct, honest, modest, obtuse, rustic, stupid 7 artless, foolish, natural, sincere 8 absolute, innocent, not fancy, ordinary, peaceful, straight, workaday 9 downright, elemental, guileless, ingenuous, out-and-out, unadorned, unfeigned, untrimmed, unworldly 10 elementary, manageable, not complex, unaffected, uninvolved 11 commonplace, fundamental, plain-spoken, rudimentary, thick-witted, undecorated, unvarnished 12 not difficult, not elaborate, uncompounded 13 inexperienced, uncomplicated, unembellished, unpretentious 15 straightforward, unsophisticated

simple house 3 cot, hut 5 shack 6 chalet 7 cottage 8 bungalow

simpleminded 4 dull, dumb, slow 5 dense, silly, thick 6 stupid 7 asinine, fatuous, foolish, idiotic, moronic, witless 8 retarded 9 brainless, dimwitted, imbecilic 10 dull-witted, halfwitted 11 empty-headed, harebrained, lamebrained 12 feeble-minded

simpleton 3 ass, oaf 4 dolt, dope, fool, hick, jerk, rube 5 booby, dummy, dunce, goose, idiot, ninny, stupe 6 donkey, rustic 7 dullard, jackass 8 dumbbell, imbecile, numskull 9 blockhead, greenhorn, ignoramus, numbskull 10 nincompoop

simplicity 6 candor, purity 7 clarity, honesty, naivete 8 easiness, openness, serenity 9 austerity, clearness, innocence, plainness, restraint, sincerity 10 directness 11 artlessness, cleanliness, naturalness, obviousness 12 truthfulness 13 guilelessness, unworldliness 19 straightforwardness

simply 7 clearly, lucidly, plainly, starkly 8 directly, modestly 9 naturally 10 explicitly 11 ingenuously 12 intelligibly, unaffectedly 15 uncomplicatedly, unpretentiously 17 straightforwardly

Simpson, O J (Orenthal James)
nickname: 5 Juice
sport: 8 football
position: 11 running back
team: 10 USC Trojans 12 Buffalo Bills 23 San Francisco Forty-Niners
film: 11 The Naked Gun
wife: 6 Nicole
accused of: 6 murder 15 murdering Nicole
verdict: 9 acquittal

Simpsons, The
creator: 12 Matt Groening
roles: 3 Apu, Moe 4 Bart, Lisa, Otto 5 Homer, Marge 6 Barney 7 Mr Burns 8 Smithers 11 Chief Wiggum 12 Mrs. Krabappel

simulate 3 act, ape 4 copy, fake, play, pose, sham 5 feign, mimic, put on 6 affect, assume, invent 7 imitate, playact, pretend 9 dissemble, fabricate 11 counterfeit, make believe

simulated 4 fake, sham 5 phony 6 forged 7 manmade, pretend 9 imitation, synthetic 10 artificial, fabricated 11 counterfeit, make-believe

simultaneous 6 coeval 10 coexistent, coexisting, coincident, concurrent, synchronal, synchronic 11 concomitant, synchronous 12 accompanying, contemporary 15 contemporaneous

sin 3 err 4 evil, fall, slip, vice 5 crime, error, lapse, shame, stray, wrong 6 breach, do evil, offend 7 do wrong, misdeed, offense, scandal 8 disgrace, evil deed, iniquity, trespass, villainy 9

violation 10 infraction, transgress, wrongdoing 13 transgression

Sin
origin: 8 Akkadian
god of: 4 moon

Sinatra, Frank
real name: 20 Francis Albert Sinatra
nickname: 8 The Voice 11 Old Blue Eyes 18 Chairman of the Board
born: 9 Hoboken NJ
wife: 9 Mia Farrow 10 Ava Gardner
daughter: 12 Nancy Sinatra
son: 14 Frank Sinatra Jr
leader of: 7 Rat Pack
roles: 8 Tony Rome 12 Angelo Maggio, Guys and Dolls, The Detective 14 The Joker Is Wild 17 The First Deadly Sin 18 From Here to Eternity 22 The Man with the Golden Arm

Sinbad the Sailor
character in: 27 Arabian Nights' Entertainments

since 2 as 3 ago, for, yet 4 ergo, from 5 after, hence, later 6 thence, whence 7 because, whereas 8 in as much 9 therefore 10 afterwards 11 accordingly, considering 12 subsequently
archaic: 4 sith
prefix: 3 cis
Scottish: 4 syne

sincere 4 real 5 frank 6 candid, honest 7 artless, earnest, genuine, natural, serious 8 truthful 9 authentic, guileless, heartfelt, ingenuous, unfeigned 10 forthright, unaffected 11 in good faith, undeceitful 12 wholehearted 15 straightforward

sincerely 5 truly 6 really 8 honestly 9 earnestly, genuinely, seriously 10 truthfully 14 wholeheartedly

sincerity 6 candor 7 honesty, probity 8 openness 9 frankness, good faith 11 artlessness, earnestness, genuineness, seriousness 12 truthfulness 13 guilelessness, ingenuousness 14 forthrightness, unaffectedness 16 wholeheartedness 19 straightforwardness

Sinclair, Upton
author of: 9 The Jungle, World's End 12 Dragon's Teeth
character: 9 Lanny Budd

Sindhi
language family: 12 Indo-European
branch: 11 Indo-Iranian
group: 5 Indic
spoken in: 13 Northern India

sine die 17 without fixing a day (for future action or a future meeting)
literally: 13 without the day

sine prole 14 without progeny 16 without offspring

sine qua non 15 without which not 18 something essential 22 indispensable condition

sinew, sinews 4 grit, thew 5 fiber, nerve, power, vigor 6 muscle, tendon

7 stamina **8** ligament, strength, virility, vitality **10** resilience, strengthen

sinewy 4 wiry **5** beefy, nervy, thewy, tough **6** brawny, robust, strong **7** fibrose, stringy **8** muscular, powerful, vigorous

sinful 3 bad **4** evil, vile **5** wrong **6** errant, unholy, wicked **7** corrupt, heinous, immoral, impious, ungodly, wayward **8** criminal, depraved, shameful **9** miscreant **10** degenerate, despicable, iniquitous, profligate, villainous **11** disgraceful, irreligious, unrighteous

sing 3 hum **4** lilt, pipe **5** carol, chant, chirp, croon, trill, tweet **6** intone, warble **7** chir rup, whistle **8** melodize

Sing Along with Mitch
  regulars: 10 Diana Trask **11** Mitch Miller **12** Leslie Uggams, Louise O'Brien, Sandy Stewart **13** Gloria Lambert, Sing Along Gang, Sing Along Kids

Singapore
  other name: 8 Singa Pur
  name means: 13 city of the lion
  capital/largest city: 9 Singapore
  others: 4 Tuas **6** Changi, Jurong **7** Nee Soon **9** Paya Lebar, Woodlands **10** Bukit Timah, Queenstown **12** Bukit Panjang **15** Toa Payoh New Town
    medieval town: 7 Temasek
  school: 7 Nanyang **8** National **9** Singapore
  monetary unit: 4 cent **6** dollar
  island: 4 Ubin **5** Brani, Bukum, Pesek **7** Semakau **8** Merlimau, Southern **10** Ayer Chawan, Ayer Merbau **11** Blakang Mati, Tekong Besar **12** Tekong Kechil
  mountain: 6 Mandai **7** Panjang
  highest point: 10 Bukit Timah
  river: 6 Jurong, Sungei **7** Kallang, Seletar **9** Singapore
  sea: 6 Indian **10** South China
  physical feature:
    harbor: 6 Keppel **9** Serangoon
    strait: 6 Johore, Pandan **8** Sembilan **9** Singapore
  people: 5 Malay **6** Indian **7** Chinese **9** Malaysian, Pakistani, Sri Lankan
    founder: 7 Raffles
    leader: 10 Lee Kwan Yew
  language: 5 Malay, Tamil **7** Chinese, English **8** Mandarin
  religion: 4 Sikh **5** Hindu, Islam **6** Taoism **8** Buddhism **12** Christianity, Confucianism
  place:
    amusement park: 8 New World **10** Great World, Happy World
    aquarium: 8 Van Kleef
    cathedral: 9 St Andrews
    gardens: 7 Botanic
    hall: 16 Victoria Memorial
    industrial park: 6 Jurong
    mosque: 6 Sultan

    park: 6 Farber **7** Merlion **12** Raffles Place
    street: 16 Raffles Boulevard
    temple: 17 One Thousand Lights
  feature:
    boat: 4 junk **6** sampan
    clothing: 4 sari

singe 4 burn, char, sear **5** brand **6** scorch

singer 4 alto, bard, bass, diva, lark **5** tenor **6** canary **7** crooner, soprano **8** baritone, minstrel, songbird, songster, vocalist **9** chanteuse, chantress, contralto **10** cantatrice, songstress, troubadour **11** nightingale **12** countertenor, mezzo-soprano

Singer, Isaac Bashevis
  author of: 6 Shosha **7** Old Love **8** The Manor **9** The Estate **13** Gimpel the Fool **15** The Family Moskat **16** In My Father's Court **24** The Spinoza of Market Street

singing group 4 trio **5** choir, nonet, octet **6** chorus, sextet **7** quartet, quintet **8** glee club **13** choral society **17** barbershop quartet

Singin' in the Rain
  director: 9 Gene Kelly **12** Stanley Donen
  cast: 9 Gene Kelly, Jean Hagen **11** Cyd Charisse **13** Donald O'Connor **14** Debbie Reynolds
  song: 11 Make 'em Laugh

single 3 one **4** lone, sole **5** unwed **6** maiden **7** only one **8** bachelor, singular, solitary, spinster, wifeless **9** unmarried **10** individual, spouseless **11** husbandless

single file 8 one by one **10** Indian file, one at a time **13** in a single line **16** one behind another

single-handedly 5 alone **7** unaided **9** by oneself, on one's own **10** unassisted **11** without help

single-minded 4 firm **6** dogged **7** devoted, intense, staunch, zealous **8** resolved, tireless, untiring **9** dedicated, steadfast, tenacious **10** determined, inflexible, persistent, relentless, unswerving, unwavering **11** persevering, unflinching

singleness 12 bachelorhood, spinsterhood **14** unmarried state **17** single blessedness

single out 4 pick, take **6** choose, opt for, select **7** call out, extract, fix upon, pick out **8** decide on, set apart, settle on **11** distinguish

sing the praises of 4 hail, laud, tout **5** boost, cheer, exalt, extol, honor **6** praise **7** acclaim, applaud, approve, commend **8** eulogize **9** celebrate **10** compliment

singular 3 odd **4** rare **5** queer **6** choice, quaint, select, unique **7** bizarre, curious, strange, unusual **8** aberrant, abnormal, atypical, freakish,

peculiar, peerless, superior, uncommon, unwonted **9** anomalous, different, eccentric, fantastic, marvelous, matchless, unequaled, unnatural, wonderful **10** noteworthy, outlandish, prodigious, remarkable, surpassing, unfamiliar **11** exceptional, uncustomary **12** unparalleled **13** extraordinary, unaccountable, unprecedented **14** unconventional **16** out-of-the-ordinary

Sinhalese
  language family: 12 Indo-European
  branch: 11 Indo-Iranian
  group: 5 Indic
  spoken in: 6 Ceylon **8** Sri Lanka

sinister 4 dark, dire, evil, foul, rank, vile **5** black **6** cursed, malign, wicked **7** adverse, fearful, hellish, ominous, unlucky **8** accursed, alarming, damnable, devilish, infernal, menacing, rascally **9** dismaying, insidious, malignant **10** despicable, detestable, diabolical, disturbing, malevolent, perfidious, villainous **11** disquieting, frightening, threatening, treacherous, unfavorable, unpromising **12** blackhearted, inauspicious, unpropitious **13** Machiavellian, reprehensible

sink 3 dig, dip, ebb, lay, sag, set **4** bore, bowl, bury, drop, fall, seep, slip, soak, tilt, wane **5** basin, drill, drive, droop, drown, gouge, lower, slant, slope, slump, stoop, yield **6** engulf, go down, lessen, plunge, reduce, shrink, worsen **7** decline, descend, give way, go to pot, go under, put down, regress, subside, succumb **8** diminish, excavate, languish, lavatory, scoop out, submerge, submerse, washbowl **9** hollow out, wash basin **10** degenerate, depreciate, go downhill, retrogress **11** deteriorate, go to the dogs

sinless 4 good, holy, pure **6** chaste **7** upright **8** innocent, spotless, virtuous **9** reputable, righteous

sinner 8 apostate, evildoer, offender **9** miscreant, misfeasor, reprobate, wrongdoer **10** backslider, malefactor, malfeasant, recidivist, trespasser **12** transgressor

Sinon
  pretended to be: 13 Greek deserter
  told Trojans of: 11 Trojan Horse

Sino-Tibetan
  language branch: 7 Sinitic **12** Tibeto-Burman
  includes: 4 Naga **5** Karen **7** Burmese, Chinese **8** Kuki-Chin, Mandarin

Sins, Seven 4 envy, lust **5** anger, pride, sloth **8** gluttony **12** covetousness

sinuosity 10 slinkiness **11** convolution, sinuousness **12** tortuousness

sinuous 6 curved, folded, volute, zigzag **7** bending, coiling, curving, twisted, winding **8** indirect, mazelike, rambling, tortuous, twisting **9** wandering **10** circuitous, convoluted, meandering, roundabout, serpentine, undulating **12** labyrinthine

sinuousness 9 sinuosity **10** slinkiness **11** convolution **12** tortuousness

Siouan
tribe: **4** Crow, Iowa **5** Ioway, Omaha, Osage, Sioux **6** Dakota, Mandan **7** Hidatsa **8** Minitari, Wazhazhe **10** Assiniboin, Gros Ventre **11** Assiniboine

Sioux see **6** Dakota

Sioux State
nickname of: **11** North Dakota

sip 3 lap, nip, sup **4** dram, drop **5** drink, savor, taste **6** sample **7** soupcon, swallow **10** thimbleful

siphon 4 tube **5** drain **7** draw off

siphonaptera
class: **8** hexapoda
phylum: **10** arthropoda
group: **4** flea

Sippar residents 11 Sepharvites

Siqueiros, David Alfaro
born: **6** Mexico **9** Chihuahua
artwork: **12** New Democracy **13** Echo of a Scream **14** Trial of Fascism **15** Ascent of Culture, Burial of a Worker **16** Towards the Cosmos **17** Death to the Invader **18** Polyforum Siqueiros **22** March of Humanity on Earth **24** Cuauhtemoc Against the Myth

sir see **6** mister

sire 4 king, lord **5** beget, breed **6** create, father **7** creator **9** originate **10** originator, progenitor

siren, Siren 4 horn, vamp **5** alarm, nymph, witch **6** sexpot **7** charmer, whistle **8** deceiver, sea nymph **9** temptress **10** seductress **11** enchantress **13** warning signal **15** bewitching woman
French: **11** femme fatale
form: **5** nymph
location: **3** sea
lured sailors by: **7** singing

Sir Gawain and the Green Knight
character: **10** King Arthur **22** Sir Bernlak de Hautdesert
horse: **9** Gringalet

sissified 6 prissy **7** unmanly **8** womanish **10** effeminate

sissy 6 coward **8** weakling **9** fraidy-cat **10** scaredy-cat

sister 3 nun, kin, sib **5** nurse **6** female **7** sibling **8** feminist, relation, relative
nautically: **6** secure **10** strengthen
society: **8** sorority

Sister Carrie
author: **15** Theodore Dreiser
character: **11** G W Hurstwood **12** Carrie Meeber **13** Charles Drouet

Sister Woman
character in: **16** Cat on a Hot Tin Roof
author: **8** Williams

Sisyphean 4 hard **5** tough **6** uphill **7** arduous, onerous **8** toilsome **9** demanding, difficult, strenuous, wearisome **10** exhausting

Sisyphus
king of: **7** Corinth
father: **6** Aeolus
mother: **7** Enarete
brother: **9** Salmoneus
wife: **6** Merope
son: **5** Almus **7** Glaucus **8** Ornytion **10** Thersander
founded: **6** Ephyra **7** Corinth
rolled: **11** stone uphill

sit 3 lie **4** loll, meet, mind, rest, rule, stay **5** abide, chair, nurse, perch, reign, roost, squat, stand, teach, watch **6** attend, endure, gather, govern, linger, remain, reside, settle, sprawl **7** baby-sit, care for, convene, preside **8** assemble, be placed, be seated, chaperon **9** have a seat, officiate **10** deliberate **11** be in session

site 4 area, post, spot, zone **5** field, locus, place, point, scene **6** ground, locale, region, sector **7** section, setting, station **8** district, locality, location, position, province **9** territory **11** whereabouts

sit in judgment 5 judge **6** decide, settle **7** adjudge, mediate **9** arbitrate, reconcile **10** adjudicate **12** bring to terms

situ 5 place

situate 3 put, set **4** post **5** build, house, lodge, place, plant, stand **6** billet, locate, settle **7** install, station **8** ensconce, position **9** construct, establish

situation 3 fix, job **4** case, duty, post, role, seat, site, spot, work **5** berth, place, state **6** locale, office, plight, status **7** dilemma, posture, station **8** capacity, function, locality, location, position, quandary **9** condition **10** assignment, livelihood **11** predicament **13** circumstances **14** state of affairs

sit upon 5 brood, cover, hatch **8** incubate

Sivan 16 third Hebrew month

Six Characters in Search of an Author
author: **15** Luigi Pirandello

six cubits 4 reed

Six Feet Under
network: **3** HBO
cast: **10** Lili Taylor (Lisa Kimmel Fisher) **11** Jeremy Sisto (Billy Chenowith), Peter Krause (Nate Fisher) **12** Michael C Hall (David Fisher) **13** Frances Conroy (Ruth Fisher), James Cromwell (George Sibley), Lauren Ambrose (Claire Fisher) **14** Justina Machado (Vanessa Diaz) **15** Freddy Rodriguez (Federico Diaz), Rachel Griffiths (Brenda Chenowith) **16** Matthew St Patrick (Keith Charles)

Six Million Dollar Man

character: **11** Dr Rudy Wells, (Col) Steve Austin **12** Oscar Goldman
cast: **9** Lee Majors **13** Martin E Brooks **15** Alan Oppenheimer, Richard Anderson
spinoff: **11** Bionic Woman

Sixth Sense, The
director: **15** M Night Shyamalan
cast: **11** Bruce Willis (Malcolm Crowe) **12** Mischa Barton (Kyra Collins), Toni Collette (Lynn Sear) **14** Donnie Wahlberg (Vincent Grey), Olivia Williams (Anna Crowe) **15** Haley Joel Osment (Cole Sear)

Sixty Minutes
correspondent: **9** Dan Rather, Ed Bradley **10** Andy Rooney, Steve Kroft **11** Diane Sawyer, Leslie Stahl, Mike Wallace, Morley Safer **13** Harry Reasoner

sizable 5 ample, broad, large, roomy **7** immense **8** spacious **9** capacious, good-sized

size 3 sum **4** area, bulk, mass, sort **5** array, grade, group, scope, total **6** amount, extent, spread, volume **7** arrange, bigness, content, expanse, stretch **8** capacity, classify, quantity, totality **9** aggregate, amplitude, greatness, largeness, magnitude **10** dimensions **11** measurement, proportions

sizzle 3 fry **4** hiss, spit **7** crackle, frizzle, hissing, sputter **8** splutter **10** sputtering

skate 3 nag, ray **4** skid, skim, slip **5** blade, coast, glide, horse, slide **6** rotter
female: **4** maid
genus: **4** Raja
mark: **4** cusp

skein 4 coil, hank, reel, yarn **5** twist **6** tangle, thread **9** filaments, twistings
members: **4** fowl **5** ducks, flock, geese **6** flyers

skeletal 4 bony, thin **5** gaunt **6** wasted **9** emaciated **10** cadaverous

skeleton 4 hulk **5** bones, frame, shell **9** framework
purpose: **7** support **8** protects **9** framework

Skelton, Red
real name: **21** Richard Bernard Skelton
born: **11** Vincennes IN
roles: **7** I Dood It **8** Ship Ahoy **12** Panama Hattie **16** Neptune's Daughter **17** The Fuller Brush Man **18** Clem Kadiddlehopper, Whistling in the Dark **20** Freddie the Freeloader

skeptic, sceptic 7 atheist, doubter, scoffer **8** agnostic **10** questioner, unbeliever **14** doubting Thomas

skeptical, sceptical 6 unsure **7** cynical, dubious **8** doubtful, doubting, scoffing **9** uncertain **11** incredulous, questioning, unbelieving, unconvinced **12** disbelieving **13** hypercritical

skepticism 5 doubt **7** dubiety **8** distrust, mistrust, unbelief **9** disbelief, suspicion **11** agnosticism, incredulity **12** doubtfulness **13** faithlessness

sketch 3 map **4** draw, plot, skit **5** chart, draft, graph, scene **6** depict, digest, precis, satire **7** drawing, lampoon, mark out, outline, picture, portray, summary, takeoff **8** abstract, rough out, synopsis, vignette **9** blueprint, burlesque, delineate, short play, summarize **11** preliminary **16** characterization

sketchy 4 bare, hazy **5** brief, crude, light, rough, short, vague **6** meager, skimpy, slight **7** cursory, outline, shallow, slender **9** essential, rough-hewn, unrefined **10** incomplete, undetailed, unfinished, unpolished **11** preliminary, preparatory, provisional, superficial

skewed 5 slued **6** veered, warped **7** oblique, sheered, slanted, swerved, twisted **9** distorted

skewer 3 pin, rod **4** spit, stab **5** truss **6** pierce, skiver **7** impale **9** brochette **10** run through

skid 3 ski **4** drag, dray, skim, skip, sled, slip **5** coast, glide, skate, slide **6** runner, sledge **7** skitter **8** glissade, platform, sideslip

Skidbladnir
  origin: 12 Scandinavian
  ship of: 4 Frey **5** Freyr
  feature: 11 collapsible

Skidmore, Owings, and Merrill
  partners: 13 John Merrill Sr, Louis Skidmore **15** Nathaniel Owings
  architects of: 10 Lever House (NYC) **11** AEC town site (Oak Ridge TN) **13** Banque Lambert (Brussels) **16** John Hancock Tower (Chicago) **17** Terrace Plaza Hotel (Cincinnati), US Air Force Academy (CO) **18** Mauna Kea Beach Hotel (Kamuela HI) **19** Istanbul Hilton Hotel (Turkey) **23** Beinecke Rare Book Library (Yale) **26** Chase Manhattan Bank Building (NYC) **33** American Republic Insurance Building (Des Moines IA)
  world's tallest building: 10 Sears Tower (Chicago)

skiff 4 boat **6** dinghy **7** rowboat

skiing
  athlete: 9 Phil Mahre **10** Bode Miller **11** Bill Johnson, Cindy Nelson **12** Alberto Tomba, Hermann Maier **13** Gustavo Thoeni, Robert Cochran **14** Marilyn Cochran, Martha Rockwell **15** Debbie Armstrong, Ingemar Stenmark, Jean Claude Killy **16** Michael Gallagher, Rosie Mittermaier ·**17** Barbara Ann Cochran **20** Annemarie Proell Moser

skill 4 gift **5** craft, knack **6** acumen, tal-

ent **7** ability, cunning, faculty, knowhow, mastery, prowess **8** artistry, capacity, deftness, facility **9** adeptness, dexterity, expertise, handiness, ingenuity **10** adroitness, cleverness, competence, experience, expertness **11** proficiency **12** skillfulness **13** inventiveness

skilled 6 adroit, expert **7** trained **8** skillful **9** competent, masterful, practiced **10** proficient **12** accomplished

skilled worker 7 artisan **9** craftsman **10** technician **15** master craftsman

skillful 3 apt **4** able, deft, keen **5** adept, handy, sharp, slick **6** adroit, clever, expert, facile, gifted **7** capable, cunning, skilled, trained, veteran **8** masterly, talented **9** competent, dexterous, ingenious, masterful, practiced, qualified **10** proficient, well-versed **11** experienced **12** accomplished, professional

skim 3 fly **4** flip, ream, sail, scan, scud, skid, skip **5** coast, float, glide, skate, sweep **6** bounce, scrape **7** dip into **8** glissade **10** glance over **11** leaf through, move lightly **12** thumb through

skimp 5 pinch, stint **6** scrimp, slight **8** be frugal, be stingy, hold back, withhold **9** economize **11** cut expenses, scrape along

skimpy 5 close, scant, small, spare, tight **6** frugal, meager, modest, scanty, slight, sparse, stingy **7** miserly, scrimpy, sparing, wanting **8** exiguous, grudging, smallish, stinting **9** illiberal, niggardly, penurious, scrimping **10** inadequate, incomplete, too thrifty **11** close fisted, tightfisted **12** insufficient, parsimonious **13** pennypinching **14** inconsiderable

skin 3 fur, pod **4** bark, case, coat, flay, hide, hull, husk, peel, pelt, rind **5** shell **6** abrade, casing, fleece, jacket, scrape, sheath **7** lay bare **9** epidermis **10** complexion, integument **12** body covering, outer coating
  outer layer: 9 epidermis
  contains: 3 fat **4** hair, pore, root **5** nerve **6** vessel **8** oil gland **10** sweat gland
  body's largest: 5 organ
  sense of: 4 cold, heat, pain **5** touch **8** pressure, tickling

skinflint 5 miser **7** hoarder, niggard, scrooge **8** tightwad **10** pinchpenny **12** penny pincher

Skinner, Cornelia Otis
  author of: 23 The Pleasure of His Company (with Samuel Taylor) **24** Our Hearts Were Young and Gay (with Emily Kimbrough)

skinny 4 lank, lean, thin, wiry **5** gaunt, gawky, lanky, spare **6** slight **7** angular, scraggy, scrawny, slender, spindly

8 gangling, rawboned, shrunken, skeletal **9** emaciated

Skin of Our Teeth, The
  author: 14 Thornton Wilder

skip 3 bob, cut, hop **4** flee, flit, jump, leap, miss, omit, romp, shun, trip **5** bound, caper, dodge, elude, evade **6** bounce, escape, eschew, gambol, ignore, prance, spring **7** abscond, make off, neglect **8** leap over, leave out, overlook, pass over **9** disappear, disregard, do without, play hooky, skedaddle **10** fly the coop **12** be absent from

skirmish 4 fray, tilt **5** brush, clash, joust, run-in, scrap, set-to **6** action, affray, battle, fracas, tussle **7** scuffle **8** struggle **9** encounter, firefight, scrimmage **10** engagement

skirt 3 hem, rim **4** edge, gird, kilt, maxi, mini, ring, shun **5** avoid, evade, flank, hem in, verge **6** border, bounds, circle, dirndl, fringe, girdle, margin **7** enclose, envelop **8** boundary, encircle, go around, lie along **9** crinoline, outer area, perimeter, periphery **10** circumvent, fight shy of **12** circumscribe, detour around

skittish 3 shy **4** wary **5** chary, jumpy, leery, shaky, timid **6** fitful, unsure **7** bashful, fearful, fidgety, flighty, guarded, jittery, nervous, restive **8** cautious, restless, unstable, unsteady, volatile **9** demurring, excitable, impulsive, mercurial, reluctant **10** suspicious **11** distrustful

skittles
  equipment: 4 pins **6** cheese
  also called: 5 closh **6** cloddy **8** rolypoly **10** Dutch bowls
  tabletop version: 15 Enfield skittles

Skrymir
  also: 10 Utgardloki
  origin: 12 Scandinavian
  form: 5 giant
  took to Jotunheim: 4 Loki, Thor **7** Thialfi

Skuld 4 Norn
  origin: 12 Scandinavian
  form: 5 dwarf
  personifies: 6 future
  developed from: 5 Urdar
  companions: 3 Urd **8** Verdandi

skulduggery, skullduggery 7 knavery **8** trickery **9** chicanery, deception **10** dirty trick **12** pettifoggery

skulk 4 hide, lurk **5** cower, creep, prowl, slink, sneak **9** pussyfoot

skull
  contains: 5 brain

Skull place 7 Calvary **8** Golgotha

sky 5 space **9** firmament **10** atmosphere, outer space, the heavens **12** arch of heaven
  goddess of: 3 Fri, Nut **5** Frigg, Frija **6** Frigga

sky blue 5 azure 8 cerulean, pale blue 9 clear blue, light blue

Sky King
character: 5 Penny 7 Clipper
cast: 10 Kirby Grant 11 Ron Haggerty 13 Gloria Winters
ranch: 11 Flying Crown
plane: 8 Songbird

skylarking 5 sport 6 antics 7 hijinks, romping 10 frolicking

skypilot 5 padre, rabbi 6 cleric, parson, priest 8 chaplain, minister 9 clergyman

skyward 2 up 6 upward 8 to the sky 10 heavenward 12 to the heavens

slab 3 wad 4 hunk, slat 5 block, board, chunk, plank, slice, wedge 10 thick slice

slack 3 lax 4 dull, easy, free, lazy, limp, slow, soft 5 baggy, loose, quiet, relax 6 easily, flabby, freely, limply, loosen, pliant, remiss, slowly, untied 7 flaccid, let up on, loosely, not busy, not firm, not taut, offhand, relaxed, slacken 8 careless, dilatory, flexible, heedless, inactive, indolent, listless, not tight, slapdash, slipshod, slothful, sluggish 9 leisurely, lethargic, negligent, slow-paced, unmindful, untighten 10 neglectful, nonchalant, permissive, slow-moving, sluggishly, unexacting, unfastened, unthinking 11 inattentive, indifferent, thoughtless, unconcerned, undemanding

slacken 4 curb, ease, flag, free, slow 5 abate, check, let go, let up, limit, loose, relax, slack 6 arrest, go limp, lessen, loosen, reduce, retard, soften, temper, weaken 7 dwindle, inhibit, release 8 decrease, diminish, keep back, mitigate, moderate, restrain, slow down, taper off 9 untighten

slacker 5 idler 6 dodger, loafer, truant 7 dallier, dawdler, goof-off, laggard, quitter, shirker 9 do-nothing, goldbrick 10 malingerer 14 good-for-nothing, procrastinator

slag 5 dross 6 cinder, scoria 8 clinkers

slake 4 calm, cool, curb, ease, hush, sate 5 allay, quell, quiet, still 6 modify, quench, soothe, subdue, temper 7 appease, assuage, compose, gratify, mollify, relieve, satiate, satisfy 8 decrease, mitigate, moderate 9 alleviate 11 tranquilize 14 take the edge off

slake off 4 wane 5 abate 6 lessen, reduce, weaken 7 decline, subside 8 diminish, fade away, slack off

slam 3 hit 4 bang, bump, slap 5 crash, smack, smash, throw

slammer 3 jug, pen 4 jail, stir 5 clink 6 cooler, lockup, prison 8 big house, hoosegow 9 calaboose, jailhouse 12 penitentiary

Slammin' Sammy
nickname of: 8 Sam Snead

slander 4 soil 5 libel, smear, sully 6 defame, malign, revile, vilify 7 calumny 8 besmirch 9 falsehood 10 defamation, distortion 12 vilification 14 false statement 17 misrepresentation

Slaney, Mary see 10 Decker, Mary

slang 4 cant, jive 5 argot, idiom, lingo 6 jargon 7 dialect

slant 4 bias, lean, list, rake, tilt, view 5 angle, color, pitch, slope 7 distort, incline, leaning 8 attitude 9 prejudice, viewpoint

slanted 4 awry 6 biased, tilted 7 colored, crooked, leaning, pitched, sloping 8 inclined 9 on an angle, on the bias 10 prejudiced

slanting 4 bias 5 alean, atilt 7 oblique, sloping 8 diagonal, glancing, inclined 10 distorting

slap 3 cut, hit 4 blow, clap, cuff, snub, swat 5 smack, whack 6 insult, rebuff, strike, wallop 9 rejection

slapdash 6 casual, sloppy 8 careless, slipshod, slovenly 9 haphazard

Slapsie Maxie
nickname of: 15 Maxie Rosenbloom

slash 3 cut, rip 4 drop, gash, mark, pare, rend, rent, slit, tear 5 lower, slice 6 reduce, stroke 8 decrease, lacerate, lowering 9 reduction 10 laceration

slate 4 list 6 ballot, tablet, ticket 10 blackboard, chalkboard

slattern 4 drab, slob, slut 5 bitch, frump 6 harlot, sloven 7 trollop

slatternly 6 frowsy, frumpy, sloppy, untidy 7 unkempt 8 slipshod, slovenly

slaughter 4 kill, slay 6 pogrom 7 butcher, destroy, killing, wipe out 8 decimate, massacre 9 bloodbath 10 annihilate, butchering, mass murder 11 exterminate

Slaughterhouse Five
author: 12 Kurt Vonnegut
character: 12 Billy Pilgrim
setting: 7 Dresden

Slav 4 Pole, Serb, Sorb, Wend 5 Croat, Czech 6 Bulgar, Slovak 7 Russian, Serbian, Slovene, Sorbian 8 Bohemian, Croatian, Moravian 9 Bulgarian, Ruthenian, Slavonian, Slovadian, Ukrainian

slave 4 prey, serf, toil 6 addict, drudge, menial, thrall, toiler, vassal, victim 7 chattel, plodder 8 bondsman 9 workhorse 11 bond servant

slaver 5 drool 6 drivel 7 slobber

slavery 4 toil 5 grind, labor, sweat 6 strain 7 bondage, serfdom, travail 8 drudgery, struggle 9 captivity, treadmill, vassalage 11 enslavement, impressment, subjugation 12 enthrallment

Slavic
language family: 12 Indo-European

group: 11 Balto-Slavic
subgroup: 12 Old Bulgarian 13 Eastern Slavic, Western Slavic 14 Southern Slavic 15 Old Church Slavic

slavish 5 exact 6 strict 7 literal, servile 9 imitative, slavelike 10 derivative, obsequious, submissive, unoriginal 11 subservient 13 unimaginative

slay 4 do in, kill 6 murder 7 destroy, execute 8 massacre 9 slaughter 10 annihilate

slayer 6 hit man, killer 7 butcher 8 assassin, murderer 11 executioner 12 exterminator

slaying 6 murder 7 killing 8 homicide 9 execution

sleazy 5 cheap, tacky 6 flimsy, shabby, shoddy, trashy, vulgar 7 schlock 13 insubstantial

sleek 4 oily 5 shiny, silky, slick, suave 6 glossy, satiny, smooth 7 fawning, velvety 8 lustrous, unctuous 12 ingratiating

sleep 3 nap 4 doze, rest 5 death, peace 6 repose, snooze 7 slumber
god of: 6 Hypnos, Hypnus, Somnus

sleeping 6 asleep, dozing 7 dormant, napping, resting 8 snoozing 9 quiescent, somnolent 13 hibernating 19 in the arms of Morpheus

Sleeping Beauty, The
composer: 11 Tchaikovsky

sleeping car (railroad)
invented by: 7 Pullman

sleeping infants
goddess of: 6 Cunina

sleeping place 3 bed, cot 4 bunk 5 berth 6 pallet 7 bedroom 9 dormitory 10 bedchamber

sleepless 5 alert 7 wakeful 8 restless, watchful 9 insomniac, wide awake 11 industrious

sleeplessness 8 insomnia 9 alertness, attention 11 wakefulness 12 restlessness

sleep lightly 3 nap, nod 4 doze 6 catnap, snooze 15 catch forty winks

sleepy 4 dull 5 quiet, tired, weary 6 drowsy 8 fatigued, inactive 9 exhausted

sleigh 4 dray, sled 6 cutter, sledge, troika 8 transport

Sleipnir
origin: 12 Scandinavian
horse of: 4 Odin 5 Othin
legs: 5 eight

slender 4 lean, poor, slim, thin, weak 5 faint, scant, small, spare 6 feeble, little, meager, narrow, remote, skinny, slight 7 willowy 8 delicate

Slender
character in: 22 The Merry Wives of Windsor
author: 11 Shakespeare

Sleuth
director: 17 Joseph L Mankiewicz

based on play by: 14 Anthony Shaffer
cast: 12 Michael Caine **15** Laurence Olivier

slew 3 lot, ton **4** gang, heap, load, lots, peck, pile, raft **5** batch, did in **6** killed **8** murdered **12** assassinated

Slezak, Walter
born: 6 Vienna **7** Austria
father: 9 Leo Slezak
roles: 5 Fanny **8** Lifeboat **11** Dr Coppelius

slice 3 cut **4** pare **5** carve, piece, sever, shave **6** cut off, divide **7** portion, section, segment, whittle **8** separate **9** dismember

slick 3 sly **4** coat, film, foxy, oily, scum, waxy, wily **5** sharp, shiny, sleek **6** clever, glassy, glossy, greasy, satiny, smooth, tricky **7** coating, cunning **8** slippery **10** make glossy **11** fast-talking **13** smooth-talking

slicker 8 raincoat **9** sou'wester **10** mackintosh, waterproof

slide 4 fall, pass, ramp, skid, slip, veer **5** chute, coast, glide, lapse, slope **7** slither **8** sideslip **11** diapositive **12** transparency

slide by 4 go by **5** lapse **6** elapse, roll by, slip by **7** glide by **8** slip away

slight 3 cut **4** lean, slap, slim, snub, thin, tiny **5** frail, small, spare **6** insult, little, modest, rebuff **7** fragile, limited, slender **8** moderate **10** incivility, negligible, restricted **11** unimportant **13** imperceptible, inappreciable, infinitesimal

slight amount 3 bit **4** dash, drop **5** pinch, touch, trace **6** little **7** smidgen, smidgin, soupcon **8** smidgeon **9** little bit **10** smattering

slightly 6 feebly, rarely **8** meagerly, scantily, scarcely, somewhat **10** negligibly **13** superficially **15** insignificantly

slim 4 lean, thin **5** faint, small **6** meager, remote, skinny, slight, svelte **7** distant, slender, thready, willowy **10** negligible

slime 3 mud **4** mire, muck, ooze **6** sludge

slimy 4 foul, vile **5** gummy, mucky, nasty **6** creepy, putrid, sticky **7** viscous **9** glutinous, loathsome, obnoxious, offensive, repulsive

sling 3 net **4** cast **5** fling, throw **9** slingshot **10** arm support

Slingin' Sammy
nickname of: 10 Sammy Baugh

slingshot 5 sling **8** catapult

slink 4 slip **5** creep, prowl, skulk, sneak, steal **6** tiptoe

slip 3 put **4** dock, drop, fail, fall, leak, pass, sink, skid **5** berth, error, glide, lapse, scrap, shoot, shred, slide, sneak, sprig, steal, strip **6** escape,

sprout, ticket, worsen **7** blunder, chemise, cutting, decline, faux pas, receipt, sapling, voucher **9** petticoat, stripling, youngling, youngster **10** be revealed, get clear of, imprudence, underdress **12** indiscretion

slip away 4 go by **5** lapse **6** elapse, escape **7** run away, slide by **8** creep off **9** tiptoe off

slip by 4 go by, pass **5** lapse **6** elapse, pass by, roll by **7** glide by, slide by

slip of the tongue, a
Latin: 13 lapsus linguae

slipper 4 mule, shoe **5** scuff **6** sandal

slippery 4 foxy, oily, waxy, wily **5** slick, soapy **6** crafty, glassy, greasy, shifty, smooth, sneaky, tricky **7** devious **9** deceitful **10** contriving, unreliable **11** treacherous **13** untrustworthy

slipshod 3 lax **5** loose, messy **6** casual, sloppy, untidy **7** offhand **8** careless, slovenly **11** thoughtless

slip-up 4 flub, goof **5** botch, error, gaffe, lapse **6** boo-boo, bungle, foul-up, mess-up, miscue **7** blooper, blunder, clinker, faux pas, mistake, screw-up **9** oversight

slit 3 cut **4** gash **5** crack, slash **7** crevice, fissure **8** incision

slither 5 glide, slide **25** move with a side-to-side motion

sliver 5 crumb, shred, slice, snick **6** morsel **8** splinter

slivovitz
type: 6 brandy **7** liqueur
origin: 10 Yugoslavia
flavor: 4 plum

Sloan, John F
born: 11 Lock Haven PA
artwork: 12 McSorley's Bar **14** Wake of the Ferry **18** Hairdresser's Window **25** Backyards Greenwich Village

slob 6 sloven **8** slattern

slobber 4 slop **5** drool **6** drivel, slaver **7** dribble, sputter **8** salivate, splutter

sloe gin
type: 7 liqueur
flavor: 9 sloe berry **15** blackthorn berry
drink: 11 Sloe Gin Fizz
with bourbon: 9 Black Hawk
with rum: 11 Shark's Tooth
with vermouth: 10 Blackthorn

slogan 5 motto **6** byword **9** battle cry, catchword, watchword

sloop 4 boat, brig, ship **5** smack **8** sailboat, schooner

slop 3 mud **4** mire, muck, ooze **5** filth, slosh, slush, spill, swash, swill, waste **6** refuse, sludge, splash **7** garbage, spatter **8** splatter

Slop, Dr
character in: 14 Tristram Shandy
author: 6 Sterne

slope 3 tip **4** bank, bend, lean, tilt **5**

angle, pitch, slant **7** descent, incline **9** downgrade **11** inclination

sloping 5 alean, steep **6** aslant **7** leaning, oblique, tilting **8** diagonal, inclined, on a slant, slanting **9** slantways **11** declivitous

sloppiness 5 chaos, mix-up, upset **6** jumble **7** clutter **8** disarray, disorder, shambles **9** messiness **10** disharmony, untidiness **12** dishevelment **14** disarrangement **15** disorganization

sloppy 3 wet **5** dirty, messy, muddy **6** marshy, sloshy, slushy, sodden, soiled, swampy, untidy, watery **7** unclean **10** disorderly

sloppy person 4 slob **6** sloven

slosh 3 lap **4** drop, mire, stir **5** slush, spill, swash **6** splash **8** flounder

slot 3 gap **4** slit **5** crack, niche, notch
machine: 14 one-armed bandit

sloth 6 phlegm, torpor **7** languor **8** idleness, laziness, lethargy **9** indolence, lassitude, torpidity **12** listlessness, sluggishness **13** do-nothingness, shiftlessness

slothful 3 lax **4** idle, lazy **5** inert **6** drowsy, otiose, supine, torpid **8** indolent, listless, sluggish **9** do-nothing, lethargic, negligent, shiftless **10** sluggardly **11** unambitious

slouch 4 bend **5** droop, hunch, idler, slump, stoop **6** loafer **7** laggard, shirker, slacker **8** sluggard **9** goldbrick, lazybones

Slovakia
formerly part of: 14 Czechoslovakia
capital/largest city: 10 Bratislava
others: 6 Kosice
head of state: 9 president
government: 8 republic
monetary unit: 5 crown **6** koruna
mountain: 7 Sudetes **8** Low Tatra **9** High Tatra, Slovak Ore **10** Carpathian, Nizke Tatry **11** Visoke Tatry **15** White Carpathian
river: 2 Uh **3** Vah **4** Hron **5** Nitra, Slana **6** Danube, Hornad, Ondava, Poprad **7** Laborec **8** Latorica
people: 5 Czech **6** Slavik, Slovak **9** Hungarian
language: 6 Slavik, Slovak
religion: 9 Christian **13** Roman Catholic

Slovenia
capital/largest city: 9 Ljubljana
others: 5 Celje, Koper, Kranj **7** Maribor
head of state: 9 president
government: 8 republic
monetary unit: 5 tolar
river: 4 Sava **5** Drava
sea: 8 Adriatic
people: 8 Slovenes
language: 9 Slovene
religion: 13 Roman Catholic

slovenly 5 dirty, dowdy, messy **6** frowzy, sloppy, untidy **7** unclean, unkempt **8** careless, slapdash, slipshod **10** disorderly, slatternly **11** indifferent, unconcerned

slow 3 dim, off **4** curb, dull, dumb, flag, late, long **5** brake, check, dense, heavy, loath, quiet **6** averse, boring, falter, hinder, hold up, impede, obtuse, retard, stupid, torpid **7** belated, delayed, laggard, lumpish, not busy, overdue, tedious, unhasty **8** backward, cautious, dawdling, dilatory, dragging, drawn out, extended, hesitant, inactive, obstruct, sluggish, tarrying **9** dim-witted, leisurely, lingering, ponderous, prolonged, reluctant, snaillike, unhurried **10** behind time, decelerate, deliberate, dull-witted, indisposed, protracted, unexciting, unpunctual

slowdown 4 curb, flag **5** brake, delay, letup, slump **6** ease-up, falter, hinder, impede, lessen, retard, slow-up **7** decline, fall off, letdown, setback, slowing, subside **8** diminish, downturn, flagging **9** grind down **10** decelerate, slackening, stagnation **11** reduce speed, retardation **12** deceleration

slow-moving 4 poky **5** pokey **6** idling **8** crawling, creeping, dawdling, sluggish **9** leisurely, snaillike **10** turtlelike **12** tortoiselike
  creature: 4 slug **5** loris, sloth, snail **6** turtle **8** tortoise

slowness 6 tedium **8** dullness **9** torpidity **10** snail's pace **12** backwardness, sluggishness

slow-paced 4 easy **7** gradual, laggard **8** sluggish **9** leisurely, lethargic, unhurried **10** deliberate

slowpoke 4 slug **5** idler, snail **7** dallier, dawdler, laggard, lie-abed, plodder **8** lingerer, slugabed, tortoise **9** saunterer, straggler **11** foot-dragger

slow to learn 4 dull **5** dense, inapt **6** stupid **8** retarded **10** slow-witted

slow up 4 stem **5** delay **6** detain, hinder, impede, retard **8** slow down

slow-witted 4 dull **5** dense **7** doltish, idiotic, moronic **8** backward, retarded **9** imbecilic

sludge 3 mud **4** mire, muck, ooze, slop **5** dregs, slime, slush **8** sediment

slug 3 bat, hit **4** bash, belt, sock **5** baste, clout, pound, punch, smite, thump, whack, whale **6** batter, strike, wallop **7** clobber **8** lambaste

sluggard 4 lazy **5** drone, idler, sloth, snail **6** loafer, truant, turtle **7** dawdler, laggard **8** loiterer, slothful, slowpoke, tortoise **9** do-nothing, lazybones **11** couch potato **12** lounge lizard **13** stick-in-the-mud

sluggish 4 lazy, slow **5** inert **6** torpid **7** languid **8** inactive, indolent, lifeless, listless, slothful **9** leisurely, lethargic, soporific, unhurried **10** phlegmatic, protracted, spiritless

sluggishness 6 torpor **7** inertia **8** lethargy, slowness **9** lassitude **10** inactivity **12** listlessness

slum
  Portuguese: 6 favela

slumber 3 nap **4** doze **5** sleep **6** snooze **8** vegetate **9** hibernate **10** be inactive, lie dormant

slump 3 dip, sag **4** drop, fall, slip **5** droop, lapse **6** plunge, slouch, tumble **7** decline, give way, reverse, setback **8** collapse

slur 3 cut, dig **4** mark, skip, spot **5** smear, stain, sully, taint **6** defame, ignore, insult, malign, mumble, mutter, slight **7** affront, blacken, blemish, let pass **8** mumbling, overlook, pass over **9** disregard, gloss over, muttering **11** run together

slush 4 slop **6** bathos **9** soppiness **11** mawkishness, melting snow **14** sentimentalism, sentimentality

slushiness 5 slush **10** sponginess **11** mawkishness **14** sentimentalism, sentimentality

slut 4 doxy, jade **5** bimbo, frump, hussy, tramp, wench, whore **6** floozy, harlot, sloven, wanton **7** jezebel, trollop **8** slattern, strumpet **10** prostitute

sly 4 foxy, wily **6** artful, covert, crafty, secret, shrewd, sneaky, tricky **7** cunning, furtive, playful, private **8** stealthy **9** conniving **11** dissembling, mischievous **12** confidential

Slye, Leonard
  real name of: 9 Roy Rogers

slyness 5 craft **7** cunning, stealth **8** archness, foxiness, subtlety, wiliness **10** artfulness, craftiness, shrewdness, trickiness **11** furtiveness **15** underhandedness

smack 3 bit, hit, rap **4** blow, buss, clap, cuff, dash, hint, kiss, slap **5** savor, smell, smite, spank, taste, tinge, touch, trace, whack **6** buffet, flavor **7** suggest

small 4 mean, tiny, weak **5** faint, minor, petty, scant **6** feeble, lesser, little, meager, modest, narrow, petite, slight **7** bigoted, fragile, ignoble, trivial **8** not great, trifling **10** diminutive, provincial, undersized **11** of no account, opinionated, superficial, unimportant **13** insignificant **15** inconsequential

Small, Lennie
  character in: 12 Of Mice and Men
  author: 9 Steinbeck

small details
  Latin: 8 minutiae

smaller 4 less **5** lower **6** lesser, tinier **7** dinkier, littler, pettier, reduced, shorter **8** inferior

smallest 5 least **6** lowest **7** tiniest **8** dinkiest, pettiest, shortest **9** slightest

small intestine

part of: 15 digestive system
  lined with: 5 villi

small-minded 4 mean **5** petty **6** narrow **7** bigoted **9** parochial **10** prejudiced **12** mean-spirited

smallness 8 meanness, tininess **9** pettiness **10** meagerness, triviality **12** dwarfishness **14** insignificance **18** inconsequentiality

small piece 3 bit, dab **4** chip, drop, snip **5** crumb, grain, piece, pinch, scrap, shred, speck **6** dollop, morsel **7** granule, smidgen, smidgin **8** fragment, particle, smidgeon

small quantity 3 bit, dab, few **5** touch **7** smidgen, smidgin, soupcon **8** smidgeon **9** little bit

small round window
  French: 11 oeil-de-boeuf

small spot 3 dab, dot **5** fleck, speck

small talk 6 banter, gossip **7** chatter, prattle **8** chitchat, idle talk, repartee **9** bavardage, prattling **12** tittle-tattle

Smallville
  network: 2 WB
  cast: 10 John Glover (Lionel Luthor), Tom Welling (Clark Kent) **11** Allison Mack (Chloe Sullivan) **12** Erica Durance (Lois Lane), Kristin Kreuk (Lana Lang) **13** Annette O'Toole (Martha Kent), John Schneider (Jonathan Kent) **16** Michael Rosenbaum (Lex Luthor)

smart 4 ache, burn, chic, hurt, keen, neat, trim **5** brash, brisk, quick, sassy, sharp, sting, wince, witty **6** astute, blench, brainy, bright, clever, flinch, modish, shrewd, suffer **7** elegant, stylish **8** feel pain, vigorous **9** be painful, energetic **10** smart-aleck **11** fashionable, intelligent

smart aleck 6 smarty **7** show-off, windbag, wiseass, wise guy **8** blowhard, braggart, saucebox, wiseacre **9** know-it-all **11** smarty-pants **12** grandstander **13** exhibitionist

smarten up 7 dress up, improve **8** beautify, spruce up

smartness 6 acumen, wisdom **8** keenness, sagacity **9** acuteness **10** astuteness, cleverness, perception, shrewdness **12** intelligence, perspicacity

smash 3 hit **4** bang, bash, beat, blow **5** break, clout, crack, crash, crush **6** batter, strike, winner **7** clobber, crack-up, destroy, shatter, success, triumph **8** accident, demolish, splinter **9** collision, sensation **12** disintegrate

smash against 4 beat, lash **5** crash, pound, smite **6** batter, buffet **7** break on

smashed 5 drunk **6** soused, wasted, zapped, zonked **7** crashed, crushed **8** squashed **9** plastered, shattered **10** inebriated **11** intoxicated **17** under the influence **20** three sheets to the wind

smashing 5 great, super **6** superb **8** fabulous, terrific **9** fantastic, marvelous, wonderful **10** stupendous **11** magnificent, sensational **13** extraordinary

smashup 5 crash, wreck **7** crackup **8** accident **9** collision **12** fender bender

smattering 3 bit, dab **4** dash, drop **5** scrap **7** smidgen, smidgin, snippet **8** smidgeon **10** sprinkling

smear 3 mar, rub **4** blur, coat, daub, soil **5** cover, lay on, libel, stain **6** blotch, injure, malign, smirch, smudge, spread, streak **7** blacken, blemish, degrade, slander, splotch, tarnish **8** besmirch, besmudge **9** denigrate **10** accusation, obliterate

smell 4 feel, nose, odor, reek **5** aroma, fetor, scent, sense, sniff, stink **6** detect, stench **7** bouquet, perfume, suspect **8** perceive **9** emanation, fragrance, get wind of

smelly 4 rank **5** fetid **6** putrid **7** noisome, odorous, reeking **8** stinking **10** malodorous

Smetana, Bedrich
  born: 7 Bohemia **8** Litomysl **11** Leitomischl **14** Czechoslovakia
  composer of: 7 Ma Vlast **9** My Country **10** From My Life **11** Czech Dances **12** The Two Widows **16** The Bartered Bride

smidgen, smidgin, smidgeon 3 bit, dab **4** mite, snip **5** crumb, pinch, scrap, shred, speck, trace **6** dollop, morsel

smile 4 beam, grin **5** favor, shine, smirk **6** simper

Smiles of a Summer Night
  director: 13 Ingmar Bergman
  cast: 11 Eva Dahlbeck **13** Ulla Jacobsson **15** Margit Carlquist **16** Harriet Andersson
  remade as: 17 A Little Night Music

Smiley's People
  author: 11 John Le Carre

Smintheus
  epithet of: 6 Apollo

smirch 4 blot, mark, soil, spot **5** dirty, smear, stain, sully, taint **6** blotch, damage, smudge, stigma **7** begrime, blacken, blemish, slander, tarnish **8** besmirch, besmudge, dishonor **9** discredit

smirk 4 grin, leer **5** sneer **6** simper **7** grimace

Smirke, Sir Robert
  architect of: 12 King's College (U of London) **13** British Museum (London) **19** Covent Garden Theater (London)
  style: 12 Greek Revival

smite 3 hit **4** swat **5** knock, smack, whack **6** enamor, strike, wallop **7** clobber

Smith, Adam
  author of: 18 The Wealth of Nations

Smith, Al
  creator/artist of: 11 Mutt and Jeff

Smith, Betty
  author of: 20 A Tree Grows in Brooklyn

Smith, Charles Aaron
  nickname: 5 Bubba
  sport: 8 football
  team: 14 Baltimore Colts

Smith, David
  born: 8 Decatur IN
  artwork: 3 Zig **4** Cubi **6** Oculus **8** Agricola, Main View, Sentinel, Star Cage **9** Australia, Royal Bird, Tank Totem **10** The Banquet **12** Detroit Queen **15** Lectern Sentinel **17** Medals for Dishonor **20** Hudson River Landscape **23** Song of an Irish Blacksmith

Smith, Lillian
  author: 12 Strange Fruit

Smith, Maggie
  born: 6 Ilford **7** England
  husband: 13 Beverley Cross **14** Robert Stephens
  roles: 4 Hook **7** Othello **11** Gosford Park, Harry Potter (series) **15** California Suite, The Pumpkin Eater, The Secret Garden **16** Tea with Mussolini **17** Travels with My Aunt **24** The Prime of Miss Jean Brodie (Oscar)
  character: 17 Minerva McGonagall

Smith, Winston
  character in: 18 Nineteen Eighty-Four
  author: 6 Orwell

smithereen 3 bit **4** atom **5** crumb, shard **8** fragment, particle **9** scintilla

Smithson, James
  field: 9 chemistry
  nationality: 7 British
  discovered: 11 smithsonite **13** zinc carbonite
  funded: 22 Smithsonian Institution

smitten 8 enamored **9** bewitched **10** enraptured, infatuated

smoke 4 draw, fume, pipe, puff, reek, suck **5** cigar, fumes **6** billow, inhale **7** light up, smolder **9** cigarette, have a drag

Smoke
  author: 12 Ivan Turgenev
  character: 5 Irina **7** Potugin **13** Tanya Shestoff **16** General Ratmiroff, Grigory Litvinoff **18** Kapitolina Shestoff

smoke screen 4 ruse **5** cover, dodge, front **6** screen **9** deception **10** camouflage, subterfuge

smoky 5 dingy, grimy, sooty **6** fuming, smudgy **7** reeking **10** smoldering

smolder 4 burn, fume, rage **5** smoke **6** seethe

Smollett, Tobias George
  author of: 14 (The Expedition of)

Humphry Clinker, Roderick Random **15** Peregrine Pickle

smooch 3 pet **4** buss, kiss, neck **5** smack, spoon **7** make out

smooth 4 calm, ease, easy, even, flat, glib, help, mild, open, pave **5** allay, level, silky, sleek, suave **6** facile, mellow, placid, polish, refine, serene, soften, soothe, steady **7** appease, assuage, flatten, mollify, orderly, perfect, prepare, velvety **8** civilize, composed, make even, mitigate, peaceful, pleasant **9** collected, cultivate, easygoing, make level **10** facilitate, flattering, harmonious, methodical, uneventful **11** well-ordered **12** ingratiating **13** self-possessed, well-regulated

smoothness 8 evenness, fineness, flatness **9** silkiness, sleekness

smooth the feathers 4 calm **6** pacify, soothe **7** appease, assuage, mollify, placate **10** conciliate

smooth-tongued 4 glib **5** suave **6** fluent **8** unctuous **10** flattering **11** fast-talking **12** hypocritical, ingratiating

smother 4 hide, mask, wrap **5** choke, quash, snuff **6** deaden, quench, shower **7** conceal **8** keep down, strangle, suppress, surround **9** choke back, envelop in, suffocate **10** asphyxiate, extinguish

Smothers Brothers Comedy Hour, The
  regulars: 10 Don Novello, Pat Paulsen **11** Bob Einstein, Leigh French, Steve Martin, Tom Smothers **12** Betty Aberlin, Dick Smothers, John Hartford, Nino Senporty, Spencer Quinn **13** Mason Williams **14** Jennifer Warren, Sally Struthers **16** Anita Kerr Singers **17** Jimmy Joyce Singers **18** Louis DaPron Dancers **19** Marty Paich Orchestra **20** Denny Vaughn Orchestra, Ron Poindexter Dancers **21** Nelson Riddle Orchestra

smudge 4 blot, mark, soil, spot **5** dirty, smear, stain **6** smutch

smudgy 5 dirty, messy **6** filthy, grubby, smeary **7** sullied **8** befouled, unwashed **9** besmeared

smug 8 superior, virtuous **10** complacent **13** self-righteous, self-satisfied

smuggle 5 sneak **15** export illegally, import illegally

smuggled goods 10 contraband **14** illegal exports, illegal imports **18** prohibited articles

smuggler 6 runner **9** gunrunner, rumrunner **10** bootlegger **13** contrabandist

smugness 7 egotism **9** immodesty **11** superiority **12** virtuousness **16** self-satisfaction **17** self-righteousness

smut 4 dirt, porn, soot **5** filth, grime **6** smudge **9** obscenity, scatology **11** pornography

smutty 4 lewd 5 dirty, grimy, sooty 6 filthy, soiled, vulgar 7 obscene 8 indecent 12 pornographic

Smyrna *see* 6 Myrrha

Smythe, Reginald
creator/artist of: 8 Andy Capp

snack 3 eat, tea 4 bite, nosh 5 munch 6 nibble, tidbit 7 take tea 8 lap lunch, munchies, nibbles, pick-me-up, snackies 9 collation, crunchies, elevenses 10 finger food, light lunch 11 cassecroute, coffee break, light repast, refreshment

snag 3 bar, rip 4 grab, stub, tear 5 block, catch, hitch, stump 7 barrier 8 obstacle 9 hindrance 10 difficulty, impediment, projection, protrusion 11 encumbrance, obstruction 14 stumbling block

Snagsby
character in: 10 Bleak House
author: 7 Dickens

snail
French: 8 escargot

snake 5 sneak, viper 7 reptile, serpent, traitor 8 ophidian 9 reptilian
combining form: 4 ophi 5 ophio, ophis 6 herpes 7 herpeto
expert: 13 herpetologist
fear of: 13 herpetophobia
genus: 7 Ophidia
kind: 3 asp, boa, sea 4 file, habu, wart, whip 5 aboma, adder, cobra, coral, krait, mamba, tiger, viper 6 bongar, elapid, garter, gopher, python, taipan 7 rattler, sunbeam 8 anaconda, cerastes, moccasin, pit viper, ringhals 9 boomslang, colubrina, mole viper, puff adder 10 black mamba, bushmaster, copperhead, fer-de-lance, sidewinder 11 cottonmouth, diamond back, Gaboon viper, rattlesnake 12 slender blind 13 elephant-trunk, water moccasin 14 boa constrictor
shedding: 7 ecdysis 8 moulting
skin: 6 exuvia
snake killer: 8 mongoose

Snake *see* 8 Shoshone

snake, poisonous 9 Coactrice

Snake, the
nickname of: 10 Ken Stabler

Snake Pit, The
author: 12 Mary Jane Ward, Sigrid Undset

snap 3 nip, pop 4 bark, bite, grab, lock, yelp 5 break, catch, cinch, clasp, click, close, crack, growl, hasty, latch, quick, snarl, spell 6 breeze, period, secure, snatch, sudden 8 careless, fastener, fracture 9 impulsive 11 thoughtless

snapdragon 11 Antirrhinum
varieties: 4 wild 5 dwarf 6 common, garden, lesser 7 spurred 8 withered

snappish 4 edgy 5 cross, huffy, surly, testy 6 crabby, cranky, shirty, touchy 7 grouchy, huffish, peevish, waspish 8 captious, petulant 9 irascible, irritable, querulous 10 ill-humored, illnatured, out of sorts 11 hot-tempered 12 cantankerous 13 quick-tempered, short-tempered

snappy 4 fast, tony 5 hasty, quick, rapid, ritzy, sharp, smart, swank, swift, swish 6 classy, dapper, jaunty, speedy, spiffy 7 stylish 12 lickety-split

snare 3 net 4 bait, hook, lure, ruse, trap 5 catch, decoy, noose, seize, trick 6 entrap 7 capture, ensnare, pitfall 9 deception 12 entanglement

snarl 4 mat 4 bark, clog, kink, knot, mess, snap 5 chaos, growl, ravel, twist 6 hinder, impede, jumble, muddle, tangle 7 confuse, lash out 8 disorder, entangle 9 confusion

snatch 3 bit, nab 4 grab, part, pull, take 5 catch, grasp, piece, pluck, seize, wrest 7 snippet 8 fragment

Snead, Sam
nickname: 12 Slammin' Sammy
sport: 4 golf
won: 7 Masters

sneak 3 sly 4 slip 5 creep, knave, rogue, scamp, steal 6 lurker, rascal, secret, spirit 7 bounder, furtive, skulker, slinker, smuggle 8 scalawag, surprise 9 miscreant, scoundrel, secretive, underhand 11 rapscallion 13 surreptitious

sneak attack 4 raid 6 ambush 7 assault 9 ambuscade, incursion

sneak off 5 elope 6 decamp 7 abscond 9 steal away

sneaky 3 sly 4 mean 7 devious, furtive, vicious 9 malicious, secretive, underhand 10 traitorous 11 treacherous

sneer 4 jeer, leer, mock 5 scoff, scorn, smirk 6 deride, rebuff 7 disdain 8 belittle, ridicule

sneer at 5 knock, scorn 6 deride, malign 7 disdain, put down, run down 8 pooh-pooh 16 cast aspersions on

Sneerwell, Lady
character in: 19 The School for Scandal
author: 8 Sheridan

snicker 5 snort 6 cackle, giggle, simper, titter 7 snigger

snide 5 nasty 7 mocking 8 scoffing 9 malicious, sarcastic 11 insinuating 12 contemptuous

Snider, Edwin
nickname: 4 Duke
sport: 8 baseball
team: 7 Dodgers

sniff 4 jeer, mock, odor 5 aroma, scoff, smell, snort, snuff, whiff 6 snivel 7 disdain, sniffle, snuffle 9 disparage

snip 3 bit, bob, cut, lop 4 brat, clip, crop, punk, snap, trim 5 clack, click, piece, prune, scrap, shear, twerp 6 sample, shrimp, swatch 7 cutting 8 fragment

snippy 4 curt, rude 5 sassy, saucy, short 6 cheeky, snotty 7 brusque 8 flippant, impudent, insolent, snippety 11 ill-mannered, impertinent, smartalecky

snivel 3 cry 5 sniff, whine 6 boohoo 7 sniffle 8 complain

sniveler 6 coward, whiner 7 crybaby 10 complainer

snob 7 elitist 13 social climber

snobbish 4 vain 6 snooty, snotty 7 haughty, high-hat, stuck-up 8 arrogant, superior 10 disdainful 11 overbearing, patronizing, pretentious 13 condescending

snoop 3 pry 7 meddler, Paul Pry 8 busybody 10 Nosy Parker 12 eavesdropper

Snoopy 6 beagle
brother: 5 Spike
creator: 6 Schulz
friend: 9 Woodstock
master: 12 Charlie Brown

snooze 3 nap 4 doze 5 sleep 6 catnap, drowse, siesta 7 slumber 10 forty winks

Snopes family
characters in: 9 The Hamlet
members: 2 Ab 4 Flem, Mink 5 Isaac
author: 8 Faulkner

snort 4 blow, gasp, huff, jeer, pant, puff, rage 5 blast, grunt, scoff, sneer, storm

snout 3 neb 4 beak, bill, nose 5 snoot, spout 6 muzzle, nozzle 9 proboscis

Snow, C P (Charles Percy Snow, Lord Snow)
author of: 9 The New Men 10 Last Things, The Masters 14 A Coat of Varnish 16 Corridors of Power 20 Strangers and Brothers

snowfall 4 firn, neve 6 flurry 8 blizzard
Scottish: 6 onding

Snow Queen, The
author: 21 Hans Christian Andersen

Snows of Kilimanjaro, The
author: 15 Ernest Hemingway

snow-white 4 pure 5 snowy 9 lilywhite, pure white 11 white as snow

Snow White and the Seven Dwarfs
character: 3 Doc 5 Dopey, Happy, Queen 6 Grumpy, Sleepy, Sneezy, mirror 8 Bashful 14 Prince Charming

snowy 4 pure 5 white 7 nievous 8 pristine, spotless 9 blizzardy

snub 3 cut 5 blunt, check, scorn, short 6 ignore, rebuff, slight, stubby 7 disdain 9 retrousse 11 repudiation 12 cold shoulder 16 turn up one's nose at 19 give the cold shoulder

snuff 5 scent, smell, sniff, whiff 7 sniffle, snuffle

snuff out 5 crush **8** suppress **10** extinguish, put an end to

snug 4 cozy, neat, safe **5** close, tight **6** secure **7** compact **8** tranquil **9** sheltered, skin-tight **11** comfortable **12** close-fitting, tight-fitting **13** well-organized

snuggle 3 hug **4** nest **6** cuddle, curl up, enfold, nestle, nuzzle

so
 Latin: **3** sic

soak 3 wet **4** seep **5** bathe, enter, steep **6** absorb, drench, sink in, take in, take up **7** immerse, pervade **8** permeate, saturate **9** penetrate

soaked 5 soggy **6** sodden, soused **7** sopping **8** drenched **9** saturated **11** waterlogged, wringing wet

soak up 4 blot **6** absorb, take up **8** sponge up

soak up warmth 4 bask **11** warm oneself **12** toast oneself

Soames Forsyte
 character in: **14** The Forsyte Saga
 author: **10** Galsworthy

Soap
 character: **5** Major **6** Benson **9** Billy Tate **10** Eunice Tate **11** Chester Tate, Corrine Tate, Danny Dallas, Jessica Tate, Jodie Dallas **12** Burt Campbell **18** Mary Dallas Campbell
 cast: **7** Ted Wass **9** Jimmy Baio **11** Diana Canova **12** Billy Crystal, Cathryn Damon, Jennifer Salt, Robert Mandan **14** Arthur Peterson **15** Richard Mulligan, Robert Guillaume **16** Katherine Helmond

soar 3 fly **4** rise, wing **5** climb, float, glide, mount, tower **8** take wing

soave
 music: **6** gentle

sob 3 cry **4** howl, wail, weep **6** lament, plaint, snivel **7** blubber, whimper

so be it 4 amen **7** let it be **9** let it be so

sober 3 dry, sad **4** cool, drab, dull, grim, sane **5** grave, sound, staid **6** dreary, sedate, solemn, somber, steady **7** joyless, prudent, serious, subdued **8** moderate, not drunk, rational **9** judicious, realistic, sorrowful, temperate **10** abstemious **11** level-headed **13** dispassionate

So Big
 author: **10** Edna Ferber

sobriety 10 abstention, abstinence, continence, temperance **13** nonindulgence **14** abstemiousness

sobriquet 7 epithet, pet name **8** nickname **11** appellation

so-called
 French: **9** soi-disant

soccer
 athlete: **4** Pele **12** David Beckham
 players/team: **6** eleven
 position: **6** goalie **7** forward **8** full-

back, halfback **10** goalkeeper
 championship: **8** World Cup **11** European Cup, National Cup **13** Cup Winner's Cup
 violation: **5** hands **7** hacking, offside **11** obstructing
 gaining control of ball: **4** trap

sociable 6 social **7** affable, cordial **8** friendly, gracious, outgoing **9** agreeable, congenial, convivial **10** gregarious, neighborly **11** extroverted **13** companionable

social 2 in **5** smart **7** stylish **8** friendly, pleasant, sociable **9** agreeable **10** gregarious, neighborly **11** cooperative, fashionable **14** interdependent

Social Contract, The
 author: **19** Jean-Jacques Rousseau

social order
 goddess of: **4** Hour **5** Horae

society 4 body, club **5** elite, group **6** circle, gentry, league **7** mankind **8** alliance, humanity, nobility **9** community, humankind **10** blue bloods **11** aristocracy, association, high society, social order **12** organization **14** the four hundred **16** the general public

sociologist
 American: **4** Mead, Park, Ward **5** Coser, Gerth, Mills, Small, Wirth **6** Bendix, Cooley, Merton, Speier, Sumner, Thomas **7** Parsons, Sorokin **8** Eberhard **10** Lazarsfeld
 British: **4** Webb **8** Hobhouse, Mannheim **12** Carr-Saunders
 Danish: **6** Geiger
 French: **4** Aron **5** Comte **8** Durkheim, Gurvitch **9** Friedmann
 German: **5** Konig, Weber, Wiese **6** Simmel **9** Habermas, Luckmann **10** Dahrendorf, Horkheimer
 Hungarian: **6** Lukacs **8** Mannheim
 Israeli: **5** Buber **10** Eisenstadt
 Norwegian: **6** Aubert **7** Galtung
 Swedish: **8** Carlsson

sociopathic 9 alienated **10** antisocial, rebellious

sock 3 box, hit, sox **4** belt, blow, slap **5** punch, smack, smash **6** strike, wallop **7** clobber **8** knee sock **9** ankle sock **13** short stocking

Socrates
 born: **6** Athens
 taught using: **5** irony **6** method
 disciple: **5** Plato **8** Xenophon
 wife: **9** Xanthippe
 death potion: **7** hemlock

sod 4 soil, turf **5** divot, earth, grass, sward **10** greensward

soda 3 pop **4** base, cola **5** tonic **6** bicarb, sodium **7** barilla, seltzer **8** beverage, root beer **9** ginger ale, soft drink **11** bicarbonate **12** sarsaparilla
 ash: **6** alkali
 in faro: **9** first card
 maker: **4** jerk

sodden 4 dull **5** heavy, lumpy, mushy,

pasty, soggy, soppy **6** doughy, soaked **7** sopping **8** besotted, drenched, dripping, listless **9** saturated **10** wet through **14** expressionless

Soddy, Frederick
 field: **9** chemistry
 nationality: **7** British
 discovered: **8** isotopes
 worked with: **13** William Ramsay **16** Ernest Rutherford
 awarded: **10** Nobel Prize

sodium
 chemical symbol: **2** Na

Sodom
 destroyed with: **5** Admah **6** Zeboim **8** Gomorrah

sofa 5 couch, divan **6** canape, lounge, settee **8** love seat **9** davenport **12** chesterfield

Sofia
 Roman name: **12** Ulpia Serdica
 Byzantine name: **9** Triaditsa
 capital of: **8** Bulgaria
 landmark: **13** Buyuk Dzhamiya **16** Saint Sofia Church **17** Saint George Church **24** Alexander Nevsky Cathedral **32** Cyril and Methodius National Library

soft 4 easy, kind, mild, pale, weak **5** downy, faint, furry, muted, quiet, silky, sleek **6** feeble, gentle, hushed, pliant, satiny, shaded, silken, smooth, supple, tender **7** lenient, not hard, pitying, pliable, restful, subdued, velvety **8** delicate, not sharp, shadowed, tolerant, tranquil, twilight **9** malleable, not strong **10** harmonious **11** sentimental, sympathetic **12** easily molded, low intensity **13** compassionate, pleasantly low **16** easily penetrated **19** having a breathy sound **21** requiring little effort **25** incapable of great endurance

soften 5 lower **6** lessen, subdue, temper **7** cushion, mollify **8** make soft, mitigate, moderate, palliate, tone down, turn down **10** ameliorate, make softer

softhearted 4 kind, soft, warm **6** benign, gentle, humane, kindly, tender **8** generous **9** forgiving, indulgent **10** benevolent **11** considerate, kindhearted, sympathetic, warmhearted **13** compassionate, tenderhearted

softly 6 easily, gently, mildly, weakly **7** quietly

softness 8 mildness **9** downiness, silkiness **10** fluffiness, gentleness, smoothness, tenderness **11** tranquility **12** tranquillity

soft soap 7 blarney **8** cajolery, flattery **10** persuasion

sogginess 7 wetness **8** dampness **9** mushiness **10** soddenness

soggy 5 heavy, mushy, pasty, soppy **6** doughy, soaked, sodden **7** sopping **8** drenched, dripping **9** saturated

Soglow, Otto
creator/artist of: **13** The Little King

soi-disant 8 so-called **9** pretended **10** self-styled **18** calling oneself thus

soigne, soignee 4 chic, neat, tidy **5** sleek, smart **6** classy, modish **7** elegant **11** well-groomed

soil 4 dirt, foul, land, loam, ruin, soot, spot **5** dirty, earth, grime, humus, muddy, smear, stain, sully **6** debase, defile, ground, region, smudge **7** blacken, country, tarnish **8** disgrace

soiled 5 dirty, grimy, messy **6** filthy, grubby, smudgy **7** muddied, sullied, unclean **8** begrimed, unwashed **9** besmeared

soiree 4 ball, prom **5** dance, party **9** cotillion, promenade

sojourn 4 stay **5** abide, pause, visit **6** stay at **7** holiday, layover **8** stay over, stopover, vacation

sojourner 6 lodger, tenant **7** pilgrim, tourist, visitor **8** traveler **9** transient, weekender **10** daytripper, vacationer

Sol
origin: **5** Roman
form: **3** god
personifies: **3** sun
corresponds to: **6** Helios **7** Mithras **8** Hyperion

sola, solus 5 alone **9** by oneself

solace 4 calm **5** cheer **6** soothe **7** assuage, comfort, console **8** reassure **10** help in need **11** consolation, reassurance **18** relief in affliction

Solaris
author: **12** Stanislaw Lem
director: **16** Steven Soderbergh
cast: **10** Viola Davis (Gordon) **11** Ulrich Tukur (Gibarian) **12** Jeremy Davies (Snow) **13** George Clooney (Chris Kelvin) **16** Natascha McElhone (Rheya)

solder 4 fuse, join, weld **5** braze, stick

soldier 2 GI **3** PFC **5** GI Joe, major **6** worker, zealot **7** captain, colonel, dogface, general, private, servant, trooper, veteran, warrior **8** corporal, follower, partisan, sergeant **10** lieutenant, serviceman, specialist **11** enlisted man, military man **14** militant leader **16** brigadier general

Soldier of Orange
director: **13** Paul Verhoeven
based on novel by: **13** Erik Hazelhoff
cast: **10** Peter Faber **11** Derek De Lint, Eddy Habbema, Rutger Hauer **12** Jeroen Krabbe **15** Susan Penhaligon
setting: **14** The Netherlands

soldiery 4 army **6** legion, troops **7** legions, militia **8** military, soldiers **11** fighting men

sole 4 lone, only **6** single **8** solitary **9** exclusive

solely 5 alone **6** merely, purely, singly **8** uniquely **11** exclusively **14** single-handedly

solemn 4 dark, drab, grim, holy **5** grave, sober, staid **6** formal, gloomy, sacred, sedate, somber **7** earnest, serious, sincere **8** absolute **9** dignified, religious, spiritual, steadfast **10** ceremonial, depressing, determined **11** ceremonious **12** awe-inspiring

solemnity 3 awe **7** dignity **8** ceremony **9** formality, reverence **11** seriousness **12** circumstance

solemnize 4 mark **5** honor **6** hallow **7** observe **9** celebrate **10** consecrate **11** commemorate

solicit 3 ask **4** seek **5** plead **7** entreat, request **9** appeal for, importune

solicitation 6 appeal **7** request **8** entreaty **11** importuning

solicitor 6 beggar, lawyer **7** counsel **8** salesman **10** supplicant

solicitous 4 avid, keen **5** eager **6** ardent, intent **7** anxious, intense, longing, mindful, zealous **8** desirous **9** attentive, concerned, regardful **10** thoughtful **12** enthusiastic

solicitude 4 care, zeal **5** worry **7** anxiety, avidity, concern **9** attention **10** enthusiasm, inquietude, uneasiness **11** disquietude, fearfulness, overconcern **12** apprehension

solid 4 firm, hard, pure, real **5** dense, massy, sober, sound, tough **6** rugged, stable, steady, strong, sturdy **7** durable, genuine, lasting, unmixed **8** complete, concrete, constant, rational, reliable, sensible, tangible, thorough, unbroken **9** not hollow, unalloyed, unanimous, undivided, well-built **10** continuous, dependable, solidified **11** impermeable, levelheaded, substantial, trustworthy **12** impenetrable **13** uninterrupted **15** well-constructed

solidarity 5 union, unity **7** harmony **9** closeness **11** cooperation, unification

solidify 3 fix, gel, set **4** cake, jell **6** cement, harden **7** congeal, stiffen, thicken **9** coagulate **11** crystallize **12** agglomerate

soliloquy 9 monologue **10** solo speech

Solinus
character in: **17** The Comedy of Errors
author: **11** Shakespeare

solitariness 8 solitude **9** aloneness, seclusion **13** reclusiveness

solitary 4 lone **6** hidden, lonely, remote, single **8** desolate, isolated, lonesome, secluded **9** concealed **10** cloistered **11** out-of-the-way, uninhabited **13** companionless

solitude 9 aloneness, isolation, seclusion, wasteland **10** desolation, loneliness, remoteness, wilderness

solo 5 alone **8** solitary **9** by oneself **10** unattended **12** singlehanded **13** unaccompanied
operatic: **4** aria

solo dance
ballet: **7** pas seul

Solomon
father: **5** David
mother: **9** Bathsheba
wife: **6** Naamah
son: **8** Rehoboam
brother: **5** Amnon **7** Absalom, Chileab **8** Adonijah
sister: **5** Tamar
visitor: **5** Sheba
wrote: **8** Proverbs **12** Ecclesiastes **13** Song of Solomon
built: **6** temple

Solomon Islands
capital/largest city: **7** Honiara
others: **4** Auki, Bina, Gizo, Luti **5** Kieta, Munda **6** Tulagi **7** Yandina **8** Kira Kira **9** Tangarare **10** Sasamungga
head of state: **14** British monarch **15** governor-general
member of: **14** Spearhead Group
monetary unit: **4** cent **6** dollar
island: **4** Buka, Gizo, Savo **5** Ndeni, Ulawa **6** Tulagi **7** Malaita, Rennell, Solomon, Vangunu **8** Choiseul, Sikaiana, Vanikoro **9** Santa Cruz **10** New Georgia, Ontong Java **11** Guadalcanal, Santa Isabel **12** Bougainville, San Cristobal
mountain: **5** Balbi
highest point: **11** Popomanasiu
ocean: **7** Pacific
physical feature:
gulf: **4** Huon, Kula
sound: **10** New Georgia
strait: **13** Indispensable
people: **7** Chinese **8** European **10** Melanesian, Polynesian
explorer: **14** Mendana de Neyra
leader: **8** Mamaloni **9** Kenilorea
language: **7** English **13** Pidgin English **16** Melanesian pidgin
religion: **8** Anglican **13** Roman Catholic

so long
Spanish: **12** hasta la vista

solution 3 key **5** blend **6** answer, cipher **7** mixture, solving **8** emulsion **9** resolving **10** resolution, suspension, unraveling **11** explanation

solve 7 resolve, unravel, work out **8** decipher, unriddle, untangle **9** figure out **10** find the key **13** find the answer

solvent 7 diluent, soluble **9** dilutable **10** dissoluble, dissolvent **11** dissolvable **16** financially sound

Solymi
origin: **9** Asia Minor
occupation: **8** warriors

Solzhenitsyn, Aleksandr
author of: **13** The Cancer Ward **14** The First Circle **19** The Gulag Archi-

pelago **22** August Nineteen-Fourteen
31 One Day in the Life of Ivan Denisovich

Somalia
   other name: 4 Punt **10** Somaliland
   12 Horn of Africa
   capital/largest city: 9 Mogadishu **10**
   Mogadiscio
   others: 5 Burao, Merca **6** Mereka **7**
   Berbera, Galkayu, Kismayu **8** Belet
   Uen, Hargeisa **9** Chisimaio
   division: 6 Hawiya **9** Mijirtein **10**
   Midjirtein
      colonial: 17 British Somaliland,
      Italian Somaliland
   measure: 3 top **4** caba **5** chela, darat,
   tabla **6** cubito **8** parsalah
   monetary unit: 4 besa **6** somalo **8**
   shilling **9** centesimi
   weight: 8 parsalah
   mountain: 5 Guban **11** Migiurtinia,
   Ogo Highland
   highest point: 7 Surud Ad
   river: 4 Juba **5** Daror, Nogal **9** Nug-
   aaleed **11** Webi Shebeli **13** Webi
   Shabeelle
   sea: 6 Indian
   physical feature:
      bay: 5 Negro
      cape: 9 Guardafui
      desert: 4 Aror
      gulf: 4 Aden
      plateau: 3 Ogo **4** Haud
   people: 3 Sab **4** Asha **5** Galla **6**
   Hawiya, Isbaak, Somali **7** Danakil,
   Hamitic, Marehan, Samaale, Shuhali
   8 Rahanwin
      leader: 9 Siad Barre **12** Ali Sher-
      marke
   language: 6 Arabic, Somali **7** English,
   Italian
   religion: 5 Islam
   feature:
      boat: 4 dhow
      cloth: 7 banadir
      clothing: 4 futa, toga **6** sarong
      tree: 6 acacia, baobab **7** incense

Somaliland *see* **7** Somalia

somber 4 dark, drab, gray, grim **5**
grave, sober **6** dreary, gloomy, solemn
7 serious **8** funereal, mournful, toneless **9** cheerless **10** depressing, melancholy

Some Like It Hot
   director: 11 Billy Wilder
   cast: 9 Joe E Brown, Pat O'Brien **10**
   George Raft, Jack Lemmon, Tony
   Curtis **13** Marilyn Monroe

Somers Islands *see* **7** Bermuda

something essential
   Latin: 10 sine qua non

something for something
   Latin: 10 quid pro quo

Something Happened
   author: 12 Joseph Heller

Something's Gotta Give
   director: 11 Nancy Meyers

cast: 10 Amanda Peet (Marin), Jon
Favreau (Leo) **11** Diane Keaton (Er-
ica Barry), Keanu Reeves (Julian
Mercer) **13** Jack Nicholson (Harry
Sanborn) **16** Frances McDormand
(Zoe Barry) **17** Paul Michael Glaser
(Dave)

sometime 4 late, once **5** later **6** former **7** quondam **8** formerly, previous
9 erstwhile **10** occasional

sometimes 7 at times **10** now and
then, on occasion **12** occasionally,
once in a while

somewhat 6 fairly, kind of, partly,
sort of **8** passably **9** tolerably **10** moderately, more or less, reasonably **13**
approximately

somnolent 4 dozy, dull **5** dopey **6**
drowsy, groggy, sleepy, torpid **7** languid, nodding, out of it, yawning **8**
hypnotic, sluggish **9** half-awake, lethargic, soporific **10** half-asleep,
slumberous **11** heavy-lidded **13** semi-
conscious

Somnus
   origin: 5 Roman
   god of: 5 sleep
   mother: 3 Nyx
   brother: 4 Mors
   corresponds to: 6 Hypnos, Hypnus

son
   French: 4 fils

sone
   unit of: 8 loudness

song 4 call, poem, tune **5** ditty, lyric,
verse **6** ballad, melody, number, piping
   French: 7 chanson

songbird 4 chat, lark, wren **5** robin,
veery, vireo **6** canary, singer, thrush
7 warbler **11** nightingale

Song of Bernadette, The
   author: 11 Franz Werfel
   character: 13 Dean Peyramale **18** Sister Marie Therese **19** Bernadette Sou-
   birous
   director: 9 Henry King
   cast: 8 Lee J Cobb **12** Vincent Price,
   William Eythe **13** Jennifer Jones **15**
   Charles Bickford
   Oscar for: 7 actress (Jones)

Song of Hiawatha *see* **8** Hiawatha

Song of Roland, The *see* **15** Chanson
de Roland

Song of Solomon
   author: 12 Toni Morrison

Song of Solomon
   bride: 9 Shulamite

Sonnets from the Portuguese
   author: 24 Elizabeth Barrett Browning

Sonny
   nickname of: 13 Charles Liston

sonorous 4 deep, rich **6** florid **7** ringing, vibrant **8** eloquent, resonant **9**
full-toned, grandiose **10** flamboyant,

impressive, resounding **13** reverberating

Sons and Lovers
   author: 10 D H Lawrence
   character: 10 Clara Dawes **11** Baxter
   Dawes **13** Miriam Leivers
      Morel family: 4 Paul **5** Annie **6** Ar-
      thur, Walter **7** William **8** Gertrude

Sons of thunder 4 John **5** James
   also: 9 Boanerges

Soo
   canals at: 13 Sault Ste. Marie

soon 4 anon **6** pronto **7** betimes, by
and by, early on, ere long, quickly,
shortly **8** directly **9** any minute, forthwith, instantly, presently, right away
10 before long **12** without delay **14** in
a little while

sooner 6 before, in time **7** earlier **9** before now, in advance **10** beforehand
11 ahead of time

sooner or later 6 one day **7** finally,
someday **8** in the end, sometime **10**
eventually, ultimately **17** in the course
of time, sometime or another

Sooner State
   nickname of: 8 Oklahoma

soot 4 dirt, smut **5** crock, grime **6** carbon, smudge, smutch **7** residue **9**
lampblack

soothe 4 calm, ease **6** lessen, pacify **7**
appease, comfort, console, mollify,
placate, relieve **8** mitigate, moderate **9**
alleviate **11** tranquilize

soothing 4 mild **7** calming, healing,
salving **9** appeasing, consoling, emollient, pacifying, placating **10** comforting, mitigating **13** tranquilizing

soothsayer 4 seer **5** sibyl **7** diviner,
prophet **10** forecaster **13** fortune-teller

soothsaying 6 augury **8** divining,
prophecy **10** divination, predicting,
prediction **11** foretelling, prophesying

sooty 4 inky **5** black, dingy, dirty,
grimy **6** smudgy, smutty **9** coal-black

sop 3 dip, tip, wet **4** dunk, soak **5**
bribe **6** absorb, drench, payoff, payola, take up **8** gratuity, saturate **9**
baksheesh, become wet, hush money

Sophie's Choice
   author: 13 William Styron

Sophisms
   author: 9 Aristotle

sophisticate 8 civilize **11** cosmopolite,
disillusion, make worldly **12** cosmopolitan

sophisticated 6 subtle **7** complex,
studied, worldly **8** advanced, cultured,
highbrow, mannered, precious, seasoned **9** difficult **10** artificial, cultivated **11** complicated, experienced,
worldly-wise **12** cosmopolitan, intellectual

sophistry 6 deceit **7** fallacy **8** subtlety
9 casuistry, chicanery, deception **10**
distortion **12** speciousness

Sophocles
author of: **4** Ajax **7** Electra, Oedipus **8** Antigone **10** Oedipus Rex, Trachiniae **11** Philoctetes **16** Oedipus at Colonus **18** The Trachinian Women

sophomoric 6 callow **7** foolish, puerile **8** childish, immature, juvenile **9** infantile **10** adolescent **12** schoolboyish

soporific 4 lazy **5** balmy, heavy **6** drowsy, sleepy **8** hypnotic, sedative, sluggish **9** lethargic, somnolent **10** slumberous **11** somniferous **12** sleep-inducer **13** sleep-inducing

soppiness 4 corn, mush **5** slush **6** bathos **7** wetness **9** mushiness **10** slushiness **11** mawkishness **14** sentimentalism, sentimentality

sopping 3 wet **5** soggy, soppy **6** soaked, sodden **8** drenched, dripping **9** saturated **10** bedraggled, soaking wet

Sopranos, The
network: **3** HBO
creator: **10** David Chase
cast: **9** Edie Falco (Carmela Soprano) **10** Robert Iler (A J Soprano), Tony Sirico (Paulie "Walnuts" Gualtieri) **12** Aida Turturro (Janice Soprano), Steve Buscemi (Tony Blundetto) **13** Joe Pantoliano (Ralph Cifaretto), Nancy Marchand (Livia Soprano) **14** Lorraine Bracco (Jennifer Melfi), Steven Van Zandt (Silvio Dante), Vincent Pastore ("Big Pussy" Bonpensiero) **15** Dominic Chianese (Corrado "Uncle Junior" Soprano), James Gandolfini (Tony Soprano), Jamie-Lynn Sigler (Meadow Soprano), John Ventimiglia (Artie Bucco) **16** Michael Imperioli (Christopher Moltisanti)

sorcerer 5 witch **6** shaman, wizard **7** warlock **8** magician **11** medicine man

sorceress 5 siren, witch **11** enchantress

sorcery 8 witchery, wizardry **9** shamanism **10** black magic, necromancy, witchcraft **11** enchantment

sordid 3 low **4** base, rank, vile **5** dirty, gross **6** filthy, putrid, rotten, vulgar, wicked **7** corrupt, ignoble, squalid, unclean **8** degraded, depraved **9** debauched **12** disreputable

sordino, con
music: **11** with the mute

sore 4 hurt **5** acute, angry, great, harsh, irked, sharp, upset, wound **6** aching, pained, severe, tender **7** bruised, extreme, grieved, hurting, painful **8** agonized, critical, grievous, smarting, sorespot, wounding **9** agonizing, desperate, indignant, irritated, sensitive **10** distressed, unbearable **11** distressing **12** inflammation

Sorel, Julien
character in: **17** The Red and the Black
author: **8** Stendhal

sorely 5 badly **7** greatly **8** severely **9** extremely **10** critically **11** desperately

soreness 4 ache, pain **10** discomfort, irritation, tenderness

sorrel 3 bay **4** herb, roan, weed **5** brown, plant, Rumex **8** chestnut **12** reddish-brown
varieties: **3** red **4** dock, tree, wood **5** lady's, sheep **6** common, French, garden, Indian **7** redwood **8** Jamaican, mountain **10** violet wood **12** European wood

sorrow 3 woe **4** loss, weep **5** be sad, mourn, trial **6** grieve, lament **7** despair, sadness, travail, trouble **8** disaster, hardship **10** affliction, bad fortune, misfortune **11** catastrophe, unhappiness
French: **9** tristesse

sorrowful 3 sad **6** woeful **7** unhappy **8** affected, grieving, mournful **9** lamenting

Sorrows of Young Werther, The
author: **6** Goethe
character: **6** Albert **9** Charlotte (Lotte)

sorry 3 sad **6** woeful **7** grieved, pitiful, unhappy **8** contrite, pathetic, pitiable, wretched **9** miserable, regretful, repentant, sorrowful **10** deplorable, melancholy, remorseful, ridiculous **11** crestfallen **13** brokenhearted

sort 4 kind, list, make, sift, type **5** brand, class, grade, group, index, order **6** divide, person **7** arrange, catalog, species, variety **8** classify, organize, separate, take from **9** segregate **10** categorize, individual **11** systematize **14** classification

sortie 4 rush **5** onset **6** attack, charge **7** assault **8** storming **9** onslaught

sortilege 6 augury **7** auspice, sorcery **10** divination, witchcraft

sorting 8 dividing, grouping **9** arranging **10** organizing **11** classifying **12** categorizing

so-so 4 blah, fair **5** ho-hum **6** casual, modest **7** average, humdrum **8** adequate, bearable, mediocre, middling, ordinary, passable **9** tolerable **10** second-rate **11** commonplace, indifferent **12** run-of-the-mill **13** unexceptional **15** undistinguished

sot 4 lush, soak **5** drunk, rummy, souse, toper **8** drunkard, rumhound **9** alcoholic, inebriate **11** dipsomaniac

Soter
epithet of: **4** Zeus
means: **6** savior

Sothern, Ann
real name: **13** Harriette Lake
born: **12** Valley City ND
husband: **10** Roger Pryor **14** Robert Sterling
roles: **6** Maisie **8** Cry Havoc **10** Lady Be Good **16** Private Secretary **19** A Letter to Three Wives

so throughout
Latin: **9** sic passim

sotto voce
music: **11** in a low voice **13** in an undertone, under the voice

sought 6 hunted **7** pursued, quested **9** attempted, looked for **10** endeavored

soul 5 being, force **6** person, spirit **7** essence **8** creature, vitality **9** inner core **10** embodiment, individual, vital force **11** inspiration **12** quintessence

soul-searching 10 discontent, insecurity, uneasiness **15** dissatisfaction, self-questioning

soul-stirring 7 rousing **8** electric, exciting, stirring **9** inspiring, thrilling **11** galvanizing

sound 3 fit **4** deep, firm, good, seem, tone, wise **5** drift, hardy, noise, range, sober, solid, tenor, utter, voice **6** intact, robust, severe, signal, stable, strong, sturdy **7** durable, earshot, healthy, lasting, perfect, solvent **8** announce, rational, reliable, sensible, thorough, unmarred **9** come off as, competent, enunciate, pronounce, undamaged, well-built **10** articulate, dependable, make a noise, reasonable, suggestion, untroubled **11** implication, penetrating, responsible, substantial **13** thoroughgoing **15** hearing distance, well-constructed

Sound and the Fury, The
author: **15** William Faulkner
character: **6** Dilsey **17** Sydney Herbert Head
Compson family: **5** Jason **7** Candace (Caddy), Quentin **8** Benjamin (Benjy)

Sounder
director: **10** Martin Ritt
cast: **8** Taj Mahal **10** Kevin Hooks **11** Cicely Tyson **12** Paul Winfield **13** Carmen Mathews
sequel: **13** Sounder Part II

sound measure 7 decibel

sound mind in a sound body
Latin: **21** mens sana in corpore sano

soundness of mind 6 reason, sanity **9** normality **12** mental health

Sound of Music, The
director: **10** Robert Wise
cast: **9** Peggy Wood **12** Julie Andrews (Maria Von Trapp) **13** Eleanor Parker **18** Christopher Plummer
setting: **7** Austria
score: **21** Rodgers and Hammerstein
Oscar for: **7** picture **8** director
song: **5** Maria **6** Do-Re-Mi **9** Edelweiss **16** My Favorite Things

sound out 7 ask **8** approach **15** make a proposal to, make overtures to, put out feelers to

soup

clear: 5 broth **8** bouillon, consomme
server: 6 tureen
spoon: 5 ladle
thick: 5 cream, gumbo **6** bisque, potage **7** chowder **10** minestrone

soupcon 3 bit, dab, jot, tad **4** clue, dash, drop, hint **5** pinch, shade, taint, taste, tinge, touch, trace, whiff **6** little, trifle **7** smidgen, smidgin, vestige **8** smidgeon **9** little bit, suspicion **10** smattering, sprinkling, suggestion **12** slight amount

Soupy Sales

character: 9 White Fang **10** Black Tooth **13** Herman the Flea, Hippy the Hippo, Pookie the Lion, Willie the Worm **14** Marilyn Monwolf

sour 3 bad **4** acid, dour, keen, tart, turn **5** nasty, sharp, spoil, surly, tangy, testy **6** crabby, cranky, curdle, rancid, sullen, turned **7** acerbic, bilious, crabbed, curdled, ferment, grouchy, peevish, spoiled, turn off, uncivil, waspish **8** alienate, choleric, embitter, jaundice, petulant, unsavory, vinegary **9** acidulous, clabbered, fermented, irritable, jaundiced, offensive, prejudice, repugnant **10** astringent, ill-dispose, ill-humored, unpleasant **11** bad-tempered, distasteful, ill-tempered **12** disagreeable

sourball 4 crab **5** crank, grump **6** grouch **9** hard candy **10** curmudgeon

source 4 font, head, root **5** basis, cause, fount **6** author, father, origin, rising, spring **8** begetter, fountain **9** authority, beginning, headwater **10** antecedent, derivation, foundation, prime mover, wellspring

source and origin

Latin: 11 fons et origo

Sourdough State

nickname of: 6 Alaska

sourness 7 acidity, vinegar **8** acerbity, acrimony, ill humor, pungency, tartness **9** acridness, greenness **10** bitterness

sourpuss 4 bear, crab **5** crank, grump **6** griper, grouch **7** grouser, killjoy **8** grumbler, sorehead **10** bellyacher, complainer, crosspatch, curmudgeon, spoilsport

Sousa, John Philip

born: 12 Washington DC
composer of: 9 El Capitan **14** Washington Post **25** The Stars and Stripes Forever

souse 3 dip, sot **4** duck, dunk, lush, soak **5** douse, drunk, rummy, steep, toper **6** barfly, boozer, drench, pickle **7** immerse, tippler **8** drunkard, inundate, marinate, saturate, submerge **9** alcoholic, inebriate **11** dipsomaniac

soused 5 drunk **6** dunked, potted, zapped, zonked **7** pickled, sloshed, smashed **8** immersed **9** plastered **10**

inebriated **11** intoxicated **17** under the influence **20** three sheets to the wind

South Africa

capital: 8 Cape Town, Pretoria **12** Bloemfontein
largest city: 12 Johannesburg
others: 3 Aus **4** Mara, Stad **6** Benoni, Bononi, Braker, Durban, Garies, Severn, Soweto, Umtata, Untata **7** Brakpan, Kokstad **8** Kaapstad, Mafeking, Modjadji **9** Germiston, Kimberley **10** East London, Oudtshoorn **11** Krugersdorp, Vereeniging **13** Port Elizabeth **16** Pietermaritzburg
school: 5 Natal **8** Capetown **13** Witwatersrand **15** Orange Free State
division: 5 Natal **8** Backveld **9** Transvaal **10** Basutoland **12** Cape Province **14** Cape of Good Hope **15** Orange Free State
  independent homelands: 5 Venda **6** Ciskei **8** Transkei **10** bantustans **14** Bophuthatswana
goverment:
  legislature: 4 Raad
measure: 4 vara
monetary unit: 4 cent, pond, rand **5** pound **6** florin **7** daalder **9** kruge-rand
mountain: 3 Aux, Kop **5** Table **7** Kathkin **9** Stormberg **10** Devil's Peak, Sneeuwberg **11** Drakensberg **12** Giant's Castle **13** Witwatersrand **14** Mont-aux-Sources **15** Great Escarpment
highest point: 8 Injasuti
river: 3 Hex **4** Vaal **5** Nosob **6** Modder, Molopo, Orange, Tugela **7** Caledon, Kurumam, Limpopo **8** Olifants **9** Crocodile, Great Fish
ocean: 6 Indian **8** Atlantic
physical feature:
  bay: 5 Algoa, False, Table **6** Mossel, Walvis **7** Walfish **8** Richard's, Saldanha **11** Saint Helena
  cape: 7 Agulhas **8** Good Hope
  current: 8 Benguela
  desert: 5 Namib **8** Kalahari
  plateau: 6 Karroo
  region: 8 Highveld, Zululand **9** Kaffraria **11** Great Karroo **12** Little Karroo
people: 3 San **4** Boer, Yosa, Zulu **5** Asian, Bantu, Namas, Nguni, Pondo, Sotho, Swazi, Tembu, Venda, Xhosa **6** Damara, Kaffir **7** African, British, Bushmen, English, Swahili **8** Bechuana, Khoikhoi **9** Afrikaner, Hottentot
  author: 5 Paton **7** Luthuli **8** Gordimer
  civil rights advocate: 6 Gandhi
  explorer: 8 Riebeeck
  leader: 4 Biko, Tutu **5** Botha, Malan, Smuts, Tomba **6** Kruger, Rhodes **7** de Klerk, Hertzog, Mandela, Vorster **8** Verwoerd **9** Buthelezi, Pretorius
language: 4 Taal, Zulu **5** Bantu,

Hindi, Nguni, Sotho, Swazi, Tamil, Venda, Xhosa **6** Telegu, Thonga **7** English, Khoisan, Ndebele, Sesotho **8** Bujarati, Fanakalo **9** Afrikaans
religion: 5 Hindu, Islam **7** animism, Judaism **8** Anglican **9** Methodist **12** Episcopalian, Presbyterian **13** Dutch Reformed, Roman Catholic
place:
  Cecil Rhodes' estate: 11 Groote Shuur
  game reserve: 5 Mkuze **6** Kruger **8** Hluhluwe
  monument: 11 Voortrekker
feature:
  bird: 4 taha
  bride price: 6 lobolo
  flower: 5 coral **6** clivia, protea **7** cowslip, fuchsia **9** phygelius **10** lachenalia
  oganization: 3 ANC **7** Inkatha **23** African National Congress
  segregation: 9 apartheid
  tree: 7 assagai **9** jacaranda
food:
  corn: 6 mealie
  drink: 9 sundowner
  meat: 7 biltong **8** sosaties **9** boerewors

South America

bird: 5 macaw **7** seriema, tinamou **8** caracara
cape: 4 Horn
country: 4 Peru **5** Chile **6** Brazil, Guyana **7** Bolivia, Ecuador, Surinam, Uruguay **8** Colombia, Paraguay **9** Argentina, Venezuela **12** French Guiana
desert: 7 Atacama
explorer: 16 Francisco Pizarro **18** Pedro Alvares Cabral
hero: 12 Simon Bolivar **15** Jose de San Martin **16** Bernardo O'Higgins **18** Antonio Jose de Sucre
highest mountain: 9 Aconcagua
islands: 8 Falkland **9** Galapagos
lake: 8 Titicaca **9** Maracaibo
mountain range: 5 Andes
native: 2 Ge **3** Ona **4** Inca **5** Carib, Mayan **7** Quechua **10** Araucanian
plain: 5 llano, pampa
region: 9 Patagonia
river: 3 Apa **5** Plata **6** Amazon **7** Orinoco

South Carolina

abbreviation: 2 SC
nickname: 7 Calinky **8** Palmetto
capital/largest city: 8 Columbia
others: 5 Aiken, Greer, Union **6** Belton, Camden, Cheraw, Conway, Dillon, Seneca, Sumter **7** Bamberg, Laurens, Manning **8** Beaufort, Florence, Newberry, Rock Hill, Walhalla **9** Greenwood **10** Charleston, Greenville, Orangeburg **11** Spartanburg
college: 5 Allen, Coker **6** Furman, Lander **7** Claffin, Clemson, Erskine, Wofford **8** Benedict, Bob Jones, Co-

lumbia, Winthrop **13** Francis Marion **15** Citadel Military

explorer: 6 Ayllon, Ribaut

feature:
  beach: 6 Myrtle
  dam: 6 Saluda
  fort: 6 Sumter
  gardens: 7 Cypress

tribe: 5 Pedee, Sewee **6** Cusabo, Santee, Waxhaw, Yamasi **7** Catawba, Shawnee, Sugeree, Wateree **8** Congaree

people: 11 James Byrnes **12** Althea Gibson, John C Calhoun **13** Bernard Baruch, Francis Marion **14** Dizzy Gillespie

island: 3 Sea **6** Parris **10** Hilton Head

lake: 6 Marion, Murray **7** Catawba, Wateree **8** Hartwell, Moultrie **9** Clark Hill

land rank: 8 fortieth

mountain: 5 Kings **6** Little **9** Blue Ridge, Sassafras

physical feature:
  bay: 8 Carolina
  plateau: 8 Piedmont

president: 13 Andrew Jackson

river: 5 Broad **6** Edisto, Pee Dee, Saluda, Santee **7** Ashepoo **8** Savannah

state admission: 6 eighth

state bird: 12 Carolina wren

state flower: 13 yellow jasmine **17** Carolina jessamine

state motto: 18 While I Breathe I Hope **26** Prepared in Mind and Resources

state song: 8 Carolina

state tree: 8 palmetto

South Dakota

abbreviation: 2 SD **4** S Dak

nickname: 6 Coyote **8** Blizzard, Sunshine

capital: 6 Pierre

largest city: 10 Sioux Falls

others: 4 Lead, Leap **5** Huron **6** Custer, Eureka, Lemmon, Miller, Winner **7** Sturgis, Webster, Yankton **8** Aberdeen, Deadwood, Sisseton **9** Brookings, Rapid City **10** Vermillion

college: 5 Huron **7** Yankton **9** Augustana **10** Mount Marty, Sioux Falls **14** Dakota Wesleyan

explorer: 8 Varennes **13** Lewis and Clark

feature: 8 Deadwood
  battlefield: 11 Wounded Knee
  dam: 4 Oahe
  mine: 9 Homestake
  monument: 13 Mount Rushmore
  national park: 8 Badlands, Wind Cave

tribe: 5 Brule, Sioux **6** Dakota, Sutaio **8** Cheyenne

people: 10 Crazy Horse **11** Sitting Bull **14** George McGovern, Hubert Humphrey

lake: 4 Oahe **5** Sharp **8** Big Stone,

Traverse **11** Francis Case **13** Lewis and Clark

land rank: 9 sixteenth

mountain: 4 Bear **5** Sheep, Table **6** Crook's, Moreau
  highest point: 6 Harney
  hills: 5 Black **7** Prairie

physical feature:
  butte: 7 Thunder **9** Deer's Ears **10** Castle Rock
  cave: 5 Jewel

river: 3 Bad **5** Grand, James, White **6** Moreau **8** Big Sioux, Cheyenne, Missouri **10** Vermillion

state admission: 8 fortieth **11** thirty-ninth (with North Dakota)

state bird: 18 ring-necked pheasant

state flower: 12 pasqueflower

state animal: 6 coyote

state motto: 21 Under God the People Rule

state song: 15 Hail South Dakota

state tree: 11 white spruce **16** Black Hills spruce

southeast wind

associated with: 5 Eurus **9** Volturnus

Southern Comfort

type: 7 liqueur

origin: 10 New Orleans

flavor: 5 peach

base: 7 bourbon

drink: 13 Scarlett O'Hara **15** Plantation Punch

with bourbon: 14 Blended Comfort

Southern Cross

constellation of: 4 Crux

Southern Crown

constellation of: 15 Corona Australis

Southerner, The

director: 10 Jean Renoir

cast: 10 Betty Field **11** Beu lah Bondi **12** Zachary Scott **13** Bunny Sunshine

Southern Fish

constellation of: 15 Piscis Austrinus

Southern Fly

constellation of: 5 Musca

Southern Rhodesia *see* **8** Zimbabwe

Southern Slavic

language family: 12 Indo-European

group: 11 Balto-Slavic

branch: 6 Slavic

language: 7 Slovene **9** Bulgarian **10** Macedonian **13** Serbo-Croatian

Southern Triangle

constellation of: 18 Triangulum Australe

South Korea *see* **5** Korea

South Park

network: 13 Comedy Central

creator: 9 Matt Stone **10** Trey Parker

cast: 9 Matt Stone (Kyle Broslofsky/Kenny McCormick/Jimbo Kearn/Tweek) **10** Isaac Hayes (Jerome "Chef" McElroy), Trey Parker (Stan Marsh/Eric Cartman/Randy Marsh/Timmy/Herbert Garrison/Philip Niles Argyle) **14** Mary Kay Bergman (Prin-

cipal Victoria/Nurse Gollum/Sharon Marsh)

catchphrase: 15 they (we, you, I) killed Kenny

South Vietnam *see* **7** Vietnam

South West Africa *see* **7** Namibia

south wind

associated with: 5 Notus

South Wind

author: 13 Norman Douglas

South Yemen *see* **5** Yemen

souvenir 4 scar **5** relic, token **6** emblem, memory, trophy **7** memento **8** keepsake, reminder **11** remembrance

sovereign 4 czar, free, king, lord, main, tsar **5** chief, major, prime, queen, regal, royal **6** kingly, potent, prince, ruling, utmost **7** emperor, highest, leading, monarch, queenly, supreme **8** absolute, autocrat, dominant, foremost, imperial, overlord, powerful, princely, reigning **9** chieftain, governing, paramount, potentate, prepotent, principal, uppermost **10** autonomous, self-ruling **11** all-powerful, crowned head, independent, monarchical **12** supreme ruler **13** self-directing, self-governing

sovereignty 4 sway **5** crown, power **6** throne **7** command, control, freedom, primacy, scepter **8** autonomy, dominion, home rule, kingship, lordship, self-rule **9** authority, supremacy **10** ascendancy **11** paramountcy **12** independence, jurisdiction, predominance **14** self-government **17** self-determination

Soviet Union *see* **6** Russia

sow 4 cast, seed **5** lodge, plant, set in, strew **6** inject, spread **7** implant, instill, scatter **8** disperse, sprinkle **9** broadcast, establish, introduce **11** disseminate

space 3 gap, sky **4** area, part, rank, room, seat, span, spot, term, time **5** berth, blank, break, chasm, ether, field, order, place, range, reach, scope, sweep, swing, width **6** hiatus, lacuna, line up, margin, period, set out, spread **7** arrange, breadth, compass, expanse, mark out, the void **8** distance, duration, infinity, interval, latitude, omission, organize, schedule, separate **9** amplitude, emptiness, keep apart, territory **10** distribute, interspace, interstice, outer space, separation, the heavens **11** nothingness, reservation, the universe **12** interruption, the firmament **13** accommodation

Space

author: 13 James Michener

spacecraft 4 ship **6** rocket **7** orbiter, shuttle **9** satellite **10** rocketship

space flight

agency: 3 ESA **4** NASA

US mission: 6 Apollo, Gemini, Skylab **7** Mercury

US rocket: 5 Atlas, Titan **6** Saturn **8** Redstone

US space shuttle: 8 Columbia **9** Discovery **10** Challenger

Soviet mission: 5 Soyuz **6** Salyut, Vostok **7** Voskhod

Soviet astronaut:
> **first man in space: 11** Yuri Gagarin

> **first woman in space: 19** Valentina Tereshkova

> **first space walk by: 13** Aleksei Leonov

American astronaut: 9 John Glenn, John Young, Sally Ride **11** Alan Shepard, Edward White, Edwin Aldrin, Frank Borman, James Lovell **12** Roger Chaffee, Wally (Walter) Schirra **13** Charles Conrad, L Gordon Cooper, Virgil (Gus) Grissom **14** Scott Carpenter, Thomas Stafford
> **first man on moon: 13** Neil Armstrong

> **oldest person in space: 9** John Glenn

> **Challenger seven: 12** Michael Smith, Ronald McNair **13** Francis Scobee, Gregory Jarvis, Judith Resnick **14** Ellison Onizuka **16** Christa McAuliffe

> **Columbia seven: 9** Llan Ramon **10** David Brown **11** Laurel Clark, Rick Husband **13** Kalpana Chawla, William McCool **15** Michael Anderson

Spacek, Sissy
real name: 19 Mary Elizabeth Spacek
born: 9 Quitman TX
roles: 6 Carrie **7** Missing **8** Badlands, The River **10** Raggedy Man **12** In the Bedroom **15** Tuck Everlasting **16** Crimes of the Heart, The Straight Story **18** Coal Miner's Daughter (Oscar)

spacious 4 vast, wide **5** ample, broad, large, roomy **7** immense, sizable **8** enormous **9** capacious, expansive, extensive, uncrowded **10** commodious

spaciousness 9 amplitude, largeness, roominess **13** capaciousness **14** commodiousness

Spade, Sam
character in: 16 The Maltese Falcon
author: 7 Hammett

Spain
other name: 6 Iberia **8** Hispania
capital/largest city: 6 Madrid
others: 4 Adra, Aspe, Baza, Elda, Horo, Irun, Jaen, Leon, Noya, Olot, Reus, Rota, Sama, Vigo **5** Baena, Bejar, Cadiz, Cieza, Cueta, Ecija, Eibar, Elche, Gades, Gadir, Gijon, Ibiza, Jerez, Jodar, Liego, Lorca, Oliva, Palma, Palos, Ronda, Siero, Ubeda, Xeres, Yecla, Zafra **6** Abdera, Aviles, Azuaga, Bilbao, Burgos, Coruna, Duenca, Gandia, Gerona, Getafe, Guadix, Hellin, Huelva, Huesca, Jativa, Lerida, Lucena, Malaga, Mataro, Merida, Murcia, Orense, Oviedo, Termel, Toledo, Utrera, Zamora **7** Almeria, Badajos, Cordoba, Daimiel, Granada, Jumilla, Linares, Logrono, Manresa, Segovia, Sevilla, Seville, Tarrasa, Vitoria **8** Alicante, Badalona, Figueras, Pamplona, Sabadell, Santiago, Torrente, Valencia, Zaragoza **9** Barcelona, Las Palmas, Saragossa

school: 6 Ciudad, Madrid
division: 4 Jaen, Leon, Lugo **5** Alava, Avila, Cadiz, Soria **6** Basque, Burgos, Coruna, Cuenca, Gerona, Huelva, Huesca, Lerida, Madrid, Malaga, Murcia, Orense, Oviedo, Teruel, Toledo, Zamora **7** Almeria, Caceres, Cordoba, Granada, Logrono, Navarra, Segovia, Sevilla, Vizcaya, Zadajoz **8** Albacete, Alicante, Baleares, Palencia, Valencia, Zaragoza **9** Catalonia
> **kingdom: 4** Leon **6** Aragon **7** Castile, Galicia, Granada, Navarre **8** Asturias **9** al-Andalus, Catalonia **12** Spanish March

government: 8 monarchy
> **legislature: 6** Cortes

head of state: 4 king
measure: 3 pie **4** codo, dedo, paso, vara **5** braza, cahiz, carga, legua, medio, palmo, sesma **6** cordel, cuarta, fanega, racion, yugada **7** azumbre, celemin, estadel, pulgada **8** fanegada

monetary unit: 3 cob **4** duro **5** dobla **6** cuarto, dinero, escudo, peseta **7** alfonso, centimo, pistole **8** doubloon

weight: 4 onza **5** frail, libra, marco, tomin **6** arroba, dinero, dracma **7** arienzo, quilate, quintal **8** tonelada

island: 5 Ceuta, Ibiza, Iviza, Palma **6** Canary, Gomera, Hierro **7** Alboran, Majorca, Melilla, Minorca **8** Balearic, Mallorca, Tagomago, Tenerife **9** Lanzarote **13** Fuerteventura

lake: 4 lago **8** Albufera
mountain: 4 Gata **5** Aneto, Rouch **6** Cuenca, Estats, Europa, Gredos, Magina, Morena, Nethou, Nevada, Teleno, Toledo **7** Alcaraz, Banuelo, Catalan, Cerredo, Demanda, Iberian, La Sagra, Moncayo, Perdido **8** Almanzor, Asturias, Galician, Maladeta, Monegros, Montseny, Penalara, Pyrenees **10** Albarracin, Cantabrian, Guadarrama, Torrecilla

highest point: 5 Teide **8** Mulhacen
river: 3 Sil, Ter **4** Cega, Ebro, Esla, Lima, Mino, Muga, Tajo, Ulla **5** Adaja, Cinca, Douro, Duero, Genil, Jalon, Jucar, Navia, Odiel, Riaza, Segie, Tagus, Tinto, Turia **6** Alagon, Aragon, Eresma, Huerva, Jarama, Orbigo, Segura, Torote **7** Almeria, Almonte, Arlanza, Barbate, Cabriel, Gallego, Henares, Mijares, Perales **8**

Duration, Guadiana **12** Guadalquivir
sea: 8 Atlantic, Balearic **13** Mediterranean
physical feature:
> **bay: 5** Bahia **6** Biscay
> **cape: 9** Trafalgar
> **gulf: 5** Cadiz **8** San Jorge, Valencia
> **peninsula: 7** Iberian
> **plateau: 6** meseta
> **strait: 9** Gibraltar

people: 5 Diego, Gente, Latin **6** Basque, Espana **7** Catalan, Espanol, Iberian **8** Galician, Gallegos, Maragato
> **architect: 5** Gaudi
> **artist: 4** Dali, Goya, Gris, Miro **6** Ribera **7** El Greco, Murillo, Picasso **8** Zurbaran **9** Velazquez
> **author: 4** Cela, Vega **5** Barea, Cueva, Rojas **6** Aleman, Alonso, Azorin, Baroja, Castro, Encina, Felipe, Ibanez, Miguel **7** Alarcon, Becquer, Cernuda, Ercilla, Gongora, Guillen, Jimenez, Machado, Unamuno **8** Montalvo, Zorrilla **9** Benavente, Cervantes, Goytisola **10** Aleixandre, Espronceda, Lope de Vega, Pardo Bazan **11** Garcia Lorca **12** Lopez de Ayala **13** Tirso de Molina **17** Calderon de la Barca
> **cellist: 6** Casals
> **composer: 7** Albeniz **8** Granados, Victoria **13** Manuel de Falla
> **converted Moslem: 7** morisco
> **dynasty: 7** Almohad, Umayyad **9** Almoravid
> **explorer: 6** Balboa, Cortes **7** Pizarro **8** Columbus
> **Jesuit founder: 14** Ignatius Loyola
> **king: 6** Pelayo, Philip, Ramiro, Sancho, Witiza **7** Alfonso, Charles **8** al-Mansur, Reccared, Roderick **9** Ferdinand, Leovigild **10** Juan Carlos **11** Abd al-Rahman, Reccosvinth
> **leader: 4** Prim **5** Godoy **6** Franco **7** Canovas **11** Calvo Sotelo **13** Primo de Rivera **14** Suarez-Gonzalez
> **queen: 8** Isabella **16** Elizabeth Farnese
> **ruler: 4** Rome **5** Celts, Moors **6** Greece **7** Almeria, Vandals **8** Carthage **9** Phoenicia, Visigoths
> **scholar: 8** Averroes
> **singer: 7** Domingo **8** Iglesias
> **warrior: 14** El Cid Campeador

language: 6 Basque **7** Catalan, Spanish **8** Balearic, Galician **9** Castilian, Valencian
expressions: 5 adios **10** buenos dias **11** que sera sera **12** hasta la vista
religion: 7 Judaism **10** Protestant **13** Roman Catholic
place:
> **aqueduct: 7** Segovia
> **bridge: 7** Cordoba
> **castle: 7** Alcazar **12** Santa Barbara
> **cathedral bell tower: 7** Giralda

center of Madrid: 12 Puerto del Sol

church/cathedral: 4 Leon **6** Burgos, Gerona, Toledo **7** Seville **9** Barcelona, San Isidro **10** Santa Maria **14** Sagrada Familia

fountain: 6 Cibele

library: 8 Columbus

minaret: 7 Seville

mosque: 11 Great Mosque **19** Santo Cristo de la Cruz

museum: 5 Prado **15** Museo de Pinturas

palace: 7 Granada, Naranco **8** Alhambra, Escorial **9** Real Mayor

park: 6 Retiro

resort: 8 Marbella **10** Costa Brava **12** Torremolinos

shrine: 32 Saint James at Santiago de Compostela

street: 7 Ramblas **13** Paseo del Prado **16** Plaza de la Cibeles **19** Paseo de la Castellana

synagogue: 10 El Transito

theater: 6 Merida

wall paintings/caves: 8 Altamira

possession: 5 Ceuta **6** Melill

feature:

bar: 6 tascas

dance: 5 tango **8** fandango, flamenco

estate: 10 latifundia

matador's suit: 12 traje de luces

political party: 7 Falange

food:

dish: 6 cocido, paella **8** zarzuela

soup: 8 gazpacho

span 4 arch, area, last, term, wing **5** cover, cross, range, reach, scope, spell, sweep, vault **6** bridge, endure, extent, length, period **7** archway, breadth, measure, stretch, survive, trestle **8** distance, duration, interval **9** extension, reach over, territory **10** bridge over, dimensions **11** proportions, reach across, stretch over **12** extend across

spangle 4 star **5** bedew **6** sequin **7** glisten, glitter, shimmer, twinkle **9** bugle bead, coruscate, paillette

spaniel

dog breed: 5 field **6** cocker, Sussex **7** clumber, Tibetan **8** Brittany **10** Irish water **13** American water, English cocker, Welsh springer **15** English springer **19** Cavalier King Charles

Spanish (language, person) 7 espanol

Spanish Guinea *see* **16** Equatorial Guinea

Spanish Sahara *see* **13** Western Sahara

Spanish Tragedy, The

author: 9 Thomas Kyd

character: 7 Horatio, Lorenzo, Villupo **9** Alexandro, Balthazar, Hieronimo **10** Bel-Imperia **16** Ghost of Don Andrea

spank 3 hit, tan **4** beat, belt, blow, cane, flog, hide, lick, slap, whip, whop **5** birch, strap, whale **6** paddle, strike, switch, thrash, wallop **8** paddling **10** flagellate

spanking 4 very **5** brisk, fresh **7** beating **8** paddling, whipping **9** extremely, thrashing **10** punishment **12** chastisement

spanking new 5 fresh **6** unused **8** brand new **9** untouched

spar 4 boom, mast, pole **5** argue, fight, sprit **6** bicker **7** dispute, quarrel, wrangle **8** crossbar **10** crosspiece

spare 3 odd **4** bony, cede, free, give, keep, lank, lean, save, thin **5** amass, extra, forgo, gaunt, grant, guard, hoard, lanky, lay up, limit, pinch, rangy, scant, stint, weedy **6** acquit, afford, defend, donate, excess, exempt, forego, let off, meager, not use, pardon, scanty, shield, skimpy, skinny, slight, unused **7** forgive, haggard, husband, let go of, protect, release, relieve, reserve, scraggy, scrawny, shelter, skimp on, slender, surplus **8** conserve, hold back, leftover, liberate, part with, reprieve, set aside, skeletal, withhold **9** auxiliary, emaciated, exonerate, fleshless, safeguard, show mercy **10** additional, extraneous, relinquish, substitute, unconsumed **11** economize on, have mercy on, superfluous, unnecessary, use frugally **12** be merciful to, dispense with, supplemental **13** supernumerary, supplementary

spared 5 freed **6** exempt, immune **7** excused **8** absolved, excepted, relieved

sparing 4 near **5** close, scant **6** frugal, meager, saving, scanty, stingy **7** careful, miserly, thrifty **8** grudging, stinting **9** niggardly, penurious **10** economical, ungenerous **11** closefisted, tightfisted **12** parsimonious

spark 3 bit, jot **4** atom, beam, fire, iota, life **5** brand, ember, flash, gleam, pique, trace **6** arouse, excite, incite, spirit **7** flicker, glimmer, glitter, inspire, provoke, sparkle **8** vitality **9** animation, instigate, stimulate **10** get-up-and-go

Spark, Muriel

author of: 11 Memento Mori **14** The Driver's Seat, The Only Problem **17** The Mandelbaum Gate, Territorial Rights **19** Loitering with Intent **21** A Far Cry from Kensington **24** The Prime of Miss Jean Brodie

sparkle 3 pep, pop, vim **4** dash, elan, fizz, foam, glow, life **5** be gay, brand, cheer, ember, flash, froth, gleam, glint, light, shine, verve **6** bubble, dazzle, fizzle, gaiety, spirit **7** be witty, flicker, glimmer, glisten, glitter, jollity, rejoice, shimmer, twinkle **8** radiance, vitality, vivacity **9** alertness, animation, briskness, coruscate, quickness **10** be cheerful, brilliance, ebullience, effervesce, effulgence, exuberance, liveliness, luminosity **11** be vivacious, scintillate **12** cheerfulness, exhilaration, luminousness **13** effervescence, scintillation

sparkling 5 fizzy **6** bubbly **7** fizzing, twinkly **8** bubbling, dazzling, glittery **9** twinkling **10** glistening, glittering **11** coruscating **12** effervescent **13** scintillating

sparse 3 few **4** thin **5** scant, spare **6** meager, scanty, scarce, skimpy, spotty, strewn **7** diffuse, exiguous, sporadic **9** dispersed, scattered, spaced-out, uncrowded **10** infrequent **16** few and far between

sparseness 7 paucity **8** sparsity, thinness **10** meagerness, scantiness

Spartacus

director: 14 Stanley Kubrick

cast: 8 Nina Foch **9** John Gavin **10** Tony Curtis **11** Jean Simmons, Kirk Douglas **12** Peter Ustinov **15** Charles Laughton, Laurence Olivier

setting: 4 Rome

score: 9 Alex North

spartan 4 hard **5** plain, stark, stern, stiff **6** frugal, severe, simple, strict **7** ascetic, austere **8** exacting, rigorous **9** stringent **10** abstemious, inexorable, inflexible, restrained, restricted **11** disciplined, self-denying **15** self-disciplined

Sparti

occupation: 8 warriors

spasm 3 fit, tic **4** grip, jerk, pang **5** burst, cramp, crick, flash, onset, spell, spurt, start, storm, throe **6** access, attack, frenzy, twitch **7** seizure, shudder, tempest **8** eruption, paroxysm **9** explosion **10** convulsion

spasmodic 6 fitful **7** erratic, flighty **8** fleeting, periodic, sporadic **9** desultory, irregular, mercurial, transient **10** capricious, inconstant, occasional **12** intermittent **13** discontinuous

spat 4 tiff **5** argue, fight, scrap, set-to **6** bicker, differ **7** contend, dispute, dissent, quarrel, wrangle **8** disagree, squabble **10** difference **11** altercation **12** disagreement **16** misunderstanding

spatter 4 slop, soil, spot **5** fleck, plash, spray, spurt, stain, swash **6** mottle, shower, splash **7** speckle, stipple **8** splatter, sprinkle

spawn 4 eggs, seed, teem **5** beget, breed, brood, fruit, yield **7** lay eggs, produce, product **8** engender, generate, multiply **9** offspring, propagate, reproduce **10** bring forth, give rise to **11** deposit eggs, give birth to, proliferate

speak 3 air, say 4 call, chat, deal, talk, tell 5 imply, orate, refer, shout, sound, state, treat, voice 6 advise, confer, convey, cry out, dilate, impart, mumble, murmur, mutter, preach, recite, relate, remark, report, reveal 7 bespeak, comment, consult, declaim, declare, discuss, divulge, expound, express, lecture, mention, suggest, whisper 8 announce, converse, disclose, harangue, indicate, proclaim, vocalize 9 discourse, enunciate, expatiate, hold forth, make known, pronounce, sermonize 10 articulate 11 communicate, give a speech

speakeasy 3 bar 6 saloon, tavern 7 gin mill 14 cocktail lounge

speaker 5 voice 6 orator, reader, talker 7 reciter 8 advocate, lecturer, preacher 9 declaimer, spokesman 10 discourser, monologist, mouthpiece, sermonizer 11 rhetorician, speechmaker, spokeswoman 13 valedictorian

speak highly of 4 laud 5 exalt, extol 6 praise 7 commend 8 eulogize 10 compliment 16 sing the praises of

speak ill of 4 slur 5 curse, knock, libel 6 defame, insult, malign, vilify 7 slander 8 bad-mouth 9 criticize, denigrate, discredit, disparage 13 find fault with 14 inveigh against

speak loudly 3 cry 4 bawl, call, hail, roar, yell 5 shout 6 bellow, clamor, cry out, halloo, holler 7 call out, speak up

speak of 7 mention, refer to 8 allude to 9 talk about, touch upon

speak to 6 talk to 7 address, lecture

speak together 3 gab, jaw, rap 4 chat, chin, talk 6 confer 7 chatter, palaver 8 chitchat, converse 10 chew the fat, chew the rag 11 communicate, confabulate

speak well of 4 laud 5 boost, extol 6 praise 7 acclaim, approve, commend, flatter, root for 8 eulogize 9 sweet talk 10 compliment, stick up for 13 speak highly of 16 sing the praises of 17 put in a good word for

spear 4 bolt, dart, gaff, gore, pike, spit, stab 5 lance, prick, shaft, spike, stick 6 impale, pierce 7 harpoon, javelin 8 puncture, transfix 9 penetrate 10 run through

spearhead 4 iron, lead 5 begin, found, start 6 launch, leader 7 creator, develop, founder, pioneer 8 begetter, conceive, initiate 9 establish, initiator, institute, originate, spokesman 10 inaugurate, instituter, prime mover 11 establisher, inaugurator, spokeswoman 12 avant-gardist

Spears, Britney
husband: 14 Kevin Federline 19 Jason Allen Alexander
roles: 3 MMC (The Mickey Mouse Club) 8 Longshot 9 In the Pink 10 Crossroads 22 Britney and Kevin Chaotic
songs: 5 Toxic 15 Baby One More Time, Oops! . . . I Did It Again, You Drive Me Crazy 17 Me Against the Music

special 4 fast, good, rare 5 close, great, novel 6 ardent, proper, select, signal, unique 7 bargain, certain, devoted, endemic, feature, staunch, typical, unusual 8 distinct, especial, intimate, peculiar, personal, sale item, singular, specific, uncommon 9 headliner, high point, highlight, important, momentous, specialty, steadfast 10 attraction, individual, noteworthy, particular, remarkable 11 distinctive, exceptional, outstanding, specialized 12 extravaganza 13 distinguished, extraordinary 14 representative, unconventional 16 out of the ordinary 17 piece de resistance

specialist 4 buff 5 adept, maven 6 expert, master 9 authority 10 past master 11 connoisseur

specialization 5 focus, forte, major 6 metier 8 province 10 speciality 13 concentration

specialize 5 adapt, focus, major 6 pursue 10 narrow down 11 concentrate

specialty 4 bent, mark, turn 5 badge, focus, forte, hobby, major, stamp 6 genius, talent 7 earmark, faculty, feature, pursuit, special 8 aptitude 9 endowment, trademark 10 competence, profession 11 claim to fame, distinction

species 4 form, kind, make, sort, type 5 breed, class, genre, group, order 6 kidney, nature, stripe 7 variety 8 category, division 11 designation, subdivision 14 classification

specific 5 exact, fixed 6 minute, stated, unique 7 bounded, certain, endemic, limited, pointed, precise, special, typical 8 clear-cut, concrete, confined, definite, detailed, especial, peculiar, personal, relevant, singular, tied-down 9 intrinsic, pertinent, specified 10 individual, particular, pinned-down, restricted 11 categorical, determinate, distinctive, unequivocal 13 circumscribed 14 characteristic

specification 6 detail 7 clarity 9 condition, precision, substance 11 enumeration, itemization, requirement, stipulation 12 concreteness 13 particularity, qualification 17 particularization

specifics 4 cure, fact, item 5 datum 6 detail, physic 10 medication, particular 12 circumstance

specify 4 cite, name 5 order 6 adduce, define, denote, detail 7 call for, focus on, itemize 8 describe, indicate, set forth 9 designate, enumerate, stipulate 13 particularize

specimen 4 case, type 5 model 6 sample 7 example 8 exemplar, instance 9 prototype 14 representative 15 exemplification

specious 5 false 6 faulty, tricky, untrue 7 dubious, in valid, unsound 8 slippery, spurious 9 casuistic, deceptive, illogical, incorrect, unfounded 10 fallacious, inaccurate, misleading 11 sophistical 12 questionable 15 unsubstantiated

speck 3 bit, dot, jot, pin 4 drop, hair, iota, mark, mite, mote, spot, whit 5 fleck, grain, pinch, trace 6 shadow, trifle 7 glimmer, modicum, speckle 8 farthing, flyspeck, particle 9 scintilla

speckled 4 pied 6 dotted 7 flecked, spotted, studded 8 freckled, peppered 9 sprinkled

spectacle 5 scene, sight 6 marvel, parade, rarity, wonder 7 display, exhibit, pageant 9 curiosity, rare sight 10 exhibition, exposition, phenomenon, production 12 extravaganza, presentation 13 demonstration

spectacles 6 lenses, shades 7 glasses 8 bifocals, pince-nez 10 eyeglasses

spectacular 4 gala, rich 5 grand, showy 6 daring 7 jeweled, opulent, stately 8 dramatic, fabulous, glorious, gorgeous, splendid, striking 9 daredevil, elaborate, marvelous, spectacle, sumptuous, thrilling 10 astounding, bespangled, eye-filling, impressive, theatrical 11 ceremonious, hairraising, magnificent, sensational 12 extravaganza, overwhelming 16 ostentatious show 19 elaborate production

spectator 3 fan 5 house 6 viewer 7 gallery, witness 8 audience, beholder, kibitzer, observer, onlooker 9 bystander, sightseer 10 aficionado, eyewitness 11 afficionado, theatergoer 12 rubbernecker

Spectator, The
author: 13 Joseph Addison, Richard Steele

specter 5 demon, ghost, ghoul, shade, spook 6 spirit, sprite, vision, wraith 7 banshee, fantasy, phantom 8 phantasm, presence, revenant 9 hobgoblin 10 apparition

spectral 4 airy 5 eerie, weird 6 creepy, spooky, unreal 7 ghastly, ghostly, phantom, shadowy, uncanny 8 ethereal, gossamer, vaporous 9 unearthly 10 chimerical, phantasmal, wraithlike 11 incorporeal 12 otherworldly, supernatural 13 insubstantial

speculate 4 muse 5 brood, dream, fancy, guess, study, think, wager 6 chance, gamble, hazard, ponder, reason, wonder 7 imagine, reflect, suppose, surmise, venture 8 cogitate, consider, meditate, ruminate, theorize 10 conjecture, deliberate, excogitate, play a hunch 11 contemplate, hypothesize, take a chance **13** play the market

speculation 4 risk **7** venture **8** gambling **9** guesswork **10** conjecture, estimation **11** supposition

speculative 4 iffy **5** dicey, risky **6** chancy **8** academic **11** conjectural, theoretical **12** experimental, hypothetical **13** suppositional

speculator 7 gambler, plunger **8** investor, operator, theorist **10** adventurer, arbitrager **11** arbitrageur

speech 4 talk **5** idiom, lingo, slang, voice **6** appeal, gossip, homily, jargon, sermon, tirade, tongue **7** address, chatter, comment, dialect, diction, lecture, oration, palaver, prattle, remarks, talking **8** chitchat, colloquy, converse, dialogue, diatribe, harangue, language, parlance, rhetoric, speaking **9** discourse, elocution, monologue, soliloquy, statement, utterance **10** discussion, expression, recitation, salutation **11** declamation, declaration, enunciation, exhortation, observation, valedictory **12** articulation, conversation, dissertation, vocalization **13** colloquialism, confabulation, pronouncement, pronunciation, verbalization

speechless 3 mum **4** dumb, mute **6** silent **7** aphonic **8** wordless **9** stupefied **10** tongue-tied

speed 3 aid, hie, run, zip **4** dart, dash, help, race, rate, rush, tear, zoom **5** boost, favor, gun it, haste, hurry, impel, speed, tempo **6** assist, barrel, gallop, hasten, hurtle, hustle, pick up, plunge, propel, scurry, step up **7** advance, further, hurry up, promote, quicken, tear off **8** alacrity, celerity, dispatch, expedite, high tail, make time, momentum, rapidity, step on it, velocity **9** bowl along, briskness, fleetness, give a lift, hastiness, make haste, move along, quickness, rapidness, swiftness **10** accelerate, expedition, get a move on, go hell-bent, lose no time, promptness, spurt ahead **11** push forward **12** acceleration **13** burn up the road

speedily 4 fast **5** apace, quick **6** pronto **7** hastily, rapidly, swiftly **8** in no time, promptly **9** post haste, right away, summarily **11** on the double **12** lickety-split

speed up 4 rush **5** hurry **6** hasten, step up **7** hop to it, quicken **8** expedite, multiply, step on it **9** encourage, intensify **10** accelerate, facilitate, get a move on **12** step on the gas

speedy 4 fast **5** brisk, early, fleet, hasty, quick, rapid, ready, swift **6** abrupt, lively, sudden **7** express, hurried, running, summary **8** headlong **9** quick-fire, rapid-fire **10** not delayed **11** precipitate

Spelaites

epithet of: 6 Hermes
means: 9 of the cave

spell 2 go **3** bit, hex **4** bout, free, lull, mean, omen, snap, term, time, tour, turn, wave **5** augur, break, charm, hitch, imply, magic, pause, round, stint, trick, while **6** allure, course, denote, herald, hoodoo, make up, period, recess, tenure, typify, voodoo **7** bespeak, betoken, connote, glamour, portend, presage, promise, purport, rapture, release, relieve, respite, signify, sorcery, stretch, suggest **8** amount to, cover for, duration, forebode, forecast, foretell, indicate, interval, stand for, witchery **9** form a word, influence, interlude, represent, symbolize **10** assignment, invocation, mumbo jumbo, open-sesame **11** abracadabra, bewitchment, enchantment, fascination, incantation, pinch-hit for, take over for **12** magic formula

spellbind 5 charm **7** bewitch, enchant **8** enthrall, entrance, intrigue, transfix **9** enrapture, fascinate, hypnotize, mesmerize, transport

spellbound 4 rapt **5** agape **7** charmed **8** wordless **9** awestruck, bewitched, enchanted, entranced, possessed **10** breathless, dumbstruck, enraptured, enthralled, fascinated, hypnotized, mesmerized, speechless, tongue-tied, transfixed **11** openmouthed, transported

Spellbound
director: 15 Alfred Hitchcock
cast: 9 John Emery **11** Gregory Peck, Leo G Carroll **13** Ingrid Bergman **14** Michael Chekhov
score: 11 Miklos Rosza
Oscar for: 5 score
dream sequences by: 12 Salvador Dali

spell out 6 define, detail **7** clarify, clear up, explain, expound, specify **8** describe, delineate, designate, elucidate, explicate, interpret, make plain **10** illustrate

Spemann, Hans
field: 7 zoology
nationality: 6 German
worked in: 20 embryonic development
awarded: 10 Nobel Prize

Spencer, Sir Stanley
born: 7 Cookham, England **9** Berkshire
artwork: 22 Resurrection of Soldiers, The Resurrection Cookham **31** Christ Preaching at Cookham Regatta **43** Double Nude Portrait the Artist and His Second Wife

spend 3 pay, use **4** dole, fill, give, pass **5** drain, empty, use up, waste **6** devote, employ, expend, invest, occupy, outlay, pay out, take up **7** burn out, consume, deplete, destroy, exhaust,

fork out, scatter, wear out **8** allocate, disburse, dispense, shell out, squander **9** dissipate, while away **10** impoverish

spendable 9 available **10** expendable **13** discretionary

spend foolishly 5 waste **8** misspend, squander **9** dissipate, throw away **11** fritter away

spendthrift 6 lavish, waster **7** wastrel **8** prodigal, spend-all, wasteful **10** big spender, profligate, squanderer **11** extravagant, improvident **12** overgenerous

Spengler, Oswald
author of: 19 The Decline of the West

Spenser, Edmund
author of: 8 Amoretti **12** Epithalamion **15** The Faerie Queene **22** The Shephearde's Calendar

spent 4 beat, done, weak **5** faint, weary **6** bushed, done in, used up **7** laid low, wearied, worn out **8** drooping, fatigued, tired out **9** enfeebled, exhausted, fagged out, played out, powerless, prostrate **11** debilitated, ready to drop **12** strengthless **14** on one's last legs

Sperry, Elmer Ambrose
invented: 11 gyrocompass **22** airplane automatic pilot

spew 5 eject, expel, heave, vomit **6** cast up **7** spit out **8** disgorge, throw out **11** regurgitate

spew up 4 spew **5** eject, expel, spout, vomit **6** cast up **7** cough up, throw up **8** disgorge **11** regurgitate

sphere 3 orb **4** area, ball, beat, pale **5** globe, orbit, range, realm, scope **6** domain **7** compass, globule **8** province, spheroid **9** bailiwick, round body, territory **10** experience

spherical 5 orbic, round **6** global, rotund **7** globate, globose, orbical **8** globular **9** orbicular **11** globe-shaped
nearly: 8 obrotund

spheroid 3 orb **4** ball **5** globe **6** sphere **7** globule

spherule 4 ball, bead, drop **6** pellet **7** droplet, globule

Sphinx
form: 7 monster
bust of: 5 woman
body of: 4 lion
father: 6 Typhon **7** Orthrus
mother: 7 Echidna **8** Chimaera
proposed: 7 riddles
location: 4 Giza **6** Thebes
answered by: 7 Oedipus

spice 3 zip **4** herb, kick, snap, tang, zest **5** savor **6** accent, flavor, relish, stacte **7** pizzazz **8** piquancy, pungency **9** condiment, flavoring, seasoning **10** excitement

spicule 4 barb **5** point, spine **7** prickle

spicy 3 hot **4** keen, racy **5** acute,

bawdy, fiery, nippy, pithy, salty, sharp, tangy, witty, zippy **6** clever, ribald, risque, snappy, strong **7** gingery, peppery, piquant, pungent **8** aromatic, improper, incisive, indecent, off-color, piercing, redolent, spirited **9** sparkling, trenchant **10** indelicate, scandalous, suggestive **11** provocative **12** questionable **13** scintillating

spider
 black widow marking: **9** hourglass
 class: **9** Arachnida
 combining form: **6** arachn **7** arachno
 family: **7** Attidae **8** Drassidae **10** Citigradae, Pisauridae
 famous: **9** Charlotte
 fear of: **13** arachnophobia
 kind: **4** crab, wolf **5** taint **7** jumping **8** trap-door **9** orb weaver, solpugida, tarantula **10** black widow **13** daddy longlegs
 mythology: **7** Arachne
 nest: **5** nidus
 order: **7** Araneae
 part: **4** claw, coxa **5** femur, tibia **6** tarsus **7** abdomen, mammula, patella, pedicel, scopula **9** chelicera, protarsis, spinneret **10** pedipalpus, trochanter **11** calamistrum **13** cephalothorax
 study of: **10** araneology **11** arachnology
 young: **11** spiderlings

Spielberg, Steven
 wife: **11** Kate Capshaw
 former wife: **9** Amy Irving
 company: **13** Dreamworks SKG
 director of: **4** Jaws **7** Amistad **11** Poltergeist **12** Jurassic Park, The Lost World **14** Minority Report, Schindler's List (Oscar), The Color Purple, War of the Worlds **15** Catch Me If You Can **17** Saving Private Ryan **19** Raiders of the Lost Ark **21** ET The Extra Terrestrial **29** Close Encounters of the Third Kind, Indiana Jones and the Last Crusade **30** Indiana Jones and the Temple of Doom

spike 3 peg, pin **4** barb, nail, spur, tine **5** briar, point, prong, rivet, spine, stake, thorn **6** needle, skewer **7** bramble, bristle, hobnail **8** spikelet

spill 3 run **4** blab, drip, drop, dump, fall, flow, shed, slop, tell, toss **5** slosh, throw, waste **6** reveal, splash **7** let flow, pour out **8** disclose, overflow, overturn

Spillane, Mickey
 real name: **13** Frank Morrison
 author of: **8** I the Jury **12** Kiss Me Deadly **14** The Girl Hunters **15** The Death Dealers
 character: **10** Mike Hammer

spin 4 roll, tell, turn **5** swirl, twirl, wheel, whirl **6** gyrate, invent, relate, render, rotate, unfold **7** concoct, narrate, recount, revolve **8** rotation, spinning **9** fabricate, pirouette

spinach 3 rot **4** bull, bunk **5** hokum, hooey, stuff **6** bunkum, hot air, humbug **7** baloney, blather, hogwash, potherb **8** claptrap, nonsense, tommyrot **9** poppycock, vegetable **10** applesauce **11** foolishness **16** stuff and nonsense

spinach 16 Spinacia oleracea
 varieties: **4** wild **5** Cuban **6** Indian **7** Malabar **8** mountain **10** New Zealand **11** round-seeded **13** pricklyseeded

spinal column 4 back **5** spine **8** backbone

spindly 4 puny **5** frail, leggy **6** skinny **7** scraggy **8** skeletal

spine 4 barb, horn, spur **5** briar, point, prong, quill, spike, thorn **6** needle **7** bramble, bristle, prickle **8** backbone **9** vertebrae **12** spinal column

spinel
 source: **5** Burma, Mogok
 color: **3** red **5** mauve

spineless 4 weak **5** timid **7** fearful **8** cowardly, cowering, cringing, timorous, wavering **10** indecisive, irresolute, spiritless, weak-willed **11** lily-livered, vacillating **12** fainthearted **13** pusillanimous **14** chickenhearted

spinelessness 8 timidity, weakness **9** cowardice **10** indecision **11** fearfulness **12** cowardliness, irresolution **13** pusillanimity

spine-tingling 7 rousing **8** exciting **9** thrilling **11** hair-raising, sensational **12** breathtaking, electrifying

spinning jenny
 invented by: **10** Hargreaves

spinoff 5 issue **6** result **7** adjunct, outcome **8** offshoot **9** byproduct, outgrowth **10** descendant, side effect, supplement **11** aftereffect, consequence

spin out 4 skid **7** draw out **8** lengthen **9** attenuate

spinster 6 virgin **7** old maid **14** unmarried woman

spinsterhood 8 celibacy **9** virginity **11** old maidhood

spiral 4 coil, curl, gyre **5** helix, screw, whirl, whorl **6** coiled, curled **7** helical, ringlet, spiroid, whorled, winding **8** curlicue, twisting **9** corkscrew **11** screw-shaped

Spiral Staircase, The
 director: **13** Robert Siodmak
 based on story by: **14** Ethel Lina White (Some Must Watch)
 cast: **9** Kent Smith **11** George Brent **13** Rhonda Fleming **14** Dorothy McGuire, Ethel Barrymore

spire 3 cap, tip **4** apex, cone, peak **5** crest, point, shaft, tower **6** belfry, summit, turret, vertex **7** minaret, obelisk, steeple **8** pinnacle **9** bell tower, campanile

spirit 3 elf **4** mind, soul, urge, will **5**

fairy, ghost, ghoul, heart, shade, spook **6** animus, dybbuk, goblin, psyche, sprite, wraith **7** banshee, bugaboo, bugbear, impulse, phantom, resolve, specter **8** phantasm, presence **9** hobgoblin, intellect **10** apparition, motivation, resolution
 German: **5** Geist

spirited 4 bold **5** fiery, nervy **6** frisky, lively, plucky **8** fearless, intrepid **10** courageous, mettlesome

spiritless 4 dull, limp, tame **6** abject **8** cowardly, lifeless, listless **9** apathetic, spineless **10** unanimated, world-weary **11** passionless

spirit of the time
 German: **9** Zeitgeist

spirits 3 aim, vim **4** bond, elan, fire, gist, glow, grit, guts, mood, sand, tone, vein, zeal, zest **5** ardor, drive, humor, pluck, sense, spunk, tenor, valor, verve, vigor **6** daring, effect, elixir, energy, fervor, intent, liquor, mettle, morale, stripe, temper, warmth **7** alcohol, avidity, bravery, courage, essence, extract, feeling, loyalty, meaning, purport, purpose, sparkle **8** attitude, audacity, backbone, boldness, devotion, emotions, feelings, tincture, vitality, vivacity **9** animation, eagerness, fortitude, intention, sentiment, stoutness, substance **10** allegiance, attachment, enterprise, enthusiasm, liveliness **11** disposition, doughtiness, staunchness **12** fearlessness, significance **13** dauntlessness, sprightliness **16** stoutheartedness **17** alcoholic solution

spiritual 4 holy **5** godly, inner, moral, pious **6** divine, mental **7** blessed, churchy, ghostly, phantom, psychic **8** cerebral, hallowed, heavenly, platonic, priestly, spectral, supernal **9** celestial, Christian, innermost, of the soul, religious, unearthly, unfleshly, unworldly **10** devotional, immaterial, intangible, sacrosanct, sanctified **11** consecrated, incorporeal **12** metaphysical, otherworldly, supernatural **13** insubstantial, psychological **14** ecclesiastical

spirituality 5 piety **8** devotion, holiness **9** godliness, reverence **10** devoutness

spirituous 4 hard **6** strong **9** alcoholic, distilled **12** intoxicating

spit 3 bar, pop, rod **4** foam, hiss, reef, spew **5** atoll, drool, eject, fling, froth, shoal, throw **6** saliva, shower, shriek, skewer, slaver, sputum **7** dribble, scatter, slobber, spatter, spittle, sputter **8** headland, sandbank, turnspit **9** brochette, peninsula **10** promontory **11** expectorate

spite 3 irk, vex **4** gall, hate, hurt, pain **5** annoy, odium, sting, venom, wound **6** animus, enmity, grudge, harass, hatred, injure, malice, misuse, nettle, put out, rancor **7** ill will, mortify, provoke **8** bad blood, ill-treat, irritate, loathing, meanness **9** animosity, antipathy, hostility, humiliate, malignity, nastiness, vengeance **10** bitterness, resentment **11** detestation, malevolence **12** vengefulness **13** maliciousness, slap in the face **14** revengefulness, vindictiveness

spiteful 4 evil **5** nasty **6** bitter, malign, wicked **7** caustic, envious, hateful, hostile, vicious **8** grudging, vengeful, venomous **9** malicious, merciless, rancorous, resentful, sarcastic, splenetic **10** ill-natured, malevolent, vindictive **11** acrimonious, unforgiving **12** antagonistic

spitting image (spit and image) 4 copy, mate, twin **6** double **9** duplicate **15** perfect likeness

splash 3 ado, hit **4** cast, dash, daub, soil, stir, toss, wash **5** bathe, break, fling, plash, slosh, smack, smear, stain, strew, surge, swash **6** batter, blazon, buffet, effect, impact, paddle, plunge, shower, spread, streak, strike, uproar, wallow, welter **7** bestrew, scatter, spatter, splotch **8** besmirch, discolor, disperse, splatter, sprinkle **9** bespatter, broadcast, commotion, sensation **10** spattering **11** splattering

splashy 5 jazzy, showy **6** flashy **10** glittering **11** spectacular **12** ostentatious

splatter 4 dash **6** splash **7** spatter

splay 4 awry **5** askew, broad **6** aslant, clumsy, extend, tilted, warped **7** awkward, crooked, fanlike, slanted, sloping, turn out **8** inclined, slanting **9** distorted, fan-shaped, irregular, outspread, spread out **10** stretch out

spleen 4 bile, gall **5** anger, spite, venom **6** animus, enmity, hatred, malice, rancor **7** ill will **8** acrimony, ill humor, vexation **9** animosity, bad temper, hostility **10** bitterness, resentment **11** malevolence, peevishness **12** irritability, spitefulness

splendid 4 fine, high, rare, rich **5** grand, lofty, noble, regal, royal **6** august, costly, ornate, superb **7** elegant, eminent, exalted, stately **8** dazzling, elevated, flashing, gleaming, glorious, gorgeous, imposing, majestic, palatial, peerless, terrific **9** admirable, beautiful, brilliant, effulgent, estimable, excellent, marvelous, sumptuous, wonderful **10** glittering, preeminent, remarkable, surpassing **11** exceptional, illustrious, magnificent, outstanding, resplendent, splendorous **12** transcendent **13** distinguished, splendiferous

Splendid Splinter
nickname of: **11** Ted Williams

splendor 4 fire, pomp **5** gleam, glory, light, sheen, shine **6** beauty, dazzle,

luster, renown **7** burnish, glitter **8** grandeur, nobility, opulence, radiance **9** intensity, sublimity **10** augustness, brilliance, effulgence, irradiance, luminosity **11** preeminence, stateliness **12** gorgeousness, luminousness, magnificence, resplendence **13** incandescence

Splendor in the Grass
director: **9** Elia Kazan
based on story by: **11** William Inge
cast: **9** Pat Hingle **11** Natalie Wood **12** Sean Garrison, Warren Beatty **14** Audrey Christie

splenetic 4 cross, nasty, surly, testy **6** cranky, malign **7** bilious, hostile, peevish **8** choleric, spiteful, venomous **9** irascible, rancorous **11** acrimonious, ill-tempered **12** cantankerous, disagreeable

splice 3 wed **4** join, knit **5** graft, merge, plait, unite **7** connect **8** dovetail **9** interlace **10** intertwine, interweave **12** interconnect

splinter 4 chip **5** smash, split **6** needle, shiver, sliver **7** break up, crumble, explode, shatter **8** fly apart, fracture, fragment **9** pulverize **12** disintegrate

split 3 hew **4** deal, dole, dual, mete, part, rent, rift, rive, snap, tear, torn **5** allot, break, burst, cleft, crack, halve, mixed, riven, sever, share **6** bisect, breach, broken, cleave, differ, divide, ripped, schism, shiver, sunder, varied **7** be riven, cracked, diverge, divided, divorce, divvy up, fissure, give way, opening, portion, quarrel, rupture, severed, twofold **8** alienate, allocate, cleavage, disagree, dispense, disperse, dissever, disunion, disunite, division, fracture, ruptured, splinter **9** apportion, fractured, parcel out, partition, segmented, segregate, separated, set at odds, subdivide, undecided **10** alienation, ambivalent, break apart, difference, dissension, dissevered, distribute, divergence, falling out, separation, splintered **11** come between, part company, tear asunder **12** disagreement, estrangement

split off 7 deviate, diverge **8** separate **9** draw apart

split the difference 5 agree **6** settle **9** make a deal **10** compromise **11** come to terms, meet halfway **14** strike a bargain

splitting off 9 diverging **10** separating **12** drawing apart

splitting up 8 dividing **9** divorcing **10** breaking up, separating **11** subdividing **12** partitioning

splotch 4 blot, daub, mark, spot **5** smear, stain **6** blotch, smudge **13** discoloration

splurge 5 binge, spree **6** bender **8** live it up **10** indulgence, showing off **12** showy display **13** be extravagant,

shoot the works **14** indulge oneself, self-indulgence **22** throw caution to the winds

splutter 4 hiss, spew, spit **5** burst, spray **6** gibber, jabber, mumble, seethe **7** bluster, slobber, spatter, sputter, stammer, stumble, stutter **9** hem and haw **11** expectorate

spoil 3 mar, rot **4** baby, flaw, harm, mold, ruin, sour, turn **5** addle, botch, decay, go bad, humor, taint **6** blight, bungle, coddle, damage, deface, foul up, impair, injure, mess up, mildew, muddle, pamper **7** blemish, destroy, disrupt, putrefy **8** mutilate **10** decompose, disfigure **11** deteriorate, mollycoddle, overgratify, overindulge

spoiled 3 bad, off **6** putrid, rotten, ruined **7** coddled, corrupt, decayed, gone bad, went bad **8** indulged, overripe, pampered **9** putrefied **10** decomposed, frustrated **12** deteriorated **15** rotten to the core

spoiler 6 vandal **8** underdog **9** deflector

spoils 4 haul, loot, swag, take **5** booty **6** bounty, prizes, quarry **7** plunder, profits **8** benefits, comforts, pickings **9** amenities, patronage **11** perquisites **12** acquisitions

spoilsport 4 drag **10** wet blanket **11** party-pooper

spoken 4 oral, said **5** parol **6** verbal, voiced **7** uttered **8** expressed **10** pronounced **11** articulated

spokesman 5 agent, PR man, proxy **6** backer, deputy **7** speaker **8** delegate, promoter **9** middleman, proponent, supporter, surrogate **10** mouthpiece, negotiator, press agent **11** protagonist

sponge 3 bum, dry, mop, rub **4** blot, swab, wash **5** cadge, clean, leech, mooch, towel **6** borrow, live on **7** cleanse, moisten **8** freeload, impose on, scrounge **9** panhandle

sponger 5 leech **6** cadger, sponge **7** moocher **8** barnacle, borrower, deadbeat **9** scrounger **10** freeloader **11** bloodsucker

sponsor 4 back **5** angel, set up **6** backer, patron, uphold **7** finance, promote, support **8** advocate, champion, defender, financer, guardian, partisan, promoter, start out, upholder, vouch for, warranty **9** guarantee, financier, guarantor, proponent, protecter, protector, supporter **10** advertiser, stand up for, underwrite

sponsorship 5 aegis **7** support **8** advocacy, auspices **9** patronage **12** championship

spontaneity 7 freedom **11** impetuosity, naturalness **12** unconstraint **13** impulsiveness, offhandedness **18** extemporaneousness

spontaneous 4 free **5** ad lib **7** natural, offhand, willing **8** unbidden **9** au-

tomatic, extempore, impetuous, impromptu, impulsive, ingenuous,
unplanned, unstudied, voluntary **10**
gratuitous, improvised, off the cuff,
unprompted **11** independent, instinctive, uncontrived **12** unhesitating **13**
unconstrained **14** extemporaneous,
unpremeditated

spoof 3 kid **4** joke, josh, twit **6** parody, satire, sendup **7** joshing, kidding,
lampoon, mockery, ribbing, takeoff **8**
satirize, travesty **9** burlesque, take off
on **10** caricature

spook 5 alarm, bogey, ghost, haunt,
scare, shade **6** goblin, shadow, spirit
7 disturb, phantom, specter, startle,
terrify, unnerve **8** disquiet, frighten,
unsettle **9** hobgoblin, terrorize **10** apparition, intimidate

spooky 5 eerie, jumpy, scary, weird **6**
creepy **7** ghostly, nervous **8** skittish
10 mysterious

sporadic 3 few **4** rare, thin **6** fitful,
meager, random, scarce, sparse,
spotty **8** isolated, periodic, uncommon
9 haphazard, irregular, scattered,
spasmodic **10** infrequent, now and
then, occasional **11** fragmentary **12**
intermittent, widely spaced **13** discontinuous **16** few and far between

sport 3 fun, toy **4** bear, butt, game,
goat, jest, joke, lark, play, romp, trip
5 abuse, caper, carry, chaff, dally,
frisk, hobby, mirth, revel **6** antics, cavort, frolic, gaiety, gambol, misuse,
monkey, take in, trifle **7** buffoon, contest, display, disport, exhibit, gambler,
jesting, jollity, kidding, mockery, rollick, show off, skylark **8** badinage, derision, fair game, flourish, hilarity, ill-
treat, raillery, ridicule, scoffing, trifling
9 amusement, athletics, daredevil, diversion, festivity, joviality, make
merry, play games, scapegoat **10** persiflage, pleasantry, recreation, relaxation, skylarking **11** competition, distraction, merrymaking **12** depreciation
13 entertainment, laughingstock **14**
divertissement

sporting house 4 stew **5** house **6**
bagnio, bordel **7** brothel **8** bordello,
cathouse **10** bawdy house, fancy
house, whorehouse **14** house of ill
fame **16** house of ill repute **19** house
of prostitution

sportive 6 blithe, frisky **7** playful **8**
animated **9** frolicsome

sportsman 6 hunter **9** fisherman

Sportsman's Notebook, A
    author: **12** Ivan Turgenev

sporty 6 casual, flashy, jaunty **8** informal

spot 3 dot, fix, see, spy **4** area, bind,
blot, daub, espy, flaw, mark, part,
seat, site, slur, soil **5** brand, fleck,
grime, locus, patch, place, point,
smear, space, speck, stain, sully, taint,

tract **6** blotch, defect, detect, locale,
locate, plight, region, sector, smirch,
smudge, splash, stigma **7** blemish, dilemma, discern, light on, pick out,
quarter, section, spatter, speckle,
splotch, station **8** discolor, discover,
disgrace, district, flyspeck, locality, location, position, premises, reproach,
sprinkle **9** aspersion, discredit, recognize, situation, territory **10** difficulty,
imputation **11** predicament **12** bad situation, neighborhood **13** discoloration

spotless 4 pure **5** clean, snowy **7** perfect, shining **8** flawless, gleaming,
pristine, unflawed, unmarred, unsoiled **9** faultless, stainless, unspotted,
unstained, unsullied, untainted **10** immaculate, impeccable **11** unblemished, untarnished **14** irreproachable
15 unexceptionable

spotted 3 saw **6** dotted, espied, soiled
7 dappled, located, mottled, stained **8**
detected, speckled **9** blemished, discerned, spattered **10** discovered **13**
caught sight of

spotty 6 fitful, pimply, random, uneven **7** blotchy, dappled, erratic,
flecked, mottled, spotted **8** episodic,
freckled, splotchy, sporadic, unsteady,
variable, wavering **9** broken out, desultory, irregular, spasmodic, uncertain
10 capricious, inconstant, unreliable,
variegated **11** full of spots **12** disorganized, intermittent, undependable,
unmethodical, unsystematic

spouse 4 mate, wife **7** consort, husband, partner **8** helpmate **10** better
half

spout 3 jet, lip **4** beak, flow, go on,
gush, nose, pipe, rant, spew, tube,
vent, well **5** eject, erupt, expel, exude,
issue, mouth, shoot, snout, spray,
spurt, surge, vomit **6** nozzle, outlet,
sluice, squirt, stream, trough **7** bluster, carry on, channel, conduit, pour
out **8** disgorge, fountain, harangue **9**
discharge, hold forth **10** waterspout
11 pontificate **12** emit forcibly **14**
speak pompously

sprawl 4 flop, lean, loll, wind **5** slump
6 branch, extend, lounge, slouch **7**
gush out, meander, recline **8** languish,
reach out, straggle **9** spread out **10**
stretch out **11** spread-eagle

spray 4 coat, mist, posy, twig **5** bough,
burst, shoot, sprig, treat, vapor **6**
dampen, nozzle, shower, splash,
switch, volley **7** atomize, barrage,
blossom, bouquet, drizzle, moisten,
nosegay, scatter, spatter, sprayer, syringe **8** atomizer, disperse, droplets,
moisture, sprinkle **9** discharge, fusillade, sprinkler, vaporizer

spread 3 air, lay **4** area, cast, coat,
open, pave, shed, span, vent **5** apply,
bruit, cloak, cover, feast, field, issue,
range, reach, scope, smear, spray,

story, strew, sweep, table, tract, width
6 bedaub, beshed, blazon, extend, extent, herald, length, notice, repeat, report, unfold, unfurl, unroll **7** account,
advance, article, banquet, besmear,
bestrew, breadth, circuit, compass, declare, diffuse, divulge, expanse, overlay, overrun, pervade, plaster, publish, radiate, scatter, spatter, stretch,
suffuse, trumpet, untwine, write-up **8**
announce, coverage, disperse, distance, increase, permeate, proclaim,
sprinkle **9** broadcast, circulate, diffusion, expansion, extension, make
known, penetrate, pervasion, propagate, publicize, radiation, spreading,
suffusion, ventilate **10** dispersion, distribute, make public, permeation,
promulgate, stretch out **11** communicate, disseminate, noise abroad, proliferate **13** amplification, dissemination,
proliferation

spread out 5 broad, widen **6** expand,
extend **7** broaden, diffuse, enlarge, radiate, stretch **8** expanded, extended,
open wide **9** dispersed, outspread,
scattered **10** distribute, unhampered
11 unconfirmed **12** unrestricted **14**
unconcentrated

spree 4 bout, orgy, toot **5** binge,
drunk, fling, revel **6** bender **7** carouse, debauch, revelry, splurge, wassail **8** carousal **9** bacchanal **10** saturnalia

sprightliness 8 buoyancy, spryness,
vivacity **9** animation, briskness **10**
breeziness, liveliness **16** lightearted-
ness

sprightly 3 gay **4** keen, spry **5** agile,
alive, brisk, jolly, merry **6** active,
blithe, breezy, cheery, jaunty, jovial,
lively, nimble **7** buoyant, chipper,
dashing, dynamic, playful **8** animated,
cheerful, spirited, sportive **9** energetic,
vivacious **10** blithesome, frolicsome
12 lighthearted

spring 3 hop, jet, pop, spa **4** come,
dart, flow, gush, jump, kick, leap,
loom, pool, pour, rise, rush, stem,
well **5** arise, baths, begin, bound, caper, ensue, fount, issue, lunge, shoot,
spout, spurt, start, surge, vault **6** appear, bounce, derive, gambol, recoil,
reflex, result, sprout, stream **7** burgeon, crop out, descend, emanate,
proceed, release, shoot up, start up,
stretch, trigger **8** buoyancy, commence, fountain, mushroom **9** come
forth, entrechat, germinate, originate,
saltation, waterhole **10** break forth,
burst forth, elasticity, resiliency **11**
flexibility
    goddess of: **4** Hebe **5** Venus

spring back 6 bounce, recoil **7** rebound **8** ricochet

spring flowers
    goddess of: **6** Thallo

springlike 4 mild, soft, warm 5 balmy

springs
  god of: 4 Fons 6 Palici
  goddess of: 4 Idun 5 Idura, Ithun 6 Ithunn

spring up 4 grow, rise 5 arise, occur, pop up 6 crop up, emerge, happen, sprout 9 originate 10 burst forth

springy 6 bouncy, spongy, supple 7 elastic 9 resilient 10 rebounding

sprinkle 4 dash, dust, rain 5 spray, strew, water 6 powder, shower, splash, spread, squirt 7 bestrew, diffuse, drizzle, moisten, scatter, spatter 8 splatter

sprinkling 4 dash, drop, hint 5 pinch, touch 7 droplet, minimum, modicum, soupcon 8 sprinkle 10 smattering

sprint 3 run 4 dart, dash, kick, race, rush, tear, whiz 5 burst, shoot, spurt, whisk 7 scamper

sprit 3 bar 4 spar 8 crossbar 10 crosspiece

sprite 3 elf 5 fairy, pixie 10 leprechaun

sprout 3 bud, wax 4 grow 5 bloom, shoot, sprig 6 come up, flower, spread, thrive 7 blossom, burgeon 8 multiply, offshoot, put forth, spring up 9 germinate, outgrowth

spruce 4 chic, neat, tidy, trim 5 kempt, natty, sharp, smart 6 dapper 7 conifer, elegant 9 evergreen, shipshape 11 well-groomed 12 spick-and-span
  French: 6 soigne

spruce 5 Picea
  varieties: 3 bog, cat, red 4 blue 5 black, Hondo, Sitka, snake, white, Yeddo 6 double, Norway 7 Alberta, big-cone, Finnish, hemlock 8 Colorado, Sakhalin, Siberian 9 Himalayan, tiger-tail 10 Black Hills 12 Colorado blue, Japanese bush

spry 4 deft, hale 5 agile, brisk, quick 6 active, frisky, hearty, jaunty, lively, nimble, supple 7 buoyant, chipper, playful 8 animated, spirited, sportive, vigorous 9 energetic, sprightly, vivacious 11 lightfooted

spunk 4 fire, grit, guts, salt, sand 5 heart, nerve, pluck 6 daring, ginger, mettle, pepper, spirit 7 bravery, courage 8 backbone, boldness, gumption 10 feistiness

spur 3 arm, leg 4 fork, goad, prod, whet, whip, wing 5 prick 6 branch, feeder, fillip, hasten, motive, siding 7 impetus, impulse 8 excitant, stimulus 9 boot spike, encourage, incentive, stimulant, stimulate, tributary 10 incitement, inducement 11 instigation, provocation, stimulation 13 encouragement

spurge 9 Euphorbia 11 Pachysandra
  varieties: 5 caper, leafy, melon 6 ipecac, myrtle, tramp's 7 cypress, mottled, seaside, slipper 8 fiddler's, Jap-

anese 9 Allegheny, flowering 10 Indian tree

spurious 4 fake, mock, sham 5 bogus, false, phony 6 faulty, forged, hollow 7 feigned, unsound 8 specious 9 imitation, simulated 10 fallacious, fraudulent, not genuine 11 counterfeit, make-believe, unauthentic 12 illegitimate

spurn 4 mock, snub 5 flout, repel, scorn 6 rebuff, refuse, reject, slight 7 condemn, decline, disdain, dismiss, repulse, scoff at, sneer at 8 turn down 9 cast aside, disparage, repudiate 12 coldshoulder, look down upon 16 turn up one's nose at

spur-of-the-moment 5 ad-lib 7 offhand 9 extempore, impromptu 10 improvised, unprepared 11 extemporary, spontaneous, unrehearsed 14 extemporaneous, unpremeditated

spurt 3 jet 4 dart, dash, emit, flow, gush, gust, rush, tear, whiz 5 burst, flash, issue, lunge, scoot, shoot, speed, spout, spray, surge 6 access, spring, sprint, squirt, stream 7 pour out 8 disgorge, ejection, eruption, fountain, outbreak, outburst 9 discharge, explosion, spring out 10 outpouring

spy 3 pry, see 4 find, peep, spot, view 5 scout, sight, snoop 6 behold, descry, detect, notice, shadow 7 discern, glimpse, make out, observe 8 discover, informer, Mata Hari, perceive, saboteur 9 keep watch, operative, recognize 11 reconnoiter, secret agent 12 catch sight of 13 undercover man, watch secretly 14 espionage agent, fifth columnist 16 agent provocateur 17 intelligence agent
  famous: 4 Abel, Hale 5 Andre, Caleb, Pitts 6 Arnold, Dulles, Philby, Powers, Smiley 8 Mata Hari 9 James Bond, Nicholson, Philbrick, Pinkerton, Rosenberg

Spy, The
  author: 19 James Fenimore Cooper

Spy Who Came In from the Cold, The
  director: 10 Martin Ritt
  based on novel by: 11 John LeCarre
  cast: 11 Claire Bloom, Oskar Werner 12 Peter Van Eyck 13 Richard Burton

Spy Who Loved Me, The
  author: 10 Ian Fleming
  director: 12 Lewis Gilbert
  cast: 10 Bernard Lee (M), Roger Moore (James Bond) 11 Barbara Bach, Curt Jurgens (Stromberg), Richard Kiel (Jaws)

squabble 3 row, war 4 spat, tiff 5 argue, brawl, clash, fight, run-in, scrap, set-to, words 6 battle, bicker, differ 7 contend, contest, dispute, quarrel, wrangle 8 argument 9 have words,

lock horns 10 bandy words, contention, difference, dissension 11 altercation, controversy 12 disagreement

squadron 5 fleet 6 armada 8 flotilla 9 naval unit 10 escadrille 11 cavalry unit 12 military unit

squalid 4 foul, mean 5 dirty, nasty 6 abject, filthy, horrid, rotten, shabby, sloppy, sordid 7 decayed, reeking, run-down, unclean 8 battered, degraded, slovenly, wretched 9 miserable 10 broken-down, disheveled, ramshackle, slatternly, tumbledown 11 dilapidated 12 deteriorated

squalor 4 dirt 5 filth 6 misery 7 neglect, poverty 8 fulness, meanness, ugliness 9 dinginess, dirtiness, nastiness, seediness 10 abjectness, grubbiness, sordidness 11 squalidness, uncleanness 12 wretchedness 13 uncleanliness

squander 4 blow 5 spend, waste 6 lavish, misuse 7 consume, deplete, exhaust 8 misspend 9 dissipate, throw away 10 run through 11 fritter away 14 spend like water

squanderer 6 waster 7 wastrel 8 prodigal 10 dissipater, profligate 11 spendthrift

squandering 7 wasting 8 prodigal, wasteful 9 imprudent 10 profligate 11 dissipating, extravagant, improvident, spendthrift 12 overspending, throwing away 14 frittering away 17 spending like water

square 3 box, fit 4 even, fogy, heal, hick, jerk, jibe, just, mend, park, prig 5 agree, align, blend, block, close, equal, green, match, place, plane, plaza, prude, tally 6 accord, adjust, candid, circus, cohere, common, concur, even up, fall in, honest, pay off, settle, smooth 7 arrange, balance, clear up, compose, conform, even out, flatten, mediate, patch up, rectify, resolve 8 block out, cornball, make even, quadrate, set right, settle up, truthful 9 arbitrate, discharge, equitable, harmonize, liquidate, make level, reconcile 10 clodhopper, correspond, quadrangle, straighten 11 marketplace 12 apple knocker, conservative 13 quadrilateral, stick-in-the-mud 15 straightforward
  type: 1 T 3 try 11 combination

Square
  character in: 8 Tom Jones
  author: 8 Fielding

Square
  constellation of: 5 Norma

square centimeter
  abbreviation: 4 sq cm

square decimeter
  abbreviation: 4 sq dm

square dekameter
  abbreviation: 5 sq dam

square foot
abbreviation: **4** sq ft

square hectometer
abbreviation: **4** sq hm

square inch
abbreviation: **4** sq in

square kilometer
abbreviation: **4** sq km

square meter
abbreviation: **3** sq m

square mile
abbreviation: **4** sq mi

square millimeter
abbreviation: **4** sq mm

square rod
abbreviation: **4** sq rd

square yard
abbreviation: **4** sq yd

squash 3 jam **4** cram, mash, pulp **5** crowd, crush, level, quash, quell, smash, upset **6** dispel, squish **7** compact, destroy, flatten, put down, ram down, repress, squeeze, squelch, trample **8** compress, suppress **9** dissipate, overthrow, prostrate, undermine **10** annihilate, obliterate **11** concentrate

squash 9 Cucurbita
varieties: **4** bush **5** acorn **6** autumn, banana, summer, turban, winter **7** Hubbard, scallop **8** pattypan, zucchini **9** cocozelle, crookneck **12** Boston marrow **13** sweet dumpling **15** Canada crookneck, summer crookneck, winter crookneck

squat 5 cower, dumpy, dwell, kneel, pudgy **6** chunky, cringe, crouch, encamp, hunker, lie low, locate, move in, shrink, square, stocky, stubby, stumpy **8** thickset

squawk 5 blare, croak, gripe **6** scream, squall **7** grumble, protest, screech **8** complain

squeak 3 cry **4** peep, yelp **5** cheep, chirp, creak, grate **6** shriek, shrill, squeal **7** screech

squeal 3 cry **4** bawl, blab, fink, peep, sing, wail, yell, yelp **5** cheep, whine **6** inform, scream, shriek, shrill, squeak **7** screech

squealer 3 pig, rat **4** fink **6** canary, piglet, snitch **7** stoolie, tattler, traitor **8** informer **10** tattletale **11** stool pigeon **12** blabbermouth

squeamish 3 coy **4** prim, sick **5** fussy **6** demure, modest, proper, queasy **7** finical, finicky, mincing, prudish, sickish **8** delicate, nauseous, priggish, qualmish **9** finicking **10** fastidious **11** puritanical, straitlaced **13** sanctimonious

squeeze 3 hug, jam, pry, ram **4** butt, cram, edge, grip, hold, pack, push **5** clasp, cramp, crowd, drive, elbow, grasp, press, shove, stuff, wedge, wrest, wring **6** clutch, coerce, compel,

defile, elicit, extort, jostle, thrust, wrench **7** compact, draw out, embrace, extract, passage, pull out, tear out **8** compress, crowding, crushing, force out, pinching, press out, pressure, shoulder, withdraw **9** extricate, narrowing, stricture **10** bottleneck **11** compression, concentrate, consolidate **12** constriction

squelch 4 hush **5** abort, crush, quash, quell, quiet, smash **6** retort, squash **7** put down, riposte, silence **8** silencer, suppress

squire 4 date, take **5** court **6** attend, escort **7** consort, gallant, planter **8** cavalier, chaperon **9** accompany, attendant, boyfriend, chauffeur, companion, landowner **14** lord of the manor **16** country gentleman

Squire
character in: **18** The Canterbury Tales
author: **7** Chaucer

squirm 4 bend, jerk, toss, turn **5** pitch, shift, smart, sweat, twist, wince **6** blench, fidget, flinch, shrink, twitch, wiggle, writhe **7** agonize, contort, wriggle **8** flounder

squirt 3 jet **4** dash, gush, punk, runt **5** piker, shoot, spout, spray, spurt **6** shower, splash, stream **7** spatter **8** sprinkle **9** discharge, pipsqueak **10** besprinkle

Sri Lanka
other name: **6** Ceylon **8** Serendib **9** Taprobane
capital/largest city: **7** Colombo
ancient capital: **11** Polonnaruwa **12** Anuradhapura
others: **3** Uva **5** Galle, Kandy **6** Jaffna, Mannar, Matale, Matara **7** Badulla, Kegalle, Negombo **8** Kalutara, Mankulem, Moratuwa, Puttalam **9** Ratnapura **10** Batticaloa, Mullaitivu **11** Ambalangoda, Trincomalee
division: **8** Dambulla, Sri Lanka **9** Taprobane
measure: **4** para, seer **5** parah **6** amunam, parrah
monetary unit: **4** cent **5** rupee
island: **5** Delft **6** Mannar **8** Sri Lanka
mountain: **5** Pedro **7** Sri Pada **9** Adam's Peak
highest point: **14** Pidurutalagala
river: **4** Kala **6** Deduru, Gal Ova **8** Aruvi Aru **9** Deburu Ova **11** Kelani Ganga **13** Mahaweli Ganga
sea: **6** Indian
physical feature:
bay: **6** Bengal **8** Koddiyar
falls: **8** Lazapana
gulf: **6** Mannar
peninsula: **6** Jaffna
plateau: **6** Hatton
strait: **4** Palk
people: **5** Malay, Tamil, Vedda **6** Veddah, Weddah **7** Burgher, Mahinda, Malabar **8** Eurasian **9** Cingalese, Dravidian, Sinhalese **10** Sin-

ghalese
leader: **11** Jayawardene **12** Bandaranaike
rebels: **11** Tamil Tigers
ruler: **5** Dutch **7** British, Chinese **10** Portuguese
language: **4** Pali **5** Tamil **7** English **9** Sinhalese
religion: **5** Hindu, Islam **8** Buddhism
place:
fortress: **8** Sigiriya
gardens: **8** Hakgalle **10** Peradiniya
national park: **6** Ruhuna **8** Wilpattu
temple: **5** Tooth **6** Gal Oya **7** Kelanya **8** Runaweli **9** Ruanvelli **10** Dankahlaka **12** Asokharamaya
feature:
animal: **5** loris **12** wild elephant
clothing: **4** sari **5** camba **6** sarong **7** cambaya **8** sherwani
dancer: **7** Kandyan
drama: **5** kolam **7** nadagam
festival: **8** Perahera
shrine: **6** dagoba
tree: **4** doon, hora, palu, tala **5** domba, ebony **7** talipot **8** halmilla, ironwood **9** satinwood **11** allaeanthus **12** shimohabodhi

SS-GB
author: **11** Len Deighton
SS troops, chief of 12 Reichsfuhrer
stab 2 go **3** cut, jab, try **4** ache, bite, gash, gore, hurt, pain, pang, pass, shot, spit **5** essay, gouge, knife, lance, lunge, prick, qualm, slash, spear, spike, stick, sting, trial, wound **6** cleave, dagger, effort, impale, pierce, shiver, stroke, thrill, thrust, twinge **7** attempt, bayonet **8** endeavor, lacerate, transfix **10** laceration, run through

stability 5 poise **6** aplomb, fixity **7** balance **8** evenness, firmness, security, solidity **9** constancy, fixedness, solidness, soundness **10** continuity, durability, permanence, stableness, steadiness, sturdiness **11** abidingness, equilibrium, reliability **13** steadfastness **14** changelessness **16** unchangeableness

stabilize 7 balance **8** hold firm, make firm **10** hold steady, make steady

stabilizer 7 balance, ballast **8** additive **9** equipoise, gyroscope **10** ballasting **12** airplane part **14** counterbalance

stable 4 barn, byre, even, firm, mews, safe, true **5** fixed, loyal, solid, sound **6** moored, secure, steady, sturdy **7** abiding, durable, staunch, uniform **8** anchored, constant, cowhouse, cowshed, enduring, faithful, reliable, resolute, stalwart **9** immovable, steadfast **10** dependable, persisting, stationary, unchanging, unwavering **11** established, unfaltering **12** indissoluble, unchangeable

Stabler, Ken
nickname: **8** the Snake
sport: **8** football

staccato
music: **12** disconnected **16** each note separate

stack 4 bank, flue, heap, load, lump, mass, pile, rick **5** amass, batch, bunch, clump, hoard, mound, sheaf **6** bundle, funnel, gather **7** chimney **8** assemble, mountain **9** amassment **10** accumulate **11** aggregation **12** accumulation

Stack, Robert
born: **12** Los Angeles CA
roles: **9** Eliot Ness **13** Name of the Game **15** The Untouchables **16** Written on the Wind **19** The High and the Mighty **24** The Bullfighter and the Lady

Stacte 5 spice

stadium 4 bowl, park **5** arena, field, stade **6** circus **8** ballpark, coliseum **9** palaestra **10** hippodrome **12** amphitheater

Stael, Madame de
author of: **7** Corinne **8** Delphine **9** On Germany **35** The Influence of Literature upon Society

staff 3 bat, man, rod **4** cane, crew, help, pole, team, tend, wand, work **5** cadre, force, group, stave, stick **6** crutch, cudgel, manage **7** retinue, scepter, service, support **8** advisors, bludgeon, flagpole **9** billy club, employees, flagstaff, personnel **10** alpenstock, assistants, shillelagh **12** walking stick

staff member 4 aide **6** worker **8** employee

stage 3 act **4** dais, play, spot, step **5** arena, drama, grade, level, phase, put on, sight, stump **6** acting, locale, period, podium, pulpit **7** perform, present, produce, rostrum, setting, show biz, soapbox, theater **8** bearings, locality, location, position, scaffold **9** dramatize, the boards

Stagecoach
director: **8** John Ford
cast: **9** John Wayne **10** Andy Devine **11** Louise Platt **12** Claire Trevor **13** John Carradine **14** George Bancroft, Thomas Mitchell
Oscar for: **15** supporting actor (Mitchell)

stagecraft 5 drama **7** theater **9** theatrics **10** dramaturgy **11** thespianism **12** dramatic arts

Stage Door
author: **10** Edna Ferber **14** George S Kaufman
director: **13** Gregory La Cava
cast: **11** Andrea Leeds, Gail Patrick **12** Ginger Rogers **13** Adolphe Menjou **16** Katharine Hepburn

stage setting
French: **11** mise en scene

stagger 3 jar **4** jolt, reel, stun, sway **5** amaze, lurch, shake, shock, waver **6** hobble, totter, wobble **7** astound, blunder, nonplus, overlap, shamble, startle, stumble, stupefy **8** astonish, bewilder, bowl over, confound, flounder, unsettle **9** alternate, dumbfound, give a turn, overwhelm, spread out **10** disconcert, knock silly, strike dumb **11** cause to reel, cause to sway, consternate, flabbergast, take in turns **12** make unsteady **15** throw off balance

staggering 7 amazing **8** shocking, stunning **9** startling **10** astounding **11** astonishing **12** breathtaking

stagnant 4 dead, dull, foul, lazy, slow **5** close, inert, quiet, slimy, stale, still **6** filthy, leaden, putrid, static, supine, torpid **7** dormant, dronish, languid, tainted **8** inactive, lifeless, listless, polluted, sluggish, standing **9** lethargic, ponderous, putrefied, quiescent **10** monotonous, motionless, not flowing, not running, stationary, unstirring, vegetative **13** uncirculating

stagnate 7 go to pot, lie idle, putrefy **8** go to seed, lie still, vegetate **10** stand still **11** cease to flow, deteriorate, stop growing **14** become inactive, become polluted, become sluggish

stagy 5 phony **8** affected, mannered **9** unnatural **10** artificial, factitious, theatrical

staid 5 grave, quiet, sober, stiff **6** decent, demure, proper, sedate, seemly, solemn, somber **7** earnest, prudish, serious, settled, subdued **8** decorous, priggish, reserved **9** dignified **10** complacent **15** undemonstrative

stain 3 dye, mar **4** blot, daub, flaw, foul, mark, ruin, slur, soil, spot, tint **5** brand, color, dirty, grime, libel, patch, shame, smear, speck, spoil, sully, taint **6** befoul, blotch, debase, defile, impair, malign, smirch, smudge, stigma, vilify **7** blacken, blemish, pigment, slander, splotch, subvert, tarnish **8** besmirch, coloring, discolor, disgrace, dishonor, dyestuff, tincture **9** denigrate, discredit, disparage, undermine **10** imputation, stigmatize **13** discoloration

stainless 5 clean, moral **6** chaste, decent **8** spotless, unsoiled **9** exemplary, unspotted, unsullied, untainted **11** unblemished

Stairway to Heaven
director: **13** Michael Powell **17** Emeric Pressburger
cast: **9** Kim Hunter **10** David Niven **12** Roger Livesey **13** Raymond Massey
original title: **21** A Matter of Life and Death

stake 3 bar, bet, peg, pot, rod **4** ante, back, grab, haul, lash, loot, moor, pale, pawn, pile, play, pole, post, prop, risk, stay, take **5** booty, brace, hitch, kitty, prize, purse, share, spike, stand, stick, treat, wager **6** chance, column, define, fasten, fetter, hazard, hold up, marker, picket, pillar, reward, secure, spoils, tether **7** delimit, finance, jackpot, mark off, mark out, outline, peg down, returns, sponsor, support, trammel, venture **8** interest, make fast, pickings, standard, winnings **9** delineate, demarcate, speculate, subsidize **10** investment, jeopardize, underwrite **11** involvement, speculation

Stalag 17
director: **11** Billy Wilder
cast: **9** Don Taylor **11** Peter Graves **12** Neville Brand **13** Harvey Lembeck, Otto Preminger, Richard Erdman, Robert Strauss, William Holden
Oscar for: **5** actor (Holden)

stale 4 dull, flat **5** banal, close, fusty, musty, trite, vapid **6** common **7** humdrum, insipid, prosaic, tedious, worn-out **8** mediocre, not fresh, ordinary, stagnant, unvaried **9** hackneyed, savorless, tasteless **10** monotonous, pedestrian, threadbare **11** commonplace **13** unimaginative, uninteresting

stalemate 3 tie **4** draw, halt **7** dead end, impasse **8** blockage, cul-de-sac, dead heat, deadlock, standoff **10** standstill

stalk 4 hunt, lurk, stem **5** haunt, march, prowl, shaft, spire, stamp, steal, stomp, strut, track, tramp, trunk **6** column, menace, stride **7** pedicel, pervade, swagger **8** hang over, threaten **9** creep up on, go through, sneak up on

stall 3 box, pen **4** cell, coop, halt, shed, shop, stop **5** block, booth, check, delay, kiosk, stand **6** arcade, arrest, hobble, impede, pull up, put off **7** bed down, confine, cubicle, disable, trammel **8** obstruct, paralyze, postpone **9** be evasive, interrupt, stop short, temporize **10** equivocate **11** compartment, play for time, stop running **12** incapacitate **13** orchestra seat

Stallone, Sylvester
born: **9** New York NY
nickname: **3** Sly
roles: **4** FIST **5** Rambo, Rocky (Oscar), Shade **7** Copland **9** Assassins **10** First Blood, Judge Dredd, Rhinestone **11** Cliffhanger **15** Rambo: First Blood **18** The Lords of Flatbush

stalwart 4 bold, firm, hale **5** beefy, brave, hardy, hefty, husky, manly, sound **6** brawny, gritty, heroic, mighty, plucky, robust, rugged, spunky, stable, strong, sturdy **7** gallant, staunch, valiant **8** constant, intrepid, muscular, powerful, resolute, valorous, vigorous **9** steadfast, strapping, unbending, undaunted **10** ablebodied, courageous, persistent, unflagging, unshakable, unswerving, unwavering, unyielding **11** indomitable, lionhearted, undeviating, unfaltering, unflinching, unshrinking **12** intransigent, stouthearted, strong-willed **14** uncompromising

stamina 4 pith **5** vigor **6** energy **8** vitality **9** endurance, hardiness, stoutness **10** ruggedness, sturdiness **12** perseverance, staying power

stammer 6 falter, fumble, mumble **7** sputter, stumble, stutter **8** splutter **9** hem and haw

stamp
  block: 4 pane
  collecting: 9 philately
  first: 10 Penny Black
    issued by: 12 Great Britain
    inscribed with: 8 One Penny
    picture of: 13 Queen Victoria
  first-day hand stamper: 6 cachet
  hole measurer: 16 perforation gauge
  mounting paper: 5 hinge
  not perforated: 11 imperforate
  paper design: 9 watermark
  rolls: 4 coil
  tear holes: 12 perforations
  tear slit: 8 roulette
  unseparated group: 5 block
  used mark: 8 postmark **12** cancellation
  value suspended: 11 demonetized

stamp, stamp out 2 OK **3** die, tag **4** cast, kind, make, mark, mint, mold, seal, sort, type **5** brand, breed, clump, crush, erase, genre, label, march, order, print, pound, punch, quash, smash, stalk, stomp, strut, thump, tramp **6** banish, betray, emblem, expose, matrix, nature, put out, reveal, rub out, signet, step on, strain, stride, trudge **7** abolish, blot out, display, engrave, exhibit, impress, imprint, put down, squelch, trample, variety, voucher **8** get rid of, hallmark, identify, inscribe, intaglio, manifest, suppress, typecast **9** character, eliminate, engraving, eradicate, personify, signature, trademark **10** annihilate, do away with, extinguish, imprimatur, stigmatize, validation **11** attestation, certificate, demonstrate, distinguish, endorsement, exterminate, **12** characterize, official mark, ratification **13** certification **14** authentication, characteristic, identification

stampede 4 bolt, dash, flee, race, rout, rush **5** chaos, flood, panic **6** engulf **7** overrun, retreat, scatter **8** inundate **10** take flight **11** crowd around, pandemonium **12** beat a retreat
  French: 12 sauve qui peut

stanchion 4 post, prop, stay **5** brace, strut **7** support, upright

stand 2 be **3** put, set **4** draw, face, hold, last, move, rank, rear, rest, rise, stay, step, take, tent **5** abide, argue, booth, brook, erect, exist, get up, hoist, honor, kiosk, mount, place, put up, raise, shift, stall, treat **6** bear up, effort, endure, obtain, pay for, policy, remain, remove, stance, suffer, uphold **7** carry on, commend, counter, defense, endorse, finance, hold out, opinion, persist, posture, prevail, provide, stick up, stomach, support, survive, sustain, undergo, weather **8** advocate, be placed, champion, continue, pavilion, position, sanction, submit to, tolerate **9** be located, be present, be upright, persevere, put up with, sentiment, undertake, viewpoint **10** resistance, set upright **11** be permanent, countenance, disposition, point of view **13** remain in force, take a position

Stand, The
  author: 11 Stephen King

standard 3 leg **4** base, flag, foot, jack, post **5** basic, canon, guide, ideal, stock, usual **6** banner, column, common, ensign, normal, pillar **7** measure, pennant, regular, support, typical, upright **8** accepted, ordinary, streamer **9** criterion, customary, guideline, principle, prototype, stanchion, universal, yardstick **10** foundation, touchstone **11** requirement **13** specification

stand behind 4 back **7** endorse, support **8** champion, vouch for **9** recommend

standby 6 backup **9** alternate, available **10** substitute, understudy **11** old reliable **12** tried-and-true

stand by 4 keep **5** cling **6** adhere, be true, defend, hold to, keep to **7** be loyal, stick by **8** cleave to, maintain **10** be constant, be faithful, stick up for

stand fast 4 hold **6** resist **8** stand pat

stand for 4 bear **5** abide, favor, stand **6** embody **7** signify **8** advocate, submit to, tolerate **9** personify, put up with, represent, symbolize

stand-in 3 sub **5** agent, proxy **6** backup, deputy, double, fill-in **9** alternate, assistant, surrogate **10** substitute, understudy **11** pinch hitter, replacement

standing 3 age **4** life, rank, term, time **5** erect, fixed, grade, inert, order, place, still **6** at rest, static, status, tenure **7** dormant, footing, lasting, station, upended, upright **8** duration, inactive, position, stagnant, vertical **9** immovable, permanent, perpetual, quiescent, renewable **10** continuing, importance, motionless, reputation,

stationary, unstirring **11** continuance **13** perpendicular

standoff 7 impasse **8** deadlock

standoffish 4 cool **5** aloof **6** formal, remote **7** distant, haughty **8** detached, reserved, solitary, taciturn **9** reclusive, withdrawn **10** antisocial, restrained, unfriendly, unsociable **12** inaccessible, misanthropic, unresponsive **14** unapproachable **15** uncommunicative, uncompanionable

standpoint 4 side **5** angle, slant **6** aspect **9** viewpoint **11** point of view

standstill 3 end **4** halt, stop **5** pause **6** hiatus **7** dead end, impasse **8** abeyance, deadlock, dead stop, full stop **9** breakdown, cessation, stalemate **10** suspension **11** termination **14** discontinuance

stand up for 4 back **5** boost **6** defend **7** further, promote, support **8** advocate, champion

stand up to 4 defy, face **5** brave **6** resist **8** confront **9** challenge

Stan the Man
  nickname of: 10 Stan Musial

Stanwyck, Barbara
  real name: 11 Ruby Stevens
  born: 10 Brooklyn NY
  husband: 8 Frank Fay **12** Robert Taylor
  roles: 9 Big Valley, The Colbys **10** Ball of Fire, The Lady Eve **11** Meet John Doe **12** Stella Dallas **15** Double Indemnity **16** Sorry Wrong Number **20** Cattle Queen of Montana **22** Christmas in Connecticut

staple 3 key **4** main **5** basic, chief, major, prime, vital **6** leader **7** feature, primary, product **8** resource, vendible **9** commodity, essential, necessary **11** fundamental, raw material **13** indispensable

Stapleton, Jean
  real name: 12 Jeanne Murray
  born: 9 New York NY
  roles: 7 Dingbat **11** Edith Bunker **14** All in the Family

Stapleton, Maureen
  born: 6 Troy NY
  roles: 7 Airport **9** Interiors **12** Lonelyhearts **13** The Rose Tattoo **18** A View from the Bridge

star, stars 3 god, sun, VIP **4** diva, fate, hero, idol, lead, lion, name **5** comet, excel, giant, great, omens, shine **6** big wig, do well, galaxy, meteor, nebula, planet **7** destiny, feature, fortune, goddess, heroine, notable, soloist, starlet, succeed, top draw **8** asteroid, cynosure, eminence, immortal, luminary, mainstay, Milky Way, portents, showcase, stand out, virtuoso **9** celebrity, headliner, meteoroid, principal, satellite, top banana **10** prima donna **11** All-American, drawing card, play the lead, protagonist **12** famous person, gain approval, heavenly body **13** celestial body, constellation **14** main attraction, predestination, prima ballerina

brightest: 6 Sirius

brightness measure: 9 magnitude **10** luminosity

color: 3 red **4** blue **5** black, white **6** orange, yellow

distance measure: 6 parsec **9** light year

double star: 6 binary

exploding star: 4 nova **9** supernova

French: 6 etoile

name: 4 Mira, Ross, Vega, Wolf **5** Cygni, Deneb, Rigel, Spica **6** Altair, Luyten, Pollux **7** Antares, Canopus, Capella, Lalande, Polaris, Procyon, Regulus, Tau Ceti **8** Achernar, Arcturus, Barnard's, Lacaille, Pleiades **9** Aldebaran, Fomalhaut **10** Beta Crucis, Betelgeuse **11** Delta Cephei, Epsilon Indi, Groombridge **12** Beta Centauri **14** Epsilon Eridani

nearest: 13 Alpha Centauri

position/motion: 7 azimuth **8** parallax **11** declination

type: 5 dwarf, giant **6** pulsar **7** cluster, neutron **8** variable **9** black hole, collapsed

Starbuck

character in: 8 Moby Dick

author: 8 Melville

starch 5 vigor **6** sizing **8** backbone, gumption **10** stiffening

starched 5 crisp, sized, stiff **7** starchy **9** stiffened

starchy 5 rigid, stiff **6** formal, proper **7** correct **10** meticulous

stare 3 eye **4** gape, gawk, gaze, ogle, peep, peer **5** glare, lower, watch **6** gaping, glower, goggle, ogling, regard **7** staring **8** once-over, scrutiny **9** fixed look **10** inspection, rubberneck

stare at 3 eye **4** ogle **5** watch **6** behold, gaze at, look at, regard **7** inspect, observe **10** scrutinize **11** contemplate

Stargate: Atlantis

network: 5 SciFi

cast: 11 Joe Flanigan (John Sheppard) **12** David Hewlett (Rodney McKay), Mitch Pileggi (Steven Caldwell) **13** Paul McGillion (Carson Beckett) **14** Rachel Luttrell (Teyla Emmagan), Torri Higginson (Elizabeth Weir) **17** Rainbow Sun Francks (Aiden Ford)

Stargate SG-1

network: 5 SciFi

cast: 9 Don S Davis (George Hammond) **10** Ben Browder (Cameron Mitchell), Corin Nemec (Jonas Quinn) **11** Beau Bridges (Hank Landry) **12** Claudia Black (Vala Maldoran), Teryl Rothery (Janet Fraiser) **13** Amanda Tapping (Samantha Carter), Michael Shanks (Daniel

Jackson) **14** Louis Gossett Jr (Gerak) **16** Carmen Argenziano (Jacob Carter/Selmak), Christopher Judge (Teal'c) **19** Richard Dean Anderson (Jack O'Neill)

Star Is Born, A

director:

1937 version: 14 William Wellman

1954 version: 11 George Cukor

1976 version: 12 Frank Pierson

cast:

1937 version: 11 Janet Gaynor **13** Adolphe Menjou, Frederic March

1954 version: 10 Jack Carson, James Mason **11** Judy Garland **15** Charles Bickford

1976 version: 9 Gary Busey **11** Oliver Clark **15** Barbra Streisand **17** Kris Kristofferson

Oscar for:

1937 version: 5 story

song:

1954 version: 17 The Man That Got Away

stark 4 bare, bold, cold, grim, pure **5** bleak, blunt, clean, empty, fully, gross, harsh, naked, plain, plumb, quite, sheer, total, utter **6** arrant, barren, chaste, patent, severe, simple, vacant, wholly **7** austere, evident, forlorn, glaring, obvious, staring, utterly **8** absolute, complete, deserted, desolate, entirely, flagrant, forsaken, outright, palpable **9** abandoned, downright, out-and-out, unadorned, unalloyed, veritable **10** absolutely, altogether, completely, consummate **11** conspicuous, unmitigated **12** unmistakable

Stark, Johannes

field: 7 physics

nationality: 6 German

described: 11 Stark Effect **14** dispersed light

awarded: 10 Nobel Prize

starlet 7 actress, ingenue **9** bit player, pinup girl

Starsky and Hutch

character: 5 Hutch (Ken Hutchinson) **7** (Dave) Starsky **9** Huggy Bear **11** (Capt) Harold Dobey

cast: 9 David Soul **13** Antonio Fargas **14** Bernie Hamilton **17** Paul Michael Glaser

car: 10 Ford Torino

start 3 aid, shy **4** dawn, drop, edge, form, gush, jerk, jolt, jump, lead, leap, odds, rush, turn **5** beget, begin, birth, blink, bound, eject, erupt, evict, flush, forge, found, issue, leave, leg up, onset, rouse, set up, shoot, spasm, spurt, wince **6** blench, broach, chance, create, depart, embark, emerge, fall to, father, flinch, ignite, kindle, launch, origin, outset, pop out, propel, recoil, set off, set out, spring, take up, twitch **7** advance, backing, disturb, genesis, make off, opening,

push off, scatter, set sail, support, take off, turn out, usher in **8** advocacy, commence, creation, displace, embark on, engender, generate, get going, initiate, organize, priority, set about, set going, touch off **9** advantage, beginning, establish, fabricate, first step, inception, institute, introduce, originate, propagate, undertake, venture on **10** assistance, break forth, bring about, buckle down, burst forth, give rise to, inaugurate, initiation, plunge into, sally forth, venture out **11** break ground, put in motion, set in action **12** commencement, inauguration, introduction **14** set in operation

starting point 5 onset, start **8** zero hour **9** beginning

Latin: 12 terminus a quo

startle 3 jar **4** faze **5** alarm, scare, shake, shock, upset **7** perturb, unnerve **8** disquiet, frighten, surprise, unsettle **9** give a turn **10** discompose, disconcert, intimidate

Star Trek

character: 4 Sulu **5** Uhura **6** Scotty (Engineer Montgomery Scott), (Ensign Pavel) Chekov **7** Mr Spock **10** (Captain) James T Kirk, (Yeoman) Janice Rand **12** (Dr) Leonard McCoy **15** (Nurse) Christine Chapel

cast: 11 George Takei, James Doohan **12** Leonard Nimoy, Majel Barrett, Walter Koenig **13** DeForest Kelly **14** William Shatner **15** Grace Lee Whitney, Nichelle Nichols

ship: 10 (USS) Enterprise

aliens: 8 Klingons, Romulans

Spock's planet: 6 Vulcan

pet: 7 tribble

starve 3 yen **4** burn, deny, fast, gasp, long, lust, pine **5** crave, raven, yearn **6** aspire, cut off, famish, hunger, refuse, thirst **7** deprive **8** be hungry, go hungry, languish

Star Wars

director: 11 George Lucas

cast: 10 Kenny Baker, Mark Hamill (Luke Skywalker) **11** David Prowse (Darth Vader) **12** Alec Guinness, Carrie Fisher (Princess Leia), Harrison Ford (Han Solo), Peter Cushing **14** Anthony Daniels

voice of Darth Vader: 14 James Earl Jones

score: 12 John Williams

Oscar for: 5 score

sequel: 15 Return of the Jedi **20** The Empire Strikes Back

prequels: 16 Revenge of the Sith, The Phantom Menace **17** Attack of the Clones

sequel casts: 7 Frank Oz (voice of Yoda) **12** Ian McDiarmid (Emperor Palpatine) **13** Sebastian Shaw (Anakin Skywalker) **16** Billy Dee Williams (Lando Calrissian)

prequel casts: 7 Frank Oz (voice of

Yoda) **9** Jake Lloyd (young Anakin Skywalker) **10** Jimmy Smits (Senator Organa), Liam Neeson (Qui-Gon Jinn) **11** Daniel Logan (Boba Fett) **12** Ewan McGregor (Obi-Wan Kenobi), Ian McDiarmid (Senator/Chancellor/Emperor Palpatine) **14** Natalie Portman (Queen Padme Amidala), Samuel L Jackson (Mace Windu) **17** Hayden Christensen (Anakin Skywalker)

stasimon 9 choral ode
literally: 8 standing

state 3 put **4** form, land, mind, mode, mood, pass, pomp **5** guise, offer, phase, realm, shape, stage **6** aspect, luxury, morale, nation, people, plight, recite, relate, report, ritual, status **7** comfort, country, declare, explain, expound, express, kingdom, narrate, posture, present, recount, spirits **8** attitude, ceremony, describe, dominion, monarchy, official, position, propound, republic, set forth **9** condition, elucidate, formality, full dress, high style, situation, structure **10** ceremonial, government **11** body politic, frame of mind, predicament, state of mind **12** commonwealth, constitution, governmental, principality **13** circumstances

state abbreviations
Alabama: 2 AL **3** Ala
Alaska: 2 AK **4** Alas
Arizona: 2 AZ **4** Ariz
Arkansas: 2 AR **3** Ark
California: 2 CA **3** Cal **5** Calif
Colorado: 2 CO **4** Colo
Connecticut: 2 CT **4** Conn
Delaware: 2 DE **3** Del
Florida: 2 FL **3** Fla
Georgia: 2 GA
Hawaii: 2 HI
Idaho: 2 ID **3** Ida
Illinois: 2 IL **3** Ill
Indiana: 2 IN **3** Ind
Iowa: 2 IA
Kansas: 2 KS **4** Kans
Kentucky: 2 KY
Louisiana: 2 LA
Maine: 2 ME
Maryland: 2 MD
Massachusetts: 2 MA **4** Mass
Michigan: 2 MI **4** Mich
Minnesota: 2 MN **4** Minn
Mississippi: 2 MS **4** Miss
Missouri: 2 MO
Montana: 2 MT
Nebraska: 2 NE **4** Nebr
Nevada: 2 NV **3** Nev
New Hampshire: 2 NH
New Jersey: 2 NJ
New Mexico: 2 NM **4** N Mex
New York: 2 NY
North Carolina: 2 NC **4** N Car
North Dakota: 2 ND **4** N Dak
Ohio: 2 OH
Oklahoma: 2 OK **4** Okla

Oregon: 2 OR **4** Oreg
Pennsylvania: 2 PA **4** Penn **5** Penna
Rhode Island: 2 RI
South Carolina: 2 SC
South Dakota: 2 SD **4** S Dak
Tennessee: 2 TN **4** Tenn
Texas: 2 TX **3** Tex
Utah: 2 UT
Vermont: 2 VT
Virginia: 2 VA
Washington: 2 WA **4** Wash
West Virginia: 2 WV **3** W Va
Wisconsin: 2 WI **3** Wis
Wyoming: 2 WY **3** Wyo

state admittance
first: 8 Delaware
second: 12 Pennsylvania
third: 9 New Jersey
fourth: 7 Georgia
fifth: 11 Connecticut
sixth: 13 Massachusetts
seventh: 8 Maryland
eighth: 13 South Carolina
ninth: 12 New Hampshire
tenth: 8 Virginia
eleventh: 7 New York
twelfth: 13 North Carolina
thirteenth: 11 Rhode Island
fourteenth: 7 Vermont
fifteenth: 8 Kentucky
sixteenth: 9 Tennessee
seventeenth: 4 Ohio
eighteenth: 9 Louisiana
nineteenth: 7 Indiana
twentieth: 11 Mississippi
twenty-first: 8 Illinois
twenty-second: 7 Alabama
twenty-third: 5 Maine
twenty-fourth: 8 Missouri
twenty-fifth: 8 Arkansas
twenty-sixth: 8 Michigan
twenty-seventh: 7 Florida
twenty-eighth: 5 Texas
twenty-ninth: 4 Iowa
thirtieth: 9 Wisconsin
thirty-first: 10 California
thirty-second: 9 Minnesota
thirty-third: 6 Oregon
thirty-fourth: 6 Kansas
thirty-fifth: 12 West Virginia
thirty-sixth: 6 Nevada
thirty-seventh: 8 Nebraska
thirty-eighth: 8 Colorado
thirty-ninth/fortieth: 11 North Dakota, South Dakota
forty-first: 7 Montana
forty-second: 10 Washington
forty-third: 5 Idaho
forty-fourth: 7 Wyoming
forty-fifth: 4 Utah
forty-sixth: 8 Oklahoma
forty-seventh: 9 New Mexico
forty-eighth: 7 Arizona
forty-ninth: 6 Alaska
fiftieth: 6 Hawaii

state capitals
Alabama: 10 Montgomery
Alaska: 6 Juneau

Arizona: 7 Phoenix
Arkansas: 10 Little Rock
California: 10 Sacramento
Colorado: 6 Denver
Connecticut: 8 Hartford
Delaware: 5 Dover
Florida: 11 Tallahassee
Georgia: 7 Atlanta
Hawaii: 8 Honolulu
Idaho: 5 Boise
Illinois: 11 Springfield
Indiana: 12 Indianapolis
Iowa: 9 Des Moines
Kansas: 6 Topeka
Kentucky: 9 Frankfort
Louisiana: 10 Baton Rouge
Maine: 7 Augusta
Maryland: 9 Annapolis
Massachusetts: 6 Boston
Michigan: 7 Lansing
Minnesota: 6 St Paul
Mississippi: 7 Jackson
Missouri: 13 Jefferson City
Montana: 6 Helena
Nebraska: 7 Lincoln
Nevada: 10 Carson City
New Hampshire: 7 Concord
New Jersey: 7 Trenton
New Mexico: 7 Santa Fe
New York: 6 Albany
North Carolina: 7 Raleigh
North Dakota: 8 Bismarck
Ohio: 8 Columbus
Oklahoma: 12 Oklahoma City
Oregon: 5 Salem
Pennsylvania: 10 Harrisburg
Rhode Island: 10 Providence
South Carolina: 8 Columbia
South Dakota: 6 Pierre
Tennessee: 9 Nashville
Texas: 6 Austin
Utah: 12 Salt Lake City
Vermont: 10 Montpelier
Virginia: 8 Richmond
Washington: 7 Olympia
West Virginia: 10 Charleston
Wisconsin: 7 Madison
Wyoming: 8 Cheyenne

State Fair
author: 9 Phil Stong
movie composers: 7 Rodgers **11** Hammerstein

state in detail 7 explain, expound **8** describe, spell out **9** explicate **16** give a full account

stateliness 7 dignity, majesty **10** augustness

stately 5 grand, lofty, noble, proud, regal, royal **6** august, formal, lordly **7** awesome, elegant, eminent **8** glorious, imperial, imposing, majestic **9** dignified, grandiose **10** ceremonial, impressive **11** magnificent

statement 3 tab **4** bill **5** check, claim, count, tally **6** avowal, charge, record, remark, report, speech **7** account, comment, invoice, mention, recital **8** relation, sentence **9** assertion, manifesto, reckoning, testimony, utterance, valuation **10** accounting, allegation, communique, exposition, profession, recitation **11** declaration, delineation, explanation, observation **12** announcement, balance sheet **13** pronouncement, specification

state of affairs 5 state **6** status **9** condition, situation **13** circumstances

State of the Union
   director: **10** Frank Capra
   cast: **10** Van Johnson **12** Spencer Tracy **13** Adolphe Menjou **14** Angela Lansbury **16** Katharine Hepburn

stateroom 5 cabin **8** quarters **11** compartment

statesman 8 diplomat **15** political leader

statesmanship 9 diplomacy **19** political leadership

static 5 fixed, inert, still **8** immobile, inactive, stagnant, unmoving **9** crackling, suspended **10** changeless, motionless, stationary, unchanging **12** interference

station 4 post, rank, site, spot, stop **5** caste, class, depot, grade, level, place **6** assign, degree, locate, sphere, status **7** footing, install **8** ensconce, facility, location, position, prestige, terminal, terminus **9** condition, firehouse, place ment **10** dispensary, guardhouse, importance **11** emplacement, whistle-stop **12** headquarters

stationary 4 even, firm **5** fixed, inert **6** intact, moored, stable, steady **7** riveted, uniform **8** constant, immobile, standing **9** dead-still, immovable, immutable, unchanged, unvarying **10** motionless, stock-still, transfixed **11** not changing, undeviating **12** unchangeable **13** standing still

Statius
   author of: **6** Silvae **10** The Thebaid **12** The Achilleid

statue 8 monument **9** sculpture **14** representation

statuesque 5 regal **7** stately **8** majestic **9** dignified

stature 4 rank, size **5** place **6** height, regard **8** eminence, position, prestige, standing, tallness **9** elevation **10** importance, prominence, reputation **11** distinction

status 4 rank **5** caste, class, grade, place, state **6** degree **7** caliber, footing, station **8** eminence, position, prestige, standing **9** condition, situation **10** estimation **11** distinction

statute 3 law **7** precept **9** prescript

statute law
   Latin: **10** lex scripta

staunch, stanch 3 dam **4** firm, stem, true **5** check, loyal, solid, sound, stout **6** impede, rugged, steady, strong, sturdy **7** contain, zealous **8** constant,

faithful, hold back, obstruct, resolute, stalwart **9** steadfast, well-built **10** watertight **11** substantial

stave off 7 beat off, fend off, keep off, ward off **9** keep at bay

stay 3 aim, guy, rib, rod **4** bunk, curb, foil, halt, live, pole, prop, rest, room, stem, stop **5** abide, block, brace, check, delay, dwell, lodge, quell, shore, stick, tarry, visit **6** endure, keep in, linger, rein in, remain, reside, splint, stifle, thwart **7** carry on, hold out, holiday, last out, persist, sojourn, support, ward off **8** abeyance, buttress, continue, hold back, mainstay, postpone, reprieve, restrain, standard, stopover, suppress, vacation, withhold **9** deferment, frustrate, persevere, staunchion **10** hang around, see through, suspension **12** postponement, reinforcement

stay put 4 stay **6** remain **8** stand pat

St Clare, Eva
   character in: **14** Uncle Tom's Cabin
   author: **5** Stowe

steadfast 4 keen, rapt **5** fixed **6** direct, intent, steady **8** resolute **9** attentive, obstinate, tenacious, undaunted **10** deep-rooted, deep-seated, inflexible, unchanging, unflagging, unwavering, unyielding **11** indomitable, persevering, unalterable, undeviating, unfaltering, unflinching **12** intransigent, single-minded, unchangeable, undistracted **14** uncompromising

steadfastness 8 tenacity **10** resolution **11** persistence **12** perseverance, resoluteness **13** determination

steadiness 4 care **5** poise **6** aplomb **8** calmness, coolness, evenness, firmness **9** composure, sangfroid, stability **10** equanimity, resolution **11** carefulness, persistence, self-control, tranquility **12** resoluteness, tranquillity **13** dependability, steadfastness **14** presence of mind, self-possession **16** imperturbability

steady 4 even, firm, sure **5** sober **6** secure, stable **7** balance, careful, devoted, regular, serious, staunch **8** constant, faithful, frequent, habitual, hold fast, reliable, resolute, unending, untiring **9** ceaseless, confirmed, dedicated, immovable, incessant, stabilize, steadfast, tenacious, unceasing **10** continuing, continuous, coolheaded, deliberate, dependable, methodical, persistent, unflagging, unwavering **11** levelheaded, persevering, substantial, undeviating, unfaltering, unremitting **12** single-minded **13** conscientious

steal 3 buy, cop **4** copy, crib, flit, flow, lift, slip, take **5** creep, drift, filch, glide, pinch, skulk, slide, slink, sneak, swipe, usurp **6** borrow, elapse, escape, extort, filter, pilfer, pocket, rip off, snatch, snitch, thieve **7** bargain,

defraud, diffuse, good buy, imitate, purloin, swindle **8** abstract, embezzle, good deal, liberate **10** burglarize, plagiarize **11** abscond with, appropriate, make off with **14** misappropriate

steal away 3 fly **4** bolt, flee, skip **5** elope **6** escape **7** get away, make off, slip out **8** creep off, slip away, sneak off **9** break free, tiptoe out **10** break loose, fly the coop **12** make a getaway

stealth 7 secrecy, slyness **10** covertness, sneakiness, subterfuge **11** furtiveness **12** stealthiness **13** secretiveness **15** unobtrusiveness **17** surreptitiousness

stealthy 3 sly **5** shady **6** covert, shifty, sneaky **7** devious, furtive **8** slippery, sneaking **9** secretive, underhand **11** clandestine, underhanded **12** huggermugger **13** surreptitious

steamboat
   invented by: **6** Fulton **9** Symington

steamed up 5 angry, het up, irate **6** raging **7** enraged, furious, riled up **8** heated up, inflamed **10** infuriated **12** mad as a wet hen **14** hot and bothered **17** hot under the collar

steamer 4 boat, clam, ship **5** liner, trunk **10** paddleboat **11** side-wheeler **12** stern-wheeler **13** paddle-wheeler

steel 4 dirk, foil, gird **5** blade, brace, knife, nerve, saber, sword **6** dagger, rapier **7** bayonet, cutlass, fortify, machete **8** falchion, scimitar **10** broadsword
   process invented by: **8** Bessemer

Steele, Sir Richard
   pseudonym: **16** Isaac Bickerstaff
   author of: **9** The Tatler (with Joseph Addison) **10** The Funeral **12** The Spectator (with Joseph Addison) **13** The Lying Lover **16** The Tender Husband **18** The Conscious Lovers

steely 4 hard **5** stony **6** flinty **9** heartless, unfeeling **10** forbidding **11** coldhearted

Steen, Jan
   born: **6** Leiden, Leyden **14** The Netherlands
   artwork: **7** Cabaret **11** The Egg Dance **12** Merry Company **14** Garden of the Inn **15** The Doctor's Visit, The Rhetoricians **16** The Morning Toilet **17** The Skittle Players **18** The World Topsy-Turvy, Young Woman Dressing

Steenburgen, Mary
   roles: **10** Cross Creek **12** Dead of Winter **13** Joan of Arcadia, Time After Time **22** Attic: Hiding of Anne Frank

steep 4 brew, bury, fill, soak **5** imbue, sharp, sheer, souse **6** abrupt, drench, engulf, infuse, plunge **7** immerse, pervade, suffuse **8** marinate, saturate, submerge **10** impregnate **11** precipitous

steeple 5 spire, tower **6** belfry **9** campanile

steer 3 aim, lay, run **4** bear, head, lead, make, sail **5** coach, guide, pilot **6** direct, govern, manage **7** conduct, proceed **8** navigate **9** supervise

steer clear of 4 shun **5** avert, avoid, dodge, evade, forgo, skirt **6** escape, eschew, forego **8** sidestep **9** keep shy of **11** abstain from, refrain from **16** give a wide berth to

Steerforth
  character in: **16** David Copperfield
  author: **7** Dickens

Steffens, Lincoln
  author of: **19** The Shame of the Cities

Steiger, Rod
  real name: **20** Rodney Stephen Steiger
  born: **13** Westhampton NY
  wife: **11** Claire Bloom
  roles: **8** Waterloo **13** The Longest Day, The Pawnbroker, W C Fields and Me **15** On the Waterfront **19** In the Heat of the Night (Oscar)

Stein, Clarence S
  architect of: **13** Temple Emanu-El (NYC)

Stein, Gertrude
  author of: **10** Three Lives **13** Tender Buttons **20** The Making of Americans **27** Autobiography of Alice B Toklas
  coined phrase: **14** lost generation

Steinbeck, John
  author of: **8** The Pearl **10** Cannery Row, East of Eden, The Red Pony **12** Of Mice and Men, Tortilla Flat **15** In Dubious Battle **16** The Grapes of Wrath **18** Travels with Charley **24** The Winter of Our Discontent

Steinmetz, Charles P
  field: **11** engineering
  developed: **2** AC **18** alternating current

Stella, Frank
  born: **8** Malden MA
  artwork: **4** Jill **5** Itata **14** Jasper's Dilemma **15** Guadalupe Island

Stella, Joseph
  born: **5** Italy **6** Naples
  artwork: **8** Full Moon (Barbados) **9** Sunflower, The Bridge **14** Brooklyn Bridge **16** Pittsburgh Winter **18** New York Interpreted **28** Battle of the Lights Coney Island

Stella Dallas
  director: **9** King Vidor
  cast: **9** John Boles **11** Anne Shirley **12** Barbara O'Neil **15** Barbara Stanwyck

stellar 6 astral, starry **7** leading **8** starring **9** brilliant, celestial, principal **11** outstanding

stem 3 dam **4** buck, cane, come, curb, grow, halt, rise, stay, stop **5** arise, block, check, deter, ensue, issue, quell, shank, shoot, speak, spire, stalk, stall, stock, trunk **6** arrest, derive, hinder, impede, oppose, resist, result, retard, spring, stanch, thwart **7** counter, pedicel, petiole, prevent, proceed, tendril **8** hold back, obstruct, peduncle, restrain, surmount **9** leafstalk, originate, withstand

stem from 5 arise, begin, start **6** derive **9** originate

stench 4 odor, reek **5** fetor, stink **8** bad smell **9** fetidness

Stendhal (Henri Marie Beyle)
  author of: **17** The Red and the Black **18** Memoirs of an Egotist **22** The Charterhouse of Parma

Stengel, Charles Dillon
  nickname: **5** Casey
  sport: **8** baseball
  position: **7** manager
  team: **11** New York Mets **14** New York Yankees **15** Brooklyn Dodgers

Stentor
  vocation: **6** herald
  characteristic: **10** loud-voiced
  voice as loud as: **8** fifty men

step 3 act **4** clip, gait, move, pace, rank, rung, span, walk **5** notch, phase, point, riser, stage, stair, strut, track, tramp, tread **6** action, degree, hobble, period, remove, stride **7** footing, measure, process, shamble, shuffle, swagger, trample **8** footfall, foothold, maneuver, purchase **9** footprint, gradation, procedure **10** proceeding

step down 4 quit **5** leave **6** resign, retire

Stephens, James
  author of: **7** Deirdre **14** The Crock of Gold **21** The Charwoman's Daughter

Stephenson, George and Robert
  nationality: **7** English
  developed: **15** steam locomotive

Steppenwolf
  author: **12** Hermann Hesse
  character: **5** Maria, Pablo **7** Hermine **11** Harry Haller

Steps
  author: **13** Jerzy Kosinski

step up 4 spur **6** come up **7** quicken, speed up **8** ap proach, escalate, expedite, increase **9** intensify **10** accelerate

stereotype 4 type **6** cliche **7** formula **8** typecast **10** categorize, pigeonhole **13** preconception

stereotyped 5 stale, trite **9** hackneyed **11** commonplace **13** unimaginative

sterile 4 bare, pure, vain **5** empty **6** barren, fallow, futile **7** aseptic, useless **8** abortive, bootless, impotent, infecund, sanitary **9** childless, fruitless, infertile, worthless **10** antiseptic, profitless, sterilized, unavailing, unfruitful,

uninfected **11** disinfected, ineffective, ineffectual, unrewarding **12** unproductive, unprofitable **13** free from germs **14** uncontaminated

sterilize 6 purify **9** autoclave, disinfect **13** decontaminate

sterling 4 pure, true **5** noble **6** silver, superb, worthy **7** genuine, perfect **8** flawless, superior **9** admirable, estimable, first-rate, honorable **10** invaluable **11** meritorious, superlative

stern 4 cold, grim, hard **5** cruel, grave, harsh, rigid, sharp, stiff **6** brutal, gloomy, severe, somber, strict, unkind **7** austere, serious **8** coercive, despotic, frowning, pitiless, rigorous, ruthless, ungentle **9** reproving, stringent, unfeeling **10** forbidding, implacable, ironfisted, ironhanded, tyrannical, unmerciful **11** admonishing, cold-blooded, reproachful **12** unreasonable **13** unsympathetic **14** unapproachable

Sterne, Laurence
  author of: **14** Tristram Shandy **19** A Sentimental Journey
  character: **9** Uncle Toby **12** Parson Yorick, Walter Shandy

sternum
  bone of: **6** breast

Steve Canyon
  creator: **12** Milton Caniff
  character: **7** Cheetah **9** Madam Lynx **10** Doe Redwood, Miss Mizzou **11** Savannah Gay **13** Copper Calhoun **14** Herself Muldoon **17** Princess Sun Flower
    wife: **6** Summer
    ward/cousin: **12** Poteet Canyon
    Summer's son: **13** Leighton Olson

Stevens, George
  director of: **5** Giant (Oscar), Shane **8** Gunga Din **9** Swing Time **13** I Remember Mama, Penny Serenade **14** A Place in the Sun (Oscar), Woman of the Year **16** The Talk of the Town **19** The Diary of Anne Frank

Stevens, James
  author of: **10** Paul Bunyan

Stevens, Wallace
  author of: **7** The Rock **9** Harmonium **13** Sunday Morning **17** Transport to Summer **23** Peter Quince at the Clavier, The Idea of Order at Key West, The Man with the Blue Guitar

Stevenson, Robert
  director of: **8** Jane Eyre **10** Back Street **11** Mary Poppins

Stevenson, Robert Louis
  author of: **9** Kidnapped **13** The Black Arrow **14** Treasure Island **18** Travels with a Donkey **21** A Child's Garden of Verses, Doctor Jekyll and Mr Hyde, The Master of Ballantrae

St Evremond, Marquis
  character in: **16** A Tale of Two Cities
  author: **7** Dickens

stew 4 fret, fume, fuss **5** chafe, gripe,

steep, tizzy, worry **6** grouse, ragout, seethe, simmer **7** agonize, fluster, flutter, grumble, mixture **10** miscellany

steward 5 agent, proxy **6** deputy, factor, waiter **7** bailiff, manager, trustee **8** executor, overseer **10** controller, supervisor **11** comptroller **13** administrator **14** representative, ship's attendant **15** flight attendant

Stewart, James
  born: 9 Indiana PA
  roles: 4 Rope **6** Harvey **7** Vertigo **10** Rear Window, Shenandoah **11** Elwood P Dowd **14** Cheyenne Autumn **16** Anatomy of a Murder, Destry Rides Again, The Stratton Story **17** Bell Book and Candle, It's a Wonderful Life **18** It's a Wonderful World, The Spirit of St Louis **19** The Glenn Miller Story **20** The Philadelphia Story (Oscar), You Can't Take It with You **22** The Greatest Show on Earth **23** Mr Smith Goes to Washington

Stewart, Mary
  real name: 22 Florence Rainbow Stewart
  author of: 11 Crystal Cave **14** The Hollow Hills **15** The Moon-Spinners **16** My Brother Michael, The Gabriel Hounds **18** Airs Above the Ground, The Last Enchantment

St George's
  capital of: 7 Grenada

stick 3 bar, bat, cue, dig, fix, jab, pin, put, rod, set **4** balk, bind, cane, club, curb, fuse, glue, hold, join, last, mire, nail, pink, poke, pole, seal, snag, stab, stop, tack, twig, wand, weld **5** abide, affix, baton, billy, block, catch, check, fagot, leave, lodge, paste, place, plant, prick, punch, shift, snarl, spear, spike, staff, stall, stake, stand, stave, stump **6** adhere, attach, boggle, branch, burden, cement, cudgel, detain, endure, fasten, hamper, hinder, hog-tie, impede, insert, pierce, puzzle, scotch, skewer, stymie, switch, thrust, thwart **7** confuse, crosier, inhibit, perplex, shackle, trammel **8** bewilder, bludgeon, caduceus, continue, obstruct, puncture **9** checkmate, constrain, perforate, truncheon, victimize **10** immobilize, shillelagh

stick fast 4 hold **5** cling, stick **6** adhere, cleave

stickler 3 bug, nut **5** crank, poser **6** enigma, purist, puzzle, riddle, zealot **7** devotee, dilemma, fanatic, mystery, stumper **8** martinet **10** enthusiast, monomaniac

sticks 4 skis **5** bonds, glues, twigs **6** pastes, Podunk **7** adheres, boonies, catches, cements, country **8** kindling **9** backwoods, boondocks, golf clubs, provinces **10** hicksville, hinterland **11** countryside, hinterlands

stick together 4 bind, fuse, glue,

hold, join **5** cling, stick, unite **6** cement, cohere

stick-to-itiveness 8 tenacity **9** endurance **10** resolution **11** persistence **12** perseverance, resoluteness **13** determination, tenaciousness

stickum 3 gum **4** glue **5** paste **6** cement **8** adhesive, mucilage **12** rubber cement

stick up for 5 boost **6** defend **7** root for **11** speak well of **17** put in a good word for

stick with 4 stay **5** abide **6** keep at **7** stand by **9** accompany, persevere

sticky 3 wet **4** damp, dank **5** gluey, gooey, gummy, humid, moist, muggy, pasty, tacky **6** clammy, clingy, steamy, sultry, viscid **7** viscous **8** adherent, adhesive, clinging, cohesive, sticking **9** glutinous, tenacious **10** gelatinous **12** mucilaginous

stiff 4 body, cold, cool, firm, grim, hard, high, iron, keen, prim, sore, taut **5** aloof, awful, brave, brisk, crisp, cruel, dense, fixed, gusty, harsh, heavy, rigid, sharp, smart, solid, steep, stern, tense, thick, tight, tough, undue **6** bitter, brutal, chilly, clumsy, corpse, dogged, forced, formal, raging, severe, steady, steely, strong, uneasy, viscid, wooden **7** austere, awkward, cadaver, clotted, decided, distant, drastic, extreme, fearful, intense, jellied, labored, precise, remains, settled, starchy, stately, staunch, steeled, stilted, uptight, valiant, violent, viscous **8** affected, constant, dead body, exacting, forceful, grievous, mannered, pitiless, pounding, powerful, resolute, resolved, rigorous, ruthless, spanking, stubborn, ungainly, unlimber, unshaken, vigorous **9** difficult, draconian, excessive, graceless, inelastic, inelegant, laborious, merciless, obstinate, resistant, steadfast, stringent, tenacious, unnatural **10** artificial, courageous, determined, exorbitant, formidable, gelatinous, immoderate, inflexible, inordinate, persistent, solidified, unswerving, unyielding **11** ceremonious, constrained, extravagant, indomitable, straitlaced, unfaltering, unflinching, unwarranted **12** strong-willed, unreasonable **14** uncompromising

stiff-necked 6 mulish **7** willful **8** contrary, obdurate, stubborn **9** obstinate, pigheaded, unbending **10** bullheaded, refractory, self-willed, unshakable, unyielding **11** intractable **12** intransigent, pertinacious

stiffness 7 tension **8** firmness, rigidity **9** aloofness, formality, tenseness, tightness **10** constraint **11** starchiness

stifle 3 gag **4** curb **5** check, choke **6** muffle, subdue **7** garrote, inhibit, repress, smother, squelch, swelter **8**

keep back, restrain, strangle, suppress, throttle **9** suffocate **10** asphyxiate

stifling 3 hot **6** stuffy **7** airless **10** overheated

stigma 4 blot, flaw, mark, scar **5** brand, odium, shame, stain, taint **6** smirch, smudge **7** blemish, tarnish **8** disgrace, dishonor **11** mark of shame **12** besmirchment

stigmatize 5 brand, smear **6** debase, defame, smirch **7** villify **9** discredit, disparage

still 4 calm, hush **5** inert, quiet **6** at rest, hushed, pacify, settle, silent **7** appease, as suage, gratify, put down, repress, silence, turn off **8** immobile, overcome, restrain, suppress, unmoving **9** noiseless, soundless **10** motionless, put an end to, stationary, unstirring

stillness 4 calm, hush **5** quiet **6** repose **7** silence **8** calmness, inaction, quietude **9** composure **10** immobility, inactivity, quiescence **11** tranquility **12** tranquillity

Stillness at Appomattox, A
  author: 11 Bruce Catton

Still Standing
  network: 3 CBS
  cast: 8 Mark Addy (Bill Miller) **9** Jami Gertz (Judy Miller) **10** Taylor Ball (Brian Miller) **11** Soleil Borda (Tina Miller) **12** Renee Olstead (Lauren Miller) **13** Jennifer Irwin (Linda)

stilted 4 cold, prim **5** rigid, stiff **6** forced, formal, stuffy, wooden **7** awkward, labored, pompous, starchy, studied, uptight **8** mannered, priggish, starched **9** graceless, unnatural **10** artificial **11** ceremonious, constrained

Stilwell, Joseph W
  nickname: 10 Vinegar Joe
  served in: 3 WWI **4** WWII
  chief of staff for: 13 Chiang Kai-shek
  driven out of: 5 Burma

stimulant 5 tonic, upper **6** bracer **8** excitant **9** energizer

stimulate 3 fan **4** spur, stir, wake **5** alert, rouse **6** arouse, awaken, excite, incite, prompt, vivify **7** actuate, animate, inflame, inspire, quicken, sharpen **8** activate, enkindle, initiate, inspirit

stimulating 5 tonic **7** piquing **8** arousing, exciting, spurring, stirring, whetting **9** animating, provoking **10** energizing, refreshing **11** interesting, provocative

stimulus 4 goad, spur, whet **5** tonic **6** bracer, fillip, motive **7** impetus **8** excitant **9** activator, energizer, incentive, quickener, stimulant **10** incitement, inducement **11** provocation **13** encouragement

sting 3 cut, nip, rub, vex **4** ache, barb, bite, blow, burn, fire, gall, gnaw, goad, grip, hurt, itch, lash, move, pain, prod, rack, rasp, rile, sore, spur, stab, whip **5** anger, chafe, cross, egg on, grate, impel, pinch, pique, prick, shake, shock, smart, venom, wince, wound **6** arouse, awaken, excite, harrow, incite, insult, kindle, madden, nettle, offend, pierce, prompt, propel, stir up, tingle, twinge **7** actuate, agonize, disturb, incense, inflame, prickle, provoke, quicken, scourge, stinger, torment, torture **8** irritate, motivate, vexation **9** infuriate, instigate, penetrate **10** affliction, irritation

Sting, The
 director: 13 George Roy Hill
 cast: 10 Paul Newman, Ray Walston, Robert Shaw **13** Eileen Brennan, Robert Redford **14** Charles Durning
 score: 11 Scott Joplin
 Oscar for: 7 picture **8** director

stinginess 6 penury **9** parsimony **11** miserliness **13** niggardliness, penny-pinching **15** tight-fistedness

stinging 4 acid **5** harsh, sharp **6** biting, bitter **7** burning, caustic, cutting, pungent **8** piercing **9** sarcastic, satirical **10** astringent

stingy 4 lean, mean, thin **5** close, scant, small, tight **6** frugal, meager, modest, paltry, scanty, skimpy, sparse **7** miserly, scrimpy, slender, sparing **8** piddling, stinting **9** illiberal, niggardly, penurious **10** inadequate, ungenerous **11** closefisted, tightfisted **12** cheeseparing, insufficient, parsimonious **13** penny-pinching

stink 4 odor, reek **5** fetor **6** stench **8** bad smell **17** smell to high heaven

stint 3 job **4** curb, duty, part, save, task, term, turn **5** check, chore, limit, quota, shift **6** reduce, scrimp **8** hold back, restrain, restrict, withhold **9** constrain, cut down on, economize **10** assignment, engagement **12** circumscribe, pinch pennies

stipend 5 grant, wages **6** income, salary **7** pension **8** fixed pay **9** allowance, emolument **10** honorarium, recompense **11** scholarship **12** compensation, remuneration

stipulate 4 cite, name **5** agree, allow, grant, state **6** assure, insure, pledge **7** promise, provide, specify, warrant **8** indicate, set forth **9** designate, guarantee

stipulation 4 term **7** proviso **9** condition **10** limitation **11** requirement, restriction

stipulative 7 limited **9** qualified, tentative **10** contingent, restricted **11** conditional, provisional **16** with reservations

stir 3 act, mix **4** beat, fire, goad, jolt, move, prod, rush, spur, to-do, whip **5** blend, rouse, shake, sough, start **6** arouse, awaken, bustle, commix, ex-

cite, flurry, hasten, hustle, kindle, mingle, mixing, moving, pother, quiver, rustle, shiver, tumult, twitch, uproar, vivify, work up **7** agitate, animate, enflame, flutter, inspire, provoke, quicken, scamper **8** energize, inspirit, intermix, mingling, movement, prodding, rustling, scramble, stirring **9** agitation, commingle, commotion, electrify, stimulate **10** get a move on, step lively **11** set in motion **12** exert oneself, make an effort

stirred up 5 riled, upset **7** aroused, excited, kindled, ruffled **8** agitated, inflamed **9** disturbed **10** stimulated

stirring 5 astir, awake **6** moving **7** rousing **8** electric, exalting, exciting, in motion, spirited **9** inspiring, thrilling **10** up and about **11** galvanizing, stimulating **12** electrifying

stir up 5 upset **6** arouse, awaken, excite, kindle, ruffle **7** agitate, disturb **9** call forth, stimulate **10** antagonize

stir vigorously 3 mix **4** beat, whip **7** agitate

stitch 3 bit, jot, sew **4** ache, iota, kink, mend, pain, pang, seam, tack **5** baste, cramp, crick, piece, scrap, shoot, shred **6** suture, tingle, twinge, twitch **7** article, garment **8** particle **9** embroider **12** charley horse

St John's
 capital of: 17 Antigua and Barbuda

St Louis
 baseball team: 9 Cardinals
 football team: 4 Rams
 founded by: 13 Pierre Laclede
 hockey team: 5 Blues
 landmark: 11 Gateway Arch
 newspaper: 12 Post-Dispatch
 river: 11 Mississippi
 site of: 10 Exposition (1904)
 university: 10 Washington

stock 4 butt, clan, form, fund, haft, herd, hold, kind, line, pull, race, root, type **5** array, basic, birth, blood, breed, broth, cache, caste, equip, goods, grasp, hoard, house, offer, shaft, store, tribe, wares **6** cattle, family, fit out, formal, handle, origin, people, shares, source, staple, strain, supply **7** appoint, capital, descent, dynasty, furnish, lineage, provide, regular, reserve, routine **8** accoutre, ancestry, bouillon, heredity, pedigree, pro forma, quantity, standard **9** forebears, genealogy, inventory, livestock, ownership, parentage, provision, reservoir, selection **10** assortment, background, extraction, family tree, investment **11** merchandise, nationality, progeniture **12** accumulation **13** capital shares

Stockhausen, Karlheinz
 born: 7 Germany, Modrath
 composer of: 5 Cycle, Tempi **6** Groups, Hymnen, Mantra, Zyklus **7** Anthems, Gruppen, Momente **8** At-

tuning, Gold Dust, Kontakte, Stimmung **9** Goldstaub, Zeitmasze **10** Procession, Prozession **12** Kontrapunkte **13** Klavierstucke **16** From the Seven Days **17** Aus den Sieben Tagen

Stockholm
 nickname: 16 Venice of the North
 capital of: 6 Sweden
 sea: 6 Baltic
 lake: 7 Malaren
 section: 8 Norrmalm **9** Sodermalm **11** Gamla Staden
 landmark: 7 Skansen **8** City Hall **11** Great Church
 site of: 10 Nobel Prize

stockpile 5 cache, hoard, stock, store **10** accumulate

stocky 5 dumpy, husky, pudgy, solid, squat, stout **6** blocky, chunky, stubby, stumpy, sturdy **8** thickset

stodgy 4 dull, flat **5** dated, heavy, lumpy, passe, staid, thick **6** boring, clumsy, dreary, narrow, prolix, stuffy **7** humdrum, pompous, prosaic, serious, starchy, tedious **8** lifeless, pedantic, tiresome **9** laborious, lumbering, wearisome **10** antiquated, inflexible, monotonous **12** indigestible, old-fashioned **13** uninteresting

stoic 4 calm **8** detached, fatalist, quietist, tranquil **9** impassive, unruffled **11** philosophic **13** dispassionate, imperturbable, unimpassioned

stoicism 8 fatalism **9** fortitude **11** impassivity, tranquility **12** tranquillity **16** imperturbability

Stoker, Bram
 author of: 7 Dracula

stole 3 fur **4** cape, robe, took, wrap **5** crept, orary, scarf **6** swiped **7** filched, pinched, sneaked, tiptoed **8** mantilla, pilfered, snatched, vestment **9** embezzled, purloined

stolen 3 hot **5** taken **6** swiped **7** filched, pinched **8** pilfered, snatched **9** embezzled, ill-gotten, purloined

stolid 4 dull **5** dense **6** bovine, obtuse **7** lumpish **8** sluggish **9** apathetic, impassive, lethargic **10** phlegmatic **11** insensitive, unemotional

stolidity 6 apathy **8** lethargy **9** inertness **11** impassivity **12** sluggishness

stomach 3 maw, pot **4** bear, bent, bias, craw, crop, guts, mind, take **5** abide, belly, brook, fancy, humor, stand, taste, tummy **6** desire, endure, hunger, liking, middle, paunch, relish, retain, suffer, temper, thirst **7** abdomen, gizzard, leaning, midriff, swallow **8** affinity, appetite, bear with, keenness, overlook, pass over, pleasure, potbelly, sympathy, tolerate **9** put up with **10** attraction, midsection, partiality, proclivity, propensity **11** breadbasket, countenance, disposition, inclination **12** predilection

stone 3 gem, nut, pip, pit 4 rock, seed 5 bijou, jewel 6 kernel, pebble 9 brilliant 10 throw rocks

Stone, Edward Durell
architect of: 9 US Embassy 17 Museum of Modern Art 33 Kennedy Center for the Performing Arts

Stone, Irving
author of: 9 The Origin 11 Lust for Life 12 Those Who Love 17 Sailor on Horseback, The President's Lady 19 Adversary in the House 21 The Agony and the Ecstasy

Stone, Oliver
born: 9 New York NY
profession: 6 writer 8 director
films: 3 JFK 5 Nixon, U-Turn 7 Platoon (Oscar) 9 Alexander 10 Wall Street 12 Patriot Games 14 Any Given Sunday, Heaven and Earth 15 Midnight Express 18 Natural Born Killers 21 Born on the Fourth of July

stonefly
varieties: 5 giant, green 6 spring, winter 8 perlodid 9 roachlike 11 green-winged 12 rolled-winged

Stone of Scone
location: 8 Scotland
purpose: 12 crowning king
moved to: 16 Westminster Abbey

stoneware 5 china 7 ceramic, pottery 8 crockery

stony 3 icy 4 cold 5 blank, bumpy, chill, rocky, rough, stern 6 coarse, craggy, flinty, frigid, jagged, marble, pebbly, rugged, severe, steely, stolid, uneven 7 austere, callous, granite, lithoid, stoical 8 concrete, deadened, gravelly, hardened, indurate, obdurate, ossified, pitiless, rocklike, soulless, uncaring 9 bloodless, heartless, merciless, petrified, unfeeling, untouched 10 adamantine, forbidding, fossilized, hard-boiled, inexorable, insensible, unaffected, unyielding

stool 5 bench 7 cricket, hassock, ottoman

stool pigeon 3 rat, spy 4 fink 5 decoy, patsy 6 snitch 7 peacher, stoolie, tattler 8 informer, squealer 10 talebearer, tattletale

stoop 3 bow, sag 4 bend, fall, sink 5 deign, droop, porch, slump, steps, yield 6 resort, slouch, submit 7 concede, descend, succumb 8 doorstep 9 acquiesce 10 condescend 11 entranceway 19 round-shoulderedness

stooped 4 bent 5 bowed 7 deigned, hunched 9 contorted 12 condescended

stop 3 ban, bar, end 4 curb, fill, halt, hold, idle, plug, quit, rest, seal, stay, stem, wait 5 abide, block, brake, break, caulk, cease, check, close, depot, deter, dwell, lapse, lodge, pause, put up, spell, stall, stand, tarry, visit 6 alight, arrest, cut off, desist, draw

up, expire, falter, finish, hamper, hiatus, hinder, pull up, recess, rein in, repose, run out, stanch, stop up, thwart 7 close up, halting, layover, occlude, prevent, respite, sojourn, station, suspend 8 abeyance, break off, conclude, cut short, hold back, intermit, interval, leave off, obstruct, pass away, peter out, postpone, preclude, restrain, suppress, surcease, terminal, terminus, wind down 9 cessation, frustrate, interlude, stand fast, terminate 10 desistance, drop anchor, put an end to, standstill, suspension 11 come to a halt, come to an end, destination, discontinue, prohibition, termination 12 intermission, interruption 17 come to a standstill 18 bring to a standstill

stopgap 7 stand-by 9 contrived, emergency, expedient, impromptu, makeshift, temporary, tentative 10 improvised, substitute 11 provisional
Latin: 5 ad hoc 6 pro tem

stop in 4 call 5 visit 6 drop in, look in

stop off 4 call 5 visit 6 drop in, look in, stop by

stoppage 4 halt 5 check, tieup 6 arrest 7 barrier, embargo, staying 8 blockage, checking, clogging, gridlock, obstacle 9 checkmate, hindrance, restraint, stricture 10 disruption, impediment 11 curtailment, obstruction 12 interruption

Stoppard, Tom
author of: 7 Jumpers 10 Travesties 12 The Real Thing 18 The Invention of Love 33 Rosencrantz and Guildenstern Are Dead

stopper 3 lid 4 bung, cock, cork, plug 5 spile

Stopping by Woods on a Snowy Evening
author: 11 Robert Frost

Stop the Music
host: 9 Bert Parks
orchestra: 11 Harry Salter
vocalist: 9 June Valli 11 Jaye P Morgan, Jimmy Blaine 12 Marion Morgan 13 Betty Ann Grove, Estelle Loring

stop up 3 jam 4 clog 5 block, choke 8 obstruct

store 3 lot 4 fund, hold, host, keep, mart, pack, pile, save, shop 5 amass, array, cache, faith, hoard, lay by, lay in, lay up, stash, stock, trust, value, wares 6 credit, esteem, gather, heap up, legion, market, plenty, regard, riches, scores, supply, volume, wealth 7 deposit, effects, husband, put away, reserve, satiety 8 emporium, lay aside, overflow, plethora, quantity, reliance, richness, salt away, sock away, stow away 9 abundance, inventory, multitude, profusion, provision, reservoir, stockpile 10 accumulate, confi-

dence, cornucopia, dependence, estimation, exuberance, luxuriance 11 copiousness, full measure, prodigality, supermarket 12 accumulation 13 establishment

storehouse 4 bank, silo 5 depot, vault 7 arsenal, granary 8 elevator, magazine, treasury 9 stockroom, warehouse 10 depository, repository

storied 4 epic 6 fabled 8 fabulous 9 legendary

storm 3 ado, row 4 blow, fume, fuss, gale, rage, rant, rave, roar, rush, stir, tear, to-do 5 burst, furor, snarl, stalk, stamp, stomp, tramp 6 assail, attack, charge, clamor, deluge, flurry, hubbub, pother, ruckus, squall, strike, tumult, uproar 7 assault, besiege, bluster, carry on, cyclone, rampage, tempest, tornado, torrent, turmoil, twister, typhoon 8 blizzard, brouhaha, downpour, eruption, fall upon, outbreak, outburst, upheaval 9 agitation, commotion, explosion, fulminate, hurricane, raise hell 10 cloudburst, hullabaloo 11 blow one's top, disturbance 12 blow one's cool, vent one's rage

storm and stress
German: 13 Sturm und Drang
name of 18th century: 16 literary movement

storm troopers
German: 14 Sturmabteilung

stormy 4 foul, wild 5 rainy, rough, snowy, windy 6 raging, rugged 7 howling, roaring, squally, violent 8 blustery 9 inclement, turbulent 10 blustering 11 tempestuous

story 3 fib, lie 4 news, plot, tale, word, yarn 5 alibi, fable, piece 6 excuse, legend, report, sketch 7 account, article, parable, romance, tidings, version 8 allegory, anecdote, argument, dispatch, news item, white lie 9 falsehood, narrative, statement, testimony 10 allegation 11 fabrication, information 13 prevarication

Story of G I Joe, The
director: 14 William Wellman
cast: 13 Freddie Steele, Robert Mitchum 15 Burgess Meredith (Ernie Pyle)

Story of Louis Pasteur, The
director: 15 William Dieterle
cast: 8 Paul Muni (Pasteur) 11 Anita Louise 19 Josephine Hutchinson
Oscar for: 5 actor (Muni)

stout 3 big, fat, fit 4 able, bold, firm, true 5 brave, bulky, burly, hardy, heavy, hefty, husky, large, obese, plump, pudgy, round, solid, tough, tubby 6 brawny, chubby, daring, fleshy, heroic, mighty, plucky, portly, robust, rotund, rugged, spunky, steady, stocky, strong, sturdy 7 doughty, gallant, staunch, valiant 8 athletic, constant, enduring, faithful, fearless, intrepid, leathery, muscular, resolute, resolved, stalwart, thickset, untiring, valorous, vigorous **9** confident, corpulent, dauntless, steadfast, strapping **10** able-bodied, courageous, determined, inflexible, unshakable, unswerving, unwavering **11** indomitable, lionhearted, unfaltering, unflinching, unshrinking

Stout, Rex
author of: **10** Fer-de-Lance **12** Too Many Cooks **16** If Death Ever Slept
character: **5** Fritz **9** Nero Wolfe **13** Archie Goodwin

stouthearted 4 bold **5** brave, gutsy, hardy **6** heroic, plucky, spunky **7** valiant **8** fearless, intrepid, resolute, spirited, stalwart, unafraid, valorous **9** dauntless, undaunted **10** courageous **11** indomitable, lionhearted, unblenching, unflinching

stouteheartedness 4 grit, guts, sand **5** nerve, pluck, spunk, valor **6** daring, mettle **7** bravery, courage **8** boldness **12** fearlessness **13** dauntlessness

stoutness
French: **10** embonpoint

stow 3 jam, put, set **4** cram, load, pack, tuck **5** cache, crowd, place, stash, store, stuff, wedge **7** deposit, squeeze **8** ensconce, salt away

Stowe, Harriet Beecher
author of: **4** Dred **12** Oldtown Folks **14** Uncle Tom's Cabin

Strachey, Lytton
author of: **13** Queen Victoria **17** Elizabeth and Essex, Eminent Victorians
member of: **15** Bloomsbury Group

strafe 7 bombard **8** fire upon **10** machine-gun

straggle 4 rove **5** drift, stray **6** sprawl, wander **7** deviate, meander **8** divagate

straight 4 even, neat, tidy, true **5** clear, frank, right, solid, sound **6** candid, direct, evenly, honest, square, unbent **7** aligned, erectly, in order, orderly, upright **8** accurate, adjusted, arranged, directly, on a level, reliable, squarely, truthful, unbroken **9** ceaseless, forthwith, incessant, instantly, not curved, shipshape, sorted out, sustained, veracious **10** aboveboard, continuous, forthright, four-square, methodical, persistent, straightly, successive, unrelieved, unswerving, unwavering **11** consecutive, coordinated, immediately, trustworthy, undeviating **13** uninterrupted

straighten 4 tidy **5** align **6** adjust, neaten, unbend **7** even out **8** level out, square up **9** put in line **10** put in order, stand erect

straightening 7 tidying **9** adjusting, alignment, evening up, unbending **10** evening out **11** leveling out **13** putting in line **14** putting in order

straighten out 6 unbend **7** realign **8** redirect **10** discipline

straighten up 4 tidy **5** align, clean, order **6** neaten, tidy up **7** arrange, stand up **8** organize

straightforward 4 open **5** blunt, frank **6** candid, direct, honest, square **7** ethical, upright **8** straight **9** guileless, honorable **10** aboveboard, creditable, forthright, scrupulous **11** plainspoken, trustworthy

straightforwardness 6 candor **7** honesty **12** truthfulness **14** forthrightness

straight from the shoulder 4 open **5** frank **6** candid, direct, openly **7** bluntly, frankly, sincere **8** candidly, directly **9** downright

straightness 7 honesty **8** evenness **10** directness **11** uprightness

strain 3 air, tax, tug **4** kind, line, pull, sift, song, sort, toil, tune, type, vein **5** blood, breed, drain, force, grain, grind, group, heave, labor, people, press, sieve, streak, stock, trait, twist **6** burden, drudge, effort, extend, family, filter, genius, injure, injury, melody, overdo, purify, refine, screen, sprain, stress, weaken, winnow, wrench **7** descent, distend, exhaust, fatigue, lineage, overtax, species, stretch, tension, tighten, try hard, variety, wear out **8** ancestry, bear down, elongate, exertion, hardship, heredity, make taut, overwork, pressure, protract, struggle, tendency **9** draw tight, make tense, overexert, parentage **10** buckle down, derivation, extraction, overburden **11** disposition, huff and puff, inclination **12** do double duty, drive oneself, exert oneself **14** predisposition, work like a horse, work like a slave

strained 5 tense **6** touchy **8** volatile **9** explosive **10** precarious

strait 7 channel, narrows, passage

straitened 5 broke, needy **6** hard-up **7** pinched **8** bank rupt, indigent, strapped, wiped-out **9** destitute, penniless, penurious **10** distressed, pauperized, restricted **11** embarrassed **12** impoverished **15** poverty-stricken

straitlaced 4 prim **5** rigid, stiff **6** formal, narrow, proper, severe, strict **7** austere, prudish, uptight **8** reserved **9** inhibited **11** puritanical **14** overscrupulous **15** undemonstrative

straits 3 fix **4** hole **6** pickle, plight **8** distress **9** extremity **10** difficulty **11** predicament **13** embarrassment

strand 4 bank, cord, lock, rope **5** beach, braid, coast, fiber, leave, shore, tress, twist **6** desert, ground, maroon, string, thread **8** filament, necklace, seacoast, seashore **9** component, go aground, riverside, shipwreck

10 ingredient, run aground **15** leave high and dry, leave in the lurch

stranded 5 stuck **6** ashore **7** aground, beached **8** grounded **9** foundered **11** shipwrecked **14** left high and dry, left in the lurch

strange 3 new, odd **4** lost **5** alien, queer **6** uneasy, unused **7** awkward, bizarre, curious, erratic, foreign, unknown, unusual **8** aberrant, abnormal, freakish, peculiar, singular, uncommon **9** alienated, anomalous, eccentric, estranged, fantastic, ill at ease, irregular, unnatural **10** bewildered, farfetched, out of place, outlandish, unexplored, unfamiliar **11** discomposed, disoriented, out-of-the-way **12** unaccustomed, undiscovered, unhabituated **13** extraordinary, unaccountable, uncomfortable **14** unconventional

Strange Fruit
author: **12** Lillian Smith

Strange Interlude
author: **12** Eugene O'Neill

strangeness 7 anomaly, oddness **9** queerness **10** aberration **11** abnormality, peculiarity **12** eccentricity, idiosyncrasy, irregularity, unconformity **13** nonconformity

stranger 5 alien **8** newcomer, outsider **9** auslander, foreigner, immigrant, outlander

Stranger, The
author: **11** Albert Camus

Strangers on a Train
director: **15** Alfred Hitchcock
cast: **9** Ruth Roman **11** Leo G Carroll, Marion Lorne **12** Robert Walker **13** Farley Granger **17** Patricia Hitchcock
remade as: **20** Once You Kiss a Stranger

strange to say
Latin: **13** mirabile dictu

strangle 3 gag **4** stop **5** burke, check, choke, crush, quell **6** muzzle, stifle **7** garrote, put down, repress, smother, squelch **8** choke off, snuff out, suppress, throttle **9** suffocate **10** asphyxiate, extinguish

strangulate 8 choke off, compress, strangle **9** constrict

strap 3 tie **4** band, beat, belt, bind, cord, flog, lash, whip **5** flail, leash, thong, truss **6** tether, thrash **7** scourge

strapped 8 bankrupt, wiped out **9** insolvent, penniless **12** impoverished, without funds

strapping 5 burly, hardy, husky, stout **6** brawny, robust, strong, sturdy **8** muscular, powerful, stalwart

stratagem 4 game, plan, plot, ploy, ruse, wile **5** blind, dodge, feint, trick **6** deceit, device, scheme, tactic **8** artifice, intrigue, maneuver, trickery **9** deception **10** subterfuge **11** contrivance, machination

strategic 3 key **4** wary **5** vital **6** clever **7** careful, crucial, cunning, guarded, planned, politic, prudent, turning **8** cautious, critical, decisive, military, tactical, vigilant **9** important, momentous, principal **10** calculated, deliberate, diplomatic **11** significant **13** consequential, precautionary

strategy 4 game **5** craft, wiles **6** policy, scheme **7** cunning, devices, tactics **8** artifice, art of war, game plan, plotting **9** war policy **10** artfulness, craftiness **11** grand design, machination, maneuvering **12** military plan **15** military science

stratosphere 3 sky **5** ozone **7** heavens **8** upper air **12** high altitude **14** wild blue yonder

stratum 4 band, belt, seam, zone **5** layer

Strauss, Johann (the Elder)
  composer of: **13** Radetzky March

Strauss, Johann (the Younger)
  composer of: **6** The Bat **13** Die Fledermaus, The Gipsy Baron **16** Der Zigeunerbaron
    waltz: **12** Emperor Waltz **13** The Blue Danube **23** Tales from the Vienna Woods

Strauss, Joseph
  composer of: **17** Music of the Spheres **27** The Village Swallows in Austria

Strauss, Levi
  make of: **5** jeans **9** dungarees

Strauss, Richard
  born: **6** Munich **7** Germany
  composer of: **6** Salome **7** Don Juan, Elektra **8** Arabella **9** Capriccio **10** Don Quixote **14** Ein Heldenleben **15** Ariadne auf Naxos **16** Der Rosenkavalier, Domestic Symphony, Till Eulenspiegel **19** Die Frau ohne Schatten **20** Die Aegyptische Helena, Thus Spake Zarathustra **21** Also Sprach Zarathustra **23** Death and Transfiguration

Stravinsky, Igor Feodorovich
  born: **6** Russia **11** Oranienbaum
  composer of: **4** Agon **6** Threni **7** Orpheus **8** The Flood **9** Card Party, Fireworks **10** Oedipus Rex, Petrouchka, Petruschka, Pulcinella **11** Jeu de Cartes, The Firebird **13** Dumbarton Oaks, Psalm Symphony **14** The Nightingale **15** Abraham and Isaac, The Rite of Spring **16** Requiem Canticles, The Rake's Progress **18** Le Sacre du Printemps

straw 3 hay **4** tube **5** chaff **7** pipette

strawberry 8 Fragaria
  varieties: **4** mock **5** beach **6** barren, Dunlap, garden, Indian **7** sow-teat **8** Klondike, Rosacean, Virginia, wood-

land
  liqueur: **13** creme de fraise

Straw Dogs
  director: **12** Sam Peckinpah
  cast: **9** T P McKenna **11** Susan George **12** Peter Vaughan **13** Dustin Hoffman

straw man 6 effigy **9** scapegoat, scarecrow

stray 4 lost, roam, rove, waif **5** drift **6** random, wander **7** digress, drifter **8** go astray, sepa rate, set apart, straggle, straying, vagabond, wanderer **9** itinerant, misplaced, scattered, straggler **10** lost animal, lost person **11** lose one's way

straying 5 lapse **8** drifting, rambling **9** departure, deviation, wandering **10** abberation, digression, divergence

streak 3 bar, bed, fly **4** band, blot, blur, cast, dart, dash, daub, line, lode, race, rush, seam, tear, vein, whiz, zoom **5** layer, level, plane, smear, speed, strip, touch **6** blotch, hurtle, smirch, smudge, strain, stripe **7** portion, splotch, stratum

stream 3 jet, run **4** blow, file, flow, flux, gush, pour, race, rill, rush, teem, tide, waft, wave **5** brook, burst, creek, float, flood, issue, river, shoot, spate, spill, spout, spurt, surge **6** abound, branch, course, deluge, extend, feeder, onrush, sluice **7** current, flutter, freshet, rivulet, torrent **8** effusion, fountain, overflow **9** profusion, tributary **11** watercourse

streamer 4 flag **6** banner, burgee **7** pennant

streamlet 3 run **4** rill **5** brook, creek **7** rivulet

streamlined 4 racy **5** clean, sleek **7** compact **8** up-to-date **9** organized **10** futuristic, modernized, simplified **11** aerodynamic

stream of abuse 6 tirade **8** diatribe, harangue **9** contumely, invective **12** vituperation

Streep, Meryl
  real name: **16** Mary Louise Streep
  born: **14** Basking Ridge NJ
  roles: **8** Ironweed, Silkwood, The Hours **10** Adaptation **11** Marvin's Room, Out of Africa **13** Falling in Love, Sophie's Choice (Oscar), The Deer Hunter **14** Before and After, Kramer vs Kramer **17** Dancing at Lughnasa **20** Postcards from the Edge, The House of the Spirits **25** The Bridges of Madison County, The French Lieutenant's Woman

street 3 way **4** lane, mews, road **5** alley, block, route **6** avenue **7** highway, roadway, terrace, thruway **8** turnpike **9** boulevard **10** expressway **12** thoroughfare

Streetcar Named Desire, A
  author: **17** Tennessee Williams

director: **9** Elia Kazan
  cast: **9** Kim Hunter (Stella Dubois Kowalski) **10** Karl Malden **11** Vivien Leigh (Blanche Dubois) **12** Marlon Brando (Stanley Kowalski)
  setting: **10** New Orleans
  score: **9** Alex North
  Oscar for: **7** actress (Leigh) **15** supporting actor (Malden) **17** supporting actress (Hunter)

Streets of San Francisco, The
  character: **9** (Det Lt) Mike Stone **10** (Inspector) Dan Robbins **11** (Inspector) Steve Keller
  cast: **10** Karl Malden **12** Richard Hatch **14** Michael Douglas

strega
  type: **7** liqueur
  origin: **5** Italy
  flavor: **6** spices **10** orange peel
  with brandy: **10** Strega Flip

Streisand, Barbra
  real name: **20** Barbara Joan Streisand
  born: **10** Brooklyn NY
  husband: **11** Elliot Gould, James Brolin
  roles: **5** Yentl **9** Funny Girl (Oscar), Funny Lady **10** Fanny Brice, Hello Dolly, What's Up Doc? **11** A Star Is Born **12** The Main Event, The Way We Were **13** The Prince of Tides **14** Meet the Fockers **20** The Mirror Has Two Faces
  recordings: **10** The Concert **11** A Star Is Born **23** The Barbra Streisand Album

strength 4 beef, grit, kick, pith, sand, size **5** brawn, force, forte, might, pluck, power, sinew, spice, vigor **6** anchor, mettle, number, purity, spirit, succor, virtue **7** bravery, muscles, potency, stamina, support **8** backbone, buttress, efficacy, firmness, mainstay, security, solidity, tenacity, vitality **9** endurance, fortitude, hardiness, intensity, lustiness, puissance, stoutness, toughness, viability **10** robustness, sturdiness, sustenance **13** concentration, effectiveness **16** stoutheartedness
  Latin: **3** vis

strengthen 4 prop **5** brace, renew, steel **6** harden **7** build up, enhance, fortify, improve, restore, shore up, support, sustain **8** buttress **9** reinforce

strength of character 4 grit, guts **5** pluck, spunk **6** mettle **7** resolve **8** backbone **9** fortitude **10** resolution **12** resoluteness **13** steadfastness

strenuous 4 hard **5** eager **6** active, ardent, dogged, taxing, uphill **7** arduous, dynamic, earnest, intense, zealous **8** animated, diligent, sedulous, spirited, untiring, vigorous **9** assiduous, difficult, energetic, laborious, punishing **10** exhausting, on one's toes **11** hardworking, industrious, painstaking **12** enterprising **13** indefatigable

stress 4 beat, mark **5** force, value, worth **6** accent, affirm, assert, burden, moment, repeat, strain, weight **7** anxiety, concern, feature, gravity, meaning, sawdust, tension, urgency **8** emphasis, pressure **9** emphasize, necessity, underline **10** accentuate, importance, insist upon, oppression, prominence, underscore **11** consequence, seriousness **12** accentuation, significance **13** consideration

stretch 4 span, term, tire **5** cover, reach, spell, stint, tract, while, widen **6** burden, deepen, expand, extend, period, sprawl, spread, spring, strain **7** distend, draw out, expanse, fatigue, lie over, overtax, pull out **8** distance, draw taut, duration, elongate, interval, lengthen, overtask, overwork, protract, put forth, reach out, tautness, traverse **9** be elastic, draw tight, make tense, make tight, overexert **10** elasticity, exaggerate, overburden, overcharge, overstrain, push too far, resiliency **11** carry too far **12** be expandable, be extendable **14** push to the limit

stretchable 7 elastic, rubbery **8** flexible **9** resilient

stretching 9 extending, extension **10** drawing out, elongation **11** attenuation, enlargement, lengthening, protraction **12** prolongation **13** amplification

stretching out 8 outreach **9** expansion, extending, extension **10** elongation **11** attenuation, lengthening **12** prolongation

stretch out 6 expand, extend **7** amplify, augment, draw out **8** elongate, lengthen, protract

Strether
character in: **14** The Ambassadors
author: **10** Henry James

strew 3 sow **6** litter **7** scatter **8** disperse **9** broadcast **11** disseminate

stricken 3 ill **4** hurt, sick **7** injured, smitten, wounded **8** blighted, diseased **9** afflicted, taken sick **13** incapacitated

strict 4 nice **5** exact, rigid, stern **6** severe **7** austere, perfect **8** absolute, complete, exacting, rigorous, unerring **9** stringent **10** fastidious, inflexible, meticulous, scrupulous, unyielding **13** authoritarian, conscientious **14** uncompromising

strictly required
French: **9** de rigueur

stride 4 gait, lope, pace, step **5** march, stalk **7** advance, headway **8** long step, progress **11** advancement, improvement **13** take long steps

strident 5 harsh **6** shrill **7** grating, jarring, rasping, raucous **8** clashing, grinding, jangling, piercing, twanging **9** dissonant **10** discordant, screeching **11** cacophonous, high-pitched

Striebel, John H
creator/artist of: **10** Dixie Dugan

strife 6 unrest **7** discord, trouble, turmoil, warfare **8** conflict, disquiet, fighting, struggle, upheaval, violence **10** contention, convulsion, disharmony, dissension **11** altercation, disturbance

Strife
author: **14** John Galsworthy

strike 3 bat, box, hit, run, tap **4** bang, beat, belt, bump, clap, clip, club, come, cuff, drub, find, flog, lash, make, meet, pelt, ring, slam, slap, slug, sock, toll, whip, wipe **5** chime, clout, erase, flail, knell, knock, light, pound, punch, reach, smash, smite, sound, thump, tie-up, whack, whale **6** affect, arrive, assail, attack, batter, buffet, cancel, chance, charge, cudgel, delete, effect, fold up, hammer, pommel, remove, seem to, thrash, wallop **7** achieve, arrange, assault, boycott, impress, occur to, protest, put away, ram into, run into, scourge, scratch, stumble, unearth, walk out **8** appear to, bump into, come upon, cross out, dawn upon, discover, fall upon, lambaste, pull down, take down **9** burst upon, devastate, eliminate, encounter, eradicate, knock into, take apart **10** come across, flagellate, meet head-on **11** beat against, collide with, dash against **12** labor dispute, work stoppage

strike a bargain 5 agree **6** settle **9** make a deal **10** compromise **11** come to terms, meet halfway **18** split the difference **20** reach an understanding

strike back 7 counter, get even, hit back, pay back, riposte **9** fight back, retaliate **13** counterattack

strike dumb 4 daze, stun **5** amaze, shock **7** astound, stagger, stupefy **8** astonish, dumfound **9** dumbfound, electrify **11** flabbergast

strike noisily 4 bang, beat, clap, slam **5** thump

strike out 6 delete, fan out, set off, set out **7** take out **10** sally forth

strike sharply 3 rap **4** slap **5** crack

striking 6 marked **7** notable **9** prominent **10** astounding, impressive, noteworthy, noticeable, remarkable, surprising **11** conspicuous, outstanding **13** extraordinary

Strindberg, August
author of: **9** Miss Julie, The Father **10** A Dream Play **12** The Creditors **14** The Ghost Sonata **15** The Dance of Death

string 3 row **4** cord, file, line, rope **5** chain, queue, train, twine **6** column, extend, parade, series, spread, strand, thread **7** binding, stretch **8** necklace, sequence **10** procession, succession

stringent 5 close, harsh, spare, stern, stiff, tight **6** cogent, frugal, severe, strict **7** sparing **8** exacting, forceful, rigorous **9** demanding, effectual, unbending **10** inflexible, unyielding **14** uncompromising

strip 3 rob **4** band, flay, loot, peel, raid, sack, skin, slip, tear **5** field, flake, rifle, shave **6** denude, divest, length, ravage, remove, ribbon, stripe, unwrap **7** deprive, despoil, disrobe, draw off, lay bare, measure, plunder, pull off, ransack, uncover, undrape, undress **8** airstrip, desolate, lay waste, spoliate, unclothe **9** steal from **11** disencumber

stripe 3 bar **4** band, line, tape **5** braid, strip, swath **6** ribbon, streak **7** chevron **8** insignia **9** striation

stripling 3 boy, lad **5** minor, youth **8** teenager, young man **9** schoolboy, youngster **10** adolescent

stripped 4 bare, nude **5** naked **6** peeled, unclad **7** denuded, exposed, unrobed **8** disrobed, divested **9** unclothed, uncovered, undressed

strive 3 vie **4** push **5** essay, fight, labor **6** battle, strain **7** contend, try hard **8** endeavor, struggle **9** take pains, undertake **10** do one's best **12** apply oneself, do one's utmost, exert oneself, spare no pains **15** work like a Trojan **18** move heaven and earth **20** leave no stone unturned

striving 4 toil **5** exert, labor **6** effort, strain **7** toiling, travail **8** exertion, struggle **9** straining **10** struggling

stroke 3 bat, hit, pat, pet, tap **4** blow, chop, coup, deed, feat, poke, slap, sock, swat **5** brush, chime, fluke, punch, whack **6** caress, chance, wallop **7** massage, ringing, seizure, tolling **8** accident, apoplexy, flourish, movement, sounding, striking **11** achievement, coincidence, piece of luck, transaction **15** brain hemorrhage

stroll 4 tour, turn, walk **5** amble, mosey **6** ramble, wander **7** meander, saunter **9** poke along, promenade **14** constitutional

stroller 4 pram **5** buggy **6** ambler, walker **7** rambler **8** carriage **9** itinerant, pushchair, saunterer **10** promenader **12** perambulator

strong 3 hot **4** able, bold, deep, keen, tart **5** burly, clear, close, fiery, hardy, nippy, sharp, solid, sound, stout, tangy, tough, vivid **6** ardent, biting, brawny, bright, cogent, fervid, fierce, gritty, hearty, mighty, moving, plucky, potent, robust, savory, severe, sinewy, sturdy **7** buoyant, capable, devoted, earnest, fervent, healthy, intense, piquant, pungent, skilled, violent, zealous **8** animated, athletic, definite, dili-

gent, distinct, emphatic, faithful, forceful, muscular, powerful, puissant, sedulous, spirited, stalwart, tireless, vehement, vigorous **9** assiduous, competent, confirmed, effective, energetic, herculean, resilient, tenacious, undiluted **10** compelling, convincing, courageous, deep-seated, persistent, proficient **11** impassioned, persevering, resourceful **12** advantageous, concentrated, highly spiced, high-spirited, unmistakable **13** indefatigable, well-qualified **14** highly flavored, highly seasoned
Spanish: 5 macho

strong-arm 3 cow **5** bully, force **6** coerce, compel **8** browbeat, threaten **10** intimidate

strong feeling 4 fear, hate, heat, love, zeal **5** anger, ardor **6** fervor, sorrow, warmth **7** despair, emotion, passion, sadness **8** jealousy **9** happiness, vehemence **12** satisfaction

stronghold 4 fort, hold, home, keep **6** bunker, center, locale, refuge **7** bastion, bulwark, citadel, rampart, redoubt **8** fastness, fortress, safehold, stockade **10** battlement, blockhouse **13** fortification

strongly committed 4 true **5** loyal **6** ardent **7** devoted, staunch, zealous **8** adhering, faithful **9** dedicated, steadfast **10** passionate, unwavering

strong point 5 forte **6** anchor **8** mainstay, strength

strong-willed 5 pushy **8** forceful, positive **9** assertive **10** aggressive **11** domineering, self-assured **13** self-assertive

structural support 3 bar **4** beam, prop, stud **5** brace, joist **6** girder, rafter, timber **7** trestle **12** underpinning

structure 4 form, plan **6** design, makeup **7** arrange, edifice, pattern **8** assemble, building, conceive, organize **9** construct, formation **11** arrangement, composition, put together **12** conformation, construction, organization **13** configuration

struggle 3 vie, war **4** duel, feud, pull, push, spar, tilt **5** argue, brawl, brush, clash, fight, grind, joust, labor, match, scrap, trial **6** action, battle, combat, differ, effort, engage, jostle, oppose, resist, strain, stress, strife, strive, tussle **7** compete, contend, contest, grapple, quarrel, scuffle **8** conflict, endeavor, exertion, long haul, skirmish, work hard **9** encounter, lock horns, take pains **10** engagement **11** altercation, cross swords **15** work like a Trojan **18** move heaven and earth **20** leave no stone unturned

strut 4 sail **6** parade, sashay **7** peacock, swagger **9** promenade

Struthiomimus
type: 8 dinosaur, theropod

known as: **15** ostrich dinosaur
period: **10** Cretaceous
characteristic: **9** toothless

Stuart, Gilbert
born: **15** North Kingston RI
artwork: **16** George Washington

Stuart, J E B
served in: **8** Civil War
side: **11** Confederate
commander of: **7** cavalry
battle: **7** Bull Run **8** Antietam **10** Gettysburg **14** Fredericksburg **16** Chancellorsville **18** Peninsular campaign

Stuart Little
author: **7** E B White

stub 3 end **4** bump, butt, dock, tail **5** crush, knock, snuff, stump **6** fag end, scrape **7** receipt, remains, tamp out, voucher **10** extinguish, torn ticket **11** counterfoil

stubble 5 beard **6** stumps **8** bristles, whiskers **9** cut stalks **16** five-o'clock shadow

stubborn 6 dogged, mulish, strong, sturdy **7** willful **8** forceful, obdurate, perverse, resolute **9** concerted, immovable, obstinate, pigheaded, resistant, tenacious, unbending, unmovable **10** bullheaded, headstrong, inflexible, persistent, purposeful, refractory, self-willed, unshakable, unyielding **11** indomitable, intractable, opinionated, uncompliant **12** hard to handle, recalcitrant, ungovernable, wholehearted

stubbornness 10 mulishness, obstinancy, resistance **11** willfulness **13** intransigence, pigheadedness

stubby 5 dumpy, pudgy, squab, squat, tubby **6** chubby, chunky, stocky, stodgy, stumpy **7** squatty **8** thickset

stuck 3 dug, put **4** held **5** bound, fixed, fused, glued, mired, poked **6** balked, curbed, jabbed, joined, nailed, pasted, pinned, placed, sealed, spiked, tacked, thrust, welded **7** adhered, affixed, boggled, impeded, planted, pricked, punched, saddled, snarled, speared, stabbed, stalled, stumped, stymied **8** attached, burdened, cemented, fastened, inserted **9** punctured **10** obstructed, perforated **11** immobilized

stuck-up 4 vain **5** cocky **6** snooty, uppish, uppity **7** haughty, high-hat **8** arrogant, snobbish **9** bigheaded, conceited **10** disdainful, egocentric, hoity-toity **11** overbearing, swellheaded **13** self-important, self-satisfied

stud 3 dot **4** beam, buck, dude, sire **5** board, rivet **6** button **7** upright **8** fastener, macho man, nailhead

student 4 coed **5** pupil **6** reader **7** analyst, learner, scholar, watcher **8** disciple, examiner, follower, observer, reviewer **9** collegian, schoolboy, spectator **10** schoolgirl **11** commentator, interpreter, matriculant **13** undergraduate

studied 8 measured **10** calculated, deliberate, purposeful **11** intentional **12** premeditated

studious 6 brainy, intent **7** bookish, earnest, erudite **8** academic, cerebral, diligent, literate, well-read **9** laborious, scholarly **10** determined, purposeful, scholastic **11** painstaking **12** intellectual

Studs Lonigan
series includes: **11** Judgment Day **12** Young Lonigan **29** The Young Manhood of Studs Lonigan
author: **13** James T Farrell

study 3 den **4** cram, read **5** grind, probe **6** office, peruse, review, search, studio, survey **7** examine, explore, inquiry, library, observe, reading **8** analysis, consider, learning, pore over, read up on, research, scrutiny **9** delve into, education **10** glance over, inspection, scrutinize **11** examination, exploration, hit the books, inquire into, instruction, investigate, read closely, reading room, scholarship **13** consideration, investigation, school oneself, search through

Study in Scarlet, A
author: **19** Sir Arthur Conan Doyle
character: **12** Dr John Watson **13** Jefferson Hope, Tobias Gregson **14** Sherlock Holmes **17** Inspector Lestrade

stuff 3 act, bit, jam, pad, wad **4** best, bosh, bunk, cram, fill, gear, heap, load, pack, pile, sate, stow **5** cache, crowd, gorge, hokum, hooey, stash, store, thing, trash, wedge **6** burden, fill up, humbug, matter, staple, tackle, things, thrust, tricks, utmost **7** effects, essence, hogwash, overeat, rubbish, satiate, spinach, twaddle **8** darndest, falderal, material, nonsense **9** component, empty talk, substance **10** balderdash, belongings, gluttonize, ingredient, make a pig of **11** constituent, foolishness, overindulge, performance, possessions, raw material **12** quintessence **13** paraphernalia

stuff-and-nonsense 3 rot **4** bosh, bull, bunk **5** hokum, hooey, trash **6** bunkum, drivel, humbug **7** baloney, hogwash, spinach, twaddle **8** buncombe, claptrap, nonsense, tommyrot **9** poppycock **10** applesauce, balderdash, tomfoolery **11** foolishness **12** fiddlesticks **13** horsefeathers

stuffed 4 full **6** filled, jammed, loaded, packed, rammed, wadded **7** crammed, crushed, replete **8** overfull, satiated, squeezed **10** sandwiched

stuff in 4 cram, pack **6** devour **8** bolt down, compress, gobble up, wolf down

stuffing 5 farce **7** filling, packing, padding, wadding **8** dressing **9** forcemeat

stuffy 4 cold, smug **5** close, fusty,

heavy, muggy, musty, staid **6** stodgy, sultry **7** airless, pompous **8** reserved, stagnant, stifling **9** clogged-up, congested, high-flown, stopped-up, stuffed-up **10** old-fogyish, oppressive, sweltering **11** pretentious, straitlaced, suffocating **12** supercilious, unventilated **13** ill-ventilated, self-satisfied, stale-smelling

stultify 4 balk **6** hinder, impair, impede, thwart **7** cripple, inhibit, nullify, vitiate **8** suppress **9** frustrate, hamstring **11** make useless

stumble 3 hit **4** fall, reel, roll, sway, trip **5** botch, lurch, pitch, spill **6** bungle, falter, happen, hash up, hobble, mess up, slip up, sprawl, topple, totter **7** blunder, misstep, shamble, stagger **8** flounder **10** take a spill **12** come by chance, make mistakes, pitch forward

stumble upon 4 find **7** learn of **8** come upon, discover **10** chance upon, happen upon **14** find by accident

stumbling block 3 bar, rub **4** snag **5** block, catch, hitch **6** hamper, hurdle **7** barrier, problem **8** drawback, obstacle **9** detriment, hindrance **10** difficulty, impediment **11** obstruction **12** complication, interference

stump 3 end **4** butt, foil, stub, thud **5** befog, clomp, clonk, clump, clunk, stamp, stomp, tramp **6** baffle, nubbin, stymie **7** confuse, mystify, nonplus, perplex **8** bewilder, confound, dumfound, footfall, stomping, tramping **9** bamboozle, dumbfound

stun 4 daze, numb **5** amaze, shock **7** astound, stagger, startle, stupefy **8** astonish, dumfound **9** dumbfound

stunner 4 doll **5** beaut, Venus **6** beauty, eyeful **8** knockout **9** dreamboat **10** good-looker

stunning 6 dazing, lovely **7** amazing, numbing **8** shocking, striking **9** beautiful, exquisite, startling **10** astounding, staggering, stupefying **11** astonishing, dumfounding **12** dumbfounding, electrifying

stunt 3 act **4** curb, feat **5** abort, check, cramp, dwarf, limit, stint, trick **6** impede, number, stifle **7** curtail, delimit **8** restrain, restrict, suppress

stunted 5 dumpy, runty **6** bantam **7** dwarfed, squatty, wizened **9** pint-sized **13** foreshortened

Stunt Man, The
    director: **11** Richard Rush
    cast: **9** Alex Rocco **11** Peter O'Toole (Eli Cross) **13** Allen Goorwitz, Sharon Farrell **14** Barbara Hershey, Steve Railsback

stupefaction 5 shock **8** numbness, surprise **9** amazement **12** astonishment

stupefied 5 dazed **6** amazed **7** shocked, stunned **8** benumbed **10**

dumbstruck, dumfounded **11** dumbfounded **13** flabbergasted, thunderstruck

stupefy 4 daze, stun **5** amaze, shock **7** astound, nonplus, stagger **8** astonish, confound, dumfound, surprise **9** dumbfound, overwhelm **11** flabbergast

stupefying 8 shocking, stunning **11** dumfounding **12** dumbfounding, electrifying, overwhelming **14** flabbergasting

stupendous 3 big **4** huge, vast **5** giant, great, jumbo **6** mighty **7** amazing, immense, mammoth, massive, titanic, unusual **8** colossal, enormous, fabulous, gigantic, imposing, stunning, terrific **9** cyclopean, herculean, marvelous, monstrous, very great, very large, wonderful **10** astounding, gargantuan, incredible, monumental, phenomenal, prodigious, remarkable, surprising, tremendous, unexpected **11** astonishing, elephantine **13** extraordinary

stupid 4 dull, dumb **5** dense, inane, inept, silly **6** absurd, oafish, obtuse, simple, unwise **7** aimless, asinine, boorish, doltish, fatuous, foolish, idiotic, moronic, witless **8** backward, childish, heedless, mistaken, reckless, tactless **9** brainless, cretinous, dimwitted, duncelike, foolhardy, ill-judged, imbecilic, imprudent, pointless, senseless **10** half-witted, ill-advised, indiscreet, irrelevant, weak-minded **11** empty-headed, meaningless, nonsensical, purposeless, thoughtless **12** absentminded, muddleheaded, preposterous, simpleminded, slow-learning, unreasonable **13** ill-considered, inappropriate, irresponsible, rattlebrained, unintelligent

stupor 4 daze **5** faint **6** apathy, torpor **7** inertia **8** blackout, lethargy, numbness **9** inertness **10** somnolence **12** stupefaction **13** insensibility

sturdy 4 able, firm **5** brave, burly, gutsy, hardy, heavy, solid, sound, stout, tough **6** daring, dogged, gritty, heroic, mighty, plucky, robust, rugged, secure, sinewy, spunky, strong **7** defiant, doughty, durable, gallant, lasting, valiant **8** enduring, fearless, forceful, intrepid, muscular, powerful, resolute, spirited, stalwart, stubborn, vigorous, well-made **9** dauntless, strapping, unabashed, undaunted, well-built **10** courageous, determined, invincible **11** indomitable, substantial, unshrinking **12** high-spirited, stouthearted **15** well-constructed

Sturges, John
    director of: **14** The Great Escape **19** The Magnificent Seven

Sturges, Preston
    director of: **10** The Lady Eve **16** Sul-

livan's Travels **17** The Palm Beach Story, Unfaithfully Yours **21** Hail the Conquering Hero **24** The Miracle of Morgan's Creek

Sturmabteilung 13 storm troopers

Sturm und Drang 22 German literary movement (18th century)
    literally: **14** storm and stress

stygian 3 dim **4** dark **5** black, murky **6** dreary, gloomy, somber **7** hellish **8** funereal, infernal, starless **9** tenebrous, unlighted

style 3 fad **4** call, elan, kind, mode, name, pomp, rage, sort, type **5** charm, class, craze, favor, flair, grace, model, taste, trend, vogue **6** design, luxury, manner, polish **7** arrange, comfort, fashion, pattern **8** currency, elegance **9** affluence, designate **10** smoothness **11** savoir-faire
    French: **4** gout

stylish 3 hip, new **4** chic **5** natty, smart, swank **6** dapper, latest, modern, modish, with-it **7** a la mode, elegant, in vogue, voguish **8** up-to-date **9** in fashion **11** fashionable **13** sophisticated, up-to-the-minute

stymie 4 balk **5** block, check, stump **6** baffle, hinder, puzzle, thwart **7** confuse, mystify **8** confound, obstruct **9** frustrate

Styracosaurus
    type: **8** dinosaur **10** ceratopsid
    location: **12** North America
    period: **10** Cretaceous
    characteristic: **6** horned

Styron, William
    author of: **12** The Long March **13** Sophie's Choice **15** Darkness Visible **17** Lie Down in Darkness **18** Set This House on Fire **25** The Confessions of Nat Turner

Styx
    form: **5** river
    location: **5** Hades **10** underworld
    father: **7** Oceanus
    ferryman: **6** Charon

suave 6 silken, smooth, urbane **7** affable, elegant, politic **8** charming, gracious, mannerly, polished, unctuous **9** civilized **10** diplomatic, flattering **12** ingratiating **13** smooth-tongued

sub 5 below, proxy, under **6** backup, deputy, second **7** beneath, standby, stand-in **9** alternate, submarine, surrogate **10** substitute, understudy **11** pinch-hitter

subaltern 4 aide **6** helper **9** assistant **10** lieutenant **11** subordinate

subconscious 3 dim **7** dawning **9** intuitive **10** subliminal **11** instinctive

subdivide 6 divide **7** split up **8** separate **9** partition

subdivision 3 arm **4** wing **6** branch **7** chapter, section **8** offshoot **11** development **12** neighborhood

subdue 3 bow 4 calm, curb, down, drub, ease, foil, mute, rout, trim, whip 5 allay, break, check, crush, floor, quell, salve, smash, still 6 deaden, defeat, master, mellow, muffle, reduce, soften, soothe, temper, thrash 7 appease, assuage, conquer, mollify, oppress, overrun, put down, relieve, slacken, subject, trample 8 mitigate, moderate, overcome, palliate, surmount, tone down, vanquish 9 meliorate, overpower, overwhelm, quiet down, soft-pedal, subjugate 10 ameliorate 11 triumph over 12 tranquillize

subdued 4 dull 5 cowed, muted, quiet 7 abashed, crushed, humbled, muffled, quelled 8 deadened, overcame 10 humiliated, indistinct, lackluster 11 intimidated, overpowered

subduer 6 victor, winner 9 conqueror, overcomer 10 subjugator, vanquisher 11 intimidator

subject 4 bare, case, gist, open, pith, text 5 field, issue, liege, motif, prone, study, theme, topic 6 affair, expose, liable, matter, submit, thesis, vassal 7 bound by, citizen, concern, exposed, lay open 8 business, disposed, follower, obedient, question 9 dependent, subjected, substance 10 answerable, discipline, in danger of, make liable, put through, vulnerable 11 stipulatory, subordinate, subservient, susceptible

subjection 11 subjugation 12 subservience 13 regimentation, subordination

subjective 5 inner 6 biased 7 partial 8 partisan, personal 9 emotional 10 individual, prejudiced 12 nonobjective

subjoin 5 add on, affix, annex 6 append, attach, tack on

subjugate 4 tame 5 crush, quell 6 subdue 7 conquer, put down 8 dominate, suppress, vanquish 10 overmaster

subjugation 6 chains, thrall 7 bondage, slavery 9 dominance, mastering, servitude, thralldom 10 conquering, domination 11 enslavement, vanquishing

subjugator 6 master, victor 7 subduer 9 conqueror, dominator 10 vanquisher 11 slavemaster

sublimate 4 turn 5 exalt, shift 6 divert, purify 7 channel, convert, elevate, ennoble 8 redirect, transfer 9 transform, transmute 12 spiritualize

sublime 4 high 5 grand, great, lofty, noble 6 superb 7 exalted, stately 8 elevated, imposing, majestic, splendid, terrific, very good 9 estimable, excellent, marvelous, wonderful 12 awe-inspiring, praiseworthy

submarine
invented by: 7 Holland

even keel: 4 Lake
torpedo: 8 Bushnell

submerge 4 dive, sink 5 douse, drown, flood, souse 6 deluge, engulf, go down, plunge 7 go under, immerse 8 inundate, pour over, submerse

submerse 5 drown 6 engulf 7 immerse 8 inundate, submerge

submersion 7 sinking 8 drowning 9 immersion 10 inundation 11 submergence

submission 8 giving in, meekness, tameness, yielding 9 handing in, obedience, passivity, surrender, tendering 10 compliance, remittance, submitting 11 passiveness 12 acquiescence, capitulation, presentation, subservience, tractability 13 nonresistance 14 submissiveness

submissive 4 meek, mild 6 docile, humble, pliant 7 dutiful, fawning, passive, servile, slavish 8 crawling, obedient, toadying, yielding 9 compliant, malleable, tractable, truckling 10 obsequious 11 acquiescent, bootlicking, complaisant, deferential, subservient, unassertive 12 capitulating, ingratiating, nonresisting 13 accommodating

submissiveness 8 docility, meekness 9 passivity 10 compliance 11 resignation 12 complaisance, tractability

submit 3 bow 4 bend, cede 5 agree, argue, claim, defer, kneel, offer, stoop, yield 6 accede, assert, commit, comply, give in, give up, resort, tender 7 contend, hold out, present, proffer, propose, succumb, suggest 8 back down, put forth 9 acquiesce, surrender, volunteer, put forward 12 knuckle under

submit an offer 3 bid 6 tender 7 proffer, propose

submit to 4 bear, take 5 abide, brave, brook, stand 6 endure, suffer 7 stomach, undergo 8 stand for, tolerate 9 put up with

subnormal 3 bad, low 5 seedy, sorry 6 crummy, dismal, shabby, sleazy, subpar 7 abysmal 8 below par, inferior, mediocre, wretched 9 defective, deficient 10 inadequate, second-rate 11 below normal, substandard 12 insufficient

subordinate 4 help 5 lower 6 junior, lackey, lesser, menial, worker 7 servant, subject 8 hireling, inferior 9 ancillary, assistant, attendant, auxiliary, dependent, of low rank, outranked, secondary, subaltern, underling 10 subsidiary 11 subservient

subordination 10 subjection 11 inferiority, subjugation 12 subservience 13 regimentation

suborn 5 bribe 6 buy off, pay off

sub rosa 8 covertly, in secret, on the sly, secretly 9 in private, privately 12

off-the-record 14 confidentially 15 behind-the-scenes 17 behind closed doors

subscribe 4 help, sign 6 assent, chip in, donate 7 consent, endorse, support 8 hold with 9 undersign 10 contribute

subsequent 4 next 7 ensuing 9 following, proximate 10 consequent, succeeding, successive

subsequently 2 so 5 after, later, since 9 afterward, following 10 succeeding 12 consequently

subservient 6 docile, menial 7 fawning, servile, slavish, subject 8 cringing, toadying, truckling 9 accessory, ancillary, auxiliary, prostrate, truckling 10 obsequious, subsidiary 11 bootlicking, subordinate, sycophantic 12 contributory, ingratiating

subside 3 ebb, sag 4 calm, drop, ease, sink, wane 5 abate, let up 6 cave in, lessen, recede, settle, shrink 7 descend, dwindle 8 decrease, diminish, level off, melt away, moderate

subsidence 5 letup 6 easing, ebbing, waning 7 calming 9 abatement, dwindling, lessening, recession, shrinking 10 decreasing, inactivity, moderation 12 diminishment

subsidiary 5 extra, lower, minor 6 branch, junior, lesser 7 adjunct 8 addition, division, inferior 9 accessory, affiliate, auxiliary, secondary 10 additional, supplement 11 subordinate 12 supplemental 13 supplementary

subsidy 3 aid 4 gift 5 award, grant 7 backing, support 9 allotment, provision 10 fellowship, grant-in-aid, honorarium, subvention 11 scholarship, sponsorship 13 appropriation, assistantship

subsist 4 live 5 exist 7 survive 9 stay alive 11 feed oneself, support life 12 make ends meet 23 keep body and soul together

subsistence 6 living, upkeep 7 support 8 survival 10 livelihood, sustenance 11 maintenance, nourishment

substance 4 body, core, germ, gist, pith, soul 5 force, heart, means, money, sense, stuff 6 burden, import, intent, marrow, matter, riches, thrust, wealth 7 element, essence, keynote, purport, reality 8 backbone, material, property, solidity 9 actuality, affluence, basic idea, main point 10 ingredient 11 connotation, constituent, corporality 12 corporeality, quintessence 13 corporealness

substandard 3 bad 4 poor 5 awful, lousy 6 crummy, shoddy 8 below par, inferior, terrible 9 imperfect 10 second-rate 11 second-class 12 below average

substantial 3 big 4 firm, full 5 ample, bulky, large, massy, solid, sound 7 massive, sizable 8 abundant 9 plenteous, plentiful **10** monumental **12** considerable

substantiate 5 prove **6** verify **7** confirm, support, sustain **11** corroborate, demonstrate **12** authenticate

substantiated 6 proved, proven **7** factual **8** verified **9** supported **11** well-founded **12** corroborated, demonstrated, well-grounded **13** authenticated

substantiation 5 proof **8** evidence **11** affirmation **12** verification **13** corroboration, demonstration, documentation **14** authentication

substitute 3 act **6** backup, change, ersatz, fill in, switch **7** standby, stand in, stopgap **8** deputize, exchange, pinch-hit, take over **9** alternate, makeshift, surrogate, temporary **10** understudy **11** alternative, pinch hitter, replacement

substitution 5 shift **6** change, switch **8** exchange, swapping **9** variation **10** alteration **11** replacement

substructure 4 base **6** ground **10** foundation, groundwork **12** underpinning

subsume 5 cover **6** assume, deduce **7** explain, include, involve **8** consider **13** subcategorize

subterfuge 4 ruse, sham, wile **5** blind, dodge, guile, shift, trick **6** scheme **7** evasion **8** artifice, intrigue, pretense, scheming **9** casuistry, chicanery, deception, duplicity, imposture, sophistry, stratagem **10** camouflage, sneakiness **11** deviousness, evasiveness, game-playing, machination, make-believe, smoke screen

subtle, subtile 3 sly **4** cagy, deft, fine, foxy, keen, wily **5** light, quick, sharp, slick **6** artful, astute, clever, crafty, expert, shifty, shrewd, tricky **7** cunning, devious, elusive, refined **8** delicate, indirect, masterly, skillful **9** deceptive, designing, ingenious, underhand **10** discerning **11** understated **13** perspicacious, sophisticated **14** discriminating

subtleties 7 nuances **10** fine points **11** refinements **12** distinctions

subtract 6 deduct, detach, lessen, reduce, remove **8** decrease, diminish, take away, withdraw

subtraction 7 removal **8** decrease **9** deduction, lessening, reduction **10** diminution, taking away, withdrawal **11** diminishing

suburbs 8 environs, vicinity **9** outskirts, periphery, precincts

sub verbo 12 under the word **15** under the heading

subversion 4 fall, ruin **6** defeat, mutiny **8** disorder, sabotage **9** overthrow, rebellion **10** corruption, disruption **11** destruction

subversive 7 traitor **8** quisling **9** insurgent, seditious **10** incendiary, traitorous, treasonous **11** seditionary **12** collaborator **13** revolutionary **14** fifth columnist **15** insurrectionary **16** collaborationist

subvert 3 mar **4** ruin, undo **5** smash, spoil, upset, wreck **6** defile, poison, ravage **7** despoil, destroy, disrupt, shatter **8** demolish, overturn **9** devastate, overthrow, undermine **11** contaminate

sub voce 21 under the specified word literally: **13** under the voice

subway 2 El **4** tube **5** metro, train **11** underground
New York City line: **3** BMT, IND, IRT
San Francisco: **4** BART
overhead lines: **3** els

succeed 3 hit, win **5** avail, catch, click **6** accede, do well, follow, move up **7** inherit, prevail, prosper, replace, triumph **8** make a hit, make good, supplant, take over **9** bear fruit, strike oil

succeed at 2 do **6** attain **7** execute, fulfill, perform, realize **8** carry out **9** make a go of **10** accomplish

succeeding 5 later **6** coming, future **7** ensuing **8** oncoming **9** following, impending, posterior **10** consequent, subsequent, successive

succeed to 6 follow **7** inherit **15** ascend the throne

succes d'estime 15 critical success

success 3 hit **4** fame **5** smash **7** triumph, victory **8** conquest **9** affluence **10** ascendancy, attainment, prosperity **11** achievement, advancement, fulfillment, good fortune

successful 4 rich **6** proven **7** perfect, wealthy, well-off **8** achieved, affluent, complete, fruitful, thriving **9** effective **10** prosperous, triumphant **11** efficacious, flourishing **12** accomplished, acknowledged

successful completion 7 success, victory, winning **9** execution **10** making good **11** achievement, culmination, fulfillment, realization **12** consummation **14** accomplishment

succession 3 run **5** chain, cycle, round, train **6** course, series **8** sequence **9** accession **10** assumption, procession, stepping-up, taking over **11** inheritance, progression

successive 7 ensuing **10** continuous, succeeding **11** consecutive

successor 4 heir **5** donee **7** devisee, heiress, heritor, legatee **8** follower, parcener **9** heritress, joint heir **10** coparcener, substitute **11** beneficiary, replacement, reversioner **12** heir apparent

succinct 4 neat **5** brief, crisp, pithy, short, terse, tight **6** direct, gnomic **7** clipped, compact, concise, summary **9**

condensed **10** aphoristic, to the point **12** epigrammatic

succinctness 7 brevity **9** crispness, terseness **11** compactness, conciseness **12** condensation

succor 3 aid **4** help **5** nurse **6** assist, back up, relief, shield, wait on **7** comfort, nurture, protect, relieve, support, sustain **8** befriend **10** assistance, minister to, sustenance, take care of **11** give a lift to, helping hand, lend a hand to, maintenance **13** accommodation

succulent 5 juicy **6** fleshy **9** toothsome **10** appetizing

succumb 3 die **5** yield **6** accede, expire, give in, submit **7** defer to, give way, go under **8** pass away **9** surrender **10** capitulate, comply with **12** fall victim to

such as
Latin: **2** eg **13** exempli gratia

such is life
French: **9** c'est la vie

sucker 3 sap **4** boob, butt, dupe, fool, goat, gull, jerk, mark **5** chump, patsy **6** pigeon, victim **7** cat's-paw, fall guy **8** easy mark, fair game, pushover **9** schlemiel, soft touch **11** sitting duck

suck up 6 absorb, soak up **7** drink in **8** sponge up **9** swallow up

Sucre
legal capital of: **7** Bolivia

Sudan
capital/largest city: **8** Khartoum
others: **3** Waw, Yei **4** Juba **5** Kosti, Meroe, Nyala, Obeid, Opari, Segon **6** Atbara, Suakin **7** Aluboyd, Elobeid, Geneina, Kassala, Malakal **8** Elfasher, Omdurman **9** al-Ubayyid, Elgeneina, Port Sudan, Wad Medani
division: **7** Jonglei **9** Upper Nile **12** Bahr el Ghazal **16** Eastern Equatoria, Western Equatoria
  ancient kingdom: **4** Alwa, Funj, Kush **7** Maqurra
measure: **2** ud
monetary unit: **5** pound **8** piastres
weight: **5** habba
lake: **2** No **4** Chad, Toad **6** Nasser
mountain: **4** Nuba **7** Imatong **9** Dongotona **10** Jabal Marra, Jebel Marra **18** Ethiopian Highlands
highest point: **7** Kinyeti
river: **4** Nile **5** Sobat **6** Atbara **8** Blue Nile **9** White Nile **10** Bahr el-Arab **11** Bahr el-Jebel **12** Bahr el-Ghazal
sea: **3** Red
physical feature:
  desert: **6** Libyan, Nubian
  gum forest: **8** Kordofan
  plain: **6** Gezira
  sandstorm: **6** haboob
  plateau: **8** Kordufan
  swamp: **4** Sudd
people: **3** Bor, Dor, Fur **4** Arab, Bari, Beri, Bobo, Daza, Egba, Fula, Golo,

Nuba, Nuer, Poul, Sere **5** Anuak, Bongo, Dinka, Fulah, Hausa, Joluo, Junje, Mosgu, Mossi, Negro, Tibbu, Volta **6** Acholi, Azande, Gurusi, Hamite, Lotuho, Makari, Nilote, Nubian, Senufo, Surhai, Tuareg **7** Balante, Baqqara, Gubayna, Jaaliin, Nilotes, Shilluk, Songhai, Songhay, Songhoi, Sourhai **8** Kababish, Mandingo, Menkiera **9** Sarakille **10** Gurmantshi, Shaiquiyya

    leader: 5 Mahdi **9** al-Nimeiry **10** Mehemet Ali **22** Jaafar Mohammed al-Nemery

    language: 2 Ga **3** Efe, Ewe, Ibo, Kru, Vak, Vei **4** Efik, Mole, Tshi **6** Arabic, Nubian, Yoruba **7** English **8** Mandango, Mandingo **9** Ta Bedawie

    religion: 5 Islam **7** animism **12** Christianity

    place:
        canal: 7 Jonglei
        dam: 6 Sennar **8** Roseires **10** Jebel Aulia
        temple: 4 Lion
        tomb: 5 Mahdi

    feature:
        boat: 6 murkab
        food: 4 dura **5** dukhn, kisra

Sudanese Republic *see* **4** Mali

sudden 4 rash **5** hasty, quick, rapid **6** abrupt, speedy **7** instant **9** immediate, impetuous **10** surprising, unexpected, unforeseen **11** precipitate, unlooked-for **13** instantaneous, unanticipated, unforeseeable

sudden development
    French: 10 coup de main

suddenly 7 quickly **8** abruptly, in no time **9** all at once, instantly, on the spot **11** in an instant **12** all of a sudden, unexpectedly **13** at short notice **14** without warning **20** on the spur-of-the-moment **21** in the twinkling of an eye

Suddenly Susan
    network: 3 NBC
    cast: 8 Eric Idle (Ian Maxtone-Graham) **10** Judd Nelson (Jack Richmond) **12** Kathy Griffin (Vicki Groener Rubenstein) **13** Barbara Barrie (Helen "Nana" Keane), Brooke Shields (Susan Keane Browne) **15** David Strickland (Todd Stites), Nestor Carbonell (Luis Rivera)

sudden movement 4 dart, jolt **5** flash, spurt

sudden noise 3 pop **4** bang, clap, slam **5** burst, crash **6** report **9** explosion

Sudermann, Hermann
    author of: 5 Honor **8** Dame Care **14** The Song of Songs

suds 3 ale **4** beer, brew, foam **5** draft, froth, lager **10** malt liquor

sue 3 beg **4** pray **5** plead **6** appeal **7** beseech, entreat, implore **8** petition **9** importune **10** supplicate

Sue, Eugene (Marie-Joseph)
    author of: 15 The Wandering Jew **19** The Mysteries of Paris

suffer 4 ache, bear, hurt, pine **5** stand **6** endure, grieve, lament **7** agonize, despair, drop off, fall off, stomach, sustain, undergo **8** bear with, feel pain, tolerate **9** go through, put up with, withstand **10** be impaired **11** deteriorate

suffer for 6 pay for **8** atone for **9** answer for

suffering 3 woe **4** ache, care, hurt, pain, pang **5** agony, dolor, grief, throe, trial **6** misery, sorrow, twinge **7** anguish, anxiety, torment, torture, travail **8** distress, soreness **9** heartache **10** affliction, discomfort, heavy heart, irritation **11** tribulation

suffice 2 do **4** last, meet, pass **5** avail, get by, serve **6** answer, make do **7** fulfill, qualify, satisfy

sufficiency 6 enough, plenty **7** surfeit **8** adequacy **9** abundance, ampleness, profusion

sufficient 5 ample **6** enough, plenty **7** copious, minimal **8** abundant, adequate **9** plenteous, plentiful **11** up to the mark **12** satisfactory

suffocate 3 gag **5** choke **6** quench, stifle **7** garrote, smother **8** snuff out, strangle, throttle **10** asphyxiate, extinguish

suffuse 4 fill, soak **5** cover, steep **6** infuse **7** diffuse, overrun, pervade **8** overflow, permeate, saturate **9** transfuse **10** impregnate, infiltrate, overspread

Sugar State
    nickname of: 9 Louisiana

sugary 5 mushy, sweet **6** syrupy **7** cloying, fulsome, gushing, honeyed, mawkish **8** cajoling, unctuous **10** flattering, saccharine

suggest 3 bid **4** move, urge **5** imply, posit **6** advise, hint at, submit **7** advance, counsel, propose **8** advocate, indicate, intimate, propound **9** give a clue, recommend **16** lead one to believe

suggested 6 hinted **7** implied, oblique **8** implicit, indirect, possible, proposed

suggestion 3 dab, tip **4** dash, hint, tint **5** grain, shade, taste, tinge, touch, trace **6** advice, urging **7** counsel, feeling, pointer, soupcon **9** prompting, suspicion **10** intimation, sprinkling **11** exhortation **14** recommendation

suggestive 4 lewd, racy **5** bawdy, loose **6** risque, sexual, wanton **8** allusive, improper, indecent, off-color, prurient, unseemly **9** evocative, reminding, seductive, shameless **10** expressive, indelicate, licentious **11** provocative, reminiscent, stimulating

sui generis 6 unique **10** one of a kind

sui juris 14 of one's own right **31** capable of managing one's own affairs **36** capable of assuming legal responsibility

suit 3 fit **4** duds, garb, plea, togs **5** befit, court, getup, habit, match **6** appeal, attire, become, beseem, follow, livery, oblige, outfit, please, prayer, wooing **7** apparel, begging, clothes, content, costume, delight, gladden, gratify, raiment, satisfy, uniform **8** clothing, entreaty, jell with, make glad, petition **9** addresses, agree with, conform to, courtship, do one good, overtures, tally with, trappings **10** accord with, attentions, comply with, fall in with, habiliment, lovemaking, square with **11** accommodate, go along with **12** be becoming to, blandishment, correspond to, dovetail with, solicitation, supplication **13** accoutrements, be agreeable to, harmonize with **14** be acceptable to, be convenient to **15** be appropriate to **16** be appropriate for

suitable 3 apt, fit **4** meet **5** right **6** proper, seemly, worthy **7** apropos, fitting, germane **8** adequate, becoming, relevant **9** befitting, congruous, cut out for, pertinent, qualified **10** applicable, seasonable **11** appropriate **12** commensurate

suitcase 3 bag **4** grip **6** valise **7** satchel **8** knapsack, rucksack **9** duffel bag, gladstone, two-suiter **11** portmanteau **12** overnight bag, traveling bag

suite 3 set **4** flat **5** chain, court, group, rooms, round **6** convoy, series **7** company, cortege, retinue **8** servants **9** apartment, followers, following **10** attendants **11** progression

suited 3 fit **7** adapted, attired, clothed, dressed, good for, matched **8** adjusted, agreeing, becoming **9** agreeable **11** appropriate, harmonizing

suit of armor 4 mail **5** armor **9** chain mail **10** coat of mail

suitor 4 beau, love **5** flame, lover, swain, wooer **6** fellow **7** admirer, gallant **8** young man **9** boyfriend **10** sweetheart

sulfur
    chemical symbol: 1 S

sulk 4 crab, fret, fume, mope, pout **5** brood, chafe, frown, grump, scowl **6** glower, grouch **7** grumble **8** be in a pet, be miffed, be put out, be sullen, look glum **9** be in a huff **11** be resentful **12** be out of humor

sulky 6 morose, sullen **7** pouting **8** petulant

sullen 4 blue, dark, glum, grim, sore, sour **5** cross, heavy, moody, sulky, surly **6** crabby, dismal, dreary, gloomy, grumpy, morose, somber, touchy **7** crabbed, doleful, forlorn, grouchy, peevish **8** brooding, desolate, dolorous, funereal, mournful, petulant, scowling **9** cheerless, glowering, resentful, saturnine, splenetic, unamiable **10** depressing, foreboding, ill-humored, ill-natured, melancholy, out of humor, out of sorts, unsociable **11** ill-tempered **13** temperamental **French: 8** farouche

sullied 5 dirty **6** impure, soiled **7** defiled, stained, unclean **9** tarnished

Sullivan, John L (Lawrence)
    nickname: 15 Boston Strong Boy
    sport: 6 boxing
    class: 11 heavyweight
    fought: 12 bareknuckled

Sullivan, Louis H
    architect of: 16 Guaranty (now Prudential) Building (Buffalo NY) **18** Auditorium Building (Chicago), Wainwright Building (St Louis MO) **21** Carson Pirie Scott Store (Chicago), Stock Exchange Building (Chicago), Merchants' National Bank (Grinnell, IA), National Farmers' Bank (Owatonna, MN)
    principle: 21 "form follows function"
    student: 16 Frank Lloyd Wright

Sullivan, Pat
    creator/artist of: 11 Felix the Cat

Sullivan's Travels
    director: 14 Preston Sturges
    cast: 10 Joel McCrea **12** Veronica Lake **13** Robert Warwick **15** William Demarest

sully 4 ruin, soil, spot **5** dirty, spoil, stain **6** befoul, defame, defile, smudge **7** begrime, besmear, blemish, corrupt, pollute, tarnish **8** disgrace, dishonor **10** adulterate **11** contaminate

Sully, Thomas
    born: 7 England **10** Horncastle
    artwork: 13 Queen Victoria **23** The Passage of the Delaware **28** Colonel Thomas Handasyd Perkins **29** Washington Crossing the Delaware

sultan 4 king **5** ruler **7** emperor, monarch **9** sovereign

sultana 5 grape **6** raisin **7** empress **11** sultan's wife

sultry 3 hot **4** sexy **5** close, humid, muggy **6** erotic, stuffy, sweaty **7** sensual **8** stifling **10** oppressive, sweltering, voluptuous **11** provocative, suffocating

sum 4 cash, coin, jack **5** bread, bucks, dough, funds, score, tally, whole **6** amount, moolah **7** lettuce, measure **8** currency, entirety, quantity, sum total, totality **9** aggregate, summation **12** entire amount **13** amount of money

sumac 4 Rhus
    varieties: 5 dwarf, lemon, scrub, sugar, swamp **6** desert, laurel, poison, smooth, velvet **7** scarlet, shining, tanner's, tobacco, wing-rib **8** fragrant, lemonade, Sicilian, staghorn, Venetian **9** elm-leaved, evergreen, Virginian **11** small-leaved **12** sweet-scented

sum and substance 4 core, crux, gist, guts, meat **5** heart **7** essence **10** brass tacks **11** nitty-gritty

Sumatra
    chevrotain: 4 napu
    city: 5 Medan **6** Padang **9** Palembang
    country: 9 Indonesia
    crop: 3 tea **6** coffee, rubber
    currency: 6 rupiah
    empire: 9 Srivijaya
    highest point: 10 Mt Kerintji
    inhabitant: 5 Batak, Malay **11** Minangkabau
    mountain range: 7 Barisan
    river: 4 Musi, Siak **6** Asahan
    squirrel shrew: 4 tana
    strait: 5 Sunda **7** Malacca

Sumerian Mythology see **19** Babylonian Mythology

Summa Catholicae Fidei Contra Gentiles
    author: 13 Thomas Aquinas

summa cum laude 17 with highest praise

summarily 6 at once **7** quickly **8** directly, promptly, speedily **9** forthwith, on the spot **11** arbitrarily, immediately, straightway **12** straightaway, with dispatch, without delay **13** at short notice, precipitately **14** unhesitatingly **20** on the spur of the moment

summarize 5 sum up **6** digest **7** abridge, outline **8** abstract, compress, condense **9** capsulize, epitomize, synopsize **10** abbreviate **11** concentrate **12** recapitulate

summary 4 curt **5** brief, hasty, rapid, short, terse, token **6** apercu, digest, precis, resume, sketch, sudden, survey **7** concise, cursory, epitome, hurried, rundown **8** abridged, abstract, analysis, succinct, syllabus, synopsis **9** breakdown, condensed **10** abridgment, peremptory **11** perfunctory **12** abbreviation, condensation, short version **13** instantaneous

Summa Theologiae
    author: 13 Thomas Aquinas

summation 5 total **6** review **7** summary **8** addition **9** reckoning **19** concluding statement

Summer and Smoke
    author: 17 Tennessee Williams
    director: 14 Peter Glenville
    cast: 9 Una Merkel **10** Rita Moreno **12** Earl Holliman **13** Geraldine Page **14** Laurence Harvey

summerhouse 5 arbor, cabin, kiosk **6** cabana, gazebo, pagoda **7** cottage

Summertime
    director: 9 David Lean

    based on story by: 14 Arthur Laurents (The Time of the Cuckoo)
    cast: 10 Isa Miranda **13** Darren McGavin, Rossano Brazzi **16** Katharine Hepburn
    setting: 6 Venice

summery 3 hot **4** warm **5** balmy, close, humid, muggy, sunny **6** stuffy, sultry, torrid, vernal **8** aestival, roasting, stifling, sunshiny **9** scorching, temperate **10** oppressive, summerlike

summit 3 tip, top **4** acme, apex, peak **5** crest, crown **6** apogee, climax, height, vertex, zenith **8** pinnacle **11** culmination **12** highest point **13** crowning point

summon 4 call **5** rouse **6** beckon, call on, draw on, gather, invoke, muster, strain **7** call for, call out, command, send for **8** activate, subpoena **9** call forth **12** call together **14** call into action, serve with a writ

summons 4 call **8** citation, subpoena **12** notification

summon up 4 stir **5** evoke **6** arouse, excite **7** collect, marshal, provoke **8** assemble **9** call forth, stimulate

summum bonum 9 chief good **11** highest good

sumptuous 4 dear, posh, rich **5** grand, plush, regal **6** costly, deluxe, lavish, superb **7** elegant **8** splendid **9** elaborate, expensive, luxurious **10** exorbitant, munificent **11** extravagant, magnificent, spectacular

sumptuousness 4 luxe **6** luxury **8** elegance, grandeur, richness, splendor **12** magnificence **13** expensiveness, luxuriousness

sum total 6 amount **8** totality **9** aggregate **11** final result

sum up 3 add **5** tally, total, tot up **6** reckon **7** compute, count up **9** calculate, enumerate, summarize

sun
    god of: 2 Ra, Re **3** Sol, Utu **5** Horus **6** Apollo, Helios **7** Shamesh **8** Hyperion

Sun Also Rises, The
    author: 15 Ernest Hemingway
    character: 10 Bill Gorton, Jake Barnes, Robert Cohn **11** Pedro Romero **15** Lady Brett Ashley, Michael (Mike) Campbell

sunbathe 3 tan **4** bask **12** soak up the sun **13** catch some rays

Sunday
    means: 11 day of the sun
    heavenly body: 3 sun
    day of: 4 rest **7** worship **8** blue laws
    observance: 16 Christian Sabbath
    French: 8 dimanche
    Italian: 8 domenica
    Spanish: 7 domingo
    German: 7 sonntag

Sunday best 6 finery 8 glad rags 11 fine clothes 16 best bib and tucker

sunder 4 rend, rive 5 crack, sever 6 cleave, divide 8 separate 9 tear apart 10 break in two 11 break in half

sundown 4 dusk 6 sunset 7 evening 8 eventide, twilight 9 nightfall

Sundowners, The
    director: 13 Fred Zinnemann
    cast: 11 Deborah Kerr, Dina Merrill, Glynis Johns 12 Peter Ustinov 13 Robert Mitchum
    setting: 9 Australia

sundry 4 many 5 mixed 6 divers, motley, myriad, varied 7 diverse, several, various 8 assorted, manifold, numerous 9 different 10 dissimilar 12 multifarious 13 heterogeneous, miscellaneous

sun-filled 4 fair 5 clear, sunny 6 bright, cheery 8 cheerful 9 cloudless

sunfish 5 dwarf, perch, pigmy, sunny 6 redear 7 lepomis, longear, teleost 8 bluegill, sailboat 9 blackband 10 Sacramento 11 bluespotted, centrarchid, pumpkinseed, yellowbelly

sunflower 10 Helianthus 12 Balsamorhiza
    varieties: 4 ashy 5 giant, showy, stiff, swamp 6 common, desert, Oregon 7 dark-eye, Mexican 8 thin-leaf 10 Maximilian 12 cucumber-leaf

Sunflower State
    nickname of: 6 Kansas

sunless 4 dark, dull, gray, hazy 5 bleak, foggy, misty, murky, rainy 6 cloudy, dismal, dreary, gloomy, leaden, somber 8 overcast 9 cheerless 10 depressing

sunny 4 fair, fine 5 clear, happy, jolly, merry 6 blithe, breezy, bright, cheery, genial, jovial, joyful, joyous, sunlit 7 affable, amiable, buoyant, shining, smiling 8 cheerful, sunshiny 9 brilliant, cloudless, sparkling, unclouded 10 optimistic 12 lighthearted

sunrise 4 dawn 5 sunup 6 aurora 7 dawning 8 cockcrow, daybreak, daylight 10 break of day, crepuscule, newborn day 15 dawn's early light 16 rosy-fingered dawn

sunset 4 dusk 7 sundown 8 blue hour, eventide, gloaming, twilight 9 nightfall 10 close of day, crepuscule

Sunset Boulevard
    director: 11 Billy Wilder
    cast: 8 Jack Webb 9 Fred Clark 11 Hedda Hopper 12 Buster Keaton 13 Cecil B DeMille, Gloria Swanson (Norma Desmond), William Holden 16 Erich von Stroheim

Sunset State
    nickname of: 6 Oregon

sunshade 3 hat 5 visor 6 awning 7 parasol, roundel 8 sombrero, umbrella 9 sunscreen

Sunshine State
    nickname of: 7 Florida 9 New Mexico

sunstone
    species: 8 feldspar

suntan 3 tan 5 brown 6 bronze 7 sunburn

suo jure 14 in one's own right

suo loco 14 in one's own place 19 in one's rightful place

Suomi see 7 Finland

sup 3 eat, sip 4 dine, feed 5 drink, feast, supra 6 absorb, supper, supply 7 consume 8 superior 10 supplement 11 superlative 13 supplementary

super 4 A-one, fine 5 grand, great, prime, prize, swell 6 grade-A, superb, tip-top 7 capital 8 peerless, superior, terrific, top-notch 9 excellent, fantastic, first-rate, marvelous, matchless, non pareil, superfine, wonderful 10 first-class, tremendous, unexcelled, world-class 11 outstanding, superlative 12 incomparable 13 extraordinary

superabound 4 teem 5 swarm 6 thrive 7 burgeon 8 be rich in, flourish, overflow

superabundance 4 glut, riot 5 flood, spate 6 deluge, excess, plenty 7 surfeit, surplus 8 overdose, overflow, pleonasm, plethora 9 avalanche 10 inundation, oversupply, redundance 11 superfluity 12 extravagance 13 overabundance 14 more than enough
    French: 19 embarras de richesses

superabundant 4 lush 6 lavish 7 copious, profuse, teeming 8 swarming, thriving 9 exuberant, luxuriant 10 burgeoning 11 flourishing, overflowing

superb 4 A-one, rare, rich 5 elect, grand, regal 6 choice, costly, deluxe, golden, lordly, select, tip-top 7 elegant, stately 8 gorgeous, imposing, laudable, majestic, peerless, precious, princely, splendid, top-notch, very fine 9 admirable, excellent, expensive, exquisite, first-rate, luxurious, marvelous, matchless, priceless, sumptuous, top-drawer 10 first-class 11 crackerjack, magnificent 12 breathtaking, praiseworthy 15 of the first water

Super Bowl
    1967:
        winner: 15 Green Bay Packers
        loser: 16 Kansas City Chiefs
        site: 8 Coliseum 10 Los Angeles
    1968:
        winner: 15 Green Bay Packers
        loser: 14 Oakland Raiders
        site: 5 Miami 10 Orange Bowl
    1969:
        winner: 11 New York Jets
        loser: 14 Baltimore Colts
        site: 5 Miami 10 Orange Bowl
    1970:
        winner: 16 Kansas City Chiefs
        loser: 16 Minnesota Vikings
        site: 10 New Orleans 13 Tulane Stadium
    1971:
        winner: 14 Baltimore Colts
        loser: 13 Dallas Cowboys
        site: 5 Miami 10 Orange Bowl
    1972:
        winner: 13 Dallas Cowboys
        loser: 13 Miami Dolphins
        site: 10 New Orleans 13 Tulane Stadium
    1973:
        winner: 13 Miami Dolphins
        loser: 18 Washington Redskins
        site: 8 Coliseum 10 Los Angeles
    1974:
        winner: 13 Miami Dolphins
        loser: 16 Minnesota Vikings
        site: 7 Houston 11 Rice Stadium
    1975:
        winner: 18 Pittsburgh Steelers
        loser: 16 Minnesota Vikings
        site: 10 New Orleans 13 Tulane Stadium
    1976:
        winner: 18 Pittsburgh Steelers
        loser: 13 Dallas Cowboys
        site: 5 Miami 10 Orange Bowl
    1977:
        winner: 14 Oakland Raiders
        loser: 16 Minnesota Vikings
        site: 8 Pasadena, Rose Bowl
    1978:
        winner: 13 Dallas Cowboys
        loser: 13 Denver Broncos
        site: 9 Superdome 10 New Orleans
    1979:
        winner: 18 Pittsburgh Steelers
        loser: 13 Dallas Cowboys
        site: 5 Miami 10 Orange Bowl
    1980:
        winner: 18 Pittsburgh Steelers
        loser: 14 Los Angeles Rams
        site: 8 Pasadena, Rose Bowl
    1981:
        winner: 14 Oakland Raiders
        loser: 18 Philadelphia Eagles
        site: 9 Superdome 10 New Orleans
    1982:
        winner: 23 San Francisco Forty-Niners
        loser: 17 Cincinnati Bengals
        site: 7 Pontiac 10 Silverdome
    1983:
        winner: 18 Washington Redskins
        loser: 13 Miami Dolphins
        site: 8 Pasadena, Rose Bowl
    1984:
        winner: 17 Los Angeles Raiders
        loser: 18 Washington Redskins
        site: 12 Tampa Stadium
    1985:
        winner: 23 San Francisco Forty-Niners
        loser: 13 Miami Dolphins
        site: 8 Palo Alto 15 Stanford Stadium

1986:
  winner: 12 Chicago Bears
  loser: 18 New England Patriots
  site: 9 Superdome **10** New Orleans
1987:
  winner: 13 New York Giants
  loser: 13 Denver Broncos
  site: 8 Pasadena, Rose Bowl
1988:
  winner: 18 Washington Redskins
  loser: 13 Denver Broncos
  site: 8 San Diego **17** Jack Murphy Stadium
1989:
  winner: 23 San Francisco Forty-Niners
  loser: 17 Cincinnati Bengals
  site: 5 Miami **16** Joe Robbie Stadium
1990:
  winner: 23 San Francisco Forty-Niners
  loser: 13 Denver Broncos
  site: 9 Superdome **10** New Orleans
1991:
  winner: 13 New York Giants
  loser: 12 Buffalo Bills
  site: 5 Tampa **12** Tampa Stadium
1992:
  winner: 18 Washington Redskins
  loser: 12 Buffalo Bills
  site: 9 Metrodome **11** Minneapolis
1993:
  winner: 13 Dallas Cowboys
  loser: 12 Buffalo Bills
  site: 8 Pasadena, Rose Bowl
1994:
  winner: 13 Dallas Cowboys
  loser: 12 Buffalo Bills
  site: 7 Atlanta **11** Georgia Dome
1995:
  winner: 23 San Francisco Forty-Niners
  loser: 16 San Diego Chargers
  site: 5 Miami **9** Joe Robbie
1996:
  winner: 13 Dallas Cowboys
  loser: 18 Pittsburgh Steelers
  site: 5 Tempe **8** Sun Devil
1997:
  winner: 1 Green Bay Packers
  loser: 18 New England Patriots
  site: 9 Superdome **10** New Orleans
1998:
  winner: 13 Denver Broncos
  loser: 15 Green Bay Packers
  site: 8 Qualcomm, San Diego
1999:
  winner: 13 Denver Broncos
  loser: 14 Atlanta Falcons
  site: 5 Miami **9** Pro Player
2000:
  winner: 11 St Louis Rams
  loser: 15 Tennessee Titans
  site: 7 Atlanta **11** Georgia Dome
2001:
  winner: 15 Baltimore Ravens
  loser: 13 New York Giants

  site: 5 Tampa **12** Raymond James
2002:
  winner: 18 New England Patriots
  loser: 11 St Louis Rams
  site: 9 Superdome **10** New Orleans
2003:
  winner: 18 Tampa Bay Buccaneers
  loser: 14 Oakland Raiders
  site: 8 Qualcomm, San Diego
2004:
  winner: 18 New England Patriots
  loser: 16 Carolina Panthers
  site: 7 Houston, Reliant
2005:
  winner: 18 New England Patriots
  loser: 18 Philadelphia Eagles
  site: 6 Alltel **12** Jacksonville

supercilious 5 proud **6** lordly, snooty, uppity **7** haughty, pompous, stuck-up **8** arrogant, prideful, snobbish **10** disdainful **11** egotistical, magisterial, overbearing, patronizing **12** vainglorious **13** condescending, high-and-mighty, self-important

superciliousness 4 airs **7** hauteur **8** snobbery **9** arrogance, pomposity **10** lordliness, snootiness **11** haughtiness **12** snobbishness **14** disdainfulness

superficial 4 slim **5** faint, outer, silly, trite **6** flimsy, hollow, myopic, slight **7** cursory, minimal, nodding, partial, passing, shallow, summary, surface **8** exterior, mindless, skin-deep **9** desultory, frivolous **10** incomplete **11** empty-headed, perfunctory **12** lacking depth, narrow-minded, on the surface

superficiality 6 myopia **9** frivolity **11** cursoriness, shallowness **13** desultoriness **16** narrow-mindedness, short-sightedness

superfine 4 A-one **6** choice, grade-A, superb, tip-top **8** superior, top-notch **9** excellent, extra fine, first-rate **10** first-class **11** outstanding, overrefined, superlative **13** extraordinary

superfluity 3 fat **5** extra, frill **6** excess, luxury **7** greater, surfeit, surplus **8** overflow, overmuch, plethora **11** gingerbread **12** extravagance **13** embellishment **14** superabundance

superfluous 5 extra, spare **6** excess **7** surplus **8** needless **9** excessive, redundant **10** extraneous, gratuitous, pleonastic **11** inessential, unnecessary **12** nonessential, overgenerous **13** superabundant, supernumerary **14** supererogatory

superhuman 4 epic **5** great **6** divine, heroic **7** godlike, supreme **8** superior **9** herculean, unearthly **10** miraculous, omnipotent **12** otherworldly, supermundane, supernatural, supranatural, transcendent **13** preternatural

superintend 3 run **4** boss **6** direct, govern, manage **7** oversee **9** supervise, watch over **10** administer **12** administrate, have charge of

superintendence 6 charge **7** bossing, running **9** direction, governing **10** leadership, management, overseeing **12** jurisdiction **14** administration

superintendent 4 boss, head **5** chief **6** warden **7** foreman, headman, manager, proctor, steward **8** director, guardian, overseer **9** custodian **10** supervisor

superior 4 boss, fine **5** chief **6** better, choice, deluxe, leader, lordly, senior **7** greater, haughty, notable **8** arrogant, foremost, higher-up, peerless, snobbish **9** commander, excellent, first-rate, imperious, matchless, nonpareil, unrivaled **10** inimitable, noteworthy, preeminent, supervisor **11** exceptional, illustrious, patronizing **12** incomparable, more advanced, vainglorious **13** condescending, distinguished, high-and-mighty
  French: 13 par excellence

superlative 4 best **5** crack, prime **6** expert **7** supreme **8** foremost, greatest, peerless, superior **9** exquisite, first-rate, matchless, nonpareil, paramount, unequaled, unmatched, unrivaled **10** consummate, preeminent, surpassing **11** magnificent, unsurpassed **12** incomparable, transcendent, unparalleled **15** of the first water **17** of the highest order

superman
  German: 10 Ubermensch

Superman
  artist: 11 Jerry Siegel
  creator: 10 Joe Shuster
  character: 4 Lara **5** Jor-el, Kal-el **8** Eben Kent, Lois Lane, Superman, Sy Horton **9** Clark Kent **10** Jimmy Olsen, Martha Kent, Perry White **22** Inspector Bill Henderson **23** Professor JJ Pepperwinkle
  place: 7 Krypton **10** Metropolis, Smallville **14** telephone booth
  nickname: 10 Man of Steel
  director: 13 Richard Donner
  cast: 9 Glenn Ford, Ned Beatty **11** Gene Hackman **12** Jackie Cooper, Margot Kidder (Lois Lane), Marlon Brando **14** Valerie Perrine **16** Christopher Reeve (Superman)

supernatural 6 mystic, occult **7** psychic **9** spiritual, unearthly **10** miraculous, paranormal **12** otherworldly, supranatural **13** preternatural, superphysical **14** transcendental

superpatriotism 8 jingoism **10** chauvinism **11** nationalism

supersede 7 discard, replace, succeed **8** displace, set aside, supplant

supervise 4 boss, head **5** guide **6** direct, govern, handle, manage, survey **7** conduct, control, oversee **8** regulate **9** look after, watch over **10** administer **11** preside over, superintend **12** have charge of

supervision 6 orders 7 control 8 guidance 9 direction 10 governance, government, management, regulation 12 surveillance 15 superintendence

supervisor 4 boss, head 5 chief 7 foreman, manager, steward 8 director, overseer 9 commander 13 administrator 14 superintendent

supper club 4 cafe 6 bistro 7 cabaret 9 nightclub, night spot

supplant 6 depose 7 replace 8 displace 9 supersede 14 take the place of

supple 5 lithe 6 limber, pliant 7 elastic, lissome, plastic, pliable 8 amenable, bendable, flexible, graceful, yielding 9 adaptable, compliant, malleable, tractable 10 submissive 11 acquiescent, complaisant, coordinated

supplement 5 add to, annex, extra, rider 6 extend, insert 7 adjunct, augment, codicil, section 8 addendum, addition, appendix, increase 9 added part, corollary, extension 10 attachment, complement, postscript 12 augmentation

supplementary 5 added, extra 6 backup 7 added on, reserve 8 appended, attached, expanded, extended 9 ancillary, auxiliary, enlarging, secondary 10 additional, amplifying, augmenting 11 subordinate 13 complementary

suppliant 5 asker 6 beggar, cadger, seeker, suitor 7 almsman 8 claimant 9 almswoman, appellant, beseecher, entreater, mendicant 10 petitioner, supplicant 11 supplicator

Suppliants, The
 author: 9 Aeschylus
 character: 6 Danaus 8 Pelasgus 19 Fifty Sons of Aegyptus 20 Fifty Maiden Daughters

Suppliants, The
 author: 9 Euripides
 character: 6 Aethra, Evadne 7 Theseus 8 Adrastus

supplicate 3 ask, beg 4 pray 5 plead 6 ask for 7 entreat 8 appeal to, call upon, petition

supplication 3 cry 4 plea, suit 6 appeal, orison, prayer 7 bumming, cadging, request 8 entreaty, mooching, petition 10 invocation 11 application, beseechment, imploration, imprecation, panhandling 12 solicitation

supplies 4 gear 5 goods, items 8 material 9 equipment, foodstuff, trappings 10 provisions 13 accoutrements

supply 4 fund, give 5 cache, equip, grant, quota, stock, store, yield 6 bestow, outfit, render 7 deal out, deliver, furnish, present, provide, reserve 9 providing, provision, reservoir 10 allocation, come up with, contribute, furnishing 12 provisioning

support 3 aid 4 base, bear, help, hold, keep, lift, pile, post, prop, stay 5

abide, boost, brace, brook, carry, favor, means, shore, stand 6 assist, back up, bear up, clinch, column, defend, endure, foster, hold up, pay for, pillar, ratify, second, succor, suffer, uphold, upkeep, verify 7 backing, bear out, bolster, comfort, confirm, defense, endorse, espouse, finance, further, keeping, nurture, shore up, sustain, warrant 8 abutment, accredit, advocacy, advocate, buttress, champion, espousal, maintain, pedestal, pilaster, sanction, strength, tolerate, vouch for 9 establish, guarantee, patronage, patronize, promotion, put up with, reinforce, stanchion, subsidize 10 assistance, livelihood, provide for, stand up for, stick up for, strengthen, sustenance, underwrite 11 buttressing, consolation, corroborate, countenance, furtherance, go along with, involvement, maintenance, subsistence 12 substantiate, underpinning 13 encouragement

supportable 9 endurable 10 defensible, verifiable 11 sustainable 12 demonstrable, maintainable

supporter 4 ally 6 backer, helper, patron 8 adherent, advocate, champion, defender, disciple, follower, partisan, upholder 10 benefactor, well-wisher 11 sympathizer

supposable 8 credible 9 thinkable 10 believable, imaginable 11 conceivable, perceivable

suppose 5 fancy, guess, judge, posit 6 assume, divine, gather, reckon 7 believe, imagine, presume, surmise, suspect 8 conceive, consider 9 predicate 11 hypothesize 14 take for granted

supposed 5 given 7 alleged, assumed 8 probable, putative 9 imaginary 11 conjectural, speculative, theoretical 12 hypothetical

supposition 4 idea, view 5 given, guess 6 belief, notion, theory, thesis 7 opinion, surmise 9 guesswork, postulate, suspicion 10 assumption, conjecture, hypothesis 11 predication, presumption, proposition, speculation

suppress 4 bury, curb, hide 5 check, crush, quash, quell, still 6 keep in, muffle, quench, squash, stifle, subdue 7 conceal, control, cover up, inhibit, put down, repress, silence, smother, squelch 8 hold back, keep back, overcome, restrain, restrict, snuff out, withhold 9 overpower 10 extinguish, keep secret, put an end to 11 hold in leash, keep private 12 put a damper on 13 put under wraps

suppressant 4 curb 5 brake 7 control 9 restraint

suppressed feelings 7 reserve 9 restraint 10 constraint, diffidence

supremacy 5 power 7 mastery, primacy 10 ascendancy, domination,

precedence 11 omnipotence, paramountcy, preeminence, sovereignty, superiority 13 transcendency

supreme 4 tops 5 chief, first, prime 6 ruling 7 extreme, highest, leading, perfect, topmost 8 absolute, dominant, foremost, peerless 9 matchless, nonpareil, paramount, principal, sovereign, unequaled, unlimited, unmatched, unrivaled, uppermost 10 commanding, consummate, unexcelled 11 all-powerful, superlative, unqualified, unsurpassed 12 front-ranking, immeasurable, incomparable, second to none, unparalleled

Supreme Court
 Chief Justices: 3 Jay (John) 4 Taft (William Howard) 5 Chase (Salmon), Stone (Harlan Fiske), Taney (Roger Brooke), Waite (Morrison), White (Edward) 6 Burger (Warren), Fuller (Melville), Hughes (Charles Evans), Vinson (Frederick), Warren (Earl) 8 Marshall (John), Rutledge (John) 9 Ellsworth (Oliver), Rehnquist (William)
 Associate Justices: 5 Black (Hugo), Story (Joseph), White (Byron) 6 Breyer (Stephen), Fortas (Abe), Holmes (Oliver Wendell), Powell (Lewis), Scalia (Antonin), Souter (David), Thomas (Clarence) 7 Brennan (William), Cardozo (Benjamin), Douglas (William O), Kennedy (Anthony), O'Connor (Sandra Day), Stevens (John), Stewart (Potter) 8 Blackmun (Harry), Brandeis (Louis), Ginsburg (Ruth Bader), Goldberg (Arthur), Marshall (Thurgood) 11 Frankfurter (Felix)
 Cases: 15 Marbury v Madison 17 Gideon v Wainwright 18 McCulloch v Maryland 20 Griswold v Connecticut
 abortion: 8 Roe v Wade
 antitrust: 8 E C Knight 11 Standard Oil 15 Swift and Company 22 American Tobacco Company
 civil rights: 9 Bakke Case 15 Plessy v Ferguson 30 Brown v Board of Education of Topeka
 Japanese internment: 22 Korematsu v United States 24 Hirabayashi v United States
 rights of accused: 15 Miranda v Arizona 17 Escobedo v Illinois
 slavery: 13 Dred Scott Case 14 Scott v Sandford

surcease 4 quit, rest, stop 5 abate, cease, pause 7 die away, respite 8 conclude, leave off 11 come to an end, discontinue 17 come to a standstill

surcharge 3 tax 4 levy 6 excise, impost

surcingle 4 band, belt 5 girth 6 girdle 8 cincture

sure 4 fast, firm, true 5 solid, sound 6 stable, steady 7 assured, certain 8 accurate, fail-safe, faithful, flawless, positive, reliable, surefire, unerring **9** confident, convinced, unfailing **10** dependable, infallible, undoubting **11** trustworthy **12** never-failing

sure bet 4 fact **5** cinch **7** reality **9** actuality, certainty, sure thing **13** inevitability **14** inescapability

surely 7 no doubt **8** of course, to be sure **9** assuredly, certainly, doubtless **10** by all means, definitely, for certain, infallibly, positively **11** come what may, indubitably, undoubtedly, without fail **12** emphatically, without doubt **14** unquestionably

sureness 6 surety **9** assurance, certainty, certitude **10** confidence **11** assuredness **12** positiveness **13** self-assurance **14** conclusiveness, self-confidence, self-possession

sure thing 4 fact **5** cinch **7** reality, sure bet **9** actuality, certainty **13** inevitability **14** inescapability

surety 4 bail, bond **8** sureness **9** certainty, certitude, guarantee **10** confidence **12** positiveness

surface 3 top **4** coat, face, skin **5** crust, shell **6** facade, finish, veneer **7** coating, outside **8** covering, exterior **11** superficies

Surface family
  characters in: 19 The School for Scandal
  member: 6 Joseph **7** Charles **9** Sir Oliver
  author: 8 Sheridan

surfeit 4 cloy, glut, sate **5** gorge, stuff **6** excess **7** satiate, satisfy, surplus **8** overmuch, plethora **9** plenitude, profusion, repletion, satiation **10** oversupply, surplusage **11** exorbitance, overindulge, prodigality, superfluity **12** extravagance **13** overabundance **14** more than enough, superabundance **15** supersaturation

surfeited 4 full **5** sated **6** gorged **7** glutted, replete, stuffed **8** overfull, satiated **9** satisfied

surge 4 rush, wave **5** flood, swell **7** torrent

Suriname
  other name: 7 Surinam **11** Dutch Guiana
  capital/largest city: 10 Paramaribo
  others: 6 Albina **7** Totness **9** Groningen **10** Brokopondo, Onverwacht **13** Nieuw Nickerie **14** Nieuw Amsterdam
  measure: 7 ketting
  monetary unit: 4 cent **7** guilder
  lake: 14 Van Blommestein
  mountain: 4 Emma **6** Kayser, Oranje **10** Tumuc-Humac, Wilhelmina **13** Eilerts Il Haan, Van Ach Van Wyck **15** Guiana Highlands
  highest point: 10 Julianatop
  river: 6 Maroni **7** Surinam **8** Nickerie,

Suriname **9** Coppename **10** Courantijn, Courantyne, Tapanahoni
  ocean: 8 Atlantic
  physical feature:
    falls: 7 Kaiteur
  people: 4 Boni, Bush, Trio **5** Djuka, Dutch **6** Creole, Wayana **7** African, Chinese Amerindian, Boschneger, West Indian **11** Asian Indian
    settler: 22 Lord Willoughby of Parham
  language: 5 Carib, Dutch, Hindi **6** Arawak **7** English **8** Javanese, Taki-Taki **10** Hindustani **11** Sranan Tongo **12** Sranang Tongo
  religion: 5 Hindu, Islam **10** Protestant **13** Roman Catholic
  feature:
    canoe: 6 corial
    clothing: 4 sari **5** dhoti **6** kamisa, sarong **10** kotomissie
    hat: 3 fez
    hut: 5 benab
    scarf: 9 selendong
    tree: 4 dali, lana, mora **5** dalli, genip, icica **7** acuyari, quassia **9** bethabara
  food:
    drink: 7 paiwari

surliness 8 ill humor, rudeness **9** bad temper **11** discourtesy, grouchiness **12** irascibility

surly 4 rude, sour **5** cross, gruff, harsh, testy **6** abrupt, crusty, grumpy, sullen, touchy **7** bearish, crabbed, grouchy, hostile, peevish, uncivil, waspish **8** choleric, churlish, insolent, petulant, snappish, snarling **9** irascible, splenetic, unamiable **10** ill-humored, ill-natured, unfriendly **11** bad-tempered **12** discourteous

surmise 4 deem, idea **5** guess, infer, judge, opine, posit, think **6** belief, notion **7** believe, imagine, opinion, presume, suppose, suspect, thought **8** conclude, consider, theorize **9** suspicion **10** assumption, conjecture, hypothesis, presuppose **11** hypothesize, presumption, speculation, supposition **13** shot in the dark

surmount 3 top **4** best **5** clear, climb, scale, worst **6** defeat, master **7** conquer, get over **8** overcome, vanquish **11** prevail over, triumph over **14** get the better of

surpass 3 top **4** beat, best **5** excel, outdo **6** exceed, outrun **7** eclipse **8** go beyond, outclass, outshine, outstrip, override **9** rise above, transcend **10** overshadow **11** go one better, leave behind, outdistance, triumph over **12** be better than, be superior to **13** have it all over

surplus 4 glut **5** extra **6** excess **7** overage, surfeit **8** leftover, overflow, plethora, residual **10** oversupply, surplusage **11** superfluity, superfluous **14** overproduction

surprise 4 stun **5** amaze, shock **6** ambush, wonder **7** astound, nonplus, set upon, stagger, startle, stupefy **8** astonish, confound, discover, dumfound, fall upon **9** amazement, bombshell, burst in on, dumbfound, take aback **10** defy belief, pounce upon, revelation, wonderment **11** flabbergast, incredulity **12** astonishment, take unawares **13** boggle the mind

surprise attack
  French: 10 coup de main

surrender 4 cede **5** forgo, let go, waive, yield **6** accede, forego, give up, render, submit, vacate **7** abandon, concede, forsake **8** delivery, forgoing, give over, giving up, hand over, part with, renounce, turn over, yielding **9** deliver up, foregoing **10** capitulate, relinquish, submission **11** lay down arms **12** capitulation, renunciation **14** relinquishment **15** throw in the towel **16** show the white flag

surreptitious 6 covert, hidden, secret, veiled **7** furtive **8** hush-hush, stealthy **9** concealed, secretive **10** undercover

surrogate 6 acting, deputy **7** interim, stand-in **9** temporary **10** substitute **11** provisional

surround 4 belt, ring **5** hedge, hem in **6** circle, enfold, engird, girdle, shut in **7** close in, compass, enclose, envelop, fence in, hedge in **8** encircle **9** encompass **12** circumscribe

surrounding area 7 suburbs **8** environs, vicinity **9** outskirts, precincts

surroundings 5 scene **6** milieu **7** habitat, setting **8** ambience, environs **10** atmosphere, conditions **11** environment **13** circumstances
  French: 11 mise en scene

surveillance 5 vigil, watch **8** scrutiny, trailing **11** observation **13** eavesdropping

survey 4 plot, poll, scan **5** gauge, graph, plumb, probe, scout, study **6** fathom, review **7** canvass, delimit, examine, inspect, measure, observe **8** analysis, block out, consider, look over, overview **10** scrutinize **11** contemplate, reconnoiter **12** pass in review **13** investigation

survival 5 relic **6** living **7** atavism, vestige **8** hangover **9** carry-over, throwback **11** subsistence **12** continuation, keeping alive

survive 4 last **5** abide, exist **6** endure, hang on, live on **7** hold out, outlast, outlive, persist, prevail, subsist **8** be extant, continue **9** keep alive **11** live through

surviving 6 extant **7** abiding, lasting **8** enduring, existent, existing, living on **9** hanging on, outliving, to be found **10** continuing, holding out, outlasting, persistent, persisting, subsisting **11** in existence **13** living through

Survivor

network: 3 CBS
creator: 11 Mark Burnett
genre: 11 reality show
host: 10 Jeff Probst
winner: 9 Ethan Zohn **10** Tina Wesson, Tom Westman **11** Amber Brkich, Brian Heidik **12** Jenna Morasca, Richard Hatch **13** Rupert Boneham, Vecepia Towery **14** Chris Daugherty **15** Sandra Diaz-Twine
locale: 5 Palau **6** Africa, Borneo, Panama **7** Vanuatu **8** Thailand **9** Australia, Guatemala, Marquesas, Pulau Tiga, the Amazon **10** the Outback **12** Pearl Islands
motto: 20 outwit outplay outlast

Susann, Jacqueline

author of: 14 The Love Machine **15** Once Is Not Enough **16** Valley of the Dolls

Susanna

husband: 6 Joakim
accused of: 8 adultery
saved by: 6 Daniel

susceptible 4 open **5** prone **7** alive to, subject **8** liable to, sensible **9** sensitive **10** disposed to, responsive, vulnerable **11** conducive to, receptive to, sensitive to, sympathetic

suspect 5 doubt, fancy, guess, judge, opine, posit, think **7** believe, imagine, presume, suppose, surmise **8** distrust, misdoubt, mistrust, question, theorize **9** speculate **10** conjecture **11** hypothesize, wonder about **14** alleged culprit, be suspicious of **19** have one's doubts about

suspend 4 halt, hang, quit, stay, stop **5** cease, check, defer, delay, sling, swing, table **6** append, arrest, dangle, put off, shelve **7** reserve **8** break off, cut short, leave off, postpone, withhold **9** interrupt, stop short **10** put an end to **11** discontinue **12** bring to a stop **18** bring to a standstill

suspenders 6 braces, straps **7** gallows, garters, hangers **8** elastics, galluses **10** supporters

suspense 7 anxiety, tension **8** edginess **9** curiosity **10** indecision **11** expectation, incertitude, uncertainty **12** anticipation **15** indetermination

suspenseful 7 anxious **8** dramatic, exciting **9** climactic, uncertain

suspension 4 stay **5** pause **6** hiatus, recess **7** tabling **8** abeyance, deferral **12** postponement **14** discontinuance

suspicion 4 idea **5** guess, hunch **6** notion **7** feeling, surmise **8** distrust, mistrust **10** conjecture, hypothesis **11** supposition

Suspicion

director: 15 Alfred Hitchcock
cast: 9 Cary Grant **10** Nigel Bruce **12** Joan Fontaine **13** Dame May Whitty

15 Cedric Hardwicke
Oscar for: 7 actress (Fontaine)

suspicious 4 wary **5** shady **7** dubious, suspect **8** doubtful, doubting, slippery **9** ambiguous **10** untrusting **11** distrustful, incredulous, mistrustful, open to doubt **12** disbelieving, questionable **13** untrustworthy

sustain 4 bear, feed, prop **5** abide, brave, brook, stand **6** bear up, endure, hold up, keep up, suffer, uphold **7** nourish, nurture, prolong, support, undergo **8** maintain, protract, tolerate, underpin **9** keep alive, withstand **10** experience **12** carry on under **14** hold out against

sustenance 4 food, gear **5** bread, means **6** living **7** aliment, support **9** provender **10** provisions **11** maintenance, nourishment, subsistence
heaven-sent: 5 manna

sustineo alas 16 I sustain the wings
motto of: 10 US Air Force

Sutherland, Donald

born: 6 Canada, St John **12** New Brunswick
son: 16 Kiefer Sutherland
roles: 4 MASH **5** Klute **8** Instinct **12** Cold Mountain, Fierce People, Space Cowboys **13** Hawkeye Pierce, The Italian Job **14** Eye of the Needle, Ordinary People **16** Fellini's Casanova **17** The Eagle Has Landed **26** Invasion of the Body Snatchers

Sutherland, Kiefer

born: 6 London **7** England
father: 16 Donald Sutherland
roles: 8 Dark City **10** Flatliners, Twenty-Four **11** A Few Good Men **16** Behind the Red Door **18** The Three Musketeers

Sutpen, Colonel Thomas

character in: 14 Absalom Absalom
author: 8 Faulkner

Suva

capital of: 4 Fiji

svelte 4 fine, lean, neat, slim, thin, trim **5** lithe, spare **7** elegant, lissome, shapely, slender, willowy **8** graceful **9** sylphlike

Svengali

character in: 6 Trilby
author: 9 Du Maurier

Sverige see **6** Sweden

swab 3 dab, mop **4** daub, lout, wipe **5** clean, cloth, patch, scrub **6** cotton, sponge **7** cleanse **8** specimen
brand name: 4 Q-tip

swagger 5 strut, sweep **6** parade, sashay, stride **7** saunter **11** swashbuckle

swaggerer 6 gascon **7** boaster, bragger **8** blowhard, braggart, strutter **11** braggadocio

swain 4 beau **6** fellow, suitor **7** admirer, gallant **8** cavalier, young man **9** boyfriend **10** sweetheart

swallow 3 bit, nip, sip **4** down, gulp, swig **5** drink, quaff, swill, taste **6** credit, devour, gobble, guzzle, hold in, imbibe, ingest, tipple **7** believe, fall for, repress **8** gulp down, hold back, keep back, mouthful, suppress, withhold

swallow up 5 drown, eat up, swamp **6** absorb, engulf **7** consume, envelop **8** inundate **9** overwhelm **10** assimilate

swallow words 6 mumble, mutter

swamp 3 bog, fen **4** fill, mire, moor, ooze, quag, sink, slew, slue **5** bayou, beset, flood, marsh, swale **6** deluge, engulf, morass, slough **7** besiege, bottoms, envelop **8** inundate, quagmire, submerge, wash over **9** everglade, marshland, overwhelm, snow under, swallow up

swamped 7 deluged, flooded, glutted, overrun **9** inundated **11** overwhelmed

Swan

constellation of: 6 Cygnus

swan

young: 6 cygnet
group of: 4 bevy

swank 4 airs **5** ritzy **6** la-di-da, snooty, swanky **9** high-class, top-drawer **11** pretensions, pretentious **12** affectations, ostentatious **15** pretentiousness **16** superciliousness

Swank, Hilary

born: 7 Lincoln **8** Nebraska
husband: 8 Chad Lowe
roles: 11 Boys Don't Cry **16** The Next Karate Kid **17** Million Dollar Baby

swanky 4 chic, posh, rich **5** fancy, grand, jazzy, plush, ritzy, sharp, showy, smart, swank **6** flashy, snazzy, spiffy, sporty **7** dashing, elegant, splashy, stylish **9** sumptuous **11** fashionable

Swan Lake

composer: 11 Tchaikovsky

Swanson, Gloria

real name: 25 Gloria Josephine Mae Swenson
born: 9 Chicago IL
husband: 12 Wallace Beery
roles: 13 Sadie Thompson, The Trespasser **15** Sunset Boulevard

swap 5 trade **6** barter, dicker, switch **7** bargain **8** exchange **11** give and take

sward 3 sod **4** lawn, rind, skin, turf **5** grass

swarm 4 herd, host, mass, rush, teem **5** cloud, crowd, drove, flock, horde, press, surge **6** abound, legion, myriad, stream, throng **7** cluster, overrun **8** stampede **9** multitude

swarthy 4 dark **5** dusky, swart, tawny **6** brunet **8** brunette **11** dark-skinned **12** brown-colored, brown-skinned, olive-skinned **14** dark-complected **16** dark-complexioned

swashbuckler 9 buccaneer, daredevil 10 adventurer

swashbuckling 4 bold 7 dashing 8 boasting 9 audacious, daredevil

swat 3 hit, tap 4 bash, belt, slam, slap, slug, sock 5 clout, knock, smack, smite, whack 6 buffet, strike, thwack, wallop 7 clobber

swathe 4 bind, wrap 5 cloak, cover 6 encase, enfold, enwrap 7 envelop, sheathe, swaddle

sway 4 bend, grip, hold, lead, list, move, reel, rock, roll, rule, spur, vary, wave 5 alter, clout, impel, power, reign, rouse, shift, swing, waver 6 change, domain, incite, induce, prompt, swerve, totter, waving, wobble 7 command, control, dispose, mastery, stagger, swaying 8 hesitate, iron hand, motivate, persuade, swinging, to-and-fro, undulate 9 authority, direction, encourage, fluctuate, influence, oscillate, pendulate, pulsation, stimulate, vacillate 10 domination, government, predispose, suzerainty, undulation 11 fluctuation, oscillation 12 back and forth, dictatorship, jurisdiction, manipulation

Swaziland
capital/largest city: 7 Mbabane
others: 5 Bunya, Hluti, Mpaka, Nsoko, Stegi 6 Gollel, Mhlume 7 Big Bend, Lobamba, Manzini 8 Havelock, Malkerns 9 Geodgegun, Hlatikulu, Mankaiana, Mankayana, Nhlangano, Pigg's Peak, Rocklands
government: 22 constitutional monarchy
head of state: 4 king
monetary unit: 4 rand 9 lilangeni
mountain: 8 Highveld 11 Drakensberg
highest point: 7 Emlembe
river: 5 Usutu 6 Komati, Lomati 8 Mhlatuze, Ngwavuma, Umbeluzi, Umbuluzi
physical feature:
  forest: 5 Usutu
  plateau: 7 Lebombo, Lubombo
people: 5 Asian, Bantu, Swazi 11 Eurafricans
  king: 3 Kbe 5 Nyama 6 Mswati 7 Sobhuza
  prince: 6 Sozisa
language: 5 Ngumi 7 English, Siswati 9 Afrikaans 10 Portuguese
religion: 7 animism 10 Protestant 13 Roman Catholic
feature:
  bride payment: 6 lobolo
  god: 14 Mkhulumngcandi
  ritual dance: 7 Incwala

swear 3 vow 4 aver, avow, cuss 5 curse, vouch 6 adjure, assert, attest, pledge 7 certify, promise, warrant 9 blaspheme 10 take an oath, utter oaths 11 bear witness

swear by 7 believe, count on 9 believe in 10 put faith in

sweat 4 ooze, toil 5 exude, worry 6 effort 7 agonize 8 drudgery, hard work, perspire 9 exudation 12 perspiration

sweaty 3 wet 6 clammy, sticky 10 perspiring

Sweden
other name: 7 Sverige
capital/largest city: 9 Stockholm
others: 4 Lund, Umea 5 Boden, Boras, Edane, Falun, Gavle, Lulea, Malmo, Pitea, Visby 6 Arvika, Kiruna, Orebro 7 Uppsala 8 Goteborg, Jokkmokk, Vasteras 9 Jonkoping, Linkoping, Sundsvall 10 Eskilstuna, Gottenburg, Norrkoping, Skelleftea 11 Halsingborg
school: 4 Lund 7 Uppsala 8 Goteborg 9 Stockholm
division: 3 Lan 4 Laen 5 Skane 6 Kalmar, Orebro 7 Dalarna, Gotland, Lapland 8 Alvsborg, Blekinge, Elfsborg, Gotaland, Jamtland, Malmohus, Norrland, Svealand
government: 22 constitutional monarchy
  legislature: 7 Riksdag
head of state: 4 king
measure: 3 aln, fot, ref 4 alar, amar, famn, kapp, last, stop 5 carat, foder, kanna, linje, nymil, spann 6 fathom, jumfru 7 oxhuvud, tunland 8 fjarding, koltunna, tunnland
monetary unit: 3 ore 5 krona, krone 7 carolin 8 skilling 9 rigsdaler
weight: 3 ass, lod 4 last, mark, sten 5 carat 6 nylast 7 centner, lispund 8 skalpund, skeppund 9 shippound
island: 5 Oland 7 Gotland
lake: 4 Ster 5 Asnen, Malar, Silja, Vaner 6 Vanern, Vetter, Wenner 7 Hielmar, Malaren, Vattern 8 Dalalven 9 Hjalmaren
mountain: 4 Sarv 5 Ammar 6 Helags, Kjolen, Ovniks, Sarjek 7 Kjollen
highest point: 5 Kebne 10 Kebnekaise
river: 3 Dal 4 Gota, Klar, Lule, Pite, Umea 5 Indal, Kalix, Lulea, Pitea, Ranea, Torne 6 Lainio, Muonio 7 Ljusnan 8 Angerman
sea: 6 Baltic 8 Atlantic
physical feature:
  canal: 4 Gota
  gulf: 7 Bothnia
  sound: 6 Kalmar
  strait: 7 Oresund 8 Kattegat 9 Skagerrak
people: 4 Lapp 5 Norse, Swede 6 Viking
  actress: 9 Liv Ullman 10 Greta Garbo 13 Ingrid Bergman
  astronomer: 7 Celsius 8 Angstrom
  author: 8 Lagerlof 10 Lagerkvist, Strindberg
  diplomat: 12 Hammarskjold
  director: 13 Ingmar Bergman 14

Arne Sucksdorff
  inventor: 5 Nobel
  king: 4 Vosa, Wasa 5 Oscar 6 Gustav 8 Gustavus 10 Carl Gustav 12 Gustav Adolph 13 Charles Gustav 22 Jean Baptiste Bernadotte
  philosopher/scientist: 10 Swedenborg
  queen: 9 Christina
  scientist: 8 Linnaeus
language: 4 Lapp 7 Swedish
religion: 19 Evangelical Lutheran
place:
  castle: 9 Gripsholm
  center of Stockholm: 11 Gamla Staden
  park: 7 Skansen 12 Millesgarden
  theater: 18 Drottningholm Court
  walled city: 5 Visby
food: 11 smorgasbord
  cheese: 7 fontina 8 jarlberg 9 jarlsberg
  dish: 10 kottbullar
  drink: 5 glogg 7 aquavit

Swedish Punch
type: 7 liqueur
origin: 6 Sweden
base: 3 rum
with gin: 5 Biffy
with vermouth: 9 Grand Slam

sweep 3 arc, fly 4 dart, dash, race, rush, scud, tear, zoom 5 hurry, spell, swing, swish, swoop, whisk 6 charge, gather, scurry, stroke 7 stretch 8 distance

sweeping 5 broad 7 blanket, radical 9 extensive, out-and-out, wholesale 10 exhaustive, large-scale, widespread 11 far-reaching, wide-ranging 12 all-inclusive 13 comprehensive, thoroughgoing

sweepings 4 dirt, dust 6 refuse

sweep off one's feet 7 enchant 8 bedazzle 9 captivate, overpower, overwhelm

sweet 4 dear, kind, nice 5 candy, fresh 6 dulcet, mellow, smooth, sugary 7 amiable, cloying, darling, dessert, lovable, nonsalt, not salt, tuneful 8 fragrant, pleasant, pleasing 9 agreeable, melodious, sweetmeat, wholesome 10 attractive, confection, euphonious, saccharine 11 good-natured, mellifluous, silver-toned, sympathetic 12 nonfermented

Sweet Bird of Youth
director: 13 Richard Brooks
based on play by: 17 Tennessee Williams
cast: 8 Ed Begley 10 Paul Newman 13 Geraldine Page, Shirley Knight 17 Madeleine Sherwood
Oscar for: 15 supporting actor (Begley)

sweetheart 4 beau, dear, love 5 flame, honey, lover, swain 6 fiance, old man, steady, suitor 7 beloved,

darling, fiancee, old lady **8** ladylove, mistress, true love **9** boyfriend, inamorata, valentine **10** girlfriend, lady friend **15** gentleman friend
French: 6 cherie

sweet life
Italian: 9 dolce vita

Sweet Mama Stringbean
nickname of: 11 Ethel Waters

sweetmeats 5 candy **6** sweets **7** bonbons **10** sugar candy **11** confections **13** confectionery

sweet-natured 5 sweet **6** benign, gentle, kindly **7** likable, lovable **8** pleasant **13** compassionate

sweetness
French: 7 douceur

sweet roll 3 bun **6** Danish **7** cruller **8** doughnut **10** coffee cake **11** cinnamon bun

sweets 5 candy **7** goodies **8** desserts **10** sugar candy, sweetmeats **11** confections **13** confectionery

sweet-scented 8 aromatic, fragrant, perfumed, redolent

sweet-smelling 5 spicy **7** scented **8** aromatic, fragrant, perfumed, redolent **9** odiferous

sweet talk 6 cajole, praise **7** blarney, flatter **8** cajolery, flattery, soft soap **10** compliment **11** endearments, loving words **13** blandishments **14** fond utterances

sweet words 7 blarney **8** flattery, soft soap **9** sweet talk **12** honeyed words

swell 3 fop, wax **4** A-one, fine, good, grow, okay, puff, rise, wave **5** bloat, bulge, dandy, great, heave, mount, super, surge, throb, widen **6** billow, blow up, comber, expand, extend, fatten, puff up **7** amplify, breaker, burgeon, distend, inflate, stretch, thicken **8** fabulous, heighten, increase, lengthen, splendid, terrific **9** excellent, first-rate, intensify, marvelous, spread out **10** delightful, first-class, tremendous, undulation **11** pleasurable **12** clotheshorse, fashion plate, smart dresser

swell-headed 8 egoistic, puffed up **9** conceited **10** egoistical **11** egotistical **12** vainglorious **13** self-important

swelling 4 bump, lump **5** bulge, swell **8** dilation **9** puffiness **10** distension **11** enlargement **12** protuberance

swell out 5 bloat, bulge **6** billow, expand **7** distend, inflate, puff out

swelter 3 fry **4** boil, cook **5** be hot, broil, sweat **8** languish, perspire

sweltering 3 hot **5** humid, muggy **6** sultry, torrid **7** burning **8** sweating **10** oppressive, perspiring

sweltry 3 hot **4** dank **5** humid, muggy **6** baking, clammy, steamy, sticky, sultry, torrid **7** boiling **8** broiling, roast-

ing, sizzling, stifling **9** scorching **10** blistering **11** suffocating

Swept Away
subtitle: 38 by an unusual destiny in the blue sea of August
director: 14 Lina Wertmuller
cast: 16 Mariangela Melato **17** Giancarlo Giannini

swerve 3 shy, yaw **4** tack, turn, veer **5** avert, dodge, sheer, shift, stray **6** careen, change **7** deviate, digress, diverge **9** turn aside

swift 4 fast **5** brisk, fleet, hasty, quick, rapid **6** abrupt, flying, prompt, speedy **8** headlong **9** immediate **11** expeditious, precipitate

Swift, Jonathan
author of: 11 A Tale of a Tub **15** A Modest Proposal **16** Battle of the Books, Gulliver's Travels
fictional places: 6 Laputa **8** Lilliput **11** Brobdingnag
character: 6 Yahoos **10** Houyhnhnms **14** Lemuel Gulliver

swiftness 5 haste, speed **8** alacrity, celerity, dispatch, rapidity **9** quickness

swill 4 mash, slop, swig **5** quaff, waste **6** guzzle, refuse, scraps, soak up, tipple **7** garbage **8** chugalug, gulp down

swimming
athlete: 9 Diana Nyad, John Naber, Mark Spitz **10** Dawn Fraser, Kim Linehan, Linda Jezek **11** Claudia Kolb, Debbie Meyer, John Hencken **12** Brian Goodell, Bruce Furniss, Greg Louganis, John Kinsella **13** Jim Montgomery, Kornelia Ender, Michael Burton, Tracy Caulkens **14** Charles Hickcox, Duke Kahanamoku, Esther Williams, Gertrude Ederle **15** Cynthia Woodhead **16** Shirley Babashoff **17** Johnny Weissmuller

Swinburne, Algernon Charles
author of: 16 Hymn to Perserpine **17** Atalanta in Calydon **18** Songs Before Sunrise

swindle 2 do **3** con, gyp **4** bilk, dupe, gull, hoax, rook **5** cheat, cozen, fraud, mulct, steal, trick **6** delude, fleece, racket, rip-off **7** con game, deceive, defraud **8** embezzle, hoodwink **9** bamboozle, defalcate **12** embezzlement **14** confidence game

swindler 3 gyp **5** cheat, crook, faker, fraud **6** con man **7** sharper **8** chiseler, deceiver **9** charlatan, embezzler **10** mountebank **12** rip-off artist

swine 3 cad, cur, rat **4** pigs **5** beast, brute **6** animal
group of: 5 drift **7** sounder

swing 4 drop, hang, loop, move, rein, rock, sway, turn **5** pivot, rally, scope, sweep, whirl **6** dangle, decide, handle, manage, rotate, seesaw, stroke, wangle **7** compass, extract, freedom, inveigh, liberty, license, listing, pull off, rocking, rolling, suspend, swaying

8 maneuver, pitching, undulate **9** determine, influence, oscillate **10** accomplish, manipulate **11** be suspended, oscillation

Swing Time
director: 13 George Stevens
cast: 9 Eric Blore **11** Fred Astaire, Victor Moore **12** Betty Furness, Ginger Rogers **14** Helen Broderick
score: 10 Jerome Kern **13** Dorothy Fields
Oscar for: 4 song
song: 12 A Fine Romance **14** Pick Yourself Up **20** The Way You Look Tonight

swirl 4 bowl, eddy, reel, roll, spin, swim, turn **5** churn, twirl, twist, wheel, whirl **6** gyrate, rotate **7** revolve

Swiss Family Robinson
director: 10 Ken Annakin
cast: 9 John Mills **10** Janet Munro **14** Dorothy McGuire, James MacArthur, Sessue Hayakawa
author: 16 Johann Rudolf Wyss
character: 13 Emily Montrose
Robinson family: 4 Jack **5** Fritz **6** Ernest **7** Francis

switch 3 box, rod, tan **4** cane, jerk, lash, move, whip **5** birch, lever, shift, shunt, stick, swing, trade, whisk **6** button, change, handle **8** exchange **9** sidetrack **11** alternation

Switzerland
also: 6 Suisse (French) **7** Schweiz (German) **8** Helvetia (Latin)
capital: 4 Bern(e)
largest city: 6 Zurich
others: 3 Zug **4** Bale, Bern, Biel, Brig, Chur, Nyon, Sion, Thun **5** Basel, Basle, Berne, Coire, Surat, Vevey **6** Geneva, Geneve, Glarus, Lugano, Sarnen, Schwyz **7** Altdorf, Fyzabad, Herisau, Locarno, Lucerne, Luzerne, Zermatt **8** Lausanne, Montreux, St Moritz **9** Neuchatel, Solothurn **10** Bellinzona, Interlaken, Winterthur **12** Schaffhausen
school: 4 Bern **5** Basel **8** Catholic, Lausanne **28** Federal Institute of Technology
division: 3 Uri, Zug **4** Bern, Chur, Nyon, Vaud **5** Aarau, Basel, Basle, Berne, Sankt, Waadt **6** Aargau, canton, Gallen, Geneva, Geneve, Glaris, Glarus, Luzern, Obwald, Schwyz, St Gall, Tessin, Ticino, Valais, Wallis, Zurich **7** Atldorf, Grisons, Lucerne, Nidwald, Thurgau **8** Fribourg, Obwalden, St Gallen **9** Appenzell, Neuchatel, Neuenberg, Solothurn **10** Graubunden **11** Unterwalden **12** Schaffhausen
measure: 3 imi, pot **4** aune, fuss, muid, pied, zoll **5** lieue, linie, maass, pouce, staab, toise **6** perche, strich **7** klafter, viertel **9** quarteron **10** holzlafter **11** holzklafter

monetary unit: 5 franc, rappe **6** hallar, rappen **7** centime, duplone **8** baetzner

weight: 4 fund **5** pfund **7** centner, quintal **12** zugthierlast

lake: 3 Uri, Zug **4** Biel, Thon, Thun **5** Ageri, Leman, Morat **6** Bienne, Brienz, Geneva, Lugano, Sarnen, Wallen, Zurich **7** Hallwil, Lucerne, Lungern **8** Maggiore, Viervald **9** Bielersee, Constance, Neuchatel, Sarnersee, Thunersee

mountain: 3 Dom **4** Alps, Jura, Rigi, Rosa, Todi **5** Adula, Blanc, Cenis, Eiger, Genis, Karpf, Righi **6** Linard, Pizela, Sentis **7** Bernina, Beverin, Grimsel, Pilatus, Rotondo **8** Balmhorn, Jungfrau **9** Weisshorn **10** Diablerets, Matterhorn, St Gotthard, Wetterhorn **11** Burgenstock **12** Dufourspitze **13** Rheinwaldhorn **14** Finsteraarhorn

  mountain pass: 5 Cenis, Furka, Gemmi **6** Albula, Kinzig, Maloja, Usteri **7** Bernina, Brenner, Grimsel, Simplon, Splugen **8** Lotschen **10** St Gotthard

highest point: 12 Dufourspitze

river: 2 Po **3** Aar, Inn **4** Aare, Arve, Thur, Toss **5** Broye, Doubs, Linth, Reuss, Rhine, Rhone, Saane **6** Limmat, Maggia, Safane, Sarine, Ticino **8** Engadine, Pratigau

physical feature:
  glacier: 5 Rhone
  plateau: 5 Swiss
people: 5 Swiss
  artist: 4 Klee
  author: 5 Hesse, Spyri **6** Keller **8** Gotthelf, Rousseau **10** Durrenmatt
  educational reformer: 10 Pestalozzi
  hero: 4 Tell
  psychologist: 4 Jung **6** Piaget
  religious leader: 6 Calvin **7** Zwingli
  scientist: 9 Bernoulli
language: 5 Ladin **6** French, German **7** Italian **8** Romansch **14** Switzerdeutsch
religion: 9 Calvinism **10** Protestant **13** Roman Catholic
place:
  castle: 7 Chillon
  fountain: 7 Jet d'Eau
  playhouse: 6 Zurich
  resort: 5 Arosa, Davos **6** Gstaad **7** Zermatt **8** St Moritz **9** Schwagalp **10** Interlaken
  street: 14 Bahnhofstrasse
  tower: 5 Clock
feature:
  animal: 4 ibex **7** chamois **12** Saint Bernard
  flower: 9 edelweiss
  industry: 7 banking
  pageant: 9 Alpenfest
food:

cheese: 6 bagnes, sbrinz **7** Gruyere **10** Emmentaler **11** Appenzeller

dish: 5 rosti **6** fondue **8** raclette **11** grisons beef **14** bundnerfleisch

drink: 11 cheri-suisse **14** marmotchocolat

swollen 5 puffy **7** bloated, bulging, swelled **8** inflated, puffed-up **9** distended

swoon 5 faint **8** collapse, keel over **13** fall prostrate **17** become unconscious

swoop 4 dive, drop, rush **5** pitch, sweep **6** plunge, pounce, spring **7** descend, plummet **8** nose-dive, swooping **9** sweep down **12** rush headlong

sword 4 epee, foil **5** blade, saber, steel **6** rapier **7** cutlass **8** scimitar **10** broadsword

sybarite 8 hedonist **10** sensualist, voluptuary

sybaritic 4 rich **6** lavish **7** sensual **9** dissolute, epicurean, luxurious **10** dissipated, hedonistic, voluptuous **12** luxury-loving, pleasure-bent **13** self-indulgent **14** pleasure-loving **15** pleasure-seeking

sycamore 8 Platanus **18** Acer pseudoplatanus
  varieties: 7 eastern **8** Egyptian

sycophant 4 tool **5** slave, toady **6** fawner, flunky, jackal, lackey, puppet, stooge, yes-man **7** cat's-paw **8** hanger-on, parasite, truckler **9** brown-nose, flatterer **10** bootlicker **11** lickspittle, rubber stamp **13** apple-polisher

Sydney
  bay: 5 Walsh **11** Rushcutter's **13** Woolloomooloo
  capital of: 13 New South Wales
  cove: 4 Farm
  founder: 7 Phillip
  harbor: 7 Darling **11** Port Jackson
  island: 4 Goat **6** Garden
  landmark: 10 Opera House **11** Wynyard Park **13** Harbour Bridge **14** Fitzroy Gardens **15** Mitchell Library **16** Australian Museum, Hyde Park Barracks, Saint James Church **18** Rushcutter's Bay Park **21** Royal Botanical Gardens
  river: 10 Parramatta
  university: 9 Macquarie **13** New South Wales

sylvan 5 bushy, leafy, woody **6** wooded, woodsy **8** arcadian, forested, timbered, woodland **9** luxuriant, overgrown **10** forestlike

Sylvanus *see* **8** Silvanus

Sylvia
  character in: 20 Two Gentlemen of Verona
  author: 11 Shakespeare

symbol 4 mark, sign **5** badge, token **6** emblem, figure, signal **10** indication **14** representation **15** exemplification

symbolize 4 mean **5** imply **6** denote, embody, symbol **7** betoken, connote,

express, signify **8** stand for **9** emblemize, exemplify, personify, represent, signalize **10** allegorize **11** emblematize

symmetrical 7 orderly, regular **8** balanced **9** congruent **12** well-balanced **16** well-proportioned

symmetry 4 form **5** order **7** balance, harmony **9** congruity **10** conformity, regularity **11** equilibrium, orderliness, parallelism, shapeliness **15** proportionality

sympathetic 6 benign, humane, kindly **7** feeling, pitying **8** friendly, merciful **9** agreeable, approving, benignant, sensitive **10** benevolent, comforting **11** soft-hearted, warmhearted **12** sympathizing, well-disposed **13** commiserative, compassionate, tenderhearted, understanding

sympathize 4 back, pity, side **5** agree, favor **7** approve, feel for, go along, support **8** sanction **9** empathize **10** appreciate, be in accord, be sorry for **11** condole with, have pity for, stand behind

sympathy 4 pity **5** amity, favor, grief **6** accord, regard, sorrow **7** concern, concert, concord, empathy, feeling, harmony, rapport, support **8** advocacy, affinity, approval, sanction **9** agreement, communion, patronage, unanimity **10** compassion, consonance, fellowship, friendship, tenderness **11** well-wishing **12** congeniality, partisanship **13** commiseration, fellow feeling, understanding

Symplegades
  form: 5 rocks
  location: 8 Bosporus **9** Euxine Sea
  characteristic: 8 clashing, dark-blue

symposium 5 forum, synod **6** debate, parley, powwow **7** meeting **8** colloquy, congress **10** conference, discussion, round table **12** deliberation **15** panel discussion

Symposium
  author: 5 Plato
  character: 7 Agathon **8** Phaedrus, Socrates **9** Pausanias **10** Alcibiades **11** Aristodemus **12** Aristophanes

symptom 4 mark, sign **5** token **6** signal **7** earmark, warning **8** evidence, giveaway **10** indication **15** prognostication

synagogue
  Yiddish: 4 shul **5** schul

synchronal 11 concomitant, synchronous **12** contemporary, simultaneous

synchronous 10 synchronal **11** concomitant **12** contemporary, simultaneous

syndicalist 5 rebel **9** anarchist, insurgent **13** revolutionary

syndicate 5 group, trust, union **6** cartel, league, merger **7** combine **8** alliance **9** coalition **10** consortium, federation **11** association

Synge, John Millington
  author of: **14** Riders to the Sea **19** Deirdre of the Sorrows **20** In the Shadow of the Glen **27** The Playboy of the Western World

synod 4 diet **13** governing body **15** advisory council **21** ecclesiastical council

synonym 8 analogue **10** equivalent **11** another name

synonymous 4 like, same **5** alike, equal **7** coequal **10** equivalent

synopsis 5 brief **6** apercu, digest, precis, resume **7** epitome, outline, rundown, summary **8** abstract, argument **11** abridgement

synopsize 6 digest **7** abridge, outline **8** abstract, condense **9** summarize

Synoptist 12 Gospel writer

synthesize 3 mix **4** fuse **5** blend **7** combine **8** compound **10** amalgamate

synthetic 4 fake, sham **5** phony **6** ersatz **7** man-made **9** unnatural **10** artificial **11** counterfeit **12** manufactured

Syria
  other name: **4** Aram
  capital/largest city: **8** Damascus
  others: **4** Hama, Homs, Nawa **5** Busra, Calno, Derra, Emesa, Halab, Hamah, Idlib, Jerud, Raqqa **6** Aleppo, Calneh, Dumeir, Fajami, Tadmor, Ugarit **7** Antioch, Latakia, Palmyra **8** Seleucia **9** Ghabaghib
  school: **6** Aleppo, Syrian **11** Arab Academy
  measure: **5** makuk **6** garava
  monetary unit: **4** lira **5** pound **6** tal-

ent **7** piaster
  weight: **4** cola **5** artal, ratel **6** talent
  lake: **5** Merom **7** Djeboid **8** Tiberias
  mountain: **6** Carmel **7** Alawite, Libanus **10** Nusairiyya **11** Anti-Lebanon
  highest point: **6** Hermon
  river: **3** Asi **6** Balikh, Barada, Jordan, Khabur, Yarmuk **7** Orontes **9** Asi Knabur, Euphrates
  sea: **13** Mediterranean
  physical feature:
    desert: **5** Hamad **6** Hauran, Syrian
    heights: **5** Golan
  people: **4** Arab, Kurd, Turk **5** Alawi, Aptal, Druse, Druze **6** Afshar, Aissor, Aushar, Avshar, Awshar **7** Amorite, Ansarie, Bedouin, Nosaris, Saracen, Shemite **8** Ansarieh, Armenian **9** Ansariyah **10** Circassian **12** Khachaturian
    king: **5** Rezin **6** Faisal, Hazael **8** Benhadad **9** Antiochus
    leader: **10** T E Lawrence **12** Hafiz al-Assad **13** Bashar al-Assad **16** Lawrence of Arabia
    queen: **7** Zenobia
    ruler: **4** Rome **5** Arabs **6** France, Greeks, Persia **7** Mongols **8** Abbasids **9** Mamelukes, Phoenicia, Seleucids **11** Seljuk Turks **12** Ottoman Turks
  language: **6** Arabic, French, Syriac **7** Aramaic, English, Kurdish, Turkish **8** Armenian
  religion: **5** Druze, Islam **7** Alawite **12** Christianity **13** Greek Orthodox **23** Eastern Rite Christianity
  place:

    dam: **5** Tabqa **9** Euphrates
    ruins: **7** Palmyra
    square: **7** Martyrs'
  feature:
    animal: **9** dromedary
    clothing: **3** aba **4** abah **7** abayyah **8** kafiyyah
    marketplace: **4** souk
    tent: **8** bayt shar
    village common: **6** maidan

Syrinx
  form: **5** nymph
  location: **8** mountain
  transformed into: **4** reed
  transformed by: **3** Pan
  made into: **7** panpipe
  pipes called: **6** syrinx

system 4 body, unit **5** setup **6** method, scheme, theory **7** program, regimen, routine **8** organism **9** procedure, structure **10** hypothesis **11** arrangement **12** constitution, organization **13** modus operandi **15** mode of operation

systematic 4 neat, tidy **7** ordered, orderly, planned, precise, regular **8** constant **9** organized **10** methodical **12** businesslike, systematized **13** well-organized, well-regulated

systematization 5 order **8** ordering **9** gradation **10** organizing **11** arrangement **12** categorizing, codification, organization **13** methodization **14** categorization, classification

systematize 5 order **7** arrange **8** classify, organize **9** methodize

systematized 7 ordered **8** arranged, codified **9** organized **10** classified, methodized, systematic

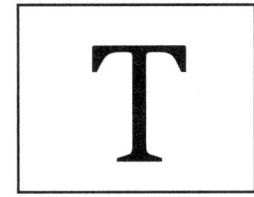
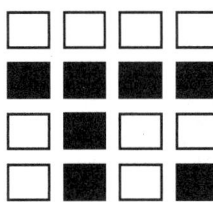

tab 3 lip **4** bill, cost, flap, loop **5** check, PC key, price, strip, tally **6** tongue **7** eyehole **10** projection

tabard 4 cape, coat **5** cloak, tunic

Tabard Inn
  starting point in: 18 The Canterbury Tales

tabernacle 6 church, temple **14** house of worship

Tabeth 16 tenth Hebrew month

Tabitha
  also called: 6 Dorcas
  revived by: 5 Peter
  hometown: 5 Joppa

table 4 fare, list, roll **5** board, chart, index **6** record, roster, shelve, spread **7** catalog **8** lay aside, postpone, put aside, register, schedule, syllabus, synopsis **9** inventory **10** tabulation

Table
  constellation of: 5 Mensa

tableau 4 view **5** scene **7** pageant, picture, setting **8** grouping **9** depiction, spectacle, still life **11** arrangement, delineation **12** illustration **13** picturization

tableau vivant 13 living picture

tablespoon
  abbreviation: 3 tbs **4** tbsp

tablet 3 pad **4** leaf **5** bolus, panel, sheet, wafer **6** pellet, plaque, troche **7** lozenge, memo pad, surface **8** flat cake, thin slab **9** tablature **10** pad of paper, writing pad

tableware 5 china **6** dishes, plates **7** cutlery **8** crockery, utensils **9** chinaware, glassware **10** dinnerware, silverware **14** cups and saucers

taboo, tabu 3 ban **4** no-no **6** banned **8** anathema, outlawed, verboten **9** forbidden, social ban **10** in bad taste, prohibited, proscribed **11** disapproved, prohibition, unthinkable **12** interdiction, proscription, religious ban, unacceptable **13** unmentionable

tabulate 4 file, list, rank, rate, sort **5** chart, grade, group, index, order, range **6** codify **7** arrange, catalog, compute, diagram, sort out **8** classify, organize **9** methodize **10** categorize, make a table **11** systematize

tace
  music: 6 silent

tacit 7 assumed, implied **8** implicit, inferred, unspoken, unstated, wordless

10 undeclared, understood **11** unexpressed **15** taken for granted

taciturn 5 aloof, quiet **6** silent **7** laconic **8** reserved, reticent **9** secretive **11** tight-lipped **12** close-mouthed **15** uncommunicative

tack 3 add, peg, pin, way **4** clap, nail, slap, veer **5** affix, sheer, shift, spike, thole **6** append, attach, change, fasten, method, swerve, switch, zigzag **7** go about **8** approach, tholepin **9** short nail **12** change course **14** course of action

tackle 3 try **4** gear, lift **5** assay, begin, crane, hoist, jenny, throw, tools, winch **6** accept, assume, attack, take on, take up **7** attempt, capstan, derrick, embrace, go about, halyard, rigging **8** endeavor, engage in, material, set about, windlass **9** apparatus, enter upon, equipment, trappings, undertake **10** appliances, embark upon, implements **11** instruments **12** appointments **13** accoutrements, paraphernalia

tack on 3 add **5** annex **6** adjoin, append, attach **7** stick on, subjoin **8** fasten to

tacky 5 dowdy, gluey, gooey, gucky, gummy, messy, ratty, seedy, tatty **6** grubby, shabby, shoddy, sloppy, sticky, untidy, viscid **7** stringy, unkempt, viscous **8** adhesive, frazzled, slipshod, slovenly **10** disordered

tact 7 finesse, suavity **8** delicacy **9** diplomacy, suaveness **10** discretion **11** savoir faire, sensibility **13** consideration **14** circumspection
  French: 11 savoir-faire

tactful 5 suave **6** polite, smooth, subtle **7** politic **8** decorous, delicate, discreet, mannerly **9** sensitive **10** diplomatic, thoughtful **11** considerate

tactic 3 way **4** line, plan, tack **6** method, policy, scheme **8** approach **9** stratagem **14** course of action

tactics 9 maneuvers **18** battle arrangements, military operations

tactless 4 curt, rude **5** blunt, brash, rough **6** abrupt, clumsy, gauche, stupid **7** boorish **8** impolite **9** hamhanded, impolitic, imprudent, untactful **10** blundering, indelicate, indiscreet **11** insensitive, thoughtless **12**

undiplomatic **13** ill-considered, inconsiderate
  French: 6 gauche

tactlessness 8 curtness **9** bluntness, gaucherie **10** abruptness, clumsiness, indelicacy **13** insensitivity, tastelessness

taedium vitae 5 ennui **12** tedium of life **22** feeling life is wearisome

Taft, William Howard
  presidential rank: 13 twenty-seventh
  party: 10 Republican
  state represented: 2 OH
  defeated: 4 (Eugene Victor) Debs **5** (William Jennings) Bryan **6** (Daniel Braxton) Turney, (Eugene Wilder) Chafin, (Thomas Edward) Watson, (Thomas Louis) Hisgen **8** (August) Gillhaus
  vice president: 7 (James Schoolcraft) Sherman
  cabinet:
    state: 4 (Philander Chase) Knox
    treasury: 8 (Franklin) MacVeagh
    war: 7 (Henry Lewis) Stimson **9** (Jacob McGavock) Dickinson
    attorney general: 10 (George Woodward) Wickersham
    navy: 5 (George von Lengerke) Meyer
    postmaster general: 9 (Frank Harris) Hitchcock
    interior: 6 (Walter Lowrie) Fisher **9** (Richard Achilles) Ballinger
    agriculture: 6 (James) Wilson
    commerce and labor: 5 (Charles) Nagel
  born: 12 Cincinnati OH
  died: 12 Washington DC
  buried: 25 Arlington National Cemetery
  education:
    university: 4 Yale
    law school: 10 Cincinnati
  religion: 9 Unitarian
  interests: 4 golf
  political career: 18 US Solicitor General
    judge: 19 Federal Circuit Court
    president of: 21 Philippines Commission
    civil governor of: 11 Philippines
    secretary of: 3 War
    US Supreme Court: 12 Chief Justice

civilian career:
  law professor: **4** Yale
  president: **22** American Bar Association
notable events of lifetime/term: **19** Postal Savings System
  Act: **10** Webb-Kenyon **11** Mann-Elkinst **12** Payne-Aldrich
  sinking of: **7** Titanic
father: **8** Alphonso
mother: **6** Louisa (Maria Torrey)
siblings: **5** Fanny **11** Henry Waters **12** Horace Dutton **15** Samuel Davenport
  half-brothers: **11** Peter Rawson **13** Charles Phelps
wife: **5** Helen (Herron)
  nickname: **6** Nellie
children: **11** Helen Herron **13** Charles Phelps **14** Robert Alphonso

tag 3 add, dog, tab **4** card, heel, mark, name, slip, stub, tail, term **5** add on, affix, annex, hound, label, title, trail **6** append, attach, attend, fasten, follow, handle, join to, marker, shadow, tack on, ticket **7** earmark, moniker, pendant **8** cognomen, identify, nickname **9** accompany, appendage, sobriquet

Tahiti
artist: **7** Gauguin
author: **9** Stevenson
capital: **7** Papeete
formerly: **8** Otaheite
island group: **7** Society
isthmus: **7** Taravao
ocean: **7** Pacific
volcano: **5** Roniu **7** Orohena

tail 3 dog **4** butt, seat **5** fanny, stalk, track, trail **6** follow, shadow **7** back end, rear end **8** buttocks

tail end, tail-end 4 back, butt, rear, rump, tail **6** caudal **7** hind end, rear end **8** backside, buttocks, last part **9** posterior

tailor 3 fit, sew **4** make, redo **5** adapt, alter, build, shape **6** change, create, design, devise, modify **7** convert, fashion, produce **8** clothier, costumer **9** construct, couturier, fabricate, transform **10** dressmaker, seamstress

taint 3 mar, rot **4** blot, flaw, ruin, soil, spot, turn **5** dirty, fault, go bad, smear, spoil, stain, sully **6** damage, debase, defect, defile, smudge, stigma **7** blemish, putrefy, tarnish **8** besmirch **12** imperfection

tainted 4 dirty **6** impure, rotten **7** spoiled, stained, unclean **9** blemished, tarnished **10** besmirched

Taipei
capital of: **6** Taiwan

Taiwan
name means: **11** terraced bay
other name: **7** Formosa **11** Ilha Formosa **15** Republic of China
capital/largest city: **6** Taipei

others: **4** Suao **5** Shoka, Takao **6** Tainan **7** Chilung, Hualien, Keelong, Keelung, Taoyuan **8** Fengshan, Kaohiung, Taichung **9** Kaohsiung
school: **7** Soochow, Tunghai **14** National Taiwan
monetary unit: **4** yuan **6** dollar
island: **5** Matsu **6** Lan Hsu, Penghu, Quemoy, Taiwan **7** Hungtou, Huoshao **10** Pescadores
mountain: **5** Tatun **6** Tzukao **7** Taitung **15** Chungyang Shanmo
highest point: **6** Yu Shan **8** Morrison **10** Sinkao Shan **11** Hsin-Kao Shan
river: **5** Wuchi **6** Tachia **7** Choshui, Hualien, Tanshui
sea: **7** Pacific **9** East China **10** Philippine, South China
physical feature:
  cape: **7** Olwanpi
  channel: **5** Bashi
  gorge: **6** Taroko
  storm: **7** monsoon, typhoon
  strait: **6** Taiwan **7** Formosa
people: **4** Yami **5** Hakka, Hoklo **7** Chinese, Malayan **9** Fukienese, Taiwanese **10** Indonesian, Polynesian **12** Kwangtungese
  goddess: **5** Matsu
  leader: **7** Koxinga **9** Sun Yat-sen **10** Yen Chia-Kan **13** Chiang Kai-shek **14** Cheng Cheng-Kung, Chiang Ching-kuo
language: **4** Amon, Amoy **5** Hakka, Kuo Yu **6** Minnan **9** Taiwanese **15** Mandarin Chinese
religion: **6** Taoism **7** animism **8** Buddhism **12** Christianity, Confucianism
place:
  museum: **14** National Palace
  square: **12** Presidential
feature:
  festival: **5** Ghost
  political party: **10** Kuomintang
food:
  feast: **6** pai-pai

Tajikistan
other name: **12** Tadzhikistan
capital/largest city: **8** Dushanbe
head of state: **9** president
government: **8** republic
monetary unit: **5** ruble
mountain: **13** Communism Peak
people: **5** Tajik, Uzbek **7** Tadzhik
language: **7** Tadzhik
religion: **11** Sunni Muslim

Taj Mahal 4 tomb **9** mausoleum
location: **4** Agra **5** India
built by: **9** Shah, Jahan
for: **4** wife

take 3 buy, get, lug, nab, net, see, use **4** bear, bilk, deem, draw, feel, gain, grab, grip, haul, have, heed, hire, hold, know, lead, loot, mark, mind, move, need, obey, read, rent, sack, tote, work **5** bring, brook, carry, catch, cheat, claim, clasp, filch, grasp,

gross, guide, infer, lease, seize, stand, steal, use up, usher, usurp **6** accept, assume, attain, clutch, convey, deduce, deduct, demand, derive, divest, employ, endure, escort, fleece, follow, look on, obtain, pilfer, pocket, profit, regard, remove, secure, snatch, suffer **7** acquire, agree to, believe, call for, capture, conduct, consume, deliver, make out, observe, pillage, plunder, purloin, receive, require, respect, stomach, succeed, suppose, undergo **8** accede to, assent to, conceive, conclude, consider, listen to, perceive, proceeds, purchase, shoulder, submit to, subtract, take away, tolerate, transfer **9** ascertain, be ruled by, consent to, deprive of, eliminate, get hold of, interpret, lay hold of, put up with, respond to, transport, undertake **10** commandeer, comply with, comprehend, confiscate, experience, lay hands on, take effect, understand **11** appropriate, begin to work, go along with, necessitate **13** help oneself to **14** avail oneself of, misappropriate

take aback 5 amaze **7** astound **8** astonish, surprise **9** overwhelm

take a crack at 3 try **5** essay **6** hazard, tackle, take on **7** attempt, venture **9** have a go at, undertake **11** make a stab at

take advantage of 3 use **5** avail **7** exploit, utilize **10** profit from

take after 4 copy, echo **6** follow, repeat **7** imitate **8** resemble, simulate **9** duplicate, reproduce

take apart 7 destroy **8** demolish **9** dismantle, knock down **11** disassemble

take a powder 4 blow, exit **5** go out, leave, scram, split **6** cut out, depart, escape **8** withdraw

take away 5 seize **6** lessen, reduce **7** abridge, bear off, curtail, detract **8** carry off, decrease, subtract **9** deprive of **11** make off with

take a whack at 3 try **5** essay **6** hazard, tackle **7** attempt, venture **8** give a try **9** have a go at **10** give a whirl **12** take a crack at

take back 6 abjure, recall, recant, renege **7** disavow, retract, reverse **8** forswear, withdraw

take captive 3 bag **4** snag, take, trap **5** catch, seize, snare **7** capture, ensnare **9** apprehend, lay hold of **12** take prisoner

take care 6 beware, be wary **9** be careful **10** be cautious **17** look before you leap

take care of 4 tend **6** assume **7** nurture **8** attend to, shoulder **10** minister to

take exception 5 demur **6** object, resent **11** look askance

take flight 3 fly 4 flee 6 escape, run off 7 abscond, fly away, run away, run free, take off 9 make a dash 10 fly the coop 12 make a getaway

take for granted 6 assume 10 undervalue

take heed 4 mind 6 beware 7 look out 8 take care, watch out 11 take warning

take hold 4 bite, grab, grip 5 grasp 6 clutch 7 catch on

take in stride 12 not skip a beat 13 be unperturbed

take into custody 3 bag, nab 4 book, bust, hold 5 catch, pinch, seize 6 arrest, collar, detain, secure 7 capture 9 apprehend 12 take prisoner

take into service 4 hire 6 employ, engage, retain, secure, take on

take issue 5 demur 6 differ 8 disagree 12 be at variance, stand opposed

take no notice of 6 ignore 9 disregard 11 pay no heed to 15 fail to recognize 16 pay no attention to 17 fail to acknowledge

take notice
Latin: 8 nota bene

take notice of 3 see 4 heed, mark, note 6 call on, regard 7 observe 8 call upon 9 recognize 10 get a load of 11 acknowledge 14 pay attention to

take nourishment 3 eat 4 feed 10 break bread 14 take sustenance

takeoff 5 spoof 6 parody, satire 7 lampoon 9 burlesque 10 caricature

take off 4 doff, lift 5 leave 6 decamp, depart, detach, remove 7 lift off, peel off, run away 8 strip off 14 leave the ground

take off guard 5 catch 8 surprise 14 take by surprise

take on 4 bear, hire 6 accept, assume, engage 8 shoulder 9 undertake

take one's breath away 4 daze, stun 5 shock 7 stupefy 8 astonish, dumfound 9 dumbfound, electrify 11 flabbergast 15 make one's eyes pop

take out 4 date 5 court 6 delete, escort, remove 7 extract, isolate 8 abstract, separate, take home, withdraw 9 strike out

take over 4 take 5 seize 6 assume, take on, take up 8 shoulder 10 commandeer, confiscate 11 appropriate, expropriate, gain control

take pains 6 strive 7 attempt, try hard 8 endeavor, go all out 10 do one's best 11 give one's all 12 make an effort 15 knock oneself out 16 give one's best shot

take pleasure in 4 like, love 5 adore, eat up, enjoy, fancy, savor 6 dote on, relish, relish 7 revel in 9 rejoice in 10 appreciate 13 be pleased with, get a kick out of

take possession of 5 claim 10 confiscate 11 appropriate, expropriate

take prisoner 3 bag, nab 4 book, bust 5 catch, pinch, seize 6 arrest, collar 7 capture 9 apprehend 11 take captive 15 take into custody

take sick 3 ail 6 sicken 8 collapse 9 become ill 10 be stricken

take stock of 5 audit, check 6 assess, review, survey 7 examine, inspect 8 look over 9 inventory

take sustenance 3 eat 4 feed 10 break bread 15 take nourishment

take the cake 5 excel 7 beat all, surpass 12 beat the devil, win hands down

take the edge off 6 lessen, pacify, soothe, temper 7 appease, assuage, lighten, mollify 8 tone down

take the first step 5 begin, start 6 launch, set out 8 commence, embark on, initiate 9 undertake 10 inaugurate

take the place of 7 replace 8 displace, supplant 9 supersede

take to be 4 deem, hold 5 count, judge, think 6 assume, regard, view as 7 account, believe 8 consider 10 look upon as

take to heart 4 heed, mind 6 attend 8 consider 9 hearken to 13 give thought to 14 pay attention to

take to one's heels 3 fly 4 flee 6 escape 7 get away, run away 10 fly the coop, make a break, take flight 12 make a getaway 15 head for the hills

take to task 4 chide, scold 6 accuse, berate, charge, rail at, rebuke 7 bawl out, censure, chasten, chew out, reprove, upbraid 8 admonish, chastise, reproach 9 castigate, criticize, dress down, reprimand 10 tongue-lash 11 remonstrate 13 call to account

take turns 5 share 6 rotate 9 alternate

take under one's wing 6 assist, defend 7 protect 8 befriend 9 look after

take unfair advantage of 5 abuse 6 misuse 7 exploit

take up 4 lift 6 absorb, accept, assume, occupy, pick up, resume, soak up, suck up 7 discuss, drink in 8 consider, continue, sponge up, talk over 9 cultivate, swallow up

taking a siesta 6 dozing 7 napping 8 snoozing 10 taking a nap 18 catching forty winks

takings 4 loot 5 booty 6 spoils 7 plunder 8 pickings

Talaria
form: 7 sandals
owner: 6 Hermes 7 Mercury
characteristic: 6 winged

tale 3 fib, lie 4 epic, myth, saga, yarn 5 fable, novel, rumor, story 6 legend, report 7 account, fiction, hearsay, recital, romance, scandal, untruth 8 anecdote 9 falsehood, fish story, narra-tion, narrative, tall story 10 short story 11 fabrication, scuttlebutt 12 tittle-tattle 13 falsification, piece of gossip 16 cock-and-bull story

talebearer 6 gossip 7 blabber, reciter, tattler 8 busybody, informer, reporter, telltale 10 newsmonger, tattletale 11 storyteller 12 blabbermouth 13 scandalmonger

talent 4 bent, gift, turn 5 flair, forte, knack, skill 6 genius 7 faculty 8 aptitude, capacity, facility, strength 9 endowment 10 capability 11 proficiency

Talent 14 Biblical weight

talented 4 able 5 adept 6 expert, gifted 7 born for, capable, endowed, skilled 8 artistic, polished 9 brilliant, competent 10 proficient 11 well-endowed 12 accomplished

Talented Mr. Ripley, The
author: 17 Patricia Highsmith
director: 16 Anthony Minghella
cast: 7 Jude Law (Dickie Greenleaf) 9 Matt Damon (Tom Ripley) 13 Cate Blanchett (Meredith Logue) 14 Gwyneth Paltrow (Marge Sherwood) 20 Philip Seymour Hoffman (Freddie Miles)

Tale of a Tub, A
author: 9 Ben Jonson 13 Jonathan Swift

Tale of Genji
author: 19 Lady Murasaki Shikibu

Tale of Two Cities, A
author: 14 Charles Dickens
character: 7 Gaspard, Stryver 9 Dr Manette, Miss Pross 11 Jarvis Lorry, John Barstad 12 Lucie Manette, Sydney Carton 13 Charles Darnay, Jerry Cruncher, Madame Defarge 18 Marquis St Evremonde
director: 10 Jack Conway
cast: 12 Blanche Yurka, Isabel Jewell, Reginald Owen, Ronald Colman (Sydney Carton) 13 Basil Rathbone, Edna May Oliver 14 Elizabeth Allan
setting: 16 French Revolution

Tales Before Midnight
author: 19 Stephen Vincent Benet

Talese, Gay
author of: 9 The Bridge 11 Unto the Sons 14 Honor Thy Father 16 Thy Neighbor's Wife 21 The Kingdom and the Power

Tales of a Wayside Inn
author: 24 Henry Wadsworth Longfellow

Tales of Hoffmann, The
also: 18 Les Contes d'Hoffmann
opera by: 9 Offenbach
character: 6 Stella 7 Antonia, Olympia 9 Dr Miracle, Giulietta 11 E T A Hoffmann 14 mechanical doll

talisman 4 tiki 5 charm 6 amulet, fetish, grigri 10 lucky piece

Talisman, The
author: **14** Sir Walter Scott
character: **7** Conrade, El Hakim **10** Sir Kenneth **15** Queen Berengaria **19** Theodorick of Engaddi **20** Lady Edith Plantagenet **21** Richard the Lion-Hearted **31** Grand Master of the Knights Templars

talk 3 gab, jaw, rap, say **4** cant, chat, word **5** argot, idiom, lingo, noise, prate, rumor, slang, speak, state, utter **6** babble, bunkum, confab, confer, gossip, hot air, intone, jargon, parley, patois, powwow, preach, report, sermon, speech, take up, tirade **7** address, blarney, blather, chatter, consult, declare, deliver, dialect, discuss, express, hearsay, lecture, oration, palaver, prattle, twaddle **8** chitchat, colloquy, converse, dialogue, harangue, language, proclaim, rattle on, verbiage **9** discourse, enunciate, negotiate, pronounce, tete-a-tete, utterance **10** bandy words, conference, discussion, rap session, recitation, speak about **11** declamation, exhortation, pontificate, scuttlebutt **12** blatherskite, consultation, conversation, tittle-tattle **13** confabulation

talkative 5 gabby, talky, windy, wordy **6** babbly, chatty, prolix **7** gossipy, verbose, voluble **8** effusive **9** garrulous **10** long-winded, loquacious

talk big 4 brag, crow **5** boast, vaunt **13** puff oneself up **15** blow one's own horn **19** pat oneself on the back

talk down to 9 patronize **10** condescend

talker 6 gabber, gossip, magpie, orator **7** babbler, speaker, windbag **8** lecturer, prattler **9** chatterer, converser **10** chatterbox, mouthpiece **11** rumormonger, speechifier, speechmaker **12** blatherskite, spokesperson **13** scandalmonger **17** conversationalist

talk nonsense 6 babble, drivel, ramble

Talk of the Town, The
director: **13** George Stevens
cast: **9** Cary Grant **10** Jean Arthur **12** Ronald Colman **13** Edgar Buchanan, Glenda Farrell

talk out of 4 balk **6** thwart **8** dissuade **10** discourage

talk over 6 confer, review **7** consult, discuss, hash out

Talk-show hosts 5 Leeza **7** Jay Leno, Geraldo **8** Cristina **9** Ricki Lake **10** Carson Daly, Jenny Jones **11** Phil Donahue, Conan O'Brien, Arsenio Hall, Maury Povich, Regis & Kelly **12** Craig Kilborn, Johnny Carson, Oprah Winfrey **13** Rosie O'Donnell, Jerry Springer **14** David Letterman, Ellen DeGeneres, Montel Williams **17** Sally Jessy Raphael

talk to 7 address, lecture, speak to **12** converse with

talk together 4 talk **6** confer **7** discuss **8** converse **9** discourse

tall 3 big **4** high **5** lanky, lofty, rangy **6** absurd **7** soaring, stringy **8** elevated, gangling, towering **10** incredible, long-limbed **11** embellished, exaggerated, implausible **12** preposterous, unbelievable **13** hard to believe, hard to swallow

tallow 3 fat, tip **5** taper **6** bougie, candle, cierge **9** rushlight

Tall State
nickname of: **8** Illinois

tall story 3 fib, lie **4** yarn **5** fable **7** fiction, untruth, whopper **9** fairy tale, falsehood, fish story, invention **11** fabrication **16** cock-and-bull story

tally 3 add, sum **4** jibe, list, mark, poll, post **5** agree, count, match, score, sum up, total **6** accord, census, concur, muster, reckon, record, square **7** catalog, compute, conform **8** coincide, mark down, register, scorepad, tabulate **9** calculate, harmonize, reckoning, scorecard **10** correspond **11** enumeration

talon 4 claw, nail, spur

Talos
form: **5** youth **7** monster
calling: **8** inventor
made of: **5** brass **6** bronze
made by: **10** Hephaestus
guarded: **5** Crete
destroyed by: **5** Medea
uncle: **8** Daedalus
killed by: **8** Daedalus
because of: **8** jealousy

talus
bone of: **5** ankle
connected to: **5** tibia **6** fibula

Tamar
father: **5** David
mother: **6** Maacah
husband: **2** Er **4** Onan **5** Judah, Uriah
brother: **5** Amnon **7** Absalom, Chileab, Solomon **8** Adonijah
son: **5** Zarah **6** Pharez
daughter: **8** Maachiah
father-in-law: **5** Judah

Tamburlaine the Great
author: **18** Christopher Marlowe
character: **6** Cosroe **7** Mycetes, Orcanes **8** Bajazeth **9** Callepine, Techelles, Zenocrate **10** Theridamas, Usumcasane

tame 4 curb, damp, dull, flat, meek, mild, rein **5** break, check, quiet, timid, train **6** boring, bridle, broken, docile, gentle, govern, manage, master, placid, pliant, serene, subdue **7** conquer, control, pliable, prosaic, repress, subdued, tedious **8** amenable, domestic, dominate, lifeless, overcome, regulate, restrain, suppress,

timorous, tranquil **9** tractable **10** make docile, submissive, unexciting **11** complaisant, domesticate, unresisting **12** domesticated **13** uninteresting

tameness 8 docility **9** placidity **10** gentleness, insipidity **12** complaisance, tractability **13** domestication **14** submissiveness

Taming of the Shrew, The
author: **18** William Shakespeare
character: **6** Bianca, Gremio, Tranio **8** Baptista, Lucentio **9** Hortensio, Katharina, Petruchio, Vincentio
director: **16** Franco Zeffirelli
cast: **11** Michael York, Natasha Pyne **13** Richard Burton (Petruchio) **14** Michael Hordern **15** Elizabeth Taylor (Katharina), Vernon Dobtcheff
score: **8** Nino Rota

Tammuz
origin: **8** Sumerian
god of: **9** shepherds
Hebrew month: **6** fourth

Tam O'Shanter
author: **11** Robert Burns

Tampa Bay
football team: **7** Bandits **10** Buccaneers
baseball team: **9** Devil Rays

tamper 3 mix **4** muck **6** butt in, fiddle, horn in, meddle, tinker **7** intrude, obtrude **9** interfere, intervene **10** fool around, mess around **12** monkey around

tamper with 5 alter **6** change, doctor **7** falsify

tan 4 roan **5** beige, brown, khaki, sandy, tawny **6** bronze, sorrel, suntan **7** bronzed **8** brownish, cinnamon, sunburnt **9** sunburned, suntanned **10** light brown **11** yellow-brown

Tanah Airkita see **9** Indonesia

Tan, Amy
author: **14** The Joy Luck Club **18** The Kitchen God's Wife **22** The Bonesetter's Daughter, The Hundred Secret Senses

Tananarive, Antananarivo
capital of: **10** Madagascar

Tanaquil
origin: **5** Roman
form: **5** queen
husband: **7** Tarquin **17** Tarquinius Priscus

Tandy, Jessica
born: **6** London **7** England
husband: **10** Hume Cronyn **11** Jack Hawkins
roles: **8** The Birds **10** The Gin Game **12** Forever Amber **16** Driving Miss Daisy (Oscar) **21** A Streetcar Named Desire

tang 3 bit **4** bite, hint, odor, reek **5** aroma, punch, savor, scent, smack, smell, sting, tinge, touch, trace **6** flavor **8** acridity, piquancy, pungency,

tartness 9 acridness, sharpness, spiciness **10** suggestion

Tange, Kenzo
  architect of: 11 Press Center (Kofu) **16** Shizuoka Building (Tokyo) **19** Olympic Sports Stadia (Tokyo) **24** Kagawa Prefectural Offices (Takamatsu) **30** Imabara Municipal Office Building

tangibility 11 materiality, palpability **12** touchability

tangible 4 real **5** solid **6** actual **7** obvious **8** clear-cut, concrete, manifest, material, palpable, physical, positive **9** corporeal, touchable **10** verifiable **11** indubitable, substantial

tangle 3 fix, net, web **4** knot, maze, mesh, muss **5** ravel, skein, snarl, twist **6** jumble, jungle, ruffle, rumple, tousle **7** impasse, network **8** dishevel, disorder **9** labyrinth **10** disarrange

tangled 6 knotty **7** chaotic, complex, jumbled, mixed-up, snarled **11** complicated, intertwined

Tanguy, Yves
  born: 5 Paris **6** France
  artwork: 4 Fear **17** Mama Papa is Wounded, Untitled Landscape **18** Rose of the Four Winds **20** Slowly Toward the North **22** Four O'Clock in Summer Hope, Indefinite Divisibility **23** Multiplication of the Arcs **25** Extinction of Useless Lights

tank 3 vat **6** boiler **7** cistern **8** aquarium, fish tank **9** container, reservoir **10** armored car, receptacle **11** storage tank

Tannhauser and the Tournament of Song at Wartburg
  opera by: 6 Wagner
  also: 41 Tannhauser und der Sangerkrieg auf dem Wartburg
  character: 5 Venus **7** Wolfram **9** Elizabeth

Tanoan
  tribe: 4 Tuei **5** Kiowa **6** Isleta

tantalize 4 bait **5** charm, taunt, tease, tempt **6** entice, lead on **7** bewitch, provoke, torment **8** intrigue **9** captivate, fascinate, titillate **15** whet the appetite **18** make one's mouth water

tantalizing 7 teasing **8** inviting, tempting **9** appealing, leading on **10** intriguing **11** fascinating

Tantalus
  king of: 4 Pisa **7** Phrygia
  father: 8 Thyestes
  wife: 12 Clytemnestra
  son: 6 Pelops
  daughter: 5 Niobe
  punishment in Hades: 6 hunger, thirst

tantamount 4 like **5** equal **9** analogous **10** comparable, equivalent, on a par with **12** commensurate **13** commensurable

tantrum 3 fit **5** storm **7** flare-up, rampage **8** outburst, paroxysm **9** explosion **12** fit of passion **13** burst of temper, conniption fit

Tanzania
  other name: 12 isle of cloves
  capital/largest city: 11 Dar es Salaam
  new capital: 6 Dodoma
  others: 4 Wete, **5** Kilwa, Lindi, Moshi, Tanga, Ujiji **6** Arusha, Kigoma, Mwadui, Mwanza, Tabora **7** Korogwe, Mtawara **8** Morogoro, Zanzibar **12** Kwasemangube, Zanzibar Town
  division: 8 Zanzibar **17** union of Tanganyika
  monetary unit: 4 cent **8** shilling
  weight: 8 farsalah
  island: 5 Mafia, Pemba **6** Latham **8** Zanzibar
  lake: 5 Eyasi, Nyasa, Rukwa **6** Malawi, Natron, Nyassa **7** Manyara **8** Victoria **10** Tanganyika
  mountain: 4 Kibo, Mero **8** Usambara
  highest point: 11 Kilimanjaro
  river: 4 Lupa, Ruvu, Wami **5** Ruaha **6** Kagera, Luwegu, Mbaesa, Rufiji, Rungwa, Ruvuma **7** Nkululu, Pangani **8** Mbenkuru **11** Mbarangandu
  sea: 6 Indian
  physical feature:
    crater: 10 Ngorongoro
    gorge: 7 Olduvai
    national park: 9 Serengeti
    plains: 9 Serengeti
    steppe: 5 Masai **8** Iwembere
    valley: 9 Great Rift
  people: 2 Ha **4** Arab, Gogo, Goma, Haya, Hehe **5** Asian, Bantu, Masai **6** Arusha, Chagga, Sukuma, Wagogo, Wagoma **7** African, Makonde, Sambara, Sandawe, Shirazi, Swahili, Wabunga, Zongora **8** Nyakyusa, Nyamwezi
    early man: 13 zinjanthropus
    explorer: 6 Da Gama **7** Rebmann **11** Livingstone
    leader: 5 Sayid **6** Karume **7** Nyerere **16** Sultan of Zanzibar
  language: 5 Bantu **6** Arabic **7** English, Khoisan, Nilotic, Swahili **8** Cushitic, Gujarati
  religion: 5 Islam **7** animism **12** Christianity
  feature:
    animal: 6 dik-dik
    cattle barn: 4 byre
    clothing: 4 sari **6** bui bui
    fly: 6 tsetse
    holiday: 8 Saba Saba
    homestead: 8 manyatta
  food:
    dish: 5 ugali

Tao Te Ching
  author: 6 Lao-tzu

Taotieh

origin: 7 Chinese
form: 6 animal

tap 3 pat, rap, use **4** cock, drum, peck, thud **5** spout, touch, valve **6** broach, employ, faucet, hammer, spigot, stroke, uncork, unplug **7** draw off, exploit, utilize **8** draw upon, stopcock **9** put to work, unstopper

taper 3 dip, wax **4** wick **5** light **6** candle, cierge, narrow **8** decrease **9** narrowing **10** diminution **12** come to a point

taper off 4 wane **5** abate **6** weaken **7** slacken, subside **8** decrease, diminish, fade away, slack off

tapestry 3 rug **5** arras, tapis **6** Bruges, fabric, mosaic **7** Gobelin, hanging, montage, weaving **8** Aubusson **12** wallcovering

Taprobane *see* **8** Sri Lanka

taproom 3 bar, pub **6** lounge, saloon, tavern **8** alehouse **11** bar and grill, public house **14** cocktail lounge

Taras Bulba
  author: 12 Nikolai Gogol
  character: 5 Ostap **6** Andrii, Yankel **26** Daughter of the Polish Waiwode

Tarascans, Tarascos
  location: 6 Mexico **9** Michoacan **14** Central America
  leader: 8 Zincicha **9** Tangaxoan, Tariacuri

Tarawa
  capital of: 8 Kiribati

Tar Baby
  author: 12 Toni Morrison

Tarchetius
  king of: 9 Alba Longa

tardy 4 late, slow **5** slack **6** remiss **7** belated, languid, overdue **8** crawling, creeping, dilatory, slowpoke, sluggish **9** leisurely, not on time, reluctant, slow-paced, snail-like **10** behindhand, behind time, unpunctual **14** slow as molasses **15** procrastinating

tare 12 Biblical weed **15** weight deduction

target 3 aim, end **4** butt, dupe, goal, goat, gull, mark, plan, prey **5** patsy **6** design, intent, object, pigeon, victim **7** purpose **8** ambition **9** intention, objective **13** laughingstock

Targitaus
  father: 4 Zeus
  first inhabitant of: 7 Scythia

Tar Heel State
  nickname of: 13 North Carolina

tariff 3 fee **4** cost, duty, fare, levy, rate, rent **5** price **6** charge, excise, impost **7** expense **8** input tax **9** excise tax, export tax **10** assessment, commission, freightage

Tarkington, Booth
  author of: 6 Penrod **9** Seventeen **10** Alice Adams **13** Kate Fennigate **14**

The Man from Home **17** Monsieur Beaucaire **19** The World Does Not Move **23** The Magnificent Ambersons

tarnish 3 dim **4** blot, dull, foul, soil, spot **5** dirty, erode, stain, sully, taint **6** befoul, darken, defame, defile, smirch, vilify **7** blacken, blemish, corrode, degrade, oxidize **8** besmirch, discolor, disgrace, dishonor **9** denigrate, discredit **10** lose luster, stigmatize **17** drag through the mud

tarnished 5 dirty **6** soiled **7** stained, sullied **8** oxidized **10** discolored

Tarnkappe
origin: **8** Germanic
mentioned in: **14** Nibelungenlied
form: **5** cloak
gives wearer: **8** strength **12** invisibility
stolen by: **9** Siegfried
stolen from: **8** Niblungs **9** Nibelungs

tarot
Italian: **6** naibes **7** attutti **8** tarocchi
German: **5** tarok
French: **5** tarau, tarot
cards/deck: **12** seventy-eight
division: **11** major arcana, minor arcana **12** lesser arcana **13** greater arcana
suit: **3** cup **4** coin, wand **5** baton, money, sword **6** cudgel **8** pentacle
face card: **4** king, page **5** knave, queen, valet **6** knight
major arcana: **4** Fool, Moon **5** Death **7** Justice **8** Judgment **9** Hanged Man **14** Wheel of Fortune

tarpaulin 4 tarp **6** canvas **9** dropcloth **15** waterproof cover

Tarpeia
form: **12** vestal virgin
father: **15** Spurius Tarpeius
betrayed: **4** Rome
betrayed to: **7** Sabines
killed by: **7** Sabines

Tarquin
king of: **4** Rome
origin: **8** Etruscan
also called: **17** Tarquinius Priscus **18** Tarquinius Superbus
wife: **8** Tanaquil

tarragon
botanical name: **20** Artemisia dracunculus
means: **6** dragon **12** little dragon
Arab: **7** tarkhum
French: **8** estragon
origin: **7** Siberia
used as: **8** purifier
flavor: **8** licorice
use: **4** fish **5** salad, sauce **10** mayonnaise **14** Bearnaise sauce

tarry 3 lag **4** bide, rest, stay, wait **5** abide, dally, delay, pause, stall **6** dawdle, linger, put off, remain **7** be tardy **8** hang back, postpone, stave

off, take time **9** temporize **10** hang around **13** cool one's heels, procrastinate

tarsal
bone of: **5** ankle

tart 3 pie **4** acid, sour **5** acerb, acrid, sharp, spicy, tangy **6** acetic, barbed, biting, bitter, crusty **7** caustic, cutting, piquant, pungent, sourish **8** vinegary **10** astringent **11** pastry shell

tartan
fabric: **6** woolen
pattern: **5** plaid
identifies: **4** clan
in: **8** Scotland **9** Highlands
skirt: **4** kilt
trousers: **5** trews

Tartarean see **8** infernal

Tartarin of Tarascon
author: **14** Alphonse Daudet

Tartarus
form: **5** abyss
below: **5** Hades
imprisoned: **6** Titans

tartness 7 acidity, sarcasm **8** acerbity **9** sharpness **11** astringency

Tartuffe
author: **7** Moliere
character: **5** Damis, Orgon **6** Dorine, Elmire, Valere **7** Cleante, Mariane **14** Madame Pernelle

Tarzan
author: **18** Edgar Rice Burroughs
character: **3** Boy **4** Jane **7** Cheetah
Tarzan also called: **15** Lord of Greystoke, Lord of the Jungle
comic strip creator: **9** Hal Foster **12** Burme Hogarth
played by: **6** Ron Ely **9** Lex Barker **11** Elmo Lincoln **12** Buster Crabbe **17** Johnny Weissmuller

task 3 job **4** duty, work **5** chore, labor, stint **6** charge, errand **7** mission **8** business **10** assignment **11** undertaking **14** responsibility

taskmaster 4 boss **6** despot, master, tyrant **7** foreman, headman, manager **8** director, martinet, overseer, stickler **10** supervisor **11** Simon Legree, slave driver **14** disciplinarian, superintendent

Tasmania
bay: **5** Storm **6** Oyster
capital: **6** Hobart
city: **10** Launceston
country: **9** Australia
formerly: **14** Van Diemen's Land
island: **4** Echo **6** Sorell
mountain: **4** Ossa **6** Cradle
river: **3** Esk
strait: **4** Bass
birthplace of: **10** Errol Flynn

Tasso, Torquato
author of: **6** Aminta **7** Rinaldo **18** Jerusalem Delivered

taste 3 bit, nip, sip, try, yen **4** bent,

bite, feel, meet, tang, test, whim **5** crumb, enjoy, fancy, savor, smack **6** desire, flavor, hunger, liking, morsel, relish, sample, thirst **7** craving, decorum, discern, forkful, insight, leaning, longing, savor of, smack of, swallow, undergo **8** appetite, delicacy, fondness, judgment, mouthful, penchant, piquancy, spoonful, yearning **9** encounter, hankering, partake of, propriety **10** experience, partiality, propensity, take a sip of **11** correctness, discernment, disposition, inclination, take a bite of **12** eat a little of, predilection **14** discrimination, drink a little of
French: **4** gout

tasteful 7 elegant, refined **8** artistic, becoming, cultured, esthetic, handsome, suitable **9** beautiful, exquisite **10** attractive, well-chosen

tasteless 3 low **4** flat, mild, rude, weak **5** bland, cheap, crass, crude, gaudy, gross, tacky **6** coarse, common, flashy, garish, ribald, watery **7** insipid, uncouth **8** improper, indecent, unseemly **9** inelegant, offensive, unrefined **10** disgusting, flavorless, indecorous, indelicate, uncultured, unesthetic, unflavored, unsuitable **11** distasteful, insensitive

tastemakers 7 leaders **10** avant-garde, innovators **12** stylesetters, trendsetters

tasty 3 hot **5** spicy, tangy, yummy **6** savory **7** piquant, zestful **8** luscious **9** delicious, flavorful, palatable, toothsome **10** appetizing, delectable, flavorsome **11** good-tasting, scrumptious **12** full-flavored, well-seasoned

Tatius
also: **5** Titus
co-ruler with: **7** Romulus

Tatler, The
author: **13** Joseph Addison, Richard Steele

tattered 4 torn **6** broken, ragged, ripped, shabby, shaggy **10** disheveled **11** dilapidated

tatters 4 rags **6** shreds **7** patches

tattle 3 rat **4** blab **5** prate **6** gabble, gossip, snitch, squeal, tell on **7** blather, chatter, hearsay, prattle, twaddle **8** inform on **9** loose talk **11** mudslinging **12** tittle-tattle **13** tonguewagging

tattletale 3 rat **4** fink **5** sneak **6** gossip, snitch **7** ratfink, stoolie, tattler **8** betrayer, busybody, informer, squealer, telltale **8** informer **10** newsmonger, talebearer **11** rumormonger, stool pigeon **12** blabbermouth, troublemaker **13** scandalmonger

Tatum, Edward Lawrie
field: **8** genetics **12** biochemistry

discovered: 19 gene characteristics
awarded: 10 Nobel Prize

taunt 3 guy, rag **4** gibe, jeer, jive, mock, slur, twit **5** scoff, sneer, tease **6** deride, harass, insult, jeer at **7** provoke, ragging, sneer at, snigger, torment **8** chaffing, derision, ridicule **9** make fun of, poke fun at, snigger at **10** harassment, make game of, tormenting **11** provocation

Taura
form: 3 cow
attribute: 6 sacred

taurobolium
rite of: 7 baptism

Taurog, Norman
director of: 6 Skippy (Oscar) **8** Boys Town

Taurus
symbol: 4 bull
planet: 5 Venus
rules: 5 money **9** resources
born: 3 May **5** April

taut 4 neat, snug, tidy, trig, trim **5** rigid, smart, tense, tight **6** spruce **7** orderly **8** not loose, not slack **9** shipshape, unbending, unrelaxed **10** drawn tight, inflexible, no-nonsense **11** under strain **12** businesslike **13** well-regulated **15** well-disciplined

tavern 3 bar, pub **4** dive **6** bistro, saloon **7** barroom, gin mill, taproom **8** alehouse, drinkery, grogshop **9** beer joint, brasserie, honky-tonk, roadhouse **10** restaurant **11** public house **12** watering hole **14** cocktail lounge
French: 7 auberge
German: 8 Brauhaus

tawdry 4 loud **5** cheap, crass, gaudy, showy, tacky **6** flashy, garish, tinsel, vulgar **7** raffish **8** gimcrack **9** inelegant, obtrusive, tasteless **10** flamboyant **11** conspicuous, pretentious **12** meretricious, ostentatious

tawny 3 tan **4** fawn **5** beige, dusky, olive, sandy **6** bronze **7** swarthy **8** brownish **10** light brown **14** yellowish-brown

tax 3 sap, try **4** duty, lade, levy, load, tire, toll **5** drain, weigh **6** assess, burden, charge, custom, excise, impost, saddle, strain, tariff, weight **7** deplete, exhaust, stretch, wear out **8** exertion, overwork **10** assessment, obligation, overburden
kind: 4 city **5** sales, state **6** county, excise, income, luxury **8** property **11** inheritance **12** excess profit

Taxi
character: 9 John Burns, Tony Banta **10** Alex Rieger **11** Elaine Nardo, Latka Gravas **12** Bobby Wheeler, Louie De Palma
cast: 9 Carol Kane, Tony Danza **10** Judd Hirsch **11** Andy Kaufman, Danny DeVito, Jeff Conaway **12** Marilu Henner **13** Randall Carver
company: 11 Sunshine Cab

taxicab 4 hack **6** jitney **7** droshky, hackney **8** hired car, rickshaw **10** automobile **11** jinrickshaw

Taxi Driver
director: 14 Martin Scorsese
cast: 10 Peter Boyle **11** Jodie Foster **12** Albert Brooks, Harvey Keitel, Robert De Niro **13** Leonard Harris **14** Cybill Shepherd
setting: 11 New York City
score: 15 Bernard Herrmann
script: 12 Paul Schrader

taxon 5 class, genus, order **6** family, phylum **7** kingdom, species

taxonomy
study of: 17 structure contrast **19** structure comparison

Taylor, Elizabeth
born: 6 London **7** England
husband: 8 Mike Todd **10** John Warner **11** Eddie Fisher, Nicky Hilton **13** Richard Burton **14** Michael Wilding
roles: 5 Giant **7** Ivanhoe **9** Cleopatra **11** Little Women **12** The Sandpiper **14** A Place in the Sun, National Velvet, Raintree County **16** Butterfield Eight (Oscar), Cat on a Hot Tin Roof, Father of the Bride **18** Suddenly Last Summer **19** The Taming of the Shrew **25** Who's Afraid of Virginia Woolf (Oscar)

Taylor, Robert
real name: 22 Spangler Arlington Brugh
wife: 12 Ursula Thiess **15** Barbara Stanwyck
roles: 7 Camille, Ivanhoe **8** Quo Vadis **11** Billy the Kid **14** Waterloo Bridge **20** Magnificent Obsession

Taylor, Zachary
nickname: 16 Old Rough and Ready
presidential rank: 7 twelfth
party: 4 Whig
state represented: 2 LA
defeated: 4 (Lewis) Cass **8** (Martin) Van Buren
vice president: 8 (Millard) Fillmore
cabinet:
  state: 7 (John Middleton) Clayton
  treasury: 8 (William Morris) Meredith
  war: 8 (George Walker) Crawford
  attorney general: 7 (Reverdy) Johnson
  navy: 7 (William Ballard) Preston
  postmaster general: 8 (Jacob) Collamer
  interior: 5 (Thomas) Ewing
born: 12 Montebello VA **12** Orange County
died: 12 Washington DC
buried: 12 Louisville KY
education: 9 no college **16** privately tutored

religion: 12 Episcopalian
political career: 21 none prior to presidency
civilian career: 7 planter, soldier
military service: 6 US Army **12** major general
  War: 7 Mexican **9** Black Hawk **19** War of Eighteen-Twelve **14** Second Seminole
notable events of lifetime/ presidency:
  treaty: 13 Clayton-Bulwer
father: 7 Richard
mother: 5 Sarah (Dabney Strother)
siblings: 6 George **7** Hancock **11** Sarah Bailey **12** Elizabeth Lee, Emily Richard **13** Joseph Pannill **21** William Dabney Strother
wife: 8 Margaret (Mackall Smith)
children: 7 Richard **9** Sarah Knox **10** Ann Mackall **13** Margaret Smith, Mary Elizabeth, Octavia Panill

Tchad see **4** Chad

Tchaikovsky, Peter (Piotr Ilyich Chaikovsky)
born: 6 Russia **8** Votkinsk
composer of: 7 Manfred, Mazeppa **8** Iolanthe, Pathetic (symphony No 6), Swan Lake **9** Joan of Arc **10** Nutcracker **12** Eugene Onegin, Winter Dreams **14** Italian Caprice, Romeo and Juliet, The Enchantress **16** The Queen of Spades **17** Francesca da Rimini, The Sleeping Beauty **22** Eighteen-Twelve Overture

tea 16 Camellia sinensis
varieties: 4 chai **5** Assam, Bohea, China, green, pekoe, Yerba **6** Ceylon, Oolong, Oswego, Tisane **7** African, Arabian, cambric, crystal, Lapsang, Mexican, redroot, Spanish **8** bergamot, camomile, Earl Grey, Labrador, mountain, Paraguay, Siberian, Souchong, Woodruff **9** gunpowder, lemon balm, New Jersey, sassafras **10** Darjeeling, Philippine **11** Appalachian, Orange Pekoe **14** Irish breakfast **16** English breakfast

teach 5 coach, drill, edify, prime, tutor **6** inform, school **7** educate, implant, prepare **8** exercise, instruct **9** enlighten, inculcate **10** discipline **12** indoctrinate

Teach
character in: 21 The Master of Ballantrae
author: 9 Stevenson

teacher 3 don **5** coach, tutor **6** master, mentor **7** maestro, trainer **8** educator **9** preceptor, professor **10** instructor, schoolmarm **12** schoolmaster **13** schoolteacher **14** schoolmistress

teaching 5 dogma, tenet **6** belief **7** nurture, precept **8** doctrine, pedagogy, training, tutelage, tutoring **9** education, principle, schooling **10** conviction, philosophy **11** inculcation, instructing, instruction, preparation **14** indoctrination

tea dance
French: **10** the dansant

teal
group of: **5** ducks
color: **4** blue **5** green

team 3 rig, set **4** ally, band, crew, five, gang, join, nine, pair, side, unit, yoke **5** force, group, merge, party, squad, staff, unify, unite **6** circle, clique, couple, eleven, league, tandem **7** combine, company, coterie, faction **8** alliance, federate **9** coalition, cooperate **10** amalgamate, federation, sports team, yoked group **11** association, consolidate, get together, incorporate **12** band together, join together **13** confederation

teammate 4 ally **7** partner **8** coplayer, coworker **9** associate, colleague, co-partner **11** confederate **12** collaborator

team spirit 10 group pride, solidarity **13** esprit de corps

team up 4 ally **5** unite **9** cooperate **10** join forces **11** collaborate

tear 3 fly, gap, hie, rip, run **4** bolt, dart, dash, grab, hole, mist, pull, race, rend, rent, rift, rive, rush, scud, slit, snag, swim, whiz, yank **5** abuse, break, crack, fault, pluck, scoot, seize, sever, shoot, shred, speed, split, spurt, sweep, whisk **6** breach, cleave, damage, divide, gallop, hasten, hustle, injury, plunge, ravage, scurry, snatch, sprint, sunder, wrench **7** disrupt, fissure, hard use, opening, rupture, scamper, scuttle **8** disunite, teardrop, scramble, splinter **9** come apart, hotfoot it, pull apart, skedaddle **10** impairment, make tracks **11** destruction **12** pull to pieces

tear down 4 raze **5** level, smash, wreck **7** destroy, flatten **8** demolish **9** dismantle, take apart

tearful 5 teary, weepy **6** crying **7** bawling, crushed, sobbing, wailing, weeping **8** mournful **9** lamenting, sniveling **10** blubbering, lachrymose, whimpering **11** heartbroken **12** inconsolable **13** brokenhearted

tear off 5 sever **6** detach, rip off **7** pull off **8** break off, separate **10** wrench away

Teasdale, Sara
author of: **8** Love Song **11** Helen of Troy **13** Dark of the Moon **14** Flame and Shadow, Rivers to the Sea, Strange Victory

tease 3 guy, irk, nag, rag, vex **4** bait, gall, gibe, goad, haze, jeer, josh, mock, pest, rile, twit **5** annoy, chafe, harry, mimic, pique, scoff, sneer,

taunt, worry **6** badger, bother, harass, hazing, heckle, hector, mocker, needle, pester, plague, teaser **7** bedevil, chafing, laugh at, needler, provoke, razzing, snigger, taunter, torment, worrier **8** derision, heckling, irritate, needling, ridicule **9** aggravate, make fun of, mimicking, persecute, tantalize, tormentor **10** harassment, tantalizer **11** persecution

teaspoon
abbreviation: **3** tsp

Teazle, Sir Peter and Lady
characters in: **19** The School for Scandal
author: **8** Sheridan

technical 5 trade **10** mechanical, vocational **11** complicated, nonacademic **13** technological

technique 3 art, way **4** form **5** craft, knack, style **6** manner, method, system **7** formula, know-how **8** approach, facility **9** procedure **10** adroitness, expertness, technology **11** proficiency **12** skillfulness

tedious 3 dry **4** drab, dull, long, slow **5** vapid **6** boring, dismal, dreary, jejune, tiring **7** humdrum, insipid, irksome, onerous, prosaic **8** drawn-out, lifeless, tiresome, wearying **9** fatiguing, laborious, wearisome **10** burdensome, exhausting, monotonous, oppressive, unexciting **13** time-consuming, unimaginative, uninteresting

tediousness 5 ennui **7** boredom **8** dullness, monotony

tedium 3 rut **5** ennui **7** boredom **8** drabness, dullness, monotony, sameness **10** dreariness **11** routineness **12** tiresomeness

tedium of life
Latin: **12** taedium vitae

teem 4 brim, gush **5** swarm **6** abound **8** be full of, overflow **9** be overrun **15** burst at the seams

teeming 4 full **7** crowded **8** swarming **9** abounding, bounteous **11** overflowing

teeny-weeny 3 wee **4** tiny **5** dwarf **6** little, minute, petite **9** miniature, minuscule **10** diminutive, pocket-size **11** lilliputian, microscopic, pocket-sized

teeter 4 reel, sway **5** lurch, waver **6** seesaw, totter, wobble **7** stagger **8** hesitate **9** vacillate

teetotaler 3 dry **9** abstainer **10** nondrinker **14** prohibitionist

Tegucigalpa
capital of: **8** Honduras

Tegyrius
king of: **6** Thrace

Tehani
character in: **17** Mutiny on the

Bounty
authors: **4** Hall **8** Nordhoff

Tehran, Teheran
capital of: **4** Iran
landmark: **10** Melaat Park **12** Marble Palace, Marmar Palace **14** Azadai Monument, Gulestan Palace, Saadabad Palace **15** Freedom Monument, Hosseineh Mosque, Shahyad Monument **23** Center for Islamic Studies
means: **9** warm place
mountain: **6** Elburz **8** Demavend
ruler: **8** Khomeini **23** Muhammad Reza Shah Pahlavi

Telamon
king of: **7** Salamis
member of: **9** Argonauts
father: **6** Aeacus
mother: **6** Endeis
brother: **6** Peleus
half-brother: **6** Phocus
wife: **6** Glauce **7** Eriboea
son: **4** Ajax **6** Teucer
friend: **8** Hercules

Telegonus
father: **7** Proteus **8** Odysseus
mother: **5** Circe
wife: **2** Io **8** Penelope
killed: **8** Odysseus
killed by: **8** Hercules

telegraph
invented by: **5** Morse, Woods **6** Edison **7** Marconi

Telemachus
father: **8** Odysseus
mother: **8** Penelope
son: **7** Latinus

Telemann, Georg Philipp
born: **7** Germany **9** Magdeburg
composer of: **9** Fantasias **10** Times of Day **12** Don Quichotte **14** Die Tageszeiten, Musique de Table

Telemus
vocation: **4** seer
father: **7** Eurymus
warned: **10** Polyphemus

telepathy 3 ESP **10** sixth sense **11** second sight **12** clairvoyance **19** spirit communication, thought transference **22** extrasensory perception

telephone
invented by: **4** Bell
type: **3** cell, pay, TDD **6** mobile, rotary **8** cellular, portable, princess, wireless **9** extension, touch-tone **10** push-button

Telephone, The
opera by: **7** Menotti

telescope
invented by: **7** Galileo **10** Lippershey
astronomical: **6** Kepler

telesterion
form: **8** building
purpose: **8** religion **11** celebration

television
  invented by: 5 Baird **8** Zworykin **10** Farnsworth

tell 3 ask, bid, own, say, see **4** blab **5** bruit, count, order, speak, spout, state, utter, weigh, write **6** advise, babble, betray, blazon, depict, detail, direct, figure, impart, inform, number, recite, reckon, relate, report, reveal, sketch, unfold **7** apprise, command, compute, confess, declare, discern, divulge, express, find out, mention, narrate, portray, predict, publish, recount, request **8** acquaint, count off, describe, disclose, estimate, forecast, foretell, identify, instruct, perceive, register, set forth **9** apprehend, ascertain, broadcast, calculate, chronicle, enumerate, enunciate, influence, make known, pronounce, recognize **10** take effect **11** communicate, distinguish **12** discriminate **17** breathe a word about

Teller, Edward
  field: 7 physics
  developed: 8 atom bomb **12** hydrogen bomb

telling 5 solid, valid **6** cogent, potent **7** decided, weighty **8** decisive, definite, forceful, material, positive, powerful, striking **9** effective, effectual, important, momentous, trenchant **10** conclusive, definitive, impressive **11** efficacious, influential, significant **13** consequential

telltale 6 gossip **7** tattler **8** busybody, giveaway, informer, squealer **9** affirming, betraying, divulging, revealing, verifying **10** confirming, disclosing, newsbearer, talebearer, tattletale **11** informative **12** blabbermouth, enlightening **13** scandalmonger

Tellus
  called: 10 Terra Mater
  origin: 5 Roman
  goddess of: 5 earth **8** marriage **9** fertility **11** agriculture
  corresponds to: 4 Gaea

temerity 4 gall **5** brass, cheek, nerve **8** audacity, boldness, chutzpah, rashness **9** brashness, freshness, impudence, insolence, pushiness, sauciness **10** brazenness, effrontery **11** forwardness **12** impertinence, indiscretion **13** foolhardiness, intrusiveness

Temin, Howard Martin
  field: 8 genetics, oncology
  discovered: 20 reverse transcriptase
  awarded: 10 Nobel Prize

temper 3 ire **4** bile, calm, fury, gall, mood, rage **5** allay, anger, humor, pique, quiet, still, wrath **6** animus, anneal, choler, dander, harden, pacify, soften, soothe, spleen **7** appease, balance, compose, dudgeon, emotion, ferment, passion, toughen, umbrage **8** acrimony, bad humor, calmness, mitigate, moderate, palliate, vexation **9** annoyance, composure, huffiness **10** irritation, strengthen **11** displeasure, disposition, equilibrium, frame of mind, indignation, peevishness, tranquilize **12** churlishness, irascibility, irritability

temperament 4 bent, cast, mood, soul, tone **5** humor, tenor **6** makeup, nature, spirit, temper **7** leaning, quality **8** tendency **9** character **10** complexion **11** disposition, frame of mind, personality

temperamental 5 fiery, moody **6** fickle **7** erratic, peppery, willful **8** unstable, volatile **9** emotional, excitable, explosive, hotheaded, mercurial, sensitive, turbulent **10** capricious, headstrong, high-strung, hysterical, mettlesome, passionate, unreliable **11** tempestuous, thin-skinned **12** undependable **13** unpredictable

temperance 8 prudence, sobriety **9** restraint **10** abstention, abstinence, discretion, moderation, self-denial **11** forbearance, prohibition, self-control, teetotalism **14** abstemiousness, self-discipline

temperate 4 calm, cool, even, mild, sane, soft, warm **5** balmy, sober, sunny **6** gentle, mellow, sedate, steady **7** clement, patient, sparing **8** composed, moderate, pleasant, rational, tranquil **9** collected, easygoing, unruffled **10** coolheaded, reasonable **11** levelheaded **13** dispassionate, self-possessed, unextravagant, unimpassioned **14** self-controlled, self-restrained

temperature measurement 6 degree, Kelvin **7** Celsius **10** Fahrenheit

tempest 5 chaos, furor, storm **6** hubbub, tumult, uproar **8** brouhaha, outbreak, upheaval **9** agitation, cataclysm, commotion **10** hurly-burly, turbulence **11** disturbance

Tempest, The
  author: 18 William Shakespeare
  character: 5 Ariel **6** Alonso **7** Antonio, Caliban, Gonzalo, Miranda **8** Prospero **9** Ferdinand, Sebastian

Tempestates
  origin: 5 Roman
  goddesses of: 6 storms

tempestuous 3 hot **5** fiery **6** raging, stormy **7** excited, frantic, furious, violent **8** agitated, feverish, frenzied **9** emotional, explosive, turbulent, wrought-up **10** hysterical, passionate, tumultuous **11** impassioned, overwrought

Templar, Simon
  character in: 8 The Saint
  author: 9 Charteris

temple 4 fane, kirk **6** chapel, church, mosque, pagoda, priory, shrine **7** convent **8** basilica, pantheon **9** cathedral, joss house, monastery, sanctuary, synagogue **10** house of God, tabernacle **12** meeting house

Temple, Shirley
  married name: 18 Shirley Temple Black
  born: 13 Santa Monica CA
  roles: 5 Heidi **10** Bright Eyes **15** Wee Willie Winkie **16** Little Miss Marker, The Little Colonel, The Littlest Rebel **18** Poor Little Rich Girl **21** Susannah of the Mounties **23** Rebecca of Sunnybrook Farm

tempo 4 clip, gait, pace, rate, time **5** meter, speed **6** pacing, stride, timing **8** momentum, velocity

tempo giusto
  music: 10 strict time

temporal 3 lay **5** civil **6** mortal **7** mundane, passing, profane, secular, worldly **8** day-to-day, fleeting, fugitive **9** ephemeral, temporary, transient **10** evanescent, noneternal **11** impermanent, nonclerical **12** nonspiritual **17** nonecclesiastical

temporary, temporarily 5 brief, fleet **7** interim, passing, stopgap **8** fleeting, fugitive **9** ephemeral, momentary, provisory, transient **10** evanescent, short-lived, transitory **11** impermanent, provisional **13** flash-in-the-pan
  Latin: 10 pro tempore

temporary dwelling
  French: 10 pied-a-terre

temporize 5 delay, hedge, stall, tarry, waver **8** hang back, maneuver **9** hem and haw, vacillate **10** equivocate **11** play for time **12** drag one's feet, tergiversate **13** procrastinate

tempt 3 try, woo **4** bait, draw, goad, lure, pull, risk **5** charm, decoy, prick, rouse **6** allure, arouse, entice, incite, invite, seduce **7** attract, bewitch, provoke **8** appeal to, intrigue, inveigle **9** captivate, tantalize **12** put to the test **13** take one's fancy **14** fly in the face of **15** whet the appetite

temptation 4 bait, draw, lure, pull, urge **5** charm, snare, spell **8** stimulus, tempting **9** incentive, seduction **10** allurement, attraction, enticement, incitement, inducement **11** captivation, fascination, provocation

tempter 5 Satan **7** enticer, seducer **8** the Devil

temptress 4 vamp **5** Circe, flirt, siren **7** charmer, Delilah, Jezebel, Lorelei, vampire **8** coquette **9** odalisque, sorceress **10** seductress **11** enchantress, femme fatale

tempus fugit 9 time flies

Ten (10)
  director: 12 Blake Edwards

cast: 7 Bo Derek **11** Dudley Moore **12** Julie Andrews

tenable 6 viable **8** arguable, rational, sensible, workable **9** excusable **10** condonable, defendable, defensible, vindicable **11** justifiable, warrantable **12** maintainable

tenacious 3 set **4** fast, firm, hard, iron **6** dogged, mulish **7** adamant, staunch **8** clinging, constant, obdurate, resolute, stalwart, stubborn **9** immovable, obstinate, pigheaded, steadfast, unbending **10** determined, inexorable, inflexible, persistent, relentless, unswerving, unwavering, unyielding **11** persevering, undeviating, unfaltering, unremitting **12** intransigent, unchangeable **14** uncompromising

tenaciousness 8 tenacity **9** endurance **10** resolution **11** persistence **12** perseverance, resoluteness **13** determination **16** stick-to-itiveness

tenacity 8 strength **9** toughness **10** resolution **11** persistence **12** cohesiveness, perseverance, resoluteness **13** determination, tenaciousness **16** stick-to-itiveness

tenant 6 lessee, lodger, renter, roomer **7** boarder, denizen, dweller **8** occupant, resident **10** inhabitant **11** householder, leaseholder, paying guest

Ten Commandments
also: 9 Decalogue
given to: 5 Moses
where given: 10 Mount Sinai
inscribed on: 12 stone tablets
first: 32 Thou shalt have no other Gods before me
second: 37 Thou shalt not bow down before graven images
third: 44 Thou shalt not take the name of the Lord thy God in vain
fourth: 34 Remember the Sabbath Day and keep it holy
fifth: 26 Honor thy father and thy mother
sixth: 16 Thou shalt not kill
seventh: 26 Thou shalt not commit adultery
eighth: 17 Thou shalt not steal
ninth: 46 Thou shalt not bear false witness against thy neighbor
tenth: 17 Thou shalt not covet

Ten Commandments, The
director: 13 Cecil B DeMille
cast: 8 Nina Foch **9** John Derek **10** Anne Baxter, Debra Paget, Yul Brynner **11** Martha Scott **12** Vincent Price **13** John Carradine, Yvonne De Carlo **14** Charlton Heston (Moses), Judith Anderson **15** Cedric Hardwicke, Edward G Robinson

tend 3 aim **4** bear, head, lead, lean, mind, move **5** be apt, guide, nurse, point, watch **6** extend, foster, manage, wait on **7** care for, nurture **8** attend to, be liable, be likely **9** bid fair to, gravitate, look after, supervise, watch over **10** minister to, predispose, take care of **11** keep an eye on

tendency 3 aim, set **4** bent **5** drift, drive, habit, trend **6** course **7** heading, impulse, leaning, turning **8** penchant **9** direction, proneness, readiness **10** proclivity, propensity **11** disposition, gravitation, inclination **14** predisposition

tender 3 raw **4** fond, give, good, kind, soft, sore, weak **5** frail, green, place, young **6** aching, benign, callow, caring, dainty, extend, feeble, gentle, hand in, loving, prefer, submit, weakly **7** advance, fragile, hold out, painful, present, proffer, propose, suggest, swollen **8** delicate, generous, immature, inflamed, juvenile, merciful, propound, underage, youthful **9** lay before, sensitive, volunteer **10** benevolent, put forward, thoughtful, vulnerable **11** considerate, sentimental, softhearted, sympathetic, warmhearted **12** affectionate **13** compassionate, inexperienced, understanding **14** impressionable **15** unsophisticated

tenderfoot 4 tyro **6** novice, rookie **8** beginner, neophyte **9** fledgling, greenhorn **10** apprentice

tenderhearted 4 mild **6** benign, gentle, humane **8** generous, merciful **10** altruistic, benevolent, responsive, thoughtful **11** considerate, kindhearted, softhearted, sympathetic, warmhearted **13** compassionate, understanding

tenderheartedness 4 pity **5** heart **7** empathy **8** sympathy **10** compassion

tendering 6 giving **8** offering **9** advancing, extending, proposing **10** holding out, preferring, proffering, submitting, suggesting **11** propounding **12** volunteering

Tender Is the Night
author: 16 F Scott Fitzgerald
character: 7 Abe North **9** Dick Diver **11** Nicole Diver, Tommy Barban **12** Rosemary Hoyt

tenderness 4 love **6** aching, warmth **7** rawness **8** delicacy, fondness, goodness, humanity, kindness, mildness, smarting, softness, soreness, sympathy **9** affection **10** compassion, gentleness, humaneness, kindliness, lovingness **11** beneficence, benevolence, painfulness, sensitivity **12** mercifulness **14** loving kindness

tendon 4 cord **5** sinew
connects: 4 bone **6** muscle

tendril 4 coil, curl **5** crook, shoot, sprig, twist **6** winder **7** climber, ringlet

tenebrous 3 dim **4** dark **5** murky **6** gloomy **7** obscure, shadowy **8** darkened, obscured **13** unilluminated

tenet 4 rule, view **5** canon, credo, creed, dogma, maxim **6** belief, thesis **7** opinion **8** doctrine, ideology, position, teaching **9** principle **10** conviction, persuasion

Tennessee
abbreviation: 2 TN **4** Tenn
nickname: 7 Big Bend **9** Volunteer **11** Old Franklin
capital: 9 Nashville
largest city: 7 Memphis
others: 5 Alcoa, Paris **6** Camden, Sparta **7** Bristol, Dickson, Pulaski **8** Franklin, Gallatin, Oak Ridge **9** Cedar Hill, Cleveland, Inglewood, Kingsport, Knoxville, Lexington **10** Greenbrier, Morristown, Old Hickory **11** Chattanooga, Clarksville, Springfield **12** Fayetteville, Murfreesboro **14** Hendersonville
college: 4 Fisk, Lane **5** Bryan, Siena **6** Bethel **7** Belmont, Lambuth, Lemoyne **8** Milligan, Tusculum **10** Vanderbilt **12** Southwestern **13** David Lipscomb **14** Meharry Medical **17** Tennessee Wesleyan
feature: 12 The Hermitage
  dam: 6 Norris, Wilson **7** Douglas
  football team: 6 Titans **15** Tennessee Titans
  fort: 5 Henry **8** Donalson, Nashboro
  national park: 6 Shiloh **13** Cumberland Gap **19** Great Smoky Mountains (with North Carolina)
  national parkway: 12 Natchez Trace
tribe: 7 Shawnee **8** Cherokee **9** Chickasaw
people: 6 Al Gore **7** Sequoya **8** John Bell **9** James Agee **10** Grace Moore **11** Bessie Smith, Cordell Hull **12** Davy Crockett, Elvis Presley **13** Estes Kefauver **23** Alvin Cullum "Sergeant" York **32** Ernest Jennings "Tennessee Ernie" Ford
  explorer: 6 Arthur, De Soto **7** Jolliet, La Salle, Needham **9** Marquette
lake: 7 Douglas **8** Barkeley, Cherokee, Reelfoot, Watts Bar **10** Center Hill **11** Chickamauga
land rank: 12 thirty-fourth
mountain: 5 Guyot **7** Lookout, Smokies **9** Blue Ridge **10** Cumberland, Great Smoky
  highest point: 13 Clingman's Dome
physical feature:
  basin: 9 Nashville
  highlands: 11 Appalachian
  plain: 7 Coastal
  plateau: 10 Cumberland
president: 10 James K Polk **13** Andrew Jackson, Andrew Johnson
river: 3 Elk **4** Duck **5** Caney, Obion, Stone **6** Clinch **7** Hatchie, Holston **8**

Hiwassee **9** Tennessee **10** Cumberland **11** French Broad, Mississippi **15** Little Tennessee

state admission: 9 sixteenth

state bird: 11 mockingbird

state flower: 4 flag, iris **6** maypop **13** passion flower

state motto: 16 America at Its Best **22** Agriculture and Commerce

state song: 11 My Tennessee **17** The Tennessee Waltz **19** My Homeland Tennessee **26** When It's Iris Time in Tennessee

state tree: 11 tulip poplar **12** yellow poplar

tennis
athlete: 8 Don Budge, Rod Laver **9** Bjorn Borg, Ivan Lendl, Stan Smith **10** Arthur Ashe, Bill Tilden, Jack Kramer, Maria Bueno, Roy Emerson, Steffi Graf **11** Alice Marble, Andre Agassi, Andy Roddick, Boris Becker, Ilie Nastase, John McEnroe, Ken Rosewall, Monica Seles, Pete Sampras, Rafael Nadal, Tracy Austin **12** Althea Gibson, Jimmy Connors, John Newcombe, Mats Wilander, Roger Federer, Virginia Wade **13** Dennis Ralston, Lleyton Hewitt, Martina Hingis, Venus Williams **14** Guillermo Vilas, Hana Mandlikova, Maria Sharapova, Pancho Gonzalez, Rosemary Casals, Serena Williams **15** Chris Evert Lloyd, Maureen Connolly **16** Lindsay Davenport **18** Margaret Smith Court, Martina Navratilova **20** Helen Wills Moody Roark **21** Billie Jean Moffitt King, Evonne Goolagong Cawley

cup: 5 Davis

Tennyson, Alfred, Lord
author of: 4 Maud **7** Mariana, Ulysses **10** Enoch Arden, In Memoriam (A H H) **12** Locksley Hall, Morte d'Arthur **16** The Lady of Shalott **18** The Idylls of the King **26** The Charge of the Light Brigade

tenor 4 gist **5** drift, sense, trend **6** course, import, intent, nature, object **7** content, essence, meaning, purport, purpose **8** argument, tendency **9** direction, intention, substance **11** connotation, implication **12** significance

tense 4 taut **5** brace, drawn, rigid, shaky, stiff, tight **6** braced, draw up, on edge, uneasy **7** anxious, excited, fearful, fidgety, jittery, nervous, restive, stiffen, uptight **8** agitated, make taut, restless, strained, timorous **9** tighten up, tremulous, wrought-up **10** high-strung, inflexible, unyielding **12** apprehensive

tension 5 dread **6** spring, strain, stress **7** anxiety, pulling, tugging **8** bad

vibes, exertion, pressure, rigidity, tautness, traction **9** hostility, misgiving, stiffness, straining, tightness **10** stretching **11** fearfulness, nervousness, restiveness, trepidation **12** apprehension, elastic force, perturbation **13** bad vibrations, combativeness

tent 3 pup **4** care, hard **5** gauze, probe, tepee **6** bigtop, canvas, search, teepee, wigwam **7** shelter **8** pavilion **10** tabernacle

tentacle 3 arm **6** feeler **9** appendage

tentative 4 iffy **5** trial **6** acting **8** not final, proposed **9** ad interim, temporary, undecided, unsettled **10** contingent, indefinite, not settled **11** conditional, probational, provisional, speculative, unconfirmed **12** experimental, probationary **15** subject to change **18** under consideration

tentative procedure 4 test **5** flier, trail **6** feeler, tryout **7** venture **10** experiment **12** trial balloon

tenuous 4 slim, thin, weak **5** frail, shaky **6** flimsy, paltry, slight **7** fragile, shallow, slender **8** delicate, gossamer **9** uncertain **10** indefinite **11** halfhearted, unsupported **12** unconvincing **13** unsubstantial

tenure 4 rule, term, time **5** reign **7** tenancy **9** occupancy, retention **10** incumbency, occupation, permanency, possession **11** entitlement, job security **14** administration

tepee, teepee 4 chum, tent **5** lodge **6** wigwam **7** wickiup

tepid 4 cool, mild **7** languid, warmish **8** lukewarm, moderate **9** apathetic, impassive, temperate **10** nonchalant, phlegmatic **11** halfhearted, indifferent, unemotional **13** lackadaisical **14** unenthusiastic

tequila
type: 6 spirit
origin: 6 Mexico
made from: 5 agave **6** maguey
used with: 4 lime, salt **5** lemon
drink: 7 Chapala **8** El Diablo
with creme de cacao: 8 Toreador
with kahlua: 9 Brave Bull
with orange juice: 7 Sunrise
with Tia Maria: 9 Brave Bull
with triple sec: 9 Margarita

Teraphim
origin: 6 Hebrew
form: 4 idol

Ter Borch, Gerard
born: 6 Zwolle **14** The Netherlands
artwork: 8 Flea Hunt **10** The Concert **14** Peace of Munster **21** The Parental Admonition

Terbrugghen, Hendrick
born: 8 Deventer **14** The Netherlands
artwork: 14 The Flute Player **19** Liberation of St Peter **21** The Calling of St Matthew

Tereshkova, Valentina
first: 12 woman in space

terete 7 tapered **11** cylindrical

tergal 4 back **6** dorsal

Terkel, Studs
author of: 4 Race **7** Working **9** Hard Times **10** "The Good War" **14** American Dreams, Division Street **15** Talking to Myself

term, terms 3 age, dub, era, tag **4** call, cite, item, name, span, time, word **5** catch, cycle, epoch, idiom, reign, spell, stage, state, style, while **6** clause, course, detail, period, phrase, status, string **7** dynasty, footing, proviso **8** duration, interval, position, standing **9** condition, designate, provision, relations, requisite **10** expression, span of time **11** appellation, designation, requirement, stipulation **12** characterize, circumstance, prerequisite **14** administration

termagant 3 nag **4** fury **5** scold, shrew, vixen **6** ogress, virago **7** hellcat, hellion, she-wolf, tigress **8** battle-ax, fishwife, harridan, spitfire **9** Xanthippe

Termagant
character in: 21 medieval morality plays

terminal 3 end **4** last **5** depot, fatal, final, stand **6** deadly, lethal, mortal **7** station **8** terminus **10** concluding

terminate 3 end **4** stop **5** cease, close, lapse **6** expire, finish, run out, wind up **8** complete, conclude **11** come to an end, discontinue **12** bring to an end

termination 3 end **4** halt **5** close, finis, lapse **6** ending, finale, finish, windup **7** closing **8** stoppage **9** cessation **10** completion, concluding, conclusion, expiration **15** discontinuation

Terminator, The
director: 12 James Cameron
cast: 12 Michael Biehn (Kyle Reese), Paul Winfield (Ed Traxler) **13** Linda Hamilton (Sarah Connor) **14** Lance Henriksen (Vukovich) **20** Arnold Schwarzenegger (the Terminator)

Terminator 2: Judgment Day
director: 12 James Cameron
cast: 8 Earl Boen (Peter Silberman) **9** Joe Morton (Miles Bennett Dyson) **13** Edward Furlong (John Connor), Linda Hamilton (Sarah Connor), Robert Patrick (T-1000) **16** S Epatha Merkerson (Tarissa Dyson) **20** Arnold Schwarzenegger (the Terminator)

Terminator 3: Rise of the Machines
director: 14 Jonathan Mostow
cast: 8 Earl Boen (Peter Silberman) **9** Nick Stahl (John Connor) **11** Claire

Danes (Kate Brewster) **12** David Andrews (Robert Brewster) **14** Kristanna Loken (T-X) **15** Mark Famiglietti (Scott Petersen) **20** Arnold Schwarzenegger (the Terminator)

terminus 3 end **4** stop **5** depot, limit **6** ending **7** extreme, station **8** boundary, last stop, terminal **9** extremity **10** conclusion

Terminus
   origin: **5** Roman
   god of: **9** landmarks **10** boundaries

terminus ad quem 10 end to which, final limit **11** ending point

terminus a quo 9 beginning **12** end from which **13** starting point

termite
   variety: **6** desert **7** dry wood **8** damp wood **10** powderpost, rotten wood **11** soldierless **12** subterranean

Terms of Endearment
   director: **12** James L Brooks
   based on novel by: **13** Larry McMurtry
   cast: **11** Debra Winger **13** Jack Nicholson **15** Shirley MacLaine
   Oscar for: **7** actress (MacLaine), picture **8** director **15** supporting actor (Nicholson)

Terpsichore
   member of: **5** Muses
   personifies: **7** dancing **10** choral song

Terra
   goddess of: **5** Earth
   Greek: **4** Gaea
   mother: **5** Chaos
   offspring: **6** Pontus, Titans, Uranus **7** Erinyes, Oceanus **8** Cyclopes **9** mountains **13** Hecatonchires

terrace 4 roof **5** level, patio, plane, porch **6** street **7** balcony, plateau **9** esplanade, promenade **10** embankment

Terraced Bay *see* **6** Taiwan

terra-cotta 4 clay **6** russet **8** brownish **12** reddish-brown **14** brownish-orange

terrain 4 area, zone **5** tract **6** ground, milieu, region **7** setting **8** district **9** territory **10** topography **11** countryside, environment **12** surroundings

terra incognita 11 unknown land **14** unexplored land, unknown subject **16** unknown territory

terrapin 3 box **4** emyd, emys **6** slider, turpin, turtle **8** tortoise **11** diamondback
   family: **8** Emydidae
   female: **6** heifer
   male: **4** bull

terrestrial 4 land **6** earth's, global, ground **7** earthly, mundane, worldly **8** riparian **10** earthbound

terrible 3 bad **4** dire, huge **5** awful, great, harsh, rough, scary **6** brutal, fierce, horrid, odious, severe, strong

7 beastly, extreme, fearful, ghastly, hateful, heinous, hideous, intense **8** alarming, dreadful, enormous, fearsome, horrible, shocking, terrific **9** appalling, excessive, harrowing, monstrous, obnoxious, offensive, repulsive, revolting, upsetting **10** disturbing, formidable, horrifying, immoderate, inordinate, terrifying, tremendous, unpleasant **11** distasteful, distressing, frightening, intolerable **12** insufferable **13** objectionable

terrier
   dog breed: **3** fox **4** bull, Skye **5** Cairn, Irish, Welsh **6** border, Boston **7** Norfolk, Tibetan, wire fox **8** Airedale, Lakeland, Scottish, Sealyham **9** Kerry Blue **10** Australian, Bedlington, Manchester **13** Dandie Dinmont **17** soft-coated wheaten, Staffordshire bull, West Highland white **18** miniature schnauzer **21** American Staffordshire

terrific 3 fab **4** fine, good, huge **5** awful, great, harsh, marvy, scary, super **6** bang-up, fierce, severe, superb **7** extreme, fearful, intense, sensash **8** alarming, dreadful, enormous, fabulous, fearsome, smashing, splendid, terrible **9** excellent, excessive, fantastic, harrowing, marvelous, monstrous, upsetting, wonderful **10** disturbing, horrifying, immoderate, inordinate, remarkable, stupendous, superduper, terrifying, tremendous **11** distressing, exceptional, frightening, sensational **13** extraordinary **14** out of this world

terrified 6 afraid, scared **7** alarmed, panicky **9** petrified **10** frightened **11** scared stiff **13** panic-stricken **14** terror-stricken **17** frightened to death

terrify 3 cow **5** abash, alarm, daunt, panic, scare, unman, upset **6** appall, dismay **7** agitate, disturb, horrify, overawe, petrify **8** disquiet, frighten **10** intimidate **17** make one's skin crawl **20** make one's blood run cold **22** make one's hair stand on end

terrifying 5 awful, dread **7** fearful **8** alarming, dreadful **9** frightful **11** frightening, hair-raising

territory 4 area, land, pale, zone **5** clime, realm, state, tract **6** bounds, colony, domain, empire, limits, locale, nation, region, sector **7** acreage, kingdom, mandate, terrain **8** confines, district, dominion, province **9** bailiwick **10** dependency **11** countryside **12** commonwealth, principality, protectorate

terror 3 awe **4** fear **5** alarm, dread, panic **6** dismay, fright, horror **7** anxiety **8** affright, disquiet **9** agitation **11** disquietude, trepidation **12** apprehension, perturbation **13** consternation **16** fear and trembling

terrorize 3 cow **5** abash, force **6** menace **7** terrify **8** browbeat, bulldoze, threaten **10** intimidate

terror-stricken 6 afraid, scared **7** alarmed, panicky **9** horrified, petrified, terrified **11** scared green, scared stiff **13** panic-stricken, scared to death

Terry and the Pirates
   creator: **12** Milton Caniff
   character: **7** Pat Ryan **8** Terry Lee **10** Dragon Lady

terse 4 curt, neat **5** brief, clear, crisp, pithy, short **6** abrupt **7** clipped, compact, concise, laconic, pointed, summary **8** clearcut, incisive, succinct **9** axiomatic, condensed, trenchant **10** compressed **11** unambiguous **12** epigrammatic **18** brief and to the point

terseness 7 brevity **8** curtness **9** crispness **10** abruptness **11** compactness, conciseness **12** succinctness

Tess (of the D'Urbervilles)
   author: **11** Thomas Hardy
   director: **13** Roman Polanski
   cast: **8** John Bett **10** Peter Firth, Tom Chadbon **14** Rosemary Martin **15** Nastassia Kinski (Tess)

test 4 exam, quiz **5** check, final, flyer, probe, proof, prove, trial **6** dry run, feeler, try out, verify **7** analyze, confirm, examine, midterm **8** analysis, validate **9** catechism **11** corroborate, examination, investigate, questioning **12** confirmation, substantiate, verification **13** comprehensive, corroboration, investigation, questionnaire

Testament 5 Bible **7** the Book **10** Scriptures **12** New Testament, Old Testament

testament 6 legacy **7** bequest **10** settlement

tester 6 canopy **8** examiner **10** questioner

testify 4 show **5** prove, swear **6** affirm, attest, evince **7** declare, signify **8** evidence, indicate, manifest **11** bear witness, demonstrate **12** give evidence

testimonial 5 medal **6** ribbon, trophy **7** tribute **8** citation, memorial, monument **9** affidavit, reference **10** deposition **11** certificate, endorsement **12** commendation **14** recommendation

testimony 5 proof **6** avowal **7** witness **8** averment, evidence **9** affidavit, statement **10** deposition, indication, profession **11** affirmation, attestation, endorsement **12** confirmation, verification **13** certification, corroboration, demonstration, documentation, manifestation **14** acknowledgment

testy 5 cross, moody **6** crabby, cranky, crusty, filthy, grumpy, snappy, sullen, touchy **7** fretful, peevish, waspish **8** captious, caviling, choleric, churlish, perverse, petulant, snappish, snarling

9 fractious, impatient, irascible, irritable, splenetic **10** ill-humored **11** acrimonious, contentious **12** cantankerous, faultfinding, sharp-tongued **13** quick-tempered, temperamental

tete-a-tete 4 chat, talk **6** parley **9** interview **12** conversation **13** confabulation

tether 3 tie **4** cord, rein, rope **5** chain, leash **6** fasten, halter, hobble, secure

Tethys
member of: 6 Titans
father: 6 Uranus
mother: 4 Gaea
husband: 7 Oceanus
mother of: 8 Oceanids **9** river gods
daughters: 13 three thousand
foster child: 4 Hera

Tetragrammaton
consonants in: 10 name for God **4** JHVH, IHVH, JHWH, YHVH, YHWH

Teutonic 5 Dutch **6** German, Gothic, Nordic **7** British, English **8** Germanic **12** Scandinavian
alphabet character: 4 rune
demon: 3 alp
goddess of death: 3 Hel, Ran
goddess of peace: 7 Nerthus
god of peace: 6 Balder
god of thunder: 4 Thor
god of war: 3 Tiu, Tyr
god of wisdom: 4 Odin

Teutonic Mythology see **17** Germanic Mythology

Texas
abbreviation: 2 TX **3** Tex
nickname: 8 Lone Star
capital: 6 Austin
largest city: 7 Houston
others: 4 Gail, Rice, Vega, Waco **5** Bryan, Marfa, Ozona, Pampa, Tyler, Wiley **6** Baylor, Borger, Dallas, Denton, El Paso, Kileen, Laredo, Odessa, Quanah, Sonora **7** Abilene, Denison, Lubbock **8** Amarillo, Beaumont, Floydada **9** Fort Worth, Galveston **10** San Antonio **13** Corpus Christi
college: 3 SMU, TCU **4** Rice **5** Lamar, Wiley **6** Austin, Baylor **7** St Mary's, Trinity **10** Texas A and M **12** Southwestern **14** Texas Christian **16** Abilene Christian **17** Southern Methodist
feature:
  fort: 5 Alamo
  national park: 7 Big Bend **18** Guadalupe Mountains
  national seashore: 11 Padre Island
  state park: 10 San Jacinto
tribe: 4 Adar, Waco **5** Caddo, Lipan **6** Apache, Biloxi, Jumano, Kichai, Shuman, Tejano **7** Alabama, Hasinai, Tonkawa **8** Comanche, Querecho **9** Coushatta, Karankawa
people: 10 James S Hogg **12** Edward M House, Thomas C Clark **13** John B Connally, Samuel Houston **14** Chester W Nimitz, Mirabeau B Lamar,

Samuel T Rayburn, Stephen F Austin, William B Travis **15** John Nance Garner, Thomas T Connally **19** Katherine Anne Porter
  explorer: 4 Vaca **7** La Salle
island: 5 Padre
lake: 6 Falcon, Sabine, Texoma **7** Amistad
river: 3 Red **5** Pecos **6** Brazos, Neches, Nueces, Sabine **7** Trinity **8** Colorado **9** Rio Grande **10** San Jacinto
land rank: 12 second
physical feature:
  bay: 13 Corpus Christi
  port: 7 Houston **9** Galveston **13** Corpus Christi
president: 11 George W Bush **12** George HW Bush **14** Lyndon B Johnson **17** Dwight D Eisenhower
  Republic of Texas: 10 Sam Houston
state admission: 12 twenty-eighth
state bird: 11 mockingbird
state flower: 10 bluebonnet, yellow rose
state motto: 10 Friendship
state song: 13 Texas Our Texas
state tree: 5 pecan
baseball team: 7 Rangers

text 5 motif, theme, topic, verse, words **6** manual, primer, sermon, thesis **7** content, passage, subject, wording **8** argument, sentence, textbook, workbook **9** paragraph, quotation **10** schoolbook **13** subject matter

textile 4 yarn **5** cloth, fiber **6** fabric **8** filament, material **9** yard goods **10** piece goods

texture 3 nap **4** feel, look **5** grain, touch, weave **6** makeup **7** quality, surface **8** fineness **9** character, structure **10** coarseness **11** composition

Tey, Josephine
real name: 19 Elizabeth MacKintosh
author of: 10 Brat Farrar **15** Miss Pym Disposes, The Singing Sands **17** The Daughter of Time **19** A Shilling for Candles
character: 9 Alan Grant

Thackeray, William Makepeace
author of: 9 Pendennis **10** Vanity Fair **11** Barry Lyndon, Henry Esmond, The Newcomes **13** The Virginians

Thaddeus of Arimathea see **5** Judas

Thai-Austronesian
language branch: 9 Thai-Kadai **12** Austronesian
includes: 5 Batak, Malay **6** Fijian, Samoan **7** Tagalog **8** Hawaiian, Javanese **15** Bahasa Indonesia
spoken in: 4 Fiji, Java **5** China, Samoa **6** Hawaii, Taiwan **7** Sumatra **9** Indonesia, Polynesia **10** Madagascar **11** Philippines **12** Easter Island

Thailand
name means: 13 land of the free
other name: 4 Siam **11** Prathet Thai
capital/largest city: 6 Bankok **7** Bangkok
  old capital: 8 Thonburi **9** Ayutthaya
others: 4 Ubon **5** Puket **6** Nakhon, Ranong **7** Ayudhya, Ayuthea, Lampang, Lamphur, Lopburi, Rahaeng, Singora, Songkla **8** Khonkaen, Kiangmai, Songkhla, Sukhotai, Thonburi **9** Ayutthaya, Chiangmai, Chiengmai **10** Ratchasima **11** Phitsanulok **14** Ubonratchthani
kingdom: 5 Funan **6** Khymer **8** Thonburi **9** Ayutthaya, Chiang Mai, Dvaravati, Sukhothai **12** Subarnabhumi
school: 9 Thammasat **13** Chulalongkorn
head of state: 4 king
measure: 2 wa **3** can, ken, niv, rai, sat, sok, wah **4** cohi, keup, niou, tang **5** kwien, leeng, sesti, vouah **6** kabiet, kanahn **7** chaimeu **8** changawn **9** anukabiet
monetary unit: 2 at **3** att **4** baht **5** cutty, fuang **6** pynung, salung **11** bullet money
weight: 3 bat, hap, pay, sen, sok **4** baht, haph, kati, klam **5** catty, chang, fuang, picul, pilul, tical **6** fluang, graini, salung, **7** tamlung
island: 2 Ko **3** Kut, Tao **4** Chan, Rawi **5** Chang, Lanta, Samui, Thalu **6** Libong, Phuket **7** Phangan, Terutao
lake: 9 Nong Lahan
mountain: 5 Dawna, Khieo **6** Phanom **8** Dang Raek, Kao Prawa, Maelamun **9** Khao Luang **11** Bilauktaung
highest point: 8 Inthanon **11** Doi Inthanon
river: 3 Chi, Mun, Nan, Yom **4** Ping **5** Menam **6** Mekong, Meping **7** Salween **10** Chaophraya
sea: 7 Andaman
physical feature:
  gulf: 4 Siam **8** Thailand
  isthmus: 3 Kra
  pass: 12 Three Pagodas
  peninsula: 5 Malay
  plateau: 5 Korat **6** Khorat
people: 3 Lao, Mon **4** Lawa, Shan, Thai **5** Malay **6** Indian, Khymer **7** Chinese, Siamese **9** Cambodian **10** Vietnamese
  king: 4 Rama **7** Chakkri, Mongkut **10** Chao Phraya **12** Prahjadhipok **13** Chulalongkorn **17** Bhumibol Adulyadej
  leader: 9 Phraruang **12** Kukrit-Pramoj
language: 3 Lao, Tai **4** Ahom, Shan, Thai **5** Kadai, Malay **7** Bangkok, Chinese, English **9** Krung Thep

religion: 5 Islam **8** Buddhism **12** Christianity, Confucianism **17** Theravada Buddhism

place:
  dam: 8 Bhumibol
  palace: 5 Grand
  ruins: 7 Ayuthia **9** Ayutthaya
  street: 7 Yawarai
  temple: 4 Dawn **7** Trimitr **10** Wat Phra Keo **11** Royal Chapel **13** Emerald Buddha

feature:
  canal: 5 klong
  clothing: 6 panung, sarong **12** saffron robes
  festival: 12 Surin Round Up
  houseboat: 6 sampan
  temple: 3 wat
  tree: 4 teak

food:
  fruit: 5 camut **6** durian, litchi, pomelo **8** rambutan **10** mangosteen

Thais
  author: 13 Anatole France
  character: 8 Athanael
  composer: 8 Massenet

Thalassa
  personifies: 3 sea

thalassic 6 marine **7** aquatic, deep-sea, neritic, oceanic, pelagic

Thales
  field: 11 mathematics
  nationality: 5 Greek
  discovered: 18 geometry principles
  predicted: 11 sun's eclipse

Thalestris
  character in: 16 The Rape of the Lock
  author: 4 Pope

Thalia
  member of: 5 Muses **6** Graces
  personifies: 6 comedy **13** idyllic poetry
  lover: 4 Zeus
  killed by: 5 Erato

Thallo
  member of: 5 Horae
  goddess of: 13 spring flowers

Thamyris
  vocation: 4 poet **8** musician
  father: 9 Philammon
  mother: 7 Argiope
  punished for: 9 arrogance
  punished by: 5 Muses
  punishment: 7 maiming **8** blinding

thanatophobia
  fear of: 5 death

Thanatos
  personifies: 5 death

thank 5 bless **12** be grateful to **13** be much obliged **18** express gratitude to

thankful 7 obliged **8** beholden, grateful **10** indebted to **12** appreciative, full of thanks **16** feeling gratitude **22** expressing appreciation

thankfulness 6 thanks **9** gratitude **12** appreciation, gratefulness

thankless 4 vain **7** ingrate, useless **8** bootless, caviling, critical, heedless **9** fruitless, unmindful, unwelcome **10** profitless, ungracious, ungrateful, uninviting, unpleasant, unrewarded, unthankful **11** distasteful, thoughtless, undesirable, unrewarding **12** disagreeable, faultfinding **13** inconsiderate, unappreciated **14** unacknowledged, unappreciative

thanks 5 grace **8** blessing **9** gratitude **11** benediction **12** appreciation, gratefulness

thanks be to God
  Latin: 10 Deo gratias

thanksgiving 6 thanks **8** blessing

Thanksgiving
  started by: 8 Bradford, Pilgrims
  traditional food: 4 corn, yams **6** turkey **10** pumpkin pie **13** sweet potatoes **14** cranberry sauce
  symbol: 9 ear of corn **12** horn of plenty

thank you
  French: 5 merci
  German: 5 danke
  Spanish: 7 gracias
  Italian: 6 grazie
  Japanese: 4 domo

Thank You, Jeeves
  author: 11 P G Wodehouse

thank you very much
  French: 9 merci bien **13** merci beaucoup
  German: 10 danke schon
  Japanese: 11 domo arigato
  Spanish: 13 muchas gracias

Thatcher, Becky
  character in: 9 Tom Sawyer
  author: 5 Twain

Thatcher, Judge
  character in: 15 (The Adventures of) Huckleberry Finn
  author: 5 Twain

That Girl
  character: 8 Ann Marie, Lou Marie **10** Helen Marie, Ruth Bauman **11** Jerry Bauman **12** Don Hollinger, Judy Bessemer **14** Dr Leon Bessemer
  cast: 9 Lew Parker **10** Ted Bessell **11** Alice Borden, Bonnie Scott, Marlo Thomas **12** Bernie Kopell **13** Dabney Coleman **14** Carolyn Daniels, Rosemary DeCamp

that is
  Latin: 2 ie **5** id est

that is to say
  Latin: 3 viz **9** videlicet

That '70s Show
  network: 3 FOX
  cast: 8 Don Stark (Bob Pinciotti) **9** Mila Kunis (Jackie Burkhart) **11** Debra Jo Rupp (Kitty Forman), Laura Prepon (Donna Pinciotti), Topher Grace (Eric Forman) **13** Ashton Kutcher (Michael Kelso), Kurtwood Smith (Red Forman) **14** Danny Masterson (Steven Hyde) **16** Wilmer Valderrama (Fez)

that's life
  French: 9 c'est la vie

thaw 4 melt, warm **5** relax **6** soften, unbend, warm up **7** liquefy, melting, thawing **8** dissolve **11** break the ice

Thea
  companion of: 7 Artemis
  ravished by: 6 Aeolus
  changed into: 4 mare
    mare named: 6 Euippe

theater 4 site **5** arena, drama, house, movie, odeum, place, scene, stage **6** cinema, lyceum **7** gallery, setting **8** assembly, audience, coliseum **9** colosseum, music hall, playhouse **10** assemblage, auditorium, movie house, spectators **11** histrionics, lecture hall, theatricals **12** amphitheater, show business

theatrical 4 film **5** hammy, movie, showy, stage, stagy **6** flashy **7** fustian, show-biz, stilted **8** affected, dramatic, mannered, thespian **9** grandiose, unnatural **10** artificial, histrionic **11** exaggerated, extravagant, pretentious, spectacular **12** magniloquent, ostentatious, show-business **13** entertainment, grandiloquent **14** larger-than-life

theatrical trick
  French: 13 coup de theatre

Thebaid
  author: 7 Statius
  character: 4 Atys **5** Creon **6** Ismene, Tydeus **7** Jocasta, Theseus **8** Antigone, Capaneus, Eteocles, Opheltes, Tiresias **9** Menoeceus, Polynices **10** Amphiaraus, Hippomedon, Melanippus

the bottle 5 booze, drink, sauce **6** liquor **7** alcohol **8** demon rum

the dansant 8 tea dance

thee therefore
  Latin: 8 te igitur

theft 5 fraud **7** larceny, looting, robbery **8** burglary, filching, rustling, stealing, thievery **9** hijacking, pilfering, swindling **10** purloining **11** shoplifting **12** embezzlement
  god of: 6 Hermes **7** Mercury

Theia
  also: 4 Thia
  member of: 6 Titans
  father: 6 Uranus
  mother: 4 Gaea
  brother: 8 Hyperion
  mother of: 8 Cercopes
  son: 6 Helios
  daughter: 3 Eos **6** Selene

the life of the land is maintained by righteousness
Hawaiian: **52** ua mau ke ea o ka aina i ka pono
motto of: **6** Hawaii

Thelma & Louise
director: **11** Ridley Scott
cast: **8** Brad Pitt (J. D.) **10** Geena Davis (Thelma) **12** Harvey Keitel (Hal) **13** Michael Madsen (Jimmy), Susan Sarandon (Louise) **17** Stephen Tobolowsky (Max) **19** Christopher McDonald (Darryl)

Them
author: **15** Joyce Carol Oates

theme 3 air **4** song, text, tune **5** essay, focus, motif, point, topic, tract **6** melody, report, review, strain, thesis **7** keynote, premise, subject **8** argument, critique, question, treatise **9** discourse, leitmotif, monograph **10** commentary **11** composition, proposition **12** dissertation

thence 6 whence **9** from there, therefore **11** accordingly, in due course **13** from that place

the next world 6 Heaven **8** eternity, paradise **12** the hereafter **14** the world to come

the norm 7 the mean, the rule **9** the median **10** the average **14** the common thing

the Occident 7 the West **20** the western hemisphere

theologian *see* **22** philosopher/theologian

theological 4 holy **6** sacred **8** Biblical, dogmatic **9** apostolic, canonical, doctrinal, religious, spiritual **10** scriptural **14** ecclesiastical

theology 5 dogma **8** divinity, doctrine, religion

Theophane
bore: **3** ram
fleece of ram: **6** golden

theoretical 8 abstract, academic, putative **11** conjectural, postulatory, speculative **12** hypothetical, nonpractical **13** suppositional

theorize 5 infer, posit, think **6** assume **7** imagine, presume, propose, suppose, surmise **8** propound **9** formulate, postulate, predicate, speculate **10** conjecture **11** hypothecate, hypothesize

theory 3 law **4** idea, view **5** guess **6** belief, notion, thesis **7** concept, opinion, science, surmise, thought **8** doctrine, ideology, judgment **9** deduction, postulate, principle **10** conclusion, conjecture, hypothesis, persuasion, philosophy **11** presumption, speculation, supposition

therapeutic, therapeutical 7 healing **8** curative, remedial, salutary, sanative **11** restorative **12** ameliorative

therapy 7 healing **9** treatment **14** rehabilitation

thereafter 5 later **9** after that, afterward **10** afterwards, from then on **11** thenceforth **12** subsequently **14** from that time on

therefore 2 so **4** ergo, thus **5** hence **11** accordingly **12** consequently, on that ground **13** for that reason, in consequence, on that account **14** for which reason

there is no disputing about tastes
Latin: **27** de gustibus non est disputandum

there it is
French: **5** voila

Therese Raquin
author: **9** Emile Zola
character: **7** Camille, Laurent

thereupon 4 then **6** at once **7** thereon **8** directly, suddenly, upon that **9** forthwith, in a moment, upon which **11** immediately **12** straightaway, without delay

thermometer
invented by: **7** Galileo, Reaumur
mercury: **10** Fahrenheit

Thero
nurse of: **4** Ares

theropod
type of: **8** dinosaur
member: **10** Allosaurus, Antrodemus **11** Coelophysis, Gorgosaurus **13** Albertosaurus, Compsognathus, Struthiomimus, Tyrannosaurus

Theroux, Paul
author of: **9** Saint Jack **12** The Cold World **13** Blinding Light, Hotel Honolulu **16** The Mosquito Coast **19** To the Ends of the Earth **20** Riding the Iron Rooster **21** The Great Railway Bazaar **23** The Old Patagonian Express

Thersites
mentioned in: **5** Iliad
origin: **5** Greek
characteristics: **4** ugly **8** deformed **11** quarrelsome
accused Agamemnon of: **5** greed
accused Achilles of: **9** cowardice
fought in: **9** Trojan War
killed by: **8** Achilles

the same as 4 like **7** equal to **9** a match for **12** comparable to, equivalent to, tantamount to **16** commensurate with

thesaurus 8 synonymy **10** word finder **11** synonymicon **12** word treasury **13** synonym finder **17** synonym dictionary **18** semantic dictionary

Thescelosaurus
type: **8** dinosaur **10** ornithopod
location: **6** Canada **12** United States
period: **10** Cretaceous

These Three
director: **12** William Wyler

based on play by: **14** Lillian Hellman (The Children's Hour)
cast: **10** Alma Kruger, Joel McCrea **11** Merle Oberon **13** Miriam Hopkins **15** Bonita Granville, Catherine Doucet

Theseus
king of: **6** Athens
father: **6** Aegeus **8** Poseidon
mother: **6** Aethra
wife: **7** Phaedra
consort: **9** Hippolyta
lover: **7** Ariadne
son: **6** Acamas **8** Demophon **10** Hippolytus, Melanippus
helmsman: **10** Nausithous
killed: **5** Sinis **6** Sciron **8** Minotaur **10** Cretan bull, Procrustes

thesis 5 essay, paper, tract **6** notion, theory **7** article, concept, surmise **8** argument, critique, proposal, treatise **9** discourse, monograph, postulate, term paper **10** commentary, conjecture, hypothesis **11** composition, proposition, speculation, supposition **12** disquisition, dissertation

Thesmia
epithet of: **7** Demeter
means: **12** goddess of law

Thesmophorus
epithet of: **7** Demeter
means: **8** lawgiver

thespian 3 ham **4** star **5** actor, extra **6** co-star, player, walk-on **7** actress, ingenue, trouper **8** juvenile **9** bit-player, guest star, performer, tragedian **10** leading man **11** leading lady, stage player

Thespis 9 Greek poet
originator of: **12** Greek tragedy

Thessalus
king of: **8** Thessaly
father: **5** Jason **8** Hercules
mother: **5** Medea **9** Chalciope

the state
Latin: **10** res publica

Thetis
member of: **7** Nereids
husband: **6** Peleus
sister: **8** Eurynome
son: **8** Achilles

the very words
Latin: **14** ipsissima verba

the world over 10 every place, everywhere, far and wide, near and far **11** in all places

They Shoot Horses, Don't They?
director: **13** Sydney Pollack
cast: **8** Gig Young **9** Bruce Dern, Jane Fonda **10** Red Buttons **12** Susannah York **13** Bonnie Bedelia **15** Michael Sarrazin
Oscar for: **15** supporting actor (Young)

They Won't Forget
director: **11** Mervyn LeRoy
cast: **10** Lana Turner, Otto Kruger **11**

Allyn Joslyn, Claude Rains **12** Elisha Cook Jr **13** Gloria Dickson

thiasus
also: **7** thiasos
group worshipping: **11** patron deity
followers of: **8** Dionysus
followers called: **6** satyrs **7** maenads

thick 3 big, fat **4** deep, dull, dumb, slow, wide **5** broad, bulky, close, dense, fuzzy, great, heavy, husky, piled, solid **6** chummy, heaped, hoarse, lavish, obtuse, packed, strong, stupid, viscid, wooden **7** blurred, clotted, compact, copious, crowded, decided, devoted, doltish, extreme, intense, liberal, muffled, profuse, teeming, throaty, viscous **8** abundant, familiar, friendly, generous, guttural, intimate, profound, sisterly, swarming **9** brotherly, condensed, fatheaded, glutinous, plenteous, unstinted **10** coagulated, dull-witted, gelatinous, indistinct, munificent, pronounced, slow-witted **11** inseparable, overflowing **12** concentrated, impenetrable, inarticulate

thicken 3 set **4** cake, clot, jell **5** muddy **6** darken, deepen, muddle **7** compact, congeal, jellify **8** condense **9** coagulate, intensify **10** gelatinize

thicket 4 bush, wood **5** brake, brush, copse, grove, scrub **6** bushes, covert, forest, shrubs **7** bracken **9** shrubbery **10** underbrush **11** undergrowth

thickheaded 4 dull, dumb, slow **5** blank, dense, dopey, thick **6** obtuse, stupid **8** ignorant **9** dim-witted, fatheaded **10** boneheaded, dull-witted, half-witted, slow-witted **11** blockheaded, thick-witted **12** dunderheaded, thick-skulled **13** chuckleheaded, knuckleheaded

thickset 5 bulky, close, dense, dumpy, husky, solid, squat, stout, tubby **6** chunky, packed, stocky, stubby, stumpy, sturdy **8** close-set, heavyset, roly-poly

thickskinned 4 hard **5** horny, tough **6** inured **7** callous **8** callused, hardened **9** unfeeling, unmovable **10** impervious, insensible **11** insensitive, unconcerned **13** imperturbable, unsusceptible **14** pachydermatous

thick-skulled 4 dull **5** dense **6** stupid **11** thickheaded **12** dunderheaded

thick-witted 4 dull, slow **5** dense **6** stupid **7** idiotic, moronic **9** dim-witted, imbecilic **11** thickheaded **12** dunderheaded, simple-minded

thief 5 crook **6** bandit, mugger, robber **7** burglar, filcher, rustler **8** hijacker, pilferer, swindler **9** defrauder, embezzler, holdup man, larcenist, purloiner, racketeer **10** highwayman, pickpocket, shoplifter **12** housebreaker, kleptomaniac **13** confidence man, pursesnatcher **14** second-story man

Thief of Bagdad, The
director: **9** Tim Whelan **12** Ludwig Berger **13** Michael Powell
cast: **4** Sabu **9** Rex Ingram **10** John Justin, June Duprez **11** Conrad Veidt

Thieves' Carnival
also: **15** Le Bal des Voleurs
author: **11** Jean Anouilh

thievish 3 sly **6** sneaky **7** furtive **8** stealthy, thieving **9** dishonest, larcenous, secretive, thieflike **13** light-fingered, surreptitious **14** sticky-fingered

thigh 3 ham, leg **4** hock **5** femur, flank, ilium **6** gammon
pain: **8** meralgia

Thimbu, Thimphu
capital of: **6** Bhutan

thin 4 fine, lank, lean, slim, weak **5** faint, gaunt, lanky, prune, runny, scant, sheer, spare, water **6** dilute, feeble, narrow, not fat, reduce, skinny, slight, sparse, watery **7** curtail, diluted, fragile, scrawny, slender, spindly **8** delicate, diminish, finespun **9** emaciated, water down **10** inadequate, threadlike **11** transparent **12** insufficient **13** unsubstantial

thin-blooded 3 wan **4** pale, weak **6** anemic, sickly

thing, things 3 act **4** deed, feat, gear, item **5** event, gizmo, goods, point **6** action, affair, aspect, detail, dingus, entity, gadget, matter, object, person **7** article, clothes, concern, effects, feature, thought **8** business, clothing, creature, movables **9** doohickey, equipment, happening, statement **10** belongings, human being, occurrence, particular, proceeding **11** eventuality, living being, possessions, thingamabob, thingamajig, transaction **12** circumstance **13** paraphernalia

Thing
legislative body of: **11** Scandinavia
thing already done
French: **12** fait accompli
thingamajig 5 gizmo **6** doodad, gadget **11** contraption, contrivance, thingamabob **15** whatchamacallit
thing of no value
Latin: **5** nihil
things done
Latin: **9** res gestae
think 4 deem, mean, plan **5** brood, fancy, guess, judge **6** design, expect, intend, ponder, reason, recall, reckon **7** believe, dwell on, imagine, presume, propose, purpose, reflect, suppose, surmise **8** cogitate, conceive, conclude, contrive, meditate, mull over, remember, ruminate **9** recollect, speculate **10** anticipate, deliberate, have in mind, keep in mind **11** con-

template, use one's mind, use one's wits **13** rack one's brain

thinkable 8 knowable **10** imaginable **11** conceivable, perceivable

think about 4 mull **6** debate, ponder **7** reflect **8** consider, mull over **10** deliberate

think alike 5 agree **11** be of one mind, see eye to eye

thinker 4 sage **6** savant, wizard **7** egghead, scholar **9** intellect **10** mastermind **11** mental giant, philosopher **13** metaphysician

Thinker, The
by: **5** Rodin

think fit 4 deem **5** deign, stoop **7** consent **10** condescend

think highly of 5 favor, honor, value **6** admire, esteem, revere **7** approve, respect **8** look up to, venerate **10** set store by

think ill of 4 hate **5** decry **6** detest **7** condemn, deplore, despise, dislike **8** object to **9** abominate, disparage, frown upon **10** disapprove **13** look askance at **14** discountenance **15** take exception to **16** find unacceptable, view with disfavor

thinking 4 view **5** smart, stand, study **6** belief, bright **7** concept, surmise, thought **8** cultured, educated, judgment, position, rational, studious **9** brainwork, deduction, inference, reasoning **10** conclusion, cultivated, impression, meditation, meditative, reflection, reflective, rumination, thoughtful **11** intelligent, speculation **12** deliberation **13** consideration, contemplation, contemplative, philosophical, sophisticated, using one's head **15** paying attention

think over 5 study, weigh **8** cogitate, consider, mull over **11** reflect upon **12** deliberate on

think through 5 weigh **6** ponder **7** analyze **8** appraise, consider, evaluate

think up 5 frame, hatch **6** create, invent **7** concoct, dream up **8** conceive, contrive

think well of 4 like **6** admire **8** look up to **10** appreciate

Thin Man, The
author: **15** Dashiell Hammett
character: **4** Asta (pet terrier) **7** Morelli **11** Nick Charles, Nora Charles **13** Arthur Nunheim, Mimi Jorgensen **15** Herbert Macaulay **18** Christian Jorgensen
Wynant family: **5** Clyde **7** Dorothy, Gilbert
director: **11** W S Van Dyke II
cast: **4** Asta **8** Myrna Loy (Nora Charles) **13** William Powell (Nick Charles)
thin man is: **6** victim
sequel (film): **14** Another Thin Man **15** After the Thin Man **16** Song of

the Thin Man **18** The Thin Man Goes Home

thin out 5 prune **6** dilute, reduce, weaken **7** weed out **9** water down **10** adulterate

Thin Red Line, The
author: **10** James Jones
director: **14** Terrence Malick
cast: **8** Sean Penn (Edward Welsh) **9** Dash Mihok (Doll), Jared Leto (Whyte), Nick Nolte (Gordon Tall) **10** Ben Chaplin (Jack Bell), John Cusack (John Gaff) **11** Adrien Brody (Fife), Elias Koteas (James Staros), Jim Caviezel (Witt), John C Reilly (Storm) **12** John Travolta (Quintard) **13** George Clooney (Charles Bosche) **14** Tim Blake Nelson (Tills), Woody Harrelson (Keck)

thinskinned 5 cross, huffy, sulky, testy **6** grumpy, sullen, touchy **7** crabbed, peevish **8** petulant, snappish **9** irascible, irritable, sensitive, squeamish **11** ill-tempered, quarrelsome, susceptible **12** cantankerous **13** oversensitive **14** hypersensitive

third estate
French: **9** tiers etat

Third Man, The
director: **9** Carol Reed
based on story by: **12** Graham Greene
cast: **10** Alida Valli **11** Orson Welles (Harry Lime) **12** Joseph Cotten, Trevor Howard **16** Wilfrid Hyde-White
setting: **6** Vienna

Third Watch
network: **3** NBC
cast: **7** Nia Long (Sasha Monroe) **8** Coby Bell (Tyrone Davis Jr), Kim Raver (Kim Zambrano) **9** Tia Texada (Maritza Cruz) **10** Amy Carlson (Alex Taylor), Chris Bauer (Fred Yokas), Jason Wiles (Maurice Boscorelli), Molly Price (Faith Yokas) **12** Eddie Cibrian (Jimmy Doherty), Michael Beach (Monte "Doc" Parker), Skipp Sudduth (John Sullivan) **15** Anthony Ruivivar (Carlos Nieto)

Third Wave, The
author: **12** Alvin Toffler

thirst 3 yen **4** itch, lust, pant **5** ardor, covet, crave, yearn **6** desire, fervor, hunger, relish **7** craving, passion, stomach **8** appetite, keenness, voracity, yearning **9** hanker for, hankering **11** thirstiness

thirsty 3 dry **4** avid **5** eager **7** parched **9** thirsting

Thirteen O'Clock
author: **19** Stephen Vincent Benet

Thirty-Nine Steps, The (The 39 Steps)
author: **10** John Buchan
director: **15** Alfred Hitchcock
cast: **11** Robert Donat **13** Godfrey

Tearle, Lucie Mannheim, Peggy Ashcroft **16** Madeleine Carroll

Thisbe
loved: **7** Pyramus
location: **7** Babylon
death by: **7** suicide
death at tomb of: **5** Ninus

this is
Latin: **6** hoc est

This Is Your Life
host: **12** Ralph Edwards
announcer: **9** Bob Warren

thistle 7 Cirsium
varieties: **3** Oat **4** Bull, Holy, Milk, Star **5** Glove, Plume, White **6** Canada, Cotton, Golden, Scotch, Silver **7** Blessed, St Mary's **8** Fishbone, Mountain, Plumless **9** Argentine, Thornless **10** Great globe, Small globe **11** Mountain sow **14** Acanthus-leaved
emblem of: **8** Scotland

Thomas 7 apostle
means: **4** twin
also called: **7** Didymus, Doubter **8** Doubting

Thomas, Ambroise
born: **4** Metz **6** France
composer of: **6** Mignon

Thomas, Danny
real name: **16** Amos Muzyad Jacobs
born: **11** Deerfield MI
daughter: **11** Marlo Thomas
roles: **13** The Jazz Singer **16** Make Room for Daddy **19** I'll See You in My Dreams

Thomas, Dylan
author of: **8** Fern Hill **13** Under Milk Wood **23** A Child's Christmas in Wales

Thomas, George H
nickname: **20** The Rock of Chickamauga
served in: **8** Civil War **10** Mexican War
side: **5** Union
commander of: **19** Army of the Cumberland
battle: **9** Nashville **11** Chattanooga, Chickamauga

Thomas, Marlo
real name: **14** Margaret Thomas
born: **9** Detroit MI
father: **11** Danny Thomas
husband: **11** Phil Donahue
roles: **8** That Girl

Thomas, W Morgan
creator/artist of: **22** Sheena Queen of the Jungle

Thomas a Kempis
author of: **20** The Imitation of Christ

Thomson, Joseph John
field: **7** physics
nationality: **7** British
discovered: **8** electron
awarded: **10** Nobel Prize

Thomson, Thomas John

born: **6** Canada **9** Claremont
artwork: **9** Spring Ice **11** The Jack Pine **12** Northern Lake **13** Northern River

Thomson, Virgil
born: **12** Kansas City MO
composer of: **9** Portraits **16** The Mother of Us All **21** Four Saints in Three Acts

thong 4 band **5** strap, strip **6** sandal **7** binding **8** swimsuit **9** underwear

Thor
origin: **12** Scandinavian
god of: **4** rain **7** farming, thunder
rode: **7** chariot
chariot pulled by: **5** goats
wielded: **6** hammer **7** Miolnir
father: **4** Odin **5** Othin

thorax 5 chest, trunk **6** breast, cavity **8** forebody

Thoreau, Henry David
author of: **6** Walden (Life in the Woods) **17** Civil Disobedience

thorium
chemical symbol: **2** Th

thorn 2 th **4** rune

thorn 3 woe **4** bane, barb, care, gall, spur **5** cross, curse, spike, spine, sting **6** plague **7** prickle, scourge, torment, trouble **8** nuisance, vexation **9** annoyance, sore point **10** affliction, bitter pill, infliction, irritation

thorn 9 Crataegus
varieties: **3** Box **4** Lily, Pear **5** Camel, Hedge, White **6** Christ, Karroo, Mysore, Sallow, Sickle, Winter **7** Thirsty **8** Cockspur, Egyptian, Kangaroo, Quick-set **9** Jerusalem, Paper-bark **10** Washington **11** Crucifixion **13** Yellow-fruited

Thornbirds, The
author: **17** Colleen McCullough

Thornburg, Betty June
real name of: **11** Betty Hutton

thorn in the side 4 bane **7** torment **9** annoyance **10** irritation

thorny 4 dire, hard **5** spiny, tough **6** barbed, spiked, sticky, trying **7** arduous, brambly, complex, crucial, irksome, prickly **8** annoying, critical, involved, ticklish **9** bristling, dangerous, difficult, vexatious **10** formidable, nettlesome, perplexing **11** complicated, troublesome

thorough 4 full, pure **5** sheer, total, utter **6** entire **7** careful, perfect, uniform **8** absolute, complete, of a piece **9** downright, out-and-out **10** consistent, definitive, exhaustive, meticulous **11** painstaking, unmitigated, unqualified **12** all-embracing, all-inclusive

thoroughbred 7 unmixed **8** purebred **9** blueblood, pedigreed, racehorse **10** aristocrat **11** full-blooded, pure-blooded **12** silkstocking

thoroughfare 4 road **6** avenue, street

7 freeway, highway, parkway, roadway, thruway **8** main road, turnpike **9** boulevard, concourse **10** expressway, interstate **12** superhighway **13** through street

thoroughgoing 5 utter **6** arrant **7** extreme **8** outright **9** confirmed, notorious, out-and-out **11** undisguised, unmitigated

thoroughly 5 fully **7** totally, utterly **8** entirely **9** carefully, downright, out-and-out, perfectly, uniformly **10** absolutely, completely, throughout **11** inclusively **12** consistently, exhaustively, meticulously **13** in all respects **15** from top to bottom **17** through and through **18** from beginning to end

Thorpe, Jim (James Francis)
  sport: 8 baseball, football **13** track and field
  won: 8 Olympics **9** decathlon
  named: 11 All-American

Thorvaldsen, Albert Bertel
  born: 7 Denmark **10** Copenhagen
  artwork: 4 Hope **9** Lord Byron **14** Cupid and Psyche **16** The Lion of Lucerne **22** Cupid and the Three Graces **24** Jason with the Golden Fleece

Thoth
  origin: 8 Egyptian
  god of: 5 magic **6** wisdom **8** learning
  scribe of: 4 gods
  inventor of: 6 letter **7** numbers
  corresponds to: 6 Hermes
  head of: 3 dog **4** ibis

though 3 tho, yet **4** even, that **5** still **6** albeit, even if **7** granted **8** although, granting **9** admitting **12** nevertheless **15** notwithstanding

thought 3 aim, end **4** goal, idea, plan, view **5** credo, dogma, fancy, tenet **6** belief, caring, design, intent, musing, notion, object, regard, scheme **7** concept, concern, opinion, purpose, reverie, surmise **8** doctrine, judgment, kindness, thinking **9** attention, intention, objective, sentiment **10** brown study, cogitation, conception, conclusion, meditation, reflection, rumination **11** expectation, imagination, speculation, supposition **12** anticipation, deliberation **13** consideration, contemplation, introspection
  French: 6 pensee

thoughtful 4 kind **6** caring, loving, musing **7** pensive, probing, serious, wistful **8** thinking **9** attentive **10** meditative, neighborly, reflective, solicitous **11** considerate, kindhearted **13** contemplative, introspective

thoughtfulness 7 probing, thought **8** kindness, thinking **10** meditation, reflection **11** questioning **13** attentiveness, consideration, contemplation **14** solicitousness **15** kindheartedness

thoughtless 4 dumb, rash, rude **5**

silly **6** stupid, unkind **7** foolish **8** careless, heedless, impolite, reckless **9** imprudent **10** ill-advised, indiscreet, neglectful, unthinking **11** harebrained, improvident, inadvertent, inattentive, insensitive **12** absent-minded, unreflecting **13** ill-considered, inconsiderate, rattlebrained **14** scatterbrained

thoughtlessness 7 neglect **8** rashness, rudeness **9** oversight, unconcern **10** imprudence, negligence, unkindness **11** inattention **12** carelessness, heedlessness, impoliteness, recklessness **13** insensitivity **15** inattentiveness **16** absentmindedness

Thousand Clowns, A
  director: 7 Fred Coe
  based on play by: 11 Herb Gardner
  cast: 11 Barry Gordon **12** Jason Robards, Martin Balsam **13** Barbara Harris
  setting: 11 New York City
  Oscar for: 15 supporting actor (Balsam)

Thousand Days, A
  author: 20 Arthur M Schlesinger Jr

thou too
  Latin: 8 tu quoque

thrall 4 serf **5** slave **6** chains **7** bondage, serfdom, servant, slavery **9** servitude **11** enslavement, subjugation

thralldom 6 chains **7** bondage, serfdom, slavery **9** servitude **11** enslavement, subjugation

thrash 4 beat, cane, drub, flog, jerk, lash, maul, toss, whip **5** birch, flail, heave, solve, spank, strap **6** jiggle, joggle, plunge, pommel, squirm, switch, thresh, tumble, wiggle, writhe **7** flounce, resolve, scourge, trounce **8** argue out, lambaste **9** thresh out **10** flagellate

threadbare 4 dull, worn **5** banal, stale, stock, tacky, trite **6** boring, frayed, jejune, ragged, shabby **7** cliched, humdrum, napless, prosaic, raveled, routine, worn-out **8** bromidic, everyday, pileworn **9** hackneyed, well-known **11** commonplace, stereotyped **12** conventional, overfamiliar **15** the worse for wear

threads 4 duds, togs **6** attire **7** apparel, clothes, strands, strings **8** clothing, garments **9** filaments

threat 4 omen, risk **5** peril **6** danger, hazard, menace **7** ill omen, portent, warning **8** jeopardy **10** foreboding **11** commination, premonition **12** intimidation

threaten 3 cow **4** warn **6** impend, menace **7** imperil **8** endanger, forewarn, hang over **9** terrorize **10** be imminent, intimidate, jeopardize

threatening 4 grim **7** baleful, ominous, warning **8** alarming, imminent, menacing, sinister **9** ill-omened, impending **10** forbidding, foreboding **11**

approaching, forewarning, terrorizing **12** inauspicious, intimidating, unpropitious

three
  French: 5 trois

Three-Cornered Hat, The
  author: 21 Pedro Antonio de Alarcon

Three Faces of Eve, The
  director: 15 Nunnally Johnson
  cast: 8 Lee J Cobb **9** Nancy Kulp **10** David Wayne **12** Vince Edwards **14** Joanne Woodward
    narration by: 13 Alistair Cooke
  Oscar for: 7 actress (Woodward)

Three Kings
  director: 13 David O Russell
  cast: 7 Ice Cube (Elgin) **8** Nora Dunn (Adriana Cruz) **10** Spike Jonze (Conrad Vig) **11** Cliff Curtis (Amir Abdullah) **12** Jamie Kennedy (Walter Wogaman), Mark Wahlberg (Troy Barlow) **13** George Clooney (Archie Gates), Said Taghmaoui (Said) **17** Mykelti Williamson (Horn)

Three Lives
  includes: 9 Melanctha **11** The Good Anna **13** The Gentle Lena
  author: 13 Gertrude Stein

Three Men in a Boat
  author: 13 Jerome K Jerome

Three Musketeers, The
  author: 14 Alexandre Dumas (pere)
  director: 13 Richard Lester
  character: 5 Athos **6** Aramis **7** Porthos **8** Planchet **9** D'Artagnan **12** Lady de Winter **17** Cardinal Richelieu **18** Constance Bonacieux
  cast: 10 Oliver Reed **11** Faye Dunaway (Milady), Michael York (D'Artagnan), Raquel Welch **12** Frank Findlay **14** Charlton Heston, Christopher Lee **16** Geraldine Chaplin **18** Richard Chamberlain
  sequel: 17 The Four Musketeers

Threepenny Opera, The
  author: 6 Brecht
  composer: 5 Weill
  based on: 15 The Beggar's Opera
  by: 7 John Gay
  song: 11 Mack the Knife

three R's 6 'riting **7** reading **9** 'rithmatic

Three's Company
  character: 5 Larry **9** Janet Wood **10** Helen Roper **11** Chrissy Snow, Jack Tripper **12** Stanley Roper
  cast: 10 John Ritter, Norman Fell **11** Joyce DeWitt **12** Audra Lindley, Richard Kline **13** Suzanne Somers

Three Sisters
  director: 10 John Sichel **15** Laurence Olivier
  author: 12 Anton Chekhov
  character: 13 Fyodor Kuligin **14** Baron Tusenbach, Vassily Solyony **17** Alexandr Vershinin
    Prozorov family: 4 Olga **5** Irina,

Masha **6** Andrey **7** Natasha
cast: 9 Alan Bates **11** Derek Jacobi,
Jeanne Watts **13** Joan Plowright,
Louise Purnell **15** Laurence Olivier

threnody 5 dirge, elegy **6** lament **7**
requiem

threshold 4 dawn, door, edge, sill **5**
brink, limen, onset, start, verge **6** portal **7** doorway, gateway, opening,
prelude **8** doorsill, entrance **9** beginning, groundsel, inception **10** ground-
sill **11** entranceway **12** commencement **13** starting point

thrift 7 economy **8** prudence **9** frugality, husbandry, parsimony **10** moderation **11** sparingness, thriftiness **14** reasonableness **15** closefistedness **16**
parsimoniousness

thriftiness 5 tight **6** thrift **7** economy
8 prudence **9** frugality, parsimony **13**
penny-pinching **15** closefistedness,
tightfistedness **16** parsimoniousness

thriftless 6 lavish **8** feckless, prodigal,
wasteful **11** extravagant, improvident

thrifty 6 frugal, saving, stingy **7** sparing **9** niggardly, penny-wise **10** economical **11** closefisted, economizing,
tightfisted **12** parsimonious **13** penny-
pinching

thrill 4 fire, glow, kick, stir **5** flush,
rouse, throb **6** arouse, excite, quiver,
tickle, tingle, tremor **7** delight, impress, inspire, tremble **9** adventure,
electrify, enrapture, galvanize, stimulate, transport **12** satisfaction

thrilled 4 agog **7** excited **9** delighted,
overjoyed **11** transported

thrilling 7 awesome **8** engaging, exciting, riveting, stirring **9** absorbing, exquisite **10** delightful **11** fascinating,
pleasurable, provocative, sensational,
tantalizing, titillating **12** electrifying

thrip
variety: 6 banded **10** tube tailed **11**
heterothrip, merothripid

thrive 3 wax **4** boom **5** bloom, get on
6 fatten **7** burgeon, prosper, succeed
8 flourish, get ahead, grow rich

thriving 4 busy, lush, rank, rich **7**
wealthy, well-off **8** blooming, in clover, vigorous, well-to-do **9** flowering,
luxuriant **10** blossoming, prospering,
prosperous, succeeding, successful **11**
flourishing

throat 3 maw **4** craw, gula, neck **5**
gorge **6** gullet **7** chamber, jugulum,
passage, pharynx
lozenge: 6 pastil
nautical: 3 jaw **4** jaws, nock
part: 6 fauces, larynx, tonsil **7** glottis,
trachea
pertaining to: 5 gular
seizing: 4 knot **5** hitch **12** cuckold's
knot
swelling: 6 goiter

throaty 3 dry, low **4** base, deep **5**
gruff, husky, thick **6** hoarse **7**

cracked, grating, rasping **8** croaking,
guttural, resonant, sonorous **9** full-
toned

throb 4 beat, jerk, pant **5** heave, pulse,
shake **6** quiver, tremor, twitch **7** beating, flutter, pulsate, shaking, tremble,
vibrate **9** palpitate, pulsation, quivering, throbbing, trembling, vibration **10**
fluttering **11** oscillation, palpitation **13**
reverberation

throes 5 agony, chaos, pangs **6** ordeal,
spasms, tumult **7** anguish, turmoil **8**
disorder, paroxysm, upheaval **9** confusion, paroxysms **10** convulsion, disruption

thrombus 4 clot **9** blood clot **11** coagulation

throng 3 jam **4** army, cram, herd,
host, mass, mill, pack, rush **5** bunch,
crowd, crush, flock, flood, horde,
press, surge, swarm **6** deluge, gather,
huddle, stream **7** cluster, collect **8** assemble, converge **9** multitude **10** assemblage, congregate

thronged 4 full **6** jammed, mobbed,
packed **7** crammed, crowded, flocked,
swarmed, teeming **8** swarming **9** congested, jampacked **11** overflowing

throttle 3 gag, gas **4** stop **5** block,
burke, check, choke **6** stifle **7** garrote,
seal off, shut off, silence, smother **8**
choke off, gas pedal, strangle **9** fuel
lever, fuel valve **11** strangulate

through, thru 4 done, past **5** ended **6**
direct **7** express **8** finished, from A to
Z, to the end **9** all the way, completed, concluded **10** terminated **12**
long-distance **15** from first to last **18**
from beginning to end **20** from one
end to the other

through and through 5 total **6**
wholly **7** totally, utterly **8** complete
10 completely, thoroughly **15** from
top to bottom **18** from beginning to
end **20** from one end to the other

through my fault
Latin: 8 mea culpa

throughout 7 all over **10** all the time,
everywhere **11** in every part **16** all
the way through **18** from beginning
to end

Through the Looking Glass
sequel to: 28 Alice's Adventures in
Wonderland
author: 12 Lewis Carroll
character: 4 Gnat, Lion **5** Alice, Di-
nah **7** Red King, Unicorn **8** Red
Queen **9** Red Knight, White King **10**
Tweedledee, Tweedledum, White
Queen **11** Black Kitten, White Kitten,
White Knight **12** Humpty Dumpty

throw 3 lob, pit, put, shy **4** cast, hurl,
shot, toss **5** chuck, fling, floor, heave,
impel, pitch, place, put in, put on,
sling **6** hurtle, launch, let fly, propel,
unseat **7** project **8** delivery **9** knock
down, put around

throw away 7 cast off, discard **8** get
rid of

throw down 5 let go **8** drop hard,
hurl down, toss down **9** fling down

throw into disorder 5 upset **7** agitate, disrupt **10** disarrange

throw off 4 emit, gush **5** exude **7**
abandon, cast off, mislead **8** get rid
of, shake off, shrug off **9** cast aside,
discharge, give forth, pour forth

throw off the scent 7 confuse, mislead **8** confound **19** throw out a red
herring

throw out 4 beam, emit, oust **5** eject,
evict, expel, exude **6** banish, bounce,
remove **7** discard, dismiss, toss out **8**
get rid of, jettison **9** cast aside, throw
away

throw overboard 4 dump **7** cast off,
discard **8** jettison, toss over

throw suspicion upon 11 cast doubt
on **17** bring into question

throw up 4 barf, spew **5** eject, expel,
spout, vomit **6** cast up, spew up **7**
cough up **8** disgorge **9** discharge **11**
regurgitate

thrust 3 jab, jam, ram **4** butt, pass,
poke, prod, push, raid, stab **5** boost,
drive, foray, force, impel, lunge,
press, sally, shove, swipe **6** attack,
charge, pierce, plunge, propel, sortie,
strike, stroke **7** assault, impetus, impulse, riposte **8** momentum **9** incursion **10** aggression

thrust aside 4 dump **6** shelve **7** discard **8** get rid of, throw off, throw out
9 cast aside, dispose of, throw away

thrust at 6 assail, attack **7** lunge at **8**
strike at

thrust out 4 spew, spit **5** eject, expel,
vomit **6** extend, propel **7** protrude

Thucydides
author of: 28 History of the Pelopon-
nesian War

thud 4 bang **5** clunk, knock, smack,
thump

thug 4 hood **6** bandit, gunman, hit
man, killer, mugger, robber **7** hoodlum, mobster, ruffian **8** assassin,
gangster, murderer **9** cutthroat

thumb 5 hitch **6** finger, handle **9**
hitchhike **10** catch a ride, hitch a ride
11 flip through, leaf through

Thumbelina
author: 21 Hans Christian Andersen

thumbnail 5 brief, short **7** compact,
concise

thump 3 hit, jab, rap **4** bang, beat,
clip, cuff, poke, slam, slap, swat, thud
5 clout, clunk, knock, pound, punch,
smack, whack **6** batter, bounce, buffet, pommel, strike, thwack **8** collapse, lambaste

thunder 4 boom, clap, echo, peal,
roar, roll **5** crack, crash **6** rumble **7**
explode, resound **8** rumbling **9** dis-

thunderbolt
charge, explosion **11** reverberate, thunderbolt, thunderclap
god of: 4 Thor **5** Donar **7** Taranis

thunderbolt 4 dart **5** flash, shaft **6** stroke

Thunderstorms, god of 8 Summanus

thunderstruck 4 agog, awed **5** agape **6** aghast, amazed **8** confused, overcome **9** astounded, awestruck, perplexed, surprised **10** astonished, bewildered **11** dumbfounded **13** flabbergasted

Thurber, James
author of: 12 The New Yorker **14** Is Sex Necessary (with E B White), The Catbird Seat **16** The Owl in the Attic **18** My Life and Hard Times, The Thurber Carnival **26** The Secret Life of Walter Mitty

Thurio
character in: 20 Two Gentlemen of Verona
author: 11 Shakespeare

Thursday
French: 5 jeudi
from: 4 Thor
German: 10 donnerstag
heavenly body: 4 Jove **7** Jupiter
Italian: 7 giovedi
Latin: 9 Dies Jovis
observance: 12 Holy Thursday, Thanksgiving **13** Corpus Christi **14** Maundy Thursday **17** Ascension Thursday
Scandinavian: 7 torsdag
Spanish: 6 jueves

thus 2 so **4** ergo **5** hence **6** like so **8** like this **9** as follows, in this way, therefore, wherefore **11** accordingly **12** consequently, in this manner **13** for this reason
Latin: 3 sic

thus always to tyrants
Latin: 17 sic semper tyrannis
motto of: 8 Virginia

thus passes away the glory of this world
Latin: 21 sic transit gloria mundi

Thus Spake Zarathustra
also: 21 Also Sprach Zarathustra
author: 18 Friedrich Nietzsche

thwack 3 box, hit, rap **4** bang, blow, slam, slap **5** baste, clout, knock, smack, thump, whack **6** buffet, paddle, strike, wallop

Thwackum
character in: 8 Tom Jones
author: 8 Fielding

thwart 3 bar **4** balk, foil, stop **5** check, cross **6** baffle, hinder, oppose **7** inhibit, prevent, ward off **8** obstruct, stave off **9** frustrate **10** contravene

Thyestean banquet
meal of: 10 human flesh

Thyestes
author: 6 Seneca

Thyestes
father: 6 Pelops
mother: 10 Hippodamia
brother: 6 Atreus
half-brother: 10 Chrysippus
sister-in-law: 6 Aerope
son: 9 Aegisthus
daughter: 7 Pelopia

Thyiad see **9** bacchante

Thymbraeus
father: 7 Laocoon

thyme
botanical name: 6 Thymus **9** T vulgaris
varieties: 4 Wild **5** Basil, Lemon, Water **6** Common, Garden, Golden **7** Caraway, Spanish
symbol of: 8 activity
attracts: 4 bees
conjures: 9 fairy folk
use: 4 fish **7** poultry **8** stuffing **10** Creole food **21** New England clam chowder

Thyrus
staff of: 8 Dionysus
tipped with: 8 pine cone
twined with: 3 ivy **5** vines

thysanoptera
class: 8 hexapoda
phylum: 10 arthropoda
group: 5 thrip

thysanura
class: 8 hexapoda
phylum: 10 arthropoda
group: 8 firebrat **10** silverfish **11** bristletail

Tia Maria
type: 6 brandy **7** liqueur
origin: 7 Jamaica
flavor: 6 coffee
with rum: 10 Black Maria
with tequila: 9 Brave Bull
with vodka: 12 Black Russian

tiara 4 band **5** crown, miter **6** diadem **7** coronet **8** frontlet, ornament **9** headdress

Tibet
other name: 3 Bod **4** Bhot **5** Tobet **8** Hsitsang **10** Land of Snow **14** Roof of the World
capital: 5 Lassa, Lhasa
city: 3 Noh **5** Karak **6** Chamdo, Gartok **7** Changtu, Totling **8** Gyangtse, Jihkatse, Shigatse **9** Chiangtzu
government: 23 autonomous region of China
monetary unit: 5 tanga
lake: 3 Aru, Bam, Bun, Nam **4** Mema, Tosu **5** Jagok, Tabia **6** Dagtse, Garhur, Kashun, Nam Iso, Seling, Tangra, Yamdok **7** Kyaring, Teriman, Tsaring, Zilling **8** Jiggitai **9** Tengrinor **11** Manasarowar
mountain: 5 Kamet, Sajum **6** Kailas, Kunlun **7** Bandala **8** Himalaya **9** Karakoram

highest point: 7 Everest
river: 3 Nak, Nau, Sak **4** Song **5** Hwang, Indus **6** Mekong, Sutlej, Yellow **7** Hwang Ho, Matsang, Melsang, Salween, Tsangpo, Yangtze **11** Brahmaputra

physical feature:
plain: 4 Kham **9** Chang Tang
valley: 7 Tsangpo

people: 5 Asian, Balti, Bodpa, Drupa **6** Bhotia, Champa, Drokpa, Khamba, Khambu, Panaka, Sherpa, Tangut **7** Bhotiya, Bhutani, Gyarung, Taghlik, Tibetan **9** Mongoloid
patron god: 14 Avalokitesvara
ruler: 4 Yuan **6** Mongol **9** dalai lama **13** Songtsan Gampo
language: 5 Balti **6** Ladkhi **7** Bhutani, Bodskad **8** Sanskrit **9** Bhutanese

religion: 5 Bonko **7** Lamaism

place:
Indian border: 11 McMahon Line
palace: 7 Potalaf
temple: 7 Jokhang **10** Tashi Lumpo **11** Tashi Lhunpo

feature:
animal: 3 dzo, yak **5** kiang **7** mastiff **8** musk deer **10** giant panda
clothing: 5 chuba
dance: 4 cham **9** achelhamo
dog: 9 lhasa apso
leader: 9 dalai lama
legend: 4 yeti **17** abominable snowman
monastery: 8 lamasery
monk: 4 lama

food:
dish: 6 tsamba, tsampa
drink: 5 chang

tibia
bone of: 4 shin

tic 5 spasm **6** twitch **12** facial twitch **13** tic douloureux **19** trigeminal neuralgia

tick 3 dot, tap **4** beat, line, list, mark, nick, note **5** blaze, check, clack, click, enter, notch, swing, throb **6** record, slight, stroke, vibrate **8** mark down, register, ticktock **9** checkmark, chronicle, oscillate, pulsation, vibration

ticket 3 tag **4** card, mark, pass, slip, stub **5** label, slate **6** ballot, coupon, marker, roster **7** sticker, voucher **14** list of nominees, traffic summons
type: 4 trip **7** parking, traffic **9** admission
free: 11 Annie Oakley

tickle 4 itch **5** amuse, cheer, prick, sting, throb **6** divert, please, regale, stroke, thrill, tingle, twitch **7** delight, enchant, enliven, gladden, gratify, prickle, rejoice **8** enthrall, entrance **9** captivate, fascinate, titillate **12** scratchiness **15** do one's heart good

ticklish 4 hard **5** itchy, tough **6** knotty, thorny, tickly, touchy, tricky **7** awkward, prickly **8** critical, delicate, scratchy, tingling **9** difficult, intricate, sensitive, uncertain **11** complicated

tidal basin 3 bay **5** inlet, sound **6** lagoon **7** estuary **11** arm of the sea

tidbit 3 bit **4** item **5** treat **6** morsel **8** delicacy, mouthful **9** choice bit

tide 4 flow, neap, wave **5** drift, state **7** current **8** movement, tendency, undertow **9** direction **10** ebb and flow, wax and wane **11** rise and fall

tidings 4 news, word **6** advice, notice, report **8** good word **11** declaration, information **12** announcement, intelligence, notification

tidy 4 neat, trig, trim **5** ample, array, clean **6** goodly, neaten, tidy up **7** arrange, careful, clean up, orderly, precise, regular, sizable **8** neaten up, spotless, spruce up **9** organized, regulated, shipshape **10** immaculate, methodical, meticulous, put in order, straighten, systematic **11** substantial **12** businesslike, considerable, straighten up **15** in apple-pie order

tidy up 5 clean **6** neaten **9** freshen up **10** put in order, straighten

tie 3 rod **4** ally, band, beam, belt, bind, bond, cord, draw, duty, join, knot, lash, line, link, rope, sash, yoke **5** brace, cable, cinch, limit, marry, match, truss, unite **6** attach, bow tie, clinch, couple, cravat, engage, fasten, girdle, hamper, hinder, ribbon, secure, string, tether **7** confine, connect, kinship, necktie, support **8** affinity, cincture, dead heat, make a bow, make fast, relation, restrain, restrict, tied vote **9** constrain, crossbeam, fastening **10** allegiance, connection, cummerbund, obligation **11** affiliation, come out even **12** relationship **13** connecting rod **15** divide the honors

Tiepolo, Giovanni Battista (Giambattista)
    born: 5 Italy **6** Venice
    artwork: 10 Kaisersaal (salon) **11** Treppenhaus (staircase) **14** The Crucifixion **16** Ronaldo and Armida **20** Madonna of Mount Carmel **21** The Communion of St Lucia, The Triumph of Aphrodite **24** St Thekla and the Pestilence **28** Apotheosis of Francesco Barbaro **28** The Worship of the Bronze Serpent

tier 3 row **4** bank, file, line, rank, step **5** layer, level, range, story **7** stratum **14** stratification

Tierney, Gene
    born: 10 Brooklyn NY
    husband: 11 Oleg Cassini
    roles: 5 Laura **10** Belle Starr **11** Tobacco Road **13** A Bell for Adano **16** Leave Her to Heaven **18** The Ghost and Mrs Muir

tiers etat 11 third estate
    in French politics: 7 commons

tie-up 3 jam **4** snag **5** block, hitch, snarl **6** slow-up **7** failure **8** blockage, gridlock, stop page **9** breakdown **10** bottleneck, disruption **11** malfunction **13** embouteillage

tie up 3 tie **4** bind, gird, lash, rope **5** hitch, snarl, strap, truss **6** engage, fasten, hinder, impede, occupy, secure, tangle **8** entangle

tiff 4 huff, miff, rage, snit, spat **5** clash, run-in, scrap, tizzy, words **6** hassle **7** dispute, quarrel, rhubarb, wrangle **8** argument, ill humor, squabble **10** difference **11** altercation **12** disagreement **16** misunderstanding

tiger 3 cat **6** cougar, jaguar **7** fighter, wildcat
    young: 5 whelp

tiger's-eye
    species: 6 quartz

Tigger
    character in: 13 Winnie-the-Pooh
    author: 5 Milne

tight 4 busy, firm, full, hard, high, snug, taut **5** blind, close, dense, drunk, exact, happy, harsh, lit up, rigid, scant, solid, stern, stiff, tense, tipsy, tough **6** firmly, frugal, gorged, hard-up, jammed, juiced, loaded, scarce, secure, severe, skimpy, sloppy, soused, stewed, stingy, stoned, strict, trying, zonked **7** austere, closely, compact, crammed, crowded, drunken, miserly, onerous, pickled, pie-eyed, smashed, solidly, sparing, stuffed **8** grudging, rigorous, securely, too small **9** deficient, difficult, illiberal, jam-packed, niggardly, penurious, plastered, skintight, stringent, worrisome **10** burdensome, compressed, glassy-eyed, impassable, inadequate, inebriated, inflexible, in one's cups, nip-and-tuck, nose-to-nose, tyrannical, ungenerous, unyielding **11** closefisted, constricted, dictatorial, impermeable, intoxicated, troublesome, well-matched **12** closefitting, impenetrable, insufficient, parsimonious **13** closely fitted, feeling no pain **14** fitting closely, uncompromising **20** three sheets to the wind

tighten 5 pinch **6** anchor, fasten, narrow, secure **7** squeeze **8** contract, make fast, make taut **9** constrict **14** take up the slack

tighten one's belt 4 save **5** skimp, stint **6** scrimp **8** conserve, cut costs **9** economize **11** cut expenses **12** pinch pennies

tightfisted 5 cheap, mingy, tight **6** greedy, stingy **7** miserly **9** illiberal, niggardly, penurious **10** avaricious **11** closefisted **12** cheeseparing, parsimonious **13** penny-pinching

tightfistedness 6 penury **9** parsimony **10** stinginess **11** miserliness **13** niggardliness, penny-pinching

tight-fitting 4 snug **5** tight **8** too small **9** skintight **11** constricted **12** constricting **15** like a second skin

tight-laced 4 prim **6** prissy, stuffy **7** prudish **8** priggish **9** inhibited, repressed, Victorian **11** puritanical, standoffish, straitlaced **13** selfrighteous

tight-lipped 3 mum **4** curt **5** brief, quiet, short, terse **8** discreet, reserved, reticent, taciturn **10** unsociable **11** untalkative **12** close-mouthed **15** uncommunicative

tightly packed 5 dense **6** jammed **7** compact, crammed, stuffed **10** compressed **12** concentrated

tightwad 5 miser, piker **7** niggard, Scrooge **9** lickpenny, skinflint **10** cheapskate, pinchpenny **12** moneygrubber

Tiki
    Polynesian: 8 first man **6** amulet

till 3 sow **4** even, farm, plow, seed, tray, unto up to **6** before, coffer, drawer, harrow, plough **7** as far as, develop, prepare **8** moneybox, treasury **9** cultivate **12** cash register
    geological: 5 drift

tillable 6 arable **8** farmable, plowable **10** cultivable

tillage 7 farming, plowing **11** agriculture, cultivation

Till Eulenspiegel
    also: 16 Tyll Eulenspiegel
    origin: 8 Germanic
    means: 14 practical joker

Tillie the Toiler
    creator: 12 Russ Westover
    character: 3 Mac **7** Mr Chase

tilt 3 row, tip **4** cant, lean, list, rake, spar, tiff **5** brawl, fence, fight, grade, joust, pitch, slant, slope **6** affray, battle, combat, oppose **7** contest, dispute, incline, quarrel **8** argument, skirmish, squabble **9** encounter **10** tournament **11** altercation

Timaeus
    author: 5 Plato

Timandra
    father: 9 Tyndareus
    mother: 4 Leda
    brother: 6 Castor, Pollux
    sister: 5 Helen **12** Clytemnestra
    husband: 7 Echemus, Phyleus
    son: 5 Meges
    cursed by: 9 Aphrodite

timber 4 bush, logs, wood **5** copse, trees, woods **6** boards, forest, lumber **7** thicket

timberland 5 woods **6** forest, sticks **8** woodland

timbre 4 tone **5** pitch **9** resonance

time, times 3 age, day, eon, era **4** beat, days, hour, term, week, year **5** clock, cycle, epoch, event, match, month, phase, spell, stage, tempo, while, years **6** adjust, chance, decade, moment, period, rhythm, season **7** century, episode, freedom, instant, liberty, measure, stretch **8** duration, incident, interval, occasion **10** experience, generation **11** opportunity, synchronize

time flies
Latin: **11** tempus fugit

time-honored 6 common, normal **7** regular, revered **8** accepted, standard **9** customary, respected, universal

timeless 7 abiding, durable, endless, eternal, lasting, undying **8** enduring, immortal, infinite, unending **9** boundless, ceaseless, deathless, immutable, incessant, permanent, perpetual **10** continuous, persistent **11** everlasting, never-ending **12** interminable, unchangeable **13** never-stopping **14** indestructible

timely 6 prompt **8** punctual **9** opportune, well-timed **10** convenient, felicitous, seasonable **12** providential

Time Machine, The
author: **7** H G Wells
character: **4** Eloi **5** Weena **8** Morlocks **12** Time Traveler

Time of Your Life, The
author: **14** William Saroyan
director: **8** H C Potter
cast: **8** Ward Bond **11** James Cagney, Wayne Morris **12** Jeanne Cagney **13** William Bendix **17** Broderick Crawford

timepiece 5 clock, watch **8** horologe **11** chronometer

Time Remembered
author: **11** Jean Anouilh

timesaving 5 quick **6** speedy **9** efficient **11** expeditious

time without end 7 forever **8** eternity, infinity

timeworn 3 old **4** aged, worn **5** dated, hoary, passe, stale, trite **6** age-old, beat-up, old-hat, shabby **7** ancient, antique **8** battered, dog-eared, obsolete, overused **9** hackneyed, out of date, venerable, weathered **10** antiquated **12** antediluvian

timid 3 coy, shy **6** afraid, humble, modest, scared **7** bashful, fearful **8** cowardly, retiring, sheepish, timorous **9** diffident, shrinking, spineless, weakkneed **10** unassuming **12** apprehensive, fainthearted **13** pusillanimous

timidity 7 modesty, shyness **8** cold feet, humility **9** cowardice, timidness **10** diffidence **11** bashfulness, fearfulness, trepidation **12** sheepishness, timorousness **13** spinelessness **16** faint-heartedness

timidness 7 shyness **8** meekness, timidity **10** diffidence, insecurity **11** bashfulness **12** timorousness **14** submissiveness **15** unassertiveness **16** faintheartedness

Timon of Athens
author: **18** William Shakespeare
character: **6** Lucius **7** Flavius **8** Lucullus **9** Apemantus, Ventidius **10** Alcibiades, Sempronius

Timor
capital: **4** Dili
country: **8** Portugal **9** Indonesia
islands: **5** Sunda **11** Lesser Sunda
strait: **5** Ombai

timorous 3 shy **4** meek **5** timid **6** afraid **7** anxious, bashful, fearful **8** retiring **9** shrinking **10** submissive **12** fainthearted

timorousness 7 shyness **8** cold feet, meekness, timidity **9** cowardice **11** fearfulness, trepidation **16** faintheartedness

Timothy
mother: **6** Eunice
grandmother: **4** Lois
companion: **4** Paul **8** Silvanus

tin
chemical symbol: **2** Sn

tincture 6 elixir **7** essence, extract, spirits **8** solution **11** concentrate

Tinder Box, The
author: **21** Hans Christian Andersen

Tin Drum, The
author: **11** Gunter Grass
director: **17** Volker Schlondorff
character: **14** Oskar Matzerath
cast: **10** Mario Adorf **12** David Bennent (Oskar) **13** Angela Winkler **16** Daniel Olbrychski **17** Katharina Tahlbach
Oscar for: **11** foreign film

tine 3 die, tip **4** barb, lose, tyne **5** point, prong, spike **6** bodkin, branch, perish, skewer **7** destroy, forfeit

tinge 3 dye **4** cast, dash, hint, lace, tint, tone, vein **5** color, imbue, shade, smack, stain, taste, touch, trace **6** flavor, infuse, nuance, season **7** instill, soupcon **9** suspicion

tingle 5 sting, throb **6** thrill, tickle, tremor **7** flutter, prickle **9** prickling, pulsation **11** palpitation

Tinker, Tailor, Soldier, Spy
author: **11** John Le Carre

Tinker Bell
character in: **8** Peter Pan
author: **6** Barrie

tinkle 4 ding, peal, ping, ring **5** chime, chink, clank, clink, plink **6** jingle **9** ting-a-ling

tin lizzie 3 car **4** auto, heap **5** motor **6** jalopy, wheels **7** flivver, machine, vehicle **8** motorcar **10** automobile **12** motor vehicle

Tin Man, Tin Woodsman
character in: **13** The Wizard of Oz
author: **4** Baum

tinsel 4 sham, show **5** gloss **6** sequin **7** glitter, spangle **8** pretense **9** gaudiness **10** camouflage, decoration, masquer-

ade **11** affectation, false colors, make-believe, ostentation

tint 3 dye, hue **4** hint, tone, wash **5** color, frost, shade, stain, tinge, touch, trace **6** nuance **7** pigment **8** coloring, tincture **10** suggestion

Tintern Abbey
author: **17** William Wordsworth

tintinnabulate 4 peal, ring, toll **5** chime, clang, knell, sound **6** jingle, tinkle

tintinnabulation 4 gong, peal, ring, toll **5** chime, knell **6** jingle **7** clangor, pealing, ringing **8** clanging, ding-dong, jingling, tinkling **11** peal of bells

Tintoretto, Jacopo
real name: **13** Jacopo Robusti
born: **5** Italy **6** Venice
artwork: **8** Paradise **13** The Last Supper **14** The Crucifixion **16** The Road to Calvary **17** Bacchus and Ariadne **18** Apotheosis of St Roch, The Flight into Egypt **20** Susanna and the Elders **21** The Temptation of Christ **26** St Mark Frees a Christian Slave **27** The Finding of the Body of St Mark **32** The Miracle of St Mark Rescuing a Slave

tiny 3 wee **5** pygmy, runty, small, teeny **6** bantam, little, midget, minute, petite **8** dwarfish **9** itsy-bitsy, miniature, minuscule, pint-sized **10** diminutive, teeny-weeny, undersized **11** Lilliputian, microscopic, pocket-sized **12** teensy-weensy

Tiny Tim
character in: **15** A Christmas Carol
author: **7** Dickens

tip 3 cap, pat, tap, top **4** acme, apex, barb, brow, cant, clue, head, hint, hook, lean, list, peak, rake, tilt **5** crest, crown, pitch, point, prong, slant, slope, spike, upend, upset **6** advice, reward, stroke, summit, tip-off, topple, upturn, vertex, zenith **7** capsize, incline, leaning, lowdown, pointer, sharpen, tilting, tipping, warning **8** gratuity, over turn, pinnacle, slanting **9** baksheesh, lagniappe **10** admonition, inside dope, perquisite, suggestion, turn turtle **11** forewarning **13** word to the wise
French: **7** douceur

tipcart 4 cart **8** dumpcart, pushcart

Tiphys
member of: **9** Argonauts
occupation: **9** steersman

tip off 3 tip **4** warn **5** alert **6** caveat **7** caution, warning **8** forewarn **11** forewarning

tip over 5 upend, upset **7** capsize **8** flip over, keel over, overturn, turn over **10** turn turtle

Tippett, Michael Kemp
born: **6** London **7** England
composer of: **9** King Priam **13** The Knot Garden **15** A Child of Our Time

20 The Midsummer Marriage **22** The Vision of St Augustine **32** Concerto for Double String Orchestra

tipple 5 drink, quaff **6** guzzle, imbibe, liquor **8** beverage

tippler 3 sot **4** lush, soak, wino **5** drunk, rummy, souse, toper **6** bibber, boozer, sponge **7** guzzler, imbiber, swiller, tosspot **8** drunkard **9** alcoholic, inebriate **10** boozehound **11** dipsomaniac

tipsy 4 high **5** awash, blind, drunk, happy, lit-up, stiff, tight **6** juiced, loaded, sloppy, sodden, soused, stewed, stoned **7** drunken, pickled, pie-eyed, smashed **9** inebriate, plastered **10** glassy-eyed, inebriated, in one's cups **11** intoxicated **12** half seas over **13** feeling no pain **20** three sheets to the wind

tip-top 4 A-one **5** elite, super **7** supreme **8** very fine **10** consummate **11** exceptional, superlative **13** extraordinary

tirade 5 curse **6** screed **7** lecture **8** diatribe, harangue, jeremiad, scolding **9** invective, reprimand **11** castigation, fulmination **12** condemnation, denunciation, dressing-down, vilification, vituperation

tirailleur 10 skirmisher **12** sharpshooter

Tirane, Tirana
    capital of: 7 Albania

tire 3 fag, irk **4** bore **5** annoy, weary **6** bother, tucker **7** disgust, exhaust, fatigue, wear out **8** be sick of **10** make sleepy **11** be fed up with **12** lose interest, lose patience

tire
    invented by: 6 Dunlop **7** Thomson

tired 4 beat **5** all in, weary **6** bushed, drowsy, fagged, pooped, sleepy **7** wearied, worn out **8** dog-tired, fatigued, tuckered **9** enervated, exhausted, played out

tireless 6 steady **7** devoted, staunch **8** constant, faithful, resolute, untiring **9** steadfast, unceasing, unwearied **10** determined, unflagging, unswerving **11** hard-working, industrious, nevertiring, persevering, unfaltering, unremitting **13** indefatigable

Tiresias
    also: 9 Teiresias
    vocation: 4 seer **7** prophet
    father: 6 Everes
    mother: 8 Chariclo
    grandfather: 6 Udaeus
    home: 6 Thebes
    struck: 5 blind
    character in: 7 Odyssey **10** Oedipus Rex
    characteristic: 9 blind seer

tiresome 4 drab, dull, hard **6** boring, deadly, dismal, tiring, trying, vexing **7** arduous, fagging, humdrum, irksome,

tedious, wearing **8** annoying, wearying **9** difficult, fatiguing, laborious, wearisome **10** bothersome, exhausting, monotonous **13** uninteresting

Tishri 18 seventh Hebrew month

Tisiphone
    member of: 6 Furies

'Tis Pity She's a Whore
    author: 8 John Ford
    character: 6 Donado, Florio, Putana **7** Soranzo, Vasques **8** Bergetto, Giovanni, Grimaldi **9** Annabella, Hippolita **11** Richardetto **16** Friar Bonaventura

tissue
    kind: 4 bone, skin **5** nerve **6** muscle

titan 5 giant, great, mogul **7** magnate

Titan
    race of: 4 gods
    father: 6 Uranus
    mother: 2 Ge **4** Gaea
    names: 5 Coeus, Crius **6** Cronus **7** Iapetus, Oceanus **8** Hyperion
    sisters: 8 Titaness
        names of sisters: 4 Rhea **5** Theia **6** Phoebe, Tethys, Themis **9** Mnemosyne

Titan, The
    sequel to: 12 The Financier
    author: 15 Theodore Dreiser
    character: 13 Peter Laughlin **15** Berenice Fleming, Stephanie Platow **16** Aileen Cowperwood **23** Frank Algernon Cowperwood

Titan, the see **6** Helios

Titaness see **5** Titan

Titania
    character in: 21 A Midsummer Night's Dream
    author: 11 Shakespeare

titanic 4 huge, vast **5** giant, great, stout **6** mighty, strong **7** immense, mammoth **8** colossal, enormous, gigantic, whopping **9** herculean, humongous, monstrous **10** gargantuan, monumental, prodigious, stupendous

Titanic
    director: 12 James Cameron
    cast: 8 Suzy Amis (Lizzy Calvert) **9** Billy Zane (Cal Hockley) **10** Bill Paxton (Brock Lovett), Kathy Bates (Molly Brown) **11** Bernard Hill (Captain Smith), David Warner (Spicer Lovejoy), Kate Winslet (Rose Bukater) **12** Gloria Stuart (Rose Dawson Calvert), Jonathan Hyde (Bruce Ismay), Victor Garber (Thomas Andrews) **13** Francis Fisher (Ruth Bukater) **16** Leonardo DiCaprio (Jack Dawson)

titanium
    chemical symbol: 2 Ti

tit for tat 8 exchange **10** quid pro quo **13** an eye for an eye

Titian
    real name: 15 Tiziano Vecellio

born: 5 Italy **13** Pieve di Cadore
artwork: 5 Pieta **12** The Bacchanal, Tribute Money **13** Noli Me Tangere **15** Diana and Actaeon, The Rape of Europa **16** The Pesaro Madonna, The Venus of Urbino **17** Bacchus and Ariadne, The Death of Actaeon, The Girl in a Fur Wrap, The Three Ages of Man **18** Charles V at Muhlberg, The Adrian Bacchanal, The Young Englishman **19** Francis I Roi de France **20** Sacred and Profane Love **21** Venus and the Lute Player **23** The Madonna of the Cherries **24** Pope Paul III and his Nephews, The Assumption of the Virgin

titillate 5 charm, rouse, tease, tempt **6** allure, arouse, excite, seduce, tickle, turn on **7** attract, provoke **8** entrance **9** captivate, fascinate, stimulate **15** whet the appetite

titillating 8 alluring, exciting, tempting **9** seductive **10** suggestive **11** provocative

title 3 dub **4** deed, name, rank, term **5** claim, crown, grade, label, place, right **6** status, tenure **7** entitle, epithet, station **8** christen, nobility, position **9** condition, designate, ownership **10** legal right, lordly rank, noble birth, possession **11** appellation, designation **12** championship

titled 5 named, noble, regal, royal **6** called, lordly **7** courtly **8** entitled **10** designated **11** blue-blooded **12** aristocratic

Titograd 9 Podgorica
    capital of: 10 Montenegro

titter 5 chirp, smirk **6** cackle, giggle, simper, teehee **7** chuckle, snicker, snigger

tittle 3 bit, dot, jot **4** atom, iota, mite **5** speck **8** particle

Tittle, Y A (Yelberton Abraham)
    sport: 8 football
    position: 11 quarterback
    team: 13 New York Giants **14** Baltimore Colts **23** San Francisco Forty-Niners

titular 7 known as, nominal **8** so-called **10** in name only, ostensible **11** in title only

Titus
    surname: 6 Justus
    hometown: 7 Corinth
    companion: 4 Paul

Titus see **6** Tatius

Titus Andronicus
    author: 18 William Shakespeare
    character: 5 Aaron **6** Chiron, Marcus, Tamora **7** Alarbus, Lavinia **9** Bassianus, Demetrius **10** Saturninus

Tiu
    Germanic god of: 3 sky, war
    Norse: 3 Tyr
    eponym of: 7 Tuesday

tizzy 4 snit **6** dither, swivet **7** dudgeon **8** tailspin
British: 8 sixpence

to 2 ad, on **3** for **4** into, near, unto, upon, with **5** about, until **6** at hand, closed, toward **7** against, forward **8** together **10** concerning, included in **11** contained in
prefix: 2 ac, ad
Scottish: 3 tae

toad
group of: 4 knot

toady 4 fawn **6** fawner, flunky, stooge, yes-man **8** hanger-on, kowtow to, parasite, truckler **9** flatterer, sycophant **10** bootlicker, curry favor **11** apple-polish, lickspittle **13** apple-polisher, backscratcher

To Althea, From Prison
author: 15 Richard Lovelace

to a man 3 all **8** every one **9** one and all **10** completely **12** to the last man

To a Skylark
author: 18 Percy Bysshe Shelley

toast 3 dry **4** heat, warm **5** brown, grill, honor **6** salute, warm up **9** celebrate **10** compliment **11** commemorate **12** browned bread, clink glasses **15** drink one's health

tobacco
varieties: 4 tree, wild **6** Indian **7** jasmine, Turkish **9** broadleaf, flowering, Nicotiana **12** long-flowered **16** Nicotiana rustica, Nicotiana tabacum

Tobacco Road
author: 15 Erskine Caldwell
character: 3 Ada **4** Dude **5** Pearl **6** Bessie **8** Ellie May **9** Lov Bensey **12** Jeeter Lester

To Be or Not To Be
director: 13 Ernst Lubitsch
cast: 9 Jack Benny **11** Robert Stack **12** Lionel Atwill **13** Carole Lombard, Felix Bressart
setting: 6 Poland

To Catch a Thief
director: 15 Alfred Hitchcock
cast: 9 Cary Grant **10** Grace Kelly **12** John Williams **17** Jessie Royce Landis
setting: 13 French Riviera

Tocqueville, Alexis de
author of: 18 Democracy in America

tocsin 4 bell **5** alarm **7** warning

today 3 now **7** this day, this era **8** nowadays, this time **9** in this era, on this day, this epoch **10** the present **11** in this epoch, modern times **13** in modern times, the present age, the present day **15** in this day and age

Todd, Richard
real name: 27 Richard Andrew Palethorpe-Todd
born: 6 Dublin **7** Ireland
roles: 13 The Hasty Heart, The Long-

est Day **14** The Virgin Queen **15** A Man Called Peter

toddle 6 waddle, wobble **14** take short steps, walk unsteadily

toddler 3 tot **4** babe, baby, tyke **5** child **6** infant **9** little one

to-do 3 ado **4** fuss, stir **5** furor, noise **6** bustle, flurry, hubbub, hustle, pother, racket, ruckus, rumpus, tumult, uproar **7** turmoil **8** activity **9** agitation, commotion **10** excitement, hullabaloo, hurly-burly **11** disturbance

Toe, The
nickname of: 8 Lou Groza

to err is human
Latin: 16 errare humanum est

toff 3 nob **4** beau **5** dandy, swell **10** young blood

Toffler, Alvin
author of: 10 Powershift **11** Future Shock **12** The Third Wave

toga 3 aba **4** garb, gown, robe **6** trabea **7** garment **12** outergarment
virilis: 9 white robe **11** manhood robe

Togo
other name: 14 French Togoland
capital/largest city: 4 Lome
others: 5 Badon, Kpeme **6** Anecho, Ansoho, Blitta, Klonto, Nuatja, Palime, Sokode **7** Bassari, Dopango, Pagonda **8** Atakpame, Tabligbo **10** Niamtougou
school: 5 Benin **6** Mawull
monetary unit: 5 franc **7** centime
mountain: 4 Togo **7** Atakora, Koronga
highest point: 7 Baumann
river: 3 Oti **4** Anie, Haho, Mono, Ogou
sea: 8 Atlantic
physical feature:
   bight: 5 Benin
   gulf: 6 Guinea
   plain: 4 Mono
people: 3 Ana, Ewe, Twi **4** Mina **5** Hausa **6** Akposa, Kabrai **7** Bassari, Cabrais, Kabrais, Ouatchi **8** Konkomba, Kotokoli, Lotokoli
   leader: 9 Eyadema **15** Sylvanus Olympio **16** Nicolas Grunitzky
language: 3 Ana, Ewe, Twi **4** Mina **5** Hausa **6** French, Kabrai, Kabrie **7** Bassari, Dagomba, Ouatchi **8** Kotokoli, Lotocoli
religion: 5 Islam **7** animism **12** Christianity

togs 4 duds **6** attire, outfit **7** apparel, clothes, threads **8** clothing, garments

To Have and Have Not
director: 11 Howard Hawks
based on novel by: 15 Ernest Hemingway
cast: 12 Dolores Moran, Lauren Bacall **13** Walter Brennan **14** Humphrey Bogart **15** Hoagy Carmichael
remade as: 13 The Gunrunners **16** The Breaking Point

To His Coy Mistress
author: 13 Andrew Marvell

toil 4 grub, moil, work **5** grind, labor, pains, slave, sweat **6** drudge, effort **7** travail **8** drudgery, exertion, hardship, hard work, industry, struggle, work hard **11** application, elbow grease **12** apply oneself, exert oneself **14** work like a horse

toiler 4 peon, serf, swot **5** navvy, prole, slave **6** drudge, flunky, menial, slavey, worker **7** grubber, laborer, servant, slogger **9** workhorse **10** wage earner **11** galley slave

toilet 2 WC **3** can, loo **4** john **5** privy **7** commode, latrine **8** facility, lavatory, men's room, outhouse, rest room, washroom **10** ladies' room **11** convenience, water closet

toilet water 5 scent **7** cologne, essence, perfume **9** fragrance

toilsome 4 hard **5** tough **6** tiring, uphill **7** arduous, onerous, tedious **8** wearying **9** difficult, effortful, fatiguing, herculean, laborious, strenuous, wearisome **10** burdensome, exhausting **12** backbreaking

token 4 mark, sign **5** index, proof **6** jetton, symbol **7** for show, memento, minimal, nodding, nominal, passing **8** evidence, keepsake, reminder, souvenir, symbolic **9** vestigial **10** expression, indication **11** perfunctory, remembrance, superficial, testimonial **13** manifestation

To Kill a Mockingbird
director: 14 Robert Mulligan
based on novel by: 9 Harper Lee
cast: 9 John Megna **10** Mary Badham **11** Gregory Peck **12** Philip Alford
Oscar for: 5 actor (Peck)

Tokyo
airport: 6 Haneda
capital of: 5 Japan
district: 5 Ginza **6** Keihin **7** Chiyoda **8** Yokohama **10** Marunouchi **18** Tama New Town Project
former name: 3 Edo
island: 6 Honshu
landmark: 8 Ueno Park **11** Meiji Shrine **12** National Diet **14** Imperial Palace, Kitanomaru Park **19** Komazawa Olympic Park
means: 14 Eastern capital

tolerable 4 fair, so-so **7** allowed, average **8** abidable, accepted, adequate, bearable, mediocre, middling, ordinary, passable **9** allowable, endurable, innocuous, permitted **10** acceptable, admissible, fairly good, sufferable **11** commonplace, indifferent, permissible **12** run-of-the-mill **14** fair-to-middling

tolerance 7 charity **8** fairness, goodwill, patience, sympathy **9** endurance **10** compassion, sufferance **11** forbearance **13** brotherly love, fair treatment, fellow feeling, power to endure **15** lack of prejudice

tolerant 4 easy, fair, soft **7** lenient, liberal, patient, sparing **8** moderate **9** easygoing, forgiving, indulgent, unbigoted **10** charitable, forbearing, permissive **11** broad-minded, kindhearted, softhearted, sympathetic **12** unprejudiced **13** compassionate, uncomplaining, understanding

tolerate 3 let **4** bear, take **5** abide, admit, allow, brook, stand **6** endure, permit, suffer, wink at **7** indulge, stomach, undergo **8** be easy on, be soft on, sanction, submit to **9** consent to, put up with, recognize, vouchsafe

To Let
   author: 14 John Galsworthy

to life
   Hebrew: **7** lehayim **8** lechayim

Tolkien, J R R
   author of: **9** The Hobbit **15** The Silmarillion **17** The Lord of the Rings
   creature: **3** ent orc
   fictional setting: **11** Middle Earth

toll 3 fee, tax **4** duty, levy, loss **6** charge, impost, tariff **7** payment, penalty, tribute, undoing **8** exaction **9** depletion, sacrifice **10** assessment, disruption, extinction **11** destruction **12** annihilation **13** extermination

Tolstoy, Leo
   author of: **11** War and Peace **12** Anna Karenina, Resurrection **17** The Kreutzer Sonata **18** Death of Ivan Ilyitch

Toltec
   city: **4** Tula
   preceded: **5** Aztec
   tribe: **4** Itza

To Lucasta, Going to the Wars
   author: **15** Richard Lovelace

tom 3 cat **6** tomcat **10** male turkey

tomato 12 Lycopersicon **24** Lycopersicon lycopersicum
   varieties: **4** Husk, Pear, Tree **6** Cherry **7** Currant **10** Gooseberry, Strawberry **11** Mexican husk
   soup: **8** gazpacho
   sauce: **6** catsup **7** ketchup

tomb 5 crypt, grave, vault **8** monument **9** mausoleum, sepulcher **11** burial place **12** resting place **13** burial chamber

tomboy 3 meg **4** girl, romp **5** rowdy **6** female, gamine, hoiden, hoyden, tomrig **8** strumpet

Tom Brown's School Days
   author: **12** Thomas Hughes

tombs
   god of: **6** Anubis

tomcat 3 cat, tom **9** womanizer

tomfoolery 4 play **6** antics **8** drollery, nonsense **9** high jinks, horseplay, silliness **10** goofing off, skylarking **11** foolishness **12** lollygagging,

monkeyshines, prankishness **13** fooling around, messing around, playing around

Tom Jones
   also: **29** The History of Tom Jones Foundling
   author: **13** Henry Fielding
   character: **6** Square **7** Bridget, Western **8** Mrs Honor, Thwackum **9** Mrs Miller, Partridge **11** Black George, Nightingale **12** Master Blifil **13** Lady Bellaston, Sophia Western **15** Squire Allworthy
   director: **14** Tony Richardson
   cast: **11** Joyce Redman **12** Albert Finney, Diane Cilento, Hugh Griffith, Susannah York **14** Dame Edith Evans
   score: **11** John Addison
   Oscar for: **5** score **7** picture **9** direction **10** screenplay

Tomlin, Lily
   real name: **14** Mary Jean Tomlin
   born: **9** Detroit MI
   roles: **6** The Kid **7** Laugh-In **8** Edith Ann **9** Ernestine, Nashville, The Player **11** The Late Show **14** Moment By Moment **15** I Heart Huckabees **16** Tea with Mussolini **20** Flirting with Disaster **27** The Incredible Shrinking Woman

tommyrot 3 rot **4** bosh, bull, bunk, crap, tosh **5** bilge, hokum, hooey, trash **6** bunkum, drivel, humbug **7** baloney, hogwash, spinach, rubbish, twaddle **8** buncombe, claptrap, folderol, malarkey, nonsense **9** poppycock **10** applesauce, balderdash, tomfoolery **11** foolishness **12** bullfeathers, fiddle-faddle **13** horsefeathers **16** stuff-and-nonsense

tomorrow 9 the future, the morrow **11** in the future **12** in days to come **16** the day after today **17** the next generation
   Spanish: **6** manana

Tom Sawyer
   author: **9** Mark Twain
   character: **8** Huck (Huckleberry) Finn, Injun Joe **9** Aunt Polly, Joe Harper **10** Muff Potter **13** Becky Thatcher

ton
   abbreviation: **1** t

tone 3 hue **4** cast, lilt, mood, note, tint **5** color, pitch, shade, sound, style, tenor, tinge **6** accent, chroma, firm up, manner, soften, spirit, stress, subdue, temper **7** cadence, quality **8** attitude, harmonic, make firm, moderate, modulate, overtone, tonality **10** inflection, intonation, make supple, modulation

Tone, Franchot
   real name: **27** Stanislas Pascal Franchot Tone
   born: **14** Niagara Falls NY
   wife: **11** Jean Wallace **12** Joan Craw-

ford **13** Barbara Payton **15** Dolores Dorn-Heft
   roles: **10** Uncle Vanya **11** Phantom Lady **13** Three Comrades **16** Advise and Consent **17** Five Graves to Cairo, Mutiny on the Bounty **23** The Lives of a Bengal Lancer

tone up 7 make fit, shape up **9** condition **10** put in shape

Tonga
   other name: **15** Friendly Islands
   capital/largest city: **9** Nukualofa
   others: **3** Mua, Pea **6** Neiafu **7** Haakame, Kolonga, Kolovai **8** Fuaamotu
   division: **5** Vavau **6** Haapai **9** Tongatapu
   government: **8** monarchy
   head of state: **4** king
   monetary unit: **6** paanga, seniti
   island: **3** Eua, Kao, Ono **4** Kotu **5** Tofua, Vavau **6** Haapai, Lifuke, Nomuka **7** Otu Tolu **9** Tongatapu
   highest point: **3** Kao
   sea: **7** Pacific
   people: **10** Polynesian
      explorer: **4** Cook **5** Bligh **6** Tasman
      king: **11** George Tupou **14** Taufaahau Tupou
      missionary: **12** Shirley Baker
      queen: **6** Salote
   language: **6** Tongan **7** English
   religion: **9** Methodist **12** Christianity **25** Wesleyan Free Church of Tonga
   feature:
      fabric: **4** tapa
      spiritual king: **8** tui tonga

tongue 3 lap **4** flap, lick, spit **5** point, shaft **6** lingua, patois, speech **7** dialect, lingula **8** language **10** promontory, vernacular, vocabulary **13** organ of speech, power of speech, style of speech
   tastes: **4** salt, sour **5** sweet **6** bitter

tongue-lash 5 scold **6** berate, rail at, rebuke **7** bawl out, chew out, reprove, upbraid **8** reproach **9** castigate, reprimand **10** take to task

tongue-lashing 6 rebuke **7** censure, chiding, reproof **8** reproach, scolding **9** reprimand **10** bawling-out, chewing-out, upbraiding **11** castigation, reprobation **12** dressing-down, remonstrance

tonic 6 bracer, pickup **7** keynote **8** pick-me-up **9** analeptic, refresher, stimulant **10** invigorant **11** restorative

tonsure 3 cut **4** trim **8** bald spot **11** shaven patch

too
   French: **4** trop

tool 4 dupe, pawn **5** agent, means **6** device, medium, puppet, stooge **7** cat's-paw, machine, utensil, vehicle **8** hireling **9** apparatus, appliance, implement, mechanism **10** instrument **11** contrivance, wherewithal **12** intermediary **15** instrumentality

carpenter's: 3 adz, awl, bit, peg, saw **4** adze, nail, rasp, vise **5** auger, brace, edger, gouge, knife, lathe, plane, ruler, screw **6** bodkin, chisel, gimlet, hammer, pliers, router, sander **7** bradawl, scraper **9** hand drill, try square **11** screwdriver

cutting/shaping: 2 ax **3** adz, axe, saw **4** adze, burr, file, froe, frow, rasp **5** burin, croze, gouge, knife, plane, razor, shave, wedge **6** chisel, sander, shears, trepan **7** hatchet, scraper **8** scissors

drilling/boring: 3 awl, bit, zax **4** pick **5** chuck, drill **6** gimlet, wimble **7** bradawl **11** countersink

farmer's: 2 ax **3** axe, hoe **4** plow, rake **5** spade **6** cradle, harrow, pickax, plough, scythe, seeder, shovel, sickle, tiller, trowel **7** hayfork **9** plowshare **10** cultivator

gripping/turning: 6 pliers, wrench **11** screwdriver

holding: 4 vise **5** clamp

measuring: 4 rule **5** gauge, level **6** square **7** caliper **8** dividers **10** micrometer

mechanic's: 3 awl, zax **4** burr, file, vise **5** bevel, lathe **6** bodkin, pliers **7** bradawl, crowbar **8** calipers **9** jackscrew **11** screwdriver **12** monkey wrench

pounding/striking: 4 maul **5** punch, wedge **6** hammer, mallet

too little 4 lack **6** dearth, scanty, scarce **7** paucity **8** scarcity, shortage **9** deficient, not enough, scantness **10** deficiency, inadequacy, inadequate **12** insufficient **13** insufficiency

too many
French: **6** de trop

too much 4 glut **5** flood **6** excess **7** profuse, surfeit, surplus **8** fullness, overflow, plethora **9** avalanche, excessive, profusion, repletion **10** inundation, oversupply **12** overabundant **13** overabundance **14** superabundance
French: **4** trop

Toonerville Folks
creator: **11** Fontaine Fox
character: **7** skipper **13** Aunt Eppie Hogg **15** Little Scorpions, Powerful Katrina, Suitcase Simpson **20** Mickey Himself McGuire **22** Terrible Tempered Mr Bang
rode on: **7** trolley

to one side 4 over **5** aloof, apart, aside **6** aslant **14** on the sidelines

to one's liking 7 fitting **8** pleasant, pleasing, suitable **9** agreeable **10** acceptable, gratifying **11** appropriate, to one's taste **12** satisfactory

toot 4 blow, honk **5** binge, blare, blast, spree **6** bender **7** trumpet **8** winging

tooth 3 cog, nib **4** barb, cusp, fang, spur, tang, tine, tusk **5** molar, point,

spike, thorn **6** canine, cuspid **7** grinder, incisor **8** bicuspid, sprocket **9** serration

toothed 6 fanged, tusked **7** dentate, notched, serrate, virgate

toothsome 6 savory **8** luscious **9** delicious, palatable **10** appetizing

Toots
character in: **12** Dombey and Son
author: **7** Dickens

Tootsie
director: **13** Sydney Pollack
cast: **8** Teri Garr (Sandy Lester) **10** Bill Murray (Jeff Slater), Geena Davis (April Page) **12** George Gaynes (John Van Horn), Jessica Lange (Julie Nichols) **13** Dabney Coleman (Ron Carlisle), Dustin Hoffman (Michael Dorsey/Dorothy Michaels), Sydney Pollack (George Fields) **14** Charles Durning (Les Nichols)

top 3 cap, lid, van **4** acme, apex, best, brow, cork, fore, head, lead, peak **5** chief, cover, crest, crown, excel, front, noted, outdo, upper **6** better, exceed, famous, summit, tiptop, vertex, zenith **7** eclipse, eminent, highest, notable, put over, stopper, surpass, topmost **8** complete, fore most, greatest, outshine, outstrip, pinnacle, renowned **9** paramount, principal, put a top on, transcend, uppermost, upper part **10** celebrated, first place, overshadow, preeminent

topaz
color: **4** blue **5** brown **6** yellow
source: **5** Japan **6** Brazil, Mexico, Saxony **13** Ural Mountains **18** Cairngorm Mountains
month: **8** November

Topaz
director: **9** Hitchcock
book by: **4** Uris

Topaze
author: **12** Marcel Pagnol

topaz quartz
species: **6** quartz
color: **4** blue, pink **5** brown, green **6** sherry

toper 3 sot **4** lush, soak **5** drunk **6** boozer **7** tippler **8** drunkard **9** alcoholic **11** dispomaniac

Top Hat
director: **12** Mark Sandrich
cast: **9** Eric Blore **11** Fred Astaire **12** Ginger Rogers **14** Helen Broderick **19** Edward Everett Horton
score: **12** Irving Berlin
song: **12** Cheek to Cheek **22** Top Hat White Tie and Tails

topic 4 text **5** theme **6** thesis **7** keynote, subject

topical 5 local **6** timely **7** current, limited **9** localized, parochial **10** particular, restricted **12** contemporary

Topkapi
director: **11** Jules Dassin

cast: **12** Peter Ustinov, Robert Morley **14** Melina Mercouri **16** Maximilian Schell
book by: **6** Ambler
setting: **8** Istanbul
Oscar for: **15** supporting actor (Ustinov)

topknot 4 comb, tuft **5** crest **9** cockscomb, headdress, headpiece

topmost 3 top **4** head **5** chief **7** highest, leading, supreme **8** foremost **9** paramount, principal, uppermost **10** preeminent

topnotch 3 ace **4** best **5** prime **6** choice, finest, tip-top **7** supreme **8** superior, very fine **9** excellent, first-rate, nonpareil, unequaled, unrivaled **10** preeminent **11** outstanding, unsurpassed **12** incomparable, unparalleled

top of the head 4 dome, pate **5** crown **6** noggin, noodle

Topper
director: **13** Norman Z McLeod
based on novel by: **11** Thorne Smith
cast: **9** Cary Grant **11** Alan Mowbray, Billie Burke, Hedda Hopper, Roland Young **16** Constance Bennett
sequel: **13** Topper Returns **16** Topper Takes a Trip

topple 4 fall **5** crush, quash, quell, smash, upset **6** defeat, sprawl, tumble **7** abolish, shatter, tip over **8** fall over, over come, overturn, turn over, vanquish **9** bring down, overpower, overthrow **12** pitch forward

tops 4 aces, A-one, fine **5** great, prime, super, swell **6** choice, grade-A, superb, tip-top **7** capital **8** peerless, sterling, superior, terrific, top-notch **9** excellent, first-rate, marvelous, matchless, superfine, wonderful **10** first-class, inimitable, out-of-sight, tremendous **11** outstanding, superlative **12** incomparable **13** extraordinary

top-secret 5 privy **7** private **8** eyesonly, hush-hush **12** confidential

topsoil 4 dirt, loam **5** earth

Topsy
character in: **14** Uncle Tom's Cabin
author: **5** Stowe

topsy-turvy 5 messy **6** untidy **7** chaotic **8** confused, inverted, reversed **9** confusing, inside out **10** disorderly, upside down **11** disarranged, wrong side up **12** disorganized

Torah 10 law of Moses

torch 5 brand **7** cresset **8** arsonist, flambeau **9** firebrand **9** set fire to **10** flashlight

torment 3 nag, vex **4** bane, pain, rack **5** agony, annoy, curse, worry **6** harass, harrow, misery, pester, plague **7** afflict, agonize, anguish, despair, scourge, torture, trouble **8** distress, irritate **9** annoyance, persecute, suffering **10** irritation

tormenter 5 bully, tease 6 despot, tyrant 7 coercer 9 oppressor 10 browbeater 11 intimidator

tormenting 7 painful, racking 9 agonizing, torturous 10 unbearable 11 unendurable 12 excruciating, insufferable

torn 4 rent, slit 5 split 6 ragged, ripped 8 ruptured, shredded 9 unraveled

tornado 4 wind 5 storm 6 funnel, squall, vortex 7 cyclone, twister, typhoon 8 outburst 9 hurricane, whirlwind, windstorm 10 waterspout 12 thunderstorm
   belt: 7 Midwest
   cloud: 4 tuba

torn apart 4 rent 6 ripped 7 asunder 8 in pieces, in shreds, shredded

toro 4 bull

Toronto
   baseball team: 8 Blue Jays
   bay: 6 Humber
   football team: 9 Argonauts
   former name: 4 York
   harbor: 5 Inner
   hockey team: 10 Maple Leafs
   lake: 7 Ontario
   landmark: 7 CN Tower 12 Ontario Place, O'Keefe Centre 13 Dufferin Grove 14 Dominion Centre 15 Roy Thompson Hall 16 Maple Leaf Stadium, St Lawrence Centre 17 Commerce Court West 18 Royal Ontario Museum 20 Nathan Phillips Square
   park: 7 Chorley, Stanley, Trinity 8 Winthrow 9 Cedarvale 12 Center Island 16 Winston Churchill
   street: 5 Yonge
   university: 4 York

torpedo 4 sink 5 wreck 7 destroy, missile, scuttle 9 explosive 10 projectile

torpedo (marine)
   invented by: 6 Fulton

torpid 4 dull, lazy 5 inert 6 drowsy, sleepy 7 dormant, languid, passive 8 inactive, indolent, listless, sluggish 9 apathetic, lethargic, somnolent 10 half asleep, languorous, slow-moving, spiritless 12 slow-thinking 13 lackadaisical

torpor, torpidity 6 apathy 7 inertia, languor 8 dullness, laziness, lethargy 9 indolence, lassitude 10 drowsiness, inactivity, sleepiness, somnolence 11 languidness, passiveness 12 listlessness, sluggishness

torrent 4 gush, rain, rush 5 burst, flood, salvo 6 deluge, rapids, stream, volley 7 barrage, cascade, Niagara 8 cataract, downpour, effusion, eruption, outburst 9 discharge, heavy rain, rapid flow, waterfall 10 cloudburst, outpouring, white water

Torrey, John
   field: 6 botany
   developed: 16 botanical library

Torricelli, Evangelista
   nationality: 7 Italian
   discovered concept leading to development of: 9 barometer

torrid 3 hot 4 sexy 5 fiery 6 ardent, erotic, fervid, heated, sexual, sultry 7 amorous, boiling, burning, excited, fervent, intense, lustful 8 broiling, desirous, parching, sizzling, spirited, tropical, vehement 9 hot and dry, scorching 10 passionate, sweltering 11 hot and heavy, impassioned

torte 4 cake 7 dessert 9 layer cake

tortilla 7 tostada 8 corncake 11 Mexican cake
   griddle: 5 comal

Tortilla Flat
   author: 13 John Steinbeck

tortuous 4 bent 5 snaky 6 spiral, zigzag 7 crooked, devious, sinuous, turning, winding, wriggly 8 indirect, involved, twisting, wrongful 9 ambiguous 10 circuitous, convoluted, meandering, roundabout, serpentine 11 complicated 12 full of curves, hard to follow, labyrinthine

tortuousness 9 sinuosity 11 indirection, sinuousness 12 convolutions 14 circuitousness

torture 4 pain, rack 5 abuse, agony, prick, smite, trial, wring 6 harrow, ordeal 7 anguish, cruelty, torment 8 distress, maltreat, mistreat 9 brutality, suffering 10 infliction, punishment 11 tribulation 12 put to the rack

torturous 4 cruel 7 galling, irksome, painful, racking 8 annoying 9 agonizing, anguished, harrowing, miserable, tormented, torturing 10 anguishing, distressed, tormenting, unpleasant 11 distressful, distressing 12 disagreeable, excruciating

tory 8 loyalist, royalist 12 conservative

Tosca
   opera by: 7 Puccini
   character: 7 Scarpia 9 Angelotti 11 Floria Tosca 16 Mario Cavaradossi

To Sir With Love
   director: 12 James Clavell
   cast: 4 Lulu 10 Judy Geeson 11 Suzy Kendall 13 Sidney Poitier 16 Christian Roberts
   setting: 6 London

toss 3 lob 4 cast, flip, hurl, jerk, rock, roll, sway 5 churn, fling, heave, pitch, shake, sling, throw 6 joggle, let fly, propel, tumble, wiggle, writhe 7 agitate, flounce, wriggle 8 flourish, undulate 9 oscillate

toss about 4 roil 5 bandy 6 jostle, jounce

toss back and forth 5 bandy 8 exchange

total 3 add, sum 4 full 5 add up, gross, sheer, solid, sum up, utter, whole 6 entire, figure, reckon, tote up

7 add up to, compute, perfect, total up 8 absolute, combined, complete, entirety, figure up, integral, outright, sum total, sweeping, thorough, totality 9 aggregate, calculate, down right, out-and-out, unlimited, wholesale 10 full amount, undisputed, unmodified 11 unqualified, whole amount 13 comprehensive, unconditional

totaling 8 addition, coming to 9 reckoning 10 adding up to

totalitarian 7 fascist 8 despotic 9 fascistic, tyrannous 10 autocratic, tyrannical 11 dictatorial 12 undemocratic 16 unrepresentative

totally 7 solidly, utterly 8 entirely 9 downright, out-and-out, perfectly 10 absolutely, completely, thoroughly, throughout 15 unconditionally 18 from beginning to end 20 without qualification

tote 3 lug 4 bear, cart, drag, haul, move, pack, pull 5 carry, fetch 6 convey 7 schlepp 9 transport

to the city and the world
   Latin: 10 urbi et orbi
   form of address used on: 10 papal bulls

to the four winds 7 all over 10 everywhere, far and wide 26 to the four corners of the world

to the letter 5 exact, right 7 correct, precise 8 accurate, explicit, specific 9 on the nose

To the Lighthouse
   author: 13 Virginia Woolf
   character: 4 Prue 5 James 7 Camilla 8 Mr Ramsey 9 Mr Tansley, Mrs Ramsey 11 Lily Briscoe 12 Mr Carmichael

to the point 6 direct 7 apropos, germane 8 explicit, relevant 9 pertinent 12 to the purpose

to the rear 3 aft 4 back 5 abaft 6 astern, behind 8 backward, rearward 9 backwards, sternward 10 to the stern 14 toward the stern

to the stern 6 astern, behind 8 rearward 9 sternward 10 to the stern

to the word
   Latin: 8 ad verbum

to this extent
   Latin: 8 quoad hoc

Toto
   dog in: 13 The Wizard of Oz
   author: 4 Baum

totter 4 reel, rock, sway 5 lurch, shake, waver 6 falter, teeter, waddle, wobble 7 shuffle, stagger, stumble 9 oscillate, vacillate

tottering 5 shaky 6 wobbly 7 rickety, shaking 8 insecure, topheavy, unstable, unsteady, wobbling 9 doddering, quivering, trembling 10 ramshackle, staggering

Toucan
constellation of: **6** Tucana

touch 3 art, bit, paw, pet, rub, use **4** abut, cite, dash, feel, fire, form, gift, hand, hint, join, meet, melt, move, note, stir, sway, tint, work **5** equal, flair, match, pinch, rival, rouse, skill, smack, speck, style, taste, thumb, tinge, trace, unite **6** adjoin, affect, arouse, border, broach, caress, excite, finger, finish, fondle, handle, hint at, manner, method, pawing, polish, sadden, soften, strike, stroke, thrill **7** concern, consume, contact, feeling, finesse, impress, inflame, inspire, mastery, mention, quality, refer to, soupcon, surface, texture, utilize **8** allude to, artistry, bear upon, come near, come up to, converge, deal with, deftness, fineness, fondling, handling, inspirit, resort to, thumbing **9** awareness, direction, electrify, fingering, influence, palpation, pertain to, suspicion, technique **10** adroitness, intimation, manipulate, perception, sprinkling, suggestion, virtuosity **11** be in contact, compare with, familiarity, guiding hand, realization **12** acquaintance, manipulation **13** communication, comprehension, understanding

touched 3 mad **4** daft, felt, nuts **5** crazy, moved, nutty **6** insane, joined **7** abutted, cracked, handled **8** demented, deranged, unhinged **10** unbalanced **12** mad as a hatter **13** off one's rocker, out of one's head **14** off one's trolley **15** mad as a March hare

Touched by an Angel
network: **3** CBS
cast: **7** John Dye (Andrew) **10** Della Reese (Tess), Roma Downey (Monica) **17** Valerie Bertinelli (Gloria)

touching 3 sad **6** moving, tender **7** pitiful **8** dramatic, pathetic, poignant, stirring **9** affecting, emotional, heartfelt, saddening, sorrowful **11** distressing, sentimental **12** heartrending **13** heartbreaking

touch me not
Latin: **13** noli me tangere

Touch of Evil
director: **11** Orson Welles
cast: **10** Janet Leigh, Ray Collins **11** Joanna Moore, Orson Welles, Zsa Zsa Gabor **12** Akim Tamiroff, Dennis Weaver **13** Joseph Calleia **14** Charlton Heston
cameo: **15** Marlene Dietrich **19** Mercedes McCambridge

touch off 5 shoot **6** set off **7** explode, fire off, trigger **8** activate, detonate **9** discharge

touch on 4 pose **6** broach, submit **7** advance, bring up, mention, propose, suggest **9** introduce

touchstone 4 norm, rule **5** basis,

gauge, guide, model, proof **7** example, measure, pattern **8** standard **9** benchmark, criterion, guideline, precedent, principle, yardstick

Touchstone
character in: **11** As You Like It
author: **11** Shakespeare

touch upon 7 apply to, concern, mention, refer to **8** allude to, bear upon, relate to **9** appertain

touchy 5 cross, huffy, surly, testy **6** bitter, crabby, grumpy **7** awkward, fragile, grouchy, peevish, waspish **8** captious, critical, delicate, petulant, snappish, ticklish **9** concerned, difficult, irascible, irritable, querulous, resentful, sensitive **10** precarious **11** thinskinned **12** cantankerous **13** quick-tempered

tough 4 cold, firm, hard, hood, lout, mean, punk, wily **5** bully, cagey, canny, cruel, hardy, rigid, rough, rowdy, solid, stern **6** brutal, crafty, dogged, knotty, mulish, rugged, savage, strict, strong, sturdy, thorny, trying **7** adamant, arduous, callous, complex, durable, hoodlum, inhuman, irksome, lasting, onerous, ruffian, vicious **8** baffling, barbaric, enduring, exacting, grievous, hooligan, involved, leathery, obdurate, perverse, pitiless, puzzling, ruthless, stubborn, ticklish, toilsome **9** barbarian, confusing, difficult, enigmatic, heartless, heavy-duty, intricate, laborious, obstinate, pigheaded, resistant, roughneck, strenuous, unbending, unfeeling **10** bullheaded, delinquent, exhausting, formidable, hardheaded, inflexible, perplexing, unyielding **11** bewildering, calculating, cold-blooded, complicated, hardhearted, hard-to-solve, infrangible, insensitive, troublesome **12** bloodthirsty, impenetrable **13** unsympathetic **14** uncompromising

toughen 4 firm **5** inure, steel **6** firm up, harden, season, temper **7** fortify, stiffen **8** accustom **9** acclimate, habituate **10** discipline, strengthen **11** acclimatize

Toulouse-Lautrec, Henri Marie Raymond de
born: **4** Albi **6** France **8** Albigois
artwork: **7** Friends **13** The Inspection **16** At the Moulin Rouge **24** Au Salon de la Rue des Moulins **27** Jane Avril at the Jardin de Paris **29** Cirque Fernando The Equestrienne **29** In the Parlor at the Rue des Moulins **29** The English Girl at Le Star Le Havre **30** La Goulue Entering the Moulin Rouge

toupee 3 rug, wig **6** carpet, peruke **7** periwig **9** hairpiece

tour 4 trek, trip **5** jaunt, visit **6** junket, safari, travel, voyage **7** inspect, journey **8** sightsee **9** excursion, itinerary

tourist 7 pilgrim, tripper, voyager **8** traveler, vagabond, wanderer, wayfarer **9** journeyer, sightseer **10** rubberneck **12** excursionist, globetrotter

tourmaline
color: **3** red **4** blue, pink **5** green

tournament 4 game **5** event, match **7** contest, rivalry, tourney **11** competition

tourney 4 game **5** event, joust, match **7** contest, rivalry **10** tournament **11** competition

tousled 5 messy **6** mussed, untidy **7** rumpled, tangled, unkempt **8** mussed-up, uncombed **10** disheveled, disordered

tout 4 plug, push **5** boost, exalt, extol, vaunt **6** praise, talk up **7** acclaim, commend, glorify, promote, tipster **8** ballyhoo, eulogize, give a tip **9** advertise, brag about, celebrate, publicize, recommend **10** aggrandize, noise about

tout a fait 8 entirely
literally: **12** wholly to fact

tout a l'heure 7 just now **8** very soon **9** presently **14** just a moment ago
literally: **15** wholly to the hour

tout de suite 6 at once **11** immediately
literally: **19** wholly consecutively

tout ensemble 11 all together

tout le monde 8 everyone **9** everybody **13** the whole world

tovarich 7 comrade

tow 3 lug **4** drag, draw, haul, lift, pull **5** hoist, trail

toward the end
Latin: **5** ad fin

toward the front 5 ahead **6** before **7** forward **9** to the fore **13** in the vanguard **14** in the forefront

toward the rear 4 back **6** astern **8** backward, rearward **9** sternward

toward the stern 6 astern **8** rearward **9** sternward **10** to the stern

tower 4 keep, loom, rock, soar **5** mount, outdo, spire, surge **6** ascend, belfry, castle, column, exceed, pillar, refuge, turret **7** bulwark, eclipse, minaret, obelisk, overtop, shoot up, steeple, surpass **8** mainstay, outclass, outshine, overhang, rise high **9** bell tower, rise above, transcend **10** foundation, overshadow, skyscraper, stronghold, wellspring **12** fountainhead

towering 4 high, tall **5** lofty **6** alpine **7** soaring, sublime, supreme **8** dominant, foremost, mounting, peerless, snowclad, superior **9** ascending, matchless, paramount, principal, unequaled, unmatched, unrivaled **10** cloud-swept, preeminent, surpassing, unexcelled **11** cloud-capped, overhanging **12** incomparable, second to none, transcendent, unparalleled **13** extraordinary

tower over 5 dwarf **7** surpass **8** dominate **9** rise above

Townes, Charles Hard
field: **7** physics
invented: **5** maser
awarded: **10** Nobel Prize

town hall
German: **7** Rathaus

town house 8 row house **10** brownstone, pied-a-terre **13** city residence

township 4 town **7** village **11** subdivision **12** municipality

toxic 5 fatal **6** deadly, lethal, mortal **7** noxious **8** poisoned, venomous **9** poisonous, unhealthy **10** pernicious

toxin 4 bane **5** venom **6** poison **8** pathogen

toy 4 play, tiny, yoyo **5** dally, pygmy, sport **6** bantam, bauble, fiddle, gadget, gewgaw, little, midget, trifle **7** dwarfed, for play, stunted, trinket **8** gimcrack **9** miniature, plaything, small-size **10** diminutive, small-scale **11** Lilliputian

Toy Bulldog
nickname of: **12** Mickey Walker

Toynbee, Arnold
author of: **15** A Study of History

to your health
French: **11** a votre sante

toy with 8 play with **9** flirt with **10** trifle with **16** amuse oneself with

trace 3 bit, jot, map **4** draw, drop, find, hint, hunt, iota, mark, seek, sign **5** dig up, relic, shade, tinge, token, touch, track, trail **6** depict, flavor, trifle **7** diagram, hunt for, look for, mark out, nose out, outline, remains, uncover, unearth, vestige **8** describe, discover, draw over, evidence **9** delineate, ferret out, footprint, light upon, little bit, search for, suspicion, track down **10** come across, indication, suggestion **11** small amount

trace to 6 credit **7** ascribe **8** charge to **9** attribute

Trachiniae
author: **9** Sophocles
characters: **4** Iole **6** Hyllus, Nessus **8** Deianira, Heracles

track 3 way **4** mark, path, rail, sign, tack **5** dirty, route, scent, spoor, trace, trail **6** course, follow **9** footprint, guide rail

track and field
athlete: **7** Jim Ryun **8** Al Oerter, Lee Evans, Zola Budd **9** Ben Jonson, Bob Beamon, Carl Lewis, Jim Thorpe **10** Bob Mathias, Bob Seagren, Edwin Moses, Grete Waitz, Jesse Owens, John Carlos, Lasse Viren, Mac Wilkins, Paavo Nurmi, Peter Snell, Steve Ovett, Wyomia Tyus **11** Bill Rodgers, Bruce Jenner, Marty Liouri, Dick Fos-

bury, Emil Zatopek, Ralph Boston, Randy Matson, Tommie Smith **12** Dwight Stones, Frank Shorter, Harvey Glance, Jay Silvester, Rafer Johnson, Sebastian Coe, Willie B White, Wilma Rudolph **13** Kipchoge Keino, Rodney Milburn, William Toomey **14** Alberto Salazar, Francie Larrieu, Kenenisa Bikele, Roger Bannister **15** Renaldo Nehemiah, Willie Davenport **16** Mary Decker Slaney, Steve Prefontaine **17** Alberto Juantoreno **18** Jackie Joyner-Kersee **21** Babe Didrikson Zaharias **22** Florence Griffith-Joyner

tract 3 lot **4** area, plot, zone **5** essay **6** parcel, region **7** booklet, expanse, leaflet, quarter, stretch **8** brochure, district, pamphlet, treatise **9** monograph, territory **12** disquisition

tractable 4 tame **6** docile **8** amenable, obedient, yielding **9** compliant, teachable, trainable **10** governable, manageable, submissive **12** controllable, easy to manage **13** easy to control

tractate 8 treatise **9** discourse, monograph **12** disquisition, dissertation

Tracy, Spencer
born: **11** Milwaukee WI
costar: **16** Katharine Hepburn
roles: **7** Desk Set **8** Adam's Rib, Boys Town (Oscar) **10** Pat and Mike **12** San Francisco, Tortilla Flat **13** The Last Hurrah **14** Cass Timberlane, Inherit the Wind, Woman of the Year **15** State of the Union **16** Father of the Bride, Keeper of the Flame **17** Bad Day at Black Rock **18** Captains Courageous (Oscar), The Old Man and the Sea **19** Judgment at Nuremberg **23** Guess Who's Coming to Dinner

trade 3 buy **4** deal, line, shop, swap **5** craft **6** barter, buyers **7** calling, patrons, pursuit **8** business, commerce, exchange, shoppers, vocation **9** clientele, customers, patronize **10** buy and sell, do business, employment, handicraft, line of work, occupation, profession **12** transactions **13** merchandising **16** business dealings, buying and selling

trade commodity 5 goods, wares

trademark 6 emblem **7** feature **8** property **9** specialty **11** peculiarity **14** characteristic

trade off 4 swap **5** trade **6** barter **8** exchange

trader 6 dealer, monger, seller **7** drummer **8** merchant, retailer **10** shopkeeper, trafficker, wholesaler **11** salesperson, storekeeper **12** merchandiser, tradesperson **14** businessperson

tradesman 6 dealer, seller **8** merchant, retailer **9** craftsman **10** shopkeeper **11** storekeeper

Trading Spaces

network: **3** TLC **18** The Learning Channel
host: **10** Alex McLeod, Paige Davis
carpenter: **10** Faber Dewar **12** Ty Pennington **13** Amy Wynn Pastor **17** Carter Oosterhouse
designers: **7** Dez Ryan, Vern Yip **9** Barry Wood **11** Frank Bielec, Laurie Smith **12** Edward Walker **13** Douglas Wilson, Roderick Shade **14** Christi Proctor **15** Genevieve Gorder, Hilda Santo-Tomas **18** Kia Steave-Dickerson

tradition 4 lore, myth, saga, tale **5** habit, usage **6** custom, legend **8** folklore, practice **10** convention **12** superstition

traditional 3 old **5** fixed, usual **7** typical **8** habitual, historic **9** ancestral, customary **10** accustomed, inveterate **11** established **12** acknowledged, conventional

traduce 5 abuse, libel, smear, sully **6** defame, malign, vilify **7** run down, slander **8** backbite, bad-mouth, besmirch **9** deprecate, disparage **10** calumniate

traffic 4 cars, deal **5** buses, ships, trade **6** barter, doings, planes, riders, trains, trucks **7** bootleg, contact, freight, smuggle **8** business, commerce, dealings, exchange, tourists, voyagers **9** commuters, relations, smuggling, travelers **10** buy and sell, enterprise, passengers **11** bootlegging, intercourse, pedestrians, proceedings **12** transactions, vacationists **13** excursionists

Traffic
director: **16** Steven Soderbergh
cast: **9** Amy Irving (Barbara Wakefield), D W Moffett (Jeff Sheridan) **10** Don Cheadle (Montel Gordon), Luis Guzman (Ray Castro) **11** Dennis Quaid (Arnie Metzger), Jacob Vargas (Manolo Sanchez), James Brolin (Ralph Landry), Steven Bauer (Carlos Ayala), Tomas Milian (Arturo Salazar), Topher Grace (Seth Abrahms) **12** Albert Finney (Chief of Staff), Miguel Ferrer (Eduardo Ruiz) **14** Benicio Del Toro (Javier Rodriguez), Michael Douglas (Robert Wakefield) **16** Erika Christensen (Caroline Wakefield) **18** Catherine Zeta-Jones (Helena Ayala)

tragedy 3 woe **4** blow **5** grief **6** misery, sorrow **7** anguish, setback **8** accident, calamity, disaster, reversal, sad thing **9** heartache **10** affliction, heartbreak **11** catastrophe

tragic 3 sad **4** dire **5** awful, fatal **6** deadly, dreary, woeful **7** piteous, pitiful, ruinous, serious, unhappy **8** dramatic, dreadful, grievous, horrible, mournful, pathetic, pitiable, shocking, terrible **9** appalling, frightful **10** calamitous, deplorable, disastrous, lamentable **11** destructive, devastating, unfortunate **12** catastrophic **13** heartbreaking

trail 3 dog, tow, way **4** drag, draw, fall, flow, hunt, mark, path, poke, sign, tail **5** float, hound, scent, spoor, trace, track **6** be down, course, dangle, dawdle, follow, lessen, shrink, stream **7** dwindle, pathway, subside **8** decrease, diminish, footpath, grow weak, hand down, peter out, taper off **9** drag along, grow faint, grow small, lag behind **10** bridle path, drag behind, footprints, move slowly **11** beaten track **14** bring up the rear

trailblazers 7 leaders **8** pioneers **10** avant-garde, innovators **11** forerunners, originators, tastemakers **12** trendsetters

train 2 el **3** aim, set **4** line **5** break, chain, drill, focus, level, point, queue, sight, teach, trail, tutor **6** column, direct, escort, school, series, subway **7** caravan, cortege, educate, prepare, retinue **8** elevated, exercise, instruct, practice, rehearse, sequence **9** afterpart, appendage, entourage, followers **10** attendants, discipline, get in shape, procession, succession **11** bring to bear, domesticate, progression **12** continuation

Train, The
director: **17** John Frankenheimer
cast: **10** Albert Remy **11** Michel Simon **12** Jeanne Moreau, Paul Scofield **13** Burt Lancaster

trained 4 able **6** expert, master **7** capable, skilled **8** schooled, seasoned **9** competent, qualified **11** experienced **12** accomplished

trainee 4 boot **5** cadet **6** rookie **7** private, rookie, student **9** greenhorn **10** apprentice

trainer 5 coach, tutor **7** teacher **16** athletic director

training 5 drill **8** coaching, drilling, practice, teaching **9** education, schooling **10** discipline **11** preparation **14** apprenticeship, indoctrination

traipse 3 gad **4** roam, walk **5** range, tramp, tread **6** stroll, trapes, wander **7** meander, saunter **8** gadabout **9** gallivant

trait 4 mark **5** quirk **7** earmark, feature, quality **8** hallmark **9** attribute, mannerism **11** peculiarity **12** idiosyncracy **14** characteristic

traitor 5 rat **5** Judas, rebel **6** ratter **7** ratfink, serpent **8** apostate, betrayer, deceiver, deserter, mutineer, quisling, renegade, turncoat **9** hypocrite **11** false friend **12** double-dealer **13** double-crosser, revolutionary **14** fifth columnist **15** snake in the grass **20** wolf in sheep's clothing

traitorous 5 false **7** corrupt **8** disloyal, renegade **9** betraying, faithless **10** perfidious, treasonous, unfaithful **11** treacherous

tramp 3 bum **4** hike, hobo, roam, rove, slog, trek, walk **5** march, prowl, stamp, stomp **6** ramble, trudge, wander **7** floater, meander, traipse, trample, vagrant **8** derelict **9** gallivant, itinerant **10** panhandler **11** perambulate, peregrinate **15** knight-of-the-road

trample 5 crush, stamp, stomp **6** squash **7** flatten, run over **14** grind under foot **15** step heavily upon

trance 4 coma, daze **5** dream, spell **6** stupor, vision **7** reverie **8** daydream, hypnosis **9** pipe dream **10** absorption, brown study **11** abstraction **12** sleepwalking **13** concentration, preoccupation, woolgathering

tranquil 4 calm, cool, mild **5** quiet, still **6** gentle, placid, serene **7** halcyon, restful **8** composed, peaceful **9** unexcited, unruffled **11** undisturbed, unperturbed **13** self-possessed

tranquility 4 calm, hush **5** peace, quiet **6** repose **7** concord, harmony **8** quietude, serenity **9** composure, placidity, stillness **11** restfulness **12** peacefulness

tranquilize 4 calm, drug, lull **5** allay, quiet, relax, still **6** becalm, pacify, sedate, settle, soothe **7** appease, assuage **9** alleviate

transact 2 do **5** exact **6** handle, manage, settle **7** achieve, carry on, conduct, execute, perform **8** carry out, exercise **9** discharge **10** accomplish, take care of **12** carry through

transaction 4 deal **6** affair **7** bargain, dealing, venture **8** exchange **9** operation **10** enterprise, settlement **11** negotiation **15** business dealing, piece of business

transcend 5 excel, outdo **6** exceed **7** eclipse, outrank, surpass **8** go beyond, outrival, outshine, outstrip, overleap, overstep, surmount **9** rise above **10** overshadow **11** outdistance

transcendence 5 merit **8** eminence **9** exceeding, greatness **10** exaltation, excellence, surpassing **11** distinction, preeminence, superiority

transcendental 5 great **6** mental **7** supreme, unusual **8** elevated, peerless, superior, uncommon **9** exceeding, intuitive, matchless, spiritual, unequaled, unrivaled **10** surpassing **11** unsurpassed **12** incomparable, metaphysical **13** extraordinary

transfer 4 cede, deed, move, send **5** bring, carry, shift **6** change, convey, moving, remove **7** consign, deeding, removal, sending **8** bringing, carrying, hand over, make over, relegate, relocate, shifting, shipment, transmit, turn over **9** conveying, transport **10** delivering, relegation, relocating, relocation

11 consignment, transmittal **12** transporting **14** transportation

transferable 8 catching **10** contagious, infectious **12** communicable **13** transmissible, transmittable

transferal 8 delivery, transfer **10** giving over **11** handing over, transmittal **12** transmission

transference 5 shift **6** change **7** passage, removal **9** transport **11** transmittal **12** dislodgement, displacement, transmission **13** transmittance

transfiguration 10 conversion **13** metamorphosis, transmutation **14** transformation

transfigure 6 change **9** transform **12** metamorphose

transfix 3 pin **4** hold, stab, stun **5** rivet, spear, spike, stick **6** absorb, impale, pierce, skewer **7** astound, bewitch, enchant, engross, fix fast, terrify **8** astonish, hold rapt, intrigue **9** captivate, fascinate, hypnotize, mesmerize, penetrate, spellbind **10** run through

transform 4 turn **5** alter **6** change, recast, remold **7** convert, remodel **8** make over **9** refurbish, transmute **11** reconstruct, transfigure **12** metamorphose, transmogrify

transformation 6 change **9** restyling **10** alteration, conversion, remodeling **13** metamorphosis, transmutation **15** transfiguration

transgress 3 err, sin **4** slip **5** break, cross, fault, lapse, wrong **6** exceed, impose, offend **7** digress, infract, violate **8** infringe, trespass

transgression 3 sin **5** crime, error, lapse, wrong **6** breach **7** misdeed, offense **8** evil deed, iniquity, trespass **9** violation **10** immorality, infraction, wrongdoing **11** lawbreaking **12** encroachment, infringement, overstepping **13** contravention

transgressor 5 felon **6** sinner **7** culprit **8** criminal, evildoer, offender, violator **9** miscreant, wrongdoer **11** lawbreaker, malefactor, trespasser

transience 7 brevity **11** evanescence **12** ephemerality, impermanence

transient 5 brief **7** passing **8** fleeting, soon past, temporal **9** ephemeral, momentary, short-term, temporary **10** evanescent, perishable, short-lived, transitory, unenduring **11** impermanent **14** passing through **24** here today and gone tomorrow

transistor
invented by: **7** Bardeen **8** Brattain, Shockley

transition 4 jump, leap **6** change **7** passage, passing **8** shifting **9** gradation, variation **10** alteration, changeover, conversion, graduation **11** progression **13** transmutation **14** transformation

transitory 5 brief **7** passing **8** fleeting, fugitive **9** ephemeral, temporary, transient **10** evanescent, not lasting, short-lived, unenduring **11** impermanent **24** here today and gone tomorrow

translate 4 turn **5** alter, apply **6** change, decode, recast, render, reword **7** clarify, convert, explain **8** decipher, rephrase, simplify, spell out **9** elucidate, interpret, make clear, transform, transmute **10** paraphrase

translucence 7 clarity **8** lucidity **10** luminosity **12** transparency **16** semitransparency

translucent 8 pellucid **10** semiopaque, translucid **15** semitransparent

transmissible 8 catching **10** contagious, infectious **12** communicable, transferable **13** transmittable

transmission 4 note **7** message, passage, passing, sending **8** delivery, dispatch, transfer **9** broadcast **10** conveyance, forwarding, remittance **11** handing over, transmittal **12** transference, transferring **13** communication **14** transportation

transmit 4 send, ship **5** carry, issue, relay, remit **6** convey, pass on, spread **7** deliver, forward **8** dispatch, televise, transfer **9** broadcast **11** communicate, disseminate

transmittable 8 catching **10** contagious, infectious **12** communicable, transferable

transmittal 7 sending **8** delivery, transfer **10** giving over, transferal **11** handing over **12** transmission

transmutation 6 change **10** conversion **13** metamorphosis **14** transformation **15** transfiguration

transmute 5 alter **6** change **7** convert **9** transform **12** metamorphose

transparency 6 purity **7** clarity **8** lucidity **9** clearness, sheerness **11** obviousness **14** diaphanousness

transparent 4 thin **5** gauzy, lucid, plain, sheer **6** glassy, limpid, patent **7** evident, obvious, visible **8** apparent, clear-cut, distinct, explicit, manifest, palpable, peekaboo, pellucid **10** diaphanous, see-through **11** perceptible, self-evident, translucent, unambiguous, unequivocal **12** crystal-clear, unmistakable

transpire 5 arise, occur **6** appear, befall, chance, crop up, evolve, happen, turn up **7** come out, leak out **9** be met with, eventuate, take place **10** be revealed, come to pass, make public **11** become known, be disclosed, come to light, show its face

transplant 5 graft, repot, shift **7** re-plant **8** displace, relocate, resettle, transfer **9** transport, transpose

transport 3 bus, lug **4** bear, cart, lift, move, send, ship, take, tote **5** bring, carry, charm, fetch, train, truck **6** convey, moving, remove, thrill **7** bearing, bewitch, carting, delight, deliver, enchant, freight, removal, sending, vehicle **8** airplane, carrying, delivery, dispatch, enthrall, entrance, shipment, shipping, transfer, transmit, trucking **9** captivate, cargo ship, carry away, conveying, electrify, enrapture, freighter, overpower **10** cargo plane, conveyance **12** freight train

transportation 7 cartage, haulage, portage, removal, transit **8** delivery, dispatch, movement, shipment **9** transport **10** conveyance, transferal **12** transference, transmission **13** transmittance

transported 5 moved **6** lifted **7** charmed **8** ecstatic, thrilled, uplifted **9** bewitched, entranced **10** captivated, enthralled **11** carried away, electrified **13** beside oneself

transverse 5 cross **6** across **7** athwart, oblique, transom **8** crossbar, crossing, diagonal, traverse **9** crosswise **10** crosspiece, horizontal

transversely 9 crossways, crosswise, laterally

Transylvania
region of: 7 Romania
city: 4 Cluj
fictional home of: 7 Dracula

trap 3 net, pit **4** lure, ploy, ruse, seal, stop, wile **5** catch, feint, snare, trick **6** ambush, device, enmesh, entrap, lock in **7** ensnare, pitfall, springe **8** artifice, entangle, hold back, hunt down, maneuver **9** booby trap, stratagem **11** machination **16** compartmentalize

trappings 4 garb, gear **5** array, dress **6** attire, outfit, things **7** apparel, clothes, costume, effects, raiment, vesture **8** adjuncts, clothing, fittings **9** ornaments, trimmings **10** adornments, habiliment, investment **11** decorations **13** accoutrements, paraphernalia **14** embellishments

trash 3 rot **4** bums, crap, junk, scum **5** dregs, dross, tripe, waste **6** debris, drivel, idlers, litter, refuse, rubble, tramps **7** garbage, hogwash, loafers, residue, rubbish, twaddle **8** castoffs, leavings, nonsense, riffraff **9** poppycock, sweepings **10** balderdash **11** foolishness, ne'er-do-wells, odds and ends **15** good-for-nothings, unsavory element

trashy 4 vile **5** cheap, inane, junky, tacky **6** flashy, flimsy **7** rubbish, trivial, useless **8** riff-raff, trumpery, wasteful **9** worthless **13** insignificant

trauma 4 hurt **5** shock, wound **6** injury, stress

travail 4 pain, toil **5** labor, worry **6** strain, stress **7** anguish **8** delivery, distress, drudgery, exertion, hard work, hardship **9** suffering **10** birth pains, childbirth, labor pains **11** parturition **12** accouchement

travel 2 go **4** be on, move, roam, rove, sail, tour, trek, wend **5** cross, drive, range, visit **6** cruise, junket, voyage, wander **7** journey, proceed **8** pass over, progress, sightsee, traverse **9** globetrot, hitchhike, take a trip **11** pass through, press onward

traveler 5 gypsy, nomad, rover **7** drummer, migrant, pilgrim, tourist, trekker, tripper, voyager **8** vagabond, wanderer, wayfarer **9** itinerant, journeyer, sightseer **10** vacationer **12** excursionist, globetrotter

travel through 2 do **5** cover, cross, visit **8** traverse **9** negotiate **11** pass through

traverse 4 span **5** cross **6** bridge, travel **8** go across, move over, overpass **9** cross over, cut across, intersect, move along, negotiate, reach over **10** extend over, run through, travel over **11** move through, pass through, reach across

travesty 4 sham **5** farce, spoof **6** parody, satire **7** lampoon, mockery, take-off **8** disgrace **9** burlesque **10** caricature, distortion, perversion **17** misrepresentation

Traviata, La
also: 9 The Misled **23** The Woman Who Was Led Astray
opera by: 5 Verdi
based on a story by: 14 Alexandre Dumas (fils)
     called: 7 Camille **17** La Dame aux Camelias
character: 8 Violetta **14** Alfredo Germont

Travolta, John
born: 11 Englewood NJ
roles: 6 Be Cool, Carrie, Grease **7** Face/Off, Mad City **9** Get Shorty **10** Tony Manero **11** Pulp Fiction, Urban Cowboy **12** A Civil Action, She's So Lovely, Staying Alive **13** Primary Colors **14** Moment By Moment **15** Ladder Forty-Nine, Vinnie Barbarino **17** Welcome Back Kotter **18** Saturday Night Fever **19** The General's Daughter

trawl 3 net **4** drag, fish, haul, line **5** seine, troll **6** dredge **7** dragnet

Treacher, Arthur
real name: 11 Arthur Veary
born: 7 England **8** Brighton
roles: 11 Mary Poppins **14** National Velvet, Thank You Jeeves **16** David Copperfield **20** Magnificent Obsession

treacherous 5 false, risky **6** tricky, unsafe, untrue **7** devious **8** disloyal, perilous, two-faced **9** dangerous, deceitful, deceptive, faithless, hazardous **10** misleading, perfidious, precarious, traitorous, treasonous, unfaithful **12** falsehearted **13** untrustworthy

treachery 5 guile **6** deceit **7** perfidy, treason **8** apostasy, betrayal, trickery **9** deception, duplicity, falseness **10** disloyalty, infidelity **11** double cross **13** breach of faith, deceitfulness, double-dealing, faithlessness **15** underhandedness **17** untrustworthiness

tread 4 gait, hike, pace, roam, rove, step, walk **5** prowl, range, stamp, stomp, tramp **6** step on, stride, stroll, trudge, walk on **7** trample **8** footfall, footstep

treason 6 mutiny, revolt **7** perfidy **8** apostasy, betrayal, sedition **9** duplicity, rebellion, treachery **10** conspiracy, disloyalty, insurgence, revolution, subversion **11** lese majesty **12** insurrection

treasonable 9 faithless, seditious **10** perfidious, subversive, traitorous **11** treacherous

treasure 3 gem **4** gold **5** hoard, jewel, prize, store, value **6** esteem, jewels, regard, revere, riches, silver **7** cherish, deposit, paragon **8** bank upon, dote upon, gold mine, hold dear **11** pride and joy **14** apple of one's eye **17** pearl of great price

treasure chest 3 box **4** case **5** chest, trunk **6** coffer

treasured 4 dear **5** loved **6** adored, valued **7** beloved **8** precious **9** cherished

Treasure Island
author: **20** Robert Louis Stevenson
character: **7** Ben Gunn **8** Smollett **9** Dr Livesey **10** Jim Hawkins **14** Long John Silver **15** Squire Trelawney
director:
  1934 version: **13** Victor Fleming
  1950 version: **11** Byron Haskin
based on novel by: **20** Robert Louis Stevenson
cast:
  1934 version: **10** Lewis Stone **12** Jackie Cooper (Jim Hawkins), Wallace Beery (Long John Silver) **15** Lionel Barrymore
  1950 version: **11** Basil Sydney **12** Robert Newton (Long John Silver) **13** Bobby Driscoll (Jim Hawkins) **16** Walter Fitzgerald

Treasure of the Sierra Madre, The
director: **10** John Huston
cast: **7** Tim Holt **12** Bruce Bennett, Walter Huston **13** Alfonso Bedoya, Barton MacLane **14** Humphrey Bogart
Oscar for: **8** director **10** screenplay **15** supporting actor (Huston)

treasurer 6 banker, bursar, purser,

teller **7** auditor, cashier **9** financier **10** accountant, bookkeeper, cash-keeper, controller **16** financial officer **17** minister of finance **22** secretary of the treasury **24** Chancellor of the Exchequer

Treasure State
nickname of: **7** Montana

treasury 4 bank, safe, till **5** funds, purse, vault **6** coffer **8** money box **9** anthology, exchequer, strongbox, thesaurus **10** collection, compendium, depository, repository, storehouse **11** bank account, compilation

treasury note 4 bill **8** bank note **9** greenback **12** currency note **17** silver certificate

treat 3 joy **4** blow, coat, give **5** apply, cover, favor, grant, imbue, stand **6** attend, divert, doctor, handle, manage, remedy, spring, thrill **7** comfort, delight, discuss, patch up, take out **8** consider, deal with, look upon, medicate, pleasure, relate to **9** act toward, small gift, try to cure, try to heal **10** impregnate, minister to, speak about, write about **12** prescribe for, satisfaction **13** gratification

treat as inferior 7 disdain **9** patronize **12** condescend to **18** look down one's nose at **19** discriminate against

treatise 4 text **5** essay, study, tract **6** manual, memoir, report, thesis **8** textbook, tractate **9** discourse, monograph **12** dissertation

treatment 3 way **4** cure **6** course, remedy **7** conduct, process, regimen, therapy **8** antidote, approach, handling, treating **9** doctoring, operation, procedure **10** management, medication **11** application, medical care **12** manipulation

treaty 4 deal, pact **6** accord **7** bargain, compact, entente **8** covenant **9** concordat **13** understanding **15** formal agreement **22** international agreement

tree 3 ash, elm, fir, oak **4** bush, palm, pine, wood **5** beech, birch, chase, maple, plane, plant, scrub, staff, stake, stick **6** corner, cudgel, redbud, spruce, timber, willow **7** gallows, lineage, live oak, sapling **8** ancestry, chestnut, hardwood, mahogany, pedigree, seedling **9** ailanthus, evergreen **10** cottonwood, eucalyptus

Tree Grows in Brooklyn, A
author: **10** Betty Smith
character:
  Nolan family: **5** Katie **6** Neeley **7** Francie, Johnnie
director: **9** Elia Kazan
cast: **9** James Dunn **10** Lloyd Nolan **12** Joan Blondell **14** Dorothy McGuire, Peggy Ann Garner
Oscar for: **7** special (Garner) **15** supporting actor (Dunn)

treeless 4 bald, bare **6** barren **7** denuded **8** unwooded **10** unforested

tref 9 not kosher

trek 4 hike, plod, roam, rove, sail, slog, trip **5** jaunt, march, range, tramp **6** junket, outing, travel, trudge, voyage, wander **7** journey, odyssey, passage **8** traverse **9** excursion, migration **10** expedition, pilgrimage **11** peregrinate **13** peregrination

trellis 5 arbor, bower, cross, frame, grill, trail **6** gazebo, screen **7** lattice, network, pergola **8** espalier **10** interweave **11** summerhouse

tremble 5 quail, quake, shake, waver **6** quaver, quiver, shiver **7** flutter, pulsate, shudder **9** palpitate

trembling 5 shaky **7** quaking, shaking **8** unsteady **9** doddering, quavering, quivering, shivering **10** shuddering **11** palpitating

tremblor 5 quake, seism, shock **6** tremor **8** upheaval **10** earthquake

tremendous 4 fine, huge, vast **5** giant, great, major **7** amazing, awesome, immense, mammoth, sizable, titanic, unusual **8** colossal, enormous, fabulous, gigantic, terrific, towering, uncommon **9** excellent, fantastic, first-rate, humongous, important, marvelous, monstrous, wonderful **10** formidable, gargantuan, incredible, noteworthy, stupendous **11** elephantine, exceptional **12** considerable **13** consequential, extraordinary

tremolo
music: **9** trembling, vibrating **30** rapid reiteration of a single pitch

tremor 3 jar **4** jolt **5** quake, shake, shock, spasm, throb, waver **6** quiver, shiver **7** flutter, shaking, shudder, tremble **8** paroxysm **9** pulsation, quavering, quivering, shivering, trembling, vibration **10** convulsion **11** palpitation

tremulous 5 jumpy, shaky, timid **6** wobbly **7** aquiver, excited, fearful, jittery, keyed-up, nervous, panicky, quaking **8** aflutter, agitated, atremble, hesitant, restless, wavering, worked-up **9** faltering, impatient, quivering, trembling, uncertain **10** irresolute, stimulated **13** on tenterhooks, panic-stricken

trench 3 cut, rut **4** scar **5** canal, ditch, drain, fosse, slash, slice **6** dugout, furrow, gutter, trough **7** channel, wrinkle **8** aqueduct **9** earthwork **10** depression

trenchant 4 acid, keen, tart **5** crisp **6** bitter **7** acerbic, caustic, concise, mordant, probing **8** clear-cut, distinct, incisive, scathing **9** sarcastic, scorching **10** razor-sharp **11** acrimonious, penetrating, well-defined

trend 4 bent, flow, mode **5** drift, style **7** fashion, impulse, leaning **8** movement, tendency **9** direction **10** proclivity, propensity **11** inclination

trendsetters 7 leaders **8** trendies, vanguard **10** avant-garde, innovators **11** pacesetters, tastemakers **12** advance guard, stylesetters, trailblazers

trendy 2 in **4** chic, tony **5** swank **6** modern, modish, with-it **7** current, faddish, popular, stylish, voguish **8** up-to-date **10** all the rage **11** fashionable **13** up-to-the-minute

trepidation 4 fear **5** alarm, dread, panic, worry **7** anxiety, jitters **8** cold feet, disquiet **10** uneasiness **11** butterflies, disquietude, jitteriness, nervousness **12** apprehension **13** consternation

trespass 3 sin **5** error, wrong **6** invade **7** impinge, intrude, misdeed, offense **8** encroach, infringe, iniquity, invasion **9** evildoing, intrusion, violation **10** immorality, infraction, misconduct, wrongdoing **11** delinquency, misbehavior **12** encroachment, infringement, overstepping **13** transgression, unlawful entry, wrongful entry

tress 4 curl, hair, lock, mane **5** braid, plait **6** strand **7** ringlet, wimpler **8** spitcurl

trestle 4 beam **5** board, brace, frame, table **6** timber **9** framework

trial 2 go **3** try, woe **4** care, pain, shot, test **5** agony, essay, flyer, whirl, worry **6** burden, effort, misery, ordeal, trying, tryout **7** anguish, attempt, bad luck, hearing, testing, test run, torment, trouble, venture **8** accident, distress, endeavor, hardship, vexation **9** adversity, court case, heartache, suffering **10** affliction, litigation, misfortune **11** cross to bear **12** misadventure, wretchedness

Trial, The
   author: 10 Franz Kafka
   character: 4 Leni **8** Joseph K **9** Titorelli **11** The Advocate

trial and error 10 experiment **13** investigation **15** experimentation **20** process of elimination

tribe *see* **11** ethnic group

Tribes of Israel *see* **6** Israel

tribulation 3 woe **4** care, pain **5** agony, grief, trial, worry **6** misery, ordeal, sorrow **7** anguish, bad luck, torment, trouble **8** distress, hardship, vexation **9** adversity, heartache, suffering **10** affliction, ill fortune, misfortune **11** unhappiness **12** wretchedness

tribunal 3 bar **5** bench, court, forum **6** judges **9** authority, judiciary **10** ruling body **11** judge's bench, judge's chair **14** seat of judgment

tributary 6 branch, feeder, source, stream **7** helping, subject **8** affluent **9** ancillary, auxiliary, confluent, secondary **10** subjugated, subsidiary **11** subordinate **12** contributing, contributory

tribute 3 tax **4** duty, levy, toll **5** bribe, honor, kudos **6** esteem, eulogy, excise, impost, payoff, praise, ransom **7** payment, respect **8** accolade, encomium, memorial **9** extolling, gratitude, laudation, panegyric **10** assessment, blood money, compliment, settlement **11** recognition, testimonial **12** commendation, pound of flesh **13** consideration, peace offering **14** acknowledgment

trice 3 sec **4** jiff, wink **5** blink, flash, jiffy, shake **6** minute, moment, second **7** instant **9** coup d'oeil, twinkling **11** split second

trichophobia
   fear of: 4 hair

trichoptera
   class: 8 hexapoda
   phylum: 10 arthropoda
   group: 3 fly **6** caddis

trick 3 art, gag **4** bait, dupe, feat, gift, gull, have, hoax, joke, ploy, ruse, trap, wile **5** antic, blind, bluff, caper, cheat, dodge, feint, fraud, knack, prank, put-on, skill, stunt **6** deceit, device, number, outfox, outwit, resort, secret, take in **7** deceive, gimmick, know-how, mislead, swindle **8** artifice, deftness, flimflam, hoodwink, maneuver **9** bamboozle, chicanery, deception, dexterity, imposture, sophistry, stratagem, technique **10** adroitness, hocus-pocus, manipulate, subterfuge **11** contrivance, machination, outmaneuver **13** practical joke, sleight of hand **16** prestidigitation

trickery 5 guile **6** bunkum, deceit **8** artifice, flimflam, pretense, quackery, wiliness **9** chicanery, deception, duplicity, imposture, rascality, stratagem **10** artfulness, craftiness, hocus-pocus, shiftiness **11** crookedness, deviousness **12** charlatanism, skullduggery, slipperiness **13** deceitfulness

trickiness 6 deceit **7** cunning, slyness **8** trickery **9** duplicity **10** craftiness **15** underhandedness

trickle 4 drip, leak, ooze, seep **5** exude **7** dribble, seepage **9** percolate

trickster 5 cheat, joker **6** dodger, rascal **8** deceiver, impostor, sleeveen **9** prankster

tricky 3 sly **4** foxy, wily **5** risky **6** artful, crafty, shifty, unsafe **7** cunning, devious **8** rascally, slippery, unstable **9** dangerous, deceptive, difficult, hazardous **10** touch-and-go, unreliable **11** complicated, underhanded **12** hard to handle, undependable **13** temperamental, unpredictable

trident
   form: 5 spear
   number of prongs: 5 three
   scepter of: 7 Neptune **8** Poseidon

trifle 3 bit, dab, jot, nip, toy **4** dash, drop, idle, iota, mite, play **5** crumb,

dally, pinch, scrap, speck, tinge, touch, trace **6** bauble, dawdle, gewgaw, linger, little, morsel, sliver **7** modicum, nothing, trinket **8** fragment, gimcrack, kill time **9** bagatelle, plaything, waste time **10** dillydally, knickknack, sprinkling, triviality **11** deal lightly, small matter **12** amuse oneself, treat lightly **13** small quantity

trifler 5 flirt, idler **6** coquet **7** dabbler, dallier **8** coquette **10** dilettante

trifling 4 puny **5** petty, small, sorry, token **6** paltry, slight **7** nominal, trivial **8** beggarly, niggling, nugatory, picayune, piddling **9** worthless **10** negligible **11** unimportant **13** beneath notice, inappreciable, insignificant **14** inconsiderable **15** inconsequential

trifling circumstances
   Latin: 8 minutiae

trifling matter
   French: 10 peu de chose

trigger 5 shoot **6** set off **7** fire off **8** activate, detonate, touch off **9** discharge

trikerion 11 candelabrum, candlestick **12** candleholder

Trilby
   author: 15 George du Maurier
   character: 5 Gecko, Sandy, Taffy **8** Svengali **12** Little Billee **14** Trilby O'Ferrall

trill
   music: 7 shaking, tremolo **9** quavering

trim 3 cut, fit, lop **4** clip, crop, deck, form, lean, pare, slim, thin **5** adorn, array, lithe, prune, shape, shave, shear, shift, sleek, state **6** adjust, bedeck, border, change, fettle, kilter, limber, paring, piping, supple, svelte **7** arrange, balance, bedizen, compact, cutting, fitness, furbish, garnish, lissome, pruning, shapely, slender, willowy **8** athletic, beautify, clipping, cropping, decorate, equalize, ornament, shearing, trick out, trimming **9** adornment, condition, embellish, embroider, shipshape **10** decoration, distribute **11** streamlined **13** embellishment, ornamentation

trimming 4 trim **5** frill **7** cutting, pruning, slicing **8** clipping **9** adornment **10** decoration, shortening, truncation **11** abridgement, contraction, curtailment **12** abbreviation **13** embellishment

Trinacria *see* **6** Sicily

Trinidad and Tobago
   capital/largest city: 11 Port of Spain
   others: 4 Debe, Toco **5** Arima **6** Canaan, Coryal, Labrea **7** San Juan, Siparia **8** Rio Claro, Tunapuna **10** Roxborough **11** San Fernando, Scarborough **12** Princess Town, Sangre Grande **14** Charlotteville
   school: 6 Fatima **7** St Mary's **11**

Queen's Royal
head of state: 14 British monarch **15** governor general
monetary unit: 4 cent **6** dollar
island: 12 Chacachacare, Little Tobago **14** Bird of Paradise
lake: 5 Pitch
mountain:
  hills: 7 Trinity **10** Montserrat **12** Three Sisters
highest point: 5 Aripo
river: 6 Caroni **7** Ortoire **8** Oropuche, Trinidad
sea: 8 Atlantic **9** Caribbean
physical feature:
  bay: 5 Cocos, Guapo **6** Matura, Mayaro
  channel: 12 Dragon's Mouth **13** Serpent's Mouth
  gulf: 5 Paria
  point: 5 Radix **6** Arenal, Galera **7** Chupara, Galeota **8** Columbus
people: 5 Irish **6** French, Syrian **7** African, Chinese, English, Spanish **8** European, Lebanese **10** East Indian, Portuguese, Venezuelan **11** Asian Indian **13** Latin American
  explorer: 8 Columbus
  leader: 8 Williams
language: 6 French **7** Chinese, English, Spanish **10** Portuguese **12** French Patois
religion: 5 Hindu, Islam **8** Anglican **10** Protestant **12** Christianity **13** Roman Catholic
place:
  asphalt lake: 9 Pitch Lake
  mansions: 16 Magnificent Seven
  park: 18 Queen's Park Savannah
feature:
  bird: 7 oilbird **8** cocorico
  clothing: 4 sari **5** dhoti
  dance: 6 Dragon, Shango
  festival: 6 Hosein, Lights
  fish: 5 guppy
  music: 7 calypso, goombay
  tree: 4 mora
food:
  drink: 16 Angostura Bitters
trinket 3 toy **5** bijou, charm, jewel **6** bauble, gewgaw, notion, trifle **8** gimcrack, ornament **9** bagatelle, plaything **10** knickknack
trip 3 bob, err **4** flip, flub, fool, muff, pull, skip, slip, tour, trek, undo **5** caper, catch, dance, fluff, foray, jaunt, outdo, throw, upset **6** bungle, cruise, frolic, gambol, junket, outfox, outing, prance, safari, set off, slip up, voyage **7** blunder, commute, confuse, flounce, journey, misstep, release, scamper, stumble **8** activate, fall over, flounder, hoodwink, throw off **9** excursion **10** disconcert, expedition, pilgrimage **11** step lightly
Triple Crown 7 Belmont **9** Preakness **13** Kentucky Derby
  winner: 5 Omaha **7** Assault **8** Af-

firmed, Citation **9** Sir Barton, Whirlaway **10** Count Fleet, Gallant Fox, War Admiral **11** Seattle Slew, Secretariat
Triple Sec *see* **9** Cointreau
Tripoli
  capital of: 5 Libya
Triptolemos, Triptolemus
  favorite of: 7 Demeter
  inventor of: 4 plow **5** wheel
  patron of: 11 agriculture
Triquetra *see* **6** Sicily
triskaidekaphobia
  fear of: 14 number thirteen
Trismegistus *see* **5** Thoth
Tristan and Isolde
  also: 16 Tristan und Isolde
  opera by: 6 Wagner
  character: 5 Melot **8** Brangane, Kurwenal **18** King Mark of Cornwall
triste 3 sad **10** melancholy
tristesse 6 sorrow **7** sadness **10** melancholy
Tristram
  author: 22 Edwin Arlington Robinson
  character in: 16 Arthurian romance
Tristram Shandy
  author: 14 Laurence Sterne
  character: 6 Dr Slop **8** Mr Yorick **10** Toby Shandy **11** Widow Wadman **12** Corporal Trim, Walter Shandy
trite 5 banal, silly, stale **6** common **7** cliched, humdrum, routine, shallow, worn-out **8** bromidic, everyday, ordinary, overdone, shopworn **9** frivolous, hackneyed **10** pedestrian, threadbare **11** commonplace, oft-repeated, stereotyped, unimportant **12** run-of-the-mill **13** platitudinous
Tritogeneia *see* **6** Athena
Triton
  god of: 3 sea
  father: 8 Poseidon
  mother: 10 Amphitrite
  shape: 6 merman
  trumpet: 10 conch-shell
triumph 3 hit, win **4** best, coup **5** smash **6** subdue **7** conquer, mastery, prevail, succeed, success, surpass, victory **8** conquest, overcome, smash hit, vanquish **9** overwhelm **10** ascendancy, attainment, gain the day **11** achievement, superiority **12** come out on top, take the prize **14** accomplishment, get the better of
triumphal 5 proud **6** joyous **8** exultant **9** ascendant, rewarding **10** fulfilling, gratifying, successful, triumphant, victorious **11** spectacular
triumphant 6 elated, joyful **7** winning **8** exultant, jubilant **9** rejoicing **10** conquering, first-place, successful, victorious **11** celebrating **12** prizewinning
trivia
  Latin: 8 minutiae

trivial 4 idle, puny, slim **5** banal, petty, small, trite **6** common, flimsy, little, meager, paltry, slight, two-bit **7** foolish **8** beggarly, everyday, niggling, nugatory, ordinary, picayune, piddling, trifling **9** rinky-dink, worthless **10** incidental, pedestrian **11** commonplace, meaningless, unessential, unimportant **13** inappreciable, insignificant, of little value **14** inconsiderable **15** inconsequential
triviality 5 frill **6** trifle **9** frivolity **10** paltriness **12** nonessential, unimportance **14** insignificance **18** inconsequentiality
troglodyte 5 brute **6** hermit **9** barbarian **11** cave dweller
Troilus
  father: 5 Priam
  mother: 6 Hecuba
Troilus and Cressida
  author: 18 William Shakespeare
  character: 4 Ajax **5** Priam **6** Hector **7** Ulysses **8** Achilles, Diomedes, Pandarus **9** Agamemnon
Troilus and Criseyde
  author: 15 Geoffrey Chaucer
  character: 8 Diomedes, Pandarus
trois 5 three
Trojan Horse
  made of: 4 wood
  made by: 7 Epeiosk
  contained: 8 Odysseus, warriors
Trojans, The
  also: 10 Les Troyens
  opera by: 7 Berlioz
  part one: 14 La Prise de Troie **16** The Capture of Troy
  part two: 19 Les Troyens a Carthage **20** The Trojans in Carthage
  character: 4 Dido **6** Aeneas, Hector
Trojan War
  length: 8 ten years
  combatants: 6 Greeks **7** Trojans
  cause: 5 Helen, Paris **14** Apple of Discord
Trojan Women, The
  author: 9 Euripides
  character: 5 Helen **6** Hecuba **8** Astyanax, Menelaus, Odysseus, Polyxena **9** Agamemnon, Cassandra **10** Andromache, Talthybius **11** Neoptolemus
troll 3 imp **4** ogre **5** dwarf, gnome **6** goblin
  origin: 12 Scandinavian
  form: 12 supernatural
  inhabits: 10 subterrain
trollop 4 doxy, slut **5** bitch, doxie, frump, hussy, trull, whore **6** floozy, harlot, wanton **7** baggage **8** slattern, strumpet **10** prostitute
Trollope, Anthony
  author of: 9 Orley Farm, The Warden **15** The Way We Live Now **16** Barchester Towers, Framley Parsonage
  character: 11 Phineas Finn

troop, troops 4 army, band, file, gang, herd, step, unit **5** bunch, crowd, crush, drove, flock, horde, march, press, swarm, tramp **6** parade, stride, throng, trudge **7** cavalry, company, militia **8** infantry, soldiers, soldiery, troopers **9** aggregate, gathering **10** armed force, assemblage **11** cavalry unit, fighting men, police force **12** congregation **13** military force

trop 3 too **7** too many, too much

Trophonius
  vocation: 7 builder
  father: 7 Erginus
  brother: 8 Agamedes
  god of: 5 earth
  killed: 8 Agamedes
  became: 6 oracle
    oracle called: 14 Zeus Trophonius

trophy 4 palm **5** award, booty, honor, kudos, medal, prize, relic, spoil **6** wreath **7** laurels, memento **8** citation, souvenir **9** loving cup **10** blue ribbon **11** testimonial

tropical 5 muggy **6** sultry, torrid **8** stifling **10** sweltering **11** hot and humid

troppo, non
  music: 10 not too much

Tros
  king of: 4 Troy
  father: 12 Erichthonius
  mother: 8 Astyoche
  wife: 10 Callirrhoe
  son: 4 Ilus **8** Ganymede **9** Assaracus

trot 3 jog **9** go briskly **11** step quickly, walk smartly

troth 8 fidelity **9** betrothal **10** affiancing, engagement **12** faithfulness

trouble 3 fix, row, vex, woe **4** blow, care, fuss, heed, mess, pain, pass, snag, work **5** agony, annoy, grief, harry, labor, pains, pinch, think, trial, upset, worry **6** affect, attend, badger, bother, burden, crisis, defect, dismay, effort, grieve, harass, misery, ordeal, pester, pickle, plague, pother, put out, scrape, sorrow, strain, strait, stress, strife, unrest **7** afflict, agitate, ailment, attempt, concern, depress, dilemma, discord, disturb, ferment, ill wind, oppress, perturb, reverse, setback, torment **8** disaster, disorder, disquiet, distress, disunity, exertion, hardship, hot water, quandary, rainy day, struggle, take time, unsettle, vexation **9** adversity, agitation, annoyance, attention, breakdown, challenge, commotion, deep water, hard times, suffering **10** affliction, convulsion, difficulty, disability, discommode, discompose, disconcert, discontent, dissension, irritation, make uneasy, misfortune, opposition **11** competition, disturbance, embroilment, instability, malfunction, predicament, tribulation **12** entanglement, exert oneself **13** inconvenience, make the effort **14** discontentment **15** dissatisfaction

troubled 5 upset **7** worried **8** bothered, careworn **9** disturbed, perturbed **10** distressed **12** heavyhearted

troublemaker 6 gossip **7** inciter **8** agitator, fomenter, provoker **9** miscreant **10** incendiary, instigator **11** rumormonger, scaremonger **12** rabble-rouser **13** mischief-maker, scandalmonger **16** agent provocateur

troublesome 4 hard **5** heavy, pesky, tough **6** cursed, knotty, taxing, thorny, tiring, trying, vexing **7** arduous, irksome, onerous, tedious **8** annoying, tiresome, unwieldy **9** demanding, difficult, fatiguing, harassing, herculean, laborious, wearisome, worrisome **10** bothersome, burdensome, cumbersome, disturbing, irritating, oppressive, tormenting, unpleasant **11** disobedient, distressing **12** disagreeable, exasperating, inconvenient, uncontrolled **13** undisciplined

troublesomeness 5 trial **10** difficulty **11** arduousness **13** inconvenience, laboriousness, vexatiousness, worrisomeness **14** bothersomeness

Trouble with Harry, The
  director: 15 Alfred Hitchcock
  cast: 11 Edmund Gwenn **12** John Forsythe **14** Mildred Dunnock, Mildred Natwick **15** Shirley MacLaine

troubling 6 vexing **8** worrying **9** worrisome **10** bothersome, disturbing, unsettling

trough 4 duct, moat, race, tray **5** canal, ditch, flume, gorge, gully **6** furrow, hollow, ravine, trench **7** channel **8** aqueduct **10** depression

trounce 4 beat, drub, lick, trim, whip **5** cream, skunk **6** humble **7** clobber **8** vanquish **9** overpower, overwhelm **10** take care of **11** carry the day **14** get the better of

troupe 4 band, cast **5** group, troop **6** actors **7** company, players **10** performers **11** road company

trouper 5 actor **7** actress **8** thespian **9** performer **13** touring player **15** repertory player

trousers 5 jeans, pants **6** chinos, slacks **7** drawers **8** breeches, britches, jodhpurs, knickers, overalls **9** dungarees **10** pantaloons **11** bellbottoms **12** pedal pushers **14** knickerbockers

Trovatore, Il
  also: 13 The Troubadour
  opera by: 5 Verdi
  character: 7 Azucena, Leonora, Manrico **11** Count di Luna

Troy
  abducted queen: 5 Helen
  archaeologist: 6 Blegen **8** Dorpfeld **10** Schliemann
  defender: 5 Eneas **6** Aeneas

  Greek name: 5 Ilion
  hero: 6 Hector
  king: 5 Priam
  Latin name: 5 Ilium
  modern name: 9 Hissarlik
  mountain: 3 Ida
  neighboring city in NY: 6 Albany **10** Watervliet
  river: 6 Hudson
  city in: 7 Alabama, New York **8** Michigan
  story: 5 Iliad **7** Odyssey
  surrounding region: 5 Troad, Troas

Troy
  director: 16 Wolfgang Petersen
  cast: 8 Brad Pitt (Achilles), Brian Cox (Agamemnon), Eric Bana (Hector), Sean Bean (Odysseus) **9** Rose Byrne (Briseis), Tyler Mane (Ajax) **10** James Cosmo (Glaucus) **11** Diane Kruger (Helen), Nathan Jones (Boagrius), Peter O'Toole (Priam), Siri Svegler (Polydora) **12** John Shrapnel (Nestor), Julian Glover (Triopas), Orlando Bloom (Paris) **13** Julie Christie (Thetis) **14** Brendan Gleeson (Menelaus), Garrett Hedlund (Patroclus), Saffron Burrows (Andromache)

truancy 3 cut **7** absence **11** absenteeism, nonpresence **12** playing hooky **13** nonappearance, nonattendance **14** cutting classes, skipping school

truant 4 gone **5** idler **6** absent, dodger, evader, loafer, no show **7** drifter, goof-off, missing, not here, shirker, slacker, vagrant **8** absentee, deserter, layabout **9** goldbrick **10** delinquent, malingerer, nonpresent, not present **11** boondoggler, hooky-player **12** nonattendant, playing hooky

truce 4 halt, lull, rest, stay, stop **5** break, pause **7** respite **9** armistice, cease-fire **12** interruption **14** breathing spell, discontinuance **23** suspension of hostilities

Trucial Oman, Trucial States see **18** United Arab Emirates

truck 3 rig, van **5** lorry **15** eighteen-wheeler
  type: 5 panel **6** pickup **7** trailer **8** delivery

truckle 3 bow **4** fawn **5** court, defer, yield **6** grovel, pander, submit **7** flatter **8** bootlick, butter up, suck up to **9** shine up to **10** curry favor, take orders **11** apple-polish, fall all over **12** knuckle under **17** ingratiate oneself

truculence 8 defiance, ill humor **9** hostility, ill temper, pugnacity, surliness **10** fierceness **11** bellicosity **12** belligerence, churlishness **14** aggressiveness

truculent 4 rude, sour **5** cross, nasty, sulky, surly **6** fierce, touchy **7** defiant, hostile, peevish **8** churlish, insolent, petulant, snappish, snarling **9** bellicose **10** aggressive, ill-humored, ill-natured, pugnacious, ungracious **11** bad-tempered, belligerent, ill-tempered

Trudeau, Garry
wife: **10** Jane Pauley
creator/artist of: **10** Doonesbury
play: **10** Doonesbury **15** A Partisan Review (with Elizabeth Swados)

Trudeau Pierre
home: **6** Canada
office: **13** prime minister

trudge 4 drag, limp, plod **5** clump, march, tramp **6** hobble, lumber **7** shamble

true 4 even, firm, full, just, pure, real **5** exact, legal, loyal, right, usual, valid **6** actual, lawful, normal, proper, steady, strict, trusty **7** correct, devoted, factual, genuine, literal, precise, regular, staunch, typical **8** absolute, accurate, bona fide, constant, faithful, official, positive, reliable, rightful, true-blue, truthful **9** authentic, simon-pure, steadfast **10** dependable, legitimate, unswerving, unwavering **11** trustworthy **14** unquestionable

true being 4 core, soul **6** nature, psyche, spirit **7** essence

True Grit
director: **13** Henry Hathaway
based on novel by: **13** Charles Portis
cast: **8** Kim Darby **9** John Wayne **11** Jeremy Slate **12** Glen Campbell, Robert Duvall **14** Strother Martin
Oscar for: **5** actor (Wayne)

Truffaut, Francois
director of: **11** Day for Night, Jules and Jim **19** Shoot the Piano Player, The Four Hundred Blows

truism 3 saw **5** adage, axiom **6** cliche, dictum, saying **9** platitude

truly 6 indeed, in fact, really, surely, verily **7** exactly, in truth, no doubt **8** actually, honestly, to be sure **9** assuredly, certainly, correctly, factually, genuinely, literally, precisely, sincerely **10** absolutely, accurately, definitely, faithfully, positively, truthfully, upon my word **11** beyond doubt, in actuality, indubitably, so help me God **12** indisputably **13** incontestably, unequivocally **14** beyond question, unquestionably **15** all kidding aside, without question

Truman, Harry S
nickname: **15** Give Em Hell Harry
presidential rank: **11** thirty-third
party: **10** Democratic
state represented: **8** Missouri
succeeded upon death of: **9** Roosevelt
defeated: **5** (Farrell) Dobbs, (Thomas Edmund) Dewey **6** (Claude A) Watson, (Norman) Thomas **7** (Henry Agard) Wallace **8** (Edward A) Teichert, (James Strom) Thurmond
vice president: **7** (Alben William) Barkley

cabinet:
state: **6** (James Francis) Byrnes **7** (Dean Gooderham) Acheson **8** (George Catlett) Marshall **10** (Edward Reilly) Stettinius (Jr)
treasury: **6** (Frederick Moore) Vinson, (John Wesley) Snyder **10** (Henry) Morgenthau (Jr)
war: **6** (Kenneth Claiborne) Royall **7** (Henry Lewis) Stimson **9** (Robert Porter) Patterson
defense: **6** (Robert Abercrombie) Lovett **7** (Louis Arthur) Johnson **8** (George Catlett) Marshall **9** (James Vincent) Forrestal
attorney general: **5** (Thomas Campbell) Clark **6** (Francis) Biddle **7** (James Howard) McGrath **9** (James Patrick) McGranery
navy: **9** (James Vincent) Forrestal
postmaster general: **6** (Frank Comerford) Walker **8** (Robert Emmet) Hannegan **9** (Jesse Monroe) Donaldson
interior: **4** (Julius Albert) Krug **5** (Harold LeClaire) Ickes **7** (Oscar Littleton) Chapman
agriculture: **7** (Charles Franklin) Brannan, (Claude Raymond) Wickard **8** (Clinton Presba) Anderson
commerce: **6** (Charles) Sawyer **7** (Henry Agard) Wallace **8** (William Averell) Harriman
labor: **5** (Maurice Joseph) Tobin **7** (Frances), Perkins (Wilson) **13** (Lewis Baxter) Schwellenbach
born: **2** MO **5** Lamar **8** Missouri
died: **2** MO **8** Missouri **10** Kansas City
buried: **2** MO **8** Missouri **12** Independence
education:
law school: **21** Kansas City School of Law (did not graduate)
religion: **7** Baptist
interests: **5** piano **7** history
vacation spot: **2** FL **7** Florida, Key West
author: **14** Year of Decision **19** Years of Trial and Hope
political career: **8** US Senate **13** Vice President
presiding judge of: **13** Jackson County
civilian career: **6** farmer
owned: **9** men's store **12** haberdashery
military service: **5** major **9** World War I **15** MO National Guard **18** Army Reserve colonel
notable events of lifetime/term: **4** NATO **5** V-E Day **8** Fair Deal **9** Korean War **17** iron-curtain speech **20** assassination attempt **31** North Atlantic Treaty Organization
act: **11** Taft-Hartley **12** Bretton-Woods
airlift to: **6** Berlin

conference: **7** Potsdam
dropping of first: **5** A-bomb **8** atom bomb
plan: **8** Marshall **9** Point Four
signing of: **9** UN charter
Treaty of: **12** Rio de Janeiro
trial of: **9** Alger Hiss
father: **12** John Anderson
mother: **6** Martha (Ellen Young)
siblings: **8** Mary Jane **10** John Vivian
wife: **9** Elizabeth (Virginia Wallace)
nickname: **4** Bess
children: **12** Mary Margaret

Trumbull, John
born: **9** Lebanon CT
artwork: **21** The Battle of Bunker Hill **26** The Resignation of Washington **28** The Declaration of Independence **29** The Surrender of General Burgoyne **32** The Capture of the Hessians at Trenton **38** The Surrender of Lord Cornwallis at Yorktown **46** The Death of General Montgomery in the Attack of Quebec, The Death of General Warren at the Battle of Bunker Hill

trumpery 5 showy, trash **6** deceit, trashy, trivia **7** rubbish, twaddle, useless **8** frippery, nonsense, trifling **9** deception, worthless **11** nonsensical

trumpet 4 honk, horn **5** blare, bugle **6** cornet **7** clarion **8** proclaim **10** hearing aid

Trumpet of the Swan, The
author: **7** E B White

trump up 4 fake **6** invent, make up **7** concoct, falsify **9** fabricate

truncate 3 bob, lop, nip **4** clip, crop, dock, snub, trim **5** prune **7** abridge, curtail, shorten **8** amputate, condense, cut short **10** abbreviate

truncheon 3 bat **4** club **5** baton, billy, stick **6** cudgel **8** bludgeon **9** billyclub

trunker 3 box, die **4** body, bole, dado, line, main **5** chief, pants, shaft, snout, stock, torso **6** coffer, engine, locker, shut up, thorax **7** baggage, close in

truss 3 tie **4** beam, bind, prop, stay **5** brace, hitch, shore, strap, tie up **6** bind up, fasten, girder, pinion, secure **7** confine, support **8** make fast **9** constrict, framework, stanchion **12** underpinning

trust 4 care, duty, hope **5** faith, hands **6** accept, assume, belief, charge, credit, expect, look to, rely on **7** believe, count on, custody, keeping, presume, swear by **8** credence, feel sure, reliance, sureness **9** certainty, certitude, count upon **10** anticipate, confidence, conviction, depend upon, obligation, protection **11** assuredness, contemplate, have faith in, safekeeping, subscribe to, take on faith, take stock in **12** guardianship **14** give credence to, responsibility, take for granted

trusted 6 trusty 8 reliable 9 unfailing 10 dependable 11 trustworthy

trustee 8 guardian 9 caretaker, custodian, protector

trusteeship 4 care 6 charge 7 custody 10 protection 11 safekeeping 12 guardianship

trusting 8 gullible, trustful 9 believing, credulous 12 unsuspicious

trustworthy 4 true 5 loyal 6 honest 7 ethical, trusted, upright 8 faithful, reliable, true-blue 9 honorable, steadfast 10 aboveboard, dependable, scrupulous 11 responsible 12 tried and true 13 incorruptible, unimpeachable 14 high-principled

trusty 7 trusted 8 reliable 9 unfailing 10 dependable 11 trustworthy

trusty companion 3 pal 5 buddy, crony 6 friend 8 intimate, sidekick 9 confidant 10 bosom buddy, confidante

truth 3 law 4 fact 5 facts 6 verity 7 reality 8 accuracy, fidelity, trueness, veracity 9 actuality, exactness, integrity 11 reliability 12 authenticity, faithfulness, truthfulness 15 proven principle, trustworthiness
Russian: 6 Pravda
also name of: 9 newspaper
god of: 7 Mithras

truth conquers all things
Latin: 18 vincit omnia veritas

truthful 4 open, true 5 exact, frank 6 candid, honest 7 artless, correct, factual, precise, sincere 8 accurate, faithful, reliable 9 authentic, guileless, veracious 10 aboveboard, meticulous, scrupulous 11 trustworthy, undeceitful, unvarnished 13 unadulterated 15 straightforward

truthfulness 6 candor 7 honesty 8 veracity

Truth or Consequences
host: 10 Jack Bailey, Steve Dunne 12 Ralph Edwards

try 2 go 3 aim, use 4 risk, seek, shot, test, turn 5 crack, essay, fling, prove, trial, whack 6 effort, sample, strain, strive, tackle 7 adjudge, attempt, venture 8 endeavor 9 have a go at, partake of, undertake 10 adjudicate, deliberate, put to a test 11 opportunity 12 have a fling at, make an effort, take a crack at

trying 4 hard 5 pesky, tough 6 taxing, vexing 7 arduous, irksome, onerous, tedious 8 tiresome 9 difficult, fatiguing, harrowing, wearisome 10 bothersome, burdensome, exhausting, irritating 11 aggravating, distressing, troublesome 12 exasperating

tryout 4 test 5 trial 7 hearing 8 audition 10 experiment

try out 3 fry 6 render 7 compete 8 audition 9 give a test 11 performance

tryst 4 date 7 meeting, vis-a-vis 9 tete-a-tete 10 engagement, rendezvous 11 appointment, assignation

try the patience of 5 annoy 7 provoke 8 irritate 10 exasperate

try to equal 5 rival 7 compete, emulate

Tuatha De Danann 4 gods
origin: 5 Irish
mother: 4 Danu

tub 3 keg, kit, pot, tun, vat 4 bath, boat, butt, cask, ship, tank, tram, wash 5 barge, bathe, fatso, fatty, keeve, tramp 6 barrel, bucket, firkin, ore car, vessel 7 cistern, tankard 8 cauldron, slow boat 9 container, freighter

tube 4 duct, hose, pipe 7 conduit 8 cylinder

tuber 3 anu, yam 4 beet, bulb, corm, eddo, root, taro 5 jalop, shoot 6 potato, turnip 8 rutabaga, swelling 11 enlargement

Tuchman, Barbara W
author of: 14 A Distant Mirror, The First Salute 15 The Guns of August, The March of Folly 17 Practicing History

tuck 3 put 4 cram 5 pleat, shove, stick, stuff 6 enwrap, gather, insert, pucker, roll up, ruffle, shroud, swathe, thrust 7 crinkle, swaddle

tucker 3 fag 4 bush, poop, tire 5 weary 7 exhaust, fatigue

tuckered out 5 all in, tired, weary 6 bushed, done in, pooped 8 fatigued 9 exhausted, fagged out

Tudor
dynasty of: 7 England
rulers: 8 Henry VII 9 Henry VIII 8 Edward VI 5 Mary I 10 Elizabeth I

Tudor, Antony
choreographer of: 11 Lilac Garden 12 Pillar of Fire

tuebor 11 I will defend

Tuei see 6 Isleta

Tuesday
from: 3 Tiw
heavenly body: 4 Mars
French: 5 mardi
Italian: 7 martedi
Spanish: 6 martes
German: 8 dienstag

tuft 4 wisp 5 batch, brush, bunch, clump, crest, plume, sheaf 6 bundle, tassel 7 cluster, topknot

tug 3 lug, tow 4 drag, draw, haul, jerk, pull, yank 6 wrench 7 wrestle

tulip 6 Tulipa
varieties: 4 lady, star 5 globe 7 Turkish 9 butterfly, guinea-hen, waterlily 10 Sierra star 11 golden globe, purple globe 16 common late garden 17 common early garden

Tullia
father: 14 Servius Tullius
husband: 7 Tarquin

Tullius see 14 Servius Tullius

Tulsa
football team: 7 Outlaws

tumble 3 mix 4 dive, drop, fall, flip, roll, toss 5 whirl 6 bounce, jumble, plunge, stir up, topple 7 descend, shuffle, stumble 9 cartwheel 10 somersault

tumbledown 5 shaky 7 rickety, rundown 8 decaying, decrepit, unstable 9 crumbling, tottering 10 broken-down, jerry-built, ramshackle 11 dilapidated, falling-down 14 disintegrating

tumbler 3 cog, dog 5 drier, glass, lever 6 goblet, vessel 7 acrobat, athlete, gymnast, juggler 12 somersaulter

tumbrel 4 cart 5 wagon 7 tipcart 8 dumpcart

tumbril
French: 7 fourgon

tumid 5 puffy 6 turgid 7 bloated, bulging, dilated, pompous, swollen 8 enlarged, expanded, inflated 9 bombastic, distended, edematous, tumescent 11 protuberant 12 magniloquent 13 grandiloquent

tummy 3 gut 5 belly 6 paunch, tumtum 7 abdomen, midriff, stomach 9 bay window 11 breadbasket

tumor 3 wen 4 cyst, lump, wart 5 pride 6 cancer, growth 7 bombast, sarcoma 8 hematoma, neoplasm, swelling, tubercle 9 carcinoma, papilloma, pomposity 11 tumefaction

tumult 3 ado, din 6 bedlam, bustle, clamor, hubbub, racket, uproar 7 turmoil 8 disorder, upheaval 9 agitation, commotion, confusion 10 excitement, hullabaloo 11 disturbance, pandemonium

tumultuous 4 loud 5 noisy, rough, rowdy 6 stormy, unruly 7 chaotic, furious, lawless, raucous, riotous, violent 8 agitated, confused 9 clamorous, disturbed, turbulent 10 boisterous, disorderly, uproarious 11 tempestuous

tun 3 keg, tub, vat 4 butt, cast, drum 6 barrel 8 hogshead

tune 3 air 4 aria, line, song, step 5 adjust, ditty, motif, pitch, theme 6 accord, adjust, melody, number, strain, unison 7 concert, concord, harmony 9 agreement 10 conformity

tuneful 6 catchy, dulcet 7 lyrical, musical 9 melodious

tungsten
chemical symbol: 1 W

tunic 4 robe 5 cloak 6 jacket, mantle, poncho, tabard 7 garment, surcoat

Tunica
tribe: 10 Chitimacha

Tunis
capital of: 7 Tunisia

Tunisia
other name: 8 Carthage 9 Ifriqiyah
capital/largest city: 5 Tunis

others: 4 Beja, Sfax, Susa 5 Gabes, Gofsa 6 Djerba, Mateur, Nabeul, Remada, Sousse, Tozeur 7 Bizerte, Kairwan 8 Carthage, Jendouba, Kairouan, Monastir, Tebourba, Zaghouan 9 Grombalia 10 Ferryville

empire: 8 Carthage 13 Barbary States

school: 5 Tunis 16 Pasteur Institute

measure: 3 saa 4 saah 5 cafiz 6 mettar 8 milerole

monetary unit: 5 dinar 6 dollar 7 millime

weight: 3 saa 4 rotl 5 artal, ratel, uckia

island: 6 Djerba, Galite

lake: 6 Achkel, Djerid 7 Bizerte

mountain: 5 Atlas 6 Mrhila 7 Tebessa 8 High Tell, Zaghouan 12 Northern Tell 17 Dorsale Tunisienne

highest point: 6 Chambi

river: 8 Medjerda, Mellegue

sea: 13 Mediterranean

physical feature:
> **cape:** 3 Bon 5 Blanc 8 Rasaddar
> **desert:** 6 Sahara
> **gulf:** 5 Gabes, Tunis 8 Hammamet
> **oasis:** 5 Gabes, Gafsa, Nefta 6 Djerba, Tozeur 9 El Oudiane 13 El Hamma Djerid
> **plains:** 5 Sahel
> **salt lake:** 11 Chott Djerid, Shatt Djerid
> **valley:** 8 Medjerda
> **wind:** 5 chile 6 chilli 7 sirocco

people: 3 Jew 4 Arab 6 Berber

artist: 5 Gorgi, Turki

dynasty: 6 Hafsid 7 Fatimid 8 Aghlabid, Almohade 10 Husseinite

leader: 6 Ben Ali 9 Bourguiba

language: 6 Arabic, Berber, French

religion: 5 Islam 7 Judaism 12 Christianity

place:
> **center of Tunis:** 13 Place d'Afrique
> **mosque:** 5 Great 7 Zitouna
> **museum:** 5 Bardo, Kouba 6 Sousse
> **palace:** 14 Dar Ben Abdallah
> **ruins:** 8 Carthage
> **street:** 14 Habib Bourguiba

feature:
> **cap:** 7 chechia
> **clothing:** 5 jebba 7 safasri 9 babbouche
> **market:** 4 souk

food:
> **dish:** 7 mesfouf 8 couscous
> **drink:** 4 iban 5 legmi
> **fruit:** 12 deglet en nour

Tunney, Gene
real name: 17 James Joseph Tunney
nickname: 14 Fighting Marine
sport: 6 boxing
class: 11 heavyweight

Tuonela
also: 6 Manala
origin: 7 Finnish
name of: 10 afterworld

form: 6 island
lacked: 3 sun 4 moon

tu quoque 7 thou too

Turandot
opera by: 7 Puccini
character: 3 Liu 4 Pang, Ping, Pong 5 Calaf, Timur 8 Turandot (Princess of China)

turbid 5 muddy, murky 6 cloudy, opaque, roiled 7 clouded, unclear 8 agitated 9 disturbed, stirred up, unsettled

turbulence 4 fury 6 frenzy, hubbub, tumult, unrest, uproar 7 ferment, rioting, torrent, turmoil 8 disorder, violence 9 agitation, commotion 10 excitement, unruliness 11 disturbance

turbulent 5 rowdy 6 fierce, raging, stormy, unruly 7 chaotic, furious, riotous, violent 8 agitated, restless 9 clamorous, disturbed 10 blustering, boisterous, disorderly, tumultuous, uproarious 11 tempestuous

tureen 4 bowl, dish 9 casserole, container 10 receptacle

turf 3 sod 4 area, peat, plot, soil 5 divot, grass, haunt, sward, track 7 verdure 9 racetrack, territory 10 greensward

Turgenev, Ivan
author of: 5 Smoke 9 First Love 10 Virgin Soil 14 Fathers and Sons 18 A Month in the Country 19 A Sportsman's Notebook, A Sportsman's Sketches, The Torrents of Spring

turgid 5 puffy, showy 6 florid, ornate 7 flowery, pompous, swollen 8 inflated, puffed up 9 bombastic, grandiose, overblown 10 hyperbolic

Turkey
capital: 6 Angora, Ankara
largest city: 8 Istanbul
others: 4 Enos, Troy, Urfa 5 Adana, Bursa, Izmir, Konya, Maras, Siirt, Sivas 6 Aintab, Edessa, Edirne, Elaziz, Marash, Samsun, Smyrna 7 Antakya, Antioch, Erzurum, Kayseri, MMersin, Scutari, Trabzon, Uskudar 8 Stamboul 9 Byzantium, Eskisehir, Gaziantep 10 Adrianople 14 Constantinople
school: 6 Aegean, Ankara 8 Istanbul
division: 4 Pera, Sert 5 Siirt, Troad 6 Angora, Eyalet, Thrace 7 Anadolu, Beyoglu, Cilicia 8 Anatolia 9 Asia Minor, Kurdistan
measure: 3 dra, oka, pik 4 draa, khat, kile, zira 5 berri, kileh, zirai 6 arshin, chinik, fortin, halebi 7 nocktat
monetary unit: 4 lira, para 5 akcha, asper, kurus, pound, rebia 6 akcheh, zequin 7 aetilik, beshlik, piaster 8 medjidie
weight: 3 oka, oke 4 aqui, dram, rotl 5 artal, cheke, kerat, obolu, ratel 6 batman, dirhem, kantar, maunch, miskal 7 drachma, quintal, yusdrum

island: 6 Cyprus, Kibris
lake: 3 Tuz, Van 7 Egridir 8 Beysehir
mountain: 2 Ak 3 Ala 4 Alai, Dagh, Kara 5 Hasan, Hinis, Honaz, Murat, Murit 6 Ala Dag, Bingol, Bolgar, Pontic, Suphan, Taurus 7 Aladagh, Erciyas 8 Karacali 10 Kackar Dagi
highest point: 6 Ararat
river: 4 Aras, Kura 5 Araks, Dicle, Firat, Gediz, Goksu, Halys, Irmak, Kizil, Mesta, Murat, Sarus 6 Araxes, Ceyhan, Seihun, Seyhan, Seylan, Tigris 7 Kurucay, Muradsu, Orontes, Sakarya 8 Granicus, Macestus, Maeander, Menderes 9 Euphrates 13 Buyukmenderes
sea: 4 Aral 5 Black 6 Aegean 7 Marmara 13 Mediterranean
physical feature:
> **cape:** 4 Baba, Ince 5 Bafra 6 Anamur, Helles, Hinzir 7 Karatas, Kerempe
> **gulf:** 3 Cos 5 Izmir 7 Antalya
> **inlet:** 10 Golden Horn
> **peninsula:** 9 Anatolian, Gallipoli
> **plateau:** 9 Anatolian
> **strait:** 8 Bosporus 9 Bosphorus 11 Dardanelles

people: 4 Arab, Kurd, Turk 6 Seljuk
king: 8 Mausolus
leader: 5 Inonu, Osman 6 Ecevit 7 Demirel 8 Menderes, Suleiman 12 Kemal Ataturk
poet: 5 Homer
language: 6 Arabic 7 Kurdish, Turkish
religion: 5 Islam 7 Judaism 12 Christianity 13 Greek Orthodox, Roman Catholic
place:
> **bridge:** 6 Galata
> **dam:** 9 Gokcekaya
> **mosque:** 4 Blue, Yeni 8 Selimiye 11 Hagia Sophia, Sultan Ahmed
> **museum:** 7 Topkapi
> **ruins:** 4 Troy 7 Ephesus 8 Pergamum
> **tomb:** 12 Kemal Ataturk
feature:
> **cap:** 3 fez 6 calpac 7 calpack
> **clothing:** 6 caftan, dolman, jelick 7 yashrak 8 charshaf, maharmah, shakseer
> **goat hair:** 6 mohair
> **grill:** 6 mangal
> **harem:** 5 serai 8 seraglio
> **musical instrument:** 5 canum, kanum 6 canoon, johnie, kussir, zither 8 crescent, jingling
> **pipe:** 10 meerschaum
food:
> **dish:** 5 halva, pilaw 10 doner kebab, shish kebab
> **drink:** 4 boza, raki 5 airan, pasha, rakee 6 mastic
> **pastry:** 7 baklava
> **turkey:** 4 hind

Turkic
- language family: **6** Altaic
- group: **5** Kazak, Nogai, Uigur, Uzbek, Yakut **7** Chuvash, Kirghiz **8** Turkoman **10** Karakalpak **11** Azerbaijani **14** Osmanli Turkish

Turkmenistan
- capital/largest city: **9** Ashkhabad
- head of state: **9** president
- government: **8** republic
- monetary unit: **5** ruble
- river: **8** Amu Darya
- sea: **7** Caspian
- physical feature: **13** Kara Kum Desert
- people: **7** Turkmen **10** Turkmenian
- language: **6** Turkic **10** West Turkic
- religion: **11** Sunni Muslim
- feature: **9** Altyn Depe

turmeric
- botanical name: **12** Curcuma longa
- also called: **7** tumeric **13** Crocus indicus, Indian saffron
- family: **6** ginger
- color: **6** yellow
- used as: **3** dye **6** amulet **8** cosmetic, medicine
- origin: **4** Asia **9** Caribbean, East India
- charm against: **5** ghost **10** tree spirit

turmoil 4 mess **5** chaos **6** tumult, uproar **7** ferment **8** disorder **9** agitation, commotion, confusion **10** convulsion **11** disturbance, pandemonium French: **14** bouleversement

turn 2 do, go **3** act, arc, lie, put **4** bend, coil, come, deed, flex, hang, look, loop, make, rest, ride, roll, send, shot, sour, spin, time, veer, walk, wing **5** alter, apply, crack, curve, drive, eject, fling, hinge, pivot, round, scare, shift, shock, spell, spoil, start, stint, swing, throw, twist, whack, wheel, whirl **6** action, become, chance, change, curdle, depend, direct, effort, fright, gyrate, invert, period, reside, rotate, sprain, stroll, swerve, swivel, wrench, zigzag **7** acidify, attempt, convert, deliver, execute, ferment, perform, reverse, revolve, service, winding **8** gyration, overturn, roll over, rotation, surprise **9** cause to go, deviation, discharge, transform **10** accomplish, alteration, revolution

turn a deaf ear to 6 ignore, slight **9** disregard

turn aside 5 avert **6** divert **7** deflect, deviate **8** turn away

turn away 5 avert **6** give up **8** alienate, estrange, send away **9** turn aside **12** turn one's back

turnback 4 fold, quit, tack **5** repel **6** defect, desert, return, revert **7** forsake, regress, relapse, repulse, retrace, retreat, reverse **9** backslide

turncoat 5 Judas **6** bolter **7** traitor **8** apostate, betrayer, defector, deserter, quisling, renegade **12** double-dealer

turn down 5 spurn **6** refuse, reject **14** lower the volume, refuse to accept

Turner, Joseph Mallord William
- born: **6** London **7** England
- artwork: **12** The Shipwreck, The Slave Ship, Tintern Abbey **17** Dawn After the Wreck **20** Dido Building Carthage **22** Venice S Giorgio Maggiore **24** The Sun of Venice Going to Sea **25** The Thames near Walton Bridge, Ulysses Deriding Polyphemus **30** Burning of the Houses of Parliament **32** Snowstorm Hannibal Crossing the Alps **32** The Falls of the Rhine at Schaffhausen **34** The Bay of Baiae with Apollo and the Sibyl **37** Fighting Temeraire Tugged to her Last Berth **47** The Parting of Hero and Leander from the Greek of Musaeus **50** The Shipwreck Fishing Boats Endeavoring to Rescue the Crew

Turner, Kathleen
- roles: **8** Body Heat **9** Serial Mom **12** Prizzi's Honor **13** The Real Blonde, War of the Roses **17** Romancing the Stone, The Jewel of the Nile, The Virgin Suicides **18** Peggy Sue Got Married

Turner, Lana
- real name: **29** Julia Jean Mildred Frances Turner
- nickname: **11** Sweater Girl
- born: **9** Wallace ID
- discovered at: **16** Schwab's Drugstore
- husband: **9** Artie Shaw, Lex Barker **10** Bob Topping **12** Stephen Crane
- roles: **7** Madame X **11** Peyton Place **15** By Love Possessed, Imitation of Life **26** The Postman Always Rings Twice

turning 4 bend **5** curve **7** bending, curving, winding **8** pivoting, rotating, spinning, twisting, whirling **9** revolving, swiveling

turnip 12 Brassica rapa
- group: **8** Rapifera
- varieties: **6** Indian **7** Italian, Swedish **8** rutabaga, seven-top

turn off 4 bore, exit **5** douse, leave, repel **6** revolt, sicken **7** disgust, repulse **8** alienate, turn away **9** switch off **10** deactivate

turn of phrase 5 idiom **8** locution, phrasing **10** expression **11** phraseology

Turn of the Screw, The
- author: **10** Henry James
- character: **5** Flora, Miles **7** Mr Quint **8** Mrs Grose **10** Miss Jessel **12** The Governess

turn on 5 start, tempt **6** allure, attack, entice, excite **7** actuate, attract **8** activate, energize, interest, switch on

turn one's stomach 6 revolt, sicken **7** disgust **8** nauseate

turnout 5 crowd **6** output, throng **8** assembly, audience **9** gathering **10** assemblage, production

turn out 4 garb, oust **5** array, dress, eject, end up, evict, exile, expel **6** appear, attend, attire, banish, clothe, evolve, fit out, invest, rig out, show up, unfold **7** cast out, come out, costume, develop, kick out **8** drive out, send away **9** switch off **11** come to light

turn over 4 flip **5** upset **6** bestow, rotate **7** deliver **8** flipflop, give over, hand over, overturn **9** surrender **10** relinquish, somersault

turn pale 4 fade **6** blanch, whiten **7** lighten

turn tail 4 flee **7** retreat, run away **8** back away **12** beat a retreat

turn to account 7 exploit, utilize **8** profit by, put to use **9** make use of **12** capitalize on

turn topsy turvy 5 upset **7** capsize, confuse, tip over **8** flip-flop, overturn, put askew **10** disarrange, turn turtle **11** disorganize

turn turtle 5 upset **7** capsize, tip over **8** flip over, keel over, overturn, turn over **14** turn upside down

turn up 4 come **6** appear, arrive, crop up, drop in, emerge, loom up, show up **7** develop, surface **11** come to light

Turpentine State
- nickname of: **13** North Carolina

turpitude 4 evil, vice **8** baseness, lewdness, vileness **9** depravity **10** corruption, debauchery, defilement, degeneracy, immorality, perversion, sinfulness, wickedness, wrongdoing **13** dissoluteness **14** licentiousness

turquoise 4 aqua **5** stone **7** mineral, sky-blue **10** aquamarine **12** greenish-blue, Prussian-blue
- source: **12** United States

turret 5 tower **6** belfry, cupola, garret, gazebo, louver, terret **7** minaret, rotator, steeple **8** gunhouse, gunmount **9** belvedere, pepperbox **10** watchtower
- tool: **5** lathe

turtle 3 box **4** musk, wood **6** slider **7** painted, reptile, snapper, spotted **8** slowpoke, terrapin, tortoise **10** turtledove **11** leatherback
- dorsal shell: **8** carapace
- nautical: **5** upset **6** pocket **7** capsize **8** overturn
- order: **8** Chelonia
- ventral shell: **8** plastron
- young: **7** turtlet

tussle 4 fray **5** brawl, fight, melee, scrap, set-to **6** battle, fracas **7** grapple, scuffle, wrestle **8** conflict, struggle **10** donnybrook, free-for-all **11** altercation

tussock 4 hair, tuft **5** brush, bunch, clump, grass, sedge **7** bulrush, cluster, thicket **8** feathers

tutelage 8 coaching, guidance, teaching, training, tutoring 9 direction, education, schooling 10 discipline 11 inculcation, instruction, supervision, trusteeship 12 guardianship 14 indoctrination

tutor 4 guru 5 coach, drill, teach 6 master, mentor, school 7 prepare, teacher 8 instruct 10 instructor 11 give lessons

tutorial 5 class 8 didactic, edifying 11 educational, instructive 12 prescriptive

tutti
  music: 3 all 18 all players together, all singers together

Tuvalu
  other name: 13 Ellice Islands, Lagoon Islands
  capital: 8 Funafuti
  head of state: 14 British monarch 15 governor general
  monetary unit: 4 cent 6 dollar
  island: 3 Nui 6 Niutao 7 Nanumea, Vaitupu 8 Funafuti 9 Nanumanga, Niulakita, Nukufetau 10 Nukulaelae
  highest point: 5 Nuwak
  sea: 7 Pacific
  people: 6 Samoan 10 Polynesian
    leader: 5 Lauti
  language: 6 Samoan 7 English 8 Tuvaluan 10 Polynesian
  religion: 10 Protestant 12 Tuvalu Church

twaddle 3 rot 4 bosh, bunk 5 trash, tripe 6 babble, drivel, gabble, jabber, piffle 7 chatter, prattle, rubbish 8 claptrap, idle talk, nonsense, tommyrot 9 jabbering, silly talk 10 balderdash 16 stuff-and-nonsense

Twain, Mark
  real name: 13 Samuel Clemens
  author of: 9 Tom Sawyer 10 Roughing It 12 A Tramp Abroad, The Gilded Age 15 (Adventures of) Huckleberry Finn 18 The Innocents Abroad 20 Life on the Mississippi 21 The Mysterious Stranger, The Prince and the Pauper 29 The Man That Corrupted Hadleyburg 36 A Connecticut Yankee in King Arthur's Court 41 The Celebrated Jumping Frog of Calaveras County

twang 9 resonance, vibration 10 nasal sound 13 reverberation

Tweedledee
  character in: 22 Through the Looking Glass
  author: 7 Carroll

Tweedledum
  character in: 22 Through the Looking Glass
  author: 7 Carroll

tweet 4 peep 5 cheep, chirp 7 chirrup, chitter, twitter

Twelfth Night
  author: 18 William Shakespeare

  character: 5 Feste, Maria, Viola (Cesario) 6 Olivia, Orsino 7 Antonio 8 Malvolio 9 Sebastian 12 Sir Toby Belch 18 Sir Andrew Aguecheek

Twelve Angry Men
  director: 11 Sidney Lumet
  cast: 8 Ed Begley, Lee J Cobb 10 E G Marshall, Henry Fonda, Jack Warden 11 Jack Klugman, John Fiedler 12 Martin Balsam

Twelve O'Clock High
  director: 9 Henry King
  cast: 10 Dean Jagger 11 Gary Merrill, Gregory Peck, Hugh Marlowe 15 Millard Mitchell
  Oscar for: 15 supporting actor (Jagger)

Twentieth Century
  director: 11 Howard Hawks
  based on play by: 8 Ben Hecht 16 Charles MacArthur
  cast: 11 Roscoe Karns 13 Carole Lombard, John Barrymore 14 Walter Connolly

Twentieth Century, The
  narrator: 14 Walter Cronkite

Twenty-Four (24)
  network: 3 FOX
  cast: 8 Kim Raver (Audrey Raines) 10 Leslie Hope (Teri Bauer) 11 Sarah Clarke (Nina Myers) 13 Alberta Watson (Erin Driscoll), Carlos Bernard (Tony Almeida), William Devane (James Heller) 14 Dennis Haysbert (David Palmer), Elisha Cuthbert (Kim Bauer), James Badge Dale (Chase Edmunds) 15 Mary Lynn Rajskub (Chloe O'Brian), Reiko Aylesworth (Michelle Dessler) 16 Kiefer Sutherland (Jack Bauer) 18 Penny Johnson Jerald (Sherry Palmer)

twenty-one see 9 blackjack

Twenty Questions
  host: 10 Bill Slater, Jay Jackson
  panelist: 11 Herb Polesie 12 Bobby McGuire 13 Johnnie McPhee 14 Dickie Harrison, Florence Rinard 15 Fred Van De Venter

Twenty Thousand Leagues Under the Sea
  author: 10 Jules Verne
  character: 7 Conseil, Ned Land 11 Captain Nemo 22 Professor Pierre Aronnax
  submarine: 8 Nautilus

Twenty Years After
  author: 14 Alexandre Dumas (pere)

Twice-Told Tales
  author: 18 Nathaniel Hawthorne

twilight 3 ebb, eve 4 dusk 6 sunset 7 decline, evening, sundown 8 eventide, gloaming, moonrise 9 half-light, last phase, nightfall 14 edge of darkness

Twilight of the Gods 8 Ragnarok
  German: 15 Gotterdammerung

Twilight Zone, The
  host: 10 Rod Serling

twin 4 dual, like 5 alike 6 double, paired 7 matched, twofold 9 duplicate, identical

Twin 6 Thomas

twine 4 coil, cord, rope, wind 5 braid, cable, plait, twist, weave 6 string, thread 7 binding, entwine 9 interlace 10 intertwine

twinge 4 pain, pang, stab 5 cramp, spasm, throb 6 stitch, tingle, twitch

twinkle 4 glow 5 blaze, flare, flash, gleam, shine 7 flicker, glimmer, glisten, shimmer, sparkle 11 scintillate

Twins
  constellation of: 6 Gemini

twirl 4 spin 5 pivot, twine, wheel, whirl 6 gyrate, rotate 7 revolve 9 pirouette

twist 3 arc, way 4 bend, coil, curl, idea, kink, knot, pull, roll, spin, turn, veer, wind, wrap, yank 5 curve, pivot, ravel, slant, snake, swing, twine, whirl, wrest 6 change, method, notion, rotate, spiral, sprain, swerve, swivel, system, tangle, wrench, zigzag 7 contort, distort, entwine, meander 8 approach, rotation, surprise 9 corkscrew, interlace, treatment 10 intertwine, involution 11 convolution, development

twisted 4 bent 6 warped 7 crooked, gnarled 8 deformed 9 contorted, distorted, misshapen

twisting 7 crooked, curving, turning 9 contorted, revolving, spiraling, swiveling

twist out of shape 4 warp 6 deform 7 contort, distort

twitch 3 tic 4 jerk 5 shake, spasm, throb 6 quaver, quiver, squirm, tremor, wiggle, writhe 7 tremble 8 paroxysm 10 convulsion

twitter 4 fuss, peep, stew 5 cheep, chirp, tizzy, tweet, whirl 6 bustle, flurry, pother, uproar, warble 7 chatter, chirrup, ferment, fluster, flutter 8 chirping 10 turbulence 11 chirruping

Two and a Half Men
  network: 3 CBS
  cast: 9 John Cryer (Alan Harper) 11 Angus T Jones (Jake Harper), Marin Hinkle (Judith Harper) 12 Charlie Sheen (Charlie Harper) 13 Holland Taylor (Evelyn Harper) 14 Melanie Lynskey (Rose)

two-faced 5 false 7 devious 8 slippery 9 deceitful, deceptive, dishonest, insincere 10 perfidious 11 dissembling, double-faced, duplicitous, fork-tongued, treacherous, underhanded 12 dishonorable, disingenuous, false-hearted, hypocritical 13 double-dealing, untrustworthy

twofold 4 dual 6 double 7 two-part

Two Gentlemen of Verona, The
  author: 18 William Shakespeare
  character: 5 Julia **6** Silvia, Thurio **7** Proteus **9** Valentine **11** Duke of Milan

Two Lands, The *see* **5** Egypt

two of a kind 4 pair **5** twins **6** couple **7** doublet

two-part 4 dual, twin **6** double, paired **9** bipartite

twosome 3 duo **4** pair **5** brace **6** couple

2001: A Space Odyssey
  author: 13 Arthur C Clarke
  director: 14 Stanley Kubrick
  character: 4 Dave **5** Steve
  computer: 3 HAL
  cast: 3 HAL **10** Keir Dullea **12** Gary Lockwood **16** William Sylvester
  song: 20 Thus Spake Zarathustra (Richard Strauss)
  sequel: 24 Two Thousand Ten: Odyssey Two

two-time 6 betray **10** be disloyal **11** double-cross **12** be unfaithful **13** be treacherous, play false with **14** break faith with

two-timing 5 false **6** tricky **7** perfidy **8** bad faith, betrayal, disloyal, trickery **9** deceiving, deception, duplicity, falseness, treachery **10** disloyalty, perfidious **11** double-cross, duplicitous, treacherous **13** breach of faith, double-dealing, faithlessness **14** double-crossing

two-wheeler 4 bike **5** cycle **7** bicycle

Two Years Before the Mast
  author: 18 Richard Henry Dana Jr

Tybalt
  character in: 14 Romeo and Juliet
  author: 11 Shakespeare

Tyche
  origin: 5 Greek
  goddess of: 7 fortune
  corresponds to: 7 Fortuna

tycoon 4 boss **5** mogul, nabob **6** big gun, bigwig **7** big shot, magnate **8** big wheel **9** potentate **12** entrepreneur **13** industrialist **17** captain of industry

tyke 3 kid, tad, tot **5** child **6** shaver, squirt, wee one **9** little one

Tyler, John
  presidential rank: 5 tenth
  party: 4 Whig **20** Democratic-Republican
  state represented: 2 VA **8** Virginia
  defeated: 5 no-one
    succeeded upon death of: 8 Harrison
  vice president: 4 none
  cabinet:
    state: 6 (Abel Parker) Upshur **7** (Daniel) Webster, (John C) Calhoun
    treasury: 4 (George Mortimer) Bibb **5** (Thomas) Ewing **7** (John Canfield) Spencer, (Walter) Forward

  war: 4 (John) Bell **7** (John Canfield) Spencer, (William) Wilkins
  attorney general: 6 (Hugh Swinton) Legare, (John) Nelson **10** (John Jordan) Crittenden
  navy: 5 (John Young) Mason **6** (Abel Parker) Upshur, (George Edmund) Badger, (Thomas Walker) Gilmer
  postmaster general: 7 (Francis) Granger **9** (Charles Anderson) Wickliffe
  born: 2 VA **8** Greenway, Virginia **17** Charles City County
  died/buried: 2 VA **8** Richmond, Virginia
  education: 14 William and Mary
  religion: 12 Episcopalian
  vacation spot: 2 VA **7** Hampton **8** Virginia
  political career: 8 US Senate **12** State Council **13** vice president **24** US House of Representatives
    delegate to: 13 State Assembly
    governor of: 8 Virginia
  civilian career: 6 farmer, lawyer
  military service: 19 War of Eighteen-Twelve
  notable events of lifetime/term:
    act: 6 Tariff (of 1842)
    annexation of: 5 Texas
    treaty: 16 Webster-Ashburton
  father: 4 John
  mother: 4 Mary (Marott Armistead)
  siblings: 7 William **8** Wat Henry **10** Maria Henry **12** Anne Contesse **14** Christina Booth **15** Martha Jefferson **18** Elizabeth Armistead
  wife: 5 Julia (Gardiner) **7** Letitia (Christian)
  children: 4 John, Mary **5** Alice, Julia, Pearl **6** Robert **7** Lachlan, Letitia **8** Tazewell **9** Elizabeth **12** Anne Contesse, Lyon Gardiner **13** David Gardiner, John Alexander **16** Robert FitzWalter

Tyll Eulenspiegel *see* **16** Till Eulenspiegel

Tyndall, John
  field: 7 physics
  nationality: 5 Irish
  studied diffusion of: 5 light

Tyndareus
  wife: 4 Leda
  daughter: 6 Phoebe **8** Philonoe, Timandra **12** Clytemnestra

Tyndaridae *see* **15** Castor and Pollux

type 4 font, kind, race, sort **5** brand, class, genus, group, model, order, print **6** design, family, phylum, sample **7** pattern, species, variety **8** category, division, specimen, typeface **9** archetype, prototype **10** typography

type, movable
  invented by: 9 Gutenberg

Typee
  author: 14 Herman Melville

  character: 3 Tom (Melville) **4** Toby **6** Marnoo, Mehevi **7** Fayaway **8** Kory-Kory

typewriter
  invented by: 5 Soule **6** Sholes **7** Glidden

Typhoeus
  form: 7 monster
  father: 8 Tartarus
  mother: 2 Ge
  number of heads: 10 one hundred

typhoon 4 gale, gust, wind **5** storm **7** cyclone, tempest, tornado, twister **9** hurricane, whirlwind

Typhoon
  author: 12 Joseph Conrad

typical 5 model, stock, usual **6** normal **7** average, regular **8** ordinary, orthodox, standard **9** exemplary, in keeping **10** individual, prototypal, true to type **11** distinctive, in character **12** conventional, to be expected **14** characteristic, representative

typify 5 sum up **6** embody **7** betoken, connote, pass for **8** instance, stand for **9** epitomize, exemplify, incarnate, personify, represent **10** illustrate **12** characterize

typography measure 2 em, en **4** pica **5** point

Tyr
  origin: 12 Scandinavian
  god of: 7 victory
  father: 4 Odin **5** Othin
  mother: 3 Fri **5** Frigg, Frija **6** Frigga
  killed by: 4 Garm

tyrannical 7 fascist **8** despotic **9** imperious **10** oppressive **11** dictatorial, domineering **13** authoritarian

tyrannize 7 oppress **8** domineer, overlord **10** slave drive

tyrannized 9 exploited, oppressed **11** downtrodden, subservient **12** harshly ruled

Tyrannosaurus
  type: 8 dinosaur, theropod
  location: 7 Montana **12** North America
  period: 10 Cretaceous

tyrannous 8 despotic **9** imperious **10** iron-handed, oppressive, repressive, tyrannical

tyranny 7 cruelty, fascism **8** coercion, iron fist, iron hand, iron rule, severity **9** despotism, harshness **10** domination, oppression, repression **11** persecution **12** dictatorship **13** reign of terror **15** totalitarianism

tyrant 5 bully **6** despot **8** dictator, martinet **10** persecutor, taskmaster **11** cruel master, slave driver

Tyre
  king of: 5 Hiram

tyro 6 intern, novice, rookie **7** learner, recruit, trainee **8** beginner, initiate, neophyte, newcomer **9** greenhorn **10** apprentice, tenderfoot

Tyro
father: **9** Salmoneus
loved by: **8** Cretheus, Poseidon
son: **5** Aeson **6** Neleus, Pelias
grandson: **5** Jason **6** Nestor

Tyrrheus
occupation: **8** shepherd

Tyson, Cicely

born: **9** New York NY
roles: **5** Roots **7** Sounder **18** Because of Winn-Dixie **33** The Autobiography of Miss Jane Pittman

Tyson, Mike
original name: **7** Michael
nickname: **8** Iron Mike
born: **2** NY **8** Brooklyn **17** Bedford-Stuyvesant
wife: **11** Robin Givens

manager: **9** Cus D'Amato **10** Bill Cayton **11** Jimmy Jacobs
trainer: **12** Angelo Dundee
promoter: **7** Don King
boxing title: **3** IBF, WBA, WBC **11** heavyweight
defeated: **6** Holmes, Spinks, Thomas, Tillis, Tucker **7** Berbick

tzimmes 4 fuss **6** uproar **10** hullabaloo
literally: **4** stew **9** mixed dish

Ubangi-Shari *see* **22** Central African Republic

Ubermensch **8** superman

ubiquitous **7** allover **9** pervading, pervasive, prevalent, universal, worldwide **10** everywhere, widespread **11** everpresent, omnipresent **12** allpervading

ubiquitously **10** everywhere **11** extensively

ubi supra **19** where mentioned above

Ucalegon
    counselor to: **5** Priam

Uccello, Paolo
    real name: **11** Paolo di Dono
    born: **5** Italy **8** Florence
    artwork: **8** The Flood **12** The Night Hunt **15** Sir John Hawkwood **18** The Rout (Battle) of San Romano **20** St George and the Dragon

Udall, Nicholas
    author of: **19** Ralph Roister Doister

Uganda
    capital/largest city: **7** Kampala
    others: **4** Arua, Gulu, Lira **5** Atiak, Jinja, Mbale, Mengo **6** Kasese, Kiboga, Kitgum, Masaka, Moroto, Pajule, Soroti, Tororo **7** Entebbe, Kachung, Kilembe, Mbarara, Mombasa **8** Kyenjojo **11** Port Masindi
    school: **8** Makerere
    division: **4** Toro **6** Ankole, Busoga **7** Buganda, Bunyoro
    monetary unit: **4** cent **8** shilling
    island: **4** Sese
    lake: **5** Kioga, Kyoga **6** Albert, Edward, George **8** Victoria
    mountain: **4** Oboa **5** Elgon **7** Virunga **9** Mufumbiro, Ruwenzori **18** Mountains of the Moon
    highest point: **10** Margherita
    river: **4** Aswa, Kafu **5** Pager **7** Katonga **9** White Nile **10** Albert Nile **12** Victoria Nile
    physical feature:
        falls: **5** Owens **8** Kabalega **9** Murchison
        plateau: **6** Ankole **11** East African
        valley: **9** Great Rift
    people: **4** Alur, Gisu, Soga, Teso **5** Ateso, Bantu, Chiga, Ganda, Langi, Lango, Nkole, Pygmy **6** Acholi, Ankole, Bagisu, Bakega, Basiga, Batoro **7** Baganda, Banyoro, Bunyoro, Hamitic, Lugbara, Nilotic, Sudanic **9** Nyoro-Toro **10** Banyankole, Karamojong
    explorer: **5** Baker, Speke **7** Stanley
    king: **6** Mutesa, Mwanga **8** Kabarega
    leader: **5** Obote **6** Mutesa **7** Omukama **8** Museveni, Nsibambi **11** Idi Amin Dada
    language: **5** Ateso, Ganda **7** English, Luganda, Swahili
    religion: **5** Islam **7** animism **8** Anglican **10** Protestant **13** Roman Catholic
    place:
        airport: **7** Entebbe
        dam: **10** Owens Falls
        national park: **6** Kidepo **14** Murchison Falls, Queen Elizabeth
    feature:
        clothing: **7** busuuti
        council of chiefs: **6** lukiko
        dance group: **17** Heart Beat of Africa
        king: **6** kabaka
    food:
        drink: **6** waragi

ugliness **8** ill-favor **9** grossness **10** homeliness **11** hideousness, monstrosity **12** unseemliness **13** frightfulness, grotesqueness, monstrousness, repulsiveness, unsightliness **14** unpleasantness **16** unattractiveness

ugly **4** foul, mean, vile **5** nasty **6** homely, horrid, odious **7** hideous, hostile, ominous **8** dreadful, horrible, menacing, unseemly **9** abhorrent, dangerous, difficult, frightful, grotesque, monstrous, obnoxious, offensive, repellent, repugnant, repulsive, sickening, unsightly **10** abominable, disgusting

ugly as sin **7** hideous **9** frightful, grotesque, monstrous, repulsive

Ugly Duckling, The
    author: **21** Hans Christian Andersen

ukase **4** fiat **5** edict, order **6** decree, dictum, ruling **7** command, mandate, statute **9** directive, manifesto, ordinance **10** injunction **12** proclamation **13** pronouncement

Ukraine
    capital/largest city: **4** Kiev
    others: **4** Lviv (Lvov), **6** Odessa **7** Donetsk, Kharkov, Lugansk (Voroshilovgrad) **8** Mariupol (Zhdanov) **9** Krivoi Rog, Zaporozhe **14** Dnepropetrovsk
    head of state: **9** president
    government: **8** republic
    monetary unit: **6** grivna **10** karbovanet
    mountain: **7** Crimean **10** Carpathian
    river: **3** Bug **6** Donets **7** Dnieper
    sea: **5** Black
    people: **7** Russian **9** Ukrainian
        leader: **6** Kuchma **10** Tymoshenko, Yushchenko
    language: **9** Ukrainian
    religion: **17** Ukrainian Catholic, Ukrainian Orthodox
    feature: **25** Askaniya Nova Nature Reserve

Ulan Bator
    capital of: **8** Mongolia

ulcer **4** sore **6** canker

Uller
    also: **4** Ullr
    origin: **8** Teutonic
    god of: **12** winter sports
    stepfather: **4** Thor

Ullmann, Liv
    born: **5** Japan, Tokyo
    nationality: **9** Norwegian
    roles: **7** Persona **10** Face to Face **11** Forty Carats, Lost Horizon **12** The Emigrants **16** Cries and Whispers **19** Scenes from a Marriage

ulna
    bone of: **8** lower arm
    neighbor: **6** radius

ulterior **6** covert, hidden, secret **7** selfish **9** concealed **10** undivulged, unrevealed **11** self-serving, undisclosed, unexpressed **13** opportunistic

ultimate **3** end **4** acme, apex, last, peak **5** final **6** height, utmost **7** extreme, maximum, supreme **8** crowning, eventual, greatest, terminal **9** at the peak, high point, last straw, longrange, resulting **10** conclusive, definitive
    French: **7** dernier

Ultima Thule **12** far-off region **15** uttermost degree

Ultor
    epithet of: **7** Jupiter
    means: **7** avenger

ultra **7** extreme **9** excessive, extremist

ultramodern **8** advanced, brand-new **10** avant-garde, newfangled **13** in the vanguard, up-to-the-minute

ulu **5** knife
    used by: **11** Eskimo women

ululate 4 hoot, howl, wail 6 lament

Ulysses
   author: 10 James Joyce
   character: 10 Molly Bloom 12 Blazes Boylan, Buck Mulligan, Leopold Bloom 14 Stephen Dedalus

Ulysses *see* 8 Odysseus

umber 5 brown 7 pigment 9 dark-brown 14 yellowish-brown

umbilicus 5 navel 11 belly button

umbrage 5 pique, shade 6 leaves, shadow 7 foliage, offense, outrage 10 resentment

umbrella 6 brolly 7 parasol 11 bumbershoot

Umbrellas of Cherbourg, The
   director: 11 Jacques Demy
   cast: 10 Anne Vernon 15 Nino Castelnuovo 16 Catharine Deneuve
   score: 13 Michel Legrand

Umbrian
   language family: 12 Indo-European
   branch: 6 Italic

umpire 5 judge 7 arbiter, mediate, referee 8 mediator, moderate 9 arbitrate, go-between, moderator 10 adjudicate, arbitrator, negotiator 11 adjudicator, intercessor

umpteen 4 many, slew 5 loads (of)

Una
   character in: 15 The Faerie Queene
   author: 7 Spenser

unabbreviated 5 uncut 8 complete, undocked, unpruned 9 uncropped, unreduced, unsnipped, untrimmed 10 full-length, unabridged 11 uncondensed, uncurtailed, unshortened 12 uncompressed, unexpurgated

unable 5 unfit 6 cannot 8 helpless, impotent 9 incapable 10 inadequate, unequipped 11 incompetent, unqualified
   to tell pitch: 8 tone deaf

unabridged 5 uncut 6 entire, intact 8 complete 10 full-length 11 uncondensed

unacceptable 8 below par, improper, unseemly, unworthy 9 deficient, out of line, unwelcome 10 disallowed, inadequate, unsuitable 11 displeasing, intolerable 12 inadmissible, not allowable, not up to snuff 13 insupportable 14 unsatisfactory 15 not up to standard

unacceptableness 8 disfavor, disgrace, ignominy 18 unsatisfactoriness

unaccommodating 4 rude 8 churlish 9 difficult, unhelpful 10 inflexible, intolerant, unyielding 11 disobliging 13 inconsiderate

unaccompanied 4 lone, solo 5 alone, apart 6 single, singly 8 isolated, lonesome, separate, solitary 9 a cappella, by oneself 10 unattended, unescorted 12 all by oneself 13 companionless

unaccountable 3 odd 4 free 5 clear, queer, weird 6 exempt, immune 7 bizarre, curious, excused, strange, unusual 8 baffling, innocent, peculiar 9 blameless, not liable, unheard-of 10 inculpable, intriguing, mysterious, surprising 11 astonishing, unexplained 12 inexplicable, unfathomable 13 extraordinary, not answerable 14 not responsible 16 incomprehensible

unaccustomed 3 new, odd 4 rare, wild 5 green, new to, novel, queer 6 quaint, unique, unused 7 amazing, bizarre, curious, foreign, not used, strange, ungiven, untried, unusual 8 original, peculiar, singular, uncommon 9 fantastic, startling, unheard-of 10 remarkable, surprising, unfamiliar, unversed in 11 astonishing, out-of-the-way, unpracticed 12 unacquainted, unhabituated, unimaginable 13 extraordinary, inexperienced 14 unfamiliar with 16 out of the ordinary

unacknowledged 9 anonymous 10 unanswered 11 disregarded 12 unidentified, unrecognized

unadorned 4 bald, bare 5 naked, plain, stark 6 simple 7 austere 11 undecorated 12 unornamented 13 unembellished 15 straightforward

unadulterated 4 pure, true 5 clear, uncut 7 genuine 9 unalloyed, untainted 14 untampered-with

unadventurous 5 chary, timid 7 careful 8 cautious, hesitant 11 circumspect

unadvisable 5 silly 6 stupid, unwise 8 unseemly 9 imprudent 11 inadvisable, inexpedient, injudicious, undesirable 15 disadvantageous

unaesthetic 9 tasteless 10 inartistic 11 insensitive 16 undiscriminating

unaffected 4 open 5 frank, naive, plain 6 candid, direct, honest, simple 7 genuine, natural, sincere, unmoved 8 innocent 9 childlike, guileless, ingenuous, unfeeling, unstirred, untouched, unworldly, wholesome 10 impervious, unbothered, unreserved 11 indifferent, insensitive, openhearted, plain-spoken, unconcerned, undesigning, undisturbed 12 unresponsive 13 unsympathetic 15 straightforward, unsophisticated

unaffectedness 4 ease 11 naturalness 12 unconstraint

unafraid 4 bold 5 brave 6 daring, heroic, plucky 7 valiant 8 fearless, intrepid, stalwart, valorous 9 audacious, daredevil, dauntless 10 courageous 11 indomitable, lionhearted, venturesome 12 stouthearted 13 adventuresome

unaggressive 3 shy 4 meek 5 timid 7 passive 8 peaceful, timorous 9 peaceable, shrinking 11 unambitious 14 unenterprising

unagitated 4 calm 6 gentle, placid, serene 8 composed, tranquil 9 collected, unexcited, unruffled 10 un-

troubled 11 undisturbed, unperturbed 13 self-possessed

unalloyed 4 pure 7 unmixed 11 unqualified 13 unadulterated

unalterable 5 fixed, rigid 6 stable 8 constant 9 immutable, indelible, obstinate, permanent, perennial 10 inflexible, persistent 11 irrevocable 12 indissoluble, unchangeable 13 irretrievable

unambitious 4 easy, lazy 6 humble, modest, simple 8 slothful 10 unaspiring 12 unaggressive 14 unenterprising

unamiable 4 sour 5 cross, surly, testy 6 sullen 7 grouchy, hostile, peevish 8 churlish 9 irascible 10 ill-humored, unfriendly, unpleasant, unsociable 11 bad-tempered, uncongenial 12 disagreeable

unamorous 4 cold, cool 6 frigid 8 unloving 11 passionless

unanimated 4 dull, flat, limp 5 inert, vapid 7 insipid 8 lifeless 10 insentient 11 unconscious

unanimity 6 accord 7 concord, harmony 9 agreement, consensus 11 concordance, concurrence 17 meeting of the minds

unanimous 6 allied, united 9 accordant, consonant, of one mind 10 harmonious, like-minded

unannounced 6 secret, sudden 8 surprise, withheld 10 suppressed, unheralded 11 undisclosed, unlooked for, unpublished 12 unadvertised 13 unanticipated

unanticipated 6 sudden 8 surprise 10 unexpected, unforeseen, unheralded 11 unannounced, unlooked-for, unpredicted

unappealing 10 disgusting, uninviting, unpleasant 11 displeasing 12 disagreeable, unappetizing, unattractive

unappetizing 6 horrid 7 insipid 10 bad-tasting, disgusting, uninviting 11 unpalatable 12 disagreeable

unapproachable 4 cold, cool 5 aloof 6 remote, unique 7 austere, awesome, distant, supreme 8 foremost, peerless, superior 9 matchless, nonpareil, unequaled, unrivaled 10 forbidding, inimitable, preeminent 11 beyond reach, stand-offish, unreachable 12 inaccessible, incomparable, intimidating, second to none, unattainable, unparalleled 13 beyond compare

unasked 6 wanton 8 unbidden, unsought, unwanted 9 uninvited, unwelcome 10 gratuitous 11 uncalled-for, undesirable, unrequested, unsolicited

unassertive 3 shy 5 timid 6 humble, modest 7 bashful 8 sheepish 9 diffident, shrinking

unassertiveness 7 modesty, shyness 8 docility, timidity 9 timidness 10 diffidence, humbleness 11 bashfulness 12 sheepishness

unassuming 5 muted, plain **6** homely, modest, simple **7** natural **9** easygoing **11** unassertive, unobtrusive **13** unpretentious **14** unostentatious

unattached 5 apart, split **6** single **8** detached, separate **9** separated **11** unconnected **12** disconnected

unattractive 4 dull, ugly **5** plain **6** homely **8** frumpish **11** unappealing, undesirable **12** unappetizing

unauthentic 4 fake, mock, sham **5** bogus, false, phony **6** untrue **7** dubious **8** doubtful **9** imitation, synthetic **10** fraudulent **11** counterfeit **12** questionable

unauthenticated 8 disputed **10** apocryphal, unverified **15** unsubstantiated

unauthorized 6 banned, covert **7** furtive **8** outlawed, unlawful **9** concealed, unallowed, underhand **10** prohibited, unapproved, unofficial **11** clandestine, uncertified, unpermitted, unwarranted **12** unaccredited, unsanctioned **13** under-the-table

unavailable 5 taken **6** scarce **7** lacking, married **9** not at hand **10** nonpresent **11** nonexistent

unavailing 4 idle, vain, weak **5** empty, inept **6** futile, no good **7** invalid, useless **8** bootless, impotent **9** fruitless, worthless **11** ineffective, ineffectual **12** unproductive, unsuccessful

unavoidable 4 sure **5** fated, fixed **7** certain **9** necessary, requisite **10** compulsory, imperative, inevitable, obligatory **11** inescapable **13** unpreventable **14** uncontrollable

unaware 8 heedless, ignorant, unwarned **9** in the dark, unalerted, unknowing, unmindful **10** unappraised **11** incognizant, unconscious **12** off one's guard, unacquainted, unsuspecting **13** unenlightened

unawares 8 abruptly, by chance, suddenly **9** by mistake **10** by accident, by surprise, mistakenly **11** unknowingly, unwittingly **12** accidentally, out of nowhere, unexpectedly, unthinkingly **13** inadvertently, involuntarily, unconsciously **14** without warning **15** unintentionally **16** like a thunderbolt **20** like a bolt from the blue, like a thief in the night

unbalanced 3 mad **4** daft, loco **5** batty, nutty, wacky **6** crazed, uneven, warped **7** bonkers, cracked, leaning, unequal, unglued, unsound **8** demented, deranged, lopsided, unhinged, unpoised, unstable, unsteady **9** disturbed, illogical, psychotic, unsettled **10** irrational, unadjusted **11** not all there **12** psychopathic

unbearable 11 intolerable, unendurable, unthinkable **12** inadmissible, insufferable, unacceptable **13** insupportable

unbecoming 4 ugly **6** homely, vulgar **8** improper, unfitted, unseemly, unsuited **9** offensive, tasteless, unsightly **10** indecorous, unsuitable **11** unappealing, unbefitting **12** unattractive **13** inappropriate

unbelief 5 doubt **7** dubiety **9** disbelief **10** skepticism **11** incredulity **12** doubtfulness

unbelievable 5 false **6** absurd, insane **7** amazing, asinine, idiotic **10** astounding, farfetched, incredible, irrational, remarkable, ridiculous **11** astonishing **12** preposterous, unimaginable, unreasonable **13** hard to swallow

unbeliever 7 atheist, heathen infidel, skeptic **8** apostate **10** godless one **11** disbeliever, nonbeliever

unbelieving 7 dubious **8** doubting **9** quizzical, skeptical **10** suspicious **11** distrustful, incredulous, questioning, unconvinced **12** disbelieving, nonbelieving

unbend 5 relax **6** relent, unflex **10** straighten **12** straighten up **13** straighten out

unbending 4 firm **5** rigid, stiff, tough **6** severe, strict **8** stubborn **9** obstinate **10** inflexible, stone-faced, unyielding **11** hard as nails **14** uncompromising

unbent 5 erect **7** relaxed, unbowed, upright, yielded **8** relented, straight, uncurved, unflexed **9** unstooped **12** straightened

unbiased 4 fair, just **7** liberal, neutral **8** detached, tolerant **9** impartial, unbigoted **10** fair-minded, open-minded, undogmatic **11** broad-minded **12** uninfluenced, unprejudiced **13** disinterested, dispassionate

unbigoted 8 tolerant, unbiased **10** open-minded **11** broad-minded **12** unprejudiced

unbind 4 free, undo **5** loose, untie **6** detach, loosen, ungird **7** deliver, release, undress **8** let loose, unfasten

unblamable 5 clear **8** innocent **9** blameless, guiltless, not guilty **10** inculpable, not at fault **14** not responsible

unblemished 4 pure **7** perfect **8** flawless, spotless, unmarred, unsoiled **9** unsullied **10** immaculate, unvitiated **11** white as snow **13** unadulterated **14** uncontaminated **15** clean as a whistle

unblock 4 free, open **5** unbar, unjam **6** unclog, unstop

unborn 5 fetal, later **6** coming, future, to come **7** in utero **9** embryonic **10** subsequent, succeeding **11** prospective

unbosom oneself 7 confess, confide, lay bare **15** unburden oneself

unbound 4 free **5** freed, loose **6**
loosed, untied **8** detached, let loose, loosened, released **10** unconfined, unfastened **12** unrestrained

unbounded 8 absolute **9** boundless, unbridled, unlimited **12** uncontrolled, unrestrained, unrestricted **13** unconditional, unconstrained

unbreakable 5 tough **6** strong

unbroken 5 whole **6** entire, intact **7** endless **8** complete **9** ceaseless, continual, incessant, uncracked, undivided, unsmashed **10** continuous, sequential, successive, unruptured **11** consecutive, progressive, unremitting, unshattered **12** undiminished **13** uninterrupted

unbuckle 4 undo **6** loosen **7** release, unhitch, unstrap **8** uncouple, unfasten

unburden 4 free **6** reveal **7** confess, confide, relieve, unbosom **8** disclose **9** disburden **10** unencumber **11** disencumber **15** get off one's chest **18** get out of one's system

unbusinesslike 6 casual, sloppy **8** informal **11** impractical, inefficient

uncalculated 9 unplanned **10** accidental, unintended **11** inadvertent **14** unpremeditated

uncalled-for 6 wanton **7** unasked **8** needless, unneeded, unsought, unwanted **9** redundant, uninvited **10** gratuitous, unprompted **11** unjustified, unnecessary, unsolicited **12** nonessential **14** supererogatory

uncanny 5 eerie, weird **6** spooky **7** curious, strange **8** inspired **9** fantastic, intuitive, marvelous, unearthly, unheard-of, unnatural **10** incredible, mysterious, prodigious, remarkable, unexampled **11** astonishing, exceptional **12** unbelievable, unimaginable **13** extraordinary, uncomfortable

uncanonical 12 unauthorized, unscriptural

Uncas
character in: **20** The Last of the Mohicans
author: **6** Cooper

unceasing 7 endless, eternal **8** constant **9** continual, incessant, perpetual, sustained **10** continuous, persistent, without end

uncelebrated 6 unsung **7** obscure, unknown **9** anonymous **14** uncommemorated

unceremonious 4 curt, rude **5** hasty, rough **6** abrupt **7** brusque **8** informal **11** precipitate

uncertain 4 hazy **6** fitful, unsure **7** dubious, erratic, not sure, obscure, unclear **8** doubtful, hesitant, nebulous, not fixed, variable, wavering **9** debatable, undecided, unsettled **10** disputable, indefinite, indistinct, in question, irresolute, unresolved, up in the air **11** conjectural, fluctuating, not definite, speculative, unconfirmed, vacillating **12** not confident, questionable, undetermined **13** indeterminate, unpredictable

uncertainty 4 odds, risk **5** doubt **6** chance, gamble **8** quandary **9** ambiguity, confusion, hesitancy, vagueness **10** hesitation, indecision, perplexity, unsureness **11** ambivalence, vacillation **12** equivocation, irresolution, shilly-shally **14** indefiniteness

unchain 4 free **7** release, set free **8** liberate, unfetter **9** unshackle

unchangeable 5 rigid **6** stable **7** uniform **8** stubborn **9** immutable, obstinate, permanent **10** inflexible, invariable **11** unalterable **12** intransigent

unchanging 4 fast, firm **5** fixed **6** stable, static **7** abiding, durable, lasting **8** constant **9** immutable, permanent, steadfast **10** monotonous **11** everlasting **12** indissoluble

unchaperoned 10 unattended, unescorted **12** unsupervised **13** unaccompanied

uncharacteristic 8 atypical **12** out of keeping **16** unrepresentative

uncharitable 5 tight **6** stingy, unkind **7** miserly **9** illiberal, niggardly, unfeeling **10** unfriendly, ungenerous, ungracious **11** closefisted, insensitive, tightfisted **12** parsimonious **13** unsympathetic **15** uncompassionate

unchaste 4 lewd **5** loose **6** erotic, impure **7** corrupt, immoral **8** immodest **9** abandoned, debauched **10** dishonored

unchecked 4 free **5** loose **6** unruly **7** liberal, rampant **8** reinless, unreined **9** out of hand, unbridled, unmuzzled **10** unhindered **12** out of control, unrestrained, unsuppressed

uncial 6 script
  form: **5** large, round
  used in: **5** Greek, Latin

unciform 10 hook-shaped

uncivil 4 curt, rude **5** blunt, surly **6** abrupt, gauche **7** boorish, brusque **8** impolite **10** ungracious **11** ill-mannered **12** disagreeable, discourteous

uncivilized 4 rude **6** savage, vulgar **7** boorish, brutish, ill-bred, uncouth, untamed **8** barbaric, churlish **9** barbarous, obnoxious, ungenteel **10** uncultured, unpolished **12** uncultivated

unclad 4 bare, nude **5** naked **7** exposed, unrobed **8** disrobed, in the raw, starkers, stripped **9** in the nude, unclothed, uncovered, undressed **10** stark-naked **15** in the altogether

unclean 4 evil, foul, tref, vile **5** dirty, dusty, grimy, messy, muddy, sooty **6** filthy, impure, soiled **7** defiled, immoral, obscene, smutted, stained **8**

polluted, unchaste **9** blemished **10** besmirched

unclear 3 dim **4** hazy **5** blear, faint, foggy, fuzzy, misty, vague **6** bleary, cloudy, vapory **7** clouded, obscure, shadowy **8** shrouded, vaporous **9** ambiguous, uncertain **10** indefinite, indistinct

Uncle Remus
  author: **18** Joel Chandler Harris

Uncle Sam
  personification of: **7** America

Uncle Tom's Cabin
  author: **19** Harriet Beecher Stowe
  character: **5** Eliza, Topsy **10** Eva St Clare **11** Simon Legree

Uncle Vanya
  author: **12** Anton Chekhov
  character: **6** Marina **12** Mihail Astrov **13** Ivan Voynitsky (Uncle Vanya) **14** Marya Voynitsky **15** Sonya Andreyevna **16** Yelena Andreyevna **19** Alexandr Serebryakov

unclose 4 open **6** reveal, unclog, unfold, unshut, unstop, unwrap **7** unblock
  poetic: **3** ope

unclothed 4 bare, nude **5** naked **6** unclad **7** exposed, unrobed **8** stripped **9** in the nude, uncovered, undressed

unclouded 5 clear, light, sunny **6** bright, serene **10** unobscured

uncollected 4 owed **5** owing, upset **6** shaken **8** agitated, troubled **9** disturbed, perturbed **11** discomposed, outstanding

uncolored 4 bald, bare, true **5** plain, stark **6** simple **9** unadorned **11** unvarnished **12** unelaborated **13** unembellished **15** straightforward

uncombed 5 messy **6** blowsy, frowzy, matted, mussed, untidy **7** ruffled, rumpled, snarled, tangled, tousled, unkempt **11** disarranged

uncomfortable 4 edgy **5** tense, upset **6** on edge, uneasy **7** awkward, keyed up, nervous, painful **8** confused, strained, troubled **9** ill at ease **10** bothersome, disquieted, irritating, out of place **11** discomfited, discomposed, distressful **13** on tenterhooks

uncommitted 9 unpledged **11** undedicated

uncommon 4 rare **5** novel **6** scarce, unique **7** bizarre, curious, notable, supreme, unusual **8** peculiar, peerless, superior **9** matchless, unmatched **10** infrequent, remarkable, unexcelled, unfamiliar **11** exceptional, outstanding, superlative **12** incomparable, unparalleled **13** extraordinary **14** unconventional **15** once in a lifetime **16** few and far between

uncommunicative 3 mum, shy **4** dumb, mute **5** quiet **6** silent **8** reserved, reticent, retiring, taciturn **9** se-

cretive, withdrawn **10** speechless, tongue-tied, unsociable **11** untalkative **12** close-mouthed, inexpressive

uncomplicated 4 easy **5** clear, plain **6** simple **10** uninvolved

uncomplimentary 8 critical, derisive, negative **9** insulting **10** unadmiring **11** disparaging **12** disapproving, unflattering

uncompromising 4 firm **5** rigid, stiff **6** strict **8** exacting, hardline, obdurate **9** immovable, unbending, unvarying **10** inexorable, inflexible, scrupulous, unyielding **11** unrelenting

unconcealed 4 bald, bare, open **5** overt **6** in view **7** exposed, in sight, obvious, visible **8** apparent, manifest, revealed **9** uncovered **11** discernible, perceivable, perceptible **12** in plain sight, out in the open

unconcentrated 4 weak **7** diffuse, diluted, thinned **9** dispersed, scattered, spread out **11** watered down

unconcern 10 dispassion **11** insouciance, nonchalance **12** indifference

unconcerned 4 cold **5** aloof **6** serene **7** distant, unaware, unmoved **8** composed, uncaring **9** apathetic, oblivious, unfeeling, unmindful **10** impervious, nonchalant, uninvolved, untroubled **11** indifferent, insensitive, passionless, unperturbed **12** unresponsive **13** unsympathetic

unconditional 5 utter **6** entire **8** absolute, complete, outright **9** downright, unlimited **10** conclusive **11** categorical, unqualified **12** unrestricted **13** thoroughgoing

unconfident 3 shy **5** timid **7** bashful **8** reticent, retiring, timorous **9** diffident, shrinking, uncertain

unconfirmed 7 dubious **8** unproved **10** unapproved, unverified **11** unvalidated **12** questionable **14** uncorroborated **15** unsubstantiated

unconformity 7 anomaly **9** deviation **10** aberration, divergence **11** abnormality, peculiarity **12** eccentricity, idiosyncrasy, irregularity **13** nonconformity

uncongenial 9 ill-suited, unamiable **10** dissimilar, unfriendly, unpleasant **12** disagreeable, incompatible **13** unsympathetic

unconnected 7 severed **8** detached, discrete, separate **9** uncoupled, unhitched, unrelated **12** disconnected

unconquerable 6 innate **9** ingrained **10** inveterate, invincible, unbeatable **12** impenetrable, invulnerable, undefeatable **14** insurmountable, unvanquishable

unconscionable 7 extreme **9** excessive **10** immoderate, inordinate, outrageous **11** inexcusable, unjustified, unwarranted **12** indefensible, preposterous, unforgivable, unpardonable, unreasonable **13** unjustifiable

unconscious 3 out **6** latent **7** in a coma, out cold **8** comatose, in a faint **9** insensate, senseless, unknowing, unmindful **10** suppressed, unrealized **11** incognizant **12** unsuspecting **14** dead to the world

unconstitutional 7 illegal **8** unlawful **12** unauthorized

unconstrained 4 bold, easy **7** natural, relaxed **8** unforced **9** abandoned **10** unaffected **11** spontaneous, uninhibited
French: **6** degage

unconstraint 4 ease **7** abandon **8** boldness, free will, openness **9** frankness **11** naturalness, spontaneity

uncontrollable 6 unruly **7** wayward **12** ungovernable, unmanageable

uncontrolled 4 free, wild **8** absolute **9** abandoned, unlimited **10** ungoverned **12** unrestrained

unconventional 3 odd **4** rare **5** crazy, kinky, nutty, queer, wacky, weird **6** far-out, quaint, unique **7** bizarre, curious, offbeat, strange, unusual **8** aberrant, atypical, bohemian, freakish, original, peculiar, singular, uncommon **9** different, eccentric, fantastic, irregular **10** newfangled, outlandish, unorthodox **11** exceptional **12** unaccustomed **13** extraordinary, idiosyncratic, nonconforming, nonconformist **15** individualistic

unconvinced 7 dubious **8** doubtful **9** skeptical, uncertain, unsettled

unconvincing 5 false, fishy **7** dubious, suspect **10** suspicious **11** implausible **12** questionable, unbelievable

uncooked
French: **9** au naturel

uncooperative 6 ornery **7** selfish **8** perverse, stubborn **9** difficult, unhelpful, unwilling **11** intractable **12** intransigent

uncoordinated 6 clumsy **7** awkward **8** ungainly **9** graceless

uncouple 4 undo **6** detach, loosen, unhook **7** release, unhitch **8** unbuckle

uncoupled 8 detached, loosened **9** separated, unhitched **10** disengaged **11** unconnected **12** disconnected

uncourageous 5 timid **8** cowardly, timorous **9** dastardly, shrinking **13** pusillanimous

uncourtly 7 ill-bred, uncivil, uncouth **9** ungallant **10** ill-behaved, ungracious, unmannerly **11** uncourteous **12** discourteous **13** ungentlemanly

uncouth 4 rude **5** crass, crude, gross, rough **6** callow, coarse **7** boorish, brutish, ill-bred, loutish, uncivil **8** barbaric, churlish, impolite **9** unrefined **10** indelicate, uncultured, unmannerly

11 ill-mannered, uncivilized **12** uncultivated

uncover 4 bare, undo **5** dig up, strip **6** denude, dig out, expose, reveal, unmask, unveil, unwrap **7** disrobe, lay bare, uncloak, undrape, undress, unearth **8** disclose, unclothe **9** make known, unsheathe **11** make visible **12** bring to light

uncovered 4 bare **5** bared, dug up, naked **7** exposed, noticed **8** detected, revealed **9** disclosed, made known **10** discovered **13** brought to view **14** brought to light

uncovering 8 exposure **9** divulging, unmasking **10** disclosure, divulgence, laying open, revelation **15** bringing to light **20** bringing out in the open

uncritical 4 dull, dumb **6** casual, obtuse, stupid **7** inexact, offhand, shallow **8** careless, ignorant, slipshod **9** imprecise, untutored **10** inaccurate, uneducated, unschooled, unthinking **11** perfunctory, superficial **12** unreflecting **16** undiscriminating

unctuous 4 oily, smug **6** smarmy **7** fawning, honeyed, servile **8** slippery, too suave **9** pietistic, too smooth **10** flattering, obsequious **11** sycophantic **12** honey-tongued, ingratiating **13** sanctimonious, self-righteous

uncultivated 3 raw **4** wild **7** uncouth **8** unfarmed, unplowed, untilled **9** unrefined **10** unimproved **11** undeveloped

uncultivated land
god of: **8** Silvanus, Sylvanus

uncultured 5 crass **6** coarse, common, vulgar **7** low-bred **9** inelegant, unrefined **10** unpolished **12** uncultivated

uncustomary 4 rare **6** unique **7** amazing, unusual **8** singular, uncommon, unwonted **9** unheard-of **10** incredible, unexpected **11** astonishing, exceptional **12** unaccustomed, unbelievable **13** extraordinary, unanticipated

undaunted 5 brave **6** gritty, heroic, plucky **7** unfazed, valiant **8** fearless, intrepid, resolute, stalwart, valorous **9** not put off **10** courageous, undismayed **11** indomitable, unflinching, unperturbed, unshrinking **12** stouthearted **13** undiscouraged

undeceive 8 disabuse **10** disenchant **11** disenthrall, disillusion **12** open one's eyes **13** break the spell **15** burst one's bubble **19** bring one down to earth **20** shatter one's illusions

undecided 4 open **5** vague **6** unsure **7** dubious, pending **8** not final, wavering **9** tentative, uncertain, unsettled **10** indecisive, indefinite, in abeyance, in a dilemma, irresolute, of two minds, open-minded, unresolved, up in the air **11** fluctuating, vacillating **12** undetermined, unformulated **16**

hemming and hawing **17** blowing hot and cold **20** going around in circles

undecorated 4 bare **5** blank, plain, stark **6** simple **7** austere **9** unadorned **13** unembellished

undedicated 11 indifferent, uncommitted

undefiled 4 pure **5** clean **6** chaste, intact, virgin **7** natural **8** innocent, spotless **9** stainless, unsullied **10** unpolluted

undemanding 4 easy **6** low-key, simple **7** patient, relaxed **9** easygoing **10** submissive **12** easy to please, laissez-faire **14** live-and-let-live

undemonstrative 3 shy **4** cold **5** aloof **7** distant, stoical **8** reserved **9** impassive **11** unemotional **12** inexpressive, unresponsive **14** self-controlled

undeniable 4 sure **6** patent, proven **7** certain, obvious **8** decisive, manifest **10** conclusive **11** established, indubitable, irrefutable **12** beyond a doubt, demonstrable, indisputable **13** incontestable **14** unquestionable **16** incontrovertible

undeniably 6 surely **9** certainly **10** decisively, definitely **11** irrefutably **12** conclusively, demonstrably, indisputably **13** incontestably **14** beyond question, unquestionably **16** incontrovertibly

undependable 6 fickle **7** erratic, flighty **8** unstable, variable, wavering **10** capricious, changeable, inconstant, unreliable **13** irresponsible, unpredictable, untrustworthy

under 3 sub **5** below, lower, neath, short **7** beneath, sedated **8** inferior, less than **9** because of **11** subordinate, unconscious

undercover 3 sly **6** covert, hidden, secret **7** furtive, sub rosa **8** hush-hush, stealthy **9** concealed, disguised, incognito **10** unrevealed **11** clandestine, undisclosed **12** confidential **13** surreptitious
French: **8** a couvert

undercurrent 4 aura, hint, mood **5** sense, tinge, vibes **7** quality, riptide **8** undertow **9** undertone **10** atmosphere, intimation, suggestion, vibrations **12** crosscurrent

undercut 9 discredit, undermine, undersell **10** compromise

underestimate 7 dismiss, put down **8** belittle, minimize, misjudge **9** deprecate, discredit, disparage, disregard, sell short, underrate, undersell **10** depreciate, undervalue **11** detract from **12** miscalculate

undergarment 3 bra **4** BVDs, slip **5** pants, shift, teddy, thong **6** boxers, corset, girdle, shorts **7** chemise, panties **8** bloomers, camisole, knickers, lingerie, skivvies **9** brassiere, petticoat, union suit **12** jockey shorts

undergo 5 brave, stand **6** endure, suffer **7** sustain, weather **8** submit to **9** encounter, go through, withstand **10** experience

undergraduate 4 coed, soph **5** frosh, plebe **6** junior, senior **7** scholar, student **8** freshman **9** sophomore, undegreed **10** degreeless, nondegreed **13** underclassman, upperclassman

underground 6 buried, covert, secret **7** sub-rosa **10** undercover **11** belowground, clandestine **12** subterranean **13** surreptitious **15** below the surface

underground chamber 4 tomb **5** crypt, vault **6** cellar **8** catacomb **9** sepulcher

underhand, underhanded 6 covert, crafty, sneaky, tricky **7** corrupt, crooked, cunning, devious, evasive, furtive, illegal **8** sneaking, stealthy **9** conniving, dishonest, unethical **10** fraudulent **12** unprincipled, unscrupulous **13** surreptitious

underhandedness 5 guile **6** deceit **7** slyness **8** trickery **9** chicanery, deception, duplicity **10** sneakiness, trickiness **13** secretiveness

underline 6 accent, stress **7** dwell on, point up **9** emphasize, press home **10** accentuate, underscore **15** bring into relief

underling 4 serf **6** flunky, lackey, menial, minion, thrall, vassal **7** servant, subject **8** employee, hireling, inferior **9** attendant, hired hand **11** subordinate

underlying 5 basic **6** covert **7** beneath, radical **8** implicit **9** elemental, essential **10** subtending **11** fundamental

undermine 4 foil, ruin **5** erode **6** injure, riddle, scotch, thwart, weaken **7** cripple, destroy, subvert, torpedo **8** sabotage **9** eat away at, frustrate, hamstring **10** neutralize **11** burrow under, tunnel under

underneath 5 below, lower **6** bottom, hidden **9** disguised, subject to **14** misrepresented

undernourished 8 starving, underfed **12** malnourished

under obligation 5 bound **6** liable **7** obliged **8** beholden, indebted **9** obligated **10** answerable, in one's debt **11** accountable, responsible

underpart 4 sole **5** belly, tails **6** bottom **9** lower side, underside

underpin 4 bear **7** bolster, support **10** strengthen **12** substantiate

underpinning 4 base **5** basic **6** ground **7** support **9** essential **10** foundation, groundwork **11** fundamental **12** substructure

underplay 8 play down **11** deemphasize

underprivileged 4 poor **5** needy **6** in need **7** hapless, unlucky **8** badly-off, deprived, ill-fated, indigent **9** destitute, penniless, penurious **10** illstarred, pauperized **11** handicapped, unfortunate **12** impoverished **13** disadvantaged **22** in adverse circumstances

underrate 6 slight **8** belittle, derogate, minimize **9** denigrate, deprecate, disparage **10** depreciate, undervalue **13** underestimate

underscore 4 mark **6** accent, deepen, play up, stress **7** feature, point up **8** heighten **9** emphasize, intensify, press home, underline **10** accentuate **15** draw attention to

underscoring 6 stress **8** emphasis **11** underlining

underside 4 back, sole **5** belly, tails **6** bottom **7** reverse **9** lower side, underpart

undersized 4 tiny **5** elfin, short, small **6** little, petite, slight **7** stunted **8** dwarfish **10** diminutive **11** lilliputian

underskirt 4 slip **7** pannier **9** crinoline, hoopskirt, petticoat

understand 3 dig, get, see **4** hear, know, read, take **5** grasp, learn **6** absorb, accept, assume, can see, fathom, gather, take it **7** be aware, discern, make out, presume, realize **8** conclude, perceive **9** apprehend, interpret, recognize **10** appreciate, comprehend **14** sympathize with, take for granted

understandable 8 apparent **12** recognizable, unmistakable **14** comprehensible

understanding 4 pact **5** grasp **7** empathy, insight, knowing **8** sympathy, tolerant **9** agreement, awareness, intuition, knowledge, sensitive **10** cognizance, compassion, compromise, discerning, perception, perceptive, responsive **11** concordance, sensitivity, sympathetic **12** appreciation, appreciative, apprehension **13** compassionate, comprehension **17** meeting of the minds

understate 8 minimize **11** deemphasize

understated 9 minimized **10** restrained **12** conservative, deemphasized

understatement 7 litotes **10** minimizing **20** conservative estimate

understudy 3 sub **6** backup, double, fill-in, relief **7** stand-by, stand-in **9** alternate, surrogate **10** substitute **11** pinch hitter, replacement

undertake 3 try **5** begin, essay, start **6** assume, strive, tackle, take on **7** attempt **8** commence, embark on, en-

deavor, set about, shoulder **9** agree to do, enter upon **11** promise to do **13** get involved in

undertaking 3 job **4** task **6** effort **7** concern, project, pursuit, venture **8** endeavor **10** commitment, enterprise

under the influence 5 drunk **6** sodden, soused, wasted, zapped, zonked **7** smashed **8** besotted **9** plastered **10** inebriated **11** intoxicated **20** three sheets to the wind

under the weather 3 bad, ill **4** sick **6** ailing, sickly, unwell **9** unhealthy **10** indisposed

undertone 4 aura, hint, mood **5** scent, sense, tinge, trace **6** flavor, mumble, murmur, nuance **7** feeling, inkling, low tone, quality, whisper **8** coloring **10** atmosphere, intimation, suggestion **11** connotation, implication **12** subdued voice, undercurrent

undervalue 6 slight **8** belittle, derogate **9** discredit, disparage, underrate **10** depreciate **13** underestimate

underwear 3 bra **4** BVDs, slip **5** pants, teddy, thong **6** boxers, briefs, corset, girdle, shorts **7** chemise, panties **8** bloomers, camisole, knickers, lingerie, skivvies **9** brassiere, petticoat, union suit **12** jockey shorts, smallclothes **14** unmentionables

underweight 4 bony, lank **5** gaunt, lanky **6** skinny **7** scrawny, spindly **8** skeletal, underfed **9** emaciated **12** skin-and-bones **13** hollow-cheeked **14** spindle-shanked, undernourished

underworld 4 Hell **5** Hades, limbo **6** the mob **8** mobsters, the Mafia **9** criminals, gangsters, purgatory **10** Cosa Nostra **11** shades below **12** the syndicate **13** bottomless pit, nether regions **14** organized crime **15** criminal element, infernal regions **16** abode of the damned

god of: 3 Dis **5** Hades, Orcus, Pluto **8** Dis Pater

under wraps 6 hidden, secret **9** concealed **10** suppressed, under cover

underwrite 3 aid **4** back **7** approve, endorse, finance, sponsor, support, warrant **8** invest in, sanction, validate **9** guarantee, subsidize **11** countersign

underwriter 5 angel **6** backer, patron **7** sponsor **8** investor **9** financier, guarantor

undeserving 3 bad **8** inferior, unworthy

undesirable 5 unfit **8** disliked, improper, unbidden, unsavory, unseemly, unwanted, unworthy **9** offensive, unpopular **10** unbecoming, uninviting, unsuitable, unwelcomed **11** distasteful, unbefitting, unwished-for **12** disagreeable, inadmissible, unacceptable, unattractive **13** inappropriate, objectionable **14** unsatisfactory

undetectable 12 unnoticeable, unobservable **13** imperceptible, unsubstantial

undetermined 6 chance **7** unfixed, unknown **8** unproved, unproven **9** uncertain, undecided **10** indefinite, irresolute **13** indeterminate, unascertained

undeveloped 3 raw **5** crude, green **6** callow, unripe **8** immature, inchoate, unformed **9** embryonic, half-baked **10** unfinished **11** rudimentary, unexploited **12** uncultivated

undignified 3 low **7** boorish **8** improper, shameful, unseemly, unworthy **9** degrading, inelegant, tasteless, unrefined **10** beneath one, indecorous, indelicate, in bad taste, unbecoming, unladylike, unsuitable **11** unbefitting **13** discreditable, inappropriate, ungentlemanly **18** beneath one's dignity **Latin: 8** infra dig **15** infra dignitatem

undiluted 4 neat, pure **5** sheer **7** unmixed **8** straight **11** unfortified **12** full-strength **13** unadulterated

Undine
  form: **6** spirit
  location: **5** water
  sex: **6** female

undiscerning 11 insensitive **12** unperceptive **14** indiscriminate

undisciplined 4 wild **6** fickle, fitful **7** erratic, wayward, willful **8** unsteady, untaught **9** mercurial, untrained, untutored **10** capricious, changeable, inconstant, uneducated, unfinished, unreliable, unschooled **11** unpracticed **12** obstreperous, uncontrolled, undependable, unrestrained **13** unpredictable

undisclosed 6 hidden, secret **7** private **9** concealed **10** unrevealed **12** confidential

undisguised 4 open **5** clear, utter **7** evident, obvious **8** complete, distinct, manifest, unhidden **9** out-and-out **10** plain as day, pronounced, unreserved **11** unconcealed **12** unmistakable, wholehearted **13** thoroughgoing **24** plain as the nose on one's face

undismayed 7 uncowed **8** unafraid, unscared **9** confident, unabashed, unalarmed, undaunted **12** unfrightened **13** undiscouraged, unintimidated

undisputed 4 sure **7** certain, granted **8** accepted **9** undoubted **10** conclusive, undeniable **11** beyond doubt, indubitable, irrefutable, past dispute, uncontested **12** acknowledged, indisputable, unchallenged, unquestioned **13** a matter of fact, incontestable **14** beyond question, freely admitted, unquestionable **15** without question **16** incontrovertible

undistinguished 5 plain, usual **6** common **7** prosaic **8** everyday, mediocre, ordinary **10** pedestrian, unexciting **11** commonplace **12** run-of-the-

mill, unremarkable **13** unexceptional **18** nothing to rave about

undistracted 4 calm **6** serene, stolid **7** unfazed **9** impassive, unruffled **10** untroubled **11** undisturbed

undisturbed 4 calm, cool **5** quiet **6** placid, serene, steady **7** equable, unmoved **8** composed, peaceful, tranquil **9** collected, inviolate, unexcited, unruffled, untouched **10** of solitude, unagitated, unbothered, untroubled **11** left in order, unperturbed **13** imperturbable, self-possessed, uninterrupted

undivided 5 solid, whole **6** entire, united **7** unified, unsplit **8** complete **9** of one mind, unanimous **10** not divided, unstinting **12** wholehearted

undo 3 end **4** free, open, ruin, void **5** annul, erase, loose, quash, untie **6** cancel, defeat, loosen, offset, repair, unbind, unfold, unhook, unknot, unlace, unlock, unwrap **7** destroy, nullify, rectify, reverse, subvert, unchain, unravel, wipe out **8** demolish, overturn, unbutton, unfasten **9** disengage, eliminate, make up for, undermine **10** counteract, invalidate, neutralize **11** disentangle **13** compensate for **14** counterbalance

undogmatic 7 liberal **8** flexible, tolerant **10** open-minded **11** broad-minded

undoing 4 doom, jinx, ruin **5** upset **6** defeat **7** erasure, nemesis **8** collapse, downfall, negation, reversal, weakness **9** annulment, breakdown, overthrow, ruination, thwarting, wiping out **11** cause of ruin, destruction **12** Achilles' heel, cancellation, invalidation **13** counteraction, nullification **14** neutralization

undomesticated 4 wild **5** feral **6** ferine, savage **7** untamed **8** barbaric **9** barbarous **11** uncivilized

undone 6 ruined **9** come apart, destroyed **10** incomplete, unfastened **12** not completed

undoubted 4 sure **5** utter **7** certain **8** absolute, complete, definite, positive **11** indubitable, unequivocal **12** indisputable **13** unimpeachable **14** unquestionable

undoubtedly 6 surely **7** no doubt **9** assuredly, certainly, decidedly, doubtless **10** absolutely, definitely, positively, undeniably **11** indubitably **12** beyond a doubt, unmistakably, without doubt **13** unequivocally **14** beyond question, unquestionably **15** without question

undress 5 strip **6** nudity **7** disrobe, uncover, undrape **8** disarray, unclothe **9** nakedness **10** dishabille **18** take off one's clothes

undressed 4 bare, nude **5** naked **6** unclad **7** denuded, exposed, unrobed **8** disrobed, stripped, undraped **9** unclothed, uncovered

Undset, Sigrid
  author of: **6** The Axe **20** Kristin Lavransdatter, The Master of Hestviken

undue 6 unmeet **8** impolite, improper, needless, overmuch, too great, unseemly, unworthy **9** excessive, tasteless **10** ill-advised, indiscreet, in bad taste, inordinate, not fitting, unbecoming, unsuitable **11** superfluous, uncalled-for, unjustified, unnecessary, unwarranted **13** inappropriate, objectionable

undulate 4 coil **5** slink, weave **9** fluctuate **11** rise and fall

undulating 4 wavy **5** bumpy **6** uneven

undulation 7 coiling **8** slinking, twisting **10** contortion **11** convolution **16** rising and falling

undutiful 6 remiss **8** disloyal **11** disobedient

undying 6 steady **7** abiding, endless, eternal, lasting **8** constant, enduring, immortal, unending, unfading, untiring **9** continual, deathless, incessant, perennial, permanent, perpetual, unceasing **10** continuing **11** everlasting, never-ending, unfaltering, unrelenting, unremitting **12** imperishable, never-failing, undiminished **13** uninterrupted **14** indestructible

unearth 4 find, show **5** dig up **6** dig out, exhume, expose, reveal **7** display, divulge, exhibit, root out, uncover **8** disclose, discover, disinter, dredge up, excavate **9** disentomb, ferret out **10** come across, come up with **12** bring to light

unearthly 5 awful, eerie, weird **6** absurd **7** extreme, ghostly, phantom, strange, uncanny, ungodly, unusual **8** abnormal, ethereal, spectral, terrible **10** horrendous, unpleasant **11** disembodied, incorporeal, unspeakable **12** disagreeable, extramundane, supernatural **13** extraordinary, preternatural

unease 5 worry **7** tension **8** disquiet **9** misgiving **10** discomfort, uneasiness **11** disquietude **12** apprehension

uneasiness 5 dread **6** dismay **7** anxiety **9** agitation, misgiving **10** discomfort, foreboding **11** disquietude, distraction, nervousness **12** apprehension, discomfiture, discomposure, perturbation **16** apprehensiveness

uneasy 4 edgy **5** nervy, tense, upset **6** on edge, queasy, unsure **7** awkward, irksome, nervous, uptight, worried **8** strained, troubled, worrying **9** disturbed, ill at ease, perturbed, upsetting **10** bothersome, disquieted, disturbing, unpleasant **11** constrained, disquieting **12** apprehensive **13** uncomfortable

uneatable 8 inedible **11** not fit to eat

uneconomical 4 dear **6** costly **8**

wasteful **9** expensive **10** exorbitant, high-priced, immoderate, overpriced **11** extravagant **12** unreasonable

uneducated 8 ignorant, untaught **9** unlearned, untrained, untutored **10** illiterate, uncultured, unlettered, unschooled **12** uncultivated, uninstructed **13** unenlightened

unelaborated 4 bald, bare **5** plain, stark **6** simple **9** essential, unadorned, uncolored **11** fundamental, unvarnished **13** unembellished **15** straightforward

unembellished 4 bald, bare **5** naked, plain, stark **7** austere **9** unadorned **11** undecorated **12** unornamented

unemotional 4 cold, cool **6** formal, remote **7** distant **8** lukewarm, reserved **9** apathetic, impassive, unfeeling **11** indifferent, passionless, unconcerned **12** unresponsive **15** undemonstrative

unemployed 4 axed, idle **5** fired **6** canned, sacked, unused **7** bounced, jobless, laid-off **8** workless **9** at leisure, at liberty, booted-out, dismissed, on the dole, on welfare, out of a job, out of work **10** discharged, unoccupied **11** pink-slipped

unencumbered 4 free **6** vacant **7** unladen **8** expedite **10** unburdened, unhindered **13** unhandicapped

unending 6 steady **7** endless, eternal, lasting **8** constant, enduring **9** continual, incessant, perennial, permanent, perpetual, unceasing **10** continuous, unwavering **11** everlasting, neverending, unremitting **12** undiminished **13** uninterrupted

unendurable 7 racking **9** agonizing, torturous **10** tormenting, unbearable **11** intolerable **12** excruciating, insufferable

unenlightened 8 ignorant **9** in the dark, unlearned **10** uneducated, uninformed **11** uninitiated **12** uninstructed

unenterprising 4 lazy **11** unambitious **12** unaggressive

unenthusiastic 8 lukewarm **10** unspirited **11** halfhearted, indifferent **13** unimpassioned

unequal 6 biased, uneven, unfair, unjust, unlike **7** bigoted, partial **9** different, disparate, unmatched **10** dissimilar, not uniform, prejudiced **11** inequitable

unequaled 7 supreme **8** peerless **9** matchless, paramount, unmatched, unrivaled **10** consummate, unexcelled **11** ne plus ultra, unsurpassed **12** incomparable, second to none, unapproached, unparalleled **13** beyond compare **16** beyond comparison

unequivocable 4 bald **5** utter **8** outright **9** out-and-out **11** categorical, unqualified

unequivocal 5 clear, final **7** certain **8** absolute, clear-cut, decisive, definite, emphatic **11** unambiguous **12** indisputable **13** incontestable **16** incontrovertible

unequivocally 7 clearly **9** certainly, downright **10** completely, decisively, definitely, thoroughly **12** emphatically, indisputably, unmistakably **13** incontestably **14** unquestionably, wholeheartedly **16** incontrovertibly

unerring 4 sure **7** certain, precise **8** constant, faithful, reliable **9** faultless, unfailing **10** infallible, unchanging

unessential 8 nonvital **9** accessory, extrinsic **10** disposable, expendable **11** dispensable, superfluous, unimportant, unnecessary **12** nonessential

unethical 5 dirty, shady, wrong **6** shoddy, unfair **7** devious **8** unworthy **9** dishonest, underhand **10** unladylike **12** dishonorable, disreputable, questionable, unprincipled **13** ungentlemanly **14** unconscionable

uneven 4 awry, bent **5** bumpy, lumpy, rough **6** angled, coarse, craggy, curved, jagged, tilted, unfair, unjust, unlike **7** crooked, not flat, slanted, sloping, unequal **8** lopsided, not level, not plumb, one-sided, unsmooth **9** different, disparate **10** dissimilar, illmatched, unbalanced

unevenness 7 oddness **9** bumpiness, lumpiness, roughness **10** jaggedness, ruggedness **11** crookedness **12** irregularity **14** changeableness

uneventful 4 dull **5** quiet, usual **6** boring **7** average, humdrum, prosaic, routine, tedious **8** ordinary, standard, tiresome **10** monotonous **11** commonplace **12** conventional **13** insignificant, unexceptional, uninteresting

unexcelled 7 supreme **8** flawless, peerless, superior, unbeaten **9** faultless, matchless, unequaled, unmatched, unrivaled **10** consummate **11** unsurpassed **12** incomparable, second to none, transcendent, unapproached, unparalleled **13** beyond compare

unexceptional 5 usual **6** normal **7** mundane, typical **8** ordinary, standard **9** customary **12** conventional, run of the mill

unexcited 4 calm, cool **6** placid, serene **7** unmoved **8** composed, detached **9** collected, unruffled **11** undisturbed, unemotional **13** dispassionate, unimpassioned

unexciting 4 dull, flat **5** vapid **6** boring **7** insipid **10** lackluster

unexpected 6 sudden **9** startling, unplanned **10** accidental, surprising, undesigned, unforeseen, unintended **11** astonishing, unlooked-for, unpredicted **12** out of the blue **13** unanticipated, unintentional

unextinguished 5 alive **10** unquenched **12** still burning

unfaded 5 fresh **6** bright **8** undimmed **10** unwithered

unfailing 4 true **5** loyal **6** steady **7** endless **8** constant, enduring, faithful, reliable **9** continual **10** continuous, dependable, infallible, unchanging, unwavering **12** never-failing **13** inexhaustible

unfair 4 foul **5** dirty **6** biased, unjust **7** corrupt, crooked, partial, unequal **8** not right, onesided, partisan **9** dishonest, underhand, unethical **10** not cricket, prejudiced **11** inequitable **12** dishonorable, unprincipled, unreasonable, unscrupulous **14** unconscionable

unfaithful 5 false **6** faulty, untrue **7** inexact **8** disloyal, unchaste **9** deceitful, distorted, erroneous, faithless, imperfect **10** adulterous, inaccurate, inconstant, perfidious **11** not accurate, treacherous **12** falsehearted **13** untrustworthy

Unfaithfully Yours
    director: 14 Preston Sturges
    cast: 10 Rudy Vallee **11** Rex Harrison **12** Edgar Kennedy, Linda Darnell **15** Barbara Lawrence

unfaithfulness 7 falsity, perfidy **9** falseness, treachery **10** disloyalty, fickleness, infidelity **11** inconstancy **13** faithlessness **14** perfidiousness

unfaltering 4 firm, sure **6** steady **8** enduring, resolute **9** obstinate, steadfast, unfailing **10** dependable, persistent, unflagging, unswerving, unwavering **11** persevering, undeviating **12** never-failing, wholehearted

unfamiliar 3 new **5** novel **6** exotic, unique **7** curious, foreign, strange, unknown, unusual **9** different **10** ignorant of, unversed in **11** a stranger to, little known, out-of-the-way, unexposed to, uninitiated, unskilled in **12** not well-known, unacquainted, unconversant **13** not acquainted, unpracticed in **14** unaccustomed to **15** inexperienced in, uninformed about **18** unenlightened about

unfamiliarity 9 ignorance **11** strangeness **12** inexperience **15** lack of knowledge

unfashionable 5 dated, dowdy, passe **6** frumpy, old-hat **8** outmoded **9** out-of-date, unstylish **12** old-fashioned

unfasten 4 undo **5** unpin, untie **6** detach, unbind, unbolt, unhook, unlace, unlash, unlink, unlock **7** unclose, unhitch, unlatch, unstick **8** unbutton, uncouple

unfastened 5 apart, undid **6** undone, untied **7** severed, unlaced, unstuck **8** detached, unhooked **9** unbuckled, uncoupled, unhitched **11** unconnected **12** disconnected

unfathomable 4 deep, vast **6** arcane,

remote, subtle **7** complex, extreme, obscure **8** abstract, abstruse, esoteric, profound, puzzling **9** enigmatic **10** bottomless, perplexing **16** hard to understand, incomprehensible

unfavorable 3 bad **4** poor **7** adverse, unhappy **8** unsuited, untimely **9** ill-suited **10** ill-favored, regretable **11** inopportune, regrettable, unfortunate, unpromising **12** inauspicious, inconvenient, infelicitous, unpropitious, unseasonable **15** disadvantageous

unfeasible 10 impossible, infeasible, unsuitable, unworkable **11** impractical **12** unachievable **13** impracticable

unfeeling 4 cold **5** cruel **9** heartless **11** hardhearted, insensitive **13** unsympathetic

unfeigned 4 real, true **7** genuine, sincere **10** unaffected

unfetter 4 free **7** release, set free, unchain **8** liberate **9** unshackle

unfilled 4 open **5** blank, empty **6** hollow, vacant **7** drained **9** available **10** unoccupied

unfinished 5 crude, rough **6** undone **7** lacking, sketchy, wanting **8** immature **9** deficient, imperfect, unnatural, unpainted, unrefined, unstained **10** incomplete, unexecuted, unpolished **11** uncompleted, unfulfilled, unlacquered, unvarnished

unfit 4 sick, weak **5** frail **6** infirm, not fit, sickly **7** not up to, unequal, unready, unsound, useless **8** delicate, disabled, unsuited **9** incapable, not suited, unhealthy, unskilled, untrained **10** inadequate, ineligible, not equal to, unequipped, unprepared, unsuitable **11** debilitated, ill-equipped, incompetent, ineffective, inefficient, not designed, unqualified **12** ill-contrived, not cut out for **13** inappropriate, incapacitated

unflagging 4 firm **5** fixed **6** steady **7** staunch **8** constant, enduring, resolute, tireless, unshaken, untiring **9** steadfast, tenacious, undaunted **10** determined, persistent, relentless, undrooping, unswerving, unwavering, unyielding **11** indomitable, persevering, undeviating, unfaltering, unremitting **13** indefatigable **14** uncompromising

unflappable 4 calm, cool **6** placid, serene **8** composed **9** collected **10** coolheaded **11** unexcitable **13** imperturbable, self-possessed

unflinching 4 firm, game **6** gritty, plucky, steady, strong **7** staunch **8** fearless, resolute, stalwart, unshaken **9** steadfast, tenacious, unabashed, undaunted **10** persistent, unswerving, unwavering, unyielding **11** indomitable, unfaltering, unshrinking **12** unhesitating

unfold 4 bare, show, tell **6** open up,

reveal, unfurl, unroll, unveil, unwrap **7** divulge, explain, expound, lay open, open out, present, recount, uncover **8** describe, disclose, set forth **9** elucidate, explicate, make known, spread out **10** stretch out

unfolding 4 rise **5** birth, start **9** beginning, evolution, inception, unfurling **10** revelation **11** development

unforced 4 easy **5** frank **6** candid, casual **7** natural, relaxed **8** informal **9** easygoing **10** unaffected **13** unconstrained

unforeseen 6 abrupt, sudden **8** surprise **9** unplanned **10** accidental, surprising, unexpected, unintended **11** unlooked-for, unpredicted **12** out of the blue **13** unanticipated

unforeseen danger 7 pitfall **8** exigency **9** emergency **11** contingency

unforgettable 7 notable **8** eventful, exciting **9** important, memorable, thrilling **10** noteworthy **11** significant

Unforgiven, The
    director: **13** Clint Eastwood
    cast: **11** Gene Hackman (Little Bill Daggett), Saul Rubinek (W W Beauchamp) **13** Clint Eastwood (Bill Munny), Frances Fisher (Strawberry Alice), Jaimz Woolvett (Schofield Kid), Morgan Freeman (Ned Logan), Richard Harris (English Bob)

unfortunate 5 sorry **6** cursed, jinxed, woeful **7** hapless, unblest, unhappy, unlucky **8** ill-fated, ill-timed, luckless, untimely, wretched **10** disastrous, ill-advised, ill-timed **11** inopportune, regrettable, unfavorable **12** inauspicious, infelicitous, unpropitious, unprosperous, unsuccessful

unfounded 4 idle **5** false **6** untrue **8** baseless, spurious **9** erroneous **10** fabricated, groundless

unfrequented 5 empty **6** lonely **7** remote, uncouth **8** isolated, solitary **9** unvisited **11** out-of-the-way **16** off the beaten path

unfriendly 4 cold **5** aloof **6** at odds, chilly **7** distant, haughty, hostile, warlike **8** inimical, snobbish **9** on the outs, reclusive, withdrawn **10** ungracious, unsociable **11** belligerent, contentious, quarrelsome, uncongenial **12** antagonistic, disagreeable, disputatious, inhospitable **13** at loggerheads, at sword's point, unsympathetic

unfruitful 4 vain **6** barren, fallow, futile **7** useless, worn-out **8** infecund **9** fruitless **10** unavailing **11** purposeless, unrewarding **12** impoverished, unproductive, unprofitable **14** unremunerative

unfulfilled 8 thwarted **10** frustrated, unrealized **11** unsatisfied
    French: **6** manque

unfurl 4 open **6** expand, spread, un-

fold, unroll **7** develop, roll out **8** shake out **9** spread out

ungainly 5 stiff **6** clumsy, klutzy **7** awkward **9** lumbering, maladroit **10** ungraceful **13** uncoordinated

ungallant 4 rude **7** boorish, uncivil, uncouth **8** impolite **9** uncourtly **10** ill-behaved, ungracious, unmannerly **11** ill-mannered, uncourteous **12** discourteous **13** ungentlemanly

ungenerous 4 mean, near **5** close, cruel, petty, small, venal **6** greedy, shabby, sordid, stingy **7** miserly, selfish, sparing **8** churlish, covetous, cowardly, grudging **9** illiberal, mercenary, niggardly, penurious, rapacious **10** avaricious **11** small-minded **12** narrow-minded, parsimonious, uncharitable

ungifted 8 mediocre **9** unskilled **10** amateurish, unskillful, untalented **14** unaccomplished

unglue 6 unseal **7** peel off, unstick **9** pull apart

ungodly 4 base, vile **5** awful **6** rotten, sinful, wicked **7** corrupt, ghastly, godless, heinous, immoral, impious **8** depraved, dreadful, terrible **9** dissolute **10** degenerate, horrendous, iniquitous, outrageous, villainous **11** blasphemous **12** dishonorable, unreasonable

ungovernable 6 unruly **7** defiant, froward, naughty, wayward **8** contrary, mutinous, perverse, stubborn **9** fractious, obstinate **10** disorderly, rebellious, refractory **11** disobedient, intractable **12** noncompliant, recalcitrant, unmanageable, unsubmissive

ungraceful 5 inept **6** clumsy **7** awkward **9** inelegant

ungracious 4 rude **5** bluff, blunt, gruff, harsh, short **6** abrupt, coarse, crusty, vulgar **7** boorish, brusque, loutish, uncivil, uncouth **8** churlish, grudging, impolite **9** uncourtly, ungallant **10** ill-behaved, unladylike, unmannerly **11** bad-mannered, ill-mannered, impertinent, uncourteous **12** disagreeable, discourteous, inhospitable **13** disrespectful, ungentlemanly

unguarded 6 unwary **7** careless, tactless, too frank **9** imprudent, unmindful, unwatched **10** incautious, indiscreet, undefended **11** defenseless, unpatrolled, unprotected **12** undiplomatic, unrestrained **13** ill-considered, uncircumspect

unguent 4 balm **5** cream, salve **6** lotion **8** ointment **9** emollient

ungula 4 hoof, nail

ungulate 2 ox **3** cow, gnu, hog, pig, yak **4** boar, calf, deer, goat, ibex **5** camel, daman, horse, llama, tapir **6** hoofed, vicuna **7** buffalo, caribou, giraffe, peccary **8** antelope, elephant, hooflike, ruminant **9** dromedary **10**

hartebeest, rhinoceros, wildebeest **12** hippopotamus

unhampered 4 free **8** expedite **9** unimpeded **10** unconfined **12** unencumbered, unrestrained, unrestricted

unhandy 5 inept **6** clumsy, gauche, klutzy **7** awkward **8** bumbling, fumbling, inexpert, unwieldy **9** all thumbs, ham-handed, maladroit, unskilled **10** cumbersome, unskillful **11** inefficient **12** inconvenient, unmanageable **14** butterfingered

unhappiness 3 woe **5** grief **6** misery, sorrow **7** anguish, sadness **8** distress **9** heartache

unhappy 3 bad, sad **4** blue, poor **5** inapt, sorry **6** gloomy, somber, unwise **7** adverse, awkward, doleful, foolish, forlorn, hapless, joyless, unlucky **8** dejected, downcast, luckless, unseemly **9** depressed, imprudent, longfaced, sorrowful, woebegone **10** despondent, dispirited, ill-advised, melancholy, unbecoming, unsuitable **11** crestfallen, injudicious, regrettable, unbefitting, unfortunate **12** heavyhearted, infelicitous, unsuccessful **13** inappropriate **14** down in the mouth

unharmed 5 whole **6** unhurt **9** uninjured, unscathed, untouched **10** in one piece, unaffected **14** with a whole skin

unhealthy 3 bad **4** sick, weak **6** ailing, feeble, infirm, morbid, poorly, sickly, unwell **7** harmful, hurtful, invalid, not well, noxious, unsound **8** depraved, diseased, negative, perilous **9** dangerous, degrading, hazardous **10** corrupting, indisposed, morally bad **11** destructive, detrimental, undesirable, unhealthful, unwholesome **12** demoralizing, in poor health, insalubrious **13** contaminating

unheard-of 3 odd **4** rare **6** unique **7** amazing, curious, unknown, unusual **8** freakish, original, singular, uncommon **9** irregular, matchless **10** incredible, outlandish, outrageous, phenomenal, unexpected **11** exceptional **12** incomparable, preposterous, unbelievable, unparalleled, unreasonable **13** extraordinary, inconceivable, unprecedented

unheated 3 icy **4** cold **6** chilly, drafty, frosty **7** ice-cold **8** unwarmed

unheeding 7 ignored **8** mindless **12** disregarding

unhelpful 7 of no use, useless **8** in the way **9** hindering **11** disobliging **13** inconsiderate, uncooperative

unheralded 6 unsung **10** unexpected, unforeseen **11** unacclaimed, unannounced, unlooked-for **12** unproclaimed, unpublicized, unrecognized **13** unanticipated

unhesitating 5 eager, quick, ready **6** direct, prompt **9** immediate **10** unre-

served **11** unflinching **12** wholehearted, without delay **13** instantaneous **18** without reservation

unhinge 6 detach **7** disrupt **8** separate, unsettle **9** disengage, dislocate, disorient, unbalance **10** disconnect **13** disarticulate

unhitch 6 detach **8** separate, uncouple, unfasten **9** disengage **10** disconnect

unhitched 8 detached **9** uncoupled **10** unfastened **12** disconnected

unholy 4 base, evil, vile **5** awful **6** rotten, sinful, wicked **7** corrupt, heinous, immoral, ungodly **8** depraved, dreadful, shocking **9** dishonest **10** horrendous, iniquitous, outrageous, villainous **12** dishonorable, unreasonable

unhurried 4 easy, slow **7** gradual **9** leisurely **10** deliberate, slow-moving

unicorn
form: 5 horse
feature: 4 horn
symbolizes: 6 purity **8** chastity
constellation of: 9 Monoceros

unidentified 5 vague **7** unknown, unnamed **8** nameless **9** anonymous, unlabeled **11** unspecified **12** undesignated, unrecognized

unification 5 union, unity **6** fusion, merger **7** uniting **8** alliance, junction **9** coalition, combining **11** coalescence, combination, confederacy **12** amalgamation **13** confederation, consolidating, consolidation, incorporation

uniform 4 even, garb **5** alike, array, at one, dress, equal, habit **6** attire, in line, in step, livery **7** apparel, costume, regalia, regular, similar, the same **8** agreeing, constant, in accord, of a piece, unvaried, vestment **9** consonant, identical, of one mind, unaltered, unvarying **10** conforming, consistent, harmonious, unchanging **11** regimentals, undeviating

uniformity 8 equality, monotony, sameness **10** consonance **11** consistency, equivalency, homogeneity **15** standardization

unify 3 wed **4** ally, fuse, join **5** blend, merge, unite **6** couple, link up **7** combine **8** coalesce, federate **10** amalgamate **11** confederate, consolidate, form into one, incorporate **12** lump together **13** bring together

unilluminated 3 dim **4** dark **5** murky, unlit **6** gloomy **7** obscure **8** darkened **9** lightless, unlighted

unimaginable 10 incredible **12** unbelievable **13** inconceivable **16** incomprehensible

unimaginative 4 dull **5** stale, stock, trite, usual, vapid **6** dreary **7** cliched, humdrum, prosaic, routine, tedious **8** everyday, mediocre, ordinary **9** hackneyed **10** pedestrian, uncreative, unexciting, uninspired, unoriginal, unromantic **11** commonplace, predictable

12 run-of-the-mill, unremarkable **13** uninteresting

unimpaired 4 good **5** clear, sound **6** intact, unhurt **8** unbroken, unharmed **9** uninjured, unscathed, unspoiled **10** undeformed

unimpassioned 4 calm, cool **6** placid, serene, stolid **7** unmoved **8** detached, unloving **9** apathetic, impassive, objective, unexcited **11** indifferent, unemotional **13** dispassionate

unimpeachable 4 pure **5** clean, solid **7** perfect **8** reliable, spotless, unmarred **9** blameless, faultless, inviolate, stainless, undefiled, untainted **10** immaculate, impeccable, inculpable, infallible **11** trustworthy, unblemished **12** unassailable **13** above reproach, totally honest **14** beyond question, irreproachable, unquestionable **15** beyond criticism, unchallengeable

unimportant 5 minor **6** lesser, meager, paltry, slight **7** trivial **8** inferior, mediocre, not vital, nugatory, piddling, trifling **10** immaterial, irrelevant, low-ranking, negligible, of no moment, second-rate **11** subordinate **12** nonessential, not important **13** insignificant **14** inconsiderable **15** inconsequential, of no consequence

uninformed 6 unread **7** unaware **8** ignorant **9** in the dark, not with it, unadvised, unknowing, unlearned **10** uneducated, unschooled **12** unconversant, uninstructed **13** unenlightened

uninhabited 5 empty **6** vacant **8** deserted, forsaken **9** abandoned, unlived in, unpeopled, unsettled **10** unoccupied, untenanted **11** unpopulated

uninhibited 4 fast, free, open, rash **5** frank **6** candid, daring, madcap, not shy, unwary **8** careless, heedless, immodest, reckless, uncurbed, unreined **9** abandoned, impetuous, impulsive, outspoken, unbridled, unchecked, unguarded, unimpeded, unstopped **10** capricious, flamboyant, forthright, headstrong, incautious, indiscreet, unhampered, unhindered, unreserved **11** instinctive, plainspoken, spontaneous **12** free-spirited, uncontrolled, unobstructed, unrestrained, unrestricted **13** unconstrained **15** straightforward, unself-conscious

uninjured 5 whole **6** intact, unhurt **8** unharmed **9** unscathed, untouched **10** in one piece **14** with a whole skin

uninspired 4 dull **5** stale, stock, trite, vapid **7** cliched, humdrum, prosaic, unmoved **8** ordinary **9** hackneyed, unexcited, unstirred, untouched **10** pedestrian, unaffected, unexciting, unoriginal **11** commonplace, indifferent, predictable, unemotional, unimpressed **12** run-of-the-mill, uninfluenced, unstimulated **13** unimaginative, uninteresting

uninspiring 4 dull **5** bland, stale **6** boring **7** insipid, prosaic **10** lackluster **13** uninteresting

uninstructive 6 barren **9** unhelpful **10** unedifying **12** unproductive **13** uninformative

unintelligent 4 dull, dumb, slow **5** blank, dense, dopey, thick **6** obtuse, stupid **7** asinine, doltish, idiotic, moronic **8** retarded **9** cretinous, dim-witted, imbecilic **10** dull-witted, half-witted, slow-witted **11** blockheaded, thickheaded **12** simpleminded

unintelligible 4 baffling, puzzling **9** confusing, illegible, insoluble **10** incoherent, perplexing **11** meaningless **12** impenetrable, inarticulate, unfathomable **14** undecipherable **16** incomprehensible

unintentional 9 unplanned, unwitting **10** accidental, fortuitous, undesigned, unintended, unthinking **11** inadvertent, involuntary, unconscious **14** unpremeditated

uninterested 5 aloof, blase **6** remote **8** heedless, listless, uncaring **9** apathetic, incurious, unmindful **10** above it all, uninvolved **11** indifferent, unconcerned **13** unimpressible

uninteresting 3 dry **4** drab, dull **5** trite, vapid **6** boring, dreary, jejune **7** humdrum, insipid, prosaic, tedious **8** lifeless, ordinary, tiresome, unmoving **9** colorless, wearisome **10** monotonous, pedestrian, uneventful **11** uninspiring **12** unsatisfying **13** insignificant

uninterrupted 8 unbroken **9** ceaseless, continual, incessant **10** continuous **11** unremitting

uninviting 8 annoying **9** offensive **10** unalluring, unpleasant, untempting **11** displeasing, distasteful, unappealing, undesirable, unwelcoming **12** disagreeable, unappetizing, unattractive

uninvolved 4 easy **5** clear **6** simple **7** neutral, obvious, outside **8** detached **9** impartial **10** unaffected **13** disinterested, dispassionate, uncomplicated

union 5 blend, guild, unity **6** fusion, league, merger **7** amalgam, joining, mixture, oneness, uniting, wedding **8** alliance, marriage, unifying **9** synthesis **10** federation, fraternity **11** affiliation, association, combination, corporation, partnership, unification **12** amalgamation **13** confederation, consolidation
　　type: 5 craft, labor, trade

Union of Soviet Socialist Republics
　　abbr: 4 CCCP, USSR
　　see **Russia**

unique 8 by itself, peerless, singular **9** matchless, nonpareil, unequaled, unmatched, unrivaled **10** inimitable, one of a kind, surpassing, unexampled,

unexcelled 11 distinctive, unsurpassed **12** incomparable, unapproached, unparalleled

unit 4 part **5** group, whole **6** entity, member **7** element, measure, package, section, segment **8** category, division, quantity **9** component **10** detachment **11** constituent, measurement **12** denomination

Unitas, Johnny
　　nickname: 7 Johnny U
　　sport: 8 football
　　position: 11 quarterback
　　team: 14 Baltimore Colts

unite 4 ally, fuse, join, pool **5** blend, merge, unify **6** couple **7** combine **8** coalesce, federate, lock arms, organize **10** amalgamate, homogenize, join forces **11** confederate, consolidate, incorporate **12** join together, lump together **13** stand together

united 3 one **5** fused **6** allied, joined, merged, pooled **7** blended, coupled, leagued, unified **8** combined **9** federated, of one mind, unanimous **10** collective **11** amalgamated, in agreement **12** consolidated, incorporated **14** joined together, lumped together

United Arab Emirates
　　other name: 11 Pirate Coast, Trucial Oman **13** Trucial States
　　capital/largest city: 8 Abu Dhabi
　　others: 5 Ajman, Dubai, Kalba, Tarif **6** Sharja **7** Fujaira **11** Ras al Khaima **12** Umm al Qaiwain
　　division: 5 Ajman, Dibai, Dubai **6** Sharja **7** Fujaira, Sharjah **8** Abu Dhabi, Fujairah **11** Ras al Khaima, Umm al Qaiwan **12** Ral al Khaimah, Umm al-Qaiwain
　　monetary unit: 3 fil **6** dirham
　　highest point: 5 Hafit
　　physical feature:
　　　　desert: 10 Rub al Khali
　　　　gulf: 4 Oman **7** Persian
　　　　oasis: 7 Buraimi **9** Al Buraymi
　　　　peninsula: 7 Arabian
　　people: 4 Arab **6** Indian **7** African, Iranian **9** Pakistani **10** South Asian
　　　　leader: 22 Zaid Bin Sultan al-Nahayan **23** Maktum bin Rashid al-Maktum **25** Khalifa bin Zayid Al Nuhayyan
　　language: 5 Farsi **6** Arabic **7** English, Persian
　　religion: 5 Islam
　　war: 4 Gulf **11** Desert Storm

United Arab Republic 3 UAR
　　onetime union of: 5 Egypt, Syria

United Kingdom
　　union of: 12 Great Britain **15** Northern Ireland

United States
　　capital: 12 Washington DC
　　largest city: 11 New York City
　　others: 4 Nome **5** Miami **6** Boston, Dallas, El Paso **7** Chicago, Detroit,

Houston, Memphis, Phoenix, San Jose, Seattle **8** Columbus, Honolulu, San Diego **9** Anchorage, Baltimore, Cleveland, Milwaukee **10** Los Angeles, New Orleans, San Antonio **12** Indianapolis, Jacksonville, Philadelphia, Salt Lake City, San Francisco
　　school: 3 MIT **4** Penn, Yale **5** Brown **6** Baylor, Drexel, Vassar **7** Amherst, Colgate, Cornell, Fordham, Harvard, Oberlin **8** Bryn Mawr, Columbia, Stanford, Wesleyan **9** Dartmouth, Princeton, Radcliffe **10** Bennington **12** Johns Hopkins, Mount Holyoke
　　division: 4 Iowa, Ohio, Utah **5** Idaho, Maine, Texas **6** Alaska, Hawaii, Kansas, Nevada, Oregon **7** Alabama, Arizona, Florida, Georgia, Indiana, Montana, New York, Vermont, Wyoming **8** Arkansas, Colorado, Delaware, Illinois, Kentucky, Maryland, Michigan, Missouri, Nebraska, Oklahoma, Virginia **9** Louisiana, Minnesota, New Jersey, New Mexico, Tennessee, Wisconsin **10** California, Puerto Rico, Washington **11** Connecticut, Mississippi, North Dakota, Rhode Island, South Dakota **12** New Hampshire, Pennsylvania, West Virginia **13** Massachusetts, North Carolina, South Carolina **18** District of Columbia
　　island: 4 Guam, Long, Maui, Oahu **5** Block, Ellis, Kauai, Lanai, Umnak **6** Hawaii, Kodiak, Niihau, Unimak, Virgin **7** Baranof, Key West, Long Key, Molokai, Nunivak, Sanibel **8** Aleutian, Hawaiian, Key Largo, Shumagin, Unalaska **9** Atka Amlia, Canal Zone, Chichagof, Kahoolawe, Nantucket, Snipe Keys **10** Islamorada, Oyster Keys, Puerto Rico, St. Lawrence **11** Longboat Key **12** Santa Barbara **13** American Samoa, Marquesas Keys, Prince of Wales, Santa Catalina, Summerland Key **15** Martha's Vineyard **16** Cantout Enderbury **26** Trust Territory of the Pacific
　　lake: 4 Erie, Mead **5** Huron, Tahoe **6** Cayuga, Finger, George, Itasca, Oneida, Seneca **7** Iliamma, Ontario **8** Michigan, Superior **9** Champlain, Great Salt, Salton Sea, Teshekpuk, Winnebago **10** Okeechobee **11** Yellowstone **13** Pontchartrain, Wallenpaupack, Winnipesaukee **14** Lake of the Woods
　　mountain: 4 Hood **5** Coast, Green, Kenai, Ozark, Rocky, White **6** Alaska, Brooks, DeLong, Elbert, Helena, Mesabi, Pocono, Shasta **7** Cascade, Chugach, Foraker, Harvard, Kilauea, Massive, Olympic, Olympus, Rainier, St Elias, Whitney **8** Catskill, Davidson, Endicott, Katahdin, Mauna Loa, Mitchell, Ouachita, St Helens, Wrangell **9** Allegheny, Blue Ridge, Kuskokwim, North Peak, Pikes Peak **10** Black Hills, Blanca Peak, Grand

Teton, Washington, Williamson **11** Appalachian, Santa Monica **12** Sierra Nevada **14** Berkshire Hills
highest point: 6 Denali **8** McKinley
river: 3 New, Red **4** Gila, Iowa, Milk, Ohio, Rock **5** Black, Cedar, Coosa, Flint, Grand, Green, James, Neuse, Osage, Pearl, Pecos, Snake, White, Yukon **6** Brazos, Hudson, Neches, Neosho, Nueces, Owybee, Pee Dee, Platte, Powder, Sabine, Salmon, Wabash **7** Alabama, Big Horn, John Day, Klamath, Potomac, Roanoke, San Juan, St Johns, Trinity **8** Arkansas, Big Black, Canadian, Cheyenne, Cimarron, Colorado, Columbia, Delaware, Humboldt, Illinois, Kentucky, Kootenay, Missouri, Niabrana, Ouachita, Savannah **9** Allegheny, Deschutes, Des Moines, Minnesota, Rio Grande, Smoky Hill, St Francis, Tennessee, Tombigbee, Wisconsin **10** Cumberland, Republican, Sacramento, San Joaquin, St Lawrence, Tallapoosa **11** Connecticut, Mississippi, North Platte, South Platte, Susquehanna, Yellowstone **12** Tallahatchie **14** Little Colorado, Little Missouri
sea: 6 Arctic, Bering **7** Pacific **8** Atlantic, Beaufort
physical feature:
   bay: 5 Tampa **7** Bristol, Prudhoe **8** Biscayne, Monterey **9** Apalachee **10** Chesapeake **11** San Francisco
   desert: 4 Gila **6** Mojave **7** Painted **8** Colorado, Vizcaino **9** Black Rock **11** Death Valley
   falls: 7 Niagara
   gulf: 6 Alaska, Mexico **10** California
   plain: 5 Great
   plateau: 8 Colorado, Piedmont **10** Cumberland **11** Appalachian
   strait: 6 Bering **7** Florida
people:
   architect: 4 Root **5** Davis **6** Upjohn, Wright **7** Burnham, Downing, Furness, Gilbert, Gropius, Latrobe **8** Bogardus, Holabird, Sullivan **9** Bullfinch, Jefferson **10** Richardson **14** Mies van der Rohe
   artist: 5 Henri, Homer, Leutz, Moses, Peale, Wyeth **6** Copley, Durand, Millet, Rothko, Stuart **7** Audubon, Cassatt, O'Keeffe, Pollock, Sargent **8** Whistler
   author: 3 Poe **4** Grey, Inge, King, Loos, Luce, West, Wouk **5** Aiken, Albee, Beach, Benet, Brown, Crane, Eliot, Frost, Guest, Harte, Hecht, James, Lewis, Oates, Odets, O'Hara, Paine, Pound, Steel, Stowe, Twain, Vidal, Welty, Wolfe, Wylie **6** Bellow, Bierce, Bryant, Cabell, Capote, Cather, Clancy, Cooper, Cullen, Ferber, Holmes, Hughes, Irving, Kilmer,

Lanier, London, Lowell, Mather, Millay, Miller, Norris, O'Neill, Porter, Styron, Updike, Wilder **7** Angelou, Baldwin, Clemens, Costain, Dreiser, Emerson, Gallico, Hammett, Hellman, Howells, Jeffers, Kerouac, Lardner, Malamud, Nabokov, Roberts, Roethke, Stevens, Thoreau, Webster, Wharton, Whitman **8** Anderson, Bradbury, Caldwell, Cornwall, Cummings, Faulkner, Macleish, McCarthy, Melville, Michener, Mitchell, Morrison, Rawlings, Robinson, Sandburg, Schwartz, Sherwood, Sinclair, Teasdale, Whittier, Williams **9** Burroughs, Dickinson, Dos Passos, Evanovich, Hawthorne, Hemingway, McCullers, Steinbeck **10** Fitzgerald, Longfellow, McCullough, Tarkington
   composer: 4 Ives, Kern **5** Cohan, Loewe, Sousa **6** Berlin, Foster, Joplin, Lerner, Porter **7** Copland, Gilbert, Rodgers **8** Gershwin, Sullivan **9** Bernstein **11** Hammerstein
   explorer: 4 Byrd, Pike **5** Boone, Cabot, Clark, Lewis, Perry **6** Hudson, Joliet **7** Jolliet **8** Columbus **9** Marquette **10** Eric the Red
   leader: 3 Jay **4** Clay, King, Penn **5** Bryan, Davis, Henry, Paine **6** Revere, Sumner **7** Stevens, Webster **8** Franklin, Humphrey **9** Goldwater
   military leader: 3 Lee **4** Pike **5** Clark, Gates, Grant, Meade, Tyler **6** Austin, Custer, Marion, Patton **7** Bradley, Houston, Jackson, Sherman **8** Marshall, Pershing **9** MacArthur, Roosevelt, Stillwell **10** Eisenhower, Vandenburg, Washington **11** Schwarzkopf
   president: 4 Bush, Ford, Polk, Taft **5** Adams, Grant, Hayes, Nixon, Tyler **6** Arthur, Carter, Hoover, Monroe, Pierce, Reagan, Taylor, Truman, Wilson **7** Clinton, Harding, Jackson, Johnson, Kennedy, Lincoln, Madison **8** Buchanan, Coolidge, Fillmore, Garfield, Hamilton, Harrison, McKinley, Van Buren **9** Cleveland, Jefferson, Roosevelt **10** Eisenhower, Washington
   sculptor: 4 Rush **6** Calder, French, Rogers **7** Borglum **9** Greenough, Remington **12** Saint-Gaudens
   language: 7 English, Spanish
   religion: 5 Amish **6** Mormon **7** Baptist, Judaism, Shakers **8** Lutheran **9** Methodist **10** Protestant **11** Pentacostal **12** Episcopalian, Presbyterian **13** Roman Catholic **14** Church of Christ, Congregational **15** Eastern Orthodox, Latter Day Saints **19** Seventh Day Adventist
   place:
   national park: 4 Zion **5** Platt **6**

Acadia, Denali, Katmai **7** Big Bend, Glacier, Olympic, Redwood, Saguaro, Sequoia **8** Biscayne, Congaree, Wind Cave, Yosemite **9** Haleakala, Lake Clark, Mesa Verde, Multnomah **10** Crater Lake, Everglades, Glacier Bay, Grand Teton, Great Basin, Hot Springs, Isle Royale, Joshua Tree, Shenandoah **11** Bryce Canyon, Canyonlands, Death Valley, Dry Tortugas, Grand Canyon, Kenai Fjords, Kobuk Valley, Mammoth Cave, Yellowstone **12** Mount Rainier **13** Virgin Islands **14** Great Sand Dunes, Lassen Volcanic, Rocky Mountains **15** Carlsbad Caverns, Petrified Forest **16** Gates of the Arctic **19** Great Smoky Mountains **24** Black Canyon of the Gunnison
   possession: 4 Guam **10** Puerto Rico **13** American Samoa, Virgin Islands **14** Mariana Islands **15** Caroline Islands, Marshall Islands
   feature:
   colony: 7 Roanoke **8** Plymouth **9** Jamestown **11** Rhode Island **12** New Amsterdam, New Hampshire **14** New Netherlands **16** Massachusetts Bay
   festival: 9 Mardi Gras
   national symbol: 9 bald eagle
   tree: 7 redwood, sequoia
unity 5 peace, union **6** accord, entity, fusion, league, merger **7** concord, harmony, joining, oneness, rapport **8** alliance, goodwill **9** synthesis, unanimity, wholeness **10** federation, fellowship, friendship **11** affiliation, association, cooperation, partnership, unification **12** amalgamation, amicableness **13** compatibility, confederation, consolidation, understanding **14** likemindedness
universal 7 general **9** worldwide **10** ubiquitous, widespread **11** omnipresent **12** affecting all, all-embracing, all-inclusive **13** international
Universal creator
   Egyptian: 4 Ptah
universality 8 currency **10** prevalence **12** predominance **17** comprehensiveness
universe
   god of: 6 Amen Ra, Amon Ra
university 6 campus, school **7** academy, college **11** institution
   English: 6 Oxford **9** Cambridge
   Cambridge: 7 Harvard
   former: 9 alma mater
   French: 8 Sorbonne
   Hanover: 9 Dartmouth
   lecturer: 9 prelector
   New Haven: 4 Yale
   New Jersey: 9 Princeton
   New York: 8 Columbia
   Providence: 5 Brown

session: 4 term 7 seminar 8 semester

Wit: 4 Lyly, Nash 5 Peele 6 Greene

unjust 6 biased, unfair, warped 7 partial 8 one-sided, partisan, wrongful 9 unmerited 10 prejudiced, unbalanced, undeserved 11 inequitable, unjustified, unwarranted

unjustifiable 11 inexcusable 12 indefensible

unjustly 7 falsely, wrongly 8 unfairly 10 wrongfully 11 dishonestly, faithlessly, inequitably 12 undeservedly

unkempt 5 messy 6 sloppy, untidy 7 rumpled, tousled 8 mussed-up, slovenly, uncombed 9 ungroomed 10 disheveled, disordered 11 disarranged

unkind 4 mean 5 nasty 7 abusive 8 uncaring 9 malicious, unfeeling 10 unfriendly, ungenerous, ungracious 11 insensitive, thoughtless 12 inhospitable, uncharitable 13 inconsiderate, unsympathetic

unknot 5 untie 7 unsnarl 8 untangle 11 disentangle

unknowable 12 inaccessible 13 inconceivable

unknown 7 obscure, unnamed 8 nameless 9 anonymous, unheard-of 10 unrenowned 12 uncelebrated, undesignated, undetermined, undiscovered, unidentified

unknown authors

  abbr.: 4 anon

  author of: 4 Edda (elder) 7 Beowulf 8 Everyman, King Horn, Stasimon 10 Cinderella 11 Poema del Cid 12 Panchatantra, Vercelli Book, Volsunga Saga 14 Gesta Romanorum, Sibylline Books 15 Chanson de Roland, The Forty Thieves, The Song of Roland 16 Grettir the Strong 17 The Nibelungenlied 20 Aucassin and Nicolette, Robin Hood's Adventures 23 The Dream of the Red Chamber, The Thousand and One Nights 26 Sir Gawain and the Green Knight 29 Collection of Ten Thousand Leaves 29 The Arabian Nights' Entertainment

unladylike 4 rude 6 coarse, common, vulgar 7 ill-bred, uncouth 8 impolite 10 unmannerly 12 discourteous

unlawful 7 illegal, illegit, illicit, lawless 8 criminal 9 forbidden 10 prohibited, unlicensed, unofficial 12 unauthorized 13 against the law 16 unconstitutional

unlawful act 5 crime 6 felony 10 wrongdoing 11 lawbreaking, malfeasance, misdemeanor

unleash 4 free 5 let go 7 release, set free 8 let loose, liberate 12 give free rein

unlettered 8 ignorant, untaught 9 unlearned, untutored 10 illiterate, uneducated, unschooled 11 unscholarly

unlighted 3 dim 4 dark 5 murky, unlit

6 gloomy 7 stygian, sunless 8 moonless 9 lightless 13 unilluminated

unlikable, unlikeable 7 hateful 9 offensive, unlovable 10 hard to like, unloveable, unpleasant 11 displeasing, unappealing 12 disagreeable

unlike 7 diverse, unalike, unequal 9 different, disparate 10 dissimilar

unlikelihood 12 doubtfulness, unlikeliness 13 improbability

unlikely 8 hopeless 10 improbable 11 unpromising 12 questionable, unbelievable, unpropitious 19 scarcely conceivable

unlikeness 8 contrast, variance 9 disparity, variation 10 difference, divergence 13 dissimilarity, dissimilitude

unlimited 4 huge, vast 5 total 7 endless, immense 8 absolute, complete, infinite 9 boundless, limitless, unbounded, unchecked 11 unqualified 12 immeasurable, totalitarian, uncontrolled, unrestrained, unrestricted 13 comprehensive, inexhaustible, unconstrained 15 all-encompassing

unload 4 dump 7 off-load 8 get rid of, unburden 9 dispose of 10 unencumber

unlooked for 6 sudden 7 unasked 8 surprise 10 unexpected, unforeseen, unheralded 11 unannounced, uncalled for, unpredicted, unsolicited 13 serendipitous, unanticipated

unlovable, unloveable 7 hateful 9 unlikable 10 hard to like, unlikeable, unpleasant 11 displeasing, unappealing 12 disagreeable

unloving 4 cold, cool 6 frigid 11 indifferent, passionless 13 unimpassioned

unlucky 6 cursed, jinxed 7 hapless, unhappy 8 ill-fated, luckless, untoward 9 ill-omened 10 ill-starred 11 star-crossed, unfortunate 12 inauspicious, misfortunate

unman 7 unnerve 8 castrate 10 discourage, emasculate

unmanageable 5 balky, bulky 6 mulish, unruly 7 awkward, unhandy, wayward, willful 8 ungainly, unwieldy 9 fractious, pigheaded 10 cumbersome, rebellious, refractory 11 disobedient, intractable, troublesome 12 incorrigible 14 uncontrollable

unmanly 5 timid 6 yellow 8 cowardly, sissyish, womanish 9 sissified, weak-kneed 10 effeminate 11 lily-livered, unmasculine, weakhearted 12 fainthearted 13 pusillanimous 14 chickenhearted

unmannerly 5 crude, gross, surly 6 coarse 7 boorish, ill-bred, loutish, uncivil, uncouth 8 impolite 10 ungracious, unladylike 11 ill-mannered 12 badly behaved, discourteous 13 ungentlemanly

unmarked 5 clean, clear 9 undam-

aged, undefaced, unnoticed 10 unobserved 11 unblemished 15 undistinguished

unmarried 4 free 5 unwed 6 maiden, single 7 old maid, widowed 8 bachelor, divorced, spinster, unwedded, virginal, wifeless 9 available, fancy free 10 spouseless, unattached 11 husbandless 21 footloose and fancy-free

unmarried girl

  French: 10 jeune fille

  German: 8 fraulein

  Spanish: 8 senorita

unmask 4 bare, show 6 betray, expose, reveal, unveil 7 lay open, uncover 8 disclose, discover 12 bring to light

unmasking 6 baring 8 betrayal, exposure 9 discovery, unveiling 10 disclosure, laying open, revelation, uncovering 15 bringing to light

unmatched 6 unlike 7 diverse, supreme, unequal 8 peerless, variable 9 differing, disparate, matchless, unequaled 10 dissimilar 12 second to none, unparalleled 13 beyond compare

unmerciful 4 cold, evil 5 cruel, harsh 6 brutal, severe, unkind 7 brutish, extreme, inhuman 8 inhumane, pitiless, ruthless 9 excessive, heartless, inclement, merciless, unfeeling, unpitying, unsparing 10 malevolent, relentless 11 hardhearted 14 unconscionable

unmindful 3 lax 6 remiss 7 unaware 8 careless, derelict, heedless 9 forgetful, negligent, oblivious, unheeding 11 thoughtless, unconscious

unmistakable 5 clear, plain 6 patent 7 evident, glaring, obvious 8 apparent, distinct, manifest, palpable 9 prominent 10 pronounced, undeniable 11 conspicuous, unequivocal 12 indisputable 14 unquestionable

unmistakably 7 clearly, plainly 8 palpably, patently 9 certainly, decidedly, downright, evidently, glaringly, obviously 10 definitely, distinctly, manifestly, positively, thoroughly, undeniably 11 prominently 12 indisputably 13 conspicuously, unequivocally 14 unquestionably 17 beyond all question

unmitigated 6 arrant 8 absolute, unabated, unbroken 9 downright, out-and-out 10 persistent, unrelieved 11 unqualified 12 unalleviated 13 uninterrupted

unmixed 4 neat, pure 5 sheer 6 simple 8 straight 9 unalloyed, unblended, undiluted, unmingled 13 unadulterated

unmoved 4 calm, cold, firm 5 aloof 6 dogged 7 devoted, staunch 8 resolute, resolved, uncaring, unshaken 9 dedicated, obstinate, steadfast, unfeeling, unpitying, unstirred, untouched 10 determined, inflexible, not shifted, persistent, relentless, unaffected, unswerving, unwavering **11** indifferent, unconcerned, undeviating, undisturbed, unfaltering **12** stonyhearted, uninterested, unresponsive **14** uncompromising

unmoving 4 dead, dull **5** fixed, inert, still **6** boring, serene **8** immobile **9** powerless **10** motionless, stationary **11** emotionless **13** at a standstill

unnamed 8 nameless, unsigned **9** anonymous, incognito **10** innominate, uncredited, unreported, unrevealed **11** undisclosed, unspecified **12** pseudonymous, undesignated, undiscovered, unidentified **14** unacknowledged

unnatural 4 fake **5** phony, put-on **6** forced **7** assumed, stilted, studied, unusual **8** aberrant, abnormal, affected, freakish, mannered, peculiar **9** anomalous, contrived **10** artificial, theatrical **13** self-conscious

unnecessary 5 extra **6** excess **7** surplus **8** needless, overmuch **9** auxiliary, excessive **10** expendable, gratuitous, unrequired **11** dispensable, superfluous, uncalled-for, unessential **13** supplementary

unnerve 5 daunt, scare, upset **7** agitate, unhinge **8** frighten, unsettle **10** intimidate

unnerving 5 scary **8** daunting **9** upsetting **10** enervating, unsettling **11** frightening

unnoticeable 3 dim **5** faint **6** hidden **7** obscure **9** concealed **10** indistinct, unassuming, unemphatic, unobserved **11** unobtrusive **12** undetectable **13** imperceptible, inconspicuous, insignificant, undiscernible **14** unostentatious

unnoticed 6 unfelt, unseen **7** unheard, unnoted **8** unheeded, untasted **10** not smelled, overlooked, unobserved **11** disregarded, unperceived **12** undiscovered

unobservant 4 dull **5** blind **8** unseeing **9** unmindful **11** incognizant

unobstructed 4 fair, free, open **5** clear **8** apparent **9** unimpeded **10** unhampered, unhindered **11** unprevented

unobtainable 9 hard to get **10** impossible, out of reach, out of touch **11** unavailable, unreachable **12** improcurable, inaccessible

unobtrusive 3 shy **6** humble, modest **7** bashful **8** reserved, reticent, retiring **9** diffident **10** unassuming **11** unassertive **13** inconspicuous, unpretentious **14** unostentatious

unoccupied 4 idle **5** empty **6** vacant **8** unfilled **9** abandoned, unengaged **10** untenanted **11** uninhabited

unofficial 8 informal **12** unauthorized

unorganized 5 loose **6** casual, random

7 aimless, chaotic **8** confused **9** haphazard, orderless, unordered **10** disjointed, unarranged, undirected **11** harum-scarum **12** unclassified, unsystematic **13** helter-skelter **14** unsystematized

unornamented 4 bald, bare **5** blank, naked, plain, stark **6** simple **7** austere **9** unadorned **11** undecorated **13** unembellished

unorthodox 7 erratic **9** eccentric, irregular **14** unconventional

unostentatious 3 shy **5** plain, quiet **6** humble, modest, simple **9** unadorned, unaffected **10** unassuming **11** constrained **13** inconspicuous, unpretentious **14** unpresumptuous

unpaid 3 due **4** owed **5** owing **9** in arrears **11** outstanding

unpaid debt 5 debit **7** arrears **9** liability **10** balance due, obligation **12** indebtedness

unpalatable 5 nasty **8** inedible, unsavory **9** repellent, repulsive **10** bad-tasting, unpleasant **11** displeasing, distasteful **12** disagreeable, unappetizing **13** hard to swallow

unparalleled 4 best, rare **5** alone, crack, elect **6** unique **8** gilt-edge, peerless, singular **9** matchless, superfine, unequaled, unmatched, unrivaled **10** crackajack, inimitable, unimitated **11** unsurpassed **12** unapproached **13** unprecedented **15** of the first water

unperceptive 5 blind **9** unfeeling **11** insensitive, unobservant **12** imperceptive, impercipient **13** unsympathetic

unperturbed 4 calm, cool **6** poised **8** composed, tranquil **9** collected, unexcited, unruffled **10** coolheaded, nonchalant, unagitated, undismayed, untroubled **11** levelheaded, undisturbed **13** unimpassioned

unplanned 9 impromptu **10** accidental, fortuitous, improvised, unexpected, unforeseen **11** spontaneous **12** uncalculated **13** unintentional **14** extemporaneous, unpremeditated **15** spur-of-the-moment

unpleasant 5 nasty, pesky **7** irksome, noisome **8** annoying, churlish **9** obnoxious, offensive, repugnant, repulsive, unlikable, vexatious **10** ill-humored, ill-natured **11** displeasing, distasteful **12** disagreeable, unattractive **13** objectionable

unpleasantness 8 ugliness **9** ill nature, nastiness **12** churlishness **13** obnoxiousness, offensiveness, repulsiveness **15** distastefulness **16** disagreeableness, unattractiveness

unpointed 4 dull **5** blunt **6** dulled **11** unsharpened

unpolished 3 raw **5** gawky, inept, rough **6** cloudy, clumsy **7** amateur, awkward, unwaxed **8** inexpert, unbuffed, unglazed, unshined **9** inele-

gant, unrefined, unskilled **10** uncultured, unfinished, unskillful **11** unburnished, unpracticed **12** uncultivated **13** inexperienced **14** unaccomplished **15** unsophisticated

unpopular 7 snubbed **8** disliked, rebuffed, rejected, slighted, unwanted **9** disdained, neglected, unwelcome **10** unaccepted **11** disapproved, undesirable **12** looked down on, unacceptable

unpopulated 5 rural **9** backwoods, unpeopled, unsettled

unprecedented 5 novel **6** unique **9** unheard-of **10** unexampled **11** exceptional **12** unparalleled **13** extraordinary **15** hitherto unknown

unpredictable 6 fitful **7** erratic **8** fanciful, unstable, variable **9** arbitrary, eccentric, impulsive, mercurial, uncertain, whimsical **10** capricious, changeable, inconstant

unprejudiced 4 fair, just **8** unbiased, unswayed **9** impartial, objective, unbigoted **10** even-handed, fair-minded, open-minded, undogmatic **11** broadminded **12** uninfluenced **13** disinterested

unpremeditated 5 ad-lib **9** impetuous, impromptu, impulsive, unplanned **10** accidental, improvised, unintended **11** involuntary, spontaneous **12** uncalculated, unthought-out **13** unintentional **14** extemporaneous **15** spur-of-the-moment

unprepared 5 ad-lib **7** offhand, unready **8** off guard **9** extempore, impromptu **10** flat-footed, improvised **11** spontaneous, unrehearsed **14** extemporaneous **15** spur-of-the-moment

unprepossessing 4 grim **5** seedy **10** ill-favored, ill-looking **12** unattractive

unpressed 5 baggy **6** mussed, sloppy **7** creased, rumpled **8** unironed, wrinkled **9** shapeless, uncreased

unpretentious 5 plain **6** homely, humble, modest, simple **10** unassuming, unimposing **11** unelaborate, unobtrusive **14** unostentatious

unprincipled 6 amoral **12** unscrupulous **14** conscienceless, unconscionable

unproductive 4 poor **6** barren **7** sterile, useless **8** bootless **9** infertile **10** unfruitful, unyielding **11** ineffective, ineffectual, inefficient **12** unprofitable

unprofessional 6 shoddy, sloppy **7** amateur **8** bungling, careless **9** negligent, unethical **10** amateurish **11** incompetent, inefficient, unpracticed **12** unprincipled **13** inexperienced, undisciplined, unworkmanlike **14** unbusinesslike

unprofitable 4 vain **7** useless **8** bootless **11** ineffective, ineffectual

unprogressive 7 diehard **8** backward, standpat, stubborn **9** benighted, right-wing **11** reactionary, reactionist **12** conservative **17** ultraconservative

unprolific **6** barren **7** sterile **9** infertile, unfertile **10** nonbearing **12** unproductive

unpromising **5** bleak **9** ill-omened **10** forbidding **11** unfavorable **12** inauspicious, unpropitious

unpropitious **7** adverse **8** contrary **9** unfitting **10** unsuitable **11** unfavorable **12** antagonistic, inauspicious, infelicitous

unprotected **4** open **5** naked **6** unsafe **7** exposed, unarmed **8** helpless, insecure, perilous **9** dangerous, hazardous, unguarded **10** undefended, vulnerable **11** defenseless

unproven **7** in doubt **8** arguable, doubtful **10** indefinite, in question, up in the air **11** open to doubt, unconfirmed **12** experimental, inconclusive, questionable **13** unestablished **14** open to question

unpunctual **4** late **5** tardy **7** belated **10** behindhand, behindtime

unqualified **5** total, unfit, utter **8** absolute, complete, inexpert, positive, thorough, unsuited **9** downright, out-and-out, unskilled, untrained **10** consummate, undisputed, uneducated, unprepared, unschooled **11** ill-equipped, incompetent **13** inexperienced, unconditional

unquenched **8** unslaked **11** unsatisfied **14** unextinguished

unquestionable **4** sure **5** clear, plain **6** proven **7** certain, evident, obvious, perfect **8** definite, flawless **9** blameless, errorless, faultless **10** impeccable, undeniable **11** beyond doubt, irrefutable, self-evident, unequivocal **12** indisputable, uncensurable **13** uncontestable, unimpeachable **14** irreproachable

unquestionably **6** surely **7** totally **9** certainly, doubtless **10** absolutely, completely, definitely, positively, unarguably **12** conclusively, indisputably, without doubt **13** unequivocally

unravel **4** undo **5** feaze, solve **6** unfold, unfurl, unknit **7** clear up, resolve **8** decipher, separate, untangle **9** pull apart **10** disinvolve **11** disentangle

unreachable **10** impossible, out of touch **11** out of the way, unavailable, unrealistic **12** inaccessible, unobtainable **14** unapproachable

unreal **4** airy **5** dream **6** dreamy **7** ghostly, not real, phantom, shadowy **8** ethereal, illusive, illusory, imagined, spectral **9** dreamlike, fantastic, imaginary, legendary **10** chimerical, fictitious, idealistic, intangible **11** nonexistent **13** insubstantial **16** phantasmagorical

unrealistic **4** wild **5** crazy, silly **6** absurd **7** asinine, foolish **8** crackpot, de-

lusory, fanciful **9** illogical **10** idealistic, improbable, infeasible, starry-eyed **11** impractical **12** unreasonable

unrealized **8** thwarted **10** frustrated, incomplete **11** nonexistent, unfulfilled, unsatisfied **14** unaccomplished

unreasonable **5** undue **6** absurd, biased, mulish, unfair **7** bigoted **8** obdurate, stubborn, too great **9** excessive, fanatical, illogical, obstinate, pigheaded, senseless, unbending **10** bullheaded, exorbitant, far-fetched, headstrong, immoderate, inflexible, inordinate, irrational, prejudiced, unyielding **11** extravagant, intractable, nonsensical, opinionated, uncalled-for, unwarranted **12** closed-minded, preposterous, ungovernable, unmanageable **13** unjustifiable

unreasoning **8** careless, heedless **9** impulsive **10** irrational, unthinking **11** thoughtless **13** unintelligent

unrecognizable **9** disguised, incognito **10** in disguise **11** camouflaged **14** unidentifiable

unrecognized **6** unsung **7** cryptic, unknown **9** incognito, unnoticed

unrefined **3** raw **5** crude, rough **6** coarse, vulgar **7** boorish, low-bred **9** inelegant

unrehearsed **7** offhand **8** informal **9** extempore, impromptu, impulsive, unplanned, unstudied **10** improvised, off-the-cuff, unprepared **11** extemporary, spontaneous **14** extemporaneous, unpremeditated **15** improvisational, spur-of-the-moment **19** off the top of one's head

unrelated **6** not kin, unlike **7** foreign **8** unallied **10** dissimilar, extraneous, irrelevant, non-germane **11** unconnected **12** inapplicable, incompatible, unassociated **13** inappropriate

unrelenting **5** rigid **6** steady **7** adamant, endless **8** constant, unabated, unbroken **9** ceaseless, incessant, tenacious, unbending **10** implacable, inexorable, inflexible, relentless, unrelieved, unswerving, unwavering, unyielding **11** undeviating, unremitting **14** uncompromising

unreliable **4** fake **5** false, phony **6** fickle **8** fallible, mistaken, unstable **9** deceitful, erroneous, uncertain **10** capricious, changeable, inaccurate, inconstant **12** questionable, undependable **13** irresponsible, untrustworthy

unremarkable **5** usual **6** common **7** average **8** everyday, mediocre, ordinary **11** commonplace **12** unimpressive, unsurprising **13** insignificant, unexceptional **15** undistinguished

unremitting **6** dogged **8** constant, tireless, untiring **9** ceaseless, continual, incessant, unceasing **10** continuous, persistent **11** persevering

unrepentant **7** callous **8** hardened,

obdurate, unatoned **9** unashamed **10** uncontrite, unexpiated **11** remorseless **12** incorrigible, unregenerate

unrepressed **4** free, open **7** liberal **8** effusive, outgoing **9** expansive, exuberant **11** extroverted, uninhibited **12** unrestrained

unreserved **4** full, open **5** frank **6** entire **11** unqualified **12** wholehearted

unresolved **4** moot **5** vague **7** pending **8** doubtful, unsolved **9** tentative, uncertain, undecided, unsettled **10** disputable, unanswered **11** contestable, speculative **12** questionable, undetermined **13** problematical, unascertained

unresponsive **4** cold, cool, dull, limp **5** inert **6** frigid **7** passive **8** lifeless **9** apathetic, unfeeling **11** cold-blooded, inattentive, indifferent, unemotional **13** dispassionate, unsympathetic

unresponsiveness **6** apathy **7** inertia **9** lassitude, passivity **11** inattention, passiveness **12** indifference

unrest **5** chaos **6** tumult **7** anarchy, discord, ferment, protest, turmoil **8** disorder, disquiet, upheaval **9** agitation, rebellion **10** discontent, turbulence **12** restlessness **15** dissatisfaction

unrestrained **8** uncurbed **9** abandoned, boundless, excessive, unbridled, unchecked, unlimited **10** immoderate, inordinate, unfettered, ungoverned, unhampered, unhindered, unreserved **11** extravagant, intemperate, uninhibited, unrepressed **12** uncontrolled, unrestricted, unsuppressed **13** irrepressible

unrestraint **6** excess **7** abandon **9** uncontrol **10** unruliness **12** extravagance, immoderation, recklessness **13** excessiveness, impulsiveness

unrestricted **8** absolute, complete **9** out-and-out, unbounded, unlimited **11** unqualified **12** unrestrained **13** unconditional

unrigid **3** lax **4** easy, limp, soft **5** loose **6** giving, limber, mobile, pliant, supple **7** elastic, lenient, plastic, pliable **8** flexible, informal, merciful, tolerant, yielding **9** indulgent, malleable **11** conformable

unrigorous **4** easy **5** loose, slack **6** casual, sloppy **7** inexact **8** careless, slapdash **9** imprecise

unripe **5** green **8** immature **10** unseasoned **11** undeveloped **14** underdeveloped

unrivaled **8** superior, topnotch **9** unequaled **10** undisputed **11** unsurpassed

unroll **6** reveal, uncoil, unfold, unfurl, unwind **7** display, lay open, play out **9** spread out

unruffled **4** calm, cool, even, mild **5** quiet, still **6** placid, serene, smooth **8**

composed, tranquil **9** collected **10** coolheaded, nonchalant, unagitated, untroubled **11** undisturbed, unperturbed **13** self-possessed

unruly 4 wild **5** rowdy **7** restive, wayward, willful **9** contrary, perverse **9** fractious, unbridled **10** boisterous, disorderly, headstrong, refractory **11** disobedient, intractable **12** obstreperous, ungovernable, unmanageable **13** undisciplined **14** uncontrollable

unsafe 5 risky **7** exposed **8** insecure, perilous **9** dangerous, hazardous, unguarded **10** undefended, unreliable, vulnerable **11** defenseless, treacherous, unprotected **13** untrustworthy

unsatisfactory 4 poor **5** inept, unfit **8** below par, inferior, unworthy **9** deficient **10** inadequate, ineligible, unsuitable **12** inadmissible, unacceptable **13** inappropriate

unsavory 3 bad **4** flat, foul **5** nasty **7** insipid, tainted **9** tasteless **10** badtasting, nauseating, unpleasant **11** distasteful, unpalatable **12** disagreeable, unappetizing

unscathed 5 sound, whole **6** entire, intact, unhurt **7** perfect **8** unharmed **9** uninjured, untouched **10** unimpaired **11** unscratched **13** all in one piece

unscholarly 8 ignorant **9** unlearned **10** illiterate, uneducated, uninformed **11** ill-informed **13** unintelligent

unschooled 3 raw **5** green **6** callow **8** ignorant, untaught **9** unlearned **10** illiterate, uneducated, uninformed, unlettered, unseasoned **11** uninitiated **13** inexperienced

unscrupulous 5 sharp **6** amoral **7** crooked, devious, immoral **9** unethical **12** dishonorable, unprincipled

unseasonable 6 too hot **7** too cold, too warm **8** abnormal, untimely

unseasoned 3 raw **5** bland, green, plain **6** callow **7** untried **8** immature **13** inexperienced

unseeing 5 blind **7** unaware **9** oblivious, sightless **11** unobservant

unseemly 4 rude **5** crude, gross **6** coarse, vulgar **7** boorish, loutish **8** churlish, improper, indecent, unworthy **9** incorrect, offensive, tasteless **10** indecorous, indelicate, out of place, unbecoming, unladylike, unsuitable **11** distasteful, ill-mannered, unbefitting, undignified **12** discourteous, disreputable **13** discreditable, inappropriate, reprehensible, ungentlemanly

unselfconscious 7 artless **10** unaffected **13** unpretentious

unselfish 7 liberal **8** generous, handsome, princely, selfless **10** altruistic, benevolent, big-hearted, charitable, open-handed **11** considerate, magnanimous, magnificent **12** humanitarian **13** philanthropic **15** self-sacrificing

unserviceable 7 useless **8** unusable

unsettle 5 upset **6** bother, rattle, ruffle **7** agitate, confuse, disturb, fluster, perturb, trouble, unhinge **8** bewilder, confound, disorder **9** unbalance **10** disconcert **13** throw off guard

unsettled 5 fazed **7** anxious, nervous, ruffled **8** agitated, confused, doubtful **9** disturbed, nonplused, perturbed, undecided **10** disquieted, distracted, nonplussed, up in the air **11** discomfited **12** disconcerted **16** at sixes and sevens

unshackle 4 free **7** release, set free, unchain **8** liberate, unfetter

unshakable 4 fast **6** stable **7** abiding, staunch **8** constant, enduring **9** dauntless, permanent, steadfast, unruffled **10** changeless, inflexible, unsinkable, unwavering **11** levelheaded, unflappable **13** imperturbable

unshaken 4 calm, cool **6** poised, serene, stable **7** staunch, unmoved **8** composed, constant, resolved **9** steadfast, tenacious, undaunted, unexcited, unruffled **10** controlled, determined, inflexible, relentless, unaffected, unswerving, untroubled, unwavering **11** levelheaded, undeviating, undisturbed, unemotional, unfaltering, unflinching, unperturbed **13** self-possessed **14** uncompromising

unshapely 5 baggy **9** amorphous, shapeless

unshaven 5 hairy **7** bearded, bristly, hirsute, stubbly, unkempt **9** whiskered **11** bewhiskered

unsheathe 4 bare **6** expose **7** pull out **8** withdraw

unsightly 4 ugly **6** horrid, odious **7** hideous u **9** obnoxious, offensive, repellent, repulsive, revolting, sickening **11** distasteful **12** unattractive

unsigned 9 anonymous **13** bearing no name

unskilled 5 green, inept **7** untried **9** untrained **10** amateurish, apprentice **11** incompetent, unqualified **13** inexperienced

unskillful 5 inept **6** clumsy, unable **7** awkward **8** inexpert **9** incapable, maladroit, untrained **10** amateurish **11** incompetent, ineffective, unpracticed **13** inexperienced

unsmiling 3 sad **4** glum, grim **5** grave **6** dismal **7** austere, joyless, serious **9** cheerless, grim-faced

unsociable 7 haughty **9** withdrawn **10** antisocial, unfriendly, ungracious **11** introverted **14** unapproachable

unsoiled 4 pure **5** clean, fresh, white **6** chaste **8** innocent, pristine, spotless **9** unstained, unsullied **10** immaculate **11** unblemished, untarnished

unsolicited 4 free **8** unforced, unsought, unwanted **9** undesired, uninvited, unwelcome, voluntary **10** gratuitous, unasked for **11** spontaneous, unnecessary, unrequested, unwished for, volunteered

unsophisticated 4 open **5** green, naive **6** candid **7** artless, natural **8** homespun, innocent, trusting **9** ingenuous, unstudied, unworldly **10** unaffected, unassuming **11** uncontrived **13** undissembling, unpretentious **15** straightforward

unsound 3 mad, off **4** weak **5** risky, shaky, unfit, wrong **6** absurd, ailing, faulty, feeble, flawed, infirm, insane, marred, sickly, unsafe **7** foolish, invalid, rickety, tottery **8** confused, crippled, decrepit, deranged, diseased, drooping, impaired, insecure, not solid, not valid, perilous, specious, spurious, unhinged, unstable, unsteady **9** blemished, dangerous, defective, erroneous, hazardous, illogical, imperfect, incorrect, senseless, uncertain, unfounded, unhealthy, unsettled, untenable **10** disordered, fallacious, groundless, irrational, precarious, unbalanced, unreliable **11** languishing, mentally ill **12** in poor health **13** off one's rocker, unsubstantial

unsoundness 7 frailty **8** delicacy, weakness **9** fragility, frailness, shakiness **11** decrepitude, derangement, instability **12** unsteadiness

unsparing 4 full **6** giving, lavish **7** copious, liberal, profuse **8** abundant, generous **9** bountiful, plenteous, plentiful, unlimited **10** big-hearted, munificent, ungrudging, unstinting **11** extravagant, magnanimous, unqualified **13** unconditional

unspeakable 4 huge, vast **5** awful, great **6** odious **7** fearful, immense **8** enormous, shocking **9** abhorrent, frightful, loathsome, monstrous, repellent, repulsive, revolting, sickening, unheard-of **10** abominable, disgusting, incredible, nauseating, prodigious **11** astonishing, unutterable **12** overwhelming, unimaginable **13** extraordinary, inconceivable, inexpressible, undescribable

unspecified 5 vague **7** general, unnamed **9** undefined, unsettled **10** indefinite **11** unannounced, unindicated, unmentioned **12** undesignated, undetermined, unpublicized, unstipulated

unspoiled 4 open **7** artless, natural, perfect **8** pristine, spotless, trusting, unharmed, unmarred **9** preserved, undamaged, unscarred, unspotted, unstudied, unworldly **10** unaffected, unassuming, unimpaired, unpampered **11** unblemished, uncorrupted **13** unpretentious **15** unself-conscious, unsophisticated

unspoken 5 tacit **6** silent **7** implied **8**

implicit **9** ineffable, not voiced, unuttered **10** understood **11** unexpressed

unspotted 5 clean **8** spotless, unsoiled **9** undefiled, unstained, unsullied **11** unblemished

unstable 4 weak **5** frail, shaky, tippy **6** fickle, fitful, flimsy, wobbly **7** erratic, fragile, rickety **8** changing, insecure, shifting, unsteady, volatile **9** emotional, mercurial, tottering **10** capricious, changeable, fly-by-night, irrational **11** fluctuating, vacillating **12** inconsistent **13** irresponsible, unpredictable, unsubstantial

unstained 5 clean **8** spotless **9** unspotted, unsullied, untainted **11** unblemished, uncorrupted

unsteady 6 fickle, wobbly **7** rickety **8** doubtful, unstable **10** unreliable **12** questionable, undependable **13** untrustworthy

unstinting 11 unqualified **12** enthusiastic, unrestrained, wholehearted

unstooped 5 erect **6** unbent **7** upright **8** straight, vertical

unstudied 4 glib **6** casual **7** artless, natural **8** informal, unforced, unversed **9** guileless, unuttered **10** unaffected **11** spontaneous **12** uncalculated

unsubmissive 6 unruly **7** defiant, froward, naughty, wayward **8** contrary, mutinous, perverse, stubborn **9** fractious, insurgent, obstinate, seditious, undutiful **10** disorderly, rebellious, refractory, unyielding **11** disobedient, intractable **12** noncompliant, recalcitrant, ungovernable, unmanageable **13** insubordinate

unsubstantial 4 airy, weak **5** filmy **6** feeble, flimsy **7** unsound **8** ethereal, fanciful, illusory **9** idealized, imaginary **10** jerrybuilt **11** lightweight **12** undetectable **13** imperceptible **17** indistinguishable

unsubstantiated 8 disputed **10** unverified **15** unauthenticated

unsuccessful 4 poor, vain **6** foiled, futile, hard up **7** baffled, hapless, unlucky, useless **8** abortive, badly off, luckless, strapped, thwarted **9** fruitless, moneyless, penniless **10** illstarred, profitless, unavailing, unfruitful **11** ineffectual, unfortunate **12** unproductive, unprofitable, unprosperous **14** unremunerative

unsuitability 9 unfitness, wrongness **11** impropriety, uselessness **12** unseemliness **13** inconsistency **15** incompatibility, unacceptability **17** inappropriateness

unsuitable 5 inapt, unfit **7** unhappy, useless **8** improper, unseemly **9** unfitting, worthless **10** inadequate, indecorous, out of place, unbecoming, unsuitable **11** incongruous, unbefitting **12** inadmissible, incompatible, incon-

sistent, infelicitous, out of keeping, unacceptable **13** inappropriate

unsuited 5 inapt, wrong **9** unfitting **10** out of place **13** inappropriate

unsullied 5 clean **8** spotless, unsoiled **9** undefiled, uninjured, untainted **10** unpolluted **11** unblackened, unblemished, uncorrupted, untarnished **14** uncontaminated

unsupportable 6 faulty **9** unfounded, untenable **12** indefensible

unsure 3 shy **5** timid **7** bashful **8** hesitant, insecure, reserved **9** unassured, uncertain, undecided **11** in a quandary, unconfident, unconvinced **12** self-doubting **15** self-distrustful

unsurpassed 4 best **7** highest, supreme **8** greatest, peerless, superior **9** matchless, nonpareil, paramount, unequaled, unmatched, unrivaled **10** consummate, unexcelled **11** exceptional **12** incomparable, transcendent, unparalleled

unsuspecting 5 naive **6** unwary **7** unaware **8** gullible, off guard, trusting **9** believing, credulous **12** overtrustful, unsuspicious **13** overcredulous

unsuspicious 5 naive **8** gullible, trustful, trusting **9** credulous **12** unsuspecting **13** unquestioning

unswerving 4 firm **6** steady, strong **7** devoted, staunch **8** faithful, resolute, resolved, unshaken, untiring **9** dedicated, steadfast, undaunted **10** determined, inflexible, unflagging, unwavering, unyielding **11** undeviating, unfaltering, unflinching, unremitting **12** single-minded **14** uncompromising

unsympathetic 7 callous **8** pitiless, uncaring **9** heartless, repellent, repugnant, unfeeling, unlikable **10** hardboiled, unlikeable, unmerciful, unpleasant **11** coldhearted, displeasing, hardhearted, indifferent, uncongenial **12** antipathetic, unattractive **15** uncompassionate

unsystematic 6 sloppy **7** chaotic, jumbled, muddled **8** confused **9** haphazard, unplanned **10** disordered, disorderly **12** disorganized, unmethodical

untainted 4 pure **5** clear **9** unsullied **11** uncorrupted **13** unadulterated

untalented 5 inept **8** mediocre, ungifted **9** unskilled **10** amateurish, unskillful **14** unaccomplished

untamed 4 wild **5** feral **6** savage **9** unsubdued **11** uncivilized **12** uncultivated

untangle 5 solve **7** clear up, unravel, unsnarl, untwist **9** extricate **11** disentangle **13** straighten out

untarnished 6 bright **7** perfect, shining **8** flawless, polished, spotless, unsoiled **9** faultless, undefiled, unstained, unsullied, untainted **10** immaculate, impeccable, undisputed, un-

oxidized **11** unblackened, unblemished **12** unbesmirched **13** unimpeachable

untaught 6 unread **7** natural **8** ignorant **9** untutored **10** illiterate, uneducated, unlettered, unschooled **11** spontaneous **12** unstructured

untenable 4 weak **6** faulty, flawed **7** invalid, unsound **8** baseless, specious, spurious **9** debatable, erroneous, illogical **10** fallacious, groundless, unreliable **11** contestable **12** indefensible, questionable **13** insupportable, unjustifiable, unsustainable **14** unmaintainable

unthinkable 11 unwarranted **12** unimaginable **13** inconceivable, insupportable, unjustifiable **16** incomprehensible, out of the question

unthinking 7 witless **8** careless, heedless, mindless, tactless **9** imprudent, negligent, senseless **11** inadvertent, insensitive, thoughtless **12** undiplomatic **13** inconsiderate, uncircumspect

untidiness 5 chaos, mix-up, upset **6** jumble **7** clutter **8** disarray, disorder, scramble, shambles **9** confusion, messiness **10** sloppiness **12** dishevelment **14** disarrangement **15** disorganization

untidy 5 dowdy, messy **6** frowsy, mussed, sloppy **7** chaotic, rumpled, tousled, unkempt **8** careless, confused, littered, mussed up, slipshod, slovenly **9** cluttered **10** bedraggled, disarrayed, disheveled, disorderly, slatternly, topsy-turvy **12** unmethodical **13** helter-skelter

untie 4 free, undo **5** loose **6** loosen, unbind, unlace **7** unchain, unstrap **8** make free, unfasten **11** disentangle

untilled 6 fallow **8** unplowed **12** uncultivated

until we meet again
    French: 5 adieu **8** au revoir
    German: 14 auf Wiedersehen
    Hawaiian: 5 aloha
    Italian: 4 ciao **5** addio **11** arrivederci
    Japanese: 8 sayonara
    Spanish: 5 adios

untimely 5 inapt **7** unhappy **8** illtimed, mistimed, unseemly **9** imprudent, premature, unfitting **10** illadvised, malapropos, out of place, unbecoming, unexpected, unsuitable **11** inopportune, unbefitting, unfortunate **12** inconvenient, infelicitous **13** inappropriate

untiring 5 fresh **6** steady **7** devoted, earnest, patient, staunch, zealous **8** constant, diligent, resolute, sedulous, tireless **9** assiduous, dedicated, steadfast, tenacious, unceasing, unwearied **10** determined, persistent, relentless, unflagging **11** never tiring, persevering, unfaltering, unremitting **12** wholehearted **13** indefatigable

untold 6 myriad, secret, unsaid 7 endless, private, unknown 8 hushed up, infinite, numerous, unspoken, withheld 9 concealed, countless, limitless, unbounded, uncounted, unrelated 10 numberless, suppressed, unnumbered, unreported, unrevealed 11 innumerable, undisclosed, unexpressed, unpublished 12 immeasurable, incalculable, undetermined

Untouchables, The
character: 7 Rossman 9 Eliot Ness, Lee Hobson 10 Cam Allison, Frank Nitti 11 Enrico Rossi 14 Martin Flaherty 18 William Youngfellow
cast: 10 Jerry Paris 11 Bruce Gordon, Paul Picerni, Robert Stack, Steve London 13 Abel Fernandez, Anthony George, Nick Georgiade
narrator: 14 Walter Winchell

untouched 3 new 4 pure 5 alone 6 intact, virgin 8 pristine, unharmed 9 uninjured 10 unaffected, unmolested

untoward 5 amiss 6 unruly 7 adverse 8 contrary 9 difficult 11 unfavorable 12 inauspicious, unpropitious

untrainable 6 unruly 11 intractable, unteachable 12 ungovernable

untrained 3 raw 5 green 7 untried 9 unskilled 11 unqualified 13 inexperienced

untried 3 raw 5 green 6 callow 8 immature, untested 10 unseasoned 13 inexperienced

untroubled 4 calm 6 placid, serene 7 halcyon, relaxed 8 carefree, careless, peaceful, tranquil 9 easygoing, unworried 10 unbothered 11 free-and-easy, undisturbed, unperturbed 12 happy-go-lucky, lighthearted

untrue 4 fake, sham 5 false 6 made up 7 not true 8 disloyal, spurious, unchaste 9 dishonest, erroneous, faithless, falsified, incorrect, unfounded 10 adulterous, fallacious, fictitious, fraudulent, groundless, inaccurate, inconstant, perfidious, unfaithful, untruthful 11 promiscuous, treacherous 12 meretricious 13 double-dealing

untrustworthy 5 false 6 fickle, shifty, untrue 7 corrupt, crooked, devious 8 disloyal, fallible, slippery, two-faced 9 corrupted, deceitful, dishonest, faithless, insincere, uncertain, unethical 10 capricious, inconstant, perfidious, unfaithful, unreliable, untruthful 11 treacherous 12 dishonorable, disreputable, questionable, undependable, unprincipled, unscrupulous 13 irresponsible 15 unauthenticated

untruth 3 fib, lie 4 hoax, tale, yarn 5 fable, story 6 canard, humbug 8 flimflam 9 deception, falsehood, fish story, invention 11 fabrication 12 equivocation 13 falsification, prevarication 16 cock-and-bull story 17 misrepresentation

untruthful 5 false, lying 8 specious, spurious 9 deceptive, dishonest 10 fraudulent, mendacious

untutored 5 naive 6 native, unread 8 ignorant, untaught 10 illiterate, uneducated, unlettered, unschooled 12 uninstructed 15 unsophisticated

untypical 3 odd 4 rare 5 alien 7 bizarre, deviant, strange, unusual 8 aberrant, abnormal, atypical, uncommon 9 anomalous, irregular, unnatural 10 unfamiliar 16 unrepresentative

unused 3 new 7 strange, untried 8 left over, not given, pristine, unopened 9 remaining, untouched 10 unemployed 12 unaccustomed, unacquainted, unhabituated

unusual 4 rare 5 novel 6 unique 7 curious, offbeat, strange 8 atypical, peculiar, singular, uncommon 9 unequaled, unheard-of, unmatched, untypical 10 noteworthy, one of a kind, phenomenal, remarkable, surprising, unfamiliar 11 exceptional 12 incomparable, unparalleled 13 extraordinary, unprecedented 16 out of the ordinary

unvaried 4 even 5 fixed 6 steady 7 regular, uniform 8 all alike, constant 9 identical, unchanged 10 all the same, invariable, monotonous, unchanging 11 homogeneous, unalterable, undeviating

unvarnished 3 raw 4 bald, bare 5 blunt, crude, frank, naked, plain, stark 6 candid, direct, honest, simple 7 sincere 8 straight 9 unadorned, uncolored 10 unfinished 11 fundamental, undisguised 13 unembellished 15 straightforward 23 straight-from-the-shoulder

unvarying 4 even 6 steady 7 regular, uniform 8 constant 10 unwavering

unveil 4 bare 6 reveal 7 divulge, publish, uncloak, uncover 8 announce, disclose 9 broadcast, make known, unsheathe 12 bring to light

unveiled 5 bared 8 divulged, laid bare, revealed 9 announced, broadcast, disclosed, made known, published, uncovered 14 brought to light

unveiling 4 show 5 array 7 display, exhibit, showing 10 exhibition, exposition 13 demonstration

unverified 7 alleged, rumored 8 disputed 15 unauthenticated, unsubstantiated

unwarranted 7 illegal 8 culpable, unlawful 9 arbitrary, unfounded 10 censurable, groundless, unapproved 11 inexcusable, uncalled-for, unjustified 12 indefensible, unauthorized, unreasonable, unsanctioned

unwary 4 rash 5 hasty 7 unalert 8 careless, headlong, heedless, reckless 9 imprudent, unguarded 10 incau-

tious, indiscreet, unwatchful 11 precipitate 12 disregardful 13 uncircumspect

unwashed 4 foul 5 dirty, grimy, muddy 6 filthy, grubby, smudgy, soiled 7 unclean 8 begrimed

unwasteful 6 frugal 7 thrifty 9 effective, effectual, efficient 10 productive

unwavering 4 firm 6 steady, strong 7 staunch 8 faithful, resolute, unshaken, untiring 9 dedicated, steadfast, tenacious 10 determined, persistent, unflagging, unswerving 11 persevering, undeviating, unfaltering, unflinching, unremitting 12 single-minded 14 uncompromising

unwelcome 7 outcast 8 excluded, rejected, unwanted 9 thankless, uninvited, unpopular 10 uncared for, unpleasant, unrequired 11 displeasing, distasteful, undesirable, unessential, unnecessary, unwished for 12 disagreeable, unacceptable

unwell 3 ill, low 4 sick 5 frail 6 ailing, infirm, laid up, poorly, queasy, sickly 7 run-down 8 delicate, qualmish 10 indisposed 11 off one's feed 15 under the weather

unwholesome 3 bad 4 evil, foul 5 toxic 6 deadly, filthy, sinful, wicked 7 baneful, harmful, hurtful, immoral, noxious, ruinous 8 depraved, venomous 9 corrupted, dangerous, degrading, poisonous, polluting, unhealthy 10 corrupting, pernicious 11 deleterious, detrimental, undesirable, unhealthful 12 demoralizing, dishonorable, insalubrious, unnourishing 13 contaminating

unwieldy 5 bulky, heavy 6 clumsy 7 awkward, weighty 8 not handy 10 burdensome, cumbersome 12 hard to handle, incommodious, inconvenient 13 uncomfortable

unwilled 6 reflex 9 automatic 11 involuntary, unconscious 12 uncontrolled 13 nonvolitional

unwilling 5 loath 6 averse 7 against, opposed 9 demurring, reluctant, resistant 10 dissenting, indisposed, undesirous 11 disinclined 12 not in the mood, recalcitrant 14 unenthusiastic

unwillingness 8 aversion 10 opposition, reluctance, resistance 13 indisposition 14 disinclination

unwise 4 dumb 5 crazy, silly 6 stupid 7 foolish, unsound 8 reckless 9 foolhardy, imprudent, senseless 10 ill-advised 11 improvident, inadvisable, injudicious 12 shortsighted, unreasonable 13 irresponsible, unintelligent

unwitting 7 unaware, unmeant 9 unknowing, unplanned 10 accidental, undesigned, unexpected, unthinking 11 inadvertent, involuntary 12 unconsenting **13** unintentional **14** unpremeditated

unwonted 4 rare **7** unusual **8** atypical, uncommon **10** infrequent, remarkable, unexpected, unfamiliar **11** exceptional **12** unaccustomed **13** extraordinary

unworkmanlike 6 clumsy, sloppy **11** inefficient

unworldly 4 holy, pure **5** godly, green, moral, naive, pious **6** callow, devout, divine, sacred, solemn **7** ethical **8** ethereal, heavenly, innocent, trusting **9** aesthetic, celestial, religious, spiritual, unearthly **10** idealistic, immaterial, provincial **12** intellectual, metaphysical, overtrusting **13** inexperienced, philosophical **14** transcendental **15** unsophisticated

unworried 4 calm **6** serene **7** relaxed **8** carefree, composed, peaceful, tranquil **9** easygoing, unruffled **10** untroubled

unworthy 5 unfit **7** ignoble **8** improper, shameful, unseemly **9** degrading, unethical **10** unbecoming, unsuitable **11** unbefitting **12** dishonorable, disreputable, unacceptable **13** discreditable, inappropriate, objectionable

unwrap 4 open **6** loosen, unbind **7** uncover

unwrinkled 4 even, flat **6** ironed, smooth **7** unlined **8** smoothed **9** uncreased, unrumpled

unwritten 4 oral **5** tacit, vocal **7** assumed, implied **8** implicit, inferred, unstated **9** customary **10** spoken only, understood, unrecorded **11** traditional, unexpressed **12** unformulated, unregistered **13** by word of mouth

unwritten law
Latin: **13** lex non scripta

unyielding 4 firm, hard **5** rigid, stiff, stony, tough **6** wooden **8** resolute, rocklike, stubborn **9** obstinate, steadfast, unbending, unpliable **10** determined, inexorable, inflexible, persistent, unswerving, unwavering **11** undeviating **14** uncompromising

up 4 atop, lift, over, rear **5** about, above, aloft, along, aside, astir, at bat, built, close, equal, erect, raise **6** apiece, ascend, higher, lifted **7** abreast, batting, forward, promote, skyward, through **8** advanced, cheerful, increase, out of bed, overhead, standing, together, windward **9** northward **10** optimistic **11** constructed

up and about 5 afoot, astir **6** active, mobile, roused **7** walking **8** out of bed **10** ambulatory, on one's feet

up-and-down 6 fitful, seesaw, uneven **7** bobbing **8** jouncing, wavering **11** alternating, fluctuating, vacillating

upbraid 5 scold **6** berate, rebuke, revile **7** bawl out, censure, chew out, reprove **8** admonish, chastise, de-

nounce, reproach **9** castigate, dress down, reprimand **10** tongue-lash

upbringing 7 rearing **8** breeding, training **10** background

upcoming 6 coming, nearby **7** looming, nearing, pending **8** imminent **9** impending, momentary **11** approaching, drawing nigh, forthcoming, in the offing, prospective

update 5 amend, emend, renew **6** recast, revamp, revise, rework **7** restore, touch up, upgrade **8** overhaul, renovate **9** refurbish **10** rejuvenate, reorganize, streamline

up for grabs 4 open **9** available

upgrade 5 raise, slope **6** ascent, better **7** advance, dignify, elevate, incline, inflate, promote **8** gradient

upheaval 5 flood, quake **6** blowup, tumult **7** turmoil **8** disorder, upthrust **9** cataclysm, explosion, tidal wave **10** disruption, earthquake, revolution **11** catastrophe, disturbance

uphill 4 hard **5** tough **6** rising, taxing, tiring, upward **7** arduous, onerous **8** toilsome, wearying **9** ascending, difficult, fatiguing, strenuous, wearisome **10** burdensome, enervating, exhausting **12** backbreaking

uphill work 8 struggle, tough job **10** difficulty, rough going **11** arduousness **12** hard sledding **13** laboriousness

uphold 4 bear, prop **5** brace, carry, raise, shore **6** defend, hold up, prop up **7** approve, bolster, confirm, elevate, endorse, protect, shore up, support, sustain **8** advocate, buttress, champion, maintain, preserve, underpin **9** encourage **10** stand up for, underbrace **11** acknowledge, corroborate

upholder 7 devotee **8** adherent, advocate, defender, partisan **9** supporter

up in the clouds 6 elated, joyful, joyous **8** ecstatic, euphoric **9** exuberant, rapturous **11** on cloud nine **15** in seventh heaven

Upis
goddess of: **10** childbirth

Upjohn, Richard
architect of: **13** Trinity Church (NYC)
style: **13** Gothic Revival

upkeep 4 keep **6** living **7** support **8** expenses, overhead **10** management, sustenance **11** maintenance, subsistence **12** conservation, preservation

upland 4 high, rise **5** ridge **6** height **7** plateau **8** eminence, highland **9** elevation, high place, high point **10** prominence

uplift 5 edify, raise **6** better, refine **7** advance, bracing, elevate, improve, inspire, lifting, shoring, support, upgrade **8** civilize, propping **9** cultivate, elevation **10** betterment, bolstering, enrichment, refinement **11** advancement, buttressing, cultivation, edifica-

tion, enhancement, improvement **12** underpinning

uplifting 9 elevating, elevation, improving, inspiring **11** improvement **12** enlightening **13** enlightenment, inspirational

upon 2 at, on **4** atop **5** about **6** toward **7** against, thereon **9** by means of, thereupon **10** after which, thereafter

upper 3 top **4** high **5** major **6** higher, inland **7** eminent, greater, topmost **8** elevated, northern, superior **9** important

upper-case letter 7 capital **9** majuscule **13** capital letter

upper class 5 elite **6** gentry, uptown **7** (high) society **8** highborn, highbred, wellborn **9** beau monde, haut monde, high-class, patrician, top drawer **10** upper crust **11** aristocracy, blue-blooded **12** aristocratic, silk-stocking **14** creme de la creme, to the manor born **15** to the manner born

upper crust 5 elite **6** gentry **7** (high) society **9** beau monde, haut monde, top drawer **10** upper class **11** aristocracy **14** creme de la creme

upper hand 4 edge, sway **5** power **7** command, control, mastery **8** whip hand **9** advantage, authority, supremacy **10** domination **12** predominance

upper house 6 Senate **12** House of Lords

uppermost, upmost 3 top **4** main **5** chief, first, major, prime **7** highest, leading, primary, supreme, topmost **8** crowning, dominant, foremost, greatest, loftiest **9** essential, paramount, principal **10** preeminent **11** predominant **12** transcendent **13** most important

Upper Volta see **11** Burkina Faso

uprightness 5 honor **7** dignity, honesty **8** morality **9** integrity **13** righteousness **15** trustworthiness

uprising 4 riot **6** mutiny, revolt **8** outbreak **9** rebellion **10** insurgence, revolution **12** insurrection

uproar 3 ado **4** stir, to-do **5** furor **6** clamor, tumult **7** turmoil **9** agitation, commotion **11** disturbance, pandemonium **16** state of confusion

uproarious 4 loud, wild **5** noisy **6** raging, stormy **7** furious, intense, riotous **9** clamorous, hilarious, turbulent, very funny **10** boisterous, disorderly, hysterical, tumultuous **11** tempestuous **13** sidesplitting

uproot 6 banish **7** abolish, cast out, destroy, root out, wipe out **8** dislodge, displace, force out **9** eliminate, extirpate **10** annihilate, do away with **11** exterminate

upset 3 ire, irk, mad, vex **4** beat **5** anger, annoy, crush, irked, messy, mix up, pique, quash, smash, upend, vexed, worry **6** bother, cancel, change, defeat, enrage, grieve, invert, jumble, muddle, mussed, rattle, thrash, untidy **7** agitate, angered, annoyed, capsize, chaotic, confuse, conquer, disturb, enraged, fluster, furious, grieved, incense, jumbled, mixed-up, perturb, reverse, tip over, trouble, trounce, unnerve, upended, worried **8** agitated, bothered, capsized, confused, demolish, disorder, distress, incensed, inverted, overcome, overturn, slovenly, troubled, turn over, unnerved, upturned, vanquish **9** discomfit, disturbed, infuriate, overpower, overthrow, overwhelm, perturbed **10** discompose, disconcert, disheveled, disordered, disorderly, disquieted, distressed, hysterical, overturned, tipped over, topple over, topsy-turvy, turned over, upside-down **11** disarranged, disorganize, overwrought, wrong side up **12** disorganized **13** make miserable **14** turn topsy-turvy

upsetting
French: **14** bouleversement

upshot 3 end **6** effect, payoff, result, sequel **7** outcome **8** offshoot **9** aftermath, outgrowth **10** conclusion **11** aftereffect, consequence, culmination, eventuality **16** final development

upside down 7 chaotic **8** reversed **10** disorderly **11** topsy turvey **12** bottomside up **16** at sixes and sevens

upstairs 2 up **11** above stairs, second floor

upstanding 4 good, tall, true **5** erect, moral, on end **6** honest **7** ethical, upright **8** straight, truthful, vertical, virtuous **9** honorable, righteous **11** trustworthy **13** incorruptible, perpendicular

upstart 4 snip, snob, snub **6** nobody **7** bounder, parvenu **8** mushroom **9** conceited, newly-rich **10** adventurer **12** nouveau riche **13** self-assertive

upsurge 4 gain, push, rise **5** spurt **6** pickup, thrust, upturn **7** advance, upswing **8** increase **11** improvement

upswing 4 rise **6** pickup **7** upsurge **11** improvement, upward trend

uptight 5 tense **7** anxious, fearful, nervous, worried, wound up **8** insecure, neurotic, troubled **9** unbending **10** unyielding **12** apprehensive

up-to-date 2 in **3** new **5** today **6** modern, modish, timely, trendy, with-it **7** current, stylish **9** in fashion **12** contemporary **13** up-to-the-minute
French: **9** au courant

upturn 4 gain, push **6** thrust **7** advance, upsurge **8** increase **9** expansion **11** improvement

upward 4 high, more **5** above, aloft **7** skyward **9** ascending, uppermost

upward movement 4 rise **5** climb **6**

ascent, rising, upturn **7** scaling, take-off **8** climbing, mounting **9** ascension

upward trend 4 rise **5** boost **6** pickup **7** advance, upsurge, upswing **8** increase **11** improvement

uraeus
figure of: **3** asp **5** cobra
on: **9** headdress
of: **7** pharoah

Uralic
language branch: **7** Samoyed **10** Finno-Ugric

Urania
member of: **5** Muses
personifies: **9** astronomy

uranium
chemical symbol: **1** U

Uranus
mother: **4** Gaea
wife: **4** Gaea
father of: **6** Giants, Titans **8** Cyclopes **10** Titanesses **13** Hecatonchires
castrated by: **6** Cronos, Cronus Kronos

Uranus
position: **7** seventh
satellite: **5** Ariel **6** Oberon **7** Miranda, Titania, Umbriel
color: **9** blue-green
characteristic: **5** rings

Urartu *see* **7** Armenia

urban 4 city, town **5** civic **8** citified **9** municipal **11** worldly-wise **12** cosmopolitan, metropolitan **13** sophisticated

urban area 3 urb **4** city **9** inner city **10** metropolis **11** megalopolis **16** metropolitan area

urbane 5 civil, suave **6** polite, smooth **7** courtly, elegant, gallant, genteel, politic, refined, tactful **8** debonair, gracious, mannerly, polished, well-bred **9** civilized, courteous **10** chivalrous, cultivated, diplomatic **11** gentlemanly **12** cosmopolitan, well-mannered **13** sophisticated

urchin 3 boy, imp, lad **4** brat, waif **5** gamin, stray, whelp, youth **6** gamine, laddie **8** young pup **9** stripling, young punk, youngster **10** young rogue, young tough **11** guttersnipe

Urd 4 Norn
origin: **12** Scandinavian
form: **8** giantess
personifies: **4** past
developed from: **5** Urdar
companion: **5** Skuld **8** Verdandi

Urey, Harold Clayton
field: **9** chemistry
isolated: **9** deuterium
awarded: **10** Nobel prize

urge 3 yen **4** back, coax, goad, itch, poke, prod, push, spur, sway, wish **5** drive, egg on, fancy, force, press, prick, speed **6** advise, desire, exhort, hasten, hunger, motive, reason, thirst **7** beseech, counsel, craving, dictate,

entreat, implore, impulse, longing, passion, push for, quicken, request, solicit, suggest **8** advocate, appeal to, argue for, champion, convince, persuade, petition, pressure, stimulus, yearning **9** hankering, importune, incentive, plead with, prescribe, prompting, recommend **10** accelerate, inducement, motivation, supplicate **11** prevail upon, provocation

urgency 4 need, urge, want **5** press **6** stress **8** exigency, pressure **9** necessity **10** importance, insistence **11** persistence **14** imperativeness **15** importunateness

urgent 5 grave **6** ardent **7** crucial, earnest, fervent, intense, serious, weighty, zealous **8** critical, pleading, pressing, required, spirited **9** demanding, essential, heartfelt, important, insistent, momentous, necessary **10** beseeching, compelling, compulsory, imperative, obligatory, passionate **12** wholehearted **13** indispensable

urge on 4 push **5** boost **7** cheer on, pull for, root for

urging 7 bidding, counsel, goading **8** egging on **9** prompting **11** exhortation

Uri 6 canton
in: **11** Switzerland
home of: **11** William Tell

Uriah
father: **7** Shemiah
wife: **9** Bathsheba
served: **5** David

urinary system
component: **6** kidney, ureter **7** bladder, urethra
rids body of: **5** salts, waste, water **8** minerals

Uris, Leon
author of: **5** Topaz **6** Exodus, The Haj **7** Trinity **9** Battle Cry, Mitla Pass **10** Armageddon, Redemption

urn 3 jar, pig **4** ewer, kist, tomb, vase **5** grave, steen **6** teapot **7** samovar **9** coffeepot
botanical: **7** capsule **11** spore-bearer
in keno: **5** goose

Ursa Major 9 Great Bear
contains: **9** Big Dipper

Ursa Minor 10 Little Bear
contains: **7** Polaris **12** Little Dipper

Uruguay
other name: **10** Purple Land
capital/largest city: **10** Montevideo
others: **4** Fray, Melo **5** Minas, Rocha, Salto **6** Bentos, Rivera **7** Artigas, Colonia, Dolores, Durazno, Florida, San Jose **8** Mercedes, Paysandu, Trinidad **9** Maldonado **10** Las Piedras, Santa Lucia, Tacuarembo **12** Treinta y Tres **13** San Jose de Mayo
measure: **4** vara **6** cuadra, suerte
monetary unit: **4** peso **9** centesimo, centisimo
weight: **7** quintal

island: 5 Lobos
lake: 5 Merin, Mirim **18** Embalse del Rio Negro
mountain: 6 Animas **10** Grand Hills **14** Cuchilla Grande
highest point: 15 Mirador Nacional
river: 4 Malo **5** Mirim, Negro, Plata **6** Parana, Ulimar **7** Cuareim, Queguay, Uruguay **8** Yaguaron **9** Cebollati **10** Tacaurembo
sea: 8 Atlantic
physical feature:
   estuary: 5 Plata
people: 4 Yaro **5** Swiss **6** Indian **7** Italian, mestizo, Russian, Spanish **8** Charruas
   artist: 6 Figari
   author: 4 Rodo **5** Reyes **6** Onetti **7** Sanchez **9** San Martin **10** Ibarbourou
   leader: 5 Oribe **6** Rivera **7** Artigas, Vazquez **9** Lavelleja **10** Bordaberry **14** Batlle y Ordonez
language: 7 Italian, Spanish
religion: 13 Roman Catholic
place:
   resort: 12 Punta del Este
   square: 13 Independencia
feature:
   animal: 4 puma **6** jaguar **8** capybara **9** armadillo
   bird: 4 rhea **5** nandu **7** hornero, ostrich
   cattle ranch: 8 estancia
   cowboy: 6 gaucho
   dance: 5 tango **7** milonga
   festival: 8 Carnival **13** Semana Criolla
   lasso: 10 boleadoras
   metal straw: 8 bombilla
   music: 9 candomble
   musical drama: 7 tablado
   ruling class: 10 Patriciado
food:
   barbecue: 5 asado
   dish: 7 puchero **9** churrasco **13** asado con cuero
   drink: 4 mate

U S A
author: 13 John Dos Passos
character: 10 Ben Compton, Mary French **11** Joe Williams **12** Margo Dowling **13** Fainy McCreary (Mac), Janey Williams **14** J Ward Morehouse **15** Charley Anderson, Eleanor Stoddard, Eveline Hutchins **18** Anne Elizabeth Trent **22** Richard Ellsworth Savage
usable 5 handy **6** useful **9** adaptable **10** functional **11** serviceable
usage 3 use **4** care, mode **5** habit **6** custom, manner, method, system **7** control **8** good form, habitude, handling, practice **9** etiquette, operation, tradition, treatment **10** convention, employment, management **12** manipulation
use 3 aid, ply, sap **4** good, help, work

5 apply, avail, drain, exert, spend, treat, usage, value, waste, wield, worth **6** devour, employ, expend, handle, profit **7** benefit, consume, deplete, exhaust, exploit, operate, service, utilize **8** deal with, exercise, function, handling, profit by, put to use, resort to, squander **9** act toward, advantage, dissipate, enjoyment, make use of, operation, swallow up, throw away **10** employment, manipulate, run through, usefulness **11** application, convenience, fritter away, utilization **12** behave toward, capitalize on **13** make the most of **14** serviceability
used 3 old **5** eaten, spent **7** applied, treated **8** actuated, consumed, depleted, employed, occupied, operated, utilized **9** customary, exercised, exhausted, exploited, practiced **10** accustomed, habituated, secondhand **11** implemented, manipulated
used up 4 beat, shot **5** all in, spent **6** wasted **7** worn out **8** depleted, tired out **9** exhausted
useful 5 handy, utile **7** helpful **8** valuable **9** effective, practical, rewarding **10** beneficial, convenient, functional, profitable, time-saving, worthwhile **11** serviceable, utilitarian **12** advantageous
usefulness 5 avail, value, worth **6** profit **7** benefit, purpose, utility **9** advantage **11** convenience, helpfulness, suitability **12** adaptability, practicality **13** effectiveness **14** serviceability
useless 4 vain **6** futile **7** of no use **8** bootless, unusable **9** fruitless, unhelpful, worthless **10** inadequate, profitless, unavailing **11** incompetent, ineffectual, inefficient **12** unproductive **13** impracticable, inefficacious, nonfunctional, unserviceable
uselessness 6 vanity **8** futility, idleness **9** inutility **10** inefficacy **13** fruitlessness, worthlessness
Uses of Enchantment, The
   author: 15 Bruno Bettelheim
use sparingly 4 save **5** hoard, stint **6** scrimp **7** cut back, dole out **8** conserve, not waste, preserve
use to advantage 7 exploit **8** profit by **12** capitalize on **13** turn to account
use up 5 drain, spend **6** expend, finish **7** consume, deplete, exhaust **9** dissipate **10** run through
Ushant
   author: 11 Conrad Aiken
usher 4 lead, show **5** guide, steer **6** attend, convoy, direct, escort, herald, launch, leader, porter, ring in, squire **7** conduct, precede, preface **8** announce, director, proclaim **9** conductor, introduce **10** doorkeeper, gatekeeper, inaugurate
Usnech *see* **6** Usnach

USSR *see* **6** Russia
Ustinov, Peter
   born: 6 London **7** England
   roles: 7 Topkapi **8** Quo Vadis? **9** Billy Budd, Spartacus **11** Lorenzo's Oil **12** We're No Angels **13** Hercule Poirot
usual 5 stock, trite **6** common, normal, wonted **7** popular, regular, routine, typical **8** expected, familiar, habitual, ordinary, orthodox, standard **9** customary, hackneyed **10** accustomed, prescribed, threadbare **11** commonplace, established, oft-repeated, traditional **12** conventional, run-of-the-mill **15** well-established
Usual Suspects, The
   director: 11 Bryan Singer
   cast: 8 Suzy Amis (Edie Finneran) **9** Dan Hedaya (Jeff Rabin) **11** Kevin Pollak (Todd Hockney), Kevin Spacey (Roger "Verbal" Kint) **12** Gabriel Byrne (Dean Keaton) **14** Benicio Del Toro (Fred Fenster), Stephen Baldwin (Michael McManus) **15** Chazz Palminteri (Dave Kujan) **17** Giancarlo Esposito (Jack Baer), Pete Postlethwaite (Kobayashi)
   villain: 10 Keyser Soze
usurer 9 loan shark **11** money lender
usurp 4 grab **5** steal **7** preempt **8** arrogate **10** commandeer **11** appropriate **12** encroach upon, infringe upon
usurpation 6 taking **7** seizure **8** grabbing, stealing **10** arrogation, preemption **13** appropriation
Utah
   abbreviation: 2 UT
   nickname: 6 Mormon **7** Beehive
   capital/largest city: 12 Salt Lake City
   others: 3 Roy **4** Moab, Orem **5** Delta, Heber, Kanab, Logan, Magna, Manti, Nepli, Ogden, Price, Provo **6** Beaver, Eureka, Kearns, Layton, Murray, Tooele, Vernal **7** Bingham **8** American **9** Bountiful **11** Brigham City
   college: 4 Utah **5** Weber **11** Westminster **12** Brigham Young
   feature:
     basketball team: 4 Jazz
     bridge: 7 Rainbow
     dam: 6 Hoover **10** Glen Canyon
     gorge: 7 Flaming
     national historic site: 11 Golden Spike
     national monument: 8 Dinosaur **14** Natural Bridges
     national park: 4 Zion **6** Arches **11** Bryce Canyon, Canyonlands, Capital Reef
     reef: 7 Capital
   tribe: 3 Ute **5** Piute, Uinta(h), Yampa **6** Navajo, Paiute **7** Gosiute **8** Paviotso, Shoshoni
   people: 7 Mormons **10** Maude Adams **11** Karl G Maeser **12** Brigham Young **13** John M Browning **15** Latter-Day Saints **16** George Sutherland **19** Dan-

iel Cowan Jackling
  explorer: 9 Dominguez, Escalante
lake: 4 Mead, Swan, Utah **6** Powell, Sevier **9** Great Salt
land rank: 8 eleventh
mountain: 4 Lena, Lion, Waas **5** Cedar, Henry, Hogup, Peale, Rocky, Trail, Uinta **6** Frisco, Navajo, Swasey, Wahwah **7** Granite, Griffin, Hawkins, Pennell, Terrace, Wasatch **8** Linnaeus **9** Confusion
  highest point: 9 Kings Peak
physical feature:
  basin: 5 Great
  canyon: 4 Echo
  desert: 6 Sevier
  plateau: 7 Wasatch **8** Colorado, Tavaputs
river: 4 Bear **5** Grand, Green, Weber **6** Jordan, Sevier, Virgin **7** San Juan **8** Colorado
state admission: 10 forty-fifth
state bird: 7 seagull
state flower: 8 sego lily
state motto: 8 Industry
state song: 14 Utah We Love Thee
state tree: 10 blue spruce
utensils 4 gear **5** tools **6** outfit, silver, tackle **8** flatware **9** apparatus **10** implements, silverware **11** instruments **13** paraphernalia
utilitarian 5 handy **6** usable, useful **8** sensible, valuable, workable **9** effective, efficient, practical, pragmatic **10** beneficial, convenient, functional, profitable **11** serviceable **12** advantageous
utility 3 aid, gas, use **4** help **5** avail, extra **6** backup **7** benefit, reserve, service **8** function **9** accessory, advantage, alternate, auxiliary, secondary, surrogate, telephone **10** additional,

substitute, usefulness **11** convenience, electricity **12** availability, supplemental **13** public service **14** serviceability
utilization 3 use **10** employment **11** application **12** exploitation
utilize 3 use **6** employ **7** exploit **8** profit by, put to use, resort to **9** make use of **12** capitalize on **13** bring into play, make the most of, turn to account **14** avail oneself of, have recourse to, put into service **15** take advantage of
utmost, uttermost 4 acme, best, main, peak, tops **5** chief, first, major, prime **6** tiptop, zenith **7** capital, highest, leading, maximum, primary, supreme, the most **8** cardinal, foremost, greatest, last word, ultimate **9** paramount, principal, sovereign **10** preeminent **11** predominant
Uto-Aztecan (Nahuatl)
  tribe: 4 Pima **5** Aatam, Aztec, Nahua **6** Mexica, Papago **8** Pima Alto
utopia 4 Eden **6** heaven **7** Erewhon **8** paradise **9** ideal life, Shangri-la **12** perfect bliss, perfect place **13** seventh heaven
utopian 9 visionary **10** idealistic, unfeasible, unworkable **11** unrealistic **12** otherworldly, unattainable, unrealizable **13** impracticable, insubstantial, unfulfillable
Utrillo, Maurice
  born: 5 Paris **6** France
  mother: 14 Suzanne Valadon
  artwork: 16 The Church at Deuil, The Church of Blevy **17** Church at St Hilaire **19** La Petite Communiante **22** Sacre Coeur de Montmartre
ut supra 7 as above
utter 3 say **4** emit, pure, talk, tell, yell

5 sheer, shout, speak, state, total, voice **6** entire, mutter, reveal **7** declare, deliver, divulge, exclaim, express, perfect, whisper **8** absolute, complete, disclose, outright, proclaim, thorough, vocalize **9** downright, enunciate, out-and-out, pronounce, unchecked **10** articulate, unmodified, unrelieved **11** categorical, unequivocal, unmitigated, unqualified
utterance 4 talk, word **6** answer, remark, speech **7** opinion **9** discourse, statement **10** expression **11** declaration, exclamation **12** articulation, proclamation, vocalization **13** pronouncement, verbalization
utterly 4 just **5** fully **6** wholly **7** totally **8** entirely, outright **9** downright, extremely, perfectly **10** absolutely, completely, thoroughly **14** to the nth degree
uttermost 6 utmost **7** extreme, maximum, supreme **9** outermost, sovereign **12** extreme limit
uxorious
  doting on: 8 one's wife
  from Latin: 4 uxor, wife
Uzbekistan
  capital/largest city: 8 Tashkent
  others: 9 Samarkand
  head of state: 9 president
  government: 8 republic
  monetary unit: 5 ruble
  river: 8 Amu Darya, Syr Darya
  sea: 4 Aral
  people: 5 Uzbek
    leader: 7 Karimov **10** Mirziyayev
  language: 5 Uzbek
  religion: 5 Islam **11** Sunni Muslim
Uzi 10 Israeli gun, machine gun

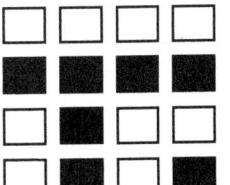
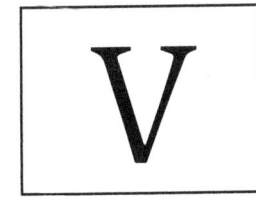

vacancy 3 gap **4** hole, void **5** abode, place **6** breach, cavity, hollow **7** crevice, fissure, housing, lodging, opening **9** emptiness, situation **10** empty space, vacantness **11** room for rent **12** house for rent

vacant 4 dull, free, idle, open **5** aloof, blank, blase, clear, empty, vapid **6** unused, wooden **7** deadpan, for rent, leisure, vacuous **8** deserted, detached, for lease, forsaken, not in use, unfilled **9** abandoned, apathetic, incurious, oblivious, poker-face, unengaged **10** tenantless, unemployed, unoccupied, untenanted **11** indifferent, unconcerned, unfurnished, uninhabited **12** unencumbered **14** expressionless **15** uncomprehending

vacate 4 quit **5** empty, leave **6** give up, resign **8** abdicate, evacuate, hand over **9** surrender **10** depart from, relinquish

vacate the throne 4 cede, flee, quit **5** yield **6** give up, resign, retire **7** abandon **8** abdicate **10** relinquish

vacation 4 rest **5** leave, R and R **6** recess **7** holiday **8** furlough, holidays **10** sabbatical **12** intermission **13** take a vacation **14** leave of absence **17** rest-and-recreation
French: 8 vacances

vaccine 5 serum **8** antitoxin
inventor: 4 Salk **5** Sabin **6** Jenner **7** Pasteur

vacillate 4 reel, rock, roll, sway, toss **5** pitch, shift, waver **6** falter, teeter, totter, wobble **7** flutter, vibrate **8** hesitate **9** fluctuate, hem and haw, oscillate **12** shilly-shally **14** blow hot and cold

vacillating 7 swaying **8** wavering **9** diffident, uncertain, vibrating **10** hesitating, irresolute, on the fence **11** fluctuating, uncertainty **12** irresolution **15** shilly-shallying

vacillation 7 swaying **8** wavering **9** faltering, vibration **10** indecision **11** fluctuation, uncertainty **12** irresolution **15** shilly-shallying

Vacuna
origin: 6 Sabine
goddess of: 11 agriculture

vacuous 4 dull, idle, void **5** blank, empty, inane, silly **6** stupid, vacant **7** fatuous, foolish **8** indolent, unfilled

9 senseless **11** empty-headed, purposeless

Vaduz
capital of: 13 Liechtenstein

vae victis 18 woe to the vanquished

vagabond 4 hobo **5** gypsy, nomad, rover, tramp **6** roamer, roving **7** drifter, floater, migrant, nomadic, rambler, roaming, vagrant **8** bohemian, carefree, homeless, rambling, wanderer, wayfarer **9** footloose, itinerant, transient, traveling, wandering, wayfaring **10** journeying **11** beachcomber

Vagabond Lover
nickname of: 10 Rudy Vallee

vagary 4 kink, whim **5** fancy, humor, quirk **6** notion, oddity, whimsy **7** caprice, fantasy, impulse **8** crotchet, daydream **10** brainstorm, erraticism **11** peculiarity **12** eccentricity, idiosyncrasy, passing fancy

vagrant 3 bum **4** hobo **5** nomad, rover, tramp **6** beggar, loafer, roamer, roving **7** floater, migrant, nomadic, roaming **8** homeless, rambling, vagabond, wanderer **9** itinerant, transient, wandering **10** panhandler, peripatetic **15** knight-of-the-road

vague 4 hazy **5** fuzzy, loose **6** casual, random, unsure **7** general, unclear **8** confused, nebulous **9** imprecise, uncertain, unsettled **10** ill-defined, indefinite, inexplicit, undetailed, unspecific **11** not definite, unspecified **12** undetermined

vaguely 5 dimly **6** hazily **7** loosely **8** dreamily, slightly, vacantly **9** obscurely, sketchily **10** nebulously **11** ambiguously **12** indistinctly

vagueness 8 haziness **9** ambiguity, confusion, fuzziness **11** uncertainty **13** lack of clarity **14** indefiniteness

vain 4 idle **5** cocky, proud, silly **6** futile **7** foolish, pompous, stuck-up, useless **8** arrogant, boastful, bootless, dandyish, egoistic, nugatory, puffed-up, trifling **9** conceited, egotistic, fruitless, pointless, worthless **10** disdainful, profitless, swaggering, unavailing **11** egotistical, ineffective, ineffectual, superficial, time-wasting **12** self-admiring, supercilious, unprofitable, unsuccessful, vainglorious **13** self-important, self-satisfied

Vainamoinen
origin: 7 Finnish
hero of: 8 Kalevala
form: 8 magician
opposes: 5 Louhi **11** Joukahainen

vainglorious 5 cocky **7** haughty, pompous, stuck-up **8** affected, arrogant, boastful, bragging, insolent **9** conceited **10** egoistical, pretentious, swaggering **11** egotistical, swellheaded **12** narcissistic, supercilious **13** full of oneself, self-important

vainglory 6 vanity **7** conceit, swagger **9** cockiness **10** pretension **11** braggadocio **14** self-importance **16** overbearing pride

vale 6 good-by **8** farewell

valedictory 4 last **5** final **7** parting **8** farewell, terminal, ultimate **9** departing **10** conclusive **11** leavetaking **14** farewell speech **19** commencement address

Valentine
character in: 20 Two Gentlemen of Verona
author: 11 Shakespeare

Valentino, Rudolph
real name: 16 Rodolfo (Alfonzo Raffaele Pierre Philibert) Guglielmi
born: 5 Italy **12** Castellaneta
wife: 9 Jean Acker **14** Natasha Rambova
roles: 8 The Sheik **12** Blood and Sand **16** The Son of the Sheik **17** Monsieur Beaucaire **30** The Four Horsemen of the Apocalypse

valerian 9 Valeriana
varieties: 3 red **5** Greek **6** common **7** African **8** American **11** long-spurred

Valery, Paul
author of: 7 Cahiers, Charmes **12** The Young Fate **13** Le Jeune Parque **16** Sketch of a Serpent **20** The Graveyard by the Sea

Valhalla
origin: 8 Teutonic
hall of: 4 Odin **5** Othin

valiant 4 bold **5** brave, noble **6** daring, heroic **7** gallant **8** fearless, intrepid, knightly, resolute, stalwart, unafraid, valorous **9** audacious, dauntless, undaunted **10** chivalrous, courageous **11** lionhearted, unflinching **12** boldspirited, great-hearted, stouthearted

valid 4 good **5** legal, licit, sound

6 lawful, proper, strong 7 fitting, genuine, logical, weighty 8 accurate, decisive, forceful, official, powerful, suitable, truthful 9 authentic, effective, legalized, realistic 10 acceptable, applicable, compelling, convincing, legitimate 11 substantial, well-founded 12 well-grounded 13 authoritative, being in effect 14 constitutional, legally binding

validate 5 enact, prove, stamp 6 ratify, verify 7 certify, confirm, sustain, warrant, witness 8 legalize, sanction 9 authorize, make legal, make valid 10 make lawful 11 corroborate, countersign 12 authenticate, make official, substantiate

validation 8 sanction 12 confirmation, legalization, ratification 13 authorization, certification

validity 5 force, logic, power, right 6 weight 7 grounds, potency 8 accuracy, legality, strength 9 authority, soundness, substance 10 legal force, legitimacy, properness 11 suitability 12 authenticity, truthfulness 13 acceptability, applicability, effectiveness 14 conclusiveness, convincingness

valise 3 bag 4 grip 7 handbag, luggage, satchel 8 suitcase 9 briefcase, Gladstone 11 portmanteau

Valjean, Jean
    character in: 13 Les Miserables
    author: 4 Hugo

Valkyrie
    origin: 8 Teutonic
    home: 8 Valhalla
    attendant of: 4 Odin 5 Othin
    queen: 8 Brunhild, Brynhild 10 Brunnhilde

Vallee, Rudy
    real name: 17 Hubert Prior Vallee
    nickname: 16 The Vagabond Lover
    born: 13 Island Point VT
    played: 9 saxophone
    wife: 9 Jane Greer
    roles: 16 The Vagabond Lover 17 The Palm Beach Story, Unfaithfully Yours 41 How to Succeed in Business Without Really Trying

Valletta
    capital of: 5 Malta

valley 3 cut, dip, gap 4 dale, dell, glen, vale 5 basin, chasm, glade, gorge, gulch, gully 6 bottom, canyon, divide, hollow, ravine 8 water gap

Valley of the Dolls
    author: 16 Jacqueline Susann

valor 4 grit, guts 5 nerve, pluck, spunk 6 daring, mettle 7 bravery, courage, heroism 8 boldness, chivalry 9 fortitude, gallantry 11 intrepidity 12 fearlessness 13 dauntlessness

valorous 4 bold 5 brave, gutsy 6 heroic, plucky 7 valiant 8 fearless, intrepid, stalwart, unafraid 9 daunt-

less 10 courageous 11 indomitable, lionhearted 12 stouthearted

valse 5 waltz

valuable 4 dear, good 6 costly, prized, useful, valued 7 admired, helpful 8 esteemed, fruitful, precious 9 expensive, important, priceless, respected, treasured 10 beneficial, high-priced, invaluable, profitable, worthwhile 11 serviceable, significant, utilitarian 12 advantageous

valuation 9 appraisal 10 assessment, evaluation 14 estimated value

value, values 3 use 4 cost, help, rate 5 assay, count, judge, merit, price, prize, rules, weigh, worth 6 admire, amount, assess, charge, esteem, ideals, profit, reckon, revere, size up 7 beliefs, benefit, cherish, compute, customs, respect, service, utility 8 appraise, evaluate, prestige, treasure 9 advantage, appraisal, greatness, moral code, practices, standards 10 admiration, appreciate, assessment, estimation, excellence, importance, set store by, usefulness 11 conventions, market price, superiority 12 code of ethics, institutions, significance

valued 6 prized 7 revered 8 esteemed 9 cherished, respected, treasured 11 appreciated 14 highly regarded

valueless 7 trivial, useless 9 worthless 11 of no account, unimportant 13 insignificant 14 good for nothing 15 inconsequential

vamoose 3 out 4 away, scat, shoo 5 be off, leave, scram 6 beat it, begone, depart, get out, go away 7 get lost

vamp 5 siren 9 temptress 10 seductress 11 enchantress, femme fatale 12 introduction

Vamp
    nickname of: 9 Theda Bara

vampire 3 bat 7 Dracula 11 bloodsucker

van 4 cart, dray, head 5 lorry, scout, truck, wagon 6 camper, picket 7 trailer 8 sentinel, vanguard 9 first line, forefront, front rank 10 avantgarde, large truck 12 advance guard, covered truck 13 front of an army 16 foremost division
    french: 7 fourgon

Van, Bobby
    real name: 10 Robert King
    born: 9 New York NY
    roles: 10 Kiss Me Kate, On Your Toes 11 No No Nanette 12 It's Only Money, The Ladies' Man 13 Small Town Girl 23 The Affairs of Dobie Gillis

Van Allen, James Alfred
    field: 7 physics
    invented: 18 radio proximity fuse
    discovered: 22 Van Allen radiation belts

Van Buren, Martin
    nicknames: 9 The Red Fox 17 The Little Magician 18 The Careful Dutchman
    presidential rank: 6 eighth
    party: 8 Democrat
    state represented: 7 New York
    defeated: 5 (Hugh Lawson) White 6 (William Person) Mangum 7 (Daniel) Webster 8 (William Henry) Harrison
    vice president: 7 (Richard Mentor) Johnson
    cabinet:
        state: 7 (John) Forsyth
        treasury: 8 (Levi) Woodbury
        war: 8 (Joel Roberts) Poinsett
        attorney general: 6 (Benjamin Franklin) Butler, (Felix) Grundy, (Henry Dilworth) Gilpin
        navy: 8 (James Kirke) Paulding 9 (Mahlon) Dickerson
        postmaster general: 5 (John Milton) Niles 7 (Amos) Kendall
    born/died/buried: 12 Kinderhook NY
    education:
        Academy: 10 Kinderhook
        studied: 3 law
    religion: 13 Dutch Reformed
    vacation:
        toured: 6 Europe (1853-1855)
    political career: 8 US Senate 11 state Senate 13 vice president 20 state Attorney General
        governor of: 7 New York
        secretary of: 5 State
        minister: 12 Great Britain
    civilian career: lawyer
    notable events of lifetime/term: 5 Panic (of 1837)
        treaty: 16 Webster-Ashburton
        war: 9 Aroostook
    father: 7 Abraham
    mother: 5 Maria (Hoes Van Alen)
    siblings: 6 Derike, Hannah 7 Abraham 8 Lawrence
    wife: 6 Hannah (Hoes)
    children: 4 John 6 Martin 7 Abraham 13 Smith Thompson

Vance, Vivian
    real name: 11 Vivian Jones
    born: 12 Cherryvale KS
    roles: 9 I Love Lucy 10 Ethel Mertz

Vancouver
    hockey team: 7 Canucks

vandal 6 looter, raider 7 ravager, wrecker 8 marauder, pillager, saboteur 9 barbarian, despoiler, destroyer, plunderer 10 demolisher

vandalism 6 damage 10 defacement 11 destruction 17 malicious mischief

vandalize 3 mar 5 trash, wreck 6 damage, deface 7 despoil, destroy

Vanderlyn, John
    born: 10 Kingston NY
    artwork: 14 Ariadne on Naxos 20 The Death of Jane McCrea 28 Marius Amid the Ruins of Carthage 31 Ariadne Asleep on the Island of Naxos

Van Dyck, Sir Anthony
    born: 7 Antwerp 8 Flanders
    artwork: 8 Charles I (in Hunting
    Dress) 11 Iconography 18 Madonna
    of the Rosary 19 Blessed Herman Jo-
    seph, Cardinal Bentiroglio 20 Ecstasy
    of St Augustine 21 Marchesa Elena
    Grimaldi

Van Dyke, Dick
    born: 12 West Plains MO
    roles: 11 Mary Poppins 12 Bye Bye
    Birdie 15 Diagnosis Murder, Dick
    Van Dyke Show
    brother: 5 Jerry
    son: 5 Barry

Vane, Sutton
    author of: 12 Outward Bound

Van Gogh, Vincent
    born: 12 GrootZundert 14 The Neth-
    erlands
    artwork: 10 Pere Tanguy 11 Cafe at
    Night, L'Arlesienne 13 The Olive
    Grove 14 The Starry Night 15 The
    Potato Eaters 16 The Bridge at Arles
    18 Portrait of Dr Gachet, The Chair
    and the Pipe 22 Cornfield with
    Cypresses

vanguard 3 van 7 leaders 8 forerank
    9 first line, forefront, front line, front
    rank, spearhead 10 avant-garde, in
    novators, leadership, modernists 11
    pacesetters, tastemakers 12 advance
    guard, trailblazers, trendsetters

vanish 3 die, end 5 cease 6 die out,
    expire, perish 7 die away 8 dissolve,
    fade away, melt away, pass away 9
    disappear, evaporate, terminate 13 de-
    materialize 15 become invisible

vanished 4 dead, gone, lost 7 defunct,
    died out, extinct 11 disappeared

vanishing 8 dying out 10 extinction,
    fading away 11 passing away 12 dis-
    appearing 13 disappearance 15 dema-
    terializing

vanitas vanitatum 16 vanity of vani-
    ties

vanity 4 sham 5 folly, pride 6 mirage
    7 compact, conceit, egotism, falsity,
    inanity 8 de lusion, futility, idleness,
    self-love 9 emptiness, powder box,
    vainglory, vanity bag 10 hollowness,
    narcissism, self-praise, vanity case
    11 makeup table, mirror table, self-
    conceit, uselessness 13 dressing table,
    fruitlessness, worthlessness 14 self-
    admiration, superficiality

Vanity Fair
    author: 25 William Makepeace
    Thackeray
    character: 10 Becky Sharp 11 Miss
    Crawley 12 Amelia Sedley, Joseph
    (Jos) Sedley 13 George Osborne,
    Rawdon Crawley 14 Sir Pitt Crawley
    20 Captain William Dobbin

vanity of vanities
    Latin: 16 vanitas vanitatum

vanquish 4 beat, best, drub, lick, rout

5 crush 6 defeat, master, subdue,
thrash 7 conquer 8 overcome 9 overpower, overthrow, overwhelm, subjugate 11 triumph over

vanquisher 6 master, victor, winner 7
    subduer 8 champion 9 conqueror 10
    subjugator

vanquishment 6 defeat 7 mastery,
    triumph, victory, winning 8 conquest
    10 conquering, overcoming

Van Tassel, Katrina
    character in: 23 The Legend of Sleepy
    Hollow
    author: 6 Irving

Vanuatu
    other name: 11 New Hebrides
    capital/largest city: 4 Vila
    others: 5 Santo 6 Forari 10 Lugan-
    ville
    school: 7 Malapoa
    monetary unit: 5 franc 7 centime
    island: 3 Api, Epi 4 Aoba, Gaua,
    Malo, Tana, Vate 5 Banks, Efate,
    Maewo, Santo, Tanna 6 Ambrym,
    Mabrim, Torres 8 Anei tyum,
    Malekula 9 Erromanga, Pentecost,
    Vanua Lava 13 Espiritu Santo
    mountain: 6 Lopevi
    highest point: 11 Tabwemasana
    sea: 7 Pacific
    people: 8 European 10 Melanesian,
    Polynesian 11 Micronesian
        explorer: 4 Cook 7 Queiros
        leader: 4 Lini 8 Kelekele
    language: 6 French 7 Bislama, Eng-
    lish 16 Melanesian Pidgin
    religion: 7 animism 8 Anglican, John
    Frum 10 Protestant 12 Presbyterian
    13 Roman Catholic
    feature:
        cult: 5 cargo

vapid 4 dull, flat, lame, tame 5 bland,
    empty, stale 7 insipid 8 lifeless 9 col-
    orless, pointless 10 flavorless, wishy-
    washy 11 meaningless, uninspiring 12
    unsatisfying 13 characterless

vapor 3 dew, fog 4 haze, mist, smog
    5 fumes, smoke, steam 6 miasma 8
    moisture

vaporize 5 dry up 7 distill 8 condense,
    melt away 9 dissipate, evaporate

Vargas Llosa, Mario
    author of: 13 The Green House, Per-
    petual Orgy 15 Death in the Andes
    16 The Time of the Hero, The Way
    to Paradise 17 The Feast of the Goat
    24 The War of the End of the World
    26 Conversation in the Cathedral 27
    Aunt Julia and the Scriptwriter 28
    The Temptation of the Impossible 34
    Captain Pantoja and the Special Serv-
    ice

variable 6 fickle, fitful, uneven, unlike
    7 diverse, mutable 8 changing, shift-
    ing, unstable, wavering 9 alterable,
    different, spasmodic, unsettled 10 ca-

pricious, changeable, inconstant, indefinite 11 fluctuating

variance 4 odds 6 change 7 dispute,
    quarrel 9 deviation, disparity 10 con-
    tention, difference, dissension, diver-
    gence, unlikeness 11 discrepancy, in-
    congruity 12 disagreement,
    modification 13 dissimilarity, incon-
    sistency

variant 7 altered, derived, take off 8
    modified 9 departure, different, diver-
    gent, variation 10 alteration 11 trans-
    formed 12 modification 14 transfor-
    mation

variation 6 change 7 variant, variety 8
    mutation, variance 9 departure, devia-
    tion, diversity 10 aberration, altera-
    tion, difference, divergency, innova-
    tion 11 discrepancy 12 disagreement,
    modification 13 metamorphosis 14
    transformation

varicolored 6 calico, motley, tartan 7
    dappled, flecked, marbled, mottled,
    piebald 9 multi-hued 10 iridescent,
    opalescent, variegated 11 rainbowlike,
    technicolor 12 multicolored, parti-
    colored 13 polychromatic

varied 5 mixed 6 motley, sundry 7 di-
    verse, various 8 assorted 9 different
    10 variegated 11 diversified 13 heter-
    ogeneous, miscellaneous

variegated 4 pied 6 motley 7
    checked, dappled, mottled, piebald 9
    checkered 12 parti-colored

variety 4 hash, kind, race, sort, type 5
    brand, breed, class, genre, genus,
    group, stock, tribe 6 change, family,
    jumble, medley, motley, strain 7 me-
    lange, mixture, species 8 category,
    division, pastiche 9 diversity, patch-
    work, variation 10 assortment, collec-
    tion, difference, hodgepodge, innova-
    tion, miscellany, subspecies 11
    subdivision 12 denomination, multi-
    plicity, unconformity 13 dissimilarity,
    heterogeneity, nonuniformity 14 clas-
    sification, omnium-gatherum 15 diver-
    sification

various 3 few 4 many, some 5 other 6
    divers, myriad, sundry, varied
    7 diverse, several 8 assorted, mani-
    fold, numerous 9 countless, different
    10 dissimilar 11 innumerable 12 mul-
    tifarious 13 miscellaneous, multitudi-
    nous

varlet 3 cur 6 rascal, wretch 7 villain
    9 scoundrel 10 blackguard

Varner, Will
    character in: 9 The Hamlet
    author: 8 Faulkner

varnish 4 gilt 5 adorn, cover, gloss,
    stain 6 excuse, soften 7 conceal, lac-
    quer 8 disguise, mitigate 9 embellish,
    gloss over 10 smooth over

vary 4 veer 5 alter, shift 6 change, de-
    part, differ, modify 7 deviate, dissent,
    diverge 8 be unlike, contrast, disagree

9 alternate, disaccord, diversify, fluctuate

vase 3 jar, jug, pot, urn **5** crock, diota **8** canister **9** container **10** jardiniere

Vashti
> **husband: 9** Ahasuerus
> **replaced by: 6** Esther

vassal 4 serf **5** helot, liege, slave **6** tenant, thrall **7** bondman, servant, subject, villein **8** retainer **9** bondslave, bondwoman, dependent **11** subordinate

vassalage 4 yoke **7** bondage, serfdom, slavery **9** servitude **11** enslavement

vast 4 huge, wide **5** great, jumbo **7** endless, immense, titanic, very big **8** colossal, enormous, far-flung, gigantic, infinite, spacious **9** boundless, capacious, extensive, limitless, monstrous, unbounded, unlimited, very large **10** monumental, prodigious, stupendous, tremendous, voluminous, widespread **11** far-reaching, measureless, significant, substantial **12** immeasurable, interminable

vastness 7 bigness **8** enormity, hugeness **9** immensity, largeness **12** enormousness

Vatican City 10 papal state
> **enclave in: 4** Rome
> **includes: 7** Vatican **13** Sistine Chapel **16** St. Peter's Basilica
> **retreat: 14** Castel Gandolfo
> **statue: 7** Laocoon

Vaughan Williams, Ralph
> **born: 7** Britain **10** Down Ampney
> **composer of: 3** Job **8** The Wasps **9** Flos Campi **10** Antarctica (symphony No 7), **11** Old King Cole **12** A Sea Symphony **13** Hugh the Drover, On Wenlock Edge, Sir John in Love, Songs of Travel **14** Riders to the Sea, The House of Life, The Sons of Light **15** A London Symphony, The Poisoned Kiss **16** The Lark Ascending **17** A Pastoral Symphony **18** Five Tudor Portraits, Sinfonia Antartica **19** The Pilgrim's Progress **22** Toward the Unknown Region

Vaughn, Robert
> **born: 9** New York NY
> **roles: 7** Bullitt **12** Napoleon Solo **15** The Man from UNCLE **19** The Magnificent Seven **22** The Young Philadelphians

vault 4 arch, dome, jump, leap, safe, tomb **5** bound, clear, crypt **6** arcade, cupola, hurdle, spring **7** ossuary **8** catacomb, jump over, leapfrog, leap over, wall safe **9** mausoleum, polevault, sepulcher, strongbox **10** arched roof, spring over, strongroom **13** arched ceiling, burial chamber

vaunt 5 strut **6** brag of, flaunt **7** exult in, show off, swagger **9** crow about, gasconade, gloat over **10** boast about

vaunted 7 exalted, praised **11** gloated over, overpraised **12** boasted about

veer 3 yaw **4** jibe, tack, turn **5** curve, dodge, drift, shift, wheel **6** swerve, zigzag **7** go about **9** come round, turn aside **15** change direction

Vega$
> **character: 5** Angie **6** Binzer **8** Beatrice, Dan Tanna **10** Bernie Roth **11** (Sgt) Bella Archer
> **cast: 10** Tony Curtis **11** Judy Landers, Robert Urich **12** Naomi Stevens, Phyllis Davis **13** Bart Braverman

vegetable 3 pea **4** bean, beet, corn **6** carrot, greens, legume, squash, turnip **7** cabbage, lettuce, parsnip, produce, spinach **8** broccoli, eggplant, lima bean, rutabaga, zucchini **10** string bean **11** cauliflower

vegetarian 5 vegan **8** meatless **9** herbivore **11** herbivorous

vegetation 5 flora, grass, sloth, weeds **6** leaves, plants, torpor **7** foliage, herbage, languor, loafing, verdure **8** dormancy, idleness, lethargy **9** flowerage, indolence, plant life, shrubbery **10** inactivity **11** hibernation, languidness, rustication **12** sluggishness
> **god of: 6** Dumuzi

vehemence 4 heat, zeal **5** ardor **6** fervor, warmth **7** passion **9** intensity

vehement 3 hot **4** wild **5** eager, fiery, rabid **6** ardent, fervid, fierce, heated, stormy **7** earnest, excited, fanatic, fervent, furious, intense, violent, zealous **8** agitated, forceful, frenzied, vigorous **9** emotional, fanatical, hotheaded **10** passionate **11** impassioned, tempestuous **12** enthusiastic

vehemently 5 hotly **6** wildly **7** eagerly **8** ardently, fiercely, strongly **9** earnestly, excitedly, fervently, furiously, intensely, violently, zealously **10** vigorously **11** emotionally, fanatically **12** passionately **13** tempestuously **16** enthusiastically

vehicle 3 bus, car **4** tool **5** agent, means, organ, plane, train, truck **6** agency, device, medium **7** bicycle **9** mechanism **10** automobile, conveyance, instrument, motorcycle, rocket ship **12** intermediary **14** transportation

veil 3 dim **4** hide, mask **5** cloak, cloud, cover **6** enwrap, mantle, screen, shroud **7** blanket, conceal, curtain, envelop, obscure **8** covering **10** camouflage

veiled 3 dim **5** murky **6** draped, hidden **7** muffled **8** obscured, shrouded **9** concealed, covered up, disguised, enveloped, enwrapped **11** camouflaged

veiling 3 net **4** mesh **8** cloaking, covering **9** obscurity **10** concealing

vein 3 rib, web **4** bent, hint, line, lode, mark, mood, seam, tone **5** fleck,

layer, stria, style, touch **6** furrow, manner, marble, nature, strain, streak, stripe, temper, thread **7** stratum **8** tendency **9** capillary, character **10** complexion, propensity **11** blood vessel, disposition, inclination, temperament **12** predilection **14** predisposition

Velazquez (Velasquez), Diego Rodriguez de Silvay
> **born: 5** Spain **7** Seville
> **artwork: 8** Philip IV **10** Las Meninas **13** Luis de Gongora, Pope Innocent X, Venus and Cupid **14** Cardinal Borgia **17** Don Gaspar de Guzman, Isabella of Bourbon **18** Adoration of the Magi, The Tapestry Weavers **19** The Infanta Margarita, The Surrender of Breda **20** Infanta Maria Theresia **21** An Old Woman Cooking Eggs **22** Portrait of a Court Jester, Portrait of Juan de Pareja **23** The Immaculate Conception **30** Prince Balthasar Carlos at the Hunt

veloce
> **music: 4** fast

velocity 4 pace **5** haste, speed **8** alacrity, celerity, rapidity **9** fleetness, quickness, swiftness **10** expedition, speediness

venal 5 shady **6** greedy **7** corrupt, crooked, selfish **8** bribable, covetous, grasping **9** dishonest, mercenary, rapacious **10** avaricious **11** corruptible **12** unprincipled, unscrupulous **13** money-grubbing

venality 7 avarice **10** corruption **11** bribe-taking **13** mercenariness, money-grubbing

vend 4 hawk, sell **5** trade **6** barter, deal in, market, peddle, retail **7** auction, trade in **8** huckster **11** merchandise

vendor, vender 6 dealer, hawker, monger, seller, trader **7** peddler **8** huckster, merchant, purveyor, retailer, salesman, supplier **9** tradesman **10** wholesaler **12** merchandiser **13** street peddler

veneer 4 coat, mask, show **5** front, layer **6** casing, facade, facing, jacket, sheath **7** coating, overlay, wrapper **8** covering, envelope, pretense **10** outer layer

venerable 3 old **4** aged **5** hoary **6** august **7** admired, ancient, elderly, honored, revered **8** esteemed **9** respected, venerated **11** patriarchal, white-haired

venerate 5 adore, extol, honor **6** admire, esteem, hallow, revere **7** cherish, glorify, idolize, respect, worship **8** look up to **9** reverence **11** pay homage to

venerated 4 holy **5** loved **6** adored, sacred **7** honored, revered **8** hallowed

9 respected **10** reverenced, worshipped **12** paid homage to

veneration 3 awe **5** honor **6** esteem, homage, wonder **7** respect, worship **8** devotion **9** adoration, adulation, reverence **10** admiration, exaltation **11** idolization **13** glorification

venereal 6 carnal, sexual **7** genital

Venezuela
name means: 12 little Venice
capital/largest city: 7 Caracas
others: 4 Aroa, Coro **6** Atures, Cumana, Merida **7** Barinas, Barines, Cabello, Guaware, Maracay, Maturin **8** Asuncion, Carupano, La Guaira, La Gyayra, Tacupita, Valencia **9** Barcelona, Maracaibo, Tacarigua **12** Barquisimeto, Puerto La Cruz, San Cristobal **13** Cuidad Bolivar, Puerto Cabello **18** Santo Tome de Guayana
division: 4 Lara **5** Apure, Sucre, Zulia **6** Aragua, Falcon, Merida **7** Barinas, Bolivar, Cojedes, Guarico, Monagas, Tachira, Yaracuy **8** Carabobo, Trujillo
measure: 5 galon **6** fanega **7** estadel
monetary unit: 4 peso **5** medio **6** fuerte **7** bolivar, centimo **8** morocota **10** venezolano
weight: 3 bag **5** libra
island: 4 Aves **7** Cubagua, Tortuga **9** La Orchila, Los Roques, Margarita **11** Los Hermanos **12** La Blanquilla
lake: 9 Maracaibo, Tacarigua
mountain: 3 Pao **4** Pava, Yair **5** Andes, Duida, Icutu **6** Concha, Cuneva, Merida, Parima, Sierra, Yumari **7** Imutaca, Masaiti, Roraima **8** Gurupira **9** Pacaraima **10** Auyan-Tepui **11** Turimiquire **18** Cordillera del Norte
highest point: 7 Bolivar
river: 3 Oro, Pao **4** Meta **5** Apure, Caura, Negro, Suata, Tigre, Unare, Zulia **6** Amazon, Arauca, Caroni, Cuyuni **7** Guanare, Guanipa, Guarico, Orinoco, Oritueo, Paragua, Suapure, Vichada, Yuruari **8** Guaviare, Manapire, Ventuari **9** Cuchivero **10** Casiquiare, Portuguesa
sea: 8 Atlantic **9** Caribbean
physical feature:
  falls: 5 Angel
  gulf: 5 Paria **6** Triste **9** Venezuela
  highlands: 6 Guiana **7** Guayana, Segovia
  plains: 6 Llanos
people: 4 Bare, Pume **5** Bello, Carib, pardo, zambo **6** Arawak, Creole, Timote **7** Charoya, Guahibo, Kaliana, mestizo, mulatto, Otomaca, Timotex **8** Caquetio, Guarauno, Matilone **11** Maquiritare
  artist: 7 Marisol
  author: 5 Bello **8** Gallegos **13** Diaz-Rodriguez
  explorer: 8 Columbus
  god: 5 Tsuma
  leader: 4 Paez **5** Gomez, Leoni **6**

Castro **7** Bolivar, Miranda **10** Betancourt **11** Chavez Frias **12** Guzman Blanco **14** Herrera Campins
language: 4 Pume **7** Spanish
religion: 5 Islam **7** Judaism **10** Protestant **13** Roman Catholic
feature:
  animal: 4 puma **5** sloth **6** jaguar, ocelot **7** manatee, peccary **8** anteater, capybara **9** armadillo
  cowboy: 7 llanero
  dance: 6 joropo **16** diablos danzantes
  folk entertainment: 10 burriquita
  musical instrument: 6 cuatro **7** maracas
  street performance: 8 parranda
food:
  black beans: 8 caraotas
  bread: 5 arepa
  dish: 7 hallaca **8** cachapos, pabellon
  soup/stew: 8 sancocho

vengeance 7 revenge **8** avenging, reprisal, requital **11** malevolence, retaliation, retribution **12** ruthlessness **13** an eye for an eye, implacability **14** revengefulness, vindictiveness **15** a tooth for a tooth

veni, vidi, vici 19 I came I saw I conquered
author: 12 Julius Caesar

venial 5 minor **6** slight **7** trivial **9** allowable, excusable **10** defensible, forgivable, not serious, pardonable **11** justifiable, unimportant, warrantable

Venice
art exhibition: 8 Biennale
artist: 7 Bellini, Codussi **8** Fabriano, Longhena, Mantegna, Palladio, Scamozzi, Veronese **9** Canaletto, Carpaccio, Giorgione, Sansovino **10** Tintoretto
capital of: 6 Veneto **15** Venezia province
church: 18 San Giorgio Maggiore, Santa Maria dei Frari **19** Santi Giovanni e Paolo
Italian: 7 Venezia
landmark: 6 Ca' d'Oro **9** Campanile **10** Grand Canal **11** Doge's Palace **13** Bridge of Sighs **15** Libreria Vecchia **16** Palazzo Rezzonico, Saint Mark's Church **17** Accademia di Belle Arti **21** Palazzo dei Procuratori **22** Scuola Grande di San Rocco **23** Palazzo Vendramin-Calergi
port: 8 Marghera
resort: 9 Lido Beach
sea: 8 Adriatic
small canal: 3 rii
tomb: 5 Titan
traveler: 9 Marco Polo

venom 3 ire **4** gall, hate **5** anger, spite, toxin, virus **6** choler, enmity, grudge, hatred, malice, poison, rancor, spleen **7** ill will **8** acrimony, savagery **9** animosity, barbarity, brutality, hostility

10 bitterness, resentment **11** malevolence **12** spitefulness **13** maliciousness, rancorousness

venomous 5 cruel, fatal, toxic **6** bitter, brutal, deadly, lethal, malign, savage **7** abusive, caustic, hostile, noxious, vicious **8** spiteful, virulent **9** malicious, malignant, poisonous, rancorous, resentful **10** malevolent **11** ill-disposed **12** bloodthirsty

vent 3 air, tap **4** bare, drip, emit, flue, gush, hole, ooze, pipe **5** exude, spout, utter, voice **6** effuse, escape, faucet, let out, outlet, reveal, spigot **7** air hole, chimney, debouch, declare, divulge, express, opening, orifice, release **8** aperture, disclose, exposure, venthole **9** discharge, let escape, pour forth, utterance **10** disclosure, expression, revelation, smoke stack, ventilator **11** communicate, declaration

ventilate 3 air, sow **5** voice **6** aerate, air out, report, review, spread **7** analyze, declare, discuss, dissent, divulge, examine, express **9** broadcast, circulate, comment on, criticize, oxygenate, publicize, talk about **10** bandy about **11** disseminate, noise abroad

ventilator 3 fan **4** flue **7** aerator **10** exhaust fan, smoke stack **14** air conditioner

venture 2 go **3** bet, try **4** dare, risk **5** flyer, offer, wager **6** chance, gamble, hazard, plunge, submit, tender, travel **7** advance, attempt, hold out, presume, proffer, project **8** endeavor, make bold **9** adventure, risk going, strive for, undertake, volunteer **10** enterprise, put forward, take a flyer **11** speculation, uncertainty, undertaking

venturesome, adventuresome 4 bold, rash **5** risky **6** daring, tricky, unsafe, unsure **7** dubious **8** doubtful, insecure, perilous, reckless, ticklish **9** ambitious, audacious, dangerous, daredevil, energetic, foolhardy, hazardous, impetuous, impulsive, uncertain **10** aggressive, precarious **11** adventurous, speculative **12** enterprising, questionable

venturesomeness 6 daring **8** audacity, boldness **9** derring-do **11** impetuosity **12** recklessness

Venus
origin: 5 Roman **7** Italian
goddess of: 4 love **6** beauty, spring **7** gardens
son: 6 Aeneas
grandson: 5 Iulus
epithet: 7 Erycina **8** Gene trix **10** Erticordia
see **9** Aphrodite

Venus (planet)
position: 6 second
closest to: 5 Earth
named after: 7 goddess **12** Roman goddess

nickname: 11 evening star, morning star

characteristics: 6 clouds

space probes: 6 Venera **7** Galileo, Pioneer **8** Magellan

Venus and Adonis

author: 18 William Shakespeare

veracious 4 true **6** honest **7** sincere **8** accurate, faithful, truthful **10** scrupulous **11** punctilious

veracity 5 truth **6** candor, verity **7** honesty, probity **8** accuracy, openness **9** exactness, frankness, integrity, sincerity **10** exactitude **11** correctness **12** truthfulness **13** guilelessness, ingenuousness **14** verisimilitude

Vera-Ellen

real name: 13 Vera-Ellen Rohe

born: 12 Cincinnati OH

roles: 9 On the Town **14** White Christmas

veranda

Hawaiian: 5 lanai

verbal 4 oral, said **5** vocal **6** spoken, voiced **7** in words, of verbs, of words, uttered **9** expressed, unwritten

verbal exchange 6 dialog **8** dialogue **10** discussion **12** conversation

verbalize 5 speak, utter, voice **7** express **10** articulate **12** put into words

verbal thrust 3 dig **4** gibe, jeer **5** taunt **13** cutting remark

verbatim 5 exact **7** exactly, literal, precise **8** accurate, faithful **9** literally, literatim, precisely **10** accurately, faithfully **11** to the letter, word for word **15** chapter and verse, letter for letter

Latin: 14 ipsissima verba

verbatim et literatim 21 in exactly the same words **29** word for word and letter for letter

verbena

varieties: 4 moss, rose, sand **5** clump, lemon, shrub **7** red sand **8** pink sand **9** beach sand **10** desert sand, Mojave sand, yellow sand **12** common garden

verbiage 9 logorrhea, loquacity, prolixity, verbosity, wordiness **10** volubility **11** verboseness **12** effusiveness **14** circumlocution, grandiloquence, long-windedness

verbose 5 gabby, wordy **6** prolix **7** voluble **8** effusive **9** garrulous, talkative **10** longwinded, loquacious **13** grandiloquent **14** circumlocutory

verbosity 9 diffusion, prolixity, talkiness, wordiness **11** diffuseness **13** talkativeness **14** long-windedness

verboten 9 forbidden **10** prohibited

Verdandi 4 Norn

origin: 12 Scandinavian

form: 3 elf

personifies: 7 present

developed from: 5 Urdar

companions: 3 Urd **5** Skuld

verdant 4 lush **5** green, leafy, shady, turfy **6** grassy **7** meadowy **8** blooming, thriving **9** luxuriant **10** burgeoning, springlike **11** flourishing

Verdi, Giuseppe

born: 5 Italy **7** Busseto

composer of: 4 Aida **6** Otello **7** Macbeth, Nabucco, Othello **8** Falstaff **9** Don Carlos, Il Corsaro, Rigoletto, The Misled **10** La Traviata **11** Il Trovatore **13** The Trouhadour **14** Manzoni Requiem **15** Simon Boccanegra

verdict 6 answer, decree, ruling **7** finding, opinion **8** decision, judgment, sentence **9** valuation **10** assessment, estimation **11** arbitrament, arbitration **12** adjudication **13** determination

Vere, Captain

character in: 9 Billy Budd

author: 8 Melville

Vereen, Ben

born: 7 Miami FL

roles: 5 Roots **6** Pippin **11** All That Jazz **13** Chicken George **20** Jesus Christ Superstar

verge 3 end, hem, lip, rim **4** brim, edge **5** bound, brink, ledge, limit, skirt **6** be near, border, flange, fringe, margin **7** confine, extreme **8** approach, boundary, frontier, terminus **9** threshold **11** approximate **12** be on the brink

verge upon 4 abut **5** flank **6** adjoin, border **8** be next to **10** neighbor on

Vergil, Virgil

author of: 6 Aeneid **8** Bucolics, Eclogues, Georgics

verification 5 proof **7** support **9** guarantee **10** validation **12** confirmation **13** accreditation, certification, corroboration, documentation **14** authentication, substantiation

verify 5 prove **7** certify, confirm, support, sustain, witness **8** accredit, attest to, document, validate, vouch for **9** establish, guarantee, testify to **11** corroborate **12** authenticate, substantiate

verily 4 amen **5** truly **6** really **9** certainly, yes indeed **10** positively

veritable 4 real, true **5** utter, valid **6** actual **7** genuine, literal **8** absolute, bona fide, complete, positive, true-blue **9** authentic **13** incontestable, unimpeachable **14** unquestionable **17** through-and-through

Verlaine, Paul

author of: 6 Wisdom **7** Sagesse **8** Langueur **17** Songs Without Words **19** Romances sans Paroles

Vermeer, Jan

born: 5 Delft **7** Holland

artwork: 11 View of Delft **12** The Lace Maker, The Procuress **13** Drinking Scene **14** A Street in Delft, The Head of a Girl **15** Allegory of Faith,

Girl with a Red Hat **16** The Artist's Studio **18** Girl Reading a Letter, Girl with a Wine-glass **19** A Girl Asleep at a Table, A Painter in his Studio **20** A Woman Weighing Pearls **22** Maidservant Pouring Milk **23** Young Woman with a Water Jug **24** A Soldier and a Laughing Girl **31** Christ in the House of Mary and Martha

vermilion 3 red **7** scarlet **8** cinnabar **9** bright red **15** mercuric sulfide

vermin 4 ants, lice, mice, owls, rats **5** crows, fleas, foxes, pests **6** snakes, wolves **7** bed bugs, coyotes, roaches, spiders, weasels **8** termites, varmints **9** water bugs **10** centipedes, silverfish **11** birds of prey **18** pestiferous insects

Vermont

abbreviation: 2 VT

nickname: 13 Green Mountain **20** Four-Season Recreation

capital: 10 Montpelier

largest city: 10 Burlington

others: 5 Barre, Stowe **7** Grafton, Newfane, Newport, Rutland **8** St Albans, Winooski **9** Bountiful, Vergennes **10** Bennington **11** Brattleboro

college: 3 UVM **7** Goddard, Norwich, Trinity, Vermont, Windham **8** Marlboro **10** Bennington, Middlebury, St Michaels

feature:

covered bridge: 5 Scott

house: 15 Old Constitution

monument: 2 Battle

people: 9 John Deere, John Dewey **10** Ethan Allen, Howard Dean **12** Brigham Young **13** Warren R Austin **15** Stephen A Douglas

lake: 7 Caspian, Dunmore, Seymour **8** Bomoseen **9** Champlain **10** Willoughby **12** Memphremagog

land rank: 10 forty-third

mountain: 5 Green, White **7** Bromley, Hogback, Taconic **8** Prospect, Stratton

highest point: 9 Mansfield

physical feature:

uplands: 10 New England

valley: 9 Champlain

president: 14 Calvin Coolidge, Chester A Arthur

river: 4 West **5** Otter, White **7** Saxtons **8** Lamoille, Nulhegan, Winooski **10** Missisquoi **11** Connecticut

state admission: 10 fourteenth

state bird: 12 hermit thrush

state animal: 11 Morgan horse

state flower: 9 red clover

state motto: 15 Freedom and Unity

state song: 11 Hail Vermont

state tree: 10 sugar maple

vermouth

type: 4 wine **6** brandy **8** aperitif

origin: 5 Italy **6** France

varieties: 3 dry **5** sweet

drink: 9 Boomerang **11** Bittersweet

with bourbon: 9 Allegheny

with brandy: 3 BVD
with Dubonnet: 3 BVD
gin: 5 Bijou, Bronx, Tango **6** Caruso **7** Bermuda, Caberet, Martini **10** Bloodhound
with rum: 6 Bolero **8** Apple Pie **10** Black Devil **11** Shark's Tooth
with rye: 8 Brooklyn **9** Algonquin
with scotch: 8 Affinity **10** Bobby Burns
with sherry: 6 Bamboo, Brazil
with sloe gin: 10 Blackthorn
with vodka: 8 Kangaroo **9** Corkscrew
with whiskey: 9 Manhattan

vernacular 4 cant **5** idiom, lingo, slang **6** jargon, patois **7** dialect **8** parlance, shoptalk **9** the vulgar **12** common speech, native tongue **13** natural speech **14** informal speech, native language

vernal 3 new **5** fresh, green **6** spring **8** youthful **10** springlike

Verne, Jules
author of: 19 Five Weeks in a Balloon **21** From the Earth to the Moon **26** Around the World in Eighty Days **32** Twenty Thousand Leagues Under the Sea
character: 11 Captain Nemo, Phineas Fogg **12** Passepartout

Veronese, Paolo (Cagliari)
born: 5 Italy **6** Verona
artwork: 12 Book of Esther **13** The Last Supper **14** Supper at Emmaus **15** The Rape of Europa, Triumph of Venice **17** Mary with the Saints, The Finding of Moses, The Marriage at Cana, Wisdom and Strength **19** Martyrdom of St George, The Choice of Hercules **21** Esther before Ahasuerus **22** Feast at the House of Simon **24** Mars and Venus United in Love, The Feast in the House of Levi, The Temptation of St Anthony **31** Jesus and the Centurion of Capernaum **32** The Family of Darius before Alexander

Verrocchio, Andrea del
real name: 31 Andrea di Michele di Francesco Cione
born: 5 Italy **8** Florence
artwork: 5 David **15** Boy with a Dolphin **17** Christ and St Thomas **18** The Baptism of Christ **19** Bartolommeo Colleoni **23** Christ and Doubting Thomas **25** Beheading of John the Baptist

versatile 3 apt **4** able **5** handy **6** adroit, clever, expert, gifted **7** protean **8** talented **9** adaptable, all-around, ingenious, many-sided **10** proficient **11** many-skilled, resourceful **12** accomplished, multifaceted

verse 4 poem **5** meter, rhyme, stave **6** jingle, poetry, stanza **7** measure, strophe

versed 4 able **5** adept **6** expert, taught

7 erudite, learned, skilled, tutored **8** lettered, schooled, skillful, well-read **9** competent, practiced, scholarly **10** at home with, instructed, proficient **11** enlightened, experienced **12** accomplished, familiar with, well-informed **14** acquainted with, conversant with

versifier 4 bard **6** rhymer, writer **8** minstrel, poetizer, poetling, rhymster **9** poetaster, rhymester **10** rhymesmith, troubadour, versemaker, versesmith **11** versemonger **12** balladmonger

version 4 side **5** story **6** report **7** account **9** depiction, rendering **10** adaptation, paraphrase, re-creation **11** description, re statement, translation **14** interpretation

vers libre 9 free verse

vertebral column
bone of: 5 spine **8** backbone

vertex 3 cap, tip **4** apex, peak **5** crown **6** summit, zenith **8** pinnacle **12** highest point **13** crowning point

vertical 5 plumb, sheer **7** upright **12** ninety-degree **13** perpendicular

vertiginous 5 dizzy, giddy, shaky **6** whirly **7** reeling **11** lightheaded

vertigo 7 reeling **8** fainting **9** dizziness, giddiness **12** unsteadiness **15** lightheadedness

Vertigo
director: 15 Alfred Hitchcock
cast: 8 Kim Novak **12** James Stewart **16** Barbara Bel Geddes
setting: 12 San Francisco
score: 15 Bernard Herrmann

verve 3 vim, zip **4** dash, elan, fire, zeal **5** ardor, drive, force, gusto, punch, vigor **6** energy, fervor, relish, spirit, warmth **7** abandon, feeling, passion, rapture, sparkle **8** vitality, vivacity **9** animation, eagerness, vehemence **10** enthusiasm, liveliness

very 4 bare, mere, most, much, pure **5** exact, extra, plain, quite, sheer, truly **6** deeply, highly, hugely, mighty, really, simple, vastly **7** awfully, exactly, fitting, greatly, notably, perfect, precise, totally **8** actually, entirely, markedly, specific, suitable, terribly **9** assuredly, certainly, decidedly, eminently, essential, extremely, immensely, intensely, necessary, obviously, perfectly, precisely, unusually, veritably **10** abnormally, absolutely, abundantly, completely, definitely, especially, particular, profoundly, remarkably, strikingly, thoroughly, uncommonly, undeniably **11** appropriate, exceedingly, excessively **12** emphatically, surpassingly, tremendously **13** exceptionally, significantly **14** unquestionably

very best
French: 14 creme de la creme

Very Easy Death, A
author: 16 Simone de Beauvoir

very great 4 huge **6** severe **7** extreme, intense, mammoth, titanic **8** colossal, enormous, gigantic **9** excessive, monstrous **10** gargantuan, immoderate, inordinate, prodigious **11** magnificent, spectacular **14** Brobdingnagian

very nearly 6 almost **7** close to **9** just about **10** more or less, not far from **13** approximately

very old 4 aged **6** primal **7** ancient, antique, archaic **8** primeval **10** antiquated, primordial **11** prehistoric **12** antediluvian

very soon
French: 11 tout a l'heure

vessel 3 cup, jar, jug, keg, mug, pot, tub, vat **4** boat, bowl, butt, cask, dish, duct, scow, ship, tube, vase, vein **5** barge, craft, crock, flask, glass, liner, plate, yacht **6** artery, barrel, beaker, carafe, flagon, goblet, packet, tanker, whaler **7** caldron, collier, cruiser, platter, tankard, trawler, tugboat, tumbler, utensil **8** decanter, paquebot, sailboat **9** capillary, container, ferry boat, freighter, houseboat, steamboat, steamship **10** ocean liner, receptacle

vest 3 rig **4** garb, robe **5** array, drape, dress **6** attire, clothe, enwrap, fit out, jacket, jerkin **7** apparel, deck out, doublet, envelop **8** accouter **9** waistcoat

Vesta
origin: 5 Roman
goddess of: 6 hearth
festival: 8 Vestalia
corresponds to: 4 Caca **6** Hestia

vestal 4 pure **6** chaste, maiden, simple, virgin **8** maidenly, virginal, virtuous **9** pure woman, undefiled, unmarried, unworldly **10** immaculate **15** unsophisticated

vested 5 fixed **7** settled **8** absolute, complete **9** permanent **10** guaranteed **11** established, inalienable **12** indisputable **14** unquestionable

vestibule 4 hall **5** entry, foyer, lobby **6** lounge **7** hallway, passage **8** anteroom, corridor **10** passageway **11** antechamber, entrance way, waiting room **12** entrance hall

vestige 4 sign **5** relic, token, trace **6** record **7** memento, remnant **8** evidence, souvenir

vestment 3 alb **4** garb, gear **5** amice, dress **6** livery, outfit **7** apparel, clothes, costume, raiment, regalia, uniform **8** clothing **9** trappings **13** accoutrements

vesture 4 robe **5** robes **7** apparel, clothes, garment, raiment **8** clothing, garments **9** vestments

vetch 5 Vicia
varieties: 3 cow **4** bard, bird, milk **5**

crown, hairy, Sitka **6** bitter, common, kidney, purple, smooth, spring, tufted, winter **8** Narbonne **9** horseshoe, Hungarian, woolly-pod **12** large Russian

veteran 3 vet **6** expert, master **7** old hand **8** old-timer, seasoned **9** ex-soldier **10** campaigner, old soldier, war veteran **11** experienced **12** ex-serviceman **13** long-practiced

veto 4 deny, void **6** denial, enjoin, forbid, negate, reject **7** nullify, prevent, refusal **8** disallow, prohibit, turn down **9** rejection **10** prevention **11** disallowing, prohibition **12** disallowance **16** turn thumbs down on

vex 3 bug, irk **4** fret, gall, miff, pain, rile **5** anger, annoy, chafe, harry, pique, upset, worry **6** badger, bother, grieve, harass, hassle, nettle, pester, plague, ruffle **7** chagrin, disturb, provoke, torment, trouble **8** distress, irritate **9** displease **10** exasperate **18** ruffle one's feathers

vexation 5 pique, trial **6** hassle **7** torment **8** headache, nuisance **9** annoyance **10** affliction, harassment, irritation **11** aggravation **13** pain in the neck

vexatious 5 pesky **6** thorny, vexing **8** annoying, nettling **9** badgering, harassing, hectoring, provoking, troubling, worrisome **10** bothersome, irritating **11** disquieting, pestiferous, troublesome

vexed 5 irked, riled, testy **6** galled, miffed, piqued **7** annoyed, nettled, peevish **8** provoked **9** irritated **11** disgruntled, exasperated

viable 6 usable **8** feasible, workable **9** adaptable, practical **10** applicable **11** practicable

viaduct 4 ramp, span **8** overpass

vial 5 ampul, flask, phial **7** ampoule

via media 10 a middle way

viands 4 cate, diet, eats, fare, food **7** cuisine, edibles, vittles **8** victuals **9** provender **10** foodstuffs, provisions

vibrancy 4 fire **5** ardor **7** elation **8** vitality, vivacity **9** animation **10** enthusiasm **11** high spirits

vibrant 4 deep, loud **5** alive, eager, vital, vivid **6** ardent, bright, florid, lively **7** fervent, glowing, intense, orotund, pealing, pulsing, radiant, ringing **8** animated, bell-like, colorful, forceful, luminous, lustrous, resonant, sonorous, spirited, vehement **9** brilliant, deep-toned, energetic, quivering, thrilling, throbbing, vibrating, vivacious **10** fluttering, glittering, resounding, shimmering **11** full of vigor, resplendent, reverberant **12** electrifying, enthusiastic

vibrate 4 beat, sway **5** quake, swing, throb, waver **6** quaver, quiver, ripple, wobble **7** flutter, pulsate, tremble **8**

undulate **9** oscillate, palpitate, pendulate **11** reverberate

vibration 5 quake **6** quiver, tremor **7** quaking **9** quivering, throbbing, trembling

vicar 6 cleric, parson, pastor **8** preacher **9** churchman, clergyman **12** ecclesiastic

vicarious 6 mental **7** by proxy **8** imagined, indirect **9** imaginary, surrogate **10** empathetic, fantasized, secondhand **11** at one remove, sympathetic

Vicar of Wakefield, The
  author: **15** Oliver Goldsmith
  character: **6** George, Olivia, Sophia **7** Deborah **10** Dr Primrose, Mr Burchill **14** Arabella Wilmot **15** Squire Thornhill **19** Sir William Thornhill

vice 4 flaw **5** fault **6** defect **7** blemish, failing, frailty **8** iniquity, weakness **9** depravity, weak point **10** corruption, debauchery, degeneracy, profligacy, wantonness, wickedness **11** shortcoming **12** imperfection **14** licentiousness

vice president
  resigned: **10** Spiro Agnew **12** John C Calhoun
  accused of treason: **9** Aaron Burr **17** John C Breckinridge
  youngest elected: **17** John C Breckinridge
  elected by Senate: **14** Richard Johnson
  elected but did not serve: **11** William King
  rejected nomination: **11** Frank Lowden, Silas Wright
  lived longest: **15** John Nance Garner
  succeeded to presidency: **9** John Tyler **10** Gerald Ford **12** Harry S Truman **13** Andrew Johnson **14** Calvin Coolidge, Chester A Arthur, Lyndon B Johnson **15** Millard Fillmore **17** Theodore Roosevelt

vice versa 9 in reverse **10** conversely **12** contrariwise **16** the other way round **18** in the opposite order

vicinity 4 area **6** region **8** environs, locality, vicinage **9** adjoining, precincts, proximity **11** environment, propinquity **12** neighborhood, surroundings

vicious 3 bad **4** base, evil, foul, mean, vile, wild **5** awful, cruel, gross, nasty, surly **6** brutal, fierce, horrid, savage, sullen, wicked **7** hateful, heinous, hellish, immoral, inhuman, untamed, violent **8** churlish, depraved, fiendish, libelous, shocking, spiteful, terrible, venomous **9** abhorrent, atrocious, barbarous, dangerous, ferocious, invidious, malicious, monstrous, nefarious, offensive, predatory, rancorous **10** abominable, defamatory, diabolical, ill-humored, ill-natured, malevolent, pernicious, slanderous, villainous, vindictive **11** acrimonious, ill-tempered, treacherous **12** bloodthirsty

viciousness 4 evil **6** malice **7** cruelty **8** ferocity, savagery, villainy, violence **9** barbarity, brutality, ill nature **10** fierceness, wickedness **11** heinousness

vicissitude 6 change **8** mutation **9** variation **10** difficulty, mutability, succession **11** fluctuation

victim 4 butt, dead, dupe, gull, mark, pawn, prey, tool **5** patsy **6** pigeon, quarry, sucker, target **7** injured, wounded **8** casualty, fatality, innocent **9** scapegoat

victimize 3 con **4** dupe, gull, hoax **5** bully, cheat, cozen **6** betray, delude **7** deceive, defraud **8** hoodwink **9** bamboozle

victor 6 winner **8** champion, medalist **9** conqueror **10** vanquisher **11** prizewinner

Victoria, Queen
  realm: **13** British Empire
  House of: **7** Hanover
  Prince Consort: **6** Albert
  son; successor: **9** Edward VII

Victoria
  capital of: **8** Hong Kong **10** Seychelles

Victoria
  origin: **5** Roman
  goddess of: **7** victory
  corresponds to: **4** Nike

Victorian 4 prim, smug **6** narrow, proper, stuffy **7** insular, prudish **8** priggish **9** pietistic **10** tight-laced **11** puritanical, straitlaced **12** conventional, hypocritical **13** sanctimonious

victorious 7 winning **8** champion **10** conquering, successful, triumphant **11** vanquishing **12** championship, prizewinning

Victor Victoria
  director: **12** Blake Edwards
  cast: **10** Alex Karras **11** James Garner **12** Julie Andrews **13** Robert Preston **14** John Rhys-Davies **15** Lesley Ann Warren
  setting: **5** Paris

victory 7 laurels, success, the palm, triumph **8** conquest, the prize **9** supremacy **10** ascendancy **11** superiority
  god of: **3** Tyr
  goddess of: **4** Nike **8** Victoria

Victory
  author: **12** Joseph Conrad
  character: **4** Lena, Wang **5** Jonas, Pedro **8** Davidson **9** Axel Heyst, Schomberg **13** Martin Ricardo

victuals 4 chow, diet, eats, fare, feed, food, grub, meat **5** meals **6** fodder, forage, repast, stores, viands **7** cooking, cuisine, edibles, rations, vittles **8** supplies **9** groceries, provender **10** foodstuffs, provisions **11** comestibles, nourishment, refreshment

Vidal, Gore
  author of: **4** Burr **5** Kalki **6** Julian **8** Creation **16** Myra Breckinridge **18**

Eighteen-Seventy-Six, The Judgment of Paris **19** Visit to a Small Planet

Vidar
  origin: 12 Scandinavian
  father: 4 Odin **5** Othin
  killed: 6 Fenrir, Fenris

vide 3 see

vide ante 9 see before

vide infra 8 see below

videlicet 6 namely **11** that is to say
  abbreviation: 3 viz

vide post 8 see after **10** see further

vide supra 8 see above

vide ut supra 10 see as above **16** see as stated above

Vidor, King
  director of: 8 The Crowd **12** Stella Dallas, The Big Parade **16** Northwest Passage

vie 4 life **5** fight **6** strive **7** compete, contend, contest **8** be a rival, struggle, tilt with **9** challenge

Vienna
  airport: 9 Schwechat
  area: 11 Innere Stadt
  capital of: 7 Austria
  early name: 4 Wena **9** Vindobono
  German: 4 Wien
  landmark: 6 Prater **7** Hofburg **10** Stadtsoper **13** Saint Stephen's **15** Albertina Museum, Belvedere Palace **16** Historical Museum, Schonbrunn Palace
  river: 6 Danube
  ruler: 8 Hapsburg
  street: 11 Ringstrasse

Vientiane, Viengchan
  capital of: 4 Laos

vi et armis 20 with force and with arms

Vietnam
  other name: 5 Annam **15** French Indochina
  former colony of: 6 France
  capital: 5 Hanoi **6** Saigon
  largest city: 6 Saigon **13** Ho Chi Minh City
  others: 3 Hue, Ron **4** Ngai, Vinh **5** Dalat, Hoa Da, Hoian **6** Annhon, Cholon, Danang, Hongay **7** Bacninh, Cam Ranh, Caobang, Donghoi, Hoabinh, Namdinh, Quinhon, Songoan, Tayninh, Viettri, Vinhloi **8** Binhdinh, Haiphong, Nhatrang, Panthiet, Phan Rang, Quangtri, Quangyen, Thanhhoa, Vinhlong **9** Haiphoang, Longxuyen **11** Dienbienphu
  school: 3 Hue **5** Hanoi **9** Ho Chi Minh
  division: 5 Annam, North, South **6** Tonkin **11** Cochin China
  measure: 4 gang, phan, thon
  monetary unit: 2 xu **4** dong **7** piaster
  weight: 3 can, yet **4** uyen
  mountain: 6 Badinh, Badink **7** Nindhoa, Ninhhoa **8** Fansipan, Knontran, Ngoklinh, Ngoolink, Tchepone, Tcle-

pore **18** Annamese Cordillera
  highest point: 8 Fan Si Pan
  river: 2 Bo, Ca, Da, Lo, Ma **3** Chu, Gam, Koi, Red **4** Chay **5** Nhiha **6** Mekong **7** Dongnai
  sea: 10 South China
  physical feature:
    delta: 6 Mekong **8** Red River
    gulf: 4 Siam **6** Tonkin **7** Tonking **8** Thailand
    peninsula: 11 Indochinese
  people: 3 Hoa, Man, Meo, Tai, Tay **4** Cham, Kinh, Nung, Thai **5** Khmer, Malay, Muong **7** Chinese **8** Annamese, Annamite **9** Cambodian **10** montagnard, Vietnamese
    leader: 5 Le Loi **8** Le Duc Tho **9** Ho Chi Minh **11** Ngo Dinh Diem, Pham Van Doug, Phan Van Khai **12** Tran Duc Luong **14** Nguyen Van Thieu
  language: 3 Yue **4** Cham **5** Khmer, Rhade **6** French **7** Chinese, English **9** Cantonese **10** Vietnamese
  religion: 6 Cao Dai, Hoa Hao, Taoism **7** animism **8** Buddhism **12** Christianity, Confucianism **13** Roman Catholic
  place:
    ruins: 10 Nguyen tomb
  feature:
    army: 4 ARVN **5** COSVN **8** Communsi, Viet Cong, Viet Minh
    clothing: 5 ao dai
    new year: 3 Tet

view 3 eye, ken, see **4** gaze, look, note, peek, peep, scan **5** judge, scene, sight, study, vista, watch **6** behold, belief, gaze at, glance, look at, notion, regard, survey, take in, theory, vision **7** diorama, examine, explore, feeling, glimpse, inspect, observe, opinion, outlook, picture, scenery, thought, witness **8** attitude, consider, glance at, judgment, panorama, perceive, pore over, prospect **9** landscape, sentiment, spectacle **10** conception, conviction, scrutinize, think about **11** contemplate, perspective

view as 4 deem, hold **5** count, judge, think **6** regard **7** account, believe **8** consider, take to be **10** look upon as

viewpoint 4 bias, side **5** angle, slant **6** aspect, belief **7** feeling, opinion **8** attitude, position **9** sentiment **10** conviction, standpoint **11** orientation, perspective **12** vantage point **16** frame of reference

view with disfavor 7 condemn, dislike **8** object to **9** frown upon **10** disapprove, think ill of **13** look askance at, regard as wrong **14** discountenance **15** take exception to

view with horror 5 abhor **6** eschew **8** sicken at **9** abominate, shudder at **10** recoil from, shrink from

vif
  music: 6 lively

vigilance 4 care, heed **7** caution, concern **8** prudence **9** alertness, attention **10** precaution **11** carefulness, forethought, guardedness, heedfulness **12** cautiousness, watchfulness **14** circumspection

vigilant 4 wary **5** alert, chary **7** careful, guarded, heedful, on guard, prudent **8** cautious, watchful **9** attentive, observant, wide-awake **10** on one's toes, on the alert **11** circumspect, on one's guard **12** on the lookout, on the qui vive

vigor 3 pep, vim, zip **4** dash, elan, fire, zeal **5** ardor, drive, force, might, power, verve **6** energy, fervor, spirit **7** passion, stamina **8** haleness, strength, vitality, vivacity **9** animation, hardiness, intensity, vehemence **10** enthusiasm, liveliness, robustness **11** earnestness **12** forcefulness

vigorous 4 bold, hale **5** hardy, lusty, vital **6** active, ardent, brawny, lively, mighty, robust, strong, sturdy, virile **7** dynamic, intense, vibrant **8** forceful, muscular, powerful, spirited **9** assertive, energetic **10** aggressive

vigorously 4 hard **7** briskly, lustily **8** actively, cogently, forcibly, robustly, strongly, sturdily **9** with force **10** forcefully, powerfully **11** strenuously **13** energetically

Vigrid
  origin: 12 Scandinavian
  final battlefield of: 4 gods

Viking, viking 4 Dane **6** pirate **7** mariner **8** Norseman, Northman, searover **9** plunderer **12** Scandinavian
  boat: 8 long ship
  burial: 9 ship grave
  chieftain: 4 jarl
  exploration: 5 Italy, Spain **6** France, Russia **7** England, Germany, Iceland, Ireland, Vinland **9** Greenland
  famous: 4 Eric **8** Eirikson, Ericsson **10** Eric the Red **11** Leif Ericson
  governing council: 4 Ting **5** Thing **8** Folkmoot
  legend: 4 Edda, saga
  origin: 6 Norway, Sweden **7** Denmark, Finland
  warrior: 7 beserk **9** berserker
  writing: 4 rune

Vila
  capital of: 7 Vanuatu

vile 3 bad, low **4** base, evil, foul, lewd, mean, ugly **5** awful, gross, nasty **6** coarse, filthy, odious, sinful, smutty, sordid, vulgar, wicked **7** beastly, hateful, heinous, ignoble, immoral, obscene, vicious **8** depraved, shameful, shocking, wretched **9** abhorrent, degrading, execrable, invidious, loathsome, nefarious, obnoxious, offensive, perverted, repellent, repugnant, repulsive, revolting, salacious **10** abominable, degenerate, despicable, detestable, disgusting, iniquitous, unpleasant, villainous **11** disgraceful, foul mouthed, humiliating **12** contemptible **13** objectionable

vileness 4 evil **8** foulness, iniquity, villainy **9** depravity, nastiness **10** immorality, odiousness **11** degradation, heinousness, viciousness **12** wretchedness **13** offensiveness

Vili
origin: **12** Scandinavian
brother: **4** Odin **5** Othin

vilification 5 libel **7** calumny, slander **10** defamation **13** disparagement

vilifier 5 scold **6** carper, critic **7** reviler **9** backbiter

vilify 5 abuse **6** defame, revile **7** slander **8** bad-mouth, dis honor **9** criticize, disparage **14** inveigh against

vilifying 7 abusive **8** libelous **9** malignant **10** calumnious, defamatory, slanderous

villa, Villa 5 aldea, dacha **6** castle, Pancho **7** chateau, mansion **9** residence **13** coun try estate

village 4 burg **6** hamlet, suburb **8** hick town **9** smalltown **11** whistlestop **12** municipality

villain 3 cad, cur, rat **5** knave, louse, rogue **6** rascal, rotter, varlet **7** caitiff, stinker **8** evil doer, scalawag **9** miscreant, scoundrel **10** blackguard, malefactor **11** rapscallion **12** transgressor, wicked person **15** snake in the grass

villainous 4 base, evil, foul, vile **6** wicked **7** caddish, heinous **8** horrible, infamous **9** monstrous, nefarious **10** abominable, despicable, detestable, maleficent **12** blackguardly **13** reprehensible

villainy 4 evil **8** vileness **9** depravity, rascality **10** wickedness **11** viciousness, maleficence

Villa-Lobos, Heitor
born: **6** Brazil **12** Rio de Janeiro
composer of: **6** Choros **20** Bachianas Brasileiras

villein 4 carl, esne, serf **5** ceorl, churl, slave **6** drudge **7** bondman, peasant **9** bondwoman

Villon, Francois
author of: **9** The Legacy **16** Le grand testament, Le petit testament
quote: **25** Mais ou sont les neiges d'antan **31** But where are the snows of yesteryear

Villuppo
character in: **17** The Spanish Tragedy
author: **3** Kyd

vim 2 go **3** pep, zip **4** dash, fire, snap, zeal **5** ardor, drive, force, might, power, punch, verve, vigor **6** energy, fervor, spirit **7** passion, potency **8** strength, vitality, vivacity **9** animation, intensity, vehemence **10** enthusiasm, liveliness

vin, vino 4 wine

Vincentio
character in: **17** Measure for Measure
author: **11** Shakespeare

vincit omnia veritas 16 truth conquers all **22** truth conquers all things

vindicate 4 free **5** clear **6** acquit, assert, defend, excuse, uphold **7** absolve, bear out, bolster, justify, support **8** advocate, champion, maintain **9** discharge, exculpate, exonerate **11** corroborate **12** substantiate

vindication 6 excuse **7** apology, defense **11** explanation **13** justification

vindictive 6 bitter, malign **8** avenging, punitive, spiteful, vengeful **9** malicious **10** malevolent, revengeful **11** retaliative, retaliatory, unforgiving

vinegarish 4 acid, sour, tart **5** harsh **6** acidic, biting **7** acerbic, pungent **9** acidulous **10** astringent

vin ordinaire 12 ordinary wine **20** inexpensive table wine

vintage 3 era, old **4** aged, date, fine, rare **5** epoch, great, prime, prize **6** choice, period **7** ancient, antique **8** sterling, superior **9** excellent, out-of-date, wonderful **11** outstanding **12** old-fashioned

Viola (Cesario)
character in: **12** Twelfth Night
author: **11** Shakespeare

violate 4 rape **5** abuse, break **6** defile, invade, ravish **7** disobey, outrage, profane **8** dishonor, infringe, trespass **9** blaspheme, desecrate, disregard, trample on **10** contravene, transgress **12** encroach upon

violation 5 abuse **6** breach **8** trespass **9** sacrilege **10** defilement, infraction **11** desecration, dishonoring **12** encroachment, infringement **13** contravention, nonobservance, transgression

violence 4 fury, rage **5** force, might, power **6** impact **7** out rage **8** ferocity, savagery, severity **9** brutality, intensity, onslaught **10** bestiality, fierceness **11** desecration, profanation **13** ferociousness, physical force **16** bloodthirstiness

violent 3 hot **4** wild **5** cruel, fiery **6** brutal, fierce, insane, raging, savage, severe, strong, unruly **7** berserk, furious, intense, rampant **8** maniacal, vehement **9** explosive, ferocious, hotheaded, murderous, unbridled **10** passionate **11** full of force, intractable, tempestuous **12** ungovernable **14** uncontrollable

Violent Land, The
author: **10** Jorge Amado

violet 5 Viola
varieties: **3** dog, red **4** bush, pale, pine, rock, tree, wood **5** coast, cream, dame's, false, flame, green, marsh, pansy, sweet, water **6**

Alaska, alpine, Canada, garden, German, horned, plains, stream **7** African, English, Mexican, Olympic, Persian, redwood, scarlet, striped, two-eyed **8** bird-foot, crowfoot, dogtooth, florist's, hook-spur, Labrador, larkspur, Missouri, trailing **9** early blue, evergreen, ivy-leaved, marsh blue, sage brush, tall white **10** Australian, great basin, Philippine, sweet white, western dog, woolly blue, yellow wood **11** Alpine marsh, American dog, arrow-leaved, Confederate, downy yellow, early yellow, lance-leaved, long-spurred, northern bog, strap-leaved **12** eastern water, great-spurred, kidney-leaved, northern blue, smooth yellow **13** common African, Halberd-leaved, northern downy, northern white, purple prairie, southern coast, white dog-tooth, yellow prairie **14** primrose-leaved, triangle-leaved **16** California golden, large-leaved white **17** round-leaved yellow, western sweet white **18** western round-leaved

violin family
instruments: **3** kit **5** cello, rebec, viola **7** baryton **8** bass viol, lyra viol, violetta **10** hurdy-gurdy **11** viola d'a more, violoncello **12** tromba marina, viola pomposa **13** lira da braccio **14** violino piccolo **15** hardanger fiddle

viper 3 asp, boa **5** adder, krait **9** puff adder **10** copperhead, fer-de-lance **11** rattlesnake
group of: **4** nest

virago 3 nag **4** fury **5** harpy, scold, shrew, vixen **6** dragon, gorgon **7** she-wolf **8** battle-ax, fishwife, harridan **9** termagant, Xanthippe

Virbius
origin: **5** Roman
god of: **6** forest **7** hunting

Virchow, Rudolf
field: **8** medicine **9** pathology
nationality: **6** German
completed formulation of: **10** cell theory

Virgil see **8** Vergil

virgin 4 girl, lass, maid, Mary, pure **6** chaste, damsel, maiden, unused **7** unmixed **8** pristine **9** unalloyed, undefiled, unsullied, untouched **10** unpolluted **13** unadulterated **14** uncontaminated
constellation of: **5** Virgo

Virgin see **4** Mary

Virginia
abbreviation: **2** VA
nickname: **11** Old Dominion
capital: **8** Richmond
largest city: **7** Norfolk
others: **5** Galax, Luray, Salem **6** Marion **7** Bedford, Bristol, Emporia, Fairfax, Pulaski, Roanoke **8** Danville, Hopewell, Manassas, Staunton, St Al-

bans, Tazewell, Yorktown **9** Arlington, Lexington, Lynchburg **10** Alexandria, Appomattox, Petersburg, Portsmouth, Waynesboro, Winchester **11** Newport News **12** Hampton Roads, Martinsville, Williamsburg **13** Virginia Beach **14** Fredericksburg **15** Charlottesville

college: 3 Lee **7** Hampton, Madison, Radford **8** Longwood, Richmond, Virginia **10** Washington **11** Mary Baldwin, Old Dominion **13** Randolph Macon **14** Averett Hollins, Mary Washington, William and Mary

feature:

battle site: 7 Bull Run **8** Fair Oaks, Manassas, Richmond, Yorktown **10** Petersburg, Seven Pines, Wilderness **12** Spotsylvania **14** Fredericksburg **16** Chancellorsville

dam: 4 Kerr

historical site: 10 Monticello **11** Mount Vernon **12** Williamsburg **13** Stratford Hall

national monument: 26 George Washington Birthplace

national park: 10 Shenandoah **26** Colonial National Historical

tribe: 6 Saponi, Tutelo **7** Monacan **8** Manahoac, Meherrin, Nottaway, Pamunkey, Powhatan **9** Matchotic **10** Appomuttoc

people: 9 Henry Clay, John Rolfe, John Smith **10** Robert E Lee, Walter Reed **11** George Mason **12** John Marshall, Patrick Henry **13** Samuel Houston **14** Cyrus McCormick **15** Meriwether Lewis **17** Booker T Washington, Richard Evelyn Bird **18** Light-Horse Harry (Henry) Lee

lake: 4 Kerr **5** Smith

land rank: 11 thirty-sixth

mountain: 5 Cedar **6** Clinch, Elliot **8** Baldknob **9** Allegheny, Blueridge

highest point: 6 Rogers

physical feature:

bay: 10 Chesapeake

bridge: 7 Natural

caverns: 5 Luray

port: 7 Norfolk **8** Richmond **10** Portsmouth **11** Newport News

tunnel: 7 Natural

valley: 10 Shenandoah

president: 9 John Tyler **11** James Monroe **12** James Madison **13** Woodrow Wilson, Zachary Taylor **15** Thomas Jefferson **16** George Washington **20** William Henry Harrison

river: 3 Dan **4** York **5** James **7** Potomac, Rapidan, Roanoke **10** Appomattox, Shenandoah **12** Rappahannock

state admission: 5 tenth

state bird: 8 cardinal

state flower: 16 flowering dogwood

state motto: 17 Thus Ever To Tyrants

state song: 24 Carry Me Back to Old Virginia

state tree: 7 dogwood

Virginian, The

author: 10 Owen Wister

character: 5 Betsy, Randy, Steve **6** Shorty **7** Trampas **9** Molly Wood **10** Judge (Henry) Garth

cast: 8 Lee J Cobb **10** Gary Clarke, James Drury, Pippa Scott, Randy Boone **11** Doug McClure **12** Roberta Shore

setting: 11 Shiloh Ranch **16** Wyoming Territory

Virgin Mary

ingredient: 11 tomato juice

Virgin Soil

author: 12 Ivan Turgenev

Virgo

symbol: 6 virgin

planet: 7 Mercury

rules: 7 service

zodiac: 5 sixth

born: 6 August **9** September

virile 4 bold **5** brave, hardy, husky, lusty, macho, manly **6** brawny, heroic, manful, mighty, potent, robust, strong **7** valiant **8** fearless, forceful, muscular, powerful, resolute, stalwart, vigorous **9** audacious, masculine, masterful, strapping, undaunted **10** courageous **12** stouthearted

virtual 5 tacit **7** implied **8** implicit, indirect **9** essential, practical **11** substantial

virtually 8 in effect **9** in essence **11** essentially, in substance, practically **13** substantially **14** for the most part **23** for all practical purposes, to all intents and purposes

virtue 5 honor, value **6** purity, reward **7** benefit, decency, honesty, modesty, probity **8** chastity, goodness, morality, strength **9** advantage, good point, innocence, integrity, principle, rectitude, virginity **11** strong point, uprightness

virtuosity 7 mastery **8** artistry, wizardry **14** accomplishment

virtuoso 4 whiz **6** expert, genius, master, wizard **7** artiste, prodigy **10** master hand

virtuous 4 good, just, pure **5** moral **6** chaste, decent, modest **7** ethical, upright **8** innocent, laudable, virginal **9** continent, exemplary, honorable, righteous, unsullied **11** commendable, meritorious **12** praiseworthy **14** high-principled

virtuous person

Hebrew: 6 zaddik

Virtus

personifies: 7 courage

virtute et armis 15 by virtue and arms

motto of: 11 Mississippi

virulent 5 toxic **6** bitter, deadly, lethal, malign **7** harmful, hostile, hurtful, noxious, vicious **8** spiteful, venomous **9** injurious, malicious, poisonous, rancorous, resentful, unhealthy **10** malevolent, pernicious **11** acrimonious, deleterious

virus 3 bug **4** germ **7** microbe **11** computer bug **13** microorganism

vis 5 force, power **8** strength

visage 3 air **4** face, look, mien **5** image **6** aspect **7** profile **8** demeanor, features **9** semblance **10** appearance **11** countenance, physiognomy

vis-a-vis 8 eye to eye, together **9** in company, privately, tete-a-tete **10** face-to-face, side by side **11** as opposed to **12** in contrast to **14** as compared with, confidentially **19** as distinguished from

viscera 4 guts **6** bowels **7** innards, insides **8** entrails **10** intestines

visceral 3 gut **5** crude **6** earthy **11** instinctive

viscous 5 gluey, gooey, gummy, slimy, tacky, thick **6** sticky, syrupy, viscid **9** glutinous

Vishnu

in trinity of: 4 Siva **5** Shiva **6** Brahma

religion: 8 Hinduism

called: 9 Preserver

avatar: 7 Krishna

visibility 7 ceiling, clarity, horizon **10** definition, prominence **11** range of view **12** distinctness **14** perceptibility **15** conspicuousness, discernibleness

visible 4 open **5** clear, plain **6** in view, marked, patent **7** blatant, evident, glaring, in focus, in sight, obvious, pointed, salient, seeable **8** apparent, distinct, manifest, palpable, revealed **9** prominent **10** noticeable, observable, pronounced **11** conspicuous, discernible, inescapable, perceivable, perceptible, well-defined **12** unmistakable

vision 4 idea **5** dream, fancy, ghost, sight **6** notion **7** concept, fantasy, phantom, specter **8** daydream, eyesight, illusion **9** foresight **10** apparition, conception, perception, revelation **11** discernment, imagination **15** materialization

visionary 4 seer **6** dreamy, unreal, zealot **7** dreamer, fanatic, fancied, utopian **8** delusive, fanciful, idealist, illusory, romantic, theorist **9** imaginary, unfounded **10** chimerical, daydreamer, idealistic, starry-eyed **11** imaginative, impractical **13** insubstantial

visit 4 call, stay **5** haunt, smite **6** affect, assail, attack, befall, call on, punish **7** afflict, assault, go to see, sojourn **8** drop in on, frequent, happen to, look in on, stay with **9** sojourn at **10** be a guest of

visitant 5 alien **7** arrival, visitor

visitor 5 guest **6** caller **7** company,

tourist, tripper, voyager **8** traveler **9** journeyer, sightseer, sojourner, transient **10** houseguest, vacationer

vista **4** view **5** scene **6** vision **7** outlook, picture, scenery **8** panorama, prospect **9** landscape **11** perspective

visual **5** optic **6** ocular **7** optical, seeable, visible **9** for the eye **10** noticeable, observable, ophthalmic **11** perceptible

visualize **5** fancy, image **7** dream of, foresee, imagine, picture **8** envision **10** conceive of, daydream of **16** see in the mind's eye

vita **3** bio **6** resume **9** biography **13** autobiography **15** curriculum vitae

vital **4** life, live **5** alive, basic, chief, quick **6** lively, living, urgent, viable **7** animate, crucial, dynamic, primary, serious, vibrant **8** animated, cardinal, critical, existing, forceful, foremost, material, pressing, spirited, vigorous **9** breathing, energetic, essential, important, necessary, paramount, requisite, vivifying **11** fundamental, significant **13** indispensable

vitality **3** pep, vim, zip **4** zeal, zest **5** verve, vigor **6** energy **8** dynamism, strength, vivacity **9** animation, life force **10** ebullience, enthusiasm, exuberance, liveliness **13** animal spirits

vitalize **6** excite, vivify **7** animate, quicken **8** activate, energize **9** stimulate **10** invigorate, strengthen **11** bring to life

vital part **9** essential, necessity, requisite **10** key element, sine qua non **11** requirement

vital principle **5** blood **6** source **9** lifeblood **10** sine qua non

vitals **5** belly **6** bowels **10** intestines **11** vital organs **14** liver and lights

Vita Nuova
　　author: **14** Dante Alighieri

vitiate **3** mar **4** thin, undo, void **5** spoil, taint **6** blight, cancel, debase, defile, dilute, impair, infect, injure, poison, weaken **7** abolish, corrupt, pervert, pollute **8** sabotage **9** discredit, undermine **10** adulterate, depreciate, invalidate, make faulty, obliterate **11** contaminate

vitriolic **4** acid **5** acerb, nasty, sharp **6** biting **7** abusive, acerbic, caustic, cutting **8** sardonic, scathing **9** sarcastic, satirical, withering **11** acrimonious **13** hypercritical

vituperate **5** abuse **6** carp at, defame, malign, rail at, rebuke, revile, vilify **7** censure **9** castigate **10** speak ill of **14** inveigh against

vituperation **5** abuse, blame, scorn **6** insult, rebuke, tirade **7** censure, obloquy, slander **8** acrimony, scolding **9** invective **10** defamation, revilement, scurrility **11** castigation, deprecation

12 calumniation, denunciation, faultfinding, vilification **13** tongue-lashing

vituperative **5** harsh **7** abusive **8** scornful **9** insulting, maligning, vilifying **10** censorious, defamatory, scurrilous, slanderous **11** acrimonious, deprecatory

vivace
　　music: **5** quick **9** vivacious

vivacious **3** gay **5** jolly, merry, sunny, vital **6** active, bright, bubbly, cheery, genial, lively **7** buoyant **8** animated, bubbling, cheerful, spirited **9** convivial, ebullient, sparkling, sprightly **10** frolicsome, full of life **12** effervescent, lighthearted

vivacity **3** zip **4** dash, elan **5** gaity, verve, vigor **6** energy, spirit **8** buoyancy, vitality **9** animation **10** ebullience, liveliness **13** effervescence

Vivaldi, Antonio
　　born: **5** Italy **6** Venice
　　composer of: **10** Gloria Mass **14** L'Estro Armonico, The Four Seasons **16** Judith Triumphant **17** Juditha Triumphans, Le Quattro Stagioni **19** Harmonic Inspiration

viva voce **5** aloud **6** orally

Viva Zapata!
　　director: **9** Elia Kazan
　　cast: **10** Jean Peters **12** Anthony Quinn, Marlon Brando
　　Oscar for: **15** supporting actor (Quinn)
　　script: **13** John Steinbeck

vive **8** long live (whomever)
　　opposite: **4** a bas

vive valeque **15** live and keep well

Vivian
　　also: **16** The Lady of the Lake
　　character in: **16** Arthurian romance
　　lover: **6** Merlin

vivid **3** gay **4** deep, loud, rich **5** clear, shiny, showy **6** bright, florid, garish, lively, moving, strong **7** glowing, graphic, in tense, radiant, shining **8** colorful, definite, distinct, dramatic, emphatic, forceful, lifelike, luminous, lustrous, powerful, stirring, striking, true-life, vigorous **9** brilliant, effulgent, energetic, marvelous, memorable, pictorial, realistic **10** astounding, expressive, impressive, remarkable **11** astonishing, conspicuous, descriptive, inescapable, luminescent, picturesque, resplendent **12** unmistakable **13** extraordinary

vividness **9** intensity **10** brightness, brilliance

vivified **7** revived **8** animated, awakened **9** enlivened, quickened, vitalized **11** invigorated

vivify **6** revive, wake up **7** animate, enliven, quicken **8** vitalize **10** invigorate

vixen **4** fury **5** scold, shrew, witch **6**

virago **8** fishwife, harridan, spitfire **9** female fox, termagant

Vladimir
　　character in: **15** Waiting for Godot
　　author: **7** Beckett

Vlaminck, Maurice de
　　born: **5** Paris **6** France
　　artwork: **8** Red Trees, The Storm **15** Hamlet in the Snow, Winter Landscape **17** The Bridge at Chatou **18** Picnic in the Country, Street at Marly-le-Roi **21** Landscape with Red Trees

vocabulary **4** cant **5** argot, idiom, lingo, slang, style **6** jargon, patois, speech, tongue **7** dialect, lexicon **8** language, glossary, phrasing **9** word stock **10** vernacular **11** phraseology, terminology

vocal **4** open, oral, sung **5** blunt, frank, lyric **6** candid, choral, direct, spoken, voiced **7** uttered, voluble **8** operatic, viva-voce **9** outspoken, vocalized **10** forthright, of the voice **11** articulated, plainspoken

vocalize **3** air, say **4** sing, vent **5** speak, utter **7** express **9** ventilate **10** articulate **12** put into words

vocation **3** job **4** line, post, role, task **5** berth, field, stint, trade **6** career, estate, metier **7** calling, pursuit, station **8** business, lifework **9** situation **10** assignment, employment, line of work, occupation, profession

vocational **3** job **5** trade **6** career **9** technical **11** specialized **12** occupational

vociferate **4** howl, yell, yelp **5** shout, shout **6** bellow, clamor, cry out, holler, shriek, squeal **7** bluster, call out, exclaim, screech **9** ejaculate **11** make a racket **12** raise a rumpus

vociferation **3** cry **4** howl, yell, yelp **5** noise, shout **6** bellow, clamor, outcry, shriek, squeal, uproar **7** screech **11** ejaculation, exclamation

vociferous **4** loud **5** noisy, vocal **6** shrill **7** blatant **8** piercing, shouting, strident, vehement **9** clamorous, outspoken **10** boisterous, loud-voiced, uproarious **11** importunate

vodka
　　origin: **6** Poland, Russia
　　drink: **10** Moscow Mule **12** Cosmopolitan
　　with amaretto: **9** Godmother
　　with bouillon: **8** Bullshot
　　with cider: **15** Brewster Special
　　with Cognac: **7** Cossack
　　with cranberry juice: **10** Cape Codder
　　with creme de cacao: **7** Barbara **9** Ninotchka **11** Russian Bear **12** Velvet Hammer, White Russian
　　with curacao: **8** Aqueduct
　　with Galliano: **16** Harvey Wallbanger
　　with gin: **15** Russian Cocktail
　　with kahlua or Tia Maria: **12** Black

Russian
with kirsch: 12 Volga Boatman
with orange juice: 11 screwdriver
with tomato juice: 10 Bloody Mary
with vermouth: 8 Kangaroo **9** Corkscrew

vogue 3 fad **4** mode, rage **5** craze,
style, trend **6** custom **7** fashion **8** currency, practice, the thing **10** acceptance, popularity **11** the last word **12**
popular favor **14** the latest thing **15**
prevailing taste

voguish 4 chic **5** smart **6** modish **7**
faddish, stylish **11** fashionable

voice 3 air, say **4** alto, bass, part, role,
tone, vent, vote, will, wish **5** speak,
state, tenor, utter **6** choice, desire, option, reveal, singer, speech **7** declare,
divulge, express, opinion, singers, soprano **8** announce, baritone, delivery,
disclose, proclaim, vocalize **9** contralto, enunciate, pronounce, ventilate
10 articulate, intonation, modulation,
prefer ence, vocal sound **11** communicate **12** articulation, mezzo-soprano
13 participation, power of speech

voiceless 3 mum **4** deaf, mute, surd **6**
silent **7** anaudia, aphonic, spirate

voice of the people
Latin: 9 vox populi

void 4 bare, emit, free, null, pass **5** annul, blank, clear, drain, eject, empty,
purge **6** barren, cancel, devoid, recant, repeal, revoke, vacant, vacuum
7 abolish, drained, emptied, exhaust,
invalid, lacking, nullify, pour out, rescind, reverse, vacuity, wanting **8** depleted, evacuate, nugatory, renounce,
throw out **9** destitute, discharge, emptiness, exhausted, repudiate **10** empty
space, invalidate, not in force **11**
countermand, inoperative

voidance 7 voiding **8** ejection, emission **9** discharge, expulsion

Voight, Jon
born: 9 Yonkers NY
daughter: 13 Angelina Jolie
roles: 3 Ali **4** Heat **5** Holes **7** Joe
Buck **8** The Champ **9** Zoolander **10**
Coming Home (Oscar) **11** Deliverance, Pearl Harbor **12** The Rainmaker **13** The Odessa File **14** Catch
Twenty-Two, Midnight Cowboy **16**
National Treasure **17** Mission: Impossible **19** Lara Croft: Tomb Raider

voila 3 see **4** look **9** there it is

volatile 4 rash, wild **5** brash, giddy,
moody **6** fickle, fitful **7** erratic, flighty,
gaseous **8** eruptive, reckless, unstable,
unsteady, vaporous, variable **9** explosive, frivolous, mercurial, spasmodic,
unsettled **10** capricious, changeable,
evaporable, inconstant, irresolute,
vaporizing **12** undependable **13** temperamental, unpredictable

volition 4 will **6** choice, option **8**

choosing, decision, free will **10** discretion, resolution **13** determination

volley 5 burst, salvo **6** shower **7** barrage **8** outbreak, outburst **9** broadside,
discharge, fusillade **10** outpouring

Volpone (The Fox)
author: 9 Ben Jonson
character: 5 Celia, Mosca **7** Bonario,
Corvino, Voltore **9** Corbaccio, Peregrine **18** Lady Politic Would-Be, Lord
Politic Would-Be

Volsung
origin: 12 Scandinavian
mentioned in: 8 Volsunga
grandfather: 4 Odin **5** Othin
son: 7 Sigmund
daughter: 5 Signy

Volsunga
origin: 9 Icelandic **12** Scandinavian
form: 4 saga
time: 17 thirteenth century
subject: 8 Volsungs

Volta, Alessandro, Count
nationality: 7 Italian
invented: 15 electric battery
discovered: 10 methane gas

Voltaic
also: 3 Gur
language family: 16 Niger-
Kordofanian
group: 10 Niger-Congo
includes: 5 Mossi

Voltaire, Francois
real name: 19 Francois Marie Arouet
author of: 5 Zadig, Zaire **6** Alzire,
Merope **7** Candide, L'Ingenu,
Mahomet **11** The Henriade **16** The
Maid of Orleans **23** Philosophical
Dictionary
member of: 11 Philosophes

Volturnus
origin: 5 Roman
personifies: 4 wind **8** east wind **13**
southeast wind

voluble 4 glib **5** wordy **6** chatty, fluent
7 twining **8** effusive, flippant, rotating, twisting **9** garrulous, talkative **10**
loquacious

volume 4 book, bulk, heap, mass, size,
tome **5** folio, sound, tract **6** amount,
extent, quarto **7** measure **8** capacity,
loudness, quantity, treatise, vastness **9**
abundance, aggregate, magnitude,
monograph **10** dimensions

voluminous 5 ample, large **7** copious,
massive, sizable **8** abundant **9** extensive

Volund *see* **7** Wayland

voluntary 6 willed **8** free-will, intended, optional, unforced **10** deliberate **11** intentional, volunteered **13** discretionary, noncompulsory

volunteer 5 offer **6** extend, tender, unpaid **7** advance, present, proffer, recruit **8** enlistee **9** voluntary **10** put
forward **11** step forward **12** unpaid
worker **13** charityworker

Volunteer State
nickname of: 9 Tennessee

Voluptas
origin: 5 Roman
goddess of: 8 pleasure

voluptuary 4 rake, roue **7** epicure,
gourmet, seducer **8** gourmand, hedonist, sybarite **9** bon vivant, debauchee,
high liver, libertine, womanizer **10**
gastronome, sensualist **14** pleasure
seeker

voluptuous 4 soft **6** carnal, erotic,
sexual, smooth, wanton **7** fleshly,
lustful, sensual **8** sensuous **9** debauched, dissolute, luxurious, sybaritic **10** dissipated, hedonistic, lascivious, licentious, profligate **13** self-
indulgent **14** pleasure-loving **15**
pleasure-seeking

vomit 4 barf, emit, puke **5** eject, expel,
heave, retch **7** bring up, throw up,
upchuck **8** disgorge **9** discharge, spew
forth **10** belch forth **11** regurgitate **15**
toss one's cookies

Vonnegut, Kurt, Jr
author of: 8 Jailbird **9** Slapstick,
Timequake **10** Cat's Cradle, Palm
Sunday **11** Player Piano **18** Slaughterhouse Five **20** Breakfast of Champions **22** Happy Birthday Wanda
June

Von Sternberg, Josef
director of: 12 The Blue Angel

Von Sydow, Max
real name: 18 Carl Adolph von Sydow
born: 4 Lund **6** Sweden
roles: 12 The Emigrants **14** The Seventh Seal **15** The Virgin Spring **16**
Wild Strawberries **24** The Greatest
Story Ever Told

voracious 6 greedy **7** hoggish **8** edacious, ravenous **10** gluttonous, insatiable, omnivorous

vortex 4 eddy **7** cyclone, twister **9**
maelstrom, whirlpool, whirlwind

votary 3 fan **4** buff **6** zealot **7** admirer,
devotee, fanatic, habitue **8** adherent,
champion, disciple, follower, partisan
10 aficionado, enthusiast **11** afficionado

vote 3 say **4** poll **5** voice **6** ballot,
choice, option, ticket **8** approval, decision, election, judgment, suffrage **9**
franchise, selection **10** plebiscite, preference, referendum **11** cast a ballot
13 determination

vouch 4 back **6** affirm, attest, back up,
uphold, verify **7** certify, confirm, endorse, support, sustain, swear to, warrant, witness **8** attest to, maintain **9**
guarantee **11** corroborate **12** authenticate

voucher 4 chip, chit **5** check, proof **6**
surety, ticket **7** receipt, warrant **8**
warranty **9** affidavit, debenture **10**

credential **11** certificate **12** verification **14** authentication

vouchsafe 4 give **5** allow, deign, favor, grant **6** bestow, convey, tender **7** concede **10** condescend

vow 4 oath, word **5** swear, troth, vouch **6** affirm, assert, assure, parole, pledge, plight, stress **7** declare, promise, resolve **8** contract **9** emphasize **11** word of honor **13** solemn promise

vox populi 14 popular opinion **16** voice of the people

voyage 4 sail **6** cruise **7** passage **8** crossing, navigate **9** ocean trip **10** sea journey

Voyage of the Beagle, The
  author: 13 Charles Darwin

voyager 5 rover **7** cruiser, pilgrim, rambler, tourist **8** traveler, wayfarer **9** jet-setter, journeyer, sightseer **10** adventurer **12** excursionist, globe-trotter, peregrinator **13** world traveler

Voyage to the Bottom of the Sea
  character: 6 Doctor **8** Kowalsky, Stu Riley, (Cdr/Capt) Lee Crane **9** Patterson **10** (Lt Cdr) Chip Morton **11** (Chief Petty Officer) Curley Jones **12** Chief Sharkey **14** (Adm) Harriman Nelson
  cast: 9 Allan Hunt, Del Monroe **10** Henry Kulky, Paul Trinka **11** Richard Bull, Terry Becker **12** David Hedison **13** Robert Dowdell **15** Richard Basehart
  submarine: 7 Seaview
  explorer: 7 Sea Crab
  mini-sub: 10 Flying Fish

Vronsky, Count Alexei
  character in: 12 Anna Karenina
  author: 7 Tolstoy

Vulcan
  origin: 5 Roman
  god of: 4 fire **12** metalworking
  epithet: 8 Mulciber
  corresponds to: 10 Hephaestus, Hephaistos

vulgar 3 low **4** base, rude **5** crude, dirty, gross, rough **6** coarse, common, filthy, ribald, risque, smutty **7** boorish, ill-bred, lowbrow, obscene, uncouth **8** impolite, indecent, off-color, ordinary, plebeian **9** offensive, tasteless, unrefined **10** suggestive **11** ill-mannered, proletarian **12** pornographic, uncultivated

vulgarian 3 oaf **4** boor, lout **5** brute, yahoo **7** Babbitt **9** ignoramus **10** philistine **16** anti-intellectual

vulgarity 8 bad taste, rudeness **9** crudeness, grossness, indecency, indecorum, obscenity **10** coarseness, ill manners, indelicacy, smuttiness **11** boorishness, pornography **12** impoliteness **13** tastelessness

vulnerable 4 weak **7** exposed **8** helpless, insecure **9** sensitive, unguarded **10** easily hurt, undefended **11** defenseless, susceptible, thin-skinned, unprotected

Vye, Eustacia
  character in: 17 Return of the Native
  author: 5 Hardy

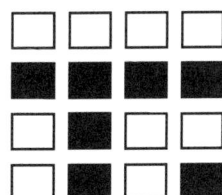

wacky, whacky 3 odd **4** nuts **5** crazy, kooky **6** cuckoo, insane, kookie **7** cracked, foolish, touched **9** eccentric, senseless **10** irrational **12** crack-brained

wad 3 bat, pad **4** cram, head, heap, lump, mass, tuft **5** money, stuff **6** bundle, riches, stop up **7** fortune **8** bankroll, plumbago

waddle 3 wag **4** sway **6** hobble, toddle, totter, wobble

wade 4 ford, plod, plow, toil, trek **5** labor **6** drudge, trudge **9** walk in mud **11** walk in water

wafer 4 chip **5** candy, flake **6** cookie **7** cracker **15** unleavened bread

waft 4 blow, puff **5** drift, float

wag 3 bob, wit **4** card, move, stir, wave **5** clown, droll, flick, joker, shake **6** jester, jiggle, switch, twitch, waggle, wiggle, wigwag **7** buffoon, farceur, flicker, flutter **8** comedian, humorist, jokester **9** oscillate **11** wisecracker **14** life of the party

wage 3 fee, pay **6** income, salary **7** carry on, conduct, payment, revenue, stipend **8** earnings, engage in, maintain, practice **9** emolument, undertake **10** recompense **12** compensation, remuneration

wage earner 6 worker **8** employee **9** job holder **12** hourly worker

wager 4 bet, pot **5** ante, pool, risk **5** fancy, guess, stake **6** assume, gamble, hazard **7** imagine, jackpot, presume, suppose, surmise, venture **8** make a bet, theorize **9** speculate **10** conjecture, take a flyer **11** speculation, try one's luck **12** tempt fortune **15** hazard an opinion

wages 3 bet, fee, pay **4** gage, hire **6** fights, reward, return, salary **7** engages, payment, stipend **8** conducts, earnings **9** emolument **10** prosecutes, recompense **12** remuneration

wage war 5 fight **6** combat **7** contend, make war **8** do battle **12** march against

waggery 5 chaff **6** banter, riding **7** joshing, kidding, ragging, ribbing **8** chaffing, drollery, raillery, twitting **French: 8** badinage

waggish 5 droll, funny **7** comical, puckish **8** humorous

waggle 4 wave **5** wield **8** brandish

Wagner, Honus
  real name: 15 John Peter Wagner
  nickname: 14 Flying Dutchman
  sport: 8 baseball
  position: 9 shortstop
  team: 17 Pittsburgh Pirates

Wagner, Richard
  born: 7 Germany, Leipzig
  composer of: 5 Faust **6** Rienzi **7** Die Feen **8** Parsifal **9** Lohengrin **10** Tannhauser, The Fairies **14** Siegfried Idyll **16** The Mastersingers, Tristan and Isolde, Wesendonck Lieder **17** The Flying Dutchman **20** Der Ring des Nibelungen, The Ring of the Nibelungs **27** Die Meistersinger von Nurnberg
    the Ring Cycle Part 1: 12 Das Rheingold, The Rhine Gold
    the Ring Cycle Part 2: 10 Die Walkure **11** The Valkyrie
    the Ring Cycle Part 3: 9 Siegfried
    the Ring Cycle Part 4: 15 Gotterdammerung **17** Twilight of the Gods

Wagner, Robert
  born: 9 Detroit MI
  wife: 11 Natalie Wood
  roles: 6 Switch **10** Hart to Hart **12** Austin Powers **13** It Takes a Thief, Prince Valiant, The Longest Day **24** All the Fine Young Cannibals

wagon 3 car, van **4** cart, dray, tram, wain **5** coach, lorry, tonga, truck **7** caisson **10** automobile, battleship
  covered: 15 prairie schooner
  maker: 10 wainwright
  police: 10 Black Maria
  Russian: 6 telega
  sideless: 6 rolley
  track: 3 rut

Wagon Train
  character: 9 Bill Hawks **11** Barnaby West, Cooper Smith, Duke Shannon **14** Charlie Wooster, Major Seth Adams **15** Christopher Hale, Flint McCullough
  cast: 8 Ward Bond **11** Scott Miller, Terry Wilson **12** Frank McGrath, John McIntire, Michael Burns, Robert Fuller, Robert Horton

waif 5 gamin, stray **6** gamine, urchin **7** mudlark **9** foundling **10** ragamuffin, street arab **11** guttersnipe **13** homeless child **14** tatterdemalion

wail 3 cry **4** bawl, howl, keen, moan, roar, weep, yell **5** groan, shout, whine **6** bellow, bemoan, bewail, cry out, lament, outcry, plaint **7** keening, moaning, wailing **9** caterwaul **10** rend the air **11** lamentation

waist 3 top **5** shirt **6** blouse, bodice, middle **7** midriff **9** mid-region, waistband, waistline **10** middle part, midsection, shirtwaist

waistband 4 belt, sash **5** cinch **6** girdle

waistcoat 4 vest **5** benjy **6** jacket, jerkin, veskit, vestee, weskit **7** singlet **French:** gilet

wait 4 halt, stay, stop **5** dally, delay, pause, tarry **6** linger, put off **7** suspend **8** postpone, stopover **9** deferment **10** suspension **11** continuance **12** postponement

wait for 6 expect **10** anticipate

Waiting for Godot
  author: 13 Samuel Beckett
  character: 8 Estragon, Vladimir

wait on 5 serve **6** assist, attend

waive 4 stay **5** defer, forgo, let go, table, yield **6** give up, not use, put off, shelve **7** forbear, lay over **8** disclaim, forswear, postpone, renounce **9** surrender

waiver 9 dismissal **10** abdication, disclaimer **11** abandonment **12** renunciation **14** relinquishment

wake 4 fire, path, stir, wash **5** rally, rouse, trail, train, vigil **6** arouse, course, excite, kindle, revive **7** enliven, provoke, quicken **8** backwash **9** galvanize, stimulate **11** resuscitate

wakeful 4 wary **5** alert, astir **7** careful, heedful **8** cautious, restless, vigilant, watchful **9** insomniac, observant, sleepless **10** unsleeping **11** circumspect

wake up 4 rise **5** arise **6** vivify **7** animate, enliven **8** vitalize **9** stimulate

Walcott, Joe
  real name: 18 Arnold Raymond Cream
  nickname: 9 Jersey Joe
  sport: 6 boxing
  class: 11 heavyweight

Walden, or Life in the Woods
  author: 17 Henry David Thoreau

Wales
  other name: 5 Cymru **7** Cambria
  part of: 13 United Kingdom

title of British heir apparent: 13
Prince of Wales
capital: 7 Cardiff
cities: 4 Rhyl, Ross **5** Flint, Towyn **6**
Amlwch, Bangor, Brecon, Sidney **7**
Cwmbran, Herford, Newport, Rhon-
dda, Swansea **8** Aberdare, Caerleon,
Holyhead, Pembroke **9** Fishguard,
Glamorgan **10** Caernarvon, Caerphilly, Carmarthen **11** Aberystwyth
12 Milford Haven **13** Kidderminster,
Merthyr-Tydfil
division: 5 Clwyd, Dyfed, Flint,
Gwent, Powys **6** Radnor **7** Denbigh,
Gwynedd **8** Anglesey, Cardigan,
Monmouth, Pembroke **9** Brecknoch,
Glamorgan, Merioneth **10** Caernarvon, Carmarthen, Montgomery
emblem: 4 leek
government: 29 constituent part of
Great Britain
measure: 5 cover **7** cantred, crannoc,
listred
island: 4 Mona **5** Caldy **8** Anglesey,
Holyhead
lake: 4 Bala **6** Vyrnwy
mountain: 6 Berwyn **8** Cambrian **9**
Prescelly **13** Brecon Beacons
highest point: 7 Snowdon
river: 3 Dee, Usk, Wye **4** Alun, Taff,
Tawe, Teme, Towy **5** Clwyd, Conwy,
Dovey, Neath, Teifi **6** Conway, Severn, Vyrnwy
sea: 5 Irish **8** Atlantic
physical feature:
  bay: 7 Swansea **8** Cardigan, Tremadoc, Tremadog
  channel: 7 Bristol **9** St George's
  hills: 7 Malvern
  peninsula: 5 Lleyn
  strait: 5 Menai
  valley: 7 Rhondda
people: 4 Celt, Kelt **5** Cymry, Kymry,
Welsh **7** Brython, Silures, Taffies **8**
Awabokal, Cambrian **9** Siluridan
  actor: 6 Burton **8** Williams **13**
  Richard Burton, Emlyn Williams
  artist: 4 John
  author: 3 Map **5** Jones, Lewis,
  Mapes, Parry **6** Machan, Thrale **9**
  Llewellyn **11** Dylan Thomas **14**
  Dafydd ap Gwylym
  god: 3 Deu, Dew **4** Bran, Gwyn **5**
  Dylan **7** Gwydion
  leader: 5 Bevan **6** Rhodri **8** Hywel
  Dwa **11** Cadwallader **12** Bishop
  Morgan **13** Owen Glendower **16**
  David Lloyd George **18** Llewelyn
  ap Gruffydd
language: 5 Welsh **6** Celtic, Cymric,
Keltic, Kymric **7** Cymraeg, English
religion: 8 Anglican **9** Methodist **10**
Protestant **12** Presbyterian
place:
  bridge: 6 Severn
  castle: 6 Conway **7** Harlech **9**
  Beaumaris **10** Caernarvon, Caerphilly **11** Aberystwyth

feature:
  festival: 10 Eisteddfod
  stories: 10 Mabinogion
food:
  dish: 8 flummery
Walesa, Lech
  award: 10 Nobel Peace
  born: 6 Poland
  leader of: 10 Solidarity
  political office: 7 premier
wander aimlessly 5 amble, stray **6**
ramble, stroll **7** meander, saunter
wandering 5 lapse **8** rambling, straying **9** deviation **10** aberration, digressive, discursive, maundering, meandering, roundabout **11** abnormality **12**
idiosyncrasy **13** nonconformity **14** circumlocutory
Wanderings
  author: 10 Chaim Potok
wane 3 ebb **4** fade, sink **5** abate,
droop, waste **6** ebbing, fading, lessen,
weaken, wither **7** abating, decline,
dwindle, subside **8** decrease, diminish, fade away **9** dwindling, lessening,
recession, subsiding, weakening, withering
wangle 4 worm **5** trick **6** jockey,
scheme **7** finagle, wheedle **8** engineer,
intrigue, maneuver **9** machinate **10**
manipulate
wanness 6 pallor **8** grayness, paleness
9 ashenness **10** sallowness, sickliness
13 colorlessness
want 4 hunt, lack, need, seek, wish **5**
covet, crave, fancy **6** dearth, demand,
desire, hunger, penury **7** be needy,
craving, hope for, long for, paucity,
pine for, poverty, require, wish for **8**
scarcity, shortage, yearn for, yearning
9 indigence, necessity, pauperism, privation, requisite **10** deficiency, insolvency **11** destitution, requirement **13**
impecuniosity, insufficiency, pennilessness **14** impoverishment
Wanted: Dead or Alive
  character: 11 Josh Randall
  cast: 12 Steve McQueen
  job: 12 bounty hunter
  gun: 8 Mare's Leg
wanting 5 short **6** absent **7** lacking,
missing **9** defective, deficient, imperfect **10** inadequate **11** substandard **12**
insufficient
wanton 4 bawd, fast, jade, lewd, rake,
roue, slut, tart **5** gross, hussy, loose,
satyr, whore **6** chippy, harlot, lecher
7 bestial, immoral, lustful, obscene,
seducer, trollop, willful **8** careless,
heedless, mindless, needless, strumpet, sybarite, unchaste **9** abandoned,
adulterer, concubine, debauched, debauchee, dissolute, lecherous, libertine,
malicious, senseless, womanizer **10**
deliberate, fornicator, groundless, licentious, malevolent, profligate,
prostitute, sensualist, unprovoked, vo-

luptuary **11** fornicatrix, promiscuous,
unjustified, whoremaster **13** inconsiderate, irresponsible
wapiti 3 elk **4** deer **11** American elk
  female: 3 cow
  literally: 9 white rump
  male: 4 bull
  species: 16 Cervus canadensis
Wapshot Chronicle
  author: 11 John Cheever
war 5 clash, fight **6** attack, battle, combat, invade **7** contend **8** conflict,
fighting, struggle **10** opposition **11**
hostilities
  god of: 4 Ares, Odin **5** Othin **8** Quirinus
  goddess of: 4 Enyo **6** Athena,
  Athene, Inanna, Ishtar, Pallas, Saitis
  7 Bellona, Mylitta **11** Tritogeneia **12**
  Pallas Athena **18** Alalcomenean
  Athena
War and Peace
  author: 10 Leo Tolstoy
  character: 7 Kutuzov **8** Napoleon **13**
  Natasha Rostov, Nikolay Rostov, Pierre Bezuhov **14** Anatole Kuragin **15**
  Andrey Bolkonsky **19** Ellen Kuragin
  Bezuhov **22** Princess Marya Bolkonsky
War and Remembrance
  author: 10 Herman Wouk
warble 4 lump, purl, sing **5** carol,
larva, trill, tumor, yodel **6** growth,
quaver, ripple **7** twitter, vibrate, whistle
war cry 6 slogan **8** Geronimo
ward 4 zone **5** avert, block, repel **6**
charge, thwart **7** beat off, fend off,
prevent, quarter **8** pavilion, precinct,
stave off, turn away **9** dependent,
forestall
  French: 7 protege
warden 5 guard **6** keeper, ranger, sentry **7** curator, manager **8** guardian,
watchman **9** protector **14** superintendent
ward off 5 avert **7** prevent
wardrobe 4 togs **5** chest **6** attire,
closet, outfit **7** apparel, clothes **8**
clothing, garments **10** cedar chest **12**
clothespress
  French: 6 bureau **7** armoire, commode **10** chiffonier **11** habillement
wares 4 line **5** stock **7** staples **8** supplies **9** inventory **11** commodities,
merchandise
warfare 5 fight **6** battle, combat **8**
conflict, fighting **11** hostilities
Warhol, Andy
  born: 14 Philadelphia PA
  artwork: 9 Brillo Box, Liz Taylor **13**
  Marilyn Monroe **16** Campbell's Soup
  Can **20** Green Coca-Cola Bottles
  protegee: 12 Edie Sedgwick
wariness 7 caution **9** alertness, suspicion, vigilance **11** carefulness, guard-

edness, heedfulness **12** watchfulness **14** circumspection

warlike 7 hostile, martial, valiant **8** inimical, militant, military **9** bellicose, combative **10** unfriendly **11** belligerent, contentious, threatening
Indian: 8 Arapahoe

warlike attitude 9 hostility, pugnacity **11** bellicosity **12** belligerence, belligerency **13** combativeness **14** aggressiveness

warm 3 hot **4** cook, heat, kind, melt, thaw **5** cheer, happy, sunny, tepid, vivid **6** bright, heated, heat up, joyful, joyous, kindly, lively, loving, simmer, tender **7** affable, cordial, earnest, fervent, glowing, intense **8** animated, cheerful, friendly, gracious, outgoing, pleasant, spirited, vehement, vigorous **9** brilliant **10** passionate **11** kindhearted, sympathetic **12** affectionate, enthusiastic **13** compassionate, tenderhearted

warmhearted 4 kind **6** genial, kindly, loving **7** cordial **10** solicitous **11** sympathetic **12** affectionate **13** compassionate

warm-hued 3 red **4** rosy **5** ruddy, vivid **6** golden, orange, yellow **7** crimson, roseate, scarlet **8** blushing

warmish 5 tepid **7** cooling

warm oneself 4 bask **12** soak up warmth, toast oneself

warmth 3 joy **4** fire, heat, zeal **5** ardor, cheer, verve, vigor **6** fervor, spirit **7** hotness, passion **8** kindness, sympathy **9** animation, happiness, intensity, vehemence **10** affability, compassion, cordiality, enthusiasm, excitement, joyfulness, kindliness, liveliness, lovingness, tenderness **11** earnestness **12** cheerfulness, friendliness, graciousness **15** kindheartedness **17** tenderheartedness

warn 5 alert **6** advise, inform, notify, signal **7** apprise, caution, counsel **8** admonish

warning 4 hint, omen, sign **5** alarm, token **6** advice, notice, signal **7** portent, presage **8** apprisal **9** foretoken **10** intimation **12** notification

War of the Worlds, The
author: 7 H G Wells
invasion by: 8 Martians
radio broadcast: 11 Orson Welles
director:
    1953: 11 Byron Haskin
    2005: 15 Steven Spielberg
cast:
    1953: 9 Gene Barry (Clayton Forrester) **11** Ann Robinson (Sylvia Van Buren), Les Tremayne (General Mann)
    2005: 9 Tom Cruise (Ray Ferrier) **10** Tim Robbins (Harlan Ogilvy) **13** Dakota Fanning (Rachel), Justin Chatwin (Robbie)

war of words 7 dispute, quarrel **8** argument **11** altercation, controversy **12** disagreement

warp 4 bend, bent, bias **5** quirk, twist **6** debase, deform, infect **7** contort, corrupt, distort, leaning, mislead, pervert **8** misguide, misshape, tendency **9** prejudice, proneness **10** contortion, distortion, partiality, proclivity, propensity **11** deformation, disposition, inclination **14** predisposition

warrant 3 vow **4** aver, avow **5** swear **6** affirm, assert, assure, attest, permit, pledge **7** certify, declare, justify, license, promise **9** authorize, guarantee **10** asseverate, permission **13** authorization

warranty 6 pledge **9** agreement **11** certificate

Warren, Robert Penn
    author of: 5 Flood **7** Audubon **8** Promises **11** Now and Then **12** Incarnations **14** All the King's Men **18** World Enough and Time
    member of: 12 the Fugitives

warring 7 hostile **8** battling, clashing, fighting, opposing **9** combatant **10** contending **11** belligerent, conflicting, contentious

warrior 7 fighter, soldier, veteran **9** combatant, man-at-arms **10** campaigner **11** legionnaire

Warsaw
    area: 11 Stare Miasto
    capital of: 6 Poland
    landmark: 14 Kazimierzowski **25** Palace of Culture and Science
    Polish: 8 Warszawa
    river: 7 Vistula
    square: 5 Rynek

warship 5 Maine, U-boat **6** corvet **7** Alabama, cruiser, frigate, gunboat, Monitor **8** Bismarck, corvette, Graf Spee, ironclad, man-of-war **9** destroyer, ironsides, Merrimack, submarine **11** dreadnought, torpedo boat **12** Constitution, Old Ironsides **13** Constellation **15** aircraft carrier **16** superdreadnought
    fleet: 6 armada
    part: 6 turret
    plating: 5 armor

wary 5 alert **7** careful, guarded, heedful, mindful, prudent, wakeful **8** cautious, discreet, vigilant, watchful **10** suspicious **11** circumspect

wash 3 mop, rub, wet **4** bath, lave, soak, swab, wipe **5** bathe, clean, float, flood, rinse, scour, scrub **6** drench, shower, sponge **7** cleanse, immerse, launder, laundry, moisten, mopping, shampoo **8** ablution, cleaning, inundate, irrigate, lavation, scouring **9** cleansing **10** laundering

washbasin 3 tub **4** bowl **5** laver **6** lavabo **8** lavatory

washed out 4 drab, dull, pale **5**
dingy, faded, white **6** dreary, grayed **8** bleached **9** colorless

washed up, washed-up 4 lost, shot **6** bathed, broken, ruined, undone **7** done for, preened, through **8** bankrupt, done with, fatigued, finished, scrubbed **9** played out, showered

washing 6 laving **7** bathing, laundry, purging, rinsing, soaking **8** cleaning, scouring **9** ablutions, drenching, scrubbing, showering **10** laundering, shampooing

Washington
    abbreviation: 2 WA **4** Wash
    nickname: 7 Chinook **9** Evergreen
    capital: 7 Olympia
    largest city: 7 Seattle
    others: 4 Omak **5** Pasco **6** Renton, Tacoma, Yakima **7** Ephrata, Everett, Hoquiam, Othello, Pullman, Spokane **8** Aberdeen, Bellevue, Longview, Puyallup, Richland **9** Anacortes, Bremerton, Kennewick, Vancouver, Wenatchee **10** Bellingham, Burlington, Walla Walla **11** Port Angeles
    college: 7 Gonzaga, Seattle, Whitman **9** Evergreen, Whitworth **10** Puget Sound, Washington **14** Seattle Pacific **15** Pacific Lutheran
    feature:
        dam: 10 Bonneville, **11** Grand Coulee
        fort: 5 Lewis
        national park: 7 Olympic **12** Mount Rainier **13** North Cascades
        tribe: 3 Hoh **5** Lummi, Makah, Twana **6** Cayuse, Samish, Skagit, Yakima **7** Chinook, Clallam, Clatsop, Cowlitz, Dwamish, Nooksak, Palouse, Quaitso, Sanpoil, Spokane, Squaxon, Tulalip **8** Chehalis, Chimakum, Colville, Nespelim, Nez Perce, Okanagon, Pishquow, Puyallup, Quileute, Quinault, Sahaptin, Salishan, Sinkiuse **9** Nisqually, Quinaielt, Semiahmoo, Skokomish, Swinomish **10** Senijextee, Shoalwater **11** Shahaptaine
    people: 7 Seattle **10** Bing Crosby **11** Hank Ketcham **12** Elisha P Ferry **13** Marcus Whitman **15** William O Douglas **19** Isaac Ingalls Stevens
        explorer: 4 Cook, Gray **6** Heceta **9** Vancouver **13** Lewis and Clark
    lake: 4 Soap **5** Moses, Union **6** Chelan, Ozette **7** Cle Elum, Cushman, Kachess **8** Crescent, Quinault **9** Keechelus, Wenatchee **10** Washington
    land rank: 9 twentieth
    mountain: 4 Blue, Jack, Tunk **5** Adams, Baker, Lemei, Logan, Moses, Sloan **6** Kettle, Quartz, Simcoe, Stuart **7** Shuksan **8** Cascades, Olympics, St Helens **11** Kettle River
        highest point: 7 Rainier
    physical feature:
        falls: 10 Snoqualmie
        port: 6 Tacoma **7** Everett, Seattle

10 Bellingham
sound: 5 Puget **7** Rosario
river: 5 Snake, White **6** Yakima **7**
Spokane **8** Columbia, Quinault **9**
Snohomish **10** Snoqualmie **11** Pend
Oreille
state admission: 11 forty-second
state bird: 15 willow goldfinch
state fish: 14 steelhead trout
state flower: 17 coast rhododendron
19 western rhododendron
state motto: 7 By and By (Alki)
state song: 16 Washington My Home
state tree: 14 western hemlock

Washington, George
nickname: 18 Father of His Country
presidential rank: 5 first
party: 10 Federalist
state represented: 2 VA
elected: 11 unanimously
vice president: 5 (John) Adams
cabinet:
state: 9 (Thomas) Jefferson
treasury: 8 (Alexander) Hamilton
war: 4 (Henry) Knox **7** (James)
McHenry **9** (Timothy) Pickering
attorney general: 3 (Charles) Lee
8 (Edmund Jennings) Randolph,
(William) Bradford
born: 2 VA **9** Wakefield **18** Westmoreland County
died/buried: 11 Mount Vernon
religion: 12 Episcopalian
interests: 7 fishing, hunting, theater
17 scientific farming
vacation: 11 Mount Vernon
political career: 9 president **16** House
of Burgesses **24** First Continental
Congress **25** Second Continental
Congress
signed: 12 Constitution
civilian career: 6 farmer **8** surveyor
military service:
war: 13 Revolutionary **15** French
and Indian
notable events of lifetime/term: 18
American Revolution
crossed: 13 Delaware River
rebellion: 7 Whiskey
winter at: 11 Valley Forge
father: 9 Augustine
mother: 4 Mary (Ball)
siblings: 5 Betty **6** Samuel **7** Charles,
Mildred **13** John Augustine
half-brother: 6 Butler **8** Lawrence
9 Augustine
half-sister: 4 Jane
wife: 6 Martha (Dandridge Custis)
children:
stepchildren: 15 John Parke Custis
17 Martha Parke Custis

Washington DC
airport: 6 Dulles **8** National
baseball team: 9 Nationals
basketball team: 7 Mystics, Wizards
capital of: 12 United States
designed by: 7 L'Enfant
football team: 8 Redskins

hockey team: 8 Capitals
landmark: 4 Mall **7** Capitol, Ellipse **8**
Pentagon **10** White House **11** National Zoo **12** Ford's Theatre, Franklin Park, Supreme Court **13** Lafayette
Park, Rock Creek Park **14** Farragut
Square, Reflecting Pool, Watergate
Hotel **15** Lincoln Memorial, McPher-
son Square **16** National Archives **17**
Jefferson Memorial, Library of Congress, National Arboretum **18** Washington Monument **21** Frederick
Douglass Home, Robert F Kennedy
Stadium **22** Smithsonian Institution
23 National Sculpture Garden **25** Arlington National Cemetery **33** Kennedy Center for the Performing Arts
museum: 5 Freer **7** Renwick **8** Corcoran **9** Hirshhorn **10** African Art **11**
Smithsonian **13** Dumbarton Oaks **15**
National Gallery **17** Folger Shakespeare **18** Phillips Collection **23** National Portrait Gallery
river: 7 Potomac **9** Rock Creek
street/avenue: 4 Ohio **7** New York,
Potomac **12** Constitution, Independence, Pennsylvania **13** Massachusetts
university: 6 Howard **8** American,
Catholic **10** Georgetown **11** George
Mason **16** George Washington

Washington Square
author: 10 Henry James

wash one's hands of 4 deny, quit **6**
give up **7** abandon, decline, disavow,
forsake **8** abnegate, cast away, disclaim, forswear, renounce **9** repudiate
10 relinquish

washout 6 fiasco, fizzle **7** failure, letdown **8** disaster **14** disappointment

wash out 4 fade, fail **6** bleach **7** deplete, fatigue **8** enervate, enfeeble **10**
debilitate, devitalize

wasp 5 vespa **6** vespid
variety: 5 paper **6** cuckoo, ensign,
hornet, potter, spider **12** yellow
jacket

waspish 5 huffy, testy **6** crabby,
cranky, ornery, shirty **7** bearish, fretful, peevish, pettish **8** petulant, snappish **9** crotchety, fractious, irascible,
irritable, querulous **12** cantankerous

Wasps, The
author: 12 Aristophanes
character: 10 Bdelycleon, Philocleon
dog: 5 Labes

wassail 5 drink, punch, revel, toast **6**
liquor, tipple **7** carouse, revelry **8**
beverage, carousal

waste 3 die, ebb, rob **4** fade, loot,
melt, rape, raze, ruin, sack, sink,
void, wane **5** abate, crush, decay,
drain, dregs, droop, empty, offal,
smash, spoil, strip, trash, wreck **6**
barren, burn up, debris, devour, litter,
misuse, ravage, razing, refuse, scraps,
steppe, tundra, weaken, wither **7**
crumble, decline, deplete, despoil, de-

stroy, dwindle, exhaust, garbage, looting, pillage, plunder, rubbish, shatter,
subside **8** badlands, decrease, demolish, diminish, leavings, misapply, misspend, needless, prey upon, remnants,
squander, wrecking **9** devastate, disappear, dissipate, emptiness, evaporate, excrement, leftovers, misemploy,
ruination, sweepings **10** demolition,
plundering, remainders, wilderness **11**
destruction, devastation, dissipation,
expenditure, fritter away, prodigality,
squandering **12** despoliation, extravagance **14** misapplication

waste away 4 fail, rust **7** corrode, decline, eat into

wasted 5 spent **6** used-up **7** ravaged **9**
emaciated, exhausted **12** unproductive

wasteful 8 prodigal **9** unthrifty **10**
thriftless **11** extravagant, improvident,
spendthrift, squandering **12** uneconomical

wastefulness 10 imprudence, lavishness **11** prodigality, squandering **12**
extravagance, improvidence

wasteland 6 desert

Waste Land, The
author: 7 T S Eliot
editor: 9 Ezra Pound

waste time 5 dally **6** dawdle, loiter
10 dillydally

watch 3 eye, see **4** heed, look, mark,
mind, note, ogle, save, tend **5** alert,
guard, scout, stare **6** attend, be wary,
gaze at, guards, look at, look on, notice, patrol, peep at, peer at, picket,
regard, sentry, survey, tend to **7** be
chary, care for, examine, lookout, observe, oversee, protect, stare at **8** pore
over, preserve, sentinel, sentries, take
heed **9** attention, patrolman, vigilance
10 observance, scrutinize **11** contemplate, observation, superintend, supervision **15** superintendence

watch fire 6 beacon
kinds: 4 bale **6** signal

watchful 4 wary **5** alert, aware,
canny, chary **6** shrewd **7** careful,
guarded, heedful, mindful, prudent **8**
cautious, open-eyed, vigilant **9** attentive, observant **11** circumspect

watchfulness 4 care, heed **9** attention, diligence, vigilance **13** attentiveness

watchman 5 guard, scout **6** patrol,
picket, sentry **7** lookout **8** sentinel **9**
patrolman

Watch on the Rhine
director: 13 Herman Shumlin
based on play by: 14 Lillian Hellman
cast: 9 Paul Lukas **10** Bette Davis **19**
Geraldine Fitzgerald
Oscar for: 5 actor (Lukas)

watch over 5 guard **6** attend **7** oversee, protect **11** superintend

847

Wayne, John

watchtower 6 beacon, pharos, signal
7 seamark 8 landmark 10 lighthouse

watchword 5 motto 6 byword, slogan

water 3 cut, dip, sea, wet 4 damp,
lake, pond, pool, soak, tear, thin 5
douse, flood, H two O, ocean, river,
souse 6 dampen, deluge, dilute,
drench, lagoon, splash, stream 7 immerse, moisten 8 inundate, irrigate,
sprinkle, submerge 10 adulterate
　goddess of: 4 Enki

Water Carrier (Water Bearer)
　constellation of: 8 Aquarius

watercolor
　French: 9 aquarelle

watercourse 5 canal, river 6 strait 7
channel, conduit, narrows, passage 8
aqueduct

water down 3 cut 6 censor, dilute,
weaken 7 thin out 9 expurgate 10
adulterate

watered down 4 weak 6 dilute 7 diluted 8 weakened 11 adulterated

waterfall 7 cascade, Niagara 8 cataract

waterfront 4 dock, mole, pier, quay 5
basin, jetty, levee, wharf 6 marina 7
landing

waterless 3 dry 4 arid, sere 6 barren
7 parched, thirsty 10 desertlike

Waterloo Bridge
　director: 11 Mervyn LeRoy
　cast: 11 Vivien Leigh 12 Lucile Watson, Robert Taylor 13 Virginia Field
　remade as: 4 Gaby

Water Monster (Sea Serpent)
　constellation of: 5 Hydra

water of life
　Latin: 9 aqua vitae

Waters, Ethel
　nickname: 19 Sweet Mama Stringbean
　born: 9 Chester PA
　roles: 5 Pinky 6 Beulah 21 The Member of the Wedding

Watership Down
　author: 12 Richard Adams

Water Snake
　constellation of: 6 Hydrus

watertight 9 nonporous 10 impervious 11 impermeable

waterway 5 canal, inlet, river, route 6
gutter, strait, strake, stream 7 channel

Water Wonderland
　nickname of: 8 Michigan

watery 3 wet 4 damp, thin, weak 5
fluid, moist, teary 6 liquid, rheumy 7
aqueous, diluted, tearful, tearing 11
adulterated

Watt, James
　nationality: 8 Scottish
　developed: 11 steam engine 12 piston engine

Watteau, Jean Antoine
　born: 6 France 12 Valenciennes

artwork: 6 Gilles 8 Mezzetin 9 La Fi-
nette 10 La Toilette 12 Joys of
Living, L'indifferent 13 La Gamme
d'Amour 16 Company in the Park,
La Lecon de Musique 18 Enseigne de
Gersaint, Gersaint's Signboard, La
Comedie Francaise, La Concert de
Famille 20 Le Dejeuner en plein air,
L'assemblee dans un parc 21 Harle-
quin and Columbine 23 Embarque-
ment pour Cythere, Italian and
French Theater, Jupiter Surprises An-
tiope, Les Amusements Champetres
24 Conversation in the Open Air,
The Embarkation for Cythera

wattle 6 Acacia
　varieties: 5 black, broom, cedar,
glory, green, hairy, oven's, Sally,
swamp 6 frosty, golden, mudgee, orange, silver, sticky 7 bramble, buffalo, coastal, prickly, weeping,
Wyalong 8 blue-leaf, cinnamon,
graceful, screw-pod, sunshine 9 red-
leaved 10 golden-rain, needle-bush
11 Cootamundra, Mount Morgan,
Wallangarra 12 Sydney golden 14
Peppermint-tree 16 Queensland silver

Watts, Sir George Frederic
　born: 6 London 7 England
　artwork: 4 Hope 14 Physical Energy
17 Paolo and Francesca 19 Anastasio
degl'Onesti 45 Caractacus Led in Triumph Through the Streets of Rome
54 Alfred Inciting His Subjects to
Prevent the Landing of the Danes

Waugh, Evelyn
　author of: 9 Men at Arms 10 Vile
Bodies 11 The Loved One 13 Black
Mischief, Edmund Campion 14 A
Handful of Dust, Decline and Fall 15
A Little Learning 19 Brideshead Re-
visited 20 Officers and Gentlemen 22
Unconditional Surrender

wave 4 coil, curl, file, flap, line, rank,
rise, roll, rush, sway, tier 5 curve,
flood, pulse, shake, surge, swell,
swing, train, twirl, wield 6 billow,
column, comber, deluge, motion,
quiver, ripple, roller, signal, spiral,
string 7 breaker, flutter, gesture, pulsate, tremble, vibrate, winding 8 brandish, flourish, increase, undulate,
whitecap 9 advancing, oscillate, pulsation, vibration 10 salutation, undulation 11 gesticulate, heightening 13
gesticulation

wave at 4 hail 6 signal 7 gesture

wave on 6 beckon, signal 7 gesture 11
gesticulate

waver 4 flap, reel, sway, vary 5 pause,
shake, swing, weave 6 careen,
change, falter, quiver, totter, wobble
7 flutter, stagger, tremble 8 hesitate,
undulate 9 fluctuate, vacillate 10 dillydally 12 shilly-shally

wavering 8 hesitant, waffling 9 unde-

cided 10 hesitating, indecisive, irresolute 11 vacillating

Waverley
　author: 14 Sir Walter Scott
　character: 12 Flora MacIvor 14 Donald Bean Lean, Edward Waverley 15
Rose Bradwardine 16 Baron Bradwardine 17 Evan Dhu MacCombich
24 Fergus MacIvor Vich Ian Vohr 25
Prince Charles Edward Stuart

wavy 4 onde, unde 5 curly 6 coiled,
curved 7 rolling, sinuous, winding 8
mazelike, rippling, tortuous 10 meandering, serpentine, undulating 11 cur-
vilinear 12 labyrinthine

wax 4 grow 5 swell, widen 6 become,
blow up, dilate, expand, extend,
thrive 7 balloon, develop, enlarge, fill
out, inflate, puff out 8 increase

way 3 far, off 4 area, form, lane, pass,
path, road, room, wont 5 habit,
means, route, space, trail, usage 6
course, custom, far off, manner,
method, nature, region, system 7 conduct, passage, pathway, process 8 behavior, distance, practice, remotely,
vicinity 9 direction, procedure, technique 12 neighborhood

wayfarer 8 traveler, wanderer
9 sojourner

Wayfaring Stranger
　nickname of: 8 Burl Ives

way in 4 door, gate 5 entry 6 access,
portal 7 doorway, gateway, ingress 8
approach, entrance

Wayland
　also: 6 Volund 7 Wieland
　origin: 8 European
　king of: 5 elves

waylay 4 lure 5 decoy 6 ambush,
assail, attack, entrap 7 assault,
ensnare, set upon 8 inveigle

Wayne, Anthony
　nickname: 10 Mad Anthony
　served in: 10 Indian Wars 16 Revolutionary War
　captured: 10 Stony Point
　battle: 10 Brandywine, Germantown
13 Fallen Timbers

Wayne, David
　real name: 13 Wayne McMeekan
　born: 14 Traverse City MI
　roles: 6 Sakini 8 Adam's Rib 12 The
Front Page 13 Mister Roberts,
Tonight We Sing 15 Huckleberry
Finn 16 Portrait of Jennie 26 The
Teahouse of the August Moon

Wayne, John
　real name: 21 Marion Michael Morrison
　nickname: 4 Duke
　born: 11 Winterset IA
　roles: 5 Hondo 6 Chisum 8 Ringo
Kid, Rio Bravo, The Alamo, True Grit
(Oscar) 9 McLintock, Rio Grande 10
Stagecoach 11 The Quiet Man, The
Shootist 12 The Searchers 14

Rooster Cogburn, The Green Berets **16** How the West Was Won **17** The Sands of Iwo Jima **27** The Man Who Shot Liberty Valance

Way of All Flesh, The
author: **12** Samuel Butler
character: **9** Mr Overton
Pontifex family: **5** Ellen **6** Althea, Ernest, George **8** Theobald **9** Christina

Way of the World, The
author: **15** William Congreve
character: **6** Foible **7** Fainall, Witwoud **8** Mirabell, Waitwell **10** Mrs Fainall, Mrs Marwood **12** Lady Wishfort, Mrs Millamant **17** Sir Wilfull Witwoud

way of thinking 7 beliefs **9** principle **10** conviction **11** persuasions

way out 4 exit **6** egress, escape, outlet

wayward 5 balky **6** fickle, fitful, mulish, unruly **7** erratic, restive, willful **8** contrary, perverse, stubborn, variable **9** mercurial, obstinate, whimsical **10** capricious, changeable, headstrong, inconstant, rebellious, refractory, self-willed **11** disobedient, fluctuating, intractable, troublesome **12** inconsistent, incorrigible, recalcitrant, undependable, ungovernable, unmanageable **13** insubordinate

weak 4 lame, poor, puny, soft, thin **5** faint, frail, shaky, spent **6** feeble, flimsy, unsafe, wasted, watery **7** brittle, diluted, exposed, fragile, insipid, lacking, unmanly **8** cowardly, delicate, helpless, timorous, unsteady, wide open **9** breakable, enervated, exhausted, frangible, powerless, spineless, tasteless, unguarded, untenable **10** assailable, effeminate, irresolute, namby-pamby, vulnerable, wishy-washy **11** adulterated, debilitated, defenseless, ineffective, ineffectual, inefficient, unprotected, unsupported **12** unconvincing **13** inefficacious, unsubstantial, untrustworthy **14** unsatisfactory

weaken 3 sap **4** fade, fail, flag, thin, wane **5** abate, droop, lower, unman, waste **6** dilute, expose, impair, lessen, soften **7** cripple, dwindle, exhaust, thin out **8** diminish, enervate, mitigate, moderate **9** undermine **10** devitalize, emasculate

weakened 5 frail **6** dilute, faulty, flawed, watery **7** diluted **8** delicate, disabled **9** enfeebled **10** undermined **11** adulterated, debilitated, watered down

weakling 4 twit, wimp **5** mouse, sissy **6** coward **7** chicken, milksop **9** cream puff, jellyfish **10** namby-pamby, pantywaist **11** milquetoast, mollycoddle

weak-minded 4 daft, dull **7** foolish **8** backward, mindless **10** irresolute **11** addleheaded, vacillating **12** feebleminded, muddleheaded, thick-skulled

weakness 4 bent, bias **5** fault **6** defect, hunger, thirst **7** failing, frailty, leaning, passion **8** appetite, debility, fondness, lameness, penchant, tendency **9** prejudice, proneness, shakiness **10** deficiency, feebleness, flimsiness, proclivity, propensity **11** inclination **12** debilitation, imperfection, unsteadiness **13** vulnerability **14** susceptibility **15** ineffectiveness **16** unconvincingness, unsubstantiality

weak point 4 flaw **5** break, crack, fault **6** defect **10** deficiency **11** shortcoming **12** Achilles heel

weak position 8 handicap **12** disadvantage

weak-willed 8 hesitant, wavering **10** hesitating, indecisive, irresolute

wealth 4 fund, mine **5** goods, means, money, store **6** assets, bounty, estate, luxury, mammon, riches **7** capital, fortune **8** chattels, fullness, opulence, property, richness **9** abundance, affluence, amplitude, plenitude, profusion, resources **10** easy street, prosperity **11** copiousness **12** independence **13** luxuriousness

wealthy 4 rich **5** flush **6** loaded **7** moneyed, well-off **8** affluent, well-to-do **9** well-fixed **10** prosperous, well-heeled

weapon 3 arm **5** guard, means **6** attack, resort **7** bulwark, defense, measure, offense **8** armament, resource, security **9** offensive, safeguard **10** protection **14** countermeasure

weaponry 4 arms, guns **8** armament, materiel, ordnance

wear 3 don, tax, use **4** duds, fray, last, tire, togs, wrap **5** drain, erode, put on, shred, weary **6** abrade, attire, damage, endure, injury, shroud, slip on, swathe **7** apparel, clothes, corrode, dress in, eat away, exhaust, fatigue, frazzle, rub away, service, swaddle, utility **8** clothing, costumes, garments, overwork, wash away **9** disrepair **10** employment, overburden **11** application, consumption, utilization **12** dilapidation **13** deterioration **14** disintegration

wear away 4 rust **5** erase, erode **7** corrode, eat into

weariness
French: **5** ennui

wearing apparel 4 duds, garb, rags, togs, wear **5** dress **6** attire, finery **7** clothes, costume, raiment, regalia, threads **8** clothing, ensemble, garments, wardrobe
French: **11** habillement

wearing away 7 erosion **8** abrasion, friction, grinding, scraping **9** corrosion

wearing down 6 tiring **7** eroding,

erosion **8** abrasion, friction, grinding, scraping **10** overcoming

wearisome 4 dull **6** boring, dreary, tiring, trying **7** arduous, irksome, tedious **8** annoying, tiresome, toilsome **9** fatiguing, laborious, vexatious **10** bothersome, burdensome, exhausting, irritating, monotonous, oppressive

wear out 4 tire **7** exhaust, fatigue **8** enervate, enfeeble **10** debilitate

weary 4 fag **4** beat, dull, tire **5** all in, blase, bored, fed up, jaded, spent, tired **6** boring, bushed, done in, drowsy, pooped, sleepy, tiring, tucker **7** annoyed, drained, exhaust, fatigue, humdrum, overtax, play out, routine, tedious, tire out, worn-out **8** dog tired, fatigued, overwork, tiresome **9** disgusted, exhausted, fatiguing, impatient, soporific, wearisome **10** dispirited, exhausting, monotonous, overburden **11** somniferous **12** discontented, dissatisfied

weather 3 dry, tan **4** face, rust **5** brave, clime, stand **6** bleach, season **7** climate, oxidize, toughen **8** confront, windward **9** withstand **11** temperature
god of: **4** Jove **7** Jupiter

weather line 6 isobar

weave 4 fuse, join, knit, lace, link, loom, meld, wind **5** blend, braid, curve, plait, snake, twist, unify, unite **6** mingle, writhe, zigzag **7** combine, entwine, meander, texture **9** interlace **10** crisscross, intertwine **11** incorporate

Weaver, Dennis
born: **8** Joplin MO
roles: **4** Duel **7** Chester, McCloud **8** Gunsmoke **9** Gentle Ben **10** Centennial **12** Duel at Diablo **13** Kentucky Jones

Weaver, Earl
nickname: **15** Earl of Baltimore
sport: **8** baseball
position: **7** manager
team: **16** Baltimore Orioles

Weaver, Sigourney
born: **12** Los Angeles CA
roles: **5** Alien, Holes **6** Aliens **7** Tadpole **10** Eyewitness **11** The Ice Storm **12** Ghostbusters **15** Imaginary Heroes **17** Gorillas in the Mist **26** The Year of Living Dangerously

web 3 net **4** maze, mesh, trap **5** snare **6** screen, tangle, tissue **7** complex, netting, network **8** gossamer **9** labyrinth, screening

Web and the Rock, The
author: **11** Thomas Wolfe
character: **10** Esther Jack **12** George Webber

Webb, Jack
born: **13** Santa Monica CA
wife: **11** Julie London
roles: **6** The Men **7** Dragnet **9** Joe Friday **15** Sunset Boulevard

Webber, George
  character in: **16** The Web and the Rock **18** You Can't Go Home Again
  author: **5** Wolfe
Weber, Karl Maria Friedrich Ernst von
  born: **6** Lubeck **7** Germany
  composer of: **6** Oberon **9** Euryanthe **13** Der Freischutz **20** Invitation to the Dance
Weber, Max
  born: **6** Russia **9** Bialystok
  artwork: **11** The Geranium **17** Chinese Restaurant **18** Adoration of the Moon
Webfoot State
  nickname of: **6** Oregon
Webster
  character: **6** George **7** Webster **9** Katherine
  cast: **10** Alex Karras, Susan Clark **13** Emmanuel Lewis
Webster, John
  author of: **13** The White Devil **17** The Duchess of Malfi
we cannot
  Latin: **11** non possumus
we command
  Latin: **8** mandamus
wed 3 tie **4** bind, fuse, link, mate, meld **5** blend, hitch, marry, merge, unify, unite, weave **6** attach, commit, couple, devote, pledge, splice **7** combine, espouse, make one, win over **8** dedicate **11** incorporate
wedded 4 tied **5** bound, fused **6** joined, linked, melded, merged, united **7** blended, devoted, marital, married, pledged, unified **9** committed, connected **12** incorporated
wedding 8 marriage, nuptials
wedding anniversaries
  first: **5** clock, paper
  second: **5** china **6** cotton
  third: **5** glass **7** crystal, leather
  fourth: **4** silk **5** linen **20** electrical appliances
  fifth: **4** wood **10** silverware
  sixth: **4** iron, wood
  seventh: **4** wool **6** copper **8** desk sets **16** pen and pencil sets
  eighth: **4** lace **6** bronze, linens
  ninth: **5** china **7** leather, pottery
  tenth: **3** tin **8** aluminum **14** diamond jewelry
  eleventh: **5** steel **11** accessories **14** fashion jewelry
  twelfth: **4** silk **6** pearls **11** colored gems
  thirteenth: **4** furs, lace **8** textiles
  fourteenth: **5** ivory **11** gold jewelry
  fifteenth: **7** crystal, watches
  twentieth: **5** china **8** platinum
  twenty-fifth: **6** silver **21** sterling silver jubilee
  thirtieth: **5** pearl **7** diamond
  thirty-fifth: **4** jade **5** coral

  fortieth: **4** ruby
  forty-fifth: **8** sapphire
  fiftieth: **4** gold **13** golden jubilee
  fifty-fifth: **7** emerald
  sixtieth: **7** diamond
weddings
  god of: **8** Talassio
wedge 3 jam, ram **4** cram, pack, rend, rive **5** chock, chunk, crowd, force, press, split, stuff **6** cleave **7** squeeze
wedlock 8 marriage **9** matrimony
Wednesday
  Dutch: **8** woensdag
  French: **8** mercredi
  German: **8** mittwoch
  heavenly body: **7** Mercury
  Italian: **9** mercoledi
  name comes from: **4** Odin **5** Woden
  observance: **12** Ash Wednesday
  Spanish: **9** miercoles
  Swedish: **6** onsdag
wee 4 tiny **5** dwarf, scant, teeny **6** little, minute, petite, scanty **9** itty-bitty, miniature, minuscule **10** diminutive, teeny-weeny, undersized **11** Lilliputian, microscopic
weed 3 bur, hoe, nag, pot **4** burr, butt, cull, dock, hemp, rake **5** cigar, joint, vetch **6** darnel, harrow, pull up, root up, uproot **7** tobacco **8** nuisance, plantain, purslane, toadflax **9** cigarette, crabgrass, cultivate, dandelion, eliminate, extirpate, marijuana **12** mourning band
weed out 6 banish **7** abolish, discard **8** get rid of, throw out **9** eliminate
weeny 3 wee **4** tiny **5** frank, small, teeny **6** hotdog, little, teensy, wiener **11** frankfurter
weep 3 cry, orp, sob **4** bawl, bend, drip, leak, lerm, ooze, shed, tear, wail **5** exude, mourn **6** bewail, boohoo, lament, shower **7** blubber, lapwing, whimper **8** sweating **9** exudation
  genus: **8** Vanellus
weep over 5 mourn **6** bemoan, bewail, lament
weevil
  variety: **4** boll, rice
Wegener, Alfred L
  field: **10** geophysics **11** meteorology
  nationality: **6** German
  theory of: **16** continental drift
weigh 4 lift **5** count, hoist, raise, scale **6** burden, charge, ponder, regard **7** balance, compare, measure **8** consider, encumber, evaluate, ruminate **11** contemplate **12** counterbalance
weigh anchor 4 sail **7** cast off, set sail, ship out
weigh down 4 load **6** anchor, burden **7** oppress **8** encumber, obligate, overload
weight 3 tax **4** heft, load, mass **5** value **6** burden, import, saddle, strain, stress **7** ballast, concern, oppress, ton-

nage, urgency **8** emphasis, encumber, poundage, pressure **9** heaviness, influence, magnitude **10** importance **11** consequence **12** significance **13** consideration, ponderousness
weight, unit of
  of Afghanistan: **3** pau, paw, ser, sir
  of Algeria: **4** rotl
  of Argentina: **4** last **5** grano, libra **7** quintal **8** tonelada
  of Austria: **4** marc, saum, unze **5** denat, karch, pfund, stein **7** centner, pfennig **8** vierling **9** quantchen
  of Belgium: **4** last **5** carat, livre, pound **6** charge **7** chariot **9** esterling
  of Bolivia: **5** libra, marco
  of Borneo: **4** para **6** chapah
  of Brazil: **3** bag **4** onca, onza **5** libra **6** arroba, oitava **7** arratel, quilate, quintal **8** tonelada
  of Bulgaria: **3** oka, oke **5** tovar
  of Cambodia: **4** mace, tael
  of Chile: **5** grano, libra **7** quintal
  of China: **3** fan, fen, hao, kin, ssu, tan, yin **4** chee, chin, dong, shih, tael, tsin **5** catty, chien, picul, tchin, tsien **6** kungli **7** haikwan, kungfen, kungssu, kungtun **8** kungchin **9** candareen **10** kupingtael
  of Colombia: **3** bag **4** saco **5** carga, libra **7** quilate, quintal
  of Costa Rica: **3** bag **4** caja **5** libra
  of Cuba: **5** libra **6** tercio
  of Ecuador: **5** libra
  of Egypt: **3** kat, ket, oka, oke **4** dera, heml, khar, okia, rotl **5** artal, artel, deben, kerat, minae, minas, okieh, pound, ratel, uckia **6** hamlah, kantar **7** drachma, quintal
  of El Salvador: **3** bag **4** caja **5** libra
  of England: **3** bag, kip, tod, ton **4** keel, last, mast, maun **5** barge, fagot, grain, maund, pound, score, stand, stone, truss **6** bushel, cental, fangot, firkin, fother, fotmal, pocket **7** quarter, quintal, sarpler
  of Estonia: **4** lood, nael, puud
  of Ethiopia: **3** pek **4** kasm, natr, oket, rotl **5** alada, artal, mocha, neter, ratel, wakea **6** wogiet **8** farasula **9** mutagalla
  of France: **3** sol **4** gros, kilo, marc, once **5** carat, livre, pound, tonne, uckia **6** gramme, passir **7** tonneau **8** esterlin **9** esterling
  of Greece: **3** mna, oka, oke **4** mina, obol **5** litra, livre, maneh, pound **6** diobol, dramme, kantar, obolos, obolus, stater, talent **7** chalcon, chalque, drachma **8** diobolon, talanton
  of Guatemala: **4** caja **5** libra
  of Guinea: **4** akey, piso, uzan **5** benda, seron **6** quinto **8** aguirage
  of Hungary: **7** vamfont **8** vammazsa
  of Iceland: **4** pund **5** pound, tunna **6** smjors
  of India: **3** mod, pai, ser, vis **4** dhan, drum, hoen, kona, myat, pala, pank,

pice, raik, ruay, tael, tali, tank, tola, wang, yava **5** adpad, bahar, hubba, masha, maund, tical **6** abucco, karsha **8** mangelin

of Indonesia: 5 catty, ounce, thail **6** soekoe

of Iran: 3 ser **4** dram, dung, rotl, sang, seer **5** abbas, artel, maund, pinar, ratel **6** dirhem, gandum, karwar, miscal, nakhod, nimman **7** abbassi **8** tcheirek

of Italy: 5 carat, libra, oncia, pound **6** carato, denaro, libbra, ottava

of Japan: 2 mo **3** fun, kin, kon, rin, shi **4** kati, kwan, niyo **5** carat, catty, momme, picul **6** kwamme **8** hiyakkin

of Java: 4 amat, pond, tali **5** pound **6** soekel

of Korea: 3 won

of Latvia: 9 liespfund

of Libya: 3 pik, saa **4** kele **5** teman, uckia **6** gorraf, misura **7** mattaro, termino **8** kharouba

of Malaysia: 4 chee, mace, tael, wang **7** tampang

of Mexico: 3 bag **4** onza **5** carga, libra, marco **6** adarme, arroba, ochava, tercio **7** quintal

of Mongolia: 3 lan

of Morocco: 4 rotl **5** artal, artel, gerbe, ratel **6** dirhem, kintar **7** quintal

of Myanmar: 2 ta **3** can, mat, moo, pai, vis **4** binh, dong, kyat, ruay, viss **5** bahar, behar, candy, tical, ticul **6** abucco **7** peiktha

of the Netherlands: 3 ons **4** last, lood, pond **5** bahar, grein **6** korrel **7** wichtje **8** esterlin

of Nicaragua: 3 bag **4** caha, caja **8** tonelada

of Norway: 3 lod **4** mark, pund **9** skaalpund **10** bismerpund

of Pakistan: 4 seer, tola **5** maund

of Paraguay: 7 quintal

of Peru: 3 libra **7** quintal

of the Philippines: 5 catty, fardo, picul, punto **6** lachsa **7** quilate **8** chinanta

of Poland: 3 lut **4** funt **5** uncya **6** kamian **7** centner, skrupul

of Portugal: 4 grao, onca, once **5** libra, marco **6** arroba, oitava **7** arratel, quintal **9** excropulo

of Russia: 3 lof, lot **4** dola, funt, lana, last, loof, loth, once, pood, poud **5** dolia

of Saudi Arabia: 3 oke

of Scotland: 4 boll, drop **5** trone **6** bushel

of Somalia: 8 parsalah

of Spain: 4 onza **5** frail, grano, libra, marco, tomin **6** adarme, arroba, dinero, dracma, ochava **7** arienzo, quilate, quintal **8** caracter, tonelada

of Sudan: 5 habba

of Sweden: 3 ass, lod, ort **4** last,

mark, sten **5** carat **6** nylast **7** centner, lispund **8** skalpund, skeppund **9** shippound

of Switzerland: 4 fund **5** pfund **7** centner, quintal **12** zugthierlast

of Syria: 4 cola, rotl **5** artal, artel, ratel **6** talent

of Tanzania: 8 farsalah

of Thailand: 3 bat, hap, pai, pay, sen, sok **4** baht, haph, kati, klam, klom **5** catty, chang, coyan, fuang, picul, pilul, tical **6** fluang, graini, salung, sompay **7** tamlung

of Tunisia: 3 saa **4** rotl **5** artal, artel, ratel, uckia **6** kantar

of Turkey: 3 oka, oke **4** aqui, dram, kile, rotl **5** artal, artel, cheke, kerat, obolu, ratel **6** batman, dirhem, kantar, maunch, miskal **7** drachma, quintal, yusdrum

of Uruguay: 7 quintal

of Venezuela: 3 bag **5** libra

of Vietnam: 3 can, yet **4** uyen

of Yugoslavia: 3 oka **5** dramm, tovar, wagon **7** satlijk

weightlessness 8 buoyancy **9** lightness **11** zero gravity

weighty 5 grave, heavy, hefty, vital **6** solemn, taxing, trying, urgent **7** arduous, crucial, earnest, massive, onerous, serious **8** critical, crushing, cumbrous, pressing **9** difficult, essential, important, ponderous **10** burdensome, cumbersome, oppressive **11** significant, substantial, troublesome **12** considerable **13** consequential

Weill, Kurt
  born: 6 Dessau **7** Germany
  composer of: 8 Happy End **13** Lady in the Dark **15** Down in the Valley **18** The Lindbergh Flight, The Threepenny Opera **19** Die Dreigroschenoper **31** Rise and Fall of the City of Mahagonny **32** Aufstieg und Fall der Stadt Mahagonny

Weir, Peter
  director of: 7 Witness **9** Gallipoli, Green Card **11** The Last Wave **13** The Truman Show **16** Dead Poets Society **18** Master and Commander **26** The Year of Living Dangerously

weird 3 odd **4** wild **5** crazy, eerie, kooky, nutty, queer **6** far-out, mystic, spooky **7** bizarre, curious, ghostly, magical, strange, unusual **8** abnormal, freakish, peculiar **9** eccentric, grotesque, irregular, unearthly, unnatural **10** mysterious, outlandish, phantasmal, unorthodox **12** supernatural **14** unconventional

weirdo 3 nut **4** kook **5** flake, freak **6** looney **7** lunatic, oddball **8** crackpot, original **9** character, eccentric, screwball **10** one-of-a-kind

Weird sisters 5 Fates, Norns

Weisenfreund, Muni
  real name of: 8 Paul Muni

Weismuller, Johnny
  real name: 20 Peter John Weissmuller
  born: 9 Windbar PA
  Olympic sport: 8 swimming
  Olympic gold medals: 4 five
  wife: 9 Lupe Velez
  roles: 6 Tarzan **9** Jungle Jim

Weiss, Peter
  author of: 10 Marat/Sade **14** Vanishing Point

welcome 4 meet **5** admit, greet **6** at home, salute, wanted **7** embrace, receive, usher in, winning **8** accepted, admitted, charming, engaging, enticing, greeting, inviting, pleasant, pleasing **9** agreeable, entertain, reception **10** delightful, gratifying, salutation **11** comfortable

Weld, Tuesday
  real name: 12 Susan Ker Weld
  born: 9 New York NY
  husband: 11 Dudley Moore
  roles: 11 Falling Down **12** I Walk the Line **14** Play It as It Lays **16** The Cincinnati Kid, Wild in the Country **19** Looking for Mr Goodbar **22** Once Upon a Time in America

welfare 4 good **6** health, profit, relief **7** benefit, success, the dole **9** advantage, happiness

well 3 jet, run **4** flow, fund, good, gush, hale, mine, ooze, pool, pour, rise **5** amply, fount, fully, issue, lucky, right, shaft, sound, spout, spurt, store, surge **6** easily, fairly, hearty, justly, kindly, nicely, proper, robust, source, spring, stream, strong, warmly **7** chipper, fitting, healthy, readily, rightly **8** famously, fountain, laudably, properly, suitably, very much, vigorous **9** agreeably, capitally, carefully, correctly, favorable, favorably, fortunate, promising, quite well **10** abundantly, acceptably, adequately, auspicious, completely, familiarly, felicitous, intimately, personally, prosperous, splendidly, successful, thoroughly **11** approvingly, commendably **12** advantageous, auspiciously, considerably, propitiously, satisfactory, successfully, sufficiently **13** substantially **14** advantageously, satisfactorily **15** sympathetically **16** enthusiastically
  hole drilled in ground for: 3 gas, oil **5** water

well-adjusted 6 normal, secure **8** sensible

well-behaved 6 polite, sedate **8** decorous

well-being 4 ease, good, luck, weal **6** health, profit **7** benefit, comfort, fortune, success, welfare **8** felicity, good luck **9** advantage, affluence, happiness **10** prosperity

wellborn 8 highbred **9** patrician **10**

upper-class **12** aristocratic, silk-stocking

well-bred 5 civil, suave **6** polite, urbane **7** elegant, gallant, genteel, refined **8** cultured, ladylike, mannerly, polished **9** civilized, courteous **10** cultivated **11** gentlemanly **13** sophisticated

well-chosen 3 apt **4** fine **5** prize **6** choice, seemly, select **7** apropos, correct, fitting, special **8** superior **9** excellent **11** appropriate

well-considered 7 careful, prudent **8** cautious **10** thoughtful **11** circumspect

well-coordinated 6 smooth **8** graceful **9** dexterous **10** effortless

well-defined 5 clear, plain **8** clear-cut, definite, distinct, palpable **10** pronounced

well-dressed 4 chic **5** natty, smart **6** dapper **11** fashionable

well-educated 7 erudite, learned **8** cultured, literate **9** scholarly **10** cultivated **13** knowledgeable

Welles, Orson
  real name: 17 George Orson Welles
  born: 9 Kenosha WI
  wife: 9 Paola Mori **12** Rita Hayworth
  formed: 14 Mercury Theatre
  radio show: 14 War of the Worlds
  roles: 8 Jane Eyre **11** Citizen Kane, The Third Man, Touch of Evil
  director of: 7 Macbeth, Othello **8** Falstaff **11** Citizen Kane, The Stranger, Touch of Evil **23** The Magnificent Ambersons

well-favored 4 fair **5** bonny **6** comely, pretty **7** sightly, winsome **8** fetching, handsome **9** beautiful **10** attractive **11** good looking

well-fed 5 hefty, plump, stout **6** portly, rotund **9** corpulent

well-fixed 4 rich **7** moneyed, wealthy **8** affluent **10** prosperous

well-founded 7 factual **9** supported **12** corroborated **13** substantiated

well-groomed 4 neat, tidy **5** natty **6** spruce **10** impeccable

well-grounded 5 valid **7** factual **8** reliable **9** supported **10** undeniable, undisputed, unshakable **11** irrefutable **12** corroborated, indisputable **13** incontestable, substantiated **16** incontrovertible

well-heeled 4 rich **7** moneyed, wealthy **8** affluent **10** in the chips, in the money, prosperous

Wellington
  capital of: 10 New Zealand

Wellington, Duke of
  also: 15 Arthur Wellesley
  nickname: 6 Hookey **12** The Great Duke
  nationality: 7 British
  served in: 5 India **14** Napoleonic Wars

battle: 6 Assaye **7** Vitoria **8** Talavera, Waterloo **9** Salamanca
  served as: 13 prime minister
  memoirs: 20 Wellington Dispatches

well-kept 4 heat, neat, tidy **7** orderly **9** organized **10** systematic **11** disciplined, uncluttered

well-known 4 open **5** famed, noted **6** common, famous **7** big-time, eminent, evident, leading, obvious, popular **8** familiar, infamous, renowned **9** important, notorious, prominent **10** celebrated, scandalous, understood **11** established, illustrious, outstanding

well-lighted 5 lit up **6** ablaze, bright **11** illuminated

well-made 4 fine **7** perfect **8** executed, flawless **9** faultless **11** beautifully

Wellman, William
  director of: 5 Wings **9** Beau Geste **11** A Star Is Born **13** Nothing Sacred **15** The Story of GI Joe **16** The Ox-Bow Incident

well-mannered 6 polite **7** genteel, refined **8** cultured, decorous, ladylike, polished **9** courteous, dignified **10** cultivated **11** gentlemanly

well-matched 5 close **10** nip-and-tuck

well-off 4 rich **5** flush **6** loaded **7** moneyed, wealthy **8** affluent **10** prosperous **11** comfortable

well-padded 5 plump, stout **6** chubby, fleshy, portly, rotund **9** corpulent

well-proportioned 7 classic, elegant, shapely **8** graceful **11** symmetrical

well-read 7 erudite, learned **8** cultured, literate **9** scholarly **10** cultivated

well-reasoned 4 wise **10** perceptive, thoughtful **11** intelligent

well-rehearsed 6 smooth **7** planned **8** prepared **9** practiced

Wells, H G (Herbert George)
  author of: 5 Kipps **10** Tono-Bungay **11** Ann Veronica **14** The Time Machine **15** The Invisible Man **16** Outline of History **17** Love and Mr Lewisham, The War of the Worlds **19** The History of Mr Polly **22** The Shape of Things to Come **23** Mr Britling Sees It Through

wellspring 4 font **6** origin, source **9** beginning **10** birthplace **12** fountainhead

well-stocked 4 full **11** overflowing

well-suited 6 proper **7** correct, fitting **8** suitable **9** congenial, congruous **10** compatible, harmonious **11** appropriate

well-to-do 4 rich **7** moneyed, wealthy **8** affluent **10** in the chips, in the money, prosperous

well up 4 boil, rise **6** bubble **7** surface

well-ventilated 4 airy **5** windy **6** breezy, drafty

well-versed 7 knowing **9** qualified **10** conversant **11** experienced **13** knowledgeable
  French: 9 au courant

well-wisher 6 friend **8** advocate, champion **9** supported

Welsh Mythology
  goddess: 3 Don
  goddess of fire/fertility/agriculture/ household/wisdom: 6 Brigit
  king: 4 Bran, Llud, Ludd, Nudd
  magician: 5 Lloyd
  paradise: 5 Annwn **6** Annfwn
  prince: 5 Pwyll **7** Kilwich
  princess: 5 Olwen
  romantic tales: 10 Mabinogian

welt 4 bump, lump, mark, wale, weal **6** bruise, streak, stripe **8** swelling **9** contusion

Weltanschauung 25 manner of looking at the world

Weltansicht 9 world view

Weltschmerz 6 sorrow **9** world pain **10** melancholy **20** sentimental pessimism

Welty, Eudora
  author of: 12 Delta Wedding, Golden Apples **13** Losing Battles **14** The Ponder Heart **15** A Sweet Devouring **19** The Robber Bridegroom **20** The Optimist's Daughter

wench 4 doxy, girl, lass, maid, slut **5** whore **6** damsel, lassie, maiden **8** strumpet **10** prostitute

Wend 4 Slav, Sorb
  in: 7 Germany

wend 4 make **5** hie to

went 3 ran **4** flew, left **5** faded, got on **6** flew by, lapsed, passed **7** elapsed, sallied **8** departed, filed off, passed by, took wing, vanished **9** proceeded, took leave **10** shuffled on, took flight **11** disappeared, forged ahead **12** sallied forth **13** pressed onward

Werfel, Franz
  author of: 9 Mirror Man **19** Forty Days of Musa Dagh, The Song of Bernadette

Werner, Oskar
  real name: 24 Oskar Josef Bschliessmayer
  born: 6 Vienna **7** Austria
  roles: 11 Jules and Jim, Ship of Fools **17** Voyage of the Damned **22** Fahrenheit Four Fifty One, The Shoes of the Fisherman **26** The Spy Who Came in from the Cold

Wertmuller, Lina
  director of: 9 Swept Away (by an unusual destiny in the blue sea of August) **13** Seven Beauties

Wescott, Glenway
  author of: 14 The Grandmother, The Pilgrim Hawk **16** The Apple of the Eye **17** Apartment in Athens

Wessex
fictional place created by: **5** Hardy
West, Benjamin
born: **13** Springfield PA
artwork: **17** Death on a Pale Horse
19 Death of General Wolfe **22** Saul
and the Witch of Endor
West, Dame Rebecca
real name: **28** Cicily Isabel Fairfield
Andrews
author of: **8** The Judge **11** Harriet
Hume **13** Birds Fall Down **15** The
Thinking Reed **19** The Strange Necessity **20** The Fountain Overflows
21 The Return of the Soldier **22**
Black Lamb and Grey Falcon
West, Jessamyn
author of: **11** Leafy Rivers **13** A Matter of Time **18** Except for Me and
Thee **21** The Friendly Persuasion **22**
The Massacre at Fall Creek
West, Mae
born: **10** Brooklyn NY
roles: **3** Sex **8** Sextette **9** I'm No An-
gel **10** Diamond Lil **13** Klondike An-
nie **14** Go West Young Man **15**
Night After Night, She Done Him
Wrong **16** Myra Breckinridge **17** My
Little Chickadee
autobiography: **28** Goodness Had
Nothing To Do With It
quote: **18** Beulah peel me a grape **22**
Come up and see me sometime
West, Morris L
author of: **7** Cassidy, Proteus **9** Harlequin **13** The Salamander **14** The
Clowns of God, Vanishing Point **15**
The Tower of Babel **17** The Devil's
Advocate **22** The Shoes of the Fisherman
West, Nathanael
author of: **12** A Cool Million **16** Miss
Lonelyhearts **17** The Day of the Locust
Westcott, Edward Noyes
author of: **10** David Harum
Westenra, Lucy
character in: **7** Dracula
author: **6** Stoker
Western, Sophia
character in: **8** Tom Jones
author: **8** Fielding
Western Sahara
other name: **13** Spanish Sahara
claimed/occupied by: **7** Morocco
capital: **6** Al Aiun **7** El Aaiun
city: **3** Zug **5** Daora, Smara **6** Aargub,
Dakhla, Tichla **9** Asqueimat, Bir
Gandus **10** Bir Enzaran **12** Guelta
Zemmur
river: **7** Uad Atui **8** Uad Assag **13**
Saguia el Hamra
sea: **8** Atlantic
physical feature:
cape: **6** Barbas **7** Bojador
desert: **6** Sahara
wind: **5** leste **6** gibleh

people: **4** Arab **6** Berber
language: **16** Hassaniyya Arabic
religion: **5** Islam
feature:
political group: **14** Polisario Front
Western Samoa
other name: **17** Navigator's Islands
capital/largest city: **4** Apia
others: **6** Safotu, Sataua **7** Faleolo,
Palauli, Poutasi, Tuasivi **8** Fagamalo,
Falelima, Lufilufi **9** Falealupo, Muli-
fanua **10** Samalaeulu, Satupaitea
monetary unit: **4** sene, tala
island: **5** Upolu **6** Manono, Savaii **7**
Apolima
mountain: **4** Fito, Vaea
highest point: **13** Mauga Silisili
sea: **7** Pacific
physical feature:
bay: **4** Asau, Salu **6** Safata **7** Lafanga, Matautu **8** Fangaloa, Salealua **9** Saluofata
strait: **7** Apolima
people: **6** Samoan **10** Melanesian,
Polynesian
author: **20** Robert Louis Stevenson
(Tusitala, Teller of Tales)
explorer: **6** Wilkes **9** Roggeveen **12**
Bougainville
language: **6** Samoan **7** English
religion: **9** Methodist **10** Protestant
13 Roman Catholic **14** Congregational
place:
observatory: **4** Apia
tomb: **9** Stevenson
feature:
chief: **5** matai
clothing: **5** pareu **8** lavalava, puletasi
dance: **4** siva
daughter of chief: **5** taupo
house: **4** fale
food:
dish: **8** palusami
drink: **3** ava
Western Star
author: **19** Stephen Vincent Benet
West Indies 11 archipelago
bird: **4** tody **6** mucaro
channel: **7** Jamaica **9** Old Bahama
component: **4** Cuba **5** Haiti **6** Tobago
7 Bahamas, Curacao, Grenada, Jamaica, St Lucia **8** Anguilla, Barbados, Dominica, Trinidad **10** Guadeloupe, Montserrat, Saint Lucia, Saint
Barts, Hispaniola, Puerto Rico **11**
Saint Martin **12** St Kitts-Nevis **13**
Cayman Islands, Virgin Islands **14**
Leeward Islands, Lesser Antilles,
Turks and Caicos **15** Greater Antilles, Windward Islands **17** Antigua
and Barbuda, Dominican Republic
crop: **6** coffee **9** sugarcane
fish: **4** pega **5** pelon
formerly: **10** federation
fruit: **5** papaw **6** pawpaw **7** genipap
islands: **5** Turks **6** Caicos, Cayman,

Virgin **7** Bahamas, Leeward **8** Windward
kale: **7** malanga
lizard: **6** arbalo
music: **7** calypso
passage: **4** Mona **8** Windward
rodent: **5** hutia
sea: **9** Caribbean
shark: **4** gata
sorcery: **3** obi **5** obeah
tree: **5** genip **6** aralie
tribesman: **5** Carib **6** Arawak **7** Ciboney
vessel: **6** droger, drogher
volcano: **5** Pelee
Westinghouse, George
nationality: **8** American
invented: **8** air brake **12** railroad frog
20 railroad signal system
Westlake, Donald E
author of: **5** The Ax **8** Bank Shot **10**
The Hot Rock **13** Dancing Aztecs,
Watch Your Back!, The Road to Ruin
15 Brothers Keepers
as Richard Stark: **8** Comeback **9**
Backflash, Flashfire, The Hunter
10 The Seventh
as Tucker Coe: **19** Murder Among
Children
Westover, Russ
creator/artist of: **15** Tillie the Toiler
West Side Story
director: **10** Robert Wise **13** Jerome
Robbins
cast: **10** Rita Moreno **11** Natalie
Wood, Russ Tamblyn **13** Richard
Beymer **14** George Chakiris
score: **15** Stephen Sondheim **16** Leonard Bernstein
Oscar for: **7** picture **8** director **15**
supporting actor (Chakiris) **17** supporting actress (Moreno)
West Virginia
abbreviation: **2** WV **3** W Va
nickname: **8** Mountain **9** Panhandle
capital: **10** Charleston
largest city: **10** Huntington
others: **5** Logan **6** Elkins, Keyser, Ripley, Vienna, Weston **7** Beckley,
Grafton, Spencer, Weirton **8** Fair-
mont, Wheeling **10** Clarksburg **11**
Moundsville, Parkersburg
college: **5** Salem **7** Bethany, Concord
8 Marshall, Wheeling **9** Bluefield **10**
Charleston **12** West Virginia **14** Davis and Elkins **16** Alderson Broaddus
20 West Virginia Wesleyan
feature:
historical site: **12** Harper's Ferry
national road: **10** Cumberland
tribe: **7** Moneton
people: **9** Pearl Buck **14** Arthur I
Boreman **19** Walter Philip Reuther
24 Thomas "Stonewall" Jackson
explorer: **12** Morgan Morgan
island: **14** Blennerhassett
lake: **4** Lynn
land rank: **10** forty-first

mountain:
  highest point: 10 Spruce Knob
physical feature:
  cavern: 6 Seneca
  plateau: 9 Allegheny
  rock: 6 Seneca
  spring: 8 Berkeley **12** White Sulphur
river: 3 Elk **4** Ohio **6** Gauley **7** Kanawha, Potomac, Tug Fork **8** Big Sandy, Guyandot **11** Monongahela
state admission: 11 Thirty-fifth
state bird: 8 cardinal
state fish: 10 brook trout
state flower: 11 great laurel **15** big rhododendron **17** great rhododendron
state motto: 25 Mountaineers Are Always Free
state song: 17 West Virginia Hills **20** This Is My West Virginia **27** West Virginia My Home Sweet Home
state tree: 10 sugar maple
Westward Ho!
  author: 15 Charles Kingsley
west wind
  associated with: 8 Favonius, Zephyrus
West Wing, The
  network: 3 NBC
  creator: 11 Aaron Sorkin
  cast: 7 Rob Lowe (Sam Seaborn) **8** Alan Alda (Arnold Vinick), Dule Hill (Charlie Young) **10** Jimmy Smits (Matt Santos), Moira Kelly (Mandy Hampton) **11** John Spencer (Leo McGarry), Martin Sheen (Jed Bartlet) **12** Janel Moloney (Donna Moss), Joshua Malina (Will Bailey) **13** Allison Janney (C J Craig), Richard Schiff (Toby Ziegler) **15** Bradley Whitford (Josh Lyman) **16** Stockard Channing (Abbey Bartlet)
wet 3 dip **4** damp, dank, rain, soak **5** humid, moist, rainy, soggy, steep, storm, water **6** clammy, dampen, drench, liquid, shower, soaked, sodden, splash, stormy, watery **7** immerse, moisten, showery, soaking, sopping, squishy, wetness **8** dampened, dampness, dankness, drenched, dripping, inundate, irrigate, moisture, sprinkle, submerge **9** exudation, liquified, moistness, rainstorm **10** clamminess **11** waterlogged **12** condensation **13** precipitation
wet blanket 4 drag **6** damper **10** spoilsport **11** party-pooper
wet down 5 spray **6** dampen **7** moisten **8** sprinkle
wettish 4 damp **5** moist **6** clammy
we who are about to die salute thee
  Latin: 19 morituri te salutamus
  said by: 15 Roman gladiators
  said to: 13 Roman emperors
whack 2 go **3** box, hit, rap, try **4** bang,

belt, blow, cuff, slam, slap, slug, sock, stab, turn **5** baste, clout, crack, knock, pound, punch, smack, smite, thump, trial **6** strike, wallop **7** attempt, venture **8** endeavor
whale 4 beat, cane, drub, flog, orca, whip **6** baleen, thrash **9** bastinado
  constellation of: 5 Cetus
  group of: 3 gam, pod
  swallowed: 5 Jonah
  Melville: 8 Moby Dick
whammy 3 hex **4** jinx **5** curse **7** evil eye **9** evil spell
wharf 3 key **4** dock, pier, quai, quay, slip **5** jetty **6** marina **7** landing **10** breakwater
Wharton, Edith
  author of: 10 Ethan Frome, The Old Maid **15** The House of Mirth **17** The Age of Innocence **21** The Custom of the Country
Whatever Happened to Baby Jane?
  director: 13 Robert Aldrich
  cast: 10 Bette Davis **11** Victor Buono **12** Joan Crawford **15** Marjorie Bennett
What Every Woman Knows
  author: 12 James M Barrie
  character: 9 John Shand **15** Charles Venables **18** Comtesse de la Briere, Lady Sybil Tenterden
    Wylie family: 5 Alick, David, James **6** Maggie
what it takes 5 knack, skill **7** ability, know-how, mastery **9** expertise **10** capability, competence, expertness **11** proficiency **13** the right stuff
What's Happening!!
  character: 5 Rerun **6** Dwayne **7** Shirley **9** Dee Thomas, (Mama) Mrs Thomas **11** Roger (Raj) Thomas
  cast: 9 Fred Berry, Mabel King **12** Ernest Thomas **13** Haywood Nelson **15** Danielle Spencer, Shirley Hemphill
What's My Line?
  host: 8 John Daly
  panelist: 8 Hal Block **9** Fred Allen **10** Steve Allen **11** Bennett Cerf **13** Arlene Francis **15** Louis Untermeyer **16** Dorothy Kilgallen
wheat 8 Triticum
  varieties: 4 club, rice **5** durum, dwarf, India, river **6** Alaska, common, German, Polish, starch **7** English, poulard **8** hedgehog **10** onegrained, two-grained **13** Mediterranean
  product: 4 bran **5** bread, flour, pasta **6** cereal **8** macaroni **9** spaghetti
Wheat State
  nickname of: 6 Kansas
wheedle 4 coax, lure **5** charm **6** cajole, entice, induce **7** beguile, flatter **8** butter up, inveigle, persuade, soft soap
wheel 4 disk, drum, hoop, ring, roll,

spin **5** pivot, round, swirl, twirl, whirl **6** caster, circle, gilgal, gyrate, roller, rotate, swivel **7** revolve **9** pirouette
Wheel of Fortune
  host: 8 Pat Sajak
  assistant: 10 Vanna White
wheels 3 car **4** auto, heap **5** motor **6** jalopy **7** flivver, vehicle **8** motorcar **9** tin lizzie **10** automobile
wheeze 4 gasp, hiss, pant, puff **7** panting, whistle
whelp 3 boy, cub, kid, lad, pup **4** brat **5** child, puppy, youth **6** urchin **9** stripling, youngster **14** whippersnapper
whence 9 from where **10** antecedent **14** from what source
Where Eagles Dare
  director: 12 Brian G Hutton
  based on novel by: 15 Alistair MacLean
  cast: 7 Mary Ure **12** Robert Beatty **13** Clint Eastwood, Patrick Wymark, Richard Burton **14** Michael Hordern
wherefore 2 so **3** why **7** because **13** for what reason
where I may stand
  Greek: 6 pou sto
where mentioned above
  Latin: 8 ubi supra
whereupon 8 upon what **10** after which **14** upon which point
wherewithal 4 cash **5** funds, means **6** assets **7** capital **9** financing, resources
whet 4 edge, hone, stir **5** grind, pique, strop, tempt **6** allure, arouse, awaken, entice, excite, induce, kindle **7** animate, provoke, quicken, sharpen **9** stimulate **11** put an edge on
whether willing or not
  Latin: 12 nolens volens
which see
  Latin: 2 qv **8** quod vide
which was to be demonstrated
  Latin: 3 QED **21** quod erat demonstrandum
which was to be done
  Latin: 17 quod erat faciendum
which was to be shown
  Latin: 3 QED **21** quod erat demonstrandum
whiff 4 hint, odor, puff **5** aroma, draft, scent, smell, sniff, trace **6** breath, breeze, zephyr **7** bouquet
  French: 7 soupcon
Whig Party
  president belonging to: 5 Tyler **6** Taylor **8** Fillmore, Harrison
while 2 as **3** yet **4** idle, till, time, when **5** until **6** during, effort, whilst **7** filling, interim, trouble, whereas **8** although, occasion
whim 4 urge **5** fancy, quirk **6** notion, vagary **7** caprice, conceit, impulse **8** crotchet **11** inspiration **12** eccentricity

whimper 3 sob 4 pule 5 whine 6 snivel 7 blubber, sniffle, sobbing 9 cry softly, sniveling 11 sob brokenly 16 whine plaintively

whimsical 5 droll 6 fickle, fitful, quaint 7 amusing, erratic, waggish 8 fanciful, notional, quixotic 9 eccentric 10 capricious, changeable, chimerical 12 inconsistent

whimsy, whimsey 4 bent, wish 5 fancy, humor, prank, quirk 6 notion, vagary 7 caprice, fantasy 8 escapade, drollery 11 make-believe

whine 3 cry, sob 4 fret, mewl, moan, wail 6 grouse, murmur, mutter, snivel 7 grumble, whimper 8 complain 9 complaint 11 gripe meekly 12 plaintive cry 14 cry plaintively

whip 3 rod 4 beat, cane, drub, flap, flog, jerk, jolt, lash, lick, maul, rout 5 birch, flick, spank, strap, thong, whisk 6 rattan, snatch, switch 7 cowhide, rawhide, scourge, trounce 8 birch rod, vanquish 9 horsewhip, toss about 10 blacksnake, flagellate 13 cat-o'-nine-tails, defeat soundly, move violently 14 beat decisively, beat into a froth

Whip 8 scorpion

whip hand 4 sway 5 power 7 control, mastery 9 advantage, authority, dominance, supremacy, upper hand 10 ascendancy, domination

whipped 5 caned, waled 6 beaten, darted, flayed, frothy, lashed, roused 7 flogged, frothed, incited, revived, spanked, subdued, swished, whisked 8 defeated, overlaid, punished, scourged, switched 9 chastised 10 vanquished

whir 3 hum 4 buzz, purr 5 drone 7 whisper

whirl 2 go 3 try 4 reel, spin, stab, turn 5 crack, fling, pivot, swirl, trial, twirl, whack, wheel 6 circle, dither, flurry, gyrate, rotate 7 attempt, revolve, turning 8 circling, gyration, pivoting, rotation, spinning, swirling, twirling, wheeling 9 feel dizzy, feel giddy, pirouette, revolving, turn round 10 dizzy round, rapid round, revolution 12 merry-go-round 17 state of excitement 18 dizzying succession

whirlpool 4 eddy 5 swirl, whirl 6 vortex 9 maelstrom 15 whirling current

whirlwind 4 rash 5 hasty, quick, rapid, short, swift 7 cyclone, tornado, twister 8 headlong 9 breakneck, impetuous, impulsive 10 waterspout

whirly 5 dizzy, giddy, shaky 7 reeling 8 spinning 11 vertiginous

whisk 3 fly, zip 4 beat, bolt, dart, dash, race, rush, tear, whip, whiz 5 bound, brush, flick, hurry, scoot, shoot, speed, spurt, sweep 6 hasten, scurry, spring, sprint
type: 4 wire 6 French 8 omelette

whiskbroom 5 brush

whiskered 5 bushy, hairy 6 shaggy 7 bearded, bristly, hirsute 8 unshaven 11 bewhiskered, mustachioed

whiskers 3 awn 5 beard 7 stubble 8 bristles

whiskey, whisky 3 gin, rum, rye 4 corn, shot 5 booze, hooch, Irish, juice, vodka 6 liquor, red eye, rotgut, Scotch 7 alcohol, aquavit, blended, bourbon, spirits 8 eau-de-vie 9 aquavitae, firewater, moonshine, unblended 10 sneaky pete, usquebaugh 11 mountain dew 14 John Barleycorn, white lightning
type: 3 rye 6 Scotch 7 bourbon
drink: 8 hot toddy 14 Klondike Cooler
with beer: 11 Boilermaker
with Benedictine: 10 Frisco Sour
with Cointreau: 16 Canadian Cocktail
with vermouth: 9 Manhattan

whisper 3 hum 4 blab, buzz, hint, purr, sigh, tell 5 blurt, bruit, drone, rumor 6 gossip, murmur, mutter, reveal, rustle 7 breathe, confide, divulge, inkling 8 disclose, innuendo, intimate 9 undertone 10 suggestion 11 insinuation

whist
derived from: 8 triomphe
descendant: 6 bridge
number of players: 4 four
six tricks: 4 book

Whistler, James Abbott McNeill
born: 8 Lowell MA
artwork: 6 Etudes 9 Harmonies, Nocturnes 10 Rosa Corder 12 Arrangements, The White Girl 13 Thomas Carlyle 15 Cicely Alexander, Wapping-on-Thames 24 Venetian Palaces Nocturnes 28 Arrangement in Grey and Black No 1 (The Artist's Mother) 29 Chelsea Nocturne in Blue and Green 31 Princess of the Land of the Porcelain 35 Falling Rocket Nocturne in Black and Gold 37 Cremorne Lights Nocturne in Blue and Silver

whistle-stop 5 stump 8 campaign 11 electioneer

whit 3 dab, dot, jot 4 chip, dash, drop, iota, mite, snip 5 crumb, grain, pinch, speck 6 morsel, tittle, trifle 7 modicum, smidgen 8 fragment, particle, splinter 9 scintilla

white 3 wan 4 ashy, fair, gray, pale, pure 5 ashen, blond, clean, filmy, hoary, ivory, milky, pasty, pearl, smoky, snowy 6 benign, chalky, chaste, cloudy, frosty, leaden, pallid, pearly, sallow, silver 7 ghostly, silvery 8 blanched, bleached, grizzled, harmless, innocent, spotless, virtuous 9 alabaster, bloodless, Caucasian, colorless, stainless, undefiled, unspotted, unstained, unsullied 10 cadaverous, immaculate 11 translucent, unblemished, unmalicious

White, E B (Elwyn Brooks)
author of: 11 One Man's Meat 12 Stuart Little 13 Charlotte's Web 14 Is Sex Necessary? (with James Thurber) 19 The Trumpet of the Swan
column: 13 Talk of the Town

White, Stanford see 17 Mead McKim and White

White, T H (Terence Hanbury)
author of: 15 The Book of Merlyn 16 The Ill-Made Knight 17 The Witch in the Wood 18 The Candle in the Wind, The Sword in the Stone 20 The Once and Future King

White Company, The
author: 19 Sir Arthur Conan Doyle

White Heat
director: 10 Raoul Walsh
cast: 11 James Cagney 12 Edmond O'Brien, Virginia Mayo 16 Margaret Wycherly

whiten 4 pale 5 clean, frost 6 blanch, bleach, silver 7 lighten

whiteness 6 pallor 7 wanness 8 paleness 9 snowiness 10 sallowness 13 colorlessness

White Nights
director: 14 Taylor Hackford
cast: 12 Gregory Hines 18 Mikhail Baryshnikov
choreographer: 10 Twyla Tharp

White Rabbit
character in: 28 Alice's Adventures in Wonderland
author: 7 Carroll

whitewash 6 excuse 7 absolve, cover up, justify 8 downplay, minimize, play down 9 calcimine, exonerate, vindicate
paint made by mixing: 12 lime and water

whitish 4 buff, pale 6 chalky, creamy 7 grayish

Whitman, Bert
creator/artist of: 14 The Green Hornet

Whitman, Walt
author of: 12 Song of Myself 13 Leaves of Grass 18 Oh Captain My Captain 33 When Lilacs Last in the Dooryard Bloom'd

Whitmore, James
born: 13 White Plains NY
roles: 4 Them 5 Bully 8 Oklahoma 9 Battlecry 10 Will Rogers 11 Black Like Me 12 Battleground, Harry S Truman, Tora Tora Tora 15 Command Decision, Give 'em Hell Harry 19 The Next Voice You Hear

Whitney, Eli
nationality: 8 American
invented: 9 cotton gin
pioneered use of: 14 mass production

Whittier, John Greenleaf
author of: 9 Snow-Bound 10 Maud

Muller **14** The Barefoot Boy **16** Barbara Frietchie

whittle 3 cut **4** clip, pare **5** carve, shave, slash **7** curtail, shorten **8** decrease

whiz 3 fly, hum, zip **4** bolt, buzz, dart, dash, hiss, race, rush, scud, tear, whir, zoom **5** adept, drone, scoot, shark, shoot, speed, spurt, sweep, swish, whine, whisk **6** expert, genius, hasten, master, scurry, sizzle, sprint, wizard **7** prodigy, scuttle, whistle **11** crackerjack

who goes there?
French: 7 qui vive

who knows?
Spanish: 9 quien sabe

whole 4 body, bulk, full, hale, unit, well **5** sound, total, uncut **6** entire, intact, robust, system **7** essence, healthy, perfect **8** complete, ensemble, entirety, totality, unbroken, unharmed, vigorous **9** aggregate, undivided, uninjured **10** assemblage, unabridged **12** completeness, quintessence, undiminished

wholehearted 4 true **7** earnest, serious, sincere, zealous **8** complete, emphatic **9** unfeigned **10** unreserved, unstinting **12** enthusiastic

wholesome 4 hale, nice, pure, well **5** clean, fresh, hardy, moral, sound **6** decent, honest, worthy **7** chipper, dutiful, ethical, healthy, upright **8** blooming, hygienic, innocent, sanitary, vigorous, virtuous **9** exemplary, healthful, honorable, uplifting **10** nourishing, nutritious, principled **11** meritorious, responsible **12** invigorating **13** strengthening

whole world, the
French: 11 tout le monde

wholly 5 fully, quite **7** totally, utterly **8** as a whole, entirely **9** perfectly **10** altogether, completely, thoroughly
Latin: 6 in toto

whoop 3 cry **4** hoot, howl, roar, yell **5** cheer, hollo, shout **6** bellow, cry out, holler, hurrah, outcry, scream, shriek **7** screech **9** hue and cry

whopper 3 fib, lie **6** big one **7** fiction **9** falsehood, fish story, tall story **16** cock-and-bull story

whopping 4 huge **5** giant, large **8** thumping, whacking, whapping **10** incredible **13** extraordinary

whore 3 pro **4** bawd, doxy, jade, slut, tart **5** hussy, tramp **6** chippy, harlot, hooker, prosty, wanton **7** demirep, hustler, trollop **8** call girl, mistress, strumpet **9** concubine **10** prostitute **12** streetwalker
French: 9 courtesan **12** demimondaine

whorl 4 coil, curl, roll **5** helix **6** circle, spiral **9** corkscrew **11** convolution

Who's Afraid of Virginia Woolf?
author: 11 Edward Albee
director: 11 Mike Nichols
cast: 11 George Segal, Sandy Dennis **13** Richard Burton **15** Elizabeth Taylor
Oscar for: 7 actress (Taylor) **17** supporting actress (Dennis)

Who Said That?
host: 8 John Daly **11** Robert Trout **13** Walter Kiernan
panelist: 9 Bill Henry **12** Bob Considine, H V Kaltenborn, June Lockhart **14** John Mason Brown, Morey Amsterdam **17** John Cameron Swayze

Who's on First?
comedy routine by: 6 Abbott **8** Costello
first base: 3 who
second base: 4 what
third base: 9 I don't know
shortstop: 9 I don't care
catcher: 5 today
pitcher: 8 tomorrow
left field: 3 why
center field: 7 because

Who's on First?
author: 17 William F Buckley Jr

wicked 3 bad, low **4** base, evil, foul, vile **5** acute, awful, gross, rowdy **6** cursed, fierce, impish, raging, severe, sinful **7** corrupt, extreme, fearful, galling, heinous, hellish, immoral, intense, knavish, naughty, painful, rampant, Satanic, serious, vicious **8** depraved, devilish, dreadful, fiendish, infamous, rascally, shameful **9** atrocious, malicious, monstrous, nefarious **10** abominable, bothersome, degenerate, iniquitous, malevolent, scandalous, villainous **11** disgraceful, mischievous, troublesome **12** blackhearted, dishonorable, incorrigible **13** reprehensible

wickedness 4 evil **6** infamy **8** baseness, foulness, iniquity, vileness **9** depravity, malignity **10** immorality, sinfulness **11** malevolence **13** maliciousness, nefariousness

Wicked Witch of the West
character in: 13 The Wizard of Oz
author: 4 Baum

wide 4 vast **5** ample, broad, fully, great, large, roomy **7** dilated, immense **8** expanded, extended, spacious **9** boundless, capacious, distended, extensive, outspread **10** commodious, completely

wide-awake 2 up **5** alert, aware, quick **8** vigilant, watchful **9** attentive, insomniac, observant, sleepless

widely 3 far **5** broad **6** abroad **7** broadly, greatly, largely **10** by and large, far and near **11** extensively

widely known 5 famed, noted **6** common **7** popular **8** familiar **9** universal, worldwide

widen 6 expand, extend, spread **7** broaden, enlarge, stretch

widened 7 swelled, swollen **8** enlarged, expanded, extended **9** broadened, distended, stretched

wide open 4 ajar, vast **5** agape **6** gaping **7** exposed, yawning **8** extended, unfenced **9** cavernous, expansive, outspread, unbounded **12** outstretched, unobstructed

wide open spaces 7 boonies, country **9** boondocks **11** countryside, hinterlands

wide-ranging 5 broad **7** immense **8** sweeping **9** extensive, universal, unlimited **10** exhaustive **11** diversified, far-reaching **12** encyclopedic **13** comprehensive

widespread 5 broad **9** extensive, outspread, pervasive, worldwide **10** nationwide **11** far-reaching

Widmark, Richard
born: 9 Sunrise MN
roles: 4 Coma **7** Madigan **8** The Alamo **11** Kiss of Death **12** The Long Ships **16** Halls of Montezuma, How the West Was Won **19** Judgment at Nuremberg

Widow Douglas
character in: 15 (The Adventures of) Huckleberry Finn
author: 5 Twain

wie geht's 9 how are you?

wield 3 ply, use **4** wave **5** apply, exert, swing **6** employ, handle, manage **7** display, utilize **8** brandish, exercise, flourish **10** manipulate

wife 3 rib **4** mate **5** bride, squaw, woman **6** missus, spouse **7** consort, old lady **8** helpmate, helpmeet **9** companion
French: 5 femme
German: 4 frau

Wife of Bath
character in: 18 The Canterbury Tales
author: 7 Chaucer

Wifey
author: 9 Judy Blume

wig 3 rug **4** fall **6** carpet, peruke, switch, topper, toupee, wiglet **7** periwig **9** hairpiece

Wiggin, Kate Douglas
author of: 23 Rebecca of Sunnybrook Farm

wiggle 3 wag **4** jerk **5** shake, twist **6** quiver, squirm, twitch, writhe **7** flutter **8** writhing **9** squirming

wigwam, Wigwam 3 hut **4** tent, tipi **5** hogan, lodge, tepee **6** teepee **7** weekwam, wickiup **11** Tammany Hall

wild, wilds, the wild 3 mad **4** bush, rash **5** bleak, feral, giddy, madly, nutty, rabid, rough, waste **6** choppy, crazed, fierce, insane, madcap, raging, raving, rugged, savage, unruly, wooded **7** berserk, bizarre, flighty, frantic, furious, howling, lawless, natural, untamed, violent **8** barbaric, blustery, demented, desolate, fanciful, forested, frenzied, insanely, maniacal, reckless, unbroken, unhinged **9** abandoned, fanatical, fantastic, ferocious, furiously, illogical, lawlessly, naturally, overgrown, primitive, rampantly, screwball, turbulent, violently, wasteland **10** disorderly, maniacally, uninformed **11** harebrained, impractical, tempestuous, uncivilized, uninhabited **12** uncultivated, ungovernable, unrestrained **13** rattlebrained, undisciplined **14** undomesticated

wild animal 5 beast, brute

Wild Bunch, The
director: **12** Sam Peckinpah
cast: **10** Ben Johnson, Robert Ryan **11** Warren Oates **12** Edmond O'Brien **13** William Holden **14** Ernest Borgnine

wildcat 3 cat **4** lynx **6** ocelot

Wild Duck, The
author: **11** Henrik Ibsen
character: **5** Werle **8** Old Ekdal **9** Gina Ekdal **12** Gregers Werle, Hjalmar Ekdal **13** Hedvig Relling

Wilde, Cornel
real name: **19** Cornelius Louis Wilde
born: **9** New York NY
wife: **11** Jean Wallace
roles: **9** Maracaibo **11** Omar Khayyam **12** Forever Amber, The Naked Prey **15** A Song to Remember **21** A Thousand and One Nights **22** The Greatest Show on Earth

Wilde, Oscar
author of: **6** Salome **17** The Critic as Artist **18** Lady Windermere's Fan **22** The Ballad of Reading Gaol, The Picture of Dorian Gray **27** The Importance of Being Earnest

Wilder, Billy
director of: **11** One Two Three **12** The Apartment (Oscar) **13** Some Like It Hot **14** The Lost Weekend (Oscar) **15** Double Indemnity, Stalag Seventeen, Sunset Boulevard **16** The Seven Year Itch **18** Love in the Afternoon **24** Witness for the Prosecution

Wilder, Gene
real name: **15** Jerome Silberman
born: **11** Milwaukee WI
wife: **10** Karen Boyer **11** Gilda Radner
roles: **9** Stir Crazy **10** Willy Wonka **12** Silver Streak, The Producers **14** Blazing Saddles, Bonnie and Clyde **17** Young Frankenstein **22** The World's Greatest Lover **27** Start the Revolution Without Me **43** The Adventures of Sherlock Holmes' Smarter Brother

Wilder, Laura Ingalls
author of: **26** The Little House on the Prairie

Wilder, Thornton
author of: **7** Our Town **9** The Cabala **13** The Matchmaker **14** The Ides of March **16** The Woman of Andros **17** The Skin of Our Teeth **20** Heaven's My Destination **21** The Bridge of San Luis Rey

wilderness 4 bush **5** waste **6** barren, desert, forest, plains, tundra **7** barrens **8** badlands, wasteland **9** mountains

Wildeve, Damon
character in: **17** Return of the Native
author: **5** Hardy

Wild Is the River
author: **14** Louis Bromfield

Wild Kingdom
host/narrator: **9** Jim Fowler, Stan Brock **13** Marlin Perkins

Wild One, The
director: **12** Laslo Benedek
cast: **9** Lee Marvin **10** Mary Murphy **12** Marlon Brando

Wild Strawberries
director: **13** Ingmar Bergman
cast: **12** Ingrid Thulin **13** Bibi Andersson **14** Victor Sjostrom **17** Gunnar Bjornstrand

Wild Wild West
character: **10** James T West **13** Artemus Gordon
cast: **9** Will Smith **10** Ross Martin, Kevin Kline **12** Robert Conrad
traveled by: **5** train

wile, wiles 4 coax, lure, ploy, ruse, trap **5** charm, guile **6** cajole, entice, gambit, seduce **7** cunning **8** artifice, maneuver, persuade, subtlety, trickery **9** chicanery, expedient, stratagem **10** artfulness, craftiness, subterfuge **11** contrivance, machination

Wilhelm, Kate
author of: **10** City of Cain, Fault Lines **11** The Planners **14** The Infinity Box **16** The Clewiston Test **19** More Bitter than Death **26** Where Late the Sweet Birds Sang

Wilhelm Meister
author: **6** Goethe

Wilhelm Tell
also: **11** William Tell
author: **17** Johann von Schiller

wiliness 5 guile **7** cunning, slyness **8** artifice, foxiness, scheming, trickery **10** artfulness, craftiness **11** machination

Wilkes family
characters in: **15** Gone With the Wind
members: **4** John **5** Honey, India **6** Ashley **15** Melanie Hamilton
author: **8** Mitchell

will 4 want, wish **5** endow **6** bestow, confer, desire **7** craving, feeling, longing, resolve, wish for **8** attitude, bequeath, pleasure, yearning **9** hankering, testament **10** conviction,

preference, resolution **11** disposition, inclination **12** resoluteness **13** determination

Will and Grace
network: **3** NBC
cast: **9** Sean Hayes (Jack McFarland) **12** Debra Messing (Grace Adler) **13** Eric McCormack (Will Truman), Megan Mullally (Karen Walker) **14** Harry Connick Jr (Leo Markus) **15** Shelley Morrison (Rosario Salazar-McFarland)

Willard, Frank
creator/artist of: **11** Moon Mullins

willful 6 mulish, unruly **7** planned, studied **8** designed, intended, obdurate, perverse, stubborn **9** obstinate, pigheaded **10** bullheaded, deliberate, determined, headstrong, inflexible, persistent, purposeful, unyielding **11** intentional, intractable **12** contemplated, premeditated, ungovernable **13** undisciplined **14** uncompromising

Williams, Esther
nickname: **13** Mermaid Tycoon **14** Queen of the Surf **17** Hollywood's Mermaid
born: **12** Los Angeles CA
husband: **13** Fernando Lamas
roles: **13** Bathing Beauty **15** Jupiter's Darling, Ziegfeld Follies **16** Dangerous When Wet, Neptune's Daughter **20** Million Dollar Mermaid

Williams, Robin
born: **9** Chicago IL
roles: **4** Jack **6** Popeye **7** Aladdin, Jumanji **8** Insomnia **10** Patch Adams **11** The Birdcage **12** Mork and Mindy, Mrs Doubtfire, One Hour Photo **14** Death to Smoochy **15** Good Will Hunting (Oscar) **17** What Dreams May Come **18** Good Morning Vietnam **22** Artificial Intelligence **23** The World According to Garp

Williams, Ted
nickname: **6** the Kid **16** Splendid Splinter
sport: **8** baseball
position: **8** outfield
team: **12** Boston Red Sox

Williams, Tennessee
author of: **10** Camino Real **13** The Rose Tattoo **14** Summer and Smoke **16** Cat on a Hot Tin Roof, Night of the Iguana, Sweet Bird of Youth **17** Orpheus Descending, The Glass Menagerie **18** Small Craft Warnings, Suddenly Last Summer **21** A Streetcar Named Desire **24** The Roman Spring of Mrs Stone

Williams, William Carlos
author of: **7** Tempers **8** Paterson **9** White Mule **11** Al Que Quiere **20** Pictures from Brueghel

William Tell
also: **13** Guillaume Tell

opera by: **7** Rossini
character: **6** Arnold **7** Gessler

William the Conqueror
also: **17** William of Normandy **21** William I King of England
fought against: **8** Harold II
battle: **8** Hastings
succeeded by: **6** Henry I **9** William II

Willie and Joe
creator: **11** Bill Mauldin

willing 4 game **5** ready **7** content **8** amenable **9** agreeable, compliant, not averse **10** responsive

willingly 4 gain, lief, soon **6** freely, gladly, liefly **7** eagerly, happily, readily **8** by choice **10** cheerfully, graciously **11** voluntarily **12** with pleasure

willingness 4 zeal **8** alacrity **9** eagerness, readiness **10** enthusiasm **11** inclination

willow 5 Salix
varieties: **3** bay, red **4** bush, goat, gray, seep **5** black, crack, false, Niobe, Pekin, pussy, silky, water, white **6** Arctic, arroyo, basket, desert, golden, laurel, puzzle, woolly, yellow **7** brittle, prairie, sandbar, scouler, shining, weeping **8** creeping, florist's, polished, Virginia **9** bay-leaved, bearberry, flowering, sprouting **10** cricket-bat, dragon-claw, large pussy, small pussy **11** green-scaled, heart-leaved, peach-leaved, Port Jackson **13** halberd-leaved **16** Wisconsin weeping

willowy 5 lithe **6** limber, pliant, supple, svelte **7** lissome **8** flexible **9** sylphlike

Wills, Chill
born: **12** Seagoville TX
group: **26** Chill Wills and the Avalon Boys
voice of: **21** Francis the Talking Mule
roles: **5** Giant **8** The Alamo **10** Way Out West **11** The Yearling **15** Meet Me in St Louis

Wills, Garry
author of: **14** Nixon Agonistes, Reagan's America **16** Inventing America

Will Scarlet
character in: **9** Robin Hood

willy-nilly 8 perforce **10** helplessly, inevitably **11** inescapably, unavoidably **12** compulsively, irresistibly **14** uncontrollably
Latin: **12** nolens volens

Wilmer
character in: **16** The Maltese Falcon
author: **7** Hammett

Wilson, Edmund
author of: **11** Axel's Castle **19** To the Finland Station

Wilson, Sloan
author of: **26** The Man in the Gray Flannel Suit

Wilson, Woodrow
name at birth: **19** Thomas Woodrow Wilson
nickname: **5** Tommy
presidential rank: **12** twenty-eighth
party: **10** Democratic
state represented: **2** NJ
defeated: **4** (Eugene Victor) Debs, (William Howard) Taft **5** (James Franklin) Hanly **6** (Allen Louis) Benson, (Arthur Edward) Reimer, (Charles Evans) Hughes, (Eugene Wilder) Chafin **9** (Theodore) Roosevelt
vice president: **8** (Thomas Riley) Marshall
cabinet:
state: **5** (Bainbridge) Colby, (William Jennings) Bryan **7** (Robert) Lansing
treasury: **5** (Carter) Glass **6** (William Gibbs) McAdoo **7** (David Franklin) Houston
war: **5** (Newton Diehl) Baker **8** (Lindley Miller) Garrison
attorney general: **6** (Alexander Mitchell) Palmer **7** (Thomas Watt) Gregory **10** (James Clark) McReynolds
navy: **7** (Josephus) Daniels
postmaster general: **8** (Albert Sidney) Burleson
interior: **4** (Franklin Knight) Lane **5** (John Barton) Payne
agriculture: **7** (David Franklin) Houston **8** (Edwin Thomas) Meredith
commerce: **8** (William Cox) Redfield **9** (Joshua Willis) Alexander
labor: **6** (William Bauchop) Wilson
born: **2** VA **8** Staunton
died/buried: **2** DC **10** Washington
education:
college: **8** Davidson **18** College of New Jersey (later known as Princeton U)
law School: **20** University of Virginia
university: **12** Johns Hopkins
religion: **12** Presbyterian
political career:
governor of: **9** New Jersey
civilian career: **6** lawyer
professor of history: **15** Bryn Mawr College **18** Wesleyan University
professor of jurisprudence: **9** Princeton
president of: **9** Princeton
notable events of lifetime/term: **14** Fourteen Points **15** League of Nations
Act: **7** Adamson **8** Sedition **9** Espionage **10** Child Labor **11** Liberty Loan, Panama Canal **14** Federal Reserve **15** Federal Farm Loan **16** Clayton Antitrust, Selective Service **22** Federal Trade Commission

conference: **3** ABC **10** Paris Peace
18th Amendment: **11** Prohibition
program: **10** New Freedom
sinking of: **9** Lusitania
Treaty: **10** Versailles
won: **15** Nobel Peace Prize
quote: **34** The world must be made safe for democracy
father: **13** Joseph Ruggles
mother: **5** Janet (Woodrow)
siblings: **13** Joseph Ruggles **14** Annie Josephson **16** Marion Williamson
wife: **5** Edith (Bolling Galt), Ellen (Louise Axson)
children: **13** Jessie Woodrow **15** Eleanor Randolph, Margaret Woodrow

wilt 3 die, ebb, sag **4** fade, flag, sink, wane **5** droop **6** recede, weaken, wither **7** decline, dwindle, shrivel, subside **8** decrease, diminish, languish **10** degenerate **11** deteriorate

Wilt the Stilt
nickname of: **15** Wilt Chamberlain

wily 3 sly **4** foxy **5** alert, sharp **6** artful, crafty, shifty, shrewd, tricky **7** crooked, cunning, devious **8** guileful, scheming **9** deceitful, deceptive, designing, underhand **10** intriguing **11** calculating, treacherous

Wimbledon
suburb of: **6** London
site of: **16** tennis tournament
court surface: **5** grass
noted for: **20** strawberries and cream

win 3 bag, get, net **4** earn, gain, sway **6** attain, induce, master, obtain, pick up, secure **7** achieve, acquire, collect, conquer, convert, prevail, procure, realize, receive, success, triumph, victory **8** conquest, convince, overcome, persuade, vanquish **9** influence **10** accomplish

win acceptance 9 establish **10** ingratiate

wince 5 cower, quail **6** cringe, flinch, recoil, shrink **7** grimace, shudder **8** cowering, cringing, draw back, quailing **9** shrinking

wind 3 air, lap **4** bend, blow, clue, coil, curl, fold, gale, gust, hint, loop, news, puff, roll **5** blast, bluff, curve, draft, scent, smell, snake, twine, twirl, twist, whiff **6** breath, breeze, hot air, ramble, report, wander, zephyr, zigzag **7** bluster, bombast, cyclone, entwine, inkling, meander, sinuate, tempest, tidings, tornado, twaddle, twister, typhoon, whisper **8** boasting, idle talk **9** aerophone, hurricane, knowledge, whirlwind **10** intimation, suggestion **11** braggadocio, fanfaronade, information **12** intelligence
god of: **5** Eurus, Niord, Njord, Notus **6** Aquilo, Auster, Boreas **8** Favonius, Zephyrus
father: **8** Astraeus
mother: **3** Eos

windfall 7 bonanza
Windhoek
  capital of: **7** Namibia
Wind in the Willows, The
  author: **14** Kenneth Grahame
  character: **4** Mole, Toad **6** Badger **8** Water Rat
windless 4 calm **5** still **8** stifling
window 3 bay **5** oriel **6** dormer **7** opening, orifice, transom **8** aperture, casement, porthole, skylight
Winds of War, The
  author: **10** Herman Wouk
windstorm 4 gale **6** squall **7** cyclone, tempest, tornado, twister, typhoon **9** hurricane, whirlwind
windswept 4 bare **5** bleak **6** barren **8** desolate **13** weatherbeaten
windup 3 end **5** close **6** ending, finish **10** completion, conclusion, expiration **11** termination
wind up 3 end **4** halt, stop **5** cease, close **6** finish, settle **8** complete, conclude **9** terminate
windy 5 blowy, empty, gabby, gusty, wordy **6** breezy **7** verbose **8** blustery, rambling **9** bombastic, garrulous, talkative **10** loquacious, meandering, rhetorical **13** grandiloquent
wine
  French: **3** vin
  Italian: **4** vino
  god of: **7** Bacchus
  goddess of: **6** Libera
wine-colored 6 claret **8** burgundy, cardinal
winemaking
  god of: **9** Aristaeus
Winesburg, Ohio
  author: **16** Sherwood Anderson
Winfrey, Oprah
  born: **12** Kosciusko MS
  host of: **19** The Oprah Winfrey Show
  author of: **17** Make the Connection **20** Oprah An Autobiography **21** In the Kitchen with Rosie
  roles: **7** Beloved **14** The Color Purple **23** The Women of Brewster Place
wing 3 ala, fly, set **4** band, clip, flap, knot, nick, soar, zoom **5** annex, graze, group **6** circle, clique, pennon, pinion **7** adjunct, aileron, coterie, faction, section, segment **8** addition, coulisse **9** appendage, extension **10** fraternity
Winged Horse
  constellation of: **7** Pegasus
Winger, Debra
  husband: **13** Timothy Hutton
  roles: **10** Black Widow, Cannery Row **11** Forget Paris, Shadowlands, Urban Cowboy **17** Terms of Endearment **22** An Officer and a Gentleman
Wingert, Dick
  creator/artist of: **6** Hubert

Wingfield family
  characters in: **17** The Glass Menagerie
  member: **3** Tom **5** Laura **6** Amanda
  author: **8** Williams
Wings
  director: **15** William A Wellman
  cast: **8** Clara Bow **10** Gary Cooper **12** Richard Arlen **18** Charles Buddy Rogers
  Oscar for: **7** picture
Wings
  network: **3** NBC
  cast: **7** Tim Daly (Joe Hackett) **11** Steven Weber (Brian Hackett) **12** David Schramm (Roy Biggins), Tony Shalhoub (Antonio Scarpacci) **13** Rebecca Schull (Fay Cochran) **14** Crystal Bernard (Helen Chapel) **17** Thomas Haden Church (Lowell Mather)
  setting: **9** Nantucket
Wings of the Dove, The
  author: **10** Henry James
  character: **8** Kate Croy, Lord Mark **9** Mrs Lowder **11** Milly Theale **12** Mrs Stringham **13** Merton Densher, Sir Luke Strett
wink at 6 ignore **7** condone, let pass **8** overlook **9** disregard
Winkle
  character in: **14** Pickwick Papers
  author: **7** Dickens
winner 5 champ **6** master, victor **8** champion **9** conqueror **10** vanquisher
Winnie-the-Pooh
  author: **7** A A Milne
  character: **3** Owl **5** Kanga **6** Eeyore, Piglet, Rabbit, Tigger **7** Baby Roo **16** Christopher Robin
winning 7 amiable **8** charming, engaging, pleasing **9** appealing, beguiling, disarming **10** attractive, bewitching, entrancing **11** captivating **12** ingratiating, irresistible
win over 4 beat, best **5** charm **6** defeat, seduce **7** convert **8** overcome, vanquish **9** captivate, overpower
winsome 5 sweet **6** comely **7** amiable, likable, lovable **8** charming, cheerful, engaging, pleasing **9** agreeable, appealing, endearing **10** attractive, bewitching, delightful
Winterbourne
  character in: **11** Daisy Miller
  author: **5** James
Winter of Our Discontent, The
  author: **13** John Steinbeck
Winters, Shelley
  real name: **14** Shirley Schrift
  born: **9** St Louis IL
  husband: **13** Tony Franciosa **15** Vittorio Gassman
  roles: **11** A Double Life **12** A Patch of Blue **14** A Place in the Sun **16** A House Is Not a Home **19** The Diary

of Anne Frank **20** The Poseidon Adventure
winter sports
  god of: **4** Ullr **5** Uller
Winter's Tale, The
  author: **18** William Shakespeare
  character: **7** Camillo, Leontes, Paulina, Perdita **8** Florizel, Hermione **9** Autolycus, Polixenes
Winter Wonderland
  nickname of: **8** Michigan
wintry 3 icy, raw **4** cold **5** bleak, chilly, harsh, polar, snowy, stark **6** arctic, chilly, dreary, frigid, frosty, frozen, gloomy, stormy **7** glacial **8** Siberian **9** cheerless
wipe 3 dry, mop, rub **4** swab **5** apply, brush, clean, erase, rub on, scour, scrub, swipe, towel **6** banish, remove, rub off, sponge, stroke
wiped out 5 broke **6** failed, ruined **8** bankrupt, indigent, strapped **9** destitute, insolvent, penniless **12** impoverished
wipe out 4 ruin **5** erase **7** abolish, destroy, eclipse **8** bankrupt **9** devastate, eliminate, eradicate, extirpate, liquidate **10** annihilate, obliterate **11** exterminate
wiping out 7 erasing **9** eclipsing, expunging **10** abolishing, destroying **11** eliminating, eradicating **12** annihilating, obliterating
wire 5 cable **8** filament, telegram **9** cablegram, telegraph
wiry 4 lean **5** agile, kinky, lanky, spare, stiff **6** limber, pliant, sinewy **7** brittle
Wisconsin
  abbreviation: **2** WI **3** Wis
  nickname: **6** Badger
  capital: **7** Madison
  largest city: **9** Milwaukee
  others: **5** Ripon **6** Antigo, Beloit, Cudahy, Neenag, Racine, Wausau **7** Ashland, Baraboo, Bloomer, Kenosha, Menasha, Oshkosh, Portage, Shawano **8** Appleton, Boscobel, Green Bay, Lacrosse, Superior, Waukesha **9** Eau Claire, Fond du Lac, Sheboygan, Shorewood, Wauwatosa, West Allis **10** Brookfield, Janesville **12** Steven's Point
  college: **5** Ripon **6** Beloit **7** Alverno, Carroll, Viterbo **8** Carthage, Lawrence **9** Marquette, Northland, Wisconsin
  feature:
    fort: **6** Howard **8** Crawford **9** Winnebago
    national lakeshore: **14** Apostle Islands
  tribe: **3** Fox, Sac **4** Sauk **5** Huron **6** Oneida, Ottawa **8** Chippewa, Kickapoo **9** Winnebago **10** Potawatomi
  people: **11** Orson Welles **12** Fredric March, Harry Houdini, Spencer Tracy

13 Hamlin Garland **14** Joseph McCarthy, Georgia O'Keeffe, Thornton Wilder **16** Frank Lloyd Wright **17** Robert M LaFollette
explorer: 6 Joliet **7** Allouez, Nicolet **8** Radisson **9** Marquette **12** Groseilliers
island: 8 Madeline
lake: 6 Geneva, Poygan **7** Kenosha, Mendota, Wissota **8** Michigan, Superior **9** Winnebago
land rank: 11 twenty-sixth
mountain: 7 Baraboo **9** Sugarbush **10** Blue Mounds
highest point: 9 Timm's Hill
physical feature:
glacial hills: 13 Kettle Moraine
rock formations: 8 The Dells
river: 3 Fox **4** Wolf **7** St Croix **8** Chippewa **9** Black Rock, Wisconsin **11** Mississippi
state admission: 9 thirtieth
state bird: 5 robin
state fish: 11 muskellunge
state flower: 5 pansy **6** violet **10** wood violet
state motto: 7 Forward
state song: 11 On Wisconsin
state tree: 10 sugar maple

wisdom 6 brains **8** sagacity **9** teachings **10** philosophy, principles, profundity **11** discernment, penetration **12** apperception, intelligence **13** comprehension, judiciousness, understanding
god of: 2 Ea **4** Enki, Odin **5** Othin, Thoth
goddess of: 6 Athena, Athene, Brigit, Pallas, Saitis **7** Minerva **11** Tritogeneia **12** Pallas Athena **18** Alalcomenean Athena

wise 3 way **4** sage **6** manner **7** knowing, respect, sapient **8** profound **9** judicious, sagacious **10** discerning, perceptive **11** intelligent **13** knowledgeable, perspicacious, understanding

Wise, Robert
director of: 4 Star! **11** I Want to Live **13** West Side Story (with Jerome Robbins, Oscar) **14** The Sand Pebbles **15** The Sound of Music (Oscar) **18** The Andromeda Strain **24** Star Trek: The Motion Picture

wiseacre 4 fool, sage **5** idiot **7** tomfool **9** know-it-all, simpleton **10** smart aleck

wisecrack 4 jest, joke, quip **5** flash, sally **8** cut jokes **9** witticism **11** smart saying

Wise men see **4** Magi

wise up 5 edify **6** advise, in form **7** apprise **9** enlighten, make aware

wish 3 yen **4** hope, long, love, pine, want, whim, will **5** crave, yearn **6** aspire, desire, hunger, thirst **7** command, craving, leaning, longing, re-quest **8** ambition, appetite, fondness, penchant, yearning **10** aspiration, partiality **11** inclination **12** predilection

wishes 11 compliments **13** felicitations **15** congratulations

wish for 4 want **5** covet, crave **6** desire

wishful 4 avid **5** eager **6** keen on, pining **7** anxious, craving, hopeful, longing, wanting, wistful **8** aspiring, bent upon, desirous, fanciful, yearning **9** ambitious, expectant

wish well 10 felicitate **12** congratulate

wishy-washy 4 blah, dull, weak **5** inane, vapid, wimpy **6** jejune **7** insipid **8** wavering **10** indecisive, irresolute **11** ineffective, ineffectual, vacillating **12** equivocating, noncommittal **14** tergiversating **15** shilly-shallying

wisp 4 lock, tuft **5** bunch, shred, torch, twist **6** bundle, rumple **8** fragment **10** whisk broom **11** ignis fatuus **13** friar's lantern

wispy 4 thin **5** frail **6** slight **8** fleeting, nebulous

wistaria, wisteria
varieties: 4 pink, wild **5** silky, water **7** Chinese **8** Japanese **9** Rhodesian

Wister, Owen
author of: 12 The Virginian

wistful 3 sad **6** musing, pining **7** craving, doleful, forlorn, longing, pensive **8** desirous, mournful, yearning **9** hankering, sorrowful, woebegone **10** meditative, melancholy, reflective **12** disconsolate **13** contemplative, introspective

wit 3 wag **4** gags **5** comic, humor, joker, jokes, quips, sense **6** acumen, banter, brains, jester, joking, levity, wisdom **7** cunning, funster, gagster, insight, punster, sparkle, waggery **8** comedian, drollery, humorist, jokester, judgment, raillery, sagacity, satirist, vivacity **9** funniness, intellect **10** astuteness, brightness, cleverness, jocularity, perception, shrewdness, witticisms **11** discernment, penetration, wisecracker **12** intelligence, perspicacity **13** comprehension, epigrammatist, sagaciousness, understanding
French: 8 badinage **9** bel-esprit **10** persiflage

witch 3 hag **4** fury **5** crone, scold, shrew, vixen **6** beldam, ogress, virago **7** seeress **8** battle-ax, harridan **9** sorceress, temptress, termagant **10** prophetess **11** enchantress

witchcraft 5 obeah **6** hoodoo, voodoo **7** sorcery **8** black art, witchery, wizardry **9** diabolism, fetishism, voodooism **10** black magic, divination, necromancy **11** conjuration, enchantment

with
French: 4 avec, chez

with a grain of salt
Latin: 13 cum grano salis

with a lawsuit pending
Latin: 12 pendente lite

with authority
Latin: 10 ex cathedra

withdraw 2 go **5** leave, split **6** depart, go away, recall, recant, remove, retire **7** extract, rescind, retract, retreat, take off, vamoose **9** disappear, unsheathe

withdrawal 4 exit **6** egress **7** leaving, retreat **9** departure **10** retirement, retraction **14** discontinuance

withdrawn 3 shy **5** quiet **8** reserved, retiring, unsocial **9** reclusive **10** unfriendly **11** introverted **15** uncommunicative

wither 4 fade, wilt **5** abash, blast, droop, dry up, shame **7** cut down, mortify, shrivel **9** dehydrate, desiccate, humiliate

withered 3 dry **4** arid, sere **5** dried, faded **6** shrunk, wilted **7** decayed, dried up, drooped, stunned, wizened **9** petrified, shriveled **10** languished

withering 6 biting **7** caustic **8** scathing **9** shrinkage, shrinking, wrinkling **10** shriveling **11** contracting, contraction, devastating

with few words
Latin: 12 paucis verbis

with force and with arms
Latin: 9 vi et armis

with great praise
Latin: 13 magna cum laude

withheld 4 kept **7** checked, forbore, refused, starved **8** kept back **9** boycotted, refrained

with highest praise
Latin: 13 summa cum laude

withhold 4 hide, keep **6** hush up, retain **7** conceal, cover up **8** suppress

withhold from 4 deny **6** refuse

within 2 on **4** into **5** inner **6** during, inside **7** indoors **8** inwardly
combining form: 3 eso **4** endo
prefix: 5 intra

within an inch of 4 near **6** all but, almost, nearly

with-it 7 current **8** up-to-date
French: 9 au courant

with one's own two hands 7 oneself, unaided **10** unassisted

without 4 save **5** minus **6** beyond, except, unless **7** lacking, nowhere, outside, wanting **8** exterior, external, free from, outdoors **9** excepting **10** externally
appointment: 7 sine die
care: 8 sine cure
charge: 4 free **6** gratis **8** sine cure
combining form: 4 ecto
doubt: 9 sine dubio
feet: 4 apod **6** apodal
French: 4 sans
horns: 7 acerous

Latin: 4 sine
law: 8 anarchic
light: 7 aphotic
life: 5 amort **9** inanimate
luster: 3 mat **5** matte
offspring: 9 sine prole
prefix: 2 in
roads: 7 invious
saddles: 8 asellate, bareback
subcalyx leaves: 9 bractless
teeth: 5 morne **8** edentate
this: 7 sine hoc
tongue, teeth, or claws: 5 morne
which not: 10 sine qua non
wings: 7 apteral **8** apterous
without a doubt 6 surely **8** of course
9 certainly **10** absolutely, positively
11 indubitably **12** indisputably
14 unquestionably
Without a Trace
network: 3 CBS
cast: 9 Eric Close (Martin Fitzgerald)
12 Martin Landau (Frank Malone)
15 Anthony LaPaglia (Jack Malone),
Enrique Murciano (Danny Taylor),
Poppy Montgomery (Samantha
Spade) **20** Marianne Jean-Baptiste
(Vivian Johnson)
without basis 7 unsound **9** unfounded **10** groundless, ungrounded
11 unjustified, unsupported **15** unsubstantiated
without care
French: 9 sans souci
without charge 4 free **10** gratuitous,
on the house **13** complimentary
Latin: 6 gratis
without doubt
French: 9 sans doute
without end 7 endless, eternal, forever **8** immortal, infinite, timeless, unending **9** ceaseless, continual, endlessly, eternally, perpetual **10**
immortally, infinitely, timelessly, unendingly **11** ceaselessly, continually,
everlasting, never-ending **13** everlastingly **14** lasting forever
without equal
French: 10 sans pareil
without error 4 true **5** exact, right **7**
correct, perfect, precise, sinless **8** accurate, truthful, unerring **9** faultless
10 infallible
without exception 5 never **6** always,
wholly **8** entirely **10** absolutely, completely, invariably, positively
**without fear and without re-
proach**
French: 22 sans peur et sans reproche
Without Feathers
author: 10 Woody Allen
without funds 5 broke **6** ruined **8**
bankrupt, indigent, strapped, wiped
out **9** destitute, flat broke, insolvent,
penniless **10** stone broke **12** impoverished
without light 3 dim **4** dark **5** black,

dusky, murky, shady **6** opaque **7** obscure, shadowy, stygian, sunless
without limit
Latin: 11 ad infinitum
without limitation 6 wholly **7** totally, utterly **8** entirely **9** endlessly **10**
absolutely, completely, definitely, positively, thoroughly **11** boundlessly **13**
unequivocally **15** unconditionally
French: 12 carte blanche
without notice 5 ad-lib **9** impromptu
10 improvised **11** extemporary **14** extemporaneous
Latin: 9 extempore
**without offspring, without prog-
eny**
Latin: 9 sine prole
without the day
Latin: 7 sine die
without which not
Latin: 10 sine qua non
with praise
Latin: 8 cum laude
withstand 4 bear, defy **5** brave **6** endure, resist, suffer **7** weather **8** confront, cope with, tolerate
witless 3 mad **5** crazy **6** insane, stupid
7 fatuous, foolish, unaware **9** slap-
happy
witness 3 see **4** mark, note, sign, view
5 proof **6** attend, behold, look on, notice, verify **7** bear out, certify, confirm, endorse, initial, observe **8** attester, attest to, beholder, deponent,
document, evidence, looker-on, observer, onlooker, perceive, validate,
vouch for **9** establish, spectator, testifier, testimony **10** validation **11** corroborate, countersign **12** authenticate,
confirmation, substantiate, verification
13 corroboration, documentation **14**
authentication, substantiation
Witness for the Prosecution
director: 11 Billy Wilder
based on play by: 14 Agatha Christie
cast: 11 Tyrone Power **14** Elsa Lanchester **15** Charles Laughton, Marlene Dietrich
wits 4 mind **6** sanity **9** composure **14**
coolheadedness
witticism 4 jest, joke, quip **5** sally **7**
epigram
French: 6 bon mot **10** jeu d'esprit
witty 5 comic, droll, funny **6** bright,
clever, jocose **7** amusing, jocular,
waggish **8** humorous, mirthful **9** brilliant, sparkling, whimsical **11** quick-
witted **13** scintillating
witty saying 4 jest, quip **6** bon mot **7**
epigram **9** witticism **13** clever comment
wizard 4 sage, seer, whiz **5** adept,
shark **6** expert, genius, oracle
7 diviner, prodigy, wise man **8** conjurer, magician, sorcerer, virtuoso **9**

enchanter **10** soothsayer **11** clairvoy-
ant, necromancer
Wizard of Id, The
creator: 10 Johnny Hart **11** Brant
Parker
character: 4 King **5** Spook **6** jester,
Rodney, Tyrant
Wizard of Oz, The
director: 13 Victor Fleming
author: 10 L Frank Baum
cast: 4 Toto **8** Bert Lahr (Zeke, Cowardly Lion) **9** Jack Haley (Hickory,
Tin Woodsman), Ray Bolger (Hunk,
Scarecrow) **11** Billie Burke (Good
Witch of the North), Frank Morgan
(wizard), Judy Garland (Dorothy
Gale) **13** Clara Blandick **15** Charley
Grapewin **16** Margaret Hamilton (Almira Gulch, Wicked Witch of the
West), The Singer Midgets (Munchkins)
other roles: 6 Aunt Em **10** Uncle
Henry
score: 9 E Y Harburg **11** Harold Arlen
remade as: 6 The Wiz
place: 6 Kansas **8** Land of Oz
11 Emerald City
Dorothy wore: 8 red shoes
wizened 3 dry **5** dried **7** dried up **8**
shrunken, withered, wrinkled
9 shriveled
WKRP in Cincinnati
character: 10 Andy Travis, Herb Tar-
lek, Les Nessman **12** Venus Flytrap
13 Arthur Carlson, Dr Johnny Fever
14 Bailey Quarters **15** Jennifer Marlowe
cast: 7 Tim Reid **9** Gary Sandy **10**
Gordon Jump **11** Frank Bonner, Jan
Smithers **12** Loni Anderson **14** Howard Hesseman, Richard Sanders
wobble 4 reel, sway **5** quake, shake,
waver **6** shimmy, teeter, totter **7**
quaking, shaking, stagger, swaying **8**
wavering **9** shimmying, teetering,
tottering **12** unsteadiness
wobbly, Wobbly 5 loose, shaky **7**
doubtful **8** hesitant, insecure, unstable,
unsteady, wavering **9** quavering,
trembling **11** vacillating
union: 17 Industrial Workers
**Wodehouse, P G (Pelham Gren-
ville)**
author of: 8 Full Moon **14** Thank
You Jeeves **15** The Mating Season
character: 6 Jeeves, Psmith **13** Bertie
Wooster
Woden
origin: 10 Anglo-Saxon
chief of: 4 gods
woe 5 agony, gloom, grief, trial, worry
6 misery, sorrow **7** anguish, anxiety,
despair, torment, torture, trouble **8** calamity, distress **9** adversity, dejection,
heartache, suffering **10** affliction, depression, melancholy, misfortune **11**
tribulation **12** wretchedness

woebegone 3 sad 4 glum 6 gloomy 7 doleful, forlorn 8 dejected, funereal, mournful, tortured, troubled, wretched 9 agonizing, anguished, miserable, sorrowful, suffering 10 distressed

woeful 3 bad, sad 5 awful, cruel 6 tragic 7 doleful, painful, unhappy 8 crushing, dreadful, grievous, hopeless, horrible, terrible, unlikely, wretched 9 agonizing, appalling, miserable, sorrowful 10 calamitous, deplorable, depressing, disastrous, lamentable 11 distressing, unpromising 12 catastrophic, heartrending 13 disheartening, heartbreaking

woe to the vanquished
  Latin: 9 vae victis

Wofford, Chloe Anthony
  real name of: 12 Toni Morrison

Wojtyla, Karol
  real name of: 14 Pope John Paul II 18 Archbishop of Krakow

wolf 4 bolt, gulp 5 scarf 6 devour, gobble 7 consume
  constellation of: 5 Lupus
  group of: 4 pack

Wolfe, Nero see 8 Stout, Rex

Wolfe, Thomas
  author of: 14 The Hills Beyond 16 The Web and the Rock 17 Look Homeward Angel, Of Time and the River 18 You Can't Go Home Again
  character: 10 Eugene Gant 12 George Webber

Wolfe, Tom
  author of: 10 A Man in Full 11 Radical Chic 13 The Right Stuff 14 The Painted Word 16 The Pump House Gang 19 I Am Charlotte Simmons 21 From Bauhaus to Our House 23 The Bonfire of the Vanities 24 Maumauing the Flak Catchers 26 The Electric Kool-Aid Acid Test 43 The Kandy Kolored Tangerine Flake Streamline Baby

Wollstonecraft, Mary
  husband: 13 William Godwin
  daughter: 25 Mary Wollstonecraft Shelley
  author of: 30 A Vindication of the Rights of Women

Wolverine State
  nickname of: 8 Michigan

woman 4 girl, lady, maid, wife 5 flame, lover 6 damsel, maiden, matron 7 beloved, darling, dowager, females, fiancee, sweetie 8 ladylove, mistress 9 charwoman, concubine 10 girlfriend, hand maiden, sweetheart, sweetie pie 11 chambermaid, housekeeper, maidservant
  French: 5 femme 8 paramour
  Latin: 9 inamorata

Woman, first 3 Eve 5 Embla 7 Pandora

Woman in White, A
  author: 13 Wilkie Collins

womanish 7 unmanly 8 feminine, ladylike 9 sissified 10 effeminate

womanlike 8 feminine 10 effeminate

womanly 8 feminine, matronly

Woman of the Year
  director: 13 George Stevens
  cast: 10 Fay Bainter 12 Reginald Owen, Spencer Tracy 16 Katharine Hepburn

Women, The
  director: 11 George Cukor
  based on play by: 15 Clare Boothe Luce
  cast: 11 Hedda Hopper 12 Joan Crawford, Joan Fontaine, Marjorie Main, Norma Shearer 15 Paulette Goddard, Rosalind Russell
  remade as: 14 The Opposite Sex

Women in Love
  director: 10 Ken Russell
  based on novel by: 10 DH Lawrence
  character: 11 Gerald Crich 12 Rupert Birkin 14 Gudrun Brangwen, Ursula Brangwen
  cast: 9 Alan Bates 10 Oliver Reed 11 Eleanor Bron 12 Jennie Linden 13 Glenda Jackson
  Oscar for: 7 actress (Jackson)

wonder 3 awe 4 gape 5 sight, stare 6 marvel, ponder, rarity 7 miracle 8 cogitate, meditate, question 9 amazement, spectacle, speculate 10 conjecture, phenomenon 11 fascination 12 astonishment, stupefaction

wonder child
  German: 10 wunderkind

wonderful 4 fine, good 5 great, super 6 divine, superb, tiptop, unique 7 amazing, capital 8 fabulous, singular, smashing, striking, terrific 9 admirable, excellent, fantastic, marvelous 10 astounding, incredible, miraculous, phenomenal, staggering, surprising 11 astonishing, crackerjack, fascinating, magnificent, sensational, spectacular 13 extraordinary

Wonderland State
  nickname of: 5 Maine

wonderstruck 5 agog 6 amazed 8 thrilled 9 astounded, stupefied 10 astonished, enthralled, spellbound 11 dumbfounded 13 flabbergasted

Wonder Woman
  character: 9 (Corp) Etta Candy 11 Diana Prince, Joe Atkinson, (Maj) Steve Trevor 12 Gen Blankenship
  cast: 11 Lynda Carter 12 Lyle Waggoner 13 Beatrice Colen, Normann Burton 14 Richard Eastham

wont 3 apt, use 4 used, vain 5 habit, haunt, usage 6 custom, desire 8 accustom, inclined, practice 10 accustomed

wonted 3 apt 5 prone 6 likely 7 given to 10 accustomed, habituated

woo 3 sue 5 chase, court 6 cajole, pur-

sue 7 address, entreat, solicit 8 petition 9 importune

wood 3 log 4 bush 5 brake, brush, copse, grove 6 boards, forest, lumber, planks, siding, timber 7 thicket 8 firewood, kindling 9 clapboard, wallboard 10 timberland

Wood, Grant
  born: 9 Anamosa IA
  artwork: 12 Spring in Town 13 Stone City Iowa 14 American Gothic 15 Woman with Plants 16 Parson Weems' Fable 18 Dinner for Threshers, John B Turner Pioneer 21 Daughters of Revolution

Wood, John, Sr
  architect of: 6 Circus (Bath)

Wood, Natalie
  real name: 13 Natasha Gurdin
  born: 14 San Francisco CA
  husband: 12 Robert Wagner
  roles: 5 Gypsy 10 Brainstorm 12 The Great Race, The Searchers 13 West Side Story 17 Inside Daisy Clover 18 Rebel Without a Cause, Splendor in the Grass 19 Sex and the Single Girl 23 This Property Is Condemned 25 Love with the Proper Stranger 27 Miracle on Thirty-Fourth Street

wooded 5 treed 8 forested

wooden 4 dull 5 frame, rigid, stiff 6 clumsy, vacant 7 awkward, deadpan 8 lifeless, ungainly 9 impassive, unbending 10 inflexible, ungraceful 11 unemotional 14 expressionless

Woodhouse, Emma
  character in: 4 Emma
  author: 8 Austen

woodland 5 copse, grove, treed 6 forest 7 coppice, thicket 8 forested

wood of life
  Latin: 11 lignum vitae

woods
  god of: 8 Silvanus, Sylvanus

Woods, Sara
  real name: 13 Sara Bowen-Judd
  author of: 11 Done to Death 12 My Life Is Done 13 Yet She Must Die 15 A Show of Violence, Knives Have Edges 16 And Shame the Devil 17 The Third Encounter, Trusted Like the Fox 18 Bloody Instructions
  character: 15 Anthony Maitland

Woodstock
  also called: 11 The Cavalier
  author: 14 Sir Walter Scott

Woodstock
  director: 15 Michael Wadleigh
  cast: 6 The Who 7 Santana 8 Joan Baez 9 Joe Cocker 12 Richie Havens 13 John Sebastian, Ten Years After 17 Jefferson Airplane 19 Crosby Stills and Nash 20 Country Joe and the Fish, Sly and the Family Stone
  Oscar for: 11 documentary

Woodward, Bob
  author of: 4 Veil 7 Maestro 9 Bush

at War, The Agenda **11** The Brethren **12** Plan of Attack, The Final Days (with Carl Bernstein), The Secret Man **19** All the President's Men (with Carl Bernstein)

Woodward, Joanne
born: **13** Thomasville GA
husband: **10** Paul Newman
roles: **12** A Fine Madness, Philadelphia, Rachel Rachel **14** From the Terrace **15** Three Faces of Eve (Oscar) **16** The Long Hot Summer

woodwind instrument 4 oboe **5** flute **7** bassoon, piccolo **8** clarinet **9** bass flute **10** cor anglais **12** bass clarinet **13** double bassoon

wooer 4 beau, love **5** flame, lover, swain **6** adorer, suitor **7** admirer, courter **8** para mour **10** sweetheart

wool
fabric: **4** felt **5** crepe, llama, serge, tweed, twill **6** alpaca, angora, boucle, covert, faille, melton, vicuna, woolen **7** challis, doeskin, Donegal, worsted **8** cashmere, homespun, shetland **9** Astrakhan, camelhair, gabardine, sharkskin **10** hopsacking **11** Harris tweed, herringbone

Woolf, Virginia
author of: **7** Orlando **8** The Waves, The Years **10** Jacob's Room **11** Mrs Dalloway **14** A Room of One's Own **15** To the Lighthouse
member of: **15** Bloomsbury Group

wool-gather 8 daydream, muse idly

woolly, wooly 5 downy, furry, fuzzy, hairy, sheep, vague **6** fleecy, lanate, lanose **7** blurred, muddled, unclear **8** confused, floccose, peronate **10** flocculent, indistinct **12** disorganized

woozy 4 hazy **5** dizzy, faint, foggy, fuzzy, giddy, shaky **6** punchy **7** muddled **9** befuddled **11** light-headed

word, words 3 vow **4** chat, dirt, news, poop, term **5** edict, order, rumor, set-to, voice **6** advice, avowal, decree, gossip, letter, notice, phrase, pledge, remark, report, ruling, signal **7** command, comment, dictate, dispute, explain, express, hearsay, lowdown, mandate, message, promise, quarrel, summons, tidings **8** argument, audience, bulletin, chitchat, colloquy, decision, describe, dialogue, dispatch, locution, telegram **9** assertion, assurance, bickering, direction, discourse, interview, sobriquet, ultimatum, utterance, wrangling **10** articulate, communique, conference, contention, discussion, expression **11** altercation, appellation, declaration, designation, information, scuttlebutt **12** consultation, intelligence, tittle-tattle **13** communication, pronouncement
French: **9** tete-a-tete

word for word and letter for let-
ter
Latin: **19** verbatim et literatim

wordiness 9 diffusion, prolixity, verbosity **11** diffuseness, profuseness

wording 8 language, phrasing **11** phraseology

wordless 4 dumb, mute **5** tacit **6** silent **8** implicit, taciturn **10** speechless **11** unexpressed

word of honor 3 vow **4** oath **6** pledge **9** assurance

word play 6 banter **7** jesting, kidding
French: **8** badinage, repartee

Words, The
author: **14** Jean-Paul Sartre

Wordsworth, William
author of: **7** Michael **9** Ode to Duty **10** The Prelude **12** Tintern Abbey **14** Lyrical Ballads (with Coleridge) **16** The Ruined Cottage **24** Intimations of Immortality **25** Resolution and Independence
home: **11** Dove Cottage

wordy 5 windy **6** prolix, turgid **7** fustian, gushing, verbose **8** effusive, mumbling **9** bombastic, garrulous, redundant, talkative **10** discursive, loquacious, rhetorical, roundabout **12** tautological **13** grandiloquent

work, works 2 do, go **3** act, job, run, win **4** book, deed, duty, feat, form, gain, line, make, mill, mold, move, shop, song, task, toil, yard **5** beget, cause, chore, craft, enact, labor, opera, piece, plant, shape, slave, solve, sweat, trade **6** drudge, effect, effort, office, output **7** achieve, calling, drawing, execute, exploit, factory, fashion, foundry, innards, insides, operate, perform, produce, product, pursuit, succeed, trouble **8** building, business, concerto, contents, creation, drudgery, endeavor, engender, exertion, function, industry, maneuver, painting, progress, symphony, transmit, vocation **9** originate, sculpture, structure **10** assignment, employment, enterprise, manipulate, occupation, production, profession **11** achievement, composition, performance, transaction
Latin: **4** opus **5** opera
French: **6** metier

work, artistic or literary
French: **6** oeuvre

workaday 5 plain **6** common **7** humdrum, prosaic, routine **8** ordinary **10** unexciting **11** commonplace

work at 3 try **5** essay **6** tackle **7** attempt **8** endeavor

workbench 5 board, table **7** counter

work conquers all
Latin: **16** labor omnia vincit
motto of: **8** Oklahoma

worker 4 doer, hand **5** grind **6** drudge, toiler **7** artisan, hustler, laborer, plodder **8** achiever, employee, producer **9** craftsman, performer **11** breadwinner, eager beaver, proletarian

work for 6 assist **7** support **8** champion

working 3 job **4** duty, toil **5** labor, tasks **6** action, chores, fluent, usable, useful **8** business, drudgery, employed, exertion, industry, laboring **9** effective, operation, operative, practical **10** employment, occupation, profession **11** assignments, functioning, performance

Working
author: **11** Studs Terkel

working-class 5 labor **8** plebian **10** blue-collar **11** proletarian

working class 4 Non-U **9** commoners, common man **10** lower class **11** blue collars, proletariat
Greek: **9** hoi polloi

workmanlike 5 adept **8** skillful **9** efficient **10** productive

workmanship 5 skill **9** handcraft, handiwork, technique **10** handicraft **11** manufacture **12** construction

work out 5 solve, train **6** figure, reckon **7** compute, resolve **8** exercise, practice **9** ascertain, calculate, determine

Works and Days
author: **6** Hesiod

work saver 9 appliance **11** convenience

work-saving 4 easy **6** simple **9** efficient

worktable 4 desk **5** bench, board, table **7** counter

work together 5 unite **7** pitch in, share in **8** take part **9** cooperate **11** collaborate, participate

work toward 3 try **4** seek **6** aim for **7** attempt **8** aspire to, endeavor, reach for

work up 4 goad, urge **5** upset **6** excite **7** agitate, ferment, provoke

work with 5 coach, drill, teach, train **6** assist, exercise, instruct **9** cooperate **11** collaborate

world 3 age, era, orb **4** gobs, lots, star **5** class, Earth, epoch, globe, group, heaps, realm, times **6** domain, nature, oodles, people, period, planet, sphere, system **7** mankind, society **8** creation, division, duration, everyone, humanity, industry, universe **9** everybody, humankind, macrocosm **10** profession
Latin: **6** cosmos
Russian: **3** mir

World According to Garp, The
author: **10** John Irving
director: **13** George Roy Hill
cast: **10** Glenn Close, Hume Cronyn **11** John Lithgow **12** Jessica Tandy, Mary Beth Hurt **13** Robin Williams

worldly 5 blase **6** astute, shrewd, urbane **7** callous, earthly, fleshly, knowing, mundane, profane, secular **8** material, physical, temporal **9** corporeal, mercenary **11** experienced, terrestrial **12** cosmopolitan **13** sophisticated

world pain
German: **11** Weltschmerz

world view
German: **11** Weltansicht

world-weary 5 blase, bored, jaded **9** unexcited

worldwide 4 rife **6** global **8** catholic, ecumenic, globular, planetal, sweeping **9** universal

worm 4 edge, inch **5** crawl, creep, steal **6** writhe **7** wriggle **9** penetrate **10** infiltrate
kinds: **4** inch, tape **5** angle, earth

worn 4 weak **5** dingy, drawn, faded, seedy, spent, tired, weary **6** frayed, shabby, wasted **7** abraded, haggard, pinched, rickety, wearied **8** battered, decrepit, dog-tired, drooping, fatigued **9** enfeebled, exhausted **10** threadbare, tumbledown **11** debilitated, dilapidated

worn-out 4 dead, shot **5** spent, tired **6** beat-up, effete, shabby, used-up **7** run-down **9** exhausted **10** threadbare **11** dilapidated **12** deteriorated

worn thin 9 motheaten **10** threadbare **11** dilapidated

worried 6 afraid, scared **7** anxious, fearful **9** concerned **10** distressed **12** apprehensive

worrisome 5 fussy, pesty **6** trying, uneasy, vexing **7** anxious, fretful, irksome **8** annoying **10** bothersome, despairing, disturbing, irritating, tormenting **11** aggravating, troublesome **12** apprehensive

worry 3 vex, woe **4** care, fret, stew **5** agony, beset, dread, grief, harry, upset **6** badger, bother, dismay, harass, hector, misery, pester, plague **7** agitate, agonize, anguish, anxiety, bugaboo, concern, despair, disturb, perturb, problem, torment, trouble **8** distress, vexation **9** misgiving, persecute **10** difficulty, uneasiness **12** apprehension **13** consternation

worsen 4 fail, slip **5** erode, lapse, slide **7** decline **10** degenerate, retrogress **11** deteriorate **12** disintegrate

worsening 7 setback **9** inflaming **10** increasing, regressing, regression **11** aggravating, heightening **12** exacerbating, intensifying **13** retrogressing, retrogression

worship 5 adore, exalt, extol **6** admire, esteem, praise, pray to, revere **7** adulate, glorify, idolize, lionize **8** dote upon, venerate **9** adoration, reverence **10** exaltation, veneration **11** devotionals

worshipful 5 pious **6** devout **8** reverent

worshiping 7 adoring **8** exalting **9** adoration, adulation, adulating, idolizing, reverence **10** exaltation, glorifying, magnifying, venerating, veneration **11** idolization **13** glorification, magnification

worst 3 bad **4** beat, best, rout **5** floor, outdo **6** defeat, lowest, outwit **7** conquer, poorest, triumph **8** inferior, overcome, vanquish **9** discomfit **10** overmaster, unpleasant

worth 3 use **4** cost, good **5** merit, price, value **6** assets, estate, wealth **7** benefit, effects, utility **8** holdings **9** appraisal, resources, valuation **10** importance, usefulness **11** consequence, possessions

worth having 8 valuable **9** desirable

worthless 6 futile, paltry **7** trivial, useless **8** bootless, piddling, unusable **9** fruitless, meritless, pointless **10** unavailing **11** ineffectual, undeserving, unimportant **12** meretricious, unproductive **13** insignificant **14** good-for-nothing

worthless objects 4 junk **5** trash **7** garbage, rubbish **8** discards **11** odds and ends

worthwhile 4 good **6** usable, useful **8** valuable **9** rewarding **10** beneficial, profitable

worthy 3 fit, VIP **4** good, name **5** moral, noble **6** bigwig, decent, honest, leader, proper **7** big shot, ethical, fitting, notable, upright **8** big wheel, great man, immortal, laudable, luminary, official, reliable, suitable, virtuous **9** admirable, befitting, deserving, dignitary, estimable, excellent, honorable, personage, reputable **10** creditable **11** appropriate, commendable, meritorious, respectable

worthy of imitation 5 model **9** emulative, exemplary

Wotan
origin: **8** Germanic
chief of: **4** gods
corresponds to: **4** Odin **5** Othin

Wouk, Herman
author of: **7** The Hope **8** The Glory **13** The Winds of War **14** The Caine Mutiny **17** War and Remembrance **19** Marjorie Morningstar
character: **12** Captain Queeg

wound 3 cut **4** gash, harm, hurt, pain, slit, tear **5** slash, sting **6** bruise, damage, grieve, injure, injury, lesion, offend, pierce, trauma **7** anguish, mortify, torment **8** distress, lacerate, vexation **9** contusion **10** affliction, irritation, laceration **11** provocation

wounded 3 cut **4** hurt **6** mauled **7** damaged, injured, pierced, stabbed **8** impaired, ruptured, stricken **11** traumatized

wrack 4 kelp, ruin **5** ruins, trash **6** clouds, refuse **7** destroy, seaweed, torment **8** downfall, eelgrass, wreckage **9** cloud rack **11** destruction, storm clouds

wraith 5 ghost, shade, spook **6** spirit **7** phantom, specter **8** phantasm **10** apparition **15** materialization
Irish: **7** banshee
German: **12** doppelganger
French: **8** revenant

wrangle 4 tiff **5** argue, brawl **6** bicker **7** dispute, quarrel **8** squabble

wrangling 6 strife **7** arguing, discord **8** clashing, friction **9** bickering **10** contention **11** quarrelling

wrap 4 bind, cape, coat, fold, gird, hide, mask, veil, wind **5** cloak, cover, scarf, shawl, stole **6** bundle, clothe, encase, enfold, girdle, jacket, mantle, shroud, swathe **7** conceal, enclose, envelop, sweater **8** surround

wrapper, wrapping paper 4 case **6** casing, jacket, sheath **8** covering, envelope, slipcase **9** container

wrapping 6 caping, hiding **7** veiling **8** cerement, bundling, swathing **9** embracing, packaging, shrouding **10** engrossing, enswathing, enveloping **11** enshrouding, surrounding

wrap up 3 end **4** pack **6** finish, wind up **7** engross, envelop, involve, package **8** bundle up, complete, conclude **9** polish off **11** dress warmly

wrath 3 ire **4** bile, fury, gall, rage **5** anger **6** animus, choler, rancor, spleen **8** vexation **9** animosity, hostility **10** irritation, resentment **11** displeasure, indignation **13** irritableness

wrathful 3 mad **5** angry, irate **6** bitter, raging **7** furious **8** incensed, virulent

wreak 4 vent, work **5** visit **7** execute, indulge, inflict, unleash

wreak vengeance 6 avenge **7** get even, revenge **9** retaliate

wreath 5 crown **6** diadem, laurel **7** chaplet, coronet, festoon, garland
Hawaiian: **3** lei

wreathe 4 bend, coil, wind **5** curve, twist **7** entwine, envelop **8** encircle **10** intertwine, interweave

wreck 3 end **4** mess, raze, ruin **5** break, crash, death, level, ruins, smash, total, up set **6** finish, ravage, wretch **7** breakup, crack-up, destroy, shatter, undoing **8** demolish, derelict **9** devastate, over throw **10** disruption **11** destruction, devastation, dissolution **12** annihilation

wreckage 4 ruin **5** ruins **6** jet sam **7** flotsam, remains **8** shambles **11** destruction

Wren, P C
author of: **9** Beau Geste

wrench 3 rip **4** jerk, pull, tear, warp **5** force, twist, wrest, wring **6** sprain, strain **7** distort, pervert **12** misrepresent

type: **6** monkey, socket **7** spanner

wrest **3** get, rip **4** earn, gain, grab, jerk, make, pull, take, tear **5** force, glean, twist, wring **6** attain, obtain, secure, wrench **7** achieve, extract, squeeze

wrestle **4** toil **5** labor **6** battle, strive, tussle **7** contend, grapple, scuffle **8** struggle **10** struggling

wrestling
athlete: **8** Dan Gable

wretch **3** cur, pig, rat **4** hobo, waif, worm **5** knave, louse, rogue, swine, tramp **6** misfit, rascal, rotter, varlet **7** castoff, outcast, stinker, villain **8** derelict, scalawag, sufferer, vagabond **9** scoundrel **10** blackguard **11** unfortunate

wretched **3** low **4** base, mean, vile **5** awful, lousy, sorry **6** abject, gloomy, rotten, shabby, sleazy **7** crushed, doleful, forlorn, hapless, pitiful, scruffy, unhappy, worried **8** dejected, downcast, dreadful, hopeless, inferior, pathetic, pitiable, terrible **9** cheerless, depressed, miserable, niggardly, sorrowful, woebegone, worthless **10** abominable, despairing, despicable, despondent, melancholy **11** crestfallen, unfortunate **12** contemptible, disconsolate, disheartened, inconsolable **13** brokenhearted

wretchedness **4** pain **6** misery, sorrow **7** despair, torment, trouble **8** distress, hardship **9** adversity **10** affliction, melancholy, misfortune **11** unhappiness **12** hopelessness

wriggle **5** twist **6** squirm, wangle, writhe **7** meander

Wright, Frank Lloyd
architect of: **8** Taliesin (Spring Green WI) **10** Robie House (Chicago) **11** Martin House (Buffalo NY), Unity Church (Oak Park IL) **12** Fallingwater (Kaufmann House Bear Run PA), Taliesin West (near Phoenix AZ) **13** Imperial Hotel (Tokyo) **16** Guggenheim Museum (NYC) **22** Marin County Civic Center (CA) **35** Larkin Company Administration Building (Buffalo NY) **45** S C Johnson and Son Wax Company Administration Center (Racine WI)
style: **6** Modern **7** Organic, Prairie

Wright, Orville and Wilbur
invented: **8** airplane
first plane: **6** Flyer I **9** Kitty Hawk

Wright, Richard
author of: **8** Black Boy **9** Native Son **17** Uncle Tom's Children

wring **4** hurt, pain, rend, stab **5** choke, force, press, twist, wrest **6** coerce, grieve, pierce, sadden, wrench **7** agonize, extract, squeeze, torture **8** compress, distress

wrinkle **4** fold, idea **5** crimp, fancy, pleat, slant, trick **6** crease, device, furrow, gather, notion, pucker, rimple, rumple **7** crumple, gimmick **9** crow's-feet, viewpoint **11** corrugation

wrinkled **3** old **4** aged **5** lined **6** folded, ridged, rucked, rugate, rugose, rugous, seamed **7** creased, crimped, rimpled, rippled, ruckled, rumpled **8** crimpled, furrowed, puckered **9** shriveled

writ **10** court order **11** sealed order **14** mandatory order

write **3** pen **4** copy, show **5** draft **6** author, draw up, record, scrawl **7** compose, dash off, jot down, make out, produce, set down, turn out **8** inscribe, scribble **10** transcribe

write down **3** jot **4** note, post **5** enter **6** record

write in full **5** add to **6** expand, extend, pad out **7** amplify, augment, stretch **9** expatiate

write out **6** expand, extend **7** amplify, enlarge, stretch **8** lengthen

writer **4** hack, poet **6** author, critic, penman, scribe **7** copyist **8** essayist, novelist, reporter, reviewer, scrawler **9** columnist, dramatist, scribbler **10** journalist, librettist, playwright, songwriter **11** penny-a-liner **12** calligrapher, newspaperman **13** correspondent **14** newspaperwoman
French: **11** litterateur

write to **7** address **8** send word **9** drop a line, send a card, send a note **10** correspond **11** send a letter

write-up **4** item **5** piece, story **7** article

write up **5** cover **6** report

writhe **4** jerk **5** flail **6** squirm, thrash, thresh, wiggle **7** contort, wriggle

writing **4** book, play, poem, tome, work **5** diary, essay, novel, print, story **6** column, letter, report, script, volume **7** article, copying, journal, penning **8** critique, document, drafting, libretto, longhand **9** authoring, composing, editorial, recording **10** inscribing, manuscript, penmanship **11** calligraphy, composition, publication **12** transcribing
Latin: **4** opus

writings
Hebrew: **7** Ketubim

written agreement **6** treaty **7** compact **8** contract

written law
Latin: **10** lex scripta

written-out form **9** extension **12** augmentation **13** amplification

wrong **3** bad, sin **4** awry, bilk, evil, harm, hurt, ruin, vice **5** abuse, amiss, cheat, crime, false, inapt, kaput, unfit **6** faulty, fleece, injure, injury, ruined, sinful, unfair, unjust, untrue, wicked **7** crooked, defraud, illegal, illicit, immoral, inexact, inverse, misdeed, offense, reverse, swindle, unhappy, unsound **8** criminal, dishonor, evil deed, ill-treat, immodest, improper, iniquity, maltreat, mistaken, mistreat, opposite, trespass, unlawful, unseemly, villain **9** dishonest, erroneous, felonious, illogical, incorrect, injustice, unethical, unfitting **10** dishonesty, fallacious, illegality, immorality, inaccurate, indecorous, indelicate, iniquitous, malapropos, mistakenly, sinfulness, unbecoming, unfairness, unsuitable, wickedness, wrongdoing **11** blameworthy, erroneously, incongruous, incorrectly, inexcusable, unbefitting, undesirable, unwarranted **12** dishonorable, inaccurately, infelicitous, unlawfulness **13** inappropriate, reprehensible, transgression, unjustifiable **15** unrighteousness

wrongdoer **5** crook, felon, knave, rogue **6** rascal, sinner **7** culprit, misdoer, villain **8** evildoer, offender **9** miscreant, scoundrel **10** blackguard, delinquent, lawbreaker, malefactor, trespasser **11** perpetrator **12** transgressor

wrongdoing **3** sin **4** evil, vice **5** crime **8** misdeeds **10** misconduct **11** delinquency, malfeasance, misbehavior

wrongful **3** bad **6** unfair, unjust **7** illegal **8** criminal, unlawful **10** iniquitous, inequitable **12** illegitimate
act: **4** tort
dispossession: **6** ouster

wrongheaded **3** wry **8** perverse, stubborn **9** misguided

wrong side out **9** backwards **10** topsy-turvy

wrought **4** made **6** beaten, formed, worked **7** crafted **8** hammered **9** fashioned **11** constructed, handcrafted

wrought-up **7** excited **8** agitated **9** emotional **10** hysterical

wry **3** dry **5** askew, droll **6** bitter, ironic, warped **7** amusing, caustic, crooked, cynical, satiric, twisted **8** perverse, sardonic **9** contorted, distorted, sarcastic

Wunderkind **11** wonder child **12** child prodigy

Wurster, William
architect of: **13** Cowell College (UC Berkeley) **17** Ghirardelli Square (San Francisco CA)

Wuthering Heights
character: **9** Ellen Dean **10** Heathcliff, Mr Lockwood **11** Edgar Linton **14** Isabella Linton **15** Catherine Linton, Frances Earnshaw, Hareton Earnshaw, Hindley Earnshaw **16** Linton Heathcliff **17** Catherine Earnshaw
director: **12** William Wyler
author: **11** Emily Bronte
cast: **10** David Niven **11** Donald Crisp, Flora Robson, Leo G Carroll,

Merle Oberon (Cathy) **15** Laurence Olivier (Heathcliff) **19** Geraldine Fitzgerald

Wyatt, James
  architect of: 8 Pantheon (London) **9** Lee Priory (Kent) **10** Stoke Poges (Buckinghamshire) **13** Fonthill Abbey (Wiltshire) **14** Dodington House Gloucestershire) **15** Heveningham Hall (Suffolk) **16** Sandleford Priory (Berkshire)
  style: 13 Gothic Revival

Wyatt, Jane
  born: 9 Campgaw NJ
  roles: 9 Boomerang **11** Lost Horizon **15** Father Knows Best **17** Great Expectations **19** Gentleman's Agreement **21** None But the Lonely Heart

Wyatt Earp, The Life and Legend of
  character: 10 Morgan Earp, Virgil Earp **11** Ben Thompson, Doc Holliday **12** Bat Masterson, Bill Thompson **13** Old Man Clanton
  cast: 9 Hal Baylor **10** Denver Pyle, Dirk London, Hugh O'Brien **12** John Anderson **13** Douglas Fowley **14** Trevor Bardette **20** Mason Alan Dinehart III
  setting: 8 OK Corral **9** Dodge City, Ellsworth, Tombstone
  Wyatt's pistols: 15 Buntline Special

Wyeth, Andrew Newell
  born: 2 PA **10** Chadds Ford
  father: 7 N C Wyeth
  son: 10 Jamie Wyeth
  artwork: 9 Grape Wine, River Cove **12** Nick and Jamie **14** Christina Olson, Distant Thunder **15** Christina's World **22** Winter Nineteen-Forty-six

Wyler, William
  director of: 6 Ben Hur (Oscar) **7** Jezebel **9** Dodsworth, Funny Girl, The

Letter **10** Mrs Miniver (Oscar), The Heiress, These Three **12** Roman Holiday **14** The Little Foxes **15** Counsellor-at-Law **16** Wuthering Heights **18** Friendly Persuasion **22** The Best Years of Our Lives (Oscar)

Wylie, Philip
  author of: 13 Opus Twenty-one **19** A Generation of Vipers

Wyman, Jane
  real name: 14 Sarah Jane Fulks
  born: 10 St Joseph MO
  husband: 12 Ronald Reagan
  daughter: 13 Maureen Reagan
  son: 13 Michael Reagan
  roles: 5 So Big **9** Pollyanna **11** Falcon Crest, The Blue Veil, The Yearling **13** Johnny Belinda (Oscar) **14** Angela Channing, The Lost Weekend **17** The Glass Menagerie **20** Magnificent Obsession

Wyndham, John
  real name: 16 John Beynon Harris
  author of: 14 The Kraken Wakes **15** Consider Her Ways **17** The Midwich Cuckoos, Trouble with Lichen **19** The Day of the Triffids

Wyoming
  abbreviation: 2 WY **3** Wyo
  nickname: 8 Equality
  capital: 8 Cheyenne
  largest city: 6 Casper
  others: 4 Cody, Lusk **7** Bighorn, Buffalo, Laramie, Rawlins, Worland **8** Gillette, Greybull, Kemmerer, Riverton, Sheridan, Sundance **11** Rock Springs
  college: 7 Wyoming
  feature:
    center: 11 Buffalo Bill
    dam: 8 Shoshone
    fort: 7 Laramie
    historical preserve: 11 Fort Bridger

national grassland: 11 Tunder Basin
national monument: 11 Devil's Tower, Fossil Butte
national park: 10 Grand Teton **11** Yellowstone
reservoir: 12 Flaming Gorge
tribe: 4 Crow **5** Kiowa, Sioux **7** Arapaho, Bannock **8** Cheyenne
people: 10 Dick Cheney **11** Buffalo Bill **14** Jackson Pollock **16** Nellie Tayloe Ross **18** Francis Emroy Warren
  explorer: 6 Colter, Stuart **7** Bridger **10** Bonneville
lake: 7 Jackson **11** Yellowstone
land rank: 5 ninth
mountain: 3 Elk **5** Cloud, Moran **6** Absaro, Hoback, Tetons **7** Bighorn, Fremont, Laramie, Rockies **8** Atlantic, Sheridan **9** Wind River **10** Black Hills **11** Rattlesnake
  highest point: 11 Gannett Peak
physical feature: 11 Jackson Hole
  basin: 7 Wyoming
  cave: 8 Shoshone
  hot springs: 11 Thermopolis
  plains: 5 Great
river: 4 Bear, Wind **5** Green, Snake **6** Platte, Powder, Tongue **7** Bighorn **8** Cheyenne, Shoshone **10** Sweetwater **11** Yellowstone **12** Belle Fourche
state admission: 11 forty-fourth
state bird: 17 western meadowlark
state flower: 10 painted cup **16** Indian paintbrush
state motto: 11 Equal Rights
state song: 7 Wyoming
state tree: 10 cottonwood

Wyss, Johann Rudolf
  author of: 22 The Swiss Family Robinson
    inspired by: 14 Robinson Crusoe

Xanthippe, Xantippe 3 hag 4 fury 5 scold, shrew, vixen 6 dragon, virago 7 scolder 8 spitfire 9 termagant
husband: 8 Socrates
Xanthus and Balius
horses of: 8 Achilles
trait: 8 immortal
Xenia
epithet of: 6 Athena
means: 10 hospitable
xeno- 6 prefix 7 foreign, strange
Xenoclea
form: 9 priestess
xenon
chemical symbol: 2 Xe
xenophobia
fear of: 9 strangers
Xerox 4 copy
Xerxes see 9 Ahasuerus
X-Files
creator: 11 Chris Carter
director: 11 Chris Carter
characters: 3 Mr. X (Steven Williams) 9 Fox Mulder (David Duchovny) 10 Alex Krycek (Nick Lea), Dana Scully (Gillian Anderson), Deep Throat (Jerry Hardin) 13 Walter Skinner (Mitch Pileggi) 19 Cigarette-Smoking Man (William B. Davis)
x-ray 9 radiogram 10 radiograph 13 roentgenogram 14 roentgenograph
X-ray tube
invented by: 8 Coolidge
yacht 4 boat, race, sail, ship, yawl 5 ketch, sloop 6 cruise, cutter 7 catboat 8 schooner
race: 11 America's Cup
yachting
athlete: 9 Ted Turner 11 Lowell North
competition 11 America's Cup
yahoo 4 lout 5 brute, yokel 7 lowbrow 9 barbarian, ignoramus, vulgarian
Yahoos
fictional people in: 16 Gulliver's Travels
author: 5 Swift
Yahweh 3 God 4 Lord 5 Jahve, Jahwe, Yahve 6 Author, I am I am, Jahveh 7 Creator, Eternal, Jehovah 8 Absolute, Almighty, Infinite
component: 2 he 3 yod, vav
pronunciation: 6 Adonai, Elohim 9 forbidden
transliteration: 4 YHVH

Yale, Linus, Jr
invented: 12 cylinder lock 27 dial-operated combination lock
Yalta
in: 7 Ukraine
conference participant: 6 Stalin 9 Churchill, Roosevelt
yam 9 Dioscorea 14 Ipomoea batatas
varieties: 4 wild 5 Negro, water, white 6 Attoto, potato, yellow 7 Chinese 11 sweet potato
Yamasaki, Minoru
architect of: 14 St Louis Airport (MO) 16 World Trade Center (NYC) 21 Woodrow Wilson Building (Princeton NJ)
yammer 3 cry 4 carp, harp, howl, wail, yell 5 whine 7 grumble, whimper 8 complain
Yangon
capital of: 5 Burma 7 Myanmar
former name: 5 Dagon 7 Rangoon
founder: 10 Alaungpaya
landmark: 10 Sule Pagoda 15 Shwe Dagon Pagoda
name means: 11 end of strife
river: 5 Rangoon
square: 12 Independence
yank 3 tug 4 jerk, pull 5 pluck, wrest 6 snatch, wrench 7 draw out, extract, pull out
Yankee, Yank 2 GI 5 teddy 6 gringo 8 American, doughboy 10 Northerner
Spanish: 6 yanqui
Yankee Doodle Dandy
director: 13 Michael Curtiz
cast: 10 Joan Leslie 11 James Cagney (George M Cohan) 12 Irene Manning, Walter Huston
Oscar for: 5 actor (Cagney)
yanqui 6 Yankee 9 US citizen
Yaounde
capital of: 8 Cameroon
yap 3 yip 4 blab, gush, rave, talk, yawp, yelp 5 scold 6 babble, gabble, gossip, jabber, rave on, tattle 7 blather, chatter, lecture, palaver, prattle 8 complain, converse
Yaqui
language family: 6 Cahita
location: 6 Mexico, Sonora 7 Arizona
yard 4 lawn 5 close, court 6 garden 7 confine, grounds, pasture 8 compound 9 enclosure, three feet
abbreviation: 2 yd

yardbird 3 con 5 felon 7 convict 8 prisoner
yard goods 5 cloth 6 fabric 8 material, textiles
yardstick 4 rule 7 measure 8 standard 9 criterion
Yaren District
capital of: 5 Nauru
yarn 4 tale 5 story 7 account 8 anecdote 9 adventure, narrative 10 experience
Yastrzemski, Carl
nickname: 3 Yaz
sport: 8 baseball
team: 12 Boston Red Sox
Yates, Peter
director of: 7 Bullitt 12 Breaking Away
yawn 3 gap 4 bore, gape 5 chasm 8 open wide, oscitate
yawp 4 roar, yelp 5 noise 6 clamor, squawk, yammer
Yaz
nickname of: 15 Carl Yastrzemski
year, years 3 age, era 4 time 5 cycle, epoch 6 period
abbreviation: 2 yr
Yearling, The
director: 13 Clarence Brown
author: 22 Marjorie Kinnan Rawlings
cast: 9 Jane Wyman 10 Chill Wills 11 Gregory Peck 14 Claude Jarman Jr
character: 9 Ora Baxter 10 Jody Baxter 11 Oliver Hutto, Penny Baxter 12 Grandma Hutto 14 Twink Weatherby 19 Fodder-Wing Forrester
yearn 4 ache, long, pine, sigh, want, wish 5 crave 6 hanker, hunger, thirst 8 languish
yearning 3 yen 4 ache, want, wish 5 fancy 6 desire, hunger, thirst 7 craving, longing, passion 9 hankering 10 aspiration 11 inclination
Year of Living Dangerously, The
director: 9 Peter Weir
cast: 9 Linda Hunt (Billy Kwan), Mel Gibson 15 Sigourney Weaver
setting: 7 Jakarta
Oscar for: 17 supporting actress (Hunt)
year of wonders
Latin: 14 annus mirabilis
Yeats, William Butler
author of: 7 A Vision 8 The Tower 9 Last Poems 14 Leda and the Swan

15 The Winding Stair **18** Sailing to Byzantium **19** Among School Children, The Wild Swans at Coole **21** Easter Nineteen Sixteen **22** The Lake Isle of Innisfree **29** An Irish Airman Foresees His Death

yegg 6 bomber **9** cracksman **11** safe-cracker

yell 3 boo, cry **4** bawl, hoot, howl, roar, yowl **5** cheer, hollo, shout, whoop **6** bellow, clamor, cry out, holler, hurrah, huzzah, outcry, scream, shriek, squall, squeal **7** screech

yellow 4 gold **5** blond, lemon, ocher **6** afraid, canary, craven, flaxen **7** chicken, fearful, saffron **8** cowardly, timorous **10** frightened **12** apprehensive, fainthearted **13** pusillanimous **14** chickenhearted

yellow-belly 6 coward **7** caitiff, chicken, dastard **8** poltroon

Yellowhammer State
nickname of: **7** Alabama

yellowish 4 buff **5** blond, cream **6** blonde, creamy, flaxen

Yellow Kid, The
creator: **10** R F Outcault
trademark: **10** nightshirt
place: **5** slums **11** Hogan's Alley
coined term: **16** yellow journalism
first: **10** comic strip

yelp 3 yap, yip **4** bark, howl **5** shout **6** clamor, holler, scream, shriek, squeal **7** screech

Yemen
other name: **4** Sana
capital/largest city: **4** Sana **5** Sanaa
others: **4** Aden, Moka, Taiz **5** Ahwar, Dahhi, Damar, Jibla, Mocha, Mukha, Shihr, Taizz, Tarim, Umram **6** Balhaf, Damqut, Seiyun, Shabwa, Shibam, Zamakh **7** Hodeida, Hudayda, Mukalla
monetary unit: **4** fils, rial **5** dinar, riyal
island: **5** Perim, Zugar **6** Hanish **7** Kamaran, Socotra
highest point: **6** Shuayb
mountain: **7** Djehaff
river: **4** Bana **5** Abrad, Zabid **6** al-Jawf, Surdud, Tibban **7** Masilah **9** Hadramaut
sea: **3** Red **6** Indian **7** Arabian
physical feature:
　desert: **10** Rub al Khali **12** Empty Quarter
　gulf: **4** Aden
　lowlands: **6** Tihama
　peninsula: **7** Arabian
　strait: **11** Bab el Mandeb
　valley: **9** Hadramawt
people: **4** Arab **5** Zaidi **6** Shafai, Yemeni **8** Yemenite
　leader: **16** Ali Abdallah Salih **19** Abd al-Aziz Abd al-Ghani
language: **6** Arabic
religion: **5** Islam

place:
　ruins: **5** Marib
feature:
　animal: **4** ibex, oryx
　clothing: **4** futa
　dagger: **7** jambiya
　king: **4** imam
　kingdom: **4** Saba **5** Sheba **11** Arabia Felix
　tree: **3** fig **5** carob, mango, myrrh
food:
　coffee: **5** mocha

yen 4 ache, long, pine, sigh, want, wish **5** crave, fancy, yearn **6** aching, desire, hanker, hunger, relish, thirst **7** craving, longing, passion **8** appetite, languish, yearning **9** hankering **10** aspiration **11** inclination

yenta 3 hen **6** gossip **8** busybody **12** blabbermouth

Yentl
director: **15** Barbra Streisand
based on story by: **19** Isaac Bashevis Singer
cast: **13** Mandy Patinkin **15** Barbra Streisand

Yeobright, Thomasin and Clym
characters in: **17** Return of the Native
author: **5** Hardy

yeoman 4 chap, exon **5** churl, clerk, swain **6** farmer, fellow **7** granger, plowman, servant **8** graycoat, retainer **9** beefeater **10** freeholder **12** petty officer

Yerby, Frank
author of: **8** Fair Oaks **10** Health Card **11** Griffin's Way **12** Pride's Castle **16** The Foxes of Harrow **21** Hail the Conquering Hero

yes 3 aye, yea **4** amen, okay, true **5** truly **6** assent, indeed, it is so, just so, really, so be it, surely, verily **7** consent, exactly, granted, no doubt **8** approval, of course, to be sure **9** agreement, assuredly, certainly, doubtless, precisely **10** acceptance, positively **11** affirmation, undoubtedly **12** acquiescence, emphatically **13** affirmatively, authorization
French: **3** oui
German: **2** ja
Spanish: **2** si

Yes, Dear
network: **3** CBS
cast: **10** Liza Snyder (Christine Hughes) **11** Mike O'Malley (Jimmy Hughes) **12** Anthony Clark (Greg Warner) **15** Jean Louisa Kelly (Kim Warner)

yesterday 7 the past **10** bygone days, days of yore, olden times, time gone by **11** former times **13** the recent past **14** the good old days **17** the day before today **22** on the day preceding today

yet 3 but **4** also, even, then, up to **5** again, still, while, until **6** no less,

though **7** besides, earlier, even now, further, however, thus far **8** although, hitherto, moreover **9** presently **10** eventually, ultimately **12** nevertheless **15** notwithstanding

yew 5 Taxus
varieties: **4** plum **5** Irish **6** golden **7** Chinese, English, Florida, Western **8** American, Japanese, Southern **11** Chinese plum, Plum-fruited **12** Japanese plum, Prince Albert **14** Harrington plum

Yggdrasil
also: **9** Iggdrasil
origin: **12** Scandinavian
kind of tree: **12** evergreen ash
roots: **5** three
binds: **6** Asgard **7** Midgard **8** Niflheim **10** Mithgarth

yield 3 pay, sag **4** bear, crop, earn, gain, give **5** beget, break, burst, defer, droop, forgo, grant, spawn, split, waive **6** accede, cave in, give in, give up, kowtow, render, return, submit, supply **7** bow down, concede, forbear, furnish, give way, harvest, payment, premium, produce, product, provide, revenue, succumb, truckle **8** collapse, cry uncle, earnings, generate, interest, proceeds, renounce **9** acquiesce, gleanings, procreate, surrender **10** capitulate, relinquish

yielding 3 lax **4** soft **6** ceding, spongy **7** sagging **8** flexible, obedient **9** compliant **11** complaisant **13** accommodating

Yigdal 22 Jewish liturgical prayer
literally: **12** becomes great

Yizkor 33 Jewish service to commemorate the dead
literally: **9** be mindful

Ymir
origin: **12** Scandinavian
progenitor of: **6** giants
earth made from: **5** flesh
water made from: **5** blood
heavens made from: **5** skull

yoga, yogi 5 Hindu **6** mystic **7** ascetic

Yogi Bear
creator: **12** Hanna-Barbera
character: **6** BooBoo
setting: **14** Jellystone Park

yoke 3 tax **4** bond, join, link, load, pair, span, team **5** brace, clasp, hitch, trial, unite **6** attach, burden, collar, couple, fasten, strain, weight **7** bondage, coupler, harness, serfdom, slavery **8** distress, pressure, troubles **9** servitude, thralldom, vassalage **10** oppression **11** enslavement, tribulation

yokel 4 clod, hick, rube **7** bumpkin, hayseed, peasant, plowboy **10** clodhopper, provincial

yolk 6 yellow

yonder 3 yon **5** there **6** far-off **7** faraway, farther, thither

Yorick
skull in: **6** Hamlet
author: **11** Shakespeare

Yorick, Mr
character in: **14** Tristram Shandy
author: **6** Sterne

York, Michael
born: **6** Fulmer **7** England
roles: **6** Tybalt **7** Cabaret **11** Lost Horizon **12** Austin Powers, The Omega
Code **14** Four Musketeers, Romeo
and Juliet, The Forsyte Saga **15**
Three Musketeers **19** The Island of
Dr Moreau **24** The Last Remake of
Beau Geste

York, Susannah
real name: **23** Susannah Yolande
Fletcher
born: **6** London **7** England
roles: **5** Freud **6** Images **8** Jane Eyre,
Tom Jones, Visitors **12** The Awakening
author of: **18** In Search of Unicorns

Yossarian
character in: **14** Catch Twenty-two
author: **6** Heller

You Asked for It
host: **8** Art Baker **9** Jack Smith

You Bet Your Life
host: **11** Groucho Marx
announcer: **14** George Fenneman

You Can't Go Home Again
author: **11** Thomas Wolfe
character: **10** Esther Jack **11** Lloyd
McHarg **12** George Webber **13** Else
von Kohler **14** Foxhall Edwards

You Can't Take It With You
author: **8** Moss Hart **14** George S
Kaufman
director: **10** Frank Capra
cast: **10** Jean Arthur, Mischa Auer **12**
Edward Arnold, James Stewart **15** Lionel Barrymore
Oscar for: **7** picture **8** director

young 3 cub, pup **4** baby, kids **5** child,
issue, minor, whelp **6** boyish, callow,
junior, kitten, youths **7** budding, girlish, growing, progeny, puerile, teenage **8** childish, children, immature,
juvenile, underage, youthful **9** beardless, infantile, juveniles, offspring,
teenagers **10** adolescent, descendant,
sophomoric, youngsters **11** adolescents, undeveloped **13** inexperienced
god of: **7** Angus Og
goddess of: **4** Hebe

Young, Chic
creator/artist of: **7** Blondie

Young, Denton True
nickname: **2** Cy **7** Cyclone
sport: **8** baseball
position: **7** pitcher
team: **12** Boston Braves, Boston Red
Sox **16** Cleveland Indians, St Louis
Cardinals

Young, Loretta
real name: **13** Gretchen Young
husband: **12** Grant Withers
roles: **13** Cause for Alarm **14** The
Bishop's Wife **15** Come to the Stable
18 The Farmer's Daughter (Oscar)
20 Rachel and the Stranger

Young, Robert
born: **9** Chicago IL
roles: **10** Relentless **11** H M Pulham
Esq **13** Marcus Welby M D **15** Father Knows Best **16** Strange Interlude

Young Frankenstein
director: **9** Mel Brooks
cast: **8** Teri Garr **10** Gene Wilder, Peter Boyle **11** Gene Hackman **12**
Madeline Kahn, Marty Feldman **14**
Cloris Leachman
score: **10** John Morris

young girl
French: **10** jeune fille

young lady
German: **8** fraulein

youngster 3 boy, kid, tot **4** baby, girl
5 child, minor, youth **7** progeny **8** juvenile, teenager **9** fledgling, offspring
10 adolescent

young Turks 6 rebels **8** radicals, up-
starts **9** activists **10** insurgents **15** re-
volutionaries

young woman
French: **10** demoiselle

you're welcome
German: **5** bitte

Your Show of Shows
regular: **9** Bill Hayes, Jerry Ross, Sid
Caesar **10** Carl Reiner **11** Imogene
Coca **12** Howard Morris, Nellie
Fisher **13** James Starbuck, Robert
Merrill **16** Marguerite Piazza

youth 3 boy, kid, lad **4** kids **5** bloom,
child, minor, prime, teens **6** heyday **7**
boyhood **8** children, girlhood, juvenile, minority, teenager **9** childhood,
fledgling, juveniles, schoolboy, stripling, teenagers, youngster **10** adolescent, pubescence, youngsters **11** adolescence, adolescents

youthful 5 fresh, young **6** boyish, callow **7** girlish, puerile, teenage **8** childish, immature, juvenile **10** adolescent,
sophomoric **12** enthusiastic, light
hearted **13** inexperienced

yowl 3 bay, cry **4** bawl, roar, wail,
yelp **5** shout, whine **6** bellow, holler,
scream, shriek, squeal **7** screech **9**
caterwaul

Ypres
in: **7** Belgium
WWI: **10** battle site

yuan
currency of: **5** China

yucca 5 agave
varieties: **4** blue **6** banana **9** San Angelo, spineless **11** twisted-leaf

Yugoslavia see **19** Serbia and Montenegro

Yuit see **6** Eskimo

Yukon Territory
border: **6** Alaska **15** British Columbia,
Selwyn Mountains **18** Mackenzie
Mountains
capital: **10** Whitehorse
country: **6** Canada
event: **8** gold rush (1897)
Indian: **4** Dene **6** Eskimo **7** Kutchin **8**
Loucheux **9** Athabasca
lake: **6** Kluane **9** Great Bear
mineral: **4** gold **6** silver
mountain: **3** Joy **5** Logan **6** Harper **7**
Kennedy **8** Campbell
region: **8** Klondike
river: **5** Pelly **9** Porcupine
sea: **8** Beaufort
town: **4** Elsa, Faro, Mayo, Snag **5**
Rocky **6** Dawson **8** Franklin, Wer-
necke **9** Mackenzie

yule 4 Noel **9** Christmas

Yule, Joe, Jr
real name of: **12** Mickey Rooney

Yuman
tribe: **6** Mohave, Mojave **8** Hualapai

Zachariah
father: **4** Babi, Elam **9** Barachias
wife: **9** Elizabeth
son: **3** Abi **14** John the Baptist
succeeded: **8** Jeroboam
visitor: **7** Gabriel

zaddik 14 virtuous person **15** righteous
person

Zadkine, Ossip
born: **6** Russia **8** Smolensk
artwork: **4** Stag **6** Christ **7** Orpheus
9 Musicians **10** The Prophet **13**
Woman with a Fan **14** Mother and
Child **16** The Destroyed City

Zadok
father: **5** Baana, Immer **6** Ahitub
son: **7** Shallum
daughter: **7** Jerusha
served: **5** David

zaftig 5 buxom, plump **6** bosomy

Zagreus
form: **5** child, deity
father: **4** Zeus
mother: **6** Semele **10** Persephone

Zaire see **26** Congo, Democratic Republic of

Zambia
other name: **16** Northern Rhodesia
capital/largest city: **6** Lusaka
others: **4** Kafu **5** Choma, Isoka,
Kabwe, Kitwe, Mansa, Mbala,
Mongu, Mpika, Mumba, Ndola **6**
Mwenda **7** Chipata, Luapula,
Mankoya **8** Balovale, Chingola, Lu-
anshya, Mazabuka, Mufulira, Mulo-
bezi **11** Livingstone
division: **7** Puapula **10** Copperbelt **11**
Barotseland
monetary unit: **5** ngwee **6** kwacha
lake: **5** Mweru **6** Kariba **9** Bangweulu
10 Tanganyika
mountain: **8** Muchinga
highest point: **12** Mafinga Hills

river: 5 Congo, Kafue 7 Luangwa, Luapula, Zambezi 8 Chambezi 9 Chambeshi

physical feature:
  cave: 5 Nsalu 14 Chifabwa Stream
  falls: 7 Kalambo 8 Victoria
  gorge: 6 Kariba
  plateau: 7 Zambian
  swamp: 7 Lukanga 9 Bangweulu 12 Mweru Wantipa
  valley: 8 Chambezi 9 Great Rift

people: 4 Lozi 5 Bantu, Bemba, Ngoni, Tonga
  developer: 6 Rhodes
  explorer: 11 Livingstone
  hero: 11 Chitimukulu
  leader: 6 Kaunda 9 Mwanawasa

language: 4 Lozi 5 Bemba, Lunda, Tonga 6 Luvale, Nyanja 7 English 9 Afrikaans

religion: 5 Hindu, Islam 7 animism 10 Protestant 13 Roman Catholic

place:
  botanical garden: 10 Munda Wanga
  dam: 5 Kafue 6 Kariba
  game reserve: 6 Valley
  library: 20 Hammerskjold Memorial
  museum: 11 Livingstone
  national park: 5 Kafue, Sumbu 12 South Luangwa

feature:
  canoe: 10 nalikwanda
  king: 7 litunga
  king's aide: 5 sungu, twite 8 inabanza
  taxi: 6 zamcab

zany 3 nut 4 wild 5 balmy, batty, booby, buffo, clown, comic, crazy, cutup, daffy, dizzy, goofy, inane, nutty, silly, wacky 6 jester, nitwit, screwy, weirdo 7 buffoon, half-wit, lunatic 8 bonehead, clownish, imbecile, lunkhead, numskull 9 blockhead, eccentric, harlequin, ludicrous, pantaloon, simpleton, slapstick 10 nincompoop, noodlehead, outlandish 11 nonsensical person
French: 7 farceur

Zapotec
  language family: 5 Otomi 6 mixtec
  location: 6 Mexico, Oaxaca

zapped 5 drunk 6 killed, soused, wasted, zonked 7 smashed 9 destroyed, plastered 10 inebriated 11 annihilated, intoxicated

zeal 4 fire, zest 5 ardor, gusto, verve, vigor 6 fervor, relish 7 passion 8 devotion, industry 9 animation, eagerness, intensity, vehemence 10 enthusiasm, fanaticism, fierceness, intentness 11 earnestness

zealot 3 fan, nut 4 buff 5 bigot, crank 6 pusher 7 devotee, fanatic, hustler 8 believer, champion, crackpot, gogetter, livewire, partisan 9 extremist 10 enthusiast

zealous 5 eager, rabid 6 ardent, fervid,

fierce, gung ho, raging, raving 7 devoted, earnest, fanatic, fervent, intense 8 animated, vehement, vigorous 10 passionate 11 impassioned, industrious 12 enthusiastic

Zebedee
  wife: 6 Salome
  son: 4 John 5 James

Zeboim
  destroyed with: 5 Admah, Sodom 8 Gomorrah

Zebulun
  father: 5 Jacob
  mother: 4 Leah
  brother: 3 Dan, Gad 4 Levi 5 Asher, Judah 6 Joseph, Reuben, Simeon 8 Benjamin, Issachar, Naphtali
  sister: 5 Dinah
  descendant of: 10 Zebulunite

Zechariah
  father: 5 Bebai, Hosah 6 Jehiel, Pashur 7 Isshiah 8 Jehoiada, Jonathan 9 Berechiah 11 Jeberechiah, Meshelemiah
  grandfather: 4 Iddo
  mother: 6 Merari
  son: 8 Jahaziel
  daughter: 6 Abijah

Zeffirelli, Franco
  director of: 6 Hamlet 14 Romeo and Juliet 16 Tea with Mussolini 19 The Taming of the Shrew 20 Brother Sun Sister Moon

Zeitgeist 18 the spirit of the time

Zelos
  origin: 5 Greek
  personifies: 4 zeal 9 emulation
  father: 11 Titan Palles
  mother: 4 Styx
  brother: 3 Bia 6 Cratus
  sister: 4 Nike

Zemeckis, Robert
  director of: 15 Back to the Future 17 Romancing the Stone

zenith 4 acme, apex, best, peak 6 apogee, climax, summit, vertex 7 maximum 8 pinnacle 11 culmination

Zenobia (Zeena)
  character in: 10 Ethan Frome
  author: 7 Wharton

zephyr 8 west wind 9 puff of air 10 gentle wind 11 breath of air, light breeze

Zephyrus
  personifies: 8 west wind
  father: 8 Astraeus
  mother: 3 Eos
  loved: 10 Hyacinthus
  son: 6 Balius 7 Xanthus

Zeppelin, Ferdinand Graf von
  nationality: 6 German
  invented: 9 dirigible 21 rigid dirigible airship
  famous ship: 10 Hindenberg

zero 2 no 3 nil, zip 5 aught, nadir, zilch 6 cipher, naught 7 nothing 8 goose egg 11 nonexistent, nothingness

zero hour 5 onset, start 7 liftoff 9 beginning 12 commencement

zest 3 joy, zip 4 salt, tang, zeal, zing 5 gusto, savor, spice, taste, verve 6 flavor, relish, thrill 7 delight, passion 8 appetite, piquancy, pleasure 9 eagerness, flavoring, seasoning 10 enthusiasm, excitement 12 exhilaration, satisfaction

zestful 6 active, lively 7 dynamic, vibrant 8 animated, spirited, vigorous 9 vivacious 12 invigorating

zesty 5 spicy, tangy 7 piquant

Zeus
  also: 7 Cenaean 9 Atabyriam, Ithomatas 10 Anchesmius 11 Panomphaeus 12 Cithaeronian
  birthplace: 5 Crete
  brother: 5 Hades 8 Poseidon
  corresponds to: 4 Amen, Amon, Jove 5 Ammon 6 Amen Ra, Amon Ra 7 Jupiter
  daughter: 4 Hebe 6 Athene 10 Eileithyia, Persephone
  epithet: 5 Areus, Arius, Sotor 6 Aqueus, Nemean, Philus 7 Alastor, Apemius, Ctesius, Lycaeus, Polieus, Stenius 8 Agoraeus, Aphesius, Apomyius, Catharius, Chthonius, Coccygius, Hecaleius, Lecheates, Mechaneus 10 Cataebates, Coryphaeus, Homagyrius, Laphystius, Meilichius 11 Eleutherius 12 Panhellenius
  father: 6 Cronus
  form: 5 deity
  god of: 7 heavens
  lover: 4 Leto 7 Demeter
  mother: 4 Rhea
  position: 7 supreme
  sister: 4 Hera 6 Hestia 7 Demeter
  son: 4 Ares 6 Apollo, Hermes
  wife: 4 Hera 5 Metis

zigzag 4 awry, tack 6 angles, forked, jagged 7 chevron, crankle, crooked, notched, sinuous, stagger 8 crotched, serrated, sideling, traverse 9 bifurcate 10 circuitous, deflection

Zilpah
  slave of: 4 Leah
  concubine of: 5 Jacob
  son: 3 Gad 5 Asher

Zimbabwe
  other name: 8 Rhodesia 16 Southern Rhodesia
  capital/largest city: 6 Harare 9 Salisbury
  others: 5 Gwelo, Gweru 6 Kariba, KweKwe, Mutare, QueQue, Umtali 7 Gatooma, Rusambo, Selukwe, Shabani 8 Bulawayo, Zimbabwe 10 Beitbridge
  monetary unit: 4 cent 6 dollar
  lake: 4 Kyle 6 Kariba
  mountain: 5 Vumba 6 Manica 7 Inyanga 11 Chimanimani, Matopo Hills
  highest point: 9 Inyangani
  river: 4 Sabi, Save 5 Lundi 6 Shashi

7 Limpopo, Umniati, Zambezi
physical feature:
  falls: 8 Victoria
  grassland: 4 veld
  plateau: 8 Highveld **11** Mashonaland
people: 3 Ila **4** Sena **5** Asian, Bantu, Bemba, Sotho, Tongo, White **6** Indian **7** Barotse, Chinese, English, Mashoma, Mashona, Ndebele **8** Coloured, Japanese, Matabele **9** Afrikaner **10** Balokwakwa
  developer: 6 Rhodes
  explorer: 11 Livingstone
  king: 9 Lobengula, Mzilikaze
  leader: 5 Nkomo **6** Mugabe **7** Sithole **8** Muzorewa **9** Ian D Smith
language: 3 Ila **5** Bantu, Shona **7** English, Ndebele
religion: 7 animism **8** Anglican **12** Christianity, Presbyterian **13** Dutch Reformed, Roman Catholic
place:
  dam: 6 Kariba
  national park: 6 Hwange, Wankie **7** Matopos **9** Inyangani **13** Victoria Falls
  ruins: 5 Khami **6** Temple **8** Zimbabwe **9** Acropolis **13** Valley of Ruins
feature:
  cattle pen: 5 kraal
  game: 5 tsoro **7** mandani
  hut: 4 kaia
  kingdom: 5 Rozwi **10** Monomotapa
  tree: 4 teak **6** baobab, mopani
Zimbalist, Efrem, Jr
born: 9 New York NY
father: 14 Efrem Zimbalist
mother: 9 Alma Gluck
daughter: 18 Stephanie Zimbalist
roles: 3 FBI **13** Wait Until Dark **15** By Love Possessed **16** The Chapman Report **23** Seventy-Seven Sunset Strip
zinc
chemical symbol: 2 Zn
zing 3 pep, vim, zap, zip **4** dash, snap, tang, whiz, zest **5** gusto, speed, vigor, whine **6** energy, spirit **7** liven up

8 satirize, vitality **9** animation, criticize **10** enthusiasm, liveliness
zingara, zingaro 5 gypsy
Zinnemann, Fred
director of: 5 Julia **8** High Noon, Oklahoma **9** The Search **12** The Nun's Story **13** The Sundowners **17** A Man for All Seasons (Oscar) **18** From Here to Eternity (Oscar)
Zion 6 utopia **9** city of God **11** City of David **13** ancient Israel
  hill in: 9 Jerusalem
  built on the hill: 6 Temple
zip 3 fly, nil, pep, run, vim **4** buzz, dart, dash, hiss, life, nada, rush, zero, zest **5** aught, close, drive, force, gusto, hurry, power, punch, speed, verve, vigor, whine, zilch **6** cipher, energy, impact, naught, spirit, streak **7** nothing, whistle **8** goose egg, strength, vitality, vivacity **9** animation, intensity **10** enthusiasm, exuberance, liveliness **13** effervescence
zipper
  invented by: 6 Judson
Zipporah
  father: 5 Reuel **6** Jethro
  husband: 5 Moses
  son: 7 Eliezer, Gershom
zircon
  source: 5 Burma **6** Ceylon **8** Cambodia, Sri Lanka **9** Kampuchea
zirconium
  chemical symbol: 2 Zr
zloty
  currency of: 6 Poland
zodiac 4 belt, zone **5** stars **7** circuit
  fire sign: 3 Leo **5** Aries **11** Sagittarius
  earth sign: 5 Virgo **6** Taurus **9** Capricorn
  air sign: 5 Libra **6** Gemini **8** Aquarius
  water: 6 Cancer, Pisces **7** Scorpio
  division: 4 sign **5** decan **6** trigon
  number of houses: 6 twelve
  falling between two signs: 4 cusp
Zola, Emile
  author of: 4 Nana **7** The Soil **8** Germinal **10** L'Assommoir **11** The

Downfall, The Dram Shop **13** Therese Raquin **14** The Human Animal **20** The Experimental Novel
zone 4 area, belt, ward **5** tract **6** region, sector **7** quarter, section, terrain **8** district, locality, location, precinct **9** territory
zonked 5 drunk **6** soused, wasted, zapped **7** smashed **9** plastered **10** inebriated **11** intoxicated
zoo 8 vivarium **9** menagerie
zoom 3 fly, zip **4** buzz, race, rise, soar **5** climb, flash, shoot, speed **6** ascend, rocket, streak **7** advance, take off **9** skyrocket
zoophobia
  fear of: 7 animals
Zophar
  friend: 3 Job **5** Elihu **6** Bildad **7** Eliphaz
Zorba the Greek
  director: 17 Michael Cacoyannis
  based on the story by: 11 Kazantzakis
  cast: 9 Alan Bates **11** Irene Pappas, Lila Kedrova **12** Anthony Quinn
  score: 16 Mikis Theodorakis
  Oscar for: 17 supporting actress (Kedrova)
zori 14 Japanese sandal
zucchini 5 gourd **6** squash **12** summer squash
Zuckerman Unbound
  author: 10 Philip Roth
Zurich
  festival: 12 Sechselanten
  landmark: 8 Rietberg **9** Kunsthaus **15** CG Jung Institute **17** Centre Le Corbusier, Fraumunster Kirche **21** Grossmunster Cathedral
  religious figure: 7 Zwingli **9** Bullinger
  river: 6 Limmat
  Roman name: 7 Turicum
Zweig, Arnold
  author of: 7 Claudia **24** The Case of Sergeant Grischa